# The Prisons Handbook 2023

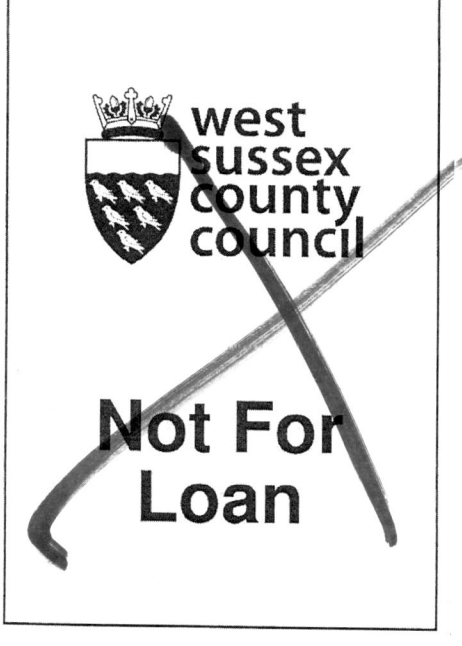
www.PrisonOracle.com

# The Prisons Handbook 2023

## Twenty-Fourth Edition

*The Definitive Annual Guide to Prisons in England and Wales*

Editor

Mark Leech

prisons org uk

Opening up the Closed World of Prisons

3

# The Prisons Handbook 2023

*TWENTY-FOURTH EDITION*

**Published October 2022 by**
PRISONS.ORG. UK LTD,
PO BOX 679
BURY BL8 9RU
Email: customer.services@prisons.org.uk
Web Site: www.prisons.org.uk

**Map of Prison Service Establishments**
© Internal Communications HM Prison Service

**ISBN: 978-1-916082465**

Printing & Binding: Hobbs The Printers, Brunel Road, Southampton SO40 3WX

Cover design: Mark Leech.

Reproduction rights have been assigned to PRISONS.ORG.UK LTD for the purposes of this edition. Photograph of Mark Leech, copyright © Mark Leech. Setting & design: Prisons Org UK Ltd.

Previous editions:
First Edition: OUP 1995
Second Edition: Pluto Press, 1997
Third Edition: Waterside Press, 1998
Fourth Edition: Waterside Press, 1999
Fifth Edition: Waterside Press, 2001
Sixth Edition: Waterside Press, 2002
Seventh Edition: prisons.org.uk, 2003
Eighth Edition: prisons.org.uk, 2004
Ninth Edition: prisons.org.uk, 2005
Tenth Edition: prisons.org.uk 2006
Eleventh Edition: prisons.org.uk 2008
Twelfth Edition: prisons.org.uk 2009
Thirteenth Edition: prisons.org.uk 2010
Fourteenth Edition: prisons.org.uk 2011
Fifteenth Edition: prisons.org.uk 2012
Sixteenth Edition: prisons.org.uk 2013
Seventeenth Edition: prisons.org.uk 2015
Eighteenth Edition: prisons.org.uk 2016
Nineteenth Edition: prisons.org.uk 2017
Twentieth Edition: prisons.org.uk 2018
Twenty-first Edition: prisons.org.uk 2019
Twenty-second Edition: prisons.org.uk 2020
Twenty-third Edition: prisons.org.uk 2021

www.PrisonOracle.com

# THE PRISONS HANDBOOK 2023
## CONTENTS

Prison Privatisation Timeline 1970-2023, 6
Prisons Strategy White Paper 2021, 7
Employment on Release - April 2022, 7
Summary - September 2022, 8
Background: Concerns about conditions, 8
Government prison estate programmes, 8
Responses to the Government's approach, 8
Understanding the prison estate
England and Wales, 9
Scotland and Northern Ireland, 9
The HMPPS estate, 9
Prisons and Young Offenders Institutions, 9
Immigration Removal Centres, 9
Secure Training Centres & Secure School, 9
Prisoner categories, 10
Types of prison and YOIs, 11
Adult male prisons, 11
Types of prison, 12
Reconfiguration, 12
Adult female prisons, 12
Prisons for children and young adults, 12
Private sector prisons, 12
Timeline: Prison Privatisation 1970-2023, 12
Which prisons are operated by the private sector, 13
Age of the prison estate, 13
£500 million boost to prison building, 13
Prisons Inspectorate: Assessment of living conditions, 13
Sanitation, 14
Lighting, 14
Heating, 14
Ventilation, 15
Fittings, 15
Communication with an officer, 15
Maintenance of prisons, 16
Performance of maintenance contracts, 16
Costs of Maintenance, 16
Sending in money & gifts, 16
New ID Rules, 16
The prison estate in England & Wales, 18-26
Map of Prison Service Establishments 2023, 27
CEO, DG and Director structure, 30
Governing Governors, 31
Private Sector Prison Contractors, 33
Other UK Prison Addresses, 34
Mark Leech Biography, 43
Prisoner Location Service, 44
HMPPS Contact Details, 44
Ministry of Justice Press Office, 44
Dedication, Frances Crook, OBE., 44
Foreword, Andrea Coomber QC (Hons), Chief Executive of The Howard League: "A Quarter of a Millennium - and What Has Changed?", 45
Acknowledgements, 47

Introduction to the 2023 Edition, 48
MOJ Directory of Service Specifications, 50
Glossary of Terms, 51
Offender Management Statistics, 54
Editorial, Mark Leech FRSA, Editor of The Prisons Handbook: "The Prisons Ombudsman: Cause for Complaint?", 62

SECTION 1: PRISONS
1.1 Prison Service Establishments in England and Wales 2023, 67-730

SECTION 2 – ADVICE
2.1 Early days in Custody, 731
2.2 Offending Behaviour Programmes, 763
2.3 Criminal Cases Review Commission, 766
2.4 Requests and Complaints, 770
2.5 Prisoner Communications, 780
2.6 Drugs and Alcohol in Prison, 797
2.7 The Prison Disciplinary System, 801
2.8 Who Can Help?, 817
2.9 Healthcare, 821
2.10 Religion, 831
2.11 Equality: Age, Gender, Disability & Race, 840
2.12 Social Security and Discharge Grants, 843
2.13 Release and Recall, 846
2.14 Indeterminate Sentences, 896
2.15 Women Prisoners, 905
2.16 Young Offenders (18-21 year olds), 916
2.17 Young People (15-17 year olds), 922
2.18 Foreign Nationals, 927
2.19 Disability in Prison, 935
2.20 Employment, Training & Skills, 938
2.21 Work and Pay, 943
2.22 Incentives and Earned Privileges, 951
2.23 Civil Partnerships & Equal Marriage, 963
2.24 Elderly Prisoners, 968
2.25 Segregation, 970
2.26 Security Categorisation, 987

SECTION 3 - THE DIRECTORY
3.1 Government & Statutory Agencies, 1001

SECTION 4 - LEGAL
4.1 Prisoners & The Law, 1007
4.2 Prison & YOI Rules, 1008
4.3 A-Z Subject Index, 1010
4.4 Appeals, 1139
4.5 Websites of interest, 1165

SECTION 5 - FORUM: Something to Say?
5.1 Gordon Brockington Managing Director G4S Care & Rehabilitation: Forward Thinking, 1167
5.2 Charlie Taylor, HM Chief Inspector of Prisons. The Musings of a Chief Inspector, 1170
5.3 Dr Varinder Panesar, Lead Forensic Psychologist HMP Pentonville: Change is coming: the mental health needs and experiences of young adults in two London remand prisons, 1175

5.4 Dr Tim Kerr: *Prison Medicine: On The Critical List? A health professional, service-user's, view of prison medicine*, 1181

5.5 Professor Karen Harrison et al, Lincoln & Hull Universities *A decency agenda of a different sort: the health and wellbeing of prison governors and operational managers*, 1184

SECTION 6 - REPORTS

6.1 Introduction to the Prisons Inspectorate, 1189

6.2.1 His Majesty's Prison & Probation Service Annual Report and Accounts, 1192

6.2.2 Prison & Probation Ombudsman's Annual Report, 1192

6.2.3 His Majesty's Chief Inspector of Prisons Annual Report, 1192

6.2.4 Parole Board For England & Wales Annual Report, 1196

6.2.5 Criminal Justice Joint Inspection - *The impact of the Covid-19 pandemic*, 1198

6.2.6 Criminal Justice Joint Inspection - *Individuals with mental health needs and disorders*, 1200

SECTION 7 - ANNEXES

7.1 Parliamentary Questions, 1205

7.2 Transparency & FOI Releases, 1231

7.3 Deaths in Prison Service Custody 1990-2022, 1236

7.4 Policy Frameworks, PSIs, PSOs, 1259

7.5 Staff Awards & Prizes 2022, 1283

7.6 Basic Custody Screening Tool, 1287

SECTION 8 - PRISON STAFF 2022/2023 OFFICERS & GOVERNORS

8.1. Officers - Custody & Detention - Professional Apprenticeships, 1303

8.2. Governors - Justice Leaders Course, 1319

8.3. Promotion, 1321

8.4. HMPPS - Workforce Statistics, 1322

8.5. HMPPS - Annual Staff Equalities Report, 1330

8.6. Pay Scales 2022/2023, 1344

8.7 Statement by the Justice Secretary, 1349

SECTION 9 - RESEARCH BRIEFINGS

*Details of almost 200 research papers ranging from Accusation of Racism in the Metropolitan Police, through to Youth Custody - dip into and out of it at your leisure - fully referenced, it contains parliamentary information fully licensed under the Open Parliament Licence; we have done all the hard work so you don't have to. You can view full versions of these research papers at prisonoracle.com*, 1369

Index, 1525

## Prison Privatisation Timeline 1970-2023

1970 Labour government contracts with Securicor for custody of immigration detainees

1987 Home affairs committee recommends private sector tendering of prisons

1991 Criminal Justice Act introduces competition into offender management services

1992 HMP Wolds, the U.K.'s first privately run prison opened. It closed in 2014 when it merged with HMP Everthorpe, next door, to become the publicly operated HMP Humber

1997 Conservative government announces its private finance initiative (PFI)

1997 New Labour government comes to power and adopts PFI approach

2000 Two privately run prisons are returned to the public sector

2003 Carter Review recommends greater use of competition in the prisons sector

2004 National Offender Management Service (NOMS) is established

2010 Coalition government comes to power and pushes ahead with a policy of privatisation

2011 HMP Doncaster the first prison to be run on a payment by results basis

2011 HMP Birmingham becomes the first public sector prison to be privatised

2011 Coalition government announces competition for nine prisons

2012 HMP Oakwood opens managed by G4S - it is the first privately Designed, Constructed, Managed and Financed prison (DCMF).

2017 HMPPS replaces NOMS

2019 G4S contract to run HMP Birmingham cancelled

2019 Government says rebuilt Wellingborough and Glen Parva to be privately operated

2020 G4S announced as preferred bidder for Wellingborough

2020 Government announces four new prisons to be built; two in the north and two in the south

2022 HMP Five Wells, G4S, Wellingborough, opened February 2022.

2023 HMP Fosse Way, opens May 2023 in Leicestershire, managed by Serco, its Director will be Wyn Jones.

# PRISONS STRATEGY WHITE PAPER

**Published 21st December 2021**
*Foreword to the White Paper*
We're carrying out the biggest prison building programme in more than 100 years to meet demand as we bring in tougher sentencing rules and the courts clear the backlogs brought about by COVID-19.

Prisons keep people safe by taking dangerous criminals off our streets, but they can only bring down crime and keep the public safer in the longer-term if they properly reform and rehabilitate offenders. In this White Paper we've set out our new strategy to support prisons to do both more effectively.

We will provide 20,000 new prison places to protect the public through punishment and incapacitation of offenders. The new estate will be more modern and secure, to keep our staff safe and provide the most productive environment to reform offenders.

Effective sanctions for prisoner misconduct and a zero-tolerance approach to weapons, drugs and contraband will enable prisons to maintain good order, so that offenders can focus on purposeful activity.

A new Prisoner Education Service will make sure offenders can improve their basic literacy and numeracy, as well as acquire further vocational qualifications, like construction and computing, to make them more employable when they leave prison.

We will transform work in prisons and on Release on Temporary Licence to improve job prospects for offenders. We will hold Governors to account for the opportunities and outcomes to participate in work-related activity they achieve for prisoners.

We will bring in earlier assessments and the full range of mental health and drug treatments, including abstinence-based methods, to support more prisoners to address their addictions and other clinical barriers to their rehabilitation.

We will introduce resettlement passports to bring together the essentials that offenders need to live crime-free lives after their release – identification, a CV, and a bank account – in one place and make sure that they are easily accessible.

In order to drive this ambitious strategy forward, we will invest £200m per year by 2024-25 to transform our approach to rehabilitation, including improving prison leavers' access to accommodation.

We will also set clear expectations of prisons and empower the highest performing ones to drive innovation and spread best practice.

We will regularly publish key performance indicators, targets, and league tables to increase transparency around prison performance, shining a light on how we can most effectively rehabilitate offenders.

The best performing prison Governors will be empowered with greater autonomy to innovate for their own prison populations, while continuing to be assessed against clear outcomes aligned to government priorities.

We know that this strategy cannot be delivered without our dedicated workforce. So, we will recruit an extra 5,000 prison officers and upskill our existing staff by enhancing training, supervision, and qualifications. We will hire the next generation of governors through an HMPPS fast-track scheme.

In order to deliver the vision set out in this White Paper, we will harness the latest technology to improve performance, and reduce the bureaucratic burden on staff.

This White Paper sets out our strategy for prisons over the next two years, as well as our longer-term 10-year vision. It seeks views on how the proposals can bring down stubbornly high rates of reoffending, cut crime and protect the public from harm.

It's part of the government's plan to build back better, stronger and fairer.

**Rt Hon Dominic Raab MP Justice Secretary**

**Employment on Release - April 2022**
*According to the Employment on Release statistical release to March 2022, published 30 April 2022:*
Employment at 6 weeks following release has increased: The proportion of persons released from custody who were employed at six weeks from their release rose by 6 percentage points to 16% between April 2021 and March 2022. This is an increase of more than half (57%).
504 persons released from custody were employed at six weeks after release in March 2022 compared to 335 in April 2021, an increase of 169.
Employment at 6 months following release has increased: The proportion of persons released from custody who were employed at six months from their release rose by 9 percentage points to 23% between April 2021 and March 2022. This is an increase of almost two thirds (66%).
581 persons released from custody were employed six months after release in March 2022, compared to 394 in April 2021, an increase of 187.

## Summary - September 2022

The prison estate in England and Wales contains 119 prisons holding people who have been sentenced or are on remand awaiting trial for a range of crimes. The prison estate has a mixture of publicly and privately-run institutions some of which are newly built - HMP Five Wells operated by G4S opened in February 2022, while HMP Fosse Way operated by Serco is due to open in May 2023 - while others date back to the Victorian era.

## Background: Concerns about conditions

There has been growing concern that the prison estate is unfit for purpose. The estate includes many dilapidated and overcrowded prisons. There is a backlog of maintenance work in prisons that has been estimated at around £1 billion.

Reports from the Chief Inspector of Prisons in 2017-19 said that conditions in this period were some of the most disturbing and squalid the inspectorate had ever seen. The inspectorate reported that in 2019-20, prior to the Covid- 19 pandemic, some prisons had improved living conditions, but conditions remained poor and overcrowded for many prisoners. The current Chief Inspector of Prisons in his 2021-22 annual report published in July 2022 again stated that the pandemic had exacerbated underlying problems and unacceptable conditions that inspections have previously criticised.

## Government prison estate programmes

The Government ran a 'Prison Estate Transformation Programme' from 2016-2019 with the aim of building 10,000 new prison places, investing in repairs and renovations and reorganising the functions of individual prisons.

In 2020 the National Audit Office and Public Accounts Committee published reports that were critical of the attempts made by the Ministry of Justice and HM Prison and Probation Service (HMPPS) to improve the prison estate. The Public Accounts Committee said that despite promises to create 10,000 new-for-old prison places by 2020, just 206 new places had been delivered, and prisoners continued to be held in unsafe, crowded conditions that did not meet their needs.

A New Prison Programme was created in 2019. In August 2019, the Government announced that it would spend up to £2.5 billion to create 10,000 prison places. In the 2020 Spending Review the Government stated it would spend more than £4 billion towards delivering 18,000 prison places across England and Wales by the mid-2020s. The 18,000 places would include the 10,000 places at four new prisons, the expansion of a further four prisons,

and the refurbishment of the existing prison estate along with the now opened HMP Five Wells and the completion HMP Fosse Way at Glen Parva in Leicestershire in May 2023.

The 2020-21 Spending Review also included £315m capital funding which HMPPS said would be used to make a start on critical refurbishment projects. The Public Accounts Committee has said the £315 million is significantly below what is required to maintain the prison estate.

## Responses to the Government's approach

Prison reform organisations have been critical of the Government's approach. They argue that instead of increasing prison places the Government should reduce the prison population thereby reducing overcrowding and freeing up resources for rehabilitation.

In January 2021, the Government announced that up to 500 prison places would be built in existing women's prisons. The plans have been criticised by prison reform organisations who have commented that they undermine the Government's commitments to reduce the women's prison population and go against the Government's own evidence that most women in prison do not need to be there.

On 28th April 2022 MPs called on the government to 'finally put the money where its mouth is' after revealing that it had spent just £9.5m on community services for women over the last four years despite promising £200m to provide 500 new prison places for women - *https://tinyurl.com/3baj2f2m*

The Public Accounts Committee (PAC) in April 2022 said that it was 'clear to us' that implementing the female offender strategy has been 'a relatively low priority' for the Ministry of Justice. The MoJ published its strategy in 2018 after years of concern about the experience of women in the criminal justice system, as set out in the 2007 Corston Report, and committed to cut the number of women in prison and increase support in the community. However the PAC reports the strategy was not designed in a way 'which would allow [the MoJ] to be held to account'.

The MPs said that the MoJ's recent funding settlement specifically included £550m over the next three years to reduce reoffending by men and women which provided 'a clear opportunity' to 'spend to save' by investing in community services for women.

'Once again we see a situation where government is unwilling or unable to prioritise the investment needed to reduce the ruinous financial, social and human costs of our creaking criminal justice system,' commented Dame Meg

Hillier MP, PAC's chair. 'Imprisoning a vulnerable woman who perhaps has children – who may then also fall between the cracks – is the very picture of the cost-shunting that became the hallmark of our criminal justice system long before the massive new challenges of the pandemic. The result of this gap between rhetoric and reality is an unacceptable human and economic toll. Government must finally put the money where its mouth is on criminal offending and 'spend to save' for the benefit to all society, families and individuals.'

## Understanding the prison estate
### England and Wales
His Majesty's Prison & Probation Service (HMPPS) has responsibility for running prison services in England and Wales. It manages public sector prisons and the contracts for private sector prisons. HMPPS is an executive agency, sponsored by the Ministry of Justice. HMPPS operates a directorate in Wales which coordinates prison and probation services there.

His Majesty's Inspectorate of Prisons is the independent body which reports on conditions and the treatment of those in held in custody.

### Scotland and Northern Ireland
Prisons in Scotland are managed by the Scottish Prison Service. Prisons in Northern Ireland are managed by the Northern Ireland Prison Service.

### The HMPPS estate
In 2022/2023 HMPPS manages an estate of 119 prisons (including the new HMP Five Wells and the newly returned Immigration Removal Centre HMP Morton Hall) and one Secure Training Centre (STC Oakhill. Outside the HMPPS estate, there are further immigration removal centres.

### Prisons and Young Offenders Institutions
There are several different types of prisons which nominally serve different categories of prisoner. Most prisons are managed directly by HMPPS, but some are run by private sector companies through contracts.

### Immigration Removal Centres
Separate from prisons, Immigration Removal Centres (IRCs) are used solely for the detention of people detained under the Immigration Act 1971 or under section 62 of the Nationality, Immigration and Asylum Act 2002. Prior to 2003, IRCs were called 'detention centres'.

Until December 2021 most IRCs were managed by private sector companies under contract to the Home Office. Only one, Morton Hall, was within the HMPPS estate but in July 2020 it was announced that Morton Hall would close as an IRC in July 2021 and would revert to being used as a prison.

Morton Hall reopened as a Category C prison for adult male Foreign National prisoners in December 2021 - it is now part of the Foreign National estate consisting of three prisons - HMPs Huntercombe and Maidstone being the other two.

HMP The Verne was also an IRC but that was converted to a public-sector prison in 2018.

### Secure Training Centres & Secure Schools
Secure Training Centres (STCs) are institutions for children up to the age of 17.

In July 2022 the House of Commons Public Accounts Committee published a highly critical Report on STCs and 'Secure Schools' [https://tinyurl.com/3nkxvpkb] in which it said:

"Youth custody provision is failing children. Our inquiry has shown that The Ministry of Justice (the Ministry) and Her Majesty's Prison & Probation Service (HMPPS) have not fixed poor provision at secure training centres (STC), where vulnerable children have been persistently held in unsafe conditions. The closure of all but one STC has led to children being sent to alternative places that are less suitable for their needs. While the number of children is custody is relatively low—560 on average in 2020 –21—the Committee is concerned that these children are receiving substandard care. Their needs are diverse, and many are highly vulnerable, particularly girls. Suitable provision is needed to help them to get their lives back on track.

"Following a long-term decline in the number of children in custody, the Ministry and HMPPS now expect this number to more than double by 2024. Meanwhile, HMPPS faces significant delays and cost increases in progressing the first of a new type of custody, a secure school. It now intends the first secure school to be a 'pathfinder', and it does not plan to launch the second secure school until it has evaluated the first. We are unconvinced of the Ministry's and HMPPS's commitment to delivering the secure school vision of small, local, educationally focused establishments. The first secure school may not open until February 2024 — more than seven years after the Ministry accepted the Taylor review 's vision for secure schools — and plans for the second have not been made.

"Meanwhile, the Ministry and HMPPS have an estate that is totally unsuited to meeting the complex needs of children in custody.

| NAME | OPERATOR | FUNCTION |
|---|---|---|
| Altcourse | G4S | Local |
| Ashfield | Serco | Cat C Trainer |
| Askham Grange | Public | Female |
| Aylesbury | Public | LTHSE |
| Bedford | Public | Local |
| Belmarsh | Public | LTHSE |
| Berwyn | Public | Cat C Trainer |
| Birmingham | Public | Local |
| Brinsford | Public | YOI |
| Bristol | Public | Local |
| Brixton | Public | Cat C Trainer |
| Bronzefield | Sodexo | Female |
| Buckley Hall | Public | Cat C Trainer |
| Bullingdon | Public | Local |
| Bure | Public | Cat C Trainer |
| Cardiff | Public | Local |
| Channings Wood | Public | Cat C Trainer |
| Chelmsford | Public | Local |
| Coldingley | Public | Cat C Trainer |
| Cookham Wood | Public | YJB |
| Dartmoor | Public | Cat C Trainer |
| Deerbolt | Public | YOI |
| Doncaster | Serco | Local |
| Dovegate | Serco | Cat B Trainer |
| Downview | Public | Female |
| Drake Hall | Public | Female |
| Durham | Public | Local |
| East Sutton Park | Public | Female |
| Eastwood Park | Public | Female |
| Elmley | Public | Local |
| Erlestoke | Public | Cat C Trainer |
| Exeter | Public | Local |
| Featherstone | Public | Cat C Trainer |
| Feltham | Public | YOI |
| Five Wells | G4S | Cat C Trainer |
| Ford | Public | Open |
| Forest Bank | Sodexo | Local |
| Fosse Way | Serco (2023) | Cat C Trainer |
| Foston Hall | Public | Female |
| Frankland | Public | LTHSE |
| Full Sutton | Public | LTHSE |
| Garth | Public | LTHSE |
| Gartree | Public | LTHSE |
| Grendon | Public | Cat B Trainer |
| Guys Marsh | Public | Cat C Trainer |
| Hatfield | Public | Open |
| Haverigg | Public | Open |
| Hewell | Public | Local |
| High Down | Public | Local |
| Highpoint | Public | Cat C Trainer |
| Hindley | Public | Cat C Trainer |
| Hollesley Bay | Public | Open |
| Holme House | Public | Cat C Trainer |
| Hull | Public | Local |
| Humber | Public | Cat C Trainer |
| Huntercombe | Public | Cat C FNP |
| Isis | Public | Cat C Trainer |
| Isle of Wight | Public | LTHSE |
| Kirkham | Public | Open |
| Kirklevington | Public | Open |
| Lancaster Farms | Public | Cat C Trainer |
| Leeds | Public | Local |
| Leicester | Public | Local |
| Lewes | Public | Local |
| Leyhill | Public | Open |
| Lincoln | Public | Local |
| Lindholme | Public | Cat C Trainer |
| Littlehey | Public | Cat C Trainer |
| Liverpool | Public | Local |
| Long Lartin | Public | LTHSE |
| Low Newton | Public | Female |
| Lowdham Grange | Serco | Cat B Trainer |
| Maidstone | Public | Cat C FNP |
| Manchester | Public | LTHSE |
| Moorland | Public | Cat C Trainer |
| Morton Hall | Public | Cat C FNP |
| Mount, The | Public | Cat C Trainer |
| New Hall | Public | Female |

| NAME | OPERATOR | FUNCTION |
|---|---|---|
| Dovegate | Serco | Cat B Trainer |
| Grendon | Public | Cat B Trainer |
| Lowdham Grange | Serco | Cat B Trainer |
| Rye Hill | G4S | Cat B Trainer |
| Huntercombe | Public | Cat C FNP |
| Maidstone | Public | Cat C FNP |
| Morton Hall | Public | Cat C FNP |
| Ashfield | Serco | Cat C Trainer |
| Berwyn | Public | Cat C Trainer |
| Brixton | Public | Cat C Trainer |
| Buckley Hall | Public | Cat C Trainer |
| Bure | Public | Cat C Trainer |
| Channings Wood | Public | Cat C Trainer |
| Coldingley | Public | Cat C Trainer |
| Dartmoor | Public | Cat C Trainer |
| Erlestoke | Public | Cat C Trainer |
| Featherstone | Public | Cat C Trainer |
| Five Wells | G4S | Cat C Trainer |
| Fosse Way | Serco (2023) | Cat C Trainer |
| Guys Marsh | Public | Cat C Trainer |
| Highpoint | Public | Cat C Trainer |
| Hindley | Public | Cat C Trainer |
| Holme House | Public | Cat C Trainer |
| Humber | Public | Cat C Trainer |
| Isis | Public | Cat C Trainer |
| Lancaster Farms | Public | Cat C Trainer |
| Lindholme | Public | Cat C Trainer |
| Littlehey | Public | Cat C Trainer |
| Moorland | Public | Cat C Trainer |
| Mount, The | Public | Cat C Trainer |
| Northumberland | Sodexo | Cat C Trainer |
| Oakwood | G4S | Cat C Trainer |
| Onley | Public | Cat C Trainer |
| Parc | G4S | Cat C Trainer |
| Portland | Public | Cat C Trainer |
| Ranby | Public | Cat C Trainer |
| Risley | Public | Cat C Trainer |
| Rochester | Public | Cat C Trainer |
| Stafford | Public | Cat C Trainer |
| Stocken | Public | Cat C Trainer |
| Stoke Heath | Public | Cat C Trainer |
| Swinfen Hall | Public | Cat C Trainer |
| Usk | Public | Cat C Trainer |
| Verne, The | Public | Cat C Trainer |
| Warren Hill | Public | Cat C Trainer |
| Wayland | Public | Cat C Trainer |
| Wealstun | Public | Cat C Trainer |
| Whatton | Public | Cat C Trainer |
| Wymott | Public | Cat C Trainer |
| Askham Grange | Public | Female |
| Bronzefield | Sodexo | Female |
| Downview | Public | Female |
| Drake Hall | Public | Female |
| East Sutton Park | Public | Female |
| Eastwood Park | Public | Female |
| Foston Hall | Public | Female |
| Low Newton | Public | Female |
| New Hall | Public | Female |
| Send | Public | Female |
| Styal | Public | Female |
| Altcourse | G4S | Local |
| Bedford | Public | Local |
| Birmingham | Public | Local |
| Bristol | Public | Local |
| Bullingdon | Public | Local |
| Cardiff | Public | Local |
| Chelmsford | Public | Local |
| Doncaster | Serco | Local |
| Durham | Public | Local |
| Elmley | Public | Local |
| Exeter | Public | Local |
| Forest Bank | Sodexo | Local |
| Hewell | Public | Local |
| High Down | Public | Local |
| Hull | Public | Local |
| Leeds | Public | Local |
| Leicester | Public | Local |
| Lewes | Public | Local |

| | | |
|---|---|---|
| North Sea Camp | Public | Open |
| Northumberland | Sodexo | Cat C Trainer |
| Norwich | Public | Local |
| Nottingham | Public | Local |
| Oakhill | G4S | STC |
| Oakwood | G4S | Cat C Trainer |
| Onley | Public | Cat C Trainer |
| Parc | G4S | Cat C Trainer |
| Pentonville | Public | Local |
| Peterborough | Sodexo | Local M/F |
| Portland | Public | Cat C Trainer |
| Prescoed | Public | Open |
| Preston | Public | Local |
| Ranby | Public | Cat C Trainer |
| Risley | Public | Cat C Trainer |
| Rochester | Public | Cat C Trainer |
| Rye Hill | G4S | Cat B Trainer |
| Send | Public | Female |
| Springhill | Public | Open |
| Stafford | Public | Cat C Trainer |
| Standford Hill | Public | Open |
| Stocken | Public | Cat C Trainer |
| Stoke Heath | Public | Cat C Trainer |
| Styal | Public | Female |
| Sudbury | Public | Open |
| Swaleside | Public | LTHSE |
| Swansea | Public | Local |
| Swinfen Hall | Public | Cat C Trainer |
| Thameside | Serco | Local |
| Thorn Cross | Public | Open |
| Usk | Public | Cat C Trainer |
| Verne, The | Public | Cat C Trainer |
| Wakefield | Public | LTHSE |
| Wandsworth | Public | Local |
| Warren Hill | Public | Cat C Trainer |
| Wayland | Public | Cat C Trainer |
| Wealstun | Public | Cat C Trainer |
| Werrington | Public | YJB |
| Wetherby | Public | YJB M/F |
| Whatton | Public | Cat C Trainer |
| Whitemoor | Public | LTHSE |
| Winchester | Public | Local |
| Woodhill | Public | LTHSE |
| Wormwood | Public | Local |
| Wymott | Public | Cat C Trainer |

| | | |
|---|---|---|
| Lincoln | Public | Local |
| Liverpool | Public | Local |
| Norwich | Public | Local |
| Nottingham | Public | Local |
| Pentonville | Public | Local |
| Preston | Public | Local |
| Swansea | Public | Local |
| Thameside | Serco | Local |
| Wandsworth | Public | Local |
| Winchester | Public | Local |
| Wormwood | Public | Local |
| Peterborough | Sodexo | Local M/F |
| Aylesbury | Public | LTHSE |
| Belmarsh | Public | LTHSE |
| Frankland | Public | LTHSE |
| Full Sutton | Public | LTHSE |
| Garth | Public | LTHSE |
| Gartree | Public | LTHSE |
| Isle of Wight | Public | LTHSE |
| Long Lartin | Public | LTHSE |
| Manchester | Public | LTHSE |
| Swaleside | Public | LTHSE |
| Wakefield | Public | LTHSE |
| Whitemoor | Public | LTHSE |
| Woodhill | Public | LTHSE |
| Ford | Public | Open |
| Hatfield | Public | Open |
| Haverigg | Public | Open |
| Hollesley Bay | Public | Open |
| Kirkham | Public | Open |
| Kirklevington | Public | Open |
| Leyhill | Public | Open |
| North Sea Camp | Public | Open |
| Prescoed | Public | Open |
| Springhill | Public | Open |
| Standford Hill | Public | Open |
| Sudbury | Public | Open |
| Thorn Cross | Public | Open |
| Oakhill | G4S | STC |
| Cookham Wood | Public | YJB |
| Werrington | Public | YJB |
| Wetherby | Public | YJB M/F |
| Brinsford | Public | YOI |
| Deerbolt | Public | YOI |
| Feltham | Public | YOI |

"The recent MacAlister review of children's social care [tinyurl.com/y7mu4r4x] described Youth Offender Institutions (YOIs) and STCs as "wholly unsuitable" for accommodating children in the criminal justice system. The Ministry is reviewing its position on the remaining STC, Oakhill, and is also considering reopening another (Rainsbrook), while progressing a first secure school and seeking to improve YOIs.

"The Ministry and HMPPS urgently need a clear and convincing plan for youth custody options that can meet children's diverse and complex needs and help them escape a vicious cycle of reoffending. They say that their vision is to be more outcomes-led and to focus on early intervention, but we are concerned by the absence of a clear strategy for evaluating what works and for ensuring appropriate placements are available for children in custody."

## Types of prison and YOIs

The *PrisonOracle.com* website contains a comprehensive information page for each prison in the prison estate. The pages describe the types of prisoners that are held in each prison and the services which are provided to them, along with details of the latest reports on the prison and links to such things as its Facility List. and also details of deaths in custody within it.

**Adult male prisons**
Prisoner categories
Nominally, prisoners are assigned to a prison based on their personal security category. However, HMPPS may transfer a prisoner to another prison with a different security category at any time.

Adult male prisoners are assigned an alphabetical categorisation between A and D (where 'A' signifies highest risk and 'D' signifies lowest risk). The risk factors assessed when categorising an individual to a particular security category are the prisoner's risks of:
• escape or abscond;
• harm to the public;
• ongoing criminality in custody;

- violent or other behaviour in prison; and
- control issues that disrupt the security and good order of the prison.

### Types of prison

There are four types of prison for adult males prisoners:

**1. Training:** Category 'C' and Category 'B' 'training' prisons are designed to house offenders at their corresponding category. Some category 'C' training prisons are "resettlement prisons" which hold prisoners on shorter sentences to prepare them for release.

**2. Local:** holding those on short sentences, those awaiting trial or sentencing, and those awaiting allocation to another establishment.

**3. Open** prisons: housing category 'D' prisoners, considered to be lowest risk. Sometimes these are prisoners who have worked their way down the prisoner categories coming to the end of their sentence.

**4. High Security:** There are two types of high security prison. *'Core locals'* hold a high security population, as described above under the 'Local' heading who are awaiting trial but they can also hold sentenced Category 'A' prisoners.

*'Dispersal Prison'* spread Category 'A' prisoners to ensure that the most dangerous prisoners are not held in a single establishment.

### Reconfiguration

HMPPS is undertaking a project to reconfigure the adult male prison estate that aims to reduce surplus local prison places and increase Category B and C capacity and access to resettlement places to ensure there is a sufficient supply of suitable prison places to meet demand.

This project continues work started by the (now failed) Prison Estates Transformation Programme which originally set out to simplify and reorganise the prison estate into three models: reception, training and resettlement.

### Adult female prisons

There are 12 prisons in England and Wales which house adult female offenders. Two of the twelve operate as 'open' prisons (Askham Grange and East Sutton Park).. In a report published 26th July 2022 - see section 2.15 - The Justice Committee warned that limited progress has been made in developing alternatives to custodial sentences for women amid concerns that the female prison population may rise by a third in the next three years.

### Prisons for children and young adults

Young offenders are housed in three types of institution: 'Young Offender Institutions' (YOIs), 'Secure Training Centres' (see above) and 'Secure Children's Homes'. The Youth Custody Service (part of the Ministry of Justice) decides on the type of institution in which a young offender will be held.

YOIs house young male offenders aged between 15-17 and 18-20 in separate institutions. Secure Training Centres are institutions for children up to the age of 17. Secure Children's Homes are run by local authorities and house children aged 10-14. They are not part of the HMPPS estate, but places are commissioned by the Youth Custody Service.

The Prison Oracle pages on Youth Custody provides more information.

### Private sector prisons

There has been private sector involvement in the custodial detention system in England and Wales since 1970. The timeline below, updated from an Institute for Government research paper, which details the early history of private sector involvement in the prison estate:

### Timeline: Prison Privatisation 1970-2023

1970 Labour government contracts with Securicor for custody of immigration detainees

1987 Home affairs committee recommends private sector tendering of prisons

1991 Criminal Justice Act introduces competition into offender management services

1992 HMP Wolds, the U.K.'s first privately run prison opened. It closed in 2014 when it merged with HMP Everthorpe, next door, to become the publicly operated HMP Humber

1997 Conservative government announces its private finance initiative (PFI)

1997 New Labour government comes to power and adopts PFI approach

2000 Two privately run prisons are returned to the public sector

2003 Carter Review recommends NOMS

2004 National Offender Management Service (NOMS) is established

2010 Coalition government comes to power and pushes ahead with a policy of privatisation

2011 HMP Doncaster the first prison to be run on a payment by results basis

2011 HMP Birmingham becomes the first public sector prison to be privatised

2011 Coalition government announces competition for nine prisons

2012 HMP Oakwood opens managed by G4S - it is the first privately Designed, Constructed, Managed and Financed prison (DCMF).

2017 HMPPS replaces NOMS

2019 G4S contract to run HMP Birmingham cancelled

2019 Government says rebuilt Wellingborough and Glen Parva to be privately operated

2020 G4S announced as preferred bidder for Wellingborough

2020 Government announces four new prisons to be built; two in the north and two in the south

2022 HMP Five Wells, G4S, Wellingborough, opened February 2022.

2023 HMP Fosse Way is due to open in May 2023, managed by Serco, at Glen Parva, Leicestershire; its Director will be Wyn Jones.

## Which prisons are operated by the private sector?

There are 14 (soon to be 15) prisons in England and Wales that are managed by private sector companies. Three different companies operate these prisons: G4S (Altcourse, Five Wells, Oakwood, Parc and Rye Hill), Serco (Ashfield, Doncaster, Lowdham Grange, Dovegate, Thameside and Fosse Way (opening in 2023) and Sodexo (Bronzefield, Forest Bank, Northumberland and Peterborough).

Most privately managed prisons in England and Wales hold adult male prisoners. Only Bronzefield and Peterborough (female unit), which are both managed by Sodexo, are prisons for female prisoners.

Private sector prisons tend to be new and large. There are no open or high security private sector prisons whereas public prisons which are a mix of prisons of different size, age and functions.

## Age of the prison estate

There have been three major periods of prison construction during which the vast majority of the current prison estate was built: the Victorian era, the mid- 20th century and the turn of the 21st century. Around a third of the prison estate was built during the Victorian era. Victorian prisons tend to be 'purpose built'. Many Victorian prisons are located in town centres and many now function as 'local prisons'.

A little under a third of the prison estate dates from the mid-20th century (1940s-1970s). Whilst many of these buildings are 'purpose built', some have been repurposed, often from military bases or internment camps used during (or after) World War Two.

Around a quarter of the prison estate dates from the late 20th and early 21st century. These buildings tend to be 'purpose built'.

## £500 million boost to prison building

On 20th June 2022 the Government announced a £500 million boost to create thousands of new prison places, with new houseblocks to be built at six prisons - accommodating more than 2,600 prisoners.

Ministry of Justice and His Majesty's Prison and Probation Service, said this was a significant step in Government's £4 billion programme to build 20,000 new places – boosting public safety and making the streets safer. Thousands of new prison places will be built at prisons across England under this £500 million construction deal, announced by the then by Prisons Minister Victoria Atkins on 20th June 2022.

It was announced that construction companies Kier and Wates had been awarded contracts to lead an alliance of hundreds of small businesses in constructing the new houseblocks.

They will also build state-of-the-art workshops at the six locations - HMPs Bullingdon, Channings Wood, Elmley, Highpoint, Hindley and Wayland – which will add further momentum to the Government's drive to cut reoffending and crime by getting more ex-offenders into jobs.

This push, the Ministry of Justice said, has already seen the proportion of ex-prisoners employed 6 months after release increase by two-thirds (66 per cent) between April 2021 and March 2022.

Designed with security and rehabilitation in mind, the innovative design of the new houseblocks will include x-shaped buildings with wider landings to increase visibility of multiple wings – helping officers to maintain order. The designs will also mean easier access to supporting facilities such as additional healthcare and kitchens, promoting rehabilitation and helping prisoners to turn their lives around.

It is estimated that the construction of the houseblocks and refurbishment works will generate over 2,000 jobs through the construction phase and over 750 jobs within the new prison facilities.

## Prisons Inspectorate assessment of living conditions

The then Chief Inspector of Prisons, Peter Clarke, in his 2017-18 and 2018-19 annual reports said that conditions in these periods were some of the most disturbing and squalid the inspectorate had ever seen.

In his 2019-20 annual report, which dealt mainly with the period before the Covid-19 pandemic, Peter Clarke said that while some prisons had improved living conditions, conditions remained poor and overcrowded for many prisoners. He said too many prisoners were spending much of their lives locked in shared, overcrowded, insanitary cells.

The current Chief Inspector of Prisons, Charlie Taylor, in his 2021-22 annual report published in July 2022 again stated that the pandemic exacerbated some underlying problems and unacceptable conditions that inspections have previously criticised.

The Inspectorate reported:

*With few exceptions, we found prisoners living together in cramped conditions in cells designed for one occupant. This was particularly a problem given the extended periods of lock-up under the COVID-19 restrictions. (…) Many shared cells were just too small and had unscreened washing and toilet facilities. Regime restrictions meant that there was little opportunity to alleviate these pressures and use communal facilities, which were often more private. The design of some single cells also meant toilets were unscreened and sometimes next to beds.*

*We found the poorest accommodation in some of the older prisons, with Leicester, Pentonville and parts of Erlestoke among the worst. Cold, dark and shabby cells were often plagued by damp and cockroaches, leaking pipes and toilets, and broken or missing furniture and windows.*

**Measuring accommodation standards**

In April 2022 a Certified Prisoner Accommodation (CPA) Policy Framework was introduced that cancelled Prison Service Instruction 17 of 2012; you can view all current Policy Frameworks and other regulatory documents on *prisonoracle.com.*

Certification is the responsibility of the Prison Group Director (for Public Sector Prisons), Executive Directors (for Wales and YCS), Deputy Director (for Long Term High Security) or Head of Custodial Contracts (for contracted prisons) and cannot be delegated. In the CPA Policy Framework the term *Authorising Director* is used to represent these roles. The CPA Policy Framework sets out the minimum requirements for certification and the mandatory actions for Authorising Directors to ensure that all accommodation they are responsible for is properly certified.

It is a legal requirement under the Prison Act 1952 (section 14), the Prison Rules (Rule 26) and the Young Offender Institution Rules (Rule 22), that no cell shall be used for the confinement of a prisoner or young offender unless it is certified by an inspector that its size, lighting, heating, ventilation and fittings are adequate for health and that it allows the prisoner to communicate at any time with a prison officer. References to an inspector to be construed as references to an officer (not being an officer of the prison) acting on behalf of the Secretary of State, by virtue of the Prison Commissioners Dissolution Order 1963, SI 1963 No 597, art 3(2), Sch.1.

The CPA sets minimum standards for the certification of prison and YOI

accommodation. Accommodation must not be certified or used as sleeping accommodation unless the Authorising Director is satisfied that it meets these standards.

The table below sets out the required attributes for uncrowded and crowded accommodation.

| Requirement | Uncrowded accommodation | Crowded accommodation |
|---|---|---|
| Space to Sleep | Y | Y |
| Space to dress and undress | Y | Y |
| Washbasin | Y | Y |
| Space for circulation, movement and seating | Y | Y |
| Space to eat Meals | Y | Y |
| Storage space | Y | Amount subject to space available – fittings may be compacted or combined |
| Personal pursuits | Y | Subject to space |
| Use of WC | In private with full body screening and ventilation | Partial privacy screening is acceptable. Separate ventilation is not required. |

Uncrowded accommodation is defined as accommodation where its occupancy matches the Certified Normal Accommodation (CNA) figure provided upon certification.

Crowded accommodation is defined as accommodation where its occupancy is required to exceed the CNA (i.e. 2 prisoners sharing a cell with a CNA of 1 or, more rarely, 3 prisoners sharing a cell with a CNA of 2).

**Sanitation**

Prisoners must have 24 hour a day access to sanitation and, where in-cell sanitation is provided, be able to use it with at least some privacy from other prisoners. Where there is no integral sanitation in the cell or room, there must be a process in place to allow the prisoner to access communal facilities 24 hours a day, and this process must be identified on the cell certificate.

**Lighting**

Electric lighting must be installed and functional, and there must be natural light. For the purposes of certification, the Authorising Director can assume that lighting and windows were designed to the standards which prevailed at the time of the original build and/or any subsequent major refurbishment. The standard is met if:
a. The diffuser is not damaged or defaced such that it would significantly reduce light output.
b. All lighting including the night-light can be switched on and off.
c. There is an external window in the cell or room.

**Heating**

A heating system must be installed and fully functional. It should not lead to the overheating of individual cells during warm weather. For the purposes of certification, the

Authorising Director can assume that this was designed to the standards which prevailed at the time of the original build and/or any subsequent major refurbishment.

The standard is met if:

a. The heat emitter (pipe coil [with or without shroud], radiator, radiant panel or under-floor heating) is clear from obstructions (but note that beds and lockers that have been fitted adjacent to radiator pipes can be disregarded); and:

b. The heating system operates when required. Where this can only be physically checked during the 'heating season', records that the building's heating system operated during the previous heating season are sufficient for certification outside of this period.

## Ventilation

The accommodation must be adequately ventilated and must not be certified if inadequate ventilation is likely to put health at risk (i.e. the risk of transmission of airborne disease). If visual inspection shows signs of mould growth and dampness on walls and other surfaces, before certifying the accommodation the Authorising Director should seek advice from Prison Maintenance Group (or equivalent in privately managed prisons), taking into account whether the previous occupant had blocked air vents or whether the cell has been recently subjected to flooding. Otherwise, the standard is met if:

a. For accommodation with openable windows: the windows open and close.

b. For accommodation with fixed window ventilators: the perforated grilles operate correctly between open and closed positions.

c. For accommodation with a separate ventilator through the wall: the perforated grille is clear and, where fitted with an integral fan, the fan operates.

d. For accommodation with mechanical extract ventilation: the extract system is operating (this can be checked by holding a sheet of A4 paper close to the grille - it should remain stuck to the grille by the suction of the extract).

## Fittings

Requirements for cell furniture are set out at Annex A of the National Standard for the Cleanliness and Physical Decency of Prisons, alongside other resources for Clean and Decent Prisons. Authorising Directors must have systems in place to fulfil these requirements before certifying the accommodation for use.

Other services which may be found in some cells, such as in-cell power, IT, telephony, TV or radio aerial outlets, showers, and in-cell fire detection, do not form part of the cell certification process but may be subject to other requirements. For further information on these or any other accommodation standard issues, please contact MoJ Property Directorate Technical Standards at:

moj_ed_technicalstandards@justice.gov.uk.

## Communication with an officer

There must be a functional mechanism for attracting the attention of staff, and this must provide both a visual and audible means of alert. The standard is met if either:

a. The prisoner is not confined to their cell or room, for example in open prison accommodation, or

b. A cell call system is installed and operating sufficiently well to be capable of attracting the attention of staff.

Certification is a legal requirement under Section 14 of the Prison Act 1952 that must be completed for all prison and young offender institution accommodation before it can be used to confine prisoners overnight.

The CPA Policy Framework avoids specific measurements or cell dimensions. It states that the Accommodation Standard (contained in Annex A of the CPA) sets out minimum requirements for certification and, "in summary" all accommodation must:

• Be of adequate size for the maximum number of prisoners it will hold.

• Have adequate lighting, heating, ventilation and fittings.

• Have 24-hour access to water and sanitation.

• Allow prisoners to communicate at any time with a prison officer.

There are however also international human rights standards for accommodation in prison. The UN Standard Minimum Rules for the Treatment of Prisoners and the European Prison Rules both include expectations that prisoners' accommodation should be clean, well ventilated, that prisons should have enough space and that they should have access to private WC facilities. Both sets of standards expect single occupancy cells to be the norm.

The European Committee for the Prevention of Torture and Inhuman Degrading Treatment or Punishment (CPT) has published minimum standards for living space per prisoner:

• 6m² of living space for a single-occupancy cell plus sanitary facility

• 4m² of living space per prisoner in a multiple-occupancy cell plus fully- partitioned sanitary facility

• at least 2m between the walls of the cell at least 2.5m between the floor and the ceiling of the cell.

## Background: Maintenance of prisons

Prior to 2012, prison maintenance of public sector prisons was managed by HMPPS (then NOMS). Private sector prisons have always managed their own maintenance contracts.

In 2012, Mitie was awarded the contract for prison facility management of HMP Brixton. Mitie later took over the provision of facilities management at two other sites. In June 2015, the facility management of the rest of the public-sector prison estate was contracted out. Amey won the contracts for the North of England, the Midlands and Wales; Carillion won the contracts for London and the South of England.

Following the liquidation of Carillion in January 2018 the Government set up 'Gov Facility Services Ltd', a government owned company, to manage the contracts in London and the South of England. This, in effect, brought the maintenance of these prisons back into the public sector.

## Performance of maintenance contracts

The National Audit Office (NAO), in January 2020, reported that HMPPS had failed to achieve the expected savings of £79 million by contracting-out to Amey and Carillion. It also reported that providers' performance against targets had been below HMPPS's expectations. It said that for the two areas which have the biggest impact on prison maintenance – high-priority planned and reactive maintenance jobs – they did not meet HMPPS's expectations.

HMPPS has recognised concerns regarding the quality of service being provided by facility management companies. Its 2019-20 annual report stated that it had acted to strengthen contract management arrangements for the facilities management contracts.

## Costs of Maintenance

The Government in 2018 stated that prison service maintenance contracts had not delivered the savings they had anticipated owing to an underestimation of historical costs. The NAO said that HMPPS did not have a clear picture of facilities management services in prisons before outsourcing the service, commenting that its approach contained common mistakes made in first- generation outsourcing.

The Ministry of Justice in November 2019 estimated the size of the priority maintenance backlog as £900 million. The Ministry said that a figure for each individual establishment was not available and would represent disproportionate cost to obtain.

The cost of the backlog had increased from around £750m in 2018. The Ministry explained that the cost increases each year owning largely to degradation of an aging estate. The then Justice Secretary in October 2019 said that 500 places a year would be lost due to dilapidation if investment was not made. In March 2021 the Public Accounts Committee described the backlog of maintenance work at an estimated £1 billion as 'eye-watering'.

## IMPORTANT CHANGES: SENDING IN MONEY AND GIFTS

Since 26th August 2021 no-one send money to a prisoner by bank transfer, cheque, postal order or send cash by post – but instead use the free and fast online service at the website address below to send money to someone in prison.

**https://www.gov.uk/send-prisoner-money**

If you cannot use the online service, you may be able to apply for an exemption at the following website address:

*https://send-money-to-prisoner.service.gov.uk/help/apply-for-exemption/*

if you:
• are unable to use a computer, a smart phone or the internet
• do not have a debit card

This will allow you to send money by post.

Prisoners can buy permitted books from Ministry of Justice Approved Book Retailers – Prisons Org UK, publishers of The Prisons Handbook, are an MOJ approved retailer which means we can source and send books in to prisoners for you.

Just email *books@prisons.org.uk* with full details of the books you want to order (title, author, ISBN) along with full details of the inmate you want them sent to (full name, prison number and name of the prison) we will source the books for you, send you a secure link for payment and then send the books you have ordered and paid for direct to the prisoner.

## New ID rules for visitors' entry to prisons
### Management of Security at Visits

Visits must be well managed, monitored, and where necessary due to suspected or proven inappropriate behaviour, terminated to maintain the good order and discipline of the prison.

All visitors to prisons in England and Wales, other than accompanied children under the age of 16, whether visiting for social, or official purposes, must be required to prove their identity before entry.

On 26th August 2021, a new list of acceptable ID was issued that defines the accepted forms of ID when visiting a prison in England and Wales.

Visitors under the age of 16 must be

accompanied by an adult, who must adhere to the ID requirement set out below. The accompanying adult has responsibility for the child, supporting the child's relationship with the prisoner, and for giving assurances of the child's identity.

To gain entry to the prison for a family visit you may use any one form of ID from List A.

If you are unable to do this, you can use one document from List B together with one document from List C.

If you are unable to produce any forms of ID from these lists, you may still be able to apply for entry under exceptional circumstances. You are likely to be turned away from the prison if you are unable to produce any of the required ID documents at the time of your visit, or if you have not made arrangements with the prison, prior to your visit.

## 1. List A

- *passports*
- *identity cards from an EU or European Economic Area (EEA) country*
- *UK photocard driving licences*
- *EU or EEA driving licences*
- *NI Electoral identity cards*
- *a US passport card*
- *a proof of age card recognised under PASS with a unique reference number (This includes the Citizen ID card)*
- *an armed forces identity card*
- *a UK biometric residence permit (BRP)*

## 2. List B

*One form of ID from this list, together with list C.*
- *a Home Office travel document (convention travel document, stateless person's document, one-way document or certificate of travel)*
- *an older person's bus pass*
- *a Freedom Pass*
- *a proof of age card recognised under the Proof of Age Standards Scheme (PASS) without a unique reference number (please refer to List A where a unique reference number is present)*

## 3. List C

*One form of ID from this list, together with list B.*
- *a birth or adoption certificate*
- *an education certificate from a regulated and recognised educational institution (such as an NVQ, SQA, GCSE, A level or degree certificate)*
- *a rental or purchase agreement for a residential property (signed and dated)*
- *a marriage or civil partnership certificate*
- *a bank, building society or credit union current account card (on which the claimed identity is shown)*

## 4. Exceptional Circumstances

If you do not have access to the above listed ID, you may still be able to attend a visit with *advanced permission* from the prison. Please contact the prison direct to arrange this.

The following documents are examples of acceptable forms of identification for Professional Visitors – such as lawyers:

*1. Members of either House of Parliament: Houses of Parliament ID card or HMG ID cards;*

*2. Legal advisers: Identification document from the above List A, or from Lists B and C. This must be in conjunction with either a. a headed document from their legal practice stating that they are representing the prisoner they are requesting to visit, or b. should they not yet be representing the prisoner, a headed document from their legal practice explaining the purpose of the visit;*

*3. Police, UK Border Agency and HM Revenue & Customs officers: warrant card;*

*4. Probation and Youth Offending Team officers: probation / YOT department ID card;*

*5. Staff from other prisons, HQ, the Children's & Young People's Secure Estate, the inspectorates (including Lay Observers) or Home Office: photo security pass issued by (or on behalf of) Ministry of Justice, HMPPS, or Home Office;*

*6. Consular officials: consular ID card;*

*7. Other public officials: departmental or local authority pass or ID card (but must show the name of the visitor and the name of the department or local authority);*

*8. Social workers: social worker identification cards;*

*9. Researchers: Security Photo pass or official letter (visits must be pre-arranged); and*

*10. Healthcare staff: NHS photographic identification badge/card or independent sector healthcare photographic identification badge/card.*

The prison estate in England and Wales, including public and contracted prisons and secure training centres. Revised September 2022

HM Prison & Probation Service

| Prison | HMPPS Region | Operator | Predominant Function | Cohort of Prisoners Held | Designation | Notes | Postal Address | Telephone | Probation Service Region | Expected Resettlement Region |
|---|---|---|---|---|---|---|---|---|---|---|
| ALTCOURSE (HMP & YOI) | #N/A | G4S | Reception | #N/A | Dual Designated Prison | #N/A | Higher Lane, Liverpool L9 7LH | (0151) 522 2000 | Region B - North West | Region B - North West Region L - Greater Manchester National Resource |
| ASHFIELD (HMP) | #N/A | Serco | Cat C | #N/A | Prison | #N/A | Shortwood Road, Pucklechurch, Bristol BS16 9QJ | (0117) 303 8000 | Region G - South West | National Resource |
| ASKHAM GRANGE (HMP & YOI) | #N/A | PSP | Female | #N/A | Dual Designated Prison | #N/A | Main Street, Askham Richard, York YO23 3FT | (01904) 772 000 | Region C - Yorkshire and Humberside | National Resource |
| AYLESBURY (HMYOI) | South Central Group | PSP | YOI | #N/A | Dual Designated Prison | Age limit increased to 27 (inclusive) from Nov 21 | Bierton Road, Aylesbury HP20 1EH | (01296) 444 000 | Region H - South Central | National Resource |
| BEDFORD (HMP & YOI) | #N/A | PSP | Reception | #N/A | Dual Designated Prison | #N/A | St Loyes Street, Bedford MK40 1HG | (01234) 373 000 | Region I - East of England | Region I - East of England |
| BELMARSH (HMP & YOI) | #N/A | PSP | High Security | #N/A | Dual Designated Prison | #N/A | Belmarsh Road, London SE28 0EB | (020) 8334 4400 | Region J - London | Region J - London National Resource (Reception A) |
| BERWYN (HMP & YOI) | #N/A | PSP | Cat C | #N/A | Dual Designated Prison | #N/A | HMP Berwyn, Bridge Road, Wrexham Industrial Estate, Wrexham LL13 9QE | (01978) 523 000 | Region D - Wales | Region D - Wales National Resource (Trainer) |
| BIRMINGHAM (HMP) | #N/A | PSP | Reception | #N/A | Prison | #N/A | Winson Green Road, Birmingham B18 4AS | (0121) 345 2500 | Region E - West Midlands | Region E - West Midlands |
| BRINSFORD (HMP & YOI) | #N/A | PSP | YOI | #N/A | Dual Designated Prison | #N/A | New Road, Featherstone, Wolverhampton WV10 7PY | (01902) 533 450 | Region E - West Midlands | Region E - West Midlands |
| BRISTOL (HMP & YOI) | #N/A | PSP | Reception | #N/A | Dual Designated Prison | #N/A | 19 Cambridge Road, Bristol BS7 8PS | (0117) 372 3100 | Region G - South West | Region G - South West |
| BRIXTON (HMP) | #N/A | PSP | Cat C | #N/A | Prison | #N/A | Jebb Avenue, London SW2 5XF | (020) 8588 6000 | Region J - London | Region J - London |
| BRONZEFIELD (HMP & YOI) | #N/A | Sodexo | Female | #N/A | Dual Designated Prison | #N/A | Woodthorpe Road, Ashford TW15 3JZ | (01784) 425 690 | Region K - Kent, Surrey and Sussex | Region K - Kent, Surrey and Sussex Region J - London Region H - South Central National Resource |
| BUCKLEY HALL (HMP) | #N/A | PSP | Cat C | #N/A | Prison | #N/A | Buckley Farm Lane, Rochdale OL12 9DP | (01706) 514 300 | Region L - Greater Manchester | National Resource |
| BULLINGDON (HMP & YOI) | #N/A | PSP | Reception | #N/A | Dual Designated Prison | #N/A | Patrick Haugh Road, Arncott, Bicester OX25 1PZ | (01869) 353 100 | Region H - South Central | Region H - South Central |
| BURE (HMP) | #N/A | PSP | Cat C | #N/A | Prison | #N/A | Jaguar Drive, Bardersfield, Norwich NR10 5GB | (01603) 326 000 | Region I - East of England | National Resource |
| CARDIFF (HMP & YOI) | #N/A | PSP | Reception | #N/A | Dual Designated Prison | #N/A | Knox Road, Cardiff CF24 0UG | (029) 2092 3100 | Region D - Wales | Region D - Wales |

| Prison | HMPPS Region | Operator | Predominant Function | Cohort of Prisoners Held | Designation | Notes | Postal Address | Telephone | Probation Service Region | Expected Resettlement Region |
|---|---|---|---|---|---|---|---|---|---|---|
| CHANNINGS WOOD (HMP) | #N/A | PSP | Cat C | #N/A | Prison | #N/A | Denbury, Newton Abbot TQ12 6DW | (01803) 814 600 | Region G - South West | Region G - South West |
| CHELMSFORD (HMP & YOI) | #N/A | PSP | Reception | #N/A | Dual Designated Prison | #N/A | 200 Springfield Road, Chelmsford CM2 6LQ | (01245) 552 000 | Region I - East of England | Region I - East of England |
| COLDINGLEY (HMP) | #N/A | PSP | Cat C | #N/A | Prison | #N/A | Shaftesbury Road, Bisley, Woking GU24 9EX | (01483) 344 300 | Region K - Kent, Surrey and Sussex | Region K - Kent, Surrey and Sussex National Resource (Trainer) |
| COOKHAM WOOD (HMYOI) | #N/A | PSP | YJB | #N/A | Young Offender Institution | #N/A | Sir Evelyn Road, Rochester ME1 3LU | (01634) 202 500 | Region K - Kent, Surrey and Sussex | National Resource |
| DARTMOOR (HMP) | #N/A | PSP | Cat C | #N/A | Prison | #N/A | Princetown, Yelverton PL20 6RO | (01822) 322 000 | Region G - South West | National Resource |
| DEERBOLT (HMYOI) | Tees and Wear Group | PSP | YOI | #N/A | Dual Designated Prison | #N/A | Bowes Road, Barnard Castle DL12 9BG | (01833) 633 200 | Region A - North East | National Resource |
| DONCASTER (HMP & YOI) | #N/A | Serco | Reception | #N/A | Dual Designated Prison | #N/A | Marshgate, Doncaster DN5 8UX | (0808) 196 8814 | Region C - Yorkshire and Humberside | Region C - Yorkshire and Humberside |
| DOVEGATE (HMP) | #N/A | Serco | Cat B | #N/A | Prison | #N/A | Uttoxeter ST14 8XR | (01283) 829 400 | Region E - West Midlands | Region E - West Midlands National Resource (Trainer) |
| DOWNVIEW (HMP & YOI) | #N/A | PSP | Female | #N/A | Dual Designated Prison | #N/A | Sutton Lane, Sutton SM2 5PD | (020) 8196 6300 | Region J - London | Region J - London National Resource |
| DRAKE HALL (HMP & YOI) | #N/A | PSP | Female | #N/A | Dual Designated Prison | #N/A | Eccleshall, Stafford ST21 6LQ | (01785) 774 100 | Region E - West Midlands | Region E - West Midlands National Resource |
| DURHAM (HMP & YOI) | #N/A | PSP | Reception | #N/A | Dual Designated Prison | #N/A | Old Elvet, Durham DH1 3HU | (0191) 332 3400 | Region A - North East | Region A - North East |
| EAST SUTTON PARK (HMP & YOI) | #N/A | PSP | Female | #N/A | Dual Designated Prison | #N/A | Sutton Valence, Maidstone ME17 3DF | (01622) 785 000 | Region K - Kent, Surrey and Sussex | National Resource |
| EASTWOOD PARK (HMP & YOI) | #N/A | PSP | Female | #N/A | Dual Designated Prison | #N/A | Eastwood Park, Falfield, Wotton-Under-Edge GL12 8DB | (01454) 382 100 | Region G - South West | Region G - South West Region E - West Midlands Region H - South Central Region D - Wales |
| ELMLEY (HMP & YOI) | #N/A | PSP | Reception | #N/A | Dual Designated Prison | #N/A | Church Road, Eastchurch, Sheerness ME12 4DZ | (01795) 802 000 | Region K - Kent, Surrey and Sussex | Region K - Kent, Surrey and Sussex National Resource (Trainer) |
| ERLESTOKE (HMP & YOI) | #N/A | PSP | Cat C | #N/A | Dual Designated Prison | #N/A | Erlestoke, Devizes SN10 5TU | (01380) 814 250 | Region G - South West | Region G - South West Region H - South Central National Resource (Trainer) |
| EXETER (HMP & YOI) | #N/A | PSP | Reception | #N/A | Dual Designated Prison | #N/A | New North Road, Exeter EX4 4EX | (01392) 415 650 | Region G - South West | Region G - South West |
| FEATHERSTONE (HMP) | #N/A | PSP | Cat C | #N/A | Prison | #N/A | Featherstone, Wolverhampton WV10 7PU | (01902) 703 000 | Region E - West Midlands | Region E - West Midlands National Resource (Trainer) |

| Prison | HMPPS Region | Operator | Predominant Function | Cohort of Prisoners Held | Notes | Designation | Postal Address | Telephone | Probation Service Region | Expected Resettlement Region |
|---|---|---|---|---|---|---|---|---|---|---|
| FELTHAM (HMYOI) | #N/A | PSP | YOI | #N/A | #N/A | Young Offender Institution | Bedfont Road, Feltham TW13 4ND | (020) 8844 5000 | Region J - London | Region J - London |
| FIVE WELLS (HMP & YOI) | #N/A | G4S | Cat C | #N/A | #N/A | Dual Designated Prison | Millers Park, Doddington Rd, Wellingborough NN8 2NH | (01933) 718 888 | Region I - East of England | Region I - East of England Region F - East Midlands Region E - West Midlands Region H - South Central |
| FORD (HMP) | #N/A | PSP | Open | #N/A | #N/A | Prison | Ford Road, Arundel BN18 0BX | (01903) 663 000 | Region K - Kent, Surrey and Sussex | National Resource |
| FOREST BANK (HMP & YOI) | #N/A | Sodexo | Reception | #N/A | #N/A | Dual Designated Prison | Forest Bank, Swinton, Manchester M27 8FB | (0161) 925 7000 | Region L - Greater Manchester | Region L - Greater Manchester |
| FOSTON HALL (HMP & YOI) | #N/A | PSP | Female | #N/A | #N/A | Dual Designated Prison | Foston, Derby DE65 5DN | (01283) 584 300 | Region F - East Midlands | Region F - East Midlands |
| FRANKLAND (HMP) | #N/A | PSP | High Security | #N/A | #N/A | Prison | Brasside, Durham DH1 5YD | (0191) 376 5000 | Region A - North East | National Resource |
| FULL SUTTON (HMP) | #N/A | PSP | High Security | #N/A | #N/A | Prison | Full Sutton, York YO41 1PS | (01759) 475 100 | Region C - Yorkshire and Humberside | National Resource |
| GARTH (HMP) | #N/A | PSP | Cat B | #N/A | #N/A | Prison | Ulnes Walton lane, Leyland PR26 8NE | (01772) 443 300 | Region B - North West | National Resource |
| GARTREE (HMP) | #N/A | PSP | Cat B | #N/A | #N/A | Prison | Gartree, Market Harborough LE16 7RP | (01858) 426 600 | Region F - East Midlands | National Resource |
| GRENDON (HMP) | South Central Group | PSP | Cat B | #N/A | #N/A | Prison | Grendon Underwood, Aylesbury HP18 0TL | (01296) 445 000 | Region H - South Central | National Resource |
| SPRING HILL (HMP) | South Central Group | PSP | Open | #N/A | Category D | Prison | Grendon Underwood, Aylesbury HP18 0TL | (01296) 445 000 | Region H - South Central | National Resource |
| GUYS MARSH (HMP) | #N/A | PSP | Cat C | #N/A | #N/A | Prison | Shaftesbury SP7 0AH | (01747) 856 400 | Region G - South West | Region G - South West National Resource (Trainer) |
| HATFIELD (HMP & YOI) | #N/A | PSP | Open | #N/A | #N/A | Dual Designated Prison | Thorne Road, Hatfield, Doncaster DN7 6EL | (01405) 746 500 | Region C - Yorkshire and Humberside | National Resource |
| HAVERIGG (HMP) | #N/A | PSP | Open | #N/A | #N/A | Prison | North Lane, Haverigg, Millom LA18 4NA | (01229) 713 000 | Region B - North West | National Resource |
| HEWELL (HMP) | #N/A | PSP | Reception | #N/A | #N/A | Prison | Hewell Lane, Redditch B97 6QS | (01527) 785 000 | Region E - West Midlands | Region E - West Midlands |
| HIGH DOWN (HMP & YOI) | #N/A | PSP | Cat C | Trainer & Resettlement | Category C or lower | Dual Designated Prison | Highdown Lane, Sutton SM2 5PJ | (020) 7147 6300 | Region J - London | Region J - London Region K - Kent, Surrey and Sussex National Resource (Trainer) |
| HIGHPOINT (HMP) | #N/A | PSP | Cat C | #N/A | #N/A | Prison | Highpoint, Stradishall, Newmarket CB8 9YG | (01440) 743 100 | Region I - East of England | Region I - East of England Region J - London National Resource (Trainer) |
| HINDLEY (HMP & YOI) | #N/A | PSP | Cat C | #N/A | #N/A | Dual Designated Prison | Gibson Street, Bickershaw, Wigan WN2 5TH | (01942) 663 100 | Region L - Greater Manchester | Region L - Greater Manchester Region B - North West National Resource (Trainer) |

| Prison | HMPPS Region | Operator | Predominant Function | Cohort of Prisoners Held | Designation | Notes | Postal Address | Telephone | Probation Service Region | Expected Resettlement Region |
|---|---|---|---|---|---|---|---|---|---|---|
| HOLLESLEY BAY (HMP & YOI) | #N/A | PSP | Open | #N/A | Dual Designated Prison | #N/A | Rectory Road, Hollesley, Woodbridge IP12 3JW | (01394) 412 400 | Region 1 - East of England | National Resource |
| HOLME HOUSE (HMP & YOI) | #N/A | PSP | Cat C | #N/A | Dual Designated Prison | #N/A | Holme House Road, Stockton-on-Tees TS18 2QU | (01642) 744 000 | Region A - North East | Region A - North East National Resource (Trainer) |
| HULL (HMP & YOI) | #N/A | PSP | Reception | #N/A | Dual Designated Prison | #N/A | Hedon Road, Hull HU9 5LS | (01482) 282 200 | Region C - Yorkshire and Humberside | Region C - Yorkshire and Humberside National Resource (Trainer) |
| HUMBER (HMP) | #N/A | PSP | Cat C | #N/A | Prison | #N/A | 4 Sands Lane, Everthorpe, Brough, East Yorkshire. HU15 2JZ HU15 2JZ | (01430) 273 000 | Region C - Yorkshire and Humberside | Region C - Yorkshire and Humberside National Resource (Trainer) |
| HUNTERCOMBE (HMP) | #N/A | PSP | Cat C | #N/A | Prison | #N/A | Huntercombe Place, Nuffield, Henley-on-Thames RG9 5SB | (01491) 643 100 | Region H - South Central | National Resource |
| ISIS HMP/YOI | #N/A | PSP | Cat C | #N/A | Dual Designated Prison | #N/A | Western Way, London SE28 0NZ | (020) 3356 4000 | Region J - London | Region J - London National Resource |
| ISLE OF WIGHT (HMP & YOI) | #N/A | PSP | Cat B | #N/A | Dual Designated Prison | #N/A | 55 Parkhurst Road, Newport PO30 5RS | (01983) 556 300 | Region H - South Central | National Resource |
| KIRKHAM (HMP) | #N/A | PSP | Open | #N/A | Prison | #N/A | Freckleton Road, Kirkham, Preston PR4 2RN | (01772) 675 400 | Region B - North West | National Resource |
| KIRKLEVINGTON GRANGE (HMP & YOI) | #N/A | PSP | Open | #N/A | Dual Designated Prison | #N/A | Kirklevington, Yarm TS15 9PA | (01642) 792 600 | Region A - North East | National Resource |
| LANCASTER FARMS (HMP) | #N/A | PSP | Cat C | #N/A | Prison | #N/A | Stone Row Head, Lancaster LA1 3QZ | (01524) 563 450 | Region B - North West | Region B - North West |
| LEEDS (HMP) | #N/A | PSP | Reception | #N/A | Prison | #N/A | Gloucester Terrace, Armley, Leeds LS12 2TJ | (0113) 203 2600 | Region C - Yorkshire and Humberside | Region C - Yorkshire and Humberside |
| LEICESTER (HMP) | #N/A | PSP | Reception | #N/A | Prison | #N/A | 116 Welford Road, Leicester LE2 7AJ | (0116) 228 3000 | Region F - East Midlands | Region F - East Midlands |
| LEWES (HMP & YOI) | #N/A | PSP | Reception | #N/A | Dual Designated Prison | #N/A | 1 Brighton Road, Lewes BN7 1EA | (01273) 785 100 | Region K - Kent, Surrey and Sussex | Region K - Kent, Surrey and Sussex |
| LEYHILL (HMP) | #N/A | PSP | Open | #N/A | Prison | #N/A | Wotton-Under-Edge GL12 8BT | (01454) 264 000 | Region G - South West | National Resource |
| LINCOLN (HMP & YOI) | #N/A | PSP | Reception | #N/A | Dual Designated Prison | #N/A | Greetwell Road, Lincoln LN2 4BD | (01522) 663 000 | Region F - East Midlands | Region F - East Midlands |
| LINDHOLME (HMP) | #N/A | PSP | Cat C | #N/A | Prison | #N/A | Lindholme, Doncaster DN7 6EE | (01302) 524 700 | Region C - Yorkshire and Humberside | National Resource |
| LITTLEHEY (HMP) | #N/A | PSP | Cat C | #N/A | Prison | #N/A | Perry, Huntingdon PE28 0SR | (01480) 333 000 | Region 1 - East of England | National Resource |
| LIVERPOOL (HMP) | #N/A | PSP | Reception | #N/A | Prison | #N/A | 68 Hornby Road, Liverpool L9 3DF0 | (0151) 530 4000 | Region B - North West | Region B - North West |

| Prison | HMPPS Region | Operator | Predominant Function | Cohort of Prisoners Held | Designation | Notes | Postal Address | Telephone | Probation Service Region | Expected Resettlement Region |
|---|---|---|---|---|---|---|---|---|---|---|
| LONG LARTIN (HMP) | #N/A | PSP | High Security | #N/A | Prison | #N/A | South Littleton, Evesham WR11 8TZ | (01386) 295 100 | Region E - West Midlands | National Resource |
| LOW NEWTON (HMP & YOI) | #N/A | PSP | Female | #N/A | Dual Designated Prison | #N/A | Brasside, Durham DH1 5YA | (0191) 376 4000 | Region A - North East | Region A - North East National Resource |
| LOWDHAM GRANGE (HMP) | #N/A | Serco | Cat B | #N/A | Prison | #N/A | Lowdham, Nottingham NG14 7DA | (0115) 966 9200 | Region F - East Midlands | National Resource |
| MAIDSTONE (HMP) | #N/A | PSP | Cat C | #N/A | Prison | #N/A | 36 County Road, Maidstone ME14 1UZ | (01622) 775 300 | Region K - Kent, Surrey and Sussex | National Resource |
| MANCHESTER (HMP & YOI) | #N/A | PSP | Cat B | #N/A | Dual Designated Prison | #N/A | Southhall Street, Manchester M6 9AH | (0161) 817 5600 | Region L - Greater Manchester | National Resource |
| MOORLAND (HMP & YOI) | #N/A | PSP | Cat C | #N/A | Dual Designated Prison | #N/A | Bawtry Road, Hatfield Woodhouse, Doncaster DN7 6BW | (01302) 523 000 | Region C - Yorkshire and Humberside | Region C - Yorkshire and Humberside National Resource (Trainer) |
| MORTON HALL (HMP) | #N/A | PSP | Cat C | #N/A | Prison | #N/A | Swinderby, Lincoln LN6 9PT | (01522) 666 700 | Region I - East of England | National Resource |
| THE MOUNT (HMP) | #N/A | PSP | Cat C | #N/A | Prison | #N/A | Molyneaux Avenue, Bovingdon, Hemel Hempstead HP3 0NZ | (01442) 836 300 | Region I - East of England | Region I - East of England National Resource (Trainer) |
| NEW HALL (HMP & YOI) | #N/A | PSP | Female | #N/A | Dual Designated Prison | #N/A | New Hall Way, Flockton, Wakefield WF4 4XX | (01924) 803 000 | Region C - Yorkshire and Humberside | Region C - Yorkshire and Humberside National Resource |
| NORTH SEA CAMP (HMP) | #N/A | PSP | Open | #N/A | Prison | #N/A | Croppers Lane, Freiston, Boston PE22 0QX | (01205) 769 300 | Region F - East Midlands | National Resource |
| NORTHUMBERLAND (HMP) | #N/A | Sodexo | Cat C | #N/A | Prison | #N/A | Acklington, Morpeth NE65 9XG | (01670) 382 100 | Region A - North East | Region A - North East National Resource (Trainer) |
| NORWICH (HMP & YOI) | #N/A | PSP | Reception | #N/A | Dual Designated Prison | #N/A | Knox Road, Norwich NR1 4LU | (01603) 708 600 | Region I - East of England | Region I - East of England National Resource (Trainer) |
| NOTTINGHAM (HMP & YOI) | #N/A | PSP | Reception | #N/A | Dual Designated Prison | #N/A | 112 Perry Road, Nottingham NG5 3AG | (0115) 872 4000 | Region F - East Midlands | Region F - East Midlands |
| OAKHILL (STC) | Secure Training Centre | G4S | STC | | Secure Training Centre | | Chalgrove Field, Oakhill, Milton Keynes MK5 6AJ | (01908) 866 000 | NA | National Resource |
| OAKWOOD (HMP) | #N/A | G4S | Cat C | #N/A | Prison | #N/A | Featherstone, Wolverhampton WV10 7QD | (01902) 799 700 | Region E - West Midlands | Region E - West Midlands National Resource (Trainer) |
| ONLEY (HMP) | #N/A | PSP | Cat C | #N/A | Prison | #N/A | Willoughby, Rugby CV23 8AP | (01788) 523 400 | Region I - East of England | Region I - East of England Region J - London National Resource (Trainer) |

| Prison | HMPPS Region | Operator | Predominant Function | Cohort of Prisoners Held | Designation | Notes | Postal Address | Telephone | Probation Service Region | Expected Resettlement Region |
|---|---|---|---|---|---|---|---|---|---|---|
| PARC (HMP & YOI) | #N/A | G4S | Cat C | #N/A | Dual Designated Prison | #N/A | Heol Hopcyn John, Coity, Bridgend CF35 6AP | (01656) 300 200 | Region D - Wales | Region D - Wales / National Resource (Trainer) |
| PENTONVILLE (HMP & YOI) | #N/A | PSP | Reception | #N/A | Dual Designated Prison | #N/A | Caledonian Road, London N7 8TT | (020) 7023 7000 | Region J - London | Region J - London |
| PETERBOROUGH (HMP & YOI) | Privately Managed Prisons | Sodexo | Reception | #N/A | Dual Designated Prison | #N/A | Saville Road, Peterborough PE3 7PD | (01733) 217 500 | Region I - East of England | Region I - East of England / Region F - East Midlands |
| PETERBOROUGH FEMALE (HMP & YOI) | | | Reception | Reception & Resettlement | Dual Designated Prison | Female prisoners suitable for closed conditions or lower | | | | |
| PORTLAND (HMPYOI) | #N/A | PSP | Cat C | #N/A | Dual Designated Prison | #N/A | The Grove, Grove Road, Portland DT5 1DL | (01305) 715 600 | Region G - South West | Region G - South West / National Resource (Trainer) |
| PRESTON (HMP & YOI) | #N/A | PSP | Reception | #N/A | Dual Designated Prison | #N/A | Ribbleton Lane, Preston PR1 5AB | (01772) 444 550 | Region B - North West | Region B - North West |
| RANBY (HMP) | #N/A | PSP | Cat C | #N/A | Prison | #N/A | Retford DN22 8EU0 | (01777) 862 000 | Region F - East Midlands | Region F - East Midlands / National Resource (Trainer) |
| RISLEY (HMP) | #N/A | PSP | Cat C | #N/A | Prison | #N/A | Warrington Road, Risley, Warrington WA3 6BP | (01925) 733 000 | Region L - Greater Manchester | Region L - Greater Manchester |
| ROCHESTER (HMP & YOI) | #N/A | PSP | Cat C | #N/A | Dual Designated Prison | #N/A | Rochester ME1 3QS | (01634) 803 100 | Region K - Kent, Surrey and Sussex | Region K - Kent, Surrey and Sussex / National Resource (Trainer) |
| RYE HILL (HMP) | #N/A | G4S | Cat B | #N/A | Prison | #N/A | Onley Park, Willoughby, Rugby CV23 8SZ | (01788) 523 300 | Region I - East of England | National Resource |
| SEND (HMP) | #N/A | PSP | Female | #N/A | Prison | #N/A | Ripley Road, Send, Woking GU23 7LJ | (01483) 471 000 | Region K - Kent, Surrey and Sussex | Region K - Kent, Surrey and Sussex / Region H - South Central / National Resource |
| STAFFORD (HMP) | #N/A | PSP | Cat C | #N/A | Prison | #N/A | 54 Gaol Road, Stafford ST16 3AW | (01785) 773 000 | Region E - West Midlands | National Resource |
| STANDFORD HILL (HMP & YOI) | #N/A | PSP | Open | #N/A | Dual Designated Prison | #N/A | Church Road, Eastchurch, Sheerness ME12 4AA | (01795) 884 500 | Region K - Kent, Surrey and Sussex | National Resource |
| STOCKEN (HMP) | #N/A | PSP | Cat C | #N/A | Prison | #N/A | Stocken Hall Road, Stretton, Oakham LE15 7RD | (01780) 795 100 | Region F - East Midlands | National Resource |
| STOKE HEATH (HMPYOI) | #N/A | PSP | Cat C | #N/A | Dual Designated Prison | #N/A | Market Drayton TF9 2JL | (01630) 636 000 | Region E - West Midlands | Region E - West Midlands / National Resource (Trainer) |
| STYAL (HMP & YOI) | #N/A | PSP | Female | #N/A | Dual Designated Prison | #N/A | Styal Road, Wilmslow SK9 4HR | (01625) 553 000 | Region L - Greater Manchester | Region L - Greater Manchester / National Resource |
| SUDBURY (HMP & YOI) | #N/A | PSP | Open | #N/A | Dual Designated Prison | #N/A | Sudbury, Ashbourne DE6 5HW | (01283) 584 000 | Region F - East Midlands | National Resource |

| Prison | HMPPS Region | Operator | Predominant Function | Cohort of Prisoners Held | Designation | Notes | Postal Address | Telephone | Probation Service Region | Expected Resettlement Region |
|---|---|---|---|---|---|---|---|---|---|---|
| SWALESIDE (HMP) | #N/A | PSP | Cat B | #N/A | Prison | #N/A | Church Road, Eastchurch, Sheerness ME12 4AX | (01795) 804 100 | Region K - Kent, Surrey and Sussex | National Resource |
| SWANSEA (HMP & YOI) | #N/A | PSP | Reception | #N/A | Dual Designated Prison | #N/A | 200 Oystermouth Road, Swansea SA1 3SR | (01792) 485 300 | Region D - Wales | Region D - Wales |
| SWINFEN HALL (HMP & YOI) | #N/A | PSP | Cat C | #N/A | Dual Designated Prison | #N/A | Swinfen, Lichfield WS14 9QS | (01543) 484 000 | Region E - West Midlands | National Resource |
| THAMESIDE (HMP & YOI) | #N/A | Serco | Reception | #N/A | Dual Designated Prison | #N/A | Griffin Manor Way, London SE28 0FJ | (020) 8317 9777 | Region J - London | Region J - London |
| THORN CROSS (HMP & YOI) | #N/A | PSP | Open | #N/A | Dual Designated Prison | #N/A | Arley Road, Appleton, Warrington WA4 4RL | (01925) 805 100 | Region B - North West | National Resource |
| USK | HMPPS Wales | PSP | Cat C | Trainer & Resettlement | Dual Designated Prison | Category C or lower | 47 Maryport Street, USK NP15 1XP | (01291) 671 600 | Region D - Wales | Region D - Wales National Resource (Trainer) |
| PRESCOED (HMP & YOI) | | | Open | | | Category D only / Young Offenders suitable for open conditions | | | | National Resource |
| THE VERNE (HMP) | #N/A | PSP | Cat C | #N/A | Prison | #N/A | Portland DT5 1EQ | (01305) 825 000 | Region G - South West | National Resource |
| WAKEFIELD (HMP) | #N/A | PSP | High Security | #N/A | Prison | #N/A | 5 Love Lane, Wakefield WF2 9AG | (01924) 612 000 | Region C - Yorkshire and Humberside | National Resource |
| WANDSWORTH (HMP & YOI) | #N/A | PSP | Reception | #N/A | Dual Designated Prison | #N/A | PO Box 757, London SW18 3HS | (020) 8588 4000 | Region J - London | Region J - London |
| WARREN HILL (HMP & YOI) | #N/A | PSP | Cat C | #N/A | Dual Designated Prison | #N/A | Rectory Road, Hollesley, Woodbridge IP12 3JW | (01394) 633 400 | Region I - East of England | Region I - East of England National Resource (Trainer) |
| WAYLAND (HMP) | #N/A | PSP | Cat C | #N/A | Prison | #N/A | Griston, Thetford IP25 6RL | (01953) 804 100 | Region I - East of England | Region I - East of England National Resource (Trainer) |
| WEALSTUN (HMP) | #N/A | PSP | Cat C | #N/A | Prison | #N/A | Walton Road, Wetherby LS23 7AZ | (01937) 444 400 | Region C - Yorkshire and Humberside | Region C - Yorkshire and Humberside National Resource (Trainer) |
| WERRINGTON (HMYOI) | #N/A | PSP | YJB | #N/A | Young Offender Institution | #N/A | Werrington, Stoke-on-Trent ST9 0DX | (01783) 463 300 | Region E - West Midlands | National Resource |
| WETHERBY (HMYOI) | #N/A | PSP | YJB | #N/A | Young Offender Institution | #N/A | York Road, Wetherby LS22 5ED | (01937) 544 200 | Region C - Yorkshire and Humberside | National Resource |
| WHATTON (HMP) | #N/A | PSP | Cat C | #N/A | Prison | #N/A | New Lane, Whatton, Nottingham NG13 9FQ | (01949) 803 200 | Region F - East Midlands | National Resource |
| WHITEMOOR (HMP) | #N/A | PSP | High Security | #N/A | Prison | #N/A | Longhill Road, March PE15 0PR | (01354) 602 350 | Region I - East of England | National Resource |
| WINCHESTER (HMP & YOI) | #N/A | PSP | Reception | #N/A | Dual Designated Prison | #N/A | Romsey Road, Winchester SO22 5DF | (01962) 723 000 | Region H - South Central | Region H - South Central Region G - South West |

| Prison | HMPPS Region | Operator | Predominant Function | Cohort of Prisoners Held | Designation | Notes | Postal Address | Telephone | Probation Service Region | Expected Resettlement Region |
|---|---|---|---|---|---|---|---|---|---|---|
| WOODHILL (HMP & YOI) | Long Term & High Security | PSP | Cat B | Trainer & Reception | Dual Designated Prison | #N/A | Tattenhoe Street, Milton Keynes MK4 4DA | (01908) 722 000 | Region H - South Central | National Resource |
| WORMWOOD SCRUBS (HMP & YOI) | #N/A | PSP | Reception | #N/A | Dual Designated Prison | #N/A | Du Cane Road, London W12 0AE | (020) 8588 3200 | Region J - London | Region J - London |
| WYMOTT (HMP & YOI) | #N/A | PSP | Cat C | #N/A | Dual Designated Prison | #N/A | Ulnes Walton Lane, Leyland PR26 8LW | (01772) 442 000 | Region B - North West | National Resource |

**Probation Service Regions**

| | |
|---|---|
| Region A - North East | Region G - South West |
| Region B - North West | Region H - South Central |
| Region C - Yorkshire and Humberside | Region I - East of England |
| Region D - Wales | Region J - London |
| Region E - West Midlands | Region K - Kent, Surrey and Sussex |
| Region F - East Midlands | Region L - Greater Manchester |

**Key**

| Cat | Category (see next page) |
|---|---|
| Dual Designated Site | If a prison holds prisoners in the YOI (18-20) and Adult (21+) age range category, in separate accommodation it is classed |
| PSR | Probation Service Region |
| PSP | Public Sector Prison |
| STC | Secure Training Centre |
| YJB | Youth Justice Board |
| YOI | Young Offender Institution |

**Summary**

There are 119 prisons and YOIs, of which 14 are operated by the contracted sector.

In addition there is one STC, that is operated by the contracted sector.

Each description represents a cohort type within a prisons function; a prison can have more than one cohort in their prison and this is reflected in each Population Specification.
In times of population pressure all prisons would be expected to accept prisoners who are next best fit to allow reception prisons to service the courts.

| Function (Type) | Description |
|---|---|
| Foreign National Hub | Sentenced offenders who are subject to immigration proceedings by the Home Office with more than 3 months and less than 30 months to serve to conditional release date. |
| Local Foreign National Hub | Local Hubs hold men of interest to the Home Office on remand or those serving less than 3 months |
| Children | Holds boys under the age of 18 both on remand and sentenced, appropriately allocated using YCS placing principles. |
| Local (female estate) | Holds female adult and Young Offenders on remand. Appropriately allocates on all offenders depending on interventions required, sentence length and Probation Service Region. |
| Resettlement (Female Estate) | Receives offenders categorised for closed conditions for the last period of custody for resettlement purposes and release into correct Probation Service Region subject to security review and capacity. |
| Resettlement Open (Female Estate) | As a national resource, receives adults and Young Offenders from closed prisons following suitability assessment for open conditions, including indeterminate offenders recommended for open conditions by the Parole Board. |
| Trainer (Female Estate) | Holds sentenced female adults and Young Offenders. Appropriately allocates on all offenders depending on interventions required, sentence length, and home Probation Service Region. |
| Reception (Adult Male and YOI) | A reception prison's main function is to serve the courts, holding people on remand and convicted unsentenced. |
| Resettlement | A resettlement prison holds Cat C offenders who have more than 28 days but equal to or less than 16 months time left to serve at the point of transfer from a reception prison. |
| Cat C (Adult Male and YOI Closed) | Resettlement prisons will also accept men transferring from the training estate when they have more than 10 months but equal to or less than 24 months time left to serve at the point of transfer. Transfers with less than 10 months time left to serve must be agreed with the POMs (Prison Offender Manager) at both establishments prior to transfer (including the COM (Community Offender Manager) if appointed). |
| Training | A Cat C training prison is a national resource and holds offenders with more than 16 months time left to serve at the point of transfer. |
| Cat C (Adult Male and YOI Closed) | Once offenders have spent at least 6 months in the training estate, and have between 10 months and 24 months time left to serve, they can transfer to a Resettlement Prison in the appropriate Probation Service Region. If transferring with less than 10 months time left to serve transfers must be in liaison with the POM (Prison Offender Manager) at both establishments (including the COM (Community Offender manager) if appointed). |
| | Includes Indeterminate Sentenced Prisoners. |
| Trainer | As a national resource, and part of the LT&HSE (Long Term & High Security Estate), Cat B training prisons population comprises offenders who have been categorised B and who have more than 28 days time left to serve at the point of transfer, including indeterminate sentence offenders. |
| Cat B (Adult Male and YOI Closed) (including Dispersal A/B) | The LT&HSE estate is made up of two different types of training prisons, these are Cat B Trainer and Cat A & B Trainer (Dispersal). When allocating into the LT&HSE, consideration should be given to the level of threat & risk each prisoner poses to the public. Those who are deemed the most risk to the public based on offence profile, age and significant time left to serve should be directed to the Cat A & B Trainer (Dispersal) prisons. |
| Cat B Specialist Units (Adult Male and YOI Closed) | As a national resource and part of the LT&HSE the Specialist Units in this establishment holds anyone deemed appropriate following specific referral into these units. Allocations for these units is co-ordinated by LTHSE centrally. |
| Resettlement Open (Adult Male and YOI Open) | A resettlement Cat D prison holds offenders who have more than 28 days but equal to or less than 36 months time left to serve. Transfers outside this timeframe may be necessary at times of population pressures or in agreement with the receiving establishment. |
| Cat D (Adult Male and YOI Open) | Transfers with more than 36 months time left to serve must be in agreement with the PGD |
| Probation Service Region - Geographical Location of the Prison | All prisons have a geographical location which dictates which Probation Service Region they're in. This column states which Probation Service Region the prison is located in, but does not necessarily dictate where or if the prisons will resettle into. For Example, an open prison will sit in the geographical location of a Probation Service Region, however, they are still a National Resource and can resettle men to any area. |
| Probation Service Regions - Expected Resettlement Region and/or National Resource | This column indicates where the prisons are expected to resettle. Resettlement services are no longer limited to specific areas due to the changes made by Probation Reform. Where prisons are a National Resource or have an expected resettlement area, this has been indicated in this column (some prisons have more than one expected resettlement area and/ or due to multiple cohorts within the same prison, may also include National Resource). |

# 2023 Prisons Map

## Public Sector Prisons North

### Cumbria & Lancashire
Prison Group Director:
John Illingsworth

HMP Haverigg
HMP Kirkham
HMP Lancaster Farms
HMP & YOI Preston
HMP & YOI Wymott

### East Midlands
PGD: Paul Cawkwell

HMP Leicester
HMP/YOI Lincoln
HMP Morton Hall
HMP North Sea Camp
HMP Onley
HMP Whatton

### Yorkshire
Prison Group Director:
Helen Judge

HMP/YOI Hatfield
HMP/YOI Hull
HMP Humber
HMP Leeds
HMP Lindholme
HMP/YOI Moorland
HMP Wealstun

### Greater Manchester, Merseyside & Cheshire
Prison Group Director:
Tim Allen

HMP Buckley Hall
HMP/YOI Hindley
HMP Liverpool
HMP Risley
HMP/YOI Thorn Cross

### West Midlands
Prison Group Director:
Teresa Clarke

HMP Birmingham
HMP/YOI Brinsford
HMP Featherstone
HMP Hewell
HMP Stafford
HMP/YOI Stoke Heath
HMP/YOI Swinfen Hall

### North East
Prison Group Director
Susan Howard

HMYOI Deerbolt
HMP Durham
HMP Holme House
HMP Kirklevington Grange

### North Midlands
Prison Group Director:
Alison Clarke

HMP/YOI Nottingham
HMP Ranby
HMP Stocken
HMP & YOI Sudbury

### Women
Prison Group Director:
Pia Sinha

HMP/YOI Drake Hall
HMP/YOI Downview &
HMP/YOI East Sutton Park
HMP/YOI Eastwood Park
HMP/YOI Foston Hall
HMP/YOI Low Newton
HMP/YOI Send
HMP/YOI Styal
HMP/YOI New Hall &
HMP/YOI Askham Grange

### Wales
Prison Group Director:
Giles Mason

HMP Berwyn
HMP/YOI Cardiff
HMP/YOI Swansea
HMP Usk &
HMP/YOI Prescoed

Contracted:
HMP/YOI Parc (YP)

### Youth Custody Service
Executive Director:
Helga Swidenbank

#### Public Youth Custody Estate

Group Director-Youth Custody:
Cathy Robinson

HMYOI Cookham Wood
HMYOI Feltham
Medway STC
HMYOI Werrington
HMYOI Wetherby

#### Contracted Youth Custody Estate

Deputy Director of Contracts:
Fiona Parker (interim)
Rainsbrook STC
Oakhill STC

#### Secure Children's Home
Adel Beck
Aldine House
Aycliff
Barton Moss
Clayfields House
Hillside
Lincolnshire
Vinney Green

### Contracted
Head of Custodial
Contracts: Neil Richards

HMP/YOI Altcourse
HMP Ashfield
HMP/YOI Bronzefield (F)
HMP/YOI Doncaster
HMP Dovegate
HMP Five Wells
HMP Fosse Way
HMP/YOI Forest Bank
HMP Lowdham Grange
HMP Northumberland
HMP Oakwood
HMP/YOI Peterborough (M/F)
HMP Rye Hill
HMP Thameside

## Public Sector Prisons South

### Avon & South Dorset
Prison Group Director:
Paul Woods

HMP Bristol
HMP Leyhill
HMP/YOI Portland
HMP The Verne

### Bedfordshire, Cambridgeshire & Norfolk
Prison Group Director:
Gary Monaghan

HMP & YOI Bedford
HMP Bure
HMP Littlehey
HMP & YOI Norwich
HMP Wayland

### Devon & North Dorset
Prison Group Director:
Jeannine Hendrick

HMP Channings Wood
HMP Dartmoor
HMP/YOI Exeter
HMP Guys Marsh

### South Central
Prison Group Director:
Andy Lattimore

HMP/YOI Bullingdon
HMP Erlestoke
HMP Grendon/Springhill
HMP Winchester

### Hertfordshire, Essex & Suffolk Group
Prison Group Director:
Simon Cartwright

HMP Chelmsford
HMP Highpoint
HMP & YOI Hollesley Bay
HMP The Mount
HMP & YOI Warren Hill

### Kent, Surrey & Sussex
Prison Group Director:
James Lucas

HMP Coldingley
HMP/YOI E\lmley
HMP Ford
HMP Lewes
HMP/YOI Rochester
HMP Standford Hill

### London
Prison Group Director:
Ian Bickers

HMP Brixton
HMP & YOI High Down
HMP/YOI Isis
HMP/YOI Pentonville
I IMP Wandsworth
HMP/YOI Wormwood Scrubs

### Immigration & Foreign National Prisons
*Prisons now absorbed into regional prison groups*

HMP Huntercombe (FNP)
*South Central*
HMP Maidstone (FNP)
*Kent, Surrey & Sussex*
IRC Morton Hall *East Midlands*

### Long Term/High Security
Prison Group Directors
Will Styles (South)
Gavin O'Malley (North)

HMYOI Aylesbury
HMP/YOI Belmarsh
HMP Frankland
HMP Full Sutton
HMP Garth
HMP Gartree
HMP Isle of Wight
HMP Long Lartin
HMP/YOI Manchester
HMP Swaleside
HMP Wakefield
HMP Whitemoor
HMP/YOI Woodhill

# 2023
# Prisons Map

**COMBINATIONS & CLUSTERS**
Acklington and Castington = HMP Northumberland
Albany and Parkhurst = HMP Isle of Wight
Sheppey Cluster = HMPs Elmley, Standford Hill & Swaleside
Wolds and Everthorpe = HMP Humber

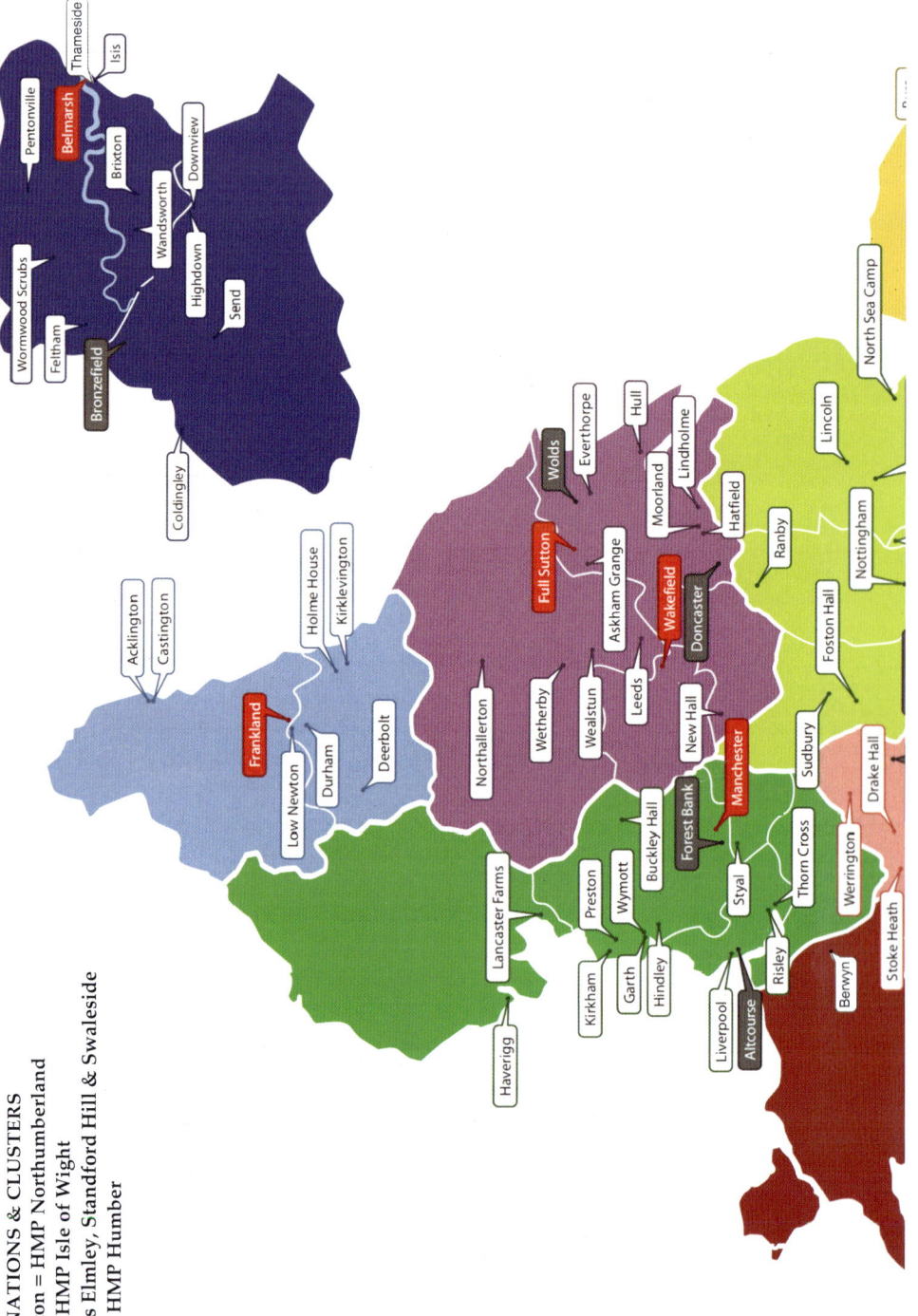

Bure
Norwich
Hollesley Bay
Warren Hill
Chelmsford
Sheppey Cluster
Highpoint South
Maidstone
Highpoint North
North Sea Camp
Wayland
Whitemoor
Lewes
East Sutton Park
Peterborough
Rochester
Lincoln
Morton Hall
Stocken
Littlehey
Bedford
The Mount
Cookham Wood
High Down
Downview
Ford
Woodhill
Aylesbury
Nottingham
Whatton
Gartree
Winchester
Foston Hall
Leicester
Five Wells Prison
Rye Hill
Grendon/Springhill
Fosse Way
Onley
Lowdham Grange
Sudbury
Bullingdon
Huntercombe
Isle of Wight Cluster
Drake Hall
Dovegate
Birmingham
Long Lartin
Leyhill
Erlestoke
The Verne
Thorn Cross
Swinfen Hall
Oakwood
Eastwood Park
Ashfield
Werrington
Hewell
Guys Marsh
Stoke Heath
Brinsford
Featherstone
Usk/Prescoed
Portland
Stafford
Channings Wood
Berwyn
Bristol
Cardiff
Parc
Exeter
Swansea
Dartmoor

# CEO, DG and Director Structure

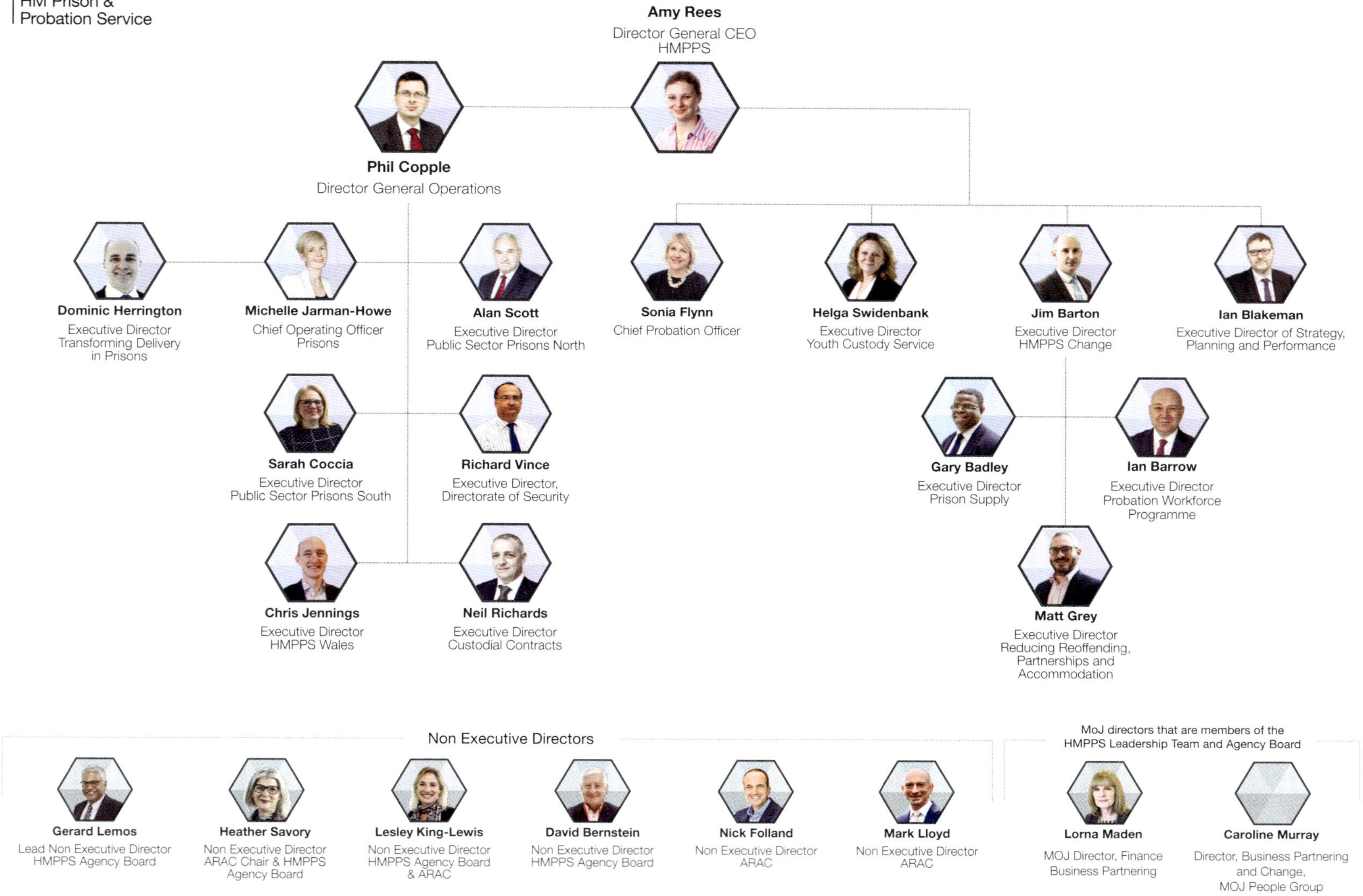

HM Prison & Probation Service

**Amy Rees**
Director General CEO HMPPS

**Phil Copple**
Director General Operations

**Dominic Herrington**
Executive Director Transforming Delivery in Prisons

**Michelle Jarman-Howe**
Chief Operating Officer Prisons

**Sarah Coccia**
Executive Director Public Sector Prisons South

**Chris Jennings**
Executive Director HMPPS Wales

**Alan Scott**
Executive Director Public Sector Prisons North

**Richard Vince**
Executive Director, Directorate of Security

**Neil Richards**
Executive Director Custodial Contracts

**Sonia Flynn**
Chief Probation Officer

**Helga Swidenbank**
Executive Director Youth Custody Service

**Jim Barton**
Executive Director HMPPS Change

**Gary Badley**
Executive Director Prison Supply

**Matt Grey**
Executive Director Reducing Reoffending, Partnerships and Accommodation

**Ian Blakeman**
Executive Director of Strategy, Planning and Performance

**Ian Barrow**
Executive Director Probation Workforce Programme

## Non Executive Directors

**Gerard Lemos**
Lead Non Executive Director HMPPS Agency Board

**Heather Savory**
Non Executive Director ARAC Chair & HMPPS Agency Board

**Lesley King-Lewis**
Non Executive Director HMPPS Agency Board & ARAC

**David Bernstein**
Non Executive Director HMPPS Agency Board

**Nick Folland**
Non Executive Director ARAC

**Mark Lloyd**
Non Executive Director ARAC

MoJ directors that are members of the HMPPS Leadership Team and Agency Board

**Lorna Maden**
MOJ Director, Finance Business Partnering

**Caroline Murray**
Director, Business Partnering and Change, MOJ People Group

## KEY OFFICIALS: 1st September 2022

*(c) = HMPPS Controller*

| Prison | Governor/Director |
|---|---|
| Altcourse | Sarah Elliott (c) |
| Altcourse | Steve Williams |
| Ashfield | Eryl Drew (c) |
| Ashfield | Martin Jones |
| Askham Grange | Julia Spence |
| Aylesbury | Mark Allen |
| Bedford | PJ Butler |
| Belmarsh | Jenny Louis |
| Berwyn | Nick Leader |
| Birmingham | Paul Newton |
| Brinsford | Amanda Hughes |
| Bristol | Vanessa Prendergast |
| Brixton | Sonia Brooks (Interim) |
| Bronzefield | Gary Crossly (c) |
| Bronzefield | Ian Whiteside |
| Buckley Hall | Robbie Durgan |
| Bullingdon | Laura Sapwell |
| Bure | Simon Rhoden |
| Cardiff | Amanda Corrigan |
| Channings Wood | Huw Sullivan |
| Chelmsford | Garry Newnes |
| Coldingley | Niall Bryant |
| Cookham Wood | Simon Drysdale |
| Dartmoor | Steve Mead |
| Deerbolt | Andy Hudson |
| Doncaster | Karen Serdet (c) |
| Doncaster | John Hewitson |
| Dovegate | Sarai Kam (c) |
| Dovegate | Mark Hanson |
| Downview | Amy Dixon |
| Drake Hall | Carl Hardwick |
| Durham | Phil Husband |
| East Sutton Park | Amy Dixon |
| Eastwood Park | Zoe Short |
| Elmley | Andy Davy |
| Erlestoke | Tim Knight |
| Exeter | Richard Luscombe |
| Featherstone | Laura Whitehurst |
| Feltham | Natasha Wilson |
| Five Wells | Lynne Hardy (c) |
| Five Wells | John McLaughlin |
| Ford | Graham Spencer |
| Forest Bank | Mohammed Elmugadam (c) |
| Forest Bank | Jonathan French |
| Foston Hall | Helen Clayton-Hoar |
| Frankland | Darren Finley |
| Full Sutton | Gareth Sands |
| Garth | Andy Lund |
| Gartree | Babafemi Dada |
| Grendon/Spring Hill | Becky Hayward |
| Guys Marsh | Ian Walters |
| Hatfield | Mick Mills |
| Haverigg | Adam Connolly |
| Hewell | Ralph Lubkowski |
| High Down | Emily Martin |
| Highpoint | Nigel Smith |
| Hindley | Natalie McKee |
| Hollesley Bay | David Daddow |
| Holme House | Sean Ormerod |
| Hull | Shaun Mycroft |
| Humber | Marcella Goligher |
| Huntercombe | David Redhouse |
| Isis | Emily Thomas |
| Isle of Wight | Dougie Graham |
| Kirkham | Alli Black |
| Kirklevington Grange | Rebecca Newby |
| Lancaster Farms | Pete Francis |
| Leeds | Simon Walters |
| Leicester | Jim Donaldson |
| Lewes | Hannah Lane |
| Leyhill | Steve Hodson |
| Lincoln | Matt Spencer |
| Lindholme | Rob Kellett |
| Littlehey | Olivia Phelps |
| Liverpool | Mark Livingston |
| Long Lartin | Steve Cross |
| Low Newton | Rob Young |
| Lowdham Grange | Trudy McCaffery (c) |
| Lowdham Grange | Martin Booth |
| Maidstone | Dawn Mauldon |
| Manchester | Rob Knight |
| Medway STC | (now closed - Secure School being constructed on site) |
| Moorland | Jennifer Willis |
| Morton Hall | Karen Head |
| New Hall | Julia Spence |
| North Sea Camp | Colin Hussey |
| Northumberland | Mark Johnstone (c) |
| Northumberland | Samantha Pariser |
| Norwich | Declan Moore |
| Nottingham | Paul Yates |
| Oakwood | Andy Walls (c) |
| Oakwood | Sean Oliver |
| Onley | Matthew Tilt |
| Parc | Janet Wallsgrove |
| Pentonville | Ian Blakeman |
| Peterborough | Hayley Folland (c) |
| Peterborough | Damian Evans |
| Portland | Rob Luxford |
| Preston | Dan Cooper |
| Ranby | Andy Sleight |
| Risley | Nicki Smith |
| Rochester | Dean Gardiner |
| Rye Hill | Mick Mullen (c) |
| Rye Hill | Peter Small |
| Send | Mark Creaven |
| Stafford | Ian West |
| Standford Hill | Gary Price |
| Stocken | Neil Thomas |
| Stoke Heath | John Huntington |
| Styal | Michelle Quirk |
| Sudbury | Craig Smith |
| Swaleside | Mark Icke |
| Swansea | Brian Ward |
| Swinfen Hall | Mark Greenhaf |
| Thameside | John Hyde (c) |
| Thameside | David Bamford |

| | |
|---|---|
| The Mount | Paul Crossey |
| The Verne | David Bourne |
| Thorn Cross | Richard Suttle |
| Usk/Prescoed | Rob Denman |
| Wakefield | Tom Wheatley |
| Wandsworth | Katie Price |
| Warren Hill | Dave Nicholson |
| Wayland | Ali Barker |
| Wealstun | Diane Lewis |
| Werrington | Keith Attwood |
| Wetherby | Pete Cormley |
| Whatton | Caroline Vine |
| Whitemoor | Ruth Stephens |
| Winchester | James Bourke |
| Woodhill | Nicola Marfleet |
| Wormwood Scrubs | Amy Frost |
| Wymott | Graham Beck |

## PRISONS: DIRECTORS
**Director General Prisons:** Phil Copple
**COO Prisons:** Michelle Jarman-Howe
**Deputy Director Prisons:** Ed Cornmell
**Public Sector South:** Sarah Coccia
**Public Sector North: Alan Scott**

## PRISON GROUPS & DIRECTORS
1. Avon, South Dorset & Wiltshire
2. Beds, Cambs & Norfolk
3. Cumbria & Lancashire
4. Custodial Contracts
5. Devon & North Dorset
6. East Midlands
7. Gtr Manchester, Mersey & Cheshire
8. Herts, Essex & Suffolk
9. IRC & FNP
10. Kent, Surrey & Sussex
11. London
12. Long Term High Security Estate
13. North East
14. North Midlands
15. South Central
16. Wales
17. West Midlands
18. Women's Directorate
19. Yorkshire
20. Young People

## 1 Avon & South Dorset
Prison Group Director: Paul Woods
HMP Bristol
HMP Leyhill
HMP/YOI Portland
HMP The Verne

## 2 Bedfordshire, Cambridgeshire & Norfolk
Prison Group Director: Gary Monaghan
HMP & YOI Bedford
HMP Bure
HMP Littlehey
HMP & YOI Norwich
HMP Wayland

## 3 Cumbria & Lancashire
Prison Group Director: John Illingsworth
HMP Haverigg
HMP Kirkham
HMP Lancaster Farms
HMP & YOI Preston
HMP & YOI Wymott

## 4 Custodial Contracts Group
Head of Custodial Contracts: Neil Richards
HMP/YOI Altcourse
HMP Ashfield
HMP/YOI Bronzefield (F)
HMP/YOI Doncaster
HMP Dovegate
HMP/YOI Forest Bank
HMP Fosse Way (Opens May 2023)
HMP Lowdham Grange
HMP Northumberland
HMP Oakwood
HMP/YOI Peterborough (M/F)
HMP Rye Hill
HMP Thameside

## 5 Devon & North Dorset
Prison Group Director: Jeannine Hendrick
HMP Channings Wood
HMP Dartmoor
HMP/YOI Exeter
HMP Guys Marsh

## 6 East Midlands
Prison Group Director: Paul Cawkwell
HMP Leicester
HMP/YOI Lincoln
HMP North Sea Camp
HMP Onley
HMP Whatton

## 7 Greater Manchester, Merseyside & Cheshire
Prison Group Director: Tim Allen
HMP Buckley Hall
HMP/YOI Hindley
HMP Liverpool
HMP Risley
HMP/YOI Thorn Cross

## 8 Hertfordshire, Essex & Suffolk Group
Prison Group Director: Simon Cartwright
HMP Chelmsford
HMP Highpoint
HMP & YOI Hollesley Bay
HMP The Mount
HMP & YOI Warren Hill

## 9 Immigration & Foreign National Prisons
*Prisons now absorbed into regional prison groups*
HMP Huntercombe (FNP) *South Central*
HMP Maidstone (FNP) *Kent, Surrey & Sussex*
IRC Morton Hall *East Midlands*

**10 Kent, Surrey & Sussex**
Prison Group Director: James Lucas
HMP Coldingley
HMP/YOI Elmley
HMP Ford
HMP Lewes
HMP/YOI Rochester
HMP Standford Hill

**11 London**
Prison Group Director: Ian Bickers
HMP Brixton
HMP & YOI High Down
HMP/YOI Isis
HMP/YOI Pentonville
HMP Wandsworth
HMP/YOI Wormwood Scrubs

**12 Long Term High Security**
Prison Group Director: Will Styles (South)
Prison Group Director: Gavin O'Malley (North)
HMP Aylesbury (S)
HMP Belmarsh (S)
HMP Isle of Wight (S)
HMP Long Lartin (S)
HMP Swaleside (S)
HMP Whitemoor (S)
HMP Woodhill (S)
HMP Frankland (N)
HMP Full Sutton (N)
HMP Garth (N)
HMP Gartree (N)
HMP Manchester (N)
HMP Wakefield (N)

**13 North East**
Prison Group Director: Susan Howard
HMYOI Deerbolt
HMP Durham
HMP Holme House
HMP Kirklevington Grange

**14 North Midlands**
Prison Group Director: Alison Clarke
HMP/YOI Nottingham
HMP Ranby
HMP Stocken
HMP & YOI Sudbury

**15 South Central**
Prison Group Director: Andy Lattimore
HMP/YOI Bullingdon
HMP Erlestoke
HMP Grendon/Springhill
HMP Huntercombe
HMP Winchester

**16 Wales**
Prison Group Director: Giles Mason
HMP/YOI Cardiff

HMP/YOI Swansea
HMP Usk
HMP & YOI Prescoed
HMP & YOI Parc

**17 West Midlands**
Prison Group Director: Teresa Clarke
HMP Birmingham
HMP/YOI Brinsford
HMP Featherstone
HMP Hewell
HMP Stafford
HMP/YOI Stoke Heath
HMP/YOI Swinfen Hall

**18 Women's Directorate**
Director Women HMPPS: Pia Sinha
HMP/YOI Drake Hall
HMP/YOI Downview
HMP/YOI East Sutton Park
HMP/YOI Eastwood Park
HMP/YOI Foston Hall
HMP/YOI Low Newton
HMP/YOI Send
HMP/YOI Styal
HMP/YOI New Hall
HMP/YOI Askham Grange

**19 Yorkshire**
Prison Group Director: Helen Judge
HMP/YOI Hatfield
HMP/YOI Hull
HMP Humber
HMP Leeds
HMP Lindholme
HMP/YOI Moorland
HMP Wealstun

**20 Young People**
Executive Director: Helga Swidenbank
Public Youth Custody Estate Group
PGD Young People: Heather Whitehead
HMYOI Cookham Wood
HMYOI Feltham
Medway STC
HMYOI Werrington
HMYOI Wetherby

## PRIVATE SECTOR PRISON CONTRACTORS 2023

**G4S JUSTICE SERVICES**
105 VICTORIA STREET
LONDON SW1E 6QT
Tel: +44 (0)208 770 7000
Email: info@uk.g4s.com

**SERCO**
ENTERPRISE HOUSE
11 BARTLEY WOOD BUSINESS PARK

BARTLEY WAY
HOOK
HAMPSHIRE RG27 9XB
T: +44 (0)1256 745900  F: +44 (0)1256 744111
E: generalenquiries@serco.com

**SODEXO JUSTICE SERVICES**
1 SOUTHAMPTON ROW
LONDON WC1B 5HA
Tel: 020 7404 0110
Email: enquiries@sodexojusticeservices.com

# OTHER UNITED KINGDOM PRISON ADDRESSES

**SCOTTISH PRISON SERVICE HEADQUARTERS:**
SCOTTISH PRISON SERVICE
CALTON HOUSE
5 REDHEUGHS RIGG
EDINBURGH. EH12 9HW
http://www.sps.gov.uk/
General Enquiries
gaolinfo@sps.pnn.gov.uk
Tel. 0131 330 3500 (HQ switchboard)
Media Enquiries spsnews@sps.pnn.gov.uk
Tel. 0131 330 3606/3609 (media only)
(out of hours contact 07919303290)

The Scottish Prison Service (SPS) is an agency of the Scottish Government and was established in April 1993. The SPS Framework Document sets out the policy and resources framework set by Scottish Ministers within which the SPS operates. As an Executive Agency, the SPS is funded by the Scottish Government.

In line with the Framework Document, the SPS sets out its business objectives in the three year Corporate Plan for the current period 2019-2022 and an annual Delivery Plan which is published in the spring of each year.

*Our Principal Activities*
The SPS is a public service-led delivery agency which is legally required to deliver custodial and rehabilitation services for those sent to it by the courts. The SPS continues to deliver a range of operational services that contribute to the strategic outcomes, objectives and policies of the Scottish Government.

Our principal objective is to contribute to making Scotland Safer by Protecting the Public and Reducing Reoffending. The SPS aims to achieve this by ensuring delivery of secure custody, safe and ordered prisons, decent standards of care and opportunities for prisoners to develop in a way that help them reintegrate into the community on release.

To support this objective, SPS agrees a service framework with each public sector prison and also manages private sector providers.
*www.sps.gov.uk/Corporate/Prisons/Prisons.aspx*
There are 13 publicly managed prisons and two privately managed prisons (HMP Kilmarnock and HMP Addiewell).

**HMP Addiewell**
9 Station Road
Addiewell
West Lothian
EH55 8QA
Tel: 01506 874500
Director: Fraser Munro

Addiewell is operated by Sodexo Justice Services and opened in 2008. It houses all offender types with the exception of females and convicted young offenders.

The prison is situated in the village of Addiewell, which is in the central belt of Scotland, between the two largest cities, Glasgow and Edinburgh. The prison was built on a site formerly known as Addiewell chemical works which produced paraffin oil. It was an active site for nearly 100 years, opening in 1860s and finally closing in 1956.

Addiewell is designed as a "learning" prison, where offenders can address their offending behaviour and the circumstances which led to their imprisonment. The learning aspect aims to improve their employability prospects, their wellbeing and community support networks, leading to a reduction in reoffending.

Addiewell provides 40 hours of purposeful activity, per offender, per week. Purposeful Activity is divided into three main areas: Learning and Skills, Jobs and Programmed Interventions. We also adopt an effective Peer Support Model, where offenders are identified for support roles throughout the prison. They act as positive role models for fellow offenders and assist staff in the delivery of classes, programmes, sports activities, induction and offender support services.

**HM Prison Barlinnie**
81 Lee Avenue
Riddrie
Glasgow
G33 2QX
Tel:(0141) 770 2000
Governor: Michael Stoney

Barlinnie Prison, for which funding in 2022 was secured for re-build in 2023, is situated on the outskirts of Glasgow but still close to the busiest courts in Scotland and close to population centres and public transport routes that allow ease of access for family visits.

Barlinnie is Scotland's largest, most complex penal establishment and holds all categories of prisoners. However, its main purpose is to hold remand and short term prisoners sent by the West of Scotland courts. We also hold a significant number of long term prisoners who have just been sentenced, are awaiting transfer to another establishment or are here for a specific management reason.

Barlinnie also has a facility that holds protection prisoners and sex offenders who are separate from the main population. The segregation unit is available for both local prisoners and national prisoners from other establishments for a variety of management reasons.

## HM Prison Castle Huntly

Longforgan
Nr Dundee
DD2 5HL
Tel: (01382) 319333
Governor: Gerry Michie

Castle Huntly is Scotland's only open prison accommodating a capacity of 285 low supervision adult male offenders from any Local Authority area. Following a robust risk management process and a period in closed conditions offenders can progress to Castle Huntly where the emphasis is on careful preparation for release. Activity focuses on enhanced personal responsibility, job readiness and positive citizenship with the aim of reducing the risk of re-offending and contributing to safer communities.

### History

It is perhaps hardly surprising that Castle Huntly ranks amongst Scotland's lesser known strongholds, despite its great antiquity, when one considers the use to which it has been put since the Second World War. A girl's probationary school, a Borstal for boys, a Young Offenders Institution and currently an Open Prison for adults! Inevitably, accessibility to the general public has been severely restricted and it seldom features in any guidebooks for obvious reasons.

The exact date of construction is uncertain but, in 1452, the first Baron Gray of Fowlis obtained a licence from James II permitting the building of a fortalice on any part of his land and it is generally agreed that Castle Huntly was completed in the second half of the 15th Century. The earliest surviving record, in the "Register of the Great Seal", records a charter granted by James IV, dated at St. Andrews 7th January, 1508, in which the monarch concedes to Andrew, 3rd Baron Gray, then Justiciary of

Scotland "the land and barony of Langforgund, with the dependencies, tenants and tenantries- viz, the lands of Langforgund, Huntlie with the tower and fortalice…"

Built by the 1st Lord Gray of Fowlis, Castle Huntly stands on an outcrop of volcanic rock just south from the village of Longforgan. Stone from Kingoodie Quarry, on the banks of the River Tay was used in its construction. Being exceptionally hard stone, it was built to work with but it was extremely durable as evidenced by the condition of the castle building, now nearly 560 years old.

Over the next 200 years there were a number of additions to the castle. In 1660, an additional storey was added by Earl Patrick of Strathmore, in 1776, a major reconstruction was carried out by the Paterson family, when the building was given a new roof, a central tower or "lantern" was added and two wings, each of two storeys, with an entrance hall in between, were erected so forming what is now seen as the front of the castle.

During the war years, the castle was used as a girl's probation school before being purchased in 1946 by the Scottish Home and Health Department for use as a borstal and, today, it still belongs to the Scottish Prison Service.

## HM Prison Cornton Vale

Cornton Road
Stirling
FK9 5NU
Tel:(01786) 832591
Governor: Jacqueline Clinton

HMP YOI Cornton Vale is the national facility for female offenders for both remand and convicted prisoners.

Cornton Vale has the design capacity to hold a maximum of 119 prisoners, along with a separate Mother and Baby Unit with 7 spaces. There are two house blocks, Ross and Peebles Houses as well as 18 spaces in our Independent Living Units in the community.

Cornton Vale will receive admissions from court and prisoners will be transferred to other establishments who hold females, Edinburgh, Greenock and Polmont. Grampian is the only other establishment who will receive admissions direct from court to service the northern areas of Scotland.

## HM Prison Dumfries

Terregles Street
Dumfries
DG2 9AX
Tel:(01387) 261218
Governor: Linda Dorward

Dumfries prison serves the local courts of Dumfries and Galloway. It holds up to 80 male offenders who are remanded in custody for trial and those convicted but remanded for reports. Short-term convicted male offenders may be retained at Dumfries or transferred to another establishment according to their length of sentence and the availability of spaces.

Dumfries prison also provides a national mainstream facility for holding up to 100 long-term and short-term offenders who require to be separated from mainstream offenders because of the nature of their offence, termed as offence related protection offenders.

*History*
Built in 1863 as a local prison to serve the catchment area of South West Scotland, in 1951 it was converted for use as a borstal and in 1965 was changed to a Young Offenders Institution.

**HM Prison Edinburgh**
33 Stenhouse Road
Edinburgh
EH11 3LN
Tel:(0131) 444 3000
Governor: David Abernethy

Edinburgh is a large community facing prison receiving offenders predominantly from courts in Edinburgh, the Lothians and Borders, but also offenders from the Fife area. The current design capacity is 870 and we hold on average 900 offenders per day. The prison manages adult male and female offenders for those on remand, short term offenders (serving less than 4 years), long term offenders (serving 4 years or more), life sentence offenders and extended sentence offenders (Order of Life Long Restrictions).

*History*
Tolbooth 1386 to 1817: The Old Tolbooth was used as a gaol where judicial torture and executions were routinely carried out. A projecting permanent platform was built on its west side, so that the public could view beheadings and hangings.

Calton Gaol 1817 to 1924: Calton Jail (Gaol) opened in 1817 amidst some controversy. Lord Cockburn remarked: 'It had been a piece of undoubted bad taste to give so glorious an eminence to a prison.' Jules Verne who visited Edinburgh in 1859 described the gaol as resembling a small-scale version of a medieval town.

HM Prison Edinburgh 1924: The building of the prison started around 1914 with the first prisoner being received about 1920 replacing Calton gaol, the current site of St Andrews House on Regent Road Edinburgh. The prison has been completely rebuilt in recent years and was the first prison to complete a refurbishment programme. The opening of Ratho House in January 2009 represented the completion of 10 years of redevelopment work. The oldest building within the grounds of the Prison is Glenesk House which opened in 1998.

**HM Prison Glenochil**
King O'Muir Road
Tullibody
Clackmannanshire
FK10 3AD
Tel: (01259) 760471
Governor: Natalie Beale

Glenochil manages adult male offenders who are short term offenders, long term offenders, life sentence offenders and extended sentence offenders (Order of Life Long Restrictions).

The prison has been completely rebuilt in recent years and is a large community facing prison, giving priority to Forth Valley and Fife ("FK" and "KY" postcodes). It is one of the major sites in Scotland for managing sex offenders and those with an Order of Lifelong Restriction (OLR). Offenders are not committed to Glenochil direct from the courts but are admitted following conviction from other local prisons around Scotland. The current design capacity is 670 and we hold on average a daily population of 660.

*History*
The land was purchased from the Coal Board in the 1960s and a detention centre was subsequently built.

In the 1980s four house blocks were built housing adult male long term offenders. The detention centre became a Young Offenders Institution which continued until the modernisation of Polmont in 2010.

**HMP YOI Grampian**
South Road
Peterhead
AB42 2YY
Tel: 01779 485 600
Governor: Mike Hebden

Grampian was opened on 3rd March 2014 and is the first purpose built community facing prison within Scotland, capable of housing over 500 offenders, both male and female, adult and young offenders from the North of Scotland Community Justice Authority.
History - On 4 June 2008, it was announced that HMP Aberdeen and HMP Peterhead were to close and one new prison would be built on part

*36*

of the old Peterhead site, to be known as HMP & YOI Grampian.

HMP Aberdeen 1890 to 2014 known locally known as Craiginches, was sited in the Torry area of Aberdeen, on the banks of the River Dee and was designed to hold 155 offenders.

HMP Peterhead 1888 to 2013 was designed to hold 208 offenders and to be Scotland's only convict prison. In 1911 occupancy averaged at around 350, until peaking at 455. Additional buildings were completed in 1909, 1960 and 1962, bringing the capacity of to 362. Peterhead supplied the labour force to work in Stirlinghill Quarry and the Admiralty Yard. The convicts supported the work of a civilian labour force employed by the Admiralty to construct the Harbour of Refuge breakwater. At the time of closure in 2013 it has capacity for 142 offenders.

Clearance of the site began in February 2012, to prepare land for the building of the new HMP & YOI Grampian.

## HM Prison Greenock
Old Inverkip Road
Greenock
PA16 9AJ
Tel:(01475) 787801
Governor: Karen Smith

Greenock's range of offenders is one of the most diverse in the SPS. We manage adult male and female offenders for those with short term sentences, long term sentences and on remand. We also manage long term males in our national Top End facility, Chrisswell House.
Accommodation comprises of three main residential areas:
· Ailsa Hall has 133 cells and accommodates a male, predominantly local, population including remand and short term convicted offenders.
· Darroch Hall accommodates a mix of short term female convicted and untried female offenders. It has 54 single cells and one safe cell.
· Chrisswell House accommodates long term males who are low supervision. There are 64 single cells over two floors.

### History
Greenock was built between 1907 and 1910, replacing the Nelson Street prison which was adjacent to the existing Sheriff Court building. The local newspaper of the day reported taking its first prisoners on 28 August 1910; "The prisoners in Nelson Street will flit to their new abode on Tuesday. The prison, which stands majestically on Knowe on the High Inverkip Road, has been medically inspected and found in fit condition".

Greenock received its prisoners on 23 August 1910.The prison was opened with just

two residential buildings, Ailsa Hall and Darroch Hall, with a third unit, Chrisswell House, opening in 1996. Chrisswell was built with the specific needs of long-term offenders in mind. Greenock had always been a male prison until the introduction of females in 2002.

Greenock is generally a local community facing prison, receiving offenders predominately from the courts in Greenock, Campbelltown, Oban, Dunoon and surrounding Inverclyde and North Strathclyde areas. The current design capacity is 249 and hold on average 242 offenders per day.

## HM Prison Inverness
Duffy Drive
Inverness IV2 3HH
Tel: (01463) 229000
Governor: Brian McKirdy

Inverness serves courts in the Highlands, Islands and Moray – a large and diverse catchment area embracing rural and urban communities. We have a design capacity of 103, but currently average population of 117. The prison manages remand prisoners both adult and young persons, convicted adults serving up to 4 years and various other offenders who are awaiting to go to their prison of allocation or need to spend time with us as a management support. The offenders in this category tend to be serving long term sentences including life.

We also have a small community integration unit (C.I.U.) which holds females at the point of their sentence where they are considered suitable to be introduced to community activities and employment as part of their progression towards eventual release.

The present prison was opened in 1902, having relocated from nearby Inverness Castle to what was, at that time, the rural parish of Porterfield.

There were 25 male and 10 female offenders in accommodation comprising of 49 cells. Throughout its subsequent history the prison has had a mixed population of men and women, convicted and untried offenders.

The accommodation halls within the confines of the original wall have changed internally over the past 100 years, although their facades have remained the same. A number of extensions and extra buildings have been incrementally added to cope with rising and changing demands. Examples include the new Gate complex, the workshops and laundry. Other areas, such as facilities for healthcare and catering have been modernised.

The original cells were barely furnished. Now they have in-cell sanitation, bunk-beds, fitments, electric power and TVs - reflecting modern standards of living.

Prison labour was used to build the establishment. Subsequent employment included oakum-picking, sack sewing and mat-making, as well as maintenance of the prison estate and further building work. Physical drills and Bible classes punctuated the week. There is no mention in the records of 1903 of learning centres nor fitness centres such as those provided today. Programmes to address offending behaviour did not feature either, although perhaps the Chaplain (who "states that he spends upwards of 2 hours weekly in the prison") and Mrs Werner, the "Lady Visitor" took such a role upon themselves.

The working environment for staff has also changed. The first Governor, John Nicol, had a house built for himself within the walls. Two houses were additionally erected for "married warders" and "female warders" had quarters provided too - supplied with drainage, gas, water and service pipes. Prison Officers now work an average of 37 hours a week and the concept of tied housing has been abandoned since the 1980s. Their job has evolved away from that of turnkey to actively engaging with offenders in pursuit of the Scottish Prison Service model of correctional excellence.

### HM Prison Kilmarnock
Mauchline Road
Kilmarnock
KA1 5AA
Tel:(01563) 548800
Director: Craig Thomson

Kilmarnock is a 500 cell prison facility operated by Serco Ltd on behalf of the Scottish Prison Service under a contract with the Scottish Ministers. It is situated approximately three miles south-east of Hurlford in East Ayrshire. Housing a range of prisoner types, Kilmarnock is the local receiving establishment primarily taking prisoners from the Sheriff Courts of Ayr and Kilmarnock. Contracted to provide purposeful activity for the prisoners, Kilmarnock has an industries department comprising six work units, and provides work opportunities for both remand and convicted prisoners. The proportion of convicted prisoners makes up approximately 80% of our population. In providing some of these purposeful activities Kilmarnock, where possible, takes the opportunity to incorporate vocational training with the intention of providing prisoners with externally recognised qualifications.

Serco Ltd is a company incorporated under the Companies Acts and has a registered address at Serco House, 16 Bartley Wood Business Park, Bartley Way, Hook, RG27 9UY.

The land on which the prison is built was used for agricultural purposes prior to construction starting; however before this it was the location of a munitions factory for the Air Ministry. In 1968 the site was abandoned by the government and its agricultural use commenced.

### HM Prison Low Moss
Crosshill Road
Bishopbriggs
Glasgow
G64 2PZ
Tel: (0141) 762 9500
Governor: Paula Arnold

Low Moss opened in March 2012. This prison's design capacity is 784 and it manages male offenders on remand, short term offenders (serving less than 4 years), long term offenders (serving 4 years or more), life sentence offenders and extended sentence offenders (Order of Life Long Restriction) primarily from the North Strathclyde Community Justice Authority area.

The facilities include a link centre where offenders are able to deal with matters relating to employment, housing, social work, throughcare addiction services, etc. as well as facilities to help offenders address their re-offending and support them to re-integrate back into the community on their release.

*History*
The establishment replaced the dated prison accommodation that had previously occupied most of the site and had started out as a barrage balloon station at the beginning of the Second World War. After the war, RAF Bishopbriggs was used by the Royal Military Police as a training school.

In 1968 the site was converted into a temporary low security prison. The original Low Moss accommodated up to 327 prisoners in mainly dormitory accommodation much of which was in the form of wooden buildings. The prison was closed in May 2007. The buildings were subsequently demolished and the site cleared ready for a new prison to be built. Construction started on the site in February 2010.

### HM Prison Perth
3 Edinburgh Road
Perth PH2 8AT
Tel: (01738) 622293
Governor: Andy Hodge

Perth is a large community facing prison receiving offenders predominantly from courts in Perth and Kinross, Dundee, Angus and Fife.

The current design capacity is over 630 and we hold on average 678 prisoners per day. The prison manages adult male offenders on remand, short term offenders (serving less than 4 years), long term offenders (serving 4 years or more), life sentence offenders, sexual offenders and extended sentence offenders (Order of Long Restrictions).

## History

Perth was built on land purchased from the Moncrieff family, under the direction of Robert Reid (1774-1856) between 1810 and 1812 by French Napoleonic Prisoners of War. During that time it was used as a depot for some 7000 offenders from the War. During their captivity in Perth Depot they were relatively well treated. The offenders would make dolls from straw and carve beautiful ornaments from animal bones which sell to the people of Perth at a market held every Wednesday at the Depot. French Officers were usually 'paroled' into the City and would stay with local families. They had to sign a promise that they would not try to run away, indeed, the few that did escape back to France were sent back by their own side to ensure that the conditions of parole were maintained on both sides of the Channel. All of the French prisoners were repatriated after the Battle of Waterloo on 1815 and thousands of Perth people turned out to wave them off!

Between 1815 and 1839 the depot was used as a military store for uniforms and weapons. In 1839 it was decided to build a central civilian prison on the site of the Perth Depot. The first phase, C Hall, was completed in 1840 and became The General Prison at Perth. It is the oldest occupied prison in Scotland.

In 1870 the prison had the dubious distinction of being the site of Britain's first private (or non public) execution when George Chalmers, a vagrant from Braco, was hanged within its walls after public executions were abolished in 1868.

The General Prison gained further notoriety around 1914 as the only prison with the facilities to force feed hunger striking suffragettes.

The prison was partially closed between the years 1922 & 1927 when it was used solely as a reception for adult males before they were sent "up the river" to Dundee Prison. Perth fully reopened after Dundee prison closed in 1927.

The prison's B Hall was demolished in 1948 after a major fire and later the cookhouse was built on the site. The central tower was removed c1965.

A new purpose built execution shed was completed in 1965. Known as the Hanging Block, it was never used as the Murder Act 1965 abolished Capital Punishment for the crime of murder. It was subsequently used as offices and a training facility until it's demolition in 2006.

There was very little refurbishment or improvement made to the prison until 1996 when 'D' hall was closed for a complete upgrade.

From 1996 the prison was in a constant state of upgrade. The most recent refurbishment was carried out in three stages over five years and was completed in 2007 making HMP Perth a modern, fit for purpose facility.

## HMYOI Polmont

Brightons
Falkirk
FK2 0AB
Tel: (01324) 711558
Governor: Brenda Stewart

Polmont is Scotland's national holding facility for male young offenders aged between 16 - 21 years of age. Sentences range from 6 months to Life. The average sentence length is between 2 - 4 years.

## History

Polmont first opened as a Borstal in 1911.

Blairlodge Academy opened in 1843 by Robert Cunningham, a Church of Scotland minister, who also played a significant part in the Free Church breakaway in Polmont in the same year. The new school was for boy boarders and flourished under an innovative and dynamic headmaster J Cooke-Gray who took over in 1874.

At the turn of the century Blairlodge was the largest school of its kind in Scotland and was the first to use electric lighting - it had nearly nine hundred bulbs at the same time as the people of Falkirk were being shown electric light as a novelty.

The pupils who left Blairlodge entered the privileged world of the Colonial Service, Oxford or Cambridge or into the upper echelons of the commercial world.

After the death of Cooke-Gray in 1902 the school experienced financial difficulties and when it was forced to close in 1908 by an outbreak of an infectious disease, it never reopened.

The buildings were purchased by the Prison Commissioners in 1911 and shortly afterwards opened as Scotland's first Borstal. It is now, of course, Polmont Young Offenders Institution.

## HM Prison Shotts

Canthill Road
Shotts
ML7 4LE
Tel: (01501) 824000
Governor: William Stuart

Shotts prison was built in 2012 and is a prison for long term adult male offenders with a capacity of

553. The prison is situated in countryside south of the M8 motorway near the Lanarkshire village of Shotts. The prison seeks to provide a secure, safe, caring and productive environment, while providing opportunities for offenders to come to terms with their sentences and address their offending behaviour.

Shotts also houses the National Integration Centre (NIC) within its boundary. The NIC holds approximately 60 adult male offenders who are in the initial stages of sentences of eight years or over and prepares them for eventual movement to mainstream prisons. It provides a supportive regime for those sentenced to life or eight years or over during the first six to nine months of their sentences.

## History

The original prison, purpose built in 1978, catered for long term male offenders (sentences of 4 years & over) who are transferred from other prisons and who require to be kept secure conditions. The prison was extended in 1987 and has since been completely rebuilt on the same site.

## NATIONAL INTEGRATION CENTRE

Located within the boundary of HMP Shotts The National Integration Centre (NIC), is a national facility and holds approximately 60 adult male prisoners who are in the initial stages of sentences of 8 years or over and prepares them for eventual movement to mainstream establishments. It provides a supportive regime for all prisoners (excluding sex offenders) sentenced to life or 8 years or over during the first six to nine months of their sentences, and other prisoners may be taken where a spell in the NIC is considered beneficial.

The regime is intended to assist prisoners to cope with the personal consequences of their offending behaviour and the impact of their sentence. It seeks to prepare them for transfer to mainstream within the context of the Sentence Management model. That process is informed by risk and needs assessment work carried out, with the prisoners' involvement, during their time in the NIC.

Information on topics such as stress management, inter-personal and social skills and the prison system are delivered in Groupwork settings. Considerable emphasis is placed on building the prisoner's relationship with his Personal Officer in order to help him adjust to and plan out his sentence. While industry forms an integral part of the regime, it is orientated towards Crawford type activities and is supported by personal fitness programmes.

## KERR HOUSE

Kerr House became the National Top End Facility in March 2007. The facility is situated within the perimeter of the establishment. This facility offers low supervision prisoners an opportunity of participating in a less structured and regimented regime earlier than under the previous arrangements. Our aim is to provide prisoners with appropriate opportunities in preparing for release. Kerr House holds approximately 52 Adult male prisoners. This facility also holds its own visit room. Visits within Kerr House are of a relaxed nature with the aim of providing good quality family time.

## NORTHERN IRELAND PRISON SERVICE HEADQUARTERS:
PRISON SERVICE HQ
DUNDONALD HOUSE
UPPER NEWTOWNARDS RD
BELFAST BT4 3SU
TEL: 028 9052 2922
FAX: 028 9052 5284
Email: info@niprisonservice.gov.uk
https://www.justice-ni.gov.uk/topics/prisons

The Northern Ireland Prison Service (NIPS) is an agency within the Department of Justice. It is responsible for the operation and delivery of services within the Northern Ireland prison system. Its main statutory duties are set out in the Prison Act (Northern Ireland) 1953.

## Aim of the prison service

The overall aim of the Northern Ireland Prison Service is to improve public safety by reducing the risk of reoffending through the management and rehabilitation of offenders in custody. Its main statutory duties are set out in the Prison Act (Northern Ireland) 1953.

The Prison Service, through its staff, serves the community by keeping in secure, safe and humane custody those committed by the courts and, by working with prisoners and with other organisations, seeks to reduce the risk of re-offending and in so doing aims to protect the public and to contribute to peace and stability in Northern Ireland.

## Prison service establishments

The Prison Service headquarters is located at Dundonald House in the Stormont estate. There are three prison establishments, namely, Maghaberry, Magilligan and Hydebank Wood College and Women's Prison. The Prison Service College is located at Millisle.

**BELFAST:**
HYDEBANK WOOD PRISON
HOSPITAL ROAD
BELFAST. BT8 8NA
TEL: 028 9025 3666
FAX: 028 9025 3668

The college which has a focus on education, learning and employment accommodates young people between the ages of 18 and 21.
It also accommodates female remand and sentenced prisoners in Ash House, a house block within the complex.

**MAGHABERRY:**
MAGHABERRY PRISON
OLD ROAD
BALLINDERRY UPPER
LISBURN BT28 2PT
Tel: 028 9261 1888
Fax: 02892 614961 (9am-5pm Monday to Friday) and 02892 613292 (out of hours, weekends and bank holidays)

Maghaberry Prison is a modern high security prison housing adult male long term sentenced and remand prisoners, in both separated and integrated conditions.

**MAGILLIGAN PRISON**
POINT ROAD
LIMAVADY
CO LONDONDERRY
BT49 0LR
TEL: 028 7776 3311
FAX: 028 7772 0307
Magilligan Prison is a medium to low security prison which holds male prisoners with six years or less to serve and who meet the relevant security classification.

**STATES OF JERSEY**
**HM PRISON LA MOYE,**
LA RUE BAAL
ST BRELADE
JE3 8HQ
TEL: 01534 441800
FAX: 01534 441880

La Moye prison holds all prisoners detained in Jersey. The prison has a total of six wings, with a total population of 255 inmates, including 35 females, 26 young offenders, 62 vulnerable prisoners, 118 main stream adult males and 14 prisoners in G Wing who work outside the prison. The latest inspection report on La Moye was published by HM Chief Inspector of Prisons on 27th February 2017.

**STATES OF GUERNSEY PRISON SERVICE**
GUERNSEY PRISON
LES NICOLLES,
ST SAMPSONS, GY2 4YF,
GUERNSEY
TEL: +44 1481 248376 FAX: +44 1481 247837
EMAIL: prison.gov@gov.gg
The States of Guernsey Prison has a Certified Normal Accommodation (CNA) capacity of 130 prisoners; however the Prison's operational capacity is 139. The prison Governor is John De Carteret and his 2019 Annual Report stated that the average population throughout 2019 was 91 inmates. The majority of priorities identified in the 2019 delivery plan have been completed and 75% of prisoners engaged with education learning and skills, with an average of 99% of eligible prisoners employed in work whilst in custody throughout the year. HM Chief Inspector of Prisons only inspects Channel Island prisons by invitation, the last inspection was on 5th November 2014. You can find all the latest annual reports on Guernsey Prison here: https://gov.gg/Prison

**ISLE OF MAN PRISON SERVICE**
**DOUGLAS:**
Isle of Man Prison
Jurby
Isle of Man
IM7 3JP
Telephone: 01624 891000

Douglas prison is the only prison on the Isle of Man, it opened in August 2008 - the old Victoria Prison which opened in 1891 closed on 14th August 2008 and was finally demolished and covered with topsoil in March 2013.

EVERYONE'S GUIDE TO SERVING & SURVIVING A PRISON SENTENCE
EDITED & PUBLISHED BY EX-OFFENDERS!

# THE CELL COMPANION 2023

The #1 Bestselling Prisoners' Guide!

prisons.org.uk

Book Retailer APPROVED Ministry of Justice

Published in Association with

**Youngs**

The Prison Law & Personal Injury Solicitors

**MARK LEECH**

The Cell Companion 2023
Sixth Edition. November 2022.
prisons.org.uk

# Mark Leech FRSA

## Editor: The Prisons Handbook

Mark Leech was taken into 'Care' at the age of 8 and like many Care-leavers he later became involved in crime serving 14 years in a prison career that was characterised by roof-top protests, riots, and successful Supreme Court legal cases that changed British prison law.

While in prison Mark wrote a series of feature articles on the prison system for The Guardian newspaper, for whom he still writes today, and he also wrote three award-winning plays – "The Facts Speak For Themselves", Directed by Ned Chaillet for BBC Radio 4's *Saturday Night Theatre*, won him the BBC Radio Drama Award.

Mark was released from prison in March 1995 and has since then risen to become the country's foremost ex-offender expert on the policy and practice of the penal system.

Mark is the founder and former Chief Executive of the award-winning national charity for people with convictions UNLOCK, he is the Managing Editor of The Prisons Handbook, the Editor of *prisonoracle.com* the definitive prisons website and the Editor of Converse; the largest circulation national monthly prisons newspaper. Mark is the Editor of Prison Law Index, the definitive annual A-Z guide to prison law, the 6th edition of which - along with the 6th edition of his best selling 'Cell Companion' everyone's guide to serving and surviving a prison sentence - are both published in November 2022.

Mark is the Director of The Institute of Prison Law, whose acclaimed Certificate of Competency in Prison Law is the only one of its kind, he is an elected Fellow of the Royal Society of Arts and a member of the National Union of Journalists.

In 2018 Mark's investigation *"Grenfell Prisons"* into fire safety, revealed how every prison inspected by the Fire Regulator in 2017/2018 had failed every inspection - a fact that had not previously been made public.

A welcome by-product of his August 2017 investigation into the Prisons Inspectorate, published in The Independent revealing how the vast majority of the Prison Inspectorate's recommendations were being routinely ignored by prisons, saw an *Urgent Notification* Protocol signed between the Ministry of Justice and the Inspectorate ensuring public accountability for failing prisons by the Justice Secretary.

Today Mark lives with his partner and their two children among the beautiful mountains of Northern Thailand.

Outside of work his interests are in aviation – Mark is a qualified helicopter pilot.

**www.prisons.org.uk**

---

prisons org uk

Opening up the Closed World of Prisons

---

**What people say about Mark Leech**

*"A thoroughly offensive, dangerous and disruptive man"*
John Thompson, Governor, HMP Dartmoor 1985

*"One of the most sensitive, resourceful, humane, energetic, intelligent, dynamic and tenacious prisoners I have ever met"*
Roger Kendrick, Governor HMP Glenochil 1995.

*"I consider myself very lucky as Director General to have had you around, I consider you not only as a colleague but also as a friend"*
Sir Martin Narey, HM Prison Service Director General, 1998-2005

*"One of the sanest and best informed commentators on prison issues."*
Phil Wheatley, HM Prison Service Director General, 2005-2010

*"One of the very best speakers on the prison system his knowledge and experiences have given him answers to those questions other so-called 'experts' can only guess at."*
Baroness Scotland QC, HM Attorney General 2005-2010

## PRISONER LOCATION SERVICE

Use the Prisoner Location Service to find people in prison when you don't know which prison they are in.
**Prisoner Location Service**
**prisoner.location.service@noms.gsi.gov.uk**
**PO Box 2152, Birmingham. B15 1SD**
https://www.gov.uk/find-prisoner

## HMPPS

Her Majesty's Prison & Probation Service (HMPPS)
Ministry of Justice
Clive House
102 Petty France
London SW1H 9AJ
Tel: 01633 630941
Email: public.enquiries@noms.gsi.gov.uk

## MOJ: PRESS OFFICE

Journalists with enquiries can call the news desk on 0203 334 3536.

**Head of News**
Sam Haq

**Deputy head of news**
Richard Jones & Ben Stack

**Chief press officers – specialist desks:**
Contact specialist desks via the news desk for filming and visit requests, and long lead enquiries.
**Justice (victims, courts and law):** Seb Walters
**Prisons:** Anna Rutter
**Probation, female and young offenders:** Richard Mellor
**News desk:** Rebecca Gough

## DEDICATION

### THE PRISONS HANDBOOK 2023
### *is Dedicated to*

### *FRANCES CROOK, OBE.*

The Prisons Handbook 2023 is dedicated to **Frances Crook OBE,** who retired at the end of 2021 as Chief Executive of the Howard League for Penal Reform, after over 30 years at the helm of what is the world's oldest penal reform charity. Frances was a familiar name for anyone working in the criminal justice sector, and a frequent contributor to public debate on prisons and sentencing. She was a fearless campaigner who presented a genuine thorn in the side of successive governments, opposing expansion of the prison estate at every turn.

While Frances was unable to stop the 'prison works' mantra that has underpinned most public policy since the days of Michael Howard as Home Secretary, she did enjoy some notable campaign successes. The Books For Prisoners campaign in 2014 exposed the absurdities of Chris Grayling's crackdown on prisoner 'perks and privileges' when he was Secretary of State for Justice. The Howard League also overturned Grayling's criminal courts charge and eventually saw the government relent on his failed attempts to part-privatise probation – which the League correctly warned from the start would prove a disaster.

Frances also came up with some genuinely radical ideas, such as 'real work in prison'. This involved the Howard League launching Barbed, a graphic design studio in HMP Coldingley – the first such social enterprise to be run in a UK prison – which enabled prisoners to develop skills, receive a real wage, and pay tax and national insurance. Barbed remains a blueprint for a totally different way of conceiving work – and indeed day-to-day life – for long-sentenced prisoners.

The greatest achievements of Frances Crook were associated with services to youth justice, for which she received an OBE in 2010. She took a landmark legal case in 2002 which found that the Children Act applies to children in custody, leading to a raft of child protection policies and procedures being introduced to youth prisons. As a result, the Howard League set up a specialist team of lawyers which now offers legal advice and representation to both under-18s and young adults in custody. More recently, the League has campaigned to improve the policing of children in England and Wales – which has played an important role in the number of child arrests falling by two-thirds over the last decade.

In turn, the numbers of children in custody have fallen dramatically in the same period.

Now that Frances has retired, it is fitting that this year's Handbook carries a foreword by her successor, Andrea Coomber, outlining what the Howard League sees as the challenges ahead.

As anyone working in prison reform will know, there is always more work to be done.

# FOREWORD

## Andrea Coomber QC (Hon)

### *A quarter of a Millenium - and what has changed?*

In 1773, the High Sheriff of Bedfordshire, John Howard, walked out of Bedford Prison in disgust at the conditions he found there and started out on what was to become, for him, a life-long journey of penal reform; indeed, The Howard League for Penal Reform, the oldest penal reform charity in the world of which I am privileged and proud to be its Chief Executive, is named after this remarkable man.

I am both pleased and honoured to have been invited to write this foreword to The Prisons Handbook 2023 – a year that marks the 250th anniversary of John Howard walking out of Bedford Prison in disgust at its conditions; and what, I wonder, would Howard make of our prison conditions today?

What would he make of the fact that, nigh on 250 years after he walked out of Bedford prison and slammed the prison gates shut behind him in disgust, the then Chief Inspector of Prisons Peter Clarke, in September 2018, did exactly the same thing when he walked out of Bedford Prison and was equally so disgusted by what he found there that he issued one of his exceptionally rare Urgent Notifications?

It's been a quarter of a Millennium, and yet what has changed?

Were he alive today, I expect that Howard would despair that recommendations from his tours of prisons in England and beyond have failed to be implemented and embedded within our penal system over the last 250 years. In his 1777 seminal work, 'The State of the Prisons in England and Wales' (a copy of which is available on The Prison Oracle (prisonoracle.com) free to members), he called for clean and healthy accommodation, proper healthcare, meaningful employment and adequate segregation.

Where Howard demanded clean and healthy accommodation, we instead have leaking roofs and infestations of rats and cockroaches. Cells made to house one Victorian woman are now pushed beyond their limits, often crammed with two grown men. Where Howard demanded proper healthcare, we instead have access so poor that babies are dying to mothers giving birth alone in their cells. Where Howard demanded meaningful employment, we instead have the current Chief Inspector decrying such stark lack of purposeful activity that prisoners are spending 23 hours of their day in cells.

Perhaps the most damning similarity is Howard's railing against indefinite sentences, where people were held in prison unless able to pay the jailer's fee for release. Today, far too many people are remanded to custody, with alarmingly high rates of self-harm and suicide. The inequities Howard sought to address have simply evolved, becoming all the more insidious in nature, now incorporating the credibility crisis of an overwhelmingly white justice system often failing to understand and then criminalising and imprisoning disproportionate numbers of black and Asian people, many of whom are children.

A country with the second-highest rate of imprisonment in Western Europe should step back and see that current approaches are not working. We have more than 80,000 people in prison, and as recently as 2021 saw the highest death toll behind bars since current recording practices began. Of the huge numbers in custody, 51 per cent of men and 76 per cent of women have mental health difficulties, and more than two-thirds of the children have special educational needs. One in five people say they feel unsafe in prison, while as many as 43 per cent say they have felt unsafe at some point in their sentence.

Far from alleviating the issues faced by people in custody, prisons are instead exacerbating existing problems and creating new ones. The Chief Inspector's most recent annual report outlined a system that was failing in too many aspects, where drug "misuse and lack of purposeful activity contributed to violence and self-harm and had a negative impact on prisoner well-being." And while the government has a strategy to imprison fewer women, the Justice Committee has recently observed that insufficient progress has been made – while self-harm in women's prisons remains disproportionately high.

Our prisons are not representative of, nor proportionate to, our society; rather, they represent the problems the state does not want to acknowledge and are over-saturated by cohorts of people who have been failed consistently. Rather than solve social problems, prisons have become warehouses for them, disappearing from sight and public conscience people who have failed society, but who, very often, have been failed by it.

The difficult truth is that crime is primarily the by-product of social failure. Rather than invest to solve and address the unmet needs of society and its vulnerable people, governments of both colours have sought to punish and imprison their way out of a mental health crisis, a drug addiction crisis, and now the beginnings of the cost-of-living crisis. Rather than engage on the widely understood drivers of crime, it is easier to engage in cheap talk about a law-and-order crisis.

And we are reaping the seeds of this now, because across the system – but particularly in the courts and in prisons – there is a crisis of the gravest order. The challenges faced are immediate but also likely to be far-reaching. Only a fundamental review of the pipeline between courts and custody, and a sweeping reassessment of what the system's priorities should be, is going to steer us from a future doomed to decades of sclerotic, failing justice and prisons that continue to damage people and moulder at the fabric of society.

Unfortunately, there is little to no sign that our politicians understand this. None of the political parties have a serious programme of reform when it comes to criminal justice. The two main parties appear committed to an arms race of political rhetoric that puts us back decades. Both the Conservatives and Labour seem content to rely on naïve assumptions that the answer to crime is ever-lengthening prison sentences, for an ever-lengthening roll-call of offences, with no accounting for what that means – not just for the criminal justice system, but for wider societal responses to the poverty, addictions and poor mental health that drive so much of what comes before the courts.

This is the atmosphere that the Howard League has been working within.

Nonetheless, we have made important strides and delivered critical results in trying times. The Howard League has brought focus to child arrests and helped deliver a programme that has contributed to a 74 per cent reduction in the arrests of children over the last decade. Work to end the criminalisation of children living in residential care has been similarly successful; children living in children's homes are now three times less likely to be criminalised. We have worked to reduce arrests of women, campaigned against the use of remand for someone's "own protection", and produced an anti-racist guide for lawyers, setting out practical steps that can be taken to change outcomes and challenge sentencing.

Our free and confidential legal advice line is the only such service in the country for children and young people aged 21 and under in custody. During the pandemic, where people were often locked in their cells for 23 hours per day, the advice line was a lifeline, receiving more than 10,000 calls a year.

The Howard League has continued to bring legal cases, sometimes in our own name, or through interventions, to help shape the law, and in the context of huge reductions in legal aid over recent years that have meant overwhelming demand for our services. As a strategic response, we will be looking to broaden the scope of our legal services to significant cases that impact people in prison of all ages, thus enabling us to change and influence wider policy and secure better outcomes for those caught up in the system.

In the months and years to come, the Howard League will join our voices with others in the sector to create hard-hitting and targeted campaigns for penal reform. I am working with our staff, trustees and members to refine the best possible contribution for the Howard League in this space, but you can expect us to be calling for intellectual honesty and moral courage in the political discourse, to be reinforcing the evidence base through research and litigation, and to help open windows for the public into life in prison, communicating why prison is not the answer to crime. We need more members to draw on and to help amplify our voice, so please do consider joining the Howard League.

John Howard's achievements did not begin and end with his role as High Sheriff. His most critical role was in opening the doors to previously hidden prison life and exposing it to the public. He believed, as I and so many other people do, that what happens in prisons, to its last detail, ought to be public knowledge, and ought to represent the values and standards of the societies in which those prisons exist. At the

Howard League, we will be continuing this legacy to empower the public with reliable and rigorous research and information, and equip them with the means and power to contest the penal system where it falls short.

For what it's worth, I suspect that politicians overstate the public's punitive bent. I am not privy to the framing of questions in the polling, but if you provide people with information about what causes crime, what prevents crime and how prison works I have little doubt that the dial will move. There are people in communities up and down this country that know what it's like to experience crime, but equally know the damage that prison wreaks. With one third of adult men in this country living with a criminal conviction, there are many people who understand that we all walk a fine line. I believe that the public fundamentally suffer not from a lack of compassion, but from a lack of information.

And, in honour of John Howard, you can expect to see the Howard League continuing to bridge that gap, and continuing the journey of penal reform that John Howard himself embarked upon exactly 250 years ago.

*Andrea Coomber QC (Hon) was appointed the Chief Executive of The Howard League for Penal Reform on 1st November 2021. Prior to that Andrea was the Director of JUSTICE, a position she held since February 2013. Andrea is a Lay Member of the Conduct Committee of the House of Lords and previously held positions including: Legal Director and Senior Equality Lawyer at Interights; Head of Information and Training at the International Service for Human Rights in Geneva, Switzerland; and Legal Officer at the South Asia Human Rights Documentation Centre in New Delhi, India. Andrea qualified as a Barrister and Solicitor with Minter Ellison in Perth, Australia, she has a BA/LLB (Hons) from the University of Western Australia and an LLM (Dist.) from the London School of Economics, where she was awarded the Rosalynn Higgins Prize for topping public international law. Andrea is a Board Member of the British and Irish Legal Information Institute (BAILII); an Honorary Master of the Bench of Middle Temple; an Affiliate Member of the Centre for Law & Social Justice at Leeds University; and Advisory Council Member of the Initiative for Strategic Litigation in Africa. In 2022, Andrea was appointed Queens Council (Honoris Causa) for a major contribution for the development in law in England and Wales.*

## ACKNOWLEDGMENTS

**To the vast majority of people who read books this, the Acknowledgments Page, is often the least important one in the entire book – but to the author it is the most important page of all.**

For it is this page that alone provides the wonderful opportunity to say 'thank you' in print to those special people without whose input this book could not have been written; and paradoxically it is also the hardest one for most authors to pen.

Editing a work of this length incurs a debt of gratitude to well over 200 people and it's impossible to name them all here. You know who you are and I am very grateful for all your help, advice and assistance.

My thanks must go first to Andrea Coomber QC (Hons), Chief Executive of The Howard League for Penal Reform, for her excellent foreword - and to Frances Crook OBE Andrea's predecessor at the Howard League for agreeing that we could dedicate this edition to her.

I am also very grateful to Dr Tim Kerr for his excellent insight into prison medicine, to Gordon Brockington Managing Director G4S Care & Rehabilitation for his thought-provoking article *Forward Thinking*; to Charlie Taylor HM Chief Inspector of Prisons for his *Musings of a Chief Inspector*; to Dr Varinder Panesar. Lead Forensic Psychologist HMP Pentonville for her *'Change is coming: the mental health needs and experiences of young adults in two London remand prisons'* and to Professor Karen Harrison, Lincoln University for her (and he colleagues at Lincoln University) article *'Just Get On With It' A qualitative exploration of the health and wellbeing of prison operational managers and governor grades.*

As ever I am also very much indebted to Andy Simpson for his help in creating the new edition.

Finally I want to save my biggest 'thank you' for my partner Oui for his typical Thai patience, and of course to our son Alex and our daughter Maisie who both have become seriously adept at wrapping me around their little fingers - often in an unforeseen exercise that later events prove was a joint conspiracy from the start lol, but who have proved to be such wonderful additions to our family they have all made my life so utterly complete.

*MARK LEECH*
*Chiang Mai,*
*Thailand.*
*September 2022*

# INTRODUCTION

### The Prisons Handbook: The Back Story
### By Mark Leech FRSA
### Editor: The Prisons Handbook

**I once had a dream - well two dreams really, but I'll come to the second in a moment.**

The first 'dream', which became the book that you now hold in your hands, started life over 30 years ago, sitting in the large caged Reception cubicle at Wandsworth prison in south London. At that time I was waiting for my prison escort to arrive to take me to Parkhurst Prison on the Isle of Wight - a journey that was destined to end in the House of Lords and change British prison law forever, but that's another story.

It was as I was sitting in that caged cubicle that I found myself surrounded by a mixture of prisoners who had just arrived at Wandsworth and others, like myself, who were lucky enough to be leaving.

Quietly I sat there and just and listened to the questions that went back and forth - between the worried new arrivals concerned at what lay ahead, and the old-hand *Norman Stanley Fletcher* replies of those like myself who couldn't wait to get out of there.

*What's it like here? What are the visits like? Is there any work available, and what are the wages like? What are the cells like? How long are we banged up, What about the food? Is it true they have a painting and decorating course? What's the doctor like? Can I see a dentist while I'm here, and is there a waiting list?*

These of course were exactly the same questions I had asked when I arrived at Wandsworth six months before - and they were exactly the same questions I would be asking again later that day when I arrived at Parkhurst.

Suddenly a penny dropped: *I wonder if there's a book that gives details about every prison and what it has to offer?*

During the journey that afternoon to Parkhurst Prison I asked the Prison Officer I was shackled to: *"Is there a reference book on Prisons?"*

"No" came the terse reply, in a way that made it clear questions were not invited and comments were equally unwelcome.

Secretly though, right there and then, I decided that I was going to write *that* book.

"What?"

"You?"

"You're going to write a book on Prisons Leech?!"

The Parkhurst Wing Governor laughed and shook his head in disbelief as I told him of my plan during my Induction Interview a few days later.

Well today, 24 annual editions later, 'that book' - The Prisons Handbook you now hold in your hands - has become the definitive annual reference book on the prison system of England and Wales that is sold all over the world.

One dream delivered - and now let me tell how the second one, connected to it, was born; The Prison Oracle web site.

In May 2018, having spent hours on the internet trying to locate a copy of *The Woolf Report* for some research I was doing, and having had to give up exasperated at my inability to find it, I had another dream.

*One place, where everything on prisons was brought together, that was user-friendly, time-saving, comprehensive, totally independent, and where full access cost less than a cup of coffee a week;*

**The Prison Oracle** was born.

Fifteen months later, in October 2019, the dream became reality when The Prison Oracle opened its cyber doors and won outstanding reviews from those who have spent a lifetime working and living in prisons.

Today, three years later, The Prison Oracle has over 10,000 members, it covers 44,000 pages, it employs over a dozen ex offender page editors who keep the site up to date - and yes it contains a copy of The Woolf Report, along with almost every other valuable and vintage publication on prisons going right back to The State of The Prisons published by John Howard in 1777.

## WHAT'S IN THE PRISONS HANDBOOK?

The Prisons Handbook is the definitive annual guide to every prison and YOI in England and Wales. Section One is the 700-page A-Z of prisons in England and Wales, using all the latest truly independent inspection reports published by the Prisons Inspectorate and the Independent Monitoring Boards as the basis for each entry - and the content of The Prisons Handbook, and particularly the Establishment Section is updated daily via a range of memberships and subscriptions that start from as little as 99p a week at the time of going to press (September 2022).

## FROM RECEPTION TO RELEASE

The Handbook contains 26 comprehensive advice chapters that authoritatively spans reception through to release; covering *Early Days in Custody; Offending Behaviour Programmes; Criminal Cases Review Commission; Requests and Complaints; Prisoner Communications; Drugs and Alcohol in Prison Institutions; The Prison Disciplinary System; Who Can Help?; Healthcare; Religion; Equality: Age, Gender, Disability & Race; Social Security and Discharge Grants; Release* and Recall; Indeterminate Sentences; Women Prisoners; Young Offenders (18-21 year olds); Young People (15-17 year olds); Foreign Nationals; Disability in Prison; Employment, Training & Skills; Work and Pay; Incentives and Earned Privileges; Civil Partnerships & Equal Marriage; Elderly Prisoners; Segregation; and Security Categorisation.

## THE DIRECTORY
Section 3 contains details of Government & Statutory Agencies, such as the Ministry of Justice and HM Prison & Probation Service.

## PRISON LAW: THE LEGAL SECTION
This important section has since been completely revised and updated to June 2022 by Barrister Grace Cowell and her **Crime & Prison Law Team at 1 Pump Court Chambers in London.**
The 150-page A-Z tour of prison law gives an authoritative account of the legal rights of prisoners and legislation applicable to prisoners.
From Access to Justice, through to Zoonotic Infections, the Team at 1 Pump Court have done a magnificent job and has produced a definitive guide to prison law that brings together all the relevant rules and regulations in an easy to understand way that will be essential reading for prisoners and their lawyers alike.
Also fully updated is an authoritative section on the subject of criminal appeals.

## FORUM - Something to Say?

**5.1 Gordon Brockington Managing Director G4S Care & Rehabilitation:** *Forward Thinking.*

**5.2 Charlie Taylor HM Chief Inspector of Prisons.** *The Musings of a Chief Inspector.*

**5.3 Dr Varinder Panesar. Lead Forensic Psychologist HMP Pentonville:** *Change is coming: the mental health needs and experiences of young adults in two London remand prisons.*

**5.4 Dr Tim Kerr:** *Prison Medicine: On The Critical List? One health professional's view of prison medicine - as a service user.*

**5.5 Professor Karen Harrison, Lincoln University:** *Just Get On With It: A qualitative exploration of the health and wellbeing of prison operational managers and governor grades.*

## INSPECTION REPORTS AND MORE
The pandemic effected the entire country so it's no surprise that it did not leave criminal justice system alone. Only now is the prison system starting to really get back into operation but there has been the inevitable shift in the publication dates of most of the major annual reports - last year the annual report of HM Prison Probation Service did not appear until December 2021, a shift from its usual July publication date, and this year, 2022, the report is not expected until October - so it is destined to be a year or two before annual reports return to anything a normal schedule.
The summaries of annual reports we carry are those which were delayed last year but we also include the web site address from where the report can be downloaded when it is published and, for prisoners without internet access, we have set out the address they can write to in order to obtain a printed copy on publication.

**Reports:**
Introduction to the Prisons Inspectorate
HM Prison & Probation Service Annual Report 2020/2021 - *published December 2021*
Prison & Probation Ombudsman's Annual Report 2020/2021 - *published September 2021*
HM Chief Inspector of Prisons Annual Report 2021/2022 - *published July 2022*
Prison Inspectorate Reports *published June 2021 to August 2022*
Parole Board For England & Wales Annual Report 2021/22 - *published July 2022*

## PEOPLE AND POLICIES
Section 7 gives details of selected Parliamentary Questions and, Freedom of Information Act requests and responses from the Ministry of Justice and HMPPS on prisons in the last 12 months. This section also contains details of Deaths in Prison Service Custody 1990-2022, details of the latest Policy Frameworks that are replacing Prison Service Orders and Instructions, Butler Trust Awards and we set out the vital *Basic Custody Screening Tool* used by HMPPS to assess everyone who arrives in custody.

## PRISON SERVICE STAFF
Section 8 has been completely updated, providing the latest information on pay, and the new prison officers level 3 Custody and Detention Professional Apprenticeship and the Professional Vocational Diploma in Custodial Care.

## RESEARCH BRIEFINGS
This section lists over 170 research briefings you can dip into and out of on various prison and crime related subjects.

### GENERAL FEEDBACK

The Prisons Handbook offers a comprehensive sweep of a complex system, providing detailed information not elsewhere drawn together. If there are general comments you would like to make about the content then please write to the Editor at *directors.office@prisons.org.uk*

## MOJ SERVICE SPECIFICATIONS

**Editor's Note:**
The Ministry of Justice 'Directory of Service Specifications.'
*https://www.gov.uk/government/collections/noms-directory-of-service-specifications*
The Service Specifications below, available on the above link, are still extant and in force in September 2022. However, as new Policy Frameworks are issued to replace Prison Service Instructions, Prison Service Orders and Probation Instructions, policy owners (previously called Policy Leads) will consider any relevant Service Specification and if it is still required, incorporate it into the new Policy Framework.
Consequently, once this has been done, the relevant Service Specification (or specific output in the Specification) will then be cancelled.
If it is determined that the Specification (or specific output in the Specification) is no longer required, then it will be cancelled.
According to the Ministry of Justice it intends, at some future point it says, to start reissuing the documents contained in the Directory of Service Specifications but with cancelled elements removed where they've been replaced.

*What are Service Specifications?*
The service specifications define what should be delivered as part of the service (the desired outcomes and outputs for services), rather than details of how the service should be provided which is what happened previously.
This ensures that legal, safe and decent services can be commissioned and delivered. It also allows providers to deliver the rehabilitative aspects of sentences in the way they believe is most likely to reduce reoffending.
Each service specification sets out:
• the minimum mandatory outputs and outcomes to be delivered by the provider
• the legal and policy context of the service
The full set of services that the Ministry of Justice commissions, covering all offender management services in prisons and probation, are listed in the Directory of Services.
These are available for the public from the above web site and via the library for serving prisoners.

• NOMS directory of services
• NOMS service specifications for secure and decent custody
• NOMS service specifications for regimes
• NOMS service specifications for external prisoner movements
• MoJ service specifications for offender management
• MoJ service specifications for interventions
• MoJ service specifications for bail court and victim work
• MoJ service specifications for approved premises

**SERVICE SPECIFICATIONS:**
*https://www.gov.uk/government/publications/national-offender-management-service-noms-service-specifications-for-secure-and-decent-custody*
From the above link you can download service specifications on the following:
• provision of secure operating environment: communication and control rooms
• catering
• services for visitors
• specialist units (HSE)
• visits booking
• processing and resolution of prisoner complaints
• prisoner discipline and segregation: prisoner discipline procedures
• prisoner discipline and segregation: segregation of prisoners
• conduct visits
• enablers of national co-commissioned services in prisons
• manage prisoner finance
• prisoner communication services
• prisoner property services
• early days and discharge: reception in
• early days and discharge: discharge
• early days and discharge: first night in custody
• mandatory drug testing
• nights
• provision of a secure operating environment: gate services
• provision of a secure operating environment: internal prisoner movement
• residential services
• security management
• early days and discharge: induction to custody
• cell and area searching
• mother and baby units

# GLOSSARY OF TERMS

**A**

| | |
|---|---|
| AA | Alcoholics Anonymous |
| ABH | Actual Bodily Harm |
| AC | Attendance Centre |
| ACL | Adult Community Learning |
| ACR | Automatic Conditional Release |
| ACCT. | Assessment, Care in Custody and Teamwork. |
| AP | Approved Premises: previously referred to as a Probation or Bail Hostel |
| ART | Aggression Replacement Training |
| ASBO | Anti-Social Behaviour Order |
| ASPIRE | Assess, Plan, Implement, Review, Evaluate (in the context of Probation's work) |
| ATR | Alcohol Treatment Requirement |

**B**

| | |
|---|---|
| BASS | Bail Accommodation Support Scheme |
| BBRP | Building Better Relationships programme |
| BCS | British Crime Survey |
| BME | Black and Minority Ethnic |
| Brief Interventions Screening | and brief advice delivered by the Offender Manager to identify a real or potential alcohol problem and motivate an individual to do something about it |
| BSR | Building Skills for Recovery programme |

**C**

| | |
|---|---|
| CAB | Citizens Advice Bureau |
| CAP | Communities Against Poverty |
| CARAT | Counselling, Assessment, Referral, Advice and Throughcare programme in prisons |
| CBT | Cognitive Behavioural Therapy |
| CDA | Crime and Disorder Act |
| CDAS | Community Drug and Alcohol Service |
| CE | Chief Executive |
| CEOP | Child Exploitation and On-Line Protection |
| CIC | Community Interest Company |
| CJA | Criminal Justice Act |
| CJS | Criminal Justice System |
| CJMHT | Criminal Justice Mental Health Team |
| CMHT | Community Mental Health Team |
| CNA | Certified Normal Accommodation. Section 14(2) Prison Act 1952 requires that prisoner accommodation must be 'certified' by an inspector as being suitable for the purpose. Certified Normal Accommodation (CNA), or uncrowded capacity, is the Prison Service's own measure of accommodation. CNA represents the good, decent standard of accommodation that the Service aspires to provide all prisoners. Baseline CNA: Baseline CNA is the sum total of all certified accommodation in an establishment except, normally Cells in punishment or segregation units, Healthcare cells or rooms in training prisons and YOIs that are not routinely used to accommodate long stay patients. In-Use CNA:  In-use CNA is baseline CNA less those places not available for immediate use, for example: damaged cells, cells affected by building works. In April 2022 a new Certified Prisoner Accommodation Policy Framework came into force. See also OP.CAP |
| CPA | Care Plan Approach |
| CPN | Community Psychiatric Nurse |
| CRB | Criminal Records Bureau |
| CRC | Community Rehabilitation Company |
| CRD | Conditional Release Date |
| CRE | Commission for Racial Equality |
| CSA | Child Support Agency |
| CSP | Community Safety Partnership |
| CO | Community Order (made by the courts to which are added a variety of extra requirements) |
| CP | Community Payback. An Unpaid Work requirement ordered by the courts to be undertaken for the benefit of the community: a punitive intervention used as a creative resource for improving the local environment, teaching offenders skills, and improving their work ethic. |
| CPC | Community Payback Coordinator |
| CPS | Crown Prosecution Service |
| CRD | Conditional Release Date |
| Criminogenic Need | The needs and priorities identified by the OASys (Offender Assessment) process as contributing to offending. These are defined as Accommodation /Education, training & employability/ Financial management and income/ Relationships/Lifestyle and associates/ Drug misuse/Alcohol misuse /Emotional wellbeing/ Thinking and behaviour/ Attitudes. |

**D**

| | |
|---|---|
| D & D | Drunk and Disorderly |
| DA/DV | Domestic Abuse/Domestic Violence |
| DAAT | Drug and Alcohol Action Teams (working locally to deliver the UK drug strategy) |
| DALO | Domestic Abuse Liaison Officer (Police) |
| DCA | Department of Constitutional Affairs |
| DD | Drink Driving |
| DDA | Disability Discrimination Act |
| DHR | Domestic Homicide Review |
| DIDP | Drunk Impaired Drivers Programme |
| DPA | Data Protection Act |

| | |
|---|---|
| DRR | Drug Rehabilitation Requirement |
| DU | Delivery Unit (Probation) See LDU |
| DV/DA | Domestic Violence/Domestic Abuse |
| DWD | Driving While Disqualified |
| DWP | Department of Work and Pensions |

**E**

| | |
|---|---|
| EDR | Earliest Date of Release |
| ECJB | Essex Criminal Justice Board |
| EHRC | Equality and Human Rights Commission |
| EIA | Equality Impact Assessment |
| EP | Essex Probation |
| EOS | Essex Offender Services (CIC) |
| ESOL | English for Speakers of Other Languages |
| ETE | Education, Training and Employment |
| ETS | Enhanced Thinking Skills programme |

**F**

| | |
|---|---|
| FDR | Fast Delivery Report (for courts) |
| FOIA | Freedom of Information Act: usually referred to in the context of requests for information |
| FNP | Foreign National Prisoner |
| FTA | Failure to attend |
| FTR | Failure to report |
| FPN | Fixed Penalty Notice |

**G**

| | |
|---|---|
| GBH | Grievous Bodily Harm |
| GOVERNOR | |
| | All prisons must have a prison Governor - these range in grade from Grade 6 to Grade 11. The Governing Governor of a prison is known as 'The Governor' - all other Governor grades are known as Managers and referred to by their role titles (for example, Head of Security or Head of Regimes.) See section 8 for more information. |

**H**

| | |
|---|---|
| H&S | Health and Safety |
| HDC | Home Detention Curfew |
| HLO | Housing Liaison Officer (Probation) |
| HMCS | Her Majesty's Courts Service |
| HMIP | Her Majesty's Inspectorate of Prisons |
| HMP | Her Majesty's Prison |
| HMPPS | HM Prison & Probation Service |
| HMP & YOI | |
| | HMP & Young Offenders Institution (15-17 & 18-21 year olds) |
| HR | Human Resources |

**I**

| | |
|---|---|
| IM | Interventions Manager |
| IOM | Integrated Offender Management: with Police and Probation working together in Probation offices and drawing in the expertise of other agencies. Using a 'carrot and stick' approach, they work not only with |

currently convicted prolific offenders, but those who we know are at risk of, or committing offences, but who are not yet convicted.

| | |
|---|---|
| IPP | Indeterminate Sentence for Public Protection |
| iSOTP | Internet Sex Offender Treatment Programme |
| ISP | Initial Sentence Plan |
| IT | Information Technology |

**J**

| | |
|---|---|
| JCC | Joint Consultative Committee |
| JCP | Job Centre Plus |
| JDATT | Joint Domestic Abuse Triage Team |
| JNCC | Joint National Consultative Committee |
| JP | Justice of the Peace (Magistrate) |

**K**

| | |
|---|---|
| KPI | Key Performance Indicator |

**L**

| | |
|---|---|
| LAA | Local Area Agreement |
| LAGIP | Lesbians, Gay Men, Bisexual and Transgendered staff in Probation |
| LCJB | Local Criminal Justice Board |
| LDU | Local Delivery Unit, which provides Probation services across a geographical area, and is located in a town central to that area |
| LED | Licence Expiry Date |
| LGBT | Lesbian, Gay, Bisexual and Transgender |
| LSCB | Local Safeguarding Children Board |

**M**

| | |
|---|---|
| MAPPA | Multi–Agency Public Protection Arrangements-providing the statutory framework for inter–agency cooperation in assessing and managing violent and sex offenders in England and Wales |
| MARAC | Multi–Agency Risk Assessment Conference provides inter– agency cooperation to support and protect victims of domestic abuse |
| MARI | Medium Alcohol Requirement Intervention (a 12–day Specified Activity) |
| MDO | Mentally Disordered Offender |
| MOJ | Ministry of Justice |
| M–OM | Manager of Offender Management |
| MSS | Manager – Support Services |

**N**

| | |
|---|---|
| Napo | National Association of Probation Officers |
| NAAPS | National Association of Asian Probation Staff |
| NAVSS | National Association of Victim Support Schemes |
| NOMS | National Offender Management Service: responsible for commissioning and delivering Prison and Probation services across England and Wales |

Non-stat Non-Statutory Offenders: not subject to supervision by the Probation Service (see IOM)

NOTA National Organisation for the Treatment of (sexual) Abusers

NPD Non-Parole Date (release date at the end of sentence, with no parole period)

**O**

OASys Offender Assessment System used by both Prison and Probation Services to help determine the causes of someone's offending and what work and interventions are necessary to address that behaviour and cut reoffending

ODR Oral Delivery Report (for courts)

OS Offender Supervisor (prisons)

OGRS Offender Group Reconviction Score

OLASS Offender Learning and Skills Service

OM Offender Management, Offender Manager

OMiC Offender Management in Custody Model

OMU Offender Management Unit (prisons)

OP. CAP Operational Capacity. The operational capacity of a prison is the total number of prisoners that an establishment can hold taking into account control, security and the proper operation of the planned regime. It is determined by the PGD on the basis of operational judgement and experience. Useable Operational Capacity, UOC, of the estate is the sum of all establishments' operational capacity less 2250 places. This is known as the operating margin and reflects the constraints imposed by the need to provide separate accommodation for different classes of prisoner i.e. by sex, age, security category, conviction status, single cell risk assessment and also due to geographical distribution. Governing governors and Controllers and Directors of contracted out prisons must ensure that the approved operational capacity is not normally exceeded other than on an exceptional basis to accommodate pressing operational need.

OTO One-to-One programme

**P**

PAR Parole Assessment Report

P-ASRO Prisons – Addressing Substance Related Offending

PED Parole Eligibility Date

PF Policy Framework

PGD Prison Group Director (Area Manager)

P-NOMIS the information system for the combined prisons and probation services. It has completely replaced obsolete computer systems and now

gives all prison and probation staff instant access to offender records; consisting of biometric id of offenders and their visitors (so banned visitors can be instantly identified), cell allocation, self harm flags, security information and sentence plans.

POA Prison Officers' Association

PPO Prisons and Probation Ombudsman

PPO Prolific and Priority Offenders. A CSP-led initiative with criminal justice agencies and others working together to catch, convict, monitor, manage and work towards rehabilitating this group of offenders. Now superseded by IOM (Integrated Offender Management).

PSA Public Service Agreement

PCC Police and Crime Commissioner

PCCA Powers of the Criminal Courts Act

PCMH Plea and Case Management Hearing

PCSC Police, Crime, Sentencing Courts Act 2022

PSR Pre-Sentence Report prepared by Probation for the courts

PTRS Probation Trust Rating System

**Q**

QA Quality Assurance

**R**

RAMP Resource and Management Planner

RCU Reverse Cohort Unit

RIC Remanded in custody

RMP Risk Management Planner

ROB Remanded on Bail

ROH Risk of Harm

ROP Referral Order Panel

ROsH Risk of Serious Harm

RoTL Release on Temporary Licence

RR Reducing Reoffending

RRA Race Relations Act

RSO Registered Sex Offender

**S**

SCR Serious Case Review

SDR Standard Delivery Report

SED Sentence Expiry Date

SEU Social Exclusion Unit

SFA Skills Funding Agency

SFO Serious Fraud Office

SFO Serious Further Offence

Sentence/Supervision Plan A plan which sets out the needs of an offender and how they will be managed during their time in custody or on community sentences; what interventions will be provided, by whom and when.

SLA Service Level Agreement

SMART Specific, Measurable, Agreed, Realistic, Timely, in the context of

setting the right targets
SMB        Strategic Management Board
SOPO       Sexual Offences Prevention Order:
           Order to stop certain activities that
           might place the public at risk.
SOSJ       Secretary of State for Justice
SOVA       Society of Voluntary Associates
SP         Sentence Plan
SPR        Sentence Plan Review
SPOC       Specific Point of Contact
SSO        Suspended Sentence Order
SSR        Specific Sentence Report
           for courts

**T**
TACT       Terrorism Act Offence
TIC        Taken into Consideration
TM         Treatment Manager
TSP        Thinking Skills Prog
TPO        Trainee Probation Officer
TWOC       Take (vehicle) without
           owner's consent TVP
           Thames Valley
           Programme for sex
           offenders

**U**
UNISON     The Public Service union
UPW/       Unpaid Work. Now often
           referred to as Community
           Payback. Work ordered
           by the courts to be
           undertaken for the benefit
           of the community: a
           punitive intervention used as a
           creative resource for improving the
           local environment, teaching offenders
           skills, and improving their work ethic.
USI        Unlawful Sexual Intercourse
UWS        Unpaid Work Supervisor

**V**
VCS        Voluntary Community Sector
ViSOR      Violent and Sex Offender Register:
           national database
VLO        Victim Liaison Officer
VOO        Violent Offender Order
VSS        Victim Support Services

**W**
WACB       Whole Area Community Budget
WNB/WWOB
           Warrant issued, with no bail
WME        White Minority Ethnic
WSW        Womens Safety Worker

**Y**
YJB        Youth Justice Board
YOI        Young Offender Institution
YOP        Youth Offender Panel
YOS        Youth Offending Service

## OFFENDER MANAGEMENT STATISTICS JANUARY-MARCH 22

**Quarter: January to March 2022**
**Published 28th July 2022**
**Prison population: 30 June 2022**
**Main Points - Published 28 July 2022**

Quarterly: January to March 2022

Prison population: 30 June 2022

Main Points

| | |
|---|---|
| 80,659 prisoners in England and Wales as at 30 June 2022 | This represents a **rise** of 3% compared to the same period in the previous year. |
| 15,354 first receptions into prison between January and March 2022 | This is a **rise** of 9% compared to the same period in 2021. |
| 11,324 releases from sentences between January and March 2022 | This is 1% **lower** than the same period in 2021. As the prison population shifts towards those serving longer sentences, we expect fewer releases in each period. |
| 37,102 adjudication outcomes between January and March 2022 | This has remained unchanged compared to the same period in 2021. Additional days were awarded as punishment on 582 occasions. |
| 5,544 licence recalls between January and March 2022 | This is a 5% **increase** on the same quarter in 2021. |
| 240,922 offenders on probation at the end of March 2022 | This number **increased** by 7% compared to the number of offenders supervised as at 31 March 2021. |

### MAIN POINTS
In this publication we are reporting on the prison population as at 30 June 2022, with comparisons to the same point in 2021. Over this 12-month period, the total prison population has risen by around 2,350 (which represents a 3% increase) to 80,659. This quarter the prison population has exceeded 80,000 for the first time since April 2020.

The increasing remand population trend that we have seen since early 2020 has continued (a 5% increase between 30 June 2021 and 30 June 2022). There were increases over the past 12 months in both elements of the remand population - the 'untried' population increased by 4% and the 'convicted unsentenced' population increased by 8%. This likely reflects the impact of partial court recovery following COVID-19 restrictions, resulting in an increase in the number of prisoners held on remand.

Between June 2021 and 2022, there was an increase of 3% in the sentenced prison population. This is the largest annual increase in the sentenced prison population we have seen since 2016 – which (as with the increasing remand population highlighted above) reflects that the normal flow of individuals from the remand to the sentenced population (after sentencing at court) is continuing to recover following COVID-19 restrictions.

On the topic of COVID-19 recovery, the prison population has not yet returned to pre-pandemic levels; the 30 June 2022 prison population is still around 2,300 below the level of 31 Mar 2020.

The prisoner flows data in this publication cover the period January to March 2022, which means that we are comparing prisoner flows data between two quarterly 'COVID-19 periods' (the comparison period being January to March 2021). In England, there was a COVID-19 lockdown in early 2021 which impacted on normal Criminal Justice System operations. The number of prisoner first receptions from January to March 2022 was 9% higher than this equivalent period in 2021.

In each of the last four quarterly periods (from April 2021 to March 2022) there have been around 15,000 prisoner first receptions per quarter; this is lower than the level of around 17,000 per quarter seen pre-pandemic.

As COVID restrictions on normal prison regime are relaxed we will see very large percentage changes in certain areas. For example, there were around 85,000 incidences of Release on Temporary Licence (ROTL) between January and March 2022 – this is a 189% increase (around three times the level) compared to the same quarter in 2021 (during which there was a national COVID-19 lockdown in England), but only a partial return towards pre-COVID levels of around 110,000 per quarter.

Large percentage changes can also be seen in a number of ROTL sub-types, for example the number of ROTL incidences for 'Training & Education' has increased from 274 (between January and March 2021) to 2,772 in the latest quarter. This represents a percentage change of more than 900% (i.e. around 10 times as high as the same quarter in 2021). This is associated with changes in operational practices, moving away from COVID-19 restrictions that had been imposed on the prison regime.

## 1. POPULATION

The prison population stood at 80,659 on 30 June 2022.

The sentenced prison population stood at 66,480 (82% of the total); the remand prison population stood at 13,409 (17%) and the non-criminal prison population stood at 770 (1%). This is the first quarter since March 2020 (the start of the COVID-19 pandemic) that the total prison population has passed 80,000.

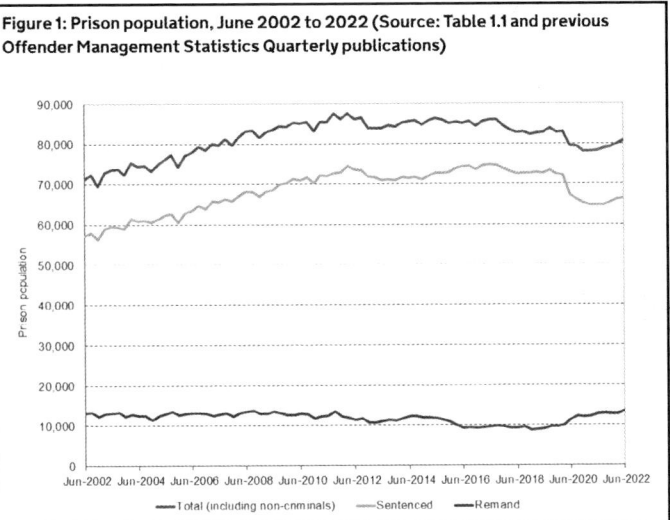

**Figure 1: Prison population, June 2002 to 2022 (Source: Table 1.1 and previous Offender Management Statistics Quarterly publications)**

### Remand prison population

Between June 2016 and the start of the COVID-19 pandemic in 2020, the remand population was under 10,000. Since the start of the pandemic, it increased and this quarter's figure of 13,409 is the highest June remand prison population since 2008. The untried prison population rose by 4% (to 8,763) when compared to the end of June 2021 whilst the convicted unsentenced population rose by 8% (to 4,646) over the same period.

Most of those in custody on remand were being held for either: violence against the person (27% of the untried population and 18% of the convicted unsentenced population); or drug offences (25% of the untried population and 34% of the convicted unsentenced population).

### Sentenced prison population

The sentenced population was 66,480 which is a 3% increase from the same point 12 months earlier. Broadly speaking, there were increases in the sentenced population serving sentence bands of 'less than 4 years' and decreases in the numbers of those serving '4 years or more' (apart from a 3% rise in those serving the longest determinate sentences of 14 years or more and a 11% rise in those serving an Extended Determinate Sentence).

### Population and Offence group

The number of prisoners serving immediate custodial sentences for drug offences has increased by 5% over the past year to 10,775 as at 30 June 2022.

While sexual offences is one of the largest groups amongst prisoners serving immediate custodial sentences, the population had been falling since it peaked in mid-2018. However, over the past year, the number has risen gradually again, with a 6% increase (to 12,455) in the 12 months to 30 June 2022. There were also 53% and 9% increases in the number of untried and convicted-unsentenced prisoners respectively in this offence group over the same period.

Three in every ten (31%) inmates serving an immediate custodial sentence have been convicted of a Violence Against the Person (VATP) offence. This proportion has increased from the 'one in four' (25%) level seen in recent years.

### Changes by offence group in relation to the COVID-19 pandemic

Due to the ongoing recovery of the courts following the COVID-19 pandemic (the number of outstanding Crown Court cases increased by 43% percent between the end March 2020 and March 2022 [footnote 1]. it is difficult to discern whether longer term changes in the prison population associated with particular offence groups are a reflection of incidences of these crimes.

The number of prisoners with associated Robbery and Theft offences has fallen by 16% and 26% respectively between 31 March 2020 and 30 June 2022 largely due to falls in the sentenced populations for these offences. Concurrently, there have only been very modest increases in the number of outstanding Crown Court cases for these offences. It is therefore possible that we are seeing a reflection of the reduced opportunity for these offences during the pandemic lockdowns, a theory supported by the published crime figures [footnote 2].

The number of prisoners with associated Possession of Weapons and Miscellaneous crimes against society offences has also fallen (by 13% and 16% respectively) since the start of the pandemic, again primarily due to decreases in the sentenced populations for these offences. These falls have been matched or exceeded by the increase in the number of outstanding Crown Court cases for these offences. However, when a conviction ratio of between eight and nine in ten and a custody rate of around three in ten is factored in [footnote 3], it is possible that the modest decreases may be attributable to the pandemic.

https://www.gov.uk/government/statistics/criminal-justice-system-statistics-quarterly-december-2021 The number of prisoners associated with VATP and Drug offences has increased since the start of the pandemic (5% and 10% respectively), primarily due large increase in their remand populations. Moreover, there has been an even larger increase in the number of outstanding Crown Court cases for these offences so it is possible that the number of prisoners associated with these offences will continue to rise for some time.

### Extended Determinate Sentences (EDS)

EDSs constitute a custodial term, the majority of which is served in prison, followed by an additional extended period of licence in the community. They can be imposed if the offender is found guilty of, or has a previous conviction for, a specific sexual, violent or terrorist offence. On 30 June 2022, 6,864 prisoners were serving such sentences; an 11% increase compared to the same time last year.

### Indeterminate sentences

As at 30 June 2022, there were 8,576 (8,245 male; 331 female) prisoners serving indeterminate sentences (Imprisonment for Public Protection (IPP) and life sentences). This represents a slight overall decrease (-1%) when compared with 30 June 2021.

The number of unreleased prisoners (7,084) serving life sentences has increased by 2% compared to one year ago whereas the number of unreleased IPP prisoners fell by 13% to 1,492. At point of sentencing, offenders are given a minimum time period ("tariff") that they must serve in prison before they can apply to the Parole Board for release. The majority (52%) of the remaining unreleased IPP prisoners have been held for more than nine years beyond the end of their tariff.

The number of recalled prisoners serving life sentences increased by 12% to 681 when compared to March 2021 whilst the number of recalled Imprisonment for Public Protection (IPP) prisoners saw an 8% increase to 1,434.

### Recall to custody

The overall population who have been recalled to custody (9,892 prisoners) has increased by 9% relative to the total a year earlier. This is the highest monthly figure since at least 2009. The increasing recall population is likely driven by a combination of factors such as a longer-term increase in the average length of determinate sentences and an increase in the number of people serving indeterminate sentences or sentences with an extended licence, which result in an increase in the size of the population released on licence from which the recall population arises.

**Foreign National Offenders (FNOs)**
There were 9,682 (2,743 remand, 6,214 sentenced and 725 non-criminal) foreign nationals held in custody as at 30 June 2022; representing 12% of the total prison population. The number of FNOs in the prison population has decreased by 1% compared to 30 June 2021, driven by a 19% fall in the number of non-criminal foreign national prisoners. The most common nationalities after British Nationals in prisons are Albanian (14% of the FNO prison population), Polish (9%), Romanian (8%), Irish (7%), Lithuanian (4%), and Jamaican (4%).

**Prison Age**
There were decreases in the number of prisoners in each age group under 30 whereas there was an increase in all the age groups above 30. For example, there was an 8% (-280 prisoners) decrease in the number of prisoners aged 18-20, and a 6% increase (+935 prisoners) in the number aged 40-49 when compared to June 2021. This pattern of an ageing population is consistent with the longer-term changes seen over the last twenty years.

**2. RECEPTIONS & ADMISSIONS**
**15,354 prisoners were received into custody as first receptions in the latest quarter.**
9,581 were remand first receptions, 5,698 were sentenced first receptions and 75 were civil non-criminal first receptions.

**Prisoner First receptions**
The total number of first receptions between January and March 2022 was 9% higher than the same quarter in 2021. The number of first receptions has increased this quarter but remains lower than pre-pandemic levels. Between January and March 2022, the number of remand first receptions was 11% higher than the same quarter in 2021. This reflects the court processes that have improved since the pandemic but not recovered to pre-pandemic levels yet.

There were 2,520 first receptions of foreign nationals during Q1 2022, which is 2% higher compared to the same quarter in 2021. The representation of foreign nationals amongst first receptions has remained similar since 2020, with around 16% of first receptions being foreign nationals. The five foreign nationalities with the highest numbers of first receptions in the latest quarter were: Albanian (428), Romanian (329),

Polish (284), Lithuanian (128) and Irish (114). When taken together, these five nationalities accounted for around half (51%) of the 2,520 first receptions of foreign nationals in Q1 2022.

**Prison admissions**
Compared to the same quarter in 2021, the number of untried admissions increased by 10%. The number of convicted unsentenced admissions increased by 11% and sentenced admissions increased by 9%. This can be attributed to the increased number of court outcomes arising from court recovery following an easing of the impacts of COVID-19 on court functions.

When considering immediate custodial sentenced admissions by offence group, violence against the person and drug offences had the largest number of sentenced admissions overall. The largest increase in admissions as compared to Q1 2021 occurred in the sexual offences group, up by 25%. Compared to females, males made up a larger proportion of sentenced admissions across each offence, but there are certain offences where this difference was more pronounced-sexual offences, drug offences, possession of weapons and summary motoring (see figure 2 below). The largest representation of females was in the fraud offence group (they accounted for 21% of all immediate custodial sentenced admissions for fraud offences).

**Figure 2: (next page) Representation (percentage) of male and female immediate custodial sentenced prisoner admissions in each offence group between January and March 2022.**
When compared with the same quarter last year, the sentence length band with the largest increase in the number of admissions was 4 years or more (excluding indeterminate sentences), with a 33% increase, which can also be attributed to the prioritisation of prosecutions for more serious offences that carry longer sentences, as mentioned above.

**Former Members of the Armed Forces**
When individuals are first received into custody, they complete a Basic Custody Screening (BCS) process. This serves to identify their needs in areas including employment, childcare and healthcare. As part of this process, they are asked whether they had served in the armed services. Between January and March 2022, 147 matched individuals first received into custody answered that they had served in the armed services - this represented 2% of those who provided a response to the question at the point of their first reception during the latest quarter.

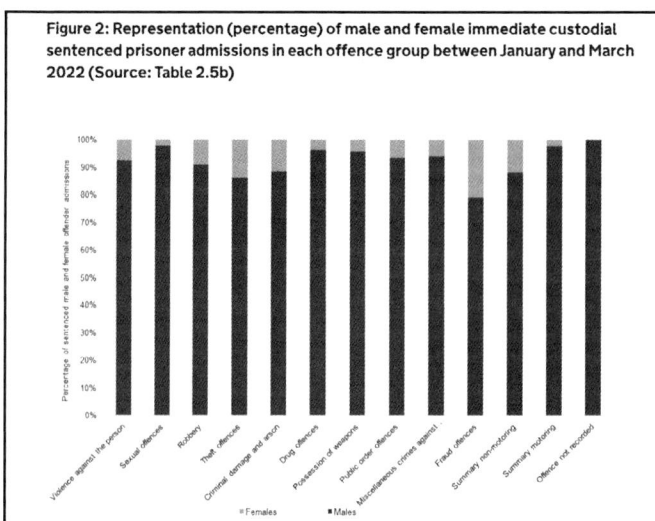

Figure 2: Representation (percentage) of male and female immediate custodial sentenced prisoner admissions in each offence group between January and March 2022 (Source: Table 2.5b)

to re-introduce access to ROTL [footnote 5] when and where it is safe to do so, and accounting for the changing national restrictions.

As a result of these changes to prison regimes, ROTL numbers have continued to increase. There were 84,824 incidences of ROTL during the quarter ending March 2022, which represents a 189% increase compared to the same quarter in 2021. This figure remains below pre-pandemic levels. Of the ROTL incidences in the latest quarter 68% were for 'Work Related' reasons.

The number of individuals receiving at least one incidence of ROTL between January and March 2022 continued to rise following the changes to prison regimes, up 273% from the same quarter in 2021. 3,984 individuals were released on temporary licence in the latest quarter.

There were 144 Temporary Release Failures between January and March 2022. This is a fall of 34 compared with the previous quarter, and a rise of 130 compared with the same period in 2021. TRFs as a proportion of temporary release incidences stood at 1 in 588 between January and March 2022.

**Prisoner transfers**
Between January and March 2022 there were 18,424 incidences of prisoner transfer, with 15,847 prisoners having at least one incidence of transfer. Both figures represent increases since the same period of 2021, with rises of 22% and 17% respectively meaning that transfers continue to recover towards pre-pandemic levels.

**4. ADJUDICATIONS**
**There were 37,102 adjudication outcomes between January and March 2022.**
This has remained almost unchanged compared with the same quarter a year ago. Additional days were awarded as punishment on 582 occasions in this quarter.
*Two thirds (67%) of adjudications were proven.*
The number of proven adjudications has remained almost unchanged (at 24,980) from the same quarter in 2021, but there was a 2% rise in the number of punishments (to 43,258).

## 3. RELEASES
**11,324 offenders were released from custody in the latest quarter.**
11,198 releases from determinate sentences and 126 from indeterminate sentences.

**Prison releases from custodial sentences**
The number of prisoner releases between January and March 2022 was 1% lower than the same quarter in 2021. The number of releases from sentences of 12 months to less than 4 years between January and March 2022 was unchanged as compared to the same period in 2021. Throughout the COVID-19 pandemic the prosecution of more serious offences has been prioritised, meaning that fewer prisoners have been received into prison and thus been released from the shorter sentences handed out for less serious offences [footnote 4].

Between January and March 2022, there was a decrease of 4%, in the number of prisoners released from sentences of 4 years or more (excluding indeterminate sentences), as compared to the same period in 2021. A larger decrease was seen for releases from indeterminate sentences, with a fall of 9%.

**Releases on Home Detention Curfew (HDC)**
The number of offenders released on HDC in the latest quarter dropped by 6%, to 2,270. The number potentially eligible for HDC over the same period was 9,500, up 4% compared to the same quarter in 2021.

**Releases on Temporary Licence (ROTL)**
Most ROTL was suspended for much of the pandemic period. HMPPS has, however, worked closely with public health authorities

A third (34%) of proven adjudications were for offences of 'disobedience and disrespect', with the next largest category being 'unauthorised transactions' (29%). The number of proven adjudications for 'unauthorised transactions' and 'violence' offences rose by 13% (to 7,189) and 2% (to 3,691) respectively on the same quarter of the previous year. This has been offset by a fall in other categories, in particular 'wilful damage' and 'disobedience and disrespect'. They fell by 19% (to 2,572) and 1% (to 8,601) respectively on the same quarter of the previous year.

Although the number of proven adjudications for violence increased in comparison to Q1 2021, this is still lower than the figures recorded up until 2019 where quarterly averages exceeded 5,000 offences. This increase is largely driven by the relaxing of measures implemented since March 2020 to reduce physical interactions amongst inmates and prison staff due to Covid-19.

Additional days were awarded as punishment on 582 occasions between January and March 2022; this is a 22% fall compared with the same period in 2021. A total of 9,218 days were awarded in the latest quarter – this is a 23% fall compared with the same quarter in 2021 (11,959 days between January and March 2021).

The overall number of adjudication outcomes has remained almost unchanged in comparison to Q1 2021.The quarterly volume of adjudication outcomes has continued to be below 40,000 since the start of the lockdown.

A number of policy interventions were made to suspend discipline hearings requiring an Independent Adjudicator (IA) between 23 March and 22 June 2020. Referrals to IAs have now resumed but are still held virtually and are subject to new guidelines. This impacted the number of referrals (876 for the quarter), which is far below the averages recorded before the lockdown.

In addition, other changes to the prison regime have been implemented to support operational delivery. These include new rules for governors, enabling them to: limit the movement of prisoners; implement social distancing; compartmentalise prisons to isolate symptomatic prisoners; quarantine new entrants; and so forth. These measures remain in place and taken together have reduced interactions between prisoners and staff, hence reducing the number of adjudications and related punishments.

In addition, other changes to the prison regime have been implemented to support operational delivery. These include new rules for governors, enabling them to: limit the movement of prisoners; implement social distancing; compartmentalise prisons to isolate symptomatic prisoners; quarantine new entrants; and so forth. These measures remain in place and taken together have reduced interactions between prisoners and staff, hence reducing the number of adjudications and related punishments [footnote 5].

More information about the trends in Adjudications between 2011 and 2018 can be found in 'The Adjudications Story' publication.

## 5. LICENCE RECALLS

**The number of licence recalls between January and March 2022 was 5,544, of which 369 were recalls from Home Detention Curfew (HDC).**
The total number of recalls increased by 5% compared to the same quarter in 2021.

The total number of quarterly recalls trended upwards between October-December 2016 and July-September 2019. There was a marked increase in the number of quarterly recalls from early 2018 to July-September 2019, mostly due to increases in the number of HDC recalls and recalls of offenders from determinate sentences of 12 months or more. These numbers then began to fall, and the downward shift was accelerated by the introduction of COVID-19 restrictions. Although relaxation of COVID-19 restrictions in early 2021 led to increases in the number of quarterly recalls, the latest figure is a decrease of 4% from the previous quarter. The latest figure does represent a 5% increase from a year ago when COVID-19 restrictions were fully in place.

The guidance for courts and prisons implemented in 2020 has remained in place so as to assist courts, custodial and detention staff in addressing Covid-19 hence reducing the rate of transmission within prisons. This has had a continuing effect on the number of court proceedings and new entrants into custody.

Following relative stability up to January-March 2020, the number of quarterly recalls of offenders released from a sentence of under 12 months noticeably began to fall, falling below 2,000 for the first time since July-September 2016, partly due to the introduction of COVID-19 restrictions. Although relaxation of COVID-19 restrictions led to increases in these numbers, they have continued to stay below 2,000. The latest figure (1,850) represents a decrease of 2% from the previous quarter and an increase of 9% from a year ago when COVID-19 restrictions were fully in place.

The pattern in quarterly recalls of offenders with a sentence of 12 months or more (including those with indeterminate sentences) more closely mirrors that of the overall quarterly recalls as this group usually constitute about 2/3 of overall recalls. Between January and March 2022, there were 3,694 recalls of such offenders, representing a decrease of 5% from the previous quarter and an increase of 3% from a year ago when COVID-19 restrictions were fully in place.

Ethnicity proportions in quarterly recalls have remained relatively stable, with about 8 in 10 recalls being white, 9% being black and 4% being Asian.

There usually is more than one reason for recalling an offender on licence. Of recalls in January-March 2022, about 33% involved a charge of further offending, 70% involved non-compliance, 28% involved failure to keep in touch, and 24% involved failure to reside.

Between January and March 2022, 120 IPP prisoners and 69 prisoners serving a life sentence were rereleased, having previously been returned to custody for a breach of licence conditions. These together represent an increase of 14% from the same quarter a year ago.

Offenders not returned to custody
Of all those released on licence and recalled to custody due to breaching the conditions of their licence between April 1999 and March 2022, there were 2,118 who had not been returned to custody by the end of June 2022.

A further 16 offenders had not been returned to custody as of June 2022 after recall between 1984 and April 1999, meaning the total number of offenders not returned to custody at the end of June 2022 was 2,134. These figures include some offenders believed to be dead or living abroad but who have not been confirmed as dead or deported.

Of the 2,134 not returned to custody by 30 June 2022, 348 had originally been serving a prison sentence for violence against the person offences and a further 64 for sexual offences.

## 6. PROBATION
**The total number of offenders on probation (i.e. court orders and pre/post-release supervision) at the end of March 2022 was 240,922.**
This represents a 7% increase compared to the end of March 2021.

Latest figures on probation starts are levelling out after increasing since operational restrictions [footnote 7], introduced in response to the COVID-19 pandemic, were lifted in late spring 2020. This had an ongoing knock-on effect on caseload figures whereby the number of offenders supervised by the Probation Service overall continued to increase and so recover to pre-pandemic levels [footnote 8], but has now slowed to a more gradual increase than in the initial periods following the lifting of restrictions.

As at 31 March 2022, there were 240,922 offenders supervised by the Probation Service (Figure 2), representing a 7% increase compared to 31 March 2021 and a 1% increase compared to 31 December 2021.

Between the end of March 2021 and the end of March 2022, court order caseload increased by 19% from 95,127 to 113,378, with the number of offenders on a community order (CO) and those on a suspended sentence order (SSO) with requirements both increasing by 19% and 21% respectively.

The total caseload of offenders supervised before or after release from prison at the end of March 2022 was 132,098, representing a decrease of less than 1% compared to the end of March 2021.

**Figure 3: Number of offenders under Probation Service supervision, 31 March 2012 to 31 March 2022 (source for 2018 to 2022: Table 4.6; source for years prior to 2018: Table 4.7)**
Between January and March 2022, 41,116 offenders started court order or pre-release probation supervision (Figure 3), representing increases of 6% on the previous quarter and of 2% compared to the same quarter a year ago.

Between January to March 2022, the number of offenders starting court orders, specifically, increased by 10% following the previous quarter. This figure also saw a 3% increase compared to the same quarter a year ago. The number of offenders starting COs increased 11% to 16,794 compared to the previous quarter and increased by 3% compared to the same quarter a year ago. Meanwhile, the number of offenders starting SSOs with requirements increased 10% to 8,671 compared to the previous quarter and increased by 5% compared to the same quarter in the previous year. Additionally, over the latest quarter, there was a small increase in the number of offenders starting pre-release supervision compared to the previous quarter (from 15,445 to 15,525) but a slight decrease since the same quarter in the previous year (from 15,744 to 15,525).

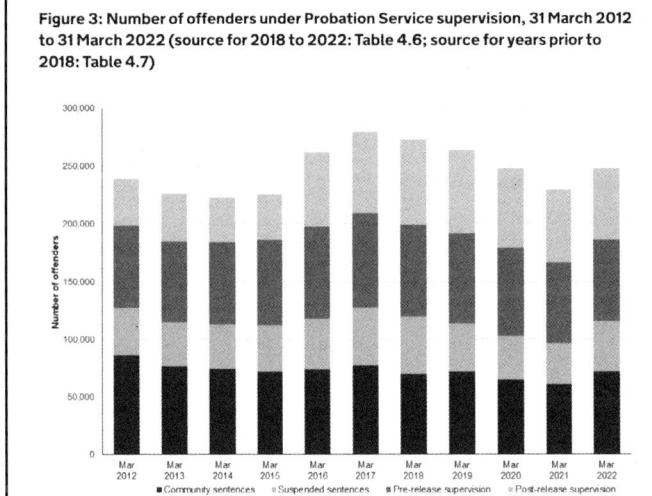

Figure 3: Number of offenders under Probation Service supervision, 31 March 2012 to 31 March 2022 (source for 2018 to 2022: Table 4.6; source for years prior to 2018: Table 4.7)

The numbers of offenders starting Probation Service supervision due to committing a violent offence against a person have seen large increases for both COs and SSOs since January to March 2021, with those starting COs increasing by 51% to 2,284 and SSOs increasing by 25% to 1,662 in January to March 2022. Consequently, the number of offenders on the Probation Service supervision caseload for a violence against the person offence as at 31 March 2022 also increased by 75% to 8,297 for COs and by 33% to 7,831 for SSOs.

**Figure 4: Number of offenders starting supervision under the Probation Service, April to June 2019 to January to March 2022 (source: Table 4.1)**

Between January and March 2022, 26,700 requirements started under COs and 15,561 requirements started under SSOs, representing increases of 6% and 11% respectively compared to the same period in the previous year. Over the same period, rehabilitation requirements started under COs and SSOs increased by 2% to 10,899 and by 5% to 6,789 respectively and remains the most common requirement included within a CO or SSO. Under COs and SSOs, there were increases across most requirement types compared to the same quarter in 2021. Most notably, under COs, mental health, alcohol treatment, and unpaid work requirements increased by 54% to 251,

by 28% to 958, and by 18% to 8,200 respectively. However, accredited programme requirements decreased by 15% to 1,485. Under SSOs, mental health, drug treatment and unpaid work requirements increased by 49% to 146, by 26% to 601, and by 20% to 4,007 respectively.

In terms of the most frequently used combinations of requirements, rehabilitation requirements combined separately with alcohol treatment, drug treatment, and unpaid work requirements increased by 35%, 14% and 10% respectively under COs in January to March 2022 compared to the same period a year ago. Under SSOs, rehabilitation requirements combined separately with drug treatment, unpaid work and alcohol treatment requirements increased by 23%, 15% and 4% respectively.

Of the 12,786 COs and 6,396 SSOs terminated between January and March 2022, 72% and 78% respectively were terminated successfully, i.e., ran their full course or were terminated early for good progress.

In the quarter January to March 2022, the total number of pre-sentence reports (PSRs) prepared by the Probation Service decreased by 3% to 20,858 compared to the previous quarter and by 2% compared to the same quarter in 2021.

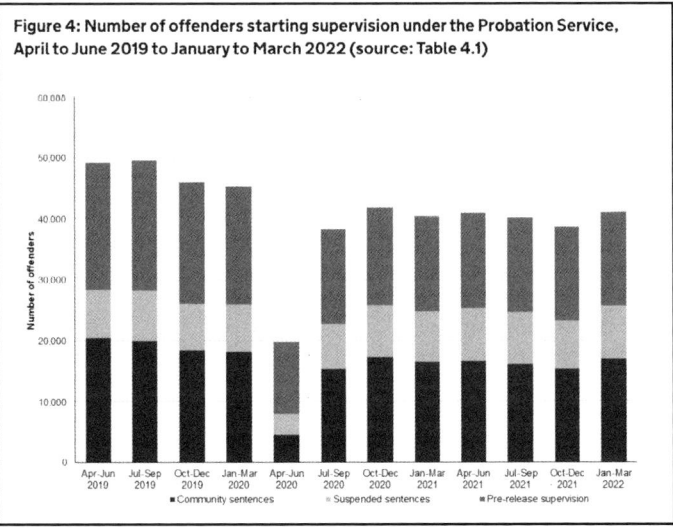

Figure 4: Number of offenders starting supervision under the Probation Service, April to June 2019 to January to March 2022 (source: Table 4.1)

Offender Management Statistics

Furthermore, 89% of immediate custodial sentences proposed in PSRs resulted in that sentence being given in the year ending March 2022, representing the highest concordance between sentence proposed and sentence given.

## EDITORIAL: MARK LEECH FRSA
## THE PRISONS OMBUDSMAN:
### Cause For Complaint?

**Any Prison Complaints process:**

## "...must be independent, and be _seen_ to be so."

**Thus, wrote Lord Woolf at paragraph 14.309 of his landmark Report into the Strangeways Riots of 1990.**

Harry Woolf's was a Report that gave birth to the Office of Prisons Ombudsman but today, over 30 years later, I ask how truly independent can this vital Office really be _seen_ to be, when its last two substantive occupants have, between them, spent almost 50 years employed by the very same Prison Service they were, as the Prisons Ombudsman, expected to subsequently independently investigate?

In this Editorial last year, I turned to the subject of The Prisons Ombudsman and particularly deaths in custody; I make no apology for returning to this subject again this year - if only for the fact that the last Prisons Ombudsman also briefly (blink and you would have missed it) repeated this year in her annual report exactly the same criticisms she made last year and which once again remain unaddressed.

But, more importantly, I return to the subject of the Prisons Ombudsman because as I write this, in September 2022, we stand on the cusp of what could be either a new dawn in the Office of Prisons Ombudsman – or which is perhaps more likely (and why I return to the subject again) more of the same pathetic failures where yet another candidate carefully selected by the Justice Secretary and viewed as a safe pair of hands on the Prison Ombudsman's helm, is advanced as the 'preferred candidate' to the Justice Committee who, bless them, will once again go through the motions of providing a veneer of independent scrutiny to the selection process of the next Prisons Ombudsman before rubber stamping the appointment however inappropriate the candidate is obviously seen to be.

On 1st July 2022 Sue McAllister, the Prisons and Probation Ombudsman since 2017 retired and we now stand at the door and wait the appointment of her successor; a new substantive Prisons and Probation Ombudsman who, hopefully for the first time since June 2011, will be seen to be truly independent.

It is vitally important to remind ourselves why we have a Prisons Ombudsman (the 'Probation part of the title came later) and from what ashes of destruction this Office was created. More saliently why, going forward, the diminution of its reputation over the last decade has to stop - or why we instead risk a repetition of the chaos that led to creation of the Prisons Ombudsman in the first place.

Let's take a step back over 30-years in time.

On Sunday 1st April 1990 Strangeways Prison in Manchester, which was then the largest prison in England and Wales and one of the largest in Europe, exploded in an almost month-long orgy of violence, destruction and death.

The riot, which spread to five other prisons (Glen Parva (soon to reopen as Fosse Way), HMPs Dartmoor, Cardiff, Bristol and Pucklechurch (now rebuilt as HMP Ashfield) lasted for 25 days and was the longest prison riot in British prison history – and, at £60million in 1990 figures, was also the most expensive.

The Strangeways series of riots lead to the establishment of the Woolf Inquiry (a copy of whose Reports can be found on The Prison Oracle - _https://prisonoracle.com_) that concluded, for the most part, that the riots were the result of appalling overcrowded, insanitary, brutalising prison conditions and a complaints process that was nothing more than a joke in appallingly bad taste.

These conditions, said Woolf, were exacerbated by the failed complaints system which meant prisoners felt they had no independent, fair or legitimate means to obtain redress of their complaints – leading them ultimately to ventilate their grievances by writing them on bedsheets draped across riot-torn prison rooftops for the public, rather than on paper for the Governor in whom they had no confidence at all.

The Strangeways series of riots was a catalyst for change, a turning point that demonstrated like no other that prisoners refused any longer to be mistreated, no more would their complaints be ignored, ripped up and ridiculed, never again would they be forced to urinate and defecate in plastic pots in overcrowded Victorian prison cells designed for one person and into which three people were crammed living with the stench of their human waste for up to 23 hours a day.

Never again.

Woolf accepted that the system of prisoner complaints had to change, accepting that nothing was more likely to cause unrest among ordinary prisoners than a sense that they had been treated unfairly and had no effective, independent, means of redress.

Woolf therefore recommended that a prisoner complaints system must be introduced which had a truly independent element to it, one in which independence existed not only in theory but more importantly was *seen* and accepted to be truly independent in practice too.

Here is what Woolf said – the numbers are the appropriate paragraph numbers in his Report:

**14.297** .....*Within a prison in particular, it is an important requirement of justice that justice should not only actually be done but should be seen to be done. It will not be seen to be done ....if there is not, at least at the final stage of the process, recourse to an independent element.*

**14.309.** *If a grievance procedure is to be of value, the procedure must:.. iv) be independent. And it must be seen to be so.*

**14.351** [By independent we mean] *"The person appointed would need to be someone of independence and standing."*

**14.345** *.... the presence of an independent element within the Grievance Procedure is more than just an "optional extra". The case for some form of independent person or body to consider grievances is incontrovertible. There is no possibility of the present system satisfactorily meeting this point... A system without an independent element is not a system which accords with proper standards of justice.*

So just how 'independent' then is *independent?*

'Independent' is a word that is used for a specific reason, with a clear and very well-understood meaning.

I start from the very basic position that the word 'independent' means *exactly* what it says.

It is a word that is not open to interpretation, personal intuition, gut feelings, hairs on the back of the neck, we are all very well aware of what it means, it is defined in the Oxford English Dictionary as *"disconnected, not influenced by something"* and so it contains no ambiguity; moreover, we recognise when something is *seen* to be independent – and we can often spot a mile off too when something that is claimed to be independent just isn't *seen* to be truly independent at all.

Independence is not just a clever form of words, used to gloss over a situation or course of events, it does not exist to give the false impression that justice is being done, that something is at arm's length when its actually seen to be in the pocket: rather independence is a *state of mind* and people who are part of the whole process that leads to an independent public appointment all have to possess it – or it fails in its entirety.

In my view the current system of Prisons Ombudsman is not one that passes the 'independence' test at all.

I impute no bad faith in respect of any of the individuals who have held the Office of Prisons Ombudsman but the fact is that whilst the first two substantive occupants of the Office, Sir Peter Woodhead and, later, Dr Stephen Shaw, were indeed *seen* to be clearly independent – having no previous employment relationship with the Prison Service - the same cannot be said of those who followed and who, between them, had around half a century of Prison Service employee experience; that, in my opinion, completely fails the crucial test of being *seen* to be independent.

Nigel Newcomen, who was Prisons Ombudsman from June 2011 to July 2017 was employed by HM Prison Service for 21 years, rising within it to the rank of Assistant Director.

Following Nigel Newcomen as substantive Ombudsman was Sue McAllister who previously not only spent decades working for HM Prison Service as a Prison Governor but who subsequently later became Director General of the Northern Ireland Prison Service before becoming Prisons Ombudsman on the mainland.

Throughout Mrs McAllister's whole tenure as Prisons Ombudsman her son, Daniel McAllister, was a serving Senior Prison Officer in HM Prison and Probation Service (which she disclosed at her pre-appointment scrutiny hearing with the Justice Committee and which at that point ought to have ruled her out as a candidate for the post completely but didn't) and, more than that, Mrs McAllister's husband, Danny McAllister, was himself a former Director of the Prison Service - which was never mentioned during the Justice Committee hearing at all.

Again, I impute no bad faith – the fault here lay jointly with Mrs McAllister in believing that with her background and continuing close personal family associations with the Prison Service that she was ever suitable for the post but, by far the most censure has to be directed at the Justice Committee in their decision to approve her appointment; they must have known (and if they didn't they ought to have done) that she was, with her background and disclosed current and personal family associations with the Prison Service, never the right person for the post in a million years.

I repeat, I impute no bad faith, but how on any view can those facts ever amount to being *'seen'* to be independent?

Remember what Woolf wrote:

**14.309.** *If a grievance procedure is to be of value, the procedure must:...*

*iv) be independent. And it must be **seen** to be so.*

Perceptions matter – lest we forget, it was the perception of prisoners at Strangeways prison that they had been treated unfairly and had no effective means of redress that led to the riot in the first place – and subsequently the creation of the Office of Ombudsman.

The Prison Ombudsman not only deals with complaints about such things as lost property but, more importantly, it is an Office also charged with investigating each death that occurs both in custody and those deaths that take place a short time after release.

It is here, in this most important aspect of their work, that the failings of the Prisons Ombudsman are the most clear and gross.

When a prisoner dies in custody or immediately after release the Ombudsman is notified and they commence an investigation into the death of the individual in the expectation, it is claimed, that the Prison Service or Private Sector operator can *learn lessons* from how it happened, what the response to it was and, where it is deemed appropriate, make recommendations to reduce the chance of the same identified errors being repeated again.

It is a forlorn hope.

The transparency of the *independent* Prisons Ombudsman is flawed from the start when it comes to deaths in custody.

The fact is that while the Prison Ombudsman is made aware of every death in custody, it is something they keep strictly to themselves; I thought it was only in China or North Korea that people died secretly in prison but the facts show that it actually happens here too.

Neither the Ministry of Justice or the Prisons Ombudsman proactively announce that a prisoner has died in the custody of the State – instead the public has to wait until a journalist is told about the death by a member of staff or a prisoner's family before the Ministry of Justice reluctantly admits to it – but this is information any independent Prisons Ombudsman should release as a matter of course - and it could easily be done without prejudicing their investigation, the Inquest or distressing the next of kin with a simple announcement along the lines of:

*"Today, in HMP Somewhere, a 34-year old convicted male prisoner died. We are conducting an investigation into the circumstances of this death, we have attributed the reference number F123456/2022 to it, and will issue a report under that reference number in due course."*

What would be wrong with that?

Instead they say nothing.

Absolutely nothing at all - and they steadfastly refuse to do so.

That silence is not the action of a Prisons Ombudsman *seen* to be independent of the State. Rather this silence is indicative of an organisation that bears on its face all the classic hallmarks of a Prisons Ombudsman that is in cahoots with the State from whom it ought to be seen to be at obvious arm's length – but is instead viewed as being in its pocket.

When it comes to investigating deaths in the custody of the State, what have we learnt?

Little or nothing at all - and certainly nothing that has made real changes.

For donkey's years, the Ombudsman has been making exactly the same recommendations in published death in custody reports, directed at exactly the same prisons, concerning the deaths of prisoners in identical circumstances and which are claimed to be made in the name of 'learning lessons' – but the truth is no one takes a blind bit of notice of them at all - and this is not just me saying this, successive Ombudsmen have, quietly, made the same complaint.

It is not uncommon for exactly the same death in custody recommendations to be made six times or more to exactly the same prison, in exactly the same deathly circumstances and for those recommendations to be ignored in exactly the same way each and every time – and the Ombudsman does nothing but write polite letters to another *Sir Humphrey* as any civil servant would be expected to do, but nothing more and nothing changes.

In each and every death in custody report the Ombudsman makes the same glib disingenuous statement that *"I offer my condolences to the deceased's family and friends"* – excuse me?

No, you don't - and nothing like it.

If the Ombudsman genuinely meant this expression of condolence they would take a stand and refuse to accept the ignorance of their recommendations – and if they had the courage they would take further action too.

For a start, they would put in place a mechanism for monitoring the implementation of their recommendations, but no such mechanism exists.

We have Independent Monitoring Boards in every prison, with whom the Ombudsman could and should if they so desired arrange virtual conferences every quarter, to obtain first-hand reports and feedback from these 'monitors' as to how the Ombudsmen's death in custody recommendations were being implemented in that establishment – or more often not implemented, as the case may be.

But the truth is such meetings never, ever take place.

The Prison Ombudsman's Office has told me personally that they rely on a visit every four or five years from the Prisons Inspectorate to assess whether their recommendations are being implemented in any particular prison – by which time it is too often a lifetime too late for those who have died in the meantime and in circumstances that had the recommendations been implemented may well have been saved.

In establishments that persistently ignore death in custody recommendations the Ombudsman could arrange an *Urgent Notification* protocol, exactly the same as that enjoyed by the Prisons Inspectorate, in which they could issue a public letter setting out which prison is persistently ignoring their death in custody recommendations and demand action that is made public by the Justice Secretary within 28 days; but not a bit of it.

This is precisely what happens when you appoint career Civil Servants to an Independent watchdog role.

Individuals, who no doubt have the best of intentions, find themselves torn and conflicted between doing what I suspect they know is necessary but which would if actioned cause public embarrassment to the very body they have spent their entire careers being groomed by to behave in a Civil Service sort of way; so they shut up, say little or nothing – because, well, after all, it's not their loved one who is dangling dead at the end of a bedsheet is it?

Any *independent* Ombudsman worthy of the title, charged with investigating deaths in the custody of the State, whose recommendations were consistently ignored, would surely say *enough is enough,* publicly stand up, resign and walk away; but I can never see that happening.

Instead their recommendations continue to be ignored and all the Ombudsman has been seen to do is to make a nod towards that ignorance in their annual reports with what appears to me to be semantic frustration.

In the Annual Report of the Prisons Ombudsman for 2019/2020 the Ombudsman wrote of the failure to implement their recommendations:

*"We remain frustrated at the number of repeat recommendations we have to make, sometimes where changes have been promised (in an action plan from the prison or from HMPPS HQ) but not delivered."*

In the Annual Report of the Prisons Ombudsman for **2020/2021** the Ombudsman wrote of the failure to implement their recommendations:

*"This remains a key challenge for us as repeat failings, and the associated need to make the same recommendations in response to what we find, continue to frustrate our work."*

There is another deeply troubling aspect to the operation of the Prisons Ombudsman and it is this; the Ombudsman's failure to refer cases of seriously defective healthcare provision to the appropriate regulatory authority - such as the General Medical Council or Nursing and Midwifery Council.

In those death in custody cases where the investigation by the Ombudsman's independent Clinical Reviewer reveals the standard of healthcare provided in an individual case was so low as to be professionally unacceptable, the current practice of the Ombudsman is **not** to refer those cases to the regulator themselves but, instead, to pass-the-buck by asking the prison's Governor if they will do it - and what's more, thereafter the Ombudsman never bothers to check back to see whether the referral has in fact been done at all.

It is wrong, in so many ways, to expect a Prison Governor to "Grass up"' one of his staff in this way. All Governors need to carry their staff with them on a daily basis and it is unfair to say the least to ask a Governor to do this and deal with the industrial fall-out such a referral would inevitably bring with it.

The Prisons Ombudsman needs to take ownership of their Report and its findings; not pass the buck. They should themselves refer cases to the professional regulatory authorities and allow those bodies the opportunity to consider for themselves if it is necessary to root out and remove individuals from healthcare practice where their conduct has resulted directly or indirectly in the death of another person.

Will the next Prisons and Probation Ombudsman do any better?

Time will tell.

My hope is that when I write this editorial next year I will be able to record that, for the first time in well over a decade, we have in post a Prisons Ombudsman totally independent of the Prison Service - and prepared to stand up to it.

An Ombudsman who has the courage to demand action when death in custody recommendations are ignored, one who understands that *'independent'* means exactly what it says - and one who would rather walk away than be a part of a corrupting system where 'independent' means *staying inside the tent* whatever the cost in human life may be.

Mark Leech FRSA
Chiang Mai
Thailand.
September 2022

# THE PRISON ORACLE - PRISONORACLE.COM

Trusted by

# THE DEFINITIVE UK PRISONS WEBSITE GIVING YOU ALL THE PRISONS INFORMATION YOU NEED FROM THE PUBLISHER EXPERTS TRUST

| News Desk Membership | Basic Membership | Standard Membership | Enhanced Membership Best Value | Corporate Membership |
|---|---|---|---|---|
| £0.99 | £4.99 | £7.99 | £9.99 | £29.99 |
| per week paid monthly | per month paid quarterly | per month paid quarterly | per month paid quarterly | per month paid annually |

## LESS THAN THE COST OF A CUP OF COFFEE A WEEK: CANCEL ANYTIME!

**The Prison Oracle:**
*I'm impressed at how comprehensive it is.*
An excellent collection of Data and Information, I'm impressed at how comprehensive it is. A bonus is access to Reports like Woolf, Woodcock, May, Learmont and others before the Internet and difficult to otherwise access. The data is user-friendly, useful for research and easy to use with access to data on the Prison Population, Safety in Custody, and Workforce Statistics easier to access and use than on the Government's own website. A very helpful, comprehensive, user friendly source of information on prison issues.

**Phil Wheatley, CB.**
Former Director General: HM. Prison Service and NOMS

**The Prison Oracle:**
*'The' Go-To Place for Everything Prison Related.*
The sheer depth of available information, coupled with a simple user interface, makes The Prison Oracle *'the'* go-to place for everything that is in any way prison related. There's a vast array of publications, alongside historic reports that you simply can't find anywhere else online.
Having such a wealth of data at your fingertips, without the need to trawl the internet for hours, is exactly why I subscribed. The Prison Oracle is a tangible learning resource for anyone with an interest in the justice section; I urge you to take a look for yourself.

**Richard Rowley**
Managing Director: Census Life

**The Prison Oracle:**
*An excellent collection of information, data and reports*
The Prison Oracle, with everything about prisons all in one place, has long been needed and I'm delighted it's finally arrived – I 've subscribed and it's such an excellent collection of information, data and reports for practitioners, justice professionals or anyone with an interest in justice issues or reform, I've no hesitation in recommending The Prison Oracle to all my Correctional Services colleagues. An added advantage is the simple access to reports that shaped the modern Prison Service – Woodcock, Woolf, Learmont, May, Carter, and Corston.

**Tony Hassall**
Commissioner: Corrective Services Western Australia

# Section 1 Prison Establishments
*COVID ALERT: Visits may be cancelled without notice*

## 1.1 PRISON ESTABLISHMENTS ENGLAND & WALES

**ALTCOURSE
PRISON**

BROOKFIELD DRIVE
LIVERPOOL
L9 7LH

**Tel: 0151 522 2000**

*For the latest reports on this prison please visit:*
https://tinyurl.com/bdfh26rv

*Important Changes:* **(1) Visits:** the identification necessary to access this prison and visit for social or professional purposes has changed; (2) **Money and Gifts** new rules now apply to these. See page 16 for full details of the above.

**Task of the establishment**
A category B men's local prison.

**Certified normal accommodation / Op.Cap**
Prisoners held at the time of inspection: 1,158
Baseline certified normal capacity: 780
In-use certified normal capacity: 780
Operational capacity: 1,164

**Population of the prison**
• 4,576 new prisoners received each year (about 380 per month).
• 106 foreign national prisoners.
• Over 40% of prisoners were unsentenced.
• 2,082 prisoners released into the community over the previous 12 months.
• 183 prisoners receiving support for substance misuse.
• 209 prisoners receiving support from the mental health team.

**Prison status and key providers**
Private: G4S
Prison Group: Custodial Contracts

Prison Group Director: Neil Richards
Governor/Director: Sarah Elliott / Steve Williams
IMB Chair: Terry Welby
Physical and mental health and substance misuse treatment provider: G4S
Health Services Secondary mental health services: CRG (Castle Rock Group)
Prison education framework provider: Novus
Escort contractor: GeoAmey

**Brief history** The prison opened in 1997 as a category A prison. It was turned into a category B core local prison in June 2003. It subsequently expanded in 2007 when a further house block holding an additional 180 prisoners opened.

**Short description of residential units**
Melling Brown – vulnerable prisoner accommodation, induction wing and reverse cohort unit (RCU) (see Appendix II Glossary of terms)
Melling Blue – vulnerable prisoner accommodation
Bechers Green – induction wing and RCU
Bechers Blue – induction wing and RCU
Furlong Red – induction wing, RCU and detoxification unit
Furlong Green – substance misuse recovery unit
Canal Green and Blue – general accommodation
Reynoldstown Brown and Blue – general accommodation
Valentines Red and Green – general accommodation
Foinavon Green – general accommodation
Foinavon Blue – family unit.
Foinavon Red – unit for enhanced level prisoners.

**Visiting Information**
HMP Altcourse is offering visits for family and friends. Visiting times and availability may change at short notice. You should contact the prison direct for any queries.

For legal visits please check with the prison for the latest information.

**INSPECTIONS & REPORTS**
**Date of last inspection:** 1–2 & 8–12 Nov 2021.
Located in Liverpool, HMP Altcourse is a category B local prison serving courts in the Merseyside and Cheshire regions. A modern institution, Altcourse is a privately run facility that has been managed by G4S since it first opened in 1997. At the time of our inspection 1,158 men were being held, just short of the

prison's capacity. The establishment experienced a significant turnover of new receptions, with just under 400 new prisoners arriving each month and about half the population either unsentenced and on remand or serving very short sentences.

We last inspected Altcourse in 2017 when, in keeping with earlier visits to the prison, we reported very positive outcomes. In the context of the restrictions created by the prison's response to the Covid-19 pandemic, this report, although critical of some aspects of the prison's performance, continues to highlight some very encouraging findings.

Overall, we assessed safety outcomes as not sufficiently good, a deterioration since the last inspection. To a great extent this reflected the fact that since 2017, eight prisoners had taken their own lives, with four of the deaths in the last 12 months. We were critical of some aspects of the prison's approach to safeguarding, but staff seemed to be responding to learning from reviews that followed these deaths. The prisoners in crisis we spoke to told us they felt well cared for, and although recorded instances of self-harm remained too high, the number had reduced over the last year.

In general, the prison was calm and well-ordered with staff working hard to ensure prisoners' experience of custody was respectful. The quality of staff/prisoner relationships remained a great strength and in our survey 83% of prisoners told us they felt respected by staff. Key worker arrangements were working reasonably well, consultation was effective and complaints and applications procedures were better than we normally see. Leaders had retained focus on the promotion of equality and were responsive to the advice provided by inspectors. Time out of cell had improved recently and most prisoners were unlocked for at least five hours a day and participating in some form of activity. Again, this was much better than most prisons we have visited this year. However, Ofsted found weaknesses in the curriculum and identified the need to maximise attendance in education, both of which required greater leadership attention. We also concluded that there was scope for more radical thinking about how the prison could improve outcomes in work to support rehabilitation and release planning.

The Director and most other leaders we met during the inspection were proactive and committed. There was evidence to suggest they could have improved planning and decision-making through more sophisticated use of data. That said, leaders had managed some significant Covid-19 outbreaks well, and there was a confidence about their approach to the management of recovery. There was a greater sense of pre-pandemic normality in the prison than we have seen elsewhere.

Altcourse is already one of the better local prisons in the country in terms of outcomes for prisoners, the capability of leadership and staff culture. Leaders responded well to our scrutiny and we were confident that they would tackle the deficits we identified and commit to further improvement.

Charlie Taylor HM Chief Inspector of Prisons
January 2021

**Safety**

At the last inspection of Altcourse in 2017 we found that outcomes for prisoners were reasonably good against this healthy prison test. At this inspection we found that outcomes for prisoners were now not sufficiently good.

Reception staff were welcoming, and the safer custody team conducted a private interview, which was designed to focus on prisoner care. Despite this, we identified several new prisoners whose needs had not been identified or addressed sufficiently following their arrival, this despite their age or background suggesting likely vulnerabilities. The frequent redeployment of staff delayed important elements of prisoners' induction.

During our visit, the prison was calm and well ordered. Recorded levels of violence, while still too high, had reduced since the previous inspection. The analysis of available safety data was limited and not applied usefully to inform a meaningful violence reduction strategy. Investigations into violent incidents did not focus on detail and did not always lead to action to address issues identified. The prison provided an enhanced unit as well as a family unit, both of which could have been used more proactively to promote good behaviour.

The use of force had increased substantially since the previous inspection, but it was still low compared with other similar prisons. Over half of incidents were attributed to low-level guiding holds, which were used to steer prisoners back to their cells following non-compliance. It was positive that there had been no use of special accommodation during the previous 12 months, and prison staff did not use batons or PAVA incapacitant spray to maintain control.

Segregation was used less frequently than at the previous inspection. Prisoners we spoke to in the unit were generally positive about the care they received, and staff knew most prisoners well. However, the use of segregation was not always fully justified, and, for example, the decision logs used to outline the reasons for segregating prisoners who were at risk of suicide or self-harm were poor.

Physical security arrangements were proportionate and aligned to the identified risks facing the prison. Managers were aware of the key threats of drugs and mobile phones. Despite this, not all intelligence-led searching that was identified took place, and there was no suspicion-led mandatory drug testing.

There had been eight self-inflicted deaths since the previous inspection, which was a significant concern. The prison was using early learning reviews to improve its practice, but we identified some weaknesses in support systems that still created unnecessary risks. Although self-harm had decreased over the previous 12 months, rates remained higher than in similar prisons. Most prisoners at risk of suicide or self-harm received support through the assessment, care in custody and teamwork (ACCT) case management process for at-risk prisoners and reported good care. Despite local quality assurance, some aspects of ACCT case management had ongoing weaknesses. The prison's analysis of safety data was too limited to inform an effective self-harm reduction strategy or action plan specific to Altcourse. Respect At the last inspection of Altcourse in 2017 we found that outcomes for prisoners were reasonably good against this healthy prison test. At this inspection we found that outcomes for prisoners remained reasonably good.

Staff-prisoner relationships remained a real strength and we observed supportive and caring interactions between staff and prisoners across all units. Key work took place more frequently than in similar prisons and was of a better standard. Some peer mentors were training to be information, advice and guidance advisers, which provided them with excellent opportunities for the future and enhanced the support they could provide to fellow prisoners.

Communal areas and cells were clean and graffiti free. Prisoners experienced few problems accessing cleaning materials and laundry facilities. During association time, which had recently been increased, prisoners could shower, exercise, and take part in recreational activities. The kitchen provided a varied and balanced menu, and the food was of reasonable quality.

Prisoner consultation was good and had continued throughout the pandemic, leading to some better outcomes for prisoners. Both the complaint and application systems were well managed and effective.

The prison had developed a comprehensive equality strategy although only some elements were being delivered. Disproportionate outcomes for prisoners with protected characteristics were not always identified or acted on. The number of discrimination incident reporting forms submitted was low. Investigations into allegations of discrimination were not always thorough, and not all responses were appropriate. Consultations with prisoners who shared protected characteristics had resumed, some of which had led to better outcomes.

The chaplaincy was well integrated and provided good spiritual and pastoral support. Almost all prisoners had access to a chaplain of their own faith, and corporate worship had resumed for a limited number of prisoners.

Effective partnership working between the prison and health care partners meant five outbreaks of Covid-19 since the pandemic began had been successfully managed. Health care services were well led, and providers had demonstrated resilience in maintaining core services. However, the pace of recovery had slowed significantly due to severe staffing shortages.

A dedicated team provided an integrated primary and secondary mental health service. Low staffing levels and recruitment difficulties affected service delivery. Too many prisoner referrals to external hospitals under the Mental Health Act exceeded the NHS guideline on waiting times.

The clinical substance misuse team provided treatment options to support prisoners, but psychosocial support had been severely reduced because of the redeployment of non-clinical staff. There remained some weaknesses in the oversight and governance of medicines management arrangements.

**Purposeful activity**
At the last inspection of Altcourse in 2017 we found that outcomes for prisoners were good against this healthy prison test.

At this inspection we found that outcomes for prisoners were now reasonably good.

Time out of cell had improved and prisoners could participate in more part-time work or education. As a result, two thirds of prisoners had a minimum of five hours out of their cells on weekdays, which was better than in most other prisons inspected recently.

The library remained closed, and the ongoing remote service did not provide prisoners with an adequate long term alternative to a full library service. The prison had expanded its physical education provision, which now included inter-wing football and running sessions.

Leaders and managers secured high-quality education and training for most prisoners, who developed their knowledge and skills over time. Prisoners took pride in their work and enjoyed their learning experience. However, leaders did not make sure that the provision of outreach education was sufficiently consistent to help prisoners achieve the qualifications they needed for employment in prison and on release. They had not implemented appropriate support for all prisoners who had additional learning needs.

Leaders did not sufficiently consider the impact on the education and vocational training curriculum when they adjusted the prison's regime from full-time to part-time activities.

Attendance at vocational training and industry workshops was good, but in education attendance was poor in too many lessons. Leaders provided a suitable range of learning programmes so prisoners could develop their personal and social skills, but they did not make sure that the advice and guidance prisoners received was sufficiently focused on their longer-term career or educational goals.

Leaders developed the curriculum to meet local and regional employment needs, introducing, for example, new vocational training in barbering and multi-trade construction. However, leaders did not have an ambitious enough vision to provide high-quality education, skills and work for all prisoners. Vulnerable prisoners did not have the same appropriate opportunities for education and vocational training as the general population.

Leaders had increased the number of education, skills and work spaces to provide enough part-time opportunities for most prisoners. They made sure that remand prisoners had the same access to activities as those who were sentenced. However, one third of available spaces were not filled at the time of the inspection, and an additional third of prisoners were unemployed. Even with increases in education spaces, there remained insufficient places to meet the demand.

### Rehabilitation and release planning

At the last inspection of Altcourse in 2017 we found that outcomes for prisoners were not sufficiently good against this healthy prison test. At this inspection we found that outcomes for prisoners remained not sufficiently good.

Visits were only available Monday to Friday and prisoners, including those on remand, could only have two social visits a month. All visitors we spoke to said booking had been straightforward and they had been treated with respect at the prison. The family unit was still in operation albeit with a restricted regime. The family intervention programme had started again recently.

The management of reducing reoffending work had been neglected since early 2020. The strategy was not suitable, and there was no action plan or strategic meeting to steer the delivery of work or drive improvements. Resettlement work to meet the needs of the significant number of unsentenced prisoners was limited.

Too often prison offender managers (POMs)

were redeployed to other operational tasks and were unable to undertake their core jobs. Recorded levels of contact between POMs and prisoners were among the lowest we have seen in 2021. Most prisoners had an up-to-date offender assessment system report, although few of them knew they had a custody plan. Most prisoners had a monthly key work session, which focused well on prisoner welfare but not on progression or sentence planning. Risk management plans that POMs prepared were reasonably good, and we saw them communicate well with community offender managers to manage potential risk on release.

The interdepartmental risk management team (IRMT) meeting considered prisoners with complex risk management issues before their release. It was not clear if the action set at this meeting had been implemented.

There was no managerial oversight of phone call monitoring for those who posed a risk, and there was a substantial backlog of calls that had yet to be dealt with.

The prison delivered one accredited programme – the Thinking Skills Programme – and some in-cell work to promote victim awareness.

Release plans we reviewed were reasonable, but finance, benefit and debt support was very limited, and prisoners could not open a bank account. The prison reported that one in five prisoners were released without suitable accommodation, although recent work with partner agencies to provide an accommodation service was promising.

### Key concerns and recommendations

Key concerns and recommendations identify the issues of most importance to improving outcomes for prisoners and are designed to help establishments prioritise and address the most significant weaknesses in the treatment and conditions of prisoners.

During this inspection we identified some areas of key concern and have made a small number of recommendations for the prison to address those concerns.

Key concern: Despite a review of early days procedures, there was evidence that amongst newly arrived prisoners not all risk factors were always identified or adequately addressed. Some new prisoners were allocated to cells that were not equipped with basic furniture or equipment, such as a working telephone or kettle. The frequent redeployment of safer custody staff meant that a significant number of new arrivals had not received important elements of their induction.

Recommendation: The vulnerabilities and risks of newly arrived prisoners should be properly assessed, and adequate support and interventions offered. All new prisoners should be properly inducted into the requirements of prison life. (To the director.)

Key concern: Although the rates of violence and self-harm had reduced since our last inspection, there had been a recent spike in incidents of violence and four self-inflicted deaths in the previous 12 months. Too many assault investigations were categorised as gang-related violence, without the analysis or evidence to support this assumption. Quality assurance data did not identify weaknesses in early days procedures, such as prisoners who had not received an induction. There had been no analysis of the poor quality of defensible decision logs justifying the segregation of prisoners at risk of suicide and self-harm. Overall, the quality and analysis of data was not used well to understand and reduce violence and self-harm.

Recommendation: Leaders should conduct a detailed analysis of data on a regular basis to inform more effective plans to improve the safety of prisoners and staff. (To the director.)

Key concern: Although leaders had identified the drug supply as one of the prison's main threats, their response was not robust. Random drug testing had only recently resumed, returning a 19% positive rate. There was still no intelligence-led drug testing and requests for intelligence-led searches often failed to happen because of staff shortages. There was no documented discussion at key meetings about the impact of this or plans to address it. Recommendation: Leaders should resume intelligence-led drug testing and ensure that all intelligence-led searches are carried out to further reduce the supply of illicit items. (To the director.)

Key concern: Levels of self-harm remained high and there had been eight self-inflicted deaths since the previous inspection. Actions identified in early learning reviews following self-inflicted deaths were not transferred into a longer-term safety plan or processes to prevent further failures. On residential units, cell emergency bells often went unanswered for long periods of time. A prisoner being supported on ACCT had their level of observations amended without an appropriate multidisciplinary case review. Safer custody staff were frequently redeployed to other duties which affected the support they could provide to vulnerable prisoners.

Recommendation: There should be action to reduce self-harm and self-inflicted deaths, drawing on previous learning and quality assurance findings. (To the director.)

Key concern: Staffing challenges had a detrimental impact on the delivery of primary care, mental health and pharmacy services. This meant prisoners experienced long delays for a mental health assessment, and reviews of their ongoing treatment and prescribed medicines did not take place. Medicines administration was prioritised, which led to frequently cancelled mental health and primary care appointments. The lack of structured clinical supervision meant that the safety and effectiveness of care was not being addressed.

Recommendation: Prison leaders should make sure there are sufficient health care staff to meet the health needs of the population in line with national guidelines. (To the director.)

Key concern: Patients requiring a transfer to secure mental health inpatient services so they could receive specialist care continued to wait far too long for a bed, often in conditions that were worsening their mental health and well-being.

Recommendation: The local delivery board, in conjunction with NHS England and NHS Improvement, should take urgent steps to make sure prisoners requiring a transfer to hospital are moved within the national timescale of 28 days. (To the director.)

Key concern: Leaders and managers had not allocated all the education, skills and workplaces that were available and there were insufficient education spaces to meet demand. Attendance in too many education classes was poor and staff absences meant that not all classes were running.

Recommendation: Leaders should make available sufficient education, skills, and work spaces to meet the demand and allocate spaces promptly. They should make sure that attendance improves significantly in education and that they have enough staff to run all the classes outlined in their curriculum plan.

Key concern: POMs were regularly redeployed which affected their ability to support the prisoners on their caseloads. Recorded levels of contact with prisoners were among the lowest we have seen in 2021, and many prisoners we interviewed could not name their POM. Most prisoners had a custody plan, although in our survey, only 14% of prisoners knew they had one. We found no evidence of POMs undertaking one-to-one work to help prisoners make progress with their plan.

Recommendation: All eligible prisoners must receive regular, meaningful contact from POMs to help them make progress against their sentence plan. (To the director.)

Key concern: Many prisoners were subject to restraining orders or child contact restrictions, yet very few were subject to monitoring arrangements. There was no oversight of call monitoring and the calls of some prisoners had not been dealt with for two months. This meant the prison's ability to identify when prisoners might use the phone to cause harm was limited,

undermining other risk-based decision making. POMs had not attended the IRMT meeting for many months and the staff could not confirm if action set at this forum had been implemented.
Recommendation: The prison should immediately put in place robust arrangements to make sure that the public protection risks posed by prisoners are identified and managed effectively. (To the director.)
Key concern: Changes within the probation service meant that unsentenced prisoners were no longer provided with formal resettlement support. In our survey, more than half of those who expected to be released in the following three months said they needed support with accommodation and finances, yet only very few said they were receiving support. Despite promising recent work to improve accommodation support, too many prisoners were still being released without an address to go to. Support to help prisoners with their finances, benefits and debts was limited to informal advice from the resettlement team and prisoners could not open bank accounts.
Recommendation: All prisoners, including those who are unsentenced, should be able to access resettlement advice and support to prepare them for their release into the community. (To the director.)

### Notable positive practice

We define notable positive practice as innovative work or practice that leads to particularly good outcomes from which other establishments may be able to learn. Inspectors look for evidence of good outcomes for prisoners; original, creative or particularly effective approaches to problem-solving or achieving the desired goal; and how other establishments could learn from or replicate the practice.
Inspectors found two examples of notable positive practice during this inspection.
The introduction of information, advice and guidance (IAG) mentors provided prisoners with an increased level of support with day-to-day issues and more complex matters. The mentors received training across a wide range of subjects, including neurodiversity and customer service. Other mentors were trained by the Shannon Trust, a charity helping prisoners to read and write through peer support. Mentors gained a national vocational qualification (NVQ) level 2 in IAG mentoring and an NVQ level 1 in mentorship.
A 'residence decency timetable' scheduled maintenance, such as the descaling of toilets, and the replacement of items like mattresses and pillows. This resolved many of the problems we regularly encounter at other prisons.

## INDEPENDENT MONITORING BOARD: Annual Report

The law requires every prison to be monitored by an independent Board appointed by the Justice Secretary; these are known as Independent Monitoring Boards (IMBs). The IMB must satisfy itself as to the humane and just treatment of those held in custody within its prison and the range and adequacy of the programmes preparing them for release; it must report annually to the Justice Secretary on how well the prison has met the standards and requirements placed on it.

### HMP Altcourse IMB Annual Report, 1 July 2020 – 30 June 2021; Published November 2021
### Background to the report
### Executive summary

The Covid-19 outbreak continues to have an impact on the Board's ability to gather information for this annual report. However as restrictions start to relax a more direct monitoring role is resuming. In addition the Board's ability to speak to prisoners has inevitably fluctuated as infection levels rose and fell within the prison and in the wider community, so at times a mix of remote and direct monitoring was adopted. The Board has therefore tried to cover as much ground as it can in these circumstances, but inevitably there is less detail in some areas than usual. Ministers are aware of these constraints. Regular information continues to be collected specifically on the prison's response to the pandemic and that is being collated nationally.

### Main judgements
### How safe is the prison?

In the judgement of the Board, Altcourse remains a safe prison, and this is evidenced, particularly during the challenges of the continuing lockdown, by the low levels of self-harm and violence, which have remained stable during this reporting year. It is too early to comment on the impact of restrictions starting to relax although there is already some evidence of an increase in the incidence of violence and an apparent self-inflicted death, the only one in this reporting year, in April. Towards the end of this reporting year, the Board has become aware of a number of out of area prisoners being placed at Altcourse from prisons where conditions may not be as settled. We are concerned about this uneasy mix of prisoners from establishments where different cultures pertain and the potential to impact on stability here.

### How fairly and humanely are prisoners treated?

In the context of the current Covid-19 lockdown, the Board considers that prisoners have been treated as fairly and humanely as is possible, despite the severe constraints upon their movement and access to family visits and activities. Prisoners have appreciated some additional benefits, such as extra telephone credit and no television rental fees. Prisoners also understand that the slow progress in the return to the normal regime is not always within the Director's control.

Morale has been enhanced by the very positive attitude of all staff and good channels of communication across the establishment. Of particular note is the weekly notice to prisoners (NTP) from the Director, giving information about plans for each lockdown stage, providing some positive news and a degree of hope to prisoners such as the planned resumption of family visits, or reopening of workshops. These communications always include messages of thanks to specific groups of prisoners whose work in keeping units clean and safe has contributed to prison stability.

Food has assumed an even more important focus of the daily routine, and it is pleasing to be able to report that, since last year, the quality and quantity of the food has continued to improve. This is confirmed by both staff and prisoners on units.

### How well are prisoners' health and wellbeing needs met?

Overall, in this reporting year the Board considers that prisoners' health and wellbeing needs are largely being met. At times waiting lists for GP and dentist consultations have been lengthy and prisoners did not fully appreciate the limitations of the triage system. Additionally there are still concerns about the specific needs of older prisoners, those requiring social care and prisoners with serious mental health needs.

Inevitably there will be long term effects on prisoners' mental health and wellbeing as a consequence of enforced isolation, limited contact with family and lack of social interaction and purposeful activity.

However the Board is pleased to note that the 0800 phone line set up at the start of the pandemic to enable prisoners to contact the IMB has been very much championed by the prison. The ability for prisoners to ring IMB members and talk about their concerns has provided a much welcome voice to the outside world during these difficult times.

### How well are prisoners progressed towards successful resettlement?

In general terms, prisoners progress well towards release, despite their reduced access to education and vocational courses. However the

limited input by the Probation Service has created significant problems in the completion of sentence planning and risk assessment work. Although the percentage of prisoners released with no fixed abode has been pleasingly low due to local authority hotel provision, this is unlikely to be a permanent arrangement, with an anticipated return to the pre- lockdown difficulty of housing Merseyside prisoners with complex needs, a number of whom have been excluded from existing placements.

The Board is greatly concerned about future resettlement planning following the termination of the Shelter/Purple Futures contract in June. It has become increasingly apparent that the new providers, Seetec Interventions Alliance, have seriously underestimated the scale of the task in hand and the volume of work involved.

### Main areas for development
### TO THE MINISTER

The transfer of seriously mentally ill prisoners to appropriate healthcare facilities continues to be a problem, with one particular prisoner spending over 300 days in segregation this year. This case was escalated to a national level. In addition we are concerned about the long-term legacy of the pandemic on prisoners' mental health. Altcourse is already seeing more seriously ill men arriving from the community where services have been stretched.

### TO THE PRISON SERVICE

The use of rigid handcuffs has been partially introduced in Altcourse. As SPEAR training, a necessary prerequisite, has been suspended due to the pandemic, they cannot be widely used but the intention is to roll out their use more widely. The Board was therefore concerned to learn, during the compilation of this report, that the use of such cuffs will no longer be recorded as a use of force but treated as a de- escalation technique and thus will no longer be monitored as such. We would describe the use of rigid cuffs as a physical intervention and thus it should be monitored: in terms of frequency, by particular officers on particular units, and the age, ethnicity profile etc. of those prisoners on whom it is used.

A continuing complaint from prisoners relates to their personal property, which has assumed much greater significance during the pandemic where photographs and personal items maybe the only remaining contact prisoners have with their families. We understand that this remains a persistent problem nationally, and although the subject of much discussion, nothing seems to change. This issue has been reported in previous annual reports.

In the latter stages of this reporting year, the resettlement function at Altcourse has been contracted to the national probation service and Seetec Interventions Alliance. Morale within this department is low: staff are uncertain about their future and only able to deal with emergency referrals. There appears to have been little handover preparation by the new provider and we are concerned that the consequences may be more prisoners being released unsupported and unprepared with a greater risk of reoffending.

It has recently come to our notice that a number of 'out of area' prisoners are starting to be placed at Altcourse with the potential for a clash of cultures which could impact on the relative stability at Altcourse.

## TO THE DIRECTOR

The quality and quantity of food provided for prisoners has consistently improved over the reporting year with the welcome addition of homemade soup and a bakery on site producing bread and rolls. Also kitchen equipment is maintained in a more timely matter. However there still remains a problem with the newly installed flooring which floods frequently despite a number of visits and attempts to resolve this by contractors. This must cause difficulties particularly for prisoners working and cleaning there.

The long standing librarian has now retired and a replacement is yet to be recruited. Regular access to books for those prisoners able to read has been an important factor when confined to cells for long periods and is a service much valued by prisoners.

This year has seen a succession of complaints clerks (four in number) and the Board has expressed concern regarding the importance of continuity and consistency in this fundamental role.

### Progress since the last report

In a difficult and challenging year all areas highlighted in last year's report have continued to improve. The excellent staff/prisoner relationships and open and regular communication from the Director have contributed to the effective management of violence and self-harm during lockdown.

Worthy of particular mention is the significant improvement in the quality of the food and the introduction of a more imaginative menu, both of which have been appreciated by prisoners.

It has been pleasing to see the counsellor placed on a permanent contract and the engagement of psychological therapists. It is hoped that these improvements may go some way to addressing the mental health issues experienced by many prisoners in the forthcoming months.

| serco | SHORTWOOD ROAD PUCKLECHURCH BRISTOL BS16 9QJ |
|---|---|
| ASHFIELD PRISON | Tel: 0117 303 8000 |

*For the latest reports on this prison please visit:*
https://tinyurl.com/bdfh26rv

*Important Changes:* **(1) Visits:** the identification necessary to access this prison and visit for social or professional purposes has changed; (2) **Money and Gifts** new rules now apply to these. See page 16 for full details of the above.

**Task of the establishment** HMP Ashfield is a category C prison for men who have been convicted of sexual offences.

**Certified normal accommodation / Op.Cap**
Number held 397
Certified normal accommodation 408

**Prison status and key providers**
Private – managed by Serco
Prison Group: Custodial Contracts
Head of Custodial Contracts: Neil Richards
Governor/Director: Martin Jones/Eryl Drew
IMB Chair: Ann Morton
Physical health provider: Bristol Community Health
Mental health provider: Avon and Wiltshire Mental Health Partnership NHS Trust
Substance misuse provider: Avon and Wiltshire Mental Health Partnership NHS Trust
Learning and skills provider: Serco
Escort contractor: GeoAmey

**Brief history** HMP Ashfield opened in November 1999, following the award of a contract to Premier Prison Services Ltd. It is built on the site of the former Pucklechurch remand centre. The establishment was re-roled in 2005 to accommodate juveniles after investment from the Youth Justice Board. In July 2013, HMP Ashfield was re-roled again to accommodate category C adult men convicted of sexual offences.

**Short description of residential units** There are two main house blocks, Avon and Severn, each with four wings housing between 40 and 60 prisoners, and the early days centre, where newly received prisoners complete five days of induction.

**Visiting Information**
HMP Ashfield is offering visits for family and friends. Visiting times and availability may change at short notice. You should contact the prison direct for any queries.

For legal visits please check with the prison for the latest information.

## INSPECTIONS & REPORTS
**Date of last inspection:** 25 March – 12 April 2019
**HMCIP Report May 2019**
HMP Ashfield is a category C prison for men who have been convicted of sexual offences. It is operated by Serco and situated in Pucklechurch a few miles to the east of Bristol, and has been fulfilling its current role since 2013.

At the time of this inspection it held some 400 prisoners, of whom 85% had been assessed as presenting a high or very high risk of harm to the public. This fact is directly relevant to the main concerns that we had as a result of this inspection, and our judgement that in terms of rehabilitation and release planning, the outcomes for prisoners were not sufficiently good. In all other areas the prison inspected well, and we had no hesitation in awarding our highest grade of good for safety, respect and purposeful activity.

The prison was very safe, with only one fight and seven assaults recorded in the six months prior to the inspection. As one would expect, the use of force was similarly low, with six incidents in the same period. However, and perhaps as a consequence of the rarity of violence, the oversight of the use of force was poor and needed focused management attention.

Similarly, the response to the few violent incidents was not as thorough as it should have been. It was also notable that in our survey around a third of prisoners told us that they had felt unsafe at some point during their time in Ashfield. This was somewhat at odds with the reality that the prison was generally a very safe place, and the reasons for these perceptions need to be understood so that they could be addressed.

We found that the prison provided a respectful environment, and relationships between staff and prisoners were particularly strong, with 86% of prisoners saying that the staff treated them with respect. This was an exceptionally high figure, and was reflected in the positive views prisoners held about the way in which applications and complaints were dealt with. The buildings were in good condition, there was no overcrowding, and there were areas devoted to gardens and animal husbandry. The food was well liked by the prisoners, health and social care provision was good, as was consultation with prisoners. In light of all this, it was slightly surprising to find that the strategic management of equality and diversity was weak, and was in need of senior management intervention. As with the management

weaknesses in the area of safety, this was perhaps due to the fact that there were no obvious negative outcomes. However, of course this did not absolve management from the need to maintain monitoring and oversight.

Purposeful activity had improved significantly since the last inspection in 2015. Our colleagues from Ofsted found that provision across the board in education, skills and work was good. When this was combined with high quality facilities for sports and exercise, a good library and exceptionally good time out of cell, we concluded that the outcomes justified the award of our highest grade, good, in this area. This was two levels up from the previous inspection, and was a significant achievement.

However, this was to some extent balanced by some disappointing findings in rehabilitation and resettlement planning. The section of this report that sets out in detail our findings is worthy of scrutiny as we believe the weaknesses we found were serious, and were exacerbated by the specialist requirements of the prisoner population at Ashfield. We found that the level and quality of contact between offender supervisors and prisoners had declined since 2015. The ability of the prison to reduce the risk posed by this high risk group of prisoners was inhibited by the fact that some 45% of them did not have an up to date OASys assessment. To make matters worse, offender supervisors were not sufficiently trained or properly supervised in working with prisoners convicted of sexual offences. In addition, the number and range of interventions to enable prisoners to address their offending behaviour and to make progress through their sentence towards the eventual point of release was insufficient. There was very little provision for those who maintained their innocence. This was all very concerning, particularly as these issues had been the subject of recommendations at the last inspection, and they had not been addressed in the intervening four years. The problems had been made worse by some systemic failures, such as the fact that there were insufficient category D places for prisoners to move to in open prisons. This meant that Ashfield, a prison with no formal resettlement function, was having to release prisoners back into the community. At the time of the last inspection the prison was releasing on average around four prisoners each month, but by the time of this inspection the figure had doubled. Given the high risk nature of the vast majority of the prisoners at Ashfield, this was an issue of great concern.

With the exception of the serious problems in rehabilitation and release planning, we found that there had been an unusually good

response from the prison to the last inspection. Of the recommendations that we made in 2015, 71% had been fully or partially achieved. The progress in purposeful activity was particularly noteworthy, as was the maintenance of high standards in safety and respect. The prison is aware of what needs to be done to address the risks presented by the weaknesses highlighted in our main recommendations, and my hope is that on this occasion they will be properly addressed.
Peter Clarke CVO OBE QPM
HM Chief Inspector of Prisons

## INDEPENDENT MONITORING BOARD ANNUAL REPORT

The law requires every prison to be monitored by an independent Board appointed by the Justice Secretary; these are known as Independent Monitoring Boards (IMBs).

The IMB must satisfy itself as to the humane and just treatment of those held in custody within its prison and the range and adequacy of the programmes preparing them for release; it must report annually to the Justice Secretary on how well the prison has met the standards and requirements placed on it.

### HMP Ashfield IMB Report 1 July 2019 – 30 June 2021. Published November 2021
### Executive summary
### Background to the report

The Covid-19 outbreak has had a significant impact on the Board 's ability to gather information and discuss the contents of this annual report. The Board has therefore tried to cover as much ground as it can in these circumstances, but inevitably there is less detail and supporting evidence than usual. Ministers are aware of these constraints. Regular information is being collected specifically on the prison 's response to the pandemic, and that is being collated nationally.

### Main judgements

It is the judgement of the Board that, particularly in the light of the significant challenges posed by the pandemic, HMP Ashfield is a well-managed prison with high standards where prisoners are treated fairly and humanely in a safe environment.

### How safe is the prison?

In the view of the Board, Ashfield has provided a safe environment in what has been a more challenging twelve months than the last reporting period.
• Levels of self-harm are relatively low, and assessment, care in custody and teamwork (ACCT) processes are particularly well managed and embedded.

• Support for individuals who struggle with the prison environment and particularly lockdown has been good through the use of personal intervention plans (PIPs), targeted key work, care plans and access to safer custody prisoner representatives and staff.
• Levels of violence have, however, increased with 13 physical assaults (compared to four in the last report) over the last 12 months, three of which were against staff (none in the last report).
• Since the ending of regime stage 4, evidence of illicit substances in the prison has emerged through a number of prisoners failing drug tests. Increased security measures have been brought in to address the problem. As at the end of the reporting year, the situation was being closely monitored.

### How fairly and humanely are prisoners treated?

The Board's considered view, based on the evidence available, is that prisoners at Ashfield are treated fairly and humanely.
• The relationship between staff and prisoners has been good, despite a more difficult environment with the restricted regimes and a changing population of prisoners, and a turnover of approximately a third of custodial staff.
• There has been a more challenging 12 months for the catering department including staffing shortages (due to sickness absences and prisoner cohorting requirements), constraints due to Covid-19 and a change of supplier.
• Regular fora/meetings and prisoner engagement have been disrupted by the restricted regimes and the monitoring of equality and diversity has similarly been limited. However, no evidence has been found that there is discrimination in relation to protected characteristics, but the Board would urge Ashfield to resume equality and diversity fora as soon as possible.

### How well are prisoners' health and wellbeing needs met?

The Covid-19 restrictions have created challenges for the provision of healthcare services but despite this, prisoners have received reasonable levels of care. The healthcare service is generally assessed as being equal to that provided in the community, but the Board has some concern over the level of mental health support.
Outbreaks of Covid-19 were very well managed and only six prisoners contracted the virus during the reporting period which is a testament to the effective safety measures implemented and the hard work of all staff to minimise the risk of the virus spreading.
• Ashfield is to be commended for maximising the opportunities within the Covid-19

pandemic restrictions in relation to time out of cell and exercise.

• Mental health support has been affected by Covid-19 restrictions and staff shortages.

• Group sessions during lockdowns ceased but when limited sessions did resume, the Covid-19 restrictions meant much smaller numbers of participants.

**How well are prisoners progressed towards successful resettlement?**

Covid-19 restrictions have continued to affect some aspects of progression to successful resettlement but Ashfield staff continue to work hard to support prisoners within those constraints and prepare them for resettlement.

• The delivery of intervention programmes has been particularly impacted by Covid-19 restrictions. The potential for adverse consequences on prisoners with programmes forming part of their sentence plan has increased.

• The number of prisoners transferring to open conditions (category D prison) has for a second year been significantly higher than pre-pandemic numbers which is welcomed by the Board, as open prison conditions are seen by many prisoners as an important stage in their successful resettlement. It is of concern though that the indications are that these numbers will not be sustained going forward.

• The release of prisoners from Ashfield continues to be a highly stressful process for prisoners due to the difficulties in securing suitable accommodation, including approved premises.

• The Board commends the initiatives by Ashfield to secure, where appropriate, external bank accounts for prisoners and to encourage them to save regularly towards their release.

**Main areas for development**
**TO THE MINISTER**

The difficulties securing appropriate accommodation in a timely fashion for prisoners released from Ashfield continue to be a major concern exacerbated by the Covid-19 restrictions. Many prisoners due to be released do not have accommodation confirmed (including approved premises) until the week prior to their release and that only after extensive work by offender management staff. Two prisoners were only found accommodation when they met with their community offender manager on the day of their release.

• The Board welcomes the response to last year's report on this issue but the accommodation challenges facing prisoners convicted of sexual offences continue unabated. Can the Minister confirm how many of the 200 approved premises new placements can be used for prisoners convicted of sexual offences and the timescale for delivery of these placements?

**TO THE PRISON SERVICE**

Covid-19 restrictions have severely reduced the number of offending behaviour programme (OBP) places available. For a large percentage of the population at Ashfield, OBPs feature on their sentence plan and the reduced availability of places is causing anxiety and concerns that, where relevant, the chances of parole have decreased if OBPs have not been completed.

• In the light of the backlog of prisoners awaiting places on OBPs, are there any plans for HMPPS to increase further, beyond current strategies, the number of OBP places to address the problem? The Board notes that the number of category D places in the only open prison in the south west, HMP Leyhill, is set to reduce in coming years; it also notes that the only other open prisons accepting prisoners convicted of sexual offences are located in Suffolk, Lincolnshire and Cumbria.

• Does HMPPS have plans to create further category D places for prisoners convicted of sex offences in the south of the country or the Midlands?

**TO THE DIRECTOR**

The Board appreciates that Covid-19 restrictions have significantly disrupted normal activity in equality and diversity but considers it is an area for attention as soon as easing of restrictions allow.

• Incentive warnings data captured does not hold ethnic information. As there was a view from the survey of black, Asian, and minority ethnic prisoners that they received more warnings proportionately than white prisoners, this view ought to be investigated. Can consideration be given to identifying ethnicity when reviewing incentive warnings?

• The scheduling of diversity and equality action team (DEAT) meetings four to five weeks after the quarter to be reviewed is, in the Board's view, not conducive to timely action to address emerging issues and the brevity of the minutes is not helpful to record the work being undertaken in this area. Can action be taken to improve the DEAT meetings?

ASKHAM RICHARD
YORK
YO23 3FT

**HMP & YOI
ASKHAM
GRANGE**   Tel: 01904 772000

*For the latest reports on this prison please visit:*
https://tinyurl.com/bdfh26rv

*Important Changes:* **(1) Visits:** the identification necessary to access this prison and visit for social or professional purposes has changed; (2) **Money and Gifts** new rules now apply to these. See page 16 for full details of the above.

**Task of the establishment** Women's open prison for sentenced prisoners and young adults.

**Certified normal accommodation / Op.Cap**
Certified normal accommodation 128
Operational capacity 128

**Prison status and key providers**
Public Sector
Prison Group: Women
Prison Group Director: Pia Sinha
Governor/Director: Julia Spence
IMB Chair: Stephen Beyer
Physical and mental health provider: Care UK
Substance use provider: Inclusion (part of the Midlands Partnership NHS Foundation Trust) and Care UK
Learning and skills provider: Novus
Escort contractor: Geoamey

**Brief history** HMP/YOI Askham Grange is a women's open prison in the rural village of Askham Richard just south of York. The overriding ethos is for resettlement and preparation of the prisoners for their return to the community via its 'interventions and pathways' regime, which encompasses all aspects of the needs of the residents. The prison has provision for up to 10 mothers with their babies, enabling them to maintain full time care of their child up to 18 months whilst in prison, and it is complemented by a nursery which is run by Barnardo's. A family team works with them and all other mothers in Askham to prepare for life on release.
The baseline certified normal accommodation (CNA) is 128, and Askham Grange has an operational capacity of 128.
The regime is focused on reducing reoffending by developing a wide range of skills to enhance the women's opportunities on release. All departments contribute to this in their separate ways.

**Short description of residential units** There were 45 single and 27 shared rooms in the prison. Accommodation in the main house comprised a mix of single rooms and dormitories, housing up to a maximum of six residents in each room. Acorn House, a standalone building within the prison grounds, provided women and their families with the opportunity to spend time together overnight in a domestic environment in single occupancy rooms. In addition, two annexes consisted of single rooms for women eligible to work outside the prison or who needed to be alone in a room. The mother and baby unit offered 10 single rooms.

**Visiting Information**
You can book your visit by telephone.
Booking line: 0300 060 6513
Monday to Friday, 9.15am to 4pm
**Visiting times**
Saturday and Sunday: 2pm to 3pm

**Legal and professional visits**
Email: HMPPSvisitbooking@justice.gov.uk
**Visiting times:**
Monday to Friday, 9am to 11:30am & 1pm to 3pm.

**INSPECTIONS & REPORTS**
**HMCIP Report 1–5 April 2019, published 16 July 2019**
HMP & YOI Askham Grange is a women's open prison situated in a rural village setting a few miles outside York. At the time of this inspection it held around 110 women. At the heart of the prison sits a large late Victorian house. Other units have been added over the years, including additional living accommodation, a well-equipped mother and baby unit and a health care unit. Immediately outside the grounds is a farm shop and café that sell produce and goods grown or produced by the prisoners.
At the last inspection in 2014 we awarded our highest grading of 'good' in all four of our healthy prison tests. On this occasion we again awarded our highest grades for all four tests. However, it was particularly pleasing to see that the leadership and staff had not simply relied upon what we found last time, nor just continued along the same path. On the contrary, there had been new initiatives and innovations in many areas. The ethos of rehabilitation and resettlement that dominated the establishment seemed to be stronger than ever, and the extraordinarily strong nature of the relationships between staff and prisoners was clear to see. There can be no doubt whatsoever that this played a huge part in achieving the goals of building women's confidence and self-esteem en route to eventual release.

From the moment that prisoners arrived at Askham Grange, they found themselves in a welcoming and safe environment. Very few prisoners indeed said they had felt unsafe, and the reception process, first night dormitory and good use of peer supporters all contributed to this. There was hardly any violence, and levels of self-harm were very low. This was a welcome finding when the levels of self-harm elsewhere in the women's estate are so troubling. Those prisoners who did need support received it appropriately. Our survey suggested that drugs and alcohol were not easily available, and there was little demand for clinical management of substance misuse. The numbers of women being returned to closed conditions seemed broadly comparable with the only other women's open prison (HMP East Sutton Park), but more needed to be done to record the detailed reasons for the returns, and to analyse the data to identify any trends. The establishment was clean, the living conditions were good and the grounds extensive. Acorn House enabled prisoners to look after their children for overnight stays, and the onsite mother and baby unit, complete with well-equipped nursery, was an excellent facility. It was clear that both mothers and babies thrived in the environment. The provision of healthcare was good. However, more needed to be done at the strategic level to monitor and analyse equalities work and the outcomes for those with a range of protected characteristics.

Prisoners were never locked in their rooms and had free access to most of the site throughout the day. For the visitor to Askham Grange, it was sometimes not immediately obvious at times whether an individual was a member of staff or prisoner, which is testament to the ethos of the establishment being turned into reality. There was a wide range of recreational and social activities available, but it seemed to us that more could be done to match what was available with prisoners' individual interests. Ofsted judged the provision of learning and skills to be outstanding. In terms of helping prisoners to progress, the links to voluntary organisations and employers were a key strength. In particular, the use of release on temporary licence (ROTL), with nearly half of such events being into paid employment, and good connections to national employers meant that even if prisoners came from a part of the country well away from Yorkshire, there was a very good chance of them finding employment on release.

As with any establishment, there will always be room for improvement in some areas, and these are detailed in the relevant section of this report, including the one main recommendation about public protection. However, it would be wrong to detract from the overall excellence of Askham Grange. I would only sound two notes of caution. One is that in the weeks following the inspection, the acting governor and deputy governor were both due to leave, and as we have seen elsewhere, maintaining consistency in leadership energy and ethos can be vital to maintaining good performance. The second issue is potentially more worrying, and it is that Askham Grange has been under threat of closure for some six years. This uncertainty needs to be resolved as soon as possible. This is one of the best performing prisons in the country. The prisoners clearly benefit enormously from what it can provide. It would be good to think that in the future Askham Grange might remain as an example of what can be achieved, and not fade away into a memory of what was once an exceptional establishment.

Peter Clarke CVO OBE QPM
HM Chief Inspector of Prisons

## INDEPENDENT MONITORING BOARD: Annual Report

The law requires every prison to be monitored by an independent Board appointed by the Justice Secretary; these are known as Independent Monitoring Boards (IMBs). The IMB must satisfy itself as to the humane and just treatment of those held in custody within its prison and the range and adequacy of the programmes preparing them for release; it must report annually to the Justice Secretary on how well the prison has met the standards and requirements placed on it.

### HMP Askham Grange IMB Report 1 July 2019 to 30 June 2021: Published 28th March 2022
### Executive summary
### Background to the report

This report covers two reporting years. It is based on observations made on visits, contact with prisoners and staff and scrutiny of records. Where visits have been unable to take place because of Covid restrictions, information has been gleaned from the daily orderly officer reports and telephone contact with staff.

The threat of possible closure remains, with no final decision being made by the Minister.

### Main judgements
### How safe is the prison?

The Board considers that Askham Grange is a safe establishment for both prisoners and staff. Incidents of violence or self-harm are rare, due in no small part to the good working relationships between staff and the women in their care. The buildings and surrounding grounds are kept in a good state of repair, ensuring that prisoners are physically safe within the establishment.

**How fairly and humanely are prisoners treated?**
It is the view of the Board that prisoners are treated both fairly and humanely. Where issues arise, they are dealt with by staff and prisoners working together, wherever possible, to achieve an acceptable solution. Staff have been particularly sensitive to the extra difficulties caused by the pandemic (including the restrictions on visits, illness or death of family members, loss of outside work due to closure of businesses) all of which can have a detrimental impact on prisoners' wellbeing.

**How well are prisoners' health and wellbeing needs met?**
Healthcare provision has been assessed as being at least as good as that found in the community. The pandemic has forced some restrictions (mainly in dental treatment) which mirrors what has happened in the community, but everyday healthcare services have continued to provide a good service to the women at Askham. There are very few concerns regarding treatment or service provision from the prisoners.

**How well are prisoners progressed towards successful resettlement?**
HMP/YOI Askham Grange has a good record of success in preparing prisoners for resettlement. This was greatly disrupted by the Covid pandemic and the lockdown measures imposed both in the community and in prisons. In 2021 the employment hub started to rebuild contacts with potential employers and the voluntary sector. However, the situation has not been helped by the low number of prisoners transferring to Askham.

**Main areas for development**
**TO THE MINISTER**
A decision concerning the future of HMP/YOI Askham Grange is long overdue and should be a priority in order that Askham Grange can formulate plans for its future appropriately.

**TO THE PRISON SERVICE**
The arrival of pods at the beginning of the pandemic meant that no one had to share rooms and that women were kept as safe as possible. The contract for keeping the pods runs out in February 2022 and they are, we are told, to be removed from the prison. The pandemic has not gone away and the women are rightly concerned about moving back into shared accommodation. Whilst accepting that there is a budgetary concern in prolonging the contract, would it not be circumspect to do so in the circumstances? Despite this being raised in previous reports, there are still prisoners with very little time left to serve being transferred in to Askham Grange. This has an impact on the level of work that can be undertaken with them prior to release and is not to their benefit. Would the Prison Service ensure that only those with sufficient time left to serve are transferred to open conditions in order that resettlement plans can be fully implemented?

**TO THE GOVERNOR**
There are no issues to raise with the Governor.

**Progress since the last report**
Progress has been hampered by the imposition of restrictions relating to Covid-19.

**BIERTON ROAD, AYLESBURY BUCKS HP20 1EH**

**HMP & YOI AYLESBURY**

Tel: 01296 444000

*For the latest reports on this prison please visit:* https://tinyurl.com/bdfh26rv

*Important Changes:* **(1) Visits:** the identification necessary to access this prison and visit for social or professional purposes has changed; (2) **Money and Gifts** new rules now apply to these. See page 16 for full details of the above.

**Task of the establishment** HMYOI Aylesbury is a closed young offender institution holding 18 to 20-year-old males serving from four years to life imprisonment.

**Certified normal accommodation / Op.Cap**
Certified normal accommodation 410
Operational capacity 444

**Prison status and key provider**
Public
Prison Group: Long Term/ High Security
Prison Group Director: Will Styles
Governor/Director: Mark Allen
IMB Chair: Colin Lambert
Physical health provider: Care UK Health and Rehabilitation Services Ltd
Mental health provider: Barnet, Enfield & Haringey Mental Health NHS Trust
Substance use psychosocial services: Inclusion, part of Midland Partnership NHS Foundation Trust Prison education framework provider: Milton Keynes College
Escort contractor: GeoAmey

### Brief history

Aylesbury Young Offender Institution (YOI) is housed in a mixture of buildings, ranging in age from Victorian to early 21st century. It has seven residential units, of differing sizes and ages. There is a refurbishment programme under way for four of the residential blocks.

The three oldest wings are of traditional Victorian pattern but have been modernised over the years. The two wings which are the next oldest, dating from, we believe, the 1930s, were also modernised over 20 years ago. The two newest units date from 1997.

The care and separation Unit (CSU), otherwise known as the segregation unit (or 'seg'), is 10 years old. A modern healthcare building, which included the reception unit, was also built at that time. There is a modern, well-equipped gym. Gov Facilities Services Limited (GFSL) holds the contract for maintenance of the prison fabric. Care UK provided healthcare, until this rebranded to Practice Plus on 1 October 2020.

When fully operational, the prison can hold a maximum of about 402 prisoners. All the cells are designed for single occupancy.

In February 2019, the prison was put into 'special measures' by Her Majesty's Prison and Probation Service (HMPPS). This was a reflection of the prison's poor performance at that time. One of the results of this was a temporary reduction in the number of prisoners to 209. Three wings were taken out of use, allowing for a project of refurbishment.

Through this reporting year, one of these wings became fully operational again. Two others were almost completed, and readied again for use. Refurbished cells, a new shower block and a modernised servery in the completed wing have all helped to make this accommodation cleaner and more comfortable.

Once the refurbishment of one of the wings was complete, the prison was then ready to start taking in more prisoners, with the aim of ultimately returning it to full occupancy. This is expected to happen gradually. As a result of Covid-19, the courts were sentencing fewer young people and there was also less movement of prisoners between prisons.

By the start of this reporting year, the prison was out of special measures. With the previous Governor having taken a new post in January, the Deputy Governor assumed the role of Governor until the new appointee assumed the role in June. A new substantive Governor took up his post on 8 June 2020 and the Deputy Governor reverted to his substantive role.

The prison is a member of the long-term and high-security estate (LTHSE) and holds the longest-sentenced young adult males in the English prison system. Prisoner intake covers most of England and Wales. The prisoners have usually begun their sentences at other YOIs or secure institutions for children under 18.

The prisoners are some of the most disruptive and challenging young men in the prison system. For our reporting period, their sentence length ranged between four years and life.

The day-to-day regime at Aylesbury would normally mirror that of similar prisons. However, along with the whole country, Covid-19 entirely dominated life in the prison for management, staff and prisoners alike throughout the reporting year. Every section of this report reflects this.

In terms of Covid-19 infection, the prison performed well through to the end of 2020, with few cases among staff or prisoners. Staff were hit severely in the first two months of 2021, when the prison was technically rated as a centre of infection. Prisoner infection was very well controlled, even at this time – the age of the prisoners being a positive factor. Embedding essential protective protocols among wing staff took consistent effort on behalf of management but eventually became systematically observed.

### Visiting Information

Book a visit on line: https://www.gov.uk/prison-visits or by phone: 01296 444302
Monday to Friday, 9:30am to 1:30pm excluding Bank Holidays
**Visiting Times**
Monday, Tuesday, Thursday, Saturday, Sunday: 2pm - 4pm.

### Legal visits

Booking line: 01296 444312 or 01296 444301
Monday to Friday, 9am to 1:30pm. Alternative booking lines: 01296 444207 or 01296 444097
Monday to Friday, 9am to 3:30pm.
**Visiting times**
Wednesday, 9am to 11am and 2pm to 4pm.

### INSPECTIONS & REPORTS

**Date of last inspection:** 30 Sept – 11 Oct 2019
*Notable features from this inspection:*
• Since May 2019, more than half the population had been moved out of Aylesbury and placed in other prisons.
• 84% of the population was assessed as high or very high risk of harm.
• 60% of the population were from a black or ethnic minority background.
• 99% of prisoners were serving long sentences of four years or more.
• The Aylesbury pathway service provided a good range of therapeutic interventions for up to 45 prisoners.

**HMCIP Report published 25 February 2020**

HMYOI Aylesbury is a young offender institution (YOI) holding male prisoners aged between 18 and 20. The overwhelming majority are serving sentences from four years to life imprisonment. The establishment was last inspected in 2017, at which time we raised serious concerns across a range of issues, but expressed particular worry about safety, for which we awarded our lowest grading of poor. The YOI has since been placed into special measures by HM Prison and Probation Service (HMPPS), and as a consequence of this the roll has been halved from around 400 to just over 200. At the time of the previous inspection, we judged performance in the remaining three of our healthy prison tests to be not sufficiently good.

On this occasion we found that in all four tests, the appropriate grade was not sufficiently good, so while there had been an improvement in safety, the rest of the grades remained the same. However, it would be quite wrong to infer that there had been no progress made in the time since the last inspection. What we found was that there had been some distinct movement and indeed some improvements within the gradings, but not sufficient to raise any of them to the acceptable standard of reasonably good.

In terms of safety, the overall rate of violence had increased, but the seriousness of most of it had declined. It is quite possible that this was a consequence of introducing some 'freeflow' in the prison. This has made it easier for prisoners to gain access to one another and fight, but at the same time more likely to be in the sight of officers who are able to intervene and de-escalate situations before they become very serious. This is a phenomenon that we have seen elsewhere. However, it was not possible to say whether this was definitely the case at Aylesbury because there was insufficient analysis of the violence and no clear violence reduction action plan. This was one of our key concerns flowing from this inspection. We were also concerned by the quality of the relationships between staff and prisoners, with a significant number of the latter saying they had been verbally abused or victimised by staff. There was some evidence that key working was beginning to have an impact, but it remained the case that far more needed to be done to improve consultation, focus properly on issues of equality and diversity, handle complaints more effectively and improve the regime so that there could be far greater opportunity for meaningful contact and relationships to develop between staff and prisoners. The regime had been inadequate at Aylesbury for many years, and it remained the case that, for much of the week, there was no evening association, time out of cell was poor and often

unpredictable and there was no opportunity at all for prisoners to eat together. For these very basic socialisation processes to be absent or poor in a prison holding young adults was clearly unacceptable and needed to be addressed. The fact that the population had halved while staff levels had remained the same should have enabled more positive changes to have been made. There had been some progress, but more needed to be done.

At the last inspection we found that the nationally mandated process for assessing the risks presented by, and the needs of, prisoners (OASys) was not working as it should. We made a main recommendation that concerted action should be taken to reduce the OASys backlog but inexplicably, considering the risks presented by the population at Aylesbury, this had not been acted upon. We found that over a quarter of the prisoners did not have an OASys at all, and too few of the remainder had received proper or timely reviews. Staff tried to work around these failures in a pragmatic way, but could not replicate the comprehensive nature of the approved but failing national process. In recent times HM Inspectorate of Prisons has frequently reported that as a process of risk management and sentence progression, OASys is showing worrying signs of systemic failure, in some places verging on collapse. We have been told on many occasions that when the Offender Management in Custody (OMiC) programme is fully implemented, with responsibility for completion transferred to Aylesbury, the situation will improve. I had little confidence that this would be the case. It was clear that the Offender Management Unit did not have the resources to absorb the extra work. These weaknesses form one of the key concerns identified by this inspection, and I trust that, unlike our main recommendation at the last inspection, it will not be ignored.

It was clear to me that Aylesbury was an institution in transition. It was reassuring that in this instance I was able to see some positive impact from the prison being in 'special measures'. The halving of the roll, closure of wings pending refurbishment and attempts to relax the regime had had a positive impact. It was easy for me to see a real sense of ownership and teamwork in support of the measures that were being taken to improve performance. However, I was concerned by suggestions that there might be plans to return the roll to its previous number of around 400, but without increasing staff numbers. If this were to happen, and I hope it does not, at least in the short term, I would be very worried about the potential impact on the treatment of and conditions experienced by the prisoners. There were some positive signs of progress at Aylesbury, an establishment that has experienced some very challenging times. It would be a pity if that progress were to be put in jeopardy. For the moment, I would encourage the leadership there to continue on their current path and to build the findings of this inspection into their current plans.

Peter Clarke CVO OBE QPM
HM Chief Inspector of Prisons

## Safety

The experience for new arrivals of reception and first night was reasonably good but induction needed to be better organised. In our survey, 27% of prisoners currently felt unsafe, and violence remained high. However, the number of serious incidents had reduced significantly. The incentives and earned privileges scheme remained ineffective. Use of force was high but governance had improved. The segregation unit was a decent environment, but the regime was basic and some stays were very long. Management of security had improved and was good. Self-harm had reduced and was low. ACCT (Assessment, care in custody and teamwork case management of prisoners at risk of suicide or self-harm.) management had improved but care maps remained variable. The safeguarding of vulnerable adults was underdeveloped. Outcomes for prisoners were not sufficiently good against this healthy prison test.

At the last inspection in 2017, we found that outcomes for prisoners in Aylesbury were poor against this healthy prison test. We made 15 recommendations in the area of safety. (This included recommendations about substance use treatment, which in our updated Expectations (Version 5, 2017) now appear under the healthy prison area of respect.) At this inspection we found that six of the recommendations had been achieved and nine had not been achieved.

Reception and first night processes were reasonably good, but only 58% of prisoners in our survey said they felt safe on their first night. There were no specific first night cells or peer mentor support. Induction was not always timely and prisoners frequently missed sessions. Prisoners on induction were locked up for long periods.

In our survey, 53% of prisoners said they had felt unsafe during their time at Aylesbury. The number of fights per 100 prisoners had increased since our last inspection and the rate of assaults remained high. However, far fewer of these incidents were serious in nature. There was no analysis of the reasons for violence and no plan to reduce it. Challenge support and intervention plans (CSIPs) (CSIPs (challenge, support and intervention plans) are used by all adult prisons to manage those prisoners who are violent or pose a heightened risk of being violent. These prisoners are managed and supported on a plan with individualised targets and regular reviews. Some prisons also use the CSIP framework to support victims of violence.) had been introduced to manage perpetrators of violence and antisocial behaviour. However, staff on residential units did not know which prisoners were on a CSIP or what their targets were.

The incentives and earned privileges (IEP) scheme did not provide enough incentive for good behaviour and managerial oversight was poor. The number of adjudications had increased and was much higher than in comparable establishments. We found many low-level charges that could have been better dealt with through the IEP scheme. Adjudication tariffs were disproportionately severe for some more minor offences. Governance had improved with better enquiry and very few outstanding hearings. Use of force was high and had increased since our last inspection. In our survey, nearly half the prisoners said they had been physically restrained at Aylesbury. Oversight had improved, with very few outstanding use of force reports. Good levels of de-escalation were evident in nearly all the incidents that we reviewed.

The use of segregation had increased and was higher per 100 prisoners than comparable establishments. A small but significant number of prisoners were segregated for long periods. Communal areas were generally clean and bright, but many cells and exercise yards contained graffiti and toilets required lids and descaling. The segregation regime was basic. It was positive that managers had made efforts to deliver gym sessions and contributions from psychology and offending behaviour programmes to prisoners in the segregation unit. Authorisation for segregation was missing from some prison records and prison group director authority for continued segregation was often late. Reintegration planning remained poor.

Security was better managed and more proportionate than at the time of the last inspection. Intelligence was handled promptly. There was a very small backlog of intelligence reports and far fewer than we have seen elsewhere. The gang database was kept up to date and staff knew how to access it. The random mandatory drug test rate was about 12% which was higher than comparable establishments. However, the local drug reduction policy was robust. The prison was conducting intelligence-based suspicion drug tests and cell searches were better than we see at comparable sites.

Self-harm had reduced since the last inspection and was lower than other establishments. The monthly safer prisons meeting was reasonably well attended but key managers were not always represented. Some data were discussed at the meeting but did not always inform tangible actions. ACCT reviews took place on time and were well attended. However, they did not all have care maps and some ACCTs had been closed before all the actions had been fully addressed. Constant watch had been used five times in the previous six months. We observed one prisoner on a constant watch who received good support from staff, but his cell was filthy. Local safeguarding procedures were underdeveloped and many staff we spoke to were unaware of how or to whom to report safeguarding concerns.

## Respect

Prisoners continued to have some poor perceptions about staff and the regime allowed little time for staff to build meaningful relationships with prisoners. Cleanliness had improved across the prison and most cells were reasonably well furnished. Access to showers and other essentials had improved and was good. However, there was still some graffiti. Consultation had improved. The complaints system was not always effective. Equality and diversity work was in disarray which was a significant concern in a prison holding such a diverse population. The enthusiastic chaplaincy offered a very good service. Health and substance misuse services were reasonably good, but access required further improvement. Outcomes for prisoners were not sufficiently good against this healthy prison test.

At the last inspection in 2017, we found that outcomes for prisoners in Aylesbury were not sufficiently good against this healthy prison test. We made 24 recommendations in the area of respect. At this inspection we found that four of the recommendations had been achieved, two had been partially achieved and 18 had not been achieved.

In our survey, 59% of prisoners said that most staff treated them with respect. However, we had concerns about the large number of prisoners who reported victimisation by staff. We observed examples of positive interactions by staff on some residential units, but the restricted regime limited the opportunity and time for staff to build good relationships with prisoners in their care. There was evidence that frequent key work sessions were starting to have a positive impact on relationships between staff and prisoners.

External exercise areas were well maintained and communal areas were reasonably clean, although some were worn. All prisoners now lived in single cells. Most cells were clean and adequately furnished, but some needed painting and graffiti remained on cell doors and walls. Showers had been refurbished on two wings and access was now good. In our survey, prisoners were positive about their access to everyday essentials which was a significant improvement since the previous inspection.

The quality and variety of the food remained reasonably good. The cleanliness of wing serveries had improved. There were still no facilities for prisoners to cook for themselves or eat together.

Consultation had improved and changes had been carried out for prisoners as a result of this. Organisation and oversight of the applications process had recently improved. Most prisoners said that it was easy to make an application, but responses still took too long. The number of complaints had increased and was very high. The complaints system was not always effective and some responses did not address the issues raised. We submitted two complaints as part of the inspection process, and they did not receive a response. Provision for legal rights was adequate, but legal visits still took place in the open visits room which compromised confidentiality.

Equality work was inadequate. There was no up-to-date policy or action plan and equality meetings lacked purpose and direction. Management of the discrimination complaints process was chaotic. Complaints boxes on the wings did not contain any blank forms. Discrimination complaints often did not receive a response and many that were responded to had not been adequately investigated.

There were no consultation forums for prisoners in protected groups which left the establishment poorly placed to understand some negative perceptions held by black and minority ethnic and Muslim prisoners, from our survey and focus groups. Equality monitoring data were not routinely analysed and disproportionality had not been investigated. The establishment was not meeting the needs of foreign national prisoners and appropriate immigration advice and guidance were not provided. Faith provision was very good. The chaplaincy provided compassionate and consistent pastoral care. All prisoners had access to a chaplain of their faith.

The quality of health provision was reasonably good, although further work was needed to ensure consistent and prompt access to health care. There had been a lack of progress in completing appropriate alterations to health care treatment rooms which affected patient care. There was a positive approach to health promotion and wellbeing and good collaboration with the gym and other areas of the prison. There was a suitable range of primary health care services with reasonable waiting times. The few patients with long-term conditions were managed well. The dental service delivered an appropriate range of treatments. New patients waited six weeks for an initial appointment and up to three months for treatment, which was too long. The management of medicines was reasonable, but supervision of medicine queues and the waiting area was inconsistent.

Although their work was of good quality, mental health services lacked the breadth of specialisms required to work with this population. Funding had been agreed to increase provision and there was a new focus on joint work with other health teams. The Pathways service had a well-resourced, multidisciplinary team who delivered an impressive range of therapeutic interventions in individual and group sessions.

The drug and alcohol recovery team provided a responsive service and offered good psychosocial support.

## Purposeful activity

Time out of cell remained poor and too many prisoners were locked up during the working day. Access to the gym and library had improved since the previous inspection. Teaching and learning in education had improved and behaviour in most sessions was good. Outcomes in key subjects including English and mathematics had also improved since our last inspection, although there remained significant areas for improvement. There was not enough activity to engage the population fully and there were few opportunities for prisoners to achieve qualifications in prison work. Outcomes for prisoners were not sufficiently good against this healthy prison test.

At the last inspection in 2017, we found that outcomes for prisoners in Aylesbury were not sufficiently good against this healthy prison test. We made 10 recommendations in the area of purposeful activity. At this inspection we found that seven of the recommendations had been achieved and three had not been achieved.

Time out of cell for most prisoners remained poor, despite a 50% reduction in the population. During our roll checks we found that a third of prisoners were locked up during the core day which was too many for a prison holding a young, long-term population. Association periods were still not provided on weekday evenings and were regularly reduced or cancelled at weekends.

Improvements had been made in engaging unemployed prisoners during the core day with weekly visits to the gym and library. However, some prisoners were still unlocked for less than an hour each day. Access to the library had improved since our last inspection with additional time allowed for each visit. The library was well managed with a good range of books. Gym facilities were good and PE staff were passionate in supporting a range of health and wellbeing activity for prisoners and staff. The classes reflected the needs of the population. Attendance during the week was not high enough.

Effective joint working between prison and college managers had resulted in improvements in the quality of education, learning and skills. College leaders had been particularly effective in supporting teachers in English and mathematics to improve their professional practice. There were not enough full-time activity places for the population and the number of unemployed prisoners was too high. No accredited qualifications were offered to prisoners engaged in prison work.

Most teachers planned interesting lessons which engaged and motivated prisoners. Teachers questioned prisoners carefully to check what they knew and adapted learning to enable them to consolidate their understanding. Prisoners enjoyed learning and could explain the practical skills that they had gained. Teachers' feedback on prisoners' written work did not always identify how prisoners could improve their work to achieve higher grades.

Most prisoners developed very useful personal, social and work skills which aided their transition to the adult estate. Prisoners demonstrated a good work ethic and behaved well during purposeful activities. Teachers improved prisoners' awareness of equality topics such as discrimination and Black History Month was celebrated. Punctuality had improved and was now good, but attendance required further improvement.

Qualification achievement rates in English and mathematics courses had improved since the last inspection and were now high. The proportion of prisoners who completed their courses was high.

## Rehabilitation and release planning

Work to support prisoners to maintain contact with family and friends had improved and visits now started at the advertised time. Rehabilitation work was fundamentally undermined by the inability of the National Probation Service to complete assessments of risk and need. A simple screening for prisoners devised locally only partially addressed this deficit. Staff shortages affected contact between prisoners and prison offender managers. Public protection work was good. Prisoners had access to a wide range of interventions, including offending behaviour programmes and the Aylesbury Pathways Service. Outcomes for prisoners were not sufficiently good against this healthy prison test.

At the last inspection in 2017, we found that outcomes for prisoners in Aylesbury were not sufficiently good against this healthy prison test. We made nine recommendations in the area of resettlement. (This included recommendations about reintegration planning for drugs and alcohol and reintegration issues for education, skills and work, which in our updated Expectations (Version 5, 2017) now appear under the healthy prison areas of respect and purposeful activity respectively.) At this inspection we found that four of the recommendations had been achieved, four had not been achieved and one was no longer relevant.

The Prison Advice and Care Trust (PACT) were contracted to provide support for prisoners to maintain family ties. A recent family forum had generated actions that were being progressed jointly by the prison and PACT. Visits started more promptly than at the previous inspection. We observed respectful interactions between staff and visitors but fewer prisoners than the comparator said that visitors were usually treated respectfully. Visits facilities were adequate, apart from closed visits. Prisoners benefited from in-cell telephones which was an improvement since the previous inspection.

The reducing reoffending strategy had been reviewed recently and a range of partners contributed to the delivery of reducing reoffending work. The strategy lacked assessment of the population to inform identification of need and the development of an action plan was based solely on a prisoner survey. Eighty-four per cent of the population was assessed as high or very high risk of harm, many of whom had not had a comprehensive initial assessment of risk and need to inform their sentence progression. Only 32 of those who had had an assessment had been reviewed following a significant event such as a move to Aylesbury. Responsibility for carrying out most of these assessments (OASys) lay with the National Probation Service but, in the cases that we reviewed, requests for assessments from offender management unit (OMU) staff had not led to completion of these assessments.

Managers continued to use locally devised systems to manage the absence of these assessments but, as we reported in 2017, these pragmatic initiatives could not fully replace the comprehensive and nationally approved assessment tool. The future transfer to the prison of responsibility for preparing OASys assessments as part of offender management in custody (The offender management in custody (OMiC) model was introduced in 2017. In the first stage, prison officer keyworkers were introduced with the aim of having regular contact with named prisoners.

The second phase sees the introduction of core offender management and prison offender managers.) (OMiC) would lead to a significant increase in workload in the OMU at Aylesbury. We found that current and realistic future resources in the department were not sufficient to manage this increase.

There were vacancies at most levels in the offender management team and caseloads were too high, even with a reduced population. Levels of contact between prison offender managers and prisoners were low and largely focused on processes rather than sentence progression.

It was creditable that all the prison offender managers received regular supervision from a senior probation officer (SPO). Good progress had been made with the introduction of OMiC keyworkers and there was evidence of them contributing to prisoners' progression and liaising well with other staff involved in reducing reoffending work.

Family days were held twice a year, but there was otherwise nothing to differentiate the management of the 17% of prisoners serving indeterminate sentences from their peers.

Re-categorisation processes were reasonably prompt, but transfers to the adult estate remained slow for some 21-year old prisoners.

Internal public protection processes were effective. The identification of multi-agency public protection arrangements (MAPPA) categories and confirmation of levels were prompt and there remained effective systems to track, monitor and escalate risk of harm issues. The probation officers prepared MAPPA F reports which were of a good standard and countersigned by the SPO. The interdepartmental risk management team meeting was a good forum for discussing and sharing understanding of the risks posed by prisoners, although in many cases the lack of an OASys risk assessment hindered the identification of risk.

Few prisoners were released from Aylesbury. There were suitable services when necessary to support their release into the community, including through-the-gate mentoring.

The prison offered a wide range of accredited interventions and other programmes. Access to interventions was determined by an assessment of need and discussion at a monthly meeting where the most suitable option and timeframe for the intervention were decided. Prisoners also benefited targeted work by resettlement partners which supported their progression, including substance misuse, dealing with the effects of violence and mentoring. The Aylesbury Pathways Service continued to support some of the more complex prisoners in the system.

## Key concerns and recommendations

Key concern: Adjudications were used to manage low-level poor and antisocial behaviour. The incentives and earned privileges scheme was largely ineffective. Measures to address this type of behaviour took place slowly and were excessively punitive.

Recommendation: A motivational and transparent rewards and sanctions scheme should be put in place to promote good behaviour and to address poor and antisocial behaviour swiftly and proportionately.

Key concern: Violence was increasing and several multi-agency meetings and procedures were used to review perpetrators, victims and antisocial behaviour. No strategy or action plan was derived from these meetings or the data provided. The drivers for violence were not understood by the prison and there was no plan to reduce it.

Recommendation: A violence reduction action plan should be developed from all available data and used to reduce levels of violence.

Key concern: The segregation regime was very poor and prisoners spent too much time locked up with little to do. Prisoners were bored and frustrated and the education offered to them was limited to worksheets. There was no procedure for recording and monitoring regime activities when they did take place.

Recommendation: The governor should improve the regime for prisoners who are segregated: risk assessments should be carried out for prisoners who can be reintegrated; activities, including education, should be properly scheduled; and records should be kept of activities undertaken by prisoners.

Key concern: Prisoners' perceptions of the quality of their relationship with staff were poor. A significant number said that, at some point, they had felt victimised by staff. The limited regime enabled them to move prisoners or unlock them for basic daily tasks rather than build and develop relationships with prisoners. This inhibited the potential for staff-prisoner relationships to be fully effective.

Recommendation: Managers should ensure there is enough time for staff to develop meaningful and effective relationships with prisoners.

Key concern: Systems for redress were weak. The number of complaints had risen significantly since the previous inspection. Responses to complaints did not always address the issues raised and not all confidential complaints received a sufficiently good response. Prisoners lacked confidence in the complaints system. The discrimination incident report form (DIRF) system did not function well and responses to DIRFs were inadequate.

Recommendation: The management of all types of complaints should be improved and meaningful investigations should be carried out to ensure that prisoners receive focused responses and redress.

Key concern: The management of equality work was inadequate. There was no up-to-date policy and equality meetings lacked purpose and direction. Prisoners in some protected groups were identified inaccurately, for example sexual orientation and disability. There was no consultation with prisoners in any protected group. Analysis of equality monitoring data was limited and disproportionality had not been addressed. Foreign national prisoners were not supported.

Recommendation: A new equality policy and action plan should be implemented with effective consultation and analysis of data and oversight by purposeful equality meetings, so that the needs of prisoners in all protected characteristic groups are understood and met.

Key concern: Attendance at health care was not prioritised sufficiently and the reasons for non-attendance were not fully understood. There had been a lengthy delay in separating the medicine administration room from the main waiting area and an inconsistent approach by officers supervising these areas which had led to a lack of privacy and the potential for bullying and altercation. Some prisoners did not attend health care for fear of confrontation on the way or in the waiting area. This situation was having a detrimental effect on prisoners' health and wellbeing.

Recommendation: All prisoners should have appropriate and prompt access to health services.

Key concern: Time out of cell for most prisoners remained poor and too many were locked up during the core day. The unlock and lock-up times were not adhered to and prisoners were not receiving association on weekdays and had significantly reduced association at weekends.

Recommendation: Prisoners should have a predictable regime throughout the week, with at least 10 hours out of their cell including evening association time.

Key concern: There was a lack of clear feedback from teachers to help prisoners improve their written work. A few teachers failed to ensure that all prisoners, including those lacking in confidence, made good progress.

Recommendation: Leaders and managers should improve the feedback that prisoners receive on their written work and ensure that teachers help all prisoners, including those lacking in confidence, to progress as well as their peers.

Key concern: Managers were still not providing opportunities for prisoners working in industries to study for an accredited qualification relevant to their job role.

Recommendation: Leaders and managers should provide opportunities for prisoners working in industries to gain a qualification related to their job.
Key concern: There was poor attendance at purposeful activity and insufficient activity spaces for the population, which had resulted in a high prisoner unemployment rate.
Recommendation: Leaders and managers should improve attendance, reduce unemployment, and provide sufficient and purposeful high-quality learning, skills and work activities that meet the needs of the population.
Key concern: A quarter of prisoners did not have any OASys assessment of their risks and needs. Responsibility to complete many assessments had lain with the National Probation Service who had not provided them despite requests from the offender management unit. The lack of assessments using the comprehensive and nationally approved assessment tool reduced the certainty that all risks had been identified. Prisoners lacked comprehensive sentence plans and focused objectives to ensure that all necessary steps were taken in a timely manner to address offending behaviour.
Recommendation: All prisoners should have an up-to-date assessment of risk and need using the nationally approved assessment tool (OASys).
Key concern: There were vacancies in the prison offender manager (POM) group which were having a negative impact on the contact that prisoners had with their POM. Caseloads were too high for the probation officers managing the high and very high risk of harm prisoners to see them regularly or do any proactive work with them. The team was taking on responsibility for completion of OASys assessments for all prisoners as part of OMiC arrangements. This would necessitate more individual work which the team was not resourced to deliver.
Recommendation: All prisoners should have regular contact with their prison offender manager to support their sentence progression.

## INDEPENDENT MONITORING BOARD ANNUAL REPORT

The law requires every prison to be monitored by an independent Board appointed by the Justice Secretary; these are known as Independent Monitoring Boards (IMBs).
The IMB must satisfy itself as to the humane and just treatment of those held in custody within its prison and the range and adequacy of the programmes preparing them for release; it must report annually to the Justice Secretary on how well the prison has met those standards.

**IMB Report April 2020 – March 2021, published December 2021**
**Executive summary**
**Background to the report**
Covid-19 dominated the reporting year. Keeping the prison functioning meant prioritising the health of prisoners and staff at all times. As the virus was better understood, particularly that close contact in closed environments encouraged its transmission, the regime in a secure prison had to change significantly.
'Gold Command' (top prison service managers) at the centre of HMPPS led most decisions on the prison regime. Risk assessments became a regular and challenging task for management in Aylesbury, and changes of protocol could occur with almost no notice. It was a very demanding year for leadership.
As with life in the outside world, Covid-19 restrictions were lifted slightly between July and October 2020. More stringent controls, limiting movement, visits, education and other aspects of a normal regime, were maintained right up until the end of our reporting year.
The report following the most recent inspection of Aylesbury by Her Majesty's Inspectorate of Prisons (HMIP) was published in February 2020. There were 13 key concerns noted. Covid-19 has delayed a measurable response to almost all of these, with the exception of S51 – '[t]he management of equality work was inadequate'. In this area, we note that good progress has been made.
The Board introduced remote monitoring right at the start of the reporting year. Two members attended the prison throughout the year and at times three or four members monitored in person. This report should be read in the light of this unparalleled state of affairs.

**Main judgements**
**How safe is the establishment?**
The data for the year shows a predictable reduction in both prisoner-on-prisoner and prisoner-on-staff violence. This was because the Covid-19 regime provided far fewer opportunities for violence, with the vast majority of prisoners confined to their wings. Less predictably, there has been a reduction in self-harm over this reporting year. It is worth noting that prisoner-on-prisoner violence rose in the middle of the reporting year, when Covid-19 restrictions loosened and movement of prisoners across the estate began to return to normal.
Disappointingly, the year has not allowed a more strategic approach to violence in the prison to be established.
The prison adopted appropriate Covid-19 protocols, although some of the changes took

repeated and insistent communication from management to ensure compliance. Infection rates among prisoners stayed at a very low level. The prison maintained stability and order, even when up to 35% of staff were absent with Covid-19, or through self-isolation.

**How fairly and humanely are prisoners treated?**
The prison maintained a stable and predictable environment for the prisoners, helping them to manage anxieties concerning the virus. A daily shower and daily outside exercise were provided throughout the year, based on a structure of social 'bubbles'. This was demanding on staff, particularly at the point of highest staff absence in January/February 2021.

The loss of much of the normal regime, including social visits, and access to the gym and to education, made life for the prisoners dull and unstimulating. Speaking to prisoners, we found that, for some, Covid-19 restrictions meant fewer demands on them, which was quite bearable. The in-cell telephone became a lifeline. The provision of free credit, allowing prisoners to afford more calls, is to be commended. The introduction of screen-based family contact, Purple Visits, came on stream slowly and remains poorly used. However, some prisoners have enjoyed this service.

Board members visiting the prison found many examples of supportive interactions between staff and prisoners. In particular, staff working in the segregation team showed marked patience and engagement with the lives of prisoners temporarily in their care. Regrettably, the positive key worker scheme established last year was much weaker this year. Many prisoners, when asked, no longer know who their key worker is or recognise a special relationship with a key worker.

**How well are prisoners' health and wellbeing needs met?**
The number of cases of Covid-19 among the prisoners was kept at a low level. In part, this reflects the ages of the prisoners, but sound prison planning and embedded protocols also contributed. Early in the year, as the virus became a material factor, the psychology team acted fast. Led by this professional team, the prison focused systematically on the potential effects of increased lockdown and ' Covid-19 anxiety' on the most vulnerable prisoners. Cross-disciplinary discussions established under the case management model of a 'challenge, support, intervention plan' (CSIP) were converted to cover a list of the most vulnerable prisoners. This allowed the prison to focus support, and resources, where most needed. Much support

was delivered by in-cell telephones. Face-to-face contact was reserved for extreme cases of need. It is much harder for us to measure the effects of this year on the majority of prisoners – that is, the less vulnerable, the less violent – in other words, the silent majority. Even the Board monitors visiting the prison had much less contact with these prisoners. Their resignation to the situation, and their recognition that the outside world was recognisably limited in some of the ways that they were, kept things calm. However, for all, a year of education, of potential rehabilitation, of growing in skills, was lost.

**How well are prisoners progressed towards transfer or successful resettlement?**
The principal provider of education services in the prison is Milton Keynes College (MKC). Education provision has been poor throughout the year. In the first six months of the year, there was almost no education on offer, except to those few prisoners following certificated distance education – for example, A levels or Open University courses.

In the autumn, when schools and colleges were open again outside, education had still not started again in the prison. MKC then organised a more systematic offer: staff provided prisoners with a series of workbooks following different subjects. Even practical subjects, such as horticulture, were reduced to paper exercises only and, unfortunately, no tie-up was made with the few prisoners on the gardening team at that time.

Education induction, measuring the capability of new arrivals, continued on a reduced basis, paper only. Prisoners completed the forms in their cells, so there was no certainty that the prisoner in question had actually completed them. Education, beyond in-cell packs, had not started again by the end of the reporting year.

Covid-19 limited almost all services which enable successful transfer and resettlement of prisoners. However, the prison managed to maintain some of the most essential support for vulnerable and/or priority prisoners. Transfers continued, subject to required quarantining.

HMPPS psychology services continued to support and engage in the delivery of high-intensity programmes, and in assessing the risk and need of prisoners for accredited interventions, as well as parole hearings.

Prisoners were still able to access support provided by certain departments: for example, support for those close to the end of their sentence ('programmes'), as well as some other specialist psychology services ('Pathways'). The in-cell telephones allowed essential contact between staff and prisoners but were not suitable for sensitive service delivery to the most vulnerable. Staff access to wings was limited to those who directly managed them.

### Main areas for development
### TO THE MINISTER

• Advocate across Whitehall for a stronger national commitment to young adult prisoner rehabilitation, backed by research evidence, shared best practice and sufficient resourcing.

• To make prison sentences more purposeful, and to diminish reoffending rates, set higher requirements for basic training within the whole Prison Service.

• Reduce the number of the seriously mentally ill being sentenced to incarceration; at the same time, ensure that a greater number of emergency mental health beds are available for prisoners in extreme need.

### TO THE PRISON SERVICE

• In post-pandemic opening up, support institutions to rebalance strategic priorities toward a more demanding focus on prisoner outcomes, diminishing the focus on risk management.

• Set national, publicly shared, targets for educational and training outcomes in young offender institutions, backed by professionally informed practice and proper data analysis.

• Set high-quality targets, and appropriate penalties, in third-party contracts for education, training and vocational skill delivery. Maintain business-like contract management to ensure proper delivery.

### TO THE GOVERNOR

• Set out a clear vision for the prison which puts improvement in prisoner outcomes first; build on the strong interdepartmental cooperation existing in the prison to realise this vision.

• Celebrate the achievements of prisoners more publicly within the prison, to help raise staff and prisoner expectations of success.

• Create a regime which sets out to resolve interpersonal threats and disagreements (non-associates), using professional interventions where needed, and in this way allow other aspects of prison life, such as education and exercise, to work more effectively.

• Negotiate resources to ensure that all prisoners (not just a high proportion) have purposeful activities every working day, including education, training and employment.

### Progress since the last report

Direct comparison with last year's report is largely inappropriate, given the unique conditions arising from the pandemic. The data shows a decrease in violence and self-harm this year, which, we would suggest, is largely a result of the increased containment of the prisoners in their cells for so much of the time.

In the period of the last report, the prison was under 'special measures' and expected to make accelerated improvements. It made some of those improvements. We now know that when the prison is once again full, a process which is under way, it will not be able to maintain the more advantageous staff/prisoner ratio established last year. This ratio will revert to that prior to the period of special measures, and the decant.

This is a severe disappointment to the Board. We now have little reassurance that, as the number of prisoners increases, and the pandemic restraints are lifted, the prison will be able to maintain improvements gained last year. The focus now is increasingly on risk management and too little on prisoner outcomes.

One notable difference this year, led by the new Governor, has been a greater focus on improving the working conditions of staff, and wider communication of staff dedication and successes.

**ST LOYES STREET
BEDFORD
MK40 1HG**

**HM PRISON
BEDFORD**   Tel: 01234 373000

*For the latest reports on this prison please visit:*
https://tinyurl.com/bdfh26rv

*Important Changes:* **(1) Visits:** the identification necessary to access this prison and visit for social or professional purposes has changed; (2) **Money and Gifts** new rules now apply to these. See page 16 for full details of the above.

**Task of the establishment** Category B male local with a reception and resettlement function.

**Certified normal accommodation / Op.Cap**
Prisoners held at the time of inspection: 359
Baseline certified normal capacity: 268
In-use certified normal capacity: 257
Operational capacity: 377

**Population of the prison**
• 17% of prisoners were foreign nationals.
• Just over 40% of prisoners were from black and minority ethnic backgrounds.
• 40% of prisoners were under the age of 30.
• The substance misuse psychosocial team was supporting about a third of the population.

**Prison status and key providers**
Public
Prison Group:
Bedfordshire, Cambridgeshire & Norfolk
Prison Group Director: Gary Monaghan
Governor: Patrick J Butler
IMB chairs: Vicky Stevenson & Anne McDonald
Leadership changes since last full inspection:
Helen Clayton-Hoar, Governor to January 2019
Physical health provider: Northamptonshire Healthcare NHS Foundation Trust
Mental health provider: Northamptonshire Healthcare NHS Foundation Trust
Substance misuse treatment provider: Westminster Drug Project
Prison education framework provider: People Plus
Escort contractor: Government Facility Services Ltd (GFSL)

**Brief history** HMP Bedford is a category B reception and resettlement prison for young adult and adult men. It has stood on its current site in the centre of Bedford since the early 19th century. It was enlarged in 1849 and in the early 1990s a new gate lodge, house block and health care centre were added. It mainly accepts prisoners from the local crown and magistrates' courts.

**Short description of residential units**
A, B and C wings are gallery-style Victorian three-storey landings.
B1 is the segregation unit.
C1 has some segregation cells and accommodation for vulnerable prisoners.
D wing is a more modern house block, on three storeys which is used as the first night unit and for induction.
F wing is a Victorian two-storey wing, with gallery landings accommodating vulnerable prisoners.
The health centre is on a single landing of a new purpose-built building.

**Visiting Information**
**Covid-19; visits can change abruptly so check before leaving**
Visits Telephone 01234 373196 Monday - Friday 9am to 12.30pm
**Visiting Times**: Wed and Thurs 2pm to 3:30pm; Sun 1:45pm to 2:45pm or 3:15pm to 4:15pm
Legal visits: You can make a booking by email at: legalvisits.bedford@justice.gov.uk

**INSPECTIONS & REPORTS**
**HMCIP Report 10 Jan and 21 – 24 Feb 2022**
**Published 8 June 2022**
In 2018, the introduction to the HMP Bedford inspection report described a prison on a "seemingly inexorable decline that is evident through the results of the four inspections carried out since 2009." At that time, the healthy prison tests scores were amongst the lowest ever awarded by the Inspectorate and my predecessor invoked the Urgent Notification process.
We returned to inspect the prison in February 2022 and I am pleased to report that the decline had been arrested and real progress had been made against our tests, with a one-point increase in each.
Huge credit for this transformation must go to the governor, who took over a prison that was dangerous, understaffed and dilapidated. Over the last three years he had developed a vision for the prison, alongside clear plans for improvement that he and his team had pursued relentlessly.
The prison's self-assessment report showed that leaders maintained an accurate understanding of the state of the prison and that they had priorities in place supported by refreshingly clear plans, targets, and measures of progress. These priorities were communicated and understood by staff on the wing and by prisoners.
The culture of the prison had considerably improved even since the scrutiny visit we conducted in March 2021. There was a focus on consistency in the way officers interacted with prisoners and we saw many skilled officers doing an excellent job. There remained a small minority of staff members whose attitude to prisoners brought down standards in the prison. Recruitment and retention were an ongoing challenge and leaders were actively seeking ways to support officers in their first year in post. Staff shortages continued to affect the running of the jail and the situation had become acute during a recent Covid-19 outbreak.
The under-25 population was overrepresented in statistics concerning negative behaviour and violence. As a result, leaders decided to create a specific wing with a bespoke regime aimed at settling and supporting younger prisoners. It will be interesting to see the effect of this initiative during future visits.
Leaders had also sought to improve the experience of treatment for the large minority of black, Asian and minority ethnic prisoners, including by being more transparent about the way that work is allocated and making a concerted effort to deal more sensitively with discrimination incident reporting forms.
Conditions in the jail continued to be unacceptable, particularly on A and B wings where most prisoners shared shabby, cramped cells designed for one person, although improvements to showers were welcomed by prisoners.
Despite the considerable progress we saw at Bedford, the levels of violence in the jail remained some of the highest in the country and, although there were welcome signs in our survey

to suggest that prisoners felt safer than in 2018, these were not yet reflected in the data on assaults on prisoners or staff. A determined attempt to reduce the use of force had been successful, but it was unacceptable that many officers still did not routinely turn on their body-worn cameras.

The governor and his team should be proud of their achievements at HMP Bedford. There had been excellent progress, although outcomes for prisoners were not yet good enough in any of our healthy prison tests. Provided that the prison can retain the many effective staff members and the strong leadership team, there is good reason to believe that further, substantial improvements can be made, particularly in reducing violence and improving living conditions.

Charlie Taylor

HM Chief Inspector of Prisons April 2022

### Safety

At the last inspection of Bedford in 2018 we found that outcomes for prisoners were poor against this healthy prison test.

At this inspection we found that outcomes for prisoners were now not sufficiently good.

All arriving prisoners received private interviews to identify vulnerability and health concerns, and reception staff and prisoner peer supporters - known as welfare partners - provided useful information. The rate of self-harm was lower than at the last full inspection. The support given to prisoners at risk had improved and there had been good progress on implementing Prison and Probation Ombudsman recommendations.

While fewer prisoners than at the last inspection told us they felt unsafe, recorded violence was still very high and violent incidents were not fully investigated. The active citizenship scheme was a promising initiative to encourage positive behaviour and a number of prisoners spoke positively of the scheme.

Technology had been used well to disrupt the supply of illicit items and the availability of illicit drugs had reduced. Prison managers worked effectively with the police when staff wrongdoing was suspected, and this had yielded some positive results.

Use of force was lower than at the last inspection but still high compared to similar prisons. Reviews of baton use lacked detail and did not give assurance of proportionality. Not all use of special accommodation had been recorded or was justified. There had been some concerning examples of staff violence towards prisoners, which were dealt with robustly when discovered. However, body-worn cameras were not routinely worn or turned on by staff and not

all planned incidents were recorded.

Despite efforts to improve the segregation environment, it remained run down and unsuitable for use. Segregation staff were friendly, capable and compassionate in their management of some challenging individuals.

### Respect

At the last inspection of Bedford in 2018 we found that outcomes for prisoners were poor against this healthy prison test.

At this inspection we found that outcomes for prisoners were now not sufficiently good.

While there had been improvements in staff-prisoner relationships, too many officers were dismissive of prisoners' concerns and lacked a focus on prisoner care. In our survey, many staff reported poor morale and said they did not feel that they had the time or skills to perform their roles effectively.

Despite refurbishment of some cells, accommodation on A and C wings provided a poor living environment, particularly in overcrowded cells. Toilets were inadequately screened and cell furniture was often in poor repair. Cleanliness in communal areas had improved and there were new shower rooms and laundries on all wings. About a third of emergency cell bells were not answered promptly. Prisoners appreciated the installation of telephones in all cells, which relieved isolation during long periods of lock-up. The quality of food was better than we usually see and canteen arrangements were effective.

Managers had introduced robust systems to monitor the timeliness and quality of responses to complaints, but too many remained unhelpful and did not answer the underlying concerns. Responses to applications could be slow and they often appeared to be delayed in wing offices. There was a good focus on consultation with prisoners which had been sustained throughout the pandemic. The appointment of a bail officer had been very beneficial in improving the risk information available to courts considering bail applications.

Discrimination incident investigations and responses were extremely thorough and were supported by external scrutiny from the Zahid Mubarek Trust. There had been a good leadership focus on equality work, particularly on improving outcomes for black and minority ethnic prisoners and young adults. However, support for prisoners with disabilities was weak, professional interpreting was underused and gay and bisexual prisoners were under-identified.

Chaplains were highly visible and had provided good support to prisoners throughout the pandemic. The chaplaincy had strong links with the community, which were used to support prisoners on release. The ongoing suspension of corporate worship was a concern for prisoners and the chaplaincy, but there were plans to reinstate this imminently.

There was a suitable range of primary care health services with reasonable waiting times. The inpatient unit delivered good patient- centred care but, while it was clean, it was tired, run down and in need of decoration and refurbishment. Social care needs were met well. There was a high level of mental health need. Although the integrated mental health team delivered a range of services and responded promptly to referrals once received, only a few prisoners said they had received prompt support. Medicines and pharmacy services were generally well managed, but officer support for medicines administration could be poor, which increased the risk of diversion.

## Purposeful activity

At the last inspection of Bedford in 2018 we found that outcomes for prisoners were poor against this healthy prison test.

At this inspection we found that outcomes for prisoners were now not sufficiently good.

Ofsted carried out a progress monitoring visit of the prison alongside our full inspection and the purposeful activity judgement incorporates their assessment of progress.

Time out of cell remained limited. Prisoners who were in education, training or work activity usually had just under six hours out of their cell each day. About 40% of prisoners were not occupied in any purposeful activity and spent nearly 22 hours locked in their cell.

Very few prisoners said they were able to exercise outside or associate together for at least five days a week. Prisoners could attend the gym at least twice weekly, but until recently their ability to use the gym had been severely affected by regular closures and redeployment of PE staff. The library was readily accessible and provided a good service.

There were enough activity places for the whole population, but most were part time and fewer than a third were available in education and training activities. The majority of prisoners were in work roles that did not occupy or challenge them sufficiently. Vulnerable prisoners had very limited access to any form of education, skills and work activity.

Attendance at education and training sessions remained too low and punctuality was variable. The majority of tutors and instructors knew the prisoners well and were able to set clear expectations for behaviour. Pay was incentivised for prisoners to encourage self- improvement and engagement in education and training. Careers advice and guidance were well planned, with a range of useful resources available to prisoners.

## Rehabilitation and release planning

At the last inspection of Bedford in 2018 we found that outcomes for prisoners were not sufficiently good against this healthy prison test. At this inspection we found that outcomes for prisoners were now reasonably good.

The visits room was reasonably welcoming, but the children's play area was still closed. A few family courses were being delivered and in-cell telephones helped prisoners to stay in contact with their families and friends. There were regular delays with sending and receiving mail.

Work to reduce the risk of reoffending was underpinned by a well- organised strategy and action plan and an unusually thorough needs analysis. Although the offender management unit (OMU) was not yet at full strength, the number of staff had increased and they worked well together to deliver core work on time. The level of contact between OMU staff and prisoners had been good throughout the pandemic. OASys assessments were completed within timescales and to a good quality. Some useful non-accredited courses were running, especially in support of young adults. Key workers were also being trained to deliver a one-to-one intervention. Home detention curfew (HDC) was managed well. About a third of approved HDC applications were past the eligibility date, usually because too short a time remained to complete the HDC process after sentencing.

The monthly public protection meeting covered all relevant areas of risk. The high number of calls made on in-cell phones made it difficult to keep up to date with phone monitoring with existing staff levels. Although individuals posing the highest risk were prioritised, there had been some long gaps and no calls had been translated. Accommodation outcomes were not good enough: 57% of those released in the previous 12 months had gone to sustainable accommodation on the first night. Outcomes had been improving in recent months because OMU staff had recognised some gaps in provision following changes in probation contracts and were working hard to fill them. A number of local community and voluntary sector groups had also given valuable help in terms of housing provision and mentoring in the Bedford area. Resettlement plans were being completed and the reintroduced 'departure lounge' provided a useful service.

**Key concerns and recommendations**

Key concerns and recommendations identify the issues of most importance to improving outcomes for prisoners and are designed to help establishments prioritise and address the most significant weaknesses in the treatment and conditions of prisoners.

During this inspection we identified some areas of key concern and have made a small number of recommendations for the prison to address those concerns.

Key concern: The incidence of violence was still too high. Incidents were not routinely investigated, which meant that leaders were unable to understand fully the drivers of violence. Challenge, support and intervention plans (CSIPs) were not used widely or effectively enough to manage perpetrators and victims of antisocial behaviour.

Recommendation: All violent incidents should be investigated and findings should inform the strategy to reduce violence. CSIPs should be used to address violence and antisocial behaviour, and to support victims.
(To the governor)

Key concern: Use of force documentation was not always fully completed and, although body-worn video cameras were readily available, many staff failed to activate them during an incident to provide evidence and support de-escalation.

Recommendation: Body-worn cameras should be routinely switched on during incidents, and both footage and written records should demonstrate the use of de-escalation before and during use of force. (To the governor)

Key concern: The environment in the segregation unit rendered it unfit for purpose. The unit was dark and confined and many cells had damaged furniture.

Recommendation: Prisoners on the segregation unit should be held in decent conditions. (To the governor and HMPPS)

Key concern: While staff-prisoner relationships had improved, some officers remained dismissive and lacked focus on prisoner care. In our survey, many staff reported poor morale and some said they did not feel they had the time or skills to perform their roles effectively.

Recommendation: Managers should investigate the causes of poor morale and the lack of focus on prisoner care among some staff and should ensure that staff development initiatives address these concerns. (To the governor)

Key concern: Many of the cells on A and C wings were not fit for occupation. Conditions were particularly poor in cells designed for one prisoner, which were holding two. There was not enough space for two people, the screening of toilets was inadequate and bunk beds were too small and in poor condition. Many cells had continuing problems with cockroaches.

Recommendation: Managers should implement a programme of renovation to improve the quality and decency of cells designed for single occupancy and these cells should be used to accommodate one prisoner only. (To the governor and HMPPS)

Key concern: Despite good monitoring information, about a third of emergency cell bell calls were not answered within the target time. Many prisoners told us that cell bells could ring for very long periods before they were answered.

Recommendation: Managers should investigate the reasons for the failure to respond to emergency cell bells and implement measures to make sure that they are answered within the target time. (To the governor)

Key concern: Despite some good work on equality, not all protected characteristics had been given priority during the previous 12 months. Notably, the basic needs of prisoners with physical disabilities were not being met and the management of personal emergency evacuation plans was poor. Professional interpreting was underused and staff and prisoners were used to interpret for confidential matters. The specific needs of prisoners of all sexual orientations were not being met.

Recommendation: Leaders should ensure that prisoners with protected characteristics are systematically identified and given consistent and good quality support. (To the governor)

Key concern: Too many prisoners were locked in their cells for nearly 22 hours a day with little to keep them occupied, and there was evidence that this was having a detrimental effect on their well-being. The ability to expand the regime was limited, partly by staff shortages, and it was unclear when a fuller regime could be delivered.

Recommendation: Leaders should ensure that during the working day all prisoners are able to spend a substantial period out of their cells and in purposeful activity. (To the governor and HMPPS)

Key concern: Many prisoners were waiting too long to attend education where they could gain valuable skills and qualifications to help them progress into further education, skills and work in another prison or in the community.

Recommendation: Leaders should make sure that more prisoners can access the education they need promptly and that waiting lists are reduced significantly. (To the governor)

Key concern: In-cell telephones had inevitably led to greater need for monitoring of calls where public protection risks had been identified. Even among prisoners who had been prioritised, no monitoring had taken place for several months. No translation had been carried out of calls in different languages, even though this included a prisoner on the priority list.

Recommendation: Monitoring of telephone calls for public protection purposes should be carried out regularly, with translation where the call is not in English. (To the governor)

Key concern: Accommodation was the most pressing issue for prisoners approaching release. Only 57% had gone to sustainable accommodation during 2021 and the housing outcomes for many prisoners were not known. The support available had reduced sharply with the changes to resettlement services in mid-2021.

Recommendation: Managers should design and implement a comprehensive system of practical support to make sure that all prisoners go to the most suitable accommodation possible on release, with clear measures of success or failure. (To the governor and HMPPS)

## Notable positive practice

We define notable positive practice as innovative work or practice that leads to particularly good outcomes from which other establishments may be able to learn. Inspectors look for evidence of good outcomes for prisoners; original, creative or particularly effective approaches to problem-solving or achieving the desired goal; and how other establishments could learn from or replicate the practice.

Inspectors found 16 examples of notable positive practice during this inspection.

The Active Citizenship scheme was a promising initiative which encouraged prisoners to make positive contributions to prison life and the wider community.

The installation of CCTV around the prison and the working relationship with the local police and council were very effective in tackling the ingress of illicit items.

Bedford had appointed three members of staff to act as single case managers for all ACCTs. These officers had a comprehensive knowledge of their cases and this made it more likely that they could provide consistent and good quality care to vulnerable prisoners.

Managers had recognised that the large number of relatively inexperienced staff sometimes had difficulty in answering prisoners' questions. They consulted prisoners to identify the most common areas of enquiry and produced a very helpful pocket-sized 'FAQ' booklet of these questions and suitable answers.

The governor had led the development of a range of measures for consulting prisoners, which allowed managers to understand better their concerns and frustrations. These included an annual survey, monthly wing councils chaired by prisoners and a fortnightly meeting between the governor, senior managers and the council chairs.

The external scrutiny from the Zahid Mubarek Trust of investigations into allegations of discrimination had been taken seriously by prison leaders and had significantly improved the process and outcomes for prisoners.

There was a strong focus on supporting young adults in custody. Several programmes were being delivered to young people and there were plans to provide more age-specific activities and tailored support for them. Staff were being given trauma-informed training to help them work more effectively with this group and young adult ambassadors had been appointed.

Chaplains had been highly visible and accessible throughout the pandemic and had continued their support for prisoners due for release. The chaplaincy made good use of tablet computers to enable prisoners to attend funerals virtually.

The multidisciplinary approach to pain management was impressive and patients received a comprehensive service to help manage their pain in the most effective way.

Through-the-gate social care arrangements into nursing/residential homes and packages of domiciliary care were very well organised, leading to effective continuity of social care.

Support plans drawn up by custody staff enabled the recipients of social care to be more in touch with reality by use of displayed reminders, including place, time and family connections. Regular conversations about the reminders demonstrably benefited the patients.

The location in the dental surgery of equipment and supplies for use in a medical emergency increased the potential for survival of a collapsed patient.

Promising work with prisoners who had been in care had been launched, with a named offender manager working with this group and with young adults. Working relationships with four local authorities had become stronger, and managers were improving contact between prisoners who had been in care and their statutory personal advisers.

Weekly discharge boards had been reintroduced for prisoners due for release in the next four weeks. A DWP work coach, a Jobcentre Plus worker, Westminster Drug Project and other professionals attended regularly to speak to individual prisoners and offer tangible help.

The probation resettlement team gave an individualised 'discharge pack' to each sentenced prisoner on release with a suggested release day itinerary and travel options.

The 'departure lounge' had been reintroduced in reception or the visits area. A range of donated supplies was available, including sets of basic domestic items for those being released homeless or to temporary accommodation.

**Scrutiny Visit 2 February and 16–17 March 2021**
**Published 21 April 2021**

HMP Bedford is a category B reception and resettlement prison for young adult and adult men. It has stood on its current site in the centre of Bedford since the early 19th century and accepts prisoners mainly from the local Crown and magistrates' courts. At the time of this scrutiny visit, it held about 372 prisoners, which was fewer than at the time of our last full inspection in 2018.

Outcomes for prisoners at the time of our 2018 inspection were poor on three out of the four healthy prison tests, which led my predecessor to issue an urgent notification to the Secretary of State. An independent review of progress was undertaken in 2019, in which we found a mixed picture, with insufficient progress made against achieving many of our recommendations.

Bedford has been under considerable pressure, owing to the impact of Covid-19. The prison returned to level 4 of the national recovery framework (see Glossary of terms) in January 2021 and had experienced two large-scale outbreaks of the virus in December 2020 and February 2021. At its peak, the second outbreak saw 20% of prisoners testing positive and a large proportion of staff absent from work. Leaders were committed to managing the spread of Covid-19 and worked hard to apply guidance on isolating prisoners. At the time of our scrutiny visit, no further prisoners had tested positive, but some staff absences continued.

The governor had a clear understanding of the issues facing Bedford before and during the pandemic and was committed to taking steps out of the restricted regime at the earliest opportunity. Communication with prisoners about the pandemic and the restricted regime was thoughtful and proactive and peer workers were used creatively to inform and support others. Our survey showed that most prisoners were aware of the Covid-19 restrictions.

Improvements in living conditions had been made, including extensive and good-quality refurbishment of communal shower rooms. The prison was cleaner and the provision of basic items such as bedding, clean clothing and cell cleaning materials was now more reliable. The work on equality and diversity had seen some recent improvements. Health care provision was reasonably good, but medicines administration on the wings needed to be improved.

Efforts to improve outcomes for prisoners continued to be made throughout the pandemic, such as increasing the size of the safer custody team, but these had not yet been fully effective in making the prison safer and many of our previous concerns persisted. The reported level of assaults between prisoners and on staff was the highest of all similar prisons over the last year. In our survey, 30% of prisoners said that they currently felt unsafe and nearly half said that they had been bullied or victimised by staff. We saw some dedicated staff who interacted with prisoners well in order to provide good care and support. However, we also saw many examples of rule breaking going unchallenged, which fed the perception that prisoners could behave badly without fear of repercussion. The quality of staff–prisoner relationships remained mixed, with not all staff buying into the vision of a rehabilitative approach set out by the governor. Formal key work support had been suspended at the start of the pandemic, which was a shame, given the positive start that the establishment had made in this area. Recorded rates of self-harm had reduced over recent months, but some weaknesses in the care and support given to those who were vulnerable or at risk of self-harm continued.

Senior leaders had an ambitious and clear vision for education, skills and work. They spoke confidently about how they intended to return to a full regime once restrictions allowed. Leaders recognised that the current regime did not meet the needs of the whole prison population. Only around a third of the prisoners accessed in-cell education. A large proportion of prisoners continued to work, to make sure that essential services were maintained, and two additional workshops had been opened during the pandemic. The important focus on rehabilitation and release planning to reduce reoffending and improve successful resettlement had largely been lost at the start of the pandemic. While the offender management unit maintained its focus on completing essential tasks linked to progression, face-to- face support was rare. Direct support aimed at promoting positive family relationships had also ended a year ago and the slow implementation of in-cell telephones did not help in promoting contact with loved ones.

Overall, many of the key concerns that we identify in this report reflect the challenges that leaders at Bedford have faced for many years. While improvements were evident under our test of respect, the more systemic issues of high levels of violence and underdeveloped staff–prisoner relationships persisted. The challenge of Covid-19 had led to poorer outcomes in rehabilitation and release planning and a lack of progress in our test of purposeful activity.

Charlie Taylor, HM Chief Inspector of Prisons
March 2021

## Summary of key findings

### Key concerns and recommendations

Key concerns and recommendations identify the issues of most importance to improving outcomes for prisoners and are designed to help establishments prioritise and address the most serious weaknesses in the treatment and conditions of prisoners.

During this visit we identified some areas of key concern and have made a small number of recommendations for the prison to address.

Key concern: Safety at the prison continued to be a concern. For example, 30% of prisoners responding to our survey reported feeling unsafe currently and the level of assaults against staff and prisoners had been the highest among comparable prisons over the last year. Basic rules were not enforced consistently by all staff and we saw some failing to provide appropriate challenge of antisocial behaviour.

Recommendation: Prisoners' perceptions of safety should be improved through clear and sustained reductions in the levels of violence and more consistent enforcement of rules by staff. (To the governor)

Key concern: In our survey, only 45% of prisoners who had been on an assessment, care in custody and teamwork (ACCT) document said that they felt well cared for. The ACCT process had too many weaknesses and lacked effective oversight by managers. The work of Listeners had been suspended since the start of the Covid-19 restrictions. Well-being checks designed to identify individuals in need of support during the restricted regime were not undertaken at regular intervals and were completed by different officers, which undermined their effectiveness.

Recommendation: Support given to vulnerable prisoners, including those at risk of self-harm, should be improved. (To the governor)

Key concern: In our survey, 59% of prisoners said that staff treated them with respect and only 31% that a member of staff had checked on them in the last week. Almost half said that they had been victimised by staff. While some prisoners felt that many officers worked hard and were helpful, they also said that others were harsh in their attitudes, resorted too readily to using force and were abrupt and uncaring in their dealings with them. Almost a quarter of officers had not worked in prison before the Covid-19 pandemic and we were concerned about their lack of skills in managing prisoners once the restricted regime was eased.

Recommendation: The reasons for prisoners' negative perceptions about staff should be explored and the prison must improve staff-prisoner relationships, including taking action to improve

the capability of new officers. (To the governor)

Key concern: Prisoners residing on A, B and C wings collected medicines from the central hub, but there was not always enough time afforded to enable them to do this for evening medications, owing to other regime pressures or shortages of prison staff. This meant that health care staff administering medicines were obliged to prioritise access to treatment based on which prisoners could 'safely' miss a dose. This potentially placed prisoners at risk.

Recommendation: All prisoners should receive their prescribed medication at the appropriate time intervals and in line with the prescribing instructions. (To the governor)

Key concern: Face-to-face family support work had not been available for the last year, which undermined prisoners' ability to establish and maintain positive relationships with the outside world.

Recommendation: Prisoners should be supported through proactive, face-to-face family support work, including establishing and maintaining positive relationships with their children and others where this is appropriate. (To the governor)

Key concern: Most prisoners had not received direct support from the resettlement team for almost a year. Face-to-face reviews of resettlement plans before release had not been taking place either and many prisoners received information about the arrangements for their release at the last minute. Practical release support was far too limited.

Recommendation: Prisoners should receive comprehensive support and all the resettlement help they need well ahead of their release date. (To the governor)

### INDEPENDENT MONITORING BOARD: Annual Report

The law requires every prison to be monitored by an independent Board appointed by the Justice Secretary; these are known as Independent Monitoring Boards (IMBs).

The IMB must satisfy itself as to the humane and just treatment of those held in custody within its prison and the range and adequacy of the programmes preparing them for release; it must report annually to the Justice Secretary on how well the prison has met the standards and requirements placed on it.

### IMB Report 1 July 2020 – 30 June 2021. Published November 2021

### Background to the report

This report has been written during a global pandemic, with the prison, for most of the time, in some sort of lockdown or severely restricted operation. In making the judgements below, we have tried to assess how the prison has operated within that context.

## Main judgements
### How safe is the prison?
The prison has performed well in keeping prisoners safe from Covid-19. There were two outbreaks and, in total, 138 prisoners tested positive. There was just one hospitalisation and no deaths resulted. This is a very creditable achievement.

However, the level of prisoner-on-prisoner violence has continued to increase and, while there has been some decrease in the number of assaults on staff, this remains very high in comparison with other prisons. Prisoners have also reported feeling unsafe.

There have been four deaths in custody in the last 18 months and we are concerned that there are repeated criticisms in the way that the processes for managing those at risk were delivered in HMP Bedford.

The prison has made progress in the provision of new scanning machines and systems to detect drugs coming into the prison. There has also been good work with the police around activities near the perimeter. However, the lack of mandatory drug testing during the pandemic means that it is difficult to judge the impact.

How fairly and humanely are prisoners treated?
The problems of an old prison – cramped and overcrowded conditions – have been exacerbated by prisoners being locked up for up to 23 hours a day. In the words of one prisoner: 'I for one found this quite hard going; you never have any privacy, which is something you need, and having to use a toilet in such a small space I find dehumanising and depressing'. Despite some improvements, the segregation unit remains a deeply unpleasant place and we look forward to the promised relocation to the main wings.

'Fair and humane' depends to a great extent on the quality of staff/prisoner relationships, particularly as judged from a prisoner perspective. Our observations – and prisoners' reports – suggest that these relationships are still mixed – some good, some not so good. The prison is also still operating with a significant number of relatively inexperienced officers.

There have been improvements in the complaints system and addressing diversity and inclusion issues. The faith team continues to play a really important role in supporting prisoners.

### How well are prisoners' health and wellbeing supported?
The healthcare team has provided a good level of service during the pandemic, with waiting times generally being better than those in the outside

community. Covid-19 vaccinations have been made available to all who request it, but it is concerning that there are high levels of refusals, particularly among younger prisoners.

The drug rehabilitation team has continued to provide a full range of services, except for group work, throughout the pandemic.

While we recognise the resourcing issues, we continue to have concerns about the effectiveness of the mental health services within the prison.

The gym was unavailable between March 2020 and June 2021. With time out of cell very limited, this has undoubtedly had a consequential impact on both the physical and mental health of prisoners.

### How well are prisoners progressed towards successful resettlement?
After a slow start, the education service has been able to provide a reasonable range of options, based on in-cell work. The library has worked effectively through a trolley service. In addition, there has been good work in providing green environmental improvements to the outside areas. Although physical visits were not possible during the reporting period, the prison has provided the opportunity for Zoom calling and provided special 'Covid-19 mobile phones'. This has been appreciated by prisoners, for whom family contact is so important.

Unfortunately, resettlement planning has not been effective during the pandemic. There has been no face-to-face work and the system of doing everything by questionnaires pushed through the cell door simply has not worked.

## Main areas for development
### TO THE MINISTER
We find it surprising that prison officers were not prioritised to received Covid-19 vaccines, and see this as indicative of the service being largely unrecognised and unappreciated. We would like to see the minister take the lead in raising the national profile of the Prison Service.

### TO THE PRISON SERVICE
The management of prisoners' property remains bedevilled by an antiquated paper system, a lack of any clear inter-establishment protocols and the absence of any performance measures. It is unclear whether there is any will to resolve these issues and so address a real ongoing problem for prisoners.

The performance of the new contract for accommodation on release is less than encouraging, and the management arrangements make it difficult for the prison, locally, to influence outcomes. As with all the outsourced services, the prison Governor is accountable for the outcomes without the responsibility for delivery.

Clear and quick mechanisms need to be in place

for the resolution of local performance issues.

It is very surprising that the removal of the community rehabilitation companies (CRCs) and the reintegration of probation services in June 2021 could not be coordinated with the letting of new finance, debt and benefits contracts, which, we understand, will not be in place until February 2022, some eight months later. Without support in these key areas, released prisoners are much more likely to find themselves back in prison.

The removal of the CRCs and the integration of many probation and resettlement services gives, in our view, an opportunity for improved effectiveness, but it does require clear leadership and a strong focus on outcomes.

## TO THE GOVERNOR

Reception is still an area that appears untidy and disorganised, which does nothing to suggest to new prisoners that they are coming into somewhere that is well managed and efficient.

While there is a steady decrease in self-harm incidents, we feel that a better system of investigation of incidents, to understand the causal links, would lead to further improvements. We echo the concerns of Her Majesty's Inspectorate of Prisons (HMIP) regarding the implementation of the assessment, care in custody and teamwork (ACCT) process and would hope that the new version might lead to improvements. We can also see real value in involving prisoners in assessing the effectiveness of the ACCT system. The interim Prisons and Probation Ombudsman (PPO) reports on two deaths in custody raise some significant issues and we would ask that a clear action plan is put in place in response to the final reports.

Despite some improvements, levels of violence remain unacceptably high.

The move of the CSU to B wing has been promised for some time and, although it is understandable that it was postponed by the pandemic, it is important that it happens in the next 12 months.

We feel that there would be considerable benefits in integrating the performance reporting of the main prison complaints and complaints to healthcare, so that there is a full picture across the establishment.

There are issues around the dispensing of medication that need resolving. Some prisoners are not receiving their medication, while others may be selling it on, as there has been inadequate supervision at the pharmacy.

Over a quarter of health appointments were missed because the prison was unable to deliver prisoners to the healthcare area, which is both a waste of healthcare resources and really unhelpful for prisoners.

We regret that the education arts specialist has left and that there is no intention to replace the role.

## Progress since the last report

The circumstances of the prison's operation during the pandemic mean that we could not expect progress in all areas (for example, the key worker scheme was not operational). We comment below on those functions where we believe that progress was possible.

## In Areas For Development Identified To The Minister

We have not seen any evidence of more money or resources invested to address educational needs and meaningful activities within prisons. The issue of the availability of stable accommodation for prisoners on release seems as problematic as ever.

## In Areas For Development Identified To The Prison Service

A new version of the ACCT process has been introduced nationally and we hope it will address the previous problems.

## In Areas For Development Identified To The Governor

There have been improvements in security, with airport-style scanning and checking at the main gate and a full body scanner introduced for prisoners at reception.

The quality of reporting and analysis of use of force incidents has improved dramatically, which should enable the whole process to be more effective.

The introduction of the Governor's weekly newsletter has been very effective in keeping prisoners informed, particularly about the pandemic, and has been very much appreciated.

The wings are generally much cleaner, which has contributed to the prison being able to get a grip on the rodent and pigeon problems.

The introduction of a well-stocked clothing exchange store has addressed the problems around the availability of basic items.

The provision of telephones direct to the cells is a great improvement.

The new diversity and inclusion manager seems to have made a huge difference, with a far better use of data resulting.

There appears to have been a significant improvement in the management of complaints.

We are pleased to note the external environmental improvements, including planters, evergreens and flowering shrubs.

The introduction of the 'departure lounge' seems a good step forward, although as access is from outside the prison gates (that is, after the prisoner has left), it may not be as effective as hoped for.

**THAMESMEAD
LONDON SE28 0EB**

**Tel: 020 8331 4400**

HM PRISON
BELMARSH

*For the latest reports on this prison please visit:*
https://tinyurl.com/bdfh26rv

*Important Changes:* **(1) Visits:** the identification necessary to access this prison and visit for social or professional purposes has changed; (2) **Money and Gifts** new rules now apply to these. See page 16 for full details of the above.

### Task of the establishment
A local prison holding adult and young adult men, some of whom require a high level of security. Certified normal accommodation and operational capacity

### Certified normal accommodation / Op.Cap
Prisoners held August 2021: 675
Baseline certified normal capacity: 792
In-use certified normal capacity: 792
Operational capacity: 773

### Population of the prison
• 1,481 new prisoners received each year (around 124 per month).
• 150 foreign national prisoners.
• 57% of prisoners from black and minority ethnic backgrounds.
• Unsentenced prisoners make up almost 60% of the population.
• 212 prisoners receiving support for substance misuse.
• Up to 240 prisoners a month referred for mental health assessment.

### Prison status and key providers
Public
Prison group: Long term and high security
Prison Group Director: Will Styles
Governor: Jenny Louis
IMB chairs: Fiona Neale
Leadership changes since last full inspection: Rob Davis, governor from 2016 until July 2020.
Physical/Mental health provider:
Oxleas NHS Foundation Trust
Substance misuse treatment provider:
Change Grow Live (CGL)
Prison education framework provider:
Milton Keynes College
Escort contractor: Serco
Prison department: Long term & high security estate

### Brief history
Belmarsh is in Thamesmead, South East London and was opened in 1991. It is one of 12 long term and high security prisons, but the only core local prison in the high security estate. It also operates a high secure unit (HSU) for prisoners presenting the very highest risk of escape.

### Short description of residential units
House block 1 – 174 older prisoners, life sentence and mixed population. House block 2 – 174 on short sentences, remands and mixed population. House block 3 – 174 on first night centre/induction and remand prisoners. House block 4 – 171 on vulnerable prisoners spur and mixed population. High secure unit (HSU) – a self-contained unit holding up to 47 prisoners who require a high level of security (including a small discrete segregation unit for HSU prisoners only).
Segregation unit – holding up to 16 prisoners serving periods of punishment or needing to be separated from others. It also contains two designated prison rule 46 cells used for the temporary management of close supervision centre (CSC) system.
Health care inpatients – a 33-bed inpatient facility staffed jointly by Oxleas NHS Foundation Trust and HMPPS.

### Visiting Information
Belmarsh is running a limited visits schedule. Visits are also happening differently than normal, observing strict guidelines, which must be followed. You can book your visit by telephone. You can also register to use the secure video calls service. There is no online booking service available.
Booking line: 0208 331 4750
The booking line is open Monday to Friday, 9:30am to 3pm. You can arrive 30-40 minutes before the time of your visit to go through security and check in.
**Visiting times:** Tuesday to Thursday: 9:15am to 10am, 11am to 11:45am. Friday: 9:15am to 10am
Saturday: 9:15am to 10am, 11am to 11:45am
How to book legal and professional visits
You can book face-to-face legal visits by calling 0208 331 4750 or email legalvisits.belmarsh@justice.gov.uk.
The booking line is open Monday to Friday, 9:30am to 15:00pm
To book legal visits via Videolink, email videolinkbelmarsh@justice.gov.uk

### INSPECTIONS & REPORTS
**HMCIP IRP Report 11–13 April 2022**
**Published 26th May 2022**
**Independent Review of Progress Report**
HMP Belmarsh is a high-security prison in south-

east London that held approximately 660 prisoners at the time of our inspection, most of whom were unsentenced. It is one of 13 long term and high security prisons, but the only reception prison in the high security estate. It also operates a high secure unit (HSU) for prisoners presenting the very highest risk of escape. At our previous inspections of HMP Belmarsh in 2018 and 2021, we made the following judgements about outcomes for prisoners.

At the full inspection in July-August 2021, staff-prisoner relationships had improved, health care was good, and the prison was calm and well-ordered. Safety had deteriorated, however: the rate of violence was high, use of force had increased and there was insufficient attention to the growing level of self-harm. There was largely inadequate use of data to support the development of effective strategies for safety or equality, and leadership oversight of these areas lacked rigour and focus. A major concern was that, notwithstanding the undoubted challenges of the pandemic, not enough had been done to increase the level of purposeful activity for prisoners who remained locked up for very long periods each day.

During this independent review of progress, we examined 10 key recommendations, and our colleagues in Ofsted addressed progress against three themes. It was clear that leaders had taken the report of the inspection seriously and, in most areas, our findings were encouraging, with reasonable progress found against most recommendations.

The governance of use of force and violence were much better and there was some early evidence of improving outcomes. Violence and self-harm had reduced and we saw some good initiatives, for example, a conflict resolution team interviewed every new arrival to identify concerns and minimise potential clashes. There had been very little progress, however, in increasing the effective use of body-worn cameras and a different approach by leadership was clearly required.

Constant supervision arrangements for prisoners at risk of self-harm were improving and there were now enough Listeners (see Glossary) for the population. Assessment, care in custody and teamwork (ACCT) case management for prisoners at risk of suicide or self-harm was also used more effectively to support those in crisis, but it was still implemented inconsistently and reviews were often not multidisciplinary.

The equality and diversity strategy had been updated and there was good progress against many of the priorities set out in the equality action plan. The diversity and inclusion meeting had just restarted and was more focused than it had been, but it was too early to assess its

effectiveness in achieving positive change. Data were being gathered and used more effectively in several areas, but there was still a considerable distance to travel to make sure they were consistently informing improvement planning. For example, we were surprised to find that leaders could not tell us how many prisoners were engaged in activities on any given day, or how frequently individual prisoners were in activity.

There had been some improvement to time out of cell and purposeful activity from a low base. We were told that most prisoners were now engaged in some form of purposeful activity, the gym and library had reopened, and corporate worship and social visits had resumed. However, too many prisoners still spent very long periods locked behind their doors with little to do. Leaders were planning to increase activities further, but there was no timetable for this and it remained unclear when the improvements would be seen.

Rehabilitation and release planning had been a generally positive area at the full inspection with the significant exceptions of poor resettlement support for the large population of unsentenced prisoners, and inadequate public protection phone monitoring. It was a concern that we saw no meaningful progress in either of these areas and there was no clear plan to address the identified problems.

Overall, there had been encouraging progress towards meeting most of our recommendations, although there were a few exceptions, and in some areas the advances were recent and fragile.

Charlie Taylor
HM Chief Inspector of Prisons April 2022

**HMCIP Report published 12th November 2021**
**Date of last inspection:** 2-6 August 2021
Belmarsh is a high-security, men's prison in south-east London that held 675 men at the time of our inspection, of whom nearly 60% were unsentenced and 17% were category A prisoners. Within the jail there is also high secure unit. The prison services the London courts, particularly Woolwich and the Old Bailey, but because of reduced courtroom space created by Covid-19 restrictions, prisoners had been attending courts further afield. This had led to a strain on resources in the prison because more staff were required for escort duty.

While maintaining a strong security focus, the governor had set out to improve relationships between officers and prisoners and to create a more representative and caring staff team. Although this change was not manifested in our survey results, inspectors commented on the many positive interactions they saw in the jail and prisoners often told us about supportive staff members. Leaders recognised there was further work to be done to improve the culture in the prison: for example, many staff routinely failed to collect or turn on body- worn cameras and we saw officers who were supposed to be supervising the most vulnerable prisoners, sitting reading the paper.

Although the prison felt generally well-ordered and calm, levels of violence had risen since our last inspection despite Covid-19 restrictions limiting the time most prisoners were out of their cells. While the prison collected data on violence and use of force, it was not being used to support the development of an effective strategy for reducing violence. It was concerning that there had been no violence reduction meeting for more than a year.

The underuse of data was something of a theme of this inspection – leaders did not have an adequate plan to consider outcomes for different groups such as the disproportionate use of force on black and younger prisoners, and neither data nor consultation were used to understand and address these or other disparities. While the prison's self-assessment report (SAR) suggested violence had reduced because there were fewer incidents, in reality, with fewer prisoners in the jail, rates were actually increasing.

The prison had not paid sufficient attention to the growing levels of self-harm and there was not enough oversight or care taken of prisoners at risk of suicide. Urgent action needed to be taken in this area to make sure that these prisoners were kept safe.

The 52% of prisoners who were not working were spending 23 hours a day locked in their cells while the education block, gym and library had sat empty and unused for more than a year. The provider was finally running some face- to-face education on the wing, though access was limited, and some prisoners were getting taught through their cell doors during the lunchtime lockdown. In- cell work packs were being offered to prisoners, but engagement had been low and prisoners in the high secure unit received no regular education. Two men who had volunteered to be reading mentors had received no training, materials or support.

The governor had a strong vision for the future of the prison, but for this to be realised she will need to strengthen her senior team and make sure that there is more rigorous oversight of some of the key areas – such as care for the most vulnerable prisoners, effective safety strategies and a better understanding of disparities between different groups – and use data to understand the challenges, set targets and measure progress.

Charlie Taylor Chief Inspector September 2021

**Summary of key findings**
We last inspected Belmarsh in 2018 and made 40 recommendations, six of which were about areas of key concern. The prison fully accepted 31 of the recommendations and partially (or subject to resources) accepted six. It rejected three recommendations.

**Progress on key concerns and recommendations from the full inspection**
Our last inspection of Belmarsh took place before the Covid-19 pandemic and the recommendations in that report focused on areas of concern affecting outcomes for prisoners at the time. Although we recognise that the challenges of keeping prisoners safe during COVID- 19 will have changed the focus for many prison leaders, we believe that it is important to report on progress in areas of key concern to help leaders to continue to drive improvement.

At our last full inspection, we made one recommendation about a key concern in the area of safety. At this inspection we found that this recommendation had not been achieved.

We made three recommendations about key concerns in the area of respect. At this inspection we found that one of those recommendations had been achieved, one had been partially achieved and one had not been achieved.

We made two recommendations about key concerns in the area of purposeful activity. At this inspection we found that one of those recommendations had been partially achieved. Ofsted carried out a progress monitoring visit alongside our inspection to assess the progress that leaders and managers had made towards reinstating a full education, skills and work curriculum. They judged it was too early to assess whether recommendations made at the last inspection had been achieved.

**Outcomes for prisoners**
We assess outcomes for prisoners against four healthy prison tests. We also include a commentary on leadership in the prison.

At this inspection of Belmarsh, we found that outcomes for prisoners had stayed the same in two healthy prison areas, improved in one and declined in one.

These judgements seek to make an objective assessment of the outcomes experienced by those detained and have taken into account the prison's recovery from Covid-19 as well as the 'regime stage' at which the prison was operating, as outlined in the HM Prison and Probation (HMPPS) National Framework for prison regimes and services.

## Safety

Reception was clean and functional, and the first night centre was a comfortable environment that provided some good support. New arrivals could not routinely discuss any immediate anxieties in private with an officer or a Listener (prisoners trained by the Samaritans to provide confidential emotional support to fellow prisoners) on their first night, but officers did conduct overnight safety checks. The induction programme was delivered in person to every prisoner. However, the content was delivered in English, including to those who did not understand English. Although prisoners were provided with a useful induction booklet translated into commonly used languages, this did not give them the opportunity to interact or ask questions at a crucial point in their prison journey. Delivery of the induction programme required greater staff oversight and the regime on the unit was limited.

In our survey, one in four prisoners said they felt unsafe. Incidents of violence had increased since our last inspection. Challenge, support and intervention plans (CSIPs, see Glossary of terms) were used appropriately to manage the most serious perpetrators of violence, but support for victims was underdeveloped. The violence reduction strategy did not address the specific issues relevant to Belmarsh. A weekly safety intervention meeting was well attended and discussed prisoners of concern. The strategic meeting to discuss wider issues of violence had stopped in early 2020 and it was not clear how leaders were driving the action plan to make the prison safer.

The use of force had increased since our last inspection. Staff did not routinely activate body-worn video cameras during incidents. Due to the lack of video footage to support staff statements, we could not be assured that the use of force was necessary in all cases. A comprehensive monthly report contained a useful range of data, but there had been no use of force governance meetings to provide adequate scrutiny and assurance.

The segregation unit was clean and well staffed. Prisoners were offered a daily regime, although those who refused to relocate back to the main prison were still deprived of a daily shower, which was unjustifiable. Prisoners and staff on the unit benefited from support from a forensic psychologist and there had been efforts to reintegrate a few very complex prisoners. However, overall, governance of segregation was relatively weak.

The security team identified appropriate security objectives. The introduction of dedicated staff to oversee prisoners affiliated to gangs was a positive initiative. There was a robust approach to the monitoring of extremism and corruption prevention. Drug testing had recently resumed and the use of suspicion testing was effective. Leaders were sighted on the risks of illicit items coming into the prison and made effective use of technology to reduce supply.

There had been four self-inflicted deaths since the last inspection. There was a good action plan to embed Prisons and Probation Ombudsman recommendations from investigations into the deaths, but the quality of suicide attempt investigations was very poor. Recorded levels of self-harm were lower than at most similar prisons, but were nearly four times higher than at the last inspection. The written strategy and action plan were not used effectively to reduce self-harm. Prisoners most at risk had been identified for welfare checks, but there was only a limited range of wider support. The quality of support delivered through assessment, care in custody and teamwork (ACCT) case management was weak. We were not assured that prisoners subject to constant supervision were always kept safe. The prison did not check the safer custody hotline frequently enough. There were no adult safeguarding processes in place.

## Respect

Staff-prisoner relationships had improved since our last inspection and many staff treated prisoners with respect. Most had a reasonable knowledge of the prisoners under their care and we observed good interactions. The absence of key work affected the development of more productive relationships.

Communal areas and facilities were generally clean and outside areas were well maintained. Double cells were no longer used to accommodate three prisoners. Cells were furnished and equipped with basic items, but some needed redecoration. Some showers were in a very poor condition, although work was under way to replace them. The high secure unit (HSU) was uncomfortably hot during hot weather and portable air conditioning units only partially addressed this. Most exercise areas were reasonable and equipped with fixed exercise machines, but the yard on the HSU had none and was comparatively austere.

The food was of reasonable quality and quantity, but meals were served too early. Prisoners had very limited opportunities to prepare their own food. There were weaknesses in the systems to provide prisoners with property and catalogue orders.

General consultation arrangements were good and had led to positive changes. Complaints were properly tracked to monitor completion and were quality assured, but there were major weaknesses in the applications process. Prisoners had good access to legal visits and there had been a significant increase in the use of video-link for judicial proceedings.

Equality work was undermined by an out-of-date strategy and lack of a multi-discipline meeting to develop and drive action planning. This was further compounded by limited consultation with prisoners with protected characteristics and poor use of data. Support for foreign national prisoners was poor and telephone interpreting services were not well used. Equality peer representatives had been identified but they lacked training and purpose. The chaplaincy had continued to provide good support to prisoners throughout the pandemic, although the return to corporate worship had taken time.

Health services had improved and were very good. They were well led and partnership working with the prison was strong. Clinical governance was robust, including improved management of complaints, and assertive oversight of care delivery in prisoners' early days. Primary care services remained comprehensive and most had continued during the regime restrictions. The non-attendance rates for appointments were low and waiting lists relatively short. As at the last inspection, too many prisoners resided in the inpatient unit for non- clinical reasons, which led to the disruption of a therapeutic regime. Mental health services were responsive, but there were unacceptable delays in transferring prisoners to hospitals under the Mental Health Act. Social care was exemplary and substance misuse services provided a good range of interventions. Pharmacy services and medicines management were good, and dental services were very good.

### Purposeful activity

Ofsted carried out a progress monitoring visit of the prison alongside our full inspection and the purposeful activity judgement incorporates their assessment of progress. Ofsted's full findings and the recommendations arising from their visit are set out in Section 5.

The majority of prisoners spent up to 23 hours a day locked in their cells and some did not receive a full hour of outdoor exercise or daily shower. The regime on the HSU was often reduced further due to staff shortages.

The library had been closed since the beginning of the pandemic, and there was no timescale for reopening it, but a remote lending service was operating. The gym had also closed and had still not reopened. Most prisoners could only access weekly outdoor PE.

Education, skills and work had been available to only a small number of prisoners during the restricted regime. Leaders and managers had provided some in-cell work, but too few prisoners were participating in education in this way. HSU prisoners had no routine access to education.

New arrivals received an in-cell education induction pack that included an initial assessment of their English and mathematics skills and the identification of any learning difficulties or disabilities. Prisoners with entry-level literacy skills or whose first language was not English struggled with these packs and too many were not completed. As a result, staff did not have sufficient information to allocate prisoners to the most appropriate purposeful activity.

Prisoners had very recently started to benefit from one-to-one, face-to- face education support. However, they could not phone education staff and had to rely on making requests for help in writing, which limited support. A few prisoners had recently been able to sit examinations leading to qualifications, but, overall, the proportion of accredited qualifications available to prisoners was too low.

Leaders had identified the education and skills programmes they planned to implement, but could not provide sufficient detail of how they would return to classroom-based teaching.

Staff from education, the prison and the newly appointed information, advice and guidance service worked in partnership to prioritise prisoners in most need of support. This service was still in its infancy, but was starting to benefit the small number of prisoners who had accessed it. Training in commercial workshops was appropriately planned and delivered. Prisoners identified as having a learning difficulty or disability had started to receive face-to-face support on an individual basis.

### Rehabilitation and release planning

Visits had recommenced in May 2021 and now allowed limited physical contact. Secure video calling had been well promoted and take-up was excellent. In-cell telephones enabled prisoners to call home regularly.

Reducing reoffending work was not based on a recent needs analysis and the monthly meeting was not sufficiently strategic or action- focused. Prison offender managers (POMs) had more manageable caseloads than at the previous inspection. This should have enabled greater in-depth support, but the recorded contact with prisoners was infrequent. The prison did not transfer prisoners out until their initial OASys (offender assessment system) assessment report had been completed, which was positive. Recategorisation decisions were prompt and prisoners were generally moved to the most appropriate establishments quickly.

There was effective oversight of prisoners subject to multi-agency public protection arrangements (MAPPA). Risk management for the release of high-risk prisoners was generally good and subject to regular scrutiny and guidance from the senior probation officer. However, there was no oversight of phone monitoring arrangements and too many calls had not been listened to.

The prison delivered two accredited programmes, which were appropriate to the population, and waiting lists were small. The psychology team had developed meaningful one-to-one interventions for prisoners who were unsuitable for programmes.

Recent national changes meant that resettlement work (previously the responsibility of the community rehabilitation company) no longer included support for the 60% of unsentenced prisoners at Belmarsh, which was a significant loss of provision. The job coach was still working remotely and there had been little careers provision, so many prisoners did not have a development plan for education, training or employment on release. In the previous 12 months, 18% of sentenced prisoners had been released without settled accommodation, which was a significant concern.

### Key concerns and recommendations

Key concerns and recommendations identify the issues of most importance to improving outcomes for prisoners and are designed to help establishments prioritise and address the most significant weaknesses in the treatment and conditions of prisoners.

During this inspection we identified some areas of key concern and have made a small number of recommendations for the prison to address those concerns.

Key concern: Levels of violence had continued to increase since the last inspection and too many prisoners felt unsafe. Despite available prison data, leaders did not analyse the indicators of violence in detail. The prison's strategy and associated action plan did not reflect the risks it faced and there had been no formal strategic meeting to address violence for over 18 months.

Recommendation: Safety data should be used to inform a strategy and action plan to reduce increasing levels of violence, which leaders monitor and drive effectively.

Key concern: Governance of use of force had lapsed. Most incidents were spontaneous, but staff did not routinely activate body-worn video cameras. Despite good local data, there was no effective analysis or detailed scrutiny of force to make sure that incidents were necessary, justified and proportionate.

Recommendation: There should be robust scrutiny of the use of force, including data, camera footage and staff statements, to make sure that force is necessary, justified and proportionate.

Key concern: The quality of case management support for prisoners at risk of suicide and self-harm was weak: risk was not always assessed correctly; some case reviews were too infrequent; and care plans were missing or poorly completed. Records of prisoners' interactions were often missing. It was clear that staff had struggled to implement the new version of ACCT.

Recommendation: Prisoners at risk of suicide and self-harm should receive additional support through the use of good quality assessment, care in custody and teamwork (ACCT) case management that includes an accurate assessment of their risk, sufficiently frequent case reviews, appropriate support actions recorded in a care plan and a consistent record of their daily interactions.

Key concern: Constant supervision arrangements for prisoners at the highest risk of suicide and self-harm were unsafe. Staff read newspapers rather than observing the prisoners, who were also sometimes left unsupervised and unobserved. Supervising staff worked long shifts, which affected their concentration, and they did little to encourage prisoner interaction and participation in anything purposeful.

Recommendation: Constant supervision arrangements should keep prisoners at risk safe and encourage them to engage with a purposeful regime wherever possible.

Key concern: There were substantial weaknesses in equality work. The equality strategy was out of date and there was no multidisciplinary meeting to develop and drive action planning. There was limited consultation of prisoners in protected groups and little consideration of equality monitoring data.

Recommendation: Equality data and effective consultation should inform an effective strategy and action plan that leaders drive proactively to address disproportionate outcomes for prisoners from protected groups.

Concern: Prisoners who were not working spent up to 23 hours a day locked in their cells. Only 23% prisoners were engaged in out-of-cell purposeful activity. Most prisoners had around 45-50 minutes outdoor exercise each day, although some got as little as 30 minutes. Association had not been available in the main prison since the restricted regime commenced in March 2020. The library remained closed and there were no developed plans to reopen it. Unlike in other prisons, the gym was still closed.

Recommendation: The core day should provide adequate time out of cell for purposeful activity, domestic tasks and recreation to assist with the rehabilitation of prisoners and to improve their well-being.

Key concern: The decision to stop resettlement workers providing advice and support to unsentenced prisoners was a significant loss to these prisoners, who made up almost 60% of the population. While the decision was outside the control of the prison, it had not put in place any measures to mitigate this.

Recommendation: All prisoners, including those who are unsentenced, should be able to access resettlement advice and support to prepare them for their release into the community. (To HMPPS)

### Notable positive practice

We define notable positive practice as innovative work or practice that leads to particularly good outcomes from which other establishments may be able to learn. Inspectors look for evidence of good outcomes for prisoners; original, creative or particularly effective approaches to problem-solving or achieving the desired goal; and how other establishments could learn from or replicate the practice.

Inspectors found five examples of notable positive practice during this inspection.

A useful induction booklet had been translated into commonly spoken languages.

The monthly use of force data pack contained a range of information that could be used to identify good practice and areas of concern so that immediate action could be taken, practice improved and learning shared.

The weekly security intelligence assessment and associated report enabled the prison to respond appropriately to emerging security and safety concerns.

Consistent monitoring of actions arising from health screening and assessment of new patients meant they were supported at a vulnerable point in their prison lives.

Belmarsh placed a transfer hold on prisoners who required completion of an OASys assessment to make sure that this process was not passed on to other establishments.

### INDEPENDENT MONITORING BOARD: Annual Report

The law requires every prison to be monitored by an independent Board appointed by the Justice Secretary; these are known as Independent Monitoring Boards (IMBs). The IMB must satisfy itself as to the humane and just treatment of those held in custody within its prison and the range and adequacy of the programmes preparing them for release; it must report annually to the Justice Secretary on how well the prison has met the standards and requirements placed on it.

### HMP Belmarsh IMB Report 1 July 2020 – 30 June 2021; Published November 2021

**Background to the report**

Undoubtedly a main feature of the monitoring during our reporting year has been Covid-19. It has had a deleterious effect on our being able to monitor as effectively as we should. It has also dominated the way the prison carried out its functions.

Below is a description of one period during the past year and how the prison managed the pandemic.

In November 2020, HMP Belmarsh was declared an outbreak site. Up to that time the prison had managed to keep numbers of infected prisoners very low – to no more than five at any one time. The vast majority of infections were brought into the prison by transferred prisoners. There were occasions when staff were responsible. The most notable of these was when an employee of a contractor entered the prison in mid-November, suffering symptoms and having had a test but awaiting the results. It was soon declared that he was positive and the consequence was a large number of officers had to self-isolate.

The outbreak started in Houseblock 1 with 15 prisoners. The prison was quick to introduce measures. All social visits were cancelled but Purple Visits (a secure video link with family, legal advisers and authorised others) continued except in the affected houseblock. Masks were made compulsory across the prison. A gatekeeper at Houseblock 1 was set up and attendance in the houseblock was restricted to staff working there and the rota ensured it was the same staff.

On Houseblock 1, prisoners were retained in their cells. Food was served at the cell door. The regime for the houseblock was for 30 minutes' exercise in groups of 12 and for each prisoner to have three showers per week. All showers were cleaned after each cohort of prisoners. Medications were received at the nurses' hatch but this greatly increased the time taken because of the need for very strict social distancing. Consequently, some medications were not received at the appropriate time. All staff had weekly testing, and for Houseblock 1 full personal protective equipment (PPE) was required.

By late November 2020, the number of positive prisoners had risen to 44. Some prisoners had been transferred to a special wing but accommodation there was limited. Three prisoners were hospitalised. Over subsequent days numbers continued to rise, reaching 71 by the end of November 2020.

Of course, prisoners were not the only ones infected. There was a toll on staff. Numbers off either sick or self-isolating rose to over 100 at one point. This put pressure on the regime. The staffing problem was acerbated by the need for remand and other prisoners to attend court, sometimes in faraway places (such as Bristol). As these were category A prisoners, transport and accompanying staff came out of the Belmarsh complement, causing further shortages. The number of category A prisoners increased significantly at this time. This put an additional strain on staffing.

Phones had been fixed in all cells across the prison and prisoners were allowed additional phone credit in order to phone home in lieu of the lack of social visits. The phones also allowed prison staff to phone in to prisoners and this was useful when conducting assessment, care in custody and teamwork (ACCT) reviews.

On 7 December 2020, it was noted that no further positive cases were recorded. On 15 December 2020 social visits recommenced. The prison was then able to move to a more normal regime, but only for a short time.

We now know that the events following this period were equally challenging. The Board continued to function, attending meetings remotely and reading all information such as daily briefings on a regular basis, but it became clear that triangulation was not possible without interaction with prisoners. Therefore, those members who could continued with visits until at the height of the pandemic there was an agreement with the prison that the Board would not visit due to the risk of bringing infection in. Physical Board visits resumed in March 2021.

## Main judgements
### How safe is the prison?

Conflicting information and factors such as changes in prison capacity as well as the effects of lockdown have made it difficult to ascertain levels of violence during the past year, but data suggest it remains similar to the previous year. The prison's strong reaction to Covid-19 kept the majority of prisoners safe from infection, and this is commendable. Also, the care of those prisoners who are most vulnerable was welcomed. However, more generally, the fear of violence from gangs remains in the form of conflicts across the prison. Plans to involve outside agencies to engage with gang members and improve relationships are promising, and the Board is hopeful that these will materialise in the near future.

The reduction in key worker support has left some prisoners unable to share their concerns on a regular basis or find out basic information that would lessen their stress. While some officers go out of their way to be supportive, others have been seen to be dismissive.

There have been discussions concerning a new regime, which it is hoped will reduce violent encounters as prisoners move about the prison but the Board has yet to hear how this will be arranged or when it will commence.

### How fairly and humanely are prisoners treated?

The Board is concerned that the prison has insufficient knowledge of the experiences of those with protected characteristics to ensure that outcomes and opportunities are equal for all. It has been difficult to access meaningful figures and comparative data in these areas, which could drive improvements in the fair treatment of some prisoners. Therefore it is not possible to state that all prisoners are treated fairly and humanely.

Some prisoners have been seen to be treated with care, especially those identified as most vulnerable, but this is not the case for all prisoners. Efforts to treat prisoners humanely are reflected in improvements in the fabric of the prison including the cleanliness of outside areas. However the slow progress of the shower installations is of concern, especially as some of the new areas are out of use due to plumbing issues. The shower units available for use by most prisoners are still in a wholly unacceptable condition.

The removal of three-man cells is at long last complete and the Board would be strongly against any reintroduction of this inhumane practice in the future.

In-cell telephony gave prisoners the opportunity to maintain vital contact with families when visits were suspended.

The majority of prisoners have a TV in their cell, which helped to pass the time during lockdown, but many prisoners are now keen to get out of their cells more and take part in activities. The provision of various activities has been slow to restart and this has caused some frustration for prisoners.

Staff shortages, and staff redeployment for cover, has meant that prisoners have sometimes missed out on basics such as showers and exercise.

Staffing issues in the business hub have meant unacceptable waits for canteen, responses to complaints and other requests, which have caused unnecessary frustration for prisoners.

Prisoners who do not speak English have been at a disadvantage, having to rely on others to support basic issues for example ordering meals and to speak up for them if they have a problem.

The Board is satisfied that prisoners in the segregation unit are treated humanely, with complaints to us being few, and relationships between staff and prisoners appearing to be generally good. Good order or discipline (GOOD) reviews have taken place throughout the year and the majority of prisoners have only remained in the unit for a short time.

Prisoners in the high security unit have suffered

due to a lack of ventilation since new windows were installed. The in-cell telephony is not available to them; their exercise time is short; and adherence to a full regime is thwarted by staff shortages.

Despite the lack of collective worship over the year, the chaplaincy is to be commended for its good work amongst the prisoners on houseblocks including support with online funerals.

**How well are prisoners' health and wellbeing needs met?**

While efforts have been made to meet prisoners' health and wellbeing needs, provision has not been consistent across the prison.

The provision of healthcare services at Belmarsh by Oxleas NHS Foundation Trust is of a satisfactory standard, and liaison between prison discipline staff and healthcare staff works well. The healthcare centre is a busy, noisy and challenging area where staff have been seen to be patient and caring even when under great pressure. Mental health issues among prisoners in healthcare, the segregation unit and on houseblocks is of similar concern to last year. The length of time taken to assess patients and move them on to a more suitable environment is unacceptable. While prison and healthcare staff do all they can to support these very sick prisoners, it is not of a sufficient standard to aid recovery.

Concerns raised last year regarding cancellation of hospital appointments, non- attendance at outpatient clinics and medicines given out at inappropriate times appear to continue according to prisoners, but there are no figures or data to evidence this.

Patient Council meetings and audits of prisoner complaints have not yet restarted. This is unfortunate as both evidence the prisoner voice, which would have been useful.

Prisoners receiving social care are identified and monitored, as are those on ACCTs, constant watch and in self-isolation. The wellbeing of these vulnerable prisoners is regularly reviewed in weekly meetings where staff are seen to be involved and caring.

Drug use remains a problem in the prison, in particular 'spice'.

There have been no soft skills available in the past year to occupy or interest prisoners apart from items such as origami or simple art materials provided to individuals in cells by officers or the library.

**How well are prisoners progressed towards successful resettlement?**

Progress in prisoner progression and resettlement was severely hampered during the past year as outside agencies did not come in, were working remotely or not at all. The majority of purposeful activity ceased, family contact was limited and staff shortages restricted the work of the offender management unit (OMU).

Gains made in purposeful activity were lost and the revival of these seems a long way off. Prisoners were initially happy to work through education packs in their cells but more recently they are keen to receive a more supportive and personal approach to learning. Those prisoners who do not speak English have been at a disadvantage during this period, although support for ESOL prisoners is about to restart on houseblocks.

Resettlement meetings restarted earlier this year and there is a strong commitment from many agencies to get things moving again in areas such as finance, housing, health and employment. Many practical and straightforward ideas have been put forward; these are yet to be seen in action. New workshops, such as textiles and horticulture, show great promise as they are well equipped and instructors are in place ready to begin as soon as they are given the go-ahead. The fact that category A prisoners can attend the textiles workshop is also promising. The Board is hopeful that the ambitions around matching provision to employability on release will result in positive action.

The impact of the new Probation Service is yet to be seen but it is unfortunate that St. Mungo's is no longer contracted to support remand prisoners with housing and the Board is concerned that this will have a detrimental effect on those remand prisoners who have lost their home after a prolonged stay due to court backlogs.

The work of the library over the year, supporting education, providing distraction packs and facilitating regular reading, and helping prisoners with little or no English, is to be commended.

**Main areas for development**
**TO THE MINISTER**

Will the minister discuss with colleague health ministers the provision of proper appropriate service outside of prison for those prisoners suffering from severe mental ill-health and the need for this to increase as a matter of urgency in order to provide the best opportunity for recovery?

Will the minister look urgently at the provision for those prisoners on remand in order to:

• speed up the courts process so that prisoners are not kept on remand for a prolonged period

• ensure that those prisoners on remand who stand to lose their accommodation due to longer stays in prison, have housing support from St. Mungo's or another suitable agency Resettlement planning)?

## TO THE PRISON SERVICE

Will HMPPS confirm that there are no plans to reintroduce the use of three-man cells in Belmarsh under any conditions?

Will HMPPS improve the length of time those prisoners who are very unwell wait for mental health assessments and the transfer to more suitable accommodation?

Will HMPPS reform the system of handling prisoners' property throughout the prison estate, so that it works effectively at ensuring that prisoners are united with their property swiftly and correctly whenever they move in the prison system?

## TO THE GOVERNOR

Will the prison appoint champions in each houseblock to be responsible for care leavers?

Will the prison ensure that the key worker scheme reverts to the initial planned level, whereby all prisoners have a named key worker, time is allocated for key worker duties and key workers remain constant even when prisoners transfer within the prison?

Will the prison ensure that diversity and inclusion is given a much higher focus than in recent years, and that detailed measures are introduced to ensure equality of outcome and opportunity for all relevant protected characteristics?

Will the prison ensure that updated prisoner induction packs are made available as a priority and the means to translate these as necessary are readily available?

Will the prison review conditions in the HSU regarding the following issues:

• Temperature due to lack of ventilation after window refurbishment
• Use of in-cell telephony
• Staffing and regime
• Education and activities
• The provision of suitable interpretation services for ESOL prisoners

Will the prison review the prisoner complaints process, as suggested in the IMB Annual Report of last year?

**BRIDGE ROAD
WREXHAM, LL13 9QS**

**HMP & YOI
BERWYN**   **Tel: 01978 523000**

*For the latest reports on this prison please visit:*
https://tinyurl.com/bdfh26rv

*Important Changes:* **(1) Visits:** the identification necessary to access this prison and visit for social or professional purposes has changed; (2) **Money and Gifts** new rules now apply to these. See page 16 for full details of the above.

### Task of the establishment
A category C training and resettlement establishment holding adult males.

### Certified normal accommodation and operational capacity
CNA: 2106
Op. Cap: 2106

### Prison status and key providers
Public
Prison Group: North Wales
Executive Director: Giles Mason
Governor/Director: Nicholas Leader
IMB Chair: Eileen Darbyshire
Physical, Mental, Substance health provider: Betsi Cadwaladr University Health Board
Learning and skills provider: Novus Cambria
Escort contractor: GeoAmey

**Brief history** HMP Berwyn is located on Wrexham Industrial Estate in North Wales. It is a reception, category C resettlement and training prison, with a capacity to hold 2,106 prisoners. During the Covid-19 pandemic this was reduced to 1,801. During 2021 a unit was established for vulnerable prisoners, including a number of men convicted of sexual offences (MCOSO). It was the first time the prison had experienced near full operational capacity since it opened in 2017 (the average monthly population for the period covered by this report being 1725 prisoners). The prison consists of three main houses: Alwen, Bala and Ceiriog. Each house is divided into eight communities. The accommodation in each community is a combination of double- and single-occupancy cells. Across the prison, 30% of cells are single occupancy and 70% are double occupancy. Alongside the main communities, the prison has a care and separation unit (CASU; Ogwen) which can hold 21 prisoners.

**Short description of residential units** There are three houses. Alwen, Bala and Ceiriog, each divided into eight communities that can accommodate up to 88 general population residents, including the following.

Alwen C Uppers: life-sentenced/indeterminate sentence for public protection

Alwen D Uppers: enhanced life-sentenced

Bala B Lowers: healthy living

Bala C Lowers: Glyndŵr: progressive unit

Bala D Lowers: Gobaith: resettlement unit

Bala B Uppers: Menai: assisted living

Bala C Uppers: Shaun Stocker: veterans and first-timers

Bala D Uppers: improving family futures

Ceiriog A Lowers: Snowdon: mature residents

Ceiriog D Lowers: induction and first night unit.

Ogwen: care and support (segregation) unit (up to 21 prisoners)

### Visiting Information
Booking line: 01978 523300
The booking line is open Monday to Friday, 8am to 5pm

### Visiting times
Monday: 8:45am to 9:45am, 10:30am to 11:30am, 2pm to 3pm and 3:45pm to 4:45pm
Tuesday: 8:45am to 9:45am, 10:30am to 11:30am and 2pm to 4pm
Wednesday: 8:45am to 9:45am, 10:30am to 11:30am, 2pm to 3pm and 3:45pm to 4:45pm
Thursday: 8:45am to 9:45am, 10:30am to 11:30am and 2pm to 4pm
Friday: 8:45 to 9:45am, 10:30am to 11:30am
Saturday: 9am to 10am, 10:45am to 11:45am, 2pm to 3pm and 3:45pm to 4:45pm
Sunday: 9am to 10am, 10:45am to 11:45am, 2pm to 3pm and 3:45pm to 4:45pm

### Legal visits
Legal visits can be booked by calling: 01978523 300
Visiting times: Tuesday to Friday: 9am to 12pm and 2pm to 5pm

### INSPECTIONS & REPORTS
**Date of last inspection:** 4–14 March 2019
**HMCIP Report published 11 July 2019**
This report records our first inspection of HMP Berwyn. Located near Wrexham in North Wales, Berwyn opened in 2017. It is the first prison to open under the management of the public sector for several years and will be the largest prison in the country. Designated a category C training prison, the establishment held 1,273 prisoners at the time of the inspection. They were held in three residential units, which in turn were subdivided in to a total of eight communities. In time the prison will be able to hold 2,106 prisoners, although we were told that currently numbers are capped to allow for the build up of

staff as well as additional activity for prisoners. Opening a new prison is a big challenge especially when that process is the subject, quite rightly, of significant public interest. The challenges can be practical, but they can also be cultural. The prison opened with a very clear rehabilitative vision which has faced resistance at times. The leadership team are still working hard to find and maintain the right balance between rehabilitation and security, freedom and control, and sanctions and reward. As this report will show, some mistakes have been made and we identify some important weaknesses, but we also acknowledge the great effort that has been made to give this prison a good start. The prison is generally ordered and settled, and when measured against our tests of a healthy prison we found Berwyn to be a reasonably respectful place. Against our other tests there was more to do.

Despite Berwyn being a Welsh prison, about 75% of those held were from England. Arrangements for the reception and induction of new arrivals were impressive and the clear majority felt safe on their first night. Our survey, however, revealed that about 23% of prisoners felt unsafe at the time we asked them; a figure comparable with other training prisons. Prisoner-on-prisoner assaults were lower than expected, but in contrast, prisoner on staff assaults were higher. Both measures seemed to be on a downward trajectory. Some work was being done to reduce violence. However, other than an interesting initiative on Glyndwr community aimed at supporting some challenging prisoners, delivery often lacked drive and needed to be implemented more effectively. We found, for example, 25 self-isolating prisoners who were completely unsupported. Schemes to incentivise good behaviour were similarly ineffective.

Use of force was higher than in similar prisons and incidents usually involved the full application of restraints. Oversight was satisfactory and new strategies to minimise the need for force were being developed. The environment and quality of supervision in the segregation unit was generally good, but the regime was limited. Security arrangements were proportionate and supported by good police liaison. Drugs had been too readily available, but actions by the prison to reduce drugs supply seemed to have had some impact, and the drug testing rate had reduced to 21.49%. This was, however, still too high and supply reduction initiatives required greater coordination and drive. There had been no self-inflicted deaths since the prison opened and self-harm was comparatively low, but arrangements to support and safeguard those who were vulnerable were not very good. Strategic leadership was weak, case management of those in crisis needed improvement and those at risk we spoke to did not feel well cared for.

Most staff at Berwyn were inexperienced but those we observed were doing their best and contributing to a relaxed and positive atmosphere. Many prisoners felt frustrated by staff inconsistency and uncertainty. We also observed some poor behaviour go unchallenged. The prison had, however, recognised the need to support staff with their attention to the basics of prisoner management. Formal consultation with prisoners, prisoner applications and formal complaints were delivered with similar inconsistency and reflected the staff's inexperience. Except for poor toilet screens in double cells, the quality of accommodation and the general environment were very good. In-cell showers, telephones and access to amenities and equipment were all very positive. The prison had been successful in its aim to make such a large prison feel small. There was a real sense of community in most of the wings, and staff teams and prisoners spoke of their 'community' rather than their 'wing'. The promotion of diversity and equality in contrast was poor, although health care provision was good overall.

Employed prisoners had reasonable time out of cell, but it was much worse for those without employment, who had about two and a half hours per day. During spot checks we found 28% of prisoners locked up during the working day, which for a new training prison was very disappointing. Routines were rarely curtailed, but often delayed, and not all staff and prisoners understood fully the requirements of the daily schedule or regime.

One of the greatest challenges facing the prison was the lack of activity places. It is difficult to understand how and why the procurement of work and training places for a new prison could be so delayed. Facing a rising population and too few activity places, prison managers had created a range of activities and there were sufficient places for the current population, but some were of inadequate quality and lacked challenge. Even those that were available were not fully used. Many prisoners were unemployed or failed to attend, and staff did too little to support a sound work ethic. In contrast, those attending education or vocational training generally received excellent teaching, made useful progress and achieved well. Our partners in Estyn assessed provision to be 'good' or 'excellent' in four of their measures and 'adequate and requiring improvement' in just leadership and management.

The prison was struggling to develop its approach to offender management and resettlement. The make-up of the population was not as had been originally envisaged; there had been no assessment of the current need. Many prisoners were serving long sentences, presented a high risk of harm and too many prisoners did not have an up-to-date assessment of risk (OASys). Offender management caseloads were too high and case management was inconsistent and reactive. Public protection measures were similarly weak and the prison lacked sufficient offending behaviour interventions to meet the needs of the population. Work to resettle prisoners was better, but about half of those currently being released returned to England. At the time of the inspection resettlement support for these prisoners was due to end in April which was a concern.

At this inspection we met many managers and staff who were working hard to make a success of this new prison. Senior managers described themselves as 'being on a journey' and we saw lots of work, many policies and numerous plans. What was needed was better oversight, better coordination and more sustained delivery. The staff seemed to us to be a strength of the prison, but they needed support in delivering the basics consistently. We thought the prison had made a good start. We were impressed by the energy and optimism we observed and there was clearly the potential to move on rapidly. We hope that our encouragement to focus on the basics and the few recommendations we make will assist that process, and guide Berwyn to becoming an enduringly safe and rehabilitative prison.

Peter Clarke CVO OBE QPM May 2019
HM Chief Inspector of Prisons

## INDEPENDENT MONITORING BOARD: Annual Report

The law requires every prison to be monitored by an independent Board appointed by the Justice Secretary; these are known as Independent Monitoring Boards (IMBs). The IMB must satisfy itself as to the humane and just treatment of those held in custody within its prison and the range and adequacy of the programmes preparing them for release; it must report annually to the Justice Secretary on how well the prison has met the standards and requirements placed on it.

## IMB Report 1 March 2020 to 29 February 2021; Published September 2021

### Executive summary

### Background to the report

The Covid-19 outbreak has had a significant impact on the Board's ability to gather information. IMB evidence usually comes from observations made on visits, scrutiny of records and informal contact with staff and prisoners as well as through applications from men to the IMB. However, within this reporting year limited physical monitoring has taken place. This has meant a greater reliance on information being relayed to the IMB by staff or men, rather than personal observation by Board members. The Board has therefore tried to cover as much ground as it can in these difficult circumstances, but inevitably there is less detail and supporting evidence than usual. Where the evidence has not been directly observed by a member, the source of the information is stated. Ministers are aware of these constraints. Regular information is being collected specifically on the prison's response to the pandemic, and that is being collated nationally. Most of the Board's time has been taken up with collating, investigating, and answering the applications received by the 0800 free phone number, which was made available to men during the Covid-19 pandemic by the IMB Secretariat. The Board also continued to receive some paper applications. A total of 826 applications were received against a total of 598 in the last reporting year.

It is the opinion of the Board that the Governor and his staff worked hard to minimise the effects of a curtailment of the usual rehabilitative regime at Berwyn and to manage the unsettling effect that Covid-19 caused, especially when the relaxation of measures inside the prison happened at a slower rate than those on the outside.

As stated above the Board has had to adopt different strategies for monitoring and we thank the Governor and all his team for answering our phone calls and emails to support our work. This cooperation has enabled the Board to report our findings set out below.

**Main judgements**
**How safe is the prison?**
The Board believes the establishment to be safe. In keeping with all establishments, men have been confined to their rooms for long periods. For more information see section 4.

**How fairly and humanely are prisoners treated?**
The Board believes that there is a generally courteous and respectful regime and staff-prisoner relationships are generally very good. However, the Covid-19 restrictions have caused some prisoners to consider that their treatment has been unfair and inhumane. On our limited rota visits, it was noted that staff at all levels were very visible, and most men knew whom to approach for help and support. The Board believes that the accommodation offered is of a good standard.

**How well are prisoners' health and wellbeing needs met?**
The Board notes that the level of healthcare provision is generally as good as that in the community and in some cases better when reviewing patient to healthcare professional ratios. However, equivalence of service is important, and consideration must be given to the concentration of physical, psychological, and dental problems within the prison population. Therefore, the services offered may not be adequate, with the wait times for dental care for instance operating at 12 months.

**How well are prisoners progressed towards successful resettlement?**
The Board notes that sentence management has been particularly difficult under the restrictions Covid-19 has presented. The resettlement team have worked with men before release to adequately support their needs.

The majority of men are released to some form of settled accommodation and we understand that the prison compares favourably with other establishments in achieving this. Nevertheless, there remains some work to do.

It is considered that despite the difficult conditions and restricted regime, every effort was made to provide access to education. Furthermore, it is our opinion that during Covid-19 lockdown periods, efforts were made to put men into essential work.

**Main areas for development**
**TO THE MINISTER**
The Board would wish to be provided with assurance that the wider issues related to the serious paint defects and ineffective heating systems will be resolved in the near future. Not solving, or delaying this work carries major challenges in terms of capacity and the operation of the establishment and the core issues do pose a detriment to the men housed there.

The Board notes that the prison experienced significant delays in being able to transfer men to more appropriate establishments and settings, especially those relating to mental ill-health. The Board considers that this lack of secure mental health facilities needs to be addressed as a matter of urgency.

**TO THE PRISON SERVICE**
Berwyn has benefited this year by having a generally stable senior management team, which has helped them navigate the establishment through these very difficult and challenging times. There is a need to resolve the serious issues surrounding paint defects and ineffective heating systems. The Board has been informed that

contractual negotiations could take some time and whilst that is understood, the core issues do pose a detriment to the prison and men housed there. The Board notes the lengthy wait time for dental care and improvements to the service provision to reduce this would be in the interest of the men. Furthermore, many applications have been received from men who have achieved category D status. There is considerable frustration from these men at the lack of available places to transfer, probably due to a restriction in the operational capacity for the open prison spaces during Covid-19.

## TO THE GOVERNOR

It has been identified that many issues which became formal complaints could and should have been dealt with at community level. Responses to these complaints (that is, Comp 1 and Comp 1A) are still an issue in the establishment, both in timescale and quality of the reply.

The Board is concerned about the high levels of self-harm, assaults and use of force.

As a Board, we have been kept well informed of the day-to-day events, by the orderly officers' report.

## Progress since the last report

The Board notes that in our previous report, the lack of meeting room and interview space was a concern. This provision was strengthened during the reporting year, with significant numbers of staff being relocated to work from the industry area. Planning work was underway to convert a workshop into a resettlement hub, where meeting pods will be available. The hub was due to open after the reporting period ended.

The Board also noted the need for more specialist communities, with a particular need for vulnerable prisoners (VPs) to be housed safely, reducing self-isolation. With the introduction of MCOSOs, Berwyn has since been able to offer vulnerable prisoners a separate regime. However, the effects of Covid-19 have meant some specialist communities have reverted to general population.

There were some improvements in terms of the long-standing issue with the heating system during the reporting period.

**WINSON GREEN ROAD
BIRMINGHAM
B18 4AS**

**HM PRISON BIRMINGHAM**   **Tel: 0121 598 8000**

*For the latest reports on this prison please visit:*
https://tinyurl.com/bdfh26rv

*Important Changes:* **(1) Visits:** the identification necessary to access this prison and visit for social or professional purposes has changed; (2) **Money and Gifts** new rules now apply to these. See page 16 for full details of the above.

**Task of the establishment** HMP Birmingham is a Category B adult male local prison serving the West Midlands courts.

**Certified normal accommodation and operational capacity**
Number held 1,443
Certified normal accommodation 1,093
Operational capacity 1,450

**Prison status and key providers**
Public
Prison Group: West Midlands
Prison Group Director: Teresa Clarke
Governor/Director: Paul Newton
IMB Chair: Jane Perera
Physical health provider:
Birmingham Community Hospitals (BCHC)
Mental health provider: Birmingham and Solihull Mental Health NHS Foundation Trust
Substance misuse treatment provider: Midlands Partnership NHS Foundation Trust (Psychosocial) and Birmingham and Solihull Mental Health Foundation Trust (Clinical)
Prison education framework provider: Novus
Escort contractor: GeoAmey

**Brief history** HMP Birmingham is a large local prison based in the city centre. The original Victorian wings were built in 1849 and these have been added to with more modern accommodation, most recently in 2004, which includes four new wings, a health centre, a gym, an education centre and workshops.

**Short description of residential units**
K & L wings - remanded and convicted prisoners
M wing - integrated drug treatment service detoxification
D wing - sex offenders
J wing - shielding unit and older/more vulnerable unit

N & P wings - reverse cohorting units for new arrivals
A, B & C wings - closed at the time of the inspection
G wing - enhanced prisoners

### Visiting Information
Booking enquiries: 0121 598 8170
The booking line is open Monday to Friday: 8:15am to 4pm
**Visiting times:** Tuesday, Wednesday, Saturday and Sunday: 9am to 11am and 2pm to 4pm

**Legal visits** There are currently no legal visits taking place.

### INSPECTIONS & REPORTS
**Date of last inspection:** 24 November 2020 and 5–6 January 2021
**Scrutiny Visit**
**Published 16 February 2021**
HMP Birmingham is a category B local prison serving courts across the West Midlands that we have heavily criticised in recent years. At our 2018 inspection, our findings were so poor we felt compelled to issue an Urgent Notification to the Secretary of State, seeking immediate improvements. At our subsequent Independent Review of Progress in 2019, we were pleased to report that prison leaders had made progress against many of our recommendations, with significant work done to restore order to the prison. Historically, Birmingham has held around 1,500 prisoners, but at the time of our scrutiny visit the capacity had been reduced to 977, with three of the older Victorian wings currently closed. We found that much of the progress seen in 2019 had been sustained, although in a few important areas oversight needed improvement to make sure this continued.

The Covid-19 pandemic had created significant challenges for leaders at Birmingham, and the prison had experienced three outbreaks. In the most recent, more than 100 prisoners had tested positive for Covid-19, and the establishment remained an outbreak site at the time of our visit. In addition, it had been returned to level four of the national recovery framework (see Glossary of terms) the day before our visit, restricting regimes significantly.

Leaders had made sure that there was effective communication with staff and prisoners throughout the period of restrictions, and they were visible on all wings, which contributed to a sense of order. Frontline staff were also visible when prisoners were unlocked, and we observed good relationships between staff and prisoners. Maintaining decent living conditions and providing a consistent, if limited, regime for all prisoners were clear priorities, and it was also encouraging to see useful work to actively promote equality and diversity, something many establishments have neglected during this

period. Health care was reasonably good, but prisoners waited too long to see a GP or dentist. Rehabilitation and release planning work was also reasonable; prison offender managers (POMs) and community rehabilitation company staff had maintained face-to-face contact with prisoners, making sure that key assessments were meaningful. Release planning was well organised, prisoners could access through-the-gate support and the new 'departure lounge' for prisoners on their day of release was a promising initiative. Around 90% of prisoners were released to sustainable accommodation, which is better than we have found at other local prisons.

In contrast, the reverse cohorting arrangements (see Glossary of terms), designed to prevent new prisoners potentially transmitting Covid-19 to the main population, were weak. Prisoners who arrived up to seven days apart were placed in the same cell, and some social bubbles (where prisoners associated and exercised in groups) included prisoners who had just arrived mixing with those about to move into the main population. This increased the risk of outbreaks across the prison.

We saw some good work to promote safety although this was undermined by the safety team's failure to record accurately all acts of violence and self-harm. Incidents were reported and investigated, but at this stage some data was missing, limiting its value to managers in seeking to monitor trends or make improvements.

The provision of education was not good enough. The provider had taken six months to deliver in- cell packs to prisoners and at the time of our visit provision was limited and badly organised. Prisoners waited for long periods to receive work, and when it came, the in-cell packs were sometimes not at the correct level. Prisoners were also uncertain about when they would see teachers or get support. Consequently, many were unenthusiastic about learning and very few had completed a course.

Overall this is an encouraging report. Given Birmingham's recent history, its continued provision of decent living conditions and a calm, well-ordered environment suggest improvements are being embedded. However, oversight of safety arrangements, practice in the reverse cohorting unit (RCU) and education provision require some immediate attention.
Charlie Taylor, HM Chief Inspector of Prisons
January 2021

### Key concerns and recommendations
Key concerns and recommendations identify the issues of most importance to improving outcomes for prisoners and are designed to help establishments prioritise and address the most significant weaknesses in the treatment and conditions of prisoners.
During this visit we identified some areas of key

concern, and have made a small number of recommendations for the prison to address.

Key concern: Reverse cohorting arrangements were poorly managed and were failing to safeguard against the spread of Covid-19 into the main population. Prisoners who had arrived up to a week apart shared cells, and prisoners about to be discharged into the main prison population were allowed to exercise and associate with prisoners who had just arrived.
Recommendation: Reverse cohorting arrangements should be implemented correctly and safely. (To the governor)

Key concern: Data around assaults and self-harm were not reported accurately and presented a misleading picture. This use of incorrect data limited managers' ability to understand or analyse correctly causal factors of violence and self-harm.
Recommendation: The prison should record incidents of violence and self-harm accurately and make sure this information is analysed and presented in a way that supports improvements in safety. (To the governor)

Key concern: The prison had been running a restricted regime for ten months to minimise the spread of Covid-19. This had the potential to affect the well-being of the prisoners. The majority did not receive any regular meaningful contact from staff unless they were in crisis. We were concerned that the gradual deterioration of prisoners could go unnoticed due to the lack of meaningful welfare checks or contact with staff.
Recommendation: Staff should interact with all prisoners regularly and meaningfully to make sure that their welfare is not deteriorating under the continued restrictions in their daily life. (To the governor)

Key concern: Work with the Health Partnership Board was lacking and more needed to be done to ensure meaningful governance and oversight of GP and dentist waiting lists. Prisoners waited too long for appointments.
Recommendation: Patients must be able to see the dentist or GP more quickly. (To the governor)

### HMCIP 2018, published 04 December 2018
HMP Birmingham is a category B local prison serving courts in the country's second largest city as well as other parts of the West Midlands. Holding up to 1,450 adult men ranging from those recently remanded to others serving significant sentences, it is a large, complex and extremely important institution. For the last seven years the prison has been operated under contract by G4S. This was the fourth time we had inspected the prison while the company was in charge.
Our previous visit was in February 2017, an inspection complicated by the fact that two months earlier the prison had experienced a major disturbance. At the time, we found a prison clearly still reeling from the shock of that

event, but also took encouragement from what we observed to be a clear determination to recover and rebuild. The contrast with our findings at this unannounced inspection could not have been starker. Far from recovering, the prison had deteriorated dramatically and was in an appalling state. Against all four of our healthy prison tests – safety, respect, purposeful activity and rehabilitation and release planning – we assessed outcomes as poor, our lowest assessment. This is only the second time we have made such judgements, a fact that speaks clearly to the seriousness of my concerns. Put simply, the treatment of prisoners and the conditions in which they were held at Birmingham were among the worst we have seen in recent years.

As a consequence, and in accordance with the protocol I have with the Ministry of Justice (The urgent notification protocol with the Ministry of Justice states that if, during the inspection of prisons, young offender institutions and secure training centres, HM Chief Inspector of Prisons (HMCIP) identifies significant concerns regarding the treatment and conditions of those detained, HMCIP will write to the Secretary of State within seven calendar days of the end of the inspection, providing notification of and reasons for those concerns. The Secretary of State must then publish an action plan within 28 days. The protocol and the HMP Birmingham urgent notification letter can be found here: https://tinyurl.com/y42ju4fu On 16 August 2018 I wrote to the Secretary of State invoking the Urgent Notification (UN) process regarding HMP Birmingham (see Appendix III). In that letter, and in the inspection debriefing paper that accompanied it, I out set out in detail my concerns and the judgements that had caused me to follow that course of action. Under the protocol, the Secretary of State commits to respond publicly to the UN within 28 days, explaining how outcomes for those detained will be improved. The Secretary of State's response, for which I am grateful, is detailed in Appendix III of this report.

I do not intend to use this introduction to repeat the details of my concerns. Suffice to say, at this inspection, we found an institution that was fundamentally unsafe, where many prisoners and staff lived and worked in fear, where drug taking was barely concealed, delinquency was rife and where individuals could behave badly with near impunity. Control in the prison was tenuous, staff were poorly led and many lacked the confidence or the competence to set about retrieving this situation. Many prisoners were living in squalor, little was being done to adequately occupy individuals and the prison was failing in its responsibility to protect the public by preparing prisoners adequately for release. I repeat, the prison was in an appalling state.

In my letter of 16 August, I made clear that a factor in my decision to invoke the UN was my lack of confidence in the prison to make improvements. I also referred to the failure of the prison to implement previous recommendations made by this Inspectorate and, perhaps most importantly, I referred to the inertia that seemed to have gripped those responsible for monitoring and managing the contracts and those meant to be delivering action on the ground. In my letter I called for an honest appraisal of how the prison had been allowed to slip into crisis. Why was it that those with responsibility for Birmingham either did not see these problems unfolding or seemed incapable of acting decisively when they did? Through the process of improvement and rectification that I trust will now follow, I hope that this call is not lost. The challenges facing this prison are huge. Managers and staff need support if they are to turn the establishment around. The helpful action plan published by the Secretary of State provides an important framework for progress and is a start, but there also needs to be accountability among those implementing the plan. It is crucial for there to be transparent, open conversations about the state of the prison and the progress being made. It will undoubtedly take some time for Birmingham to make the improvements needed, and as an Inspectorate we leave the prison with a number of recommendations that set out the priorities as we see them.

Peter Clarke CVO OBE QPM September 2018
HM Chief Inspector of Prisons

## INDEPENDENT MONITORING BOARD ANNUAL REPORT

The law requires every prison to be monitored by an independent Board appointed by the Justice Secretary; these are known as Independent Monitoring Boards (IMBs).

The IMB must satisfy itself as to the humane and just treatment of those held in custody within its prison and the range and adequacy of the programmes preparing them for release; it must report annually to the Justice Secretary on how well the prison has met the standards and requirements placed on it.

**IMB Report 01 July 2020 – 30 June 2021; Published November 2021**
**Executive summary**
**Background to the report**
The Covid-19 outbreak has had a significant impact on the Board's ability to monitor the prison on-site and to discuss the contents of this annual report. The Board has therefore tried to

obtain as accurate a picture as possible in these difficult circumstances, but inevitably there is less observed supporting evidence than usual. The prison has made all their statistical data available to the Board.

Evidence for this report comes from observations made on a reduced number of visits, attendance at meetings, scrutiny of records and data, applications and good order or discipline (GOOD) reviews. Members of the Board have gathered evidence from regular contact with senior leaders, managers and prisoner representatives. From March 2020 through to July 2020, monitoring was conducted remotely via teleconferences with the Governor, senior leaders and managers, and prisoner representatives. From August 2020 onwards, the Board has attended all GOOD reviews three times a week, directly monitoring the care and separation unit (CSU). There have been limited visits to some wings in recent months.

At the time of writing, the prison has almost 25% of staff off work, largely as a result of the pandemic.

**Main judgements**
**How safe is the prison?**
It is the Board's view that Birmingham prison is the safest it has been for a number of years. Two years into public management and new leadership, there is ongoing improvement and stability, although the pandemic makes it harder to identify trends and make comparisons.

The Covid-19 pandemic has impeded, but not fully prevented, progress. Violence has reduced, possibly artificially, under a restricted regime with less mixing and more time in cell, but a general improvement in safety had been noted before the pandemic, when prisoners were out of cell for much of the day. There has been a slight increase in violent incidents in the last three months, as prisoners tire after more than 16 months of a regime of 22 and a half hours a day lock-up, knowing at the same time that restrictions in the community are easing. The number of assaults on staff is lower than in previous, non-pandemic times but assaults on other prisoners have risen in the last three months.

Good use of data has helped improve safety. Analysis is systematic, rigorous and used to identify areas of concern. The senior leadership team (SLT) aims to prevent problems before they arise, as opposed to having to react to them. Prison self- evaluation is detailed and informs targeted interventions.

Communication between prisoners and management is good, and builds confidence and stability. Consultation in the form of surveys, forums and the involvement of prisoner representatives in key meetings leads to positive actions.

The installation of the body scanner in reception in August 2020 and enhanced security searches at the gate from May 2021 have seen a reduction in the ingress of illicit items, although there has been an increase in 'throw- overs'.

It has been challenging for the prison to manage 'keep aparts', as Covid-19 cohorting arrangements and the temporary closure of three Victorian wings leave few options for separating prisoners. At the same time, the prison has received a relatively high number of prisoners convicted of very serious crimes, and many involved in organised crime groups and factions. Although levels of self-harm are always a concern, they have remained fairly constant in recent months, which the Board considers to be a reflection on the work done to understand the drivers of self-harm, in order to keep prisoners safe.

**How fairly and humanely are prisoners treated?**
Long stays in the segregation unit continue to give rise for concern. The prison provides good care and support for prisoners in the CSU, and personalised interventions provided by the psychologist for those in need, but external provision beyond that which the prison can offer does not exist and the most challenging cases remain stranded in segregation. The prison has no alternative for these prisoners because it is not safe to house them on the wings and there is nowhere else for them to go. There is no obvious solution at present for these challenging cases. The Board believes that prolonged segregation is inhumane. The Board does not consider that the regime, locking individuals up for 22 and a half hours per day, is humane, although prisoners have tolerated this for 16 months and ongoing, knowing that the community has also been in lockdown, and knowing that the prompt action taken around Covid-19 has kept them safe. Given the challenges, the prison leaders have managed the situation well and continuously look for ways of providing a better regime, but the constraints of the pandemic and their potential longer-term impact on mental health are not yet known.

Levels of unplanned use of force are very high when compared with those in similar prisons, and there is a lack of consistency in using body-worn video cameras (BWCs). The prison leaders are aware of this and regularly issue reminders to staff at daily briefings, but are also aware that more cameras and rigour are required for improvement with BWC use.

The Board has observed prisoners being treated fairly and with respect. On occasion, where there is evidence of staff wrongdoing, there is an investigation, suspension and, if appropriate a dismissal. While being supportive of staff and applying the principle of fair process, the SLT has a zero tolerance of any activity which is unjust.

The expectations hub and wellbeing navigators, trained in basic mental health first- aid, along with community information lead (CIL) wing workers, are all examples of the excellent employment of prisoners who are able to demonstrate leadership and represent constructively the voice of all prisoners to the SLT, and vice versa.

Refurbishments, both completed and planned, are providing prisoners with better living conditions. There has been substantial investment in improving accommodation, with, for example, over £1 million spent on updating all showers.

**How well are prisoners' health and wellbeing needs met?**
Healthcare provision is good, and possibly better than that in the community under Covid-19 conditions. Prisoners' wellbeing is a priority.

Nursing, psychiatric and psychology provision has operated without interruption. GP services have been triaged, and non-aerosol-generating dental treatment resumed in January. All emergency treatment has been possible externally. Covid-19 has been managed well in the prison. There have been three Covid-19 outbreaks, without any individuals falling seriously ill. Only one prisoner, a 99-year- old with comorbidities, who died while in custody, has had a reference to Covid-19 on his death certificate. During remote monitoring, teleconferences with prisoner representatives from all wings gave regular feedback that provision was good.

The chaplaincy has, without interruption, supported prisoners during the Covid-19 restrictions, visiting the wings and seeing them at cell doors.

Peer support is a strength evidenced by the work of the wellbeing navigators, the expectations hub, Listeners and CIL workers.

The Board has concerns for the ongoing mental health impact of long hours in-cell, with purposeful activity, for some prisoners, limited to distraction packs.

**How well are prisoners progressed towards successful resettlement?**
Offending behaviour programmes were totally shut down by the Covid-19 restrictions from March 2020 onwards, and almost all purposeful activity, including classroom- based education, was suspended for several months. Rehabilitation has thus been interrupted and the long-term effects are yet to be seen.

However, the community rehabilitation company (CRC) continued working on-site throughout the pandemic. Its provision for prisoners on the wings and at the point of release has been good at all times. All prisoners have been seen on the day of their release, and accommodation on release continues to be at well above 90%.

The Board has concerns about support for finding accommodation on release, with the new contract with Nacro.

Issues continue with immediate and late releases from court to no fixed abode. In every such case, the CRC staff have to find accommodation with no advance notice.

There have been problems for prisoners in opening bank accounts on release, which is important for the receipt of benefit payments.

Family contact has been limited to telephone calls and virtual visits, and social visits only restarted in June 2021).

The prison leads excellent partnership collaborative working by convening monthly meetings, bringing together most partner and external agencies involved in resettlement. There is a wide range of interventions and support structures in place to promote reducing reoffending.

**Main areas for development**

Plans, in line with national Her Majesty's Prison and Probation Service (HMPPS) guidance for a revised regime post-Covid-19, indicate fewer hours out of cell, but with a greater focus on purposeful activity. The quality of those activities will be of crucial importance. There is a risk of prisoners being locked up for longer without opportunities for social interaction and personal responsibility, which may not adequately prepare them for release.

Learning difficulties and autism are not particularly well addressed at present in the prison, and greater awareness and training will be required. However, a nurse specialist in learning difficulties has been appointed.

When Birmingham prison reaches full reception prison status, with a population of 80% remand and 20% resettlement prisoners, offending behaviour programmes and education courses will need to be tailored to better meet the needs of short-stay prisoners on remand. Currently, the prison is assessed in the same way as training prisons, although its designation and context are not the same.

**TO THE MINISTER**

Homelessness is a concern, and a frequent issue in repeat offending. Will the Minister improve the management of immediate releases from court to "no fixed abode" and will he ensure that the Courts have a role to play to help ensure better communication and co-ordination with their local resettlement services so that no- one is immediately released to sleep on the streets?

What will the minister do to ensure that prisoners on remand, on short sentences, reaching the end of their sentence and those released out of their home area who are not on probation are given access to accommodation on release, as at present, as this will not be covered by the new contract with Nacro?

How will the minister ensure that foreign national prisoners are released or deported at the end of their sentence, and that they are not held in custody beyond the expiry of their sentence?

**TO THE PRISON SERVICE**

Will the Prison Service make better provision for the rehabilitative needs and resources required for prisoners who are long stay in the CSU, for whom normal location is not suitable?

What is provided in close supervision centres for prisoners who, having already spent excessive times in segregation, are transferred to such units? Will the Prison Service commit to ensuring that isolation is balanced with rehabilitation and human, social needs and rights?

Many prisoners are subject to repeated stays in isolation in the CSU, as well as those who remain there for excessively long periods of time. Why is the number of days that a prisoner spends in the CSU not calculated cumulatively and continued on transfer from one prison to another?

How will the Prison Service plan a more coordinated, consistent and fair system of recording and tracking provision for prisoners with autism and learning difficulties, and how will they ensure that staff are fully trained and competent at recognising, working and interacting with prisoners with these conditions? Her Majesty's Inspectorate of Prisons recommends that every prisoner should have 10 hours out-of-cell each day. How will the Prison Service ensure that prisoners have access to a humane regime, with fair access to exercise, fresh air and purposeful activity post-Covid-19?

Does HMPPS accept that personal and social skills are part of a prisoner's preparation for release, and that limited social interactions in a restricted regime post-Covid-19 may in the long term inhibit reducing reoffending, even if in the immediate term it improves stability in the prison?

**TO THE GOVERNOR**

As the prison moves to a new regime post-Covid-19, what assurance can the Governor give that the work provided will be genuinely purposeful and, in education, matched to individual capabilities?

Will the Governor assure a more robust system of ensuring that agreed actions in good order and/or discipline reviews are written down, communicated and acted upon?

How can officers be certain of using body-worn video cameras if they do not have access to one each, and can a more robust, reliable and accountable system be introduced to ensure that all radios are collected, deployed and returned every day?

How will the Governor ensure parity between ethnic groups when enhanced incentives and earned privileges status is applied?

Following the redeployment of the property officer from reception, how will the Governor ensure that all prisoners' property is correctly logged, held securely and does not go missing within the prison and on transfer on from the prison?

**NEW ROAD,
FEATHERSTONE
WOLVERHAMPTON
WV10 7PY**

**HMYOI
BRINSFORD**

**Tel: 01902 533450**

*For the latest reports on this prison please visit:*
https://tinyurl.com/bdfh26rv

*Important Changes:* **(1) Visits:** the identification necessary to access this prison and visit for social or professional purposes has changed; (2) **Money and Gifts** new rules now apply to these. See page 16 for full details of the above.

### Task of the establishment
HMYOI Brinsford accommodates men aged 18–21 on remand, and men aged 18–25 (temporarily adjusted to 29) who are sentenced and have between 28 days and 16 months left to serve. HMYOI Brinsford also accepts men transferring from the training estate with between 10 and 24 months left to serve at the point of transfer. Its primary function is a resettlement prison and it is also a reception establishment. It offers a resettlement service for young adults and category C adults who live in Staffordshire and the West Midlands.

Certified normal accommodation and operational capacity

Prisoners held August 2021: 466

Baseline certified normal capacity: 539

In-use certified normal capacity: 539

Operational capacity: 577

### Population of the prison
• 920 admissions were received last year, broken down as 442 new prisoners from court, 368 transfers, 63 licence recalls and 47 HDC recalls.
• There were 69 foreign national prisoners (14.8% of the population).
• 48.7% of prisoners were from a black and minority ethnic background.
• 70 prisoners were released into the community each month.
• Three prisoners were currently receiving support for substance use.
• 36 prisoners had been referred for mental health assessment in the previous month.

### Prison status and key providers
Public

Prison Group: West Midlands

Prison Group Director: Teresa Clarke

Name of Governor/Director: Amanda Hughes

IMB Chair: Pauline Hirons

Physical health provider: Practice Plus Group

Mental health provider: Inclusion

Substance use treatment provider: Inclusion

Prison education framework provider: Novus

Escort contractor: GeoAmey

Prison group/Department: West Midlands

### Brief history
Brinsford opened as a young adult offender institution and remand centre in November 1991. It is on the same site as HMPs Featherstone and Oakwood. In 2008, residential unit 5 was opened. In 2009, the Rowan activities centre opened. Following an unannounced HM Inspectorate of Prisons inspection in November 2013, Brinsford underwent a programme to refurbish residential units 1 to 4. In 2016, the establishment re-roled to a mixed population of young adults and sentenced category C adults.

### Short description of residential units
Residential unit 1 – development progression unit

Residential unit 2 – standardised unit

Residential unit 3 – half reverse cohort unit (see Glossary of terms) and early days in custody, and half standardised unit

Residential unit 4 – standardised unit

Residential unit 5 – full-time workers/enhanced status unit

First night centre – currently not in use as being used as a reverse cohort unit Health care centre – 14 beds

Segregation unit – 16 beds

### Visiting Information
Brinsford is currently operating a limited visits schedule for family and friends. You can book your visit by telephone.

Booking line: 0300 060 6500 Monday to Friday, 9:15am to 12pm and 1pm to 4pm

**Visiting times:**

Monday, Tuesday, Thursday, Saturday and Sunday: 2pm to 4pm

Booking slots are allocated to specific wings each day. This will be explained upon booking.

**Legal visits:** There are currently no legal visits taking place.

**INSPECTIONS & REPORTS**
**HMCIP Report**
**Date of last inspection:** 16, 23-27 August 2021
**Published 30 November 2021**
**Summary of key findings**
We last inspected HMYOI Brinsford in 2017 and made 56 recommendations, four of which were about areas of key concern. The establishment fully accepted 47 of the recommendations and partially (or subject to resources) accepted four. It rejected five of the recommendations.

**Progress on key concerns and recommendations**
Our last inspection of HMYOI Brinsford took place before the COVID- 19 pandemic and the recommendations in that report focused on areas of concern affecting outcomes for prisoners at the time. Although we recognise that the challenges of keeping prisoners safe during COVID- 19 will have changed the focus for many prison leaders, we believe that it is important to follow up on recommendations about areas of key concern to help leaders to continue to drive improvement.
At our last full inspection, we made one recommendation about key concerns in the area of safety. At this inspection, we found that this recommendation had been achieved.
We made one recommendation about key concerns in the area of respect. At this inspection, we found that this recommendation had not been achieved.
We made one recommendation about key concerns in the area of purposeful activity. At this inspection, we found that this recommendation had not been achieved.
We made one recommendation about key concerns in the area of rehabilitation and release planning. At this inspection, we found that this recommendation had been achieved.
Outcomes for prisoners
We assess outcomes for prisoners against four healthy prison tests. We also include a commentary on leadership in the prison.
At this inspection of HMYOI Brinsford, we found that outcomes for prisoners had stayed the same in one healthy prison area, improved in one and declined in two.
These judgements seek to make an objective assessment of the outcomes experienced by those detained and have taken into account the prison's recovery from Covid-19 as well as the 'regime stage' at which the prison was operating, as outlined in the HM Prison and Probation (HMPPS) National Framework for prison regimes and services.
**Safety**

Reception staff treated new arrivals decently and respectfully, but prisoners often waited in reception for long periods. First night risk assessments were not always held in private and records of concerns lacked detail. First night cells were of a poor standard. The recently improved induction process provided key information to newly arrived prisoners and included the use of a peer worker and translated and adapted materials. Overall, levels of violence had reduced since the last inspection, but the number of assaults between prisoners was higher than at comparable prisons. The actions generated both to challenge perpetrators and support victims of violence through the safety intervention meetings and challenge, support and intervention plans (CSIPs) were well managed and effective. Families often took part in CSIP reviews.
Supervision of prisoners on most wings was limited. Staff did not challenge poor behaviour, including loud music, graffiti and threatening language, consistently. The rewards and sanctions scheme did little to promote good behaviour.
Levels of use of force had reduced since the previous inspection. The use of force that we viewed on-site was proportionate, but we witnessed abusive language by incident managers during restraints. Oversight of use of force was poor; leaders could not assure themselves that all force used was necessary. Too few staff used body- worn cameras, there was little footage available and some footage that should have been retained was missing.
The cells on the segregation unit were dirty and contained large amounts of graffiti. The regime on the unit was limited to 30 minutes' exercise and a shower every day. The lack of radios and the practice of not giving prisoners an in-cell telephone until they had had a segregation review or adjudication were inappropriate, but both issues were addressed during the inspection. Staff–prisoner relationships on the unit were good, as was reintegration planning, with most prisoners returned to the wings within five or six days.
Staff did not account accurately for the whereabouts of prisoners during the day and could not tell us how many were on the units during our roll checks, which undermined security. There was a good flow of intelligence to the security department which was appropriately acted on. Gang-related information was particularly well managed and there were strong links with West Midlands Police. The strip-searching of all new arrivals could not be justified if used in addition to the body scanner.
Levels of self-harm had reduced considerably since the last inspection but remained high when compared with similar prisons. There had been one self-inflicted death since the previous inspection, and the safety team had good

oversight of the response to recommendations from the Prisons and Probation Ombudsman. Most of the prisoners who had been subject to assessment, care in custody and teamwork (ACCT) case management for those at risk of suicide or self-harm had felt well cared for by staff, but there were weaknesses in care planning and recorded interaction. Families were engaged as part of the ACCT process, including attendance at reviews. Access to Listeners (prisoners trained by the Samaritans to provide confidential emotional support to fellow prisoners) was poor.

## Respect

In our survey, 75% of respondents said that staff treat them with respect. However, we observed mostly functional interactions because of the limited regime. The formal schemes to support regular engagement between staff and prisoners were ineffective.

Cells and communal areas were generally shabby and in need of refurbishment. Some cells were missing essential items, such as curtains and chairs. A programme of redecoration had begun recently, but oversight needed to improve to maintain standards in refurbished cells. External areas and gardens were attractive and well maintained, but prisoners had limited access to them.

Regular consultation meetings took place, but many prisoners did not know who their unit representatives were. The complaints system was reasonably effective, but records showed that many applications were not responded to.

Since the beginning of 2021, there had been an increased focus on, and resources for, equality work, but insufficient attention was being given to some important areas. Analysis of needs was limited, and equality monitoring data, indicating inequitable outcomes for some prisoners with protected characteristics, had not been explored or acted on. The equality lead had identified that the quality of responses to discrimination complaints had been inadequate and had taken steps to address this. Forums on protected characteristics had recently resumed but some of these had not been sufficiently focused on the identification of unmet need. Most prisoners had access to a chaplain of their faith, and the chaplaincy provided good pastoral support. However, access to corporate worship was extremely limited.

Health care provision was well led, and a range of age-appropriate primary care services was available. Reception processes were thorough, and prompt secondary screening enabled early identification of any underlying conditions and access to ongoing treatment. The inpatient environment and care provided had improved since the previous inspection, but amenities were not used to their full potential and the regime

was too often curtailed because of prison officers being withdrawn from the unit.

Integrated mental health and substance misuse services supported the prison effectively in caring for prisoners with complex mental health and addiction problems.

## Purposeful activity

Ofsted carried out a progress monitoring visit of the prison alongside our full inspection and the purposeful activity judgement incorporates their assessment of progress.

Senior leaders told us that prisoners were provided with a minimum of 75 minutes out of cell each day. However, we found that most prisoners who were unemployed received between 45 minutes and one hour out of their cell, and those who were employed had up to six hours. Managers were also unaware of the regime being delivered for prisoners with potential Covid-19 symptoms and those testing positive. In practice, this was limited to a daily shower, but even this didn't happen consistently.

The library had reopened in June 2021, but most prisoners were still not able to visit it. Although the remote library service had played a useful role in the pandemic, it did not provide an adequate long-term alternative to library access. Most prisoners could only use the gym every other week.

Senior leaders had developed a detailed vision for the curriculum that was appropriate for the prison's role (reception and resettlement). However, the curriculum at the time of the inspection was too narrow and did not meet the needs of the prisoners.

Leaders had made slow progress in returning to face-to-face lessons and had not prioritised learning for those who would benefit most from this form of teaching. Too few prisoners were engaged in enough meaningful education, training and work. Leaders did not ensure that all prisoners received high-quality information, advice and guidance at induction or that subsequent allocations to education, training and work were based on prisoner need. Most teachers taught the curriculum well through face-to-face teaching. They enabled prisoners to build on their existing knowledge and learn and remember more.

While education staff screened the small number of prisoners who attended education classes, to assess their support needs, the majority who attended in industry and work were not assessed and did not receive a support plan.

## Rehabilitation and release planning

The introduction of in-cell telephony and secure video calls had been valued by prisoners. Visits had restarted in April 2021. The visits hall was clean and bright and been sensitively adapted to allow social distancing. Lateral flow testing, to enable contact between prisoners and families, if they so chose, had been introduced recently.

There was a clear focus on reducing reoffending work, with a detailed action plan overseen by a regular strategic meeting. There was good joint working between reducing reoffending and offender management unit managers. Prison offender manager (POM) caseloads were manageable. Contact between POMs and prisoners was generally good and focused on progression. Most eligible prisoners had an offender assessment system (OASys) assessment and a sentence plan. The quality of sentence plans that we reviewed was mostly good and risk management plans ranged from adequate to very good.

Remanded prisoners received some POM input, which made sure that their risks and needs were identified, and necessary actions taken. The distinct needs of prisoners who had previously been in local authority care or had transitioned from the youth estate were recognised, with enthusiastic staff involved in developing provision.

Public protection arrangements had been strengthened since the previous inspection. The release management planning meeting was a good forum for reviewing high-risk prisoners who were due to be released, but was undermined, in part, by inconsistent attendance. Contact restrictions and arrangements to conduct and review telephone and mail monitoring for public protection purposes were managed well. The delivery of accredited programmes had restarted recently with reduced group sizes. There were insufficient places planned to meet the needs of the population. POMs were using the Choices and Changes work pack and Probation Service workbooks for structured work with prisoners. Nearly all prisoners had been released to accommodation during the previous year.

### Key concerns and recommendations

Key concerns and recommendations identify the issues of most importance to improving outcomes for prisoners and are designed to help establishments prioritise and address the most significant weaknesses in the treatment and conditions of prisoners.

During this inspection we identified some areas of key concern and have made a small number of recommendations for the prison to address those concerns.

Key concern: Leaders and managers lacked visibility on the residential units, and delivery in key areas did not reflect their understanding or expectations. Morale among frontline staff was low and too many reported that communication from managers was poor.

Recommendation: Leaders and managers should be more visible to support staff, assure themselves that practice reflects their intentions and make

sure that progress is made in priority areas.

Key concern: The supervision of prisoners and challenge of poor behaviour were inadequate. We witnessed many incidents of low-level bad behaviour going unchallenged by staff, and groups of prisoners left unsupervised for long periods.

Recommendation: Prisoners should be subject to suitable levels of supervision and be challenged appropriately by staff when behaving poorly.

Key concern: Due to the lack of body-worn camera footage available for incidents, leaders could not assure themselves that every use of force was justified.

Recommendation: Leaders should make sure that staff use body- worn cameras when responding to incidents; where this has not been possible, a reason should be given in the use of force report.

Key concern: Prisoners on the segregation unit were locked up all day, except for 30 minutes' exercise and a shower, with little to occupy themselves.

Recommendation: Prisoners on the segregation unit should have access to a regime that engages them with purposeful activity while segregated. (To the governor)

Key concern: Living conditions on the wings were not good enough, with cells, showers and communal areas on all wings in need of refurbishment or repair. The programme of weekly cell checks was not effective, as some cells still lacked basic furniture, and some toilets needed deep cleaning. Prisoners reported issues, but improvements were slow to happen. There was also a lack of furniture in association areas.

Recommendation: Accommodation and communal areas should be well maintained, suitably equipped and cleaned regularly. Staff and prisoners should play an active role in maintaining these standards, and monitoring should be robust.

Key concern: The prison did not have a good understanding of the needs of its prisoners in relation to equality. There was limited analysis of data, and inadequate efforts had been made to gather the views of prisoners with protected characteristics. This meant that all equality work being undertaken was not targeted specifically to the circumstances and needs of the prisoners.

Recommendation: Leaders should consult regularly with prisoners and use data to identify, investigate and address potential discrimination.

Key concern: Too many prisoners spent most of their day in their cells sleeping or watching television, which was not conducive to the well-being or the prospects for rehabilitation of – mostly young – prisoners. The reopening of the library and the gym had not had much of an impact on the amount of time that many prisoners spent out of their cell.

Recommendation: There should be a concerted effort to maximise both the amount of time that prisoners spend out of their cell and the available purposeful and recreational activity across the prison.

Key concern: Senior leaders did not provide education, training and work opportunities to meet the needs of the prisoners.

Recommendation: Leaders and managers should provide an appropriate offer in education, training and work, so that prisoners acquire new knowledge, skills and behaviour, in line with their sentence plans.

Key concern: Too few prisoners were engaged in enough meaningful education, training and work. Prisoners did not receive high-quality information, advice and guidance at induction, while allocation to activity was not based on the needs of prisoners. Many prisoners were not screened for additional learning needs, and those in industry and work did not receive a support plan. While there was a detailed and ambitious vision for an improved education, skills and work offer, this would require investment in staffing and workshops that had not been secured.

Recommendation A: Leaders and managers should raise prisoners' participation in education, skills, and work rapidly and substantially, according to the advice and guidance that they receive.

Recommendation B: Managers should make sure that face-to-face and remote learning reflect the needs of the prisoners, and that this priority is reflected in the allocation process.

Recommendation C: Leaders should make sure that there is sufficient resource to support the new curriculum vision, in terms of both staffing and capital investment.

Recommendation D: Leaders should make sure that, on arrival, prisoners receive an assessment of their additional learning needs, where appropriate, and that this information is used and updated, so that they can progress well in education, skills and work.

Key concern: There was insufficient capacity to meet the needs of the number of prisoners identified to complete one of the accredited interventions offered at Brinsford. This was exacerbated by new programmes facilitators having long waits to access training to be able to deliver an intervention.

Recommendation: Managers should make sure that prisoners who are assessed as needing an accredited intervention are able to access it while in custody.

## Notable positive practice

We define notable positive practice as innovative work or practice that leads to particularly good outcomes from which other establishments may be able to learn. Inspectors look for evidence of good outcomes for prisoners; original, creative or particularly effective approaches to problem-solving or achieving the desired goal; and how other establishments could learn from or replicate the practice.

Inspectors found two examples of notable positive practice during this inspection.

The practice of inviting families in to support prisoners during reviews of both the CSIP and ACCT processes was very good. This provided additional support for these prisoners, many of whom were vulnerable; increased the amount of information available for staff; and added greater meaning and benefit to the actions that were generated jointly between the family and staff present.

Patients had a care plan for each mental health and substance misuse problem, and this was individualised, focused and up to date. Additionally, some care plans addressed both mental health and substance misuse treatment needs simultaneously, so that actions were unified and more efficient.

## INDEPENDENT MONITORING BOARD ANNUAL REPORT

The law requires every prison to be monitored by an independent Board appointed by the Justice Secretary; these are known as Independent Monitoring Boards (IMBs).

The IMB must satisfy itself as to the humane and just treatment of those held in custody within its prison and the range and adequacy of the programmes preparing them for release; it must report annually to the Justice Secretary on how well the prison has met the standards and requirements placed on it.

### IMB Report 1 July 2020 to 30 June 2021
### Published December 2021

This report presents the findings of the Board for the period 1 July 2020 to 30 June 2021. For the period prior to the Covid-19 restrictions, our evidence comes from observations made during visits, scrutiny of records and data, informal contact with prisoners and staff, and prisoner applications. The Covid-19 outbreak has had a continuing impact on the Board s ability to gather information, with normal visits not resuming until May 2021. Some members continued to participate in segregation reviews and others retained contact with the prison via remote monitoring and telephone calls. Inevitably, there is less detail and supporting evidence than usual. Regular information is being collected specifically on the prison s response to the pandemic.

The education contract did not meet the needs of the prison for most of the time but started to improve later in the lockdown, and some in-cell activities commenced, resulting in a considerable number of qualifications being achieved. Before that, Novus failed to deliver any meaningful service to prisoners, who were behind their doors for up to 23 hours a day. The way the contract has been written makes it very hard to challenge.

Before the lockdown, the number of activity places was far too low, which meant that many prisoners were unemployed. When the Covid-19 regime ends, the Board will need to conduct a detailed review of access to education places and the number of courses available, with checks relevant to the needs of the prisoners.

However, similar to last year, the Board has determined that the staff are running a safe prison and that, overall, despite a very restricted regime since March 2020, prisoners are treated fairly. As noted in previous reports, there continue to be ongoing incidents of violence, self-harm and substance misuse, although the Board notes that these are all reducing because of the Covid-19 restrictions limiting time out of cell.

Gang culture remains a problem that causes friction between prisoners, and is often a cause of premeditated violence.

The training and rehabilitation of prisoners were both good prior to March 2020 but were reduced during lockdown, picking up to an acceptable level later in the period.

There remains a problem in relocating prisoners with mental health problems to more suitable treatment centres. Healthcare staff do an excellent job but it takes too long to find a bed elsewhere for those prisoners assessed as requiring one. This has improved during the reporting period, which is a benefit, but the number of prisoners in custody with mental health issues is still too high.

## Main judgements
### How safe is the prison?

In the judgement of the Board, Brinsford remains a safe prison, and this is evidenced, particularly during the challenges of lockdown, through the low levels of self-harm and violence. There remains a minority of prisoners who self-harm but credit must go to staff who work really hard with these individuals to improve the situation. The overall level of self-harm has been a priority, and good progress has been made in reducing this. There are a few prisoners who still self-harm, even after the best efforts of staff, and we feel that they often need specialist support in another establishment.

Violent incidents were relatively rare during lockdown but increased a little when things opened up a bit. Gang-related issues make it difficult to place prisoners in the safest location.

### How fairly and humanely are prisoners treated?

In the context of the current Covid-19 lockdown, the Board considers that prisoners have been treated as fairly and humanely as is possible, despite the severe constraints on their movement and access to family visits and activities. Prisoners have appreciated some additional benefits, such as extra telephone credit and televisions, and understand that the slow progress in the return to the normal regime is not within the local management's control.

### How well are prisoners' health and wellbeing needs met?

The Board believes that the healthcare needs of the prisoners are well met by Practice Plus Group. The challenges of the pandemic were handled well and the number of infections was low. Those that were infected were isolated and levels of transmission were low. There was an effective system of bubbles and isolation of new entrants, which was well managed.

### How well are prisoners progressed towards successful resettlement?

The deficiencies of rehabilitative work and preparations for release have both been commented on frequently in recent reports. Little has changed and details of these deficiencies can be found in the Board's reports in 2019 and 2020. Limited face-to-face visiting, socially distanced, has restarted, and Purple Visits were becoming more popular.

### Main areas for development
### TO THE MINISTER

The information technology (IT) at Brinsford is old and failing, and needs to be updated. Long periods without a working network are potentially dangerous and, even at its best, this makes it difficult for staff to do their jobs well. Investment in a good IT system would improve many outcomes for staff and prisoners.

Prisoners held on immigration status are kept far too long before transfer to an immigration removal centre or their home country.

### TO THE PRISON SERVICE

The fabric of Brinsford is in a poor state and therefore needs a great deal of investment to return it to a reasonable state.

There are too few activity places, particularly for those prisoners who are over the age of 21. Every prisoner should have the opportunity to work or have education, and Brinsford is around 100 places short of being able to deliver that.

There have been far too many transfers between establishments, particularly during the pandemic, for what appear to be operational reasons; however, when Brinsford staff members feel that a prisoner needs to be moved urgently, it seems to be very difficult to find a place elsewhere. Bringing in a number of prisoners from other establishments makes the gang problem more difficult to manage, although it needs to be understood that these moves have to be in the best interests of the prisoner concerned.

When prisoners are recategorised, it is often a long time before they are moved. This was evident when Brinsford had a number of category D prisoners who were frustrated while waiting for a place in an open establishment.

The education contract is not fit for purpose. It has always proved very difficult to hold the provider to account, to ensure that the prison gets good education provision. Any new contracts need to be much tighter in what must be provided and how prisons can be compensated for services not provided.

The management of prisoner property in the establishment and the transfer of property between establishments continues to cause many problems, including prisoner anger and claims for compensation. A new policy and procedure have been many years in the development stage and need to be implemented urgently.

## TO THE GOVERNOR

More places are needed in both education and work-based activities. Quicker entry onto courses would make a big difference to our short-sentence prisoners and would provide a better way forward.

Visits need to return to pre-pandemic levels as soon as it is safe. Purple Visits have been useful and should be continued for any prisoners who cannot receive face-to-face visits.

The key worker scheme needs to be brought back to at least its pre-pandemic levels, and further improved. It was understandably reduced owing to staff shortages. Officers need support and, possibly, further training to get the scheme to work as it should, to support prisoners.

### Progress since the last report

Several areas which were highlighted in the last few annual reports have continued to improve. These include:
• The number and level of prisoners self-harming has reduced but there is still a small number of repeat offenders that are proving difficult to help.
• The level of violence has reduced further, with some good programmes in place to support the perpetrators of violence.
• Mentally unwell prisoners are not waiting as long for transfers to specialist accommodation.
Other issues have not improved or have got worse. These are:
• The education provision is still not delivering the service that we would expect.

• Prisoners' property is still going missing and is the major issue in their complaints. • The fabric of the prison is still poor. Some painting has been done but considerably more is required to return it to a reasonable standard. Cells are in a particularly poor state.

**19 CAMBRIDGE ROAD BISHOPSTON BRISTOL BS7 8PS**

**HM PRISON BRISTOL**

**Tel: 0117 372 3100**

*For the latest reports on this prison please visit:* https://tinyurl.com/bdfh26rv

*Important Changes:* **(1) Visits:** the identification necessary to access this prison and visit for social or professional purposes has changed; (2) **Money and Gifts** new rules now apply to these. See page 16 for full details of the above.

**Task of the establishment** HMP Bristol is a category B local and resettlement prison holding adult and young adult males.

### Certified normal accommodation / Op.Cap
Prisoners held at the time of this visit: 489
Baseline certified normal capacity: 406
In-use certified normal capacity: 406
Operational capacity: 505

### Prison status and key providers
Public
Prison Group: Avon & South Dorset
Prison Group Director: Paul Woods
Name of Governor: Vanessa Prendergast
IMB Chair: Eleanor Agar
Physical health provider: Bristol Community Health and Hanham Secure Health
Mental health provider: Avon and Wiltshire NHS Partnership Trust (Prime Contract holder)
Substance use treatment provider: Avon and Wiltshire NHS Partnership Trust
Prison education framework provider: Weston College
Escort contractor: Serco

**Brief history** The prison was built in 1883. B and C wings were added in the 1960s.

### Short description of residential units
A wing: 126-bed wing, general population.
B wing: 99 single cells, mainly enhanced or super-enhanced prisoners. No in-cell sanitation.
C wing: 148-bed wing, incorporating the first night centre, integrated drug treatment

system/drug recovery and a dedicated detoxification unit on C3. Reverse cohort unit and PIU are also located on C wing.

D wing and F wing annex: 116-bed wing containing the induction centre. D wing is for vulnerable prisoners.

E wing: 11-bed dedicated segregation wing, with two additional unfurnished cells.

G wing: 125-bed wing, general population.

Brunel unit: reintegration unit holding prisoners with complex mental and physical health needs

### Visiting Information

Visits: Telephone booking line: 0300 060 6510, Monday to Friday, 9am to 6pm

**Visiting times:** Monday to Sunday: 2pm to 4pm (except bank holidays)

**Legal visits:** Legal and professional visits are offered by video link only.

Email: VideoLink-Bristol@justice.gov.uk

You can also book by telephone.

Booking line: 0117 942 4074

Monday to Friday, 9am to 6pm

### INSPECTIONS & REPORTS
**Scrutiny Visit**

14 and 22-23 September 2020

**Published 23rd October 2020**

This report presents the findings from our scrutiny visit to HMP Bristol and reports on the conditions and treatment of prisoners during the Covid-19 pandemic. Bristol is a category B local and resettlement prison holding approximately 500 young and adult male prisoners.

Following our most recent inspection of Bristol, in May – June 2019, I was so concerned at the outcomes we observed that I wrote to the Secretary of State on 11 June 2019 invoking the Urgent Notification (UN) process. That inspection was, at the time, the latest in a series of visits to Bristol where we had reported on declining standards and either poor or insufficiently good outcomes across all our tests of a healthy prison. At the time, and following our protocol with the Ministry of Justice, the Secretary of State responded publicly to the UN, explaining how outcomes for those detained would be improved. A scrutiny visit does not have the scope or capacity to fully follow up a situation such as this one, but I am pleased to report that we saw enough to be confident that, in our view, Bristol was a much-improved institution. We found a now well-led establishment that had taken a more thoughtful approach to regime restrictions than we have seen in other prisons. Given the high levels of suicide and self-harm in the prison, appropriate care had been taken to balance the risk of the virus against the impact on prisoners' mental well-being of a very restricted regime. Within the limitations of the national

restrictions, the governor had used some local initiative to keep activities open and maximise time unlocked, which had reduced prisoners' frustration. Although the time prisoners could spend outside their cells was limited for some to a minimum of one hour 45 minutes a day, almost half the prisoners were out for considerably longer, engaging in a variety of purposeful activities.

All workshops had remained open during the pandemic, albeit with reduced numbers to enable safe social distancing. A proactive group of PE staff had provided frequent access to structured outside physical activity throughout the period. The new and impressive education facility had very recently reopened to allow small groups of prisoners to access direct learning. Good use was made of peer mentors to provide support, and prisoner work parties had continued to improve living conditions and the cleanliness of the environment.

These efforts to maximise the time that prisoners could be unlocked and engaged in activity were underpinned by a robust approach to cleanliness and social distancing. We saw effective social distancing by prisoners and staff, despite staff reporting in our survey that it was difficult to do so. Communal areas were cleaned frequently by trained 'COVID cleaners' and there were hand sanitising stations at the entrance to buildings to minimise the risk of transmission of the virus.

There had been no confirmed Covid-19 cases among prisoners since the start of the pandemic. The management team had applied appropriate restrictions to manage the risks associated with the Covid-19 virus and had implemented quarantine and shielding arrangements in accordance with national directives.

Strategic and partnership meetings and various initiatives had not been suspended at the start of regime restrictions as we have found in some other prisons. On the contrary, a dynamic and motivated management team had maintained good oversight and taken the opportunity to innovate during this period. There was evidence of recent improvements in important areas of safety, respect and purposeful activity.

Managerial oversight and governance of safety were very good. A significant effort had been made to understand the causal factors of violence and self-harm which took into consideration the impact of the restricted regime. There were encouraging trends in the level of violence but use of force was at a similar level to the period before March. High levels of suicide and self-harm, however, remained a concern, with two self-inflicted deaths in 2020 and one further very recent unexplained death which was under investigation. Recorded self-harm incidents were three times higher than at comparator prisons. Considerable effort had been made to reduce self-harm, and there were very early indications that these initiatives might be having an impact.

We witnessed many positive interactions between staff and prisoners. These observations were reflected in our survey where 72% of prisoners said that staff treated them with respect. Key work was limited to the most vulnerable prisoners, but weekly welfare checks were in place for all. In our survey, the majority of prisoners said they had been treated fairly under the new incentives scheme, and we were impressed by the focus on positive behaviour that it provided. The recent introduction of a prison shop supplying snack items, and another for prisoners to purchase smart and casual clothes at affordable prices, was also positive.

Communication had been good, with 81% of prisoners in our survey saying that the restrictions had been explained to them. An elected prisoner council had continued to meet senior managers throughout the pandemic. Several surveys had been conducted for prisoners with protected characteristics to understand their needs and concerns during the pandemic. The support for prisoners with disabilities and those requiring social care had improved significantly since our previous inspection in 2019. However, our survey found some concerning perceptions among prisoners from a black, Asian, mixed or minority ethnic background, which needed to be addressed.

Significant improvements, which included new showers and serveries, had been made to the living conditions in some areas. A local decency team of staff and prisoners was involved in the ongoing refurbishment of residential accommodation. Although mostly clean, tidy and free of graffiti, some accommodation remained poor in areas that had not yet been refurbished.

Good partnership work had ensured that emergency health care and an increasing level of routine care had remained available. However, dental needs were not being fully met due to national restrictions and local access issues. At the time of our visit, 99 prisoners were on the waiting list for treatment, and some had been waiting for more than six months. As a result, outcomes were deteriorating. We were told, for example, that teeth were being extracted that might otherwise have been treatable.

Social visits had resumed earlier than in many prisons. Visits were managed with sensitivity and suitable exercise of discretion, while reflecting Public Health England advice. The introduction of video calling (Purple Visits, see Glossary of terms) to family and friends was appreciated by prisoners.

Sentence planning and risk assessment processes were up to date, but we found deficiencies in some public protection work which was a concern. An increase in the use of in-cell telephones during the pandemic had led to a substantial backlog of phone monitoring which the prison urgently needed to address.

Release planning by the community rehabilitation company was mostly conducted through written correspondence with the prisoner, but face-to-face work was expected to increase with the opening of the new resettlement centre. The percentage of prisoners released without settled accommodation had reduced since our last inspection (when it was 47%) but, at 25% during the pandemic, was still far too high.

It was evident during this visit that at long last there had been important changes at Bristol. Not only had the response to the pandemic been very well managed with the support of the prison group director, but strong and energetic leadership had kept work going during this period to improve the prison. We found a more purposeful, safe and decent establishment than at the time of our previous inspection, despite the regime restrictions. The prison now needs the opportunity to embed and sustain this progress with continued additional support from HM Prison and Probation Service.

Peter Clarke CVO OBE QPM

HM Chief Inspector of Prisons September 2020

## HMCIP Report

**Date of last inspection:** 20–21 May, 3–7 June 2019
**Published 18 September 2019**

HMP Bristol is a category B local and resettlement prison, holding male adult and young adult prisoners. At the time of this inspection 464 men were resident, a slightly reduced roll, caused by the temporary closure of the prison's D wing for refurbishment.

Following this inspection of HMP Bristol, and because of our findings, in accordance with the protocol I have with the Ministry of Justice, I wrote to the Secretary of State invoking the Urgent Notification (UN) process (see Appendix V) on 11 June 2019. (The protocol is available at https://tinyurl.com/y42ju4fu). In that letter, and in the inspection debriefing paper that accompanied it, I set out in detail my concerns and the judgements that had caused me to follow that course of action. Under the protocol, the Secretary of State commits to respond publicly to the UN within 28 days, explaining how outcomes for those detained will be improved. The Secretary of State's response, for which I am grateful, is also detailed in Appendix VII of this report.

As I indicated in my letter of 11 June, prior to this inspection we last inspected Bristol in March 2017 when we reported on declining standards and either poor or insufficiently good outcomes across all our tests of a healthy prison. These findings followed similarly poor inspections in both 2013 and 2014. Despite expressing some optimism at the time of the last inspection and despite subsequent important initiatives within the prison (including the recruitment of many staff, some new investment and the designation of Bristol by Her Majesty's Prison and Probation Service (HMPPS) as a prison under 'special measures'), at this inspection we were again unable to report on any significant improvement to overall outcomes.

We last reported more positively about this prison some nine years ago in 2010, but since then, as the chart shows, it has been a record of seemingly intractable failure.

Outcomes in safety for example, have been poor for two consecutive inspections, as they have been in the provision of purposeful activity. It was striking that of the 76 recommendations we made in 2017 we found that only 23 had been achieved or partially achieved; some 52 (68%) having not been achieved. Moreover, the prison met all seven of our criteria for invoking a UN.

My detailed findings for this inspection are contained within the summary and body of this report, and were similarly summarised in my letter to the Secretary of State. I will not repeat them here. As I have indicated previously, Bristol may not have reached the extreme lack of order and crisis seen in some other prisons and this report acknowledges some developments and some improvements, but many initiatives were poorly coordinated, applied inconsistently or not well embedded. Our repeated requests for the prison to provide us with meaningful objectives or an assessment of the impact of 'special measures' in driving improvement were unsuccessful. We were left with little confidence that the prison had a coherent and robust plan to impact and improve outcomes meaningfully. In 2017 the cautious optimism to which I referred gave me grounds to think that the leadership at Bristol, supported regionally and nationally, might be able to make progress. The current reality however, shows this did not happen. I hope this report and the UN that preceded it constitute a timely reminder that HMP Bristol needs to be gripped and supported at all levels of management in HMPPS.

Peter Clarke CVO OBE QPM July 2019
HM Chief Inspector of Prisons

**INDEPENDENT MONITORING BOARD ANNUAL REPORT**

The law requires every prison to be monitored by an independent Board appointed by the Justice Secretary; these are known as Independent Monitoring Boards (IMBs). The IMB must satisfy itself as to the humane and just treatment of those held in custody within its prison and the range and adequacy of the programmes preparing them for release; it must report annually to the Justice Secretary on how well the prison has met the standards.

**IMB Report 1 August 2020 – 31st July 2021**
**Published December 2021**
**Executive summary**
**Background to the report**

This is the second annual report produced during the period of Covid-19, and during this time various levels of an exceptional delivery model (EDM) have been in force. While many restrictions were in place during this period, there were also many new practices of quarantine, testing and vaccination being implemented. It is of great credit to the management, staff and prisoners that there were only two small outbreaks of Covid-19 infection during this time, which were short lived, and there were no serious illness or deaths from Covid-19 in the prison population.

The operational capacity at Bristol was maintained at a reduced level, agreed following the urgent notification by HM Inspectorate of Prisons (HMIP) in 2019, to facilitate progress in areas of safety and decency. The HMIP scrutiny visit in September 2020 was very positive about progress made, and the prison has since come out of the urgent notification. Although this is just out of the reporting period, we feel it is worth noting and celebrating.

**Main judgements**
**How safe is the prison?**

Since the HMIP inspection of 2019, safer custody has remained rated at level 1, the lowest rating given by HMIP. Several initiatives have been introduced over the last 18 months. These include not unlocking a whole wing at one time, food only being served one landing at a time at supervised serveries, wellbeing buddies, and weekly safety action (SAM) and safety intervention (SIM) meetings to support those who are at risk of self-harm or perpetrating violence. All prisoners have access to a safety hotline from their in-cell phone line. The usage is monitored by staff, and welfare checks on prisoners are made if any concerns arise. Main concerns raised were recorded as mental health, medication and transfers. There is an external safety line, where family or friends can leave messages concerning the welfare of prisoners. This is also monitored, and welfare checks are carried out if necessary. All these initiatives have seen an improved downward trend of self-harm and violence, with data to support this.

The Board has the perception, and has heard from prisoners, that the prison has felt safer in the last year. This is supported by the HMIP scrutiny visit survey, which found that 28% of prisoners felt unsafe, a significant reduction from 62% reported in 2019. The safer custody team has carried out focus groups and surveys on feeling unsafe, and these concerns can also be expressed at prison council meetings attended by wing representatives.

## How fairly and humanely are prisoners treated?

On returning to the prison as restrictions began to be lifted in spring 2021, the Board has noticed that the general environment has significantly improved on the wings and in the grounds. As noted in last year's report, the wings feel calmer and prisoners have free access to basic toiletries and prison clothing. Staff consistency on the wings has led to better communication with the prisoners.

There is still a problem with disability access, especially to the healthcare building, due to the Victorian buildings and layout of the prison.

Key working has been adapted during the year, and has not been consistently delivered.

## How well are prisoners' health and wellbeing needs met?

Healthcare provision is generally good and there has been successful management of Covid-19 infection, prevention and vaccination.

A variety of wellbeing resources are available for prisoners and staff.

There is an increasing number of older and disabled prisoners with medical, mobility and social care needs in the prison. Typically, around 30 prisoners are classified as needing personal emergency evacuation plans (PEEPs). While these needs are mostly being met, this can impact on staffing, due to hospital attendances and increasing numbers of bed watches. At its peak, there were nine prisoners on 24- hour bed watches requiring one-to-one supervision.

The Criminal Justice Inspectorates joint inspection report, 'Neurodiversity in the criminal justice system: A review of evidence', published in July 2021, estimated that half of people entering prison could reasonably be expected to have some form of neurodivergence, and this impacts their ability to engage. Support for neurodivergence in HMP Bristol is an area of concern for the Board.

## How well are prisoners progressed towards successful resettlement?

There is a high number of remand prisoners who have spent long periods in Bristol and who may be released without having been fully prepared when they do finally get to court.

The improvement in the number of prisoners released to settled accommodation has been maintained and there are several initiatives now running to improve outcomes on release.

Education delivered in-cell during the EDM restrictions was well received and is gradually returning to a blended face-to-face and in-cell learning approach.

## Main areas for development
### TO THE MINISTER

What initiatives – for example, training for prison staff – are planned to improve outcomes for prisoners with neurodivergent conditions, which, as we have observed and a recent review outlined, impacts their ability to engage?

How is the Ministry of Justice working with other agencies to consider alternatives to prison for elderly and vulnerable prisoners who could be better managed in non- custodial environments?

Why was Covid-19 vaccination not carried out as a pan-prison programme to protect vulnerable prisoners in crowded environments and also staff, many of whom should be considered equal to care staff in their role? Is this being reviewed for the future?

### TO THE PRISON SERVICE

Can you provide further resources and guidance as to how key work should be delivered and how well it is achieving its strategic intentions?

The reduction in the operational capacity following the urgent notification in 2019 has facilitated the progress in safety and decency observed in our report. We hope that the numbers will not be increased too quickly or too high to enable this progress to be consolidated.

Please encourage HM Prison and Probation Service (HMPPS) and other visitors to the establishment to make contact with the Board. As independent volunteers carrying out a statutory role, we are a vital set of eyes and ears, and can provide valuable information and insights into the prison.

Property delay or loss during transfers from other establishments remains a problem locally and nationally. What is being done to improve this?

### TO THE GOVERNOR

The Board has welcomed Governor attendance at our Board meetings, and useful communication between meetings including with the Deputy Governor. We hope that we will be invited to meet visitors to the prison and attend appropriate debriefings, which did not happen consistently during this year.

It would also be useful to share details of how various initiatives are aligned to key areas for improvement, so we can better monitor and report on developments.

Can you facilitate access to appropriate room allocations, so that the mental health, substance misuse and other teams can deliver their full range of programmes effectively?

## Progress since the last report

### Safety

The safety team has put in place processes to improve safety and wellbeing, and this is evidenced by the reduction in self-harm and violence. The Board is grateful that while monitoring remotely, the governor of safer custody was available for a weekly telephone update and always responded to questions or concerns by email.

### Fair and humane treatment

Accommodation and general environment improvements have continued and built on last year's progress, which has had a positive impact on the mood within the prison. Prisoners have continued to report positively about the management of the regime, with smaller groups out on the wings for meals and domestics.

Disability access has still not improved, including access to the healthcare building. Issues regarding loss of property and delays in receiving property when transferred to and from other establishments continue to be a problem, although reduced in number this year.

### Health and wellbeing

Cooperation between healthcare and prison staff reported last year has continued. As in the community, there are still delays for some services, such as dental treatment.

Time taken to transfer prisoners with severe mental ill-health to a secure hospital placement has improved slightly but varies significantly between different hospitals.

### Progression and release

Last year's improvements in numbers release d into settled accommodation have been sustained despite the cessation of the government funding for hotel accommodation. The prison has been proactive in working with outside organisations and has been successful in starting new initiatives aiming to improve outcomes on release.

There are, however, some prisoners in Bristol who seem to be inappropriately placed. This includes individuals with significant mobility and social care needs, those recalled or remanded waiting for court dates, and vulnerable immigration detainees.

JEBB AVENUE
BRIXTON
LONDON
SW2 5XF

**HM PRISON BRIXTON**

Tel: 020 8588 6000

*For the latest reports on this prison please visit:*
https://tinyurl.com/bdfh26rv

*Important Changes:* **(1) Visits:** the identification necessary to access this prison and visit for social or professional purposes has changed; (2) **Money and Gifts** new rules now apply to these. See page 16 for full details of the above.

**Task of the establishment** HMP Brixton is a category C resettlement prison.

### Certified normal accommodation and operational capacity

Prisoners held at the time of inspection: 720
Baseline certified normal capacity: 530
In-use certified normal capacity: 509
Operational capacity: 778

### Population of the prison

- 660 new prisoners received each year (an average of 55 per month).
- 215 prisoners convicted of a sexual offence.
- 51 foreign national prisoners.
- 49% of prisoners are from a black and minority ethnic background.
- An average of 74 prisoners is released into the community each month.
- 267 prisoners are receiving support for substance misuse.

### Prison status and key providers

Public
Prison Group: London
Prison Group Director: Ian Bickers
Governor/Director: Sonia Brooks
IMB Chair: Mike Howes
Physical health provider: Practice Plus Group Health & Rehabilitation Services Limited
Mental health provider: Barnet, Enfield and Haringey NHS Trust
Substance misuse treatment provider: Forward Trust
Prison education framework provider: Novus
Escort contractor: Serco

**Brief history** HMP Brixton opened in 1819 as the Surrey House of Correction, subsequently becoming a prison for women and then a military prison. In 1898, it became an adult male local prison, serving the whole of the London area and particularly focusing on South London.

In July 2012, it became a category C and D resettlement prison for the local area. However, the role of the prison was changed in February 2017 to house solely category C prisoners.

## Short description of residential units
A wing: category C prisoners, including 34 prisoners on the London Pathways Unit (for prisoners with personality disorders)
B wing: first night/induction accommodation for category C prisoners
C wing: enhanced prisoners
D wing: drug recovery and well-being wing
G wing: prisoners convicted of a sexual offence
Segregation unit

## Visiting Information
### How to book family and friends visits
Brixton is running a limited visits schedule. Visits are also happening differently than normal, observing strict guidelines, which must be followed.
You can book your visit online.
You can also book your visit by telephone.
Booking line: 0208 678 1433
Monday to Friday, 1:15pm to 4pm
### Visiting times
• Monday: B wing - 4pm to 5pm, D wing - 2:15 to 3:15pm
• Tuesday: G wing - 2:15pm to 3:15pm and 4pm to 5pm
• Wednesday: A wing - 2:15pm to 3:15pm and 4pm to 5pm
• Thursday: C wing - 2:15pm to 3:15pm and 4pm to 5pm
• Friday: No visits
• Saturday: A wing - 2:15pm to 3:15pm, C wing - 3:45pm to 4:45pm, D wing - 9:15am to 10:15am and G wing - 10:45am to 11:45am
• Sunday: A wing - 9:15am to 10:15am, B wing - 2:15pm to 3:15pm, C wing - 10:45am to 11:45am and G wing - 3:45pm to 4:45pm.
You should arrive at the prison 30 minutes before your visit to allow time to get through security.

### How to book legal and professional visits
Legal and professional visits are offered face to face, via videolink or telephone.
You can book your visit by emailing: legalvisits.brixton@justice.gov.uk
Or you can book by telephone.
Booking line: 0208 588 6230 or 0208 588 6231
Monday to Friday, 8:30am to 4:00pm.
Only legal visits will be booked on this line, social visitors calling this number will be directed to the social visits booking line.

### Legal visit times
A, B, C, D Wing:
• Monday, Wednesday and Thursdays: 8:30am to 9:30am, 10:15am to 11:15am, 2:15pm to 3:15pm, 4pm to 5pm
G wing:
• Tuesday: 8:30am to 9:30am, 10:15am to 11:15am, 2:15pm to 3:15pm, 4pm to 5pm

## INSPECTIONS & REPORTS
**HMCIP Report 14 and 21–25 March 2022**
**Published 30 June 2022**
This report into HMP Brixton revealed a prison that was in trouble. With a temporary governor recently in post and an inexperienced leadership team, this category C London resettlement prison will need considerable support and investment from HMPPS to get back on track.
The behaviour on the wings was not good enough with prisoners breaking the rules without challenge from staff members who either did not have high enough expectations or who turned a blind eye. Prisoners were free to vape around the jail, the dress code was not enforced, and some prisoners appeared to be permitted to spend much longer on the phone than others. This lack of proper oversight had led to some individuals isolating on the wing without anyone noticing. There was inadequate care for some of the most vulnerable who, even when placed on an ACCT (assessment, care in custody, and teamwork), were not given the support that they needed.
The system for applications had broken down meaning many were ignored or unanswered. This led to prisoners putting in complaints which were often dismissed. It took inspectors a long time to walk from one end of a wing to the other because they were stopped by so many prisoners eager to express their exasperation with life at the prison and their inability to get the support they needed to complete their sentence and prepare for release. ROTL had been suspended meaning that the prisoners – particularly those who had category D status, could not go out to work while they suffered interminable waits for transfer to an open prison.
There were not nearly enough activities for the 724 prisoners, and only a lucky few were allocated to the high-quality workshops such as drywalling or painting. Those that were able to get prison jobs were often working part time or were not using skills that would be useful after release. Standards of education were poor with the quality of teaching in English and maths not good enough for the small number of prisoners who attended.
On G wing, which held vulnerable prisoners, there was even less to do. The regime was

restrictive and apart from the kitchen (which produced excellent food), there was little work or training. Prisoners on this wing told me they had made a mistake in opting to come to Brixton, and many compared it to a category B establishment. If this wing is to remain, leaders in the prison and at HMPPS will have to give some serious thought to how they improve provision to this largely compliant but frustrated group of prisoners some of whom, if they are not given suitable support or access to treatment programmes, could pose a risk to the public when they are released.

The standards of accommodation were often very poor. Many prisoners shared tiny, cramped, and dilapidated cells with inadequate furniture and graffiti on the walls. Despite being rerolled in 2012 as a category C prison, Brixton had the feel of a local prison, but one in which prisoners were spending much longer periods of time.

The experienced and effective temporary governor is in no doubt about the scale of the task of improving standards which had, unusually, fallen in three of our four healthy prison tests. If given enough time, she will certainly be able to address many of our concerns, but progress will be very constrained if the prison service does not provide material support in refurbishing cells and reducing the headcount so that there is enough meaningful activity to go round. HMPPS will need to consider whether there is any future for a vulnerable prisoners wing in such a small site. Ultimately, the only way that this prison can be more successful with so little space is if a substantial proportion of prisoners are going to work every day outside the wall.

Charlie Taylor
HM Chief Inspector of Prisons April 2022

**Safety**

At the last inspection of HMP Brixton, in 2019, we found that outcomes for prisoners were reasonably good against this healthy prison test. At this inspection, we found that outcomes for prisoners were now not sufficiently good.

The establishment had started to receive more new prisoners than it was prepared for. This meant that prisoners often spent too long in reception holding rooms, waiting to be processed. First night cells on B wing were in poor condition, with many dirty, missing furniture and containing graffiti. While better for prisoners going to G wing, induction into prison life had deteriorated since the last inspection.

In our survey, 24% of prisoners said that they currently felt unsafe. Recorded levels of violence against staff had increased since the last inspection and were high, and likely to be a result of prisoners' frustrations with an inability to resolve day-to-day problems. The number of recorded assaults on prisoners had decreased. Strategic violence reduction work had considerable weaknesses. Meetings lacked focus and did not result in action to reduce violence. Violent incidents were not always investigated and the investigations that did take place were poor. Residential and safety managers were unaware of prisoners isolating for their own protection. There were limited incentives to encourage positive behaviour, and staff were ineffective. in challenging low-level poor behaviour.

There had been 220 recorded use of force incidents in the last 12 months. Most of those we reviewed had been de-escalated successfully. Scrutiny of use of force was weak. We found evidence of some poor use of techniques, inappropriate language from staff and concerning practice that was not identified during the monthly meetings. Leaders were unaware of how often body-worn video cameras were used.

Security intelligence was well managed, and there were good processes to mitigate risks. Leaders were taking appropriate action to combat staff corruption, which was a key risk for the establishment.

Self-harm levels had reduced and were comparable to those at similar prisons. Too few prisoners at risk of self-harm felt cared for and concerns identified in assessment, care in custody and teamwork (ACCT) case management reviews for those at risk of suicide or self- harm were not always captured on care maps. Attendance by residential managers at the weekly safety intervention meeting was poor and the meeting was ineffective in addressing the needs of the most vulnerable prisoners. The constant observation cell in use on A wing during the inspection was in poor condition and staff interactions were conducted through a locked gate.

**Respect**

At the last inspection of HMP Brixton, in 2019, we found that outcomes for prisoners were reasonably good against this healthy prison test. At this inspection, we found that outcomes for prisoners were now poor.

In our survey, only 58% of respondents said that most staff treated them with respect. We found that some relationships between staff and prisoners were dysfunctional, with staff failing to challenge poor behaviour. Many prisoners reported unequal treatment by staff, and that the only way to get attention was to behave badly. Too many prisoners shared very cramped cells designed for one. Living conditions were poor;

many cells were missing furniture, curtains and screening for toilets, and contained large amounts of graffiti. Despite the prison holding adequate supplies of cleaning equipment and toilet paper, prisoners on some wings found staff reluctant to obtain these necessities for them. Laundry facilities were inadequate on all wings, with too few washers and dryers for the size of the population, and several of these either inoperative or in a state of disrepair. The quality of the food was excellent, and many prisoners said that it was the most positive part of life at the prison.

The application and complaint systems were inadequate, which meant that prisoners were unable to resolve legitimate requests. Very few applications received a reply at all. The complaint system was equally chaotic; in 2022 to date, 46% of all submitted complaints had been returned late, were still outstanding or had been returned unanswered. Many responses, both to applications and complaints, were poor and there were no quality assurance processes to help improve standards.

Oversight of equality provision had been overlooked in 2021. In recent months, a renewed focus by the governor had led to some improvements. Use of data to identify areas of disproportionality had started, but the action plan to address equality issues was weak. In our survey, prisoners from some protected groups, such as younger prisoners and those from a black and minority ethnic background, reported worse treatment than the rest of the population. The discrimination incident report form (DIRF) system was underused, which could have been because of a lack of trust in the system and difficulty in submitting DIRFs. Quality assurance of DIRF investigations had improved. Faith provision was weak and prisoners wishing to attend group worship could only do so once every five to six weeks.

The quality of health services was reasonably good. However, access to services within the health care centre was hindered by regime restrictions and inefficient officer escort arrangements. Prisoners were highly dissatisfied with access to health services. A suitable range of services was offered and waiting times for most clinics were reasonable, although patients waited too long to see an optician, podiatrist and dentist. Responses to health care complaints were late and lacked detail. There were no prisoners in receipt of a social care package (see Glossary) at the time of the inspection, but there were good systems to identify and provide this when needed.

Mental health services provided a range of support to patients with mild to moderate and more complex needs. Groups were yet to restart and access to psychology services was limited because of staff shortages. Prisoners with addiction problems were well supported.

Medicines management arrangements were generally effective. However, the management of medicine queues by officers and the observation of compliance were inconsistent.

## Purposeful activity

At the last inspection of HMP Brixton, in 2019, we found that outcomes for prisoners were not sufficiently good against this healthy prison test. At this inspection, we found that outcomes for prisoners were now poor.

Most prisoners spent too little time unlocked; unemployed prisoners spent an average of only one and a half hours per day unlocked, with much less on Fridays. Those who were fortunate enough to have a job received up to 10 hours on a day that they worked. During our roll checks, we found 55% of prisoners locked up during the day. All prisoners could visit the library at least once a week. Access to the gym was good. Outdoor facilities were very limited, but gym staff ran regular sports session on a shared exercise yard.

There were too few activity spaces to meet the needs of the population. Many of the spaces were part time, with very few hours of face-to-face activity. Prisoners rightly felt frustrated at the lack of opportunity to gain accredited qualifications while at the prison. Allocation was ineffective and did not make full use of the limited provision, or make sure that prisoners attended the activities that most met their needs. As a result, a large number of prisoners were unemployed and unmotivated. The curriculum did not provide equal access to courses for vulnerable prisoners. Information, advice and guidance was not delivered effectively.

Teaching in English and mathematics did not support prisoners to develop their knowledge and skills at a rapid enough pace. Few had achieved accredited qualifications. By contrast, the small number of prisoners in vocational training had a good understanding of the skills they were gaining and how these would be useful to them on release. Prisoners' practical work was of a high standard and they received useful support to get jobs on discharge from the prison.

Punctuality was poor as a result of delays to unlocking on the wings. Attendance of prisoners at training and work sessions was disrupted by other prison activities, including gym sessions. Prisoners were set clear expectations for behaviour in the workshops, classrooms and work areas, and most behaved well.

Teachers did not receive information about the outcomes of prisoners' assessments for learning difficulties and/or disabilities swiftly enough. As a result, they did not know whether prisoners had specific needs or how to support them.

### Rehabilitation and release planning

At the last inspection of HMP Brixton, in 2019, we found that outcomes for prisoners were not sufficiently good against this healthy prison test. At this inspection, we found that outcomes for prisoners remained not sufficiently good.

Prisoners had reasonably good access to visits. Provision for secure video calls (see Glossary) were better than we see in other prisons. The Prison Advice and Care Trust families team continued to provide support to prisoners with family issues and broader resettlement needs. Facilities to enable prisoners to maintain telephone contact with the outside world were not good enough. There was a limited number of telephones on the wings, and many of these were broken.

The most recent needs analysis had been completed in December 2020, based on the prison's resettlement role. Plans to improve the support provided to prisoners were well developed. There was a large backlog of initial assessments of risk and need. Many prisoners had justifiable frustrations with their inability to communicate with the offender management unit. Prisoners we interviewed had a very low awareness of their sentence plans and most could not name their prison offender manager (POM). POM activity was task driven and reactive, and levels of recorded contact were disappointing. Work undertaken by POMs was of reasonable quality and we saw some proactive work to support progression. Prisoners experienced delays to their release on home detention curfew. Over 40 prisoners had been released over the previous year without having their multi-agency public protection arrangements (MAPPA) management level confirmed.

Recategorisation reviews were not always completed on time and prisoners assessed as suitable for open conditions could experience long waits for transfer. No use was made of release on temporary licence to mitigate this.

No accredited interventions were available, despite the large population of prisoners convicted of sexual offences. Other interventions were offered by Forward Trust, and POMs carried out some one-to-one work and provided in-cell work packs. The London Pathways Unit provided effective support for prisoners with complex personality difficulties.

Resettlement planning was undermined by inconsistent probation service provision in the London area. Over the last year, an average of 74 prisoners were released each month; 35% had been released without accommodation being recorded and only 6.75% had had employment on release. Prisoners could open bank accounts before release, get copies of their birth certificates for identification purposes and see Jobcentre Plus staff for benefits advice. Links with an external partner to support gang exit were being rebuilt after the pandemic. 'Through-the-gate' mentoring was provided to a few prisoners and the 'departure lounge' offered practical support on the day of release.

### Key concerns and recommendations

Key concerns and recommendations identify the issues of most importance to improving outcomes for prisoners and are designed to help establishments prioritise and address the most significant weaknesses in the treatment and conditions of prisoners.

During this inspection we identified some areas of key concern and have made a small number of recommendations for the prison to address those concerns.

Key concern: Prisoners often spent too long in reception holding rooms, waiting to be processed. First night cells on B wing were ill-prepared for new arrivals. Many cells were dirty, missing furniture and contained graffiti. Induction into prison life had deteriorated since the last inspection.

Recommendation: Leaders should make sure that prisoners are safe and treated with respect during their reception, first night and induction. (To the governor)

Key concern: Scrutiny of use of force was weak. We found evidence of poor use of techniques, inappropriate language from staff and concerning practice that was not identified during monthly meetings.

Recommendation: There should be appropriate routine scrutiny of use of force incidents, with effective management oversight. (To the governor)

Key concern: Support for prisoners at risk of self-harm or suicide required improvement. Case reviews did not translate into meaningful care maps, which meant that prisoners' concerns and risks were not always fully addressed.

Recommendation: Prisoners at risk of self-harm should have an effective plan that directs their care. (To the governor)

Key concern: Staff–prisoner relationships were dysfunctional and lacked professional boundaries in some cases. Staff did not challenge low-level poor behaviour and failed to promote prosocial behaviour in prisoners. Prisoners told us that the only way to get any issues resolved was to become aggressive, and that staff were less responsive to the needs of those prisoners who behaved.

Recommendation: Staff should model prosocial

behaviour, set appropriate boundaries and ensure that good behaviour is rewarded. (To the governor)

Key concern: Too many prisoners lived in cells which were poorly equipped, dirty and contained graffiti. Many cells were overcrowded and poorly ventilated. Access to basics, such as toilet rolls, cleaning materials, clean bedding, clothing and stored property, was too often very poor.

Recommendation (a): Prisoners should not be held in overcrowded conditions. (To the governor)

Recommendation (b): Prisoners should live in decent conditions, with access to everyday basics. (To the governor)

Key concern: The application and complaint systems were not working, with too many prisoners receiving answers late or not at all. When they did receive an answer, it often did not adequately address the issue that was being raised.

Recommendation: Prisoners should receive a timely response to applications and complaints that fully addresses the issue raised. (To the governor)

Key concern: Regime restrictions and inefficient officer escort arrangements contributed to long waits to see the dentist, optician and podiatrist. Some external hospital appointments were cancelled by officers without consultation with health care staff. The management of medicine queues by officers was inconsistent and increased the risk of diversion. We also found some weaknesses with the health care application process, which meant that some appointments had not been booked, contributing to the delays.

Recommendation: Prisoners should have timely access to health interventions, assisted by adequate officer support, clear communication and a functional health care appointment system. (To the governor)

Key concern: There were too few activity spaces available to meet the needs of the prison population, and too many vacancies within the spaces available. Many prisoners were under-occupied and demotivated, and when they attended activities, too many arrived late.

Recommendation: Leaders should take rapid action to make sure that a large proportion of prisoners have access to, and can punctually attend, education, skills and work activities. (To the governor)

Key concern: Leaders did not use data effectively to evaluate the impact of education, skills and work activities. They did not routinely collect information on prisoners' employment pathways and could not pinpoint exactly how many prisoners were unemployed.

Recommendation: Leaders should make more effective use of data to scrutinise the curriculum that they offer, and to make alterations to it accordingly. (To the governor)

Key concern: Prisoners did not receive effective careers information, advice and guidance, and career aspirations were not linked well to prisoners' education, skills and work activities.

Recommendation: Leaders should make sure that the prison's staff work productively to meet individual prisoners' resettlement needs, and that careers advice and guidance is effective. (To the governor)

Key concern: The quality of English and mathematics education had not improved since the last inspection, and too few prisoners had gained accredited qualifications in these subjects.

Recommendation: Leaders should make sure that the quality of English and mathematics provision improves, so that prisoners develop their knowledge more rapidly and achieve qualifications in these subjects. (To the governor)

Key concern: There was limited support for prisoners to progress while at the establishment. Many did not have regular contact with their prison offender manager, and key work was not supportive of progression. The lack of accredited interventions was a particular issue, given the population of prisoners convicted of sexual offences.

Recommendation: Prisoners should receive the support they need from prison offender managers to be able to make progress while at the establishment. (To the governor)

Key concern: Too few prisoners had, or knew about, a sentence plan.

Recommendation: Concerted action should be taken to make sure that all prisoners who need one have a complete and up-to-date offender assessment system (OASys) document. (To HMPPS)

Key concern: The prison's public protection database showed that over 40 prisoners had not had a MAPPA management level confirmed before their release. The reasons for this needed to be understood and addressed by managers.

Recommendation: MAPPA levels should be confirmed and recorded in good time for release. (To the governor)

Key concern: Accommodation and employment support and outcomes for released prisoners needed attention. Prisoners felt unsupported in these areas, and HMPPS data showed that too many were released without accommodation identified and too few had education, training or employment to go to. There was no systematic follow-up of these outcomes to inform future provision.

Recommendation: Prisoners should have accommodation and education, training or employment on release. (To the governor)

**Notable positive practice**

We define notable positive practice as innovative work or practice that leads to particularly good outcomes from which other establishments may be able to learn. Inspectors look for evidence of good outcomes for prisoners; original, creative or particularly effective approaches to problem-solving or achieving the desired goal; and how other establishments could learn from or replicate the practice.

Inspectors found no examples of notable positive practice during this inspection.

## INDEPENDENT MONITORING BOARD: Annual Report

The law requires every prison to be monitored by an independent Board appointed by the Justice Secretary; these are known as Independent Monitoring Boards (IMBs). The IMB must satisfy itself as to the humane and just treatment of those held in custody within its prison and the range and adequacy of the programmes preparing them for release; it must report annually to the Justice Secretary on how well the prison has met the standards and requirements placed on it.

**IMB Report 01 September 2020–31 August 2021 Published 17 March 2022**

**Background to the report**

This year was dominated by Covid-19. As the regime was starting to open up, positive cases began to appear, and by early October 2020 an outbreak had been declared. Initially, track and trace efforts kept the numbers low, but as cases peaked nationally, the situation worsened, becoming very difficult – with around 200 prisoners affected in total and many staff absent – in December and January. On 11 and 12 January, there were 132 prisoners positive and isolating, and about 90 staff absences. Prisoners refusing to take a test also had to isolate. There were five bed watches, and 11 mobile phones out of action. Prisoners had to wear a face covering when out of cell, and staff in contact with positive or isolating men wore full personal protective equipment (PPE). A mass testing the following week also produced high positive numbers for men and staff.

The prison had been working in the autumn to open up the regime. This meant producing detailed documentation for HMPPS Gold Command, for instance assessing the number of men from a cohort who could safely use a classroom (with or without an officer present), and details of the cleaning regime. What progress there had been was ended, and time out of cell (for those not isolating) reduced.

Although three rotating bubbles of kitchen staff were formed, to increase resilience against infection, in one week wing staff and the Clink had to step in to keep the meal service going. Activities, gym, and some support work on the wings, from the offender management unit (OMU), Forward Trust, the Prison Advice and Care Trust (PACT) and induction groups stopped. However, Routes to Change (R2C) triaged seven prisoners a day and completed casework via remote call appointments and the Email A Prisoner Service with support from OSG staff. Those in need of urgent support were offered appointments and telephone support; other low-level cases were given support via the Email a Prisoner Service. In addition, the Family and Significant Others Service contacted families via emails, newsletters and by telephone. Legal visits and assessment, care in custody and teamwork (ACCT) reviews continued, and chaplains and offender managers were visiting the wings.

Some men who were new receptions had to be housed on A wing in the LPU, which was disruptive. Collective worship, suspended in March 2020, did not resume till June 2021. Meals were delivered to cell doors, denying even the limited association with others in the servery queue. Mobile phones (supplementing the limited number on the wings) were withdrawn for a time in October, until better cleaning between use could be put in place. Key workers were reassigned to work on their 'home' wing (to reduce cross-infection), instead of being with the same men until their release.

This, combined with the lack of time out of cell, meant that men had possibly less confidence in finding support. The safer custody team continued to work on the wings until their officer members (and gym staff) were redeployed for wing cover.

With the resumption of court hearings and pressure on the local prisons, the offender flow to Brixton had changed in September, with men arriving from local prisons without passing through training prisons, some very soon after being sentenced.

This, and the restrictions on the regime, meant that Brixton could no longer function effectively as a resettlement prison. Men arrived with only a few weeks to serve before release, for which no preparation had been made; without the basic educational qualifications; without having started courses required in their sentence plans (courses not offered at Brixton); or with long sentences to serve. Initial efforts to provide some support for the latter two groups had to be given up because of the lack of staff resource. Induction and assessment were suspended for months in the winter. Coupled with the increased shortage of places within the prison estate for D category prisoners, this had the effect of creating a significant group of men whose needs could not be met or were not identified. The Board's perception was that the number of recategorisations to B also increased; certainly, there were more men who were very disruptive, taking up a disproportionate amount of staff time, and the number of men posing a high risk for cell-sharing increased by about half, from under 40 to over 70, and had not returned to its former level in August 2021.

The impact on prisoners, back in lockdown after a few months, was severe; particularly since in October there were few national restrictions. Against all expectations, reported incidents of self-harm almost halved during lockdown compared to the period immediately before its implementation. Men seemed more resigned than angry about the limited regime, as IMB members found when they were able to visit, and one Listener reported in September that family problems were more of an issue then than the restrictions. More understandably, given the reduced opportunities, there was a large reduction in violence within the prison. Over the year, however, mental health problems increased significantly and stretched capacity. At the end of May, violence also increased, and there were more recategorisations to B.

The Board recognises some of the findings contained in the Chief Inspector of Prisons' report of February 2021, What happens to Prisoners in a Pandemic. It also recognises the significant efforts made by prison staff, led by the safer custody team, and by healthcare and agencies, to support men in difficulties and to provide as much extra as they could – gym work on the exercise yards, for instance, the activities committee, and excellent food. In the spring, the kitchen team started providing cooked breakfasts to small groups of men, on a rotating pattern.

Staff were under severe pressure in the lockdown months, with many absences. Although there was a reduction in prisoner-on-prisoner violence, assaults on staff increased, and there was more disruptive behaviour. Nationally, staff training was interrupted – for instance, control and restraint training could not be done. It was recognised that relatively new officers, of whom there was a high proportion, had little experience of supervising large numbers of men out of their cells at the same time, and exercising authority. Advice and training was implemented on the wings when possible.

The Governor and staff at all levels did their best to fulfil their duty of care towards the men in the prison, even in the worst weeks. They anticipated difficulties and planned ahead whenever it was possible, winning funding for significant accommodation improvements in the autumn, and producing a new strategy in April. The Board recognises and applauds their commitment, their skill in dealing with difficult and changing conditions, and their efforts to make life for the men in Brixton as decent as possible.

For the second year, the Board has been unable to visit the prison regularly for months on end. This report is based to a much larger extent than we would wish on the prison's reports and data. We believe it does give some reflection of the conditions experienced by prisoners during the year.

## Main judgements How safe is the prison?

The prison has been a physically safer place with slightly fewer incidents of self- harm, and of those that did occur, 82 (of the 192 incidents) were by 12 men. There were fewer prisoner on prisoner assaults than in the corresponding period last year, but prisoner on staff assaults and their seriousness increased. One man was severely ill-treated by his cellmate during lockdown over a period of several months.

## How fairly and humanely are prisoners treated?

The restricted regime during lockdown could not be described as humane. In the Board's resettlement survey, 57% of men reported that they were fairly and humanely treated by staff. For comparison, in the last HMIP inspection in March 2019, 72% of men said they were treated with respect by staff, and 78% said they could ask staff if they had a problem. Inevitably, during the lockdown and the restricted regime, men had less contact with staff, and the key worker system was disrupted. The focus had to be on prisoners with obvious problems: there was less attention paid to men who were quiet and resigned.

The changes in the offender flow system were not fair and humane, because they prevented a significant number of prisoners in Brixton from being prepared for release.

## How well are prisoners' health and wellbeing needs met?

Prisoners have been protected from Covid as well as possible in the crowded conditions. They have had the opportunity to shield (which some refused), and cohorts to provide for new arrivals have worked well. Covid vaccinations have been offered in line with community provision and the vaccine refusal rate has been broadly consistent, for the age ranges. The healthcare teams have been very stretched, particularly during the outbreak, but there has been no disruption in treatment on the wings, including GP visits when movement to the healthcare building was not possible in lockdown. Outpatient appointments were resumed as soon as possible. Within the constraints of lockdown, there has been good support from the chaplaincy team, Forward Trust and PACT. PE instructors were available on the yards during lockdown, and the food remained excellent.

**How well are prisoners progressed towards successful resettlement?**
For the second year, resettlement work was severely disrupted. There was no education or training from August 2020 until the limited provision starting in June 2021, except for in-cell work and some distance learning, and work in the kitchen and the Clink. PACT continued working, remotely during lockdown and until June, on family ties and support, as did the CRC on pre-release needs. The departure lounge continued operating until summer 2021, and there was through the gate support for some men from RECONNECT, an NHS project, and Forward Trust. A smaller proportion of men than in 2019 and 2020 surveyed in summer 2021 before release had accommodation.

As noted above, the changes in the offender flow system worked against resettlement.

**Main areas for development**
**TO THE MINISTER**
The already inadequate number of places in category D prisons has been exacerbated by remedial works at existing open prisons taking a number of places out of commission. The absence of the benefits of experiencing open conditions before release for prisoners who have earned them not only increases the likelihood of re-offending but also removes the incentive for good behaviour for men still working towards D categorisation. An increase in the number of D category places is urgently required.

As in previous years, the Board is concerned at the number of men revealed by our annual survey (29% in 2021 compared with 36% in 2019) as having no accommodation to go to upon release. The impact of homelessness on reoffending was con- firmed in a study published in July 2021 undertaken by Royal Holloway, University of London; and PACT data showed that 68% of prisoners released to rough sleeping and 55% of prisoners released to other forms of homelessness re-offend within one year, compared to 42% released to settled accommodation. Those who are home- less at the beginning of their sentence are at a higher risk of reoffending and 79% reoffend within a year. 60% of prisoners believe having a home would help them to stop reoffending. Accordingly, and to help the prison fulfil its rehabilitative mission, increasing the supply of accommodation for men released from prison is urgently required.

**TO THE PRISON SERVICE**
The introduction of the offender flow process has resulted in men who do not meet the profile being sent to Brixton which is not equipped to support men very recently convicted, or those who have not been in a training prison, or men with substantial sentences still to serve. The process is setting up both these prisoners and the prison to fail and needs to be amended to ensure that only men who do meet the profile are directed to Brixton.

Brixton continues to manage a prison population that includes a number of men over 70. The infrastructure of the prison is not geared to men with mobility impairments, nor does it have appropriate residential accommodation for the elderly and infirm. Better living conditions appropriate for frail men and those with mobility impairments is urgently required.

Prisoner pay varies across the estate depending on the other pressures on a prison's budget. This should be reviewed so that a standard amount can be provided across the estate, to match the standard costs of items available through canteen and of telephone calls.

sodexo
JUSTICE SERVICES

WOODTHORPE ROAD
ASHFORD, MIDDLESEX
TW15 3JZ

**HMP & YOI**
**BRONZEFIELD** Tel: 01784 425690

*For the latest reports on this prison please visit:*
https://tinyurl.com/bdfh26rv

*Important Changes:* **(1) Visits:** the identification necessary to access this prison and visit for social or professional purposes has changed; (2) **Money and Gifts** new rules now apply to these. See page 16 for full details of the above.

**Task of the establishment** Bronzefield is a women's resettlement and reception prison that also holds restricted status prisoners (those considered to require specific management arrangements). It is also the national hub for female offenders held under the Terrorism Act.

**Certified normal accommodation and operational capacity**
Women held at the time of inspection: 468
Baseline certified normal capacity: 527
In-use certified normal capacity: 527
Operational capacity: 542

**Population of the prison**
• An average of 120 new women received each month.

- 118 foreign national women.
- 31% of women from black and minority ethnic backgrounds.
- 114 women released into the community each month.
- 450 women receiving support for substance misuse.
- 300 women referred for mental health assessment each month.

### Prison status and key providers
Private – managed by: Sodexo
Prison Group: Custodial Contracts
Prison Group Director: Neil Richards
Director: Ian Whiteside / Gary Crossly (c)
IMB Chair: Alice Lean
Physical health provider: Sodexo
Mental health provider: Central and North West London NHS Foundation Trust
Substance misuse treatment provider: Sodexo
Prison education framework provider: Sodexo
Escort contractor: GeoAmey and Serco

**Brief history** Bronzefield opened in June 2004 and was the first purpose-built, privately operated prison for women. In 2016, it increased its capacity following the closure of HMP Holloway. It accepts women directly from over 90 courts.

### Short description of residential units
The prison comprises four house blocks:
House block 1: drug recovery unit, including reverse cohort unit (RCU) spaces
House block 2: early days in custody unit, including RCU spaces
House block 3: sentenced prisoners
House block 4: life-sentenced and enhanced level prisoners.
There are also a 12-bed mother and baby unit, an 18-bed health care inpatient facility and a 12-bed segregation unit.

### Visiting Information hmpbronzefield.co.uk
Booking: Residents make booking arrangements via the POD system on their house blocks.
Visiting Times - due to the Covid-19 pandemic visiting times are changing frequently so you will be advised when your visit is booked.

**Legal visits:** check with the prison for the latest information.

### INSPECTIONS & REPORTS
**HMCIP Report**
**Date of last inspection:** 24th January, 31st January - 4th February 2022
**Published 11th May 2022**
Bronzefield, the largest women's prison in the country, was badly affected by the death of a baby born to a mother in the prison in 2019. Since that tragedy and after the recent publication of the Prisons and Probation Ombudsman report into the case, there had been impressive action from leaders, particularly the deputy director, to respond to recommendations. This included setting clear standards within the prison and stronger partnership working with local maternity services.

At the time of our inspection there were 468 women held on four main house blocks. House block 1, which contained the drug treatment and detoxification wing, was noisy and unsettled, and the women housed there reported twice the levels of intimidation from their peers and abuse from staff than elsewhere in the jail.

Sodexo, which ran the prison, was also the education provider. This made for a much stronger connection than we often see, with the head of education sitting on the senior management team. Teachers had stayed on site throughout the pandemic, working on the wings when they were not allowed to open classrooms. Health care services, also run by Sodexo, needed to improve the management of medicines: it was disorganised and understaffed, which meant that some women did not get the right medication on time.

Leaders had shown impressive ambition in reopening services and increasing the amount of time women were spending out of their cells, with a recognition of the deleterious effects of protracted lockdowns on the mental health of prisoners. There remained, however, a large proportion of women who did not have jobs or attend education and were locked up for 20 hours a day, with further regime slippage at the weekend often leading to even less time out of cell.

The prison had worked hard to care for the many women with serious mental health difficulties. On the health care wing 11 of the 13 women had mental health problems and of those, three had already been assessed as requiring a place in a mental health facility and were waiting for a space. A dedicated team worked very hard to support these women, but they were not able to provide the treatment that they needed. The prison was collecting useful data on the number of women who had come to prison as a 'place of safety', either on remand or recall to custody. Many of these women should not have been in prison and were only there because there was insufficient provision in the community. This is a national problem that is worse in the women's estate and, because of its location, even more pronounced in Bronzefield.

Like all prisons that are in or close to London, Bronzefield struggled to recruit and hold on to prison officers. The director was aiming to make the selection process stronger so potential trainees had a better understanding of the job. He was also aiming to create a mentoring system that would offer support to officers in their first or second year in the job. Staff who filled out our survey, particularly those in their first year, were critical of the support they had had so far. The prison needed to dedicate considerable time and resource to improving the officer retention rate.

Far too many women left the prison without safe and stable accommodation and this meant that some were reluctant to leave, preferring prison to the uncertainties of freedom. One had even slept in the gatehouse for two nights

because she had nowhere else to go. Finding adequate housing and support for the many women with complex needs leaving Bronzefield must be a priority for the mayor of London, probation services and local authorities. Without stable, safe accommodation many women are liable to have mental health relapses, return to substance misuse and become involved in crime on release, creating more victims and, at great cost to the taxpayer, repeating the cycle and undoing the good work of the prison.

Bronzefield is a well-run prison with a strong, experienced director and leadership team who are committed to improving outcomes for women. They have shown a willingness to consider innovative ways to do this and desire to influence national policy. As Covid-19 restrictions are finally lifted, leaders will need to focus on supporting officers in front line roles to reassert clear behaviour management systems that challenge rule-breaking and provide meaningful incentives to promote good behaviour. Leaders will benefit from making better use of the data they collect to set targets and drive forward improvement. They will inevitably be disappointed with the scores in this inspection which have declined in the areas of respect and rehabilitation and release planning, but there is much to build on after a difficult two years.

Charlie Taylor HM Chief Inspector of Prisons
March 2022

## Safety

At the last inspection of Bronzefield in 2018 we found that outcomes for women were reasonably good against this healthy prison test.

At this inspection we found that outcomes for women remained reasonably good.

Women arriving at the prison received good individual support and interviews were appropriately focused on safety. Peer workers provided valuable help, which continued after women had left the induction unit.

Most officers knew women in their care well and interactions were positive. However, 54% of women on house block 1 reported verbal abuse from staff compared with 25% of women living on other house blocks. We saw minor rule breaking on most house blocks, such as vaping outside cells, which staff did not challenge. Some staff seemed to have accepted that rules would be broken or chose not to cause conflict by challenging them. Many women complained about staff's lack of consistency in their application of the rules. They also felt that staff overlooked quiet and compliant women and rewarded louder and more disruptive prisoners. Recorded rates of self-harm were 72% higher than at our previous inspection, but a small number of women accounted for almost two thirds of all incidents. Staff provided care for women at risk of self-harm proactively, appropriately focusing on enhanced support for those who repeatedly self-harmed. Data showed a reduction in the number of incidents over the previous few months.

The standard of assessment, care in custody and teamwork case management documents for prisoners at risk of suicide or self-harm was reasonably good, but the Listener scheme (in which prisoners trained by the Samaritans provide confidential emotional support to fellow prisoners) was well used, and women had good access to the Samaritans helpline. Lessons learned from women's attempts to take their own lives were shared to inform improvements.

In the previous two years, 86 women who were acutely unwell had been sent to the prison because of a lack of appropriate mental health provision in the community. Leaders at Bronzefield collected good quality data to demonstrate the extent of the problem.

The atmosphere in the prison was calm and, in our survey, 16% said they felt unsafe at the time of the inspection. The total number of assaults on staff had reduced by 40% and assaults between prisoners had reduced by 64% since the previous inspection. However, too many women reported having been victimised by other prisoners (61%) and staff (47%). The safer custody team focused on investigating and understanding the causes of violence, but a broader range of interventions to help further promote the safety of victims and to challenge perpetrators could have been introduced. The daily regime in the segregation unit was limited, but this was offset by prisoners being able to attend risk-assessed activities in the main prison. Reintegration planning took place, but some plans lacked detail and did not record prisoners' progress or outcomes. Quarterly meetings to monitor the use of segregation were held but were not multidisciplinary and generated little action.

The number of times force had been used in the

previous year had increased by approximately 25% compared to the same period before the previous inspection. The use of force committee provided limited oversight and did not do enough to identify or implement improvements. The availability of drugs remained a risk, and the prison did not have sufficient measures in place to detect drugs being brought in by new arrivals or staff.

## Respect

At the last inspection of Bronzefield in 2022 we found that outcomes for women were good against this healthy prison test.

At this inspection we found that outcomes for women were now reasonably good.

Visiting facilities were among the best we have seen. External areas of the prison were pleasant and well maintained, but exercise yards were bare. The prison was not overcrowded, and cells were relatively spacious and well equipped. Far more women than in other prisons said their cell bell was answered promptly. Although cell bells could be answered by phone, we were not confident that women who needed to be seen face-to-face always had this opportunity. The prison council was limited. Applications and complaints were managed reasonably well.

There were no self-catering facilities. In our survey, 47% of women thought the food was good; meanwhile, only 53% said the range of products available from the prison shop catered for their needs, which was significantly lower than at similar prisons (67%).

Leaders had shown a genuine commitment to addressing Prisons and Probation Ombudsman health recommendations related to the death of a baby born at the prison – they had developed a mental health perinatal team and enhanced working links with maternity services in the community.

Women had access to an appropriate range of primary care and gender specific services, which had reasonable waiting times. However, some aspects of long-term conditions management were weak, for example, some patients were not monitored effectively.

Mental health support had improved. The number of acutely mentally unwell women arriving at the prison had led to an increase in referrals to hospital under the Mental Health Act, but some transfers took too long. The social care needs of women were met well, and women with addiction problems received good support.

Many women experienced delays in receiving their medication. There were staff shortages in the pharmacy team as well as delays in the delivery of medicines. The governance of stock management was poor.

Waiting times for routine dental appointments had been reduced to about three weeks and emergency dental care continued to be provided throughout the pandemic.

Strategic oversight of diversity and equality had declined during the pandemic and the analysis and use of data were limited. Consultation with women with each protected and minority characteristic was limited. Discrimination incident reporting forms were readily available, and responses were appropriate but too often late.

In our survey, foreign national women were significantly more negative than other prisoners when they were asked if there was a member of staff they could turn to. Hibiscus, a social justice charity, helped them with various issues, and the prison made use of professional interpreting services. Support for transgender prisoners was good and the prison was in the process of creating more adapted cells to cater for women with physical disabilities.

The chaplaincy was involved in a range of work and had forged strong links with the local community to provide support on release. Corporate worship and faith-based classes had resumed but on a smaller scale.

## Purposeful activity

At the last inspection of Bronzefield in 2018 we found that outcomes for women were reasonably good against this healthy prison test.

At this inspection we found that outcomes for women remained reasonably good.

Ofsted carried out a progress monitoring visit of the prison alongside our full inspection and the purposeful activity judgement incorporates their assessment of progress.

Women who were involved in education, training or work had a reasonable amount of time out of their cells during the week. Unemployed women had a more negative experience as did those in the reverse cohort units (see Glossary) for whom time out of cell was poor. Weekend regimes were regularly curtailed due to staff shortages. In our survey, more women said they could go to the gym compared to those in other women's prisons, and access to the library was good.

Leaders enabled women to access purposeful activities throughout the Covid-19 restrictions and had pushed the provision as far as possible. There were sufficient education, skills and work places available for the whole population and waiting lists were very short. Most women benefited from a challenging curriculum, but attendance and punctuality at sessions was not consistently high. Peer mentors provided good support. The induction to education, skills and work was limited, as were careers advice and guidance for those due for release. Most women who took accredited courses in education and vocational training achieved them.

### Rehabilitation and release planning

At the last inspection of Bronzefield in 2018 we found that outcomes for women were good against this healthy prison test.

At this inspection we found that outcomes for women were now reasonably good.

The offender management, rehabilitation and resettlement strategy was up-to-date and based on a thorough needs analysis. The impact of trauma and abuse on women was increasingly being taken into account across many aspects of the support on offer, but only one domestic abuse support adviser was in post (instead of three). The Freedom Programme for survivors of abuse had restarted and training – to make sure staff and peer workers were trauma informed – was delivered, but the Street Safe forum for those connected with the sex industry had not yet resumed.

The offender management team provided good support with practical issues relating to finance, benefits and debt, but about 65% of sentenced women did not have sustainable accommodation on release. Home detention curfew processes were efficient, but external factors delayed some releases. 1.32 Despite the government's aim to improve women's access to open prison places nearer home, HM Prison and Probation Service (HMPPS) leaders had closed Bronzefield's semi-open prison unit. Use of release on temporary licence to promote family ties had been suspended for much of the pandemic and was slow to restart.

The standard of risk-management and sentence plans developed by the offender management unit was good. However, in some cases those managed by the National Probation Service did not relate directly to prisoners' risks or progression while in prison. Offender managers had maintained good contact with women throughout the Covid-19 restrictions. Women's resettlement needs were generally assessed soon after their reception, but there were too few staff to address them.

Women, including those with restricted status and some serving long sentences, lacked the opportunity to demonstrate progression at Bronzefield. However, the Eos programme (part of the national offender personality disorder services for women with highly complex needs) supported risk reduction for some of the highest risk women. Categorisation and allocation work was up to date, although women still could not provide direct input at board level. Public protection systems were robust and multi-

agency public protection arrangements were used effectively.

There was limited evidence of contact between the community offender manager and women to prepare for their release. The probation resettlement team in the prison was understaffed. Not all community through-the-gate services were up to speed with the volume of work. However, we saw some very good practical support offered to women being released: for example, community workers walked leavers to the railway station.

### Key concerns and recommendations

Key concerns and recommendations identify the issues of most importance to improving outcomes for women in prison and are designed to help establishments prioritise and address the most significant weaknesses in the treatment and conditions of women.

During this inspection we identified some areas of key concern and have made a small number of recommendations for the prison to address those concerns.

Key concern: In the previous two years, 86 women who were acutely mentally unwell had been sent to Bronzefield because of the lack of appropriate mental health provision in the community. The prison was not an appropriate place for these women as it was not equipped to manage their risks or needs.

Recommendation: Acutely mentally unwell women should be able to access appropriate assessment and diversion to mental health services instead of being sent to prison. (To the secretary of state)

Key concern: Low staffing levels within the pharmacy team were having an adverse effect on provision. The service had reverted to using stock medication instead of named-patient medicines. This, along with other issues, had caused delays in patients receiving their medication. Poor medicines stock control on the wings increased the risk of potential errors in administration. There were no reconciliation procedures for stock control, for example, the use of medicines stored in the out-of-hours cupboard was not audited. There was limited patient access to a pharmacist.

Recommendation: An adequately staffed pharmacy team should administer medicines to women on time and make sure medicines are managed safely and effectively. (To the director)

Key concern: There was a lack of management oversight of several aspects of health care. This included responses to health care complaints, checks on emergency equipment and the management of long-term conditions. Clinical oversight of external hospital appointments was not

sufficient to identify or address delays in treatment.
Recommendation: Oversight of responses to health care complaints and checks on emergency equipment should be improved, and long-term health conditions and access to external hospital appointments should be monitored to make sure women receive appropriate care. (To the director)
Key concern: Two full-time housing workers had been withdrawn from the prison following changes in the probation service and there had been a severe reduction in the size of the resettlement team and the loss of domestic abuse support workers.
Recommendation: Women's resettlement needs, including overcoming the impact of domestic abuse, should be addressed through comprehensive support from a well-resourced team. (To HMPPS)
Key concern: Based on the prison's data, about 65% of sentenced women did not have sustainable accommodation on release (lasting longer than 12 weeks), which was a concern, given the risks and needs of so many of the women.
Recommendation: All women should have sustainable accommodation on release.
(To HMPPS)
Key concern: Some women posing a high risk of harm to others, particularly restricted status women and those serving long or indeterminate sentences, found it difficult to progress. There was only one accredited programme available, and women found it hard to show progression by undertaking other structured interventions. Transfers to other prisons to complete interventions were not always easy to achieve.
Recommendation: Restricted status women and those serving long sentences should be able to demonstrate progression by completing accredited programmes or other structured therapeutic interventions. HMPPS should make sure that women are transferred to other prisons to complete risk-reduction work as part of an agreed progression plan. (To HMPPS)

**Notable positive practice**
We define notable positive practice as innovative work or practice that leads to particularly good outcomes from which other establishments may be able to learn. Inspectors look for evidence of good outcomes for women; original, creative or particularly effective approaches to problem-solving or achieving the desired goal; and how other establishments could learn from or replicate the practice.
Inspectors found five examples of notable positive practice during this inspection.
Early days peer workers offered women good support, which continued for up to 20 days after they had finished their induction and had left the

unit. Peer workers were also available in the library, while peer mentors were particularly effective in education, skills and work. They underwent rigorous training, and mentors were proud of their work. They provided excellent academic, practical and emotional support and women were extremely positively about them.
A weekly complex case meeting provided frontline staff with practical support in managing women with very complex needs.
The prison had good systems in place for identifying women who had been sent to the prison because of a lack of appropriate mental health provision in the community. Data collection was much better than we have found anywhere elsewhere.
The health care service had continued to provide testing and treatment for hepatitis C throughout the pandemic and had achieved hepatitis C micro-elimination status.
Through-the-gate support for women with mental health issues provided emotional and practical assistance on the day of their release and up to three months afterwards, enabling women to establish positive links and access help in the community.

## INDEPENDENT MONITORING BOARD: Annual Report
The law requires every prison to be monitored by an independent Board appointed by the Justice Secretary; these are known as Independent Monitoring Boards (IMBs). The IMB must satisfy itself as to the humane and just treatment of those held in custody within its prison and the range and adequacy of the programmes preparing them for release; it must report annually to the Justice Secretary on how well the prison has met the standards and requirements placed on it.

### IMB Annual Report 1 August 2020 – 31 July 2021
### Published December 2021
Executive summary
### Background to the report
The Covid-19 national framework for prison regimes and services has been in place throughout the reporting year. For around four months, between December and April, the prison was in stage 4 (lockdown).
At the end of the reporting year, the prison was in stage 3 (restricted) regime, with two positive Covid-19 cases in the prisoner population and two cases amongst staff. Insufficiently high levels of staff testing were one of the factors preventing a move to stage 2 (reduced) regime.

## Main judgements
### How safe is the prison?

It is the Board's perception that HMP/YOI Bronzefield is a physically safe environment.

The prison has managed the spread of Covid-19 within the prisoner population efficiently. A total of 58 prisoners tested positive in the reporting year and it is believed that the majority contracted the virus in the community.

There have been further steep increases in the incidences of self-harm. The incidences have increased from a monthly average of 91 in 2017/18 and 141 in 2018/19 to 175 incidents in 2019/20 and 220 in this reporting year with a monthly peak of 375 incidents in August 2020. The average number of self-harmers has also increased from 28 in 2017/18 to 42 in 2019/20 and 44 in this reporting year.

### How fairly and humanely are prisoners treated?

The effect of the severe Covid-19 pandemic restrictions in place for most of the reporting year has been amplified by staff absences and inexperienced officers. This has compromised the prison's ability to treat prisoners fairly and humanely at all times.

Many prisoners reported to the Board that they have felt 'safe' and 'well-cared' for by the staff during the Covid crisis.

### How well are prisoners' health and wellbeing needs met?

The prison continues to be used as a place of safety for women with serious complex and enduring mental health conditions. These women put severe pressure on the healthcare unit and residential houseblock staff.

The prison continues to carry out a comprehensive Covid-19 vaccination programme in line with the community. Prisoners are strongly encouraged to participate. At the end of the reporting year 48% of the prisoners at HMP/YOI Bronzefield had had their first vaccination and 29% their second vaccination.

### How well are prisoners progressed towards successful resettlement?

The number of sentenced prisoners released without safe and secure accommodation increased from 60% (findings in an IMB survey in February 2020) to 77% (as recorded by the prison) in July 2021.

## Main areas for development
### TO THE MINISTER

Given the importance to rehabilitation of safe and secure accommodation on release, why, with the termination of community rehabilitation company (CRC) contracts at the end of June 2021,

have in-prison accommodation services been removed from HMP/YOI Bronzefield? What urgent action is being taken to address this issue? Why has the Minister not considered the problem of drugs getting into prisons in the women's estate sufficient to introduce enhanced gate security?

### TO THE PRISON SERVICE

The number of self-harm incidents has escalated to an average of 220 incidents each month in the reporting year. How is the prison service supporting the prison to manage this high level of risk on an urgent and long-term basis?

### TO THE DIRECTOR

Following the comparison of a sample of canteen prices with two other prisons, HMP/YOI Bronzefield's prices were shown to be the highest, with products up to 15% more expensive. What steps are being taken to remedy this issue?

### TO THE MAYOR OF LONDON

The Board wishes to restate the question from our 2017/18, 2018/19 and 2019/20 annual reports: What has the mayor's office for policing and crime done in the last year to increase the availability of accommodation for those women who leave prison with no fixed abode?

### Progress since the last report

60 in-cell telephones have been replaced during the reporting year. This has enabled consistent communication for prisoners with their family, friends and prison staff during the pandemic.

There has been an improvement in the transfer of severely mentally unwell prisoners to secure inpatient mental health hospitals.

Following the death of the newborn baby of a prisoner in custody in September 2019 a comprehensive pregnancy action plan has been put in place. All confirmed and suspected pregnant women are referred into the revised perinatal pathway.

The prison received an award for achieving elimination of hepatitis C amongst the prisoners and for exceeding the national average for hepatitis C testing.

**BUCKLEY HALL ROAD**
**ROCHDALE**
**LANCS**
**OL12 9DP**

**Tel: 01706 514300**

*For the latest reports on this prison please visit:*
https://tinyurl.com/bdfh26rv

*Important Changes:* **(1) Visits:** the identification necessary to access this prison and visit for social or professional purposes has changed; (2) **Money and Gifts** new rules now apply to these. See page 16 for full details of the above.

**Task of the establishment** Category C adult male training prison holding prisoners sentenced to four years and over.

### Certified normal accommodation and operational capacity
Prisoners held at the time of inspection: 448
Baseline certified normal capacity: 409
In-use certified normal capacity: 409
Operational capacity: 459

### Prison status and key providers
Public
Prison Group: Greater Manchester, Merseyside & Cheshire
Prison Group Director: Tim Allen
Governor/Director: Robbie Durgan
IMB Chair: John Warburton
Mental health provider: Greater Manchester Mental Health NHS Foundation Trust
Substance use treatment provider:
Delphi Medical Ltd
Learning and skills provider: Novus
Escort contractors: GeoAmey

### Brief history
HMP Buckley Hall is a training prison for male prisoners, on the edge of the Pennines, near Rochdale, Lancashire.
The prison has four residential blocks and an operational capacity of 459. Although this makes it relatively small in numbers, the Board regards this as a strength and not a weakness of the prison. Before the onset of lockdown, Buckley Hall was operating overall as a level 3 prison in the annual prison performance ratings.
The induction unit for new prisoners is on one side of C Wing, and the Aspire unit on the other. The Aspire unit houses some 60 prisoners who are either complex or serving an indeterminate prison sentence and celebrated its second anniversary in October 2020. The prison is in the process of developing the drug recovery work already taking place on A wing and establishing an incentivised substance-free living unit.
The prison opened in 1994 as one of four contracted-out prisons and was managed by Group 4 for a period of five years. In 2000, a 10-year contract was put out for tender and won by the Prison Service. During this period, the prison held category C men, then women for two years and then category C men again. In 2011, the Prison Service was successful in its bid to continue providing a category C male prison. In October 2019, the prison celebrated its 25th anniversary.
In 2014, Buckley Hall was designated as a non-resettlement training prison, holding male prisoners with sentences of four years or more. According to the Bromley Briefing papers, 16% of the sentenced prison population are serving an indeterminate sentence whereas the figure for Buckley Hall is twice this number.
A number of services within the prison are subcontracted and among them are: Education and Library: Novus (formerly The Manchester College) Healthcare: Greater Manchester Mental Health NHS Foundation Trust (GMMH)
Visitors Reception: Partners of Prisoners and Families (POPS)
Drug & Alcohol Recovery: Delphi
Facilities: Amey.

### Short description of residential units
A wing - 110 beds; one spur is normal accommodation and the other is the drug and alcohol recovery unit
B wing - 120 beds, normal accommodation
C wing - 120 beds, one spur is the first night centre and induction and the other is the Aspire unit
D wing- 59 beds, normal accommodation.

### Visiting Information
Visits Telephone 01706 514350
**Visits:** Monday to Thursday: 2pm to 4pm, Saturday and Sunday: 9:30am to 11:30am and 2pm to 4.30pm

### Legal visits:
Email: legalvisits.buckleyhall@justice.gov.uk
Booking line: 01706 514 350
Monday, Wednesday and Friday, 9:30am to 11:30am and 1pm to 4pm, Tuesday and Thursday, 9:30am to 11:30am

### INSPECTIONS & REPORTS
**Date of last inspection:** 15–26 July 2019
**Published 05 November 2019**
Notable features from this inspection
• Levels of violence had halved in the last 12 months.
• Almost 60% of prisoners were serving sentences of more than 10 years.

• Almost 70% of prisoners were assessed as high risk of harm to others.
• The Aspire unit was one of four national progression regimes for indeterminate sentence prisoners.

HMP Buckley Hall is a category C training prison located near Rochdale in Lancashire. A relatively modern facility, the prison was rebuilt and reopened in 1995. Comprising four house blocks, the prison can hold just over 450 adult male prisoners (459) and, at the time of our inspection, was full, with a population ranging in age and sentence length. Of those held, however, nearly a third were serving indeterminate sentences and 45 men were serving life.

This was an excellent inspection and we are pleased to report that we judged outcomes for prisoners to be 'good' – our highest assessment – in three of our four tests of a healthy prison. Our one concern was that more work was still needed to improve the quality and outcomes of education and work. Our assessments also recognised and recorded significant improvement since our last inspection in 2016.

Buckley Hall is a very safe prison. Reception and induction arrangements were thorough and our survey suggested they were appreciated by prisoners. Our survey also indicated that just 7% of respondents reported feeling unsafe, which was very low and much lower than in comparable establishments. Recorded violence and use of force had reduced since our previous inspection and work to reduce it further was robust and multi-disciplinary, with initiatives informed by good data and leading to good practice. The rehabilitative ethos that pervaded the prison was, in our view, key to the quality of engagement seen among prisoners, which in turn was reflected in the calm and settled atmosphere in the prison and the sense of well-being expressed by many of those we spoke to.

The application of security was generally proportionate but more needed to be done to reduce the availability of illicit substances. The number of positive mandatory drug tests for the six months prior to our inspection stood at 15%, although notably comparatively few were for psychoactive substances, reflecting some very good multidisciplinary work and health promotion initiatives intended to combat this problem.

Self-harm had increased since our last inspection but remained comparatively low. Tragically there had also been one self-inflicted death. Work to reduce self-harm and support those in crisis was very good. The prison's approach was multidisciplinary, based on evidence and good supervision but, most importantly, afforded men in need of support good quality of care.

Staff-prisoner relationships were a strength.

Some 88% of prisoners told us they felt respected and we saw lots of evidence of a confident, caring and supportive staff group. The key worker scheme was embedded and effective with nearly all prisoners telling us they had a personal officer and 78% telling us they thought their personal officer was useful. Living conditions were generally very good, the prisoners were very positive about the food and work to deal with complaints or ensure meaningful consultation with prisoners was effective. The promotion of equality and diversity was similarly much improved and based on a good understanding of need and useful consultation, while ensuring reasonably equitable outcomes and perceptions among groups with protected characteristics. Primary health care, substance misuse services and mental health support was good, with some excellent elements.

Time out of cell for prisoners remained very good and much better than we often see. Daily routines, including evening association four times a week, were delivered in accordance with published routines and access to library and gym facilities was also good. The quality of education, work and skills provision had, however, deteriorated and our colleagues in Ofsted rated the overall effectiveness of provision as 'requires improvement'. Engagement by prisoners in activity and learning was excellent, but recent improvements to provision had yet to have sufficient impact and the quality of teaching and learning, as well as achievements and progress made by learners, needed to be better.

Work to support and promote family ties was excellent. Work to reduce the risk of reoffending was similarly very good and despite many prisoners presenting a high risk of harm, assessments (OASYs) were reasonably up to date, and all prisoners had a sentence plan. Most men understood their objectives and contact with prison offender managers was better than we often see. In our survey prisoners indicated that they thought their experiences at the prison had made them less likely to offend in the future. Buckley Hall was not a resettlement prison but for the few who were released there was good one-to-one engagement and resettlement support. Re-categorisation arrangements were managed well and men who qualified could move on to open prisons promptly. Public protection arrangements were robust.

Buckley Hall is a very good prison. It had got the basics right and there was meaningful attention to detail that supported good outcomes for those detained. Prisoners could see this, and were personally incentivised to respond positively. Work undertaken throughout the prison was usually multi-disciplinary, and often based on useful evidence and an effective use of data and subject to effective governance and oversight. A culture of respect and rehabilitation, led from the top, permeated all aspects of the prison's work and culture, and was a quality that seemed to be embraced by all departments. Good leadership and a confident and respectful staff had achieved much through hard work, underpinned by an ethos and culture they had created. They should be congratulated.

Peter Clarke, HM Chief Inspector of Prisons
September 2019

## INDEPENDENT MONITORING BOARD: Annual Report

The law requires every prison to be monitored by an independent Board appointed by the Justice Secretary; these are known as Independent Monitoring Boards (IMBs). The IMB must satisfy itself as to the humane and just treatment of those held in custody within its prison and the range and adequacy of the programmes preparing them for release; it must report annually to the Justice Secretary on how well the prison has met the standards and requirements placed on it.

### IMB Report 1 August 2020 – 31 July 2021
### Published November 2021
### Executive summary
### Background to the report

This reporting year to July 2021 on HMP Buckley Hall has been dominated and defined by Covid-19. Prison management has managed a turbulent and uncertain reporting year which began with a lockdown, followed by a period where some of the restrictions were relaxed, then the reintroduction of lockdown and, finally, some easing again of restrictions. In the judgement of the Board, the prison is ably led by an experienced, approachable and committed Governor and Deputy Governor. However, in this uncertain and changing environment they have been far from in control of their own destiny. Staff and managers at Buckley Hall have coped by drawing heavily on their traditional reserves of 'can do' and 'getting on with it'. A senior manager summed the prevailing attitude neatly as 'all in its stride'.

Nevertheless, the effect of Covid on staff should not be under-estimated and during the reporting year, a number have expressed some degree of physical and emotional fatigue and drop in resilience. Those who manage the staff detail have told the Board that it has become increasingly difficult to find replacement cover for absent staff, even with the offer of Payment Plus overtime.

Between April 2020 and July 2021, there were 105 positive Covid-19 tests among staff. In the peak months of October 2020 to February 2021, there were an average of 18.6 positive tests per month, with the peak in January 2021 of 37. These numbers inevitably impacted on the daily regime and it is to the credit of the vast majority of the prisoners at Buckley Hall that they accepted the restrictions with fortitude and good grace.

No aspect of prison life has been unaffected by Covid-19 and, looking to the future, it seems likely that some of the lessons learned during the reporting year will have a permanent impact on the prison landscape. For example, a return to HMIP's ambition for prisoners to be out of cell for at least 10 hours a day seems a most unlikely possibility. In addition, a number of officers and prison managers believe that most prisoners prefer an earlier evening lock-up. It is said the men prefer the quiet and safety of their own cell and will accept a reduced time out of cell in the evenings as long as their contact with family, showers, telephone, food and work/employment is sufficient. The Board's own random survey of prisoners revealed that the majority asked concur with this view.

From April 2020 to July 2021, there were 87 positive Covid-19 tests among the prisoners and in the peak months of January and February 2021, 39 and 26 positive cases were recorded. Fortunately, there have been no fatalities. Healthcare staff have been proactive in encouraging the men to have the Covid vaccine and at the end of the reporting year, 59% of the prisoners had received their second dose. There has been some resistance to receiving the vaccine among the men and on the same date it was reported that 30% of the men had declined the vaccine. As in the community the decline rate tends to be higher among younger prisoners.

During the reporting year, senior management introduced, a significant change to the format of the daily briefing and as a consequence, these briefings have become far more detailed and informative. The meetings between governors and prisoner Covid representatives have continued throughout the reporting year and provided a valuable two-way channel of communication. In addition to using the electronic kiosk for community notices, the prison has also made effective use of the Wayout TV channel to communicate information and updates to the men.

In the last four months of the reporting year, the prison incurred Covid-related costs in excess of £25,000 and the Board is concerned because this will not attract any additional funding and a considerable sum of money will have to be resourced locally from the existing prison's budget.

**Main judgements**
**How safe is the prison?**
The Board judges Buckley Hall to be a safe environment for the prisoners.

**How fairly and humanely are prisoners treated?**
Positive and constructive relationships between staff and prisoners have been an undoubted strength of the prison in the past. Because of Covid restrictions over the reporting year, this contact between staff and prisoners has been reduced but, it is to be hoped, this situation will improve as lockdown conditions are eased. The emphasis in the prison from the top down on treating prisoners with 'fairness and decency' remains central to its mission.

**How well are prisoners' health and wellbeing needs met?**
The Board considers the provision of health and wellbeing to have been good over the reporting year.

**How well are prisoners progressed towards successful resettlement?**
The lack of movement to open prisons and the restricted numbers on the courses in programmes have led to some considerable frustration for men wishing to progress during the reporting year. Unfortunately, any resolution of this situation has not been within the prison's control.

**Main areas for development**
**TO THE MINISTER**
Ensure the return of the independent adjudicator.
Endeavour to reduce the number of prisoners with indeterminate public protection (IPP) sentences.

**TO THE PRISON SERVICE**
Ensure the speedy resumption of moves to open and resettlement prisons.
Provide sufficient additional funding for the new integrated drug recovery wing.
Install in-cell telephony.
Provide secure medication in-cell facilities.
Improve the transfer of prisoners' monies between prisons in the private and public sector.

**TO THE GOVERNOR**
Review the criteria for prisoners to reside on D wing.
Ensure that all prisoners have ready access to a cell courtesy key.
Improve the playback facilities for the use of force assurance committee.
Increase the number of key work sessions as soon as is practical.
Install CCTV in the healthcare waiting area.
Increase the number of prisoners enrolled on programmes courses.

Review the decision to confiscate Sony Giga Jukes from newly arriving prisoners.
Review the operation of the current challenge, support and intervention plan (CSIP) scheme.
Ensure that the cell-bell call data is downloaded and monitored.
Improve the prisoner showers on the wing.
Provide newly arriving prisoners with a means of transporting their property to the wings.

**Progress since the last report**
• The introduction of a body scanner in reception to reduce the number of illegal items being smuggled into Buckley Hall by prisoners
• The efforts made to improve the cleanliness of the wings
• The erection of a car park barrier and fob entry system to reduce the likelihood of vandalism to staff cars noted in last year's annual report
• The detailed and informative daily briefings
• Increased use of body-worn video cameras by staff.
• Improved monitoring of prisoner complaints

PATRICK HAUGH ROAD
BICESTER
OXON
OX25 1PZ

**HM PRISON BULLINGDON**    Tel: 01869 353100

*For the latest reports on this prison please visit:*
https://tinyurl.com/bdfh26rv

*Important Changes:* **(1) Visits:** the identification necessary to access this prison and visit for social or professional purposes has changed; (2) **Money and Gifts** new rules now apply to these. See page 16 for full details of the above.

**Task of the establishment** HMP Bullingdon is a local and resettlement prison for Thames Valley and Hampshire. It serves the courts of Oxfordshire, Berkshire and Wiltshire.

**Certified normal accommodation and operational capacity**
Prisoners held at the time of inspection: 1,060
Baseline certified normal capacity: 869
In-use certified normal capacity: 869
Operational capacity: 1,114

**Prison status and key providers**
Public
Prison Group: South Central
Prison Group Director: Andy Lattimore
Governor/Director: Laura Sapwell
IMB Chair: Vicki Talbot

Physical health provider: Care UK
Mental health provider: Care UK
Substance use treatment provider: Inclusion
Learning and skills provider: Milton Keynes College
Escort contractor: GeoAmey

**Brief history** HMP Bullingdon is a local and resettlement prison situated near Bicester in Oxfordshire. During the reporting year the process of reconfiguration has continued. This means that it now holds a larger number of prisoners on remand (up to 45% of its population) than it did before reconfiguration began. Most of these prisoners will transfer to other establishments if they are convicted. Many will appear at court hearings by video-link from the prison. It also means that Bullingdon now serves a larger number of courts than before reconfiguration. Therefore, an increasing number of prisoners who will be released to the areas served by those courts are moved back to Bullingdon for the end of their sentences, provided that they have at least three months to serve. This means that an increasing number of prisoners are serving shorter stays in the prison. The high level of turnover ('churn') leads to various problems, in particular with regard to progression and resettlement.

The prison continues to hold some young adults and sex offenders under treatment. About 15% of the prisoners are foreign national prisoners (FNPs). The prison's certified normal accommodation is 869, but its normal operational capacity (permitted maximum number of prisoners) was 1,077, increased to 1,081 on 27 June 2021. It is planned to return it to its pre-pandemic level of 1,114 by January 2022. Average occupancy during the reporting year was 1,034. This is to be compared with 1,057 for April-June 2020 (after the onset of Covid-19) and 1,068 for July 2020-March 2021. The averages were 1054 for the year to June 2019 and 1,109 for the year to June 2018. These high levels mean that many prisoners share cells that were designed for only one occupant.

**Short description of residential units**
Arncott unit – general population, including the support and mentoring unit on A3 spur
Blackthorn unit – general population
Charndon unit – general population, including the drug recovery unit on C2 spur
Dorton unit – general population
Edgcott unit – prisoners convicted of sexual offences Finmere unit – the first night centre
Segregation unit
Health care inpatient unit

**Visiting Information**
You can book your visit by email or telephone.
Email: socialvisits.bullingdon@justice.gov.uk
Telephone: 01869 353 176, Monday to Friday (except Public Holidays) 9:30am to 11:30am, 1:30pm to 4pm.
**Visiting times:** Every day except Friday: 1.45pm to 4pm

**Legal visits:** Available to book.

**INSPECTIONS & REPORTS**
**Date of last inspection:** 1–12 July 2019
**HMCIP Report, published 15 October 2019**
HMP Bullingdon is a local and resettlement prison for men and young adult male prisoners, situated some 15 miles north of Oxford. At the time of this inspection, it held around 1,050 prisoners, around a quarter of whom were unsentenced. The prison was last inspected in May 2017, when we found that outcomes for prisoners were not sufficiently good in all four of our healthy prison tests. At this inspection, we found that our judgements in safety and respect had both improved, to reasonably good. It was notable that since the last inspection, when chronic staff shortages had led to the prison struggling to deliver even basic services, an injection of new staff had arrived. Although this meant that some 75% of staff had less than two years' service, our sense was that new staff were being well supported, and their presence was contributing to the prison being under control and feeling well ordered. Seventy per cent of prisoners told us that they were treated respectfully by staff.

Levels of violence had risen substantially overall since the last inspection, but there had been some welcome reductions in recent months. More needed to be done to understand precisely which aspects of violence reduction work were having an impact. Our survey also showed that 61% of prisoners had felt unsafe at some point during their time at Bullingdon, and 32% felt unsafe at the time of the inspection. These are high figures, and the perceptions need to be understood.

Even though there were indications that illicit drugs were becoming harder to obtain, the fact remained that more than half of the prisoners believed it was easy to get hold of them, and around one in five said that they had acquired a drug habit since coming into Bullingdon. An overarching drug supply reduction strategy needed to be implemented, and more suspicion testing carried out.

There was too much overcrowding at the prison. Some 23% of cells which were designed to hold one prisoner were actually holding two. This meant that around 400 prisoners were in cramped and overcrowded accommodation, which, when combined with the fact that we found around a third of prisoners locked up during the working day, had a highly damaging impact on living conditions.

It was disappointing to see that there was very little focus on equality. There was a real need for senior leaders to take personal responsibility for driving this forward, initiating action and ensuring that every aspect of prison life was scrutinised for signs of disproportion or inequality. Alongside this work, there needed to be regular monitoring of data and focused efforts to understand the more negative perceptions held by minorities.

It was heartening to find that health care had improved since the last inspection, and now provided a generally very good service.

Our colleagues from Ofsted found that, overall, the provision of education, skills and work required improvement. The details of their findings can be seen in the report, but it was particularly concerning to find that there were insufficient activity places for the population, with a shortfall of around 400 places. Some 140 prisoners were unemployed, and only 65% of all prisoners were allocated to an activity, either full- or part-time.

In terms of rehabilitation and release planning, it was good to find that arrangements for visits had improved. However, we had some very serious concerns about other aspects. For instance, the situation at Bullingdon in terms of the use of the offender assessment system (OASys) was yet another example of a prison failing to adhere to this vital corporate policy requirement. OASys documentation sits at the heart of offender management, sentence planning and progression, risk management and preparation for release. Despite this, we found that only half of eligible prisoners had OASys documentation, meaning that some 300 prisoners had none at all. There was a shortage of probation officers at the prison, and little realistic prospect of either recruiting more or dealing with the huge backlog of forms. I have often said that the OASys procedures appear to be at risk of collapse across the Prison Service, and the weaknesses at Bullingdon gave a stark example of this.

The situation was made worse by the fact that many high-risk prisoners received little or no offender supervisor contact. To compound matters, public protection arrangements were poor. The interdepartmental risk management team was ineffective, and multi-agency public protection arrangements (MAPPA) risk levels were often not confirmed before a prisoner was released. The danger that high-risk prisoners could be released in an unsafe way was very real,

and heightened by failures to monitor and restrict inappropriate communications, and the fact that a third of prisoners were released to accommodation that was not considered to be sustainable.

Despite these very serious issues, we found that Bullingdon was a prison that had made some significant improvements. It can continue to do so, as it now has far more staff than at the time of the last inspection. The achievement of our recommendations since the last inspection was at a level that we have come to recognise as reasonable, at around half being achieved or partly achieved. I would of course encourage prison leaders, drawing on the energy and enthusiasm of new staff and the experience of existing colleagues, to aim higher, and give themselves a realistic chance of making further progress.

Peter Clarke CVO OBE QPM August 2019
HM Chief Inspector of Prisons

### INDEPENDENT MONITORING BOARD: Annual Report

The law requires every prison to be monitored by an independent Board appointed by the Justice Secretary; these are known as Independent Monitoring Boards (IMBs). The IMB must satisfy itself as to the humane and just treatment of those held in custody within its prison and the range and adequacy of the programmes preparing them for release; it must report annually to the Justice Secretary on how well the prison has met the standards and requirements placed on it.

**IMB Report 1 July 2020 – 30 June 2021**
**Published December 2021**
**Executive summary**
**Background to the report**

The Covid-19 outbreak has had a significant impact on the Board's ability to gather information and discuss the contents of this annual report. The Board has therefore tried to cover as much ground as it can in these difficult circumstances, but inevitably there is less detail and supporting evidence than usual. Ministers are aware of these constraints. Regular information was collected specifically on the prison's response to the pandemic, and that was collated nationally.

**Staff matters**

As of 30 June 2021, Bullingdon had 316 uniformed staff, operational support staff, prison officers, supervisory officers and custodial managers. Twenty-three of these officers were either in their first (probationary) year, having completed the initial 12-week training course Prison Officer Entry Level Training (POELT)), or were waiting to begin the course. Thirty officers had experience of under two years, and 263 officers (including supervisory officers and custodial managers) had experience of two or more years. Between 1 July 2020 and 30 June 2021, 59 prison officers left Bullingdon: 36 of these officers resigned, and the other 23 either transferred to other establishments, retired, or were dismissed.

Eight members of staff received awards for long service and good conduct.

Information technology (IT) systems in the prison continued to be slow and unreliable, and often made it very difficult for staff to carry out routine tasks. This had a bearing on safety and security, and on sentence progression, since it was an impediment to keeping records up-to-date. The recent introduction of electronic recording of use of force (UoF) and complaints has put even greater strain on the prison's IT systems.

Review of safety in the prison by the regional safety team

A review was carried out by the regional safety team in September 2020. One of the principal findings was that the prison had failed to implement the majority of the recommendations which the Prisons and Probation Ombudsman (PPO) had made in its reports on cases of alleged suicide in the prison. Although several enquiries have been made by the IMB, it has not been possible to identify an action plan or what actions have been taken by the prison to address the recommendations made since the report was published (October 2020).

### Audit of safe custody

This audit was carried out in May 2021 by the central performance group. In most respects the judgements made were no better than 'adequate', although it was acknowledged that allowances were needed because of the impact of Covid-19. The main aspects identified as in need of improvements were quality assurance (QA) (better application of available processes), induction (need for more local relevance), risk assessment on entry (better information required), and higher standards of monitoring and managing those most at risk of self-harm.

### Ofsted interim visit

An Ofsted interim visit was conducted remotely on 23-24 February 2021. Ofsted noted that leaders and managers had responded appropriately to providing education, training and work where lockdown restrictions permitted and had well- developed plans to restart face-to-face-teaching. Recommendations included the need to improve the quality of learning packs and to provide training for teachers in delivering remote blended learning.

### Prison life during a pandemic

The IMB's annual report for the year to 30 June 2020 explained how changes to the running of the prison, arising from the need to prevent the spread of Covid-19, had been introduced in the period from March to June 2020. There had been three significant changes: firstly, the ending of social visits and of access to the library and the gym, secondly the curtailment of outside agencies providing education and vocational training and work, and thirdly the implementation of a very restrictive national regime to help to maintain social distancing as far as possible for both prisoners and staff; this resulted in many prisoners having to spend 23 hours a day in their cells.

These restrictions continued to apply in this reporting year although there was a certain amount of variation in the severity of the restrictions. The prison was successful in keeping the prison largely free from Covid-19 until January 2021.

Social visits were suspended periodically during the reporting year. In July, a system of visits by video link (Purple Visits) was established. After a slow start the popularity of such visits increased. It is intended that after the Covid-19 restrictions have been lifted, these visits will continue and operate alongside in-person social visits.

Education and vocational training and work opportunities continued to be adversely affected by the Covid-19 restrictions during the reporting year. Until December 2020, education packs were delivered and returned to prisoners by tutors at the cell door, but between January and April 2021 the tutors were not able to go on to the wings. From April to June 2021 the packs were once again delivered and returned to prisoners by tutors at the cell door.

Many prisoners continued to have to spend 23 hours a day in their cells. In many cases they left their cells only to collect meals and medication, and to take showers and exercise on a restricted basis. Staff continued to make daily welfare checks on prisoners with the cell door open to provide direct communication with the prisoners, but this led to long periods of isolation for many prisoners with minimal access to facilities and much reduced scope for exercise and social interaction. The pressure for prisoners to share cells designed for single occupancy is likely to continue.

The pressures outlined above led to an exceptionally difficult week beginning on 12 April about which the Bullingdon IMB Chair wrote to the IMB regional representative. Following a difficult weekend, there had been 42 men on assessment, care in custody and teamwork (ACCTs), five prisoners on constant watch and five incidents of serious self-harm on one day. The separation, segregation and care unit (SSCU) had reached its maximum capacity of 20 prisoners. Healthcare held 16 prisoners but 10 of these were on ACCTs. Nine ambulances were called to the prison and there were serious staff shortages in healthcare. This unsafe situation was attributable to a range of factors: frustration of prisoners who had been under lockdown for months, exhausted and inexperienced staff, and poor healthcare provision due to staff shortages. These staff shortages had been exacerbated by a dispute with agency staff arising from recent national changes to tax regulations. The regional representative shared these concerns with the National Chair of the Independent Monitoring Boards who forwarded them to the Minister in a letter in May 2021. Since then, the situation has improved: the dispute with the healthcare agency staff has been resolved and the Governor has put in place a recruitment strategy for mental health staff. However, the broad concerns of the IMB remain.

On the more positive side, the recently installed in-cell telephones (with extra personal information number (PIN) credits for prisoners for the duration of the pandemic) and additional telephones on the main wings and elsewhere have continued to work well. These helped to facilitate contact between the prisoners and their families and between the prison staff and prisoners.

There has been little success in decreasing the prison population, despite the reduction of its operational capacity because of Covid-19. Significant numbers have been brought back into prison on recall, often for very short periods of between seven and 14 days, so that they never leave the part of the induction unit in which all newly arrived prisoners are quarantined.

Some prisoners were appointed as Covid-19 peer representatives. They have met regularly with the deputy governor, and then spoken with other prisoners, helping to inform and reassure them. Prison television and radio were also used to communicate messages to prisoners.

## Main judgements
### How safe is the prison?

This is the sixth consecutive year in which the Board has reported concerns about safety in the prison. Levels of violence increased marginally in the reporting year when they might have been expected to reduce because of the Covid-19 restrictions, and are still far too high. A large number of drugs was found in the prison. On the positive side, in September 2020 a body scanner was installed in reception, and this has been successful in reducing the number of drugs coming into the prison. Also, in April 2021 an airport-style scanner was installed at the gate used on entry by all staff and visitors. However, the number of drugs coming into the prison is still high.

In early April 2021, owing to a combination of factors, the prison was in such an unsafe situation that the IMB Chair wrote to the IMB regional representative to set out the Board's concerns at the situation. These concerns were passed on to the Minister in a letter in May 2021.

### How fairly and humanely are prisoners treated?

Although the prison has made efforts to treat prisoners as fairly and humanely as possible, these efforts have been frustrated by the Covid-19 restrictions. The Board questions whether it is fair or humane for prisoners to have to share cells which were designed for single occupancy, especially since prisoners eat meals and use the toilet in their cells. This chronic problem arising from overcrowding has been exacerbated by measures that the Prison Service introduced as part of its attempt to minimise the spread of infection during the pandemic, which meant that most prisoners spent 23 hours in their cells each day.

The Board is not fully confident that the prison has done all that it could to eliminate discrimination, although recent revisions in procedures are starting to improve the collection and interpretation of data related to equality issues.

There is a poor level of written communication with prisoners. When notices to prisoners (NTPs) are sent out, they are put on a noticeboard on the wings, but during Covid-19 some prisoners found it difficult to look at noticeboards, and some prisoners are unable to read. Also, some NTPs have been sent out giving very little notice of actions which are about to take place.

### How well are prisoners' health and wellbeing needs met?

The efforts of the prison to meet prisoners' health and wellbeing needs have been severely hampered by the Covid-19 restrictions.

The recruitment and retention of healthcare staff have remained an issue. National changes to tax regulations also impacted on and decreased the supply of agency and bank staff during the latter part of the reporting year.

An internal audit in August 2020 identified too many cases of mislaid prescriptions and delays in administration of medications. Waiting lists for dentistry and for both urgent and routine appointments with GPs and nurses have been unacceptably long, although to some extent this has been caused by Covid-19 restrictions and is therefore a direct consequence of the pandemic. The mental health team does not offer counselling. Volunteer counsellors have not been able to visit the prison during much of the year due to Covid-19 restrictions.

There are some prisoners whose mental health is such that the prison is not equipped to cope with them; it is very likely that they need to be sent to secure psychiatric institutions instead.

### How well are prisoners progressed towards successful resettlement?

Covid-19 restrictions have frustrated the prison's efforts in this regard. Education courses were suspended for the period July-September 2020. A programme of in-cell learning was then implemented, with most education having to be conducted remotely, although some education classes were reintroduced from May 2021.

Vocational training and work also suffered in so far as some workshops remained closed and numbers of prisoners working in the remaining workshops and on the wings were reduced in order to meet social distancing requirements.

The offender management in custody (OMiC) system continued to function on a reduced scale within Covid-19 restrictions, but offending behaviour programmes were severely curtailed for most of the year because of the restrictions.

The increasing number of prisoners on remand or serving shorter sentences leading to greater churn has frustrated the prison's efforts to progress prisoners towards successful resettlement. In many cases, prisoners are not able to complete education courses before release. Also, in many cases prisoners are not able to progress from unskilled work to skilled work or, if they do, to finish any training courses that they undertake as part of that skilled work. On a more positive note, the prison has been selected to take part in the reducing reoffending accelerator (RRA) project and it is hoped that this will result in improved job prospects for prisoners upon release.

### Main areas for development

There are some prisoners in Bullingdon whose state of mental health is such that the prison is not equipped to cope with them; it is very likely that they need to be sent to secure psychiatric institutions instead. Some of these prisoners have spent far longer in the SSCU than 42 days, after which continued segregation has to be reported to regional management, and some of them have repeatedly self-harmed. What steps will the Minister take to ensure that such prisoners are no longer sent to the prison?

There continues to be a high proportion of staff with limited experience. How will the Minister ensure that experienced staff levels are maintained at adequate levels, and what can the Minister do to enhance the training that all staff receive?

The continuing reconfiguration of the prison has led to an increasing number of prisoners on remand or serving shorter sentences. The increasing churn has caused the prison problems, in particular with regard to progression and resettlement. The selection of the prison to take part in the RRA project is welcomed, but what other steps can the Minister take so that the prison can improve its provision of progression and resettlement services?

The prison continues to be chronically overcrowded, despite repeated representations by the Board that the overcrowding is unacceptable. There are 521 cells designed for single occupancy, most of which are occupied by two prisoners. This overcrowding puts great pressure on communal spaces and facilities. It is incompatible with the fair and decent treatment of prisoners who are doubled up in cells designed for single use, particularly when, owing to Covid-19 restrictions, many prisoners have to spend 23 hours per day in their cells What steps can the Minister take to reduce the chronic overcrowding?

The Board understands that there are plans for a new building at the prison which is to accommodate 240 more prisoners. Does the Minister intend that the new building be used to reduce the chronic overcrowding in the existing prison?

### Progress since the last report

Following the suspension of social visits, a system of Purple Visits (video link) was established. After a slow start, the success of these visits grew and it is intended that they will continue after the Covid-19 restrictions have been lifted.

The reduction of the number of outstanding offender assessment system (OASys) plans continued. This was a positive development as better and quicker sentence planning is needed to improve prospects for the rehabilitation of prisoners for their release.

A new x-ray body scanner for prisoners was installed in reception in September 2020. This proved successful in detecting illicit items.

An airport-style scanner was installed in April 2021 at the gate used for entry by visitors and staff. The prison has been selected to take part in the RRA project. This means that it has started to receive additional support to improve rehabilitative support to prisoners particularly as regards employment and accommodation. Two new temporary staff were appointed in June 2021 specifically to support the RRA project.

**JAGUAR DRIVE
BADERSFIELD
NORWICH
NR10 5GB**

**HM PRISON BURE**

**Tel: 01603 326000**

*For the latest reports on this prison please visit:*
https://tinyurl.com/bdfh26rv

*Important Changes:* **(1) Visits:** the identification necessary to access this prison and visit for social or professional purposes has changed; (2) **Money and Gifts** new rules now apply to these. See page 16 for full details of the above.

**Task of the establishment** HMP &is a category C prison for sentenced men convicted of sexual offences.

**Certified normal accommodation and operational capacity**
Prisoners held at the time of this visit 585
Baseline certified normal capacity: 604
In-use certified normal capacity: 604
Operational capacity: 624

**Prison status and key providers**
Public
Prison Group: Bedfordshire, Cambridgeshire & Norfolk
Prison Group Director: Gary Monaghan
Governor/Director: Simon Rhoden
IMB Chair: Maggie Dixon
Physical health provider: Practice Plus Group
Mental health provider: Practice Plus Group
Substance misuse treatment provider: Phoenix Futures
Prison education framework provider: People Plus

**Brief history** HMP Bure is built on part of the former RAF Coltishall site, seven miles north of Norwich. Constructed in 2009, the prison is a mix of new buildings and converted RAF accommodation and service buildings. A new unit, built for 101 prisoners, was constructed in September 2013. The unit temporarily increased to 120 prisoners in 2020, but it had reverted back to 101 by the time of the inspection.

**Short description of residential units** There are seven residential units, comprising mostly single cells. Residential units 1, 3, 4, 5 and 6 each have four double cells and residential unit 7 has one. Residential units 1–6 have communal showers and residential unit 7 has integral showers in every cell. All units serve as purely residential accommodation, except for residential unit 6, which has one landing of 10 cells assigned as induction cells. Residential unit 7's ground floor

accommodation is allocated to prisoners with identified medical needs.

Under Covid-19 arrangements, there is additional accommodation in the form of 19 portable cabins, all of which have integral showers. In addition, residential unit 6 has been realigned to encompass 20 reverse cohort unit spaces and 20 protective isolation spaces. Those prisoners who are shielding are located on residential unit 7, unless they have requested to remain in their own cells.

**Visiting Information**
Visits Telephone 01603 326252, Tues/Weds 8:30am to 12pm, Thurs 10am- 12pm, Sat/Sun 8:30am to 12pm
**Visiting Times** Sat and Sun 1:30pm to 2:30pm, 3pm to 4pm

**Legal visits**
Booking line: 01603 326 231, open Monday to Friday 9:30am to 11:30am and 2pm to 3pm
Legal and professional visits are available on Tuesday only: 8:30am - 11:30am, 1:45pm - 3:45pm

**INSPECTIONS & REPORTS**
**Scrutiny Visit** 16 and 23–24 March 2021
**Date of last full inspection** 27 March–7 April 2017
**Scrutiny Visit: Date of publication 30 April 2021**
This report presents the findings from our scrutiny visit to HMP Bure to report on the conditions and treatment of prisoners during the Covid-19 pandemic. Situated on the former RAF Coltishall base in Norfolk and opened in 2009, HMP Bure is a category C training prison and a national resource for around 600 prisoners convicted of sexual offences. At the time of our visit, about three-quarters of the population had been assessed as presenting a high risk of harm and nearly all were serving long sentences of four years or more. More than half the prisoners were aged over 50 and a third were considered clinically vulnerable to Covid-19.
The prison was well led and attention to Covid-19-safe procedures was particularly impressive. Shielding and quarantine arrangements had been applied rigorously to minimise the spread of the virus. The potentially more serious consequences for an older and, in many cases, frailer population had been avoided during a recent Covid-19 outbreak. Although one prisoner had died of a COVID- 19-related illness, there had been no confirmed cases on the residential unit where the most clinically vulnerable and many shielding prisoners were located. Communal areas were kept very clean and face masks were worn by staff and prisoners alike. Staff uptake of regular Covid-19 testing was high and the prison operated its own robust internal

'test and trace' system to help contain the virus. At the time of our visit, more than 40% of prisoners had received their first vaccination and almost all of who had been offered the vaccine had taken it. Health care provision was also good.

Prison leaders had taken swift action to limit access to the regime at times of increased risk of Covid-19, but had also acted quickly to ease restrictions when possible. As one of the first prisons to have a recovery plan approved by HM Prison and Probation Service following the most recent national lockdown, the prison had progressed to 'regime stage 3' during the week of our visit. Group worship, indoor gym, workshops and classrooms were in the process of reopening. However, plans were still in preparation for increasing the time unlocked on the residential units and for outside exercise. The amount of time unlocked for most prisoners remained limited to less than two hours a day, which included 45 minutes' access to the exercise yard. Without in-cell telephony, there was not enough time or privacy for calls, which were limited to only five minutes, on the communal telephones.

The prison was calm and well ordered, with low levels of violence and use of force, and a very sparing use of disciplinary measures during the period of restrictions. The segregation unit had been shut for the past three months. Staff-prisoner relationships were a strength, with 91% of prisoners in our survey saying that staff treated them with respect. Most also said that they had a staff member to turn to if they had a problem and we observed supportive and helpful interactions. This caring ethos was also evident in the additional support given to the most vulnerable during the pandemic, although we found some weaknesses in assessment, care in custody and teamwork (ACCT) case management. Levels of self-harm had reduced in the past 12 months, but the rate was still higher than at some similar prisons and we found examples of serious self harm among the population. There had been two self-inflicted deaths during the pandemic. The demand for Listeners (prisoners trained by the Samaritans to provide confidential emotional support to fellow prisoners) was very high.

Only around a fifth of prisoners had accessed any form of in-cell education and only a small proportion had remained in their work roles during the pandemic. More positively, some offending behaviour programme work had continued. However, the need to adapt delivery for one-to-one sessions or small groups had delayed completion rates and, ultimately, progression for some prisoners, which was an understandable source of frustration.

We found public protection procedures to be reasonable, although a lack of communication from community offender managers had had an impact on the timeliness of some risk management and release planning arrangements. Unlike at our 2017 inspection, dedicated resettlement resources were now available. However, the community rehabilitation company providing the 'through-the-gate' support had withdrawn all face-to-face contact with prisoners at the start of the pandemic until the week of our visit.

In conclusion, the prison had managed well in protecting its frail and older population from the virus. The committed and caring leadership and staff group had maintained a safe, decent and very respectful prison despite the challenges of the pandemic. With national approval to move forward with its plan for recovery, the prison is in a strong position now to increase time unlocked and give much needed access to more purposeful activity.

Charlie Taylor, HM Chief Inspector of Prisons
April 2021

**Key concerns and recommendations**

Key concerns and recommendations identify the issues of most importance to improving outcomes for prisoners and are designed to help establishments prioritise and address the most significant weaknesses in the treatment and conditions of prisoners.

During this visit we identified some areas of key concern, and have made a small number of recommendations for the prison to address.

Key concern: There had been two self-inflicted deaths during the Covid-19 restrictions, the first at Bure since its opening. Overall levels of self-harm had reduced but there were still some serious incidents and demand for the Listeners was high. Assessment, care in custody and teamwork (ACCT) case management procedures had too many weaknesses and these had also been identified by Prisons and Probation Ombudsman investigations. We found examples of unresolved care map actions causing anxiety, unachievable care map goals and the premature withdrawal of support.

Key recommendation: Prisoners at risk of suicide or self-harm should receive effective support which delivers prompt actions to reduce their risk and continues until that risk has lowered. (To the governor)

Key concern: Most referrals for social care assessments had not been responded to within three months and one had been outstanding for over two years.

Key recommendation: Response times to referrals for social care assessments should be monitored, to make sure that these are prompt and that prisoners are able to live independently. (To the governor)

Key concern: The prison did not have in-cell telephony. Prisoners could only use the landing-based communal telephones and the prison's supply of mobile devices during their daily periods of unlock, or apply to use one during the evening. Calls made on landing telephones were limited to only five minutes and lacked privacy.

Key recommendation: All prisoners should have access to in-cell telephones. (To HMPPS)

Key concern: The lack of communication from community offender managers (COMs) was having an impact on the timeliness of the prison's risk management and release planning arrangements. Clarification from COMs of critical information, such as multi-agency public protection arrangements (MAPPA) levels, accommodation arrangements and licence conditions, was too often confirmed only in the last few weeks, and in some cases days, before a prisoner's release.

Key recommendation: COMs should ensure prompt communication and confirmation of critical information to the offender management unit, to enable timely risk management and release planning arrangements to be put in place before a prisoner's release. (To HMPPS)

## INDEPENDENT MONITORING BOARD: Annual Report

The law requires every prison to be monitored by an independent Board appointed by the Justice Secretary; these are known as Independent Monitoring Boards (IMBs). The IMB must satisfy itself as to the humane and just treatment of those held in custody within its prison and the range and adequacy of the programmes preparing them for release; it must report annually to the Justice Secretary on how well the prison has met the standards and requirements placed on it.

**IMB Report 1 August 2020 – 31 July 2021**
**Published 5th May 2022**
**Background to the report**

The report presents the findings of the Independent Monitoring Board for the period 1 August 2020 – 31 July 2021. Evidence comes from the observations made on visits, scrutiny of records and data, informal contact with prisoners and staff, surveys and prisoner applications. The reporting period has been extraordinary due to the challenge of the Covid-19 pandemic. The Board has worked closely with staff and residents using remote ways of monitoring to safeguard all those who live and work at HMP Bure. The Board communicates regularly with the Governors and staff and despite long hours

of lock down for residents morale remained high. At the time of writing we have resumed face to face contact with residents who have been able to provide a comprehensive account of how they have been affected during the reporting year.

The ongoing Covid-19 pandemic has had a significant impact on the Board's ability to gather information and monitor in person during the first half of the period covered by this annual report, as Board members were unable to attend the prison. Ministers are aware of these constraints. The Board understands that regular information is being collected specifically on the prison's response to the pandemic, and that is being collated nationally.

There have also been incidents of illness of Board members and the resignation of one member, plus two members on sabbatical. Despite these difficult circumstances, the Board has tried to cover as much ground as possible, but inevitably there is less detail and supporting evidence than is usually to be expected. Such detail as there is has necessarily largely been sourced from report of the scrutiny visit undertaken by Her Majesty's Inspectorate of Prisons (HMIP) on 16 and 23-24 March 2021 and from the prison's own statistics. We should like to record our gratitude to those members of staff at HMP Bure who have willingly taken time out of their busy schedules to respond to our several and varied requests for information.

**Main judgements**
**How safe is the prison**

Assaults on prisoners – 18
Assaults on staff – 10
Violence levels generally reduced, mainly due to reduced association.
Self-harm levels have generally decreased, as per section 4.2 of this report.

**How fairly and humanely are prisoners treated?**

Overall prisoners continue to receive fair and humane treatment in the establishment. The introduction of the residents' council during the last reporting period has proved invaluable in the current situation. The council meets once a month and has been attended by governors, including the governing Governor. With residents being on lock down for up to 23 hours a day, the council has made the wellbeing of all residents their priority ensuring steps to prevent the spread of Covid19. The mental and physical health of everyone has been a concern and ideas were generated by both the residents' council and staff to minimise harm. In a recent survey, 84% of residents felt they were treated humanely and fairly. Thirty-two cells on residential unit 7 remain equipped for double occupancy;

however, the IMB would like a commitment from Her Majesty's Prison and Probation Service (HMPPS) that these won't be used again.

*Quote from a resident who canvassed the opinions of fellow residents:*
"while 23.5 hours locked up alone with almost no human contact certainly reduced the risks of catching covid, one wonders whether the long-term damage to our mental health and physical health will only emerge in time. The need for in-cell telephone and IT surely must become a top priority; access to communication and education must never again be allowed to be curtailed".

## How well are prisoners' health and wellbeing needs met?
During the reporting year, there were eight deaths in custody.
The safer custody team is considered outstanding in their delivery of support to both prisoners and families. Listeners selected from residents by the prison staff and trained by the Samaritans have become a well-respected group who have worked diligently to support those seriously affected by long hours of lockdown and increased anxiety for their families.
Healthcare is fully staffed and has not needed to use 'bank' staff. Healthcare, including the mental health team, has delivered a service equal to that expected in the local community during the current Covid-19 pandemic. Clinics had to be cancelled, but the healthcare team have had face to face meetings with residents using the appropriate personal protective equipment (PPE) in urgent cases.

## Main areas for development
### TO THE MINISTER
Will the Minister explain why, as at July 2021, 58 prisoners were serving indeterminate sentences for public protection (IPP) without provision for any offending behaviour programmes or accredited interventions to allow progression towards release?
For example, HMP Bure has one individual who has served five times more than his original tariff. In the Board's view this is neither fair or humane.
The Board notes that in the Minister's letter dated 30 May 2019 to the National Chair of the IMB he stated that "HMPPS remains committed to the safe progression of prisoners serving IPPs and ensuring prioritisation of post-tariff prisoners in accessing rehabilitative interventions'.

### TO THE PRISON SERVICE
Will HMPPS make funding available to the prison to enable prisoners to have access to in-cell telephony? We notice that no progress has been made to the provision of in-cell telephony. Telephony facilities for prisoners are principally landing-based communal telephones, which lack privacy and are limited to five minutes' use only. There is in addition a limited supply of mobile telephones available to prisoners when unlocked or which they can apply to use in their cell during the evening.
We notice that the heating situation was improved on residential units 1-6 but problems still remain on residential unit 7, where the boiler and whole heating system needs replacement. It is necessary that a fixed date is given for the resolution of this problem.

### Progress since the last report
In last year's report, published in November 2020, we noted concerns that had been raised with the Board regarding ventilation in residential units1 to 6. Despite work that had been done on cell windows to improve ventilation in the cells, we noted that some prisoners were still experiencing very hot conditions at times during the summer months. We asked the Governor to ensure that work on the ventilation system in those residential units was undertaken as a matter of priority.
The report of an investigation by the Prisons and Probation Ombudsman following the death of a prisoner on 1 August 2020, published in April 2021, concluded that high temperatures in prisoner accommodation during a heatwave could have contributed to the dehydration linked to his death.
The Board is pleased to note that during March 2021, work was undertaken to improve ventilation to the residential units, allowing the outer windows to be opened independently of the smoke extraction system. Individual fans were also made available to all residents for further ventilation, if required. Further funding to improve the in-cell air circulation was also secured and maintenance work is expected to commence during 2021. Installing further insulation above each residential unit is also being explored to better control the rise in temperature during very hot weather.

**KNOX ROAD**
**CARDIFF, CF24 0UG**

**HM PRISON SERVICE**

**HMP & YOI CARDIFF**

**Tel: 02920 923100**

*For the latest reports on this prison please visit:*
https://tinyurl.com/bdfh26rv

*Important Changes:* **(1) Visits:** the identification necessary to access this prison and visit for social or professional purposes has changed; (2) **Money and Gifts** new rules now apply to these. See page 16 for full details of the above.

**Task of the establishment** A category B local prison for adult male prisoners serving the courts in southeast Wales.

**Certified normal accommodation and operational capacity**
Prisoners held at the time of inspection: 738
Baseline certified normal capacity: 539
In-use certified normal capacity: 539
Operational capacity: 779

**Prison status and key providers**
Public
Prison Group: Wales
Prison Group Director: Giles Mason
Governor/Director: Amanda Corrigan
IMB Chair: Jaci Rankmore
Physical health provider: Cardiff and Vale University Health Board
Mental health provider: Cardiff and Vale University Health Board
Substance misuse (services) provider: G4S and Cardiff and Vale University Health Board
Learning and skills provider: HM Prison and Probation Service in Wales
Escort contractor: GeoAmey

**Brief history** HMP Cardiff was built in 1827 so the accommodation was predominately Victorian. The prison held unconvicted and remand prisoners from local courts and short-term prisoners serving up to 12 months. New units were built in 1996, comprising a first night centre and two further wings. A health care centre was opened in May 2008, providing a 22-bed inpatient facility.

**Short description of residential units**
A wing: General population
A1: Mainly prisoners working in the kitchen and on recycling
B wing: General population
B1: Vulnerable prisoners
C wing: Induction and first night centre
D wing: Enhanced level prisoners
E wing: General population
F wing: General population
F1: Prisoners suspected of secreting illicit items on or in their body/self-isolators and Safer Custody referrals who have raised concerns over personal safety in the general population
H wing: Health care unit

**Visiting Information**
*Covid-19: visits can change abruptly so check before leaving*
Visits telephone: 029 2092 3327
Visiting Times: Mon, Wed, Fri, Sat 1400-1500

Legal visits are generally not operating at the time of publication (November 2021) but check with the prison for the latest information.

**INSPECTIONS & REPORTS**
**Date of last full inspection:** 15–26 July 2019
**HMCIP Report, published 05 November 2019**
HMP Cardiff is a category B local prison for men. At the time of this inspection it held a little under 750 prisoners. It is a traditional local prison, situated in the heart of the city, and serving the courts of south-east Wales. The prison consists predominantly of Victorian buildings, but there have been some more modern additions in recent decades. The prison was last inspected in the summer of 2016 when we found that outcomes for prisoners were not sufficiently good in two out of four of our inspection areas. Purposeful activity and resettlement were judged to be reasonably good.

I had also been present during the 2016 inspection, and was pleased to find that in the intervening period the prison had made real progress. The grades had improved in all but one of our healthy prison tests, rising in safety, respect and purposeful activity. In view of the challenging context in which prisons, particularly local prisons, have been operating in recent years, this represents a very significant achievement. It is my judgement that much of the improvement can be ascribed to the excellent relationships that existed between staff and prisoners, and the obviously energetic and well-focused leadership of the senior team. These positive relationships had, in turn, contributed to the ability of the prison to address some of the basics that shaped the character of a jail, such as levels of violence, the prevalence or otherwise of drugs, and the living conditions experienced by prisoners. Importantly, the prison was relatively safe. Fewer prisoners than in similar establishments told us they felt unsafe, which is an enormously important indicator that affects so much else that happens in a jail. We often see the corrosive impact of violence on many aspects of prison life when the prisoners themselves are living in fear. It is much to Cardiff's credit that while violence figures across the prison estate have generally been rising at an alarming rate in recent years, they had managed to buck the trend. Violence had not increased since the last inspection.

The comprehensive drug supply reduction strategy had undoubtedly had an impact. At the last inspection there were very real concerns about the flow of drugs entering the establishment and in, particular, the role played in this by prisoners being recalled to prison. Illicit drugs were still a very real problem, but the positive mandatory drug testing rate had dropped, and at least there was a sense that there was a degree of control over the situation. The prison would undoubtedly benefit from more technology to assist them in their efforts, and the lack of a body scanner was a significant gap in their defences. In the meantime, they cannot afford to relax their vigilance in any way, and it is our view that although it should be subject to regular review, the current searching regime for new prisoners entering the jail remained proportionate. Alongside the stabilisation of violence and drug supply, living conditions had improved significantly since the last inspection. Communal areas and cells were cleaner, there was a programme of renewing cell furniture, showers had been improved on some wings, there was now much easier access to basic kit and bedding than at the last inspection thanks to the prison now having its own laundry, and lavatories were better screened. It was certainly true that there were still overcrowded cells, but in general, for a local prison of its type and age, a great deal of progress had been made.

Cardiff prison was, of course, not immune from the social problems that affect wider communities. Some 65% of prisoners arriving at the prison reported having mental health problems. Over half of new arrivals reported drug problems, and a third said they had problems with alcohol. In the six months prior to our inspection more than 350 prisoners required alcohol detoxification. There was also the worrying statistic that since the last inspection, levels of self-harm had risen threefold. More needed to be done to understand why this had happened. All of this placed enormous demands on health care provision, the details of which can be seen in the body of this report. It was a mixed picture, and some of our key concerns and recommendations focus on the provision of services to meet very high demand.

A further social issue that had a significant impact on the prison, and the service it could give to those in its care, was that of homelessness on release. Over the six months prior to the inspection an extremely high figure of 47% of the prisoners being released from the prison did not have any form of accommodation to go to. The community rehabilitation company (CRC) did not follow through with prisoners adequately after their release, and so it was not known how many prisoners eventually found appropriate accommodation. The well-established correlation between homelessness in these circumstances and the risk of reoffending is well known. This was a problem that is clearly beyond the ability of the prison service to address on its own. I have therefore taken the unusual step of making a recommendation to both HMPPS and the Welsh Government that they should work together to find solutions to this very serious problem.

Overall, this was an enormously encouraging inspection as it showed what can be achieved in a traditional local prison. HMP Cardiff disproves the clichés about inner-city Victorian prisons inevitably being places of squalor, violence and despair. The improvements since the last inspection were incredibly encouraging to see, and were testimony to the hard work that had brought them about. On this, my second inspection of Cardiff, it was also clear to me that many prisoners had responded positively to the improvements and wanted to make their own contribution to the prison and thereby to their own futures.

Peter Clarke CVO OBE QPM September 2019
HM Chief Inspector of Prisons

## INDEPENDENT MONITORING BOARD: Annual Report

The law requires every prison to be monitored by an independent Board appointed by the Justice Secretary; these are known as Independent Monitoring Boards (IMBs). The IMB must satisfy itself as to the humane and just treatment of those held in custody within its prison and the range and adequacy of the programmes preparing them for release; it must report annually to the Justice Secretary on how well the prison has met the standards and requirements placed on it.

**IMB Report 1 September 2020 – 31 August 2021
Published 4th March 2022
Summary
Background to the report**
The Covid-19 outbreak has had a significant impact on the Board's ability to gather information and discuss the contents of this annual report. The Board has therefore tried to

cover as much ground as it can in these difficult circumstances, but inevitably there is less detail and supporting evidence than usual. Ministers are aware of these constraints. Regular information is being collected specifically on the prison's response to the pandemic, and that is being collated nationally.

The Board was able to provide limited 'in person' visits to the prison from September 2020; this gradually increased over the reporting year. In April 2021, in order to increase our understanding of prisoners' experience of conditions, the Board undertook a survey. Questionnaires were sent out to all men, except those on the reverse cohorting unit (RCU). We received 149 replies.

Despite any issues noted in this report, the Independent Monitoring Board (IMB) based at HMP Cardiff applauds the management and staff of the establishment in continuing to provide a reasonably safe and humane environment for the men in their care.

### Main judgements How safe is the prison?

The Board believes that HMP Cardiff is a relatively safe prison. This belief is based on the fact that both use of force and incidents of self-harm reduced this year.

Although there were four deaths, only one is thought to be self-inflicted. Incidents of violence remained at a similar low level to the previous year. In addition to this, the survey completed by the Board suggested that 58% of men felt safe in the prison, although this percentage dropped to 46% for non- workers.

### How fairly and humanely are prisoners treated?

It is the Board's view that most men in HMP Cardiff are treated fairly and humanely. However, the effects of the restricted regime have had, we believe, an adverse effect on relationships between men and officers. This has been exacerbated by the staffing pressures that officers and staff have had to work under at times during the year. However, it must be noted that men have made positive comments about staff.

Efforts were made by the prison to ensure men are not held in the care and separation unit (CSU) unnecessarily.

The age of the building causes some issues. Staffing issues within the business hub have an adverse effect on the complaints procedure. Finally, there are still some concerns about the disproportionate use of force on young prisoners and those from a Caribbean or mixed-race Caribbean background. Additionally the Board again wishes to highlight the disproportionate number of men from a black, Asian and minority ethnic background (BAME) who are labelled as dangerous.

### How well are prisoners' health and wellbeing needs met?

There has been an improvement in staffing in both physical healthcare and mental healthcare. The Board believes that this has led to an improvement in the service offered. The physical healthcare team continued to operate a service despite the added pressures put on them by the pandemic and the mental health team has expanded its services).

Unfortunately, there were some exceptions to this, notably in relation to pharmacy services and during lockdown optician and dentistry services. In addition, it has been noted that extra GP hours are required.

As part of the process to provide a humane regime during the pandemic, in July 2021 the prison was able to increase time out of cell to two hours a day.

### How well are prisoners progressed towards successful resettlement?

Through the entire reporting year, the education and learning skills department provided opportunities at a reduced level, only opening education and training as Covid-19 restrictions allowed. This understandably impacted progression toward successful resettlement.

There were some initial issues when the CRC staff became contracted under the NPS and resettlement services outside the prison have been managed by phone calls with other agencies.

Accommodation remained an issue for men leaving with no settled home and despite the Welsh Government agreeing to fund support until April 2022 there remains a lack of available and affordable housing.

Positively, as a large proportion of prisoners within HMP Cardiff are on remand, a new bail information scheme was piloted, managed by a member of staff and using bail peers on the RCU.

### Main areas for development
### TO THE MINISTER

The Board is concerned about the increase, this year, in men requiring transfer to mental health establishments. We have noted the recommendations of the House of Commons Justice Committee report Mental health in prisons of September 2021, particularly the recommendation that 'The MoJ and the NHS should accelerate plans to increase the availability of Community Sentence Treatment Requirement orders, so these orders are available options for sentencers in all parts of England and Wales by 31 March 2023.'1 Although we realise that this recommendation relates to England, we would ask whether any discussions are taking place with the Welsh Government to implement this recommendation. The Board continues to have concerns about men being held in custody on IS91s and their access to Home Office representatives. This issue has been raised in the last two reports. In March and April 2021, one man who was held under an IS91 began to refuse food because he was held in custody past his release date. Whilst understanding the pressures on the immigration removal centres (IRCs), men held in prison do not have access to the same facilities as those in IRCs. The Board would ask that this issue is again raised with the Home Office.

## TO THE WELSH GOVERNMENT

The Board has two concerns in relation to healthcare which we would ask the Health Minister to consider with Cardiff and the Vale Health Board. Both relate to staffing: the first is the ongoing issue with lack of cover for pharmacists, which can lead to locum pharmacists being brought in on an emergency basis and affects the planning of the team in their attempts to improve the service. This difficulty was also noted last year.

The second has been raised by the temporary clinical director who has identified the need for increased GP hours to cover the health needs of the men.

The Board was pleased to hear that support for men who are leaving prison without settled accommodation is being extended until April 2022. However, there appears to be a lack of available and suitable accommodation, particularly in certain areas, and we would be interested to see what steps the Welsh Government is able to take, jointly with local authorities, to address this problem.

## TO THE PRISON SERVICE

Staff and men in HMP Cardiff have made efforts to keep the prison clean and of a good standard during the pandemic. The Board also acknowledges the work that has been done on refurbishing wings. However, some of the older wings have annual issues with heating, problems with accessing TV channels and the rats are having an effect on the infrastructure. Some of these problems (the heating and TV channels) have been occurring for several years and the prison in conjunction with Amey has tried to remedy the problems. The Board would ask the service to consider what long term remedies could be found.

Allied to the infrastructure is the concern the Board has in relation to access for wheelchair users and those with mobility problems to some areas of the prison. We are aware that refurbishment of one wing is making some

adaptations to aid access, but difficulties still remain for men who may not be accommodated on that wing.

The Board is pleased that the regime in HMP Cardiff is easing and realises all relaxing of the regime is dependent on infection rates. However, from our monitoring of the prison we believe that men were finding life increasingly difficult under this regime and would hope that a return to normal regime could be considered as soon as practicable, in line with Covid-19 protocols.

The Board is concerned that the use of body worn cameras (BWC) is being affected by the need to service and replace cameras. We understand that HMP Cardiff will have cameras replaced in February 2022: we hope that will not be delayed further.

## TO THE GOVERNOR

We have been concerned by the staffing pressures the business hub appears to have been under, which in turn affects issues which directly affect the men.

Therefore we would ask whether there is any way to ensure sufficient trained staff are available to cover shortfalls.

Our concern noted in the last report in relation to the disproportionate number of BAME prisoners labelled as dangerous remains. In addition to this, the Board has noticed a perception amongst BAME prisoners that they are being discriminated against in the allocation of work and education and we would ask that further investigation of any apparent discrimination be considered.

**GREENHILL LANE
DENBURY
NEWTON ABBOT
TQ12 6DW**

**HM PRISON CHANNINGS WOOD**

**TEL: 01803 814600**

*For the latest reports on this prison please visit:*
https://tinyurl.com/bdfh26rv

*Important Changes:* **(1) Visits:** the identification necessary to access this prison and visit for social or professional purposes has changed; (2) **Money and Gifts** new rules now apply to these. See page 16 for full details of the above.

**Task of the establishment** Category C adult male training and resettlement prison.

**Certified normal accommodation and operational capacity**
Prisoners held at the time of inspection: 667

Certified normal capacity: 698
In-use certified normal capacity: 698
Operational capacity: 724

**Prison status and key providers**
Public
Prison Group: Devon & North Dorset
Prison Group Director: Jeannine Hendrick
Governor/Director: Huw Sullivan
IMB Chair: Gerald Hine-Haycock
Physical health provider: Care UK
Mental health provider: Care UK
Substance misuse provider: Care UK – EDP Drug and Alcohol Services
Learning and skills provider: Weston College
Escort contractor: GeoAmey

**Brief history** Channings Wood prison was built on the site of a Ministry of Defence base in 1973 and opened in July 1974. Further building programmes have taken place over the last two decades with the addition of 104 prisoner places in living blocks 7 and 8.

**Short description of residential units** The establishment has eight residential units, known as living blocks (LBs). LB1 to LB5 are similar in layout, with two spurs of 56 cells over two floors. LB1 accommodates 138 prisoners and is the only unit with single cells that are holding two prisoners. LB2 to LB5 each accommodates 112 prisoners, and are designated as single occupancy. LB6 and LB7 accommodate prisoners on the highest level of privileges, holding 34 and 40 prisoners respectively. LB8 accommodates 64 prisoners in double cells.

**Visiting Information**
Booking line: 01803 812 060
The booking line is open Monday to Friday (except Bank Holidays) 10am to 2:30pm
**Visiting times:** Wednesday, Friday, Saturday, Sunday: 2pm to 4pm
Saturday and Sunday visits alternate between prisoners in the main prison and the vulnerable prisoners unit. The booking line can advise you on the appropriate weekend day to visit.

**Legal visits:** There are currently no legal visits taking place.

**INSPECTIONS & REPORTS**
**Date of last inspection:** 10, 11, 17–20 Sept 2018
**HMCIP Report published 05 February 2019**
HMP Channings Wood is a category C training and resettlement prison near Newton Abbott in Devon. Holding up to 724 adult men, the prison's campus comprises eight residential units, some dating back to the early 1970s when

the prison first opened, others added more recently. Those held represented the full range of sentences, with the majority serving between two and 10 years and a small number serving indeterminate sentences. A sizeable proportion of those held were located separately as vulnerable prisoners, either because of the nature of their offence or because they were seeking protection. Channings Wood was last inspected in late 2016 when we assessed outcomes as being not sufficiently good against all four of our healthy prison tests. At this inspection we were made aware of the problems the prison had faced in recent years and the view expressed that improvements had been made more recently. This was probably the case, although the picture remained very mixed and we again assessed outcomes in all four of our healthy prison tests – safety, respect, purposeful activity and rehabilitation and release planning – as being not sufficiently good.

There had been efforts to improve safety at the prison but these were often uncoordinated, which undermined their effectiveness. Our survey of prisoners revealed that nearly two-thirds had felt unsafe in the prison in the past, with a third still feeling unsafe at the time of the inspection. The reception and induction of mainstream prisoners was good but was in sharp contrast to the induction experienced by vulnerable prisoners, who were subject to squalid conditions and intimidation from others. Violence was rising in the prison but the quality and understanding of related data, as well as the unsatisfactory quality of investigations, undermined the prospects for improvement. We were not assured that the well-being of vulnerable prisoners was always sufficiently safeguarded and the prison lacked a coordinated approach to the reduction of violence linked to the problem of drugs. Testing indicated a positive rate for drug usage in the prison of around 30% and over three-quarters of prisoners thought illicit drugs were easy to access. Inadequate supervision of prisoners, for example, meant there were repeated opportunities for drug misuse and associated violence.

Since we last inspected, two prisoners had tragically taken their own lives and the number of self-harm incidents had doubled. Despite this, important recommendations following investigation of these deaths had not been implemented and case management support was often poor. The support from peer workers for those in crisis was better.

The environment in Channings Wood reflected stark contrasts. Much of the accommodation was of a good standard and prisoners appreciated their access to the pleasant surrounding grounds. On three units, however, in our view, failures of leadership had led to some very poor standards with prisoners living in often bleak and dirty cells. In addition, access to general amenities was at best mixed. Kit and cleaning materials were usually accessible but many showers, although again accessible, were in a poor condition. Prisoners expressed some negative perceptions concerning the quality of the food and the fairness of complaints arrangements, but our observations overall were more positive in these areas.

Most prisoners felt respected by staff and indicated that they knew who to turn to for help. Our own observations, however, suggested variability and polarisation. We saw much positive work being undertaken by staff of all disciplines working appropriately to set and maintain standards. On the poorer wings, in contrast, we found staff congregating in offices, failing to set standards or maintain supportive living conditions and failing to challenge delinquent behaviour on the part of prisoners. It was our view also that the significant number of newer, less experienced officers needed greater support. Work to promote equality had deteriorated since we last inspected. Team meetings were poorly attended and action planning was weak. Consultation among prisoners with protected characteristics varied greatly, as did outcomes. Health care provision was stretched and was largely reactive, although waiting times to see clinicians were reducing.

Prisoners had reasonable access to time out of cell, although we found about 16% locked in their cells during the working day. Slippage in daily routines was a further source of frustration to many prisoners. The prison had sufficient full-time activity places for most but the management of attendance and punctuality was poor. Similarly, the quality of teaching, learning and assessment required improvement. That said, the provision benefited from some realistic working environments and peer mentors made a valued contribution. Most prisoners completed their qualifications and a small number could progress to higher learning. Our colleagues in Ofsted, however, judged the overall effectiveness of provision as 'requires improvement'.

The prison's reducing reoffending strategy was limited and needed review. Oversight lacked rigour and consistency, and many prisoners did not have an up-to-date offender assessment system (OASys) assessment or sentence plan. Added to this, contact between prisoners and their supervisors was often reactive and unfocused, which undermined the achievement of objectives. Public protection measures, as well as release and resettlement planning, were similarly weak and inconsistent.

Inconsistency of outcomes was a recurrent theme of our findings at this inspection. This was best exemplified in varying standards being accepted across the different accommodation wings, but

also in the way initiatives to bring about improvement were often implemented in a partial or uncoordinated way. Managers were enthusiastic and open about making progress, but optimism and energy needed to be harnessed in a way that ensured leaders at all levels were visible, demanding consistent standards, and ensuring improvement was embedded and sustainable. We leave the prison with several recommendations which we hope will assist that process.

Peter Clarke CVO OBE QPM November 2018
HM Chief Inspector of Prisons

## INDEPENDENT MONITORING BOARD: Annual Report

The law requires every prison to be monitored by an independent Board appointed by the Justice Secretary; these are known as Independent Monitoring Boards (IMBs). The IMB must satisfy itself as to the humane and just treatment of those held in custody within its prison and the range and adequacy of the programmes preparing them for release; it must report annually to the Justice Secretary on how well the prison has met the standards and requirements placed on it.

### IMB Report 1 September 2020 – 31 August 2021

Executive summary

Background to the report

The Covid-19 outbreak has had a significant impact on the Board's ability to gather information and discuss the contents of this annual report. The Board has therefore tried to cover as much ground as it can in these difficult circumstances, but inevitably there is less detail and supporting evidence than usual. Ministers are aware of these constraints. Regular information is being collected specifically on the prison's response to the pandemic, and that is being collated nationally.

In order to hear the men's voice while monitoring remotely, for the first time the Board conducted two surveys – a general questionnaire on safety, fairness and decency and a second on progression and resettlement. The general questionnaire was issued at the annual report six-month point to all prisoners and over 100 responded. The resettlement survey went to men who, in the period June to August, had entered their 12-week window for discharge. Of 105 men surveyed, 46 (44%) responded.

The Board recognises the demands that operating the prison throughout the pandemic have put on staff and prisoners and notes that the prison has largely remained settled despite the significant restrictions.

## Main judgements
### How safe is the prison?

The Board still judges that the prison remains largely safe. Following the trends of the previous year, the number of incidents of self-harm and assaults both continued to decrease. Anecdotally, prisoners and staff reported that these reductions had been the result of limitations in the amount of movement and free association. This was reflected in the IMB survey, when over 70% of those who responded said they felt safe most of the time. Incidents of substance misuse more than halved, most likely because of limited access to illicit substances during the pandemic restrictions. The Board will continue to monitor the situation and the measures the prison management put in place once the regime permits more movement and visiting returns to normal.

Use of force incidents dropped by just over a quarter. There was only one use of a baton and although staff were trained to use pelargonic acid vanillylamide (PAVA), it was not used on the only occasion that it was drawn. The Board's judgement is that force does not appear to be overused and seems to be used proportionately.

### How fairly and humanely are prisoners treated?

During the reporting period, the prison regime was determined by the relevant stage of the exceptional delivery model (EDM). Within the restrictions that this imposed, the Board judges that prisoners were treated with fairness and humanity.

### How well are prisoners' health and wellbeing needs met?

The EDM significantly limited the time that prisoners had out of their cell and, although prisoners reported the difficulties in using the restricted time to carry out basic tasks, including showering and making phone calls, it is to their huge credit that most men remained tolerant and positive about these severe limitations. Additional 'comfort packs' were supplied by the kitchen providing some treats. As the changes in regime impacted on work and education opportunities, distraction packs and remote learning packs were made available. Healthcare adapted its distribution of medication and, where appropriate, men were given their own drugs. The Board believes that, as far as was possible, men's health and wellbeing needs were met.

### How well are prisoners progressed towards successful resettlement?

The Covid-19 pandemic and the prolonged adoption of the EDM has significantly impacted those areas where one to one work is so vital. The measures required to minimise the risk to prisoners, taken together with the resultant staff shortages, has seen education, offender management and resettlement particularly hard hit. Despite some of the concerns noted, the Board applauds the successes that have been achieved and recognised in this report, in particular the very encouraging judgement of significant progress given by Ofsted on the provision of education, skills and work, and the 'outstanding' grading awarded for through the gate services by HM Inspectorate of Probation. The Board is also aware that a return to 'normal service' will take both time and a sustained effort and will look to see it over the coming year.

## Main areas for development
### TO THE MINISTER

What measures are planned to address the backlog in the provision of offending behaviour programmes? What is being done in order to minimise the detrimental effect on men awaiting courses prior to parole board hearings while at the same time ensuring that public safety requirements are met?

### TO THE PRISON SERVICE

The Board restates the question it posed last year: Why are the Prison Service and its contractors unable to manage the efficient and secure movement and storage of prisoners' property, particularly during transfers? The loss of personal items causes a great deal of frustration and unhappiness for the individuals concerned that often detracts from their ability to settle. The costs to the Prison Service in replacing lost items must be significant.

### TO THE GOVERNOR

What can be done to ensure that men arriving at Channings Wood late on a Friday receive the same level of support during the reception process as those arriving during the working week?

### Progress since the last report

Concern: Significant delays in making arrangements requiring secure mental health provision, despite concerted efforts by prison and healthcare staff?

Response: The Minister acknowledged that despite the concerted efforts from prison and healthcare staff, there were often significant delays in transferring prisoners diagnosed with mental ill health to a secure hospital when the transfer is outside the Devon, Cornwall and Wiltshire clinical commissioning group (CCG) catchment 7 area. Mention was made of work to establish an effective escalation protocol and that an Early Days Mental Health Practitioner pilot was taking place across six sites which will be evaluated to inform future provision. Some progress on waiting times has been noted in the Board's monitoring.

Concern: Why are the Prison Service and its contractors unable to manage the efficient and secure movement and storage of prisoners' property, particularly during transfers? The loss of personal items causes a great deal of frustration and unhappiness for the individuals concerned that often detracts from their ability to settle. The costs to the Prison Service in replacing lost items must be significant.

Response: Little evidence of progress has been seen during monitoring.

Concern: While the Board very much welcomes the continued downward trend in many key safety indicators, progress in reducing levels of selfharm and the use of psychoactive substances (PS) is slower. What steps are planned to further reduce the number of prisoners selfharming at Channings Wood? Despite successes in the interception of drugs, can even more effective measures be taken to reduce the availability of drugs in the prison?

Response: Further significant reductions in psychoactive substance (PS) related incidents and self-harm have been noted.

**200 SPRINGFIELD ROAD**
**CHELMSFORD**
**ESSEX, CM2 6LQ**

**HMP & YOI CHELMSFORD**   Tel: 01245 552000

*For the latest reports on this prison please visit:*
https://tinyurl.com/bdfh26rv

*Important Changes:* **(1) Visits:** the identification necessary to access this prison and visit for social or professional purposes has changed; (2) **Money and Gifts** new rules now apply to these.

### Task of the prison/establishment
A category B local reception and resettlement prison holding adult men and a small number of young adults.

### Certified normal accommodation and operational capacity
Prisoners held August 2021: 712
Baseline certified normal capacity: 550
In-use certified normal capacity: 550
Operational capacity: 720

### Population of the prison
• Over 200 new prisoners arrived and an average of 83 prisoners were released each month.

• The proportion of unsentenced prisoners had increased to almost 60%.
• A quarter of prisoners were from black and minority ethnic backgrounds.
• The prison held 96 foreign national prisoners.
• 10% of the population were aged under 21.
• 125 prisoners were receiving antipsychotic medication and there was a high level of mental health need.
• 41% of the population received care from the substance misuse psychosocial team.
Prison status and key providers

### Prison status and key providers
Public
Prison group: Hertfordshire, Essex and Suffolk
Prison Group Director: Simon Cartwright
Governor/Director: Garry Newnes
IMB chair: Martin Burchett
Date of last inspection 21 May 2018 – 7 June 2018
Physical health and mental health provider: Castle Rock Group Medical Services Limited
Substance misuse provider: Forward Trust
Prison education provider: PeoplePlus
Escort contractor: Serco

### Brief history
HMP and YOI Chelmsford was built in the 1830s. E and F residential units were added in 1996 and G wing was opened in 2006. The prison serves local courts and holds those who are sentenced or on remand.
Short description of residential units
Old Victorian-built wings
A wing – includes segregation unit
B wing – reverse cohort and induction units
C wing – general population
D wing – general population
E wing – drug interventions unit
F wing – general population
G wing – vulnerable prisoners on one side and enhanced prisoners on the other side.
Enhanced care unit – 12 beds for unwell prisoners, including those with mental health needs. Heath care staff attend the unit as needed to provide care for prisoners.

### Visiting Information
Booking lines: 01245 552 265 and 01245 552 240
Monday to Friday, 8:15am to 11am and 12:30pm to 3:30pm.
**Visiting Times:** Mon to Thurs: 1:40pm to 3:40pm

**Legal visits:** There are currently no legal visits taking place.
**INSPECTIONS & REPORTS**
**Urgent notification issued August 2021**
**Inspection Report Published 24 November 2021**
HMP Chelmsford is a category B local and

resettlement prison for adult and young adult men. At the time of this inspection 712 prisoners were held in a sprawling institution, comprising older wings from the Victorian era and more modern facilities added from the late 1990s.

Following this inspection, I wrote to the Secretary of State on 26 August 2021 invoking the Urgent Notification (UN) protocol (see Appendix IV: Further resources). I set out in detail my concerns about the prison and the judgements that had caused our course of action. Under the protocol, the Secretary of State commits to respond publicly to the UN within 28 days, explaining how outcomes for those detained will be improved. The Secretary of State's response, for which I am grateful, is also detailed in the further resources for this report.

We had last inspected Chelmsford prison in June 2018 and reported our serious concerns about the conditions we found. At that time, we assessed outcomes in safety and purposeful activity as poor, our lowest assessment, and in respect, not sufficiently good. Only in rehabilitation and release planning did we judge outcomes to be reasonably good. Despite this, the then Chief Inspector was reassured by both local management and HM Prison and Probation Service (HMPPS) that they were aware of the problems at the prison and would implement strategies for improvement. Sadly, that optimism was misplaced. At this inspection we found no improvement in outcomes in safety and purposeful activity, both of which remained poor; no improvement in respect where outcomes remained not sufficiently good, and a deterioration in rehabilitation and release planning to not sufficiently good. In reaching these judgements I took full account of the additional pressures placed on the prison due to the Covid-19 pandemic, but also the failure of the special measures programme and other initiatives introduced by HMPPS to drive improvement. These had not worked.

As at our last inspection in 2018, a new governor had been appointed a few months before we arrived. We were encouraged by his vision and enthusiasm for the establishment, but we were also struck by the seeming intractability of the failings at Chelmsford. The last time we were able to write a positive report about this prison was 10 years ago and it was clear to us that the jail was failing in its basic duty to keep those it held safe. This report also highlights our concern about the negative and damaging staff culture. Many staff were new or inexperienced, their morale was low and they were disengaged from their work and dismissive of the men in their care. Prisoners found it very difficult to access even the most basic entitlements and were

frustrated that they could not get things done. We were told that this frustration had led to an increase in assaults on staff.

The negative culture among some staff was compounded by a lack of management oversight or accountability, which allowed poor staff behaviour and practice to go unchallenged. Other very serious concerns included the inadequacy of the prison's response to the high levels of suicide and self-harm, and the similarly deficient response to some of the highest levels of violence in the prison estate. The paucity of the daily regime meant that many prisoners spent extended periods locked up and isolated in their cells. It was no surprise that many prisoners told us that they felt unsafe at the prison.

Such factors, combined with the inherent risks and vulnerabilities associated with Chelmsford's status as a frontline local establishment and the failure to grip the prison's problems over recent years, meant that Chelmsford met our criteria for an Urgent Notification. I concluded my letter to the Secretary of State by saying that HMP Chelmsford would not improve without a sustained drive to make sure that all staff members take responsibility for creating a safer, more decent environment, a meaningful regime and greater engagement with training and education. I argued that this will require strong and consistent leadership at all levels within the prison and much more effective support from HMPPS. As we indicated in 2018 and repeat now, the drift and decline at this prison must be addressed.

Charlie Taylor Chief Inspector September 2021

**Urgent Notification**

HM Chief Inspector of Prisons demands urgent action from Secretary of State over continued safety concerns at Chelmsford Prison

HM Chief Inspector of Prisons Charlie Taylor is so troubled by the lack of progress to address violence, safety and poor conditions at HMP & YOI Chelmsford, a men's local prison in Essex, that he has issued a rare Urgent Notification (UN) requiring immediate action from the Secretary of State for Justice.

Inspectors from HM Inspectorate of Prisons (HMI Prisons) visited the jail in August 2021 and identified numerous significant concerns about the treatment and conditions of prisoners. Performance at Chelmsford has been assessed as deteriorating in a series of inspections since 2014, with inspectors finding "chronic and apparently intractable failings".

Mr Taylor said the 2021 findings were particularly disappointing as his predecessor, Peter Clarke, had decided against instigating the UN protocol at the last full inspection in 2018, despite evidence of many worrying failings. Mr. Clarke thought there may be grounds for some "cautious optimism" but, Mr Taylor commented: "We found that the optimism expressed three years ago was misplaced. The latest inspection has shown that these improvements have not materialised."

Since 2018, HM Prison and Probation Service (HMPPS) has supported Chelmsford in what were termed 'Special Measures' and then with a proposed Prison Performance Support Plan (PPSP), which had barely begun by August 2021. A new governor has also been appointed. However, Mr Taylor said: "It was too early to confirm any real improvements and it was clear to us that he and his team would need significant support."

Among key concerns were:

Safety. Mr Taylor said Chelmsford had "sadly failed in its responsibility to keep prisoners safe." It was found to be one of the country's most violent local prisons. There had also been eight self-inflicted deaths since 2018 and a further four non-natural deaths in three years. In addition, self-harm had continued to rise for the fourth successive inspection.

A negative staff culture. Although some staff were committed and constructive, many others described very low morale, disillusionment and disengagement. Many staff, for example, failed to respond to even basic requests from prisoners and too many were dismissive in their dealings with prisoners or evidenced only limited empathy. Almost half of the prisoners said that they had been victimised by staff, particularly those prisoners with disabilities and mental health problems.

Lack of accountability and management oversight. This enabled poor performance and behaviour to go unchallenged. Many staff had witnessed poor behaviour among their peers and too few took responsibility for the duties to which they had been deployed. Emergency cell bells were often only answered after long delays. A poor daily regime. Many prisoners were locked in their cell for almost 23 hours a day. This reflected Covid-19 restrictions but even in 2018 many prisoners had been locked in their cell for 22 hours a day. Plans to reintroduce a meaningful regime were limited and being implemented far too slowly.

The Chelmsford Urgent Notification is the ninth time the protocol has been used since it was introduced in 2017. It is used rarely, in inspections which identify significant concerns. The Chief Inspector writes publicly to the Secretary of State for Justice who is required to respond within 28 days with plans to improve the prison.

Mr Taylor concluded his letter by saying: "HMP & YOI Chelmsford is a violent, unsafe prison in which conditions for prisoners have declined disturbingly over recent years, despite attempts by HMPPS to support improvement. Many failings stem from a negative and demoralised staff culture which results in little apparent concern for (or attention to) the welfare and basic needs of a complex and, at times, vulnerable population. "Chelmsford will not improve without a sustained drive to make sure that all staff members take responsibility for ensuring safety, decency and engagement with training and education in a meaningful regime. This will require strong, consistent leadership at all levels within the prison and much more effective support from HMPPS than the approach it has taken in recent years, which failed completely to arrest the drift and decline which must have been obvious to the service."

**Debriefing paper for the inspection of HMP & YOI Chelmsford 9–20 August 2021**
**by HM Inspectorate of Prisons**
**Healthy prison assessments**

Outcomes for prisoners are good against this healthy prison test.

There is no evidence that outcomes for prisoners are being adversely affected in any significant areas.

Outcomes for prisoners are reasonably good against this healthy prison test.

There is evidence of adverse outcomes for prisoners in only a small number of areas. For the majority there are no significant concerns. Procedures to safeguard outcomes are in place.

Outcomes for prisoners are not sufficiently good against this healthy prison test.

There is evidence that outcomes for prisoners are being adversely affected in many areas or particularly in those areas of greatest importance to the well- being of prisoners. Problems/ concerns, if left unattended, are likely to become areas of serious concern.

Outcomes for prisoners are poor against this healthy prison test.

There is evidence that the outcomes for prisoners are seriously affected by current practice. There is a failure to ensure even adequate treatment of and/or conditions for prisoners. Immediate remedial action is required.

**Leadership**

Our judgements about leadership take a narrative form and do not result in a score.

• A previous programme of support from HMPPS known as Special Measures had been largely ineffective in improving outcomes at Chelmsford and none of our key concerns from our last inspection in 2018 had been fully achieved.

• In the autumn of 2020 HMPPS recognised the need to provide further support to improve outcomes through the introduction of a Prison Performance Support programme but this had experienced delays and one year later had barely begun.

• Significant changes within the leadership team at the prison had taken place over recent months including a new governor and deputy. They had clear ambitions to drive performance and were committed to improvements, but there was still a need for fuller engagement from the wider staff group in taking forward the priorities. It was clear to us that the governor and his team would need significant support in improving outcomes.

• The use of data was weak in many key functions and action to make improvements was lacking, even when data suggested it was needed.

• Leaders and staff paid insufficient attention to analysing, understanding and addressing poor outcomes, including those relating to safety. The key concerns found at our last inspection persisted.

• The dominant culture among staff was one of disillusionment and disengagement, issues that had been evident at Chelmsford for years. The culture was negative and damaging and failed to support or promote safety.

• There had been a clear lack of accountability and management oversight of practice at all levels, which enabled some poor performance and behaviour to go unchallenged. For example, many staff failed to respond to even basic requests from prisoners and too many were dismissive in their day-to-day dealings or evidenced only limited empathy for those in their care.

• Staff training had been neglected during the Covid-19 restrictions. Nearly a third of staff had been in post for less than two years and had not yet received adequate mentoring or support. There was no current training plan, but a new manager had taken up post recently and was seeking to rectify this.

• Partnership working between health care and the prison needed improving to ensure services were delivered as intended.

• Leaders had neglected Prisons and Probation Ombudsman (PPO) and HMI Prisons action plans which was poor given the areas of repeated concern including, for example, the high number of self-inflicted deaths over the last three years.

• Like other prisons, Chelmsford had been hit hard by the Covid-19 restrictions and a large-scale outbreak in the first few months of 2021 made it difficult for the prison to deliver even the very basic regime for about two months. This outbreak was managed well but since then the pace of recovery from the restrictions had been far too slow. For example, most prisoners were still locked in cell for almost 23 hours a day.

**Safety**

Outcomes for prisoners against this healthy prison test remained poor. Early days in custody

• Chelmsford remained a busy local prison receiving around 48 new arrivals each week.

• Despite some redecorating, the reception area was in need of further improvement. Holding rooms were stark and some toilets were unscreened.

• Prisoners were interviewed in private both during the reception process and when located on the first night centre.

• The regime on the first night centre was poor. Some prisoners spent too long there before being moved to another wing. They waited too long to get their basic needs met.

• Cells approved for occupation were often poorly prepared and prisoners spent too long locked in their cells.

• The full induction programme had been suspended at the start of the pandemic and had not restarted, which was a gap.

**Managing behaviour**

**Encouraging positive behaviour**

• In our survey, 27% of prisoners said that they currently felt unsafe which remained similar to our 2018 finding.

• Violence levels remained among the highest of all local prisons since 2018.

• Almost half of the prisoners in our survey said that they had been victimised by staff and those with disabilities and mental health problems were significantly more negative.

• Leaders placed too much reliance on the safer custody team to address violence, but the team were not provided with consistent resources to deliver these priorities and there was insufficient support for this work from staff and leaders.

• The challenge, support and intervention plan (CSIP) process was not used effectively. There was insufficient challenge of the behaviour of perpetrators of violence and support for victims was poor.

• The use of data was limited and did not inform the violence reduction strategy. There was no associated plan to drive and monitor actions to reduce violence and make the prison safer.

• There was no strategy to use incentives to improve the culture and the regime. The use of basic privileges had been reintroduced to challenge poor behaviour but was not being applied consistently.

**Adjudications**

• The number of adjudications over the previous 12 months was similar to our last inspection, although we found that some charges could have been dealt with by more informal responses.

• Poor quality report writing meant that some

charges had had to be abandoned, although it was more positive that work had taken place to reduce the number of adjourned charges.

### Use of force
• The number of times use of force had been used had reduced slightly since our last inspection but remained higher than many similar prisons.
• Most incidents of force were unplanned, and they often involved younger prisoners.
• In the cases we reviewed, we were satisfied that incidents were proportionate and there was evidence of de-escalation. However, staff did not routinely activate body-worn video cameras in response to unplanned incidents.
• A monthly report contained a useful range of data, but despite analysis, actions were not identified to further reduce the use of force.

### Segregation
• The segregation unit was reasonably clean, but some cells were damp, and we were told about poor drainage issues.
• The daily regime was poor and more could have been done to encourage those who failed to engage.
• There had been good focus on the reintegration of a few very complex prisoners into the general population.
• Despite a useful range of available data for all aspects of disciplinary procedures (segregation, force and adjudications), there was no systematic analysis to drive improvements in practice and promote positive outcomes.

### Security
• Security arrangements were generally proportionate and aligned to the risks. However, some procedures were disproportionate, such as the routine use of handcuffs for prisoners being escorted to hospital and strip-searching in reception.
• Awareness of key threats was good, but there was little analysis of data or identification of actions to ensure progress. Intelligence reports were not analysed quickly enough so there was a large backlog and it was not always clear what action had been taken as a result.
• The supply of illicit drugs and other items remained a clear threat. Some positive steps had been taken to try to manage this, but we were surprised to find that the body scanner was often not used, and drug testing was yet to recommence.
• Leaders had worked effectively with the police when staff corruption was suspected, and this had yielded some positive results.

### Safeguarding
Suicide and self -harm prevention
• Despite some serious failings identified by the

PPO and others, the key concerns and recommendations from our last inspection had not been achieved.
• There had been eight self-inflicted deaths and four non-natural deaths since 2018.
• There had also been a large increase in the number of self-harm incidents since 2018, reflecting an increase across four successive inspections.
• The PPO action plan was out of date and implementation of some of the recommendations had been too slow.
• During our night visit we observed serious flaws in safety practice.
• Staff lacked confidence in using the new ACCT document and felt they had received too little training. We found many weaknesses in its completion. Prisoners we spoke to were mixed in their views about support provided while on an ACCT.
• The strategic approach to self-harm was limited and there had been no detailed analysis of data to fully understand the causes and drivers.
• There were too few Listeners for the population and access to them was poor, with only 34% of prisoners in our survey reporting it was easy to speak to a Listener if they wanted to.

### Protection of adults at risk
• The adult safeguarding policy was brief and links with the local safeguarding adults board had lapsed.
• Most staff we spoke to were unfamiliar with safeguarding procedures and associated procedures, which increased the risk of needs being missed.

### Respect
Outcomes for prisoners against this healthy prison test remained not sufficiently good.

### Staff -prisoner relationships
• In our survey, about two-thirds of prisoners said that most staff treated them with respect and that there were staff they could turn to if they had a problem; both of these were significantly more negative than at our last inspection. Some groups of prisoners, including younger adults were even more negative in their views than others.
• Many prisoners we spoke to could name good staff and we observed some friendly and supportive interactions. However, the most common theme reported by prisoners was of staff not responding to basic requests, being dismissive and not showing care or compassion. This led to high levels of frustration and prison leaders suggested this was linked to an increase in assaults on staff. This negative and damaging staff culture undermined the focus on

rehabilitation and had been allowed to go unchallenged for far too long.
• Other factors such as poor time out of cell and the high use of force presented further barriers to effective staff-prisoner relationships.
• As in our last inspection, there were plans to provide additional support and training for staff, but none of this work was yet in place. The lack of staff training in mental health and trauma were significant gaps.
• The key worker scheme was not working as intended by the Offender Management in Custody (OMiC) model and plans to restore it were not ambitious.

### Daily life
### Living conditions
• The older part of the prison was cramped and remained significantly overcrowded. The newer wings were better laid out, brighter and more open.
• Standards of cleanliness on most wings had improved since our last inspection. However, many cells across the site were very grubby and in poor repair. We saw many cells with graffiti and inadequate furniture. There was a shortage of some key amenities, including pillows, decent mattresses, and kettles.
• Only 55% of prisoners in our survey said they normally had enough clean, suitable clothes for the week. Only 50% said they had clean sheets every week. Wing laundry facilities were inadequate and weekly kit change did not always happen.
• Despite work to control the issue, there was still a significant problem with rats, including on wings and in food servery areas.
• There was inadequate oversight of staff response times to emergency cell bells. In logs we looked at, there were delays of up to 39 minutes.
• Staff appeared to have become inured to the poor conditions and some inexperienced staff did not have the benefit of comparing conditions at Chelmsford to conditions found in other prisons.

### Residential services
• In our survey, only 19% of prisoners said the food was very or quite good and only 16% reported they had enough to eat at mealtimes. We also saw lunch being served at cell doors which was unnecessary.
• The main kitchen was unkempt and grubby. Some equipment was in poor repair and poor drainage left water pooling in cooking areas.
• Most prisoners told us the prison shop sold what they needed, although new arrivals still had to wait almost two weeks for their first order.
### Prisoner consultation, applications and redress
• Prisoners had not had chance to attend the prison council since the start of the pandemic.

• Application forms were widely available on wings, but prisoners' confidence in the system was low and the prison had no quality assurance process in place.
• The number of complaints was high, and the responses we reviewed did not always address the problem raised.

### Equality, diversity and faith
### Strategic management
• Strategic oversight of equalities work had improved since the last inspection. However, some weaknesses remained, and provision had been further adversely impacted by Covid-19 restrictions.
• There was now a monthly meeting to oversee equality work, and good partnership working with Ipswich and Suffolk Commission for Race Equality (ISCRE). The meeting was informed by some particularly good consultation with black and minority ethnic prisoners. It was much less focused on the needs of prisoners in other protected groups.
• A wide range of equality data was collated but analysis of data was generally weak. There was insufficient discussion and action on some areas of disproportion, such as the use of force against black and minority ethnic and younger prisoners.
• The quality of most discrimination incident reporting form (DIRF) investigations and responses was good.
• On the whole, prisoners in protected groups reported similar treatment and conditions in their responses to most questions in our survey.
• Some reasonable efforts had been made to provide translated material, but professional telephone interpretation was not always used when required.
• There had been insufficient attention to the needs of prisoners with disabilities and not enough adjustments had been made to meet their needs. Arrangements for their evacuation were inadequate. Informal 'buddy' arrangements were not supervised.
• Although the Youth Council continued to meet throughout much of 2020, it was currently suspended. The younger persons strategy was predicated on the provision of a good regime and had not been adjusted to account for Covid-19 restrictions.
• In our survey, fewer prisoners than in our last inspection said their religious beliefs were respected. Religious classes and communal worship remained suspended, although chaplains had continued to see prisoners face-to-face, and pastoral support remained strong. The multi-faith room was run down.
### Health, well-being and social care
• Some aspects of health care had improved but significant staffing issues within the pharmacy

and mental health teams had a negative impact on service delivery.
- We found too many examples of patients missing doses of their medication or waiting too long for medication to arrive, which was poor.
- There remained some weaknesses in partnership working between the prison and health care services, with longstanding issues such as inconsistent officer support to effectively manage medicine administration and the cancellation of external hospital appointments happening too frequently.
- Effective communication between key stakeholders was evident in the management of Covid-19. The rollout of the Covid-19 vaccination programme had been progressing well but had been delayed due to an error in administration.
- The management of long-term health conditions and complex needs had generally improved since the last inspection, with evidence-based care plans and patients receiving regular reviews.
- All prisoners aged over 50 were screened by health care staff to assess their ability to complete daily living activities and were offered additional support, which was notable positive practice.
- Partnership working between the prison and Essex County Council in relation to social care needed improvement. Despite this, social care outcomes for prisoners were generally good.
- Officers on the enhanced care unit knew the prisoners well and were caring. Most of the prisoners had mental health needs but the unit lacked an overall therapeutic approach and its function was unclear.
- Forward Trust substance misuse clinical and psychosocial services were very good.
- The prison was one of two national pilot sites for the prescribing of Buvidal (buprenorphine by depot injection) in prisons, which was innovative.
- The mental health team was mostly made up of agency nurses which meant that continuity of service may have been compromised. They provided good support on a needs basis rather than having individual caseloads to cover the staffing deficits within the team.
- The Improving Access to Psychological Therapies (IAPT) service was providing good support and had been commissioned to make contact with a specific cohort of prisoners to reduce the risks of suicide, which was a promising initiative.
- Patients requiring transfer to secure mental health facilities continued to wait too long for a place.
- There was a long waiting list for the dentist. The provision of AGP treatment was delayed because officers didn't have the correct PPE to enter the room in an emergency.

**Purposeful activity**
Outcomes for prisoners against this healthy prison test remained poor.

**Time out of cell**
- Prisoners were not sure when they would be unlocked as the core day was not published and there were inconsistencies in the account different staff gave about the daily regime.
- Only 15% of prisoners were in full-time employment. They could spend up to seven hours out of their cell.
- Over 16 months after the pandemic began, almost half the population was unemployed. They were locked in the cells for almost 23 hours a day, which placed an inevitable toll on their well-being.
- Our roll checks found 50% of prisoners locked in cells during the working day.
- Although regular, exercise periods were still too short.
- There was little creative use of peer workers to promote constructive activity. Library and PE
- The library had been closed since the beginning of the pandemic and was only reopened during our inspection. The remote library service was not well promoted by prison staff and its use had been limited.
- Covid-19 had led to the closure of the gym and it didn't reopen until June 2021, which was later than many other prisons.
- There were credible plans for the reintroduction of accredited learning through the gym and links to the community such as the FA Twinning project.

**Education, skills and work activities**
- Leaders and managers had worked closely with the education provider to ensure that prisoners had access to in-cell education through a variety of learning packs during the national restrictions.
- Leaders and managers had successfully put in place their plans to bring back the full curriculum in education, skills and work. This allowed small groups of prisoners to return to face-to-face teaching and instruction in almost all subject areas.
- Leaders recognised that they did not maximise the number of prisoners accessing the available activity places and more places were needed to meet the needs of the population. Attendance was often too low, and prisoners' punctuality was not always good.
- Since the previous inspection and moving into stage 3 of the recovery programme, leaders had introduced new courses. Prisoners had completed new courses in food hygiene and had recently started a course in barbering.
- The courses and work available for vulnerable

171

prisoners and those in the drug rehabilitation unit were limited.

• Tutors and instructors provided good support to prisoners to develop their skills and gain new knowledge. Prisoners understood how they could use these newly acquired skills outside of the prison.

• Most prisoners enjoyed their learning. In-cell learning packs helped them to develop their knowledge in a logical way.

• Tutors marked prisoners' work frequently and gave prisoners useful feedback about how well they completed assessments. However, in a few instances tutors did not give prisoners precise feedback on how they could improve their work, such as in grammar and punctuation.

• The information, advice and guidance prisoners received at their induction was generally effective. However, the ongoing advice and guidance was not planned and developed well enough to help prisoners move on to their chosen next steps.

• Most prisoners felt well supported by staff. Tutors supported those prisoners identified as needing extra help, such as those with dyslexia, appropriately. However, prisoners with more complex needs, such as autism, did not benefit from clear, individualised support plans to help them.

**Rehabilitation and release planning**
Outcomes for prisoners against this healthy prison test were now not sufficiently good.
Children and families and contact with the outside world

• In our survey, only 18% of prisoners said staff had encouraged them to keep in touch with their family and friends, which was significantly lower than in 2018. However, the prison had, very recently, developed a positive strategy and action plan to promote this.

• At the time of the inspection face-to-face social visits were not available at the weekend, which was a significant gap.

• Family days and parenting courses had stopped at the start of the pandemic and there were no clear plans to reintroduce them.

• All visitors we spoke with said they had been treated with respect during the visit, but all also said they had experienced significant delays in getting through to the booking office by telephone.

• In our survey, almost all prisoners said they could use the phone every day, but we found some prisoners who did not have a phone in cell and one prisoner had not had one for a month.
Reducing risk, rehabilitation and progression

• Management of reducing reoffending work had been neglected last year but it had recently improved and looked promising, with a good needs analysis, strategy and action plan to drive forward improvements.

• Resettlement agencies had recently returned to working on site but were still not always seeing prisoners face to face.

• About 40% of the population were eligible for offender management support. As a result, offender management unit caseloads were relatively small. However, uniformed prison offender managers (POMs) often lost most of their time through cross deployment to other duties within the prison.

• Most eligible prisoners had an initial OASys and we found that initial resettlement plans were being completed on time. However, in our survey only 14% of prisoners knew they had a plan.

• Contact between prisoners and POMs varied greatly. In addition, the key worker scheme was not operating.

• Home detention curfew (HDC) was managed reasonably well within the prison but almost a third of prisoners were released late, often for reasons outside the control of the prison.

**Public protection**
• Public protection arrangements were not robust. For example, the inter- departmental risk management team (IDRMT) had not been functioning since the start of the pandemic, although there was evidence of reasonable risk management planning by individual POMs.

• The number of prisoners under mail and phone monitoring to protect the public was not excessive. However, there was a backlog of phone calls waiting to be monitored and we were concerned that requirement to monitor could be removed without the evidence to do so.

**Categorisation and transfers**
• Initial categorisation and reviews were timely, and most prisoners were promptly moved to another prison following sentencing.

• However, there were some difficulties in transferring category B prisoners and sometimes those convicted of sexual offences.

**Interventions**
• In 2018 we saw an innovative range of interventions to address offending behaviour, so it was disappointing that these had ended.

• The psychology department supported some prisoners on a one-to-one basis but POMs were not trained to deliver bespoke interventions for those convicted of sexual offending or domestic violence.

**Release planning**
• In our survey, only 43% of prisoners said someone was helping them to prepare for release.

• Too many prisoners were released without a suitable or sustainable address to go to and monitoring of this issue was poor.

- Despite a high level of need, support for finance, benefit and debt problems was weak.
- The positive resettlement 'drop -in centre' six weeks prior to release had not yet fully reopened.
- Resettlement planning in all the cases we reviewed was reasonably good, but there was little basic support on the day of release.

## INDEPENDENT MONITORING BOARD: Annual Report

The law requires every prison to be monitored by an independent Board appointed by the Justice Secretary; these are known as Independent Monitoring Boards (IMBs). The IMB must satisfy itself as to the humane and just treatment of those held in custody within its prison and the range and adequacy of the programmes preparing them for release; it must report annually to the Justice Secretary on how well the prison has met the standards and requirements placed on it.

### IMB Report 1st Sept 2020 – 31st August 2021
### Published 16th February 2022
### Executive Summary

As a category B local prison, HMP Chelmsford houses men that are sent directly from courts in the South Essex area (sentenced, on remand or on trial). Depending on the length of sentence and the individual prisoner's security category (established after initial assessment), it is possible a convicted prisoner may spend his entire sentence at Chelmsford. However, the majority will not. The average stay at HMP Chelmsford is 56 days. This means that the prison population constantly changes, with a monthly average of 57 men transferred to other establishments and 92 released. Stability is therefore very difficult to achieve.

The effect of Covid added to the pressure, with new arrivals spending their first 14 days in strict isolation, and most men spending up to 23 hours a day in a shared cell for much of the year.

### Main judgements How safe is the prison?

In our judgement, most of the prisoners, for most of the time, are safe. However, the prison is not without its problems. There were four deaths in custody during the reporting period and the number of self-harm incidents remained high. The prison has been criticised at inquests for failures in the way those at risk of suicide or self-harm have been supported. Bullying, debt and gang activity were, arguably, the underlying causes of much of the violence.

### How fairly and humanely are prisoners treated?

We witnessed many examples of good interaction between staff and prisoners, and good care and attention given to prisoners in need of support. Our most significant areas of concern were the infestation of rats in the older parts of the prison, the time it takes for the prison to deal with complaints, the process for safeguarding prisoners' property, and overcrowding – more than 70% of prisoners sharing cells designed for one person.

### How well are prisoners' health and wellbeing needs met?

Healthcare-related IMB applications were down 32% compared with the previous year and men were able to contact healthcare and pharmacy by phone from their cells. The most pressing problems are the time it takes for men to see the dentist, insufficient psychiatric support, and the difficulty in getting prisoners transferred from the enhanced care unit to more appropriate establishments.

### How well are prisoners progressed towards successful resettlement?

The lockdowns had an adverse effect, e.g. there were fewer opportunities for purposeful activity, there were fewer transfers to more appropriate locations, notably for category D prisoners and many areas were not always fully staffed, although towards the end of the year there were noticeable improvements.

### Main areas for development

To continue to improve the physical condition of the prison buildings.

To improve processes so that everyone can have confidence that prisoners' property does not get lost.

### TO THE MINISTER
### We urge the minister:

To make every effort to eliminate overcrowding, which is in conflict with the requirements of decency and respect and is in contravention of the United Nations Standard Minimum Rules for the treatment of prisoners

To ensure adequate funding for the ongoing improvement of the prison's buildings and facilities.

To work with other government agencies to ensure that IS91 prisoners (those detained by the immigration authorities) are informed of the intention to deport at the earliest possible moment, not at the end of their term, which inevitably means that they are detained beyond the end of their sentence.

To exert influence to ensure provision of suitable permanent accommodation for prisoners upon release, so that no prisoner ends up on the street.

## TO THE PRISON SERVICE
**We urge the prison service:**

To support the Governor and staff in making the changes and improvements highlighted by Her Majesty's Inspectorate of Prisons' inspection in August 2021, and those noted by us.

We would welcome a decrease in the OpCap and additional staffing during the transitional period to ensure that business as usual is not adversely affected by a concentration of effort on improvements.

## TO THE GOVERNOR
**We urge the Governor:**

To continue to take steps to reduce the levels of violence, self-harm, bullying, drug taking and drug smuggling.

To make it difficult for prisoners not to attend purposeful activity, so that they get the maximum opportunity to make themselves employable upon release.

To ensure that offender supervisors and key workers are given the time to perform their vital role, rather than being allocated to other duties at a moment's notice.

To continue to make every effort to ensure a clean and decent environment, including the elimination of accumulated rubbish around the exterior of prison wings.

To ensure that when staff assess whether newly arrived prisoners should be put on an assessment, care in custody and teamwork (ACCT) document, they are guided not just by the prisoner's presentation on the day but by an understanding of the prisoner's known risk factors.

## Progress since the last report

The Covid-19 pandemic had an adverse effect for much of the year, with a restricted regime, reduced opportunities for work and education, suspension of social visits and closure of the gym. Things improved when the prison moved to stage 3 of the Covid-19 restrictions roadmap. Prisoners were allowed more time out of their cells, workshops, classroom teaching, the library and the gym began to open up, and social visits were allowed again.

The refurbishment of the segregation unit on A wing was completed, allowing the use of the temporary segregation unit on D wing to return to normal use.

**SHAFTESBURY RD
BISLEY, WOKING
SURREY, GU24 9EX**

**HM PRISON
COLDINGLEY**   **Tel: 01483 344300**

*For the latest reports on this prison please visit:*
https://tinyurl.com/bdfh26rv

*Important Changes:* **(1) Visits:** the identification necessary to access this prison and visit for social or professional purposes has changed; (2) **Money and Gifts** new rules now apply to these. See page 16 for full details of the above.

## Task of the establishment

Coldingley is a category C training and resettlement prison for adult males, holding mostly long-term, including life-sentenced, prisoners.

## Certified normal accommodation and operational capacity

Prisoners held January 2022: 431
Baseline certified normal capacity: 493
In-use certified normal capacity: 483
Operational capacity: 433

## Population of the prison

• 418 new prisoners received in 2021.
• 56 foreign national prisoners.
• 43% of prisoners from black and minority ethnic backgrounds.
• Around 11 prisoners released into the community each month.
• 170 prisoners had been transferred to open conditions in the last 12 months.
• 134 prisoners receiving support for substance misuse.
• Up to 10 prisoners referred for mental health assessment each month.

## Prison status and key providers

Public
Prison group: Kent, Surrey and Sussex
Prison Group Director James Lucas
Governor/Director: Niall Bryan
IMB chair Heather Cook
Physical health provider: Central and North West London NHS Foundation Trust
Mental health provider: Central and North West London NHS Foundation Trust Substance misuse treatment provider: Forward Trust
Prison education provider: Weston College
Escort contractors: Serco; GeoAmey

## Brief history

Coldingley opened in 1969 as a category B industrial training prison. In 1993, it became a category C prison. E wing was opened in 2009 and an additional temporary unit, G wing, in 2020.

## Short description of residential units

A–D wings 93 prisoners each, mostly in single cells; none have internal sanitation, except for three double cells on each landing/wing.

E wing 115 single cells and eight double cells with internal sanitation, including a shower.

G wing 60 prisoners; all pods have internal sanitation, including a shower.

## Visiting Information

You can book your visit online:
https://www.gov.uk/prison-visits
**Visiting times:**
Monday - Thursday: 10am to 11am and 2:30pm to 3:30pm, Friday: 10am to 11am

**Legal visits:** There are currently no legal visits taking place.

## INSPECTIONS & REPORTS
### HMCIP Report
**Date of last inspection:** 6 & 10-14 January 2022
**Published 20th April 2022**

The prisoners at Coldingley, a category C training prison in Surrey, were spending up to seven hours a day unlocked; this was in contrast with other jails we had recently inspected, where prisoners were lucky if they got out of their cells for more than a couple of hours. Our visit came as the prison was recovering from a recent Covid-19 outbreak, but leaders had kept the regime open while successfully managing the risk for the 431 prisoners who were being held there.

Levels of violence at Coldingley were around average for the category C estate and the prison generally had a calm and friendly atmosphere. A consistent regime was presided over by a strong cadre of dedicated and skilled prison officers, though the oversight of support for prisoners at risk of suicide or self- harm needed improvement. At times it seemed to inspectors that the atmosphere was a little too laid back and there a tolerance of some low-level behaviour that should have been addressed. It was disappointing to see from our survey how readily drugs were available in the prison and there needed to be a concerted effort from leaders to reduce the supply.

Since I came into post in November 2020, I have rarely visited a jail about which prisoners spoke so positively. This was particularly impressive because the fabric of the prison in the older parts was poor, with cold, dark cells and shabby communal areas. A night sanitation system remained in place on A–D wings and waits to use the lavatories were so long that prisoners often had to revert to using a bucket in their cell and were unable to wash their hands. Inspectors were encouraged to hear that a much needed, extensive refurbishment plan was in place.

Considering the time prisoners were unlocked, it was disappointing that the provision of education was so poor, with Ofsted colleagues awarding it their lowest rating. This was a huge missed opportunity to get prisoners onto productive leaning pathways that would help them to resettle when released. There was also a lack of work opportunities available for prisoners, which meant that some did not have enough to do during the day and were not able to get used to normal working habits. Prisoners were not being sufficiently incentivised or challenged to go to work or attend education and during this inspection, we found too many either in their cells watching daytime television or socialising on the wings during working hours.

The effective and thoughtful governor knew his prison well and had well- developed plans in place to make improvements. As the disruption of the pandemic receded, he and his team had the opportunity to build on the excellent staff-prisoner relationships and to focus on making sure that all prisoners spend their time productively, either working or in education. There was also scope for building relationships with local employers, in a part of the country with a buoyant jobs market, to offer release on temporary licence for those prisoners who met the threshold. This would further prepare them for working life and incentivise good behaviour and attendance among the rest of the population.

Coldingley was a well-run and decent prison, but with renovation of the buildings, the development of a comprehensive, challenging work and education offer, and the reduction in the supply of drugs there was scope for further improvements. The governor and his team should be ambitious in aiming to make this prison a model for other category C establishments in the country.

## Safety

At the last inspection of Coldingley in 2017 we found that outcomes for prisoners were reasonably good against this healthy prison test. At this inspection we found that outcomes for prisoners remained reasonably good.

New arrivals experienced generally good reception procedures with several opportunities for staff to identify any vulnerability. First night cells were in poor condition and some contained offensive graffiti. Induction was comprehensive and conducted in person.

Most prisoners were unlocked, and the wings remained calm and settled during our inspection. Prisoner-on-prisoner assaults were 20% lower than at the previous inspection, and much lower than at similar prisons. Drug-related debt remained the leading cause of violence; the most serious perpetrators being subject to adjudication and monitored through challenge, support and intervention plans (see Glossary). There was good support for victims and those identified as potentially at risk from violence. Sufficient time out of cell, positive staff-prisoner relationships, extensive work opportunities and the ability to progress to better accommodation on E and G wings encouraged prisoners to behave well. However, the prison's response, tackling some low-level poor behaviour was not robust enough.

The use of force was low compared with similar prisons. Very few incidents led to full restraint and there was evidence of good de-escalation. The average length of stays in the segregation unit was relatively short. Staff and prisoner relationships in the unit were positive, but the regime was poor and reintegration planning was inadequate.

Security arrangements were broadly proportionate for a category C prison. The security team had effective measures to manage the entry of illicit mobile phones and weapons, but the response to drugs was less robust. There was no mandatory or suspicion drug testing, and inadequate CCTV coverage and supervision on residential wings. The prison lacked a coordinated drug supply reduction plan to improve outcomes in this area.

Levels of self-harm were lower than in most comparable prisons. Investigations into incidents of serious self-harm were good, as were complex case reviews that sought to support prisoners with the highest levels of risk. There was an effective and well-supported Listener scheme (prisoners trained by the Samaritans to provide confidential emotional support to fellow prisoners). However, levels of self-harm had increased since our last visit and there was no coordinated plan to address this. The quality of assessment, care in custody and teamwork (ACCT) casework documentation was variable and quality assurance processes were yet to address identified issues effectively.

### Respect

At the last inspection of Coldingley in 2017 we found that outcomes for prisoners were not sufficiently good against this healthy prison test. At this inspection we found that outcomes for prisoners were now reasonably good.

In our survey, 82% of prisoners reported that staff treated them with respect and had someone to turn to, which was higher than at similar prisons. We observed good relationships between staff and prisoners, and most staff had good knowledge of those in their care. However, staff did not always challenge low-level poor behaviour. The quality and frequency of key work (see Glossary) was inconsistent.

Despite some efforts to keep wings clean, accommodation on the older units remained poor. Prisoners did not have a toilet or sink in their cells and sometimes waited for hours before being unlocked to use communal facilities. Many prisoners reported continued issues with inadequate heating, compounded by broken windows in cells. Living accommodation on E and G wings was better; cells were more spacious, well equipped, and benefited from in-cell toilets and showers.

In our survey, prisoners were more positive about the quantity and quality of the food than at similar prisons, and they could access some self-catering facilities.

Prisoner council meetings were chaired by the governor, but it was not clear if consultation led to positive change. There were weaknesses in the prisoner complaints and application processes.

In our survey, prisoners with protected characteristics reported similar outcomes to others and it was clear that some staff had provided informal support to meet individual needs. However, the promotion of equality had not been prioritised by leaders and there were weaknesses in the identification and support for prisoners with protected characteristics. The provision and facilities for corporate worship were very good and the chaplaincy provided valuable support to prisoners.

Leadership and strategic oversight of health care were good and made sure there was effective monitoring of the provision. A dedicated primary care team delivered a wide range of health services, although waiting times for podiatry and optometry were too long. Early days mental health provision exemplified good practice, and substance misuse services were safe and effective. Gaps in the provision of psychological therapy had resulted in some unmet patient need. There was a reasonable pharmacy service and dental services were sufficient.

### Purposeful activity

At the last inspection of Coldingley in 2017 we found that outcomes for prisoners were reasonably good against this healthy prison test. At this inspection we found that outcomes for prisoners were now not sufficiently good.

Prisoners at Coldingley had more time out of cell than at most other closed prisons. Almost all prisoners were unlocked for around seven hours a day and those on G wing were unlocked all day. They could visit the library and go to the gym twice a week.

Despite sufficient time out of cell, too few prisoners were engaged in education, skills or work activities and too many were unemployed. Prisoners in education made slow progress in developing new knowledge and skills. Very few of those with additional needs received the support they needed to engage in learning effectively. However, prisoners on distance learning programmes benefited from dedicated tutor support in education, which enabled them to make good progress in their studies.

There were insufficient accredited programmes available to prisoners through work roles and workshops. The range of provision was too narrow in employer-led workshops, and the work prisoners completed was mundane and lacked challenge. Too few prison instructors were qualified in teaching or training.

Prisoners in education and work activities behaved well and had a good rapport with staff, and those engaged in vocational workshops worked effectively and productively.

Allocation to education, skills and work was not linked to prisoners' aspirations or needs, and they did not receive advice and guidance about future employment plans. It was too early to see the impact of the recently improved induction, and advice and guidance service.

There were sufficient activity spaces for the population and leaders made sure that the curriculum was well informed by local labour market intelligence and prisoner needs. They had identified accurate strengths and areas for development for education and vocational training. However, they had not considered the quality of teaching and curriculum content and had done too little to address known weaknesses. There was insufficient oversight of the quality of activities outside of education. Professional development for teachers was too focused on operational matters and did not help them improve their teaching and assessment practices. Leaders did not make sure that there was sufficient capacity in education to help the high proportion of prisoners with low levels of literacy and numeracy to improve their skills in these subjects. The prisoner pay policy did not provide incentives to take part in education and they could earn more from most other roles in the prison.

### Rehabilitation and release planning

At the last inspection of Coldingley in 2017 we found that outcomes for prisoners were good against this healthy prison test.

At this inspection we found that outcomes for prisoners were now reasonably good.

Social visits had resumed in May 2021 with sensible infection control protocols in place. Video call visits facilities on each unit allowed easy and unlimited access for prisoners. Family days had recently recommenced and were popular.

Reducing reoffending work lacked clear direction and there was insufficient focus on sentence progression. There was no credible action plan or evidence that data were used to monitor and improve outcomes. Prison offender manager (POM) contact with prisoners was reasonable with more frequent contact in high-risk cases. POM activity was task-driven and reactive, but overall was of good quality. Most of the sentence plans and risk management plans we reviewed were reasonably good.

The inter-departmental risk management team had an appropriate focus on managing prisoner risk in preparation for their release. The quality of reports prepared for multi-agency public protection arrangements (MAPPA) meetings was good, as was information sharing with community offender managers.

In the previous 12 months, 170 prisoners had been moved to open conditions. There were some delays to recategorisation due to out of date offender assessment system (OASys) reports and because prisoners had not completed offending behaviour work. Coldingley had stopped delivering all offending behaviour programmes and in the previous 12 months only one prisoner had been transferred to complete a programme elsewhere. Some prisoners had not sufficiently reduced their risk of harm or reoffending due to the lack of accredited offender behaviour work.

There were about 10 releases into the community each month, about half of whom were high risk and therefore released to approved premises. The prison was unable to provide data on the number of prisoners released without a suitable address. Every release was considered at the monthly resettlement meeting to make sure that all relevant action had been taken to meet prisoners' needs before they left.

### Key concerns and recommendations

Key concerns and recommendations identify the issues of most importance to improving outcomes for prisoners and are designed to help establishments prioritise and address the most significant weaknesses in the treatment and conditions of prisoners.

During this inspection we identified some areas of key concern and have made a small number of recommendations for the prison to address those concerns.

Key concern: In our survey, 38% of prisoners said drugs were easy to get hold of at the prison and most safety issues related to debt were associated with the use of illicit substances. Drug testing and aspects of searching were inadequate. The prison lacked an effective multidisciplinary strategy to reduce the supply of drugs and manage associated problems.

Recommendation: Leaders should develop a coordinated prison wide strategy to detect and reduce the supply of illegal drugs and associated debt, bullying and violence. (To the governor)

Key concern: The quality of some assessment, care in custody and teamwork (ACCT) casework management documents for at-risk prisoners was poor. Actions agreed at case reviews were not always identified on care plans, which left staff ill equipped to follow them through. The quality assurance system and subsequent action plan had not addressed the problem.

Recommendation: A robust quality assurance system should make sure that actions agreed at assessment, care in custody and teamwork (ACCT) reviews are clearly recorded on care plans and then completed by staff to help prisoners through their period of crisis. (To the governor)

Key concern: Over half the prisoners lived on the older wings in poor conditions. The outdated sanitation system meant there were no toilets or running water in cells. Prisoners faced long waits to use the communal toilets or were forced to use buckets in their cells with no facilities to wash their hands. Cells were cramped, dingy and cold, which was compounded by broken and moulding windows.

Recommendation: All prisoners should live in suitable accommodation with reliable heating, a toilet and hand washing facilities. (To the governor)

Key concern: Work to ensure equality at the prison had not been prioritised during the pandemic. Leaders did not monitor disproportionality, the equality action plan had been closed and consultation with prisoners with protected characteristics was very limited.

Recommendation: There should be effective consultation and monitoring to make sure that the needs of prisoners with protected characteristics are identified and met, and that disproportionate outcomes are addressed. (To the governor)

Key concern: Psychological therapy provision did not meet patient need, with staff shortages resulting in approximately 40 waiting for their treatment to start, some for many months.

Recommendation: Patients diagnosed with a need for psychological therapy should be treated promptly. (To the governor)

Key concern: Leaders and managers had not considered the quality of teaching and assessment, the appropriateness of the content of learning programmes or how effectively education and training courses were designed. No effective action had been taken to make sure that the quality of education, skills and work improved, and too many prisoners were not successful in their learning.

Recommendation: Leaders should identify accurate areas for improvement in teaching and assessment practices, and in curriculum design and content. They should also identify and implement actions to make sure that teachers and instructors improve their skills in teaching, and enable prisoners to build on, and make progress in, developing their skills and knowledge. (To the governor)

Key concern: A high proportion of prisoners chose not to attend their allocated education, skills or work activity, and too many remained unemployed and not engaged in any purposeful activity.

Recommendation: Leaders and managers should ascertain the reasons why prisoners do not wish to engage in education and work, and take effective action to improve attendance and the proportion of prisoners allocated to appropriate activities. Prison staff should consistently promote the benefits of education to prisoners in their rehabilitation and future employability. (To the governor)

Key concern: The prison induction did not provide prisoners with useful information about their options for activities at the prison and to make informed and appropriate choices. Prisoners did not receive impartial careers advice and guidance to establish their aspirations or help make suitable choices about future employment.

Recommendation: Information about prisoners' aspirations and long-term employment goals should be used to inform allocations to education, skills and work activities, and they should receive impartial advice and guidance that promotes career development. (To the governor)

Key concern: There was no effective oversight of education, skills and work and the quality of prison-led activities was not monitored. Most prisoners in prison-led workshops were not challenged by their work roles and instructors did not help them to learn new skills. The progress that prisoners made in these areas was not recognised or recorded effectively, and too few prison-led activities resulted in accreditation.

Recommendation: The quality of prison-led activities should be monitored. Prisoners should be sufficiently challenged in all workshops, instructors should recognise and record the progress they make, and the number of accredited programmes in prison led activities and prisoners who achieve these should be increased. (To the governor).

Key concern: The prison lacked an adequate needs analysis to clearly identify the resettlement needs of the population. The reducing reoffending strategy and associated meeting did not identify and drive actions to make sure that support was available across all pathways. There was no evidence that data were used to monitor and improve outcomes.

Recommendation: Leaders should identify and understand the resettlement needs of the population and make sure that interventions and services are provided to meet those needs. (To the governor)

Key concern: There was insufficient focus on, and opportunities for, sentence progression by prisoners. Coldingley had stopped delivering accredited offending behaviour programmes and prisoners were not transferred to complete these elsewhere. There was little one-to-one offending behaviour work with prisoners, and sentence plans often failed to identify specific offending behaviour targets. Some prisoners had not reduced their risk of harm or reoffending sufficiently before release.

Recommendation: Prisoners' offending behaviour needs should be identified and met to reduce their risk of reoffending on release. (To the governor)

## Notable positive practice

We define notable positive practice as innovative work or practice that leads to particularly good outcomes from which other establishments may be able to learn. Inspectors look for evidence of good outcomes for prisoners; original, creative or particularly effective approaches to problem-solving or achieving the desired goal; and how other establishments could learn from or replicate the practice.

Inspectors found seven examples of notable positive practice during this inspection.

The work undertaken by the charity 'Belong', such as restorative justice training, mediation, and one-to-one sessions on conflict resolution, promoted positive ways of resolving disputes and preventing future violence.

The deputy governor scrutinised all incidents of force used against black and minority ethnic prisoners, which provided additional assurance and oversight.

The provision of an extended range of visiting health consultants, including a gastroenterology consultant, pain consultant and muscular skeletal specialist, enhanced confidentiality, enabled multidisciplinary working and improved waiting times for specialist care.

A mental health professional saw all new arrivals, which is not a practice that we routinely see in category C establishments. This made sure that all arrivals had an early opportunity to discuss their mental health and well-being, which enabled prompt referrals to appropriate services.

Prison leaders had prioritised time out of cell for prisoners, making sure that cohorting arrangements provided around seven hours a day, which was better than most prisons during the pandemic.

The uptake of video call visits was better than we often see. Facilities were located on each wing to maximise access. Visits could be booked by either the family or the prisoner, and there was no restriction on the number of calls each prisoner could make.

All prison offender managers now received regular supervision from the senior probation officer, and a monthly team meeting included speakers from other departments to improve awareness of how departments could work together more effectively.

## INDEPENDENT MONITORING BOARD: Annual Report

The law requires every prison to be monitored by an independent Board appointed by the Justice Secretary; these are known as Independent Monitoring Boards (IMBs). The IMB must satisfy itself as to the humane and just treatment of those held in custody within its prison and the range and adequacy of the programmes preparing them for release; it must report annually to the Justice Secretary on how well the prison has met the standards and requirements placed on it.

**IMB Report 1 August 2020 – 31 July 2021**
**Published October 2021**
**Executive summary**
**Background to the report**

The Covid-19 pandemic has continued to impact on the Board's ability to gather information and discuss the contents of this annual report. The Board has therefore tried to cover as much ground as it can in these difficult circumstances, but inevitably there is less detail and supporting evidence than usual. Ministers are aware of these constraints. Regular information is being collected specifically on the prison's response to the pandemic, and that is being collated nationally.

**Main judgements**
**How safe is the prison?**

The volume of drugs and mobile phones that continue to be found in the prison are of great concern to the Board. Large quantities of alcoholic liquid ('hooch') are also frequently found. Inevitably, the availability of these illicit items gives rise to increased levels of violence and bullying.

Significant positive efforts are made by staff, prison orderlies, Listeners, the chaplaincy, the restorative justice organisation, Belong, and representatives of voluntary organisations to support prisoners and deal with the consequences for prisoners' safety. It is to be hoped that the installation of a body scanner in May 2021 will improve the situation.

There are a number of health and safety issues, the most important of which is the absence of in-cell sanitation.

In addition, the fabric of the four older wings and the flooring on the newer (E) wing are in an extremely unsatisfactory state and repairs are still taking far too long to be implemented.

It is to the credit of the Governor and staff that the Covid-19 outbreak in the prison in September 2020 was effectively contained.

**How fairly and humanely are prisoners treated?**

The Board's view of staff -prisoner relations is a positive one. The supportive approach to prisoners is shared by non-uniformed staff, including workshop instructors.

Prisoners with complex needs are assigned a case manager and reviewed fortnightly. Assessment, care in custody and teamwork (ACCT) reviews are given due time and priority. Throughout the Covid-19 outbreaks prisoners have been able to attend their ACCT reviews.

The absence of in-cell sanitation impacts significantly on any assessment of how fairly and humanely prisoners are treated. No amount of humane treatment by staff can overcome the basic indignity for grown men, many of whom are elderly, having to ring a bell and wait in a queue to use the lavatory.

**How well are prisoners' health and wellbeing needs met?**

A restricted regime operated throughout much of the reporting period, but the Governor and staff are to be congratulated on organising prisoners into 'household bubbles' on a landing basis in January 2021, so that for the greater part of the lockdown, prisoners were out of their cells for five hours or more. Throughout, daily welfare checks were maintained.

Social visits were suspended in line with lockdown requirements, but video calls (Purple Visits) gained in popularity with the distribution of laptops to all wings. Several prisoners commented that they had never before seen their children opening their Christmas presents.

Healthcare provision continued to be largely well-regarded by prisoners and the Covid-19 vaccination programme was effectively handled, with efforts made to allay concerns that prisoners expressed.

**How well are prisoners progressed towards successful resettlement?**

Unsurprisingly, this area of activity has suffered as a result of infection control restrictions.

The lack of face-to-face education provision has impacted significantly on prisoners. This is particularly regrettable in view of the time that was available while prisoners were not engaged in their usual work activities, but which was effectively wasted.

The Board would however wish to commend the efforts made by the head of learning and skills to fill the gap left by the education providers by distributing in-cell packs, running competitions and inspiring the establishment of a library in the education department. The prison orderly responsible for organising this resource has done an excellent job. The main prison library remains closed at the end of the reporting period, but the librarian is delivering books to prisoners on request.

Work opportunities have of necessity been restricted during the pandemic.

Parole hearings by phone and recategorisation reviews continued to take place during the restricted regime.

**Main areas for development**

**TO THE MINISTER**

Absence of in-cell sanitation

As recorded in last year's annual report, the Board was delighted to be advised of the significant planned investment to improve conditions at the prison, including the provision of in-cell sanitation in the older accommodation blocks. The Board has been informed that major refurbishment, including the provision of in-cell sanitation, will commence in January 2022.

The Board is delighted to note the Minister's continuing commitment to this vital work.

**Indeterminate sentences for public protection (IPP)**

The Board continues to be concerned about the number of IPP prisoners serving many years beyond their tariff. Last year there were nine IPP prisoners at HMP Coldingley. As at 24 June 2021 there were five IPP prisoners, of whom two have served 11 years beyond their tariff date.

Would the Minister please advise the Board what the current plans are for addressing this issue?

**TO THE PRISON SERVICE**

**Violence and bullying**

There is continuing evidence in the daily reports of bullying and unexplained injuries which do not seem appropriate in a category C training prison. The Board is interested to hear of the 'Cuckooing' guidance and accepts that efforts are being made to combat this damaging behaviour. 'Cuckooing' is the term used to describe the taking over of a cell by a more dominant prisoner, usually for the storage of illicit items. Would the Prison Service please confirm that priority will be given in terms of resource allocation (such as effective CCTV) to keeping prisoners safe and free from bullying?

### The road to recovery

The Board is aware that it has been a difficult balancing act to keep prisoners and staff safe while considering the impact of infection control on other aspects of wellbeing, in particular mental health needs. The Board recognises that account needs to be taken of infection levels within the wider community as well as within the prison. However, where there have been no recorded cases of Covid-19 among prisoners for some time and levels in the surrounding areas are at an appropriately low level, it would seem that more rapid progress along the road to recovery might be appropriate.

Would HMPPS consider allowing individual prison Governors increased delegated powers to progress more rapidly if local infection levels allow?

### TO THE GOVERNOR

The Board recognises the work undertaken by the Governor, the senior management team (SMT) and prison staff to continue to provide a decent and humane regime in the face of considerable challenges, not least the Covid-19 pandemic and the absence of in-cell sanitation.

The Board applauds the significant efforts that have been made at HMP Coldingley to provide prisoners with as much time out of cell as they can have while adhering to infection control protocols, and ensuring that there was adequate provision for phone calls and video calls to maintain family contacts when social visits were suspended.

The Board trusts that the Governor will continue to press for commencement of the major refurbishment promised for the prison.

The Board also hopes that the option of video calls will be maintained once social visits return to full capacity as many relatives, particularly those with young children, find it difficult to access the prison.

### Progress since the last report

The installation of over 60 accommodation pods last year appears to have worked well, with prisoners generally appreciating the more relaxed environment and enhanced facilities provided. Work is proceeding to improve the pathways, construct canopies and to provide some gardening opportunities as requested by prisoners.

At the end of the reporting period, plans were proceeding to establish an incentivised substance free living (ISFL) community within the prison. The Board welcomes this positive initiative to reduce addiction and the associated debt and bullying problems.

In this difficult year, the Board has appreciated the time given by the Governor to attend Board teleconferences and the willingness of all staff to share information.

The Board resumed face-to-face monitoring on 17 May 2021.

SIR EVELYN ROAD
ROCHESTER
KENT
ME1 3LU

**HMP & YOI COOKHAM WOOD**

Tel: 01634 202500

*For the latest reports on this prison please visit:*
https://tinyurl.com/bdfh26rv

*Important Changes:* **(1) Visits:** the identification necessary to access this prison and visit for social or professional purposes has changed; (2) **Money and Gifts** new rules now apply to these. See page 16 for full details of the above.

### Task of the establishment

HMYOI Cookham Wood is a young offender institution for boys aged 15 to 18.

### Certified normal accommodation and operational capacity

Children held August 2021 87
Baseline certified normal capacity: 193
In-use certified normal capacity: 188
Operational capacity: 188

### Population of the establishment

• Approximately 29 new children were received each month.
• There were 16 foreign national children.
• 79% of children were from black and minority ethnic backgrounds.
• 50% of children were on remand.
• Around 15 children were released into the community each month.
• 62% would become adults while in custody on their current sentence or remand (33% remand, 29% sentenced).
• 75% of children had been excluded from mainstream education before coming into custody.
• 22% of children had experienced being in the care of their local authority at some point before coming into custody.

181

### Establishment status and key providers

Public
Prison group/Department: Youth Custody Service
Prison Group Director: Helga Swidenbank
Governor/Director: Simon Drysdale
IMB chair: Keith Morrison
Physical health provider:
Oxleas NHS Foundation Trust
Mental health provider: Central and North West
London Foundation Trust
Substance use treatment provider: Open Road
Prison education framework provider: Novus
Escort contractor: Serco

### Brief history

HMYOI Cookham Wood was built in the 1970s, originally for young men, but its use was changed in the late 1990s, to meet the growing need for secure female accommodation at the time. In 2007/08, it changed its function again, to accommodate 15–17-year-old male prisoners, to reduce capacity pressures in London and the South-East for this age group.

In January 2014, a new purpose-built residential unit was opened, incorporating integrated facilities and designed to meet the needs of the young people and improve safety.

### Short description of residential units

One main residential unit is split into A and B wings, with 176 single cells, each with an integral telephone and shower, spread over six self-contained landings. There is one room to accommodate a young person with a disability.

B1 aims to provide additional support to those young people identified as posing a risk to and/or from themselves and others.

B3 is the reverse cohort unit/induction unit.

Cedar unit is separate to the main residential building, holding some children who access release on temporary licence, and enhanced children in full-time education.

### Visiting Information

Booking line: 01634 202 557. The booking line is open Monday to Friday, 9am to 3pm

**Visiting times:**

Monday & Thursday: 2:30pm to 4pm
Saturday & Sunday: 10am to 11:30am and 2:30pm to 4pm

**Legal visits:** Please check with the prison for the latest information.

### INSPECTIONS & REPORTS

**Date of last full inspection** 9-13 August 2021
**HMCIP Report, published 16 November 2021**
Providing relatively new accommodation, Cookham Wood in Kent is a well- established young offender institution (YOI) that has been largely redeveloped in recent years. The institution can hold up to 188 boys between the ages of 15 and 18, but due to reductions in the population of children in custody during the Covid-19 pandemic, at the time of our inspection there were just 87 boys in residence. Coming from the greater part of south and south-east England, these boys had varying status, ranging from those recently remanded to those serving indeterminate sentences for the most serious of offences. The risks associated with the detention of such young people mean that this is the latest in a series of annual inspections, although there was some interruption during the pandemic.

When we last fully inspected Cookham Wood in 2019, we were concerned to find that outcomes for children were not sufficiently good against any of our four tests of a healthy institution. At this inspection we found they had not improved and had in fact worsened in our purposeful activity test, where outcomes were now poor. For an institution providing services to children this inability to address failings was completely unacceptable. Admittedly the restrictions imposed by the pandemic had not helped, but it was hard to understand why the institution had not been more ambitious in, for example, providing a better regime, perhaps adopting an approach that mirrored more closely that adopted for children in the community or at other YOIs. As it was, we found parts of the prison where more than half of children were locked in cell during the school day and typically spent as little as four hours a day out of cell, and just two hours at weekends.

We found low morale among staff, low standards, low expectations and a lack of energy and creativity that could engage and motivate children to use their time at Cookham Wood usefully, despite holding only half the young people it was resourced to hold. The response to difficulties found between children was invariably limited to keeping them apart, placing further restrictions on the regime. Leaders needed to find ways to move beyond this reactive and limiting approach, starting with energetic and motivational engagement with children, as well as the clear demarcation and enforcement of standards.

The key to this is good local leadership and national leadership through HM Prison and Probation Service (HMPPS). Since we last inspected a new governor and a further six senior managers had been appointed. The governor was beginning to implement a business plan which prioritised reducing violence, the creation of communities and investing in staff. These priorities seemed reasonable, although it was too early to discern progress and we were not convinced that staff were fully aware or engaged with this vision. Their engagement was not, however, optional. Staff needed clarity about what was expected of them and leaders needed to show greater rigour in ensuring policies were understood and delivered. Poor practice and behaviour needed to be challenged consistently, and staff needed to make sure basic standards were maintained.

We encourage close scrutiny by HMPPS, and the provision of support to assist the new governor of Cookham Wood. There needs to be a shared and collective determination that establishes how and when improvements will be made.

Charlie Taylor Chief Inspector September 2021.

### Summary of key findings

We last inspected HMYOI Cookham Wood in 2019 and made 32 recommendations, 14 of which were about areas of key concern. The establishment fully accepted 26 of the recommendations and partially (or subject to resources) accepted six.

### Progress on key concerns and recommendations

Our last inspection of HMYOI Cookham Wood took place before the Covid-19 pandemic and the recommendations in that report focused on areas of concern affecting outcomes for children at the time. Although we recognise that the challenges of keeping children safe during Covid-19 will have changed the focus for many prison leaders, we believe that it is important to report on progress in areas of key concern to help leaders to continue to drive improvement.

At our last full inspection, we made four recommendations about key concerns in the area of safety. At this inspection, we found that one of those recommendations had been achieved, and three had not been achieved.

We made three recommendations about key concerns in the area of care.

At this inspection, we found that all three had not been achieved.

We made four recommendations about key concerns in the area of purposeful activity. At this inspection, we found that one had not been achieved. Ofsted carried out a progress monitoring visit alongside our inspection, to assess the progress that leaders and managers had made towards reinstating a full education, skills and work curriculum. They judged that it was too early to assess whether three recommendations made at the last inspection had been achieved.

We made three recommendations about key concerns in the area of resettlement. At this

inspection, we found that one of those recommendations had been achieved and two had not been achieved.

### Outcomes for children

We assess outcomes for children against four healthy establishment tests (see Appendix I for more information). We also include a commentary on leadership in the establishment.

At this inspection of HMYOI Cookham Wood, we found that outcomes for children had stayed the same in three healthy prison areas, improved in none and declined in one.

These judgements seek to make an objective assessment of the outcomes experienced by those detained and have taken into account the establishment's recovery from Covid-19 as well as the 'regime stage' at which the establishment was operating, as outlined in the HM Prison and Probation (HMPPS) National Framework for prison regimes and services.

### Safety

The new escort provision from police and court custody had led to fewer children arriving at the prison late at night and had stopped unnecessarily long journeys to multiple destinations, as children were no longer transported with adults. Procedures were in place to ensure the safety of children on arrival and during their first night in custody. Good introductory information about the establishment was provided by staff on the first night unit. However, the remainder of the induction programme, which included important information, was rarely completed by children before they left the unit.

Children's perceptions of safety had improved, but in our survey 18% of respondents said that they had felt unsafe at some point during their time at Cookham Wood. Child protection and safeguarding referrals were well managed and there were good relationships with the local authority. Safeguarding officers conducted daily checks on the children who were identified as the most vulnerable. However, because of regular cross-deployment of staff to other units, officers had insufficient time to have meaningful engagement with the children.

The number of incidents of self-harm had reduced and was low. The quality of assessment, care in custody and teamwork (ACCT) case management documents for children at risk of suicide or self-harm had deteriorated. Oversight of this process was poor, and the quality assurance process was ineffective. However, children we spoke to who were at risk of self-harm felt supported by staff.

Levels of violence had increased since the

previous inspection and were very high. Some of these incidents were serious in nature. Staff set low standards on the living units and did not adequately challenge anti-social behaviour, endemic graffiti or the high levels of noise throughout the day and at night. Many residential staff were unaware of the multiple plans, targets and case formulations that children were subject to. There was an over-reliance on keeping children apart in small groups to manage conflict. This and the poor provision of activities and time unlocked for many created an uninspiring living environment.

Levels of use of force had reduced since the previous inspection. Oversight was good and appropriately challenged poor practice. In many incidents a large number of officers responded and were not swiftly stood down when the situation was under control. On occasion this led to confusion and hindered attempts to deescalate incidents. Body-worn video cameras were well used during incidents.

Appropriately, the segregation unit had been closed since the previous
inspection and children were now separated in their own cell. However, oversight of self-isolation and Rule 49 (good order or discipline) was lacking. The regime that separated children received was not recorded regularly, and when it was it the regime provided was poor. In one case over a nine-day separation, the child did not leave his cell for four days, and on two other days he had left it for just 30 minutes.

**Care**

In our survey, more children than at the time of the previous inspection said that most staff treated them with respect. We found relationships to be better on the specialist units (B1, B3 and Cedar) than elsewhere, but expectations of children generally were too low and we saw too many examples of staff not engaging with children during exercise or association. There was no system to make sure that children had regular, meaningful contact with a named officer, and most residential staff we spoke to were not aware of children's progress in areas such as education and sentence plans. Peer support was underdeveloped.

Although the accommodation was modern, communal areas and cells were grubby and untidy. The extensive and offensive graffiti in cells, communal areas and exercise yards was emblematic of the generally poor standards. Most cells were furnished adequately, and children had reasonable access to cleaning materials. Managers had recently introduced laptop computers for children in their cells, which enabled them to submit shop orders,

applications and food choices. The quality and quantity of food were reasonable, but children ate most of their meals alone in their cell. Consultation with children had recently restarted, but was not yet effective or influencing meaningful change.

The promotion of strategic management of equality and diversity remained weak. Equality monitoring data to identify differences in treatment did not lead to action, and investigations into discrimination complaints were either poor or did not take place at all. Equality officers were regularly cross-deployed, so were unable to fulfil their role successfully. We were, however, told that the appointment of a new manager for this team was imminent. The chaplaincy provided good pastoral support and delivered a suitable range of religious services.

Partnership working and governance structures were in place across the health care providers. Primary care services were well led and the provision was efficient. Primary mental health care interventions were delivered by a well-resourced nursing and multidisciplinary team. However, access to children was limited by the complicated unlock procedures and a lack of suitable rooms to deliver mental health interventions. Despite substantial investment, the Framework for Integrated Care (Secure Stairs) (see Glossary of terms) was not operating effectively. The substance misuse team delivered a range of psychosocial interventions, including 'through-the-gate' support for up to three months post-release. Clinical substance misuse interventions were available if the need arose. Pharmacy services were well organised, with improved oversight since the last inspection. Dental provision was good.

**Purposeful activity**

Ofsted carried out a progress monitoring visit of the establishment alongside our full inspection, and the purposeful activity judgement incorporates their assessment of progress. Ofsted's full findings and the recommendations arising from their visit are set out in Section 5.

The amount of time that children could expect to spend out of their cell was poor, at around four and a half hours a day on weekdays and two hours at weekends. Those who were segregated or isolating received even less, with a maximum of two hours out of their cells per day throughout the week.

Access to the library was good, with each child having 30 minutes' access each week. Children who were segregated, isolating because of Covid-19 or had just arrived did not have access and had to order books from a list through wing staff. There were good indoor and outdoor gym facilities. Most children spent three hours a week in the gym and had a good variety of activity.

Children were not able to access enough hours of education. They could attend classes for a maximum of only 12 hours a week, but in many cases they received far less than this. Too many learners attended activities that did not match their career aspirations or next steps. Attendance at education classes was poor. Children did not undertake enough learning outside formal education lessons. They felt frustrated, justifiably, that they spent too much time in their cell without doing anything purposeful.

Too many vocational training courses were not delivered or ran intermittently. This was, in part, due to staff vacancies and shortages, both from the prison and the education provider. Too few children developed their mathematics, information and communications technology, or English skills at satisfactory rates. By contrast, there were good standards of learning and work in food hygiene and music technology. Learning support practitioners were used well to support learners with special educational needs and disability.

The quality of children's written work was, too often, not good enough. Teachers did not correct learners' errors thoroughly.

### Resettlement

Despite good in-person and remote visits provision, few children accessed either. In addition, they were frustrated, justifiably, by delays in receiving mail, and in approving telephone numbers.

Leadership of resettlement had improved. A needs analysis was in place, with an action plan that drove improvement. Case workers held an average caseload of nine children, which was not excessive. However, the allocation of children to case workers by unit created unnecessary inconsistency when children moved units. Leaders had restarted release on temporary licence in late 2020 and there had been 136 events since then, but risk assessments were not good enough.

There had been considerable improvements in support for children transitioning to adult prisons, including the open estate.

All of the children we reviewed had a sentence or remand plan, although many residential staff and children were unaware of them. Some plans were too generic and not individualised to the child. Review meetings took place regularly, with most being timely, and contact with children was reasonable. However, records of meetings and of contact with children were poor and did not reflect the work undertaken. The limited use of the Youth Justice Assessment Framework system undermined effectiveness and created unnecessary risk.

There were weaknesses in oversight of public protection. While public protection meetings took place monthly, attendance was limited. Multi- agency public protection arrangements (MAPPA) management levels were not always confirmed before children were released.

The number of children with current or previous involvement with children's social care was high. Provision on site was good, but community social workers did not always attend the establishment for reviews or sentence planning meetings.

Release planning for accommodation and education started on arrival, but more work was needed to coordinate release planning across all the pathways. The prison had good oversight of accommodation a month before release.

The delivery of interventions had restarted following the pandemic

restrictions. While interventions were prioritised based on release dates and level of need, some children were released without having their identified offending behaviour needs met.

### Key concerns and recommendations

Key concerns and recommendations identify the issues of most importance to improving outcomes for children and are designed to help establishments prioritise and address the most significant weaknesses in the treatment and conditions of children.

During this inspection, we identified some areas of key concern and have made a small number of recommendations for the establishment to address those concerns.

Key concern: The number of violent incidents was high. The response to this was invariably to keep children apart from each other, which had a negative impact on their regime and reinforced the violent behaviour. Staffing unavailability, lack of engagement and redeployment of specialist conflict resolution staff to support the regime compounded the problem.

Recommendation: An effective violence reduction strategy, with a robust action plan, should be implemented to reduce the incidence of violence.

Key concern: Too much poor behaviour went unchallenged by staff. This included banging of doors, the blocking of observation panels and shouting out of doors and windows. Expectations of behaviour were not enforced robustly and there was an inconsistent approach to ensuring that even the most basic of standards were met. There was a lack of immediate or longer-term rewards or incentives to reward good behaviour and make sure that children who engaged could consistently progress and attain long-term goals both within the prison – for example, with a more trusted status – or as they moved toward release.

Recommendation: Consistent expectations of behaviour should be set and communicated to children.

Recommendation: There should be clear pathways for children that properly incentivise education, rehabilitation work and prosocial behaviour.

Key concern: The arrangements for separating children did not safeguard children's well-being. Local managers had failed to prevent children from being subject to potentially harmful regimes for extended periods. Oversight arrangements did not enable managers to be better informed of the interactions, education or health care input that these children were receiving. Safeguards for separated children involved a large number of cursory checks, rather than meaningful and dynamic engagement.

Recommendation: Leaders and managers should make sure that children subject to separation can access a regime that is equivalent to that of their non-separated peers.

Key concern: Extensive and offensive graffiti in cells, communal areas and exercise yards remained a significant problem and was emblematic of generally poor standards across the prison. During the inspection, children told us that graffiti was a 'normal' feature of the prison. Poor standards of cleanliness in cells and communal areas were not challenged effectively by staff and managers.

Recommendation: The establishment should be well maintained, clean and free of graffiti.

Key concern: The promotion of equality and diversity remained weak.

Equality monitoring data did not lead to actions or thorough investigations into disproportionate outcomes for some children in protected groups. Investigations into discrimination following receipt of incident report forms were poor and some did not take place at all.

Recommendation: Leaders should make sure that all incidences of discrimination are identified, investigated and addressed.

Key concern: The well-resourced mental health services continued to struggle with accessing the children in confidential and therapeutic rooms with allocated officer escorts, resulting in frequently aborted appointments.

Recommendation: Children should be able to access planned mental health care appointments in clinically appropriate and therapeutic environments.

Key concern: Time out of cell was too limited, at a daily average of about four and half hours on weekdays and two hours at weekends. Regime restrictions and controlled movement were responsible for many delays affecting the time available to children for education classes, work or recreation.

Recommendation: Opportunities for children to spend time out of their cell in education or other constructive activities, including social time together, should be increased, particularly at the weekend.

Key concern: Children were not able to access enough hours or a broad enough range of face-to-face education, and many were justifiably frustrated that they had too few in-cell learning tasks to complete.

Recommendation: Leaders should make sure that they maximise opportunities for children to study, including in-cell study.

Key concern: Leaders were not able to offer the subjects that they had planned as part of the curriculum because of shortages of teachers and prison officers. Too often, classes that were offered were delivered intermittently. As a result, not enough children developed their vocational, mathematics, English, and information and communications technology (ICT) skills at satisfactory rates.

Recommendation: Leaders should make sure that the curriculum includes sufficient opportunities for children to develop vocational, mathematics, English and ICT skills.

Key concern: Too many children did not attend their allocated classes, or arrived late to lessons.

Recommendation: Leaders across the prison should make sure that they work collaboratively to prioritise education and increase children's attendance at classes.

Key concern: Children's written work was, in many cases, of low quality. They wrote answers to theory-based questions that were partially incorrect. In a few cases, children did not take tasks seriously, and their answers to questions were of an inappropriate tone. Teachers usually marked this work as correct, without challenging the children to produce more detailed or accurate answers.

Recommendation: Leaders should make sure that teachers provide children with constructive feedback that helps them to improve their work.

Key concern: Despite good in-person and remote visits provision, take-up was low. In addition, children faced long delays in getting telephone numbers approved and receiving letters from their family and friends.

Recommendation: Children should receive support to enable them to maintain contact with their family and friends in the community.

Key concern: We found several areas where there was an absence of adequate risk management. ROTL risk assessments were not sufficiently robust; they failed to acknowledge any potential risk of harm posed by the child. MAPPA management levels were not routinely confirmed before release, and contributions to MAPPA meetings were variable. Case workers had no formal training in risk management.

Recommendation: Risk management processes, including ROTL and public protection, should identify and action risks adequately.

## Notable positive practice
We define notable positive practice as innovative work or practice that leads to particularly good outcomes from which other establishments may be able to learn. Inspectors look for evidence of good outcomes for children; original, creative or particularly effective approaches to problem-solving or achieving the desired goal; and how other establishments could learn from or replicate the practice.

Inspectors found one example of notable positive practice during this inspection.

Leaders and minimising and managing physical restraint (MMPR) coordinators alike challenged staff who did not turn on their body-worn video cameras. Staff had to provide justification for not turning their camera on, or turning it on after the incident had started, in their use of force report. Any staff who did not do this or could not justify their actions were challenged appropriately. MMPR coordinators told us that they had seen a rise in the use of body-worn cameras by about 30% since this policy began.

## INDEPENDENT MONITORING BOARD: Annual Report
The law requires every prison to be monitored by an independent Board appointed by the Justice Secretary; these are known as Independent Monitoring Boards (IMBs). The IMB must satisfy itself as to the humane and just treatment of those held in custody within its prison and the range and adequacy of the programmes preparing them for release; it must report annually to the Justice Secretary on how well the prison has met the standards and requirements placed on it.

## IMB Report 1 September 2020 – 31 August 2021
**Published 15 February 2022**
### Background to the report
This report presents the findings of the IMB at HMYOI Cookham Wood for the period 1 September 2020 to 30 August 2021. Following the pandemic, some Board members returned to visiting the establishment from August 2020 but stopped again in December when a local Covid-19 outbreak occurred. All members resumed visiting in May 2021. When they were not visiting Cookham, members performed remote monitoring, contacting staff by email and telephone, and reading daily bulletins and prison documents.

## Impact of the Covid pandemic
Boys at Cookham Wood were generally well protected from Covid infection, but an outbreak of Covid in the institution from 10 December forcefully demonstrated the need for vigilance. At the height of this outbreak, 60 staff had tested positive for Covid and over 90 were self-isolating. Twenty-two boys were quarantined after positive tests (though they recovered quickly and did not require hospitalisation). Strict and effective control measures were introduced, and the outbreak was contained within three weeks. From 1 January to 31 August, no boys tested positive for Covid.

For much of the year, the Medway area had one of the highest community infection rates in the country and the impact of this on the number of available staff was marked – particularly during and after the December outbreak, and again in July (with the spread of the Delta variant) when many staff were required to self-isolate following Test and Trace 'pings'. These shortages were compounded by attrition (officers resigning to take jobs outside the Service, e.g. with Border Force) and the need to clear accumulated annual leave.

By August, there were 17 band 3 officer vacancies and 28 officers still in initial training – a total shortfall of 45. It was little surprise that average daily time out of room for boys dropped steadily from 5.11 hours in February to 3.86 hours in August. Reduced officer numbers together with ongoing Covid regime restrictions, the high number of small group bubble movements daily, and regular ad hoc movement of officers between landings and duties (to fill gaps) led to significant inconsistencies in the way landings were managed.

As the daily regime was opened out to include timetabled 'integrated care and landing activities' (from March: two half days per week) and 'community learning' (landing-based educational activity) pilots, it became clear that the existing (pre-Covid) staffing profile no longer matched demand. A new staffing profile was prepared, increasing the number of staff during the core day and allowing landing officer to work in consistent teams (one team for two landings). It was still under negotiation at the end of August.

During this reporting period, the population of Cookham Wood has been well below the pre-lockdown operational capacity of 188:

## Main judgements
The published aim of the Youth Custody Service (YCS) is to create a safe, decent, and nurturing environment that provides outstanding levels of care and support for children in custody.

### Its stated priorities are:
* to be a provider of high-quality children's services, where skilled, enthusiastic staff have the tools and capability to work with children in

order to meet their individual needs, so that they are better able to lead rewarding, constructive lives upon their release.
* to ensure that children in custody are protected from being harmed and prevented from causing harm; that youth custody is an educational and supportive environment, helping to reduce risky behaviour and improve the life chances upon release.

The IMB recognises that Cookham Wood, being a closed community, was rightly deemed to be a high-risk environment when the Covid pandemic struck. However, very tight restrictions on the boys' activity and association have continued for far too long. These restrictions have had a detrimental impact on the boys' wellbeing and personal and social development, and indeed on staff morale. Crucially they have led to a complete failure of the service to deliver its aims and stated priorities as they relate to boys held in Cookham Wood.

Despite the best efforts of staff, Cookham Wood sadly did not provide a 'nurturing, supportive environment' this year. On average, boys were locked in their rooms for 20 hours a day during the week, and 21 hours at weekends. They had 10 hours' education (plus two hours PE) per week. Structured one-to-one support (custody support programme (CUSP), SECURE STAIRS, intervention programmes) for boys who were not considered vulnerable or high risk was substantially reduced or curtailed completely.

The key reason for these failures in service, in the IMB's view, was the restriction of association between boys to small group 'bubbles' (typically six to nine boys, with two or three bubbles per landing). This made the management of the regime much more complicated and difficult. 'Bubble working' was introduced to protect the boys from Covid infection, and to reduce opportunities for violence and group disorder in a time of crisis. While this strategy proved successful at limiting infections in the early stages of the pandemic, it was sustained, in the IMB's view, far beyond what was necessary or humane. The number of violent incidents remained high. This was not surprising, because bubble working, and the associated limitation of time out of room, fragmented the community; was boring and frustrating for the boys; and tied up prison officers, who became little more than 'unlock and movement agents' with little or no time to have meaningful conversations with the boys in their care.

The IMB believes that the continuation of 'bubble' restrictions on the boys' association and activity for a full 17 months after the initial outbreak of the Covid pandemic, albeit in line with Prison Service and YCS guidance and directions, was unjustified and oppressive. Continuing to keep boys locked in their rooms for much of their time was most definitely not 'an educational and supportive environment, helping to reduce risky behaviour and improve the life chances upon release'.

By the end of the reporting year, there were well-developed and very encouraging plans to 'rebuild landing communities' and increase access to education. However, the IMB believes these plans should have been developed and implemented much sooner.

### How safe is the establishment?
* The number of boy-on-boy, boy-on-staff and group assaults increased in January when there were staff shortages.
* During their short time out of room each day, boys generally mixed comfortably in small 'family' groups; some said that they felt safer mixing in these small groups. They developed trusting relationships with their landing officers.
* Despite this, the protracted lockdown had many other negative impacts on their wellbeing.
* The introduction of 'family bubbles' (small groups of six to nine boys) appears to have recreated a gang culture mentality in some boys, resulting in often violent incidents. There were multiple incidents throughout the year of 'many on one' assaults.
* The Board has no evidence that the use of physical restraint by staff has been anything other than necessary, proportionate, and tightly controlled throughout the year.

### How fairly and humanely are young people treated?
Staff are caring in their work, with a sympathetic understanding of the boys' needs. We do not believe there is, and have not observed, any deliberately inhumane treatment by staff; however, certain aspects of life at the establishment are inhumane:

### Physical environment.
The Phoenix segregation unit was unfit for purpose. The Board had serious concerns about the impact of the segregation regime, including the accommodation and facilities, on the boys who were held there. This was highlighted in the previous reports by the Board. This unit was closed for refurbishment and re-designation in December and was not yet open in August 2021.

### Treatment of prisoners.
Staff are fair and their relationships with the boys are generally good, but:
There is a significant sub-group of the prison population who have endured extremely long

stays isolated in their rooms. The lockdown has meant that boys were locked in their rooms for up to 20 hours per day (see section 6.5). As outlined above, staff are caring in their work, with a sympathetic understanding of the boys' needs. The Board has seen no deliberately inhumane treatment by staff.

However:

* A significant number of boys aged 18+, with long sentences and complex needs, waited months for their transfer to adult or young adult prisons.
* The delay in organising transfers to the adult estate in such cases is inhumane. The Board is pleased to note that there has been a significant improvement in the timing of transfers of 18+ boys over the last six months.
* The chronic lack of secure mental health hospital beds nationally for children has resulted in boys with significant mental health issues being placed in Cookham Wood for several months, which the Board considers inhumane. The boys do not receive the therapeutic treatment they need. The national shortage of suit able secure mental health accommodation for such boys is in humane.
* A group of adult men, one of whom admitted to being aged 30 years, were sent to Cookham Wood and could have posed a significant safety risk. Fortunately, staff handled the situation well and demonstrated that they could work imaginatively in a challenging situation.
* During this reporting year, staff have struggled to provide a consistent regime for the boys and there has been insufficient time out of room or purposeful activity. Gym sessions were restricted by a shortage of physical education instructors (PEIs).
* During the lockdown period, boys were well protected from Covid-19 infection. But their welfare suffered because of the tight and protracted restrictions on their activity and social contact. Relaxation of the lockdown restrictions was overly cautious, and there appeared to be little scope for local management discretion or flexibility.

## How effective is the education provision for young people?

* Education delivery has deviated from pathway-based learning since March 2020 to a restricted common curriculum offering for all boys. This has meant that boys have not had access to their chosen pathway, and education impact has therefore been less effective. Access to pathways has been restricted due to the limits on class sizes and in mixing of family bubbles.
* Schools in the wider community returned to full-time attendance in March. However, restricted access to education remained in place at Cookham Wood (in August 2021 it was still only offering 12 hours per week plus three hours PE).

* The education department has kept the maximum class size at six boys. They say the boys do not feel safe in larger groups.
* Despite the difficulties caused by lockdown restrictions, boys at Cookham Wood have achieved several positive results.

## How well are young people progressed towards transfer or successful resettlement?

* The situation in July 2020 was that no resettlement meetings had been held for more than a year, no reviews were being held, no interventions were being delivered, a significant number of 18+ boys with long sentences were stuck in Cookham Wood without plans for transition, and the sentence plans were Covid focussed. Since then, the resettlement team at Cookham Wood has been transformed. Previously the IMB had serious concerns at its lack of impact; it is now well led and managed, and we are starting to see an impact on the boys.
* During the Covid-19 lockdown, the resettlement team worked hard to maintain good working relationships with families, carers, youth offending team (YOT) workers and legal teams; but these relationships were very seriously handicapped by Cookham Wood's lack of information technology (IT) and telephone capacity limiting the quantity and range of contacts with external agencies.
* The Covid-19 lockdown seriously disrupted sentence planning; this was exacerbated by the large number of boys held on remand and the number of 18-year-olds awaiting transfer to the young adult estate.

## Main areas for development
## Outstanding issues from last year

There has been limited progress in the following areas since our report of last year – our comments then, sadly, are largely still as relevant now as they were a year ago.

There continues to be a chronic lack of secure mental health hospital beds for children nationally, and the time taken to transfer boys with significant mental health issues to hospital from a YOI is inhumane. Boys who have been transferred to institutions with better facilities should not have been initially sent to Cookham Wood.

Any delay in organising transfers to the adult estate for boys who have reached the age of 18 years is inhumane.

The lockdown highlighted Cookham Wood's serious lack of IT facilities and telephone capacity. This greatly inhibited effective communication and planning with both parents and external agencies. The Purple Visits video call facility has not proved popular.

**Development is required in the following areas:**

**TO THE MINISTER**

What urgent steps will be taken to work with ministerial colleagues in the Department of Health to provide more secure mental health services for children?

The percentage of boys at Cookham Wood who are there while being held on remand has increased over the reporting year.

An urgent review of court procedures is required, to avoid children enduring long periods in prison while being held on remand – with the potential for at least some of them being found not guilty at the end of their long stay on remand.

**TO THE YOUTH CUSTODY SERVICE**

Boys at Cookham Wood were still subjected to a severely restricted regime and were locked in their room for long periods. They were restricted to 'family bubbles' and not allowed to mix for purposes of education or recreation.

The IMB believes that the continuation of 'bubble' restrictions on the boys' association and activity for a full 17 months after the initial outbreak of the Covid pandemic was unjustified and oppressive. By the end of the year, there were well -developed and very encouraging plans to 'rebuild landing communities' and increase access to education. However, the IMB believes this should be developed and implemented urgently.

Additional care and support are needed for long-sentenced boys (specifically those with extended or life sentences). Violent and/or disruptive 18-year-olds in YOIs can become 'stuck' awaiting transfer.

Sentence planning is required to ensure that young adults do not get stuck in YOIs pending transfer to the young adult estate.

Is there end-to-end sentence planning and support for these boys?

Do they carry their sentence plan with them when they transition to a young adult institution? Or do they have to start afresh?

What steps will be taken to arrange transfers to the adult estate for young adults who are aged 18+ and have long sentences and/or needs?

At the end of August 2021, there were no plans to return to full-time education at Cookham Wood. Schools in England returned to full-time education in March 2021.

When will the YCS all ow full-time education to resume for boys in Cookham Wood so they can return to pathway-based education?

The service was unable to recruit a substantive Governor last year as a permanent replacement. Both the acting Governor and the deputy governor are temporary appointments. Cookham Wood will face further leadership churn in the future, suggesting a lack of leadership continuity.

Is the YCS confident that an appointment of a substantive post-holder to the role of Governor at Cookham Wood can be made? And will there be adequate plans in place to support a smooth leadership transition when this eventually takes place?

What will be done to increase IT and telephone communication facilities in YOIs?

Youth offending teams in certain London boroughs were not always helpful in resolving issues regarding young people placed at Cookham Wood. This has caused difficulties for the resettlement team on several occasions throughout the reporting year.

What can the YCS do to monitor and support YOIs when dealing with youth offending teams? Is the staffing level for youth offending teams adequate?

**TO THE GOVERNOR**

When will there be a revised timetable offering boys significant time out of room, a full education timetable and more purposeful activity time in larger groups?

As the lockdown restrictions are removed and a full regime is offered, there will be more opportunities for boy-on-boy assaults and bullying. How will the behaviour management policy be developed to address this?

What is the plan and timescale for the provision of full SECURE STAIRS support for all boys and staff? When will the refurbished Phoenix unit be opened as a functioning integrated care unit?

What will be done to improve the opportunities for boys of all faiths to attend collective / collegiate worship?

**Progress since the last report**

* The Phoenix segregation unit has undergone major redevelopment and refurbishment. It is planned to use the new facility as a breakout/outreach area for boys who have complex needs. The addition of such a facility at Cookham Wood will represent a significant step forward. (The unit was not open at the end of this reporting period, although it had been closed for almost 12 months).

* The resettlement team at Cookham Wood has been transformed. Previously the IMB had serious concerns at its lack of impact; it is now well led and managed, and we are starting to see an impact on the boys.

* A new visitors centre has been installed outside the entrance to Cookham Wood. This promises to provide enhanced facilities for visitors when it is fully operational.

* The continued operation of the Woody's Barista Cafe has given boys the opportunity to be

trained in the skills required to prepare professional quality food and beverages for staff and visitors in the prison, and to earn a City & Guilds qualification.

**PRINCETOWN**
**YELVERTON**
**DEVON**
**PL2O 6RR**

**HM PRISON DARTMOOR**

Tel: 01822 322000

*For the latest reports on this prison please visit:*
https://tinyurl.com/bdfh26rv

*Important Changes:* **(1) Visits:** the identification necessary to access this prison and visit for social or professional purposes has changed; (2) **Money and Gifts** new rules now apply to these. See page 16 for full details of the above.

**Task of the establishment** Category C training prison.

**Certified normal accommodation and operational capacity**
Prisoners held at the time of this visit: 615
Baseline certified normal capacity: 642
In-use certified normal capacity: 642
Operational capacity: 640

**Prison status and key providers**
Public
Prison Group: Devon & North Dorset
Prison Group Director: Jeannine Hendrick
Governor/Director: Bridie Steve Mead
IMB Chair: Colin Stares
Physical health provider: Care UK
Mental health provider: Devon Partnership NHS Foundation Trust
Substance use treatment provider:
Exeter Drugs Project
Prison education framework provider:
Weston College
Escort contractor: Serco

**Brief history** HMP Dartmoor is a category C training prison for up to 640 adult male prisoners. 2.2 The prison is situated in Princetown, on the western edge of Dartmoor National Park, eight miles from Tavistock and 16 miles from Plymouth (the nearest main- line railway station). Access is difficult, with very limited public transport. The local environment is harsh and can be particularly bleak in the winter months.
The prison comprises six residential wings (known in HMP Dartmoor as tors), a care and separation unit (CSU), a healthcare suite, a chapel, and education facilities and workshops. In addition, there is a large gym, a well-equipped kitchen and other facilities to support the life of the prison. A fully integrated smoke-free regime is in operation; all wings are integrated and accommodate main and vulnerable prisoners, including those who have committed sexual offences, in single cells. The prison and prisoners are supported by contractors and charities, either working in the prison or visiting on a regular basis.
The buildings are leased from the Duchy of Cornwall, and the Prison Service is responsible for their upkeep. Notice of termination of the lease has been given and the prison will close in 2023 unless the lease is renewed.
Most of the buildings in the prison are old but kept clean, built of granite and prone to damp. There are well-maintained and attractive garden areas. The prison is one of the major employers in the town, alongside agriculture, tourism and a brewery.

**Short description of residential units**
The prison comprises six residential wings:
Arch Tor, Burra Tor and Granite Tor: integrated mainstream units
Down Tor: an integrated mainstream unit, D1 is the PIU but is not used
East Tor: an integrated enhanced mainstream unit, including the RCU
Fox Tor: an integrated social care unit, including the shielding unit.
CSU: the segregation unit

**Visiting Information**
Visits booking line: 01822 322 022. The booking line is open: Monday to Friday: 9am to 12pm
**Visiting times:** Friday: 9:30am to 11:30am, Saturday & Sunday 9:30am to 11:30am and 2pm to 4pm

**Legal visits:** Legal Visits operate on Monday to Friday from 9am to 3:15pm. We can offer CVP (Cloud Video Platform) visits, telephone calls and in person visits. Please contact 01822 322408 or email LegalVisits.Dartmoor@justice.gov.uk for more information.

**INSPECTIONS & REPORTS**
**Scrutiny visit** 22 & 29–30 Sept 2020
**Scrutiny Visit Report, published 03 Nov 2020**
This report outlines the findings from our scrutiny visit to HMP Dartmoor, a category C training prison holding around 600 prisoners. The prison runs an integrated regime where prisoners who are vulnerable because of the nature of their offence are located with mainstream prisoners. At the time of our visit

just over half the population were convicted of sexual offences and 84% were serving sentences of more than four years.

Managers had been operating under a closure notice since 2013 and the 'planning blight' mentioned at the last inspection had continued. Many of the buildings needed capital investment to stop water ingress, equipment was needed to reduce the supply of illicit drugs and facilities such as the visits hall were outdated. In addition, it was clear that the closure notice had affected staff morale. This was made worse by the Covid-19 pandemic. In our survey, 55% of staff who responded to it said that morale had declined during the pandemic compared to just 5% who said it had improved.

The restricted time out of cell meant that there were very few meaningful incentives for prisoners who engaged well with staff and the regime. Levels of violence remained low and violence against prisoners had reduced, although there had been an increase in assaults against staff since the start of the restrictions. Safer custody peer workers provided good support to prisoners who were victims of bullying and violence. In contrast to the fall in violence, use of force had doubled during the restrictions. Oversight had been maintained but there were too many occasions where body-worn video cameras were not turned on at the start of incidents for managers to be confident that this significant rise in use of force was justified.

There had been one self-inflicted death in May 2020 which was subject to a Prisons and Probation Ombudsman investigation. While self-harm had reduced, the number of ACCT documents (see Glossary of terms) opened had increased during the pandemic as wing staff were identifying increasing numbers of prisoners struggling with the restrictions. A safety intervention team had been established with officers detailed each day to see every prisoner identified as vulnerable, which was positive. However, there was no management oversight of the ACCT process and documents that we reviewed were poor. Demand for Listeners (prisoners trained by the Samaritans to provide emotional support to fellow prisoners) had tripled during the restrictions and there were too few for a prison of this size.

In our survey, 82% of prisoners said that staff treated them with respect, and we found that relationships were generally good. Many prisoners were trusted to work in peer support roles although these were operating a restricted service. The key work scheme had been suspended which was a significant gap in provision.

All prisoners lived in single cells and staff and prisoners ensured that dilapidated wings were cleaned to a high standard. Outside areas were also clean and tidy. Responses to complaints were timely and generally addressed the issues raised. Prisoners were positive about the food and our findings supported these views.

Equality and diversity work had stopped at the start of the pandemic which left managers unable to explain poor perceptions among prisoners with disabilities and poor mental health. Discrimination complaints were not adequately investigated and many of the responses were dismissive. At the time of our visit there was no plan to reinstate this work.

Partnership working between the establishment, the main health provider and Public Health England was managing the risks of Covid-19 effectively. There had been no confirmed positive cases since April. Health care services were limited at the start of the pandemic and an appropriate triage system was in place to enable prisoners to access a GP. About a third of the population was over 50 and many prisoners had long-term health conditions. It was positive that services were being restored but we had concerns about very long waiting lists for the dentist, optician, podiatrist and physiotherapist.

The mental health service had worked remotely at the start of the pandemic and was now undertaking one-to-one work with prisoners. The 57 prisoners receiving opiate substitution treatment continued to receive regular joint reviews with a specialist prescriber and a member of the psychosocial team. Medicines administration was reasonable but lacked privacy on some wings.

The prison continued to make social care referrals but the local authority had not carried out any assessments during the pandemic.

Time out of cell was very limited, and most prisoners were only unlocked for one hour a day. Managers were preparing further improvements and if the prison gained approval to move into stage two of the national recovery plan (see Glossary of terms) the regime would be significantly improved. However, there was no justification for the very limited time out of cell prisoners could access while the prison remained in stage three. It was positive that work had continued for about a third of the population in the kitchens and gardens and in wing work roles. However, many of the workshops and all the education classrooms remained closed. After an initial absence, the education provider was now distributing a wide range of in-cell workbooks, about 4,500 of which had been completed. There had been more than 600 course completions by nearly 500 prisoners. Gym staff offered prisoners at least two circuit sessions a week and the library offered a limited outreach service for prisoners.

There was limited provision to help prisoners maintain contact with their friends and family. There were no in-cell telephones and prisoners could only access telephones on the landings during the hour they were unlocked. Staff did accommodate requests to make important calls at other times of the core day. For most prisoners, however, calls with children at school or adults who worked could only be made at the weekend. Despite the lack of in-cell phones the prison had not been prioritised for video calling technology, which had only been installed in August. It had been well received by prisoners who had used the service. Social visits had been reinstated but restrictions had significantly reduced demand.

The offender management unit (OMU) had benefited from stable leadership since the last inspection and had worked hard to ensure that nearly all prisoners had an up-to-date assessment of risk and a sentence plan. Offender management work was focused on time bound events such as release, recategorisation and parole. Face-to-face contact with prison offender managers (POMs) was limited for most prisoners and this was compounded by the lack of key worker support. Delivery of offending behaviour interventions was very limited and the programmes needed by many prisoners were not offered at Dartmoor. Transfers to other prisons had almost ceased during the pandemic and moves to category D prisons had only recently started to reduce the increasing number of prisoners suitable for open conditions. The low number of progressive moves was not helped by the lack of consistent staffing for the observation, classification and allocation (OCA) (see Glossary of terms) function.

Public protection measures were broadly sound and there were no backlogs in monitoring. It was concerning that four prisoners had been released during the pandemic without confirmation of the level of their multi-agency public protection arrangements (MAPPA).

Dartmoor was not a designated resettlement prison but had released about 20 prisoners each month. Resettlement work diverted POMs from the offence-focused work that many of the population needed. On-site community rehabilitation company (CRC) resettlement provision had been introduced since the last inspection. The CRC was not providing face-to-face resettlement support, although records showed that contact was being made in good time for release and action was being taken to try to resolve accommodation and other issues. Despite this, eight prisoners released in the previous six months had not had accommodation to go to on their day of release and others had gone to transient accommodation.

Despite the planned closure, Dartmoor continues to hold more than 600 prisoners in accommodation and facilities that need significant investment to make them fit for purpose. Staff have been working under notice of closure for seven years with a predictable impact on morale. The pandemic has made a difficult situation worse. Managers had worked well to implement national guidance, which was positive, and the prison remained reasonably safe and respectful. However, there were significant shortfalls that needed addressing including the poor infrastructure, limited regime and the lack of equality and diversity provision.

Peter Clarke CVO OBE QPM
HM Chief Inspector of Prisons, October 2020

## INDEPENDENT MONITORING BOARD: Annual Report

The law requires every prison to be monitored by an independent Board appointed by the Justice Secretary; these are known as Independent Monitoring Boards (IMBs). The IMB must satisfy itself as to the humane and just treatment of those held in custody within its prison and the range and adequacy of the programmes preparing them for release; it must report annually to the Justice Secretary on how well the prison has met the standards and requirements placed on it.

### IMB Report 1 October 2020 – 30 September 2022
### Published December 2021
### Executive summary
### Background to the report

The Covid-19 pandemic has continued to have a significant impact on the Board's ability to carry out its duties. During most of the reporting year, members' access to the prison was more limited than usual, although prisoner applications were collected and limited onsite monitoring undertaken at least every week. This was supplemented by data provided by the prison in regular management reports, rather than from independent monitoring. In some areas, there was less supporting evidence collected. Until July 2021, the Board met once a month via telephone conference. Since July 2021, the Board has met in-person in the prison again.

Ministers are aware of these constraints. Regular information is being collected specifically on the prison's responses to the pandemic, and that is being collated nationally.

### Main judgements

Throughout the reporting year, HMP Dartmoor has been under central Her Majesty's Prison and Probation Service (HMPPS) Gold Command, with measures to assist in managing the estate through the pandemic. The Board is pleased to report that these measures, coupled with the commitment and hard work of management and officers, have been successful for Dartmoor in limiting Covid-19 infections. Apart from one limited outbreak over Christmas 2020, which was soon contained, there have been no significant outbreaks in the prison. There was one death in the prison within 28 days of a positive Covid-19 test during the reporting year. We commend management and staff for the support offered to prisoners during the pandemic. This is particularly notable in an environment where there has been a change of Governor following retirement, and a striking lack of continuity in the senior management team and wing management following retirement, other absences and a number of acting-up positions. There have been, for example, three Deputy Governors, three heads of residence and safety, and several officers acting up to senior officer/custody manager/governor grade in the year.

However, the Covid-19 measures have come at a price for prisoners and staff alike and the year has been atypical. For prisoners, there have been extensive lock- up times, no face-to-face visits for much of the year and restrictions on activities, which have had their own, largely detrimental, impact on prisoners and their wellbeing, as highlighted in the rest of this report. For staff, there have been the stresses and difficulties with coping with the prison environment during the pandemic, alongside concerns about the safety of their families, and all in the context of needing to cope with the uncertainties about closure and a frequently changing management team.

**Since the last Annual Report:**
• The closure notice and the current lack of clarity on how it is to be implemented have led to a situation in HMP Dartmoor that is now impacting negatively on many sections of prison life. This has been a theme of the last two reports and is a major theme of this latest report too. We have raised this with ministers in our previous reports but do not consider our concerns to have been addressed in the replies.
• The closure notice continues to affect staff recruitment and retention, both operational and non-operational. We are also being told by functional management that recruitment in non-operational grades has become problematic. Over the course of the reporting year, the Board learnt of difficulties in filling vacancies in the kitchens, industries and healthcare teams.
• The Board's findings last year also show that, before lockdown, the lack of investment in buildings, staff and equipment was resulting in a

shortage of work placements for the prisoners and increased their time in cells and on the wing. This has not changed, even as the regime has been relaxed.
• The number of times that the prison has been on a red or red/amber regime, resulting in prisoners being locked up for excessively long periods, especially at weekends, has increased, despite a relaxation in the restrictions imposed during lockdown, and is a matter of grave concern for the Board. Although some of this is caused by the number of bed watches and constant watches, staffing levels also have an impact here.

**How safe is the prison?**
We find that the prison is generally a safe place, a view generally supported by the many prisoners we have spoken to throughout the year. The uncertainties around closure and the lack of capital investment over recent years continue to raise several safety issues for prisoners and staff alike, including, for example, stretched staffing levels and the lack of drug scanners on entry, both of which have been reported in previous years. However, to its credit, the prison manages to work round the issues that arise, although the Board is concerned about how long these workarounds can be sustained.

**How fairly and humanely are prisoners treated?**
The prison works hard to ensure that prisoners are treated fairly and humanely. All areas of the prison have striven hard to support prisoners during lockdown, with in-cell education and faith packs, welfare visits for those considered vulnerable and, in the absence of physical visits, promotion of family contact through Purple Visits (a video-calling platform).
In the early part of the reporting year, prisoners continued to tell us that they only had less than 60 minutes a day out of their cell. Prison management have worked hard to extend this, and by the end of the year a minimum of 90 minutes was being targeted, with further significant extensions of unlock times planned beyond year-end. The Board has concerns that the lack of operational staff at certain times means that prisoners are still locked up on some days for far too long. This is a particular problem at weekends.
Monitoring evidence as the Covid-19 regime relaxes points strongly to prisoners now not being afforded the level of regime, amenities and equipment that they should expect. Examples include: a lack of staff, impacting on unlock times and on wing regime restrictions, including access to showers and telephones; under- investment in the infrastructure, with frequent outages of

television services and telephones; and the impact on prisoners of frequent breakdowns in kitchen and laundry equipment. The Board increasingly questions how HMPPS proposes to address these issues in a prison due to close in 2023.

### How well are prisoners' health and wellbeing needs met?

Supported by prisoner comments during the year, the Board commends the professionalism of the healthcare teams, who have continued to treat prisoners face- to-face at a time of high-risk and challenging staffing levels, through the Covid-19 pandemic.

Based on our monitoring, the Board is of the opinion that healthcare provision to prisoners is generally of a good standard and is provided in a professional and timely manner. However, we are concerned about limitations on the mental health support available to prisoners, particularly in an environment of extended times locked up in cells. We also have concerns about the long waiting times for non- emergency dental support.

### How well are prisoners progressed towards successful resettlement?

Dartmoor is not a resettlement prison but has released 220 prisoners back into the community during the reporting year. Before lockdown, and within the resource limitations of a training prison, staff tried hard to give prisoners adequate preparation for release. During lockdown, it was even harder to ensure adequate preparations. Since the regime has been relaxed, these preparations have started to be put back in place, but the Board remains concerned that some prisoners are being released back into very temporary accommodation, with only limited support being offered.

The Board understands that inter-prison transfers were minimised nationally during the pandemic but, with transfers resuming, the Board remains of the opinion that it would be better if prisoners due for release were transferred in adequate time to a resettlement prison where they can be given the full resources and advice that HMP Dartmoor is unable to provide.

### Main areas for development
### TO THE MINISTER

Concerns raised to the minister in the previous report have, in the opinion of the Board, not been addressed adequately, even when follow-up clarifications were sought by the Board. In particular, the lack of clarity on closure is having a detrimental effect on the prisoner experience (lack of investment, staff shortages impacting on the regime) and on staff (impact of uncertainties on

home life, turnover, recruitment). What measures does the minister plan, to ensure that concerns raised in this report are meaningfully addressed? What reassurance can the minister offer that until HMP Dartmoor closes in 2023, prisoners currently in the establishment will not be harmed or discriminated against, compared with other prisoners elsewhere in the national prison estate, due to a lack of staff and a failure to invest in the infrastructure, security, kitchens, laundry and other equipment?

HMP Dartmoor still had 29 prisoners serving indeterminate sentences for public protection (IPPs) at the end of the reporting year. Most are substantially over tariff or have been subject to recall. What changes are in the pipeline for these individuals? How will their release be achieved and how will they be supported on release, so that they do not endlessly return to prison under recall? The long wait for psychiatric hospital placements (96 days in one case this reporting year) is of concern to prisoners, staff and the Board. What measures are being taken by the MoJ, working with other Departments, to reduce these waiting times?

### TO THE PRISON SERVICE

What is the path for Dartmoor prisoners who require 24-hour health or social care support?
When is the prison going to receive the funding necessary to help return towards fuller employment?
What measures are planned to help ensure that the release planning model is fully implemented, to support prisoners coming towards release, including the timely community offender manager/prison offender manager handover?

### TO THE GOVERNOR

How will the Governor continue to track the recommendations from last year's IMB annual report, which have been in abeyance because of the Covid-19 regime?
What measures are in place to ensure that all wings (tors) always have complaint forms available, to protect a prisoner's right to complain?
What steps will be taken to strengthen the discrimination incident report form system and ensure adequate and timely responses to all submissions?
Given Dartmoor's remote location, can the Purple Visits system be expanded to the benefit of more prisoners and their families?
Given the importance of family communications, when will the prison take forward in-cell telephony, including completing the required asbestos survey?
On a small number of occasions, prisoners have not been able to access Listeners and the Samaritans at night. What steps is the prison

taking to ensure that these services are available at all times of the day and night, including making sure that all staff understand that access to these services should be allowed?

### Progress since the last report

Given the Covid-19 lockdown, there has understandably been limited progress on many of the issues raised to Governor in the last IMB annual report. As the prison progressively unlocks, it is fair to say that prison managers are mindful of, and beginning to address, the questions raised last year, concerning equality, support to prisoners who have been shielding for a long period, the dialogue road mapping scheme, body-worn cameras and the library service. For example, although the situation has somewhat improved, there is still inconsistency regarding the use of body-worn cameras, and this needs addressing as a matter of urgency. In addition, the Board notes the continued lack of library stock refresh and inter-library loans.

**BOWES RD
BARNARD CASTLE
Co DURHAM, DL12 9BG**

**Tel: 01833 633200**

*For the latest reports on this prison please visit:*
https://tinyurl.com/bdfh26rv

*Important Changes:* **(1) Visits:** the identification necessary to access this prison and visit for social or professional purposes has changed; (2) **Money and Gifts** new rules now apply to these. See page 16 for full details of the above.

### Task of the prison/establishment

**March 2022:** At a baseline level, a maximum of 529 sentenced male prisoners aged 18-24 can be accommodated at HMP/HMYOI Deerbolt, near Barnard Castle in County Durham.

Operational capacity was reduced to 387 from June 2019 and later to 337 in September 2021. The reductions in number were partly to restore an acceptable staff-to- prisoner ratio, but also to allow residential wings to be taken out of service for major refurbishment. Deerbolt was first established as a young offender institution (YOI) for 18- to 21-year-olds on sentences of up to four years, and has education, work training and activities to suit this prisoner group. However, it now takes men up to the ages of 24. There is no restriction on the length of prisoners' sentences, and the population now includes lifers and those on long indeterminate sentences.

The purpose-built establishment was opened in 1973. It includes an administration centre, ten residential wings with exercise yards (including the new K wing and segregation unit), substantial industrial workshops and education classrooms, a gymnasium, reception and a chapel, a reducing reoffending unit and visitors' centre. The buildings have been maintained over the years and have regularly been refurbished by the prison to both meet the latest regulations for fire safety and general standards. The prison has recently benefited from a new tarmacked through road, and the removal of asbestos has begun on some wings. Such recent improvements include new windows and better showers. The external CCTV units have been improved, the gymnasium has been refurbished and a new car park offers better access for staff and visitors alike.

There are extensive areas of grass, and cultivated plots of flowers and vegetables, which are generally well kept and constitute an attractive environment. That said, Deerbolt also benefits from many green areas that are unused, such as at the top of the site, where there are historical sports pitches that have not been used for many years.

Prisoners are received from a wide catchment area so that young adults from the local north-east region are in a minority and many prisoners find themselves far from home. Since the Covid lockdown, new prisoners have mainly come from the local region. Some face to face visits have been allowed for the last several months of this reporting period, but with reduced numbers to enable social distancing. However, visits via video link are now been readily offered which have been helpful for families who live a long distance away.

### Certified normal accommodation and operational capacity

Baseline certified normal capacity: 529
In-use certified normal capacity: 347
Operational capacity: 337

### Prison status and key providers

Public
Prison Group: North East
Prison Group Director: Susan Howard
Governor/director: Andy Hudson
IMB chair: Charlies Ing
The main providers of services in the prison are Novus (education), Amey (works/maintenance), Spectrum (healthcare) and Tees, Esk and Wear Valleys NHS Foundation Trust (mental health). Visitor care and support is provided by the voluntary agency the North East Prison Aftercare Society (NEPACS), which also offers provision for family visits and group work with young fathers.

**Short description of residential units**

I wing: The induction and first night wing and current reverse cohort unit, consisting of 60 cells.

K wing: A small unit used to transition prisoners from youth custody, holding up to 16 prisoners.

A, D and F wings: Currently closed for refurbishment.

A and C wings: 60 cells.

E wing: 66 cells.

G wing: 36 cells.

J wing: 39 cells.

Segregation unit: 13 cells and two special accommodation cells.

**INSPECTIONS & REPORTS**

**Date of latest inspection: 7-9 March 2022**

**HMCIP IRP Report published 12 April 2021**

**Independent Review of Progress Report**

Located near Barnard Castle in County Durham, HMP/YOI Deerbolt is a closed male young offender institution (YOI) and category C training prison for young adults aged 18 to 24. It receives prisoners from across the country, some serving long sentences. At the time of our visit, just as at the July 2021 inspection, Deerbolt held about 270 prisoners, which was much lower than its usual occupational capacity due to the ongoing refurbishment of some wings.

At our previous inspections of HMP/YOI Deerbolt in 2018 and 2021 we made the following judgements about outcomes for prisoners.

At our July 2021 inspection, our overriding concern had been the lack of time out of cell and purposeful activity for such a young population. Eight months later, at this review we found no improvement and progress had been much too slow. The aspiration as Covid-19 restrictions lifted was much too limited for a training prison, with just 3.5 hours a day out of cell planned for most. But even this part-time regime, in its infancy when we visited, was unreliable despite the reduced population. The prison faced major staff shortages, which affected most aspects of the regime.

We saw workshops sitting empty because there were no staff available to unlock and escort prisoners. There were tiny numbers of prisoners in classrooms. Places in work and education had often not been allocated and many prisoners had not had initial assessments to determine the most appropriate activity for them. Those who were not in work or education places still spent 23 hours in their cells each day, and we found nearly two-thirds of prisoners locked up during the working day, more than at the 2021 inspection.

Leaders had made better progress in addressing our concerns about safety. There were clear improvements to the segregation unit and there had been reasonable moves to manage better

perpetrators of violence and strengthen oversight of the use of force. But even this progress required a note of caution. Violence between prisoners was higher than at the 2021 inspection and some of it was very serious. Use of force was also high. With so little constructive time unlocked to engage or tire them out, we saw prisoners with their backs to the perimeter of the exercise yards, clearly anxious for their safety. Some of the footage of incidents we viewed left us deeply concerned.

The challenge of managing conflict while getting prisoners to activity safely was a huge hurdle for managers. The prison's policy to incentivise good behaviour did not offer sufficient rewards relevant to the young age group, and was irrelevant in any case while prisoners had so little to lose in terms of their daily regime. Attempts to build staff-prisoner relationships through key work had not made meaningful advance and very few prisoners had any reliable support from a key worker.

There had been better progress against some of our other recommendations. A substantial improvement had been the introduction of in-cell phones on all but one wing. Medication queues were now better supervised, and consultation, both prison-wide and with protected groups, showed early promise.

Deerbolt remains a prison with some excellent facilities and great potential, but there was far too little for the young prisoners to do. We left without any assurance that managers would be able to deliver the safe and reliable full-time regime their population needed. They will need to move quickly to address staff shortages, restore purposeful activity and reduce the high levels of violence.

**Date of last inspection: 21 June - 9 July 2021**

**HMCIP Report published 12 October 2021**

Deerbolt is a prison and young offender institution located near to Barnard Castle in County Durham. The establishment is normally capable of holding more than 500 young adult prisoners aged 18 to 24 years old, but a rolling programme of refurbishment and upgrades meant that this number had been dramatically reduced and only 265 prisoners were held at the time of our visit. Of these, nearly two-thirds were under the age of 21.

When we last inspected Deerbolt in 2018 we found a prison that was reasonably safe and respectful, but one that surprisingly, bearing in mind the resources available, needed to improve the regime experienced by those detained and its approach to the rehabilitation and resettlement of prisoners about to be released. At this inspection we again found a mixed picture, showing a deterioration in safety outcomes and the quality of regime, but improvement in work towards resettlement.

Deerbolt had been impacted significantly by the Covid-19 pandemic which partly explained the deterioration of the regime. Leaders and managers had taken effective action to minimise the spread of the virus, although at the time of our visit the prison had been declared an outbreak site for the third time in recent months. One prisoner and six members of staff had tested positive and a larger group of staff were isolating after being contacted by NHS test and trace. All prisoners and staff had been offered the vaccine and regular testing was available. This is important context, but it remained the case that the experience was very poor for these young prisoners who were typically spending 23 hours a day locked in cell with little structured activity. The impact of this on prisoners was stark and much more needed to be done, and greater ambition shown, in making sure that more work, education and recreational activity was reintroduced as a priority. This was particularly disappointing given the large amounts of outdoor space at the prison.

In contrast, the prison had made commendable improvements to sentence planning and risk management arrangements and we were confident there were plans in place to develop this work further. Similarly, we noted some good work to support care leavers and the introduction of a new and interesting initiative to support young people as they transitioned to Deerbolt from juvenile facilities during their sentence. Outcomes in health care, mental health care and social care were likewise much improved and ensured some positive outcomes.

It was clear to us that the governor had a vision for Deerbolt's future, but it was perhaps less clear how progress would be measured or how and when the vision could be realised. During the inspection itself, leaders did make some improvements in response to our feedback and findings. While welcome, this confirmed to us a somewhat reactive approach to issues and the absence of a useful plan which identified priorities and timeframes for progress. Oversight of violence reduction measures, for example, was poor, which led to a response that was reactive and limited rather than one which dealt with the underlying conflict and issues. This will need to be addressed as the regime improves.

Deerbolt is a prison which retains great potential. We encourage leaders and managers to show greater confidence in the restoration and development of the regime and makes better use of the extensive space. We also encourage them to develop a more consultative and ambitious approach with prisoners that expects more of them and incentivises their engagement with what the prison is able to offer.

Charlie Taylor Chief Inspector July 2021

**Summary of Key Findings**

We last inspected HMP/YOI Deerbolt in 2018 and made 52 recommendations, three of which were about areas of key concern. The prison fully accepted 38 of the recommendations and partially (or subject to resources) accepted 10. It rejected four of the recommendations.

**Progress on key concerns and recommendations**

Our last inspection of HMP/YOI Deerbolt took place before the COVID- 19 pandemic and the recommendations in that report focused on areas of concern affecting outcomes for prisoners at the time. Although we recognise that the challenges of keeping prisoners safe during COVID- 19 will have changed the focus for many prison leaders, we believe that it is important to follow up on recommendations about areas of key concern to help leaders to continue to drive improvement. At our last full inspection, we made one recommendation about a key concern in the area of safety. At this inspection, we found that this recommendation had been achieved.

We made one recommendation about a key concern in the area of purposeful activity. At this inspection, Ofsted carried out a progress monitoring visit alongside our inspection to assess the progress that leaders and managers had made towards reinstating a full education, skills and work curriculum. They judged that it was too early to assess whether recommendations made at the last inspection had been achieved.

We made one recommendation about key concerns in the area of rehabilitation and release planning. At this inspection, we found that this recommendation had been achieved.

**Outcomes for prisoners**

We assess outcomes for prisoners against four healthy prison tests. At this inspection of HMP/YOI Deerbolt, we found that outcomes for prisoners had stayed the same in one healthy prison area, improved in one and declined in two. These judgements seek to make an objective assessment of the outcomes experienced by those detained and have taken into account the prison's recovery from Covid-19 as well as the 'regime stage' at which the prison was operating, as outlined in the HM Prison and Probation (HMPPS) National Framework for prison regimes and services.

## Safety

The reception area had been improved by the provision of private space for interviews. Reception processes were relatively swift, and staff were welcoming. Cells for new arrivals were clean and adequately equipped but looked shabby. The regime for new arrivals during their 14 days on the reverse cohort unit was limited to one hour's mixing each day with others who had arrived within 24 hours of their admission. In our survey, fewer prisoners than at the time of the previous inspection said that they had had an induction, and only just over half of these said that this had told them all they needed to know about the prison. The transitions unit, while a promising addition to the support offered to prisoners coming from the youth custody estate, needed further development.

Levels of violence had reduced and were similar to those at comparator prisons. Systems for challenging perpetrators and supporting victims of bullying and violence were in disarray and had resulted in some prisoners being held in segregation conditions without the appropriate safeguards. There were very few meaningful incentives for prisoners who engaged with the regime and behaved well.

Despite attempts to improve governance of use of force, there remained weaknesses. We reviewed a sample of incidents and raised concerns with senior leaders over practice observed in several of these incidents. Special accommodation had been used six times in the last six months, but prison records did not always justify adequately its use.

The number of prisoners segregated had fallen in line with the population. Prisoners in segregation spoke well of the staff on the unit, although the regime and environment were poor.

The number of incidents of self-harm had reduced during the pandemic and was lower than at similar prisons. The generally good support for prisoners on assessment, care in custody and teamwork (ACCT) case management for those at risk of suicide or self-harm was undermined by the poor regime, which reduced opportunities for spontaneous supportive interaction with staff and other prisoners. The constant supervision cells provided a very poor environment. There had been little use of Listeners (prisoners trained by the Samaritans to provide confidential emotional support to fellow prisoners).

## Respect

In our survey, more prisoners than at the time of the previous inspection said that most staff treated them with respect. Meaningful interaction between staff and prisoners was limited by the regime and some opportunities were missed. However, we saw examples of personalised, supportive input from staff and some relaxed informal conversations. Key work was very limited.

A programme of refurbishment was under way and included the installation of in-cell telephony. External areas were pleasant, but exercise yards were stark. Prisoners were not provided with coats and we saw some using bin bags to protect them from the rain. Cell conditions were generally reasonable. However, toilets were dirty and most remained unscreened. The flooring in too many cells needed repair. The process to allow prisoners access to their property was poor and many were frustrated by this. Arrangements for consulting prisoners were poor and the resolution of matters raised was slow.

Prisoners' perceptions of the food had improved and the new healthy options were well received. Prisoners had no access to self-catering facilities, and they continued to eat all meals in their cells. Strategic oversight of equality and diversity had been impacted adversely by Covid-19 restrictions. The diversity equalities monitoring team (DEMT) had continued to meet, but there had been no consultation with prisoners in protected groups and there was little analysis of data, both of which undermined its effectiveness. Work to raise awareness of protected characteristics had been limited, but the quality assurance of responses to discrimination incident report forms was good. A third of the population was from a black and minority ethnic background. In our survey, these prisoners reported more negatively than their white counterparts across a range of questions. There was insufficient support for the 25 foreign national prisoners at the establishment. Faith provision was good and corporate worship had recently restarted.

In our survey, 75% of respondents said that the overall quality of health services was good, and prisoners we spoke to were positive about health care provision. The prison and health care providers had worked diligently, in close collaboration with Public Health England, to make sure that prisoners' health needs continued to be met during the Covid-19 restrictions. Primary care services were very good and all services had resumed following the Covid-19 restrictions.

The prison, Durham County Council and Spectrum provided exemplary access to social care assessments and packages of care and support to those meeting the threshold.

The responsive mental health team was easily accessible and the prisoners we spoke to valued the support it offered. However, those needing transfer to secure mental health inpatient services continued to wait far too long for a bed. Substance misuse services were very good but subject to inefficiencies due to the lack of access to electronic clinical records, and failures to attend appointments because of regime and allocations limitations.

Medicines management arrangements were generally safe. However, medicine queues were not sufficiently well supervised and health care staff's observation of compliance was poor.

## Purposeful Activity

Ofsted carried out a progress monitoring visit of the prison alongside our full inspection and the purposeful activity judgement incorporates their assessment of progress.

The regime was inadequate and prisoners were frustrated by the slow pace of change. Most prisoners spent 23 hours each day locked in their cells with little useful activity to fill their time. Access to time in the fresh air was limited to 30 minutes a day. The lack of meaningful activity meant that many prisoners spent most of their days bored or asleep in their cells. We had concerns about the impact of the lack of normal social interaction on the well-being of a long-term young adult population.

Prisoners could not attend the library in person, but there was good use of the order and delivery service that it operated. Gym sessions were appreciated by prisoners, but staffing issues had resulted in some being cancelled.

Leaders and managers had made sure that most prisoners had access to some form of education, skills or work, although this was mostly limited to in-cell education packs. The prison appropriately had prioritised the participation in remote learning of prisoners with learning needs and/or disabilities and those who need to improve their English or mathematics skills.

Induction was undermined by an over-reliance on written information being sent to prisoners. Many of the induction packs were not returned by prisoners.

Information, advice and guidance arrangements were relatively new and not yet effective. As a result, not all prisoners enrolled on education courses that related to their interests or career aspirations.

The small number of prisoners in industry workshops took pride in their work and developed well their life skills and the vocational knowledge and behaviour needed to succeed following release.

Most learning packs were of a good standard. However, reinforcement of prisoners' learning through the linking of theory with practical application was not possible for many. In addition, these packs did not challenge more able prisoners sufficiently. Prisoners in education classes did not have routine access to the relevant information technology and telephony needed to support their development.

## Rehabilitation and release planning

A full-time family support worker had provided a good service to prisoners. This service had stopped when the community rehabilitation company contract ended, but it had been recommissioned and was due to restart. Social visits had restarted recently but were very limited in number. Access to telephones was limited on those wings without in- cell telephony. Secure Video Calls (see Glossary of terms) were popular and leaders had made them available during the evenings, when prisoners' families were most accessible.

Strategic oversight of offender management was good. The strategy was effective and well informed and linked to an action plan that was well managed and drove change. Every prisoner had an assessment of their needs and risk, and a sentence plan. Around two-thirds of these had been reviewed in the last 12 months. The quality of sentence plans that we reviewed was mostly good; there was good engagement between the prison and community offender managers before release. Home detention curfew processes were timely and external housing support was effective. Re-categorisation reviews were well managed and most prisoners were moved on within reasonable timescales.

Public protection arrangements were effective. The interdepartmental risk management team meeting routinely considered those due for release at appropriate intervals, to make sure that their risks were managed appropriately.

Delivery of accredited programmes had restarted following the pandemic restrictions, and there were plans to address the backlog that this had caused. However, some prisoners had been discharged without being able to complete needed offending behaviour work. The care leaver support worker provided a good service to prisoners.

There was a 'through-the-gate' service, which engaged with every prisoner and provided good support with their resettlement needs. Employment, training and education outcomes were not fully coordinated through the prison offender manager, which meant that the prison and probation service may not have been aware of all aspects of a prisoner's release arrangements.

## Key concerns and recommendations

Key concerns and recommendations identify the issues of most importance to improving outcomes for prisoners and are designed to help establishments prioritise and address the most significant weaknesses in the treatment and conditions of prisoners.

During this inspection we identified some areas of key concern and have made a small number of recommendations for the prison to address those concerns.

Key concern: There were few meaningful incentives to motivate positive behaviour among young adult prisoners. The regime offered few opportunities for progress to be supported or recognised among those who engaged constructively with their sentence plan or the wider custodial experience. The existing and limited incentives scheme was not applied equitably.

Recommendation: Managers should review the prison's approach to incentives in all aspects of prison life. Rewards and incentives that are meaningful to prisoners and which recognise and support those who engage with the regime and behave well should be introduced.

Key concern: Processes to manage victims and perpetrators of violence (challenge, support and intervention plans) were in disarray. Only serious incidents of violence were investigated. Subsequent plans to manage victim and perpetrators lacked detail, wing staff were unsure of who was subject to monitoring and why, and there was no managerial oversight of the process, including reviews. As a result, some prisoners were locked up for several weeks without meaningful human contact, welfare checks or any indication as to when the restrictions would end. There was no system to resolve conflicts between prisoners swiftly, which meant that the default response was to keep prisoners apart, rather than help them resolve their issues.

Recommendation: Oversight of violence reduction measures should make sure that all incidents of violence are investigated swiftly and that victims and perpetrators are challenged and supported appropriately.

Key concern: Despite some improvements in governance, weaknesses in use of force practice were not always identified by the prison or referred subsequently to the governor for further investigation. Due to poor recording and accountability, some footage of incidents from body-worn cameras was now unavailable. Special accommodation had been used six times in the last six months, and prison records did not demonstrate that there had been adequate justification or that it had been necessarily used as a last resort.

Recommendation: Use of force and use of special accommodation should be more accountable with concerning incidents promptly and

properly investigated and opportunities for learning and improvement usefully exploited.

Key concern: The segregation unit was bleak. Cells, showers and exercise yards were in poor condition and there was no in-cell electricity. It required urgent refurbishment. Apart from a basic regime entitlement of a daily shower, telephone call and half an hour's outdoor exercise, there was little to engage, stimulate or encourage positive behaviour. Multi-unlock staffing levels were routine, without documented authority or daily reviews to check if they remained appropriate.

Recommendation: The purpose of segregation, and the regime and environment that support it, should be to prioritise meeting the specific needs of individuals, provide support to improve their behaviour and develop an approach that encourages and incentivises their re-engagement with the prison regime.

Key concern: The key work scheme was not functioning at the time of the inspection. This lack of regular meaningful interaction was of concern, given the potential impact of continuing restrictions on prisoners' well-being and progression.

Recommendation: Managers should make sure that every prisoner has regular contact with a key worker who can address their welfare needs and progression goals.

Key concern: Consultation arrangements were poor and the resolution of issues was very slow. Prisoners had become disengaged from the consultative process as they felt that they were not taken seriously, and that the prison failed to act on the concerns they raised.

Recommendation: There should be ongoing, meaningful consultation with prisoners, with their issues and concerns addressed and resolved in an accountable way.

Key concern: There had been no consultation with prisoners in protected groups, which undermined the DEMT's effectiveness, and there was little work with prisoners to promote protected characteristic groups. Black and minority ethnic prisoners reported more negatively than their counterparts in our survey. There was little analysis of data relating to the treatment and experience of those with protected characteristics. Actions from the DEMT meeting often took too long to resolve.

Recommendation: There should be consultation with prisoners in protected groups, and detailed analysis of the data relating to the treatment and experience of these prisoners. This should be used to identify and address any differences in treatment leading to more equitable outcomes.

Key concern: Prisoners needing a transfer to hospital under the Mental Health Act waited far too long for a bed.

Recommendation: The local delivery board, in conjunction with NHS England and Improvement, should make sure that transfers to secure mental health inpatient units under the Mental Health Act take place within the national timescale of 28 days.

Key concern: Continuing integration of the work of the substance misuse team with physical health, clinical management and mental health teams and the efficiency of joint care delivery were being hampered by lack of access to SystmOne, the inability to co-locate mental health and drug and alcohol recovery teams, and lost appointments due to regime and allocations challenges.

Recommendation: Challenges to the continuing integration of the work of Spectrum, Tees, Esk and Wear Valleys, and Humankind staff should be resolved by the local delivery board.

Key concern: Many prisoners spent up to 23 hours in their cells each day with too little to do. Progress to improve the poor regime had been slow. We were concerned about the impact on the well-being and progression of young prisoners, who had limited opportunities to talk to staff, socialise with peers or maintain their relationships with loved ones; were not kept physically or mentally active; and spent only 30 minutes each day in the fresh air.

Recommendation: Time out of cell and access to activity should be improved and increased.

Key concern: At the time of the inspection, no prisoners could access group lessons, either on the wing or in classrooms. This hindered substantially the development of those prisoners who learnt best through direct teacher contact.

Recommendation: Leaders and managers should expand the learning offer by introducing wing- and classroom-based learning sessions as soon as is practically possible. They should provide prisoners with access to relevant information technology resources and enough mentoring support to help them progress.

Key concern: Most prisoners had limited access to the telephone, with only 10 minutes allowed each day. There was no availability on some wings for prisoners to make telephone calls in the evenings, when their families were most accessible.

Recommendation: All prisoners should have access to the telephone at least once a day, for a duration and at a time that supports meaningful family contact.

**Notable positive practice**

We define notable positive practice as innovative work or practice that leads to particularly good outcomes from which other establishments may be able to learn. Inspectors look for evidence of good outcomes for prisoners; original, creative or particularly effective approaches to problem-solving or achieving the desired goal; and how other establishments could learn from or replicate the practice.

Inspectors found three examples of notable positive practice during this inspection.

Health care staff spoke to all prisoners who had been subject to the use of force, to gather their views on the incident and the aftercare they received. This information was shared, with consent, with health and prison leaders, and informed practice.

Community offender managers were invited to dial in as part of the interdepartmental risk management team meeting, which supported strong risk management and information sharing.

There was a care leavers support worker, who provided excellent one- to-one bespoke support for prisoners who had recently left local authority care. A large number of prisoners had been identified as needing this service, with each seen individually to assess their need. Advocacy services, resettlement planning and support, housing and help with forming links in the community were all provided, as well as group work and peer support outside of the pandemic restrictions.

## INDEPENDENT MONITORING BOARD: Annual Report

The law requires every prison to be monitored by an independent Board appointed by the Justice Secretary; these are known as Independent Monitoring Boards (IMBs). The IMB must satisfy itself as to the humane and just treatment of those held in custody within its prison and the range and adequacy of the programmes preparing them for release; it must report annually to the Justice Secretary on how well the prison has met the standards and requirements placed on it.

### IMB Report 1 October 2020 – 30 September 2021 Published 11th March 2022

The Covid-19 outbreak has continued to have a significant impact on the Board's ability to gather information and discuss the contents of this annual report. While the Board has therefore tried to cover as much ground as it can in these difficult circumstances, a level of caution should be considered due to the overreliance on objective data and not as much 'on the ground' monitoring for supporting evidence as usual. We hope ministers are aware of these constraints. These are particularly impactful on both our education and resettlement sections.

HMP/YOI Deerbolt has since the pandemic adopted a strict protocol for entry and a one-way system into the prison. These new changes, and the great work of staff within the prison, have minimised the risk of the virus and provided a safe environment for the prisoners. Prisoners in Deerbolt have been fearful of the unknown, yet staff have been quick to reassure and educate the prison population. With this, the IMB would like to commend the efforts shown to keep the prisoners of Deerbolt safe. There have also been low Covid-19 rates in prisoners when compared with the normal population.

As a consequence of the Covid-19 outbreak, the Board has adopted a range of approaches to maintain contact with prisoners and to receive information about the prison at regular intervals. The Board worked remotely, held fortnightly meetings with governors, and additional information was shared with the Board by email on a daily basis (i.e. daily stability reports). The prison management are to be commended for facilitating the sharing of documentation and for promoting our presence in the prison by inviting us to meetings, and granting us the opportunity to send a message to prisoners via the prison's own educational television channel (WayoutTV). However, despite this, with a lack of visibility in inductions and presence around the prison, the Board notes that the total number of applications received are significantly lower than pre-lockdown. While the Board recognise the enormous difficulties facing the Prison Service at the onset of the Covid-19 pandemic, and as the Prison Service continues to recover from the pandemic, the Board continues to be concerned with the lack of purposeful activity at a time when prisoners can still be locked up for up to 22/23 hours a day. Staff shortages have had an effect on this process; however, the Board has been disappointed that the prison has not thought outside the box to find novel ways to challenge and engage prisoners during this period of time. Following a recent Her Majesty's Inspectorate of Prisons (HMIP) inspection, Deerbolt management were justifiably critiqued for the outcomes for the prisoners at their establishment. While the inspection focused on the direction of the senior management team, one must consider the recent changes to the prison demographic before the management team joined (prior to June 2018) and while they have been in post for the last few years (i.e. an older population). This was exacerbated by the many newly trained staff recruited to deal with shortages and Deerbolt's overall provision, with facilities specialised for the needs of young offenders and not slightly older, more complex prisoners. These factors should be considered when critiquing the very restrictive regime witnessed at the time of the inspection. That said, just like the HMIP team, the IMB expected some progression of activity towards pre-lockdown levels during this

reporting period, but believes that a sudden increase in freedom for prisoners may hamper the good work staff are performing on a daily basis; thus, a more progressive movement out of the pandemic is advised.

### Main judgements
#### How safe is the establishment?
As per our previous reports, Deerbolt has long had a good safety record relative to comparator prisons. The data from this reporting period would support this premise. However, there are still many prisoners who feel under threat, often because of debts incurred when locked up or because of inter-gang rivalries (these are gangs based in prisoners' home cities with which they may have been in some way involved). Deerbolt staff continue to call upon their skills and experience to seek intelligence about prisoners' gang affiliations in order to promote safety in the establishment. However, while this has had short term successes, due to the background of many prisoners the IMB has been told that other prisoners are often forced to join prison gangs for their own safety, and this only exacerbates the issue.

That said, while the numbers of assaults by prisoners on other prisoners and on staff were lower than in the previous reporting period, this is most probably because there were fewer opportunities for prisoners to interact. However, the IMB wishes to outline that the practice of locking prisoners up does not always mean that prisoners will feel more safe, particularly when gang affiliations start to become widespread and when prisoners develop anxieties with regard to potentially moving back to normal regimes with their peers.

Despite this, the IMB would also like to praise Deerbolt staff for their passion and commitment to more complex prisoners. Given the difficulties in moving out prisoners who are at risk at Deerbolt because of such gang-related issues, mistakes they have made in their time at the establishment or their complex needs, Deerbolt regularly houses a number of prisoners who either would like to be kept in the segregation unit for their own safety. This year, there have been several very difficult prisoners; despite Deerbolt not having suitable facilities to deal with their complex needs, the staff have understood challenges and have built relationships, showed patience and have directly communicated with the IMB to keep the Board in the loop as to their circumstances.

#### How fairly and humanely are prisoners treated?
As per our last reporting period, there is no doubt that the regime and the vast majority of

staff, both individually and collectively, do their best to treat the prisoners fairly and humanely. Moreover, the Board is convinced that prison staff hold quality one to one communication with the most vulnerable. However, the Board is concerned by the interaction with the wider population in Deerbolt. The cessation of key worker sessions and the low number of wellbeing checks would highlight this.

While exceptional delivery models (EDMs) stipulate that given low staff numbers, Deerbolt has to attend to the most vulnerable, the IMB feels that the population at Deerbolt would benefit from increased dialogue on a regular basis. The IMB would hate to think that some prisoners may feel as if they have been forgotten by the establishment, although this may not be the case.

The IMB has also received a record low number of applications to speak to us and to use our services. This itself could imply that prisoners are indeed being treated fairly and humanely. However, our inability in this reporting year to be visible may explain this, although the IMB feels as if the prison has done all that they can do to promote our presence in a bid to promote fair and humane treatment.

In August 2021, the Bilsdale transmitter fire, with the subsequent loss of TV signal, provided Deerbolt with huge challenges. However, Deerbolt staff should be commended for their quick responses to this by issuing prisoners with alternative provision. That acknowledged, while distraction techniques are being provided, being locked up for long periods is not fair or humane. However, the IMB are hopeful and confident that Deerbolt management understand the challenges and are ready to learn lessons from the past 18 months.

## How well are prisoners' health and wellbeing needs met?

In the recent HMIP inspection, healthcare staff were commended for their high-level service. The IMB is confident that health and wellbeing needs are indeed being met. A qualified nurse is on site seven days a week and the drug and alcohol recovery team (DART) provide one to one support throughout the pandemic, despite there still being no healthcare beds at the establishment. Deerbolt and HMP/YOI Wetherby have also improved the transitions from the children's estate into the youth/adult estate. Over the years, the IMB has received numerous comments on how tough Deerbolt is compared to their previous establishment, so we are glad that this issue has been focused on.

That said, the time taken for prisoners to gain a transfer to hospitals under the Mental Health Act

or due to other concerns is still too long. Moreover, the extended periods of inactivity and prisoners being locked up for long periods of time would justify the view that mental health needs are being overlooked, though the care itself is of a very high standard.

## How well are prisoners progressed towards transfer or successful resettlement?

As per our last reporting year, the Covid-19 lockdown has meant that most of this reporting year was affected by no education or craft training, with no progressive methods for rehabilitation. In-cell packs were distributed to prisoners. While the prison was able to deflect the attention of prisoners away from their current circumstances, the method's suitability as a rehabilitation tool can surely be questioned. That said, in the spring/summer of 2021, education classes began opening, with in- cell distance working characterising this provision. While Novus staff have endeavoured to provide education services, the prison is perhaps focused on quantity of allocation rather than quality of provision.

The IMB is therefore concerned about the effectiveness of the current education in HMP/YOI Deerbolt. That said, there are some notable successes: the bike workshop and the horticulture academy continue to be an impressive resource in Deerbolt. For example, the horticulture academy has provided floral displays for the centre of Barnard Castle after developing a strong link with the local town council.

The IMB has long had concerns regarding the lack of dialogue between case managers to successfully progress young adults through their complementing sentence plans. However, as the Inspectorate correctly reports, a full-time family support worker provides a good service to prisoners. Social visits had recommenced following the Covid-19 pandemic and there have been many benefits witnessed from Purple (video) Visits. The prison is also able to effectively utilise action plans to progress prisoners towards transfer. Resettlement planning is also successfully applied at the establishment by good quality staff.

## Main areas for development
## TO THE MINISTER

As members of the local community, we understand that staffing is difficult in all sectors in our region. We also acknowledge that many jobs are going to big retail companies as they are simply paying more money. Have ministers understood the challenges with regard to employing new recruits in the north-east of England? In our past decade of reporting, staff shortages have continued to be key to our concerns at the establishment.

## TO THE PRISON SERVICE

The IMB at Deerbolt has been concerned with regard to the definitions of key worker sessions, wellbeing checks etc. Could there be an easier and less time-consuming way of prison staff logging prisoner interactions so that independent groups such as the IMB can be aware of prisoner interactions?

In 2021, the topic of prisoner transfers is again a concern at Deerbolt. There have been instances when prisoners have been held within the segregation unit for very long periods of time. When transfers are the logical conclusion but other prisons with greater provision are reluctant to facilitate moves, does the prison service have powers to be able to force transfers of prisoners to more suitable establishments?

At Deerbolt, we have also found it difficult to quantify what constitutes good practice in the prison when we are unable to objectively compare this establishment with others. While the safer custody team share statistics with us at meetings, is there any way in which there can be increased information from the prison service on statistics between similar prisons? (statistics such as education services, regime restrictions, staffing level, Covid-19 level etc).

## TO THE GOVERNOR

The IMB understands and completely respects the hard work the management team have put in through difficult circumstances and challenges this year. However, do you think there is more that could have been achieved this year to reduce prisoner lock-up time?

The IMB also understands that there are always security/safety risks with launching new initiatives within the prison. However, are there things that can be done to use the green space within the prison, particularly on the outer perimeter of the establishment?

In our 2018/19 annual report, the IMB was excited about the proposition of monitoring the effectiveness of the key worker system following its launch at Deerbolt. However, the Board did also have concerns regarding the enthusiasm and dedication of your team to this task over time. Of course, there have been so many factors impacting on the allocation of key worker provision, but what do you see as the future of key worker sessions and other official logged methods for important prisoner interactions?

### Progress since the last report

Since the last report, it is difficult not to acknowledge the current challenges the Deerbolt

management team have faced in the past 12 months. While morale had improved going into 2020, staff shortages, exacerbated by issues in gaining new recruits, low Covid-19 vaccine uptake in staff and the direct impact of the Covid-19 pandemic, have led to difficulties for the prison in successfully progressing the regime into 2021.

However, one must acknowledge the fact that the prison, when compared to other establishments, has been slow to move through the stages and ease restrictions during this reporting period. This, complemented by frustrations of some prisoners with being locked up for such long periods of time, has meant that some new staff were perhaps anxious about taking up their new posts, and at times morale between prisoners/staff has been very low.

In our last report, we cited that the Covid-19 lockdown meant that prisoners were kept in their cells for large periods of time, which reduced prisoner interaction, and we surmised that this reduced violence, with some prisoners feeling safer. In 2020, the prison carried on with this premise but also provided extra televisions/other forms of stimulation to occupy the prisoners. However, we did say in the longer term this may cause difficulties, and sadly this may have been the case during this reporting period. The perception of our members visiting the establishment is that the restrictive regimes have lasted too long and with this we have even had some prisoners state to us that 'being locked up, doesn't mean that you are safe'. In addition, without forms of meaningful rehabilitation, some prisoners feel as if they are not able to improve their life prospects on release from the establishment.

This all said, the prison's response to the Bilsdale transmitter fire and the HMIP inspection has allowed our members to be encouraged by the keenness to learn from the past 18 months and we are confident that the senior management team will unite prison staff and we hope, steer them towards their targets.

MARSHGATE
DONCASTER
SOUTH YORKS
DN5 8UX

Tel: 01302 760870

*For the latest reports on this prison please visit:*
https://tinyurl.com/bdfh26rv

*Important Changes:* **(1) Visits:** the identification necessary to access this prison and visit for social or professional purposes has changed; (2) **Money and Gifts** new rules now apply to these. See page 16 for full details of the above.

**Task of the establishment** HMP & YOI Doncaster is a category B local and resettlement prison accommodating young adult (18–20 years) and adult male prisoners.

**Certified normal accommodation and operational capacity**
Prisoners held at the time of inspection: 1,107
Baseline certified normal capacity: 738
In-use certified normal capacity: 738
Operational capacity: 1,145

**Population of the prison**
• 3,042 new prisoners are received each year (around 254 per month).
• 165 foreign national prisoners.
• 21% of prisoners from black and minority ethnic backgrounds.
• 2,251 prisoners are released each year into the community (around 188 per month).
• 199 young offenders.
• 171 prisoners convicted of sexual offences. • 35% remand prisoners.
• 41% resettlement prisoners.
• 24% of prisoners are waiting for transfer.

**Prison status and key providers**
Private: Serco
Prison Group: Custodial Contracts
Prison Group Director: Neil Richards
Director: John Hewitson / Karen Serdet (c)
IMB Chair: Steve Clark
Physical health provider: Practice Plus Group
Mental health provider: Practice Plus Group
Substance misuse treatment provider: Practice Plus Group Prison education framework provider: Novus
Escort contractor: GeoAmey

**Brief history** The prison opened its doors in 1994, and was originally contracted to Premier Prison Services Ltd (owned by Serco and Wackenhut Corrections). In 2005, the prison management was contracted to Serco.

**Short description of residential units** The current configuration of the residential units is as follows:
Houseblock 1A: wing for prisoners convicted of sexual offences (PCOSOs)
Houseblock 1B: general population
Houseblock 1C: PCOSO wing
Houseblock 1D: general population
Houseblock 2A: general population (evolving to reintegration unit)
Houseblock 2B: general population/off-wing workers
Houseblock 2C: general population
Houseblock 2D: general population
Houseblock 3A: general population
Houseblock 3B: stabilisation unit
Houseblock 3C: early days centre/induction
Houseblock 3D: general population
The Loft: complex needs unit
Social care unit
Segregation unit

**Visiting Information**
HMP Doncaster is offering visits for family and friends. Visiting times and availability may change at short notice. You should contact the prison direct for any queries.
Visitors aged 12 and over need to take a lateral flow device test (LFD) before coming for their visit.
You can also contact the Prisoners' Families Helpline on 0808 808 2003. You will not be able to book a visit using this number.

**Legal visits:** Monday to Friday (except Bank Holidays) 9.15am to 11.45am, 1.15pm to 4.45pm

**INSPECTIONS & REPORTS**
**HMCIP Report 21–22 Feb & 28 Feb – 4 Mar 2022 Published 16 June 2022**
Doncaster prison is a category B Reception and Resettlement Prison in South Yorkshire. At the time of our inspection the prison held just over 1,100 men and young adults, a third of whom were on remand. A busy and complex prison, the establishment was receiving in excess of 250 new prisoners every month, held about 165 foreign nationals and provided separate accommodation for over 170 men convicted of sexual offences. Opening in 1994, the prison had been privately run since 2005 under a contract delivered by the company SERCO.
Doncaster prison is a challenging institution, and the Inspectorate has, in the past, been highly critical of the outcomes we have observed there. It is pleasing therefore to report that, overall, the findings of this inspection are very encouraging. Doncaster was now a much safer prison and remained 'reasonably good' in the area of respect. Outcomes in our healthy prison test for

rehabilitation and release planning were judged 'good' and only in the provision of purposeful activity were outcomes identified as 'not sufficiently good', but even here the prison's work to support the regime was better than we have seen in similar establishments.

Very good arrangements were in place to receive new prisoners and most told us they were treated well and properly inducted on arrival. Nearly every measure of safety that we assess, such as the amount of violence, the number of disciplinary proceedings, use of segregation and use of force were falling, and fewer prisoners now told us they felt unsafe. There had been eight self-inflicted deaths since our last inspection, although the recorded incidents of self-harm had remained constant. Despite this, the work undertaken to support those in crisis seemed to us to be useful and effective. We spoke to prisoners currently receiving support through crises, who told us they felt well cared for.

The prison remained overcrowded, but the environment was generally much improved. We observed an engaged and committed, albeit inexperienced, staff group who were both proactive and supportive in their dealings with prisoners. Engagement was, however, inhibited by a limited time unlocked as the prison emerged from the restrictions of Covid-19. This, in turn, was having a detrimental impact on the take-up of purposeful activity, such as education and work. Improving this situation was arguably the prison's most immediate priority. Support for prisoners to help maintain their family ties and work in general to deliver rehabilitative and resettlement services were impressive.

Doncaster was a very well led prison. The director and his management team were responsible for a capable and confident culture despite the former only taking up his role at the beginning of the pandemic. An important component of this culture was their visible leadership. They had taken very effective action in response to a formal improvement notice issued by the Ministry of Justice in 2020 following concerns about safety. The general sense of order and calm in the prison was a testament to the success of this action. Leaders had also taken advantage of the time made available to staff by the pandemic to support them with training and to oversee improvements to the governance of the prison. This capability and creativity in the prison was further evidenced by the nine examples of notable practice we identified.

Doncaster is not an easy prison to run. Leaders and their staff are to be congratulated on the progress they have achieved even during challenging times.

Charlie Taylor
HM Chief Inspector of Prisons March 2022

## Safety

At the last inspection of HMP Doncaster, in 2019, we found that outcomes for prisoners were not sufficiently good against this healthy prison test. At this inspection, we found that outcomes for prisoners were now reasonably good.

The reception area was clean and welcoming, but prisoners spent too long there on arrival. There was excellent peer support during the early days at the prison and induction was comprehensive. The levels of assaults, against staff and prisoners alike, had decreased substantially since the last inspection and were now lower than the average for similar prisons. In our survey, fewer prisoners than at the time of our last inspection said that they had felt unsafe during their stay. The safety strategy identified key areas of focus and safety meetings interrogated a wide range of data.

The challenge, support and intervention plan process (CSIP) (see Glossary) was used usefully to provide support but was not yet sufficiently embedded or applied consistently. The number of adjudication hearings had reduced since the last inspection and they were mostly timely and proportionate.

Use of force had also reduced since the last inspection and was lower than the average for the type of prison. Use of force paperwork was comprehensive and supported accountability, but too few incidents were recorded on body-worn cameras. Incidents were not reviewed at use of force meetings to identify learning and good practice. The number of prisoners segregated had reduced since the last inspection. Living conditions on the segregation unit were bleak, but relationships between staff and prisoners were good.

Security arrangements were generally proportionate, and the flow of intelligence was good. In our survey, fewer prisoners than at the time of our last inspection said that it was easy to get illicit drugs and alcohol.

There had been eight self-inflicted deaths since the last inspection. Actions in response to Prisons and Probation Ombudsman recommendations had been implemented and were regularly reviewed. The number of recorded self-harm incidents had remained at a consistent level for the last 12 months but was higher than at comparable prisons. Recent analysis of data had been used effectively to develop a strategy to reduce levels of harm. The prison had developed some excellent initiatives for prisoners in crisis and the quality of assessment, care in custody and teamwork (ACCT) case management documents for prisoners at risk of suicide or self-harm had improved overall.

**Respect**

At the last inspection of HMP Doncaster, in 2019, we found that outcomes for prisoners were reasonably good against this healthy prison test. At this inspection, we found that outcomes for prisoners remained reasonably good.

Staff control of the wings had improved since the last inspection and we saw appropriate challenge of prisoners. Interactions between staff and prisoners appeared generally positive. Key worker sessions were recorded more regularly than we normally see, but the content was limited. The prison remained overcrowded, with about 700 prisoners living two to a cell designed for one. The cells were in reasonably good condition and wing workers reported any faults, which were rectified quickly. Most showers were in poor condition, with a lack of ventilation and a fly infestation. The communal areas were clean and well maintained.

Food provision was reasonable, and the on-site shop provided early access to the full selection of goods.

Prison-wide consultation arrangements were adequate and improving with the easing of regime restrictions. Prisoners could easily make applications using the touchscreen kiosks around the prison and most were responded to promptly. Complaints were managed reasonably well, and analysis of data was robust.

Video-conferencing facilities were impressive and used for a variety of purposes, including court hearings and contact with community offender managers (COMs), immigration officials and health care professionals.

The strategic management of equality and diversity had been neglected during much of the pandemic, but recent progress was promising. However, analysis of data to identify potential disproportionate treatment remained limited. Responses to discrimination incident report forms were reasonable but not always timely.

Support for foreign nationals was impressive, including the innovative use of on-site technology to translate legal documentation.

The chaplaincy provided good pastoral support, but corporate worship remained suspended and not all prisoners had access to a chaplain of their own faith because of staffing shortfalls.

Health services were well led by a strong leadership team and clinical governance processes were robust. Patients were seen promptly for urgent GP and nurse appointments, but clinical oversight of triage arrangements was not sufficient. Mental health services were responsive to demand, with prompt assessment and prioritisation of crisis support. However, there were delays in transferring patients to hospital under the Mental Health Act.

There was a continuous demand for social care for those with complex needs, but service provision was very good.

Medicines management arrangements were good, but there was no on-site pharmacist to provide clinical advice and medicine use reviews. Demand for substance misuse and alcohol detoxification services was high, but patients could easily access the services, which met their needs sensitively. Dental services were good, but patients waited too long for treatment.

**Purposeful activity**

At the last inspection of HMP Doncaster, in 2019, we found that outcomes for prisoners were not sufficiently good against this healthy prison test. At this inspection, we found that outcomes for prisoners remained not sufficiently good.

Time out of cell was very limited, at around two and a half hours per day for most, but this was better for full-time workers, who had about seven hours a day unlocked. In our roll checks, we found just under 39% of prisoners locked up and only 150 in off-wing activity.

The library was yet to reopen fully and, in our survey, only 9% of respondents said that they were able to visit the library once a week or more. Gym provision was impressive, but we were not confident that all prisoners had equitable access. The number and range of qualifications delivered were much higher than we normally see.

Too few prisoners were benefiting from education, skills and work – through face-to-face or remote delivery – and attendance at education in the classrooms was not consistently high.

Although leaders had a clear vision for the development of the curriculum, there was more to do to meet the needs of the population, given the revised purpose of the prison. There was too much reliance on wing work roles, insufficient workshop space, and there was no specific provision to support the skills needed for self-employment. However, an attractive and welcoming environment had been created, where a small number of prisoners developed their vocational skills and interacted with internal customers in a street market.

The quality of education was not consistently good. There were some areas of strength – for example, in barbering, horticulture, catering and graphics – but there were weaknesses in the planning and teaching of English, mathematics and support for those learning English for speakers of other languages. This was compounded in English teaching by the shortage of staff. A personal development curriculum was also needed.

While prisoners' additional needs were identified, vocational tutors did not make sufficient use of this information to support these prisoners to progress. The small number of prisoners on distance learning courses were also not sufficiently supported.

### Rehabilitation and release planning

At the last inspection of HMP Doncaster, in 2019, we found that outcomes for prisoners were reasonably good against this healthy prison test. At this inspection, we found that outcomes for prisoners were now good.

Social visits had restarted in 2021, but, with no refreshments or play facilities, the experience was less rewarding than in pre-pandemic times. However, the 'Families First' team was doing some excellent work in spite of the Covid-19 restrictions.

The strategies and policies were good across the whole range of reducing reoffending activity and an ambitious change programme had begun to remodel the offender management unit to meet the needs of the reconfigured prison population. Almost all offender assessment system (OASys) assessments were up to date and most were comprehensive. Sentence plans contained relevant and achievable objectives. Contact levels between prison offender managers and prisoners were good and large caseloads had begun to reduce with additional staff.

There was good communication with COMs, often by three-way video- link meetings involving the prisoner, enabling discussion of release plans and licence conditions. Some useful support was given to those on remand and those recalled to prison. Recategorisation reviews were carried out fairly and on time, and transfers were being carried out more readily.

Public protection processes had been tightened in all important areas since the last inspection. Monitoring of mail and telephone calls was kept up to date and the flow of information was much improved. Multi- agency public protection arrangements (MAPPA) processes were supported well.

The psychology team had been strengthened and added considerable value to the work of the prison. A range of programmes was offered, in groups and one to one. Restorative justice interventions were provided. Help with finance and debt matters had been withdrawn following the reunification of probation services, and not fully replaced.

Resettlement needs on arrival were captured and followed up well. A weekly multidisciplinary meeting discussed forthcoming releases. The new 'departure lounge' had produced a far better service on the day of release than at the time of our last inspection.

Despite a dip in service delivery following the reunification of probation services in mid-2021,

staff had worked hard to sustain support for those without a release address.

### Key concerns and recommendations

Key concerns and recommendations identify the issues of most importance to improving outcomes for prisoners and are designed to help establishments prioritise and address the most significant weaknesses in the treatment and conditions of prisoners.

During this inspection we identified some areas of key concern and have made a small number of recommendations for the prison to address those concerns.

Key concern: The prison was overcrowded and almost 700 prisoners were doubled up in cells designed for one prisoner.

Recommendation: Two prisoners should not be held together in cells designed for one. (To the director)

Key concern: There was no tailored equality strategy setting out a clear vision to improve outcomes for prisoners with protected characteristics. The analysis of data was limited and engagement with protected groups was not frequent enough for the prison to fully understand and address their needs, especially given the high turnover of the population.

Recommendation: Equality data and effective consultation should inform a tailored strategy that leaders drive proactively to address disproportionate outcomes for prisoners from protected groups. (To the director)

Key concern: Prisoners needing a transfer to secure mental health inpatient services continued to wait far too long for a bed.

Recommendation: Patients requiring admission to hospital under the Mental Health Act should be transferred expeditiously, and within current Department of Health guidelines. (To the director)

Key concern: There was insufficient activity or time unlocked for most of the population. Many prisoners spent around 21 and a half hours in their cells, and some even longer. There was too little purposeful activity for the population and too many prisoners were under- employed in wing-based work.

Recommendation: Leaders should urgently prioritise increasing time unlocked and the provision of regular education, skills and work activities to enable a larger number of prisoners to attend them. (To the director and HMPPS)

### Notable positive practice

We define notable positive practice as innovative work or practice that leads to particularly good outcomes from which other establishments may be able to learn. Inspectors look for evidence of good outcomes for prisoners; original, creative or particularly effective approaches to problem-solving or achieving the desired goal; and how other establishments could learn from or replicate the practice.

Inspectors found nine examples of notable positive practice during this inspection.

The prison had developed some excellent initiatives for prisoners in crisis and at risk of self-harm. These included a theory-based toolkit programme called 'Break the Cycle', and 'one-page plans', completed by psychologists – both designed for those who self-harmed prolifically. These had resulted in positive outcomes and had reduced harm.

A locally produced online catalogue improved prisoners' access to purchases.

The innovative use of technology to translate important legal documents and information on daily prison life was impressive and greatly appreciated by the many who found it difficult, or were unable, to understand English.

A wide range of PE-based qualifications, delivered by a PE instructor permanently assigned to the task, was consistently achieved.

Some innovative small-scale businesses had been developed in a welcoming and attractive environment known as 'Market Street', located within 'Enterprise City'. Here, prisoners designed, made and sold soft toys, repaired televisions and bicycles, and produced high-quality paintings on canvas.)

The 'Families First' team was very active, in spite of Covid-19 restrictions. Its activities included 'Daddy Newborn', offering a supervised, well-equipped nursery room for a parent to bond with their child; a relationships course; and a 'family album' scheme in preparation for Mother's Day, with the family support worker taking photographs of prisoners with their mothers. Family events had been held over the Christmas period, and a programme of regular special events in visits was being prepared for the coming months.

There was good communication with community offender managers, often by three-way video-link meetings involving the prisoner, providing the opportunity to discuss release plans and licence conditions.

A monthly interdisciplinary meeting considered, individually and in depth, the progress of those on indeterminate sentences for public protection (IPP). This had recently shown success, enabling the progression of some IPP prisoners.

The new 'departure lounge' included a large number of practical items, mainly donated by large retailers, for the basic needs of those leaving the prison, including food, toiletries and clothing. The two skilled staff, helped by volunteers, were also able to give personal help, such as direct telephone access to statutory housing and benefits teams as well as liaison with community offender managers.

## INDEPENDENT MONITORING BOARD: Annual Report

The law requires every prison to be monitored by an independent Board appointed by the Justice Secretary; these are known as Independent Monitoring Boards (IMBs). The IMB must satisfy itself as to the humane and just treatment of those held in custody within its prison and the range and adequacy of the programmes preparing them for release; it must report annually to the Justice Secretary on how well the prison has met the standards and requirements placed on it.

**IMB Report 1 October 2019 to 30 September 2020**
**Published November 2021**
**Executive summary**
**Background to the report**
**Covid**

As with all prisons and all IMBs, the dominant factor during the year has been the impact of the coronavirus (Covid). The need to manage Covid risks to prisoners has very significantly affected many aspects of the prison regime, day to day life and some non-routine activities.

The IMB at HMP Doncaster has been reduced in the number of members able to visit the prison (reduced to one person for much of the period from March to September 2020) and this has had a significant effect on the board's ability to monitor. As a board, we took a decision to concentrate on certain aspects of our monitoring and to largely suspend those aspects that could not be resourced. Distant/virtual monitoring has been a feature of some IMBs during Covid but our board has only had very limited impact via monitoring from outside and almost all that follows in our report is the outcome of the much reduced in-person visits. Our board will seek out examples of good practice from other boards who were able to carry out more remote monitoring. In particular, to see whether some of the barriers our board encountered, such as difficulty to join meetings taking place in the prison via IT links, can be overcome by different technology and / or by improved IT skills among our team.

The areas that the Board decided to prioritise were
• individual applications (complaints to the IMB) by prisoners. These were received via written applications, requests to contact a prisoner while within the prison and via the IMB (0800) line
• healthcare
• safer custody

The report is limited to those areas monitored during this period and those things not monitored (the majority of the prison's work) are not dealt with below.

### New management team
The previous Director retired in April 2020. He was always accessible to the IMB and supportive of the Board's role and work and we wish him well for his retirement.

The new Director has made changes to the senior management team, including some changes in roles, capacity and priorities. Although Covid has been impactful since he took up his post, the changes to day to day and longer term, strategic running of the prison are evident and, in the Board's opinion, positive.

### Main judgements
### How safe is the prison?
The restrictions of the Covid regime have meant a significant reduction in the association of men within the prison and this has had an effect on some of the potential points of contact and prisoner-on-prisoner and prisoner-on-staff violence. The Board is concerned about self-harm. Although self-harm is a risk that the prison has to address at all times, Covid or non-Covid, the negative impact of a restricted regime (especially reduced contact with family and friends through visits) must create additional risks. The Board is aware and supportive of work being done in the prison to identify men at risk, to engage with them to reduce risk, the recording of incidents (in a timely way) and work with men who have self-harmed.

There is drug use in the prison. This creates acute and longer-term health issues and, at its most severe, can be an immediate risk to life. Security measures are in place both routinely and targeted. The Board is aware of and supportive of the prison's drug strategy. There were deaths in custody during the period of this report. These received immediate and longer-term "lessons-learnt" attention by the prison and have had support from safer custody colleagues from other prisons. All the deaths were subject to investigation by the Prisons and Probation Ombudsman (PPO), with final reports being issued for some. The PPO has made recommendations for action and improvement and the Board will monitor to be assured of progress to action those recommendations

### How fairly and humanely are prisoners treated?
Doncaster received its last monitoring the quality of prison life (MQPL) survey in March 2020 and it is a notable improvement on the previous survey of 2015; an improved score for safety, going from a 1 to a 2 and retaining a level 3 for decency is notable, though this was before lockdown restrictions were implemented. The report does not provide any singular standout or exceptional finding that would cause concern to the management team beyond what they were already aware of and resolving.

### Discrimination incident report form (DIRF)
The Board and the prison both observed that issues and complaints were being raised which included some comment by the prisoner about inequality of treatment related to a protected characteristic but that these complaints were not always made via the DIRF process and therefore not dealt with according to the DIRF protocols or timetable. Potentially useful information from DIRFs about common issues and patterns could also be missed.

The Board is pleased to see the renewed process in the prison to encourage and enable men to complete a DIRF where this is the right way to raise an issue and to investigate and reply to DIRFs within an improved timescale.

The Board predicts that for the 2020/21 year there will be more DIRFs and would regard that as a positive thing (more issues being raised and then receiving attention) rather than a negative indicator.

### Use of force / ethnicity or religion
Planned and unplanned use of force is monitored and shows no patterns of concern in terms of use of force on prisoners by ethnicity or religion.

### How well are prisoners' health and wellbeing needs met?
Key issues
• Capacity of mental health staffing ie the number of professional on-site staff available for prisoners in a timely manner
• Access/agency – the ability of all prisoners (including those less confident with appointment-making systems) to get the care they need when they need it. The access to healthcare is a shared responsibility ie prisoners using the appointment system effectively, officers enabling men to leave their residential wing to go for an appointment and healthcare handling the appointment. From our conversations with prisoners, it is the Board's view that not all of these worked together effectively in all cases and some men missed out on attention that they should have received.
• Complaints – it was the Board's view that the prison/healthcare were not receiving all complaints about health issues that should have been made. Some prisoners were unaware of healthcare complaints procedures and some were raising complaints informally (and less effectively) eg making verbal complaints to officers. The Board is pleased to see that an

improved healthcare complaints process has been established for 2020 /21 including complaints forms and healthcare complaints boxes being accessible on all wings. The Board predicts that there will be an increase in the number of healthcare complaints in 2020/21 but this (and the opportunities for informing improvements) would not be a negative.

• Prisons and Probation Ombudsman (PPO) findings in reports into deaths in custody. There have been recommendations included in PPO reports into deaths in custody during the 2019 /20 year. It is important that all learning from such findings and recommendations is taken and this has been discussed by the board with prison and healthcare senior management.

## Main areas for development
### TO THE MINISTER

Our Board recommends that work be done to research the impact of Covid and Covid precautions on prisoners and on their families to make sure that their experiences are fully understood and their voices on the impact of Covid and Covid precautions are captured.

Our Board sees some similarities with other areas of high risk (such as hospitals) where very difficult decisions about safety and infection control have had to be made. We are not critical of those decisions, but given that Covid may be with us in some form for some time yet and there will be a risk of future pandemics, we believe that it is important that what prisoners experienced and what their families experienced needs to be recorded, understood and inform planning for any future.

We would particularly emphasise the need to understand impact on prisoners'
families, for example, on limited in-person contact by children with their parent.

We believe research should include contact with a representative sample of those prisoners who have since been released from prisons.

### TO THE PRISON SERVICE

We would make a similar recommendation to that above but with the scope being research with people in prisons. As mentioned above, our Board understands the very difficult decisions that have had to be made to reduce Covid spread and to keep people safe but we feel that prisoners' experiences need to be captured in a systematic manner and those findings used to inform plans for future risks

UTTOXETER
ST14 8XR

DOVEGATE (MAIN) PRISON

Tel: 01283 829400

*For the latest reports on this prison please visit:*
https://tinyurl.com/bdfh26rv

*Important Changes:* **(1) Visits:** the identification necessary to access this prison and visit for social or professional purposes has changed; (2) **Money and Gifts** new rules now apply to these. See page 16 for full details of the above.

**Task of the establishment** A long-term high security men's prison with remand and therapeutic community facilities for category B prisoners.

**Certified normal accommodation and operational capacity**
Prisoners held March 2022: 960
Baseline certified normal capacity: 960
In-use certified normal capacity: 960
Operational capacity: 960

**Prison status and key providers**
Private – managed by: Serco
Prison Group: Contracted
Head of Custodial Contracts: Neil Richards
Governor/Director: Mark Hanson/Sarai Kam (c)
IMB Chair: John Haley
Physical health provider: Care UK
Mental health provider: Care UK
Substance use treatment provider: Care UK
Prison education framework provider: Serco
Escort contractor: GeoAmey

**Brief history and residential** March 2022: HMP Dovegate is located near Uttoxeter, Staffordshire, and is a category B training prison holding male residents aged 21 and over.

The main prison consists of convicted residents, mainly serving determinate sentences, a remand facility and about 130 local prison places.

There is also a purpose-built therapeutic community (TC), which takes repeat and mainly violent offenders, who come from any prison in the country and volunteer to address their offending behaviour through group and individual therapy. All residents go through an assessment before being accepted as suitable for the challenges which come with the therapy on the TC.

The certified normal accommodation of the main prison is 960, and that of the TC is 200, giving a combined total of 1,160.

The number of residents held in the main prison during 2020/2021 has been at, or close to, the operational capacity.

**Houseblock 1 Category B trainer**
Sentences over 10 years and enhanced incentives and earned privileges (IEP) status. B-W wings sentenced residents engaged in employment, education.

**Houseblock 2 Category B trainer**
Sentenced residents engaged in employment/education. Long-term sentences (over 10 years) and enhanced IEP status. Sentenced residents engaged in employment/education Sentenced residents engaged in employment/education
Social responsibility unit (SRU)

**Houseblock 3 Local prison**
Sentenced/remand residents serving less than two years. Early days centre, and interventions and substance misuse team (ISMT) detoxification. Dovegate induction wing. (P wing is for Vulnerable residents (including those convicted of a sexual offences).

The TC, which is separated from the main prison by an internal fence, consists of three house blocks, all having single occupancy cells, with in-cell toilets and showers. The fourth block houses the education department and a small TC visits hall with a family room. It shares some of the main prison facilities – for example, the health centre and gym.

The care and separation unit (CSU - segregation) is a separate block and has 18 cells and two special cells.

Automated teller machines (ATMs) (kiosks), are installed in all the residential areas, allowing residents to check their accounts, order meals, make medical and dental appointments, access the prison complaints system, and arrange visits. Other functions are added on a regular basis.

The prison has its own kitchen and laundry.

The health centre has two waiting rooms and a range of treatment and consulting rooms for outpatient clinics. The inpatient facility has accommodation for 11 residents. Each room has a toilet and washbasin. There is one bath/shower room in the unit.

The prison has a large education and training facility (Dovegate College), four workshops, a gym, and a multi-faith centre.

The library services are provided by Serco, in partnership with Staffordshire Library Services. The Shannon Trust are active in the prison as an additional support to prisoners with poor reading skills.

The prison kitchen produces all meals in-house for residents, as well as for staff in a small bistro. The prison has a contract with Serco Integrated Services for facilities management.

The prison has well-maintained and attractive gardens, with productive vegetable and flower growing areas. TC grounds are exceptional, with ponds and ducks cared for by residents. These have been looked after well throughout the whole year despite lockdowns.

The hedgehog preservation scheme began in summer 2018. Constructed by residents, the project has increased the population of this endangered species, who are still very much in evidence.

Staff vacancies became an increasing concern throughout 2020/2021, both in administrative and operational roles. A significant number of the newer staff members moved on during the year. Combined with staff illness and self-isolation this proved a challenge for management at times. Attempts to address the issue through offering overtime were only partially successful. The Board were pleased to see management take new innovative measures to aid recruitment, including visiting local universities and placing adverts at sporting venues.

**Visiting Information**
To book a social visit email:
visits.dovegate@serco.com with as much information as possible.
Call the Visits Booking Team on 0800 8778951 between the hours of 10am and 12pm and 1pm to 3pm, Monday to Friday
**Visiting Times:** 09.00-11.30, 13.30-16.00

**Legal visits:** To book a legal/video link visit email visits.dovegate@serco.com with as much information as possible

**INSPECTIONS & REPORTS**
**Date of last inspection:** 30 Sept–11 Oct 2019
*Notable features from this inspection*
• Dovegate was an unusual category B training prison as it held a number of prisoners on remand and serving very short sentences.
• 70% of the population were serving sentences of 10 years or more and nearly a third were serving indeterminate sentences.
• Three-quarters of the population were assessed as presenting either a high or very high risk of serious harm to others and half were convicted of violence as their main offence.
• 17% of those responding to our survey reported that they had an alcohol problem when they arrived at Dovegate compared to 9% in other category B training prisons.
• 73% of prisoners were under 40 years old.
• 10% of prisoners were foreign nationals.

**HMCIP Report, published 13 February 2020**

Located near Uttoxeter in Staffordshire and built in 2001, HMP Dovegate, a privately-run prison operated by SERCO, is a modern and complex institution that comprises a self-contained therapeutic community (TC), a separate training prison for category B prisoners and a small local prison function. It holds up to 960 adult men. This inspection concerned only the training and local prison functions at the establishment as the TC is inspected separately.

In comparison to our inspection in 2017, we are pleased to report that this inspection found some notable improvements. Outcomes in safety and rehabilitation and release planning, like respect, were now reasonably good, although they remained insufficiently good in purposeful activity. Dovegate is a safer prison than in 2017. Appropriate attention was given to individual risk among newly arrived prisoners, and reception procedures and induction arrangements were generally good. More prisoners in our survey told us they felt safe on their first night than we usually find in similar prisons, with other survey evidence suggesting this positive sense of safety continued throughout their stay. Work was in place to address violence, although more needed to be done to ensure it was sufficiently impactful, as the number of violent incidents, some of them serious, continued to fluctuate. However, after a recent peak in 2018, violence had fallen in the months before our visit and was now more in keeping with the level seen in similar prisons.

The evidence suggested that prisoners felt reasonably incentivised to behave and engage with the prison, and the number of formal adjudications had halved since we last inspected. The use of force had similarly fallen, although oversight of it was weak and paradoxically the use of segregation was increasing. Prisoners were reasonably positive about their treatment and their relationships with staff while in segregation, although we found some aspects of the way the unit was managed to be restrictive and unnecessary. Security procedures were proportionate, and a comprehensive and joined-up approach to combating the misuse of drugs was now in place. But despite this, drug availability remained a key concern. We were told that since we last inspected there had been two deaths linked to the use of illicit substances and a further three self-inflicted deaths. The level of self-harm, in contrast, was relatively low. The prison seemed to have responded adequately to recommendations made following enquiries into the deaths and those in crisis we spoke to told us they felt supported.

Except for some inertia in respect to minor rule breaking, supervision was generally good and staff-prisoner relationships constructive. The prison was clean and well maintained, and prisoners' access to amenities and kit was good. There were good prisoner consultation arrangements in place, although some improvement needed to be made in regard to how complaints were dealt with. More prominence was now given to the promotion of equality but there needed to be greater determination to improve the work of the equality action team in addressing negative perceptions among some minority groups. Health provision was good overall.

We found about a quarter of prisoners locked in cell during the working day although this was the case predominantly in the local part of the prison, with the proportion falling to 16% on the training wings. There were enough activity places for most prisoners although fewer for vulnerable prisoners. The availability of education was better than the more limited availability of vocational provision, but attendance generally was not good enough. Productive links with external employers ensured some demanding commercial standards in workshops, although there were missed opportunities in terms of recording skills acquisition and achievements. Most learners in education were making progress but our colleagues in Ofsted judged the overall effectiveness of provision as 'requires improvement', their second lowest level of assessment.

The support prisoners were given to maintain their family ties was encouraging, with very good visits and enhanced family visits arrangements. Family support and parenting courses were also available.

The prison held many high risk of harm prisoners serving long sentences. The majority had an offender assessment (OASys) although sentence plan reviews were often missed. Contact between offender supervisors and prisoners was reasonable. Public protection arrangements, including planning for release, were robust. Offending behaviour work was well managed but provision for vulnerable prisoners and one-to-one interventions was more limited. Support for the considerable number of prisoners being released needed to be better, with meaningful reviews of resettlement needs and plans prior to departure currently lacking and many individuals being released without a settled address.

Despite this, we found the prison settled. Prisoners were confident and engaged, and staff were knowledgeable. The Director and his team were ensuring the prison was well run and we had every confidence that the establishment would continue to improve. This report provides a number of recommendations which we hope will assist in that process.

Peter Clarke CVO OBE QPM October 2019
HM Chief Inspector of Prisons

## INDEPENDENT MONITORING BOARD: Annual Report

The law requires every prison to be monitored by an independent Board appointed by the Justice Secretary; these are known as Independent Monitoring Boards (IMBs). The IMB must satisfy itself as to the humane and just treatment of those held in custody within its prison and the range and adequacy of the programmes preparing them for release; it must report annually to the Justice Secretary on how well the prison has met the standards and requirements placed on it.

## IMB Report 1 Oct 2020 – 30 Sept 2021. Published March 2022

### Background to the report

As with last year, due to the Covid situation, at times during 2020/2021 only one or two members made limited visits and from November through to February only two members visited the prison. This was principally to attend CSU reviews and answer applications, including those received in the prison and through the 0800 line.

The Director was well established in post at the start of the year and continued to appoint new members to her senior management team and make new appointments in all areas of the prison. Board members have had access to all areas of the prison. The Board has had full cooperation from the Director and her senior management team. We would like to express our thanks to them for their help, especially through the difficult months of lockdowns during the pandemic. The Director and her deputy make themselves available to the Board at any time and are open and frank in our discussions.

We also greatly appreciate the guidance and support received from the controller and her team, who also make themselves available to the Board at any time.

### Main judgements

#### How safe is the prison?

The prison was generally calm and settled, and residents had good relationships with each other and staff. Managers actively work to address gang culture and be aware of vulnerable residents who may be taken advantage of.

A weekly stability meeting was introduced, attended by senior staff from all houseblocks, safer custody and security. The HMPPS controller and chair of the Board also attend. After contributions are received by all interested parties, each wing is assessed and given a 'traffic light' stability rating for the week. Areas and/or individuals of note are highlighted.

#### How fairly and humanely are prisoners treated?

Accommodation and facilities in Dovegate are good. The reporting system from the Board's weekly rota visits works well, and issues of cleanliness or disrepair were generally acted on quickly.

However, during the year, it was clear that there were 'wear and tear' issues in the fabric of the prison, specifically leaking roofs and smelly, blocked drains. There was a leaking roof in the kitchen which threatened to affect the electric supply. This was dealt with as an emergency. Repairing other leaking roofs will need a long-term plan with consideration of security issues involved in employing outside contractors working at height.

Staff treated residents with respect and the Board saw generally positive relationships between them. Although the successful key worker scheme had to be limited to the most vulnerable there was excellent communication between management, staff, and residents. The Board sensed a level of acceptance amongst the prisoners that the restrictions were necessary to keep them as safe as possible.

The lack of availability of body-worn cameras (BWCs) had been an issue for the Board for several years and had been raised in previous reports. The Board is pleased to report that new BWCs started to be rolled out to frontline staff at the start of the year and it is now rare to see these staff members without them. This is particularly the case in the CSU where their lack of availability had been an on-going concern for the Board.

The food is of a consistently high standard, with every dietary need catered for. Residents also have access to a wide range of products in the prison shop.

#### How well are prisoners' health and wellbeing needs met?

Health and social care are provided by Practice Plus, which subcontracts to Midland Partnership Foundation Trust for the delivery of mental health services.

The Board has found that good cooperation between the healthcare and custodial teams produces positive outcomes for residents' health, and any concerns that the Board raises are generally dealt with immediately.

## How well are prisoners progressed towards successful resettlement?

'Through the gate' work was undertaken by the Reducing Reoffending Partnership (RRP), under contract to the community rehabilitation company until July 2021. RRP provided the seven resettlement pathway assessments and courses. These continued during lockdown and, although group work courses had to stop, the courses were adapted for one-to-one work using booklets and in-cell telephone contact.

In July 2021, national changes to the probation services resulted in much of the work being the responsibility of the prison. The Board has not been able to monitor this, but plans are in place to give time to this in the current year.

## Main areas for development
### TO THE MINISTER

The Board looks for positive timely action from the Prison Service regarding the point raised below: prisoners' property during transfer. This has been highlighted in at least our last three annual reports. Far more urgency needs to be applied to this problem.

There should be focus on reviewing the sentences of imprisonment for public protection (IPP) prisoners, enabling them to progress and move towards a safe release. It is against natural justice that so long after this sentence was abolished so many prisoners are still in prison.

### TO THE PRISON SERVICE

The Board continues to deal with a substantial number of property issues resulting from transfers from other establishments. More effort needs to be made to find a national solution to this problem. Despite a framework being developed in April 2020, nothing very significant seems to have happened and the IMB still chases property that has not arrived with the prisoner or is incomplete. No electronic system exists across the estate and prisoners still arrive with property cards.

### TO THE DIRECTOR

The Board would like to thank the Director for her availability and openness, especially during the various lockdowns due to Covid-19. We are hopeful that what we highlight here, especially the points raised in previous annual reports, will see action in the present reporting year.

Accelerate plans for the conversion of the in-patient unit in healthcare to provide consultation and treatment rooms adequate for the number of residents in the prison.

Should it be decided not to proceed with the above, then urgently upgrade the inpatient bath/shower room.

Liaise with the head of healthcare to reinstate escorts to outside hospital appointments to the levels in place the previous reporting year.

Continue to encourage staff to make proper use of the BWCs which are now available and worn by frontline staff. Staff should be reminded that their value as de-escalation and evidential tools is only useful if they are turned on. This is essential for in-cell interaction where no other CCTV source is available.

## Progress since the last report

The Board acknowledges the continuation of improvements made to the fabric and general cleanliness of the prison, which impacts on the health and welfare of residents. Every opportunity was taken throughout the year to upgrade many areas of the prison, highlighted elsewhere in the report.

The Board at last, after many years of reporting, was pleased to see the unhygienic toilet in the main healthcare waiting room boarded up and put out of action.

New BWCs are now available and being used by frontline staff, including in the CSU.

The ongoing improvements to healthcare provision in the prison which the Board has recognised in previous reports, and the cooperation between custodial and healthcare staff, undoubtedly contributed to the successful implementation of measures to combat the Covid-19 pandemic.

| serco | UTTOXETER ST14 8XR |
|---|---|
| DOVEGATE THERAPEUTIC PRISON | Tel: 01283 829400 |

*For the latest reports on this prison please visit:*
https://tinyurl.com/bdfh26rv

*Important Changes:* **(1) Visits:** the identification necessary to access this prison and visit for social or professional purposes has changed; (2) **Money and Gifts** new rules now apply to these. See page 16 for full details of the above.

**Task of the establishment** A category B trainer custodial therapeutic prison (TP) for men.

**Certified normal accommodation and operational capacity**
Prisoners held March 2022: 200
Baseline certified normal capacity: 200
In-use certified normal capacity: 200
Operational capacity: 200

## Prison status and key providers

Private – managed by: Serco
Prison Group: Custodial Contracts
Prison Group Director: Neil Richards
Governor/Director: Mark Hanson/Sarai Kam (c)
IMB Chair: John Haley
Physical health provider: Primary Practice Group (PPG) - formerly Care UK Health and Rehabilitation Services
Mental health provider: South Staffordshire and Shropshire Healthcare NHS Foundation Trust, under a sub-contract from PPG
Substance misuse provider: Care UK Health and Rehabilitation Services
Learning and skills provider: HMP Dovegate
Escort contractor: GeoAmey

**Brief history** HMP Dovegate was built in 2001 as a category B training prison. It had the first purpose-built custodial TP holding up to 200 residents. A small local prison servicing the courts also existed within the main prison.

A TP consists of several distinct therapeutic communities (TCs) in which people choose to live together, support each other, challenge others and be challenged on all aspects of their offending. It aims to alter people's way of thinking, enabling them to change their lives for the better.

The TCs were run democratically, which meant that where possible all members of the community were involved in making decisions that affected the community. Prisoners were encouraged to play an active role in their community and a variety of roles and representative jobs were available.

Communities were learning experiences and everything was designed to have therapeutic value and provide men with an opportunity to develop within a safe environment.

## Short description of residential units

Avalon, Camelot, Endeavour and Genesis – therapeutic communities of 40 residents each
Venture TC+ – 20 residents with learning difficulties
Destiny – induction unit accommodating 20 prisoners.

## Visiting Information

To book a social visit email:
visits.dovegate@serco.com with as much information as possible.
Call the Visits Booking Team on 0800 8778951 between the hours of 10am and 12pm and 1pm to 3pm, Monday to Friday
**Visiting Times:** 09.00-11.30, 13.30-16.00

**Legal visits:** To book a legal/video link visit email visits.dovegate@serco.com with as much information as possible

## INSPECTIONS & REPORTS
**Date of last inspection:** 12–22 March 2018
**HMCIP Report, published 17 July 2018**

Dovegate Therapeutic Prison (TP) held up to 200 men in one of five therapeutic communities (TCs) and an induction unit. Although managed as part of Dovegate prison, its functions are very specific, most facilities are discrete to the TP site and it is largely self-contained. We inspect Dovegate main prison separately.

Men held in the TP were referred or referred themselves for the accredited TC process, which aims to help them reduce their risk of harm to others by providing them with a structured community and a range of therapeutic work. The underlying ethos of TCs is that both staff and prisoners have a real say in how the communities are run. Men involved must be willing to be open about their offending and related institutional behaviour and to being challenged by their peers and staff. Therapy is embedded into all TC activities, not just in individual and group therapy sessions. It is a structured, externally validated intervention, and for men who go through the whole process, it lasts approximately two and a half years. Most men in the TP were serving very long determinate or indeterminate sentences and the TCs had to operate within the security imperatives of a category B prison.

Dovegate TP was a safe prison. There was very little violence, and when incidents occurred, appropriate formal disciplinary action was taken, including deselection if the matter was serious. Most incidents, however, related to minor antisocial behaviour or verbal exchanges, and they were mostly managed within the communities themselves through community challenge, individual self-reflection or community sanctions. Men received good support on arrival, including the small number who felt vulnerable and were at risk of self-harm. There had been no self-inflicted deaths since our last inspection.

Dovegate TP was also a respectful prison. Good staff-prisoner relationships were at the core of the therapeutic approach and held the communities together. After a short induction, all men lived on one of five TCs, where physical conditions were excellent, as was the external environment. Men felt well cared for, both by staff and their peers. Consultation arrangements were very strong, and the food provided was good. Some strategic arrangements relating to equality and diversity were being developed, but support for those with protected characteristics and faith provision were very strong. Health care was reasonably good, but there were some issues, particularly with waiting lists, which were too long.

Time out of cell was good and delivered reliably, although outside exercise opportunities were somewhat restricted. Leadership and management of learning, skills and work activities were not effective in ensuring that the provision was sufficient to meet prisoners' needs or that it fully supported the therapeutic process. The range and breadth of work and the curriculum was not wide enough, teaching and learning was not consistent and activities were not regarded as essential to supporting the therapeutic process.

Most men felt they were making progress through the work they were undertaking in the TCs and we were struck by the insights they had about their past behaviour and offending and about how different and productive their future could be. This was testament to the impact of the therapy and the hard work of the men and staff. However, the clinical model used to support therapy was undergoing significant change, and many specialist staff were not yet in post, which was having an impact on what could be done. Therapy staff did not have a good enough understanding of why so many men dropped out of therapy or how they could retain them, and some aspects of the work to prepare men for progressive moves was not coordinated well enough. Very few men were directly released from the TP, but overall staff were undertaking excellent work to reduce the risks and doing their best at an individual level to assist progression.

Dovegate TP was impressive. A national resource, it was part of the offender personality disorder pathway. It worked with men intensively over a period of years to better understand their problematic behaviour, attitudes and thinking patterns and to help them change. Most men who reached the end of the process made progress, and over 80% of respondents in our survey said they felt they had done something at the prison to make it less likely they would reoffend in the future. Learning, skills and work activities needed to better complement the prison's therapeutic aims, and the clinical model underpinning therapy work needed to be implemented in full. However, in nearly all other respects the work the prison was carrying out was excellent.

## INDEPENDENT MONITORING BOARD:
## Annual Report

The law requires every prison to be monitored by an independent Board appointed by the Justice Secretary; these are known as Independent Monitoring Boards (IMBs). The IMB must satisfy itself as to the humane and just treatment of those held in custody within its prison and the range and adequacy of the programmes preparing them for release; it must report annually to the Justice Secretary on how well the prison has met the standards and requirements placed on it.

### IMB Annual Report

The therapeutic community is separated by an internal fence within the HMP Dovegate grounds. Residents must make a request to the admittance committee and are discussed to see if they are likely to benefit from the therapeutic and group work that is fundamental to the workings of this area.

There are three blocks with two wings on each, holding a maximum of 200 prisoners in total. Each wing has a wing chairman and deputy who are elected, and all residents sign up to the community constitution before they enter the therapeutic system.

As the community is based on group work, Covid-19 has had a major impact on the progress of all residents in this area. The initial complete lockdown meant that the psychology-based group work was halted, and residents received only two exercise sessions of 45 minutes per day. As time progressed, with the realisation that Covid was continuing, the prison became more inventive in its delivery of in-cell phone therapy. Once Stage 3 was reached, group work for ten residents was allowed twice a week and education once a week.

The accommodation has been improved over the lockdown period with more cleaning and painting taking place, and with fewer residents on the wing at a time less mess occurs. The TC remains one of the cleanest areas in the whole of HMP Dovegate, the community charter increasing the pride that residents take in their communal areas.

For more information see HMP Dovegate (Main) IMB Report above.

**SUTTON LANE**
**SUTTON**
**SM2 5PD**

**HM PRISON**
**DOWNVIEW**     **Tel: 020 8196 6300**

*For the latest reports on this prison please visit:*
https://tinyurl.com/bdfh26rv

*Important Changes:* **(1) Visits:** the identification necessary to access this prison and visit for social or professional purposes has changed; (2) **Money and Gifts** new rules now apply to these. See page 16 for full details of the above.

## Task of the prison/establishment
A women's closed training prison.

## Certified normal accommodation and operational capacity
Women held July 2021: 210
Baseline certified normal capacity: 356
In-use certified normal capacity: 356
Operational capacity: 356

## Population of the prison
- 18 new prisoners per month.
- 25 foreign national women.
- 30% of women were from BAME backgrounds.
- 85 women were receiving support for substance use.
- 65 women were referred for mental health assessment each month.

## Prison status and key providers
Public
Prison department: Women's estate
Prison group director: Pia Sinha
Name of governor: Amy Dixon
IMB chair: Beverley Rexstrew
Physical and mental health provider: Central and North West London NHS Foundation Trust
Substance use treatment provider: Forward Trust
Prison education framework provider:
Weston College
Escort contractor: Serco

## Brief history
HMP Downview is a closed women's prison, housing adult and young adult females. When it first opened in 1979, it was a category C men's prison. In 2001, it was converted into an establishment for women. However, in 2013, the Ministry of Justice announced its intention to turn it back into a men's prison. Shortly afterwards, it closed for two years and eight months. Following the closure of HMP Holloway, it was decided to retain Downview within the women's estate. The prison reopened in May 2016.

## Short description of residential units
A wing – induction unit, including peer workers
B wing – general population
C wing north – enhanced level prisoners and the general population
C wing south – protective isolation units (accommodation for known or probably Covid-19 cases), reverse cohort units and accommodation for the general population
D wing – resettlement prisoners
E wing – high-risk transgender unit.

## INSPECTIONS & REPORTS
Date of last full inspection 12-23 July 2021
HMCIP Report, published 27 October 2021.

Downview is a closed training prison in south London that held 210 women at the time of our inspection, nearly three-quarters of whom were serving sentences of over four years and 40% were assessed as presenting a high risk of harm to others. The site was well looked after and women lived in cells that were generally in good condition, although in somewhat tired-looking accommodation blocks. The prison had successfully come through a challenging Covid-19 outbreak earlier in the year and was beginning to lift some restrictions.

Leaders had prioritised opening up education and workshops had begun to operate, with women attending lessons in classrooms or outreach sessions on the wing. Though plans for the further rollout of education were not fully developed, Downview had made considerably more progress than we have seen elsewhere, and enthusiastic staff members were helping to drive this forward.

Although inspectors saw many friendly interactions, relations between staff and women were not as good as we have seen in other women's prisons. My colleagues and I were given many examples of staff members being rude, dismissive or unhelpful. This was particularly worrying in a prison that holds such a vulnerable population and was in marked contrast to the quality of relationships we reported in our inspection of nearby HMP Send. It was also concerning that local and national leaders had not identified improving the quality of relationships in the prison as a priority.

The governor had recognised the need for development of middle leaders and that relationships between middle and senior leaders was strained. In response, an externally-run programme had been brought in to help address these issues, but the impact was not yet apparent and further work was required to change what seemed to be some deep-seated cultural issues.

The women held at Downview generally behaved well and levels of violence were low, but more could have been done to encourage good behaviour. As Covid-19 restrictions are lifted, the prison should make sure that the incentives scheme rewards those who have earned their enhanced status.

At the start of the second week of our inspection, the prison introduced a new regime that was designed to make sure that women had more time to complete domestic tasks, socialise and exercise, particularly those who were in work. Leaders had failed to communicate this change clearly and during the week both staff and women often did not know what they were supposed to be doing or where they were supposed to be, which they said was consistent with a pattern of poor communication in the prison. Leaders needed to make sure that there was adequate consultation and more thorough communication, through a wider range of channels, before changes were made.

Inspectors saw some excellent partnerships between professionals in health care, but there were not always enough officers to escort women, which meant that a quarter of GP appointments were missed.

Though many women were still locked in their cells for too long, with some only getting out for an hour-and-a-half a day, it was heartening to see workshops open and flourishing after so many months of restrictions. The prison has the opportunity to build on this and begin to provide a fully operational service. All plans to improve Downview will be dependent on senior leaders strengthening their own relationships with middle leaders, and between officers and the women. This must be a priority for the prison and leaders should plan to spend more time on the wings modelling the behaviour they want to see and, where necessary, addressing inappropriate staff conduct.

HM Chief Inspector of Prisons
September 2021.

### Summary of Key Findings

We last inspected HMP & YOI Downview in 2017 and made 60 recommendations, four of which were about areas of key concern. The prison fully accepted 48 of the recommendations and partially (or subject to resources) accepted 10. It rejected two of the recommendations.

### Progress on key concerns and recommendations from the full inspection

Our last inspection of HMP & YOI Downview took place before the Covid-19 pandemic and the recommendations in that report focused on areas of concern affecting outcomes for women prisoners at the time. Although we recognise that the challenges of keeping prisoners safe during Covid-19 will have changed the focus for many prison leaders, we believe that it is important to follow up on recommendations about areas of key concern to help leaders to continue to drive improvement.

We made one recommendation about a key concern in the area of respect. At this inspection we found that this recommendation had been partially achieved.

We made one recommendation about a key concern in the area of purposeful activity. Ofsted inspectors carried out a progress monitoring visit alongside our inspection to assess the progress

that leaders and managers had made towards reinstating a full education, skills and work curriculum. They judged it was too early to assess whether recommendations made at the previous inspection had been achieved.

We made two recommendations about key concerns in the area of resettlement. At this inspection we found that one of those recommendations had been achieved and one had not been achieved.

### Outcomes for women prisoners

We assess outcomes for women in prison against four healthy prison tests (see Appendix I for more information about the tests). At this inspection of HMP & YOI Downview, we found that outcomes for women had stayed the same in two healthy prison areas, improved in one and declined in one.

These judgements seek to make an objective assessment of the outcomes experienced by those detained and have taken into account the prison's recovery from Covid-19 as well as the 'regime stage' at which the prison was operating, as outlined in the HM Prison and Probation Service (HMPPS) National Framework for prison regimes and services.

### Safety

Women were treated well in reception and the induction was comprehensive. Covid-19 cohorting arrangements hindered a promising initiative, which paired new arrivals with enhanced peer support workers in the induction unit.

In our survey, 77% of women reported that staff treated them with respect but, as at the previous inspection, some said staff were rude, inconsistent and spoke to them inappropriately. We also observed some staff addressing women by their surname and interactions that did not reflect a trauma-informed approach. In our survey, more women (59%) than at the previous inspection (37%) reported that a member of staff had talked to them in the previous week to see how they were getting on. Intimate relationships between women were managed appropriately.

Following a reduction in the level of self-harm before Covid-19, rates had increased over the previous year. The safer custody strategic meeting was held regularly and examined a good range of data, but there was no strategy in place to reduce self-harm. Assessment, care in custody and teamwork (ACCT) case management documents for women at risk of suicide or self-harm were reasonable, although only 48% of women in our survey who had thought about self-harming said they felt cared for by staff. There was a reasonable mix of interventions, including counselling and one-to-one support, to help women manage their emotions and the Listener scheme (in which prisoners trained by the Samaritans provide confidential emotional support to fellow prisoners) had restarted.

There had been two self-inflicted deaths since the previous inspection. Recommendations following investigations conducted by the Prisons and Probation Ombudsman were taken seriously, and progress was monitored well.

The incentives scheme had become largely ineffective – there was little distinction between the enhanced and standard levels, which frustrated many women. Although marginally higher than at the previous inspection, the level of violence remained low and comparable to similar prisons. Violent incidents were not always recorded accurately, and leaders were unaware of the reasons for much of the violence. The challenge support and intervention plan process (see Appendix II: Glossary of terms) was underdeveloped.

The small number of adjudications were well managed in the prison. Despite having been recently redecorated, the segregation unit was bleak, but fewer women were now being segregated. Force was used infrequently, but more often than at the previous inspection. Security procedures were proportionate, but the prison's drug strategy was weak.

**Respect**

Support to help women maintain contact with their family had been limited during the pandemic, affecting the well-being of many women. There was now a promising family strategy, but no action plan. Women valued the in-cell phones, which had recently been installed. However, family days and group-work sessions were not available due to COVID-19 restrictions and the Prison Advice and Care Trust family engagement worker provided a very limited service. Social visits had restarted but uptake was low. The video calling facility was reasonably well used.

Some consultation had continued throughout most of the pandemic, but many women told us that communication and consultation relating to changes that affected them was poor. A new applications process had been introduced, but was not yet effective enough. Although responses to complaints were mostly timely, they did not always address the issues prisoners raised well enough. The provision for legal advice and representation was appropriate.

All women had their own cells, which were in good condition and well-furnished, but some toilets were unscreened. The communal areas and facilities on the wings were well maintained, although many were not currently in use. External areas were clean and well kept. Women

had few opportunities to prepare their own food. The shop was running well, although many black and minority ethnic women said it did not meet all their needs.

Health care partnership working had weaknesses, and problems getting women to their appointments were unresolved. Lack of prison escorting staff often delayed or prevented women from accessing health provision. Oversight of applications and waiting lists was inconsistent, which meant women's health needs might not have been triaged appropriately.

Mental health services provided women with good outcomes, but the psychologist was on secondment, which meant there was a gap in the mental health team. There was a memorandum of understanding between the prison and Surrey County Council to support the delivery of social care. Peer supporters provided non-personal care. The integrated clinical and psychosocial substance use service provided a good standard of care. Medicines were well organised, but women had their access to basic pain relief restricted. Dental services were good and waiting lists were short.

Equality and diversity work had improved since the previous inspection, but this area was still not fully developed. Although a good policy was now in place and meetings had resumed, equality data were not monitored sufficiently and disproportionalities, although identified, were not acted on. Consultation with prisoners with specific protected characteristics was limited. Our survey found that black and minority ethnic prisoners had a more negative view of several aspects of prison life, compared with their white counterparts. The support provided to foreign nationals was limited. Transgender women, who had been accommodated on E wing, had progressed to other sites, although one woman had been living there on her own for the previous six months. Responses to discrimination incident reporting forms were mixed, but staff training was planned. Faith provision had adapted well to the challenges of the pandemic and chaplains provided good pastoral care.

**Purposeful activity**

Ofsted carried out a progress monitoring visit of the prison alongside our full inspection and the purposeful activity judgement incorporates their assessment of progress.

Time out of cell, which had been reduced significantly due to Covid-19 restrictions, was a minimum of one and a half hours each day. The amount of time women were unlocked for domestic activities varied, and most could only exercise outside for half an hour a day, which was insufficient. However, at the time of our visit, more than 90% of the women had been allocated to an activity, although only part time in some cases.

The library had reopened and provided a good service. Physical education provision had been well adapted to the restricted regime but was not available during the evenings.

Education, skills and work provision had re-opened effectively and there were more than enough activity places for the population. The curriculum was informed by the needs of the women, with external partners providing popular work roles and qualifications. However, women did not receive enough information, advice and guidance (IAG) to help inform their education, skills and work choices. Women were frustrated about movements preventing them from arriving at prison activities on time.

Leaders had not considered how to help women retain the learning gained from in-cell work packs, and women were repeating lessons during face-to-face sessions. Women in most work areas developed useful skills for employment, as well as achieving relevant qualifications. Teachers and instructors were patient with women and most checked their understanding in face-to-face sessions effectively. However, most teachers provided purely positive feedback, which did not help women improve their skills or expand their knowledge. Education staff identified women with learning difficulties or disabilities effectively, but strategies to support women were not shared with staff across the prison.

### Rehabilitation and release planning

Nearly three-quarters of the population were serving long sentences of over four years, and 40% were assessed as presenting a high risk of harm to others. A good recent analysis of the needs of the women had not yet resulted in a strategy or action plan. The prison's interventions lacked coordination and were not promoted well enough. The range of interventions available was reasonable, but some were not yet being delivered face to face or to full group capacity, and some waiting lists were long. There was a considerable need for support for women who had experienced trauma and abuse. Not all women had an assessment of their risks and needs, and about a third of existing assessments were over a year old. The standard of some up-to-date assessments that we viewed was not good enough. While it was positive that no women had been released without an address in the previous six months, 16% were released into temporary or transient accommodation. Home detention curfew processes were well managed. Women had been unable to access

release on temporary licence (ROTL) for education or work or to build family ties during the pandemic. Progress to reinstate ROTL opportunities was slow.

Probation officer prison offender managers (POMs) held reasonable caseloads and managed their cases well. Operational POMs were still being cross-deployed, which meant their contact levels did not support lower risk women to be motivated or to progress. Key working had started well. Women whose cases were complex did not have a key worker but received more time from their probation POM along with some good input from mental health and psychology staff.

Progression opportunities were limited and there had been very few transfers to other prisons in the previous year to help women access treatment and courses. There was little extra support for about 20 women serving indeterminate sentences. Most women categorised for open conditions benefited from living on D wing, the resettlement unit, but otherwise their opportunities were limited.

Work to protect the public from harm was good. The inter-departmental risk management team meeting provided effective oversight of high-risk women in the six months before their release. Reports that prison staff shared with probation staff in the community about the highest risk women nearing their release were very good. Monitoring arrangements continued to be sound and processes for managing prisoners who were not allowed contact with children were proportionate.

The number of women released had decreased since the previous inspection to about 10 a month. There was a well-staffed resettlement team, whose members provided a good service, but there was no clear plan for the provision after the summer. Practical release arrangements were sound, and good 'through-the-gate' mentoring provision was in place.

### Key concerns and recommendations

Key concerns and recommendations identify the issues of most importance to improving outcomes for women in prison and are designed to help establishments prioritise and address the most significant weaknesses in the treatment and conditions of women.

During this inspection we identified some areas of key concern and have made a small number of recommendations for the prison to address those concerns.

Key concern: As at the previous inspection, women reported that some staff were rude, unsupportive and inconsistent, leaving them feeling they had been dealt with unfairly. We observed some staff inappropriately addressing women by their surname and interactions that were not supportive of a trauma-informed and rehabilitative culture.

Recommendation: Staff's relationships with women should reflect a rehabilitative and trauma-responsive approach.

Key concern: Support to help women maintain or develop positive relationships with their children or families had been severely limited during the pandemic. Family days and group-work sessions were no longer available and the number of prisoners receiving social visits had declined significantly. Many women we spoke to reported that long periods of time without contact with their loved ones had adversely affected their well-being.

Recommendation: The prison should ensure that women receive sufficient support to help them maintain and develop positive relationships with their children, family members and other people significant to them.

Key concern: Inconsistencies in how the daily regime was applied caused frustration among many women and staff. Recent changes to the regime had taken place without sufficient consultation and were poorly communicated to staff and prisoners.

Recommendation: The prison should improve consultation and communication to ensure women and staff are aware of changes that affect their daily lives.

Key concern: The prison failed to consult the local health quality board sufficiently about changes affecting patient care. Although the board identified limited patient access to services, the problem had not been resolved 12 months on. We saw approximately a quarter of GP appointments being missed because there were not enough officers to escort prisoners to their appointments.

Recommendation: Local partners and prison leaders should use the local quality and delivery board and contracts meetings to improve communication and consultation. Assurances that health services are effective should be sought, including ensuring sufficient staff to escort women to their appointments.

Key concern: There was insufficient clinical oversight of patient applications, electronic tasks, the GP waiting list and long-term conditions, which meant that women might not have had their needs met promptly.

Recommendation: Enough clinically qualified staff should be available every day to oversee patient applications, electronic tasks, the GP waiting list and long-term conditions, to optimise women's health outcomes.

## Notable positive practice

We define notable positive practice as innovative work or practice that leads to particularly good outcomes from which other establishments may be able to learn. Inspectors look for evidence of good outcomes for women; original, creative or particularly effective approaches to problem-solving or achieving the desired goal; and how other establishments could learn from or replicate the practice.

Inspectors found two examples of notable positive practice during this inspection.

Some women benefited from the photography service in the Max Spielmann workshop, where photos of prisoners and their visitors could be taken and which were later available to buy.

Joint working was in place in several areas. Complex case reviews involved all relevant clinicians, which improved consistency and provided joined-up health outcome targets. Other examples of joint working were evident, such as assessments undertaken by mental health and learning disability nurses, when dual diagnosis and underlying neurodivergent needs were addressed. Prison records demonstrated that psychiatrists regularly undertook assessments, which were noted in offender management plans. Prisoners benefited from joint working by having a diagnosis and treatment.

## INDEPENDENT MONITORING BOARD: Annual Report

The law requires every prison to be monitored by an independent Board appointed by the Justice Secretary; these are known as Independent Monitoring Boards (IMBs). The IMB must satisfy itself as to the humane and just treatment of those held in custody within its prison and the range and adequacy of the programmes preparing them for release; it must report annually to the Justice Secretary on how well the prison has met the standards and requirements placed on it.

**IMB Report 1 May 2020 – 30 April 2021**
**Published September 2021**
**Executive summary**
**Background to the report**

Since the end of March 2020, the prison has been significantly impacted by the measures taken in response to the Covid-19 pandemic. There were three phases over the course of the reporting year: the initial lockdown in March 2020 (prior to the start of the reporting year), in which all prisoners were locked in their cells for around 23 hours a day; some minor relaxations to the regime over the summer as 2020 progressed (then halted in November by the prison being in community tier 4); and then the return to tight restrictions during the national lockdown in early 2021. During these periods of lockdown, the regime has been severely restricted, with many activities and functions suspended: many women have remained in their cells for 22.5 hours a day throughout the reporting period (their time out of cell taking into account time for meals and medication distribution, where necessary). At various stages in the reporting period, the population dipped to below 200 (as fewer admissions took place from the courts and, consequently, from other prisons during the pandemic). There was a population average over the reporting period of 219 (compared to 287 in the previous reporting period). It may be helpful to review certain information in this report against the backdrop of this lower population for the period.

There appeared to be minimal local flexibility granted in terms of managing progression through the various stages of the HMPPS exceptional delivery models (EDMs). Senior staff spent considerable amounts of time in often 'unrealistically' short timescales, drafting and agreeing local operating procedures which were submitted for central HMPPS approval and redrafting in various iterations (referred to as 'going around the houses with the wording' by one staff member). Trade union input sometimes appeared to stymie progress. The regime was further impacted by certain contractors and support agencies (e.g., PACT, Weston College, Max Spielmann, the Clink kitchens, Hibiscus, CXK, Shaw Trust, Jobcentre Plus, Home Office Immigration Enforcement) either choosing not to attend or being instructed by their own central management not to attend the prison; for example, staff from the Department of Work and Pensions (DWP) had still not returned to the prison as of May 2021. We observed this to be a source of frustration to prison staff who felt it created additional operational challenges and decreased opportunities for prisoners, as well as being unfair that prison staff should be put at risk from Covid-19 when partners did not attend in person.

Downview was declared an outbreak site in late January 2021, leading to full lockdown on A Wing (following the discovery that all prisoners on the wing were contacts for track and trace purposes). By way of a snapshot to illustrate the extraordinary pressure which the prison was under at times: on 28 January 2021 (at a time when over 80 other prisons were also facing an outbreak situation), Downview had 40 women on isolation in the protective isolation unit (PIU) and reverse cohorting unit (RCU) and five women shielding; 56 staff absent (46 for Covid-related reasons) and eight staff on restricted

duties; two women on bed-watch in a local hospital (one seriously ill in ICU with Covid-19, involving the full-time equivalent of nine staff absent from the prison daily), and many WAMITAB deep-cleaning workers unavailable. As of mid-April 2021, Downview was no longer a designated outbreak site: local operating procedures moving to level 3 were awaiting sign off at the end of the reporting period (after a significant number of other prisons had been permitted to move to level 3).

Against this backdrop, whilst the prison in recent years was on the verge of becoming a level 1 prison and placed on a performance improvement plan, progress was made with regard to many of the HMPPS performance measures and the prison moved up to a level 3. Between April and November 2020, Downview was one of only two prisons in the women's estate to achieve a level 4 in performance measures for both self-harm and assaults.

The pandemic has had an impact on the Board's ability to gather information for this report. Since the end of March 2020, monitoring by the Board has been undertaken remotely, although for most of the reporting year, at least one member has visited in person regularly. Board engagement with the prison has, however, been extensive during this period, and we have sought creative ways to triangulate the information which we were receiving from the prison (see section 8 below). There was a short scrutiny visit by HMIP in July 2020, for which the outcomes were broadly positive: the report highlighted the need to move to a more purposeful regime at a time when the outside community was re-opening and how recovery planning was being hampered by HMPPS guidance.

Staff have worked extremely hard under extraordinary circumstances to keep prisoners and staff safe and should be highly commended for this. Whilst the introduction of a staff bonus scheme helped in the first lockdown and again in March 2021, there have been times when staff absences have been so high that the Governor, senior management and also non-operational staff have been required to work, for example, in the servery and carrying out accommodation fabric checks, and at times during allocated time off. Staff were drafted in on detached duty from other prisons (continuing as of the end of the reporting period, and which has been well-received by prisoners), and early in the reporting period some senior staff were seconded from central HMPPS. Many custodial managers and senior officers were redeployed to the wings and operational support grade (OSG) numbers were severely impacted. One staff communication from a governor in early 2021, thanking staff for their efforts, gave an articulate insight into the extraordinary challenges faced: 'the [newly created protective isolation wing] was literally set up overnight in response to a large number of positive results and associated contact traces. We have all been learning as we go. Building new regimes. Finding new cleaners. Staff serving the meals on the wing and ferrying them up and down the stairs three meals at a time..... every time we blink there seems to be a new test result to deal with, or additional gaps in the detail'.

As the prison moves towards opening up the regime after lockdown, the view has been expressed that this will create its own difficulties for the women, with more noise, activity and attendant bullying / debt issues to which to become accustomed. To factor into this readjustment, many new officers who joined in lockdown (28 in total) may have not had experience of a pre-Covid regime. The low average unlock numbers over the reporting period have contributed to more flexibility in the regime. Pressures will increase as the courts and transfers revert to full capacity and planning continues for a new post-Covid regime.

## Main judgements
### How safe is the prison?
The Board considers that Downview is a safe prison, although it continues to receive a high number of challenging women, with complex backgrounds and specific needs.

### How fairly and humanely are prisoners treated?
The impact of the regime imposed by HMMPS on the mental and physical health of prisoners was of significant concern to the Board. However, given that this regime was largely unavoidable during the majority of the reporting period due to the pandemic, we are of the view that during the reporting period, Downview treated prisoners in a fair and humane way.

### How well are prisoners' health and wellbeing needs met?
Despite healthcare staff's ongoing commitment to support prisoners, the restricted healthcare regime has inevitably had a significant effect on prisoners' healthcare needs. However, given the extraordinary constraints faced by healthcare during the reporting year, the Board is satisfied that prisoners' primary medical health needs have been met, with external hospital appointments continuing to be facilitated.

There is, however, some concern about the degree to which mental health needs have been addressed, since empirically tested psychological therapies were (in the main) replaced with brief interventions, such as 20-minute wellbeing checks and in- cell distraction packs. Many psychological services were either fully suspended, including all group-based therapy activities, or cut back such as in the case of and one-to-one services. The more recent loss of senior psychology and psychotherapy staff has further reduced capacity for one-to-one therapy towards the end of the reporting year.

### How well are prisoners progressed towards successful resettlement?
During lockdown, CRC staff worked remotely, which created difficulties in maximising opportunities in the short window of engagement prior to release.

Release on temporary licence (ROTL) was cancelled and education and offending behaviour interventions were less available because of the lockdown. Accommodation options upon release were more available owing to extra Covid-19- funding.

## Main areas for development
### TO THE MINISTER
• We are concerned that the easing of the restricted regime may be delayed across the entire estate. What steps are being taken to end the current severe lockdown regime in prisons, taking into account its significant and long-term impact on the mental health of prisoners?

• It was disappointing that the Ministry did not support prisons receiving special vaccination status (given their recognised status as 'epidemiological pumps'), and contrary to SAGE's recommendations. It was then contradictory to this position when families were not permitted to hug their loved ones in visits after the May 2021 unlock in the community, on the stated grounds that prisons are 'high risk, closed environments where the virus can spread quickly' (HMP Downview Notice to Residents, May 2021).

• The Board is concerned to hear of the programme to create an extra 500 prison places for women (equivalent to two and a half times the roll of Downview at the end of the reporting period). How does the Minister justify this in the context of the reassurances and support for women's community sector services and supervision in the community outlined in Lucy Frazer's response to our previous report (dated November 2020)?

• We are also concerned that, despite previous public assurances by the Minister and HMPPS to rectify this, there is still no data collated centrally regarding the numbers of dependent children of prisoners. It would seem to be virtually impossible to provide effective family engagement without having accurate data available.

**TO THE PRISON SERVICE**
• What steps will be taken to ensure that purposeful activity and opportunities for rehabilitation and progression can be built into the post-lockdown regime? And how will the input of trade unions be managed in a constructive fashion?

• We are concerned about the centralised management of contracting processes. Certain contracts are negotiated centrally between HMPPS and third-party providers, with minimal input from local establishments. At Downview, operational information regarding the PACT contract was not provided (being retained at HMPPS level or otherwise remotely) which limits the ability of the establishment to performance manage operation of the contract effectively. Given the forthcoming procurement exercise regarding family engagement (albeit delayed due to Covid-19), will measures be taken to incorporate robust contract management processes?

• During lockdown, there appeared to be large numbers of third-party providers unable or unwilling to attend the prison (for example, Weston College, PACT, CRC, Jobcentre Plus, CXK, Shaw Trust, DWP, Home Office Immigration Enforcement) – this left prison staff exposed and frustrated, and prisoners denied appropriate support. How can this be managed in a more consistent way in the future if required?

• The Board is extremely concerned about the reduced capacity and headcount for psychology interventions and subsequent waiting list – particularly during a time of increased demand. What support can be provided to enable prompt recruitment to these critical roles?

• The pandemic has thrown into sharp relief the significant obstacles placed in prisoners' way regarding access to IT for education purposes. What progress has been made with plans for the Prison Service to develop an effective digital strategy for education, to ensure that digital devices are available within prisons and to ensure safe and secure access to the internet in the women's estate?

• Likewise, internal IT systems often appear out of date and challenging to work with, wasting significant amounts of staff time – what are the plans for updating these across the estate?

**TO THE GOVERNOR**
• The Board is concerned about predictions of fewer opportunities for association in the future and, if this is to be the case, we hope that it can be replaced by purposeful activity. We will closely monitor this area – the fact remains that association managed well is a positive activity.

• We look forward to seeing a more family-centred approach. The Board will also welcome

further proactive management of the contracted-out resource in the prison.

• The Board will look forward to monitoring the operation of the Weston College contract during the next reporting period as more face-to-face teaching takes place.

• The Board continues to be disappointed to find frequent inaccuracies in presented data (whether in daily operational records, or other prison-generated management information) - usually minor, but on occasions significant.

• Some healthcare complaints appear to be subjectively treated as concerns, and dealt with accordingly, on a more informal basis than a formal complaint would demand. How can this be more effectively managed in the future?

• The Board recognises and acknowledges the efforts to promote positive wellbeing amongst the prisoners and staff during this year. Although not entirely successful in the difficult circumstances, there was genuine effort in evidence and this is welcomed by the Board for the future.

**Progress since the last report**
• Following on from our previous report, significant changes have been made to prisoners' menus to provide healthier options and prisoner wellbeing features in menu design (although, obviously, selecting those healthier options remains a matter of individual choice).

• During the past year, efforts have continued to improve the standard of the prisoner environment with the refurbishment of several wing bathrooms and a comprehensive programme of painting and decoration on wings and other areas.

ECCLESHALL
STAFFORD
ST21 6LQ

HMP & YOI DRAKE HALL    Tel: 01785 774100

*For the latest reports on this prison please visit:* https://tinyurl.com/bdfh26rv

*Important Changes:* **(1) Visits:** the identification necessary to access this prison and visit for social or professional purposes has changed; (2) **Money and Gifts** new rules now apply to these. See page 16 for full details of the above.

**Task of the establishment** A women's resettlement prison and young offender institution.

## Certified normal accommodation and operational capacity
Prisoners average population 2021: 257
Baseline certified normal capacity: 340
In-use certified normal capacity: 340
Operational capacity: 340

## Prison status and key providers
Public
Prison Group: Women
Prison Group Director: Pia Sinha
Governor/Director: Carl Hardwick OBE
IMB Chair: Patrick Sullivan
Physical health provider and clinical substance misuse: Care UK
Mental health and substance misuse provider: Inclusion (Psychosocial and mental health)
Learning and skills provider: People Plus
Escort contractor: GeoAmey

## Brief history
April 2022: Drake Hall is situated in rural Staffordshire, about a mile from Eccleshall and 10 miles from Stafford. The prison is a training and resettlement prison and does not take remand prisoners.

Although designated as a closed prison, the layout provides significant freedom of movement for prisoners within the perimeter fence. In this sense, the environment is unique within the women's closed estate, and comparisons with other prisons must account for these differences.

The prison takes both adult women and young adults The prison has a capacity of 340. The prisoners are accommodated in 15 individual houses, each with around 20 rooms. Most are single rooms, with a small number of doubles. The closed element of the prison has a capacity of 315. An additional house lies beyond the perimeter fence of the prison. This open unit provides additional capacity for 25 prisoners and the unit aims to prepare the prisoners for a productive life after release.

The prison also has a care and support unit (CSU), which contains six cells and is used in situations where a prisoner must be segregated from the main population for disciplinary or safety reasons.

During the pandemic, the prison introduced an additional facility: Truro is a temporary facility that consists of 10 spaces for prisoners shielding because of the Covid-19 virus.

Prisoners at the establishment come from a wide geographical area across England and Wales to serve a variety of sentences, ranging in length from a few months to life. Their ages range from 18 to 70 years.

The prison population averaged just over 75% capacity (257) in this reporting year, a reduction from over 82% (280) in 2019/20 and 97% (330) in 2018/19 prior to the pandemic.

Many of the women have complex needs associated with their mental or physical health, substance misuse, history of trauma or abuse, or experience of the care system.

The prison is accredited as an enabling environment by the Royal College of Psychiatrists.

## Short description of residential units
There were 15 residential units within the prison's perimeter fence, accommodating up to 315 prisoners, with most units holding approximately 20 people.

Norwich unit – general non-vaping unit
Bristol unit – for the general population and those with complex needs
Canterbury, Durham, Exeter, Folkestone, Gloucester, Ipswich, Margate, Oxford and Richmond units – for the general population with some double rooms
Keele unit – a 19-room induction unit
Plymouth unit – for prisoners on the enhanced level
Lancaster unit – mostly housing long-term prisoners and lifers
St David's unit – 16 single rooms for prisoners with social care or mobility needs.

The prison also has an open unit outside the perimeter fence that has an operational capacity of 25, enabling prisoners to work in the local community and prepare for release. The open unit has a facility for overnight children's visits (subject to prisoners meeting the required criteria).

## Visiting Information
Drake Hall is currently operating a limited visits schedule for family and friends. You can book your visit by telephone.
Visits booking line: 0300 060 6501
The booking line is open Monday to Friday, 9.15am to 4pm.
Email bookings:
socialvisits.drakehall@hmps.gsi.gov.uk
**Visiting Times:** Tuesday: 1:30pm to 3:45pm, Saturday: 9.30am - 11.30am and 1:30pm to 3.45pm, Sunday: 1:30pm - 3.45pm

**Legal visits:** Visits booking line: 0300 060 6501
The booking line is open Monday to Friday, 9.15am to 4pm. Drake Hall offers the option to book a Virtual Meeting Room or a face-to-face visit. Please confirm when booking.

## INSPECTIONS & REPORTS
**Date of last inspection:** 27 Jan–6 Feb 2020
*Notable features from this inspection*
• Prisoners were never locked in their rooms and had good access to the prison grounds throughout the day.
• In our survey, 62% of prisoners said they had a mental health problem on arrival at the prison.

• In the previous six months, release on temporary licence had been used over 5000 times to support a variety of resettlement activities, including contact with children.

• The prison had an open unit outside the prison, which accommodated up to 25 prisoners who were all in full-time employment.

## HMCIP Report published 22 May 2020

HMP/YOI Drake Hall is a training and resettlement prison in Staffordshire holding 324 adult and young adult women. While being a closed prison, Drake Hall has an open regime within the perimeter of the fence. Prisoners are never locked in their rooms and have free access around the site during the day; at night they are only locked in their house blocks leaving them able to move around their unit. Just outside the main prison is a fully open facility that accommodates up to 25 prisoners. Drake Hall promoted a community ethos where prisoners lived together, were involved in the running of the prison and were given the responsibility to behave well and determine their own progression. We last inspected Drake Hall in the summer of 2016 and judged that outcomes for prisoners were good in three of four of our healthy prison tests, with outcomes under respect judged to be reasonably good. At this inspection we made similar judgements, with outcomes under respect having improved to good, our highest grade. However, outcomes in purposeful activity had deteriorated to reasonably good under Ofsted's inspection framework.

Drake Hall remained a safe place to live with hardly any serious violence, and prisoners were positive about the community ethos and their role in developing this. However, in our survey, half of the prisoners said they had been intimidated, bullied or victimised by others and we found that some anti-social or violent incidents noted by wing staff had not been reported to the safer custody team for investigation. Some house units were not staffed and we found that the level of staff engagement with the prisoners was too limited at times. It did not always provide adequate protection for the more vulnerable or challenge those involved in bullying others. It also meant that prisoners found it more difficult to get simple tasks done and this was the most common complaint we heard from prisoners throughout our inspection weeks.

The availability of illicit drugs was one of our key concerns. Much of the evidence suggested that drugs were too easily available and the prison needed to do more to stem the flow. The proportion of prisoners who said they had developed a drug problem while at Drake Hall had increased since our last inspection and was higher than in similar prisons. Although use of force had increased over recent months, incidents were very low level and did not involve the use of full restraint. The use of segregation was appropriate but had some weaknesses around the quality of reintegration planning. The proportion of self-harm incidents was lower than we have seen in similar prisons and care provided was good.

Progression opportunities within the prison community stemmed from the use of release on temporary license (ROTL) and Drake Hall far exceeded other closed prisons in the number of events completed each year. The open unit provided a further incentive to behave well, although other incentives were not very effective in this. Interactions between staff and prisoners were good but were not supported by an effective personal officer scheme. The use of peer workers, however, was good overall which further promoted the community ethos and empowered prisoners to support each other. Management of equality and diversity work was well established but consultation with prisoners from every protected characteristic was not very effective and there was too little direct support for some groups.

Living conditions were reasonable overall but were poor on two units. Richmond and Plymouth units were World War II prefabricated buildings which had been in need of replacement for many years. Some refurbishment to the showers had been made but it is our view that these two buildings were not fit for purpose and were in urgent need of demolition and replacement. It was disappointing that Her Majesty's Prison and Probation Service (HMPPS) had not committed resources to this despite previous promises to do so. The food provided was good and some positive steps had been taken to enable prisoners to buy clothing and accessories from the prison-based charity shop.

Healthcare provision had improved since our last inspection and was now good, which is especially important in a women's prison. Prisoners had good access to a range of primary care services which now included a female GP. The addition of specialist counselling was very good, enabling prisoners to address the impact of trauma on their lives and develop coping skills for the future.

Ofsted considered Drake Hall's education, skills and work activity as good. There were enough activity places, with good attendance and punctuality. Most prisoners achieved their qualifications. However, there was no strategic oversight of the curriculum and a lack of data made it difficult to evidence useful outcomes after release.

Offender management and resettlement work remained good overall and was supported by an effective CRC provision. Work to help prisoners maintain contact with children and family members remained positive and most of the other resettlement pathways were well developed. However, this work was not yet informed by a comprehensive analysis of needs across the population. ROTL continued to be well managed and used effectively, including good links with national employers so that prisoners could continue their employment upon release. Some home detention curfew (HDC) releases were hindered by the lack of Bail, Accommodation and Support Service (BASS) places. Few prisoners were released homeless but there was a lack of monitoring of longer term outcomes which made it difficult to evidence the effectiveness of this work.

Peter Clarke CVO OBE QPM
HM Chief Inspector of Prisons April 2020

## INDEPENDENT MONITORING BOARD: Annual Report

The law requires every prison to be monitored by an independent Board appointed by the Justice Secretary; these are known as Independent Monitoring Boards (IMBs). The IMB must satisfy itself as to the humane and just treatment of those held in custody within its prison and the range and adequacy of the programmes preparing them for release; it must report annually to the Justice Secretary on how well the prison has met the standards and requirements placed on it.

### IMB Report 1 Nov 2020 to 31 Oct 2021
### Published 1st April 2022

The Board believes that HMP Drake Hall provides a safe and secure environment for prisoners and that they are treated decently and with humanity. The prison offers sufficient structure and control to ensure the environment is safe but provides a level of empowerment expected in an enabling environment.

The Board remains concerned about some of the prisoner accommodation: two units, Plymouth and Richmond, both constructed during World War 2, are not of an acceptable standard. **The Board has raised this issue in every report for nearly 20 years.** Her Majesty's Inspectorate of Prisons (HMIP) takes a similar view, suggesting that they should be demolished and replaced.

The Board does not criticise the local prison managers, as they have worked consistently to improve these units. Unfortunately, fundamental structural difficulties remain and the units should be replaced. An infestation of rats illustrates this point. This is unacceptable and the women should not be expected to live in a damp, cold and rat-infested environment. The prison should not have to work constantly to try and mitigate the issues these problems cause. The Board again draws this matter to the minister's attention and hopes that this year its view will not fall on deaf ears.

The Board continues to be concerned about the transfer of property. Prisoners can arrive at the prison without all their belongings and there are often delays in rectifying the situation. Some of the property lost can be replaced but some is irreplaceable, often of sentimental value. This is a national issue that urgently needs resolution. Despite regular assurances that a solution is pending, this remains an important and ongoing problem.

The pandemic affected, and continues to affect, Drake Hall. It has impacted the everyday running of the prison and has altered work, learning and exercise. A restricted regime has now been in operation since March 2020 and it has affected the prison's rehabilitation ethos and the preparation of the prisoners for release.

The overriding objective during the pandemic has been to keep prisoners and staff safe. This objective has been achieved. This is in no small measure due to the hard work and commitment of the prison staff, and they must be commended. Throughout the pandemic the prison staff and management have displayed considerable flexibility, innovation and compassion in ensuring that the needs of the women are met and that a humane, secure and effective regime is maintained.

The role of the prisoners must also be mentioned: without their cooperation and support, the measures put in place by the prison would have been far less effective.

They have adapted to a continually changing environment with good grace and understanding. This deserves recognition.

### Background to the Report

The pandemic has been ever-present during the reporting period. Prisons are prone to outbreaks with higher rates of infection, hospitalisation and mortality than in the wider community. Intensive control measures are necessary to reduce infection and these measures must be robust. There is a constant balance to be struck between the implementation of restrictions to minimise the risk to life and health and the harm that such control measures can cause due to prolonged isolation.

The environment and the approach taken have meant the prison is far more restricted than pre-Covid-19 but less restrictive than many other closed women's prisons. The process has been managed well, although this has inevitably been at the expense of some of the rehabilitation ethos of the prison.

## Main judgements
### How safe is the prison?
Drake Hall provides a safe environment. However, we accept that there will always be some prisoners who do not feel safe and others who may be vulnerable and subject to bullying. Nevertheless, levels of violence against staff and between the prisoners remain low, and rates of self-injury are lower than in other closed prisons in the women's estate. The Board commends the proactive approach to the reduction of self-harm for women at risk which has been in evidence during the reporting period.

### How fairly and humanely are prisoners treated?
Prisoners are treated fairly and humanely. This approach has continued despite the restrictions associated with the pandemic. These restrictions have always been approved through the relevant command structures and followed the guidance provided by Public Health England. Any limits imposed have been both proportionate and necessary.

### How well are prisoners' health and wellbeing needs met?
The healthcare needs of the prisoners are generally well met. Systems for accessing health appointments and receiving treatment mirror arrangements outside the prison. The management of the Covid 19 outbreaks has been excellent.

### How well are prisoners progressed towards successful resettlement?
The pandemic has affected this element of the prison's work. Many activities have had to be curtailed for long periods, while opportunities for employment and educational activities have been reduced. This has had an impact on the prison's ability to maintain its resettlement ethos. Significant policy changes in the delivery of probation services are also a concern. The outcome of these changes is yet to become apparent.

## Main areas for development
### TO THE MINISTER
The Board again draws attention to the condition of Richmond and Plymouth houses. They are not fit for purpose. Allowing prisoners to live in sub-standard accommodation is detrimental to their physical and mental wellbeing. The provision of new accommodation is long overdue. The problems associated with an infestation of rats during the reporting period provide more evidence, if needed, that this remains an ongoing problem. The Board is increasingly frustrated that these concerns have been ignored. It is appreciated that there are worse environments in the prison system. However, this does not provide any justification for failing to address this issue. Allowing women to live in this way cannot be defended.

### TO THE PRISON SERVICE
In our last report, the Board drew the attention of the prison service to four main issues. Unfortunately, three of these remain problematic. In addition, we raise two additional matters.

Delayed or lost property on transfer to Drake Hall remains a significant problem and causes unnecessary distress to prisoners. It is a systemic issue that requires action across the Prison Service.

The number of mental healthcare staff has increased. With the potential to increase the range of therapeutic interventions available. However, there is a lack of private and confidential interview space available to allow the team to work effectively and for women to engage in therapeutic work.

Additionally, during the year the prison had to deal with a prisoner experiencing difficulties associated with an eating disorder. However, no facility existed that could provide specialist services for this individual. As a result, the prison was forced to manage the situation without specialist support. This constitutes a service deficit. Due to operational pressure, increasing numbers of prisoners are transferred shortly before their release date. This has the potential to harm their successful transition from prison.

Prison Service guidance means that the prisoner banking programme is only available for prisoners who are within six months of release and who do not have an existing bank account. This can impact on the rehabilitative experience in the open unit.

### TO THE GOVERNOR
Drug ingress into the prison appears to have been low during the pandemic. It is hoped that these improvements can be maintained.

The showers on the open unit are covered in mould and damp. The cause is structural. A long-term solution is required to resolve this problem. The Board participated in an equality and diversity survey undertaken across the women's estate. It is hoped that addressing the findings will lead to improvements in the experience of some ethnic minority women.

The Board looks forward to seeing an increase the number of social visits, pandemic permitting.

**OLD ELVET
DURHAM
DH1 3HU**

**HM PRISON
DURHAM**    Tel: 0191 332 3400

*For the latest reports on this prison please visit:*
https://tinyurl.com/bdfh26rv

*Important Changes:* **(1) Visits:** the identification necessary to access this prison and visit for social or professional purposes has changed; (2) **Money and Gifts** new rules now apply to these. See page 16 for full details of the above.

### Task of the prison
A reception prison for adult and young adult men, with a small resettlement function.
Certified normal accommodation and OpCap
Prisoners held November 2021: 959
Baseline certified normal capacity: 600
In-use certified normal capacity: 578
Operational capacity: 980

### Population of the prison
• 5,000 new prisoners received in the previous year (around 420 per month).
• 62% of prisoners are on remand.
• 120 foreign national prisoners.
• 12% of prisoners from black and minority ethnic backgrounds.
• Around 140 prisoners released into the community each month.
• 348 prisoners receiving support for substance misuse.
• 96 prisoners with complex mental ill health being supported.

### Prison status and key providers
Public
Prison group: North East
Prison Group Director: Susan Howard
Name of governor: Phillip Husband
IMB chair: Therese Quincey
Physical health provider:
Spectrum Community Health CIC
Mental health provider: Tees, Esk and Wear Valleys NHS Foundation Trust Substance misuse treatment provider: Humankind
Prison education framework provider: Novus
Escort contractor: GeoAmey

### Brief history
Opened in 1819 and rebuilt in 1881, Durham prison's primary role from May 2017 was as a reception prison holding adult men aged 21 and over and young adults aged 18 and over. It serves the courts of Tyneside, Teesside, Durham and Cumbria.

### Short description of residential units
A, B, C D wings – general population E wing – first night and induction unit F wing – vulnerable prisoner unit
Integrated support unit (ISU) based on I wing (11 beds and two cells for cleaners) for prisoners with significant mental health problems
G wing – segregation unit
Health care inpatient unit – six beds

### Visiting Information
Visits are booked by prisoner-led application. You will then be contacted your visit directly by the prison. You can also register to use the secure video calls service. There is no telephone or online booking service available.
**Visiting times:**
Visits happen every day, including weekends at the following times: 10:45am to 11:30am, 2:00pm to 2:30pm

**Legal visits:** Times are constantly changing so check with the prison for the latest information.

### INSPECTIONS & REPORTS
**Date of last inspection:** 24 26 November 2021
**HMCIP Report, published 11 March 2022**
Largely rebuilt in 1881, HMP Durham is a men's category B reception prison that accepts prisoners from across the north of England. At the time of our inspection there were 959 prisoners, of whom 606 were on remand. More than a third of the prison's population were receiving support for substance misuse.
Much credit must go to the impressive governor and to what was a generally strong leadership team, who had worked together to reduce the supply of drugs into the prison. This had contributed to a more than 60% fall in violence since our last inspection, making the prison one of the safer locals in the country.
Throughout the inspection the prison felt calm and generally well-ordered.
We also saw a commensurate fall in the use of physical intervention, but during the inspection we uncovered some examples of staff appearing to use force in improper and disproportionate ways. Leaders needed to take urgent action to make sure that staff were sufficiently trained and had effective systems for reviewing incidents.
Like most local prisons the jail had a large population of prisoners who came in with often serious mental health difficulties or who misused drugs or alcohol.
This meant that, particularly in their first days in custody, they could be at risk of suicide or self-harm. We were therefore concerned that late in the evening or at particularly busy times, the prison was not able to offer full health care

screenings to new arrivals. These prisoners often had to be dispersed around the jail because the induction unit was full, which meant they did not always get the care and the attention they needed. The quality of health care in every area, from GP appointments to mental health provision, was suffering from some serious staff shortages. Prisoners frequently complained to inspectors about the difficulties in getting treatment or medication. These issues were compounded by problems with the application system that meant prisoners could not submit a second application to a department before a previous application had been resolved – for example, a prisoner who had put in an application for a visit could not make an application to see the GP until the visit had been agreed. This issue also impacted on family contact: slots for visits remained unfilled, with families often only being told the day before that there was an available time.

Many prisoners remained locked in their cells for too long, particularly those on the induction wing. The prison could have done more to provide activities and work, but they were hampered by an education provider that had been slow to restore services.

The prison had worked to refurbish much of the indoor and outdoor communal areas in this historic prison, but many cells were overcrowded and dilapidated. While staff from the former community rehabilitation company continued to provide some support to prisoners on remand, the future of this provision was uncertain with the reunification of probation services. This and the fact that the senior probation officer was leaving to be replaced by a temporary appointment, meant the provision of resettlement work and sentence planning was fragile. Inspectors were very concerned that 43% of prisoners left the jail without suitable accommodation.

Durham prison has showed some impressive improvements since our last inspection and the governor and his team should be proud of the progress the jail has made, particularly considering the challenges caused by the pandemic. The inspection team left optimistic that if senior leaders remain in post and the issues raised in this report are addressed, the prison can continue to make good progress.

### Safety

At the last inspection of Durham in 2018 we found that outcomes for prisoners were poor against this healthy prison test.

At this inspection we found that outcomes for prisoners were now reasonably good.

Reception was a busy environment. Staff were welcoming but late admissions affected the quality of provision. There was good opportunity for new arrivals to discuss any anxieties or concerns as a robust vulnerabilities assessment was completed on admission. The first night centre was also busy and at times this resulted in a lack of action on important requests from prisoners, and the regime was not good enough. Population pressure meant that many prisoners spent their first night on other wings, creating additional risk. First night cells were unwelcoming, and some were missing essentials, such as pillows or blankets. Induction was weak and many prisoners did not receive key information.

Work to improve security and reduce the supply of drugs and associated violence had been successful. Violence had fallen by 61% since the last inspection and the number of incidents was low. The monthly safety meetings were effective and examined a wide range of data, which were used to inform the violence reduction strategy and take appropriate actions. Weekly safety intervention meetings focusing on individual prisoners and incidents also led to useful actions. Plans to challenge perpetrators and support victims of violence were undermined by poor targets and a lack of engagement from frontline officers.

Use of force had reduced by 69% since our last inspection and was low. The monthly use of force meetings discussed relevant data, but scrutiny of CCTV footage required improvement. We saw several examples of poor practice during use of force and referred these to managers for further investigation. Unfurnished accommodation had been used 20 times in the last year. Records were poor and did not always justify its use.

Use of segregation remained similar to the last inspection. The reasons for segregation were not always documented appropriately. At the time of our inspection, two prisoners had been in the segregation unit for over 100 days. There was an absence of reintegration planning, which frustrated prisoners we spoke to. Cells were bare; many lacked tables and chairs. The regime was poor.

There had been five self-inflicted deaths since our last visit. There was evidence that the prison had taken action in response to Prisons and Probation Ombudsman recommendations following investigations into these. Recorded levels of self-harm were lower than similar prisons and were on a downward trend. There was good interrogation of selfharm data at the monthly safety meeting. The quality of support delivered through assessment, care in custody and teamwork (ACCT) case management for at-risk prisoners varied. Most we spoke to were positive about the care they received; however, care maps were poorly completed and staff records of daily interaction with prisoners were often missing. Changes in risk levels were not always explained. Staff supervising prisoners on constant supervision did little to encourage purposeful interaction and participation for them.

## Respect

At the last inspection of Durham in 2018 we found that outcomes for prisoners were reasonably good against this healthy prison test. At this inspection we found that outcomes for prisoners were now not sufficiently good.

In our survey, two-thirds of prisoners said that they were treated with respect by staff and those we spoke to were generally positive. The key worker scheme was operating better than we have seen in similar establishments. We observed mostly positive interactions, including some effective staff challenge of low-level poor behaviour.

Over three-quarters of prisoners were living in crowded conditions. The standard of cells needed improvement; many were poorly ventilated, lacked furniture and some were in a state of disrepair. Some showers were also in poor condition and not adequately screened. The cleanliness of communal and outside areas was good.

The number of complaints had reduced since our last inspection and was low. Responses to complaints did not always address the issues raised, particularly when the complaint was about staff. The electronic kiosk applications system was well used, but it had restrictions that were a frustration for prisoners. Prisoner consultation arrangements were good and led to positive change.

Leaders did not have a complete picture of prisoners with protected characteristics and were therefore not able to make sure their needs were met. Consultation with protected characteristic groups had not yet resumed, although equality representatives for each wing had recently been appointed. Many prisoners were not aware of how to report discrimination. Some prisoners who struggled to speak English were overlooked. There was promising work to support younger prisoners. Corporate worship and faith-based study classes had resumed.

Prisoners who arrived late did not receive health care reception screening and health care risk management was not sufficient to ensure patient safety. Staffing shortages were having a detrimental impact on the provision of health care in all areas. There were 264 prisoners on the waiting list for the GP, with the longest wait at eight weeks, and there was no evidence of risk management in the clinical records. An audit of

medicines management had identified that medications were frequently not available, there was a failure to follow-up patients who did not collect their medication and poor recordkeeping. Officer supervision of medication queues continued to be inconsistent or absent. The quality of dental provision was good, although waiting times were too long.

## Purposeful activity

At the last inspection of Durham in 2018 we found that outcomes for prisoners were not sufficiently good against this healthy prison test. At this inspection we found that outcomes for prisoners remained not sufficiently good.

Time out of cell varied from about 30 minutes a day in the open air for prisoners on the reverse cohort unit (RCU) to 6.5 hours for fully employed prisoners. Leaders had started a programme that increased prisoners' time out of cell under the new regime delivery plan. Our roll checks found that 56% of prisoners were locked behind their doors during the core day and 25% were at work or in out-of-cell education. Prisoners who worked full time were not offered exercise on weekdays. The library provision was reasonably good and supported literacy initiatives. The gym timetable was too restrictive and it was underused.

Leaders had a clear and appropriate curriculum plan for education, skills and work, but the return to face-to-face education and vocational training workshops was slow. While there were sufficient activity places in the plan, a combination of staff shortages and unavailability of facilities meant that too many prisoners were not benefiting from purposeful activity.

Prisoners who attended education, skills or work worked well in a calm and respectful environment. However, attendance was too low and prisoners were not routinely punctual at activities.

Prisoners in full-time wing work did not benefit from the planned development of skills or acquisition of vocational qualifications. Some were not busy enough and would have benefited from combining work with in-cell learning, but this option was not available.

The availability of full-time jobs and additional responsibilities on the wing were a disincentive to prisoner participation in education. During the Covid-19 restrictions, the induction and allocation process had not operated effectively and a large backlog of prisoners needed to complete the induction.

The quality of education was not consistently good. There were some areas of strength in creative community projects (IT), social enterprise, 'think family' and horticulture courses. However, the quality of education in

English for speakers of other languages (ESOL) and multiskills required improvement. With the support of peripatetic tutors, prisoners in work made good progress in English and mathematics. Where prisoners with learning difficulties and disabilities were assessed, they made good progress. However, there was a backlog of prisoners with additional needs awaiting assessment who had yet to benefit from the available support.

### Rehabilitation and release planning

At the last inspection of Durham in 2018 we found that outcomes for prisoners were not sufficiently good against this healthy prison test. At this inspection we found that outcomes for prisoners remained not sufficiently good.

The prison had three family workers who provided valuable support to prisoners.

The visits booking system was in disarray with delays in processing applications, resulting in many prisoners missing their entitlement, including prisoners on remand.

The reducing reoffending action plan was focused on Covid-19 recovery and did not link to any offender management strategy or action plan. There was limited provision to meet the resettlement needs of the significant number of unsentenced prisoners. Backlogs in the court system meant that many of these prisoners were released having served their time.

The quality and timeliness of most offender assessment system (OASys) assessments that we viewed were good, but there was little management oversight or quality assurance. Recording of contact with prison offender managers was poor; about half the cases we viewed did not record any contact.

Most prisoners had regular key work sessions, but these were focused on their welfare rather than progression and sentence planning. Risk management plans were good, and we saw some good communication with community offender managers for managing potential risk on release. Home detention curfew was well managed with most prisoners released on time.

Categorisation decisions were timely and appropriate. Most prisoners were moved within 10 days of sentence.

Public protection arrangements were good. The dedicated team collated critical risk management information on high-risk prisoners effectively despite the high turnover of the population.

Before release, the inter-departmental risk management team considered prisoners with complex issues appropriately. The monitoring of phone calls and mail for prisoners who posed a risk was managed well and there was no backlog. The resettlement team assessed the needs of every prisoner irrespective of status within five days of arrival, which was positive. The release plans that we viewed were good. Records showed that 43% of sentenced prisoners and nearly all remand prisoners who were directed for release left Durham without suitable accommodation, including some prisoners regarded as high risk.

### Key concerns and recommendations

Key concerns and recommendations identify the issues of most importance to improving outcomes for prisoners and are designed to help establishments prioritise and address the most significant weaknesses in the treatment and conditions of prisoners.

During this inspection we identified some areas of key concern and have made a small number of recommendations for the prison to address those concerns.

Key concern: Due to population pressures, prisoners usually arrived into an environment at the prison that was chaotic and busy, and were allocated to wings not equipped for providing an introduction to Durham. Some new arrivals went into cells that were not adequately furnished, missing basic items such as pillows and blankets or with torn or worn-out mattresses. The early days regime was poor and induction did not cover essential information about life at Durham.

Recommendation: All aspects of prisoners' arrival into the establishment should be effective and fit for purpose, including standards of accommodation and the quality of induction and regime. (To the governor)

Key concern: Review of use of force footage was inadequate and in several incidents, leaders had missed actions by staff that needed to be addressed. Much of the footage we observed had been recorded inadequately and provided limited scope to observe clearly what had taken place.

Recommendation: Leaders should make sure that all use of force is necessary and proportionate. (To the governor)

Key concern: Governance of the segregation unit was weak and we were not assured that segregated prisoners would be kept safe. The justification for segregating prisoners, especially those on at-risk case management or with mental health concerns, was not always documented appropriately and safety screens were not reviewed routinely.

Recommendation: Prisoners should be kept safe at all times while segregated, and their needs should be recognised and given proper attention. (To the governor)

Key concern: The prison was overcrowded, with over three-quarters of prisoners living in cramped conditions, sharing cells designed for one. Most shared cells did not have adequate screening to the toilet or sufficient lockable cabinets. Many cells had insufficient furniture and equipment, and some were in a state of disrepair.

Recommendation A: Prisoners should not live in overcrowded conditions. (To the governor)

Recommendation B: Cells should be equipped and furnished to a decent standard.
(To the governor)

Key concern: The prison did not have a complete picture of prisoners with protected characteristics. Data were incomplete and had not been reconciled with those from various sources across the prison. Analysis of data was rudimentary and mostly limited to ethnicity and age.

Recommendation: Leaders and managers should use data to construct a clear picture of prisoners with protected characteristics in order to meet their needs. (To the governor)

Key concern: Significant staffing shortages had had a detrimental impact on the delivery of primary care, mental health and pharmacy services, with long delays for routine GP appointments and mental health assessment, and the absence of reviews of ongoing treatment and prescribed medicines.

Recommendation: The prison should work with NHS England and NHS Improvement to make sure there are sufficient health care staff to meet the health needs of the population, in line with national guidelines. (To the governor)

Key concern: The late arrival of prisoners into reception meant that not all received a first night reception health care screening. This created the risk that the health needs of new arrivals were left unassessed before they were transferred to their cells.

Recommendation: All new arrivals should receive a first night health care reception screening before they are moved to the induction wing. (To the governor)

Key concern: Prisoners were prioritising full-time work on the wings, where they were not explicitly developing and recording skills, at the expense of education and vocational training.

Recommendation: The delivery of education, work and skills should allow for a combination of face-to-face and in-cell learning to engage more prisoners in purposeful activity, and the activities, allocations and pay policies should be aligned to motivate prisoners to work towards their long-term goals. (To the governor)

Key concern: Prisoners with needs for provision in English for speakers of other languages were not receiving the quality of education they needed and too many were not getting any support at all.

Recommendation: Leaders should assess, meet the need and improve the quality of provision in English

for speakers of other languages. (To the governor)

Key concern: The visits booking process was failing. Applications from prisoners to arrange a visit were being processed two weeks after they had been submitted and many prisoners told us they could often get no more than one visit a month, including prisoners on remand who were entitled to three visits a week.

Recommendation: Managers should make sure that prisoners can access the visits they are entitled to. (To the governor)

Key concern: Some remand prisoners spent long periods in custody due to backlogs in the courts. There was little in place to support these prisoners or occupy them while in custody, and their resettlement needs were not assessed or met.

Recommendation: Managers should assess the needs of the remand population to make sure appropriate support is provided while they are in custody and after release. (To the governor)

Key concern: Nearly all prisoners due for unplanned release and 43% of all sentenced prisoners released, including some high-risk prisoners, did not have suitable housing to go to.

Recommendation: Prisoners should have suitable and stable accommodation on their release. (To the governor)

**Notable positive practice**

We define notable positive practice as innovative work or practice that leads to particularly good outcomes from which other establishments may be able to learn. Inspectors look for evidence of good outcomes for prisoners; original, creative or particularly effective approaches to problem-solving or achieving the desired goal; and how other establishments could learn from or replicate the practice.

Inspectors found one example of notable positive practice during this inspection.

Prisoners held in segregation under the secreted items policy were seen by psychosocial practitioners daily to encourage engagement with their service and to provide education on the potential risks associated with having secreted items.

**INDEPENDENT MONITORING BOARD: Annual Report.** The law requires every prison to be monitored by an independent Board appointed by the Justice Secretary; these are known as Independent Monitoring Boards (IMBs). The IMB must satisfy itself as to the humane and just treatment of those held in custody within its prison and the range and adequacy of the programmes preparing them for release; it must report annually to the Justice Secretary on how well the prison has met the standards and requirements placed on it.

**IMB Report for reporting year 1 November 2020- 31 October 2021**
**Published 24th March 2022**
**Summary**

This report presents the findings of the IMB at HMP Durham for the period 1 November 2020 to 31 October 2021. Evidence comes from observations made on visits, scrutiny of records and data, informal contact with prisoners and staff, surveys and prisoner applications. Whilst IMB members were only able to physically monitor five months of the previous year because of the first national lockdown, this year members have been visiting the prison since November 2020, following the national safety guidance and the exceptional delivery models (EDMs) of the prison.

HMP Durham is a Georgian prison for adult prisoners and young offenders. In May 2017, the prison changed its function to that of a reception prison and primarily serves the courts. In 2020, a further change was made into a reception and resettlement prison for adult males and young offenders. The model for this is 65% on remand and 35% sentenced. Prisoners who have 16 months or less to serve of their sentence may complete their sentence in Durham. At the end of 2021, 69% of prisoners were on remand, compared to 73% last year.

The change to and the ongoing management of such a prison (with its rapid churn) has presented many challenges especially in the area of safety. The prison has continuously reviewed its working practices in order to address these issues. The Governor and staff are to be commended for the positive way in which they have approached this. The alignment of Durham court's catchment area (Carlisle to North Yorkshire) means the prison normally holds most prisoners close to their home. Last year, 65% of prisoners came from the area. This year, as Covid 19 has affected other prisons nationally, Durham has taken men out of area. For example, between May and October Durham took over 300 prisoners from the north west. Durham is a large sprawling prison made up of several wings with up to five landings. This limits mobility access. In 2017 a 12-bed integrated support unit (ISU) was opened, offering inpatient mental health support to Tees and Wear prisons. The prison also houses a six-cell healthcare unit.

During the pandemic HMP Durham continued with its role as a reception prison, including managing men through the courts, receiving newly convicted prisoners and facilitating increasingly high numbers of video courts. The prison has faced many challenges, but it is a credit to the Governor and his team that they have fulfilled its obligations to provide the necessary spaces to meet the courts and the population management needs.

Prison capacity is measured by two figures, namely the certified normal accommodation (CNA) and the operational capacity (OpCap). The CNA figure records the ideal maximum population of the prison without overcrowding. The CNA for HMP Durham is 596 and the OpCap was 995, then reduced to 980 in October 2021. However, for most of the year a flexible OpCap of 950 has been used to allow for the fact that, due to the high churn, cell sharing is not safe for some prisoners.

In November 2021 the prison population had turned over 5.8 times and the average length of stay was 9 weeks. This is in line with the previous year and continues to be influenced by the number of prisoners with short sentences.

During the monitoring year the prison has experienced two national lockdowns, impacting greatly upon regime: November 2020 and January to April 2021. Prisoners have experienced varying restrictions under different stages in the prison.

At the start of the monitoring year, the prison faced Stage 3 restrictions (introduced on 18 August 2020), then a return to Stage 4 from January to May 2021. It returned to Stage 3 on 4 May 2021, until Stage 2 was introduced on 17 September 2021. At the time of writing this report at the end of the monitoring year, Stage 1 was gradually being introduced. Unfortunately, restrictions were subsequently re-imposed. In January, the large outbreak of Covid 19 across the prison led to HMP Durham being under the outbreak control team from January to April 2021.

**Main judgements**
**How safe is the prison?**

The Board believes HMP Durham to be a safe environment. It is a credit to the Governor and his team that achieving this has remained one of the prison's key objectives despite the challenges presented by the pandemic. The prison has implemented systems to support vulnerable men on entry, and supports prisoners at risk of suicide or self-harm through a robust ACCT system (assessment, care in custody and teamwork – a planning process for prisoners identified at risk of suicide, resulting in actions to mitigate risk of suicide). However, the Board has concerns about the impact on prisoners of the lack of induction, particularly as men have had limited communication with peers due to the pandemic. In addition, the Board remains concerned about the length of time prisoners remain in Durham because of the court backlogs. Systems including the scanner and the new drugs strategy continue to tackle drugs with a positive impact. The Board would like to see the use of body worn cameras (BWVC) embedded in the culture of the prison.

## How fairly and humanely are prisoners treated?

During the difficulties and the restricted regime caused by the pandemic, the Board is reassured from survey and observation that the prison has prioritised humane and dignified treatment. The Board does remain concerned about overcrowding and the state of some cells, whilst acknowledging the work of the Governor in driving the introduction of men having their own clothing. Whilst work has developed in terms of equality and diversity, there is still work to be done on embedding appropriate information in meetings through a more robust reporting system. The Board's view is that men held under IS91s (immigration warrants) continue to be held too long in HMP Durham.

## How well are prisoners' health and wellbeing needs met?

The Board is not convinced that prisoners are satisfied with the level of healthcare in HMP Durham. Prisoners coming into the prison are not guaranteed to see a nurse in reception; secondary screening is low and waiting times are long.

Prisoners do find the nursing staff supportive; are well supported by the drug, alcohol and recovery team (DART) and DART's interventions are informed by prisoner voice. The mental health team offer an 'Integrated Support Unit' (ISU), a valuable regional resource, which celebrated four years open in October 2021. Despite staffing shortages in the mental health team, adaptations have been made to support men in isolation.

## How well are prisoners progressed towards successful resettlement?

Education staffing has impacted on the personal development of prisoners. Support has been given in-cell during the pandemic, but the complete withdrawal of face-to-face learning in November 2021, is a concern for men with more defined needs. The prison has only recently introduced qualifications. It is a concern that vocational qualifications are not offered and that there are no offending behaviour programmes. The Board is also concerned that some prisoners are choosing not to work. It is good to evidence progress in providing external job opportunities.

## Main areas for development
### TO THE MINISTER
The Board continues to be concerned:
By the level of overcrowding and its impact on the dignity of prisoners. We ask again what, specifically for HMP Durham, can be done to alleviate this problem?
IS91 men are not being moved on fast enough.

## How does the Minister intend to solve this problem?
Of concern is the rise in the number of unsentenced prisoners: there has been a 100% increase in the numbers who have been in Durham for more than one year. The Board awaits the Minister's response on what else can be done to reduce the backlog in criminal cases and hence reduce time on remand.

### TO THE PRISON SERVICE
The Board is concerned at the loss of local control and accountability to the Governor of third-party providers to push with pace the work needed in the local context, for example healthcare and education. How can the Prison Service strengthen this line of accountability?
The Board looks forward to a response from the Prison Service as to its intentions to improve resources and the impact of contractors:
In improving accommodation.
Healthcare provision - with particular reference to waiting lists and secondary screening.
Healthcare attendance at GOoD reviews remains woefully inadequate. What will be done to ensure attendance?
In our 2019 / 2020 report the question was asked "Why were the numbers of prisoners missing 3 days or more of medication no longer reported?". The response was: "This is not part of the HJIP (Healthcare Joint Initiative Partnership)". The Board considers this unsatisfactory and wants to know if this metric will be re-introduced.
In terms of education, how can the contractor improve provision for qualifications and support further men with defined needs?

### TO THE GOVERNOR
What more can the Governor do to embed the use of body worn video cameras (BWVC) in the prison? The Board is interested in understanding how the Governor intends to develop further the work in equality and diversity by improving attendance at diversity and inclusion action team (DIAT) meetings and strand reports.
Use of force is disproportionate in the age groups 18–21 and 22–29. Other than actively pursuing the young adult strategy, what else can be done to address the behaviour of this demographic?
The Board is concerned at the length of time it takes for actions to be enacted in the minutes of prison meetings, e.g. DIAT and use of force.
The Board is concerned that prisoners are working as cleaners before checks are completed and they are not receiving back-pay.

SUTTON VALENCE
MAIDSTONE
KENT
ME17 3DF

HM PRISON SERVICE

HMP & YOI
EAST SUTTON
PARK

Tel: 01622 785000

*For the latest reports on this prison please visit:*
https://tinyurl.com/bdfh26rv

*Important Changes:* **(1) Visits:** the identification necessary to access this prison and visit for social or professional purposes has changed; (2) **Money and Gifts** new rules now apply to these. See page 16 for full details of the above.

**Task of the establishment** East Sutton Park is a women's open establishment with a resettlement function.

## Certified normal accommodation and operational capacity
Prisoners held at the time of this visit: 81
Baseline certified normal capacity: 96
In-use certified normal capacity: 96
Operational capacity: 96

## Prison status and key providers
Public
Prison Group: Women
Prison Group Director: Pia Sinha
Governor/Director: Amy Dixon
IMB Chair: Peter Judges
Physical and mental health provider: Oxleas NHS Foundation Trust
Substance misuse treatment provider: Forward Trust
Prison education framework provider: Weston College
Escort contractor: Serco Prison group

**Brief history** East Sutton Park opened as a female borstal in 1946 and has been a female establishment ever since. The prison is a 15th century manor house set in 80 acres of land with a working farm.

## Short description of residential units
Short description of residential units
Main house – 32 bedrooms, 15 of which had two beds and the largest of which normally had six beds; however, no bedrooms had more than three residents due to Covid-19 measures. The reverse cohort unit was also based here.
The Oaks unit – temporary accommodation, consisting of 20 pods each accommodating one resident.
The Willows unit – four separate flats, each accommodating four residents in two single rooms and one double room.

## Visiting Information
You can book your visit online:
https://www.gov.uk/prison-visits
You can book your visit by telephone. Booking line: 0300 303 0630. The booking line is open Monday to Friday: 9.30am to 1.30pm
**Visiting times:** Saturday/Sunday: 9:30am to 11:30am and 2pm to 4pm

**Legal visits:** There are currently no legal visits taking place.

## INSPECTIONS & REPORTS
**Scrutiny visit 12–13 and 20–21 April 2021**
**Date of last full inspection** 8–18 August 2016
**Scrutiny Visit: published 27 May 2021**
HMP/YOI East Sutton Park in Kent, which was holding 81 women at the time of our visit, is one of only two dedicated women's open prisons in England. The prison has been under threat of closure since an announcement by HM Prison and Probation Service (HMPPS) in October 2013, but this has subsequently been delayed following a legal challenge. The main building is a grade II-listed Jacobean manor house, located in extensive grounds with a working farm. At our last inspection, in 2016, we found East Sutton Park to be an excellent prison, where very strong staff-prisoner relationships underpinned safety and where there was a respectful and purposeful approach to preparing women for release.
During this visit, we found the prison had largely maintained its strong rehabilitative function despite the pandemic. Women continued working both in and outside the prison during the national restrictions. Almost a third of the population was released on temporary licence (ROTL) every day to carry out essential work in the community, which was impressive. Extra work placements in the prison gardens and farm were available for women who did not have essential worker roles and were unable to benefit from ROTL. This had led to more women achieving qualifications in these areas and more women had also enrolled on distance learning and Open University courses.
At the start of the pandemic, prison leaders had gone to considerable lengths to put appropriate measures in place to manage the risk of Covid-19. Social distancing and keeping cohorts of women apart in the main house, which had dormitory accommodation, had been especially problematic. New accommodation, including four flats offering independent living and 20 temporary single-occupancy pods, had opened so women going out to work could live separately. The dormitory accommodation in the main building had been reduced from six to a maximum of three women per room to minimise

the spread of the virus. A separate unit for new arrivals and others required to quarantine had been set up in the main house and extra portable toilets/showers installed outside. New transfers to the prison had been suspended at the start of the pandemic until September 2020 when the changes had been completed.

Despite these measures, there were 34 confirmed cases – more than 40% of the population – during a Covid-19 outbreak starting in December 2020. Prison leaders had worked in partnership with the health care department, NHS England and NHS Improvement and Public Health England to make sure appropriate steps were taken to contain further spread of the virus. Covid-19-safe procedures were strictly enforced. This included wearing face masks inside buildings and sanctions being applied to women for breaching social distancing rules.

During the pandemic, violent incidents had remained very low, although women reported an increase in bullying as relations became strained during the Covid-19 outbreak when regime restrictions were tightened. Recorded levels of self-harm were also low. However, vulnerable women who had been on an assessment, care in custody and teamwork (ACCT) case management plan for prisoners at risk of suicide or self-harm, said staff did not always give them the extra support they needed. Relationships were generally good, although more mixed than at the last inspection, especially in the main house, where only 60% in our survey said that most staff treated them with respect. This appeared to reflect, in part at least, frustrations that had built up during the period of restrictions. Women spoke very highly of some staff, but identified a small number as unhelpful. In our survey, women from minority ethnic groups were also less positive about the way they were treated by staff.

Opportunities for women to leave the prison temporarily to see their children and families had been suspended, in line with Covid-19 restrictions. The prison had promptly introduced the option for women to FaceTime their families and friends on a weekly basis using a mobile phone. Resettlement planning was generally timely but, until recently, plans had been developed remotely via questionnaire, which was not an adequate substitute for face-to-face contact. As one of the first prisons to receive HMPPS approval to progress to 'regime stage three' following the most recent national lockdown, recovery plans (see Appendix III: Glossary of terms) were comparatively well advanced. Social visits, education classes and day release for resettlement purposes and to see family members had now re-started.

In summary, the prison had continued to be a safe and purposeful place during the pandemic. Opening new accommodation to minimise the risk of virus transmission had brought considerable improvements, and living conditions were better in the former dormitory accommodation. The challenge remains for prison leaders to address the decline in the previously very strong staff- prisoner relationships and improve support for women as they prepare for their release.

Charlie Taylor

HM Chief Inspector of Prisons May 2021

**Key concerns and recommendations**

*Key concerns* and recommendations identify the issues of most importance to improving outcomes for prisoners and are designed to help establishments prioritise and address the most significant weaknesses in the treatment and conditions of prisoners.

During this visit we identified some areas of key concern, and have made one recommendation for the prison to address.

*Key concern:* The recording of medication administration did not meet the required standard. We found entries written on the consultation page of the record that were not linked to the prescription because the information was not also recorded on the medicines administration chart. Essential details, such as the dose administered, were missing. When a patient was on a repeat prescription it was not possible to determine which prescription was being used. The failure to record medicines administration on the chart meant the health care provider could not ensure its records were clear or accurate.

Recommendation: The health care partnership board should review how medicines administration is recorded to ensure that best practice standards and continuity of clinical information are maintained. (To the governor)

**INDEPENDENT MONITORING BOARD: Annual Report**

The law requires every prison to be monitored by an independent Board appointed by the Justice Secretary; these are known as Independent Monitoring Boards (IMBs). The IMB must satisfy itself as to the humane and just treatment of those held in custody within its prison and the range and adequacy of the programmes preparing them for release; it must report annually to the Justice Secretary on how well the prison has met the standards and requirements placed on it.

**IMB Report 1 November 2020 – 31 October 2021**
**Published January 2022**
**Executive summary**
**Background to the report**
This report presents the findings of the Board at ESP for the period 1 November 2020 to 31 October 2021. The Board's conclusions are based on observations made on rota visits, daily briefing reports, examination of records and documents, attendance at some internal meetings (though this was limited due to Covid-19 restrictions), and conversations with staff and prisoners.

**Main judgements**
**How safe is the prison?**
It is the Board's view that the prison is a safe place to be. Overall, the Board judges that the prison is well run, with prisoners, for the most part, enjoying a good relationship with staff and each other.

**How fairly and humanely are prisoners treated?**
The prisoners are treated fairly, with an efficient key worker scheme operating. They are encouraged by staff to make the most of their time at the establishment.
Prisoners are treated with great consideration, in a disciplined environment. Staff offer support and encouragement as prisoners prepare for release into the community.

**How well are prisoners' health and wellbeing needs met?**
Healthcare works very well within the limitations of the Monday to Friday service. Staff work very closely with the residents picking up and dealing with any wellbeing issues quickly and efficiently. There is a fully supportive professional service in place to deal with mental health issues.

**How well are prisoners progressed towards successful resettlement?**
Generally, prisoners are prepared well for release. Few leave without accommodation to go to, and some continue with the employer with whom they have been released on temporary licence (ROTL) for paid work. However, although much improved, some prisoners still arrive with too little time to serve, allowing insufficient time to prepare them properly for release. Those arriving with several months to serve undertake a structured programme, with an emphasis on improving their education, obtaining accommodation, and gaining employment. They are encouraged to take responsibility for their sentence plans, which are discussed and agreed at sentence planning boards within two or three weeks of arrival.

Sadly, these boards were run on a much-reduced basis since the beginning of the pandemic, losing the benefit of group discussion of the prisoners' needs. We are pleased to note that they are now operating as in the past.

**Main areas for development**
**TO THE MINISTER**
To urge/direct the Prison Service to continue to ensure that prisoners coming to ESP have enough time left to serve, in order to ensure that the greatest benefit in resettlement can be achieved, and therefore representing value for money.

**TO THE PRISON SERVICE**
To ensure that closed female establishments progress women, who are suitable for the resettlement regime, to come to East Sutton Park. To approve an application the prison has made for a further 24 pods.

**TO THE GOVERNOR**
To continue with the prompt and careful steps taken to combat Covid-19.
To make greater use of the incentives and earned privileges (IEP) scheme for prisoners who are disruptive or whose behaviour falls short of the standards expected by the prison.

**Progress since the last report**
Occupation of the flats and pods has allowed prisoners to gain a measure of self-sufficiency, which should stand them in good stead at their release. It has also given those residents in the house something to aspire to.
The success of the jobs fairs has led to potential new employers for those prisoners in outside paid employment.
The return of full sentence planning boards allowing full discussion of the prisoner's needs.
It is pleasing that the maintaining of Prison Service Orders and Instructions has been resolved.

 FALFIELD
WOTTON-UNDER-EDGE
GLOUCESTERSHIRE
GL12 8DB

HMP & YOI EASTWOOD PARK
Tel: 01454 382100

*For the latest reports on this prison please visit:*
https://tinyurl.com/bdfh26rv

*Important Changes:* **(1) Visits:** the identification necessary to access this prison and visit for social or professional purposes has changed; (2) **Money and Gifts** new rules now apply to these. See page 16 for full details of the above.

**Task of the establishment** HMP Eastwood Park is a closed women's resettlement prison.

**Certified normal accommodation and operational capacity**
Prisoners held at the time of inspection: 388
Baseline certified normal capacity: 430
In-use certified normal capacity: 430
Operational capacity: 430

**Prison status and key providers**
Public
Prison Group: Women
Prison Group Director: Pia Sinha
Governor/Director: Zoe Short
IMB Chair: Di Askwith
Physical health provider: InspireBetterHealth
Mental health provider: Avon and Wiltshire Partnership
Substance misuse provider: Avon and Wiltshire Partnership
Learning and skills provider: Weston College
Escort contractor: GEO Amey

**Brief history** Eastwood Park opened as a women's prison in March 1996, admitting prisoners from HMP Pucklechurch. The prison opened a mother and baby unit in 2004 and the Mary Carpenter Unit for 17-year-old girls in 2005. The Mary Carpenter Unit closed in 2013 and reopened as the Nexus Programme Unit in 2015. The Kinnon Unit, a substance use unit, opened in 2009.

**Short description of residential units**
Residential 1 – Closed prisoners
Residential 2 – Closed prisoners
Residential 3 – Closed prisoners
Residential 4 – Mental health/crisis intervention unit
Residential 5 – Drug recovery and transition unit
Residential 6 – Transition unit
Residential 7 – Open environment
Residential 8 – First night induction unit for all prisoners, including those requiring detoxification for substance use
Residential 9 – Mother and baby unit
Residential 10 – Nexus programme unit (personality disorder unit)

**Visiting Information**
You can book your visit online:
https://www.gov.uk/prison-visits
You can also book by telephone or email:
socialvisits.eastwoodpark@hmps.gsi.gov.uk
Booking line: 0300 303 0631
Monday to Friday, 9am to 6pm
**Visiting times:** Tues, Wed, Fri, Sat and Sun: 2pm to 3pm and 3:30pm to 4:30pm.

**Legal visits:** Booking line: 0300 303 0631
Monday to Friday, 9am to 6pm.

**INSPECTIONS & REPORTS**
**Date of last HMCIP inspection** 3–17 May 2019
**HMCIP Report, published 28 August 2019**
HMP Eastwood Park is a closed women's prison situated in a semi-rural area to the north of Bristol. At the time of this inspection, it held slightly fewer than 400 prisoners. It was last inspected in November 2016. At this inspection our findings resulted in similar gradings to 2016, with the exception of 'Resettlement' where the outcomes had declined from being 'reasonably good' to 'not sufficiently good'. It is notable that Eastwood Park has a huge catchment area, including much of Wales. Consequently, half the women were being held more than 50 miles from home, and over one-third never received any visits. As with all women's prisons, the population included many with very complex needs, and many who had been victimised in a variety of ways before coming into custody. Overall, we found that Eastwood Park remained a safe, respectful and purposeful prison.

In terms of safety, there was a need for the prison to think very carefully about the arrangements for those women being segregated for extended periods, and indeed whether it was necessary to do so. More attention needed to be given to planning for reintegrating such women back into the mainstream of the prison. The practice of segregating women on residential wings also had a detrimental knock-on effect on the regime of the rest of the prisoners who were not in segregation. Despite the fact the use of force by staff had declined since the last inspection, we had concerns about its oversight. Although we had to alert the prison to an incident that had some worrying aspects, it is important to note that this did not have any influence on the grade awarded for 'Safety' as it had yet to be fully investigated. Nevertheless, the incident was only going to be properly investigated after inspectors brought it to the attention of senior managers, and so was perhaps symptomatic of our broader concerns over the governance of the use of force.

As in other women's prisons, the complexity and vulnerability of many of the prisoners meant that there were a high number of women subject to assessment, care and casework teamwork (ACCT) documents. However, we formed a clear view that far more attention needed to be paid to the documents' quality, although we found the actual levels of care received by women was good. Although, by and large, living conditions in the prison were good, the accommodation provided on Units 1-3 were completely inappropriate for a women's prison. These units were poor in comparison with the rest of the prison. Women were locked in their cells for far too long, and there was a backlog of repair jobs to bring the decaying fabric back up to acceptable standards. On entering these units, I was immediately struck by the sight of rows of women's faces pressed against the open observation hatches of their locked doors, peering out into the narrow, dark, cell block corridor. It was as if they were waiting for something or indeed anything to happen, however mundane, to relieve the monotony of their existence. It is my belief that unless something radical can be done to improve the conditions on these units, then serious consideration should be given to closing them. At present they are simply not fit for purpose.

Most prisoners told us that staff treated them with respect, increasingly they were being consulted about their experiences in the prison, and we saw many positive interactions with staff. It was noticeable that the number of complaints had significantly decreased since the last inspection.

The details of why our judgement for 'resettlement' had declined are set out in the report, and the complexity of the population clearly has an impact on the provision of effective offender management and resettlement services. For instance, 73% of prisoners told us they had mental health problems, and around half had problems with illicit drug use. These issues were compounded by the fact that many women were serving short sentences of less than six months, reducing the opportunity for effective interventions. Of particular concern was the fact that in the months leading up to the inspection, about a half of women had been released homeless and were left either to live on the streets or to go to temporary emergency accommodation. I spoke to several prisoners who had previously experienced this and had either re-offended or felt it was inevitable that they would do so if released again in similar circumstances. In many ways this is an issue that is beyond the control of the prison, but more support does need to be given before release.

Finally, I would encourage the leadership to look very carefully at the recommendations contained in this report. On the last occasion we made 48 recommendations, of which only 19 were fully achieved. Although we neither reward nor penalise prisons for their success or failure to implement inspection recommendations, it remains the fact that it is possible to see a correlation between achievement of recommendations and performance.

Peter Clarke CVO OBE QPM July 2019
HM Chief Inspector of Prisons

## INDEPENDENT MONITORING BOARD: Annual Report

The law requires every prison to be monitored by an independent Board appointed by the Justice Secretary; these are known as Independent Monitoring Boards (IMBs). The IMB must satisfy itself as to the humane and just treatment of those held in custody within its prison and the range and adequacy of the programmes preparing them for release; it must report annually to the Justice Secretary on how well the prison has met the standards and requirements placed on it.

### IMB Report 1 November 2020 – 31 October 2021. Published 22nd March 2022
### Background to the report

This has been another exceptional year because of the impact of the Covid-19 pandemic on the way that prisons have been run and on the ability of the Board to carry out face-to-face monitoring. The IMB suspended monitoring visits between 11 December 2020 and 5 April 2021. In this respect, it was difficult to make realistic comparisons with previous years. However, the Board at Eastwood Park has scrutinised what has been happening at the prison and continued to take and look into applications from prisoners, both on paper and from the national applications helpline. In April 2021, the Governor was seconded to the Prison Group Director's team without prior notice and the Deputy Governor moved to a new post elsewhere in the estate in October 2021. Senior managers have been seconded from elsewhere in the service and management has continued seamlessly. Our enquiries were dealt with promptly, and satisfactory responses received. We commend management and staff on the professional and humane manner that they have undertaken their duties during this challenging period. Sadly, there was one death in custody on 24 July 2021 of a prisoner who had recently been remanded. The Coroner's inquest was awaited.

### Main judgements
### How safe is the prison?

Overall HMP/YOI Eastwood Park was safe for most women most of the time. We have been, as with previous years, concerned about the levels of self-harm and violence. There have been comprehensive efforts to reduce levels but they have proved difficult to change. The high numbers of women with mental health issues has been compounded by the impact of lockdown.

### How fairly and humanely are prisoners treated?

We continue to be impressed with the professionalism of staff and have observed many examples of this in practice. However, as with last year, we have to stop short of reporting that prisoners were treated humanely because of the impact of Covid and the lengths of time for which prisoners were locked up.

## How well are prisoners' health and wellbeing needs met?
We had a continued concern about the long-term effect on prisoners' mental and physical wellbeing due to long times in cells due to coronavirus restrictions, albeit we have seen the efforts that the prison and healthcare teams have made to keep women safe from the virus. For example, Eastwood Park was among the prisons with the highest uptake of Covid vaccinations in England and Wales. We also note that there has been a steady decrease in the number of applications received by the IMB relating to health. We took this as a sign that there has been a steady improvement.

## How well are prisoners progressed towards successful resettlement?
The changes to the service provider and challenges of finding suitable accommodation provided a difficult framework within which to deliver a comprehensive resettlement service. The failure of the prison regime to match the changes in the prison population meant that women's offending-related needs were hardly met. The new reducing reoffending strategy that appeared towards the end of the reporting year gave the Board some hope that these matters would be addressed. The Board welcomes the beginning of the long-awaited construction of the activity centre which should offer the opportunity to address some of the deficits.
The Board also welcomed the opening of Eden House, an approved premises for the resettlement of prisoners. Several women from Eastwood Park benefitted from this new accommodation option.

## Main areas for development
### TO THE MINISTER
Our concerns continue about a prisoner with an acquired brain injury who has been continuously segregated at Downview and Eastwood Park prisons for 1,202 days by the end of this reporting period. In response to correspondence your predecessor stated that 'the truth is that the right environment simply doesn't exist within the prison system to cater for her unique needs'. Why is it acceptable to discriminate against women when specialist facilities are available for men with a similar condition?
Women with mental health issues and complex needs who would be better treated in the health rather than criminal justice system continue to be

sent to Eastwood Park. When will the Minister take action to reduce this significantly? In response to a question in our last annual report about the establishment of a women's centre in Wales, your predecessor responded by advising that seed funding had been made available. What progress has been made with this project?

### TO THE MINISTRY OF JUSTICE
In response to a question in our last annual report about the establishment of a women's centre in Wales, the Minister responded by advising that seed funding had been made available. When is the centre likely to open?

### TO THE PRISON SERVICE
When will the longstanding dampness on two wings be addressed?
Given the fluctuations in staffing levels caused by this pandemic, which are likely to continue for some time, will HMPPS ensure that prisons are staffed sufficiently to cope with this ongoing situation?
Will HMPPS confirm what actions they are taking to improve the accommodation options for women leaving prisons and when this is likely to have an impact on outcomes?

### TO THE GOVERNOR
Construction of the new activities centre is due for completion by June 2022. When is this important training facility due to become operational? What action is being taken to improve officer recruitment and retention at Eastwood Park?
This year has been exceptional because of the impact of the Covid-19 pandemic on the way that prisons have been run and on the ability of the Board to carry out face-to-face monitoring. In this respect, it is difficult to make realistic comparisons with previous years. However, the Board at Eastwood Park has scrutinised what has been happening at the prison and continued to take and look into applications from prisoners, both on paper and from the national applications helpline. The early release scheme had little impact on the population at Eastwood Park, and the Board was surprised that more prisoners in the MBU were not released early. There were many versions of the criteria applying to early release and it was disappointing that all of these revisions took managers' time away from other important tasks. Her Majesty's Inspectorate of Prisons (HMIP) did not carry out a full inspection at Eastwood Park during this reporting year. However, the establishment was inspected, along with other prisons for women, with a specific focus on the response to the Covid-19 pandemic, and the report was published in June 2020. This was

243

broadly positive, and six out of seven mentions of good practice related to Eastwood Park. There were some concerns, including the lack of separation of new prisoners in the reverse cohorting unit (the unit where new prisoners were quarantined for 14 days); this was addressed immediately by the prison.

Around a third of prisoners at Eastwood Park come from Wales. The Prison Reform Trust published a report in December 2020, having analysed 2019 sentencing data by police force area. In the South Wales Police Force area, the imprisonment rate per 100,000 was 62. This was 19 more than the next highest and 48 higher than in Devon and Cornwall, the lowest in Eastwood Park's catchment area. Although the Board does not report on sentencing, these findings are of great concern as they relate to the delivery of justice.

CHURCH ROAD
EASTCHURCH
SHEERNESS
KENT, ME12 4DZ

**HM PRISON
ELMLEY**

Tel: 01795 802000

*For the latest reports on this prison please visit:*
https://tinyurl.com/bdfh26rv

*Important Changes:* **(1) Visits:** the identification necessary to access this prison and visit for social or professional purposes has changed; (2) **Money and Gifts** new rules now apply to these. See page 16 for full details of the above.

**This prison operates the new Digital Categorisation System, pursuant to the Security Categorisation Policy Framework as such PSIs 40 and 41 of 2011 do not apply to prisoners being categorised in this establishment. See section 2.26 for more information.**

**Task of the establishment** Category B reception and category C training prison for adult males.

**Certified normal accommodation and operational capacity**
Prisoners held at the time of inspection: 1,095
Baseline certified normal capacity: 1,007
In-use certified normal capacity: 1,007
Operational capacity: 1,137

**Population of the prison**
• 2,793 new prisoners received each year (around 232 per month).
• 194 foreign national prisoners (18%).
• 19.8% of prisoners from black and minority ethnic backgrounds.

• 129 prisoners released into the community each month.
• Around 38% of the population were known to the substance misuse service.
• 350 prisoners referred for mental health assessment each month.

**Prison status and key providers**
Public
Prison Group: Kent, Surrey & Sussex
Prison Group Director: James Lucas
Governor/Director: Andy Davy
IMB Chairs: Pam Spindlow, John Cunningham
Physical health provider: Integrated Care 24
Mental health provider:
Oxleas NHS Foundation Trust
Substance misuse treatment provider: Forward Trust
Prison education framework provider:
Weston College
Escort contractor: Serco

**Brief history** Elmley opened in 1992 and is the largest of the three prisons on the Isle of Sheppey. Since the 2019 inspection it has changed its role; while its primary function is to receive remand prisoners from the courts, its secondary purpose is now as a training establishment for a large population of sentenced category C prisoners (almost 500 currently).

**Short description of residential units**
House block 1 first night and induction, currently also operating as reverse cohort unit.
House block 2 remand and convicted prisoners.
House block 3 substance recovery, working in partnership with Forward Trust.
House block 4 remand and convicted prisoners.
House block 5 enhanced and category C prisoners and full-time workers.
House block 6 foreign nationals and sex offenders. Planning permission has recently been granted for house block 7.

**Visiting Information**
You can book your visit online:
https://www.gov.uk/prison-visits
Or by telephone: Booking line: 0300 060 6605 open Monday to Friday, 9am to 4pm
**Visiting times:** Monday to Friday: 2pm to 3pm
**Legal visits:** Monday to Friday: 9am to 11:30am

**INSPECTIONS & REPORTS**
**HMCIP Report**
**Date of last inspection** 28 February–1 March and 7–11 March 2022
**Published 21 June 2022**
HMCIP Elmley is a Category B reception and category C training prison located on the Isle of Sheppey. The category C prisoners, which made

up 45% of the population, were housed on a separate wing.

The relationships between staff and prisoners were better than we usually see in this sort of prison and during the inspection we were impressed by the way most officers interacted with the men. In spite of ongoing Covid-19 cases in prisoners arriving at the jail, the prison had worked hard to keep the regime going and those in work were out of their cells for more than seven hours a day. Even unemployed prisoners could expect to be unlocked for at least five hours. It was therefore disappointing that the provision of education was so poor, with Ofsted inspectors awarding their lowest grade in two areas and their second lowest in two more, with the quality of teaching and the lack of a proper needs assessment being particularly disappointing.

The governor, who was well-liked by both staff and prisoners, had only been in post since August 2021, but she had made some progress in building a more rehabilitative culture as the risk from Covid-19 began to recede.

Levels of violence were slightly below the average for similar prisons, although prisoners' perception of their own safety had not improved since our last inspection. In spite of this, the use of force had gone up significantly and the leaders had not done enough to understand the reasons for this rise. The processes for assessing, addressing and monitoring the behaviour of the more serious perpetrators of violence was not yet effective enough. We were concerned that at Elmley, a much larger number of incidents than we usually see were routinely being classed as "miscellaneous" rather than being put in a more suitable category. We also found that the use of data in measuring outcomes between different groups was not sophisticated enough to understand and act where these were disproportionate.

We were disappointed to hear that the excellent early days mental health screening pilot was coming to an end. This had aimed to identify those prisoners whose mental health was at risk and was valued by both prisoners and staff. We were assured that the new service model would incorporate the same level of service and support. In healthcare more generally, there were not enough staff members to be able to provide a stable, high-quality service, leading to delays and a lack of consistency.

The prison received more complaints than any other local prison, to which its responses were often neither timely nor helpful. This is partly because the system for making applications was not working, leading to greater prisoner frustration.

We were very pleased to see that the prison was offering visits every day of the week. This was much better than we often see in other jails, where Covid-19 restrictions or staffing shortages tend to result in provision being curtailed.

Staffing levels at the prison have deteriorated in recent months, but they are not yet at a critical level. The way staff are deployed is not always as creative as it could be. Consequently, key work has largely been lost and prisoner offender managers (POM) in the offender management unit are often cross deployed, directly affecting prisoner progression.

There is much to build on at Elmley with many good staff members and a leadership team that has grown in confidence. The prison will need to continue to be led effectively and creatively if it is to build on the findings of this inspection.

Charlie Taylor

HM Chief Inspector of Prisons April 2022

**Safety**

At the last inspection of Elmley in 2019 we found that outcomes for prisoners were not sufficiently good against this healthy prison test.

At this inspection we found that outcomes for prisoners remained not sufficiently good.

Reception was a busy environment. New arrivals were treated well and the process was relatively swift. First night cells were unwelcoming and some new prisoners missed important aspects of induction.

One in four prisoners in our survey said they currently felt unsafe. Prisoner-on-prisoner violence had decreased but levels of violence against staff and serious assaults were broadly comparable to the last inspection. Not all violent incidents were investigated, which meant that leaders were unable to fully understand the causes and drivers of violence at Elmley.

There were weaknesses in the systems to address violence and behaviour issues, including challenge, support and intervention plans (CSIPs, see Glossary), the Incentives Policy and adjudications. In addition, serious cases referred to the police were not progressed and had a limited deterrent effect. There was little distinction between what was offered on the house blocks, which meant that the category C enhanced spur was not effective as a tool to motivate good behaviour and encourage progression.

The use of force had increased since the last inspection, even though prisoners were locked up for longer and so spent less time in contact with others. The incidents of force we were able to review demonstrated some good de-escalation by staff, but too many, including serious incidents involving batons or PAVA incapacitant spray, were not recorded on body-worn video cameras. Investigations into the use of force were not always thorough so it was difficult to be assured that it had been reasonable and proportionate.

245

Segregation to manage the most challenging prisoners was used proportionately. Relationships between officers and prisoners on the unit were good and prisoners had good access to mental health staff. The cells were hot and not always sufficiently clean, and until recently prisoners could not shower every day. Reasonable reintegration planning made sure that prisoners were not segregated for too long.

Security arrangements were proportionate. Intelligence reports were of reasonable quality, but staff redeployment had reduced the department's ability to respond. Too many incident reports were recorded as 'miscellaneous', rather than ascribed to specific indicators of security breaches, which left the prison poorly placed to understand the full extent of problems relating to safety. The strategic approach to drug supply reduction had greatly improved.

There had been four self-inflicted deaths since our last visit. The prison had begun implementing recommendations from the two Prisons and Probation Ombudsman (PPO) investigation reports received to date, but implementation was not monitored over time to ensure ongoing compliance. Reported self-harm was lower than in most comparable prisons but had increased since our last visit and was on an upward trend. Data analysis of self-harm was poor. The safer custody team was well resourced and had recently introduced some good initiatives and safeguards to identify and support prisoners at risk. Prisoners supported through assessment, care in custody and teamwork (ACCT) case management were generally positive about the care they received, although there were some weaknesses in the process itself. There was an action plan to improve the quality of case management. The prison operated an effective Listener scheme to provide peer support to those in need.

**Respect**

At the last inspection of Elmley in 2019 we found that outcomes for prisoners were not sufficiently good against this healthy prison test.

At this inspection we found that outcomes for prisoners remained not sufficiently good.

The majority of staff were visible and approachable. In our survey, prisoners were more positive about staff relationships than in similar prisons. However, there was too little key work to develop relationships and make them more constructive. Peer work was established, but there were opportunities to develop this to greater effect.

Around 30% of prisoners lived in overcrowded conditions, with two occupying cells designed for one. These were often untidy and not adequately equipped, but the prison had begun to address this. Although some showers had been refurbished to a good standard, many remained grubby and lacked sufficient privacy. Prisoners had good access to clean clothing and bedding each week.

Despite efforts to improve the food, many prisoners complained about the quality and size of meals. The prison shop catered for most prisoner needs, but there were also many valid complaints relating to missing items and problems receiving refunds.

The Elmley community consultation group met regularly but was not yet fully effective, and many prisoners were unsure if consultation had led to improvement. There were weaknesses in the application system and, despite improvements, responses to prisoner complaints did not always address the issue fully; some had waited months for a response.

Monthly diversity and inclusion meetings provided a focus for equality work and were attended by prisoner representatives. The meetings examined data and leaders had compiled an action plan to address some identified shortfalls. However, in the absence of a needs analysis and clear strategy setting out the main objectives, it was difficult to monitor outcomes or assess progress in equality and diversity work.

There were inconsistencies in the focus and support given to prisoners with protected characteristics. For example, consultation with prisoners from some, but not all, protected groups had recently restarted, and senior managers had been appointed as leads for most groups. However, there had been no consultation with prisoners with disabilities and no senior lead appointed to ensure appropriate support for foreign national prisoners. It was too early to assess the impact of some recent initiatives to address the needs of protected groups.

A dedicated and well-managed chaplaincy provided important pastoral support and care, particularly for prisoners in crisis. While opportunities for corporate worship remained too limited, prisoners greatly valued the multi-faith team.

Many prisoners expressed frustration about access to health care, another department that had experienced notable staff shortages during the pandemic. The primary care service had prioritised essential services and was now running clinics on the wings where possible. GPs were covering gaps in the provision, which had extended waits for routine GP appointments to four weeks, which was too long. A range of allied health professionals and external services were providing clinics, but prisoner attendance was variable due to factors such as lack of officer escorts. Attendance at external hospital appointments was also affected by prison arrangements for hospital escorts and long delays in access to community provision. The inpatient department provided good care for patients with complex mental health needs. Social care was good, including continuity of care on release.

Against a background of significant workforce challenges, mental health services had responded positively to prisoners in need of urgent support. Prisoners waited longer than before the pandemic to access routine psychological care, but caring staff provided alternative support while they waited. Support for prisoners with substance misuse needs was reasonably good.

Most aspects of pharmacy services were adequate, although inconsistent officer supervision of medicine queues increased the risk of medicines being diverted. Dental services were good with waits for routine appointments reduced to four weeks.

**Purposeful activity**

At the last inspection of Elmley in 2019 we found that outcomes for prisoners were not sufficiently good against this healthy prison test.

At this inspection we found that outcomes for prisoners remained not sufficiently good.

The new, less restricted regime had increased prisoner time out of cell to up to seven hours on a weekday for the few prisoners working full time. During our roll checks we found one-third of prisoners locked behind their doors which, although still too many, was better than in similar prisons. Only half of those prisoners who were unlocked were actually in education or work. Prisoners on the house block 5 enhanced spur benefited from evening association, which meant they had up to nine hours a day out of cell, which was good. At weekends, most prisoners were unlocked for only three hours a day.

After a long period of closure, prisoners could now visit a well-stocked, welcoming library twice a week. This was also complemented by an outreach service. PE facilities were very good, including a large sports hall, well-equipped gym and weights annex. Monitoring of attendance data was limited, leaving the prison poorly equipped to target non- attenders and encourage wider participation.

Leaders and managers had correctly identified weaknesses in the education provision, but the overall quality of education, particularly in classroom-based subjects, was inadequate. Recent actions to address this had not yet had the necessary impact.

Too few prisoners attended the education, skills, and work activities they were assigned to. The induction sessions offered by the learning and skills provider did not motivate prisoners to attend activities or provide sufficient information about the options on offer. Teachers did not focus closely enough on what prisoners most needed to learn and did not do enough to support those with learning difficulties or disabilities.

Teachers did not provide targeted feedback that supported prisoners to progress in their learning, and too few achieved the qualification they were working towards. Prisoners did not receive sufficient careers advice and guidance. The use of data was weak, and leaders did not adequately track trends in recruitment, retention and achievement on education courses.

Leaders offered a suitable range of provision to prisoners. Behaviour was good and prisoners valued their education and work activities. Support from the new employer adviser had steadily increased the number of prisoners going into work. Leaders made sure that the curriculum included valuable programmes, such as music, mindfulness and art, which enabled some prisoners to make progress with their mental health.

**Rehabilitation and release planning**

At the last inspection of Elmley in 2019 we found that outcomes for prisoners were not sufficiently good against this healthy prison test.

At this inspection we found that outcomes for prisoners remained not sufficiently good.

Prisoners had better opportunities to have in-person social visits than we had seen at most other prisons since the start of the pandemic. The Spurgeons charity provided some good family initiatives that prisoners greatly appreciated. All prisoners had in-cell telephones, enabling them to maintain contact with families.

A recently revised strategy and improvements to governance arrangements to coordinate better reducing reoffending work looked positive. In addition to its primary function serving the courts, Elmley was now also a training prison for the 40% of sentenced prisoners who were category C. There was little distinction between the prison's category B and category C functions, with too few opportunities for category C prisoners to demonstrate a reduction in risk or progress through their sentence.

Prison officer in prison offender managers (POM) roles were still cross- deployed to other duties too often, which affected their ability to maintain regular contact with prisoners on their caseload. There was still a backlog of prisoner assessments (OASys) to be completed, and some of the sentence plans we reviewed were not good enough to support sentence progression. There were weaknesses in the administration of home detention curfew.

Public protection arrangements remained inadequate. The interdepartmental risk management team meeting focused only on prisoners on the higher levels of multi-agency public protection arrangements (MAPPA) and missed the opportunity to manage the risks of some other high-risk prisoners. Delays in the monitoring of phone calls made by prisoners identified as posing a risk to the public was a concern.

COVID restrictions and staff shortages had severely affected the delivery of interventions to address offending behaviour. Prisoners had benefited from the support of the new employment adviser under the 'Accelerator' pilot (see Glossary), which had already led to employment for a small number of prisoners on release. The scheme also provided an accommodation adviser. But despite concerted efforts by prison staff to secure accommodation, many prisoners were discharged from Elmley without an address to go to.

The resettlement team assessed the resettlement needs of all new arrivals and then reviewed all low- and medium-risk prisoners 12 weeks before release to help them with their release plan. The weekly resettlement meeting provided assurance that action was being taken to support those being released.

**Key concerns and recommendations**

Key concerns and recommendations identify the issues of most importance to improving outcomes for prisoners and are designed to help establishments prioritise and address the most significant weaknesses in the treatment and conditions of prisoners.

During this inspection we identified some areas of key concern and have made a small number of recommendations for the prison to address those concerns.

Key concern: Systems to understand and respond to the causes of violence were underdeveloped. Not all violent incidents were investigated and there was little evidence that lessons were learned from those that were. In the sample of investigations we reviewed, there was usually a lack of inquiry into why the incident happened and how it could have been prevented.

Recommendation: Investigations into incidents of violence should be sufficiently thorough to understand and respond to the causes of violence, ensuring that perpetrators and victims are managed and supported appropriately. (To the governor)

Key concern: Use of force documentation was not always fully completed and, although body-worn video cameras were readily available, too many staff failed to activate them during an incident to provide evidence and support de-escalation.

Recommendation: Leaders should make sure that staff routinely switch on body-worn cameras during use of force incidents, and there is proper oversight of documentation. (To the governor)

Key concern: There were weaknesses in the governance of adjudications, segregation and security. Records of the key meetings providing scrutiny in these areas did not give assurance that important issues were discussed or that the right people were in attendance. Poor assessment of data undermined the prison's understanding of some of the challenges it faced.

Recommendation: There should be effective oversight of all aspects of safety in the prison. Governance meetings should be well attended, and discussion and action should focus on key priorities in each area informed by good data analysis. (To the governor)

Key concern: The absence of a needs analysis and clearly defined equality strategy left leaders without a sense of direction or the ability to monitor progress or assess outcomes for prisoners with protected characteristics. There was little evidence that the needs of these prisoners were understood or met. Recent consultation with protected groups lacked purpose, direction and focus.

Recommendation: The prison should have a clear strategy to identify and meet the needs of prisoners from all protected characteristic groups, ensuring there is no disproportionate treatment. (To the governor)

Key Concern: Staffing shortages in primary health care had led to weaknesses in governance, a reduction in the services available and long waiting times. Staffing shortfalls across the prison also affected prisoner access to internal and external health appointments.

Recommendation: Staffing levels should be sufficient to ensure that prisoners have timely access to the full range of primary health services and appointments. (To the governor and the health provider)

Key concern: Prisoners received a low quality of education, particularly in classroom and outreach settings. They did not develop substantial new knowledge and skills, and they achieved accredited qualifications at low rates.

Recommendation: Leaders should take rapid action to address the poor quality of teaching in classroom-based education, for example through improved training and quality assurance. They should make sure that prisoners have opportunities to develop substantial new knowledge and skills and, as a result, to achieve accredited qualifications at high rates. (To the governor)

Key concern: Leaders did not use data effectively to monitor the quality of education. For example, they did not adequately track trends in recruitment, retention and achievement, and use this information to tackle weaknesses in the education provision.

Recommendation: Leaders should make more effective use of data to scrutinise the performance of learners on education courses. (To the governor)

Key concern: Prisoners did not receive a thorough induction to education, skills and work or enough information about their education, skills and work options. Staff inhibited prisoners from making choices by discussing their confidential information in front of other prisoners. Leaders did not make sure that allocations to activities matched prisoners' career goals.

Recommendation: Leaders should make sure that prisoners benefit from a good-quality induction, carried out sensitively, that helps them to make informed choices about their work or study options, and that allocations to courses match prisoners' career aspirations. (To the governor)

Key concern: Prisoners with learning difficulties and/or disabilities received inadequate support and support plans did not identify appropriate strategies. Prisoners who required a more in-depth assessment of their needs had to wait too long for an assessment. Too many teachers lacked the confidence to support prisoners with learning difficulties and/or disabilities effectively.

Recommendation: Leaders should make sure that prisoners with learning difficulties and/or disabilities needs receive appropriate support that enables them to make good progress in education, skills and work activities. (To the governor)

Key concern: There was insufficient focus on, and opportunities for, sentence progression by prisoners. Contact between prison offender managers and prisoners was too infrequent, and many of the targets in prisoners' sentence plans were not specific about the work they needed to do to reduce their risk. Very few prisoners had been able to complete accredited offending behaviour programmes at Elmley or elsewhere, and POMs did not undertake one-to-one offending behaviour work with prisoners.

Recommendation: Prisoners should be able to access appropriate offending behaviour interventions to reduce their risk and progress through their sentence. (To the governor)

Key concern: Public protection arrangements were inadequate. The scope of the inter-departmental risk management meeting was too limited to consider all high-risk prisoners approaching release. There was a six-week backlog of phone calls made by high-risk prisoners waiting to be monitored.

Recommendation: Leaders should enforce robust arrangements to protect the public by identifying and managing effectively the risks posed by all high-risk prisoners in custody and before their release. (To the governor)

**Notable positive practice**
We define notable positive practice as innovative work or practice that leads to particularly good outcomes from which other establishments may be able to learn. Inspectors look for evidence of good outcomes for prisoners; original, creative or particularly effective approaches to problem-solving or achieving the desired goal; and how other establishments could learn from or replicate the practice.

Inspectors found three examples of notable positive practice during this inspection.

Segregation reviews were multidisciplinary and could involve the prisoner's family. In one case, the mother of a prisoner was invited to a review to help staff understand his needs better.

A nurse-led multidisciplinary chronic pain clinic helped patients to manage and overcome the challenge of suffering with long-term pain. This positive approach to pain management meant that patients received a comprehensive service to help them cope in the most effective way.

The social care team was compassionate and provided exemplary care and support to prisoners with an identified social care need. Continuity of care was achieved by well-organised and effective pathways, including the smooth transition of released prisoners into community nursing/residential homes.

**INDEPENDENT MONITORING BOARD: Annual Report**
The law requires every prison to be monitored by an independent Board appointed by the Justice Secretary; these are known as Independent Monitoring Boards (IMBs). The IMB must satisfy itself as to the humane and just treatment of those held in custody within its prison and the range and adequacy of the programmes preparing them for release; it must report annually to the Justice Secretary on how well the prison has met the standards and requirements placed on it.

**IMB Report 1 November 2020 – 31 October 2021**
**Published 3rd March 2022**
**Background to the report**
At the beginning of this reporting period HMP Elmley was a Covid-19 outbreak site and following the Stage 4 exceptional delivery model (EDM). This meant a very restricted regime for prisoners and a cautious approach to monitoring by the Board. Three members were able to visit

the prison during this four-month period, establishing distanced contact with prisoners when responding to their applications to the Board and gathering what information they could. Members joined the Board meetings by phone during this time. Blended monitoring was not very satisfactory as it was difficult to maintain contact with prison staff from outside the prison.

For the last six months of the reporting period, restrictions gradually eased with the implementation of Stages 2 and 3, and members began to feel able to return to visiting the prison. Preparation was made for Stage 1, the new normal, although it had yet to be achieved by October 2021.

### Main judgements
### How safe is the prison?
In response to the survey question 'How safe do you feel with the Covid rules in Elmley?', 33 percent said that they did feel safe, and 67 percent said that being locked down did not make sense. They were tested at reception and only moved on to normal location when they had a negative test. They were acutely aware that it was staff that introduced infection in the prison and criticised officers for not wearing masks or maintaining social distancing. This could be understood as an expression of their resentment at their further loss of liberty but is a fact which the Board has observed.

### How fairly and humanely are prisoners treated?
On the whole prisoners are treated fairly within the limits that have been set for the establishment by HMPPS.

It is questionable whether locking men up for 23 hours a day in small spaces, often confined with another man, feeding off each other's anxieties, is humane.

### How well are prisoners' health and wellbeing needs met?
Health provision has been patchy due to staffing difficulties.

The quality and quantity of the food is poor, largely because of the budget allowed for food. The complaints about favouritism at the serveries is in part another expression of resentment.

The service provided by DHL in the delivery of the canteen is disappointing. Prisoners rely on the canteen to supplement their prison diet with fresh fruit and vegetables.

### How well are prisoners progressed towards successful resettlement?
The Accelerator project, which is being piloted at Elmley, shows good prospects of success in its ambition to co-ordinate all the relevant agencies that a newly released prisoner needs help with. It is still to be fully assessed. Unfortunately, because of the current long delays in court listings, some remanded prisoners have completed the sentence they receive before their case is heard. They are then released from court without the benefit of the resettlement service.

The surgeries that have been set up on a house block by the offender management unit (OMU) have been a success in responding promptly to prisoners' issues and are due to be rolled out in other areas of the prison.

### Main areas for development
### TO THE MINISTER
We hope that the minister will give careful thought to the notion of confining men for long periods in small spaces, with little in the way of facilities, in order to protect them from infection. More thought should be given to the effect on their physical and mental health.

### TO THE PRISON SERVICE
Difficulties in recruitment have meant that Elmley has been short of staff in this reporting year. The pandemic has further impacted on staffing and highlighted the need to recruit more officers. The situation for prisoners could have been ameliorated to some extent if staffing had allowed more flexibility in managing the bubbles. There need to be incentives to help recruit and retain staff.

The budget for food needs an overhaul. The budget of £2.14 per man per day is inadequate. The contract with DHL needs to be reviewed and reinforced to ensure that the company abides by their contractual obligations.

### TO THE GOVERNOR
The poor management of the unlock list on the house blocks is disrupting education and healthcare appointments as well as work in industries. The number of missed appointments in outpatients wastes the time of staff in healthcare who are already overstretched. Prisoners benefit from being encouraged to engage but they need to be let off the house block and directed to the right resource. The discipline derived from work and education could play an important part in their rehabilitation and resettlement.

There should be greater, more formal analysis of self-harm. The assessment, care in custody and teamwork (ACCT) documents are valuable for recording such events and their possible triggers, but the underlying causes seem never to be identified in their relation to the prison environment, which could be modified.

Prisoners' property getting lost in the system is

a perennial problem. Staff should be encouraged to have more care and respect for property when relocating prisoners, particularly in terms of cell clearance.

**DEVIZES**
**WILTSHIRE**
**SN10 5TU**

**HM PRISON ERLESTOKE**   Tel: 01380 814250

*For the latest reports on this prison please visit:*
https://tinyurl.com/bdfh26rv

*Important Changes:*
**(1) Visits:** the identification necessary to access this prison and visit for social or professional purposes has changed;
**(2) Money and Gifts** new rules now apply to these. See page 16 for full details of the above.

### Task of the establishment
Category C adult males and young offenders.

### Certified normal accommodation and operational capacity
Prisoners held August 2021: 440
Baseline certified normal capacity: 444
In-use certified normal capacity: 436
Operational capacity: 444

### Population of the prison
• 315 new prisoners received each year.
• 20 foreign national prisoners.
• 30% prisoners from BAME backgrounds.
• 14 prisoners released each month.
• The majority of prisoners were serving long sentences of four years or more.
• 33% were serving indeterminate sentences.
• Nearly two-thirds of prisoners were assessed as high/very high risk of harm to others.

### Prison status and key providers
Public
Prison group: South Central
Prison Group Director: Andy Lattimore
Name of governor: Tim Knight
IMB chair: Nicholas Rheinberg
Physical health provider: Hanham Secure Health
Substance and Mental health provider: Avon and Wiltshire Mental Health Partnership NHS Trust
Prison education framework provider:
Milton Keynes College
Escort contractors: Serco; G4S

### Brief history
HMP Erlestoke was built on the former grounds of Erlestoke manor house. The site was taken over by the then Prison Commissioners in 1960 for use as a detention centre. In 1977 it became a young prisoners' centre and was converted to a category C adult male training prison in 1988. Life-sentenced prisoners were first received in the 1990s. Since 2018, it has held closed young offenders and adult category C males.

### Short description of residential units
Alfred – 64-bed unit, 58 single cells and three doubles
Wessex – 66-bed unit, 58 single cells and four doubles
Imber – progression regime, 40 single cells.
Marlborough – drug rehabilitation unit, up to 60 prisoners in 30 double cells.
Sarum – 54-bed enhanced unit, 50 single cells and two double cells.
Silbury A1 – progression regime/social care, 28 single cells and two adapted cells.
Silbury A 2– super enhanced unit, 34 single cells.
Silbury B – first night/induction, 30 double cells and 30 single cells.
Wren – 24-bed super enhanced unit, all single cells.
Care and separation unit – eight cells for segregated prisoners, two orderly cells, one strip cell and one constant supervision cell.

### Visiting Information
You can book your visit online:
https://www.gov.uk/prison-visits
You can book your visit by telephone:0300 303 0634, Monday to Friday, 9:15am to 5pm

**Legal visits:** To book Legal visits please email: LegalVisits.Erlestoke@justice.gov.uk.

### INSPECTIONS & REPORTS
**IRP: 24–26 May 2022**
**Published 05 July 2022**
HMP Erlestoke, built on the former grounds of Erlestoke manor house, became a young prisoners centre in 1970 and was converted to a category C adult male prison in 1988. Since 2018, it has been an adult category C training prison, with many serving long and/or indeterminate sentences.
At our previous inspections of HMP Erlestoke in 2017 and 2021, we made the following judgements about outcomes for prisoners.
Our full inspection in August 2021 followed a scrutiny visit in 2020, at the height of the pandemic, at which we had found a serious deterioration in safety, poor living conditions and a lack of purposeful relationships between staff and prisoners. In 2021, we found little improvement, and, indeed, deterioration in the areas covered by our 'respect' healthy prison test.

Frustration among prisoners was linked to rising levels of violence and of self-harm, as well as to an unduly impoverished regime. Leadership was not strong and many of the staff lacked confidence in the absence of active support from managers.

During this independent review of progress, we examined 13 key recommendations, and our colleagues in Ofsted addressed progress against three themes. There had been a serious attempt to address the growing concerns of our previous two visits, with the result that we found reasonable or good progress against all but two of our key recommendations, while Ofsted assessed progress against all three of their themes as reasonable. In the two areas where progress was judged insufficient, there had been a start on measures to address the deficiencies, but their impact was not yet clear.

The quality of leadership had improved, with some energetic new senior managers, and some new posts had been created, targeted to key priorities such as the up-skilling of new staff, better use of data on matters of safety (both violence and self-harm), and development of equality work.

There had been improvements in work to understand and counter the sources of violence, especially debt, focusing especially on young adults. Self-harm had reduced considerably, and better support was being given to those at risk of it. Scrutiny of use of force had improved, although the shortage of working body-worn cameras was problematic. The segregation unit was beginning to work more positively towards reintegration of its occupants into the wider prison community. Problems with drugs and alcohol remained acute, and this was an area of insufficient progress.

The very mixed living environment had been further improved and was cleaner, including the reception area as well as the less congenial of the residential blocks. The relationships between staff and prisoners, however, had not improved sufficiently. Work and training were going into this, but the inexperience of a number of staff members and a lack of real engagement by some officers were illustrated by tolerance of some low-level rule-breaking behaviour. Equality work was improving from a fairly low base, but some complex issues needed to be grasped. The specific issues about health care appointments, similarly, were being addressed practically, but without yet having solved the capacity issues that caused some delays.

Leaders (see Glossary) had moved fairly quickly to take advantage of the freedoms resulting from the recent lifting of the Covid-19 restrictions, in opening up the regime. Time out of cell (see Glossary), and the numbers in activities, had improved markedly, although there was still some way to go before the ethos of a 'normal' category C training prison could be re-established.

Work with families, especially visits, had been maintained reasonably through the pandemic and was quickly gaining momentum. The offender management unit was another area which had been strengthened recently, through some key probation appointments in particular, and it was commendable that a pattern of monthly contact with every prisoner had been established.

After a few years when Erlestoke had not been moving in the right direction, it was encouraging to see that it was now doing so across most areas. The improvements were in many cases recent, and resulted, in part, from new managers and newly funded roles. There is no reason why these improvements should not become embedded, if the resourcing in key areas and the leadership momentum can be sustained.

Charlie Taylor
HM Chief Inspector of Prisons June 2022

**Date of last HMCIP inspection** 6–27 August 2021
**Report published 7 December 2021**

HMP Erlestoke is a category C training and resettlement prison near Devizes in Wiltshire. Holding just over 440 adult men the prison fulfils an important function with most prisoners serving long sentences of over four years and nearly two- thirds assessed as high or very high risk of harm to others. About a third of the population were serving indeterminate sentences - including 80 prisoners serving life - and the prison also held young adults. Part of the establishment's remit was to provide a national resource for offending behaviour programmes.

The prison itself was a campus-style establishment with different accommodation types set in the grounds of a former country house. The prison held a challenging but generally stable population but had many advantages, not least its clarity of purpose and a group of prisoners who knew they would need to engage fully with their sentence objectives and the regime of the prison if they were to progress. In this context, our findings at Erlestoke were disappointing. When we last inspected in 2017, we assessed outcomes for prisoners as not sufficiently good against our healthy prison tests of safety, purposeful activity and rehabilitation and release planning. Only in the healthy prison area of respect were outcomes reasonably good. Similarly, our findings from a scrutiny visit to the prison a year ago, at the height of the pandemic, were so concerning that my predecessor raised his concerns directly with the Secretary of State. A deterioration in safety, poor living conditions and a lack of purposeful relationships between staff and prisoners were among the serious issues identified. At this inspection we found little improvement, and respect had deteriorated to the extent that it too was now not sufficiently good. The prison had undoubtedly been impacted by Covid-19 outbreaks in addition to the general restrictions imposed by the pandemic, but it was clear that prisoners were becoming increasingly frustrated at what they perceived to be a growing divergence between their experience and the general easing of restrictions in the community. Some restrictions in the prison were applied inconsistently and the prison leadership needed to be more ambitious about the pace for opening up the regime safely - which might have overcome the sense of aimlessness that we observed.

This frustration among prisoners was linked to some concerning outcomes, for example increasing violence and high levels of self-harm. Basic standards were not upheld and opportunities were missed. Examples included: limited reception and induction arrangements and a lack of motivational and rehabilitative culture; both were opportunities that could have been used to encourage and connect constructively with longer-term prisoners. Leaders were not visible, oversight arrangements lacked rigour and priorities were not communicated. Forums for the oversight of operational practice were often poorly attended and the leaders did not use data effectively to inform decision making. In a survey we undertook, staff (many of whom were inexperienced) told us that their well- being was not supported, and that morale was low. A clear agenda aimed at practical steps to build confidence and competence among staff, as well as some supervisors, was needed.

The end of the pandemic offers Erlestoke an opportunity to review and reinvent its approach and culture. Like all prisons it faces challenges, but the establishment also has some advantages. While Erlestoke is not the worst prison we have inspected it should be performing better. With effective leadership and a more engaged staff group, who maintain standards and have higher expectations of prisoners, it could quickly improve.

Charlie Taylor Chief Inspector October 2021

## Summary of key findings

We last inspected Erlestoke in 2017 and made 71 recommendations, five of which were about areas of key concern. The prison fully accepted 57 of the recommendations and partially (or subject to resources) accepted 12. It rejected two of the recommendations.

In August 2020, during the Covid-19 pandemic, we conducted a scrutiny visit at the prison. We made nine recommendations about areas of key concern.

Our last inspection of Erlestoke took place before the Covid-19 pandemic and the recommendations in that report focused on areas of concern affecting outcomes for prisoners at the time. Although we recognise that the challenges of keeping prisoners safe during COVID- 19 will have changed the focus for many prison leaders, we believe that it is important to report on progress in areas of key concern to help leaders to continue to drive improvement.

At our last full inspection, we made two recommendations about key concerns in the area of safety. At this inspection we found that both those recommendations had not been achieved.

We made one recommendation about key concerns in the area of respect. At this inspection we found that this recommendation had been partially achieved.

We made one recommendation about key concerns in the area of purposeful activity. Ofsted carried out a progress monitoring visit alongside our inspection to assess the progress that leaders and managers had made towards reinstating a full education, skills and work curriculum. They judged it was too early to assess whether recommendations made at the last inspection had been achieved.

We made one recommendation about key concerns in the area of rehabilitation and release planning. At this inspection we found that this recommendation had not been achieved.

### Progress on recommendations from the scrutiny visit

During the pandemic we made a scrutiny visit to Erlestoke. Scrutiny visits (SVs) focused on individual establishments and how they were recovering from the challenges of the Covid-19 pandemic. They were shorter than full inspections and looked at key areas based on our existing human rights-based Expectations. For more information on SVs, visit *prisonoracle.com*

As part of this inspection we have followed up those recommendations to help assess the continued necessity and proportionality of measures taken in response to Covid-19, how well the prison is returning to a constructive rehabilitative regime, and to provide transparency about the prison's recovery from Covid-19.

We made nine recommendations about areas of key concern. At this inspection we found that four of the recommendations had been achieved and five had not been achieved.

### Outcomes for prisoners

We assess outcomes for prisoners against four healthy prison tests. We also include a commentary on leadership in the prison.

At this inspection of Erlestoke, we found that outcomes for prisoners had stayed the same in three healthy prison areas and declined in one. These judgements seek to make an objective assessment of the outcomes experienced by those detained and have taken into account the prison's recovery from Covid-19 as well as the 'regime stage' at which the prison was operating, as outlined in the HM Prison and Probation (HMPPS) National Framework for prison regimes and services.

**Safety**

At the last inspection of Erlestoke in 2017 we found that outcomes for prisoners were not sufficiently good against this healthy prison test. At this inspection we found that outcomes for prisoners remained not sufficiently good against this healthy prison test.

Prisoners in our survey reported being treated well in reception, although not all initial assessments took place in private. First night and induction cells were dirty, ill-equipped, graffitied and in a generally poor condition. The regime for new arrivals who isolated in line with COVID- 19 guidance was poor, allowing only 30 minutes a day unlocked. Induction was limited, with a lack of focus on prisoners' progression and rehabilitation.

In our survey, over half of prisoners said they had felt unsafe at some point during their stay and almost a third felt unsafe now, which was much higher than at our previous inspection. Half reported verbal abuse from other prisoners and 45% from staff. Assaults on staff were double the rate for similar prisons and were rising. Prisoner-on-prisoner assaults had increased since May 2021 but were lower than comparable prisons. The safety meetings had too little focus on understanding the causes of violence and lacked a plan to make the prison safer. The challenge, support and intervention plan (CSIP) casework model was not operating effectively and a small number of prisoners self-isolating for their own safety lacked support.

A new incentives scheme had been launched recently, but few staff were able to explain how it worked. The primary incentive for good behaviour was access to better living conditions on the enhanced units. Monitoring of the few prisoners on basic was reasonable, but generic targets undermined the review process. There was insufficient oversight of adjudications and too many were outstanding.

Use of force had increased significantly since 2017, but there was insufficient oversight and accountability concerning its deployment. We were not convinced that it was necessary or proportionate in every case we reviewed. There was insufficient justification for the high use of special accommodation and not all incidents involving the drawing of batons were investigated. Although treatment and living conditions in segregation had improved since our scrutiny visit a year ago, the regime and reintegration planning remained insufficient.

In our survey, almost half of prisoners said that it was easy to get illicit drugs and alcohol and there were frequent medical emergencies caused by psychoactive substances. The reopening of the drug recovery unit was positive, but not enough was being done to tackle the supply of illicit drugs. There had been one self-inflicted death since the last inspection. Recorded levels of self-harm were much higher than most similar prisons. In our survey, only a third of prisoners subject to assessment, care in custody and teamwork (ACCT) case management felt cared for by staff, and there were gaps in the quality of support delivered through the new version of ACCT. Revised case management arrangements had been introduced without any formal, in-person staff training. Listeners (prisoners trained by the Samaritans to provide confidential emotional support to fellow prisoners) had continued to operate throughout the pandemic, but staff did not always grant access to them.

**Respect**

Significantly fewer prisoners than in 2017 said that they were treated respectfully by staff. All too often we saw staff congregated in offices, reluctant to assist with reasonable requests and failing to challenge poor behaviour. The key worker scheme (see Glossary in Appendix II) was not yet operating fully and few staff entries in prisoner electronic case notes recorded any useful contact.

Although most communal areas on the enhanced units were clean and well maintained, those on Alfred, Wessex and Silbury B wings were dirty. The standard of some accommodation had improved since our last visit, but cells on Silbury B were overcrowded and in very poor condition. Few prisoners thought responses to cell bells were prompt, and access to stored property was not good enough.

Cleaning regimes were inconsistent across the prison and some units struggled to obtain necessary materials and equipment. COVID-safe procedures were inadequate. Many areas in the grounds were overgrown and there was a significant rat infestation - we were told that rats frequently entered the residential units.

Meals were still served too early, but the opportunity for prisoners to comment on the food on their weekly meal request sheet was a good initiative. Although prisoners appreciated the self-catering facilities, they were dirty, unhygienic and used inappropriately. Prisoner consultation through the prison council was reasonably good, but outcomes were not promoted widely. In our survey, prisoners were negative about the fairness and timeliness of responses to complaints and applications.

The promotion of equality and diversity remained inadequate and the work had not been sufficiently resourced. In our survey, prisoners from protected groups had some poor perceptions across a range of important outcomes. Many from a racial minority described racist and discriminatory treatment by staff and there was evidence to support these perceptions. The discrimination complaints process was inadequate, there was poor use of data and consultation with protected and minority groups had lapsed. Prisoners appreciated the support offered by the chaplaincy.

Health care provision was reasonably good, but the prison failed to provide enough staff to escort prisoners to appointments, resulting in lost clinical time and many cancelled hospital appointments. All health services had resumed following a significant Covid-19 outbreak between January and April 2021. Clinical staff had good oversight of waiting lists, and prisoners on all wings had access to a health care professional every morning. Social care arrangements were much improved and there was good oversight of a new prisoner 'buddy' scheme to support prisoners with care needs. The well-being team provided an integrated service for prisoners with mental health and substance misuse needs, but there was a lack of clinical psychological interventions.

Medicines management arrangements were generally safe, but there was poor supervision of queues by officers. The management of prisoners with multiple prescriptions for sedating medications created some negativity, but was good practice. The quality of dental services was good, but waiting lists were far too long.

### Purposeful activity

Ofsted carried out a progress monitoring visit of the prison alongside our full inspection and the purposeful activity judgement incorporates their assessment of progress.

Time unlocked for many prisoners remained very limited at around two hours a day on weekdays and just an hour at the weekend. Although those on the enhanced units had up to 10 hours a day unlocked, there was a lack of purposeful activity and association equipment was limited. Around 140 prisoners were allocated to activities, but our checks found just 12% in work or education off the wing and a further 12% working on the wing, for example,

cleaning. The number of peer support workers had reduced.

The library had operated a good mobile service and some reading initiatives during the pandemic, and prisoners now had two indoor gym sessions a week.

The curriculum had been adapted using printed work packs to engage prisoners with in-cell education. Teachers supported the in-cell learning through face-to-face visits to the wing and most prisoners praised the support they received. A very few were also engaged in face-to-face practical learning for accredited qualifications in forklift operating, cleaning and peer mentoring. Prisoners were working in areas such as maintenance, recycling, the kitchen and waste management, but the numbers involved were very low due to the pandemic restrictions.

There were plans to increase activities as the prison moved to stage 2 of the HMPPS recovery plan (see Glossary in Appendix II). However, leaders had been too slow to maximise the opportunities to increase places for face-to-face activities through stage 3, such as those that could take place in large workshops or the open air.

The careers advice and guidance and support in preparation for release was insufficient and too many prisoners were released with little or no support.

### Rehabilitation and release planning

The prison did not do enough to encourage prisoners to maintain contact with their children and families, and family engagement provision was too limited. Take-up of social visits was very low, although the recent easing of some restrictions, such as physical contact during visits, was welcomed. Difficulties with technology, booking slots and limited call times meant that take-up of secure video calls had also been low.

Access to the limited number of communal phones was a source of prisoner frustration, but it was positive that in-cell phones were being installed. The 'email a prisoner' scheme was well used.

The reducing reoffending strategy had been refreshed, informed by an updated needs analysis and was underpinned by a relevant action plan. The offender management unit was, however, under-resourced with too few probation offender managers, others due to leave and several prison officer offender managers who were very new in post. Contact was insufficient to drive positive outcomes for prisoners and focused instead on time-limited tasks, such as preparation of parole reports and recategorisation reviews.

The progression regime, which had been an important support for up to 80 life and indeterminate sentence prisoners, had lost its focus following the recent closure of one unit delivering this work; the remaining unit required substantial investment.

Category D prisoners waited too long to transfer to open conditions. Home detention curfew processes were managed well.

Public protection arrangements were adequate. The release management planning meeting generally considered prisoners in sufficient time before release, and arrangements with community offender managers were managed effectively. The prison's contributions to multi-agency public protection arrangements (MAPPA) meetings in the community were of good quality and on time, and public protection monitoring was managed appropriately.

Delivery of accredited offending behaviour programmes had resumed at the earliest opportunity following their suspension in March 2020. Waiting lists were prioritised appropriately and the level of delivery went beyond the nationally set guidance.

Since our last inspection, Erlestoke had been reconfigured as both a training and resettlement prison. Until recently, a community rehabilitation company had provided good and timely support for all prisoners in preparation for release. However, the unification of the National Probation Service in June 2021 had produced a lack of clarity about the delivery of services and the risk that some prisoners would not have their resettlement needs met during this transition.

### Key concerns and recommendations

Key concerns and recommendations identify the issues of most importance to improving outcomes for prisoners and are designed to help establishments prioritise and address the most significant weaknesses in the treatment and conditions of prisoners.

During this inspection we identified some areas of key concern and have made a small number of recommendations for the prison to address those concerns.

Key concern: The reception area was small with only one functioning holding room and no designated private space, limiting the ability to undertake safety assessments confidentially. First night and induction cells were in poor condition, dirty and ill-equipped. There was a limited induction with a lack of focus on prisoners' progression and rehabilitation. The regime during prisoners' early days was inadequate, with each receiving only 30 minutes a day out of their cell.

Recommendation: Early days arrangements should be reviewed so that all aspects of prisoners' arrival to the establishment are decent, fit for purpose and have a focus on progression and rehabilitation.

Key concern: Over half of respondents in our survey reported feeling unsafe and prisoners who had chosen to self-isolate because they feared other prisoners were unsupported. Violence towards staff was high and increasing, but the prison had no plan to tackle the violence. Poorly attended safer custody meetings did not analyse information effectively or identify actions to improve safety. The management of the perpetrators of violence and support for victims were weak and too many investigations into incidents were incomplete.

Recommendation: The prison should develop a plan to reduce violence with clear criteria for how it will be reduced and by when.

Key concern: The use of force and special accommodation was high.

Staff did not always demonstrate the use of de-escalation techniques and not all incidents involving the drawing of batons were investigated. Too much use of force documentation was missing and scrutiny by leaders was insufficient. We were not convinced that use of force was necessary or proportionate in every case we reviewed.

Recommendation: Use of force and the use of special accommodation should only happen as a last resort. Leaders should develop alternative approaches which will reduce the need for such interventions.

Key concern: The day-to-day regime for prisoners in the segregation unit was poor. Too many prisoners were seeking protection there and wanted a transfer to another prison. Reintegration planning was poor and meetings to monitor the use of segregation were too infrequent.

Recommendation: The segregation unit should provide a safe, decent and purposeful regime that promotes improved behaviour for prisoners held there and their reintegration with the wider prison.

Key concern: Prisoners reported that drugs and alcohol were easily available. There were frequent medical emergencies resulting from the suspected use of psychoactive substances and other unknown substances. Many prisoners said that the availability of drugs made it difficult for them to maintain recovery. Not all staff were confident about the searching procedures for detecting the concealment of contraband items. There was a lack of a whole prison approach to tackling drug supply.

Recommendation: The prison should take robust action to reduce the availability of illicit drugs and alcohol.

Key concern: Recorded levels of self-harm had increased considerably and were significantly higher than most similar prisons. Despite this, leaders had not identified suicide and self-harm prevention as a key priority, and the safety action plan was not shared or reviewed to direct work to reduce self-harm. There were gaps in the quality of support delivered through the new assessment, care in custody and teamwork (ACCT) case management model.

Recommendation: The prison should develop an effective plan to reduce self-harm and deliver consistently good care for at-risk prisoners.

Key concern: Staff interaction with prisoners lacked consistency, leading to insufficient engagement and low behavioural expectations. Prison officers spent much of their time in unit offices rather than supervising and actively engaging with prisoners on the landings. Poor prisoner behaviour often went unchallenged. We saw staff failing to enforce even the most basic of behavioural expectations, such as music volume, the inappropriate use of cooking equipment and dress codes. There was a lack of leadership in supporting staff to develop the confidence to challenge poor behaviour.

Recommendation: Staff should be supported to positively engage with prisoners and where necessary to challenge poor prisoner behaviour.

Key concern: Too many areas of the prison were dirty and unkempt, with too few prisoners actively engaged in keeping the prison clean, a lack of cleaning materials on some units and insufficient managerial oversight of standards.

Recommendation: Basic standards of cleanliness and decency should be set and maintained consistently across the prison.

Key concern: Work to promote equality remained too limited, a concern we had raised in our two previous visits. Protected characteristic and minority prisoners had negative perceptions. Data was not used effectively to identify or address areas of inequality or discriminatory treatment. Prisoners told us of racist behaviour on the part of staff, but this was not always effectively identified or acted on.

Recommendation: The prison should take robust action to promote equality and eliminate discriminatory treatment and racist behaviour.

Key concern: The lack of custody staff to escort patients to the health care department and to external hospital visits had significantly affected the delivery of health services in the prison and had led to the cancellation of 17 out of 38 hospital appointments in the month of our inspection, including two patients who had prepared for surgery.

Recommendation: Health care and hospital appointments should not be cancelled or delayed. Prisoners should be able to attend appointments at the time and date set by health care staff to best meet the prisoners' health needs.

Key concern: Time unlocked for many prisoners remained very limited at around two hours a day on weekdays and just an hour at the weekend. Although those on the enhanced units had up to 10 hours a day unlocked, few prisoners were actively engaged in any purposeful activity for any length of time, fostering a sense of aimlessness across the prison. Leaders had not maximised the opportunities to increase places for such activities through stage 3 of the HMPPS recovery plan, in particular those that could have taken place in the open air or large workshops. On a walk-through of activity places, we found only five prisoners engaged in workshops and four in the whole of the education building, three of whom were cleaners or orderlies.

Recommendation: Leaders should urgently prioritise increasing time unlocked and the number of in person places in education, skills and work activities to enable a larger number of prisoners to attend them.

Key concern: Not enough was done to encourage prisoners to maintain contact with their children and families, and family engagement provision was too limited. Take-up of social visits was very low, and difficulties with technology, booking slots and limited call times had also led to low take-up of secure video calls.

Recommendation: Prisoners should be encouraged to build and maintain positive relationships with their families and friends.

Key concern: The offender management unit was acutely under- resourced with too few probation offender managers, and caseloads were too high. Frequency of contact between both prison and probation offender managers and prisoners was inadequate and did not drive their sentence progression effectively.

Recommendation: Probation offender manager staffing levels should be increased sufficiently to provide manageable caseloads and effective case management of prisoners' sentence planning and progression.

## Notable positive practice

We define notable positive practice as innovative work or practice that leads to particularly good outcomes from which other establishments may be able to learn. Inspectors look for evidence of good outcomes for prisoners; original, creative or particularly effective approaches to problem-solving or achieving the desired goal; and how other establishments could learn from or replicate the practice.

Inspectors found two examples of notable positive practice during this inspection.

Prisoners had the opportunity to comment on food provision and make suggestions on the back of their weekly menu request sheets.

Although not always initially welcomed by some prisoners, and challenging for those initiating the changes, there was comprehensive review, consultation and safer prescribing for prisoners arriving with combinations of sedating medicines.

## INDEPENDENT MONITORING BOARD: Annual Report

The law requires every prison to be monitored by an independent Board appointed by the Justice Secretary; these are known as Independent Monitoring Boards (IMBs). The IMB must satisfy itself as to the humane and just treatment of those held in custody within its prison and the range and adequacy of the programmes preparing them for release; it must report annually to the Justice Secretary on how well the prison has met the standards and requirements placed on it.

**IMB Report 1st April 2020 to 31st March 2021**
**Published 15 October 2021**
**Executive summary**
**Background to the report**

During the early part of lockdown, monitoring was carried out remotely with the result that there was less direct contact with prisoners and staff apart from regular meetings with the Governor. However, by June the segregation unit (CSU) was visited regularly in person by members who were not shielding. A serious outbreak of Covid-19 infection among prisoners curtailed visits to the wings but by the end of the reporting period face-to-face monitoring had been restored. Applications by prisoners were dealt with through correspondence.

### Main judgements
### How safe is the prison?

Ironically with Covid-19 restrictions keeping prisoners in their cells for up to 22 hours a day, many prisoners have felt safer than when there was an open regime. In general terms the Board is satisfied that prisoners at HMP Erlestoke remain relatively safe and has been pleased to note a significant decrease in incidents of violence although self-harm has shown a troubling increase. A survey of prisoners was carried out by the Board at the end of the reporting year. A total of 77 prisoners responded to the survey, a response rate of 18%. 25% of prisoners said that they felt unsafe whilst 75% of prisoners reported feeling safe.

### How fairly and humanely are prisoners treated?

At the beginning of the reporting period the social care needs of a number of elderly and infirm prisoners were neglected.

In early August 2020 conditions in the CSU fell well below acceptable standards of decency. A group of three particularly recalcitrant prisoners caused extensive damage to their cells, smashing their lavatories and washbasins. As a result of ineffectual efforts to repair the damage, prisoners were left without proper sanitation and running water for up to three weeks. However, the Board is satisfied that this particularly unfortunate episode does not characterise normal conditions on the CSU where prisoners are dealt with in a caring and professional way.

For the most part prisoners are treated humanely and senior management have taken steps to ease lockdown restrictions to the best of their ability, enhancing time out of cells in excess of the norm in other prisons.

### How well are prisoners' health and wellbeing needs met?

Healthcare has faced serious challenges during lockdown and is to be particularly congratulated with the way that they managed a very serious outbreak of Covid-19. In general terms healthcare has performed well in difficult times. However, the Board have two concerns. First, a lack of IT capability means that patient safety is being put at risk at reception when newly arrived prisoners receive their healthcare screening and on the wings when nurses attend to patients, in each case through a lack of access to patients' healthcare records (see 6.1.3). Secondly, the Board is troubled by a relatively high turnover of healthcare staff.

### How well are prisoners progressed towards successful resettlement?

With the Covid-induced cessation of programmes, training, education, employment and indeed any purposeful activity, it has been difficult for prisoners to progress their sentence causing understandable anger and frustration. Nevertheless, resettlement planning has seen considerable improvement during the reporting year. However, many prisoners sent to Erlestoke in order to complete courses have effectively been marking time with no course work undertaken.

### Main areas for development
### TO THE MINISTER

For much of the reporting year a prisoner has languished in segregation. The prisoner in question has special needs, probably driven by autism, which means that he has been unwilling to be moved to a normal location. Although he resides in segregation of his own volition, his continued confinement is inhumane and derives from a lack of suitable accommodation within the prison system for prisoners who do not meet the criteria for a hospital order. Will the Minister consider providing more facilities to meet the needs of those within the autistic spectrum, unsuitable for location in a normal prison environment?

As is the case throughout the penal system, there are a number of IPP prisoners, most many years over their original sentence tariff. This has produced a cohort of men who are left without hope and are in danger of becoming institutionalised and dehumanised. Some are suffering from mental illness. What steps are proposed to alleviate this national tragedy?

### TO THE PRISON SERVICE

Two residential units were closed during the year. Plans to replace the units appear to have faltered. Long-term planning for the prison cannot be undertaken until positive decisions are made with a timetable for implementation. When will the units be replaced?

A substantial number of prisoners place very considerable importance on the ability to carry out weight training. The existing weight training gym has been considerably enhanced by the provision of new flooring and new equipment. However, all of this has been put in peril by a leaking roof which urgently requires replacement. Will funds be put in place to achieve this goal?

### TO THE GOVERNOR

This is the second year in which improvements have been noted in the attendance of a healthcare representative at the first ACCT review. However, it is still the case that a healthcare representative is absent in 40% of cases. Will further efforts be made to ensure that firstly, prison staff liaise with healthcare staff to inform them of forthcoming reviews and secondly that better arrangements are made to schedule reviews for healthcare operating hours?

There is currently no clear communication with the IMB regarding prisoners segregated on their own location. Will this be rectified?

Prisoners and staff complain regularly over lack of consistency from management about the application of rules. Will action be taken to address this issue?

Function heads take scant part in diversity and inclusion meetings and monitoring equality and fairness requires a more robust regime with appropriate analysis of trends (see 5.4.1). This is a recurring theme and will action now be taken? The complaints system lacks independence in terms of investigation (see 5.7). What steps do you intend to take to improve this situation?

To the Governor and Avon and Wiltshire Mental Health Partnership Trust: a lack of adequate wi-fi capability and suitable iPads means that patient healthcare records cannot be accessed at reception or on the wings thus putting patients at risk. Will steps be taken to enhance IT capabilities in this regard?

### Progress since the last report

The Board notes with pleasure the reduction in incidences of violence. The Board congratulates healthcare in their management of the Covid-19 outbreak.

The Board congratulates the Listener service for excellent work during difficult times.

The dissemination of quality distraction packs particularly within segregation, where unrest has now considerably diminished, is applauded.

The continued handling of lockdown by the Governor and his management team is acknowledged as are the efforts of physical education instructors maintaining gym sessions and the library and education department.

The prison staff are particularly commended for their work during lockdown. At a time when numbers were significantly reduced through illness and shielding, they kept the prison functioning by working excessively long hours (including on occasion living in the prison). Unvaccinated, they escorted sick prisoners to hospital Covid wards with some thereafter contracting Covid-19 with a near fatal result in one case.

Finally, we are impressed with the patience shown by so many prisoners during an exceptionally long period of restricted regime.

30 NEW NORTH ROAD
EXETER
DEVON
EX4 4EX

Tel: 01392 415650

*For the latest reports on this prison please visit:*
https://tinyurl.com/bdfh26rv

*Important Changes:* **(1) Visits:** the identification necessary to access this prison and visit for social or professional purposes has changed; (2) **Money and Gifts** new rules now apply to these. See page 16 for full details of the above.

### Task of the establishment

Category B adult male local prison serving the south west area courts.

### Certified normal accommodation and operational capacity

Prisoners held at the time of this visit: 432
Baseline certified normal capacity: 326

In-use certified normal capacity: 432
Operational capacity: 432 (reduced temporarily from 531 due to closure of D wing for replacement of fire alarms

## Prison status and key providers
Public
Prison Group: Devon and North Dorset
Prison Group Director: Jeannine Hendrick
Governor/Director: Richard Luscombe
IMB chair: Jenny Ellis
Physical health provider: Practice Plus
Mental health provider:
Devon Partnership NHS Trust
Substance misuse treatment provider:
Practice Plus
Prison education framework provider:
Weston College
Escort contractor: Serco

**Brief history** Built in 1853, HMP Exeter is a Victorian prison of radial design, with three wings positioned around the centre. In the late 20th century, D wing was added and, more recently, education blocks were built. In recent years a refurbished reception, new visits hall and a social care unit (F wing) have been introduced.

## Short description of residential units
A wing holds 194 remand or sentenced and convicted adults and young prisoners. A4 has a constant supervision cell. A1 is the segregation unit.
B wing, the vulnerable prisoner wing, holds 87 remand or sentenced and convicted adults and young prisoners.
C wing holds 189 remand or sentenced and convicted adults and young prisoners. C4 landing houses first night prisoners and prisoners requiring integrated drug treatment and alcohol detoxification.
D wing is currently closed while a new fire alarm system is installed.
F wing, a social care unit, holds 11 prisoners. It contains the Jubilee Suite, a palliative care room for terminally ill prisoners, and a constant supervision cell.

## Visiting Information
Exeter is currently operating a limited visits schedule for family and friends. You can book your visit by telephone.
Booking line: 01392 415 833
The booking line is open: Monday to Friday, 9:30am to 12pm and 1pm to 4:30pm.
**Visiting times:**
Tuesday/Thursday/Friday: 2:15pm to 4:15pm

**Legal visits:** There are currently no legal visits taking place.

## INSPECTIONS & REPORTS
**Date of last Scrutiny visit: 9 & 16–17 March 2021**
**Scrutiny visit, published 27 April 2021**
HMP Exeter is a category B local and resettlement prison which holds prisoners remanded or sentenced by the courts in south west England and those resettling in the region. At the time of this visit, about 430 prisoners were held in the prison.

The last full inspection of Exeter took place in May 2018. On that occasion outcomes for prisoners were so poor in the area of safety that we issued an Urgent Notification to the Secretary of State for Justice. At our subsequent Independent Review of Progress in 2019 we found, despite some progress, that improvement against the majority of key recommendations was 'too little too late'. Since then, further progress has been hampered by high turnover of staff at all levels. At this visit, some key leadership posts had just been filled and one-third of frontline staff had been in post for less than a year.

The governor had a clear vision for the establishment, which was focused on improving staff culture, but significant progress was still needed in order to create a safer, more decent and secure establishment. We found that relationships between prisoners and staff were not good enough and many prisoners were frustrated at the difficulties they faced, for example, when making reasonable requests. In particular, prisoners from a black or minority ethnic background had very poor perceptions of staff.

Notwithstanding these concerns, during the pandemic violence had reduced and use of force was reasonably well managed, which was encouraging. There was evidence that action taken to reduce the supply of illicit substances was beginning to have an impact, but there had been little progress in addressing long-standing deficiencies in the care of prisoners at risk of self-harm or suicide.

Health care provision was reasonable and access to clinics was improving. There were good partnership arrangements which had helped address a recent outbreak of Covid-19. The response to the pandemic was undermined by weaknesses in the cohorting of new prisoners. We found prisoners who should have been kept separate from the main population socialising in other prisoners' cells. Symptomatic prisoners were unable to leave their cell for any reason for a minimum of 10 days.

Time out of cell for most prisoners was limited to about 90 minutes on most days and less on Fridays and at weekends. Work opportunities had been confined to essential roles only and education was being delivered through work packs completed in cells. While some prisoners made good progress, others spoke of difficulties in getting access to teachers or to the resources needed to complete the work.

The offender management unit was well led and had a very small backlog of work. There was very little face-to-face contact with prisoners and prison offender managers relied on telephone calls and contact made through cell doors. Public protection arrangements were good. Prisoners valued the practical support offered immediately before their release.

Despite some progress since our last inspection and during the pandemic, outcomes for prisoners at Exeter still required improvement. All leaders and managers needed to commit fully to the governor's vision for the establishment with the development of staff capability based on good quality relationships with prisoners remaining a priority.

Charlie Taylor
HM Chief Inspector of Prisons March 2021

### Key concerns and recommendations

Key concerns and recommendations identify the issues of most importance to improving outcomes for prisoners and are designed to help establishments prioritise and address the most significant weaknesses in the treatment and conditions of prisoners.

During this visit we identified eight areas of key concern and have made a small number of recommendations for the prison to address.

Key concern: Despite a clear vision for a safe, decent and secure establishment, we found many areas where outcomes needed to improve. Many of these deficiencies were linked to the staff culture we observed and the associated lack of confidence among staff, many of whom were inexperienced. Staff-prisoner relationships were lacking. Some examples of this included unresponsiveness to prisoner requests and enquiries, insufficient care for prisoners at risk of self-harm or suicide and indifference to the needs of prisoners with physical disabilities, one of whom we found located on the fourth landing of a wing.
Recommendation: Leaders and managers should set high standards, model the culture articulated by the governor and support frontline staff to improve relationships with prisoners. Oversight of practice should be improved to ensure the needs of prisoners, particularly the most vulnerable, are met. (To the governor)

Key concern: We found newly arrived prisoners who should have been isolated from the main population socialising in other prisoners' cells. This undermined the purpose of the reverse cohort unit. In addition, arrangements for symptomatic prisoners were not decent, with prisoners unable to leave their cells for at least 10 days.
Recommendation: Leaders should make sure that the reverse cohort unit operates effectively and that prisoners subject to cohorting arrangements have opportunities to leave their cell for a shower and time in the open air. (To the governor)

Key concern: Induction for new prisoners was ineffective and prisoners told us that they did not get the information they required from induction, for example, how to perform day-to-day tasks such as using the electronic kiosks to make applications or complaints. Leaders and staff could not account for how much, if any, of the induction process individual new arrivals had completed.
Recommendation: A comprehensive induction programme should be developed to make sure that prisoners new to custody are given all the information they need in their early days at Exeter. (To the governor)

Key concern: There had been six self-inflicted deaths since our last inspection and several recommendations from the Prisons and Probation Ombudsman about the quality and effectiveness of the ACCT process. During this visit we found that the quality of ACCT documents and their management remained poor and prisoners in at risk of self-harm were not adequately supported. Care maps were superficial with too many outstanding actions. Prisoners were often assessed and supported by staff through locked cell doors and health care professionals did not always contribute to ACCT reviews.
Recommendation: Prisoners in crisis should be supported by an ACCT procedure that is multidisciplinary, thorough, caring and leads to action which addresses the needs of the individual. Leaders should make sure that meaningful supervision and rigorous quality assurance processes embed and sustain progress. (To the governor)

Key concern: Work to promote equality remained weak. Analysis was inadequate which limited the ability to identify potentially disproportionate outcomes for groups of prisoners. There was no systematic consultation with prisoners with protected characteristics. Black and minority ethnic prisoners responded less positively with, for example, only 29% of these prisoners telling us they felt respected by staff but 59% telling us they had felt bullied or victimised by staff. Prisoners from this group said they felt targeted by staff because of their ethnicity. The responses to discrimination incident report forms did not address complaints of discrimination adequately.
Recommendation: The promotion of equality should be given sufficient priority and

improved. Outcomes for prisoners from protected groups should see measurable improvements. (To the governor)

*Key concern:* The secondary health care screening covered a range of key health indicators and was undertaken by questionnaire. This process lacked the monitoring and oversight needed to make sure that all patients completed an assessment and that the health needs of patients were identified.

Recommendation: The Partnership Board should review secondary health care screening procedures to make sure that the health care needs of all patients are identified and that assessments are completed. (To the governor)

*Key concern:* The administration of medication at the cell door was observed to include 'potting up', a practice that is proscribed because it is unsafe and deviates from the required standard.

Recommendation: The Partnership Board should review the practice of administering medication at cell doors to make sure that it is undertaken in the safest possible way and meets professional and good practice standards. (To the governor)

## INDEPENDENT MONITORING BOARD: Annual Report

The law requires every prison to be monitored by an independent Board appointed by the Justice Secretary; these are known as Independent Monitoring Boards (IMBs). The IMB must satisfy itself as to the humane and just treatment of those held in custody within its prison and the range and adequacy of the programmes preparing them for release; it must report annually to the Justice Secretary on how well the prison has met the standards and requirements placed on it.

## IMB Report 1 January 2021 – 31 December 2021
Published 4th May 2022
### Introduction

This report presents the findings of the Independent Monitoring Board (IMB) at HMP Exeter for the year 2021. It is the second annual report produced during the period of Covid-19. All members of the Board returned to direct monitoring in May, but the Covid-19 pandemic has had a significant impact on the Board's ability to undertake its normal monitoring. The Board has, therefore, tried to cover as much ground as it can in these difficult circumstances, but inevitably there is less detail and supporting evidence than usual. Ministers are aware of these constraints.

The Board's report is based on:

• direct monitoring of accommodation, facilities and services

• remote review of documentation, records and data

• external reports: Prisons and Probation Ombudsman (PPO) and Her Majesty's Inspectorate of Prisons (HMIP)

• attendance at some prison meetings

• conversations with prisoners, staff and other agencies

• monitoring of prisoner complaints

• dealing with prisoners' applications to the IMB

### Background to the Report
### IMB monitoring arrangements

Until May 2021 the Board was adopting a hybrid approach to monitoring (see 3.2.2). Arrangements to enable prisoners to contact the Board, via the applications process, were continued from the previous year and Exeter also participated in the 0800 applications phoneline service. However, this was not well used by the prisoners. During the reporting period five new Board members were appointed and inducted.

### Impact of the pandemic

For the entire reporting period the prison has been operating against a background of the pandemic and various levels of an exceptional delivery model (EDM) have been in place. The prison has not yet been able to return to the pre-pandemic 'normal regime'. Although the pandemic has generally been well managed, with plans in place to control Covid-19 and risks managed at regular outbreak control meetings, there have been positive cases among the prisoners and staff. In February 2021 the prison experienced a significant outbreak of Covid-19 when more than 100 prisoners and 70 staff had to isolate. At the time of the HMIP scrutiny visit in March the prison remained an outbreak site. By the end of the reporting year the prison was again declared an outbreak site. However, it is to the credit of the management, staff and prisoners that there were only two limited outbreaks of Covid-19 infection during this time and there was no serious illness or deaths from Covid-19 in the prison population. One impact of this situation is that a number of prison processes and programmes have suffered as a result of the disruption, for example key working (see 5.3.1), challenge, support and intervention plans (CSIPs) and prisoner induction. Additionally, the restricted daily regime came at a cost to prisoners in terms of reduced opportunities to engage in education, work and training, social interaction and other routine activities including exercise and domestics. Our focussed monitoring on the impact of Covid-19 on prisoners at Exeter also suggests that the impact of this is likely to have been particularly severe because most cells are shared by two people, which not only makes them cramped, but limits opportunity for privacy and personal space.

## External inspections

The last full HMIP inspection of Exeter took place in May 2018 resulting in an urgent notification to the Secretary of State for Justice. Following this an independent review of progress was undertaken in 2019 and in March 2021 HMIP undertook a scrutiny visit. The reporting year, therefore, covers a period where the prison was still taking forward a performance improvement plan (PIP) and an action plan arising from the 2018 HMIP inspection report and 2019 independent review of progress. The scrutiny visit identified that progress had been hampered by high turnover of staff at all levels and that 'significant progress was still needed in order to create a safer, more decent and secure establishment' and 'outcomes for prisoners at Exeter still required improvement'.

## Staffing

At the beginning of the reporting period the staff-in-post position, across all officer grades, showed the prison to be fully staffed. However, this masks the staffing challenges faced by the prison again this year. Around one in three officers had been appointed in the previous year. Because of the pandemic these less experienced officers, and the new cohort of officers (POELTs) appointed, have not had the same training opportunities or experienced a normal regime and interactions with prisoners. As the prison has gradually moved through the stages in relaxing restrictions, some less experienced staff have found the transition from lockdown difficult. At times of staffing shortages, Exeter has been able to take advantage of an incentivised Payment Plus (PP) scheme providing opportunities for officers to work extra hours. While this has provided the prison with a short-term solution, it masks the more serious issue of the inability of the prison to retain officers. Job opportunities in other national services (such as the police or railways) appear more attractive and better paid. Additionally, the Board is aware that there have been instances of staff fatigue as a result of shortages and PP, which could have negative consequences for the safe and secure running of the prison. The Board believes that as a profession, prison officers do not always receive the same kind of parity as some other public servants (for example, priority with the Covid-19 vaccine roll-out) and that this often leads to perceptions of being undervalued. A lack of stability within the senior management team (SMT), raised previously by the IMB and also HMIP in 2021, has unfortunately persisted. This is reflected in a series (three) of external and internal temporary appointments or secondments at deputy governor level. A

number of temporary appointments to back-fill key posts within the SMT following resignations or promotions to other establishments has also occurred. The impact of this has slowed progress and disrupted the ability of the prison to take forward improvements in a timely, consistent and sustained manner.

During the reporting period there have also been limits on staff training and professional development. The control and restraint (C&R) qualifications of many officers are overdue and this is of particular concern in an area such as the care and separation unit (CSU).

## Violence and self-harm

There has been a steady increase in the number of violent incidents recorded each month. Variations between months tended to coincide with periods when the regime had either started to open up following some relaxation of Covid-19 restrictions or when prisoner interactions were more limited because of a more tightly restricted regime. In March HMIP reported that prisoners' perceptions of safety were poor.

Incidents of self-harm have varied across the year. They declined gently in the first eight months of the year but increased towards the end of the year to a very high monthly rate of about 70. Data shows that a small number of prolific self-harmers account for a disproportionate number of reported incidents.

## Healthcare

It has been another difficult year for healthcare because staffing problems have coincided with the ongoing need to manage the pandemic, which has exposed some vulnerabilities in the system. Healthcare appointments were restricted to urgent care and medications only, as in the community, although GP appointments were able to continue via telephone calls.

## Prison maintenance

Scheduled maintenance to residential accommodation has meant that for much of the reporting year the prison has operated with a reduced capacity and contractors on site. The refurbishment of D wing suffered a number of delays and eventual handover was significantly overdue and fraught with snagging issues including faults to the fire detection system. Work to the temporary visits hall was delayed, which pushed back demolition of the old hall and work towards the construction of a new visits complex. Towards the end of the reporting period the refurbishment of B wing, which accommodated vulnerable prisoners (VP), and their temporary relocation to A4 created a number of practical challenges for prisoners.

Some of these impacted on their perceptions of safety and opportunities.

### Information technology
The IT infrastructure does not always support effective administrative and operational functioning. The service is slow, often unreliable and a shortage of suitable equipment has limited the scope of communication with the Board during the pandemic. For example, the Board could not attend segregation review boards (SRBs) remotely, via telephone conferencing, because there was insufficient hardware available to facilitate this. Similarly, on only one occasion could a governor report via Zoom at a Board meeting because the prison had only one suitable laptop/iPad. The Board regularly encounters difficulties with the office IT system. There have also been a number of occasions where the CCTV for the prison has suddenly gone down. The Board was surprised to hear that the maintenance contract for this did not provide for, or cover, urgent repairs. This is a worrying situation, which creates unnecessary risks. The potential impact on the safety and security of the prison is obvious.

### Main judgements
### How safe is the prison?
HMP Exeter continues to experience high levels of violence and self-harm. Despite a vision and some strategies to ensure and improve the safety of prisoners there are still some vulnerabilities, at both a managerial and operational level. These can have an adverse impact on outcomes for prisoners. The Board still has concerns about the assessment, care in custody and teamwork (ACCT) and CSIP processes that are designed to keep prisoners safe. Covid has played a part in adversely affecting efforts to improve safety, along with an increasing number of prisoners with mental health issues and a significant number of prisoners with a history of self-harm. A commitment to safety requires a coordinated multi- dimensional approach and is as much about culture and effective relationships as processes. While there is clear evidence that the prison is committed to reducing violence and self-harm and interrupting the supply of illicit items, which are associated with debt, bullying and violence, there is still scope for improvements.

### How fairly and humanely are prisoners treated?
The overcrowded conditions and severely restricted regime resulting from the Covid pandemic has meant that living conditions have not always been humane. Additionally, some issues with clothing and kit have undermined the decency agenda. However, standards of communal cleanliness have improved year on year, which is an achievement in such a challenging environment. Attempts have also been made to brighten up some areas through painting parties.
Staff-prisoner relationships, with the exception of the CSU have unfortunately deteriorated, which has had an impact on how respectfully some prisoners feel they are treated. Written communications with prisoners generally reflect respect and fairness and the regular monitoring of data reveals no evidence that prisoners with protected characteristics are treated unfairly.

### How well are prisoners' health and wellbeing needs met?
Although there were some unwelcome outcomes of the prison's response to Covid, the pandemic was generally well-managed and the prison is to be commended for its success in preventing and managing internally generated infection. Arrangements for medically vulnerable prisoners followed, as far as possible, those in the community. Prisoners eligible for Covid vaccination received this in line with government priorities operating in the community. Challenges posed by the pandemic did have an impact on outcomes for prisoners and were often comparable to those experienced in the wider community. While prison is not an appropriate environment for those with mental health conditions, the restricted regime and limited purposeful activity did not help prisoners' wellbeing or mental health. Emergency care was generally managed effectively and response/waiting times appeared reasonable.

### How well are prisoners progressed towards successful resettlement?
Opportunities for prisoners to make progress towards their resettlement have been limited. This has been the case for those on short-term sentences and those in the resettlement phase of their sentence. While Covid has certainly played a part, maintenance issues and staffing shortages have also had an impact. Although the prison has a vision and plans for improvements in this area, it has still not progressed these sufficiently. Opportunities for prisoners to engage in the kind of experiences and work to support resettlement in the community are inadequate at present.

### Main areas for development
### TO THE MINISTER
Will the Secretary of State:
Exert influence to help the retention of prison officers by recognising the work they do and ensuring parity with other public servant roles. Increase the human and financial resources

required to more effectively support the rehabilitative and resettlement role of local prisons. Intensify efforts to support individuals who are at risk of homelessness on their release from prison and increase the level of expectations on local authorities and the Probation Service to improve accommodation outcomes.

## TO THE PRISON SERVICE
### Will the Prison Service:

As a matter of some urgency support Governors to reduce the backlog in staff training and particularly C&R basic, refresher and advanced training.

Invest in improving systems, processes and expectations associated with the management of prisoners' property. Current arrangements often reflect insufficient care and attention to the management of prisoners' property both internally and on transfer between prisons.

Improve the arrangements for procurement of maintenance work to enable Governors to be more confident in their scheduling of changes having an impact on prisoners and their access to services or amenities.

Invest in an IT infrastructure, hardware and technical support which enables prisons to function more effectively and communicate with stakeholders and others in a more diverse and contemporary way.

Improve the arrangements for external seconded and temporary SMT cover so that there is time for the seconded person to share their expertise, make an impact, and be involved in embedding improvements etc., before they are moved on, which often creates additional turbulence within existing staff roles.

## TO THE GOVERNOR
### Will the Governor:

Review the current arrangements for prisoners' induction (particularly support for young adults) and implement quality assurance systems to make sure that prisoners new to custody are given all the information they need in their early days at Exeter. This should include information on the IMB.

Undertake to improve the effectiveness, management and oversight of CSIPs.

Review systems and processes for the receipt, recording and distribution of prisoners' property to ensure that effective communication with prisoners takes place and that property is treated with respect and distributed in a timely manner.

Review how prisoner complaints are recorded for analytical purposes to ensure consistency of data categorisation.

Prioritise the plans for developments around prisoner progression and the resettlement role of the prison so that progress is made and results in improved outcomes for prisoners in terms of better education, training and workshop opportunities and, thereby, prospects on release. Undertake to improve communication with and feedback opportunities for prisoners.

### Progress since the last report
The Board is pleased to note improvements in the following areas since the last report:

### Safety
Use of force – the appointment of a full-time coordinator and management oversight and quality assurance.

CSU – improvements to the supervision arrangements of the CSU by providing a greater staff presence in the unit office out of hours.

Preventing illicit items – efforts made and initiatives launched to reduce and prevent illicit items entering the prison.

ACCTs – efforts made to ensure reviews are multidisciplinary and attended by appropriate representatives from other services within the prison. Improved procedures are in place for ACCT assurance checks.

### Fair and humane treatment
Cleanliness of communal areas – raised expectations and outcomes for prisoners.

Improvements to accommodation and living conditions for prisoners; for example, wing refurbishment projects (D and B wings) and repainting in communal areas.

### Health and wellbeing
Attendance at segregation review boards – healthcare/mental health staff now routinely attend and contribute to reviews.

The appointment of a custodial discharge coordinator within healthcare ensures that prisoners transferring and being released from Exeter have their health needs properly coordinated and passed on to community services.

### Progression and Resettlement
Purple Visits – increased take up of Purple (video) Visits.

**NEW ROAD
FEATHERSTONE
WOLVERHAMPTON
WV10 7PU**

**HM PRISON
FEATHERSTONE**

**Tel: 01902 703000**

*For the latest reports on this prison please visit:*
https://tinyurl.com/bdfh26rv

*Important Changes:* **(1) Visits:** the identification necessary to access this prison and visit for social or professional purposes has changed; (2) **Money and Gifts** new rules now apply to these. See page 16 for full details of the above.

**Task of the establishment** HMP Featherstone is a category C training and resettlement prison.

**Certified normal accommodation and operational capacity**
Prisoners held at the time of inspection: 607
Baseline certified normal capacity: 622
In-use certified normal capacity: 622
Operational capacity: 637

**Prison status and key providers**
Public
Prison group/Department: West Midlands
Prison Group Director: Teresa Clarke
Governor/Director: Laura Whitehurst
IMB Chair: John Credland
Physical health provider: Care UK
Mental health provider: Inclusion (Midlands Partnership NHS Trust)
Substance misuse provider: Inclusion (Midlands Partnership NHS Trust)
Learning and skills provider: Milton Keynes College
Escort contractor: GeoAmey

**Brief history** HMP Featherstone was opened in November 1976, with house blocks 5, 6 and 7 being added later. It was originally a long-term category C training prison but in 2014 became a designated training and resettlement prison for prisoners returning to Warwickshire and West Mercia.

**Short description of residential units**
House block 1 – General residential, including first night and induction House block 2 - General residential
House block 3 - General residential
House block 4 - General residential
House block 5 - Resettlement
House block 6 - Enhanced
House block 7 - General residential
Care and separation unit

**Visiting Information**
You can book your visit by telephone. There is no online booking service available.
Email: visitsbooking.westmidlands@justice.gov.uk
Booking line: 0300 060 6502
Monday to Friday, 9.15am to 4pm
**Visiting Times:** Tuesday to Thursday: 2pm to 4pm, Saturday and Sunday: 2pm to 4pm

**Legal visits:** There are currently no legal visits taking place.

**INSPECTIONS & REPORTS**
**Date of last inspection:** 1–5 October 2018
**HMCIP Report, published 07 February 2019**
HMP Featherstone is a category C training and resettlement prison near Wolverhampton. Opened in 1976, the prison has seen additional house blocks added over the years and the establishment now holds up to 637 adult male prisoners. The majority of those held were serving more than two years and usually much longer than that, with about 170 men serving over 10 years or life. The prison was last inspected in 2016 when we found very poor outcomes in safety and outcomes which were not sufficiently good in our other three tests of a healthy prison. In contrast, at this inspection we were pleased to find evidence of significant improvement. Across all four tests we found measurable improvements with outcomes in respect, purposeful activity and rehabilitation now all sufficiently good. The prison was still not safe enough but here, too, meaningful improvements were evidenced.
Staff-prisoner relationships reflected this broad improvement and were now good. A largely inexperienced staff group were well supported by supervisors and managers and most prisoners indicated that they felt respected. Residential units were calm and ordered and staff demonstrated the confidence to challenge poor behaviour. Much of the site needed refurbishment but, again, living conditions were better than when we last inspected. Cells were cleaner and properly equipped and there was good access to kit and amenities. Prisoners disliked the food and arrangements to deal with applications and complaints needed to be better, but consultation with prisoners was good. The promotion of equality and diversity was better than we usually see and outcomes for protected groups were reasonable. Health services were similarly reasonably good.
The prison's recent success was underpinned by a much more purposeful regime. Time unlocked was good and daily routines predictable. Only 29 prisoners had not been allocated to activity, and during spot checks we found just 12% of prisoners locked up during the working day. The range of education, training and work had

increased but the prison held a substantial number of prisoners with low-level skills in English and maths and more needed to be done to improve their skills – an issue to which we refer in our main recommendations. Allocation to activity was, however, working well and taking proper account of prisoner need. Teaching, learning and assessment in both education and vocational training were effective, leading to progress for most and high achievement rates. Most prisoners could develop skills and confidence in education, training or work, although the overall work ethic was undermined by frequent late attendance at activity. Our colleagues in Ofsted judged the overall effectiveness of provision as 'good'.

Help for prisoners to maintain their family ties was useful and had been recently enhanced by the recruitment of a Barnardo's family engagement worker. The visits hall was shabby and visits did not always start on time. The strategic management of reducing reoffending needed improvement, a priority in view of the high risk posed by many of those held. A recent analysis of need, for example, was too limited and had yet to influence the reducing reoffending action plan. Despite this, offender supervision was reasonable and the number of prisoners without an up-to-date offender assessment system (OASys) assessment had fallen. Public protection arrangements were sound. A key concern that we identified, and refer to in our main recommendations, was a lack of sufficient accredited offending behaviour work which would otherwise help men to reduce their risk and to progress.

More needed to be done to improve safety in the prison but, again, there was unmistakable evidence of improvement. In our survey about a quarter of respondents suggested to us they still felt unsafe and violence remained high, but it was falling, in recent times quite sharply. A range of initiatives had been put in place to confront violence and its causes and there were some encouraging indications that this work was having an impact. Linked to violence was the ready availability of illicit drugs, certainly one of the key challenges the prison still faced. The response of the prison was impressive with a whole series of active, intelligence-led measures in place to try to combat the problem. There was some early evidence that, like the initiatives to tackle violence, these measures were beginning to have an impact. In our main recommendations we argue that this work to confront drugs and violence must be sustained.

Use of force remained high but supervision and accountability was good. The use of segregation was more limited and not normally imposed for long. The facility itself was run down but the case management and care of those held was good. We considered care for those in crisis to be good

overall. Although there had been a sizable increase in the amount of recorded self-harm, relatively few prisoners accounted for a disproportionate number of incidents. However, since we last inspected, several prisoners had died with one confirmed as having taken his own life.

The key message of this inspection was one of improvement. The prison had come a considerable distance in a relatively brief period of time. Staff were supported to do their job and, despite many having been recruited quite recently, they knew the prisoners well and afforded them meaningful care and support. Energy and initiative were evidenced throughout the prison, being reflected in tangible benefits for those detained and the improved assessments. The governor, managers and the whole staff group should be congratulated for what they were achieving.

Peter Clarke CVO OBE QPM November 2018
HM Chief Inspector of Prisons

## INDEPENDENT MONITORING BOARD: Annual Report

The law requires every prison to be monitored by an independent Board appointed by the Justice Secretary; these are known as Independent Monitoring Boards (IMBs). The IMB must satisfy itself as to the humane and just treatment of those held in custody within its prison and the range and adequacy of the programmes preparing them for release; it must report annually to the Justice Secretary on how well the prison has met the standards and requirements placed on it.

### IMB Report 1 November 2020 – 31 October 2021
### Published 12th April 2022
### Background to the report

This report presents the findings of the Board at HMP Featherstone for the period 1 November 2020 to 31 October 2021. For much of the reporting year the majority of monitoring was conducted using remote monitoring arrangements, although limited direct monitoring was maintained throughout, particularly in regard to segregation. Board members received every assistance from all prison staff in attempting to gain information, but direct access to prisoners was extremely limited and hence had an impact on the evidence collected. As the year progressed more direct monitoring took place, with on-site Board meetings recommencing in June 2021.

Remote monitoring included:

teleconferencing for Board meetings and regional forums

regular telephone rota questioning of staff on the house units and in other departments

the collection of prisoner applications by prison

staff, which were then forwarded to the Board
email correspondence with the prison council
prisoner lead, facilitated by the IMB clerk
weekly telephone conversations with the Governor
participation in the IMB 0800 applications line,
accessed by prisoners from their in-cell telephones.
Despite the difficult operating circumstances
during the pandemic, staff and prisoners alike
rose to the challenges and cooperated well to
ensure that everyone remained safe. The prison
council was instrumental in communication with
prisoners, gaining feedback and securing
compliance with the new regime requirements.
The restricted regime saw reductions in the
number of assessment, care in custody and
teamwork (ACCT) documents, self-harming,
violence levels and use of force, resulting in
prisoners reporting that they felt much safer..

Covid-19 had a significant impact on the Board's
ability to gather information and discuss the
contents of this annual report with prison staff.
The Board has therefore tried to cover as much
ground as possible in these difficult
circumstances, but inevitably there is less detail
and supporting evidence than usual. Ministers
are aware of these constraints. Regular
information is being collected specifically on the
prison's response to the pandemic, and that is
being collated nationally.

The Board is appreciative of the efforts of the
Governor and all the staff for their support and
encouragement in enabling the Board to maintain
its monitoring role during the pandemic.

## Main judgements
### How safe is the prison?

The Board believes, that prisoners are, for the
most part, safe. Throughout the year the
atmosphere within the prison appeared largely
positive, with generally good relationships
between staff and prisoners creating a climate
where individuals could raise concerns. The
prison safer custody team has taken a robust
approach to collecting data, monitoring and
managing situations as they arise, and has
initiated a variety of approaches to address
problem areas. However, the prison population
includes a large number of prisoners convicted of
violent crime, often with links to organised crime
groups, so there remains a concern that there is
often pressure on more vulnerable prisoners to
hold illicit items.

There was a severe spike of psychoactive
substances (PS) use this year and the production of
'hooch' presented constant problems. The prison
tackled the issues head on and is to be commended
on the strategy used to reduce drug issues.

### How fairly and humanely are prisoners treated?

The Board feels that generally prisoners are fairly
and humanely treated. Prison officers have been
observed to behave with respect, good humour
and care, even under the most difficult of
circumstances. In particular, the care and
separation unit (CSU) faced challenges,
managing several prisoners with difficult mental
health issues. The Board observed the positive
effects these efforts have produced on the
wellbeing of these prisoners. Staff do not always
have specialist mental health training, but have
done their best and should be congratulated on
their patience and perseverance.

Despite the work done improving the fabric of
the buildings their condition is still poor. Many
cells are dark, with shoddy windows and a
heating system that is not fit for purpose. Even
before lockdown, although there are dining
facilities, most prisoners ate in their meals in
cells, close to the toilet. Substantial improvement
is urgently required to bring the accommodation
up to a decent standard.

### How well are prisoners' health and wellbeing needs met?

The provision of medical services is generally
well managed and consistent with provision in
the community. The issues arising from Covid-19
placed additional pressures on the provision of all
services, which were generally well coped with.

Throughout the reporting year the waiting list
for the dentist has been excessive and at times,
due to lack of staff, no practical provision has
been provided. Continual promises of
improvement are made, but this has been an
ongoing problem for some years.

The transfer of the pharmacy contract from
Lloyds to PPG provoked serious disruptions to
the provision of healthcare. Prisoners were
delayed in getting medication, additional drug
stocks had to be kept in the prison, staff were
seconded to the pharmacy and a data breach
occurred. There has now been an improvement,
but the prison has been fortunate not to
experience more serious outcomes.

As previously reported, the system for booking
appointments is outdated and improvements
need to be made.

### How well are prisoners progressed towards successful resettlement?

Due to the pandemic, education provision has
been extremely limited. Additionally, staffing
issues have meant that opportunities for
progression by this route have been extremely
limited. Progress has been made in preparing the
system for reopening.

Opportunities for work were also limited during

the year. Where possible, work opportunities were arranged to allow activity to be available to the maximum number of prisoners.

Resettlement provision is a cause for concern. There appears to be a lack of cohesion between different providers and prisoners are being released without bank accounts or accommodation.

### Main areas for development
### TO THE MINISTER

Featherstone was built in the 1970s and despite some improvements this shows in much of the accommodation, with showers, windows and heating which are not up to contemporary standards. We understand that the Ministry is aware of this, but consideration of improving the physical environment should urgently be made.

### TO THE PRISON SERVICE

This year again saw the transfer of another major contract (pharmacy) which caused significant issues in the supply of adequate services to prisoners. This follows on from the previous transfer of contracts, e.g. education and maintenance, which initially resulted in substandard provision for prisoners. In the light of these initial failures, the procurement process must be questioned.

The monitoring of incoming prisoners has seen significant finds of prisoners arriving with drugs, which were found on scanning, as well as some examples of positive tests for Covid-19 Why are prisons allowed to export their problems in this way?

Prisoners property, particularly on transfer, remains a significant issue for the Board. How will the prison service put systems in place to resolve these issues.

### TO THE GOVERNOR

The provision of healthcare services has generally been good this year, and management have been responsive to the IMB. However there have been a number of issues with healthcare which will require continued monitoring by the prison, i.e. the dental contract, which has continuously underperformed; the provision of medication; the operation of the complaints system; and attendance at segregation reviews and use of force incidents.

Shortly after appointment, the Governor recognised that there were some problems with the culture of some staff and took steps to improve it. More than a year on, our applications indicate that some of these problems may remain and vigilance will need to be maintained to ensure issues are addressed.

BEDFONT ROAD
FELTHAM
MIDDLESEX
TW13 4ND

HMYOI
FELTHAM    Tel: 020 8844 5000

*For the latest reports on this prison please visit:*
https://tinyurl.com/bdfh26rv

*Important Changes:* **(1) Visits:** the identification necessary to access this prison and visit for social or professional purposes has changed; (2) **Money and Gifts** new rules now apply to these. See page 16 for full details of the above.

### Feltham A
**Task of the establishment** Feltham A manages children on remand and those who have been convicted by the courts.

### Certified normal accommodation and operational capacity
Children held at the time of inspection: 75
Baseline certified normal capacity: 240
In-use certified normal capacity: 168
Operational capacity: 120

### Population of the establishment
• 206 children received in a year
• 20% foreign national children
• 75% of prisoners from black and minority ethnic backgrounds • Three children released into the community each month
• Seven children transferred to the adult estate each month

### Prison status and key providers
Public
Prison Group: Youth Custody Service
Prison Group Director: Helga Swidenbank
Governor/Director: Natasha Wilson
IMB Chair: Maggie Thurer
Physical health provider: Central and North-west London NHS Foundation Trust (CNWL)
Mental health provider: CNWL
Substance misuse treatment provider: CNWL
Prison education framework provider: Prospects
Escort contractor: Serco

**Brief history** The original Feltham was built in 1854 as an industrial school and was taken over in 1910 by the Prison Commissioners as their second Borstal institution. The existing building opened as a remand centre in March 1988.
The current HM Prison and Young Offender Institution Feltham was formed by the amalgamation of Ashford Remand Centre and Feltham Borstal in 1990/1991.

**Short description of residential units**
Alpine: Enhanced support unit (ESU)
Bittern: Currently closed for installation of shower pods
Curlew: Induction and reverse cohort unit (RCU)
Dunlin: Platinum community
Eagle: Normal location
Falcon: Reintegration unit
Heron: Normal location
Jay: Normal location
Grebe: Closed

**Visiting Information**
**How to book family and friends visits**
HMP Feltham is currently operating a limited visits schedule for family and friends. You can book your visit by telephone. There is no online booking service available.
Booking line: 020 8844 5000
The booking line is open: Monday to Sunday 8am to 11:30am and 1pm to 4:30pm
**Visiting times for Feltham A (15 to 18 year olds):**
Monday: 2:00pm to 3:00pm, 3:30pm to 4:30pm
Tuesday: 2:00pm to 3:00pm, 3:30pm to 4:30pm
Wednesday: 2:00pm to 3:00pm, 3:30pm to 4:30pm
Thursday: 2:00pm to 3:00pm, 3:30pm to 4:30pm

**Legal visits:** There are currently no legal visits taking place.

**INSPECTIONS & REPORTS**
**HMCIP Report 21 February – 4 March 2022**
**Published 14 June 2022**
Our inspection of Feltham A in 2019 revealed "a dramatic and precipitous collapse in standards". The prison had become so violent and chaotic that my predecessor decided to invoke the urgent notification (UN) process – the first time it had been used in a children's prison.
At both of our scrutiny visits in July 2020 and February 2021 we saw signs of improvement, but the transformation we found at our most recent inspection was impressive. Much credit must go to the excellent work of the governor, who remained in post after the UN and had created a strong team around her with a renewed sense of purpose and vision. As a result, the prison was safer, happier and more productive, with a more confident staff team able to meet the often complex needs and address the behaviour of what was, at times, a challenging group of children.
We saw good functional leadership in a number of areas, including education, resettlement, and safety – where we saw some of the biggest improvements. A notable success lay in the development of Alpine unit, which held children considered unable to mix with the general population due to their behaviour and level of need. A well-trained and motivated team created a supportive and inclusive culture that aimed to get the boys out of their cells and mixing with their peers in a therapeutic environment. As a result, children who in the past would have spent much of their time languishing in segregation were being given bespoke support and, where possible, helped to reintegrate back onto their wing or to make a successful transfer to adult prison.
Our reports frequently comment on the lack of motivation prisoners have toward the incentives and earned privileges (IEP) scheme, in which sanctions are harsh and desultory rewards are often not forthcoming. At Feltham, the IEP were some of the best I have seen; good behaviour was noted and rewarded while poor behaviour was usually addressed quickly. Every child I spoke to was aware of the opportunities offered in the Dunlin enhanced unit if they earned a place. Here, they got more time out of their cells and a chance to join activities such as the Duke of Edinburgh scheme, army cadets or the barbering workshop. The aim was to make this provision more widely available as the constraints from the pandemic were lifted.
The number of children on 'keep apart' lists – aimed to prevent particular children from mixing – had reduced and was lower than we had seen elsewhere. This was impressive, given that the population was largely London based and some were gang affiliated, thereby increasing the risk that conflict in the community would spill over into the prison.
Attendance in education stood at an impressive 96%, having improved noticeably since last time. It was disappointing, however, to see that children were put in lessons that did not differentiate them by ability, resulting in work being either too easy or too difficult.
The last day of our inspection coincided with the governor's last day in post, and she left for another prison having made very good progress. There remains, however, much to do at Feltham to complete the recovery from Covid-19, recruit and retain sufficient staff, improve the quality of education and continue to bear down on levels of violence which remain too high.
Even when things are going well, because of the nature of the children it serves, Feltham is a fragile place and close attention and support from the Youth Custody Service (YCS) will be essential to make sure that the transition from one leader to the next is a success.
Charlie Taylor
HM Chief Inspector of Prisons April 2022

**Safety**
At the last inspection of HMYOI Feltham in 2019, we found that outcomes for children were poor against this healthy establishment test.

At this inspection we found that outcomes for children were now reasonably good.

The reception process was swift and children's perceptions of how they were searched and treated on arrival had improved. Reverse cohort arrangements were reasonably good but all children, including those who tested negative for Covid-19, had to isolate for 10 days. Cells on the induction unit were well prepared and welfare checks for newly arrived children were frequent and detailed.

There were strong links with the local authority, safeguarding referrals were completed in a timely manner and were well investigated by social workers who referred cases to the local authority designated officer (DO) where appropriate. During the night visit we observed evidence of poor practice that needed to be addressed.

Levels of self-harm had fallen by approximately 80% and there was good assurance of processes to keep children safe. Leaders discussed relevant data at the safety meetings and were aware of incidents and rates of self-harm. Children who had been at risk of self-harm felt well supported and cared for by staff.

Children's perceptions of safety were similar to those at the previous inspection. Levels of violence, however, although still too high, had reduced considerably since our last inspection and were now similar to comparable establishments. Violence reduction and anti-bullying processes were effective and well embedded. These were underpinned by regular core support meetings which generated actions to help staff manage children's behaviour. The enhanced support unit provided good care and support for children with the most complex needs, which was good practice. The conflict resolution team was proactive and had been effective in reducing the number of children who could not mix with their peers.

Most low-level poor behaviour and play fighting was challenged effectively by staff who used immediate rewards and sanctions appropriately. Children liked the benefits of both gold and platinum regimes which were motivational and promoted good behaviour.

Levels of force used by staff had also reduced greatly and were now comparable with similar prisons. In our survey, 52% of children said that they had been restrained compared with 74% at our previous inspection. Governance of use of force was generally good.

The number of children separated had reduced considerably since our last inspection and only one child was held on Falcon unit. Most children who needed to be separated received a tailored regime and were reintegrated within 72 hours. Children were no longer routinely separated on the wings.

**Care**

At the last inspection of HMYOI Feltham in 2019, we found that outcomes for children were poor against this healthy establishment test.

At this inspection we found that outcomes for children were now reasonably good.

Relationships between staff and children had improved considerably since our last inspection. Our observations of interactions between children and staff were positive. Case formulations and regular core support meetings helped residential staff to understand the needs of the children in their care. Most frontline staff were knowledgeable about children on their unit and we saw staff adapting their practice to meet their needs.

Most communal areas and cells were clean and tidy, although some cells still had graffiti on furniture and badly stained toilets. Children benefited from improvements including in-cell telephones and laptops. In-cell showers had been installed on two units, but not all children could access a shower every day. Access to property required improvement. Children had justifiably poor perceptions of the complaints process.

The food was reasonably good and it was positive that children could sometimes eat together. Meals were served at the children's door when they were eating in their cell, which was poor practice.

Equality meetings did not identify or monitor disproportionality. Focus groups had not been taking place and leaders were not aware of the needs of children with protected characteristics. Investigations into discrimination complaints were poor and responses to children required improvement. Children felt supported by chaplains but could only attend communal worship once every eight weeks, which was poor. Governance arrangements were good, although prison representatives did not attend the local delivery board and, therefore, did not have effective oversight of services. CNWL had continued to monitor their own performance indicators and maintained their governance processes. The use of laptops had led to an increase in appointments for the sexual health clinic, which was positive. A rich skill mix of professionals worked collaboratively to provide good support to children with their mental health and substance misuse needs. The framework for integrated care was well embedded and provided a centre-wide approach in supporting children to feel safe and improve their emotional health and self-esteem. Pharmacy provision had improved, and medicines were administered safely. The carrying of medicines around the wings at 6pm was not good practice.

## Purposeful activity

At the last inspection of HMYOI Feltham in 2019, we found that outcomes for children were poor against this healthy establishment test.

At this inspection we found that outcomes for children were now not sufficiently good.

Leaders were continually aiming to improve time out of cell for children, but progress had been hindered by the pandemic and staff shortages. The average time out of cell for during February 2022 was 5.5 hours, but this ranged from 1.5 hours for those who were in isolation to up to nine hours for some children. The introduction of evening activity was good and there were plans to extend this. Children had good access to the gym, but library provision was poor.

Leaders had put an education curriculum in place that enabled children to make progress in the skills they needed for employment and to overcome their barriers to learning. Most children received at least their statutory entitlement to face-to-face education. Attendance had improved and was high, but too few children attended education full time. Leaders did not ensure that there was enough learning in subjects other than English and mathematics at level 2 or higher. Education staff contributed to children's induction, but managers did not allocate children to education pathways that reflected their aspirations and career goals.

The quality of education had improved since the previous inspection, but the quality of teaching and assessment was still inconsistent. Most learners developed knowledge in GCSE English and mathematics courses and a good proportion of children achieved grade four or above. The ICT curriculum was very limited and vocational training options were available for only a small proportion of children.

Most children produced work of an acceptable standard. Children developed good practical skills in vocational programmes. Teachers' feedback varied in its usefulness and, too often, children did not act on it. Too many teachers did not check children's understanding fully in class. Teachers identified children's learning support needs and special educational needs promptly. However, too many teachers did not adopt strategies in their teaching to support these children. Children did not receive enough careers advice and guidance.

## Resettlement

At the last inspection of HMYOI Feltham in 2019, we found that outcomes for children were not sufficiently good against this healthy establishment test.

At this inspection we found that outcomes for children were now reasonably good.

Children were much more positive about being helped to keep in touch with their families and friends than at the previous inspection. The introduction of in-cell telephones and laptops and the support from a family therapist and Spurgeons workers all contributed to improvements in enabling children to have regular contact with their families. Visits provision was too limited and underused.

Reducing reoffending work was informed by an up-to-date needs analysis and received reasonable oversight at regular meetings. Attention had been given to the increasing numbers of children with, or facing, long and indeterminate sentences and work to support them was developing well. Transitions to adult prisons were started in good time. Managers had been proactive in identifying how, subject to a risk assessment, restricted status children could be given information about the prison they would transition to. The monthly risk management meetings gave suitable oversight to public protection work.

Resettlement practitioners (RPs) had impressive knowledge of their own and colleagues' cases and children had good levels of contact with them. Most children we interviewed had a positive view of Feltham A and their RP. Regular reviews informed children's remand and sentence plans which were generally good and age appropriate. Restrictions imposed during the pandemic had reduced the number of face-to-face meetings children had with community agencies involved in their care which had been replaced by virtual meetings or conference calls. Release on temporary licence (ROTL) processes were thorough but fewer children were accessing ROTL than at the last inspection.

Over the previous year, 52 children had completed an accredited intervention and the first group intervention since the pandemic started had recently been completed. Children participated in other intervention work delivered by several teams which addressed the factors that had led to their custody.

Social services were involved in the care of most children and had good support from the on-site social work team. This often involved making sure that children received statutory entitlements from their local authority.

During the previous six months, all children had had a confirmed accommodation placement more than 10 days before their release. However, only 19% had had a confirmed education or training place on release.

## Key concerns and recommendations

Key concerns and recommendations identify the issues of most importance to improving outcomes for children and are designed to help establishments prioritise and address the most significant weaknesses in the treatment and conditions of children.

During this inspection we identified some areas of key concern and have made a small number of recommendations for the establishment to address those.

Key concern: Important safety procedures such as the protocol for entering a cell in an emergency overnight and calling an ambulance were not known by some staff who only worked nights. A cell door was left unsecured and was set up with a television and chair. This had occurred before the handover to night staff who did not have ready access to a cell key.

Key recommendation: Staff should adhere to policies which make sure that children are properly safeguarded during the night. (To the governor)

Key concern: Equality work was underdeveloped. In particular, data was not used effectively to identify and address any unequal treatment.

Key recommendation. Leaders and managers should monitor data in order to identify and address any unequal treatment. (To the governor)

Key concern: Children lacked confidence in prison procedures to redress perceived injustice. Discrimination incident report forms and complaints were not thoroughly investigated and responses were inadequate and often late. Quality assurance of DIRFs and complaints did not improve outcomes.

Key recommendation: Complaints and DIRFs should be thoroughly investigated and children should be routinely interviewed as part of the investigation. (To the governor)

Key concern: Children did not spend enough time out of their cell and plans to increase it could not be realised with the current staffing shortfalls.

Key recommendation: Children should have 10 hours a day out of their cell. (To the governor)

Key concern: Leaders and managers had not yet improved the quality of education sufficiently. Teaching and assessment practices were of inconsistent quality which adversely affected the progress children made in education. Too many teachers did not adapt their teaching to reflect known support strategies for children with special educational needs.

Key recommendation: Leaders and managers should continue to identify the weaknesses in teaching and assessment practices. They should ensure that staff development activities are targeted to improving the quality of individual teachers, and that they monitor closely the impact of these activities on improving teachers' skills so that more children, including those with special educational needs, make more rapid progress in developing their skills and knowledge. (To the governor)

Key concern: Not all children had enough time scheduled during the core day in education activities and too few children could access vocational training.

Key recommendation: Leaders should increase the time children are timetabled to spend in education and should make sure that the timetable enables more children to access vocational training. (To the governor)

Key concern: Poor ICT infrastructure was adversely affecting the experience of children in education. Children were not able to develop essential ICT skills or achieve appropriate qualifications in this subject.

Key recommendation: Leaders should urgently improve the technical resources available in education. They should ensure that the curriculum enables children to develop the essential ICT skills they need to succeed in their lives and careers, and that children are able to achieve appropriate qualifications in this subject. (To the governor)

Key concern: Children did not receive ongoing careers advice and guidance. They were not aware of how to reach their career goals and did not have any opportunities to raise their aspirations through the curriculum offered or the activities to which they were allocated.

Key recommendation: Leaders and managers should make sure that children receive careers advice and guidance during their custody at the prison. All children should be allocated to activities relevant to their career goals and should have more access to employers. Leaders should make sure that ROTL is used appropriately and that children explore the full extent of the careers available to them. (To the governor)

Key concern: Too many children were leaving custody with no confirmed education or training placement.

Key recommendation: Leaders should implement robust systems to make sure that children are supported in securing recognised educational and training placements when transitioning from custody to the community. (To the governor)

**Notable positive practice**

We define notable positive practice as innovative work or practice that leads to particularly good outcomes from which other establishments may be able to learn. Inspectors look for evidence of good outcomes for children; original, creative or particularly effective approaches to problem-solving or achieving the desired goal; and how other establishments could learn from or replicate the practice.

Inspectors found eight examples of notable

273

positive practice during this inspection.

Safeguarding procedures were very good. Complaints by children were referred to the on-site team of local authority social workers within 24 hours. Concerns were escalated appropriately to the local authority designated officer (DO), again within 24 hours. The social workers worked closely with prison staff and the DO attended the prison regularly.

The four-tier rewards and sanctions scheme was well embedded and encouraged good behaviour in children. Staff and children liked the system of immediate rewards and sanctions. These incentive schemes were complemented by staff challenging low-level poor behaviour and setting appropriate standards and boundaries for children.

Weekly core support meetings enabled a wide range of departments, including resettlement, education, psychology and residential staff, to share information and understand children's needs. These meetings focused on the factors influencing a child's negative behaviour and underpinned all behaviour management processes. Alpine unit (the enhanced support unit) provided excellent support for children with the most complex needs, and the levels of care shown by staff were impressive. This provision ensured children who would otherwise be separated received a full programme of activities from unit staff education, healthcare and psychology. The success of Alpine meant other units were disrupted less often and staff had more time to meet the needs of the children in their care.

All children were referred to the dentist on arrival for a dental assessment.

Leaders had developed a scheduling system which gave each child an individual weekly timetable and allowed departments to schedule time with a child that did not affect education or other key activities.

A lifer and long-term sentences meeting attended by departments across the establishment was an innovative approach which focused on the needs of the increasing proportion of the population facing lengthy periods in custody.

**Scrutiny visit: 9 and 17 February 2021**
**Scrutiny visit, published 23 March 2021**

HMYOI Feltham A is an establishment in West London that holds children aged 15 to 18. It is jointly managed with an adjacent establishment, Feltham B, which holds young adults.

At the time of our last full inspection of Feltham A in July 2019, outcomes for children had declined dramatically and we considered them to be poor, our lowest judgement, in three of our four tests of a healthy establishment. This decline was so acute that my predecessor invoked the

Urgent Notification (UN) process for the first time in an establishment holding children.

The Covid-19 pandemic emerged eight months later, and managers had to implement restrictions to keep staff and children safe. At this visit we found that these restrictions had been implemented appropriately and despite a significant outbreak of Covid-19 among staff, the establishment had experienced very few cases among children.

Since our last inspection, progress had been made and, remarkably in the middle of a pandemic, outcomes in some areas had improved. Children were split into groups of four in which they accessed education and other activities. We found that being in small groups had improved the quality of relationships between children and staff, with more children than at the previous inspection reporting feeling cared for or being encouraged to attend education. Self-harm had reduced dramatically with only five incidents recorded in the previous six months compared to 242 in the same period before our previous inspection. The number of violent incidents had also fallen, although one in five children felt unsafe at the time of our visit and there was a concerning rise in multi-perpetrator assaults as friction between different groups increased. The enhanced support unit had been relaunched and there was a positive ethos enabling children to spend more time out of cell, including for education and interventions, than they could have on other units.

Health services were generally good with very few waiting lists for clinics. The dental service was particularly proactive and had established itself as an urgent care centre. This ensured that children could access treatment in the early stages of the pandemic.

Time out of cell had also improved since our last inspection. On average children received about 4.5 hours a day during the week and 3.5 hours during the weekend. This included face-to-face education which had been consistently delivered since June 2020. Attendance at education had improved dramatically but punctuality remained a problem.

There were some areas where progress was not as good. Support for children to maintain contact with family and friends needed improvement to make sure video and in-person visits were accessed by all children who wanted them. Oversight of equality and diversity was also underdeveloped and many children did not feel involved in their sentence or remand plan.

While the improvement made at Feltham A is commendable, some of this reflects how bad things had been at the time of the Urgent Notification. Headway has been made with a far smaller

population than usual and the challenge for local and national leaders is to consolidate and build on this progress as the population increases.
Charlie Taylor, HM Chief Inspector of Prisons
February 2021

Key concerns and recommendations
Key concerns and recommendations identify the issues of most importance to improving outcomes for children and are designed to help establishments prioritise and address the most significant weaknesses in the treatment and conditions of children.

During this visit we identified some areas of key concern and have made a small number of recommendations for the establishment to address.

Key concern: The consistency of welfare checks on children was variable and there was little evidence that they were being carried out every day. Staff were unsure of where responsibility lay for carrying out welfare checks or the required frequency.

Recommendation: Leaders and managers should ensure that welfare checks are conducted and recorded each day for every child and that staff are aware of their responsibility to do so. (To the governor)

Key concern: Serious incident warning signs during restraint incidents were not routinely referred to the local authority designated officer.

Recommendation: Leaders and managers should ensure that all child protection concerns are promptly referred to the local authority designated officer. (To the governor)

Key concern: The increase in group assaults was concerning and contributed to the continuing high levels of use of force.

Recommendation: Leaders should investigate the rise in group assaults and put measures in place to prevent them. (To the governor)

Key concern: Resources had been allocated to improve equality work but there was no clear plan for improvement. Some monitoring of treatment and access to services by protected characteristic groups took place but there was no evidence of action taken to investigate or address discrepancies.

Recommendation: The approach to promoting equality should be underpinned by systematic monitoring and analysis of outcomes for children in each protected characteristic group and action should be taken when there is evidence of unequal treatment. (To the governor)

Key concern: Video call visits were underused which was a missed opportunity to support children to maintain contact with their family and friends.

Recommendation: Children and their families should be actively supported to make full use of the options available for video calls and visits. (To the governor)

Key concern: While attendance at education had improved, punctuality required improvement.

Recommendation: Children should arrive at education classes on time.

Key concern: Too few children attended their review meetings with youth offending teams, social workers and other community professionals. This undermined the usefulness of these meetings, leaving some children unaware of their targets in custody and not contributing to plans for their future.

Recommendation: The reasons for children not attending their review meetings should be identified and addressed so that children are familiar with their targets and contribute to their future plans. (To the governor)

## INDEPENDENT MONITORING BOARD: Annual Report

The law requires every prison to be monitored by an independent Board appointed by the Justice Secretary; these are known as Independent Monitoring Boards (IMBs). The IMB must satisfy itself as to the humane and just treatment of those held in custody within its prison and the range and adequacy of the programmes preparing them for release; it must report annually to the Justice Secretary on how well the prison has met the standards and requirements placed on it.

**IMB Report 1 September 2020 – 31 August 2021**
**Published January 2022**
**Executive summary**
**Background to the report**
This report presents the findings of the Board at HMP & YOI Feltham for the period of 1 September 2020 to 31 August 2021.

Evidence comes from a range of sources including observations made on visits, the scrutiny of records and data, attendance at prison meetings, informal contact with prisoners and staff and communication with prisoners following applications made to the Board. The Covid pandemic has continued to affect the Board's monitoring practices, and as a consequence fewer in person visits were made in the past year than previously. The Board continued a hybrid approach, monitoring remotely when necessary and attending the prison when appropriate.

As has been the case over the past three years, the Board continues to adapt its monitoring to reflect that Feltham A and Feltham B essentially operate as two discrete establishments. While there is a single management structure that oversees both Feltham A and Feltham B, the regime and many of the rules and operating procedures are unique to each. Throughout the report, the term "young people" has been used to refer to prisoners on Feltham A who are between 15 and 18 years old. The term "young adult" has been used to refer to prisoners between 18 and 21 years old on Feltham B. Where comments refer to both Feltham A and Feltham B the term "prisoners" is used. Where appropriate, this report has differentiated the Board's findings for Feltham A and Feltham B. Given the distinct nature of Feltham A and Feltham B, these findings are not intended to be compared.

The Board remains grateful for the helpful cooperation of so many prison staff at all levels within the establishment and wishes to commend them for their continued dedication and commitment in caring for some of the most complex, difficult and vulnerable young men in the country. The challenge of doing so was evident before the onset of the Covid pandemic, and the prison staff's flexibility and resilience in doing so during an extremely unpredictable period continues to be noted by the Board.

Finally, it should be noted again that the Covid outbreak has continued to have a significant impact on the Board's ability to gather information and discuss the contents of this annual report. The Board has therefore tried to cover as much ground as it can in these difficult circumstances, but inevitably there is less detail and supporting evidence than usual. Ministers are aware of these constraints. Regular information is being collected specifically on the prison's response to the pandemic and is being collated nationally.

**Main judgements**
**How safe is the establishment?**
The social distancing restrictions put in place in response to Covid have continued to make Feltham a safer establishment for prisoners and staff. Mixing in small bubbles has made prisoners feel safer and enabled staff to manage risk more effectively.

However, given the complex nature of the population at Feltham, the risk of violence remains and the degree to which prisoners feel safe varies given their individual circumstances.

**How fairly and humanely are prisoners treated?**
Prisoners are treated fairly and humanely by staff. However, the built environment has a negative impact on prisoners' living conditions and access to purposeful activity. Attendance on training programmes is severely limited by the state of disrepair of the workshops. The restrictions put in place due to Covid continued to place limits on the amount of time prisoners spent outside their rooms, although this improved significantly over the course of the reporting period.

**How well are prisoner's health and wellbeing needs met?**
Prisoners' physical health and general wellbeing needs are met well. However, the prison is not equipped to provide for prisoners with serious mental health issues. Transfers to settings where appropriate care can be provided for prisoners with serious mental health needs are difficult to arrange and often delayed.

**How effective is the education provision for prisoners?**
Many prisoners at Feltham present with a range of challenges that create barriers to their educational attainment. The education provision on Feltham A is provided by Prospects Ltd. And, while there have been improvements to attendance and delivery, there is room for improvement in educational outcomes. The education provision on Feltham B is provided by Novus, and there continued to be gaps in provision across the reporting year.

**How well are prisoners progressed towards transfer or successful resettlement?**
Young people on Feltham A have benefited from the improvements to the regime that led to the lifting of the urgent notification status. Young people cannot be released without a package of care, support and accommodation. Those who are due for transfer to the adult estate can suffer delays due to appropriate places not being available.

Most young adults on Feltham B are not adequately progressed towards successful transfer or resettlement. Despite being designated as a category C training prison in 2015, the financial support was not provided to ensure adequate infrastructure and opportunities for every young adult. With the significant physical deterioration of the workshop buildings and Covid restrictions further limiting access, the situation has become even more acute over the reporting period.

In addition, resettlement arrangements are often not confirmed until immediately before a prisoner's release. This is unsettling for all involved, most especially for the prisoners, but also for the prison staff who were often doing everything within their power but were reliant on partner organisations to progress arrangements. The Board recognises that preparation for release involves a range of outside agencies, including local authorities and the probation service, and effective joint working is critical in preparing young adults for their transition and ensuring their safety once released. As the Board is specifically charged with "satisfying itself as to the adequacy of programmes preparing prisoners for release" this remains an area of significant concern.

## Main areas for development
### TO THE MINISTER
The built environment at Feltham has a direct and deleterious effect on prisoners' lived experience. Is the current system for maintaining the prison estate and procuring refurbishment and general building work time efficient and cost effective? What is being done to ensure this? Is it current government policy to provide a rehabilitative regime in prisons? If so, will additional funding be made available to enable every young adult to receive a full regime of education, training and employment? Young prisoners returning to the community need a coordinated approach to resettlement that integrates training, employment, and accommodation, as well as social and financial support. What will you put in place to achieve this?

### TO THE YOUTH CUSTODY SERVICE / HMPPS
It was noted that during 2020-21, significant funding was made available to undertake necessary building works at Feltham, but various protracted delays beyond the control of the prison meant work did not commence within the relevant budget period, and that as a result these much-needed works could now be at risk. Will HMPPS ensure that funds will be rolled forward to enhance the built environment for the benefit of the young people and young adults at Feltham? How will the reorganisation that brings community rehabilitation companies (CRCs) back into the probation service support effective joint working across prisons, probation, and local authorities to better support young offenders upon their release? How do you feel the current provision of rehabilitation within Feltham affects the reoffending rate?

### TO THE GOVERNOR
Will the prison develop a reliable daily time out of room reporting mechanism for young adults on Feltham B which is as robust as that in place for young people on Feltham A?
Following the lifting of the urgent notification and the easing of Covid restrictions, the roll on Feltham A is expected to rise. What mechanisms are in place to ensure that the reduction in violence seen over the past two years is maintained?
Similarly, as the regime opens up and the roll increases on Feltham B, how will the young adults' feeling of increased safety from mixing in smaller groups be maintained?

## Progress since the last report
### Feltham A
The most important progress made during the reporting year was the improvements that led to the lifting of the urgent notification in June 2021. The Board would like to commend the Governor and her senior management team who, together with the staff across Feltham A, have worked tirelessly to improve the care and support provided to the young people in their custody.

### Feltham B
The planned refurbishments across residential and workshop facilities on Feltham B have not progressed as expected. Some delays were inevitable due to continuing Covid restrictions, but most were due to procurement processes and delays by the facilities provider over which Feltham staff had little or no control. The Board received regular updates from the Governor and senior management team on the progress of these projects over the course of the year and commends them for their perseverance in their ongoing efforts to ensure these improvements are eventually completed for the benefit of the young adults on Feltham B.

### Feltham B – young adults
*For the latest reports on this prison please visit:*
https://tinyurl.com/bdfh26rv

*Important Changes:* **(1) Visits:** the identification necessary to access this prison and visit for social or professional purposes has changed; (2) **Money and Gifts** new rules now apply to these. See page 16 for full details of the above.

**Task of the establishment** Feltham B accommodates 18–20-year-old convicted prisoners.

### Certified normal accommodation and operational capacity
Prisoners held at the time of inspection: 361
Baseline certified normal capacity: 529
In-use certified normal capacity: 388
Operational capacity: 388

### Prison status and key providers
Public
Prison Group: Youth Custody Service
Prison Group Director: Helga Swidenbank
Governor/Director: Natasha Wilson
IMB Chair: Caroline Langton
Physical health provider: Care UK
Mental health provider: Barnet, Enfield and Haringey Mental Health Trust
Substance use treatment provider: Addaction
Learning and skills provider: Novus
Escort contractor: Serco

**Brief history** The original Feltham was built in The original Feltham was built in 1854 as an industrial school and was taken over in 1910 by the prison commissioners as their second borstal institution. The existing building opened as a remand centre in March 1988. The current HMYOI Feltham was formed by the amalgamation. The establishment is split into Feltham A, which holds children and young people (aged 15–18), and Feltham B, which holds young adults (aged 18–21); this report relates to Feltham B.

**Short description of residential units**
Kingfisher – induction unit, 52 beds
Lapwing – closed, 48 beds
Mallard – normal location, 56 beds
Nightingale – normal location, 56 beds
Osprey – closed, 56 beds
Partridge – normal location, 56 beds
Quail – normal location, 56 beds
Raven – normal location, 56 beds
Swallow – normal location, 55 beds
Teal – closed, 38 beds
Ibis – segregation unit

**Visiting Information**
How to book family and friends visits
HMP Feltham is currently operating a limited visits schedule for family and friends. You can book your visit by telephone. There is no online booking service available.
Booking line: 020 8844 5000
The booking line is open: Monday to Sunday 8am to 11:30am and 1pm to 4:30pm

**Visiting times for Feltham B (18 to 21 year olds):**
Monday: 2:00pm to 3:00pm & 3:30pm to 4:30pm
Wednesday: 2:00pm to 3:00pm & 3:30pm to 4:30pm
Saturday: 9:00am to 10:00am, 10:30 to 11:30am, 2:00pm to 3:00pm, & 3:30pm to 4:30pm
Sunday: 2:00pm to 3:00pm & 3:30pm to 4:30pm

**HMCIP Report, published 30 October 2019**
HMYOI Feltham B holds convicted male prisoners aged between 18 and 20. It is situated adjacent to and comes under the same management as Feltham A, which hold boys aged between 15 and 17. At the time of this inspection the prison held around 360 prisoners. The prison was last inspected in January and February 2017, when we found that outcomes for prisoners in three of our healthy prison tests – safety, purposeful activity and rehabilitation and release planning – were not sufficiently good. We judged respect to be reasonably good. On this occasion we found there had been improvements in safety and rehabilitation and release planning which were now reasonably good, but a decline

in purposeful activity which was now poor. Despite this latter judgement, overall the results of this inspection mark a significant achievement for an establishment that has faced similar pressures to many others that have not been able to maintain, let alone improve, their overall level of performance in recent times.

It is also worth reflecting on the context in which this inspection took place. As a result of concerns that had been reaching HMI Prisons about conditions at Feltham, but in particular Feltham A, I decided to bring forward the scheduled inspections of both Feltham A and B and to conduct concurrent inspections of both parts of the overall establishment. The outcome of the Feltham A inspection is the subject of a separate report.

Having expressed concerns elsewhere that Feltham had been left without a governor for some five months during 2018, I am reassured to be told that the two parts of the establishment will, in future, each have their own dedicated deputy governor in an effort to ensure greater resilience and continuity. I hope that this will allow Feltham B to continue to make progress, and avoid the risk of managerial focus being diverted to address the many problems we found during the inspection of Feltham A. The progress that had been made to date at Feltham B was creditable, and was reflected in the fact that in the space of some two years, it had managed to achieve or partially achieve around half of our recommendations from the last inspection. This was a better rate of achievement than we often see.

In terms of safety, there were distinct weaknesses in the strategic management of violence, the use of disciplinary procedures through the incentives and earned privileges (IEP) scheme and oversight of the use of force. However, the weaknesses were, to some extent, ameliorated by good relationships between staff and prisoners and, compared with other similar establishments, fewer prisoners felt unsafe at the time of the inspection and fewer reported being victimised. There had been a slight rise since the last inspection in violence between prisoners, but against staff it had reduced significantly.

A feature of the establishment that needed attention was the impact that security processes were having on the ability of prisoners to access education, training, work and health care. It was telling that our colleagues from Ofsted commented that 'across the prison, managers did not do enough to ensure that all aspects of the prison regime contributed to prisoners' good attendance and punctuality'. Quite apart from whether prisoners were getting to the activities to which they had been allocated, there was also the issue that there were only sufficient full-time activity places for just over half of the population. Meanwhile, some 20% of the entire population were employed as residential unit cleaners and painters, where they were under-occupied and poorly managed. We also found, when we conducted our roll checks, that some 37% of prisoners were locked in their cells during the working day, which is far too high a figure for a training prison. Inevitably, the judgement we came to for purposeful activity was that it was poor, and the section of this report that sets out the findings in this area is worthy of close attention. Despite the weaknesses in purposeful activity, we found that respect had improved, supported by the good relationships between staff and prisoners. In particular, the keyworker scheme was making a positive contribution. Living conditions in the residential units had improved since the last inspection,

but the condition of cells was no more than adequate, there was still too much graffiti, and there was still a pressing need for refurbishment in some areas, particularly the showers.

Although the quality of health care services was generally good prisoners, as noted above, were all too often unable to get to their appointments because of regime restrictions or security measures. For instance, in June prisoners failed to attend 58% of the appointments made with the doctor, around 35% with the dentist and 80% with the optician. This was clearly an unacceptable waste of NHS resources.

It was pleasing to see that the well led and well-organised Offender Management Unit had reduced the backlog of Offender Assessment System (OASys) initial assessments from 56% to 19% in the space of six months. This was a significant achievement, and in marked contrast to what we see in many establishments. Nevertheless, all prisoners should arrive at Feltham with a completed assessment, and most did not. This was indicative of a systemic weakness that we frequently see during inspections, and clearly needs to be addressed as the OASys sits at the heart of offender management processes.

Feltham B is a complex and challenging establishment in which to achieve the outcomes that should be of real benefit to prisoners and public alike. It was reassuring that some real progress had been made since our last inspection. Clearly there was still much to do, but we were heartened by the positive attitude of many staff about what could be achieved, and the sound relationships between many staff and prisoners that underpinned much of the progress that had already been made. We have seen in the past that progress at this complex establishment has proved to be fragile. I hope that on this occasion it will prove possible to build on what

has been achieved and sustain it into the future.
Peter Clarke CVO OBE QPM September 2019
HM Chief Inspector of Prisons

**IMB Report, see Feltham A above**

**301 DODDINGTON ROAD WELLINGBOROUGH NN8 2NX**

**FIVE WELLS PRISON**    Tel: 01933 718888

*For the latest reports on this prison please visit:*
https://tinyurl.com/bdfh26rv

*Important Changes:* **(1) Visits:** the identification necessary to access this prison and visit for social or professional purposes has changed; (2) **Money and Gifts** new rules now apply to these. See page 16 for full details of the above.

HMP Five Wells, Britain's biggest prison, opened in February 2022 and will be fully open by October; its Director is Lynne Hardy.
The privately-owned jail has been built with revolutionary X-shaped wings, instead of the typical K shape.

*How many inmates does it hold?*
The prison is set to hold 1,680 inmates and is run by security firm G4S who won the contract back in October 2020.

*How much did it cost to build?*
It has cost around £253,000,000 to build. It was constructed on the site of the old HM Prison Wellingborough; demolished in 2019.

*What kind of prisoners does it hold?*
The category C jail is seen as a flagship example of the Government's aim to create a "modern, efficient prison estate that is fit for the future" and has a clear focus on rehabilitating offenders. As a Category C prison it will not hold the most dangerous prisoners.

*How has Northamptonshire reacted to the new mega prison?*
Britain's biggest ever prison has proven to be devisive among locals. Some believe that more needs to be done to keep offenders off the street, and a prison like this is the perfect image of justice, deterrence and rehabilitation for the county.
It's also created at least 700 jobs in the local area. Others believe that the £253,000,000 spent could have been better used to combat the root causes of crime, like poverty and inequality.
Back in April 2021, protestors blocked delivery

vehicles carrying construction materials to the prison, objecting to the privatisation and monetisation of the prison system.

Certified Normal Capacity: 1680
Operational Capacity: 1680
Prison Group Director: Neil Richards
Director: Lynne Hardy (c)/John McLaughlin
Number of wings: 28 communities over 7 houseblocks
Health provider: Practice Plus Group
Adult Learning provider: Weston College

Task of the prison: Category C Resettlement male establishment catering for residents from 18 years old.

### Visiting Information
HMP Five Wells is offering visits for family and friends. Visiting times and availability may change at short notice. You should contact the prison direct for any queries.

### Vision & Values
Our vision for HMP Five Wells is to be the standard bearer of the existing resettlement estate and the new prisons yet to be built. Residents will experience a safe, decent and secure environment centred on rehabilitation from day one.
Our approach is one of self-determination and normalisation; giving Residents as much control as possible over their own lives, whilst providing a normalised environment that reflects life outside of the establishment, in order to prepare Residents for successful resettlement. We will take a 'Whole Prison' approach to achieve this aim, which means every aspect of the regime will be focused on supporting successful resettlement. Drawing from our experience across our custodial estate, we created a bespoke set of values for HMP Five Wells, which are based on the principles of rehabilitative culture. These will be embedded in all our operations, will help us in decision-making and will clarify to all what HMP Five Wells stands for.
They are as follows:

### EMPOWERING LEADERSHIP
The Director and their team will take decisions and actions focused on consistently modelling and encouraging rehabilitative behaviours and attitudes.

### MEANINGFUL RELATIONSHIPS
Building and maintaining positive relationships between residents, staff, families and partners.

### BUILDING HOPE
Engendering hope amongst the population to enable successful change and helping those in our care prepare for successful resettlement.

### FAIR PROCESS
Promoting compliant and progressive behaviour through the opportunity to be heard and the delivery of fair and transparent processes. Peer Led Initiatives will be at the heart of Five Wells and Resident Led Roles such as that of Gym Support Staff, Teaching Assistants and others will allow for real life work experience with meaningful qualifications.

### NORMALISED ENVIRONMENT
Normalising the physical and personal environment, meaning that the Establishment is organised in such a way that the conditions within the walls resemble the conditions outside including that of Resident Mobile Devices.

### ENABLING POSITIVE CHANGE
Supporting Residents in taking the next successful step in their life, by encouraging and rewarding participation in rehabilitation and resettlement activities including increased ROTL opportunities.

### REFLECTING THE CORE G4S VALUES
Acting with integrity and respect, being passionate about safety, security and service excellence, and achieving this through innovation and teamwork

### Daily Life
We received our first Residents in early February 2022 and they can expect to be located on one of 28 small communities each with their own identity. They include but are not limited to Incentivised Substance Free Living, Older Residents, Motivation and Engagement and "Decompression Units" targeted at those at the end of very long sentences.
All residents can expect to have access to resettlement support delivered in a variety of methods such as peer led, group sessions, 121s and self-directed through their Resident Mobile Devices. Wider resettlement will be supported by our partner Change, Grow, Live and social prescription will be delivered by Voluntary Impact Northamptonshire who in turn call upon a directory of local services. Amongst our other partners, HALOW will support our Children, Families and Relationship provision and Residents will be able to maintain ties with loved ones through a variety of methods.
Across our vast workshop area, Residents will be able to work in an environment that mirrors the community all of which will be supported by meaningful qualifications. Examples include that of our radio and media suite, mechanics shop

and engineering workshop to name a few. All jobs are also linked with employers who will support both ROTL opportunities and employment post release.

For anyone hoping to be transferred to HMP Five Wells, they can contact us via their local OCA teams or by writing to us at our address.

**ARUNDEL**
**WEST SUSSEX**
**BN18 0BX**

**HM PRISON FORD**      **Tel: 01903 663000**

*For the latest reports on this prison please visit:*
https://tinyurl.com/bdfh26rv

*Important Changes:* **(1) Visits:** the identification necessary to access this prison and visit for social or professional purposes has changed; (2) **Money and Gifts** new rules now apply to these. See page 16 for full details of the above.

**Task of the establishment** HMP Ford is a category D adult male prison.

**Certified normal accommodation and operational capacity**
Prisoners held at the time of this visit: 418
Baseline certified normal capacity: 448
In-use certified normal capacity: 448
Operational capacity: 448

**Prison status and key providers**
Public
Prison Group: Kent, Surrey & Sussex
Prison Group Director: James Lucas
Governor/Director: Graham Spencer
IMB Chair: Ken Porter
Physical health provider: Practice Plus Group
Mental health provider: Practice Plus Group
Substance misuse treatment provider: Practice Plus Group
Prison education framework providers: Weston College, Chichester College Group, Chichester College Ford Campus School of Construction
Escort contractor: Serco

**Brief history** Formerly a Royal Navy Fleet Air Arm station, HMP Ford converted to an open prison in 1960 with an emphasis on the resettlement of prisoners into the community.

**Short description of residential units** A mixture of ex-military billets, mainly with shared rooms, single room prefabricated pods and brick-built accommodation blocks.

'A' block comprised brick-built accommodation with 11 landings of single rooms. 'B' block comprised 22 billet huts with mainly shared rooms. The billet huts were in use for much of the period of restrictions, but the recent condemnation of 'B' block saw the replacement of many billets with temporary modular units (pods). At the time of the visit, 10 billet huts and 40 modular units were in full use in addition to the 214 single rooms on 'A' block.

**Visiting Information**
You can book your visit online:
https://www.gov.uk/prison-visits
You can book your visit by telephone: 01903 663120. The booking line is open Monday-Saturday, 10am to 11am and 1pm to 3pm
**Visiting times:** Wednesday: 6pm to 8pm, Friday to Sunday: 2pm to 4pm

**Legal visits:** There are currently no legal visits taking place.

**INSPECTIONS & REPORTS**
**Scrutiny visit 29–30 March and 13–14 April 2021**
**Scrutiny visit, published 19 May 2021**
HMP Ford is a category D open prison near Arundel in West Sussex. At the time of our scrutiny visit, the prison held 418 prisoners, having reduced numbers following the closure of some old billet accommodation.

Like all prisons, Ford had been operating on a restricted regime for most of the last year due to the Covid-19 pandemic. This had a significant impact on the many prisoners who had worked hard to progress to open conditions, only for further potential progress to be frustrated by a national ban on temporary release. Prisoners who had expected to be working in the community and rebuilding family ties on resettlement licence instead found themselves, literally, confined to barracks. Less than a third of prisoners had accessed any purposeful activity for most of the last year and, even though the prison was now in stage three of the national recovery plan (see Glossary of terms), too many were still unemployed or under-employed.

The prison had not experienced an outbreak of Covid-19 and very few prisoners or staff had tested positive for the virus in the last year. However, there was the potential for a virus to spread rapidly due to some poor hygiene and cohorting practices.

Published data and our experience during the visit demonstrated that Ford remained a safe prison. Despite this, some leaders and staff had developed a narrative that suggested it was more violent and volatile than the statistics indicated. Some also expressed low expectations of prisoners, even though they were category D. Ford had one of the highest rates of return to closed conditions in the open estate, which supported the view of many prisoners who said the threat of recategorisation was used unfairly to control their behaviour and sometimes deterred them from speaking out about issues affecting them. All of this was contributing to a culture that felt far from rehabilitative.

While we acknowledge the inherent limitations of the old and worn accommodation at Ford, this did not excuse the poor cleanliness and shabby conditions we found. It was clear that there had been little oversight of standards in the residential accommodation. It was unacceptable that, during a pandemic, access to laundry facilities and the provision of soap was so poor. We saw prisoners cleaning their underwear and dishes in buckets in shared toilet areas, which we would not expect to see in a modern prison service, let alone in an open prison that should be promoting and supporting independent living skills.

The prison had recently moved to stage three of the national plan for recovery and was working to ease the previous restrictions. Despite this, at the time of our visit, there were few prisoners in education, vocational training or community placements, which indicated weaknesses in the planning for recovery. Release on temporary licence had started to ramp up, but ultimately there were too many unemployed and unoccupied prisoners who were bored, demotivated and unable to progress in the way they had expected.

Leaders asserted that their focus over the last year had been to keep people safe from the virus. This was clearly very important, but should not have been to the exclusion of progressing other priorities. Leaders at Ford were not faced with some of the challenges that the restrictions had presented in closed conditions; prisoners were grateful for their place in an open site and were mostly compliant, yet progress in some important areas had been slow. For example, although our previous reports had highlighted major weaknesses in the strategy to improve equality and diversity, work to improve this had only recently commenced.

There were several examples of promising work to help prisoners. Good family support work was greatly valued and some prisoners were now able to see their families on temporary release into the community. We also identified notable positive practice in the appointment of peer mentors who supported fathers at Ford. There were many examples of active work by some prison offender managers to support prisoners through their sentence.

This was a disappointing visit and we urge leaders at national and local levels to address the concerns we have highlighted with urgency. The first challenge is to assess the extent to which the problems have been caused by the pandemic and how much they are specific to the culture of the prison. The former will, we hope, be resolved as restrictions are lifted, but the latter will require more focused leadership and support from HM Prison and Probation Service to make sure that Ford fulfils its rehabilitative purpose in the future.
Charlie Taylor, HM Chief Inspector of Prisons
May 2021

### Key concerns and recommendations

Key concerns and recommendations identify the issues of most importance to improving outcomes for prisoners and are designed to help establishments prioritise and address the most significant weaknesses in the treatment and conditions of prisoners.

We last visited Ford for a short scrutiny visit in June 2020. During this scrutiny visit we identified some areas of key concern, and have made a small number of recommendations for the prison to address.

Key concern: Prisoners said some staff and managers were distant and not supportive of their efforts to progress. We found that some staff had low expectations of prisoners and were negative about them. Leaders did not have a good understanding of safety data and a narrative had developed that presented the prison as being more unsafe than the evidence indicated. Prisoners said they were under constant threat of a return to closed conditions and the data showed a high level of recategorisation. These factors had led to a negative rather than a rehabilitative culture, not one that encouraged and promoted success.

Recommendation: Leaders should accurately analyse and interpret the safety data to develop an accurate understanding of what is happening in their prison. Leaders should look to develop a culture among staff that is focused on the prison's rehabilitative purpose and which encourages, supports and shows confidence in prisoners' capacity to succeed. (To the governor)

Key concern: Nearly all living accommodation and communal areas were poorly maintained and lacked investment. Many prisoners still lived in overcrowded rooms. Some showers and toilets were in poor condition. Some of the small kitchen areas lacked running water, which led to prisoners cleaning their utensils in the same buckets used to wash clothing (see below).

Recommendation: The standard of accommodation should be upgraded to provide all prisoners with decent living conditions. (To HMPPS)

Key concern: A lack of oversight, supervision and quality assurance on residential units had resulted in poor cleanliness and hygiene. Prisoners could not access adequate cleaning materials; soap dispensers were often empty; laundry facilities were inadequate and prisoners could only wash their personal clothing on a monthly rota, with some having to wait up to six weeks. Prisoners resorted to washing their clothes in buckets.

Recommendation: Prisoners should have access to adequate cleaning materials and washing facilities. (To the governor)

Key concern: Prisoner consultation meetings were often cancelled or curtailed and identified actions were not always addressed. This undermined prisoner confidence in the process and compounded a view that communication with leaders was poor.

Recommendation: Prisoner consultation should be regular, provide sufficient time to discuss issues and clearly demonstrate progress against identified actions. Outcomes should be clearly communicated to all prisoners. (To the governor)

Key concern: Staff attendance at the strategic diversity and inclusion meeting was poor. There was little effective analysis of the data presented and identified actions were not progressed with rigour. The revised diversity strategy lacked detail to support the prison's vision of improving equality work. Recently introduced meetings to support prisoners with protected characteristics lacked structure and clarity of purpose.

Recommendation: The strategy to promote equality and diversity should be clear, coordinated and supported by all departments. It should incorporate effective data analysis, consultation and actions to eradicate discrimination and improve outcomes for prisoners from all protected groups. (To the governor)

Key concern: The community rehabilitation company (CRC) had continued to operate remotely throughout the pandemic, using a written questionnaire to identify prisoners' resettlement needs. This led to delays in providing support and a poor understanding by prisoners of the work being done to assist them. In our survey, only 36% of prisoners who expected to be released in the next three months said that anybody was helping them to prepare for this.

Recommendation: All prisoners should be able to engage in meaningful discussion with the relevant staff about their resettlement needs and be kept informed of progress to make sure that they are fully prepared for release into the community. (To the governor)

## INDEPENDENT MONITORING BOARD: Annual Report

The law requires every prison to be monitored by an independent Board appointed by the Justice Secretary; these are known as Independent Monitoring Boards (IMBs). The IMB must satisfy itself as to the humane and just treatment of those held in custody within its prison and the range and adequacy of the programmes preparing them for release; it must report annually to the Justice Secretary on how well the prison has met the standards and requirements placed on it.

### IMB Report 1st Nov 2020 to 31st Oct 2021
### Published April 2022
### Summary
### Background to the report

This report covers the 12-month period ending 31 October 2021 and tracks improvement and deterioration from year to year. This is not a one-off snapshot assessment of the prison.

Due to Covid-19, the Board started the year with only four members attending in person and this reduced to just two by December. However, all members participated in remote monitoring and the prison staff were helpful in facilitating this. Numbers visiting the prison to monitor in person steadily increased from March and by July all members were attending regularly. During regime restrictions most of the face to face monitoring was done by attending the Governor's and the offenders' consultative committee's (OCC's) regular forums. Remote monitoring included access to all on-site reports, telephone calls to departmental staff, review of the daily operational reports and oversight of minutes and similar documentation. Applications to see the IMB continued to be held face to face unless the issues could be resolved remotely.

### Main judgements
### How safe is the prison?

The Board believes the prison to be fundamentally safe. It is pleasing to note that, in spite of the frustrations and boredom of regime restrictions, the violence statistics in section 4 were well down on the previous year.

### How fairly and humanely are prisoners treated?

The regime at HMP Ford is generally both fair and humane and the Board believes that when genuine grievances arise they are consistently well resolved.

During the year the Governor and his team have worked hard to ensure that racial bias forms no part in the treatment of different ethnicities. This is not always reflected in the perceptions of the prisoners but when we investigated, for instance, claims that white prisoners were unfairly favoured for outside paid work the statistics did not bear this out. This is a marked improvement on the position last year. See section 5.4.

### How well are prisoners' health and wellbeing needs met?
Healthcare is well run and provides a good service to the prisoners. The Board was however concerned to note that the protocol agreed in 2019 concerning the treatment of prisoners' long-term medical conditions had not been followed in the case of a prisoner who died in 2020.

The Board congratulates the prison management and staff on the care taken to protect the prisoners from Covid. Section 6 includes further details on this.

### How well are prisoners progressed towards successful resettlement?
Good work to recover from the first set of restrictions was beginning at the start of the year, but was shortly thereafter set back by the second set of restrictions. Since those were lifted, good progress has been made in obtaining outside paid work for prisoners.

### Main areas for development
### TO THE MINISTER
It is a pity that after many years of submissions by the senior management and criticism in our last 13 annual reports, your predecessors appeared to have no plan in place for the replacement of the wooden billets on B wing when they were finally condemned following a fire inspection in November 2020. This failure to plan ahead meant that there was no structured strategy for a gradual closure and rebuild of the huts and the operating capacity of the prison had to be drastically reduced. The subsequent panic measure of trying to put two prisoners in the new pods which were designed for one was an elementary mistake and, though they were then returned to single use, by the reporting year end there still appeared to be no urgency in getting the two-tier bunks restored to single beds. Meanwhile, prisoners could not sit on their beds as there was not enough headroom in either the top or bottom bunks to allow this.

We would also draw to your attention the lack of planning for the replacement of kitchen equipment or washing machines. In the latter case we understand that, since the end of the reporting year, a leasing scheme is being planned for washing machines. However the current arrangement of putting in annual bids for funding for kitchen equipment is slow, bureaucratic and does not provide any guarantee that these essential items will be replaced in a timely manner.

The doubling of the capacity of the prison in the current year will require close monitoring to avoid further expensive mistakes.

### TO THE PRISON SERVICE
As mentioned above, we are delighted that at last the wooden accommodation billets have been condemned and are emptied. However we fail to understand why action was not taken earlier in view of the complaints made over many years. The subsequent attempt to turn the pods into double accommodation was completely unrealistic and in the opinion of the Board would undoubtedly have led to serious accidents. The policy was reversed promptly by the prison but four months later, at the end of the reporting year, the bunks had not been converted back to single beds and the occupants were left in uncomfortable and unsuitable conditions. In the Board's view the whole exercise was a complete waste of public funds.

We are concerned about the very limited importance given to IT training for the prisoners. It is now a requirement of most jobs and the reasons for not allowing a controlled access to wifi on the premises are somewhat negated by the prisoners who go out on ROTL to work or education being allowed mobiles when outside the prison.

Although we were assured last year that HMPPS was looking to increase the number of ethnic minority staff in its workforce, the proportion at HMP Ford remains totally different from that in its prisoner community. We appreciate the difficulty, given the racial balance in the local community, but we have seen little sign of any proactive moves on the part of the Prison Service to redress the balance.

Property remains an issue. Prisoners frequently arrive at HMP Ford having had to leave some of their property at their previous prison due to different practices among and within the companies transporting them. This leads to losses and corresponding claims. There also seems to be no consistency between prisons as to the rules relating to the types of property each prisoner is allowed. Prisoners frequently arrive at HMP Ford with items bought legitimately whilst at their previous prison, only to be told the items are not allowed. This is deeply demotivating given that transfer to an open prison is supposed to be a promotion. Whilst there used to be a greater fire risk at HMP Ford than elsewhere because of the wooden billets, this is no longer the case and we would urge you to bring in consistent rules.

## TO THE GOVERNOR

The Board commends the action taken by you and your staff in preventing the spread of Covid by effective safety measures. When the restrictions ended, the return of prisoners to outside work was impressive.

The Board was particularly impressed by the reaction of you and your staff to comments made in our last report concerning diversity and inclusion. Monthly diversity meetings were set up to ensure that the importance of diversity and inclusion filtered down to every aspect of prison life.

Communication has continued to be a problem. During lockdown you held regular forums attended by a representative from each corridor, delete comma but the information given out did not seem to reach the other prisoners in spite of the fact that the forums were each followed up by a notice to the community. Prisoners also reported that communication with staff, particularly the offender management unit (OMU), was a problem.

The Board is very concerned by the Prisons and Probation Ombudsman (PPO) report into the death in custody in 2020, which criticised the treatment of long-term medical conditions. We appreciate that the healthcare provider has changed since then but it is essential that the protocol is adhered to in all cases.

### Progress in the last year

This has been a difficult year for the Governor and his team at HMP Ford. For much of the year they were seeking to prevent the spread of Covid whilst coping with the risk of infection, not only from staff movements in and out of the prison but also from new prisoners transferred from other establishments. The few cases which occurred among the prisoners are a testament to their success.

The other main change was in the accommodation. The long overdue condemnation of B wing resulted in the introduction of new pods and a major reduction in the operating capacity of some 35%. This brought its own problems when outside paid work on ROTL resumed, as enough prisoners had to be kept on-site to enable the prison to function, whereas many prisoners had arrived expecting unrealistically to get paid work immediately. However, the efforts of the prison to increase effective outside employment were impressive.

The Board congratulates the Governor on the way he and his staff coped in a difficult year.

**sodexo** AGECROFT ROAD
JUSTICE SERVICES PENDLEBURY
SALFORD
M27 8FB

**FOREST BANK**
**PRISON & YOI** Tel: 0161 925 7000

*For the latest reports on this prison please visit:*
https://tinyurl.com/bdfh26rv

*Important Changes:* **(1) Visits:** the identification necessary to access this prison and visit for social or professional purposes has changed; (2) **Money and Gifts** new rules now apply to these. See page 16 for full details of the above.

**Task of the establishment** A men's reception and resettlement prison Certified normal accommodation and operational capacity.

### Certified normal accommodation and operational capacity

Prisoners held at the time of inspection: 1354
Baseline certified normal capacity: 1061
In-use certified normal capacity: 996
Operational capacity: 1366

### Population of the prison

- 3530 new prisoners received each year (about 294 per month)
- 171 foreign national prisoners •
29% of prisoners from black and minority ethnic backgrounds
- 164 prisoners released into the community each month
- 96 prisoners on average referred for mental health assessment each month

### Prison status and key providers

Private: Sodexo Justice Services
Prison group: Custodial contracts group
Prison group director: Neil Richards
Director:
Jonathan French / Mohammed Elmugadam (c)
IMB chair: Ross Hemsley
Physical health provider: Sodexo Justice Services
Mental health provider: Greater Manchester Mental Health NHS Foundation Trust
Substance misuse treatment provider: Sodexo Justice Services
Prison education framework provider: Sodexo Justice Services
Escort contractor: GeoAmey

**Brief history** HMP Forest Bank opened in 2000 as a local prison serving the courts of Greater Manchester. Accommodation was initially provided over six residential units with a further two added in 2009. Single and double cellular accommodation was available, along with an inpatient facility in the health care centre. Forest Bank held remand and sentenced adult men and young adults.

## Short description of residential units
A1, A2, B1, B2, C2, E2, F1 and F2 – convicted and un-convicted adults and under 21-year-olds
C1, D2 – convicted and un-convicted vulnerable adults and under 21-year-olds
D1 – reverse cohort unit (RCU)/induction unit
E1 – closed
G1, G2 and H2 – recovery wings
H1 – RCU/induction unit for prisoners needing drug or alcohol treatment

## Visiting Information
Visits are booked by the resident on behalf of their visitors, on a month by month basis, max of 3 visitors, consisting of 2 adults and one child or 1 adult and 2 children.

**Legal visits:** Fax 0161 925 7031 or email: fb.booked@sodexogov.co.uk

## INSPECTIONS & REPORTS
### HMCIP Report
**Date of last inspection** 14 and 21–25 Feb 2022
**Published 31 May 2022**
Forest Bank is a privately managed prison, located in Manchester, that has been operated by Sodexo for well over 20 years. Currently designated a reception prison, it can hold up to 1,366 men. The prison has three primary purposes: to receive those recently remanded to custody and hold them until their court appearances are concluded; to hold those who are serving fairly short prison sentences; and to hold those requiring resettlement support as their release date approaches. Convicted men with time to serve would be expected to be allocated to training establishments elsewhere. As an approach, the model has some merit. The evidence, however, would seem to suggest the prison was struggling to make it work, primarily because there was simply not enough space to be sure all new prisoners (about 300 a month) could be accommodated. This inevitably meant that, on an almost daily basis, significant numbers of prisoners were being diverted to other prisons out of the area, impacting the individuals and undermining the prison's core mission.
This was our first visit to Forest Bank since 2019. In our healthy prison assessments, we evidenced similar outcomes in safety and respect, but deteriorations in both purposeful activity and rehabilitation and release planning (RRP). The impact of Covid-19 measures in the prison had made the lack of purposeful activity worse. We

judged the prison's regime as 'poor', with prisoners experiencing very limited time unlocked. Leaders showed limited ambition to improve this situation. Our colleagues at Ofsted judged Forest Bank's overall learning and skills provision as 'inadequate', their lowest marking. It was clear to us that the prison needed to re-think both what constituted a useful and meaningful regime and how they approached supporting resettlement for a largely transient population.
This was not, however, the whole story. In late 2021, HM Prison and Probation Service (HMPPS) was forced to issue Sodexo with a formal rectification notice over their concerns about the safety of prisoners and the conditions in which they were being held. This was a concerning step, but there was clear evidence that the company had responded quickly and positively and had, for example, recruited a new Director and Deputy Director to lead the prison. Decisive action had seen noticeable recent improvement in living conditions and new priorities focused on improving safety had been identified. The plans to deliver these priorities, however, still needed more development to ensure their implementation was sufficiently robust.
More also needed to be done to make sure newly received prisoners were properly supported and inducted. Violence and associated measures, such as use of force, use of segregation, and the application of disciplinary procedures all remained high. Levels of recorded violence had paradoxically reduced, but violence among prisoners was still the fourth highest among comparable prisons. Combating the ingress of drugs and other illicit items – all of which likely fuelled some of the violence – also remained problematic; although again, there was some early evidence to suggest that measures to tackle this were having an impact.
In common with many prisons, a key strategic challenge for Forest Bank was staffing. We found a staff group who were committed to doing a decent job – and some 71% of prisoners told us they felt respected by them – although very limited unlock meant the building of meaningful and purposeful relationships was severely restricted. Nearly a quarter of all officers had less than a years' experience, and staff were often lacking in confidence or had a limited understanding of their role outside of the Covid-19 restricted regime. We saw repeated evidence of reticence among staff in enforcing the rules and confronting poor behaviour. Again, the prison was aware of the problem and were beginning to develop strategies to better support their staff.
Forest Bank is a prison in transition. We were told repeatedly that had we visited some months

before, we would have found a prison in real difficulties. The prison was still dealing with some significant weaknesses; however, our findings were encouraging. HMPPS and the provider had taken decisive action and it was clear to us that the decline in living conditions had been arrested, sensible priorities identified and that there were some very hopeful signs of stability and improvement.

Charlie Taylor, HM Chief Inspector of Prisons
April 2022

## Safety

At the last inspection of Forest Bank in 2019 we found that outcomes for prisoners were not sufficiently good against this healthy prison test. At this inspection we found that outcomes for prisoners remained not sufficiently good.

The reception area was clean, and processes were efficient, but we were not confident that an assessment of prisoners' risks was always explored thoroughly during initial safety meetings. Peer support provided in the first few days was good, but the induction programme was still not running in full, and too many new prisoners felt daunted and ill-prepared for prison life. Vulnerable prisoners felt significantly less safe on their first night compared with the rest of the population.

Violence between prisoners, although declining, remained very high and the fourth highest of all local prisons. Overall, 24% of men felt unsafe at the time of our inspection. Multidisciplinary meetings explored trends in violence data, but actions in response were not followed up effectively. The most serious perpetrators were managed through challenge support and intervention plans (CSIP) (see Glossary), but conflict resolution and other interventions were not yet embedded or having sufficient impact.

The number of incidents involving force was high. A range of data was reviewed and analysed but not used to make improvements. We found some concerning examples of potentially dangerous practice. Conditions in the segregation unit required improvement and the daily regime was very limited, but prisoners we spoke to were positive about their treatment.

Steps had been taken to stem the flow of drugs and other illicit items. These measures were helping to reduce availability, but not all requested cell searches were carried out, which was a missed opportunity. In our survey, 40% of prisoners said it was easy to obtain illicit drugs, which was higher than at similar prisons (26%), but lower than when we inspected Forest Bank in 2019 (61%).

The recorded level of self-harm had dropped by about 20% since our last inspection and levels were now similar to other local prisons. There had, however, been two self-inflicted deaths since the last inspection, and leaders had still to implement all of the Prisons and Probation Ombudsman's recommendations. Some staff on duty at night were not sure about how to respond to emergencies. The safety team was small and did not have a sufficient profile across the prison. Prisoners could not reliably access a Listener (prisoners trained by the Samaritans to provide confidential emotional support to fellow prisoners) and the scheme was not promoted well. The operation of the new assessment, care in custody and teamwork case management process for prisoners at risk of suicide or self-harm was not good enough. Care maps were weak and often out of date, and case files were not always easily accessible to staff.

## Respect

At the last inspection of Forest Bank in 2019 we found that outcomes for prisoners were reasonably good against this healthy prison test. At this inspection we found that outcomes for prisoners remained reasonably good.

Meaningful staff-prisoner relationships were being hampered by the extremely limited time out of cell, the lack of an effective key worker scheme (see Glossary) and the short stays at the prison that many prisoners experienced. Despite this, 71% of those responding to our survey said staff treated them with respect. In recent months, there had not always been enough officers in the units, and they did not always interact with prisoners or consistently challenge poor behaviour.

Half of the prisoners continued to live in overcrowded and cramped cells and many toilets lacked adequate privacy screening. In our survey, only 16% of prisoners said their cell bell was answered promptly, which was significantly lower than in similar prisons (26%).

All meals were taken to the cell door, which was disrespectful. As in 2019, just under half of the prisoners in our survey (43%) said the shop sold what they needed, which was lower than in similar prisons (57%).

There were some signs of recent improvements in prisoner consultation arrangements. Responses to applications were usually timely. Prisoners' access to complaints forms was inconsistent, some responses were delayed, and too many failed to address the complaint.

Prisoners had good access to legal advice, bail information and support.

Equality work was not underpinned by a comprehensive needs analysis. Focus groups had been temporarily replaced by questionnaires and in-cell calls during the pandemic, which made sure there was some ongoing consultation. Data collection and analysis was limited to a few key areas and did not always lead to changes in practice. Investigations into discrimination incident reporting form (DIRF) complaints were thorough, however responses were often delayed and not comprehensive enough.

There were few areas where prisoners reported disproportionate outcomes in our survey. However, prisoners with a disability or mental health problem were noticeably more negative about safety. There was little support available for younger or older men but provision for foreign national prisoners was good. The prison had not yet investigated black and minority ethnic prisoners' perceptions of being disadvantaged when it came to work allocations.

Health care governance and partnership arrangements were positive, and services were generally well-led, but the applications process was not efficient enough and triage arrangements were not consistent. A good range of primary health care services was available and waiting times for clinics were reasonable. Despite some improvements in the physical environment of the inpatient unit, it was not led by clinical staff and patients did not have enough access to daily activities. Mental health services were reasonable, but the range of interventions was too limited. Substance misuse services were good, as were pharmacy services, but medications were not always administered on time.

### Purposeful activity

At the last inspection of Forest Bank in 2019 we found that outcomes for prisoners were reasonably good against this healthy prison test. At this inspection we found that outcomes for prisoners were now poor.

The regime had been severely restricted because of another recent outbreak of Covid-19. However, as this outbreak subsided, the prison had been slower to restore the regime than has been seen in many other establishments. About two thirds of prisoners were locked up during the core working day and those not involved in activities only had about two hours a day out of their cell.

Ofsted awarded its lowest grade for education, skills and work. Education, skills and work were not a priority and expectations of what prisoners could achieve were not high. Leaders and managers had not aligned their curricula to meet the changing needs of the prison population. Quality assurance and improvement arrangements were not effective.

There was no induction to assess prisoners' starting points, prior knowledge and skills, or future ambitions. Prisoners did not receive effective or impartial careers advice and guidance. Planning for the English and mathematics curricula focused on prisoners working towards achieving units of qualifications that might not have been recognised by other prison colleges or community colleges. Trainers did not routinely make sure that prisoners developed their English and mathematics in vocational training and prison work.

Leaders did not make sure that allocations to activities were fair, equitable and timely. Attendance at education, skills and work activities was low. Those who acted as mentors were not suitably trained and peer workers in the residential units did not have appropriate qualifications.

### Rehabilitation and release planning

At the last inspection of Forest Bank in 2019 we found that outcomes for prisoners were good against this healthy prison test.

At this inspection we found that outcomes for prisoners were now reasonably good.

There were no family days and the number of social visits for each prisoner was not sufficient, especially for those on remand. Video calls were underused. The families team provided some good support but only to a very small number of men. Storybook Dads (in which prisoners record a story for their children to listen to at home) was available, and some parenting group work had just restarted, including a father-baby bonding session. Forest Bank was a reception prison and the only one in the Greater Manchester area to accept prisoners on remand, but delivery of the model was hindered by significant population pressures and lack of spaces to accept new arrivals. For example, the prison could not meet the demand for places, meaning many remanded prisoners and others who should have stayed at Forest Bank in the lead up to release were routinely transferred to other prisons often miles away.

The number of sentenced prisoners requiring offender management was much lower than at the last inspection. Levels of recorded contact between these prisoners and prison offender managers was, however, poor.

Too many prisoners (40%) were released after their home detention curfew eligibility (HDC) date. This was due to their lack of time left to serve, insufficient available accommodation and disproportionate Covid-19 restrictions imposed by HMPPS.

Work to protect the public was robust and information sharing with community agencies such as children's services was effective.

Prisoners' mail and telephone calls were monitored well, and child contact restrictions were managed appropriately.

Initial categorisations were mostly timely, and

reviews took into account a reasonable amount of useful information. Too many prisoners who should have moved onto other prisons to complete offending behaviour work remained at Forest Bank for too long.

There was not enough evidence to demonstrate the need for the Thinking Skills Programme and there were no structured interventions for men convicted of domestic violence or sexual offences. We found little evidence of prisoners taking part in individual offending behaviour work.

Release planning was reasonable for sentenced prisoners but not for remanded or unsentenced prisoners. Although they had a plan, they received too little support to address their problems. About 86% of sentenced prisoners left with settled accommodation, which was much better than we see elsewhere. However, remanded or unsentenced men did not receive help to find accommodation. Support for prisoners with finance, benefit and debt needs was far too limited.

**Key concerns and recommendations**

Key concerns and recommendations identify the issues of most importance to improving outcomes for prisoners and are designed to help establishments prioritise and address the most significant weaknesses in the treatment and conditions of prisoners.

During this inspection we identified some areas of key concern and have made a small number of recommendations for the prison to address those concerns.

Key concern: Early days processes did not always keep prisoners supported or informed. Holding rooms in reception lacked useful information, prisoners' safety interviews were not held in private, and staff did not always make a full assessment of the risks posed by individuals based on information received and a detailed exploration of the concerns with the man. Vulnerable prisoners were held alongside the general population and felt significantly less safe on their first night. Prisoners could not have a shower on their first night. There was very little time out of cell for those in the induction unit and most prisoners did not get a full induction. As a result, prisoners too often felt unprepared for prison life.

Recommendation: All prisoners should feel safe on their first night. Support in the first few days should prepare new arrivals for prison life and they should receive sufficient time out of cell. (To the director.)

Key concern: Levels of violence remained very high but interventions to manage perpetrators and support victims were too limited. The adjudication system was undermined by the large number of cases that had not been concluded, which meant that some poor and antisocial behaviour went unpunished. The incentives scheme focused too much on punitive measures rather than promoting good behaviour.

Recommendation: Violence should be reduced using a range of effective interventions that challenge perpetrators and support victims. Good behaviour should be promoted and those who break the rules should be held to account. (To the director.)

Key concern: Illicit items such as mobile phones and drugs had been easily available in the prison and had fuelled debt and associated violence. Steps had been taken to stem the flow but some of them, such as escorting prisoners to exercise yards away from their units were time consuming and possibly hard to sustain in the long term. Intelligence reports were processed swiftly, but not all requested cell searches were undertaken.

Recommendation: Leaders should take robust and sustainable action to reduce the availability of illicit items, including acting on all intelligence received. (To the director.)

Key concern: The lack of an effective key worker scheme, little time out of cell and the very short stays of most prisoners had a detrimental effect on staff-prisoner relationships. A quarter of prison custody officers had less than a year in post and some lacked the confidence, knowledge and experience they needed to do their jobs effectively. Some staff were still too reticent to challenge poor behaviour consistently. We too often saw them in unit offices rather than interacting with and supervising prisoners.

Recommendation: Staff should receive enough training and ongoing supervision to give them the confidence, knowledge and skills to engage meaningfully with prisoners, support those who need their help and challenge poor behaviour consistently. (To the director.)

Key concern: Despite raising significant concerns at our last two inspections, the inpatient unit remained poor. There was a lack of clinical leadership to coordinate health care input and no continuous nursing presence. Time out of cell was very limited and there was a lack of therapeutic activities. Patients could not routinely access the day room as it was constantly being used for other purposes.

Recommendation: The inpatient unit should deliver a clinically led, purposeful and therapeutic environment. (To the director and the healthcare provider.)

Key concern: Leaders had been too slow to ease some Covid-19 restrictions. Very few prisoners had access to work or education, and we found about two thirds of the population locked up during the core working day. Unemployed prisoners had only two hours out of their cell each day. Hardly any could visit the library and access to the gym was far too limited.

Recommendation: Prisoners should have more time out of cell to access purposeful activity including work, education, the gym and library. (To the director.)

Key concern: Leaders and managers did not have effective oversight of the quality of the education, skills and work provision. They were unaware of the weaknesses in the standards of teaching, training and work.

Recommendation: Leaders should have effective oversight of education, skills and work provision, to make sure that the standard of teaching, training and learning is high enough to prepare prisoners effectively for their next steps, including employment. (To the director.)

Key concern: There were too few purposeful activity places to meet the needs of the prison population and the allocations process was not fair, equitable or timely.

Recommendation: Leaders must increase the number of education, skills and work activity places to meet the needs of the prison population and make sure that allocations are fair, equitable and timely. (To the director.)

Key concern: Education and training were not planned effectively enough to enable prisoners to increase their knowledge, remember what they had learned or achieve the most appropriate qualifications that would help them in the future. Support for those with additional needs or who struggled to complete their work was poor.

Recommendation: Leaders must make sure that all prisoners receive appropriate tuition and support that is planned effectively to enable prisoners to remember what they have learned and enable them to achieve relevant qualifications that are useful in the future. (To the director.)

Key concern: There were too few social visits available for the population, especially for the large number of remanded and unsentenced prisoners. Other methods of communication, such as video-calling, were underused.

Recommendation: Prisoners, especially those on remand or unsentenced, should be able to have more visiting sessions, and video calling should be used more extensively. (To the director.)

Key concern: Forest Bank was now a reception prison and the only one in the Greater Manchester area to accept prisoners on remand. The model was not working well and had badly affected outcomes for prisoners in a range of areas. Some remanded prisoners were sent from court to other prisons often miles away because the prison had no space, while others serving shorter sentences who should have stayed at

Forest Bank in the lead up to their release were often transferred away from their resettlement area. Prisoners serving longer sentences needed to progress to training prisons but instead remained at Forest Bank.

Recommendation: The role of Forest Bank as a reception and resettlement prison should be reviewed to make sure it has the capacity to receive and retain the correct prisoners and thereby fulfil its designated function. (To HMPPS.)

**Notable positive practice**

We define notable positive practice as innovative work or practice that leads to particularly good outcomes from which other establishments may be able to learn. Inspectors look for evidence of good outcomes for prisoners; original, creative or particularly effective approaches to problem-solving or achieving the desired goal; and how other establishments could learn from or replicate the practice.

Inspectors found four examples of notable positive practice during this inspection.

A dedicated worker delivered good support and made sure prisoners' social care needs were met.

The integrated substance misuse teams organised their caseloads based on geographical areas covering the Manchester region. This resulted in more effective and sustainable partnership working, which was delivering good through-the-gate support.

Work to protect the public was robust. A dedicated and skilled monitoring team listened to a high volume of calls every day with very few delays. Prison offender managers promptly shared concerns with other agencies

Accommodation outcomes on release were very good. The prison had a dedicated housing specialist and had received funding from the Greater Manchester temporary housing scheme. Data showed that 86% of sentenced prisoners had some form of housing on the day of their release.

**INDEPENDENT MONITORING BOARD: Annual Report**

The law requires every prison to be monitored by an independent Board appointed by the Justice Secretary; these are known as Independent Monitoring Boards (IMBs). The IMB must satisfy itself as to the humane and just treatment of those held in custody within its prison and the range and adequacy of the programmes preparing them for release; it must report annually to the Justice Secretary on how well the prison has met the standards and requirements placed on it.

**IMB Report: 1st Nov 2020 to 31st Oct 2021**
**Published 14 February 2022**
**Executive Summary**
**Background to the report**

During the period under review there have been three very significant occurrences that have had a major influence on the prison.

The first has been the ongoing effect of the Covid-19 pandemic. As the reporting period commenced the prison was operating on a stage 4 regime, which was reduced to stage 3 in May and reduced again to stage 2 in October. The prison has throughout the period been extremely proactive in addressing and controlling the spread of the virus despite losing 7580 staff days to isolation and the actual infection. This obviously created extreme difficulties for other staff, who worked extremely hard along with the management team to cover this shortfall. However, this focus may have concentrated resources away from other areas, leading to the improvement notice that was served by HMPPS. August saw the departure of both the Director and deputy director, with interim leaders coming in to facilitate the SJS response to the rectification notice. So far there has been an extremely positive reaction to the new management team, with a strong focus on making the prison a more decent and humane place for residents to live in. Finally, the management team, despite the above challenges, have all worked to develop and progress the prison into a remand and resettlement prison for the area, and are around 89% towards their target of holding 60% remand and short- sentenced residents and 40% resettlement residents who are being released back into the local community.

The Covid-19 outbreak has had a significant impact on the Board's ability to gather information and discuss the contents of this annual report. The Board has therefore tried to cover as much ground as it can in these difficult circumstances, but inevitably there is less detail and supporting evidence than usual. Ministers are aware of these constraints.

**Main judgements**
**How safe is the prison?**

Once again, this has been an extremely difficult year for the prison, its residents, and its staff. The Board are satisfied however that the management team have consistently put the safety of everybody in the facility at the top of their agenda. There has been a very slight increase in the number of applications received by the Board (36 as opposed to 33 last year) concerning alleged staff and prisoner concerns, including bullying, but in the context of the much higher turnover of prisoners and,

following investigation of each application, we are satisfied that safety remains paramount.

**How fairly and humanely are prisoners treated?**

There have been considerable periods of time during the twelve months when the prison, like the rest of Greater Manchester, has had to be run in very high states of lockdown, often with reduced numbers of staff available. The Board believes that every possible effort has been made to ensure that prisoners have been treated with the utmost fairness given the circumstances. All HMPPS guidance appears to have been complied with, and all advice regarding IEP has been adhered to during the period. Every effort is now being made to get the prison back to a more normal regime, despite the ongoing levels of Covid being experienced in several areas of the prison.

**How well are prisoners' health and wellbeing needs met?**

Once again, the healthcare team have worked extremely hard in difficult conditions to deliver a service that is, possibly, in the current circumstances, better than that is available to the general public. Healthcare applications received by the Board have increased by around a third, from 35 to 47; bearing in mind the far greater turnover of men this is to be expected. All dealings between the Board and the healthcare team have been carried out promptly with patient confidentiality being respected at all times.

Residents' decency was criticised in the rectification notice, however the Board is of the opinion that as the newly refurbished wings are opened up the men will benefit from the much better facilities

**How well are prisoners progressed towards successful resettlement?**

The brand-new development of the employment hub, transforming a large industrial unit into a spacious modern open-plan centre that is well decorated and well furnished, has to be seen as an extremely positive step towards successful resettlement.

The combination of the Ingeus ('through the gate') team and the Jobcentre staff working together with the new employment hub unit, with a very positive attitude, should help in getting offenders back into employment quickly. The Board hopes to be able to report on the success of this reorganisation and investment over the coming months.

**Main areas for development**
**TO THE PRISON SERVICE**

There continue to be problems regarding the transfer, handling, storage and accessibility of prisoners' property during their time within the system. We understand that work is ongoing to improve this, but seek further reassurance that this is still being addressed.

Concerns have been expressed by several sources around the prison regarding the transfer in status to reception prison. This is being managed well internally, but there continue to be problems, as prisoners who would previously have been sent to HMP Manchester are now coming into Forest Bank, raising significant issues regarding the ongoing activity of organised crime groups. What are your views on this?

### TO THE GOVERNOR

This has been a very difficult year for Forest Bank generally, but we are pleased to report that in most key areas we have seen significant improvements, particularly in those mentioned in the HMPPS rectification notice. Given that currently things appear to be moving in the right direction in areas such as accommodation cleanliness, general refurbishment, enhanced security, staff and resident testing and Covid containment in particular, do you think that these results will be sustainable and ongoing when the prison returns to its full capacity, bearing in mind the staff shortages you have experienced and that are forecast as continuing to be a national issue in 2022?

### Progress since the last report

As they did last year, the key parameters of violence, self-harm and accidents have once again been slightly reduced, despite the additional pressures placed on both staff and residents during the period. The change in the prison's status has resulted in a much increased 'churn' of residents, which has been a major issue that the management team have addressed. The way that Covid-19 has been handled in one of the worst-hit areas of the country is a credit to the entire staff, who have learned such a lot and progressed so far from the early days of lockdown. A comprehensive testing regime developed during the period resulted in 5,130 men being isolated, with 249 positive cases being identified and treated.

As the regimes have eased from one hour exercise daily and 45 minutes for limited association, it is now encouraging to see residents being encouraged to attend education/employment and other activities; this of course depends on testing.

The exceptional partnership between the prison and Public Health England (PHE) has continued, with Forest Bank being commended for helping Salford City Council with supplies of personal protective equipment (PPE). Despite the

previously mentioned improvement notice, the Board would like to thank the entire staff and management team for their dedication and hard work during both the pandemic and the ongoing change to reception status.

One of the areas of concern raised in the improvement notice related to the amount of contraband that was getting into the prison. The security team has addressed this problem with a much more focussed and concerted effort. The lack of social visits has seen far fewer opportunities for visitors to bring contraband in, so during the period the prison has introduced airline-type security checks for every staff member and visitor that operates at all times. There have also been articles in the Manchester Evening News concerning the amount of contraband that has been thrown over the perimeter walls and fences into exercise yards. This is detailed in section 4.5 of the report.

TIGERS ROAD
WIGSTON
LEICESTER
LE18 4AE

Adult & YOI Male Category C Resettlement Prison
Operated by Serco
Prison Director: Wyn Jones
Opening: May 2023
7 Houseblocks
Op Cap/CNA 1,715
Health provider: Notts NHS Trust
L&S provider: Milton Keynes College

FOSTON HALL
FOSTON, DERBY
DERBYSHIRE
DE65 5DN

Tel: 01283 584300

*For the latest reports on this prison please visit:*
https://tinyurl.com/bdfh26rv

*Important Changes:* **(1) Visits:** the identification necessary to access this prison and visit for social or professional purposes has changed; (2) **Money and Gifts** new rules now apply to these. See page 16 for full details of the above.

**Task of the establishment** A women's resettlement and local prison

**Certified normal accommodation and operational capacity**
Prisoners held November 2021: 272
Baseline certified normal capacity: 254
In-use certified normal capacity: 254
Operational capacity: 296

**Prison status and key providers**
Public
Prison Group: Women
Prison Group Director: Pia Sinha
Governor/Director: Helen Clayton-Hoar
IMB Chair: Sue Wall
Physical and mental health provider:
Practice Plus Group
Substance use provider: Inclusion
Learning and skills provider:
Milton Keynes College
Prison education provider: People Plus
Resettlement provider: East Midlands probation
Escort contractor: GeoAmey

**Brief history** Foston Hall near Uttoxeter was built in 1863 as a family home and was acquired by the Prison Service in 1953. Since then it has been used as a detention centre, an immigration centre and a satellite prison for nearby HMP Sudbury. Shut in 1996, it reopened on 31 July 1997 as a closed women's prison following major refurbishment and building work. HMP Foston Hall is now a local women's resettlement prison serving courts in the Midlands and mid-Wales. It holds a complex mix of prisoners, from those recently remanded in custody to those with lengthy or indeterminate sentences.

**Population of the prison**
23 foreign national women
15% of women from BAME backgrounds
57 released each month
134 on substance misuse support
51 monthly referred for mental health assessment

**Prison status and key providers**
Public Sector

**Brief history**
Foston Hall near Uttoxeter was built in 1863 as a family home and was acquired by the Prison Service in 1953. Since then, it has been used as a detention centre, an immigration centre and a satellite prison for nearby HMP Sudbury. Shut in 1996, it reopened on 31 July 1997 as a closed women's prison following major refurbishment and building work. HMP Foston Hall is now a local women's resettlement prison serving courts in the Midlands. It holds a complex mix of women, from those recently remanded in custody to those with lengthy or indeterminate sentences.

**Short description of residential units**
First night and induction unit for 63 women
C wing – mainstream for 40 women
D wing – mainstream for 29 women
E wing – for 11 long-term and enhanced regime
F wing – mainstream for 63 women
T wing – mainstream for 56 women.
G wing – temporary accommodation for34 lower risk women

**Visiting Information**
You must book your first visit by telephone on: 0300 060 6516, Monday to Friday, 9am to 5pm or online at: https://www.gov.uk/prison-visits
**Visiting times:**
Wednesday and Friday: 2pm to 4pm
Sunday (morning): 9:30am to 11:30am
Sunday (afternoon): 2pm to 4pm

**Legal visits:**
All official visits (legal / social services etc.) must be booked by emailing: hmppsvisitbooking@justice.gov.uk between 9am and 1pm. Any bookings received after this will be dealt with the following day.
**Visiting times:**
Monday to Friday: 9:30am to 10:29am, 10:30am to 11:30am, 2pm to 2:59pm, 3pm to 4pm

**INSPECTIONS & REPORTS**
**Date of last inspection 5/6 November 2021**
**HMCIP Report, published 9 February 2022**
Foston Hall, in Derbyshire, is a women's prison which, at the time of our inspection, was holding 272 residents, just short of its capacity of 296. In common with other women's prisons, the establishment accommodates several categories of prisoner ranging from those recently remanded or at the beginning of their sentences, to women serving indeterminate sentences, including life, for very serious crimes. The prison itself comprises an old stately home surrounded by a mix of accommodation types that have been added over the years. Its rural setting and well-kept grounds provide an excellent external environment which supports individual well-being.
Foston Hall was last inspected in 2019 when we found outcomes to be reasonably good against all our tests of a healthy prison. This inspection, however, proved less positive and in common with many establishments emerging from the Covid-19 pandemic, we found a deterioration in the regime and the provision of purposeful activity. Of greater concern, however, were the safety outcomes which we judged to be poor, our lowest assessment. This is a rare and unexpected finding in a women's prison. While we accept that the issues in Foston Hall differ from those we might expect to see in an unsafe men's prison,

the evidence for this judgement was compelling. Neither the prison's assessment of vulnerability, nor the support offered to newly arrived women were good enough. The unpredictability of the regime was contributing to tensions on the wings and, we suspected, increased violence, particularly against staff. Violence was now very high. The use of force had doubled since the last inspection and was the highest in the women's estate. There was now far more frequent use of the poor segregation unit.

Recorded levels of self-harm were also the highest in the women's estate and two women had taken their own lives since we last inspected. As an indicator of the level of distress, women were making 1,000 calls a month to the Samaritans. The prison had no strategy to reduce self-harm or improve the care for those in crisis. Recommendations made by the Prisons and Probation Ombudsman following their investigation into deaths in custody had still to be addressed and the relatively few women who accounted for most of the incidents did not have meaningful care plans. The response to women in crisis was too reactive, uncaring and often punitive. This, taken with other safety metrics and observation, meant it was no surprise that in our survey nearly a third of women told us they felt unsafe.

It was clear that since our last visit the prison had experienced considerable instability in its leadership, with many structures and arrangements for supervising delivery and monitoring performance operating ineffectively, if at all. A new governor had been appointed a year ago and had begun to address these weaknesses, most notably by developing the effectiveness of middle managers and overseeing improvements in the work to support rehabilitation and release planning However, many deficiencies remained and despite the identification of a series of new priorities there was insufficient attention to the very obvious need to improve the safety of women or improve the quality and consistency of care they received. Managers needed to be more visible to make sure the needs of women were being met by staff. We were told repeatedly by staff that morale was low and – although the prison was near to being fully staffed at the time of our visit – nearly a third of frontline officers were non-effective and non-deployable, which undermined work to improve the establishment.

Foston Hall needs to do much better. During our inspection there was a sense that decline had been arrested but we had less confidence about how improvements would be made going forward. It was clear to us that leaders needed to get staff back to work and determine how managers could better support staff to fulfil their duties and responsibilities. Leaders also needed to reconsider their priorities. One of those priorities must be new thinking followed by action, about how to make a women's prison safer, including new strategies and greater confidence in meeting the needs of the most intractable and vulnerable women.

## INDEPENDENT MONITORING BOARD: Annual Report

The law requires every prison to be monitored by an independent Board appointed by the Justice Secretary; these are known as Independent Monitoring Boards (IMBs). The IMB must satisfy itself as to the humane and just treatment of those held in custody within its prison and the range and adequacy of the programmes preparing them for release; it must report annually to the Justice Secretary on how well the prison has met the standards and requirements placed on it.

### IMB Report 1 December 2020 to 30 November 2021. Published 18 March 2022
#### Background to the report

Once again, Covid-19 has dominated the year. It has been a difficult and challenging time for both prisoners and staff. For prisoners, many of whom are already struggling with mental health issues, it has meant having to cope with being confined to their cells for most of the day. As the year has progressed there has been a gradual easing of restrictions, with the reintroduction of more work and activity opportunities, but the regime has still not returned to normal.

Staff have not only had to cope with managing the implications of Covid-19, but they have been operating in the context of considerable staffing Factors in this have been the level of staff illness, including that linked to Covid-19, the intake of new staff, their absences for training, the proportion of inexperienced staff, and the ongoing demands for duties such as bed-watches. The consistency of leadership throughout the year is welcome, with the appointment in October 2020 of the current Governor, after a period of great The IMB recognises the many challenges faced by the management team throughout the year.

Due to the pandemic, the IMB monitored the prison remotely for the first part of the year. A gradual resumption of visits began in spring, but monitoring continued to be constrained by factors linked to Covid-19, which impacted on the extent and nature of contact with different parts of the prison. As an additional means of evidence gathering, the IMB undertook a number of surveys on different aspects of prisoners' experience. These are summarised in section 8, and are referred to throughout the report.

As noted in last year's report, the population reduced in autumn 2020. As a consequence, the balance of the population has changed, with a higher proportion of remand and unsentenced prisoners. The turnover in population is considerable, as is the number in the prison for short periods

## How safe is the prison?

In a survey of all prisoners, with a response rate of 37%, 70% of the prisoners who responded agreed or strongly agreed that they felt safe in Foston Hall, 14% were undecided, and 16% disagreed or strongly disagreed that they felt safe. It is the view of the IMB that the culture of Foston Hall keeps prisoners safe and manifestations of this are regularly seen in interactions between staff and prisoners as well as in much decision making and planning. Arrangements to manage Covid- 19 have been effective and well managed. However, it is a serious concern that the prison has such high levels of self-harm. There is a particular problem with a small number of prolific self-harmers who account for nearly 80% of self-harm. The high incidence of use of force is also a serious concern. The level of force used is usually low, and often a small number of prisoners are responsible for multiple incidents. These issues reflect in part the acute challenges of managing high numbers of prisoners with very complex needs in very difficult times.

## How fairly and humanely are prisoners treated?

The IMB does not consider that the restricted regime, confining prisoners to their cells for up to 23 hours a day, is humane, but recognises nationally imposed restrictions stemmed from the need to protect prisoners from Covid-19. While managers and staff have worked hard to ameliorate the impact where possible, the situation has been further exacerbated by additional regime curtailments due to staffing pressures, sometimes at very short

Before the pandemic, considerable progress had been made in relation to Covid-19 restrictions on the movement and mixing of prisoners meant the suspension, until October, of support groups for prisoners (linked to age, race, sexual orientation, gender reassignment, foreign nationals and Gypsy. Romany and Traveller prisoners). As activities have gradually resumed, monitoring in relation to equalities is re-emerging, but there are significant gaps, for example in relation to education.

A survey undertaken by the IMB in July of black, Asian and minority ethnic (BAME), foreign national and Gypsy, Romany and Traveller

prisoners revealed a mixed picture of their experience at Foston Hall. Concerning findings included a perceived lack of understanding of cultural needs and inadequate provision for foreign national prisoner.

## How well are prisoners' health and wellbeing needs met?

Operating in the context of staff shortages, Covid-19 and inadequate accommodation, the healthcare providers have worked hard to ensure the delivery of priority services. This includes emergency care, Covid-19 requirements and medication. Staffing pressures have impacted on the provision of services; for example, an absence of a qualified night nurse on occasion. Mental health provision has also been impacted by staffing pressures. Support from the ACCESS team (comprising a psychologist, prison officer and mental health nurse) has continued, in a limited form. Associated provision for mental health, including the CAMEO programme, has begun to resume. Throughout the year, the chaplaincy has had a much-valued role in supporting prisoners in distress and with mental health problems. The IMB is concerned that there continues to be a large volume of unmet mental healthcare need, as reflected in its survey of prisoners.

## How well are prisoners progressed towards successful resettlement?

As the year has progressed and Covid-19 restrictions have eased there has been a gradual, if sometimes halting, resumption of education and training activities, although these had to be delivered remotely or on a 1-to-1 basis until September, when small groups could meet in classrooms. It is recognised that more needs to be done to ensure the curriculum supports prisoners into future employment. Links to external employers remain dormant pending more easing of restrictions.

Considerable efforts have been made to support family contact. The national policy introduced at the start of Covid-19, to provide additional phone credit, has had a key role in helping prisoners maintain contact with their families. Take up of video and social visits remains low, although times and arrangements have been adjusted to encourage their use. Screening of prisoners for their resettlement needs has continued, as has support to open bank accounts and deal with benefits. However, the restructuring involved in the national probation service reform has fragmented provision and resulted in the loss of key services, for example the discharge lounge for prisoners to use on the day of release. The withdrawal of Covid-19 homelessness funding in April, has, as feared, led to a significant increase in the number of prisoners being released without an address, averaging 19% between June and October

### Main areas for development
### TO THE MINISTER
**Are there plans to address:**
• the inadequate provision for mental health throughout the criminal justice system, which is a serious concern? This is manifested in Foston Hall in a high level of unmet need for mental health treatment and delays in transferring prisoners to secure hospitals
• the increased number of prisoners being released without an address to go to now additional Covid-19 funding to tackle homelessness has stopped
• the implications of probation reform, including the loss of staffing for the discharge lounge, the loss of support for those on remand, the fractured/dispersed support away from prison – and huge demand on resources to implement reform

### TO THE PRISON SERVICE
**Are there plans to address:**
• the longstanding inadequacy of accommodation on D wing
• the longstanding problem of the size and layout of the CSU (despite the recent renovation), which mean the regime provided is limited and the environment is poor
• the serious shortcomings of the temporary G wing accommodation
the inadequate accommodation for the provision of healthcare
• the lack of interview rooms, which seriously undermines the delivery of rehabilitative work, in particular healthcare, mental health and offender management?
• the unmet mental healthcare need
• the continuing poor performance of Amey in undertaking maintenance and repairs
• the ongoing IT problems which result in lengthy delays in resolving problems and replacing broken equipment, undermining the efficient administration of the prison?

### TO THE GOVERNOR
The IMB recognises that the Governor is aware of the issues below and that plans to address many of them have been or are being prepared. The IMB is concerned about:

### Safety
• the continued high level of self-harm
increase in violent incidents due to an increase in assaults on staff.
• the high, if erratic, level of use of force, and

the need for improvement in the use of body worn cameras.

### Fair and humane treatment
• the high number of regime curtailments due to staffing issues.
• high use of segregation, and the increase in prisoners segregated on an open ACCT.
• the increase in use of cellular confinement.
• the absence of referrals to the independent adjudicator during the year, despite appropriate cases.
• ongoing backlogs/delays in processing prisoners' property.
• the underuse of the discrimination incident reporting form (DIRF) system and prisoner feedback which suggest it is not well understood or trusted.
• the views of black, Asian and minority ethnic (BAME) prisoners surveyed by the IMB, rating the prison's understanding of their cultural needs as low, especially regarding access to canteen products, appropriate food and clothing. lack of support to foreign national prisoners who do not speak English.

### Health and wellbeing
• staffing pressures in healthcare and mental health, impacting on services.
• the 'short-term' closure of the mental health office to facilitate the demolition of A and B wings, which by November had extended into three months, causing acute problems for the delivery of mental health services.

### Progression and release
• the ongoing absence of initial screening of prisoners for learning difficulties and disability (LDD) due to a staffing.
• the increase in the number of prisoners being released without an address.

**BRASSIDE
DURHAM
DH1 5YD**

**HM PRISON
FRANKLAND**   Tel: 0191 376 5000

*For the latest reports on this prison please visit:*
https://tinyurl.com/bdfh26rv

*Important Changes:* **(1) Visits:** the identification necessary to access this prison and visit for social or professional purposes has changed; (2) **Money and Gifts** new rules now apply to these. See page 16 for full details of the above.

**Task of the establishment** A high security prison for category A and B convicted and category A remand male prisoners.

**Certified normal accommodation and operational capacity**
Prisoners held March 2022: 849
Baseline certified normal capacity: 852
In-use certified normal capacity: 852
Operational capacity: 852

**Prison status and key providers**
Public
Prison Group: Long Term/High Security
Prison Group Director: Gavin O'Malley
Governor/Director: Darren Finley
IMB Chair: Richard Wilkinson
Physical health provider: G4S Forensic and Medical Services
Mental health provider: Tees, Esk and Wear Valleys NHS Foundation Trust
Substance misuse treatment provider: Change, Grow, Live
Prison education framework provider: Milton Keynes College
Escort contractor: GeoAmey

**Brief history** HMP Frankland was the first purpose-built dispersal prison and opened in 1983 on the outskirts of Durham city, providing a maximum-security environment for adult convicted men serving sentences of over four years and category A remand prisoners. In 2019, following the national configuration programme, Frankland was designated as a prison with a training function, its purpose being to settle prisoners into the prison environment and identify and address their offending behaviour and needs. This has resulted in little change, other than prisoners being transferred to Frankland earlier in their sentence. The prison has an operational capacity of 852 and has operated close to capacity in the reporting year. An important factor is the prison's location, particularly as the most northerly high security prison and the most distant for many families, friends and professionals visiting prisoners. In addition, public transport links from the nearest railway station to the prison are poor.

**Short description of residential units**
• Four original wings – A, B, C and D. Each can house up to 108 vulnerable prisoners.
• Two wings, F and G, which opened in 1998. They can house up to 120 and 88 ordinary location prisoners, respectively.
• The Westgate unit (capacity 65) opened in 2004 for prisoners with severe personality disorders. It includes the psychologically informed planned

environment (PIPE) unit, with a capacity of 21, which opened in May 2012.
• J wing, which opened in 2009 and can house up to 120 ordinary location prisoners.
• A separation centre which opened in 2018 and was the first in the UK prison estate exclusively to hold prisoners with extremist ideological views.
• Frankland has a segregation unit (management and progression unit: MPU), which has a capacity of 28 cells, including two designated cells which are only used for close supervision centre (CSC) prisoners.

**The following agencies provide support to the prison:**
• Healthcare services are provided by Spectrum, with a number of subcontractors.
• Learning and skills development is provided Milton Keynes College.
• Security support is provided by Durham Police (two police liaison officers).
• Escort services are provided by GeoAmey for all prisoners other than category A.
• Facilities maintenance, cleaning and other small works are provided by Amey plc.

The following organisations and volunteers help in the smooth running of the prison:
• North East Prison After Care Society (Nepacs) volunteers work alongside prison staff to assist in the day-to-day running of the visitors' centre and in providing support to families.
• The Sunderland branch of the Samaritans provides training for prison Listeners and Mind provides counselling support for prisoners with mental health issues.

**Visiting Information**
Book online: https://www.gov.uk/prison-visits or by telephone on 0191 376 5048. The booking line is open Monday to Friday, 8:30am to midday Find out about call charges
**Visiting times:**
Tuesday to Sunday: 2pm to 4pm

**Legal visits:** There are currently no legal visits taking place.

**INSPECTIONS & REPORTS**
**Date of last inspection** 13–24 January 2020
**HMCIP Report, published 05 May 2020**
HMP Frankland, near Durham, is one of the country's most secure prisons. Holding 840 convicted adult men at the time of our inspection, over 250 were classified as category A, the highest security classification, and of these, nine were considered high-risk category A. Almost all those held were serving sentences in excess of ten years, with the majority serving

indeterminate or life sentences. The majority had committed the most serious, and often violent, offences and posed very great risks to the public. The security measures applied at Frankland, as well the depth of custody experienced, reflected fully these risks.

The prison included four wings (A to D) holding mainly vulnerable prisoners, and three newer wings (F to J) holding more mainstream offenders. The most modern facility was the Westgate units, which provided psychologically-informed interventions and sought to treat complex personality disorders. The prison also contained a 'separation unit' where a small number of individuals who were judged to present a particular risk to national security were held. This facility will be inspected separately at a later date, so did not form part of this inspection. Our findings at this inspection, consistent with our findings when we last visited in 2016, showed that Frankland continued to ensure reasonable outcomes against all our tests of a healthy prison. A stable population meant daily movement through reception was limited, but new prisoners were received and inducted well. Most prisoners reported feeling safe and overall levels of violence were low, despite all the risks. Some good work was taking place to ensure this continued to be the case, and although use of force had increased, it remained lower than the level seen in similar prisons. Accountability for its use was generally good. The regime offered in segregation remained limited but relationships were good and there were credible joint working initiatives to better case manage individuals and break the cycle of long-term segregation.

The security department was extensive and well resourced. The management of intelligence was a priority and we were told of robust procedures for monitoring potential extremism and corruption. Although lower than at prisons generally, drug testing suggested that more illicit drugs were available than in comparison to other high security prisons, and prisoners suggested to us that drugs were easy to get hold of.

Since we last inspected, there had been one self-inflicted death and levels of self-harm had increased and were now higher than at similar prisons. The prison's response to this challenge was mixed and it was clear the issue needed greater prioritisation. Case management of those in crisis, for example, varied greatly, although prisoners in crisis we spoke to nevertheless felt cared for.

Frankland remained a reasonably respectful prison. Relationships were relaxed and informal, and most prisoners felt respected by staff. The environment and living conditions were satisfactory throughout most of the prison and arrangements to ensure meaningful consultation were, for the most part, adequate, as were those to deal with applications and complaints. The promotion of equality and diversity, however, needed improvement and required greater prioritisation. The chaplaincy in contrast was a strength. Outcomes in healthcare as well as in drug and substance misuse services were good.

In the context of a settled and stable training establishment we were surprised to find about 30% of prisoners locked up during the working day, including the majority of those who had reached retirement age. That aside, leaders and managers had worked well together to ensure that the quality of regime and education offered was reasonably good. The curriculum generally met need, although accreditation in workshops and prison work was lacking. The quality of teaching and learning was good and assistance from peer supporters was useful. Achievements were generally high despite low attendance in education. Our colleagues in Ofsted judged the overall effectiveness of education, skills and work provision as 'good'.

The prison had a good understanding of prisoner risk and need, but we identified some weaknesses in the prison's approach to offender management and sentence planning. Staff had high caseloads and the approach to case management was too often poorly coordinated. That said, most prisoners had an up-to-date assessment (OASys) and most were of good quality. We found public protection arrangements to be robust. The prison had enough offending behaviour interventions to meet most need, augmented by some very good psychology-led one-to-one work. The offender personality disorder pathway worked as well as other psychological approaches delivered on the Westgate units, which were recognised as centres of excellence.

Frankland is a large and complex high security prison with many challenges, managing some notable risks. The outcomes that prisoners experienced, despite this, continued to be good. We leave the prison with a number of recommendations we hope will assist further improvement.

Peter Clarke CVO OBE QPM
HM Chief Inspector of Prisons March 2020

**INDEPENDENT MONITORING BOARD: Annual Report**

The law requires every prison to be monitored by an independent Board appointed by the Justice Secretary; these are known as Independent Monitoring Boards (IMBs). The IMB must satisfy itself as to the humane and just treatment of those held in custody within its prison and the range and adequacy of the programmes preparing them for release; it must report annually to the Justice Secretary on how well the prison has met the standards and requirements placed on it.

**IMB Report 1 Dec 2020 – 30 Nov 2021**
**Published 25th March 2022**
**Executive summary**
**Background to the report**
The Covid-19 outbreak has had a significant impact on the Board's ability to gather information and discuss the contents of this annual report. The Board has therefore tried to cover as much ground as it can in these difficult circumstances, but inevitably there is less detail and supporting evidence than usual. Ministers are aware of these constraints. Regular information is being collected specifically on the prison's response to the pandemic, and that is being collated nationally.

**Main judgements**
**How safe is the prison?**
The IMB is satisfied that staff and senior managers work hard to maintain a safe environment whilst dealing with a number of prisoners with challenging behaviours. Whilst any instance of assault or self-harm is always unwelcome, the establishment compares favourably with other establishments in the long-term high security estate (LTHSE) and reflects the management focus on safety.

**How fairly and humanely are prisoners treated?**
The IMB is satisfied that the regime throughout the pandemic has been fair and humane. When the opportunity arose to reduce restrictions, this was done quickly but only when safe to do so. Measures were introduced to counteract longer periods in cells and activities were introduced as soon as it was considered safe. 'Virtual' visits were available (and remain so) and the face-to-face visiting regime was reintroduced, albeit with adaptations to limit the potential exposure to Covid.

**How well are prisoners' health and wellbeing needs met?**
The pandemic impacted prisoners' access to healthcare professionals, with serious and urgent cases prioritised. Waiting times for dental appointments were a particular concern.
The physical environment in healthcare (which was built for a prison half the size) is no longer suitable for the size of the prison. The room allocated to the mental health team is too small for the size of the team and there are insufficient rooms for members of the team to meet with prisoners.

The IMB remains concerned about the lack of an appropriate environment for prisoners diagnosed with dementia.

**How well are prisoners progressed towards successful resettlement?**
The pandemic has had a significant impact on resettlement, with extended hours of isolation in cells. It was good to see many appropriate activities being reintroduced as restrictions were eased.
Two areas of concern are staff shortages in the offender management unit (OMU) and the inconsistency of key worker input.

**Main areas for development**
**TO THE MINISTER**
Given the ageing prison population and a growing number of prisoners being diagnosed with dementia, can consideration now be given to providing an appropriate physical environment for this group of prisoners along with suitably qualified care workers (para 6.4)?

**TO THE PRISON SERVICE**
Can HMPPS now expedite the completion of the prisoners' property policy framework with particular focus on consistent, effective processes and rules that are easily understood (para 5.8)?
Can HMPPS review the physical environment for healthcare, which is no longer sufficient for the size of the establishment?

**TO THE GOVERNOR**
Can the relaunch of the key worker scheme be taken forward as soon as possible to include further staff training and additional management input where appropriate?

MOOR LANE
FULL SUTTON
YORK
YO41 1PS

**HM PRISON FULL SUTTON**    Tel: 01759 475100

*For the latest reports on this prison please visit:*
https://tinyurl.com/bdfh26rv

*Important Changes:* **(1) Visits:** the identification necessary to access this prison and visit for social or professional purposes has changed; (2) **Money and Gifts** new rules now apply to these. See page 16 for full details of the above.

**Task of the establishment** HMP Full Sutton is a high security men's establishment for category A and B prisoners.

**Certified normal accommodation and operational capacity**
Prisoners held at the time of inspection: 561
Baseline certified normal capacity: 597
In-use certified normal capacity: 597
Operational capacity: 586

**Prison status and key providers**
Public Sector
Prison Group: Long Term/ High Security
Prison Group Director: Gavin O'Malley
Governor/Director: Gareth Sands
IMB Chair: Sally Hobbs
Physical and mental health and substance misuse treatment provider: Spectrum
Prison education framework provider: Milton Keynes College

**Brief history** HMP Full Sutton opened in 1987 and is a high security dispersal establishment, which is part of the newly formed long-term and high security estate directorate, housing a complex prisoner population. The population predominantly compromises indeterminate sentence prisoners and a substantial number of longer sentenced determinate prisoners who have category A or B status.

**Short description of residential units**
A unit – residential unit
B unit – vulnerable prisoners' unit and the STEP unit
C unit – vulnerable prisoners' unit
D unit – vulnerable prisoners' unit
E unit – residential unit
F unit – residential unit
Close supervision centre unit – not inspected
Separation centre – not inspected

**Visiting Information**
Book online: https://www.gov.uk/prison-visit or by telephone on 01759 475 355 Monday to Friday, 8:30am to 4:30pm.
**Visiting times:** Friday afternoon, Saturday morning and afternoon

**Legal visits:** Booking line: 01759 475 355 Monday to Friday, 8:30am to 4.30pm
**Visiting times:** Thursdays only during Covid-19 restrictions

**INSPECTIONS & REPORTS**
**Date of last inspection:** 24 Feb–6 Mar 2020
*Notable features from this inspection*
• 59% of the population were serving indeterminate sentences.
• More than a fifth of the population (22%) had category A security status.
• 83% were as assessed as presenting a high or very high risk of harm.

• 98% of prisoners were subject to multi-agency public protection arrangements.
• Prison data showed 44% of the population had a disability.
• The supporting transition and enabling progression (STEP) unit, a national resource, accommodated a small number of long-term segregated prisoners.

**HMCIP Report, published 11 June 2020**
HMP Full Sutton is a high security dispersal prison for men, holding category A and B prisoners. It is situated near York, and at the time of this inspection held around 560 prisoners. Over 80% are assessed as presenting a high or very high risk of harm to others, and nearly 60% are serving indeterminate sentences. The prisoner population is complex, including prisoners convicted of a wide range of very serious offences.

At the last inspection, held in January 2016, we found the prison to be performing well, achieving grades of reasonably good in safety, respect and rehabilitation and release planning, and good for purposeful activity. On this occasion, the grades awarded for respect and rehabilitation and release planning remained the same, while safety improved to our highest grade of good, and purposeful activity declined to be not sufficiently good.

In terms of safety, Full Sutton had the lowest levels of violence in the high security estate, with a comparatively small proportion of prisoners (22%) reporting to us that they felt unsafe at the time of the inspection. It was pleasing to see that the segregation unit had improved considerably since the time of the last inspection. The incentives and earned privileges scheme (IEP) was used in a way that did genuinely encourage good behaviour, and it was good to find that Challenge, Support and Intervention Plans (CSIPs) were being well used. Less positively it was disappointing that drugs suspicion testing was not being used as effectively as it should be in an establishment such as Full Sutton, with only a third of requested tests being carried out, of which a third were proving positive. This represents a missed opportunity to make Full Sutton even safer than it already is.

Our survey found that those prisoners suffering with mental health problems or who were disabled (44% and 38% respectively) had more negative views of their treatment, including their safety, than others. The reasons behind these perceptions need to be properly analysed and action taken to address them. We also found that there was a lack of strategic management of equality and diversity issues, and when this is rectified it should help with addressing the negative perceptions of disabled prisoners and those with mental health problems.

Our findings in the area of purposeful activity were disappointing. There were not enough work or activity places for the population, and allocation was too slow in some cases. Our colleagues from Ofsted recognised that plans were in place to bring about improvements, but those had yet to materialise. For instance, knowledge and skills gained by prisoners were not recorded, and there was no opportunity to achieve accredited qualifications. Although the prison's plans around this were in place, they had not been implemented at the time of this inspection, and Ofsted were clear in their judgement that the provision of education, skills and work required improvement. The prison was very confident that its plans would come to fruition quite quickly, and said they would be encouraging Ofsted for an early re-appraisal of progress.

Public protection work was generally robust, which was an important finding given the high risk posed by so many of Full Sutton's prisoners. However, it was disappointing that around 40% of prisoners did not have an up to date assessment (OASys) of their risks and needs. In a prison such as this, with many prisoners serving very long sentences, it is obviously important that they should feel that their needs have been recognised and that there is an opportunity to make progress. We also found that more could be done to help prisoners maintain meaningful contact with families and friends. On a very positive note, psychology staff were well integrated across the prison, and we have identified the way in which this has been done at Full Sutton as good practice.

Overall, Full Sutton is a prison that performs its important function well. It is fundamentally a safe and decent establishment, benefitting from energetic leadership and a staff group who interact well with the prisoners in their charge. If the plans that are now in place to improve the provision of education, skills and work bear fruit, and a few key issues in other areas are addressed, there is no reason why Full Sutton could not aspire to be one of the best performing prisons in the country.

Peter Clarke CVO OBE QPM

HM Chief Inspector of Prisons, April 2020

## INDEPENDENT MONITORING BOARD:
### Annual Report

The law requires every prison to be monitored by an independent Board appointed by the Justice Secretary; these are known as Independent Monitoring Boards (IMBs). The IMB must satisfy itself as to the humane and just treatment of those held in custody within its prison and the range and adequacy of the programmes preparing them for release; it must report annually to the Justice Secretary on how well the prison has met the standards and requirements placed on it.

### IMB Report 1 January 2021 – 31 December 2021
### Published 29th April 2022
### Background to the report

This report, which covers the period January to December 2021, is written against the background of the continuing Covid-19 pandemic. A national lockdown began again on 4 January 2021; in February several wings and then the prison as a whole were declared an outbreak site by Public Health England. During the course of the year, the prison has operated at all restriction levels, from Stage 4 down to, briefly, Stage 1, but the transition was not linear. Different levels of restrictions were applied at different times during the year, when necessary, on a wing-by-wing basis, depending on levels of infection and the need to contain the spread.

2021 has, therefore, been another testing and tiring year for management, staff and prisoners, with constantly changing restrictions and regimes.

The prison has a dedicated Covid team, which has been operating since the start of the pandemic, and which monitors levels of infection in staff and prisoners, manages changing operational requirements and which oversaw the introduction of vaccination for prisoners and the regular testing of staff. This team has worked hard and professionally throughout and has made a real contribution to keeping prisoners and staff as safe as possible.

While the pandemic, and managing the prison through it, has in many ways been all-encompassing for prison management, managers have also tried to manage for the future. Improvements continued to be made to the fabric and decoration of the building, thus improving the environment for prisoners, and at the end of the year, preparatory work had been undertaken for an array of solar panels for electricity generation to be installed and operational during 2022. Additionally, six electric vehicle charging points were installed.

Staffing has at times been tight. There has been additional staff absence due to Covid, continued staff turnover, and a number of staff are new or have less that two years' experience. The Governor has sought to address staff absence and recruitment issues. The deployment of prison staff has focussed on ensuring that changing regimes ran decently and safely. This was largely achieved. It meant, however, that some functions, including drug testing regimes and the safer custody and equalities teams, had to operate on significantly reduced staffing at times. Training in some areas was curtailed due to national restrictions placed on training.

In December 2020 the IMB withdrew from visiting the prison on a regular basis in the light of national restrictions and the advice to work from home where possible. During that time, we continued the arrangements for monitoring remotely that we had established in 2020: regular attendance, by teleconference, at morning management meetings and rule 45 boards, regular telephone contact with governors, functional heads and wing custodial managers, and receipt of prison monitoring and management information. In March we conducted a prisoner survey to enable us to understand how prisoners were experiencing lockdown. We returned to visiting the prison again, on a limited basis, in June 2021. After our return, we maintained our telephone contact with prison staff, but also attended meetings involving prisoner welfare in person and met prisoners again in some units and on exercise yards. In December 2021 we withdrew again. We continued throughout to deal with applications from prisoners, made to us in writing or through the 0800 telephone application service.

The Board is grateful for the support and cooperation it received from the Governor and prison staff which enabled it to continue working remotely, and for their open and inclusive approach to communication. We have tried to cover all aspects of prisoners' welfare during this difficult time, whilst also ensuring we understood the pressures on staff and the decisions of managers. Nevertheless, in some areas, coverage may have been less than usual.

### Main judgements
### How safe is the prison?

Safety within the prison was maintained in 2021. The prison continued to manage restrictions and the effects of the pandemic professionally. Incidents of violence between prisoners were higher than in 2020, reflecting the fact that at times prisoners were again able to mix together. By contrast, the number of challenge, support and intervention plans (CSIPs) opened to investigate potential violence or bullying between prisoners reduced, as did assaults against staff. The same number of those assaults were classed as serious as in 2020. The number of incidents of self-harm rose in 2021 compared with 2020, but continued to be below pre-pandemic levels. We are satisfied that prisoners who were vulnerable or whose needs were particularly complex were regularly reviewed and supported, albeit against a backdrop of

sometimes reduced staffing levels. Overall, there was good sharing of information between staff. No prisoner in Full Sutton took their own life in 2021.The use of force increased slightly during the year.

### How fairly and humanely are prisoners treated?

Our assessment is that prisoners were treated humanely and fairly within the restrictions imposed due to the pandemic. Careful thought was given to the way regimes, which had to be restricted because of Covid, were run, and this ensured prisoners received showers, exercise and access to the telephone.

### How well are prisoners' health and wellbeing needs met?

Prisoners' health needs were generally met, with clinics continuing to run. Prisoners with mental health needs were supported by the mental health team and vulnerable prisoners supported through visits by wing officers. Access to the gym continued whenever possible. Activities designed to promote wellbeing, for example, the older prisoner's group, could not be held during times of restriction, and planned Narcotics Anonymous and Alcoholics Anonymous groups could not be held.

### How well are prisoners progressed towards successful resettlement?

The provision of education has been very patchy and irregular during the year; rostered face-to-face learning took place on the wings from April when restrictions allowed, but there has been very little classroom learning, which only restarted in September 2021 on a restricted basis. Lower than expected numbers enrolled for in-cell learning. Whilst some progress has been made, including engagement with prisoners who have been difficult to reach in the past, a culture of education and learning amongst the wider prisoner population will need to be re-established in the coming year. The ability to work was also severely restricted, with workshops, except DHL and the kitchens, closed or operating with reduced numbers for most of the year. Prisoners were furloughed while workshops were shut. Offending behaviour programmes restarted during the year but on a reduced basis; steps were taken to mitigate the impact. The prison ensured that contact between prisoners and their families was maintained by secure video calling, the availability of which increased, and by reopening face-to-face visiting as soon as safely possible.

### Main areas for development

The Board is carrying forward the areas for

development identified in its 2019 and 2020 reports, which have not been able to be implemented because of the pandemic. We will monitor progress in these areas when we can in the coming year, and report on them in our 2022 report.

## TO THE GOVERNOR

To continue to improve the provision of meaningful work and the breadth of education for prisoners. (Recommended in 2019 and 2020. Recommendation carried forward.)

Continue to develop the STEP unit, and ensure its role in the Pathways to Progression programme is adequately funded and maintains a clear referral system, so that it can resume fully its intended role of breaking the cycle of segregation. (Recommended in 2020. Recommendation carried forward.)

Ensure that the equality forum and equality action group resume, to enable equality issues to be aired, and that an equality advisory group is established to support staff understanding.

That action is taken to communicate examples of best practice in complaint handling in order to improve the quality and fairness of responses.

That action is taken to ensure that staffing levels allow all forms of drug testing, (random, suspicion and reception) to take place to the required levels.

### Progress since the last report

Despite the pandemic there has been some progress against the main areas for development and improvement identified by the Board last year. Plans are more firmly in place to open a broader range of workshops including a wood mill (which has been planned for several years), a recycling workshop, work producing LED lighting components and a barista station in the industries and college area. It will be important that there is no further delay in the establishment of these workshops, as for several years, and currently, there is insufficient work for prisoners to do.

There has been some improvement in the provision of education, even though the delivery of learning has been severely interrupted. Further progress is, however, required in 2022 to ensure that a culture of learning and education is re-established.

Some improvement has been made to the operation of the STEP unit during 2021, despite the difficult circumstances of the continuing pandemic, but its funding needs to be put on a secure footing

In our report for 2020 we made an additional two recommendations to the Prison Service:

• First, that the cost of telephone calls should be re-examined with the provider, with a view to reducing their cost. The Prison Service responded that, while the PIN phone system is not directly comparable to any other public payphone service, requiring security and monitoring which was essential to the specific requirements of HMPPS, services and cost were being reviewed. In August 2021 call charges in Full Sutton were brought into line with charges applied in prisons where there is in-cell telephony, resulting in cheaper calls for prisoners in Full Sutton.

• Secondly, that the Prison Service should improve systems for the management and tracking of prisoners' property. The Prison Service responded that the development of a new prisoner property policy framework was paused due to Covid, although consultation took place later in 2020. A new draft framework was due for further consultation in 2021. The IMB will monitor the handling of prisoner property in 2022.

**ULNES WALTON LANE**
**LEYLAND**
**PRESTON**
**PR26 8NE**

**HM PRISON**
**GARTH**

**Tel: 01772 443300**

*For the latest reports on this prison please visit:*
https://tinyurl.com/bdfh26rv

*Important Changes:* **(1) Visits:** the identification necessary to access this prison and visit for social or professional purposes has changed; (2) **Money and Gifts** new rules now apply to these. See page 16 for full details of the above.

**Task of the establishment** A category B men's training prison.

**Certified normal accommodation and operational capacity**
Prisoners held at the time of inspection: 816
Baseline certified normal capacity: 810
In-use certified normal capacity: 810
Operational capacity: 8308

**Prison status and key providers**
Public
Prison Group: Long Term/High Security
Prison Group Director: Gavin O'Malley
Governor/Director: Andy Lund
IMB Chair: Frank Holden
Physical health provider: Bridgewater Community Healthcare NHS Foundation Trust
Mental health provider: Greater Manchester Mental Health NHS Foundation Trust

Substance use provider:
Greater Manchester Mental Health NHS Foundation Trust, Phoenix Futures
Learning and skills provider: Novus
Escort contractor: GeoAmey

**Brief history** HMP Garth opened in 1988. A category B men's establishment, it is part of the newly formed long- term and high-security estate directorate, holding a complex population. The population was predominantly made up of convicted adults serving more than four years and those serving indeterminate sentences.
In addition to the mainstream residential accommodation, the prison had a number of specialist units: The Beacon Unit, offering the offender personality disorder pathway service; The Building Hope Unit, a psychologically informed therapeutic environment; a substance misuse therapeutic community and a residential support unit.

**Short description of residential units**
Residential units:
A wing – residential unit
B wing – residential support unit and The Beacon Unit
C wing – residential unit
D wing – residential unit and The Building Hope Unit
E wing – residential unit and substance misuse therapeutic community
F wing – vulnerable prisoner unit
G wing – vulnerable prisoner unit
Segregation unit.

**Visiting Information**
Book online: https://www.gov.uk/prison-visit or by telephone on 01772 443 503 Monday to Thursday, 9am to 12:30pm and 2pm to 4:30pm.
**Visiting times:** Monday to Thursday: 2pm to 4pm

**Legal visits:** Booking line: 01772 443503. The booking line is open Monday to Thursday, 9am to 12:30pm and 2pm to 4:30pm.
**Legal visiting times**
Tuesday to Thursday: 2pm to 4pm

**INSPECTIONS & REPORTS**
**Date of last full inspection** 17 December 2018–18 January 2019
**HMCIP Report, published 09 May 2019**
HMP Garth is a category B training prison situated near Leyland in Lancashire. It was originally opened in 1988, and is now part of the long-term and high-security estate. At the time of this inspection it held just over 800 prisoners, the vast majority of whom were serving sentences of more than 10 years and presented a high risk of harm. Around two-thirds of those prisoners had been convicted of serious violence and a quarter

convicted of sexual offences. At the last inspection in 2017 we found that safety at the prison was poor, violence had increased and large numbers of prisoners were living in fear. The problems were compounded by the ready availability of drugs, and although there were some good features, such as the effectiveness of the learning and skills provision, we concluded that the prison was one of the most unsafe we had been to in recent times and that 'violence and drugs dominated the prisoner experience'.
It is pleasing to be able to report that in the space of two years there had been significant improvements at the prison. Although there was still too much violence, it had not risen in line with the overall trend across the prison estate, and credit is due to the staff at Garth for working hard to understand and contain it. There is absolutely no room for complacency, but there were some early encouraging signs of improvement. As with many other prisons, the ready availability of illicit drugs drove much of the violence, and the scale of the challenge in this respect at Garth was daunting. Sixty per cent of prisoners told us it was easy to obtain drugs, 30% were testing positive for drugs and around a quarter had developed a drug habit since entering the prison. There was a drug supply reduction strategy in place and both it and the violence reduction work will need constant review if the progress that has been made is to be maintained. Our assessments of safety and respect had improved since the last inspection, but there was still much to be done. My confidence that the prison can continue to make progress was strengthened by what I saw and heard during my meeting with the senior management team. It was very clear to me that they worked together in a highly collaborative way to address the serious challenges faced by the establishment. Members of the team, from whatever specialised function, were eager to contribute to what their colleagues were trying to achieve in their particular areas of responsibility. It was heartening to see this approach and to experience the obvious enthusiasm of the team for what they were striving to achieve. After the inspection had concluded I was also not surprised to learn that, in the space of only two years, around half of the recommendations made at the last inspection had been achieved, which is highly creditable given the very real challenges faced by the prison. For the future, there will need to be a continuing focus on dealing with violence. Far too many prisoners still felt unsafe, and much of the violence was serious. Similarly, the impact of illicit drugs was still severe, and the whole-prison approach to problem solving noted above will be vital to making progress in this regard.

Although the assessment of respect had improved, and health care is an important part of that healthy prison test, there was a serious concern around the high cancellation rate of external hospital appointments, with about half of them being consistently cancelled. This placed prisoners at unnecessary risk and needed to be addressed. So too did the issue of managing the potential risks to the public posed by those few prisoners who were released from Garth. Given the profile of the population held in the prison, this was a very serious issue and needed addressing. This report, in Section 4, sets out the details of where the weaknesses rest and what needs to be done to address them.

The leadership of HMP Garth were keen to point out to me that there were early signs of improvement, and it was to their credit that what had been achieved was sufficient to raise our assessments in two of our healthy prison tests. Given the overall context in which establishments such as Garth have been operating over the past few years, this is an achievement that should not be underestimated. For the future, dealing with the twin scourges of drugs and violence will be the key to making further progress, and I hope that when we next inspect HMP Garth we will be able to report that the momentum we saw on this occasion will have been maintained.

Peter Clarke CVO OBE QPM March 2019
HM Chief Inspector of Prisons

## INDEPENDENT MONITORING BOARD:
**Annual Report**

The law requires every prison to be monitored by an independent Board appointed by the Justice Secretary; these are known as Independent Monitoring Boards (IMBs). The IMB must satisfy itself as to the humane and just treatment of those held in custody within its prison and the range and adequacy of the programmes preparing them for release; it must report annually to the Justice Secretary on how well the prison has met the standards and requirements placed on it.

**IMB Report 1 December 2020 – 30 November 2021**
**Published March 2022**
**EXECUTIVE SUMMARY**
**Background to the report**

For a second year all aspects of life in the prison have been dominated by the continuing Covid-19 pandemic and the constant changes imposed or lifted by the government. Endeavours to control the pandemic and keep infections out of the establishment have continued throughout and the Governor, with the continuing support of the senior management team and staff, has

worked tirelessly to maintain and improve on the work of the previous year. The dangers that the virus posed were clearly recognised and steps to manage the situation were taken. This was done by restricting the regime, closing down education classes, workshops, gyms and family and domestic visits and by keeping prisoner movement throughout the prison to a minimum. Some family contact was maintained via 'Purple Visits' Precautions were also taken to reduce the number of people entering the prison. As a consequence the risk of bringing the virus into the prison was much reduced. Constant testing of staff and prisoners is ongoing and continuous. The first Covid-19 case was found in Garth during October 2020; since then there have been isolated cases throughout 2021 with Garth listed by Public Health England, as an 'outbreak site on three occasions. Staff absences due to people having been in contact with others have been high, frequently with more than 65 staff absent, either with Covid-19 or having to isolate, and that situation is continuing. Staff absences have put additional pressure on staff in work. The situation has been handled effectively, although constant changes to the regime have been necessitated and on many occasions wings have had to be 'locked down'.

Throughout this period the Board recognised that it had a right to continue to enter the prison, if it was safe for members and prisoners. On three occasions the Board monitored remotely for short periods. At all times it has striven to work effectively but clearly its work has been affected by the conditions and by the fact that it has been going through a Board membership rebuilding period.

**Main judgements**
**How safe is the prison?**
In many respects the prison has been safer as a result of the pandemic restrictions than it was during periods on normal regime. Fewer than usual incidents have occurred

**How fairly and humanely are prisoners treated?**
Whilst, during the restrictions, many regular activities have been reduced or curtailed, in other respects prisoners have been well supported by staff and fewer than usual incidents have occurred. It should be noted, however, that throughout this period the prison has been actively recruiting new staff and that, consequently, there is a large number of relatively inexperienced staff in post.

### How well are prisoners' health and wellbeing needs met?

An unusually high number of applications have been received about healthcare issues during this period but it is the opinion of the Board that the regular healthcare staff have worked tirelessly to provide a full and effective service. There have been some instances where visiting practitioners have been unable to attend but, generally, the system has worked well.

### How well are prisoners progressed towards successful resettlement?

The transfer of prisoners has been reduced during this period because of Covid-19 restrictions both in Garth and in other prisons. Clearly this is a national problem which requires urgent attention. It should be noted that Garth normally holds long- sentence prisoners who are some distance from release. A small number of prisoners are released from Garth but increasingly problems are being encountered in transferring prisoners to resettlement prisons for discharge. In-cell telephony was installed in March/April 2020 and this has proved to be an important benefit for prisoners to keep them in touch with family and friends.

The in-cell telephony was installed in March/April 2020 and this has proved to be an important benefit for prisoners to keep them in touch with family and friends

### Main areas for development
### TO THE MINISTER

The Board's strong recommendation is that the contract with Amey should be investigated and reviewed as poor maintenance of the prison is impacting negatively on all aspects of life at Garth prison for both prisoners and staff.

The ongoing problem of the indeterminate sentence for public protection (IPP) continues. It is understood that the matter is subject to an inquiry by the Parliamentary Justice Select Committee and this Board has offered a contribution to the response from the IMB Management Board.

Staff retention problems throughout HMPPS have increased throughout this period in large part because of the erosion of staff salaries and conditions of service. This matter needs to be urgently addressed and rectified.

The Board regularly compliments the kitchen manager and his staff on the quality and quantity of the food provided but it is suggested that the food budget be increased as a matter of urgency Similarly the number of beds available for prisoners with special needs throughout the estate is inadequate and requires increase urgently.

Throughout the prison estate there is a serious shortage of beds for difficult and hard to manage prisoners. This all too frequently results in excessively long periods of segregation. This issue needs to be addressed as a matter of urgency.

### TO THE PRISON SERVICE

The Board continues to be concerned about the length of time some prisoners are held in the segregation unit. The three specialist units in the prison do take some of the most disturbed of these people but it may be more appropriate to move some of them elsewhere. Further work needs to be carried out to improve this process.

The recruitment of uniformed staff needs urgent attention:

• Each prison and each category of prison has its own needs in terms of staff recruitment and balance.

• Each prison should have a say in the recruitment of individual officers in order to address the above requirements. This would be facilitated by face-to-face interviews in the prison.

• Each prison should have a say as to the gender balance of recruits.

• The retention of new staff is proving to be problematic. If the above issues are addressed it is likely that retention will be improved.

There is a growing number of older prisoners, many of whom are in need of mobility and other aids. Presently there is confusion about who should provide these aids and this matter needs urgent attention because it impacts increasingly upon budgets.

The Board is very concerned that the role and involvement of the outside Probation Service has been seriously limited in that.

• The community offender manager (COM) is not now allocated to a prisoner until (s)he is within sight of release.

• Pre-sentence reports are not now routinely prepared for defendants facing custodial sentences. The offender assessment system (OASys) has been seriously diluted pre- and post- sentence and before transfer to category B and other prisons.

### TO THE GOVERNOR

• Restore the effectiveness of the key worker scheme.

• Maintain a secure and safe environment through the remainder of the Covid pandemic.

• Continue to monitor the effectiveness of Amey.

Progress since the last report

The following issues were raised in last year's report:

• indeterminate sentences for public protection (IPP)

• deaths in custody

• staffing and recruitment of prison officers

• prisoners' property

In all of these categories the problems remain very much as they were despite best efforts by staff.

**GALLOW FIELD ROAD
MARKET HARBOROUGH
LEICS
LE16 7RP**

**HM PRISON
GARTREE**

**Tel: 01858 426600**

*For the latest reports on this prison please visit:*
https://tinyurl.com/bdfh26rv

*Important Changes:* **(1) Visits:** the identification necessary to access this prison and visit for social or professional purposes has changed; (2) **Money and Gifts** new rules now apply to these. See page 16 for full details of the above.

**Task of the establishment** HMP Gartree is a category B prison holding life and indeterminate sentence male prisoners.

**Certified normal accommodation and operational capacity**
Prisoners held at the time of this visit: 645
Baseline certified normal capacity: 708
In-use certified normal capacity: 648 (population reduced for maintenance project)
Operational capacity: 648

**Prison status and key providers**
Public
Prison Group: Long Term/High Security
Prison Group Director: Gavin O'Malley
Governor/Director: Babafemi Dada
IMB Chair: Tim Norman
Physical health provider: Nottinghamshire Healthcare NHS Foundation Trust
Mental health provider: Nottinghamshire Healthcare NHS Foundation Trust
Substance use treatment provider:
Nottinghamshire Healthcare NHS Foundation Trust
Prison education framework provider:
Milton Keynes College
Escort contractor: GeoAmey

**Brief history** HMP Gartree opened in 1965 as a category C training prison but changed its role and came within the high security system, reverting to a category B prison in 1992. Since then the population of indeterminate sentence prisoners has been growing, and in 1997 the prison's role changed to that of a main life-sentenced prisoner centre. In 2017 it became part of the Prison Service's new long-term high security estate.

**Short description of residential units**
*A, B, C and D wings:* Generic residential wings that are part of the original 1960s build and have

since been refurbished. A- C wings have single cells only, and D wing also has two double cells.
*G wing:* Induction/reverse cohort unit, opened in 2005-06. It has two double cells; the remainder are single cells.
*H wing:* Opened in 2005-06, it houses prisoners aged over 50 and the psychologically informed planned environment (PIPE) unit.
*I wing:* Houses 28 prisoners in 13 double and two single cells.
*Gartree therapeutic community (GTC):* Holds up to 25 prisoners in single cells.
*Therapeutic community plus (TC+):* For prisoners with learning difficulties or low IQ who require additional assistance and guidance, with 12 single cells.
*The segregation unit:* 12 beds.

**Visiting Information**
Book online: https://www.gov.uk/prison-visit or by telephone on 01858 426 727 Monday to Friday, 9am to midday and 1pm to 2pm.
**Visiting times:** Tuesday, Thursday, Saturday and Sunday: 2pm to 3:30pm.

**Legal visits:** Book by email:
socialvisits.gartree@justice.gov.uk or by telephone 01858 426 727 Monday to Friday, 9am to midday and 1pm to 2pm.
**Legal visiting time:** Wednesdays, 9am to 11am

**INSPECTIONS & REPORTS**
**Scrutiny visit: 22 and 29-30 September 2020**
**Published 30 October 2020**
HMP Gartree is a category B adult male prison in Leicestershire. At the time of our scrutiny visit the prison accommodated 645 prisoners serving indeterminate and life sentences. The roll was lower than usual due to a wing closure for maintenance work. This had enabled the transfer out of a significant number of category C and D prisoners to appropriate prisons, and had eased the burden on staffing at a challenging time. The senior management team had implemented all relevant Covid-19 procedures as directed by the HMPPS National Framework (see Glossary of terms), and by and large prisoners and staff were being kept safe from the virus. However, as we are finding in many prisons, social distancing was not always possible or enforced. A small number of prisoners and staff had tested positive for Covid-19 since March 2020, but none at the time of our visit. Under new procedures there was no requirement for a dedicated reverse cohort unit (RCU), prisoner isolation unit (PIU) or shielding unit (see Glossary of terms). Instead, symptomatic prisoners or those transferring in from a prison where there was an outbreak of the virus were isolated on their current unit and

provided with a separate regime. Given the low numbers of transfers in and the procedures in place, this was a proportionate response.

Some of the indicators of safety were concerning. The number of prisoner assaults and the seriousness of the violence remained similar to the period before the regime was restricted, even though prisoners were locked up for most of the day. Levels of self-harm and the use of force were higher than before March, and we had some concerns about oversight of segregation. When the restrictions were first imposed, the prison had stopped most of its strategic functional meetings to focus on the emerging crisis. While this might have been proportionate at the time, there seemed to be less justification six months on. A weakened strategic oversight of safety meant that although the prison was collecting and analysing data, the results were not being used effectively to learn lessons and drive improvement. The promotion of equality and diversity had also suffered because it too had been given insufficient priority when compared to the continued focus on managing the impact of the pandemic. The governor had, however, recognised this and recently taken action to start necessary improvements.

The condition of the older residential accommodation was poor. Despite many bids to fund the refurbishment of the prison, and efforts to keep the units clean, much accommodation needed refurbishment or replacement. The showers on A to D units were unacceptably poor and, given the importance of cleanliness during a pandemic, this needed to be addressed with urgency. There was no privacy screening around most toilets, and an outdated heating system meant cells could be oppressively hot or very cold. Good staff-prisoner relationships mitigated some of the negative aspects of the restrictions in place. Staff were knowledgeable about the prisoners in their care, and most prisoners said they had someone they could turn to. Unlike some other prisons we have visited during this period, most prisoners had benefited from a key work session (see Glossary of terms) in the last month, and the quality of the interaction was good, even though some of it was by telephone.

Since the last inspection, there had been improvements to the provision of health care. We were particularly encouraged to see the use of information technology to facilitate psychiatric consultations with patients. However, we were concerned about the continued delay in reinstating a full dental service due to a national industrial relations dispute; this had created a significant backlog of appointments and put the oral health of prisoners at risk.

The prison had retained essential work for about 12% of the population and these prisoners had more time out of cell than the majority, who were locked up for over 22 hours a day. Almost every prisoner could shower daily, and PE staff made the morning exercise period more purposeful by leading circuit classes on the exercise yard. Prisoners who were studying for GCSEs and AS levels were supported through regular calls from tutors and assistance from trained peer mentors, and the success rate in the summer exams had been good. There were plans to return prisoners to work and education part time to enable social distancing, but these were not yet timetabled.

Purple Visits (see Glossary of terms) had been in place since June, but social visits were only reintroduced in early September. Take-up of both was disappointing, and adjustments were needed to make visits more attractive to prisoners and their families.

Rehabilitation and the ability for prisoners to progress were perhaps the greatest casualties of the pandemic. The prison was a national hub for programmes and therapeutic interventions, but both had been greatly affected by the restrictions. That said, it was reassuring that public protection work had not halted.

In conclusion, managers and staff at Gartree had responded well to the threats presented by the national pandemic. However, it is important that the senior team seeks to strengthen oversight and delivery of the prison's core work. This is needed to improve the outcomes for prisoners who have been subject to an extremely restricted regime for over six months. More specific and time-bound recovery plans would help the prison to do this more quickly in the move to the next stage of the national framework for easing restrictions.

Peter Clarke CVO OBE QPM

HM Chief Inspector of Prisons October 2020

## INDEPENDENT MONITORING BOARD: Annual Report

The law requires every prison to be monitored by an independent Board appointed by the Justice Secretary; these are known as Independent Monitoring Boards (IMBs). The IMB must satisfy itself as to the humane and just treatment of those held in custody within its prison and the range and adequacy of the programmes preparing them for release; it must report annually to the Justice Secretary on how well the prison has met the standards and requirements placed on it.

**IMB Report 1 December 2020 – 30 November 2021**
**Published May 2022**
**EXECUTIVE SUMMARY**
**Background to the report**
Unfortunately, much of the Board's monitoring over the past reporting period has again been

undertaken remotely, due to ongoing Covid-19 restrictions. This has meant that for some months weekly rota reports and applications have been handled remotely, our involvement in review boards and wider departmental meetings has been limited, and face to face access to prisoners restricted. For the periods where Board members have been able to enter the prison, we have adhered to Public Health England (PHE) guidelines.

However, as we stated in our annual report last year, remote monitoring is not the same as being in the prison and being visible and accessible to prisoners who may need help from the Board. The restrictions have affected our ability to monitor and communicate directly with prisoners, which will be reflected in the content of this report.

The Board thanks all staff for their continued support and help during this challenging time and praises the Governor, senior management team (SMT) and all staff who have continued to support and care for the prisoners under very difficult circumstances. On the whole Gartree has been fortunate not to have experienced major and prolonged Covid-19 outbreaks and where they have occurred, they appear to have been handled effectively. However, it is sad to note that there have been Covid-related illnesses and deaths amongst prisoners. The prison has operated a Covid suite to carry out testing of staff and visitors and to allow 'track and trace' to be undertaken for staff and monitoring of cases amongst prisoners.

The Board is concerned that the long periods of lock-up experienced by the prisoners will have a detrimental effect on their mental health and wellbeing and in some cases their ability to rehabilitate and progress. The unprecedented impact of the Covid-19 pandemic has hit the prisoners and their families hard, with them having to endure incredibly long periods of a severely restricted regime. This situation is not unique to Gartree as the regime has followed national operating 'stages' within guidelines set by the MoJ. The prisoners at Gartree have shown great tolerance and compliance, despite the fact that they and their families have suffered during this period and have been directly affected by the fact that when restrictions have been imposed, they have tightened more quickly for them but then appear to be relaxing far more slowly than for the wider community.

As with last year's annual report the Board remains concerned that many of the negative effects experienced by the prisoners because of Covid-19 restrictions, including limiting access to education, psychological and behavioural programmes, education, work, some healthcare services and clinics, will persist for years to come.

Over the past year, some physical improvements have been taking place to the fabric of the prison, with fire safety measures and roof repairs continuing. However, more still needs to be done. Some of the wings require immediate investment and the condition of the older residential accommodation needs addressing, as recommended in Her Majesty's Inspectorate of Prisons (HMIP) scrutiny report published in October 2020. These recommended actions remain outstanding.

Improvements to security on the main entrance gate have started; the physical building works have been completed but X-ray machines are still to be installed. These additional measures are welcomed as they will help to prevent unauthorised items being brought into the prison which can undermine safety and security.

The Board has noticed that a large number of new, less experienced staff (who have only worked in the prison during the restricted regime), are now in post and it welcomes the news that two apprentice coaches and one prison officer entry level trainee (POELT) mentor are supporting these new officers to ensure that they receive all necessary training and peer support to help them care for prisoners within the normal regime.

## Main judgements
### How safe is the prison?

Once again, the Board acknowledges there has been effective management of the pandemic at all levels, evidenced by the low number of Covid-19 cases. The prison's effective response to Covid has undoubtedly helped to keep the majority of prisoners safe from infection, which is commendable. Where there has been an outbreak on a wing, this was managed well. Despite staffing issues, the healthcare provider has maintained a basic level of care to the prisoners although the Board has heard some grumbles about the speed at which vaccinations were rolled out for the prisoners. The Board has been advised that vaccinations were rolled out as per PHE and National Health Service England (NHSE) guidelines and that an exception report was provided for NHSE for the prisoners who were unable to have vaccinations because they had tested positive for Covid-19 within the previous 28 days.

Inevitably, the lockdown has limited the access of prisoners to one another, and the number of violent incidents has reduced over the past year. However, there have still been assaults (prisoner on prisoner: 39 and prisoner on staff: 43) which in some instances have been linked to debt, substance misuse and frustrations with the regime.

The influx of drugs and other illegal items has continued over the past year with an increasing number of drone sightings and finds. However, effective targeted detection and searching has allowed prohibited items such as phones, drugs, weapons, and 'hooch' (illicitly brewed alcohol) to be detected and confiscated. Changes in the way that exercise has been facilitated may have helped to reduce the trading of illicit items and improve safety and the Board has been advised that there will be no return to whole-prison exercise periods on the sports field when the normal regime resumes.

Over the past year the safer custody and equality functions have benefited from additional resource, which has enabled the allocation of dedicated staff to lead on assessment, care in custody and teamwork (ACCT) and/or challenge, support and intervention plan (CSIP) reviews and documents. This information continues to be clearly noted on the daily briefing sheet (DBS), which is useful for monitoring purposes.

Issues relating to debt and violence persist and some prisoners still report being victimised or feeling vulnerable to attack, which can lead to them self- isolating and/or self-harming. The Board is pleased to note that the number of prisoners listed as socially isolating has reduced significantly over the past year and these individuals are now actively managed with CSIPs. Once again there has been a reduction in the use of long-term segregation in both the SAPU and on the wings.

The Board has heard that there has been a reduction in some key work but is also aware that some staff members have used the in-cell phones to continue working with the more vulnerable prisoners.

**How fairly and humanely are prisoners treated?**
The Board considers that on the whole prisoners at Gartree are treated fairly and humanely, although with continued Covid-19 restrictions we remain concerned about the length of time that prisoners have spent locked up in their cells over the past two years. The acceptance of this by most prisoners has been commendable and they have acknowledged that because the prison has published exercise rotas and (wherever possible) allowed prisoners time to carry out 'domestics' this has helped them to cope with the long periods in- cell.

There is still some work to be done in improving knowledge of the experience of those with protected characteristics to ensure that outcomes and opportunities are equal for all, but it is very encouraging to see that a new equalities officer has been appointed and is taking a lead on a wide range of issues. The Board looks forward to understanding how meaningful figures and comparative data will be used to help drive and inform improvements in achieving fair treatment at Gartree.

The Board is dismayed at the slow progress on improvements to showers and some other areas, which affects the humane treatment of prisoners. Many of the shower units available for use are wholly unacceptable, despite money being allocated some repairs have not been completed. The Board fails to understand that, whilst wings have been vacated to allow fire safety work to take place, other long overdue improvements have not also been carried out. The Board understands the challenges regarding pest control and acknowledges the work by Gartree to remove rubbish as quickly as possible, however the issues remain.

In-cell phones have helped prisoners to maintain vital contact with families when visits were suspended. The majority of prisoners have a TV in their cell, which helps them to pass time during lockdown, but there have been issues with the reception on some wings which has taken a long time to remedy.

Some foreign national prisoners have expressed concern about lack of access to Home Office officials and legal advice. The Board does however acknowledge that these individuals have been provided with additional PIN credits and postage facilities to enable them to maintain family ties.

The Board is satisfied that prisoners in the segregation unit are treated humanely. Relationships between staff and prisoners are generally good, the physical fabric of the unit is reasonably well maintained, and prisoners now have access to in-cell phones. Good order and/or discipline (GOOD) reviews now take place on two days a week and wherever possible are conducted by the head of safety, which has improved the consistency and management of prisoners on the unit and segregated on wings, who can be some of the most vulnerable and/or challenging prisoners in Gartree.

**How well are prisoners' health and wellbeing needs met?**
Prior to Covid the NHS provider in the prison was beginning to make progress to address some of the issues concerning the quality and access to healthcare which the Board had previously highlighted. Unfortunately, there is little progress to report and recruitment and retention of permanent staff remains a huge issue in both the physical and mental health teams.

Inevitably waiting times will have increased and access to outside services and clinics will have been affected by the pandemic, reflecting issues in the wider community as a whole.

The Board has struggled to obtain data from the health provider and whilst we acknowledge that this is probably as a result of staffing issues,* moving forward we need to find a way in which we can easily access and utilise the data, which no doubt already exists as the Board assumes the SMT and the Prison Service receives this as part of monitoring the contract services being provided. The Board is also keen to gain an understanding of what any NHS Covid-19 recovery plan will mean for the prisoners in Gartree who have had appointments/treatments cancelled and postponed and how the prisoners receiving or requiring social care will be supported in the future.

*The Board is now aware that performance data for prison healthcare and prison performance were suspended by the NHS and HMMPS for the period 1 April 2020 to 31 March 2021 as they implemented exceptional delivery models and recovery plans at the start of the pandemic.

The Board is concerned that for many prisoners there will be serious longer- term issues arising from these lockdown restrictions, which may affect both their physical and mental health. Loss of social visits and of access to purposeful activities, programmes, education, physical exercise, and wider association will inevitably have had an impact on prisoners' wellbeing.

Once again the Board acknowledges that some positive work has been done by the prison to try to manage time spent alone in cell, such as: some essential work has continued; some prisoners have been allowed to undertake purposeful activities; some gym sessions and the opportunity to do circuit activities during exercise periods; sentence reviews and parole boards continued; some key work has continued; most face-to-face education stopped but learners were still given assessed in-cell work; in-cell telephony with additional PIN credit; virtual 'Purple Visits'; and some access to mental health and substance misuse professionals.

### How well are prisoners progressed towards successful resettlement?

Understandably, many activities linked to prisoner progression and resettlement have been hampered during the past year. For the majority of prisoners all purposeful activity ceased, with only essential workers such as the prisoners who work as kitchen staff, on waste collections and as grounds workers continuing to work in small bubbles, to help maintain the wider prison function.

Prisoners were initially happy to work through education packs in their cells, but some have now advised that they are keen to receive a more supportive and personal approach to learning. Some prisoners have been able to attend in-person education sessions during both the Stage 3 and Stage 2 (lockdown) regime. The Board acknowledges that the Governor has stressed his desire to see all prisoners as fully employed or engaging in meaningful activities or education as soon at the regime can be opened up.

The Prison Reform Trust recently reported in its annual Bromley Briefing that work it had undertaken with its Prisoner Policy Network (PPN), following the publication of the government's White Paper on the future of prisons, (Prisons Strategy White Paper, 7 December 2021) highlighted how many prisoners long for a full working day and the opportunity to make decisions and take responsibility as preparation for life after release. The Board is hopeful that plans to provide wider training and employment opportunities to support future employability and promote greater self-esteem will be successful. In the past we expressed some concern about the amount and quality of purposeful activity truly available to the prisoners at Gartree, and any opportunities which help to prepare prisoners for a future release into a modern digital world are to be welcomed.

The new offender management unit (OMU) incorporating staff from the Probation Service seems to have been progressing many recategorisations over the past year and over a hundred prisoners are now awaiting places at category C or D establishments.

The work carried out by the library over the past year to help prisoners support their education and facilitate access to reading material is to be commended. The Board was also impressed with a recent exhibition held in the nearby public library showcasing the artwork and library activities of some of the prisoners at Gartree; this is a positive view of the prison which members of the public may not normally get to see.

### Main areas for development

The Board requests that answers are specific to Gartree rather than at a national level.

### TO THE MINISTER

Will the Minister confirm that the funding bid received by Gartree to address the unacceptable state of the showers will remain available to the establishment even if the work has not commenced during the financial year it was awarded?

Could the Minister confirm that investment to address the seriously declined infrastructure of Gartree will continue regardless of any options under consideration for a new prison to be built within the locality, and that Gartree will not suffer in any way should a new prison be built? The Board acknowledges the Minister's response to the question raised in our last annual report regarding the national partnership agreement for prison healthcare. The Board requests the Minister provide a further update on resources being planned post-Covid-19 to enable the delivery of measures outlined in the partnership agreement specifically for Gartree, as the Board has increasing concerns regarding the mental and physical wellbeing of the men at Gartree?

Will the Minister explain the reasons for the delay in rolling out booster Covid- 19 vaccine in Gartree (albeit that the Board has been advised that vaccinations were rolled out as per PHE and NHSE guidelines except where prisoners were unable to have vaccinations because they had tested positive for Covid-19 within the previous 28 days)? It has been acknowledged that prisoners experience a more confined environment, and therefore potentially greater vulnerability to Covid. However, despite the importance of the booster being promoted daily in the wider community from September 2021, especially for adults over 50 years and for those with underlying health conditions under 50, Gartree only offered the booster from mid-December 2021.

The Board acknowledges the Minister's response to our last annual report regarding indeterminate sentences for public protection (IPP) prisoners. However, Gartree continues to hold IPP prisoners who are now many years over their tariff. Frustration continues among these prisoners. The Board looks forward to an update from the Minister about plans that will resolve this ongoing issue, specifically for the prisoners at Gartree.

## TO THE PRISON SERVICE

The Board requests an update on the new prisoners' property policy framework which was referenced in the Prison Service's response to the query in the Board's last annual report regarding prisoners' property.

The Board is still concerned about the ongoing situation regarding the repair or replacement of equipment in the kitchens. Can the Prison Service confirm that they have engaged with contractors to create a service level agreement which will achieve more timely response to address such issues at Gartree?

The Board requests that the Prison Service confirm the structure within the service that ensures that the contracts performance is being achieved in accordance with the signed contract. Will the Prison Service work with the Board to ensure that it has access to necessary information, for example healthcare data, so that the Board is able to monitor more effectively how well the prison is meeting the standards and requirements placed on it and what impact these

have on those in its custody? Can the Prison Service confirm that Gartree will receive sufficient ongoing budget and capital funding in order both that prisoners can live and staff can work within a safe, secure, and decent environment as the establishment returns to a pre-Covid-19 regime? The Board has noted that other prisons have received substantial investment to improve their infrastructure, and the Board, based on the information provided over the years, fails to understand why Gartree has not received this level of investment.

Will the Prison Service ensure that Gartree will be sufficiently funded so that prisoners' access to employment, purposeful activity, education, and healthcare will address the impacts of Covid-19 as quickly as possible?

Can the Prison Service confirm to the Board who has overall responsibility for the health and wellbeing of the prisoners at Gartree?

Can the Prison Service share with the Board how it will ensure the recruitment of staff to Gartree when salaries in the public sector compared to private prisons appear lower? For example, HMP Five Wells in Wellingborough has recently been recruiting for officers with a starting salary of £25,164 p.a. versus Gartree at £23,144 p.a. (Source: Indeed.co.uk).

Will the Prison Service clarify the reasons why the additional weekly phone credit (£5 per week to call family and friends) ceased for Gartree in September when we have been made aware that this may not have been the case in privately operated prisons (e.g. HMP Forest Bank)?

Category D prisoners housed at Gartree are put at a serious disadvantage at parole hearings because they have been unable to prove themselves in open prison conditions. Can the Board understand how this disadvantage will be mitigated going forward for these prisoners? In addition, the Board seeks to understand the objective, and how this will be measured, of the new system of categorisations from the Prison Service as we remain unclear.

Will the Prison Service ensure that the money which has been allocated to upgrade showers is ringfenced to allow this long overdue work to take place and that there is a process put in place to test for and treat legionella in all shower blocks in the future?

## TO THE GOVERNOR

Will the Governor continue to encourage greater use of body-worn cameras throughout the establishment to help de-escalate potentially violent situations?

Can the Governor confirm that the Board will be allowed to resume dedicated use of an office without the need to allow other members of staff access to use the in-cell phone to call prisoners or for other purposes?

Will the Governor ensure that all custodial managers are aware of the occasion when the Board needs to be notified of incidents, deaths in custody, use of force and all other routine notifications which are outlined in the memorandum of understanding between HMPPS and the Management Board for the IMB, dated December 2019?

Can confirmation be given as to when the key worker scheme will revert to the initial planned level, whereby all prisoners have a named key worker, who has time allocated for key worker duties, and that key workers will remain constant even when prisoners transfer within the prison?

Will the Governor ensure the prison continues to provide resources to allow diversity and inclusion to continue with the renewed focus it has been given in the past year to promote equality of outcome and opportunity for all relevant protected characteristics?

Will the Governor ensure that all new arrivals are provided with a cell which contains all basic items of furniture and that they are given the clothing and any items they need on arrival at Gartree?

Will the Governor ensure effective pest control measures are put in place, used and reviewed to control vermin?

Will the Governor continue to ensure that monitoring and quality assurance checks of all ACCT and CSIP documents are carried out by a dedicated custodial manager, and that all post-closure reviews and documentation are of the required standard?

Can the Governor confirm that there is a simple and clear system in place to ensure that prisoners are able to understand exactly what property they can have in possession and in storage and what additional items they are allowed to order (from approved suppliers) and/or have sent in, and that staff are fully trained to support them with this and any issues which may arise?

The Board remains concerned about property going missing either on prisoners' arrival, when they are transferred to new cells or when searches take place. Please can the Governor share with the Board measures that have been or will be put in place to improve processes and procedures regarding prisoners' property, as complaints remain high.?

Can the Governor reassure the Board that any future regime design will not result in more time in their cells for the prisoners at Gartree than at pre-Covid- 19 levels?

Will the Governor work with the Board to identify ways to continue to improve engagement between the Board and the SMT? The Board acknowledges that aspects of the working relationship have improved, but there are still occasions when the flow of information relies on us asking questions. We are keen to have key information provided so that we have the knowledge and information to support us in undertaking the role assigned to us.

The key worker scheme, part of offender management in custody (OMiC), has been introduced and dedicated qualified probation staff are based in the OMU. However, it is the Board's view that Covid lockdowns have seriously impacted on this work and the Board looks forward to seeing the levels of interaction with the men achieved prior to lockdowns being restored as a matter of urgency.

**Progress since the last report**
Once again, this year the Board acknowledges that stability within the SMT continues which is welcomed by the Board. A new deputy governor has been appointed who appears to be building relationships with the prisoners and the prisoner council. The impact of this has been evidenced through the remote rota reports, where a number of staff have expressed positive comments about management and how the prison is managed/run. The Board continues to acknowledge the effective management of the challenges that Covid-19 has given Gartree. The effective management at all levels, from wing staff to the Governor, is evidenced by the limited number of Covid cases reported and the manner in which localised wing outbreaks have been managed. We continue to acknowledge the challenges that Covid-19 has had on both prisoners and staff.

Healthcare provision has continued throughout Covid lockdowns in the most challenging of circumstances although the Board does have concerns about current staffing issues and the impact on the prisoners now and in the future. However, the Board acknowledges that recruitment and retention is a challenge across the NHS.

Outbreaks of Covid have been managed well due to a close working relationship between healthcare and the prison.

Prisoners who self-isolate are now being monitored more closely and referred for proactive CSIP referrals, when appropriate.

Communication about which dedicated staff member is the lead on a prisoner's ACCT and/or CSIP is available through the DBS. The introduction of a single case management system for ACCT put this in place.

Complaint handling and quality assurance monitoring has improved; now, only dedicated administrative staff have access to the complaints box. A similar approach is being adopted for discrimination incident reporting forms (DIRFs).

The decant, within Gartree and to other establishments, of large numbers of prisoners to enable the closure of wings for fire safety works was managed well.

Wing staff and gym staff have worked hard to ensure that the short periods of exercise which have been permitted to the prisoners are beneficial. Gym staff devised circuit routes and exercise for those men using the daily exercise yard.

The Governor's emphasis on staff endeavouring to de-escalate situations before use of force is required has begun to achieve positive results. This has been evidenced through reviewing video footage, which show that de- escalation methods are now being adopted by staff and best practice is being shared.

Recategorisation and transfers have taken place but some prisoners report being 'stuck' awaiting moves. It is acknowledged that some seem to prefer to stay at Gartree.

There has been a reduction in both the number of prisoners in SAPU and the time they stay there and, in addition, far fewer prisoners segregated on the wings.

Whilst prisoners' brewing of hooch and distilled alcohol continues at a high level, there is effective proactive detection and seizure taking place in an attempt to manage the issue.

New security initiatives have started with works to the gate, which allow scanning and searching of all persons entering the establishment.

Gang activity remains a concern, but the prison is working on a new core day and regime changes that will seek to minimise the opportunity for those with conflicts to meet in communal areas off the wing.

Outbreaks of Covid have been effectively managed and contained.

The OMiC scheme, which was introduced last year and saw dedicated, qualified probation staff joining the offender management unit, has continued.

Prisoners who self-isolate are now being monitored more closely and referred for proactive CSIP referrals.

Version 6 of ACCT has been introduced, although there are still some issues with training and quality assurance.

Over the past year, improvements to the prison complaint handling and quality assurance monitoring have been maintained although the Board has experienced an increase in COMP2 (confidential) applications (most of which do not in fact meet the criteria to be considered a COMP2 complaint).

**GRENDON UNDERWOOD
AYLESBURY
BUCKS
HP18 0TL**

HM PRISON SERVICE
**HM PRISON
GRENDON**  Tel: 01296 445000

*For the latest reports on this prison please visit:*
https://tinyurl.com/bdfh26rv

*Important Changes:* **(1) Visits:** the identification necessary to access this prison and visit for social or professional purposes has changed; (2) **Money and Gifts** new rules now apply to these. See page 16 for full details of the above.

**Task of the establishment** Category B adult male training prison, therapeutic delivery.

**Certified normal accommodation and operational capacity**
Prisoners held March 2021: 164
Baseline certified normal capacity: 233
In-use certified normal capacity: 193
Operational capacity: 233

**Prison status and key providers**
Public
Prison Group: South Central
Prison Group Director: Andy Lattimore
Governor/Director: Rebecca Hayward
IMB Chair: Christoff Lewis
Physical health provider: Practice Plus Group
Mental health provider: Barnet, Enfield and Haringey Mental Health NHS Trust
Substance misuse treatment provider: Midlands Partnership Foundation Trust
Prison education framework provider: Milton Keynes College
Escort contractor: Serco

**Brief history** Opened in 1962, Grendon was initially used as an experimental psychiatric prison and psychiatric unit for prisoners with antisocial personality disorders. It developed into a therapeutic community (TC) prison based upon principles established at the Henderson Hospital in London. There are six discrete therapeutic communities, each with over 40 resident prisoners. In 2014, a small TC opened for prisoners with learning disabilities who had previously been excluded from treatment. Grendon and the adjacent HMP Spring Hill, an open prison for adult men, are managed jointly by a single senior management team.

**Short description of residential units**
A wing - TC for prisoners convicted of sex offences
B wing - assessment and TC

C wing - TC
D wing - TC
F wing - closed at the time of the visit for fire safety improvements
G wing - TC+ for prisoners with learning disabilities (also the reverse cohort unit)

**Visiting Information**
Book online: https://www.gov.uk/prison-visit or by telephone on 01296 445 243 The booking line is open Monday to Friday: 10am to 12pm.
**Visiting times:** Wednesday, Saturday and Sunday: 1:45pm to 3:15pm

**Legal visits:** There are currently no legal visits taking place.

**INSPECTIONS & REPORTS**
**Scrutiny visit: 2 and 9–10 March 2021**
**Published 13 April 2021**
HMP Grendon is a category B training prison in Buckinghamshire with a capacity of just over 200 adult male prisoners, all of whom are serving long determinate or life sentences. The buildings have not aged well and they are tired and dilapidated; it is one of only a few prisons that still does not have in-cell sanitation. At the time of our visit, the prison capacity had been reduced with the closure of a wing for fire and alarm upgrades. This, combined with fewer prisoners transferring in due to the pandemic, resulted in a population of 164 at the time of our visit.

Grendon is one of just two specialist prisons in England and Wales that function as democratic therapeutic communities (see Glossary of terms). All prisoners undertake accredited therapy to understand and address their offending behaviour and live in a collaborative setting with their peers and staff. Prisoners are given a say in the day-to-day running of the establishment to equip them with greater insight into their own behaviour and instil a greater sense of responsibility for others.

When restrictions to manage the spread of Covid-19 were introduced in March 2020, as part of the HM Prison and Probation Service (HMPPS) national framework (see Glossary of terms), the curbing of regime activities, therapy groups and the democratic community structures, while necessary to keep prisoners and staff safe, risked Grendon regressing from its specialist role into a mainstream prison for long-term offenders. This restricted regime could not fully support the well-embedded therapeutic ethos of Grendon and its role as a therapeutic community. It was, therefore, positive to find that the governor and leaders had retained a focus throughout to continue limited therapeutic support for prisoners in a way that could be managed safely. Specialist prison officers, alongside clinical and non-operational staff, remained at work to support prisoners' well-being in the absence of more formal weekly group work.

During summer 2020, successful planning allowed for progression to HMPPS stage three restrictions (the second highest level). Between July and November, the prison offered key elements of the regime, such as social visits, small group work and indoor PE. Despite the national lockdown in November 2020, the prison was able to continue to provide smaller group work delivery and indoor PE, as well as 'Purple Visits' video calling to support prisoners' family ties.

After the country was placed into a full lockdown, the prison found itself back on stage four restrictions in early January 2021 and prison leaders had to put a hold on a move to stage two and the planned reintroduction of therapeutic group work, core creative support therapies and face-to-face education. Leaders adapted recovery plans (see Glossary of terms) to maintain safe prisoner cohort sizes that enabled increased time out of cell and the continuation of outdoor PE. Small group work initially had to cease, but had recommenced in early March 2021. Partnership work between the prison and health care providers had been effective in reducing the potential spread of Covid-19 into the prison. Since restrictions were introduced in March 2020, just two prisoners had tested positive, both of whom were identified during their reception, and appropriate follow-up procedures had mitigated the spread of the virus into the prison community. Despite the reduction of therapeutic work, levels of violence and self-harm remained very low. Nevertheless, we identified several issues that required immediate attention. For example, in our survey, more than one in five prisoners said that they felt unsafe. In addition, prisoners from several protected characteristic groups identified concerns, and the experiences of some black and minority ethnic prisoners were poor. We noted that despite very good staff-prisoner relationships that were underpinned by a skilled staff group, the oversight of equality work was weak and formal equality meetings had ceased. Although Grendon was not able to offer the structured therapy that formed the core of its offending behaviour work, other essential sentence management work, such as parole assessments and recategorisation reviews, had continued throughout the period of restrictions. Leaders and staff at Grendon had responded well to the operational challenges presented by the pandemic and the prison remained a safe and respectful environment. However, while the prisoner therapeutic communities had weathered the necessary restrictions reasonably well, some outcomes were beginning to deteriorate. The longer the restrictions persist, the more the therapeutic culture will be at risk and the longer it will take Grendon to recover.

It is important for HMPPS to support the governor and staff to implement a full recovery plan as soon as is practicable to enable a safe return to being a successful therapeutic community, particularly after the successful roll-out of the vaccine in the prison.

Charlie Taylor, HM Chief Inspector of Prisons
March 2021

### Key concerns and recommendations

Key concerns and recommendations identify the issues of most importance to improving outcomes for prisoners and are designed to help establishments prioritise and address the most significant weaknesses in the treatment and conditions of prisoners.

During this visit we identified some areas of key concern, and have made a small number of recommendations for the prison to address.

Key concern: Work to promote equality and diversity was not prioritised. There were weaknesses in the monitoring and analysis of equality data and other actions to understand and address the needs of prisoners with protected characteristics. Black and minority ethnic prisoners criticised discriminatory behaviour from staff. The discrimination complaints system lacked credibility,

Recommendation: There should be robust oversight, effective monitoring and action planning for equality work so that the individual needs of prisoners with protected characteristics are consistently identified and met. The strategic management of equality and diversity work should identify and address discriminatory treatment and make sure that prisoners have confidence in the discrimination reporting system. (To the governor)

Key concern: The Covid-19 restrictions had limited the prison's therapeutic work and was in danger of affecting the management of behaviour and staff-prisoner relationships. Left unchecked, these weaknesses were likely to undermine the prison's therapeutic ethos and recovery from the effect of the restrictions.

Recommendation: HMPPS and the governor should work together to support and apply tailored measures for managing the Covid-19 pandemic at Grendon that aim to protect the ongoing viability of the therapeutic community. (To the governor and HMPPS)

### INDEPENDENT MONITORING BOARD: Annual Report

The law requires every prison to be monitored by an independent Board appointed by the Justice Secretary; these are known as Independent Monitoring Boards (IMBs). The IMB must satisfy itself as to the humane and just treatment of those held in custody within its prison and the range and adequacy of the programmes preparing them for release; it must report annually to the Justice Secretary on how well the prison has met the standards and requirements placed on it.

### IMB Report 1 January 2021 – 31 December 2021
### Published 26 April 2022
### Background to the report

For the first three months of the year, the Covid-19 outbreak had a significant impact on the Board's ability to gather information and discuss the contents of this annual report. The Board has therefore covered as much ground as it can in these difficult circumstances, but inevitably there is less detail than usual and not all supporting evidence has been triangulated due to restricted access to residents. Ministers are aware of these constraints. Regular information is being collected specifically on the prison's response to the pandemic, and that is being collated nationally.

Her Majesty's Inspectorate of Prisons (HMIP) conducted a short scrutiny visit in March 2021, (see above) and the Board has referenced several of the questions and responses to this visit, to supplement views from residents that the Board has been unable to gather.

### Main judgements
### How safe is the prison?

Many of the indicators to measure safety showed improvements over the previous year. Actual incidents and intelligence reports (IRs) of self-harm were down, as well as assaults and uses of force. The number of opened assessment, care in custody and teamwork (ACCT) documents also fell to 38, from 60 in 2020. This all points to a safe environment. There is, however, no indication for the reasons behind these statistics, given that they reflect another difficult year for staff and residents due to Covid restrictions, compounded by the ongoing disruption caused by the fire safety project.

The Board again notes the lack of data to support response times to cell bells, which is a concern. Although there is no evidence (for example, from complaints) that the required three-minute response times are not being met, the lack of reporting remains a concern.

Residents broke down locked shower doors during night sanitation and these have not been secured. Access to showers was an area of concern in the coroner's report in 2017 following a death in custody.

Finds and intelligence reports (IRs) for both drugs and phones are down and other security interventions have proved effective.

**How fairly and humanely are prisoners treated?**
Residents are treated fairly. Virtually all the prison's activities are still restricted to some degree and so are not as humane as they would be with a normal regime, despite best efforts by staff. Time out of cell improved over the year but remained restricted. Issues with the night sanitation system are again raised by the Board and it is hoped that some of the faults will be remedied as part of the fire safety work, but decency issues remain. The Board noted two significant data breaches.

There have been considerable improvements to the analysis of diversity and inclusion issues. The Board noted too many late replies to discrimination incident report forms (DIRF).

Residents' comments about the food were generally good or excellent, although the Board queries how standards can be maintained in the future on budgets that have been static for many years.

Residents report that they are treated with respect. The number of complaints was on a par with 2020 but the proportion of property issues is still too high. During the restrictions, the prison has maintained a monthly residents meeting.

**How well are prisoners' health and wellbeing needs met?**
Healthcare was able to provide nearly full access to services, with good levels of appointments and low levels of 'did not attends' (DNAs).

Outbreak control measures for Covid-19 were well managed and the vaccination rollout proved effective in mitigating more serious effects.

Fifty per cent of respondents to the HMIP questionnaire said that they had mental health issues. Some delivery of services was affected by staffing levels.

**How well are prisoners progressed towards successful resettlement?**
There was an improvement in the delivery of therapy with the return of group work and structured wing activities The Board heard evidence from some residents how the sense of community has been lost.

The merger of the assessment wing with one community created tensions for staff and residents. The assessment period was reduced from eight to six weeks. At year-end, a decision was made to restore the assessment wing to its normal roll but at the expense of losing one of the

five communities. This has reduced Grendon's capacity to deliver transforming therapy by 25% until the safety work project is completed.

There were 62 transfers out for the year, of which 31 were described as 'progressive'. This was on a par with 2020 but, given the restricted therapeutic regime, this description is not likely to be as meaningful as in pre-pandemic times.

Education provision made steady improvements through the year but remained behind what was being achieved in pre-pandemic years. Distance learning is recovering.

Family contact has been maintained through the effective use of Purple (video Visits and increased access to social visits but is still far from levels that the prison would like to deliver.

**Main areas for development**
**TO THE MINISTER**
The Board monitored one prisoner's journey over six months, illustrating how his needs were not being adequately met in prison, in spite of the good level of care he received at Grendon.

**TO THE PRISON SERVICE**
Further delays to the delivery of the fire safety project will reduce the prison's capacity to deliver the very best outcomes for residents and its therapeutic work.

It is not clear that the upgrade to the sanitation software will deliver better outcomes for residents than conditions described this year.

Is there a date for Grendon to have in-cell telephony installed?

**TO THE GOVERNOR**
Restrictions due to Covid-19 and project work notwithstanding, the Board looks forward to:
i. rebuilding the culture and the sense of collective responsibility in the communities which has been affected across so many of the activities that Grendon was able to provide pre-pandemic.
ii. continuing the good progress made this year on diversity and inclusion issues, especially when residents can be involved in the process.
iii. monitoring cell bell response times the delivery of timely training for ACCTs, and control and restraint.
iv. refresher training to minimise data breaches.

**Progress since the last report**
The fire safety work includes an upgrade to the sanitation software, but there are no plans to increase the number of cells with in-cell sanitation and the Board continues to monitor outcomes for residents that are not decent.

Monitoring of equality and diversity issues has been greatly improved.

**SHAFTESBURY
DORSET
SP7 0AH**

**HMP & YOI
GUYS MARSH**  **Tel: 01747 856400**

*For the latest reports on this prison please visit:*
https://tinyurl.com/bdfh26rv

*Important Changes:* **(1) Visits:** the identification necessary to access this prison and visit for social or professional purposes has changed; (2) **Money and Gifts** new rules now apply to these. See page 16 for full details of the above.

### Task of the establishment
April 2022: HMP Guys Marsh is a category C adult male training and resettlement prison located two miles south of Shaftesbury in rural Dorset. The operating capacity as of the end of 2021 was 466.

Numbers fluctuated to fit the fire safety refurbishment schedule as wings were emptied in rotation. The campus-style layout comprises nine wings, one of which consists of 24 separate units. There is little zonal fencing.

Fire improvement work increased the requirement for cell sharing. During 2020/2021, Mercia wing and subsequently Jubilee wing were decommissioned to allow for fire safety improvements. Jubilee wing, a former enhanced wing, was, at the end of 2021 still out of use.

Tarrant wing, the care and separation unit (CSU), has 12 cells in the main block and two adjacent special cells. It has its own exercise yard. The unit was closed for four months as a result of fire safety improvement work. The planned reflooring of the unit did not take place and needs to be rescheduled for a future date.

There is an extensive range of workshops suitable for industries, and land-based activities including horticulture, ground maintenance and egg production.

The prison has one multi-use playing area due to be the site of a future wing, a well-appointed gymnasium, a health centre and a multifaith chapel complex attached to the education and library block.

During the year, the senior management team (SMT) were much focussed on expansion plans for the prison from the current roll of 466 to 650 prisoners. By the end of the reporting period, there was some action in relation to the demolition of the former Wessex wing. The site will become the new multi-use games area; a welcome addition to the health and wellbeing of prisoners.

The visitor centre is just outside the perimeter fence. The Jailhouse Café, normally open to the public, and the regional learning centre are located nearer the entrance to the site.

The main contractors for the provision of services at Guys Marsh were:
- education and learning skills: Weston College
- healthcare: Practice Plus
- works and maintenance: GFSL
- prisoner transport: GeoAmey

**Certified normal accommodation and operational capacity**
Prisoners held at the end of 2021: 450
Baseline certified normal capacity: 454
Operational capacity: 466

**Prison status and key providers** Public
Prison Group: Devon & North Dorset
Prison Group Director: Jeannine Hendrick
Governor/Director: Ian Walters
IMB Chair: Leslie Simms

**Visiting Information**
Book online: https://www.gov.uk/prison-visit or by telephone on 01747 856 586. The booking line is open Monday to Thursday: 1pm to 3pm Friday: 11.30am to 1pm.
**Visiting times:**
Friday, Saturday, Sunday: 2pm to 3:30pm

**Legal visits:** Email socialvisitsguysmarsh@justice.gov.uk or ring 01747 856 586 Monday to Thursday, 8am to 4.30pm and Friday, 8am to 4pm.
**Visiting times** Thursdays 9am to 11:30am and 2pm to 4pm.

**INSPECTIONS & REPORTS**
**Date of last full inspection** 17, 18 December 2018, 7–11 January 2019
**HMCIP Report, published 21 May 2019**
Guys Marsh is a category C training and resettlement prison located near Shaftesbury in Dorset. Taking men from much of the South West, the prison held at the time of the inspection up to 396 prisoners. This was a reduction of about 60 compared to the last inspection, and was to facilitate a rolling programme of refurbishment. The prison held men subject to a full range of sentences but there was a preponderance of longer-term prisoners, with nearly half serving between four and 10 years, and a further 15% serving over 10 years. About 50 men were serving indeterminate sentences.

Guys Marsh is a prison the Inspectorate has considered to be high risk for a number of years. When we inspected in 2014 we found a prison we described as being out of control. Our subsequent inspection in 2016 saw only marginal improvements, when we found progress to be slow and judged outcomes for prisoners as insufficient or worse across all our assessments. It is therefore pleasing to report that, following this inspection, we found a prison where improvement was both substantial and significant. While considerable concerns about safety remained, Guys Marsh was a safer prison and our overall impression was of a calmer, more settled institution. About a quarter of the prisoners we surveyed still suggested to us they felt unsafe, although this figure was now more consistent with findings at similar prisons. Levels of violence, driven by drug use and debt, were higher than at similar prisons. The prison had been slow to formulate strategies to improve the situation, but more recently had established a firmer grip, and we saw evidence of several useful initiatives to better understand and confront violence as well as improve support for more isolated individuals.

Force had been used frequently but we were not assured that supervision and accountability concerning its use were adequate. We referred three incidents to the governor for further enquiry. The use of segregation was also up, but stays were not excessive and reintegration arrangements were satisfactory. Security was applied proportionately and considerable attention had been given to combating illicit drug use. However, many initiatives were new and untested and with the mandatory positive drug testing rate at 27%, the evidence suggested a still considerable problem.

There had been one self-inflicted death since we last inspected and a further four where evidence pointed to a connection to the use of illegal drugs. Recommendations following Prisons and Probation Ombudsman (PPO) investigations had been implemented but there remained a problem with increased self-harm among prisoners. There was a significant amount of work being done to try to improve the situation and support for those in crisis seemed good.

Staff supervision and visibility were reasonable. Staff-prisoner relationships were mostly good and the key worker scheme seemed to be helping greatly. The fabric of the prison needed renewal but this work had begun. The prison was cleaner than before and access to facilities and amenities was much improved. There was, however, still some overcrowding in cramped cells.

Consultation with prisoners was adequate and complaints were dealt with reasonably well. The management of general applications, however, needed to be better. The promotion of equality remained weak but the prison had recently begun to refocus on this work. The newly appointed equality officer was greatly valued by prisoners so it was a disappointment that he was often transferred to other duties. Four prisoner equality representatives showed great commitment and seemed to exercise a positive influence. Health service provision was very good overall. Daily routines in the prison were no longer as restricted as we have seen previously and were now far more predictable. Despite this, we still found a quarter of prisoners locked in cell during the working day. Progress in developing learning and skills provision had been slow and, despite there being sufficient activity places, punctuality and attendance were poor. Achievements for those who attended training and education were mixed and teaching was inconsistent. Our colleagues in Ofsted assessed the overall effectiveness of education, skills and work as 'requires improvement'. In contrast, the management of rehabilitation was much improved and robust. There had been a useful assessment of need and the offender management unit functioned well. Public protection work was similarly effective and resettlement work was reasonable.

This inspection of Guys Marsh evidenced tangible progress for the first time in many years. There was still much to correct and improve but managers were visible and there was good leadership, as well as commitment and enthusiasm among those who worked there. The prison was far more settled and there was an underpinning commitment to promoting well-being among all those held.

Peter Clarke CVO OBE QPM March 2019
HM Chief Inspector of Prisons

## INDEPENDENT MONITORING BOARD: Annual Report

The law requires every prison to be monitored by an independent Board appointed by the Justice Secretary; these are known as Independent Monitoring Boards (IMBs). The IMB must satisfy itself as to the humane and just treatment of those held in custody within its prison and the range and adequacy of the programmes preparing them for release; it must report annually to the Justice Secretary on how well the prison has met the standards and requirements placed on it.

## IMB December 2020 – 30th November 2021
## Published April 2022
### Background to the report

This report presents the findings of the Board from 1 December 2020 to 30 November 2021. Evidence has been derived from monitoring activities, attendance at meetings, scrutiny of data, the prison's daily reports, logs and registers, surveys, discussion with prisoners and staff, and applications to the Board.

The Covid-19 outbreak and the change to the prison regime presented challenges to monitoring (see section 8). During the reporting year the prison was on a 'red regime', with Covid numbers particularly acute during the period December 2020 to April 2021. The levels of restriction eased as the year progressed and in late August the prison moved to Stage 2, where it stayed until the end of the reporting year

## Main judgements
### How safe is the prison?

Guys Marsh is by and large a safe establishment. During the year there have been no deaths within the prison, although one prisoner died within 24 hours of his release.

Despite the pressures on the prison population created by red regimes and extended times in cell, self-harm incidents fell by 20% when compared to 2019 statistics (a more comparable year than 2020).

The safer custody team held multidisciplinary safety intervention meetings (SIM) at which prisoners of concern were assessed for action on a weekly basis. The locating of the safer custody team alongside the intelligence hub resulted in data being readily available to further safeguard those at most risk.

The Board had concerns about the number of prisoners who had severe mental health issues and the length of time it took to find a suitable placement for ill prisoners.

There was a regrettable increase in the number of assaults on staff, which averaged six a month. In part, this was the result of inexperience among prison officers, but it was also a result of increased prisoner frustration because of greater extended time in cells. The Board commends staff for operating under some very difficult circumstances. There were 45 life and IPP prisoners within the establishment, whose progression was hindered during the year by the effects of lockdown. The Board was gratified to see the Parole Board's intervention to ensure the release of one prisoner who was 16 years over tariff.

Use of force incidents increased marginally in the year. Whilst acknowledging the professionalism of officers who were charged with using force tactics, the accompanying paperwork and analysis of incidents was not always as robust as it should have been.

There was still a reluctance among staff to wear body worn cameras. (Only 60% of incidents were filmed).

The availability of illicit substances continued to be a concern. A particularly dangerous shipment of psychoactive substances (PS) circulated on two wings and resulted in several near-death incidents only prevented by vigilant staff.

The Board had concerns about how effectively cell-sharing risk assessments were made; several prisoner-on-prisoner assaults occurred during the year as a result of inappropriate cell sharing. The prison and healthcare team are to be congratulated on keeping the prison relatively free from Covid. Only one prisoner had to be hospitalised during the year as a result of the virus.

### How fairly and humanely are prisoners treated?

The prison operated on a red regime basis for the year which impacted on prisoners' time out of cell. At Stage 2 in the period from August to November, time out of cell for work and education reflected normal routines. Prior to this, prisoners were only allowed out in wing 'bubbles', which meant that time out of cells was limited.

Staff/prisoner relationships were good (5.3.1). Staff as a rule were supportive both on the wings and in the CSU.

Key working was notably absent over the year and impacted on prisoners' wellbeing. The Prisons and Probation Ombudsman (PPO), in a report on the death of a former prisoner in the last reporting year, commented on the absence of key working as being a contributory factor in the sad demise of the prisoner.

Lack of laundry facilities on the wings for long periods of the year was frustrating for prisoners and laundry orderlies. A timelier ordering of new machines would have alleviated the issues. Property that was lost either in transit or within the prison was an issue of concern. Twenty-four percent of all complaints to the prison centred on property loss.

The Board welcomed the establishment of the decency project, which allowed prisoners to order supplies a week in advance.

The DHL contract to supply canteen items was a frustrating cause for concern for prisoners. Healthy eating options were narrowed. Refunds for items not delivered took weeks to process, thus denying prisoners funds for further orders. The introduction of in-cell phones was a success. It allowed prisoners to keep in contact with families, as well as allowing prison departments such as healthcare to consult with prisoners. The Board regretted that the planned introduction of in-cell IT links was abandoned by the prison service.

The Board welcomed the new IEP policy in March, however, its management was not always even. Of particular concern were incidents where prisoners were reduced in status without appropriate communication.

The Board was disappointed to note that the Prison Service had changed the conditions for enrolling prisoners onto the 'Resolve' course to those in their final year of sentence. This debarred some prisoners from moving to category D establishments.

## How well are prisoners' health and wellbeing needs met?

The healthcare team provided good care during the restricted regime, attending to general healthcare requirements and being present at incidents on the estate.

As the prison moved into Stage 2, access to the gym increased. However, for the majority of the reporting year, access was severely curtailed.

The mental healthcare team also provided care via in-cell telephony, and in person once restrictions were lifted. It was not possible to measure the long-term impact on mental health adequately.

The Board continued to be concerned about the timely distribution of appointment slips for healthcare – this should have been addressed by good wing management.

Exercise and soft skills regimes were necessarily restricted by the epidemic, but the integrated substance misuse service team strove to maintain their service as far as was possible.

## How well are prisoners progressed towards successful resettlement?

The Board welcomed the improvement in educational provision and management by Weston College, as highlighted by the Ofsted progress visit.

Face to face teaching began in April of the reporting year. Ofsted highlighted the need to further improve on delivery of key skills subjects, notably Maths and English.

There appeared to be little effective provision for those learners with neuro-atypical learning patterns. The library was welcoming and provided support for distance learning.

Opportunities for work were severely restricted to essential activities for the majority of the year. Only moving to Stage 2 allowed work opportunities to open up.

Lack of attendance at work was an area of concern for the Board. There were too many prisoners not actively engaged with out of cell activities during the latter part of the reporting year.

Board members raised distinct concerns as to how the resettlement pathways were to be delivered given the end of the Catch22 contract in July. Post-release accommodation provision was devolved externally to the community offender manager (COM), which prisoners found difficult to manage. Board members were also concerned about the number of prisoners released to 'no fixed abode'.

Key working did not, for a number of logistical reasons, develop to planned targets, so hindering prisoners in their progression.

Visits were curtailed through the year because of restrictions on movement both within and without the prison. The Board were pleased to see the introduction of Purple (video) Visits as a way of bringing families together.

The progression of enhanced prisoners who were re-categorised to category D, was held back, since they often had to wait for too long as a result of a national shortage of category D places.

## Main areas for development
### TO THE MINISTER

In view of the increasing size of the prison population and the clear intention to prioritise rehabilitation, will the minister give significant thought to expanding category D provision in the south-west?

What steps will the minister take to ensure that the Prison Service is an attractive profession with competitive remuneration, training and professional development?

There continues to be national concerns about the increase in prisoners with poor mental health. Will the Minister continue to liaise with other Ministers to ensure a coordinated approach to the humane incarceration of such prisoners?

### TO THE PRISON SERVICE

What priority is Her Majesty's Prison and Probation Service (HMPPS) giving to investing in more efficient IT systems to improve both staff efficiency and accurate, timely communication?

What progress is HMPPS making with plans to install IT capabilities in cells to aid prisoner education and administration?

How does HMPPS propose to ensure that prisons are adequately resourced to deliver the six remaining pathways for resettlement?

### TO THE GOVERNOR

This has been another difficult year and the Governor is commended for prompt management of Covid outbreaks and progressing the regime to Stage 2. However, how is the model structure and implementation of key working going to be repaired?

After such a long period of disruption, how are plans for incentivising attendance at work and education developing?

The IEP policy is in place, but how is it going to be monitored so that it clearly acts as more of an incentive rather than being punitive?

**Progress since the last report**
Education provision supplied by Weston College improved in its scope and delivery.
A clear new IEP policy has been introduced.
Prisoner voice has been increased with the introduction of the '3Cs' meeting.
Use of force (UoF) reviews became more thorough and analytical.
There was improvement in the handling of discrimination incident reporting form (DIRFs).

THORNE ROAD
HATFIELD
DONCASTER
DN7 6EL

HM PRISON SERVICE
HMP & YOI HATFIELD

Tel: 01405 746500

*For the latest reports on this prison please visit:*
https://tinyurl.com/bdfh26rv

*Important Changes:* **(1) Visits:** the identification necessary to access this prison and visit for social or professional purposes has changed; (2) **Money and Gifts** new rules now apply to these. See page 16 for full details of the above.

**Task of the establishment** HMP/YOI Hatfield is an open resettlement prison for men.

**Certified normal accommodation and operational capacity**
Prisoners held at the time of inspection: 378
Baseline certified normal capacity: 378
In-use certified normal capacity: 378
Operational capacity: 378

**Prison status and key providers**
Public
Prison Group: Yorkshire
Prison Group Director: Helen Judge
Governor/Director: Mick Mills
IMB Chair: Chris Hilley
Physical health provider: Care UK Health and Rehabilitation Services Limited
Mental health provider: Care UK Health and Rehabilitation Services Limited
Substance use treatment provider: Care UK Health and Rehabilitation Services Limited
Learning and skills provider: Novus
Escort contractor: GeoAmey

**Brief history** Hatfield is a Category D Resettlement prison situated on the outskirts of Doncaster, South Yorkshire. The CNA is 378.
The prison is on 2 sites which are 4 miles apart. Both sites are based on former Royal Air Force bases. The smaller site Hatfield Lakes holds normally 112 prisoners and is used as a reception area where prisoners spend their first 3 months. The accommodation is in large double rooms in 2 wings holding 56 prisoners in each wing. During the Covid-19 pandemic, these numbers have reduced and there are 80 prisoners in this accommodation. At the present time (2021) extensive work is being undertaken to improve the fire safety in the buildings in line with current legislation across both sites which is very welcome. The Lakes site has extensive horticultural facilities, free range chickens, a furniture refurbishment workshop, education and IT rooms and a bicycle repair shop. There is also a well organised group of prisoners who carry out general maintenance of the site.

**Short description of residential units**
The Hatfield site comprises 6 separate accommodation blocks with 260 single rooms and a small 6 bedded unit for independent living. A major building project is to take place in 2020/2021 to replace two of the units, D and E blocks. The previous units were in constant need of repair and maintenance. The new facilities will provide an extra 60 beds in addition to those already there.
During 2020/2021 there has been an ongoing refurbishment to shower rooms and the toilet facilities on the landings and there has been an improvement to the privacy and decency in these areas. At Hatfield work opportunity is provided by the charity "recycling lives", horticulture, general recycling and maintenance. Retail experience is gained in the "Thyme Served" shop which is open to the public and the Barista coffee bar which also serves lunches and snacks. Education is provided by NOVUS with courses in IT, corporate business, welding and barbering. Outside work is in 2 stages. Stage 1 voluntary work and Stage 2 paid employment.
Health Care is provided by Practice Plus Group.

**Visiting Information**
Book online: https://www.gov.uk/prison-visit or by telephone on 01405 746 611. The booking line is open Monday to Friday 9am to 1pm.
**Visiting times:** Wednesday, Friday, Saturday, and Sunday 2pm to 2:50pm and 3pm to 3:50pm

**Legal visits:** There are currently no legal visits taking place.

**INSPECTIONS & REPORTS**
**Date of last full inspection** 5–16 August 2019
Notable features from this inspection
• The prison was spread over two sites, four miles apart.

- Most prisoners lived in single accommodation.
- A quarter of the population was assessed as presenting a high risk of serious harm to others.

**HMCIP Report, published 09 January 2020**

HMP/YOI Hatfield is a category D resettlement prison for men situated near to Doncaster in South Yorkshire. The prison is split across two sites: a main site, and a further site that used to form part of HMP Lindholme but is now used for receptions into the prison and is usually referred to as Hatfield Lakes or The Lakes site. In common with the other prisons in this cluster, it went through a failed market test some years ago, but since 2015 has been an autonomous establishment. At the time of this inspection the prison held a little under 380 men, of whom around 70 were aged over 50. Thirty per cent were from black and minority ethnic groups. The prison was last inspected in 2015, on which occasion it attracted the highest grading, of 'good', in all four of our healthy prison tests.

On this occasion, the prison again inspected very well, achieving 'good' grades across the board. A new governor was in the process of taking up post during this inspection, but the prison had benefited from consistent leadership for a number of years, which was also reflected in what appeared to be a settled, mature and very competent staff group.

The prison was unequivocally safe. Violence was very rare, the overwhelming majority of prisoners felt safe and staff struggled to recall the last time there had been an assault. No incidents of self-harm had been recorded in the year preceding the inspection and the impression I gained was of an institution that was relaxed and well ordered. The incentives scheme operated well, the numbers placed on report was lower than at other category D prisons and the use of force was rare. Around eight to 10 prisoners were returned to closed conditions each month. I was very impressed to learn that if a prisoner transgressed in some way, rather than halt his potential progression with an immediate return to closed conditions, he would typically be sent to The Lakes site for a period of assessment in order decide the best way forward. It seemed to me that this approach had much to commend it. Relationships between staff and prisoners were good and there was a clear sense of community. However, the prison was not funded for the Offender Management in Custody (OMiC) programme, which limited the amount of time available for staff to interact on a one-to-one basis with prisoners. There was also a need to conduct further work and analysis to understand inequalities and perceptions of inequality revealed both by our survey and the prison's own data. We also felt that a broader review of

consultation arrangements would be beneficial, to demonstrate the value of what was being done, as part of broader work to improve confidence in the complaints process. Although generally the sites were in good condition and living conditions reasonable, some units were showing signs of age and needed refurbishment. We were given to understand that funding for this work had been bid for, but had already been allocated elsewhere and would not become available for at least two years.

As was to be expected in an establishment of this kind, time out of cell was excellent. Our colleagues from Ofsted judged that the leadership and management of learning, skills and work were good, and the achievement of qualifications on most courses was at a very high level. One in five prisoners were released into the community on employment and training placements, although it was not always possible to see clear linkages between these placements and long-term career aspirations on release. The number of releases on temporary licence (ROTL) was dependent upon individual members of staff with extensive local knowledge, energy and expertise, rather than robust, documented processes. Nevertheless, we felt that the overall provision of purposeful activity remained good in terms of our healthy prison test.

Work with children and families was very good, and prisoners were positive about visit provision at Hatfield. It was also pleasing to see that home detention curfew processes were well managed, with all applications during the past six months having been approved and most put into action at the earliest opportunity. It was also good to see that Multi-Agency Public Protection Arrangement (MAPPA) levels were confirmed before prisoners gained access to ROTL, which is better than we often see. It was also pleasing to see that no prisoners had been released homeless during the previous six months, and that every prisoner was discussed at a discharge board prior to release, which we considered to be good practice.

This was obviously a very positive inspection, and it was good to see that after the previous excellent inspection in 2015, complacency had not been allowed to take root. Whilst it had no impact in itself on our judgements, it was notable that the achievement rate against our previous recommendations was extremely high, with 26 out of 30 recommendations being fully or partially achieved.

HMP/YOI Hatfield was a well-run and decent establishment, fulfilling its role in preparing men for their release. There was much to commend, and the leadership and staff should take pride in what they have achieved and how they have encouraged the prisoners to play an active role in making it a safe, decent and purposeful establishment. August 2019. HM Chief Inspector of Prisons

### Safety

Work to support prisoners in their early days was reasonably good. Almost all prisoners felt safe. Violence was rare and most prisoners displayed good behaviour. The adjudication system was managed effectively, and the incentives scheme operated well. Incidents requiring the use of force were also rare. Security measures were proportionate and there was a well-developed response to the supply of illicit drugs. The levels of absconds and temporary release failures were relatively low. There were few incidents of self-harm. Outcomes for prisoners were good against this healthy prison test.

At the last inspection, in 2015, we found that outcomes for prisoners in Hatfield were good against this healthy prison test. We made six recommendations in the area of safety. (This included recommendations about substance use treatment, which in our updated Expectations (Version 5, 2017) now appear under the healthy prison area of respect.) At this inspection, we found that four of the recommendations had been achieved, one had not been achieved and one was no longer relevant.

The reception environment was clean and bright. Most reception processes were efficient and staff were welcoming, which put prisoners at ease on arrival. Detailed information about the prison was provided by experienced peer workers. First night assessments with the induction officer were not always sufficiently focused on safety or completed in a confidential setting.

Almost all prisoners said that they felt safe. Incidents of violence were rare, and challenge, support and intervention plans (The challenge, support and intervention plan is a system used by some prisons to manage the most violent prisoners and support the most vulnerable prisoners in the system. Prisoners who are identified as the perpetrator of serious or repeated violence, or who are vulnerable due to being the victim of violence or bullying behaviour, are managed and supported on a plan with individualised targets and regular reviews.)were used effectively to keep prisoners safe. The formal incentives and earned privileges scheme operated well and most prisoners displayed good behaviour. The primary motivation to behave well was the opportunities available in open conditions. The number of adjudications was lower than at other category D prisons; procedures were appropriate and quality assurance of the process had improved. Incidents requiring the use of force were rare, and any force used was subject to appropriate scrutiny.

Security measures were proportionate. Intelligence was analysed by a regional intelligence hub, and the prison was sighted on its current risks. The positive mandatory drug testing rate had increased slightly since the previous inspection. The strategic approach to supply reduction was well developed through joint working between departments, and the recent introduction of risk-based testing showed early signs of being an effective deterrent. The levels of absconds and temporary release failures were relatively low.

Levels of self-harm were very low, with no such incidents in the previous year. Staff understood the procedures to follow if a prisoner was in crisis, and there were sufficient Listeners (prisoners trained by the Samaritans to provide confidential emotional support to fellow prisoners) in place.

The regional adult safeguarding policy was embedded and there were effective links with the local adult safeguarding board. The provision of information to prisoners to raise awareness of how to report safeguarding concerns using a 'community concern form' was good practice.

### Respect

Relationships between staff and prisoners were good. Prisoner mentors provided additional advice and support to their peers. Living conditions were reasonably good, and most prisoners were satisfied with their accommodation. Shared toilet and shower facilities were clean. The food provided was reasonably good and there was some provision for prisoners to prepare their own meals. Consultation arrangements were in place, although less effective than at the time of the previous inspection. More work was needed to understand and meet the needs of prisoners from a black and minority ethnic background. Faith provision was good. Health services were very good. Outcomes for prisoners were good against this healthy prison test.

At the last inspection, in 2015, we found that outcomes for prisoners in Hatfield were good against this healthy prison test. We made 14 recommendations in the area of respect. At this inspection, we found that 11 of the recommendations had been achieved, one had been partially achieved and two had not been achieved.

In our survey, more respondents than at comparator prisons said that staff treated them respectfully. Good multidisciplinary work and a sense of community were evident in the positive relationships between prisoners and staff. The establishment was not funded for key work sessions, which had an impact on residential officers' ability to provide regular private meetings with prisoners to support their progression. Case notes from 'contact and support officers' were often basic and made no reference to sentence plans, and quality assurance did not address this. Peer mentors were used effectively to provide additional support and advice.

Outside areas were clean, tidy and well maintained. Some improvements had been made to living areas since the previous inspection, and accommodation at both sites was reasonably clean and well furnished. Rooms on The Lakes site were more spacious, although most residents on both sites were satisfied with their accommodation. The communal showers and toilets were generally clean and screened for privacy. There was a reasonable range of equipment in association areas, although the television room on D and E units was too small to accommodate the number of prisoners using it, and also housed the communal telephones. Access to laundry facilities met most prisoners' needs. The food served was reasonably good, and included the option of a hot breakfast every day. There was also adequate provision for prisoners who worked outside the prison. Many prisoners raised concerns that the food choices did not fully reflect the diverse population of the prison. All units had toasters and microwave ovens, and slow cookers and toasted sandwich makers had recently been provided. However, with the exception of F wing, no units had refrigerators or cookers to support independent living fully. New arrivals still had to wait too long before they could buy basic items from the prison shop.

Consultation arrangements were in place for specific groups and issues, such as catering, but there was no longer an effective prisoner council to discuss and effect change in more general prison matters. Our survey findings and discussions with prisoners suggested a lack of confidence in the fairness of the complaints system. The complaint responses we reviewed were respectful, but some lacked sufficient investigation and were unhelpful.

The equality action team meeting, chaired by the governor, was held quarterly and maintained oversight of equality work. However, the meeting was not used well to monitor and progress the equality action plan or the prison's equality policy. Our survey results, focus groups and the prison's own data all demonstrated some inequality, and perceptions of inequality. Prisoners expressed little confidence in the discrimination incident report form (DIRF) process, and we found that only one DIRF had been submitted in the previous six months. There was some consultation with prisoners with protected characteristics, but it was inconsistent.

Faith provision was good, and most prisoners had access to a chaplain of their faith. The chaplaincy provided appropriate pastoral care and the prison had delivered numerous celebratory events based on the diversity calendar. There were strong and effective health care governance systems, and patient satisfaction with health services was high. Improvements had been made to the health centre on both sites, and clinical rooms met infection control standards. There were appropriate arrangements to provide out-of-hours care and deal with medical emergencies. Prisoners had good access to a wide range of primary care and dental services, and waiting times were good overall. Staff had direct access to advice from hospital consultants, which increased the accuracy and efficiency of care for patients. Pharmacy and mental health services were very good. Substance use services were highly effective. Pre-release health arrangements were appropriate.

**Purposeful activity**

The amount of time out of cell was excellent. There was a good library and gym on both sites. The leadership and management of learning skills and work was good, with some very effective partnership working. Teaching, learning and assessment supported rehabilitation, although not all prisoners made the progress of which they were capable. Prisoners were motivated to learn and achieve, and the standard of their work in some areas was excellent. One in five prisoners were released into the community on employment and training placements, but the quality and relevance of placements did not always link to career plans. Qualification achievement rates on most courses were very high. Outcomes for prisoners were good against this healthy prison test.

At the last inspection, in 2015, we found that outcomes for prisoners in Hatfield were good against this healthy prison test. We made three recommendations in the area of purposeful activity. At this inspection, we found that two of the recommendations had been achieved and one had been partially achieved.

The amount of time out of cell was excellent. The library was well used at both sites and supported literacy initiatives, quarterly family days and Storybook Dads (in which prisoners record stories for their children). PE staff actively supported a range of health and well-being activity. Access to the gym was good on the main site but more restricted on The Lakes site, although an additional fitness suite mitigated the impact of this.

Relationships between college and prison managers were very good, resulting in a suitably wide range of provision that met the needs of most prisoners. The college's arrangements for monitoring and improving the quality of teaching and learning were effective. Prison leaders provided enough full-time activity places to meet the population's needs. They had developed productive links with employers, resulting in a wide range of release on temporary licence (ROTL) placements and jobs. However, the quality and relevance of ROTL placements were not always related to regional skills shortages or to prisoners' long- term career plans. The prison did not hold accurate information on prisoners' employment or training destinations on release, which limited its ability to evaluate the effectiveness of the curriculum it offered.

Teachers supported prisoners' prospects of rehabilitation by promoting and developing a wide range of employability skills. They made good use of the available information on prisoners to set individualised targets that helped to prepare them for employment or further training. Teaching, learning and assessment, and work activities supported prisoners well to develop their English and mathematics skills. However, prisoners did not always make the progress of which they were capable because too many teaching and learning activities failed to challenge or motivate them sufficiently.

Prisoners' behaviour during purposeful activities was exemplary, and attendance was high. Around 20% of prisoners benefited from the opportunities offered by ROTL placements to improve their employment and training prospects. The standard of prisoners' work in welding, woodwork and in the prison's commercial recycling facility was good, and often excellent. Prisoners demonstrated an excellent work ethic and were motivated to learn and achieve.

Qualification achievement rates were very high on almost all courses. There were no marked differences in performance between different groups of prisoners.

### Rehabilitation and release planning

Children and families work was very good. The strategy to reduce reoffending was not informed by a comprehensive needs analysis. Nonetheless, the prison was clearly supporting rehabilitation through temporary release into the community within 12 weeks of arrival for almost all prisoners. Of these, 20% of prisoners were working in the community, with well-developed plans to increase this to almost a third. Risk assessment and sentence planning were managed well. Public protection arrangements were generally robust. Recategorisation back to closed conditions was proportionate. Release

planning was very good. Outcomes for prisoners were good against this healthy prison test.

At the last inspection, in 2015, we found that outcomes for prisoners in Hatfield were good against this healthy prison test. We made seven recommendations in the area of resettlement. (This included recommendations about reintegration planning for drugs and alcohol and reintegration issues for education, skills and work, which in our updated Expectations (Version 5, 2017) now appear under the healthy prison areas of respect and purposeful activity respectively.) At this inspection, we found that all seven of the recommendations had been achieved.

In our survey, most prisoners were positive about their visits experience. The visits hall on each site was welcoming. The café facility on the main site was an excellent facility, where families could buy good-quality food. Three-quarters of the population could access ROTL, which was the primary way that prisoners maintained their family ties. The Prison Advice and Care Trust provided a range of support to prisoners through group and one-to-one work, to help them to develop and maintain their relationships.

The reducing reoffending strategy covered all the resettlement pathways but was not based on a comprehensive needs analysis. However, the ROTL process was well managed. Decisions were robust and most prisoners had access to ROTL within 12 weeks of their arrival. Around 20% of prisoners were working in the community, with well-developed plans to increase this to almost a third in the near future. S31 All high-risk multi-agency public protection arrangements (M APP A) prisoners and those serving indeterminate sentences were appropriately supervised by probation officers, with regular and meaningful contact to drive sentence progression. All other prisoners were supervised by prison offender supervisors, who focused on risk assessments and ROTL progression. However, due to cross-deployment, offender supervisors had limited time to maintain regular, meaningful contact with the prisoners on their caseload. Most prisoners had an up-to-date offender assessment system (OASys) assessment which was of good quality and contained sentence plan objectives which were appropriate for open conditions. The home detention curfew process was well managed; in the previous six months, all applications had been approved and most prisoners had been released at the earliest opportunity.

Public protection arrangements were generally robust. The interdepartmental risk management team meeting discussed appropriate cases but, due to poor attendance by all appropriate departments, much of the work had to be done outside of the meeting. The prison had taken good steps to ensure that MAPPA management levels were confirmed before prisoners accessed ROTL. Support for indeterminate-sentenced prisoners (ISPs) was reasonably good. Under the new ROTL policy, ISPs had better access to ROTL, which was a valued change.

Decisions to recategorise prisoners and return them to closed conditions were appropriate, proportionate and multidisciplinary.

The establishment did not run accredited offending behaviour programmes but prisoners could complete interventions on ROTL when there was an identified need. The demand for accommodation support was low because most prisoners had established housing links before release, and no prisoners had been released homeless within the previous six months. There was a greater demand for finance, benefit and debt services to enable access to work placements, and Nacro, alongside other partnership agencies, provided a wide range of support.

Most prisoners had an established resettlement plan before their release but, for those who did not, there was appropriate support available from the community rehabilitation company. The prison also discussed every prisoner at a well-attended discharge board, ensuring that all prisoners were fully prepared for release, which was good practice.

## Key concerns and recommendations

Concern: Analysis of complaints data was cursory and limited managers' understanding of the factors leading to complaints. This, and the absence of independent scrutiny, inhibited institutional learning and action to address the poor perceptions held by some prisoners.

Recommendation: Quality assurance should be improved, to ensure that a comprehensive analysis of complaints data leads to action that improves prisoners' confidence in the complaints system.

Concern: Survey results and focus groups revealed comparatively negative perceptions from black and minority ethnic and Muslim prisoners. The prison's own data also revealed disproportionality within these groups in areas of discipline and security.

Recommendation: Consultation, action planning and communication should be improved, to provide assurance of fair treatment of prisoners from black and minority ethnic and Muslim backgrounds.

Concern: Too many prisoners released on temporary licence to do voluntary or paid work in the community were in jobs that bore little relation to their intended career path or to identified local skills shortage areas.

Recommendation: Prisoners released on temporary licence to work in the community should be able to participate in employment or voluntary work

that is closely aligned to their intended future career and to local skills shortage areas.

## INDEPENDENT MONITORING BOARD: Annual Report

The law requires every prison to be monitored by an independent Board appointed by the Justice Secretary; these are known as Independent Monitoring Boards (IMBs). The IMB must satisfy itself as to the humane and just treatment of those held in custody within its prison and the range and adequacy of the programmes preparing them for release; it must report annually to the Justice Secretary on how well the prison has met the standards and requirements placed on it.

**IMB Report May 2020-April 2021**
**Published November 2021**
**Executive summary**
**Background to the report**
This report presents the findings of the Independent Monitoring Board at HMP & YOI Hatfield for the period 1st of April, 2020 to 31 of March, 2021. IMB evidence comes from observations made on visits, scrutiny of records and of data, informal contact with prisoners, prison staff and prisoner applications. This reporting period has happened whilst the restrictions to manage the Covid-19 pandemic were in place.

The Covid-19 outbreak had a significant impact on the Board's ability to gather information and discuss the contents of this Annual Report. The Board has therefore tried to cover as much ground as it can in these difficult circumstances, but inevitably there is less detail and supporting evidence than usual. Ministers are aware of the constraints. Regular information was collected specifically on the prison's response to the pandemic, and was collated nationally.

## Main judgements
### How safe is the prison?
The Board finds that both Hatfield and The Lakes are a safe environment for both prisoners and staff.

### Fair and Humane Treatment
The prison is proactive in tackling any incidents concerning real or perceived issues relating to unfair or inhumane incidents. An Officer is responsible for Equality and Diversity and the Board members work closely with him to monitor any incidents.

### Health and Wellbeing
The Board finds that physical and mental healthcare on the two sites is well managed and is accessible to all men.

**Progression and Resettlement**

All men have coming to the prison are assessed and allocated suitable and appropriate work and education opportunities that support their progression and resettlement within the community.

**Main areas for development**
**TO THE MINISTER**

Covid-19 has had a significant impact on ROTL over the year and consequently on Parole Boards. HMP Hatfield have responded innovatively, for example, Parole Hearings were accommodated by secure video link or telephone.

The Board is pleased to report that after many years of concern, Units D and E are to be demolished in the next financial year and a new accommodation unit is to be built during 2021/22. This should not impact significantly on the population as alternative temporary accommodation will be provided.

**TO THE PRISON SERVICE**

During the pandemic HMP Hatfield maintained a number of prisoners as Key Workers in the community. The Governor and staff worked hard to protect the population and maintain daily routines for prisoners where possible. This included stringent Covid-19 testing to ensure that positive cases of COVID- 19 on both sites was kept to a minimum amongst staff and prisoners.

**TO THE GOVERNOR**

The Board would like to acknowledge the hard work and commitment of the Governor and staff during a particularly challenging year. Moral and motivation has remained high throughout the prison and staff, and prisoners have been kept well informed through daily briefings.

Prisoners have recognised the impact of strong leadership in maintaining positive working practices within the prison throughout the year.

**Progress since the last report**

Due to the COVID 19 Pandemic, it has been very difficult to measure progress in all areas as many workshops and areas of the prison have been closed for significant periods. As areas are opening up again we will resume our monitoring and assess progress.

However, despite the challenges of the Pandemic, HMP Hatfield has made every attempt to maintain as close to a normal regime as possible whilst keeping men and staff safe. This included maintaining education and workshop provision where practical and implementing strict checks to enable working in the community to be maintained in significant numbers (50+) even during peaks in the pandemic.

**NORTH LANE**
**MILLOM**
**CUMBRIA**
**LA18 4NA**

**HM PRISON HAVERIGG**

Tel: 01229 713000

*For the latest reports on this prison please visit:*
https://tinyurl.com/bdfh26rv

*Important Changes:* **(1)** **Visits:** the identification necessary to access this prison and visit for social or professional purposes has changed; (2) **Money and Gifts** new rules now apply to these. See page 16 for full details of the above.

**Task of the establishment** Category D male prison.

**Certified normal accommodation and operational capacity**
Prisoners held November 2021: 310
Baseline certified normal capacity: 488
In-use certified normal capacity: 486
Operational capacity: 490

**Population of the prison**
- 1% (four prisoners) aged 18–24 years
- 82% (253 prisoners) 35 or older
- 36% (110 prisoners) 55 or older
- 17% of the population spending time in the community each week
- 86.8% of prisoners identify as White
- 5.8% of prisoners identify as Asian
- 2.6% of prisoners identify as Black
- 4.8% of prisoners identify as Mixed Race
- 52% Christian
- 28% identify as atheist or no religion
- 8% Muslim
- 7% Buddhists

**Prison status and key providers**
Public Sector
Prison Group: Cumbria & Lancashire
Prison Group Director: John Illingsworth
Governor/Director: Adam Connolly
IMB Chair: Lynn Chambers
Cumbria Integrated Care NHS Foundation Trust – primary healthcare
Gables Medical – GP services
Tees, Esk and Wear Valley NHS Foundation Trust – mental health services
Burgess and Hyder – dental services
Northumberland, Tyne and Wear NHS Foundation Trust – substance misuse service
Cumbria County Council – adult social care
Pen Optical – Rowlands Pharmacy
Novus, education and training
Booker/DHL – prisoners' canteen

GeoAmey – prisoner transport
Department of Education– library funder
The Samaritans
Visitors and Children's Support Group (independent charity) – visitor centre
Interventions Alliance, Recoop and Careers Connect– financial advice, accommodation, employment guidance Amey – facilities management
Cancer Research UK – charity shop
Fusion21 – vocational course provider

**Brief history** Haverigg became a category D open prison in December 2019 and was designated as a national resource for men/prisoners convicted of a sexual offence (PCOSO).

Despite restrictions imposed by the Covid-19 pandemic, considerable progress was made with physical changes and improvements across the prison resulting, at the time of writing, in an environment more closely resembling an open establishment.

Except for one residence, R4, closed last year following a fire safety inspection, all the other four residences remained open throughout the year. One residence (R5) continued to function as the reverse cohorting and isolation unit for most of the year and has only, in recent weeks, returned to normal use.

The operational capacity of the prison is planned to be 490. The current roll is 310 with the speed of transfer having slowed, in part due to the pandemic, but in particular because of staff shortages in key probation, offender management and psychology roles.

Plans to build a new accommodation block on the site of R4, currently being demolished, are at an early stage and it is understood that construction may be some years away. When open, the operational capacity of the prison will increase to 570.

The prison is remote from mainline rail services and major road networks. The M6 motorway is almost 50 miles away, with much of the journey on narrow country roads. The location has an impact on the maintenance of family ties, recruitment to specialist posts in the prison and to the IMB.

The prison is on an old military site dating back to World War 2 and has 80, mainly old, buildings within the 4.5-mile perimeter. The site is large and exposed, especially to strong sea winds.

### Short description of residential units
R1 Purpose-built house block split into two wings, with 60 cells on each wing with internal sanitation and communal showers, including two secure accommodation rooms.
R2 Nine billets of 18 cells with internal sanitation

and communal showers, as well as specialised disability accommodation.
R3 Seven billets of 16 cells with a kitchen and dining area. These billets have communal showers and sanitation facilities.
R5 Purpose-built house block split into six spurs across two landings. Each cell has a shower and internal sanitation. This unit is currently used as the RCU and PIU.
R6 Two billets of 16 cells, with a kitchen and dining area. These billets have communal showers and sanitation facilities.
R4 and the segregation unit are closed.

### Visiting Information
Book online: https://www.gov.uk/prison-visit or by telephone on 01229 713 016 Monday to Friday, 1pm to 4pm
**Visiting times:** Sat/Sun: 10:30am to 4:15pm

**Legal visits:** Booking line: 01229 713 016 Monday to Friday, 1pm to 4pm
**Visiting times:** Friday: 1:30pm to 4:15pm

### INSPECTIONS & REPORTS
**Date of last full inspection:** 17–28 May 2021
**HMCIP Report, published 01 September 2021**
Situated near Millom in Cumbria, and one of the more remote establishments in the English prison system, HMP Haverigg is a sprawling former RAF station that had been a category C training prison since 1967. A prison with a troubled history and one that has been the subject of much criticism from the Inspectorate in recent years, particularly in relation to safety and control, significant change was introduced in late 2019 when HM Prison and Probation Service (HMPPS), greatly influenced by a respected former governor, re- designated Haverigg as an open prison. This, however, unfortunately coincided with the outbreak of the Covid-19 pandemic. The prison's response to the pandemic, while maintaining the momentum behind the transition, has therefore been the main strategic challenge for the establishment over the last 16 months. It is greatly to the credit of the acting governor, her management team and the staff and prisoners of Haverigg, that they have progressed so well.
Capable of holding about 480 prisoners, there were just 310 in residence during our inspection. Representing a reasonably mature age profile, most prisoners had been convicted of a sexual offence, and meeting the needs of this type of prisoner had been quickly established as the new purpose and specialism of the prison. Haverigg had made a very impressive start and at this inspection we found that outcomes for prisoners were at least reasonably good against all our tests

of a healthy prison, and in safety we judged them to be 'good'. Much of this success was predicated on good staff-prisoner relationships, a traditional strength at Haverigg, with prisoners in our survey being very positive about their experiences in the prison. Staff in turn seemed to us to be greatly relieved that the prison had gained for itself a new lease of life, one that they were embracing, although some expressed anxiety about the need to gain the new skills required for working with the particular type of prisoner now held at Haverigg.

Data and outcomes confirmed to us that the prison was very safe and we noted a general sense of well-being. We inspected as the prison was emerging from inevitable restrictions imposed during the Covid-19 pandemic, but found prisoners had very good access to the prison grounds and that nearly everyone was involved in some kind of purposeful work or education. We were similarly encouraged by the way the prison was sustaining its approach to sentence management, critical risk of harm reduction work and rehabilitative services. As the prison settles into its new role, these services will take on even greater significance.

Another striking observation of ours was the prison's sense of confidence and self-reliance. Solutions were being sought to problems as they emerged, with this perhaps best exemplified by the way the prison, using prisoner labour, had organised the removal of the now superfluous security fencing, as well as other restrictions. This was not an insignificant task. A workshop had even been created to make use of the reclaimed steel. Similarly, the prison's extensive grounds were being developed and opened for prisoner access rather than being cordoned off.

More, of course, remained to be done. Some governance arrangements needed to be tightened up and while prisoners mitigated the worst impact, many accommodation facilities required investment and renewal. The challenge of ensuring a safe but accessible offer of temporary release also needed to be met. These issues, which are supported by our recommendations, do not, however, detract from our encouraging findings. Haverigg is fast becoming a very capable establishment and is progressing to a point where it soon may well be one of the better open prisons in the estate.

Charlie Taylor, HM Chief Inspector of Prisons
June 2021

### Safety

At the last inspection of HMP Haverigg in 2017, we found that outcomes for prisoners were not sufficiently good against this healthy prison test. At this inspection we found that outcomes for prisoners were now good. The reception area was organised to minimise the risks of virus transmission. The reverse cohort unit (RCU, see Glossary of terms) was managed effectively to prevent the spread of the virus without imposing disproportionate restrictions. All newly arriving prisoners received a private risk and needs assessment. Peer-led face-to-face induction was comprehensive and prompt.

There were very few recorded violent incidents and the vast majority of prisoners told us they felt safe. There was good management oversight of violence reduction work. Use of force was rare, with only four incidents in the previous 12 months, but there was little evidence of de-escalation. There was no segregation unit but two designated secure cells had been used appropriately in the cases we examined, to hold people returning to closed conditions. Governance of secure cell use and the use of force were weak. Adjudications were usually managed adequately, but in one case a prisoner was denied legal assistance with no recorded explanation.

Procedural security was proportionate. Intelligence reports were analysed, collated and disseminated well, but we found some evidence of under-reporting. There was very little evidence of substance misuse. Thirty-nine prisoners had been returned to closed conditions in the previous 12 months, which was comparatively low.

There had been three deaths since our last inspection, including two that were self-inflicted, both of which took place when the prison was still a category C establishment. The prison had made good progress in implementing recommendations of the Prisons and Probation Ombudsman. There was very little self-harm at the time of the inspection and ACCT (assessment, care in custody and teamwork) case management processes for prisoners at risk of suicide or self- harm were carried out well. No safeguarding referrals had been made to the local adults safeguarding board in the previous year and we identified some shortcomings in the management of one case. Peer support workers gave valued help to the most vulnerable prisoners but lacked staff oversight.

### Respect

At the last inspection of HMP Haverigg in 2017, we found that outcomes for prisoners were reasonably good against this healthy prison test. At this inspection we found that they remained reasonably good.

Staff and prisoner relationships were generally positive and respectful. However, staff had received limited training in working with category D prisoners or those convicted of sexual offences, and many of those we spoke to said they were not yet fully confident to work with the population.

Prisoners all had single accommodation, and the worst unit at our last inspection (R1) had been refurbished to a good standard. However, billets were old and many needed repair to roofs and flooring, and some showers were still in poor condition. While many parts of the grounds were maintained well, the physical environment did not reflect what we would expect in an open prison. There were many internal fences and razor wire, and most cell windows still had bars. Most prisoners we spoke to were content with the food, but they could not yet cook for themselves and the kitchen was in a poor state of repair.

Consultation arrangements, in the form of regular forums and the Prison Council, were good. Prisoners found it easy to make an application, but many told us that they were not answered promptly. Prisoner orderlies had been appointed to help track applications more effectively, but departments were not consistently using them. Responses to complaints were usually prompt, polite and constructive, but property complaints redirected to other prisons were often not resolved quickly. Good quality assurance arrangements included peer representatives checking a proportion of redacted complaints.

Well-attended diversity and inclusion meetings had continued throughout much of the pandemic and provided good oversight of equality work. The few submitted discrimination incident reports were robustly and quickly investigated. Most prisoners with a disability whom we spoke to said they felt supported. The 'village hall' provided a valued hub for older prisoners to socialise and participate in activities. Transgender prisoners said they felt supported in matters relating to their transition and could access appropriate health care.

Facilities for worship were good and had improved during the pandemic. The chaplaincy provided good pastoral support and had built links with community groups. Chaplains visited the wings each day.

Health services were well led, responsive to the needs of the population and underpinned by mature partnership working. A wide range of health information and activities enabled prisoners to take responsibility for improving their health and well-being. A good range of mental health therapies was provided by a skilled team. Medicines management and pharmacy services were very good. A very high proportion of prisoners (88%) in our survey said the quality of health services was good and we saw some excellent support for patients.

## Purposeful activity

At the last inspection of HMP Haverigg in 2017, we found that outcomes for prisoners were reasonably good against this healthy prison test. At this inspection we found that they remained reasonably good.

Ofsted carried out a progress monitoring visit of the prison alongside our full inspection.

Prisoners could leave their units for about 13 hours a day. Library staff had just returned to the prison and, in the meantime, prisoners had been delivering library items to anyone who requested them. The gym was clean and well equipped and prisoners had reasonably good access to it. Prisoners could also access open spaces and nature in the extensive prison grounds.

Most prisoners were engaged in education, skills and work during the various phases of the Covid-19 pandemic and, at the time of the inspection, all eligible prisoners had some form of purposeful activity. There were realistic plans to adapt the education, skills and work offer to reflect the changing needs of the population and wider economic and social demands. The employment hub was a particularly helpful service for prisoners.

The quality of education delivered during the first phase of lockdown was not of a consistently good standard, and leaders had taken effective action to improve quality through staff development and recruitment. Prisoners had a structured induction programme and good individual learning plans.

Prisoners benefited from a high standard of technical training. They developed significant new skills, knowledge and behaviours through vocational training. Teachers planned and delivered a well-structured curriculum in mathematics and information communication technology. However, prisoners were not able to practise some of the skills they had learned because of limited access to computers.

Trainers in workshops where no qualifications were offered did not capture in writing the full range of knowledge, skills and behaviours that prisoners had developed. Prisoners' additional support needs were identified at the start of their education and training and addressed. Local employers spoke highly of the contributions made by prisoners on release on temporary licence (ROTL) to their businesses and communities.

## Rehabilitation and release planning

At the last inspection of HMP Haverigg in 2017, we found that outcomes for prisoners were reasonably good against this healthy prison test. At this inspection we found that they remained reasonably good.

Visits had restarted in April 2021, but demand

was low. Prisoners had good access to Purple Visits (see Glossary of terms), which had been used about 700 times in the previous six months. The visits room had been refurbished and provided a very welcoming environment. Monitoring by visits staff was discreet, and they were aware of prisoners with contact restrictions. Community agencies providing family support work had not yet returned to the prison.

Strategic oversight of reducing reoffending was undermined by the lack of a comprehensive needs analysis and overarching dynamic action plan. However, the offender management unit (OMU) was well led and focused on improvement. A shortage of probation officers was mitigated by employing more prison staff to act as prison offender managers (POMs). All POMs had reasonable caseloads and most prisoners benefited from regular, purposeful contact with them. Most prisoners had up-to-date sentence plans and those we spoke to were making reasonable progress. OMU staff communicated well with prisoners and ran surgeries four times a week to answer their questions.

ROTL assessments had continued through the pandemic and about half the population had been able to access ROTL opportunities since its reintroduction in April 2021. However, the range of voluntary and paid work opportunities was very limited. In our case sample, ROTL decision-making was well considered and informed by a full range of information, including prisoner participation at all boards. There had been no ROTL failures to date.

Nearly all prisoners were convicted of sexual offences and more than 80% were assessed as posing a high or very high risk of harm. Public protection work in the cases we inspected was good. The interdepartmental risk management meeting was not tracking cases from six months before release, which ran the risk of delay to necessary actions. However, all MAPPA levels in our case sample were confirmed before release. Child contact restrictions and mail and telephone monitoring processes were robust and proportionate, although there was a small backlog in telephone monitoring cases.

Decisions to re-categorise prisoners and return them to closed conditions were proportionate and multidisciplinary. Prison managers were aware of the few prisoners with outstanding needs in relation to offending behaviour interventions, and staff liaised with community offender managers to establish if these could be completed on licence or on temporary release from custody.

About 10 prisoners a month were released from Haverigg, with the majority going to approved premises. The community rehabilitation company (CRC) met prisoners 12 weeks before release to discuss resettlement plans and provide suitable support. Leaders had put systems in place to ensure continuity of release planning once the current CRC contract expired in June 2021.

**Key concerns and recommendations**
Key concerns and recommendations identify the issues of most importance to improving outcomes for prisoners and are designed to help establishments prioritise and address the most significant weaknesses in the treatment and conditions of prisoners.

During this inspection we identified some areas of key concern and have made a small number of recommendations for the prison to address those concerns.

Key concern: While safety outcomes were currently good, there were some shortcomings in assurance structures; for example, governance of the use of force and secure cells was weak, the safeguarding strategy was out of date, and there was inadequate staff supervision of the peer workers who supported particularly vulnerable prisoners.
Recommendation: Leaders should implement robust governance of key areas of safety, including use of force, secure accommodation and safeguarding of the most vulnerable prisoners. (To the governor)

Key concern: The general environment did not yet reflect that of a category D open prison, with internal fences, razor wire and bars on cell windows. Much of the prison also needed refurbishment and repair; many billets had leaking roofs and cracked floors. Some showers and the main kitchen were also in poor condition. A recent power loss in the kitchen caused by a broken part had resulted in considerable disruption and a limited menu for several weeks.
Recommendation: The prison should complete its transition to an open prison environment with proportionate physical security, and the living areas and main kitchen should be repaired and refurbished to provide consistently decent living and working conditions.
(To HMPPS and the governor)

Key concern: ROTL was a key objective for most prisoners at Haverigg. However, the range of voluntary and paid work opportunities in the community was very limited.
Recommendation: Prison leaders should expand the range of paid and voluntary work opportunities available to prisoners undertaking ROTL in the community.

**Notable positive practice**
We define notable positive practice as innovative work or practice that leads to particularly good outcomes from which other establishments may

be able to learn. Inspectors look for evidence of good outcomes for prisoners; original, creative or particularly effective approaches to problem-solving or achieving the desired goal; and how other establishments could learn from or replicate the practice.

Inspectors found 15 examples of notable positive practice during this inspection.

Records showed a measured approach to dealing with infringements that may have resulted in a return to closed conditions. Staff worked with prisoners to address concerns and decisions were made only following a comprehensive and multidisciplinary review at which relevant risk factors were considered.

The locally adapted support intervention plans provided a broad range of support to those who had additional needs or vulnerability.

The village hall encouraged community living for older prisoners, who could associate in a welcoming environment, engage in competitions or participate in art or music.

The nature trail was an excellent, creative use of unused land in the prison grounds. It had been transformed from scrubland into a nature area with bees, and rare tree plantations that attracted birds and insects. The project, entirely designed and maintained by prisoners, provided constructive activity and supported mental and physical well-being.

Prisoner representatives quality assured redacted versions of complaints. This initiative facilitated positive engagement with prisoners.

Regular and meaningful consultations were held with prisoners with protected characteristics.

The daily briefing included a reminder to prison officers of patients who were using the 'do not attempt to resuscitate' protocol.

All patients on four or more medicines were automatically reviewed by the pharmacist; this useful layer of governance promoted safe prescribing practices for prisoners with complex health needs.

Drug recovery workers kept in touch with patients for up to six months after release, which provided ongoing support and continuity of care with community agencies.

Prisoners had daily access to minor health and well-being products, which removed a wait of up to seven days for canteen deliveries.

Potential ROTL activity placements were jointly assessed by resettlement and OMU staff to ensure both health and safety and public protection risks were fully explored and considered. OMU staff communicated well with prisoners and ran surgeries four times a week to answer their questions. Prisoners could arrange scheduled meetings the same day with managers and staff from the OMU.

Prisoners were able to attend and contribute to their ROTL boards, which enhanced the quality of assessment and helped to address prisoners' anxieties, maximising the chances of successful temporary release.

Staff who undertook mail and telephone monitoring were invited to attend and contribute to monitoring review meetings, providing a potentially valuable perspective on decisions, and reinforcing an ethos of inclusivity and joint working in the prison.

The new 'last stop' resettlement facility was a promising initiative designed to give prisoners national and local information in advance of their release.

**INDEPENDENT MONITORING BOARD: Annual Report**

The law requires every prison to be monitored by an independent Board appointed by the Justice Secretary; these are known as Independent Monitoring Boards (IMBs). The IMB must satisfy itself as to the humane and just treatment of those held in custody within its prison and the range and adequacy of the programmes preparing them for release; it must report annually to the Justice Secretary on how well the prison has met the standards and requirements placed on it.

**IMB Report 1 Dec 2020 – 30 Nov 2021**
**Published 23rd February 2022**
**Background to the report**

The Covid-19 pandemic led to the Board returning to remote monitoring from December 2020 to the beginning of March 2021. However, throughout this time, the Board had fortnightly teleconferences with groups of prisoners from each of the residences. Members of the Board also remotely attended morning meetings and in addition, the chair and acting governor re-established their weekly telephone call.

Evidence for this report, therefore, comes from remote monitoring, observations made on visits from March to the end of November and scrutiny of records and data.

Throughout the lockdowns the prisoners at Haverigg benefitted from having almost unlimited freedom of movement within their own billet or wing and access to grounds and gardens surrounding each residence; however, the impact of the pandemic was experienced in other ways. Of particular concern to prisoners was a lack of purposeful activity, suspension of release on temporary licence (ROTL), and inability to make progress and prepare for release.

## Main judgements

### How safe is the prison?

The Board is of the view that the management team give safety the priority it needs, as evidenced through direct observation, discussions with prisoners and attendances at meetings.

Prisoners in all areas consistently told the Board they felt that the Covid-19 pandemic had been managed well by the prison and that they felt safe. Very low levels of self-harm and incidences of violence ensured that the prison was settled throughout much of the year. In the judgement of the Board, the prison is a safe environment.

### How fairly and humanely are prisoners treated?

The Board's view is that prisoners are treated fairly and humanely, but it is aware of a perception amongst some prisoners that different groups are treated more favourably, particularly relating to ROTL and, more generally, to employment opportunities. The Board has seen no evidence of this and monthly statistics provided by the offender management unit (OMU) demonstrate that determinate and indeterminate sentenced prisoners are progressed equally.

Although there have been limited opportunities to observe adjudications and immediate suitability reviews (ISRs), those that have been attended by members of the Board were judged to be fair, proportionate and constructive. Decisions to return a prisoner to closed conditions were taken following detailed consideration of all the evidence presented. The Board's view is that prisoners are treated fairly.

Although our judgement is that prisoners are treated humanely at Haverigg, it is regrettable that some experiences beyond the control of the Governor and his management team are less humane. Long waiting times for dental treatment, for example, left one prisoner waiting six weeks for dentures to be fitted and several accommodation billets became uninhabitable during unprecedented heavy rainfall and widespread flooding which occurred throughout Cumbria in early November, although alternative accommodation was offered and repairs to the roofs and building fabric were prioritised.

However, the Board considers that the continued imprisonment of imprisonment for public protection (IPP) prisoners, who make up approximately 30% of Haverigg's population, for many years, and in some cases over a decade, beyond their tariff, and their treatment by the wider criminal justice system, is inhumane.

### How well are prisoners' health and wellbeing needs met?

As last year, prisoners have expressed their appreciation to the Board for the primary and mental healthcare provided at the prison.

With an ageing population, the focus throughout the year has been on chronic disease management and, in partnership with gym staff, the provision of health promotion activities.

The introduction of resident support assistants has provided a strong network of support for prisoners with disabilities. However, in the view of the Board, the social care processes of assessment and provision of aids to daily living lag services provided in the community. There is also a need for a clearly defined pathway for social care support on discharge.

Prisoner anxiety on transfer from a closed establishment to an open prison and prior to discharge is, as observed by the Board, managed sensitively by officers, healthcare and civilian staff. It is evident to the Board that prisoners' health and wellbeing needs are met and that every effort is being made to improve the level of social care provision and to clarify arrangements for discharge.

### How well are prisoners progressed towards successful resettlement?

For prisoners of working age, a wide range of employment opportunities are available in the prison. Increasingly, for those with ROTL clearance, paid work within local businesses and industry is becoming available.

The employment hub provides details of vacancies across the northwest and supports prisoners in making applications and preparation for interviews.

On release, the majority of prisoners will go, initially, to approved premises. The OMU begins planning release six months before known discharge dates. A member of the Board observes the monthly release planning meetings and notes that for most prisoners accommodation is confirmed well in advance. However, the Board is aware that for two prisoners accommodation was only confirmed the day before release. This caused them considerable anxiety.

As a national resource for PCOSO, prisoners at Haverigg are from all over the UK. The Board is aware that offender managers have experienced difficulties in communicating with community managers and have faced delay in the receipt of reports from outside agencies for both release planning and preparation for Parole Board hearings. There is a perception amongst IPP prisoners that they are treated less favourably than those serving determinate sentences and vice versa. Evidence seen by the Board does not bear this out. Monthly statistics from the OMU clearly show that in all aspects of progression and resettlement, both sentence groups are treated equitably and proportionate to their populations. The Board's view is that, for prisoners of working age, there is a wide range of employment opportunities, many of which lead to vocational qualifications, placing them in a good position to secure employment on release. Prisoners of retirement age, some of whom have been in prison for several decades, are well prepared for when they are released.

Despite continuing difficulty in recruiting to key posts, the Board is satisfied that every effort is made to provide prisoners with the support, skills and experience for them to progress towards a successful resettlement.

## Main areas for development
### TO THE MINISTER

The plight of prisoners at Haverigg serving an IPP sentence continues to be a major concern of the Board and is neither fair nor humane. Although the Justice Select Committee's inquiry into IPP sentences is welcome and the Board awaits its recommendations with interest, for prisoners many years over tariff there is little, if any, confidence in a justice system which has kept them imprisoned long after the IPP sentence was abolished.

It is of concern that action proposed by a former chair of the Parole Board in 2016, in which he put forward the suggestion that the risk test for IPP-sentenced prisoners 'be reversed so that they would only remain in prison if there was evidence that they were a risk to the public, rather than evidence that they were not' has not been introduced.

A further concern of the Board is the high level of licence recalls, on occasions almost outnumbering releases.

Is the Minister able to provide assurance to the Board that he will consider legislation to commute the IPP sentence to a determinate one, to limit recall to a determinate period and to increase the level of support, particularly probation, for these prisoners on release?

The Board welcomes the Prime Minister's commitment that employment opportunities will be made available for 1,000 prison leavers by the end of 2023 and asks whether this opportunity will be available to prisoners convicted of sexual offences.

### TO THE PRISON SERVICE

Once again, the Board is concerned about the loss of property on transfer, with over 25% of IMB applications received this year related to property. Two members of the Board participated in the prison property framework (PPF) focus group and commented on the draft document, finding it disappointing that there is no evidence of any improvement in the management of prisoners' property.

At the time of writing, the Board has little confidence that the long-awaited implementation of the PPF will result in systemic improvements to prevent the distressing loss of prisoners' property, especially on transfer between establishments.

Unless or until responsibility and accountability for property are aligned with performance monitoring, it is our view that nothing will change. Is HMPPS able to reassure the Board that priority will be given to resolving this long-standing issue?

### TO THE GOVERNOR

Once again, the Board commends the Governor, his management team and staff on their efforts to effectively and sensitively manage Covid-19 and lead the prison progressively forward to the Stage 1 regime of increasing normality. A high rate of vaccination (93%) across the prison and the intensive testing programme for prisoners and staff has minimised the impact of the pandemic.

However, the Board is concerned about the impact of staff vacancies in key roles, especially the OMU, and the impact this has on prisoners' progression and resettlement. The Board is interested to learn about efforts to recruit probation officers and the measures taken to mitigate any delays in progression, particularly on arrangements for accommodation on release.

### Progress since the last report

Environmental improvements continued throughout the year, including the removal or lowering of internal fencing, tree planting and the creation of boules courts and a bowling green.

The introduction of resident support assistant and residential information officer roles, together with orderlies supporting many of the prison's operational services, increased the involvement of prisoners in all aspects of prison life.

It was particularly pleasing to the Board that concerns raised by prisoners during lockdown teleconferences were progressively addressed, with improvements made in, for example, laundry facilities in all residences and increased privacy around wing telephones. Staff and prisoner relationships continued to strengthen throughout the year, with members of the Board routinely observing constructive interactions. Prisoners have regularly made positive comments to the Board about staff, a much-improved position to those made last year ('stuck in a category C mentality').

**HEWELL LANE
REDDITCH
WORCESTERSHIRE
B97 6QS**

**HM PRISON
HEWELL**

**Tel: 01527 785000**

*For the latest reports on this prison please visit:*
https://tinyurl.com/bdfh26rv

*Important Changes:* **(1) Visits:** the identification necessary to access this prison and visit for social or professional purposes has changed; (2) **Money and Gifts** new rules now apply to these. See page 16 for full details of the above.

**Task of the establishment** Hewell is a category B adult male local prison.

**Certified normal accommodation and operational capacity**
Prisoners held at the time of this visit: 828
Baseline certified normal capacity: 1,070
In-use certified normal capacity: 998
Operational capacity: 900

**Prison status and key providers**
Public
Prison Group: West Midlands
Prison Group Director: Teresa Clarke
Governor/Director: Ralph Lubkowski
IMB Chair: Rodger Lawrence
Physical health provider: Care UK
Mental health provider: Care UK
Substance use treatment provider: Care UK
Prison education framework provider: Novus
Escort contractor: GeoAmey

**Brief history** Hewell was opened in June 2008. It consists of a closed category B male site. The open category D Grange resettlement unit, a grade ll* listed manor house built in 1894 in the Jacobean style, was decommissioned in April 2020.
House blocks 1 to 6 on the closed site hold remand (including potential category A), sentenced and vulnerable prisoners.

**Short description of residential units**
The six house blocks have single and double cells, all with in-cell sanitation.
House blocks 1, 2 A&C spur, 3 B&C spur and 6 - Convicted and unconvicted prisoners
House block 2 A&C spur 3 C Spur - Induction/first night unit
House block 4 – Prisoners with drug or alcohol issues
House block 5, 2B spur - Vulnerable prisoners
Segregation Unit - Prisoners subject to segregation rules PSO1700

Inpatients' Unit - Prisoners with health care requirements

**Visiting Information**
Book online:
visitsbooking.westmidlands@noms.gsi.gov.uk or by telephone on 0300 060 6503 Monday to Friday, 9:15am to 4pm
**Visiting times:** Mon, Wed, Fri, Sat, Sun: 8:45am to 11am and 1:15pm to 4pm.

**Legal visits:** Email
visitsbooking.westmidlands@noms.gsi.gov.uk or ring 0300 060 6503 Monday to Friday, 9am to 6pm.
**Visiting times:** Monday to Friday 9am to 11:30am and 2pm to 4:30pm.

**INSPECTIONS & REPORTS**
SSV: Section 6.2.3.1
**Scrutiny visit: 4 and 11–12 August 2020**
**Published: 15 September 2020**
This report discusses the findings of our scrutiny visit to HMP Hewell concerning the conditions and treatment of prisoners during the Covid-19 pandemic.
Hewell is a large category B local prison in Worcestershire, holding up to 900 adult male prisoners – 828 at the time of the visit. The prison had a high churn and continued to serve the courts and manage many short-term sentences throughout the national restrictions. At the time of our visit almost a quarter of prisoners had had their licences revoked, some of whom had been recalled for very short periods. This added to the challenges faced by the prison.
Our visit took place almost five months after restrictions had been imposed. At the start of restrictions, the senior team were properly focused on managing the risks associated with COVID- 19 and on safeguarding the, often transient and short-term, population. Given the type of prison and the risks it faced, it was to their credit that only nine prisoners had tested positive for the virus and none at all since late April. Attention to social distancing remained a continuing challenge but overall the prison had managed the initial stages of the crisis well and had kept prisoners and staff safe.
In the early stages the prison had appointed a senior manager to lead on Covid-19. This role focused on delivering a communication strategy to both prisoners and staff and was broadly effective in ensuring that both groups understood the reasons for the restrictions and when they were to be eased.
It is difficult to comment on how Hewell was coping with the pressures and constraints imposed by a pandemic without reflecting on our last inspection (in June 2019) when we found

that outcomes for prisoners were poor or not sufficiently good across our healthy prison assessments and significant work was required to address our concerns. The prison had started work on addressing our recommendations when the more immediate concerns of dealing with the Covid-19 crisis had understandably interrupted many of their plans.

The prison had secured some funding to improve the conditions of cells and communal areas, and this work had continued since restrictions were imposed. The prison was clean and generally well maintained, although further work was required in some areas. Health care provision, including management of the response to the virus, was good overall.

There were, however, some concerns. Almost a third of prisoners felt unsafe, though the focus of these feelings had changed somewhat to reflect the impact of Covid-19, particularly the lack of consistent attention to social distancing. It was inevitable that violence would reduce when the regime was so significantly curtailed but, despite this, the number of incidents remained comparatively high, particularly against staff. At the time of our visit Hewell could not be considered a safe prison. The structures to identify and address violence and anti-social behaviour were not yet good enough to take appropriate and consistent action where needed, which was concerning.

Key work had stopped for the majority of prisoners. Meaningful contact was difficult with limited time, and most interactions that we observed were purely transactional to meet the basic needs of prisoners. However, in our survey, 70% of prisoners said they felt respected by staff and they told us of positive experiences. In contrast, 41% of prisoners said they had been bullied or victimised by staff and we were told of negative treatment and poor staff culture.

The needs of many prisoners at Hewell were complex and more than two-thirds identified as having mental health concerns. The care for particularly vulnerable prisoners was good but many still felt that they were not supported at their time of need. There were weaknesses in the assessment, care in custody and teamwork (ACCT) process which did not provide an individual package of care for many prisoners. More needed to be done to understand and address these important issues.

The severely curtailed regime at the start of the restrictions was understandable but almost five months had passed and there had been little progress in ensuring that prisoners had sufficient time out of cell or purposeful activity. This contributed to prisoners' frustration and potentially to a deterioration in mental and emotional well-being. Prison leaders at both local and national level should take note of the fact that 70% of the prisoners we surveyed at Hewell reported problems with their mental health. One hour out of cell each day was simply not enough. The situation was often worse for prisoners on the margins, including the small number who were isolating. They could not have a shower regularly and sometimes had to wait for up to 14 days to do so.

The prison was not fully accessible for many prisoners with disabilities, including wheelchair users, who were routinely sent there. We found some prisoners with impaired mobility who had not had time in the fresh air for weeks and who experienced particular difficulty in accessing showers regularly. This was wholly unacceptable.

Efforts had been made to ensure that prisoners could maintain some contact with their families in the absence of visits. The implementation of in-cell telephones had been brought forward to April.

These were greatly appreciated by prisoners, although confidentiality and privacy of calls in shared cells could not always be achieved. The reintroduction of visits had been a priority for the prison after nearly five months without any and this was also valued by prisoners. Social distancing from visitors was clearly challenging, but threats to impose closed visits if this was not adhered to were not managed sensitively or in a proportionate fashion. Purple Visits had started two weeks before our visit but uptake had been slow.

Offender management work was mostly limited to milestone events such as parole and home detention curfew. Prisoners, including those who were suitable for open conditions, were generally unable to make progress with their sentences. Arrangements for public protection were reasonable and targeted prisoners who posed the highest risk. An unintended consequence of access to in-cell telephones had been an unprecedented rise in call volumes, which exposed the fact that there were inadequate resources to monitor calls consistently where it was appropriate to do so. This was concerning. Release planning for the large number of prisoners affected was reasonable in terms of securing housing. Only five prisoners had been released since late March with no accommodation to go to.

A new governor had arrived five weeks before our visit and had made some small changes relatively quickly, including increasing the time out of cell from half an hour to an hour, opening a workshop for a small number of prisoners and introducing an outside exercise session led by PE staff for all prisoners once a week. Yet many workshops remained empty, classroom-based education was still not permitted and only 14% of prisoners were employed. At the time of our visit recovery plans were only slowly being submitted for approval with limited progress in their implementation.

While we are acutely aware of the need to ease restrictions in a safe and measured way, we felt that progress had been too slow and the restrictions in place were no longer proportionate. Additional improvements could be made by the governor but further progress was limited by rigid national procedures which prevented a creative leadership team from implementing credible and safe plans to improve the regime.

The governor was realistic about the significant challenges that lay ahead. He described an optimistic vision for Hewell of delivering a more person-centred, purposeful and rehabilitative regime within the constraints of running a busy local prison The initial stages of the Covid-19 crisis had been managed well, and the challenge now will be to secure, as quickly as possible, a recovery plan that will enable the prison to fulfil its role safely and decently.

HM Chief Inspector of Prisons August 2020

## INDEPENDENT MONITORING BOARD: Annual Report

The law requires every prison to be monitored by an independent Board appointed by the Justice Secretary; these are known as Independent Monitoring Boards (IMBs). The IMB must satisfy itself as to the humane and just treatment of those held in custody within its prison and the range and adequacy of the programmes preparing them for release; it must report annually to the Justice Secretary on how well the prison has met the standards and requirements placed on it.

### IMB Report 1 October 2020 – 30 September 2021
### Published January 2022
### Background to the report

The Covid-19 outbreak has had a significant impact on the Board's ability to gather information and discuss the contents of this annual report. The Board has, therefore, tried to cover as much ground as it can in these difficult circumstances, but inevitably there is less detail and supporting evidence than usual. Ministers are aware of these constraints. Regular information is being collected specifically on the prison's response to the pandemic and is being collated nationally.

The prison was under the most restrictive Covid-related operating system for virtually the entire year, moving to Stage 2 on 20 September 2021.

Given the restrictions imposed, the number and experience of members, there are areas of this report that are more limited than would be optimal. This report covers the first full reporting year in the tenure of the new substantive Governor. Our evidence comes from personal observations gleaned on visits, remote monitoring contact with the prison, scrutiny of prison data and records, attendance at meetings, informal contact with both prisoners and staff and through handling applications from prisoners.

We are aware of a large number of planned initiatives to improve the prison which were due to be implemented once the prison moved to Stage 2 restrictions. In the main, as we have no direct or indirect evidence of these initiatives and how they impacted on prisoners, we have not included them in the report.

### Main judgements

The Board's overall impression is of an improving prison which is now safer and more secure than we have shown in previous reports. The Board is particularly keen to commend the agility and imagination with which the prison has managed the impact of the pandemic and the extent to which both the prisoners and staff have, largely, been protected from the direct impact of Covid.

That the very significant restrictions have been implemented so calmly, thoroughly and with the support of the population is creditable.

Effective and safe handling of the impact of the pandemic would, in and of itself, have been a major challenge for the staff and management during the year. That this has been achieved at the same time as real progress has been made towards a bold and ambitious programme to move the prison forward is a significant achievement.

The fact that the cultural change and genuine attempts to reset HMP Hewell have not yet been fully implemented should not detract from the ambition and radical nature of the vision and drive to improve the establishment.

The Board acknowledges that improvements in staff morale and, crucially, retention are beginning to have a positive impact on the stability and effectiveness of the prison. The challenge of training and building the confidence of a large proportion of inexperienced staff and filling the gaps left by the departure of a number of experienced staff is significant but the Board observes that, in this regard, the early signs are positive.

The prison is showing real signs of developing a more overt sense of community and of shared experience for those living and working there. The Board recognises the potentially positive effect of this drive to substantive cultural change, though notes that the confidence to 'do things differently' is not yet fully embedded within all the staff.

The Board commends the very real progress made during the year towards making the prison cleaner, smarter and more comfortable. That said, the challenges presented by the basic fabric of the buildings, years of neglect and the infrastructure available to the staff limit this progress. Frequent false fire alarms, broken vehicle gates, unreliable/broken keys and antiquated computer systems have a deleterious impact on the smooth running of the prison and present frustrations for prisoners and staff. Such failings are often a daily distraction from other more constructive duties and therefore affect the wellbeing of the prisoners and illustrate working conditions for staff that are unsatisfactory. The inappropriateness of the prison for prisoners (and staff) with disabilities remains a disgrace.

While commending the progress made within the prison during the year, the Board is clear that systemic failings remain a cause for concern. Challenges inherent in a local prison, which include the churn of men, the significant proportion of remand prisoners (many of whom have spent longer on remand than would have been expected pre-pandemic) and the mixture of categories of prisoners are a problem for HMP Hewell. The fact that the majority of men share cells designed for a single occupant has largely become an accepted feature of life in the prison. Such arrangements are undignified and appear to create much of the tension within the prison. That prisoners are still held under indeterminate sentences remains, in the opinion of the Board, an injustice and an inhumane system for a civilised society.

That genuine efforts are made to support such individuals in HMP Hewell does not mitigate the problem.

The paucity of, and difficulty of accessing, appropriate accommodation for the most vulnerable and unwell prisoners remains a concern for the Board. Increased emphasis on improving the wellbeing of such men at Hewell and early signs of more focused and therapeutic care for such individuals does not and will not, in the view of the Board, replace genuinely appropriate alternative arrangements for such men.

### How safe is the prison?

The prison is now safer than in our past reporting year as measured by levels of assaults, both between prisoners and against staff. The Board notes the challenge of continuing this trend once the current restrictions are eased, though has confidence that the cultural and regime changes being introduced will support this positive transformation. The Board is pleased to note the almost, but not complete, eradication of cell fires within the prison.

Levels of self-harm within the prison, though still too high, are decreasing, and the Board notes the more personalised and targeted support and interventions offered to individuals at risk of such behaviours.

The Board is aware of the early positive impact of the new and more closely managed system of using the assessment, care in custody and teamwork (ACCT) system and notes an increasingly effective use of multidisciplinary reviews. The Board would like to see a fuller implementation of the key worker scheme, currently offered only to the most vulnerable cohorts due to staffing challenges.

Data and incidents observed show a decrease in the use of force and a proactive approach to further improvement. Incidents observed and recorded indicate that use of force is administered in a safe and humane manner.

### How fairly and humanely are prisoners treated?

The Board has no evidence of active or intentional discrimination within the prison but is concerned at an apparent lack of appetite by management to investigate or question more subtle or inadvertent unfairness in the treatment of prisoners.

The much-improved data collection in the area of equalities is to be commended, though the Board would welcome more robust interrogation of that data and its implications. There are early signs (e.g., in the form of increased, though still low, levels of self-declaration) that the drive to welcome and celebrate diversity and different minorities is paying dividends, though the Board is clear that token acknowledgement of diversity is no substitute for fundamentally fair treatment. The Board notes the unrealistically low number of discrimination incident report forms (DIRFs) submitted during the year and shares the prison's assumption that this reflects a lack of confidence on the part of prisoners in the DIRF system. The Board welcomes the prison's intention to address this in the coming year and will follow progress with interest.

In terms of specific protected characteristics, the Board commends the intention to introduce forums for different groups of prisoners and acknowledges the real efforts being made to encourage engagement from minority groups. The Board welcomes the plan to work with the Zahid Mubarek Trust around issues of race within the prison but notes significant gaps in focus on other groups; for example, older prisoners, those with hidden disabilities and those with limited language skills.

Facilities for prisoners with mobility issues remain unacceptable.

The Board believes that prisoners are, on the

whole, treated compassionately and humanely. That said, we are concerned that a minority of individuals do not have their needs sufficiently met unless and until they present a disciplinary problem for the prison.

## How well are prisoners' health and wellbeing needs met?

While the Board cannot comment on clinical matters, it remains consistently struck by the level of discontent on the part of prisoners with not having their health needs met and with healthcare services in general. This discontent is particularly prevalent regarding mental health care provision. We have some evidence of tension between the prison and the healthcare provider, which is to the detriment of the prisoners.

The Board notes the conspicuous and explicit focus on wider wellbeing of prisoners and commends the adoption of a more holistic approach to the wellbeing of the men accommodated at Hewell. The development of a houseblock specifically designed to focus on men with health or wellbeing needs (including drug and alcohol issues) and the development of the Targeted Care Pathway to bring the various disparate strands of care and support together is welcomed by the Board. This specialist unit is still in its infancy and the Board looks forward to monitoring its progress and the impact it has on both the individuals housed there and on the wider prison community. The delayed opening of the much-heralded Oak Unit (in the former inpatients unit, to accommodate the most complex individuals routinely accommodated in segregation and to act as a staging post to/from specialist mental and other health facilities) is disappointing. The Board commends the ambition behind the plan and looks forward to its opening. In the meantime, the Board repeats its previously-reported view that inadequate provision is currently made for the most challenging individuals – either in the prison or in the wider criminal justice and health systems.

## How well are prisoners progressed towards successful resettlement?

The Board has little direct evidence of progress or otherwise in this area, which has been particularly impacted by the Covid-19 restrictions. Some isolated examples of activity are briefly described elsewhere in this report. However, the Board remains concerned that there are prisoners at Hewell whose status (imprisonment for public protection (IPP), life sentence, category D etc.) make it an inappropriate location for these men to be progressed towards successful resettlement.

## Main areas for development
### TO THE MINISTER

The Board again restates its previously recorded concern at the prevalence and treatment of prisoners held in custody indefinitely under indeterminate sentences for public protection. We have seen no evidence of attempts to manage the sentences of these individuals with any focus on forward progression. Nor have we seen recognition that the despair of endless detention results in self-destructive behaviour, leading to the use of segregation and challenges to discipline within the prison. This, in turn, causes these prisoners to fail at the parole board. We urge the minister to take up the issue of prisoners still being held in custody indefinitely despite the power to pass such sentences being removed eight years ago.

Similarly, the Board remains concerned about the difficulties encountered in transferring prisoners with severe mental health/behavioural issues to an environment where they can be treated effectively. Again, will the minister work with colleagues in other departments to ensure greater availability of more suitable locations for these prisoners?

### TO THE PRISON SERVICE

In the light of long remand periods, review the policy that remand prisoners are exempt from some of the obligations that go with effective resettlement and opportunities are provided.

Ensure that prisoners inappropriately located at HMP Hewell (by reason of their category, etc.) are speedily moved to appropriate prisons.

Provide funding to ensure that those with mobility issues can move around the prison e.g., lifts and widened doorways.

When the category D Hewell Grange was open prisoners were employed to maintain the approach to the prison, cut the verges and clear and tidy the car parks. Those prisoners are no longer present and funding to fulfil these requirements is necessary.

### TO THE PRISONS AND PROBATION OMBUDSMAN

Please conclude the report into the death on 14 June 2018, so that any identified lessons learned may be acted upon.

### TO THE GOVERNOR

Maintain the improvement with the early days unit, including improved transition from the induction houseblock to permanent accommodation. Improve identification of those prisoners with learning difficulties/disabilities and their consequential support.

Maintain culture change pressure to have a

consistent standard of staff behaviour towards prisoners.

Improve the handling of prison complaints and applications systems, focusing particularly on those which raise issues of discrimination, to ensure that such concerns are appropriately addressed and where necessary dealt with through the DIRF process.

Improve the cleanliness and appearance of the approach to the prison.

Maintain a focus on equality issues to ensure that all prisoners are treated fairly. For example, but not exclusively: the provision of wheelchairs in reception, translation services and information in other languages.

**HIGH DOWN LANE
SUTTON
SURREY
SM2 5PJ**

**Tel: 020 7147 6300**

*For the latest reports on this prison please visit:*
https://tinyurl.com/bdfh26rv

*Important Changes:* **(1) Visits:** the identification necessary to access this prison and visit for social or professional purposes has changed; (2) **Money and Gifts** new rules now apply to these. See page 16 for full details of the above.

**Task of the establishment** Adult male category B local prison.

**Certified normal accommodation and operational capacity**
Prisoners held at the time of this visit: 1,152
Baseline certified normal capacity: 1,001
In-use certified normal capacity: 999
Operational capacity: 1,153

**Prison status and key providers**
Public
Prison Group: London
Prison Group Director: Ian Bickers
Governor/Director: Emily Martin
Joint IMB chairs: Sheila Souchard/Andrea Coady
Physical health provider: Central and North-west London NHS Foundation Trust (CNWL)
Mental health provider: CNWL
Substance misuse treatment provider:
The Forward Trust
Prison education framework provider: Novus
Escort contractor: Serco

**Brief history** HMP High Down was built on the site of the former mental health hospital in Banstead and opened in 1992. Since 2009, two new residential houseblocks, a new gymnasium and an Educational Centre with 21 classrooms which offers a range of vocational training, personal and social development courses and traditional education opportunities have been added to the site.

**Short description of residential units**
Each houseblock can hold just under 200 prisoners.
Houseblock 1 – general houseblock with protective isolation unit
Houseblock 2 – includes reverse cohort unit for the general population
Houseblock 3 – general houseblock
Houseblock 4 – substance misuse treatment unit with reverse cohort unit for prisoners undergoing treatment on arrival
Houseblock 5 – general houseblock
Houseblock 6 – vulnerable prisoners' unit with reverse cohort unit for new arrivals from this population
Segregation unit: holding up to 21 prisoners
Inpatient health care: holding up to 23 prisoners

**Visiting Information**
Book online: www.gov.uk/prison-visits or by telephone on 020 7147 6570 Monday to Wednesday 10am to midday and 2pm to 4pm, Thursday and Friday 10am to midday.
**Visiting times:** Tuesday to Thursday: 9:30am to 10:30am and 2:30pm to 3:30pm.

**Legal visits:** Booking line: 020 7147 6570 Monday to Wednesday 10am to midday and 2pm to 4pm, Thursday and Friday 10am to midday.
**Visiting times:** Tuesday to Thursday: 10am to 11am and 3pm to 4pm.

**INSPECTIONS & REPORTS**
**Scrutiny visit 23 March and 7 – 8 April 2021**
**Published 13 May 2021**
This report presents the findings from our scrutiny visit to HMP High Down, a large prison in Surrey holding about 1,150 men. Our visit highlighted a number of significant concerns about the treatment and conditions of prisoners, but one issue above all had seriously affected the running of the prison.

At our 2018 inspection, my predecessor, Peter Clarke, expressed his serious concern over the uncertainty about the prison's future role. I include the relevant paragraph from that report:
"The area that caused us greatest concern was that of purposeful activity, and this was directly related to the uncertainty over the prison's future. We were told that there had been some delayed plans to re-role the prison to become a category C training prison. So far as the senior management

team were aware, the latest plan was that this should happen in the autumn of 2018, just a few months after the inspection. When I asked if this was definitely going to happen and what the plans were to enable it to do so, no-one could give me a clear answer. They simply did not know. This, I was told, was because they had not been given any more detail by Her Majesty's Prison and Probation Service (HMPPS). This was extraordinary."

Three years later, and five years after High Down's transition from a category B local prison to a category C training prison was first proposed, it is astonishing that this situation had still not been resolved.

The current governor had been asked to complete the recategorisation during the pandemic, which was no easy task. She had accepted category C prisoners from across the estate. Plans were advanced and a newsletter had even been sent to prisoners confirming the new direction for High Down. Then very shortly before our visit and just after this news was communicated to prisoners, senior HMPPS leaders suspended the change in function. High Down remains a local category B prison, but without the full-time activity or offending behaviour programme places that are needed by the majority of the population.

There had been no prisoner or staff deaths due to Covid-19, but quarantine arrangements for newly arrived prisoners were not well organised and risked transmitting infection across the population. Hundreds of prisoners had been isolated following possible contact with infection during the months before our visit. They had faced isolation periods of 10 days with no time out of cell at all other than a weekly shower. A good number had experienced these levels of isolation two or three times. The scale of isolation was not mitigated by welfare checks, which were irregular for most prisoners and not of sufficient quality for those identified as needing extra support. Recorded levels of self-harm had reduced during the pandemic, but the number of assessment, care in custody and teamwork (ACCT) documents was high and this had affected the quality of support for those at risk of suicide and self-harm. Sometimes there was no care map and it was not clear how staff were supposed to help the individual. Recorded levels of violence had decreased, but use of force by staff remained at pre-pandemic levels. Drugs were still a serious problem. Communal areas were clean. Many prisoners continued to share small, cramped cells designed for one. The fragility of the regime meant that prisoners did not always get a daily shower. Very little equality or diversity work had been completed in the previous 12 months and some groups such as foreign nationals who spoke little

English were struggling.

Health care provision was poor and caused us serious concern. There had been a lack of consistent leadership, with four heads of health care in the year. There had been severe staff shortages and health care staff told us they felt compromised by the unmanageable demands on their time. Basic processes, such as making sure that emergency response bags were up to date and properly equipped, had failed.

Progress had been too slow to provide prisoners with purposeful activity 12 months into Covid-19 restrictions. Most prisoners still had only one hour out of their cells each day, sometimes less when time in the open air was cancelled. It had taken five months to launch in-cell education packs. About 350 prisoners had a full-time job, but there were no clear plans to provide the rest of the population with work once the pandemic ended. The work of the offender management unit was fundamentally undermined by the decision to reverse the prison's change of function. There was little contact between prison offender managers and prisoners and there was a large backlog of assessments of prisoners' risk and needs. There was a good focus on the release of high-risk prisoners, but staffing difficulties had prevented officers from listening to the calls of prisoners who required public protection monitoring. There was a real chance that important information about risk could be missed.

We found a troubled prison confronting difficult, long-term challenges. It is a serious indictment of HMPPS leadership that the governor and her team should have been asked to spend so much of the pandemic distracted by a change in function which was ultimately suspended. The prison leadership need an early, definite and final decision on the future direction of the establishment and category C prisoners who were brought to High Down deserve to know how their needs will be met to help them emerge from prison with less risk of reoffending.

Charlie Taylor, HM Chief Inspector of Prisons
April 2021

### Key concerns and recommendations

Key concerns and recommendations identify the issues of most importance to improving outcomes for prisoners and are designed to help establishments prioritise and address the most significant weaknesses in the treatment and conditions of prisoners.

During this visit we identified areas of key concern and have made recommendations for the prison to address.

Key concern: For five years. High Down had been subject to plans to change its function from a category B local prison to a category C training prison. When we inspected in 2018, outcomes for prisoners were already being adversely affected by the uncertainty over the prison's future, and the situation was now critical. Hundreds of category C prisoners had been brought to the prison during the pandemic, but after months of planning HMPPS leaders had suddenly decided to retain High Down as a local prison for the foreseeable future. There would not be enough full-time activity or offending behaviour programme places for these category C prisoners once the pandemic ended. It was unclear what would happen to them, how they could reduce their risk or gain work skills before they were released. Offender management work at the prison had no clear direction as a result of this decision. Recommendation: A final decision should be made about the future of High Down and there should be sufficient full-time purposeful activity places and offending behaviour programme places to meet the needs of the population. (To HMPPS)

Key concern: A year into the pandemic, most prisoners still only had one hour out of their cells each day consisting of 30 minutes outside exercise and 30 minutes domestic time to have a shower, submit applications and raise any concerns they may have with staff. Hundreds of prisoners had been isolated for 10 days with no time out of cell except for a weekly shower. Most prisoners did not receive regular, meaningful, face-to-face welfare checks. Most welfare checks that were conducted were completed on in-cell phones and staff were unable to assess the prisoner's appearance and cell conditions for signs of deterioration.
Recommendation: All prisoners subject to Covid-19 regime restrictions should have regular, meaningful, face-to-face welfare checks. (To the governor)

Key concern: The number of prisoners being supported by the ACCT process was high and staff struggled to deliver good quality care. ACCT procedures had too many weaknesses, including the lack of an effective care map and very limited records of meaningful contact.
Recommendation: Prisoners at risk of suicide or self-harm should receive effective support with a regularly updated care map to deliver prompt actions to reduce their risk. ACCT documentation should demonstrate meaningful daily contact. (To the governor)

Key concern: Prisoners could not consistently shower every day because the regime was sometimes curtailed. Hundreds of prisoners isolated because of possible exposure to Covid-19 were only offered a weekly shower.
Recommendation: All prisoners should be able to shower every day. (To the governor)

Key concern: Very little strategic or operational work had been carried out during the previous 12 months to improve outcomes for protected and minority groups. Not enough had been done to support prisoners who did not speak, write or read English fluently.
Recommendation: Outcomes for prisoners in protected and minority groups should be routinely monitored and, if any adverse outcomes are identified, prompt remedial action should follow. (To the governor)

Key concern: The procedure for evacuating prisoners with disabilities in the event of an emergency was ineffective. A list of prisoners who required a personal emergency evacuation plan was kept in a folder on each houseblock. These records were inconsistent and often out of date with little or no detail about the help the prisoner needed. Residential staff could not tell us about individual prisoners' needs in any detail and did not know where to find this information.
Recommendation: Every prisoner requiring assistance during an evacuation should have an up-to-date personal emergency evacuation plan which describes the support they need. These plans should be accessible to residential staff, who should be familiar with these prisoners and their needs and locations. (To the governor)

Key concern: There had been three incidents between November 2020 and March 2021 of essential items missing from emergency resuscitation bags. Governance for checking this equipment was not robust.
Recommendation: Emergency resuscitation equipment and medicines should be in good order and ready for use. An effective monitoring system should be established which should be regularly audited to ensure compliance. (To the governor/partnership board)

Key concern: Many aspects of health care provision were poor. The primary care team had experienced significant staffing difficulties with staff having to combine different roles including responding to emergencies, completing reception screening and medication rounds. These competing demands had contributed to delays in delivering services and caused stress to staff. Clinical incident data for the previous six months described several areas of concern including poor practice. Secondary health screening was not being completed by health care staff. Waiting times to see a GP for a routine appointment were too long.
Recommendation: The full range of health services should be delivered to patients in a timely and safe manner. (To the governor/partnership board)

Key concern: Prisoners across High Down could not have an hour in the open air every day. Even the 30 minutes offered as part of the current restricted regime was sometimes cancelled. Those isolated for 10 days due to possible exposure to Covid-19 had no outdoor exercise at all.

Recommendation: All prisoners should be able to spend an hour in the open air every day.
(To the governor)

Key concern: The monitoring of telephone calls for public protection was ineffective. No calls had been listened to for many months and it was planned that only a random sample of calls would be checked in future. This meant that potentially important risk information, such as prisoners continuing to threaten or harass their victims, could be missed.

Recommendation: When public protection concerns necessitate the monitoring of prisoners' phone calls, every call should be listened to promptly to identify risk. New information indicating an increased risk should prompt immediate action to protect victims and manage the prisoner effectively in custody.
(To the governor)

### Education, skills and work (Ofsted)

During this visit Ofsted inspectors conducted an interim assessment of the provision of education, skills and work in the establishment. They identified steps that the prison needed to take to meet the needs of prisoners, including those with special educational needs and disabilities.

### Next steps

Leaders and managers should support face-to-face and remote learning to ensure that more prisoners can access education, skills and work and enhance their learning experience.

Managers should improve the quality of the feedback that learners receive on their work, so that they know what they need to do to improve and develop their knowledge and understanding of the subject they are studying.

Leaders and managers should increase support for learners who speak English as an additional language, so that they can improve their English skills.

### Notable positive practice

We define notable positive practice as innovative practice or practice that leads to particularly good outcomes from which other establishments may be able to learn. Inspectors look for evidence of good outcomes for prisoners; original, creative or particularly effective approaches to problem-solving or achieving the desired goal; and how other establishments could learn from or replicate the practice.

Inspectors found two examples of notable positive practice during this visit.

An online service recently established and run by staff and volunteers from The Forward Trust provided information, advice and support on drug and alcohol issues for recently released prisoners and their families.

Every prisoner who had not yet taken advantage of the video visits service had been identified and spoken to by staff to encourage them to book a visit. This one-off exercise was a positive initiative which should be repeated.

### INDEPENDENT MONITORING BOARD: Annual Report

The law requires every prison to be monitored by an independent Board appointed by the Justice Secretary; these are known as Independent Monitoring Boards (IMBs). The IMB must satisfy itself as to the humane and just treatment of those held in custody within its prison and the range and adequacy of the programmes preparing them for release; it must report annually to the Justice Secretary on how well the prison has met the standards and requirements placed on it.

**IMB Report1 January 2021 – 31 December 2021**
**Published June 2022**
**Executive summary**
**Background to the report**

Life at High Down has continued to be impacted by the Covid-19 pandemic throughout 2021, resulting in more limited time out of cell and restricted opportunities for sentence progression across the establishment.

High Down has continued to have a lack of continuity of leadership. After a lengthy period with an acting Governor in 2020, High Down enjoyed a period with a permanent Governor from August 2020. Unfortunately, she left post in November 2021, and although a permanent replacement was appointed, this was short-lived as her replacement announced within weeks of her arrival that she was to move to another prison. The Board has upheld its independent monitoring role to the best of its ability during a year when we have continued to have periods where some members were unable to make visits to the prison in person. The Board's capacity to hear directly from prisoners about their experience has therefore remained compromised, although to a lesser extent than in 2020.

### Main judgements
### How safe is the prison?

We are pleased to note that since last year there has been an overall reduction in the level of assaults, both prisoner-on-prisoner at 32% and prisoner-on-staff at 27%. This may in part be attributed to less time out of cell than before the pandemic.

We asked a random sample of 46 prisoners if

they feel they had been kept safe during 2021. In response 22 felt they had been kept safe, six felt mostly safe and eight felt they had not been kept safe. Ten did not know. Several men told us that they feel safer on their own in their cell. Some reported staff turning a blind eye to prisoners' behaviour which made them feel unsafe. Men who were newly arrived to High Down felt staff and peer supporters had been very supportive.

We remain concerned that there are insufficient body-worn video cameras (BWVCs) for all staff, and that those that are available are not always worn or turned on, despite continued encouragement from senior management. Prisoners report that staff often do not turn their BWVC on and that they feel safer when cameras are used.

We also remain concerned that despite enhanced gate security, body scanners and other initiatives introduced to disrupt the flow of illicit items into the prison, the men continue to report to us that there is still a ready supply of drugs available.

**How fairly and humanely are prisoners treated?**
The continued lockdown of prisons due to the pandemic has meant that the men at High Down have spent less time out of cell each day than prior to the pandemic. This has resulted in many men still living in cramped conditions, as High Down has 400 single cells being used for double occupancy, which have in-cell toilets with little or no privacy.

A large number of category C and D prisoners are now held in High Down in preparation for the prison's recategorisation (989 at the end of the reporting period). Until category C facilities are available in High Down it is understandable that many men who have earned category C status feel aggrieved at being held at or transferred into High Down.

Limited time out of cell for many months has inevitably impacted on the prison's ability to treat the men fairly and humanely. High Down is fortunate to have in-cell telephony but access to showers, exercise and domestic facilities have all been severely curtailed.

The ongoing issue with the heating on some house blocks which we have reported on for a number of years has continued and remains of concern to the Board.

Issues with missing and lost property continue to cause unnecessary anxiety and distress.

**How well are prisoners' health and wellbeing needs met?**
The Board continues to be concerned about the effect of the pandemic on the mental health and wellbeing of the men. The prison has put in place weekly wellbeing checks for every man, but we do not know how consistent or effective they are. In a survey of 46 prisoners 31 told us that they felt their mental health had been affected. The Board has been particularly concerned about the limited availability of mental health support, in view of the impact of the pandemic on prisoners' mental health.

The lack of non-urgent appointments with the dentist, optician, physiotherapist, chiropodist etc has also impacted on the health and wellbeing of prisoners.

The chaplaincy team has proactively provided regular support throughout the year, providing access to faith services and support with family contact.

**How well are prisoners progressed towards successful resettlement?**
The lack of courses to address offending behaviour is of particular concern. We are also concerned that the lack of availability of progressive transfers for most men during the pandemic has had, and will continue to have, a significant impact on sentence progression. We are concerned that the backlog of transfers across the estate will take considerable time to be cleared.

The reduced capacity for social visits has made it more difficult for the men to maintain family ties. Social video calls are not without issue but have generally been welcomed, particularly by those with family overseas or who are otherwise unable to visit. The additional funding for telephone calls and additional letters until October 2022 have continued to help prisoners maintain vital contact with the outside world.

The Board continues to be extremely concerned about the lack of activity spaces which will be available once the prison recategorises to a category C establishment, and as stated above, a part-time working model does not address the fact that many men spend excessive time without any positive or purposeful activity.

In 2021 116 men were released from High Down with 'no fixed abode'. Successful resettlement in these circumstances is very challenging, as having somewhere to live is a key foundation to enable people to rebuild their lives and stop offending.

**Main areas for development**
**TO THE MINISTER**
• What help will be provided nationally to support the additional wellbeing and mental health needs of prisoners arising as a consequence of the pandemic?
• What help will be provided nationally in order to alleviate the negative consequences of the pandemic on the ability of prisoners to make progress in their sentences? This is important both in terms of applications for parole and their

ability to successfully resettle into the community.
• When is the Minister going to address the problem of prisoners serving indeterminate sentences for public protection (IPPs)?
• What steps does the Prison Service intend to take to ensure that prisoners who require transfer to an outside secure mental health unit are assessed and transferred without delay?

## TO THE PRISON SERVICE
• What steps does the Prison Service intend to take to ensure there are sufficient body-worn video cameras and that they are worn by all officers who have contact with prisoners, and used in accordance with PSI 04/2017?
• How will the Prison Service ensure that sufficient activity and education spaces, and behavioural programmes, are available when High Down becomes a category C prison?
• What steps can the Prison Service take to tackle the issue of loss of property, both when moving cells within the establishment and being transferred to or from High Down?
• What steps can the Prison Service take to ensure that issues with the supply of canteen and refunds are resolved in a timely manner?

## TO THE GOVERNOR
• Although short-term measures have again been taken to alleviate discomfort caused by the lack of heating, when does the Governor anticipate being able to find a permanent and long-term solution?
• What is the solution for the overheating of cells in the summer months, particularly in the south-facing sections of house blocks 5 and 6? This is a recurring issue every summer at High Down.
• How can more staff be encouraged to wear and use body-worn video cameras?
• Can the prison develop a more efficient process for handling prisoners' property, particularly in relation to cell clearances for moves between house blocks? The number of complaints about property lost as a result of a move within High Down increased in 2021 by 62%.

## Progress since the last report
We are pleased to note that work has begun on the long-overdue shower refurbishment and that some showers have now been fully refurbished. However, many showering facilities remain unsanitary and require urgent remedial work, which we understand is to be completed in the current year.
We have been reporting on issues with window grilles for many years, many of which are broken, rusting, and filled with rubbish. This is both unsightly and a health and safety issue. A programme of works has now begun to remove the window grilles and we understand that this work will be completed during the current year.

STRADISHALL
NEWMARKET
SUFFOLK
CB8 9YG

HM PRISON
HIGHPOINT
NORTH &
SOUTH

Tel: 01440 743100

*For the latest reports on this prison please visit:*
https://tinyurl.com/bdfh26rv

*Important Changes:* **(1) Visits:** the identification necessary to access this prison and visit for social or professional purposes has changed; (2) **Money and Gifts** new rules now apply to these. See page 16 for full details of the above.

**Task of the establishment** A category C men's training and resettlement prison.

**Certified normal accommodation and operational capacity**
Prisoners held at the time of inspection: 1,280
Baseline certified normal capacity: 1,287
In-use certified normal capacity: 1,287
Operational capacity: 1,325

**Prison status and key providers**
Public
Prison Group: Hertfordshire, Essex & Suffolk
Prison Group Director: Simon Cartwright
Governor/Director: Nigel Smith
IMB chair: Susan Feary
Physical health provider: Care UK
Mental health provider: Care UK
Substance use treatment provider: Phoenix Futures
Prison education framework provider: People Plus
Escort contractor: Serco

**Brief history** This former Royal Air Force base and refugee camp opened as a prison in 1977. Originally, there were two prisons, one holding women and the other holding men. In 2005, the women's prison became a men's prison and in 2011, the two prisons merged to form HMP Highpoint, with a North and South site.

**Short description of residential units**
*South site*
10 units (1-10) A number of units were reserved for prisoners on the enhanced level of the IEP scheme, others enabled prisoners to spend more time out of their cells. The integrated drug treatment system and drug recovery departments were also housed in two of these units. A segregation unit was also included.
*North site*

6 units (11-16) A number of units were reserved for prisoners on the enhanced level of the IEP scheme, others enabled prisoners to spend more time out of their cells. Unit 16 accommodated a small number of prisoners involved in a pilot project providing them with additional support.

**Visiting Information**
Book online: www.gov.uk/prison-visits or by telephone on 01440 743 134 Monday to Friday, 8am to 2pm
**Visiting times:**
*Highpoint North*
Friday: 3:30pm 4.30pm
Saturday: 3:30pm 4.30pm
Sunday: 3:30pm 4.30pm

*Highpoint South visiting times:*
Monday: 2:45pm to 3:45pm
Friday: 2:45pm to 3:45pm
Saturday: 2:45pm to 3:45pm
Sunday: 10am to 11am and 2:45pm to 3:45pm

**Legal visits:** There are currently no legal visits taking place.

**INSPECTIONS & REPORTS**
**Date of last full inspection** 12–23 August 2019
*Notable features from this inspection*
Highpoint was one of the biggest category C training prisons in the country and was split across two sites.
Almost all prisoners were serving over four years and nearly half were assessed as presenting a high risk of harm.
17% of the population were foreign nationals.
18% of the population were aged under 25.
There was a clear rehabilitative approach throughout the prison and almost all prisoners were on the enhanced incentives and earned privileges (IEP) scheme level.

**HMCIP Report, published 22 January 2020**
HMP Highpoint is a category C training and resettlement prison. It is situated in Suffolk on the site of a former Royal Air Force base. It is a large establishment, holding a little under 1,300 prisoners at the time of this inspection. It is spread over two sites and uses many of the buildings from its days as an RAF facility. The prison has benefited from consistent leadership, with the current governor having been in post since 2013. The last inspection took place in 2015, when outcomes were judged to be reasonably good across the board, with the exception of Resettlement, which was still not sufficiently good, as we had found at the previous inspection in 2012. At this inspection we found that respect had risen to good, but disappointingly

rehabilitation and release planning (known as Resettlement at the time of the last inspection) was still not sufficiently good.
The maintenance of standards in most areas, and indeed the improvement in respect, had been based upon and made possible by the positive ethos that ran through the establishment. The strength of relationships between staff and prisoners had created a collaborative environment that was focused on establishing and maintaining a safe, decent and purposeful community. This marked Highpoint out from many of its comparator prisons, and there was much here from which others could learn. In particular, the visibility and active involvement of the senior leadership in checking and maintaining decent standards across the prison were notable. Within a three-week cycle, every one of the prison's 1,181 cells are checked by a member of the senior leadership team. Many prisoners commented positively to us about the leadership, and in our survey 58% of prisoners said they regularly saw senior leaders talking to prisoners. The figure for similar prisons is 10%.
In terms of safety, there was still work to do around the availability of illicit drugs in the prison. Over a third of prisoners told us it was easy to get hold of drugs in the jail and 13% said they had acquired a drug habit since coming into Highpoint. The linkage between illicit drugs, violence and debt is clear, and the supply reduction strategy needed to be reinvigorated. Some progress had been made but there was room for more drug testing to be carried out where use was suspected, better searching of mail and greater use of technology.
The award of a 'good' grade for respect reflects the excellent relationships that existed between staff and prisoners, the decent living conditions, the high levels of cleanliness and the shared respect that prisoners and staff take in their surroundings. I found that in many parts of the prison, the general atmosphere, freedom of movement and accessibility to facilities and activities made it easy to forget that this was category C and not an open prison. In many ways it felt more like the latter.
We found the overall provision of purposeful activity to be reasonably good. We found a very low 10% of prisoners locked in their cells during the working day, which compared extraordinarily well with their main comparator prisons where the figure had been around the 40% mark. The units referred to above, which basically operated as 'open' units, were exceptional and in our experience unique. Beyond the formal delivery of education, training and employment, the prison ensured that there was both a culture and the tangible

delivery of constructive community and rehabilitative activities, including life skills. One inspector remarked to me that 'It doesn't feel as if there is a minute wasted'.

The number of activity places had increased since the last inspection, but the number of full-time places needed to increase. It was concerning that attendance and punctuality at activities was not consistently good enough, and this had an impact on the ability of prisoners to gain the skills and qualifications needed for effective resettlement. Ofsted found that there needed to be more focus on individual needs, on supporting prisoners in improving their English and mathematics and on better meeting the needs of those with learning difficulties. The Ofsted judgement was that overall the provision of education, skills and work activity required improvement.

It was concerning to find that for the third successive inspection many of the fundamentals of rehabilitation and release planning were not in place. The population was complex, with around a half presenting a high risk of harm and some 150 being associated with organised crime groups. Despite this, there were serious weaknesses in work to ensure that the public was properly protected. The details of these weaknesses are set out in this report, but include an obsolescence of too many OASys reports, too few probation officers to manage high-risk prisoners and a lack of communication between offender supervisors in the prison and community-based offender managers. In addition, there was not a systematic and reliable process for ensuring that all high-risk prisoners approaching release were reviewed to ensure there were no gaps in risk management planning. Over and above these issues, there were some weaknesses in basic public protection work, potentially allowing contact between prisoners and victims. All of these issues need to be addressed as a matter of urgency and not allowed to carry on as they have in the past.

Despite the failings in rehabilitation and release planning, overall this was a very encouraging inspection of a prison that has found a way of treating high risk prisoners with respect in decent surroundings. There is still work to be done around violence, drugs and resettlement, but with the solid foundations that are in place in terms of the incredibly strong positive ethos that permeates the prison, there is no reason why the necessary improvements cannot be achieved.
Peter Clarke CVO OBE QPM August 2019 HM Chief Inspector of Prisons

**INDEPENDENT MONITORING BOARD: Annual Report**
The law requires every prison to be monitored by an independent Board appointed by the Justice Secretary; these are known as Independent Monitoring Boards (IMBs). The IMB must satisfy itself as to the humane and just treatment of those held in custody within its prison and the range and adequacy of the programmes preparing them for release; it must report annually to the Justice Secretary on how well the prison has met the standards.

**IMB Report 1 January 2021 – 31 December 2021**
**Published June 2022**
**Executive summary**
**Background to the report**
Covid-19 has continued to impact the Board's operations. When not able to visit the prison in person, members carried out monitoring by telephone, which has its limitations

**Main judgements**
**How safe is the prison?**
There was a noticeable decrease in all of the following: self-harm, violent incidents, incidents of disorder, and the number of prisoners supported by the assessment, care in custody and teamwork (ACCT) procedure. Mandatory drug testing was disrupted due to Covid, but a new drugs strategy was published at the end of the reporting year. Efforts have been made to maintain support systems for vulnerable prisoners in spite of Covid restrictions. Strategies for dealing with the issues of debt were being highlighted at the end of the year.

**How fairly and humanely are prisoners treated?**
On the whole, prisoners appear to have adapted well to the changing Covid regimes throughout the reporting year, and accepted the various restrictions. It must be highlighted that every attempt has been made by the Governor and staff to reduce the stress created during this period. Time out of cell has been curtailed as little as possible for prisoners.

**How well are prisoners' health and wellbeing needs met?**
The GP and nurse-led services have continued to meet the needs of prisoners but there have been some limitations on numbers of patients seen in clinic. Considerable effort has been put into resolving the number of patients failing to turn up for appointments. This continues to be an area requiring focus however. It is disappointing to note that the difficulty with the external provider of mental health services continues, which then impacts on the workload of the in-house team.

The Board is pleased to note that exercise periods and time out of the cell for domestics and meal collection have been as little affected as Covid restrictions would permit.

## How well are prisoners progressed towards successful resettlement?

From May 2021, education and vocational work resumed, but with reduced numbers. Library access has been restricted, which inevitably had some negative impact. There were waiting lists for vocational courses, due to reduced workshop numbers and tutor vacancies. Social visits resumed in May (again, on a reduced basis) but remote visits continued throughout the year. The offender management unit (OMU) has been working hard against a backlog of cases, and there is a waiting list for places on offending behaviour programmes. Resettlement planning underwent a change of organisation in June, and outcomes are not clear.

## Main areas for development
### TO THE MINISTER

The loss or delay of prisoners' property in transfer between establishments is still an issue of concern. The Board again asks for an urgent review into the handling of prisoners' belongings.

In the interests of reducing reoffending and supporting prisoners' progression, the Board asks for consideration of stable funding strategies for the provision of therapeutic initiatives (e.g. music/drama) across the prison estate.

### TO THE PRISON SERVICE

The service provided by GFSL is still a major cause for concern. The Board requests an urgent review of the works maintenance contract to ensure it fully meets the ongoing needs of a challenging prison environment.

The effects of under-resourcing in contracted areas is having a significant impact on outcomes for prisoners. The Board wishes to draw attention in particular to recruitment and retention of tutors (People Plus), and mental health providers (Forward Trust) within HMP Highpoint. The Board understands that while rates of pay may or may not differ from 'outside' employment, in some instances the terms and conditions of employment may vary considerably.

Prisoner progression has been badly affected by Covid restrictions. D category applications, Parole Board hearings, and the availability of offending behaviour programmes (OBPs) are examples of this. The Board asks if some form of 'catch up' strategy could be considered for prisons where there is a substantial need.

The netting that blew down in the storm over a year ago at HMP Highpoint, and which has still not been mended or replaced, remains a security and safety issue. This prison is vulnerable to throw-overs, and the increased opportunity for contraband to get into the prison has a negative impact on the health and wellbeing of the prisoners.

### TO THE GOVERNOR

The Board recommends that in the interests of fairness and safety the increased use of body-worn video cameras is strongly encouraged.

Whilst the Board is aware of successful and effective regime changes, restricted access to the library is negatively impacting on opportunities for prisoner education and progression. The Board therefore asks for consideration to be given to facilitating increased access to this area. It is hoped, with the decrease in Covid restrictions, that the key worker scheme can be reintroduced in support of the prisoners, in the way it was originally conceived.

### Progress since the last report

The Board welcomes the appointment of an advanced nurse practitioner (Healthcare) and a full-time family worker (Phoenix Futures) – both of which have had a significant effect on prisoner support in their respective departments.

There have been continued reductions in self-harm and violence, and in the number of prisoners located in the segregation unit. These figures can again be interpreted as a positive reflection on the work of the Governor and staff in reducing tension during Covid restrictions.

The return of social visits, albeit in reduced numbers, the continuation of Purple Visits (a secure video calling platform) and the facilitation by the chaplaincy team of compassionate Zoom meetings have been appreciated by the prisoners. With the loosening of Covid restrictions, the resumption of vocational courses and the return of a full-time Job Centre Plus worker from April 2021 have improved support and progression routes for prisoners.

**GIBSON STREET**
**BICKERSHAW**
**WIGAN**
**LANCS**
**WN2 5TH**

**HMP & YOI HINDLEY**

**Tel: 01942 663100**

*For the latest reports on this prison please visit:*
https://tinyurl.com/bdfh26rv

*Important Changes:* **(1) Visits:** the identification necessary to access this prison and visit for social or professional purposes has changed; (2) **Money and Gifts** new rules now apply to these. See page 16 for full details of the above.

**Task of the establishment** A category C adult male prison and young offender establishment.

**Certified normal accommodation and operational capacity**
Prisoners held at the time of this visit: 538
Baseline certified normal capacity: 590
In-use certified normal capacity: 590
Operational capacity: 590

**Prison status and key providers**
Public
Prison Group: Greater Manchester, Merseyside & Cheshire
Prison Group Director: Tim Allen
Governor/Director: Natalie McKee
IMB Chair: Maggie Maudsley
Physical and mental health provider: Greater Manchester Mental Health NHS Foundation Trust
Substance use treatment provider: Greater Manchester Mental Health NHS Foundation Trust and Phoenix Futures
Prison education framework provider: Novus
Escort contractor: GeoAmey

**Brief history** Hindley was originally opened in 1961 as a borstal and became a youth custody centre in 1983. In 1989, two additional wings – E and F – were built, and in 2019, the Acorn unit reopened as a preparation psychologically informed planned environment (PIPE), following refurbishment. The establishment has undergone a number of population changes and is now a young offender and adult male category C establishment. The two populations are housed separately.

**Short description of residential units**
A wing: up to 83 sentenced adult prisoners
B wing: up to 76 sentenced adult prisoners
C wing: up to 84 sentenced adult prisoners
D wing: up to 84 sentenced adult prisoners
E wing: up to 125 sentenced adult prisoners
F wing: up to 128 sentenced young adult prisoners (18-21)
Acorn preparation PIPE unit: up to 10 adult and young prisoners Willow unit: segregation unit for up to 11 adult and young prisoners.

**Visiting Information**
Book online: www.gov.uk/prison-visits or by telephone on 01942 663 234 Monday to Friday: 9am to midday and 1pm to 3pm.
**Visiting times:** Mon to Thurs: 9:30am to 10:30am and 2:30pm to 3:30pm, Fri: 9:30am to 10:30am

**Legal visits:** email:
LegalVisits.Hindley@justice.gov.uk or call 01942 663 492 and 01942 663 234 9am to 12pm and 1pm to 3pm
**Visiting times:**
Monday, Tuesday, Wednesday, Thursday: 9:30am to 10:30am, 10:30am to 11:30am, 2:30pm to 3:30pm and 3:30pm to 4:30pm, Friday: 9:30am to 10:30am, 10:30am to 11:30am

**INSPECTIONS & REPORTS**
**Scrutiny visit 8 and 15–16 December 2020**
**Published 26 January 2021**
This report presents the findings from our scrutiny visit to HMP/YOI Hindley on the conditions and treatment of prisoners during the Covid-19 pandemic. Hindley is a category C training and resettlement prison near Wigan, holding up to 590 adult male prisoners; at the time of our visit, nearly a quarter of the population were under 21. About half of the prisoners were serving long sentences of four years or more.
The management team had worked well with health care staff and Public Health England to control the spread of Covid-19. There had been only one confirmed case among prisoners: one had contracted the virus while in hospital at the start of the pandemic. The prison had been designated an outbreak site on 1 December following confirmed Covid-19 cases among staff on F wing. Measures that included wearing face masks, further regime restrictions and limiting prisoners' movements to and from F wing, the segregation unit and in the gate had suppressed the spread of the virus. Quarantine arrangements in the reverse cohort units (RCU; see Glossary of terms) for those in their first 14 days at the prison and shielding arrangements for prisoners vulnerable to the virus had been implemented appropriately.
Although Covid-19-safe procedures were clearly displayed throughout the prison, staff did not adhere to social distancing measures. The mandatory requirement for staff to wear fluid-

resistant face masks throughout the prison following the outbreak on F wing was withdrawn by the governor during our visit. Face masks were still mandated for some parts of the prison, including the reception and the gate, but were optional on the residential wings.

Some recovery plans had been approved, but implementation had been set back by further national and local community restrictions in response to the second wave of the virus. Social visits, which had been resumed at the end of July, were subsequently suspended on two separate occasions. The amount of time out of cell for most prisoners had increased since the start of the pandemic to a 45-minute session in the morning and another 45 minutes in the afternoon when they could shower, exercise outdoors and undertake other domestic activities. The two gyms had also recently reopened, which prisoners appreciated. Prisoners in the RCU or who were self- isolating did not get sufficient time out of their cells. The new governor, who began in September, was consulting staff and prisoners to learn lessons from the pandemic and retain positive practice for future recovery plans. Strategic meetings, which had been suspended at the start of the pandemic, were reconvened, but some still did not have enough oversight or focus. The safer custody meeting was held every two months, which was not frequent enough, and it was not sufficiently responsive. Although violence and self-harm had declined at the start of the pandemic, the number of incidents had later risen towards pre-pandemic levels. The prison did not have a cohesive strategy to tackle this. The recent reintroduction of mandatory drug tests had yielded a positive rate of 59% in the first month, which was very high. The prison was taking steps to reduce the supply of drugs, but psychosocial support for prisoners with drug and alcohol problems was very stretched.

The care of those at risk of self-harm was reasonable. Staff checked on the well-being of all prisoners regularly, and those with high risks or needs received support through regular key work sessions. In our survey, only 13% of prisoners said they felt unsafe at the time of the inspection. Prisoners who had chosen to self-isolate because they felt unsafe reported that they had few opportunities to spend time in the open air.

We noticed that relationships were good and interactions between staff and prisoners positive and, in our survey, a majority of prisoners said that most staff treated them with respect. Living conditions had improved since our last inspection in 2017. Although prisoners on the four older wings (A to D) occupied small cells that were unsuitable for adults, the residential areas were clean and well kept.

Prisoners, officers and managers carried out regular cell checks for damage, lack of equipment and cleanliness. Meetings that were held to gather prisoners' views and suggestions had been suspended at the start of the restrictions and replaced by 'decency representatives' on each wing. They met frequently with managers during the early weeks of Covid-19, and several practical improvements had been made.

Health services were well led and there was a good team ethos. A flexible response made sure core services were maintained throughout the pandemic. As a result, there were no significant waiting times for any clinical services apart from dentistry. A good range of mental health support was available, including additional welfare support, which was being provided in response to an increase in demand across the prisoner population since the pandemic had begun.

According to the prison, almost a quarter of prisoners were engaged in work outside their cells. In- cell activity packs had been provided from the start of the pandemic, at first through the chaplaincy. Once education staff had resumed work in the establishment in August, they introduced a range of in-cell learning packs covering the full range of education provision, adapted in many cases to the needs of individual prisoners. Some face-to-face classes were being held in interview rooms, which had been created on each wing. A commendable range of enrichment activities had also been organised.

The uptake of video calls and social visits, when they were able to take place, had been low. All prisoners had in-cell telephones and could use them 24 hours a day, which helped them maintain family contact. Prisoners also used iPads when there were compassionate reasons for doing so, which included contacting children with learning difficulties. Partners of Prisoners (a charity providing support for families of prisoners) had remained on site throughout the pandemic and dedicated staff had adapted and increased the support they could offer.

Some face-to-face contact between prisoners and offender managers had been resumed, so that sentence progression could be planned, and weekly surgeries had recently started on each wing. There was an extensive backlog of about five months of calls waiting to be listened to where prisoners were subject to public protection monitoring, potentially putting the public at risk. Delivery of offending behaviour programmes had been suspended since March, which meant that many prisoners left Hindley without having their behaviour needs addressed. Although the community rehabilitation company relied on prisoners completing self-assessment paper questionnaires for resettlement planning, some face-to-face contact with prisoners who were considered the most vulnerable had begun. Resettlement boards involving wider prison partners had also been reinstated.

Staff and prisoners had managed well since the start of the pandemic, balancing the need for restrictions to remain Covid-19-safe with some creative adaptations, which allowed for support to be provided where needed. Positive relationships between staff and prisoners had been a strength, and the impetus to maintain decent living conditions had continued throughout the Covid-19 period. The challenge remains for the prison to understand better and tackle rising levels of violence as well as continue to implement positive practice developed during the pandemic in future recovery plans.

Charlie Taylor, HM Chief Inspector of Prisons
December 2020

### Key concerns and recommendations

Key concerns and recommendations identify the issues of most importance to improving outcomes for prisoners and are designed to help establishments prioritise and address the most significant weaknesses in the treatment and conditions of prisoners.

During this visit we identified some areas of key concern, and have made a small number of key recommendations for the prison to address.

Key concern: The prison lacked a strategic framework for managing violence. Safer custody meetings indicated that a range of data were being collated, but they were not sufficiently analysed and the prison's response was limited.

Key recommendation: The prison should have a coherent strategy for managing violence, tailored to the population, and a local violence reduction policy, informed by an up-to-date and responsive action plan. (To the governor)

Key concern: A range of intelligence and other data indicated that there was a problem with prisoners accessing drugs in the prison and a lack of capacity to reduce the demand. The recovery wing was not operating during the pandemic. Although psychosocial support for prisoners with drug and alcohol dependencies was maintained, staffing was extremely stretched and caseloads were too high. The drug strategy group had only recently reconvened, but it was not sufficiently focused and lacked strategic oversight.

Key recommendation: The prison should adopt an integrated, strategic approach to the prison's drug problem, establish what the key operational priorities are to reduce the supply and demand for drugs and implement appropriate action. (To the governor)

Key concern: Those who were self-isolating or in the reverse cohort unit (RCU) did not have enough consistent time out of their cells, and their experience was worse than that of the rest of the population.

Key recommendation: Prisoners in the RCU and those who are isolating should have a regime that is equitable to the rest of the population. (To the governor)

Key concern: There was a backlog of about five months of calls for prisoners subject to public protection restrictions waiting to be monitored, which meant the prison did not know what risks they posed to the public. The lack of evidence to inform reviews resulted in monitoring having to be continually extended.

Key recommendation: The telephone monitoring backlog should be eliminated urgently. Monitoring arrangements should be reviewed promptly, so that prisoners' risks are appropriately managed and the public protected. (To the governor)

### Notable positive practice

We define notable positive practice as innovative practice or practice that leads to particularly good outcomes from which other establishments may be able to learn. Inspectors look for evidence of good outcomes for prisoners; original, creative or particularly effective approaches to problem-solving or achieving the desired goal; and how other establishments could learn from .

Inspectors found the following examples of notable positive practice during this visit.

• A multi-layered approach to cell checking achieved a good standard of decency across the prison. Each wing officer was a 'cell champion' for a group of cells, 'room ready' prisoner workers cleaned and prepared all cells as they became vacant, and wing managers and governors carried out regular, recorded cell checks. On some wings, continuous records were kept of the state of every cell.

• In learning and skills, a commendable range of enrichment activities had been organised from the start of the Covid-19 period. They included: a partnership with specialist creative arts group Odd Arts, working with 10 learners who were finding it hard to engage with the standard curriculum; and two projects involving social enterprise White Water Writers, which led to the production of a published book of Hindley prisoners' writing.

• Physical education staff had organised regular circuit training in the wing exercise yards from the start of the pandemic. In the summer, they offered body pump training in the open air outside the main gym, and had brought both gyms into full use as soon as they could.

• Family interventions visits for prisoners whose children had learning difficulties were carried out using iPads, which meant they did not have to struggle with the technical limitations of the Purple Visits system.

## INDEPENDENT MONITORING BOARD: Annual Report

The law requires every prison to be monitored by an independent Board appointed by the Justice Secretary; these are known as Independent Monitoring Boards (IMBs). The IMB must satisfy itself as to the humane and just treatment of those held in custody within its prison and the range and adequacy of the programmes preparing them for release; it must report annually to the Justice Secretary on how well the prison has met the standards and requirements placed on it.

### IMB Report 1 January 2021 to 31 December 2021
### Published 3rd May 2022
### Background to the report

The Covid-19 outbreaks have continued to have had a significant impact on the Board's ability to gather information and discuss the contents of this annual report. The Board has therefore tried to cover as much ground as it can in these difficult circumstances, but inevitably there is less detail and supporting evidence than usual. Ministers are aware of these constraints. Regular information is being collected specifically on the prison's response to the pandemic, and that is being collated nationally.

Throughout the year, the prison has been subject to a range of restricted regimes as management tried to maximise out of cell opportunities for the men whilst protecting them and the staff from further Covid-19 outbreaks. A rigorous, accessible testing regime, led by enthusiastic and committed staff, and clear guidance from management on the necessary precautions to be taken have helped minimise the number of positive cases amongst prisoners and staff.

The prison was classified as stage 3 at the commencement of the year, moving to stage 2 in August and was approved to move to stage 1 in December; however, the Omicron variant and the increased infection rates meant that the majority of prisons reverted to stage 3, much to the frustration and disappointment of prisoners and staff.

These regime changes and rigorous testing have undoubtedly kept the prisoners safe, and the vast majority accepted the need for them and were appreciative of the efforts taken on their behalf. As in the wider community, patience was wearing thin by the end of the year and the reintroduction of tighter controls because of the Omicron outbreak and resultant staff shortages led to some frustrations amongst prisoners. There have been two occasions when the prison was declared as an outbreak site by Public Health England (PHE). 114 men tested positive in the year, which is around 11% of the total number of prisoners held at the prison during the year.

A new Governor took up post in September 2020 and introduced a range of management changes, new appointments, and a restructure of responsibilities during 2021. These have still to have the full impact on operations, as Covid-19 continues to dominate daily decision making, restrict possible changes to the regime and hinder the introduction of new activities.

During the year the prison received a positive security audit, a good living standards audit, a good fire safety inspection and positive feedback from Ofsted on the progress of the education team.

HMP/YOI Hindley, as a resettlement prison, serves the wider northwest community, incorporating both Greater Manchester and the Liverpool City region. This produces its own challenges, with prisoner s' home and gang allegiances creating tensions, and the necessity of liaising with a wide range of community partners with varying degrees of coverage and inconsistency of provision.

### How safe is the prison?

The Board considers HMP/YOI Hindley to be overall a safe environment for prisoners. However, there has been a concerning increase in violence and self-harm, notably amongst those under 25 years old.

### How fairly and humanely are prisoners treated?

The Board considers that prisoners are treated with a high level of fairness and humanity. Positive and constructive staff/prisoner relationships are evident across the prison and there is a strong emphasis on fairness and decency. The increased lockdown was handled sensitively, but the impact of the Omicron variant at the end of the year, with the necessary reintroduction of tighter restrictions and a lockdown of up to 23 hours per day, was unwelcome and if operated for a protracted period could impact negatively on the wellbeing of prisoners.

The original living accommodation (wings A to D) and kitchens are cramped and no longer fit for purpose.

### How well are prisoners' health and wellbeing needs met?

The Board believes that the prisoners' health and wellbeing needs are met satisfactorily.

The Covid-19 testing team were particularly dedicated and committed to ensuring there was widespread, timely testing of all who attended the site, and the prisoners were encouraged to be vaccinated, despite many being reluctant to take up the offer of vaccination.

### How well are prisoners progressed towards successful resettlement?

As identified in last year's report, resettlement services have adapted working practice in response to the changing pandemic restrictions imposed, however the Board continued to have concerns regarding the robustness of systems and their application to support transition on the release of prisoners.

### Main areas for development
### TO THE MINISTER

The Board welcomes the announcement that HMP/YOI Hindley is to be expanded, subject to planning permission being granted. It is important that the funding is fully secured to complete the full project in a timely way.

### TO THE PRISON SERVICE

The Board continues to be very concerned about the amount of property lost within the system, and the negative impact on prisoners' wellbeing and the disproportionate amount of time spent on resolving matters by staff and the Board.

### TO THE GOVERNOR

As raised last year, Covid-19 and the introduction of new contracts have had a negative impact on the information advice and guidance available to men prior to and on release. Resolving this now needs to be a priority to ensure prisoners receive comprehensive support at this time of potential vulnerability.

Whilst the Board recognises the need to prevent the spread of Covid-19, it wishes to register ongoing concerns about the men being locked in their cells for 23 out of 24 hours, and on occasions longer. This is not conducive to their long-term rehabilitation or wellbeing.

The ongoing problem with litter outside F wing and behind window grilles across the prison is not only an eyesore but also a health, safety, and security risk. The Board urges the Governor to ensure that further action is taken to resolve this matter.

WOODBRIDGE
SUFFOLK
IP12 3JW

**HMP & YOI HOLLESLEY BAY**

Tel: 01394 412400

*For the latest reports on this prison please visit:*
https://tinyurl.com/bdfh26rv

*Important Changes:* **(1) Visits:** the identification necessary to access this prison and visit for social or professional purposes has changed; (2) **Money and Gifts** new rules now apply to these. See page 16 for full details of the above.

**Task of the establishment** HMP & YOI Hollesley Bay is a category D open resettlement prison.

**Certified normal accommodation and operational capacity**
Prisoners held at the time of inspection: 470
Baseline certified normal capacity: 482
In-use certified normal capacity: 480
Operational capacity: 485

**Prison status and key providers**
Public
Prison Group: Hertfordshire, Essex & Suffolk
Prison Group Director: Simon Cartwright
Governor/Director: David Daddow
IMB Chair: Guy Baly
Physical health provider: Care UK Health and Rehabilitation Services Limited Mental health provider: Care UK Health and Rehabilitation Services Limited Substance misuse provider: Phoenix Futures
Learning and skills provider: People Plus
Escort contractor: Serco Wincanton

**Brief history** April 2022: HMP/YOI Hollesley Bay is a rambling open prison with capacity for up to 495 adult and young adult (18-21) male prisoners in nine residential units. This number is expected to increase to approximately 650 before mid 2023. It is situated in East Suffolk, a mile from the North Sea, and the nearest large town is Ipswich 20 miles away.

As an open prison, Hollesley Bay only accommodates prisoners who are category D, that is prisoners assessed as least risk to the public. All prisoners, unless excused for medical or age reasons, are occupied in daytime working hours. Under normal circumstances, approximately 150 (c. 30%) will work in jobs or community service outside the prison. The remainder work at the prison or attend practical training courses or education. This figure was significantly reduced for the majority of 2021 due to the coronavirus pandemic restrictions.

For the great majority of prisoners, Hollesley Bay will be their final destination before release and emphasis is placed on rehabilitation and preparation for a return to society (see Resettlement section). Sentence planning by offender supervisors is carried out immediately upon prisoners' arrival and thereafter the main objective is for residents to assume more responsibility for themselves be it in work and/or training, and their behaviour. They are encouraged in this via the incentives scheme and progressive stages of release on temporary licence (ROTL).

The nine accommodation units are as follows: Hoxon, Stow, Cosford, Wilford, Blything, Samford, Mutford, Threadling and Plomesgate. Bosmere unit was demolished in 2021.

Most units house between 40 and 80 men, mainly in single accommodation but there are about 40-45 double occupancy rooms and a few quadruple rooms. A temporary unit, Claydon, was added in 2020. this consisted of 24 temporary residential units often referred to as 'bunkabins.'

Plomesgate (Containex type of provision) with accommodation for 48 prisoners replaced Claydon, with appropriate electricity supply, drainage, sanitation, self-cooking kitchen, communal space, etc. There will be a further expansion of these units in 2022.

The prison complex includes a dedicated and well-equipped healthcare and pharmacy facility; a range of outbuildings accommodating the practical training workshops; extensive greenhouses staffed by prisoners for fruit and vegetable production; a chapel; a multi-faith centre; a library; a large and well-equipped gymnasium; and an industrial-class kitchen which also serves nearby HMP Warren Hill. This kitchen was replaced in 2021 by a much-improved temporary 'field' kitchen. At the time of writing there is no certainty about the timing of work on the permanent replacement kitchen.

Administration, including the Governor, deputy, and assistant governors' offices and all departments involved in the management of prisoners and the prison itself, is based in the main building (St. Georges) which is in the centre of the complex.

In mid-2019, it was announced that the prison would in future begin to accept more persons convicted of sexual offences (now named PCOSO rather than the original term of MCOSO). Consideration of the required staffing numbers and profile progressed during 2020 and the first controlled intake of up to 30 PCOSO prisoners, arrived at Hollesley Bay from September 2021 A couple of months prior to this, a new Governor

was appointed, and after approximately six months they are now well established in the prison, making changes and leading the staff in a very professional manner.

**Visiting Information**
Telephone booking only: 01394 412559 Monday to Thursday, 9am to midday and 1pm to 4pm.
**Visiting times:** Saturday & Sunday: 2pm to 3:45pm

**Legal Visits:** There are currently no legal visits taking place.

**INSPECTIONS & REPORTS**
**Date of last inspection:** 22 Oct–1 Nov 2018
**HMCIP Report, published 05 March 2019**
HMP & YOI Hollesley Bay is an open prison in Suffolk holding up to 485 adult prisoners. Many of those held are serving relatively long sentences of more than four years, with just over 100 serving over 10 years or life. Those held had been convicted of a range of offences, although more than 100 were violent offenders. At the time we inspected, the prison was making plans to begin holding sex offenders, although there was much more work to do concerning this proposal. We last inspected the prison in 2014 when we reported on an impressive institution. Following this inspection, we can report that the prison continued to deliver good or reasonably good outcomes for those detained.

Hollesley Bay was a very safe prison. Those arriving were received well into the prison and in our survey most prisoners indicated that they felt safe. Violence was relatively rare and informal structures of support for those who were vulnerable or at risk were good. Use of force was similarly rare but when used its management needed to be more thorough and accountable. The application of security was proportionate, although there had been a disappointing increase in the use of drugs. Strategies were in place to try to address this concern. Self-harm incidents remained infrequent.

The prison was an overwhelmingly respectful place, underpinned by some very supportive staff- prisoner relationships. That said, there was evidence of a strong undercurrent of prisoners who felt intimidated by staff and feared that they could be arbitrarily returned to closed conditions. This was a perception that the prison needed to do more to understand and remedy. Extensive use of peer supporters was undermined by a lack of clarity concerning some of their roles and some indifferent training. General consultation with prisoners was lacklustre. Accommodation was generally good but the Bosmere unit needed further refurbishment. The grounds were well maintained and accessible. The promotion of equality was weak but evidence suggested most outcomes among those with protected characteristics were equitable. Health and substance misuse services were good.

Prisoners had significant amounts of time out of their cells and the prison offered a wide range of educational and vocational training programmes. The prison had good relationships with regional employers and this had led to many unpaid and community positions for prisoners on release on temporary licence (ROTL). Accreditation in prison industries and structured careers advice was less well developed. Teaching and prisoner achievements were generally good, with our colleagues in Ofsted assessing overall provision as 'good'.

ROTL was used extensively to support work, resettlement and family ties. The prison's approach to reducing reoffending was reasonable, although the analysis of need to support the targeting of resettlement work and the prison's improvement action plan were too limited. Offender management was improving and contact with supervisors, supported by peer workers and a drop-in surgery, was reasonable. The integration of offender management with the wider establishment was, however, weaker. Of concern, and in contrast to much that was happening in the prison, public protection work was not good enough. We have made this very significant failing the subject of our one main recommendation. Reintegration planning for those approaching release was better.

Hollesley Bay remained a successful and effective prison. The establishment was, at the time of our inspection, experiencing a time of change, with a new governor about to be appointed and plans to develop the prison's role to hold sex offenders. Outcomes were, however, reasonably good or better and those detained were treated well. We leave the prison with several recommendations which we hope will assist further improvement.

Peter Clarke CVO OBE QPM December 2018
HM Chief Inspector of Prisons

## INDEPENDENT MONITORING BOARD: Annual Report

The law requires every prison to be monitored by an independent Board appointed by the Justice Secretary; these are known as Independent Monitoring Boards (IMBs). The IMB must satisfy itself as to the humane and just treatment of those held in custody within its prison and the range and adequacy of the programmes preparing them for release; it must report annually to the Justice Secretary on how well the prison has met the standards and requirements placed on it.

**IMB Report 1 January – 31 December 2021**
**Published 7th April 2022**
**Background to this Report Covid-19**

Please note that 2021 report was compiled during the Covid-19 pandemic and the various 'lockdowns' throughout the year. Accordingly, certain evidential statistics, trends or being able to meet up with staff to discuss and verify information were considerably more difficult due to this unprecedented situation. During these times, the Governor and his staff introduced new ways of working and, although not perfect, this allowed the IMB to continue to fulfill its monitoring role – for example circulation of the routine daily briefing sheets (DBS), notices to colleagues (NTCs), notices to residents (NTRs) and notifications of adjudication hearings and the decisions made.

The IMB would also like to commend the effective way in which the Covid pandemic was managed. Plans were prepared very quickly and thoroughly for the site, including establishing an isolation unit; communications between staff and prisoners were effective; mask wearing (when compulsory) was generally upheld and the movement of prisoners from unit to unit or cell to cell was met with little resistance from the prisoners themselves. Effective communication was maintained throughout the year.

**Main judgements**

Building on the successes of the first strategy document 'Vision, Priorities and Objectives 2020 – 2021', a second strategy document for 2021 – 2022 was introduced. This built on and developed much of what was in the first document.

The priorities were identified as follows:

a) Create and develop a rehabilitative culture — by understanding the residents and promoting a culture which is safe, decent and will encourage change and make prison 'less like' prison;

b) To re-energise professional development — by working with colleagues and partner agencies to realise their full potential and be more confident in their roles. We will utilize a model of staff supervision and focus training and capability;

c) Successful reconfiguration and introduction of the PCOSO (Persons Convicted of Sexual Offences) population by developing an implementation plan. Engaging with key stakeholders. Effective delivery of the OMiC (Offender Management in Custody) model

d) Continued emphasis on increasing training opportunities, education activities and paid work opportunities for the men in custody at Hollesley Bay by working with national and local employers and focusing on what we can do. This remains a priority from last year.

e) The new regime can be summarized by the acronym — PROUD
• People • Reducing Offending • Offender Management Unit
• Unlocking Intelligence • Decency

The vision document was supported by specific ambitions which were well communicated to all staff and throughout the organisation: for example, expansion of the GFSL (Government Facilities Services Ltd. – part of the MoJ) schemes whereby prisoners would learn trades and skills by working with skilled tradespeople carrying out work on-site, better understanding of the equalities agenda and paying specific attention to the 2010 Equalities Act protected characteristics, and meeting the four HMIP 'healthy prison' tests of safety, respect, purposeful activity, and rehabilitation and release planning.

In addition to the above, Hollesley Bay prison introduced a set of five further ambitions, each championed by a senior member of staff and all underpinned by the concept of common sense 'decency.'

These were:
• Protecting the Public;
• Reducing Reoffending;
• Decent and Safe prison;
• Diverse, Skilled and Valued workforce; and
• High Quality Sentence Management.

These ambitions and values are fully on view as one enters the gate house to the prison. The IMB welcomed this approach and is fully supportive of the framework described.

### How safe is the prison?

The Board considers the prison to be a safe place for the vast majority of prisoners and staff; where incidents of bullying or aggression are detected or suspected, these are dealt with both efficiently and effectively.

To our knowledge there has been no official serious incident in the past seven years.

### How fairly and humanely are prisoners treated?

The IMB believes the prisoners are treated fairly, humanely and consistently at the prison and that there is a culture within the prison that encourages dignity and respect between staff, staff and prisoners and prisoner to prisoner. However, it is recognised that this is an area where complacency must not be allowed to set in and there has to be continual reinforcement of this approach. Staff and prisoners are continually reminded of this approach by the Governor and his senior staff.

### How well are the prisoners' health and well-being needs met?

In 2020 there was a change in the provision of healthcare at the prison. A new contract was negotiated with Leiston Surgery who provide the GP services for the prison and there is additional support provided by a self-employed GP. This service is working well, with no major issues identified by the IMB.

Out of hours care is provided by ringing NHS 111 services. Healthcare checks, including mental health and medication reviews, are completed on each prisoner by professionally qualified practitioners within 24 hours of arrival at Hollesley Bay.

Dentistry, ophthalmic and podiatry care have adhered to the Covid-19 guidelines issued by Public Health England (PHE), which has inevitably resulted in a lesser service than previously offered. However, services are now returning to the previous normal.

### How are prisoners progressed towards successful resettlement?

Following induction, all prisoners other than those who are long term sick or past retirement age are required to be purposefully engaged whilst at the establishment.

An assessment process takes place during which prisoners may express a preference as to whether they wish to take on a work role within Hollesley Bay or whether they wish to engage in a vocational training course or education.

Pre-Covid, there was a significant increase over the year in the numbers of prisoners who undertake paid employment outside of the prison. The prison has also invested in a dedicated member of staff whose primary purpose is to establish links with local employers and increase the number and range of job opportunities available to prisoners. The IMB welcomes the increased emphasis placed on prisoner employability. Outside work was the number one priority for the previous Governor and the then-senior management team.

However, since the arrival of the current Governor there has been greater emphasis placed upon 'earned progression'. This is most probably best explained by prisoners being expected to demonstrate commitment and strict involvement in working towards their planned release. So, for example, on arrival at Hollesley Bay a detailed assessment of prisoners' abilities and past achievements is undertaken along with discussions about their future work or employment. These latter discussions are tailored towards the prisoners' future ambitions, tinged with a large element of realism about the job market in their home area. This 'pathway approach' was not universally accepted by the prison population when it was first introduced. However, with the passing of time it has become accepted and prisoners can genuinely see the reasoning and philosophy underpinning the approach. The IMB welcomes this more structured approach.

However, the IMB recognises that in some cases the employment opportunities in East Anglia will be different to those available in places where the prisoners are likely to live upon release. Nevertheless, good work habits will have been established and, if possible, the staff will introduce more courses tailored to typical urban areas. There are obviously certain work opportunities that are common to both.

## Main areas for development

By way of introduction to the recommendations from the Hollesley Bay IMB, it is recognised that the year being reported on, 2021, has been a difficult year to maintain and develop services at the prison. Nevertheless, most services (albeit with reduced numbers and frequency) have been maintained and the IMB would like to pay recognition to the Governor and the staff for dealing with complex and difficult issues (which required flexibility and agility) throughout the year in a very comprehensive and effective manner. It is also recognised that cooperation from and joint working with the prisoners makes life considerably easier all round and this was achieved.

The IMB also welcomes the majority of suggestions made in the recently- published White Paper and in particular is very supportive of the stronger emphasis being placed on creating a 'rehabilitative culture' in our prisons.1 Being specific, more and a greater range of training courses and the development of a 'compact' between the prison leavers and the wider society were welcomed. The introduction of a 'resettlement passport' and further strengthening of the independent scrutiny of prisons were also supported. It is against this background that the following recommendations are made.

## To the Minister

1. That the recommendations made in the Ministry of Justice's White Paper, after consultation, are implemented and adequately resourced.

2. That particular attention is given to prisoners when they leave prison having access to suitable accommodation and employment opportunities.

3. That effective support for mental health issues is developed within prisons and after leaving should they still be required.

4. That further consideration is given to the indeterminate sentences for public protection

(IPP) regime to eradicate many of the injustices that are all too common in the system.

5. That consideration is given to the introduction of the key worker system in open prisons.

6. That the Minister, jointly with the IMB Secretariat, explore ways of broadening the numerical strength and composition of local IMBs so that they become more representative of the UK's population as a whole and the profile of our current prisoner population.

## To the Prison Service

1. The IMB at Hollesley Bay recognises the considerable investment made in 2021. There was a residential unit demolished and this was replaced by ˋContainer units, all single-person units. Based upon this experience, the IMB would urge the Prison Service to move to a situation where all multiple-occupancy cells are removed and replaced with single person accommodation.

2. That further capital investment is made into the open prison estate to allow the buildings and facilities to be improved and the backlog of maintenance requirements to be tackled in a programmed way — failing heating systems, leaking roofs, inadequate catering facilities, etc, as well as funding additional security measures, enhanced CCTV and improved security lighting.

3. To allow Governors of prisons greater budgetary flexibility to meet the priorities of their prison.

## To the Governor

1. The IMB welcomes the introduction of the more formal sequential learning approach adopted by the prison in 2021. This is beneficial to the prisoners and acts as a good motivational tool, which leads to ROTL being used in a more purposeful way.

2. The publication of a more comprehensive induction booklet is welcomed; not only does it inform the prisoners from other sending prisons what they can expect from Hollesley Bay, it provides a structured approach to learning which enables staff to better prepare prisoners in terms of their 'employability' and what to expect from life outside of prison. Considering this in slightly greater depth, outside society will have changed considerably for many prisoners during their time inside; none more so than in the of use of the internet. To this end the IMB would ask the Governor to consider introducing ways of using IT, and mobile phones in particular, that are safe and improve family contact and may well have other have other benefits as well.

3. Recognising that there are difficulties in developing an 'employers forum' for Hollesley Bay (since many of the prisoners' home addresses will be considerable distances away)

the prison should develop a two-stage approach towards prisoner employability whereby basic skills or behaviours are brought up to scratch and other labour market considerations are developed to give prisoners the best chance of employment once their sentences are completed, e.g. in street works, warehousing, construction.

4. That the efforts being put into improving the site security are continued.

**Progress since the last report**

Considerable progress has been made during the 2021 year - such as:

Improved communications with staff, prisoners and the local communities (via parish councils in the main) and considerably more openness in discussion to address issues that face Hollesley Bay, the staff of the prison and those who live there.

Continued emphasis on the equality agenda, with considerably more monitoring to identify any possible disparities between the various racial groups in the prison and much improved facilities and space for ISCRE (Ipswich & Suffolk Council for Racial Equality). The direct benefit of this approach is yet to mature, but from informal feedback from the prisoners there appears to be greater belief that the organisation is willing to tackle institutional bias, whether intentional or not. The monthly analysis of the prison's population according to race and adjudications, resettlement, education, employability, open conditions suitability assessments (OCSA) and complaints gives further assurance.

The concepts of employment progression and employment pathways were introduced in 2021 by the Governor and his senior management team. This is welcomed by the IMB, since it provides a more structured approach to learning and outside employment. The concept of earned progression is supported.

The continued emphasis on outside employment opportunities for prisoners and recruiting a dedicated staff resource to increase the number and variety of outside job employment opportunities.

More structured employment opportunities within the prison for prisoners and specifically enhancing the employability of prisoners with the opportunities afforded by the Lansbury Café, the restaurant at Marsh Farm Barn and the nearby Farm Shop. The concept of progression – from work solely within prison units, to work involving contact with the public, progressing to work in a commercial setting – via job opportunities is a most welcome improvement.

A number of prisoners have found paid work with GFSL at Hollesley Bay which we greatly welcome and we hope this kind of purposeful use of in-house skills and abilities can increase for the mutual benefit of both the residents and the prison.

Increased capital investment in buildings that have been neglected for several years and generally improving the overall appearance of the site. However, after years of neglect there is still a large backlog to be tackled.

The demolition of the former Bosmere unit and the replacement by Plomesgate 'container' units was welcome.

The transfer of the room where adjudications are held, thereby meeting Covid restrictions, was an enormous improvement and very helpful to the IMB as it enabled observations to continue.

The programmed redecoration of the prison throughout the offices and residential units has led to a much brighter and more cared-for environment. The installation of outside gym stations for each unit is a valuable addition to the prison.

The development of a prison community ethos both inside and outside of Hollesley Bay is welcomed.

The analysis of the abscond rates and the actions taken to reduce them has instilled greater confidence in the service.

Body-worn cameras have been introduced and officers, under strong encouragement, are now increasingly wearing them.

There has been a similar number of intelligence reports (IRs) in 2020 and 2021, helping management to monitor all aspects of activity at the prison.

Significant ACCT 6 training has been undertaken by the staff and the IMB members.

The IMB particularly welcomed the establishment of an IPP and lifers working group within the prison and looks forward to the implementation of many of the changes recommended by this group.

It is pleasing to see that the prison's values and priorities are clearly displayed at the main gate and throughout the site.

Although not an improvement as such, the IMB would wish to place on record the very effective way in which the Covid-19 pandemic issues were dealt with at Hollesley Bay. At the very start of the pandemic, effective communication routines were set up, with the Governor regularly talking to staff and prisoners on the outdoor sport pitches with in excess of 150 men attending; regular bulletins were issued and Wayout TV was used to good effect. When Hollesley Bay was declared an outbreak site, a unit was quickly identified for prisoner isolation. Prisoners were moved around to prevent further spread of the disease.

Measures were introduced for prisoners so that the levels of anxiety experienced by them and their families on the outside were kept to a minimum. The level of co-operation displayed by the prisoners was notably high, due in large part to the full and open communication from staff.

As the pandemic developed, the prison maintained services as well as it could. In-cell educational activities and library services were provided albeit the 'take- up' was disappointingly low.

As the coronavirus mutated from Delta to Omicron, the prison effectively mirrored the moves in the wider society with the wearing of facemasks and the introduction of testing routines. The leadership required in these situations was displayed in abundance by the Governors and their senior management teams.

**HOLME HOUSE ROAD
STOCKTON-ON-TEES
TS18 2QU**

**HM PRISON
HOLME
HOUSE**

**Tel: 01642 744000**

*For the latest reports on this prison please visit:*
https://tinyurl.com/bdfh26rv

*Important Changes:* **(1) Visits:** the identification necessary to access this prison and visit for social or professional purposes has changed; (2) **Money and Gifts** new rules now apply to these. See page 16 for full details of the above.

**Task of the establishment** HMP Holme House is a category C training and resettlement prison for male prisoners.

**Certified normal accommodation and operational capacity**
Prisoners held at the time of inspection: 1,183
Baseline certified normal capacity: 1,036
In-use certified normal capacity: 1,036
Operational capacity: 1,210

**Prison status and key providers**
Public
Prison Group: North East
Prison Group Director: Susan Howard
Governor/Director: Sean Ormerod
IMB Chair: Brenda Kirby
Physical health provider: Spectrum for GP and pharmacy services; G4S for nursing and clinical drug and alcohol team (DART); Burgess and Hyder Dental Group for dental services
Mental health provider: Tees, Esk and Wear Valley Mental Health Trust
Substance misuse treatment provider: G4S for clinical DART; Change, Grow, Live for psychosocial DART
Prison education framework provider: Novus
Escort contractor: GeoAmey

**Brief history** The prison opened in May 1992. It expanded in the late 1990s with the building of two further house blocks, providing 235 additional places. Two new workshops opened in 1997 and an additional house block, with 224 places, opened in 2010, along with two further regimes buildings, providing activity places for around 200 prisoners. In June 2016, it was announced that HMP Holme House would be one of six reform prisons. In 2017, it transitioned from a purpose-built category B prison to its current role. It now forms part of the Tees and Wear Prisons Group, alongside HMP Kirklevington Grange, HMYOI Deerbolt and HMP Durham.

**Short description of residential units**
House block 1 A and B wing  S e n t e n c e d
prisoners
House block 1 C wing 'Own protection' unit
House block 2 Sentenced prisoners
House block 3 Sentenced prisoners
House block 4 Sentenced prisoners
House block 5 Sentenced prisoners
House block 6 A wing Therapeutic community
House block 6 B wing Sentenced prisoners
House block 7 Unit for those convicted of a sexual offence
Health care unit
Segregation unit

**Visiting Information**
Book online at: www.gov.uk/prison-visits or ring 0300 060 6602 Monday to Wednesday and Friday, 8:30am to 4pm (closed Thursdays)
**Visiting times:** Mon to Fri: 2pm to 3:30pm, Sat and Sun: 9am to 11am and 1:45pm to 3:45pm

**Legal Visits:** There are currently no legal visits taking place.

**INSPECTIONS & REPORTS**
**Date of last full inspection** 24–25 February; 2–6 March 2020
*Notable features from this inspection*
• The prison will benefit from approximately £9 million over three years as part of the Drug Recovery Prison project.
• Holme House is one of only two substance misuse therapeutic communities in England and Wales. Most arrivals at the prison transferred from HMP Durham.
• Over 80% of new arrivals said that they had had a problem when they arrived at the prison.
• Over a third of prisoners were housed in overcrowded conditions.

**HMCIP Report, published 17 June 2020**
HMP Holme House, located in Stockton, is a relatively modern facility built in the early 1990s,

with space for 1,210 adult men. Originally a category B local prison, the establishment had transitioned to becoming a category C training prison at the time of our previous inspection in 2017. As part of that process Holme House was forming close links to the reception prison (HMP Durham) and the nearby open prison (HMP Kirklevington Grange).

This report refers to an inspection that took place in late February and early March 2020, just prior to the full onset of the Covid-19 crisis with all its attendant implications for the prison system and individual establishments like Holme House. As such the impact of the crisis and what this has meant for the prison are not addressed in this report, although our judgements about outcomes in the prison, as it was then, were concerning. Against all four of our tests of a healthy prison, we found outcomes for prisoners that were not sufficiently good, a situation no better than that which we found in 2017. Overall it was clear to us that the prison was falling well short of achieving its purpose as a training prison for category C prisoners.

The prison was still not safe enough. Arrangements to receive and induct new prisoners were inadequate, and while overall levels of violence were consistent with similar prisons, much more could have been done to improve the safety and well-being of prisoners and reduce violence still further. More attention was also needed to ensure that the use of force was always fully accounted for, while both the regime and relationships between staff and prisoners in the segregation unit required improvement. The management of security was, however, more encouraging, although the application of some elements lacked the proportionality commensurate with the establishment's training prison status. Significant investment and a coordinated strategy had, however, delivered some very impressive reductions in the availability of illicit substances, something that had been almost out of control in 2017. Tragically, since we last inspected there had been three self-inflicted deaths and instances of self-harm had increased. The prison's response to this priority could best be described as inconsistent.

Holme House had embedded a reasonably effective keyworker scheme, but at the heart of many of the prison's problems were poor staff-prisoner relationships which were due partly to staff indifference. There was a clear need for a more proactive culture among staff, one that was more supportive of a constructive, rehabilitative ethos. Along with this, the general environment, levels of overcrowding and the quality of accommodation, as well as other factors

associated with the quality of daily living such as the food and arrangements to support legitimate redress among prisoners, required improvement. The promotion of equality, by way of contrast, was getting better, and outcomes in health were good. The high-profile drug recovery prison (DRP) project had delivered encouraging results, and the substance misuse therapeutic community was a well-managed national resource.

Time out of cell and the general level of prisoner engagement with education and work did not reflect what is normally expected of a training prison. We found, for example, a third of prisoners locked up during the working day, while attendance and punctuality with respect to activity was, as we describe in the report, sporadic and inconsistent. The curriculum failed to fully meet the needs of prisoners and allocation arrangements to ensure the right people were in the correct class or workshop were not good enough. Our colleagues from Ofsted judged the overall effectiveness of education, skills and work as 'requires improvement', their second lowest grade.

The prison retained a well-resourced offender management unit which was now better integrated with its resettlement work. The completion of risk management casework (OASys) was more up to date than it had been in 2017, although direct contact between offender managers and prisoners was disappointing. Public protection measures were satisfactory and prisoners had good access to a range of offending behaviour interventions, although referrals needed to be more prompt. Release planning was reasonably good.

It is too soon to say how Holme House will emerge from the Covid-19 crisis and judge the longer-term impact this experience will have on the prison. Doubtless there will be new, and perhaps unforeseen, challenges to contend with going forward. That said, our criticisms relate to the prevailing culture we found when we inspected. The prison seemed to us to be reasonably well resourced and equipped, and its purpose seemed clearly defined. The key to Holme House's success will be ensuring that staff are encouraged to engage constructively and consistently with prisoners, that staff expectations of prisoners are greater and that standards generally are raised.

Peter Clarke CVO OBE QPM

HM Chief Inspector of Prisons April 2020

## INDEPENDENT MONITORING BOARD: Annual Report

The law requires every prison to be monitored by an independent Board appointed by the Justice Secretary; these are known as Independent

Monitoring Boards (IMBs). The IMB must satisfy itself as to the humane and just treatment of those held in custody within its prison and the range and adequacy of the programmes preparing them for release; it must report annually to the Justice Secretary on how well the prison has met the standards and requirements placed on it.

**IMB Report1 January 2021 – 31 December 2021**
**Published June 2022**
**Executive summary**
**Background to the report**
This annual report is set, as last year, against a background of the impact that the Covid-19 pandemic has had on the prison and the local community. During the year, the prison operated in a range of regime stages (stage 4 being the most restrictive):

January to May - stage 4
May to September - stage 3
September to November - stage 2
November to 16 December - stage 1
16 December - stage 2
22 December - stage 3

The prison leadership team worked hard to ensure that activities and the regime followed these constraints whilst enabling the prisoners to have a reasonable quality of life.
Notifications to the prisoners were timely and comprehensive. We were impressed about the way in which the sudden changes in regime two weeks before Christmas were handled and lockdown benefits, that had been removed, were reinstated expediently.

**Main judgements**
**How safe is the prison?**
There was a slight increase in self-harm during the year and there were two self-inflicted deaths. The reduction in violence starting in September 2020 has continued. The levels of violence are low compared with other establishments.

**How fairly and humanely are prisoners treated?**
The prisoners were, in the main, treated fairly.
For many periods of the year, time out of cell was constrained because of Covid-19. Despite this, officers worked hard to help prisoners cope with the situation.
Gym services were delivered throughout the year on a restricted basis with each prisoner being offered at least an hour per week.
Recovery from the Covid-19 pandemic has not been as expeditious as was expected, with prisoners still having long periods of time locked in their cells throughout the year.
Sadly, we report that there is still an unsatisfactory level of unscreened toilets in cells,

many of which are shared. This remains non-compliant with the national standard for the physical cleanliness and physical decency of prisons, published in April 2019. It cannot be considered to be a humane situation, especially considering the length of time the prisoners were locked in their cells and must eat their meals there as there are no communal dining facilities.

**How well are prisoners' health and wellbeing needs met?**
In general healthcare services have improved during the year with the community (houseblock-based) model being established. Waiting lists to consult a GP were reduced, as some consultations were held by telephone and houseblock-based nurses carried out triage.
The waiting time to see a dentist has been unacceptable with only emergencies, in the main, getting attention. This situation is not comparable with services in the local community nor our neighbouring prison, HMP Kirklevington Grange, or a similar prison, HMP Northumberland.

**How well are prisoners progressed towards successful resettlement?**
Face to face education was limited and only returned towards the end of the year, with very few prisoners being invited to attend classroom work. The library remained closed throughout the year, although red band prisoners offered a delivery service. Despite staff absences and the constraints imposed by Covid-19 the OMU team was resourceful in enabling much of their work to continue. We congratulate the team for its diligence and commitment.

**Main areas for development**
It is imperative that dental services be improved. The service was reported in our annual report for 2019 as "Dental services also provided a poor service, with waiting lists for first consultations being up to 21 weeks, with the wait for on-going treatment and oral health education, being eight weeks and dental therapy nine weeks". Sadly, almost two years of Covid-19 pandemic have left this area of care for prisoners significantly worse.
Education and training require improvement. These services are not as good as they were three to four years ago when active classrooms, with attendance in the region of 100 prisoners a week, delivered a meaningful education and prisoners were achieving level one and level two qualifications. Covid-19 arrangements were in place to accommodate in-cell learning.
There have been issues regarding access to distance learning and Open University programmes. This has resulted in some prisoners not being able to achieve their aims and aspirations.

## TO THE MINISTER

We are pleased with improvements to the prison over the year. There is still funding needed to ensure a reasonable level of decency within cells. We would however ask the Minister to take action in connection with dental services at HMP Holme House.

## TO THE PRISON SERVICE

We are concerned that the prison service has not acted expediently in connection with the poor dental services at the prison.

We would also like to comment on the cumbersome content and lack of clarity around some contracts with external service providers. The Board must monitor against standards and understanding the content of contracts is critical to this. We do not have access to those contracts and seemingly the prison does not. We do measure healthcare standards against those within the community. Some other matters, such as waiting times for repairs, are inaccessible to the Board.

The constraints about property transport are unclear and can cause distress to prisoners. This links to the issues regarding contracts detailed above where there is not clarity about what is expected. Too many prisoners arrive at Holme House not really understanding where their property is and when they will get it. Prisoners leaving the prison to move to other prisons, particularly out of the region, sometimes have considerable delays.

Some areas of education could not progress because of repairs not being carried out. These included the ventilation to the bistro and the ceilings to the toilets in the engagement centre. This situation is unacceptable as there were restrictions because of Covid-19 on some repairs in house blocks and cells. It could be reasonably expected that the resources could be redirected to those areas where they are required.

## TO THE GOVERNOR

There are improvements to be made in certain areas, such as dental care and education. The Board monitors against agreed standards and it is difficult to know what they are in some areas as contract details are not available

We would like to see the leadership team in the prison take an increased interest in healthcare complaints in a similar way to prison complaints. Responses to healthcare complaints did not meet their longer response timescales over several months and should be comparable.

## Progress since the last report

We have seen a considerable improvement in the culture and ambiance within the prison. The art work, cleanliness and atmosphere within the prison are excellent.

We were impressed by the caring way that benefits to the prisoners were implemented when Covid-19 restrictions were imposed during the year.

There has been progress regarding the living environment within the prison, with improvements in cleanliness and the living environment is now pleasant.

Improvements to new prisoner induction are welcome and it is essential that this is worked on and is sustainable.

Services provided by healthcare have significantly improved, with waiting times to see a GP or nurse no longer being an issue.

**HEDON ROAD**
**HULL**
**HU9 5LS**

**HM PRISON HULL**

**Tel: 01482 282200**

*For the latest reports on this prison please visit:*
https://tinyurl.com/bdfh26rv

*Important Changes:* **(1) Visits:** the identification necessary to access this prison and visit for social or professional purposes has changed; (2) **Money and Gifts** new rules now apply to these. See page 16 for full details of the above.

### Task of the prison/establishment
Category B local for male prisoners

### Certified normal accommodation and operational capacity
Prisoners held July 2021: 965
Baseline certified normal capacity: 723
In-use certified normal capacity: 723
Operational capacity: 1,002 at the time of the inspection. A reduction of 42 had been made to facilitate RCU arrangements and the temporary closure of wings for fire safety improvements

### Population of the prison
• 1,290 new prisoners were received each year (about 100 to 150 a month).
• 307 prisoners had been convicted of sexual offences.
• 108 prisoners were foreign nationals.
• 222 prisoners were receiving support for substance use at the time of this inspection.
• 204 prisoners were receiving support for mental health problems at the time of this inspection.

## Prison status and key providers
Public
Prison group: Yorkshire
Prison Group Director Helen Judge
Governing governor: Shaun Mycroft
IMB chair: David Gillyan-Powell
Physical/Mental Substance health provider:
City Health Care Partnership
Prison education framework provider: Novus
Escort contractor: GeoAmey

## Brief history
HMP Hull is a Victorian prison which opened in 1870 to hold men and women. In 1939 it was used as a military prison and later a civil defence depot. In 1950 it re-opened as a closed male borstal. In 1969, after extensive security work, Hull became one of the first maximum security dispersal prisons. In 1986, Hull assumed its current role as a male local prison and remand centre. In 2002 the prison expanded with four new wings, new health care centre, new sports hall and multi-faith centre and refurbishment to other parts of the prison including the kitchen, education and workshops.

## Short description of residential units
A wing - 50 single cells for the PIPE unit. The rest for prisoners with a history of drug use.
B wing – Remand and convicted prisoners. Built in 1990s.
C wing – Remand and convicted prisoners. Built in 1860s.
D wing – Remand and convicted prisoners. Built in 1860s.
G wing – Induction unit/reverse cohort unit. Opened 2002.
H wing – Vulnerable prisoners' unit/induction/reverse cohort overflow. Opened 2002
I wing – Vulnerable prisoners' unit. Opened 2002.
J wing – Vulnerable prisoners' unit. Opened 2002.
Well-being unit – Prisoners with complex care needs, includes a palliative care suite
K wing – Currently unoccupied for fire safety improvement project. Became the separation and care unit from 14 July 2021.

## Visiting Information
To book a visit ring: 01482 282 016 Monday to Friday, 8am to 12:30pm
**Visiting times:** Monday, Friday, Saturday, Sunday: 8:30am to 11:45am and 1:30pm to 4:45pm

**Legal visits:** There are currently no legal visits taking place.

## INSPECTIONS & REPORTS
**IRP Report: 14–16 March 2022**
**Published 26 April 2022**
HMP Hull is a large, inner-city prison of two halves. The older wings, built in the 19th century, receive remanded or newly convicted men from the local community, while the newer wings largely hold vulnerable prisoners, many of whom are convicted of sexual offences. At the time of this review visit, the prison had a reduced capacity of around 900 prisoners while a wing was closed for fire improvement works.

At our previous inspections of HMP Hull in 2018 and 2021, we made the following judgements about outcomes for prisoners.

At our last visit, in July 2021, we reported on a prison where standards and outcomes had slipped after a succession of more positive inspections. Our findings were disappointing, with evidence of shortcomings and deterioration in all four of our healthy prison assessments, which were judged to be not sufficiently good. Violence had begun to increase, and we were not confident that the use of force was necessary, proportionate or safe in every case. Our concern at the incidence of eight self-inflicted deaths and two non-natural deaths was compounded by a lack of evidence that important recommendations made by the Prisons and Probation Ombudsman had led to sustained change, particularly in relation to health care. In fact, health care services were failing in some critical areas. We were not confident that partnership working was providing sufficient oversight and governance, and mental health services were inadequately resourced. There were serious risks and unmet need which needed immediate attention. Disappointingly, we found most prisoners locked in their cells for 23 hours a day, which was worse than we had seen in similar prisons. Offender management had also deteriorated, with very poor contact between prison-based offender managers and prisoners, and insufficient oversight of high risk of harm prisoners approaching release.

The situation at the time, however, seemed eminently retrievable, subject to some meaningful planning which focused on improved outcomes and more rigorous oversight. The prison had retained some core strengths and generally remained a capable institution. Staff were experienced and prisoners appeared to have considerable confidence in them. With the recent arrival of a new governor, our sense was that this was a time of potential and opportunity for the prison.

During this review visit, we examined nine key recommendations and our colleagues in Ofsted addressed three themes. Our findings were encouraging. There had been good or reasonable progress against eight of the 12 recommendations and themes, although there remained insufficient progress against four of these. Health care services were still of considerable concern. While governance had been strengthened, staff shortages continued to have a negative impact on the delivery of safe patient care.

The amount of time that prisoners spent unlocked was still very poor for many prisoners. There had been little progress since the last inspection for those who were unemployed. Although a prolonged Covid-19 outbreak and national restrictions had hindered the prison's ability to improve the regime, the time unlocked for prisoners at Hull was considerably worse than we have seen recently in comparable prisons that face similar challenges.

For the minority of prisoners who were engaged in education, however, Ofsted found that there had been reasonable progress. More learners had completed qualifications and there was better information, advice and guidance. Identification and support for those with learning difficulties and disabilities had also improved.

There had been considerable effort by the senior team in response to our recommendation that clear and up-to-date strategies were needed, along with rigorous oversight, to drive improvement. We found impressive progress in outcomes for prisoner safety that was underpinned by a revised strategy and better use of data. Incidents of violence and use of force had reduced since the last inspection, and scrutiny of use of force had markedly improved. The progress we found in offender management also reflected a prison that had renewed its sense of purpose and had clearer direction.

Overall, this was a positive review. The governor, his senior team and staff should be congratulated on what they have achieved so far in addressing the shortcomings we identified at the last inspection. As Covid-19 restrictions are lifted, the renewed confidence in the prison now needs to be translated into a much greater ambition in the amount of time that prisoners are unlocked from their cells.

Charlie Taylor
HM Chief Inspector of Prisons March 2022

**HMCIP report:** 12-30 July 2021
**Published 2 November 2021**

HMP Hull is a large, inner-city male establishment holding just under 1,000 prisoners. A prison of two halves, the four older wings date from the late 19th century, with the remainder built in the early part of the 21st century. The older wings act as a local or reception establishment, receiving remanded or newly convicted men from the local community, while the newer wings largely hold vulnerable prisoners, many of whom are convicted of sexual offences.

A complex, interesting and challenging institution, Hull is a prison about which we have been able to report positively at recent inspections. At our last visit in 2018, for example, we found that outcomes for prisoners were reasonably good against all four tests of a healthy prison. Findings at this inspection have been more disappointing, with evidence of significant shortcomings and deterioration in all four of our assessments.

The prison had been impacted quite significantly by the Covid-19 pandemic and experienced more than one outbreak, although it had responded quickly and effectively to these difficulties. It was also undergoing a period of transition with the recent arrival of a new governor, as well as other changes to the senior management team. Despite this the prison seemed to have retained some core strengths and generally remained a capable institution. Staff were experienced and prisoners appeared to have considerable confidence in them. Staff culture was quite traditional, which was mostly a strength, but there was clearly a need for effective oversight, supervision and regulation to ensure relationships remained constructive and legitimate.

Our sense was that this was a time of potential and opportunity for the prison. Hull was beginning to work towards recovery as it emerged from the restrictions of the pandemic and the governor was in the process of refining his priorities. We were told this included better meeting the needs of short sentence prisoners, staff training, operational grip and safety. As priorities they were reasonable, but there was a need for more substance and clarity in the establishment's plans that detailed how improvements would be made, by whom and when. It was clear to us that current oversight arrangements and structures lacked rigour and accountability and we identified the need for improvement in several specific areas of delivery, including segregation arrangements, safer custody and the use of force. Other priorities included offender management and public protection procedures, both of which required improvement; greater ambition in improving access to activity and time out of cell; and getting a much better hold on the delivery of decent health care, an area that was failing badly.

Standards and outcomes have slipped at Hull. The situation however, seems eminently retrievable, subject to some meaningful planning which focuses on improved outcomes and is supported by rigorous oversight to ensure delivery, compliance and accountability. We have made recommendations which we hope will support that process and believe a relatively early return visit by the Inspectorate may be beneficial. HM Chief Inspector of Prisons July 2021

### Summary of key findings

We last inspected HMP Hull in 2018 and made 44 recommendations, four of which were about areas of key concern. The prison fully accepted 33 of the recommendations and partially (or subject to resources) accepted seven. It rejected four of the recommendations.

### Progress on key concerns and recommendations from the full inspection

Our last inspection of HMP Hull took place before the Covid-19 pandemic and the recommendations in that report focused on areas of concern affecting outcomes for prisoners at the time. Although we recognise that the challenges of keeping prisoners safe during COVID- 19 will have changed the focus for many prison leaders, we believe that it is important to report on progress in areas of key concern to help leaders to continue to drive improvement.

At our last full inspection, we made one recommendation about a key concern in the area of safety. At this inspection we found that this recommendation had been achieved.

We made two recommendations about key concerns in the area of respect. At this inspection we found that one of those recommendations had been achieved and one had been partially achieved.

We made no recommendations about key concerns in the area of purposeful activity. Ofsted carried out a progress monitoring visit alongside our inspection to assess the progress that leaders and managers had made towards reinstating a full education, skills and work curriculum. They judged it was too early to assess whether recommendations made at the last inspection had been achieved.

We made one recommendation about a key concern in the area of rehabilitation and release planning. At this inspection we found that this recommendation had not been achieved.

### Outcomes for prisoners

We assess outcomes for prisoners against four healthy prison tests. We also include a commentary on leadership in the prison.

At this inspection of HMP Hull, we found that outcomes for prisoners had declined in all healthy prison areas.

These judgements seek to make an objective assessment of the outcomes experienced by those detained and have taken into account the

prison's recovery from Covid-19 as well as the 'regime stage' at which the prison was operating, as outlined in the HM Prison and Probation (HMPPS) National Framework for prison regimes and services.

### Safety

Support for prisoners on arrival and during their first few days at the prison was reasonable and the attention given to assessing and addressing individuals' vulnerability had improved.

The majority of prisoners felt safe. In our survey, 15% said that they felt unsafe at the time of the inspection, although this was significantly higher for those with mental health problems. The number of recorded assaults among prisoners had reduced since the last inspection. However, in recent months both assaults on staff and assaults among prisoners had begun to increase again. The focus on the immediate emerging risks and threats was good but more needed to be done to understand the causes of violence and set targets for improvement. The challenge, support and intervention plan (CSIP) casework model was not operating effectively.

We were not confident that the use of force was necessary in every case that we reviewed and, in some cases, it was not proportionate or safe. The segregation unit remained very clean and prisoners spoke positively about their relationships with staff. However, the regime was poor, and the treatment of prisoners suspected of secreting illicit items needed immediate attention.

Security arrangements were proportionate. Measures to reduce the supply of drugs were appropriate given the risks and the use of a body scanner to detect illicit items was good.

The other principal contributory factor to the judgement about outcomes under this test was the incidence of eight self-inflicted deaths and two non-natural deaths since the last inspection. This was compounded by a lack of evidence that important recommendations made by the Prisons and Probation Ombudsman, following their investigation into these incidents, had led to sustained change, particularly in relation to health care services.

Prisoners we spoke to were positive about the care they received when subject to an ACCT (assessment, care in custody and teamwork case management of prisoners at risk of suicide or self-harm). The well- being unit, although weakened by the inadequate mental health support, provided some very vulnerable prisoners with a decent and safe place to live.

## Respect

Working relationships between staff and prisoners remained positive.

Living conditions had improved in some important areas but overcrowding continued and the conditions were exacerbated by the fact that most prisoners spent 23 hours a day locked in their cell. External and communal areas were very clean and well maintained and some of the garden areas were excellent.

In the temporary absence of a prison council, prisoner information desk workers were a good source for consultation and in our survey significantly more prisoners than at our last inspection said they were consulted about key issues. There was good oversight of complaints but responses to applications were not tracked.

1.19 Strategic oversight of equality and diversity had been limited during the pandemic, but a sound strategy had recently been developed with a clear vision for success. Diversity and inclusion action team meetings had recently resumed but there was a lack of commitment to the work by departments across the prison. Analysis of data was underdeveloped but showing signs of improvement. The quality of responses to discrimination incident report forms was good. Support for prisoners with protected characteristics was not yet fully embedded but work with young prisoners was developing well. Corporate worship remained suspended due to the pandemic, but the chaplaincy provided good support to prisoners.

Health care services had been weak well before the pandemic and were failing in some critical areas. We were not confident that partnership working with healthcare was providing sufficient oversight and governance and there were staffing vacancies across all clinical disciplines. Mental health services were not properly resourced. There were significant risks and unmet need which required immediate attention. Patients waited too long for some primary care services and there was no oversight of waiting lists. Health care staff had good relationships with patients and were caring in their approach. However, patients with long-term conditions did not always receive person-centred, holistic care.

## Purposeful activity

Ofsted carried out a progress monitoring visit of the prison alongside our full inspection and the purposeful activity judgement incorporates their assessment of progress.

The use of peer workers to deliver constructive activity and improve time out of cell had not been maximised by leaders. More than a third of prisoners were unemployed at the time of this inspection and 16 months after the start of the Covid-19 restricted regime it was disappointing that most prisoners were locked in their cells for 23 hours a day. This was worse than we have seen in similar prisons. Prisoners who were isolating because of Covid-19 had no time out of cell, which was very poor. The library remained closed, but a mobile service was operating, and the gym provision was reasonable, albeit operating with much reduced numbers.

Leaders had worked effectively to ensure that, in most cases, the restricted number of spaces in education and work activities were fully used. The range of activities met the needs of both short-term prisoners and those staying at Hull for longer.

There were too few information, advice and guidance staff and leaders recognised that too many sentenced prisoners were not engaged in education or work activities. Quality assurance of the work that tutors did remotely with learners was thorough. The small number of prisoners who attended workshops or were doing courses developed valuable new skills. In-cell learning booklets were of a reasonable quality and used by many prisoners. There were too few opportunities for prisoners to gain accredited qualifications in vocational training and education.

## Rehabilitation and release planning

Work to support prisoners' contact with children and families was good.

In-cell telephones were of great benefit and the 'family story time' was a positive and creative project. Face-to-face visits had resumed and had been increased at the earliest opportunity and the use of secure video calls (see Glossary of terms) had improved.

Following a gap for much of the Covid-19 pandemic, oversight of reducing reoffending work had recently restarted but the strategy and needs analysis were out of date. The recent reunification of probation had led to significant interruptions in the delivery of some key resettlement services.

Most eligible prisoners had had an initial assessment of their risk and need. In our survey, 34% of prisoners said they had a custody plan. Most of them knew what they needed to do to achieve their targets but only 64% said someone was helping them to achieve them. Contact between prison-based offender managers and prisoners was very poor. It was predominantly task driven and for most prisoners did not focus on sentence progression. Initial categorisation and reviews were timely and appropriate. Home detention curfew procedures were managed well given the circumstances.

There was not enough oversight of high risk of harm prisoners approaching release. In too many cases we could not see evidence that the MAPPA management level had been confirmed or reviewed in the lead up to release. The number of prisoners on mail and phone monitoring had significantly reduced and procedures were managed appropriately.

Accredited programmes had restarted in the summer of 2020 but there was a backlog of prisoners waiting for a suitability assessment. The psychologically informed planned environment (PIPE) was impressive and the delivery of the Choices and Changes programme to young prisoners was positive.

An average of 80 prisoners were released each month and there was a reasonably high demand for resettlement services. Resettlement planning for high-risk prisoners was non-existent at the time of the inspection. Basic practical arrangements were in place for the day of release, but more could be done to further enhance the support provided.

### Key concerns and recommendations

Key concerns and recommendations identify the issues of most importance to improving outcomes for prisoners and are designed to help establishments prioritise and address the most significant weaknesses in the treatment and conditions of prisoners.

During this inspection we identified some areas of key concern and have made a number of recommendations for the prison to address those concerns.

Key concern: Leadership and progress was hindered by the insufficient

or inadequate strategies and action plans to affect improvement. Some were out of date and others, such as the safety strategy, did not set out a clear vision for success or steps to be taken to improve outcomes. This meant that there was a lack of a shared vision or agreement across the prison about the priorities and next steps.

Recommendation: Outcomes for prisoners should be improved. Clear and up-to-date strategies and action plans should be implemented to achieve improvement. The strategies should be regularly reviewed to monitor progress and to ensure oversight arrangements are in place to sustain delivery and provide accountability. (To the governor)

Key concern: Management oversight of the use of force and segregation was inadequate. For example, some incidents of force we reviewed were not proportionate to the risk and they were not always carried out safely. The segregation unit provided a poor daily regime and the management of those suspected of secreting illicit items was worrying as they were denied time out of cell and access to medication.

Recommendation: The number of times force is used should be reduced. When used it should be proportionate and undertaken safely.
(To the governor)

Recommendation: Outcomes for prisoners in the segregation unit should be improved through the provision of a purposeful regime. Those suspected of secreting illicit items should not be denied access to any part of the regime or necessary support. (To the governor)

Key concern: There had been eight self-inflicted deaths and two further non-natural deaths in the previous three years. Investigations by the Prisons and Probation Ombudsman had generated a large number of recommendations and some highly negative findings about treatment and conditions. We were concerned to find that there had not been sufficient focus on achieving many of these recommendations, particularly those relating to health care.

Recommendation: All Prisons and Probation Ombudsman recommendations should be implemented and sustained over time to help prevent further self-inflicted deaths.
(To the governor)

Key concern: Prisoners with protected and minority characteristics had little direct support and the analysis of data to identify disproportionate treatment remained limited. Promoting positive outcomes for each protected characteristic group was not seen as a priority by all departments so the work was not given sufficient attention.

Recommendation: Leaders should deliver a coordinated and well-resourced approach to promoting equality and inclusion in all aspects of prison life, and make sure that prisoners are consulted frequently to strengthen the support available. (To the governor)

Key concern: The lack of clinical and operational leadership, inadequate GP capacity and chronic staff shortages meant that patients' changing needs, including the management of long-term conditions and mental health, were not being assessed or met in a timely manner. This was creating significant risk.

Recommendation: The local delivery board, in conjunction with NHS England and Improvement, should undertake an urgent health needs analysis to ensure that adequate resources are in place to meet the needs of all patients safely. (To the governor)

Key concern: The daily regime was far too restricted and most prisoners continued to spend 23 hours a day locked in their cells. Opportunities to engage in purposeful activity remained limited and too many prisoners were unemployed.

Recommendation: All prisoners should have sufficient time out of cell, including longer in the open air, and be engaged in activities that support their rehabilitation. (To the governor)

Key concern: The sharing of information and handover of responsibility for prisoners' risk management were inadequate. Multi-agency public protection arrangements were not always agreed, and some risk management plans were out of date. The interdepartmental risk management meeting was poorly conducted and there was no strategic oversight of these cases. At the time of the inspection, there was no resettlement planning for high risk of harm prisoners.

Recommendation: All MAPPA-eligible prisoners approaching release should have a multidisciplinary plan agreed in sufficient time to fully manage risks and address resettlement needs. (To the governor)

**Notable positive practice**

We define notable positive practice as innovative work or practice that leads to particularly good outcomes from which other establishments may be able to learn. Inspectors look for evidence of good outcomes for prisoners; original, creative or particularly effective approaches to problem-solving or achieving the desired goal; and how other establishments could learn from or replicate the practice.

Inspectors found three examples of notable positive practice during this inspection.

Leaders continued to fund a professional counsellor to provide specialist support to staff. The counsellor had been well used over the last year and was a positive source of additional support.

Prisoners safety representatives had been introduced to give support to their more vulnerable peers. Some selected for this role had been habitual self-harmers themselves and, with appropriate guidance from the safer prisons team, had found this a constructive way to strengthen their own recovery and to use their experience for the benefit of others.

A positive project had been established to promote contact with children. Through the 'family story time' initiative prisoners could film themselves reading bedtime stories from a range of children's books, to send to their children as a DVD.

**INDEPENDENT REVIEW OF PROGRESS**
Date of IRP: 14-16 March 2022
HMCIP IRP Report, published 26 April 2022

An independent review of progress (IRP)at HMP Hull, a category B prison holding around 900 prisoners, showed an encouraging commitment to improvement, although a lack of action in purposeful activity and health care demonstrated that more needed to be done.

Inspectors from HM Inspectorate of Prisons were following up on their visit to the jail in July 2021, where they found that outcomes for prisoners were not sufficiently good in all four healthy prison areas, having slipped considerably since the previous inspection in 2018. Violence had increased, and inspectors were not confident that use of force was always necessary, proportionate, or safe. A worrying eight self-inflicted deaths and two non-natural deaths had occurred, yet there was no evidence that recommendations by the Prisons and Probation Ombudsman (PPO) had led to improvement in prisoner safety. Inspectors found most prisoners locked in their cells for 23 hours a day.

At this IRP inspectors found encouraging signs at the prison, which held a mix of remanded or newly convicted men from the local community as well as a group of vulnerable prisoners. There had been good or reasonable progress against eight of the 12 HMI Prisons recommendations and Ofsted themes, although there remained insufficient progress against four. Charlie Taylor, Chief Inspector of Prisons, said: "There had been considerable effort by the senior team in response to our recommendation that clear and up-to-date strategies were needed, along with rigorous oversight, to drive improvement."

Insufficient progress had been made in the provision of purposeful activity. Most prisoners spent around 1.5 hours per day unlocked, which included just 30 minutes in the open air. Although a prolonged Covid-19 outbreak and HM Prison and Probation Service restrictions had hindered progress in this area, many of the plans to improve were not being followed. Only around 14% of the population were engaged in off-wing activity at any given time. The gym and workshops were not operating at full capacity.

Inspectors were impressed by improvements in prisoner safety, facilitated by a revised strategy and better use of data. The number of violent incidents, against both staff and prisoners, had fallen sharply by 60% and 55% respectively. Knowledge of the challenge, support, and intervention plan (CSIP) was widespread, thanks to the safety team's commitment to training staff and use of force was subject to improved scrutiny. The impressive achievements in managing violence and offending were not supported by improvements in health care provision. Although a monthly 'safe and secure' meeting provided greater strategic oversight of the PPO recommendations, inspectors found that health care leaders did not attend. Some health care recommendations had still not been implemented. Mr Taylor said: "The governor, his senior team and staff should be congratulated on what they have achieved so far in addressing the shortcomings we identified at the last inspection. As Covid-19 restrictions are lifted, the renewed confidence in the prison now needs to be translated into a much greater ambition in the amount of time that prisoners are unlocked from their cells."

## INDEPENDENT MONITORING BOARD: Annual Report

The law requires every prison to be monitored by an independent Board appointed by the Justice Secretary; these are known as Independent Monitoring Boards (IMBs). The IMB must satisfy itself as to the humane and just treatment of those held in custody within its prison and the range and adequacy of the programmes preparing them for release; it must report annually to the Justice Secretary on how well the prison has met the standards and requirements placed on it.

### IMB Report 1 March 2021 – 28 February 2022
### Published July 2022
### Executive Summary
### Background to the report

During the Covid-19 restrictions, the Board has had only five fully active members over the last 12 months (though its recommended complement is sixteen). Two new members started in September and October 2021, and have made rapid progress. The Board Chair does not feel that adequate support with regard to recruitment and retention has been prioritised by the IMB Management Board and Secretariat. The scope of the Board's monitoring has, therefore, been restricted. Face-to-face monitoring visits were maintained through the periods of Covid-19 restrictions. Covid secure measures for the collection and response to applications made by prisoners to the IMB were introduced to ensure the concerns of the prisoners were addressed. Healthcare was observed closely, as was segregation and safer custody, but observation of other areas was largely driven by prisoner applications.

In July 2021, HM Inspectorate of Prisons (HMIP) undertook an announced inspection at the establishment, having last undertaken an inspection in 2018. The findings of the latest inspection found that the judgement against the four healthy prison outcomes had declined from 'reasonably good' to 'not sufficiently good' in all four areas. A new Governor had been appointed shortly before the July 2021 HMIP inspection.

### Main judgements
### How safe is the prison?

Though there were two self-inflicted deaths in custody, overall, the prison is a safe place and prisoners with mental health issues are usually well cared for.

There has been an overall reduction in self-harming. Statistically, prisoner on prisoner violence has reduced from last year, as have assaults on staff.

Staff use of force has reduced, as have the number of illicit and dangerous substances coming into the prison presumably due to the restricted regime imposed as a consequence of the pandemic.

### How fairly and humanely are prisoners treated?

The quality of the buildings makes it difficult to accommodate the operational capacity in HMP Hull. Prisoners are commonly accommodated in double cells which are inadequate both in size and design. Prisoners in wheelchairs have difficulties accessing facilities such as showers. However, the existing facilities are kept clean and habitable.

Prisoners in the segregation unit and wellbeing unit are carefully managed to ensure their welfare.

Staff have continued to provide support for prisoners who have spent long periods locked in their cells, but the support from key workers has been restricted during lockdown. Religious support has continued via the prison's in house television system, and the support for diversity within the prison has been enhanced with greater scrutiny and awareness raising following the appointment a new diversity and inclusivity lead. Prisoners have raised concerns about the effectiveness of the complaints system, possibly due to reduced staff numbers during pandemic. The prison has enhanced the procedures for monitoring the effectiveness of the process.

The management of property transferred in and out of the prison has improved, but recently arrived prisoners are often unaware of what property they are allowed to access.

### How well are prisoners' health and wellbeing needs met?

Healthcare needs have generally not been consistently and satisfactorily met due to contractual failures and staff absences.

The clinical staff have worked hard to identify and meet prisoners' needs, and the support for prisoners with mental health needs has been sustained. The Board has received comments, however, about the perceived lack of support from senior management. Social care has remained effective on the wings, but access to exercise has been significantly restricted.

During the height of pandemic lockdown, distraction packs and in-cell activities/ exercise were introduced using the in-house television system to help facilitate this.

## How well are prisoners progressed towards successful resettlement?

The Covid-19 restrictions have instigated a new approach to education based on meeting individual needs either in cell or in small groups. This has reduced negative responses from prisoners who are resistant to classroom learning. A learners' forum provides feedback for the education team to respond to, though an Ofsted inspection said there were too few opportunities to gain qualifications. Support for prisoners to change their ways of thinking have continued but with lower numbers due to Covid-19 restrictions.

Opportunities to work in the well refurbished industries site have doubled since last year, and the jobs available have been seen as purposeful and satisfying.

Offender management was less effective for much of the year but the prison is training all offender management unit (OMU) staff to improve this. Ensuring that resettlement is effective has been difficult due to inconsistent communication from the outside agencies, the loss of the work of "Shelter" and the hand over from CRC; with regard to housing, finance and employment.

Family contact was difficult for much of the year, but has been improved recently with both video and face to face contacts, though contact with children is still limited.

## Main areas for development

### TO THE MINISTER

• The Board would ask the minister to:

o consider the issues of insufficient capacity within the prison estate which continues to see prisoners housed in double cells which are inadequate both in size and design for this purpose and impinge upon the right to privacy and dignity;

o improve the work of outside contractors and organisations responsible for ensuring appropriate accommodation and support is available on release to reduce the risk of re-offending as they are not communicating effectively with the in-prison resettlement team.

### TO THE PRISON SERVICE

• Prisoners' property, particularly on transfer, remains a significant issue for the Board. How will the prison service put systems in place to resolve these issues?

### TO THE GOVERNOR

Continue to develop the attitude-changing interventions with young adults.

Restore the full support from key workers.

Sustain the training for OMU staff to ensure that all prisoners get the information, advice and guidance to prepare them for transfers or release.

## Progress since the last report

*Issue raised in the last report* **Progress made**

*Improve the management structure of healthcare provision and its communication with prison management.* This has resulted in tendering for a new provider.

*Sustain some of the changes which have reportedly improved some prisoners' perception of personal safety, while allowing greater freedoms for activity and association.* The extended lockdown period restricted progress in these areas.

*Continue to build contacts with external employers to support prisoners on release.* The prison has continued with this process, and is seeking to extend this further.

*Continue to develop the attitude-changing interventions with young adults.* The initiative has continued, though some of the staff originally involved have not had the time available to continue. Discussions with prisoners and staff involved, and observation of the records of the discussions, show that the interventions are helping the young adults to reflect on their behaviour, thinking, and relationships, and giving them new targets for the future.

*Restore the full support of key workers.* The key worker support has remained limited due to the extensive pressures on the staff involved during the crisis.

EVERTHORPE
BROUGH
HU15 2JZ

HM PRISON SERVICE

HM PRISON HUMBER    TEL: 01430 273000

*For the latest reports on this prison please visit:*
https://tinyurl.com/bdfh26rv

*Important Changes:* **(1) Visits:** the identification necessary to access this prison and visit for social or professional purposes has changed; (2) **Money and Gifts** new rules now apply to these. See page 16 for full details of the above.

**Task of the establishment** HMP Humber is a category C resettlement prison for adult men.

**Certified normal accommodation and operational capacity**
Prisoners held at the time of this visit: 925
Baseline certified normal capacity: 952
In-use certified normal capacity: 952
Operational capacity: 1,062

**Prison status and key providers**
Public
Prison Group: Yorkshire
Prison Group Director: Helen Judge
Governor/Director: Marcella Goligher OBE
IMB Chair: Paul Holland
Physical health provider: City Health Care Partnership Community Interest Company
Mental health provider: City Health Care Partnership Community Interest Company
Substance use treatment provider: City Health Care Partnership Community Interest Company
Prison education framework provider: Novus
Escort contractor: GeoAmey

**Brief history** HMP Humber was formed in June 2013 by the amalgamation of two former prisons, HMP Everthorpe (originally opened as a borstal in 1958) and HMP Wolds (opened in 1992 as a category B establishment, and the first privately run prison in Europe).

**Short description of residential units**
Zone 1 comprises wings A to G. These are small, open-gallery units.
Zone 2 comprises wings H to N. Apart from a modern induction block, these are mostly older, tier-style units, and include the segregation unit.

**Visiting Information**
Book online at: www.gov.uk/prison-visits or ring 0300 060 6606 Monday to Friday: 9am to 11:30am and 1pm to 3pm.
**Visiting times:** Monday, Thursday, Friday, Saturday, Sunday: 2pm to 4pm.

**Legal visits:** To book legal visits please email: LegalVisits.Humber.Everthorpe@justice.gov.uk

**INSPECTIONS & REPORTS**
**Scrutiny visit: 27 October & 3–4 November 2020**
**Published: 08 December 2020**
HMP Humber is a large category C training prison in East Yorkshire. It is an amalgamation of the formerly privately run HMP Wolds (zone 1) and the old Everthorpe prison (zone 2). At the time of our scrutiny visit, the prison held 925 adult male prisoners, which was a slight reduction on the population held before the implementation of the Covid-19 restrictions. This meant that fewer prisoners were sharing small cells originally designed for one person, which helped in controlling the spread of the virus.
The senior management team had reacted quickly to minimise the spread of the Covid-19 virus following the announcement of the restrictions in prisons at the end of March 2020. There was an outbreak among staff in May, but this was handled well. Many prisoners we spoke to were positive about the steps taken throughout the last seven months to keep them safe, and at the time of our visit few staff had tested positive and no prisoners were currently positive. Despite a clear desire and regular reminders to maintain social distancing, this was very difficult to achieve in some parts of the prison, particularly in zone 2, where corridors and landings were much narrower. Arrangements to keep new prisoners separate from others on the two reverse cohort units were proportionate and sensible, but the use of a shared exercise yard with prisoners from other wings presented an avoidable risk of the virus being transmitted.
Senior managers had planned and taken some important steps towards recovery. However, they were frustrated at the slow pace of recovery set out by national guidance from HM Prison and Probation Service (HMPPS), which gave little room for local autonomy. In addition, plans for further recovery were in doubt following the start of a second national lockdown in the community which would come into force on the day after our visit.
Many of the strategic meetings had been suspended early on in the restricted regime, which was understandable, given the need to focus on the imminent risk of the Covid-19 virus spreading within the prison. It was good to see that these had been reinstated, and most were providing important oversight again. However, the strategic meeting for equality and diversity needed to become more fully embedded and effective over the coming months. The senior management team recognised the need to improve the focus on equality and diversity across the prison.
Data before and during the restricted regime showed that the number of incidents of violence and self-harm had fallen considerably. The number of times that force had been used against prisoners had also reduced since the end of March, and the number of prisoners placed in the segregation unit was very low. In our survey, few prisoners said that they currently felt unsafe. Few felt bullied or victimised by other prisoners but about a third felt victimised by staff. The reasons for the latter perception were unclear.
The care for those at risk of self-harm was reasonable, but we were surprised to find that the formal Listener scheme had not been fully functioning since the end of March. The peer-led support groups known as Andy's Man Club had resumed in July and were very popular. Staff regularly undertook well-being checks on all prisoners, and the safer custody team, alongside the safety intervention meeting, provided good oversight of, and support to, the most vulnerable. The use of anti-ligature clothing for prisoners in crisis was unusually high, which we

found concerning, and prisoners' negative perceptions of the care they received while in crisis needed to be explored.

Staff–prisoner interactions were positive, but the formal and structured key worker sessions had been suspended early on in the restricted regime. Consultation with prisoners was promoted by a peer-led scheme known as the 'Humber Pilot'. Living conditions were decent and clean. Prisoners had good access to essential items, and the regime was reliably delivered on the whole. The complaints process was concerning, and we found some serious complaints that had not been adequately dealt with.

Health care staff had maintained core functions during the Covid-19 restrictions, including access to GPs and nurses, emergency dentistry, mental health services and substance misuse support. Some of the clinics and therapies curtailed during the restrictions had yet to restart, and the dental service had accumulated an extensive waiting list. There had been errors within medicines management that compromised prisoner safety.

The number of prisoners in some form of purposeful activity out of their cell had increased recently to about a quarter of the population. A few workshops had reopened with a reduced capacity, and safe systems of working and some education sessions were now taking place. However, for the majority not in an activity, they remained locked in the cell for 22.5 hours a day, and some of those we spoke to clearly described the detrimental impact this was having on their health and well-being.

Social visits had restarted but would be suspended again following the imminent further restrictions in the community. Video calling was available, but the uptake was low. In-cell telephones provided a huge benefit.

Before the pandemic and the introduction of the restricted regime, HMP Humber had had a clear focus on progression and rehabilitation. For a prison of this type, where prisoners are eager to progress, the loss of many of the rehabilitative tools was a huge frustration. The delivery of offending behaviour programmes had restarted, albeit only one-to-one, and the Hope unit (a small unit aimed at supporting indeterminate sentenced prisoners in their sentence progression) had continued to provide some important progression work throughout the restricted regime. However, contact by prison offender managers with those on their caseload was variable. The quality of resettlement planning was poor, with resettlement plans still being developed without direct engagement with the prisoner, either face-to-face or by telephone. Some basic resettlement help was

available, but with too many gaps in provision for us to be confident that it was fully effective.

In conclusion, managers, staff and prisoners had responded well to the pandemic some seven months ago and were still working hard to maintain an environment safe from Covid-19. At the time of our visit, it was unclear how the new restrictions in the community would affect the prison's pathway to recovery, but it is important that the prison delivers on the improvements we identify in this report, particularly in regaining a clear focus on rehabilitation and resettlement.

Charlie Taylor, HM Chief Inspector of Prisons
November 2020

## INDEPENDENT MONITORING BOARD: Annual Report

The law requires every prison to be monitored by an independent Board appointed by the Justice Secretary; these are known as Independent Monitoring Boards (IMBs). The IMB must satisfy itself as to the humane and just treatment of those held in custody within its prison and the range and adequacy of the programmes preparing them for release; it must report annually to the Justice Secretary on how well the prison has met the standards and requirements placed on it.

### IMB Report 1 January 2021 – 31 December 2021
**Published May 2022**
### Executive Summary
### Background to the report

Over the reporting period, the ongoing Covid-19 pandemic and restrictions placed upon prisons and the general public have affected the lives of all prisoners considerably. It has had a significant impact on the Board's ability to gather information and discuss the contents of this annual report. The Board has therefore tried to cover as much ground as it can in these difficult circumstances, but inevitably there may be less detail and supporting evidence than usual. Ministers are aware of these constraints.

This report presents the findings of the IMB at HMP Humber for the period 1 January 2021 to 31 December 2021. Evidence for this report comes from applications to the Board, observations made on visits, scrutiny of records and data, attendance at meetings and also remote monitoring (that is, contact via telephone and email).

Over the reporting period, the prison has operated under various iterations of recovery – that is, stage 4 in January, with it becoming an outbreak site in February, and progressing finally to stage 1 in November, only to move back to stage 2 in December.

For the first six months of 2021, blended monitoring took place, with two members of the

Board making visits to the prison in person, when it was safe to do so, with the remaining members undertaking monitoring duties remotely. From July until December, all but one member visited the prison in person, but, again, some of the Board reverted back to blended monitoring in December as a result of the Omicron variant.

Throughout this reporting period, as previously stated, the prison transitioned through various stages of recovery, whereby prisoners were locked up for the majority of each day in a lockdown situation, to near normal circumstances of prisoners attending their place of work. The Board acknowledges that this was unavoidable, given the pressures upon the prison during the ongoing pandemic. The Board has continued to admire the professionalism and resilience of the Governor and senior management team, and commends them on their progress planning and continued management of the at times very restricted systems of working, so as to mitigate the threat of Covid-19 to the prison population.

The Board is grateful for the cooperation and assistance of all prison staff during this very challenging and, again, unpredictable year and wishes to commend them for their outstanding work, dedication and commitment to caring for the prisoners with both sensitivity and compassion.

### Main judgements
### How safe is the prison?

The Board feels that, following the imposed restrictions in all prisons at the end of March 2020, HMP Humber has continued to be extremely well managed throughout 2021, within the circumstances and constraints of the Covid-19 pandemic. The Governor and senior management team (SMT) appear to have given all possible consideration to moving forward in their planning of a revised alternative regime, in order to maintain the safety of everyone within the establishment – both staff and prisoners.

There has been very little intelligence of illicit drug supply into the prison, and the levels of violence, bullying and self-harm have remained low, which in turn makes the environment safer. The Board is concerned about how the levels will increase when the regime restrictions are lifted, as we already saw levels increase with the move to stage 2 in August 2021.

### How fairly and humanely are prisoners treated?

Prior to the Covid-19 pandemic and under a normal progressive regime, the Board agrees that prisoners are treated fairly and humanely within HMP Humber.

During the period of restrictions and the various regime stages, good relationships between staff and prisoners, and the open two-way communications, have helped prisoners' sense of personal safety and their overall trust in staff. Staffing issues, however, in relation to isolation and sickness, have themselves proved to be a huge issue at times, in relation to managing a restricted regime.

As the restrictions have continued for a further year, it must be noted that, over this extremely long period of time, minimal positive interactions cannot take the place of progression, rehabilitation, education and purposeful activity. Over time, being behind a door for the vast majority of the day will have a long-term and detrimental effect on general health and wellbeing. There continues to be a positive attitude towards supporting prisoners in maintaining good relationships with their family and friends by means of additional telephone credit and time, and the option of 'Purple Visits' in place of social visits. Gestures such as additional telephone credit and time are seen by the Board as being positive in supporting the prisoners in managing themselves through this ongoing crisis.

Despite the restrictions and limited movements between establishments, the loss and/or mismanagement of property has, surprisingly, still been a negative issue for prisoners. This has been reflected in applications to the Board and we are aware that this is still a huge ongoing issue on a nationwide level.

### How well are prisoners' health and wellbeing needs met?

It is the opinion of the Board that the prison has been extremely well managed within the circumstances and constraints of the pandemic. All possible consideration has been given to the wellbeing of prisoners, and as a result they have behaved and conformed very well. Ongoing and regular communications as to the reasons behind any new restrictions have been effective, with prisoners understanding why the restrictions have been in place.

The Board does have serious reservations over the long term with regard to prisoners being in their cell for the majority of each day and the impact on their mental health, in both the short and long term.

### How well are prisoners progressed towards successful resettlement?

The Board is very aware of the impact on resettlement objectives since the implementation of changes to probation services, in particular the loss of some six probation staff who previously worked within HMP Humber.

The ongoing reunification of the community

rehabilitation company and the probation service seems to have created specific issues while in transition, concerning the process for the organisation of post-release prisoner accommodation.

We have identified the particular challenge between obtaining confirmation of a release date and the willingness of partners to allocate or reserve accommodation without a specified date. The loss of the onsite ability to communicate and engage freely with colleagues and prisoners will, it seems, have an unintended but adverse effect on HMP Humber's drive for positive resettlement outcomes.

## Main areas for development
### TO THE MINISTER

The Prison Service, on the whole, has managed the process of safeguarding the staff and prisoners within its care well. However, the impact of the restrictions imposed upon prisons, together with those within them, cannot be overstated. The Board has grave concerns about the potential for long-term damage to the prisoners. We are keen to hear from the Minister about the proposals she has to address this, as restrictions are removed.

As a Board, we have great concerns with the Prison Service losing operational staff to similar uniformed, salaried employment within other government organisations which pay higher salaries with enhanced conditions of employment. The prison is currently losing experienced staff officers faster than it can recruit replacements. This vacancy factor was a foreseeable and preventable situation which has inevitably resulted in poorer outcomes for prisoners. We urge the minister to re-establish competitive pay and conditions for prison staff.

The reunification of probation services on 26 June 2021 has led to the transfer of the majority of staff working within the through-the-gate team from the prison to the community. This has resulted in only one person working within the prison itself, whose role is to deal only with bank accounts (see section 7.5). Although there is a new outreach service based in the community, there is little capacity for any preparation for release programmes or processes within the prison. Prison staff are currently not able to monitor the number of prisoners released into the community with suitable housing and employment. Given the vibrant nature of the resettlement provision within HMP Humber prior to the Covid-19 pandemic, the Board feels that the loss of this provision is of grave concern for those in custody at HMP Humber.

### TO THE PRISON SERVICE

The Board is disappointed to note that there has been little, if any, practical response to the comments raised in the preceding report.

As the pandemic has continued, the Board would have hoped that the Prison Service would have demonstrated greater flexibility in its approach to HMP Humber rather than retain the rigid adherence to stated stages of recovery imposed across the prison estate.

While the Board hopes that the circumstances of the pandemic are not repeated, it feels that the Governor and SMT should be afforded greater autonomy in responding to the demands of the situation. This would enable them to respond appropriately, taking into account the size and geography of the institution and the needs of the prisoners and staff, and to proceed at a pace that is right for them, rather than being constrained by a national framework.

The Board is concerned to learn that among the proposals to increase the capacity of the site is a proposal to increase the number of shared cells. The Board is strongly of the opinion that detaining prisoners in shared cells for long periods of time is not decent, and we would urge the Prison Service to reconsider.

The loss of prisoners' property, both within the prison and during prison transfers, is continuing on a regular basis. The Board believes that the current level of property losses between prisons continues to be especially unacceptable. The Board has raised concerns around property loss in our annual reports for several years. However, we have still not seen any notable improvement in performance (see section 5.8). It causes stress to the individuals affected and also significant additional work for the prison staff, together with unnecessary costs to the tax payer.

### TO THE GOVERNOR

The Board acknowledges the continued excellent and challenging work by the Governor and SMT in their ongoing commitment to building a recovery plan as a result of the Covid-19 pandemic, maintaining the stability of HMP Humber and everyone who works and resides there, and in managing the frustrations due to continued setbacks. The overall stability of the prison has been maintained because of good relationships between prisoners and staff, which demonstrates strong leadership.

As a Board, we wish to raise following areas of concern:
• Key workers: While we understand that the effectiveness of the key worker process has been compromised due to the Covid-19 restrictions and staff shortages, we would urge the Governor

to make it a high priority to re-establish this excellent initiative as soon as possible.

• Complaints: Again, while we appreciate the effect of the Covid-19 restrictions and staff shortages, we would welcome the continuation of robust assurance checks on maintaining good, quality responses to prisoners' complaints.

• Property: We are pleased to note that a more proactive approach in addressing property loss within the prison was taken in the latter part of 2021. As a Board, we continue to be concerned with property losses and cell clearance, and will continue to monitor this situation and improvements.

The Board appreciates the regular updates from the Governor and welcomes the opportunity to discuss matters on an ongoing monthly basis.

## Progress since the last report

While the Board, again, feels it inappropriate to comment on progress, as much, if any, progress made has probably been lost because of the restricted regime, we wish to mention the following positive occurrences:

• Increased use of tele-medicine (health-related services via electronic telecom technologies) has taken place over the year as a result of ongoing restrictions and trying to achieve more efficient ways of working;

• In Cell Education/Entertainment television (ICE TV) was installed and accessible over the entire prison in April 2021. It has proved itself to be an excellent communication vehicle and a very successful way of disseminating HMP Humber-specific information, education and entertainment to all prisoners, and is particularly useful at a time when movement and normal channels of communication are limited;

• Purple Visits have been an excellent way to achieve communication links with family and friends over a prolonged period, also reducing the infection risks associated with Omicron.

**NUFFIELD**
**HENLEY ON THAMES**
**OXFORDSHIRE**
**RG9 5SB**

**Tel: 01491 643100**

*For the latest reports on this prison please visit:*
https://tinyurl.com/bdfh26rv

*Important Changes:* **(1) Visits:** the identification necessary to access this prison and visit for social or professional purposes has changed; (2) **Money and Gifts** new rules now apply to these. See page 16 for full details of the above.

**Task of the establishment** Category C foreign national prison.

**Certified normal accommodation and operational capacity**
Prisoners held at the time of this visit: 403
Baseline certified normal capacity: 480
In-use certified normal capacity: 391
Operational capacity: 480

**Prison status and key providers**
Public
Prison Group: South Central
Prison Group Director: Andy Lattimore
Governor/Director: David Redhouse
IMB Chair: John Evans
Physical health provider: Practice Plus Group
Mental health provider: Practice Plus Group
Substance use treatment provider:
Practice Plus Group
Prison education framework provider:
Milton Keynes College
Escort contractor: Serco/GeoAmey for serving prisoners; Mitie for immigration detainees

**Brief history** The site was originally built as an internment camp. After World War II the site opened as a prison and was a Borstal until 1983. In 2000 Huntercombe became a prison for male juveniles aged 15 to 18. In November 2010 the establishment re-roled to an adult category C training prison and since March 2012 it has held solely category C foreign national prisoners, one of two prisons of this type.

**Short description of residential units** The establishment has eight units. Patterson, Rich, Howard and Fry Units have an older style layout, with two levels and four closed spurs. Mountbatten A and B Units have a newer open layout on two levels and Mountbatten C comprises 26 portable cabins in a horseshoe formation. The segregation unit has five cells including one constant watch suite. Patterson Unit is the induction unit, Rich Unit is for enhanced prisoners and all other units consist of regular accommodation.

**Visiting Information**
Book online at: www.gov.uk/prison-visits
**Visiting times:** Monday, Thursday, Saturday, Sunday: 2pm to 4pm.

**Legal visits:** Legal visits are on Tuesday and Thursday mornings and can be booked by email: legalvisits.huntercombe@justice.gov.uk

**INSPECTIONS & REPORTS**
**Scrutiny visit: 1 and 8–9 December 2020**
**Published: 19 January 2021**

HMP Huntercombe is a category C prison in Oxfordshire and is one of only two prisons in the country with the sole purpose of holding convicted foreign nationals. It held about 400 men at the time of our visit, 15% less than at the previous full inspection in 2017 and slightly more than the uncrowded capacity of 370 prisoners. Lower prisoner numbers contributed to the ability of staff to deliver a consistent regime throughout the pandemic and prisoners were able to have a shower and take outside exercise every day. However, most still spent 23 hours a day in their cells, and this was affecting mental health for some. About a quarter of prisoners had some form of employment, which increased time out of cell, but there were missed opportunities for further expanding activity in a safe way. This was partly because the prison had to wait for the approval of centrally managed recovery plans.

The speedy and highly effective roll-out of video-calling technology had helped prisoners to maintain family relationships throughout the pandemic and showed what the prison was capable of achieving. The governor provided visible and enabling leadership, characterised by clear communication and regular personal engagement with prisoners and staff. A high proportion of staff said that they were supported by managers. Managers and staff had met the demands of Covid-19 well and most prisoners felt that they had been kept safe during the pandemic. There had been no outbreaks since the height of the first wave of the pandemic in April until early December, when a positive test was returned. It was notable that, throughout the pandemic, senior managers had maintained focus on the recommendations for improvement that had been identified at the last full inspection in 2017.

Reception and cohorting arrangements for new arrivals appeared to be effective. Like the rest of the prison, the reception area was clean and a comprehensive assessment process was undertaken for arriving prisoners.

Recorded violence and use of force had remained reasonably low, and well-attended monthly meetings provided adequate strategic oversight of safety. However, a fifth of prisoners in our survey said they felt unsafe and a third that they had been victimised by staff. The latter proportion was higher among both younger and black and minority ethnic prisoners. The reasons for this were unclear, but prisoners made a range of comments about staff, including dismissive attitudes to their concerns about the amount of time locked up, anxiety about immigration cases and concern about inconsistent social distancing. Despite the many friendly interactions that we observed, a number of prisoners said that staff were not always proactive in supporting them and that key work sessions were often not detailed or helpful enough. We leave the prison with a recommendation to explore these findings thoroughly and take necessary action.

There had been no deaths in custody since our full inspection and levels of self-harm had remained at their traditionally low levels. Prisoners at risk of self-harm were supported through a well implemented assessment, care in custody and teamwork case management of prisoners at risk of suicide or self-harm (ACCT) process, which included multidisciplinary case reviews and regular use of professional interpreters. Access to Listeners (prisoners trained by the Samaritans to provide confidential emotional support to fellow prisoners) had been facilitated throughout the pandemic. Prisoners reported that staff usually responded quickly to emergency cell bells.

The physical environment was clean and cells were in good order. Prisoner cleaners and 'social distancing champions' were deployed to clean high contact points between cohorts of prisoners being let out of their cells. Management of complaints was effective and prisoner consultation had resumed. Access to legal advice was good. Home Office staff had remained on site and were accessible. The use of the prison incentives scheme to sanction prisoners who were considered to be non-compliant with the Home Office was inappropriate. The prison was following a national policy which allowed the prisons' incentive scheme to be used to sanction prisoners for non- compliance. Prisoners had a right to challenge the Home Office about immigration matters and should not have been sanctioned by the prison for refusing to sign immigration paperwork. This also confused the prison's role, in managing and caring for prisoners, with Home Office procedures.

Equality and diversity management structures were in place and good work had been carried out to understand potential equality concerns, although not always to deliver actions. The chaplaincy remained active and had resumed running small faith groups for religious discussion. Health care was effective. Despite staff shortages, the well managed department continued to deliver essential services. Waiting lists were short for most clinics and external hospital appointments had continued to be facilitated throughout the pandemic. The mental health team provided a responsive one-to-one service and was meeting the demand for services.

At our full inspection in 2017, a serious concern was the poor attention to addressing risk, offending- related needs and release planning. At this scrutiny visit, we were pleased to find that a changed attitude to this area of work had led to very significant and sustained progress. Contact levels between prison offender managers and prisoners had much improved and most prisoners were now well aware of their sentence plan targets. The vast majority of prisoners had an up-to-date OASys (offender assessment of risk and need). While there were still shortcomings in the specialist resettlement support available to prisoners, there were well developed and funded plans to create a resettlement hub to help prisoners manage practical problems, such as housing and debt management, which are known to increase the risk of reoffending. This support was to be available to prisoners being removed to other countries, who constituted the vast majority of discharges. Perhaps most impressively, release on temporary licence (ROTL) had become established to support rehabilitation and family contact, and it had continued during the Covid-19 period. There had been no ROTL failures.

In summary, this is one of the most positive scrutiny visits that we have so far undertaken. The prison was well led and progressive and, while we have identified some concerns that need to be addressed, prisoners generally spoke positively of their experiences at Huntercombe. The prison and HM Prison and Probation Service leadership are to be commended for the work they have done to respond to long-standing shortcomings in rehabilitation and release planning. We look forward in due course to seeing the further development of this work.

Charlie Taylor, HM Chief Inspector of Prisons
December 2020

## Key concerns and recommendations

Key concerns and recommendations identify the issues of most importance to improving outcomes for prisoners and are designed to help establishments prioritise and address the most significant weaknesses in the treatment and conditions of prisoners.

Key concern: In our survey, a third of prisoners said they had been victimised by staff; this was reported by significantly more younger prisoners and those from a black and minority ethnic background. The reasons for these findings were unclear, but prisoners commented on dismissive attitudes by staff to their concerns about the time they spent locked up, worries about immigration cases, and concern about inconsistent social distancing.

Recommendation: Managers should carry out a thorough investigation into prisoners' reports of staff victimisation, focusing in particular on black and minority ethnic and younger prisoners, and implement a suitable response. (To the Governor)

Key concern: The incentives scheme was being used inappropriately to sanction prisoners who were in dispute with the Home Office over immigration status claims. The prison's role of managing and caring for prisoners had become confused with Home Office procedures.

Recommendation: Prisoners' rights to dispute identity claims should be upheld and the incentives scheme should not be used to sanction prisoners who are in dispute with the Home Office over immigration claims.
(To Home Office immigration staff and HMPPS)

Key concern: Most prisoners were still locked in their cells for about 23 hours a day. Some progress had been made in resuming purposeful activity, but there were missed opportunities for increasing activity in a safe way. Not all workshops had reopened even though they provided adequate space for socially distanced activity.

Recommendation: Managers should ensure that opportunities for safely increasing education and employment activities are fully explored and that suitable action to increase time out of cell is implemented as soon as possible.
(To the Governor)

## Notable positive practice

We define notable positive practice as innovative practice or practice that leads to particularly good outcomes from which other establishments may be able to learn. Inspectors look for evidence of good outcomes for prisoners; original, creative or particularly effective approaches to problem-solving or achieving the desired goal; and how other establishments could learn from or replicate the practice.

Inspectors found the following examples of notable positive practice during this visit.

• The assessment, care in custody and teamwork case management of prisoners at risk of suicide or self-harm (ACCT) system was used well to support prisoners. Staff often demonstrated an understanding of the impact of the restricted regime on prisoners and responded to them with compassion. We saw documented examples of meaningful conversations showing an understanding of the prisoner's state of mind and personal circumstances. Each ACCT that we reviewed was purposeful, with a clearly documented reason for its inception and a plan to support the prisoner. Staff from the induction wing met prisoners in reception who arrived with an existing ACCT to see how they were feeling, discuss their care and offer extra support.

• The social distancing champions scheme

implemented by the prison was effective in encouraging staff and prisoners to maintain distance and reminding them of the risks. The champions also supported wing cleaners by sanitising high-contact points on the wings throughout the day.

• A legal surgery run by a local firm of solicitors had continued to offer legal advice to prisoners remotely throughout the pandemic. Although it did not provide legal advice, the charity Asylum Welcome also provided support on immigration matters using video-call.

• A range of self-help resources included a particularly helpful booklet entitled 'Living with Lockdown', which had been translated into Albanian, Romanian, Spanish and Polish to help prisoners to use coping strategies.

• There had been a speedy, safe and highly effective roll-out of video-calling technology to help prisoners to maintain family relationships throughout the pandemic. Prisoners were positive about the operation and delivery of the service. They reported fewer concerns than we have seen elsewhere about screen-freezing and loss of conversation time. Take- up was higher than anywhere else in the prison estate.

• The introduction and sustained use of release on temporary licence (ROTL) throughout the pandemic was notable and provided positive outcomes for prisoners to support their resettlement. There had been no ROTL failures.

• There had been very significant progress in rehabilitation and release planning services, including improved resources in the offender management unit and a funded resettlement service for prisoners who were being discharged to other countries.

## INDEPENDENT MONITORING BOARD: Annual Report

The law requires every prison to be monitored by an independent Board appointed by the Justice Secretary; these are known as Independent Monitoring Boards (IMBs). The IMB must satisfy itself as to the humane and just treatment of those held in custody within its prison and the range and adequacy of the programmes preparing them for release; it must report annually to the Justice Secretary on how well the prison has met the standards and requirements placed on it.

**IMB Report 1 January 2021 – 31 December 2021**
**Published June 2022**
**Executive Summary**
**Background to the report**
2021 was a difficult and sad year for the Board at Huntercombe. John Evans, our very experienced Chair of several years, whilst hopeful of making

a full recovery from an operation he had at the end of 2020, remained on extended sick leave throughout the year until his sad death in October 2021.

The ongoing situation surrounding Covid-19 continued to impact on both the management of prisons nationally and the ability of Boards to monitor flexibly and efficiently throughout 2021. Due to the Chair's ill-health the Board at Huntercombe commenced the reporting year with only three active members. Members of the Board attended the prison for monitoring throughout the year apart from a period between 23 January 2021 and 18 February 2021 when no visits took place.

Huntercombe was an outbreak prison from the beginning of the year until 12 March when it was at stage 3 of the national regime. From this point the prison gradually progressed and 'opened up' in line with Ministry of Justice (MoJ) guidance, though a limited regime has continued to operate, including wing- based association time; use of the main gym has been dependent upon the regime stage and all workshops were open in a limited capacity by August. The prison arrived at stage 1 a few days before the end of the year. Unfortunately, due to the continued transfer of prisoners from other outbreak establishments, Huntercombe was once again declared an outbreak prison on the last day of the calendar year.

Despite the fact that a considerable number of staff, both experienced and inexperienced, had not been offered a vaccination due to their age until the year was well advanced, the senior management team and prison staff are to be commended for their efforts to enable all the prisoners to attend as many activities and as much time out of cell as possible through these difficult months.

**Main judgements**
**How safe is the prison?**
The Board considers that the prison is a safe environment for prisoners.

**How fairly and humanely are prisoners treated?**
The Board believes that in general prisoners are treated fairly and humanely in so far as the Covid restrictions of the national regime have allowed throughout the year.

The exception is the ongoing incarceration of men who have passed their sentence expiry date and are held under immigration powers (IS91s) who remain under convicted criminal conditions.

**How well are prisoners' health and wellbeing needs met?**
Covid cases were dealt with well and kept to a bare minimum, enabling the prison to finally

reach stage 1 of the national regime just before the end of the reporting year, unfortunately then for the virus to exponentially take hold following the transfer into the prison of prisoners from several outbreak prisons. Staff and prisoner uptake of the national vaccination programme gradually increased throughout the year. There were some difficulties experienced by prisoners in access to NHS services, but this was similar to the situation outside the prison. During 2022 the Board will be seeking an improvement in the way information about prisoners' health is shared with prison staff in a timely and consistent way.

### How well are prisoners progressed towards successful resettlement?

A resettlement budget awarded to the prison at the end of 2020 has allowed for considerable improvements for prisoners to be progressed towards resettlement. However, due to the lack of resettlement programmes and courses which are available in the wider prison estate, which include internationally recognised accreditations, progress towards successful resettlement remains limited.

### Main areas for development
### TO THE MINISTER

Together with Home Office colleagues, to resolve the issue of men continuing to be held under immigration powers post-sentence under convicted criminal conditions.

To ensure that the Home Office and the Prison Service work together to issue prisoners with an IS91 notification in accordance with the time limits set out in the service level agreement (SLA) with Home Office Immigration Enforcement (HOIE).

### TO THE PRISON SERVICE

To formulate a standard practice across the entire prison estate for the volumetric allowance and timely transfer of property between prisons, and for all prisons to have a consistent and agreed list of the articles available in-possession according to the prisoner's incentives status.

### TO THE GOVERNOR

The Board has been informed by prisoners on multiple occasions in the past and throughout the reporting year of the unsatisfactory condition of the showers in all locations in Huntercombe, water temperature and low pressure being the constant laments.

For a more robust audit system to be operated as regards the complaints log, and for complaints beyond their response date to be consistently pursued.

To develop a process with healthcare to ensure there is documented sharing of appropriate health information with prison staff.

### Progress since the last report

By the end of the reporting year in-cell telephony had been installed and was about to be fully operational.

The resettlement budget was awarded and the hub was fully operational from the commencement of January 2021.

Video calls continue to be a particularly successful, and highly commendable facility especially for foreign nationals who might otherwise have little or no contact with family and friends overseas.

A body scanner was installed in reception in mid-July 2021.

**WESTERN WAY**
**THAMESMEAD**
**LONDON**
**SE28 0NZ**

**HMP YOI ISIS**

**TEL: 020 3356 4000**

*For the latest reports on this prison please visit:*
https://tinyurl.com/bdfh26rv

*Important Changes:* **(1) Visits:** the identification necessary to access this prison and visit for social or professional purposes has changed; (2) **Money and Gifts** new rules now apply to these. See page 16 for full details of the above.

**Task of the establishment** A young adult and category C training prison for young adult and adult males.

**Certified normal accommodation and operational capacity**
Prisoners held at the time of inspection: 612
Baseline certified normal capacity: 478
In-use certified normal capacity: 478
Operational capacity: 628

**Prison status and key providers**
Public
Prison Group: London
Prison Group Director: Ian Bickers
Governor/Director: Emily Thomas
IMB Chair: Maureen Lewis
Physical health provider: Oxleas NHS Foundation Trust
Mental health provider: Oxleas NHS Foundation Trust
Substance misuse provider: Oxleas Interventions
Learning and skills provider: Novus
Escort contractor: Serco

**Brief history** HMP/YOI Isis in South East London was the first young adult and category C training prison for young men and adults in the

London region. Constructed within the perimeter of HMP Belmarsh, it received its first prisoners on 26 July 2010. Young adult prisoners who turn 21 can remain to continue their sentence, if this in the interest of successful completion of their sentence plan and they are intending to resettle locally. Isis is the first whole-build public sector prison to be built in the last 20 years. In December 2016, the age cap of 18–30 was lifted, allowing prisoners of all ages to be transferred to Isis.

**Short description of residential units** The two house blocks, Thames and Meridian, are of a similar size, with four spurs radiating from a central hub and three landings on each spur. On average, there is accommodation for about 80 prisoners on each spur in a mixture of single and double cells. There are also a few fully-equipped cells for prisoners with disabilities.

**Visiting Information**
Isis is running a limited visits schedule. Visits are also happening differently than normal, observing strict guidelines, which must be followed.
Visits are only booked by prisoners via digital application on CMS computer.
**Visiting times:** Monday to Thursday: 2:30pm to 4:30pm, Saturday and Sunday: 2:30pm to 4pm

**Legal visits:** Legal visits are available on: Monday to Thursday: 2:30pm to 3:30pm and 3:45pm to 4:45pm. Book a legal visit by emailing legalvisitsisis@justice.gov.uk or call: 0203 356 4030 / 0203 356 4034

**INSPECTIONS & REPORTS**
**Date of last full inspection** 23 July–2 August 2018
**HMCIP Report, published 18 December 2018**
HMP/YOI Isis is a category C training prison in South East London which sits within the wall line of the high security Belmarsh prison. At the time of our inspection, Isis held just over 600 convicted prisoners. Almost 70% of the population were under 30 and 22% were under 21 years old. Nearly half of those held were serving over four years.
Our last inspection of Isis in 2016 was disappointing. At the time we recorded insufficient progress and a failure to attend to the delivery of some basic services. We were particularly critical of a restricted regime first put in place in 2013 which was still in operation when we inspected three years later. Restrictions persisted but, reassuringly, improvements had been made and the average number of prisoners locked up during the working day had reduced to 22% of the population compared to 40% last time. Prisoners also had better access to domestic

activities and association time, which included evening association for those on the enhanced wing. The prison again talked about plans to introduce and improve the regime, although at this inspection the plans seemed more credible as staffing numbers had improved significantly.
The current governor took up post shortly after our last inspection and had clearly prioritised getting the basics right, with visible leadership evident and a more positive culture beginning to emerge. The prison had been authorised to conduct a local recruitment campaign to recruit prison officers, instead of relying on the usual national campaign which sometimes displaced people from their home areas and created long commutes. The governor believed that this local recruitment had enabled her to appoint a team of officers more committed to the aims of her establishment. The influx of new staff clearly brought its own challenges, with 80% of the staff group still in their first year of service, but the governor commendably saw this as a long-term opportunity for the prison and not a hindrance.
Similar to other prisons holding significant numbers of young people, levels of violence at HMP/YOI Isis had increased and were high. One in four prisoners in our survey reported feeling unsafe, but the senior team had introduced a number of initiatives aimed at reducing violence and encouraging good behaviour. The quality of investigations of violent incidents had improved significantly, systems to identify and deal with gang activity were well managed, and relationships with the local police were very good. Additionally, the governor was clearly focused on tackling any potential staff corruption. New behaviour management processes designed to deal with the most complex individuals were promising, although it was a little too early to see their benefits. Concerted effort had been made to encourage good behaviour, including the introduction of an enhanced unit, peer support roles and opportunities for release on temporary licence (ROTL). All departments were working together to try to tackle drug misuse.
It was vital that this commendable initiative and effort was sustained. Our survey of those held was very negative around two critical areas: only 48% of respondents said that most staff treated them with respect, and only 46% could say that they had not experienced any kind of victimisation by staff. Important recent steps had been taken by the senior team to deal with staff who contributed to the negative experiences of prisoners, but more work was needed to understand and address these negative perceptions. Our own observations and discussions with prisoners about staff, in contrast, were more positive. Indeed, we were

encouraged by the energy and commitment of many staff we met. Most prisoners spoke about 'good officers' they could talk to if they needed help. Prison staff and managers had received hundreds of letters of thanks from prisoners they had helped through difficult times.

Living conditions had improved since our last inspection. Communal areas and most external areas were clean and well presented. Prisoners were encouraged to clean their cells and there was little graffiti and few offensive pictures on display. The governor and a team of her staff also hosted regular 'think tank' meetings with prisoners to discuss ways to improve conditions at the prison. However, our visit took place during the summer heatwave and inspectors were struck by the oppressive heat in some of the cells that had no curtains or fans to lower the temperature. One of our most serious concerns was around the use of force, which we were not assured was always justified. We identified a need for more rigorous scrutiny of when and how force was applied. When there had been a failure to turn on body-worn cameras, de-escalate incidents, or complete important assurance paperwork, governance arrangements did not robustly challenge this. Some of the youngest prisoners are often the most vulnerable and yet they were disproportionately represented in the statistics relating to force and segregation.

We were disappointed that very little had been done to achieve the main recommendation made at the last inspection concerning the prison's management of equality and diversity, and we have been compelled to make a similar main recommendation in this report. The diverse population at Isis demands more flexibility in the application of policy to ensure that difference is recognised and understood. We were particularly concerned about adverse outcomes for foreign national and young prisoners. The establishment needed to do more to understand the distinct needs of these groups on arrival at the prison and dedicate resources to ensuring that their needs were met. In the case of young prisoners, a greater understanding of the developmental needs of young people still going through the process of maturation was required. Prisoners still did not spend enough time in education or training, and those on vocational courses often did not have time to gain accredited qualifications. Poor attendance and punctuality contributed significantly to Ofsted's judgement that the overall effectiveness of education, skills and work required improvement. Prisoners were supported to build and maintain family ties, but a shortfall of offender assessment system (OASys) assessments impacted prisoners' ability to

progress through their sentence. Offender management and the quality of supervision were mixed and there were weaknesses in public protection arrangements. Support for care leavers and resettlement planning were, however, better.

Our assessments have remained largely unchanged since the last inspection, although this was not the whole story. We noted an encouraging change in direction since the appointment of the current governor and the culture and atmosphere in the prison were definitely improving. We left the prison confident that the senior managers and staff would use our report to effect further positive change, particularly in those areas which caused us most concern.

Peter Clarke CVO OBE QPM September 2018
HM Chief Inspector of Prisons

## INDEPENDENT MONITORING BOARD: Annual Report

The law requires every prison to be monitored by an independent Board appointed by the Justice Secretary; these are known as Independent Monitoring Boards (IMBs). The IMB must satisfy itself as to the humane and just treatment of those held in custody within its prison and the range and adequacy of the programmes preparing them for release; it must report annually to the Justice Secretary on how well the prison has met the standards and requirements placed on it.

**IMB Report 1 January 2021 – 31 December 2021**
**Published May 2022**
**Executive Summary**
**Background to the report**

Evidence comes from a range of sources including observations made on visits, the scrutiny of records and data, attendance at prison meetings, informal contact with prisoners and staff and communication with prisoners following applications made to the Board. The Covid pandemic has continued to affect the Board's monitoring practice. For the first half of the year meetings were held virtually, but the Board adopted a hybrid approach to monitoring, with some members visiting the prison and others gathering information remotely. The Board remains grateful for the helpful cooperation of prison staff at all levels within the establishment. During the year, particularly as the prison moved to Covid-19 Stage 1 in October, the prison introduced fundamental changes to prison life. The impact of these changes on outcomes for prisoners cannot yet be fully assessed. In this report we identify early progress and potential future issues.

**Main judgements**

**How safe is the prison?**

Arguably the pandemic has been the greatest risk to safety within the prison in 2021. The handling of the pandemic is determined by Her Majesty's Prisons and Probation Service (HMPPS), with the prison developing detailed exceptional delivery models (EDMs) relating to changes in the regime and the operation of the prison. Restrictions on the prison regime were in place until the prison moved to Stage 1 in October, when it was possible to relax some of the measures.

Staff in reception have been well organised for new arrivals, and prisoners are treated with decency and respect throughout the check-in and searching procedures. First night procedures are well organised. Induction sessions have been greatly affected throughout the year; many sessions by departments and agencies are conducted by telephone and some by prisoner-led mentors.

The number of assessment, care in custody and teamwork (ACCT) documents opened during 2021 decreased to an average of 12 per month (or a total of 148 for the year – down from 182 in 2020). There was a disturbing rise in self-harm during the year with 412 reported incidents compared to 277 during the same period in 2020. There were significant reports of self-harm in March (61), April (57) and May (73). The figures are somewhat distorted by a small number of prisoners with mental health conditions or personality disorders, who often self-harmed eight or more times a month.

There was a steadily increasing trend of violence during the year. On average there were 19 prisoner assaults or fights reported each month and an average of 11 assaults on staff each month. Part of this increase can be attributed to a younger population, where over 90% of the prisoners were 25 years old or younger by year end. They typically account for 98% of the violence. Use of force (staff assaults, prisoner assaults and fights) showed an increasing trend across the year, with use of force increasing by 24% over the course of the year. There was a total of 370 violent incidents during the year, considerably higher than 2020 (184 incidents) and higher than pre-lockdown 2019 (311 incidents).

During the year, 370 items of contraband, including drugs, and 159 weapons were found.

**How fairly and humanely are prisoners treated?**

The standards of hygiene and cleanliness are generally good, and the improvements reported in 2020 have been maintained.

An average of 32 prisoners were segregated each month in 2021 (the monthly average was 34 in 2020). There were 382 prisoners segregated during 2021, of whom 128 (114 in 2020) were young adults; this increase is probably a reflection of the changing age of the population. Four prisoners were held in the unit for more than 42 days. There were 62 prisoners held under GOAD rules, and of these 22 were young adults. The periods of hybrid monitoring made it difficult for an IMB member to be present at GOAD reviews during much of 2021, and this was exacerbated by the move away from a regular time for the reviews.

In most aspects of prison life, the treatment of men from Black, Asian and minority ethnic (BAME) backgrounds and other protected categories is within the expected range when compared to the prison population as a whole. In 2021 the number of discrimination incident reporting forms (DIRFs) submitted increased to 41, and of these six were upheld and two partially upheld, a significant increase on previous years and perhaps an indication of prisoners' increased confidence in the process. In 2021 the prison introduced a recruitment process for jobs that is managed centrally by allocations staff. Prisoners must apply for jobs, and those who meet the specification are interviewed.

For most of the year faith services could not be held. Where faith services have been possible, these have been restricted to one spur weekly for each faith, meaning prisoners have only been able to attend their faith service once every eight weeks. However, chaplains have continued to give pastoral care, work with prisoners with complex needs and offer time out of cell prayers in the multi-faith suite whenever possible.

The majority of prisoners' property arrives with them from other prisons but, despite the efforts of staff, there are too many occasions when prisoners' property is not recovered. In its 2020 reply to the issue of property, HMPPS said that a framework 'will be published later this year, which will provide greater direction and standardisation on a national basis and has been designed with procedural justice at its core'. This has not happened.

**How well are prisoners' health and wellbeing needs met?**

During 2021, Oxleas NHS Foundation Trust has spent a significant amount of time responding to the challenges of the pandemic, including testing staff and prisoners and encouraging and providing vaccinations. During this period services continued to be provided including: a 24-hour 7 day a week service with emergency response, GP service, pharmacy services and houseblock medication services, daily input into the segregation unit, attendance at ACCT reviews (mental health led), an internal X- ray service and a dental service. The mental health team continued to provide one to one supportive primary and secondary mental health services. There has been a steady increase during the year of prisoners accessing the range of mental health services, including the in-reach team that treats those with serious enduring illness, psychological therapies and interventions for those who misuse and or are addicted to drugs or alcohol. The total caseload grew from 387 at the beginning of the year to 439 in September.

The Board has previously expressed its concern that, though healthcare and prison staff are committed to helping and supporting prisoners with chronic and enduring mental illness, prison is not the environment that will deliver improvements in these prisoners' conditions. This continues to be the Board's view, though the psychological therapies model does support the care of those with mental illness. Despite the good practice model for the transfer of prisoners under the Mental Health Act referred to by the Minister in his response to last year's annual report, there have been examples this year of prisoners waiting too long to be moved to an NHS facility. An example is a prisoner who has had to be kept in the segregation unit for 40 days, because it is the only safe place to hold him, whilst he waits for an NHS place.

### How well are prisoners progressed towards successful resettlement?

The prison provides 192 spaces in education over 10 courses for the 600+ prisoners held at Isis. Since the Covid restrictions were introduced, education opportunities have been delivered through the provision of graded in-cell learning packs to be completed individually by the learners for 7.5 hours. The men are supported through calls made on the in-cell telephones by tutors and a 2.5 hour 1-1 or 1-2 tutor session. Education representatives have been introduced to support prisoners to access and maintain their learning. During the recent restrictions in December 202, all face-to- face teaching was again cancelled, with a total return to in-cell packs. Return of these by prisoners for assessment by teachers was minimal. Following the expected return in January 2022 to the new style of learning offered by the academy, it will be important for the prison to monitor and assess whether the removal of most face-to- face teaching results in improved academic outcomes for the prisoners.

Attendance at education or skills workshop sessions has been low, approximately 50% since returning from lockdown. For English and maths, whether prisoners need to start at entry level or a higher level qualification is normally determined through the induction process, but this process has been significantly negatively impacted by the lockdown regimes. Ofsted visited the prison in July for a progress monitoring visit. Progress was judged to be reasonable. The IMB concurs with the report's recommendations of the need to improve the induction process for prisoners so that their access to education is faster-paced and more closely aligned to their needs.

The range of work opportunities available to prisoners includes houseblock orderlies, orderlies for visits, induction and reception, serveries, library, chapel, horticulture, education, skills and gym, Listeners, wing representatives and a range of representative and mentor roles. These had all resumed during the autumn, but were removed again in December due to the Omicron outbreak.

The offender management unit (OMU) has again had to deal with prisoners arriving at Isis without an OASys report. Prisons receiving those convicted from the courts are resourced to provide an OASys report for prisoners. This is not the case for Isis. This means that prison offender managers spend time completing these rather than on pre-release or other work. At the end of 2021 there were 85 outstanding OASys reports.

Throughout the year there have been long delays moving prisoners to other establishments following recategorisation. However, the situation improved later in the year. At the end of 2021 there were 29 prisoners waiting for transfer to category D establishments. The movement between prisons and the provision of transport is managed centrally, and some additional delays have been caused by Covid-related issues. But it also appears that prisoners were not being moved as a part of wider population management across the prison estate. The IMB questions whether this is a sound reason for prisoners who have achieved category D status not being moved to open conditions where they can focus on activities that will improve the success of their resettlement on release.

A combination of limitations and restrictions within the prison and in the wider employment and housing markets because of the pandemic, together with changes in the way resettlement is managed for those leaving prison, means that it has been difficult to assess how well prisoners are prepared for and seen through release and resettlement. Within the prison there is a lack of up-to-date statistics, partly because of the difficulties of collating these figures from different organisations in the community.

## Main areas for development
### TO THE MINISTER
• Require the Prison Service to deliver the policy framework for handling prisoners' property that has been promised for so many years.
• Education and work are central to the aims of the Prisons Strategy White Paper, but an integrated and sustainable programme will be needed if prisoners are to successfully make a life outside prison.

### TO THE PRISON SERVICE
• Publish the new property policy framework referred to in the response to the 2020 annual report and which the Prison Service said would be published in 2021.
• Require prisons receiving prisoners from the courts to complete an OASys report before a prisoner is transferred.
• Put in place arrangements that allow category D prisoners to move to category D prisons without undue delay after they have been recategorised.
• Support the prison to find a long-term solution to the broken cell windows in the prison.
• Provide an assessment of the impact of the changed arrangements for the resettlement of prisoners on their prospects of securing housing, employment and education.

### TO THE GOVERNOR
• As soon as the measures relating to Covid-19 allow, reinstate an induction programme for new arrivals.
• Continue to increase the amount of time spent on key work and keep under review the effectiveness of the 'community-based' approach to key work.
• In year, evaluate whether the 'community-based model' is delivering the benefits anticipated in relation to violence, education and training, attendance at other activities and prisoners' feelings of safety. But also assess the impact of no planned time for association on prisoners.
• Continue to work effectively and proactively with education and vocational training providers to drive up levels of engagement and motivation in education and work-related skills, to ensure that prisoners are fully prepared to enter the world of work upon release.
• Reinstate as soon as possible Christian faith services, so that all denominations can worship on Sundays, and Friday prayers for Muslim prisoners.
• Complete the review of the IEP scheme and introduce any changes.

## Progress since the last report
### Issues raised with the Minister
To require concrete plans to be developed to address the continued detention of prisoners with enduring or chronic mental health problems and those with personality disorders, as a prison environment will not deliver the positive changes needed.
*Response*
The White Paper Reforming the Mental Health Act was published 13 January 2021. (Reforming the Mental Health Act, 13 January 2021, updated 24 August 2021) The Government response, August 2021, provides a commitment to introduce a statutory time limit of 28 days for the transfer to mental health hospitals from custody.
· NHS England and NHS Improvement published good practice guidance on 10 June 2021 that sets the timeframe for completing the assessment, transfer and remission of individuals detained under the Mental Health Act.
· The mental health service specification will be reviewed; due to be implemented 2021/22.
· The National Partnership Agreement for Prison Healthcare in England sets out a co-ordinated approach to deliver safe decent and effective healthcare in prison.

### Issues raised with HMPPS
1. Deliver the 'prisoners' property policy framework' that the Minister stated in response to previous annual reports that HMPPS was planning to publish. Response
The framework will be published later this year (2021), which will provide greater direction and standardisation on a national basis and has been designed with procedural justice at its core. This has not happened.
2. Commission research into the impact of the time spent in cells during the pandemic on the mental health of prisoners.
*Response*
13 studies have been approved by HMPPS National Research Committee. None had reported at time of response (30 June 2021).
3. Future arrangements for education need to reflect that tuition is often necessary with less confident learners, or for some aspects of learning, such as practical skills or complex concepts. Most learners benefit from a range of different approaches, rather than a single method.
*Response*
There are local plans to reintroduce face to face teaching as restrictions ease, but there will still be a blended approach at least in the medium term.

### Issues for the Governor and current position
1. Resume organised physical exercise and access to the gym as soon as conditions permit.

Throughout the year prisoners have had an hour for outdoor exercise in their spur exercise yard. In April the gym reopened, with 14 prisoners from the same cohort attending one session a week; this increased to 20 prisoners in June. In October prisoners had the opportunity to attend three sessions per week, including one session at weekends.

2. Ensure that plans are in place to prevent a return to the levels of self-harm over the first three months of the year (2020), when a normal regime is resumed. Normal regime has not resumed in 2021. There were significant reports of self-harm in March (61), April (57) and May (73) before the numbers started to drop as the regime was relaxed. The figures are somewhat distorted by a small number of prisoners with mental health conditions or personality disorders, who self-harmed eight or more times a month.

3. Ensure that initiatives to reduce violence are focused on the increasing number of young adults, and acknowledge the incidence of bullying.

Levels of violence are of concern and are likely to increase as restrictions are lifted and the number of young men increases as the young adult strategy continues to roll out in 2022.

4. Continue to work hard with Novus to drive up levels of engagement in remote learning during a period when classroom teaching is unlikely to return for several more months.

Attendance at education or skills workshop sessions has been low, approximately 50% since returning from lockdown. There were unfilled spaces on a number of vocational courses and prisoner jobs; there is a perceived reduction in motivation amongst the population to engage in learning or roles of responsibility.

5. Ensure that healthcare complaint forms are easily accessible to all prisoners during the period when time out of cell is severely limited.

Healthcare complaint forms have been available on both houseblocks.

6. Ensure that communication between the offender management unit (OMU) and prisoners about sentence planning, recategorisation and transfers improves as staffing levels increase.

Staffing in the OMU has been tight throughout the year and there have been some examples of poor communications between the unit staff and prisoners.

7. Respond to the findings of the equality survey carried out by the Board, and particularly:
– understand why prisoners feel that jobs are unfairly allocated
– review whether the discrimination incident report form (DIRF) system is an effective means of prisoners reporting discrimination and having their concerns investigated.
· In 2021 the prison introduced a recruitment process for jobs that is managed centrally by allocations staff. Prisoners must apply for jobs, those who meet the specification are interviewed by a panel and if suitable are allocated to the post. · In 2021 the number of DIRFs submitted increased to 41. Of these, six were upheld and two partially upheld.

ALBANY HOUSE
NEWPORT
ISLE OF WIGHT
PO30 5RS

HM PRISON
ISLE OF
WIGHT

Tel: 01983 634000

*For the latest reports on this prison please visit:*
https://tinyurl.com/bdfh26rv

*Important Changes:* **(1) Visits:** the identification necessary to access this prison and visit for social or professional purposes has changed; (2) **Money and Gifts** new rules now apply to these. See page 16 for full details of the above.

**Task of the establishment** HMP Isle of Wight is a category B male training prison predominantly for sex offenders. It also has a small local remand function. The prison holds approximately 1,100 prisoners on two sites with a central administration.

**Certified normal accommodation and operational capacity**
Prisoners held at the time of inspection: 1,029
Baseline certified normal capacity: 1,073
In-use certified normal capacity: 1,065
Operational capacity: 1,085

**Prison status and key providers**
Public
Prison Group: Long Term/High Security
Prison Group Director: Will Styles
Governor/Director: Dougie Graham
IMB Chair: Linda Johnson
Physical health provider: Care UK
Mental health provider: Care UK
Substance misuse provider: Care UK
Dental service provider: Time for Teeth
Learning and skills provider: Milton Keynes College Escort contractor: GeoAmey

**Brief history** HMP Isle of Wight opened in April 2009 with the merger of three prisons: HMP Albany, HMP Parkhurst and HMP Camp Hill. Albany was constructed in the 1960s and occupies the site of a former military barracks. Parkhurst was originally a military hospital and became a prison in 1863. Camp Hill was built in 1912 using prisoner labour from Parkhurst, but closed in April 2013.

## Short description of residential units

Albany – the five original residential units (house blocks 11 to 17) on Albany are identical in design and located off one main corridor. In 2010 a new health care facility opened, replacing the former unit in Parkhurst. House block 15 is currently uninhabited following a fire in January 2015.

Albany has no internal sanitation in cells on house blocks 11 to 15. An electronic night sanitation system is in operation in these units. The remand unit on house block 16 has internal sanitation as does the assisted living unit on house block 17.

Parkhurst – comprises eight residential units, seven of which are Victorian galleried units and the eighth a small former health care unit. There is also a recently refurbished segregation and reintegration unit in a former special secure unit.

## Visiting Information

Book a visit at: www.gov.uk/prison-visits or email: socialvisitsisleofwight@hmps.gsi.gov.uk or by phone on 01983 556573 Mon – Fri 09:00 to 10:00 and 16:30 to 18:30.

**Visiting times:** Monday, Wednesday, Friday, Saturday, Sunday 14:00-16:00

**Legal visits:** Check with the prison for the latest visiting times.

## INSPECTIONS & REPORTS

**Date of last full inspection** 15 April – 2 May 2019
**IRP visit 7–9 January 2020**
**Published: 14 February 2020**

*HMP Isle of Wight - improvements by local managers but lack of support from prison service nationally*
Inspectors revisiting HMP Isle of Wight to review improvement following a full inspection last year found a mixed picture and assessed overall that progress was not good enough.

The training prison holds about 1,000 prisoners across two separate sites, almost all serving long sentences for sexual offences but with a small number on remand. At a full inspection in April–May 2019, its purposeful activity – education, training and work – was assessed as good, but outcomes for prisoners had declined, against the previous inspection in 2015, in the areas of safety and respect and continued not to be sufficiently good in rehabilitation and release planning. At an independent review of progress (IRP) in January 2020, inspectors reviewed progress against 11 key recommendations from the full inspection.

Peter Clarke, HM Chief Inspector of Prisons, said: "Taken as a whole, progress had not been good enough in the majority of areas. There had been good progress in three, reasonable progress in two, insufficient progress in one and no meaningful progress in five areas."

There was a significant difference between how work had progressed in areas local managers had responsibility for and those that required national support from HM Prison and Probation Service (HMPPS).

Local managers had made reasonable or better progress in five out of seven recommendations. In the safety area, this included important work to determine the causes of violence and challenge or support individuals involved in violent incidents. Prison managers had also ensured that staff understood their roles and responsibilities in the event of a medical emergency. However, there continued to be significant weaknesses in the operation of the incentives and rewards policy. In the area of respect, managers had worked well to improve systems for prisoners' applications and redress. Social care had also been improved by the implementation of a Memorandum of Understanding with the local council.

In rehabilitation and release planning, there had been some work to improve oversight of the department and train prison offender managers (POMs).

In contrast to the progress made by local managers, Mr Clarke said, "all four recommendations that required external support from HMPPS had been rejected and so no progress had been made."

These included taking steps to ensure basic standards of decency by reducing overcrowding and ensuring all prisoners had access to a toilet overnight. "During this visit, we found that about 160 prisoners continued to live in overcrowded cells. In addition, most prisoners on the Albany site continued to live in cells without a toilet or sink. Instead they relied on night sanitation, an electronic system that allows prisoners out of their cells individually to use communal facilities overnight."

Mr Clarke continued: "Prisoners, including older and disabled people, were allowed seven minutes to use the facilities, which many said was not long enough. It was not uncommon for prisoners to face a wait of an hour. This meant that many resorted to using a bucket in their cell and effectively 'slopping out' in the morning. This was not an acceptable situation."

HMPPS rejected a recommendation intended to ensure sick prisoners were transferred to a mental health facility in line with national guidelines. Inspectors found that one patient who had been waiting too long for a hospital bed during the inspection was still waiting at the time of the IRP visit eight months later. HMPPS also rejected a recommendation that remand prisoners should be held at an establishment that could meet their needs.

Overall, Mr Clarke said: "This was a mixed review. Local managers had worked well and made progress in some important areas. However, HMPPS needs a change of approach to ensure accommodation meets basic standards and all prisoners receive appropriate support and health care."

**Chief Inspector's summary**

1.1 At our inspection of HMP Isle of Wight in 2019 we made the following judgements about outcomes for prisoners. Figure 3: HMP Isle of Wight healthy prison outcomes 2015 and 2019.

1.2 HMP Isle of Wight is a training prison holding about 1,000 prisoners across two separate sites. Almost all of them were serving long sentences for sexual offences, but the prison was also used to hold a small remand population from the Isle of Wight. The prison was last inspected in April/May 2019. While Ofsted judged the overall effectiveness of education training and work to be good, outcomes for prisoners had declined in the areas of safety and respect and continued not to be sufficiently good in rehabilitation and release planning.

1.3 At this visit, we reviewed progress against 11 key recommendations. Taken as a whole, progress had not been good enough in the majority of areas. There had been good progress in three, reasonable progress in two, insufficient progress in one and no meaningful progress in five areas. However, there was a significant difference between how work had progressed in areas local managers had responsibility for and those that required national support from HM Prison and Probation Service (HMPPS).

1.4 Local managers had made reasonable or better progress in five out of seven recommendations. This included important work to determine the causes of violence and challenge or support individuals involved in violent incidents. The safety team had used information from this work to inform a strategy to reduce overall levels of violence, but it had been implemented too recently for us to see any impact on outcomes. Managers had also ensured that staff understood their roles and responsibilities in the event of a medical emergency and that an ambulance was called when an emergency code was used. However, there continued to be significant weaknesses in the operation of the incentives and rewards policy.

1.5 In the area of respect, managers had worked well to improve systems for applications and redress. Social care had also been improved by the implementation of a memorandum of understanding with the local council.

1.6 In rehabilitation and release planning, there had been some work to improve oversight of the department and train prison offender managers (POMs). However, there continued to be a large backlog of assessments of prisoners' risks and needs, and infrequent contact between POMs and prisoners.

1.7 In contrast to the progress made by local managers, all four recommendations that required external support from HMPPS had been rejected and so no progress had been made. These recommendations included taking steps to ensure basic standards of decency by reducing overcrowding and ensuring all prisoners had access to a toilet overnight. During this visit, we found that about 160 prisoners continued to live in overcrowded cells. In addition, most prisoners on the Albany site continued to live in cells without a toilet or sink. Instead they relied on night sanitation, an electronic system that allows prisoners out of their cells individually to use communal facilities overnight. Prisoners, including older and disabled people, were allowed seven minutes to use the facilities, which many said was not long enough. It was not uncommon for prisoners to face a wait of an hour. This meant that many resorted to using a bucket in their cell and effectively 'slopping out' in the morning. This was not an acceptable situation.

1.8 HMPPS also rejected a recommendation intended to ensure sick prisoners were transferred to a mental health facility in line with national guidelines. I accept that this recommendation requires working in partnership with NHS commissioners, but the continued lack of action means patients remain in facilities that are unable to meet their needs for significant periods of time. One patient who had been waiting too long for a hospital bed during our inspection was still waiting at the time of this visit eight months later.

1.9 Finally, HMPPS rejected a recommendation that remand prisoners should be held at an establishment that could meet their needs. As a consequence, there continued to be no release planning for this group and none of them were participating in education or activities during our visit. In addition, the small remand population was prevented from exercising its voting rights in the general election of December 2019.

1.10 This was a mixed review. Local managers had worked well and made progress in some important areas. However, HMPPS needs a change of approach to ensure accommodation meets basic standards and all prisoners receive appropriate support and health care.

Peter Clarke CVO OBE QPM January 2020
HM Chief Inspector of Prisons

**HMCIP Report, published 13 August 2019**

HMP Isle of Wight is a training prison holding around 1,000 prisoners, almost all of whom have been convicted of sexual offences. Most of the prisoners held at the time of this inspection were serving long sentences for serious offences. Forty per cent of the population were over 50 years old and a significant proportion of these prisoners were elderly and sometimes frail. The prison continued to house a very small remand population from local courts on the island, although it was ill-suited to this role.

We last inspected HMP Isle of Wight in 2015 and since this time the number of people convicted of sexual offences has increased across England and Wales. In response to this we have changed the comparator group of prisons for the Isle of Wight from other category B training prisons to other prisons holding prisoners convicted of sexual offences.

At this inspection we found there had been a deterioration in outcomes in two of our healthy prison tests and that outcomes were not sufficiently good in the areas of safety and rehabilitation and release planning. Despite this, much positive work continued to take place at the prison.

Relationships between staff and prisoners remained good, underpinning prisoners' experience of everyday life. The overwhelming majority of prisoners said they had a member of staff they could turn to if they had a problem. With the notable exception of the widespread use of night sanitation on the Albany site, living conditions were also reasonably good. Communal areas and cells, while worn, were clean, free of graffiti and properly furnished. In addition, staff and prisoners clearly put significant effort into maintaining the attractive gardens across both sites. Equality work had received some much-needed attention in the months before our inspection. Health care was very good but stronger links with the local authority were needed to support prisoners with social care needs.

Outcomes in the area of purposeful activity were also reasonably good. Most prisoners could access 10 hours out of their cell each weekday and the gym and library provision was good. Managers had improved their use of data and had well-developed plans to improve the education, training and work provision. Teaching and learning were also good and achievement rates were very high on most courses. However, we found a large number of prisoners underemployed in a significant number of wing roles.

More concerningly, we found prisoners had very poor perceptions of safety. In our survey, more than half said they had felt unsafe during their time at HMP Isle of Wight and nearly a quarter felt unsafe at the time of the inspection. While violence was still not widespread, it had risen significantly since the previous inspection and

the response of managers was not good enough, leading to inconsistent challenge of perpetrators and little support for victims. The approach to all aspects of behaviour management was in need of attention to ensure that there were clear incentives for prisoners who engaged with the regime and behaved well. Levels of self-harm were high and there had been three self-inflicted deaths since the last inspection. It was concerning that some Prisons and Probation Ombudsman recommendations had not been implemented. The prison was caring for a small but significant number of prisoners with complex needs and good relationships between staff and prisoners led to good care. However, managers needed to use data better to understand the causes and reduce the frequency of self-harm.

Many prisoners were held a long way from home and families experienced significant travel times and expense visiting the Isle of Wight. It was therefore disappointing that support for prisoners to maintain contact with the outside world was limited to letters, phone calls and some fairly basic visits facilities, particularly at Albany. Managers had introduced 'email a prisoner', regular family days and some play work provision, but more could have been done to support prisoners to establish and maintain contact with friends and family.

The long-term, high-risk sex offender population presented significant challenges in the area of rehabilitation and release planning. We found a very similar picture to the previous inspection. Fundamentally, some good work was undermined by a lack of up-to-date assessments of risk and need, high offender supervisor caseloads and a lack of contact between offender supervisors and prisoners. This meant the one-to-one motivational work needed with the large number of prisoners who were maintaining their innocence could not take place. The programme provision had improved with the addition of non accredited programmes, but this was still not enough to meet need. Support for the small number of prisoners released from HMP Isle of Wight was poor.

HMP Isle of Wight is a respectful place where good relationships between frontline staff and prisoners result in many positive outcomes. However, there needs to be a better operational grip on safety. Managers need to address the weaknesses in offender management to ensure the prison fulfils its purpose of reducing the risks these long-term prisoners pose, both within the prison and, importantly, when they are eventually released.

Peter Clarke CVO OBE QPM June 2019

## INDEPENDENT MONITORING BOARD: Annual Report

The law requires every prison to be monitored by an independent Board appointed by the Justice Secretary; these are known as Independent Monitoring Boards (IMBs). The IMB must satisfy itself as to the humane and just treatment of those held in custody within its prison and the range and adequacy of the programmes preparing them for release; it must report annually to the Justice Secretary on how well the prison has met the standards and requirements placed on it.

### IMB Report 1 January 2020 – 31 December 2020
### Published June 2021
### Background to the report

This has been an extraordinarily difficult year for prisoners, staff and the IMB. HMP IOW was extremely successful in managing the spread of COVID 19 throughout the year.

The Board initially withdrew from physically monitoring the prison in March 2020, but continued to meet using Zoom.

The Board developed a modified version of the IMB HMP Winchester model of remote monitoring, which we started using in June 2020. The prison has two residential sites, with seven wings in Albany plus the inpatient healthcare unit, and eight wings in Parkhurst. Board members took responsibility for two wings each, keeping in contact with wing staff on a weekly basis to ascertain the issues affecting prisoners and staff. As part of the process the 'measuring the quality of prison life' prisoner representatives were asked to report on a variety of areas: food, medical provision, safety and family access, as well as commenting on issues that they wanted the Board to be aware of, and on what was going well. This information provided the Board with an overview of all 15 wings, including the inpatient healthcare unit and the SARU. When limited numbers of Board members returned to physically monitoring the prison, their reports were combined with those being prepared remotely. Throughout the pandemic the Board continued to allocate prisoner applications, 0800 calls (telephone contact via a central number to enable prisoners to raise issues and concerns), as well as confidential access requests to Board members, and these were responded to in a timely fashion. At the end of 2020 the Board had 28 detailed weekly reports, giving us an excellent perspective, and perhaps more insight than in the past, into the atmosphere in the prison throughout this stressful and anxious time.

I would like to highlight the positive approach taken by the majority of prisoners, the prison staff who have worked tirelessly and all members of the IMB who continued to carry out their monitoring functions during this difficult period.

### Main judgements
### How safe is the prison?

The inspection by Her Majesty's Inspectorate of Prisons (HMIP) in April – May 2019 identified that the areas of safety and respect had declined since the 2015 inspection. A subsequent independent review of progress (IRP) in January 2020 noted that: local managers had made reasonable or better progress in five out of seven recommendations. In the safety area, this included important work to determine the causes of violence, and challenge or support individuals involved in violent incidents.

The Board believes that the continued developments within the SARU, the use of challenge, support and intervention plans (CSIPs) and the safety intervention meetings (SIMs) have given a holistic approach to managing the most challenging of prisoners.

Figures indicate that, since last year, the level of prisoner-on-prisoner violence has reduced by 60% and prisoner-on-staff violence by 10%, and self-harm has reduced by 2%. The overall figure for violence has reduced by 39% from 2019 figures. The reduction in violent incidents is perhaps to be expected due to the restricted time prisoners were allowed out of their cells for association during the pandemic. However, the initial expectation of more self-harm was incorrect with 15% of incidents occurring in those with a history of multiple self-harm events. Force has been used on 207 occasions during 2020, 29% of which were in the SARU.

### How fairly and humanely are prisoners treated?

During the pandemic significant actions were taken to assist prisoners with the lengthy periods of confinement. The issuing of goody bags, distraction packs and weekly telephone credit, to ensure family contact, was maintained. There was excellent communication with prisoners to explain the up-to-date situation regarding the pandemic and regime changes, and they were given the opportunity to make suggestions for improvements, which the prisoners welcomed. Many prison staff were identified by prisoners highlighting how committed and positively they were working with prisoners at this stressful time.

### How well are prisoners' health and wellbeing needs met?

The health provision during 2020 has been excellent, with healthcare staff working closely with management to ensure prisoners and staff were working in a safe environment. Feedback from prisoner representatives spoke positively about the role of healthcare.

## How well are prisoners progressed towards successful resettlement?

The HMIP IRP visit in January 2020 acknowledged that oversight on rehabilitation and release planning work had improved the department, together with the training of prison offender managers.

During 2020 HMP IoW recategorised 408 prisoners from category B to C. They were also able to transfer 238 to appropriate category prisons.

## Main areas for development

### TO THE MINISTER

Again the issue of prisoners experiencing significant mental health issues has been overlooked. The HMIP recommendation to Her Majesty's Prison and Probation Service (HMPPS) to ensure that mentally ill prisoners are transferred to appropriate facilities, in line with national guidance, was rejected. What plans are in place to ensure that mentally ill prisoners are managed in line with HMIP recommendations and mental health national guidance

In 2020 there have been a number of remand prisoners requiring immediate admission to inpatient healthcare facilities in the prison and urgent referral to secure units. Are there any actions planned with HM Courts and Tribunals Service to provide appropriate psychiatric assessment in the court setting, to ensure prisoners who are significantly mentally unwell are diverted to psychiatric hospital rather than to an inappropriate remand wing.

### TO THE PRISON SERVICE

The HMIP inspection identified four areas that required external support from HMPPS; the subsequent Independent Review of Progress (IRP) report noted that: 'these were rejected and so no progress had been made'. The IRP visit in January 2020 noted improvement by local management but there was a lack of support from the Prison Service nationally – including in ensuring basic standards of decency by reducing overcrowding and ensuring all prisoners had access to a toilet overnight. Is the Prison Service reviewing the decision to reject the recommendations of HMIP? It will be impossible for HMP IOW to improve the situation of prisoners in Albany without the support and financial backing of HMPPS.

There is considerable concern that a newly refurbished wing in the prison has had a number of outstanding problems since August 2020, and four months later they were still outstanding. What mechanisms are in place to ensure refurbishment projects are completed in full and on time?

### TO THE GOVERNOR

The IMB identified concerns in 2020 that there were significantly more unsuccessful searches regarding those from the black, Asian and minority ethnic (BAME) community. The IMB was concerned that this area of invasive contact with prisoners was not monitored in terms of ethnicity. The IMB would significantly benefit from a telephone system in their office in Albany to enable them to contact prisoners in their cells; this would ensure efficient and effective use of IMB members' time. While accepting that finance is always an issue, the IMB makes limited demands on prison resources.

### Progress since the last report

• Decrease in violence and self-harm
• In line with HMIP recommendations, improvement in determining causes of violence, and challenge and support (CSIP and SIMs)
• Continued consistent improvements in the management of the SARU
• Continued improvement in equality management and prisoner-led forums
• Reduced number of discrimination incident report forms (DIRFs)
• Lammy review recommendations implemented: 11 areas 'green', with only three 'amber'
• Continued improvement in the complaints process
• Access to mental health provision seven days a week
• Development of 'Purple Visits'.

**FRECKLETON ROAD
KIRKHAM, PRESTON
LANCS, PR4 2RN**

**HM PRISON KIRKHAM**  **Tel: 01772 675400**

*For the latest reports on this prison please visit:*
https://tinyurl.com/bdfh26rv

*Important Changes:* **(1) Visits:** the identification necessary to access this prison and visit for social or professional purposes has changed; (2) **Money and Gifts** new rules now apply to these. See page 16 for full details of the above.

**Task of the establishment** HMP Kirkham is a category D open prison holding adult male convicted prisoners.

### Certified normal accommodation and operational capacity

Prisoners held at the time of inspection: 589
Baseline certified normal capacity: 657
Operational capacity: 657

## Prison status (public or private) and key providers

Public

Prison Group: Cumbria & Lancashire

Prison Group Director: John Illingsworth

Governor/Director: Alli Black

IMB Chair: Jean Adam

Physical health provider: Spectrum Community Health CIC

Mental health provider: Tees, Esk and Wear Valleys NHS Trust Substance misuse provider: Spectrum Community Health CIC

Learning and skills provider: Novus

Escort contractor: GeoAmey

**Brief history** HMP Kirkham occupies the site of a former Royal Air Force technical training centre. The facility was taken over by the Home Office in the early 1960s and has been in use as a prison since 1962. Prisoner accommodation was built over the period 1990–1999 but other parts of the prison date back to the 1940s.

## Short description of residential units

25 small residential units, known as billets

77-bed admissions unit, including a reception and first night centre

## Visiting Information

Visits can only be booked by prisoner application. **Visiting times:** Thursday to Sunday: 2.30pm to 3.15pm, 13.15 to 2pm (shielding prisoners only).

**Legal visits:** There are currently no legal visits taking place.

## INSPECTIONS & REPORTS

**Date of last inspection:** 25 June–5 July 2018

**HMCIP Report, published 06 November 2018**

HMP Kirkham is an open prison in the North West of England that holds up to 657 adult male prisoners, although at the time of inspection 589 men were held. They represented a broad spectrum of ages and the full range of sentences, but over 70% were serving more than four years. Nearly 90 prisoners were serving more than 10 years or life. The prison's primary function was to resettle men, most of whom were nearing the end of their time in custody. We last inspected Kirkham in 2013, when we found a successful prison that was delivering outcomes that were reasonably good or better across all four of our healthy prison tests. At this inspection we are pleased to report that our findings were very similar.

Prisoners were received into the prison and inducted well, and most told us in our survey that they felt safe. There was little violence or bullying among prisoners and the use of force was rare. Work to create a motivational and incentivising culture within the prison was ongoing, although some of this work was developmental and needed to be refined. Prisoners were always segregated as a prelude to their prospective return to closed conditions but we were unclear as to whether segregation in a secure cell was always needed. Security arrangements were proportionate and the rate of abscond and breaches of release on temporary licence (ROTL), although high in the previous year, appeared to be reducing.

In our survey, too many prisoners told us they felt victimised by staff and many had very negative perceptions about the attitude of some staff. Significantly fewer prisoners than at the time of our previous inspection, and when compared to those at other open prisons, felt respected by staff. There was sufficient evidence, in our view, to suggest the prisoners may have had a point, and that the approach of some, certainly too many, staff was unsupportive of the ethos to which the prison aspired. Addressing this shortcoming in the quality of staff-prisoner relationships was the key priority to emerge from this inspection.

The grounds of the prison were excellent and residential accommodation was maintained reasonably well despite signs of wear and tear. The food provided was popular with most prisoners. Monthly consultation meetings with prisoners were well attended and useful but despite an efficient complaints system, prisoners were not confident in using it for fear of being seen as problematic and of being returned to closed conditions. We found no evidence to support these views, although the prison should take them seriously and address the issue as part of its drive to improve relationships and prisoner confidence. We found little evidence of discriminatory behaviour but work to actively promote equality was variable and often quite limited. Health services were generally good.

Kirkham being an open prison meant that prisoners were never locked in their rooms. The provision of learning and skills remained reasonably good and there were sufficient activity places for the whole population, including a useful range of placements accessed on ROTL. Teaching, learning and learner achievements were all good, although there were weaknesses in the recording of skills acquisition and in embedding the development of functional skills in English and maths in vocational and work placements. Links to local employers and employment opportunities were good. Our colleagues in Ofsted assessed the overall provision at Kirkham to be 'good'.

Outcomes in the prison's core function of resettlement we judged to be reasonably good overall, although more needed to be done to ensure greater continuity, consistency and coherence in the work. Little strategy was evident, for example, and despite there being a substantial proportion of prisoners considered high risk, there had been no recent needs analysis. Notwithstanding, many prisoners were taking advantage of the opportunities presented by ROTL. Levels of contact between prisoners and their offender supervisors were reasonable, if inconsistent, and the focus on risk management was similarly reasonable overall. Public protection arrangements were prioritised and resettlement planning prior to release was good. To conclude, Kirkham continues to be an effective open resettlement prison. Good outcomes were evident and this was reflected in a good report. A cautionary note would be that the prison needed to guard against complacency. Offender management provision required some new and joined-up thinking and, in our view, staff needed to ensure they were fully committed to the prison's values and purpose.

Peter Clarke CVO OBE QPM August 2018
HM Chief Inspector of Prisons

## INDEPENDENT MONITORING BOARD:
## Annual Report

The law requires every prison to be monitored by an independent Board appointed by the Justice Secretary; these are known as Independent Monitoring Boards (IMBs). The IMB must satisfy itself as to the humane and just treatment of those held in custody within its prison and the range and adequacy of the programmes preparing them for release; it must report annually to the Justice Secretary on how well the prison has met the standards and requirements placed on it.

### IMB Report 1 January 2021 – 31 December 2021
### Published 28th April 2022

Background to the report

This report is written from a Covid-19 perspective; the Board continued to visit the establishment during the pandemic, while ensuring that prisoners were able to speak with members without them having to go into the billets. This report is not able to comment on the condition of repair of the living accommodation which is currently occupied. The Board has therefore tried to cover as much ground as it can in these difficult circumstances, but inevitably there is less detail and supporting evidence than usual. Ministers are aware of these constraints.

The reporting period started with a further period of lockdown due to the pandemic. The establishment was periodically an outbreak control site but gradually by the middle of the year, restrictions started to ease which resulted in the reintroduction of prisoners being able to access release on temporary licence (ROTL) along with work in the community and charity settings. Towards the end of the reporting period further restrictions were imposed following the spread of the Omicron variant.

Over the reporting period there have been 16 absconds, all but one of these being after the lifting of restrictions in late spring. Some of the absconds were from those who had recently transferred to the prison. There were also 19 ROTL failures, of these seven were either late back or had not complied with their licence restrictions. Nine prisoners had failed to return to the establishment and two were arrested for committing further offences.

This has been another year that has required clear and coherent handling of the communications to the IMB, staff and prisoners, to understand the constant regime changes reflecting the government announcements and rising cases of the Delta variant. The Governor, in his final year in office prior to retirement, prioritised ensuring all staff and prisoners were kept safe, as well as keeping them informed each time quick changes had to be made to the regime. Levels of drug use and drug drops were still high, the number of drug finds being similar to the previous reporting period (281 in 2020 and 279 in 2021). This figure is despite a number of factors: the improvement in CCTV, the reintroduction of ROTL and more patrols by the local constabulary.

There are plans for a new gym to be built but that is the final project on the list of work currently being undertaken to demolish old hangars and the Board is concerned that the capital allocated may not be available when this stage of the project is reached. Limited access to the current gym is available for use of some equipment but the main sports hall is not accessible due to health and safety issues with the roof.

### Main judgements
### How safe is the prison?

The prison is next to busy main roads, a small industrial site and a housing estate. This location makes it relatively easy for those who are an abscond risk to do so. Throughout the reporting period the prison has been in the main a building site with lots of external contractors and their associated vehicles being on site; areas being worked on were all marked off and had staff on patrol to ensure those who had no need to be there were kept out.

The Board receives feedback from some members of staff regarding drug use who feel insufficient corrective action is being taken by senior management. There are also concerns regarding the behaviour of some prisoners not adhering to the regime and displaying behaviours well below the standard expected in an open establishment. The Board also had the same concerns especially regarding the calibre of prisoners being sent to Kirkham.

Throughout the pandemic, changes to the regime have focused on the safety of both prisoners and staff. With the relaxing of the restrictions within the establishment, day and overnight release started again in early summer along with prisoners accessing outside work. This inevitably meant prisoners were in contact with Covid-19 within the community and further infection was brought into the establishment. A number of billets had to be regularly put into isolation for testing and track and trace purposes.

HMP Kirkham was declared an outbreak site on three occasions due to the number of infections. Testing of all prisoners who consented to being tested was introduced on a number of occasions so that the full extent of the spread of infection could be understood and managed.

**How fairly and humanely are prisoners treated?**
The Board believes that prisoners are treated both fairly and humanely. Living conditions are good, but there continue to be recurring problems with the heating and hot water supplies to some billets over the reporting period. Approval, in principle, has been received for a programme of boiler replacements to start in 2022 at the earliest. Some of this work had to be brought forward due to the number of times the boilers were failing.

All billets have now had an upgrade to the fire alarm system, although the work is still being completed in the non-residential areas. In some of the older billets there have been issues with fire breaks in the roof space impacting the new alarm system so further work is being done there.

**How well are prisoners' health and wellbeing needs met?**
Spectrum provides healthcare and recovery services at the prison, with Tees, Esk and Wear Valley NHS Trust providing mental health services. Healthcare staff have played an important part in many decisions made with regard to the pandemic. The good links and working relationships between all departments have meant that the health and wellbeing of the prisoners has been a priority.

Initial uptake of Covid vaccines by prisoners was sparse but with the easing of restrictions, coupled with the rapid spread of the different variants, uptake has improved greatly. This is mainly due to pressure from families, who wanted to keep their loved ones safe while either they were visiting the establishment or prisoners were home on temporary release. A number of prisoners have told the IMB that 'the missus says I had to have my vaccine before I went home'.

**How well are prisoners progressed towards successful resettlement?**
This has been a challenging year for a consistent rehabilitative culture due to Covid-19 and subsequent changes to the regime. With the easing of Covid-19 restrictions prisoners were once again able to access work within the community, as well as access to various courses to help with rehabilitation. The accelerator prisons project also assists prisoners in accessing employment, housing and banking on release. Kirkham is a working prison, where prisoners are expected to work either internally on the farm or businesses (Calpac, Timbers etc); however, the task of maintaining a work ethic along with assisting and preparing prisoners towards eventual release was impossible to maintain during the pandemic. Consequently, prisoners were unable to work and the expectation of turning up for work being the norm was lost. This presents a significant challenge for the senior management team (SMT) and staff in trying to instil a working ethos and environment into a largely reluctant population.

**Main areas for development**
**TO THE MINISTER**
As a Board, we understand the pressures on the Prison Service but, despite assurances for the last four years from the Minister that the categorisation of prisoners was being correctly carried out, there are still many individuals who are unsuitable for transfer to a category D establishment being sent to Kirkham. During the reporting period 149 prisoners have been returned to closed conditions, mainly due to drug issues which involved dealing, debts and assaults. This figure is a reduction from the previous year (189) but is comparable due to the reduction in capacity over the reporting period.

**TO THE PRISON SERVICE**
A number of works are underway but more still needs to be done. The lighting around the site is poor, and there appears to be delays between reporting issues and getting them fixed. Temporary lighting has been brought onto the site over the darker nights as lighting around dining hall, offender management unit and chapel is very poor.

The Board is pleased that work has eventually started on the demolition of the old hangars, however progression has been much slower than planned and additional costs are being incurred.

The funding included the building and furnishing of a new gym which is expected to be the final stage of the project. The Board wishes for a reassurance that final approval will be given for the funding for the new gym, so important for the wellbeing and mental stability of the prisoners, along with appropriate equipment.

The Board is pleased that some of the work recommended in the disability review in 2019 is eventually being undertaken as part of the funding approved to repair roadways on the site, including dropping pavements for accessibility.

The prison's IT system is in desperate need of an upgrade. Use of the latest Microsoft packages would enable a more accurate, efficient and robust administration with quicker queries of data and responses to complaints. This would be of benefit to both staff and prisoners.

## TO THE GOVERNOR

There is an urgent need to fully implement the abscond and drugs strategies to improve stability within the establishment. Recommendations from this work should be agreed and implemented without delay.

A member of staff needs to be identified to support finance, banking and debt management. This work is currently being covered by staff in the accelerator project as they identified that there was no support for setting up bank accounts or financial management, an area that is vital for prisoners on release.

The Board feels that the SMT and senior management were not operating in a cohesive manner. We are aware that the introduction of a new Governor will go some way to addressing the issues.

Kirkham are currently utilising a diversity and inclusion manager from HMP Preston on an 11-hour weekly contract. This is clearly insufficient and it is recommended that funding is made available to support a Kirkham-based post.

YARM
CLEVELAND
TS15 9PA

HM PRISON
KIRKLEVINGTON
GRANGE   Tel: 01642 792600

*For the latest reports on this prison please visit:*
https://tinyurl.com/bdfh26rv

*Important Changes:* **(1) Visits:** the identification necessary to access this prison and visit for social or professional purposes has changed; (2) **Money and Gifts** new rules now apply to these. See page 16 for full details of the above.

**Task of the establishment** The prison is a category D open prison for adult men and young people over the age of 18.

**Certified normal accommodation and operational capacity**
Prisoners held at the time of inspection: 266
In-use certified normal capacity: 283
Operational capacity: 283

**Prison status and key providers**
Public
Prison Group: North East
Prison Group Director: Susan Howard
Governor/Director: Rebecca Newby
IMB Chair: Colin Stratton
Physical health provider: G4S Health Services (UK) Limited (nursing); Spectrum Community Health CIC (GP and pharmacy)
Mental health provider: Tees, Esk and Wear Valleys NHS Foundation Trust
Substance use treatment provider: G4S (clinical); Change, Grow, Live (psychosocial)
Learning and skills provider: Novus
Escort contractor: GeoAmey

**Brief history** Kirklevington Grange was originally a detention centre for children before re-roling as a pilot resettlement prison holding mostly category D adult male prisoners, with some category C prisoners who were likely to progress to category D. It expanded more recently to include young adults to enable men between 18 to 21 to progress to open conditions in an area closer to their home.

**Short description of residential units**
All the units have single occupancy rooms; some have their own shower facilities.
A, B, C, J units - have communal showers/toilets and a kitchenette with some cooking facilities
F unit - the induction unit with communal showers, toilets and a kitchenette

G unit - has a kitchenette but no showers/toilets
H unit - has a bath and toilets but no kitchenette
R unit – has showers and toilets as well as a kitchenette
There are four 'external' units.

D unit – all rooms are en-suite; there is a kitchenette
E unit – all rooms are en-suite; there is a kitchenette
K unit – has communal shower/toilets and a kitchenette
L unit - all rooms are en-suite; there is a kitchenette

### Visiting Information

It is not possible to book your own visit to Kirklevington Grange. Prisoners must arrange visits themselves using an app.
**Visiting times:** Wednesday, Friday, Saturday: 1:45pm to 3:45pm, Sunday: 9am to 11am and 1:45pm to 3:45pm

**Legal visits:** Email:
visitsbooking.kirklevington@hmps.gsi.gov.uk
**Visiting times:**
Wednesday, Friday, Saturday: 1:45pm to 3:45pm, Sunday: 9am to 11am and 1:45pm to 3:45pm.

### INSPECTIONS & REPORTS
**Date of last full inspection** 12–23 August 2019
*Notable features from this inspection*
• There had been no violent incidents and no self-harm incidents in the previous six months.
• There was no segregation unit.
• Nearly a quarter of the population were being supported by the drug and alcohol recovery psychosocial team.
• Two-thirds of prisoners accessed release on temporary licence (ROTL), and there had been only six failures out of the 18,068 ROTLs in the previous six months.
• All prisoners were released into accommodation and with active bank accounts, and more than half left with a job or education place to go to.

### HMCIP Report, published 09 January 2020

Kirklevington Grange is an open prison near Stockton-on-Tees. A former closed detention centre for young people, the prison now holds up to 283 adult men and young adults, a significant number of whom are serving lengthy sentences, including life. We last inspected in 2015, when we found a prison that was delivering good outcomes against all four of our healthy prison tests. We are pleased to report that at this inspection we found the same good outcomes for those detained.

The prison was an overwhelmingly safe and respectful facility. Reception processes for new arrivals were good, with robust procedures in place to promote well-being. Prisoners told us they felt safe and violence was rare, and we found procedures in place to ensure this remained the case. Prisoners acted positively and were motivated to progress. Force was rarely required and the prison had dispensed with its segregation unit. Security was generally proportionate, although some elements of physical security were unnecessary for a category D prison. Temporary release failures were commendably low and the random positive drug test rate was similarly low. Acts of self-harm were rare, although one prisoner had tragically died by misadventure since we last inspected. Recommendations following an investigation into that incident had been addressed and there was generally good care for those at risk.

The positive relationships between staff and prisoners were a strength of the prison and contributed greatly to the settled atmosphere we observed. The environment was well maintained and despite some issues with older accommodation, it was mostly in good condition. Consultation arrangements were useful, with staff responsive to applications or complaints. The food was very popular. Meaningful work was being undertaken to promote diversity and equality, and outcomes for those from protected groups were generally reasonable. Prisoners were positive about the quality of health care they received, and our findings supported this view.

As an open prison, prisoners were never locked up and enjoyed good access around the prison. All were fully employed and many benefitted from access to temporary release to undertake one of the many good quality work or training placements available in the community. More needed to be done, however, to ensure men could progress quickly into paid employment in the community, and to systematically record the progress individuals made. Well over half of those released at the end of their sentence went into employment, education or training, but more needed to be done in education and vocational training to ensure achievements and qualifications could be properly recorded.

In our survey over 80% of prisoners said that their experiences in the prison had made them less likely to offend. Strategy and action planning had improved and supported the prison's rehabilitative and resettlement agenda. Sentence planning was prompt and contact with offender supervisors was regular, although recording could have been better. Almost all prisoners had an up-to-date risk of harm (OASys) assessment and most had access to temporary release to support their rehabilitation. Both public protection and resettlement work were robust and effective.

Kirklevington Grange was a safe, decent and

purposeful place where prisoners' needs were being met. The prison was well led, staff knew their prisoners well and the regime on offer was purposeful. Prisoners appeared to be responding positively to the opportunities they were being given. We left the prison with a small number of recommendations which we hope will assist with further improvements.

Peter Clarke CVO OBE QPM October 2019
HM Chief Inspector of Prisons

## INDEPENDENT MONITORING BOARD:
### Annual Report

The law requires every prison to be monitored by an independent Board appointed by the Justice Secretary; these are known as Independent Monitoring Boards (IMBs). The IMB must satisfy itself as to the humane and just treatment of those held in custody within its prison and the range and adequacy of the programmes preparing them for release; it must report annually to the Justice Secretary on how well the prison has met the standards and requirements placed on it.

**IMB Report 1 January 2021 – 31 December 2021**
**Published May 2022**
### EXECUTIVE SUMMARY
#### Background to the report

The Covid-19 pandemic continued to affect the monitoring of the establishment, with restrictions on on-site monitoring. Use was made of Zoom and other telecom services to communicate with fellow members and to attend daily briefings and other meetings. Some restrictions were lifted in April, and the Board was able to resume regular rota visits and to communicate with both prison staff and prisoners, face to face, whilst observing some restrictions.

The Governor/ staff did an excellent job at restricting Covid-19 within the establishment and were quick to react to any changes in national regulations. They are to be congratulated in their efforts in that there were only eight prisoner and 57 staff infections recorded. One prisoner was hospitalised, though this was fortunately not a serious infection and he returned to the prison.

Contracted staff also contributed to the efficient running of the establishment through this difficult period, providing the necessary services to the prison population.

Through the diligence and work of staff, no absconds were reported over the year and out of over 12,000 ROTLs there were only 31 failures recorded.

An overall view of the prison showed that it continued to be a well-run establishment and most of the prisoners continued to have a positive experience during their stay. Applications to the Board were fewer than the previous year; this may be partially due to the reduced population but also to the diligence of the Board on the regular rota visits.

### Main judgements
#### How safe is the prison?

Statistics showed that there was an increase in some monitored items, possibly as a result of Covid-19, the frustration of prisoners, and at times shortage of staff, but it was acknowledged that Kirklevington remained a safe environment.

#### How fairly and humanely are prisoners treated?

Exit interviews showed that during reception prisoners were well informed of rules and conditions, and during their stay staff had treated them with respect, being helpful with any queries. The IMB closely monitored the effect of the pandemic on staff-prisoner relationships and will continue to do so into the coming year.

#### How well are prisoners' health and wellbeing needs met?

It is the Board's view that the healthcare provision is good, and that wellbeing needs are met during a normal regime. The healthcare service is assessed as being equal to, or often exceeding, that provided in the community. Mental health provision meets normal demand, but Covid-19 restrictions did result in an increased waiting time for group sessions and outside appointments, which in a lockdown situation can lead to increased anxiety and agitation. However, telephone triage and distraction packs were being used to alleviate this.

In a normal regime, prisoners have access to a wide range of educational, vocational and sporting activities. During lockdown some essential services were being delivered, and this included the fitness suite, which could be used outside normal hours. The prisoners valued their freedom to use the suite and it helped towards their mental wellbeing.

#### How well are prisoners progressed towards successful resettlement?

Most of the prisoners appreciated the efforts of the reducing reoffending team in providing opportunities for developing new skills, accessing work placements and obtaining lasting employment opportunities. Their proactive approach contributed significantly to preparing prisoners for work on their release. Where issues arose, for example in the change from through the gate to community rehabilitation services, steps were taken promptly to mitigate any detriment to prisoners. All prisoners left Kirklevington Grange adequately prepared and with accommodation upon release. Risk is managed well and rates of abscond (0) and ROTL failure (31) represent an extraordinary success rate.

## Main areas for development
### TO THE MINISTER

Reference to our previous year's report shows the operational capacity was reduced significantly though the closure of three accommodation units. This reduction in category D capacity deprived other prisoners in the estate the opportunities provided at Kirklevington Grange. Can it be ensured that the programme for the 'new build' and the subsequent increase to full capacity is given priority?

### TO THE PRISON SERVICE

When prisoners arrive, it is often the case that not all their property arrives with them, and outstanding property often goes missing in transit, causing issues for the prisoner. Kirklevington Grange itself has a satisfactory record of property management and has recently carried out a 'prison property framework' review to improve both the efficiency and accuracy of record keeping. Are there plans to move to an electronic property management system? This could facilitate transfer between establishments and help reduce the volume of lost property.

There are still ongoing issues with obtaining debit/credit cards for prisoners, something we believe has been raised previously by the Governor. To assist prisoners on release and facing financial issues, is this something that can be resolved?

### TO THE GOVERNOR

The IMB will monitor prisoners' perceptions that "if we complain we will be returned to closed conditions". We would like to see some means of dispelling this culture.

In the last year there has been a feeling from new admissions that Kirklevington Grange does not feel like a category D establishment. We do appreciate that Covid- 19 restrictions have had a bearing on this, as they have in other establishments, with the extra policing needed to manage the estate safely. At Kirklevington the perimeter fence is a point of contention, but the Board agrees this is a sensible necessity. We realise there are plans to address this issue in your business plan and look forward to the change in attitude of prisoners.

## Progress since the last report

Demolition of the three condemned units commenced by the end of 2021 and good progress was made on K unit. Consultations took place involving officers and staff, and involving IMB members, as to the suitability of designs and fittings for the replacement units.

It has been a difficult year, especially dealing with the Covid-19 restrictions. Rigorous Covid-19 testing was carried out in line with the government's recommendations. This ensured that positive cases of Covid-19 were kept to a minimum amongst staff, prisoners and visitors. The Governor and staff worked exceptionally hard to protect the establishment and maintained the daily routines wherever possible.

Many of the issues for Kirklevington related to long term under-investment in the infrastructure and buildings, so we were pleased to see a greater investment to improve living conditions and general facilities during the year.

The new accommodation units currently under development are long overdue and we are pleased to be informed that the new units should be complete by the end of 2022.

**STONE ROW HEAD**
**Off QUERNMORE ROAD**
**LANCASTER**
**LA1 3QZ**

**HMYOI LANCASTER FARMS**

**Tel: 01524 563450**

*For the latest reports on this prison please visit:*
https://tinyurl.com/bdfh26rv

*Important Changes:* **(1) Visits:** the identification necessary to access this prison and visit for social or professional purposes has changed; (2) **Money and Gifts** new rules now apply to these. See page 16 for full details of the above.

**Task of the establishment** A category C adult male resettlement prison.

**Certified normal accommodation and operational capacity**
Prisoners held at the time of inspection: 545
Baseline certified normal capacity: 495
In-use certified normal capacity: 495
Operational capacity: 560

**Prison status and key providers**
Public
Prison Group: Cumbria and Lancashire
Prison Group Director: John Illingsworth
Governor/Director: Pete Francis
IMB Chairs: David Skinns and David Forrest
Physical health provider: Spectrum Community Health CIC
Mental health provider: Tees, Esk and Wear

Valleys NHS Foundation Trust Substance use provider: Spectrum Community Health CIC
Learning and skills provider: Novus
Community rehabilitation company: Cumbria and Lancashire CRC
Escort contractor: GeoAmey

**Brief history** The prison opened in 1993 as a remand centre and young offender institution (YOI). In 2008–2009, it became the sole dedicated YOI for the north west. In 2011, the establishment changed its role from a category B YOI to a category C YOI training prison. In 2014, the prison became a category C resettlement prison for adults.

**Short description of residential units**
The prison has four main residential units, each split into two wings. Each wing has two landings, which mainly consist of single cells and a small number of doubles on the ground floor.
Grizedale – First night centre
Coniston 1 – Well-being unit
Coniston 2 – General population
Derwent – General population
Windermere – General population
Buttermere – General population
Ullswater – Segregation unit

**Visiting Information**
Book online at: www.gov.uk/prison-visits or telephone 01524 563 636 Monday to Friday, 9am to midday.
**Visiting times:** Tuesday and Wednesday: 2pm to 3pm and 3.30pm to 4.30pm, Sunday: 1:45pm to 2:45pm and 3:15 to 4:15pm

**Legal visits:** Email LegvisLancasterFarms@justice.gov.uk to book your visit. The mailbox is monitored Monday to Friday 9am to midday.
**Visiting times:**
Tuesday and Wednesday: 2pm to 3pm and 3:30pm to 4:30pm

**INSPECTIONS & REPORTS**
**Date of last inspection:** 29 Oct, 5–8 Nov2018
**HMCIP Report, published 12 March 2019**
HMP Lancaster Farms is a category C resettlement prison serving the North West of England. Opened in 1993, the prison has an operational capacity of 560 and now holds adult male prisoners in a prison campus that contains six main accommodation units. The majority of those held were aged between 21 and 40, with most serving sentences of between two and 10 years. A smaller number of shorter-term prisoners and those serving life were also in residence. Most prisoners had arrived at the prison over the preceding 12 months.

We last inspected Lancaster Farms in 2015 when we found a prison that was reasonably safe and respectful but with more to do to improve outcomes in learning and skills as well as resettlement. At this inspection the evidence pointed clearly to some improvement, but overall our healthy prison assessments remained the same. It was disappointing that only a third of our previous recommendations had been achieved. The prison continued to be a reasonably safe place. Arrangements to receive new prisoners into the establishment were generally effective and we found a prison that was calm and ordered. Levels of violence broadly reflected those seen in similar prisons but most incidents, with some exceptions, were relatively less serious. There was some evidence of prisoners intimidating other prisoners and there were several individuals who sought sanctuary either through self-isolation or in segregation. Support for these prisoners was better than before but remained insufficient. New CSIP (Challenge, Support and Intervention Plan) (Challenge, Support and Intervention Plan (CSIP) is a system used by some prisons to manage the most violent prisoners and support the most vulnerable prisoners in the system. Prisoners who are identified as the perpetrator of serious or repeated violence, or who are vulnerable due to being the victim of violence or bullying behaviour, are managed and supported on a plan with individualised targets and regular reviews.) case management and multi-disciplinary initiatives to promote improved outcomes for victims and perpetrators were encouraging but embryonic. The use of force had increased noticeably but was poorly documented, which meant there was inadequate assurance that it was used proportionately and legitimately. Segregation was usually full, although staff were supportive and living conditions reasonable. Reintegration planning for those segregated was too limited.
Security was managed competently and proportionately. There was a good flow of intelligence, although some was not prioritised or acted upon with sufficient rigour. There was considerable evidence of a drug problem within the prison, notwithstanding a series of initiatives to combat the problem. Many prisoners thought it was easy to get hold of illicit substances and testing suggested a high but reducing positive rate. Care for those at risk of self-harm was reasonably good, but too many lived an isolated experience and levels of self-harm were now much higher than the previous inspection. Case management was, however, reasonable and efforts to include families, if possible, were a good thing. Prisoners in crisis told us they felt well supported by staff.

The prison had met all previous recommendations made by the Prison and Probation Ombudsman (PPO).

Staff-prisoner relationships in general were very good, with 84% of prisoners telling us they felt respected by staff. The lived environment was bright and spacious and outside areas were clean and well maintained. Cellular accommodation was reasonable, as was the food, and there were reasonable attempts at formal consultation with prisoners. Attempts to improve the way prisoners made applications were not yet, however, working effectively and the complaints process was undermined by delays. Work to improve the promotion of equality had started recently but it was too early to be sure whether this initiative would lead to substantive and sustained improvement. Outcomes for differing groups with protected characteristics remained mixed. The provision of health care, like many other areas, was improving and was satisfactory overall, despite often long waits for access. Drug services, aided by a new well-being unit for those recovering from drug abuse, were very good.

Time out of cell was reasonable, as was access to the gym and library. There was good support for family ties and visits, thanks in considerable measure to the work of the Prison Advice and Care Trust (PACT) and Partners of Prisoners (PoPs), and there was sufficient activity for all prisoners following recent increases to the number of places available. Despite this, many of the weaknesses identified at the previous inspection had still to be addressed. Too few prisoners attended education or work regularly or on time and cover for staff absences was insufficient, leading to the frequent cancellation of activities. Allocation to learning activity too often did not recognise a learner's abilities or experience, and learning targets were of limited use. Basic skills were not well supported in vocational training and shortcomings in teaching, learning and assessment all combined to limit learner progress. For those prisoners able to complete a course, however, the achievement of qualifications was high on most courses. Overall our partners in Ofsted judged the effectiveness of provision as 'requires improvement'.

There was some improved collaborative work between departments to support rehabilitation and resettlement, but many weaknesses persisted. Many prisoners did not have an up-to-date offender assessment system (OASys) assessment or arrived at Lancaster Farms without one. Contact with offender supervisors was too limited or reactive, and the shortage of probation staff was a concern regarding higher-risk cases and the overall quality of risk management. Some of the case work we

inspected was poor. Public protection work had improved but remained insufficiently robust, particularly concerning support for multi-agency public protection arrangements (MAPPA). Offending behaviour work was narrow but resettlement assessments and work with those about to be released were much better.

The evidence of this inspection confirmed to us that Lancaster Farms remained a competent prison enabled by a capable management team and a generally confident staff. There was a definite sense that if you were a motivated prisoner with a determination to improve your own life chances, there were opportunities and resources that were available for you in the prison. In contrast, if you were less motivated, you could easily opt out with too little challenge from the institution. This was a missed opportunity. Lancaster Farms was a decent enough place in comparison to many similar prisons, but it can do more and do it better.

Peter Clarke CVO OBE QPM January 2019
HM Chief Inspector of Prisons

## INDEPENDENT MONITORING BOARD: Annual Report

The law requires every prison to be monitored by an independent Board appointed by the Justice Secretary; these are known as Independent Monitoring Boards (IMBs). The IMB must satisfy itself as to the humane and just treatment of those held in custody within its prison and the range and adequacy of the programmes preparing them for release; it must report annually to the Justice Secretary on how well the prison has met the standards and requirements placed on it.

**IMB Report February 2021 – January 2022**
**Published June 2022**
**Executive summary**
**Background to the report**

The Covid-19 outbreak continued to have an impact on the Board's reporting activity.

While the Board recognises the enormous difficulties facing the Prison Service since the onset of the pandemic, we have raised concerns regarding the wearing of masks and social distancing within the prison. While managers have urged compliance, the implementation was sometimes limited during the reporting year. Given the particular risks affecting both prisoners and staff held or working within a confined area, it was imperative that as much could be done at the earliest opportunity to reduce virus transmission.

Unlike in 2020, the Board has maintained a full presence at the prison. In addition, for part of the year, additional information was shared with the

Board by email on weekdays. Sadly, by autumn 2021 information was no longer provided by the prison to Board members via the secure CJSM system. And from December 2021 there has been no Board clerk.

Prisoners were able to contact the Board by paper-based applications or via a national freephone telephone service. The Board was able to respond to prisoners using the 'email-a-prisoner' system. Arrangements were in place in spring 2021 and in the RCU for prisoners to submit paper-based applications to the Board, using sealed envelopes passed to prison staff. Overall, the Board notes that the total number of applications received was slightly higher than that in the previous reporting year.

For part of the reporting year, most Board members responded to requests from the prison to avoid face-to-face meetings with prisoners on the RCU or in accommodation wings with known Covid-19 infections. Throughout this period, the Board received support from prison staff, including telephone calls to units with pandemic outbreaks, in its efforts to continue monitoring the fair and humane treatment of prisoners and their preparation for release.

Responses to the Covid-19 outbreak by the Prison Service and by the Governor have had many consequences for the experience of prisoners held within HMP Lancaster Farms. These responses are reflected in many of the comments in the evidence sections of this report. The Board notes that the major impact of the pandemic on prisoners has been the policy to reduce significantly the amount of time out of cell for association or purposeful activities. While these measures were undoubtedly aimed at reducing infection risks, the Board notes that enforced confinement within cells for over 20 hours per day, for periods of many months, does not in itself appear to be consistent with humane treatment of prisoners. By the autumn, the Board was also alerted to problems in staffing the prison. Staff shortages led to further reductions in some out-of-cell activities. In summary, the Board would prefer to see more time for association and purposeful activities.

Notwithstanding the concern recorded in paragraph 3.1.7, the Board also notes that many prisoners arriving during the year have offered feedback that the regime at HMP Lancaster Farms has allowed more time out of cells than the regimes experienced at other establishments.

## Main judgements
### How safe is the prison?
The Board's monitoring of the prison continues to reveal that the Governor and prison staff work hard to offer and, to a large extent, succeed in providing a safe environment for the accommodation of prisoners at HMP Lancaster Farms. The Board has observed effective management of risks at safety intervention meetings and successful collaboration between key workers, safer custody, custodial managers, the mental health team and the chaplaincy.

From the start of the pandemic, significant steps were taken to increase the safety of prisoners by reducing infection risk, notably the introduction of the emergency regime to organise time out of cells in cohorts, the reduction of prisoner movement and activities, and the management of transfers into the prison via an RCU. During the year, measures such as temperature checking at the gate and lateral flow tests were employed also to control the pandemic. The Board acknowledges that these measures were successful at controlling the spread of the virus within the prison. However, the Board believes that the wearing of face coverings by staff and limiting the numbers of staff in wing offices at any one time could have been more rigorously implemented.

The Board notes the continuation of high levels of self-harm among a small handful of prisoners, many of whom have challenging and complex mental health needs yet continue to be accommodated at the establishment rather than transferred to more specialist and secure mental health facilities.

Levels of violence, prisoner debt and substance misuse appear to have reduced during the pandemic, in parallel with the limited time out of cells, movement around the prison and number of prisoners within each cohort out of cells. The Board welcomes the improvements in safety, but it is regrettable that this has been by default because of the pandemic and reduced time out of cell. However, it is noted that the number of instances of use of force and the number of assaults on staff and between prisoners have all reduced substantially.

### How fairly and humanely are prisoners treated?
The Board believes that, to a large extent, prisoners at HM Lancaster Farms are treated fairly and humanely, with considerable care taken by prison staff to treat prisoners with decency and respect. The Board noted the support given to prisoners during the pandemic, such as extra PIN telephone credit, diversion materials and snack packs, and wellbeing checks where appropriate. Positive acknowledgement is given to the introduction of in-cell telephony in November 2021.

Responses to the pandemic, while undoubtedly aimed at increasing the safety of prisoners and staff, raise questions as to the humane treatment of prisoners (and, possibly, consequences for prisoners' mental health), most notably in the high levels of confinement to cells, with few in-cell activities, loss of in-cell packaging employment, restricted contact with families and restricted access to telephones, until the introduction of in-cell telephony.

As in previous years' reports, the Board notes that a minority of prisoners continue to be accommodated in double cells with limited screening of the toilet and/or no toilet seats. The Board is still disturbed that eating in cells has been normalised inside/outside Covid-19 restrictions.

Steps have been taken to undertake some refurbishment of cells and association areas within both regular accommodation and the CSU. However, through its monitoring, the Board has identified some outstanding issues such as poor ventilation in some cells and the absence of some door screens, broken equipment on some exercise yards and some overflows/poor drainage in wet weather.

The Board has encountered evidence relating to the handling of complaints from prisoners. While the number of overdue complaints is relatively few, some responses to complaints are delayed (especially those related to previous prisons). Of concern also is that prisoners are sometimes not kept updated on progress.

The treatment of prisoners' property remains an issue of concern for the Board.

## How well are prisoners' health and wellbeing needs met?

Monitoring by the Board during this reporting year suggests that, to a large extent, the prison has continued to offer reasonable levels of primary healthcare to prisoners, despite the enormous challenges arising from the pandemic. We note the positive implementation of the hepatitis C elimination programme.

The provision of mental healthcare within the prison appears to have faced even greater challenges, at a time when the impact of the pandemic on prisoners might suggest a need for enhanced provision of these services. The overall level of staffing for mental health services and staff shortages are matters of concern for the Board, as is the cessation of drug rehabilitation group work and the difficulties in finding suitable alternative, specialist accommodation at other prisons for those facing serious mental health difficulties.

The Board recognises the range of initiatives deployed to provide prisoners with access to exercise equipment during the pandemic and the steps taken to offer limited use of the gym.

Other significant detriments to prisoner wellbeing arose as a consequence of measures relating to the pandemic, most notably the significant reductions to time spent out of cell, access to purposeful activities and contact with families via visits and telephone calls (the latter remedied in autumn 2021, with the introduction of in-cell telephony).

## How well are prisoners progressed towards successful resettlement?

One of the many significant and problematic consequences of the pandemic was the reduced face-to-face teaching by the education provider, Novus, and the use of education via packs delivered to prisoners in cells. This resulted in a reduction in prisoners' progress through educational courses during the year.

Similarly, most workplaces functioned at reduced capacity during the regime, to manage infection risk. This resulted in limited progress towards the completion of vocational courses and less valuable work experience than is normally offered to prisoners, although the Board notes some positive progress during 2021/22.

The Board regrets that offending behaviour programmes were much reduced, alongside other educational and vocational courses, leading to significant obstacles for prisoners seeking progression to category D status during the year, and concerns among prisoners, shared by the Board, regarding the fairness of this.

Restrictions due to the Covid-19 infection risk also affected the availability of visits for much of the year, and hence the continuation of family contact considered to be an important component of preparation for release. While the alternative online video meetings between prisoners and families were welcomed in principle, delays, technical difficulties and the lack of privacy offered to prisoners have limited their impact and effectiveness.

## Main areas for development
## TO THE MINISTER

To further improve the strategies available to the prison to manage and reduce the number of incidents of self-harm, particularly among the small number of prisoners who frequently self-harm and could be assessed as demonstrating severe mental health difficulties.

Given concerns expressed above to invite Department of Health colleagues to work with the Minister to review the capacity associated with the provision of mental health services across the prison estate for those prisoners with severe and enduring mental illness.

To reduce the number of prisoners serving indeterminate sentences for public protection (IPP).

To fund the Prison Service for the growth and maintenance of effective staffing levels.

To provide 'surge funding' for learning/skills

provision and programme provision to remedy shortcomings in the preparation for resettlement and sentence planning caused by the Covid-19 pandemic.

## TO THE PRISON SERVICE

To conduct a wide-ranging review of prison staffing, to address the loss of experienced staff and of a large percentage of new staff that leave within 12 months of recruitment.

As Covid restrictions are removed, to ensure more focus on purposeful activities including programmes to support sentence planning, and full-time education and training and 'job readiness'. To reduce losses of property as it transfers across the Prison Service.

To address shortcomings in the contracts for resettlement activity, canteen provision and education/training.

## TO THE GOVERNOR

To support growth in the amount of purposeful activity, including education, training, work and association.

As Covid restrictions are removed, to enable prisoners to eat outside their cells.

To ensure that any work in regard to toilets in double cells is addressed: broken screens, lack of toilet seats, etc.

To review and progress improvements and repairs to ventilation in residential areas and drainage outside residential areas, including exercise areas.

To improve the use of body-worn cameras by prison staff.

To improve communication with prisoners in key areas such as the progress towards resolving or responding to complaints, availability of programmes and the reasons for recategorisation.

To complete the Listener programme (started in November 2021 but halted by the pandemic) and ensure that there is a rolling programme of training for future Listeners (given the turnover of prisoners in a category C resettlement prison).

To ensure that processes previously agreed with the Board, such as that the Board will be notified immediately following the deployment of PAVA, deaths in custody and/or the use of the special cell, are implemented. In addition, to ensure that the appointment to the vacant position of Board clerk is prioritised, with a clear remit for that person to support better communication between the prison and the Board.

To ensure that contact between prisoners and their key workers becomes more effective.

To take further steps to ensure that food hygiene logs are completed for each wing at each meal, and that food temperatures are routinely logged.

## Progress since the last report

Issue raised *Response given* Action taken

Reductions in self-harm *Prison works hard to support this small percentage of prisoners* Seek beds in specialist facilities. However, the Government/Prison Service needs to extend availability of specialist facilities

Provision of mental health services *Some dedicated funding (e.g. psychology)* Psychology support available now, but mental health vacancies (e.g. in nursing) now exist at the prison

Response to the pandemic to improve the fair and humane treatment of prisoners *Learning from 2020 onwards* The Board remains concerned by the long periods of lockdown and lack of purposeful activity

Suitability and implications of making transfers between *Reduced in 2021/22.* Reduced in 2021/22 but when it does occur, problems regarding food, medication and so forth remain prisons on Friday

Management of prisoner property at transfer *Internal process at the prison is good* Problems identified by the Board, largely those related to the transfer between prisons

Toilet screening *In place.* Issue where screens are removed/toilet seats broken

Improvements to the estate *Ongoing* Overall good but some issues of ventilation and drainage

Communication with prisoners about complaints, decisions *Internal complaints: feedback within time* Feedback about some decisions could be more effective (e.g. sentence management)

Re-start equality action team and prisoner council meetings *Restarted* Ongoing monitoring

Arrange training for new Listeners *Started* Not completed

Processes to inform Board about the deployment of PAVA, special cell *Process in place* Many instances of this not working

Key worker contact *On paper, it appears largely to be in place* Evidence of it not working effectively

Wheelchair availability *In place (subject to orders/receipt)* Less need in 2021/22

Food hygiene logs *In place* Not implemented consistently

**HM PRISON SERVICE**

**HM PRISON LEEDS**

**2 GLOUCESTER TERRACE
STANNINGLEY ROAD
LEEDS
LS12 2TJ**

**Tel: 0113 203 2600**

*For the latest reports on this prison please visit:*
https://tinyurl.com/bdfh26rv

*Important Changes:* **(1) Visits:** the identification necessary to access this prison and visit for social or professional purposes has changed; (2) **Money and Gifts** new rules now apply to these. See page 16 for full details of the above.

**Task of the establishment** HMP Leeds is a local category B prison.

**Certified normal accommodation and operational capacity**
Prisoners held at the time of inspection: 1,051
Baseline certified normal capacity: 687
In-use certified normal capacity: 1,131
Operational capacity: 1,131

**Prison status and key providers**
Public
Prison Group: Yorkshire
Prison Group Director: Helen Judge
Governor/Director: Simon Walters
IMB Chair: Judith Wadsworth
Physical health provider: Care UK Health and Rehabilitation Services Limited
Mental health provider: Care UK Health and Rehabilitation Services Limited
Substance use treatment provider: Time for Teeth
Prison education framework provider: Clinical: Care UK;
Psychosocial: Inclusion (Midlands Partnership NHS Foundation Trust)
Escort contractor: GeoAmey

**Brief history** The establishment was built in 1847 and originally comprised four wings. Two further wings were added in 1993.

**Short description of residential units**
A, B, C, E wings hold adult male convicted prisoners and those on remand. A wing is an incentivised drug-free living unit, which accommodates those who wish to engage in therapeutic activities to support a substance-free lifestyle. The segregation unit is on A1 landing.
D wing accommodates adult male convicted prisoners and those on remand, along with those stabilising from the effects of drugs and alcohol.

The first night centre is on D1 landing.
F wing is the vulnerable prisoner unit

**Visiting Information**
Ring: 01132 032 995. The booking line is open Monday to Friday, 8am to 10am and midday to 2pm. Email (enquiries only):
socialvisits.leeds@hmps.gsi.gov.uk
**Visiting times:** Thursday to Sunday: 9am to 10:30am and 2pm to 3:30pm.

**Legal visits:** Email
Legal visits are only taking place by video link which can be booked by emailing:
vccleeds@justice.gov.uk

**INSPECTIONS & REPORTS**
**Date of last inspection:** 25 Nov – 6 Dec 2019
**SSV: Section 6.2.3.1**
Notable features from this inspection:
• There had been eight self-inflicted deaths and one homicide since the last inspection.
• In our survey, 92% of prisoners said that they had had problems on arrival at the prison, and 61% that they had had mental health problems.
• At the time of inspection, 56% of officers had less than two years' service, and about a quarter had less than one year.
• Around two-thirds of prisoners were living in overcrowded conditions.
• Almost a third of the population were assessed as presenting a high or very high risk of harm to others.
• There was a high turnover of prisoners, with 38% of those sentenced and 67% of those unsentenced remaining at Leeds for three months or less.

**HMCIP Report, published 24 March 2020**
HMP Leeds, originally built 1847, is a classic example of an inner city Victorian prison, with the institutional culture, risks and challenges that description implies. Holding up to 1,131 adult male prisoners, many in overcrowded conditions, the establishment is a category B local prison serving a catchment across West Yorkshire. The prison comprises six wings: four original wings and two units added in the early 1990s. The wings have a variety of designated functions including an incentivised drug-free facility, a first night centre on D1 and a wing (F) for vulnerable prisoners. The population represents a range of categories of prisoner, with about two-thirds being convicted and just under half sentenced. When we inspected, some 20% of the population were on remand and just over 11% were licence recalls. Many Leeds prisoners had significant needs and spent comparatively short periods at the establishment, which

resulted in a considerable population turnover each week.

We last inspected Leeds in 2017 when we found an establishment that was unsafe and also failing to achieve good enough outcomes in two of our healthy prison tests, respect and purposeful activity (PA). Outcomes in rehabilitation and release planning (RRP) were better. At this inspection it was true to say that Leeds continued to face many significant challenges, but we found a generally competent institution where improvement was evident in many areas. This was particularly true of safety, which was now much better, although much remained to be done. In respect we assessed outcomes to now be reasonably good. Our assessments in PA and RRP remained unchanged, although both areas had improved.

The prison's new reception provided a welcoming environment. New arrivals were seen quickly and the assessment of risk was now generally satisfactory. New prisoners taken to the first night unit received reasonable levels of support from staff and induction arrangements were generally effective. A body scanner had been introduced to the reception area, which we were told was proving effective in detecting contraband. Levels of violence had reduced and serious violence had reduced considerably, and several important initiatives were aimed at sustaining this improvement. Despite this, in our survey over a third of prisoners still told us they felt unsafe and intimidated by staff. Prisoners also suggested to us that the use of force by staff was sometimes excessive, and we found evidence to support their view. The amount of force used in the prison was high although many incidents did not involve the deployment of full restraint. The prison ensured robust action was taken where poor practice was identified, but some aspects of governance and supervision still required improvement.

The segregation unit was a reasonable facility, subject to good oversight and benefiting from some constructive staff-prisoner relationships. The daily routine remained limited, although prisoners generally did not stay long before their reintegration back in to the main prison. Security was well managed, with some competent collation and use of intelligence. This in combination with the deployment of drug detection technology had undoubtedly aided a reduction in the availability of illicit drugs. Mandatory testing now suggested a positive rate as low as 6.6% which was a substantial improvement on the last inspection.

Tragically, there had been eight self-inflicted deaths since we last inspected in Leeds. Several other deaths were under investigation. The case

management (ACCT) of those in crisis was not good enough, despite recommendations made by the Prisons and Probation Ombudsman following her investigation into some of these deaths. Similarly, the number of incidents of self-harm was much higher than in similar prisons and than at the time of the last inspection. Overall, we found that the prison's safeguarding strategy was not sufficiently effective in addressing emerging issues or risks, or the needs of individuals in crisis.

We generally observed good and relaxed staff-prisoner relationships around the prison, although this was not a consistent finding, with some observations suggesting dismissive and potentially intimidating behaviour by staff. In our survey, only just over half of prisoners told us they thought staff treated them respectfully. Despite some positive features such as a generally effective key worker scheme, the prison still had some way to go before it could claim to have established a meaningful rehabilitative culture.

The capacity of the prison had reduced slightly in recent times. Cramped living conditions were prevalent, but mitigated slightly by a proactive and effective approach to upholding standards, including cleanliness, as well as to providing cell equipment and access to basic amenities. The useful and effective prisoner maintenance team, named 'Q-branch', was a further valued support to improving living conditions. Prisoner consultation was meaningful and prisoners appreciated the peer information desk arrangements that helped provide one-to-one help for individuals. Application and grievance arrangements, however, needed to be more responsive and reliable. The outcomes experienced by prisoners with protected characteristics varied significantly, but the promotion of diversity was being prioritised and the prison was working hard to ensure meaningful improvement. The provision of health services was generally good.

The time out of cell experienced by prisoners varied greatly from about nine hours a day for a fully employed prisoner to as little as two hours for those unemployed and subject to a basic regime. The daily routine was reasonably predictable but our spot checks still found 40% of prisoners locked in cell during the working day. There remained too few activity places in work and education and those that were available were not always filled. The quality of teaching and learning needed improving, although most learners who completed their courses, with the significant exception of English, achieved their qualification. Prisoners in vocational training and work could acquire useful skills but there was little evidence that this was leading to prisoners securing work, training or education places on release.

The complex needs of the population were evident to us throughout this inspection. Nearly a third of the population, for example, were known to present a high or very high risk of harm and over 60% reported mental health problems. Partnership working to support rehabilitation services was strong and contact between prison offender managers and prisoners was better than we usually see. Despite some weaknesses, including some mixed outcomes in public protection arrangements, individual prisoners generally received good resettlement planning and support. Interventions to tackle offending behaviour needs, however, remained limited.

It is right to acknowledge again the challenges in running a prison like Leeds. The level of need among prisoners was great, the environment required constant work and attention in order that minimum standards could be maintained and the operational context required real grip. Overall, though, we were encouraged by what we saw. Leeds could not yet be described as cultivating a rehabilitative culture as aspired to by HM Prison and Probation Service (HMPPS), but we could see some very important work being done and improvements were evident. The Governor and his team deserve acknowledgement for what they have achieved so far. Priorities going forward, as we would see them, include further improvements in safety outcomes, notably safeguarding those at risk of self- harm, and getting prisoners out of cell and into purposeful activity with greater consistency. Peter Clarke CVO OBE QPM March 2020 HM Chief Inspector of Prisons

### INDEPENDENT MONITORING BOARD: Annual Report

The law requires every prison to be monitored by an independent Board appointed by the Justice Secretary; these are known as Independent Monitoring Boards (IMBs). The IMB must satisfy itself as to the humane and just treatment of those held in custody within its prison and the range and adequacy of the programmes preparing them for release; it must report annually to the Justice Secretary on how well the prison has met the standards and requirements placed on it.

### IMB Report 1 January 2020 – 31 December 2020
**Published July 2021**
**Background to the report**

The Covid-19 outbreak has had a significant impact on the Board's ability to gather information and discuss the contents of this annual report. The Board has therefore tried to cover as much ground as it can in these difficult circumstances, but inevitably there is less detail and supporting evidence than usual. Ministers are aware of these constraints. Regular information is being collected specifically on the prison's response to the pandemic, and that is being collated nationally.

At the same time, the Board has experienced considerable change. Due to reduced numbers and resignations, three dual boarding members were appointed at the time the pandemic hit, to support the induction of three new members. They then had to work remotely and develop relationships with staff and managers at the prison to obtain information remotely. By the end of the reporting year, some visits were possible, and the induction of new members was started. This situation has inevitably constrained the Board's reporting.

The 0800 telephone application line, set up by the Secretariat, and introduced at Leeds in July 2020, gave prisoners the opportunity to submit applications to the Board and have their concerns responded to, although the process may have taken a little longer than usual. Applications gave the Board an understanding of the issues that were important to the prisoners during this difficult time.

### Main judgements
### How safe is the prison?

The curtailed, strict regime with confinement necessitated by the exceptional circumstances of the pandemic has meant that the opportunity for incidents relating to debt, bullying and violent incidents amongst prisoners diminished and staff report that prisoners have generally felt safer. Against this is the number of apparently self- inflicted deaths and self-harm incidents during the reporting period.

The main risk has been from the possibility of infection brought in by people (both staff and prisoners) entering and leaving the establishment daily. Both staff and prisoners are instructed to wear masks and keep to social distancing rules, although the latter is difficult due to the narrowness of wing landings. There are extra hand washing facilities throughout the prison and hand gel is available also. Additionally, the use of reverse cohorting to keep new arrivals separate for a period of 14 days helped to ensure that the spread of the virus was kept to a minimum.

Staff are instructed to use body worn video cameras (BWVCs) at the start of any incident, yet often they are not deployed immediately. Use of Force scrutiny meetings have been held regularly and the Chair of the IMB has attended one such meeting and observed video footage of a prison officer acting in such a forceful way with a prisoner on the ground that he was suspended pending investigation and subsequently dismissed from the service. It is of great concern that the Board later found out that this matter had not been reported to the police.

**How fairly and humanely are prisoners treated?**
Generally, and from our limited observations, the Board is satisfied that prisoners were treated both fairly and humanely over the reporting period. However, Board members are concerned about the indignity of sharing a small cell in which all daily functions (eating, sleeping, using the toilet, washing and dressing) are undertaken particularly during the extreme lockdown conditions of the pandemic. Whilst we understand that the cost of single cell accommodation would be prohibitive, the Board cannot consider that it is acceptable that the consumption of food occurs in the same space as integral toilet facilities.

All prisoners have access to showers daily, although the Board noted that not all prisoners got daily showers, either because they were isolating/shielding or, and of considerable concern to the Board, as an unlawful punishment for poor behaviour although this latter practice was quickly stopped following a short scrutiny visit by HM Inspectorate of Prisons in June 2020. Information about regime changes was distributed either by notices to prisoners or via the prison video channel. Prisoners were happy to receive any information explaining changes to the regime and being informed in a timely manner gave stability throughout the establishment. In August 2020, the Acting Governor felt moved to remind staff that bullying, discrimination and harassment of any kind was not acceptable and would not be tolerated. Whilst this was an issue regarding behaviour among staff, the inference may be that if staff were subjecting colleagues to such behaviour, how might that be impacting on prisoners. Staff who felt affected by these issues were encouraged to speak out. The IMB will be able to monitor this situation more closely when they return to the prison on a more regular basis. On the few occasions that a member of the IMB has visited the prison in the latter part of the reporting year, several incidences of care, compassion and respect from staff were observed as they dealt with prisoners, and particularly when dealing with those who were anxious or uncooperative.

**How well are prisoners' health and wellbeing needs met?**
In respect of healthcare, the pandemic saw a greater use of in-cell phones for initial consultations with doctors and nurse practitioners. A number of key face-to-face contacts continued to be undertaken to meet patient needs such as wound management and the delivery of social care. This had the benefit of prisoners not having to be moved from their wing and a reduction in face-to-face contact, both of which were important in preventing the spread of Covid-19.

Exercise has been limited by the closure of the gym, although there has been the opportunity to follow in-cell exercises, courtesy of the prison video channel. All prisoners have the choice of taking half an hour for outdoor exercise and fresh air in the yard.

**How well are prisoners progressed towards successful resettlement?**
The unusual circumstances of the year have prevented significant work for successful resettlement. Most programmes were stopped. Work was limited and such education as there was, was via distance learning.

Prisoners have been able to keep in touch with family and friends by telephone and Purple Visits. There was a short time between lockdowns when visitors were able to come to the prison but take up was disappointing. The visits room had been adapted specifically to ensure safety, with screens and suitable distances between tables.

**Main areas for development**
**TO THE MINISTER**
The Minister should be aware of the disruptions that short, seven-day sentences cause in HMP Leeds, particularly in such a year as we have experienced. They create management problems within reception, for induction, administration, healthcare, cell management, education, and probation. Processing prisoners with short sentences might protect the public and punish people for a few days but little help can be provided for reoffending or resettlement.

Some prisoners requiring places in secure mental health hospitals find themselves in prison due to the lack of secure hospital places and the lack of liaison and diversion schemes to provide alternatives. It can take many weeks to establish their need through interdisciplinary team meetings and then there is a further delay whilst waiting for a bed to become available. Can the Minister seek assurances that more special hospital beds will be made available and within what timeframe? Also, that liaison and diversion schemes are fully implemented and resourced.

The plight of immigration detainees being held within the prison system, after finishing their sentences for offences committed, is of concern to the IMB. Progress appears to be slow in relation to any decision being made regarding deportation or any subsequent appeal. Is the Minister aware of this situation and could he comment on what is being done to relieve the situation of detainees?

## TO THE PRISON SERVICE

The Board has expressed concern earlier in this report about prisoners sharing cells that were originally meant for single occupancy and which perforce are the place where all normal, daily activities and bodily functions are carried out. It is degrading, unhygienic and undignified. Does the Prison Service have any plans to bring about a change to these circumstances?

## TO THE GOVERNOR

The timing and use of BWVCs has been referred to earlier in this report and is of concern to both the Governor and his senior management team (SMT) and to the IMB. The use and review of BWVCs is essential in determining what really happened in difficult situations. Will the Governor ensure that staff use BWC at the very start of any incident where use of force is likely to be employed?

In-cell telephones have proved their worth as healthcare, probation and education staff were able to contact prisoners when unable to meet face to face. Similarly, key workers are disadvantaged by finding difficulty in accessing an available computer to record their meetings. The pandemic has proved the worth of these resources and greater provision of both in-cell telephony and computers would be beneficial. Are there plans to increase the numbers of telephones for staff that can access the in-cell telephone system and increase the number of computers for staff?

The IMB are concerned that the work involved in receiving and discharging prisoners can be too much for one nurse to deal with. Practice Plus Group (PPG) are reviewing reception and triage pathways for patients and associated resources, however data indicates that primary and secondary reception screening is occurring. Is the Governor able to support the healthcare team in their request to the NHS for another nurse to work as part of the reception team?

The Board is grateful to the Governor and Deputy Governor (who was in charge while the Governor took over a regional role temporarily) for the assistance given in helping to establish the new Board in the most trying of circumstances. Staff of all grades should be commended for their efforts to ensure the smooth running of the establishment throughout the pandemic.

## Progress since the last report

The last Annual Report was in 2018 and that year saw the introduction of a body scanner in reception. This has greatly reduced the likelihood of drugs and mobile telephones finding their way on to the wings and potentially causing significant problems regarding the safety of both prisoners and staff.

As there are no members from the Board prior to March 2020 who are still serving, it is difficult for the current Board to accurately assess what progress may have been made in the intervening years. The introduction of in-cell telephony has been of significant benefit, particularly in relation to the restrictions imposed because of the pandemic.

**116 WELFORD ROAD LEICESTER LE2 7AJ**

**HM PRISON LEICESTER**

**Tel: 0116 228 3000**

*For the latest reports on this prison please visit:* https://tinyurl.com/bdfh26rv

*Important Changes:* **(1) Visits:** the identification necessary to access this prison and visit for social or professional purposes has changed; (2) **Money and Gifts** new rules now apply to these. See page 16 for full details of the above.

**Task of the establishment** HMP Leicester is a local adult male prison, supporting the courts of Leicester and Leicestershire, holding prisoners on remand as well as those sentenced, typically for resettlement purposes.

### Certified normal accommodation and operational capacity

Prisoners held at the time of this visit: 294
Baseline certified normal capacity: 214
In-use certified normal capacity: 217
Operational capacity: 300

### Prison status and key providers

Public
Prison Group: East Midlands
Prison Group Director: Paul Cawkwell
Governor/Director: Jim Donaldson
IMB Chair: Irene Peat
Physical health provider: Nottinghamshire Health Care NHS Foundation Trust
Mental health provider: Nottinghamshire Health Care NHS Foundation Trust
Substance use treatment provider: Turning Point
Prison education framework provider: People Plus
Escort contractor: GeoAmey

**Brief history** HMP Leicester is a Victorian prison built in 1874, behind a gatehouse dating back to 1825. It occupies a site of three acres, close to Leicester city centre. A visits and administration block was added in 1990.

**Short description of residential units**

HMP Leicester is predominantly made up of one large residential wing, separated into landings and units.

Landing 1: (subterranean) the Parson's Unit (enhanced/workers'), Lambert Unit (re-integration) and segregation.

Landing 2: mainstream population with the shielding unit attached.

Landing 3: mainstream population and the reverse cohort unit.

Landing 4: mainstream population, prisoner isolation unit and additional reverse cohort unit spaces. Welford Unit: prisoners convicted of sexual offences and vulnerable prisoners.

**Visiting Information**

Only prisoners can book visits via an application to the wing staff.

**Visiting times:** Mon - Sun 1:30pm to 4:30pm.

**Legal visits:** Email

Book your visit online:www.gov.uk/prison-visits

Email: hmpleicesterlegalvisits@justice.gov.uk

It is strongly recommended that you use the video link system, however, face to face visits can be arranged. If a face to face visit is authorised, social distancing must be maintained and the wearing of an issued face mask is mandatory.

**Visiting times:** Monday, Tuesday, Thursday, Friday: 9am to 4:15pm, Wednesday (except 1st Wednesday of the month): 9am to 4:15pm. Visits are 1 hour long.

**INSPECTIONS & REPORTS**

**Scrutiny visit: 8 and 15-16 December 2020**

**Published 27 January 2021**

This report presents the findings from our scrutiny visit to HMP Leicester on the conditions and treatment of prisoners during the Covid-19 pandemic. HMP Leicester is a small and ageing city-centre, local prison which opened in 1828. There were 294 prisoners at the time of our visit, slightly less than the operating capacity, but many more than the prison was designed for. Some areas of the prison were cramped and social distancing was a challenge for staff and prisoners. In areas such as wing offices, we frequently observed several staff gathered with little regard to maintaining a safe distance.

There had been welcome investment to improve conditions at the prison before the Covid-19 crisis. Improvements to communal showers were

appreciated by prisoners and the planned introduction of in-cell telephones in early 2021 will help them to maintain family contact. The recent installation of a body scanner helped to combat illicit items.

The prison had a high turnover and had continued to serve the courts and manage many short-term sentences throughout the pandemic. The challenges faced by the prison were compounded by the high rates of Covid-19 in the city and the local lockdown that had been in place since the summer.

In March 2020, several prison staff had been absent with Covid-19 symptoms and in April 2020 a prisoner with Covid-19 symptoms had died. The senior management team had taken swift action to implement quarantine and shielding arrangements shortly before the imposition of national restrictions. This had helped to keep prisoners safe from the spread of infection and there had been just eight known positive tests among prisoners since March, with the last recorded case in October.

It was acknowledged that the severely curtailed regime at the start of the pandemic was sensible to keep people safe, but 10 months later a very cautious approach remained and progress towards recovery was slow. Limited improvement in some areas had been hampered further by the second national lockdown shortly before our visit.

Oversight of areas such as safety had continued during the pandemic and the focus on the imminent risk of Covid-19 spreading in the prison was understandable. Many strategic meetings had been suspended soon after restrictions were introduced, though some key meetings such as equality and diversity had restarted during the summer but were not yet fully functioning. There had been no formal oversight of segregation procedures during 2020, which was concerning.

Arrangements had been made to make sure that reception procedures minimised the risk of transmission of the virus. Covid-19 testing was now routinely offered to all arriving prisoners and a programme had recently been implemented to offer staff testing. Some aspects of early days arrangements lacked adequate oversight by staff and time out of cell for those on the reverse cohort unit was very limited, especially at weekends.

Recorded incidents of violence and use of force had reduced during the pandemic. Prison managers attributed this to a combination of the restricted regime and positive staff-prisoner relationships. In contrast, reported incidents of self-harm had remained high compared to similar prisons and one in five prisoners who responded to our survey said that they felt unsafe. The use of the Lambert unit lacked clarity. During the restricted regime it had been used for prisoners with complex mental health needs and those with challenging behaviour, which were incompatible. We witnessed a prisoner being given an unofficial punishment following an outburst towards staff. The Lambert unit and segregation unit lacked strategic governance to make sure they were used appropriately.

Most interactions between staff and prisoners were positive, but formal, structured key worker sessions remained suspended. Prisoners who were identified as vulnerable received a daily welfare check, though these were too superficial to identify emerging issues. Senior managers were often visible during the day, but formal communication with prisoners was largely limited to printed material and there had been no consultation forums since March.

Many cells were cold with little natural light and this was even more pronounced on the prison's subterranean level. Not all cells were adequately equipped and access to clothing was a concern, for example, prisoners were only issued with two pairs of underpants a week.

In our survey, only 47% of prisoners said that health services were good. Despite this, we found that the health providers had worked well to help manage the risk of infection and were well prepared for any future outbreak. The regime restrictions and social distancing requirements had reduced access to some aspects of health care, but waiting lists for most services had been reduced. The use of a dedicated health care assistant for prompt assessment of social care needs and mental health support on release was a positive initiative.

The regime was consistent for most prisoners, but it remained severely limited and there had been very little improvement since March. Most prisoners had at most 50 minutes out of cell, including 30 minutes in the open air. The library had continued to operate, but access was limited, and the ordering system was not robust for prisoners who could not attend. The recent introduction of classroom-based education for a small number of prisoners was encouraging, but too many remained locked in their cells with little meaningful activity. The gym facilities had remained closed since March, despite work by staff to plan for the reintroduction of Covid-19 secure indoor PE.

The ability of prisoners to maintain contact with their children and families had been limited throughout the restricted regime. Social visits had not restarted until October and had then been further curtailed to reflect national restrictions. Actions taken following an infringement of

physical contact between a prisoner and his child were disproportionate and lacked compassion. The absence of face-to-face family support work also affected family engagement.

Most prisoners had an up-to-date assessment of their risks and needs, but the quality of offender management had been undermined by the lack of face-to-face contact. There was an over-reliance on a self-reporting questionnaire or outdated information to complete assessments. The lack of direct contact had also affected the quality of resettlement planning for the large number of prisoners released from Leicester. The introduction of a well-used, direct phone line for prisoners to contact the offender management unit and resettlement teams was a positive intervention to address some of these concerns.

Managers, staff and prisoners had responded well to the early stages of the pandemic with a focus on reducing the risk of transmission and maintaining an environment safe from Covid-19. The continuing local community restrictions had understandably affected some aspects of recovery, but progress had been slow in re-introducing key strategic meetings and consultations with prisoners. More focus was needed on reducing the high levels of self-harm. The reduction in violence was welcome, but an emergency restricted regime is not a long-term solution to keeping prisoners safe and strategic planning will be needed to maintain any improvement when recovery from the pandemic gathers pace.

Charlie Taylor, HM Chief Inspector of Prisons
December 2020

**Key concerns and recommendations**
Key concerns and recommendations identify the issues of most importance to improving outcomes for prisoners and are designed to help establishments prioritise and address the most significant weaknesses in the treatment and conditions of prisoners.

During this visit we identified some areas of key concern and have made a number of key recommendations for the prison to address.

Key concern: The Lambert unit was intended to provide a more focused approach for prisoners who needed additional support and care. In reality, the unit appeared to be an extension of or alternative to segregation and the unit lacked clear purpose. Prisoners with complex mental health needs, challenging and violent behaviour and those leaving segregation were all housed on the unit. Some prisoners were awarded unofficial punishments by staff, including further restrictions to their regime.

Key recommendation: The purpose of the Lambert unit should be clearly defined, and robust oversight should ensure appropriate use of the unit, segregation and special accommodation, and effective reintegration planning. (To the governor)

Key concern: The living conditions remained poor and not all prisoners lived in a clean, decent environment. Too many prisoners were held in overcrowded conditions in cells with little natural light that remained cold even when additional heaters had been provided. Many cells containing two prisoners did not have enough privacy screening round the toilet and lacked lockable cabinets. Most prisoners were unable to shower each day and were not issued with enough clean clothes or a coat to wear in the winter.

Key recommendation: All prisoners should be able to live in a clean and decent environment. (To the governor)

Key concern: Work to promote equality remained weak. There were no accurate data on prisoners with protected characteristics and no systematic consultations with prisoner groups. There was little evidence that the prison collected and analysed data to identify potentially disproportionate outcomes for groups of prisoners. Actions at the equality action team meetings were not progressed quickly. Two designated equality posts had been vacant for more than six months. The responses to discrimination incident report forms did not address adequately complaints of discrimination.

Key recommendation: The needs of prisoners with protected characteristics should be identified and addressed. (To the governor)

Key concern: Patients requiring assessment and treatment in mental health hospitals waited excessive times to progress, despite our recommendation in 2018. At the time of our visit, five patients had waited between 21 and 266 days to be transferred, which was unacceptable.

Key recommendation: Patients requiring assessment and treatment in mental health hospitals should be transferred expeditiously, and within the Department of Health target transfer time. (To the HMP Leicester health partnership board)

Key concern: Time out of cell for prisoners was inadequate. Most prisoners had at most 50 minutes to complete daily tasks and take exercise, with even less time from Friday to Sunday. Workers had more time out of cell, but three-quarters of the population remained unemployed. Prisoners who spent more than 23 hours a day in their cells had little to occupy them, group therapies had been halted and health clinics were under-used.

Key recommendation: Prisoners should have adequate time out of their cell each day to promote health and mental well-being. (To the governor)

Key concern: The ability of prisoners to maintain contact with their families was very limited. There were no social visits and no face-to-face family support work. Video calling was limited to one 30-minute call a month. Some prisoners had not been able to see their children and families for more than nine months and told us that this was adversely affecting their mental health and well-being.

Key recommendation: Prisoners who are not subject to any associated public protection restrictions should be able to re-establish and maintain relationships with their children and families. (To the governor)

Key concern: Many prisoners had not received face-to-face support from the offender management unit and resettlement team for the last 10 months. Assessments of prisoners' risks and needs were often completed without speaking to the prisoner or were based on outdated assessments. Resettlement plans were only reviewed using the internal mail. The importance of face-to-face contact to identify risks, behaviours and changes in circumstances was not recognised.

Recommendation: Prisoners should have face-to-face contact with their offender manager and resettlement worker to ensure that their risks are appropriately managed and their needs met. (To the governor)

**Notable positive practice**

We define notable positive practice as innovative practice or practice that leads to particularly good outcomes from which other establishments may be able to learn. Inspectors look for evidence of good outcomes for prisoners; original, creative or particularly effective approaches to problem-solving or achieving the desired goal; and how other establishments could learn from or replicate the practice.

Inspectors found the following examples of notable positive practice during this visit.

• A health care assistant, funded by the local authority and dedicated to social care, provided rapid assessment of and responses to physical disabilities among the prisoners.

• The new mental health CTI (critical time interventions) team ensured that patients being released from the prison were supported before leaving and for up to six weeks after release. This helped to cement their relationships with the services they needed at a vulnerable time.

• A prisoner who had difficulty reading had been supplied with a reading pen to scan text and convert it to audio to enable the prisoner to engage with education.

• Astro-turf had been installed and gazebos erected in the exercise yard to encourage

411

prisoners to engage in physical exercise during bad weather.

• A direct phone line had been introduced for prisoners to call several key departments including the offender management unit. This service was well used and prisoners told us that they valued receiving quick responses to their concerns.

## INDEPENDENT MONITORING BOARD: Annual Report

The law requires every prison to be monitored by an independent Board appointed by the Justice Secretary; these are known as Independent Monitoring Boards (IMBs). The IMB must satisfy itself as to the humane and just treatment of those held in custody within its prison and the range and adequacy of the programmes preparing them for release; it must report annually to the Justice Secretary on how well the prison has met the standards and requirements placed on it.

### IMB Report 1 February 2021 – 31 January 2022
### Published July 2022
### Executive summary
### Background to the report

The Board was fully supported in its work by the establishment during the reporting year and was able to deliver face-to-face monitoring during the whole of 2021.

The continuation of the lockdown measures introduced on 24 March 2020 to manage Covid-19 infection again had a great impact on both prisoners and staff. The severe Stage 4 restrictions in place for 2020 continued until May 2021 and are described in full in our previous report. The lifting of prison restrictions was slower than for the general public, and time out of cell continued to be low for most prisoners during 2021. It is to the credit of prisoners and staff that the establishment remained settled over the whole year.

### Main judgements

HMP Leicester continued to be a well-run establishment, with strong leadership by the energetic and strategic thinking Governor, supported by a hardworking senior management team (SMT) and an engaged body of staff. There were many examples during the year of good teamwork and of staff 'going the extra mile' to keep services running.

### How safe is the prison?

The Board judges that the prison remained safe. Covid management remained very good. Safety processes and quality assurance improved, and the important weekly multidisciplinary safety intervention meeting (SIM) continued without interruption. As usual, the establishment continued to house some prisoners with very challenging behaviour but compared with 2020 there was less violence, and less need for the use of force. There were fewer incidents of self-harm although long periods of constant watch were again required for a few individuals. Security was strengthened, and the availability and use of drugs, particularly new psychoactive substances (NPS), continued to fall (4.5). Prisoners reported feeling safe.

### How fairly and humanely are prisoners treated?

As in our last report, the Board feels that it is not humane to lock a person in a small, shared cell for 23 hours a day, and this was the situation for the majority of prisoners in HMP Leicester until May 2021, and even after that, time out of cell was severely curtailed. Nonetheless the Board judges that prisoners were treated fairly and with respect during the reporting year. Staff did their best to help prisoners cope with the restricted regime, and good staff-prisoner engagement remained a strength of the establishment. The capital investment programme started to improve the decency of the accommodation. There were fewer prisoner complaints to the establishment and fewer applications to the IMB (P.34).

### How well are prisoners' health and wellbeing needs met?

The Board believes that the establishment continued to do its best to meet prisoners' health and wellbeing needs, in the circumstances. Healthcare continued to deliver a very good service and was strengthened by the integration of substance misuse services. Prisoners were supported by an energetic chaplaincy team and were especially appreciative of the efforts of the physical education officers. The Samaritans made a valuable contribution to prisoner safety and wellbeing during 2021. The installation of in-cell telephony was a 'game-changer'.

### How well are prisoners progressed towards successful resettlement?

The progress of most prisoners towards rehabilitation and resettlement was hampered by the consequences of lockdown. The opportunities for work were very much reduced. The main purposeful activity remained in-cell education, well supported by PeoplePlus. The high reception population compromised local resettlement work, and many Leicester men were transferred to and released from HMP Lincoln. The transfer of resettlement services from the CRC to the national probation services started to embed well, but the specification did not include remand prisoners. The situation for prisoners serving an indeterminate sentence for public protection (IPP) was again of great concern to the Board during 2021.

## Main areas for development
### TO THE MINISTER
**1 The transfer of seriously mentally ill prisoners**
Although gatekeeping processes have gradually improved, the Board again has to report that two prisoners experienced very long waits for transfer to secure hospital accommodation.
Is the minister satisfied that there are sufficient secure hospital places to cope promptly with the demand?

**2.The management of prisoners serving an indeterminate sentence for public protection (IPP)**
The Board remains concerned about the management of IPP prisoners, including their recall. Does the minister agree that allowing them to make progress to safe discharge should have a higher priority?

**3 The new arrangements for resettlement services**
The Board accepts that the transfer of service provision from the CRC to the probation services will take some time to embed. The arrangements apply to convicted men, but there is no clear specification yet for those on remand, who often also need help and support with finance and accommodation issues, both on reception and release.
Can the minister reassure the Board that this will be addressed soon?

**4 The increasing number of prisoners waiting for court hearings**
The Board raised this last year, when the reception population at the end of 2020 had risen to 70%. By December 2021, there had been a further rise to 80% with many men waiting too long for court hearings. This continues to compromise Leicester's designated 45% resettlement function.
Is the minister able to work with colleagues in the criminal justice system to address this situation?

**5 The performance of Amey Commercial**
The Board has raised concerns about Amey facilities management since 2018, and previous responses from the minister have acknowledged this issue and have mentioned changes to be introduced so that contracting processes and project delivery improve.
The Board would like to draw the minister's attention to its continued concerns about the service provided.

### TO THE PRISON SERVICE
**6 Re-introduction of key working and staff recruitment and retention**
While welcoming the gradual resumption of key working, the Board notes that its delivery is critically dependent on full staffing. Recruitment and retention of staff continues to present problems for the establishment.
What plans does the prison service have to address this?

**7 The installation of in-cell information technology**
In-cell technology would be a major benefit for Leicester prisoners, in particular to support education, the main purposeful activity, and would introduce the virtual campus and the ability to expand teaching input, and link to Wayout TV. Even with the expanded regime available from March 2022, prisoners still spend considerable time in-cell, because of the cramped nature of the accommodation.
For these reasons, the Board requests that the prison service treats Leicester as a priority for its installation.

## Progress since the last report
### Capital investment
The Board is pleased to report that a number of capital investment projects has been completed, and that the introduction of in-cell telephony has been of major benefit to prisoners.

**1 BRIGHTON ROAD**
**LEWES**
**EAST SUSSEX**
**BN7 1EA**

HM PRISON SERVICE
HMP & YOI LEWES

Tel: 01273 785100

*For the latest reports on this prison please visit:*
https://tinyurl.com/bdfh26rv

*Important Changes:* **(1) Visits:** the identification necessary to access this prison and visit for social or professional purposes has changed; (2) **Money and Gifts** new rules now apply to these. See page 16 for full details of the above.

**Task of the establishment** Category B male local/resettlement prison, which also holds category C and D prisoners.

**Certified normal accommodation and operational capacity**
Prisoners held at the time of inspection: 584
Baseline certified normal capacity: 617
In-use certified normal capacity: 617
Operational capacity: 6922

**Prison status and key providers**
Public
Prison Group: Kent, Surrey & Sussex
Prison Group Director: James Lucas
Governor/Director: Hannah Lane
IMB Chair: Mary Bell
Physical health provider: Sussex Partnership NHS Foundation Trust and MEDCO
Mental health provider: Sussex Partnership NHS Foundation Trust
Substance misuse provider: The Forward Trust
Learning and skills provider: Novus
Escort contractor: GeoAmey

**Brief history** HMP Lewes was built in 1853 as the county prison for Sussex. It has a semi-radial design and is half a mile from the town centre of Lewes. In 2007, a new house block was completed, which created 174 places in two attached wings, plus a new workshop, gym, visits hall, multi-faith centre and several new classrooms. F wing was refurbished in 2012.

**Short description of residential units**
A wing: drug and alcohol support (recovery unit) for 134 prisoners
C wing: 150 places
F wing: 178 places for sex offenders and others requiring protection
G wing: first night centre for 23 prisoners
K wing: drug and alcohol stabilisation unit for 22 prisoners
L wing: 80 places
M wing: 94 places
Health care unit: 11 prisoners

**Visiting Information**
Booking line: 01273 785 277 or 01273 785 271 The booking line is open everyday, 8am to 5pm.
**Visiting times:** Monday, Tuesday, Wednesday, Thursday: 2pm to 3:30pm, Friday: 9am to 10:30am, Saturday and Sunday: 2pm to 3:30pm

**Legal visits:** There are currently no legal visits taking place.

**INSPECTIONS & REPORTS**
**Independent Review of Progress: 2–4 Dec 2019**
**Date of last full inspection** 14, 21  25 January 2019
**IRP: Published 16 January 2020**
**Chief Inspector's summary**
1.1 At our inspection of HMP Lewes in 2019 we made the following judgements about outcomes for prisoners.
1.2 HMP Lewes in East Sussex is a medium-sized category B local prison. Its main function is to serve the local courts by holding unsentenced and newly sentenced prisoners. The average length of stay is short at about nine weeks. In addition to this core function, the prison holds recalled prisoners and those with a variety of sentence lengths, including lifers and those convicted of sexual offences. Like many other local prisons, it dates from the Victorian era and much of its infrastructure is old and cramped.
1.3 When we inspected the prison in January 2019, it had been in 'special measures' for two years, but outcomes for prisoners were declining rather than improving. A great deal of urgent work was needed to improve safety. The number of assaults against staff was high, a fifth of all assaults were serious and a quarter of prisoners said they felt unsafe. Despite this, the prison lacked an effective strategy for reducing violence. Force was used frequently, but its oversight was poor, and far too much paperwork justifying its use was missing. Illicit drugs were a big security problem, yet the prison had not done enough to identify or control their supply. Self-harm was common and five prisoners had taken their own lives between our 2016 and 2019 inspections. Again, the prison lacked an adequate strategic response to this problem. Many prisoners reported that staff treated them with respect, but a number of officers lacked authority and were too passive in their interactions with prisoners. Cleanliness on wings was generally poor and there were rats and large amounts of bird droppings in outside areas. We found very real weaknesses in the leadership and management of health services. These deficiencies meant our colleagues in the Care Quality Commission issued requirement notices relating to three breaches of the commission's regulations. Mental health services, nurse-led primary care and care for prisoners with longterm conditions were poor. Ofsted judged the overall effectiveness of education, skills and work provision as inadequate, its lowest score. Teaching and prisoners' learning were not good enough. Too many prisoners were unemployed, with only enough activity places for two-thirds of the population. Prison managers were aware of these problems but did not have a clear strategy for improving learning and skills. Not enough was done to reduce the risks of prisoners reoffending after release. More than 100 assessments of prisoners' risks were out of date or had not been completed. Prison departments did not work closely to reduce prisoners' risks and had not adequately analysed the population's needs. As in many other areas of the prison, there was no overarching strategy for driving improvement in this area.
1.4 During this independent review of progress, we found a prison with a renewed sense of purpose and direction. The prison had been taken out of special measures and had discarded

the associated bureaucracy and ineffective action plan. The governor and her senior managers understood our concerns and recommendations, and had formulated a more realistic and focused plan for improvement. We were pleased to find that the prison had made good or reasonably good progress in two-thirds of the areas that we reviewed during this visit.

1.5 The prison had consulted staff and prisoners about what was causing violence in the prison. This consultation had informed a revised safety strategy and action plan. The safer custody team was now better resourced. However, these positive developments had yet to translate into reduced levels of violence. There were in fact now more assaults against staff than at the time of the inspection.

1.6 Managers now had much better oversight of the use of force than at the inspection. Nearly all planned incidents were video-recorded and the amount of outstanding paperwork justifying the use of force had been greatly reduced.

1.7 The number of prisoners testing positive in random drug tests had fallen. Prison staff were making much better use of technology and search dogs to disrupt the supply of drugs. However, staff were still not carrying out enough targeted drug tests following the receipt of intelligence.

1.8 The number of self-harm incidents in the previous six months had declined by over a third compared to a similar period before the inspection. One prisoner had taken their own life following our inspection. Managers had used an analysis of self-harm data to inform a new comprehensive strategy but had yet to publish it. Despite regular quality assurance, assessment, care in custody and team work documentation for those at risk of suicide or self-harm required improvement.

1.9 Managers assertively challenged prisoners' antisocial behaviour, but officers' approaches were not always consistent. Despite this, officers were generally supportive of prisoners in their care.

1.10 Managers now paid more attention to cleanliness and hygiene, and overall standards had improved. The problem with rats had been tackled. Offensive displays were no longer visible and graffiti had been reduced. Despite these improvements, some showers were run down and dirty, while many communal areas remained untidy.

1.11 Health governance structures had improved, and health care staff now received clinical and managerial supervision. Care for prisoners with long-term health conditions had also improved but was undermined by the large number of prisoners who did not attend their appointments. The mental health service was

better than at the inspection, and more interventions were available.

1.12 There were still insufficient activity places for the population and some prisoners remained unemployed for more than two months. Officers did not routinely challenge prisoners who chose not to attend an activity. The overall quality of teaching, learning and assessment had improved. Prisoners could now study short modules in English and mathematics, which were better suited to the prison with its high turnover of prisoners. However, not enough prisoners benefited from work-related qualifications.

1.13 The prison had published an offender management strategy and established a committee to improve joint working and information sharing between departments involved in prisoners' rehabilitation. The prison held fewer registered sex offenders than before and had implemented a sensible strategy for managing the population and ensuring prisoners progressed to a more suitable prison.

1.14 The number of prisoners without an offender assessment system (OASys) report had been reduced, but the prison could not tell us how many OASys assessments needed to be reviewed. While some offender management unit staff had frequent, good quality contact with prisoners on their caseload, others did not. Proactive interactions with prisoners were hampered by staff shortages and a lack of suitable interview rooms.

1.15 Overall, this was a promising review. The governor and her senior managers were taking the prison in the right direction. They were realistic about the scale of the challenges they faced and understood that further progress would require sustained effort and vigour. Their challenge now is to build on the progress they have made since the inspection and to translate this work into positive outcomes for prisoners. Nevertheless, they should be congratulated on what they have achieved so far.

**HMCIP Report, published 14 May 2019**
HMP Lewes is a medium-sized category B local prison. At the time of this inspection it held around 580 male prisoners, both sentenced and on remand. The prison was last inspected in January 2016. On that occasion we found it to be reasonably good in the areas of respect and resettlement, and not sufficiently good in the areas of safety and purposeful activity.
Unfortunately, the findings of this inspection were deeply troubling and indicative of systemic failure within the prison service. HM Inspectorate of Prisons found that in three areas – respect, purposeful activity and rehabilitation and release planning – there had been a decline

415

in performance to such an extent that they all attracted a lower assessment than at the last inspection. In the fourth area, the key one of safety, although performance was not so poor as to drag the assessment to the lowest possible level, it was undoubtedly heading in that direction, unless in the near future there was to be decisive intervention to halt the decline in standards. A good start would be if the findings of this inspection were to be taken more seriously than has been the case in the past. We found that in the three years since the last inspection, a mere 10 out of the 54 recommendations we made on that occasion had been fully achieved. Our experience as an inspectorate is that prisons which pay so little attention to inspection findings will inevitably fail to improve.

What makes the decline at Lewes even more difficult to understand is the fact that two years ago HM Prison and Probation Service (HMPPS) put the prison into what it described as 'special measures'. I have examined the 'Improving Lewes (Special Measures) Action Plan' agreed with senior HMPPS management in August 2018. However, of the 45 action points in the plan, 39 had not been completed and the majority were described as requiring 'major development'. There were over 50 references to reviewing activity in the plan, but a noticeable dearth of hard targets. The results of this inspection clearly showed that, far from delivering better outcomes, two years of 'special measures' had coincided with a serious decline in performance. In short, unless in the future HMP Lewes benefits from strong leadership and a realistic action plan focused on delivering clear, measurable outcomes, it is highly likely that the use of the Urgent Notification procedure will have to be considered at some point.

In terms of safety, there was a great deal of urgent work to be done. Since the last inspection there had been five self-inflicted deaths, and incidents of self-harm had tripled. Meanwhile, there had been an inadequate response to recommendations made by the Prisons and Probation Ombudsman (PPO) in response to those deaths. While levels of violence were broadly similar to those we saw at the last inspection, assaults against staff had risen and a quarter of prisoners felt unsafe at the time of the inspection. There was a backlog of investigations into acts of violence, a situation that clearly inhibited the ability of the prison to take a more informed and proactive approach to violence reduction.

The availability of illicit drugs undoubtedly sat behind much of the violence. Fifty-nine per cent of prisoners told us it was easy to get hold of drugs in the prison, and 14% had acquired a drug habit after entering the jail. Despite this, the devices to detect contraband and drugs had not been working since April 2018, and I was told this was because of 'procurement' difficulties. If 'special measures' was intended to help the prison overcome this type of bureaucratic obstacle, it had failed.

Despite the many weaknesses we found in the performance of the prison, it is notable that 78% of prisoners told us that staff treated them with respect. This was an unusually high figure for this type of prison, and added weight to the notion that the problems at Lewes were not insoluble, but did require significant management intervention. For instance, this report sets out very real weaknesses in the leadership and management of health care in the prison, and also in the provision of sufficient activity for the prisoners. Our colleagues from Ofsted were clear in their view that there was no clear strategy for the delivery of learning and skills, and indeed allocation to activities appeared to be a matter of luck. During the inspection I saw workshops and classrooms where attendance was very poor, and it was clear that there was insufficient attention being paid to getting prisoners into activities. As a result, while time out of cell was good for those attending activities, it was not so good for those not attending, and we found 40% of prisoners locked in their cells during the working day.

A similar picture emerged in the area of rehabilitation and release planning, where a lack of leadership meant that there was weak strategic management, and the reducing reoffending strategy was out of date. Notably, only one of nine recommendations made in this area at the last inspection had been fully achieved.

Overall, this was a very disappointing inspection. I would recommend readers to look carefully at the detail contained in this report, as it brings into question the utility of 'special measures' if a prison can decline so badly when supposedly benefitting from them for a full two years. It also validates the Inspectorate's new Independent Reviews of Progress, which are specifically designed to give ministers a report of progress against previous inspection reports at struggling prisons such as Lewes. A new governor had taken up post shortly before this inspection, and she will need support from her own management team and from more senior levels in HMPPS if the decline at HMP Lewes is to be arrested and reversed.

**INDEPENDENT MONITORING BOARD: Annual Report**

The law requires every prison to be monitored by an independent Board appointed by the Justice Secretary; these are known as Independent

Monitoring Boards (IMBs). The IMB must satisfy itself as to the humane and just treatment of those held in custody within its prison and the range and adequacy of the programmes preparing them for release; it must report annually to the Justice Secretary on how well the prison has met the standards and requirements placed on it.

**IMB Report 1 February 2021 – 31 January 2022**
**Published July 2022**
**EXECUTIVE SUMMARY**
**Background to the report**

Throughout this reporting year restrictions caused by the Covid-19 pandemic (Covid) have continued, dominating every aspect of the prisoner's life at HMP Lewes. As we reported last year, it is our view that these restrictions have been overwhelmingly to the detriment of prisoners. This year, progress towards unlocking prisoners more often during the day, getting them into work or in-person education or other activities, has been slow and at times set back due to local Covid outbreaks and staff shortages, including healthcare and other support staff, brought about by Covid. Keeping prisoners within 'bubbles' so that they do not mix with more than a limited number of other prisoners has also had an impact on every aspect of their lives.

At various times during this year, prisoners have only been unlocked from their cells for half an hour a day and the 'best' regime offered has been very far from ideal. As stated last year, we cannot know what the long-term impact on prisoners' physical and mental welfare will be of being kept in cells for such long periods.

We do recognise that the purpose behind such strict lockdown rules has been to keep prisoners safer from catching Covid, which has been fairly successful, and note that when there have been outbreaks they have been contained quickly. We also recognise that it is harder for a local prison such as HMP Lewes to offer decent periods of unlock when it has a constant flow of new prisoners coming from the community, who need to be kept separated from others, meaning it has had to run many separate 'regimes' within one day. Managing Covid has been an enormous undertaking for staff and prisoners alike and the Board does not doubt the efforts of senior management and many members of staff to do this or their desire to run a more open, constructive, prison. However, it is the Board's duty to consider the actual experience for prisoners, which, at a general level, has been poor.

**Main judgements**
**How safe is the prison?**

The Board has observed that prisoners who harm themselves or others are generally monitored quite closely by the prison safety team, who often work hard to assist them. However, this year the number of prisoner-on-prisoner assaults averaged around 12 a month, which is a 12% increase on last year. Reported self-harm decreased but is still an almost daily occurrence. All prisoners should be safer with the introduction of the new enhanced gate security, as everyone entering the prison is now searched, hopefully reducing the ingress of illicit substances which are often behind cases of bullying and violence. Increased 'finds' of illicit substances should also help.

The Board does not consider that the induction process at HMP Lewes is adequate and believes that a more structured process would allow prisoners to start their sentences with a better understanding of prison life and accordingly be less vulnerable to others.

**How fairly and humanely are prisoners treated?**

This reporting year has been dominated by Covid and all the complications that its management brings to everyday life for prisoners. The Board recognises that the Governor and the senior leadership team at HMP Lewes have been severely restricted in what they have been able to offer prisoners in terms of regime because of restrictions placed upon them by public health requirements. However, we do not consider that the regime during this year has been humane. For more than two months at least, the planned regime allowed prisoners to be unlocked for just half an hour a day and the 'best' regime during the year, while giving some prisoners around four hours out of their cells a day, still restricted prisoners without work or education to an hour unlocked from their cells each day.

There has been a welcome programme of refurbishment of cells but the main residential areas are often not decent, with constant problems which seemingly take a long time to fix such as broken showers and windows, no toilet lids and pigeons flying around living areas.

The Board is again concerned that prisoners from ethnic minorities (excluding White minorities) may not be being treated fairly in some areas, specifically in use of force and the incentives and earned privileges scheme, where they are disproportionately represented.

**How well are prisoners' health and wellbeing needs met?**

Last year the Board reported that it had been an 'extraordinary' year and the psychological impact on prisoners of being locked up for a long time every day over such a long period could not be overstated. Sadly, the current year has been very similar and it is observed that the numbers of prisoners being referred to mental health services is high. Some of the funding measures introduced last year to minimise the potential damage to mental health, such as extra 'comfort' food, have unfortunately been removed by HMPPS. The Board is also concerned by its understanding that HMPPS is requiring that all times that prisoners are unlocked from their cells should be 'purposeful', which ignores the mental health benefit of all people to have some unstructured time to socialise with others.

Prisoner wellbeing will have been improved by the opportunities, although fairly limited, to go to in-person education or workshops which started in May. The Board also recognises the lengths that the senior management team have gone to try and ensure a predictable regime for prisoners, which prisoners generally welcome, and to try and find enough staff to open the gym regularly. It is the Board's view that the chaplaincy department plays an important role in the wellbeing of prisoners.

Having welcomed the appointment of Practice Plus Group (PPG) last year, the Board is disappointed to report that there has been a deterioration in the delivery of physical and mental health services during this year. Essential services have still been delivered, and there has been a full programme of Covid vaccinations, but the level of complaints to the Board from prisoners has been high. The Board was extremely concerned by a period when essential medications for long-term conditions (e.g. asthma) were removed from prisoners in reception, and the unavailability of particular medicines at times. Poor communication with prisoners has also been a problem and there have been long waiting lists for services. It is the Board's view that many of these problems are because of inadequate staffing and an overdependence on agency staff.

**How well are prisoners progressed towards successful resettlement?**

Covid restrictions meant that for parts of the last year there was no face-to-face education, which is inevitably second-best, and few job opportunities. When open, the number of education and work places available to prisoners is less than 50% of the prison population. This means opportunities to gain skills are limited.

Similarly, resettlement staff spent some of the year only communicating with prisoners on paper or through their doors, again a poor second best. Staff shortages have also meant reduced or slower services by the offender management unit and the probation services. There has routinely been a backlog in prisoners

getting their sentence plans, without which they cannot progress. In addition, organising transfers to prisons which are better able to help prisoners progress through their sentences has often been difficult.

**Main areas for development**
**TO THE MINISTER**

Will the Minister do everything in her power to ensure sufficient funding for capital investment in HMP Lewes' buildings such that the basic accommodation can finally be considered uniformly decent?

Once again the Board asks that the Minister does everything she can to ensure that prisoners who have been detained very many years beyond their tariff dates under indeterminate sentences for public protection are released as soon as is possible. It is the Board's view that the treatment of these prisoners is inhumane.

**TO THE PRISON SERVICE**

Will the Prison Service recognise the importance for prisoner wellbeing of them being unlocked for unstructured association, particularly when in a prison such as HMP Lewes there are insufficient work and education places for all prisoners?

Will the Prison Service ensure sufficient funding of inter-prison transfer services so that prisoners do not get delayed moving to prisons where their rehabilitation needs can be better met?

**TO THE GOVERNOR**

The Board asks the Governor to do everything in her power to improve the amount of time prisoners are allowed out of their cells as quickly as possible.

To ensure that as Covid restrictions are eased, remand and sentence-expired foreign national prisoners are treated appropriately and differently from the main sentenced population.

**Progress since the last report**

The Board welcomes that in December 2021, HMP Lewes brought in enhanced gate security. This now means that everyone entering the prison is subject to a scan and a search of personal possessions. The Board considers this must have improved safety for prisoners.

The Board welcomes that many cells have been refurbished this year, making them cleaner and more pleasant with better standards of furniture. The Board welcomes the number of prisoners forums that have been held this year as a positive step in prison management. This gives a better understanding of prisoners who have protected characteristics and the Board encourages this to go further.

**HM PRISON LEYHILL**

WOTTON-UNDER-EDGE
GLOUCESTER
GL12 8BT

Tel: 01454 264000

*For the latest reports on this prison please visit:*
https://tinyurl.com/bdfh26rv

*Important Changes:* **(1) Visits:** the identification necessary to access this prison and visit for social or professional purposes has changed; **(2) Money and Gifts** new rules now apply to these. See page 16 for full details of the above.

**Task of the establishment** HMP Leyhill is an open prison, accommodating category D male prisoners.

**Certified normal accommodation and operational capacity**
Prisoners held at the time of this visit: 492
Baseline certified normal capacity: 515
In-use certified normal capacity: 515
Operational capacity: 497

**Prison status and key providers**
Public
Prison Group: Avon & South Dorset
Prison Group Director: Paul Woods
Governor/Director: Steve Hodson
IMB Chair: Jane Holzgrawe
Physical health provider: Inspire Better Health
Mental health provider: Inspire Better Health
Substance misuse treatment provider: Inspire Better Health
Prison education framework provider: Weston College
Escort contractor: Serco

**Brief history** The prison first opened with hutted accommodation in 1946. It was then rebuilt in the late 1970s to early 1980s, and in 1986 residents were rehoused in new living accommodation. In 2002, again, new accommodation units were added, to create C unit.
An expansion of two 60-bed units is expected to start later in 2021. At present, there is long-awaited refurbishment work ongoing to both the roofs of the industries building and washroom facilities.

**Short description of residential units**
• Ash unit holds 208 prisoners
• Beech unit holds 199 prisoners and has a facility for prisoners with disabilities and complex needs. The shielding unit, with a capacity of 24, is located here.
• Cedar unit holds 108 enhanced prisoners.
• Cedar unit 4 temporary accommodation is a reverse cohort unit, with 40 spaces.
The establishment has a purpose-built palliative care unit which can house two residents in end-of-life palliative care.

**Visiting Information**
Book at: www.gov.uk/prison-visits
**Visiting times:** Tuesday, Saturday, Sunday: 1:30pm to 3:30pm

**Legal visits:** Book legal visits by telephone on 01454 264 000 Monday to Friday, 9am to 11am, 2pm to 4pm
**Visiting times:** Monday, Wednesday, Friday: 1:30pm to 3:45pm

**INSPECTIONS & REPORTS**
**Scrutiny visit: 23 February and 2–3 March 2021**
**Published: 07 April 2021**
This report presents the findings from our scrutiny visit to HMP Leyhill to report on the conditions and treatment of prisoners during the Covid-19 pandemic. Leyhill is a category D open prison in Gloucestershire, holding almost 500 adult male prisoners in preparation for their release back into the community. With two-thirds convicted of sexual offences and the majority serving long sentences, half of which were indeterminate or for life, this is a complex population requiring careful management of risk. The prison had responded well to the threat of transmission of the virus and there had been few confirmed Covid-19 cases to date. A small outbreak involving two staff in October had been successfully controlled and five prisoners, who had tested positive on arrival at the prison, had been effectively isolated. With half of the population aged over 50 and more than a third in high-vulnerability groups, these measures had limited potentially serious consequences from the pandemic. The self-contained shielding unit for 24 prisoners provided a safe and decent environment, and Covid-19-safe procedures were evident across the prison. Communal areas were clean and face coverings were worn both indoors and outdoors by staff and prisoners. Health care provision was good. However, we found that arrangements on the reverse cohort unit for those in quarantine carried some risk of cross-infection.
There were considerably fewer restrictions on daily life than we have seen in the closed prison estate. As before the pandemic, prisoners were unlocked for more than 11 hours a day and could access the open air during this time, with free movement around the site. Leaders had kept workshops open to provide a supervised, safe environment with more space to socially distance than on the residential units. Most prisoners who were able to work were employed, which was

impressive. The number of reported incidents of violence and self-harm remained low, and absconds from the prison had reduced since the start of national restrictions. Although there were reports of an increase in illicit drug use, steps were being taken to address this.

Despite this relatively positive picture, we received many negative comments from prisoners in response to our survey. Less than two-thirds said that staff treated them with respect and almost a third reported that staff bullied or victimised them. Black and minority ethnic prisoners reported even poorer perceptions of treatment. The personal officer scheme, which had been suspended at the start of the pandemic, had been too slow to restart. The lack of release on temporary licence was also a source of much frustration. Although leaders had rightly taken a cautious approach, given the vulnerability of the prison population to the virus, only three prisoners were in essential work placements outside the prison at the time of our visit. Employer links were far too limited and, even before the start of the pandemic, were too few to fulfil the resettlement purpose of an open prison. The lack of progression opportunities had prevented some prisoners from demonstrating their suitability for release to the parole board. Over half of the parole hearings held in 2020 had been deferred. There were not enough offender supervisors in post and contact with prisoners was inconsistent. However, the pathways enhanced resettlement service (PERS) provided good support for the most complex prisoners, to help them manage in open conditions.

Poor management oversight of public protection arrangements for those prisoners approaching release was a serious concern. The planning was not sufficiently robust or timely, particularly for those convicted of sexual offences. About half of prisoners went to approved premises owing to risk concerns, but a lack of places in such accommodation meant that some prisoners waited months for release after being granted parole. Extraordinarily, one prisoner with disabilities was still being held more than a year beyond the date that his release had been approved.

In summary, the prison had managed well in shielding its ageing population from the virus. It had remained safe and continued to provide a decent daily regime. However, prison leaders had been too slow to address concerns, including deteriorating staff–prisoner relationships, poor perceptions of treatment among those from a black and minority ethnic background and frustration at the lack of progression opportunities during the pandemic. The management of public protection arrangements for the release of some high-risk prisoners also

needed urgently to improve.
Charlie Taylor, HM Chief Inspector of Prisons
March 2021

**Key concerns and recommendations**
Key concerns and recommendations identify the issues of most importance to improving outcomes for prisoners and are designed to help establishments prioritise and address the most significant weaknesses in the treatment and conditions of prisoners.

During this visit we identified some areas of key concern, and have made a small number of recommendations for the prison to address.

Key concern: Staff–prisoner relationships had deteriorated since the inspection in 2016. Only 64% of prisoners said that they felt respected by staff, and almost a third that they had experienced bullying or victimisation by staff. Prisoners spoke negatively about their experience and staff were not visible on the residential units. Black and minority ethnic prisoners had even poorer perceptions of treatment. In our survey, only 43% of these prisoners said that they felt respected by staff, and almost two-thirds that they were bullied or victimised by staff. Prisoners from this group were not engaged in equality focus groups and said that they felt targeted by staff because of their ethnicity, and were afraid to speak up for fear of repercussions.

Recommendation: Leaders should improve staff–prisoner relationships, particularly with those from a black and minority ethnic background, so that all prisoners are treated with respect. (To the governor)

Key concern: Video-call visits were proving increasingly popular but were not well enough resourced. Nearly 200 prisoners had signed up to the scheme, but only 36 prisoners could benefit each week and, when we arrived, there was a three-week wait for a visit. Without the allocation of more staff, the reintroduction of face-to-face visits could mean that video-call visits provision would be further reduced.

Recommendation: There should be enough video-call visit sessions each week to meet the needs of the population. (To the governor)

Key concern: Employer links in the local community were far too limited and, even before the start of the pandemic, were too few for an open prison. Even if the pandemic eased and restrictions on release on temporary licence were lifted, at the time of our visit the prison had confirmed plans for only 26 prisoners, about 5% of the population, to work in the community.

Recommendation: There should be a broad range of community work placements which allow prisoners to progress, develop skills and

demonstrate a reduction in their risk.
(To the governor)

Key concern: Two-thirds of prisoners were assessed as high risk, and the need for good oversight of their release had increased during the pandemic. Most prisoners had not had a chance to demonstrate any compliance while released on temporary licence, some were arriving at Leyhill with little time to serve and probation staff had been largely based off-site during the pandemic. There was no evidence of the interdepartmental risk management meeting taking actions to meet any gaps in release planning, and the meeting did not consider the release of prisoners far enough into the future to be effective. Too little was recorded by offender supervisors in prisoner electronic records to show that effective planning was under way. Where good work had been completed by the offender management unit (OMU), it could not be accessed by partner agencies also planning for release.

Recommendation: Multidisciplinary management oversight of all high-risk releases should consider cases far enough ahead of release to identify any gaps in planning and take effective remedial action. Information to assist release planning should be shared effectively by offender supervisors with partner agencies.
(To the governor)

Key concern: Prisoners granted parole on the proviso that they reside at an approved premise to help manage their risk sometimes waited several months for release because there were not enough suitable places. Extraordinarily, one prisoner with disabilities who needed an adapted room was still being held at Leyhill more than a year after his approval date. This outcome did not fulfil the parole board's decision and prevented other prisoners from accessing open conditions.

Recommendation: There should be enough suitable places in approved premises to ensure that prisoners who require this accommodation as part of their licence conditions are released without delay. (To HMPPS)

Education, skills and work (Ofsted)

During this visit Ofsted inspectors conducted an interim assessment of the provision of education, skills and work in the establishment. They identified steps that the prison needed to take to meet the needs of prisoners, including those with special educational needs and disabilities.

**Next steps**

Leaders and managers should increase substantially the number of prisoners engaging with work-pack learning and prioritise their enrolment in practical learning, once restrictions are lifted.

Leaders and managers should restart classroom-based and vocational learning as soon as it is safe to do so.

Leaders and managers should improve prisoners' access to digital learning technology, so that they are better supported in their learning and skills development as part of their resettlement plans.

Leaders and managers should restart the job club, to support prisoners into employment on release as soon as it is safe to do so.

Notable positive practice

We define notable positive practice as innovative practice or practice that leads to particularly good outcomes from which other establishments may be able to learn. Inspectors look for evidence of good outcomes for prisoners; original, creative or particularly effective approaches to problem-solving or achieving the desired goal; and how other establishments could learn from or replicate the practice.

Inspectors found four examples of notable positive practice during this visit.

Prison leaders had arranged for external support for transgender prisoners through an LGBT life coach, who regularly provided one-to-one support to these prisoners.

The pharmacy shop provided by the medicines management team was open most afternoons. This enabled prisoners to shop for a variety of daily care products, encouraging a culture of self-care of their health and well-being, and was comparable to the community pharmacy service.

Most prisoners who were able to work were employed. Leaders had created more than 350 full-time work opportunities in the prison. This was done through altering working conditions to allow for social distancing, creating new roles, adapting work times and creating split shifts to allow more prisoners the opportunity to gain employment. Workshops had stayed open throughout the pandemic to provide a supervised, safe environment with more space to socially distance than on the residential units.

The introduction of four new video-link facilities during the pandemic meant that the OMU was well resourced to conduct parole hearings and three-way conferences between prisoners, offender supervisors and community offender managers.

**INDEPENDENT MONITORING BOARD: Annual Report**

The law requires every prison to be monitored by an independent Board appointed by the Justice Secretary; these are known as Independent Monitoring Boards (IMBs). The IMB must satisfy itself as to the humane and just treatment of those held in custody within its prison and the range and adequacy of the programmes preparing them for release; it must report annually to the Justice Secretary on how well the prison has met the standards and requirements placed on it.

**IMB Report 1 February 2021 – 31 January 2022**
**Published June 2022**
**EXECUTIVE SUMMARY**
**Background to the report**

Monitoring this year has proved challenging for the Board due to the changing regime at Leyhill in response to the number of Covid cases. The Board has moved towards in person monitoring with several members visiting the site regularly. During outbreaks or increasing levels of infection, monitoring was conducted remotely by Board members. The Board acknowledged that there was a risk of members transmitting the coronavirus to prisoners and limited visits to the site during peak infection rates.

The majority of Board meetings have been held at Leyhill with limited numbers in person and teleconference access for other members.

The prison management have made prisoners' safety the top priority and prisoners have shown their appreciation by complying with the regime. Prisoner morale has been maintained despite the restrictions made necessary by Covid and by the problems caused by the ongoing, long-delayed refurbishment of the shower and toilet facilities.

**Main judgements**
**How safe is the prison?**

In a year that has again been dominated by the pandemic, Leyhill has responded swiftly and positively in order to implement the required protocols and to take its own initiatives. The use of unit C4 to isolate prisoners for reverse cohorting and also those that had tested positive has proved to be invaluable in reducing the spread of the coronavirus. Track and trace has been used effectively on staff and prisoners, with close contacts of positive cases subjected to daily LFT testing for seven days.

Staffing levels have been significantly affected by the infection rates in the community and outbreaks at Leyhill. The staff responded to the challenges and provided cover where necessary, working extended shifts and rest days.

In keeping with its emphasis on community, a spirit of inclusivity has characterised the Leyhill regime. Whilst opportunities to speak with prisoners and staff have been limited, it is noted that the atmosphere feels positive despite some obvious frustration with the restrictions of Covid-19. In the judgement of the Board, the prison is a safe environment.

Self-harm incidents have remained low and are well-monitored (section 4.2) while cases of violence have been rare.

**How fairly and humanely are prisoners treated?**

Fair and humane treatment of the prisoners is evident in the much-improved work of the equalities team; the use of Samaritan-trained prisoners as Listeners, especially during times when high levels of stress and anxiety were experienced by prisoners; and in the different ways in which prisoners' communication with their families was supported during the times of Covid restrictions.

The chaplaincy continues to provide support to all prisoners.

Failure to locate missing items of property, especially in transfer from other prisons, understandably leads to many prisoner complaints.

**How well are prisoners' health and wellbeing needs met?**

Leyhill is an open prison and prisoners are encouraged to access areas of the grounds during their free time, with subsequent benefits to both physical and mental health. The grounds and outdoor activities have been used extensively during the coronavirus restrictions.

A wide range of indoor and outdoor activities has been provided to enable the prisoners to engage in physical activity and to maintain morale.

The installation of outdoor gym equipment proved to be popular during lockdown when other facilities were closed due to Covid restrictions. The equipment continues to be used regularly by all ages.

The vaccination of 94% of the prisoners in the reporting year is to be commended.

Waiting times for healthcare services are in line with the community and it is noted that prisoner feedback gives more compliments than complaints. In a survey conducted in February 2021, 75% of the prisoners judged the overall quality of healthcare to be good.

**How well are prisoners progressed towards successful resettlement?**

Prisoners 'progress towards resettlement has been enhanced by the prison's success, during Covid times, in engaging 'the hard to reach 'in education, while a recent survey revealed a high level of appreciation of the teaching provided at Leyhill.

Vocational training and work have provided purposeful activity and developed skills which enhance prisoners 'chances of securing employment on release.

Lack of opportunities for release on temporary licence (ROTL) have delayed and limited progress made towards parole and, thus, towards resettlement. This has led to delays in release which, in the Board's opinion, is unfair and unjust. However, the residents consultative committee recognised an improvement in the situation towards the end of the year.

The community rehabilitation company has been dismantled and its responsibilities dispersed. In the judgment of the Board, this has led to a deterioration in the provision made for prisoners on their path to resettlement. The work of the Lobster Pot has made up for some of the shortfall. The lack of approved premises, which a large percentage of Leyhill prisoners require before they can be released, results in unjust, unfair treatment and, together with the delays in ROTL, can mean prisoners' release is put back many months and, in some cases, over a year

All except two of the 124 prisoners sentenced on IPP terms at Leyhill remain in prison beyond their tariff date, which in the Board's view is unfair and unjust.

## Main areas for development
### TO THE MINISTER

1.a) What further action will the Minister take to speed up the resettlement in the community of the prisoners serving IPP sentences, many of whom have spent far longer in custody than recommended in their indicative tariffs?

2.b) What action will the Minister take to remedy the lack of spaces in approved premises which leads to many prisoners facing incarceration beyond their release dates?

3.c) What action will the Minister take to restore the quality of rehabilitation lost as a result of the closing of the community rehabilitation company?

### TO THE PRISON SERVICE

a) What further action will be taken to deal with the recurring problem of property lost or mislaid during transfer from other prisons?

### TO THE GOVERNOR

a) The Board urges the Governor to continue to explore ways to give more prisoners the opportunity to experience external work placements.

b) The Board urges the Governor to build on the recent improvements made in the provision of opportunities for ROTL.

## Progress since the last report

The long-awaited refurbishment of the shower and toilet facilities has progressed but has been subject to contractual and design issues. Prisoners using refurbished facilities have acknowledged the significant improvements made.

Reviews of the ROTL application process to improve efficiency and communication have been welcomed by prisoners and staff.

Discussions on future investment and improvement plans have been welcomed by all parties.

Covid outbreaks have been well managed and the prison is moving toward a more normal regime.

**GREETWELL ROAD
LINCOLN
LN2 4BD**

**HM PRISON
LINCOLN**    Tel: 01522 663000

*For the latest reports on this prison please visit:*
https://tinyurl.com/bdfh26rv

*Important Changes:* **(1) Visits:** the identification necessary to access this prison and visit for social or professional purposes has changed; (2) **Money and Gifts** new rules now apply to these. See page 16 for full details of the above.

**Task of the establishment** Category B male local prison. However, most prisoners were category C or unsentenced and waiting to be sentenced, transferred or released to their home areas outside the local area.

**Certified normal accommodation and operational capacity**
Prisoners held at the time of inspection: 630
Baseline certified normal capacity: 408
In-use certified normal capacity: 403
Operational capacity: 664

**Prison status and key providers**
Public
Prison Group: East Midlands
Prison Group Director: Paul Cawkwell
Governor/Director: Matt Spencer
IMB Chair: Norma Krawiec/Jeremy Taylor
Physical health provider: Nottinghamshire Healthcare NHS Foundation Trust
Mental health provider: Nottinghamshire Healthcare NHS Foundation Trust
Substance misuse treatment provider: Addaction
Prison education framework provider: People Plus
Escort contractor: GeoAmey

**Brief history** Lincoln opened in 1872. Parts of the prison are grade II listed buildings, and three of the four main residential units are the original Victorian design. E wing was opened in 1992.

**Short description of residential units** All wings hold a mixture of remand, convicted and sentenced adult and young adult prisoners.
A wing: up to 216 prisoners (currently 196); includes the first night centre and induction landing
B wing: up to 150 prisoners (currently 141)
C wing: up to 198 prisoners (currently 175)
E wing: up to 165 vulnerable prisoners (currently 152)

## Visiting Information

Book at: www.gov.uk/prison-visits or by telephone on 01522 663 172 Monday to Friday: 9:30am to midday

**Visiting times:** Thursday, Saturday and Sunday: 9am to 11am and 2pm to 4pm

**Legal visits:** There are currently no legal visits taking place.

## INSPECTIONS & REPORTS

**Date of last full inspection** 9–10 December 2019, 6–10 January 2020

*Notable features from this inspection*
• The Lincolnshire Action Trust provided a range of effective services that supported prisoners and their families.
• There had been two self-inflicted deaths since the last inspection, but none in the previous year.
• Around 80% of prisoners were living in cramped and overcrowded conditions.
• About 100 prisoners were released from Lincoln every month.
• 36% of prisoners were released from Lincoln without sustainable accommodation.
• The majority of prisoners, 76%, were released outside the prison's intended resettlement area of North Yorkshire, Humberside and Lincolnshire.

## HMCIP Report published 15 April 2020

HMP Lincoln, built mostly in the late 19th century, is a category B local prison holding, at the time of our inspection, about 630 adult and young adult men. As a prison it faces not insignificant environmental and operational challenges, which are combined currently with the additional challenge of supporting and building capability among a relatively inexperienced staff complement. It is therefore pleasing to report that at this inspection we found a prison that was ensuring, in most areas, reasonably good outcomes and where, since we last inspected in 2017, improvement was clearly evident.

Lincoln was now a much safer prison. Reception and induction arrangements were very good and enhanced considerably by useful interventions from the prison's very impressive partner, the non-governmental organisation (NGO) Lincolnshire Action Trust. The amount of recorded violence had remained unchanged from that seen in 2017, but we found the prison to be calm and ordered, and prisoners' views about their own safety, as reported in our survey, were broadly positive. Initiatives to help reduce violence were meaningful and reflected useful consultation and analysis of data. Segregated prisoners reported positively on their treatment by staff and had better access to facilities than we normally see. Security arrangements were proportionate and were based on good intelligence flows that were beginning to deliver improved outcomes, particularly surrounding drug supply reduction. The positive rate for mandatory drug testing (MDT) was now down to 10%, much better than in most local prisons.

Since we last inspected, there had been two self-inflicted deaths and incidents of self-harm remained stubbornly high. However, the prison's approach to supporting those in crisis was good. Recommendations made by the Prisons and Probation Ombudsman (PPO) following their investigation of the deaths had been implemented and case management of those at risk of self-harm (ACCT) was generally good. In addition, some useful work was being done to try and understand better the factors behind self-harm, for example an initiative that sought to address the impact of debt on self-harm.

Staff-prisoner relationships were very encouraging, despite over half of all staff having been in post for less than two years. In our survey, 81% of prisoners told us they felt respected by staff and our own observations were consistent with this view. Key worker arrangements were embedded, the wings were properly supervised and rules were applied consistently. The prison was working hard to keep up standards of cleanliness and prisoners had generally good access to amenities, although maintaining old cells and ensuring they were properly equipped remained a challenge. Of concern was the fact that despite a slightly reduced roll, some 80% of prisoners were held in overcrowded cells.

Consultation arrangements with prisoners were effective and led to meaningful change, and over 80% of prisoners told us it was easy to make simple applications. We were impressed by the telephone call centre created by the prison and run by trained peer workers, which provided help and advice to prisoners who requested it. Formal complaints were similarly well managed. The promotion of equality and diversity was much improved and benefited from good leadership. Data was analysed usefully and consultation was getting better. Discrimination incidents were also investigated thoroughly. Health care provision, overall, was very good.

Daily routines were predictable. There was sufficient activity for all prisoners, and most had reasonable amounts of time out of cell. The prison's engagement with the learning and skills provider was leading to improved performance, although the recruitment of teaching staff was proving to be a struggle and was limiting progress. Overall the quality of teaching and the education curriculum needed to be better and, despite some vocational and skills acquisition, the achievement of qualifications among learners was low. Our colleagues in Ofsted judged the overall effectiveness of education, skills and work as 'requires improvement'.

The prison faced a particular challenge in managing rehabilitation and release planning, which was complicated by a great variation in the lengths of stay experienced by those held. Alongside the usually local, shorter-stay remand and convicted population, the prison also held many longer sentence prisoners, who were often brought to the prison from well out of the area. The analysis of need in the prison called for some improvement and a strategy that addressed more comprehensively the needs of all was still required. That said, most eligible prisoners had an up-to- date assessment of risk and need (OASys), although there were quite poor levels of contact between prisoners and prison offender managers. Many prisoners held in Lincoln presented quite high risks of harm and it was our view that public protection arrangement needed to be more robust: we make this issue one of our key recommendations. Far too many prisoners were released homeless, which was not helped by some complicated contractual issues among providers and restrictions that seemed to inhibit the prison's ability to grip the issue. This was, however, balanced by some very good practice that provided 'through the gate' and resettlement support. Again, Lincolnshire Action Trust proved to be an excellent partner in providing support for prisoners in maintaining contact with their children and families.

To conclude, the Governor and his team should be commended for the work they have done at Lincoln. Progress at the prison was predicated on the quality of staff-prisoner relationships and some very constructive partnerships. There was attention to getting the basics right in most areas we inspected, but also space for innovation and creativity. This combination was leading to much good practice and meaningful and sustainable improvement. There was lots still to be done and many of the problems like overcrowding had an intractability that required Her Majesty's Prison and Probation Service's (HMPPS) intervention to support the prison. We were confident, however, that the Governor and staff were committed to ensuring continuous improvement. We leave several recommendations which we hope will help support that.

Peter Clarke CVO OBE QPM
HM Chief Inspector of Prisons April 2020

## INDEPENDENT MONITORING BOARD: Annual Report

The law requires every prison to be monitored by an independent Board appointed by the Justice Secretary; these are known as Independent Monitoring Boards (IMBs). The IMB must satisfy itself as to the humane and just treatment of those held in custody within its prison and the range and adequacy of the programmes preparing them for release; it must report annually to the Justice Secretary on how well the prison has met the standards and requirements placed on it.

### IMB Report 1 February 2020 – 31 January 2021
### Published July 2021
### Executive Summary

This report presents the findings of the Independent Monitoring Board (IMB) at HMP/YOI Lincoln for the year 1 February 2020 to 31 January 2021.

We continue to observe the activities of the Governor and his team as maintaining an effective "grip" of the key areas of prison life. We are pleased to note the progress and significant improvements made over the past four years.

It is the view of this board that HMP/YOI Lincoln is a well-run prison which, notwithstanding the limitations of its Victorian buildings and the necessary restrictions consequent upon a pandemic, has delivered a humane regime and a significant reduction in violence and self-harm while keeping its prisoners safe.

### Background to the report

This reporting year has been dominated by the Covid-19 pandemic and the necessary responses to it. From mid-March 2020 onwards the prison has been in lock-down with gradual movement towards a careful loosening of restrictions stalled by the second national wave of infections. By the end of the reporting period the prison was well prepared to move towards a more "normal" situation.

The first positive prisoner Covid-19 case was recorded on 14 April 2020 and the first staff case on 23 April 2020. The prison remains a "red" outbreak site but at the time of writing there is only one case among prisoners and there are two staff off sick with confirmed covid. This was a remarkable recovery. Extraordinary efforts were made to keep the prison running smoothly throughout what might otherwise have been a real crisis, especially when at its height the pandemic had forced over 65 staff off work either with the disease or shielding.

Incoming prisoners, any showing symptoms of Covid-19 and those tested positive or ill have as far as possible been located on designated landings (cohorting units) until being tested negative when they were relocated among the general prison population. Prisoners have spent no more than 40 minutes per day out of cell for exercise and showers, except for those doing essential jobs such as cleaning or kitchen work. Visits to prisoners have been almost totally prohibited.

The regime changes consequent on the pandemic restrictions have severely limited educational opportunities. Prisoner time and numbers in those workshops which continued to function have been carefully rationed. Group religious services have been virtually non-existent. Contact between prisoners and staff has been often by telephone.

Maintenance and other work by outside bodies has continued but to a significant extent during night hours.

From 15 March to 13 September 2020 and again from 12 November 2020 to 31 January 2021 the IMB was unable to function normally due to national lockdown conditions prevailing and advice from the Ministry of Justice. Because of the pandemic and to reduce the possibility of spreading the virus most members of the board were self-shielding for parts of the reporting year and did not go into the prison but kept in touch by telephone. Nonetheless, throughout those periods we had an emergency response capability, management of prisoner applications remotely by telephone and email via the IMB clerk, and also attendance at prison meetings via Zoom and dial-in. The board itself remained in contact with telephone conference calls and Zoom meetings. In consequence of this curtailment of our work our ability to attest first-hand to all that we say is limited, and in some cases our comments represent desk-top research. In particular, for much of the year our usual physical presence, high visibility, and high engagement with individual prisoners and prisoner groups have been very limited.

**Main judgements**
**How safe is the prison?**
Safety at the establishment is a matter of great importance for all staff and, of course, prisoners. Without a safe environment, effective custody and rehabilitation cannot occur, and a lot of attention is rightly paid to this important aspect of the running of the prison. It is the opinion of the board that a range of safety measures are in place, including behaviour management, frequent reviews of and responses to incidents of violence and self-harm, and sharing of information among all relevant departments within the prison.

The principal elements of a safe environment for the prison are centred around the early days in custody, how behaviour is managed (particularly the encouragement of positive behaviour), the use of rarely applied but sometimes essential measures such as segregation and the use of force. Safeguarding features large in consideration around this area, particularly in regard to the protection of vulnerable adults and those at risk of suicide or self-harm.

The coordination of activities is overseen by the safer custody committee, which meets monthly. This committee is a multidisciplinary group, including representatives from offender management, security, mental health, We Are With You and the chaplaincy. An IMB member attended all of the meetings throughout the year. Prisoner Listener representatives, present in a normal year, were absent. The meeting is followed by shorter supplementary meetings that consider issues such as prisoner transfers, controls assurance and allocation to wings and cells.

The purpose of the meeting is to review the safer custody team reports on incidents of suicide and self-harm and incidents of violent behaviour, and the responses to these. Information is shared on ACCT (Assessment, Care in Custody and Teamwork) activity, incidents of self-harm, deaths in custody, assaults, violence reduction, constant supervision and safeguarding issues. Analyses are made against incidence reports to gauge how well the prison is doing compared with similar prisons elsewhere.

**How fairly and humanely are prisoners treated?**
Overall, it is the opinion of the board that prisoners at HMP/YOI Lincoln are treated fairly and with respect. This is demonstrated throughout the establishment, but in particular by the regime on the wings in difficult circumstances, the level of use of force, the attention given to equality and fairness, and the management of segregated prisoners in the care and separation unit (CSU).

Moreover, in the view of the board the establishment has a positive emphasis on the humane treatment of the prisoners in its care. This is evidenced by the continuing efforts to improve the cleanliness and appearance of the establishment, the attention to and focus on safety in custody, and including the ACCT process, the use of force, segregation processes, the excellent services provided by the healthcare team, and the emphasis on treating every prisoner as a unique individual. There has been a welcome reduction in self-harm.

**How well are prisoners' health and wellbeing needs met?**
The provision of healthcare services is of a standard at least comparable to that available in the community.

All prisoners are seen and assessed by healthcare staff within 24 hours of arrival. All physical, dentistry and optometry services continued to be provided throughout the reporting year with Covid-19 and flu vaccinations being implemented in line with those of the general public. Cohorting (isolation) arrangements for new and symptomatic prisoners were put in place together with regime changes to minimise the likelihood of cross-infection and spread of Covid-19; probably in consequence of this there was, as far as we can tell in the absence of coroners' inquests at this time, only one covid-related death.

The prison has a high number of prisoners with mental health problems which are well managed by the mental health team. The incidence of mental ill health is estimated at around 40% of the prison population with a similar proportion declaring that they encounter significant issues through their learning disabilities and the challenges contingent on neurodiversity. Personality disorder is a confounding factor which complicates all interventions.

Despite the necessarily restricted regime prisoners were provided with greater television access, remote learning facilities, library books and distraction packs and, whenever possible, outdoor exercise. Although visiting was not permitted for much of the reporting year, in-cell telephones and additional call credit went some way to compensating for the lack of direct contact with family and friends, and some video contact has been made possible via Purple Visits (video links).

**How well are prisoners progressed towards successful resettlement?**
The offender management unit (OMU), Lincolnshire Action Trust (LAT), Shelter and other agencies all have processes in place to support the preparation for release of prisoners. The principal concerns of the board are the very limited training opportunities available especially during the reporting year, and the number of prisoners, albeit small thanks to covid interventions, who, notwithstanding the best efforts of the various agencies, are released to homelessness or no fixed abode. The government's "Everybody In" emergency homelessness prevention strategy for covid has been a welcome safety net, but there are still some 25% of prisoners who, either by choice or due to their disruptive history with housing providers, are being discharged to "no fixed abode". Preparations for discharge programmes of work and education have been severely disrupted by the national regime having to be enforced. However, the use of written materials, Way Out TV and the maintenance of the library service have all combined to maximise the potential for discharge preparation in these extraordinary times.

**Main areas for development**
**TO THE MINISTER**
1. As in previous years, the Board remains concerned about the tardy manner in which

numerous repair and maintenance jobs across the establishment are dealt with.
2. Despite the great efforts made locally, the Board remains concerned about the high level of homelessness of discharged prisoners.
3. The Board is concerned that there is a small but nevertheless significant group of prisoners in Lincoln who are subject to indeterminate sentences for public protection (IPP) and have remained in custody well beyond their tariff date.
4. Despite best local efforts, the board is concerned that prisoners who are in need of transfer to a mental health institution sometimes wait far too long for an appropriate placement. The absence of a comprehensive and readily accessible personality disorder treatment service is a continuing concern.

**TO THE PRISON SERVICE**
1. The Board continues to question when we can expect the ceiling of the CSU to be replaced as previously advised, or is it no longer considered to be required?

**TO THE GOVERNOR**
1. Whilst acknowledging that the building structures do not lend themselves to easy access for prisoners who have mobility difficulties or are wheelchair bound, are there any further plans to improve disabled access to all parts of the establishment?
2. How soon will Samaritan training of Listeners resume?
3. How can the needs of some prisoners for education in social and interpersonal skills be identified and met in the absence of face-to-face teaching?

**Progress since the last report**
Many and various improvements are noted throughout this report but the board is particularly pleased to draw attention to the matters mentioned below.
1. A significant reduction in self-harm and violence amongst prisoners.
2. An apparent reduction in illicit drug use among prisoners.
3. The commissioning of replacement of the A Wing lift.
4. The clearing of the A Wing exercise yard which is now back in use by prisoners.
5. The installation of CCTV on E Wing.
6. More security fencing and gate alarms fitted.
7. Improvements to the appearance and fabric of the buildings.
8. Significant improvements to water treatment.
9. The prison's capacity to deal with infectious disease outbreaks, which has at times needed to be exemplary.

**BAWTRY ROAD**
**HATFIELD**
**DONCASTER**
**DN7 6EE**

**HM PRISON LINDHOLME** | **TEL: 01302 524700**

*For the latest reports on this prison please visit:*
https://tinyurl.com/bdfh26rv

*Important Changes:* **(1) Visits:** the identification necessary to access this prison and visit for social or professional purposes has changed; (2) **Money and Gifts** new rules now apply to these. See page 16 for full details of the above.

**Task of the establishment** Category C adult male prison.

**Certified normal accommodation and operational capacity**
Prisoners held at the time of this visit: 902
Baseline certified normal capacity: 935
In-use certified normal capacity: 933
Operational capacity: 935

**Prison status and key providers**
Public
Prison Group: Yorkshire
Prison Group Director: Helen Judge
Governor/Director: Rob Kellett
IMB Chair: Nigel Wood
Physical health provider: Practice Plus Group
Mental health provider: Practice Plus Group
Substance use treatment provider:
Practice Plus Group
Prison education framework provider: Novus
Escort contractor: GeoAmey

**Brief history** HMP Lindholme was previously an RAF camp and opened as a prison in 1985. It currently holds category C convicted males over 21, including life sentence prisoners.

**Short description of residential units** Ten wings with single and multi-occupancy rooms. Six of the wings are of a dormitory design and have single and multi-occupancy rooms on lockable spurs.

**Visiting Information**
Book a visit on 01302 524 980 Monday to Friday, 9am to 11am and 1:30pm to 3:30pm
**Visiting times:** Monday. Wednesday, Friday, Saturday, and Sunday: 2:15pm to 3:15pm.

**Legal visits:** There are currently no legal visits taking place.

You can book a legal phone call by email.
legal.visits.lindholme@justice.co.uk

**INSPECTIONS & REPORTS**
**Scrutiny Visit: 13 and 27-28 October 2020**
**Published: 01 December 2020**
This report presents the findings from our scrutiny visit to HMP Lindholme on the conditions and treatment of prisoners during the Covid-19 pandemic. Lindholme is a category C prison, near Doncaster, sited on an old RAF base. The prison held around 900 prisoners at the time of our visit. Over half the prisoners were high-risk offenders, with a large number (more than 200) having links to organised crime. The majority of prisoners were serving lengthy sentences, a fifth of which were indeterminate or for life.

The senior management team had implemented quarantine and shielding arrangements in accordance with national directives to manage the risks associated with the Covid-19 virus. There had been no Covid-19 cases among prisoners since the start of the pandemic, and only a small number of confirmed cases among staff. However, as we have seen in other prisons, there was little evidence of social distancing by staff or prisoners on residential units. At the time of our visit, very few staff were wearing the face masks recently made available by HM Prison and Probation Service (HMPPS). Prisoners repeatedly told us that they felt staff should wear masks to minimise transmission of the virus, especially as the local area Covid-19 alert level had moved to a higher tier.

The severely curtailed regime at the start of the pandemic restrictions in March 2020 was reasonable, but almost seven months later there had been little progress in ensuring that prisoners had adequate time out of cell or purposeful activity. The time unlocked was severely restricted to less than an hour a day for most prisoners, and it was not uncommon for time in the open air to be limited to 20 minutes in a day. Prisoners could also remain locked in their cells for 28 hours in one stretch at the weekend. There was mounting frustration among prisoners who reported that the excessive time spent locked up was having a negative impact on their well-being, including weight gain, difficulty in sleeping and a deterioration in their mental health.

The governor had plans to ease restrictions by opening the gym, and doubling the time unlocked for outdoor exercise and activity on the wing. The management team had identified the staff resource and space required to implement these changes, and Public Health England had given its support. However, negotiations with the local staff association had not reached an agreement. While we were aware of the need to ease restrictions in a safe and measured way, progress had been far too slow and the restrictions in place were not proportionate when compared with other prisons.

The failure to improve the regime during the summer meant that prisoners were now subject to a second-wave tightening of restrictions without having had much reprieve. Following the local community's recent move into a higher Covid-19 alert level, social visits had been suspended and the prison's plans to move to the next stage of the HMPPS recovery plan (stage 2, see Glossary of terms) had been put on hold.

Although the prison had made significant progress in improving safety since our inspection in 2017, with a reduction in assaults by half, incidents of violence and self-harm were now on an upward trajectory. Following a drop in violence and self-harm figures at the start of the restrictions, the number of incidents was gradually increasing back to pre-pandemic levels. In general, the wings and outside areas were kept clean and tidy, but some shower rooms were in poor condition. A programme of refurbishment and upgrade of the older wings was under way. Despite some poor living conditions, those prisoners located on the older wings liked being able to live together on a small spur, where they were not confined to their cells. However, we found too many recurring problems with heating and ventilation, damp walls, broken washing and drying machines, worn mattresses and lack of privacy screens. Prisoners also complained of insufficient cleaning materials to improve cleanliness to slow the spread of the virus.

The day-to-day frustrations reported to us by prisoners and the impact of the severe regime restrictions were too often exacerbated by a lack of meaningful engagement with staff. While we saw some good staff-prisoner interactions, in our survey only 64% of prisoners said that staff treated them with respect. A light-touch key worker system had been introduced since March, but many prisoners said that it was not working well. In our survey, only around a quarter of prisoners said that a member of staff had asked them in the last week how they were getting on. Equality work had also suffered during the period of restrictions, but there was good management attention to any evidence of possible discrimination. In our survey, prisoners from a black or minority ethnic background were more negative about staff behaviour, with fewer than half reporting that staff treated them with respect. There was, however, a creative approach to marking Black History Month under the present conditions, and the chaplaincy had responded well to the challenges of the pandemic restrictions.

Although in our survey prisoners had poor perceptions of health services, the health providers had worked effectively in managing the risks around Covid-19 and had continued to provide essential services. Restrictions on services and challenges for the prison in enabling prisoners to attend health care appointments had exacerbated waiting lists, especially for those with long-term conditions and dental needs.

Although workshops were closed and only around 10% of prisoners were engaged in the prison's essential jobs, the education team had recently been active in managing individualised in-cell learning. Tutors were now also going on to the wings to see learners and work with small groups. Considerably more prisoners were engaging with education than before the Covid-19 period.

Take-up of social visits had been low, but the prison had introduced the incentive for families to buy prisoners a pack of items after the visit to encourage more visits. The prison had requested an increase in sessions available for video calling ('Purple Visits', see Glossary of terms) following the recent suspension of social visits.

Prisoners were frustrated at the lack of contact with their prison offender manager and the inability to progress with their sentence plan. Accredited programme delivery had ceased at the start of the restrictions in March, and plans to re-start were not well developed. However, there had still been progressive transfers of a significant number of category D prisoners to open conditions.

The measures for public protection were a concern, with five high-risk prisoners released during the pandemic restrictions without confirmation of their multi-agency public protection arrangements (MAPPA). Although not a designated resettlement prison, Lindholme had released about 20 prisoners a month. Despite this, 10 prisoners released in the previous three months had no accommodation to go to on their day of release.

Since the previous inspection there had clearly been progress, with significant improvements in prison safety. It was especially disappointing, therefore, to find such an excessively poor regime exacerbating mounting frustration, and the deterioration of well-being for many prisoners. There was a clear need for managers and local staff associations to come to an agreement about safe and credible plans that would allow the prison regime to develop and ensure outcomes for those detained improved.

Charlie Taylor, HM Chief Inspector of Prisons
November 2020

## Key concerns and recommendations

Key concerns and recommendations identify the issues of most importance to improving outcomes for prisoners and are designed to help establishments prioritise and address the most significant weaknesses in the treatment and conditions of prisoners.

During this visit we identified some areas of key concern, and have made a small number of key recommendations for the prison to address.

Key concern: Staff had limited individual contact with prisoners. In our survey, only 64% of respondents said that most staff treated them with respect. Despite some good interactions, officers held themselves apart from prisoners and did not take the initiative to engage with them. Many prisoners said that staff did not regularly ask them about their individual welfare. Key recommendation: Key worker sessions should resume for all prisoners. Staff should engage positively with each prisoner by checking on their well-being and any concerns or needs, at least weekly, noting the outcome in the prisoner's electronic case record. (To the governor)

Key concern: There were too many recurring problems with basic living conditions, including very poor shower rooms, broken washing and drying machines, problems with heating and ventilation, and no privacy screen for the in-cell toilet in double cells. Too many mattresses were past their useful life and too thin, a problem sometimes compounded by bent metal bed bases. The prison had begun to address some of these problems, but progress was insufficient. Key recommendation: There should be investment to bring living conditions on the wings up to an acceptable standard, and make sure that all residential services and facilities are in good working order. (To HMPPS and the governor)

Key concern: Prisoners from black and minority ethnic backgrounds had much more negative perceptions about staff behaviour than white prisoners. Fewer than half (48%) of black and minority ethnic prisoners, compared with 73% of white prisoners, said that most staff treated them with respect, and 58% said they had experienced bullying or victimisation by staff. Black and minority ethnic prisoners were much less likely to say that it was easy to get a job in the prison. Key recommendation: The prison should address the poor perceptions of black and minority ethnic prisoners and ensure fair and positive treatment. Outcomes and perceptions should be measured and the needs of black and minority prisoners understood and, where possible, met. (To the governor)

Key concern: Prisoners with long-term health conditions did not receive any ongoing support or annual reviews, and waiting times for prisoners to use dental services had lengthened significantly, which could lead to a deterioration in prisoner health.

Key recommendation: The prison should work with the health care partnership board to ensure coordinated action to reduce the health care waiting lists, and enable prisoners to attend appointments without delay. (To the governor)

Key concern: Many prisoners had less than an hour a day out of cell on four days a week, and 45 minutes on the other days, and they could be locked up for 28 hours at a stretch over the weekend. It was not uncommon for their time in the open air to be limited to 20 minutes a day, and no prisoner received more than 30 minutes outdoors.

Key recommendation: Time out of cell for prisoners should be increased to enable more purposeful activity and more time in the open air. (To the governor)

Key concern: A backlog in OASys (offender assessment system) assessments meant that not all prisoners had an up-to-date sentence plan, and prisoners were not always involved in their sentence planning. Prisoners were frustrated with the lack of contact with offender managers and the lack of opportunity to progress through their sentence. Accredited programmes had been suspended at the start of the Covid-19 restrictions, and there were no immediate plans to resume their delivery.

Key recommendation: All prisoners should have an up-to-date sentence plan in which they are involved. Prison offender managers should engage with prisoners more frequently and discuss the impact of the regime restrictions on their progression. If accredited interventions are not available, alternative support for progression should be detailed and realistic objectives set to meet key dates in a prisoner's sentence. (To the governor)

Key concern: There were significant weaknesses in the management of public protection. The weekly interdepartmental risk management team meetings were poorly attended, and high-risk prisoners were not always discussed in enough time to complete all key elements of their release; this meant that some were released without confirmation of a multi-agency public protection management level. The prison had a substantial backlog of prisoner telephone calls waiting to be monitored, but although there were plans to address this and safeguard the public, these depended on adequate staff resources forthcoming.

Key recommendation: There should be regular and consistent multidisciplinary attendance at the interdepartmental risk management team meeting, and all high-risk prisoners should be discussed well enough in advance of their release to make sure that all key elements, including multi-agency public protection management levels, are confirmed. Telephone call monitoring should take place promptly. (To the governor)

### Notable positive practice

We define notable positive practice as innovative practice or practice that leads to particularly good outcomes from which other establishments may be able to learn. Inspectors look for evidence of good outcomes for prisoners; original, creative or particularly effective approaches to problem-solving or achieving the desired goal; and how other establishments could learn from or replicate the practice.

Inspectors found the following example of notable positive practice during this visit.

• The education team had been active in providing in-cell learning materials to prisoners and responding to them promptly, through daily collection of work, delivery of marked work and tracking of all achievements. Tutors were delivering some one-to-one sessions, and working with small groups of up to three learners. Remote learning had been provided through iPads, under supervision. Considerably more prisoners were engaging with education than before the Covid-19 period.

### INDEPENDENT MONITORING BOARD: Annual Report

The law requires every prison to be monitored by an independent Board appointed by the Justice Secretary; these are known as Independent Monitoring Boards (IMBs). The IMB must satisfy itself as to the humane and just treatment of those held in custody within its prison and the range and adequacy of the programmes preparing them for release; it must report annually to the Justice Secretary on how well the prison has met the standards and requirements placed on it.

1 February 2021 to 31 January 2022
Published May 2022
### EXECUTIVE SUMMARY
### Background to the report

The prison has continued to be in some form of lockdown throughout this year. Although the stringent measures were eased in the middle of the year, in order to avoid spreading the Covid virus, prisoners still spent long periods of the day inside their cells or in small cohorts of limited numbers.

It was possible to re-commence some work and education in classes during the year, but that had to be ceased again in December because of the resurgence of the Omicron variant. However, the need for prisoners to spend time outside their cells is well recognised and every effort has been made to allow as much time as possible for

exercise, including gym sessions, and association. During the course of the year a digital infrastructure has been introduced throughout the prison, providing all prisoners with their own laptop computer. This gives them access to a wide variety of information about the prison, access to approved entertainment and allows them to undertake a variety of requests of their own, such as daily meal choices, canteen orders, and requests for new approved phone numbers. This facility is only available within the confines of the prison and does not enable prisoners to submit formal complaints. The introduction of this service has been enthusiastically welcomed by the vast majority of the prisoners and provides a significant step forward in their preparation for returning to life outside the prison, which has become ever more digitally focussed.

### Main judgements
### How safe is the prison?

The majority of prisoners (79%) consider the prison to be safe although 54% are aware of victimisation, racism or bullying.

Some 33% of prisoners consider the drug problem in the prison to be serious, while some 13% consider the alcohol problem to be serious. Both these figures are lower than the figures for 2019, although there remains a high percentage (49%) who describe the drug problem as 'moderate'.

### How fairly and humanely are prisoners treated?

The proportion of cells designed for single occupancy which are authorised for double occupancy has not reduced and it is disappointing that there are no plans to reduce the number in the foreseeable future, even though additional capital funding has been committed to provide additional prison places by the mid 2020s. It is commendable that at HMP Lindholme considerable funds have been spent over the past year to bring the accommodation back to its authorised state, although there remains a constant demand to replace privacy curtains.

### How well are prisoners' health and wellbeing needs met?

The pandemic has continued to present a major challenge to the delivery of healthcare in the prison. The Board welcomes the efforts made by the staff to undertake the Covid vaccination programme of prisoners and it is encouraging to see that waiting times have fallen in all areas except dentistry. It is disappointing to note from the survey of prisoners that more than half still express the opinion that it is not easy to access healthcare, only a slightly smaller proportion than in the previous survey two years ago (56.6%). Although the wellbeing of prisoners has continued to suffer throughout the year because of the lengthy lockdown regime, the Board notes that while mental health referrals have risen, those referred have been seen promptly.

While prisoners were given the appropriate time outside their cells during each stage of the lockdown, the regime necessitated limited prisoner association to the detriment of their socialisation.

The Board is grateful for the introduction of the in-cell phone facility for prisoners, for not only improving their wellbeing by giving them much needed access to the outside world, but also enabling Board members to deal quickly with prisoners' concerns.

### How well are prisoners progressed towards successful resettlement?

There has been little progress towards improving successful resettlement over the past year. HMP Lindholme is not a designated resettlement prison and lacks the resource to provide a satisfactory resettlement service. It is of concern that 222 prisoners were released into the community last year without the full benefit of a structured pre-release programme.

That said, the Governor is well aware of this shortcoming and measures have been taken recently to address the problem and we look forward to a significant improvement over the next year.

### Main areas for development
### TO THE MINISTER

We are still concerned at the number of men who remain in prison with indeterminate Imprisonment for public protection (IPP) sentences. Although the numbers in this prison have dropped from 53 to 38 over the past year, we continue to urge the Minister to maintain efforts to get rid of what we consider to be an iniquitous sentence altogether.

### TO THE PRISON SERVICE

We are aware that the problems of overcrowding are caused by a lack of capacity in the prison estate, however the problem remains a very real one which is causing difficulties for prison staff, as well as having a detrimental effect on the mental health of prisoners. More needs to be done in the short term to address the problem, rather than waiting for a long-term building plan to provide the necessary additional capacity.

We note that if this prison is to develop as a training prison, many of the buildings in the industrial area require significant investment.

### TO THE GOVERNOR

The initiative to provide a satisfactory resettlement service should be continued until such time as men can be transferred to resettlement prisons before the end of their sentence.

A large proportion of prisoners who were surveyed said that their complaints were not handled in a timely manner. We recommend that the matter be reviewed in order to improve prisoners' confidence in the complaints system.

Following a large increase in the number of complaints about the way that prisoners' property is handled, a better system of dealing with the matter was initiated towards the end of our reporting year. We would urge that this initiative is reinforced in order to further reduce the dissatisfaction that arises amongst prisoners. Consider ways to reintegrate library attendance into the weekly regime.

### Progress since the last report

o The prison digital infrastructure has been introduced throughout the prison and has been well received by the majority of prisoners.

o While the number of double occupancy cells has not reduced, there has been considerable improvement in bringing all cells back to their authorised state.

o Considering the constraints caused by the pandemic, the provision of healthcare has improved with waiting times returning to pre-Covid times, apart from dentistry.

o The blended learning approach to education has enabled many prisoners to take up the opportunity of education courses during the pandemic.

PERRY
HUNTINGDON
CAMBS
PE28 0SR

HM PRISON SERVICE

HMP & YOI LITTLEHEY

Tel: 01480 335000

*For the latest reports on this prison please visit:*
https://tinyurl.com/bdfh26rv

*Important Changes:* **(1) Visits:** the identification necessary to access this prison and visit for social or professional purposes has changed; (2) **Money and Gifts** new rules now apply to these. See page 16 for full details of the above.

**Task of the establishment** HMP Littlehey is a category C training prison specialising in holding prisoners convicted of sexual offences.

**Certified normal accommodation and operational capacity**
Prisoners held at the time of inspection: 1,210
Baseline certified normal capacity: 1,154
In-use certified normal capacity: 1,154
Operational capacity: 1,220

## Prison status and key providers
Public

Prison Group: Bedfordshire, Cambridgeshire & Norfolk

Prison Group Director: Gary Monaghan

Governor/Director: Olivia Phelps

IMB Chair: Harry Chandlers

Physical health provider: Northamptonshire Healthcare NHS Foundation Trust

Mental health provider: Northamptonshire Healthcare NHS Foundation Trust

Substance use treatment provider: Phoenix Futures

Learning and skills provider: PeoplePlus

Escort contractor: Serco

**Brief history** HMP Littlehey, located in the village of Perry in Cambridgeshire, is a category C training prison for men convicted of sex offences. It is the largest prison in Europe for men convicted of sexual offences, and at the end of the reporting year, 94% of its population had been convicted of a sexual offence as their index offence.

In 2021:

48% of prisoners were aged 50 years and over at the end of the reporting period, compared with a national figure of 17%. Sixteen percent were under the age of 30.

Of the 527 people over 50, 32.8% (173) were in their 60s and 26.4% (139) were 70 or older (compared with national prison figures of 24.7% and 12.8% respectively).

The prison housed over 45 nationalities and 26 religious denominations, not including those stating 'no religion', atheist or agnostic.

The prison held 1,098 prisoners at the end of 2021 (compared with an operational capacity of 1,180 and an average end-of-month population of 1,136). 925 prisoners were accommodated in single-occupancy cells and 173 in double-occupancy cells, of whom 41 were the sole occupants. 66 cells designed for single occupancy are allocated for sharing by two prisoners.

There are four constant watch cells.

Healthcare services, including mental health care, were provided by the Northampton Health NHS Foundation Trust, with support from the charity Phoenix Futures for delivering substance misuse programmes.

From August 2020 dental services were provided by Prison-Centred Dental Care. Social care was provided by Cambridgeshire County Council, as were library facilities until April 2020 when the contract was awarded to Suffolk Libraries. Education was delivered by PeoplePlus.

The contract for facilities management was held by Government Facilities Services Limited (GFSL).

The visitors centre and visits hall were run by the Ormiston Trust.

Other providers to the prison included the Samaritans, Prison Visitors, Prison Fellowship, Peace Partners, Relate, Shannon Trust, Sue Ryder, Christians Against Poverty, and the Mothers Union.

There were 13 residential wings at the start of the period, including a dedicated reception wing, two enhanced wings, an accredited enabling environment wing, a progressive wing, a small wing dedicated to prisoners with indeterminate sentences for public protection (IPP), and two wings dedicated to older prisoners.

An additional wing was added during the year to accommodate the social distancing demands of the Coronavirus pandemic. Inadequate foundations led to its subsequent removal from service. One of the two enhanced wings was also removed from service after being condemned by HMPPS. HMP Littlehey therefore ended the period with 12 residential wings.

The residential accommodation, set in extensive well-maintained gardens, is supported by two kitchens, two healthcare centres, an education facility, workshops, two libraries, two gyms, two multi-faith rooms, a CSU with nine operational cells, two all-weather sports pitches and a visits hall.

## Short description of residential units

| | |
|---|---|
| A wing | General population |
| B wing | General population |
| C wing | Community wing, run on rehabilitative culture principles |
| D wing | General population |
| E wing | Induction unit |
| F wing | Progression unit for enhanced residents |
| G wing | Progression unit for enhanced residents |
| H wing | Accredited enabling environment |
| I wing | Elderly unit with support |
| J wing | Elderly unit with support |
| K wing | General population |
| L wing | General population |
| M wing | Indeterminate sentence for public protection (IPP) unit |

Wings A–H are on the original site and are referred to locally as Lakeside. Wings I–M are on the newer site and are referred to locally as Woodlands.

## Visiting Information

Booking line: 01480 335 650 Tuesday to Sunday: 8:30am to 4:30pm or email:

socialvisits.littlehey@hmps.gsi.gov.uk

**Visiting times:** Tuesday to Friday: 2pm to 4pm
Saturday and Sunday: 9am to 11am & 2pm to 4pm.

**Legal visits:** There are currently no legal visits taking place.

## INSPECTIONS & REPORTS
**Date of last inspection** 22 July – 2 August 2019
**SSV: Section 6.2.3.1**
**HMCIP Report, published 17 December 2019**
Located near Huntingdon in Cambridgeshire, Littlehey is a category C training prison, holding up to 1,220 adult male prisoners. With a specialist function and holding men from across the country, the prison is one of a very small number that holds only those convicted of a sexual offence and as such the profile of prisoners held is unusual. Forty-four per cent of prisoners were serving lengthy sentences of between four and 10 years, with over a third serving more than 10 years. Around 150 prisoners were serving indeterminate sentences, including life. Among the population nearly half were over the age of 50 and of all those held, some 78% presented a high or very high risk of harm.

When we last inspected Littlehey in 2015, we found a prison that was both safe and respectful, but where outcomes in purposeful activity and rehabilitation and release planning were insufficiently good. At this inspection we were pleased to find that outcomes in safety and respect remained good, and had improved in purposeful activity, but disappointingly remained insufficient in the important test of rehabilitation. Littlehey continued to be an overwhelmingly safe prison. New prisoners were received well into the prison and helped to settle. The prison was calm and prisoners reported to us that they felt safe. Very little violence was recorded and a culture that incentivised good behaviour helped greatly. There had been some increase in the use of force but oversight was satisfactory and the use of segregation had decreased since our last inspection. The segregation regime was also much better with re-integration actively supported. Security arrangements were proportionate and the use of illicit drugs remained low. Self-harm had increased in recent years but again remained low. There had tragically been one self-inflicted death since we last visited but care for those in crisis was generally very good.

In our survey of prisoners, the majority indicated that they felt respected by staff and the interactions we observed were relaxed although not always particularly proactive. They were improving, however, following the successful introduction of the keyworker scheme. The internal and external areas of the prison were clean and well-maintained, although some overcrowding and ongoing problems with heating systems were significant issues. Access to kit and other amenities was good, as was the quality of the food. General consultation arrangements were also good and while the promotion of equality had weaknesses, outcomes for prisoners across most protected characteristics were reasonably equitable. Prisoners were positive in their views about the quality of healthcare they received.

Time out of cell for most prisoners in full-time activity was good, although we found a surprisingly high 17% locked in cell during the working day. There was sufficient activity for all, but allocation arrangements were inflexible and unresponsive. The quality and range of education, training and work was good and prisoners could gain qualifications up to level 3. Many made satisfactory progress and were clearly engaged and motivated. Our colleagues in Ofsted judged the overall effectiveness of education, skills and work to be good. Physical education was impressive.

The area where outcomes were weakest was in rehabilitation and release planning. The promotion of family ties needed improvement. About half of prisoners did not have an up-to-date offender assessment system (OASys) assessment, many having arrived without such an assessment. This was concerning given the high level of risk the population presented. Contact between offender supervisors and prisoners was inconsistent and often reactive, with very little one-to-one sentence planning work taking place. There were also quite limited opportunities for those prisoners who did not meet the threshold for participation in offending behaviour programmes. Those who were eligible could normally access programmes prior to release. Public protection arrangements were not sufficiently robust and the prison had only recently introduced resettlement initiatives capable of supporting sufficiently the approximately 30 men discharged each month.

Overall, and despite some criticisms, this report reflects some very good findings and some excellent outcomes for prisoners at Littlehey. The prison had a clearly defined function and held a substantial number of elevated risk men in safe and respectful conditions. Prisoners benefited from a very good daily regime and we saw examples of good practice. Going forward, the prison's main priorities are to assess and reduce the risks of the prisoners it holds, and to prepare those being released for successful resettlement into the community.

Peter Clarke CVO OBE QPM July 2019
HM Chief Inspector of Prisons

## INDEPENDENT MONITORING BOARD: Annual Report
The law requires every prison to be monitored by an independent Board appointed by the Justice Secretary; these are known as Independent

Monitoring Boards (IMBs). The IMB must satisfy itself as to the humane and just treatment of those held in custody within its prison and the range and adequacy of the programmes preparing them for release; it must report annually to the Justice Secretary on how well the prison has met the standards and requirements placed on it.

**IMB Report February 2020 to January 2021**
**Published October 2021**
**Executive summary**
**Background to the report**
This report presents the findings of the Independent Monitoring Board (IMB) at HMP Littlehey for the period 1 February 2020 to 31 January 2021. It should be noted that for 11 months of that period i.e. March 2020 – Jan 2021 the prison has undergone severe restrictions in its normal regime and activities due to the necessary response to the Coronavirus pandemic.

The normal monitoring activities of the Board have been extremely limited with many members unable to visit the prison in person, either through guidance from the Secretariat or from personal concerns. Attempts to monitor remotely were met with variable success. The focus of the report is therefore about how the prison was able to operate a regime and fulfil statutory expectations given the regime it was obliged to adopt.

**Main judgements**
**How safe is the prison?**
Overall HMP Littlehey continues to be a safe and secure prison. There has only been one major incident when the command suite was opened during the last 12 months and a low rate of prisoner-on-prisoner violence.

**How fairly and humanely are prisoners treated?**
With few exceptions prisoners are treated with respect, decency and humanity. In some cases, the prison has found it difficult to provide the specialist interventions needed for those with complex issues, such as the prolific self-harmers and those repeatedly housed, or housed long-term, in the care and separation unit (CSU).

**How well are prisoners' health and wellbeing needs met?**
The coronavirus pandemic has significantly impacted the health and wellbeing needs of the prisoners. The prison has managed the challenges provided by the pandemic well. It was initially designated as an outbreak site in March 2020 and in recognition of this, and the fact that 48% of its population are aged 50+ and therefore particularly vulnerable to the virus, it immediately instigated protocols to protect all the prisoners. This included designating two wings as isolation wings and enforcing strict PPE and social distancing adherence.

The cessation of most non-essential prison activities including much education and all workshops and gym, together with the restrictions in prisoner association and time out of cells, has inevitably impacted negatively on prisoners' mental wellbeing. However, the prison has managed these restrictions as positively as possible.

**How well are prisoners progressed towards successful resettlement?**
As stated in last year's report, HMP Littlehey is not a resettlement prison and is not funded for this activity although it typically releases 25-30 prisoners each month.

Within the limited resources available the prison makes good efforts to support the resettlement of prisoners; however, due to the offences of those being released their resettlement often has to be to a new rather than their home area. This creates complications for both the prisoners and those charged with supporting their resettlement.

The enforced closure of G Wing, which was a progression unit housing enhanced prisoners, is a backward step. It has significantly reduced the opportunities for prisoners to develop their personal independence and decision-making skills with the prisoners being moved back to general population wings.

**Main areas for development**
**TO THE MINISTER**
The Board was advised during the annual reporting period that the residential wing to be built to replace the closed G wing will consist of double cells. The Board believes this contravenes Ministry of Justice strategy and would be a retrograde step in terms of safety and decency. The Board believes that appropriate accommodation for the aged and disabled prison population needs to be a significant consideration in the final decision of the replacement for G wing.

As stated in last year's report, there continue to be too many prisoners forced to share cells, some of which are designed as single cells.

**TO THE PRISON SERVICE**
Property continues to be the area most complained about and recognised as such across the prison estate. The HMPPS property group has not yet introduced any changes to address this issue and as far as the Board is aware the promised policy framework for prisoner's

property has still not been published.

In addition, the slow, or lack of, response from some prisons in responding to prisoner complaints about their missing or damaged property after their transfer to HMP Littlehey continues to be an area of frustration for all concerned.

The Board reiterates the questions we asked last year – when will the new policy framework for prisoners' property be published? And, when issue s do arise, how will the prison service ensure complaints to other establishments are dealt with in a timely manner?

## TO THE GOVERNOR

Given its large elderly population, HMP Littlehey should continue to provide opportunities for physical activity, mental stimulation and to encourage mobility. In addition, the provision of suitable accommodation, including wheelchair access where appropriate, needs to be given priority.

While the Board recognises the progress made during the year on understanding the equality issues at HMP Littlehey it believes this area needs further development to fully understand any underlying factors or issues which may be leading to the over-representation of different groups within such areas as adjudications.

With the high number of deaths in custody the Board asks whether the Governor will be focussing on the learning points from those that have occurred and, whether she will be addressing the number of trained family liaison officers (FLOs).

## Progress since the last report

The Board is pleased that the ongoing issues with the heating and hot water infrastructure are now being addressed through the funded programme of work that has been agreed. It recognises that this will be an ongoing project.

The publication of the older persons strategy in December 2020 is to be welcomed and the Board looks forward to seeing it implemented once the prison is able to move to a post-pandemic regime.

The Board has observed an increased focus on diversity and inclusion within the prison during the year. It is particularly noted that senior prison leadership have promoted equalities as a priority and have made efforts to continue to involve prisoner representatives for protected characteristics despite regime restrictions. The Board feels positive regarding the progress made to date.

**68 HORNBY ROAD**
**LIVERPOOL**
**L9 3DF**

**HM PRISON SERVICE**

**HM PRISON LIVERPOOL**   **Tel: 0151 530 4000**

*For the latest reports on this prison please visit:* https://tinyurl.com/bdfh26rv

*Important Changes:* **(1) Visits:** the identification necessary to access this prison and visit for social or professional purposes has changed; (2) **Money and Gifts** new rules now apply to these. See page 16 for full details of the above.

**Task of the establishment** HMP Liverpool is a local category B prison serving the Merseyside area.

**Certified normal accommodation and operational capacity**
Prisoners held 2021: 800
Baseline certified normal capacity: 1,173
In-use certified normal capacity: 700
Operational capacity: 700

**Prison status and key providers**
Public
Prison Group: Greater Manchester, Merseyside & Cheshire
Prison Group Director: Tim Allen
Governor/Director: Mark Livingston
IMB Chair: John Hudson
Physical health provider: Spectrum
Mental health provider: Merseycare
Substance use treatment provider: Change, Grow, Live (CGL)
Learning and skills provider: Novus
Escort contractor: GeoAmey

**Brief history** HMP Liverpool is a category B local adult male prison. It was opened in 1855 and, as a Victorian prison, faces many challenges with the infrastructure of the original building.

At the start of 2020, the operational capacity had been reduced to 700, in order to facilitate an extensive programme of refurbishment. Due to the pandemic, the capacity has remained reduced, but at the end of 2020 the population was around 800.

The residential accommodation consists of eight living units, including first night/ induction, drug rehabilitation and vulnerable prisoner units. The healthcare inpatient facility is provided by Spectrum Healthcare UK Limited, and Mersey Care NHS Trust.

Education is provided by Novus. This includes English, maths and information technology, plus vocational training courses in a number of skills including plastering, painting and decorating, catering, construction and industrial cleaning. Unfortunately, during the restricted Covid period these workshops have ceased to operate. There are industrial workshops, including leather goods (for prisons) and laundry. The prison works in partnership with resettlement agencies to help prisoners find employment, education, housing and other resettlement areas on release. Again, these workshops have remained closed during the restricted regime.

Partners of prisoners (POPS) and the chaplaincy provide individual support, and under normal conditions Samaritans train prisoners to act as 'Listeners' to support other prisoners through difficult periods. The prison has a weights room, sports hall and outdoor sports pitches, and provides a full programme of fitness activities. Facilities management services by Amey.

## Short description of residential units

A Wing: Drug dependency unit with five landings
B Wing: First night centre with four landings, care and separation unit located on B1
F Wing: Generic with five landings, cell accommodation on landing 1 out of use
G Wing: Generic with five landings, cell accommodation on landing 1 out of use
H Wing: 2021 Closed for refurbishment
I Wing: Generic with five landings, cell accommodation on landing 1 out of use
J Wing: Wellbeing unit with two landings
K Wing: Vulnerable prisoner unit with five landings

## Visiting Information

Book online at: www.gov.uk/prison-visits or by telephone 0151 530 4050 Monday to Friday: 8:30am to 4:30pm
**Visiting times:** Monday to Friday: 1:30pm to 2:30pm, 1:45pm to 2:45pm, 3:15pm to 4:15pm and 3:30pm to 4:30pm.

**Legal visits:** Tuesday, Thursday: 8:50am, 9:06am, 10:21am, 10:35am, 1:50pm, 2:05pm, 3:20pm, 3:35pm. All slots are 1 hour long.

## INSPECTIONS & REPORTS

**Date of last full inspection** 27 Aug – 6 Sept 2019
Notable features from this inspection
• There had been six self-inflicted deaths since our last inspection in 2017
• The population had been reduced by approximately 500 prisoners
• 22% of cells had been taken out of use to improve decency
• The approach taken by the weekly resettlement board and the resettlement hub represented good practice
• There were very few outstanding OASys reports

**HMCIP Report, published 14 January 2020**
**HMCIP Report** HMP Liverpool is a category B local prison that serves the Merseyside area. For historical reasons it is known locally and indeed beyond as Walton prison, and it is situated just to the north of the city centre. The prison has a very strong local identity, and newly arrived prisoners are greeted by large murals depicting scenes of the city and its surroundings. It is, in every sense of the word, a local prison.

It was last inspected in September 2017, at which time it held around 1,150 prisoners. That inspection found that conditions had deteriorated from a previous poor inspection in 2015. In 2015 our judgement had been that the treatment and conditions of prisoners was 'not sufficiently good' in all four of our healthy prison tests. By the time of the 2017 inspection, there had been no improvements, but on the contrary our judgements in respect and purposeful activity had declined to the lowest possible result, poor.

However, the grades themselves do not tell the full story of what we found in 2017. At that time I described the 'abject failure of HMP Liverpool to offer a safe, decent and purposeful environment' and concluded that 'leaders at all levels, both within the prison and beyond, had presided over the failure to address the concerns raised at the last inspection'. Following the 2015 inspection we had made 89 recommendations, 53 of which had not been achieved and 14 of which had been partially achieved.

Some of the specific issues that we reported in 2017 included the living conditions that were among the worst inspectors had ever seen. There were hundreds of broken windows, filthy blocked lavatories, graffiti, damp, dirt and infestations of rodents and insects. Violence had increased, drugs were readily available, the regime was poor and there were serious failings in health care and purposeful activity. We could see no credible plans to address any of these issues. The inspection was so troubling that I took the unusual step of writing to the Chief Executive of the Prison Service to express my concerns. (This inspection pre-dated the introduction of the Urgent Notification protocol in November 2017.) In January 2018 the Parliamentary Justice Select Committee held an unprecedented evidence session devoted solely to exploring the issues raised by the inspection. A new governor was appointed to the prison, the population was reduced by between 450 and 500 prisoners, an extensive programme of refurbishment was started and health care services changed to a different provider.

The impact of these and other measures has been dramatic. At this latest inspection we found that

49 out of 72 recommendations made in 2017 had been fully achieved, and a further four partially achieved. This is an exceptionally high achievement rate and is particularly creditable in light of the dire situation at the prison only two years before. I should make clear that the increase in grades in three of our healthy prison tests was not a reward for implementing recommendations. It was quite simply a reflection of what we found, which is set out in the summary and in the report itself. I shall not therefore recount them in detail in this introduction.

The finding that safety was still 'not sufficiently good' at Liverpool was not because there were no plans or actions being taken to address violence. It was simply that those plans had not yet had the desired impact on the outcomes being experienced by prisoners. There were still too many drugs entering the prison, despite a comprehensive supply reduction strategy. The strategy clearly needed to be reviewed and refined. Although instances of violence had been subject to analysis, they were still too high. The measures implemented under CSIP (challenge, support and intervention plans) had yet to move from a process to delivering clear outcomes, and did not address low-level poor behaviour. Levels of self-harm were also a continuing concern and, although there were some good plans, more analysis was needed if the recent signs of a decline in incidents was to be maintained. The improvement from poor to good for respect represented a remarkable achievement since the last inspection. The squalor and filth we saw in 2017 had gone, replaced by clean and decent living conditions for the vast majority of prisoners. It is important to understand that this had not been brought about simply as a result of the population being reduced and resources channelled towards the prison. That had of course helped, but the real change had been in the quality of leadership and teamwork within the prison and with other partners. There was now a culture of care that I simply could not see in 2017. The following example illustrates this and is emblematic of the change that had taken place.

In 2017 I reported that: 'In one extreme case, I found a prisoner who had complex mental health needs being held in a cell that had no furniture other than a bed. The windows of both the cell and the toilet recess were broken, the light fitting in his toilet was broken with wires exposed, the lavatory was filthy and appeared to be blocked, his sink was leaking and the cell was dark and damp. Extraordinarily, this man had apparently been held in this condition for some weeks. The inspectors had brought this prisoner's circumstances to the attention of the prison, and it should not have needed my personal intervention for this man to be moved from such appalling conditions'.

During this inspection I saw this same man. He was now living as an inpatient in the health care unit. His surroundings were bright and clean. He was still showing clear signs of illness but was alert and responsive – a complete change from the person I had met two years before. He was now receiving proper care and treatment and not being neglected in a squalid, filthy cell.

The judgement for purposeful activity remained at not sufficiently good. While the time prisoners spent out of their cells had improved since the last inspection, too many were still locked up during the working day. There were not enough activity places and attendance rates were too low. There were some good plans to improve, but an injection of pace was needed to give real impetus to what leaders and managers knew needed to be done.

The improvement in rehabilitation and release planning was a very real achievement. There were some weaknesses in public protection arrangements and in risk management. However, the offender assessment system (OASys) was well managed, with no backlog, which is unusual in this type of prison and a solid achievement. The introduction of in-cell phones had made a huge difference to the ability of prisoners to maintain family contact, and the visitors' centre had improved. We saw examples of good practice in the work done to prepare prisoners for release, and these are detailed in the report. It was also notable that, unlike at so many other establishments, the vast majority of prisoners were released to sustainable accommodation. During a meeting with the governor and senior management team, I was asked to recognise the enormous amount of work that had been done since 2017, and I hope both the words of this report and the grades awarded by the inspection show that recognition. There was still a huge amount of work to do to implement, embed and refine the many plans that were in place. As we have seen in other establishments, improvements can prove to be fragile, and I very much hope this will not prove to be the case at Liverpool, with the necessary support continuing to be provided by HMPPS. Encouragingly, despite all that has been achieved, I saw no signs of complacency within the establishment. It was very clear to me that senior managers were operating as a cohesive team in support of enormously energetic and respected leadership, and not as a group of individuals focusing only on their functional responsibilities. I am sure this has been the key to their success so far and will need to be maintained into the future if the work of transforming HMP Liverpool is to be completed.

Peter Clarke CVO OBE QPM August 2019
HM Chief Inspector of Prisons

# INDEPENDENT MONITORING BOARD: Annual Report

The law requires every prison to be monitored by an independent Board appointed by the Justice Secretary; these are known as Independent Monitoring Boards (IMBs). The IMB must satisfy itself as to the humane and just treatment of those held in custody within its prison and the range and adequacy of the programmes preparing them for release; it must report annually to the Justice Secretary on how well the prison has met the standards and requirements placed on it.

## IMB Report 1 January 2021 – 31 December 2021 Published July 2022

Executive summary

Background to the report

The impact of Covid restrictions has reduced the amount of monitoring by the Board. The prison was on varying levels of regime restrictions for the whole reporting period.

## Main judgements
### How safe is the prison?

The Board considers HMP Liverpool to be a safe environment for prisoners. The continued Covid-19 lockdown throughout 2021 has meant the majority of prisoners have spent around one hour a day out of cell on many days throughout the year. The limited weekly on-site monitoring by IMB members confirmed the view of prison staff that all wings have remained calm, and most prisoners have felt safe. Incidents of self-harm have not increased significantly. The Board feels that future regimes should take account of the obvious benefits in reducing levels of unstructured socialising for prisoners whilst ensuring that as many prisoners as possible return to full-time purposeful activity as quickly as possible as restrictions are eased.

The Board continues to have concerns about the insufficient use of body-worn cameras. There have been technical difficulties and the Board recognises that prison managers are taking steps to train staff and address the negative views some staff have of the use of body-worn cameras. This will be a continued focus for the Board in 2022.

### How fairly and humanely are prisoners treated?

The Board feels that the prison leaders have done their best to ensure prisoners have been treated as fairly as possible considering the severe restrictions that Covid lockdown continued to have throughout 2021. The Board is satisfied that the regime restrictions, whilst far from ideal for most prisoners, are nonetheless not inhumane. Prisoners appreciated the extra benefits given to them and maintained through 2021. The Board

has received fewer applications regarding issues with regime e.g. showers as the year went on. The few applications the IMB received about the regime and the conversations members had with prisoners indicate that prisoners have accepted and adapted to the situation. The Board feels that some in-depth work to investigate the long-term impact of the prolonged restricted regime on prisoners could inform future planning by prison leadership and healthcare providers.

The rubbish accumulating in gullies around I wing remained a cause for concern throughout the year, although there were periods when they remained clear. The Governor has been candid with the Board in how the prison has continued to address the drone activity associated with I wing. The Board was informed late in the year that I wing will be refurbished in spring 2022 which is a year ahead of the original planned date.

### How well are prisoners' health and wellbeing needs met?

The Board felt that the healthcare services were maintained to an appropriate level. Staff were open about the challenges associated with the restricted regime which has impacted on the number of missed and rescheduled appointments. Prisoners' applications regarding healthcare did not reflect any major issues as a result of regime issues. The most common theme was that of prisoners expressing that they had not been listened to by healthcare staff. IMB did not find evidence that this was the case and issues were resolved in due course. The Board has continued concerns regarding seriously mentally ill prisoners being kept in the prison and especially in the care and separation unit (CSU). Healthcare staff acknowledge that this situation is not ideal and that those prisoners should be in appropriate mental hospitals.

### How well are prisoners progressed towards successful resettlement?

Opportunities to complete education and offending behaviour courses have continued to be impacted by lockdown. The information received by the Board would indicate that resettlement targets are being met. There has been little face-to-face contact between professionals and prisoners. Transport between prisons and pandemic restrictions have delayed the movement of re-categorised prisoners.

## Main areas for development
### TO THE MINISTER

The impact of Covid restrictions on the rehabilitation, personal development and wellbeing of prisoners should be considered at a national level and where possible action taken to mitigate any impact on possible increase on reoffending and to support reintegration into the community. The positive impact of Covid regime restrictions should be reviewed and guidance issued to the Prison Service. Examples of best practice should be shared in managing unstructured socialisation and how to maximise purposeful activity to impact on rehabilitation outcomes for prisoners.

## TO THE PRISON SERVICE

The system of managing the collection, storage and issue of prisoner property and the transport of property during transfer is an ongoing issue that leads to extra work for staff and increased levels of anxiety for those prisoners affected. Can the Prison Service look at improving the systems involved?

## TO THE GOVERNOR

The prison should engage all prisoners in purposeful activity as soon as is practicable. The IMB believes that the prison should analyse the impact of lockdown on prisoner outcomes and where possible take remedial action to mitigate such impact. The role of the key worker should be developed, particularly in supporting prisoners who find it difficult to access prison systems. The use of body-worn cameras should remain an area of development for the prison.

## Progress since the last report

The work of the prison has been constrained by regime restrictions imposed during Covid lockdown periods. The prison remains settled. Mentally ill prisoners are still waiting too long for a hospital bed reflecting the national shortage. Problems relating to prisoner property at the prison and during transfer remain an ongoing issue. The building work on H wing has been completed and the refurbishment of I wing is underway. Significant investment will be required to develop workshops in order for all prisoners to have access to purposeful activity as part of their rehabilitation. The prison has not been able to make significant progress in engaging all prisoners in purposeful activity. The Governor has continued to plan for re-categorisation and there are positive signs that there will be greater opportunity for prisoners to engage in a wider range of activities as part of their rehabilitation.

**SOUTH LITTLETON**
**EVESHAM**
**WORCS**
**WR11 8TZ**

## HM PRISON
## LONG LARTIN  Tel: 01386 295100

*For the latest reports on this prison please visit:*
https://tinyurl.com/bdfh26rv

*Important Changes:* **(1) Visits:** the identification necessary to access this prison and visit for social or professional purposes has changed; (2) **Money and Gifts** new rules now apply to these. See page 16 for full details of the above.

**Task of the establishment** Long Lartin is a dispersal prison in the long term high security estate. It holds category A and category B male prisoners.

**Certified normal accommodation and operational capacity**
Prisoners held December 2021: 546
Baseline certified normal capacity: 613
In-use certified normal capacity: 533
Operational capacity: 533

**Prison status and key providers**
Public Sector
Prison Group: Long Term/High Security
Prison Group Director: Will Styles
Governor/Director: Steve Cross
IMB Vice Chair: Sue Harrop
Physical health provider: Practice Plus Group
Mental health provider: Inclusion (Midlands Partnership Foundation Trust)
Substance misuse treatment provider: Inclusion (Midlands Partnership Foundation Trust)
Prison education framework provider:
Milton Keynes College
Escort contractor: GeoAmey

**Brief history** Long Lartin was built in the 1960s as a war department ordnance depot and opened as a prison in 1971. Originally a category C prison, it was upgraded to provide dispersal-level security in 1973. Further improvements in security were made between 1995 and 1997 and an additional wing, Perrie, was opened in June 1999. In 2009, a new purpose-built unit, Atherton (E and F wings), replaced older-style wings, increasing the capacity of the prison.

**Short description of residential units**
A and B Older-style wings without in-cell sanitation, currently holding vulnerable prisoners. C and D Older-style wings without in-cell sanitation, currently holding mainstream prisoners.

E and F Two wings in a modern unit with accommodation for 184 mainstream prisoners.

Perrie A Modern unit with accommodation for up to 112 mainstream prisoners. Perrie Red has 74 single cells.

Segregation Accommodation for 40 prisoners. There are two designated cells for R46/close supervision centre prisoners.

Health care Accommodation for seven prisoners, including one cell that can provide end-of-life care if required.

PIPE unit A 'psychologically informed planned environment' unit providing accommodation for 14 prisoners, both vulnerable and mainstream, who mix subject to risk assessment

### Visiting Information

Booking line: 01386 295 188 Monday to Friday, 9am to 2pm.

**Visiting times:** Tuesday: 2pm to 4pm, Thursday, Saturday, Sunday: 2pm to 4:30pm.

**Legal visits:** To book a legal visit please email: legalvisits.longlartin@justice.gov.uk

**Visiting times:** Tuesday, Thursday: 9:30am to 11:30am

### INSPECTIONS & REPORTS

**Scrutiny visit: 2 and 9 February 2021**

**Published: 16 March 2021**

Located near Evesham in Worcestershire, HMP Long Lartin is part of the long term and high security prison estate. It holds some of the country's most dangerous and serious offenders, with two-thirds of the population serving life sentences and almost all of the rest serving more than 10 years. At the time of our visit, over 20% of those held were category A, the highest security classification, indicative of the risk being managed. In the previous two months, an outbreak of Covid-19 had affected a large number of staff and prisoners, three of whom had died after testing positive for the virus. Leaders had also been faced with staff shortages, which had affected the provision they could offer prisoners.

The governor and his team had focused on the management of the pandemic, and the partnership working between the establishment, the main health provider and Public Health England was effective. Managers had established 'cohorting' arrangements (see Glossary of terms) for new arrivals, symptomatic prisoners and those who were particularly vulnerable to the virus. They had provided good communication about the restrictions to both staff and prisoners, with regular updates. Most prisoners said that the measures to prevent the spread of the disease were necessary, but the recent outbreak had affected their perceptions of their own safety,

which were poor despite falls in recorded violence and self-harm.

This report outlines weaknesses in other areas of prison life. The segregation unit subjected prisoners to a very austere regime for long periods without any reintegration planning. Planned use of force was very high, largely because of excessive use of handcuffs in the segregation unit, much of which went unrecorded. The prison's investigations into prisoner complaints were poor and sometimes carried out by the member of staff about whom the prisoner had complained. The system for investigating complaints into discrimination was in disarray and nearly half of allegations made in the previous three months had not received a response. Health care waiting lists were undermanaged, resulting in some waits of over a year to see the GP. There had been long delays in telephone monitoring of prisoner calls for public protection reasons.

Our concerns about these practices was compounded by the failure of leaders to establish effective oversight to identify or address any of them. We had little confidence that sustained progress was possible without a major improvement to governance and management across many areas of prison life.

Charlie Taylor, HM Chief Inspector of Prisons
February 2021

### Key concerns and recommendations

Key concerns and recommendations identify the issues of most importance to improving outcomes for prisoners and are designed to help establishments prioritise and address the most significant weaknesses in the treatment and conditions of prisoners.

During this visit we identified some areas of key concern, and have made a small number of recommendations for the prison to address.

Key concern: There were many areas where oversight by leaders needed to improve. Governance meetings across the prison were not effective in monitoring practice, setting actions or checking if actions set were completed. For example, in the area of safety some actions dated back over a year and a recent safety intervention meeting (SIM) had nearly 50 outstanding actions dating back four months. These shortcomings were a problem given the number and extent of our concerns, where action was needed to improve outcomes for prisoners.

Recommendation: Leaders and managers should revise the oversight arrangements across the establishment so that their purpose is clear and their oversight sufficiently robust to ensure improved practice. (To the governor)

Key concern: Some prisoners in the segregation

unit were routinely handcuffed if they were placed on to a handcuffing 'protocol'. They remained on these protocols for long periods with insufficient oversight and justification. Not all use of force was recorded.

Recommendation: Force should only be used as a last resort and when necessary and proportionate. All force should be recorded accurately and subject to oversight. (To the governor)

Key concern: Prisoners were held in segregation for too long, had no reintegration plans and rarely attended reviews. Record-keeping on the segregation unit needed improvement. The regime on the unit was poor with prisoners only receiving a telephone call and shower on alternate days. Staff-prisoner relationships were weak and prisoners we spoke to had poor perceptions of their treatment by staff.

Recommendation: Prisoners who require segregation should only be segregated for as long as is necessary and have a reintegration plan. Relationships between staff and prisoners should be improved and prisoners should have daily access to telephones and showers. (To the governor)

Key concern: Some responses to prisoner complaints were very poor and responses to complaints against staff were especially weak, demonstrating a lack of respect for prisoners' concerns. We saw insufficient investigation and failure to address the main issue or even speak with the prisoner. Junior officers responded to complaints about their peers and in one case the officer complained against had answered the complaint.

Recommendation: All prisoner complaints should be investigated thoroughly. The issues should be appropriately addressed and the response should be transparent and independent. (To the governor)

Key concern: The was little evidence that the prison monitored access to elements of the regime by protected characteristic (groups protected from discrimination by the Equality Act 2010), except for incentives levels and complaints. The available data were not sophisticated enough to compare outcomes for different groups and provided no assurance that potential discrimination would be identified. There had been responses to only half the discrimination incident report forms submitted from October to December 2020 by the time of our inspection in February 2021. Most responses were late and some were inadequate, and oversight of this process was ineffective. These failings contributed to prisoner perceptions that Long Lartin's staff had scant regard for equality and diversity.

Recommendation: The governor should take immediate action to make sure his approach to promoting equality is underpinned by systematic monitoring and analysis of outcomes for prisoners in each protected characteristic group, supporting an effective system for the reporting and investigation of complaints about discrimination. (To the governor)

Key concern: Health care waiting times were long, the allocation of urgent clinic appointments was not always based on risk and prisoner access to services was not facilitated effectively. This situation created risks to patients' health outcomes that were not adequately mitigated.

Recommendation: The prison should work with health providers to manage prisoner access to health professionals and individual patient risks safely, and to reduce health care waiting times. (To the governor)

Key concern: Medications were now administered in the segregation unit through the cell door. This prevented clear observation and increased the risk of hoarding and diversion.

Recommendation: Medicines should be administered to patients in the safest way, meeting professional and good practice standards. (To the governor)

Key concern: There had been no consistent public protection telephone monitoring in the previous three months because of staff shortages; this risked harm to the public.

Recommendation: Prison leaders should make sure that all public protection monitoring takes place promptly. (To the governor)

**Education, skills and work (Ofsted)**

During this visit Ofsted inspectors conducted an interim assessment of the provision of education, skills and work in the establishment. They identified steps that the prison needed to take to meet the needs of prisoners, including those with special educational needs and disabilities.

**Next steps**

Leaders should finalise their plans to resume face-to-face education, skills and work activities quickly to enable as many prisoners as possible to access activities safely and swiftly when restrictions are lifted.

Leaders and managers should implement swiftly a safe approach to providing prisoners with appropriate additional learning and skills support on the wings.

Leaders should support prison instructors to plan a seamless return to work for prisoners in the workshops. They should identify any extra training and support prisoners need to enable them to be effective at work.

Leaders and managers should make sure that all prisoners are fully aware of the educational opportunities available to them for when they resume face-to-face learning. This should include information about the benefits of non-accredited learning and how in-cell work packs are aligned to qualifications.

Leaders and managers need to make sure that prisoners who speak English as a second language have priority when they resume the allocation of prisoners to face-to-face lessons. Tutors should assess thoroughly the knowledge and skills these prisoners have retained. They will also need to plan and teach appropriate activities that help prisoners who have fallen behind to catch up.

### Notable positive practice

We define notable positive practice as innovative practice or practice that leads to particularly good outcomes from which other establishments may be able to learn. Inspectors look for evidence of good outcomes for prisoners; original, creative or particularly effective approaches to problem-solving or achieving the desired goal; and how other establishments could learn from or replicate the practice.

Inspectors found two examples of notable positive practice during this visit.

Listeners (prisoners trained by the Samaritans to provide confidential emotional support to fellow prisoners) were given an additional £10 telephone credit every two weeks and the direct contact number of a designated Samaritans worker. This gave them an opportunity to debrief and gain support, and was a positive initiative. Exercise yards were open throughout prisoners' time unlocked enabling them to access time in the open air for over two hours a day during the week.

### INDEPENDENT MONITORING BOARD: Annual Report

The law requires every prison to be monitored by an independent Board appointed by the Justice Secretary; these are known as Independent Monitoring Boards (IMBs). The IMB must satisfy itself as to the humane and just treatment of those held in custody within its prison and the range and adequacy of the programmes preparing them for release; it must report annually to the Justice Secretary on how well the prison has met the standards and requirements placed on it.

### IMB Report 1 January 2021 – 31 December 2021 Published 22nd April 2022

Background to the report

The Board monitored the prison throughout 2021 but, due to the Covid-19 pandemic precautions, the monitoring was periodically carried out remotely. The prison regime began the reporting year in Covid-19 stage 3 and, through a series of steps, progressed to stage 2 on 16 June. On 1 November the regime progressed to stage 1 but, due to the impact of the Omicron variant, regressed to enhanced stage 3 on 20 December.

The Board has followed the operational management process by remote attendance at the Governor's daily briefings.

Special attention has been paid to:
• prisoner regimes in light of the fluctuating Covid-19 situation and staffing levels
• levels of violence and safety for both prisoners and staff
• the night sanitation (nightsan) facilities and their associated risk to health and safety
• the population and challenges in the CSRU
• the effects of Covid-19 measures on prisoners' mental health

A severely restricted regime with long periods of lockdown, cessation of most activities and reduced association, continued through the year. Whenever the rules permitted, the restrictions were eased.

The prison received a Her Majesty's Inspectorate of Prisons (HMIP) scrutiny visit (SV) in February and an Operational and System Assurance Group (OSAG) security audit in October.

### Main judgements

Judgements are made against a background of Covid-19 challenges faced by the prison and the constantly changing situation during the reporting year.

### How safe is the prison?

HMP Long Lartin is an orderly and disciplined prison committed to keeping prisoners and staff as safe as is reasonably practical with the ever-present threat of violence. Nevertheless, violence to staff and other prisoners has occurred and there have been incidents of self-harm. Recent inquests have highlighted the need for better resourcing to support a stand-alone safety group of officers, including assessment, care in custody and teamwork (ACCT) assessors, and training is planned for 2022. The Board would like to see continued focus on serious incidents of violence and greater use of multidisciplinary meetings to address the needs of the most violent offenders.

### How fairly and humanely are prisoners treated?

The Board believes that treatment by staff has been largely fair, humane and consistent. The cells on four wings lack running water and sanitation, falling below modern standards of decency for about half of all prisoners. The Board is concerned that prisoners remain in the CSRU for extended periods for lack of more suitable alternatives. The Board recognises the knowledge and understanding of staff of prisoners in their care and their receptiveness to prisoners' everyday needs. However, the number of prison complaints remains high, especially those relating to property.

### How well are prisoners' health and wellbeing needs met?

Covid-19 measures, shortages of discipline staff and difficulties in obtaining hospital appointments have adversely affected all aspects of the delivery of healthcare. Healthcare and Inclusion staff have done their best to overcome these limitations and prisoners have in the main been patient and have accepted shortcomings with good grace. Opportunities to follow a healthy lifestyle have been very limited and health champions have had little opportunity to give help and encouragement. However, access to the gym has been possible for most of the year. Restricted activities, association, education and movement, together with long periods in cells, have caused much frustration but it is the opinion of the Inclusion managers that this has not had an unduly damaging effect on the mental health of most of the population.

### How well are prisoners progressed towards successful resettlement?

Education provision has been responsive and was maintained throughout the year, but vocational training and work have been limited. The number of prisoners re- categorised and transferred out has increased. Very few prisoners are released directly from Long Lartin and the prison is managing an increasing number of prisoners beyond retirement age.

**BRASSIDE
DURHAM
DH1 5YA**

HM PRISON SERVICE

HMP & YOI
LOW NEWTON **Tel: 0191 376 4000**

*For the latest reports on this prison please visit:*
https://tinyurl.com/bdfh26rv

*Important Changes:* **(1) Visits:** the identification necessary to access this prison and visit for social or professional purposes has changed; (2) **Money and Gifts** new rules now apply to these. See page 16 for full details of the above.

**Task of the establishment** HMP & YOI Low Newton is a women's local and resettlement prison in County Durham, serving courts from the Scottish Borders to Cumbria and North Yorkshire. It holds women on remand and those serving a custodial sentence.

### Certified normal accommodation and operational capacity

Prisoners held at the time of inspection: 229
Baseline certified normal capacity: 304
In-use certified normal capacity: 267
Operational capacity: 344

### Population of the prison

• About 10 new receptions arrived each week.
• About 6% of women were from black and minority ethnic backgrounds.
• Seven women were foreign nationals.
• In our survey, 50% of women said they had a disability.
• 127 women were receiving support for substance use problems.
• On average, 45 to 50 women a month were referred for a mental health assessment.
• On average, 31 women a month were released into the community.

### Prison status and key providers

Public
Prison Group: Women
Prison Group Director: Pia Sinha
Governor/Director: Rob Young
IMB Chair: David Randall
Physical health provider: Spectrum Community Health CIC
Mental health provider: Tees, Esk & Wear Valleys NHS Foundation Trust
Substance use treatment providers: Spectrum Community Health CIC; Humankind
Prison education framework provider: Novus
CRCs: Changing Lives; Durham Tees Valley
Escort contractor: GeoAmey

**Brief history** HMP &YOI Low Newton, on the outskirts of Durham City, was built in 1965 as a small remand centre for men and women. Additional accommodation was added in 1975 and the prison changed its role to a male young offender institute in 1976 with a small self-contained unit holding remand women. The prison became a women's prison in 1998.

### Short description of residential units

A wing – 30 spaces
B wing – 31 spaces
C wing – 51 spaces
D wing – 52 spaces
E wing – 59 spaces; early days in custody unit, including the safety and support and substance misuse units
F wing – 40 spaces; long-term and indeterminate sentence women, restricted status women and Primrose unit (high-risk women)
G wing – recently decommissioned
Health care – 12 spaces and palliative care suite

I wing – 39 spaces, psychologically informed planned environment (PIPE).

### Visiting Information
Book at: www.gov.uk/prison-visits or ring 0300 303 0632 Monday to Friday: 9.15am to 4pm
**Visiting times:** Tuesday, Thursday: 2:15pm to 4:15pm, Friday 2:15pm to 4:30pm, Saturday, Sunday: 2pm to 4pm.

**Legal visits:** Telephone line 0300 303 0632 Monday to Friday: 9.15am to 4pm.
**Visiting times:** Tuesday, Thursday, Friday: 2:15pm to 4:15pm

### INSPECTIONS & REPORTS
**Date of last inspection: 2–18 June 2021**
**HMCIP Report, published 07 September 2021**
HMP & YOI Low Newton is a woman's local and resettlement prison that services the courts across a large swathe of northern England. At inspection, it held 229 women with 45 unsentenced and the rest sentenced to anything from a few months to life. The excellent relationships between staff and the women, many of whom have complex needs, have helped to carry this prison through the last, difficult year.

The many examples of notable positive practice that we highlight in this report show the effort that staff members make to provide innovative support for the many vulnerable women, some of whom present a risk to themselves or to the public. The comfortable Achieving Best Evidence Suite was created to allow women, who have been victims of crime, to give evidence in a safe environment without needing to go out to the police station, and the recently decorated adjudications room was a contrast to the spartan environments that we usually see. Video calling had been expanded well beyond the limits of Purple Visits to mean that families living in different households were able to come together on screen. The chaplaincy was exceptional even when compared to the many good examples we see and family support was also excellent with a strong team helping women to maintain relationships at every stage of their sentence.

Given these many impressive initiatives, it was disappointing that the Listener scheme had been allowed to wither at a time when women needed peer support more than ever. There was a similar anomaly with clothing, where women were able to buy new clothes from the prison shop or choose from an extensive second hand range, while a ban on receiving parcels from home was a source of much frustration, particularly as the reasons for this policy were not clear to the women. Levels of self-harm were lower than at most similar prisons and there was a very good range of support available to help women manage their feelings and avoid potential crisis.

It was very concerning to see that the prison is regularly being used as a 'place of safety' for women with acute mental health difficulties. These women should not be kept in prison where, out of sight, they exist in an environment that does not begin to address their needs. Health care and prison staff do their best to support women who are in profound distress, but they do not have the training, skills or resources to provide for patients who are so unwell. The unintended consequence of the well-intentioned policy designed to prevent seriously mentally ill women from languishing in police cells, has led to the problem being passed onto prisons, which are themselves an equally unsuitable environment. These women should be in hospital where they can be treated, not left in prison where they put an additional burden on already stretched resources. Women attending the health care department for their GP appointments could hear the constant screaming of one of the women. Despite the many examples of good practice we saw at the prison, women continue to be locked in their cells for far too long and leaders must urgently begin to extend significantly the amount of time women are unlocked. There was very limited education provision, meaning that women who need to improve their basic learning, earn qualifications and acquire the skills that will help them to get work when they are released are not getting the help that they need to live safe, crime-free lives.

There is much that the team at Low Newton can be rightly proud of, and coherent planning from leaders with clear timescales and targets will help this prison to build on its many successes and provide more effectively for the often-troubled women in its care.

Charlie Taylor, HM Chief Inspector of Prisons
July 2021

#### Safety
At the last inspection of Low Newton in 2018 we found that outcomes for women were reasonably good against this healthy prison test.
At this inspection we found that outcomes for women were now good.
At the last inspection of Low Newton in 2018 we found that outcomes for women were reasonably good against this healthy prison test.
At this inspection we found that outcomes for women were now good.
Early days arrangements were reasonably good, but escort arrangements for transferring women to the prison remained very unsatisfactory. Rubdown searching in reception needed to be reinstated to avoid the use of strip searching. A

445

project worker from NEPACS (formerly North East Prisons After Care Society) provided excellent help to women in their first few days at the prison and this was supported by a DVD created by the chaplaincy to introduce new arrivals to many aspects of prison life.

Leaders and staff knew women well and we saw many examples of good care, encouragement and support. Key work (see Glossary of terms) was rolling out and those with the highest need had been prioritised for contact.

Work to reduce self-harm was not underpinned by a coherent strategy and measures of success were unclear. There was good day-to-day support for women at risk of self-harm and the safety interventions meeting was effective, but the Listener scheme (prisoners trained by the Samaritans to provide confidential emotional support to fellow prisoners) was no longer fully operational. Our main concern was that courts continued to send acutely mentally unwell women to Low Newton as a 'place of safety' due to the lack of appropriate support and residential placements in the community.

The prison was safe, although women with disabilities had a significantly more negative perception about this. Assaults by women on staff had increased since our last inspection. There were few formal incentives to encourage positive behaviour, but the policy was currently under review. The new adjudications room was excellent. The segregation unit was clean, but cells were inadequately equipped. The daily regime provided in the unit was limited and there was no formal reintegration planning.

Management of security was good. In our survey, far fewer women than in 2018 said it was easy to get illegal drugs in the prison. Despite this, drug supply remained a significant risk. In the absence of a body scanner to identify women arriving at the prison who were secreting drugs internally, a new monitoring unit, the safety and support unit (SSU) had been opened. There was a clear vision and credible action plan for the unit in the longer term, but at the time of the inspection the daily regime amounted to segregation.

**Respect**

At the last inspection of Low Newton in 2018 we found that outcomes for women were good against this healthy prison test.

At this inspection we found that outcomes for women remained good.

There was now a very impressive team of family engagement workers. The introduction of in-cell phones was hugely valued. Social visits had been badly affected by Covid-19 restrictions and consequently they were not well used. The regular use of the 'cloud' video platform to allow

parents to have video calls with their children and continue parenting when Purple Visits (see Glossary of terms) proved too restrictive, represented best practice.

Consultation with women remained good and the prisoner council had continued to function throughout the pandemic. However, many other peer support roles had stopped.

Applications submitted were not tracked or quality assured. The number of complaints had reduced since our last inspection and there were good governance arrangements. There was adequate legal provision and the availability of a parental legal rights adviser was excellent.

Living conditions were good and, due to a reduced population, all women now had their own cell. There was a reasonable choice of food, although meals were served too early. Most women had no opportunities to prepare their own meals. The prison's Rags to Riches shop provided a good service, but sentenced women were no longer able to have parcels sent in.

Health care partnership working was effective. Health and well-being screening had continued throughout the pandemic, including vaccinations and immunisations, blood-borne virus screening and cervical smears. Social care provision had also continued. Despite staffing shortages, Spectrum Community Health Care in Custody provided effective primary care services. Patients with long-term conditions were managed by a small group of experienced staff who knew their patients well. However, most patients were unaware of a health care appointment when it was scheduled for them on the day.

Some treatment rooms did not meet the required infection-control standards. An onsite colposcopy unit for cervical screening was excellent. The mental health team delivered a diverse and comprehensive range of treatments for primary and secondary care. The location of highly disturbed women with acute mental health problems on the health care unit caused distress to other patients and staff.

Clinical and psychosocial substance misuse teams were well integrated. Arrival and discharge arrangements were robust and prescribing arrangements were flexible. Medicines and pharmacy services were well managed, but we observed administration of medication that did not meet best practice standards. Naloxone was provided on release to manage substance overdose.

The priority given to equality work had diminished over the last year. There was no comprehensive strategy setting out the priorities and measures of success and the analysis of data was very limited. Support for prisoners with protected and minority characteristics was good overall. A range of consultation forums had recently restarted, but attendance was limited.

Faith provision was very innovative and we have rarely found a chaplaincy of such high quality. The team's efforts and creativity in supporting women were very impressive.

### Purposeful activity

At the last inspection of Low Newton in 2018 we found that outcomes for women were good against this healthy prison test.

At this inspection we found that outcomes for women were now not sufficiently good.

Ofsted carried out a progress monitoring visit of the prison alongside our full inspection and the purposeful activity judgement incorporates their assessment of progress.

Time out of cell had deteriorated significantly due to the Covid-19 restrictions, but leaders had credible plans to improve this. Too many women were locked in their cells during the core working day. The restricted regime was delivered reliably. Very few women were employed as peer workers to encourage and promote more time out of cell.

Library provision had deteriorated and access was limited, but the mobile book delivery service developed in the pandemic was effective and highly valued. Current gym provision was limited, but there were firm plans for improving it.

Ofsted judged that the prison was making reasonable progress in restoring the full delivery of education, skills and work activity. Leaders and managers had continued to offer a range of education, skills and work activities throughout the pandemic, although on reduced hours. The proportion of women completing in-cell education packs was at a reasonable level and they received helpful feedback from tutors.

Some women had resumed classroom attendance at the end of April 2021, although on a restricted basis. Leaders and managers continued to offer accreditation for the majority of courses and more substantial qualifications for women working in the kitchens were about to start. Activity places for women in certain areas of work were limited by the lack of instructors. Leaders and managers had recently reduced significantly the backlog of women awaiting induction that had built up during the pandemic restrictions.

### Rehabilitation and release planning

At the last inspection of Low Newton in 2018 we found that outcomes for women were reasonably good against this healthy prison test.

At this inspection we found that outcomes for women remained reasonably good.

There had been very limited oversight of the reducing reoffending work. The strategy lacked a meaningful action plan to evidence success.

Covid-19 restrictions had affected the opportunities for women to achieve their sentence plan targets and some had been released without completing the offending behaviour work they needed. The range of one-to-one support had begun to improve. Women living on the psychologically informed planned environment (PIPE, see Glossary of terms) and Primrose specialist unit (providing intensive treatment for high-risk individuals) were especially positive about the support they received.

Over the last year, there had been limited support for women's finance, benefit and debt needs. While most women were released to stable accommodation, a concerning proportion still left the prison without a sustainable and suitable place. Home detention curfew (HDC) processes were well managed, but some were concluded late, mainly due to poor availability or suitability of release accommodation. It was positive that a bail information officer now provided help for women on remand.

Nearly all women who required a sentence plan had one, but a third had not been reviewed for over a year and this was much longer for some of the indeterminate sentence women. Implementation of Offender Management in Custody (OMiC, see Glossary of terms) looked positive. Most women had adequate contact with their prison offender manager.

There was evidence of good pre-release risk management planning for women who presented a high risk of serious harm to others. A small number of women were subject to mail and phone monitoring for public protection concerns and this was well managed. Child contact restrictions were applied appropriately.

Staff from the community rehabilitation companies (CRCs, see Glossary of terms) were now seeing women in person well ahead of time to discuss their needs and plan for their release. All women were given essential basic items for release and the Reconnect pilot scheme was good.

### Key concerns and recommendations

Key concerns and recommendations identify the issues of most importance to improving outcomes for women in prison and are designed to help establishments prioritise and address the most significant weaknesses in the treatment and conditions of women.

During this inspection we identified some areas of key concern and have made a small number of recommendations for the prison to address those concerns.

Key concern: Too many of the prison's priorities, such as reducing self-harm, improving outcomes for protected groups and reducing reoffending, were not underpinned by comprehensive strategies and action plans. These were either missing or limited in scope and detail. They did not provide an evidence-based way of measuring progress or demonstrating success.

Recommendation: The delivery of each of the key priorities for the prison should be supported by comprehensive strategies and detailed action plans that set out the vision for success, how this would be achieved and by when. (To the governor)

Key concern: There were some key weaknesses in assessment, care in custody and teamwork (ACCT) case management for women at risk of suicide or self-harm. Some new arrivals were not placed on an ACCT despite evidence of significant risk factors. Care maps were not always proactive or used well, and some had not been added to for months and did not address the woman's current concerns.

Recommendation: All risk factors should be considered when deciding to open assessment, care in custody and teamwork (ACCT) case management on a woman, particularly those new to custody. Care maps should be regularly updated to reflect current risks and needs. (To the governor)

Key concern: Acutely mentally unwell women who were at risk of taking their own lives were still being sent to Low Newton because of the lack of appropriate provision in the community. In the previous two months, six women had been admitted from the courts for their own protection, due to seeing prison as a place of safety. The prison was clearly not the appropriate place for these women as it was not properly resourced to manage their risks and needs.

Recommendation: Acutely mentally unwell women should not be sent to prison as a place of safety. (To the Secretary of State)

Key concern: It was extremely unsatisfactory that the inpatient unit and primary care services remained co-located. Highly disturbed inpatients lived next to outpatient clinic rooms, the main waiting area, visiting specialist services and the palliative care suite. Some of their behaviour, such as repeated screaming and banging, was very upsetting to others. Inpatients who needed a quiet environment instead had to cope with a daily stream of visiting outpatients. We highlighted these problems at previous inspections.

Recommendation: Primary care and inpatient facilities should not be co-located. (To the Partnership Board and the governor)

Key concern: Too many women remained locked in their cell during the core working day. Many valuable peer support roles had stopped during Covid-19 restrictions, reducing opportunities for women to have more time out of cell, and very few

creative or recreational activities were available.

Recommendation: Women should have more time out of cell through better access to peer support and opportunities for recreational and social activities that enable them to use their time constructively and creatively. (To the governor)

Key concern: The Covid-19 restrictions had limited opportunities for women to achieve their sentence plan targets and some were released without completing the offending behaviour work they needed.

Recommendation: All women should be able to complete the offending behaviour work needed before their release. (To the governor)

**Notable positive practice**

We define notable positive practice as innovative work or practice that leads to particularly good outcomes from which other establishments may be able to learn. Inspectors look for evidence of good outcomes for women; original, creative or particularly effective approaches to problem-solving or achieving the desired goal; and how other establishments could learn from or replicate the practice.

Inspectors found 12 examples of notable positive practice during this inspection.

An 'early days in custody' project worker from NEPACS offered excellent individual and practical help to new arrivals to address their main worries and reduce the likelihood of self-harm.

The chaplaincy had produced an innovative induction DVD to introduce new arrivals to the full range of prison staff and departments in an accessible, friendly way. Women could watch it on their TVs during their two-week induction.

A local charity, Junction 42, provided packs containing essential toiletries and sanitary items to every woman arriving at and being released from Low Newton.

The 'achieving best evidence' suite was a private, comfortable, trauma- informed room set away from the main prison that allowed women who had been victims of crime to give formal evidence to the police without the need to leave the prison.

Whenever possible, adjudications were now held away from the segregation unit in a room that provided a comfortable, calming and pleasant environment.

A very impressive, expanded multidisciplinary team of five family engagement workers, including a full-time parental rights adviser, met need and supported women at all stages of custody.

When the Purple Visits system proved too restrictive, women could use the 'cloud' video platform to continue parenting via video calls. This was compassionate and creative.

The decision to test all new arrivals for hepatitis

C on arrival was an excellent initiative. This was done on an 'opt-out' basis to improve take-up and led to prompt identification and treatment of the virus.

An onsite colposcopy suite enabled women to receive prompt checks and care for possible cervical cancer. It had significantly improved the uptake, early diagnosis and outcomes for women. Naloxone, a drug to manage substance misuse overdose, was offered to women leaving prison on an opt-out basis and consequently a higher number of women than usual left the prison with an emergency kit.

Redacted discrimination complaints were shared with the prisoner council to raise awareness and promote transparency.

The chaplaincy was very visible and accessible through an array of services that improved outcomes for women, including personalised birthday cards, the production of DVDs and exceptional pastoral support.

## INDEPENDENT MONITORING BOARD: Annual Report

The law requires every prison to be monitored by an independent Board appointed by the Justice Secretary; these are known as Independent Monitoring Boards (IMBs). The IMB must satisfy itself as to the humane and just treatment of those held in custody within its prison and the range and adequacy of the programmes preparing them for release; it must report annually to the Justice Secretary on how well the prison has met the standards and requirements placed on it.

### IMB Report 1 March 2021 – 28 February 2022
### Published August 2022
### Executive summary
### Background to the report

The Covid-19 outbreak has had an impact on the Board's ability to gather information and discuss the contents of this annual report. The Board has therefore tried to cover as much ground as it can in these difficult circumstances, but inevitably there is less detail and supporting evidence than usual. Ministers are aware of these constraints. Regular information is being collected specifically on the prison's response to the pandemic, and that is being collated nationally.

The Board has been able to return to the prison for most of the reporting year but for a while the regime has been restricted either due to the national Covid-19 situation or the fact that at times HMP/YOI Low Newton has been classed as an outbreak site.

## Main judgements
## How safe is the prison?

It is the Board's opinion that the prison provides an environment that protects the safety of the prisoners. Levels of self-harm and violence are relatively low. The Board is impressed by the in-depth knowledge the staff have of the prisoners. This is demonstrated at the regular safety meetings which are monitored by the Board.

## How fairly and humanely are prisoners treated?

It is the view of the Board that the prisoners are treated fairly and humanely. Interactions between staff and prisoners are normally good and friendly. The prison regime has been supportive of the prisoners despite the limitations due to Covid. The chaplains have in particular been innovative in supporting the prisoners. The establishment is kept very clean and tidy inside and out by both prisoners and staff.

## How well are prisoners' health and wellbeing needs met?

The Board considers that prisoners' health needs are generally well met. The last year has been difficult and ways of providing healthcare have had to be changed. Appointments with outside healthcare providers have restarted following their postponement during the lockdown period, although there are still some delays outside the prison's control. There are still some women in the prison who have serious mental health issues and for whom prison is not the most appropriate place. Plans are being made for the development of a new healthcare centre and mental health unit.

## How well are prisoners progressed towards successful resettlement?

A wide range of interventions is provided to assist in resettlement, but areas of concern are finding appropriate accommodation and dealing with mental health issues. Low Newton's priority has always been to offer every prisoner opportunities and support to plan for their successful, crime-free release and future. A number of new initiatives are being developed which are welcomed by the Board. The Board is concerned that the prison system is in general geared to male prisoners and does not always take account of the particular needs of women prisoners. This is particularly true of women serving short sentences.

## Main areas for development
## TO THE MINISTER

What progress is being made to increase the number of places available nationally in secure psychiatric units, since it remains the case that some women are being placed inappropriately in prison?

What assessment has been made of the effectiveness of current contracts for the resettlement of prisoners who have no permanent home to go to upon release, given the importance of this issue in reducing re-offending?

## TO THE PRISON SERVICE
Could the CCTV system be replaced to assist in monitoring incidents around the prison?

## TO THE GOVERNOR
How can the Governor ensure that targets are consistently met for delivery of the key worker scheme?
How can the Governor ensure that body worn cameras are used more consistently during use of force incidents?

### Progress since the last report
**Issue raised** *Comment*
Women with severe mental health issues being housed inappropriately *This is still happening and there is often a delay getting them into a secure hospital.*
Additional funding for new educational and vocational initiatives *New initiatives are being developed.*
Review of mental health services in the prison and possible creation of mental health unit *Plans are being developed for a new healthcare unit. Should this be successful the prison is considering a number of options for the current healthcare unit which will include the creation of a mental health unit*

**OLD EPPERSTONE ROAD
LOWDHAM
NOTTINGHAM
NG14 7DA**

**Tel: 0115 966 9200**

**THIS PRISON WILL BE MANAGED BY SODEXO FROM 16 FEBRUARY 2023**

*For the latest reports on this prison please visit:*
https://tinyurl.com/bdfh26rv

*Important Changes:* **(1) Visits:** the identification necessary to access this prison and visit for social or professional purposes has changed; (2) **Money and Gifts** new rules now apply to these. See page 16 for full details of the above.

**This prison operates the Digital Categorisation System, pursuant to the Security Categorisation Policy Framework as such PSIs 40 and 41 of 2011 do not apply to prisoners being categorised in this establishment. See section 2.26 for more information.**

**Task of the establishment** Male category B.
**Certified normal accommodation and operational capacity**
Prisoners held at the time of this visit: 884
Baseline certified normal capacity: 894
In-use certified normal capacity: 888
Operational capacity: 888

**Prison status and key providers**
Private - managed by: Serco
Prison Group: Custodial Contracts
Prison Group Director: Neil Richards
Governor/Director:
Martin Booth/Trudy McCaffery (c)
IMB Chair: Barbara Morgan
Physical health provider: Nottinghamshire Healthcare NHS Foundation Trust
Mental health provider: Nottinghamshire Healthcare NHS Foundation Trust
Substance misuse treatment provider: Nottinghamshire Healthcare NHS Foundation Trust
Prison education framework provider: Serco
Escort contractor: GeoAmey

**Brief history** The prison opened in February 1998 as an 'industrial prison' employing 300 prisoners in workshops with commercial partner companies. New house blocks expanded the prison by 128 additional prisoner places in 2007 and 260 in 2010.

**Short description of residential units**
Houseblock 1 Four residential wings
Houseblock 2 Four residential wings
House block 3 Two residential wings
House block 4 Two residential wings
House block 5 Two residential wings

**Visiting Information** Booked by the prisoners themselves via internal processes.
**Visiting times:** Thursday, Friday 13:15 - 14:45, 15:15 - 16:45, Saturday, Sunday 10:00 - 11:30, 13:15 - 14:45, 15:15 - 16:45

**Legal visits:** Ring 01159 669321 to book a visit.

**INSPECTIONS & REPORTS**
**Scrutiny report: 12 January and 2 February 2021**
**Published: 05 March 2021**
This report presents the findings of our scrutiny visit to HMP Lowdham Grange and the conditions and treatment of prisoners during the Covid-19 pandemic. Lowdham Grange is a category B prison located near Nottingham and is privately managed by Serco. The prison is part of the long-term high security estate and at the time of our visit held around 880 prisoners, the majority of whom were serving sentences of 10 years or more.

We found a well-led prison that had faced some considerable challenges during the pandemic, including a serious outbreak of Covid-19 in late September 2020 in which nearly 200 prisoners and 160 staff had tested positive for the virus. One prisoner subsequently died with Covid-19-related symptoms. This outbreak was one of the biggest in a prison at that time. The leadership team had worked effectively in partnership with health care providers and an outbreak control team, which included the NHS and Public Health England (PHE), to bring it under control. Arrangements to have all prisoners and staff tested were introduced promptly to support a local track-and-trace scheme to isolate asymptomatic cases. Prison leaders had identified lessons to be learned from the outbreak and had taken a robust approach to minimising the risks of transmission, which meant that a smaller outbreak shortly before our visit was well managed and swiftly contained.

Communication with staff and prisoners about the current restrictions was effective and social distancing was well promoted. The prison had invested in technology such as proximity sensors to alert staff who inadvertently breached distancing protocols. Further innovative use of technology to normalise prison life was being trialled at the time of our visit and showed promise. In addition to testing of new prisoner arrivals, staff were offered weekly Covid-19 testing, and all wore fluid-resistant face masks.

Frontline staff were clearly visible when cells were unlocked, and we observed good relationships between staff and prisoners. This was reflected in our survey in which 79% of prisoners said staff treated them with respect. However, while the prison's data recorded that violence between prisoners had reduced between July and December 2020, compared with the same period in 2019, violence towards staff had increased. Leaders felt that this was due to growing frustration with regime restrictions, although there had been no detailed analysis to understand the causes.

Living conditions were reasonable and there was a programme to improve the flooring on the older units. Nearly all cells contained telephones and many also had integral showers.

Work to promote equality had continued throughout the pandemic period, although a promising race equality taskforce, established as a response to wider concerns raised by prisoners around Black Lives Matter, had to be suspended due to the September outbreak of Covid-19.

Health care provision was reasonably good and partnership working to address local outbreaks of Covid-19 was impressive. Despite this, GP waiting times were too long and some prisoners had excessive waits for transfer to mental health hospitals under the Mental Health Act. A Covid-19 vaccination programme for prisoners eligible under the government priority groups was being implemented at the time of our visit.

The prison had introduced a tier system to support prisoners having longer periods out of their cell to offset the impact if an individual prisoner tested positive or displayed symptoms of Covid-19. Prisoners in tier one or two could have 90 minutes a day out of cell, while those who were symptomatic or awaiting test results went into tier three and received at least 45 minutes out of cell, including access to the open air. Prolonged periods locked in cells were clearly taking their toll and many prisoners raised concerns about the impact of restrictions on their well-being.

Prisoners' access to the library was poor and the prison did not promote it enough as a resource, which was concerning given the need to promote in-cell activity to improve their well-being.

Education staff were directly employed by Serco and had remained on site since March. Education leaders recognised that they had been too slow to reinstate a broad curriculum and, while it was good that the proportion of prisoners engaging in education had increased during this period, too few had had their new skills and knowledge accredited.

The prison had taken far too long to introduce some critical aspects of prison life, such as family contact through Purple Visits video calling.

Lack of staffing had limited the contact between prisoners and their prison offender manager for several months, and over half of the population had not received a review of their risk and sentence plan in the previous year. Recategorisation reviews were timely, but population pressures in other prisons often affected moves of prisoners to lower category prisons.

Overall this is an encouraging report. The prison had learned from the serious Covid-19 outbreak, and partnership working between prison and health leaders was a real strength. Despite the requirement for national approval of recovery plans, the prison had been active in easing restrictions before the outbreak and had been able to reopen several key work activity areas during the summer. Nearly all strategic meetings had continued throughout this period and, while the two outbreaks combined with wider national restrictions had stalled progress, the prison was in a strong position to widen the regime when it becomes safe to do so.

Charlie Taylor

HM Chief Inspector of Prisons

February 2021

**Key concerns and recommendations**

Key concerns and recommendations identify the issues of most importance to improving outcomes for prisoners and are designed to help establishments prioritise and address the most significant weaknesses in the treatment and conditions of prisoners.

Key concern: Induction procedures lacked coordination and there was evidence of gaps in delivery. Incomplete records suggested the first night induction programme was not always delivered, and the recording of participation in induction from disciplines such as education, the offender management unit and gym highlighted the gaps in provision. Induction was also sometimes delivered informally by a member of staff or a key worker.

Recommendation: All prisoners should receive a full, comprehensive and prompt induction to make sure that they fully understand the regime and facilities available. (To the director)

Key concern: The restricted regime had greatly reduced prisoner access to peer mentoring schemes such as 'buddies' (peer supporters) just at the time when effective peer support should have been available to promote safeguarding and better support vulnerable prisoners.

Recommendation: All prisoners should have prompt access to a peer mentor in a private setting. (To the director)

Key concern: Waiting times for all health services had been affected by the pandemic, but the wait for a routine GP appointment was too long, with some prisoners waiting up to 14 weeks. This had also been a concern at the last full inspection. The waiting times for aerosol generating procedures (see Glossary of terms) in the dental suite had also been further delayed pending delivery of a ventilation machine, adding to the excessive dental waiting list.

Recommendation: Routine GP appointments and treatment for dental patients should be provided promptly in timescales equivalent to those in the community. (To the HMP Lowdham Grange health partnership board)

Key concern: Despite attempts by the mental health team to address the issue, patients requiring assessment and treatment in mental health facilities under the Mental Health Act had waited far too long to be transferred. Four patients had waited between 76 and 230 days for transfer.

Recommendation: Patients requiring assessment and treatment in mental health hospitals should transferred promptly and within the Department of Health target transfer time. (To the HMP Lowdham Grange health partnership board)

Key concern: The library provision was underused even though the pandemic restrictions meant that increased in-cell activity was of even greater importance. Although tutors had been assigned to wings to oversee prisoner access to library services, there had been little take-up, and some officers were not aware of how prisoners could access the library.

Recommendation: The library should be accessible and well promoted to encourage in-cell activity. (To the director)

Key concern: About 80% of the population had been assessed as high risk, but offending behaviour programmes to help prisoners reduce their risk had been suspended and most prisoners had also not received any structured support from their prison offender manager (POM). Over half the population had not had their risk and sentence plan reviewed in the previous 12 months to make sure that it was current and appropriate.

Recommendation: The prison should make sure that every prisoner has support to allow them to reduce their risk level and make progress against their sentence plan. (To the director)

**Education, skills and work (Ofsted)**

During this visit Ofsted inspectors conducted an interim assessment of the provision of education, skills and work in the establishment. They identified steps that the prison needed to take to meet the needs of prisoners, including those with special educational needs and disabilities.

**Next steps**

Leaders and managers need to make sure that learners with needs in English for speakers of other languages (ESOL) and those with lower levels in English are supported effectively to improve their skills.

Managers and tutors should make sure that learners with a learning difficulty or disability are promptly identified and suitably supported to make good progress.

Managers should check the quality of tutors' work rigorously to make sure that they are implementing the planned curriculum effectively. Leaders should make sure that effective careers advice and guidance is available for all prisoners so that they are able to make informed choices about their careers both inside prison and upon release. Leaders and managers should recognise the new skills and knowledge that learners achieve through in-cell learning and other activities, and accredit them as appropriate.

**Notable positive practice**

We define notable positive practice as innovative practice or practice that leads to particularly good outcomes from which other establishments may be able to learn. Inspectors look for evidence of good outcomes for prisoners; original, creative or particularly effective approaches to problem-solving or achieving the desired goal; and how other establishments could learn from or replicate the practice. Inspectors found four examples of notable positive practice during this visit.

Staff wore proximity sensors to provide alerts and reminders when social distancing guidelines were breached due to the limitations of the prison's working environment.

The prisoner advice line (PAL) was staffed seven days a week by knowledgeable peer representatives with access to appropriate information and communications technology facilities. Prisoners could call the PAL from their in-cell telephone for information on a range of matters.

The well-being centre was a promising initiative overseen by the mental health team providing a therapeutic group room for when groups restarted, and a sensory room to help regulate physiological and emotional responses for patients assessed as benefiting from this form of therapy.

The use of technology, including the media suite, supported prisoner learning and improved communication, while also improving family contact by providing over 500 video recordings from prisoners to their families.

## INDEPENDENT MONITORING BOARD: Annual Report

The law requires every prison to be monitored by an independent Board appointed by the Justice Secretary; these are known as Independent Monitoring Boards (IMBs). The IMB must satisfy itself as to the humane and just treatment of those held in custody within its prison and the range and adequacy of the programmes preparing them for release; it must report annually to the Justice Secretary on how well the prison has met the standards and requirements placed on it.

### IMB Report 1 February 2021 – 31 January 2022
### Published June 2022
### EXECUTIVE SUMMARY
#### Background to the report

The Covid-19 outbreak has continued to have a significant impact on the Board's ability to visit the prison, gather information, and to talk to prisoners in order to prepare this annual report. The Board members endeavoured to cover as much ground as they could in these difficult circumstances but inevitably, there may be less detail and supporting evidence than in previous reports.

In the period February-April 2021, while the roll-out of the vaccination programme had not yet been completed in the prison or the community, Board members could not visit the prison or talk to prisoners. The regime was relaxed a little more in May and June and some members of the Board

(those who were double-vaccinated) took the opportunity to visit the prison, talk to prisoners and monitor conditions in the house block wings. At the end of June there was a significant Covid-19 outbreak and visiting ceased again for two months. From September onwards the prison started to 'open up' and Board visits began to take place. This was paused again in December when the site (and the country) was again subjected to restrictions and these continued to the end of the reporting period.

Despite the visiting restrictions, the Board is pleased to report that its members continued to attend video and telephone meetings, and in particular those meetings concerning health provision, segregation reviews and the daily morning briefings.

The current contract for the operation of the prison expires in February 2023 and during the period of this report, the procurement process for the new contract started. While the Board does not have any role in this, it is very much aware of the need to ensure that the new contract recognises the best possible outcome for the prisoners in terms of their safety, fair and humane treatment, physical and mental health and their progression towards release.

### Main judgements
#### How safe is the prison?

The prison leadership has continued to focus on the risks from Covid-19 to ensure that prisoners, members of staff, and visitors to the prison were kept safe during times of increased infection rates in the community. This approach has been successful in controlling infections.

The negative impact of the continued restrictions on prisoners has been significant and total prisoner-on-prisoner assaults show a marked increase of almost 50%. Self-harm amongst prisoners has increased by 10% and there have been four deaths in custody. Therefore, it cannot be said that the prison feels as safe as in the previous reporting year.

#### How fairly and humanely are prisoners treated?

Prisoners at HMP Lowdham Grange are generally treated fairly. Although the prison houses some very challenging prisoners, the regime is built on a positive ethos and the HM Inspectorate of Prisons (HMIP) scrutiny visit of January 2021 commented on positive communication and relationships between staff and prisoners. HMIP also commented favourably on the prison's management of the Covid-19 outbreaks in the previous year. The Board does not feel that this has deteriorated but it has been concerned that prisoners were not given adequate opportunities to attend their adjudications in person for 11 months of this reporting year.

## How well are prisoners' health and wellbeing needs met?

Healthcare services continued to be under great pressure throughout the period and prisoners' physical and mental health was seen as a priority. The service responded very efficiently to requirements for vaccination programmes and treatment and it is the view of the Board that the service has been equivalent to that provided in the wider community.

The mental and emotional wellbeing of prisoners remains a significant concern due to the effect of prolonged periods of time spent by prisoners in their cells.

The shortages of healthcare staff have increased the risk to the wellbeing of prisoners. Although it is appreciated that this reflects the situation throughout the NHS, every effort has been made by the on-site team to provide care and support to all prisoners.

## How well are prisoners progressed towards successful resettlement?

Continued restrictions in the prison have compromised the overall progression of prisoners in their sentences. Nevertheless, by the end of the reporting period, 83 prisoners had progressed to category C status, and were awaiting transfer. Once again, there was no reduction in the number of indeterminate sentenced prisoners.

There has been some progress on learning through the provision of in-cell packs from the education department. A small number of prisoners continued to work on the production of scrubs for the NHS but otherwise the workshops and other vocational training opportunities were not available for much of the year.

The significant shortage of probation staff in the offender management unit (OMU) has meant that many prisoners have not received their sentence planning/reviews required this year.

## Main areas for development
### TO THE MINISTER

In its 2020-2021 report, the Board requested priority be given to holding coroners' inquests for deaths in custody to provide bereaved families with an understanding of the circumstances of the deaths of their relatives. No inquests into deaths in custody at HMP Lowdham Grange have been held in the reporting period and this means that some families have been waiting four years for the answers to their questions. The Board considers that this is grossly inconsiderate to a prisoner's family and disrespectful to the deceased. Moreover, it does not allow the prison and healthcare partners to learn any lessons in avoiding and preventing other deaths in custody. The Board believes there should be a greater focus on reviewing the sentences of indeterminate sentenced prisoners, enabling them to progress and move towards a safe release.

There is a compelling need for all government departments to work together to ensure that appropriate facilities are available for those prisoners with severe mental health disorders; this will avoid the need for prisons to hold such prisoners in segregation for extended periods.

### TO THE PRISON SERVICE

To provide a framework in the post-Covid structured regime that supports and funds innovative programmes of rehabilitation, mental health provision, education, skills development and self-improvement for prisoners instead of requiring them to be locked in their cells for long periods.

To give priority to resourcing of probation services to the required levels within the prison estate and in the community, so that prisoners have adequate support and guidance before and after their release.

To give renewed emphasis to the development of a national system of storage and retrieval of prisoners' property when prisoners are moved between prisons. Despite a framework being developed in April 2020, nothing significant appears to have happened and greater efforts are needed to find a national solution to this problem.

To give priority for the training of family liaison officers (FLOs) in 2022 so that appropriate resources are allocated for this important role and to support those volunteer prison staff already undertaking it.

### TO THE DIRECTOR

To continue to support the fair treatment of all prisoners by ensuring that adjudication hearings are held in person with the prisoner(s) present in the room.

To implement a post-Covid structured regime that gives all prisoners the opportunity to progress through their sentences with sufficient and high-quality support and programmes of learning.

To exert pressure on the commissioners of Nottinghamshire Healthcare NHS Trust to secure and maintain staffing at a level to provide the service required for all prisoners' health and wellbeing needs.

### Progress since the last report

Having reported on the following issues in year 2020-2021, the Board is disappointed that there is no evidence to suggest there has been progress or significant improvement during the year on the following items:

- There continue to be significant delays in finding appropriate treatment/beds in secure units for prisoners who have very serious mental health disorders.
- Analysis of the complaints log and the applications received by the Board indicates that there has been no improvement in the management and handling of prisoners' property when transferring between establishments.

**The Board is encouraged to note the following positives:**
- Since the introduction of new body-worn video cameras the number issued daily has been consistent for both day and night shifts, and the video evidence is logged and reviewed for each incident recorded.
- The continued use of the body scanner and X-ray equipment together with searches and the use of drug dogs has been consistent throughout the reporting period. This shows a continuing commitment to curb the entry of drugs and other prohibited items to HMP Lowdham Grange.
- The response by the on-site healthcare team members and prison staff has been remarkable in their handling of the serious outbreaks of Covid-19 and the demands for vaccination programmes, together with the need for tuberculosis screening and treatment of an outbreak of scabies during the year.

**36 COUNTY ROAD**
**MAIDSTONE**
**KENT**
**ME14 1UZ**

Tel: 01622 775300

*For the latest reports on this prison please visit:*
https://tinyurl.com/bdfh26rv

*Important Changes:* **(1) Visits:** the identification necessary to access this prison and visit for social or professional purposes has changed; **(2) Money and Gifts** new rules now apply to these. See page 16 for full details of the above.

This prison operates the Digital Categorisation System, pursuant to the Security Categorisation Policy Framework as such PSIs 40 and 41 of 2011 do not apply to prisoners being categorised in this establishment. See section 2.26 for more information.

**Task of the establishment** Category C prison holding male foreign national prisoners.

**Certified normal accommodation and operational capacity**
Prisoners held at the time of inspection: 595
Baseline certified normal capacity: 565
In-use certified normal capacity: 565
Operational capacity: 600

**Prison status and key providers**
Public
Prison Group: Kent, Surrey & Sussex
Prison Group Director: James Lucas
Governor/Director: Dawn Mauldon
IMB Chair: Lynn Jessop
Physical health provider:
Oxleas NHS Foundation Trust
Mental health provider: Oxleas NHS Foundation Trust
Substance misuse provider: Forward Trust
Learning and skills provider: Novus
Escort contractor: GeoAmey, Serco, Mitie Care and Custody

**Brief history** Maidstone prison was originally built in 1819. The prison underwent a re-role in 2013 and is now a designated foreign national prison.

**Short description of residential units**
There are four residential units and one segregation unit.
Kent unit - built in 1850, holds up to 178 prisoners in single cells
Medway unit - built in 1966, holds 101 prisoners in single cells
Thanet unit - built in 1909 and extended in the 1970s to hold 174 prisoners in single cells
Weald unit - built in 2009, holds 149 prisoners in single and double cells

**Visiting Information** You can book your visit by telephone. There is no online booking service available. Booking line: 01622 775621. The booking line is open Monday to Friday: 9am to 12:30pm.
**Visiting times:** Tues & Thurs: 2pm to 3:30pm.

**Legal visits:** Email:
legalvisits.maidstone@hmps.gsi.gov.uk You can also book by sending a fax to 01622 775660.
**Visiting times:** Mon to Thurs, 9am to 11am.

**INSPECTIONS & REPORTS**
**Date of last inspection:** 8, 9, 15–19 October 2018
**SSV: Section 6.2.3.1**
**HMCIP Report, published 19 February 2019**
HMP Maidstone is a category C prison that holds exclusively foreign national prisoners, and has done since 2013. At the time of this inspection it held just under 600 prisoners. It had a young population, with some 40% being under 30 years of age. The prison itself dates back to 1819 and is situated near to the centre of Maidstone. In many

respects it is like a typical Victorian jail, with high walls dominating the surrounding streets, and has been a feature of the life of the town for many generations. The current governor has been in post since 2013, which is a longer tenure than we often see. The prison was last inspected in August 2015.

In terms of safety, the prison was calm and well ordered but it was noticeable that the initial risk assessment of prisoners carried out on their arrival was not adequate and needed to be addressed as a matter of some urgency.

The use of force in the prison had increased since the last inspection but was lower than at other category C prisons and the seriousness of incidents was mostly low level. In terms of behaviour management, it was good to see what we have recorded as good practice in the use of incentives and earned privileges (IEP) forums, where the use of the IEP scheme was regularly reviewed and prisoner participation was included. I would sound a note of caution about the situation at HMP Maidstone insofar as the impact of illicit drugs is concerned. The prison, unlike so many others, had not been destabilised by an influx of drugs, but there were some worrying signs. Despite the fact that the random drug testing carried out on prisoners was predictable, the positive test rate had risen and now stood at 14.5%. This was too high to be taken lightly. Shortly after this inspection some 15 parcels containing contraband, including drugs, were thrown over the wall into the prison in the space of a single night. Despite the clear indications that drugs were a growing problem, the response to intelligence was poor, with backlogs and suspicion searches not being carried out in a timely fashion or at all. There was clearly a need to refocus on the strategy for reducing the supply of illicit drugs, and there is certainly no room at all for complacency.

Generally speaking, we found that relationships between staff and prisoners were good, and a higher than usual proportion of prisoners told us they were treated with respect by staff. There were also good consultation arrangements with prisoners. The food in the prison was unusually well regarded by prisoners, with some 60% telling us it was good. However, as in too many prisons, it was served far too early, and we observed lunch being served at 11.20am and the evening meal at 4.20pm. A major issue for the prison was that much of the residential accommodation was old, shabby and in need of refurbishment. Living conditions were also adversely affected by the fact that the sports hall had been condemned and closed. There were serious problems with laundry arrangements, causing prisoners to have to wash and dry

clothes in their cells. Overall, though, our judgement was that HMP Maidstone was a more respectful prison than when we last inspected, thanks in no small part to the quality of the relationships between staff and prisoners.

One of the most serious concerns brought to light by this inspection was the decline in terms of the purposeful activity available to prisoners. For those in employment the amount of time out of cell was perfectly adequate, but there were only sufficient activity places for around three-quarters of the population. There did not appear to be a strong culture of promoting teaching, learning or work within the prison. Indeed, inspectors concluded that much of the workshop activity was geared towards income generation for the prison rather than developing skills for prisoners to assist with their release and resettlement. Far too much of the work that was available was mundane and menial, and I was surprised to see large numbers of prisoners in workshops playing games rather than being engaged in work. In one case, prisoners were being allocated to an activity that did not actually exist. Ofsted judged the provision of education, work and skills to be inadequate in all of the areas they inspected, and it was inevitable that our overall judgement in the area of purposeful activity declined compared to the last inspection to the lowest assessment, 'poor'.

In contrast, we found that rehabilitation and release planning had improved since the last inspection, although more still needed to be done. There was a need to develop a single, coherent system that would be capable of addressing the needs of each and every prisoner. The needs of foreign national prisoners can be very different from those of the majority of the prison population, and it is fair to say there had been some improvements in recent times, but there were still too many inconsistencies and errors, such as prisoners being incorrectly allocated to a Community Rehabilitation Company instead of to the National Probation Service, and it proving hugely difficult to get the error corrected. About half of prisoners did not have an up-to-date offender assessment system (OASys) assessment. More also needed to be done to support the significant number of prisoners who received no social visits at all.

Those prisoners who were destined to be held in detention under immigration powers at the conclusion of their sentence should have been told that this was going to happen sooner rather than later, and certainly not left until very close to the time when they anticipated that they would be released. Although the problems with education and employment needed to be taken very seriously and resolved as soon as possible, it was good to see that there had been improvements in two of our healthy prison tests. The prison was completely aware of the distinct needs of their population, although more needed to be done to understand the more negative perceptions of their treatment and conditions held by prisoners with protected characteristics. The establishment also needed support in terms of investment to get the fabric of the buildings back to an acceptable standard and facilities such as the sports hall restored.

Peter Clarke CVO OBE QPM December 2018
HM Chief Inspector of Prisons

## INDEPENDENT MONITORING BOARD: Annual Report

The law requires every prison to be monitored by an independent Board appointed by the Justice Secretary; these are known as Independent Monitoring Boards (IMBs). The IMB must satisfy itself as to the humane and just treatment of those held in custody within its prison and the range and adequacy of the programmes preparing them for release; it must report annually to the Justice Secretary on how well the prison has met the standards and requirements placed on it.

**IMB Report 1 March 2021 – 28 February 2022**
**Published August 2022**
**Executive summary**
**Background to the report**
All prisons in England have been under the direct control, known as command mode, of Her Majesty's Prison and Probation Service (HMPPS) since March 2020. For the reporting period, Maidstone's regime has been directed by HMPPS commanders rather than Maidstone's Governor and the usual autonomy of the Governor has been restricted. The Board is of the opinion that an early return to local Governor control would allow more nuanced decisions to be made, informed by local conditions, and that this will be beneficial for Maidstone's prisoners and staff. As with other prisons, Maidstone has undergone various regime stages of lockdown as a result of the pandemic.

| Date | Regime |
|------|--------|
| March 2021 | stage 3 |
| July 2021 | stage 2 |
| September 2021 | stage 3 |
| November 2021 | stage 1 |
| December 2021 | stage 3 |
| February 2022 | stage 2 |

For a brief period, at the end of November 2021, Maidstone was the first prison in the region to achieve stage 1 status, until a new wave of the virus was detected, placing it back into the more restrictive stage 3 state. At the end of the reporting period the prison was at stage 2. The prison estate lags behind the wider community relative to relaxation of Covid-19 restrictions, for example mask wearing in prison remained mandated after this was made voluntary in the wider community.

Throughout the period all members have been able to attend in person for the rota sessions they have agreed to cover, although some members have needed to restrict their visits due to personal circumstances.

The pandemic has placed extreme pressures on prison management and staff. Despite the challenges, information sharing has been maintained.

## Main judgements
### How safe is the prison?
Despite a death after an apparent prisoner-on-prisoner attack on a wing in December 2021, it is the Board's view that HMP Maidstone is a safe prison. The Board judges that the prison is well run, that prisoners, for the most part, enjoy a good relationship with staff and each other and violence continues to remain at a low level.

### How fairly and humanely are prisoners treated?
During this reporting period, prisoners have been locked in their cells for long periods each day – during some parts of the year for in excess of 22 hours a day. The Board reiterates that the restrictive regime operating throughout the prison estate cannot constitute fair and humane treatment. It is problematic for health and wellbeing and provides few opportunities for rehabilitation. Maidstone staff have endeavoured to help and support individual prisoner needs within the constraints of this regime. Even when there have been significant staff shortages, prison officers have striven to deliver a fair and humane experience.

A significant concern of the Board is the reduced level of contact that Maidstone's foreign national prisoners have had with HOIE during the pandemic and the service they receive from the Home Office. Last year, the community council and chaplaincy cited this as a major cause of stress and anxiety leading to self-harm and other negative behaviours by some prisoners. The number of prisoners held under IS91 provisions (authority to detain under Immigration Act powers after completing their sentence) has significantly increased and more needs to be done to improve this situation. The Board considers it essential that HMPPS and HOIE work better together to ensure that these issues are addressed.

## How well are prisoners' health and wellbeing needs met?

As we report in section 6, the range and availability of health services has been affected by the restrictive Covid-19 regime and Covid security measures. However, primary and mental healthcare services continued to be provided as far as possible.

The Board considers that prison and healthcare staff have continued to make health and wellbeing a focus of attention particularly for vulnerable prisoners and that, within the limitations imposed by the pandemic, they have endeavoured to meet the health and wellbeing needs of prisoners.

## How well are prisoners progressed towards successful resettlement?

Although Covid-19 has severely impacted resettlement efforts, the Board commends the progress made by the resettlement management unit despite being understaffed. However, insufficient numbers of prisoners are accessing education and limited opportunities remain for vocational training or work.

Most of Maidstone's foreign national prisoners are of interest to the Home Office and destined to be removed from the UK but this year flights from the UK have again been limited. A scaled-back HOIE service to Maidstone prisoners for most of the reporting period also reduced opportunities for exit and resulted in end of sentence plans for many prisoners being incomplete or disrupted with the number of men detained under IS91 increasing.

## Main areas for development
### TO THE MINISTER

Support the restoration of local Governor control of establishments.

Work with the Home Office to ensure that HOIE documents required to be signed by foreign national prisoners are provided in languages they can fully understand.

Support, or sponsor if necessary, work to implement effective collaboration between HMPPS and HOIE so that communication and end of sentence management for foreign national prisoners are improved, the number of men detained under IS91 is reduced and that these men are no longer held in prisons.

### TO THE PRISON SERVICE

Provide more clarity about the prisoner property management framework.

Provide more category D accommodation across the estate and address the current restrictions of category D establishments accepting foreign national prisoners.

Support the re-establishment of a release on temporary licence (ROTL) facility at Maidstone.

Arrange for core material prepared for the resettlement of foreign national prisoners to be developed across the estate nationally.

Work with the Probation Service to ensure that there are mechanisms to provide feedback to Maidstone on the work they do to prepare prisoners for release in the UK. Consider what parallel arrangements might be made in respect of prisoners released overseas.

Prioritise the provision of upgraded internet bandwidth at Maidstone so that prisoners have more opportunities to communicate with family and support agencies. As we noted last year, a poor internet service continues to impact successful video calls (Purple Visits).

### TO THE GOVERNOR

Ensure the induction process is sufficiently robust. Improve communication of end of sentence arrangements.

Continue to seek ways to enhance the role of the community council.

Restart governor wing surgeries as soon as possible. Consolidate the progress made in the amount of key work undertaken and work to increase its quality. Improve delivery of education and training.

Consider the resettlement team's proposal to establish a ROTL facility.

Provide category D prisoners that cannot be moved to a category D establishment with as many category D privileges as possible.

Main areas for development Improvements
TO THE MINISTER

• Support, or sponsor if necessary, work to implement effective collaboration between HMPPS and HOIE so that communication and end of sentence management for foreign national prisoners are improved, the number of IS91 detainees is reduced and that these detainees are no longer held in closed prisons.

• Work with the Home Office to ensure that HOIE documents required to be signed by foreign national prisoners are provided in languages they can fully understand.

• Support the restoration of local governor control of establishments

• Finance appropriate technology services for IMBs as suggested by IMB Secretariat

The number of men held under IS91 has continued to rise and they are still held in closed prisons. Minister stated that 'The Home Office currently issue this documentation in English only, however a project is underway to explorer (sic) options of translating a selection of documents into a number of other languages.' No evidence of translated forms. Local Governor control has not been restored. IMB Maidstone is participating in the roll out of Kahootz.

## TO THE PRISON SERVICE
• Urgently review prisoner transfer and testing processes so that prisoners are not transferred until they have first been properly COVID tested.
• Develop a more integrated relationship with HOIE to ensure fair and humane treatment for foreign national prisoners and their families through improved communication and end of sentence management.
• Support better translation facilities for Foreign Nationals.
• Negotiate with suppliers to lower international telephone and video call charges for foreign nationals.
• Prioritise the provision of improved infrastructure including in-cell telephony and upgraded Internet bandwidth at Maidstone so that prisoners have more opportunities to communicate with family and support agencies.
• Develop systems to solve the longstanding issue of property being lost on transfer between prisons.
• Exit Command Mode as soon as possible.
HMPPS feedback suggested its strategy is kept under ongoing review and is 'regularly adapting. HMPPS did not feed back on this point. New contract signed with Big Word, but there are still problems. HMPPS commented that the service required is not comparable to public phone services and prices need to be higher. In-cell telephony delivered March 2022. Internet bandwidth has not changed. Draft framework issued but no improvements observed. HMPPS did not comment on this. Local Governor control has not been restored.

## TO THE GOVERNOR
• Work with HOIE management to improve communications and end of sentence management for prisoners destined to exit the UK
• Seek budget for the early implementation of in-cell telephony and better Internet bandwidth.
• Ensure consistent availability of Samaritans phones and better use of mobile PIN phones.
• Improve CCTV implementation to provide full prison coverage
• Restart governor wing surgeries as soon as possible
• Continue to improve keywork engagement and reintroduce OMiC (Offender Management in Custody).
• Address the unresolved issues surrounding Muslim prayer facilities highlighted in last year's report
Remains on the strategy delivery plan February 2022. In-cell telephony delivered March 2022. Internet bandwidth has not changed.
This appears to have improved.

Currently not implemented but scheduled to be delivered by December 2022.
Some success at some times during the year when the regime allowed. We expect to see all surgeries now being held regularly.
Key work meetings are happening more frequently. Restrictions during the reporting year meant these issues did not arise but the causes remain unresolved.

**1 SOUTHALL ST**
**MANCHESTER**
**M60 9AH**

**Tel: 0161 817 5600**

*For the latest reports on this prison please visit:* https://tinyurl.com/bdfh26rv

*Important Changes:* **(1) Visits:** the identification necessary to access this prison and visit for social or professional purposes has changed; (2) **Money and Gifts** new rules now apply to these. See page 16 for full details of the above.

### Task of the establishment
HMP Manchester is a category B training prison, holding a small number of category A prisoners, and a discrete close supervision centre.

### Certified normal accommodation and operational capacity
Prisoners held September 2021: 624
Baseline certified normal capacity: 695
In-use certified normal capacity: 695
Operational capacity: 744

### Population of the prison
• About 37 new prisoners had been received each month over the previous year.
• About 12 prisoners a month had been released into the community over the previous year.
• 55 foreign national prisoners were held during the inspection.
• 26.5% of prisoners were from black and minority ethnic backgrounds.

### Prison status and key providers
Public
Prison group: Long-term high security estate
Prison Group Director: Gavin O'Malley
Governor: Rob Knight
IMB chair Richard Christopherson
Physical and mental health provider: GM Mental Health NHS Foundation Trust
Substance misuse treatment provider: Delphi
Prison education framework provider:

459

Milton Keynes College
Escort contractor: GeoAmey and HM Prison and Probation Service

### Brief history
Manchester Prison opened in June 1868. Following a large-scale disturbance in 1990, the prison required major refurbishment. It was moved into the directorate of the high security estate in April 2003. In 2020, its function changed from a local to a category B training prison.
Short description of residential units
A wing: General population
B wing: General population
C wing: General population full-time workers
D wing: General population
E wing: Category A unit and category B and escape list prisoners
G wing: Drug and alcohol recovery unit and incentivised substance free living unit
H wing: Reverse cohort unit and a small social care unit on H1
I wing: General population
K wing: Vulnerable prisoner unit
M wing: Health care inpatients unit.

**Visiting Information** Book a reception visit on: 0161 817 5655 Monday to Thursday 8am to 4pm, and Friday 8am to 12pm. All other visits must be booked by the prisoner, who will need to inform you of the details. There are different visiting times for prisoners restricted to closed visits (where they are kept separate from the visitors).
**Visiting times:**
*General visiting times:*
Monday to Thursday: 2pm to 3pm and 3:30pm to 4:30pm, Saturday: 9am to 10am, 10:30am to 11:30am, 2pm to 3pm, and 3:30pm to 4:30pm, Sunday: 2pm to 3pm and 3:30pm to 4:30pm
*Closed visiting times:*
Please call the booking line for up to date information

**Legal visits:** Booking line: 0161 817 5656 Monday to Friday, 8am to 4pm.
**Visiting times:** Monday to Friday, 9:30am to 10:30am and 10:30am to 11:30am.

### INSPECTIONS & REPORTS
**Date of last inspection:** 13-17 September 2021
**HMCIP Report, published 21 December 2021**
In 2020, HMP Manchester made the transition from a local to a category B training prison, retaining a small category A function and separate close supervision centre. At the time of our visit it held 624 men, of whom a third were serving indeterminate sentences.
The governor had taken on the challenge of transforming the culture of the prison and the mindset of the staff to focus on the rehabilitation of long- sentenced prisoners rather than the needs of a transient local prison population, but much of this work had been delayed or derailed by the Covid-19 pandemic.
Some material changes had certainly supported this process – all but a few prisoners were held in single cells, showers had been improved and new kitchens on wings would soon mean prisoners could cook their own food.
With Covid-19 restrictions still in place, many prisoners were still spending too long in their cells with few jobs available, very limited offending behaviour programmes and face-to-face education practically non-existent. Staff shortages restricted the number of prisoners who could get to the library, gym or workshops.
One of the themes of this inspection was the lack of trust that prisoners had in prison staff. For example, they did not believe that complaints would be dealt with robustly, they could not get hold of their stored property, the booking line for visits rang unanswered, there was often no response to applications and the vulnerable prisoners on K wing reported high levels of victimisation from staff.
The governor had taken some active steps to address this issue, moving his office and those of senior managers onto the wings to increase their visibility to prisoners and staff. He had put in a new system for managing complaints, brought in new quality assurance to respond to allegations of discrimination and he chaired the black prisoner consultation forum. He had also held a drug summit in which staff and prisoners were consulted on how to reduce the supply of drugs, from which leaders had developed a series of actions. At the last inspection we were very critical of the segregation unit and we were pleased to see improvements not only in the physical environment, but in the way men with often very complex needs were helped back into the main prison, with some impressive input from the psychology service in formulating support plans. The governor had also prioritised improving the staff culture in the prison and the often good and caring interactions we saw with prisoners were evidence that progress was being made. Inspectors who had also been on the previous inspection noticed an improvement in the atmosphere. The prison had recently adopted a new incentive scheme that aimed to improve prisoners' behaviour, though it was too early to see the effects. Leaders had introduced targeted performance management for custodial managers to improve their confidence and competence in leading their teams; this was crucial to transforming the prison culture.

There was, however, much to be done – in some wings, inspectors were struck by the lack of engagement and poor attitudes of some officers. This along with a reluctance to turn on body-worn cameras, the unnecessary use of an aggressive, barking dog to accompany prisoners who were being relocated to the segregation unit, the unwillingness of some staff to challenge disruptive behaviour, the extraordinary strip-searching of prisoners who were being released and the often poor treatment of those at risk of suicide or self-harm, pointed to the scale of the challenge.

The board in the administrative block lists the 10 governors who have led the prison since the turn of the century, a turnover rate that explains why so many deep-set problems remain. If HMP Manchester is to make the transformation from a security-focused local prison to a category B training prison that rehabilitates the often challenging and complex men in its care, the prison service will need to make sure that this strong and effective governor has the time and money to complete the job.

Charlie Taylor Chief Inspector October 2021

### Summary of key findings

We last inspected HMP Manchester in 2018 and made 67 recommendations, five of which were about areas of key concern. The prison fully accepted 46 of the recommendations and partially (or subject to resources) accepted 12. It rejected nine of the recommendations.

### Progress on key concerns and recommendations from the full inspection

Our last inspection of HMP Manchester took place before the COVID-19 pandemic and the recommendations in that report focused on areas of concern affecting outcomes for prisoners at the time. Although we recognise that the challenges of keeping prisoners safe during COVID-19 will have changed the focus for many prison leaders, we believe that it is important to follow up on recommendations about areas of key concern to help leaders to continue to drive improvement.

At our last full inspection, we made one recommendation about key concerns in the area of safety. At this inspection we found that this recommendation had not been achieved.

We made three recommendations about key concerns in the area of respect. At this inspection we found that one of those recommendations had been achieved, one had been partially achieved and one had not been achieved.

We made one recommendation about key concerns in the area of purposeful activity. At this inspection we found that this recommendation had not been achieved.

### Outcomes for prisoners

We assess outcomes for prisoners against four healthy prison tests (see Appendix I for more information about the tests). We also include a commentary on leadership in the prison.

At this inspection of HMP Manchester, we found that outcomes for prisoners had stayed the same in two healthy prison areas, improved in one and declined in one.

These judgements seek to make an objective assessment of the outcomes experienced by those detained and have taken into account the prison's recovery from Covid-19 as well as the 'regime stage' at which the prison was operating, as outlined in the HM Prison and Probation (HMPPS) National Framework for prison regimes and services.

### Safety

The reception area was clean, and prisoners were treated well overall, but strip-searching all new arrivals in addition to using the body scanner could not be justified. There was an appropriate focus on assessing the risks posed by new prisoners as well as their vulnerabilities. About two-thirds of prisoners in our survey said they felt safe on their first night. Cells were clean and well-equipped, and staff were friendly and helpful.

In our survey, 25% of prisoners said they felt unsafe at the time of our inspection and those with mental health problems or other disabilities were significantly more negative than other prisoners. Levels of violence were lower than at our previous inspection, however, the rate of serious assaults had increased. Management oversight of violence reduction work was limited. While initial investigations into violent incidents were reasonably good, management and support plans were largely ineffective in helping perpetrators change their behaviour. Safety and violence reduction strategies had been reviewed but did not fully explore the causes of violence at the prison.

Since 2018, there had been five self-inflicted deaths and five deaths that were not from natural causes, some of which were linked to drug use. The rate of self-harm incidents in the previous year was similar to the rate leading up to our inspection in 2018. Not all serious incidents of self-harm were investigated and the standard of enquiry in those cases that were investigated was poor. The prison's strategic approach to reducing the level of self-harm had been neglected. Monthly Safer Manchester meetings were poorly attended. There had been no detailed analysis of data so that the causes of self-harming behaviour could be determined, or appropriate action planning taken to address them.

There was a death in custody action plan in response to Prisons and Probation Ombudsman recommendations, but there was little evidence showing that improvements were embedded in practice. Data analysis was too limited to inform a self-harm reduction strategy specific to Manchester. Staff we spoke to knew who was on an assessment, care in custody and teamwork (ACCT) case management document for prisoners at risk of suicide or self-harm, but many told us they had not received enough training in how to use the new version and the quality of documentation was poor. Support offered to those in crisis or at risk of self-harm needed improvement. There were too few Listeners (prisoners trained by the Samaritans to provide confidential emotional support to fellow prisoners) and in our survey, only 50% of prisoners who had been on an ACCT said they felt cared for.

Too many adjudication cases, including those for serious incidents, such as violence and use of illicit drugs, were still waiting to be concluded. Force was used less often than at the previous inspection, but de-escalation attempts were inadequate in many of the incidents we reviewed, and oversight of the use of special accommodation was weak. The use of force committee was not effective and the application of data to make continuous improvements was limited. Management of the segregation unit was now good. Reintegration planning had improved, and staff had a good understanding of the risks and triggers for those in their care.

Security procedures were broadly proportionate and the prison appropriately prioritised action to reduce the supply of illicit items. Leaders had held a 'drug summit', a meeting where staff and prisoners identified concerns, and a subsequent action plan, which looked promising, was drawn up. The effectiveness of drug testing was undermined because action was not always taken following a positive test result.

### Respect

The inspection team saw many examples of positive staff-prisoner relationships. Most staff knew prisoners well and many offered good care, compassion and support, but we also observed some who appeared distant and disengaged. Problems with basic operational systems undermined the level of trust prisoners had in staff. In our survey, only 54% of prisoners said staff had victimised or bullied them; for vulnerable prisoners on K wing the figure was higher at 81% Covid-19 restrictions had hindered the delivery of the key worker scheme (see Appendix II Glossary of terms), but prisoners with vulnerabilities, including those at risk of self-harm, were being prioritised for contact.

Almost all prisoners now lived in single cells and some important improvements had been made to living conditions. While prisoners had reasonable access to materials to keep their cells clean, some we inspected needed to be refurbished. For example, broken windows required fixing and a damp problem needed to be addressed. Communal areas and landings were reasonably clean and the installation of new showers on some wings was positive, but some outside exercise yards remained littered. Prisoners' access to their stored property was very poor.

There was a reasonable selection of food, but prisoners were negative about it and better supervision was required while meals were being served. The planned opening of kitchenettes on each wing would enable prisoners to cook for themselves.

The applications system was not always effective, and some prisoners did not receive responses to their questions, which added to prisoners' lack of trust. Despite timely responses, replies to complaints did not always address the issues, and prisoners had little confidence in the system. However, leaders were taking steps to make improvements.

The equality strategy was not specific to HMP Manchester and progress against the action plan was slow. However, the governor had taken responsibility for improving outcomes for black and minority ethnic prisoners. Consultation with prisoners from most of the protected characteristics had recently restarted and lead managers for each group had been identified to take the work forward. Data analysis to identify potential disproportionate treatment was improving.

There was a lack of trust in the discrimination incident reporting form (DIRF) system, but some steps had been taken to address this. Responses to DIRFs were poor and the quality assurance process did not identify many of the issues.

Despite having a large number of foreign national prisoners, little support was available for this group, for example, there was a lack of translated material.

Strong partnership working took place between the prison and health partners. Health and social care governance were inconsistent, and some wing medicine administration rooms were dirty and untidy. Systems for checking, cleaning and updating some equipment lacked oversight.

There was an appropriate range of primary care services, waiting times were short and urgent appointments were available every day. Inpatient services offered dedicated and compassionate care, supported by close partnership working between officers and nurses. The local authority provided suitable social care packages.

The mental health team was responsive to demand, promptly assessing patients and prioritising support. Too many patients experienced delays in being transferred to hospital under the Mental Health Act.

The drug recovery unit was providing effective support, including outreach to patients on other wings. Clinical treatment arrangements were flexible and evidence-based, responding to needs. Pharmacy services had improved. Dental services were very good.

## Purposeful activity

Ofsted carried out a progress monitoring visit of the prison alongside our full inspection and the purposeful activity judgement incorporates their assessment of progress.

Most prisoners still had far too little time out of their cells and staff shortages at weekends exacerbated this. Approximately 43% of the population were unemployed and were locked in their cells for about 22.5 hours a day during the week.

Prisoners could now attend the library in person but only in very limited numbers. An order and delivery service continued to supplement the service. Literacy skills were promoted well. During the inspection, prisoners still only received one hour of gym time each week.

Leaders and managers did not provide enough education, skills or workplaces to meet the needs of all prisoners. They identified that, although they had the capacity to provide more face-to-face education places, they did not have enough prison staff to escort prisoners to the education wing.

Leaders and managers did not make sure that all the in-cell work packs were appropriately tailored to learners. Not all men received the support they needed to make progress. Too often, prisoners' access to education, training and work was determined by the regime, the wing they were on, or informal contact with prison staff, rather than their long-term plans. Leaders and managers had kept essential workshops open during the pandemic, albeit at reduced numbers. Leaders had in place plans to expand their work provision and had continued to offer accredited courses throughout the pandemic.

## Rehabilitation and release planning

Most prisoners could only access one social visit a month for one hour and the length of time allowed on video calls was too short. Over the previous 18 months, a small number of prisoners and their families had taken part in a distance-learning relationships course. Support from family workers was good. The introduction of in-cell telephones helped prisoners stay in touch with their friends and family. Meetings to oversee and drive forward reducing reoffending

work had restarted after a long gap during the pandemic. There was no current strategy, but a needs analysis was being undertaken to inform one in the future.

Offender managers at the prison had become very task-focused in their work and their face-to-face contact with prisoners was limited. Prison offender managers' contact with too many prisoners was not sufficiently frequent and in most cases we reviewed, the focus on progression was not good enough. Only half of those in our survey knew they had a custody plan. Communication between offender managers in the prison and those in the community was effective and the quality of individual risk management plans was good.

Processes for identifying risks to the public posed by newly arrived prisoners were sound and measures to mitigate these risks were authorised and applied appropriately. However, there was a backlog of telephone calls waiting to be reviewed. The interdepartmental risk management team was not effective.

Categorisation reviews were timely, and decisions could be justified. Many prisoners who needed to be transferred to another prison so that they could progress remained at Manchester for too long.

The three types of accredited programmes on offer were appropriate for the population but the number of programme places planned for the following year would not meet the level of need.

## Key concerns and recommendations

Key concerns and recommendations identify the issues of most importance to improving outcomes for prisoners and are designed to help establishments prioritise and address the most significant weaknesses in the treatment and conditions of prisoners.

During this inspection we identified some areas of key concern and have made a small number of recommendations for the prison to address those concerns.

Key concern: Leaders had not yet made sure that the opportunities and services provided, such as offence-focused work, addressed the full range of needs among the new population of long-term category B prisoners. Staffing issues often affected prisoners' access to services because there were not enough officers to escort them from their wing.

Recommendation A: Leaders should make sure that services and progression opportunities, such as the range of offence-focused work, meet the needs of a long-term category B population – for example those convicted of violence against a partner.

Recommendation B: The staff profile and their allocation to tasks should be reviewed to ensure there are enough officers to escort prisoners to their appointments.

Key concern: Governance and oversight of the use of force was weak. Data analysis was not sufficient and there was a lack of focus on learning lessons following incidents involving force, such as the use of batons. De-escalation techniques were not always used well enough and body-worn cameras were not routinely switched on during incidents. The use of special accommodation was not always justified.

Recommendation: Leaders should improve oversight of and accountability for the use of force, including special accommodation, to make sure it is only used when necessary and justified. Body-worn cameras should always be switched on at the beginning of an incident.

Key concern: The level of self-harm remained high and there had been

five self-inflicted deaths and five deaths through non-natural causes since the previous inspection. The new assessment, care in custody and teamwork case management documentation for prisoners at risk of suicide or self-harm was poorly completed in too many cases and prisoners did not always receive a good, proactive level of care.

Recommendation: The prison should take steps to reduce the level of self-harm. Prisoners should receive proactive, meaningful day-to-day care to reduce their risk of self-harm. Weaknesses in the standard of ACCT documentation should be addressed.

Key concern: The use of key working to support prisoners and build trust in staff was poor, and some staff were not committed to promoting prisoners' progression or rehabilitation. Prisoners had negative perceptions of how some staff treated them. They did not have confidence in basic processes, such as the management of their personal property or the applications and complaints systems.

Recommendation: Leaders should implement ways of improving and measuring the levels of trust among prisoners to ensure that their perceptions about the prison are more positive. This should be supported by effective processes, such as the management of property and the applications and complaints systems. All prisoners should have a named member of staff who supports them to make positive changes in their lives.

Key concern: We observed out-of-date stock items in primary care areas and gaps in mandatory training in moving and handling patients. Staff also had few opportunities to meet as a team and there was minimal evidence of lessons learned from incidents being widely shared.

Recommendation: Managers should strengthen oversight of primary care and social care services to make sure patient care is delivered safely.

Key concern: Many prisoners were still locked in their cells for 22.5 hours a day during the working week and longer at weekends when the regime was regularly curtailed.

Recommendation: Prisoners should have regular and predictable time out of cell that is sufficient to promote rehabilitation and well-being.

Key concern: Leaders and managers did not provide enough education, training or workplaces to meet the needs of all prisoners. For example, only 16 learners attended face-to-face classes in the education unit. Leaders did not make sure that prisoners were allocated to education or work activities that reflected their personal learning plans or goals. Too often, prisoners' access to education, training and work was determined by the regime, the wing they were on or informal contact with prison staff, rather than prisoners' long-term plans.

Recommendation: The number of education, training and workplaces must be increased significantly, and the allocation process should be well coordinated and equitable to make sure that prisoners undertake activities that meet their short-, medium- and long-term plans.

Key concern: Sentenced prisoners had too few opportunities to receive visits from their family and friends and the sessions were too short. Visitors found it difficult to get through to the visits booking system by phone.

Recommendation: Leaders should make sure that prisoners are easily able to maintain links to their friends and family through regular, longer visits and an effective booking system.

Key concern: Offender management in the prison was not proactive and contact with prisoners did not take place regularly and was not always meaningful, which meant individuals' progression was not fully supported.

Recommendation: Leaders should enable all eligible prisoners to receive structured, face-to-face offender management support that enables them to achieve their targets and progress through their sentence.

**Notable positive practice**

We define notable positive practice as innovative work or practice that leads to particularly good outcomes from which other establishments may be able to learn. Inspectors look for evidence of good outcomes for prisoners; original, creative or particularly effective approaches to problem-solving or achieving the desired goal; and how other establishments could learn from or replicate the practice.

Inspectors found five examples of notable positive practice during this inspection.

The governor and most of the senior leaders had

moved out of the administration block and had relocated their offices on to the wings to improve visibility and communication.

Consultation with staff and prisoners through a 'drug summit' and survey to identify ways of addressing the use of illicit drugs had led to an effective action plan.

Patients had access to the Greater Manchester Mental Health NHS Foundation Trust complaints department via their phone where they could register their complaints at trust level if they believed local staff would be biased in their handling of the issue.

Individual needs assessments carried out by pharmacy staff encouraged patients to take responsibility and be more confident in managing their own medicines. Reminder charts helped them keep track of when they had taken their medicines.

Library services promoted literacy among prisoners well. The Shannon Trust had continued to work with prisoners by providing in-cell work packs until face-to-face work could restart. The Writing on the Wall competition was well advertised and encouraged prisoners to write short stories. The Reading Ahead programme engaged over 250 prisoners, supplying free dictionaries and grammar books to those who took part. Participants prepared written reviews of six books or articles they had read through the programme.

## INDEPENDENT MONITORING BOARD: Annual Report

The law requires every prison to be monitored by an independent Board appointed by the Justice Secretary; these are known as Independent Monitoring Boards (IMBs). The IMB must satisfy itself as to the humane and just treatment of those held in custody within its prison and the range and adequacy of the programmes preparing them for release; it must report annually to the Justice Secretary on how well the prison has met the standards and requirements placed on it.

### IMB Report 1 March 2020 to 28 February 2021
### Published December 2021
### Main judgments
### How safe is the prison?

HMP Manchester has been through a period of transition during its re-categorisation, and as a result within the reporting year the prison population had reduced by 20.9%, which continues the downward trend seen in recent years. This reduction in prisoner numbers has also resulted in a fewer number of assaults both in relation to prisoner on prisoner and prisoner on staff incidents, and violence within the prison has also decreased over the same period. The

Board has identified a reduction in the number of self-harm incidents which can often be associated with bullying and debt-related issues. Levels of violence in the prison have reduced during the Covid-19 lockdown, as prisoners were largely confined to their cells. The change of role to a Category B prison is likely to lead to a more settled regime, with prisoners staying at Manchester for longer periods. Longer term residency may mean that disagreements between prisoners are less likely to rapidly escalate into violence. Single cell occupancy is also likely to contribute to a reduction in violence.

The level of self-harm incidents, prisoner-on-staff assaults and prisoner-on prisoner assaults have all seen a positive and disproportionate drop compared with the reduction in the population. Prisoner-on-staff assaults have fallen even more than prisoner on prisoner assaults.

Throughout the pandemic, the staff have worked very hard to provide a safe and secure environment. The prison managed restrictions and the effects of the COVID-19 pandemic professionally, and managers and staff ensured that the prison remained a safe residential and working environment.

### How fairly and humanely are prisoners treated?

The Board considers that during the reporting year HMP Manchester has consistently tried to treat prisoners fairly and humanely. However, the need to respond to the Covid-19 pandemic and to carry out essential building works has compromised that effort and the outcome for prisoners has not therefore always been humane. HMP Manchester has had to prioritise reducing the spread of infection and therefore the Board has witnessed prisoners having to spend much more time than usual in their cells. Normal and purposeful activity such as work, association, gym access and education were heavily curtailed. The prison has supported prisoners in staying in contact with family and friends and the provision of in-cell phones has assisted in this process. To mitigate the effect of the Covid-19 restrictions on face to face visits, financial contributions towards prisoner's phone credits were provided so as not to deny family contact caused by the prisoner's inability to pay and the earlier reference in this report to the introduction of 'Purple Visits' has been an asset.

The physical estate at HMP Manchester has had a number of improvements over the reporting year with new showers installed on several wings and a new boiler fitted to provide regular heating to cells which had previously been the subject of complaints to the IMB in respect of cold conditions and a lack of hot water. However, the Board noted that during the period of several months whilst the work was carried out, prisoners on the wings in question were not able to have showers or heating.

The work of the Chaplaincy, in particular the support provided to prisoners of all religious faiths across the prison estate in the absence of regular weekly chapel activity has been an important resource.

### How well are prisoners' health and wellbeing needs met?

HMP Manchester has experienced a challenging year in meeting prisoners' health and wellbeing needs caused by the priority of restricting the spread of Covid-19 and treating those prisoners who did catch it. Managers and healthcare staff have however managed to maintain a reasonable standard of healthcare and wellbeing and have continued to distribute medication and arrange hospital admissions for those prisoners requiring urgent medical attention.

As part of the efforts to restrict the spread of infection, the procedure for healthcare appointments was changed, Triage calls were introduced to determine if face to face appointments were necessary, using the in cell telephones. This has significantly reduced the number of face-to-face appointments carried out we believe although we are unable to verify this as Healthcare records do not distinguish between telephone and face to face appointments.

Covid-19 restrictions on external hospital clinics have inevitably caused a reduction in the number of external hospital appointments made available to prisoners and this has eased the pressures on the prison to provide escort staff.

Last year, The Board wrote about specific case studies to evidence our concerns about the mental health and wellbeing of prisoners who spend prolonged periods on constant watch, sometimes in segregation. This formed part of the larger issue of management of prisoners in jail whilst they are waiting to be transferred to a secure hospital when the waiting time is often prolonged. From its day to day monitoring the Board notes that the situation has not improved. The Board is very concerned about the mental health of such prisoners. Prison is not a suitable environment, evidenced by the clinical decision that they need transfer to hospital, and neither segregation nor healthcare can provide the care that is necessary for such prisoners. Being managed in such unsuitable environment may further damage the prisoners' mental health that is already frail, and the Board's regular interactions with such prisoners also suggest so. It also adds a strain on the jail as such management requires more resources and can also be challenging for staff to deal with.

In the light of the above, the Board concludes that the waiting times for transfers to secure healthcare facilities are often unacceptable and unfair. The Board understands the obstacles that the Covid-19 pandemic may have introduced, however, this concern was evident prior to the pandemic.

The Board has identified the increased use of cells located on a separate landing within the Healthcare unit to provide normal accommodation for some Category A prisoners who need to be separated from other Category A prisoners. No extra prison staff to manage the Category A prisoners have been provided to the Healthcare Unit and the patients on the unit are therefore spending longer than normal periods in their cells as the staff are regularly required to manage the separate regimes for these prisoners. In addition, any duties required of healthcare staff to attend to intermittent and constant watches also places a pressure on resources in this area.

### How well are prisoners progressed towards successful resettlement?

HMP Manchester is now a Category B training prison and therefore no longer has resettlement plans as it is not envisaged that any prisoners will be released directly back into the community. Any work required is referred to as Community Offender Management, and responsibility for it lies with the Offender Management Unit but the majority of the work is undertaken by outside agencies.

During the reporting year, prisoner numbers have steadily decreased at the prison, as transfers have been arranged for moves to the neighbouring prison at HMP Forest Bank. This process will continue as the plan is for all prisoners to move to this establishment within 16 months prior to their release.

In addition, as part of the transition period HMP Manchester had a cohort of 350 Category C prisoners requiring transfers to other jails in the UK. Due to Covid-19 and the tight restrictions relating to prison transfers, the Board understands this has reduced to 127 Category C prisoners who remain at HMP Manchester awaiting transfer.

The Offender Management team is very restricted as 50% are working from home and this has created delays in the management of cases.

### Main areas for development
### TO THE MINISTER

The Board welcomed the response by the Minister to their report last year and was pleased to learn that the bid for funding to install secure windows at HMP Manchester had been successful. The Board notes however that this priority work at the time of writing this report has not commenced and would therefore ask the Minister when this will happen?

In the previous annual report, the Board raised concerns about prisoners who spend prolonged periods on constant watch, sometimes in segregation. This formed part of the larger issue of management of prisoners in jail whilst they are waiting to be transferred to a secure hospital. The waiting time often lasts months. The Board acknowledges comments made by the Minister last year outlining the current ongoing work to help make the process quicker. Unfortunately, this year the Board has not seen any progress. Whilst the Board understands that some changes will not take place immediately, the Board would like to know what action is being taken in the interim period, what support is being offered to the prisoners now and what support is offered to jail when managing prisoners who should managed in a hospital environment?

### TO HMPPS

Is HMPPS considering the introduction of a stricter process for recording prisoner property through the use of photographs as opposed to hand written descriptions by officers on property cards to address the number of complaints and provide reassurance to prisoners regarding their property?

### TO THE GOVERNOR

The Board would advise that it continues to have concerns about the security of prisoners' property. This applies particularly where prisoners are moving internally between wings at HMP Manchester and when prisoners arrive on transfer from other prisons. Although it is now a requirement for staff at HMP Manchester to use Body Worn Video Cameras (BWVCs) during cell clearances, the Board understands that this is not happening for every clearance. The Board further understands that after cells have been cleared they are left unlocked and therefore any overlooked property is unprotected, presenting an opportunity for it to go missing. Would the Governor please confirm what measures are being introduced to ensure improved practices are adopted to mitigate the loss of prisoner property?

The Board has noted an increase in applications relating to prisoners being permitted to order items directly from the catalogue but finding when these items arrive that they do not meet the criteria as permitted items in the prison. In addition, prisoners at HMP Manchester are restricted to receiving permitted additional items during their 6 month property window, causing further frustration as the same rules do not apply in other prisons from which a number have transferred. Would the Governor confirm if

existing processes in relation to prisoner property is to be reviewed to permit HMP Manchester to operate consistently with other Category B establishments?

The Board has also observed a case of a prisoner with learning difficulties and would like to clarify what the provisions are for such prisoners? The prisoner has learning difficulties and very low IQ and has been waiting for a suitable facility for over a year whilst being managed between healthcare and segregation units in the jail.

The Board notes the increase in the number of packages containing illegal substances being thrown over the perimeter wall into the prison. What measures have been implemented to reduce the risk of prisoners accessing packages whilst on exercise?

### Progress since the last report

The Board is pleased to see several improvements in the prison across a number of areas. One area of improvement during the reporting year has been general cleanliness within the prison, in particular the external areas within exercise yards with reduced volumes of litter and discarded food. There has been a particular difference in the standard of cleanliness around the serveries on the wings.

The Board is also pleased to see repairs and refurbishment taking place around the prison with wings having been painted, a new boiler installed to ensure hot water for showers, and the completion work on the installation of new showers.

The Board identified an increase in applications from prisoners on 'K' Wing during July. Prison management promptly investigated the concerns raised by prisoners and made a number of changes to operational duties and returned the wing to a settled environment.

The Board has also noted the work of the prison in responding to the impact of the Covid-19 pandemic. HMP Manchester has worked to provide conditions to mitigate the risk from the spread of infection and has introduced a range of safe working practices to ensure government guidelines on social distancing are maintained to provide as healthy an environment as possible for staff and prisoners. The use of 'Covid-19 clean team' in particular, has made a significant difference to the general cleanliness of both the internal and external areas of the prison and to the administrative block.

BAWTRY ROAD
HATFIELD WOODHOUSE
DONCASTER
DN7 6BW

**Tel: 01302 523000**

*For the latest reports on this prison please visit:*
https://tinyurl.com/bdfh26rv

*Important Changes:* **(1) Visits:** the identification necessary to access this prison and visit for social or professional purposes has changed; (2) **Money and Gifts** new rules now apply to these. See page 16 for full details of the above.

**Task of the establishment** HMP & YOI Moorland is a category C resettlement prison.

**Certified normal accommodation and operational capacity**
Prisoners held at the time of inspection: 956
Baseline certified normal capacity: 1,006
In-use certified normal capacity: 957
Operational capacity: 1,006

**Prison status and key providers**
Public
Prison Group: Yorkshire
Prison Group Director: Helen Judge
Governor/Director: Jennifer Willis
IMB Chair: Esther Beeston
Physical, Mental, Substance use health provider: Premier Plus Group
Learning and skills provider: Novus
Escort contractor (PECS): Geo Amey

**Brief history** HMP Moorland opened in 1991, with a remand and young offender institution (YOI) function. It expanded in 1998 and 2011, when it started to receive sex offenders from Yorkshire and Humberside. In September 2002, HMP/YOI Moorland merged with HMP/YOI Hatfield. In July 2011, Moorland and Hatfield were subject to market testing and placed into the 'South Yorkshire cluster', which included HMP Lindholme. This became HMP South Yorkshire. In January 2014, HMP/YOI Moorland reverted to a single prison.

**Short description of residential units**
House block 1 – substance misuse treatment
House block 2 – first night centre
House blocks 3 and 4 – prisoners convicted of sexual offences
House block 5 – includes the reintegration unit
House block 6 – drug-free environment
House block 7 – unit for older prisoners and those with poor mobility (integrated general population and prisoners convicted of sexual offences)

**Visiting Information** Book your visit online: https://www.gov.uk/prison-visits
Visits can be booked via email at:
SocialVisits.Moorland@justice.gov.uk
This mailbox is monitored from 9am to 4pm Monday to Friday but please allow up to 3 working days for a response.
**Visiting times:**
Tues, Thurs, Sat, Sun: 2pm to 3:30pm

**Legal visits:** To book legal visits please email: LegalVisits.Moorland@justice.gov.uk.
**Visiting times:** Tues, Wed, Thurs: 2pm – 4pm

**INSPECTIONS & REPORTS**
**Date of last inspection 11–21 February 2019**
**HMCIP Report, published 11 June 2019**
HMP/YOI Moorland is a category C adult and young adult men's resettlement prison situated near Doncaster. It was last inspected in February 2016, at which time it was still adapting to having been re-roled as a resettlement prison. There had also been a period of uncertainty prior to the last inspection as a result of the prison being earmarked for privatisation; a plan which was subsequently abandoned. In 2016 the prison was also suffering very badly from an influx of illicit drugs, particularly new psychoactive substances (NPS). This was causing daily medical emergencies and not enough was being done to stem the flow of drugs into the jail. At that time it was also made clear to the inspection team that the staff felt that the prison had been severely affected by the benchmarking process, leaving it desperately short of staff.
It was therefore heartening to see the progress that had been made in the past three years. In 2016 three of our healthy prison tests had been graded as 'not sufficiently good'. In contrast, on this occasion we found three to be 'reasonably good', with increases in grading for safety and respect. Given the context in which prisons such as Moorland have been operating over the past few years, this is a significant achievement, and testament to a huge amount of hard work by all the leaders and staff at Moorland.
We found Moorland to be a very different prison from the one we inspected in 2016. Levels of violence had not only stabilised, but had actually decreased – clearly bucking the national trend over that period. However, despite the fact that overall levels of violence had dropped, assaults against staff had doubled and were higher than at similar prisons. There is still more to do to deal with violence, but the way in which it was now being analysed was positive, as was the support

being offered to victims. The use of force by staff had increased since the last inspection, and recording was generally good, although some aspects of governance needed to improve.

Along with the reduction in violence, it was also notable that the prevalence of NPS seen at the last inspection has decreased. There was a comprehensive drug strategy and good work between the security department and substance misuse services.

It was concerning that levels of self-harm were very high, and in light of this it was disappointing that there were insufficient Listeners. One of our main recommendations from this inspection is around the need to analyse, understand and respond to whatever lies behind the high levels of self-harm.

Staff-prisoner relationships had improved considerably since the last inspection, and it was good to see that the keyworker scheme was being implemented. It was clear that this was having a positive impact on relationships. As in every prison where we see it happening, the introduction of in-cell telephones was an important development and beneficial in many ways.

However, there was much work to be done to understand the equality monitoring data that indicated some poorer outcomes for prisoners with protected characteristics. There was a need for more consultation and better involvement of community groups who worked in equality and diversity. Our survey indicated adverse results for black and minority ethnic and disabled prisoners, and this needed to be understood.

The reintegration unit was, in principle, a good initiative, with perfectly sensible aspirations to manage poor behaviour, incentivise good behaviour and assist prisoners in locating back onto mainstream accommodation. However, at the time of the inspection there was still much work to be done to realise the full potential of the unit, and a more meaningful regime needed to be introduced from the moment prisoners were first located onto the unit.

The most serious concern we had was around the lack of effective public protection measures. The report gives detailed evidence of how these were lacking in too many ways, and it was unacceptable that high risk prisoners approaching release were not receiving the detailed consideration that their potential risk to the public should have demanded. Moorland has now been a resettlement prison for a number of years, and this whole area of responsibility, not only to the prisoners but also to the public, needs to be addressed as a matter of urgency.

Overall, this was a good inspection, and although there were some vital areas where improvement was still needed, it was obvious that the findings of the last inspection had been taken seriously. Around two-thirds of our recommendations had been achieved, and this is more that we are used to seeing in recent times. I would urge the leadership and staff at Moorland not to feel defensive about some of the issues raised in this report, which some might interpret as criticism. It is the duty of HM Inspectorate of Prisons to report on what we see, and if there are shortcomings we will point them out, in the spirit of helping to secure further improvements through recommendations. This was a reassuring inspection, and shows what can be achieved even in difficult and testing times, but it would be unduly complacent not to acknowledge that further improvement is necessary and achievable.

Peter Clarke CVO OBE QPM April 2019
HM Chief Inspector of Prisons

## INDEPENDENT MONITORING BOARD: Annual Report

The law requires every prison to be monitored by an independent Board appointed by the Justice Secretary; these are known as Independent Monitoring Boards (IMBs). The IMB must satisfy itself as to the humane and just treatment of those held in custody within its prison and the range and adequacy of the programmes preparing them for release; it must report annually to the Justice Secretary on how well the prison has met the standards and requirements placed on it.

**IMB Report: 1 March 2021 – 28 February 2022**
**Published: July 2022**
**Executive summary**
**Background to the report**

The Covid-19 outbreak has had a significant impact on the Board's ability to gather information and discuss the contents of this annual report. The Board has therefore tried to cover as much ground as it can in these difficult circumstances, but inevitably there is less detail and supporting evidence than usual. Ministers are aware of these constraints. Regular information is being collected specifically on the prison's response to the pandemic, and that is being collated nationally.

This is the third annual report that the Moorland Board has prepared which has been impacted by the Covid-19 pandemic. However, the Board has been visiting the prison for most of this year, although this has been interrupted by members' health and lockdowns within the year. We held our April 2021 Board meeting within the prison and gradually resumed our duties, though these were initially limited, due to the restricted regimes and safe access to prisoners. The remote working we had developed during the previous year was used when necessary (e.g. telephoning in to segregation unit reviews) and prisoners continued to make use of the 0800 IMB line, with 44 prisoners making 113 applications in this way during the year, 33% of total applications.

During the year there has been a change of Governor and significant changes to the senior management team. The Governor regularly attends the Board meetings and staff have been helpful throughout the year and in providing information for this report. As part of the Board strategic work plan, compiled in August 2021 at an 'away half-day', and following a Board session with the senior probation officer in October 2021, it was decided that a piece of focused work would take place with prisoners serving indeterminate sentences for public protection (IPP). This has been illuminating and concerning work, which has extended to IMB colleagues from the Yorkshire and Humber region.

The previously anticipated population changes towards more foreign national prisoners and PCOSOs did not occur, with the ratio of different categories remaining relatively constant. There were 1,111 receptions, 169 transfers and 953 releases from Moorland during the reporting period. Although offending behaviour courses, identified in sentence plans, have had limited availability, prison offender managers (POMs) have worked on sentence progression with their community colleagues and the prisoner. However, this has been a frustrating and challenging process for some of the prisoners and staff.

The fabric and cleanliness of the prison is generally good. Work has begun to re-roof the accommodation blocks, and, as mentioned, half of houseblock 7 has been repurposed as an intermediate care unit. The visits hall has been open for most of the year with a gradual reduction of Covid-19 protective measures to improve the quality of the visits. However, the numbers remain limited and the children's play area has not reopened. However, the number of Purple Visits (remote video-calls) has increased and they remain popular, although connection issues remain a frustration on occasions.

## Main judgements
### How safe is the prison?
Self-harm has continued on a downward trend throughout the year, although the overall number of incidents is 12 higher than last year. However, there were 159 fewer assessment, care in custody and teamwork (ACCT) documents opened, due, in part, to the extensive 'post-closure' work, which can prevent the need for a further ACCT for the same prisoner.

There have been six deaths in custody, four of which were apparently from natural causes, one apparently from an accidental overdose, and one apparent suicide shortly after release.

The incidents of violence have also reduced, from 87 to 84, with fewer assaults on staff. At times during the year there has been an increase in contacts between prisoners as the prison moved through the 'stages' of the national framework, which has resulted in more potential for stress and violence between prisoners.

The focus on reducing the availability of illicit drugs and alcohol has continued via the use of the body scanner, photocopying of mail and vigilance of staff (both HM Prison and Probation Service (HMPPS) and healthcare). Generally, it has been successful, with any 'spikes' immediately interrogated and appropriate action taken.

### How fairly and humanely are prisoners treated?
There is generally good standard accommodation across the prison, with in-cell telephony in all cells except houseblock 8, where prisoners are offered the use of a mobile phone at certain times, and the segregation unit.

There were concerted complaints about the food on one occasion but usually, within the challenging constraints, the food is acceptable and meets the diverse dietary needs of the population. There have been issues with kitchen equipment, especially freezers for a period, and, as elsewhere, Covid-19 has affected the availability of prisoners and staff to work in the kitchen. Once again, the Board is requesting that the food budget is increased, and it is understood there are ongoing negotiations with the Governor. The Board has paid particular attention to the treatment of IPP sentenced prisoners. There is a sense of helplessness and hopelessness for many, especially for those detained for many years after a recall. This unfair and inhumane sentence was rescinded in 2012 but there remain 22 prisoners in Moorland who were sentenced before that date. There is reference to this issue in the report.

### How well are prisoners' health and wellbeing needs met?
The IMB's opinion is that overall the care of prisoners' health and wellbeing is equivalent to that which they could expect in the community; of course, both settings have been badly affected by the pandemic.

When deaths in custody this year have resulted in independent clinical reviews by the Prisons and Probation Ombudsman, issues have been highlighted where improvements should be made, but it was concluded that in no case would the outcome have been different.

We do have concerns about the long waiting list

for dentistry and the many cancellations of the specialist pain clinic.

The high 'did not attend' rate requires further investigation.

We remain concerned about the difficulty in arranging prompt transfers to psychiatric hospital when required.

### How well are prisoners progressed towards successful resettlement?

There remains a backlog for offender assessment system (OASys) assessments, due to failure to complete these in local prisons and staffing shortages. Sentence plans have been prepared, where possible, using in-cell telephones, and recategorisation reviews have taken place. Also, programme needs assessments are gradually being completed.

There has been significant frustration due to the lack of progress caused both by the pandemic and the shortage of trained programme staff within Moorland. Additionally, there have been reduced transfers to other establishments (either category D or for required programmes) due to Covid-19 restrictions.

There have been fewer educational opportunities, with reduced class sizes. Similarly, employment opportunities are now mostly part-time and the vocational qualifications limited. There are plans to increase and improve the employment within the prison and the availability of relevant skills and experience pre-release.

However, resettlement work, coordinated by the OMU, has been continuing within the 12-week window prior to release. This is provided by the voluntary sector organisations in the resettlement hub and by the Probation Service for the higher-risk offenders returning to the community.

### Main areas for development
### TO THE MINISTER

• There remains delay in the transfer of prisoners requiring secure psychiatric care. This appears to be a national problem. Can the minister ask cabinet colleagues in the Department of Health and Social Care and the Treasury to address this shortage of beds?

• Can the minister review and prioritise the progression and release (where appropriate) of IPP prisoners?

### TO THE PRISON SERVICE

• Can consideration be given to the implementation of the 2019 HMPPS nine 'priority' and four 'key' ideals, suggested as best practice in working with IPP prisoners, to ensure a consistent and humane offer to this cohort of prisoners?

• Can consideration be given to resourcing the backlog of programme provision, to allow

progression towards a safe release for determinate sentenced prisoners?

### TO THE GOVERNOR

• Can key worker sessions be prioritised?
• Can relationships with local employers be established to provide a pathway into employment on release?
• Can there be a general improvement in sentence progression and resettlement services for prisoners?
• Can the 2019 HMPPS IPP 'Ideals' document be adopted and implemented in Moorland?

### Progress since the last report

Although in-cell telephony, which is available to nearly all prisoners, has been of great value for both social and staff calls, there has been no progress on other digital in-cell technology, despite cabling being installed several years ago. Such technology would enhance the prisoner options to develop digital skills and speed up applications, complaints etc within the prison.

Working with other IMBs across Yorkshire and Humber, and with the senior probation officer at Moorland, the situation of IPP prisoners has been investigated and their experiences explored. This awareness raising will result in a paper with proposals to share with the Yorkshire and Humber IMB Chairs and with the Governor at Moorland.

Opportunity has been taken, as Covid-19 restrictions reduce, to embed good practice, such as more association time to mix with others. There are increasing opportunities to invite prisoner and staff suggestions for improvement, with prisoner representation in various fora.

### Issue raised in 2020/21 report, response given and action taken

Continuing national shortage of secure psychiatric beds, leading to delays in transfer of severely mentally ill prisoners. Minister said White Paper Reforming the Mental Health Act, published in January 2021, provides commitment to introduce a statutory time limit of 28 days for transfer to mental health hospitals from custody, and a new independent role to oversee the transfer process. 'Current strategic direction continues to be maintenance of existing bed capacity rather than an increase'.

Government has consulted on the White Paper and intends to bring forward a bill 'when parliamentary time allows'. In line with Government's stated intention, no action has been taken to increase the number of secure psychiatric beds.

Pilot on increasing accommodation for released prisoners to be rolled out as swiftly as possible. Minister said pilot to continue until July 2022.

£20m to provide 12 weeks of transitional accommodation in five regions. Further rollout nationally will be determined by future funding. No indication of places from pilot for Moorland prisoners – unclear as to whether rollout has taken place.

Backlog in delivery of programmes identified in prisoners' sentence plans. HMPPS stated that new programme staff due to take up post by October 2021. Data being used to understand and manage waiting lists. Focus is on addressing backlog. Some capacity but limited and only available to those within 12 months of a 'significant' sentence date. Remains a frustrating issue.

Budgetary allowance for food insufficient. HMPPS said that food budget is devolved to Governors. Recognised to be challenging, but 'catering team continues to provide nutritionally balanced meals'. No increase in budgets. Prisoners have complained about food which has supported negotiations for increased funding.

Re-establishment of key worker sessions. No written response given on this issue. Only available to the most vulnerable this reporting year, due to staffing issues, but a key priority for the Governor.

Consideration be given to increasing the number of vocational and accredited qualifications in the workshops, to enhance prisoner confidence and employment opportunities on release. Workshops have been gradually reopened and progress on vocational qualifications and improved skill development relevant to current employment opportunities is being made (for example, fork-lift truck and warehousing qualifications).

SWINDERBY
LINCOLN
LN6 9PT

Tel: 01522 666700

*For the latest reports on this prison please visit:*
https://tinyurl.com/bdfh26rv

*Important Changes:* **(1) Visits:** the identification necessary to access this prison and visit for social or professional purposes has changed; (2) **Money and Gifts** new rules now apply to these. See page 16 for full details of the above.

**This former Immigration Removal Centre ceased to operate in July 2021 and reopened as a Category C prison for Foreign National Prisoners on 6th December 2021 - it operates with HMP Maidstone and HMP Huntercombe.**

Morton Hall, near Swinderby, Lincolnshire, attracted criticism due to high levels of self-harm and violence. In 2020, the Home Office confirmed it would return to its former use as an adult male prison.

Lincolnshire's Police and Crime Commissioner (PCC) said it would house adult male foreign national offenders. It will be the third specialist prison in England dealing with foreign nationals, alongside HMP Maidstone and HMP Huntercombe.

PCC Mark Jones said in a report to the county's police and crime panel: "As a national resource the intention is that the majority of inmates will move back to their place of origin (or be deported) on release."

According to the Local Democracy Reporting Service, Mr Jones confirmed Morton Hall had ceased operating on 23 July and would reopen in "early December".

The decision to close the detention centre was taken after inspectors raised concerns about how long people were being held on the site and the impact this had on their mental health.

There were also concerns around self-harm and violence at the centre, which had seen four deaths over a five-year period.

HM Prison and Probation Service said when it reopens it would create almost 400 extra prison places at the site over a 12-month period.

The service said no compulsory redundancies were expected.

Mr Jones said meetings had taken place to discuss timelines and "understand any potential impacts to the locality" when it reopened.

**Task of the establishment** To detain adult male detainees subject to immigration control.

**Certified normal accommodation and operational capacity**
Detainees held at the time of inspection: 244
Baseline certified normal capacity: 391
In-use certified normal capacity: 391
Operational capacity: 391

**Prison status and key providers**
Public
Prison Group: East Midlands
Prison Group Director: Paul Cawkwell
Governor: Karen Head
IMB Chair: Malcolm Brock
Escort provider: Mitie Care and Custody
Health service commissioner and provider:
Nottinghamshire Healthcare NHS Foundation Trust
Learning and skills providers: People Plus sub-contracted to Lincoln College

**Brief history** Originally a Royal Air Force base, Morton Hall opened as a prison in 1985. New accommodation was added in 1996 and it was refitted in 2001 to provide facilities for women prisoners. Two more residential units were added in July 2002. In March 2009, Morton Hall, then a semi-open establishment, was turned into a closed prison, with a specialist role in managing foreign nationals, who comprised most of the population. In 2011, it became an immigration removal centre. The IRC was closed in July 2021 and the establishment is due to reopen as a prison for adult male foreign nationals in December 2021.

**Short description of residential units** Morton Hall has five units in use, all with single cells.

**Visiting Information** Booking line: 01522 666819 Monday to Sunday 9:30am to 12:30pm or email: booking: SocialVisits.MortonHall@justice.gov.uk
**Visiting times:** Tuesday, Thursday, Saturday, Sunday: 1:30pm to 4:15pm

**Legal visits:**
Booking line: 01522 666 819 9:30am to 12:30pm or email: LegalVisits.MortonHall@justice.gov.uk
**Visiting times:** Monday to Friday, 9am to 11:45am & 1:15pm to 5pm.

**INSPECTIONS & REPORTS**
**Date of last inspection 28 Oct–15 Nov 2019**
Notable features from this inspection
• About a third fewer detainees were held than at our previous inspection.
• About two-thirds of the population left the centre within a month and there had been a marked reduction in the number of lengthy detentions since the previous inspection.
• Five detainees were assessed as being level 3 adults at risk, which meant that the Home Office had accepted evidence that detention was likely to cause them harm.
• In the six months before the inspection, doctors had submitted 173 reports to the Home Office concerning detainees who might have been survivors of torture but none because they were having thoughts about suicide or had other health concerns.
• Each month, approximately 120 detainees were referred to the centre's mental health services.
• The centre provided enough activity places for all detainees.
• Good welfare services were provided by independent third sector organisation Lincolnshire Action Trust.

**HMCIP Report, published 10 March 2020**
Morton Hall is an immigration removal centre (IRC) near Lincoln that holds adult male detainees. It is the only remaining IRC operated by HM Prison and Probation Service on behalf of the Home Office. Since the previous inspection in November 2016, the number of detainees had declined by about a third while staffing levels had remained approximately the same. The centre held about 240 people and at the time of this inspection one of the units was not in use.

The centre had improved since the previous inspection. We assessed overall safety as now being reasonably good. Along with the smaller population, the marked reduction in the number of very long detentions had contributed to a calmer atmosphere. The number of detainees held for over a year had been reduced to five compared with nearly 30 at the previous inspection, and two-thirds of the population left the centre within a month.

However, most of our safety concerns remained. Uncertainty about detainees' immigration status and the potential for long-term detention continued to cause frustration. One detainee, for example, had been held for over two years, which was unacceptable. Those held for lengthy periods were often detained because of documentation problems, a lack of suitable accommodation or casework inefficiencies. For example, one detainee had been awaiting an asylum decision for 11 months. Nearly a quarter of the population arrived after serving prison sentences during which their cases should have been resolved without the need for immigration detention.

There were several clear indications of the vulnerability of the population. For example, levels of self- harm were high and over 40 detainees had been subject to constant supervision in the previous six months because they were assessed to be at risk of imminent self-harm or self-inflicted death. Care for detainees at risk of self-harm was generally good and supported by effective key working arrangements. However, as elsewhere, Rule 35 procedures1 were not being used to safeguard detainees at risk of suicide or those with other health concerns.

Levels of violence and use of force were still too high, but there were few serious incidents. Much more attention was paid to those falling under the Home Office's at risk in detention policy. In our staff survey and interviews, staff said they would report safeguarding concerns and were generally confident they would be taken seriously. A real strength of the centre was its staff-detainee relationships. In our confidential interviews, most detainees were very positive about the way staff treated them. Consultation arrangements

473

were good. Equality work was reasonably good and interpreters were used very regularly. Health services, including mental health provision, were good.

Accommodation was in an adequate condition, but the centre still looked and felt far too much like the prison it was before it was designated an IRC. This was reinforced by large quantities of razor wire, which managers themselves acknowledged was out of keeping with the generally calm environment in the centre. Detainees were also locked in cells or on landings from 8.30pm. At other times, detainees could move freely around the centre and, unlike in most other IRCs, they could go outside easily during the day and walk around a fairly large and open site.

As at the last inspection, the range of activities was very good and all detainees could participate if they wished to do so. However, take-up was low and the centre needed to do more to promote what was on offer.

Another considerable strength was the welfare service provided by the third-sector organisation Lincolnshire Action Trust, which detainees valued highly. Well-qualified workers gave detainees good support on arrival and before discharge.

We make a number of recommendations which I hope will allow the centre to further improve its care for detainees, especially in the area of safety. However, this is a largely positive report documenting significant improvements in a centre where staff from a range of agencies are doing a creditable job in mitigating the potential harms of detention.

November 2019 HM Chief Inspector of Prisons

### INDEPENDENT MONITORING BOARD: Annual Report

The law requires every prison to be monitored by an independent Board appointed by the Justice Secretary; these are known as Independent Monitoring Boards (IMBs). The IMB must satisfy itself as to the humane and just treatment of those held in custody within its prison and the range and adequacy of the programmes preparing them for release; it must report annually to the Justice Secretary on how well the prison has met the standards and requirements placed on it.

### IMB Report 1 January 2021 – 23 July 2021
### Published September 2021

Background to the report

We write following the response of your predecessor, Chris Philp MP, who wrote to us on 1 September 2021, following our 2020 Annual Report, and also sent an action plan prepared by officials in your department. Morton Hall Immigration

Removal Centre (IRC) closed on 23 July 2021 and our Board carried out independent monitoring duties throughout 2021 up to the closure date.

After consultation with Anne Owers, National Chair of Independent Monitoring Boards, we have decided to present our final report as a letter to you rather than a full annual report. Much of the description of the establishment and observations on conditions that were set out in our 2020 report, published in August 2021, remained the case during 2021 so we judge there is no need to cover the same ground. Instead, we focus this shorter letter on specific findings arising from the last 203 days of the centre's operation running up to the 23 July closure date and on a follow-up to the action plan referred to above.

### Background

Covid-19 restrictions in the first few months of 2021 meant that we continued to suspend physical visits to the centre, in line with overall health guidance to stay at home and in line with personal health decisions by Board members. Instead, a number of measures – an 0800 telephone applications line for detainees, electronic access to daily briefings, increased telephone contact with centre management and staff, and teleconference monthly Board meetings – enabled the Board to move to a system of 'remote monitoring' for this period when 'in person' onsite monitoring was suspended. Actual onsite monitoring visits to the centre were resumed in mid-April 2021.

### Main judgements

We continued to observe that Morton Hall was largely a safe environment for detainees with staff who acted in a professional and empathetic manner to support detainees. Staff worked hard to prevent violence and we raised no concerns over the use of the Care and Segregation Unit (CSU) for detainees confined under rule 40 and rule 42.

Healthcare provision by Nottinghamshire Healthcare Foundation Trust was well delivered with access to the full suite of healthcare services. However, Covid-19 restrictions meant much of the provision of well-being, faith and recreational facilities were curtailed in line with national Her Majesty's Prison and Probation Service (HMPPS) protocol s. Our view is that these restrictions had a limiting effect on the quality of life for detainees in the centre and we were concerned to see that they were not lifted at the same pace as restrictions in non-HMPPS IRCs or those in the wider community.

This was a source of frustration. For example, the multi-faith centre never reopened for individual prayer and services from 21 April onwards were limited to a maximum of ten detainees. Outdoor sports were not allowed in the centre even after the 12 April easing of community restrictions. In late April and May, staff had to manage a number of incidents to try to stop detainees playing football with improvised homemade footballs and one such incident resulted in a detainee breaking his ankle. It strikes us that the national Gold Command blanket restriction did not balance risk and outcomes appropriately and perversely penalised an outside activity in the fresh air where the risk of virus transmission is less than indoors.

Another source of frustration during this period was the continued significant delays in detainees being released from the centre even after a judge had awarded bail. Releases continued to be held up because of difficulties in the Home Office and the National Probation Service finding and checking suitable addresses. On one of our monitoring visits in mid-June 2021, for example, just over a quarter of the detainees (23 out of a total centre population of 87) were awaiting accommodation address checks with four of them having waited more than three months since their bail decision.

These delays inevitably cause a feeling of injustice among the detainees affected. They have been granted bail from a judge only to find themselves remaining in detention with no clear end date in sight. These frustrations added to the challenge of managing the centre and resulted in the centre having to declare a serious incident on the night of 18 May 2021 when a group of 20 detainees decided to stage an outside night-time protest about this issue.

The men who were involved in the incident were passive throughout with no threats to staff or attempts to breach the security of the centre, but it was a difficult situation to manage and eventually resulted in the deployment of a national tactical response group ('tornado' team) to the centre with the incident coming to a peaceful end shortly before 4 am. We assume that the delays in finding and checking bail addresses are largely due to resources, but such resources need to be balanced against the costs of continued detention and expensive exercises such as the deployment of tornado teams.

The centre closed on 23 July and the run-up to the closure necessitated considerable planning and care by staff. The closure of the centre had the potential to cause stress and anxiety among detainees or to trigger disruptive behaviour. Throughout the months running up to the closure we were impressed by the way in which management and staff at the centre conducted an open and transparent process with detainees, consulting them and keeping them updated on what was happening and what it would mean for them. This was a period when staff were themselves anxious about their own jobs and future, but this did not undermine the professionalism with which they continued to manage the centre and care for detainees.

The transfer of men from the centre proceeded in a well-managed and orderly manner and the closure did not result in any incidents of concern. We conclude our main judgements by congratulating the staff and management of the centre both for the way they approached this task and for their overall success in ensuring fair and humane treatment of detainees.

### Recommendations

1. We hope that, in the event of any future need for health pandemic (or similar) rules that the introduction and relaxation of rules in IRCs is kept in line with those in the wider community rather than moving at a different pace, as we found with football and communal worship in the centre.

We recommend that the government gathers and publishes monthly data on the number of detainees for whom a judge has granted bail but who remain in detention together with information on the length of time they have remained in detention since the judge's decision. This data should be used to understand and track delays in release from detention and inform the use of resources to reduce these delays.

Following on from (2) we recommend that the government publish data on the full cost of keeping people in detention following bail release decisions, as well as other costs such as managing serious incidents arising from the frustration of those remaining in detention. Speeding up bail address checks could reduce these costs. Such an understanding of costs would help inform policy decisions to ensure the most effective use of resources in the best interests of detainees and the implementation of justice.

### Response to the Home Office action plan following our 2021 annual report.

There is an acceptance in the action plan that in the case of foreign national offenders, wherever possible, immigration cases should be resolved in prison so as to prevent the need for follow-on detention. We note that the Home Office has introduced a new operating model with the Ministry of Justice (MoJ) to expedite appeals and ensure timely resolving of cases. Some of our members will be monitoring in the new Morton Hall FNO prison and will be in a position to monitor the effects of this new model. We hope that the Home Office and MoJ will publish data that will enable all interested parties to track case management timescales and appeal waiting times. The action plan partially accepted our suggestion that consideration be given to retaining an immigration team within the new prison. The Detention Engagement Team (DET) model improved communication between the Home Office and detainees and helped reduce frustration for detainees. We hope that there will be enough Home Office capacity in the new prison to support the foreign national offender population and determine outcomes at the end of their sentences.

We are disappointed that the action plan does not accept our recommendations on remuneration for paid activities and for education. In particular we do not accept the action plan 's claim that paid activities, such as work in the kitchens and cleaning accommodation units, are "not comparable with gainful employment in the community." Such a claim is not at all consistent with the everyday picture of life that we see inside the IRC where detainees are undertaking cleaning and kitchen work, as well as other activities, that are important for the running of the centre. Without such activity by detainees the centre would have to invest in a larger paid workforce. In these circumstances we repeat our contention that a £1 per hour rate of pay, which has remained unchanged since 2008, is derisory.

### Conclusion

With the closure of Morton Hall IRC, this is our final report as independent monitors of the centre. We have often identified concerns and made recommendations for improvement, both in our day to day monitoring and our annual reports. We have been honoured to have undertaken this important public duty. The system of independent monitoring ensures that places of detention have a set of independent fresh eyes looking at conditions to ensure they are fair and decent.
Chair IMB IRC Morton Hall

**MOLYNEAUX AVENUE
BOVINGDON
HEMEL HEMPSTEAD
HERTS
HP3 0NZ**

HM PRISON
SERVICE

HM PRISON
THE MOUNT

**Tel: 01442 836300**

*For the latest reports on this prison please visit:*
https://tinyurl.com/bdfh26rv

*Important Changes:* **(1) Visits:** the identification necessary to access this prison and visit for social or professional purposes has changed; (2) **Money and Gifts** new rules now apply to these. See page 16 for full details of the above.

**Task of the establishment** Male adult category C training and resettlement prison.

**Certified normal accommodation and operational capacity**
Prisoners held at the time of inspection: 992
Baseline certified normal capacity: 1,010
In-use certified normal capacity: 1,007
Operational capacity: 1,028

**Population of the prison**
• 20 new prisoners received each week.
• 19.7% foreign national prisoners.
• 53.4% prisoners from black and minority ethnic backgrounds.
• 46 prisoners released into the community each month.
• 244 prisoners receiving support for substance misuse.
• 55 prisoners referred for mental health assessment each month.

**Prison status and key providers**
Public
Prison Group: Hertfordshire, Essex & Suffolk
Prison Group Director: Simon Cartwright
Governor/Director: Paul Crossey
IMB Chair: Raymond Little
Physical health provider: Practice Plus Group
Mental health provider: Practice Plus Group
Substance misuse treatment provider: Forward Trust
Prison education framework provider: PeoplePlus
Escort contractor: Serco

**Brief history** Situated in Bovingdon near Hemel Hempstead on the site of a former RAF station, The Mount opened in 1987 as a young offender institution and has since been converted to a category C training prison.

## Short description of residential units
### Bottom site (older units)
The Annexe – pre-release wing for 44 prisoners

Brister – induction wing/reverse cohort unit on 2 spurs, 116 prisoners

Ellis – general population, 117 prisoners

Fowler – general population, 112 prisoners

The Lakes (also known as the Wellbeing unit) – drug support wing, 111 prisoners

Care and separation (segregation) unit – 18 prisoners.

### Top site (newer units)
Dixon – general population, 120 prisoners

Howard – general population, 110 prisoners

Narey – wing for older prisoners (over-50s), 48 prisoners Nash A – general population, 125 prisoners

Nash B – general population, 125 prisoners.

**Visiting Information** Booking line: 01442 836352 Monday to Friday 10:30am to 4pm.

**Visiting times:** Monday to Friday: 5:45pm to 6:45pm, Saturday and Sunday: 2:30pm to 3:30pm

### Legal visits:
Email: professionalvisitsthemount@justice.gov.uk

**Visiting times:** Tuesday & Thursday: 9am to 11am.

## INSPECTIONS & REPORTS
**HMCIP Report:** 14 and 21–25 March 2022

**Published 30 June 2022**

At our last inspection in 2018 of The Mount, a category C prison near Hemel Hempstead, we found a prison that was deteriorating to the extent that in every healthy prison test the establishment was judged poor or not sufficiently good. The prison held about 1,000 adult men at the time of the visit, with more than two-fifths assessed as either high or very high risk of harm to others. At this inspection, we found an improvement in the test of safety, which was now reasonably good, and a slight improvement in rehabilitation and release planning, but no improvement in outcomes for respect and purposeful activity. The senior leadership team had an appropriate vision that included improving safety, the maintenance of decent standards and developing progression opportunities for the men held there, but there remained some basic and persistent barriers to success.

Ofsted, our partners who joined us at this inspection, judged the provision of education, work and skills to be inadequate, their lowest judgement. The prison did not have a comprehensive overview or evaluation of the strengths and weaknesses of education provision and had not provided enough purposeful activity places for the population. Those prisoners who did have a place were not always fully or usefully occupied when they attended. Such failings were completely undermining The Mount's stated purpose as a training establishment.

Despite some improvements in core functioning, rehabilitation and resettlement planning was not sufficiently good overall and was the main area of complaint to us by prisoners during our inspection. We found an insufficient focus on and opportunities for sentence progression, which is crucial to men in a category C training prison. There were few interventions, besides accredited offending behaviour programmes, to help prisoners reduce their risk and make progress. Transfers to open prisons often took far too long. Officer shortages had been a problem well before the Covid-19 pandemic and at this inspection, 40% of staff could not be deployed to operational duties. As such, the regime remained severely restricted, and time out of cell was poor, with many men locked up for 22 hours a day. Prisoners were very frustrated by limited access to key areas of support, such as the library and the gym, social visits, and the ongoing suspension of corporate worship. The staff shortages caused additional pressure on those who were left to deliver the day-to-day regime, and many felt they did not have enough time to support prisoners.

Leaders had taken proactive steps to improve safety, and these were beginning to take effect. Most prisoners now said they felt safe, a sentiment backed up by the data - the rate of assaults was lower than in 2018 and fewer were serious. The site had been divided into two, which allowed for much better supervision of prisoner movements around the campus, and leaders had further improved supervision with the introduction of escorted moves which had, we were told, contributed to improved safety outcomes. However, there were also some disadvantages to this arrangement, including difficulties for prisoners on one site accessing activities on the other. Steps to disrupt the supply of drugs were also having a positive impact and far fewer men said they were easy to get hold of, but drug testing was yet to restart and less than half of the requested cell searches were completed; both major gaps. Support for those at risk of self-harm was limited and many were left locked in cell for most of the day which was not conducive to positive emotional wellbeing.

The prison continued to deal with some significant weaknesses including staff shortages, but our findings showed some signs of encouragement around safety. The prison had benefitted from some investment by HMPPS to make it clean and decent, and prisoners were more positive about many aspects. It was disappointing that some of the cells and communal areas, especially on the older site, were tired and in need of refurbishment if outcomes were to improve further. Clearly, addressing the weaknesses in purposeful activity and rehabilitation and release planning is a critical priority for a training prison - leaving men locked in a cell for most of the day surely does not lead to better citizens on release.

Charlie Taylor

HM Chief Inspector of Prisons April 2022

### Safety

At the last inspection of The Mount in 2018 we found that outcomes for prisoners were not sufficiently good against this healthy prison test. At this inspection we found that outcomes for prisoners were now reasonably good.

Most prisoners said they felt safe at The Mount. The rate of assaults was lower than in 2018 and fewer were serious. A small number of prisoners were self-isolating in their cells because of threats from others, some for a very long time and more needed to be done to engage with these prisoners, ensure their safety and promote reintegration.

The strategy for managing violence was not informed by local data and there was no action plan or means of measuring progress. Challenge, support and intervention plans (CSIPs) lacked meaningful targets. 'Belong', a restorative justice charity, provided good one-to-one support and conflict resolution, but there were few other tools to encourage prisoners to change their behaviour. The number of adjudications had decreased since the last inspection and most hearings were now held on the wings rather than in the segregation unit, which was positive, but too many were remanded or delayed.

The number of times force was used against prisoners had decreased. Most incidents that did occur were spontaneous and often stemmed from prisoners' frustrations that day-to-day issues were not dealt with. There had been significant improvements in the overall supervision and oversight of force, but special accommodation was still used too often.

The use of segregation had reduced since our last inspection and supervision by leaders was beginning to improve. The day-to-day regime was very limited but reintegration planning getting better. Cells were austere with no in-cell electricity and unscreened toilets. Communal areas were, however, clean, although the outside exercise yard was bleak.

The management of intelligence information was very good. More controlled movement of prisoners around the two sites had enabled better supervision by staff and an improved sense of order and control. Drug availability was being addressed through a variety of steps and in our survey, fewer prisoners than previously said it was easy to obtain them. Drug testing, however, had not yet resumed and less than half of the requested cell searches were completed, both major gaps.

The recorded level of self-harm was slightly higher than at the last inspection. There had been two self-inflicted deaths since 2018 and some learning from the Prisons and Probation Ombudsman (PPO) investigation into the first of these had been implemented. Work to reduce self-harm was not driven by or measured against an action plan. There was too little support for prisoners in crisis and staff had struggled to implement the new case management support process, which sometimes ended without having addressed the prisoner's risks and needs.

### Respect

At the last inspection of The Mount in 2018 we found that outcomes for prisoners were not sufficiently good against this healthy prison test. At this inspection we found that outcomes for prisoners remained not sufficiently good.

In our survey, two-thirds of prisoners said staff treated them with respect, although this figure fell to 43% for Muslim prisoners compared with almost three-quarters of non-Muslims. The quality and quantity of key working (see Glossary) were poor. We saw some good individual interactions between staff and prisoners, but some prisoners told us they felt staff were dismissive and could not be relied upon to attend to their basic requests. We saw many examples of staff not challenging rule-breaking on the wings.

The prison was split into two sites, locally referred to as the top and bottom sites. The bottom site had older units originating from when the prison was first built whilst the top site had more modern units which had been added as the prison expanded. Outdoor areas on both sites were generally well kept but some cells and communal areas, particularly on the bottom site, were tired and needed refurbishment. Many cells were not fully equipped and some had insufficient or broken furniture. In our survey, prisoners were more positive than at our last inspection about some important aspects of their daily experience, including access to clean bedding and clothing, and the cleanliness of communal areas. Staff did not always respond to cell bells quickly enough. In our survey, only 29% of prisoners thought the quality of the food was good compared with 45% in similar prisons.

The prisoner 'unity team' provided an innovative approach to consultation by undertaking checks against the HMIP expectations and feeding back their findings to leaders. The applications system was poor, and prisoners had little confidence in it. The number of complaints was high, but responses were generally prompt.

The promotion of equality and diversity was generally good, supported by a comprehensive strategy and action plan, but data were not always analysed and acted on systematically. The number of discrimination complaints was high but it was positive that there was quality assurance of complaint responses by the Ipswich & Suffolk Council for Racial Equality.

Our surveys showed few significant differences in outcomes across the protected characteristic groups and, in contrast to our last inspection, black and minority ethnic prisoners did not indicate more negative perceptions than white prisoners. However, far more prisoners with disabilities felt unsafe at the time of our inspection. Support to meet the needs of foreign national prisoners was generally good but there was insufficient use of telephone interpretation services. The recovery of faith services following Covid-19 restrictions had been slow.

There had been no population health needs assessment since 2017. Health and well-being champions offered valued peer support. There was an appropriate range of primary health care services and waiting times were reasonable for most. Patients with long-term conditions received good care, but attendance at external hospital appointments did not always take place as planned.

Mental health services had improved. The integrated substance misuse team and clinical prescribers provided evidence-based care. Pharmacy and medicines management had been professionalised and were very good. Patients waited far too long to see the dentist and the dental suite was not suitable to carry out aerosol-generating procedures.

**Purposeful activity**

At the last inspection of The Mount in 2018 we found that outcomes for prisoners were poor against this healthy prison test.

At this inspection we found that outcomes for prisoners remained poor.

Staff shortages continued to impact on the delivery of a meaningful regime. Many prisoners had very little time out of cell, being locked up for 22 hours on a weekday and longer at weekends. A range of recreational activities were in the early stages of development but needed to expand quickly. Library and gym provision also needed to increase.

Leaders and managers had a clear view of how education, skills and work could contribute to prisoners' success but had been too slow to realise this vision. The curriculum did not fully

meet all prisoners' needs and there were too few activity places. Allocations to work on the wings over-relied on the decisions of officers rather than being determined by the needs and aspirations of the prisoner. There were delays in allocation when prisoners needed to relocate between the two sites. There were long waiting lists for some activities. The prison did not have a comprehensive overview and evaluation of the strengths and weaknesses of the overall provision. Available data were not always used well enough to make improvements, and quality assurance was limited.

Education achievement rates were generally low. Teachers responded positively to prisoners' different abilities and needs. Individual coaching in workshops and vocational training was good. Many prisoners in workshops and work developed useful practical skills and knowledge, but these were not recognised or recorded. Outside of education, prisoners did not receive support to develop their English and maths skills. The relatively small number of prisoners with self-declared learning difficulties and disabilities received appropriate support in education, but very limited support elsewhere.

Prisoners in jobs on the wings were underemployed. Prisoner attendance was good in industries and vocational training but required improvement in education. In workshops and work, prisoners did not routinely start work on time and too often sessions ended early. Pre- release arrangements to prepare prisoners for resettlement were weak.

**Rehabilitation and release planning**

At the last inspection of The Mount in 2018 we found that outcomes for prisoners were poor against this healthy prison test.

At this inspection we found that outcomes for prisoners were now not sufficiently good.

Visits entitlement had deteriorated, and in our survey, only 15% of prisoners said staff encouraged them to keep in touch their family and friends. Family courses such as parenting skills had yet to resume, but there were plans to restart family days, which was a positive step.

Prisoners had too few opportunities to progress through their sentence and achieve their targets. Oversight of the delivery against all the resettlement pathways was not yet sufficiently robust.

The backlog of offender assessments (OASys) had reduced and completed assessments and sentence plans were of good quality. Prison offender manager (POM) contact with prisoners was poor in too many cases and some POMs felt that their caseloads were too high to complete regular meaningful one-to-one work, although we also saw some examples of outstanding work. Public protection arrangements were applied reasonably well.

Over 50 men were waiting to move to open prisons, and some had waited for more than six months. In some cases, category D status was not given due to the fact that an accredited programme had not been completed but failed to take into account other risk reduction work successfully done.

The prison offered a wider range of accredited offending behaviour programmes than at our last inspection but some prisoners waited too long to transfer to another prison to access accredited programmes not on offer at The Mount. Other than accredited programmes, there were few other interventions available to help prisoners progress their sentence plan targets.

Work to prepare prisoners for release was reasonably good. Data on prisoner accommodation outcomes on release were unreliable. Almost a quarter of releases on home detention curfew were late. Prisoners received reasonably good support to prepare for release. Too many HDCs were approved after the eligibility date and data to monitor prisoners' accommodation outcomes after release was not robust.

### Key concerns and recommendations

Key concerns and recommendations identify the issues of most importance to improving outcomes for prisoners and are designed to help establishments prioritise and address the most significant weaknesses in the treatment and conditions of prisoners.

During this inspection we identified some areas of key concern and have made a small number of recommendations for the prison to address those concerns.

Key concern: The shortage of officers available to deliver a meaningful day-to-day regime or ensure prisoner access to activities or appointments, meant many prisoners remained locked up most of the day and their needs unmet. Staff shortages were caused by several factors, including the high proportion of officers not deployable to operational duties and the significant percentage of new officers who had resigned within their first year.

Recommendation: Leaders should improve staff retention and significantly reduce the proportion of officers not deployable to operational duties. (To the governor)

Key concern: Continuous improvement was difficult to evidence as too many workstreams lacked a coherent strategy and action plan against which to monitor progress made.

Recommendation The focus on continuous improvement should be strengthened by having clear plans, against which progress can be monitored. These plans should be subject to rigorous oversight. (To the governor)

Key concern: Many prisoners at risk of self-harm or suicide were left locked in cell for almost the entire day with little access to support, interventions or activities to help them manage their crisis. Care plans were sometimes closed without prisoners having been given the help they needed. The Samaritans phone number was incorrectly advertised and the Listener suite was not in use.

Recommendation: Prisoners at risk of self-harm or suicide should have access to a broad range of support, interventions and activities, which are delivered through well-coordinated care plans. (To the governor)

Key concern: Many residential units needed major refurbishment. Cells were often poorly furnished, and many had broken furniture, unscreened toilets and no curtains for the windows.

Recommendation: There should be a programme of refurbishment of the residential units, prioritising the worst. (To the governor)

Key concern: The dental needs of the population were not being met due to the lack of aerosol-generating procedures, too few dental sessions and the overwhelming requirement for urgent rather than routine treatments. As a result, many patients were left in pain for several months.

Recommendation: Leaders from the prison and the health partnership board should make sure that the dental needs of prisoners are addressed immediately. (To the governor and the healthcare provider)

Key concern: Many prisoners continued to be locked in their cell for 22 hours on a weekday and longer at weekends, which affected their well-being. Prisoners were very frustrated by their limited access to some key areas of support, such as the lack of opportunities to go to the library and the gym, few social visits and the ongoing suspension of corporate worship.

Recommendation: Prisoners should have far more time out of their cell each day and be able to engage in a meaningful range of constructive activities to promote their well-being. (To the governor)

Key concern: Leaders and managers had not provided enough purposeful activity places or made sure that all prisoners were fully occupied when attending them. Allocation to activities was often delayed as the prisoner needed to move from living on one side of the prison to the other to take up the activity, and work allocation on residential units was not subject to adequate managerial oversight.

Recommendation: Leaders and managers should provide enough purposeful activity places to engage all prisoners and keep them fully occupied. Allocation arrangements should include effective scrutiny of decisions and minimise any delay in prisoners starting activities. (To the governor)

Key concern: Leaders and managers had not established a curriculum that supported prisoners' development needs, including those serving longer sentences. Prisoners, particularly in work and workshops did not routinely receive the help they needed to improve their English, mathematics and digital skills or gain recognition for the other skills and knowledge they had acquired. Managers did not have a sufficiently comprehensive oversight of the training quality in workshops and work.

Recommendation: Leaders should review and develop the curriculum so that it meets the needs of the prison population, including an effective literacy, numeracy and digital skills strategy. They need to make sure that arrangements to record and recognise prisoners' skills and knowledge development is subject to effective quality assurance and improvement processes. (To the governor)

Key concern: Leaders and managers had not ensured that prisoners were fully prepared for education, training or employment on release, including receiving effective information, advice and guidance to make informed plans. Too few prisoners could use the 'virtual campus' see Glossary) to research career opportunities and make applications as part of their resettlement plan.

Recommendation: Leaders and managers should make sure that prisoners receive suitable and effective pre-release preparation, including use of the virtual campus, where relevant. (To the governor)

Key concern: In our survey, only 15% said staff encouraged them to keep in touch with family and friends. The visits provision was still not good enough and the prison had not yet consulted prisoners or their visitors on how it could be improved. There were no additional visits for prisoners on the highest incentives level, which reduced the opportunities to motivate positive behaviour. Problems with the booking system meant that some visitors were turned away at the prison gate on the day of the visit.

Recommendation: Leaders should prioritise and encourage prisoners to maintain relationships with their family and friends and make sure they have easy access to regular visits. (To the governor)

Key concern: There was insufficient focus on, and opportunities for, sentence progression. Many prisoners waited far too long to receive a sentence plan, contact between (POMs) and prisoners was too infrequent and there was little evidence that POMs carried out structured one-to-one work with them. There were few interventions, other than accredited offending behaviour programmes, to help prisoners reduce their risk and make progress.

Recommendation: Prisoners should have a range of opportunities to demonstrate a reduction in their risk of harm and likelihood of reoffending and progress through their sentence, including structured contact with prison offender managers. (To the governor)

Notable positive practice

We define notable positive practice as innovative work or practice that leads to particularly good outcomes from which other establishments may be able to learn. Inspectors look for evidence of good outcomes for prisoners; original, creative or particularly effective approaches to problem-solving or achieving the desired goal; and how other establishments could learn from or replicate the practice.

Inspectors found four examples of notable positive practice during this inspection.

The prison's continued investment in commissioning 'Belong', a charity promoting restorative justice, provided a service that worked to bring together prisoners and staff, and promoted family ties.

Most adjudications were now held on the wing, which was an improvement and meant that the majority of prisoners did not spend unnecessary time on the segregation unit waiting for their hearing to be held.

The participation of the prisoner unity representatives in the senior leadership team meetings through videoconferencing allowed them to feed back the views of prisoners directly to senior leaders.

A senior mental health nurse spoke to all prisoners in the segregation unit every day, which enabled an assessment of vulnerabilities and contributed to independent scrutiny of care in the unit.

## INDEPENDENT MONITORING BOARD: Annual Report

The law requires every prison to be monitored by an independent Board appointed by the Justice Secretary; these are known as Independent Monitoring Boards (IMBs).

The IMB must satisfy itself as to the humane and just treatment of those held in custody within its prison and the range and adequacy of the programmes preparing them for release; it must report annually to the Justice Secretary on how well the prison has met the standards and requirements placed on it.

IMB Report 1 March 2021 – 28 February 2022
Published May 2022

## EXECUTIVE SUMMARY

### Background to the report

This was the second year of Covid. Our reporting year started at the beginning of March 2021 when the epidemic was affecting the whole country. During the year the prison went from a lockdown regime to a more relaxed regime during the summer months then back to a lockdown regime in line with the Government requirements for the rest of the country's population. At the end of the year there was the start of a more relaxed regime with some workplaces available. However, there continued to be very limited time out of cell for the majority of the prisoners.

Many feared that the virus would have a devastating impact on the prison with many deaths but to the credit of the Governor and staff this did not happen. With the introduction of regular testing of staff, managing the prisoners in small groups within their residential units and social distancing, any outbreaks were quickly isolated.

The instructions for lockdown were given by Gold Command in Head Office which has been nationally directing the position for prisons during the pandemic. Despite the effect of the virus on staffing levels, The Mount has always been able to provide prisoners with the maximum time out of cell permitted by these national restrictions. The Mount has been classified a number of times throughout the year as an outbreak site which has restricted the regime, particularly time out of cells and the movement of prisoners to education or work. The workshops, education and library were closed for nearly all the year leaving prisoners often locked down for 23 hours a day, which was damaging to their mental and physical health. There were some offending behaviour programmes but with limited numbers not all prisoners were unable to complete their sentence plans or have in-person social visits. For much of the year the prisoners have not had adequate time out of their cells for exercise, domestics and association with others.

During the year due to staffing levels the prisoners were being served with their only hot meal of the day as early as 11am. This caused a lot of frustration and complaints from the prisoners. At the end of the reporting period the hot meal was being served in the evening which has been welcomed by prisoners.

The virus has produced some gains. The introduction of Purple Visits (secure video calls), in-cell telephones and email-a-prisoner has helped prisoners to stay in touch with their families when face-to-face visits were not allowed. When face-to-face visits were resumed they were with reduced numbers and no physical contact.

Isolating spurs within the residential units helped the reduced staffing levels to manage the prisoners. It also reduced the levels of violence but it has had an effect on the prisoners' mental and general health. The lack of activities and exercise despite the introduction of in-cell work, books and education packs has taken its toll on prisoners' health generally.

Staffing levels have been a major concern during the year with prisoners being denied visits to the gym, library and limited access to showers and association time. During the year due to the national recruitment campaign a number of new starters arrived at the prison. Unfortunately, some did not stay very long as the role did not suit them and they left – some within days - a waste of money and time. Better vetting of applicants' suitability needs to be employed.

During the height of the pandemic the IMB did not want to bring the virus into the prison and so visited the prison much less frequently. However the Board continued to monitor the prison remotely during part of the year at the height of the pandemic. Zoom and Teams were used for IMB Board meetings which were also attended by the Governor. Prisoners' applications were dealt with by using the 0800 applications line and email-a-prisoner. Contact was maintained with the prison by dialling into meetings and rule 45 reviews. IMB visits to the prison resumed during the year but went back to remote monitoring when the second wave hit. A normal visit schedule is now in place and has been since December 2021.

### Main judgements

#### How safe is the prison?

There have been fewer prisoner-on-prisoner and prisoner-on-staff assaults
throughout the lockdown periods as movement of prisoners has been limited due to the separation of spurs within wings, which has limited prisoner association. Unfortunately, sometimes self-harm is used as a release from other problems and the frustrations of the lockdown which is distressing

#### How fairly and humanely are prisoners treated?

The measures required during lockdown which were directed nationally were not humane. In some wings the outside exercise areas are small and offer very little in terms of a comfortable environment. It seems that it is believed that all prisoners want is fitness equipment. Towards the end of the year the frustration with the regime was coming to the surface. The morale among staff and prisoners was low given the very difficult year.

### How well are prisoners' health and wellbeing needs met?

The new healthcare provider is now providing a satisfactory service given the limitations caused by the regime. Weekends are now covered which is welcomed. The in-cell telephone has enabled prisoners to speak with healthcare about their health concerns. Face-to-face consultations are now taking place but with reduced numbers.

### How well are prisoners progressed towards successful resettlement?

There has been little in the way of resettlement during the lockdown periods. During the year a 1-1 programme using the in-cell telephone was introduced for prisoners nearing release and towards the end of the year face-to-face appointments were resumed. However during the year, for the second year in a row, prisoners were being released without having completed the offending behaviour programmes included in their sentence plans.

### Main areas for development
### TO THE MINISTER

The Board is concerned at the lack of category D places. Prisoners are being assessed and approved but then face months waiting for a place. Some are released before being allocated a category D placement. Increasing the period that a prisoner can apply from two to three years with no extra places will increase the frustration of prisoners.

### TO THE PRISON SERVICE

On staffing levels and new recruits, the Prison Service needs to better appraise applicants as to their suitability for the role. A lot of effort and money is wasted when trainees leave because they cannot cope with the environment. Numbers recruited should not be the only measure. The number that finish their training who are still employed 12 months later is the most important measure. The loss of experienced officers that the service has experienced over the years means that there are fewer opportunities for mentoring when new recruits are in role.

Some investment has been made to improve the showers but the remaining showers need refurbishing to bring them to an acceptable standard. The heating and hot water boilers need replacing with modern energy efficiency to provide better living conditions.

Education programmes need more investment so that more prisoners can access them, together with more investment in the workshops with meaningful employment that can lead to qualifications to improve employment opportunities on release.

There continue to be many problems with the transfer of property during prison-to- prison transfers. There is insufficient room in the transfer vehicles for all prisoners' property and arrangements for any that is left behind is patchy. Frequently prisoners' property gets lost completely leading to expensive and avoidable claims on the Prison Service. This matter needs to be dealt with.

### TO THE GOVERNOR

Given the management of smaller groups of prisoners and not returning to pre- pandemic 'free flow' regime, the challenge will be to manage movement of prisoners so that prisoners are able to attend work and education every day, to make use of the library and gyms regularly and to have sufficient time out of cell. We have raised concerns that identifying set wings to house prisoners engaging in education or having a workshop place will limit prisoners' opportunities and necessitate prisoners moving wings to access new opportunities.

### Progress since the last report

Throughout the year The Mount has continued to operate a restricted Covid-safe regime under Gold Command so little comparison to previous years is possible. We accept that the management of the prisoners in small groups has helped to control the virus within the prison but in doing so has had an effect on the general health and mental health of prisoners. Staff and prisoner morale has been low during the year: prisoners because of the restricted regime, lack of activities and extended lock down times and staff due to low staffing levels and the stress that places on them.

**NEW HALL WAY**
**FLOCKTON**
**WAKEFIELD**
**WF4 4AX**

**HMP & YOI**
**NEW HALL**    Tel: 01924 803000

*For the latest reports on this prison please visit:*
https://tinyurl.com/bdfh26rv

*Important Changes:* **(1) Visits:** the identification necessary to access this prison and visit for social or professional purposes has changed; (2) **Money and Gifts** new rules now apply to these. See page 16 for full details of the above.

**Task of the establishment** A women's resettlement and local prison.

**Certified normal accommodation and operational capacity**
Prisoners held at the time of inspection: 395
Baseline certified normal capacity: 416
In-use certified normal capacity: 416
Operational capacity: 425

**Prison status and key providers**
Public
Prison Group: Women
Prison Group Director: Pia Sinha
Governor/Director: Julia Spence
IMB Chair: Tony Ogden
Physical and mental health provider: Care UK Clinical Services Limited (Care UK)
Substance use provider: Care UK (clinical), Midland Partnering Foundation Trust (psychosocial)
Learning and skills provider: Novus
Escort contractor: GeoAmey

**Brief history** New Hall, which opened in 1933, was originally populated by prisoners from HMP Wakefield who were soon due to be released. In 1961, it became a senior detention centre for male young offenders. It became a young offender institution in the 1980s, and in 1987, a women's prison.

**Short description of residential units**
Sycamore House: Segregation unit with 12 cells
Holly House: For 12 prisoners with complex issues
Rivendell House: 30 en-suite rooms for women with personality disorders and those on the enhanced regime
Larch House: A 40-bed, semi-open unit for those aiming to progress to open conditions
Maple House: Mother and baby unit for up to nine women and 10 babies
Oak House: Mainstream residential unit and detoxification unit for some prisoners
Poplar House: First night centre (Poplar 1) and mainstream residential unit (Poplar 2)
Willow House: A and B wings – mainstream residential accommodation; C wing for residents serving life and long-term sentences.

**Visiting Information** Book online at: https://www.gov.uk/prison-visits or ring 0300 060 6515 Monday to Friday, 9:15am to 4pm.
**Visiting times:** Tuesday, Thursday, Saturday: 1:45pm to 4pm.

**Legal visits:**
Email: hmppsvisitbooking@justice.gov.uk or ring 0300 060 6515 Monday, Wednesday, Thursday, 9:30am to 12:30pm and 1:30pm to 2:30pm.
**Visiting times:** Tuesday, Wednesday, Thursday: 9am to 11:30am.

**INSPECTIONS & REPORTS**
**Date of last inspection** 25 Feb–8 Mar 2019
**HMCIP Report, published 28 June 2019**
HMP & YOI New Hall is a women's prison near Wakefield. It is capable of holding 425 prisoners, but at the time of our inspection 395 prisoners were in residence. In keeping with most women's establishments, the prison fulfilled multiple functions and held prisoners ranging from those still on remand (about 13% of the population) up to those serving life (about 10% of the population). Over one-third (39%) were serving more than four years in prison.

At this inspection, our first since 2015, we found a prison that continued to be safe, respectful and purposeful, and where work to resettle and rehabilitate prisoners was improving.

Recorded violence in the prison was quite high, but nearly all incidents were very minor and overall most prisoners felt safe. Work to intervene and support those perpetrating threatening or anti-social behaviour, and the victims of such incidents, was effective. There had been three self-inflicted deaths since we last inspected. Most recommendations made by the Prisons and Probation Ombudsman following its enquires had been implemented, although one had, in our view, been interpreted disproportionately and was limiting prisoners' reasonable movement around the prison. Those at risk of self-harm and those with complex needs received good oversight and case management and those we spoke to were positive about the care they received.

A seeming over-reliance on the use of formal disciplinary processes was emergent and some punishments seemed excessive to us. Use of force had also increased substantially and several women had been in 'special accommodation' conditions on the house units, although records failed to adequately justify these decisions. The segregation unit was a clean but austere facility with a basic regime. One woman was held in segregation at the time of our visit.

The environment in the prison was good but the quality of accommodation was more variable, although reasonable overall. Staff-prisoner relationships were good although some prisoners expressed frustration at their inability to get some simple tasks done by staff. The prison would have benefited from greater visibility and support from managers. It was also our observation that the proportion of female staff was too low and was something that was a very stark and particular feature of the senior team. Work to promote equality was limited despite the best efforts of the equalities officer who was too often redeployed. Outcomes for minorities despite this, remained broadly consistent with others, and the mother and baby unit was excellent. Health care was similarly good but mental health provision was undermined by staff shortages among the mental health team. Substance misuse services were reasonable.

Prisoners experienced good time out of their cells, including association on Friday evenings which we now rarely see. The provision of learning, skills and work was improving with plans for a new curriculum and strong partnership working evident. Our colleagues in Ofsted assessed the overall effectiveness of provision as 'good', but undermined in part by quite poor levels of attendance. The coordination of resettlement work had improved greatly and offender management was clearly focused on risk reduction. Work in support of the resettlement pathways was also effective, including a range of offending behaviour initiatives – most notably Rivendell House, a self-contained unit that catered for women with a personality disorder.

New Hall remains a good prison, delivering effective outcomes for those held there. At the time of our inspection the prison was experiencing something of an interregnum with a temporary governor in post and new permanent governor about to be appointed. Our report highlights both the strengths and weaknesses of this prison. We trust the findings we detail will help the new governor to ensure momentum is maintained and continuous improvement sustained.

Peter Clarke CVO OBE QPM April 2019
HM Chief Inspector of Prisons

## INDEPENDENT MONITORING BOARD:
## Annual Report

The law requires every prison to be monitored by an independent Board appointed by the Justice Secretary; these are known as Independent Monitoring Boards (IMBs). The IMB must satisfy itself as to the humane and just treatment of those held in custody within its prison and the range and adequacy of the programmes preparing them for release; it must report annually to the Justice Secretary on how well the prison has met the standards and requirements placed on it.

## IMB Report 1 March 2020 – 28 February 2021
## Published October 2021
## Executive summary
## Background

This report presents the findings of the Board at HMP New Hall for the period 1 March 2020 to 28 February 2021. This reporting period covers the time of national and local lockdowns as a result of the Covid-19 pandemic. The Board's conclusions

are based on observations made on rota visits, reports from remote monitoring phone calls, daily report sheets during lockdown, examination of records and documents, limited attendance at some internal meetings and conversations with residents and officers.

Board members have been restricted during the lockdowns and there has been a greater reliance on remote monitoring than members would have wished. The prison is generally well run with the establishment facing the difficulties of keeping everyone safe inevitably limiting the usual activities. The Board recruited six new members who started during lockdown. They are completing the formal training online but have had few accompanied visits to the prison.

### Summary

The prison is generally well run and it is the Board's view that the prison is a safe place to be, having made appropriate regime changes to keep everyone Covid19 safe.

Risk assessments and processing of new residents is rigorous and thorough to ensure maximum safety.

Accommodation is generally appropriate for the residents' needs and there is a programme of maintenance that ensures operational capacity.

Relationships between the staff and residents are generally good although tested by the challenging situation during lockdown.

There is a fair and equal approach to working with residents and there is an appreciation of all groups, catering for and celebrating their faith and other needs.

The chaplaincy centre provides faith and pastoral support for all residents. The work of the centre was curtailed by lockdowns but volunteers were able to visit the prison and continue this work.

The pandemic has affected healthcare provision and the IMB has monitored the situation remotely. There have been challenging situations particularly when Covid-19 infection rates increased among residents and staff. Vaccinations have taken place in line with community practice. Substantive staffing posts have been filled and arrangements for temporary cover made more reliable.

Prior to the pandemic, the adult education team worked with residents to help them make progress and so be better equipped for employment after release. During the first lockdown, at the end of March 2020, there was a temporary withdrawal of the service. When restarted it was only available as prepared packs for residents to work through in their cells, and feedback via in-cell telephones. There is currently no resumption of face-to-face teaching.

## Main areas for development

### For the Minister

The Board is concerned that the government plan for 500 new prison places for women contradicts the female estate offender strategy published in 2018 which details that custody should be the final resort, received for the most serious offences. The Board remains concerned about the lack of appropriate resettlement accommodation.

### For the Prison Service

The Board hopes that the Purple Visits service will continue and appropriate funding provided. The Board is concerned that Covid-19 has created problems for some prisoners, making it difficult for them to complete their sentence plans and move towards release.

### For the Governor

Identify the good practice developed during Covid-19 enforced restrictions and continue to develop these moving forward. Wider and increased use of IT has maintained valuable contact for the residents.

Actively promote the rollout and evaluation of the new key worker system, ensuring that the staff is supported to carry out the role.

Work towards a greater representation of black, Asian and minority ethnic staff in management positions.

### Progress since the last report

It is pleasing to report that the operational staffing levels in healthcare have been addressed and a more consistent level of service is now being provided.

Senior management changes during the reporting period and beyond have had a positive impact on the prison.

Emphasis on the wellbeing of the residents during the pandemic has led to a reduction in self-harm and a lower number of ACCTs than in previous years for which the prison should be commended.

CROPPERS LANE
FREISTON
BOSTON
LINCS
PE22 0QX

HM PRISON SERVICE
HM PRISON NORTH SEA CAMP

Tel: 01205 769300

*For the latest reports on this prison please visit:*
https://tinyurl.com/bdfh26rv

*Important Changes:* **(1) Visits:** the identification necessary to access this prison and visit for social or professional purposes has changed; (2) **Money**

and Gifts new rules now apply to these. See page 16 for full details of the above.

**Task of the establishment** HMP North Sea Camp is an open male category D prison holding a large proportion of indeterminate sentence prisoners and those convicted of sexual offences.

### Certified normal accommodation and operational capacity

Prisoners held at the time of this visit: 336
Baseline certified normal capacity: 420
In-use certified normal capacity: 420
Operational capacity: 420

### Prison status and key providers

Public
Prison Group: East Midlands
Prison Group Director: Paul Cawkwell
Governor/Director: Colin Hussey
IMB Chair: Greg Cejer
Physical health provider: Nottinghamshire Healthcare NHS Foundation Trust
Mental health provider: Nottinghamshire Healthcare NHS Foundation Trust
Substance use treatment provider: We Are With You
Prison education framework provider: People Plus
Escort contractor: G4S

**Brief history** HMP North Sea Camp, which opened in 1935, was originally a Borstal. A tented camp was established at the site while the permanent buildings were constructed. A new sea bank was also built, to reclaim land from The Wash. The work was completed in 1979. In 1988, North Sea Camp became an adult male open prison.

### Short description of residential units

• North unit holds general prisoners and also those with mobility issues or disabilities.

• South 1 unit is the induction unit which holds general prisoners and also new receptions.

• South 2 unit holds general prisoners, but 4 and 5 landings are the protective isolation unit.

• Llewellin unit holds general prisoners, but currently also holds some shielding prisoners.

• Harrison unit holds general prisoners.

• Selby unit comprises 66 self-contained single bed units. This was set up during the Covid-19 pandemic to help reduce the number of double rooms in the establishment.

• Jubilee unit 1 is currently being used as the reverse cohort unit (RCU; see Glossary of terms).

• Jubilee units 2–6 hold long-term prisoners living independently and prisoners working outside of the establishment on ROTL.

**Visiting Information** Ring 01205 769368 Monday to Friday: 9:30am to 11:30am and 2:30pm to 3:30pm, Saturday and Sunday: 2:30pm to 3:30pm.

**Visiting times:** Wednesday: 1:30pm to 3:30pm Saturday and Sunday: 9:30am to 11:30am and 1:30pm to 3:30pm.

**Legal visits:**
Ring 01205 769 368 Monday-Friday: 09.30am - 11.30am & 2.30pm - 3.30pm, Saturday and Sunday: 2.30pm - 3.30pm.
**Visiting times:** Wednesday: 9.30am - 11.30am.

## INSPECTIONS & REPORTS
**Scrutiny visit: 19 and 27–28 April 2021**
**Published 02 June 2021**

HMP North Sea Camp is an open prison near Boston in Lincolnshire. At the time of our visit, it held 336 prisoners, which was below the certified normal capacity of 420. This reduction in the population and the installation of temporary accommodation units had made it easier to implement good cohorting arrangements and provide more single rooms throughout the pandemic. Although quarantining and shielding arrangements were good, the prison had had an outbreak of Covid-19 in late 2020. Leaders worked well with health care staff, the NHS and Public Health England to contain the outbreak.

A very limited regime had been in place for most of the last year. In comparison with other open prisons we have visited recently, the arrangements at North Sea Camp had seemed overly restrictive, particularly in the months either side of the outbreak. For example, prisoners had been required to confine themselves to their rooms and their unit which meant that they were only allowed outside in the fresh air for a designated exercise period each day. Two weeks before our visit, the prison had moved to stage three of the framework for recovery (see Glossary of terms – recovery plan), which meant that prisoners now had more time in the open air in the areas around the house units, which was a much-needed step forward.

The pandemic had resulted in the suspension of all release on temporary licence (ROTL) other than for those needing to go to hospital and for those in jobs in the community designated as essential. This meant that for most prisoners, one of the key incentives of being in open conditions had been lost and the impact of this on their progression had been significant. Many of the peer-led initiatives within the prison had also stopped and much of the support from partner agencies remained suspended. As a result, the prison had been unable to fulfil much of its rehabilitative function throughout the last year.

Too many staff were unaware of the prison's wider Covid-19 recovery plans and opportunities to reinstate support services had been grasped too slowly. There was a sense of frustration among prisoners and some staff that the restrictions applied to prisons generally did not take account of the unique environment of an open prison.

The prison remained safe. Violent incidents were rare and most were low level. Support for the most vulnerable was good and included regular welfare checks. Good attention was given to helping individuals maintain their commitment to living in open conditions, and the number of prisoners returned to closed conditions for poor behaviour had decreased over the last year.

Living conditions were clean and the new modular self-contained accommodation units were impressive. The use of the independent living houses located just inside the prison grounds provided an important incentive to progression. The mobile library facility was good, but the gym remained closed. Many prisoners were not in purposeful activity and they felt bored and frustrated after a year of the pandemic.

The core tasks of offender management work continued to be completed, but beyond this, the level of engagement with prisoners was too limited and many prisoners described unresponsive offender managers in the prison. Family support work had been reduced, but social visits had restarted just before our visit and the use of video calling had increased over recent months. Resettlement opportunities remained very restricted.

Many of the prisoners presented a high risk of harm to others. Public protection work was reasonable overall, but weaknesses in the monitoring of telephone calls led us to raise a key concern and recommendation in this area.

Overall, North Sea Camp, like many other open prisons, had been hit hard by the restrictions imposed nationally throughout much of the last year. However, the pace of recovery at the establishment needed review, to make sure that every possible step was being taken, at the earliest opportunity, to reinstate its focus on progression, engagement and rehabilitation.

Charlie Taylor, HM Chief Inspector of Prisons
April 2021

### Key concerns and recommendations
Key concerns and recommendations identify the issues of most importance to improving outcomes for prisoners and are designed to help establishments prioritise and address the most significant weaknesses in the treatment and conditions of prisoners. During this visit we identified some areas of key concern and have

made a small number of recommendations for the prison to address.

Key concern: Confinement of prisoners to their rooms and unit, imposed throughout much of the pandemic year, meant that they had little time in the open air each day. This was not in line with the restrictions we have seen at some other open prisons and left prisoners potentially more exposed to the virus than if they were allowed free access to open air. While recent changes to the restrictions were an improvement, conditions for prisoners still fell short of what we would expect.
Recommendation: Prisoners should have access to outside areas, subject to appropriate levels of social distancing and other Covid-19 safety measures. (To the governor)

Key concern: Resettlement support and advice had been very limited over the last year. For example, resettlement planning had not involved the prisoner in a face-to-face interview and some of the peer-led initiatives remained suspended.
Recommendation: Prisoners should meet with resettlement staff to identify the help that is needed and this should be supported by the reintroduction of the peer-led initiatives previously in place. (To the governor)

Key concern: The ongoing suspension of ROTL and the limited range of work placements in the community had a huge impact on prisoners' ability to maintain contact with children and families and demonstrate risk reduction and progression.
Recommendation: Resettlement Day Release should be resumed to enable prisoners to have contact with their children and families and also secure work, training or education (To the governor)

Key concern: Strategic oversight of equalities had stalled during the Covid-19 restrictions and work to promote equality remained limited, for example there were no support forums. Some disparities in treatment for prisoners with protected characteristics had been identified but more needed to be done to address these.
Recommendation: A comprehensive equalities strategy should be introduced, with a clear timetable for restarting forums to support prisoners with protected characteristics. Evidence of disproportionate treatment should be further explored, and action taken to address issues arising. (To the governor)

Key concern: Prisoners described the offender management unit (OMU) as unresponsive and they were frustrated about the limited support provided. Most prisoners had received little face-to-face contact with their prison offender managers in recent months and our survey results suggested only half knew their custody plan targets.
Recommendation: Leaders should explore and understand prisoners' poor perceptions about the support provided by the OMU and take steps to make sure that the work is central to the rehabilitative function of the prison. (To the governor)

Key concern: Seventy per cent of prisoners were assessed as presenting a high risk of harm to others and more than half were convicted of sexual offences, so the need for robust risk management was essential. Public protection arrangements were undermined by a large backlog of telephone calls waiting to be listened to by staff, and the lack of a system for monitoring calls made by prisoners living on Selby unit was a concern.
Recommendation: Telephone call monitoring for public protection purposes should be robust. (To the governor)

Key concern: Prisoners who were granted parole with the condition that they reside at approved premises to help manage their risk sometimes waited several months for release because there were not enough suitable places. At the time of our visit, one prisoner had been waiting since January 2021 to be released.
Recommendation: There should be enough suitable places in approved premises to make sure that prisoners who require this as part of their parole conditions are released without delay. (To HMPPS)

**Education, skills and work (Ofsted)**
During this visit Ofsted inspectors conducted an interim assessment of the provision of education, skills and work in the establishment. They identified steps that the prison needed to take to meet the needs of prisoners, including those with special educational needs and disabilities.

**Next steps**
Prison leaders and managers should make sure that prisoners who are engaged in learning make more rapid progress to complete their studies.
Prison leaders should make sure that all prisoners are engaged in meaningful education, skills and work-related activities, as soon as possible. Tutors need to provide all prisoners with feedback on their completed in-cell work packs that helps them to improve the standard and quality of their work over time.

**Notable positive practice**
We define notable positive practice as innovative practice or practice that leads to particularly good outcomes from which other establishments may be able to learn. Inspectors look for evidence of good outcomes for prisoners; original, creative or particularly effective approaches to problem-solving or achieving the desired goal; and how other establishments could learn from or replicate the practice.

Inspectors found four examples of notable positive practice during this visit.

The independent living opportunities provided by the Jubilee units provided excellent facilities to help prepare prisoners for their eventual release from custody.

Almost all prisoners rated the quality of food as good or reasonable, which we rarely see in prisons. The use of locally produced ingredients to provide a wide range of 'home cooked' food had led to this high satisfaction rating.

The mental health team had been resourceful in finding ways to support prisoners by changing their working hours to fit in with exercise times on the playing field and by visiting patients on the units. They also made themselves available to see any prisoner who needed support and guidance about their mental health and well-being.

The 'pathways enhanced resettlement service' provided responsive support for prisoners who were likely to have difficulty in managing the transition from closed to open conditions, or the transition from open conditions to the community, and was valued by prisoners.

## INDEPENDENT MONITORING BOARD: Annual Report

The law requires every prison to be monitored by an independent Board appointed by the Justice Secretary; these are known as Independent Monitoring Boards (IMBs). The IMB must satisfy itself as to the humane and just treatment of those held in custody within its prison and the range and adequacy of the programmes preparing them for release; it must report annually to the Justice Secretary on how well the prison has met the standards and requirements placed on it.

**IMB Report 1 March 2020 – 28 February 2021**
**Published September 2021**
**Executive Summary**
**Background to the report**
The Covid-19 outbreak and subsequent national lockdowns has had a significant impact on the IMB ability to gather information to inform the writing of the annual report. Some members of the IMB were over 70 years old and as a result had to shield. The IMB tried to cover as much ground as it could in these difficult circumstances, but inevitably there is less detail and supporting evidence than usual. Ministers are aware of these constraints. Regular information is being collected specifically on the prison's response to the pandemic, and that is being collated by the IMB nationally. From late March 2020 onwards, the prison was in lockdown with gradual movement towards a careful loosening of restrictions stalled by the

second national wave of infections. In writing this report the IMB notes that the prison was subject to directions from both Gold and Silver Command and was required to follow Public Health England (PHE) guidance. This meant that some of the issues raised by prisoners and as a result the IMB were not issues that the prison could address without permission from other parts of the Prison Service or PHE England.

Limited face-to-face monitoring by the IMB took place throughout the year save for three weeks in late March/early April 2020 and between late November 2020 and early January 2021. The latter break was caused by the first outbreak of Covid-19 in the prison. Regular face-to-face monitoring took place from the beginning of July to the middle of November. Throughout the year the IMB has monitored via the telephone, with IMB members phoning healthcare twice a week and listening in to one virtual morning briefing in addition to any live visits. This process has been supplemented by the IMB Chair visiting periodically to deal with prisoner applications. The IMB boxes were emptied by the IMB clerk and any applications emailed to the IMB member on rota or dealt with by the IMB Chair when on a visit.

Most incoming prisoners were isolated in the Jubilee 1 houses (reverse cohorting units) near the prison gates prior to moving into the main prison units. (Those who had isolated at the prison they came from went straight to the main units at HMP North Sea Camp.) Any prisoners showing symptoms of Covid-19 and those who tested positive or became ill remained in the reverse cohorting units until they had a negative test result at which point, they were moved. Prisoners were confined to their accommodation units, with exercise on the sports field at designated times.

Due to the pandemic, regime changes have meant that education, release on temporary licence (ROTL) and workshops, with the exception of lobster pots and recycling, did not fully function. Group religious activities did not take place. Family visits to prisoners were stopped at times, but prisoners were able to use video calling (Purple Visits) to maintain contact with their families.

The IMB at HMP North Sea Camp is satisfied that HMP North Sea Camp
• normally provides prisoners with humane and just treatment. However, the confinement of prisoners to their rooms (some were two to a small room often without a table or a chair) and their unit for most of the day during parts of the reporting year led to prisoner frustration.

One of the issues faced by the prison was that the R rate in Boston and the surrounding area was in the top five in the country for much of the reporting period. As a result, prisoner movement both within and outside the prison was limited. This was deemed necessary by the prison management to try to avoid a catastrophic outbreak of the Covid-19 virus in the early stages of lockdown.

• normally provides a wide ranging and adequate level of programmes preparing prisoners for release. This has been severely impacted by the lockdowns due to the Covid-19 pandemic.

• ensured core tasks were completed by the offender management unit (OMU) and other departments albeit often more slowly than normal. However, direct contact with prisoners especially by OMU was too limited. With the open space available at HMP North Sea Camp urgent face-to-face contact could have been maintained. All this has adversely impacted their progress towards release.

Budgets continue to be tight and HMP North Sea Camp has had to juggle priorities during the reporting year. As reported in last year's report, work has continued on the refurbishment of some disused staff housing, to add these premises to the Jubilee self-catering housing project. This work is now due for completion in early 2022 (some delay has been caused by a colony of bats). Due to the extra provision of single accommodation created by the Selby unit it has been possible to decommission the dormitories as multi-occupancy rooms. Two only share a dormitory at present. In the past four or six prisoners could be sharing a dormitory.

However, this will change if the prison returns to certified normal accommodation.

The healthcare extension (to enable the mental health team to work within the main healthcare building) and the staff changing facility are nearing completion.

The rehabilitative culture at HMP North Sea Camp continues to work well with a polite and calm atmosphere being created. There are very few violent incidents.

The staff at HMP North Sea Camp continue to create an environment which welcomes and integrates all, no matter what their offence or protected characteristic.

The recycling activity undertaken by prisoners and staff both in the prison and in the community is helping to reduce the amount of rubbish that has to be consigned to landfill. The employment opportunities generated in this area enable prisoners to obtain qualifications which will help them find employment when they leave the prison.

The IMB remains of the view that the healthcare provision at HMP North Sea Camp, at the end of the reporting year, is good, however, as in the community, healthcare did not function normally during the pandemic. The following services suffered disruption: dental care, optician and physiotherapy. There was provision to deal with emergencies.

There are however areas of concern at HMP North Sea Camp which the IMB feel should be addressed. The concerns relating to humane and just treatment are:

HMP North Sea Camp has, at the time of reporting, an aging population. Inevitably, many of them suffer from a range of medical conditions – some of them very serious. Currently, there is no facility within HMP North Sea Camp where prisoners can be suitably cared for during an end-of-life period; there are no on-site residential healthcare facilities. This means that prisoners who have chronic and other serious health issues stay on the units within the prison, surrounded by the other prisoners and the usual activities of everyday prison life. This has a very upsetting effect on those prisoners living alongside.

With the exception of the Selby units, all accommodation has been in service for several decades and in many cases requires more than the periodic repairs which the prison undertakes. The size of the double rooms in all the main accommodation units is not adequate in that it is often impossible to put a chair or table, let alone two of each, into a room. The cramped accommodation means that the accommodation listed does not comply with the Prison Service Instruction (PSI) when used by two prisoners.

Prisoners who use wheelchairs can experience difficulties travelling to and getting overnight accommodation at approved premises (APs) when going on resettlement overnight release (ROR), which can delay their ROTL programme and have a significant delaying effect on their sentence plan and parole board hearings.

Prisoners said they had issues with the offender management unit (OMU).

Although attitudes among staff in the OMU have improved since last year's report, prisoners said that they felt the OMU were slow to respond to requests and there was no face-to-face contact even in the outside during the lockdowns.

In the IMB prisoner survey, 50% (of the 99 who responded) felt that they had been inadequately prepared for release.

Additional comments: A new Governor and Deputy Governor took up their posts in early April 2021 and there have already been many changes, with the opening up of services such as the prisoner advice centre (PAC) and prisoners now being allowed more freedom across the prison site. More prisoners are at work. The 2020-2021 IMB report on HMP North Sea Camp covers an exceptionally difficult year when England was in the grip of the Covid-19 pandemic and it is expected that next year's IMB report will be very different.

## Main judgements
### How safe is the prison?
The IMB is satisfied that HMP North Sea Camp provides a safe environment for all prisoners.

### How fairly and humanely are prisoners treated?
Due to the limited opportunities to interact with the prisoners the Board sent a questionnaire to all the prisoners. 340 were sent out and 99 were returned (29%). The results showed that in many areas the needs of the prisoners were addressed well during the pandemic. However, the survey did flag up the fact that the OMU were slow to respond and that the lack of face-to-face interaction during parts of the year had a detrimental effect on progress.

The restrictions on leaving cells due to the Covid-19 lockdown meant that for a large proportion of the reporting year prisoners were confined to their cells for most of the day. Many prisoners felt this was unfair and inhumane as cells are small, some had to be shared by two prisoners and HMP North Sea Camp is an open prison with a large amount of land accessible to prisoners. The IMB survey had many prisoner comments on this.

As more information became available to the IMB from other open prisons, it became apparent that some open prisons had done things differently during the lockdowns. The open space at HMP North Sea Camp could probably have been better utilised to give prisoners more time out of their rooms, but the fear of a serious outbreak of Covid-19 with many deaths would have been the most important item staff considered and would have stopped staff doing anything but follow advice received from the Prison Service. Throughout the pandemic the Boston Borough Council Area had high levels of Covid-19 deaths in comparison with other parts of Lincolnshire.

There were a number of staff who were on long-term temporary promotion for the whole of the reporting year. Temporary promotion may have made staff hesitant to question if something mandated by the Prison Service could have been adapted to make better use of the open spaces at HMP North Sea Camp.

Even when prisoners were unable to work due to the Covid-19 restrictions they were still paid their full wages which was extremely welcome to the prisoners.

### How well are prisoners' health and wellbeing needs met?
During the reporting year, there has been a reduction in healthcare services offered, however this has generally been in line with what was available to those living in the community. As and when possible, facilities were reopened, as the establishment progressed through the various phases of lockdown. With the last national lockdown some services at HMP North Sea Camp suffered again.

The mental and physical healthcare teams are to be praised for the way they continued to look after the health of the prisoners during the pandemic.

### How well are prisoners progressed towards successful resettlement?
The IMB is concerned that the OMU were slow to respond to prisoner queries and face-to-face contact was not adequately maintained, thus severely impacting progress towards release.

Education stopped for part of the year and prisoners then did guided self-learning. Many prisoners will struggle to get the qualifications they need before they are released into the community.

Voluntary and paid outside work opportunities were severely curtailed due to the lockdown, which will disadvantage those due for release who rely on such opportunities to gain valuable experience of the workplace and also means they cannot demonstrate to prospective employers that they can be trusted in a community working environment.

## Main areas for development
### TO THE MINISTER
The IMB is concerned by the time taken to complete routine maintenance jobs, and the issues around the transfer of prisoners' property. These are issues that are provided by contracted out services and the Board is concerned that contract failures do not result in penalties to encourage compliance.

Specific examples include the maintenance contractor claiming machines that need expensive repairs which they are contracted to pay for need replacing (where the cost will be met by the prison).

With property the contractor seems to use the smallest vehicles they can which means that prisoners with a large amount of property face a long wait for their property to come and often it does not arrive at all.

The quality of some of the accommodation is poor and the space allocated to prisoners sharing rooms is close to being inhumane. The other benefits of being in an open prison would mitigate this in a normal year but this year over half of the prisoners have had to eat, sleep and live in a shared room where there is no room for a chair and a table for even one person. Although pods were sent to the prison some prisoners still had to share rooms.

### TO THE PRISON SERVICE
Opportunities should be taken to return to a regime where prisoners can have more time

away from their accommodation and resume their resettlement plans.

Offender managers in the probation service often take a long time to update their part of an offender assessment system (OASys) and to complete the paperwork to enable prisoners to sit ROTL boards. This can mean prisoners having to postpone Parole Board hearings as they have not done the required ROTLs and means prisoners may spend more time in prison than strictly necessary. Timescales for return of paperwork would be helpful.

There are some areas of the prison inaccessible to prisoners with physical disabilities, especially those who use wheelchairs. Although improvements have been made, budget needs to be allocated so that all areas are accessible to those who use wheelchairs, especially bariatric wheelchairs. This issue is also of concern to the Governor, but more budget from central resources needs to be allocated for improvements.

In order to ensure that no prisoner is asked to share with more than one other person, budget needs to be allocated to convert the current dormitories to smaller rooms so that, when HMP North Sea Camp is at full capacity, no prisoners will have to share with more than one other person.

**TO THE GOVERNOR**

Prisoners say that the OMU do not respond in a timely manner or keep appointments and that at times OMU staff could be more courteous. This needs addressing and maybe the rollout of offender management in custody (OMiC) will help with this.

There are some areas of the prison inaccessible to prisoners with physical disabilities, especially those who use wheelchairs.

To ensure that work continues on the further extension of Jubilee self-catering housing.

**Progress since the last report**

Attributable to the Covid-19 pandemic, the dormitories on South 1 and 2 are no longer in use as multi-occupancy dormitories, with a maximum of 2 prisoners in any dormitory. The phasing out of the multi-occupancy of dormitories is something the IMB has advocated for many years. However, once the prison returns to normal operating conditions, it will be necessary to allocate four prisoners to every dormitory. The current Governor has submitted a bid for the funding required to convert the dormitories to smaller two-person rooms. This is an issue the IMB has raised in previous reports expressing concerns about the need to use dormitories.

At the very beginning of the reporting year before lockdown, all healthcare clinics and services including dental treatment were functioning well.

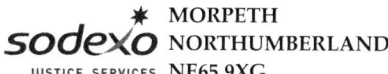

**MORPETH**
**NORTHUMBERLAND**
**NE65 9XG**

NORTHUMBERLAND
**PRISON & YOI** Tel: 01670 383100

*For the latest reports on this prison please visit:*
https://tinyurl.com/bdfh26rv

*Important Changes:* **(1) Visits:** the identification necessary to access this prison and visit for social or professional purposes has changed; (2) **Money and Gifts** new rules now apply to these. See page 16 for full details of the above.

**Task of the establishment** Category C working prison for adult males.

**Certified normal accommodation and operational capacity**
Prisoners held at the time of this visit: 1,310
Baseline certified normal capacity: 1,368
In-use certified normal capacity: 1,368
Operational capacity: 1,368

**Prison status and key providers**
Private – managed by: Sodexo
Prison Group: Custodial Contracts
Head of Custodial Contracts: Neil Richards
Governor/Director:
Samantha Pariser / Mark Johnstone (c)
IMB Chair: Lesley Craig
Physical health provider:
Spectrum Community Health
Mental health provider: Tees, Esk and Wear Valleys NHS Foundation Trust
Substance misuse treatment provider: Spectrum (clinical), Humankind (non-clinical)
Prison education framework provider: Novus
Escort contractor: GeoAmey

**Brief history** HMP Northumberland was formed from the merger of HMP Acklington and HMP/YOI Castington, completed in October 2011. It became part of the private prison sector on 1 December 2013.

**Short description of residential units** There are 16 house blocks, five holding vulnerable prisoners, including sex offenders. House blocks range from 40 to 240 beds and are of differing layouts and ages.

There are two induction house blocks (one for vulnerable prisoners), dedicated integrated drug treatment systems house blocks, a drug recovery house block, a drug-free house block, and an older vulnerable prisoner house block.

**Visiting Information** Prisoners must book their visit 48 hours prior to the visit.
**Visiting times:** Wednesday - Friday 1400 – 1600, Saturday - Sunday 0900 - 1100, 1400 – 1600.

**Legal visits:** Email: legalvisits.northumberland@hmps.gsi.gov.uk

## INSPECTIONS & REPORTS
**Scrutiny visit: 8 and 15–16 September 2020**
**Published: 16 October 2020**

HMP Northumberland is a category C male prison with a strong emphasis on constructive employment. Over 1,300 prisoners are accommodated in 16 house blocks over a large area.

There was a prompt and active response by managers at the beginning of the Covid-19 restricted regime period. Because some other prisons in the region had suffered outbreaks, Northumberland had from the start of the period taken a considerable number of new receptions, and the provisions to cohort those arriving each day had been effective. On the advice of Public Health England (PHE), prisoners who needed to be isolated were kept on their existing house block to minimise risk of cross-infection, since the buildings were well spaced out.

There had been a stream of communication throughout the period, and good signage on precautions against the spread of infection. However, social distancing was largely confined to organised settings such as queues; there was relatively little of it when staff or prisoners were grouped together. The limited opening up of the regime had gone smoothly, although most prisoners had less time unlocked than in similar prisons at this stage. We were disappointed to find that a few prisoners who showed symptoms were locked in their cells 24 hours a day for up to eight days, without access to a shower or the open air, until a test result became available.

The amount of violence and self-harm had reduced during the Covid-19 period. This was in the context of reducing trends over recent years, which had continued through the first half of 2020, although self-harm had been rising in the last two months. The prison's regular pattern of meetings to review and plan actions on safety had been paused, but it had taken reasonable measures to flex disciplinary actions in response to the risk of infection, without harming safety and good order. It was a concern that a system of locking individuals in their cells for the whole day, in effect as a form of punishment, had grown without proper authorisation or oversight.

Prisoners generally spoke positively of staff attitudes and behaviour; however, in our survey, a third said that they had experienced intimidation from staff at some time, and those with disabilities were more likely to report this. For many, the short periods of unlock prevented much meaningful interaction. Regular key work (see Glossary of terms) sessions by wing staff had ceased, although members of the programmes team had been making regular contact by in-cell telephone with those who had specific risks or needs. The residential areas were generally clean and in better condition than a few years ago. However, in a house block with several prisoners with mobility difficulties, the showers were not accessible; we met one prisoner who had not been able to shower since March, as a previous arrangement to shower in a neighbouring house block was not possible during this period.

Work on equality and diversity had in effect ceased, although there were well-formed plans to revive this work in the near future. The chaplaincy had done excellent work, maintaining face-to-face contact and support with prisoners throughout the establishment and providing faith resources.

The health care department had responded well to the pandemic situation, maintaining all essential processes in spite of staffing problems. The mental health team had continued a high level of service, including face-to-face work, as had the clinical substance misuse team, and the psychosocial substance misuse service was working creatively to maintain individual contact. Medicines management had improved, with some specific areas still needing attention.

About 30% of prisoners had jobs in the prison at the time of our visit, and some key workshops had continued to operate throughout this period, with the number increasing recently. However, most prisoners had only one hour a day out of their cell, in addition to collecting meals. This gave more limited time than at most similar prisons for basic activities, such as showering, exercising and using the electronic kiosks to make requests. Those on the induction units often had only 30 minutes rather than an hour a day out of their cell.

The learning and skills function had been unusually active from the beginning of the restricted regime, providing individualised learning materials for those already enrolled in education. Education staff were now back in the establishment and enriching the offer further, although without any classes or face-to-face work. There was innovative use of incentives for prisoners to take part in a range of activities compatible with the restricted regime. Gym staff had begun to offer structured outdoor activities on a limited scale, and the library staff had made books available while the libraries themselves were closed.

Social visits had restarted promptly in July after

*493*

the national go-ahead had been given, and the arrangements were satisfactory, but the take-up low. The prison did not use video calling for 'virtual' visits, which was attributed to deficiencies in broadband access. Legal visits had restarted more recently.

Offender management and sentence planning had continued at a reduced level, but their quality was reduced by the lack of face-to-face contact between the relevant staff and individual prisoners. The only exceptions were for the most urgent milestones, such as parole hearings. There were some backlogs, for example in recategorisation, and delays in transfers to open conditions.

There were some weaknesses in public protection processes; most seriously, the commencement of telephone and mail monitoring for those presenting specific risks was often delayed by days or even weeks at the time of our visit. One significant impact of Covid-19 for a training prison offering offending behaviour programmes was that none of these programmes or individual interventions had taken place, and there were no well-advanced preparations for bringing such work back on stream.

Although about 100 prisoners were released each month, there was too little attention to planning and support for release. In many cases, work to help prisoners plan was beginning much too close to the release date. Although clear data were hard to attain, a significant number of prisoners were not released to permanent and settled accommodation. No prisoner had been released under the available early release provision. There was an air of positivity and confidence across many aspects of the prison's life and its management; many departments had risen to the challenges of the pandemic situation well. However, in some specific areas of work, management grip was lacking; and while the regime had in many respects moved forward, the prison still needed to seek out and pursue further opportunities to provide as full a regime as possible within the current restraints.

Peter Clarke CVO OBE QPM
HM Chief Inspector of Prisons, September 2020

## Key concerns and recommendations

Key concerns and recommendations identify the issues of most importance to improving outcomes for prisoners and are designed to help establishments prioritise and address the most significant weaknesses in the treatment and conditions of prisoners.

During this visit we identified some areas of key concern, and have made a small number of key recommendations for the prison to address.

Key concern: On some house blocks, prisoners who were considered to have behaved inappropriately were punished informally by not being allowed out of their cells for the regime on the following day. There was no prison-wide oversight or control of this practice, which constituted an unofficial punishment.

Recommendation: Disciplinary action should only be taken in line with established policies and procedures, and should be subject to proper oversight. (To the director)

Key concern: The showers on the house block accommodating several prisoners with mobility difficulties were unsuitable for wheelchair users and not accessible. At least one prisoner had been unable to shower for more than seven months since the start of the restricted regime.

Recommendation: All prisoners should have access to a daily shower. (To the director)

Key concern: Most prisoners had only an hour out of their cells on a typical day to complete domestic tasks, shower and spend time outdoors and, under the unlocking rota, some spent up to 27 hours at a time locked in their cell. Prisoners were left with very little time to engage with staff or peers, especially as the key worker sessions had only restarted for the most vulnerable prisoners. Time out of cell was below several other comparable prisons.

Recommendation: Prisoners should have more than an hour a day out of their cell to give them access to constructive activity, including opportunities to engage with staff and peers. (To the director)

Key concern: The overall take-up of social visits was low, largely because of their very limited nature. Although some of the restrictions were unavoidable, the lack of any weekend visits, refreshments or play facilities and reduced time slots were gaps that the prison could explore further and address.

Recommendation: The prison should take measures as soon as possible to encourage more families and significant others to attend social visits, including longer visits, weekend sessions, facilities for children and refreshments. (To the director)

Key concern: There were delays of about three weeks in activating monitoring for new arrivals presenting potential public protection risks, and an additional backlog of calls waiting to be checked.

Recommendation: The prison should implement communications monitoring for all relevant new arrivals promptly to ensure that risks are managed appropriately and the public are protected. (To the director)

Key concern: Resettlement planning continued to be undertaken remotely with no face-to-face contact between staff and prisoners. For nearly all prisoners, plans were developed too near to the date of release to be meaningful and effective.

Recommendation: The director should work

with Northumbria Community Rehabilitation Company and resettlement agencies to enable effective and timely release planning to be safely resumed, including direct contact with each prisoner. (To the director)

## Notable positive practice
We define notable positive practice as innovative practice or practice that leads to particularly good outcomes from which other establishments may be able to learn. Inspectors look for evidence of good outcomes for prisoners; original, creative or particularly effective approaches to problem-solving or achieving the desired goal; and how other establishments could learn from or replicate the practice.
Inspectors found the following examples of notable positive practice during this visit.
• The learning and skills department had been active since the beginning of the restricted regime in ensuring that prisoners already enrolled in education received weekly individualised in-cell learning packs from the education provider.
• The learning and skills department was piloting the 'Coracle Inside' trial project in which prisoners were allocated individual laptops to access learning material and word processing.
• Arrangements had been made for some remand prisoners who had arrived from HMP Durham without a completed pre-sentence report to call their court probation officer for free via their in-cell telephone so that the report could be ready for the sentencing court. The National Probation Service bore the cost of these calls, which were sometimes lengthy.

## INDEPENDENT MONITORING BOARD: Annual Report
The law requires every prison to be monitored by an independent Board appointed by the Justice Secretary; these are known as Independent Monitoring Boards (IMBs). The IMB must satisfy itself as to the humane and just treatment of those held in custody within its prison and the range and adequacy of the programmes preparing them for release; it must report annually to the Justice Secretary on how well the prison has met the standards and requirements placed on it.

## IMB Report 1 January 2021 – 31 December 2021
### Published May 2022
### Executive summary
### Background to the report
The evidence for this report has been gathered during a global pandemic. Although some restrictions eased for periods during 2021, the Board continued to monitor with a blend of face to face and remote monitoring.

Greater use of 'dial in systems' and alternative technologies helped with accessing information. Again, this year, the prison has prioritised prisoner and staff wellbeing and safety in the light of pandemic conditions. These measures have successfully managed peaks in Covid-19 cases and yet again the difficult decisions made by the leadership of the prison have resulted in good, strong management of a difficult situation.

## Main judgements
### How safe is the prison?
The Board confirms that the prison is a safe environment where many of the prison's initiatives are supporting prisoners to ensure that they feel safe. The ongoing work led by the safer custody team has supported prisoners in reducing violent behaviour and the data demonstrates there has been a significant decline in violence which continues the trend begun before Covid imposed restrictions.

### How fairly and humanely are prisoners treated?
The Board maintains that, in its view, the prisoners at HMPN are treated fairly and humanely. Many staff continue to pay particular attention and care when dealing with those who are extremely vulnerable. This is particularly notable in the segregation unit where the team not only deal with the most challenging of prisoners but also the most vulnerable. The Board also recognises and commends the care, knowledge and expertise of staff at all levels across the prison.

### How well are prisoners' health and wellbeing needs met?
In most cases, prisoners' health and wellbeing needs are being well met. The mental health team have been supportive throughout the pandemic for those prisoners who need additional support for their mental health needs.
Where prisoners bring to our attention their concerns regarding healthcare, it is almost exclusively related to administration of prescription medication, most notably for pain relief, when they transfer from other prisons.

### How well are prisoners progressed towards successful resettlement?
The restrictions imposed by the pandemic have led to a significant lack of opportunities available in education, work and training, both here in the prison and in the wider community.
New opportunities are beginning to open up in the north east and the prison has been quick to recognise them. During 2022 we have prioritised monitoring of progress in this area as the pandemic severely compromised access to the minimal opportunities that there were.

### Main areas for development

To prioritise opportunities for men to re-engage with learning, employment and training to mitigate the disadvantages of the lockdowns and the impact of the Covid-19 pandemic on preparation for release. This remains the same as last year because the pandemic, combined with very few local opportunities, severely restricted progress.

### TO THE MINISTER

Whilst we are aware the prison has managed the pandemic very effectively, we are concerned that the full effect on prisoner mental health has yet to be seen. We would like assurance from the minister that a fully funded infrastructure of support is available to the entire prison estate to support adequate opportunity for mental health support, along with adequate education and employment opportunities on release.

Additionally, the full effect of the transition to the new probation service has yet to be evaluated, but we are aware that men are released into homeless situations and we find this unacceptable. We would seek confirmation from the minister that those agencies charged with the responsibility of housing men on release are doing just that and, more importantly, that there is adequate appropriate housing stock available.

### TO THE DIRECTOR

We continue to support the measures taken by the Director to ensure the safety and wellbeing of men in the care of HMPN. We look forward to monitoring the new initiatives for 2022 relating to employment, education and preparation for release and see these as a welcome development.

### Progress since last report

We have observed the maintenance of the higher standards of cleanliness and dignity for men in the care of the prison throughout 2021.

We recognise that, although the contract for healthcare provision is not in the gift of the organisation running the prison, every possible step has been taken to secure appropriate staffing and stabilise delivery to the residents. Given the difficulties presented by the ongoing pandemic, the location of the prison and the crisis in healthcare recruitment nationally, delivery has continued with considerable attempts to reduce waiting times for both GP appointments and dentistry.

KNOX ROAD
NORWICH
NORFOLK
NR1 4LU

**HM PRISON NORWICH**

Tel 01603 708600

*For the latest reports on this prison please visit:*
https://tinyurl.com/bdfh26rv

*Important Changes:* **(1) Visits:** the identification necessary to access this prison and visit for social or professional purposes has changed; (2) **Money and Gifts** new rules now apply to these. See page 16 for full details of the above.

**Task of the establishment** HMP/YOI Norwich is a multifunctional local prison holding remand and sentenced category B, C and D adult prisoners as well as remand and sentenced young adults.

**Certified normal accommodation and operational capacity**
Prisoners held at the time of inspection: 695
Baseline certified normal capacity: 616
In-use certified normal capacity: 770
Operational capacity: 773

**Prison status and key providers**
Public
Prison Group: Bedfordshire, Cambridgeshire & Norfolk
Prison Group Director: Gary Monaghan
Governor/Director: Declan Moore
IMB Chair: Stephanie Amey
Physical health provider: Virgin Care Limited
Mental health provider: Norfolk and Suffolk NHS Foundation Trust
Substance use treatment provider: Phoenix Futures
Prison education framework provider: People Plus
Escort contractor: Serco

**Brief history** Norwich prison was built in 1887 on the site of the Britannia barracks home of the Royal Norfolk Regiment. The establishment has a mixture of buildings dating from 1887 to 2010, when the new A wing and activity centre was built. The prison is a complex site – it is split into three areas, each serving different functions: the main prison (a local prison), the local discharge unit (LDU) (a category C unit) and Britannia House (which holds category D prisoners).

**Short description of residential units**
*Main prison site (local prison)*
A wing – induction unit, first night centre, integrated drug treatment system, stabilisation

and maintenance unit for 212 prisoners.
B wing – accommodation for 119 unconvicted and sentenced adults and young adults.
C wing – places for 123 unconvicted and sentenced adults and young adults and vulnerable prisoners (those convicted of a sexual offence).
E wing – space for 26 unconvicted and sentenced adults and young adults from the general population.
M wing – category C unit for 40 prisoners soon to become an enabling environment ethos unit.
U wing – segregation unit.
Segregation unit – accommodation for 10 prisoners.
*LDU (unit for category C prisoners)*
F and G wings – accommodation for 178 category C prisoners.
L wing – places for 15 prisoners with significant social care needs or requiring palliative care.
*Britannia House*
D wing – resettlement unit for 42 category D prisoners working both in the establishment and in the community.

### Visiting Information
Book online at: www.gov.uk/prison-visits or by telephone 01603 708790 Monday to Thursday: 10am to 12 noon and 2pm to 4pm, Friday: 10am to 12:30pm and 2pm to 3:30pm.
**Visiting times:** Visiting times are allocated depending on wing and isolation status of prisoners. Monday: 10am to 11am and 2pm to 3pm, secure video calls only.
Tuesday: 2pm to 3pm and 3:45pm to 4:45pm. Secure video calls: 8:30am to 9am, 9:15am to 9:45am, 10am to 11am, 2pm to 2:30pm, 3pm to 3:30pm, 3:45pm to 4:15pm
Wednesday: 2pm to 3pm. Secure video calls: 3:30pm to 4pm, 4:15pm to 4:45pm
Thursday: 10am to 11am (Brit House), 10:30am to 11:30pm, 2pm to 3pm and 3:45pm to 4:45pm. Secure video calls: 8:30am to 9am, 9:15am to 9:45am, 2pm to 2:30pm, 3pm to 3:30pm, 3:45pm to 4:15pm.
Friday: 10am to 11am (Brit House), 2pm to 3pm, 3:30pm to 4:30pm.
Saturday: 10:45am to 11:45am, 2pm to 3pm and 3:45 to 4:45pm.
Brit House: 10am to 11am, 2pm to 3pm and 3:30pm to 3:30pm.
Sunday: 9am to 10am, 10:45am to 11:45am, 2pm to 3pm and 3:45pm to 4:45pm.
Brit House: 10am to 11am, 2pm to 3pm and 3:30pm to 4:30pm. Secure video calls: 2pm to 2:30pm, 3pm to 3:30pm and 3:45pm to 4:15pm

### Legal visits: Email:
legalvisits.norwich@hmps.gsi.gov.uk Monday to Friday: 9am to 11:30am or 1pm 3pm

### INSPECTIONS & REPORTS
**Date of last full inspection 21 Oct–1 Nov 2019**
*Notable features from this inspection*
• Although categorised as a local prison, HMP Norwich had multiple functions, accommodating category B, C and D prisoners in three separate sites.
• Norwich had a dedicated unit that provided specialist support for elderly prisoners and those requiring social and palliative care.
• 40% of the population were under 30.
• Only 38% of prisoners were released to sustainable accommodation.
• 60% of staff were within their first two years of service.
• In our survey, 46% of prisoners in the closed site declared a disability.
• There had been six self-inflicted deaths since the previous inspection.

### HMCIP Report, published 27 February 2020
HMP/YOI Norwich is an important and complex local prison, located in central Norwich and serving East Anglia. Comprising three adjacent but separate sites, the establishment includes: the local reception prison site, holding convicted and unconvicted category B and category C prisoners; the local discharge unit (LDU), a training facility holding category C prisoners; and an open resettlement facility, Britannia House, holding category D prisoners. While this level of complexity brings with it not insignificant management challenges, this combination of facilities ought, if managed effectively, to offer real opportunities to help prisoners progress through their sentence to the point of resettlement into the local community. Our findings at this inspection suggested that the prison still had some way to go before such a vision could be fully realised.
We last inspected Norwich in 2016, when we found an improved prison delivering reasonably good outcomes across all four of our tests of a healthy prison (safety, respect, purposeful activity and resettlement (now rehabilitation and release planning)). At this inspection, managers told us that since that time they had faced considerable difficulties and that the prison had deteriorated significantly. They were also keen to tell us that the deterioration had been reduced with some recent improvement over the last year. Outcomes and assessments, which at this inspection were not sufficiently good against any of the four tests, to an extent confirmed this narrative. Norwich was now less safe. Most, but not all, new prisoners received reasonable treatment when they arrived but arrangements were inconsistent and poorly coordinated. Levels of recorded violence had increased and were

relatively high, although there were comparably fewer serious incidents. About a fifth of prisoners told us in our survey that they felt unsafe, a figure that was consistent with findings in similar prisons. Initiatives were in place to reduce violence, for example, 24 perpetrators of violence were being case managed on challenge, support and intervention plans (CSIPs) (Challenge, support and intervention plans are used by all adult prisons to manage those prisoners who are violent or pose a heightened risk of being violent. These prisoners are managed and supported on a plan with individualised targets and regular reviews. Some prisons also use the CSIP framework to support victims of violence.), but few staff were aware and it was evident that such processes needed to be applied with better coordination and greater rigour. Use of force had also increased. Procedures aimed at improving supervision and accountability in the management of use of force had been introduced recently but it was too soon to test their effectiveness. Fewer prisoners were now segregated, with those who were subject to a basic regime, but again, as at the 2016 inspection, we were told of planned improvements to the segregation unit regime. Security arrangements were applied reasonably well and the positive mandatory drug rate was now relatively low.

Tragically, there had been six self-inflicted deaths since we last inspected and in recent months the number of self-harm incidents had increased. The key recommendations identified following investigations into the deaths had been implemented and we were assured progress was kept under review. Work to individually review the activity allocation and time out of cell of those identified as being in crisis was very positive and the prison had begun piloting new case management (ACCT) arrangements. That said, we found many weaknesses in case management practice, although the prisoners themselves told us they felt well cared for.

During the inspection we were made aware of staffing shortfalls in the prison. Many of those staff in post were also very inexperienced. Three-quarters of the prisoners we surveyed told us that they felt respected by staff, but it was clear that despite much positive engagement we observed, staff inexperience was a cause of considerable frustration amongst the prisoners. In addition, much low level poor behaviour went unchallenged.

The general environment around the prison was reasonable and most wings were mostly clean, but the quality of cellular accommodation was varied and basic maintenance was behind schedule. Access to basic amenities and facilities was similarly inconsistent, and food serveries

and food trolleys were dirty. Consultation arrangements and the management of complaints, although just about adequate, needed improvement. Peer-led information desk arrangements were, however, a helpful mitigation. The promotion of equality and diversity in the prison had deteriorated markedly since our last inspection and required immediate attention to ensure the needs of minority groups were understood and met. Healthcare was satisfactory, with some good practice in the provision of social care and palliative care, but with notably poor outcomes in dentistry.

There was sufficient activity to engage about 80% of the population, but we found between 30 and 35% of prisoners locked up during the working day. English and mathematics were prioritised in the prison's education strategy and there was good vocational provision in the LDU. Demanding commercial standards were achieved in the prison workshops, influenced by the prison's productive external commercial links. Hard-to-reach individuals were supported by educational outreach, with some provided with in-cell education, but access to higher level qualifications was limited and skills acquisition was often not recognised or recorded which was a missed opportunity. Teaching standards were inconsistent and punctuality and attendance were poor. Our colleagues in Ofsted judged the overall effectiveness of provision as 'requires improvement'. The prison lacked an overarching offender needs analysis, strategy or action plan to ensure the prison became a place of meaningful and effective rehabilitation. There was a growing backlog of offender assessments (OASys) and basic screening often did not take place. Despite this, progress was being made in building an offender management team for the future, and those assessments that did take place were usually good, although routine contact with prisoners was still intermittent. There were no structured offending behaviour courses and while Britannia House provided some useful resettlement opportunities, some recent disruption had temporarily limited the availability of outside work placements. Reintegration work was organised and effective, but finding suitable accommodation for those being released remained a challenge.

The findings of this inspection indicated that local managers were right that there were improvements to be seen at Norwich. Much of this improvement was, however, recent, inconsistent and not particularly well coordinated. It was also hard to discern a coherent and considered plan for the prison, a plan consistent with the development of a rehabilitative culture. In addition, there remained a number of safety risks that needed to be addressed, prisoners needed to be supported and incentivised to engage purposefully with the regime and there was much to do in ensuring that an inexperienced staff group received the support they needed.

Peter Clarke CVO OBE QPM November 2019
HM Chief Inspector of Prisons

## INDEPENDENT MONITORING BOARD: Annual Report

The law requires every prison to be monitored by an independent Board appointed by the Justice Secretary; these are known as Independent Monitoring Boards (IMBs). The IMB must satisfy itself as to the humane and just treatment of those held in custody within its prison and the range and adequacy of the programmes preparing them for release; it must report annually to the Justice Secretary on how well the prison has met the standards and requirements placed on it.

### IMB Report 1 March 2021 – 28 February 2022
### Published July 2022
### Executive summary

The Covid-19 (Covid) pandemic continued to have a significant impact on the Board's ability to gather information and monitor in person, as for a period Board members were unable to attend the prison. The Board was also unable to attend some meetings due to the size of the rooms where they were conducted. Where this occurred, the Board monitored the paperwork. The Board has covered as much ground as possible under the circumstances but much of the detail and evidence within this report is sourced from prison and prison agencies' statistics, analysis and information. Much could not be independently verified. The Board uses analysis and quotes prisoners' responses from two IMB questionnaires conducted during the year but due to Covid these questionnaires were limited in scope and sent to a reduced number of prisoners. The continuous and overarching issue of staff shortages exacerbated by the Covid pandemic has overshadowed all aspects of prison life, undermining the ability of staff and management to make the prison 'a place of safety and reform' and to assist prisoners 'to lead law-abiding and useful lives both while they are in prison and after they are released.'

(www.gov.uk/government/organisations/hm-prison-service)

### Background to the report

In March 2020 the entire prison estate went into command mode and remained in command mode throughout the last reporting year (2020-21) and throughout this reporting year (March 2021-February 2022). Policies continued to be directed nationally by Gold command. As stated in the report of 2020-21, the Board continues to recognise the continued strong and effective local leadership during Covid at HMP/YOI Norwich through the prison governors (Bronze command). Substantial efforts continued to be made by HMP/YOI Norwich, despite huge and unpredictable shortfalls in staffing, to try to protect the prisoners in their care from Covid and to provide as humane and fair a system as possible during this unprecedented time. Successful teamwork continued to be evident between many of the prison and civilian staff and management, with many going above and beyond their duty. However, the adverse impact upon prisoners due to the continued severe but mandatory constraints upon activities, education, and time out of cell, and also the impact upon staff, cannot be underestimated. There was an outbreak of Covid at the establishment in November 2021 and the prison was declared an outbreak site. This continued all the way through to the end of the reporting year. Staff cooperated with testing procedures to try to limit exposure to Covid for the prisoners. Despite efforts to minimise transmission of the virus, there was evidence of prisoner-to-prisoner transmission and staff-prisoner and vice versa.

Time out of cell and activities have continued to be limited. When the prison was not in lockdown, the attendance at work and education was limited due to the need for social distancing in classrooms and workshops. Gym sessions were also operating with limited numbers. The compliance and acceptance by the majority of prisoners has been commendable and the various initiatives to alleviate boredom and isolation have been largely appreciated.

Governor's notices to prisoners (GNTPs) are intended to ensure that prisoners are kept informed on all significant matters, particularly on Covid restrictions and updates. However, the Board is concerned that not all prisoners see and understand these important notices.

There have been shortfalls in the prevention of infection procedures, with a lack of cleaning materials throughout the establishment. Even though masks were mandatory they were not habitually worn where necessary by all members of staff and prisoners.

As stated previously, the Board welcomes the recent funded restoration plans for the old A wing, along with further expansion projects (with the new M wing) and hopes that catering and activity/education and gym facilities will be upgraded to service the new prisoner places created.

Accommodation in L wing, the healthcare unit, E wing and the segregation unit is outdated and would benefit from refurbishment and modernisation. Accommodation fabric checks (AFCs) have been nominal, first night induction was reduced to a 'through the door conversation' when there were outbreaks on the wings, the useful key worker programme continues to be curtailed due to staff shortages, and education and workshop classes have limited numbers. This means that programmes/qualifications take longer to obtain and where reliance is made on additional work being done by prisoners in their cells, this disadvantages prisoners with low levels of literacy and numeracy.

## Main judgements
### How safe is the prison?
Statistics show HMP/YOI Norwich as having a medium to high rate of violence against comparator prisons. There has been a reduction in violence, but this may be attributed to less association amongst prisoners. Prisoner-on-prisoner assaults are too frequent. Assaults on officers have decreased, but this may again be attributable to fewer prisoners being out of their cells at any one time. The planning for safeguarding of more vulnerable prisoners is thorough and there are multi-disciplinary discussions of more complex prisoners at the weekly safety intervention meeting (SIM) which instigate good all-round support.

Self-harm in the prison population remains high and has increased during lockdown. The mental health team are overstretched. Key workers were diverted to support those prisoners suffering the most during lockdown as the prison, quite correctly, focused on supporting the prisoners with the greatest need. Prisoners are supported using the assessment, care in custody and teamwork (ACCT) process, however there is need for improvements in the training of staff, completion of documents and the management of the system.

Current induction processes during Covid are brief and inadequate, confusing some new prisoners.

### How fairly and humanely are prisoners treated?
Covid has impacted on the humane treatment at HMP/YOI Norwich, with prisoners being locked up for long hours due to Covid restrictions. New arrivals at HMP Norwich are kept behind their doors for up to five days or until testing shows they are clear of Covid. Those who are Covid positive are kept behind their doors. There is interaction with staff on a daily basis and the introduction of the in-cell phone system means it is easier for them to keep in contact with friends and family. They are not allowed out of their cells

for showers, exercise etc. Otherwise, the prisoners are treated fairly and humanely in general but there are several issues which undermine this basic principle. As reported for many years, the prison is overpopulated and toilet facilities in doubled-up cells lack essential privacy. Some accommodation is outdated and needs modernisation. There is variable provision of some basic essentials e.g. full AFCs to ensure clean and well-equipped cells and correct cleaning equipment/materials on all the wings. There are currently 11 foreign nationals at HMP/YOI Norwich whose sentences have expired. Their continued detention is neither fair nor humane.

### How well are prisoners' health and wellbeing needs met?
Observations are mainly based on a review of statistical analysis from the prison's meeting minutes provided and from prisoners' comments to the Board/responses to IMB questionnaires. The prison's minutes indicate that in the main physical and mental healthcare provision is equivalent to that in the community, apart from dentistry. Although a well-functioning triage system is in place, prisoners comment adversely about GP access but say that good nursing provision is available. Prisoners identify dental provision as inadequate. The air exchange units in the dentist's clinics have not been installed. Covid restrictions and loss of regime, including time out of cell, access to activity and exercise, have continued to impact upon prisoners' wellbeing and mental health. Education and distraction packs in English have been readily available in an attempt to mitigate this effect, but prisoners state that they have been affected by long hours locked in cells with little to do. Gym and exercise classes have been limited. Caseloads for the mental health team are very heavy. Dispensary hatches on the second floor are not easily accessible to all prisoners as there is no lift on B and C wings and the lift on A wing has frequent breakdowns. There is no accessible shower on the healthcare unit.

### How well are prisoners progressed towards successful resettlement?
The Accelerator prisons project and appointment of a dedicated member of staff to focus on employment has led to an increase in contact with local employers and more opportunities for men to gain employment on release working with KickStart (a Department for Work and Pensions scheme). There have been employment boards with businesses visiting the prison, along with hospitality industry days where employers met with prisoners. This has led to an increase in

opportunities for men on release and those residents in Britannia House. Accommodation is a big issue for some men on release and the Accelerator project staff member is working with these men to find accommodation.

Some prisoners do not have an offender assessment system (OASys) plan. There is no funding for accredited interventions and offending behaviour programmes (OBPs) at HMP/YOI Norwich and there is nothing for long-term sentenced prisoners and those serving indeterminate public protection sentences (IPPs) to help demonstrate a reduction in risk. Purple Visits (a video calling option) made a big impact on prisoners' abilities to keep in touch with their families during the pandemic when visits were limited and some families were reluctant to visit the establishment. The introduction of in-cell phones has also greatly improved prisoners' opportunities to maintain family contact. Spurgeons (the family support services charity working in Norwich prison) has also worked hard to maintain family contacts by various means.

## Main areas for development
### TO THE MINISTER
As stated in last year's report, the Minister's letter of 30 May 2019 to the IMB National Chair stated 'HMPPS remains committed to the safe progression of prisoners serving IPPs and ensuring prioritisation of post-tariff prisoners in accessing rehabilitative interventions'. Will the Minister explain why there are still eight prisoners serving indeterminate sentences for public protection (IPP) and 30 life sentenced prisoners in HMP/YOI Norwich in February 2022 without provision of any offending behaviour programmes or accredited interventions to allow progression towards release?

The Board continues to have concerns that the increase in prisoner numbers planned for HMP/YOI Norwich is being funded without additional funding for education, catering and activity provision. Will the Minister confirm that the plan for an increased prison population at HMP/YOI Norwich will ensure sufficient, decent prison spaces alongside adequate provision of rehabilitative programmes and interventions?

As stated in last year's report: "While recognising the work of court liaison and diversion services, the Board continues to encounter inhumane treatment through the incarceration of men with severe mental health issues and/or learning disabilities. These men often have to be housed in HCC or the segregation unit for the safety of other prisoners and staff. The Minister stated that he was 'determined to improve the process to ensure delays in transferring prisoners to secure mental health facilities are reduced' (letter 30 May 2019),

but the Board contends that the needs of these men have not been properly identified early enough in the criminal justice process. These men should never have been imprisoned but rather located in establishments which could properly address their issues. In the consultation on Reforming the Mental Health Act published on 13 January 2021, it states, 'When there is no hospital bed available and a defendant (meaning a person against whom a criminal or civil action is brought) requires mental health care and treatment, courts may be forced to put them in prison as a 'place of safety'." The Board asks the minister 'Why are these men still being kept in custody?'

The budget for food is £2.02 per prisoner per day. With the rapid increase in food prices, this makes it increasingly difficult for the prison to provide a balanced diet for prisoners. The Board commends the catering team who have worked so hard to continue to provide a good variety of balanced diets to the prisoners. Will the Minister please outline his plan for aligning the catering budget with the increases in the cost of living to ensure prisoners can be offered a balanced and nutritious diet?

There are currently 11 foreign national prisoners who are still in Norwich prison despite the expiry of their sentences. Will the Minister please explain why this continues to be the case and what plans there are to move them out of HMP/YOI Norwich?

### TO THE PRISON SERVICE
The Board requests again that the Prison Service looks at the care of prisoners who are located in the segregation unit for long periods of time. The reason given for this is often that there is nowhere else to take them. In the case of the prisoner referred to in section 5.2 (Segregation), the Board contacted the Prison Group Director (PGD) and HMPPS as his treatment is inhumane and there are fears for his wellbeing. This does not in any way reflect upon the care for this prisoner given by HMP/YOI Norwich which continues to be fair, but on the individual specifics of this prisoner and the impropriety of him being held at HMP/YOI Norwich. Are there plans for refurbishment of the outdated buildings e.g. the healthcare unit, L wing, E wing and the segregation unit, alongside the planned refurbishment of a previously closed wing and the installation of a new M wing?

The delays in appointing outside contractors are long and lead to unacceptable and inhumane outcomes e.g. the rats mentioned in section 5.1, the cleaning of showers etc. following dirty protests. Would the Prison Service define its policies regarding the employment of contractors outside the existing contracts when the circumstances dictate the need for extra work? What are the policies for allowing prison Governors to secure/procure such contracts when they deem them necessary?

The Board asks for confirmation that plans are in place, and asks for details, for increasing the education, activities and catering provision alongside the increase in prison spaces following refurbishment of the old A wing.

Following a fire in the catering manager's office in December, unsafe light fittings were identified in offices throughout the establishment. What resources are being allocated to replace these fittings to reduce the risk to life of fire?

Due to the number of deaths following self-harm over the last 12 months, HMP/YOI Norwich has been classed as a 'cluster site'. What additional resources could be made available to support the prison since it has been labelled as a cluster site?'

The long-standing issue of low staff numbers has led to the further curtailment of regimes on many occasions. What steps is HMPPS taking to improve recruitment and staff retention and can it outline the policies regarding local recruitment?

The prison has been operating under a Covid regime for more than two years now, with prisoners having limited time out of cell and access to activities and education is limited. As the outside community learns to live with Covid, can HMPPS please outline what steps will be taken to return the prison to a more normal regime which would enable rehabilitation and more humane conditions?

Loss of property is one of the biggest issues for prisoners. Their belongings go missing during transfers between establishments and they face long and demoralising waits to be reunited with their property. Where property is deemed lost by the Prison Service, prisoners have difficulties in claiming compensation. This takes up a huge amount of staff time and resource. Can HMPPS please outline the steps it intends to take to address this costly issue?

TO THE GOVERNOR

The Board asks the Governor to provide information on plans for the following:

• making sure that all communications especially Governor's notices to prisoners (GNTPs) are distributed to, seen and understood by all prisoners including those who do not read/speak English This concern was highlighted in the 2020-21 annual report but the Board does not see any improvement.

• ensuring that foreign nationals are better supported and that staff access the translation facilities whenever needed.

• maintaining the focus on decency and provision of basic essentials

• ensuring that scheduled forums take place and minutes are readily available for prisoners to see.

• ensuring that Prisoner representatives have time allocated in order to support their fellow prisoners.

• proper completion of ACCT documents and the management of the ACCT process.

• continued emphasis on AFCs

• managing prisoners' property effectively, particularly during cell clearances

• construction of the workshops on the category C site.

• restoring the intended role of key worker

• analysis of equalities statistics to determine whether minority groups such as those with protected characteristics, physical or mental disabilities, learning difficulties/disabilities, neurodiversity, foreign nationals, younger and elderly prisoners are properly identified and treated fairly and that adjustments are made to support their needs and to make adequate provision for those prisoners.

• controlling bullying and debt issues on the wings

**Progress since the last report**

Due to the prolonged impact of the pandemic, much of the planned improvement has been curtailed or postponed. A few highlights of the year have been:

• The safety team has worked tirelessly to support men with mental health needs inside the establishment. The numbers of men on ACCTs and those selfharming have been very high and staff have worked hard to support them.

• Dedicated staff have been identified to review ACCTs.

• Teamwork. All staff at HMP/YOI Norwich worked as a team during this difficult year e.g. the physical education instructors and civilian staff have assisted in multiple roles which has proved invaluable in helping look after prisoners.

• Installation of in-cell telephony has had a big and positive impact on prisoners' ability to maintain contact with their families

• Social video calls (delivered during the reporting period by Purple Visits) have also made a big difference to prisoners' wellbeing by allowing visual contact with their families and loved ones.

• The development of the old A wing, a video conferencing centre and the new M wing.

• The Accelerator prisons project has brought a greater focus on employment and accommodation on release and its role in reducing reoffending. The employment boards and open days with local employers, along with links to Jobcentre Plus and Department for Work and Pensions, have enabled men to gain employment while at Britannia House and on release. The focus on accommodation on release

should also assist prisoners in the transition to life outside.
• Staff reacted professionally and worked long hours to support the prisoners during the power outage on 7 January 2022.
• Spurgeons have worked hard throughout the year to encourage and enable prisoners in maintaining family contact and to support their families.
• Construction skills training offered on the category C site assists prisoners to gain vocational qualifications which can improve their opportunities of entering into employment on release.

**PERRY ROAD
SHERWOOD
NOTTINGHAM
NG5 3AG**

**HM PRISON
NOTTINGHAM** Tel: 0115 872 4000

*For the latest reports on this prison please visit:*
https://tinyurl.com/bdfh26rv

*Important Changes:* **(1) Visits:** the identification necessary to access this prison and visit for social or professional purposes has changed; **(2) Money and Gifts** new rules now apply to these. See page 16 for full details of the above.

**Task of the establishment** HMP Nottingham is a resettlement and local prison serving the courts of Nottinghamshire and Derbyshire.

**Certified normal accommodation and operational capacity**
Prisoners held at the time of inspection: 798
Baseline certified normal capacity: 718
In-use certified normal capacity: 718
Operational capacity: 1060

**Prison status and key providers**
Public
Prison Group: North Midlands
Prison Group Director: Alison Clarke
Governor/Director: Paul Yates
IMB Chair: Janet White
Physical health, mental health and substance misuse treatment provider: Nottinghamshire Healthcare NHS Foundation Trust
Prison education framework provider: PeoplePlus
Escort contractor: GeoAmey

**Brief history** HMP Nottingham opened in 1890, but the original Victorian buildings were demolished in 2008. The new prison opened in February 2010.

**Short description of residential units**
A wing – integrated drug treatment service (IDTS)
B wing – mainstream location
C wing – mainstream location
D wing – mainstream location and incentivised substance-free living unit E wing – mainstream location
F wing – first night centre and induction unit G wing – vulnerable prisoner unit

**Visiting Information** Ring 0115 962 8980 Monday and Thursday, 1pm to 4pm, Tuesday, Friday and Saturday, 9am to midday or email: socialvisits.nottingham@justice.gov.uk. You can also book your next visit in person when you're at the prison.
**Visiting times:** Monday: 2pm to 4.30pm, Tuesday: 9am to 11.30am, 2pm to 4.30pm, Wednesday: no visits, Thursday: 9am to 11.30am, 2pm to 4.30pm, Friday: 9am to 11am Saturday and Sunday: 9am to 11.30am, 2pm to 4.30pm.

**Legal visits:**
No legal visits currently taking place.

**INSPECTIONS & REPORTS**
**Date of last full inspection** 6–17 January 2020
*Notable features from this inspection:*
• Following our last full inspection in 2018, Nottingham became the first prison to be subject to HM Inspectorate of Prisons' urgent notification process.
• Nearly half the population was unsentenced, more than at other local prisons and at our last inspection.
• 12% of the population was under the age of 21.
• 60% of prisoners in our survey reported having mental health problems.
• 20% of prison officers were in their first year of service.

**HMCIP Report, published 07 April 2020**
HMP Nottingham is a local prison that at the time of this inspection held a little under 800 prisoners, the number having been reduced from around 1,000. The inspection history of Nottingham in recent years is such that an explanation of what has happened is important in order to understand the background to this most recent inspection and the overall context in which we came to our judgements.
The prison was last inspected in early January 2018, which was the third full inspection since 2014. In contrast to our usual practice of arriving unannounced, that inspection and the previous one in 2016 were both announced well in advance. Notice of an impending inspection is intended to give an opportunity to a prison to focus on improvement or on completing earlier recommendations. We therefore found it

extraordinary that, over the course of those three inspections, the prison had consistently failed to achieve standards that were sufficient in any of our four tests of a healthy prison. Most concerning of all was that, at all three inspections, we judged outcomes in safety to be poor, our lowest assessment, and that, at the 2018 inspection, we found that only two of 13 recommendations made in 2016 in the area of safety had been fully achieved. We could recall only one other occasion when we had judged safety in a prison to be poor following three consecutive inspections.

This persistent and fundamental lack of safety, together with an overall lack of improvement following previous poor inspections, led me in January 2018 to write to the Secretary of State for Justice and for the first time invoke the urgent notification (UN) protocol (see Glossary of terms), which was new at that time. In 2018 the Inspectorate also introduced a new procedure, called an independent review of progress (IRP), which was piloted at Nottingham in November 2018. An IRP is not a full inspection looking at outcomes experienced by prisoners across the full breadth of our usual inspection framework. Instead, it is intended to review progress made against key recommendations where there have been serious concerns following a full inspection. The IRP at Nottingham was disappointing and we found that the response to many of our recommendations had been far too slow. Although the Secretary of State's action plan had been issued promptly following the UN, we found that little was done before July 2018 – a full six months. The concept of 'urgency' seemed not to have been grasped by either the prison or Her Majesty's Prison and Probation Service (HMPPS). As a result, by the time of the IRP, various initiatives had yet to result in any discernible improvements in outcomes for prisoners, and a new Governor who had taken up post during the second half of 2018 had as yet been unable to effect any notable improvement.

Given the disappointing and indeed troubling history of poor inspections followed by inadequate responses, it was gratifying to find during this latest inspection that there had at long last been some real change at Nottingham. There had been improvements in three of our tests of a healthy prison, and we came away with some confidence that the improvements could be sustained and built upon if the leadership and energy that was now evident could be maintained into the future.

In terms of safety, although there was much data that was troubling and levels of violence were still far too high, we felt able to raise our judgement from poor to not sufficiently good.

Too many prisoners still felt unsafe, there was still far too much violence and not enough was yet being done to counter it effectively. However, security had now improved and was beginning to have a positive impact. In particular, a body scanner was now being used to very good effect, leading to regular finds of secreted contraband that would not otherwise have been detected. For the future it is important that the full potential of this technology, both in detecting and deterring the ingress of illicit items, should be fully exploited. There was some evidence that the availability of illicit drugs was beginning to decline, the response to intelligence was appropriate and it was good to see that there was coordination between security and substance misuse services.

It was concerning that the number of self-harm incidents had increased substantially and that there had been four self-inflicted deaths since the last inspection. Prisons and Probation Ombudsman (PPO) recommendations following self-inflicted deaths had not always been addressed adequately. Despite the fact that analysis of data had improved, it had not yet led to a clear strategy. The quality of assessment, care in custody and teamwork (ACCT) documentation for prisoners at risk of suicide or self-harm had improved, and prisoners were positive about the support they received.

It would have been quite possible for our judgement for safety to have remained at poor. However, although the raw figures had not improved, I take the view that there are occasions when new processes by their very existence can amount to positive outcomes, for instance when, as at Nottingham, they offer reassurance to prisoners, introduce safeguards and ensure improved governance. These improvements had yet to be translated into encouraging data, but we took the view that they were sufficiently important to warrant an improvement in our judgement about the overall safety of the prison. At this inspection we found that healthcare had improved and was now good, and work in equality and diversity was in the early stages of improving. We also found that relationships between staff and prisoners had improved since the previous inspection, despite the continuing problems with lack of basic kit, clothing and bedding. We were also very concerned about delays in answering cell call bells in a prison where high levels of self-harm were of such concern. It was notable that applications and complaints were now much better handled, helped by the introduction of new electronic kiosks on the wings.

There had been significant improvements in rehabilitation and release planning, but there still remained much to do. We were particularly concerned about the shortage of probation officers in the offender management unit (OMU), and about the number of prisoners being released homeless. At around 40%, the figure was far too high and speaks of a need for more joint working with the local authority.

I hope this inspection can at long last mark a watershed in the troubled history of Nottingham. For many years it had a well-deserved reputation for being an unsafe prison. There is still a huge amount to do, but it would be wrong not to recognise the impressive progress that has been made since the poor findings of the IRP in November 2018. When a previously poorly performing prison improves, I have seen how it is possible for a new and optimistic culture, offering real care for prisoners and a better chance for them to rehabilitate, can take hold. I hope that can be achieved at Nottingham, as it could underpin future progress. All too often we have seen improvements in prisons prove to be fragile. The greatest risks have come from complacency or lack of consistency in leadership. I hope that neither will be the case at Nottingham, and that the highly creditable progress at this complex and challenging prison can be sustained into the future.

Peter Clarke CVO OBE QPM

HM Chief Inspector of Prisons March 2020

## INDEPENDENT MONITORING BOARD:
### Annual Report

The law requires every prison to be monitored by an independent Board appointed by the Justice Secretary; these are known as Independent Monitoring Boards (IMBs). The IMB must satisfy itself as to the humane and just treatment of those held in custody within its prison and the range and adequacy of the programmes preparing them for release; it must report annually to the Justice Secretary on how well the prison has met the standards and requirements placed on it.

**IMB Report 1 March 2021 – 28 February 2022**
**Published July 2022**
**Executive summary**
**Background to the report**

The entire reporting period has been affected by the response to the pandemic and the restrictions persisted beyond the end of the reporting period. However, except during periods of outbreak, the restrictions have been less onerous than during the previous year. Prisoners have been able to access exercise, collect their own meals and have some time out of cell for domestic matters. Slowly the normal prison systems, such as use of the kiosks for internal communications, have been reopened and some prisoners have been able to access work. We understand that the future regime will retain elements of the pandemic response with less time off the wing, less mixing across accommodation cohorts and employment limited mainly to half-days. We are concerned that this may mean more time in cell for prisoners and we will continue to monitor this aspect of life in the establishment. National efforts to ameliorate the effects of the pandemic have been gradually scaled back, with the removal of enhanced food items for the packed evening meal and the withdrawal of the additional £5 for phone access. The availability of in-cell phones has continued to make life better than it might otherwise have been. In spite of the situation, mostly prisoners have accepted the restrictions with tolerance and good nature and have been observed supporting each other, although it has to be recognised that for many the frustrations and restrictions were very difficult to cope with, leading to violent outbursts and self-harm.

The prison spent the year in a state of management flux with the head of residence acting up as deputy governor for almost all of the period, and then when a new deputy governor was appointed, she almost immediately had to act up as Governor. We felt that throughout the pandemic restrictions, governance was effective, in spite of the changes. A new Governor, with previous experience of working at HMP Nottingham, arrived just before the end of the reporting period and we look forward to working with him.

Our own monitoring efforts have continued to be affected by low numbers, with colleagues deployed to Covid roles in the community or health service. Several members have been directly affected by Covid infection. However, we have maintained in-person monitoring throughout the period and have dealt with applications in line with our previous practice. We have been able to welcome some new colleagues and worked with them on induction into the role.

PPE has been made freely available to us, as has routine testing, and we have been both grateful for that inclusion and happy to comply with testing regimes.

### Main judgements
#### How safe is the prison?

Self-harm incidence is reduced from the previous reporting period, but incidents of violence have increased.

Much of the safety focus has related to the pandemic; we have, overall, again been impressed with the commitment of everyone at HMP Nottingham to their own and others' safety.

**How fairly and humanely are prisoners treated?**
There is a broad prison ethos to treat all prisoners humanely and fairly as individuals. Of course, there have been times when we have needed to raise basic housekeeping issues and concerns about food but we have found staff willing to listen. An increase in applications to us about staff attitudes over the final four months of the reporting period was acknowledged by prison management who advised us of various reviews of processes (for example, the discrimination incident reporting form, or DIRF, process) to improve prisoner experience. As in the past, sometimes wing staff have represented prisoners' frustrations to us for attention. Prisoners have again sometimes been deprived of basic rights and confined to cell for much longer periods of time each day than would usually be regarded as acceptable because of the pandemic. This has affected everybody some of the time and those subject to self-isolation for longer periods. There have been individual cases of lengthy deprivations but the general management of the situation has been much more refined than the previous year resulting in less onerous restrictions.

**How well are prisoners' health and wellbeing needs met?**
As in the community, the pandemic resulted in cancelled appointments, limited face-to-face access and in some cases, periods without treatment and this continued into this reporting year. This situation improved significantly as Covid restrictions eased and whilst face-to-face consultations resumed, in line with community experience, practitioners continued to conduct some consultations using the in-cell telephones.
As far as we can tell, prisoners were given ample opportunities to avail themselves of both Covid and flu vaccinations as appropriate, but it is disappointing that despite all the prison and healthcare teams' efforts, vaccination rates were relatively low.
Once again, we draw attention to the mental health needs of prisoners and we continue to be concerned that allocation of in-patient mental health facilities to prisoners does not meet their needs. We understand the pressures on mental health services overall and how this often results in individual prisoners spending very extended periods in a prison segregation unit, as it is the only location available where they and/or others can be kept safe.

**How well are prisoners progressed towards successful resettlement?**
Resettlement efforts continued to be severely curtailed because of the pandemic restrictions. In addition, there were significant changes in provision and management of these services, due to the national action to return these services back to in-house provision. Despite this, resettlement staff did all they could to support prisoners within the prevailing circumstances at any point in time. The national initiatives to prevent prisoners being released without a place of residence were most welcome but their winding down is disappointing. In June 2021 housing providers resumed responsibility for supporting clients in seeking accommodation. The prison established an accommodation hub during the autumn of 2021. We will continue to monitor progress.
There continued to be prisoners with indeterminate sentences for public protection (IPP sentences) within the prison and, as highlighted last year, maintaining hope and preparing them for what few opportunities there are for review of their situation remains incredibly difficult for all involved. We were disappointed to see that limited progress has been made, despite a change in the law that should improve the situation of these individuals; after the end of the reporting period the prison made changes to the prison organisation to increase the focus on these prisoners.

**Main areas for development**
**TO THE MINISTER**
We would again ask the minister to address the ongoing situation in relation to IPP prisoners who are many years beyond their minimum term.

**TO THE PRISON SERVICE**
The required separation of remand and convicted prisoners is so widely ignored throughout the prison estate that we suggest this is a matter requiring structural attention beyond the individual prison. It was disappointing to have a high-profile announcement that this was to change, only for that decision to be reversed.

**TO THE GOVERNOR**
We hope that lessons learned during the lockdown period will be used to inform the organisation of the prison when the restrictions are lifted and that initiatives found to be beneficial can continue, so that the overall experience of prisoners is improved.

**Progress since the last report**
A general easing of the restrictions arising from the pandemic is indicated throughout this report. The reduction in the number of prisoners transferred from Rampton Hospital and spending long periods in segregation has been welcome. The reduction in use of force has been sustained from the previous reporting period although there has been no significant further improvement.

**OAKWOOD PRISON**

OAKS ROAD
FEATHERSTONE
WEST MIDLANDS
WV10 7QD

Tel: 01902 799700

*For the latest reports on this prison please visit:*
https://tinyurl.com/bdfh26rv

*Important Changes:* **(1) Visits:** the identification necessary to access this prison and visit for social or professional purposes has changed; (2) **Money and Gifts** new rules now apply to these. See page 16 for full details of the above.

**Task of the establishment** A category C training prison.

**Certified normal accommodation and operational capacity**
Prisoners held at the time of inspection: 2,087
Baseline certified normal capacity: 1,600
In-use certified normal capacity: 1,600
Operational capacity: 2,106

**Population of the prison**
• 2,388 new prisoners received in the previous 12 months.
• 184 foreign national prisoners.
• 33.2% of prisoners from black and minority ethnic backgrounds.
• Circa 150 prisoners released into the community each month.
• 220 prisoners receiving support for substance use.
• 287 prisoners working with the mental health team.

**Prison status and key providers**
Private: G4S
Prison Group: Custodial Contracts
Head of Custodial Contracts: Neil Richards
Governor/Director: Sean Oliver / Andy Walls (c)
IMB Chair: Barbara Evans
Private: G4S
Physical and mental health and substance use provider: Practice Plus Group
Prison education framework provider: Novus
Escort contractors: GeoAmey

**Brief history** HMP Oakwood opened on 24 April 2012, as a category C men's prison holding up to 1,605 prisoners. In 2017 it increased its capacity to 2,106.

**Short description of residential units**
Ash: Vulnerable prisoner population, including vulnerable prisoners on induction, enhanced level prisoners, those serving life and long-term sentences, the over-50s and those receiving assisted living support.

Beech: General population, including Willow (a reintegration landing), a family unit, the induction unit and accommodation for long-term prisoners.
Cedar: General population, including Chestnut (a reintegration landing), an enhanced level unit and an over-40s enhanced level unit.
Douglas: Lifer and long-term population.
Elm: Drug support unit.
Fir: Segregation unit.
Oaks: 80 temporary single occupancy units.

**Visiting Information**
Prisoners are given the opportunity to book their own visits through the Kiosk.
**Visiting times:**
*Monday*
Interventions 9:45- 11:45
SOCIAL VISITS
13:45- 15.15, 16.00 – 17.00 Cedar/Beech
17.45- 18.45 Ash/Elm
*Tuesday*
Interventions 9:45- 11:45
SOCIAL VISITS
13:45- 15.15, 16.00 – 17.00 Ash/Elm
17.45- 18.45 Cedar/Beech
*Wednesday*
Interventions 9:45- 11:45
SOCIAL VISITS
13:45- 15.15, 16.00 – 17.00 Cedar/Beech
17.45- 18.45 Ash/Elm
*Thursday*
Family events
10.00-12.00 and 14.00-16.00
*Friday*
SOCIAL VISITS
9:45- 11:45 Large halls Cedar/Beech
13:45-15.45 Ash/Elm Both halls
16.30 – 17.30 Cedar/Beech Both halls
*Saturday*
SOCIAL VISITS
9:45-11:45 Ash/Elm Large Hall/Kids club
13:45-15.45 Cedar/Beech Both halls
16.30 – 17.30 Ash/Elm Both halls
*Sunday*
SOCIAL VISITS
9:45-11:45 Cedar/Beech Both halls
13:45-15.45 Ash/Elm Both halls
16.30 – 17.30 Cedar/Beech Both halls

**Legal visits:** Email on the HMP Oakwood booking form. To request a booking form please e-mail: legalvisits.oakwood@uk.g4s.com
**Visiting times:** Mon - Fri 8.45 – 9.45, 9.45 – 10.45, 10.45 – 11.45

507

## INSPECTIONS & REPORTS
### Date of last full inspection 17–28 May 2021
### HMCIP Report, published 03 September 2021

Occupying a relatively small site in near Wolverhampton, G4S-run HMP Oakwood is the biggest prison in England, housing more than 2,000 men, most of whom live in three large accommodation blocks. The prison opened as a category C training prison in 2012; it has been well-maintained and still looks clean and new. A large proportion of prisoners at Oakwood are serving more than four years and 10% are on indeterminate sentences, but despite this complex and often high-risk population, the prison was a safe and respectful place.

I was consistently struck by the positive way that prisoners talked about the prison, welcoming the levels of trust that they were given and describing, with very few exceptions, a professional and supportive staff team. Even those who were on the basic regime and were still subjected to protracted time locked in their cells because of Covid-19 restrictions, praised the prison with many, who had spent years moving round the secure estate, telling me it was the best prison they had been to.

The director succeeded a well-respected predecessor in March 2021, but despite such a significant change, leaders had a clear set of priorities for further development when pandemic restrictions are lifted.

The performance of the education provider had been disappointing. Last year, as lockdowns were imposed, there were unnecessary delays in producing any sort of in-cell learning and there had been no face-to-face education when restrictions were lifted in summer 2020. There were also inexplicable delays with the assessment of the learning needs of new prisoners. At the time of the inspection, the provider was beginning to open classrooms and workshops, but progress was slow.

In our last inspection, in 2018, we commented on the lack of programmes to address the behaviour of sex offenders, so it was disappointing to see that there was still nothing in place despite these prisoners making up a quarter of the population. We were also concerned that the governance and practice of use of force were not good enough, nor was assessment of need and risk on arrival or in preparation for release sufficient.

The prison had developed and allowed the flourishing of an extensive network of Prisoner Led Initiatives (PLI). Without direct staff supervision, prisoners ran and organised a workshop that built tables, benches, bird boxes and hanging baskets that were sold to the local community. PLI were responsible for the maintenance of the grounds and a market garden that grew food for the prison and sold plants and vegetables. Other PLI ran support networks for new arrivals that assessed need, provided support for different faiths and gave advice. Prisoners who were on a basic regime, or those with other vulnerabilities, were taken out of their cells, given a chance to talk, offered the opportunity to do some work and begin the journey to an enhanced regime. Not only had PLI been able to support the most vulnerable prisoners, but those who were leading the activities told me that it had given real meaning to their lives.

Covid-19 restrictions meant that prisoners at Oakwood were still locked in their cells for too long each day and there was not yet enough access to work or training, but if momentum is maintained, I am confident that the prison will continue to make progress when the pandemic is over.

The prison has a friendly and positive atmosphere in which people are treated with respect and expectations are high. The governor and his staff are determined to maintain the levels of trust and responsibility that are given to prisoners, because they are committed to the rehabilitation of the men in their care. Staff and prisoners should be proud of what they have achieved.

Charlie Taylor, HM Chief Inspector of Prisons
June 2021

### Safety

At the last inspection of Oakwood in 2018 we found that outcomes for prisoners were reasonably good against this healthy prison test. At this inspection we found that outcomes for prisoners were now good against this healthy prison test.

Reception was welcoming, efficient and very clean. Staff were respectful and most prisoners told us they were treated well. There was excellent use of peer support workers, although it was not always appropriate that they were used as interpreters for non-English speakers.

The regime for most new arrivals was poor. Many prisoners were only unlocked for 10 minutes every day to carry out domestic tasks and 30 minutes to exercise outside during their 14 days in quarantine. First night cells were clean and well equipped with in-cell showers and phones. A streamlined induction provided a good overview.

Most prisoners told us they felt safe. The number of assaults was lower than at the previous inspection and compared with similar prisons, but violence was on an upward trajectory. The monthly violence meeting analysed incidents well, and interventions to reduce violence had now restarted. Support for vulnerable prisoners was good, and an impressive use of peer support workers promoted a safe environment. Most prisoners were on the higher level of the incentives scheme, but the prospect of becoming involved in prisoner-led initiatives and less restrictive arrangements in some residential units were the main incentives for positive behaviour. The number of adjudications had increased since the previous inspection.

Use of force had decreased and documentation was good, but senior managers did not provide sufficient scrutiny. We were not confident that force was always used proportionately. Use of segregation had decreased. The segregation unit was clean and staff-prisoner relationships were good. The use of peer workers was positive, but the regime and reintegration planning were too limited. The use of full personal protective equipment (see Glossary of terms) while escorting some prisoners to the unit and routine strip-searching on arrival was disproportionate.

Security was generally well managed and electronic technology was used effectively to detect illicit items. However, decisions to restrict or ban a prisoner's visits were not well recorded. Over a quarter of prisoners told us it was very easy to get illicit drugs, but the prison had not restarted drug testing. The drug strategy and collaborative working were good.

Levels of self-harm were comparable to our previous inspection and average compared with similar prisons. Self-harm peaked in October 2020 and was on a slight upward trend. Almost two-thirds of prisoners who had received support through the assessment, care in custody and teamwork (ACCT) case management process for prisoners at risk of suicide or self-harm told us they felt cared for, and ACCT case management had improved. Safer prisons meetings were not held during the pandemic, but a comprehensive amount of data was analysed. Prisoners at risk were housed separately from the general population and good efforts were made to keep them safe.

### Respect

At the last inspection of Oakwood in 2018 we found that outcomes for prisoners were good against this healthy prison test.

At this inspection we found that outcomes for prisoners remained good against this healthy prison test.

Most prisoners said that staff treated them respectfully and that they had an officer they could turn to for help. Staff's electronic case notes were comprehensive, and managerial oversight was effective.

External areas were neat and tidy, and internal communal areas were impressively clean. Cells were well maintained and mostly suitably equipped, although the 500 overcrowded cells were cramped and inadequately furnished. Access to cleaning material, laundry facilities and prison kit was good. The response to cell bells had improved since the previous inspection and electronic kiosks were well used.

Meals were served too early. Self-catering arrangements in Douglas and The Oaks units were positive initiatives. Newly arrived prisoners could wait up to two weeks for their first shop order, but the availability of additional goods enhanced prisoners' everyday lives.

Consultation arrangements were good. Prisoners made applications through the unit kiosks and timeliness was monitored well. The number of complaints was low at half that of comparator prisons. Access to legal visits was adequate and they mostly took place in the video booths. There was no legal services provision, but prisoner-led legal support was good.

The strategic oversight of equality and diversity and the analysis of monitoring data were insufficient. There were delays in replying to some discrimination incident reporting forms, but responses were good. Only 58% of black and minority ethnic and 54% of Muslim prisoners said in our survey that staff treated them respectfully. Support for foreign national prisoners was insufficient – Home Office surgeries remained suspended and there was poor access to free legal representation. Provision for prisoners with hidden disabilities was better than we normally see. There was some good support for transgender prisoners. The chaplaincy continued to provide prisoners with support throughout the pandemic, and the peer-led Project Unite had restarted its innovative interventions work.

Health care services were effectively governed and well-led, and providers' resilience had meant core services could be maintained. The prisoner-led Health Advisory Service (HAS) made sure patients were well informed. The collaborative Beat Diabetes project and the Dying Well in Prison Charter were positive. Social care arrangements were working well. Mental health and substance use services were well integrated. Mental health support had been limited. There had been an increase in demand, but a skilled team could now offer a wider range of interventions. The drug recovery unit continued to provide good support. Medicine administration in the units was generally well managed, but the pharmacy's oversight of medicine management arrangements was not sufficiently robust. Dental services had been reduced during the pandemic, but a full range of treatments was now being delivered.

## Purposeful activity

At the last inspection of Oakwood in 2018 we found that outcomes for prisoners were good against this healthy prison test.

At this inspection we found that outcomes for prisoners were now reasonably good against this healthy prison test.

Ofsted carried out a progress monitoring visit of the prison alongside our full inspection. Ofsted's full findings and the recommendations arising from their visit are set out in Section 4.

Prisoners in full-time employment could spend at least nine hours out of their cell, however many prisoners were still locked up for 22 hours a day, which placed an inevitable toll on prisoner well-being. Almost all prisoners could take an hour of outside exercise. In our spot checks during the working day, we found 33% of prisoners locked in their cells.

The pandemic had had a significant impact on library services, with a big drop in the number of books being issued to prisoners compared with the previous year. Unit-based equipment had mitigated the closure of the gym, but more could have been done to make sure that access was equitable.

Face-to-face education had restarted, and the number of work roles was increasing. The education provider was too slow to reintroduce face-to-face vocational training, but there were plans for a further expansion of prison-run workshops and vocational training programmes. Leaders appropriately prioritised English and mathematics and targeted prisoners known to have lower levels in these subjects, including those for whom English was not their first language. Prisoners who arrived at the prison since March 2020 had not received an education induction or completed initial assessments. As a result, leaders and managers did not know the needs of a significant proportion of the population. Prisoners did not receive advice or guidance to help them make informed choices about learning and work activities. They could access a breadth of subjects through in-cell work packs and most of the work they produced was of a high standard. The uptake and return of in-cell work packs during the pandemic had been low, but had increased significantly very recently. Prisoners on distance learning programmes received particularly good support to continue to make progress and achieve. Learning support staff screened the needs of learners known to have learning difficulties or disabilities appropriately and used the information to provide helpful learning support strategies.

## Rehabilitation and release planning

At the last inspection of Oakwood in 2018 we found that outcomes for prisoners were reasonably good against this healthy prison test. At this inspection we found that outcomes for prisoners were now not sufficiently good against this healthy prison test.

The take up of visits was low because they were only for a short time and subject to restrictions, for example, physical contact was prohibited. Equipment for the Purple Visits system (see Glossary of terms) was only delivered to the prison in October 2020. Imaginative use of Purple Visits enabled fathers to read bedtime stories to their children. The Help and Advice Line for Offenders' Wives ran a family engagement service and had resumed face-to-face support. The family interventions unit provided a supportive environment, and the excellent range of family intervention courses had been quick to restart.

Reducing reoffending meetings had not taken place for over a year. The prison held a challenging mix of prisoners, with half assessed as presenting a high risk of harm to others, nearly three quarters serving long sentences of four years or more and about a quarter convicted of a sexual offence. Almost 40% of the population did not have an initial assessment of their risks or needs or an updated assessment to inform their sentence planning and progression. In our survey, 58% of prisoners told us they had a custody plan, but only 48% said someone was helping them to achieve their targets. Probation and prison offender manager (POM) caseloads were far too high, and contact had rarely been face-to-face. Home detention curfew processes were managed well, but there were delays in prisoners being released owing to a lack of Bail Accommodation and Support Service and approved premises accommodation.

Those posing a high risk who were due to be released were not routinely considered ahead of time at the interdepartmental risk management team meeting, but contributions to multi-agency public protection arrangement (MAPPA) meetings were very good. Mail and phone monitoring was better than we see in other prisons. Although there was a credible recovery plan (see Glossary of terms), accredited programme places were not sufficient to meet the needs of the population. Programmes and needs assessments for prisoners convicted of sex offences were not sufficient. Release on temporary licence for a small number of prisoners had restarted. Services to help prisoners manage their finances and debt had continued, and accommodation support was good. The community rehabilitation company (CRC) had remained on site and supported the majority of the approximately 150 prisoners released each month. However, plans were mostly drawn up remotely and were not always timely. The

Resettlement Advice Line and Prisoner Helpdesk and the Oakwood Community Hub provided practical support.

## Key concerns and recommendations
Key concerns and recommendations identify the issues of most importance to improving outcomes for prisoners and are designed to help establishments prioritise and address the most significant weaknesses in the treatment and conditions of prisoners.

During this inspection we identified some areas of key concern and have made a small number of recommendations for the prison to address those concerns.

Key concern: Not all force was used proportionately, and staff missed opportunities to de-escalate situations. Senior managers did not sufficiently scrutinise paperwork or camera footage and meetings took place infrequently and were not effective.

Recommendation: There should be regular managerial oversight of the use of force, which should involve routine reviews of all instances. Patterns and trends should be identified and acted on, to ensure that force is always justified and proportionate. (Directed to: the director.)

Key concern: Provision for foreign national prisoners was poor. Surgeries with immigration officials remained suspended, and unlike those held in immigration removal centres, detainees had no access to free legal advice surgeries. The Home Office had not informed the prison of four vulnerable detainees assessed to be at higher levels of risk in detention.

Recommendation: Prisoners should have access to regular surgeries with immigration officials and should be given at least one month's notice of a decision to detain them. The Home Office should inform the prison promptly of all prisoners assessed to be at risk in detention, so that appropriate arrangements for their care can be made. (Directed to: the Home Office and Ministry of Justice.)

Key concern: Managers were unaware of the educational needs of too many prisoners who had arrived at the prison since the start of the pandemic as these men had not had an education induction and had not completed any initial assessments.

Recommendation: Leaders and managers must identify rapidly the starting points and needs of prisoners who have arrived at the prison since the start of the pandemic. They must make sure that all prisoners are fully informed about the education and training options available, and that prisoners undertake learning that will benefit them. (Directed to: the director.)

Key concern: At the time of our inspection, 12% of prisoners did not have an initial assessment of their risks or needs, and a further 27% did not have an updated assessment, reviewed in the previous 12 months, to inform sentence planning and progression. Contact with prison offender managers was too infrequent and did not drive sentence progression. Caseloads were too high, which affected prison and probation offender mangers' ability to complete assessments and have meaningful contact with prisoners.

Recommendation: All prisoners should have an up-to-date assessment of their risks and needs, and prisoners should have regular meaningful contact with a prison offender manager that challenges their offending behaviour and drives sentence progression. (Directed to: the director.)

Key concern: The interdepartmental risk management meeting was not sufficiently focused on prisoners' risks and any action set was not always followed up. There was an inadequate escalation process to make sure that prisoners' MAPPA levels were confirmed six months before their release, which meant that some high-risk prisoners could be released without a robust risk management plan.

Recommendation: Public protection procedures should ensure that there is a robust risk management plan in place well in advance of the prisoner's release. (Directed to: the director.)

Key concern: HMP Oakwood was not commissioned to deliver accredited programmes or a programme needs assessment (PNA) for prisoners convicted of a sexual offence. Prisons delivering suitable interventions would not always accept prisoners without a PNA, which prevented them from progressing. The prison's most recent needs assessment showed that 90% of prisoners convicted of a sexual offence with an offender assessment system report, had not completed any intervention or was awaiting an assessment. There was a significant gap in provision for prisoners convicted of a sexual offence.

Recommendation: A strategy should be developed for delivering specific offence-focused work to sex offenders, including improved access to accredited programmes and the provision of alternative opportunities for those assessed as unsuitable. (Directed to: the director.)

## Notable positive practice
We define notable positive practice as innovative work or practice that leads to particularly good outcomes from which other establishments may be able to learn. Inspectors look for evidence of good outcomes for prisoners; original, creative or particularly effective approaches to problem-solving or achieving the desired goal; and how other establishments could learn from or replicate the practice.

Inspectors found eight examples of notable positive practice during this inspection.

The effective use of the wide range of prisoner-led initiatives contributed positively to the living experience of prisoners.

The prison had identified that prisoners might have required support following legal visits and invited prisoners to take part in a post-legal visit debrief to check on their well-being.

Processes were in place to identify on arrival prisoners with hidden disabilities, such as post-traumatic stress disorder, learning difficulties and autism, and to make appropriate referrals, for example, to health care and education departments. A group of 16 men with autism were receiving enhanced peer support. The prison was about to launch its Hidden Disabilities project, which aimed to build on this by introducing formal assessment and wing care planning processes.

The prisoner-led Health Advisory Service offered an innovative and pragmatic information and advice programme, which was well received by prisoners and supported the delivery of health services.

The Beat Diabetes project, involving the health care team and other prison departments, helped improve patients' understanding of diabetes and self-care to support well-being.

End-of-life care had been fully embedded at the prison and was offered to patients with a terminal disease. Those involved could choose to remain in prison and be cared for by staff who knew them.

The prison was using Purple Visits technology for popular evening 'bedtime story visits' enabling fathers to read stories to their children. The family intervention unit on Beech house block provided prisoners wishing to maintain family ties with a supportive environment. It offered parenting and family courses and peer mentors.

## INDEPENDENT MONITORING BOARD: Annual Report

The law requires every prison to be monitored by an independent Board appointed by the Justice Secretary; these are known as Independent Monitoring Boards (IMBs). The IMB must satisfy itself as to the humane and just treatment of those held in custody within its prison and the range and adequacy of the programmes preparing them for release; it must report annually to the Justice Secretary on how well the prison has met the standards and requirements placed on it.

**IMB Report 1 April 2021 – 31 March 2022**
**Published August 2022**
**Executive summary**
**Background to the report**

For a second year, all aspects of life in the prison have been dominated by the Covid-19 pandemic and the rigorous and fluctuating changes imposed on prisons by the government. Strong and exemplary efforts to keep infections out of the prison have continued and the Director, with the support of the SMT and staff, has worked meticulously to manage the constantly changing situation. This was done by restricting the regime, reducing interactions and adapting procedures, especially during the first and last quarter of the reporting year. As a result, the work of the IMB was frequently frustrated by the Covid-related restrictions. However, the Director and SMT have been very supportive in facilitating the Board's endeavours to maintain its monitoring role throughout.

The Board would like to highlight the following:

• The ongoing impact of the lockdown restrictions imposed on prisoners and the potential impact on their health and wellbeing has been to the fore in all aspects of the prison's Covid-19 planning.

• All levels of prison staff have continued to show exemplary commitment in their care for the prisoners, at times to the detriment of their own wellbeing.

• The written communications from the Director to both staff and prisoners at all stages of the lockdown period have been informative and honest throughout.

The impact on the prisoners of a 23-hour lockdown regime with limited exercise and association has been at best difficult and, for some, traumatic. The commitment and care of both prison.

**Main judgements**
**How safe is the prison?**

It is the Board's view that the prison is generally a safe environment for the prisoners.

The safety and wellbeing of prisoners has been under constant review to mitigate the effects of Covid-19. The guidance from HMPPS and Public Health England, in partnership with other health partners, has been scrupulously followed throughout to ensure the safety of prisoners and staff.

The SMT monitor the use of force on a weekly basis to ensure it is being used appropriately.

There is now a regular health and safety committee meeting, which the IMB are invited to observe.

**How fairly and humanely are prisoners treated?**
The Board is of the opinion that prisoners are treated humanely and fairly. The confinements imposed on prisoners have, in general, been sensitively managed. Regular, but timed, exercise has been maintained throughout the Covid-19 lockdown periods.
The video calling service Purple Visits has, in the absence of social visits, continued to take place. Key worker sessions for two priority groups of prisoners have continued under an exceptional delivery model.
Contact with the prisoners has been taking place by in-cell telephone to ensure that, as far as possible, plans are made in relation to their presenting needs.

**How well are prisoners' health and wellbeing needs met?**
The Board is of the view that the health needs of the prison population have been met and are at least equivalent to that offered in the community and sometimes better.
Prisoners were given the opportunity to have Covid-19 vaccinations to mirror the access available in the community.
Vulnerable men were placed in a section of one house block that was modified to ensure they were kept safe from the virus as far as possible.
Prisoners were tested for the virus on arrival at the prison and isolated if necessary.

**How well are prisoners progressed towards successful resettlement?**
As far as possible, prisoners have progressed but not as effectively and efficiently as they were prior to the pandemic.
The circumstances in the community have made the situation worse, as access to suitable accommodation and employment on release has been a challenge owing to the change of provider. The prison's resettlement advice line and prisoner helpdesk (RALPH), a prisoner-led initiative continued to work at a distance; face-to-face work ceased but work continued via use of in-cell telephony and written correspondence.

**Main areas for development 2021/22**
**TO THE MINISTER**
The Board has been concerned during the reporting year that, following the retirement of the Coroner in the Staffordshire area, it has not been informed of impending inquests. This has had a direct impact on the ability of the Board to monitor any recommendations within the prison. Can the Minister ask the Chief Coroner to issue guidance about the importance of notifying the IMB of inquests concerning prisoners as referred to in the IMB reference book guidance in relation to deaths in custody?

It was commented on in the Board's reports for 2018/19, 2019/20 and 2020/21 that the transfer of prisoners' property across the prison estate still remains a concern. The Minister responded in September 2021 saying the framework was due to be published in early 2022. The Board is concerned that after three years this framework has not yet been published.

**TO THE PRISON SERVICE**
The Board is concerned that the change in arrangements for resettlement has created a service that is not of a good quality for prisoners in some areas, in particular the outsourcing of accommodation support. Housing referrals now go to the charity Nacro but there appear to be problems in obtaining accommodation. Nacro, which has taken over from the community rehabilitation company (CRC), is having problems locating accommodation for prisoners (especially high-risk prisoners) and is only achieving a 40-50% success rate in comparison to the 96% recorded by the CRC. It does not deal with prisoners requiring relocation out of the local area.
The Board is concerned about the delays in transferring prisoners to category D open accommodation. We understand there is a shortage of places and this is creating waiting lists across the country. At Oakwood the waiting list for category D at the end of the reporting period was 84.
The Board is concerned about the time it can take for transfers to mental health establishments where the prisoner is deemed to have a severe mental health need. Despite the constraints of the pandemic the Board considers it was problematical during the reporting period, which meant prisoners stayed in the care and separation unit (CSU) longer than was desirable. The Board is concerned that the education service from Novus is not viewed positively by prisoners and the small survey undertaken (see appendix A) demonstrates that communication and access to courses is not as it should be.

**TO THE DIRECTOR**
The Board requests the Director to review the following areas:
• The Board continues to be concerned about prisoners in the servery not wearing the appropriate personal protective equipment (PPE) and clothing. Notwithstanding that Aramark provided continuity of a balanced menu and two cooked meals a day, the Board is still concerned about the quality, quantity and variety of the food provided and the ensuing waste that results, and that the food is not always tested for serving at the correct temperature. There is also

the problem of the time it can take for equipment to be repaired.

• The Board would like to suggest the introduction of a simplified guidance leaflet based on the HMPPS document for prisoners wishing to make a complaint. It would be helpful if this could include information on the request system that the prison currently uses, which is not always understood by prisoners transferring to Oakwood. The Board feels that the prison needs to operate a system that is transparent to prisoners which, at the present time, we feel is not fully understood, particularly in relation to requests/concerns.

• A further concern for the Board is the fact that the letter sent to explain how a request will be dealt with is long and not always clear for prisoners who cannot read easily or whose first language is not English. These multifunctional response letters are not dated and do not have any reference numbers assigned for easy identification in the future. The Board asks that this be reviewed.

• During the reporting year the Board has been concerned that the healthcare complaint boxes were not emptied on a regular basis and their location is not easily accessible to all prisoners at all times. The Board asks the Director to review this with the head of healthcare.

• The Board requests that it is invited to the equality action group meetings.

• Discrimination incident reporting form (DIRF) scrutiny meetings should take place with HMPs Brinsford and Featherstone, but these have not taken place during the reporting year due to Covid-19 restrictions. The Board understands that these meetings are yet to restart and the Board would suggest that arrangements are made for them to start as soon as possible in order to bring some external scrutiny to the process. The Board also requests that it is made aware of when the meetings take place in order that a member can attend and observe the process.

• The independent adjudicator (IA) ceased sitting shortly after the start of the lockdown period and has yet to return to the prison; hearings were held remotely. The Courts Service made a decision to continue to use remote systems, as it is more efficient and makes it easier for solicitors to join the meeting. It would be helpful if the Board could join some of the remote IA adjudications and an agreement and system of notification needs to be put in place.

• The Board is concerned about the number and experience of new staff on the house blocks. From observing some of the case notes of key worker sessions, the quality of the reporting varies. The Board suggests that senior managers

look at putting further training in place.

• The Board asks that the offender management unit (OMU) looks and reviews its communication with prisoners, using all the systems available to help to manage the prisoners' expectations.

• The Board asks that the Director reviews communication in relation to access to education and courses available. The Board also asks that consideration is given for prisoners who share a cell to be given access to a space to undertake coursework.

**Progress since the last report**

The following are responses received following issues identified as areas for development in last year's annual report.

**TO THE MINISTER**

A letter was sent from the Minister dated 15 September 2021, which acknowledged the Board's concern about the slow progress on publishing the new Prisoner Property Policy Framework. The Minister stated the framework was due to be published in early 2022. In addition, the new Prisoner Escort and Custody Services (PECS) contract has undertaken a review of the amount of property a prisoner can have transported from prison to prison.

In response to the Board's concern about support for foreign national prisoners, the Minister stated that face-to-face support will resume when it is safe to do so but support would continue virtually, with an interpreter present if necessary. The prison immigration team are in daily contact with HMP Oakwood and with prisoners when requested – all still virtually.

It was encouraging to receive comments commending HMP Oakwood's management team for their commitment and dedication during a challenging and unprecedented period. The Minister was pleased to hear that good standards of cleanliness were maintained and the reception and induction processes were delivered effectively.

**TO HMPPS**

• Education provision. It has seen a significant improvement at HMP Oakwood since the arrival of the new educational manager in April 2021. The prison is currently satisfied with the quality of teaching and learning, engagement of learners and performance of the provider. The improvement notice issued in response to concerns about the service provided by Novus will remain active.

• Access to medication/medical records. The healthcare provider stated there were no concerns with transfers from HMP Dovegate.

The concern regarding HMP Birmingham has been addressed. NHS England and NHS Improvement will continue to monitor the situation and offer support.
• Late arrivals. The PECS contract delivery manager (CDM) conducts monthly reviews of arrival times and those received very late are raised by the CDM with the contactor as official complaints.
• Contact with family and friends. The connectivity and network issues in relation to secure social video calling (Purple Visits) were resolved and no further issues identified.
• Ligature inflicted incidents. HMPPS apologised for the way in which the reporting of ligatures was communicated to the IMB. HMPPS changed its position on recording of noose making, not ligature incidents. Ligatures are still reported as self-harm incidents. Directors and Governors have been instructed to notify staff that this change does not mean noose making should be treated any less seriously.
• Testing for Covid-19. All testing is voluntary and refusal to test does not prevent a transfer from going ahead. All prisoners arriving at HMP Oakwood are routinely tested for Covid-19 on arrival and on the first and fifth day.
• Offending behaviour programmes. In August 2020 HMPPS interventions services developed an 'alternative delivery format' for the delivery of accredited programmes. As a result, a remote delivery model was developed, although this could not be relied upon in every case, nor with every prisoner and this was considered on a case-by-case basis.

TO THE DIRECTOR
• The condition and numbers of body worn video cameras (BWVC). New BWVC cameras have been ordered and additional staff have been deployed daily to ensure all cameras are functioning and staff draw cameras correctly.
• Informing IMB about planned use of force incidents. An instruction has been sent to the orderly officers by the Deputy Director to ensure the IMB member is alerted to any planned intervention.
• Lack of alternative communication options as well as kiosks on the wings. Oakwood TV has now been established with great success, including Directors/SMT announcements and faith TV, in addition to notices to prisoners, which are displayed on the kiosk and on units. Purple Visits have proved to be a valuable alternative throughout the pandemic for the prisoners to help maintain family contact during restricted regimes. The prison is currently exploring the feasibility of retaining the service as part of its future regime development post-Covid-19.
• Following up on missing property. The process has been reiterated to all managers and the

number of complaints and issues relating to missing property has reduced. A significant number of missing property issues stem from sending prisons.
• PIN numbers to be checked soon after prisoners transfer to the prison. Public Protection manage the process appropriately and within the public protection guidelines.

WILLOUGHBY
RUGBY
WARKS
CV23 8AP

HMP & YOI ONLEY

Tel: 01788 523400

*For the latest reports on this prison please visit:*
https://tinyurl.com/bdfh26rv

*Important Changes:* **(1) Visits:** the identification necessary to access this prison and visit for social or professional purposes has changed; (2) **Money and Gifts** new rules now apply to these. See page 16 for full details of the above.

**Task of the establishment** HMP Onley is a category C training and resettlement prison for men.

**Certified normal accommodation and operational capacity**
Prisoners held at the time of inspection: 738
Baseline certified normal capacity: 742
In-use certified normal capacity: 742
Operational capacity: 742

**Prison status and key providers**
Public
Prison Group: East Midlands
Prison Group Director: Paul Cawkwell
Governor/Director: Matthew Tilt
IMB Chair: Leslie Leeson
Physical health provider: Northamptonshire Healthcare NHS Foundation Trust (NHFT)
Mental health provider: Northamptonshire Healthcare NHS Foundation Trust (NHFT)
Substance use providers: Northamptonshire Healthcare NHS Foundation Trust (NHFT) and Phoenix Futures
Learning and skills provider: Novus
Escort contractor: GeoAmey

**Brief history** Built as a Borstal in 1968, Onley held young offenders until 1998. The juvenile population was replaced by sentenced adults in March 2004. The establishment was re-roled to a full adult category C training establishment in March 2010. From 2013, HMP Onley was designated as a resettlement prison for Greater London. The role of the establishment is to house a proportion of London prisoners approaching the end of their sentence, with a view to accessing community rehabilitation companies to prepare them for release into their home area. Owing to a reconfiguration of establishments in 2017, the prison has moved back into the Midlands cohort, although still largely holds a London population.

### Short description of residential units
A to H wings were the older original wings. A, B, C, D and E wings each provide general accommodation for 60 prisoners.
F wing is the segregation unit, consisting of 15 cells. G wing is the resettlement wing and H wing is the first night and induction unit, both providing accommodation for 60 prisoners.
I wing provides general accommodation, for 100 prisoners.
J wing and K wings each provide general accommodation for 76 prisoners. L wing is the enhanced wing, providing accommodation for 70 prisoners.

### Visiting Information
Book online at: https://www.gov.uk/prison-visits or phone 01788 523402 Monday to Friday, 10am to 12:45pm and 1:15pm to 4pm.
**Visiting times:** Every day except Tues: 2pm to 3:30pm

**Legal visits:** Book on: 01788 523 402 Monday to Friday, 10am to 12:45pm and 1:15pm to 4pm.

**Visiting times:** Monday, Wednesday, Thursday, Friday: 2pm to 3pm.

### INSPECTIONS & REPORTS
**HMIP conducted a short scrutiny visit on 16 June 2020 at HMP Onley and details of which are on** *prisonoracle.com.*
**Date of last HMCIP inspection: 12–23 Nov 2018**
**IRP Report:** 11 – 13 November 2019
**HMCIP Report, published 21 March 2019**
HMP Onley, situated near Rugby in Warwickshire, is a category C training prison holding, at the time of this inspection, around 740 men. It was last inspected in the summer of 2016. Some 80% of the prisoners held there come from the London area. Sixty per cent are from black and minority ethnic backgrounds, and around three-quarters are serving lengthy sentences of four years or more.
At the last inspection we found that the prison was unsafe, and judged the area of safety to be 'poor', our lowest assessment. Making this judgement is not something we do lightly, and is a reflection of the depths of our concerns when we do so. It was particularly disappointing, therefore, to find that at this latest inspection,

two and a half years later, the prison was still fundamentally unsafe, and for the second time attracted our lowest assessment. Inexplicably, of the 18 recommendations we made in 2016 in the area of safety, only five had been achieved. Time and again we find that prisons which are unsafe will struggle to make progress in other areas, and HMP Onley was no exception. On this occasion we found that the prison was offering less respectful detention than at the last inspection, and had failed to make progress in the areas of purposeful activity and resettlement and release planning.
The lack of safety at Onley was all too obvious. From the moment of their arrival, prisoners were exposed to unnecessary risks. Inspectors found that they were placed on an induction wing, in poorly prepared cells, where prisoners who had caused problems elsewhere in the jail were allowed to intimidate and be predatory towards new arrivals. Perhaps it is not surprising that in our survey only 62% of prisoners said they felt safe on the first night. Sadly, their feelings were an all too accurate reflection of what life in Onley would be like during their time there.
As is the case in many prisons, the prevalence of illicit drugs played a major role in causing destabilising factors such as violence, debt, bullying and health emergencies. At Onley we found that nearly a quarter of prisoners were providing positive random drug tests, one in six had acquired a drug habit since entering the jail, and nearly half said it was easy to get hold of drugs. During the previous three months there had been some 200 emergency health calls related to the use of new psychoactive substances (NPS). Despite this, we found that far too little was being done to obstruct the flow of drugs into the jail. The use of intelligence was poor, with some 300 reports waiting to be acted upon.
In light of this, it was almost inevitable that levels of violence would be high – and indeed they were. As a result, more than half of the prisoners told us they had felt unsafe at some time, and a quarter felt unsafe at the time of the inspection. However, there was a lack of analysis of the causes and patterns of violence, and the approach by the prison to it was largely reactive. The prison did not appear to be able to articulate the impact of drugs on the violence. Not only was their approach reactive, it was slow. There were more than 60 outstanding investigations into acts of violence, 42% of adjudications were never dealt with and some 140 referrals to the police were still awaiting a result. Some of these were many months old. The lack of effective challenge to poor behaviour, either informally or through formal processes, inevitably led to a situation where we found that far too many prisoners were self-isolating – refusing to come out of their

cells or to go to education, work and training.

HMP Onley was a clear example of where the failure to deal with drugs and violence undermined many other aspects of prison life. There was a vicious circle where fear, frustration and boredom increased the demand for drugs, which in turn fuelled the violence, and thus completed the circle.

In order for Onley to break out of this circle, there must obviously be more effective action taken to reduce violence and the availability of drugs. But at the same time, more can be done in other areas. Onley is a training prison and yet there were not enough activity places for the population, and during the inspection we found that only 50% of prisoners were engaged in purposeful activity at any one time. In contrast, during our roll checks, conducted during the working day, we found that some 39% of prisoners were locked in their cells. For the past four years the prison had operated a restricted regime, meaning that there was no evening association and no scheduled exercise. The exercise yards were open for an hour, but this was at the same time as prisoners were expected to attend to domestic issues, such as cleaning, and take their meal. It is true that the prison had never really recovered from the chronic staffing shortages brought about a few years ago by the benchmarking exercise, but now that new staff were arriving, freeing up the regime and offering sufficient activity places needed to be a prime objective.

There can also be little doubt that doing more to support family relationships would help prisoners rehabilitate and prepare for their eventual release. Although Onley had been moved administratively from the London to the Midlands group of prisons, 80% of the prisoners still came from London. There were clearly many who felt disorientated by being held so far from home, and who said they rarely received visits from friends or family. Nothing was done to help visitors, either practically or financially, to get to the prison.

While my comments in this introduction might sound highly critical of the lack of progress at Onley, I would not wish to detract from the many good things happening there that were being delivered by dedicated and skilful staff. Health care, education, training, industry and offender management leading to release were all areas where there was some very good provision. Sadly, Onley will fail to fulfil its role as a training and resettlement prison until it can deal with the inextricably linked blights of drugs and violence. This will require a greater attention to Inspectorate recommendations than has been the case in the past, and strong leadership that is focused on clear operational outcomes.

Peter Clarke CVO OBE QPM January 2019
HM Chief Inspector of Prisons

### IRP Report, published 18 December 2019
Chief Inspector's summary

HMP Onley is a category C training prison holding around 740 prisoners. It is situated near Rugby in Warwickshire but some 80% of the prisoners held there come from the London area. About three-quarters are serving lengthy sentences of four years or more.

At our inspection in November 2018, we reported our concerns about safety, where we judged (as we had at a previous inspection in 2016) outcomes for prisoners to be poor, our lowest assessment. Outcomes for prisoners were little better across our other healthy prison tests of respect, purposeful activity and rehabilitation and release planning, all of which we judged to be not sufficiently good. The lack of safety at Onley was all too obvious. From the moment of their arrival, prisoners were exposed to unnecessary risks and intimidation; levels of violence were very high and drugs were easily available. The prison was doing too little to understand the causes of violence or the impact of gang activity on the safety of prisoners. It failed to manage the risks, with an approach that was not only reactive, but slow. Underpinning nearly all our concerns were chronic staff shortages and inexperience, and staff lacked the confidence and skills to challenge poor prisoner behaviour. Prisoners had too little time unlocked and for the previous four years the prison had operated a restricted regime, meaning that there was no evening association and no scheduled exercise. Despite being a training prison, Onley had too few activity places and only half the population was engaged in anything purposeful. The prison was failing to assess prisoners' risks and needs effectively or provide opportunities for progression, despite holding a relatively high-risk, long-term population.

At this independent review of progress (IRP), we followed up 10 recommendations and three Ofsted themes.

We found that the prison's response had been good or reasonably good in half the recommendations that we reviewed and that it had made reasonable progress in one Ofsted theme. Some improvements had been achieved following an increase in staff, but this also compounded some of the challenges of staff inexperience that the prison faced.

In the area of safety, our area of greatest concern, the prison had made mostly good or reasonable progress.

Prisoners were now better supported and informed during their early days at the prison and were better protected from predatory behaviour. The prison was managing its intelligence more effectively and had a much better understanding of the gang affiliations of prisoners in order to manage them more safely. We were concerned about the risks presented by using peer workers to gather valuable and sensitive information about gangs, and this needed to be addressed immediately. The prison had worked extremely hard to address violence. The causes of violence were now well understood and a range of actions had been taken to make the prison safer.

Levels of violence against both staff and prisoners had reduced substantially since our inspection. Disappointingly, there had been no meaningful progress in tackling drug availability. A quarter of prisoners were testing positive for drugs, more than at the 2018 inspection.

Relationships between staff and prisoners had not improved overall. Increased staffing levels meant that staff supervision was often better, but about 60% of officers had less than 12 months' experience and did not have the skills and confidence to challenge poor behaviour or even respond to very basic requests from prisoners. Action to improve the external and communal areas of the prison had been minimal. Communal areas were still grubby, rats were still prevalent and showers were in a very poor state. With the arrival of new staff, a new fuller regime had been introduced, allowing for greater time unlocked, but this regime remained beset by cancellations and was not reliably delivered. This was compounded by a lack of education, work and training places and poor attendance, leaving more than a third of prisoners locked up during the working day, which is particularly unacceptable in a training prison. The prison had made insufficient progress in improving prisoners' access to recognised qualifications and in increasing the proportion of prisoners who achieved qualifications that they had started, both of which remained too low.

No meaningful progress had been made in addressing the OASys backlog or providing prisoners with regular, purposeful contact with their offender supervisor. This meant that many prisoners (most of whom were serving long sentences) struggled to progress. Some reasonable progress had been made in establishing and delivering a suitable range of interventions.

At this IRP, we found that progress was very mixed. It was clear the prison had focused on safety as a main concern and its success in reducing levels of violence should be commended. However, the lack of attention to tackling drugs was inexplicable. The lack of progress in improving education, work and skills

outcomes for prisoners, given that Onley is a training prison, is a concern. There are other considerable challenges ahead. The prison has been running with staff shortages for many years. The impact this has had on staff and prisoners has been immense, and while there have been some improvements, staff shortages continue to blight progress. If Onley is to progress further, it needs support to recruit and retain its new staff, and ensure they are skilled and confident in their role.

November 2019
HM Chief Inspector of Prisons

## INDEPENDENT MONITORING BOARD: Annual Report

The law requires every prison to be monitored by an independent Board appointed by the Justice Secretary; these are known as Independent Monitoring Boards (IMBs). The IMB must satisfy itself as to the humane and just treatment of those held in custody within its prison and the range and adequacy of the programmes preparing them for release; it must report annually to the Justice Secretary on how well the prison has met the standards and requirements placed on it.

**IMB Report 1 March 2021 – 28 February 2022**
**Published July 2022**
**Executive summary**
**Background to the report**

Throughout the reporting period, the prison operated under various pandemic national lockdown regimes. This inevitably had an impact on the Board's ability to monitor effectively and gather relevant information. Monitoring duties and visits continued in person, when safe to do so, but the opportunity to meet with prisoners was restricted.

Evidence for this report comes from applications to the Board, observations made on visits, scrutiny of records and data, attendance at meetings and discussions with staff.

The Board has been impressed with the professionalism of the Governor and senior management team (SMT). We commend them on the speed at which revised and very restricted systems of working were implemented to mitigate the threat of Covid19 to the population. The Board is grateful for the cooperation and assistance of all prison staff.

**Main judgements**
**How safe is the prison?**

There was no change in the overall number of violent incidents in comparison to 2020. This would appear to be a consequence of the restricted regime, reduced time out of cell and prisoner movement. Violence was at its lowest in December when the prison became an outbreak site for Covid-19. There was a small reduction in the number of self-harming individuals between 2020 and 2021.

Despite severe staff shortages – due partly to a high attrition rate, shielding and self-isolation – the prison remained calm. Regular patrol states, the deployment of detached duty, overtime and implementation of the operational stability payment (OSP), enabled the prison to run efficiently and effectively. Funding was approved for eight extra operational support grade (OSG) staff to create a total of 43.

Intelligence-led searches continued to identify illicit items. Rapiscan continued to find mail containing new psychoactive substances (NPS). Drone activity notably increased with the easing of regime restrictions.

Every effort by the Governor and SMT was made to ensure that all staff, visitors and prisoners followed the infection prevention measures of social distancing, mask wearing and hand hygiene. Shortly after moving to stage 1 at the end of October 2021, the prison was designated an outbreak site following a rapid increase in the number of prisoners testing positive for Covid-19. The prison worked closely with the United Kingdom Health Security Agency to manage the outbreak. Mandatory staff testing was introduced. The Board is impressed by the depth of knowledge and understanding held by safer custody about prisoners deemed particularly vulnerable.

**How fairly and humanely are prisoners treated?**
The Board is of the opinion prisoners were treated fairly and humanely. Our observations of the relationship between staff and prisoners were positive. Race continued, however, to be the main reason for prisoners submitting a discrimination incident reporting form (DIRF). The Board is aware that staff training is being rolled out to increase awareness of subtle forms of discrimination.

Prisoner representatives attend the prison council and safety and equality meetings. Their views and opinions are respectfully considered and are recorded in the meeting minutes. The prison Listeners are supported by the mental healthcare team (MHCT) and the Samaritans.

The residential wings were clean and tidy. Prisoners were provided with distraction and education packs, additional TV channels, and materials and resources for different faiths to help them keep occupied. Tutors visited the wings in the latter part of the reporting year.

Property 'lost' in the establishment, in another establishment or during transfer continues to be a major issue. This causes immense distress and

frustration for prisoners. This is compounded by the length of time it takes the Board and staff to investigate and resolve property issues.

**How well are prisoners' health and wellbeing needs met?**
The prison, in collaboration with healthcare, the MHCT, Phoenix Futures, chaplaincy, the Samaritans, education and the gym, has demonstrated a commitment to meeting the health and wellbeing needs of prisoners. A wealth of data is comprehensively collected, collated and analysed to enable the identification of trends and patterns that can support health and wellbeing interventions. Waiting times for dentistry and the optician were significant but progress in reducing these delays and hence the backlog is being made. Specialist care provision and hospital appointments following referral, as a result of the pandemic, are slowly being resolved.

**How well are prisoners progressed towards successful resettlement?**
The Board is concerned about opportunities for prisoners to undertake meaningful work. Whilst the workshops were affected by the restricted regime, the continued shortage of instructors, workshops and workshop places will have an impact on prisoner progression towards successful resettlement.

**Main areas for development**
**TO THE MINISTER**
In last year's annual report, the Board stated that there was a pressing need for increased capacity in category D (open) prisons. This situation still remains and there were a significant number of 'cat D' prisoners at HMP Onley throughout the reporting year.

The shortage of officers and probation staff needs to be addressed. Recruitment and retention of staffing is an ongoing issue at HMP Onley. Can serious consideration be given to adding HMP Onley to the enhanced payment scheme? Quality and dedicated staff are leaving, and there are difficulties in recruiting staff, due to competitive salaries within the local area.

**TO THE PRISON SERVICE**
There needs to be more prompt action in moving non-category C prisoners from HMP Onley. Prisoners who are re-categorised from C to B should be moved within 72 hours but often remain in the segregation unit for a significant period. Those recategorised from C to D are also waiting too long to move to open conditions due to the lack of available accommodation in category D prisons in the London area.

The Board has serious concerns over the lack of

access to programmes. This leads to a prisoner's inability to reduce their risk of reoffending and progress, and significantly impacts on their ability to move to a category D establishment.

The management of prisoner property remains a significant problem. There are often long delays in property being received from the sending prison even after the complaints process has been followed. If more resources were available to investigate missing property, prisoner frustration levels may be reduced.

The Board in previous reports has mentioned the poor state of the windows in the older parts of the prison. Can Her Majesty's Prison and Probation Service (HMPPS) please advise when this essential work will be carried out, as we are of the opinion this has a detrimental effect on decency standards and needs addressing as a priority.

The Board wishes to be advised when the enhanced gate security (EGS) bag scanner will arrive on site and be operational. This essential equipment this has been awaited since September 2021.

This has been a particularly difficult year for the recruitment and retention of staff and the Board would ask that HMP Onley be added to the list of establishments given a market supplement to help attract and retain staff.

**TO THE GOVERNOR**

The Board is of the opinion there would be considerable benefit in finding a way to integrate the reporting of complaints to healthcare with general prison complaints providing confidentiality is maintained. This would provide a more comprehensive overview of prisoner concerns across the establishment.

It is vital that the purpose of HMP Onley, as a training and resettlement prison, retains priority. More workshops and instructors need to become involved with the prison to support successful resettlement.

**Progress since the last report**

The Board would like to congratulate the Governor for his leadership during the pandemic and the way in which the staff have worked throughout the past year during such difficult and uncertain times.

The Board recognises that significant efforts have been made at HMP Onley to provide prisoners with as much time out of cell as possible whilst maintaining infection control protocols. They have ensured there was adequate provision for phone calls and video calls to maintain family contacts when social visits were suspended. Prisoners and families were provided with weekly updates. The impact of these actions has helped to minimise the effect on prisoners. Enhanced security measures,

implemented to reduce the number of illicit items entering the prison, are a welcome development since the last report. All staff and visitors are now searched on entry to the prison. The X-ray baggage equipment is expected to arrive during 2022. The issuing to all staff of standardised bags is a further enhanced security measure.

A green code has been implemented to alert staff to a drone flying in the vicinity of the prison. Additional fencing has been erected inside sections of perimeter fencing to deter prisoners from collecting throw overs.

Razor blades are no longer allowed in the prison and cannot be purchased from the canteen. Not only is this an additional security measure but it aims to eliminate one method of self-harm.

Cell bell response times on each wing are now constantly monitored, recorded and audited.

Telephones are being installed in all cells.

Telephone referrals to the MHCT from officers are no longer accepted. All referrals are now via paper application.

A recovery unit has been setup on J wing for prisoners undergoing drug treatment who want to rehabilitate. An incentivised substance free living unit is being embedded on K wing.

Part-time officer training is to commence during May 2022. This will complement the prison officer entry level training (POELTS) training programme (national vocational qualification (NVQ) and apprenticeship routes) that are firmly embedded.

**HEOL HOPCYN JOHN BRIDGEND CF35 6AP**

**PARC PRISON** Tel: 01656 300200

*For the latest reports on this prison please visit:*
https://tinyurl.com/bdfh26rv

*Important Changes:* **(1) Visits:** the identification necessary to access this prison and visit for social or professional purposes has changed; (2) **Money and Gifts** new rules now apply to these. See page 16 for full details of the above.

**CHILDREN'S UNIT**

**Task of the establishment** To hold sentenced and remanded children aged 15 to 17 years.

**Certified normal accommodation and operational capacity**

Children held at the time of inspection: 20
Baseline certified normal capacity: 64
In-use certified normal capacity: 60
Operational capacity: 60

## Population of the establishment
During the year March 2021 to February 2022:
• 59 children received, an average of five children a month
• One foreign national child at the time of the inspection
• Average of 53% of children from black and minority ethnic backgrounds
• An average of 17% of children on remand
• 46 children released into the community
• An average of 43% of children in the care of their local authority before custody

## Prison status and key providers
Private: G4S
Prison group: Wales
Prison Group Director: Giles Mason
Director: Janet Wallsgrove OBE
IMB chair: Kelvin Hughes
Physical health provider: G4S Health Services UK
Mental health provider:
Primary G4S Health Services UK
Substance misuse treatment provider: G4S
Prison education framework provider: G4S
Escort contractor: GeoAmey

**Brief history** The children's unit in HMP & YOI Parc opened in March 2002 as a 28-cell facility for remanded children aged 15 to 18. In October 2004, it expanded to house 36 children aged 15 to18, both remand and sentenced, with a further expansion in February 2007 to 64 children. Initially the unit housed Welsh children but since March 2013 the court catchment area has covered Wales and South-west England.

## Short description of residential units
The children's unit consists of two accommodation units with single and double occupancy cells. Echo One is a 24-bed unit split over two levels and Golf One has a capacity of 36 on one level. Both units have showers and communal spaces.

## Visiting Information
Prisoners are responsible for booking their own visits. Once a visit has been approved it is up the individual prisoner to inform his family and friends of the date and time of the visit.
**Visiting times:**
*MAIN HOUSE BLOCKS*
Monday - Thursday: 14:15 - 16:15, 17:45 - 18:45
Friday Saturday and Sunday: 09:00 - 10:00, 10:45 - 11:45, 14:00 - 16:00
*COED UNIT*
Monday - Thursday: 17:45 - 18:45
Wednesday, Thursday: 14:15 - 16:15, 17:45 - 18:45
Friday Saturday and Sunday: 09:00 - 10:00, 10:45 - 11:45, 14:00 - 16:00

*YP's*
Monday - Thursday: 17:45 - 18:45
Friday: 14:00 - 16:00
Saturday and Sunday: 09:00 - 10:00, 10:45 - 11:45, 14:00 - 16:00

**Legal visits:** Email: parclegalvisits@uk.g4s.com
**Visiting times:**
*MAIN HOUSE BLOCKS* Monday - Frida: 09:15 - 10:15, 10:45 - 11:45, 14:15 - 15:15, 15:45 - 16:45
*COED UNIT* Monday and Tuesday: 09:15 - 10:15, 10:45 - 11:45, 14:15 - 15:15, 15:45 - 16:45.
Evening Sessions (Monday to Thursday only): 17:45 - 18:45
*YP's* Monday - Friday: 09:15 - 10:15, 10:45 - 11:45, 14:15 - 15:15, 15:45 - 16:45

## INSPECTIONS & REPORTS
### HMCIP Report 28 March – 8 April 2022
### Published 20 July 2022
HMYOI Parc is a facility for up to 60 young people located within Parc prison near Bridgend in South Wales, though managed as a separate entity. Operated under contract by the private company G4S, this inspection has again shown the facility to be arguably the best performing young offender institution in the country. Against all four of our healthy prison tests, we judged outcomes to be good, our highest assessment.
Underpinning Parc's success were the excellent relationships between young people and the staff who cared for them. The culture was one of engagement, high expectations and incentivisation of good behaviour. Staff modelled high standards of behaviour themselves and were prepared to tackle delinquency among young people when they saw it. In our survey, no children reported feeling unsafe and against almost every safety measure we look at, such as the amount of violence or the application of force, levels were lower than at comparable institutions. Time out of cell was much better than we see elsewhere, with children unlocked for between eight and 11 hours a day during the week and for over four hours at weekends. Our colleagues from Estyn similarly reported very positively about both the quality of education on offer and crucially, the access young people had to this education. To the great credit of leaders and managers, this standard of regime had, following the application of sensible risk management arrangements, been sustained throughout most of the pandemic.
The institution had also prioritised the promotion of family ties, a factor of great importance to childrens' well-being and successful rehabilitation and resettlement. All but one young person held at Parc was more than 50 miles from home and yet there was a range of initiatives,

including evening and weekend visits, that encouraged family contact and sat alongside other impressive work to support sentence management and resettlement planning.

Parc YOI was a very well led institution. Managers were visible, morale was high, and the overwhelming majority of staff supported the establishment's priorities, including its commitment to the young people held. The one caveat was that, in keeping with other YOIs, the number of children held at the time of our inspection was fairly low, and with a higher roll it is likely that the maintenance of these high standards will be tested. Notwithstanding, on its current performance Parc is setting a standard for the management of children and young people in custody. The director and her staff are to be congratulated on their achievements.

Charlie Taylor HM Chief Inspector of Prisons May 2022

**Safety**

At the last inspection of HMYOI Parc in 2019, we found that outcomes for children were reasonably good against this healthy establishment test.

At this inspection we found that outcomes for children were now good.

Newly arrived children were met at reception by staff who carried out effective safety interviews. Ninety per cent of children told us they felt safe on their first night at Parc. The induction programme was good and new admissions received four to five hours out of their cells each day.

In our survey, no children said that they felt unsafe at the time of the inspection and children confirmed this in private interviews with inspectors. The positive culture in the staff group, high expectations of children, very good relationships and effective multidisciplinary working supported the safeguarding of children. Child protection and safeguarding referrals were managed well and referred appropriately for external investigation, but there had been delays in final outcomes being notified to the prison and children.

Care for children at risk of self-harm was good and appropriately focused on providing education, engagement with staff and, where appropriate, support from family members and youth offending team workers.

Staff modelled high standards of behaviour and supported children to behave well. We observed only good behaviour in all areas of life at Parc. Levels of violence were lower than at the last inspection and good attempts were made to understand and resolve conflicts between children. Children described staff stepping in quickly when violence started and mediation taking place after fights. However, the ongoing conflict between children on the two residential units was detrimental to the overall ethos and children interviewed during the inspection could not explain why there were issues between the two units. Leaders made good use of data to inform their understanding of bullying and violence.

The incentives scheme was used well to encourage participation in educational and recreational activities and community living. Most low-level poor behaviour was challenged effectively by staff and formal adjudication processes were used for more serious rule breaches.

Levels of force had reduced since the last inspection and most of the force used was relatively low level. Oversight of use of force was generally good.

Few children were separated for reasons of good order or discipline and, where possible, the impact of separation was mitigated by a bespoke daily regime which mirrored that of other children at Parc. Children separated on the intensive support unit (ISU) experienced a far more limited regime, but this facility was rarely used. We were concerned that a child who was assessed as needing a tier four mental health bed had been placed at Parc and lived on the ISU for 14 days in 2021 before a move to hospital was arranged.

**Care**

At the last inspection of HMYOI Parc in 2019, we found that outcomes for children were good against this healthy establishment test.

At this inspection we found that outcomes for children remained good.

Relationships between staff and children were good. Children we spoke to were positive about their relationships with staff and responded very well to the nurturing and caring ethos of the unit. There had been significant investment in the custody support plan (CuSP) and both officers and children found the scheme beneficial.

Communal areas were clean, and equipment was in good condition and well maintained. Cells were in good order and with encouragement from staff, children kept them clean and tidy. However, the windows were in poor condition. Access to showers, laundry facilities and property was good. There had been 12 complaints in the last six months, all of which had been investigated well, and responses to the child were respectful. Consultation with children was not responsive.

The food had improved since the last inspection. The quantity of food was good, and a hot option was available at lunch and the evening meal. Children had plenty of opportunities to cook for themselves. Children were able to eat every meal in the communal areas and engage with peers and staff. Lunch and the evening meal were served by senior managers, giving them time to engage with the children.

At the time of the inspection, there was no equality and diversity lead to take responsibility for this area, but some interesting initiatives had been developed to address this gap. Equality and diversity training for staff was well attended and the positive relationships that staff had with children mitigated the gap in provision. Good data were being gathered, but analysis and action planning were limited. There had been two complaints about discrimination in the last six months, both of which had been dealt with well. There was very limited oversight and governance of the children's unit by senior health care managers. We raised this with managers during the inspection and they responded appropriately. The two highly motivated staff nurses provided skilled clinical care to the children, with whom they had good relationships. Access to primary and secondary care services was good. After a prolonged absence, Forensic Adolescent Consultation and Treatment Service (FACTS) had returned on site in February 2022 having delivered services virtually during much of the pandemic. FACTS staff did not have consistent access to SystmOne and clinical records were not completed in a timely manner. Access to pain relief at the weekend and overnight was sometimes subject to delay.

**Purposeful activity**

At the last inspection of HMYOI Parc in 2019, we found that outcomes for children were good against this healthy establishment test.

At this inspection we found that outcomes for children remained good.

Time out of cell was much better than at other YOIs. Most children were out of their cell for between eight and 11 hours a day during the week and four to six hours a day at the weekend. Children attended education together on weekday mornings and afternoons, ate together and participated in enrichment activities such as chess, pool and football tournaments.

Children had access to a well-stocked library, and the librarian visited once a week to speak to each child. Most children visited the gym every day and four PE officers provided access to a wide range of qualifications and activities.

Nearly all children developed skills and knowledge in classes which improved their employability and enabled them to gain a good range of qualifications. They made good progress in improving their literacy and numeracy skills, often from a very low start. Learners with additional learning needs and those from minority ethnic groups performed well when compared to the unit's learners as a whole. Attendance, punctuality and behaviour in class were excellent.

Teachers were respectful to children and acted as good role models in the way they spoke and engaged with them. Staff had high aspirations for the children and nearly all children behaved respectfully. The curriculum offered a broad range of subjects and activities on release.

Teachers understood learners' needs well and worked effectively as a team with additional learning needs specialists to provide strong, individualised support to children. Teachers used a good range of teaching skills to engage, support and assess learners.

All children were assessed promptly on arrival to determine literacy and numeracy levels and identify learning needs accurately. Teachers carried out further useful diagnostic reviews to make sure that the targeted support met learners' needs.

Communication within the education team and with senior managers was highly effective in developing tailored programmes to meet children's needs. A newly developed management information system had strengthened the monitoring of performance. Leaders took appropriate account of labour market information in reviewing and planning development of the provision.

**Resettlement**

At the last inspection of HMYOI Parc in 2019, we found that outcomes for children were reasonably good against this healthy establishment test. At this inspection we found that outcomes for children were now good.

All but one child at Parc was more than 50 miles from home. Managers had prioritised impressive access to phone calls, secure video calls and visits, especially at evenings and weekends. As a consequence, children at Parc were better able to maintain relationships with family and friends than those at other YOIs. There was good support for new fathers and a programme of regular family events was planned.

Strategic management of resettlement was improving. The recent needs analysis was useful but had not yet been used to inform the reducing reoffending strategy and action plan. Planning for the increasing number of children who required transition to adult prisons was reasonable. Home detention curfew, early release and release on temporary licence (ROTL) were managed effectively. Work to support the increasing number of children with long-term sentences remained underdeveloped.

Needs, engagement and well-being team caseworkers (NEWTs) had regular and meaningful contact with children. Evidence of their work on the Youth Justice Application Framework (YJAF) was very good. There was effective and frequent communication between NEWTs, youth offending teams, probation, social workers and parents. Sentence and remand plans were reviewed regularly. Review meetings were of a good quality and often included families. Children made good progress against their sentence plans, especially in education. Leaders had plans to increase the small number of interventions.

Information sharing for the increasing number of children who were subject to multi-agency public protection arrangements (MAPPA) was effective. Most children had social services involvement in their care. The social worker post had been vacant for an extended period, during which NEWTs had done their best to challenge local authorities effectively to make sure that looked-after children received their entitlements.

Most children had their address confirmed before their release meeting, but a few late confirmations continued to affect negatively children's plans for education and health support. Outcomes in education, training and employment for children on release were reasonably good and better than we see at other YOIs.

### Key concerns and recommendations

Key concerns and recommendations identify the issues of most importance to improving outcomes for children and are designed to help establishments prioritise and address the most significant weaknesses in the treatment and conditions of children.

During this inspection we identified some areas of key concern and have made a small number of recommendations for the establishment to address those concerns.

Key concern: The unit had not had a dedicated social worker for an extended period. This had reduced the support and advocacy available to the increasingly large proportion of children who were in the care of their local authority or who had some involvement with social services. Managers responsible for safeguarding and child protection did not have a source of expertise to refer to on site. Key recommendation: The unit should have a dedicated, on-site social worker. (To the Youth Custody Service)

Key concern: A very unwell child assessed as needing a tier four mental health bed had been placed at Parc and segregated for 14 days in 2021 before a move to hospital was arranged. Key recommendation: Children who need a hospital placement should not be sent to prison as a place of safety. (To the Ministry of Justice)

Key concern: There was no oversight or responsibility for equality and diversity work at Parc and analysis of data remained limited. Children we spoke to felt supported by staff and their needs were being met, but gaps in provision could cause risks.

Key recommendation: Leaders should provide effective oversight of equality and diversity work at all times and data should be scrutinised thoroughly to ensure unequal treatment is identified and addressed. (To the director) 1

Key concern: Support for the increasing number of children with indeterminate or long-term sentences was underdeveloped and limited compared to other YOIs. More children than at the previous inspection were held on remand or were serving sentences for murder or attempted murder.

Key recommendation: There should be an appropriate range of support to meet the risks and needs of children serving indeterminate or long sentences. (To the director)

### Notable positive practice

We define notable positive practice as innovative work or practice that leads to particularly good outcomes from which other establishments may be able to learn. Inspectors look for evidence of good outcomes for children; original, creative or particularly effective approaches to problem-solving or achieving the desired goal; and how other establishments could learn from or replicate the practice.

Inspectors found 12 examples of notable positive practice during this inspection.

Leaders and staff made sure that children spent most of their time out of their cells, engaged in education, physical exercise or other purposeful activity. The time out of cell and plentiful opportunities to engage with staff prevented boredom and frustration, leading to better outcomes for children in safety and care.

Managers had created a positive culture which helped children to feel safe. They knew that staff expected high standards of behaviour from everyone and staff would intervene quickly in incidents and take steps to resolve conflicts.

The effective delivery of the custody support plan scheme had already seen positive outcomes for children. Regular meaningful work was being done with the children to meet their individual needs.

Positive staff encouragement made sure that children took responsibility for their cells and were able to live in a clean and tidy environment. Senior managers served lunch and evening meals which gave them time for effective interaction with the children.

The offer of a 'well man' check to every child with a sentence of more than four years was a positive initiative to help children develop skills and care for their own health and well-being.

Every child was referred to the optician for an assessment of their vision to determine the need for further treatment or glasses.

All children were referred to the dentist following reception screening for a dental assessment.

Most learners arrived with poor levels of literacy and numeracy. Their basic skills were assessed promptly and teachers undertook further assessments to clarify children's needs. They used this information well to help children develop their skills. Nearly all children improved their literacy and numeracy skills by at least one level while in education and many by two levels. Nearly all staff had a very good understanding of learners' progress and emerging needs in education. They updated children's learning plans regularly and shared information to determine how best to meet each learner's needs. This resulted in well-tailored provision which enabled each child to make the best possible progress.

Leaders had given priority to ensuring that children could successfully maintain relationships with family and friends. They had provided impressive access to phone calls and daily access to secure video calls and social visits. Outcomes in education, training and employment for children on release were reasonably good and better than we see at other YOIs. On release from custody, 19 children had had a placement in education, training or employment, including apprenticeships, college and, in some instances, a return to full-time education.

## MAIN PRISON

Important Changes: **(1) Visits:** the identification necessary to access this prison and visit for social or professional purposes has changed; (2) **Money and Gifts** new rules now apply to these. See page 16 for full details of the above.

**Task of the establishment** HMP Parc is a category B local prison holding convicted male adult and young offenders, convicted and remand sex offenders, and young people.

**Certified normal accommodation and operational capacity**
Prisoners held at the time of inspection. 1,612
Baseline certified normal capacity: 1,559
In-use certified normal capacity: 1,559
Operational capacity: 1,699

**Prison status and key providers**
Private – managed by: G4S
Prison Group: Wales, contracted
Prison Group Director: Giles Mason
Governor/Director: Janet Wallsgrove OBE
IMB Chair: Brian Thomas
Physical health provider: G4S Health
Mental health provider: G4S Health
Substance misuse provider: G4S Health
Learning and skills provider: G4S Education
Escort contractor: GeoAmey

**Brief history** Located in Bridgend, South Wales, HMP/YOI Parc was the first prison to be built in the UK under the private finance initiative (PFI), and opened in November 1997. G4S Care and Justice Ltd has a 25- year operating contract to manage the prison on behalf of Her Majesty's Prison and Probation Service which runs until 2022. Parc holds a complex mix of residents, including young people aged 15–17 years, young adults, life-sentenced prisoners and those who have committed sexual offences, making it one of the largest prisons in the UK.

**Short description of residential units**
A2 is the induction/early days in custody unit for main residential prisoners.
A4 (Dewis unit) provides a follow-on unit from induction.
Cynnwys unit provides assisted living conditions for prisoners who have learning difficulties or disabilities, autism spectrum disorder and/or brain injury.
B3 is the young adults unit, where there is a focus on promoting positive and respectful behaviour among younger prisoners.
D unit is the substance misuse support unit, tailored specifically for individuals experiencing dependent and/or problematic substance use.
T1 is the first time in custody/college unit, providing focused access to education in a learning environment.
T3 is the first time in custody and military veterans unit.
T4 is the families and significant others unit.
T5 (Taith unit) provides support to offenders on the thinking skills programme and Resolve accredited interventions.
Coed unit houses vulnerable prisoners – both convicted and on remand.
X1 is the induction/early days in custody unit for vulnerable prisoners.
X3 and T6 are assisted living units for prisoners who are older or clinically vulnerable.

**Visiting Information**
Prisoners are responsible for booking their own visits. Once a visit has been approved it is up the individual prisoner to inform his family and friends of the date and time of the visit.
**Visiting times:**
*MAIN HOUSE BLOCKS*
Monday - Thursday: 14:15 - 16:15, 17:45 - 18:45
Friday Saturday and Sunday: 09:00 - 10:00, 10:45 - 11:45, 14:00 - 16:00
*COED UNIT*
Monday - Thursday: 17:45 - 18:45
Wednesday, Thursday: 14:15 - 16:15, 17:45 - 18:45
Friday Saturday and Sunday: 09:00 - 10:00, 10:45 - 11:45, 14:00 - 16:00

YP's
Monday - Thursday: 17:45 - 18:45
Friday: 14:00 - 16:00
Saturday and Sunday: 09:00 - 10:00, 10:45 - 11:45, 14:00 - 16:00

**Legal visits:** Email: parclegalvisits@uk.g4s.com
**Visiting times:**
MAIN HOUSE BLOCKS Monday - Frida: 09:15 - 10:15, 10:45 - 11:45, 14:15 - 15:15, 15:45 - 16:45
COED UNIT Monday and Tuesday: 09:15 - 10:15, 10:45 - 11:45, 14:15 - 15:15, 15:45 - 16:45.
Evening Sessions (Monday to Thursday only): 17:45 - 18:45
YP's Monday - Friday: 09:15 - 10:15, 10:45 - 11:45, 14:15 - 15:15, 15:45 - 16:45

### INSPECTIONS & REPORTS
**Main Prison**
**Date of last inspection: 11–22 November 2019**
**HMCIP Report, published 17 March 2020**

HMP Parc is a category B local men's prison holding convicted adult and young adult offenders, as well as a considerable number of prisoners convicted of sexual offences. It is a very large and complex prison, with over 1,600 prisoners at the time of this inspection. Opened in 1997, it is situated near Bridgend in South Wales and is operated under contract by G4S Care and Justice Ltd.

The prison was last inspected in January 2016, on which occasion our judgement was that safety at Parc was not sufficiently good, respect was reasonably good and the remaining tests of purposeful activity and rehabilitation and release planning were both at our highest level, good. On this occasion the judgements were broadly similar, except that we now found safety to have improved to reasonably good. These are impressive findings for this kind of prison, particularly given the challenging environment in which so many prisons have been operating over the past few years.

The improved grade in safety was a significant achievement in the current context across the custodial estate. Parc had managed to buck the trend in terms of the overall and very large increases in violence that have been recorded. We were particularly impressed by the oversight of the use of force by staff. There was a robust review process, significant managerial input and a clear determination to learn from incidents and share that learning with staff. We have recognised the whole approach to this issue as good practice, and would recommend the approach taken at Parc to others who might wish to learn from it.

As well as the decline in levels of violence over the previous two years, it was pleasing to see that there had been a recent decline in the levels of self-harm, although they were much higher than at the time of the last inspection. Nevertheless, there were some good initiatives, such as the care and support offered to prisoners on their first night in custody, and the safer custody team was working hard to derive the maximum benefit from challenge, support and intervention plans (CSIPs). It was also of note that positive rates in drug tests had declined in the past year, and measures had been introduced which may have contributed to this. While it was true that drugs were still too readily available, positive action was being taken to address the problem. Overall, we took the view that the work that had been done across various areas to improve safety – probably reflected in the early signs of improvement in several areas – was sufficient to improve our rating to 'reasonably good'.

In our survey, over half the prisoners at Parc told us that they had a problem with their mental health. However, only 23% said that they had received help to address their issues, which was a lower figure than at comparable prisons. The demand was not properly quantified in a health needs assessment and, possibly because of this, while support was available for some needs, there were inadequate interventions and support for others. One of our key concerns arising from this inspection was that this weakness should be addressed, with a full range of therapeutic interventions to be made available for all psychiatric conditions.

A very positive feature of Parc was the quality of the relationships between staff and prisoners: 73% of prisoners told us that they were treated with respect by staff, and the key worker scheme appeared to be working well. While it was certainly the case that the prison was generally clean and well maintained, and there was reasonably good access to facilities such as laundry and showers, there was room for improvement in the area of food. In our survey, a mere 28% of prisoners said that the food was good, and less than a third told us that they always or on most occasions had enough to eat. It was good to see a prison where all meals were taken communally, but these very poor perceptions of the food, which were reinforced by our own observations, do need to be addressed. We have explained our concerns and made recommendations to address them, and I shall only make specific mention of a few of them in this introduction as they are clearly set out in the relevant sections of the report. It is important to note that 17% of the prisoners held at Parc had been convicted of sexual offences, but intervention provision was woefully inadequate. It was certainly the case that some prisoners were transferred to other prisons to receive appropriate interventions, but given the size of the sex offender population at Parc, there should have been provision within the establishment itself. As an inspectorate, we frequently highlight how important it is that prisoners are released to settled accommodation to begin their life back in the community. The lack of appropriate, or as we see far too often, any accommodation at all, is widely recognised as a major factor that can contribute to reoffending. At Parc, some 100 prisoners were released on average each month, and 17% of them did not have an address to go to. We saw a great deal of effort going into rehabilitation and release planning at Parc, and indeed our overall judgement in this area was that the outcomes for prisoners warranted our highest grading. However, there is a serious risk that much of this good work could be undermined by prisoners not having appropriate accommodation on their release. We have therefore made a recommendation directly to Her Majesty's Prison and Probation Service (HMPPS) that it should work with the Welsh Government to ensure that accommodation is available for prisoners on release.

Although there is a body of opinion that large prisons are inferior to smaller establishments, Parc shows that this need not be the case. In fact, I gained a clear impression of how Parc has avoided being inflexible or monolithic in its service provision, and has, in fact, used its size and breadth of resources to provide a range of services to different groups that simply could not be made available in smaller establishments. For instance, there were bespoke services for prisoners with learning disabilities or autism. There was an excellent unit focusing on veterans, and young adults had specialist provision, as did vulnerable prisoners and those with assisted living needs. Parc has, of course, also retained its international reputation for the work carried out with children and families. The result is that it does not feel like a huge establishment for the prisoners held there, and it certainly did not merit the pejorative description of a 'warehouse' that is sometimes aimed at large establishments. Parc has benefitted from consistency of leadership over many years, and it was clear during my meetings with the governor, senior management and staff at Parc that they were rightly proud of what has been achieved. Of course, as with every prison, there was room for improvement, some of it urgent and in key areas, but overall this was a prison that, as we considered it, was fulfilling its core purposes and performing well.

Peter Clarke CVO OBE QPM
HM Chief Inspector of Prisons February 2020

## INDEPENDENT MONITORING BOARD: Annual Report

The law requires every prison to be monitored by an independent Board appointed by the Justice Secretary; these are known as Independent Monitoring Boards (IMBs). The IMB must satisfy itself as to the humane and just treatment of those held in custody within its prison and the range and adequacy of the programmes preparing them for release; it must report annually to the Justice Secretary on how well the prison has met the standards and requirements placed on it.

**IMB Report 1 March 2020 to 28 February 2021**
**Published December 2021**
**Main Judgements**
**Executive summary**
**Background to the report**

The Covid-19 pandemic was active throughout the period of this report, and the Board agreed to discontinue visits immediately when the first lockdown was announced; throughout the period of this report, there were no physical visits. Almost immediately, three members resigned, with a further one transferring to another prison and another member resigning during the reporting period. This resulted in an almost complete lack of direct contact with prisoners, with only two members remote monitoring.

Both the Director and Deputy Director of the prison continued to make themselves available to the Chair and relevant contact information was provided to ensure that those remaining members could contact the appropriate staff, who were supportive in providing the required information to support remote monitoring.

During the outbreak, there were significant pressures due to staff shortages and it is important to recognise the outstanding effort and contribution that staff made throughout the period of this report.

While conditions where prisoners were locked away for up to 23 hours per day could be described as inhumane, credit must be given to management and staff for the procedures and good practices adopted that ensured that no lives, either prisoner or staff, were lost due to Covid-19 during this period. Credit must also be given to prisoners for the way they responded through an extremely difficult and challenging period.

Our observations are based solely on remote monitoring, discussions between the Board Chair and the Director/Deputy Director, and discussions between Board members and members of staff to gather information and evidence to construct this report. The Board also had access to prison data and minutes from meetings and attended review boards via video link and telephone.

## Main judgements
### How safe is the prison?

While the significant changes to the regime may be considered as a contributor to improved safety (in relation to preventing the spread of infection), it is the judgement of the Board that during the period of this report staff have worked effectively to make the prison a safe place for prisoners.

Across the prison, there were reductions in the numbers of assaults, serious assaults, proven assaults, uses of force, adjudications, reportable incidents and fights.

As stated, the period of this report mirrored the Covid-19 pandemic and it is considered that the initial and continued actions of senior management and staff in implementing appropriate protocols was recognised by prisoners as being both necessary and appropriate.

It is a concern of the Board that despite prisoners being kept in their cells for up to 23 hours per day, and the limited social visits, drugs continued to enter the prison.

### How fairly and humanely are prisoners treated?

As stated, the period of this report overlapped the Covid-19 pandemic, and throughout the period of this report the prison was subject to restrictions imposed by HMPPS, with prisoners locked in their cells for up to 23 hours per day, imposing a psychological impact which cannot go unrecognised.

It is considered that the government decision not to prioritise prisoner and operational staff vaccinations lengthened what has been described as an inhumane regime, which a prisoner questionnaire identified as a contributor to increased and sustained cases of mental health problems.

The Board recognises that the Director and the senior management team (SMT) commenced planning immediately the pandemic broke out, putting procedures in place to protect the prison population. The challenges of a regime confining prisoners to their cells for around 23 hours per day were evident and actions were taken quite early to mitigate the impact as much as possible. As part of the response to Covid-19, it was identified at an early stage that existing peer support and red-band (trusted prisoner) residents had the potential to establish the concerns of prisoners and to support the delivery of essential services.

### How well are prisoners' health and wellbeing needs met?

At the outset of this period, healthcare staff reviewed all their waiting lists. Throughout the pandemic, the GP operated telephone consultations, and those with urgent needs were seen face to face, with a GP on-site daily. Healthcare staff operated a telephone triage service which was inhibited due to an insufficient number of telephones. The wait list to see the GP was 5–7 days, which is seen as favourable compared to the community equivalent, which is up to10 days. The dentist was unable to see prisoners during the pandemic, which created excessive wait lists. The wait list for the optician and podiatrist became excessive as neither came on-site during the pandemic.

Support for those with mental health issues suffered due to the withdrawal of secondary care from the local health board.

Prisoners also received £5 per week telephone credit and 'goody packs' twice a week, in addition to any pay received.

Purple visits, which used video technology, started in September 2020, and the data about these visits was extracted weekly, in line with HMPPS reporting requirements. There were 48 30-minute sessions per day available as a maximum, with video terminals located on X block (x2) T4, T3, T2, Legals, and the visits lounge.

Prisoners were provided with distraction packs including things like crosswords, word searches, sudoku etc., during the Covid-19 regime when they were locked in their cells for up to 23 hours a day.

### How well are prisoners progressed towards successful resettlement?

As the St Giles Trust resettlement team was not on-site during lockdown, two prison offender managers (POMs) covered this resettlement work for four months, in addition to their own workload, processing housing referrals, and requests for benefits and bank accounts, and ensuring that all public protection work was completed prior to release. For the case administration/custody element of the department, business continued very much as usual, with the transactional work relating to sentence calculations, pre-release checks, home detention curfew (HDC) and parole continuing to be delivered. There was a significant increase in the use of video-link facilities by the courts and other professionals requesting this service, which was managed proficiently by the team.

### Main areas for development
### TO THE MINISTER

Should there be further need for vaccinations for any form of Covid-19 or any other such pandemic, operational staff within the Prison Service should be treated as a priority group in order to protect the integrity of the service.

## TO WELSH GOVERNMENT

Should there be further need for vaccinations for Covid-19 or any other such pandemic, operational staff within the Prison Service should be treated as a priority group in order to protect the integrity of the service. There was, at one stage, capacity within Cwm Taf Local Health Board to support vaccinations, but this was withdrawn by Public Health Wales (PHW).

The supply of vaccines to protect prisoners should be continuous, without gaps in supply from PHW, which made the risk of transmission greater in a prison environment.

## TO THE PRISON SERVICE

Procedures should be in place, during any form of pandemic, whereby prisoners transferring are tested and, where found to be positive, isolated prior to a transfer to another establishment taking place. This should be a mandatory action and not left to individual prisons to make a decision.

It was identified that a proportion of prisoners were positive about the Purple Visits service, and it is hoped that this will continue to be fully funded, with improved software to avoid random disconnections in the service.

HM Inspectorate of Prisons made a recommendation: 'Prisoners who are convicted of sexual offences should be able to access relevant offending behaviour interventions without the need to transfer to another prison'; will HMPPS provide comprehensive and adequate programmes for these individuals?

## TO THE DIRECTOR

While nursing staff attend reviews, they are often late, and sometimes unprepared in relation to the healthcare needs of the prisoner, and this means that the review is not always as robust as it should be.

There are continuing problems with prisoners not wearing the correct clothing in the serveries, and the cleanliness of equipment. What can be done to ensure consistent compliance with the Director's directives governing the availability and wearing of appropriate clothing?

There were issues surrounding the ability of healthcare staff to provide an appropriate service to prisoners as a consequence of there being insufficient telephones available. Any issue of this nature should be treated as an absolute priority.

The effectiveness of individual case reviews can be limited by poor attendance, with examples being where staff do not respond to an invitation or, having responded, fail to attend. The frustration to staff in the safer custody unit is apparent, with occasions where an individual 's

needs cannot be progressed. This is an issue that should be monitored.

### Progress since the last report

The Board at Parc did not produce a report for the year 2019/20, and the previous one was based on a different format; therefore no comparison can be made to the last report.

**CALEDONIAN ROAD
LONDON
N7 8TT**

## HM PRISON PENTONVILLE   **Tel: 020 7023 7000**

*For the latest reports on this prison please visit:*
https://tinyurl.com/bdfh26rv

*Important Changes:* **(1) Visits:** the identification necessary to access this prison and visit for social or professional purposes has changed; (2) **Money and Gifts** new rules now apply to these. See page 16 for full details of the above.

**This prison operates the Digital Categorisation System, pursuant to the Security Categorisation Policy Framework as such PSIs 40 and 41 of 2011 do not apply to prisoners being categorised in this establishment. See section 2.26 for more information.**

**Task of the establishment** Local category B resettlement prison for remand and convicted prisoners aged 18 and over.

### Certified normal accommodation and operational capacity

Prisoners held at the time of this visit: 988
Baseline certified normal capacity: 899
In-use certified normal capacity: 747
Operational capacity: 1,310 (1,000 at time of visit following a reduction in operational capacity)

### Prison status and key providers

Public
Prison Group: London
Prison Group Director: Ian Bickers
Governor/Director: Ian Blakeman
IMB Chairs: Barry Baker & Dominique Demeure
Physical health provider: Practice Plus Group
Mental health provider: Practice Plus Group, Barnet, Enfield and Haringey Mental Health NHS Trust
Substance use treatment provider: Phoenix Futures
Prison education framework provider: Novus
Escort contractor: Serco

**Brief history** HMP Pentonville is a large Victorian local prison for remand and convicted prisoners, with four wings unchanged since it was built in 1842. It is one of the busiest prisons in the country with approximately 33,000 movements a year through its reception.

### Short description of residential units

A wing – 226 spaces, general remand and convicted prisoners (currently reverse cohort unit/first night centre)

C wing – 160 spaces, general remand and convicted prisoners

D wing – 180 spaces, general remand and convicted prisoners

E1 wing – segregation unit, 12 spaces

E2-5 wings – 136 spaces, general remand and convicted prisoners (currently decanted) F 1-3 wings – 126 spaces for prisoners requiring substance misuse stabilisation

F4-5 wing – 65 spaces for vulnerable prisoners

G wing – 415 spaces, general remand and convicted prisoners

J wing – 64 space first night centre (currently protective isolation unit)

Health care – 22 beds

### Visiting Information

Book online at: www.gov.uk/prison-visits or by telephone on 0300 060 6504 Monday to Friday 9:15am to 4pm.

**Legal visits:** Book a legal or professional visit by emailing: LegalVisits.Pentonville@justice.gov.uk

### INSPECTIONS & REPORTS
**Scrutiny visit 27 October & 3-4 November 2020**
**IRP Report: 4–6 February 2020**
**Scrutiny visit: Published 04 December 2020**

This report discusses the findings from a scrutiny visit (SV) to HMP Pentonville. The SV methodology develops the 'short scrutiny visit' (SSV, see Glossary of terms) approach that HMI Prisons used to provide independent oversight of custodial establishments from April to July 2020. Our previous approach monitored outcomes for prisoners in a small number of key areas at a time when regimes were severely restricted in all prisons. While SVs are still more limited in scope than our full inspections, they increase the intensity of scrutiny. SVs examine the treatment and conditions of prisoners in greater detail and focus in particular on the pace of recovery and proportionality of treatment, while ensuring the safest possible inspection practices. HMP Pentonville is in north London and is one of the country's oldest and most famous institutions. It is largely unchanged structurally in nearly 180 years and epitomises the challenges confronting ageing, inner-city prisons with transient populations with varied needs.

Pentonville was already an institution of significant concern before the pandemic. This was reflected in poor findings at the previous full inspection in April 2019 and a subsequent independent review of progress in February 2020. At this scrutiny visit, it was pleasing to find that there had been some tangible, if fragile, progress. To the prison's credit, it had continued to focus on the key priorities we had set out at the last inspection, while managing the additional problems created by Covid-19. At the start of the pandemic, the prison had suffered some deaths among staff. At the time of our visit, there were no confirmed staff or prisoner cases. The prison's age and design limited the degree to which it could provide decent accommodation. Despite a small reduction in population and the recent arrival of some detached duty staff, the prison remained overcrowded and understaffed. Social distancing was all but impossible in some areas and we saw few attempts by staff to socially distance even where it was achievable. Prisoners had cooperated with the extreme restrictions. Many continued to feel unsafe and were acutely aware of the risks of infection being brought into the prison community from outside. The busy reception was well organised and procedures were in place to ensure a safe flow of people through the area. Covid-19 testing was now routinely offered to all arriving prisoners and was about to start for staff. Cohorting arrangements appeared to be effective, with prisoners unlocked in groups based on when they arrived. Time out of cell was very limited, and provision of showers and exercise was inconsistent. In our survey, 32% of prisoners said they felt unsafe and 40% that they were victimised by staff. We were surprised to find that the basic level of the incentives policy had been maintained for low-level transgressions, including limits on spending ability and occasional withdrawal of televisions. Given the already very restricted regime, this was unjustifiably punitive.

The level of violence was slightly lower than before the restricted regime, though with a few significant spikes in incidents. Use of force had similarly fluctuated and we were pleased to see that governance of use of force had improved significantly since our last inspection. Data were being collected more routinely, but trend analysis and subsequent actions remained limited in many areas, including violence, use of force and segregation. Self-harm had increased in the months since the restricted regime had started and there had been four self-inflicted deaths since our last full inspection. The prison was attempting to address a large number of outstanding Prisons and Probation Ombudsman (PPO) recommendations, but some critical concerns had still not been effectively resolved, including slow responses to emergency cell bells and inconsistent management of assessment, care in custody and teamwork (ACCT) case management of prisoners at risk of suicide or self-harm. However, we were pleased to find that the Listener scheme was operating well and had been sustained throughout the pandemic with support from the Samaritans. This was a significant achievement.

Staff were appreciative of the good communication and visible leadership in the prison. We heard from many staff that there was a greater sense of common purpose than in the past. However, outcomes for prisoners had so far improved little. We observed many interactions between staff and prisoners that were professional, good-natured and supportive, but we also saw staff being dismissive, unhelpful and, in one case, verbally abusive. While there was an obvious commitment to address such behaviour, this challenge required continuing focus. Managers were attempting to address the deteriorating physical conditions in the prison and poor state of many cells. The pressure on spaces made this a difficult task. One wing had been closed for redecoration, another landing had been redecorated and funding had been obtained to refurbish the many showers that were dirty, mouldy and unfit for use. The communal areas of the prison were kept reasonably clean and prisoners were employed to sanitise high-use areas throughout the day. However, it was concerning that prisoners often could not obtain cleaning materials for their cells and that, unless they were in full-time work, they could not shower every day. Meals were served very early, with the evening meal serving starting as early as 3.30pm.

Strategic oversight of equality work had recently resumed. Data were being used to understand areas of over-representation, but there were few subsequent actions. A key concern was the inadequate treatment and conditions for prisoners with disabilities. The layout of Pentonville prevented sufficient access to facilities and some prisoners, especially wheelchair users, could not go outside. This was wholly unacceptable. The use of interpreting was also poor, undermining the care of the large population of foreign national prisoners. The introduction of a bespoke intervention programme (Time 4 Change) was a positive development aimed at younger prisoners who were over- represented in discipline statistics. The chaplaincy had provided excellent support to prisoners throughout the pandemic, visiting each individual prisoner at least once a week, which was impressive.

Health care was reasonable and medicines administration was safe. However, demand was high, the provision was stretched and many prisoners complained about both access and quality. Waiting times for most health services were reasonable, but there were shortcomings in the appointments system. Over half the prisoners in our survey said they had mental health problems and waits for primary mental health support had increased.

A consistent regime was provided for most, but it was very limited for prisoners who were not in work. Unemployed prisoners generally had no more than 45 minutes a day out of their cells, and we received many comments about the impact of such confinement on prisoners' health and wellbeing. The prison had maintained some workshops with reduced attendance to maintain social distancing, and it was positive that about a quarter of prisoners were in some form of employment. In-cell activity was generally of good quality.

Family support work had been good and the reintroduction of visits had been managed well, with sensible and proportionate supervision. Take up remained low and less than a fifth of prisoners said they had seen their families in person or via video-calling in the previous month. In-cell telephones were a great help to prisoners locked up for long periods.

Sentence planning and risk assessment processes were up to date and the prison had worked hard to reduce the offender assessment system (OASys) backlog. Some risk management procedures were not working effectively. Prisoners were often frustrated at not being able to access relevant offender management staff or pre-release support. It was particularly concerning that more than half the prisoners released in the previous six months had not had settled accommodation and about 14% of these were released with no fixed abode.

Managers, staff and prisoners at Pentonville had shown resilience in managing the demands of the pandemic in an institution with many pre-existing problems. There were signs that the pandemic had focused the minds of staff and that the positive direction that the governor and senior management team had set was starting to have an effect. Prisoners already faced a challenging prison environment, and the high levels of mental health need reflected the additional negative impact of the pandemic. A sustained focus on our recommendations will be essential if the deep-rooted problems facing the prison are to be overcome.

Charlie Taylor, HM Chief Inspector of Prisons
November 2020

## Key concerns and recommendations
*Key concerns* and recommendations identify the issues of most importance to improving outcomes for prisoners and are designed to help establishments prioritise and address the most significant weaknesses in the treatment and conditions of prisoners.

*Key concern:* While a wide range of data were now collected and analysed, particularly on safety and equality, there was little evidence that the analysis had been used to improve outcomes for prisoners.

Recommendation: Managers should make sure that data are used effectively to identify concerns and take action which leads to tangible and demonstrable improvements in prisoner outcomes. (To the governor)

*Key concern:* Contrary to national guidance, the prison had decided to maintain the basic level of the incentives scheme. Given the extreme restrictions already in place for all prisoners, this was disproportionately punitive and had resulted in reduced spending ability and withdrawal of televisions in some cases.

Recommendation: Managers should use proportionate means to deal with low- level transgressions by prisoners. (To the governor)

*Key concern:* The prison was attempting to address a large number of outstanding Prisons and Probation Ombudsman (PPO) recommendations following deaths in custody, but some critical concerns had still not been effectively resolved, including slow responses to emergency cell bells and the variable quality of ACCT procedures.

Recommendation: All recommendations from death in custody reviews should be implemented swiftly. Managers should, in particular, address urgently the slow response to emergency cell bells and the inconsistent quality of ACCT processes. (To the governor)

*Key concern:* Cells were generally in a poor condition and lacking maintenance. Broken and dilapidated fixtures, graffiti, mould, and broken windows and observation panels were commonplace. Positive efforts were being made to refurbish cells on some wings, but there was a lack of attention to poor conditions in cells that were not being refurbished.

Recommendation: Managers should make sure that all cells are kept in a good state of repair and provide decent living conditions. Problems reported by prisoners should be addressed promptly. (To the governor)

*Key concern:* Meals were served very early with serving of the evening meal starting between 3.30 and 3.45pm.

Recommendation: The evening meal should not be served before 5pm. (To the governor)

*Key concern:* Treatment and conditions for many prisoners with disabilities were inadequate. In our survey, 70% of prisoners said they had been victimised by staff and often commented on poor access to facilities. Some prisoners, especially wheelchair users, did not go outside. Others were unable to shower regularly because the shower facilities were not accessible.

Recommendation: Prisoners with disabilities should not be held in Pentonville if they have no ready access to outdoor exercise areas and key provision, such as work and education. (To HMPPS)

*Key concern:* Time out of cell for unemployed prisoners was restricted to about 45 minutes a day. Showers and outdoor exercise were offered to these prisoners on alternate days except Saturdays which meant that they were not able to shower and go outside each day.

Recommendation: All prisoners should be able to have a shower and outdoor exercise every day. (To the governor)

*Key concern:* During the previous six months, 58% of prisoners had been released with no settled accommodation and 14% with no accommodation, which was far too high. Nearly a quarter of prisoners receiving support with accommodation were released with no accommodation arranged for the day of release.

Recommendation: The prison should continue to work with community partners, with appropriate support from HMPPS, to ensure that no prisoners are released without settled accommodation. (To HMPPS and the governor)

## Notable positive practice
We define notable positive practice as innovative practice or practice that leads to particularly good outcomes from which other establishments may be able to learn. Inspectors look for evidence of good outcomes for prisoners; original, creative or particularly effective approaches to problem-solving or achieving the desired goal; and how other establishments could learn from or replicate the practice.

Inspectors found the following examples of notable positive practice during this visit.

• Listeners had been able to carry out their important work throughout the pandemic. The Samaritans had initially provided the necessary training, mentoring and support remotely and, as soon as they were authorised to return to the prison, had provided that support in person.

• A bespoke 12-session intervention programme, Time 4 Change, had been developed for 18-25-year-old prisoners who were over-represented in discipline statistics. Pre- and post-programme outcomes were monitored to assess if the intervention had had any impact on behaviour. The use of mentors and a counsellor between sessions provided helpful support.

• Chaplains met every prisoner each week to provide individual support. They also undertook daily visits to vulnerable prisoners in need of additional support. These included prisoners who found social interaction difficult, those in prison for the first time, prisoners with learning support or literacy needs, and those experiencing bereavement and family illness.

• In-cell work packs provided by PACT (Prison Advice and Care Trust) on the theme of relationships were of a high quality. They were tracked and assessed, with prisoners receiving certificates after completion. This was a good initiative to help keep prisoners occupied with purposeful and rehabilitative work during long periods confined to cells.

**IRP Report, published 12 March 2020**

HMP Pentonville, an inner-city category B local male prison serving the London courts, is one of the oldest and most famous prisons in the country. It is a large, complex establishment with a transient population of more than 1,000 adult and young adult prisoners, ranging from those recently remanded to others serving significant sentences. We last inspected Pentonville in 2019 when we reported poor outcomes in our healthy prison test of safety, and not sufficiently good outcomes in the areas of respect, purposeful activity, and rehabilitation and release planning. At the time we highlighted a failure to meet the undoubted challenges faced by this prison, but were critical that only one of our 15 recommendations on safety had been achieved in full.

At that last inspection, in April 2019, we reported that violence had increased significantly and that work to analyse and address this had been inadequate. There had been a sharp rise in the use of force, and there was no strategy to reduce the high levels of illicit drugs despite their ready availability throughout the prison. There had been four self-inflicted deaths in the two years between the 2017 and 2019 inspections. Despite this, the response to recommendations made by the Prisons and Probation Ombudsman following its investigations into the deaths had been inadequate, and case management support (assessment, care in custody and teamwork, ACCT) for prisoners in crisis was poor. Living conditions for many prisoners were also poor, and a negative attitude among certain staff indicated some deep-rooted cultural problems that got in the way of delivering positive work with prisoners. Nearly a third of prisoners were locked in their cells during the working day, and attendance at activities remained poor. Ofsted

judged the overall effectiveness of education, skills and work across the prison as 'requires improvement'. The strategic approach to rehabilitation work remained weak, and prisoners did not receive enough support throughout their sentence.

At the time of the 2019 inspection we gave serious consideration to invoking the inspectorate's Urgent Notification (UN) procedures*. Our decision not to follow this path was based on us having some confidence in the plans proposed by an enthusiastic new senior management team. However, we were very clear that we would return within the year to conduct an independent review of the progress (IRP) being made against the key concerns and recommendations in the report.

Unfortunately, our findings at the end of this IRP, more than nine months after the inspection, were a cause for continued concern. The prison had made good progress in only one of the 15 key concerns and recommendations, and reasonable progress against only a further three. There had been no meaningful progress against six key concerns and recommendations, and insufficient progress against the remaining five. This was the poorest progress that we have seen in any of the IRPs that we have conducted to date.

We were joined during this IRP by our colleagues from Ofsted, who conducted a monitoring visit to follow up three themes drawn from recommendations on the education, skills and work provision at the prison. Managers had made reasonable progress against one of those themes and insufficient progress against the other two.

The IRP revealed that in terms of safety, until very recently there had been a lack of clear accountability at every level. Action planning to deliver the safety strategies that were now in place had been neither swift nor effective. Indeed, overall levels of violence had once again increased. The key strategic safety meeting that should have been an effective vehicle for driving improvements was not used well for this purpose. Despite the high levels of violence, case management delivered through the challenge, support and intervention plans (CSIPs)* had not yet been implemented effectively. There were few incentives to motivate good behaviour, and too many adjudications for serious breaches of the rules were written off. This failure to grip and manage key processes created a culture where violence and poor behaviour could all too easily go unpunished.

Data collection and analysis within the safety function were showing early signs of improvement, particularly in monitoring the use of segregation. Recently introduced quality assurance measures had the potential, if applied more robustly, to improve outcomes. However, scrutiny overall was still not rigorous, which resulted in the poor delivery of key safety processes. For example, scrutiny of the increasing use of force had only begun in earnest a few weeks before we returned to conduct this review, and managers could assure neither themselves nor us that all uses of force were justified.

ACCT processes were not managed effectively, and quality assurance had only been introduced in the weeks before the review. Tragically, there had been three self-inflicted deaths in the nine months since our last inspection. These were currently under investigation by the Prisons and Probation Ombudsman (PPO). The response to the early learning points was weak, and implementation of recommendations from previous suicides could only be described as lacklustre. A failure to discuss actions at key strategic meetings, and an over- reliance on staff information notices, characterised the prison's approach to learning from deaths in custody.

In contrast, the prison had made good progress in tackling its significant drug problem. There was now a coherent supply reduction strategy, with an action plan that was being driven through a well-attended multidisciplinary meeting. The number of prisoners testing positive for drugs, although still high, had reduced since our inspection in April 2019. Reasonable progress had also been made to improve physical security, but the prison needed ongoing funding to complete this work.

We observed some very good interactions between staff and prisoners during our visit, but some prisoners reported that staff could be rude and unhelpful. Managers and staff did not set high standards for prisoners, and we witnessed some low-level bad behaviour that staff did not challenge. It was very disappointing that key work (in which prison officers have regular contact with named individual prisoners) had stalled in August 2019 and had only just been revived in the weeks leading up to our review.

The prison had clearly placed a greater focus on environmental cleanliness, which had improved, and cell repairs and refurbishment were under way. However, the pace of improvement was slow and there was still some way to go to establish and maintain decent living conditions. Equality work remained neglected. There had been reasonable progress in the area of prisoner health and well-being.

Managers understood that boredom and inactivity contributed to bad behaviour, violence and poor well-being. Despite this, prisoners at Pentonville still spent far too long locked in their cells during the working day. Even though there were sufficient part-time activity spaces for the entire population, only just over two-thirds of the spaces were used, and over 300 prisoners were unemployed. Attendance by those who were allocated to an activity was often poor. To compound this, prisoners were given very little time out of their cell to shower, exercise and associate with their peers.

Ofsted inspectors found that there had been insufficient progress in the allocation of prisoners to education, skills and work. A high number of prisoners allocated to education never started their courses, and a third of prisoners who did start their course did not complete it, which was much higher than at the inspection.

The quality of teaching had improved, particularly for prisoners with learning difficulties or disabilities. However, too few prisoners gained qualifications in English and mathematics during their time at the jail.

Work to reduce reoffending and prepare prisoners for release was slow to progress and had not been prioritised.

I was so concerned by the findings of this IRP that immediately after it was concluded I wrote to the Secretary of State expressing my serious concern at the lack of progress since the last inspection. I was particularly disappointed to see that in many areas little or nothing had been done until very shortly before the IRP took place. I acknowledged that a change of leadership at the prison since the inspection had been problematic. I also made the point that lasting improvement would not be achieved through the simple expedient of reducing the prisoner population and giving more resources to the prison. The solution to most issues was in the gift of the prison, but would need a truly collaborative effort from all staff, clear leadership and support from Her Majesty's Prison and Probation Service (HMPPS).

I also explained to the Secretary of State that I had decided not to invoke the UN procedure, but that the Inspectorate would return in November 2020 to conduct a further full inspection. This would give the prison and HMPPS a full nine months from the time of the IRP to act upon its findings and make Pentonville a safer, more decent, purposeful and rehabilitative establishment.

Peter Clarke CVO OBE QPM

HM Chief Inspector of Prisons February 2020

**INDEPENDENT MONITORING BOARD: Annual Report**

The law requires every prison to be monitored by an independent Board appointed by the Justice Secretary; these are known as Independent Monitoring Boards (IMBs). The IMB must satisfy itself as to the humane and just treatment of those held in custody within its prison and the range and adequacy of the programmes preparing them for release; it must report annually to the Justice Secretary on how well the prison has met the standards and requirements placed on it.

## IMB Report 1 April 2020 to 31 March 2021
## Published September 2021
Background to the report:
the pandemic in Pentonville

Two prisoners, two members of staff, and a volunteer chaplain were sadly lost to the Covid-19 virus.

Pentonville was in lockdown from late March until June 2020, and also in Covid-19 outbreak mode (as defined by Public Health England (PHE)) for part of this time. Men were confined to their cells, many up to 23 hours a day, with infrequent opportunities for shower or exercise.

New prisoners had to quarantine, and showers and exercise were very limited for all prisoners. An isolation unit operated for prisoners who were symptomatic or confirmed Covid-19 cases and they were not allowed out of their cells at all. Early in the year, testing was slow and swabs had to be sent out of the prison. GPs could however contact the men via in-cell telephones.

Essential workshops/activities kept going but with fewer workers: recycling, industrial cleaning, boxer shorts and bedding production, and distribution of prison clothing. Opportunities for other work were limited. The prison recorded that overall 300 men were at work most days.

All group activities stopped including collective worship, mental health therapy, drug rehabilitation groups, education classes and skills workshops. However, one-to-one support continued throughout, including from health professionals and other key services. Members of the chaplaincy team visited most men weekly throughout the year.

Activity and education packs were provided. Games consoles were dug out of the property store. Gym staff gave tips on exercise routines for the men to follow in their cells and ran outdoor group exercise classes. The library began a book ordering service and kept book tables stocked on the wings.

In-cell telephones were a lifeline for prisoners to keep in touch with families, and for the most anxious to call the Samaritans at any time. Digital visits became popular and enabled prisoners to see family, including those overseas. Visits to the prison resumed for a period in the summer, but with social distancing and prisoners concerned for their families' wellbeing, the take-up was low.

Remand and sentencing hearings went online, as did conferences with lawyers. Legal visits at the prison resumed in person as more trials got underway. However, the backlog in the courts meant some men waited for more than a year to get to court, and many continue to do so. Parole Board hearings also went online.

Tentative plans for resuming some activities were overtaken by the autumn lockdown and then the winter surge in the virus. Pentonville was an 'outbreak' prison again in January and February, and face coverings became mandatory for staff and prisoners. Vaccinations for prisoners began in line with community criteria and were offered to all Pentonville staff by Islington Council in March.

The IMB resumed visiting from the end of June until December, and again in late February, but on fewer occasions than in previous years. Prisoners could instead contact the IMB on a free national phone line. Pentonville was the second highest user with 675 individual calls over the period, which provided the Board with a picture of their main concerns. Prisoners in distress could then be referred by the IMB for welfare checks by staff. The emailaprisoner service meant IMB responses reached men promptly. It should be noted that this IMB report is informed by our visits, although it also relies more than usual on information provided by the prison and should be read in that context and against the background of the public health and operational constraints on the prison.

## Main judgements
## How safe is the prison?

The overwhelming threat to safety this year has been Covid-19. Prison management and healthcare saved many lives by coordinating a stringent isolation and testing regime without which many more than the two prisoners who died might have perished.

However, the day-to-day safety issues which affect prison life have continued, namely violence and drugs. CCTV coverage around the prison has been boosted this year, and more staff have been wearing, and turning on, their body worn video cameras (BWVC), but violence between prisoners, or involving staff, has still been an issue. Young adult violence numbers remain too high, and notwithstanding the innovative Time 4 Change programme, much more is needed to engage this population.

Drug strategy was at last at the forefront of Pentonville's management priorities this year. More drugs dogs have been working this year than last, although there have still been gaps in cover, and there was no mandatory drug testing (MDT) during the reporting period.

## How fairly and humanely are prisoners treated?

It would be difficult to overestimate the boredom and sense of isolation and anxiety generated by conditions in Pentonville over the past year. To hold two men in a 12 x 8 feet cell with a bunk bed, a television, a badly screened toilet and a sink with precious little time out of cell is bad enough. Not to let them out at all for 10 days when isolating is inhumane, given the conditions inside cells. However, the IMB believes that the management team could not have safely provided the men with a better regime given the infection risks, the staffing numbers, the infrastructure, and the number of prisoners at Pentonville.

There will not be decency at Pentonville until it is one man to a cell. It may be that sharing a cell alleviated some of the loneliness of lockdown for some men, but their accommodation could not be judged as decent by any measure.

Data collection and analysis around use of force and adjudications have improved. Equalities is now receiving the attention that it deserves. Allegations of staff misconduct are robustly investigated. The Board believes that, in general, prisoners are treated fairly.

## How well are prisoners' health and wellbeing needs met?

Covid-19 has changed many prison systems drastically and healthcare perhaps the most. That Pentonville never had a more sustained and deadly Covid-19 outbreak (compared to other London prisons) speaks well for the prison and healthcare working together. While there were occasional coordination issues with the prison, healthcare managed their responsibilities well and, in general, the relationship between the prison and healthcare was good. Given the challenges of Covid-19 and staff shielding, it was fortunate that there was never a shortfall of healthcare staff. However, Covid-19 has reduced the mental health provision for prisoners dramatically. The care has moved from therapeutic (helping prisoners to improve) to basic monitoring (trying to ensure that patients don't get worse).

## How well are prisoners progressed towards successful resettlement?

With limited access to work and education, and the absence or curtailing of other group activities, progress toward resettlement was, inevitably, compromised. Nonetheless, some good work was established or continued. The homelessness prevention taskforce (HPT) was a major initiative enabling prisoners to secure accommodation, a key requirement for effective resettlement. Also, more drug rehabilitation places were secured. In-cell telephony enabled prisoners to maintain contact with their families. Given its limited contact with prisoners, the Board was unable to explore directly how useful they considered resettlement services to have been during the reporting period. But it is noteworthy that, in contrast with some other services, the CRC remained in the prison throughout the year and even expanded their role.

Main areas for development

### TO THE MINISTER

Will you take steps to reduce the population in Pentonville?

Will you invest in the fabric of the prison to provide a safe, decent and rehabilitative environment?

Will the investment in technology made during lockdown be sustained and developed going forward to give prisoners more technology for personal use? For example, more prisoner laptops for education, more video links for those having legal visits, and biometric kiosks on wings.

### TO THE PRISON SERVICE

Will the Prison Service fund and deliver more essential refurbishment for decency, such as toilets and showers?

In the case of further lockdowns, will the Prison Service ensure that prisoners have better access to the education staff than during this past year?

Will the Prison Service increase the capacity of offending behaviour programmes at Pentonville, so that prisoners can benefit from these programmes without needing to transfer to another prison?

Will the Prison Service commit to increasing the devolution of decision-making powers to local Governors?

### TO THE GOVERNOR

What will you do to improve the quality of assessment, care in custody and teamwork (ACCT) documents?

Will you refresh the local incentives and earned privileges (IEP) policy to give: (i) better recognition to positive behaviour and (ii) enhanced prisoners meaningful privileges that will incentivise sustained good behaviour?

Will you commit to developing a record of achievement for prisoners that they can use in job applications upon release?

Will you ensure that each equalities meeting is attended by yourself or your deputy, and commit to updating and progressing the equalities action plan?

Will you commit to improving the analysis and action driven by the equalities data that is being collected, including discrimination incident reporting forms (DIRFs)?

Will you urgently address the lack of timeliness of internal prison communication regarding prisoners' sentence management, which generates a lot of anxiety among the prisoners?

**Progress since the last report**
• More scrutiny by prison of use of force incidents
• Better focus by the prison on implementing its drugs strategy
• More data collection generally across the prison
• Better communication with prisoners through regular use of in-cell TV and newsletters
• Production by CSU staff of detailed reports on their residents
• Renewed emphasis by prison management on equalities data and work
• In-cell telephony for all prisoners
• Freephone 0800 IMB applications line and use of emailaprisoner by the Board
• Regular support from safer custody team when referring on prisoners of concern who contacted the IMB on the 0800 applications line
• Use of remote technology to facilitate prisoners' visits (so called 'Purple Visits')
• CCTV now on all wings
• Renovation of some prisoner accommodation and shower rooms
• Energy and dedication shown by chaplaincy throughout the pandemic, against a backdrop of reduced staffing and volunteer numbers and personal difficulties
• A prison officer received a Butler Trust Award for his work devising and leading Time 4 Change
• An education tutor commended by the Butler Trust Award scheme and awarded 'outstanding tutor award' at the Festival of Learning 2021

**SAVILLE ROAD**
**WESTWOOD**
**PETERBOROUGH**
**PE3 7PD**

PETERBOROUGH
PRISON          **Tel: 01733 217500**

## HMP Peterborough (Male)
*For the latest reports on this prison please visit:*
https://tinyurl.com/bdfh26rv

*Important Changes:* **(1) Visits:** the identification necessary to access this prison and visit for social or professional purposes has changed; **(2) Money and Gifts** new rules now apply to these. See page 16 for full details of the above.
**Task of the establishment** Male category B reception prison with a resettlement function.

**Certified normal accommodation and operational capacity**
Prisoners held at the time of this visit: 863
Baseline certified normal capacity: 762

In-use certified normal capacity: 762
Operational capacity: 868

**Prison status and key providers**
Private - managed by: Sodexo Justice Services
Prison Group: Custodial Contracts
Head of Custodial Contracts: Neil Richards
Governor/Director:
Damien Evans / Hayley Folland (c)
IMB Chair: Pauline Davison
Physical health provider: Sodexo Justice Services
Mental health provider: Cambridgeshire and Peterborough NHS Foundation Trust
Substance misuse treatment provider: Sodexo Justice Services
Prison education framework provider: Sodexo Justice Services
Escort contractors: Serco, GeoAmey and Mitie Care and Custody

**Brief history** The prison opened on 28 March 2005 with two residential units, House block 3 and House block 4, initially accommodating 480 prisoners. In January 2015 it opened an extension, House block 5, which provided an additional 292 prisoner places.

**Short description of residential units**
*House block 3:*
W1 wing: Early days centre
X1 wing: Integrated substance misuse service and first night centre for those requiring detoxification or stabilisation
Y1 wing: Remand/general population
Z1 wing: Remand/general population
*House block 4:*
W2 wing: Convicted prisoners
X2 wing: Convicted prisoners
Y2 wing: Convicted prisoners
Z2 wing: Mature prisoners
*House block 5:*
Burghley wing: Enhanced prisoners and those on release on temporary licence.
Royce wing: Safeguarding unit for vulnerable prisoners
Cavell wing: Convicted prisoners
Nene wing: Convicted prisoners

**Visiting Information**
Visits are booked by prisoners and visitors will be advised of the date and time to visit once the booking has been accepted.

**Legal visits:** Check with the prison for the latest information.

## INSPECTIONS & REPORTS
### Scrutiny visit: 17 and 24–25 November 2020
### Published: 06 January 2021

HMP Peterborough is a privately run, category B local prison holding both men and women. The men's and women's jails are separated but are on the same site and share a management team. During this scrutiny visit, the prison held just over 850 male prisoners.

We last inspected the men's prison in July 2018, when we assessed outcomes in safety as not sufficiently good, respect and purposeful activity outcomes as reasonably good and rehabilitation and release planning as good. Our revised methodology to assess outcomes during the Covid-19 pandemic does not include making judgements for each test as we would at a full inspection, but we have agreed several key concerns and recommendations to help the prison through the next phase of recovery.

Subject to the same HM Prison and Probation Service (HMPPS) control as public sector prisons, the prison had introduced a range of centrally-mandated measures to limit the spread of the virus. Indeed, there had been no positive tests recorded for prisoners since the start of the restricted regime, and the number of staff testing positive was low. Prison leaders had quickly established a structure to communicate information, design cohort arrangements and deliver a restricted regime. The prison was taking a very cautious route to recovery, which meant that some improvements had been slow to materialise. Work to support prisoners in their early days had improved recently, and an enthusiastic team of prisoner peer workers now delivered face-to-face induction to new arrivals. However, until very recently, prisoners had not been issued with kettles, and there had also been problems sourcing basic provisions, such as pillows and toiletries.

The prison's recorded data demonstrated a reduction in violence since the commencement of the restricted regime. Despite this, our survey indicated that around one in four prisoners felt unsafe, and a notable number said they had been victimised. There were several systems to identify and support vulnerable prisoners, but it was clear they were not always robust enough to detect everyone who needed help. During our visit we spoke to a few prisoners who clearly had some unmet needs. We also found that some safeguards were insufficient to identify and address underlying issues. For example, although key work (see Glossary of terms) was prioritised for prisoners who had been identified as vulnerable, staff interactions with them were often superficial and did not encourage discussion of their concerns.

Living conditions were generally clean and tidy, although the limited time out of cell and some procedural problems meant some prisoners found it difficult to keep themselves or their cells clean. Prisoners were consulted about minor issues affecting their daily lives, but actions from consultation meetings were carried over from meeting to meeting and, in some cases, were not resolved. Equality work had not been prioritised during much of the restricted regime, although it had started to gather some momentum recently. Again, the quality of the prison's engagement with prisoners from protected groups was basic and did not really explore the issues affecting them. The health care manager was clearly committed to improving health services for prisoners, but the 40-week waiting list for dental treatment required urgent attention.

Prisoners who were not allocated to essential work had very limited time out of cell, and were fatigued by the amount of time locked in a small cell with very little to do. The director's priority was to ease restrictions so prisoners could take part in purposeful work rather than unlock them when they had little to do. Despite this, only a third of prisoners could go to work, much of which was based on the residential wings. Unlike other prisons, Sodexo employed the education staff directly and they had remained on site throughout the restrictions providing some education for around 130 prisoners, albeit mostly in cell.

The prison had retained a reduced library service through a book trolley, and PE instructors provided some circuit training on exercise yards, though neither were provided consistently as the relevant staff were often cross-deployed to other duties. The indoor gym had reopened very recently which had improved opportunities for some prisoners.

Rehabilitation and release planning had been a strength at the last visit, and some elements of this work remained in place and had developed further. Partnership working with Nacro had resulted in the purchase of accommodation in the city centre that prioritised prisoners leaving Peterborough. Despite this, a third of prisoners leaving the prison had no settled accommodation to go to. Gaps in public protection work also created some risk, particularly in multidisciplinary work and monitoring the calls of some dangerous prisoners.

Leaders at Peterborough assured us that recovery plans (see Glossary of terms) to move into phase two of the national strategy were complete and would provide a much more purposeful regime. Given that the prison has remained mostly virus-free for eight months, we would encourage it to implement these plans as soon as it is safe to do so. This report contains several key concerns and recommendations that we hope will help it to prioritise its work as it enters this important next stage.

Charlie Taylor, HM Chief Inspector of Prisons
January 2021

## Key concerns and recommendations

*Key concerns* and recommendations identify the issues of most importance to improving outcomes for prisoners and are designed to help establishments prioritise and address the most significant weaknesses in the treatment and conditions of prisoners.

During this visit we identified some areas of key concern and have made a small number of key recommendations for the prison to address.

*Key concern:* The current systems to identify prisoners who could be vulnerable were not robust enough. We found examples of prisoners who required a higher level of support who the prison had not identified and prioritised.

Key recommendation: The prison should strengthen measures to identify vulnerable prisoners and those with additional needs to make sure that all prisoners are supported and cared for. (To the director)

*Key concern:* Work to promote equality and diversity was not prioritised. Strategic and prisoner consultation meetings had lapsed for much of the restricted regime. The equality data collected was not used well to improve outcomes for prisoners with protected characteristics. The recent equality action plan did not focus enough on identifying or meeting the needs of a diverse population.

Key recommendation: Oversight of equality work should make sure that equality data are used well to inform action planning, and that actions are effective in improving the outcomes of the diverse population. The prison should improve the ways it identifies prisoners with protected characteristics to make sure that their needs are met consistently. (To the director)

*Key concern:* There had been no routine dental service since March 2020 resulting in excessive waiting times for treatment of up to 40 weeks, with over 180 patients on the list. This risked a deterioration in oral health for some prisoners, requiring more extensive dental treatment than should have been the case. Additionally, optician and podiatry services had not yet restarted, resulting in lengthy waits of up to 40 weeks, which could also lead to a deterioration in health.

Key recommendation: The prison should provide a full range of timely health treatment and services equivalent to those in the community. (To the director and Sodexo Justice Services)

*Key concern:* The regime for the majority of prisoners had been poor for too long, with an increasing impact on well-being. Most spent less than 90 minutes out of their cell on a typical day, and they had little time to engage with staff or peers.

Key recommendation: All prisoners should have enough time out of cell each day to take part in purposeful activity, complete domestic tasks, and engage with staff and their peers.
(To the director)

*Key concern:* There were weaknesses in the management of public protection. Monthly interdepartmental risk management meetings had not been held consistently since March 2020 and were often very poorly attended. Prisoner cases were not always discussed in sufficient depth before their release. A backlog in monitoring meant that the telephone calls of prisoners subject to public protection measures had not been listened to and so the meetings could not discuss any recent arising issues.

Key recommendation: Interdepartmental risk management meetings should be multidisciplinary, regular and consider relevant, up-to-date information. They should discuss all relevant cases in enough depth to address risks before prisoners are released. (To the director)

## Notable positive practice

We define notable positive practice as innovative practice or practice that leads to particularly good outcomes from which other establishments may be able to learn. Inspectors look for evidence of good outcomes for prisoners; original, creative or particularly effective approaches to problem-solving or achieving the desired goal; and how other establishments could learn from or replicate the practice.

Inspectors found the following examples of notable positive practice during this visit.

• Working in partnership, the prison and Nacro had sourced 15 accommodation units in the city centre that were prioritised for prisoners released from Peterborough. St Giles Trust had also secured funding from Peterborough City Council to recruit a member of staff to support prisoners who had been rough sleeping before coming into custody.

• The Outside Links facility supported prisoners on their day of discharge, including practical assistance to charge mobile phones and make initial contact with families. A further facility in Peterborough city centre provided ongoing support after release.

## INDEPENDENT MONITORING BOARD: Annual Report

The law requires every prison to be monitored by an independent Board appointed by the Justice Secretary; these are known as Independent Monitoring Boards (IMBs). The IMB must satisfy itself as to the humane and just treatment of those held in custody within its prison and the

539

range and adequacy of the programmes preparing them for release; it must report annually to the Justice Secretary on how well the prison has met the standards and requirements placed on it.

**IMB Report April 2020 to March 2021**
**Published 11 October 2021**
**Main judgements**
**Are prisoners treated fairly?**
The Board believes that overall residents are treated fairly and with respect.

The offender management in custody key worker initiative has been implemented and experienced wing in charge officers appointed.

Most prison complaints are handled within time limits. The Board is concerned that handling of residents' property continues to be problematic, both within the prison and on transfer.

The prison regime is good, and time out of cell was more than 10 hours.

The standard of wing accommodation has improved but concerns remain: in-cell toilets are not adequately screened and lack of furniture means residents usually eat in their cells.

**Are prisoners treated humanely?**
The Board believes that overall residents are treated humanely and with decency.

The increased focus on safety is starting to have positive results. However, illicit substance issues remain challenging and mandatory drug testing results exceed targets. It is hoped the intelligence-led use of the body scanner and screening of post for illicit substances will produce positive results.

The Board is concerned that some residents are held in the separation and care unit for long periods.

Improvements to the healthcare provision are ongoing, and mental health and social care provision is good. There remains a reliance on agency nurses and locum doctors. The Board is concerned that there has been little evidence of health promotion activities.

**Are prisoners prepared well for their release?**
Preparation for release is very important in the prison, evidenced by the good learning and skills provision, the focus on maintaining family ties, and the effectiveness of the Outside Links service. Short sentences, however, make it difficult to deliver effective interventions (11.4). Accommodation on release remains an issue but the Board is pleased additional accommodation has been secured with a new charitable provider working jointly with the Sodexo CRC.

**Main Areas for Development**
**TO THE MINISTER**
The Board remains concerned about the lack of suitable accommodation for men on release, as proper resourcing of accommodation could be cost-effective in reducing reoffending.

**TO THE PRISON SERVICE**
The Board is concerned that some residents are held in the Separation and Care Unit for long periods.

**TO THE DIRECTOR**
The Board remains concerned at the level of illicit substance use and its consequences for residents' safety.

The Board notes the improvements to the governance and delivery of healthcare were implemented following the action plan prepared in response to the care quality commission (CQC). The prison should continue to embed these improvements into normal practice.

**Improvements**
The Board welcomes the increased emphasis on resident safety this year. There has also been a gradual improvement in the appearance of wings, which it is hoped will be enhanced by the introduction of new furniture. The daily regime has been modified and this has improved the timing of meals.

## HMP/YOI Peterborough (Women)

*For the latest reports on this prison please visit:*
https://tinyurl.com/bdfh26rv

*Important Changes:* **(1) Visits:** the identification necessary to access this prison and visit for social or professional purposes has changed; (2) **Money and Gifts** new rules now apply to these. See page 16 for full details of the above.

**Task of the establishment** HMP & YOI Peterborough is a local resettlement prison for adult and young women.

**Certified normal accommodation and operational capacity**
Prisoners held at the time of this visit: 317
Baseline certified normal capacity: 372 plus 12 mother and baby unit (MBU) places
In-use certified normal capacity: 372
Operational capacity: 396

**Prison status and key providers**
Private – managed by: Sodexo Justice Services
Prison Group: Custodial Contracts
Head of Custodial Contracts: Neil Richards
Governor/Director: Damien Evans

IMB Chair: Tani Nath
Physical health provider: Sodexo Justice Services
(GP services subcontracted to Cimmaron UK)
Mental health provider: Cambridgeshire and
Peterborough NHS Foundation Trust
Substance misuse treatment provider:
Sodexo Justice Services.
Prison education framework provider:
Sodexo Justice Services
Escort contractor: Serco, GeoAmey, and Mitie
Care and Custody

**Brief history** The prison opened on 28 March
2005 with two residential units and an MBU.

**Short description of residential units** There are
10 residential wings across houseblocks 1 and 2,
a segregation unit and a 12-place MBU.
*Houseblock 1:*
A1 – Young adults
B1 – Integrated substance misuse service and
first night centre for those requiring
detoxification or stabilisation
C1 – Early days centre
D1 – For those serving long-term sentences
E1 – Enhanced and open conditions unit
*Houseblock 2:*
A2 – Remand
B2 – Restricted status prisoners and the general
population
C2 – For those with complex needs
D2 – Non-vaping unit also accommodating the
general population
E2 – Foreign national unit (HMP & YOI
Peterborough is a designated foreign national hub)

**Visiting Information**
Visits are booked by prisoners and visitors will
be advised of the date and time to visit once the
booking has been accepted.

**Legal visits:** Check with the prison for the latest
information.

**INSPECTIONS & REPORTS**
**Scrutiny visit report HMP & YOI Peterborough
(women) (2 and 9–10 March 2021). Date of
publication 20 April 2021**
HMP & YOI Peterborough women's prison in the
east of England is a local and resettlement facility
for adult and young adult women. It shares the
same site and some resources with the adjoining
men's prison and serves the needs of women on
remand, and also encompasses the full range of
offences and sentences. This report presents the
findings from our scrutiny visit and focuses on
the treatment of women and the conditions in which
they were held during the Covid-19 pandemic.
The leadership team had managed the

consequences of the Covid-19 pandemic in the
prison effectively. There had been very few
positive cases over the year and the partnership
arrangements with health colleagues had
delivered a range of measures to contain
potential infections and protect prisoners and
staff. Cohorting arrangements were applied
inconsistently and this had the potential to
undermine the otherwise robust procedures and
guidance that existed.
In line with national guidance, the prison had
returned to a more restricted regime in January
2021. Women repeatedly described the
debilitating impact that being locked in a cell for
about 23 hours every day was having and the toll
it was taking on their mental health and
emotional well-being. Some even told us they
had considered suicide, although what we found
was a prison that was safe, calm and well
ordered. Levels of self-harm remained lower
than they were pre-Covid-19 despite a recent
slight increase. The case management
arrangements for women at risk of suicide or
self-harm appeared good, although many
women who had been in crisis reported that they
did not feel adequately supported. Anti-ligature
clothing was used to manage a small number of
women at risk more frequently than at other
women's prisons. We were not persuaded that
this was always necessary.
The number of recorded violent incidents had
declined since the beginning of the pandemic
and the environment and regime in the
segregation unit were reasonable. The use of
force had increased and was applied
disproportionately to young adults and in the
segregation unit, where generally stays were
short. We were not confident that across the
prison force was always used as a last resort or
that governance arrangements were sufficiently
robust. Previously high levels of strip-searching
had decreased considerably.
Overall, we found that the prison treated the
women respectfully, although there was
evidence to suggest that there was much more to
do to embed an approach that considered more
fully the trauma many women had experienced
and which is so often linked to their offending.
The environment was pleasant and women
appreciated being able to personalise their cells,
but toilets were not sufficiently screened.
Showers lacked privacy, deterring a number of
women from using them, and there were some
issues with the provision of menstrual care
products, soap and hand sanitiser. Relationships
between staff and women were generally
positive, but the regular meaningful contact that
is particularly important to women in prison was
less evident. Good consultation arrangements

had continued throughout the pandemic. Many women were positive about the food, but dinner was routinely served too early, from 3.30pm.

Equality and diversity needed to be promoted better, to make sure that the needs of all prisoners from protected groups were met consistently. The provision for foreign national women was good, but we found some women with disabilities who required better support. Mothers and their babies were well cared for, but concerns that the current restrictions were preventing babies and children from having face-to-face contact with their fathers were understandable.

Health services were broadly equal to those in the community. The perinatal pathway was working well and pregnant women received good support, including from a specialist midwife. However, three-quarters of women in our survey identified as having mental health problems and we were not confident that they were all getting the support they needed promptly. The regime was predictable, but at best most women could only achieve a maximum of one hour and 15 minutes out of their cell each day and this was often curtailed. The experience for the small number of women on the enhanced unit was much better. Most women did not have enough to keep them purposefully occupied – work and vocational opportunities were limited, and the education provision was too narrow, although the achievement of qualifications was high.

Women received effective support to help them maintain contact with their children and families, particularly in the absence of social visits. The Purple Visits system (see Glossary of terms) was now very well used. In-cell telephones and additional credit were valued, as was the well-used email contact scheme.

The arrangements to support women to progress through their sentences had continued. The case management of individual sentences was appropriately prioritised and included some face-to-face contact from prison offender managers. A small number of women had completed offending behaviour programmes. Some weaknesses in public protection arrangements had been identified previously but we found signs of improvement and there were now no areas of serious concern.

There was some good work to support women on their release. Despite this, many were released either without any housing or into emergency, short-term accommodation. This was not directly the fault of the prison but was symptomatic of a broader concern about the provision of suitable accommodation for women leaving prison.

Leaders described recovery plans (see Glossary of terms) that were ready to be implemented as soon as they were given permission to relax the current restrictions, although they also suggested an intent to progress with extreme caution. The management of risk will clearly need to develop as new advice is received.

This was a reasonably good visit, with a number of encouraging features. This report identifies nine areas of notable positive practice and also highlights eight key concerns and recommendations that we hope will assist the prison further to improve outcomes for the women in their care.

Chief Inspector of Prisons, March 2021

### Key concerns and recommendations

Key concerns and recommendations identify the issues of most importance to improving outcomes for prisoners and are designed to help establishments prioritise and address the most significant weaknesses in the treatment and conditions of prisoners.

During this visit we identified some areas of key concern, and have made a small number of recommendations for the prison to address.

Key concern: The environment, regime and culture in women's prisons should support an approach that assists women in prison to manage and overcome the trauma they may have experienced prior to custody. Despite some good, targeted work by dedicated staff and peer supporters, this approach was not yet fully embedded across the whole establishment. For example, a number of women said that they were partly deterred from using the showers and baths on the wings, because they were open to the landings and were not sufficiently private.

Recommendation: All practices and provision should be reviewed, to make sure that the environment, regime and culture across the prison support an approach that assists women to manage and overcome previous and current trauma. (To the director)

Key concern: The regime for the majority of women had been poor for too long and was having an increasingly negative impact on their mental health and well-being. Most spent, at best, 75 minutes out of their cell on a typical day, when competing factors such as time in the open air and domestic tasks occupied them and limited their opportunity to engage in purposeful activity or to interact with staff and their peers. This already limited time out of cell was often further curtailed.

Recommendation: All women should have consistent and sufficient time out of cell each day. They should be able to spend one hour in the open air, participate in purposeful activity, complete domestic tasks, and interact with staff and their peers. (To the director)

Key concern: In the six months prior to our visit, the overall number of incidents involving the use of force had increased and was much higher than the previous six months. The use of planned interventions was more frequent that at comparator prisons. A disproportionately large number of incidents involving the use of force either involved young adults or took place in the segregation unit. The written incident reports we examined did not always describe sufficiently attempts to de-escalate situations before force was used and some contained conflicting accounts. We were concerned that force was not always used as a last resort. There was regular oversight, but we queried its rigour.

Recommendation: Force should only be used against women in prison as a last resort. Written accounts should reflect that communication and de-escalation were attempted before force was used. Quality assurance of incidents should identify any shortfalls and action taken as a result. (To the director)

Key concern: Anti-ligature clothing was used more frequently and for longer periods than we usually see in women's prisons. We were concerned that it may have been used as a control measure for a small number of women and we were not convinced that it was always necessary. Support for women with complex needs required improvement.

Recommendation: Anti-ligature clothing should only be used as a last resort and for the shortest period possible. (To the director)

Key concern: Women reported a lack of regular, meaningful, face-to-face engagement with staff. This was a particular worry, given the detrimental impact they felt the limited regime was having on their mental health and well-being. Many women we spoke to talked about the struggles they were having, including some who had considered suicide. In our survey, only 51% of women reported that a member of staff had spoken to them in the previous week to see how they were getting on.

Recommendation: Welfare checks should be regular, face to face and provide women with a meaningful opportunity to talk about their well-being. (To the director)

Key concern: Women repeatedly told us about difficulties in ordering, and delays in accessing, menstrual care products, soap and hand sanitiser.

Recommendation: As a matter of urgency, women should have ready access to menstrual care products, soap and hand sanitiser. (To the director)

Key concern: The provision for some disabled women was inadequate and was having an impact on their well-being. One woman we spoke to had not used the exercise yard since the start of the pandemic and others told us that they were unable to access showers because of their physical disabilities.

Recommendation: All women with disabilities should have up-to-date care plans, which should ensure that reasonable adjustments are in place for them so that they are able to access the same provision within the prison as other prisoners. (To the director)

Key concern: In our survey, 75% of women said that they had a mental health problem, but only 15% that it was easy to see a mental health worker. Several women we spoke to told us that they had experienced long waits to see the mental health team and that their needs were not being met during this time. The team was stretched because of staff shortages, which included a long-standing psychologist vacancy, a staff grade psychiatrist position and a nursing vacancy. They adversely affected the timeliness of assessments for primary mental health services, which, at five weeks, was too long.

Recommendation: All women should receive timely assessment and support to meet their mental health needs. (To the director)

## Education, skills and work (Ofsted)

During this visit Ofsted inspectors conducted an interim assessment of the provision of education, skills and work in the establishment. They identified steps that the prison needed to take to meet the needs of prisoners, including those with special educational needs and disabilities.

## Next steps

Leaders and managers should ensure that the education offer during the restricted regime is broadened, so that women have more opportunities to learn new skills and gain new knowledge ahead of the full reopening of the regime. The offer should be informed by a training needs analysis of the prison population, to establish fully its needs in relation to education, skills and work.

Leaders and managers should formally monitor the quality of in-cell learning. They should work with staff to improve their skills in remote teaching and in providing developmental feedback to learners.

Leaders and managers should monitor how well women engage in the activities available to them, to assure themselves that women not allocated to education, skills and work activities are occupied and meaningfully engaged during their time in cells.

Leaders and managers should ensure that support for women with special educational needs is appropriate, effectively coordinated and provided in a timely manner.

### Notable positive practice

We define notable positive practice as innovative practice or practice that leads to particularly good outcomes from which other establishments may be able to learn. Inspectors look for evidence of good outcomes for prisoners; original, creative or particularly effective approaches to problem-solving or achieving the desired goal; and how other establishments could learn from or replicate the practice.

Inspectors found nine examples of notable positive practice during this visit.

Women were able to access free face-to-face help, advice and support with legal issues from a local solicitor. This was unusual and assisted the prison in ensuring that women could adequately access help to achieve their legal rights.

A one-stop clinic was innovative and made sure that a comprehensive health screening was undertaken on the day after a woman's arrival. This included a range of tests and access to clinicians. It was completed in one day, in contrast to the delayed and sometime disjointed arrangements we often see. This enabled the early identification and treatment of women's health needs and had reduced the non-attendance rate for secondary screening and other health appointments.

The development of a perinatal pathway was positive. It ensured that pregnant women were identified promptly, and that their needs were met as part of a structured pathway, based on good multidisciplinary work, including a specialist midwife, mother and baby unit staff and the mental health team.

The two-year peer support programme, commissioned by NHS England and NHS Improvement, saw two perinatal and two health care peer supporters offer emotional and practical support to women, with a focus on those who were eight weeks pre-release.

The enhanced unit allowed women to access much better time out of cell than elsewhere in the prison. Women valued this and it was mentioned as a key factor in supporting their overall well-being.

The prison's in-house 'family matters' team had continued to provide excellent, meaningful support for women and their families. Staff saw all women face to face soon after their arrival, identifying primary carers and those who needed help with practical and emotional matters, such as brokering and facilitating calls with families, social services, legal teams and adoption agencies.

Valuable practical support was given to women who were not eligible for prison offender manager interventions. This useful initiative ('Most in Need') worked with women on an individual basis and focused on motivating them to embrace change and to support them in reducing their risk of re-offending, delivering some targeted non-accredited interventions where relevant.

A dedicated team of prison staff and peer trauma champions provided support for women who had experienced trauma, including abuse, rape or domestic violence. Peer champions saw all new arrivals to identify their needs, and the team provided valuable, well-needed support to women in prison.

The Outside Links facility at the prison offered excellent face-to-face support to women, both on their day of discharge and after release, at a further Community Outside Links facility in Peterborough City Centre.

### INDEPENDENT MONITORING BOARD: Annual Report

The law requires every prison to be monitored by an independent Board appointed by the Justice Secretary; these are known as Independent Monitoring Boards (IMBs). The IMB must satisfy itself as to the humane and just treatment of those held in custody within its prison and the range and adequacy of the programmes preparing them for release; it must report annually to the Justice Secretary on how well the prison has met the standards and requirements placed on it.

### IMB Report April 2020 to March 2021
### Published 11 October 2021

The Board believes that overall residents are treated fairly and with respect.

The Board is concerned that the prison holds a high number of women with complex needs. The Complex Needs group carefully considers their needs but there are often limited opportunities for rehabilitation, and some remain in the healthcare or segregation unit for long periods.

Most prison complaints are handled within time limits. The Board is concerned that handling of residents' property continues to be problematic, both within the prison and on transfer.

The prison regime is good, and time out of cell was more than 11 hours.

### Are prisoners treated humanely?

The Board believes that overall, residents are treated humanely and with decency. The increased focus on safety has had positive results, with self-harm falling by approximately 10%.

The standard of accommodation is good, but it is a concern that in-cell toilets are not screened for privacy.

Improvements to the healthcare provision are ongoing, and mental health and social care provision is good. There remains a reliance on agency nurses and locum doctors (8.3). The Board is pleased the weekly well-woman clinic continues.

## Are prisoners prepared well for their release?

Preparation for release is very important in the prison, evidenced by the good learning and skills provision, the focus on maintaining family ties, and the Outside Links service. Short sentences, however, make it difficult to deliver effective interventions. Accommodation on release remains an issue but the Board is pleased additional accommodation has been secured with two new charitable providers, one in a joint project with the Sodexo CRC.

## Main Areas for Development
### TO THE MINISTER

The Board remains concerned about the lack of suitable accommodation for women on release, as proper resourcing of accommodation could be cost-effective in reducing reoffending.

### TO THE PRISON SERVICE

The Board is concerned that some very complex women have been segregated for long periods with very limited regime. The prison does not have provision for appropriate interventions for some of these cases, and the Board considers that the national complex needs team should be more proactive in considering transfers to other secure establishments with suitable programmes.

### TO THE DIRECTOR

The Board notes that improvements to the governance and delivery of healthcare were implemented following the action plan prepared in response to the Care Quality Commission (CQC). The prison should continue to embed these improvements into normal practice.

### Improvements

The Board welcomes the reduction in self harm achieved during the reporting year. There should be a continuing focus on the safety of residents.

**THE GROVE
EASTON
PORTLAND
DORSET
DT5 1DL**

**HMP & YOI PORTLAND**

**Tel: 01305 715600**

*For the latest reports on this prison please visit:*
https://tinyurl.com/bdfh26rv

*Important Changes:* **(1) Visits:** the identification necessary to access this prison and visit for social or professional purposes has changed; (2) **Money and Gifts** new rules now apply to these. See page 16 for full details of the above.

**Task of the establishment** Male closed young offender institution and male category C adults.

**Certified normal accommodation and operational capacity**
Prisoners held at the time of inspection: 492
Baseline certified normal capacity: 463
In-use certified normal capacity: 458
Operational capacity: 530

**Prison status and key providers**
Public
Prison Group: Avon & South Dorset
Prison Group Director: Paul Woods
Governor/Director: Rob Luxford
IMB Chair: Anna Knight
Physical health provider: Care UK
Mental health provider: Care UK
Substance use treatment provider: EDP
Learning and skills provider: Weston College
Escort contractor: GeoAmey

**Brief history** HMP/YOI Portland is a category C prison located on Portland Bill, Dorset. It is a historic prison, originally built in 1848. It houses around 500 adult male and young adult male prisoners.

**Short description of residential units**
Collingwood is the induction wing.
Nelson and Grenville are young offenders' wings. Benbow, Raleigh and Drake are general population wings with some young offenders. Beaufort is working towards being an enabled environment.

**Visiting Information**
Booking line: 01305 715 775 Monday to Friday, 8:30am to 12pm and 1:30pm to 3pm.
**Visiting times:** Wednesday, Saturday, and Sunday: 2pm to 3pm and 3:30pm to 4:30pm.

**Legal visits:** There are currently no legal visits taking place.

## INSPECTIONS & REPORTS

**Date of last inspections** 29 July – 9 August 2019

*Notable features from this inspection*

• Nearly two-thirds of the prison's population were under 30 years old.

• Only 11.5% of prisoners had been at Portland for a year or longer.

• The level of prisoner self-harm had doubled since the previous inspection.

• Sixteen per cent of the population were sharing cells designed to hold one person.

• A quarter of prisoners were unemployed during the core day.

• Half the prisoners released were from outside Portland's resettlement catchment area.

• Only 4% of prisoners said it was easy for family and friends to get to Portland.

### HMCIP Report, published 16 January 2020

HMP/YOI Portland is a category C closed facility holding up to 530 adult and young adult male prisoners. Originally built in 1848, the prison is in Dorset although those held generally came from a much wider catchment across southern England. The population profile as a whole was relatively young, with 25% aged under 21 and nearly 58% between 21 and 39. The vast majority of prisoners were serving more than 12 months, with nearly half serving between two and four years, and nearly a third serving longer than that.

When we last inspected Portland, in 2017, we expressed guarded optimism about the prison's future, despite finding some concerning outcomes. At the time, we found outcomes to be insufficiently good across three of our four tests of a healthy prison, and we rated safety as poor. At this inspection we found that outcomes had not improved in any of our tests and, of greatest concern, the prison remained poor in safety.

Prisoners arriving at Portland were received reasonably well into the institution but induction was often delayed or cancelled. The early experience of many prisoners consisted of extended periods locked in cell. Levels of violence had reduced following a recent increase in 2018 but remained high and comparable to the levels we saw during our last inspection. Work by staff to tackle violence, as well as to challenge poor behaviour by prisoners, was not good enough. The situation was not helped by a failure to develop any kind of incentivising culture that might motivate prisoners to engage and behave. Consistent with the level of violence in the prison, use of force had increased markedly. While we found no evidence that force had been misused, supervision and accountability were insufficient. In contrast, the number of adjudications and the use of segregation had decreased since 2017.

Indeed, the use of segregation was lower than at similar prisons and lengths of stay were comparatively brief for most. Living conditions on the unit were better, although the regime was very limited. Some security arrangements were too restrictive but the prison used intelligence well and had done some very good work to reduce an influx of illegal drugs. Data from mandatory drug tests suggested a positive rate of just over 5%.

Levels of self-harm had doubled since our last inspection and were now very high. Case management (ACCTs) of men in crisis was generally poor and many experienced protracted periods of lock-up and isolation. The prison had no safeguarding policy.

Our observations suggested a reasonable quality of personal interaction between staff and prisoners but the paucity of the regime limited the ability of staff to engage consistently. Staff were too slow to challenge poor behaviour. It was no surprise that in our survey just 59% of prisoners thought staff treated them with respect. Cleanliness and the quality of the environment were little improved since our last inspection, with some cells in a poor condition and many overcrowded. Showers were in a particularly poor condition, although access to basic items had recently improved. Consultation with prisoners was weak, as was the management of the applications and complaints processes. The promotion of equality and diversity was similarly weak but there was evidence that, with the encouragement of the Prison Group Director's office, improvements were beginning to be made. The prison provided reasonable health care but facilities were poor and prisoners had difficulty accessing the service.

The amount of time prisoners spent out of their cells was poor and reflected a limited and restricted regime prone to slippage and cancellations that ultimately undermined so much of the work of the establishment. A quarter of prisoners were not engaged in activity and could experience as little as one hour 15 minutes out of cell each day. During roll checks we found a shocking 44% of prisoners locked in cell during the working day. The curricula offered in education and vocational training opportunities were appropriate but there remained too few activity places. Those places that were available were underused, a situation compounded by continued poor punctuality and in some areas poor attendance, although generally attendance had improved since the last inspection. Those that did attend seemed motivated and made the progress expected of them. Teaching, learning and assessment were well planned and there were some improvements in prisoners' achievements.

Our colleagues in Ofsted assessed the overall effectiveness of provision as 'requires improvement'. The relative remoteness of Portland meant that promoting good family ties remained a challenge. The involvement of Barnardo's in support of family days and through their encouragement of care leavers was, however, impressive. The prison had a good reducing reoffending strategy based on a useful needs analysis and since our last inspection the prison had reduced its backlog of offender assessments (OASys) by half. The quality of many assessments, however, was not good enough and contact between offenders and their supervisors was low and almost entirely reactive. Too few prisoners said they had a sentence plan, and offending behaviour opportunities and one-to-one interventions were too limited. Public protection work was, however, good and resettlement support for the approximately 40 prisoners released each month was reasonable despite most discharged prisoners returning to other parts of the country. Overall, our findings at this inspection were troubling. Outcomes had not declined and there was some recent evidence that the impetus and initiative provided by the Prison Group Director was having some beneficial effect. This, however, was not enough. We had concerns about whether local managers had realistic, grounded plans to meet the challenges the prison faced. The prison's approach to safety was lacklustre, basic standards were not maintained and staff generally needed to have greater expectations of the prisoners they supervised. The prison also needed to re-focus on its primary function as a training and resettlement prison and ensure first that it did the basics right. It urgently needed to ensure that an active and purposeful regime was being delivered and that this met fully the needs of the men held.

Peter Clarke CVO OBE QPM August 2019
HM Chief Inspector of Prisons

## INDEPENDENT MONITORING BOARD:
## Annual Report

The law requires every prison to be monitored by an independent Board appointed by the Justice Secretary; these are known as Independent Monitoring Boards (IMBs). The IMB must satisfy itself as to the humane and just treatment of those held in custody within its prison and the range and adequacy of the programmes preparing them for release; it must report annually to the Justice Secretary on how well the prison has met the standards and requirements placed on it.

**IMB Report 01 April 2019 – 31 March 2020**
**Published July 2020** (latest available 7.8.22)
**Executive Summary**
**Background to the report**

This report is compiled according to the policy of the Board, which is not to include any item or issue which has not first been recorded in weekly rota reports, or a periodic wing or departmental report. It includes observations from meetings attended whilst performing the regular monitoring which forms our role and responsibility in Portland.

## Main judgements
### How safe is the prison?

The number of prisoner-on-prisoner assaults has reduced; however, numbers are still higher than would be anticipated based on the age range of the population. Assaults on staff continue to occur, albeit to a lesser extent than prisoner-on-prisoner assaults.

The ingress of illicit substances continues to present problems for the prison. Drug- related debt, extortion, violence, self-harm and mental health issues are a constant feature of life in Portland.

There has been some progress in relation to the oversight and management of complex offenders and vulnerable prisoners. Greater collaboration between service providers and the introduction of key workers have been beneficial. Unfortunately the roll out of the key worker scheme has been slow and this has had an impact on developments.

The initiative on Beaufort wing for self-isolating prisoners is a positive step forward in meeting the needs of this group.

### How fairly and humanely are prisoners treated?

There is evidence suggesting that prisoners in Portland are not always treated with compassion and fairness as demonstrated by:

• the lack of challenge to the poor standards of maintenance and repair of the buildings
• the seeming lack of concern from some staff regarding the conditions in which prisoners are living and working
• the unhelpful attitudes and behaviour shown by some staff towards prisoners
• evidence that some groups of prisoner are not getting equal access to opportunities

However, there is some evidence that, after several months without a fully functioning equalities lead, the diversity and race equality action team (DREAT) is starting to get a grip on the extent of the problem and is beginning to identify training needs for staff.

## How well are prisoners' health and wellbeing needs met?

Portland's struggle to reliably deliver a daily regime – including education and employment opportunities and time out of cell – has had an impact on prisoner health and well-being, as well as stability around the prison.

Problems with the appointment and retention of mental health and psychology staff have added to prisoner stress levels. Delays in diagnosis and treatments have had an impact on prisoner health and well-being. They have also put pressure on operational staff and others dealing with prisoners on a daily basis. Mental health nurses have expressed concerns that, for too long, treatment for this group of prisoners has centred on medication rather than therapeutic interventions.

## How well are prisoners progressed towards successful resettlement?

The resumption in the delivery of accredited offending behaviour programmes is a step forward for prisoners.

The slight increase in the opportunities to access release on temporary licence (ROTL) in the local community is also welcomed. Board members hope that this will be further extended, in line with the change to the profile of the prison and its status as a resettlement prison for Dorset prisoners. Unfortunately, regular shutdowns have had an impact on opportunities for prisoners to develop education and work skills and achieve qualifications to assist in securing employment on release.

The move to release more local prisoners has caused additional pressure because of the lack of accommodation available through local authorities in Dorset. There is a lack of night shelter facilities and move-on supported housing in the area, and the indications are that there will be no change in this situation.

## Main areas for development
## TO THE MINISTER

Over 50% of prisoners present as being of no fixed abode on arrival at Portland. As a consequence of changes to the prison profile, Dorset prisoners will now be released from Portland. There is a dearth of accommodation available through local authorities in the area.

Poole and Bournemouth Council has indicated to the prison that there will be no additional investment or change to their current policy, which serves to limit the availability of night-shelter facilities and move-on supported housing provision for released prisoners.

The resettlement team in Portland has been pro-active in developing links with independent housing providers. The reality is, however, that without more substantial support on release, this group is unlikely to make the changes necessary to turn their lives around.

In order to maximise the opportunities for learning and change provided to prisoners while in custody, investment needs to be put into accommodation, employment and learning opportunities in the community post-release.

## TO THE PRISON SERVICE

Structural repairs that are urgently required to the fabric of buildings, plumbing, heating and telephony systems in Portland need to be investigated and addressed accordingly. An updated assessment of health and safety conditions in the workshops also needs to be undertaken, and any failings put right.

Systems to ensure the safe storage of prisoner property whilst they are in custody, and specifically during inter-prison transfers, need addressing. The amount of property which has been logged on property cards and then goes missing is unacceptable. It causes prisoners distress and diminishes trust and confidence in the prison service. Checks need to be put in place to ensure that critically unwell prisoners, suffering significant health problems, cannot be unilaterally transferred. Should this ever be necessary, it should not happen without prior negotiation with the receiving establishment and the provision of up to date and comprehensive medical records.

## TO THE GOVERNOR

For a number of years, Portland has been unable to deliver a regime that meets the requirements of its prisoner population. Shutdowns are frequent, and last minute changes to the daily regime a regular occurrence. This is to the detriment of education and work opportunities for prisoners and the delivery of substance misuse and offending behaviour programmes. It has a destabilising impact on the prisoner population, in general, and emotionally vulnerable prisoners in particular.

Prisoners from Black, Asian and minority ethnic groups, those with mental health problems and those with other protected characteristics have indicated that they do not feel understood or supported by operational staff on the wings. Confidence in discrimination incident reporting and the complaints process is low. Prisoners have indicated that they do not feel the system in Portland is working for them. Operational staff have identified deficits in their knowledge, skills and ability when working with some prisoner groups. Collaborative work between staff and prisoner representatives has begun to identify training needs to be addressed in order to ensure that Portland delivers a fair and humane environment for all its residents.

The Board continues to have concerns about some aspects of use of force practises – specifically, the failure of staff to wear and/or switch on body-worn cameras. The recovery of closed-circuit television (CCTV) footage from the wings is still problematic. The timely and adequate completion of use of force paperwork has improved, with fewer outstanding reports, but continues to require regular monitoring.

The provision of healthcare services has suffered for lack of a psychologist and psychiatrist at times during the reporting period. The appointment and retention of psychologists and psychiatrists to posts in Portland have been problematic since the contract transferred from the local health authority. It would be helpful if the reasons for this could be explored and, where possible, addressed.

The number of prisoners failing to attend for pre-arranged healthcare appointments because operational support grade (OSG) staff have not followed agreed protocols is not acceptable. This is the second year running that this situation has ensued. The ingress of illicit drugs into Portland needs to be addressed. It is having an impact on the health and well-being of prisoners and staff, and is linked to debt, bullying, violence, isolation and overall stability in the prison.

## Progress since the last report
### Safety
Portland has worked to address criticism of its approach to Safety following a Her Majesty's Inspectorate of Prisons (HMIP) inspection last year. Whilst levels of prisoner violence remain high, the initiatives introduced by the safer custody team have seen reductions of approximately 50% in the figures for prisoner-on-prisoner assaults during the first three months of 2020, as opposed to the same period in 2019.

The number of prisoners choosing to self-isolate has seen a considerable increase in recent years. The introduction of a supportive regime on Beaufort wing aimed at re- integration is seeing early success.

It has significantly improved the regime delivered for this group and, at the same time, contributed to a reduction in its numbers.

The introduction of the 'safety hotline' for families in November 2019 is a new and positive move.

### Fair and Humane Treatment
The introduction of the key worker system, albeit slowly and ad hoc, has had a positive impact for those prisoners allocated a worker.

Prisoners on assessment, care in custody and team work (ACCT) plans and those whose progress is being monitored under a challenge, support and intervention plan (CSIP) are being motivated and encouraged to address their treatment plans, with the support and encouragement of key workers.

The re-integration strategy, devised by staff in the CSU to support prisoners reluctant or anxious about a return to life on main location, is proving to be a positive initiative.

### Health and well-being
Overall the Board are reporting similar concerns to those we raised in our last report:
- There has been a failure to address the ingress of illicit drugs and substance misuse in the prison.
- Ongoing problems recruiting and retaining a psychologist and a psychiatrist have affected the assessment and treatment of prisoners requiring these services.
- Agreed procedures to ensure that prisoners get to healthcare appointments have been ignored by operational and OSG staff, resulting in failures in the delivery of essential services.

However, the conclusion of the current reporting period coincides with the early stages of the coronavirus crisis. This period has seen improvements in collaboration and co-operation between operational and healthcare staff.

### Progression and Release
The range of education and employment opportunities on offer in Portland is good. Prisoner access to these opportunities, as well as other activities, continues to be impeded by the number of shutdowns.

**COED-Y-PAEN**
**PONTYPOOL**
**MONMOUTHSHIRE**
**NP4 0TB**

HMPYOI PRESCOED

See entry for HMP Usk

**2 RIBBLETON LANE**
**PRESTON**
**LANCASHIRE**
**PR1 5AB**

HMP & YOI PRESTON

Tel: 01772 444550

*August 2021 - Important Changes:* (1) **Visits:** the identification necessary to access this prison and visit for social or professional purposes has changed; (2) **Money and Gifts** new rules now apply to these. See page 16 for full details of the above.

**Task of the establishment** HMP Preston is a Category B local resettlement prison for young adult and adult males.

## Certified normal accommodation and operational capacity

Prisoners held at the time of this visit: 650
Baseline certified normal capacity: 426
In-use certified normal capacity: 426
Operational capacity: 715

## Prison status and key providers

Public
Prison Group: Cumbria & Lancashire
Prison Group Director: John Illingsworth
Governor/Director: Dan Cooper
IMB Chair: David Kelshaw
Physical health provider: Spectrum
Mental health provider: Tees, Esk and Wear Valleys NHS Foundation Trust
Substance misuse treatment provider: Spectrum
Prison education framework provider:
Escort contractor: GeoAmey

**Brief history** HMP Preston was built in 1790 and later enlarged as a radial prison. The four wings leading from the centre building were constructed between 1840 and 1895. Since 1790, it was used as a civil defence centre and a naval detention quarters, before becoming a training prison for category C prisoners. In 1990 it became a local prison.

## Short description of residential units

A1 – Separation and care unit
A2 – Complex prisoner unit
A3/4/5 – General population
B – Vulnerable prisoner unit
C1 – Reverse cohort unit, RCU (see Glossary of terms)/Induction and first night centre
C2 – Reverse cohort unit, RCU (see Glossary of terms)/Induction and first night centre
C3 –26 RCU spaces annex (gated off)/general population
C4 –32 RCU spaces annex (gated off)/general population
D – General population
F – Risk-assessed workers' unit accommodating prison orderlies
G – Substance misuse recovery unit
H - Health care

## Visiting Information

Book online at: www.gov.uk/prison-visits or ring 01772 444888 Monday to Thursday, 8am to 12pm and 1:30pm to 3:30pm, Friday: 8am to 12pm
**Visiting times:** Tuesday and Thursday to Sunday: 2pm to 3pm and 3:30pm to 4:30pm.

**Legal visits:** Book a legal or professional visit by emailing: Legalvisits.Preston@justice.gov.uk or ring 01772 444 777 Monday – Thursday: 8am to 12pm, 1:30pm to 3:30pm, Friday: 8am to 12pm

## INSPECTIONS & REPORTS
**Scrutiny visit: 4 and 11–12 August 2020**
**Published: 15 September 2020**

This report discusses the findings from a scrutiny visit (SV) to HMP Preston. The SV methodology develops the 'short scrutiny visit' (SSV, see Glossary of terms) approach that HMI Prisons has used to provide independent oversight of custodial establishments since April 2020. Our previous approach monitored outcomes for prisoners in a small number of key areas at a time when regimes were severely restricted. While SVs are still far more limited in scope than our full inspections, they are increasing the intensity of scrutiny as prisons enter a phase of recovery. SVs examine the treatment and conditions of prisoners in greater detail, and focus in particular on the pace of recovery and proportionality of treatment, while ensuring the safest possible inspection practices.

HMP Preston is a local prison which, at the time of our visit, held around 650 adult males drawn from Lancashire and other parts of the North West. While the population was lower than at our previous inspection in 2017, the prison was still severely overcrowded. As we have found elsewhere, the early release schemes brought in to relieve pressure on places during the pandemic had been ineffective, with no prisoners released following assessment. HM Prison and Probation Service (HMPPS) had classed the prison as a Covid-19 outbreak site until 10 July. At the time of our visit, there were no confirmed prisoner cases. A small number of staff were shielding or away from work while awaiting test results.

The prison dates from the 18th century, and some of the accommodation was deteriorating or, as in the case of the very cramped reception area, barely fit for purpose. In such areas, social distancing was all but impossible, and it was difficult in much of the rest of the prison because of its cramped design and overcrowding. We saw few attempts by staff and prisoners to socially distance even where it was achievable.

The reverse cohort unit (RCU, see Glossary of terms) was large and busy. It was evident that it could not be run practically in line with best practices – such as the consistent separation of prisoners arriving on different days – while also delivering basic facilities, such as daily showers and telephone calls. This undermined the effectiveness of the unit, as did the staff from other wings walking unnecessarily through the RCU. While most prisoners understood the reasons for the restrictions imposed in March 2020, many told us they were confused and concerned about the possible next steps. There had been a lack of investment in communications technology, and the prison had no in-cell telephones or prisoner information kiosks, and no prison television channel. This particularly disadvantaged prisoners with literacy or language difficulties. Nearly all prisoners received the restricted regime reliably, including daily access to telephones and showers, and exercise in the open air six days a week. However, most were still locked up for 22.5 hours a day, usually in shared cells that were not designed to hold more than one prisoner. Isolated prisoners (those symptomatic or positive for Covid-19, see Glossary of terms) were allowed out of their cells for only 15 minutes a week to shower. This was unacceptable and, given that there was only one such prisoner during our visit, wholly avoidable. Following an initial reduction, the incidence of violence was now starting to increase. Use of force had increased in May and June 2020 to levels above those before the regime had been restricted, but it had started to reduce again. There was evidence that some use of force had resulted from prisoners being frustrated at the prolonged restrictions and a lack of purposeful activity. While managers tackled inappropriate use of force robustly where it was identified, we were concerned to find that staff often did not switch on body-worn cameras when they should have used them. This required a stronger management response.

Self-harm was at a similar level to that before the restricted regime was imposed. Assessment, care in custody and teamwork (ACCT) case management for prisoners at risk of suicide or self-harm was generally reasonable, and Listeners were available at most times.

There was a very high level of mental health need in the prison. In our survey, two-thirds of prisoners said they had mental health problems and 11 were waiting to be transferred to a secure hospital. Some prisoners we interviewed described a decline in their mental well-being during the restricted regime.

Primary and mental health services were stretched, and there were long waits for routine and some urgent assessments. Health care staff were working hard to improve matters and there were early signs of recovery, as staff who had been shielding returned to work. The psychosocial support team had a limited presence in the main prison but had recently resumed one-to-one work in the substance misuse recovery unit. In a positive move, wing staff had also supported peer workers to resume some useful group support in the recovery unit.

We observed generally good staff-prisoner relationships, although there were routine welfare checks only for the most vulnerable groups. Prisoner consultation had recently resumed. The prison was clean and additional cleaning was being carried out daily. Prisoners also reported good access to cleaning materials for their cells.

Strategic oversight of equality work had also recently resumed; this was needed given some negative reporting by black and ethnic minority prisoners in our survey. Support for prisoners who did not speak English was generally limited, and there was little translated material about the regime. Despite significant staff shortages, the chaplaincy had maintained a presence in the establishment.

Education providers had not yet returned to the prison and few prisoners were in work. Library books and activity packs were distributed to wings, but many prisoners we spoke with did not know about the latter.

There was some good family support work. Social visits had been reintroduced, but they had been suspended shortly after as a result of local area restrictions. Video calling to family and friends was appreciated by most of the prisoners who had used it, but had only been available for just over a week. Prisoners had regular access to telephones but often at times that their families were at work or otherwise unavailable, and calls were limited to 15 minutes. The prison had not used the HMPPS- supplied mobile phones creatively to overcome this problem.

Sentence planning and risk assessment processes were up to date, which was positive, and most risk management procedures were working reasonably effectively. However, the continuing lack of face- to-face interviews limited the effectiveness of some provision. No prisoners had been released since March 2020 without some form of accommodation, which was positive. Managers and staff at Preston had shown considerable resilience in managing the changing demands of the Covid-19 period. Prisoners had shown similar fortitude, although the costs to their mental health of such an extended period of restriction were increasingly evident. There were some obvious changes that the prison should have made to improve matters, such as ensuring that prisoners in protective isolation had more time out of cell. More ambition in general would also have improved the pace of recovery, and alleviated the evident and growing strain on prisoners. This is partly a matter for local managers, but there was no doubt that they needed to feel they had the autonomy from HMPPS to innovate.

At our previous full inspection, we commented that Preston had many strengths but that with more imagination it could and should deliver more. That judgement also held true during this scrutiny visit.

Peter Clarke CVO OBE QPM

HM Chief Inspector of Prisons August 2020

### Key concerns and recommendations

*Key concerns* and recommendations identify the issues of most importance to improving outcomes for prisoners and are designed to help establishments prioritise and address the most significant weaknesses in the treatment and conditions of prisoners.

During this visit we identified some areas of key concern, and have made a small number of key recommendations for the prison to address.

*Key concern:* There was a lack of investment in the variety of communication methods that we have seen in other prisons; for example, there were no information kiosks, no dedicated prison TV channel and no in-cell telephones, which particularly disadvantaged prisoners with literacy or language difficulties. The HMPPS-supplied mobile phones were not widely used.

Key recommendation: There should be investment into communications technology and better use of existing resources to improve information flow to and communication with prisoners. (To HMPPS and the governor)

*Key concern:* The reverse cohort unit (RCU) was very large and could not be run practically in line with best practices, such as the separation of prisoners arriving on different days, while also delivering basic facilities, such as daily showers and telephone calls. The unit's effectiveness was further reduced by prisoners mixing during exercise, and staff from other wings walking through it unnecessarily.

Key recommendation: Reverse cohorting should be implemented consistently to minimise the risk of spreading infection. The unit should be resourced and organised sufficiently to achieve this objective. (To governor)

*Key concern:* Violence was increasing, and use of force had been higher than previously in the two months following the introduction of the restrictions. The relevant documents we reviewed did not always demonstrate the use of de-escalation techniques, and even though body-worn cameras were available, these were not always turned on during incidents.

Key recommendation: Staff should turn on body-worn cameras at the earliest opportunity to ensure that use of force incidents are recorded. Managers should effectively address staff reluctance to use body-worn cameras. (To governor)

*Key concern:* There was still little activity for prisoners and the pace of progress was slow, with an increasing impact on the well-being of prisoners. Most prisoners spent no more than 1.5 hours out of their cells on a typical day. The prison could have done more to alleviate this problem. Some prisoners were undertaking multiple work roles while others had none. The

one prisoner held in protective isolation (see Glossary of terms) had only 15 minutes out of cell a week, which was unacceptable and unnecessary. The HMPPS standardised recovery plans were too limiting on local discretion.

Recommendation: There should be a local, tailored prison recovery plan that outlines how and when the restrictions can be lifted, and how to provide purposeful activity to the greatest possible number of prisoners. Prisoners in protective isolation should be enabled to spend some time out of their cell every day. (To HMPPS and governor)

*Key concern:* Pressures on health care staffing and their limited access to prisoners had created long waiting times for health care appointments, with some prisoners waiting up to 13 days for an urgent appointment with a GP. There was a very high level of mental health need. In our survey, two-thirds of prisoners said they had mental health problems, and those we interviewed described a decline in their mental well-being during the restricted regime. Eleven prisoners had needs so serious that they were waiting to be transferred to a secure hospital. Only 13% of prisoners surveyed said it was easy to get a mental health appointment. Routine mental health assessments had ceased, with waiting times now at 16 weeks.

Key recommendation. The prison should work with its health partners to ensure that immediate action is taken to mitigate the deterioration in prisoners' mental and physical health during the Covid-19 crisis. This should include sufficient staffing to give prisoners prompt access to urgent and routine health care. (To governor)

*Key concern:* The vast majority of prisoners had not been seen by prison offender managers or resettlement workers employed by the community rehabilitation company. Prisoners were anxious about their progression or release, and frustrated at the lack of information and support available.

Recommendation: HMPPS and the governor should work with key partners providing offender management and resettlement services to enable their staff to resume routine and private contact with prisoners safely. (To HMPPS and governor)

### Notable positive practice

We define notable positive practice as innovative practice or practice that leads to particularly good outcomes from which other establishments may be able to learn. Inspectors look for evidence of good outcomes for prisoners; original, creative or particularly effective approaches to problem-solving or achieving the desired goal; and how other establishments could learn from or replicate the practice.

Inspectors found the following examples of notable positive practice during this visit.

• A member of the safer custody team made daily contact with prisoners on case management for risk of suicide or self-harm.

• Listeners had been given a dedicated telephone number to contact the Samaritans for support, as the Samaritans were currently unable to visit the establishment in person.

• The prison had provided tablet computers on around 14 occasions to allow prisoners to contact their families in exceptional circumstances, such as the livestream of funerals, or to see their newborn children or end-of-life relatives.

• The family liaison team had introduced a new service to allow prisoners to send and/or receive an electronic photograph each month (subject to public protection restrictions).

## INDEPENDENT MONITORING BOARD:
### Annual Report

The law requires every prison to be monitored by an independent Board appointed by the Justice Secretary; these are known as Independent Monitoring Boards (IMBs). The IMB must satisfy itself as to the humane and just treatment of those held in custody within its prison and the range and adequacy of the programmes preparing them for release; it must report annually to the Justice Secretary on how well the prison has met the standards and requirements.

### IMB Report April 2020 – March 2021
### Published September 2021
### Executive Summary
### Background to the report

The Covid-19 outbreak has been in effect for the whole of the period of this annual report. This has had a significant impact on the Board's ability to gather information and discuss the contents of this annual report. The Board has therefore tried to cover as much ground as possible in these difficult circumstances, but inevitably there is less detail and supporting evidence than usual. Ministers are aware of these constraints. Regular information is being collected specifically on the prison's response to the pandemic, and that is being collated nationally. At the start of the national outbreak the Ministry of Justice (MoJ) and Her Majesty's Prison and Probation Service (HMPPS) implemented the Covid-19: National Framework for Prisons and Services which established an estate-wide consistent basis for Governors to make decisions according to their local circumstances, and with the appropriate level of oversight. This was achieved by establishing five regime stages at which the prison could operate and placing prisons in command mode and reporting to Gold command. The prisons had to develop exceptional delivery models (EDM) for each stage approved by Gold command. This resulted in very strong day to day central control of the prisons across the country, to ensure that every prison was being treated the same.

There was naturally a lot of apprehension amongst the staff, as there was in the nation as a whole. Infection control measures were immediately put in place; social distancing enforced for staff and prisoners, and prisoners confined to their cells except for exercise, and showers and phone calls. The senior management team (SMT) had to develop new working practices as directed by the Gold command. Data needed to control an infectious outbreak had to be collected and collated.

The prison has an operational capacity of 680 prisoners. It has 305 prisoner facing staff, 57 administrative staff, and additional staff belonging to the partner agencies (healthcare, education, probation, Amey etc...). These staff and the prisoners live in the local areas, which have continually had a high number of Covid-19 cases. They have family members, and are subject to all the same risks of infection as in general society. This similarity of personal circumstances may have helped relations between prisoners and staff. The prison suffered two outbreaks of Covid-19. The first was in early June 2020 and the second started in October 2020 and lasted until February 2021. Whilst the prison was suffering the outbreaks an outbreak control team (OCT) was formed. The OCT was led by Public Health England (PHE) and met weekly to discuss the situation in the prison, agree control measures and suggest areas for improvement. Issues and recommendations that could affect the prison estate were escalated to gold command. The outbreak could only be declared over if there had been no infections for 28 days (for either prisoners or staff).

The seriousness of an outbreak in a confined institution such as a prison can be shown by the following figures. At the start of the second outbreak, it was known that there were fifteen prisoners testing positive for Covid-19 with half a dozen prisoners thought to be symptomatic but not declaring. The OCT authorised three tranches of mass testing of the prisoners, spaced at seven-day intervals. Out of a total of 590 prisoners tested, 139 returned a positive result. This resulted in 202 prisoners being placed in isolation. If the mass testing had not taken place when it did, the spread in the prison could have been total and the staff would have had difficulty in coping. The extra work involved in having a prisoner in a cell isolating involves delivering meals to the cell and delivering mobile phones to the cell. As the cells do not have showers, prisoners have to be escorted to the showers, and they require a special clean after each use. There has also been a need for special laundry provision for clothing and bedding. Each of these contacts requires the use of PPE. With over 100 cells containing prisoners who had tested positive, this was a major task. Also, during this second outbreak, for a two-week period there were 55 officers absent due to Covid-19 related illnesses. Staff levels have been a constant problem this year. There were staff shielding because of clinically vulnerable family members in June and although they returned to work in August, they had to return to shielding on 31 December, when the new government guidance was issued. At one point during the second outbreak there was a total of 65 staff off due to Covid-19 symptoms or isolating due to contact with a positive case. There have also been staff off due to having to quarantine after travelling outside of the country (six staff in total). Staff were able to work overtime (payment plus) when resources were low. This was entirely voluntary. The take-up was nowhere near enough, due to the staff being tired after months of managing the pandemic. The staffing levels were not helped by the prison having 20 prison officers on entry level (POELT). These are officers under training, but who are still counted as being on the establishment of the prison. In normal times their absence on training courses has to be covered by cross deployment. In the Covid-19 situation they are not receiving any training, but due to staff shortages are having to cover for experienced staff.

This year has shown that although prisons are a confined environment, they are not isolated environments. In a confined environment infection can spread rapidly as it did in the second outbreak. Prisons are accessed by the staff working there, who can bring in and take out the virus. Prisoners are taken to and received from courts and other prisons. Again, the virus can be taken in and taken out. The requirement that staff restrain violent prisoners, provide emergency first aid and provide escorts to hospital are examples of where non-social distanced contact is necessary. The former examples are ones where time is of the essence and PPE may not have been used. The testing has identified 139 positive cases amongst staff, and 250 amongst prisoners. This equates to just below 40% of all staff within the prison. The exact percentage of prisoners is difficult to establish due to transfers and released prisoners. The Board believes this to be a high percentage and the fact that there have been no prisoner deaths and only two staff still suffering from long Covid to be fortunate. These figures indicate that the only way to control an outbreak in the prison was to vaccinate all staff and prisoners. This was recommended by the OCT to Gold command, but not accepted.

**Main judgements**
**How safe is the prison?**
This year's restricted regime has limited contact between prisoners so has reduced certain prisoner-on-prisoner pressures. The time locked in cell has caused more low- level violence between cell mates and as time has passed it increased pressure on individual prisoners. Consequently, self-harm has increased slightly, but mainly it has been low level cutting. There have been a number of serious attacks on staff. A number of these have been caused by prisoners on the mental health wing of HMP Preston's regional hospital. Preston compares well with its comparator prisons.

**How fairly and humanely are prisoners treated?**
The physical environment of the prison does not meet modern standards due to the fact that it was built in the Victorian era. Particular areas of concern are reception, and the size of the cells. The personal relationship between the staff and the prisoners is good. This is in part due to good communications in keeping the prisoners informed of all regime changes during lockdown, and the additional facilities introduced to help prisoners maintain relations with family members.

**How well are prisoners' health and wellbeing needs met?**
The primary concern has been the control of the Covid-19 virus. Severe restrictions on time out of cell were imposed immediately. The basic contractual health functions to protect the safety of the prisoners were met throughout the year, but at times certain procedures were not functioning. The wellbeing of the prisoners was seen as important. The use of key workers was continued but at a reduced intensity, but assessment, care in custody teams and weekly safety intervention teams were functioning throughout.

**How well are prisoners progressed towards successful resettlement?**
This area has suffered this year.
The management of the prisoner's progress through their sentence has suffered through Covid-19. Many probation offender managers have been either working from home, or more recently only attending the prison on a rota basis. It is a credit to the offender management in custody (OMiC) team that the offender assessment system (OASys) assessments have been completed, oral hearings have been supported and multi-agency public protection arrangement (MAPPA) and parole reports completed.
The ability to enhance the prisoner's skills suffered with education closing down and then reopening with courses that could not give qualifications. Vocational training ceased.

In terms of accommodation and employment Shelter have been operating on a form system and no face-to-face interviews have taken place with prisoners. This, of course, is a far less effective system.

The progress towards successful resettlement has been as good as can be expected, under the present circumstances.

## Main areas for development
### TO THE MINISTER

Will the Minister do all within his power to support the White Paper on the reform of the Mental Health Act that proposes a statutory time limit of 28 days on the provision of a bed in a secure mental health unit when formally requested by the prison?

Will the Minister review the current guidelines and ensure that all personnel within the prison are vaccinated irrespective of the guidelines for the general public?

### TO THE PRISON SERVICE

Will the Prison Service secure the resources for and progress the purchase of the site of the adjacent county museum building, to secure the perimeter of the prison and to open up potential for other associated possible improvements in the prison structure such as the provision of a new reception area?

Will the Prison Service secure funds to allow the repair of telephone lines to the offender management unit (OMU)?

### TO THE GOVERNOR

It is difficult to recommend areas for development when the main wish must be "to get back to normal", which is outside the Governor's control. The pandemic has seen the introduction of some innovative uses of technology; Purple Visits, tablets for socially important meetings with families and Christmas photos. It is hoped that these will continue and be developed. The pandemic has also seen the reduction in some functions such as key workers. It is to be hoped that this function can be reinstated as soon as possible.

### Progress since the last report

The Covid-19 pandemic and the lockdown within the prison has set back rather than enhanced the work of the prison this year. The work this year has been primarily to contain the spread of Covid-19.

The full integration of the body scanner into reception has improved the detection of concealed items being brought into the prison, although reducing the physical space of reception. Following on from the previous year, a further number of cells have been re-classified as single occupancy for humane reasons.

The introduction of more electronic communications has facilitated some remote monitoring by the IMB, and has allowed prisoners access to family members whilst social visits have been cancelled.

Work to install in-cell telephones commenced in 2021.

No progress has been made to improving the reception area despite continued criticism of the physical layout.

 **RETFORD NOTTINGHAM DN22 8EU**

**HM PRISON RANBY**

**Tel: 01777 862000**

*For the latest reports on this prison please visit:* https://tinyurl.com/bdfh26rv

*Important Changes:* **(1) Visits:** the identification necessary to access this prison and visit for social or professional purposes has changed; (2) **Money and Gifts** new rules now apply to these. See page 16 for full details of the above.

**Task of the establishment** Ranby is a category C male adult training and resettlement prison.

**Certified normal accommodation and operational capacity**
Baseline certified normal capacity: 892
Operational capacity: 1025

**Prison status and key providers**
Public Sector
Prison Group: North Midlands
Prison Group Director: Alison Clarke
Governor/Director: Andy Sleight
Physical and mental health and substance misuse provider: Nottinghamshire Healthcare NHS Foundation Trust
Learning and skills provider: Milton Keynes College
Escort contractor: GeoAmey

**Brief history** HMP Ranby is situated in North Nottinghamshire, mid-way between the towns of Worksop and Retford. Ranby is a category C male training prison. Since opening as a prison in 1972, Ranby has had the accommodation capacity regularly and significantly increased due to demand including most recently 2008 when further accommodation was built. In May 2016 Ranby was named as one of six early adopter sites for autonomy where the Director of

East Midlands Reform Group was able to make business and financial decisions separately to the wider prison estate.

The certified normal accommodation (CNA) at HMP Ranby as at the end of March 2020 was 892 and its operational capacity (OC) 1,025.

The residential accommodation consists of seven house blocks. Located within the house blocks are the departments for the induction of new prisoners, resettlement, skills for life and safer custody. One house block has prisoners on integrated drug treatment system (IDTS).

There is a provision for a 24-hour healthcare service, as HMP Ranby has no hospital but has 24-hour healthcare cover on site. The single storey healthcare building accommodates other functioning departments, such as the drug and alcohol recovery team (DART), IDTS and mandatory drug testing (MDT).

The segregation unit is located in one of the older buildings and has 16 single cells. Attached to the segregation unit is a small, paved exercise area which is contained by a high wall.

Education is allocated within two buildings, one of which holds the library and one the chaplaincy. For prisoners in the segregation unit, there is in-cell learning and teachers visit them as appropriate.

The workshops, which are run both by the prison and education provider, include:

Textiles; painting and decorating; woodwork; wood assembly; plastics; industrial cleaning; officers' mess; data input; laundry; powder coating; engineering; barbering, waste management; gardens; building trades.

Physical exercise takes place within two buildings and the sports field. One building instructs prisoners mainly on weights and treats prisoners who have physical disabilities. Fitness equipment has been installed outside each house block.

### Short description of residential units

House block 1: induction wing with single and double cells.

House block 2 North: a general wing; South: the drug intervention and drug recovery unit.

House block 3 North: a general wing; South: the 'enabling environment', where the regime was more relaxed and prisoners living there were expected to live more autonomously.

House block 4: Closed during the inspection to undergo a fire protection upgrade.

### Visiting Information

Book online: www.gov.uk/prison-visits or by telephone on 01777 862 107 Mon to Thurs, 9am to 12pm and 1pm to 3pm, Fri: 9am to 12pm.

**Visiting times:**

Mon & Fri: 2pm to 4pm

Sat/Sun: 9am to 11am and 2pm to 4pm

**Legal visits:** Email: visitsbookingranby@justice.gov.uk.

**Visiting times:** Tues and Wed: 2pm to 4pm.

### INSPECTIONS & REPORTS

**HMCIP Report** 21–22 March and 4–8 April 2022

**Published 12 July 2022**

As a result of concerted efforts by prison leaders, and with the use of better technology, Ranby, a category C training and resettlement prison in Nottinghamshire, was much safer jail than at our inspections in 2016 and 2018. The flow of drugs had been a chief cause of violence but had been stemmed with better perimeter security, use of dogs and body scanners.

Leaders had taken advantage of the Covid-19 lockdowns to reset, focusing on breaking the cycle of violence. Our survey showed that prisoners felt much safer than they had at the time of our last inspection, and longer-serving staff members also said they were not experiencing anything like the levels of threat that they had suffered in the past.

We saw improvements across all parts our safety test, for which the prison was awarded our highest grade, 'good', with fewer assaults on staff and prisoners, better oversight of the use of force, good planning, and provision in place to improve the behaviour of the most violent prisoners and care for the most vulnerable.

Conditions in the prison were also gradually improving. Some of the more dilapidated wings had been refurbished and checks were in place to make sure that cells were clean and largely free from graffiti. Prisoners had recently been given laptops on which they were able to complete some of their domestic tasks, and inspectors were optimistic that once some initial issues were fixed, there would be an improvement in the response times to applications, complaints and diversity incident report forms. The functionality of the laptops was still limited, but there was scope for future expansion.

At the time of our inspection the prison had been at stage one of the HMPPS Covid-19 recovery framework for more than three weeks – this meant that most restrictions should have been lifted and the prison should have resumed its training role. While inspectors were sympathetic to the idea of a gradual return to full activities, leaders had been far too cautious in their approach and there were no dates set for when the regime was to be opened up. The very well-resourced workshops were almost empty, only a handful of prisoners attended classes, and the orderlies were usually the only ones in the library. Those prisoners who could not read were not supported by the education provider and were fortunate if they were allocated a peer mentor. More than 52% of prisoners were unemployed, and many were stuck in their cells or on their spurs with little or nothing to occupy their time.

The prison had recently introduced 'structured on wing activity' (SOWA), but the rationale was not clear to staff or to prisoners, mainly because leaders had failed to consider and communicate the outcomes they expected from this initiative. There appeared to be an eclectic mix of activities on offer to prisoners, though many – such as exercising outdoors or playing table tennis – could, in normal circumstances, have done as part of daily association time. A substance misuse workshop and an offender management surgery were also advertised, but staff from these two departments had not been told and nobody turned up.

Unemployed prisoners who did not sign up for SOWA activities were locked in their cells for an extra half hour; a shocking 23 hours a day behind their doors.

HMPPS had not done enough to prevent Ranby from becoming out of kilter with its remit as a training prison. More than 65% of prisoners transferred to the jail for resettlement as they reached the end of their sentences, but leaders had not responded to or planned for this change and were not providing adequate services for these men. Two particular community offender managers were working very hard to clear the backlog of cases, but the OMU was woefully under-resourced for the population, leading one frustrated prisoner to quip: 'OM-who?'.

At the time of our inspection, Ranby was not operating as a category C training prison. Just keeping prisoners safe is not good enough, and if it is to fulfil its essential function in giving them the skills, knowledge, confidence and work ethic to support their return to the community, leaders urgently need to get them into the workshops and classrooms which should be a thriving part of this jail. The prison must break out of its Covid-19 inertia and provide meaningful, well planned, and structured activities. It was telling that the most impressive work being done by prisoners was cooking and serving in the staff canteen – the challenge for leaders is to make the rest of the prison as productive.

Charlie Taylor HM Chief Inspector of Prisons
May 2022

## Safety

At the last inspection of HMP Ranby, in 2018, we found that outcomes for prisoners were not sufficiently good against this healthy prison test. At this inspection, we found that outcomes for prisoners were now good.

New arrivals were treated well, and access to the 'tuck shop' in reception reduced potential debt issues. Our survey showed that many prisoners faced problems in their early days at the prison, especially in contacting their family. The induction process had been cut back because of the pandemic restrictions and was not sufficiently comprehensive.

Levels of violence had fallen considerably since the last inspection. Assaults against fellow prisoners had reduced by almost half, and against staff by 39%, with few being deemed serious. Prisoner-on-prisoner assaults had gradually increased in the past 12 months, but assaults on staff had remained much lower.

The weekly violence reduction meeting provided a forum for dynamic action, and a twice-weekly safety intervention meeting focused on those who needed the most preventive action or support. Challenge, support and intervention plan (see Glossary) processes were reasonably good and most investigations were conducted swiftly. The incentives policy was being revised and was not currently being used effectively to promote good behaviour. The number of adjudications had halved since the last inspection, and a new 'supportive adjudications' approach was aiming to make formal discipline a more positive element in behaviour management.

Managerial oversight of the use of force was good, and a weekly scrutiny panel reviewed all incidents to identify positive practice and address any concerns. All paperwork was completed and showed a focus on de-escalation of incidents, although the use of handcuffs was high. Special accommodation had not been used since before the last inspection and there had been no baton strikes or use of PAVA (see Glossary) in the past year. Most segregated prisoners had a television, in-cell telephone and laptop computer, and a committed staff group looked after them well.

The prison had addressed the prevalent drug culture that we had found at the last inspection. In our survey, fewer prisoners than at our previous visit said that they had developed a drug problem at the prison or that they could easily obtain illicit drugs or alcohol.

Regular briefings ensured wider engagement in the overall security and safety of the prison. This included an additional briefing collated specifically for the weekend. A prompt response to intelligence, which was triaged twice daily, and the success of target-led searching regularly yielded large amounts of alcohol.

There had been three self-inflicted deaths since the last inspection. The focus on implementing Prisons and Probation Ombudsman recommendations was good. The level of self-harm had been at around one incident a day for the last two years, considerably lower than in previous years, and below the average for similar prisons. The well-resourced safety team carried out detailed analysis of self-harm incidents. There had been an effective focus on improving the assessment, care in custody and teamwork (ACCT) case management process for prisoners at risk of suicide or self-harm, with three layers of management checks.

## Respect

At the last inspection of HMP Ranby, in 2018, we found that outcomes for prisoners were reasonably good against this healthy prison test. At this inspection, we found that outcomes for prisoners remained reasonably good.

In our survey, 68% of respondents said that most staff treated them with respect. There was a widespread perception that while many staff were active and helpful, others were not. The key worker scheme was working to an extent, but prisoners told us that they did not generally find it sufficiently supportive.

Cells were kept in a reasonable state of repair through a rigorous system of decency checks. Unhygienic conditions persisted in some showers, but a refurbishment programme was in progress. The recent installation of in-cell technology, giving a laptop computer to every prisoner, was welcomed, but response times to cell call bells remained a concern. Many prisoners complained that access to their stored property and incoming parcels was slow.

There were some promising initiatives to enable consultation with prisoners, but it was too early to tell whether this was leading to improvements. In our survey, prisoners were more negative about the applications process than at similar prisons, although an online system, using the new in-cell technology, had been introduced recently.

A recent drive was invigorating work on equality, but the strategy was not underpinned by a needs analysis of the population. Diversity and inclusion mentors attended the recently resumed monthly equality meetings and reviewed a sample of diversity incident report forms each month. Members of the senior management team each led on one protected characteristic, but only some had held forums with their respective groups. Some prisoners from a black and minority ethnic background told us that they felt unfairly treated on certain house blocks, which needed further exploration by leaders. The prison had made some adjustments for prisoners with disabilities and it was encouraging to see a focus on neurodiversity. In our survey, fewer young adults than their older counterparts said that

staff treated them with respect. Others felt unsupported because of their sexual orientation. Corporate worship had still not fully resumed and those from larger faith groups had only fortnightly access.

Overall, we found the quality of health care services to be reasonable. However, the lack of officers to escort patients to their appointments had increased waiting times. The recent introduction of a new electronic appointment system had caused huge pressure because of an increased volume of applications. Processes to ensure clinical oversight of the applications were being established, but in the interim this posed a clinical risk that urgent issues could be missed. Service delivery in some areas, particularly substance misuse provision, were curtailed because of low staffing levels.

There was no prison-wide approach to health promotion, but a suitable range of primary care services was available and long-term conditions and complex cases were managed well. A skilled and experienced mental health team provided a range of support to prisoners with mild to moderate and more complex needs, and a recently established neurodiversity pathway was a very positive initiative. The Reconnect service was good, providing holistic 'through-the-gate' support for vulnerable individuals released from prison. Prescribing for opiate addiction was not in line with expected practice, and psychosocial interventions remained limited. Medicines management arrangements were adequate, but the management of medicine queues by officers was mostly ineffective. Dental services were good.

## Purposeful activity

At the last inspection of HMP Ranby, in 2018, we found that outcomes for prisoners were reasonably good against this healthy prison test. At this inspection, we found that outcomes for prisoners were now poor.

Time out of cell for many prisoners was extremely poor, at a little over an hour a day, despite the prison progressing to stage 1 of the HMPPS Covid-19 recovery plan. For those who were unemployed on the three larger wings, time in the open air was too limited, at 30 minutes daily. Access to the gym was too restrictive and the sports field remained out of use. Use of the library was similarly poor and we saw sessions throughout the week where almost no prisoners attended. Literacy promotion was very limited and few prisoners were being supported to learn to read.

Leaders and managers had failed to plan and implement a curriculum that addressed the needs of the population following the prison's move to the final stage of the Covid-19 recovery plan.

There were too few education, skills and work places to occupy all prisoners and the potential capacity available was not fully exploited. The unemployment rate was very high. Activity allocation arrangements were not sufficiently effective and pay rates disincentivised prisoners' participation in learning. Attendance levels at education and workshop sessions were too low and not improving.

Too few prisoners received support to improve their English and mathematics skills. Unless attending education sessions, prisoners with a learning disability or difficulty received no help to overcome their barriers to learning. In workshops and work, prisoners did not have access to accredited qualifications.

The large proportion of prisoners not allocated to education, skills and work were failing to develop the behaviour and attitudes that would prepare them for their next steps. Wing-based prisoners were underemployed and not able to develop an appropriate work ethic.

Those in education sessions and in industrial workshops generally developed their skills and knowledge well. However, in workshops information about prisoners' starting points was not routinely available to allow for effective planning of training. Prisoners who stayed on programmes achieved at a high rate, but too many did not complete their studies. Much of the curriculum was not subject to adequate quality assurance arrangements.

Planning for the introduction and development of 'structured on-wing activity' (SOWA) was weak. It did not link to prisoners' rehabilitation and resettlement needs, and prisoner participation in these activities was low.

Pre-release preparation arrangements were weak, and few prisoners received adequate information, advice and guidance. The prison had insufficient links with employers.

### Rehabilitation and release planning

At the last inspection of HMP Ranby, in 2018, we found that outcomes for prisoners were not sufficiently good against this healthy prison test. At this inspection, we found that outcomes for prisoners were now poor.

Social visits were operating at just over half the pre-pandemic capacity. Families faced considerable difficulties in booking visits and there were not enough slots to meet demand. However, the overall quality of the visits experience had improved greatly now that the café had reopened, physical contact was allowed and children had access to activities.

The prison faced considerable pressures in managing an offender flow that was out of step with its current designated function and resourcing

as a 65% trainer and 35% resettlement prison, whereas in reality these figures were reversed. These challenges were compounded by the impact of the reunification of probation services. Multidisciplinary meetings to oversee and drive forward reducing reoffending work had not taken place for at least a year and there was no strategy setting out the work that needed to be done.

Prisoners continued to express considerable frustration about their lack of contact with their offender manager. There were also inconsistencies in the quality and timeliness of offender assessment system (OASys) reviews. Too many prisoners were not assessed promptly for home detention curfew, or released on time, for reasons generally beyond the prison's control. The prison's risk management meeting did not provide enough oversight to make sure that risk and release planning arrangements for all prisoners assessed as presenting a high risk of harm were managed appropriately. Contact between community offender managers and the prison, to hand over responsibility for cases, was not always robust or timely.

Category D prisoners waited too long to transfer to open conditions, mainly because of external factors. Access to offending behaviour programmes had been suspended during the pandemic and had only recently resumed for a very few. This meant many prisoners would be discharged without having had the opportunity to address their offending behaviour needs and demonstrate a reduction in risk.

Just over 100 prisoners were released each month and demand for support was high. Many prisoners arriving at the prison had less than three months left to serve, which added to the challenges for the timeliness of effective release planning. Following the reunification of probation services, resettlement planning arrangements were fragmented, having a negative impact on outcomes for prisoners.

Too many prisoners left the establishment not knowing where they would be staying on the night of their release. However, the 'departure lounge', offering practical support for prisoners on their release, was a positive initiative.

### Key concerns and recommendations

Key concerns and recommendations identify the issues of most importance to improving outcomes for prisoners and are designed to help establishments prioritise and address the most significant weaknesses in the treatment and conditions of prisoners.

During this inspection we identified some areas of key concern and have made a small number of recommendations for the prison to address those concerns.

Key concern: Non-attendance rates were high for some clinics, including the optician and sexual health services, and there were long waits to see the podiatrist. This was due, in part, to a lack of officers to escort prisoners to their appointments, and to prisoners not being informed about these. Appointments were rescheduled but this extended waiting times for patients and wasted clinical time.

Recommendation: Prisoners should have prompt access to health services, facilitated by sufficient staff to escort them to their health care appointments, to improve attendance, reduce waiting time and optimise use of clinical time. (To the governor and the partnership board)

Key concern: Prescribing for opiate addiction was not in line with expected practice as the prescriber did not attend the prison or consult prisoners directly, and methadone was the only opiate substitution therapy available. The psychosocial interventions remained limited.

Recommendation: The integrated substance misuse service should provide treatment and interventions that are in line with national guidelines. Regular face-to-face reviews with the opiate substitution treatment prescriber, and a range of psychosocial interventions to support treatment and recovery, should be provided. (To the governor and the partnership board)

Key concern: There was insufficient activity or time unlocked for too much of the population. Access to work was still very limited and the prison had been slow to implement a new regime, despite being at stage 1 of the HMPPS recovery plan. There was too little time in the open air for many. Access to the gym was also too restricted and attendance at the library was poor.

Recommendation: Leaders should urgently prioritise increasing time unlocked and the provision of regular education, skills and work activities to fulfil the role of a training prison. (To the governor)

Key concern: Leaders and managers had not implemented an ambitious curriculum that helped all prisoners develop the skills, knowledge, behaviour and attitudes needed for successful resettlement on release. Prisoners, particularly in work and workshops, did not receive the help they needed to improve their English and mathematics skills or gain recognition for the skills and knowledge they had developed. Few prisoners with learning disabilities and/or difficulties (LDD) needs received the necessary help. Managers had insufficient oversight of the quality of training in workshops and work.

Recommendation: Leaders and managers should swiftly implement an ambitious curriculum that addresses the development needs of all the prison population, provides comprehensive support to remove barriers to learning for prisoners with LDD, and recognises and promotes all prisoners' achievements in workshops and work, with rigorous quality assurance and improvement procedures. (To the governor)

Key concern: Leaders and managers had not made sure that all prisoners were allocated, and attended, appropriately purposeful activity that met their needs. Activity allocation was not informed by sentence plans or prisoners' careers aspirations. Work on accommodation units failed to include appropriate managerial oversight to check its allocation and whether prisoners were fully occupied.

Recommendation: Leaders and managers should make sure that activity allocation supports all prisoners' rehabilitation and resettlement needs and includes effective checks on allocation decisions. All prisoners should be allocated, and attend, purposeful activity that fully occupies them throughout the working week. (To the governor)

Key concern: Leaders and managers had not made sure that prisoners received adequate pre-release preparation, including access to timely careers information, advice and guidance and the virtual campus, to research career options and apply for employment, education or employment before their release.

Recommendation: Leaders and managers should provide all prisoners with effective pre-release preparation, including ready access to careers information, advice and guidance, and the use of the virtual campus, so that prisoners can research career options and apply for employment, education or employment before their release. (To the governor)

Key concern: Although in its infancy, the introduction of 'structured on-wing activity' (SOWA), designed to provide purposeful and enriching extracurricular activity, appeared ill-conceived and had been poorly planned and implemented by leaders. It was not clear to inspectors what the objectives were of this initiative or how it would improve outcomes from prisoners. The activity sessions that we observed were largely recreational, including exercise, pool and table tennis, and would previously have been available during periods of association.

Recommendation: Structured on-wing activity should provide purposeful and enriching extracurricular activities as intended. (To HMPPS and the governor)

Key concern: The functioning of the prison was hampered by its population (65% in the 'resettlement window' before release and 35% with a longer period still to serve, needing a training prison) being contrary to that for which it was designed and resourced (65% trainer and 35% resettlement). These challenges were compounded by the impact of the reunification of probation services.

Recommendation: Population flow to the prison should reflect its design and resourcing.
(To HMPPS)

Key concern: Multidisciplinary meetings to oversee and drive forward reducing reoffending work had not taken place for at least a year. There was no strategy setting out the work and no dynamic action planning to identify and measure outcomes across the resettlement pathways.

Recommendation: A comprehensive reducing reoffending strategy, supported by a detailed action plan that is monitored and updated regularly, should be developed to improve outcomes for prisoners. (To the governor)

Key concern: Prisoners continued to express considerable frustration about their inability to see and communicate with their offender manager. Contact was often infrequent and lacked sufficient focus and support to drive prisoners' progression. The quality and timeliness of offender assessment system (OASys) reviews to inform sentence planning were inconsistent. Recommendation: All eligible prisoners should have a relevant, up-to-date sentence plan, and regular and meaningful contact with an appropriately trained offender manager, focused on promoting and enabling their progression. (To the governor)

Key concern: The risk management meeting did not provide enough timely or collaborative oversight to make sure that risk and release planning arrangements for all prisoners assessed as presenting a high very/high risk of harm were managed appropriately. The sharing of information and handover of responsibility for prisoners' risk management were not always robust or timely, and risk management plans were of variable quality.

Recommendation: Public protection assurance arrangements should make sure that all prisoners approaching release who present a high or very high risk of harm to others are managed appropriately and have a comprehensive plan in place in sufficient time to address any gaps in risk management and resettlement needs.
(To HMPPS and the governor)

Key concern: Resettlement planning arrangements were fragmented, creating gaps and confusion in what support could be offered, by whom and when. This was having a negative impact on too many outcomes for prisoners.

Recommendation: Resettlement planning for all prisoners, irrespective of their release area or

risk-of-harm status, should be timely, coordinated and comprehensive, to make sure that any outstanding needs are addressed.
(To the governor)

**Notable positive practice**

We define notable positive practice as innovative work or practice that leads to particularly good outcomes from which other establishments may be able to learn. Inspectors look for evidence of good outcomes for prisoners; original, creative or particularly effective approaches to problem-solving or achieving the desired goal; and how other establishments could learn from or replicate the practice.

Inspectors found four examples of notable positive practice during this inspection.

A new 'supportive adjudications' approach was being taken, with a well-considered approach which gave priority to supporting any prisoner who expressed a desire to improve their behaviour and compliance. This positive approach was helping to make formal discipline a more positive element in behaviour management. The weekend security briefing was an effective way of continuing the focus on security and safety. Leaders had used the in-cell technology to make meal menus more accessible, with each choice accompanied by a photograph of the food, as prepared in the prison.

The Reconnect service had provided good through-the-gate healthcare support to patients throughout the pandemic and the introduction of the 'departure lounge' was a positive initiative, offering practical support on the day of release.

**INDEPENDENT MONITORING BOARD: Annual Report**

The law requires every prison to be monitored by an independent Board appointed by the Justice Secretary; these are known as Independent Monitoring Boards (IMBs). The IMB must satisfy itself as to the humane and just treatment of those held in custody within its prison and the range and adequacy of the programmes preparing them for release; it must report annually to the Justice Secretary on how well the prison has met the standards and requirements placed on it.

**IMB Report 1 April 2021 – 31 March 2022**
**Published August 2022**
**Executive summary**
**Background to the report**
The Covid-19 outbreak has had a significant impact on the Board's ability to gather information and discuss the contents of this annual report. The Board has therefore tried to cover as much ground as it can in these difficult circumstances. Inevitably

there is less detail and supporting evidence than usual. Ministers are aware of these constraints. Regular information is being collected specifically on the prison's response to the pandemic, and that is being collated nationally.

Initially during the pandemic members monitored at a distance by phoning each houseblock and talking to officers on a weekly basis. Through the prison council a council member was able to talk with a member of the IMB over the phone to give a prisoner's perspective.

During the current reporting period the Board has had only five fully active members over the last 12 months (though its recommended complement is 16). Two other members have been on extended sabbaticals. Therefore, the scope of the Board's monitoring has been restricted.

Systems for the collection and response to paper applications were not possible at times due to Covid restrictions. Prisoners were aware of and used the 0800 system during this period.

Though some Board members attended the prison in October and November 2020 generally no Board members visited the prison between the first national lockdown in March 2020 and June 2021; even then few face-to-face meetings took place.

Covid-19 has continued to impact on prison management, staff and prisoners during this reporting period.

At times staffing levels were significantly low. This was managed by the Governor, the management team and staff who kept Covid-19 under control and avoided a major outbreak of the disease in the close society of the prison.

Towards the end of our reporting period the prison moved to Stage 1, the least restrictive stage of the Prison Service's national framework of Covid restrictions.

## Main judgements
### How safe is the prison?

The Board continued to receive statistical data from the prison which would indicate that the prison was reasonably safe, in terms of acts of violence.

HMP Ranby ranks well in the national ranking with a total number of incidents down by 60% year on year from before the pandemic.

### How fairly and humanely are prisoners treated?

It is the opinion of the Board that the prisoners within the confines of HMP Ranby are generally treated fairly and with humanity, however, there are exceptions that remain and that we repeat, including: staff communication, cell sharing, cell clearing, and canteen via DHL. The Board considers that the prison system, and not necessarily HMP Ranby, fails to provide fair and humane treatment to prisoners.

### How well are prisoners' health and wellbeing needs met?

The health service provide by Nottinghamshire NHS is in line with the service provided to the general public outside the prison. We consider that they provide a satisfactory service most of the time.

### How well are prisoners progressed towards successful resettlement?

In the later part of the reporting year the Board is aware that the resettlement department at Ranby has ceased to operate.

Some residual work is still being done via the Department for Work and Pensions and other agencies on site.

Due to Covid restrictions the Board believes that no offending behaviour courses were run. An ongoing problem continues to be the lack of courses to facilitate a prisoner's sentence plan. Also, some courses are not available to some men as they do not have sufficient time left to serve.

### Main areas for development

The Board has previously reported on the changing population of HMP Ranby.

HMP Ranby is currently designated as a category C training prison. However, it is routinely receiving many prisoners with a very short time to serve.

The Governor reports this situation has been exacerbated by Covid, which has diverted HMP Ranby and its staff away from its primary purpose which is to function as a training prison. During the reporting year the Board does not feel that there has been any progress in addressing previous issues.

### TO THE MINISTER

Although the minister answered our questions last year, the Board feels that very little has been done since then to rectify our concerns regarding prisoners who should be receiving specialist treatment for mental health issues. Prisoners are still being held for far too long when they should be in specialist mental health facilities.

Could the minister assure the Board that this situation is receiving their urgent attention and that something is being done about it?

### TO THE PRISON SERVICE

Will the Prison Service explain why several prisoners transferred from other prisons are continuing to arrive without all their property?

Will the Prison Service explain when HMP Ranby will be returned to a training prison with prisoners who are able to complete courses according to their sentence plan and with adequate funding to prepare them for release?

Prisoners are being sent to HMP Ranby needing courses required for release but when they arrive, they are not running.

## TO THE GOVERNOR
Could the Governor please explain why the Board had to read in the local press about a serious incident which took place on April 20 2019, where a coroner's report criticised Governors' actions regarding the release of a prisoner from HMP Ranby who went on to kill a person standing at a bus stop?
Could the Governor explain why the system of recording incoming property has changed? This has made it very difficult for the Board to address prisoners' concerns about their missing property. The lack of a dedicated Clerk for the IMB and functioning office equipment has been a significant problem for the IMB during this reporting period.

### Progress since the last report
The development of the ABC (activities, basics, consistency) strategy
The possibility of building category D accommodation and two new house blocks.
The introduction of new in-cell laptops and telephones has enabled prisoners to access applications containing all their personal information and communication requirements, therefore enabling them to keep contact with family more readily.

**WARRINGTON ROAD RISLEY, WARRINGTON CHESHIRE, WA3 6BP**

Tel: 01925 733000

*For the latest reports on this prison please visit:* https://tinyurl.com/bdfh26rv

*Important Changes:* **(1) Visits:** the identification necessary to access this prison and visit for social or professional purposes has changed; (2) **Money and Gifts** new rules now apply to these. See page 16 for full details of the above.

**Task of the establishment** HMP Risley is a category C resettlement prison.

### Certified normal accommodation and operational capacity
Prisoners held at the time of this visit: 1,040
Baseline certified normal capacity: 1,061
In-use certified normal capacity: 1,061
Operational capacity: 1,115

### Prison status and key providers
Public Sector
Prison Group: Greater Manchester, Merseyside & Cheshire.
Prison Group Director: Tim Allen
Governor/Director: Nicki Smith
IMB Chair: Albert Aldridge
Physical health provider: Greater Manchester Mental Health NHS Trust
Mental health provider: Greater Manchester Mental Health NHS Trust
Substance use treatment provider: Change Grow Live
Prison education framework provider: Novus
Escort contractor: GeoAmey

**Brief history** Risley opened in 1964 as a remand centre for men and women. In 1989, the male part of the prison became a training prison. Although there were plans in the early 1990s to replace all the original buildings, some are still in use. The training prison was expanded further and refurbished in 2003 with the addition of a new wing (G). The population of prisoners convicted of a sexual offence was relocated to separate residential areas in 2009 and 2020. In 2009, Risley became a hub for up to 200 foreign national prisoners.

### Short description of residential units
A wing – category C prisoners, with several foreign national prisoners
B wing – induction/first night unit for mainstream category C prisoners
C wing – developing incentivised substance-free living unit
D wing – category C prisoners
E wing – prisoners convicted of sexual offences
F wing – prisoners convicted of sexual offences; transitioning to a self-isolators support unit
G wing – prisoners convicted of sexual offences (including older prisoners and those with a disability)
R1 – independent living unit for prisoners on the enhanced level of the incentives scheme
Segregation unit

### Visiting Information
Book online at: www.gov.uk/prison-visits or ring 01925 733284 or 01925 733285 Monday to Friday: 9am to 4pm.
**Visiting times:**
Monday afternoon - A wing
Tuesday morning - B wing, F wing & CSU
Tuesday afternoon - C wing
Wednesday afternoon - D wing
Thursday morning - E wing
Thursday afternoon - G wing
Specific visiting times will be given upon booking. Visitors will be allocated a time to arrive at the Visitors Centre when they book their visit.

**Legal visits:** Booking line: 01925 733284 or 01925 733285. Professional and legal visits can also be booked by sending an email to: LegalVisits.Risley@justice.gov.uk

**Visiting times:**

Monday afternoon - A wing
Tuesday morning - B wing, F wing & CSU
Tuesday afternoon - C wing
Wednesday afternoon - D wing
Thursday morning - E wing
Thursday afternoon - G wing

Visitors will be allocated a time to arrive at the Visitors Centre when they book their visit.

### INSPECTIONS & REPORTS
**Scrutiny visit: 17 and 24–25 November 2020**
**Published: 12 January 2021**

This report presents the findings from our scrutiny visit to HMP Risley on the conditions and treatment of prisoners during the Covid-19 pandemic. Risley is a category C training and resettlement prison near Warrington in Cheshire. The prison holds more than 1,000 adult male prisoners, a mixture of mainstream prisoners, foreign nationals and prisoners convicted of a sexual offence. At the time of our visit, almost two-thirds of the population were serving sentences of more than four years.

We found a well-led prison that had continued to progress despite the pandemic. The management team had worked effectively, in partnership with health care staff and Public Health England, to control a Covid-19 outbreak at the start of the pandemic and to contain a later outbreak on G wing in September. Quarantine arrangements for those in their first 14 days at the prison and shielding arrangements for those vulnerable to the virus had been implemented in accordance with national directives.

The management team had taken a robust approach to minimising the risks of transmission of the virus by promoting social distancing and cleanliness, with frequent cleaning of communal areas by a team of prisoner 'COVID cleaners'. Communication with staff and prisoners about Covid-19 had been good, with information provided in a range of languages. Staff were now wearing fluid-resistant face masks in all areas of the prison, and weekly Covid-19 testing of staff had started on-site.

Although the requirement for national approval of recovery plans (see Glossary of terms) had been cumbersome, senior managers had been proactive in their efforts to ease restrictions. The prison had been among the first in the country to reopen social visits and had resumed delivery of offending behaviour programmes to small groups in August. However, well-developed plans to progress to HM Prison and Probation Service stage 2 of recovery had been interrupted by the recent national lockdown in response to the second wave of the virus.

The amount of violence and self-harm had reduced at the start of the restrictions. There had been a subsequent rise in the number of incidents, but this remained below pre-pandemic levels. This was in the context of improved prison safety and reducing trends in both violence and self-harm in the year up to the pandemic. Safety meetings had continued throughout the pandemic and managerial oversight of this area was good. There had been two self-inflicted deaths during the period of regime restrictions. We found evidence of a good level of support for prisoners at risk of suicide or self-harm, supported by the assessment, care in custody and teamwork (ACCT) case management process.

We saw staff engaging well with prisoners. These observations were reflected in our survey, where most prisoners (79%) said that staff treated them with respect. Key work had been well embedded in the prison before the pandemic, and weekly checks on the well-being of more vulnerable prisoners and those near to release had continued during the Covid-19 period.

Although the residential units had suffered much wear and tear, with flooring in a poor condition and some showers below a decent standard, there had been considerable efforts to improve the environment as far as was possible in the absence of funding for proper refurbishment. The wing painting programme and the 'Creating Rehabilitation, Enabling Decency' programme of refurbishment of E wing by prisoners had continued despite the pandemic. The participation of prisoners through peer support work and frequent consultation and community meetings had been a strength throughout the period of regime restrictions. The peer review of anonymised responses to complaints, discrimination incident report forms and use of force reports had been maintained. Work to promote equalities had improved considerably since our inspection in 2016, and had continued uninterrupted during the pandemic. The chaplaincy had also been visible and active.

Health care services had improved since our inspection in 2016. The full capacity of health services in the prison was underused because of social distancing and regime restrictions, which led to too many prisoners not attending for appointments and inefficient use of clinicians' time. The restrictions, which limited the dispensing of medication at the prescribed time, had also introduced unnecessary clinical risk.

For most prisoners, the regime was severely limited to around one hour a day unlocked, which was a serious concern. Although a larger proportion (30%) than we have seen in some other prisons had jobs, a lack of in-cell telephony placed further pressure on prisoners to make their calls during the short time available out of their cell. Prisoners now had weekly access to the gyms, but the sessions took place during their hour of unlock.

Social visits had stopped again because of national Covid-19 restrictions. The introduction of video calls ('Purple Visits'; see Glossary of terms) with family and friends was positive, and available capacity had allowed prisoners to access these twice a month. Welfare checks had been introduced following a Purple Visit, as this had been an emotional experience for some prisoners. There was also some good family support work, including a virtual family forum and video messages from prisoners to their families. Sentence planning and risk assessment processes were up to date, but there was a large backlog in telephone call monitoring for public protection which the prison urgently needed to address. Although offending behaviour work had resumed, there were no interventions for those convicted of sexual offences. Progressive moves of category D prisoners to open conditions had continued during the restrictions, and restorative justice sessions had also taken place.

Release planning by the community rehabilitation company (CRC) was mostly through written correspondence, and not all prisoners had completed the questionnaire sent to them. Weekly virtual resettlement boards had started, but better communication with prisoners was required for them to feel involved. The 'through-the-gate' hub outside the prison provided good support for those being released but, as a result of the restrictions, this was available only to those deemed vulnerable by the CRC.

In conclusion, we found strong leadership and a motivated management team that had risen to the challenges of the pandemic. At the same time, plans to progress the prison had not stopped. Despite the lack of some basic facilities, such as in-cell telephones and decent showers, there were ongoing efforts to improve the environment and to build on the already considerable work that had been done to make Risley a more respectful and safer place. However, the impact of lack of time unlocked for most prisoners some eight months since the start of the pandemic was a serious concern.

Charlie Taylor, HM Chief Inspector of Prisons
December 2020

**Key concerns and recommendations**

Key concerns and recommendations identify the issues of most importance to improving

outcomes for prisoners and are designed to help establishments prioritise and address the most significant weaknesses in the treatment and conditions of prisoners.

During this visit we identified some areas of key concern, and have made a small number of key recommendations for the prison to address.

Key concern: Prisoners' dental health needs were not being fully met. Too many prisoners were failing to attend appointments because of a reduction in waiting room capacity due to social distancing and the limited time out of cell. Aerosol generating procedures were unavailable despite agreement to proceed.

Key recommendation: Dental treatment should be provided promptly and be equivalent to that delivered in the community. (To the governor)

Key concern: The regime restrictions often presented prisoners with an unacceptable choice between attending their health care, dental and substance misuse appointments or taking a shower and exercise during their very limited time out of cell. The inability to release prisoners to receive not-in-possession medicines at the prescribed times was a serious concern as it increased the likelihood of medicines being ineffective or unwanted side-effects occurring, such as drowsiness in the early evening or pain in the early morning.

Key recommendation: Prisoners should be able to attend health care appointments on time and to receive their medicines at the prescribed time. (To the governor)

Key concern: Unless they had a job, prisoners were out of their cell for an hour a day, and for meal collection. Even with the full hour, this did not give them enough time for telephone calls, showers and other domestic needs, as well as outside exercise. Many prisoners spoke of the numbing and demoralising effect of being locked up for so long, especially as a 28-hour period was not uncommon from one morning to the following afternoon.

Key recommendation: Time out of cell for prisoners should be increased, to enable more purposeful activity and more time in the open air. (To the governor)

Key concern: Prisoners' contact with families was restricted by the lack of in-cell telephones. There were few telephones on the landings, and they could only be used at restricted times.

Key recommendation: Prisoners should have telephone in their cells to be able to have regular and frequent telephone contact with their families. (To HMPPS)

Key concern: As a result of staffing shortages, there was a large backlog in the number of telephone calls which needed to be listened to for public protection purposes.

Key recommendation: The backlog in telephone monitoring should be eliminated as a matter of urgency. (To the governor)

**Notable positive practice**

We define notable positive practice as innovative practice or practice that leads to particularly good outcomes from which other establishments may be able to learn. Inspectors look for evidence of good outcomes for prisoners; original, creative or particularly effective approaches to problem-solving or achieving the desired goal; and how other establishments could learn from or replicate the practice.

Inspectors found the following examples of notable positive practice during this visit.

• The interactive peer-led induction was delivered in the two 'welcome centres' on a one-to-one basis in separate booths, at a pace that ensured that each element was understood by new prisoners.

• A catalogue of official stationery from legal advisers, which had been verified with the sender, was used to make comparisons with any suspicious packages. This assisted in detecting bogus Rule 39 (legal and confidential) mail, which was a known route for the trafficking of drug-impregnated paper.

• All prisoners were promoted to the highest level of the incentives scheme at the start of the restrictions. This incentivised positive behaviour and gave prisoners greater spending power to buy additional telephone credit and items from the prison shop.

• Prisoner representatives conducted structured quality checks of a sample of records of use of force, completed complaint forms and discrimination incident report forms, with anonymisation in each case. This was useful and likely to increase trust.

• Prisoner council meetings had increased in frequency during the Covid-19 period, and were well used by the governor and senior managers to communicate and consult on developments. These, and regular wing meetings, were well organised, properly recorded and effective.

• The availability of naloxone by nasal spray in addition to by injection enabled easier administration and swifter absorption of the medicine in an emergency and increased the options to keep prisoners safe after release.

• The re-establishment of therapeutic groups within the substance misuse service enabled prisoners to support each other and receive valued mutual aid, such as Narcotics Anonymous, that had been curtailed at the beginning of the outbreak.

• The availability of well-being and substance misuse peer workers despite the restrictions enabled some harm minimisation activities to

continue and aided the delivery of health care and substance misuse programmes that would otherwise have stopped.

• The introduction of welfare checks on prisoners who had been on a 'Purple Visit' was effective in supporting their emotional well-being.

• Phoenix Futures facilitated several initiatives to support and promote family ties, which include virtual family forums and video messages from prisoners to their families.

• Despite substantial restrictions to the regime, several restorative justice sessions had taken place.

**INDEPENDENT MONITORING BOARD: Annual Report**

The law requires every prison to be monitored by an independent Board appointed by the Justice Secretary; these are known as Independent Monitoring Boards (IMBs). The IMB must satisfy itself as to the humane and just treatment of those held in custody within its prison and the range and adequacy of the programmes preparing them for release; it must report annually to the Justice Secretary on how well the prison has met the standards and requirements placed on it.

**IMB Report 1 April 2020 – 31 March 2021
Published 28th January 2022**

HMP Risley is one of the largest category C training prisons in the UK, housing an average of 1,100+ male prisoners.

The prison continues to be a hub for foreign national prisoners in the North West and Home Office Immigration Enforcement (formerly UK Border Agency) staff are permanently based in the prison. The population profile showed that, at the end of this reporting year, there were 100+ foreign nationals, 187 prisoners who have committed sexual offences, 50 prisoners serving indeterminate sentences for public protection (IPP) and 70 lifers.

The Risley site consists of seven residential wings, two of which house vulnerable prisoners. There is also a care and separation unit with its own outside exercise area. The training facilities within the establishment provide 12 workshops and 14 education classrooms, together with a library. There is also a health centre with full-time doctors and nursing staff. In addition, dental, podiatry and physiotherapy services are provided. Other facilities include a sports hall and two gyms. To cater for the various faith groups of the prison, there is a multi-faith centre, which is supported by several ministers from the various faiths.

## Executive summary
### Background to the report

The Board has covered as much ground as it could in these difficult circumstances, as the ongoing Covid-19 pandemic has continued to have an impact on the Board's ability to gather information and discuss the contents of this annual report. Ministers are aware of these constraints. The outbreak was confirmed in March 2020 and new systems and ways of working were devised and introduced. Prisoners were kept informed of developments and accepted and understood circumstances. This report presents the findings of the Board at HMP Risley for the period 1 April 2020 to 31 March 2021 and therefore there is less detail and supporting evidence within this report. Board evidence comes from observations made on visits, scrutiny of records and of data, informal contact with prisoners and staff, surveys, and prisoner applications.

### Main judgements
### How safe is the prison?

It is the opinion of the Board that the overall safety of the prison meets a high standard throughout. As the following report will demonstrate, the prison 's reception processing unit works closely with the transport contractor, with consideration being given to the risks posed by Covid-19.

Prisoners are generally positive about their treatment in the reception area. Initial health screenings for new arrivals are undertaken promptly by a registered nurse. Immediate health care needs are identified, including mental health and substance misuse, as well as completion of assessment, care in custody and teamwork (ACCT) documents if deemed necessary. Initial cell-sharing risk assessments are also carried out.

This year due to Covid 19 ACCTs provide evidence that due to limited contact between prisoners there has been a reduction in violence in respect of prisoner on prisoner.

### How fairly and humanely are prisoners treated?

It is the opinion of the Board that, overall, prisoners are treated fairly. Replacement of the roof to the laundry and workshops 1, 2 and 3 have all been completed.

The prisoners on average during the pandemic have an hour out of their cell.

The prison's ongoing focus on decent and humane treatment is demonstrated through the decency agenda introduced by the safer living department, including a 'room ready' programme and ensuring that all new prisoners receive an induction pack.

### How well are prisoners' health and wellbeing needs met?

It is the opinion of the Board that the prisoners' health and wellbeing needs are, in the main, being addressed by the health centre staff, which includes full-time doctors and nursing staff, dental, podiatry and physiotherapy services, plus a full mental health team.

On arrival at reception, procedures are adequately focused on the risks posed by Covid-19, with all new arrivals monitored for the virus, followed by prompt health screenings by a registered nurse.

Prisoners use the appointment system which is available to them. During this reporting year, improvements to attendance at healthcare appointments have been made, taking into account social distancing and Covid-19 testing.

### How well are prisoners progressed towards successful resettlement?

Prisoners are encouraged to develop skills through a good educational provision and training in a range of workshops. All agencies are aware of prisoners' imminent release. Ofsted was part of the HM Inspectorate of Prisons (HMIP) scrutiny visit in November, followed by guided planning for the future, and plans are in place for the department to move forward. The prison is in the process of setting up an employment hub, which should operate on the lines of a job centre. At the start of the year, there were still problems for families wishing to book visits. This has since dramatically improved; with the introduction of the online booking system and allocated visit times, it is a vast improvement on the previous system.

### Main areas for development
### TO THE MINISTER

What discussions are you having with colleague ministers in order to help improve the long repatriation/deportation timeframes for foreign national prisoners?

### TO THE PRISON SERVICE

There are frequent instances of prisoners being transferred to establishments that cannot facilitate the courses needed for their identified requirements with regard to sentence management and rehabilitation. Why are prisoners transferred to prisons which cannot ensure completion of sentence management requirements, and might the Prison Service consider a more efficient way of eradicating these problems, going forward?

The Board continues to receive a large number of applications regarding loss of prisoners' property. What plans does the Prison Service have to introduce a more streamlined system of handling prisoners' property when being transferred between prisons? This would avoid unnecessary distress for prisoners being transferred and also minimise the number of compensation claims.

### TO THE GOVERNOR

There have been instances where the Board has not been called to serious incidents, particularly out of hours. What are your plans, going forward, to ensure that Board members may monitor and observe serious incidents, while maintaining all appropriate safety and security protocols?

The Board still has concerns about the efficient provision of prisoners ' property. What plans does the prison have regarding developing a more efficient, consistent and streamlined approach to handling and allocating prisoners' property, on arrival, departure and movement within the prison?

### Progress since the last report

A prisoner engagement session has been introduced as part of the staff induction process. Food and catering has much improved since the last report, with prisoner 'Food forums/food focus meetings' being implemented, as well as healthy options introduced on the evening menus on Saturdays and Sundays to promote healthy living.

**1 FORT ROAD
ROCHESTER
KENT
ME1 3QS**

**HMP/YOI ROCHESTER**   **Tel: 01634 803100**

*For the latest reports on this prison please visit:*
https://tinyurl.com/bdfh26rv

*Important Changes:* **(1) Visits:** the identification necessary to access this prison and visit for social or professional purposes has changed; (2) **Money and Gifts** new rules now apply to these. See page 16 for full details of the above.

**This prison operates the Digital Categorisation System, pursuant to the Security Categorisation Policy Framework as such PSIs 40 and 41 of 2011 do not apply to prisoners being categorised in this establishment. See section 2.26 for more information.**

**Task of the establishment** A category C resettlement prison for adult men and young offenders.

### Certified normal accommodation and operational capacity

Prisoners held at the time of inspection: 658
Baseline certified normal capacity: 695
In-use certified normal capacity: 658
Operational capacity: 695

### Population of the prison

• 1,350 new prisoners received each year (about 113 per month).

• 44 foreign national prisoners representing 6.5% of the current population.

• 19.8% of prisoners from a black and minority ethnic background.

• An average of 68 prisoners released into the community each month.

• 233 prisoners receiving support for substance misuse.

• An average of 80 prisoners referred for mental health assessment each month.

### Prison status and key providers

Public
Prison Group: Kent, Surrey & Sussex
Prison Group Director: James Lucas
Governor/Director: Dean Gardiner
IMB Chair: Dr Vyra Navaratnam
Physical and mental health provider: Oxleas NHS Foundation Trust
Substance misuse treatment provider: The Forward Trust
Prison education framework provider: Weston College
Escort contractor: GeoAmey

**Brief history** Rochester prison was originally built in 1874 on a former military site above the Medway River. In 1983, Rochester was converted into a youth custody centre and, in 1988, it became a remand centre for Kent courts. In 2011, Rochester was turned into a dual-purpose site for young adult and adult category C prisoners. Following a rescinded closure notice in 2017, it held young adult and adult category C and D prisoners.

**Short description of residential units** There were eight residential units:
A wing – drug recovery unit
B, D, E, G and H wings – general accommodation
R and F wings – reverse cohort units and first night centres.

### Visiting Information

Book online at: www.gov.uk/prison-visits or ring 0300 060 6513 Monday to Friday 9am to 5pm.
**Visiting times:** Monday to Thursday: 2pm to 2:45pm and 3:30pm to 4:15pm, Friday: 9:15am to 10am and 10:45am to 11:30am.

**Legal visits:** Legal visits are running Monday to Friday from 9:30am to 12:00pm.

## INSPECTIONS & REPORTS

**Date of last full inspection** 4 & 11–15 October 2021
**HMCIP Report, published 01 February 2022**

HMP and YOI Rochester, the original borstal, is a category C training and resettlement prison for adult men and young offenders in Kent. When we last inspected in 2017, the prison was in a state of flux, with plans to close it just rescinded. At this inspection the situation had changed radically and, far from closure, there was now talk of potential plans to redevelop the site.

Whether these plans come to fruition remains to be seen, although as our report shows, a key strategic priority for the prison is the need to end overcrowding and radically improve the condition of the living accommodation in which prisoners were held. The establishment comprises a mix of very old house blocks and some relatively new. All, however, were in a very poor condition.

At the time of our inspection Rochester was holding 658 men; some way short of its capacity of just under 700. There was a significant turnover of prisoners each month, although 60% of the population were serving long or indeterminate sentences. About 40% were judged to present a serious risk of harm to others. Overall, and in the context of the restrictions imposed by the Covid-19 pandemic, this was a reasonable inspection. As we found in 2017, outcomes in safety remained reasonably good, but were not sufficiently good in respect, principally due to the very poor living environment. In purposeful activity outcomes had deteriorated and were now poor – largely a consequence of Covid-19 restrictions – but outcomes had improved in rehabilitation and release planning to the extent that they were now reasonably good.

It was clear that leaders in the prison had prioritised Rochester's response to the pandemic and had, commendably, been successful in mitigating risks. As the prison recovered however, progress to us seemed slow, even tentative. The reasons and explanations we heard for this were often unclear and inconsistent. Too few prisoners were engaged in useful activity and plans to move the prison to the next stage of the HMPPS recovery framework seemed to be fragile and unambitious. It must be acknowledged that another key strategic challenge for the prison – and one that was a significant additional limitation on progress – was the chronic shortage of staff. In common with other prisons in the Kent area, staff attrition rates were high and recruitment very slow. It was

not clear that the prison had a credible plan to resolve this.

Rochester was achieving reasonably good outcomes in some important areas. The prison was settled, and prisoners seemed generally accepting, even sanguine about their situation, despite the poor living conditions and lack of activity. It was hard to avoid the sense, however, that with greater confidence, ambition and clarity of purpose from leaders, more could have been achieved. Clearer plans about the prison's future, including how it will be redeveloped, and a robust strategy – probably led by HMPPS – to ensure effective recruitment are the two critical priorities.
Charlie Taylor HM Chief Inspector of Prisons
December 2021

### Safety

At the last inspection of Rochester in 2017 we found that outcomes for prisoners were reasonably good against this healthy prison test. At this inspection we found that outcomes for prisoners remained reasonably good.

Reception procedures were carried out well and prisoners were treated with respect on their arrival at Rochester. However, the first night safety interview needed to be confidential and new arrivals might have benefitted from structured peer support during their early days in custody. The first night cells we looked at were clean and well prepared but induction to the prison and the regime were poor.

Most prisoners at Rochester felt safe. Rates of violence were similar to the previous inspection, but fewer incidents were serious. The prison did not undertake any detailed analysis of the causes of violence to inform future planning. The safety intervention meeting was ineffective, but good support was provided to a small number of prisoners through complex case reviews. The current regime did little to promote good behaviour. Too many adjudication cases did not proceed, some of which involved serious offences. Force was used frequently, but levels were similar to comparable prisons. Governance arrangements with respect to the use of force were reasonably good. Use of the segregation unit was high, but over half of prisoners segregated were there pending adjudication. Segregation staff knew the prisoners in their care well, and the unit was settled. The regime was poor and little attention was paid to reintegration planning.

Intelligence reports were analysed, collated and disseminated well. Inter-agency work to manage staff corruption, gangs and extremism was good. Managers were aware of the key threats to the prison, one of which was the availability of drugs. Despite this threat, there was still no mandatory drug testing, and more than a third of target searches could not proceed due to staff shortfalls.

There had been one self-inflicted death since the previous inspection and the prison acted promptly to implement the Prisons and Probation Ombudsman's recommendations. The rate of self-harm had declined since the previous inspection and was lower than at other category C prisons. Assessment, care in custody and teamwork (ACCT) case management documentation for prisoners at risk of suicide or self-harm was generally completed to a reasonable standard and prisoners said they received good care from staff. However, their daily regime was usually poor, and they had limited access to some of the interventions recommended for their care, including Listeners (prisoners trained by the Samaritans to provide confidential emotional support to fellow prisoners). There was insufficient effective data analysis of self-harm, and the prison did not have a robust plan to deal with potential rises in levels once Covid-19 restrictions are eased.

## Respect

At the last inspection of Rochester in 2017 we found that outcomes for prisoners were not sufficiently good against this healthy prison test. At this inspection we found that outcomes for prisoners remained not sufficiently good.

In our survey, fewer prisoners than at the previous inspection said staff treated them with respect. During our inspection, we observed some positive interactions, but little effective key work (see Appendix II Glossary of terms) had taken place in recent months. Only a limited number of prisoners had been allocated to meaningful peer support roles.

Cells in the older accommodation were dilapidated and in need of continual repair. The newer accommodation was marginally better, and cells were equipped with in-cell showers. Rodent infestations persisted despite efforts to address the problem. Communal areas were clean and tidy, and most outside exercise areas were equipped with exercise machines. Despite evidence from numerous complaints, applications and Independent Monitoring Board reports, prisoners still experienced problems accessing their stored property. The food was reasonably good, and most wings had microwaves, a toaster and a fridge.

Prisoner consultation arrangements were in place and the main forum was reasonably good. Applications from prisoners were not tracked or overseen, and some remained unanswered for over a month. Many of the complaints submitted were upheld, which indicated that they were properly investigated. However, we also found too many responses that were unhelpful. Trends in complaints were monitored but had not led to improvements in areas such as property management.

Work to promote equality was reasonably good. Consultation with prisoners with protected characteristics was developing and had led to improvements in outcomes for some. Responses to discrimination complaints were generally satisfactory, but too many were delayed. In our survey, prisoners in most protected groups had broadly similar views, except for Muslim prisoners who were more negative about how staff treated them. Interpretation services were used to communicate with non-English speakers. Staff demonstrated a good awareness of prisoners who had personal emergency evacuation plans, but the day-to-day treatment of prisoners with physical disabilities was not monitored well enough. Those transitioning from the youth estate and care leavers (a person aged 25 or under, who has been looked after by a local authority) received good support. The chaplaincy had also continued to support prisoners throughout the pandemic.

Partnership working between health providers, Public Health England and NHS Commissioners was good. Processes in place to manage a Covid-19 outbreak and the vaccination programme were effective. However, clinical governance systems and processes were not robust. Not all incidents were being reported which meant that risks, trends and themes to identify gaps in patient care were not identified.

Primary care services were well led and the team provided a good quality service. This was hampered by the inadequate clinical space and some waiting lists were too long. Access to external hospital appointments was limited to four days per week to accommodate operational staff shortfalls.

Mental health and substance misuse services were delivered by dedicated and experienced teams. All patient assessments took place on the wings but confidential and therapeutic space was not always available which wasted clinical time, delayed care and contributed to long waits for therapeutic interventions.

## Purposeful activity

At the last inspection of Rochester in 2017 we found that outcomes for prisoners were not sufficiently good against this healthy prison test. At this inspection we found that outcomes for prisoners were now poor.

Ofsted carried out a progress monitoring visit of the prison alongside our full inspection and the purposeful activity judgement incorporates their assessment of progress.

Most prisoners spent over 22 hours locked in their cells each day and too few prisoners took part in any form of purposeful activity either remotely or face to face.

Gym staff were quick to introduce outside sessions when the pandemic began and reopen the sports hall once restrictions permitted. However, most prisoners could only attend once or twice a week, and some could not attend any sessions. The library remained closed.

Progress towards delivering a full education, skills and work curriculum had been too slow. Teachers had made suitable plans to reintroduce classroom and workshop teaching, but the expansion of the provision was limited by ongoing staff shortages.

The number of prisoners who had participated in in-cell education was extremely small. Most in-cell packs were of a suitable standard and the majority seen by inspectors had been appropriately marked. A small number of prisoners achieved their certificates in mathematics and information and communications technology.

Leaders continued to work with businesses to develop training opportunities within the prison, such as in roofing or events stewarding.

Managers had not sufficiently prioritised digital learning, and prisoners were not developing the vital digital skills they needed to support their resettlement. Prisoners' involvement with careers advice and guidance workers was limited to the short time prisoners spent out of their cells and had a limited impact.

The induction to education was not effective enough and did not meet prisoners' needs. Prisoners undertook induction and initial assessment activities unsupported in their cells, because of the requirement to self-isolate on arrival at the prison.

In the few sessions we could visit, prisoners were engaged, attentive and pleased to be with their peers, teaching staff and instructors.

### Rehabilitation and release planning

At the last inspection of Rochester in 2017 we found that outcomes for prisoners were not sufficiently good against this healthy prison test. At this inspection we found that outcomes for prisoners were now reasonably good.

Social visits had resumed in May 2021, and video calling was available, but staffing shortages limited the availability of both. Visiting sessions were only available for 45 minutes, the minimum that the prison was permitted to deliver under stage 3 of the national framework for prison regimes and service. National charity Spurgeons continued to provide support to prisoners and their families. Prisoners valued their in-cell phones, which enabled them to stay in touch with family and friends.

An up-to-date reducing reoffending strategy document was in place, but there was no action plan, and only two meetings to drive the delivery of the strategy had taken place since the start of the pandemic. Caseloads for prison offender managers (POMs) were reasonable and levels of contact between them and prisoners were sufficient to promote progress in the majority of cases we inspected.

The offender assessment system report backlog was small. Most of the prisoners whose cases we examined in depth had sentence plans that were at least of a reasonably good standard, and some were very good. In just over half of these cases, prisoners had also made sufficient progress against their plans.

Home detention curfew processes were generally sound, but too many were released after their eligibility date. Release on temporary licence remained suspended, despite the high number of category D prisoners.

In the prisoner cases we reviewed, up-to-date risk management plans were in place in virtually all cases and were of reasonable quality. Work on managing the risks of those within a few months of release was also good. Public protection monitoring arrangements were weak and there was a large backlog of calls waiting to be monitored.

A substantial number of category D prisoners (90) had not yet been transferred to open conditions, and they were not being provided with a regime that was suited to their reduced risk level.

Some offending behaviour programmes had been delivered in the previous 12 months, but with significantly reduced prisoner numbers. Waiting lists for courses continued to rise and a large number of prisoners were likely to be released from custody without having completed interventions to address their offending behaviour. Some POMs had undertaken meaningful face-to-face, offence-related work with prisoners who were unable to take part in accredited programmes.

We found good evidence of POMs liaising with external community offender managers to confirm resettlement plans. Assistance and advice were available for prisoners approaching release. Key resettlement partners had all now returned to the prison and were seeing prisoners face to face. Data supplied by the prison indicated that in the previous 12 months, 86% of prisoners had sustainable accommodation on their first night of release.

## Key concerns and recommendations

Key concerns and recommendations identify the issues of most importance to improving outcomes for prisoners and are designed to help establishments prioritise and address the most significant weaknesses in the treatment and conditions of prisoners.

During this inspection we identified some areas of key concern and have made a small number of recommendations for the prison to address those concerns.

Key concern: There were weaknesses in the support provided to new arrivals. First night interviews did not assess prisoners' immediate risks and vulnerabilities thoroughly enough to ensure that staff could provide appropriate support. The regime on the reverse cohorting units was poor, which limited opportunities for staff to identify prisoners at risk of self-harm. There was no formal induction programme, and prisoners did not have access to Listeners or other peer workers to help them understand what to expect from their early days in custody, or how to access sources of support.

Recommendation: Safeguards should be in place to ensure that all prisoners arriving at Rochester are kept safe, including a thorough risk assessment of their needs, and have access to relevant information and proactive support from staff and peer workers during their early days in custody. (To the governor)

Key concern: Rates of attrition and staff shortfalls impacted on the prison's ability to deliver a full regime. Drugs were identified as a key threat but there were insufficient staff to carry out mandatory drug testing and target searching. External hospital appointments were restricted, and some were cancelled. The prison could not deliver enough courses to meet the needs of the population. Staffing shortfalls were likely to delay progress to a full regime until at least spring 2022.

Recommendation: There should be clear measures to recruit, train, and retain operational staff to keep prisoners safe and healthy and deliver a full rehabilitative regime. (To HMPPS and the governor)

Key concern: There were weaknesses in the prisons' approach to maintaining safety. The policy was out of date, data was not analysed to determine the risks of rising violence and self-harm as restrictions eased and there were no plans to counteract these risks. There were few proactive interventions to manage the perpetrators of violence and little support for victims. There were no arrangements for logging or monitoring referrals made to the safer custody team and we found one case of bullying that was not acted on for this reason.

Recommendation: The strategy to improve safety outcomes should be informed by good data analysis and include an effective action plan to reduce violence and self-harm. (To the governor)

Key concern: In our survey significantly fewer prisoners than last time said staff treated them with respect (66% compared with 78%). Limited time out of cell restricted the time available for positive relationships to develop. Staff had little time to help prisoners with day-to-day issues. Key work duties were cancelled which compounded this problem. There was no evidence of key workers supporting prisoners on ACCT case management or challenge, support and intervention plans.

Recommendation: Staffing levels and prisoners' time out of cell should be increased to facilitate the development of productive and positive relationships. (To the governor)

Key concern: The cells in the older accommodation blocks were dingy and dilapidated and in need of continual repair, leaking plumbing was commonplace, and in some cells the electricity wiring appeared to be in a dangerous state. There was an ongoing problem with a rodent infestation that affected most prisoners. None of the single cells had toilet screens, which was undignified. Most windows across the prison needed to be repaired or replaced as the ventilation hatches could not be opened, which meant it was difficult to regulate the temperature in the cells.

Recommendation: Cells in the older part of the prison should be taken out of commission and refurbished or replaced to ensure that all prisoners live in cells that are safe, decent and comfortable. (To the governor and HMPPS)

Key concern: Prisoners told us about problems accessing their stored property, and, in 2021, almost a third of all complaints related to the issue. There were delays in processing property and answering prisoners' queries, leading to frustration. Records were not always complete, which meant it was not possible to find items. Some prisoners waited months to receive items sent in by post.

Recommendation: Prisoners should have ready access to their stored property. Requests for access should be dealt with within agreed and published time scales following consultation with prisoners. (To the governor and HMPPS)

Key concern: Clinical governance systems and processes were underdeveloped across primary care and dental services. This included the management of complaints, infection prevention and control oversight and learning lessons from incidents. We were not confident that factors affecting patient safety were identified or addressed in a timely manner.

Recommendation: Robust governance procedures, including consistent incident reporting and investigation, should be implemented to ensure that concerns affecting patient safety are promptly addressed.
(To the governor)

Key concern: Most prisoners were locked in their cells for over 22 hours a day, with little to keep them occupied, which was having a detrimental effect on their well-being. The prison had been slow to expand the regime, partly because of staff shortages. The prison did not have a clear plan for a complete regime recovery.

Recommendation: All prisoners should have adequate time out of cell to participate in a regime that includes purposeful activity, time to complete domestic chores and the opportunity to socialise with their peers. (To the governor)

**Notable positive practice**

We define notable positive practice as innovative work or practice that leads to particularly good outcomes from which other establishments may be able to learn. Inspectors look for evidence of good outcomes for prisoners; original, creative or particularly effective approaches to problem-solving or achieving the desired goal; and how other establishments could learn from or replicate the practice.

Inspectors found four examples of notable positive practice during this inspection.

Spurgeons charity had been particularly innovative in finding ways to support prisoners and their families during the pandemic. Initiatives included working with local community charities to strengthen fathers' ties with their new-born babies and supporting families with financial difficulties by providing basic items, such as toiletries and baby products.

All POMs received regular formal supervision. To inform these sessions, they completed a 'delivery report' in advance, which was a simple but effective way to record the work they had done, provide assurance to managers, and stimulate useful discussion during supervision.

Many POMs had been allocated the responsibility for developing expertise and knowledge in specific thematic areas, for example, care leavers, mental health and foreign nationals. They provided the OMU with a point of reference.

A care leaver specialist from Kent County Council visited the prison to advise and support care leavers, which promoted good partnership working and helped with effective release planning.

**INDEPENDENT MONITORING BOARD: Annual Report**

The law requires every prison to be monitored by an independent Board appointed by the Justice Secretary; these are known as Independent Monitoring Boards (IMBs). The IMB must satisfy itself as to the humane and just treatment of those held in custody within its prison and the range and adequacy of the programmes preparing them for release; it must report annually to the Justice Secretary on how well the prison has met the standards and requirements placed on it.

**IMB Report 1 April 2020 – 31 March 2021**
**Published September 2021**
**Executive Summary**
**Background to the report**

Throughout this reporting period, and the exceptional conditions in place because of the Covid-19 pandemic, HMP & YOI Rochester has continued to provide a stable, safe and decent environment for prisoners. Its prison officers deal with offenders in their care as sympathetically and effectively as resources allow, despite there being some prisoners who are especially demanding and whose needs are increasingly difficult to meet. Social distancing arrangements have worked well; there were no cases of Covid infection at the prison during the first wave. There were some outbreaks in the second wave, but considerably fewer than at other Kent prisons.

It is indicative of the positive relationship between the officers and the prisoners at Rochester that many of the expected difficulties associated with lockdown (increased violence, self-harm and mental health) did not occur to the extent anticipated. Much of this is due to the Key Worker system, which continued throughout the year. The restrictive regime in place allows for 2 hours of association per day for each prisoner. This is an extreme arrangement which is not humane, but is necessary at present. The Board strongly supports the introduction of a more normal regime as soon as is safely possible.

In the main the most demanding prisoners are those with mental health issues, including those with an underlying substance abuse issue which may be acerbated whilst in prison. The availability of contraband including new psychoactive substances (NPS) and other illicit drugs, mobile phones and tobacco has decreased during the year because of the restrictive regime in place. In turn this means incidents of violence, intimidation and, in turn, self-harming has lessened too.

Improved searching of all individuals entering the prison has proved successful in curtailing an avenue of entry for contraband into the prison. An airport style searching pod was due to be set up but building this has yet to commence.

Many of the buildings are Edwardian, structurally poor, and difficult to modernise. However, in spite of this, social distancing arrangements were introduced and are working well. There is still a vermin problem at the prison, but it has improved since the Board's last report. As a resettlement prison, preparation for release is a key feature of the regime at Rochester. However all activity connected with Work, Education, and Behavioural Programmes had to stop due to the restricted regime. In-cell work was provided, and books from the library remained available.

Arrangements for the introduction of video visits was handled successfully, and allowed prisoners to keep in contact with family members, who were unable to visit the prison in person. The Chaplaincy assisted with video funeral arrangements, given that attendance at funerals was difficult to arrange at times.

No prisoners were released on temporary licence (ROTL), and while home detention curfew (HDC) continued, there is an ongoing issue of accommodation being available to enable more prisoners with the correct profile to be released. There are too many Category D prisoners awaiting relocation to a prison with open conditions; the Board has received many applications about the disappointment and feeling of general unfairness the delay is causing. A good decision was made by the Prison Service to utilise the old Medway Secure Training Centre building for housing Category D prisoners during the Covid outbreak. Known as the Annex (as it is run by HMP Rochester), it was open from May to October. The conversion was achieved speedily, and demonstrates what can be accomplished when all parties work together coherently. The Board was duly impressed and commends all those involved in achieving this project.

## Main judgements
### How safe is the prison?
HMP Rochester was in a lockdown regime for the report period. This meant less mixing between prisoners, which impacted on violence levels and inhibited passing of illicit substances. Consequently, it has proved a safe environment for prisoners. Levels of violence had been falling prior to lockdown, and the lack of incidents reflects the generally good and co-operative relationship there is between staff and prisoners at Rochester.

### How fairly and humanely are prisoners treated?
Given that prisoners at HMP Rochester have been locked up for 22 hours per day because of the pandemic restrictions, the Board cannot report that prisoners are being treated in a humane way. However, within these necessary restrictions, the Board considers the regime has been delivered in a humane way. This is in spite of the ongoing difficulties the prison faces, such as deteriorating buildings and the availability of drugs. The Board's perception is that prisoners are being treated fairly, with adjudications conducted correctly, the conclusions reasonable and the outcomes just and fair. Assessment Care in Custody Teamwork (ACCT) and Good Order or Discipline (GOOD) reviews are undertaken within required timescales, with some positive outcomes. The Board's view is that provisions for Equalities and Safer Custody are good and the prison is operating in an equitable way. The lack of availability of open conditions means that too many prisoners are awaiting transfer to Category D establishments, which is unfair on those prisoners who work towards gaining this status change.

### How well are prisoners' health and wellbeing needs met?
Healthcare appointments are commensurate with community NHS provision. Mental healthcare and drug recovery arrangements are good. The Key Worker scheme has been introduced successfully and played a key role in the prison's stability during the lockdown period. There is good provision for exercise, which has started to resume, and the Chaplaincy team works hard to engage with all prisoners, not just those with faith. The vermin problem is less severe than reported last year.

### How well are prisoners progressed towards successful resettlement?
Unfortunately, the restricted regime impacted on all aspects of resettlement, and those prisoners leaving, while getting some basic support, did not have the usual preparedness for release which Rochester can provide. Relatively few behavioural programmes took place due to social distancing. As restrictions are relaxed, the Board hopes that meaningful occupation for the prisoners can be identified, and supports the prison is its aim to re-examine what it can provide.

### Main areas for development
### TO THE MINISTER
1. a) The Board still retains the view that in order to enable a better outcome for prisoners and reduce re-offending, increased funding for resources should be allocated across the entire prison estate for tackling drug-use by prisoners.

This includes improvements in security technology and intervention programmes.

2. b) Re-offending rates cannot be reduced unless there is suitable accommodation for all prisoners who have completed their sentence; too many prisoners are released from Rochester to become homeless rough sleepers. The Board retains the view that the recent initiative for prisons to refer those at risk of homelessness to local authorities, as referred to by the Minister in replying to previous reports, is not working and does not seem to be producing any improvement.

## TO THE PRISON SERVICE

a) Property losses on transfer: Yet again, there appears to have been no progress in resolving the problems which occur when a prisoner and their property are transferred from other establishments. Frustratingly items are still going missing and unnecessary delays occurring. This is a transport issue, not one of volumetric control. Lack of ownership over this re- occurring problem is frustrating. When will a revised framework for ensuring the effective transfer of prisoners' property come into being?

b) There are too many Category D prisoners in Rochester awaiting transfer to open conditions. The creation of the Annex mitigated this during the May to October, but this was just a temporary fix. More Category D accommodation needs to be resourced. It is unfair for prisoners to be encouraged to gain Category D status, when the opportunities for transfer to open conditions are so limited.

## TO THE GOVERNOR

The Board is still noting that cell clearance checks remain haphazard and many are not conducted properly, particularly when an individual is moved to the CSU from a double cell. Can this be addressed please?

### Progress since the last report

Key Working has proven its worth in contributing towards the stability of the prison, especially during the first lockdown period.

The introduction of video visits was challenging. The open location of Rochester with each wing in its own building meant a separate dedicated location had to be identified, and set up. It was managed well, has been a successful innovation and was implemented within the timescale required. Body searching for all incoming personnel into the prison was introduced. It has been carried out in a considerate way, and has added to the preventative security provisions at the prison.

**ONLY PARK WILLOUGHBY NR RUGBY WARKS, CV23 8SZ**

RYE HILL PRISON    Tel: 01788 523300

*For the latest reports on this prison please visit:*
https://tinyurl.com/bdfh26rv

*Important Changes:* **(1) Visits:** the identification necessary to access this prison and visit for social or professional purposes has changed; (2) **Money and Gifts** new rules now apply to these. See page 16 for full details of the above.

**Task of the establishment** HMP Rye Hill is a category B prison for men aged over 21, serving sentences of over four years who have been convicted of sexual offences.

**Certified normal accommodation and operational capacity**
Prisoners held at the time of inspection: 659
Baseline certified normal capacity: 600
Operational capacity: 664

**Prison status and key providers**
Private – managed by: G4S
Prison Group: Contracted
Head of Custodial Contracts: Neil Richards
Governor/Director: Peter Small / Mick Mullen (c)
IMB Chair: Michael Waring
Physical and mental health provider: G4S Healthcare
Secondary mental health care provider: Northamptonshire Healthcare NHS Foundation Trust
Substance use treatment provider: G4S
Prison education framework provider: Novus
Community rehabilitation company: N/A
Escort contractor: GeoAmey

**Brief history** HMP Rye Hill opened in 2001. In summer 2014, the prison was re-rolled to hold an entire population of prisoners convicted of sexual offences.

**Short description of residential units**
One unit (Andrews wing) was the induction unit and all the other seven units held sentenced prisoners.

**Visiting Information**
Prisoners book all their family and friends visits on a computer kiosk. They will then notify you of the date and time they have booked (you will not receive a visiting order).

**Legal visits:** To make a booking please call our direct number 01788 523303.

## INSPECTIONS & REPORTS

**Date of last full inspection** 1–13 September 2019

*Notable features from this inspection*

• All prisoners were convicted of a sexual offence.

• 90% of the population had been assessed as high or very high risk of serious harm to others.

• 90% of the population was serving either an indeterminate sentence or a sentence of 10 years or more.

• A fifth of the population was over the age of 60.

• Two thirds of the population had only attained level 1 or lower in English or mathematics.

## HMCIP Report, published 07 February 2020

HMP Rye Hill is a relatively modern category B training prison in the West Midlands. Capable of holding up to 664 convicted adult men, the prison is operated by the private contractor G4S. Since 2014 the prison has fulfilled a specialist function, holding only those convicted of sexual offences. The considerable risk posed by them is most easily represented by the fact that, of the 659 prisoners being held there when we inspected, some 488 were serving sentences of more than 10 years and over 100 were serving indeterminate sentences, including life. Almost all presented a high risk of serious harm to others. This was our first visit to Rye Hill since 2015. Although there was some variation in our healthy prison assessments, as on that occasion, this is basically an effective prison delivering good outcomes. Rye Hill continues to be a safe prison. New arrivals received good support on reception and were inducted well. The amount of violence recorded was not excessive and those incidents that did occur were not normally very serious. The atmosphere in the prison was settled and most prisoners seemed motivated to engage with the staff and the daily regime. In our survey prisoners did, however, raise questions about their own perceptions of safety, a finding worth further exploration by the prison. Similarly, the amount of force used and the number of adjudications initiated seemed misaligned with other findings and required better understanding by the prison. Self-harm in the prison was relatively high, although a relatively small number of prisoners accounted for a disproportionate number of incidents. Those in crisis suggested to us that they felt well cared for, aided in part by good peer support engagement. Rye Hill had become a more respectful prison. Relationships between staff and prisoners were constructive and supportive, encouraged further by well managed key worker and very useful peer worker schemes. Consultation was wide ranging and although we were concerned that not all formal complaints were properly recorded, those that were, as well as general requests and applications, were mostly properly dealt with. The prison was doing some useful and encouraging work to promote diversity, including providing good support for older prisoners and those with disabilities, but despite this there was clear evidence that perceptions among some protected groups continued to be more negative. Faith provision was a strength of the prison and the quality of health provision was reasonably good.

The prison was clean and well maintained, and cellular accommodation was very good. Access to amenities such as clothing, showers and cleaning materials was similarly good. The very impressive grounds and garden areas, to which prisoners had reasonable access, were a civilising feature of the prison's environment and was likely to have supported the sense of well-being among the men.

Rye Hill remained a purposeful place. Prisoners were unlocked for meaningful amounts of time and very few were locked up during the working day. There was good access to recreational facilities, including a valuable activity centre offering support for older, vulnerable and disabled men. Work to promote education, skills and work was not as good, with issues such as attendance and the acquisition of skills in English and maths needing improvement. Too many prisoners were not being sufficiently challenged. Our partners in Ofsted judged the overall effectiveness of education, skills and work as 'requires improvement', which was disappointing. The prison was more successful in managing and addressing one of its core tasks, that of managing the risk of harm among those being held there. Almost all had an assessment of their risk and needs (OASys) and a sentence plan, and most prisoners understood what was expected of them. Offender supervisors supported by key workers ensured reasonable levels of contact, and although one-to-one interventions were limited, access to accredited offending behaviour work was better. Public protection work was satisfactory but support for the few prisoners who were released from the prison needed to be improved. At Rye Hill we found a well-led establishment working hard to promote the well-being of its prisoners, to sustain a credible community ethos and to create a meaningful rehabilitative culture. We found some very effective outcomes and while there were gaps, there was every reason to believe that the prison was very well placed to improve still further.

Peter Clarke CVO OBE QPM October 2019
HM Chief Inspector of Prisons

**INDEPENDENT MONITORING BOARD: Annual Report**

The law requires every prison to be monitored by an independent Board appointed by the Justice Secretary; these are known as Independent Monitoring Boards (IMBs). The IMB must satisfy itself as to the humane and just treatment of those held in custody within its prison and the range and adequacy of the programmes preparing them for release; it must report annually to the Justice Secretary on how well the prison has met the standards and requirements placed on it.

**IMB Report 1 April 2021 – 31 March 2022**
**Published August 2022**
**Executive summary**
**Background to the report**

This report presents the findings of the Independent Monitoring Board at HMP Rye Hill for the period 1 April 2021 to 31 March 2022. During this period Covid-19 restrictions have continued with periods of lockdown to control the spread of the virus. These restrictions have had a material impact on the Board's ability to gather information, the Board has therefore tried to cover as much ground as it can in these difficult circumstances, and ministers are aware of these constraints.

The framework of different stages of restrictions implemented by the Ministry of Justice in March 2020 remained in place during the reporting year. This framework had five stages, from Stage 5: full lockdown to Stage 1: prepare for a return to normal operation.

At the start of the reporting year the prison was part way through a nine-week transition from Stage 3 into Stage 2 and actively moving towards a 50/50 employment model for 95% of the prison population; this involved one day on, one day off working. Activities such as the violence elimination team (VET) football league were also restarting.

Plans were worked on during June/July to expand the weekend regime with more structured activities and at the end of July the prison moved fully to Stage 2 with the reintroduction of face-to-face library sessions and the restarting of face-to-face faith groups. Being at Stage 2 also allowed for the opportunity to dine out of cell with others on alternate evenings and the restarting of face-to-face visits. During August/September focus groups were held with prisoners and staff to plan how best to move to Stage 1 with full employment and four evenings of structured activities per week for the whole prison being planned. The move to Stage 1 happened in early November but by this time cases in the community were rising quickly and on 2 December HMPPS issued a directive that all prisons should return to Stage 3.

During January and February plans were put in place to move back to Stage 2 with 50/50 employment and the return to face-to-face education and faith services. This Stage 2 regime was again in place by the end of the reporting period with plans developed for a return to Stage 1. The opening up of the regime was facilitated by the much wider accessibility of testing, with staff taking daily lateral flow tests (LFTs), reduced to three times a week at the end of the reporting period, and the possibility of testing all prisoners on a unit when a case was identified, allowing the isolation of non-symptomatic sufferers and reducing transmission.

Another key factor allowing the easing of restrictions was the vaccination programme with 554 prisoners with one vaccination, 549 with two and 503 with a third booster by the end of the reporting period. Seventy-four prisoners declined to be vaccinated. These numbers do change as people transfer in and out of the prison, but additional vaccination clinics are held if new arrivals, or previous decliners, agree to further vaccination. Although cases continue to be found there has been no serious illness inside the prison in recent months and no prisoners hospitalised due to Covid-19.

In order to try and maintain the open regime for most prisoners in spite of continuing cases, when a prisoner tests positive they are isolated in their cell with a specific daily period when they can take a shower and have 30 minutes' exercise time on their own or with other prisoners testing positive on the same unit. Staff who test positive are not allowed to return to work until they test negative even if this exceeds the 10-day period set for isolation in the community.

Although there have been many changes to the regime those prisoners spoken to by the IMB, including a sample of older prisoners, have stated they have felt safe and appreciated the level of information provided about plans for the prison and about what was happening in the community. The reduction across all categories of violence, use of force and self-harm underpins the statements from prisoners that the environment was safe.

The Board enjoys an excellent working relationship with the Director, the Deputy Director and other members of the senior management team (SMT) and appreciates the open, honest, cooperative, and transparent way in which they interact with the Board. In particular, the Board wishes to highlight the excellent work done by the SMT involving the development of an innovative communication strategy which ensured prisoners and staff were kept fully informed during the unprecedented pandemic. This method of ensuring the same message to everyone contributed to the environment remaining safe and secure. The Daily Vlog (an update transmitted to every cell other than the care and separation unit) has become a feature of life for prisoners held at Rye Hill and now forms one of the pillars of communication to all prisoners. The critical role played by the staff in maintaining a calm atmosphere within the prison should also be recognised.

## Main Judgements
### How safe is the prison?
The Board considers the prison to be a safe environment for prisoners, and this is supported by conversations with prisoners including the older population. The reduced level of violence and self-harm also supports this conclusion.

### How fairly and humanely are prisoners treated?
The Board considers that the treatment received by prisoners has been fair and humane although there have been periods of restriction due to Covid-19 cases. A lot of effort has been expended to keep the prisoners involved with, and informed about, the regime changes and the need for them.

The Board also wishes to recognise the efforts of all who are involved in managing the care and separation unit (CSU). The number housed there remains consistently low with the vast majority staying for only a very short time.

### How well are prisoners' health and wellbeing needs met?
The Board considers that the health of prisoners was adequately provided for with access to healthcare for most prisoners, most of the time. The flexible vaccination programme was a key tool in preventing serious illness. However, the Board has concerns about the time being taken to action the change in primary healthcare supplier as a delay may impact staff recruitment and motivation.

### How well are prisoners progressed towards successful resettlement?
The Board considers the delivery of programmes to have been flexible, within the restrictions, allowing a reasonable number of prisoners to complete their sentence plan requirement, but continues to have concerns about access to vocational training and higher education for those prisoners who are not suitable for programmes. It is pleasing to see some of the category C prisoners who have not been able to transfer have been given a parole-directed release, but it is still a concern that though the prison has a substantial number of releases it is not part of the estate considered as needing specific 'through the gate' resources.

## Main areas for development
### TO THE MINISTER
Progress for the IPP cohort remains a concern. This issue not only impacts Rye Hill, but the whole prison estate. Prisoners subject to this sentence often present major challenges in their management making it even harder for them to progress.

### TO THE PRISON SERVICE
The difficulties surrounding appropriate arrangements for end-of-life care and compassionate release, imposed by current HMPPS facilities and procedures, impact HMP Rye Hill disproportionately because of the higher than average age profile of the prisoners held. The current procedures do not seem to facilitate humane treatment of these prisoners.

The Board remains concerned that the stated preparation for release path of staged movements from category B to category C and then to a local or category D prison, as defined by HMPPS, represents a particular problem for prisoners convicted of sexual offences and frequently does not seem to happen in practice leaving them to be released from an establishment with no specialist 'through the gate' support.

There does not seem to be a process for managing the impact on prisoners of changes to the rules on in-possession property with items being allowed, then disallowed with no explanation or transition period leading to unfairness especially for those prisoners who have recently acquired withdrawn items.

### TO THE DIRECTOR
Based on comments from staff members, refresher training for key workers would be valuable once regimes are fully reopened.

Prisoners have asked for a specific appeal form concerning recategorisation decisions (rather than using a Comp1) and the Board considers this would be a useful upgrade to the process.

### Progress since the last report
The continuation of Covid-19 restrictions has made it hard to implement improvements, however several initiatives have been completed or are underway:
• A new gatehouse has been built providing an automated key issuance system.
• A media hub has been opened to allow the restarting of the production of the Rye Hill Times, a newspaper produced by the prisoners themselves. This facility will also allow other communication projects in the future.
• An education improvement plan has been agreed and tasks are now being actioned.
If the planned expansion building work goes ahead this is planned to include improvements in work locations, healthcare, and multi-faith facilities.

**RIPLEY ROAD
RIPLEY
WOKING
GU23 7LJ**

**HMP & YOI
SEND**

**Tel: 01483 471000**

*For the latest reports on this prison please visit:*
https://tinyurl.com/bdfh26rv

*Important Changes:* **(1) Visits:** the identification necessary to access this prison and visit for social or professional purposes has changed; (2) **Money and Gifts** new rules now apply to these. See page 16 for full details of the above.

**Task of the establishment** Closed women's prison.

**Certified normal accommodation and operational capacity**
Prisoners held at the time of inspection: 164
Baseline certified normal capacity: 202
In-use certified normal capacity: 202
Operational capacity: 202 (temporary adjustment to192 for Covid-19)

**Population of the prison**
• The number of new receptions had been lower over the last year with only 40 admissions
• 17 foreign national prisoners
• 28% of prisoners from black and minority ethnic backgrounds
• eight prisoners a month released into the community
• 80 prisoners receiving support for substance use
• nine prisoners a month referred for mental health assessment.

**Prison status and key providers**
Public
Prison Group: Women
Prison Group Director: Pia Sinha
Governor/Director: Mark Creaven
IMB Chair: Sam Coop
Physical health provider: Central and North West London NHS Foundation Trust
Mental health provider: Central and North West London NHS Foundation Trust
Substance use treatment provider: Forward Trust
Prison education framework provider: Weston College
CRCs: London CRC (part of MTC); Kent, Surrey and Sussex CRC
Escort contractors: Serco; GeoAmey

**Brief history** Originally an isolation hospital, Send first opened as a prison in 1962 when it was a junior detention centre. In 1987, it was reclassified as a category C adult men's training

prison. Re-roled in 1998 and completely rebuilt by 1999, Send currently operates as a closed women's prison. It houses a PIPE (psychologically informed planned environment) unit with a capacity of 35 and a therapeutic community with a capacity of 24.

**Short description of residential units**
A wing: PIPE (including pre and progression)
B wing: general population
C wing: enhanced prisoners
D wing: enhanced prisoners and ROTL unit
E and F wings: currently closed
J wing: induction; general population; therapeutic community

**Visiting Information**
Book online at: www.gov.uk/prison-visits or ring 0300 060 6514 Monday to Friday, 9am to 4pm
**Visiting times:** Thursday: 2pm to 3.30pm, Saturday, Sunday: 2pm to 4pm

**Legal visits:** There are currently no legal visits taking place.

**INSPECTIONS & REPORTS**
**Date of last inspection:** 10–21 May 2021
**HMCIP Report, published 26 August 2021**
HMP Send, in Surrey, is a closed training prison for women which has a complex population of up to 202, many presenting a high risk of harm to others. The prison contains the only democratic therapeutic community for women in the country with 24 places, as well as a psychologically informed planned environment (PIPE) unit with 35 places.
After a year spent with lockdown restrictions in place, a serious outbreak of Covid-19 in January 2021, in which a staff member died, and the forced closure of two wings at short notice due to fire safety concerns, Send was coping remarkably well. Women, many of whom had complex needs and were serving long sentences, felt generally well cared for and supported by staff. The excellent relationships between women and staff were evident throughout the prison, where we witnessed many friendly interactions conducted on first-name terms.
Regular meetings considered the needs of the most vulnerable, making sure that suitable support was in place for women who were distressed, self-harming or particularly vulnerable. Staff knew the women well and were able to respond quickly when difficulties arose. Women told us they felt supported by their peers, either informally or through the Listener scheme. The restrictions on social visits had hit women hard, particularly those with young children, and many had chosen not to see their families at all

because the ban on hugging during visits had been too painful for both mother and child. This meant there had been fewer visits in the last year than there usually were in a month. In-cell telephones and extra credit meant that connections had at least been maintained, but it was no substitute for physical contact. One woman movingly told me how she could feel her son beginning to drift away from her.

Women were getting out of their cells for at least three hours a day, more than we have seen in most of the men's estate, but the loss of time to socialise, and get access to peer support, education and training, meant women had suffered. Staff members had noted that self-harm tended to increase when the lifting of restrictions in the community was not mirrored in the prison. The closure of the two enhanced wings meant that some women were living in more closed conditions than they had been used to and, though an external door was kept open all day, women's time outside was unnecessarily limited and cell doors were now locked at night. The prison grounds were unkempt in places and needed more looking after.

Restrictions meant that the democratic therapeutic community was unable to operate in its usual form, but despite this, women said they were still receiving good support from officers and therapists. Similarly, activity in the specialist PIPE unit had also been constrained, but in contrast to the rest of the prison, one-to-one interventions had continued for these women. The key work session I was invited to observe showed a high level of skilled and knowledgeable support from the officer involved.

The governor had a very positive vision for the prison and a clear set of priorities that included restoring education, release on temporary licence (ROTL), visits and the therapeutic interventions. Inspectors agreed with her analysis that sentence progression, particularly for women on longer sentences, was not as good as it should be, although the outstanding chaplaincy had developed a mentoring support scheme for those who were due for release.

There was a strong, deep culture of respect and support that had been established in the prison, maintained by the visible and accessible leadership team and a dedicated staff. This perhaps explains why some women who had achieved category D status decided to stay at Send rather than transfer to open conditions. This culture had sustained the prison through the last, challenging year and inspectors were confident that as restrictions are lifted, the prison will continue to make good progress.

Charlie Taylor, HM Chief Inspector of Prisons
June 2021

## Safety

At the last inspection of Send in 2018 we found that outcomes for women were good against this healthy prison test.

At this inspection we found that outcomes for women remained good against this healthy prison test.

The use of peer support in reception had started again, which was positive. New arrivals were not locked in holding rooms and reception processes were thorough, with a focus on safety. Reverse cohorting arrangements were appropriate. The current induction programme, in development, was not yet comprehensive.

Staff-prisoner relationships remained very good, staff knew the women they cared for well and we observed positive and constructive interactions. In our survey, more than two-thirds of women said that a member of staff had talked to them in the last week to see how they were getting on. The personal officer scheme was no longer effective, but key work (see Glossary of terms) was developing.

Rates of self-harm were high and had increased since the start of the Covid-19 restrictions; a small number of women repeatedly self-harmed. Support for women on assessment, care in custody and teamwork (ACCT) case management for risk of suicide or self-harm was good. The safer custody strategic meeting was effective and supported by a weekly safety intervention meeting to review women with multiple risk factors.

The range of incentives to behave well had been limited for much of the last year, including the ongoing suspension of release on temporary licence (ROTL). The closure of E and F resettlement wings also contributed to women's perceptions of fewer incentives as they were located instead on the main prison wings, which did not yet provide the full range of incentives.

The prison remained a safe place to live. In our survey, 19% of women said they currently felt unsafe. Violence had not increased over the last couple of years and serious incidents were very rare. However, women reported a range of victimisation from other prisoners that the prison needed to explore further to understand the causes and develop solutions. The use of force had increased over the last year; most incidents related to the prevention of self-harm. Governance of use of force had improved. Security arrangements were proportionate. Despite some good work to prevent drug supply, 36% of survey respondents said that it was easy to get illegal drugs in the prison.

## Respect

At the last inspection of Send in 2018 we found that outcomes for women were good against this healthy prison test.

At this inspection we found that outcomes for women remained good against this healthy prison test.

Work to support women in maintaining contact with their children and families had been more limited due to Covid-19, but a social worker had recently been appointed to take this forward. Video calling and in- cell telephones had become important means of maintaining contact with family members. Restrictions on physical contact between women and their children during social visits was a major factor in the low take- up of visits. Women were not yet allowed ROTL to promote family ties.

Consultation with women was good, including a well-established prisoner council. However, many of the peer support groups had stopped during the national restrictions. All women had their own cell and most had in-cell showers and toilets. Communal areas on the wings were very clean and well maintained.

Health care was very good and partnership working was effective. Essential services had continued throughout the pandemic with effective daily triage by nurses and access to the GP. Routine clinics had resumed, including visiting specialists and allied health professionals. The multidisciplinary mental health team offered a good range of interventions to meet the needs of the population. The provision of social care was good.

Ambulances were not always called immediately in response to an emergency, which caused unnecessary delays. Joint work had restarted to address key health promotion issues, including tackling obesity and some excellent examples of creative health promotion activities. Screening for sexual health and reproductive needs had continued. Waits for routine dental appointments had reduced and emergency dental care had continued throughout the pandemic period.

The substance misuse service provided a good standard of care. The family worker in the substance misuse team continued to provide support to women and their families throughout the pandemic, which was good practice.

Oversight of equality and diversity work had largely been suspended when the Covid-19 restrictions were introduced. Meetings had restarted last summer but had not always been as often as intended. Data collection and analysis remained limited, but there were efforts to improve this. Work to support women with protected or minority characteristics was just restarting, with good consultation in areas such as sexual orientation. Care for prisoners with protected and minority characteristics was good overall. Faith provision was excellent and had continued throughout the Covid-19 restrictions, with corporate worship now taking place.

## Purposeful activity

At the last inspection of Send in 2018 we found that outcomes for women were not sufficiently good against this healthy prison test.

At this inspection we found that outcomes for women remained not sufficiently good against this healthy prison test.

Ofsted carried out a progress monitoring visit of the prison alongside our full inspection and the purposeful activity judgement incorporates their assessment of progress.

Time out of cell had deteriorated significantly due to the Covid-19 restrictions, but leaders were planning to deliver a new regime to improve this. Unemployed women had a minimum of two hours out of their cell each day during the working week, but many women had more than this. No indoor association was taking place and there were few opportunities for social activities. Leaders had not made sure that the culture at the prison promoted the benefits of education effectively or challenged women to achieve. Few women chose to engage with learning and those with the most need were not identified and targeted.

Leaders had meaningful long-term plans for when the full education, skills and work curriculum could be offered, but they did not have plans for further improvements in the meantime. Women did not receive advice and guidance to inform their choices for education, skills and work. Most women were not placed on the best course to meet their resettlement needs or sentence plans.

Leaders had been too slow to reintroduce face-to-face inductions and the information about education, skills and work was of an insufficient quality. There was little acknowledgment of the skills and knowledge that women developed in their work roles. Prison instructors provided effective feedback to learners on their practical work to help them improve their skills. However, education staff feedback on in-cell packs was less effective. Managers did not have a good enough understanding of the women who had learning needs and the support they required.

## Rehabilitation and release planning

At the last inspection of Send in 2018 we found that outcomes for women were good against this healthy prison test.

At this inspection we found that outcomes for women were now reasonably good against this healthy prison test.

Oversight of reducing reoffending work had resumed following the pandemic restrictions, but the new strategy lacked an action plan to drive improvements and the aggregated needs analysis was too limited.

Before the Covid-19 restrictions, work to help women address previous trauma had been excellent and there were steps to reintroduce this. Women valued the support provided by the democratic therapeutic community (DTC) and the two psychologically informed planned environment (PIPE) units (see Glossary of terms), despite the severe limitations on opportunities for group therapy under the COVID restrictions. Help for women in the general population to address their offending behaviour was limited, but the chaplaincy had started to deliver some impressive courses again.

Resettlement support was reasonable overall. Most women had stable accommodation to go to on release, but were unable to make a benefit claim in advance. Home detention curfew processes were well managed and parole hearings had continued. ROTL had remained suspended for the last year and had been slow to restart.

Opportunities to achieve sentence plan targets and progress had been severely limited by the pandemic restrictions. The offender management unit had a good mixture of staff skills and was open and accessible to women. Prison offender managers had adequate contact with women on their caseload, but staff shortages had led to long gaps in some cases. About a third of the population were serving indeterminate sentences, but they had little targeted support. Women could still progress in their categorisation and transfer to open conditions.

Public protection arrangements were reasonable with evidence of risk management planning between offender managers in the prison and the community. Prison staff did not always understand or enforce restrictions on contact with children or others.

'Making Connections', a mentoring project managed by the chaplaincy, provided very good support for those approaching parole hearings or release.

### Key concerns and recommendations

Key concerns and recommendations identify the issues of most importance to improving outcomes for women in prison and are designed to help establishments prioritise and address the most significant weaknesses in the treatment and conditions of women.

During this inspection we identified some areas of key concern and have made a small number of recommendations for the prison to address those concerns.

Key concern: Although Covid-19-related restrictions on physical contact had been relaxed in the community before the inspection, contact between prisoners and visitors during social visits remained restricted. Women were not able to have any physical contact with visitors, including a ban on hugging their children, which caused enormous upset.

Recommendation: Restrictions on physical contact during face- to- face social visits should be relaxed to be in line with those applicable in the community. (To HMPPS)

Key concern: Leaders had been slow to reintroduce face-to-face inductions for prisoner participation in education, skills and work. The information that women received about the curriculum was out of date, inaccurate and lacked detail. Most women were not placed on courses that met their resettlement needs or that were informed by their sentence plans.

Recommendation: Leaders and managers should promote the benefits of education effectively. They must rapidly increase and improve the advice and guidance women receive to enable them to make the appropriate choices about taking part in education, skills and work. (To the governor)

Key concern: Opportunities for women to demonstrate progression against their sentence plan targets remained limited due to the COVID-19 restrictions. For example, many peer worker roles had not resumed and release on temporary licence (ROTL) had remained suspended for the last year and had been slow to restart. The closure of E and F wings meant that women had lost a positive, progressive environment, which had not yet been replicated on C and D wings. Core components of the PIPE unit and the democratic therapeutic community, such as therapy groups, had yet to restart.

Recommendation: Women should have access to a full range of progression pathways that allow them to take responsibility, complete their sentence plans and learn new skills. (To the governor)

### Notable positive practice

We define notable positive practice as innovative work or practice that leads to particularly good outcomes from which other establishments may be able to learn. Inspectors look for evidence of good outcomes for women; original, creative or particularly effective approaches to problem-solving or achieving the desired goal; and how other establishments could learn from or replicate the practice.

Inspectors found seven examples of notable positive practice during this inspection.

The prison had commissioned work by the psychology team to understand the importance of healthy relationships and develop best practice approaches.

Further support was provided to the more vulnerable women through a Friday meeting to identify and manage their potential risks and triggers over the weekend.

The mental health team took an impressively active approach to promoting health and well-being that helped to improve the general welfare of women.

Women with a learning disability were given an easy-read version of their licensing conditions on release and also had this explained to them in person. This helped women to understand what they needed to do to prevent being recalled back to prison.

Surrey County Council funded additional specialist external support to help women improve their lives and maintain their health and well- being.

The family practitioner in the substance misuse service supported women and their families through a range of help with a focus on recovery. Women received good support through Making Connections, a mentoring project overseen by the chaplaincy. Every woman approaching release or their parole hearing had the opportunity to be mentored by a local community volunteer for six months. This extended to practical through-the-gate support on their day of release.

## INDEPENDENT MONITORING BOARD:
## Annual Report

The law requires every prison to be monitored by an independent Board appointed by the Justice Secretary; these are known as Independent Monitoring Boards (IMBs). The IMB must satisfy itself as to the humane and just treatment of those held in custody within its prison and the range and adequacy of the programmes preparing them for release; it must report annually to the Justice Secretary on how well the prison has met the standards and requirements placed on it.

## IMB Report 24 March 2020 to 31 March 2021
## Published August 2021
## Executive Summary
## Background to the report

The report covers the last week of the previous reporting year, however, the prison statistics provided may not include figures from the last week of March 2020. Throughout this reporting year it has been difficult to make certain comparisons to previous years due to the national restrictions imposed by Her Majesty's Prison and Probation Service (HMPPS) and the decrease in prison population.

The reporting year has been entirely during the Covid-19 pandemic, and the prisoners were kept behind their doors for up to 23 hours a day. There was no face- to-face education, no release on temporary licence and fewer prisoners in work.

In early January 2021, the prison had a Covid-19 outbreak with 95 staff and 68 women (over one third of the population) testing positive, and one staff fatality. On 11 March the prison was declared Covid-19-free (on the basis that there had been no staff or prisoner with Covid-19 in the previous 28 days).

During the outbreak period there were serious staff shortages and many staff from other prisons were sent on detached duty to Send. The Board would like to commend the staff for their outstanding effort during the outbreak and the entire year of lockdown.

Because of Covid-19, the Board only made 66 visits to the prison in person during the reporting year compared to 509 last year and 489 the year before. This impacted on our ability to monitor effectively as we received fewer first-hand accounts of issues from the prisoners. Most rota visits were conducted remotely with daily calls to the orderly officer. We instigated two prisoner-to-IMB phone calls a week from December 2020 after the installation of in-cell phones.

## Main judgements
## How safe is the prison?

The Board considers that Send is a safe prison, and prison management is continually focusing on maintaining safety. A shielding wing was implemented quickly to keep clinically vulnerable prisoners safe from Covid-19.

However, Covid-19 restrictions – though intended to protect the lives of people in custody – have compromised some elements of prisoner safety. The major risk to prisoner safety at Send is self-harm, levels of which seemed unaffected early on in the pandemic but climbed as the year progressed.

Despite limited social visits during the year and prisoners being kept in their cells for up to 23 hours per day, the Board is concerned that drugs continued to enter the prison.

## How fairly and humanely are prisoners treated?

During the whole of the reporting year the prison has been subject to national restrictions imposed by HMPPS. The Board considers that under this very restricted national regime living conditions have been inhumane, and that a government decision to only allow vaccinations to be administered to prisoners and staff in line with the community meant the length of time restrictions were in place was unfair. Classroom education did not take place all year, nor did vocational training or ROTL. Group therapy, indoor gym and faith groups were stopped for most or all of the year, work opportunities were curtailed and preparation for release was limited. Under the early release scheme set up on 4 April 2020, in which pregnant women and mothers of young children were to be a priority, of the four assessed by HMP Send as suitable only one was released. Visits from family and friends were only available from July to December 2020. No association was permitted, time out of cell was limited and many prisoners were locked in their cells 23 hours a day for some periods during the year.

Throughout the reporting year staff acted with utmost professionalism and prisoners were treated humanely in the delivery of the regime at a local level; the Board has observed many instances of kindness and consideration from staff during the Covid- 19 regime and commends this. Measures such as an 'open door policy' at the beginning of 2021 to allow prisoners social time, showed an understanding of the impact of confinement on mental health.

Living conditions for prisoners are generally decent, although two prefab blocks were declared unfit for use in January 2021 after failing fire safety regulation checks.

It is unfair that the two remaining imprisonment for public protection (IPP) prisoners at Send continue to be held for many years beyond their tariff dates, one by six years and one by 10 years. Prisoners receive fair final responses to their complaints, and the prison has made a noticeable and largely successful effort to reduce the use of interim responses, which lengthen the permitted response time from five to 14 days.

There were long delays in exchanging clothing from stored property and receiving property and mail sent in but there has been an improvement in the canteen service from DHL.

### How well are prisoners' health and wellbeing needs met?

The Board is extremely concerned about the detrimental impact that the national restrictions imposed by HMPPS have had on prisoners' physical and mental health.

In addition to the matters referred to in the above section:

• The opportunities for physical exercise were limited which could have contributed in part to a rise in obesity which is a significant problem at Send and has worsened over the last twelve months.

• During the majority of the reporting year therapeutic interventions including PIPE and DTC were severely curtailed.

• The waiting list for dental treatment lengthened. The Board would nevertheless like to acknowledge the work carried out specifically to deal with Covid-19 to ensure prisoners' health needs were met and commend the efforts of staff to work quickly to isolate positive cases, set up a shielding wing, implement prisoner and staff testing, and arrange GP and hospital phone consultations, as well as start vaccinations in line with the community.

There was outstanding continued pastoral support from chaplaincy. The Board also recognises the work undertaken by staff in the provision of in-cell activities.

### How well are prisoners progressed towards successful resettlement?

The Board regrets that, because of Covid-19 restrictions, the following areas essential to successful resettlement were curtailed for the whole reporting year:

• Classroom teaching was suspended under the first lockdown and had not resumed by the end of March. In-cell learning packs were provided but prior to the introduction of in-cell phones in November 2020 there was no one-to-one tutor input or support for prisoners with learning difficulties or disabilities.

• Rehabilitative programmes to help prisoners to address their personality disorders and addictions and help them learn to live cooperatively with others were run on a limited one-to-one basis only.

• No prisoners were released on temporary licence (ROTL) to experience work in the community or had the opportunity to reconnect with their families before release.

In addition to the work of the CRCs, Making Connections offers prisoners support as they approach release, including finding accommodation. There were five 'no fixed abode' releases at Send in 2020, one being a foreign national (FN) offender who had no access to public funds.

The provision of IT is not adequate for some learning. Lack of technology training and access to IT to enable familiarisation is woefully insufficient for reintegration into a digital society.

### Main areas for development
### TO THE MINISTER

The Board continues to have concerns about the unjust detention of the two IPP prisoners, both of whom are many years past their original short tariff date.

The Board is concerned that the government plan for 500 new prison places for women contradicts the female offender strategy (June 2018) which sets out the vision that custody should be made a last resort, reserved for the most serious offences. The Board believes that reassigning these resources into areas such as technology provision would positively impact on prisoners.

The Board urges the Ministry of Justice to learn lessons from the last 12 months to develop a strategy for a future pandemic which ensures the humane treatment of prisoners.

The Board regrets the government decision not to allow prisoners and staff early access to vaccinations given the increased risks of transmission in a prison environment.

The Board is concerned that there is a lack of appropriate resettlement accommodation.

## TO THE PRISON SERVICE

The Board is concerned that the Covid-19 restrictions have created barriers for some prisoners, making them unable to complete their sentence plans and progress towards release.

The Board is concerned that education was given a low priority in the restrictive HMPPS national regime requirements, and that a lack of digital infrastructure meant that resumption of education in the community could not be replicated.

The Board is concerned that the Prison Service is currently failing to provide prisoners with the skills required for life in a digital age.

The Board is concerned about the gaps in the care of vulnerable foreign national prisoners at risk of deportation and about the lack of clarity regarding ownership of responsibility on release.

The Board is concerned that national equality monitoring data is not current and does not allow for effective analysis of discrimination.

The Board hopes that the Purple Visits service will continue to be funded, with improved software to be more accommodating to children moving on screen.

## TO THE GOVERNOR

The Board is concerned that drugs have continued to enter the prison throughout the reporting year. This is having a negative impact on the safety of prisoners.

The Board is concerned that the issues identified in the 2018 HM Prisons Inspectorate report for the development of learning, skills and work, have not been fully addressed.

The Board is concerned that discrimination incident report forms (DIRFs) where racist behaviour between prisoners was highlighted have had inconsistent outcomes, indicating staff have been unable to establish beyond doubt racist behaviours.

The Board would like to highlight that ventilation is an issue in cells particularly during the hot summer days and has had a negative impact on the health and wellbeing of prisoners.

The Board is concerned that there are still long delays in exchanging clothing from stored property and receiving property and mail sent in. The Board has identified that complaints in March 2021 have been stamped in batches indicating that boxes on wings were not being emptied nightly: this delay would impact on true response times.

### Progress since the last report

Since November 2021 prisoners have had in-cell phones which has meant easier access to support such as Samaritans and offender managers, to healthcare, and to family contact. The Board considers this an extremely positive development. The introduction of Purple Visits has facilitated visual family contact during lockdown when social visits were on hold.

Staff made increased efforts to provide activities for prisoners during the Covid-19 regime when they were locked in their cells for up to 23 hours a day.

Canteen has improved since the last reporting period with more timely refunds and a specified staff member overseeing the service. Prisoners stated in a safer custody survey that they preferred the delivery of canteen to cell doors.

Passive and active drug dogs are now at Send two days per week, but there is not yet evidence that this has reduced the number of drugs entering the prison.

Three probation officers have been recruited so the team is fully staffed.

**GRENDON UNDERWOOD
AYLESBURY
BUCKS
HP18 0TL**

HM PRISON
SPRING HILL   Tel: 01296 445000

*For the latest reports on this prison please visit:*
https://tinyurl.com/bdfh26rv

*Important Changes:* **(1) Visits:** the identification necessary to access this prison and visit for social or professional purposes has changed; (2) **Money and Gifts** new rules now apply to these. See page 16 for full details of the above.

**Task of the establishment** HMP Spring Hill is an adult male category D open establishment with a resettlement function.

### Certified normal accommodation and operational capacity
Prisoners held at the time of inspection: 332
Certified normal capacity: 335
Operational capacity: 335

## Prison status and key providers
Public
Prison Group: South Central
Prison Group Director: Andy Lattimore
Governor/Director: Rebecca Hayward
IMB Chair: Rob Wandrak
Primary care provider Care UK
Secondary care, mental health services Barnet, Enfield and Haringey Mental Health NHS Trust
Psychosocial substance misuse services Inclusion (South Staffordshire and Shropshire Healthcare NHS Foundation Trust)
Learning and skills provider: Milton Keynes College
Escort contractor: GeoAmey

**Brief history** The establishment, opened in 1953, is the oldest of the open prisons. It forms part of a two establishment cluster with HMP Grendon.

## Short description of residential units
Accommodation in 13 huts. Nine huts (J to S) hold 22 prisoners each in shared accommodation, with a few single rooms. All huts have a communal lounge, kitchen, showers and separate toilets.
Three single-room huts (X, Y and Z) each contain 40 rooms and have a communal lounge/games room, laundry, shower and toilet facilities.
T hut is a 16-bed dedicated unit for prisoners with substance misuse support needs.

## Visiting Information
Book online at: www.gov.uk/prison-visits or ring 01296 445 082 Mon to Fri: 10am to 12pm.
**Visiting times:** Sat and Sun 1:45pm to 3:45pm

**Legal visits:** Telephone: 01296 445002.
**Visiting times:** Monday to Friday from 9:30am to 11:30am and 1pm to 4:30pm.

## INSPECTIONS & REPORTS
**Date of last full inspection 4–15 December 2017**
**HMCIP Report published 10 April 2018**
HMP Spring Hill is an open prison in Buckinghamshire holding over 300 category D prisoners. Most men were coming towards the end of long sentences, and one of the prison's main aims was to test their readiness for release and help prepare them for this step. To this end, prisoners were allowed more freedom to make their own day-to-day decisions and, critically – subject to risk assessment – were given opportunities for release on temporary licence (ROTL). Although at our last inspection in May 2014 we had found that the prison was doing some good work, its performance had been adversely affected by tragic events resulting from a prisoner reoffending in 2013 while in the community on ROTL. It was therefore heartening that at the present inspection the prison had made progress in many of the areas we looked at, although there remained a number of important issues to address.

The number of absconds had increased. An analysis done by the prison showed that the majority of absconds involved indeterminate-sentenced prisoners (ISPs) who were fairly new to living in open conditions after having spent many years in closed conditions. Some action was being taken to address this but more needed to be done to ensure these men were more supported during their first few months, to help them settle in and live confidently in open conditions. Communal and external areas were clean and prisoners were able to move freely around the pleasant grounds. Some of the residential units were dilapidated and in need of significant refurbishment or rebuilding. While the prison attempted to mitigate these problems with temporary fixes, the conditions in a few units were unacceptable. More generally, the heating system was inadequate and the hot water supply unreliable. The solutions to these deficits were not in the gift of the local management team, and the prison needed significant capital funding to resolve them.

Equality and diversity work was reasonably good overall, although more work was needed to provide sufficient additional support to those with some protected characteristics. Complaints were now reasonably well managed and health care provision was strong. However, prisoners continued to be less positive about the quality of staff-prisoner relationships than we usually see in open prisons. The reasons for this were complex but managers had taken proactive steps to improve the approach of some staff, and these efforts needed to be further improved and maintained. Education, skills and work provision had improved since our last inspection and prison leaders had provided a real impetus to developing a wide range of useful partnerships, particularly with employers, some of whom now saw the prison as a source of reliable and effective employees. ROTL was being used extensively to this end, and the day-to-day management of placements was good.

Prisoners who were not eligible for ROTL were encouraged to attend activities within the prison and there were sufficient places for all of them to do something. However, more needed to be done to motivate those who still needed to improve their functional skills to engage in education before moving on to other activities.

Children and families work had improved, and prisoners were generally well supported in maintaining contact with their children, families and friends; ROTL was, again, used well in this regard. Most offender management support was appropriate and nearly all prisoners had up-to-date offender assessment system (OASys) assessments which reflected their move to open conditions. Public protection work was generally good, and ROTL assessments were adequate. However, the ROTL board process needed to be more robust and not merely rubber-stamp recommendations made by these assessments. There was a good focus on supporting prisoners to prepare for release, and an appropriate range of practical assistance was offered.

The prison benefited from clear leadership, a motivated management team and a clear plan around how they wanted to improve the prison further. Some significant challenges remained, and it was encouraging that the governor understood and accepted the need for further work to focus on these areas. In terms of the conditions of the residential units, the prison needed external assistance to bring these up to an acceptable standard. In the key area of helping prisoners to prepare for release, the prison was doing better than previously, but needed to ensure that all supporting processes for ROTL were robust and provided sufficient reassurance. Nevertheless, this was an encouraging inspection overall, with outcomes for prisoners improving in two of our healthy prison tests and outcomes at least reasonably good or better in all four.

Peter Clarke CVO OBE QPM January 2018
HM Chief Inspector of Prisons

## INDEPENDENT MONITORING BOARD: Annual Report

The law requires every prison to be monitored by an independent Board appointed by the Justice Secretary; these are known as Independent Monitoring Boards (IMBs). The IMB must satisfy itself as to the humane and just treatment of those held in custody within its prison and the range and adequacy of the programmes preparing them for release; it must report annually to the Justice Secretary on how well the prison has met the standards and requirements placed on it.

## IMB Report 1 January 2021 – 31 December 2021
Published 27th April 2022
### Background to the report

For the first three months of the year, the Covid-19 outbreak had a significant impact on the Board's ability to gather information and discuss the contents of this annual report. The Board has therefore covered as much ground as it can in these difficult circumstances, but inevitably not all supporting evidence has been triangulated due to restricted access to residents. Ministers are aware of these constraints. Regular information is being collected specifically on the prison's response to the pandemic, and that is being collated nationally.

## Main judgements
### How safe is the prison?

Safety indicators, such as the numbers of assessment, care in custody and teamwork (ACCT) documents, and incidents of self-harm and violence remained at low levels throughout the year.

The numbers of absconds and failures to return were low, and down on 2020, although the number of transfers out increased. Reports of intruders on the camp were down on the previous year.

Intelligence reports (IRs) for drugs increased year on year but this did not translate into more finds. Apart from December, testing for alcohol was limited. IRs for phones were slightly down and finds were on a par with the previous year.

### How fairly and humanely are prisoners treated?

There were improvements for some men as additional single accommodation was provided. However, the Board continues to report on conditions for the rest of the accommodation that are not decent and not conducive to rehabilitation. The replacement 'bunkabins'/huts are temporary by design and this seems a short-term solution to an ongoing problem. The Board was particularly concerned about the late delivery of some of the new accommodation, which meant that at least 12 men were unable to start their release on temporary licence (ROTL), including five men who had places funded and reserved at Oxford Brookes University.

The Board monitored food portion sizes in the first quarter, following complaints from the men, but was satisfied that food provision was adequate. The Board queries how levels can be maintained on a daily budget of £2.10 per prisoner, which has not been altered for many years.

Diversity analysis has been greatly improved since the last report. Forums were set up with residents to discuss issues identified by more targeted analysis.

Complaints were well down on previous years but the proportion of property issues remains far too high.

### How well are prisoners' health and wellbeing needs met?

Healthcare provision improved over the year. In the two Covid-19 outbreaks, the isolation regime and the vaccination rollout proved effective in mitigating more severe outcomes; a significant number of men remain unvaccinated by choice.

A questionnaire revealed high levels of self-declared mental health issues but there remains a lack of understanding of actual levels of mental health in the prison.

### How well are prisoners progressed towards successful resettlement?

Opportunities for ROTL improved over the year, initially for men in full time work, but levels were still well short of what was being achieved before the pandemic.

Offender management in custody (OMiC) was introduced in April. Some men experienced serious delays in being granted ROTL due to communication issues with their community offender manager (COM) and issues with police checks – initially in the London area but latterly more widely. There were also some issues with COMs in relation to commissioned rehabilitation services (CRS), resulting in incomplete accommodation referrals.

Outcomes on release for employment and accommodation on self-declared data deteriorated over the year, with too many men being released to non-settled accommodation or unemployed. The prison has recognised that a more coordinated approach between sentence planning and activities is required, with each prisoner's goals clearly identified on their arrival. A job club has been set up, with the aim of encouraging local business engagement through an employment advisory board.

basic pay has not significantly increased for some time for men working on camp but plans for engagement with local enterprises will help to mitigate wages for some men.

The college increased the take-up of courses over the 12 months but, as with so many activities, it operated at levels well below what was being achieved pre-Covid- 19. Teaching was a blend of small class sizes and work in the huts by residents. The prison took a pragmatic approach to men who had not managed to achieve functional skills in literacy and numeracy.

The failure to deliver replacement accommodation on time, combined with the restrictions of national exceptional delivery models (EDMs) had an adverse effect on at least 12 men ready for work and further education.

The quality and frequency of family contact have been affected by another year of Covid-19 restrictions. Social visits did pick up through the year, albeit from a low base, and Purple (virtual) Visits' remained popular but with only a few men.

### Main areas for development
### TO THE MINISTER
Although some of the accommodation has improved, the Board has repeatedly commented on the condition of most of the huts, which are not decent and do not support Springhill's resettlement objectives. Will funding be made available to improve this?

### TO THE PRISON SERVICE
The Board has highlighted the connection between late delivery of building projects and the impact on some men being able to access ROTL.

The open estate has not been allocated body scanners. Given the relatively large number of IRs/finds compared with neighbouring Grendon, where a scanner has been used, this would seem to be an opportunity to improve the detection of illicit items.

The Board appreciates that levels of pay for residents are set by the Governor, but the budget is insufficient to support an increase that keeps pace with inflation.

The Board queries how long the prison will be able to sustain standards on food based on a budget per head that has remained unchanged for many years.

The Board has highlighted issues with outside probation that are affecting some residents' access to ROTL and securing appropriate accommodation on release.

### TO THE GOVERNOR
Restrictions due to Covid-19 and project work notwithstanding, the Board looks forward to:
• improvements to outcomes on release based on improved sequencing the development of more full time work on camp, as planned.
• a better understanding of actual levels of mental ill-health and how communication is linked to wellbeing.
• improvements to the reception area.

### Progress since the last report
Monitoring of equality and diversity issues has been greatly improved. The number of men being temporarily transferred to HMP Grendon has been significantly reduced.

**54 GAOL ROAD
STAFFORD
ST16 3AW**

**HM PRISON
STAFFORD** **Tel: 01785 773000**

*For the latest reports on this prison please visit:*
https://tinyurl.com/bdfh26rv

*Important Changes:* **(1) Visits:** the identification necessary to access this prison and visit for social or professional purposes has changed; (2) **Money and Gifts** new rules now apply to these. See page 16 for full details of the above.

**Task of the establishment** HMP Stafford is a category C training prison for prisoners convicted of sexual offences.

**Certified normal accommodation and operational capacity**
Prisoners held at the time of inspection: 744
Baseline certified normal capacity: 751
In-use certified normal capacity: 741
Operational capacity: 751

**Prison status and key providers**
Public
Prison Group: West Midlands
Prison Group Director: Teresa Clarke
Governor/Director: Ian West
IMB Chair: Clive Noak
Physical / Mental health provider: Care UK Health and Rehabilitation Services Ltd
Substance use treatment provider: PPG
Education provider: Novus
Escort contractor: Geoamey

**Brief history** There has been a prison in Stafford since the end of the 12th century. In 1793, the prison opened as the new Staffordshire Gaol but, although some of the original building remains, the present establishment is mainly Victorian, notably the main hall and crescent wings.
The present prison was built in 1794 and, apart from the period 1916 to 1940, has been in continuous use. The prison was closed between 1916 and 1940, reopening at the outbreak of the Second World War as an establishment holding both men and women. The women's section of the prison closed within a few years of reopening, and for many years afterwards HMP Stafford held young offenders as well as adult prisoners. The prison re-roled in August 2014 from a category C adult male prison to a category C prison for prisoners convicted of sexual offences.

**Short description of residential units**
The modern buildings include the reception area, visits hall, education department, kitchen, a 40-bed house block and the sports hall. A site adjacent to the prison was purchased and developed as an industrial workshop complex in 1986. There are seven wings: A, B, C, D, E, F and G. D wing is the induction unit.

**Visiting Information**
Book online at: www.gov.uk/prison-visits or ring 0300 060 6505 Mon to Fri 9:15am to 4pm.
**Visiting times:** Wed, Thurs, Sat, Sun: 2 to 4pm.

**Legal visits:** Email:
visitsbooking.westmidlands@noms.gsi.gov.uk or 0300 060 6505.
**Visiting times:** Mon - Thurs: 9:30am to 11am.

**INSPECTIONS & REPORTS**
**Date of last full inspection** 13–24 January 2020
*Notable features from this inspection*
• About 85% of prisoners were subject to some form of child contact restriction.
• About three-quarters of the population were assessed as presenting a high or very high risk of harm to others.
• 93% of prisoners were serving sentences of four years or more.
• Nearly half of the population were over 50 years of age.
• In our survey, 35% of prisoners considered themselves to have a disability.
• There had been 17 deaths due to natural causes since the previous inspection.

**HMCIP Report, published 12 May 2020**
HMP Stafford is a category C training prison for prisoners convicted of sexual offences. At the time of this inspection it held a little under 750 prisoners. Some three-quarters of them were assessed as presenting a high or very high risk of harm to others, and nearly half of them were over 50 years old. Stafford is a clear example of the phenomenon whereby the increase in recent years of the prosecution of historical and other sex offences has led to an ageing prisoner population that poses specific challenges and has distinct needs.
The prison is one of the oldest in the country. The current building was commenced in 1794, but despite its age the establishment was kept in good, clean condition and provided decent living conditions for those held there. It was last inspected in 2016, when it attracted a range of gradings from good (safety), through reasonably good (respect and purposeful activity) to not sufficiently good (rehabilitation and release planning). This inspection found that those

grades had improved in the areas of respect, which was now judged to be at our highest grade (good), and rehabilitation and release planning, which was now reasonably good. To improve in two areas was creditable, and it was pleasing to see the obvious energy that the leadership and staff were putting into the care and support offered to prisoners.

In terms of safety, although we judged it to be good, there was no room for complacency. While the prison undoubtedly provided a fundamentally safe environment, this seemed to us to be, to some extent, the result of the type of population being held, rather than of any specific initiatives being delivered by the prison. The processes and safeguards that we always expect to see in an establishment were not as consistently applied as we would have liked. If the prisoner population had not been fundamentally compliant and calm, we might well have seen some very different outcomes. There was a need for the prison to inject greater assurance and oversight in this area, and to gain a full understanding of what contributes to a safe environment, and where there could be weaknesses. The improvement in the area of respect since the last inspection owed much to the way in which healthcare was delivered, which we found met the needs of the population and had made good progress since 2016. As mentioned above, despite its age the prison was fundamentally clean and decent. It was still the case that a considerable number of cells held more prisoners than they were designed for, but at least the lavatories were recessed and the cells themselves were larger than we often find, particularly in prisons of this age. The prisoners told us that the food was good, with the exceptionally high approval rating in our survey of 86%. There was no doubt that this was in no small part due to the efforts of the hugely energetic and enthusiastic catering manager, who deserves much credit for her efforts.

Ofsted found that there had been some improvements in the overall provision of education, skills and work, and it was good to see that there were sufficient activity places for the population. While there were too few qualifications available to be worked towards, and there needed to be more high-level qualifications on offer, there was good attendance and punctuality at education. Given the age profile of the prisoners, it was pleasing to see that there was a good range of recreational activities, although it was unfortunately the case that the gym had been neglected. As we would hope to see in a prison of this kind, the time that prisoners had out of their cells each day was good.

In the area of rehabilitation and release planning

there had been some real progress since the last inspection, and resettlement support had considerably improved. Nevertheless, we did have some key concerns, including the lack of frequent, consistent and high-quality contact between prisoners and prison offender managers. We also found that planning for the release of high-risk prisoners still needed improving.

Overall, this was a very good inspection, and a gratifying number of examples of good practice, which are detailed in the body of the report and in Section 5, emerged from it. These included the information desk in the visits hall, the charity shop, the coordination of social care and the arrangement of special visits for those prisoners who would otherwise get none.

HMP Stafford is a settled establishment where, to an extent, the nature of the prisoner population is such that it contributes to their own positive outcomes. When this is combined with a positive inspection report, as this most certainly is, there can sometimes be a risk of complacency on the part of management. This has not been the case to date at Stafford, and my sense was that the leadership were aware of the risk, and were determined to avoid it and continue to make the positive progress that has been achieved to date.

Peter Clarke CVO OBE QPM

HM Chief Inspector of Prisons March 2020

**INDEPENDENT MONITORING BOARD: Annual Report**

The law requires every prison to be monitored by an independent Board appointed by the Justice Secretary; these are known as Independent Monitoring Boards (IMBs). The IMB must satisfy itself as to the humane and just treatment of those held in custody within its prison and the range and adequacy of the programmes preparing them for release; it must report annually to the Justice Secretary on how well the prison has met the standards and requirements placed on it.

**IMB Report 01 May 2020 – 30 April 2021**
**Published September 2021**
**Executive Summary**
**Background to the report**
The impact of Covid-19 and especially the "lockdowns" has shaped this report both negatively and positively.

**Negatively**
• It almost completely eliminated the ability of Board members to perform on- site monitoring and hence have direct contact with residents
• It made triangulation of information exceptionally difficult
• It made Board members extremely reliant on

the goodwill of prison staff to provide the information sought at an extremely difficult time for them

### Positively
• It has forced Board members to consider and try new ways of monitoring and communicating (e.g. Zoom Board meetings), use of the 0800 free phone telephone number for the gathering of residents' IMB applications (Apps*)
• As a result of the extremely restrictive regime the residents had to abide by (i.e. a 23 hour lock-down, so leaving only one hour to eat, shower, make phone calls and exercise) the fears Board members had of significant increases in residents self-harming, serious and violent events have not been realised
• Overall prison staff attitudes, resilience, perseverance, flexibility and understanding have all been commendable (however there were a number of negative comments regarding some staff recorded in the Residents' Survey)
[* IMB Apps – request by a resident for a personal interview or response to a query, which was not necessarily a complaint]

At the end of the reporting period, and in order to provide further data, it was decided to circulate to residents a questionnaire for their completion so the Board could ensure their voice was heard. The data generated also enabled some triangulation of that obtained from other sources. The Residents' Council representatives kindly volunteered to support and help the Board with this project by distributing and collecting the responses. The survey was anonymous, involved 24 questions and incorporated space for residents' comments.

199 questionnaire responses were received at a time when the prison complement was 690 residents, a superb 28.84% response and hence highly valid results. 117 of the 199 (59.80%) responses also contained written comments by the resident, which varied from a few words to, in most cases, several sentences.

This "Residents' Survey" will be frequently referred to during this report and some of the residents' comments quoted directly.

It should be noted that in addition to Covid-19, significant personnel changes took place, namely a new Deputy Governor, Governing Governor, Head of Healthcare and Managing Chaplain. This, in turn, created changes in other roles, especially those within the senior leadership team (SLT).

### Main judgements
### How safe was the prison?
As in previous years, violence and drugs within the prison were at very low levels, such that residents frequently commented on how "safe" the prison was. The Board's greatest concern to resident safety was with regard to all elements of medicines management within the establishment.

### How fairly and humanely are residents treated?
During the period of this report there were indications and evidence from sources such as IMB Apps, the Residents' Survey, complaints and observations that some of the residents were treated other than fairly or humanely. For example, in answer to the question from the Residents' Survey "Do most staff treat you with respect?" the answer was "Yes" in 65.6% of responses. However, many of the written responses to this question described contrary situations that, in some cases, were most worrying.

### How well are residents' health and wellbeing needs met?
All through the Covid-19 pandemic the greatest danger to residents' health was the realisation that they would become infected by the virus being brought unintentionally into the prison by a member of staff, yet the Government and its advisers did nothing to prevent this and did not even acknowledge that the risks in a prison environment were akin to those of a care home. Furthermore, when a vaccine did become available prison staff were not considered front-line workers or even a priority. Given the population dynamics of HMP Stafford this was a recipe for disaster, which, unfortunately was realised during the second wave of the pandemic with 222 cases of Covid-19 (approximately a third of the prison population at that time). Given that many of the staff themselves were ill with Covid-19 during this time the prison did exceptionally well in managing to perform any sort of regime, a situation acknowledged by the residents themselves and evidenced by the Residents' Survey and Board conversations with residents.

Other than for the situation described above and medicines management there were very few reports of anything additionally negative regarding the establishment meeting the needs of residents' health and wellbeing. Indeed, in response to the Residents' Survey questions of "Based on your experience what is the overall quality of the health services like?" 61% responded good or reasonable.

Given the amount of time residents had to spend in their cells, the Board anticipated many more issues regarding their mental health and wellbeing and it was to the credit of the prison staff that, despite the pressures they were under themselves during the Covid-19 outbreaks, this was not the situation.

**How well are residents progressed towards successful resettlement?**

With almost everything suspended during the lockdown and outbreak periods inherent within the period of this report, the Board were pleased to note that all 198 residents released had accommodation on release. Staff frustration at not being able to provide more (e.g. programme support), was clearly evident, along with resident frustration regarding contact with their Keyworker and Prison Offender Manager (POM), Keyworkers, progression" for detail. It was not clear to the Board what else could have been done during the pandemic to further support residents' progress towards successful resettlement given the constraints both within the establishment and the community as a whole.

## Main areas for development
### TO THE MINISTER

• In order to protect residents and prison staff, will the Minister seek the elevation of prison staff to the equivalent of front line healthcare workers such that, should we ever experience another pandemic, they will be amongst the first groups provided with highly effective personal protective equipment (PPE) and vaccination/treatment?

• Due to the failure of HMPPS over recent years to address the issue, will the Minister ensure that the pay inequalities between what residents can earn within a private prison versus a state run prison are removed?

• Will the Minister ensure that funding and resourcing of the 0800 telephone number that enabled residents to submit IMB Apps over the phone is maintained as this proved to be such a powerful means of communication with residents during the last 12 months?

### TO THE PRISON SERVICE

• Will HMPPS ensure that HMP Stafford and Practice Plus Group initiate, with immediate effect, a medicines management system that, unlike now, does not impair the safety of its residents and is put under close supervision until ALL previous recommendations (PPO, CQC, HMIP, etc.) have been fully and successfully delivered?

• Will HMPPS provide direction to the population management unit (PMU) that they must take more responsibility regarding the suitability of residents they transfer to HMP Stafford (e.g. residents who cannot manage stairs yet the sending prison has categorised them as fit and well)? Inappropriate transfer of the kind seen during the period of this report places unfair pressure on prison staff and is to the detriment of the transferring resident at all levels (safety, fair and humane treatment, health and wellbeing).

• Given the inability of HMPPS to deploy across much of the prison estate in- cell phones, as exampled by HMP Stafford, will they ensure that the disparity of call charges is removed so that it is no longer more expensive to make a call from a wing phone, rather than an in-cell phone? This lack of in-cell phones puts residents at a distinct disadvantage; a situation detrimental to their mental health, contacts with family and subsequent resettlement chances.

• Given that HMP Stafford is a national facility for People Convicted Of Sexual Offences (PCOSO) and hence the difficulties and long distances often experienced by residents' relatives when visiting the establishment, will HMPPS consider firstly maintaining the Purple Visit scheme and secondly extending it to incorporate evenings and weekends?

### TO THE GOVERNOR

• Will the Governor ensure that specialist debt advice is re-introduced as a service to the residents?

• Given the many negative comments of the Residents' Survey regarding staff/resident relationships will the Governor put in place an action plan that is aimed at rectifying these issues?

## Progress since the last report
### What is better?

The physical improvements being made to the prison (e.g. decoration) by the unified efforts of residents and staff (including contractors)

The regional specialist care unit (SCU) is almost completed and due to open in the summer

The low level of IMB Apps- 19 for the year as a whole

The availability of the 0800 Freephone number for the submission of IMB Apps

The provision of Purple Visits

### What remains the same?

The drive by all to deliver the vision of "proud to return active citizens, through rehabilitation, to our communities"

A prison well led by the Governor through the endeavours of all staff

The majority of residents being treated fairly, humanely and with compassion

The cleanliness of the prison and the comments by residents of how safe they feel

### What is worse?

Medicine management, from ordering to delivery

**HM PRISON SERVICE**

**HM PRISON STANDFORD HILL**

CHURCH ROAD
EASTCHURCH
SHEERNESS
KENT, ME12 4AA

Tel: 01795 884500

*For the latest reports on this prison please visit:*
https://tinyurl.com/bdfh26rv

*Important Changes:* **(1) Visits:** the identification necessary to access this prison and visit for social or professional purposes has changed; **(2) Money and Gifts** new rules now apply to these. See page 16 for full details of the above.

**Task of the establishment** HMP & YOI Standford Hill is a category D men's open resettlement prison.

**Certified normal accommodation and operational capacity**
Prisoners held at the time of inspection: 460
Baseline certified normal capacity: 464
In-use certified normal capacity: 464
Operational capacity: 464

**Prison status and key providers**
Public Sector
Prison Group: Kent, Surrey & Sussex
Prison Group Director: James Lucas
Governor/Director: Gary Price
IMB Chair: Siju Adeoye
Primary health provider: Premier Plus Group
Mental health provider:
Oxleas NHS Foundation Trust
Substance use treatment provider:
The Forward Trust
Prison education framework provider:
Weston College
Escort contractor: GeoAmey

**Brief history** Standford Hill is an open resettlement prison on the Isle of Sheppey. The buildings were redeveloped in 1986 and are on the site of a World War 1 Royal Air Force station.

**Short description of residential units**
A wing – 192 bed-unit which holds mainstream prisoners on their first night and during their induction
B wing – 192 bed-unit for mainstream prisoners
C wing – 80 bed-unit for mainstream prisoners.

**Visiting Information**
Book online at: www.gov.uk/prison-visits
Visits booked by phone only on 0300 060 6603
Monday-Friday, 9am to 4pm.
**Visiting times:** Wed, Thurs, Sat, Sun 1345-1545.

**Legal visits:** There are currently no legal visits taking place.

**INSPECTIONS & REPORTS**
**Report on an unannounced inspection of HMP & YOI Standford Hill (19–20 August, 2–5 September 2019) published 4th February 2020**

**Notable features from this inspection**
• There were no violent incidents and none of the prisoners were formally monitored using anti-bullying procedures in the six months before the inspection.
• There was no segregation unit.
• Prisoners were not required to share rooms.
• All prisoners were employed.
• About 80% of the population had access to release on temporary licence (ROTL), amounting to 28,300 incidences of ROTL in the six months before the inspection.
• 55% of prisoners had a job to go to on release.
• 96% of prisoners were released to suitable permanent accommodation.

Standford Hill is an open resettlement prison on the Isle of Sheppey in Kent. It holds category D prisoners who are coming to the end of their sentences and are being prepared for their resettlement back into the community. Many had spent long periods in closed conditions – during our inspection, 58% of prisoners were serving an indeterminate sentence or a determinate sentence of over 10 years. At our last inspection in 2015, we found that outcomes for prisoners were good in three of our healthy prison tests and reasonably good in the fourth. At this inspection, the prison had maintained these outcomes and was doing well in fulfilling its purpose as a resettlement prison.

The prison remained safe and calm, and prisoners were well behaved. There had been no fights or assaults in the previous six months. Staff rarely used force, but we were disappointed to find that officers did not routinely complete paperwork following the application of ratchet handcuffs when returning prisoners to closed conditions. This omission meant some force was effectively unaccounted for. Prisoners' good behaviour was driven not by the formal rewards or disciplinary schemes but by the establishment's positive ethos and culture. Prisoners understood the freedoms and opportunities the prison offered and did not want to risk a return to closed conditions. At the last inspection, the prison took a zero-tolerance approach to infringements of the prison rules, with about 10 prisoners a month being returned to closed conditions. At this inspection, the prison responded to poor behaviour in a more nuanced way by trying to understand the prisoners' poor behaviour and, where appropriate, offering a second chance to remain in open conditions. This innovative approach was promising and we found no evidence that the prison was taking undue risks; around five prisoners a month were still returned to closed conditions.

Relationships between staff and prisoners were strong, despite some consistent reports of a few uninterested officers. Prisoners' perception of the food was negative and may have been driven by the fact that the food was prepared in a neighbouring prison. Better management of the serveries might have mitigated some of these perceptions. Consultation, application and complaints mechanisms were reasonably good and contributed to the smooth running of the prison. At our last inspection, fewer black and minority ethnic prisoners were satisfied with their treatment than white prisoners across many areas of prison life. At this inspection, our survey suggested equality of treatment had improved. An equality and diversity manager had been appointed, but more work was still required to address some prisoners' perceptions of unequal treatment. Health services were reasonably good, but we received many credible complaints about disrespectful health care staff. The service was further undermined by poor opening times. Other than a nurse-led triage clinic once a fortnight, all services were held during the working day, which reduced access for the many prisoners working or studying outside the prison.

Appropriately for an open prison, prisoners were never locked in their rooms and were able to move around the site. A key strength of the prison was the opportunity it afforded prisoners to study, train and work. The prison had addressed most weaknesses relating to purposeful activity that we identified at our last inspection. No prisoners were unemployed and 48% regularly worked, studied or trained in the community. Prisoners of all abilities could engage in a challenging activity, from level 1 in mathematics and English, to level 3 trade qualifications, through to university courses. The prison's partnership with East Kent College was impressive, but prison managers still needed more oversight over the quality of its delivery. Prisoners could study electrical installation, plumbing and information and communications technology (ICT) with members of the community at the Old Mill Training Centre just outside the prison. Others were trained outside the prison in scaffolding, fork-lift truck driving and rail track maintenance. These and other opportunities were tailored to meet in-demand skills in the labour market. Consequently, 55% of prisoners were in employment on the day they were released from the prison. Despite this positive picture, there was still room for improvement. Prisoners' punctuality when attending activities in the prison was poor and the cumbersome 'dynamic purchasing system' meant prisoners could not study art and business enterprises at the time of our inspection.

Work to rehabilitate prisoners and plan for their release continued to be good. The prison, along with the children's charity Spurgeons, offered prisoners a wide range of opportunities to maintain and rebuild their family lives. The outstanding visitors' centre was one of the best in the prison estate and was used to host regular and constructive family days. Offender management work was good. Unusually, almost all prisoners had an up-to-date assessment of their risks and needs. Release on temporary licence (ROTL) was used appropriately and safely to reintegrate prisoners into the community. Arrangements for protecting the public were robust. The pathways enhanced resettlement service provided additional support and resources for prisoners with personality difficulties, many of them serving indeterminate sentences, and was a welcome development. The community rehabilitation company helped prisoners plan for their release, and the quality of their work was good. We were impressed to find that 96% of prisoners discharged in the previous six months went into settled and sustainable accommodation. Despite a few criticisms and the identification of a small number of areas for improvement, highlighted throughout the report, the prison fulfilled its resettlement function well. The prison's calm atmosphere, the good staff-prisoner relationships, its impressive education, training and work opportunities and the solid rehabilitative work clearly motivated and incentivised prisoners and gave them a good chance of a successful return to the community on their release.

September 2019 HM Chief Inspector of Prisons

## INDEPENDENT MONITORING BOARD: Annual Report

The law requires every prison to be monitored by an independent Board appointed by the Justice Secretary; these are known as Independent Monitoring Boards (IMBs). The IMB must satisfy itself as to the humane and just treatment of those held in custody within its prison and the range and adequacy of the programmes preparing them for release; it must report annually to the Justice Secretary on how well the prison has met the standards and requirements placed on it.

**IMB Report 1 April 2020 – 31 March 2021**
**Published October 2021**
**Background to the report**
**Covid -19 preface**

The move into lockdown because of the Covid-19 pandemic coincided almost exactly with the beginning of the reporting year. The impact of the pandemic and the steps that had to be taken by the prison management at Standford Hill to contain and manage Covid-19 are by some distance the overriding theme of any analysis of prison activity in the period under review.

One factor exacerbating this process was the recurrence of the pandemic after a relatively benign first wave. During the first outbreak community transmission in the area around the prison was never significant and the area around the prison was in the less critical tiers.

In the first wave the prison recorded the following level of infections:

Prisoner cases:

3 positive prisoners 30.03.20 and 19.04.20

The infection rate among prisoners during the first wave was low, and there were no staff cases. However, control of the prison regime was complicated because several members of staff had to self-isolate either because they had been in contact with someone who had Covid-19 or because they had Covid-like symptoms, but subsequently tested negative. Nevertheless, we were satisfied that good control was maintained in the prison, a sound process to prevent infections was in place and staff tried to reassure and educate prisoners while infections were rising in the community.

When the first wave struck and infections began, we withdrew from active monitoring and tried to monitor remotely. We met weekly as a Board via Zoom and we were delighted that ultimately the Governor could join us on a regular basis although even prior to that time she had regularly informed us of any significant developments in writing and via telephone.

As infections reduced and lockdown measures were made less onerous, we moved back to active monitoring and in September we were able to meet as a Board in the prison, albeit on a socially distanced basis. Members of the Board were keen to be physically present in the prison because it was not possible to replicate the normal contact with prisoners remotely.

Unfortunately, the second wave brought with it much more profound challenges for the prison, not least because of much higher community transmission in East Kent and the discovery in late November of the 'Kent variant', (now renamed Alpha), which during December and January saw rates of infection in the area surrounding the prison rise to the highest in the country. This had a very significant impact on the prison and during the second wave the prison recorded the following statistics:

Prisoner cases:

32 positive prisoners 16.10.20 and 06.02.21

Staff cases: 74 positive staff cases between 13.10.20 and 22.02.21

In November these statistics sadly included the Covid-related death of Mr Rahman on the prison premises following his release from hospital. Staff numbers were badly affected because of infections and a number of staff had severe complications following their infections, several of which continue at the time of writing. This severely impinged on the ability of the prison to function in the normal way and facilities such as release on temporary licence (ROTL), resettlement day release (RDR) and social visits had to be discontinued. This extended into Christmas and the situation was exacerbated by the exceptionally high community transmission prevalent in Sheppey (where large numbers of the prison staff live). The situation has eased over the last few months but Standford Hill was classified as an outbreak site in October 2020 which still obtained at the end of the reporting period.

We moved to a system of remote monitoring in the late autumn, but our Zoom meetings continued as a permanent feature throughout the year and are something we have decided to continue as a feature of our on-going monitoring. Whilst remote monitoring is a very unsatisfactory way of following events in the prison it was unavoidable.

We have been reassured by the degree of communication we have been able to maintain with the Governor, the deputy governors and senior officers in the prison. Remote monitoring only works if the degree of disclosure by the prison management is extensive and they are committed to helping us continue our monitoring role. We are satisfied that this is what has happened and we would like to record our appreciation of the dedication which the staff have shown in running the prison during the pandemic and the transparency they have maintained in allowing us to monitor their management activities.

During our weekly meetings we have talked to all parts of the prison management and some prisoners, examined statistics relating to key activities and looked at the way in which the prison authorities are seeking to run the prison. The Board is convinced that it is being kept in touch with all necessary developments. The Governor has continued to be available to us as a Board and we have been notified immediately of all major developments affecting the prison.

While the events of the last year relating to the

pandemic are far from ideal and create major obstacles to full and efficient monitoring, we believe that the co-operation the Board has received from the prison has enabled it to carry out its duties effectively, albeit, inevitably, in a limited way.

## Main judgements
### How safe is the prison?

The Board, whilst retaining its independent role, has a strong sense that over the past year HMP Standford Hill has been a very well-run prison. Morale is good among prisoners and staff in circumstances that have, particularly recently, been stressful. The 2020 HMIP report underlined that the regime was generally a good one with a strong and successful emphasis on rehabilitation, which, from the Board's observations during the past year, continues to be the case. We are aware of a strong, joint sense of purpose among prison staff driven by a well-organised and determined Governor who communicates effectively with staff and prisoners and who is also always available to us at the IMB.

### How fairly and humanely are prisoners treated?

Treatment of prisoners within Standford Hill is respectful and humane. One of the most important aspects of the regime at the prison is the ability to balance firm discipline with respect and understanding. This has continued over the last year. Whilst accusations of bullying are rare, these are, nevertheless, taken very seriously by the prison, and we are satisfied that the institutional culture within the prison is healthy and fair.

### How well are prisoners' health and wellbeing needs met?

The Covid-19 outbreak continued to test the healthcare capabilities of the prison as never before. Whilst we were concerned that, during the pandemic, 24/7 healthcare cover onsite would be necessary, both the prison management and the healthcare providers were, and continue to be satisfied with, the existing situation and the interaction with the 111 system for external healthcare. The prisoner surveys about healthcare provision have been shared with us and show an improving and significant level of satisfaction with healthcare provision among prisoners. We believe that healthcare needs are adequately catered for in every respect.

### How well are prisoners progressed towards successful resettlement?

The emphasis on resettlement and the ability and desire to rehabilitate prisoners is the most noteworthy aspect of life at Standford Hill and we believe it is the main contributor to the exceptionally low reoffending rate at the prison. Given the number of prisons that a typical prisoner may experience during his sentence, no one prison can claim complete credit for low reoffending rates. However, the startlingly good rate at Standford Hill, which has been maintained over several years, bears testament to the successful resettlement work, which is part of the preparation for life beyond prison for those leaving Standford Hill.

We are also supportive of the Governor's desire to introduce an internet room. This is a very practical prerequisite for any establishment looking to prepare prisoners to move into the outside world. In a controlled environment the ability to use digital communications effectively will help to equip men with appropriate skills to look for jobs, prepare CVs and maintain links with their families. We believe that harnessing technology appropriately is a prerequisite of any successful prison in an age of advanced digital communication.

## Main areas for development
### TO THE MINISTER

We would again commend the work done on resettlement and its success in reducing reoffending after prisoners leave Standford Hill. The proposed expansion of Standford Hill, together with the provision of its own kitchen facilities and the on-going replacement of the old C wing with individual pods, will help Standford Hill to capitalise further on the successful resettlement of prisoners.

### TO THE PRISON SERVICE

The proposed expansion of Standford Hill is to be welcomed, particularly the provision of onsite kitchen facilities. We also believe that the effectiveness of the prison and its rehabilitation programme would be enhanced if an internet room could be created for prisoners to plan their futures and communicate with future employers. We believe that, with the creation of a kitchen, prison life would be enhanced by the provision of a dining room.

### TO THE GOVERNOR

The last year has inevitably slowed the focus on instituting an NVQ qualification for staff working in the gardens, but this is an objective we believe should be pursued.

Our main concern is over the death of Mr Rahman, the oversight by healthcare and whether such an incident could occur again. While we appreciate that prison management have to trust healthcare to supervise patients according to medical practice and protocols, the system clearly did not operate properly in this case and, though it is unclear whether this may have prevented his death, we believe he did not receive the requisite care following his discharge from hospital. This is also reflected in the PPO's initial report.

**Progress since the last report**
Given the impact of the pandemic, the decision to remodel and expand the prison and the lower capacity throughout the year, the main emphasis has been on managing the prison within the constraints imposed by HM Prison Service. Nevertheless, the positive prison culture has not been diluted despite the impact of Covid.

**STOCKEN HALL ROAD STRETTON, OAKHAM RUTLAND, LEICS LE15 7RD**

**Tel: 01780 795100**

*For the latest reports on this prison please visit:*
https://tinyurl.com/bdfh26rv

*Important Changes:* **(1) Visits:** the identification necessary to access this prison and visit for social or professional purposes has changed; (2) **Money and Gifts** new rules now apply to these. See page 16 for full details of the above.

**Task of the establishment** HMP Stocken is an adult male category C training prison.

**Certified normal accommodation and operational capacity**
Prisoners held April 2021: 955
Baseline certified normal capacity: 1044
Operational capacity: 1044

**Prison status and key providers**
Public Sector
Prison Group: North Midlands
Prison Group Director: Alison Clarke
Governor/Director: Neil Thomas
IMB Chair: Ruth Bray
Physical health provider: Premier Plus Group
Mental health provider: Northamptonshire Foundation NHS Trust
Substance use provider: Inclusion–Midlands Partnership NHS Foundation Trust
Learning and skills provider: Milton Keynes College

**Brief history** HMP Stocken is a category C male training prison with an operational capacity of 1,044. It is situated in a rural location close to the A1 in Rutland. Access to public transport is very limited; the nearest trains and buses are in Oakham (nine miles away).

Most prisoners serve medium- to long-term sentences (that is, of four years or longer) but the prison also holds a number of life-sentenced prisoners and those serving indeterminate sentences for public protection (IPP).
There are seven wings – four 'small', holding about 95–120 prisoners, and three 'large', holding nearly 200 each. There are 14 workshops and a substantial education section. There is a large and well-equipped gym, library, chapel and multi-faith room, which are, generally, very well attended, although less so during the 2020/2021 pandemic. Education is provided by PeoplePlus, and healthcare and mental health services are provided by the Practice Plus Group. Inclusion (drug rehabilitation) is part of Midlands Partnership Foundation Trust. Library services are provided by Rutland County Council. Voluntary services include the Samaritans, Lincolnshire Action Trust, the Prison Fellowship, the Shannon Trust and the Sycamore Trust.

**Visiting Information**
Book online at: www.gov.uk/prison-visits or by telephone on 01780 795 156 Monday to Friday, 9am to 11am.
**Visiting times:**
Tuesday: 1:45pm to 3:45pm, Thursday, Saturday, Sunday: 9am to 11am and 1:45pm to 3:45pm.

**Legal visits:**
To book a visit please email:
officialvisits.stocken@hmps.gsi.gov.uk
**Visiting times:**
Tuesday: 1:45pm to 3:45pm, Thursday: 9am to 11am and 1:45pm to 3:45pm

**INSPECTIONS & REPORTS**
**Date of last full inspection 22 Jan – 8 Feb 2019**
**HMCIP Report, published 29 May 2019**
HMP Stocken is a category C training prison located in a rural setting near Oakham in Rutland, a few miles to the south of Grantham. At the time of this inspection it held some 833 adult male prisoners, more than 50% of whom had been convicted of crimes of violence. Nearly all of the prisoners were serving sentences of more than four years. We had last inspected the prison in July 2015.
Overall, we found a mixed picture of progress since 2015, with improvements in one area and declines in performance in two – purposeful activity and rehabilitation and release planning. The approach to implementing our previous recommendations was reasonable, and better than we sometimes see. Some 48% had been fully achieved, and a further 7% partially achieved, and it was clear that the leadership of the prison was fully committed to maintaining and

improving performance. There was also a very clear commitment from the governor to promulgating the values he wished all his staff to adhere to when going about their work.

A very obvious sign of success is that the rating we awarded for safety, so often a challenge for prisons in recent times, had risen from not sufficiently good at the last inspection to reasonably good on this occasion. This is a very real achievement. Levels of violence had not increased, and were lower than at similar prisons. HMP Stocken had managed to defy the national trend of year-on-year increases in violence. There was good analysis of violence with a strong focus on safety. There was strong leadership in this area, and this had clearly paid off. It is also notable that there had been significant improvement in the governance of the use of force by staff since the last inspection. Levels of self-harm were similar to comparable prisons, and the fact that more than 50% of the 184 incidents in the past six months were carried out by only eight prisoners showed the complex challenges posed by some of the prisoners held in the jail.

The presence of illicit drugs in prisons is often a key factor in the levels of violence, and HMP Stocken needed to review and develop its strategy in this area. The whole prison needed to be involved in this, with every function contributing as they could and recognising they had a role to play. In particular, there needed to be a focus on the threat posed by new psychoactive substances (NPS), which did not receive sufficient attention in the strategy. Nevertheless, there had been some good work carried out, and although the mandatory drug testing positive results were high for the previous six months at around 26%, there were some encouraging signs of improvement in the period leading up to the inspection, and it is to be hoped that this continues.

It was reassuring to see that relationships between staff and prisoners were generally positive, and we witnessed many constructive interactions. However, there had been insufficient attention paid to equalities since the last inspection some four years ago, and a lack of direct personal involvement from the most senior leadership of the prison in driving progress. We were concerned by some serious weaknesses in the area of health care, with some poor practice evident in medicines management, stock control and unsafe storage. There was also a worrying lack of managerial and clinical supervision of primary care staff.

It was disappointing, both for the Inspectorate and the prison, to find that performance in the area of purposeful activity had fallen away. At the previous inspection we had awarded our highest grade of 'good', but this had now declined to 'not sufficiently good'. While the quality of what was being delivered was frequently good, our colleagues from Ofsted found that the overall effectiveness of education, skills and work required improvement. Broadly speaking there were enough activity places and those that attended generally achieved well. However, we found that only 60% of prisoners actually left their wings to attend activities, and a further 16% were wing workers who for much of the time were not gainfully employed. Our assessment was that only around three-quarters of prisoners were engaged in genuinely purposeful activity. For those who did get to their allocated activities, punctuality was often poor and they frequently failed to settle into work promptly.

We also had a major concern about the risks to public protection potentially posed by the small number of prisoners, around eight each month, released from Stocken into the community. Stocken is not designated as a resettlement prison, and as such does not receive services from a community rehabilitation company (CRC). Most prisoners were transferred to a resettlement prison prior to release, but a small number were not. This created potentially serious risks, given the profile of the prisoner population at Stocken, and those risks were compounded by weaknesses in the internal assessment of risk as set out in Section 4 of this report.

In conclusion, I would recommend that this report is read very carefully to appreciate the evidence which sits behind our judgements, both those that were positive and those that were less so. Some of those judgements were finely balanced, but the main concerns we have identified will, I hope, give a clear steer for where the undoubted energy and commitment of the leadership and staff at Stocken can best be focused.

Peter Clarke CVO OBE QPM March 2019
HM Chief Inspector of Prisons

## INDEPENDENT MONITORING BOARD: Annual Report

The law requires every prison to be monitored by an independent Board appointed by the Justice Secretary; these are known as Independent Monitoring Boards (IMBs). The IMB must satisfy itself as to the humane and just treatment of those held in custody within its prison and the range and adequacy of the programmes preparing them for release; it must report annually to the Justice Secretary on how well the prison has met the standards and requirements placed on it.

IMB Report 1st May 2020 – 30th April 2021
Published 9 November 2021

## Executive summary

### Background to the report

The Covid-19 outbreak has had a significant impact on the Board's ability to gather information and discuss the contents of this annual report. The Board has therefore tried to cover as much ground as it can in these difficult circumstances, but inevitably there is less detail and supporting evidence than usual. Ministers are aware of these constraints. Regular information is being collected specifically on the prison's response to the pandemic, and that is being collated nationally.

Throughout the reporting year, the Board held monthly meetings by Zoom (for the Board meeting) and teleconferencing (with the Governor). Monitoring was done remotely via Board members' areas of special interest, meetings with the Governor and, when safe, in-person monitoring.

The Board 's triennial review took place at the end of calendar year 2020.

The Board was pleased that Stocken's outbreak of Covid-19 was formally closed by Public Health England (PHE) in April 2021, after having no positive Covid-19 cases within the prison for the previous 28 days. Procedures put in place at the start of the pandemic had kept Covid-19 out of the prison for 11 months, which is commendable. Vaccinations had been offered to all prisoners over 50 years of age by mid-April of the reporting year. Stocken was ranked second in the country (7% behind HMP Moorland) for overall vaccination rates.

### Main judgements

#### How safe is the prison?

We feel that HMP Stocken is a safe environment for prisoners and staff.

How fairly and humanely are prisoners treated?

In general, prisoners are treated fairly and humanely. Reports of unprofessional attitudes from staff are taken very seriously and thoroughly investigated. There was a necessary extended lock-up period during Covid which undoubtedly impacted on freedom of movement and association is prisoners across the establishment. However, the Board is confident that the prison took all necessary steps to preserve the humane treatment of prisoners as far as was possible.

#### How well are prisoners' health and wellbeing needs met?

Physical health is well catered for. There are too many prisoners with mental health issues in the prison system as a whole, and Stocken is no exception. The mental health team do their best but we often have concerns about the mental health of some prisoners.

#### How well are prisoners progressed towards successful resettlement?

Training and education are excellent but were disrupted for most of the reporting year. As Stocken is not a resettlement prison, it is not funded to prepare those released directly into the community as well as they would be in a resettlement prison, and the Board has some concerns about the impact of the 'offender flow' process (see 'Main areas for development' (to the Prison Service).

### Main areas for development

#### TO THE MINISTER

In last year's annual report, we reported that there was a pressing need for increased capacity in category D (open) prisons. This situation still remains and there are a significant number of 'cat D' prisoners at Stocken.

Little has changed in the past year.

#### TO THE PRISON SERVICE

##### Recategorisation

There needs to be more active and prompt action in moving non-category C prisoners from Stocken. Prisoners who are recategorised from C to B should be moved within 72 hours but often are still in the segregation unit 42 days later. Those recategorised from C to D are also waiting too long to move to open conditions.

We raised this as an issue in last year's report and little has changed in the past year.

##### Resettlement

The 'prisoner flow' system is not working effectively at Stocken. It is not a resettlement prison and, is not, therefore, funded to prepare those released directly into the community. However, there are a significant number of prisoners at Stocken who should be in resettlement establishments but are released directly from Stocken without adequate support in place. In the reporting year, 245 prisoners were directly released from Stocken, either on conditional release or on parole. The Board feels that two options need to be considered:

• increased funding for Stocken to undertake resettlement work with prisoners who are released direct from Stocken

• more urgency in moving prisoners who meet the criteria for a resettlement prison from Stocken to a resettlement prison.

### Programmes

The Board has grave concerns over the lack of access to programmes which can lead to a prisoner's inability to reduce their risk of reoffending and their progression to a category D establishment.

### TO THE GOVERNOR

The prison had moved from Level 3 to Level 2 regime during the reporting year and we look forward to plans under Level 1 with the introduction of a more structured and purposeful regime as soon as is possible. However, The Board would like to commend the leadership of the Governor during the pandemic, and the way in which the staff have worked throughout the past year under such difficult and uncertain times. This has had a positive impact on the prisoners under their care and the way in which they have reacted to the, at times, very restricted regime.

### Progress since the last report

It is difficult to assess progress, given the impact of Covid-19, with the whole reporting year being affected by Covid and different levels of lockdown in the prison

**MARKET DRAYTON
SHROPSHIRE
TF9 2JL**

**HMYOI
STOKE HEATH** **Tel: 01630 636000**

*For the latest reports on this prison please visit:*
https://tinyurl.com/bdfh26rv

*Important Changes:* **(1) Visits:** the identification necessary to access this prison and visit for social or professional purposes has changed; (2) **Money and Gifts** new rules now apply to these. See page 16 for full details of the above.

**Task of the establishment** A closed category C male prison with a small open category D unit; its main role is the training and resettlement of prisoners.

### Certified normal accommodation and operational capacity

Prisoners held at the time of inspection: 765
Baseline certified normal capacity: 662
In-use certified normal capacity: 662
Operational capacity: 782

### Prison status (public or private) and key providers

Public
Prison Group: West Midlands
Prison Group Director: Teresa Clarke
Governor/Director: John Huntington
IMB Chair: Val Meachin
Physical health provider: Shropshire Community Health NHS Trust
Mental health provider: primary, Shropshire Community Health NHS Trust; secondary, Midlands Partnership NHS Foundation Trust
Substance use provider: Forward Trust
Learning and skills provider: Novus
Escort contractor: GeoAmey

**Brief history** Stoke Heath was built in 1964 as a category C adult prison, holding both adults and young adults since July 2011. In November 2014, it began reconfiguration as a designated resettlement prison for Wales. The resettlement function was reviewed in 2017 and the prison now serves the West Midlands.

### Short description of residential units

A–E wings – residential units
F wing – designated drug treatment/ active citizenship unit
G wing – induction and longer-term prisoners
I wing – progression & ROTL unit
Clive unit – external unit holding up to 16 category D prisoners

### Visiting Information

Book online at: www.gov.uk/prison-visits or by telephone on 0300 060 6506 Monday to Friday, 9.15am to 4.00pm.
**Visiting times:**
Tues, Thurs, Sat, Sun: 2.30pm to 3.30pm

**Legal visits:** Ring: 0300 060 6506 Monday to Friday, 9.15am to 4.00pm
**Visiting times:** Mon and Fri: 9.30am-10.30am

### INSPECTIONS & REPORTS

**Date of last HMCIP inspection: 12–22 Nov 2018**
**HMCIP Report, published 19 March 2019**
HMP/YOI Stoke Heath in Shropshire is a category C training and resettlement prison with capacity for up to 782 adult men. Located in a rural setting with a long exposed perimeter, the prison campus contains a variety of accommodation, much of it added over the years to the older original facility first built in the early 1960s. Many of those held were allocated from local prisons in the West Midlands, with the population profile reflecting a comparatively even spread of age groups and sentence lengths. We last inspected Stoke Heath in 2015 when we found a prison that was delivering reasonably good outcomes against all our tests of a healthy prison. At this inspection we were pleased to find a very similar picture despite some deterioration

in the provision of purposeful activity.

The prison remained an overwhelmingly safe institution. The reception area had been improved and was bright and welcoming. Upon arrival, risk to individuals was properly assessed and first night arrangements were reasonable. Peer support during this time was useful, although induction arrangements needed to be more structured, comprehensive and expeditious. In our survey, about a quarter of prisoners told us they felt unsafe, a figure similar to our findings in 2015. Violence in the prison, unlike at many other prisons, had not increased since 2015, with an encouraging decrease since the summer of 2018 following a spike earlier in the year. Work to address violence and incentivise prisoners was reasonably good and, overall, we found a prison that was ordered and under control. Use of force, however, had increased and was high. Supervision of use of force had improved but we still believed more needed to be done to ensure that there was comprehensive governance and accountability in place. Segregated prisoners were generally treated well. Security arrangements were proportionate and effective. The combined mandatory drug testing figure of 10.6% was much better than we have seen in other prisons managing very similar risks. The supervision of mail, relationships with the local police and community, and the prison's good grip on the management of intelligence were some of the measures that seemed to be ensuring some encouraging outcomes.

Of more concern was the prison's response to self-harm, which had risen sharply. In addition, one prisoner had taken their own life since we last inspected. Recommendations made by the Prisons and Probation Ombudsman following their investigation into this death had not been implemented in full, and while prisoners in crisis told us they felt well cared for, they were often left locked up for extended periods. Some monitoring and case management arrangements were insufficient.

Prisoners expressed to us real confidence in the staff, who they saw as being in control, and work to introduce the key worker scheme and an active citizenship initiative were well advanced. The quality of cells, however, varied greatly and many were very small and cramped. Communal areas were clean and access to showers and other amenities was reasonable. Prisoners had many complaints about the quality of the food, complaints we thought were often justified. Consultation arrangements were in place but they needed to be more effective and useful. The management of complaints was inconsistent, with confidential access arrangements being a particular weakness. The promotion of equality

and diversity had improved and many aspects were good, although prisoners from a black and minority ethnic background expressed several more negative perceptions about their experiences in the prison. Outcomes in health care were more mixed, with some aspects not well integrated.

A major weakness of the prison was the number of prisoners who were inactive and locked up during the working day. During checks we found about a third of prisoners in this situation. Gym and library facilities were underused and there was insufficient activity for the whole population. In addition, many wing cleaners and workers were underemployed. The range and variety of work on offer were reasonable and in education English and mathematics were correctly prioritised. For those who attended education and vocational training, good coaching and teaching were available and, in general, quality improvement measures undertaken by the prison and providers were effective. Achievement rates for those who attended education, vocational training or work were generally good.

The prison was ensuring reasonable outcomes regarding resettlement. A useful analysis of need had taken place recently and new developments in offender management were being introduced well. Work was impacted, however, by the continuing problem of new prisoners arriving without a completed offender assessment system (OASys) assessment. The prison was working hard to clear the backlog but our review showed that many of those held had insufficient risk management plans.

Contact with key workers was regular but too often lacked focus on risk issues. Public protection arrangements, despite this, were generally sound. Prisoners were assisted with some good pre-release planning and the prison had made some recent progress in trying to ensure more accommodation was made available to those being released. Release on temporary licence (ROTL) was used well to assist the process of rehabilitation.

Overall this is an encouraging report, particularly in the context of the pressures experienced by the prison system in recent times. Stoke Heath has benefitted, in our view, from stable and competent leadership that has attended to trying to get the basics right. This is not to argue that there aren't further improvements that can be made – there are many. But Stoke Heath was dealing with the same risks and challenges that other less successful training prisons face and yet it remained a largely well-ordered place where the prisoners, for the most part, trusted the staff. Good work was being done to confront the scourge of drugs and violence. The challenge going forward is to maintain these successes and build on them in a way that also integrates improvements to the prison's regime and resettlement offer.

Peter Clarke CVO OBE QPM January 2019
HM Chief Inspector of Prisons

## INDEPENDENT MONITORING BOARD: Annual Report

The law requires every prison to be monitored by an independent Board appointed by the Justice Secretary; these are known as Independent Monitoring Boards (IMBs). The IMB must satisfy itself as to the humane and just treatment of those held in custody within its prison and the range and adequacy of the programmes preparing them for release; it must report annually to the Justice Secretary on how well the prison has met the standards and requirements placed on it.

**IMB Report 1 May 2020 – 30 April 2021**
**Published October 2021**
**Executive summary**
**Background to the report: the impact of Covid-19**
The Covid-19 outbreak has had a significant impact on the Board's ability to gather information for this annual report but we have tried to cover as much ground as possible in these difficult circumstances. Inevitably there is less supporting evidence than usual but Ministers are aware of these constraints. Regular information is being collected specifically on the prison's response to the pandemic and that is being collated nationally.

Covid-19 and the consequent change to the prison regime has presented many challenges for prisoners, prison staff, and the way in which the Board has had to work. Necessary changes were made to the prison regime to manage infection rates, but at the expense of meaningful activity. Whilst prisoners have said that they appreciated the efforts of prison staff to keep them safe, the impact on prisoners' physical and mental wellbeing of being locked in their cells for 23 hours a day is less clear.

Despite the enormous efforts made to keep prisoners safe from catching Covid-19, during the second wave HMP Stoke Heath reported one of the most serious outbreaks in the prison service. Whilst difficult to pinpoint the source of the outbreak, it was considered highly likely that it was imported mainly from the community via prison staff. Public Health England considered Stoke Heath's response to the outbreak to have been managed exceptionally well. However, the IMB questions why prisoners were still being transferred into Stoke Heath during times of major outbreak in the prison and in the general community.

The IMB hopes that reviewing the lessons learned from the prison service's response to Covid-19 will support planning going forward.

The Board would like to place on record its appreciation of the business hub team at Stoke Heath for their outstanding work in supporting the Board during this very challenging time of remote working.

**Main judgements**
**How safe is the prison?**
The Board is satisfied that the prison is safe. However, sadly, there were three deaths in custody during the reporting year, two from Covid-19. The ability to speak directly to prisoners has been severely restricted due to the pandemic and as a result the IMB is much less able to reflect the lived experience of the prisoners than in than previous years. Applications received show a minimal number of safety related concerns and where appropriate have been taken up directly with the deputy governor. Where investigation has been required on site or remotely the Board has found an open approach from governors and staff.

**How fairly and humanely are prisoners treated?**
Covid-19 regime restrictions have been very challenging for prisoners. The Board considers that the impact of these restrictions on prisoners will be far-reaching for some time in terms of successful resettlement, mental health and general wellbeing.

Outside the restricted regime, the Board remains satisfied that prisoners are treated fairly and humanely and is pleased that, despite the challenges faced, prisoner/staff relationships remain positive.

A longstanding issue remains regarding the inadequate national system for managing prisoners' property on transfer. The loss of personal items causes prisoners a great deal of distress and has a negative impact on their wellbeing.

**How well are prisoners' health and wellbeing needs met?**
Given the extremely challenging and unprecedented circumstances, the opinion of the Board is that healthcare services have been well led and responsive. The excellent relationship and involvement between the prison senior management and healthcare ensures that health services are seen as a shared priority.

**How well are prisoners progressed towards successful resettlement?**
The Board questions whether Stoke Heath can deliver the prison objective of rehabilitation with the resources at its disposal. Funding cuts over

the past three years have had a profound impact on vocational training and the potential rehabilitation of prisoners. The impact of these cuts has resulted in the loss of 102 full-time activity spaces. Whilst the prison has been able to retain some purposeful activity, when Covid-19 restrictions have allowed, it is questionable how much of this work will translate into gainful employment opportunities upon release. It is important that the prison continues to work with the private sector to sponsor key vocational skills such as in building, infrastructure and manufacture.

## Main areas for development
### TO THE MINISTER
Stoke Heath is unable to meet HMIP and Ofsted inspection requirements as a 32% cut to its education budget, over three years from April 2019, has resulted in the loss of all prisoner qualifications in engineering, tailoring, horticulture, gardens, waste management and gym. The negative impact on vocational training and meaningful activity leads us to question Stoke Heath's ability to meet its objective for the rehabilitation of prisoners.

### TO THE PRISON SERVICE
Prisoners should be encouraged to take up and work toward the achievement of maths and English qualifications at an earlier stage in their sentence, before coming to Stoke Heath, to allow more focus on their vocational training.

Only in exceptional circumstances should a prisoner come to Stoke Heath without an appropriate OASys (offender assessment). Currently, about 10% of prisoners who transfer into Stoke Heath have no OASys or OMiC (offender management in custody) plan and whilst this is an improvement compared with last year, it puts pressure on resources at Stoke Heath.

### TO THE GOVERNOR
The heating and hot water system at HMP Stoke Heath is not fit for purpose. The Board has been made aware that funding has been secured from the Ministry of Justice to replace the system and that the work is planned for next year. However, the Board sees replacement of the system as a priority and urges the Governor to start the work as a matter of priority so that the prisoners do not have to face another winter with inadequate heating.

The move towards blended learning for education courses will result in prisoners being locked up in residential units for longer periods during the working day. This will make it more difficult to develop an effective rehabilitative culture which develops the skills needed by prisoners when released.

Resettlement planning: the Board hopes that for next year the prison is able to build on its actions for resettlement and use its influence and creativity to build new opportunities for prisoners with the skills that are in demand in the workplace. This will increase their chances of meaningful employment and decrease the risk of reoffending. The Board urges the Governor to give priority to his plans to re-introduce a full key worker programme as soon as restrictions allow. The Board believes that this will be a critical tool for the successful transition to a normal regime.

### Progress since the last report
The installation of a body scanner in reception to detect illicit items being brought into the prison has impacted positively in reducing the use of illegal substances.

The installation of in-cell telephony started in January 2021. Its positive impact on prisoner welfare will be significant.

Telemedicine is in the process of being established. This will shorten waiting times for prisoners' consultations by enabling them to take place remotely (see paragraph 6.2.1). 3.4.4 There has been an improvement in the number of prisoners transferring to Stoke Heath with an offender assessment (OASys) or offender management in custody (OMiC) plan. About 10% transferred in without a plan, compared with 30% last year, but, whilst this is an improvement, it still puts pressure on resources at Stoke Heath.

The heating and hot water system is not fit for purpose. Extreme temperatures in the cells are impacting adversely on the health and wellbeing of prisoners. The Board sees replacement of the system as a priority for the fair and humane treatment of prisoners.

The Board remains concerned about the quality of some of the prison's responses to complaints but is encouraged that a senior manager has ownership of the quality assurance process for prisoner complaints.

The Board remains disappointed that there has been no discernible improvement in the management of prisoners' property. However, as Stoke Heath is now part of a regional group seeking to improve the system for managing prisoners' property, the Board hopes to see significant progress over the coming year.

Funding cuts to the education budget have resulted in the loss of 102 full-time equivalent activity spaces, a loss of qualification and a lack of progress on employment outcomes. Furthermore, the prison continues to prioritise maths and English assessment for new prisoners who should have been encouraged to take up maths and English at an earlier stage in their sentence.

**WILMSLOW
CHESHIRE
SK9 4HR**

**HM PRISON SERVICE**

**HMP & YOI STYAL**

**Tel: 01625 553000**

*For the latest reports on this prison please visit:*
https://tinyurl.com/bdfh26rv

*Important Changes:* **(1) Visits:** the identification necessary to access this prison and visit for social or professional purposes has changed; (2) **Money and Gifts** new rules now apply to these. See page 16 for full details of the above.

**Task of the establishment** Styal was originally a children's home, looking after children under 'Victorian Poor Law.' In 1956 the cottages began to hold Hungarian refugees and in 1960 Prison Commissioners purchased the site and three years later it opened as a semi-secure prison for women. In April 1999, the female wing at HMP Risley closed and in winter 2005/2006 HMP Buckley Hall re-roled to the male estate meaning HMP Styal became the only female establishment in the north-west. HMP Styal currently has capacity for up to 486 women and receives remanded and convicted adults and young adults from courts all over the north-west serving any type of sentence from a few days to life.

**Certified normal accommodation and operational capacity**
Women held October 2021: 362
Baseline certified normal capacity: 486
In-use certified normal capacity: 422
Operational capacity: 422

**Population of the prison**
Approximately 90 women received each month
Approximately 74 women released into the community each month
17 foreign national prisoners
30 prisoners from black and minority ethnic backgrounds

**Prison status (public or private) and key providers**
Public
Prison group/Department Women's estate
Prison Group Director: Pia Sinha
Governor/Director: Michelle Quirke
IMB Chair: Lynne Heath
Physical health provider: Spectrum
Mental health provider: Greater Manchester
Mental Health Substance misuse treatment provider: Spectrum
Prison education framework provider: Novus

HMPPS (Unified Probation Services)
Escort contractor: GeoAmey

**Brief history**
Styal was originally a children's home, looking after children under 'Victorian Poor Law.' In 1956 the cottages began to hold Hungarian refugees and in 1960 Prison Commissioners purchased the site and three years later it opened as a semi-secure prison for women.
In April 1999, the female wing at HMP Risley closed and in winter 2005/2006 HMP Buckley Hall re-roled to the male estate meaning HMP Styal became the only female establishment in the north-west. HMP Styal currently has capacity for up to 486 women and receives remanded and convicted adults and young adults from courts all over the north-west serving any type of sentence from a few days to life.

**Short description of residential units**
Waite Wing – First night centre/ RCU and normal accommodation
A1 - Bronte - currently closed and waiting to be reopened following refurbishment.
A2 - Gaskell - normal accommodation
B1 - Acorn - mother and baby unit
B2 - Bruce- Incentivised substance-free living
Houses B3 to E3 - general population
H1 - Valentina - A quiet space for prisoners requiring a temporary location for timeout and respite.
Care & separation unit - a small unit for segregated prisoners
ADD - Bollinwood Unit - a small open unit outside of the closed site

**Visiting Information**
Book online at: www.gov.uk/prison-visits or by telephone on 0300 060 6512 Monday to Friday, 9.30am to 5pm.
**Visiting times:** Monday to Thursday: 2pm to 4pm, Saturday and Sunday: 2pm to 4pm.

**Legal visits:** There are currently no legal visits taking place.

**INSPECTIONS & REPORTS**
**Date of last inspection:** 4-8 October 2021
**HMCIP Report, published 12 January 2022**
Located in the buildings of a former children's home, Styal is an unusual setting for a prison, with its Edwardian houseblocks situated along tree-lined avenues. At the time of our visit the prison housed 362 women, most of whom were on remand or serving short sentences, with a substantial minority serving four or more years. The site provides excellent opportunities to develop independent living, but also presents some challenges, particularly in supervising

women inside the houses and around the grounds. Covid-19 restrictions had meant that women were locked in their houses together – with up to four sharing a small room – for long periods of time. Under such conditions it was perhaps not surprising that there had been an increase in levels of violence since we last inspected as frustrations began to spill over into confrontations.

Though restrictions had begun to be lifted, the leaders had sensibly decided not to return to the previous free-flow movement around the prison. Instead they had put in place measures that allowed for better knowledge of where all the women were, with more contained movement and better roll checks. This, coupled with improved physical security, had led to a reduction in the prison's long-term problems with drugs entering the premises.

Leaders had also sought to address the high levels of self-harm among some of the women and to improve care for the most vulnerable, putting into place the learning from the four self-inflicted deaths since our last inspection. An impressive, weekly safety interventions meeting (SIM) sought to understand the needs of and provide for those most at risk, including the excellent Stepping Stones programme. This bespoke support continued to operate during the pandemic. In addition, the Valentina unit was used for women who needed higher levels of care.

Despite this strong, whole-prison approach, some women with acute mental health difficulties still ended up in the bleak segregation unit, where some caring staff did their best to support the women in completely unsuitable conditions.

On the Bollinwood house unit, outside the perimeter fence, a small number of women were living in open conditions. During the pandemic, release on temporary licence (ROTL) had been curtailed. This meant that many lost their jobs outside the prison and, for much of lockdown, they were unable to use temporary release to maintain contact with their family or put in place plans for their release. Although ROTL had restarted, an overcautious approach meant women were heavily restricted in where they could go; visits to the town were not allowed and women could not use the local park to exercise, leaving outdoor exercise space as no more than a walk around the car park at the prison. Although these women were allowed into the prison for health care, they could not go to the prison shop or get their hair cut in the salon. A priority for leaders must be to restore this provision so that women on the Bollinwood house unit have the opportunity to begin to experience life as a citizen, and women behind the fence have an incentive to move to open conditions.

One of the houses (Bronte) had recently been refurbished, and conditions were good on the more prison-like Waite wing, but much of the existing provision remained substandard. Rotting windows, leaks, damp, broken equipment and mould were ubiquitous in the houses and in some homes 20 women were sharing two lavatories and showers.

A strong and cohesive senior team left inspectors optimistic that this prison can continue to improve provision for what is a complex and often needy population. This will be dependent on building the capabilities of existing staff, while dealing with any poor behaviour that holds back progress, and critically, making sure that attrition rates do not increase. Only with a full complement of effective and dedicated staff will this prison be able to offer the care, challenge and regime that will support the rehabilitation of this group of women.

HM Chief Inspector of Prisons October 2021

### Safety

At the last inspection of HMP & YOI Styal in 2018 we found that outcomes for women were good against this healthy prison test.

At this inspection we found that outcomes for women were now reasonably good.

In our survey, almost all women said there was a member of staff they could turn to and significantly more than at our last inspection said a member of staff had checked on them in the last week to see how they were getting on. Most interactions between women and staff were respectful and some staff showed a high level of empathy and skill in dealing with women in crisis. On occasions, however, we observed unhelpful responses from staff to some very basic requests.

There had been four self-inflicted deaths since the last inspection, three of which had taken place during the early days in custody. First night arrangements had been improved considerably. Recorded rates of self-harm were higher, but three-quarters of all incidents in recent months had involved a small number of women who had repeatedly self-harmed. The rate had steadily decreased over the last eight months and the strategy of targeted support and engagement ensured very good and proactive care for women with complex needs, including the innovative Stepping Stones project. However, the quality of recordkeeping in assessment, care in custody and teamwork (ACCT) documents was poor.

Leaders had responded well to lessons learned about the vulnerability of pregnant women and unexpected births. There was a new system to identify women sent to prison for their own protection, but the collection of data was not yet systematic or focused.

Responses to our survey showed that the vast majority of women continued to feel safe. The rate of violent incidents had increased significantly since 2018, but most were not serious and reflected a build-up of frustration. All violent incidents were investigated well, and the management of perpetrators and victims was good. The safety intervention meeting provided good multidisciplinary oversight of violence and self-harm. Women were now better supervised around the grounds which had brought much needed order and control across the prison. There were plans to improve the level of supervision throughout the houses.

The five women held in the segregation unit had very complex needs and most of them were awaiting a mental health assessment to determine if they would transfer to a secure hospital. Segregation staff interacted well with them, but the unit was bleak and the regime was still too limited. No special accommodation had been used over the last year.

The number of times physical force had been used against women by staff had increased. Most incidents involved minimal force, although we reviewed some incidents where it was excessive. The focus on reducing the availability of drugs was appropriate and the investment in security measures had led to improvements but the lack of technology to identify internally secreted items was difficult to understand. Local innovation had led to the development of an incentivised substance-free living unit, which was the first in the women's estate.

### Respect

At the last inspection of HMP & YOI Styal in 2018, we found that outcomes for women were reasonably good against this healthy prison test. At this inspection we found that outcomes for women remained reasonably good.

Women now had in-cell telephones and access to video calling which helped them stay in touch with their children and family. Social visits had restarted but uptake was low. There were plans to restart family days and hold them each weekend. Women living on the mother and baby unit received reasonable support, but not enough was done to promote the welfare of babies and young children through contact with family members in the community.

The prisoner council was well established, and the house representatives' scheme was a good peer support initiative which gave women a sense of purpose and pride and promoted an ethos of community in the prison. Women lacked confidence in the application and complaints systems. There was adequate legal provision and the availability of free legal advice was good.

In our survey, about a third of women said the food was good. The choice of meals and provision for those who lived in self-catering houses were reasonable. Most women had access to a small shop on site for clothes and the weekly canteen. The grounds and outdoor areas were very pleasant and well maintained. Waite wing was clean, cells were well equipped and the refurbished showers were an improvement. Some of the houses were dilapidated, cramped and not fit for purpose.

Governance of health services was strong. Primary care was effective but there were occasional staff shortages. Services specific to the needs of women were provided, including screening, contraception and pre- and post-natal care. Appropriate packages of social care were provided. Mental health care was good and transfers under the Mental Health Act were timely. The substance misuse service delivered interventions appropriate to women's needs.

Local medicines management arrangements and pharmacy oversight of prescribing practice were robust. Supervision of medicines administration on Waite wing was poor, which created unnecessary risks.

There was no equality strategy and, in our survey, there were differences in perceptions of treatment among the protected characteristic groups. Local and national data showed disproportionate outcomes in some key areas but there was a lack of evidence that these had been fully addressed. Support for individual women with protected characteristics was adequate but responses to discrimination incident report forms were not always robust.

There was unmet need among transgender prisoners who told us that staff repeatedly misused pronouns and that they faced delays in accessing basic items. Women with physical disabilities had difficulties with access in the houses and other key buildings.

There was still no provision for corporate worship, which was poor.

### Purposeful activity

At the last inspection of HMP & YOI Styal in 2018, we found that outcomes for women were reasonably good against this healthy prison test. At this inspection we found that outcomes for women remained reasonably good.

Ofsted carried out a progress monitoring visit of the prison alongside our full inspection and the purposeful activity judgement incorporates their assessment of progress.

Most women lived in houses and were never locked in their rooms. Those on Waite wing were locked in their cells when not involved in activities and new arrivals only had about 45 minutes out of their cell each day, which was poor. Women on Waite wing who were not in purposeful activity had between two and three hours out of cell each day. At the time of the inspection, about 60% of the population were employed in full-time work or activities.

There were too few opportunities for women to benefit from peer working or recreational and social activities. The gym provision was reasonable, but the library service was poor.

From September 2021, when the prison moved to Stage 2 of the recovery plan (see Glossary of terms), face-to-face induction had been reintroduced and all education classes and workshops had reopened, with reduced numbers to enable social distancing. Many women still did not have an activity place and about 70 were waiting to complete their induction.

In-cell education packs were very popular. Prisoners found the content engaging and said that the marking and feedback on their work were good.

Prisoners' English, mathematics and additional learning needs were now assessed effectively at induction which informed their allocation to activities. Face-to-face teaching and effective quality assurance processes had restarted.

There had been a reduction in the learning and skills budget and not all the education places that had existed before the pandemic would be restored. Accredited training in workshops such as cleaning and horticulture had not yet been restored. Prison managers had developed partnerships with companies and organisations which delivered very high-quality contract work on site, for example Televerde, Recycling Lives, and Clinks. These organisations developed good employability skills and supported employment on release.

No prisoners were undertaking RoTL (release on temporary licence) for work, but three were preparing to take up placements outside the prison in the near future.

A peer mentoring training programme was about to be restarted to address the lack of trained mentors.

### Rehabilitation and release planning

At the last inspection of HMP & YOI Styal in 2018, we found that outcomes for women were good against this healthy prison test.

At this inspection we found that outcomes for women were now reasonably good.

The focus on work to reduce reoffending had been sustained during the pandemic. Good support was given to help women deal with their past experiences of trauma. However, there were no short, structured interventions for women who had been victims of domestic abuse. An impressive counselling service had continued

during the pandemic and had been expanded. The range of interventions to address attitudes, thinking and behaviour was too limited and more interventions were needed for women serving short sentences. The personality disorder service and the psychology team provided excellent support to some women with complex needs.

Remanded and unsentenced women were unable to access help with housing or finances. The extent and quality of housing and finance support available to sentenced women depended on the provider in their home or release area.

Home detention curfew procedures were well managed but there was a lack of suitable and safe BASS (Bail Accommodation Support Services) accommodation. In recent weeks, opportunities for release on temporary licence (ROTL) to help women build family ties had gathered pace.

The open unit had lost its purpose during the pandemic. The women were poorly supported and were unable to access some of the most basic services available in the main prison. Most requests by women for access to the local community, for example to go shopping, get a haircut or go swimming, were denied.

The offender management unit was well staffed with an appropriate mix of prison offender managers. Caseloads were manageable. Contact with women was regular and purposeful.

The handover from prison to community offender managers was timely and well managed. The interdepartmental risk management team meetings were frequent and well attended but did not routinely consider all high-risk women approaching release. Restrictions on contact with children were not always enforced and there was a significant backlog of phone calls waiting to be monitored.

Several months after major changes to resettlement services started, new providers were not yet all in place and the delivery model lacked clarity. Through-the-gate support on the day of release had reduced since the last inspection.

### Key concerns and recommendations

Key concerns and recommendations identify the issues of most importance to improving outcomes for women in prison and are designed to help establishments prioritise and address the most significant weaknesses in the treatment and conditions of women.

During this inspection we identified some areas of key concern and have made a small number of recommendations for the prison to address those concerns.

Key concern: Plans to improve supervision of the houses had been delayed because of staff shortages. This hindered the oversight of women at risk of self-harm and meant that staff were not always available to address violence promptly or respond to requests from women in a timely way. Recommendation: Sufficient staff should be in post to provide effective supervision of the women living in the houses so that they feel safe from harm. (To HMPPS and the governor)

Key concern: About 70% of the population lived in houses. These were kept clean by the women, but some were dilapidated and not fit for purpose. There were numerous outstanding repairs, many houses suffered from damp and window frames were rotting and damaged. Toilet and bathroom facilities were limited and some houses only had two toilets for about 20 women. Showers and baths were often unpleasant and in a poor state. Bedrooms were sometimes too small to hold three or four women comfortably. Furniture in these rooms was often in a poor condition.

Key recommendation: All residential accommodation should be decent and in a good state of repair including sufficient facilities for the numbers of women. (To HMPPS)

Key concern: Some of the practices used to administer medicines to patients unable to attend the medicine hatches were poor and presented risks to the women. The transport of controlled drugs in an insecure bag was unacceptable.

Key recommendation: The dispensing of medicines, including controlled drugs, should be carried out legally, safely and in line with established policy. (To the governor)

Key concern: There were not enough opportunities for women to progress. Release on temporary licence (ROTL) had been very slow to restart after the pandemic which had badly affected women living on the mother and baby unit and the open unit. The open unit had lost its purpose and women living there were poorly supported and rarely visited by prison staff. There were few incentives to progress to the unit which women did not regard as a worthwhile progression opportunity.

Key recommendation: All eligible women should have the opportunity to build family ties and develop links with the community through regular ROTL. The prison should take a more proportionate approach to granting ROTL, including releasing women to access provision in the local community. (To the governor)

### Notable positive practice

We define notable positive practice as innovative work or practice that leads to particularly good outcomes from which other establishments may be able to learn. Inspectors look for evidence of good outcomes for women; original, creative or particularly effective approaches to problem-solving or achieving the desired goal; and how other establishments could learn from or replicate the practice.

Inspectors found five examples of notable positive practice during this inspection.

The additional checks on new arrivals made by the safer custody team provided a further opportunity to assess individual risks and start to address them.

The Stepping Stones programme provided very vulnerable women with recreational and social activities including arts and crafts, attending the gym together and relaxation techniques. This helped to improve their confidence in interacting with staff and other women and progressing into education, skills or work.

The safety and security team worked together in an intelligence hub which produced very good coordinated data. Comprehensive analysis of the data identified emerging patterns and trends which were shared with senior leaders at a range of strategic meetings.

The prescribing pharmacist was reviewing patients' responses to antidepressant medication at regular intervals in line with the National Institute for Health and Care Excellence (NICE) guidelines. This ensured optimum benefits of the medicines for patients and prescribing to enhance outcomes.

An impressive counselling service called 'Time For Me' had delivered talking therapy to women throughout the pandemic. Women who self-referred could access 10 hours of counselling to explore their experiences of trauma. The service had expanded to meet the high demand.

### INDEPENDENT MONITORING BOARD: Annual Report

The law requires every prison to be monitored by an independent Board appointed by the Justice Secretary; these are known as Independent Monitoring Boards (IMBs). The IMB must satisfy itself as to the humane and just treatment of those held in custody within its prison and the range and adequacy of the programmes preparing them for release; it must report annually to the Justice Secretary on how well the prison has met the standards and requirements placed on it.

### IMB Report 1 May 2019 – 30 April 2020
### Published September 2021
### Background to the report

This year has been exceptional because of the impact of the Covid-19 pandemic on the way that prisons have been run and on the ability of the Board to carry out face- to-face monitoring. In this respect, it is difficult to make realistic comparisons with previous years. However, the Board at Styal has scrutinised what has been happening at the prison, through very helpful data sharing, regular conversations with prison staff and access to minutes of meetings. The Board has continued to monitor, investigate and respond to applications from prisoners, both on paper and from the national 0800 applications helpline. The management of the prison has been very effective in reducing the spread of the virus and keeping infection rates down to the minimum. Staff have worked tirelessly, despite the constrained circumstances of lockdown, to maintain a positive and supportive environment for prisoners and to keep them safe.

The early release scheme had little impact on the population at Styal, and the Board was surprised that more prisoners in the MBU were not released early.

## Main judgements
### How safe is the prison?

During this reporting period, the Governor identified the safety of the prisoners and the security of the regime as key priorities. Covid-19 has had a significant impact on the regime at Styal, leading to a number of changes which have positively affected safety, including reductions in free flow, a higher profile staff presence in the prison grounds, and an officer presence on the houses. A new induction Centre [IC] on Waite wing has been operational which allows for a 24-hour nursing presence and better monitoring of detoxing. The distribution of medication has been better controlled in smaller groups, with all prisoners being escorted to and from appointments.

The Board would usually report that the prison is safe for most prisoners, most of the time. However, given the nature of the Covid-19 restrictions on social movement and the lack of time out of cell, the Board believes that Styal has been as safe as the current situation allowed. Staff have worked hard under difficult circumstances to support prisoners.

Although there has been a reduction of the inflow of illicit substances during lockdown, we remain concerned about this issue, particularly as the lockdown restrictions begin to ease. In addition, the fire concerns identified towards the end of the reporting period constitute a serious safety issue.

### How fairly and humanely are prisoners treated?

The prison and its occupants are well served by the staff who, despite the deteriorating fabric and present testing conditions, continue to maintain a humane regime. There have been many occasions when Board members have been aware of staff working in a highly professional and caring way. Whilst the lockdown conditions have clearly impacted on fair and humane treatment, we believe the prison has worked effectively to protect prisoners from the virus and its consequences.

### How well are prisoners' health and wellbeing needs met?

During lockdown, the provision of healthcare at Styal has been as good as, if not better in some cases, than that provided in the community. The service adapted well to the challenges of Covid-19. Health promotion and prevention remains good, with most preventive clinics and campaigns taking place, including those for flu vaccinations, breast cancer screening and smoking cessation. The GP service has provided one-to-one consultations and other specialist health services have also been maintained.

However, the mental health needs of prisoners were not fully supported which is problematic, given the number of prisoners with severe and enduring mental ill health. Despite the best efforts of the prison and healthcare staff, prolonged lockdown had an inevitable impact on prisoners' mental health.

### How well are prisoners progressed towards successful resettlement?

As a result of the impact of the Covid-19 crisis, resettlement staff worked remotely, and efforts were made to continue to assess and plan for resettlement needs. Education, work opportunities and offending behaviour interventions were less available as a result of the impact of lockdown. Those prisoners on Bollinwood house were particularly affected by the restrictions placed on ROTL work placements. Short sentences allowed little time for rehabilitative efforts.

### Main areas for development
### TO THE MINISTER

There is a significant fire risk to prisoners who reside in the 16 houses which have not yet been refurbished at Styal. A recent survey has classed all of these buildings as red fire risk. These risks include the existence of false ceilings, and ceilings made of lath and plaster, which would require expensive and specialist repair to be brought within regulations. Fire doors and surrounds, which are not suitable and not fire resistant, are evident in almost 70% of the houses. Almost half of the Victorian buildings have defects related to holes caused by pipe work, internal stairs and storage areas, which are not in line with fire safety regulations.

As also reported last year, there continue to be significant failings in the maintenance of accommodation at the prison. Contracts with outside maintenance providers continue to result in excessive quotations and long delays in repairs and refurbishment, including health and safety related matters. These failings are resulting in further deterioration in the fabric and serious decency issues for the prisoners. Whilst significant additional resource has been made available to the prison, the cost and time of refurbishment, approximately £800,000 per house, is unlikely to be sustainable.

There has been a reduction in the supply, trading and use of illicit drugs during the pandemic, and this in turn has helped to reduce intimidation and bullying. As the prison returns to level 3 and level 2 the resumption of visits and more free flow is likely to impact on the amount of drugs being brought into the prison by visitors and by new and recalled prisoners. Increased resources are required to support the new Governor in tackling this problem, including better and more regular access to dogs during visits. The provision of body scanners in the female estate could also substantially help to mitigate the drugs traffic, as would the enhanced security resources more commonly found in the male estate. The prison continues to be challenged by the need to manage many prisoners with severe and enduring mental health problems and complex needs. Over the year, there has been a significant reduction in the time spent by these prisoners in long-term segregation within the prison. Nationally, there is still a pressing need for more specialist facilities that can be easily accessed.

## TO THE PRISON SERVICE

Greater consideration is needed around the issue of prison escorts. Staffing at Styal has been stretched throughout the lockdown, and it continues to be precarious at times. The cohort at Styal includes prisoners with serious mental and physical health issues, as well as pregnant prisoners and the residents of the MBU, including their children. The need for escorts exacerbates what is already a critical staffing situation, and recognition needs to be given to the different demands for hospital visits and treatment in the female estate.

The Board is concerned about the changes to the contracts for Through the Gate (TTG) Services, including the loss of Shelter who are a known and experienced partner. Whilst TTG services will now be managed by the National Probation Service (NPS), there will still be a number of new external partners, replacing the current partners and based around different geographical areas than those currently used. The impact of these changes will need to be carefully monitored at national level.

## TO THE GOVERNOR

The effectiveness of the induction centre has yet to be monitored and reviewed by the Board and it would be helpful to consider its impact, once it is no longer incorporated in the RCU provision. There has been some improvement in communications with the mental health team and other areas of the prison, which has led to a more holistic approach to mental health treatment. However, there is still not enough dialogue between healthcare and other staff in the prison, and the Board have been unable to access any analysis of complaints made by prisoners directly to the healthcare provider. Given the high number of applications to the IMB over the year related to healthcare issues, this raises concerns about the transparency and accountability of the provider.

The work of ADAPT during the last year is to be commended and we hope that this will be encouraged and supported to make even more impact in the future.

The distribution of medication during lockdown has led to far fewer incidents of bullying and intimidation from prisoners. The queues have been shorter, the cohorts awaiting medication have been much smaller and this has made many prisoners feel more secure about acquiring and storing their medication in their safes. It is hoped that this practice will continue as lockdown eases.

### Progress since the last report

Most of the recommendations from the Prisons and Probation Ombudsman (PPO) reports regarding the deaths in custody in the last reporting year have been acted upon. In particular, the refurbishment and enhanced staffing of the reception area has enabled more effective assessments of prisoners' mental and physical health, by health professionals on entry into the prison. The follow up in the induction centre has also been more consistent and regular, especially with regard to detoxing.

There has been a lot of building work in the prison, much of which is still ongoing. To date, this has resulted in the remodelling of the car park and the refurbishment of one of the houses. A new visitor centre is being built and plans for a new gatehouse with increased security measures have been developed. The new security fencing, perimeter lighting and CCTV have greatly improved security at the prison. There has been much less evidence of throw overs, which were becoming an increasing problem last year.

The development of the Stepping Stones programme is showing early signs of success with some of the most vulnerable prisoners at Styal. The programme provides alternative therapeutic and creative activities and has continued throughout lockdown, helping to stabilise the behaviour of a small number of prolific self-harmers.

There has been a continued and significant reduction in the numbers of segregated or self-isolating prisoners, and in the amount of time spent in the CSU. Referrals to the Valentina unit are considered at the weekly safety and intervention monitoring (SIM) meeting and reviewed regularly by senior managers. Staff in both of these facilities now demonstrate a level of care and professionalism that is commendable.

In relation to last year's judgement on resettlement, the figures provided to us for this reporting period indicate that Styal and partner agencies have made progress in providing accommodation on release. It seems that Styal is now exceeding its target, whereas last year it was considerably below. Some of this may be due to the improved access to temporary accommodation provided by local and national initiatives, relating to homelessness during the pandemic. However, the Board is concerned that the loss of Shelter may have an adverse effect on accommodation in the future and would urge the prison to monitor the impact of this change.

Last year the Board identified an issue regarding unauthorised absence from work and or education. During the pandemic conditions have not been strictly comparable. However, the changes to the regime during the pandemic have meant that prisoners are escorted everywhere, including to workspaces and education. All prisoners, whether in education or working full- or part-time, now have scheduled times for appointments outside working hours. These changes seem to be making a difference to workplace attendance, where these are open. We will continue to monitor this as education and more workplaces reopen.

**ASHBOURNE DERBYSHIRE DE6 5HW**

**HMP & YOI SUDBURY**    **Tel: 01283 584000**

*For the latest reports on this prison please visit:* https://tinyurl.com/bdfh26rv

*Important Changes:* **(1) Visits:** the identification necessary to access this prison and visit for social or professional purposes has changed; (2) **Money and Gifts** new rules now apply to these. See page 16 for full details of the above.

**Task of the establishment** Sudbury is an open prison accommodating category D male prisoners.

**Certified normal accommodation and operational capacity**
Prisoners held at the time of this visit: 480
Baseline certified normal capacity: 581
In-use certified normal capacity: 564
Operational capacity: 564

**Prison status and key providers**
Public
Prison Group: North Midlands
Prison Group Director: Alison Clarke
Governor/Director: Craig Smith
IMB Chair: Lis Martin
Physical health provider: Practice Plus Group
Mental health provider: Practice Plus Group
Substance misuse treatment provider:
NHS Inclusion
Prison education framework provider:
People Plus
Escort contractor: GeoAmey

**Brief history** Originally built during the late 1930s as an American Air Force hospital, the site was converted to a prison in 1948 and has been used consistently since then as an open resettlement establishment for men aged 21 and over. In 2015, it began taking men aged between 18 and 20.

**Short description of residential units** East and West 1-7 – 14 older units consisting of single and double rooms
W5 – induction unit
W7 - designated for older prisoners and those with mobility issues
P1-4 – four newer buildings mainly for prisoners working outside the prison
D wing – 80 new temporary modular accommodation of single units ('pods').
D1 – used for shielding prisoners
D5 – used for protective isolation
Secure accommodation unit (SAU) – two cells

**Visiting Information**
Book online at: www.gov.uk/prison-visits or by telephone on 01283 584175 Monday to Friday, 9am to 11am and 1.30pm-3pm.
**Visiting times:** Wednesday and Thursday: 2pm to 3pm and 4pm to 5pm, Saturday and Sunday: 9am to 10am, 11am to 12 noon, 2pm to 3pm and 4pm to 5pm.

**Legal visits:** There are currently no legal visits taking place.

**INSPECTIONS & REPORTS**
**Scrutiny visit: 27–28 April and 11–12 May 2021**
**Date of last full inspection 10–28 April 2017**
**SSV: Section 6.2.3.1**
**Scrutiny visit, published 17 June 2021**

This report presents our findings from a scrutiny visit to HMP & YOI Sudbury, an open prison in Derbyshire. At the time of our visit, the population had been reduced from 564 to 480 prisoners as a result of fewer prisoners transferring into the prison, which had previously experienced a six-week Covid-19 outbreak. This reduction, slightly off-set by the installation of temporary accommodation in autumn 2020, had made it easier to implement Covid-19 cohorting arrangements and had meant more prisoners were living in single rooms.

Although quarantining and shielding arrangements were appropriate, the prison had experienced an outbreak of Covid-19 in early March 2021. Prison leaders had worked well with health care providers and Public Health England to contain the outbreak and by the time of our visit the prison had progressed back to stage three of the national recovery plan (see Glossary of terms). One prisoner had died of Covid-19-related symptoms in April 2020.

The primary purpose of Sudbury is to prepare prisoners for their successful return to the community on release and at our last full inspection in 2017 we reported that outcomes in this regard were improving. The pandemic, however, had disrupted the prison's ability to maintain this progress and although it was encouraging that around 50 prisoners had continued to use release on temporary licence (ROTL) to access external key work employment, the numbers generally had greatly reduced. For prisoners classed as a high risk to the public, probation prison offender managers (POMs) had maintained onsite provision, including face-to-face support. For most of the population (around 60%), however, who were allocated POMs, many had not had adequate contact for several months. It was clear that prisoners' lack of access to offender management was a source of considerable frustration.

The return to the stage three regime had enabled the prison to announce the welcome resumption of social visits. Prison leaders were also planning to increase the number of opportunities for ROTL to maintain family ties from mid-May 2021, although a cautious approach meant that very few prisoners would initially benefit from this. Similarly, the re-introduction of face-to-face teaching was to be limited to small numbers, even though inspectors had identified that classroom space was available. The education provider had no effective strategy to provide

support or reinforce learning for prisoners using in-cell learning packs.

Sudbury remained generally safe with few incidents of violence or self-harm. The use of segregation and incidents of force were, however, far higher than we have seen in other open prisons. While most force involved just the use of ratchet handcuffs to escort prisoners to segregation, this high usage could be tracked back to 2019 and had continued through the period of restrictions. Leaders needed to review this to understand the reasons and make sure that all applications of force were proportionate and necessary.

Living accommodation was mixed. Many communal areas, particularly on the older units, were dilapidated and grubby and, despite a programme of scheduled remedial repairs, significant investment was needed to enable the prison to achieve acceptable standards.

Of greatest concern, in our prisoner survey, we received many negative comments about staff. Only 61%, for example, said that staff treated them with respect and a third said that they had been subjected to some victimisation from staff. Prisoner perceptions on the use of segregation, the high number of prisoners returned to closed conditions, as well as the inconsistent support from POMs had been further compounded by a local dispute with staff associations that was affecting the progress of the personal officer scheme. These issues combined to contribute to some poor prisoner perceptions and undermined the rehabilitative purpose of the prison.

Overall, and despite the recent virus outbreak, the prison had managed reasonably well throughout the period of restrictions to keep people safe. However, many aspects of daily life, including the high use of force, poor staff-prisoner relationships and the management of some key aspects of offender management, needed urgent improvement, while much of the living accommodation required significant investment.
Charlie Taylor, HM Chief Inspector of Prisons
May 2021

**Key concerns and recommendations**

*Key concerns* and recommendations identify the issues of most importance to improving outcomes for prisoners and are designed to help establishments prioritise and address the most significant weaknesses in the treatment and conditions of prisoners.

During this visit we identified some areas of key concern, and have made a small number of recommendations for the prison to address.
*Key concern:* Data on violence and the use of force were not reported accurately. This ran the risk that incidents were not investigated robustly and responded to accordingly. The use of incorrect

data limited leaders' ability to understand or analyse correctly the safety and well-being of prisoners in their care.

Recommendation: The prison should record incidents of violence and use of force accurately and make sure this information is used to support improvements in safety. (To the governor)

Key concern: Use of ratchet handcuffs was very high. Most incidents took place as prisoners were relocated from their cell to the segregation unit, when they were almost always handcuffed in their rooms before movement. Handcuffs were applied irrespective of level of risk or compliance. This had been a long-term practice and did not reflect a category D prison rehabilitative culture.

Recommendation: Ratchet handcuffs should only be used on the basis of an individual risk assessment. (To the governor)

Key concern: Many prisoners reported poor relationships with staff and a staff culture that undermined the rehabilitative purpose of the prison. In our survey, almost a third of prisoners said that they had been victimised by staff. Most we spoke to felt insecure and said that staff used the threat of recategorisation as a method of control. There were many reports of staff being abrupt, unhelpful and having a punitive approach. The disproportionate use of restraints, the frequent suspension of release on temporary licence (ROTL) and the high number of prisoners returned to closed conditions supported prisoner perceptions.

Recommendation: The prison should develop staff-prisoner relationships so that they underpin its rehabilitative purpose. Rules and policy should be applied fairly, with transparency and in a way that promotes trust and confidence among prisoners and encourages them to engage with their rehabilitation. (To the governor)

Key concern: Despite remedial work since our last inspection, much of the communal living accommodation, particularly in the older units, was gloomy, dilapidated and grubby. There was extensive mould, poor tiling and broken partitioning in some showers. Some rooms were damp, mouldy and in poor condition. Although more remedial work was scheduled, the longstanding problems with the fabric of the accommodation needed significant investment to be resolved.

Recommendation: There should be substantial investment in the fabric of the living accommodation in Sudbury to enable the prison to maintain a decent standard of accommodation. (To HMPPS)

Key concern: Many prisoners told us they had not seen their POM for many months and felt they had no support to progress. In our survey, 21% of prisoners said they did not know their sentence plan targets and of those who did only 37% said staff were helping them to meet these targets.

Recommendation: All prisoners should have regular and meaningful support to help them progress through their sentence. (To the governor)

Key concern: At the time of the visit, although 11 prisoners were subject to restrictions that meant they were not permitted to have contact with any child. There were no arrangements to monitor whether they were having contact with a child by mail.

Recommendation: There should be appropriate mail monitoring arrangements to safeguard public protection. (To the governor)

**Education, skills and work (Ofsted)**

During this visit Ofsted inspectors conducted an interim assessment of the provision of education, skills and work in the establishment. They identified steps that the prison needed to take to meet the needs of prisoners, including those with special educational needs and disabilities.

**Next steps**

Leaders should rapidly establish effective methods for teachers to be able to have contact with prisoners. Teachers should check and reinforce what prisoners are learning. They should make sure that prisoners are challenged by the content of in-cell learning and that they make progress towards their intended careers on release. Leaders and managers should ensure that teachers plan and deliver the content of the remote curriculum in education programmes sequentially. Leaders and managers should make sure that prisoners with a learning difficulty or disability receive the support they require to gain new knowledge through in-cell learning.

Leaders and managers should make sure that information, advice and guidance services are quickly re-established. The needs of prisoners who missed inductions in the last year should be ascertained to help guide them to appropriate education, skills and work activities.

Notable positive practice

We define notable positive practice as innovative practice or practice that leads to particularly good outcomes from which other establishments may be able to learn.

Inspectors look for evidence of good outcomes for prisoners; original, creative or particularly effective approaches to problem-solving or achieving the desired goal; and how other establishments could learn from or replicate the practice.

Inspectors found three examples of notable positive practice during this visit.

The kitchen supplied samples of healthier menu options to the weekly healthy living club to encourage prisoners to improve their diet. It also supplied fresh fruit as a weekly prize for the prisoner making most progress with his healthy living goals. Equality provision was well-supported by the collation and analysis of local monitoring data, which was much better than we usually see. There had been some very good consultation meetings with prisoners from several protected groups to discuss evidence of disproportionate treatment and to feed into the prison's investigation of the data.

The library service had been active in implementing a new 'share a story' project in the absence of the usual Storybook Dads scheme (where prisoners record a story for their children). It sent one copy of a children's book to the prisoner's family and also gave a copy to the prisoner to read to their child in an interactive storytelling session over the phone.

**INDEPENDENT MONITORING BOARD:**
**Annual Report**

The law requires every prison to be monitored by an independent Board appointed by the Justice Secretary; these are known as Independent Monitoring Boards (IMBs). The IMB must satisfy itself as to the humane and just treatment of those held in custody within its prison and the range and adequacy of the programmes preparing them for release; it must report annually to the Justice Secretary on how well the prison has met the standards and requirements placed on it.

**IMB Report 1 June 2020 – 31 May 2021**
**Published October 2021**
**Executive summary**
**Background to the report**

The Covid-19 outbreak has had a significant impact on the Board's ability to gather information and discuss the contents of this annual report. The Board has therefore tried to cover as much ground as it can in these difficult circumstances, but inevitably there is less detail and supporting evidence than usual. Unlike some other prisons, Sudbury does not have in-cell telephones, so the Board depends on visits to speak to prisoners about their experiences. The Board has only been able to make a total of 18 monitoring visits to the prison, mostly during a brief period in summer 2020 when restrictions were lifted, so, due to the timing of our reporting year and to HMP/YOI Sudbury being declared an outbreak site in April 2021 most of the information in this report is based on data from the prison, not on independent observation.

Ministers are aware of these constraints. Regular information is being collected specifically on the prison's response to the pandemic, and that is being collated nationally.

It should be borne in mind that, in April this year, when the total number of prisoners at Sudbury was 484, 391 of these had been there for less than 12 months. This means that the vast majority of current prisoners have only known Sudbury under Covid-19 restrictions and their views will be informed by their experience of lockdown, rather than reflecting the experience of prisoners under a normal regime.

**Main judgements**
**How safe is the prison?**

Throughout the reporting year the safety of prisoners has been primarily framed within the context of the pandemic, and everything about life in Sudbury has been atypical, but the prison continues to have low levels of self-harm despite the challenging circumstances of the past year. Managing the risk of Covid-19 infection has been a major consideration, and, despite the outbreak in April 2021, there have been no Covid-19 deaths in the prison during the reporting year.

**How fairly and humanely are prisoners treated?**

The prison has prioritised implementing social distancing and each wing has operated as a 'bubble' for the purpose of social contacts. It has been necessary to balance fairness with protection from infection, and most prisoners have accepted that some compromise is necessary within the prison as it has been outside. The suspension of home release on temporary licence has been difficult for many prisoners, but it has been implemented in a way that is seen to be fair. Most of the residential blocks comprise structures that were built to be temporary, a long time ago and, despite constant refurbishment, need significant investment.

The prison monitors equalities issues robustly, identifying and addressing issues as they arise, although the need to dedicate staff to lockdown related duties has had a negative impact on the availability of specialist staff.

**How well are prisoners' health and wellbeing needs met?**

As in the wider community, access to doctor and dentist appointments have been restricted at times, particularly during the outbreak in April; the prison has provided good access to outside space and rapidly set up an outdoor gym to encourage exercise; the prison is addressing issues relating to prisoners with diabetes through joint work between healthcare and the kitchen.

**How well are prisoners progressed towards successful resettlement?**

As a category D prison, Sudbury's main focus is successful resettlement. This has made the restrictions and limitations of movement imposed by the Prison Service over the last reporting year frustrating for staff and prisoners alike. Limited access to prison offender managers (POMs), and restricted access to outside work have put significant obstacles in the way of progression, although the prison succeeded in keeping a good number prisoners in outside work, which is a credit to the resettlement team. The suspension of ROTL and of family visits was a huge blow to prisoners, and the Christmas period, in particular, saw many hopes of a brief reunion dashed as Government policy changed. Purple visits and additional telephone credits offer a poor alternative to physical meetings.

**Main areas for development**
**TO THE MINISTER**
What measures are proposed to ensure that the return of probation services to the public sector will be managed more smoothly than the privatisation, which led to huge disruption in release on temporary licence (ROTL) planning for many prisoners?

**TO THE PRISON SERVICE**
The IMB's ongoing concerns that the lack of funding for the fundamental improvements to the fabric of the building necessary to ensure decent living conditions at the prison have yet to be acted upon by the Prison Service. The Board hopes that this vital issue will be addressed in the coming year.
Prisoners continue to experience significant problems with property when they are transferred between prisons. What can the prison service do to ensure that contractors take proper care of prisoners' property?

**TO THE GOVERNOR**
Some measures introduced because of Covid-19, such as the more regulated queuing at mealtimes, have proved popular with many prisoners. Do you anticipate retaining these after the return to 'normal' life? If there is another national lockdown, will the prison be in a better position to respond?

**Progress since the last report**
As the reporting year for this report covers an almost unbroken period of lockdown it would be both unfair and unhelpful for the Board to attempt to judge progress since our last report. This being said, the Board was pleased to observe an increase in modern single accommodation units on site.

**BRABAZON ROAD**
**EASTCHURCH**
**ISLE OF SHEPPEY**
**KENT, ME12 4AX**
**Tel: 01795 804100**

*For the latest reports on this prison please visit:*
https://tinyurl.com/bdfh26rv

*Important Changes:* **(1) Visits:** the identification necessary to access this prison and visit for social or professional purposes has changed; (2) **Money and Gifts** new rules now apply to these. See page 16 for full details of the above.

**Task of the prison**
HMP Swaleside is a category B adult male training prison.

**Certified normal accommodation and operational capacity**
Prisoners held October 2021: 964
Baseline certified normal capacity: 1,111
In-use certified normal capacity: 1,090
Operational capacity: 1,090

**Population of the prison**
• Number of new transferred prisoners received:
• 15 October 2020 – 14 October 2021: 326
• 15 October 2019 – 14 October 2020: 218
• 171 foreign national prisoners
• 44% of prisoners from BAME backgrounds
• 37 prisoners were released into the community from October 2020 to October 2021
• 431 prisoners were receiving support for substance use:
- 24 on the integrated drug treatment system
- 221 on an open care plan
- 186 on a closed care plan (still supported)
• Approximately 100–120 prisoners were on the caseload for mental health services each month

**Prison status (public or private) and key providers**
Public
Prison Group: Long Term High Security
Prison Group Director: Will Styles
Governor/director: Mark Icke
IMB chair Bob Chapman
Physical health provider: Integrated Care 24 (IC24)
Mental health provider: Oxleas NHS
Substance misuse provider: Forward Trust
Prison education framework provider:
Milton Keynes College
Escort contractor: Serco

**Brief history** HMP Swaleside is a category B adult male training prison.

### Short description of residential units
A wing – 126 prisoners of various sentences

B wing – 126 prisoners, compact-based vulnerable prisoner unit

C wing – 126 prisoners, includes the emotional well-being initiative D wing – 126 prisoners, first night centre and induction

E wing – 120 prisoners; drug, alcohol and substance misuse treatment unit F wing – 120 prisoners, 60 prisoners allocated the psychologically informed planned environment (PIPE) unit

G wing – 178 prisoners, one-half of which is a lifers unit

H wing – 178 prisoners, unit for prisoners convicted of sexual offences

### Visiting Information
Email: SocialVisits.Swaleside@justice.gov.uk

Booking line: 0300 060 6604 Monday to Friday, 8:30am to 4pm.

**Visiting times:** Tues to Thurs: 2:30pm to 4pm

**Legal visits:** Bookings can be made by emailing: LegalVisits.Swaleside@justice.gov.uk

**Visiting times:** Tues to Thurs: 2pm to 4pm

### INSPECTIONS & REPORTS
**Date of last full inspection: October 2021**

**HMCIP Report, published 22 February 2022**

HMP Swaleside is a category B training prison for adult men and is part of HM Prison and Probation Service's (HMPPS) long term and high security estate. Built mostly in the late 1980s and located on the Isle of Sheppey in Kent, the prison was holding just under 1,000 prisoners at the time of our inspection, some way short of its operating capacity of 1,090. Our last full inspection of the prison was in 2018, which was followed by an independent review of progress in 2019. Overall, and notwithstanding the very real challenges of the Covid-19 pandemic, outcomes for prisoners at Swaleside remained disappointing. In safety and purposeful activity, for example, outcomes were still not sufficiently good. They had deteriorated in respect to not sufficiently good and in rehabilitation and release planning they remained poor.

This was not, however, the whole story. The governor was enthusiastic and committed and he articulated clearly, although largely informally, his values- based vision for the prison. The energy of the leadership team was carrying the prison some distance and despite significant operational risk, it was settled and relationships were benign. Across the prison, we saw several pockets of good practice and useful endeavour.

Examples included efforts to upgrade aspects of the environment, the good work of specialist facilities such as the PIPE unit, innovative arrangements to support new staff and some useful work to encourage the promotion of equality.

The prison was less effective in harnessing its strengths in a more sophisticated way to accelerate and sustain progress. Structures to oversee and supervise operational delivery, for example, were often underdeveloped or missing. The coordination of departments was weak; data was not used sufficiently to inform decision-making and there was a lack of robust planning to identify priorities and deliver improvements.

These failings were perhaps most clearly seen in the prison's approach to rehabilitation. Most prisoners were serving over 10 years, with a third serving life or another indeterminate sentence. Nearly all presented a serious risk of harm. The progress of high-risk men, serving long sentences, was at the heart of the prison's mission, yet for the second successive inspection we saw a lacklustre and poorly coordinated service that was failing to meet the needs of the public or prisoners. It was no surprise to us that in our survey of prisoners, fewer than half of respondents thought their time at Swaleside would make them less likely to offend.

Similarly, work was needed to improve important partnerships, notably in health care provision and facilities management. Time out of cell for prisoners was better than we sometimes see, although the recovery of the regime in the wake of the pandemic lacked ambition. In addition to some weak planning and coordination, progress across many areas of delivery, including rehabilitation and release planning, was hindered by significant shortages of staff, including specialist staff. Much of this was beyond leaders' ability to influence directly, but it was a fundamental strategic risk and priority, which needed the intervention and support of HMPPS.

Despite the identification of some weak outcomes, we sensed that leaders and their staff were doing their best and working hard to take the prison forward. To aid this process we have made recommendations, which include the need for a more coordinated and evidence based approach to planning, urgently needed improvements to rehabilitation and release planning, and a clear strategy, supported by HMPPS, to increase staffing.

Charlie Taylor HMCIP November 2021

### Safety
Early days in custody were affected adversely by ongoing Covid-19 restrictions, and the regime for new arrivals was poor. Too many initial

assessments, including health care screening, took place in cells on residential units, which compromised privacy.

Although lower than at our last inspection, the number of assaults against staff was higher than at similar prisons, and the incidence of violence was on the rise. The causes of violence were not yet fully understood and there was no long-term plan to make the prison safer. In our survey, over a third of prisoners said that they felt unsafe, and those we spoke to said that there were limited incentives to encourage positive behaviour.

Several prisoners alleged to us that they had been assaulted by staff, and in our survey Muslim respondents and those who identified as being from a racial minority reported more negatively than their counterparts in relation to bullying or victimisation by staff.

Too many disciplinary adjudications had been adjourned for a long period, thereby undermining efforts to address poor behaviour. Data analysis was still too basic to identify any emerging patterns and improve processes.

The number of incidents involving the use of force had increased substantially. We saw evidence of good de-escalation of incidents, but some use of force was excessive and approved techniques were not always used in some of the closed-circuit television records we viewed. Aspects of governance arrangements were adequate, but there had been no use of force management meetings and the prison did not have enough body-worn cameras to capture valuable evidence.

The use of special accommodation had reduced considerably since the last inspection and our review visit in 2019. However, we found two cells in the segregation unit without furniture that had been used many times without authorisation by senior managers.

Although cells were grubby, the communal areas in the segregation unit were clean. The unit was usually full, and lengths of stay were long. Although a small number of prisoners were supported by Swaleside Outreach Service (see paragraph 6.41), the regime on the unit was too limited and reintegration planning was generally poor.

Most security measures were proportionate and security information was managed well. Preventing the supply of illicit items was a key priority for managers. A small dedicated team addressed the risks posed by staff corruption and threats from prisoners with extremist views.

There had been three self-inflicted deaths since the last inspection, two of which had happened a few months before this inspection. The amount of self-harm had almost doubled since the last inspection and had been rising throughout 2021,

peaking in April. Analysis by managers had identified that, over a three-month period, 10 prisoners had been responsible for almost two-thirds of self-harm incidents. The self-harm prevention strategy was specific to the establishment, but data analysis was not used sufficiently to drive improvements.

The quality of support delivered through assessment, care in custody and teamwork (ACCT) case management for prisoners at risk of suicide and self-harm was variable, with some inconsistent case management and care plans that lacked meaningful or completed actions. In our survey, only just under half of prisoners with experience of being on an ACCT said that they had felt cared for by staff.

### Respect

We saw some skillful management of prisoners by prison staff, but some low-level poor behaviour went unchallenged and it was disappointing that we often found too many staff in offices, away from the prisoners in their care. There was a lack of visible input from middle managers to support their staff and reinforce standards and practices. The key worker scheme (see Glossary of terms) was not operating fully and few electronic case notes we observed demonstrated effective support.

Communal areas were generally clean, and most cells were equipped and maintained to a decent standard, but too many toilets lacked lids and were dirty. Some showers had been refurbished and a window replacement programme had started, although prisoners repeatedly complained about a lack of ventilation. Insufficient prison-issue clothing and bedding were provided and there was no effective system for kit exchange.

Meals were served too early and often served at the prisoners' doors which was disrespectful. Self-cook facilities had been removed at the outbreak of the pandemic, which was a source of considerable prisoner complaint.

All applications were tracked using an impressive recording system, but not logged on return. The number of complaints submitted was much higher than in comparator prisons, but little had been done to explain this, although arrangements for the quality assurance of complaints was identifying areas for improvement both in relation to the decision made on a complaint and how it was communicated.

Wing-based prisoner council meetings had ended at the beginning of the pandemic, but the main consultation committee had met regularly throughout, which was positive.

Although the prison lacked a strategic approach for the promotion of equality, there was evidence of some good work in important areas. Equality monitoring data, for example, were analysed and some disproportionality highlighted was addressed. Responses to discrimination incident report forms had improved.

Our survey highlighted negative perceptions among black and Muslim prisoners, and we heard repeated complaints about racist attitudes from some staff. We were told about innovative mentoring of some black prisoners and reverse-mentoring that was being undertaken between prisoners and staff.

Support to meet the needs of foreign nationals, older prisoners and those with disabilities was too limited. A forum for LGBT prisoners was no longer taking place, although transgender prisoners were receiving individual support. There was some good care for young people who had previously been in local authority care.

The chaplaincy provided good pastoral support, but access to corporate worship remained limited because of pandemic restrictions.

A resilient health care team delivered primary care services but was overstretched because of longstanding staff shortages. Too many prisoners missed internal and external appointments because of a lack of officer escorts, leading to prisoner frustration and wasted clinical time. All services also had limited access to appropriate space on the wings to carry out assessments and interventions. There was a lack of a whole-prison approach to health promotion, and there were no nurse-led long-term condition clinics, although the GPs still managed complex cases.

The cleanliness and fabric of the inpatient unit were unsatisfactory and did not meet infection prevention and control standards, and there was a lack of therapeutic activities to support patient well-being and recovery. Some emergency resuscitation equipment had not been kept in good order and it was unclear if there were regular checks. Social care needs were identified and met, but peer mentors lacked training and oversight.

Mental health services provided a range of support, but groups were yet to restart and waiting times for counselling remained too long. Substance misuse services were reasonably good and psychosocial groups had resumed.

Aspects of medicine management were poor, including unsafe transportation of medicines and inconsistent supervision of medicine queues. Dental services were good and long waits for routine appointments had been cut to just four weeks.

**Purposeful activity**

Although time out of cell, at up to three and a half hours a day for most prisoners, was more than we had seen recently in other prisons, during our roll checks we found just 17% attending any purposeful activity. Gym provision was good, although take-up was low, and the library provided a reasonable out-reach service.

Plans for reopening education, skills and work were over-cautious. Workshops were not fully used, and there were too few work and vocational options available. Attendance and punctuality to training and work were poor. Prison staff shortages had a negative impact on the regime and workshops were closed too often.

Until recently, there had been no careers advice and guidance service and too many prisoners did not know what was on offer at the prison. Prisoners were highly frustrated at the poor communication about the recently revised pay policy, and the reduction in pay for many.

A broad and interesting education curriculum was provided through supported in-cell learning, engaging more prisoners with education than before the pandemic. Teachers produced high-quality in-cell learning packs but took too long to provide them when requested or give feedback on completion.

Those who worked in the DHL workshop completed good-quality work and gained skills that would help them on release. However, too few were able to attain accredited learning through workshops, and there was insufficient support available to meet the needs of those with the lowest levels of English and mathematics. Personal development for prisoners had also not been considered.

**Rehabilitation and release planning**

Access to social visits was insufficient and there were none available at weekends. Problems with the booking line and the scarcity of visit slots made booking a visit difficult. The visits hall was welcoming and there was a popular tea bar staffed by prisoners, but the children's play area was still closed. Secure video calls were greatly appreciated by prisoners.

Most prisoners were serving long sentences and posed a high risk of harm to the public after committing violent or sexual offences. Around a third of prisoners were serving an indeterminate or life sentence but were provided with only limited support or additional interventions. The oversight and coordination of reducing reoffending work was weak and had not improved since the last inspection.

Prisoners did not have enough in person contact with their prison offender manager (POM) to aid progression and rehabilitation. The prison struggled to recruit probation officers, which resulted in prison officer POMs being responsible for high-risk and complex cases. At the time of the inspection, most of the probation officers in post were still working mainly remotely. There continued to be a backlog in offender assessment system (OASys) assessments.

Public protection had improved and processes were now generally sound. However, for those needing monitoring, the inability to listen to all telephone calls because of a lack of resource limited the prison's ability to protect the public.

Recategorisation reviews were timely, but we were not confident that decisions were always fair, consistent or in line with the new HMPPS recategorisation policy. Although 25% of the population were category C prisoners, progressive moves were not timely, as a result of a national shortage of category C spaces and poor oversight of movement holds. This meant that some prisoners were kept at the establishment for longer than they should have been.

There was a lack of programme opportunities, which limited prisoners' ability to progress. Group programmes had stopped in March 2020 because of the pandemic and had only recently restarted for a handful of prisoners, and were restricted to wing cohorts. Completion of group programmes on a larger scale was unlikely to start before April 2022 because of staffing issues. Since the last inspection, the prison had introduced some appropriate short courses for prisoners convicted of sexual offences.

Services provided under the offender personality disorder pathway, including the psychologically informed planned environment (PIPE) unit, which ran a range of therapeutic groups, and Swaleside Outreach Service were providing a good level of support. Attending work sessions in the farms and gardens area was valued by the prisoners involved, who said that it gave them a sense of well-being and hope.

Few prisoners were released from Swaleside, but those being released could access some useful practical support.

## INDEPENDENT MONITORING BOARD:
## Annual Report

The law requires every prison to be monitored by an independent Board appointed by the Justice Secretary; these are known as Independent Monitoring Boards (IMBs). The IMB must satisfy itself as to the humane and just treatment of those held in custody within its prison and the range and adequacy of the programmes preparing them for release; it must report annually to the Justice Secretary on how well the prison has met the standards and requirements placed on it.

IMB Report 1 May 2021 - 30 April 2022
Published: July 2022

### Executive summary
### Background to the report

As previously, the Board's report concentrates on major elements of concern or required improvement, with a focus on the treatment of prisoners under the headings of 'fair and humane treatment' and 'preparation for resettlement'.

Firstly, it is worth stating that the Board has been impressed with the effort expended by the staff and governors in trying to implement worthwhile regimes for the prisoners during a reporting year made difficult, not only by the consequences of Covid-19 infections among staff and prisoners, but also the much-reduced staffing numbers as mentioned below.

This report is being written during an unprecedented period of staff shortage. This shortage has a direct and major impact on the wellbeing of both prisoners and staff and has a negative impact on the fair and humane treatment of prisoners. Inevitably, the same shortage will impact the directed move towards the improved resettlement of prisoners.

To put the shortage into context: at the time of writing, the prisoner population is 1,038 and the uniformed staff numbers are 160 (available) out of an agreed complement of 261. The problems arising from this need little explanation but will continue to be mentioned throughout the report. Over 35% of uniformed staff have less than two years' experience and it is apparent that newly arrived apprentice officers do not know what to expect and are seeing the inside of a prison for the first time.

The geographical situation of Swaleside on the Isle of Sheppey in Kent is an exacerbating feature in the staffing difficulty in that it is an 'isolated' area and has many competing opportunities for staff, and is adjacent to areas offering good links to London as well as the Kent coast. It is no consolation that most staff losses are to other Government departments, including Border Force and the police. These other agencies, inexplicably, offer better employment terms than HMPPS for all levels and grades of staff.

In the Board's view, the changes to the Swaleside population and role imposed are having a serious detrimental effect on the stability of the establishment and the wellbeing of the prisoners. Having had a long, settled period as a category B trainer, catering for prisoners with 4+ year sentences and part of the LTHSE, recent changes have seen the retention of category C prisoners (and even some category D returnees) and the arrival of young and short-term prisoners with only weeks to serve. This has had an immediate and detrimental impact on established services and causes concern and disruption to prisoners (especially the older and longer-term prisoners). The prison has had to begin to introduce costly and extensive facilities including resettlement and training services to cater for these additional releases. The impact on the reception and induction areas has already been considerable. These changes appear to be happening throughout the prison estate and the Board wonders whether the impact of these changes is fully understood.

High among the Board's other concerns is the lack of working body worn cameras (BWCs). The use of this technology is valuable for both staff and prisoners given its ability to record incidents. At the time of writing, the Board understands that only 18- 25 working BWCs are available and that these are often not to hand for essential areas of the prison such as the CSRU. It is the Board's understanding that this situation will not be remedied until 2023/24 and it finds this unacceptable. Although a short-term addition to the current style of cameras is being sought, a solution to allow implementation of 'always on' BWCs available for all operational staff must be found rapidly.

The reporting year has been a challenging one because of the continuing impact of Covid-19 and the necessity for the regime suggested by Gold Command to be followed. Thus, time out of cells for prisoners was, at one point, just 30 minutes per day and prisoners were organised into cohorts to avoid cross-contamination. The impact on the mental health and general well-being of the prisoners hardly needs explanation and the increase in self-harm, incidents and attacks on both prisoners and staff exacerbated by the restrictions is shown on page 12.

The foregoing comments should not take away from the excellent work carried out throughout the reporting period by staff and governors at all levels. Every effort has been made to implement a regime to allow as much normality as was feasible. However, the staff shortage has meant that, for most of the reporting year, a restricted regime has been in place with prisoner working limited to kitchen, DHL (canteen, from H wing), wing cleaners and, latterly, F wing prisoners. At the time of writing, plans are being made for more prisoners to resume working but this intent is seriously hampered by the low staff numbers.

The lack of meaningful activity for prisoners on all but two wings gives the Board concern and this concern is echoed by the prisoners themselves. There seems little prospect of a resumption of normal working and activities whilst the staff numbers remain a problem. It is a matter of utmost urgency to remedy this situation to alleviate these issues.

The Board was impressed by the efforts made to increase time out of cell and, generally, to improve the regime for prisoners as the threat of Covid-19 infection receded and staff numbers allowed. Staff themselves have been frustrated by their inability to implement anything approaching a full regime. Adverse comments offered by HMIP following an inspection in February 2022 had a damaging effect on staff morale and seemed to ignore the reality of the Covid-19 situation during an extremely challenging period.

A further impact of the staff shortage has been the almost total withdrawal of the key worker scheme, in itself leading to further frustration and worry for prisoners. It is possible that this could be a factor leading to the increase in deaths in custody.

The service from the education providers, Milton Keynes College, during the Covid-19 restrictions has been first class and the provision of meaningful in-cell packs during the restrictions placed them top in the country in terms of numbers issued. Results from the prisoners have been very encouraging.

In our previous report we indicated that the service from GFSL had improved and was beginning to be satisfactory. This improvement has not been fully maintained and the service provided is not yet at the level required. For example, there were 66 cells out of action during April 2022. It seems that the removal of the dedicated GFSL in-house supervisory position may be an element in the disappointing results, although part of the problem seems to be caused by incorrect and inadequate reporting of problems by wing staff.

The kitchen has maintained an impressive service during this difficult period especially given the budgetary constraint and supply difficulties. The kitchen continues to cater for Standford Hill prisoners as well as Swaleside. Given that self-cook has not existed during this period and that growing numbers of sealed meals (e.g. kosher) have had to be provided, the pressure on the budget has been immense. Staff shortages in this area have also caused pressure. The catering manager, in concert with healthcare, is examining ways in which unjustified and unnecessary F35s allowing special food orders may be justifiably reduced. The Board remains concerned at the lack of control at wing serveries, meaning that the wearing of 'whites' is not enforced and evidence of hygiene and food care controls being followed is not apparent.

Although there were some social visits earlier in 2021, regular visits resumed in October 2021 and, to date, have been restricted to 20 per session. It is expected that this number may increase to 30 per session and that, when staff numbers allow, weekend visits may resume. The use of Purple Visits (by video-link) has continued to be a success and has helped ameliorate many of the difficulties caused by the restrictions.

One of the most successful departments at Swaleside is the Swaleside outreach service (SoS) which has continued its excellent work in helping the prison's most violent and disruptive men. The personal attention and care that is put into managing these prisoners is outstanding and excellent results are achieved.

The accommodation has largely been cleaner and more acceptable, perhaps largely because of the reduced time out of cell. However, the damage to cells is noticeably higher and very costly both monetarily and in terms of operating the prison. The improvements to showers were welcomed overall but, in many cases, have been disappointing because of poor ventilation, low water pressure and drainage problems with the newly installed showers.

Litter around the establishment improved for a time following the change to the windows on E wing, although litter does reappear from time to time. The rat 'epidemic' appears largely to have abated.

Healthcare services generally have very recently been transferred from IC24 to Oxleas HealthCare Trust. Whilst it is still too early to draw any conclusions, the indications thus far are very encouraging, although staff shortages in this area still continue.

On many occasions we have raised the issue of the paraplegic prisoner who has been resident in the healthcare area long-term and who causes many problems. Swaleside is not suitable for this prisoner and that fact has been agreed at the highest level. However, despite it being agreed that a transfer is necessary, there is, as yet, no action. The Board deplores this situation.

We are pleased to note that the in-cell technology installation has commenced and look forward to the improvements that this will bring for the prisoners and for the operation of the prison.

The IMB Board members are themselves to be commended for the resumption of 'normal' working following the Covid-19 pandemic. Although there was a period prior to October 2021 when the wings were not frequently visited, nevertheless written contact was continued with any prisoner making a request and responses to applications from prisoners met the normal fast turnaround. Where needed, use was made of Zoom and telephone contact as well as face to face attendance for attendance at meetings and reviews. The Board also now regularly attends many more meetings with the staff and governors. The Board would again wish to thank staff and governors for their assistance in providing the information, assistance and co-operation as part of an excellent working arrangement.

## Main judgements
### How safe is the prison?

Focus on safety has been continued by the management team, although results have been mixed due to a number of factors including:

• reduced staffing levels lowering the number of officers on each wing

• unavailability of body-worn cameras for all staff meaning that the deterrent and evidential aspects of their use has not been apparent

• lack of key working, meaningful employment and activities which increases the frustration felt by prisoners, in turn increasing the levels of violence and self-harm

• an increase of inexperienced officers amongst the staff who, of necessity, have been called upon to fill roles normally carried out by experienced staff

• seemingly, continuing access to illegal substances, hooch and distilled liquor despite increasing efforts to prevent this.

• an increase in concern and resulting incidents especially for the older, long-term prisoners due to the arrival of short-term and younger prisoners.

Many of the reported incidents are confined to two wings, which is of concern as it gives rise to many requests from prisoners for a change of location or a transfer to avoid problems. The majority of prisoners seem to avoid 'trouble' and remain feeling safe. Nevertheless, the prison again has a considerable problem with safety.

The information relating to incidents shows the recorded incidents at Swaleside which, although showing a major increase, differ little from other LTHSE establishments.

Staff welfare checks, and the availability of the safer custody department have been instrumental in minimising problem areas although lack of staff has caused an inordinate amount of movement and instability to the detriment of all.

During the long periods of confinement to cells, the availability of in-cell packs from education has been invaluable in preventing a greater degree of problematic behaviour from a large number of prisoners. The work of the psychology team in this regard has also been of great value. The prison has been moved to phase 2 of an investigation as a result of seven deaths in custody occurring during the reporting period.

A further key point is that a large majority of the 1000+ prisoners do not cause issues or problems and follow their daily routines as expected.

### How fairly and humanely are prisoners treated?

Prisoners, in the main, continue to be treated with a great deal of respect by most staff.

However, the Board has noted that there appears to be a growing number of occasions when this respect is lacking, particularly when prisoners are interacting with less experienced staff. It is important for this aspect to be dealt with during the initial training of staff. Over 30% of uniformed staff have service of less than two years.

There are several aspects of concern in this area which have been mentioned previously and continue to give cause for concern:

• The continued occupancy of an end-of-life cell by a paraplegic prisoner who has different needs and means that this room cannot be used by those for whom it is designed. Lack of action in this case has continued for several years despite being taken to Minister level.

• The mental health of the prisoner population as a whole gives rise to concern. The lack of purposeful activity and lower wages causes a great deal of resentment and frustration.

• Unsatisfactory results of the wing shower upgrades, leaving prisoners resentful that the promised improvements have not been delivered.

• The mix of shorter-term and younger prisoners with the older long-term prisoners in itself causes issues.

### How well are prisoners' health and wellbeing needs being met?

Very recently the healthcare services as a whole for the prison were transferred from IC24 to Oxleas Healthcare Trust. It is therefore too early to pass comment on the new providers, although results so far are encouraging, albeit with a continuing shortage of qualified staff.

The problem of missed outside specialist appointments continues, as mentioned previously, and is most often caused by a lack of escort staff.

Nevertheless, the Board is content that the service provided to the prisoner population is at least to the level expected and achieved for the general public.

### How well are prisoners progressed towards successful resettlement?

Up to this year, Swaleside was not regarded as a resettlement prison and there was little resettlement help for prisoners although services were brought in as required. The prison released very low numbers annually and relied on transfer to local prisons within about three months of the prisoner's release date.

However, recent changes to population allocation by HMPPS have resulted in Swaleside (a category B trainer in the LTHSE) receiving shorter term and sometimes younger prisoners, in addition to being forced to retain a greater number of category C prisoners. This change is further

discussed in section 7 but particularly means that a greater number of prisoners are expected to be released from this prison than in previous years. This change, combined with a directive to provide more training for prisoners, has brought about relevant changes for both reception and the induction wing and to provide an employment hub identifying and training prisoners for employment in prison and on release. This hub could be providing services in 2022.

The Board is currently concerned by the lack of meaningful and rewarding work for all wings apart from F and H wing prisoners. This is regretted by management but caused by general staffing issues and lack of instructors.

### Main areas for development
### TO THE MINISTER

The Board is extremely concerned at the continuing low numbers of staff and the seeming inability to recruit. The inequality of pay and conditions when compared to other government agencies is certainly a factor in the cause of this issue together with the accessibility of the geographical area in which the prison is situated. The low numbers of staff severely impact the mental health and well-being of prisoners. Urgent action is needed to remedy this situation. The Board shares the concerns expressed by the Senior Management Team regarding the number of deaths in custody during the year and appreciates that much investigation is being conducted by the LTHSE into the root causes of these. However, a national investigation is perhaps required to establish either commonality of cause irrespective of prison type or to highlight specific issues relating to particular establishments.

The length of time spent in the CSRU by a number of prisoners is far too long and far exceeds normal recommendations. An effective means of reducing this time should be sought as a matter of urgency.

### TO THE PRISON SERVICE

The Board is concerned at the detrimental aspects of the recently introduced prisoner flow and allocation system such that Swaleside, a category B trainer within the LTHSE, is receiving young (21-24), shorter sentenced (as little as four weeks) prisoners to the detrimental effect of the well-being of older, long sentenced prisoners. This change should be re-examined and the benefit examined against its detrimental impact. Prison staff should ALL have access to up-to-date body-worn cameras as issued to police and other services. Current equipment is inadequate and inappropriate and should be replaced urgently to support the reduced number of staff.

The continued reliance of HMP Standford Hill on

the kitchen at Swaleside for the preparation of its food continues to cause major issues, as has been stated for several years. The stalled installation of kitchens at HMP Standford Hill should be restarted urgently and be completed without further delay.

The Board has seen examples of inadequacy of apprentice officer training and believes that training must at least result in those staff knowing what to expect when they arrive at their establishment. Shortage of trained staff exacerbates failings in this respect.

The inequality of opportunity for men convicted of sexual offences (MCOSO) and vulnerable prisoners still needs to be addressed, despite progress made in that direction.

The Board has concerns regarding the mental health of prisoners who have suffered long-term lockdown as evidenced by the high number of assessment, care in custody and teamwork (ACCTs) cases, self-harm cases and general violent incidents. The necessity for increased psychology and psychiatric services should be assessed.

The continued occupancy of the life limited room in healthcare by one paraplegic prisoner whose needs are different, whilst there are a number of other prisoners who qualify for the use of this room requires urgent resolution.

## TO THE GOVERNOR

A solution should be found for the lack of external gate security (EGS) staff as a matter of urgency.

Wellbeing checks for all prisoners must be increased and maintained regularly to prevent self-harm.

The Board believes that more could be done to avoid self-seclusion by prisoners and wonders whether more help should be sought from psychological services.

The Board is again concerned at the lack of discipline and cleanliness at wing serveries and believes that this should receive immediate attention. This approach should insist on the use of temperature probes and 'whites' to avoid a health risk to prisoners.

Training on the use of Planet FM should be given to senior officers (SOs) and above to ensure a correct interface is maintained with GFSL.

The number of adjudications dismissed or 'not proceeded with' has continued at a high level. Further staff training is required to remedy this situation.

Adjudication awards should be re-examined to ensure that appropriate disincentives for prisoners are available. This seems particularly pertinent for prisoners producing hooch or distilled liquor.

Challenge, support and intervention plan (CSIP) should receive more attention from custody managers (CMs) as evidenced by minutes from the weekly safety intervention meetings (SIMs).

GFSL should be tasked with improving the rate at which out of action cells are brought back into use. The installation of showers throughout the establishment should be completed. The identified faults with recently installed showers should be remedied urgently.

The IMB is concerned at the occasional failure to be invited to serious incidents and planned moves to the CSRU and would appreciate the necessity for this to be reiterated to all senior staff.

## Progress since the last report

Progress since the last report has been remarkable, bearing in mind the impact of Covid-19 during the period and the overall shortage of staff which increased pressure at all senior levels.

– The previous issue preventing access to Comp2 paperwork by the Board has been resolved.

– A start has at last been made to correct the lack of in-cell telephony for inpatient prisoners.

– The installation of in-cell technology has commenced.

– Use of dogs, the dedicated search team (DST) and other measures to control the access to contraband items.

– The Board again commends the continued work of the Swaleside outreach service (SoS) team in dealing with very demanding prisoners.

– Establishment of the community forum.

– The regular work of the drug strategy committee.

– The effectiveness of ESG for a number of weeks in the early part of the reporting period.

**200 OYSTERMOUTH ROAD SWANSEA SA1 3SR**

HM PRISON SERVICE

**HMP YOI SWANSEA** **Tel: 01792 485300**

*For the latest reports on this prison please visit:* https://tinyurl.com/bdfh26rv

*Important Changes:* **(1) Visits:** the identification necessary to access this prison and visit for social or professional purposes has changed; (2) **Money and Gifts** new rules now apply to these. See page 16 for full details of the above.

**Task of the establishment** Category B local prison.

**Certified normal accommodation and operational capacity**

Prisoners held at the time of this visit: 371
Baseline certified normal capacity: 255
In-use certified normal capacity: 255
Operational capacity: 499

**Prison status and key providers**
Public
Prison Group: Wales
Prison Group Director: Giles Mason
Governor/Director: Brian Ward
IMB Chair: Paul Baker
Physical health provider: Swansea Bay Health Board
Mental health provider: Prison In-reach Services
Substance use treatment provider: Dyfodol Swansea
Prison education framework provider: HMPPS
Escort contractor: GeoAmey

**Brief history** The prison is situated about half a mile from the city centre on the coast road. Building on HMP Swansea started in 1845 and was completed in 1861. It functioned as a prison for both male and female prisoners until 1922 when females were transferred to Cardiff Prison. Swansea has since operated as a local prison, holding prisoners up to and including category B. In the early 1980s, Swansea started the Samaritan-trained prisoner Listener scheme that has now developed into nationwide provision.

**Short description of residential units**
A wing holds 185 prisoners - General population, remand and convicted
B wing holds 51 prisoners - First night/induction
C wing holds 40 prisoners - Full-time workers, drug-free/enhanced
D wing holds 116 prisoners - General population, remand and convicted
E wing - Care and separation unit
F wing holds 59 prisoners - General population, remand and convicted
G wing holds 52 - Resettlement, predominantly men in their last three months of sentence

**Visiting Information**
Book online at: https://www.gov.uk/prison-visits or email: socvisswansea@justice.gov.uk or ring: 01792 485 322 Monday to Friday, 8:45am to 3:45pm.
**Visiting times:** Mon-Thurs & Sat-Sun: 2:30pm to 3:30pm

**Legal visits:** There are currently no legal visits taking place.

**INSPECTIONS & REPORTS**
**Scrutiny visit: 25 August and 2-3 September 2020**
**Date of last HMCIP inspection 7, 8, 14–17 Aug 2017**
**Scrutiny visit, published 06 October 2020**
This report outlines the findings from our scrutiny visit to HMP Swansea, a Victorian local prison holding around 370 prisoners. At the time of our visit most of the population were from the local area, nearly all had been at Swansea for six months or less and 38% were on remand.

We found a well led establishment that had made good progress since the start of the pandemic. There was good partnership work with the local health care provider, Public Health Wales, and the Welsh Government to ensure that every symptomatic prisoner was tested. There had not been a confirmed case of Covid-19 at Swansea since April 2020.

Managers had worked to maximise the regime available to prisoners within the rigid national restrictions. Planning was good and focused on ensuring that managers could introduce new elements to the regime quickly once national managers authorised the move to stage three of the national framework for recovery.

The governor was particularly visible and accessible to both staff and prisoners. She chaired two weekly consultation meetings with prisoners which ensured both that the population were well informed about the Covid-19 restrictions and that managers could act swiftly to address the key concerns of prisoners.

Quarantine arrangements (referred to as cohorting) were in place for symptomatic prisoners, those vulnerable to the virus and prisoners in their first 14 days at Swansea. Arrangements for those vulnerable to the virus were appropriate, but the effectiveness of quarantine for new prisoners was undermined by the practice of allowing prisoners arriving on different days to mix with each other.

The scale of mental health problems in the population was extremely high; in our survey 79% of prisoners said they had a mental health need. The relatively new crisis team of mental health practitioners had provided valuable additional resource to identify risk and need on arrival and give some immediate support during a period when existing conditions could be exacerbated by extended time locked in cell. Given the scale of need and the restricted regime it was concerning that care for and monitoring of prisoners at risk of self-harm through the assessment, care in custody and teamwork (ACCT) process required improvement. After an initial rise at the start of lockdown, levels of self-harm had fallen and were lower than during the same period last year. Commendably, the prison had started training for a new group of Listeners (prisoners trained by the Samaritans to provide confidential support to their peers) and access to Listeners, either in person or by phone, had been maintained throughout the Covid-19 period.

Violence had reduced at the start of the pandemic and, while rising, remained lower than before the restrictions were imposed. It was positive that only 13% of prisoners felt unsafe at the time of the visit. Managers had maintained challenge support and intervention plans (CSIPs, see

Glossary of terms) to challenge and support perpetrators and were aware that the quality needed improvement. Behaviour management largely relied on the adjudication system. This was reserved for more serious incidents and the number of adjudications remained much lower than before the pandemic. Use of force had also fallen, oversight of use of force had been reinstated and weekly meetings were identifying and progressing areas for remedial action.

The segregation unit was empty at the time of our visit. The regime available to segregated prisoners had not been improved in line with the rest of the establishment. This meant that segregated prisoners did not receive a daily shower or phone call. Managers committed to rectifying this during our visit.

Despite a reduction in the population, the prison remained very overcrowded and most prisoners shared a cell that was designed for one prisoner. This made implementing a safe regime, including social distancing, more of a challenge and we saw few attempts to socially distance even in areas where it was possible. More positively, staff and prisoners ensured that wings were cleaned to a high standard and outside areas were also clean and tidy. The complaints system required improvement. Many replies were inadequate and poorly investigated and did not provide an acceptable resolution.

Prisoners were positive about the food and our findings supported these views. The kitchen was clean and well organised, serveries were clean and the food was better than we normally see. In addition, prisoners had received daily snack packs throughout the restrictions.

Some equality and diversity consultation and monitoring of outcomes continued. However, discrimination complaints were not adequately investigated. There was an equality action plan, but the action points on it were not time sensitive and many had been devolved to the equality officer. We found some concerning perceptions among black and minority ethnic prisoners which needed to be addressed.

Health care services were limited at the start of the pandemic and an appropriate triage system enabled prisoners to access the GP. At the time of our visit some services were being restored but we had concerns about access to optical services, podiatry and physiotherapy. There was a lack of oversight of mental health services to ensure that sufficient services were in place to meet the significant levels of need. Medicines administration was poor and created unnecessary risks.

In common with the rest of the prison estate, the regime for most prisoners was limited to around 1.5 hours out of their cell each day. In addition,

prisoners could access circuit training once a week. It was particularly positive that managers maintained work for about a third of the population and outreach one-to-one education continued to support prisoners who had attained 163 accreditations during the pandemic. This meant that a far greater proportion of the population at Swansea was engaged in purposeful activity than at other local prisons we have visited. The library was providing an outreach service but too few prisoners and wing staff knew about it.

Swansea was among the first prisons to re-establish social visits and more than 200 had taken place by the time of our visit. Most of the restrictions were appropriate but children between the ages of eight months and 11 were unable to visit, which was an unnecessary restriction. Prisoners also had access to video calls and the 'email a prisoner' scheme had been expanded. Most prisoners said they had daily access to phone calls despite the lack of in-cell telephones. The offender management unit had continued with most aspects of rehabilitation and release planning. There was no backlog of OASys assessments and prison offender managers had limited face-to-face contact with prisoners on their caseload. Public protection arrangements were appropriate. Release planning continued and it was positive that prisoners were provided with emergency accommodation on release during the pandemic. However, this scheme had been discontinued from September 2020 which would inevitably mean that a significant proportion of prisoners would be released homeless in the coming months.

We found that managers had made significant progress during the Covid-19 pandemic despite the disadvantages of managing an overcrowded, Victorian prison lacking basic facilities such as in-cell telephones. The governor ensured that staff and prisoners were well informed and acted on concerns. Appropriate priority was given to keeping prisoners in work, maintaining some limited face-to-face education and continuing sentence and risk management. Outcomes for many prisoners at Swansea were better than at other local prisons. As the prison continues to progress, the management team need to establish appropriate oversight in the areas of self-harm prevention, equality and diversity and health care to ensure that outcomes continue to improve.
Peter Clarke CVO OBE QPM
HM Chief Inspector of Prisons September 2020

**Key concerns and recommendations**
Key concerns and recommendations identify the issues of most importance to improving outcomes for prisoners and are designed to help

establishments prioritise and address the most significant weaknesses in the treatment and conditions of prisoners.

During this visit we identified some areas of key concern and have made a small number of key recommendations for the prison to address.

Key concern: The effectiveness of the reverse cohort unit was undermined by the practice of allowing prisoners who had arrived on different days to mix during their time out of cell. This created a risk that prisoners who were about to move to the main population would become infected by new arrivals.

Key recommendation: Prisoners who arrive on separate days should not mix on the reverse cohort unit. (To the governor)

Key concern: There were weaknesses in ACCT documentation which did not demonstrate good levels of care for prisoners in crisis. This included actions that were signed off as completed before any demonstrable outcome or change for the prisoner had been achieved, actions that were not progressed quickly enough and were carried over to subsequent reviews, predictably timed observations and recorded conversations that lacked substance or evidence of real enquiry into a prisoner's well-being.

Key recommendation: Prisoners being managed on ACCTs should receive consistent, well documented care and support that addresses the factors underlying their vulnerability to self-harm or suicide. (To the governor)

Key concern: There were gaps in prison data, particularly for prisoners with disabilities, which was concerning. Experiences of safety and victimisation were not equitable across all groups.

Key recommendation: There should be robust oversight and analysis of equality and diversity to ensure that differences in treatment and access to the regime are identified, understood and addressed. (To the governor)

Key concern: The lack of secure management of controlled medication and poor medication administration practices had continued on the shielding and segregation units. The treatment rooms on A and B wings could be accessed with a general suite key and had no lockable gates. Medication cupboards were not secured on either unit and medicines were taken out of their original packaging and put into alternative pots before being taken to the units. Medication was passed through the inundation hatch which prevented clear observation and increased the risk of hoarding and diversion. Unaccompanied staff carried controlled drugs round the establishment in an insecure bag.

Key recommendation: The Partnership Board should review the poor security of medicines and administration practices on the segregation and A and B units to ensure that medicines are transported around the prison and administered safely to patients in accordance with professional and good practice standards.
(To the Partnership Board)

Key concern: Primary and crisis mental health services lacked structured monitoring and oversight of their effectiveness and outcomes for prisoners. There was evidence of unmet need in secondary in-reach services.

Key recommendation: The Partnership Board should review the provision of in- reach mental health services and the system of oversight, monitoring and effectiveness of primary and crisis mental health provision. (To the Partnership Board)

**Notable positive practice**

We define notable positive practice as innovative practice or practice that leads to particularly good outcomes from which other establishments may be able to learn. Inspectors look for evidence of good outcomes for prisoners; original, creative or particularly effective approaches to problem-solving or achieving the desired goal; and how other establishments could learn from or replicate the practice.

Inspectors found the following examples of notable positive practice during this visit.

• Consultation and communication with staff and prisoners were very good. This was led by the governor who attended staff briefings, chaired two prisoner consultation meetings a week and was available to staff and prisoners most days on the wings. This consultation led to several meaningful improvements for prisoners.

• The continued involvement of prisoner peer workers was an integral and important part of the prison's induction activity.

• The prison had its own trained counsellor who undertook one-to-one counselling sessions with prisoners.

• General cleanliness and tidiness had been maintained despite the constraints of an old Victorian building and the unusual regime restrictions.

• The prison had maintained work for around a third of the population.

• One-to-one outreach education had continued to support prisoners during the pandemic and 139 accredited qualifications had been achieved.

• All prisoners at Swansea who required it had an up-to-date assessment of their risk to others and of their offending related needs.

**INDEPENDENT MONITORING BOARD: Annual Report**

The law requires every prison to be monitored by an independent Board appointed by the Justice

Secretary; these are known as Independent Monitoring Boards (IMBs). The IMB must satisfy itself as to the humane and just treatment of those held in custody within its prison and the range and adequacy of the programmes preparing them for release; it must report annually to the Justice Secretary on how well the prison has met the standards and requirements placed on it.

**IMB Report 1 June 2020 – 31 May 2021**
**Published August 2022**
**Executive summary**
**Background to the report**
The Covid-19 outbreak had a significant impact on the Board's ability to gather information and discuss the contents of this annual report. During most of the reporting year, there were only two active members of the Board who were able to make visits to the prison. The Board therefore tried to cover as much ground as it can in these difficult circumstances, but inevitably there is less detail and supporting evidence than usual. Ministers are aware of these constraints. The Board recognised the effort by the managers and staff of HMP Swansea to protect the prisoners in their care from infection by Covid-19 and to provide a humane and fair system during this difficult time.

Since the disappointing HM Inspectorate of Prisons (HMIP) report in 2017, improvements have been made to the way HMP Swansea has been managed and the services it provides to prisoners. Successive Governors have sought to take on board the recommendations of HMIP and considerable success has been achieved in raising standards, not only environmentally but also in the relationships between staff and prisoners and the opportunities and services available to prisoners.

Respect for individuals is paramount. Relationships between staff and prisoners are central to the wellbeing of the prison. All members of staff play a vital role in maintaining a stable and, above all, safe environment. The aim of the prison, through the varied and positive programmes and activities available, is to enable prisoners to address their offending behaviour and thus reduce their risk of reoffending and to assist with resettlement. This is achieved through partnerships with a wide range of statutory, private and voluntary organisations.

**Main judgements**
**How safe is the prison?**
It is the Board's view that HMP Swansea was a safe prison. Violence continued to remain at a low level, which the Board believes reflected the

historically good relationships that staff had been able to build up with prisoners. This was clearly demonstrated during the pandemic, when prisoners have been locked in cells for far more time than is normally the case.

**How fairly and humanely are prisoners treated?**
The Board is satisfied that, generally, most prisoners were being treated fairly and humanely. The restricted regime, put in place during Covid-19, raised concerns, as did the suspension of visiting arrangements – although the new social video call arrangements were a great benefit and proved popular with prisoners and their families. It is hoped that these will continue in the future.

The prison governors held weekly meetings with representatives of the prisoners where all aspects of prison life, the Covid pandemic and the general prison regime were discussed. In general, morale amongst prisoners was good.

The Board was concerned about the length of time that prisoners were on remand and awaiting court appearances.

**How well are prisoners' health and wellbeing needs met?**
There was a slight improvement in relation to prisoners' access to mental health support, aided by a grant received from the Welsh Government. However, mental health provision continued to cause concern to the Board. During the Covid-19 pandemic, services which supported prisoners' health and wellbeing were restricted, at a time when their need for it was very high. There was concern about the level of dental provision.

**How well are prisoners progressed towards successful resettlement?**
Unfortunately, the advances made in relation to resettlement and training activities, such as the call centre and the barista workshop, were suspended during the pandemic. However, other activities such as the sewing workshop, cleaning services and multi-skill training continued. The prison continued to support prisoners with their resettlement. However, the education department has been severely curtailed, although prisoners have been provided with education packs and library books for their use on wings. The education department continued to be involved in the induction process for new prisoners.

**Main areas for development**
**TO THE WELSH GOVERNMENT**
The Board recognises the improvements in prisoners being able to access accommodation on release and welcomed the Welsh Government's initiative to house all rough sleepers during the

Covid-19 pandemic. We would make a plea that this scheme be continued for prisoners leaving custody without accommodation in future.

The Board remains concerned as to the mental health service offered to prisoners within HMP Swansea. The Board would ask the Welsh Government to raise this issue with Swansea Bay University Health Board.

## TO THE PRISON SERVICE

The Board has been concerned with the number of times where prisoners from 'out of area' are being received into HMP Swansea, whether from transfer from other Welsh prisons or from prisons in England. We fully appreciate that the Prison Service is often under pressure to accommodate prisoners but would ask that reducing the number of out of area prisoners be considered when making placement decisions.

The Board is increasingly concerned at the effect that the restricted regime will have on the prison's ability to provide a safe, humane, and positive environment which encourages prisoners' progression to resettlement. This is despite all the efforts being made by staff to support the prisoners in their care. The Board shares the concerns of other Welsh Boards that long-term continuation of regime restrictions will have a further detrimental effect on the wellbeing of the prisoners.

## TO THE GOVERNOR

We applaud the establishment in its efforts to maintain key worker sessions during the restricted regime but would ask that consideration be given to whether the cross-deployment of key workers affected the incidence of self-harm.

The Board recognises the efforts that the establishment has made in increasing its understanding of the needs of prisoners within the protected characteristics groups.

The early activation of body-worn cameras (BWCs) should continue to be encouraged.

LICHFIELD
STAFFS
WS14 9QS

HMP & YOI
SWINFEN
HALL

Tel: 01543 484000

*For the latest reports on this prison please visit:*
https://tinyurl.com/bdfh26rv

*Important Changes:* **(1) Visits:** the identification necessary to access this prison and visit for social or professional purposes has changed; (2) **Money and Gifts** new rules now apply to these. See page 16 for full details of the above.

**Task of the establishment** Young adult male training establishment and adult male category C prison Certified normal accommodation and operational capacity.
Prisoners held July 2021: 531
Baseline certified normal capacity: 604
In-use certified normal capacity: 624
Operational capacity: 624

**Population of the prison**
• 376 new prisoners received over last 12 months (about 31 a month)
• 57 foreign national prisoners
• 48% of prisoners from BAME backgrounds
• 144 prisoners released over the last 12 months
• 34 prisoners receiving substance support
• 40 prisoners referred for mental health assessment each month.

**Prison status and key providers**
Public
Prison group West Midlands
Prison Group Director Teresa Clarke CBE
Governor: Mark Greenhaf
IMB chair: Adrian Allen
Physical health provider: Practice Plus Group
Mental health provider: Midlands Partnership NHS Foundation Trust Substance use treatment provider: Midlands Partnership NHS Foundation Trust Prison education framework provider: Novus
Escort contractor: GeoAmey

**Brief history**
HMP Swinfen Hall opened in February 1963. It currently receives young adult and adult prisoners aged 18 to 28 serving from 16 months up to and including life.

**Short description of residential units**
Prisoners are housed in nine wings:
A - 64 places

B - 60 places
C - 60 places – induction/first night
D - 68 places (personality disorder treatment service enabling environment)
E - 60 places PIPE (psychologically informed planned environment)
F - 90 places
G - 90 places
I - 72 places
J - 60 places
CSU - 15 cells

## INSPECTIONS & REPORTS
### IRP Report: February 2022
**Published 1st April 2022**

HMP/YOI Swinfen Hall is a category C prison for young adult and adult men aged 18 to 28, mostly serving sentences of over four years. At the time of our visit, it held 598 prisoners, of whom almost half were from black and minority ethnic backgrounds. The prison contained two specialist wings: one supported prisoners with emerging or diagnosed personality disorders and the other provided a psychologically informed planned environment (PIPE) for 60 prisoners.

At our previous inspections of HMP/YOI Swinfen Hall in 2018 and 2021 we made the following judgements about outcomes for prisoners.

Swinfen Hall is situated near Lichfield in Staffordshire and, at the time of this independent review of progress, was holding around 598 young male prisoners serving sentences of more than four years. The prison was last inspected in July 2021 and this review was our first visit since then.

In July we found that outcomes for prisoners had improved in our healthy prison tests of respect and purposeful activity, but safety remained a concern with, for example, high rates of violence, significant use of force and an increase in the use of PAVA incapacitant spray. We also found that incentives to motivate positive behaviour or deter low-level poor behaviour were limited.

Prisoners not allocated to an activity were locked in their cell for 22 hours each day. Despite the gradual opening up of classrooms following the introduction of Covid-19 safeguards, local arrangements limited the number of prisoners able to attend. Outcomes for prisoners in the healthy prison test of rehabilitation and release planning had regressed. Too many faced lengthy delays before attending rehabilitative programmes, while the coordination of services for those due to be released was weak.

At this visit, we reviewed progress against 10 recommendations. We found that the prison had made good progress in two, and reasonable progress in a further two. There had been insufficient progress in the remaining six. Working in partnership with us, Ofsted undertook a monitoring visit, following up four themes they had identified in education, skills and work provision. Ofsted found reasonable progress in two themes and insufficient progress in the other two.

A new governor had taken up post in September 2021 with a clear intention to drive improvement and there had been several changes to the senior leadership team in the months before this visit. The governor's vision was known as 'RAISE the bar' (relationships, activities, inclusivity, self-responsibility and environment). Senior leaders had communicated the vision to staff and there was some evidence that staff understood and had embraced this vision. The strategy was realistic, and the prison seemed to us to have a renewed sense of purpose and direction.

In the area of safety, the governor had recently appointed a dedicated senior lead and an analyst to develop understanding of safety data to drive improvement. A full review of local safety strategies had been conducted and while it was yet to be launched, it was underpinned by consultation with prisoners and staff. Senior leaders had been active in securing funds to progress several key strands of work to reduce violence, including conflict resolution and age-appropriate initiatives to encourage positive behaviour.

It was concerning that the use of force, including PAVA, remained high. Senior leaders were receiving external support to understand the underlying causes and, while there had been some improvement in the staff use of body-worn cameras, oversight of force required more vigour. In contrast, it was positive that rates of recorded self-harm had reduced by over a third since our inspection and were now lower than in similar prisons.

Key work, while still requiring further development, had benefited from the arrival of a senior leader who was driving the scheme with enthusiasm. A review in January 2022 had resulted in a large increase in recorded prisoner contacts by staff; the challenge now was to continue this drive and improve quality. Work to progress equality and diversity had been slow, but the prison had very recently appointed a dedicated lead who provided evidence of advanced plans to relaunch the diversity agenda throughout the prison.

Despite ongoing staff resource issues and a significant Covid-19 outbreak in late 2021, leaders had been focused on moving to stage 2 of the HMPPS recovery plan and had developed credible plans to open the regime further. Ofsted judged there to be reasonable progress in two of its four themes, although work to improve careers guidance and progression, in addition to access to digital resources, was insufficient.

The offender management unit (OMU) was now adequately resourced. There had been good progress to address the backlog of offending behaviour programmes and prisoners were prioritised properly based on need. While not a resettlement prison, Swinfen Hall still released around 12 prisoners a month and, despite some improvements, the strategic management and oversight of resettlement work remained underdeveloped.

Overall, and despite some shortcomings, this was a promising review, recognising an improved culture and a renewed sense of purpose and progress. The revitalised senior leadership team were taking the prison in the right direction supported by the prison group director. They were realistic about the scale of the tasks ahead and understood that further progress would require sustained effort and determination.

**HMCIP Report:** 28 June - 9 July 2021
**Published 6 October 2021**

Swinfen Hall is a category C prison for young adults and adults aged 18 to 28, mostly serving sentences of over four years. At the time of our inspection, it contained 531 prisoners of whom nearly half were from black and minority ethnic backgrounds. Within the prison were two specialist wings for those with emerging or diagnosed personality disorders.

This prison continued to wrestle with the challenges that we outlined in our 2016 and 2019 inspections, but had made some noticeable progress despite dealing with the effects of the pandemic. Leaders had set up good systems to analyse data and create plans for the more troubled individuals and significantly more prisoners told us they felt safe than at the previous inspection. However, despite the Covid-19 restrictions on mixing and the limited amount of time prisoners spent out of their cells, levels of violence, often serious, between prisoners were still too high and staff assaults were on the rise. It was very concerning to see increases in the use of PAVA incapacitant spray as the regime began to open up and leaders needed to make certain that this did not become a routine way of managing challenging behaviour.

An excellent custody manager on the induction wing had made this a safe and positive place for new arrivals who were helped by more established peers to settle into the prison. On the specialist units, we saw prisoners with complex needs making good progress in a supportive environment. Elsewhere, some less experienced staff did not have high enough expectations of prisoners' behaviour and lacked the skills and confidence to create a stable and safe environment. Though inspectors saw some positive interactions between officers and prisoners, they also witnessed staff members who were ineffectual, dismissive or rude.

In a prison like Swinfen Hall, the incentives scheme should be a key tool in improving behaviour and helping leaders and staff to raise standards. It was, therefore, disappointing to hear how ineffective prisoners felt it was in motivating them, with those on an enhanced level often not getting the rewards that they had earned.

Though the prison had worked to increase the amount of time prisoners spent out of their cells, those without jobs were routinely locked up for 22 hours a day, a bleak prospect for the prison's young and energetic population. There were also long waiting lists for rehabilitation programmes that should have been helping prisoners to progress through their sentences and restarting these fully must be an urgent priority for the prison. A lack of oversight of partner agencies meant there was insufficient coordination of services to support prisoners who were due for release.

For the last year, most education had taken the form of in-cell packs and though these had improved they were no substitute for face-to-face education, particularly for those with learning difficulties. Classrooms had begun to open up, but despite desks being set apart to prevent infection, absurdly, only prisoners from the same bubble were allowed to be in education together. This meant very few prisoners were getting regular, face-to-face education.

Leaders had worked hard to improve the decency and conditions of Swinfen Hall and inspectors who had been on previous inspections noticed an improvement in the atmosphere of the prison, which felt more positive than it had in the past. The standard of accommodation was much improved since our last inspection: wings had been refurbished, showers had been upgraded, there were new clothes washing facilities and the prison was clean and well- maintained.

There remains considerable and fundamental work still to do to create an environment in which this group of young men are really incentivised and motivated to behave in an atmosphere that is safe and supportive, and provides them with meaningful and productive work, education, training and rehabilitation.

Charlie Taylor, Chief Inspector, July 2021.

**Summary of key findings**

We last inspected Swinfen Hall in 2018 and made 57 recommendations, four of which were about areas of key concern. The prison fully accepted 49 of the recommendations and partially (or subject to resources) accepted five. It rejected three of the recommendations.

## Progress on key concerns and recommendations from the full inspection

Our last inspection of Swinfen Hall took place before the Covid-19 pandemic and the recommendations in that report focused on areas of concern affecting outcomes for prisoners at the time. Although we recognise that the challenges of keeping prisoners safe during COVID-19 will have changed the focus for many prison leaders, we believe that it is important to report on progress in areas of key concern to help leaders continue to drive improvement.

At our last full inspection, we made one recommendation about a key concern in the area of safety. At this inspection we found that this recommendation had not been achieved.

We made two recommendations about key concerns in the area of respect. At this inspection we found that neither of these recommendations had been achieved.

We made one recommendation about a key concern in the area of purposeful activity. At this inspection we found that this recommendation had not been achieved. Ofsted carried out a progress monitoring visit alongside our inspection to assess the progress that leaders and managers had made towards reinstating a full education, skills and work curriculum. They judged it was too early to assess whether recommendations made at the last inspection had been achieved.

## Outcomes for prisoners

We assess outcomes for prisoners against four healthy prison tests (see Appendix I for more information about the tests). At this inspection of HMP/YOI Swinfen Hall, we found that outcomes for prisoners had stayed the same in one healthy prison area, improved in two and declined in one.

These judgements seek to make an objective assessment of the outcomes experienced by those detained and have taken into account the prison's recovery from Covid-19 as well as the 'regime stage' at which the prison was operating, as outlined in the HM Prison and Probation (HMPPS) National Framework for prison regimes and services.

## Safety

At the last inspection of Swinfen Hall in 2018, we found that outcomes for prisoners were not sufficiently good against this healthy prison test. At this inspection we found that outcomes for prisoners remained not sufficiently good against this healthy prison test.

All appropriate Covid-19 measures were in place in reception and staff on the unit were respectful and courteous. Prisoners were able to order essential items on arrival which were delivered swiftly. Some unnecessary delays in procedures resulted in prisoners spending too long in reception.

The induction unit provided a positive environment for newly arrived prisoners. First night assessments were comprehensive, and prisoners said they felt safe. A suitable face-to-face induction was delivered with good support from induction orderlies. However, the regime for most new arrivals was poor.

During the previous 12 months, the number of violent incidents among prisoners, some of them serious, remained high and violence towards staff was increasing. Data were analysed effectively to inform a structured action plan designed to improve safety. A range of collaborative safety meetings made good use of data to monitor progress and identify and address actions. Challenge, support and intervention plans were well embedded and examples that we reviewed were among the best we have seen. There were limited incentives to motivate good behaviour, but the incentives scheme did little to deter low-level poor behaviour.

Staff-prisoner relationships in the segregation unit had improved significantly since our last inspection and living conditions in the unit were generally good. The regime was still too limited, but there were some good examples of reintegration planning.

The use of force had increased since our last inspection and was high. Governance arrangements were in place and the documentation was of a reasonable quality. However, in some of the cases that we examined, force was not always justified, and we were concerned about the frequent and increasing use of PAVA incapacitant spray to deal with challenging behaviour.

Security was well managed with a good flow of intelligence analysed swiftly by a newly developed regional intelligence team. Security priorities were broadly aligned to the prevailing threats of violence and drugs. The prison had worked hard to reduce the availability of illicit substances.

Levels of self-harm had reduced but were still high in comparison to similar prisons. Self-harm rates among the young adult population remained higher than their older peers. A comprehensive range of data was available but was not used well enough to understand the full picture. The safer prisons team provided good support for prisoners being supported through the ACCT (assessment, care in custody and teamwork case management of prisoners at risk of suicide or self-harm) process. There were only three trained Listeners (prisoners trained by the Samaritans to provide emotional support to fellow prisoners) which limited access to this important scheme.

### Respect

At the last inspection of Swinfen Hall in 2018, we found that outcomes for prisoners were not sufficiently good against this healthy prison test. At this inspection we found that outcomes for prisoners were now reasonably good against this healthy prison test.

In our survey, only 64% of prisoners said that staff treated them with respect, similar to our previous inspection. Prisoners from a black and minority ethnic background responded more negatively than their white peers. Progress in developing positive staff-prisoner relationships had stalled over the last year and the delivery of quality key work was too limited. We observed supportive and caring interactions across wings but there were also examples of staff who were distant or dismissive of prisoners. Relationships remained a strength on the two specialist units and the induction unit where prisoners received additional support.

Living conditions had improved significantly since our previous inspection. Most prisoners now had their own cells which were clean and well equipped. Prisoners had good access to showers, cleaning materials and bedding.

A reasonable choice of food was available, but the quality was variable. Prisoners ate every meal in their cell and there were limited opportunities for them to cook their own food.

The number of complaints from prisoners had reduced significantly and quality assurance was good. There were weaknesses in the application system. Some consultation with prisoners had continued throughout the restricted regime.

There were significant weaknesses in the delivery of an equality strategy. Work to address this was undermined by poor consultation and poor consideration of equality monitoring data. Action planning did not focus adequately on key challenges such as disproportionate treatment of black and minority ethnic prisoners and young prisoners. Only 14 discrimination incident report forms had been submitted in the last year, suggesting little awareness of or confidence in the process. Some responses were poor, and few were quality assured. In our survey black and minority ethnic prisoners reported worse treatment and conditions, particularly in relation to staff respect. The prison was not monitoring the treatment of prisoners with disabilities.

The chaplaincy had continued to provide good support to prisoners throughout the pandemic. The team had been quick to resume corporate worship for the more numerous faith groups, although Muslim prisoners could only attend Friday prayers once every six weeks.

Health services were good overall with effective partnership working between the prison, health providers, Public Health England and health commissioners, particularly in the management of Covid-19. There had been no positive cases in the prisoner population since March 2021. Full Covid-19 vaccinations had been delivered to vulnerable groups with underlying health conditions but there was a much lower uptake by the remaining cohort, despite innovative ways of trying to increase this. Routine clinics had restarted with reasonable waiting times, with the exception of the GP whose waiting lists for routine appointments averaged three weeks. Medicines were generally well managed. The skilled, integrated multidisciplinary mental health and psychosocial substance misuse team delivered a responsive service. The three services under the offender personality disorder pathway were providing a good level of support. The enhanced support service provided a good level of support through psychologically informed interventions.

### Purposeful Activity

At the last inspection of Swinfen Hall in 2018, we found that outcomes for prisoners were poor against this healthy prison test.

At this inspection we found that outcomes for prisoners were now not sufficiently good against this healthy prison test.

Ofsted carried out a progress monitoring visit of the prison a month before our full inspection and the purposeful activity judgement incorporates their assessment of progress.

Time out of cell had improved considerably in May 2021 when regime restrictions were relaxed allowing more opportunities for prisoners to engage in work and education. However, this still left one-third of prisoners locked up for at least 22 hours a day, which placed an inevitable toll on their well-being. In our spot checks, we found 39% of prisoners locked in their cells. Inspectors also found classroom and workshop spaces that were not filled because the cohorting strategy restricted the mixing of prisoners from different bubbles, even when the rooms had been risk assessed for social distancing. As a result, classrooms held only three or four prisoners or lay empty while many were locked up on wings. PE staff had been quick to introduce outside gym sessions when the pandemic began, and also to re-open the sports hall when restrictions permitted. However, most prisoners could only attend once or twice a fortnight. The library remained closed. Some good efforts were made to mitigate the impact of this, but data suggested a huge drop in book issues.

During a progress visit to Swinfen Hall in June

2021, Ofsted judged that reasonable progress had been made in ensuring that staff taught a full curriculum and provided support to meet prisoners' needs, including the provision of remote learning. (See separate Ofsted visit report.)

## Rehabilitation & Release Planning

At the last inspection of Swinfen Hall in 2018, we found that outcomes for prisoners were reasonably good against this healthy prison test. At this inspection we found that outcomes for prisoners were now not sufficiently good against this healthy prison test.

Social visits had only resumed in May 2021 and take up of secure video calls (see Glossary of terms) was low. Prisoners did not have in- cell telephones to make calls when families were at home. Family days and relationship courses remained suspended and, until May 2021, little family engagement casework had been done.

Nearly all prisoners were serving long sentences and were high risk. The reducing reoffending strategy was ambitious but had no built-in milestones to measure progress. Attendance at the meeting to guide delivery of the strategy had continued during the pandemic but attendance by core participants was too variable for it to be fully effective. Persistent staff shortages in the offender management unit were undermining core work and caseloads for prison offender managers (POMs) were unsustainable. Approximately 25% of the population did not have an OASys assessment of need. Those that had been assessed had appropriate targets, but most prisoners did not have enough contact with their POMs to drive positive outcomes.

Up-to-date risk management plans were in place and were of a sufficiently good standard. The interdepartmental risk management meeting met monthly and all MAPPA levels (multi-agency public protection arrangements) in our case sample were confirmed before release. The application of public protection procedures to protect children and other potential victims was generally good. MAPPA F forms were well completed.

A core function of Swinfen Hall was to deliver accredited offending behaviour programmes to meet the needs of their high-risk population. Delivery had initially been paused at the start of the pandemic and, although some one-to-one work had restarted, group work was yet to start. Waiting lists had increased during the pandemic, and some prisoners were released from custody without completing interventions to address their offending behaviour.

The prison continued to release approximately 10 prisoners each month. A third were released into approved premises but a small number had no sustainable accommodation on the day of their release. In our case sample, most of the prisoners facing release in the next three months did not have an assessment of their resettlement needs. Some were close to release with unresolved housing needs and many prisoners we spoke to required additional support with financial and other matters. There was a lack of clarity about the resettlement services on offer which was compounded by the absence of some partner agencies during the restrictions, including the community rehabilitation company.

## Key concerns and recommendations

Key concerns and recommendations identify the issues of most importance to improving outcomes for prisoners and are designed to help establishments prioritise and address the most significant weaknesses in the treatment and conditions of prisoners.

During this inspection we identified some areas of key concern and have made a number of recommendations for the prison to address those concerns.

Key concern: Recorded levels of violence remained high despite prisoners being locked up for long periods due to Covid-19 restrictions. Insufficient focus had been given to how the young population could be motivated to behave well. The strategic safety meeting designed to drive this work was poorly attended by some departments, which undermined a joint approach to the reduction of violence.

Recommendation: All key departments should contribute to the development of an effective strategy to reduce violence which includes an age-appropriate rewards scheme to motivate good behaviour.

Key concern: Use of force was high and not always justified and the use of PAVA incapacitant spray was increasing. Governance meetings were often poorly attended and analysis of use of force data was poor.

Recommendation: Comprehensive data on the use of force should be analysed regularly by a multidisciplinary team to identify trends and training opportunities so that appropriate measures are put in place to reduce the use of force.

Key concern: Self-harm rates remained high in comparison to similar prisons, particularly among the young adult population.

Recommendation: Data analysis and consultation with prisoners should be used to understand the root causes of self- harm. Results should inform an effective strategy and action plan to reduce the high levels of self-harm.

Key concern: Progress in developing positive staff-prisoner relationships had stalled since the start of the pandemic and quality key work for most prisoners was now too limited.

Recommendation: Opportunities for regular and meaningful contact between staff and prisoners should be prioritised to improve relationships between staff and prisoners.

Key concern: There was no comprehensive monitoring of the treatment of prisoners in protected groups. Records indicated long-standing over- representation of black and minority ethnic and younger prisoners in segregation, disciplinary procedures and incidents of disruptive behaviour. There was no strategy to address these concerns.

Recommendation: Data, consultation and effective monitoring should address negative perceptions and disproportionate outcomes for prisoners in all protected groups.

Key concern: The cohorting strategy prevented classroom and workshop spaces from being filled even when the rooms had been risk assessed for social distancing. There were still no opportunities for about one-third of prisoners to engage in out-of-cell activities and they remained locked up for at least 22 hours a day. Poor time out of cell took a toll on prisoner well-being and access to time out of cell was not monitored.

Recommendation: Covid-19 safety measures should be reviewed nationally and locally to maximise opportunities for prisoners to spend time out of their cell. Time out of cell should be monitored to ensure equitable access for all prisoners.

Key concern: Persistent staff shortages in the offender management unit had resulted in excessively large caseloads for prison offender managers. This restricted their ability to make regular and effective contact with all the prisoners under their supervision.

Recommendation: Prison offender managers should have adequate time to maintain regular and effective contact with the prisoners on their caseload to support sentence progression. (To the governor)

Key concern: Offending behaviour programmes for small groups of prisoners, a core function of the prison, had been too slow to restart because of Covid-19 measures and too few facilitators. Too many prisoners were on waiting lists or yet to be assessed and the continued release of such prisoners into the community presented risks.

Recommendation: A full programme of key accredited offending behaviour programmes should be delivered, prioritising high-risk prisoners so that their risk is reduced before release. (To the governor)

Key concern: The resettlement outcomes for more than 100 prisoners released each year were of concern. There was no coordinated oversight of the core resettlement services delivered by partner agencies, and no quality assurance procedures. This had created uncertainty among staff and prisoners about which services were available.

Recommendation: Services delivered by resettlement partners should be effectively coordinated and quality assured so that the provision meets the need, and prisoners and staff have a clear understanding of the resettlement services available.

**Notable positive practice**

We define notable positive practice as innovative work or practice that leads to particularly good outcomes from which other establishments may be able to learn. Inspectors look for evidence of good outcomes for prisoners; original, creative or particularly effective approaches to problem-solving or achieving the desired goal; and how other establishments could learn from or replicate the practice.

Inspectors found two examples of notable positive practice during this inspection.

The enhanced support service provided very good psychological and emotional support to prisoners with challenging behaviours.

Staff and prisoners worked together to vastly improve living conditions. Prisoners were proud of their contribution and their efforts were rewarded through wing competitions and cooked breakfast from the bistro. Managers had introduced robust quality assurance to improve the standards of cleanliness and ensured that cells were appropriately equipped and regularly painted.

**INDEPENDENT MONITORING BOARD: Annual Report**

The law requires every prison to be monitored by an independent Board appointed by the Justice Secretary; these are known as Independent Monitoring Boards (IMBs). The IMB must satisfy itself as to the humane and just treatment of those held in custody within its prison and the range and adequacy of the programmes preparing them for release; it must report annually to the Justice Secretary on how well the prison has met the standards and requirements placed on it.

**IMB Report 01 May 2020 – 30 April 2021**
**Published November 2021**
**Executive Summary**
**Background to the report**

The Covid-19 outbreak has had a significant impact on the Board's ability to monitor in person, gather information and discuss the contents of this annual report. The Board has tried to cover as much ground as it can in these difficult circumstances, but inevitably there is less detail and supporting evidence than usual. Ministers are aware of these constraints. Regular information is being collected specifically on the prison's response to the pandemic, and that is being collated nationally.

• There was a mixture of remote and on-site monitoring based on official guidance and personal risk factors of board members.

• Regular contact was maintained with the prison through telephone contact with senior management team, key departments and wing staff with conversations recorded in rota reports.

• Contact with the CSU was maintained throughout the year. Where site visits were made the CSU was prioritised and most reviews were attended either in person or by telephone.

• Prisoners were able to make applications to the Board either by using the 0800 line or by making written submissions which, in the event of board members not attending site, were scanned to the chair for action on rota visits.

### Main judgements
### How safe is the establishment?

Evidence gathered during the year shows that some prisoners felt safer during the pandemic because of the restricted regime which seriously reduced time out of cell, limiting contact with other prisoners. Data from the SMT daily briefing shows that there was a sustained reduction in self-isolators during the pandemic. Members have ascertained that this was due to self-isolators coming out of cells together and feeling safer because of this. The challenge for Swinfen Hall is how this increased level of safety felt by vulnerable prisoners can be maintained as the regime re- opens.

### How fairly and humanely are prisoners treated?

The restricted regime implemented during the pandemic has the potential to have impacted mental health. However, both mental health and general wellbeing are yet to be fully assessed . In addition to a lack of time out of cell for work, education, and association, there has been very limited opportunity for visits by family and friends.

### How well are prisoners' health and wellbeing needs met?

Whilst there was understandable disruption to clinics due to Covid-19 restrictions, the healthcare provision has generally been good. However, an increase in mental health referrals and increased rates of referral to external A&E is cause for concern and the Board will continue to monitor this.

### How effective is the education provision for prisoners?

The pandemic has had a significant impact on the delivery of education programmes to prisoners, as for many months the provider, Novus, was not active in the prison. There must be a concerted effort to enable prisoners to catch up with their studies, especially where it impacts on their progression but also to aid general wellbeing by engaging with others. Out of cell workshops were also severely curtailed although waste management and tailoring were able to continue with reduced numbers in accordance with the national directive regarding essential workshops. The Board will continue to monitor this.

### How well are prisoners progressed towards transfer or successful resettlement?

The transfer of 53 prisoners to the category D estate over the year is commendable in the circumstances of reduced staff and the strictures of Covid-19. There has been a welcome improvement in the completion rate for OASys this year. However, the delivery of essential programmes has been badly affected with no possibility of delivering any group sessions; a considerable backlog has built up and must be addressed.

### Main areas for development
### TO THE MINISTER

The operational capacity has been impacted by the poor workmanship in the refurbishment of A, B and C wings. Work has been sub-standard and has had to be repeated. Will the Minister assure the Board that there will be an improvement in contract monitoring and adequate supervision of works carried out in the prison estate?

Additional mental health services, healthcare clinics, work and education opportunities, as well as staffing to facilitate association and family visits are needed to mitigate the deprivations suffered by prisoners during the pandemic. Will the necessary funding be made available to the prison to facilitate these mitigations?

### TO HMPPS

The Board remains deeply concerned at the loss of prisoners' property when they transfer to Swinfen Hall. The ministerial response to our last annual report referenced a new prisoners' property policy framework, and Her Majesty's Prison and Probation Service (HMPPS) seeking service improvements through the new prisoner escort and custody service contract. The Board has not seen any difference in property issues, which continue to cause prisoners considerable distress. How is the effectiveness of the current contract being evaluated?

The new offender flow process introduced in September 2020 means that newly sentenced prisoners now only reside at a Reception prison for a maximum of 10 days prior to being allocated to their longer-term establishment. This results in nearly all these prisoners coming to Swinfen Hall with no initial OASys assessment. What measures will be put in place to enable Swinfen Hall to continue to manage the increased number of prisoners arriving without a completed OASys assessment?

Prisoners have been deprived of education and work, programmes essential for their rehabilitation, as well as daily association and family visits. How will staffing and services be bolstered to make up for the losses suffered by prisoners?

## TO THE GOVERNOR

There is a need for additional mental health services, healthcare clinics, work and education opportunities as well as staffing to facilitate association and family visits. How will funding be made available to provide additional staffing and services to mitigate the deprivation suffered by prisoners during the pandemic?

How will the prison maintain the increased level of safety felt by vulnerable prisoners as the regime opens up?

**GRIFFIN MANOR WAY**
**THAMESMEAD**
**LONDON SE28 0FJ**

THAMESIDE
PRISON

Tel: 020 8317 9777

*For the latest reports on this prison please visit:*
https://tinyurl.com/bdfh26rv

*Important Changes:* **(1) Visits:** the identification necessary to access this prison and visit for social or professional purposes has changed; (2) **Money and Gifts** new rules now apply to these. See page 16 for full details of the above.

### Task of the prison/establishment

HMP Thameside is a local/reception category B establishment.

### Certified normal accommodation and operational capacity

Prisoners held November 2021: 1,194
Baseline certified normal capacity: 926
In-use certified normal capacity: 926
Operational capacity: 1,232

### Population of the prison

1,068 new prisoners were received each year, with around 89 per week

22% were foreign national prisoners
62% of prisoners were from black and minority ethnic backgrounds
An average of 258 prisoners were released into the community each month
292 prisoners were receiving support for substance
An average of seven prisoners were referred for mental health assessment each month

### Prison status and key providers

Private (run by Serco)
Prison group: Custodial Contracts
Prison Group Director: Neil Richards
Governor/Director: David Bamford / John Hyde (c)
IMB chair: Mike Austerberry
Physical health provider: Oxleas NHS Foundation Trust Mental health provider: Oxleas NHS Foundation Trust
Substance misuse treatment providers: Turning Point and Oxleas NHS Foundation Trust
Prison education framework provider: Novus
Community rehabilitation company (CRC): Reunified to Probation Service, previously MTC
Escort contractor: Serco

### Brief history

HMP Thameside opened on March 2012. In February 2015, an additional house block opened, creating 332 extra spaces.

### Short description of residential units

There are seven wings, split across two house blocks, each divided into two units ('uppers' and 'lowers'), with an average unit capacity of 110 prisoners.
House block 1 – A, B, C, D and E wings House block 2 – H and J wings
The first night centre is on the 'upper' unit of A wing, and the drug stabilisation unit on the 'lower' unit. A dedicated health care unit has inpatient facilities for 18 prisoners, and the segregation unit has capacity for 18 prisoners.

### Visiting Information

Prisoners at HMP Thameside book their own visits using an automated system. The prisoner will need to book a visit then inform the visitor to tell them when it is.

### Legal visits:

For current legal visiting information please contact the prison direct.

### INSPECTIONS & REPORTS
### Date of inspection: November 2021
### HMCIP Report, published 1st March 2022

Thameside is a modern category B local prison in south-east London that contained 1,194 prisoners at the time of our inspection. Around 60% of those held were on remand or unsentenced and almost a quarter were category C prisoners who were often at the end of their sentence and preparing for release.

The prison had been too slow to increase the amount of time that prisoners were unlocked, with those in the induction and drugs wing spending little more than half an hour a day out of their cells. Remand prisoners were locked up for up to 23.5 hours a day with very few activities on offer; this was particularly concerning for the 60 prisoners who had been on remand for more than a year. A Covid-19 outbreak that occurred just as the prison was entering stage two of the HMPPS five stage recovery framework meant that restrictions could not be lifted, but since then leaders should have done more to open up the regime and increase what was on offer for prisoners.

Offender management unit (OMU) staff were doing some excellent work in the prison – they proactively contacted prisoners, were a visible presence on the wings and provided good support. This was the best provision I had seen during the last year and, because the prison had outsourced offender management work to Catch 22, staff were not cross deployed to other duties as we so often see in jails. Despite this, the reunification of probation services had badly affected the large remand population, as essential support with housing, benefits and managing debt (that was previously provided by community rehabilitation companies) was removed overnight.

At our last inspection we had been critical of the segregation unit and we were pleased to see that it was now much improved. Usage had fallen and those who were there had a more predictable regime and were encouraged back into the prison by a caring and well-led staff team. Segregated prisoners were supported by a strong psychology team who offered guidance and helped to create support packages. This service provided all segregation unit staff regular, one-to-one meetings to talk about the challenges with dealing with this complex and often violent group of prisoners. Other prisons would do well to emulate and learn from this practice.

Leaders had focused on improving the use and quality of body-worn cameras to record use of force incidents and it was pleasing to see that the uptake had increased significantly in response. This is an issue that we frequently raise in our inspections and it was good to see it being addressed at Thameside.

Education at the jail had only recently restarted and could accommodate six prisoners per classroom, but in roll-checks during the inspection there were, on average, fewer than three prisoners in each lesson. Lessons were inexplicably long at three hours, and only prisoners who had been allocated their education in the morning were allowed to attend in the afternoon. This meant only a tiny proportion of the population was being taught. Education was rated inadequate by Ofsted. The education provider and prison leaders needed to apply some real control and ambition, getting many more prisoners into education and training.

There was some impressive, innovative work to incentivise better behaviour from younger prisoners and rather than separating members of different gangs, the prison was working to improve relationships and keep them living together. The strong and experienced governor, supported by some effective functional heads of department, had a clear set of priorities for the future. Inspectors were impressed to see leaders challenging some poor staff practice and disciplining or dismissing those who had seriously breached the rules. While the governor had been able to put in place some incentives, the prison's biggest, ongoing challenge will remain recruiting and retaining enough high-quality staff so that it can expand the regime and make sure that prisoners, particularly those on remand, are given opportunities for education and training.

Charlie Taylor
HM Chief Inspector of Prisons January 2022

## INDEPENDENT MONITORING BOARD: Annual Report

The law requires every prison to be monitored by an independent Board appointed by the Justice Secretary; these are known as Independent Monitoring Boards (IMBs). The IMB must satisfy itself as to the humane and just treatment of those held in custody within its prison and the range and adequacy of the programmes preparing them for release; it must report annually to the Justice Secretary on how well the prison has met the standards and requirements placed on it.

### IMB Report July 2020 – June 2021
### Published October 2021
#### Background to the report

Throughout 2020/2021 HMP Thameside has operated to a Covid-19 exceptional delivery model (EDM) regime set by HMPPS. In April 2021 it received HMPPS permission to move from EDM stage 4 (lockdown regime) into EDM stage 3 (restricted regime), the first London prison to do so.

This move allowed for some limited easing of the prisoner regime including an increase from 30 to

60 minutes' daily outdoor exercise and the reintroduction of social visits and outdoor gym in controlled groups. In early September 2021 the prison received permission to move from EDM stage 3 to a stage 2 regime, providing further incremental regime easing.

While this positive direction of travel in returning to regime normalisation is welcome, in the period covered by this annual report ending 30 June 2021 the daily norm for most prisoners has been to spend 23 hours or more in a shared cell. Board members have visited the prison throughout the year, though with less frequency and presence on the wings than in past years. Staff from important functions in the prisoner resettlement area including education, probation and housing for prisoners on release withdrew from the prison for several months. These factors have affected the level of monitoring evidence available to the Board in finalising some areas of this annual report.

### Main judgements
### How safe is the prison?

The prison has taken effective measures to contain and prevent the spread of Covid-19 in challenging circumstances. The majority of confirmed cases of the virus at Thameside were brought in by prisoners arriving at reception from other prisons or the outside community. Testing of staff was introduced once testing kits became available. No prisoners have died from the virus, but sadly one staff member died from Covid-19 during the reporting year.

Several initiatives aimed at more active and pre-emptive prisoner safety management and monitoring have been introduced this year including more targeted use of the challenge, support and intervention plan (CSIP) to tackle violence and a revised approach to gang members. A more active focus on assessment, care in custody and teamwork (ACCT) and self-harming has been introduced. The Board welcomes these positive developments though it is difficult to judge their effectiveness until the prison emerges more fully from extended lockdown. No mandatory drug testing was carried out this year. Reliable data to assess the extent and nature of the continuing problem of prisoner drug use has therefore been unavailable.

### How fairly and humanely are prisoners treated?

The lockdown measures taken to keep prisoners safe during the pandemic have unfortunately come at a cost to acceptable norms of humane treatment. The Board has considerable concerns at the longer-term impact on the mental and physical health and wellbeing of prisoners who have endured prolonged periods of confinement

and lack of socialisation. An IMB survey of prisoners found that overall the prison was felt to have handled the lockdown fairly, though there was perceived favouritism in the allocation of jobs. The majority of staff interactions with prisoners are observed by the Board to be positive and professional.

There has been a welcome drive to tackle long standing facilities management failings affecting the residential wings. Complaints to prison managers about accommodation issues increased by 59% this year. Management of the lengths of stay in the care and separation unit has improved; the Board would like to see evidence from body-worn video cameras being available in adjudications. Committed support by the chaplaincy team has been provided on the residential wings throughout the year to prisoners of all faiths and none. The prison's processes for investigating allegations of bullying and assault by staff referred by the IMB have made some improvement but remain disappointing overall.

### How well are prisoners' health and wellbeing needs met?

The incremental steps taken to ease daily regimes and provide prisoners with more out of cell time are welcomed, though the IMB regrets the frequent cancellation of gym activities since they restarted. In the prisoner survey about the prison's handling of lockdown, overwhelmingly those who responded wanted more gym and exercise classes above anything else. There has been a concerning low take-up of Covid-19 vaccines by the prisoner population.

The Board again reports the unacceptable delays in the transfer of severely mentally ill patients to secure establishments with more suitable facilities. While this is not within the healthcare provider's control, the daily dispensing of medication is, and there have been serious lapses in this regard reported to the IMB. One is the subject of an independent investigation by the NHS Commissioner. The IMB receives more applications about healthcare matters than any other issue, and considers improvement is needed by the healthcare provider in handling complaints.

### How well are prisoners progressed towards successful resettlement?

Progression towards successful resettlement was compromised in several areas by the extended lockdown and the absence from the prison of key staff, notably in education. However, positive developments included the introduction of Purple Visits that enable prisoners to meet their families by video link, innovative work by the library staff and the overdue transfer from Thameside of life sentenced and category D prisoners to more suitable establishments. The Board is unable to comment on the help given to prisoners this year to secure accommodation and employment on release due to the unavailability of information.

## Main areas for development
### TO THE MINISTER
The Board has considerable concerns at the longer-term impact on the mental and physical health and wellbeing, and potentially the future behaviours, of prisoners who have endured prolonged periods of confinement and lack of socialisation.

While staff employed by the prison operator and the healthcare provider have worked ceaselessly throughout the pandemic in the interest of prisoners, staff employed in important prisoner resettlement activities have operated remotely with varying degrees of actual engagement. The education contractor, Novus, provided almost no service to prisoners. Foreign national prisoners, and especially those subject to IS91, have suffered from an absence of Home Office immigration staff visiting the prison and progression of their cases. Many prisoners have been released from Thameside this year with far less resettlement support on accommodation and other matters than they would have received prior to the pandemic.

Delays in transferring severely mentally ill prisoners to secure establishments that provide more specialist treatment have been a longstanding concern of the Board. While the government's positive response to Sir Simon Wessely's mental health review is noted, transfer wait times for these vulnerable individuals have remained this year overall in excess of NHS England guidelines.

### TO THE PRISON SERVICE
The Board was concerned at the number of prisoners arriving at HMP Thameside on transfer from other prisons with Covid-19 symptoms. Some developed into confirmed cases. While all arrivals were subject to the prison's reverse cohorting procedures, these transfers placed other prisoners and Thameside staff at risk.

HMPPS is understood to be reviewing lessons learnt from the lockdown for post-Covid prison regimes. The Board stresses to HMPPS the importance of all prisoners having the opportunity to engage in regular purposeful out of cell activities and jobs. However there are insufficient such opportunities at present in Thameside for a prison of 1200 men. To make up this deficiency will require investment. Out of cell socialisation time (association), appropriately managed, is also essential for the welfare of prisoners, and should not be seen as optional.

### TO THE DIRECTOR
The Board welcomes the Director's strong, top-down authoritative leadership focused on positive change initiatives (such as in the management of prison safety) and reinforcing the responsibilities and accountabilities of managers and staff. Important areas of the core prison regime are now more tightly and purposefully managed, as detailed in the main evidence sections (especially in section 4).

The Board would like to see the same concentrated focus on improving the quality of the daily lives of prisoners where these can be influenced by the actions of staff, especially in the residential areas. IMB members regularly observe how poor communication between managers can stifle improved outcomes for prisoners, and how lack of empathy or thought can rob them of legitimate entitlements. Examples are contained in the report's main evidence sections.

### Progress since the last report
Positive developments noted by the Board during the year include:

• A significant shift in approach towards more active and pre-emptive management and monitoring of safety within the prison, including management of the ACCT process.

• A radical change to housing gang members in the prison.

• More collection and analysis of data and trends affecting prison safety (see introduction to section 4 and sections.

• Staff refresher instruction and upskilling in the use of force, and insistence on timely and accurate completion of use of force paperwork.

• Enforcing the wearing and use of body-worn video cameras, though evidence from them remained unavailable for prisoner adjudications.

• Decline in drugs finds, though the absence this year of data from mandatory drug testing has obscured the extent of drug availability.

• Reduced average lengths of stay in the CSU through better management in the unit.

• Investment in a new in-cell computer system (CMS) in place of existing legacy equipment.

• More focused and responsive facilities management efforts to repair damaged residential wing facilities and equipment and overhaul fire safety systems.

• Decline in complaints about property going missing within the prison, suggesting an improvement in cell clearance procedures.

• Introduction of Purple Visits providing prisoners and their families/friends the opportunity of virtual social visits.

• Thameside was the first London prison to receive permission to move out of a lockdown regime based on detailed plans submitted to HMPPS and effective control of Covid-19.

• Widening the attendance at the Director's morning meetings to all senior managers including the heads of the non-custodial and external agency teams has encouraged a more joined-up approach across the prison.

• Opening of the new video conference centre providing virtual courts. Completed to a high standard and managed with efficiency and pride, it has reduced the need for prisoner escorts to and from outside courts.

**THORN CROSS
ARLEY ROAD
APPLETON THORN
WARRINGTON
CHESHIRE, WA4 4RL**

**HM PRISON SERVICE
HMP & YOI THORN CROSS**

**Tel: 01925 805100**

*For the latest reports on this prison please visit:*
https://tinyurl.com/bdfh26rv

*Important Changes:* **(1) Visits:** the identification necessary to access this prison and visit for social or professional purposes has changed; (2) **Money and Gifts** new rules now apply to these. See page 16 for full details of the above.

**Task of the establishment** HMP/YOI Thorn Cross is a category D open resettlement prison for young adult and adult male prisoners.

**Certified normal accommodation and operational capacity**
Prisoners held at the time of this visit: 316
Baseline certified normal capacity: 327
In-use certified normal capacity: 385
Operational capacity: 325 (temporary reduction for fire safety improvement project)

**Prison status and key providers**
Public
Prison Group: Greater Manchester, Merseyside & Cheshire
Prison Group Director: Tim Allen
Governor/Director: Richard Suttle
IMB Chair: Geoffrey Thomas
Physical health provider: Greater Manchester Mental Health (GMMH) NHS Foundation Trust
Mental health provider: GMMH
Substance misuse treatment provider: Change, Grow, Live (CGL)
Prison education framework provider: Novus
Community rehabilitation company (CRC): Cheshire and Greater Manchester Escort contractor: GeoAmey

**Brief history** HMP/YOI Thorn Cross was purpose built in 1985 as an open establishment for male juvenile and young prisoners. It was re-roled in 2008 to become a prison for 18- to 25-year-old men but, due to the decrease in prisoners under 25, this upper age limit was removed in 2013.

**Short description of residential units**
Units 1-5 - Each unit has 60 single rooms. Unit 4 is currently closed to enable the installation of a new fire alarm system.
Unit 6 - An enhanced unit with 10 single rooms for prisoners who are ready to progress to outside work opportunities. An additional four rooms can be used if a prisoner needs to be held securely before being transferred back to closed conditions.
Unit 7 - Unit 7 has 33 single rooms and is a reverse cohort unit.
Unit 8 - Unit 8 has 44 individual self-contained temporary living units to accommodate prisoners on workouts and those who are shielding or isolating.

**Visiting Information**
Thorn Cross is currently running visits based on prisoner applications. Family and friends will then be contacted by the prison to arrange visits.
**Visiting times:** Friday, Saturday: 1:45pm to 3:45pm, Sunday: 9:45am to 11.45am and 1:45pm to 3:45pm

**Legal visits:** You can book a legal visit via the prisoner's legal advisor. Tuesdays and Thursdays: 9am to 12pm
Booking line: 01925 805018 Booking line opening times: 8:30am to 12pm Monday to Friday.

**INSPECTIONS & REPORTS**
**Scrutiny visit: 12–13 and 20–21 April 2021 report published 25 May 2021**
Thorn Cross is an open prison in Cheshire holding adult male prisoners, most of whom are serving lengthy or indeterminate sentences. At the time of our visit, there were 316 prisoners, 17% fewer than at our last full inspection in 2016 and slightly below the uncrowded capacity of 325.
The fundamental purpose of Thorn Cross is to prepare prisoners for their return to the community and previous full inspections found that it had performed this role consistently well. However, the pandemic had severely and understandably disrupted the prison's ability to sustain previous levels of pre-release preparation and support. While much resettlement provision remained in place and key tasks such as parole assessments were being completed, there was far less release on temporary licence (ROTL) for the

purposes of work or training than in the past. Face-to-face contact with offender managers and resettlement support services had also been very limited and prisoners were often frustrated about their inability to obtain information from the offender management unit. Prison leaders had not done enough to address this problem.

In most other respects, Thorn Cross remained an impressive establishment with a culture and physical environment that supported rehabilitative endeavour and delivered positive outcomes for prisoners. Relationships between staff and prisoners were mature and respectful. Complaints were managed well and leaders had continued to undertake a good level of prisoner consultation. Leaders were aware of prisoners' main concerns and tangible actions were usually being taken to address them. The management of equality and diversity had been improving and was reasonable, although many black and minority ethnic prisoners lacked confidence in the fairness of prison procedures. Security was proportionate and it was encouraging that relatively few prisoners were returned to closed conditions. There was little violence, use of force or self-harm, but governance of segregation and use of force was weak.

The prison had progressed to a 'level three' regime shortly before our visit. Social visits had resumed and were popular, and there had been encouraging early progress towards increasing the number of prisoners able to benefit from ROTL. Notably, subject to appropriate risk assessment, a few prisoners had been able to undertake essential community work placements since autumn 2020.

Our Ofsted colleagues concluded that prison leaders had worked flexibly and innovatively to maintain a broad education, skills and work curriculum throughout the Covid-19 restrictions. The vast majority of prisoners were engaged in some form of work, training or education, and much of it was good quality. About a third of available education and training places were unfilled and more could have been done to increase the number of prisoners taking part in full-time activity.

Health care provision was also impressive and a very high percentage of prisoners in our survey said that the quality was good. An outbreak of Covid-19 in February 2021 had been managed efficiently and was resolved quickly with the cooperation of prisoners, who understood and accepted the extra restrictions that were imposed. Reverse cohorting procedures were effective and prisoners on the unit still had access to key services and could easily use an outside exercise area.

Overall, this scrutiny visit found a prison that had coped well with the challenges of the pandemic and was making reasonably good progress in safely increasing its provision. Prison leaders had realistic plans to improve the currently insufficient rehabilitative provision, which were supported by a positive staff culture, a good physical environment and generally good safety outcomes. An immediate challenge was to improve communication and dialogue between prisoners and their offender managers.

Charlie Taylor, HM Chief Inspector of Prisons
May 2021

### Key concerns and recommendations

Key concerns and recommendations identify the issues of most importance to improving outcomes for prisoners and are designed to help establishments prioritise and address the most significant weaknesses in the treatment and conditions of prisoners.

During this visit we identified some areas of key concern and have made a small number of recommendations for the prison to address.

Key concern: Governance of use of force and segregation was weak. Use of force paperwork was not completed thoroughly or checked for quality. A questionable use of a baton had not been reviewed by managers. The use of segregation was not always properly authorised or risk assessed.

Recommendation: The use of force and segregation should be subject to rigorous management oversight which provides assurance that they are used proportionately and accountably. (To the governor)

Key concern: Although there was little self-harm, there had been three serious incidents since the start of the pandemic, which had not been subject to review to establish lessons that could be learned.

Recommendation: All serious incidents of self-harm should be reviewed so that lessons can be learned. (To the governor)

Key concern: Prisoners were frustrated at the lack of regular face-to-face engagement and communication with their offender managers. They were unable to attend the offender management unit (OMU) without an appointment and often had to resort to asking wing staff to follow up queries on their behalf. The OMU was short of staff and face-to-face work was limited.

Recommendation: Effective communication strategies should be implemented to make sure that prisoners are informed about the progression of their cases and are able to contribute to key processes involving them, such as ROTL boards and sentence plan reviews. (To the governor)

Key concern: Attendance at the interdepartmental risk-management meeting was variable. Key departments were not always represented and minutes reflected few actions. Impending high-risk releases were not systematically considered, which was a significant omission.

Recommendation: A multidisciplinary risk management meeting should review all high and very high risk-of-harm prisoners before their release and make sure that suitable actions are taken. (To the governor)

### Education, skills and work (Ofsted)

During this visit Ofsted inspectors conducted an interim assessment of the provision of education, skills and work in the establishment. They identified steps that the prison needed to take to meet the needs of prisoners, including those with special educational needs and disabilities.

### Next steps

Leaders and managers should maximise the take up of allocated places in education and training. Leaders and managers should increase swiftly the numbers of prisoners on work placements in the community, including voluntary and paid work, education and training.

### Notable positive practice

We define notable positive practice as innovative practice or practice that leads to particularly good outcomes from which other establishments may be able to learn. Inspectors look for evidence of good outcomes for prisoners; original, creative or particularly effective approaches to problem-solving or achieving the desired goal; and how other establishments could learn from or replicate the practice.

Inspectors found six examples of notable positive practice during this visit.

Despite the constraints of the pandemic and the frustration that many prisoners felt about lack of progression, Thorn Cross had retained a positive culture characterised by constructive and mature relationships between most prisoners and staff.

The pre-fabricated 'pods' provided good quality living conditions for more than 40 prisoners and were popular among prisoners.

Effective prisoner consultation had been maintained, including through weekly Prison Council meetings and forums for prisoners with protected characteristics. This consultation was appreciated by prisoners and had resulted in tangible actions; it also helped to support prisoner confidence in and communication with staff.

Safer custody and mental health staff jointly assessed and, where necessary, supported patients with complex needs and vulnerability. This coordination of care avoided duplication of effort and enhanced shared understanding of prisoners' needs.

The availability of naloxone nasal spray, in addition to injections, enabled easier administration and swifter absorption of the medicine in an emergency. The uptake of naloxone on release had increased as patients were more open to using the spray rather than needles and syringes.

Prisoners continued to be allowed to use their own mobile phones to maintain contact with their friends and family, including via video-calls, even after the reintroduction of social visits. This was a popular and effective means of promoting family ties.

### INDEPENDENT MONITORING BOARD: Annual Report

The law requires every prison to be monitored by an independent Board appointed by the Justice Secretary; these are known as Independent Monitoring Boards (IMBs). The IMB must satisfy itself as to the humane and just treatment of those held in custody within its prison and the range and adequacy of the programmes preparing them for release; it must report annually to the Justice Secretary on how well the prison has met the standards and requirements placed on it.

### IMB Report 1 May 2021 – 30 April 2022
**Published July 2022**
**Executive summary**
**Background to the report**

Unsurprisingly, this reporting year has seen the management of the pandemic dominating the work of the prison. Positive cases have been reported throughout most of the year, with 13 being the highest number amongst the prisoners at any one time. The prison has managed these cases well, ensuring that all prisoners could have as near a normal regime as possible. Level 1 (the least restrictive level of the Prison Service's Covid regime management) has been achieved but wisely the prison has reintroduced the normal regime gradually to avoid slipping back. A major challenge this year has been the level of staff absence, not all of which has been Covid related. The Acting Governor has managed this proactively and the level of absence has been gradually falling. Missing staff inevitably increased the workload of the staff who were in work, which for part of the year also affected morale. Support for staff is available from a variety of sources, which are widely advertised by way of posters, email reminders and the regular employee newsletter. As absence reduced it was possible to increase the minimum number of staff for each shift.

This year has again seen a number of staffing changes. The Governor has been on a secondment to another prison and shortly after arriving back he left to start another secondment. There have also been some vacancies in a variety of roles, which are now starting to be filled.

The level of absconds has increased from 12 to 17 in comparison with 2020- 21. Although this is lower than the 22 in 2019-20. Each abscond is thoroughly investigated to see if any lessons can be learned. This has been subject to external review by the Prison Service, the results of which are not known at the time of writing.

## Main judgements
### How safe is the prison?
Thorn Cross is a safe establishment where incidents of violence and bullying continue to be rare. The rise in absconds is being managed robustly with a clear action plan. The strong security objective to disrupt and deter drug trafficking and supply has had an impact this year.

### How fairly and humanely are prisoners treated?
The men are treated well. The staff know the men and are able to respond to their needs. The accommodation is of a good standard. Staff are visible through the estate. The relationships between the staff and the prisoners are good. The regime is courteous, respectful and good humoured.

### How well are prisoners' health and wellbeing needs met?
The healthcare services are good with services reflecting or bettering those in the community. Healthcare needs are well assessed and the range of clinics offered is impressive. The dedicated mental health service is providing an invaluable service and is appreciated by the prisoners.

### How well are prisoners progressed towards successful resettlement?
Thorn Cross has a rehabilitative culture, which permeates all areas of the establishment. There is positive partnership working with outside agencies and employers. Provision is bespoke.

## Main areas for development
### TO THE MINISTER
To ensure that the prison budget keeps pace with the inflationary pressures, which are now being felt. To ensure that the ministerial oversight of high risk prisoners transferring to the open estate does not cause undue delay.

### TO THE PRISON SERVICE
To resolve the continuing issues with the transfer of property so that less of it goes missing and when it does there is a swift remedy.
To continue the controlled use of mobile phones, as it maintains family ties and so aids rehabilitation.

To provide decent fire retardant seating consistent with the ethos of the open estate.
To ensure that sending prisons complete records fully.

### TO THE GOVERNOR
To continue to pursue initiatives that will reduce the number of absconds.
To extend the number of areas of prison activity that are analysed in terms of protected characteristics.
To increase mandatory drug testing to at least pre-pandemic levels.
To train members of the Prison Council so that they are better equipped to fulfil their role.
To ensure that the infrastructure is such that it can manage any increase in number.
To learn from the experiences of the recent introduction of extra accommodation, resulting in better planning and implementation of any future new accommodation.

### Progress since the last report
Issue raised previously *Progress since previous report*
Increase in the number of open prison places nationally *There has been no increase in places but an increase is planned for 2023*
Adequate resources to meet the needs of more complex prisoners *New working arrangements have enabled more resources to be put into supporting prisoners with more complex needs*
Lack of approved premises *By the end of the reporting year, places were available as required*
Continued authorised use of mobile phones *The use of mobile phones has been suspended pending a review of staffing*
Review of arrangements that allow for prisoners to transfer directly from a high security setting *The transfer of high security prisoners now requires more liaison between the sending prison and Thorn Cross and will be subject to prison offender manager approval*
Provision of decent fire retardant seating for prisoners' rooms *A wider range of seating is now available but has not yet been bought*
Property being lost during transfer *This is a service wide issue and a review into how the prison manages this continues*
Upgrade of IT systems *This is due to take place in June 2022 resulting in a more efficient and reliable systems*
Impact of OMiC staffing model *Staff have adjusted well to the new structure and outcomes for prisoners have improved, particularly from the increase in probation staff*
Reduction in the amount of contraband brought into the estate by intruders *Improved perimeter security and changed shift patterns has brought about a significant reduction in the amount of contraband brought in*
Reassessment of methods used to identify prisoners who are at risk of absconding so

number of absconds continues to fall *Each abscond is carefully investigated and an abscond strategy has been developed. However, the number of absconds increased this reporting year.*

Maintenance of virtual and in person visits *In person visits have become more frequent during the year and are preferred over virtual visits, which have consequently declined*

Diversity and Equality Action Team meeting regularly and provision of data on all aspects of the prison's work *Monitoring of protected characteristics across all aspects of the prison's work has not happened and DEAT meetings are not held at least quarterly*

Provision of regular complaints monitoring information *Lack of staffing has meant that although data is more frequently provided it is still sometimes incomplete*

**47 MARYPORT ST
USK, MON
NP15 1XP**

**HM PRISON
USK**    **Tel: 01291 671600**

*For the latest reports on this prison please visit:*
https://tinyurl.com/bdfh26rv

*Important Changes:* **(1) Visits:** the identification necessary to access this prison and visit for social or professional purposes has changed; (2) **Money and Gifts** new rules now apply to these. See page 16 for full details of the above.

**Task of the establishment** Usk is an adult men's category C national sex offender treatment provider and resettlement prison. Prescoed is an adult and young adult men's open resettlement prison.

**Certified normal accommodation and operational capacity**
*Usk*
Prisoners held at the time of inspection: 220
Baseline certified normal capacity: 159
In-use certified normal capacity: 159
Operational capacity: 254
*Prescoed*
Prisoners held at the time of inspection: 231
Baseline certified normal capacity: 260
In-use certified normal capacity: 260
Operational capacity: 260

**Population of the prison**
*Usk*
45% of the population was over 50 years of age.
10.45% of the prisoners were from black and ethnic minority backgrounds.

10 prisoners were foreign nationals.
12 prisoners had less than two months left to serve.
78.18% of prisoners were sentenced to five years or more.
99.09% of prisoners had been convicted of a sexual offence.
8.63% of men were working with the substance use team.
*Prescoed*
21.05% of the population were over 50 years of age.
14.91% of the prisoners were from black and ethnic minority backgrounds. There were no foreign national prisoners at HMP Prescoed.
27 (11.84%) had less than two months left to serve.
72.26% of prisoners were sentenced to five years or more.
8.33% of prisoners had been convicted of a sexual offence.
13.15% of prisoners were working with the substance use team.

**Prison status and key providers**
Public
Prison Group: Wales
Executive Director: Giles Mason
Governor/Director: Rob Denman
IMB Chair: Julian Williams
Physical and mental health provider:
Aneurin Bevan University Health Board
Substance use treatment provider: Dyfodol
Prison education framework provider:
HM Prison and Probation Service (HMPPS)
Escort contractor: GeoAmey

**Brief history** Usk opened in 1844 as a house of correction. In 1870, it became the county gaol for Monmouthshire and remained in that role until 1922, when it closed. It reopened in 1939 as a closed borstal and became a detention centre in 1964. In 1983, it was turned into a youth custody centre, and from 1988 to 1990 a young offender institution. Since May 1990, it has been an adult category C establishment largely holding men convicted of sexual offences. It became a resettlement prison in 2019.

Prescoed opened in 1939 as an open borstal. It became a detention centre in 1964, an open youth custody centre in 1983 and an open young offender institution in 1988. Some years later it also started holding category D adult men. Since 2004, it has been exclusively an open prison for adult males, including young adult men aged 18 to 21.

**Short description of residential units**
*At Usk*, the accommodation consisted of four wings:
A, B and C – each with two-storey landings. A1 landing was used as protective isolation units (PIU) (accommodation for known or probably

Covid-19 cases) and reverse cohort units (RCU) during the height of the pandemic.

D wing – a single-storey shielding unit.

*At Prescoed*, there were 10 residential units; all except the Lester unit were single storey, consisting of a mixture of single and double rooms: The Mitchell unit - larger single room accommodation for prisoners working in the community.

Two semi-detached houses – accommodation for up to eight longer term men, assisting them to prepare for release.

Forty temporary pods with their own en-suite facilities, 20 of which had been used as PIU and RCU during Covid-19, and the remainder accommodating those working outside the prison.

## Visiting Information

Book online at: www.gov.uk/prison-visits or by telephone on 01291 671 730 Monday to Friday 5pm to 7pm.

**Visiting Times:** Tuesday, Thursday, and Friday 2pm to 4pm, Wednesday 2pm to 4pm and 5pm to 7pm, Saturday, Sunday 2pm to 4pm

## Legal visits:

Book legal visits on 01291 671 730 Monday to Friday, 9am to 11am and 2pm to 4pm

**Visiting times:** Tues and Wed: 9am to midday.

## INSPECTIONS & REPORTS

**Date of last full inspection 14–25 June 2021**
**HMCIP Report, published 1 October 2021**

Usk and Prescoed, as the names suggest, are two distinct prisons, although managed as a single entity. Usk is a small establishment built in a traditional 19th century style which held 220 category C prisoners, almost all of whom were serving sentences for sexual offences. Prescoed is an open prison in a deeply rural setting about three miles away, with a clear focus on the resettlement of the 231 men it held during our inspection.

In recent years the Inspectorate has routinely reported very positively on the outcomes experienced by prisoners at the two sites and this remains the case. Making separate healthy prison assessments, we judged outcomes in safety and respect to be good (our highest mark) at both Usk and Prescoed and reasonably good or better at both for purposeful activity and rehabilitation and release planning. These are excellent results made more noteworthy in that they were achieved while the prisons were still emerging from the effects of the pandemic. It should be noted that Usk, in particular, had faced very real challenges and risks in responding to Covid-19, with a generally older and more vulnerable population and the tragic loss of two members of staff and a prisoner. The

prison had, in our view, shown remarkable resilience in its response.

Key to the continuing success of the prisons seemed to be the quality of leadership. There was a genuine sense of community within the prisons with an engaged staff and generally good consultation with those held. It was clear from our survey that prisoners felt respected and supported by staff and we observed several examples during our inspection where the well-being of prisoners was at the heart of initiatives and a clear consideration in how the prison was being taken forward. One such example was the formal endorsement of Usk as an Enabling Environment, an accreditation achieved during the pandemic (see paragraphs 1.45 and 3.5). Similarly, we observed some exemplary social care arrangements.

As the pandemic seemed to be easing, both prisons had moved quickly within the HMPPS risk management framework to open up their regimes and we were told that the prisons were among the first to advance to HM Prison and Probation Service (HMPPS) 'stage 2', a designation that defines the extent to which regimes could be opened further. In this context, it was pleasing to see that release on temporary licence (ROTL) had continued during restrictions for those Prescoed prisoners who were defined as essential workers, and that by the time of our inspection, some 60% of Prescoed prisoners were now benefiting from various forms of ROTL. More needed to be done to ensure work and education became fully operational but we had confidence in the prisons' plans and their long-established record of delivery.

Our report notes a small number of issues that require further attention. These include some refurbishment of accommodation at Prescoed and mitigating the impact of some overcrowding in Usk. We have also noted the comparatively high number of prisoners who were returned to closed conditions from Prescoed, possibly linked to the application of a so-called 'zero tolerance' policy concerning the application of rules at the site. But these issue aside, it was clear to us that the resilience being shown by Usk and Prescoed leaders, staff and prisoners was ensuring that those held continued to experience meaningful and positive outcomes.

Charlie Taylor

HM Chief Inspector of Prisons August 2021

### Safety

At the last inspection of HMP Usk and HMP and YOI Prescoed in 2017 we found that outcomes for prisoners were good against this healthy prison test. At this inspection we found that outcomes for prisoners remained good.

Peer workers provided new arrivals with good support, and staff were friendly and efficient. However, prisoners were not always able to make a phone call on their first night at Usk.

Levels of violence at both sites remained extremely low. Very few prisoners absconded from Prescoed, although the number of returns to closed conditions was higher than from most other open prisons. A 'zero-tolerance policy' meant any behaviour that might be termed violent or involve the misuse of drugs or a mobile phone led to an immediate return to closed conditions, without appearing to consider any mitigation or the impact on the individual.

Use of force was rare, and oversight was good. There was no designated segregation unit at Usk or Prescoed, but prisoners returning to closed conditions from Prescoed were placed in a holding room that had an unscreened toilet and no chair. Security systems were proportionate, information was well managed, and very good local tactical assessments were communicated well to staff. All strip-searching at Prescoed was intelligence led, but it still took place routinely following social visits at Usk.

There had been one self-inflicted death at Usk since the previous inspection. Levels of self-harm remained very low in both prisons. The standard of assessment, care in custody and teamwork case management documents for prisoners at risk of suicide or self-harm was mostly good. Access to Listeners (prisoners trained by the Samaritans to provide confidential emotional support to fellow prisoners) at both prisons was also good and the well-being garden at Prescoed was welcoming.

The safeguarding adults policy was comprehensive and there were well established links with the local authority. Staff knew about the referral process.

### Respect

At the last inspection of HMP Usk and HMP and YOI Prescoed in 2017 we found that outcomes for prisoners were good against this healthy prison test. At this inspection we found that outcomes for prisoners remained good.

Most prisoners in our survey reported respectful treatment and said they had a member of staff they could go to for help. We observed friendly and helpful interactions, and regular electronic case note entries provided good evidence of engagement.

Prisoners were also very positive about residential issues at both prisons. Shower areas had been refurbished to a decent standard. Although cells were generally in a good state of repair, too many prisoners at Usk still lived in cramped conditions, sharing cells designed for

one person. Prisoners at Prescoed were very content with their accommodation arrangements. External areas at both sites were impressive.

Self-catering facilities were too limited and available only to a small number of prisoners at Prescoed. New arrivals at Prescoed were not offered grocery packs, and prisoners at both Usk and Prescoed could wait up to nine days for their first full shop order.

Consultation arrangements at both prisons were good, and a new application process had been introduced. The number of complaints was lower than the average for similar prisons, and most responses were reasonable and timely.

The promotion of equality needed to improve, starting with an effective plan that detailed priorities for both prisons. There was reasonable and frequent consultation at Usk, leading to some better outcomes for minorities, but this was not replicated at Prescoed, where too much was left to the initiative of prisoners with insufficient support from staff and managers. Faith provision across both sites was well managed and prisoners said they received good pastoral care.

In our survey, 95% of patients said the overall quality of health services was very or quite good. Timely advice from Public Health Wales enabled leaders to manage the situation well during the Covid-19 pandemic. Primary care was very good and long-term conditions care had improved.

Social care arrangements were excellent and partnerships between the health care department, the local council and the prisons were effective. The responsive mental health team was easily accessible and offered support that the patients we spoke to valued. As in 2017, psychosocial services for patients with substance use problems were appropriate. The absence of the visiting pharmacist, due to Covid-19 redeployment, had led to a lack of professional oversight of pharmacy services. Dental services were good and waiting times for treatment were acceptable.

### Purposeful activity

At the last inspection of HMP Usk and HMP and YOI Prescoed in 2017 we found that outcomes for prisoners were reasonably good against this healthy prison test.

At this inspection we found that outcomes for prisoners remained reasonably good.

Prisoners at Usk had on average two hours and 45 minutes out of their cells a day to exercise outside, make a telephone call, have a shower and associate. This was not as good as we would have hoped but represented progress as the prison was among the first to move to stage 2 of the HMPPS recovery plan to ease Covid-19 regime restrictions. At Prescoed, access to outdoor areas was unrestricted until 8:30pm.

Libraries across both prisons operated during the pandemic despite the long absence of a librarian. Committed prisoners had kept services running, but library stocks needed replenishing. Physical education staff operated across both sites but were unable to deliver a full timetable due to insufficient staffing levels.

The prison had a clear recovery plan in place for education, enabling prisoners to resume activities, while observing social distancing. Prisoners in Prescoed had participated well in work placements in the community and at the prison farm throughout Covid-19 restrictions, while a few in Usk had been employed in essential prison jobs. Some prisoners had made progress on Open University courses or courses funded by the Prisoner Education Trust. Prisoners reported that teachers and staff had been supportive and helpful during Covid-19 restrictions, helping them to access books, internet printouts and art material, as well as worksheets. Mentors and orderlies encouraged and supported prisoners very effectively so they could take part in education sessions. Most prisoners knew what goals in their individual learning plans they had agreed and understood what they needed to do to make progress. Prisoners at both sites had reasonable access to computers, although laptops acquired for use in cells were not suitable, and material from the virtual campus (prisoner access to community education, training and employment opportunities via the internet) could not be accessed in classes.

The prison had interacted well with employers to extend the range of work placement opportunities for Prescoed prisoners. The prisons had also considered labour market information in its curriculum planning. A useful quality assurance plan was in place.

There were some bilingual displays and a few that promoted Welsh culture. However, the prison's own evaluation of its Welsh language provision was sometimes too positive and some targets within the Welsh language strategy were still to be met.

**Rehabilitation and release planning**

At the last inspection of HMP Usk in 2017 we found that outcomes for prisoners were reasonably good against this healthy prison test. At this inspection we found that outcomes for prisoners remained reasonably good.

At the last inspection of HMP and YOI Prescoed in 2017 we found that outcomes for prisoners were good against this healthy prison test. At this inspection we found that outcomes for prisoners remained good.

Face-to-face social visits had operated intermittently over the previous year in line with Public Health Wales guidance. Usk had made good use of a marquee to host visits outside. Family workers from the Prison Advice and Care Trust were back on site delivering services to prisoners and children.

Use of secure video calling (see Appendix II: Glossary of terms) at Prescoed was very good. However, at Usk uptake was much lower – in our survey, only 8% of prisoners said they had used the video calling facility. Many prisoners at Usk complained about limited access to prison phones. Comprehensive needs analyses of the population at each prison had recently been completed and used to inform a specific strategy for reducing reoffending. Nearly all prisoners had an offender assessment system report outlining their risks and needs, as well as a sentence plan, and nearly all had been reviewed in the previous 12 months. The standard of the sentence plans we examined was good.

The progress prisoners made against their sentence plans was reasonably good at Usk, but the curtailment of offending behaviour programmes during the regime restrictions had had an impact in some cases. In contrast, release on temporary licence (ROTL) had been maintained at Prescoed, so progress was good for most prisoners there.

Probation offender manager staffing levels were insufficient at Usk. Contact between prison and probation offender managers and prisoners had been adversely affected by Covid-19 restrictions in both prisons, but the impact was felt less severely at Prescoed, where many prisoners continued to be off site on ROTL. Offender management unit (OMU) clinics at Prescoed, held two evenings a week and at weekends, were appreciated.

Public protection arrangements were managed well. At Usk, the interdepartmental risk management team (IRMT) meeting routinely considered all new arrivals and those due for release, but Prescoed did not have an IRMT meeting, which meant there was a gap in oversight. However, we were confident that risk management and joint release planning with community offender managers were still being dealt with effectively.

The quality of prisoners' risk management plans was generally very good across both establishments. Prison and community offender managers worked well together to manage those subject to multi- agency public protection arrangements. Child contact restrictions and telephone monitoring for public protection purposes were well managed.

ROTL provision for prisoners at Prescoed undertaking essential work continued throughout the regime and community restrictions, which was good. Wider ROTL opportunities had been introduced as soon as restrictions allowed and, at the time of our inspection, over 60% of prisoners were on some form of ROTL.

The suspension of accredited behaviour programmes in March 2020 meant that some prisoners left Usk without having their treatment needs addressed. However, it was positive that they had resumed in September 2020, and access was prioritised appropriately. Plans to address the needs of prisoners who did not meet the threshold for programmes had been paused over the previous year.

Usk had been designated a training and resettlement prison and now also had community rehabilitation company provision in place. Prisoners across both sites received good support to make release planning arrangements, including help to address their accommodation needs.

### Key concerns and recommendations

Key concerns and recommendations identify the issues of most importance to improving outcomes for prisoners and are designed to help establishments prioritise and address the most significant weaknesses in the treatment and conditions of prisoners.

During this inspection we identified some areas of key concern and have made a small number of recommendations for the prison to address those concerns.

Key concern: Prescoed's zero-tolerance policy returned prisoners to closed conditions without due consideration of any mitigation, the overall impact on the prisoner and whether the decision was a proportionate response. The number of returns to closed conditions was higher than in most other open prisons.

Recommendation: Prisoners should only be returned to closed conditions following an appropriate re-categorisation review that fully considers all the circumstances and ensures that the decision is always a proportionate response. (To the governor)

Key concern: Aneurin Bevan University Health Board lead pharmacists had stopped providing regular input at Usk and Prescoed. This had led to: a failure to make sure that medicines were appropriate and patients knew how to take them; inadequate pharmacy staffing to make sure the supply of medicines was safe; a limited range of medicines for patients to buy to treat minor ailments or that did not require prescribing by a doctor; and gaps in the oversight of pharmacy service processes and procedures.

Recommendation: There should be more pharmacist involvement to oversee the service's professional standards, protocols and procedures to make sure the supply of medicines is safe. (To the governor)

### Notable positive practice

We define notable positive practice as innovative work or practice that leads to particularly good outcomes from which other establishments may be able to learn. Inspectors look for evidence of good outcomes for prisoners; original, creative or particularly effective approaches to problem-solving or achieving the desired goal; and how other establishments could learn from or replicate the practice.

Inspectors found four examples of notable positive practice during this inspection.

Following an assessment process which began before the pandemic, Usk had recently gained Enabling Environments accreditation, awarded by the Royal College of Psychiatrists to institutions and organisations that meet required standards for creating a positive environment and healthy relationships.

Social care arrangements were exemplary. Integrated social care staff were embedded in the prison and were driving service developments to meet the needs of the ageing population.

During pandemic restrictions, Prescoed had made highly effective use of its prison resources and its links with employers to maintain a high level of employment among prisoners. This has led to 45% of prisoners being employed in areas, such as, the farm, the market garden and the waste management unit. In addition, many prisoners were placed with employers outside the prison.

The OMU at Prescoed held evening and weekend clinics, providing prisoners with the opportunity to see offender managers out of hours, when they returned from work.

### INDEPENDENT MONITORING BOARD: Annual Report

The law requires every prison to be monitored by an independent Board appointed by the Justice Secretary; these are known as Independent Monitoring Boards (IMBs). The IMB must satisfy itself as to the humane and just treatment of those held in custody within its prison and the range and adequacy of the programmes preparing them for release; it must report annually to the Justice Secretary on how well the prison has met the standards and requirements placed on it.

**IMB Report 1 April 2020 – 31 March 2021**
**Published November 2021**
**Background to the report**
**Executive summary**
The Covid-19 pandemic has had a significant

impact on the Board's ability to research the contents of this annual report, which presents our findings for the period 1 April 2020 to 31 March 2021. The Board has covered as much ground as it can in the circumstances, but there is less detail and supporting evidence than usual – as will be noted, this period was completely covered by the varying stages of lockdown.

Ministers are aware of the constraints described but it is important to note that as far as the findings of this report are concerned:

• The Board continued to collect and analyse data throughout the period.

• Whilst regular physical monitoring was limited, we were still able to conduct some rota visits during the differing waves and stages of lockdown.

• Visits were supplemented by:

o regular weekly telephone contact with staff

o some (but infrequent) telephone contact with prisoner representatives

o attendance at weekly prison management meetings

o increased levels of data and feedback from the senior management team (SMT)

• The Board wishes to record the high level of cooperation it has received from the prisoners, staff, and the SMT in collecting information for this report.

From this the Board:

• Has triangulated our previous regular contact in the prison with the more limited monitoring we have been able to accomplish during the year.

• Derived information from data we and others have been able to collect.

• Considers its conclusions to be valid in that we have attempted to extract a realistic picture from evidence and experience. (See section 8.1 for a description of monitoring during lockdown.)

In addition, regular information is being collected on the prison's response to the pandemic, and that is being collated nationally.

Throughout this report, the Board has used phrases such as 'in general' and 'in the main', and we wish to specify what is meant by this. It is intended to indicate an informed 'real-world view' of the prison – things can occasionally go wrong, and it would be naive to suggest that any prison could get everything right all the time. The Board accepts this corrective to be true of all organisations, bodies, and individuals.

As can be seen from the entirety of this report, the Board considers HMP Usk and Prescoed to be effective, well-run prisons, following the concept of transparent review and continuous improvement. This opinion is derived from our direct observations, the views of prisoners as expressed to members and our triangulation of data supplied by the prison. It is supported by the reports of other bodies monitoring or inspecting the prison. These include Her Majesty's Inspectorate of Prisons (HMIP) and the Welsh Prison Group Director's quarterly reviews.

In addition, in 2020 the prison was awarded the College Centre for Quality Improvement's (CCQI) Enabling Environments award. This is awarded by the Royal College of Psychiatrists. See glossary section 8 for an explanation of what this means.

## Main judgements
### How safe is the prison?

The Board considers that both Usk and Prescoed are safe prisons, with low levels of violence, bullying and self-harm. Most men report feeling safe.

The prison had an effective strategy to respond to Covid-19 which was robust and well communicated. Clinically vulnerable prisoners have been shielded and its men were amongst the earliest (in the prison estate) to be vaccinated.

### How fairly and humanely are prisoners treated?

Due to Covid19, safety, fairness, and health in prisons were uniquely linked over the last year. It is the Board's view that the prison should be commended in the way it has managed the pandemic and considers this to be indicative of its wider management ethos.

Despite lockdown the Governor has managed to prioritise the principle of risk management rather than mere risk avoidance. This means that, whilst men have paid a high price for their safety, they have not seen these constraints as compromising either fairness or their humanity. Practical examples of this include:

• The prison was one of the first to be allowed to move to level 2 and increase the amount of time out of cell. (Not within the reporting period, but a useful indicator, the prison applied to move to stage 1 on 2.9.21)

• At HMP Prescoed 80 prisoners have opted to engage in the "Thursday food shopping day" – this is available to fully paid outworkers on ROTL. A step towards normality, it allows them to store a selection of sandwiches and microwavable meals for the evenings should they miss the hot meal service in the evening.

### How well are prisoners' health and wellbeing needs met?

The Board considers that the prison has coped well with the restrictions imposed by the pandemic and that it has provided healthcare comparable to that available in the community.

### How well are prisoners progressed towards successful resettlement?

Considering the restrictions operating during the reporting period, the Board considers that the prison has been successful in progressing men towards resettlement. In fact, many of its effects appear to have been ameliorated by the work of the prison and it is notable that workers from HMP Prescoed were enabled to continue their off-site placements throughout the period.

During the pandemic the prison has continued to work with the Prison Advice & Care Trust to ensure that support is available to both families and men during Covid19 restrictions.

**Main areas for development**
**TO THE MINISTER and the Minister of Health and Social Services of Wales**
Stage 4 lockdown (prisoners confined in their cells for 23 hours a day) succeeded in its aim to protect prisoner safety during the Covid19 pandemic but the consequences for these often-vulnerable people have been significant. The Board asks that the Minister recognises this and secures raised priority (through the JCVI) to enable officers and men to be included in future vaccination priority lists.

The current state of vaccine development in the UK suggests that other groups would not be disadvantaged by this policy. Future choke points are unlikely to be in vaccine design, testing, manufacturing, or the logistics of bulk delivery but in the final stage – getting it into individual arms. Prison healthcare professionals and trained officers are already in place to accomplish this task, without compromising community programmes.

**TO THE MINISTER for Education and Welsh Language**
Education is a key element in improving prisoner rehabilitation. After accounting for staff salary pay awards (mandated over the last few years) the Board is concerned that there has been an effective decrease in the value of funding the education department receives and that this will have a negative impact on prisoner outcomes.

**TO THE PRISON SERVICE**
As reported in our 2020 report, up to fifty per cent of the OASys documents received in HMP Usk vary in quality with the "start custody" section either remaining blank or the quality of recording falling short of expectation.

The Board would suggest that ways be explored to retain experienced and effective officers in HMPPS. The Board recognises the high level of skills required that enable an officer to facilitate a safe and rehabilitative culture.

With respect to the promotion of prison safety, the Board supports the concerns of Dame Anne Owers (letter to the Director General of Prisons, November 2020) regarding the decision that

making a ligature (also known as noose making) by prisoners should no longer be a nationally reportable self-harm incident.

**TO THE GOVERNOR**
Referring to our comments in the executive summary we have not much to add here other than to ask that the team expands their efforts to improve telephone access for the men in Usk.

**Progress since the last report**
Since both HMP Usk and Prescoed have operated under atypical Covid-safe regimes throughout the period of this report, making comparisons with earlier years is probably unproductive; however, the Board has noted the high level of productive cooperation between staff and men that has characterised this lockdown. Other progress includes:
• HMP Usk has gained the Enabling Environments qualification.
• Residential custody managers at Prescoed held regular update and Q & A sessions to keep men informed on what was happening during the Covid-19 lockdowns and why.
• Investment has been secured by the SMT to improve the fabric of both prisons. This has been noticeable in the refurbishment of the some of the toilets and showers in HMP Usk and the decommissioning and future replacement of the unsatisfactory Lester unit in HMP Prescoed.
• The additional 40 Bunkabin accommodation units in HMP Prescoed have worked well and allowed the prison to offer more single room accommodation during the pandemic. Twenty of these were used for stage 2 outworkers and the other 20 became a protective isolation unit (PIU). It would be good if the prison was allowed to keep these units permanently.
• In HMP Usk the prison was innovative in maximising possible exercise time for the men. For example, the sports field was split into areas to allow walking groups, group circuits and weight sessions and, depending on the weather, five sessions a day were run.
• To promote equality and diversity at Prescoed "Let's Talk" events were delivered on race and disability. Events celebrating Black History Month and Women's History Month were conducted for both staff and prisoners.
• The level of cooperation and trust between men and officers required to maintain a protracted lockdown is considerable. The fact that this has been achieved in a positive spirit is noteworthy.

HMP Prescoed had its operational capacity increased for men convicted of sexual offences (MCOSO) from 20 to 25.

**VERNE COMMON ROAD
PORTLAND
DORSET
DT5 1EQ**

**HM PRISON
THE VERNE**  **Tel: 01305 825000**

*For the latest reports on this prison please visit:*
https://tinyurl.com/bdfh26rv

*Important Changes:* **(1) Visits:** the identification necessary to access this prison and visit for social or professional purposes has changed; (2) **Money and Gifts** new rules now apply to these. See page 16 for full details of the above.

**Task of the establishment** HMP The Verne is a male category C training prison, for those convicted of sexual offences.

**Certified normal accommodation and operational capacity**
Prisoners held at the time of inspection: 576
Baseline certified normal capacity: 570
In-use certified normal capacity: 570
Operational capacity: 580

**Prison status and key providers**
Public
Prison Group: Avon & South Dorset
Prison Group Director: Paul Woods
Governor/Director: David Bourne
IMB Chair: Chris Miller
Physical health provider: Care UK Health and Rehabilitation Services Limited
Mental health provider: Care UK Health and Rehabilitation Services Limited
Substance use treatment provider: Care UK Health and Rehabilitation Services Limited
Prison education framework provider: Weston College
Escort contractor: GeoAmey Custodial Services

**Brief history** HMP The Verne is located on the Isle of Portland in Dorset. The Verne citadel, constructed using convict labour between 1857-81, served as Portland Harbour's primary defensive fortification. Many of the original buildings are still in use today and are Grade II or II* listed by Historic England. These buildings require constant upkeep and attention and cannot be altered without permission.
The Verne operated as a prison from 1949 until October 2013. It then housed an adult male immigration removal centre (IRC) from March 2014 until December 2017. On 28 July 2018, The Verne re-opened as an adult training prison, operated by Her Majesty's Prison and Probation

Service (HMPPS), for persons convicted of sexual offences (PCOSO).
The certified normal accommodation is 570; the operational capacity is 580. This will increase to 604 once Evershot wing is fully occupied following refurbishment.
Weston College provides most of the vocational and educational opportunities; these include tiling, bricklaying, barber shop, art and music. These are housed in the older 'casemates' part of the estate, as are the art room, library and multi-faith centre. Sports facilities at The Verne include:
• a well-used multi-use games area (MUGA)
• a larger playing field for football and cricket
• a well-equipped gymnasium and other outside exercise equipment.
Apart from education and health, HMPPS is responsible for all services currently offered in The Verne. Healthcare is provided by the Practice Plus Group. Social care forms part of the statutory duties of Dorset Council.
Voluntary organisations regularly entering the prison before Covid included: Age UK, Circles UK, the Samaritans, the Shannon Trust, Narcotics Anonymous and Alcoholics Anonymous (AA).

**Short description of residential units**
Constructed in the early 1970s, the greater part of the residential accommodation consists of three blocks each divided into two units. Each of the six wings - Arne, Abbotsbury, Bincombe, Blandford, Corfe and Chesil - has two spurs, each of twenty rooms, on both the first and second floors. The rooms do not have sanitation, but each spur has 24-hour access to WCs, washbasins and showers. Those residents employed in cleaning have maintained a very high standard of hygiene within all wings. On the ground floor of each unit there is a laundry, servery, dining area, communal area, and office. During lockdown a spur on Corfe was reserved for Covid positive prisoners needing to be isolated. New arrivals to the prison were housed on a spur on Bincombe until their Covid status could be determined.
Dorset wing is situated in the old 'casemate' part of the prison. All ten dormitories are on the ground floor with no stairs. This wing houses prisoners with mobility issues and social care needs. It has its own servery, WC and showers. £0.5m has recently been made available for a refurbishment of the recesses. Evershot wing comprises 24 portakabin-type pods. Each of these pods has its own WC and shower. This wing was used to house suspected Covid cases before those testing positive were moved to a dedicated spur on Bincombe.
At the beginning of 2020 there was a total loss of heating and hot water after all four boilers failed (under normal conditions, two boilers are in

operation). Portable heaters were purchased and distributed throughout the establishment, although this took some time. These did not provide an adequate level of heating in some areas and there were numerous complaints from prisoners. Extra bedding was made available for prisoners who required it. Temporary boilers were installed until the existing boilers were repaired. The boilers have now been refurbished and are working efficiently. A filtration system has now been installed which, it is hoped, will prevent a recurrence of the build-up of limescale which caused the breakdown.

The kitchen is situated within the accommodation block. During the pandemic, the kitchen ran a two-shift system to provide continuity if one team of residents tested positive. In February, infection in one of these teams meant that the second had to work for around twenty days continuously. During the pandemic, three meals per day were provided for, on average, 550 prisoners.

### Visiting Information
Book online at: www.gov.uk/prison-visits or ring 01305 825014 Monday to Friday, 2pm to 4pm (closes at 3:30pm on Friday) Visits are booked by prisoner led application.
**Visiting times:** Tuesday, Saturday and Sunday: 1:45pm to 4pm.

**Legal visits:** Email:
LegalVisits.TheVerne@Justice.Gov.uk
**Visiting times:** Tuesday: 9am to 1pm

### INSPECTIONS & REPORTS
**Date of last full inspection:** 10–21 February 2020
Notable features from this inspection
• In December 2017, the prison had re-roled from an immigration removal centre to an establishment holding prisoners convicted of sexual offences, reopening in July 2018.
• All prisoners had been allocated a key worker and there was a full complement of operational staff.
• Nearly all prisoners in our survey said that staff treated them respectfully.
• Nearly two-thirds of the population were serving 10 years or more.
• Over half of the population were over 50; the oldest prisoner was 87.
• Prisoners were never locked in their rooms on the main residential units.
• Dorset unit was a mobility and social needs support unit.

### HMCIP Report, published 03 June 2020
HMP The Verne, located in Portland in Dorset, was previously an immigration removal centre (IRC). While we inspected The Verne in 2015, this is our first inspection since the establishment was reopened as a category C training prison in July 2018. The Verne now holds prisoners convicted of sexual offences and has been fully occupied since June 2019. This is a positive report: outcomes were good, our highest judgement, in our healthy prison tests of safety and respect, not sufficiently good in purposeful activity and reasonably good in rehabilitation and release planning.

The Verne is a safe prison. We found low levels of violence and self-harm, and few prisoners reported feeling unsafe. When violence or antisocial behaviour did occur, incidents were investigated well and victims received good support. Managers had worked effectively with prisoner peer support workers to promote a safe community ethos. It was this sense of community and the positive relationships between staff and prisoners which encouraged good behaviour. As a consequence, adjudications, segregation and restraint were rarely used.

Relationships between staff and prisoners were among the best we have seen. In our survey, 97% of prisoners reported that most staff treated them with respect, 99% reported having a key worker and 86% of those said their key worker was helpful. Our findings supported this view: we observed respectful interactions and found that staff were knowledgeable about the prisoners in their care. Prisoners were able to contribute to their community in a wide range of peer worker roles and consultation with prisoners was regular and effective. Living conditions were also good: residential units were clean and well equipped. The food was better than we normally see and it was positive that prisoners ate their evening meals in well-resourced dining rooms.

Equality, diversity and faith provision was also good. There were consultation fora for all protected characteristics and a range of events, mainly organised by prisoners, were held throughout the year. In addition, a very active chaplaincy team supported a wide range of activities for prisoners from all faiths as well as those from none.

Healthcare provision was less positive. It had taken too long for NHS commissioners to carry out a health needs assessment to reflect the needs of the population. As a result, the health services team was under-resourced and was unable to meet the needs of the population.

Prisoners were never locked in their rooms and had free access around the site for over nine hours a day. However, there was not enough activity to occupy all prisoners and, in addition, the education curriculum did not meet the needs of the population. This meant too many prisoners were unemployed at the time of the inspection. While behaviour, attitudes to learning and punctuality were good, there needed to be more focus on progressing learners to the next stage of their education and better support for those with additional learning needs In the area of rehabilitation and release planning, support for prisoners to maintain contact with their family and friends was reasonable but facilities for visitors were basic. We found a well-led offender management unit. Nearly all prisoners had a high-quality assessment and sentence plan and since the introduction of offender management in custody (OMiC), key workers had seen their allocated prisoners, recorded contact well and communicated effectively with the prison offender manager. Public protection procedures were reasonable but there were weaknesses in implementing contact restrictions, which needed to be addressed. The lack of offending behaviour programmes was a gap but was mitigated, in part, by transfers to prisons with appropriate provision. Despite having no resettlement provision, a small but increasing number of prisoners were being released from The Verne. Staff were supporting this group well but this was unsustainable in the long term.

Overall this was a positive inspection of a well-run institution. Since The Verne reopened as a training prison, the Governor has established a culture where staff and prisoners treat each other with respect and legitimate concerns are responded to. However, there needs to be better partnership work and robust challenge of key partners in order to improve healthcare and activities provision.

HM Chief Inspector of Prisons April 2020

## INDEPENDENT MONITORING BOARD: Annual Report

The law requires every prison to be monitored by an independent Board appointed by the Justice Secretary; these are known as Independent Monitoring Boards (IMBs) The IMB must satisfy itself as to the humane and just treatment of those held in custody within its prison and the range and adequacy of the programmes preparing them for release; it must report annually to the Justice Secretary on how well the prison has met the standards and requirements placed on it.

### IMB Report 1 August 2020 – 31 July 2021
### Published December 2021

Executive summary

Background to the report

This report presents the findings of the Independent Monitoring Board (IMB) of HMP The Verne ('the Board') for the period 1 August 2020 – 31 July 2021. For the first half of that period, the Board was able to collect evidence from observations made on visits, scrutiny of prison records and of data, informal contact with residents and staff, and residents' applications. As in the previous year, Covid restrictions meant Board members did not enter the prison for most of the latter half of the reporting period. Monitoring was then restricted to telephone conversations with staff from across the institution. The Board also held weekly telephone conferences with the Governor or a senior staff member taking part. In addition, the clerk was able to give the Board her first-hand impression of conditions within the prison. She was also able to copy to members the (few) applications collected during this period and to pass on the Board's responses. The Board acknowledges with gratitude the clerk's important role during this period.

Although the Board participated in the scheme whereby prisoners could use an 0800 number to speak to an IMB volunteer who recorded their complaints, the Board received only one application via this route from a Verne resident.

### Main judgements
### How safe is the prison?

The Verne is very safe when compared with other prisons. Instances of violence are rare. Disruptive behaviour is dealt with promptly and firmly.

### How fairly and humanely are prisoners treated?

The prevailing ethos established at The Verne is one of mutual respect between staff and residents. The perceived fairness and humanity of the regime is perhaps best indicated by the widespread acceptance of the various restrictions which Covid has necessitated for a second year. The Board regrets that, once again, it has to point to an area where conditions might fall short of humane: the lack of 24 hour provision for an as yet small but growing number of frail, elderly residents who need regular personal care.

### How well are prisoners' health and wellbeing needs met?

The Board is satisfied that, with the exception of the oldest and frailest residents, the health and wellbeing needs of the majority are adequately met.

### How well are prisoners progressed towards successful resettlement?

The Board recognises that The Verne was set up as a training, rather than a resettlement, prison. It is aware of the considerable efforts that have been made to prepare the small number of residents who are released directly into the community. While the shortage of category D places continues to make such releases an unfortunate necessity, the Board does not consider the resettlement provision to be entirely satisfactory.

### Main areas for development
**TO THE MINISTER**
The Board invites the Minister to reflect on the need, in any future pandemic, for prison staff to be treated as a priority group in respect of vaccination.

### TO THE PRISON SERVICE
The Board urges HMPPS to expedite the establishment of the 'community hospital' and a facility enabling 24hr social care at The Verne.

### TO THE GOVERNOR
The Board hopes the Governor will continue the search for further employment opportunities for Verne residents.

### Progress since the last report
Any discussion of progress must take account of the constraints imposed by the pandemic. In addition, the Board is only too aware that progress cannot be reliably gauged when absent from the prison for over four months. However, the Board considers that Covid presented The Verne with an exceptionally serious situation. Structures built to service a Victorian artillery platform do not lend themselves to confining a dangerous pathogen. As time passes and normality slowly returns, it is easy to take the view that 'it was not that bad'. But five residents died from Covid, and more needed hospital treatment, as did several prison staff.

It is unfortunate therefore that, in the event of a recurrence of the pandemic in the immediate future, the 'community hospital' discussed in our last report will not be available. A further source of regret lies in the lack of progress in respect of the social care facility.

5 LOVE LANE
WAKEFIELD
WEST YORKS
WF2 9AG

**HM PRISON WAKEFIELD**   Tel: 01924 612000

*For the latest reports on this prison please visit:*
https://tinyurl.com/bdfh26rv

*Important Changes:* **(1) Visits:** the identification necessary to access this prison and visit for social or professional purposes has changed; (2) **Money and Gifts** new rules now apply to these. See page 16 for full details of the above.

**Task of the establishment** HMP Wakefield is a high security prison for category A and B male prisoners, almost exclusively holding those with a determinate sentence of over 10 years, lifers and prisoners with an indeterminate sentence for public protection.

### Certified normal accommodation and operational capacity
Prisoners held at the time of inspection: 709
Certified normal capacity: 750
Operational capacity: 750

### Prison status and key providers
Public
Prison Group: Long Term / High Security
Prison Group Director: Gavin O'Malley
Governor / Director: Tom Wheatley
IMB Chair: Ron Drake
Physical health provider: Care UK Health and Rehabilitation Services Limited (Care UK)
Mental health provider: Care UK Health and Rehabilitation Services Limited (Care UK)
Substance misuse provider: Care UK Health and Rehabilitation Services Limited (Care UK) (clinical), Inclusion (psychosocial)
Learning and skills provider: Novus
Escort contractor: GeoAmey and HM Prison and Probation Service

**Brief history** HMP Wakefield was built as a house of correction in 1594. The prison became a dispersal prison in 1996 and held those posing the highest security risk. It is now a lifer centre with a focus on serious sex offenders.

### Short description of residential units
Wings A-D: residential units
Wing F: segregation unit and close supervision centre
Health care centre: inpatient unit

### Visiting Information
Book online at: www.gov.uk/prison-visits or ring 01924 612 274 Monday and Friday: 9am to midday, Tuesday to Thursday: 9am to midday and 2pm to 4pm.
**Visiting times:** Monday to Thursday, Saturday: 2pm to 4pm.

**Legal visits:** Ring 01924 612 085 Monday and Friday: 9am to midday, Tuesday to Thursday: 9am to midday and 2pm to 4pm.
**Visiting times:** Tues to Thurs: 9am to 11am.

### INSPECTIONS & REPORTS
**Date of last inspection: 11, 12 & 18–22 June 2018**
**HMCIP Report, published 01 November 2018**
HMP Wakefield is a high security establishment holding category A and B prisoners. At the time

of this inspection there were some 700 being held. The vast majority were serving sentences of more than 10 years, and included some of the most challenging and complex prisoners in the country. Despite this, the prison was calm and had an atmosphere that spoke of good order, safety, security and decency. This was reflected in the assessments under our four healthy prison tests, in particular the improved assessment of purposeful activity and the continuing highest possible assessment of 'good' in the area of respect. The identification and promulgation of good practice is, I believe, a key function of the inspection process. To that end I would urge readers to pay particular attention to the examples cited in Section 5 of this report. They include a varied and impressive set of initiatives and good work drawn from across all of the healthy prison tests.

A problem that was not unique to Wakefield, but which was particularly acute there, was that of transferring prisoners under the Mental Health Act to secure accommodation. Because of the totally unacceptable delays in doing so, many prisoners across the prison estate are held in conditions that are not in any way therapeutic and indeed in many cases clearly exacerbate their condition. This is a national strategic issue to which we have made reference many times in inspection reports. The situation at Wakefield was yet another example of prisoners with severe illness not receiving the care that they needed. It is clearly something that is beyond the capability of either individual prisons or HM Prison and Probation Service (HMPPS) to resolve. Therefore, in view of the fact that to date there has been no effective response to this issue, on this occasion I am taking the unusual step of making a recommendation directly to the Prisons Minister in the hope that he can use his influence to initiate effective cross-departmental action to address the problem.

We found HMP Wakefield to be an essentially respectful prison, with many examples of good relationships and interactions between staff and prisoners. However, as in so many establishments, our survey revealed that black and minority ethnic prisoners had a poorer perception of their treatment and conditions than their white counterparts. These negative perceptions needed to be understood. Until this happened there would be no way of knowing whether the negative perceptions were justified or not, and even if they were not, the negative perceptions themselves needed to be taken seriously and addressed.

Despite the fact that we found an overall improvement in the area of purposeful activity, there was still a need to provide sufficient activity places for the entire population. This would then complement the adequate time out of cell that was already available to those who were employed. The introduction of key workers, offering an ongoing link between individual prisoners and identified officers, was a key strategic initiative. Early indications were that this could be a highly significant development, and once it was fully embedded could well offer the opportunity for further improvement in the area of rehabilitation and release planning.

By any standards this was a good inspection, which was highly creditable given the complexity of the prison. The high standards, good practice and improvements that have been achieved were the result of hard work and dedication on the part of those who clearly took very seriously their responsibilities for the safe, secure and purposeful imprisonment of those in their care.

Peter Clarke CVO OBE QPM August 2018
HM Chief Inspector of Prisons

## INDEPENDENT MONITORING BOARD: Annual Report

The law requires every prison to be monitored by an independent Board appointed by the Justice Secretary; these are known as Independent Monitoring Boards (IMBs). The IMB must satisfy itself as to the humane and just treatment of those held in custody within its prison and the range and adequacy of the programmes preparing them for release; it must report annually to the Justice Secretary on how well the prison has met the standards and requirements placed on it.

### IMB Report 01 May 2020 – 30 April 2021
### Published October 2021
### Background to the report

This report presents the Board's views on the conditions of custody at HMP Wakefield during the reporting period 01 May 2020 – 30 April 2021. In arriving at our judgments, we draw on an evidence base that includes evidence gathered through remote monitoring, attendance at 'bi-weekly' Prison Rule 45 review Boards, local management committees, prisoner representation bodies, and dealing with specific prisoner applications to the Board including those received under confidential access to the chairperson.

This report covers the period during which HMP Wakefield implemented the COVID19: National Framework for Prison Regimes and Services; this required the Board to develop a new operating model in line with agreed procedures and practices for Board operations and local restrictions in force across the city of Wakefield and in the individual Board members' places of residence.

### Remote monitoring

At the outset of the pandemic, the Board was strongly advised to review its position on face-to-face/direct monitoring. The decision as to whether to attend the establishment in person remains with the individual Board member, although this decision should seek to balance the benefits of in-person attendance with the possibility of transmission in the establishment. Individual Board members received advice that they should not feel obliged to directly monitor during the period covered by this annual report. Furthermore, the Board was asked to implement remote monitoring principles wherever possible, including:

• Receiving daily briefings and regime management plans/equivalent and updates through CJSM (secure email system)
• Receiving key statistics from the prison on a regular basis, including of prisoners segregated
• Monthly Board meetings by video conference

And, where feasible:

• Attend meetings via conference call where they would otherwise attend in person
• Maintain regular contact with the healthcare unit by telephone and with the operational manager responsible

### Remote monitoring principles *How the principles was observed*

Receiving daily briefings and regime management plans/equivalent and updates through CJSM (secure email system) *The Governor (or his delegate) provided a copy of the daily Governor's report to the Chair via CJSM.*

Receiving key statistics from the prison on a regular basis, including of prisoners segregated *SMARG, use of force and adjudication standardisation data reports were provided to the Board without exception and to an extremely high standard. Initial notification of segregation was made by telephone call to the individual Board member on duty as 'first contact'.*

Monthly Board meetings by video conference *Most Board meetings were arranged by video conference. Three socially distanced meetings were held in the HMP Wakefield training building.*

Attend meetings via conference call where they would otherwise attend in person *Teleconference was made available for the purposes of facilitating IMB attendance where appropriate, including Prison Rule 45 and 46 reviews. In numerous cases, in-person attendance by an individual Board member was deemed to be more appropriate.*

Maintain regular contact with the healthcare unit by telephone and with the operational manager responsible *Two members of the Board were assigned responsibility for the healthcare function and maintained regular contact with staff throughout.*

The Board confirms that the HMPPS operational guidance to Governors (3 April 2020), which sets out how establishments should support IMBs in remote monitoring, was implemented effectively at HMP Wakefield.

### Segregation

The Board received guidance that it should maintain active monitoring of prisoners in segregation, if not by visits, then through telephone calls to F wing and information updates made available by the Governor. Board members were asked, where possible, to monitor some segregation reviews, preferably remotely by telephone, using conference calling.

On 8 April 2020 the Board issued the following statement in its quarterly report to the HMP Wakefield segregation monitoring and review group (SMARG):

*COV-19 restrictions and 'remote' monitoring arrangements The Board has arranged, in consultation with the Governor responsible for the Segregation Unit, to trial several measures to ensure that the monitoring outcomes can be achieved. Prison Rule 45 reviews will be attended by a member of the IMB (via phone-link) with pre- and post-review paperwork shared via the Ministry of Justice 'CJSM' system – this is cleared for all communications marked 'OFFICIAL-SENSITIVE'. Board members will sign the 'Authorisation for Continued Segregation' OT025 using one of either a) a digital signature or b) an email from the individual Board member's CJSM account indicating that they agree/disagree with the statement 'I am satisfied that procedures have been followed and the decision reached is reasonable'. In the case of prisoners who are being considered at their first 14-day review, then the Board members should be provided with a copy of FORM OT024 which indicates the name of the IMB member informed of the decision to segregate.*

*The Board should also be notified of any prisoners held under Prison Rule 55 (1)(e) following adjudication. The Board has nominated two members to take specific responsibility for R45/53 related monitoring work:*

*1. Mr. (name redacted) – weekly phone call to F-Wing office for updates on individual prisoners and health/safety arrangements necessitated by COVID19.*

*2. Mr. (name redacted) – SMARG. The United Nations has issued updated guidance on monitoring of prisons during the pandemic, this is attached for reference.*

### Applications to the Board, including COMP2 (confidential access to the Chairperson of the Board)

At the outset of the pandemic, the Board was able to continue to receive applications as normal, chiefly due to the availability and willingness of the Board's clerk to collect applications from the wings on a weekly basis. The Board received 42 standard written applications and 113 oral applications via the 0800 (freephone) number during the reporting period. The Board agreed to facilitate the implementation of the 0800 applications line' and appointed an individual Board member with the responsibility for liaison with the central co-ordinating function of the IMB Secretariat. We are grateful to her for volunteering to take on this additional responsibility and for covering shifts on the call-handlers pool.

It is the view of the Board that the availability of the '0800 applications line' should be time-limited at HMP Wakefield. In the case of one prisoner, it has led to unintended disbenefits including a propensity for him to make frequent calls. This has placed unacceptable burdens on the Board. Admittedly, the prisoner has prior history of making many written applications to the Board, but this had reduced substantially following careful work by individual Board members to encourage behaviour change.

## Main judgements
### How safe is the prison?

HMP Wakefield's own data indicates a 10% reduction in acts of violence. It is entirely plausible that this reduction occurred because prisoners have spent considerable periods of time in their own cells due to the implementation of the HMPPS Covid-19 National Framework for Prison Regimes and Services. There were some isolated incidents of prisoner-on-prisoner and prisoner-on-staff violence that were of sufficient severity to warrant a referral to West Yorkshire Police.

During the reporting period, routine cell searching (referred to as accommodation fabric checks (AFCs)) was suspended for Category B prisoners in favour of intelligence-led searches – we understand that this decision was taken in the context of minimising local transmission of Covid-19. Resumption of normal AFC routines was due to be reinstated at the time of publication of the report.

HMP Wakefield was classified as an outbreak site during the reporting period, chiefly due to the number of cases recorded in the establishment. On the 25 February 2021 we wrote to the Minister (under §6(3) Prison Act 1952 (c.52)) to raise our concerns that the Government had not prioritised vaccination of HM Prison Service staff and members of the IMB at HMP Wakefield. This was deeply concerning to us, particularly in the context of a high security dispersal prison with a segregation unit and close supervision centre (F Wing) where some of the most dangerous prisoners in the country are held in conditions that are not conducive to social distancing and characterised by poor ventilation in a highly constrained physical environment.

During our visit to the segregation unit on 23 February 2021, the consequences of the virus on staffing levels was brought into stark focus; most staff on duty were drafted in from other parts of the prison due to isolation/sick leave of F wing staff. Our conversations with staff on duty revealed feelings of exhaustion and worry in dealing with prisoners who, by virtue of their offending, are extremely volatile and sensitive to regime disruption. There is no doubt that it takes exceptional courage to work in this environment, yet the absence of a vaccination programme for this specific group of public servants suggested to us that their work, and ours, was not valued, perhaps because it is practised behind closed doors and not in the public eye. Individual members of the Board made further written representations to their respective MPs.

### How fairly and humanely are prisoners treated?

Throughout the reporting period, the prison has been either subject to level 3 or level 4 lockdown requirements of the HMPPS Covid-19 National Framework. From May 2020 to July 2020 the prison operated under level 4 lockdown measures. From July 2020 to January 2021 the prison was subject to level 3 but where there were localised outbreaks of Covid-19 on wings the regime in these areas followed the level 4 protocols. From January 2021 to the end of April 2021 the prison has remained at level 4. This has had an impact on the regime and the facilities available for prisoners. Prior to the pandemic, prisoners at Wakefield experienced a period of around 11 hours a day out of their cells. The lockdown measures have meant that there has been a period of one and a half hours a day for prisoners to be out of their cells to complete their domestic tasks. This was achieved by unlocking small cohorts of prisoners at a time.

In the early stages of the pandemic, we found evidence of staff actively seeking to mitigate the impact of prolonged cellular confinement through regular communication and the provision of in-cell activity. All prisoners on Level 1 (basic) of the incentives and earned privileges (IEP) scheme were automatically upgraded to Level 2 (standard) to permit issue of an in-cell television. Distraction packs featuring word searches, puzzles etc were issued to all prisoners yet some prisoners told us that the content did not provide sufficient mental stimulation.

Towards the end of the reporting period, where a return to some in-person monitoring commenced, we were able to glean perceptions of prisoners themselves. Most conversations led us to believe that prisoners understood that their individual circumstances reflected restrictions in the wider community, although many have struggled to manage their mental health during this time, leading to some extremely distressing examples of self-harm. Isolation, extreme boredom and the monotonous nature of the regime have left a lasting impact on many prisoners at Wakefield.

### How well are prisoners' health and wellbeing needs met?

It is difficult to judge the true impact of the pandemic on prisoners' health and wellbeing given the restricted amount of time that Board members have spent in the prison. The Board remains concerned that the Governor's ability to influence healthcare service delivery in HMP Wakefield is significantly constrained by the outsourcing of healthcare provision to an external contractor. Prisoners are entitled to receive an equivalent level of care to that what might reasonably be expected in the community, but we do not believe that this is always the case at Wakefield. We have observed situations where it appears to be that the contract, rather than the individual needs of prisoners, determines service delivery.

The prison does not have access to a consultant forensic psychiatrist. We believe that this is because the contract does not specify provision for one. This is not consistent with the provision at other LTHSE establishments, to the best of our knowledge. We therefore do not believe that the mental health needs of prisoners who require forensic psychiatry services are being met at Wakefield.

The consequences of poor mental health can be harrowing; in one incident, a prisoner was taken to outside hospital following an act of extreme self-harm – one that had a profound and traumatic impact on the prisoner and the staff who provided care in the aftermath. The prisoner was taken to outside hospital for treatment, but our understanding is that he was quickly returned to prison following treatment rather than being assessed for an immediate transfer to a secure hospital under Section 47 of the Mental Health Act. Information that we have received from the prison suggests to us that the prisoner's health needs may not have been met by the NHS. This matter is now subject of a formal complaint against the NHS Trust concerned, and we are monitoring the situation very closely.

### How well are prisoners progressed towards successful resettlement?

Resettlement work is not a major emphasis of activity at HMP Wakefield. Most programmes are designed to address offending behaviour that is typical of long duration life-sentence tariffs or fixed-term sentences. Therefore, the focus at HMP Wakefield is on 'settlement' rather than 'resettlement'. Nevertheless, the assessment and interventions (AIC) team work closely with other departments in the prison including the offender management unit (OMU) and probation to ensure that prisoners are given the appropriate support, advice and guidance to progress through their sentence in a constructive way. We are concerned by one isolated case, a prisoner on Rule 45 who may be released direct from the segregation unit of HMP Wakefield having completed more than 1500 consecutive days in segregated conditions. We have low confidence of a successful reintegration to the community.

### Main areas for development
### TO THE MINISTER

We ask the Minister to explain how the Government intends to address longstanding and yet unresolved problems with the assessment and transfer of prisoners who present with serious mental health and personality disorders from HMP Wakefield to hospital (section 47, Mental Health Act 1983). This is a repeated concern that appears in our 2015/16, 2016/17, 2018/19 and 2019/20 annual reports.

We ask the Minister to act in respect of prisoners at HMP Wakefield who are substantially over tariff and subject to the consequences of the now discredited 'sentences of imprisonment for public protection' (IPP) (see Criminal Justice Act 2003).

### TO THE PRISON SERVICE

We ask HMPPS to clarify the role of HMP Wakefield in the 'Pathways to Progression' programme.

We ask HMPPS to clarify if the complaints procedure for healthcare provision at HMP Wakefield is audited in line with standard complaints made under the COMP1/2 procedures. We urge HMPPS to explore the possibility of implementing a nationally available set of legal resources for prisoners, including easy access to Prison Service Orders and Instructions.

We ask HMPPS to clarify progress on the integration of the SystmOne project led by the Ministry of Justice's digital team.

### TO THE GOVERNOR

We ask the Governor of HMP Wakefield to clarify if (or when) in-cell telephony will become available to prisoners.

The House of Commons Justice Committee published its Fourth Report of Session 2019-21 on 'Coronavirus (Covid-19): The impact on prisons' (HC 299) on 27 July 2020. The report states 'we are not clear as to why there is such wide variance across the estate in type of regime and time out of cell. We agree with the Independent Monitoring Board and recommend that the Ministry of Justice set out clear expectations of the minimum time out of cell and activity to be provided at each phase of recovery. This is not currently clearly set out in the Covid-19: National Framework for Prisons and Services'. We ask the Governor of HMP Wakefield to clarify the target minimum time out of cell for the next reporting period.

### Progress since last report
The Board continues to receive excellent resources in the form of a competent and experienced clerk, two HMPPS quantum-linked information technology terminals, a printer, document scanner and access to the prison national offender management information system (P-NOMIS).
Some members of the Board access the new HMPPS digital prison services 'core' and report on a positive experience. However, we note that the prisoner's index offence is highly visible on the opening page, whereas this is not the case with the legacy P-NOMIS system. We would prefer this to not be the case.
In April 2021, an operational support grade (OSG) staff member retired from HMPPS. It is believed that she was at the time, the longest serving member of staff in the prison service.

**HEATHFIELD ROAD
WANDSWORTH
LONDON
SW18 3HU**

HM PRISON
WANDSWORTH

Tel: 020 8588 4000

*For the latest reports on this prison please visit:*
https://tinyurl.com/bdfh26rv

*Important Changes:* **(1) Visits:** the identification necessary to access this prison and visit for social or professional purposes has changed; (2) **Money and Gifts** new rules now apply to these. See page 16 for full details of the above.

This prison operates the Digital Categorisation System, pursuant to the Security Categorisation Policy Framework as such PSIs 40 and 41 of 2011 do not apply to prisoners being categorised in this establishment.

### Task of the establishment
Local category B reception and resettlement adult male prison.

### Certified normal accommodation and operational capacity
Prisoners held September 2021: 1,364
Baseline certified normal capacity: 1,334

In-use certified normal capacity: 1,325
Operational capacity: 1,368

### Population of the prison
• 4,615 new prisoners received each year (around 88 per week).
• 613 foreign national prisoners, about 45% of the population.
• 41% of prisoners from black and minority ethnic backgrounds.
• Just under half the population were on remand and nearly three-quarters were unsentenced.
• Nearly half of sentenced and just over half of unsentenced prisoners stayed for three months or less.
• 160 prisoners released each month.
• 967 prisoners on substance misuse support.
• 531 prisoners referred to mental health services each month.

### Prison status and key providers
Public
Prison Group: London
Prison Group Director: Ian Bickers
Governor/Director: Katie Price
IMB chair Tim Aikens
Physical health provider:
Oxleas NHS Foundation Trust
Mental health provider: South London and the Maudsley NHS Trust Substance misuse treatment provider: Change Grow Live
Prison education framework provider: Novus
Escort contractor: Serco

### Brief history
Built 170 years ago, Wandsworth is a large Victorian prison serving the courts of south west London.

### Short description of residential units
Heathfield Unit
A and B wings – general population
C wing – general population; vulnerable prisoners
D wing – drug recovery unit
E wing – first night and induction unit
Trinity Unit
G, H and K wings – resettlement unit
Addison and Jones – health care inpatient units

### Visiting Information
Book online at: www.gov.uk/prison-visits or ring 0300 060 6509 Monday to Friday, 9:15am to 5pm.
**Visiting times:** Monday to Friday: 1:30pm to 2:30pm and 3:30pm to 4:30pm

**Legal visits:** Email:
LegalvisitsWandsworth@justice.gov.uk
**Visiting times:** Monday to Thursday: 8:30am to 9:30am, 10:30am to 11:30am, 1:30pm to 2:30pm, 3:30pm to 4:30pm.

## INSPECTIONS & REPORTS

**Date of last inspection: 13, 20-24 September 2021**
**HMCIP Report, published 6 January 2022**

The decision by the prison service to reduce the number of prisoners held at Wandsworth by 300, as well as the work of the dynamic and experienced governor, had stopped this busy local prison from being overwhelmed by its many challenges.

There were not enough staff to make sure prisoners received even the most basic regime; for example, they sometimes had to choose between exercise, ordering from the kiosk and having a shower. Gym sessions were regularly cancelled and much of the essential resettlement and sentence progression work was not happening because prison offender managers and PE staff were deployed on the wings to backfill staff absences. One group of prisoners from Trinity Unit, who came blinking into the sunlight, told me that it was the first time they had been outside for more than a week.

The education provider had failed to do enough to engage prisoners or develop learning opportunities for a population that was desperately bored. The education block had sat unused since March 2020 and most of the very limited provision came in the form of work packs. Education staff were barely doing any face-to-face teaching, so it was not entirely clear how their time was being spent.

Nearly half of the prisoners were foreign nationals, many of whom come from eastern Europe. The prison, the education service and, in particular, Home Office staff, were not doing enough to support this group of prisoners. There were 37 prisoners over their tariff waiting for a decision on when or if they would be deported. Some foreign national prisoners had even been told on the day of their release that they were to continue to be held in the jail. A local charity, BEST, had stayed on site during the pandemic and were doing invaluable work in supporting foreign national prisoners while, inexplicably, Home Office staff had absented themselves from the prison for more than a year. In the meantime, prison officers and other staff had to deal with the consequences of their inaction. Even since Home Office staff had returned, working what appeared to be limited hours, they were not running surgeries on the wing and prisoners were lucky if they got a phone call.

The infrastructure of the jail needed a lot of work: cells and landings were often tatty, some of the showers were awful and outside areas were strewn with rubbish. The inpatient mental health unit, due to be refurbished, was not a fit place to care for seriously unwell patients. Fortunately, there had also been some impressive improvements: the legal visits and video conferencing took place in an excellent facility and the visits hall had been decorated with prisoner-painted murals.

Communication between the governor through a range of media (including Radio Wanno) had meant that prisoners were kept well informed about the pandemic and any developments in the prison. This may have contributed to the generally calm atmosphere in the jail – which we witnessed – despite the paucity of the regime. Interactions between officers and prisoners were, because of staffing shortages, largely transactional. Key work was very limited, although prisoners recognised that often staff were trying to do their best.

Understandably, the governor had been focused on keeping the day-to-day functions of the prison going as he dealt with the extensive list of challenges that we highlight in this report. He now has the opportunity, with an improving leadership team, to put in more robust assurance systems around some crucial functions such as use of force, safeguarding and violence reduction. There had been nine self-inflicted deaths since our last inspection. The prison must continue to respond to the Prisons and Probation Ombudsman's reports to make sure that everything is done to reduce the risk to the most vulnerable prisoners.

As some of the concerns about the pandemic begins to reduce, leaders will have the opportunity to focus on developing longer-term plans for the jail that set targets and introduce effective systems for monitoring and review. This will mean that some of the more complex concerns can be addressed, such as the regime (including access to work and education), the support for foreign national prisoners and the development of the staff team.

Leaders in this crumbling, overcrowded, vermin-infested prison will need considerable ongoing support from the prison service, notably with the recruitment and retention of staff, improving the infrastructure of the jail and making sure that external agencies such as the Home Office and the education provider pull their weight. It is hard to see how HMP Wandsworth's limited progress can be sustained if prisoner numbers in this jail are allowed to increase as they are scheduled to do next April.

### Safety

At the last inspection of Wandsworth in 2018 we found that outcomes for prisoners were not sufficiently good against this healthy prison test. At this inspection we found that outcomes for prisoners remained not sufficiently good.

Reception was welcoming and processes were thorough. Procedures for identifying prisoners at increased risk following court appearances had improved, as had the first night interviews. First night cells were clean, but many had insufficient or broken furniture. Not all new arrivals were offered the opportunity to shower. Induction was good and information was available in a range of languages.

In our survey, over half of respondents said they had felt unsafe at some point during their stay and 22% said they felt unsafe now. The recorded number of assaults had increased over the last 12 months and assaults against staff were higher than at similar prisons. Although data monitoring had improved, the prison lacked a longer-term plan to reduce violence. The challenge, support and intervention plan (CSIP, see Glossary of terms) casework model for perpetrators of violence was not operating effectively and there was no formal support for victims.

There were limited incentives to encourage positive behaviour and the scheme was ineffective in addressing poor behaviour. Too many adjudications had been remanded for a long time.

Use of force incidents had increased significantly since the last inspection, but only around 20% of staff had received up-to-date training. There were strengths in some aspects of governance, but there had been no formal monitoring meetings and senior managers did not investigate all incidents involving the use of batons or PAVA incapacitant spray. Officers did not always switch on body-worn cameras early enough to provide evidence and CCTV footage was not routinely downloaded to check that force used was justified and proportionate.

Use of special accommodation in the last 12 months was high and not always in exceptional circumstances. However, leaders had taken action to address this and consequently special accommodation had not been used since April 2021. The daily regime for prisoners in the segregation unit had improved since the last inspection, but it was still too limited and reintegration planning was not meaningful. Prisoners held in the unit were positive about their relationships with staff. The unit's communal areas were clean, but cells were grubby with ingrained dirt and exercise yards remained grim.

Most aspects of security were proportionate, but new arrivals were strip-searched in addition to going through the body scanner. The flow of security information was processed efficiently, and monthly local tactical briefings were based on relevant intelligence and objectives. There was an appropriate focus on counter terrorism. The prison also had a good strategic approach to tackling drug supply.

There had been nine self-inflicted deaths since the last inspection in 2018 and two further deaths related to drug misuse. The prison had acted swiftly in response to the recommendations from the Prisons and Probation Ombudsman (PPO) investigation reports received to date.

The rate of self-harm had more than doubled during the year but remained comparatively low for the type of prison. The prison had taken action to address levels of self-harm, underpinned by daily reviews of incidents and scrutiny of data. There was no published overall safety strategy and supporting action plan to make the prison safer. The quality of assessment, care in custody and teamwork (ACCT) case management documentation for prisoners at risk of suicide or self-harm varied too widely across the prison. The large team of Listeners (prisoners trained by the Samaritans to provide confidential emotional support to fellow prisoners) was well supported and available on a rota to those requiring them.

## Respect

At the last inspection of Wandsworth in 2018 we found that outcomes for prisoners were not sufficiently good against this healthy prison test. At this inspection we found that outcomes for prisoners remained not sufficiently good.

Over 60% of prisoners in our survey said that most staff treated them with respect and that there were staff they could turn to if they had a problem. We observed some friendly and positive interactions, but the poor regime and staffing shortfalls undermined the quality of staff relationships with prisoners in providing support and rehabilitation. The key worker scheme was not working as intended by the Offender Management in Custody (OMiC) model (see Glossary). Plans to restore the scheme were neither fully developed nor realistic.

Despite a recent reduction in population, nearly three-quarters of prisoners were still sharing cells designed for one. While most cells were now adequately equipped, vandalism was a concern. Many prisoners complained to us about a lack of clean clothing and sheets, and the organisation of cleaning materials was chaotic. However, leaders had made concerted efforts to make sure that staff responded to electronic cell bells promptly, which was positive.

The refurbishment of showers in wings on the Heathfield unit was welcome, but in the Trinity unit communal showers on the wings were unsatisfactory. A combination of a poor regime and damage meant that prisoners could often go several days without a shower. Despite efforts to control vermin, there was still a major problem with rats, mice and pigeons. Despite work to control vermin, including many rats, mice and pigeons, this was still a major problem.

Over half of prisoners in our survey said that the food was good, compared with just 34% at similar prisons. However, meals were served too early and staff distributed the evening meal at cell doors, which further restricted opportunity for time out of cell. Hotplate trolleys used to transport food were filthy.

Prisoner consultation and communication were a real strength at Wandsworth. The prison broadcast information to all prisoners via Radio Wanno and there was a new prison TV channel. Prisoners could now make applications through the electronic kiosks and responses were now more prompt. Complaints were reasonably well managed. Provision for legal visits and court video-conferencing facilities were impressive.

Strategic oversight of equality and diversity work remained underdeveloped. There was no tailored strategy and meetings had only recently resumed. There was a lack of regular consultation with protected and minority groups. However, discrimination complaints were well managed. Nearly half the population identified as black or minority ethnic and in our survey they reported broadly similar perceptions to white prisoners.

Support for the many foreign national prisoners was insufficient. Wing staff did not always use professional telephone interpreting when required. Home Office immigration staff had only recently returned to the prison having left many foreign nationals unsupported throughout the pandemic. They appreciated the work of BEST, a charity befriending and supporting foreign national prisoners in Wandsworth, and, more recently, similar support from Catch 22. However, detainees spent far too long in the prison with their cases unresolved.

The chaplaincy was highly regarded by prisoners and well-integrated into prison life, but the ongoing suspension of corporate worship was a source of frustration for many. Links with community faith groups were excellent.

Health care provision was reasonably good, but the environment on the inpatient unit was unsuitable for patients. There were staffing shortages in all clinical services, affecting mental health services more severely due to the lack of available agency staff. Patients requiring transfer to secure mental health inpatient services continued to wait far too long.

Primary health care services were well led. A committed and enthusiastic staff team provided a safe and effective service, despite some long waiting times. Non-attendance rates at both internal and external hospital appointments were high. Substance misuse and dental services were both good. Pharmacy services were reasonable, although officer management of queues was ineffective in preventing potential medicines diversion.

### Purposeful activity

At the last inspection of Wandsworth in 2018 we found that outcomes for prisoners were poor against this healthy prison test.

At this inspection we found that outcomes for prisoners remained poor.

Ofsted carried out a progress monitoring visit of the prison alongside our full inspection and the purposeful activity judgement incorporates their assessment of progress.

In our survey, prisoners reported too little time spent unlocked, especially at weekends when 91% said they had less than two hours a day out of cell. Time unlocked for most prisoners was unpredictable and for some as little as 45 minutes. Access to exercise was inadequate, particularly for prisoners on Trinity unit who repeatedly complained about going for days, and sometimes weeks, without time in the open air.

The library remained closed and although prisoners could order books, relatively few were delivered each day. Covid-19 restrictions had reduced the PE programme, which was compounded by a shortage of gym staff and their frequent redeployment.

The main education block had been closed since March 2020 and few prisoners were regularly engaged in any purposeful work or learning. Too many had not completed an education induction, such as assessments of their mathematics and English abilities. There were insufficient activity spaces to meet the needs of the population and not enough prisoners had been enrolled on to even the limited number of education places available. The education provider had been slow to reintroduce vocational training to the curriculum, and prisoners had very limited opportunities to gain accredited qualifications.

Too many education courses developed prisoners' skills only to level 1, which was below the ability level of many. Tutors' written feedback to prisoners was of an inconsistent quality. Information, advice and guidance to help prisoners understand the education or work options was not good enough, and leaders had been too slow to introduce support for those with learning difficulties and/or disabilities. However, prisoners close to the end of their sentences benefited from newly introduced support.

Prison leaders had identified many of the weaknesses with the education curriculum and the quality of teaching and had worked productively with education provider leaders as they planned to make improvements.

## Rehabilitation and release planning

At the last inspection of Wandsworth in 2018 we found that outcomes for prisoners were reasonably good against this healthy prison test. At this inspection we found that outcomes for prisoners were now not sufficiently good.

Face-to-face visits had resumed in June 2021 and take-up was good. While they had been suspended the prison had redecorated the visits hall and it was now impressive. The use of secure video calls (see Glossary) was reasonable, but more could have been done to encourage foreign national prisoners to use the facility. In-cell telephones were a great help for prisoners in maintaining family contact. The prison and PACT (Prison Advice and Care Trust) staff had been creative in encouraging contact between prisoners and their families.

Nearly three-quarters of the population were unsentenced and the turnover of prisoners was high. A good prisoner needs analysis, supported by a strategy, focused on key areas for their improvement. The monthly reducing reoffending meeting was well attended and demonstrated good links with the rest of the prison.

Almost all eligible prisoners had an assessment of their needs on arrival and most had an OASys (offender assessment system) assessment that had been completed in the last 12 months. Sentence plan objectives were appropriate, and most prisoners we spoke to had a reasonable understanding of them. However, in our survey, only 6% of prisoners, against 45% in similar prisons, said that staff were helping them to achieve their targets.

Contact between prison offender managers (POMs) and prisoners was undermined by their cross-deployment to other duties. This caused much frustration and reduced opportunities for POMs to support the progression of prisoners on their caseload. Home detention curfew (HDC) processes were managed well, but some problems beyond the control of the prison led to some prisoners being released after their eligibility date.

Public protection procedures were well managed. However, the prison was not monitoring mail and telephone calls for all new arrivals, as they should have done under national guidelines. There was reasonably good information exchange between the prison and community offender managers to develop robust risk management release plans.

The demand for resettlement help was high with 160 prisoners a month released. Following unification of probation services, provision for resettlement was not yet effective. Under the new contract, the housing provider, St Mungo's, no longer provided support for prisoners on remand,

which was a significant gap. Only 45% of prisoners released in the last year had accommodation fixed for their first night in the community.

Resettlement plans lacked depth and did not always lead to a positive outcome, and prisoners we spoke to were not always aware of what was being done to address their resettlement needs. However, practical release arrangements were good and several organisations provided through-the-gate support.

## Key concerns and recommendations

Key concerns and recommendations identify the issues of most importance to improving outcomes for prisoners and are designed to help establishments prioritise and address the most significant weaknesses in the treatment and conditions of prisoners.

During this inspection we identified some areas of key concern and have made a small number of recommendations for the prison to address those concerns.

Key concern: Although leaders were making good use of data to measure daily and weekly progress, governance arrangements were not sufficient to make sure that longer term plans, targets and monitoring were taking place in a number of important areas such as violence reduction, use of force, key work, safety and equality and diversity.

Recommendation: Prison leaders need to develop longer term plans for improving the prison against their priorities. The governor and his team should introduce robust governance arrangements to give them assurance that plans are being followed, that work is taking place on time, that there are clear lines of accountability, that progress is monitored and that there is a process for reviewing plans (To the governor)

Key concern: Over half of respondents to our survey reported that they had felt unsafe at some point during their stay. There was no formal support for victims. Violence was increasing and the number of assaults on staff was high. The management of perpetrators of violence was weak, too many investigations into incidents were not thorough enough, and there was no embedded violence reduction strategy or action plan.

Recommendation: There should be a prison-wide approach to reducing violence and making prisoners feels safe. This should include setting targets for set periods, monitoring progress and reviewing, and where necessary, amending plans. (To the governor)

Key concern: The use of force was high and there were no formal governance meetings. Staff involved in incidents did not always record de-escalation techniques or switch on body-worn cameras early enough to provide sufficient scrutiny. Not all incidents involving the use of batons and PAVA incapacitant spray were investigated by senior managers and too much use of force documentation was missing.

Recommendation: Leaders should make sure that body-worn cameras are switched on at the beginning of any incident. There should be regular and effective senior management scrutiny and oversight of the use of force, including deployment of batons and PAVA, to make sure that force used is always justified and proportionate. (To the governor)

Key concern: Wandsworth remained one of the most overcrowded prisons in the country with most prisoners sharing a cell built for one. The shower areas on Trinity were poor. The physical environment in the mental health inpatient unit was unacceptable, did not meet infection control standards and had ligature points that had not been remedied to reduce the risk to patients. The control of vermin needed greater focus, including measures to prevent food waste and rubbish being thrown from cell windows.

Recommendation: All living conditions, including the inpatient unit and Trinity unit, should be improved to safe and decent standards.
(To the governor)

Key concern: The was insufficient support for the many foreign national prisoners held at Wandsworth. Home Office immigration staff had only recently returned to the prison, face-to-face contact was limited, and wing surgeries were still suspended. Legal documents were often served too late, and prisoners and detainees spent far too long in prison with their cases unresolved.

Recommendation: Foreign national prisoners and detainees should have their cases reviewed promptly and have timely access to information, help and face-to-face support.
(To the Home Office)

Key concern: The lack of primary mental health and inpatient staff resulted in patients not having their mental health needs met in a safe or timely manner. This was creating significant risks affecting the monitoring of referrals, assessments taking place within agreed timescales and ensuring that the outcome of assessments was fully documented.

Recommendation: The prison should work with the local delivery board, in conjunction with NHS England and Improvement, to make sure there are sufficient staff to meet the needs of patients with mental health problems safely.
(To the governor)

Key concern: Patients requiring transfer to secure mental health inpatient services continued to wait far too long for a bed. Only four of the 18 patients transferred to a mental health hospital under the Mental Health Act in the last six months had done so in fewer than 14 days. The remaining 14 patients waited from 15 to 226 days, which was unacceptable.

Recommendation: The prison should work with the local delivery board, in conjunction with NHS England and Improvement, to make sure that patients requiring a transfer under the Mental Health Act are transferred expeditiously and within the current transfer guidelines.
(To HMPPS and the governor)

Key concern: The daily regime remained far too limited and most prisoners continued to spend more than 22 hours a day locked in their cells, with some denied access to the open air for days at a time. Opportunities to engage in purposeful activity remained very limited and too many prisoners were unemployed. Access to the library and the gym and education were poor.

Recommendation: Time out of cell should be improved, including a daily regime that provides at least an hour in the open air for all and access to work, PE, the library, education, training or other constructive activities. (To the governor)

Key concern: Following unification of the Probation Service, the housing provider no longer supported prisoners on remand. This resulted in the large number of remand prisoners not being able to access support, for example to secure tenancies or deal with rent arrears.

Recommendation: Leaders should make sure that there is effective housing support for all prisoners, including those on remand.
(To HMPPS and the governor)

**Notable positive practice**

We define notable positive practice as innovative work or practice that leads to particularly good outcomes from which other establishments may be able to learn. Inspectors look for evidence of good outcomes for prisoners; original, creative or particularly effective approaches to problem-solving or achieving the desired goal; and how other establishments could learn from or replicate the practice.

Inspectors found six examples of notable positive practice during this inspection.

An assessment, care in custody and teamwork (ACCT) case management handover record had been introduced to identify which staff were responsible for the support of prisoners subject to ACCT.

The prison made effective use of available technology, including radio and TV, to support prisoner consultation and communication in a modern and informative manner.

A recently appointed bail information officer had worked with over 2,000 prisoners who might have been eligible to apply for bail in the last six months, which was an extremely useful resource given that almost half the population were on remand.

The assistant psychologist had delivered notable mental health training for prison officers and health care orderlies, which enabled officers and patients to come together to understand each other's responses to certain behaviours.

The provision of a dental surgeon on site enabled a wider range of dental treatment within the prison.

The public protection team regularly reviewed logs completed by staff who monitored prisoner telephone calls to provide an extra layer of quality assurance.

## INDEPENDENT MONITORING BOARD: Annual Report

The law requires every prison to be monitored by an independent Board appointed by the Justice Secretary; these are known as Independent Monitoring Boards (IMBs). The IMB must satisfy itself as to the humane and just treatment of those held in custody within its prison and the range and adequacy of the programmes preparing them for release; it must report annually to the Justice Secretary on how well the prison has met the standards and requirements placed on it.

**IMB Report 1 June 2020 to 31 May 2021**
**Published October 2021**
**Background to the report**
**– Covid -19**

The Covid-19 (Covid) pandemic had a significant impact on the Board's ability to gather information and compile this annual report. Ministers are aware of the constraints. Regular information is being collected specifically on the prison's response to the pandemic, and that is being collated nationally.

HMP Wandsworth worked to a national policy framework, the National Exceptional Delivery Model, which was underpinned by four key deliverables:

• provision of meals
• provision of healthcare
• prisoner safety, and
• welfare and continuation of family contact.

During the period under review the establishment was in stage 3 or stage 4 of the national framework. In stage 4, legal visits could be facilitated, social visits could not, the gym was closed and only external exercise was permitted. The property store was temporarily closed and was unable to take in new items. Prisoner bubbles were formed comprising groups of between 15 and 30, and they were kept separate from other groups whenever they were outside their cells.

HMP Wandsworth was in stage 4 at the start of the reporting period but moved to stage 3 in July. In January, it was moved back to stage 4, in line with increased lockdown restrictions in the community. The outbreak ended in mid-May but stage 4 restrictions continued beyond the end of the reporting year.

Public Health England (PHE) defined an outbreak as "Two or more test-confirmed cases of Covid or clinically suspected cases among individuals associated with a specific setting with illness onset dates within 14 days".

It was necessary to come out of outbreak and control the transmission of cases in the prison before it could move down to stage 3. The prison also needed to demonstrate it had the local operating procedures, risk assessment and standard operating procedures in place for each area that would be impacted by progressing to a new stage with possible increased risk. For HMP Wandsworth, stage 3 required that it could look at contact – social visits, reopening the property store, control gym access in bubbles and relax the strict social bubbles. This would allow meals to be served more efficiently, and offer gym and exercise to a greater number of men.

HMP Wandsworth, in line with the four key deliverables, during both stages 3 and 4:

• continued to offer all medical clinic appointments where possible, and Covid tested prisoners prior to movement, established a working RCU, and offered a Covid vaccination to every prisoner
• served hot meal at lunch as opposed to tea time
• issued prisoners with an additional £5 on induction to prison to be used for phone credit
• provided sentenced prisoners with workbooks to help manage behaviour
• provided all suitable prisoners with workbooks on managing substance misuse

The Governing Governor and staff operated under immense pressure and managed a protracted and extremely challenging situation with skill and imagination. New systems and ways of working were rapidly devised and introduced. Communication was enhanced with daily briefings; prisoners were kept fully informed of developments and largely accepted what, in normal circumstances, would be considered inhumane treatment, being locked up in some cases for 23.5 hours a day.

Contact with outside agencies was limited and often made using in-cell phones. Cells were called by representatives of Prison Advice and Care Trust (PACT), Change Grow Lives (CGL) and the Offender Management Unit (OMU) for key working. Isolating prisoners were phoned to take menu and canteen orders and complete welfare checks.

Considerable effort was made to reduce the strain on prisoners who were being required to comply with very tough conditions and who were suffering major restrictions on their already limited freedoms. It is inevitable that the mental and physical health and general wellbeing of prisoners were affected.

Staff absence through illness, shielding or self-isolation created further difficulties and led to additional restrictions to the regime.

Board members attended the establishment whenever conditions allowed and maintained contact with their areas of special interest. The majority of Board meetings were held online.

The Board was very impressed with the sensitive and imaginative manner in which the management team operated and the concern they showed for the welfare of everyone in the establishment. The Board commends personnel for their dedication and resolve.

### Main judgements

The Covid pandemic had an adverse impact on the running of the prison and the statements below reflect the Board's view of the year. An institution where men were locked up for up to 23.5 hours per day, with a very limited regime, was the reality for those in HMP Wandsworth over the year.

### How safe is the prison?

The prison was not safe as reflected in the level of violence with 274 (2019/2020: 270) prisoner-on-officer and 326 (2019/2020: 352) prisoner-on-prisoner assaults. Much of the violence was committed by a small minority – but it had a disproportionate impact on the operation of the whole prison. The Board was impressed by the initiatives and programmes introduced by the Governor and staff to improve safety but these could not overcome the cramped and inhumane living conditions exacerbated by the availability of drugs.

Drugs remained the principal trigger for aggressive behaviour and HMP Wandsworth made progress by installing a long-awaited X-ray body scanner in reception and the intermittent use of a Rapiscan to check incoming mail. Unfortunately, mandatory drug testing (MDT) was not carried out owing to Covid protocols.

### How fairly and humanely are prisoners treated?

Prisoners were treated fairly and with care and respect despite the restricted regime. The inhumane living conditions will only improve when there are substantial structural changes to the 170-year-old residential buildings and their occupancy. Problems with heating, hot water, showers, rodents and kit shortages were only some of the frequent and disruptive faults.

For many men, particularly those with complex behavioural issues, respecting the accommodation in which they lived, ate, slept, performed all bodily functions, two to a cramped cell with no personal space or privacy, was very challenging.

Visits were unavailable for most of the period and staff, aided by the chaplaincy, were quick to introduce initiatives to facilitate other forms of communication between prisoners and their families. These included supervised internet and video calls. Tablets were used to enable prisoners to 'attend' hospital visits and funerals.

### How well are prisoners' health and wellbeing needs met?

All contracted healthcare services were provided throughout the period, although some were adapted as a result of the restrictions. Appointments took place in clinics or by cell visits, remote prescribing or telephone, but with a significant increase in waiting times.

The Board was most concerned and surprised that the new healthcare facility, currently under construction, would not include any cell accommodation to relieve pressure on the totally inadequate Jones and Addison residential units.

The impact of the restricted regime on prisoners' wellbeing was severe. Referrals to mental health averaged 510 per month (2019/2020: 425), a significant increase.

There was a significant rise in the number of mental health assessments, due to an increase in the number of prisoners who were seriously unwell, and those who, whilst not diagnosed as psychotic, presented with worrying behaviour.

### How well are prisoners progressed towards successful resettlement?

Catch-22 replaced Penrose as the provider of resettlement services. This led to a short-lived improvement in the quality of the resettlement provision and resulted in data being supplied much more quickly and efficiently. On average 88.3% (2019/20: 30.5%) of BCST3 meetings (the assessment undertaken in the 12 weeks prior to release) took place.

The Board was greatly concerned by the planned disbanding of the community rehabilitation companies (CRCs), with no clear replacement strategy. Catch 22's contract would be terminated and its work taken over by the National Probation Service. The lack of central direction and shortage of information regarding this major change caused considerable uncertainty.

### Main areas for development
### TO THE MINISTER

The lack of adapted cells for wheelchair users remained a major concern and at times the only space available was in the Jones unit. As a result, an otherwise healthy wheelchair user became a "bed blocker" preventing an unwell prisoner from being admitted to Jones. The Board considered this unacceptable. When will the prison receive funding for more wheelchair adapted cells?

Home Office immigration enforcement officers left the prison in March 2020 and did not return for the duration of the reporting period. Their absence meant that in most cases foreign nationals relied on prison officers and the charity, Befriending Support Team (BEST), to answer questions, resolve issues and errors, and serve notices of case progress and/or removal. This was a most unsatisfactory situation and was quite often a contributor to a prisoner self-harming. When will the Immigration Service offer a full service in the prison, including being on the wings?

HMP Wandsworth continues to be severely overcrowded. Does the Government have a plan to resolve this situation?

During the year the mental health team (InReach) received an average of 510 referrals per month, up from 425 last year. The InReach team is overwhelmed. When will more resource be made available in the prison to address the increase in mental health issues?

## TO THE PRISON SERVICE

The re-role to a reception prison was originally expected to take place in 2017. The date was put back to 2018 and then again to early 2019. The change did not happen and was rescheduled for late 2020 but again did not materialise. At the period end, there were 1,097 prisoners on remand, 73% of the total population. When will the re- role take place?

The fabric of the prisoner accommodation continued to be unacceptable with broken windows, mould, leaking plumbing, leaking rooves, frequent heating failures, pigeon faeces, rodents and other issues. This is neither decent nor acceptable. What plans does the Prison Service have to address the wholly unacceptable state of the residential facilities?

The prison has complained to Novus, the education provider, repeatedly during the year and in previous years about the inadequacy of its offering. Unfortunately the prison has no management control over Novus and is therefore unable to effect improvements. When will this be rectified?

Funding for an upgrade to the CCTV system was approved over a year ago. When will this long overdue essential work be carried out?

The new healthcare facility will not include any cell accommodation to relieve pressure on the totally inadequate Jones and Addison units.

When will more residential medical capacity be made available?

## TO THE GOVERNOR

Listeners, trained to support other prisoners, provided a highly valuable role but were not always unlocked. The Board also noted that the Listener suites, which provided a private space, were often not available due to maintenance and other issues. What changes will be made to ensure a full and continuous Listener service is provided across all wings?

The lack of adequate kit was a recurrent issue. This included frequently reported shortages of kettles, bedding and clothing. The Board was also concerned about the number of complaints concerning the lack of privacy curtains in shared cells. What is being done to rectify this very unsatisfactory situation?

**GROVE ROAD
HOLLESLEY
WOODBRIDGE
SUFFOLK, IP12 3BF**

**Tel: 01394 633400**

*For the latest reports on this prison please visit:* https://tinyurl.com/bdfh26rv

*Important Changes:* **(1) Visits:** the identification necessary to access this prison and visit for social or professional purposes has changed; (2) **Money and Gifts** new rules now apply to these. See page 16 for full details of the above.

**Task of the establishment** A category C adult male closed prison with a progression regime.

**Certified normal accommodation and operational capacity**
Prisoners held at the time of inspection: 243
Baseline certified normal capacity: 258
In-use certified normal capacity: 258
Operational capacity: 264

**Prison status and key providers**
Public
Prison Group: Hertfordshire, Essex & Suffolk Group
Prison Group Director: Simon Cartwright
Governor/Director: Dave Nicholson
IMB Chair: Maggie Menzies
Physical health provider: Care UK
Mental health provider: Care UK
Substance use treatment provider: Phoenix Futures
Prison education framework provider: People Plus
Escort contractor: Serco

**Brief history** Previously an establishment holding boys aged 15 to 18, in 2014 the prison became a category C establishment holding adult men in a developing progression regime, a therapeutic community (TC)* and a psychologically informed planned environment (PIPE).* The progression regime was initially established in response to the decision by the Secretary of State for Justice on prisoners' suitability to transfer to open conditions, and it excluded a number of prisoners on indeterminate sentences (ISPs), both on life sentences and indeterminate sentence for public protection (IPP). (See Ministry of Justice. (2014). Release on Temporary Licence (ROTL) Consolidated Interim Instructions. PSO 6300.) The progression regime was established to ensure that ISPs excluded from open conditions could evidence that they had reduced their risk of serious harm sufficiently to enable them to be released from custody (PSI 22/2015: Generic Parole Process for Indeterminate and Determinate Sentenced Prisoners.). Since then, additional groups of prisoners are now also considered for the progression regime. The PIPE has places for up to 20, primarily to offer transitional support for prisoners who have completed therapy. The TC accommodates up to 40 prisoners and provides intensive group-based therapy under the guidance of psychologists and trained officers.

**Short description of residential units**
Alder: 89 beds (progression regime)
Oak: 90 beds (progression regime)
Elm: 40 beds (therapeutic community)
Maple: 20 beds (PIPE)
Sycamore: 19 beds (over-50s)

**Visiting Information**
Book online at: www.gov.uk/prison-visits or ring 01394 633 633 Mon to Thurs: 9am to midday
**Visiting times:** Fri, Sat, Sun: 2pm to 4pm.

**Legal visits:** Email:
legalvisits.warrenhill@justice.gov.uk or ring 01394 633633 Mon to Thurs: 9am to midday.
**Visiting times:** Wednesday - 2pm to 4pm.

**INSPECTIONS & REPORTS**
**Date of last full inspection** 18 Nov – 6 Dec 2019
*Notable features from this inspection*
• Warren Hill had the lowest incidence of self-harm and violent incidents among category C prisons.
• The prison comprised a therapeutic community, a psychologically informed planned environment (PIPE) and several units running a progression regime. It had recently become the only prison in England and Wales to be awarded prison-wide Enabling Environment accreditation (EE).
• All prisoners were in single cells.
• There was no segregation unit.
• Over 90% of prisoners were serving an indeterminate sentence.

**HMCIP Report, published 19 March 2020**
HMP Warren Hill is a category C male prison situated in Suffolk near the village of Hollesley. At the time of the inspection it held around 240 prisoners in closed conditions, but as this report makes clear it is a far from typical closed prison. The last inspection was carried out in October 2015, at which time it was judged to be delivering outcomes at our highest grading, good, in three of the tests of a healthy prison. Only in purposeful activity was the judgement at the lower level (by one grade) of reasonably good. On that occasion we made 27 recommendations, of which a commendably high 78% were achieved. Perhaps it is not surprising therefore that this latest inspection found that the grades to be awarded were exactly the same as in 2015, reflecting a continued commitment to the purpose and ethos of the prison.

Warren Hill is unusual among category C closed prisons in that it is entirely dedicated to delivering a range of services in specialist environments to support long term or complex prisoners towards progression into open conditions or for release into the community. It holds some of the most serious offenders in the prison estate. While to a certain extent they have been 'selected' for the unique regime the prison offers, we should not underestimate the risk they pose or the achievements of the prison in managing their behaviour.

Within the prison there is a therapeutic community, a psychologically-informed planned environment (PIPE) and other units delivering what is described as a progression regime. The purpose and features of these various units and programmes are set out in this report and so I shall not describe them in detail in this introduction. Nevertheless, it is notable that this is one of very few establishments that has such an unwavering focus on progression and on offering prisoners the opportunity to demonstrate, when being considered for re-categorisation, parole or release, how they have reduced the risk that they pose.

Warren Hill was the safest category C prison in the country, having the lowest levels of self-harm and violence among comparable establishments. It was a thoroughly respectful place, with strong staff-prisoner relationships being a defining feature. The accommodation was fit for purpose, there was excellent time out of cell and the range of activities, both educational and extracurricular, was impressive. There were more than enough activities available to keep every prisoner occupied on a full-time basis. However, the food could not be described as anything other than merely adequate, and not all prisoners could afford to supplement what was available by purchasing supplies from the prison shop.

The overwhelmingly positive aspects of the prison were such that we have made very few recommendations. There was one key concern which focused on expanding and improving the education provision, and ensuring that attendance was encouraged on a consistent basis. Otherwise, we made only 11 recommendations. Among these, we have commented on the need to improve the response to complaints, to help staff with their understanding of diversity issues, to do more for prisoners with disabilities and to more carefully monitor the timing at which medication is administered. Yet again, we have found ourselves looking at the issue of how to improve prisoners' ability to contact their families through the use of video-enabled social media. We are well aware of the potential risks associated with this, but would encourage Her Majesty's Prison and Probation Service (HMPPS) to think innovatively as to how these risks could be managed and trials conducted in appropriate circumstances. It is surely inevitable that at some point in the future this will be seen as an entirely normal feature of prison life, and Warren Hill could well be the type of environment in which the possibilities and benefits could be usefully explored. We also identified no fewer than 16 features of the prison that we considered to represent good practice. Some of these were obviously more easily delivered in a prison such as Warren Hill than in many others, but nevertheless I would encourage HMPPS to look at them with an open mind and give serious consideration to what could realistically be replicated elsewhere.

Warren Hill was an excellent facility that benefited from dedicated staff delivering a range of specialist interventions in an atmosphere that encouraged good behaviour. It offered prisoners serving long sentences, many of whom have had little hope of progressing in the past, the chance to begin the often long and difficult path towards release or being placed in open conditions. We commend the approach and achievements at Warren Hill, and hope that the approach that is taken there to underpin effective rehabilitation can be used as an example for other establishments to follow.

Peter Clarke CVO OBE QPM

HM Chief Inspector of Prisons December 2019

## INDEPENDENT MONITORING BOARD: Annual Report

The law requires every prison to be monitored by an independent Board appointed by the Justice Secretary; these are known as Independent Monitoring Boards (IMBs). The IMB must satisfy itself as to the humane and just treatment of those held in custody within its prison and the range and adequacy of the programmes preparing them for release; it must report annually to the Justice Secretary on how well the prison has met the standards and requirements placed on it.

### IMB Report 1 June 2020 – 31 May 2021
### Published October 2021
### Background to the report

The Covid-19 outbreak has again had a significant impact on the Board's ability to gather information and discuss the contents of this annual report. The Board has tried to cover as much ground as it can in these difficult circumstances, but inevitably there is less detail and supporting evidence than usual. Ministers are aware of these constraints. Regular information is being collected specifically on the prison's response to the pandemic, and that is being collated nationally.

### Main judgements
### How safe is the prison?

The Board considers that Warren Hill is a prison that feels safe for both prisoners and staff. While there are occasional incidents of low-level bullying, the prison makes good use of challenge, support and intervention plans (CSIPs) and prisoners are encouraged to engage in mediation where appropriate. There was one death in custody last year and the IMB has noted that the prison has responded rapidly to identified learning points.

How fairly and humanely are prisoners treated? The Board finds that prisoners are treated with respect. While the pandemic impacted on the operation of the key worker system, officers and managers continued to engage with the men and to explain the reasons for restrictions. The Board notes that the residents' council was very much involved in this process and where face-to-face contact was not always possible, prisoners were encouraged to voice their concerns and make suggestions in writing.

A major concern through the year has been the provision and quality of the food provided by the HMP Hollesley Bay kitchen. Staff shortages resulting from the pandemic along with food that has often been prepared too early and sometimes cold, and evidence of inadequate hygiene practices has led to a breakdown in trust. The IMB considers that this situation can only be resolved in the long term by investment in a kitchen at Warren Hill.

### How well are prisoners' health and wellbeing needs met?

The healthcare provision is generally good and of a standard similar to that in the community. It could indeed be argued that at the height of the pandemic the availability of healthcare in the prison was better than outside. When concerns have been raised about treatment or service, the IMB has found the healthcare manager to be responsive and changes have been made. The Board hopes to see the reactivation of the healthcare forum in the coming year.

The Board considers that prisoner wellbeing has been well supported in difficult and unprecedented circumstances. Staff have completed regular welfare checks with all individuals and have distributed distraction packs, DVDs and other additional items. These were provided when prisoners were confined for prolonged periods.

### How well are prisoners progressed towards successful resettlement?

The Board recognises that many aspects of the progression regime have been severely curtailed by the pandemic. It has not been possible for PeoplePlus to run education classes for almost the whole of the year to the end of May 2021 and key elements of the progression regime have similarly not functioned. The TC and PIPE have not been able to run group therapy sessions because of the need for social distancing.

### Main areas for development
### TO THE MINISTER

While this prison has received fewer complaints about the movement of property in the year to the end of May 2021, it remains a matter of concern that the long-awaited review of the handling of prisoners' property has still not been publish ed. This Board appreciates that delays in circulating a draft policy framework on property have occurred as a result of the pandemic but hopes that as restrictions ease, a comprehensive policy framework will be published in the near future.

### TO THE PRISON SERVICE

The Board is pleased that the long-awaited upgrade in telephone and information technology data lines have been undertaken and that plans are well advanced for the installation of in-cell telephony at Warren Hill. However, the Board notes with regret that the opportunity was not being taken to install in-cell laptops at the same time.

The Board has noted with much concern the ongoing difficulties with the provision of food from the Hollesley Bay kitchens and asks the Prison Service to examine the provision of a kitchen on the Warren Hill site.

### TO THE GOVERNOR

The Board fully acknowledges that the Governor has been unable to proceed with plans to extend purposeful activity and to extend the release on temporary licence (ROTL) scheme because of the pandemic. However, as restrictions ease the IMB would like to see these plans revived.

The Board also recognises that the prolonged lockdown has provided an opportunity to look at the regime at Warren Hill and hopes that the Governor will use this to implement positive changes.

### Progress since the last report

This last year has not provided many opportunities for progress. Nevertheless, the IMB notes that at long last the plan for an on-site approved premises is nearing completion, as is a cell which can accommodate a disabled prisoner. The Board has been impressed by the continuing efforts of managers and staff at Warren Hill to maintain relationships with and between prisoners at a time when so many restrictions have been in place.

GRISTON
THETFORD
NORFOLK
IP25 6RL

HM PRISON
SERVICE

HM PRISON
WAYLAND    Tel: 01953 804100

*For the latest reports on this prison please visit:*
https://tinyurl.com/bdfh26rv

*Important Changes:* **(1) Visits:** the identification necessary to access this prison and visit for social or professional purposes has changed; (2) **Money and Gifts** new rules now apply to these. See page 16 for full details of the above.

**Task of the establishment** HMP Wayland is a category C training prison with a resettlement function.

### Certified normal accommodation and operational capacity

Certified normal accommodation 914
Operational capacity: 1003

### Prison status and key providers

Public
Prison Group: Bedfordshire, Cambridgeshire & Norfolk
Prison Group Director: Gary Monaghan

Governor/Director: Ali Barker
IMB Chair: Trish Phillips
Health provider: Virgin Care Services Limited
Learning and skills provider: PeoplePlus
Escort contractor: Serco

**Brief history** HMP Wayland is a category C male training prison. The prison is 13.2 miles from the nearest railway station and three miles from the nearest bus stop, which can make visiting both difficult and expensive, as only around 15% of the prisoners are from Norfolk and Suffolk, almost all the rest being from London and the south-east of England.

The prison's certified normal accommodation is, currently, 914. At the start of the reporting year, the capacity was 1,003 but, following a fire inspection of the prison, two units, F and H wings, whose unacceptable condition this Board had raised previously with no result, were declared unsafe and are now in the process of demolition.

The original prison, built over 35 years ago, comprises:
• four, large H-blocks, mainly single cells with an integral toilet and washbasin, but with communal shower rooms
• a further, smaller, two-storey unit
• the segregation unit (locally named the reintegration unit)
• the healthcare unit,
• a kitchen
• the gym
• a large workshop/activity complex
• the prison's reception and visiting areas
• the main administration and entry building.

There have since been four expansions with now, as well as the original units above, and after the closure of F and H wings:
• five short-life, ready-to-use units of 60 prisoners each, all cells double, with full integral sanitation, including showers
• an individually designed two-wing accommodation unit of 95 single cells, all with integral sanitation
• a first night centre
• a second kitchen
• a large education centre
• a further administration building.
All of this has resulted in a very spread-out site. The Board is pleased to record that work has now started on the long-anticipated construction of a new robust, segregation unit, which is scheduled to open by the end of 2021.

The older buildings continue to have problems with their leaking flat roofs, resulting in puddles in the corridors, cells and other places. These problematic flat roofs have seen repairs, but more work is likely to be needed, especially as

the cell construction in these buildings includes poor window design and inward-opening doors, which are easy to barricade and potentially a source of difficulty for staff making an emergency entry. The Prison Service has now agreed to refurbish these cells with more modern anti-barricade doors, windows and furniture. The Board welcomes that move, although it regrets that the work will take some considerable time.

There have also been continuing severe problems with the fabric and construction of the newer builds. A refurbishment programme has taken place but the design and construction of these units will mean that further work will be an ongoing requirement; they are already beyond their original design life.

As the prison is expected to expand further, in addition to replacing the accommodation lost by the demolition of F and H wings, there will be a need to review whether expansion will be needed for the central administration and support areas, such as the reception unit, and the visits, faith and training areas, all of which were under pressure when the prison's population was at its previous certified normal accommodation of 1,003.

**Visiting Information**
Book online at: www.gov.uk/prison-visits or ring 01953 804152 everyday: 9:30am to 12pm and 2:30pm to 4pm.
**Visiting times:** Mon-Wed, Sat-Sun: 2pm to 4pm.

**Legal visits:** There are currently no legal visits taking place.

**INSPECTIONS & REPORTS**
**Date of last full inspection 19–30 June 2017**
**HMCIP Report, published 24 October 2017**
HMP Wayland – a well-led prison moving in a positive direction
HMP Wayland, near Thetford in rural Norfolk and housing many prisoners on long sentences, was a "very well-led" prison making some progress toward becoming safer after a sharp rise in violence over the last four years, according to a report by HM Inspectorate of Prisons.
The jail, with almost 1,000 men, was confronting problems of violence and illicit drugs with some apparent success, inspectors found in an unannounced visit in June 2017. They also noted that work to support learning and vocational opportunities was good and nearly two-thirds of prisoners felt Wayland had helped them become less likely to reoffend.
Peter Clarke, HM Inspector of Prisons, said the category C prison – with over two-thirds of prisoners serving more than four years and just over 100 serving life sentences – was moving in a positive direction.

Though assaults had risen sharply since the last inspection in 2013, and violence remained "very high", it had begun to fall in the months leading up to the inspection. Mr Clarke said safety was a key priority and meaningful work was being done to confront violence and reduce it, and this seemed to be having an effect, though it was yet to be reflected in improved prisoner confidence. Illicit drugs were also a problem and nearly half of prisoners surveyed thought it was easy to obtain drugs and alcohol. However, "as with the prison's approach to violence reduction, useful strategies were in place to cut off supply and there was some evidence of successes."

Ofsted inspectors who accompanied HMIP inspectors found the overall effectiveness of learning and vocational opportunities to be good. Similarly, Mr Clarke noted: "Wayland took its responsibilities as a resettlement prison seriously...Nearly two thirds of prisoners thought that the prison had assisted them in making them less likely to reoffend. Reintegration and release planning was generally good."

Offending behaviour work was also effective, and in particular the personality disorder (PDU) and psychologically informed planned environment (PIPE) units were excellent. The presence of these units was found to be helpful to the overall culture of the prison. Prisoners were assessed for around five months on the PDU to determine if they had a personality disorder; those who did then remained on the unit for around 18 months and then moved onto the PIPE unit as part of their progression.

Wayland remained a generally respectful prison, inspectors concluded. The environment was reasonable, although some cells needed to be cleaner. Access to in-cell telephones and secure laptops that eased access to administrative systems was an example of good practice. Consultation with minority groups was very good, although this had still to realise measurable improvement in outcomes for, and the perceptions of, minority groups. Many black and minority ethnic men came from London, felt far from home and regarded the lack of black or Asian staff as a problem.

Mr Clarke said: "Overall, Wayland was, in our view, making progress and this is an encouraging report. Our assessment has had to balance a number of objective measures, many of which still need to improve further, with more dynamic measures such as the clear energy and determination within the prison to improve matters. The prison was very well led, while plans for improvement were active and substantive, taking the prison forward in a positive direction."

Michael Spurr, CEO of HM Prison and Probation Service, said: "The Chief Inspector has commended the positive work being done at Wayland to tackle violence and drug use and to support effective rehabilitation. The progress being made in challenging circumstances is a credit to the Governor and the staff. We will use the recommendations in the report to achieve further improvements over the coming months."

**INDEPENDENT MONITORING BOARD: Annual Report**
The law requires every prison to be monitored by an independent Board appointed by the Justice Secretary; these are known as Independent Monitoring Boards (IMBs). The IMB must satisfy itself as to the humane and just treatment of those held in custody within its prison and the range and adequacy of the programmes preparing them for release; it must report annually to the Justice Secretary on how well the prison has met the standards and requirements placed on it.

**IMB Report 1 June 2020 – 31 May 2021**
**Published November 2021**
**EXECUTIVE SUMMARY**
**Background to the report**
Life in Wayland during the whole of the reporting year has been dominated by the Covid-19 pandemic, which has directly impoverished the regime. Prisoners have frequently been locked up for up to 22 hours a day, with occasionally less than two hours for exercise, showers and domestic activity. No employment has been taking place, other than work in wing cleaning, kitchens, the DHL packing shop, waste management and a small personal protective equipment (PPE) workshop. The unlock situation eased a bit at the end of the reporting year and also for a short time in the late summer of 2020, when face-to-face visits were allowed, although with limitations. However, during the whole of this year there have been no industrial workshops or training courses open (except those noted above), virtually no education and only remote use of the library.

Wayland has, however, been fortunate to have had a low number of positive Covid-19 cases and only one pandemic-related death, so far, in the prisoner population, bearing in mind the cramped conditions that the prisoners live under. This was despite there being occasional spikes in infections from prisoners from HMP Norwich and elsewhere, and brought in from the community, the local area having a high level at one time from an outbreak at a food factory.

Nevertheless, the lockdown has reportedly had a bad effect on some prisoners' mental health, particularly in the early stages, although this has been much less than feared. Although, due to the increased demands on their services, the mental health team may have missed the potential signs it is perhaps significant to record that there has been no increase in formal diagnoses of depression, although the number said to have 'low mood' has increased, although there has been an increase in, thankfully mostly minor, self-harming and in the number of assessment, care in custody and teamwork (ACCT) documents opened. At the end of our reporting year, with restrictions easing, with personal visits resuming, a little longer time out of cells and a little gym time, the Board trusts that prisoners' mental health issues can be given more of the attention that they need.

The Board, however, is increasingly concerned that any improvement in the treatment of prisoners, as the world, and the Prison Service, comes out of the pandemic, will be threatened by two serious issues. First, the already low staffing numbers are threatening the recovery. Second, a very high proportion of prison officers have almost no experience of the challenging management of prisoners outside of a tightly controlled pandemic-restricted environment.

The Board has been informed that the number of prison officer grade staff available for duty is often as low as two-thirds of the agreed staffing profile, although some of this lack is due to the need to temporarily promote junior staff to supervisory positions, as well as to pandemic effects. Nevertheless, it is the case that the total agreed staffing level is short by 28 band 3 (prison officer) staff. Even if, however, the staff numbers are brought up to the current agreed level, it is the Board's view, from its monitoring observations, that this is significantly fewer than would be needed to create a properly profiled organisation, committed to the rehabilitation of its prisoners. Prisoners are not in the equivalent of an Amazon warehouse, just waiting for workers to move them to the delivery vans, they are complex human beings with more than averagely complex needs. As such, there needs to be an adequate number of staff, adequately trained, to deliver on the Prison Service's commitment to rehabilitation, as well as security. In the Board's view, therefore, the Prison Service should not only review the total number of staff available in Wayland, but also ensure that they are adequately trained to carry out their demanding roles, and that their pay is such as will ensure their retention.

**Main judgements**
**How safe is the prison?**
During this year of lockdown, prisoners have undoubtedly been safer due to their restricted movements and the smaller number of prisoners able to associate during exercise or domestic duties, compared with pre-pandemic opportunities. However, there have still been assaults, prisoner on prisoner, and for a time in the early lockdown times, prisoner assaults on other prisoners, and on staff, increased, although a significant number of the latter were triggered, it seemed, by the inevitable potential for conflict during return to cell. However, the number of assaults declined as the pandemic restrictions took hold. In addition, as experience of the lockdown was gained, both by staff and prisoners, there was more acceptance of the restrictions, and reductions in assaults.

Alongside this, the number of self-isolating prisoners also reduced; many, perhaps, because there were fewer opportunities to acquire drugs, and therefore debts, which reduced reversion to self-isolation. However, assaults are, by their nature, extreme events and although it is useful to be aware of these clear indicators of a lack of safety, their lesser frequency, or absence, perhaps should not be taken as an indicator that all is well. Prisoners may feel unsafe, even if they do not feel they are exposed to such extreme events. A low level of threats to ensure compliance over small things, such as holding drugs or hooch for others if cell searches are suspected, can still result in prisoners feeling unsafe. In our recent survey of prisoners' attitudes and views, we asked three questions on the issue of safety:

1. Did you feel safe after your arrival?
2. Do you feel safe NOW?
3. How many other prisoners do you feel you can REALLY trust at Wayland?

The answers were revealing:
1. Exactly a third said that they did not feel safe on arrival.
2. This fell to 22% feeling unsafe (after an average stay of 18 months), which is still a significant minority who felt unsafe.
3. However, 40% admitted trusting nobody in the prisoner population, and the average number who admitted trusting some other prisoners was only three.

If safety is an absence of a fear of direct threat and harmful actions by others, then Wayland is not a safe prison for around one in five of its prisoners. If, however, safety is defined as a state where prisoners can feel safe in the company of others and have the opportunity to get on with their personal lives without a constant low-level anxiety of what might happen to them, then Wayland still has a way to go to be a safe prison for almost all prisoners.

**How fairly and humanely are prisoners treated?**
Despite the challenges of Covid-19, staff have made consistent efforts to manage prisoners in a fair and humane fashion in their daily interactions. When possible during the pandemic, prisoner forums have been received well, and positively, and were a significant factor in the prison community's continued acceptance of the restrictions of the lockdown. Other initiatives, such weekly 'coffee mornings' for life - sentenced prisoners and those serving an indeterminate sentence for public protection, where they could easily interact with staff at all levels, were welcomed and well attended when possible. Communication with prisoners has been uniformly very well received, with 80% of respondents in our survey agreeing that communication over the pandemic and other issues had been good.

We are also able to say, from Board members' observations and discussions with prisoners, that staff have shown consistent fairness towards prisoners, and a willingness to try to help them, in their daily interactions, despite the challenge of many being very new to the job and hard-pressed by the constant unlocking and relocking driven by the pandemic lockdown requirements.

**How well are prisoners' health and wellbeing needs met?**
Although the Board has a professional relationship with the head of healthcare, we have found it difficult to get much of an evidenced view on how the health and wellbeing of prisoners has been met. For the second year, unlike the Board's previous experience, we have been excluded from attending any healthcare meetings outwith the prison, although we are hopeful that, as this issue has now been escalated, the NHS commissioner will be more sympathetic to our attendance. Additionally, due to the pandemic, there have been no in-prison meetings. We have, therefore, been largely reliant on those prisoners we have managed to speak to, information from discussions with healthcare staff, and the results of a few questions in our prisoner survey.

**How well are prisoners progressed towards successful resettlement?**
It would not be too far off the mark to say that, in this reporting year, the only progression of prisoners towards their resettlement will have been their own self- determination, as the prison, under the effect of the pandemic, has been able to do very little with a few prisoners, and almost nothing with most to address their rehabilitative needs effectively, a situation we describe in detail in many sections of this report.

Of course, as we have been informed, and as we have observed, the necessary restrictions under the pandemic management policies have been the main source of this failure, but, as we have stated above, it is also our observation that the prison is woefully understaffed, not only by there being insufficient officers actually in post, which might be covered in time by recruitment, but also because, in the Board's view, the staffing profile needs a radical overhaul. If Wayland is to become an effective training prison which identifies prisoners' resettlement needs accurately, provides responses to those needs and ensures that their resettlement plans are positive and supported, it needs an increase in the number not just of staff, but of trained staff who are equipped to deliver the regime which underpins the plans, responses and support, at an individual prisoner level on a daily basis.

**Main areas for development**
**TO THE MINISTER**
The Board understands that the per diem allowance of prison catering has remained at £2.02 for many years. It is the Board's view that an increase per diem would create greater prisoner satisfaction with a fundamental aspect of the prison's care for its prisoners and thereby encourage their positive response to the regime as a whole.

We draw to the minister's attention, as required under our remit, our surprise at our understanding that there has been no research, actioned or contemplated, into the effect on rehabilitation and reoffending of the virtual cessation of programmed courses, vocational and employment training, and education for more than a year to date.

The Board urges the minister to charge the public sector successors to the community rehabilitation companies with ensuring that, for all prisoners, there is effective planning for, and confirmed accommodation upon, their release.

**TO THE PRISON SERVICE**
The Board believes, from its monitoring responsibilities, that Wayland is significantly short of staff, not just in numbers but, importantly, in experience and training in responding adequately to the many complex needs of its prisoners. The Board believes that this situation needs urgent action. The Board hopes, in addressing the scourge of drugs and intoxicants in prison, that innovative use of modern technology, including the use of targeted sobriety testing or tagging, and an enlargement of official ways of sourcing permitted items, could be researched as a policy initiative by the Prison Service and so recommends.

The Board believes that a comprehensive refurbishment programme is necessary in the new-build wings, in order to prevent a continuing deterioration in the living conditions of prisoners, and looks forward to confirmation that such a programme will be commenced in the coming year.

Based on our findings that a large majority of prisoners express a willingness to talk to staff about their problems, the Board urges the Prison Service to ensure that properly profiled key working, including time for training and supervision in this key prison officering skill, is included in the review of staff that we are calling for in this report.

Through our discussions with prisoners, our reviews of the prison complaints procedures and their management, and the results of our recent survey, the Board suggests to the Prison Service that a less tight timetable for responses would decrease delays in replies and increase the acceptance of replies which have had time to investigate the complaint properly. Relying on interim replies is seen as a brush-off by most prisoners.

As our monitoring has revealed a significant likelihood that cell clearance certification procedures have not always been duly followed, the Board believes that the importance of managing an accurate and timely cell clearance certificate needs reinforcement on a national basis. The Board requests that if healthcare contractors' contracts do not include a requirement to permit the Board's sight of contract documents, excluding only financial and patient confidentiality issues, they are revised to do so.

With regard to contingency planning, the Board believes that the lesson from the current pandemic is for the Prison Service to plan, on a national basis, for the maintenance of its core remit of enabling prisoners' rehabilitation, and so avoid the current position of almost complete failure to address rehabilitative needs for more than the first year of the pandemic.

The Board believes that, despite the challenges, there should be a serious attempt to identify those with the greatest need for resettlement assistance and do what is possible to provide this and so recommends to the Prison Service.

In the Board's view, the expected benefit of 'Purple Visits' has not been fully realised due, prisoners have informed us, to the conditions imposed on relatives. It therefore urges the Prison Service to review these arrangements to find consumer-acceptable alternatives to face-to-face social and family visits.

## TO THE GOVERNOR

The Board believes, from its observations, discussions with staff and prisoners, and its recent survey, that an increasingly experienced prisoner community is meeting an increasingly inexperienced staff community, with obvious implications for prisoner management. The Board believes that this change, alone, requires focused training for new staff as they develop their skills, and urges the Governor to seek such staffing and re-establish the funding that will allow this training to take place.

The Board's findings that 35% of the prisoner community respondents felt that they could trust no other prisoner and of those who could trust others, an average of only three others suggests that there is an urgent need for more detailed research, and a strategic response then identified, to this situation.

The Board has been surprised to discover how few prisoners had had cell acceptance forms provided on their reception. Proper procedural implementation of this requirement would underline the prison's acceptance of this practical demonstration of decency. The Board asks that an operational review be held into this identified failure in decency management.

The Board's findings that almost 60% of survey respondents declared that they did not normally receive weekly bedding changes was disappointing, and a worse finding than previously found, when the response was evenly split. The Board draws the Governor's attention to this finding and hopes that measures will be put in place to achieve a weekly bedding change as a matter of routine for all prisoners.

From respondents' answers to other questions we posed, and from how prisoners describe to Members their disappointment if staff do not live up to the standards they expect, the Board believes that there is a bedrock of views in which prisoners see staff as people who they want to trust. The Board hopes that this insight is built upon to provide more effective staff training.

This year, the Board has discovered that 'did not attends' for healthcare are much lower than last year's, and hopes that strategies will be developed so that these lower numbers are maintained after lockdown is eased.

With an average of only half the education packs delivered to cells being returned, the Board hopes that the Governor can remedy this situation and ensure that operational and educational arrangements are brought into harmony in future, to avoid this significant waste of resources.

The Board has been disappointed at the apparent inability to use pandemic-safe resources, such as the 'Streetworks' course, in the current operational response to the pandemic, and trusts that decisions can be taken, at both local and national levels, to plan for greater activity provision in future such emergencies.

**CHURCH CAUSEWAY
THORP ARCH
WETHERBY
YORKSHIRE, LS23 7AZ**

**HM PRISON
WEALSTUN**

**Tel: 01937 444400**

*For the latest reports on this prison please visit:*
https://tinyurl.com/bdfh26rv

*Important Changes:* **(1) Visits:** the identification necessary to access this prison and visit for social or professional purposes has changed; (2) **Money and Gifts** new rules now apply to these. See page 16 for full details of the above.

**Task of the establishment** HMP Wealstun is a category C adult training and resettlement prison for men.

**Certified normal accommodation and operational capacity**
Prisoners held April 2021: 803
Baseline certified normal capacity: 809
Operational capacity: 832

**Prison status and key providers**
Public
Prison Group: Yorkshire
Prison Group Director: Helen Judge
Governor/Director: Dianne Lewis
IMB Chair: Rebecca Major
Physical health provider: Care UK
Mental health provider: Care UK
Substance use treatment provider: Midlands Partnership NHS Foundation Trust and Care UK
Prison education framework provider: Novus
Escort contractor: GeoAmey

**Brief history** On 1 April 1995, HM Prisons Thorp Arch and Rudgate amalgamated to form HMP Wealstun. This created a category C (closed) side and category D (open) side within one establishment. In 2008, the open prison closed and the prison underwent a conversion to an entirely category C prison, which was fully operational in May 2010. Since May 2015, it has served a resettlement function for the West Yorkshire area. It has a certified normal accommodation of 809 and an operational capacity of 832. However, the latter was reduced to 809 in April 2020 to enable all prisoners to be housed in single cells during the Covid-19 pandemic.

**Short description of residential units**
There are 10 residential units and a segregation unit. A and B wings are the original 1960s remand centre buildings; A wing includes a residential support unit of self-isolators; D wing is a pre-fabricated single-cell accommodation unit; C wing accommodates the majority of prisoners on the integrated drug treatment system programme; E, F, G, H, I and J wings were converted from open category D accommodation to closed category C accommodation; G wing is the incentivised substance-free living unit; H wing is mainly for prison kitchen workers.

However, following the start of the pandemic and the need to manage different cohorts of prisoners, I and J wings are now the reverse cohort units and induction wings. The site also comprises a kitchen, visitors' centre, chaplaincy, gym, library, healthcare centre and a number of workshops. A reception area for prisoners' visitors is located outside the main gate.

The prison is part of the public sector and, although HMPPS is responsible for the operation of the establishment, the main service providers are:
- Novus, for works, learning and skills
- Practice Plus Group from 1 October 2020, for the provision of physical/mental healthcare
- GeoAmey, for escort provision
- Amey, for the provision of facilities management and site maintenance
- St Giles Trust, for resettlement services
- Jigsaw, for family intervention services.

**Visiting Information**
Booking line: 01937 444400 Open 24 hours.
**Visiting times:** Monday to Thursday, 6:30am to 8am, 11:30am to 1pm, 5:30pm to 11pm, Fridays, 6:30am to 8pm, 11:30am to 11pm, Weekends and bank holidays: 6:30am to 11pm.

**Legal visits:**
Booking line: 01937 444400 Open 24 hours.

**INSPECTIONS & REPORTS**
**Date of last full inspection 15–25 October 2019**
**HMCIP Report, published 13 February 2020**
HMP Wealstun is a category C training and resettlement prison for adult men, situated a few miles from Wetherby in Yorkshire. At the time of this inspection some 820 prisoners were being held there. The population was transient and young, with two-thirds of the prisoners having been held there for less than six months, and around a third being aged under 30.

The prison was last inspected in 2015, on which occasion it was judged to be good or reasonably good in all four of our healthy prison tests. This recent inspection showed there had been a decline in two of those areas, safety and purposeful activity, in which we found that outcomes were now insufficiently good.

The ready availability of illicit drugs undermined much of what the prison was trying to achieve. In our survey, 69% of prisoners told us it was easy to obtain drugs, and nearly a quarter of all prisoners said they had acquired a drug habit since entering the jail – a remarkable figure given the short time that many prisoners stayed there. The prison had benefitted, belatedly, from being part of the '10 Prisons Project' set up under the last but one Prisons Minister, and as a result now had some modern technology in place to help detect drugs and enhanced physical security to help keep them out. We were told that although the project had been set up in August 2018, support at a local level had not materialised until March 2019, and it could well be that the longer-term benefits of the project have yet to be felt.

The positive impact of technology and physical security improvements was compromised by the lack of response to intelligence reports. Far too little targeted searching or testing had been carried out, which, in view of the fact that the intelligence itself appeared to be of a good quality, was a missed opportunity. There was no clear overall strategy to deal with the drugs supply problem. Until such time as there is a comprehensive action plan in place, that not only requires an effective response to intelligence but is also proactive in seeking out incoming supply routes, the harms caused by the ready availability of drugs will not be reduced.

It was disturbing to find that levels of self-harm had increased six-fold since the last inspection. As in many prisons that we inspect, not enough had been done to analyse and understand what sat behind this huge increase. Until such analysis is carried out, it will not be possible to know whether the excessive amount of time that prisoners spent locked in their cells was a contributory factor or not. For a training prison such as Wealstun to have 28% of prisoners locked in their cells during the working day, as we found during this inspection, was simply counter-productive and unacceptable. Far too many prisoners failed to attend their allocated activity, which was a lost opportunity as we found that those who did attend generally had a positive attitude to learning and work, and in many cases were proud of their achievements.

I frequently refer in inspection reports to the weaknesses in the Offender Assessment System (OASys) which seem to afflict so many prisons. Given that nearly half of the prisoners were assessed as presenting a high risk of serious harm to others, it was concerning to find that Wealstun suffered from these same weaknesses, which appear to be systemic. OASys is supposed to provide the basis for managing risk, informing sentence planning, making re-categorisation decisions and planning for release. However, we found that 75% of prisoners who were arriving at Wealstun were doing so without an assessment, and more than a quarter had one that had not been updated for more than a year. There had been some creditable work carried out locally to try to devise sentence plans, but two-thirds of these were missing in the cases we looked at, and where they did exist they were ineffective. The widespread shortcomings of OASys comprise in my view a strategic failure that undermines so much good work that we see being carried out at a local level, and demands a more co-ordinated and serious response from HM Prison and Probation Service (HMPPS) than has been the case to date.

Given the failure in so many cases to properly assess the risks presented by prisoners, it was perhaps inevitable that we should find other serious weaknesses in public protection and release planning. These are set out in detail in the report, but in essence amount to failures in what should be standard procedures.

I have deliberately focused on a number of key weaknesses, because they inevitably undermined much of the very good work that was being carried out at Wealstun. The relationships between staff and prisoners were generally very good, although at times we did see poor behaviour going unchallenged. Healthcare was good, and in many cases living conditions had improved considerably. Overall, we judged that outcomes in our respect test were good, our highest grade, and that is to the credit of the establishment, given the challenges they face in so many areas. I have little doubt that if the key areas of illicit drug supply and failure to assess risks were to be addressed, Wealstun could recover from the decline in grades since the last inspection, and indeed move on to better serve the needs of its prisoners.

Peter Clarke OBE CVO QPM October 2019
HM Chief Inspector of Prisons

**INDEPENDENT MONITORING BOARD: Annual Report**

The law requires every prison to be monitored by an independent Board appointed by the Justice Secretary; these are known as Independent Monitoring Boards (IMBs). The IMB must satisfy itself as to the humane and just treatment of those held in custody within its prison and the range and adequacy of the programmes preparing them for release; it must report annually to the Justice Secretary on how well the prison has met the standards and requirements placed on it.

**IMB Report 1 June 2020 – 31 May 2021**
**Published October 2021**
**Executive summary**
**Background to the report**

The restrictions placed on prisons and the general public due to the Covid-19 pandemic have affected the lives of the prisoners considerably, as well as the ability of the Board to directly monitor the situation throughout the period of this report. The Board has therefore tried to cover as much ground as it can in these difficult circumstances but inevitably there is less detail and supporting evidence than usual. Ministers are aware of these constraints.

This report presents the findings of the Board at HMP Wealstun for the period 1 June 2020 – 31 May 2021. Board evidence comes from a variety of sources, which was especially difficult to achieve when direct monitoring was not possible. Monitoring instead had to be conducted remotely through regular telephone and email contact with the Governor, wing staff and functional heads. As soon as it was permitted, some members returned to direct monitoring and so evidence was then available from observations made on visits, scrutiny of records and data, informal contact with prisoners and staff, and prisoner applications, although this was limited at times. The restrictions have, however, caused a considerable amount of additional work for the Board and this will continue until normality returns.

Throughout the reporting period the majority of prisoners were locked up for up to 23 hours a day, which would normally be unacceptable, but the Board acknowledge that it was unavoidable given the pressures on the prison during the pandemic. A small number of essential workshops were running, with a reduced number of prisoners working in each. There was a major outbreak of Covid amongst the prisoners and staff early in 2021 which affected the regime further. However, considering how difficult the year has been for both staff and prisoners, the prison was settled and the restrictions and difficulties were accepted by all. The Board commends the prison for their handling of this situation.

**Main judgements**
**How safe is the prison?**

During the majority of the reporting period the prisoners were locked up for up to 23 hours a day. There was very little access to drugs and the level of violence and self- harm was significantly lower than in the previous reporting period. There was also little bullying and things were generally quiet, so prisoners were probably safer. However, whilst a prison might be judged to be safe in this situation, the Board is concerned about what will happen once the regime restrictions begin to be lifted and, as has already been seen, the level of violence begins to rise.

**How fairly and humanely are prisoners treated?**

Whilst the Board accepts that there have been extenuating circumstances this year as a result of the pandemic, the fact that the prisoners were locked up for most of each day could be seen as inhumane, as being locked up for 23 hours a day is clearly unsatisfactory, and would normally be unacceptable, but the Board acknowledge that it was unavoidable given the pressures on the prison during the pandemic.

However, the Board feels that the prisoners were treated fairly as there was a consistent approach across the prison and all prisoners were able to have a television and were given a £5 pin credit to enable them to keep in touch with their families, and goody bags.

**How well are prisoners' health and wellbeing needs met?**

Healthcare has managed well over this period, with prisoners having normal access to most healthcare services. However, access to dentistry was stopped for a number of months and there is now a backlog. As previously stated, the length of time out of the cell was extremely limited and, as the report highlights, there was little face-to-face access for prisoners to soft skills such as Jigsaw, although full use was made of the opportunities presented.

**How well are prisoners progressed towards successful resettlement?**

There has been little progression work during the reporting period as there was limited work and education and no accredited behaviour programmes. Transfers to category D prisons, when allowed, were delayed because of a lack of spaces and having to reverse cohort prior to transfer. Visits were cancelled for the majority of the year. The one positive aspect was the additional £5 pin credit each prisoner received and the introduction of 'purple visits' (video calling), which although not well liked initially, allowed prisoners to keep in touch with their families.

**Main areas for development**
**TO THE MINISTER**

To consider increasing the daily food allowance, as £2.02 is an extremely small amount to feed adult men and provide the nutrition they require

To consider how to encourage employers to be more supportive towards employing ex-offenders, given the shortage of labour in certain sectors.

**TO THE PRISON SERVICE**

Ensure that as prisons move out of lockdown a review is undertaken to identify any long-term effects on prisoners and plans are in place to address them (repeat area from 2019/2020 report).

Ensure that prisons are provided with detailed guidance on managing the withdrawal of the mitigations that were put in place during the pandemic (for example, the £5 pin credit) as this withdrawal is likely to cause prisoners considerable upset.

Ensure that the requirements are clear for when prisons which undertook training as part of their participation in a pilot should undertake refresher training; if it is essential training for a pilot, why isn't it refreshed?

Ensure that there is a comprehensive review of the use of body scanners, including better training for officers and consistency across the estate, so that prisoners are not segregated when the only evidence is the scan image which is subject to interpretation.

Ensure that the system used to record prisoners' learning (CURIOUS) is updated so that information is available to inform decisions.

Provide more category D open prison places, so that transfers are not delayed once a prisoner is recategorised.

**TO THE GOVERNOR**

Ensure that once approval is given to resume training, refresher training in use of PAVA and rigid-bar handcuffs is given priority (repeat area from 2019/202 report).

Ensure that the planned change for all laundry to be done in the prison laundry is managed sensitively, as prisoners may have concerns about an increased risk of personal clothing damage or loss.

Ensure that the secreted items policy is reviewed, including daily scans for segregated prisoners so that prisoners are not segregated where evidence is not clear/available or kept segregated any longer than necessary.

Ensure that when lockdown restrictions are lifted, key workers are fully in place for all prisoners.

Ensure that the Board is notified consistently when a prisoner is placed in segregation.

Ensure that funding is available to reinstate the Resolve offending behaviour programme, given the significant number of prisoners with a history of domestic violence.

Ensure that the monthly forum with the offender management unit (OMU) for IPP and life-sentenced prisoners is reinstated.

**Progress since the last report**

Due to the pandemic, several of the main areas for development from the annual report for 2019/2020 have not progressed. Where significant, they have been repeated for 2020/2021 and are included above.

**ASH BANK ROAD**
**WERRINGTON**
**STOKE-ON-TRENT**
**STAFFS, ST9 0DX**

**HM PRISON**
**WERRINGTON**

**Tel: 01782 463300**

*For the latest reports on this prison please visit:*
https://tinyurl.com/bdfh26rv

*Important Changes:* **(1) Visits:** the identification necessary to access this prison and visit for social or professional purposes has changed; (2) **Money and Gifts** new rules now apply to these. See page 16 for full details of the above.

**Task of the establishment** To hold sentenced and remanded children aged 15 to 17 years.

**Certified normal accommodation and operational capacity**
Children held at the time of inspection: 64
Baseline certified normal capacity: 94
In-use certified normal capacity: 94
Operational capacity: 118

**Population of the establishment**
• 139 new children received in 2021
• 45 sentenced, 19 on remand at the time of the inspection
• 11 foreign national children
• 63% of children from black and minority ethnic backgrounds
• Four children 15 years of age, 17 children 16 years of age, 34 children aged 17 and nine children aged 18.

**Prison status and key providers**
Public
Prison Group: Youth Custody Service
Prison Group Director: Helga Swidenbank
Governor/Director: Keith Attwood
IMB Chair: Sally Osborne
Physical health provider: Practice Plus Group
Mental health provider: Midlands Partnership NHS Foundation Trust (MPFT), Inclusion team
Psychosocial substance misuse service: MPFT, Inclusion team
Clinical substance misuse intervention: Practice Plus Group
Prison education framework provider: Novus
Escort contractor: GeoAmey

**Leadership changes since the last inspection**
Sonia Brookes OBE, until January 2021
Ian Darlington, acting governor, Jan – Mar 2021

**Brief history** The institution started life in 1895 as an industrial school and was subsequently purchased by the Prison Commissioners in 1955. Following implementation of the Criminal Justice Act 1982 it converted to a youth custody centre in 1985 and in 1988 it became a young people's centre.

**Short description of residential units**

Werrington consists of three main residential units. The Doulton unit: A wing has 52 cells; B wing has 44 cells. All cells are single occupancy, some with in-cell showers.

The Denby unit: C1 landing is the welfare and development enhancement unit: eight cells occupied by children who require extra support. C2 landing has 22 cells: 12 are allocated to children on the highest level of the rewards scheme and 10 to children on induction. All cells have showers.

**Visiting Information**

Book online at: www.gov.uk/prison-visits or ring 0300 060 6508 Monday-Friday, 9am to 6pm
**Visiting times:** Tues-Thurs: 1:30pm to 4:15pm; Sat-Sun: 1:45pm to 4:30pm

**Legal visits:** Booking line: 0300 060 6508 Mon-Fri 9am to 6pm.
**Visiting times:** Monday: 1:30pm to 4:15pm. There will be 8 sessions available for a duration of 90 minutes each.

**INSPECTIONS & REPORTS**
**HMCIP Report 24 & 31 Jan – 4 Feb 2022**
**Published 20 May 2022**

HMYOI Werrington is a facility for boys under the age of 18, located near Stoke- on-Trent. Capable of holding up to 118, at the time of our inspection just 64 children were in residence. The status of these children ranged from those recently remanded to some who were facing long and sometimes indeterminate sentences. Overall, this was a disappointing inspection which recorded a deterioration in three of our four healthy prison assessments – most notably in safety and purposeful activity, which we now judged to be poor.

Despite the prison making significant progress in reducing the amount of self- harm, the perceptions of safety (as recorded in our detainee survey) were worse than any other young offender institution (YOI). Nearly 40% of children told us that they had felt unsafe at some point during their stay. Incidents of violence were higher than any other establishment in England and Wales and a significant number were serious in nature. Force was used more frequently than comparable institutions and over 400 weapons

had been discovered in the preceding 12 months. Work had begun to reduce bullying and violence, but this was only recently initiated and was disorganised. Children had limited confidence in the ability of staff to keep them safe.

The only consistently applied strategy to try to maintain order was a process of creating 'keep apart' lists that sought to separate individuals or groups. We found an incredible 263 such non-associations among a population of just 64 individuals, and the requirements were constantly changing. This ineffective and harmful arrangement was, in effect, a reactive process of risk avoidance, rather than risk management and had come to totally dominate life in Werrington. Our colleagues in Ofsted found that, among many other failings in the education and regime provision, children were allocated to learning not on the basis of need, but on the basis of who they could or could not mix with at any particular moment in time. The approach was corrosive and completely undermined the purpose of the institution.

Despite this, Werrington remained a reasonably respectful prison, although only 60% of young people felt respected by staff. The staff we observed were enthusiastic, if inexperienced. They wanted to do a good job, but their engagement with young people was too often merely transactional. Limited time unlocked, restrictive practice and risk aversion all impeded the vital goal of helping staff to engage more purposefully with the children they were supposed to be supporting.

We were left with the sense that Werrington had lost its way and needed to rediscover a sense of purpose. The prison had managed the consequence of the COVID pandemic well and there were several capital improvement and other projects being delivered. The governor had set out a series of priorities for the establishment, but it was clear to us that more needed to be done to ensure staff were fully committed to these priorities and that plans were delivered. Nevertheless, improvement at Werrington should be expected. There are currently about 400 staff of various grades and disciplines responsible for just over 60 young people. We hope this report will assist that process of improvement.

Charlie Taylor
HM Chief Inspector of Prisons March 2022

**Safety**

At the last inspection of Werrington in 2020, we found that outcomes for children were not sufficiently good against this healthy establishment test.

At this inspection we found that outcomes for children were now poor.

There was good identification of risk and need and sharing of information about children on reception and their first night at Werrington. Induction was reasonable, but children spent lengthy periods locked up during their first few days.

Leaders and managers had a good relationship with the local authority and child protection concerns were identified and investigated. Self-harm had reduced by 43% since our last inspection, but the quality of ACCT documents required improvement.

Processing and dissemination of intelligence were good, but monthly security objectives did not reflect current threats, which was a weakness. Strip-searching of children in reception was routine and often unjustified.

Perceptions of safety were worse than in other YOIs. In our survey, 16% said they felt unsafe at the time of our inspection. Despite recent reductions, levels of violence over the previous six months were higher than in any other establishment in England and Wales. A significant number of incidents were serious in nature, including group assaults and the use of weapons. Violence had resulted in 32 children attending hospital. During the last 12 months, 399 weapons had been found.

Children told us they carried weapons because they did not have confidence in the ability of staff to keep them safe.

The conflict resolution team had been re-established, but most children continued to have at least one keep-apart issue. Time spent managing the 263 non-associations (in a population of 66 children) affected all areas of life at Werrington negatively. Efforts to reduce violence and bullying and promote pro-social behaviour were disorganised. There was no consistent process to manage bullying. New behaviour management and reward and sanction strategies had been developed but not yet implemented on the wings.

The rate of use of force by staff towards children was higher than in all other YOIs and higher than at our last inspection. Most incidents involved the full application of restraint in response to violence. All incidents of force were reviewed by managers who identified learning and good practice. A mentoring programme, which supported new and existing staff with the safe application of MMPR techniques and decision-making during incidents, was positive.

There was no designated separation unit and children were separated on their wings. Use of separation remained similar to the last inspection. Two children had been separated for more than 50 days. Access to education and other services was not equitable for this group and there was a lack of formal reintegration planning or meaningful behaviour targets.

## Care

At the last inspection of Werrington in 2020, we found that outcomes for children were good against this healthy establishment test.

At this inspection we found that outcomes for children were now reasonably good.

In our survey, only 60% of children said that most staff treated them with respect and 42% that they felt staff cared for them. Many staff were enthusiastic and wanted to provide good care for children but interaction between staff and children that we observed was often transactional. Anxiety about safety and time spent managing keep- apart issues hindered the development of effective relationships.

Custody support plan (CuSP) and personal officer work were not sufficiently embedded to ensure that all children benefited. This was not helped by the lack of spaces for private conversations.

Communal areas were clean, but the residential units needed to look less sterile and more age appropriate. Most cells were clean, free of graffiti and adequately equipped but it was noticeable that children did little to personalise their cells. The installation of showers and new toilets in some cells was an improvement since the previous inspection. Older toilets remained badly stained. Food was reasonably good, but most meals were eaten in cells. Some consultation had taken place and more recently children had been invited to respond to surveys on their laptops which was a good use of the new equipment. Management oversight and quality assurance of complaints were good.

Equality meetings were well attended and chaired by the governor. A good range of data was presented. Disproportionate treatment was identified but investigations lacked depth and did not always identify the underlying cause. An equality adviser had carried out some consultation and organised celebration events. However, the promotion of equality was too dependent on one individual and not embedded across the establishment. Corporate worship was face to face and the chaplaincy had planned extra sessions to ensure that all children had equitable access.

Health services were child centred and good. Clinical governance in health care was robust. There were several examples of learning and change following incidents and audits, including innovative and enhanced assessment of injuries to victims of group assault. Waiting times and attendance at health appointments were good, but there were still too many occasions when patients did not attend at the appointed time, which led to inefficient use of clinical time.

Health assessment had been strengthened by a new health passport approach, interface with family members during induction, and innovative sexual health screening. A full range of age-appropriate immunisations and vaccinations was available to patients, including Covid-19. The management of medicines was excellent. Mental health and substance misuse services offered good child-centred care. Dental treatments were available promptly and the range of dental treatments was good, including oral health promotion.

### Purposeful activity

At the last inspection of Werrington in 2020, we found that outcomes for children were reasonably good against this healthy establishment test.

At this inspection we found that outcomes for children were now poor.

Time spent out of cell was recovering from the impact of the Covid-19 outbreak at the end of 2021, but the weekday regime had consistently fallen far short of our expectations over the previous six months. At the time of the inspection, children were spending an average of 4.5 hours out of their cells during the week and as little as two hours at the weekend. Gym provision was good for most children. Children had very limited access to the library services.

Leaders and managers had a vision to deliver a curriculum that met the needs of children. However, instability in staffing had limited the range of courses available. Allocation of children to courses was not based on need or aspirations but on which children could mix together. This resulted in children becoming frustrated and disengaged. Despite only 15 hours of education a week, children routinely arrived late to lessons and finished early. Behaviour management in many classes was poor. Too many children refused to engage in tasks while in lessons and behaved poorly and disrespectfully towards tutors.

The curriculum in English and mathematics functional skills classes was unambitious and narrow. In some vocational areas, such as barbering, tutors introduced higher level work for those children who had achieved well. This motivated them and created ambition to further their skills and progress to higher-level studies. A majority of children achieved their qualification but achievement in mathematics and catering was too low. Kinetic Youth workers provided useful sessions that helped children to deal with their own personal barriers which prevented them from participating in education. Learning support tutors had effectively helped children who had special educational needs or disabilities to increase their confidence and their knowledge and understanding of English and mathematics.

A few children undertook a limited range of work roles instead of attending education classes. These included cleaning and servery work in the residential wings, laundry duties and litter picking in the grounds. Children's participation and development was not part of a planned and coherent programme that supported their personal development.

### Resettlement

At the last inspection of Werrington in 2020, we found that outcomes for children were reasonably good against this healthy establishment test.

At this inspection we found that outcomes for children remained reasonably good.

There was good support for families and carers to have contact with children and be kept updated with information about the establishment. Thought had been given to how children could be involved in important family events and there was good use of technology to support this. The use of exceptional circumstance visits was responsive to need and the increased use of photos for and with families was child focused. Uptake of secure video calls was good, but there was scope to extend the number of sessions.

The needs analysis was out of date and did not reflect the needs of the current population. The reducing reoffending meetings were not well attended and too many actions were not completed. Home detention curfew and early release were used effectively. It was positive that release on temporary licence (ROTL) was being used but further development was needed to ensure that ROTL was always linked to sentence planning goals. Interventions had restarted but the low level of delivery meant that children left Werrington with their identified offending behaviour not addressed. There was no additional provision for the increasing proportion of children with long or indeterminate sentences.

Remand and sentenced children had up-to-date plans with appropriate targets. Resettlement practitioners had very good relationships with children and face-to-face contact was frequent and well documented. Resettlement practitioners worked closely with other departments, but residential officers did not attend review meetings. Most children at Werrington were looked after by a local authority. Reviews were well attended, but they often took place late. Social workers ensured that children received their monetary and clothing entitlements from the local authorities. All children who were high or very high risk and those coming up to release were appropriately discussed at monthly risk management meetings. Phone and mail monitoring was managed very well. Only seven children were on public protection monitoring and there were no backlogs or overdue reviews.

During the previous six months, all children had been released with an accommodation placement that had been confirmed more than 10 days before release, which was positive. However, less than half had a confirmed education or training place.

## Key concerns and recommendations

Key concerns and recommendations identify the issues of most importance to improving outcomes for children and are designed to help establishments prioritise and address the most significant weaknesses in the treatment and conditions of children.

During this inspection we identified some areas of key concern and have made a number of recommendations for the establishment to address those concerns.

Key concern: The use of force and levels of violence among children and against staff were too high. Violence reduction strategies had either been withdrawn or were newly implemented and had only recently generated some limited impact on overall levels of violence.

Key recommendation: An informed and establishment-wide strategy should be implemented to reduce levels of violence. (To the governor)

Key concern: Behaviour management processes were confused and did not give staff across the YOI the confidence to challenge children effectively and consistently when necessary. This lack of challenge and inability to require and enforce decent behavioural standards contributed to increased incidents of violent behaviour by children. In the absence of effective behaviour management, leaders had become over-reliant on 'keep-apart' arrangements. The list of children who had to be separated had become unmanageable.

Key recommendation: Behaviour management processes should be developed that give all staff the confidence to challenge poor behaviour and promote prosocial behaviour. (To the governor)

Key concern: Interaction between staff and children was often transactional. There was limited meaningful time spent addressing children's risks and needs or the support and encouragement that they needed to progress. Opportunities for engagement were hindered by the number of keep-aparts and regime groups that staff had to manage. There was also a lack of places for private discussions on residential units. Personal officer and custody support plan work were not fully embedded.

Key recommendation: Relationships between staff and children should be meaningful and

support children's progression. (To the governor)

Key concern: The appearance of the wings, particularly Doulton wing, was stark and unwelcoming and not appropriate for children. The design of the units afforded little flexibility for activities for the number of children who could be accommodated. Rooms for private meetings with children were scarce.

Key recommendation: Children should live on age-appropriate wings that are configured and resourced so that children can engage in a full regime of activities that support their rehabilitation. (To the governor)

Key concern: Leaders were using data to identify unequal treatment amongst certain protected groups, but further enquiry and subsequent investigations did not identify the underlying cause of these disparities or resolve them.

Key recommendation: Unequal outcomes should be investigated and addressed. (To the governor)

Key concern: Patients failing to attend or arriving late for health appointments impaired efficient use of health resources, including some clinicians' time. Several factors contributed to this including reduced capacity in the waiting room during the pandemic, regime restrictions and clashes, and keep-aparts.

Key recommendation: Sustained action should be taken to make sure that health resources are fully used to optimise the health care of patients. (To the governor)

Key concern: Children did not spend enough time out of cell during the day, particularly at weekends.

Key recommendation: The time that children spend out of their cells in activity should be increased, including at weekends. (To the governor)

Key concern: The quality of education provided by leaders and managers was not good enough. The curriculum in some areas was unambitious and narrow. The focus was on preparing children for their functional skills exams rather than broadening the curriculum to build on existing skills.

Key recommendation A: Leaders should support staff to deliver a curriculum that develops children's skills in their subject.

Key recommendation B: Staff working on functional skills courses should ensure that the curriculum is ambitious and develops children's knowledge.

Key concern: Children were not sufficiently motivated to engage in their learning. Allocation to courses was made on the basis of which children could mix together, rather than on children's chosen curriculum pathway. This resulted in many children not taking their preferred course or moving between courses and becoming disengaged and lacking in motivation.

Key recommendation A: Leaders and managers

should ensure that children have the opportunity to study their chosen subject.

Key recommendation B: Staff should set high expectations for children. Children should be encouraged and supported to identify and develop the skills that will support them during their time in custody and on release.

Key concern: There was no support at all for children serving life or indeterminate sentences. Not enough interventions were available to children, many of whom were released with no support to help them reduce their risk and resettle into the community.

Key recommendation: The range of interventions should be broadened to include those aimed at children serving life or indeterminate sentences. Interventions should be sequenced to make sure that all children requiring interventions receive them. (To the governor)

Key concern: Too many children were leaving custody with no confirmed education or training placement. Systems for monitoring and addressing this in custody and after release were inadequate.

Key recommendation: Leaders should implement robust systems that ensure recognised educational and training placements are secured when transitioning from custody to the community. (To the governor)

**Notable positive practice**

We define notable positive practice as innovative work or practice that leads to particularly good outcomes from which other establishments may be able to learn. Inspectors look for evidence of good outcomes for children; original, creative or particularly effective approaches to problem-solving or achieving the desired goal; and how other establishments could learn from or replicate the practice.

Inspectors found five examples of notable positive practice during this inspection.

MMPR coordinators had developed a mentoring scheme to support staff who were not confident in the application of restraint techniques or in how to respond in a violent situation. Our review of video footage of incidents where force was used showed high levels of competence in the application of physical restraint by staff.

Sexual health screening after 14 days ensured, for new arrivals, that long-term effects of unrecognised and untreated disease at reception were minimised.

Practice Plus Group worked with the YOI family engagement officer to acquire health-related information from parents and carers to inform the health care of their children. Families were able to talk to nurses and be reassured that their children would be looked after. Other age-appropriate initiatives by the family engagement officer to keep families involved with their child included a virtual discussion forum, regular newsletters, and additional contact during times of important family events.

Nurses reviewed CCTV records within 24 hours of all group assaults to check that the victim had not received blows to the back of their bodies or heads. This made sure that post-incident assessment of injuries was comprehensive and reduced the likelihood of complications developing from unassessed injuries.

The speech and language therapist had redesigned the induction timetable given to all children, making it more accessible to those with speech and language difficulties.

**INDEPENDENT MONITORING BOARD: Annual Report**

The law requires every prison to be monitored by an independent Board appointed by the Justice Secretary; these are known as Independent Monitoring Boards (IMBs). The IMB must satisfy itself as to the humane and just treatment of those held in custody within its prison and the range and adequacy of the programmes preparing them for release; it must report annually to the Justice Secretary on how well the prison has met the standards and requirements placed on it.

**IMB Report 01 Sept 2020 – 31 Aug 2021**
**Published January 2022**
**Executive Summary**
**Background to the report**

A new Governing Governor took up post in March 2021.

The pandemic continued with Werrington operating at stage 3.

In the summer major refurbishment commenced, with the closure of initially part of one wing then the total closure of a residential block so that in-room showers could be installed.

In July/August there was a sharp and continuing increase in the level of violence and disruption.

**Main judgements**
**How safe is the establishment?**

We consider that YOI Werrington has been unsafe for the young people and the staff since the beginning of July 2021, as a result of which we escalated our concerns to the Youth Custody Service (YCS) Executive Director, Helga Swidenbank, and Philip Copple, Director General for Prisons, on 28 July 2021.

## How fairly and humanely are young people treated?

The young people are mostly treated fairly but are not treated humanely, due to the restricted time out of room and staff shortages.

## How well are young people's health and wellbeing needs met?

Young people's health is proactively and efficiently catered for. Their wellbeing needs are met by a wide variety of staff.

## How effective is the education provision for young people?

The Board does not consider the educational provision as adequate, due to some extent to the facilities available but also due to regular outbreaks of violence.

There is an improved vocational offering, but the integration of maths and English into the curriculum has yet to embedded.

## How well are young people progressed towards transfer or successful resettlement?

The Board is satisfied that the young people at Werrington are progressed well.

## Main areas for development
### TO THE MINISTER

Rule 49 is being used for young people who cannot be found a suitable placement in a group. Is this the correct use of this rule and is it fair?

Are the courts keeping to time limits when remanding young people?

### TO THE YOUTH CUSTODY SERVICE

If family is valued as an important influence, why are young people not allowed to have photographs of themselves with their family displayed in their rooms?

What steps are the Youth Custody Service (YCS) taking to improve the institutional allocation process in court to reduce the unacceptable waiting time?

### TO THE GOVERNOR

As a stabilisation plan is in progress at the end of the reporting period, what steps can you take to reassure the Board that it will regularly reviewed and acted on, not just during the implementation period but afterwards?

As Werrington has recently had worryingly low amounts of time out of room, how can the Board be reassured that this will not continue?

## Progress since the last report

The established use of in-room phones, crucial for mental health during the pandemic, allowing professionals and family to contact the young people.

The provision of in-room showers, allowing the young people more privacy and hygiene.

The MUGA pitch extending the time for external games to proceed in all weathers.

Replacement curtains in the young people's rooms. Added subjects to the vocational curriculum. Improved quality and choice of meals.

The appointment of an advanced nurse practitioner to the healthcare team.

The arrival of young staff who are keen to develop good relationships with young people and are willing to study at degree level.

The Board was pleased by the prompt and effective intervention of the YCS management team and their stabilisation plan to help Werrington deal with the violence and disruption at the end of the reporting period.

**YORK ROAD**
**WETHERBY**
**LS22 5ED**

**HMYOI WETHERBY**    **Tel: 01937 544200**

*For the latest reports on this prison please visit:*
https://tinyurl.com/bdfh26rv

*Important Changes:* **(1) Visits:** the identification necessary to access this prison and visit for social or professional purposes has changed; (2) **Money and Gifts** new rules now apply to these. See page 16 for full details of the above.

### Task of the establishment

HMYOI Wetherby is an establishment looking after children aged between 15 and 18 years. It is part of the youth custody estate.

### Certified normal accommodation and operational capacity

Children held December 2021: 142
Baseline certified normal capacity: 340
In-use certified normal capacity: 276
Operational capacity: 266

### Population of the establishment December 2021

• 174 children had arrived in the last six months
• 16 were foreign nationals
• 31% of children were from black and minority ethnic backgrounds
• 28% of children were on remand
• 20 children were released into the community on average each month
• Three-quarters of children had been in local authority care at some point before custody
• 29% of children had been excluded from school
• 32% of children were not in education, employment or training before custody.

### Establishment status and key providers

Public
Prison Group: Youth Custody Service
Prison Group Director: Helga Swidenbank
Governor/Director: Pete Gormley
IMB chair: Catherine Porter
Physical health provider: Leeds Community Healthcare NHS Trust
Mental health provider: South-west Yorkshire Partnership NHS Foundation Trust
Substance misuse treatment provider: Young People's Drug and Alcohol Support Service (YPDASS)
Prison education framework provider: Novus
Escort contractor: GeoAmey

### Brief history

A former naval base, Wetherby became a borstal in 1958 and has since changed its role from an open youth custody centre to a closed youth custody centre and is now a dedicated establishment for children between 15 and 18.

### Short description of residential units

• Anson is the separation unit.
• Benbow is a 48-bed unit and is the first night and induction centre. One spur of the unit for all restricted status boys.
• Collingwood and Drake are 60-bed units with an enhanced unit for children on gold level of the incentives and earned privileges scheme.
• Exmouth and Frobisher are 60-bed units. (Exmouth closed for renovation).
• Keppel unit is a 48-bed nationally resourced complex needs unit for children referred there by the central placements team.
• Napier is the enhanced support unit. (Three girls were held temporarily on Napier while designated female accommodation on Keppel was being refurbished.)

### Visiting Information

Visits are led by prisoner application. There is no telephone booking service available.
**Visiting times:** Mon - Fri: 6.45pm – 7.45pm.

**Legal visits:** There are currently no legal visits taking place.

### INSPECTIONS & REPORTS

**HMIP Report:** 6 and 13–17 December 2021
**Published:** 16th March 2022
Wetherby is the largest young offender institution (YOI) in the country. It held 143 children – including three girls in the Napier unit – at the time of our inspection, much reduced from its capacity of 266. Our healthy prison test scores show that ground has been lost in the last two years, in part, no doubt, due to the pandemic.

In the Keppel unit, housed within the YOI and designated as a therapeutic provision, inspectors saw a disappointing fall in standards. At the time of the inspection it felt more like another wing of the main prison rather than provision for a vulnerable group of children with a range of complex needs. The unit needed some real grip from the leadership, with the aims re-established and suitable staff selected and trained to recover its distinct purpose.

A fall from a healthy prison test score of good to not sufficiently good in the area of resettlement reflects a deterioration in this area with a team that had become dysfunctional and disaffected. The public protection arrangements – for children who pose high levels of risk to the public – also needed urgent attention to make sure they were effectively monitored.

The governor and his team had managed to get the regime to open up more quickly from Covid-19 restrictions than we have seen on other sites, particularly on the two enhanced wings. Overall though, children were still spending too long in their cells, only being unlocked for an average of six hours on a weekday and fewer than five at weekends.

Leaders had aimed to transform behaviour management systems so that they focused more on rewarding and promoting positive behaviour and less on sanctions. However, adjudications still remained high and the governor's expectations had not yet been absorbed by staff on the wing, where children did not always receive the rewards they had earned and there was still over- reliance on punishment.

Inspectors noted some improvements in the use of de-escalation of incidents and use of force had reduced since our last inspection, although it was very disappointing to see some uses of pain-inducing techniques that could not be justified.

Accommodation on the wings remained prison-like and some of the exercise yards resembled those in a high security jail. Some improvements had taken place with the introduction of showers in some cells and the refurbishment of the new girl's wing on the Keppel unit. There will, however, need to be considerable capital investment to create an environment that is suitable for children.

Leaders had begun to roll out 'community learning' as an adjunct to formal education, but the curriculum had not been sufficiently developed, expectations of the children were not communicated and there were no outcome measures in place to show progress. Leaders needed to do further work to clarify the meaning of community learning, what the objectives were and how this would be communicated to staff and children.

The closure of places elsewhere and the refusal of some secure children's homes to accept girls with more complex needs – particularly those who were violent – meant that a decision was taken by the Youth Custody Service to develop additional capacity at Wetherby. The YOI had embraced this challenge and had worked hard to provide a more suitable environment for girls. At the time of the inspection they were housed in Napier unit where staff had created a caring and supportive environment.

A leadership team of 27 seemed to far exceed what was needed to manage this prison, which contained just 140 children. A move to a flatter leadership structure would create clearer lines to the governor and his deputy, avoid duplication, improve accountability and allow resources to be deployed elsewhere.

Levels of violence had remained lower than comparator prisons and, in our survey, just 3% of children said they felt unsafe – an impressive reduction from 27% at our last inspection.

The calmer atmosphere at Wetherby should provide the opportunity for children to spend more time out of their cells and be involved in a wider range of purposeful activity. If the governor's vision for positive behaviour management is to be translated into a change in practice on the wing, there needs to be consistent and committed focus from leaders on making sure that good behaviour is recognised and rewarded. Children who are often stuck in long-term patterns of negative behaviour will need to see and feel the benefits of doing the right thing. The scores from this inspection will have been disappointing to staff at Wetherby and Keppel after what has been a difficult year. There is, however, the opportunity for this establishment to build on the many positives that we highlight in this report, particularly as the disruption from the pandemic begins to recede.

HM Chief Inspector of Prisons December 2021

## INDEPENDENT MONITORING BOARD:
## Annual Report

The law requires every prison to be monitored by an independent Board appointed by the Justice Secretary; these are known as Independent Monitoring Boards (IMBs). The IMB must satisfy itself as to the humane and just treatment of those held in custody within its prison and the range and adequacy of the programmes preparing them for release; it must report annually to the Justice Secretary on how well the prison has met the standards and requirements placed on it.

**IMB Report 1 June 2020 – 31 August 2021**
**Published 4th January 2022**
**Background to the report**

Wetherby YOI has experienced many significant changes throughout the reporting period:

A new Governor was appointed in July 2020.

The senior management team is ethnically White, British, with one exception.

The Covid-19 pandemic, which presented enormous challenges for staff and young people alike, has been well managed.

Throughout the period there has been a fluctuating availability of staff due to Covid-19, which has made regime delivery demanding.

The Board is very concerned as to the apparent lack of permanence in the senior management team. Many of the governors and acting governors are in post for a very short period before being moved again.

In mid-July 2021, a few young female prisoners were transferred at short notice to Wetherby from elsewhere. To the credit of all staff, including the stores and kitchen, this has been managed seamlessly.

There has been much needed extensive and ongoing building work to improve the amenities for the young people.

At the start of the reporting year, June 1 2020, the roll was 145, of whom 50 young people were on remand and 95 sentenced. Five young people were aged 15, 27 aged 16, 85 aged 17 and 28 aged over 18. At the end of the reporting year in August 2021, the roll was 164 with 57 young people on remand and 107 sentenced. Nine young people were aged 15, 26 aged 16, 99 aged 17, and there were 30 over-18-year-olds.

The figures for those young people held at Wetherby on remand, or sentenced for murder, including attempted murder and manslaughter: in June 2020, 13 on remand, 11 sentenced. In August 2021, 22 on remand, 10 sentenced.

## Main judgements
## How safe is the establishment?

Many of the young people held at Wetherby are on remand or sentenced for serious and violent offences. It is therefore unsurprising that their behaviour can be challenging. During periods of lockdown and reduced regime the number and severity of assaults decreased dramatically. However, as the regime eased some very serious assaults have taken place, not just between young people, but on staff. A large number of weapons were found in relation to the average population, some of which were used in assaults.

In early November a serious incident took place which meant that the colleges had to be closed and security reviewed.

Young people generally report that they feel safe, but as we have reported previously, they are less likely to talk openly about any perceived weakness, such as being fearful.

In May some very serious issues were raised by a management enquiry into the care and management of a young person at high risk of suicide and self- harm on Keppel unit.

There continues to be concern about the application and understanding of the assessment, care and custody and teamwork (ACCT) process. However, the quality assurance process has improved during the last few months.

The HMPPS psychology services withdrew from prisons during Covid, which meant a lack of intensive interventions for those young people in need. Psychologists returned for two days per week on 27 April 2020 then for two and a half days, leading to the rest of the team beginning to return in June.

The lack of routine activation, in many instances, of body-worn cameras (BWC) when using managing and minimising physical restraint (MMPR) techniques remains a concern. This means there is a failure to capture the lead-up and full incident so some MMPR reviews are unable to evaluate evidence sufficiently. This is particularly concerning when involving a child protection referral.

**How fairly and humanely are young people treated?**

Through our regular monitoring and observations of the interaction between staff and young people we have noticed this generally to be positive.

In particular young people arriving into reception and first night in custody are well catered for and treated with respect.

During the pandemic smaller groups of young people, family groups or 'bubbles' have enabled staff to develop more meaningful relationships with the young people in their care. The Board has seen cards and letters from not only families, but young people themselves, thanking the staff for the care provided.

The acute lack of secure hospital mental health beds remains a concern. It is wrong that the mental health of the young people, who are effectively 'in care', is actually deteriorating while in prison. However, these young people add to the use of force and self-harm. The officers who support these young people do their utmost, but are not trained mental health professionals.

There continues to be an unacceptable delay in transferring the small minority, four this year, of young people with severe mental health issues to the secure hospital bed that they require. The Board considers this to be inhumane and completely unacceptable.

Anson, the segregation wing, experiences extremes of temperature, too hot in summer and too cold in winter. At times, especially for young people observing Ramadan, the heat on some days was excessive and unhelpful. Benbow also has extremes of temperature.

The delay in transferring young people aged over 18 to the adult estate is, in the opinion of the Board, unacceptable. Young people, especially those with challenging behaviour, seem to be increasingly difficult to place. They are accepted at Wetherby from the courts, but the Governors in the adult estate seem to be allowed to pick and choose which of the young people they will accept. This practice must stop. Apart from any other consideration, such as the impact on the young people, it is a waste of staff time and consequently not cost effective.

**How well are young people's health and wellbeing needs met?**

Appropriate healthcare was provided for all young people during the pandemic. This was due in particular to the good working partnership which enabled all appropriate actions to be taken to keep the young people safe During the pandemic, time out of cell has been much lower than usual, partly due to young people being in small bubbles and significant prison staff shortages. Unfortunately, there continues to be a high turnover of staff with recruitment and retention a problem. As a consequence, agency staff fill the vacancies.

The Board is pleased to report that GPs are now wing based and travel round each wing. This has had a positive impact in relation to meeting their needs. As a result, 'did not attend's (DNAs) have reduced pre- and post-Covid. Covid was well managed. There were quite a high number of young people who were deemed as vulnerable and offered vaccinations at the earliest opportunity. Those infected with Covid were promptly isolated and looked after on each Covid wing. If released mid-vaccination programme, follow-up arrangements were made with the young people's local healthcare provider. The Board is pleased to report that the Covid vaccination programme was successfully rolled out with a positive response from the young people. This resulted in Wetherby delivering the highest number in the YOI estate. Again, there has been good partnership working in response to Covid requirements.

Social workers at Wetherby challenge those local authorities (LAs) who fail to provide adequate support for looked-after children. This is a perennial issue and is unacceptable. This year more issues have been escalated to the Howard League for Penal Reform, the Children's

Commissioner's office and the appropriate Director of Children's Services than last year.

## How effective is the education provision for young people?

Covid-19 has presented a demanding task for those who are responsible for providing education for the young people at Wetherby.

To some extent, the juvenile estate was bound by the same directive from HMPPS with regard to access to education. However, towards the end of July 2020 young people re-commenced some wing-based education.

Inevitably delivering a consistent regime was onerous, due to outbreaks and high numbers of staff, both teachers and officers, who were isolating. There was a gradual increase in the provision of education to young people who started back again in the colleges in September 2020. Initially this proved difficult as young people regarded the class room more as an opportunity to socialise and interact with their peers than an opportunity to learn. The specialist units such as Napier, a smaller unit with less of risk of transmission of the virus, and Anson, found it easier to re-introduce education.

Many, if not all, of the young people would, if in the community, have come under the category of vulnerable and have additional educational support. Realistically, during Covid-19 some may not have accessed education or training at all had they been in the community. It has, however, undoubtedly been a missed opportunity that the young people were unable to get back sooner into face-to-face learning.

In order for young people to progress with their education there needs to be a consistency of delivery and the belief by the education staff that they and the young people are safe in lessons. The establishment needs to work hard so that teachers feel well supported by officers, particularly when presented with challenging and, at times, violent behaviour.

## How well are young people progressed towards transfer or successful resettlement?

Covid-19 has had a significant impact on progression and transfers. However, some of the delays have been of concern to the Board for many years.

Maintaining all-important family links was established through innovative practice. Most, but not all, young people had access to a telephone in their cell, and with increased phone credit, were able to keep in touch with their families, and as necessary, legal advisers and other agencies.

During the pandemic professional visits stopped. These visits only took place face-to-face in exceptional circumstances. Video links were established, and some face-to-face visits resumed in April 2021. From June 2021 things returned to a more normal basis.

Similarly, there were no social visits to the establishment. These resumed under Covid-secure conditions, in December 2020 and were offered every weekday evening and at weekends. The introduction of Purple (video) Visits was welcomed by most young people. The significant increase in the use of Purple Visits at the end of 2020 was as a result of the appointment of a dedicated Purple Visits officer. They were responsible for liaising with young people and families and supporting them with the practicalities of technology. The establishment took the initiative to contact family members and encourage and invite to Purple Visits, removing the requirement for the young people to undertake this task and allow assurance to be provided to loved ones. The Board commends the practice.

## Main areas for development
## TO THE MINISTER

Each year we ask the Minister what is being done nationally to reduce the levels of violence amongst young people. With an ever-increasing number of victims and offenders, it would appear that what we have been told is being done is clearly not working.

The figures for those young people held at Wetherby on remand, or sentenced for murder, including attempted murder and manslaughter, make stark reading

The Board would like to know what is being done to reduce the level of serious violence by young people in the community?

The Board continues to be frustrated by the acute lack of secure mental health hospital beds and the inability of politicians to address the situation. **For the sixth year running,** we ask what is being done to increase the number of beds for those young people for whom prison is clearly not the right place?

It is inhumane to place young people where their serious mental health needs cannot be met despite the best efforts of the staff who support them.

## TO THE YOUTH CUSTODY SERVICE

Many young people already held at Wetherby who are aged 18+ continue to experience delay while waiting to transfer to the adult estate. It is unreasonable for young people to have to endure a lengthy wait while negotiations take place between establishments. These are frequently complex young people with challenging behaviour, many of whom face long sentences. The heightened anxiety created by endless delay does little to help their behaviour.

Can the Youth Custody Service reassure the Board that negotiations between establishments and subsequent transfers will take place expeditiously? Until July 2021 Wetherby YOI was a YOI for young male offenders. **The introduction of young female offenders was to many, not least the Board, a surprise.** It appears that there has been significant financial investment in order to accommodate them. Is this to be a permanent arrangement?

Is the future of Wetherby now as a mixed sex establishment?

### TO THE GOVERNOR

The sudden and relatively unexpected arrival of young female prisoners at Wetherby has been well managed. However, the male prisoners are less than happy. They feel that the females are being treated not only differently, but favourably. They do not arrive via reception but directly on to their unit: the female accommodation is perceived as superior and they can wear their own clothing. There may well be justification for this practice, but in the eyes of the male young people it is unfair.

What is being done to address their concerns?

Lengthy delays in maintenance work continue: for example, delays in repairing out of order cells and the never-ending saga of the kitchen floor. This is unacceptable. Throughout Covid the standard of cleanliness at Wetherby was excellent. However, as the pandemic seems to be easing, there is slippage. It would be unfortunate if this is allowed to continue.

Can the Governor reassure the Board that standards of cleanliness will be maintained, and that repair and maintenance is dealt with in a timely manner?

The lack of permanence within the senior management team is of great concern to the Board. Is the Governor able to offer reassurance to the Board that some level of stability will take place? Barnardo's advocacy has an important role to play in supporting the young people. They hear of Barnardo's role, along with that of many others, during the induction programme. However, since the start of Covid-19, Barnardo's have been far less visible.

How can the Governor make sure that all young people have an equal opportunity to access advocacy support?

The completion of the new ACCT v6 document presents, for many staff, a substantial challenge and too many completion errors and omissions still remain.

Can the Governor reassure the Board that sufficient quality assurance procedures are in place to improve understanding of the ACCT document across the prison?

### Progress since the last report

The Board is pleased to report that since the introduction of the new Prisoner Escort and Custody Service (PECS) contract in August 2020, there has been a reduction in the number of young people arriving into Wetherby late at night. However, as there have been fewer young people in general going through the court system due to the pandemic, we regard the data with cautious optimism.

The regime and time out of room has gradually increased as of July 2020 and at the end of our reporting year in August 2021, young people were generally out for 5.85 hours per day.

Covid-19, by necessity, brought with it a general and much needed improvement in cleanliness throughout the establishment. For example, since the start of lockdown, litter has been non-existent. This had previously been a problem due rubbish escaping from overflowing external bins and flying around the exposed and, at times, windy site

The gradual updating of the wings, including the introduction of showers in the cells, is a much-welcomed improvement. There is still much to be done.

The education colleges, which have been redecorated and furniture updated, now provide a more attractive learning environment.

While some of these changes may appear trivial, for the young people at Wetherby it does much to improve their self-esteem and encourages them to take a pride in their environment. There is little evidence of graffiti.

The use of Purple Visits, which was just starting as we wrote our last report, is now a well-established system for young people to keep in touch with family members. For those who are placed at a distance, it is an excellent way of maintaining contact.

Young people held on Anson, the segregation unit, have a more proactive regime, are better supported by psychologists and we are pleased to report that the wing itself is less austere.

**NEW LANE
WHATTON
NOTTS
NG13 9FQ**

**HM PRISON WHATTON**  Tel: 01949 803200

*For the latest reports on this prison please visit:*
https://tinyurl.com/bdfh26rv

*Important Changes:* **(1) Visits:** the identification necessary to access this prison and visit for social or professional purposes has changed;

(2) **Money and Gifts** new rules now apply to these. See page 16 for full details of the above.

**Task of the establishment** HMP Whatton is an adult male category C training prison holding exclusively people convicted of sex offences.

**Certified normal accommodation and operational capacity**
Prisoners held at the time of this visit: 777
Baseline certified normal capacity: 841
In-use certified normal capacity: 775
Operational capacity: 841

**Prison status and key providers**
Public
Prison Group: East Midlands
Prison Group Director: Paul Cawkwell
Governor/Director: Caroline Vine
IMB chair: Colin Braziel
Physical health provider: Care UK
Mental health provider: Care UK
Substance use treatment provider: Care UK
Prison education framework provider: PeoplePlus
Escort contractor: GeoAmey

**Brief history** HMP Whatton was built in 1966 as a detention centre for boys. It became a young offender institution in 1989 and re-roled in 1990 as an adult male category C training prison. During the 1990s, it developed as a prison for people convicted of sex offences. Its population more than doubled in early 2006 with the building of eight new units. The prison remains exclusively for prisoners convicted of sex offences.

**Short description of residential units**
A1–8: Newer residential wings with modern cells. The care and separation (segregation) unit is attached to A3.
B1 and B2: The original accommodation, mostly former dormitories with cubicles.
B3 landing: 35 cells
C1–3: Modular units: C2 is low security, C3 is doubled accommodation.
Palliative care unit

**Visiting Information**
Book online at: www.gov.uk/prison-visits or ring 01949 803 200 Monday to Friday 9am to midday and 1pm to 5pm.
**Visiting times:** Monday: 1:45pm to 3:15pm
Thursday, Friday: 1:45pm to 3:45pm, Saturday, Sunday: 9am to 11am and 1:45pm to 3:45pm

**Legal visits:** There are currently no legal visits taking place. Telephone calls can be made.

**INSPECTIONS & REPORTS**
**Scrutiny visit: 18 and 25–26 August 2020**
**Date of last full inspection 15–26 August 2016**
**Scrutiny visit, published 29 September 2020**
HMP Whatton is a category C training prison in Nottinghamshire and at the time of our visit held about 770 convicted male prisoners. Whatton fulfils a national function providing services to address the offending behaviour of prisoners convicted of sexual offences. The vast majority of prisoners held are serving long sentences of over four years, including some 45% serving indeterminate or life sentences.

In the five months leading up to this visit, Whatton had been operating a restricted regime that had been imposed nationally in response to the Covid-19 pandemic. At the very start of the pandemic, one prisoner had died in hospital from a Covid-19-related illness and a few staff members had been symptomatic, but there had been no further cases in the prison since then. Clear communication to staff and prisoners and the implementation of appropriate measures to reduce the spread of infection had helped to keep the prison safe.

During the restricted regime, levels of violence had reduced and the use of force remained low. However, self-harm was higher than before the restrictions were imposed. While this could be partially attributed to a small number of prolific individuals, the problem was clearly wider spread. In our survey, almost one in four prisoners reported feeling unsafe. The uncertainty created by the restricted regime and threat of a dangerous virus no doubt fed those negative perceptions. We were concerned that some of the systems in place to identify vulnerable prisoners, such as first night safety interviews and good quality key work, were not sufficiently robust, and there was no formal system to identify those who were isolating themselves from staff and peers. During a normal regime at Whatton these prisoners would possibly stand out, but at a time when prisoners spent most of their day locked up there was an increased risk that some vulnerable prisoners could be overlooked.

Staff-prisoner relationships remained positive, and although time out of cell was restricted, staff were approachable and friendly when prisoners were unlocked. Managers had taken a reasonable decision to focus what limited time for key work was available on the prisoners with the greatest need, such as those who were being supported by assessment, care in custody and teamwork (ACCT) case management. However, other one-to-one opportunities with prison offender managers (POMs) or other specialist staff were limited, providing a possible explanation for our survey findings, which although positive about relationships with staff, indicated the quality of contact needed to be better.

The mental health team and the 'intellectual and developmental disabilities' service continued to provide good support for those with the most acute need, and the social care support was a real strength. However, there were some risks in the management of medicines that required review.

The prison had maintained several important strategic meetings, including one covering equality and diversity. Good support for prisoners from the LGBT community and older prisoners had continued through the restricted regime, but many black prisoners felt that they were treated differently and as a result had a more negative experience than their white counterparts. We strongly urge the prison to explore and understand these perceptions, and to take action to address the issues identified.

Prisoners at Whatton felt the weight of the restrictions heavily because before lockdown most of them had benefited from plenty of time out of cell and reliable access to programmes, education and work. At the time of our visit, most prisoners were locked up for around 22 hours a day, which was clearly taking its toll on many of those we spoke to. The prison had retained work for around a third of the population, which was commendable and gave these prisoners more time out of their cells.

Managers believed they could deliver more but the need to comply rigidly to the national framework for recovery (https://www.gov.uk/government/publications/covid-19-national-framework-for-prison-regimes-and-services) had affected the scope of what the prison could offer, and the pace at which it could be delivered, in several areas. This was clearly a source of frustration for managers and prisoners, who felt their ability to be innovative and creative had been severely curtailed.

Prisoners had transferred to Whatton from all over the country to complete offending behaviour programmes to reduce their risk and progress through their sentence. Much of this crucial work had stopped during the restricted regime and some prisoners reported feeling stuck. The prison had maintained some useful one-to-one offending behaviour work and had well-developed plans to restart small-scale groupwork. However, it was clear that it would take some time before it could address the growing backlog of cases, and some prisoners would be released without addressing some risky behaviours. Additionally, despite local efforts, too many prisoners were released without sustainable accommodation, which undermined the otherwise good public protection work.

In conclusion, managers and staff at Whatton were keeping prisoners relatively safe and motivated during challenging times. The pace of change was being directed nationally and was slower than the prison was capable of. Managers and staff were anxious about the impact on prisoners of long-term restrictions in a prison that had previously provided a full and rehabilitative regime.

Peter Clarke CVO OBE QPM
HM Chief Inspector of Prisons, September 2020

**Key concerns and recommendations**

Key concerns and recommendations identify the issues of most importance to improving outcomes for prisoners and are designed to help establishments prioritise and address the most significant weaknesses in the treatment and conditions of prisoners.

During this visit we identified some areas of key concern and have made a small number of key recommendations for the prison to address.

Key concern: The national HMPPS framework for recovery and the exceptional delivery models (EDMs) dictated what the prison could deliver. There were numerous examples, including time out of cell and access to activity, where managers wanted, and indicated that they were able, to deliver more but were not authorised to do so. This was despite there being no recorded cases of Covid-19 since April.

Key recommendation: The national recovery framework should set out minimum standards but give governors the autonomy to deliver a fuller regime at a faster pace if they judge it safe to do so. (To HMPPS)

Key concern: Current restrictions and prolonged periods locked up increased the risk of vulnerable prisoners becoming isolated. There was no formal system to identify and support vulnerable prisoners who were withdrawing from staff and peers, which increased their risk of psychological deterioration.

Key recommendation: The prison should introduce robust measures to identify vulnerable prisoners and social isolators to ensure that these prisoners receive appropriate supervision and support. (To the governor).

Key concern: Prisoners from a black or minority ethnic background, predominantly black prisoners, reported worse outcomes than white prisoners in some important areas.

Key recommendation: Managers should actively seek to understand and address the negative experiences of black prisoners. (To the governor)

Key concern: The lack of accommodation for prisoners on their release was a growing problem, with reduced availability in the approved premises needed for many of those released from Whatton. Thirteen prisoners had been released without accommodation since April, and in some cases their first-night release address was a hotel. The offender management unit and community rehabilitation company staff worked hard to support community offender managers in finding housing wherever possible, but outcomes were not improving and the reasons for this were not confined to the impact of Covid-19.

Key recommendation: HMPPS should work with government to ensure that there is sufficient appropriate accommodation, especially in approved premises, for released prisoners who need such accommodation for reasons of public protection and their own safe resettlement. (To HMPPS)

### Notable positive practice

• We define notable positive practice as innovative practice or practice that leads to particularly good outcomes from which other establishments may be able to learn. Inspectors look for evidence of good outcomes for prisoners; original, creative or particularly effective approaches to problem-solving or achieving the desired goal; and how other establishments could learn from or replicate the practice.

Inspectors found the following examples of notable positive practice during this visit.

• The unit for older prisoners and those needing social care had maintained very good support during the restricted regime, with carers based on the unit and appropriate input from the health team. An occupational therapist provided mobility and equipment assessments, promoting a rehabilitative approach to care. The team, together with peer supporters (social care advocates, SCA) created a positive environment which enabled prisoners to do as much for themselves as possible.

• The mental health team and intellectual and developmental disabilities (IDD) service continued to provide good care to patients on their caseload and were responsive to urgent referrals. Although groupwork had been suspended, individual therapy and a range of distraction packs and anxiety management resources were provided.

• The Acorn project was a relatively recent initiative doing rigorous therapeutic work with some prisoners who had problematic personality traits causing a risk of harm, as part of the offender personality disorder pathway. This work was carried out within a clinical structure supported by NHS governance and supervision, and was a promising approach to work with a group of 30 prisoners who showed challenging behaviours.

• Two of the Safer Living Foundation's projects – circles of support and accountability in the local counties, and the in-prison volunteer support and mentoring service – were doing valuable work to prepare and support prisoners up to and following release. The support and mentoring service in the prison targeted some prisoners with the most pressing needs (such as over-55s, and those with intellectual and developmental disabilities), and had continued to work through in-cell packs during the Covid-19 period.

### INDEPENDENT MONITORING BOARD: Annual Report

The law requires every prison to be monitored by an independent Board appointed by the Justice Secretary; these are known as Independent Monitoring Boards (IMBs). The IMB must satisfy itself as to the humane and just treatment of those held in custody within its prison and the range and adequacy of the programmes preparing them for release; it must report annually to the Justice Secretary on how well the prison has met the standards and requirements placed on it.

### IMB Report 1 June 2020 – 31 May 2021
### Published October 2021
### Executive Summary
### Background to the Report

For over two-thirds of this reporting year, HMP Whatton has been operating in the context of Covid-19. This has meant drastic changes to the operation of the prison. The regime has been severely restricted, with prisoners confined to their cells for most of the day and many activities and functions suspended.

The Covid-19 pandemic has curtailed visits to the prison by Board members and significantly impacted on its ability to gather information and to discuss it in the context of this annual report. Some members have been able to make occasional visits, but the principal contacts have been made by telephone to the prison when conversations, both with staff and the wing prisoners' representatives on a regular basis, have enabled the Board to have some evidence on which to base judgements.

The Board itself has not had face-to-face meetings each month and has relied on videoconferencing to maintain contact through formal Board meetings and weekly, less formal conversations. Ministers are aware of these constraints and the national collection of information on prisoner s' reactions to the pandemic and to lockdown.

The report are the findings of the Board at HMP Whatton for the period 1 June 2020 to 31 May 2021. Until the pandemic-imposed restrictions, members of the Board had made twice weekly visits to the prison but in this reporting year the range of activities and facilities reviewed have been, accordingly, very limited. Attendance at prison meetings has been possible through telephone contact and members have attended in this way. Prisoner applications have been dealt with as and when they could be collected.

In spite of the restrictions, Board members have felt that the access to the prison staff and, wherever possible, to the life of the prison, has provided as strong a link as is possible in the circumstances. The Board has met monthly with the Governor (via videoconferencing) and has appreciated the frank discussions, co-operation and support from her and the senior management team. The Board has greatly appreciated this, especially at a time when all the staff have been under great pressure. We are also grateful for the support of the Business Hub personnel and of our Board clerk in supporting us in our work.

The Board wishes to commend the Governor, senior management team and the staff of HMP Whatton for the fair and humane manner in which the restrictions imposed by the measures to combat Covid-19 were carried out with prisoner welfare the first concern. There was a consistent regime allowing daily telephone calls and regular exercise for each prisoner and throughout this year the prison has been settled and prisoners have been understanding of the need for the severe regime.

## Main Judgements
### How safe is the prison?

It is evident to the IMB that there is a clear intention on the part of prison management and staff that all prisoners should be safe and that much effort is invested in pursuing this objective. The national regime of lockdown for 22 hours each day has given an entirely different life for prisoners. It has changed the parameters for safety for prisoners in that, whilst in lockdown, they are secure. A proportion have been working in activities outside their cells for a limited time but at the height of the pandemic facilities, food and materials were brought to the cells. There have been instances of self-harming and one critical incident, but prisoners have accepted the strictures of the regime well, perhaps appreciating that there are national restrictions faced by the general population in force.

### How fairly and humanely are prisoners treated?

Prisoners are normally treated with fairness and humanity. However, since the start of the Covid-19 pandemic, the majority of the prisoners have been locked in their cells for 22 hours per day. This regime followed the emergency regime management plan issued by Her Majesty's

Prison and Probation Service (HMPPS). This, and other directives, have constrained the Governor from relaxing the lockdown rules and any local initiatives have, in the main, been rejected by HMPPS. The Board believes that this situation is unsustainable and cannot be regarded as fair and humane treatment.

The substandard accommodation in the B wings continues to raise concerns. B Wing contains some of the smallest cells within the prison estate. The Board is aware that the Governor and prison managers have repeatedly raised concerns about the quality of this accommodation but no funding for a replacement has been made available. Board members have, on several occasions, observed the use of force, but these incidents have not raised any concerns.

### How well are prisoners' health and well being needs met?

The Board is satisfied that prisoners receive healthcare treatment that is at least equivalent to that provided in the community, and that they can access these services within a reasonable time frame. However, during the Covid-19 pandemic, many of the clinics have been suspended and there have been extended waiting times to see the dentist. The healthcare team have, however, continued to provide an outstanding service despite reduced staffing levels. They have managed the roll- out of the Covid-19 vaccination programme very efficiently. We reiterate that the standard of the accommodation in the healthcare centre remains a significant concern. The statutory requirement to provide a healthcare standard to HBN 00-03/09 is not being met, and the facilities are, therefore, deemed to be non-compliant. Furthermore, the condition of the healthcare facilities falls well below the standards that would be expected in the community.

### How well are prisoners progressed towards successful resettlement?

During the pandemic, the provision of accredited programmes has been curtailed or significantly reduced. The resettlement programmes for prisoners had to be suspended. This means that prisoners have not been well prepared for their release into the community.

The IMB is concerned about the backlog of prisoners waiting to complete the accredited programmes for which they have been transferred to HMP Whatton to undertake. Many prisoners have expressed their concerns about the impact that this will have on their sentence plan, parole hearings and subsequent release.

There continue to be delays in transferring category D prisoners to suitable prisons.

## Main areas for Development
### TO THE MINISTER
Once again, the Board has had to report that a prisoner was held for a long time in secure conditions with deteriorating mental health waiting for secure hospital accommodation. Despite regular assurances from the National Health Service (NHS) commissioners that this area of concern was being addressed nationally, there have been no improvements to the speedy resolution of such cases. Once again, we ask, will the minister intervene and address this issue directly with the Secretary of State for Health and Social Care?

### TO THE PRISON SERVICE
As we have reported annually, the Board continues to receive applications about the loss of prisoners' property, usually when being transferred from another prison. Responses to prisoners' complaints from other establishments are often late or not received at all. Each year, IMBs across the country receive assurances that something will be done about this. However, nothing happens. Can the Prison Service develop a reliable system of handling and tracking prisoners' property, to reduce these unacceptable losses and to minimise the number of compensation claims? The standard of the accommodation in the healthcare centre continues to be a significant concern (6.1.6). Will the Prison Service, once again, consider substantial refurbishment or replacement of the healthcare facilities? We repeat our previous request for the Prison Service to review, with other agencies, the timely notification of approved premises for released prisoners, to give them the best chance of resettlement and rehabilitation?

### TO THE GOVERNOR
Will the Governor review the complaints procedure to ensure it is timely, reliable, and credible?

### Progress since the Last Report
Various maintenance projects have been undertaken, including the resurfacing of pathways, refurbishment of showers and some remedial work in healthcare.

**LONGHILL ROAD**
**MARCH**
**CAMBS**
**PE15 0PR**

**HM PRISON SERVICE**
**HM PRISON WHITEMOOR** Tel: 01354 602350

*For the latest reports on this prison please visit:* https://tinyurl.com/bdfh26rv

*Important Changes:* **(1) Visits:** the identification necessary to access this prison and visit for social or professional purposes has changed; (2) **Money and Gifts** new rules now apply to these. See page 16 for full details of the above.

**Task of the establishment** HMP Whitemoor is a high-security prison for category A and B male prisoners.

### Certified normal accommodation and operational capacity
Prisoners held May 2021: 388
Baseline certified normal capacity: 514
In-use certified normal capacity: 473
Operational capacity: 458

### Prison status and key providers
Public
Prison Group: Long Term/High Security
Prison Group Director: Will Styles
Governor/Director: Ruth Stephens
IMB Chair: Jill Collins

### Brief history
HMP Whitemoor lies outside the Cambridgeshire town of March. Opened in 1992 as a maximum security prison for men in categories A and B, it is one of eight high-security prisons in England within the long-term and high-security estate (LTHSE). On 31 May 2021, the prison held 388 prisoners, against an operational capacity of 458. A total of 139 were category A, of whom 11 were high risk. All Whitemoor prisoners are accommodated in single cells, with integral sanitation but separate shared external showers. A major construction project beginning in August 2021 to replace and upgrade electrical fittings and alarms requires prisoners to be decanted from one wing at a time; the decanting process from B wing started in May 2021 and has resulted in a progressive reduction in prisoner numbers.
The prison comprises the following units:
• three main residential wings (A, B and C wings)
• the Fens unit, accommodating up to 70 prisoners diagnosed with a personality disorder and undergoing psychological treatment, delivered in partnership with the National

Health Service (NHS) and Her Majesty's Prison and Probation Service professionals (D wing)

• a close supervision centre (CSC) holding up to 10 prisoners, managed under a nationally coordinated strategy to provide a secure location for the most disruptive, challenging and dangerous prisoners (F wing)

• a psychologically informed planned environment (PIPE) unit, designed to enable prisoners to maintain and build on developments they have previously achieved in prison, holding an average of 19 full PIPE prisoners (out of a capacity of 30) and 11 lodgers at the end of the reporting year

• the Bridge unit, opened in April 2019, designed to support prisoners progressing out of segregated conditions, with a capacity of 12.

Healthcare services are provided by Northamptonshire NHS Foundation Trust and dentistry by Prison Centred Dental Care; education and the library are delivered by Milton Keynes College and maintenance by Government Facility Services Ltd. Cambridgeshire County Council provides adult social care services. Psychological services in the Fens unit are provided by Cambridgeshire and Peterborough NHS Foundation Trust.

### Visiting Information

Booking line: 01354 602 800 Monday to Friday, 9.30am to 1.30pm.

**Visiting times:**
Wednesday, Thursday: 1:30pm to 3:30pm

**Legal visits:** Booking line number: 01354 602654 Monday to Friday, 9.30am to 1.30pm
**Visiting times:** Tuesday & Wednesday: 8:30am to 9:30am and 9:45am to 10:45am.

### INSPECTIONS & REPORTS

**Scrutiny visit: 28 July and 4–5 August 2020**
**Date of last full inspection** 13–23 March 2017
**Scrutiny visit, published 08 September 2020**
This report discusses the findings from our scrutiny visit to HMP Whitemoor, a category A prison holding around 450 prisoners at the time of our visit. Most prisoners were high risk, serving indeterminate sentences, and had been at the establishment for over a year. About a third of the population were category A prisoners.

Whitemoor experienced a Covid-19 outbreak in March, before any national guidance had been issued. This presented significant challenges to managers, who imposed restrictions in consultation with the health care provider, Public Health England and the National Health Service. At the peak of the outbreak, around 250 staff were off work, which prevented the delivery of a decent regime. At the time of our visit, the prison

had not had a case of Covid-19 for 12 weeks and managers had rightly prioritised increasing time out of cell, with some success. Most prisoners could be out of their cells for two to two-and-a-half hours each day, which was better than at many other prisons.

Communication with prisoners had been good throughout the pandemic, and nearly all prisoners reported that they understood the restrictions, and that the reasons had been explained to them. However, feedback forms sent to the governor and our conversations with prisoners demonstrated clear frustrations around the variety, quality and quantity of food and contact with families.

Managers were completing the exceptional delivery models (EDMs) required by HM Prison and Probation Service (HMPPS) before resuming additional activities. The decision had been made that all of the sites in the long-term and high-security estate would move through the stages of recovery together, which would inevitably delay measures in some sites which were ready to progress earlier. Four EDMs had been approved and others were being prepared. While these would have some impact, the progress already made in improving the regime meant that significant additional improvement would be unlikely in the short term.

Arrangements (referred to as 'cohorting') were in place for symptomatic prisoners, those vulnerable to the virus and prisoners in their first 14 days at Whitemoor. Quarantine for new prisoners was undermined by the practice of allowing those who had arrived on different days to exercise together.

Levels of violence and self-harm had fallen at the start of the pandemic. However, they were now rising, and self-harm had returned to pre-restriction levels. Despite the suspension of strategic meetings, the safer custody team continued to monitor levels of self-harm, and outreach work from the Fens unit was arranged for vulnerable prisoners living elsewhere. Care for most prisoners was reasonably good, and better on the Fens unit, where an impressive 100% of prisoners with experience of being supported through the assessment, care in custody and teamwork (ACCT) process reported feeling cared for by staff.

It was concerning that 38% of prisoners felt unsafe at the time of our visit. We found that this was a combination of those who felt physically unsafe and those who had anxieties about the pandemic. Apart from oversight of the use of force, which was better than at most prisons, behaviour management processes were limited or suspended at the start of the pandemic. Downgrades to incentives and earned privileges had recently been introduced for the most disruptive prisoners. We found that in the absence of formal processes, behaviour management relied on the positive relationships we observed between prisoners and staff.

In terms of safety, our key concern was segregation. The pandemic had halted work to reintegrate segregated prisoners through the Bridge unit. As a consequence, the number of prisoners in segregation had increased, and the average length of stay had nearly doubled to an excessive 95 days.

Residential units were relatively modern and all prisoners lived in single cells. As this was a long-term and settled population, many cells were personalised and prisoners took pride in keeping them clean.

By contrast, the cleaning of communal areas required improvement. Around one in five prisoners was employed as a cleaner but these prisoners were given only 30 minutes to clean each morning. This created Covid-19-related risks and led to wings looking grubby in places. Systems for redress were in disarray and the Independent Monitoring Board remained offsite. Prisoners were very negative about the food. This was largely because the well-equipped self-catering kitchens had been closed. This meant that all prisoners relied on food cooked in the main kitchens, and they reported that the food was of poor quality and often cold when they received it.

Equality and diversity provision also needed attention; much work had been suspended at the start of the pandemic and little monitoring of access to services or outcomes was taking place. We could see no plan in place to address this, which was a gap in a prison with such a diverse population.

Good partnership work meant that key health services, including access to nurses, the GP and mental health support, continued. Managers were now reintroducing other services, including the optician and dentist, in line with community provision, and there was a clear plan for recovery. However, the continued lack of podiatry was poor. Although the cleanliness of the inpatient unit had improved, more focus was needed on a therapeutic regime. Medicines management was undermined by the continued practice of secondary dispensing on the segregation unit.

Managers and staff had worked hard to deliver a limited regime, which was better than that currently offered at most other sites we have visited. Work in other areas of purposeful activity was underdeveloped – in particular, in-cell education. It had taken four months for the education provider and prison managers to establish a way to deliver targeted education

packs to prisoners, and at the time of our visit only seven of these packs had been completed. However, we were particularly impressed with the continuation of library provision; there was a clear system to ensure that prisoners had access to books and DVDs throughout the pandemic.

Managers had put in place some innovative initiatives to support family contact, and the introduction of video calling was also positive. In-person visits were about to be restarted but the number of restrictions and lack of weekend slots made them unattractive to prisoners' families. The key barrier to family contact was a shortage of telephones. The prison had tried to source additional wing telephones but this had been refused as HMPPS was going to deliver mobile phones for use in prisons. However, by the time these phones had arrived at Whitemoor, guidance had been issued preventing their use in the high-security estate. To resolve this, HMPPS should install more wing telephones without delay.

Apart from public protection, much offender management work had been suspended. This was understandable but had the impact of delaying prisoner progression. There were plans to reintroduce offender management for some, but for most prisoners this situation was likely to continue for some time.

We found that managers at Whitemoor had made significant progress in improving regime provision, and the prison was largely safe and decent at the time of our visit. However, establishing in-cell education provision had taken too long. Planning for the recovery was well advanced in some areas but more focus was needed on the issues that mattered most to prisoners. Put simply, managers needed to buy more telephones, improve the quality of the food and implement a safe way for prisoners to cook for themselves. In addition, managers needed to address and redress shortfalls in the areas of segregation, equality and diversity.

Peter Clarke CVO OBE QPM

HM Chief Inspector of Prisons August 2020

**Key concerns and recommendations**

Key concerns and recommendations identify the issues of most importance to improving outcomes for prisoners and are designed to help establishments prioritise and address the most significant weaknesses in the treatment and conditions of prisoners.

During this visit we identified some areas of key concern, and have made a small number of key recommendations for the prison to address.

Key concern: More prisoners were segregated than the segregation unit could accommodate. As a consequence, some were segregated on the Bridge unit, which was also full, leading to one prisoner being segregated on the inpatient unit. This compromised the role of the Bridge unit in supporting prisoners to leave segregation and return to the residential units. The average length of stay on the segregation unit had nearly doubled. For those prisoners who progressed to the Bridge unit from segregation, there was little difference in the regime they experienced.

Key recommendation: Segregated prisoners should be reintegrated back to normal location as swiftly as possible. (To the governor)

Key concern: Listeners' access to prisoners had been reduced. Speaking through a clear screen or during unlock time on the units was no substitute for a private, supportive conversation with a trained peer during a time of crisis. Listeners did not receive onsite support from the Samaritans.

Key recommendation: All prisoners should have prompt access to a Listener in a private setting. (To the governor)

Key concern: Formal systems for redress were in disarray; more than 200 complaints had gone unanswered, and the responses we saw did not always address the issue raised. The Independent Monitoring Board (IMB) had not yet resumed its visits to the prison, and limited telephone access prevented prisoners from using the IMB freephone number.

Key recommendation: All complaints should be answered. Responses should address the issues raised and prisoners should be able to access the Independent Monitoring Board. (To the governor)

Key concern: The strategic management of equality and diversity was weak and the prison had done little to understand, monitor and address the impact of Covid-19 restrictions on prisoners from different groups. This was of concern, given that over half the population identified as being from a black and minority ethnic background and over a quarter had disclosed a disability. Celebration of cultural events was limited, and many complaints about inequality had been left to the equality team to deal with, which in many cases had not resolved the issue raised.

Key recommendation: The strategic management of equality and diversity should ensure that discriminatory treatment is identified and addressed. (To the governor)

Key concern: Long-standing poor medication administration practices had continued on the inpatient and segregation units. There was no treatment room on either unit, and medicines to be administered there were taken out of their original packaging in the pharmacy by nurses and put into pots, which posed a potential risk for errors, and then taken to the units. Staff described passing medication through the inundation point, which prevented clear observation and increased the risk of hoarding and diversion.

Key recommendation: Medicines should be administered to patients in the safest way, meeting professional and good practice standards. (To the governor)

Key concern: It took too long to provide targeted education packs, and the process for managing this was ineffective, with only seven packs returned since their introduction at the end of July. Systems to distribute and collect packs were weak and many packs did not reach teachers for marking.

Key recommendation: Prisoners should have access to targeted education provision in line with their individual needs, with effective processes for distributing and collecting packs. (To the governor)

Key concern: There were far too few telephones, which severely limited prisoners' family contact. There were no in-cell telephones, and far too few on the landings. On some days, prisoners' calls were restricted to just 10 minutes. Managers had been prevented from using mobile phones tied to prisoners' existing PIN telephone accounts.

Key recommendation: The prison should install more telephones on every residential unit without delay. (To the governor)

Key concern: In-person social visits were about to be reintroduced but take-up was slow among prisoners' families because almost every aspect of the experience was limited and unappealing. Although some of the restrictions were unavoidable, the lack of any weekend visits or catering were both gaps which could be addressed.

Key recommendation: Social visits provision should include weekend sessions and provide catering, to encourage more families to attend. (To the governor)

Key concern: Most prisoners would not have any ongoing offender management in the foreseeable future. Access to offending behaviour programmes was severely reduced. Sentence progression had stopped for all prisoners. The continuing absence of challenge and supervision for most indeterminate sentence prisoners risked them experiencing hopelessness and losing motivation to address their offending behaviour.

Key recommendation: Prison offender managers should speak to every prisoner, to discuss the impact of the ongoing restricted regime on their individual sentence plan, and realistic timescales for progression. (To the governor)

**Notable positive practice**
We define notable positive practice as innovative practice or practice that leads to particularly good outcomes from which other establishments may be able to learn.
Inspectors look for evidence of good outcomes for

prisoners; original, creative or particularly effective approaches to problem-solving or achieving the desired goal; and how other establishments could learn from or replicate the practice.

Inspectors found the following examples of notable positive practice during this visit:

• There were very few overdue use of force reports. Electronic report completion and use for the daily briefing sheet, to identify which reports were due from staff involved in restraint incidents, helped to achieve this.

• The sharing of self-harm trigger dates in the daily briefing sheet was a good prompt for staff that a prisoner might be at additional risk of self-harm.

• Owing to the cancellation of many face-to-face hospital appointments, telephone patient consultations with external specialists had been established and had proved successful, helping to allay prisoners' anxiety about ongoing treatment.

• Distraction packs had been created, addressing the anxiety and worries around Covid-19, which included activities, relaxation techniques and in-cell yoga, and self- help guidance had been produced for the Way-Out TV channel used within the prison.

• The continued library provision was excellent and the prison ensured that the flow of books and DVDs to prisoners was regular.

• Managers had innovated to address gaps in family contact. Photographs of over 300 prisoners had been taken and printed off, for them to send to their families. Staff had also recorded over 100 short video messages from prisoners, which were then sent to their relatives using WhatsApp.

• Video calling ('Purple visits'; see Glossary of terms) had proven popular with prisoners. About 30% of prisoners had used the service in its first month. It was positive that managers had allowed prisoners to make multiple calls to use sessions that would otherwise have gone to waste.

## INDEPENDENT MONITORING BOARD: Annual Report

The law requires every prison to be monitored by an independent Board appointed by the Justice Secretary; these are known as Independent Monitoring Boards (IMBs). The IMB must satisfy itself as to the humane and just treatment of those held in custody within its prison and the range and adequacy of the programmes preparing them for release; it must report annually to the Justice Secretary on how well the prison has met the standards and requirements placed on it.

**IMB Report 1 June 2020– 31 May 2021**
**Published November 2021**
**Background to the report**

The Covid-19 outbreak has had a significant impact on the Board's ability to gather information and discuss the contents of this annual report. The Board has therefore tried to cover as much ground as it can in these difficult circumstances, but, inevitably, there is less detail and supporting evidence than usual. Ministers are aware of these constraints. Regular information is being collected specifically on the prison's response to the pandemic, and that is being collated nationally.

Board members have not been able to visit the prison since mid-March 2020, but monitoring has continued remotely; monthly conversations have taken place between the Board and the Governor or her deputy; and Board members have been in telephone contact with many of the senior officers of the prison. The Board has taken advantage of the arrangements made nationally for email contact with prisoners and has made similar arrangements locally to communicate with prisoner representatives.

The Board recognises that members' absence from the prison may have reduced prisoners' awareness of its role and readiness to turn to the IMB for assistance. We will work hard to raise our profile during the recovery process.

Throughout the pandemic Whitemoor has operated in compliance with the requirements of the National Framework for Prison Regimes and Services Exceptional Delivery Models. These have provided a valuable framework for keeping the prison safe and secure. The amount of work required of staff at all levels to draw up, review, refresh and implement the ever-changing plans should not be under- estimated.

The anticipated inquests into the deaths at London Bridge at the end of 2019 hung over the prison for much of the year. The tragic deaths of Jack Merritt who worked with Whitemoor residents as part of the Learning Together team, and Saskia Jones who took part in Sing Inside at Whitemoor, affected members of the Whitemoor community in different ways, in some cases profoundly. The Board offers its condolences to the families of those who died and commends the professionalism of the prison staff who gave evidence at the inquests.

## Main judgements
### How safe is the prison?

Whitemoor continues to be a reasonably well-ordered prison: the constrained conditions caused by the pandemic have reduced the opportunity for bad behaviour with men having been locked in their cells for 21 and a half hours per day and released for wing activities in groups of 21 to enable social distancing on the narrow landings. The prison used a bubble system to limit contact to groups from the same wing. This was successful in keeping infection under control: prisoners recognise and appreciate the efforts made to keep them safe.

However, the impact on mental health and wellbeing is a different matter. The use of illegal substances appears to have increased. With the cessation of social visits and the use of the Rapiscan itemiser to screen mail closing (two of the habitual routes for the entry of drugs) it became increasingly clear that there was an issue of staff corruption leading to the suspension of one member of staff.

It has been suggested that the prospective review of regime conditions in prisons will draw from the lessons learned during lockdown. We hope that HMPPS will take a balanced view of the needs of all groups of prisoners. We have heard younger prisoners expressing concern about the reduced opportunities to socialise caused by the restricted conditions. The newly formed prison rehabilitation culture council will be helpful in advising on the way forward for Whitemoor.

There were two deaths in custody.

**How fairly and humanely are prisoners treated?**
The prison's commitment to a more rehabilitative culture has been maintained during lockdown. A prison rehabilitation culture council has been established, coordinated by two prisoners. The council forms an umbrella for the other consultative bodies involving prisoners and appears to have the potential to generate open and productive conversations about ways in which prison life can be made more secure and purposeful. The Governor has personally met prisoners to explain the council's role. Covid-19 restrictions mean that other consultative meetings have had to take place on a wing basis; this is time-consuming for the governor responsible for residence, who attends all such meetings, but facilitates thoughtful and constructive dialogue with the relevant wing custodial managers (CMs) present.

The amount of time that prisoners have spent in their cells is a major cause of concern with much valuable activity suspended. The inability to use wing kitchens and gyms has been felt keenly. Delivering the regime in a period of two and a half hours has led to tension and stress for both staff and prisoners. The requirements of the exceptional delivery models were scrupulously met but evening telephone calls were a constant struggle leading to the serving of food in foil containers to stop time being lost at the serveries. The response of the education provider to the

need to find appropriate alternatives to classroom learning was disappointing in the early stages of lockdown. However, with the help of HMPPS advisers, the low-level distraction packs which were initially provided evolved into learning packs specifically related to some of the courses. The librarian's commitment to ensure that books and DVDs continued to be made available was exemplary and he received good support from prison staff. The opportunity for families to send in recreational packs was welcomed.

Corporate worship was another casualty of Covid-19 with only limited services taking place in the course of the year on a wing basis. Worship took place fortnightly instead of weekly because of the need to preserve wing-based bubbles. Some residents felt it was unfair that corporate worship came out of regime time but the logistics of managing movement seemed to make that necessary.

On a more positive note, the Board noted the impact of good team-working between the new CM and a dedicated psychologist in the segregation unit. The CM has energetically shared a vision for a more humane segregation regime with his colleagues and the prison as a whole, but there is some way to go to achieve the cultural change he seeks. However, although seg numbers fell at the very end of the year, for most of the time they have been too high, far in excess of the 18 for which the segregation unit is staffed and impacting negatively on the capacity of the next-door Bridge unit to fulfil its role. Men are kept in segregation for too long. The chairing of segregation review boards and attendance by other departments has improved, but action points are not always promptly followed up, and not all attendees are appropriately prepared.

The inevitable monotony of the working day with reduced opportunities for officers to work supportively with prisoners did little to encourage staff retention. Given the recent heavy recruitment into the prison service as a result of government policy changes, the prison is inevitably reliant on less experienced officers who through no fault of their own lack the inter-personal skills and jail craft of more experienced colleagues and this sometimes led to friction with prisoners.

**How well are prisoners' health and wellbeing needs met?**
Whitemoor managed the Covid-19 pandemic extremely well with very few cases of the illness reported. An unfortunate consequence of the limitations on the cross-deployment of officers was the decrease in the number of key worker sessions delivered, though vulnerable prisoners were given priority.

Healthcare staffing increased, welcome progress in an area which has concerned the Board for a number of years. Waiting times for appointments in general healthcare were similar to those in the wider community and 80% were fulfilled, with much lower levels of complaint than in the past. Mental health was an area of particular improvement with 88% of referrals seen within the target time of five days and a weekly mental health visit introduced for segregation unit prisoners.

The review of food provision took place as planned, resulting in a wide-ranging report which referenced best practice in other prisons. The Board was pleased to note the priority given to issues like the motivation of kitchen workers and the opportunities presented by the kitchen for prisoners to train in employment skills, as well as to the fabric of the main kitchen and the quality of food produced.

## How well are prisoners progressed towards successful resettlement?

As a high security prison, Whitemoor seldom releases prisoners directly to the community but takes seriously its residents' need to take some early steps towards rehabilitation. Initiatives like the prison rehabilitation culture council are important in allowing prisoners to feel a sense of responsibility for their actions and for building the sort of community in which they feel safe and have a sense of purpose about their futures.

The Board welcomes the progress that has been made in promoting family contact through the introduction of Purple Visits video technology to enable prisoners including foreign nationals to connect with their homes. Whitemoor was proactive in seeking priority for access to the system because of limited personal identification number (PIN) phone availability. It should be regarded as a very high priority to keep this going after the pandemic is over. Equally the installation of cabling so that prisoners can use telephones inside their cells is an urgently needed improvement which would enable easier communication with families (including young children) at times convenient to them, reduce the stress caused by the competition to make calls on wing telephones during association, and lessen the temptation to trade in phones as contraband. The value of in-cell telephones emerges clearly from a report by Her Majesty's Inspectorate of Prisons on the first six months of lockdown, 'What happens to prisoners in a pandemic?'. We call on HMPPS to take the opportunity created by the major electrical works which are imminent to install in-cell telephone cabling.

The closure of education classes and workshops during the pandemic has meant significant disruption to men's learning and the prison will need to make a huge effort to restore these activities and reignite men's interest in them.

## Main areas for development
### TO THE MINISTER
Will the Minister please give personal attention to ensure:
• that HMPPS installs the cabling for in-cell telephones as part of the major electrical project currently taking place at Whitemoor?
• the continuation of Purple Visits technology to allow prisoners to communicate by video conference with their families, both in the UK and, for foreign nationals, overseas?

### TO THE PRISON SERVICE
Will the prison service please review urgently the use of specialised units in order to ensure that better and speedier arrangements can be made for prisoners whose needs are difficult or impossible to meet in a prison like Whitemoor? This would avoid the sad spectacle of men languishing for months at a time in demoralising and degrading conditions.

Will HMPPS please give urgent attention to supporting prison governors in the battle to stop the importing and manufacture of illicit substances including hooch within the prison? These substances endanger the health and wellbeing of prisoners and the safety of officers and their wide-spread use should be a cause of national concern.

Will the prison service please bring to a conclusion the protracted review of a system for managing prisoners' property, the lack of which causes so much distress and frustration at all levels of the service at present?

Will the prison service please review its approach to securing value for money in contracts for building works? Yet again a refurbishment project (this time of the main kitchen at Whitemoor) has been delayed by sub-contractors passing work from company to company until the job reached a firm whose staff did not have the necessary security clearance; the cladding appears to be of poor quality and is already breaking up before it has been fully installed.

### TO THE GOVERNOR
Will the Governor please ensure that the key worker scheme which has the potential to make a very positive contribution to staff/prisoner relations is resourced appropriately and supported from the top down to do the job it was created to do?

The Board strongly supports the establishment of the prison rehabilitation culture council and would encourage the Governor to continue the positive work she has begun to ensure that it is seen by prisoners as a significant force for the improvement of prison life in Whitemoor.

**Progress since the last report**
We are pleased to have seen the following improvements since last year:
• the introduction of Purple Visits technology to enable prisoners to make video contact with their families;
• the establishment of a prison rehabilitation culture council;
• the reduction in segregation unit numbers towards the end of the year;
• the efficiency of the complaints system with 70-75% of complaints being answered within target;
• the increased number of mental health staff and the introduction of a weekly mental health visit to the segregation unit;
• the beginning of the implementation of the recommendations of the food review;
• the refurbishment of four shower units;
• plans to install an additional phone on each wing and in the segregation unit; • preparations for a major project to refurbish electrical and alarm installations on the wings (but it is vital that this project should include the cabling for in-cell telephones).

ROMSEY ROAD
WINCHESTER
SO22 5DF

HM PRISON
WINCHESTER    Tel: 01962 723000

*For the latest reports on this prison please visit:*
https://tinyurl.com/bdfh26rv

*Important Changes:* **(1) Visits:** the identification necessary to access this prison and visit for social or professional purposes has changed; (2) **Money and Gifts** new rules now apply to these. See page 16 for full details of the above.

**Task of the establishment** HMP Winchester is a category B local men's prison with a separate category C unit. The establishment also holds young adults.

**Certified normal accommodation and operational capacity**
Prisoners held at the time of inspection: 492
Baseline certified normal capacity: 448
In-use certified normal capacity: 468
Operational capacity: 564

**Population of the prison**
• 50% of the population are unsentenced, 39% are the resettlement cohort, 8% are the training cohort

and 3% are serving an indeterminate sentence.
• 13% are foreign national prisoners.
• 21% of the population are aged 25 yrs and under.
• Approximately 80 prisoners are released into the community each month.

**Prison status and key providers**
Public
Prison group/Department: South Central
Prison Group Director: Andy Lattimore
Governor/director and date in post
James Bourke, September 2018
IMB Chair: Rob Heather
Physical health provider: Practice Plus Group
Mental health provider: Practice Plus Group
Substance misuse treatment provider:
Practice Plus Group
Prison education framework provider:
Milton Keynes College
Escort contractor: Serco

**Brief history** HMP Winchester was built in 1849 and has a radial design typical of Victorian prisons. The prison covers an area of approximately six acres. In 1908, the health care unit was built, and in 1964 another unit was added as a remand centre for young offenders. The unit, known as West Hill, continued to be used for this function until 1991, when it started housing women prisoners. In 2004, its role changed to a category C resettlement unit.

**Short description of residential units**
On the local prison site:
A wing – currently closed for refurbishment.
B wing – remand and convicted prisoners.
C wing – detoxification and integrated drug treatment system. Landing C4 was also used for additional first night cells and reverse cohorting (see Glossary) at the time of the inspection.
D wing – remand and convicted vulnerable prisoners. Landing D4 was also used for first night cells and reverse cohorting at the time of the inspection.
On the category C site:
Two units accommodating category C and a small number of category D prisoners, known as West Hill and the Hearn unit, respectively.

**Visiting Information**
Booking line: 0345 223 5514 Monday to Friday, 10am to 11:30am and 2pm to 3:30pm.
**Visiting times:** Tuesday, Thursday, Saturday: 1:30pm to 4:30pm.

**Legal Visits:** There are currently no legal visits taking place.

INSPECTIONS & REPORTS
**Date of last full inspection 31 January – 1
February and 7–11 February 2022
HMCIP Report, published 25th May 2022**

Winchester is a small, Victorian, local prison that serves the courts in south and central England. At the time of our inspection it held nearly 500 prisoners in the main category B prison and a small, separate category C facility. Over half of the prisoners were unsentenced.

At our last inspection in 2019, we found a prison struggling with high levels of violence and which was providing prisoners with very little time out of cell. On our return, we were disappointed to find that – despite some limited progress – our healthy prison test scores remained the same. Winchester continued to be one of the most violent prisons in the country.

While there had been impressive work to reduce the risk posed by some of the most violent prisoners, there was no meaningful strategy to understand and address the causes of violence within the main population. Most prisoners were locked in their cells for 22.5 hours a day, and even more at the weekend. The enthusiastic education managers were very frustrated by the prison's inability to get prisoners to classrooms and workshops, both consistently and on time. This made it impossible to plan work programmes because they did not know who, if anyone, was going turn up each day. There was no assessment of the skills of prisoners when they came into the prison, which meant that those who had been employed in the community were not provided with suitable work.

As during our 2019 inspection, men on the category C side of the prison did not have enough to do. We found a group of relatively low-risk prisoners who were bored and frustrated by the lack of activity, while workshops were underused and the gardens were out of bounds. There is huge scope to develop the offer for these prisoners and create a thriving, productive environment which will support sentence progression and provide an incentive to prisoners on the main site.

Despite some improvements to the fabric of Winchester's buildings, such as new showers on some wings, ongoing issues with the water supply meant that fewer prisoners than any prison we have visited were able to have a daily shower. Many of the cells, particularly on the C4 landing, were covered in graffiti or dilapidated, with worn out furniture and lavatories. Leaders had put up posters around the prison showing their aspiration for how cells ought to look, but there was no credible plan for how or when these improvements would be made.

The prison had struggled to recruit and retain enough staff and this problem was directly affecting the day-to-day running of the jail, where at times there were simply not enough officers to ensure even the most basic regime for prisoners. Officers were frequently cross deployed from the gym and the offender management unit which meant access to these services was further reduced. Leaders will need to develop an understanding of why so many officers (in an affluent part of the country with low levels of unemployment) are leaving the prison and put in place some meaningful support to help retain good staff members during their first year of service.

Inspectors were frequently impressed by many of the officers and staff, who showed great skill and dedication in their work, despite the many challenges that they had faced over the last two years. Leaders had managed to keep visits going during the latest lockdown and this was a real achievement, given how frequently the prison was short staffed.

There is no doubt that the pandemic has limited some of the progress at Winchester, but leaders have failed to show enough real, sustained grip. If it is to improve from this disappointing inspection, the prison will need leaders to be active and visible on the wings, and set clear, measurable targets for improvement so that prisoners are safer, kept in decent conditions and given enough to do during the day.

Charlie Taylor, HM Chief Inspector of Prisons
March 2022

### Safety

At the last inspection of Winchester, in 2019, we found that outcomes for prisoners were poor against this healthy prison test for the local site and reasonably good at the category C site.

At this inspection, we found that outcomes for prisoners remained poor on the local site and reasonably good at the category C site.

In our survey for both sites, prisoners reported more negatively than in similar prisons across several aspects of early days processes. Improvements had been made to initial safety screening to identify risk, but accommodation for prisoners in their early days was poor, and not all prisoners received important aspects of induction. The overall numbers of assaults on staff and prisoners were higher than in similar prisons. Although assaults on staff were reducing, prisoner-on-prisoner violence was not showing the same decline. The local site was far more violent than the category C site, where prisoners felt much safer. Violent incidents were not routinely investigated, so the nature of the high levels of violence was not fully understood. The most serious perpetrators of violence were managed using a challenge, support and intervention plan, and many had good plans, with a range of tailored interventions and actions. The culture of the prison did not promote hope and optimism, and there was little to incentivise good behaviour. Standards of behaviour were set too low. Monthly safety meetings discussed a wide range of useful data, but this did not lead to actions to reduce violence or promote better behaviour.

We could not be confident that all use of force was proportionate, necessary and justified as a result of weaknesses in governance. Some incidents were not recorded, documentation lacked detail, statements were missing, and body-worn cameras were not always used to capture evidence.

Living conditions in the relocated segregation unit had marginally improved, although cells remained dingy. Cells on the ground floor of the segregation unit were overlooked by prisoners on the vulnerable prisoner exercise yard. This meant unscreened toilets were in view and that some segregated prisoners could shout abuse to the vulnerable prisoners while they exercised.

Staff–prisoner relationships in the unit remained a strength and they showed good knowledge of the prisoners in their care. The average length of stay was short and there was an emphasis on reintegration, helped by good, regular and detailed input from mental health and psychology teams.

Security arrangements on the local site were broadly proportionate to the risks posed, but this was not the case on the category C site, where prisoners were locked onto landings, unable to move between locations unescorted. The prison identified drugs as its main threat – and some measures to address the problem had been put into place – but the drug strategy was too generic to be effective and lacked a specific local action plan to improve outcomes. Demand for drugs was inevitably exacerbated by a severely restricted regime.

Levels of self-harm had reduced on the local site since the last inspection but remained among the highest of all local prisons. The safety strategy was aligned with the risks that the establishment faced, but not enough use was made of the impressive range of data collated or the action plan to improve safeguarding outcomes.

### Respect

At the last inspection of Winchester, in 2019, we found that outcomes for prisoners were not sufficiently good against this healthy prison test for the local site and reasonably good at the category C site.

At this inspection, we found that outcomes for prisoners remained not sufficiently good on the local site and reasonably good at the category C site. A very restricted regime and staffing shortfalls were having a severe impact on the opportunity to develop meaningful and supportive relationships between staff and prisoners. We saw some skilful management of some challenging behaviour, but very little effective key work (see Glossary) was taking place.

Too many prisoners shared cells designed for one. Some cells were in a poor state, with insufficient furniture, large amounts of graffiti, and scaled and dirty toilets. There were not enough working showers for the population on both sites because of problems with the water supply. Too many prisoners went for days without a shower and did not have regular and reliable access to clean clothes and bedding.

In our survey, only 36% and 30% of respondents at the local and category C sites, respectively, said that the food was good, and 45% and 46%, respectively, said that the shop sold the things they needed. There was little evidence of consultation with prisoners leading to positive change.

Prisoners had little faith in the application system and there was no analysis of available data to address common issues. The complaints system was well managed and oversight was good. Access to legal services was adequate.

The strategic oversight of equality had improved with the arrival of a dedicated manager, but so far insufficient progress had been made. A strategy document identified priorities for protected groups and data analysis identified potential disproportionate treatment, but neither had led to sufficient action to improve outcomes for prisoners. Consultation with some protected groups had only recently restarted, which left the prison poorly placed to understand needs fully. Investigations and responses to discrimination incident report forms had improved. Despite being under-resourced, the chaplaincy had continued to provide strong pastoral support throughout the pandemic, but opportunities for corporate worship remained too limited.

Health care staff delivered a wide range of appropriate services and had successfully managed four Covid-19 outbreaks and the vaccination programme. There were vacancies in all clinical disciplines. Clinics and secondary care appointments were regularly cancelled due to HMPPS staff shortages, which caused delays in access to care. No progress had been made to address the environmental deficits within the health care unit and clinical rooms. There was good management of patients with long-term conditions, but there were increasing waits for mental health services, including psychology and initial assessment. The substance misuse team provided a valuable service, although group work still had not restarted after the easing of the pandemic restrictions.

## Purposeful activity

Restrictions to time out of cell were having a detrimental effect on prisoners' physical and mental health, and their motivation to progress. On the local site, most prisoners had about an hour and a half out of their cell each day, but there were also some who were unlocked for less than that. Prisoners on the category C site were unlocked onto the spurs of their landings for most of the day, but too few prisoners on either site had access to any purposeful activity.

Too many prisoners were unemployed or not yet allocated to any activity. There were insufficient activity spaces to meet the needs of the population, and the curriculum for work was too narrow. The work available to those on the local site was inadequate, both in quantity and quality. Vocational training was available only to prisoners from the category C site, and only benefited a very small proportion of prisoners.

Too few prisoners were yet to have an induction to education. The quality of in-cell learning packs was too variable and did not always match the level of learning for which they were intended. Teachers and instructors did not establish prisoners' existing skills and knowledge effectively, or plan learning sequentially. Too many prisoners with a learning difficulty or disability did not develop the skills and knowledge they needed to succeed in the future. Most prisoners were not challenged by their workshop or wing work role, or were allocated activities that did not match their needs or interests. Instructors did not monitor prisoners' progress in their subjects or in relation to employability skills adequately.

Attendance at education, vocational training and work was far too low and prisoners were often late to their lessons. Staff did not take into account the needs, abilities or aspirations of prisoners when allocating them to work and education activities.

Leaders and managers did not focus sufficiently on the quality of education, skills and work. There was too little impact from the functional skills strategy that leaders had recently put in place; too few prisoners were prepared effectively to sit examinations for functional skills English and mathematics, and only a few passed them.

## Rehabilitation and release planning

At the last inspection of Winchester, in 2019, we found that outcomes for prisoners were not sufficiently good against this healthy prison test for the local site and reasonably good at the category C site.

At this inspection, we found that outcomes for prisoners remained not sufficiently good on the local site and at the category C site.

Social visits were available to all prisoners. Access was restricted to two visits each month – including for remand and enhanced prisoners – even though there were spaces available. Spurgeons family workers provided excellent support to prisoners with family issues and broader resettlement needs, and had resumed delivery of group family interventions in December 2021.

Work to reduce reoffending was hampered by the lack of a current needs analysis, a strategy setting out the work that needed to be done and an action plan to identify and measure progress across the resettlement pathways. Multidisciplinary meetings to oversee and drive reducing reoffending work had only just restarted after the easing of the restrictions and records were poor. Vacancies and cross-deployment of operational prison offender managers had led to weaknesses in some core functions, such as delays in home detention curfew applications and recategorisations.

Oversight and timeliness of offender assessment system (OASys) assessments were good. Most eligible prisoners had a current sentence plan of reasonable quality, but prisoners' knowledge of these plans was limited in too many cases. Levels of contact with prisoners were often insufficient to support progression.

Processes for identifying prisoners who posed a risk to the public had improved and monitoring arrangements were now better coordinated. The prison's contributions to multi-agency public protection arrangements (MAPPA) meetings in the community were mostly of good quality.

Leaders had not assessed the treatment needs of their population and there were no accredited interventions on either site. However, a small number of prisoners had benefited from interventions from Spurgeons, the education team and the chaplaincy, which facilitated a victim awareness course.

On average, a total of 80 prisoners were released from the establishment each month. Leaders did not collate and review data on prisoner outcomes, such as sustainable accommodation and work on release. We saw evidence of good work to support prisoners approaching release, although details were often not settled until their last few days in the prison.

## Key concerns and recommendations

Key concerns and recommendations identify the issues of most importance to improving outcomes for prisoners and are designed to help establishments prioritise and address the most significant weaknesses in the treatment and conditions of prisoners.

During this inspection we identified some areas of key concern and have made a small number of recommendations for the prison to address those concerns.

Key concern: Delivery of priorities set at the last inspection was slow, and the plan to deliver the basics of custody had not been executed well or delivered the results intended. Standards were not set sufficiently high, and leaders had become complacent about some poor outcomes.

Recommendation: Leaders should ensure that the basics of custody are delivered consistently and to a high standard. (To the governor)

Key concern: Staffing levels were not sufficient to deliver a decent regime and current recruitment did not keep pace with staff departures. Relationships between staff and prisoners inevitably suffered because of a lack of meaningful interaction and frustration caused by the inability to get the simplest tasks done. Fragilities within the management structure limited oversight, role modelling and support for staff.

Recommendation: Recommendation: Staffing at all levels should be sufficient to deliver a full regime, support constructive relationships and facilitate leaders to carry out their line management duties. (To HMPPS)

Key concern: Winchester remained one of the least safe prisons in the country. Incidents were not always investigated to help leaders gain a full understanding of the underlying causes of violence to enable them to devise a responsive strategy. Staff were unfamiliar with some key processes and the culture of the prison did not motivate good behaviour.

Recommendation: A thorough analysis of the causes of violence should be used to devise a safety strategy that addresses deep- seated cultural issues that leads to a reduction in the high levels of violence and make the prison safe. (To the governor)

Key concern: Documentation to justify the use was force was often incomplete. Body-worn video cameras were not routinely operated during incidents, and recordings of incidents, both planned and spontaneous, were not always retained. Some incidents were not recorded through the HMPPS incident reporting system. Governance of the use of force was poor. As a result of these deficiencies, HMPPS could not be assured that all force used was proportionate, necessary and justified.

Recommendation: Leaders should provide rigorous oversight of the use of force, ensuring appropriate accountability through accurate reporting, activating body-worn cameras and retaining footage as evidence and to inform learning. (To the governor)

Key concern: Self-harm rates remained high in comparison with those at similar prisons, and the establishment was not making effective use of available data to understand the underlying causes of self-harm. There was insufficient quality assurance and inadequate peer support for prisoners who were in crisis.

Recommendation: Data analysis should be used to understand the root causes of self-harm, and the results should inform an effective action plan that leads to a reduction in incidents and support prisoners at times of crisis. (To the governor)

Key concern: Too many prisoners on the local site lived in cold, poorly equipped and dirty cells. Many cells were overcrowded. The 'decency policy' was not being implemented, and staff and many prisoners had become desensitised to the poor conditions that many prisoners were held in. Access to basics, such as a daily shower, cleaning materials, clean bedding, clothing and stored property, was too often very poor.

Recommendation: All prisoners should have access to the basics of custody, including in-cell furniture, daily showers, cleaning materials, clean bedding and clothing, and their stored property. (To the governor)

Key concern: Staffing challenges were having a detrimental impact on the delivery of mental health and pharmacy services, as well as on access to clinics and secondary care. This resulted in delays for mental health assessment, limited access to a pharmacist and delays in treatment.

Recommendation: Staffing levels in health care should be sufficient to provide appropriate support, training and clinical supervision in order to deliver good patient care. (To the health partnership board)

Key concern: Prisoners had insufficient time out of cell and access to purposeful activity. Many prisoners on the local site spent about 23 hours a day locked in their cells, and some even longer. There was insufficient activity across both sites, which led to frustration and a detrimental impact on mental and physical well-being.

Recommendation: All prisoners should have adequate time out of cell to conduct domestic tasks, engage in purposeful activities and socialise with peers. (To HMPPS and the governor)

Key concern: Leaders and managers had not considered the quality of teaching and assessment, and had focused too much on compliance and processes. They did not help teachers or instructors to improve their teaching and training practices effectively.

Recommendation: Leaders should make sure that they evaluate fully the quality of teaching and assessment. They should identify and implement actions that will improve teachers' and instructors' teaching practices. (To the governor)

Key concern: Leaders had not taken sufficient, or effective, actions to make sure that prisoners attended their education and work activities, and there were too few spaces for the size of the population. Too many prisoners had their progress disrupted by their inability to attend activities and their frequent lateness because of substantial delays to the regime.

Recommendation: Leaders should maximise prisoners' opportunities to access education and work, and enable them to attend their allocated activities on time. (To the governor)

Key concern: Leaders prioritised a minority of the population for face- to-face inductions, allocation to activities and access to advice and guidance. They did not understand the needs, experience or aspirations of most of the population.

Recommendation: Leaders should allocate prisoners to activities fairly, taking into account their needs and aspirations, and give them equal access to essential services, including induction and careers advice and guidance. (To the governor)

Key concern: Leaders and managers did not make sure that teachers and instructors provided prisoners who had a learning difficulty or disability (LDD), or for whom English was not their first language, with the support they needed to succeed. Too few prisoners with known LDD or English for speakers of other languages (ESOL) needs developed the skills and knowledge they needed for their next steps.

Recommendation: Leaders should make sure that teachers and instructors adapt their teaching practices to take account of prisoners' known learning needs. Support staff should make sure that they identify appropriate support strategies, which they share with teachers and instructors, so that prisoners make good progress in their learning and training. (To the governor)

### Notable positive practice

We define notable positive practice as innovative work or practice that leads to particularly good outcomes from which other establishments may be able to learn. Inspectors look for evidence of good outcomes for prisoners; original, creative or particularly effective approaches to problem-solving or achieving the desired goal; and how other establishments could learn from or replicate the practice.

Inspectors found two examples of notable positive practice during this inspection.

A flow-chart was provided with every complaint response, to highlight prisoners' routes of appeal if needed.

The pharmacy team contacted the patient's GP to obtain clinical information, and if no response had been received within 72 hours, a further contact was made.

## INDEPENDENT MONITORING BOARD: Annual Report

The law requires every prison to be monitored by an independent Board appointed by the Justice Secretary; these are known as Independent Monitoring Boards (IMBs). The IMB must satisfy itself as to the humane and just treatment of those held in custody within its prison and the range and adequacy of the programmes preparing them for release; it must report annually to the Justice Secretary on how well the prison has met the standards.

### IMB Report 1 June 2020 – 31 May 2021
### Published October 2021
### Background to the report

The background to this year's report has been dominated by the Covid-19 pandemic. The IMB's attendance has been minimal, with only one member continuing to visit throughout. Information has largely been collected by phone and email, with the personal touch lacking.

### Overall performance

The progress, identified as part of last year's annual report, has continued during the current reporting period and is reflected in its removal from special measures, now known as the prison performance support programme (PPSP). Improvement has been at a slower pace, due to regime and management at HMP Winchester having been dominated by the Covid-19 pandemic and its impact on the operation of the prison. Time out of cell and meaningful activity have been areas particularly negatively impacted. The IMB notes that, despite these increased restrictions, there have been no major disturbances during the current reporting period. The IMB has been kept informed by the prison management about plans for return to a more normal regime and the steps outlined to achieve this. Of particular note is the imminent reconfiguration of part of the refurbished D wing as a new CSU which encourages hope that the much criticised current arrangement on A wing will be replaced by early July 2021.

### Covid -19

HMP Winchester is to be congratulated on its professional approach to managing the Covid-19 epidemic. During the first wave of the disease, the prison took maximum precautions and isolated newly arriving prisoners. There were no cases recorded within the prison population but sadly one prisoner died in hospital, having contracted the disease whilst there. In October 2020, the situation worsened, in common with the rest of the country. Compulsory face mask wearing was introduced for all staff. A high number of staff were absent having contracted the illness or having to isolate. Prisoners were placed in small regime groups and were allowed the required exercise and showers etc. with one group at a time out of cells. The kitchen workers who normally come from Westhill and the Hearn were all relocated to the Hearn so that they could remain working in their bubbles. During this time prisoners were in their small, usually shared cells for 23 hours per day and their tolerance and understanding of the situation was impressive. Communication of regimes, bubbles and fluctuations depending on available staffing was efficiently delivered which mitigated behaviour problems. In late October cases of Covid-19 occurred in prisoners, appearing to stem from court contact. Visits were suspended.

By early December, there were 77 Covid-19 positive prisoners (16% of the population) with the numbers growing, and 54 staff sick or isolating. Two prisoners were ill enough to require bed watches and, sadly, in March, the prison recorded its second death in custody for Covid-19 related reasons.

Work for prisoners was suspended, including the 35 whose jobs were in the kitchen. The 10 stalwart prison kitchen employees and a few volunteer staff from other departments, went beyond the call of duty and provided three meals per day for each prisoner for over a month. During this time, the prison was under great strain, but with good management and hard work, cases slowly reduced and by mid-March the prison was Covid-19 free.

Gradually the very strict regime is beginning to ease with everyone only too aware that caution is still needed. Gyms opened in early December for a few people at a time and visits recommenced from the end of May.

From late March 2020, the IMB took the decision not to enter the prison because of Covid-19, both for the protection of members and to minimise the risk of introducing the disease to the establishment. Interim measures such as relying on prison staff emptying application boxes and forwarding scanned copies to the IMB via email and telephone attendance at meeting were put in place. Very limited IMB on-site monitoring was resumed from July 2020, with a focus on the areas housing the most vulnerable inmates (CSU, healthcare). On-site monitoring was gradually increased, approaching near-normal levels by late April 2021 and the phasing out of off-site activities, in favour of resuming in-person attendance of the establishment, commenced. A transition phase is envisaged where some off-site monitoring activities, such as telephone attendance at meetings, will continue while members readjust.

The drastically reduced out-of-cell time during the lockdown periods was broadly accepted among the prisoners, who were aware of the very unusual and restricted circumstances on the outside. The rationale behind the regime offered by the prison was clearly communicated to the prisoners to achieve, by HMP Winchester standards, high levels of compliance. However, with the situation normalising on the outside the restoration of a more open regime with more purposeful activities is a significant challenge ahead. IMB has frequent communications from prison management on the subject. The constraints imposed by being a local prison with an average stay time per prisoner of around 12 weeks, and the high number of daily prisoner movements, makes this one of the most pressing concerns for all involved. In addition to endeavouring to maintain a safe and rehabilitative environment for the prisoners, the task for prison senior staff is to manage things such as incidents, investigations, staff issues, and the health/educational needs of the prisoners; at times the number and unpredictability of this is extremely challenging. Her Majesty's Prison and Probation Service (HMPPS) adds to this extensive workload with such things as new and/or revamped policies, complicated action plans, statistics gathering, training requirements etc; all valid, but time consuming, sometimes overly bureaucratic and not always geared to the needs or realities of the front-line staff, whilst rarely providing extra staff to meet these demands.

Covid-19 necessitated the production, by HMPPS, of quantities of instructions for prisons, many of them helpful but some unnecessarily long, with repeated changes and rewrites, albeit done in good faith. HMP Winchester is to be congratulated on managing to establish from this, an efficient system of necessary isolation and segregation which has kept virtually everyone safe whilst allowing the prison to function efficiently in its new restricted way. More recently vaccination and encouraging reluctant prisoners.

## Main judgements
### How safe is the prison?

HMP Winchester continues to experience very high levels of violence. For much of the year the prison has been the highest in its comparator group for assaults on staff and the second highest for prisoner-on-prisoner assaults. Covid-19 has undoubtedly adversely affected efforts to improve this situation in numerous ways, with the combination of limited purposeful activity, a significant backlog in staff training and the availability of drugs and contraband frustrating effective prevention and intervention.

The lack of a facility appropriate to the housing

of prisoners with very challenging behaviour, presenting as mentally ill, who fall below the threshold for in-patient health care, presents a risk both to the prisoners and staff in the CSU. On more than one occasion prisoners and/or CSU staff have suffered physical harm due to the limitations of this accommodation.

Despite this, focused attention on improving ACCTs has seen a reduction in the number of prisoners needing to be managed under this protocol, which will have contributed to the fact that there were no self-inflicted deaths during the reporting period.

Work to improve some of the physical conditions in which the prisoners live has continued throughout the year. However, there have been incidents of pieces of the building collapsing, and prisoners damaging the sub-standard walls and windows of their cells. It cannot be said that the fundamental fabric of the prison creates a safe or progressive environment.

### How fairly and humanely are prisoners treated?
The severely restricted regime resulting from the Covid-19 pandemic, was such that a significant minority of prisoners had only 45 minutes a day out of their cell for just three days per week. 64% of prisoners surveyed stated that they spent less than an hour out of cell daily, which cannot be regarded as humane. The rapid turnover of the varied type of prisoners, a length of stay averaging only 12 weeks, the overcrowding and high number of 18-25 year-olds with a propensity for violence, also makes consistency difficult to achieve in the poor physical conditions.

### How well are prisoners' health and wellbeing needs met?
The prison is to be commended for its response to Covid-19 and its success in preventing internally generated infection. Winchester was one of the last of all the local prisons to be designated as an 'outbreak' site (in January 2021), whereupon it controlled and reduced the incidence as well as could be expected. Healthcare and prison staff are now better integrated than before, following the arrival of the new contract holders, Patient Plus Group (PPG) in July 2020. Fewer clinical appointments are being missed and mental health services - while under continual strain - are managing their large case load effectively.

### How well are prisoners progressed towards successful resettlement?
The pandemic has had a considerable impact on the ability of the prison's partnering organisations to develop prisoners' capabilities or prepare them for a more productive life upon release; finding suitable accommodation for them on leaving the prison remains problematic. The reducing reoffending department has made tremendous efforts to offer education, despite not being able to use classrooms. While commendable, it has not been able to provide the levels of service or progress that are required or expected in normal circumstances. Purposeful activities such as workshops, have been very significantly constrained, and early release and work experience schemes curtailed. Moreover, over nine months of the last year for which data have been made available, approximately two thirds of released prisoners have been categorised as having no fixed abode.

### Main areas for development
### TO THE MINISTER
What is the Minister's plan to resolve the issue of permanent cell overcrowding and the fact that prison service instruction (PSI) 17/2012 states prisoners must be 'able to use the wc with some privacy', which is impossible to achieve in HMP Winchester?

Many cells get very hot in summer due to poor ventilation, even before the impact of climate change and the resulting incidence of extreme heat. Should there be a specified limit on the upper temperature in a prison cell?

### TO THE PRISON SERVICE
What is the prison service's plan to ensure that prisoners with mobility challenges have access to all parts of the prison, including the entrance and cells? Any necessary improvements that require central budgeting approval take far too long to get through the process. What is the prison service's plan to deal with the long - standing surveillance issues which the IMB will identify in a separate letter, and the continuing problem of the defective vehicle entrance barrier?

HMP Winchester is right in its view, particularly given the state of its infrastructure, that the clean and decent project remains a vital initiative. Although the additional funding that accompanied its roll-out has been stopped, the prison is continuing to fund it. Can the extra funding be reinstated as a matter of urgent priority?

What is the prison service doing to hasten the upgrade to the healthcare bathroom and shower area which should be condemned? This work is very long overdue and the need for it was raised in our last two annual reports.

Can the prison service prioritise and reduce the extra policy initiatives and tasks that it expects senior prison staff to action, to give them more time to concentrate on progress at HMP Winchester?

In view of the apparent inconsistencies between prisons concerning which game consoles are approved for use, will the prison service review the policy on the types and availability of consoles that can be purchased and used by prisoners when transferred between establishments?

Will the prison service introduce a barcode/tracking system to identify prisoners' personal property?

Can the canteen list include more items of fresh fruit and vegetable for prisoners who wish to purchase them?

The provision of clerking to the board as agreed in the memorandum of understanding between the IMB and the Ministry of Justice (MOJ), continues to be an issue. Despite best efforts, it has not been honoured fully due to the shortage of administrative staff in the business hub. Will the prison service provide the additional resources necessary to enable this requirement to be fully accommodated?

## TO THE GOVERNOR

Can the installation of a more secure gate to the dispensary on A wing, mentioned last year, be made a priority?

When will a photocopier, able to copy all mail, be available in the prison?

More clinical space is needed on the wings, especially for confidential mental health consultations. When will this be facilitated?

Can ACCT review be planned so that daily demands on prison and healthcare staff are manageable, thereby improving the quality of reviews?

## Progress since the last report

HMP Winchester's progress is demonstrated by its removal from special measures, now known as the PPSP.

With the appointment of Practice Plus Group (PPG), the prison health care provision has improved.

The reduction in the number of ACCTs open at any one time is welcome.

During the period covered by this report there have been no self-inflicted deaths.

The provision of the new tailoring workshop has provided additional full time jobs.

The reception department, where new prisoners are processed, has enhanced both its environment and communication, providing more pleasant surroundings and an effective information booklet.

**TATTENHOE STREET**
**MILTON KEYNES**
**MK4 4DA**

**HM PRISON WOODHILL**    **Tel: 01908 722000**

*For the latest reports on this prison please visit:* https://tinyurl.com/bdfh26rv

*Important Changes:* **(1) Visits:** the identification necessary to access this prison and visit for social or professional purposes has changed; (2) **Money and Gifts** new rules now apply to these. See page 16 for full details of the above.

**Task of the establishment**
Category B training prison

**Certified normal accommodation and operational capacity**
Prisoners held September 2021: 501
Baseline certified normal capacity: 644
In-use certified normal capacity: 627
Operational capacity: 570

**Population of the prison**
• 500 new prisoners received each year
• 67 foreign national prisoners
• 43% of prisoners from BAME backgrounds
• 2-3 released into the community each month
• 450 receiving support for substance use
• 115 referred for mental health assessment over previous 12 months

**Prison status and key providers**
Public
Prison group: Long-term and high security
Prison Group Director: Will Styles
Governor/Director: Nicola Marfleet
IMB chair: Phillip Perlin
Physical, Mental, Substance health provider: Central North-west London NHS Foundation Trust (CNWL)
Prison education: Milton Keynes College
Escort contractor: GeoAmey (north), Serco (south)

**Brief history**
HMP Woodhill was opened in 1992. It started as a local prison but in the late 1990s took on a high-security role as a core local, re-roling to a long-term category B prison in 2020.

**Short description of residential units**
Each house unit, except units 5 and 6, is divided into two wings, A and B. Each wing on the main house units is designed to hold 60 prisoners in single cells. All units hold a cross-section of prisoners, including category A, category B and

young adults, following a risk assessment.
House unit 1A – convicted prisoners (a designated unit to hold remand category A prisoners if required);
House units 1B, 2A, 2B, 3A, 3B, 4A – convicted.
House unit 4B currently closed due to staff shortfalls
House unit 5–12 first night centre
House unit 6 – national close supervision centre, separation unit and protected witness unit.
Clinical assessment unit – health care inpatients
Compass unit reintegration and additional needs

### Visiting Information
Visits booking line: 01908 722329 Monday to Friday: 8am to 11.30am and 1pm to 3.30pm (except Bank Holidays).
**Visiting times:** HMP Woodhill is offering visits for family and friends. Visiting times and availability may change at short notice. You should contact the prison direct for any queries.

### Legal visits:
Request a legal visits form from: legalvisits.woodhill@justice.gov.uk

### INSPECTIONS & REPORTS
**IRP Report:** 6–8 June 2022
**Published 14 July 2022**
**Chief Inspector's summary**
HMP Woodhill is a relatively modern prison in Milton Keynes. In addition to its role as a category B training prison, it also holds several remanded category A prisoners and operates several specialist units, making it a complex and high-risk institution. At the time of the inspection, the prison held approximately 500 prisoners, which is below its operational capacity (see Glossary), as a result of the closure of one house unit to mitigate staff shortages.
At our previous inspections of HMP Woodhill in 2018 and 2021, we made the following judgements about outcomes for prisoners.
At our last inspection, in September 2021, we found a prison where standards and outcomes were not sufficiently good, and in the areas of safety and purposeful activity outcomes were judged to be poor. Against nearly all the main measures, the prison was not safe enough and there had been seven self-inflicted deaths since the previous inspection. The daily regime was inadequate, and prisoners had a legitimate lack of confidence in the effectiveness of the staff group. Despite committed and enthusiastic leadership, it was clear that the source of many problems in the prison was the inability to recruit and retain staff.
During this review visit, we examined eight key recommendations, and our colleagues in Ofsted addressed three themes. There had been reasonable progress against five of the 11 recommendations and themes, and insufficient progress against six

Staff shortfalls, access to time out of cell (see Glossary) and purposeful activity were still of considerable concern. Violence and self-harm were still too high, although we were encouraged by a renewed focus on safety, including a trauma-informed response to prisoners with complex needs. Levels of cleanliness had improved, but efforts to maintain consistently high standards were undermined by a failure to unlock cleaners every day. Wing forums and a prisoner council were once again running and there were well-developed plans to improve the effectiveness of consultation. Too many prisoners were still unemployed or underemployed, and therefore remained locked up for most of the day. Leaders (see Glossary) had taken steps to make some work part time, to occupy more prisoners, and a few more work and education areas were now open. However, not all spaces were occupied, which again left prisoners who expected to be able to progress locked in their cells. A new offender management clinic held on residential wings was welcomed by prisoners but did not compensate for the lack of sufficient good-quality contact with their own offender manager to support sentence progression.
Overall, in most areas, leaders and managers demonstrated a will and desire to improve outcomes for prisoners, and also for staff. Much of their effort was, however, thwarted by staff shortages. The pace of progress was also affected by legacy cultural issues relating to Woodhilll's former status as a category A local prison. Staff need to place more trust in prisoners if the prison is to fulfil its role as a predominantly category B training prison. For example, staffing ratios should enable greater numbers of wing workers to be unlocked on residential wings, and the high number of prisoners identified as too risky to work off-wing should be reviewed.
Following the inspection, HM Prison and Probation Service (HMPPS) had taken important steps to support local leaders and it was clear that recruitment and retention were now a fundamental strategic priority. A whole series of support measures had been introduced or were in development, but external forces and the relative affluence of the local area were having a serious impact on leaders' ability to recruit and retain staff. Indeed, the staffing position was no better than it had been at the time of the inspection, with as many staff leaving the prison as joining. The scale of the task is huge, but I would strongly urge leaders to continue in their quest to find creative and practical solutions to

make Woodhill an attractive employer. Without continued vigour, it is inevitable that outcomes for the prison and the public will deteriorate even further.

Charlie Taylor HM Chief Inspector of Prisons June 2022

**HMCIP Report:** 20–24 September 2021
**Published 14 December 2021**

Since we last inspected Woodhill in 2018 the establishment had transitioned from a core local prison to a category B training prison. It had retained several remanded category A prisoners, as well as the operation of several specialist units, and remained a complex and high-risk institution. Relatively modern – built about 30 years ago – the prison comprises a series of house blocks within a secure campus in Milton Keynes. At the time of our inspection the prison held approximately 500 men, about 70 below its operational capacity; this was a consequence of both Covid-19 mitigation and staff shortages.

Our findings at this inspection were disappointing. As in 2018, outcomes in safety and purposeful activity were poor, while outcomes in respect and rehabilitation and release planning had deteriorated and were now not sufficiently good. Against nearly all the main measures, the prison was not safe enough. Violence was higher than comparable prisons; use of force, though mostly legitimate, was also high; use of segregation was considerable; and there had been seven self-inflicted deaths since we last inspected. Self-harm was also high. It would be wrong to say the prison had done nothing to try to address these issues. There had been some useful work led by the governor to try to better understand the causes of these problems, but this had yet to translate into action that was making a difference.

Prisoners were frustrated about the confidence and competence of staff and the inconsistency of their interactions with them. In our survey only two-thirds of respondents felt respected by staff; a reflection, perhaps, of the fact that about a third of all officers had been recruited in the last 12 months, 40% were only in their second year and many supervisors were similarly inexperienced. Our own observations were largely consistent with the views of prisoners. Many staff were well-meaning and seemed to want to do a good job, but as a group they were not sufficiently effective. Standards were not maintained and poor behaviour not addressed. Many prisoners told us that staff were either unable or unwilling to deal with their reasonable requests. Whatever the problem at Woodhill, be it the safety of the prison, the confidence prisoners had in staff, the total inadequacy of the daily regime or

weaknesses in the provision of services, the source seemed to be the inability to recruit and retain staff. This was the fundamental strategic priority that needed to be addressed.

Leadership at Woodhill had huge challenges. Apart from the issue of human resources, the complexity of the prison and the risks managed were significant. The governor was both energetic and enthusiastic in her approach, she had shown considerable commitment to the establishment over time and it was clear to us that most staff were aware of her priorities. In specific departments we saw other examples of good leadership and there was evidence of initiative and effort across the prison, but this was not bearing fruit in terms of improvement.

Arguably HM Prison and Probation Service needs to take stock of what is happening at Woodhill and reflect on what it can do to support change. Local leaders need more support to address issues beyond their control and, most of all, there needs to be a deliverable local plan to recruit, retain and equip the staff needed to run the prison.

Charlie Taylor Chief Inspector October 2021

**Summary of key findings**

We last inspected Woodhill in 2018 and made 61 recommendations, three of which were about areas of key concern. The prison fully accepted 49 of the recommendations and partially (or subject to resources) accepted six. It rejected six of the recommendations.

Progress on key concerns and recommendations Our last inspection of HMP Woodhill took place before the Covid-19 pandemic and the recommendations in that report focused on areas of concern affecting outcomes for prisoners at the time. Although we recognise that the challenges of keeping prisoners safe during COVID-19 will have changed the focus for many prison leaders, we believe that it is important to report on progress in areas of key concern to help leaders to continue to drive improvement.

At our last full inspection, we made two recommendations about key concerns in the area of safety. At this inspection we found that both these recommendations had not been achieved.

We made one recommendation about key concerns in the area of purposeful activity. At this inspection we found that this recommendation had not been achieved. Ofsted carried out a progress monitoring visit alongside our inspection to assess the progress that leaders and managers had made towards reinstating a full education, skills and work curriculum. They judged it was too early to assess whether recommendations made at the last inspection had been achieved.

## Outcomes for prisoners

We assess outcomes for prisoners against four healthy prison tests (see Appendix I for more information about the tests). We also include a commentary on leadership in the prison.

At this inspection of HMP Woodhill, we found that outcomes for prisoners had stayed the same in two healthy prison areas and declined in two.

1.8 These judgements seek to make an objective assessment of the outcomes experienced by those detained and have taken into account the prison's recovery from Covid-19 as well as the 'regime stage' at which the prison was operating, as outlined in the HM Prison and Probation (HMPPS) National Framework for prison regimes and services.

## Safety

The reception environment was good and processes were sound. It was helpful for risk mitigation that each prisoner had private interviews with reception and health care staff on arrival, and with a member of the safety and mental health teams within 72 hours. They often waited too long for access to their property because of staff shortages.

The incidence of violence remained very high, 1.5 times higher than comparable prisons, and was still increasing. Almost two-thirds of all assaults were spontaneous and against staff, and assaults on staff were on the rise.

Many prisoners expressed frustration at the regime and the lack of consistency and competence among staff. They attributed much of the violence to this. The systems to monitor and intervene with those who perpetrated violence were not effective and lacked meaningful contact and day-to-day support. Considerable research and discussion on violence had taken place with community partners but with no effect on outcomes to date. Prisoners had started to work as mediators but it was too early to assess outcomes.

Oversight of adjudications, which had reduced during the pandemic, had improved. A serious backlog of adjudications referred to the police needed resolution.

The level of use of force was very high, 2.5 times higher than comparable prisons, and had been increasing in recent months. Almost all use of force was in response to spontaneous incidents. Oversight of use of force had improved, but the review of incidents was not adequate. CCTV footage of incidents was neither reviewed nor kept, and body-worn cameras were not used sufficiently.

There were many long stays in segregation. Some work was done to prepare for reintegration to normal location, but this was not reflected in regular segregation reviews. Although physical conditions were not adequate in all respects, prisoners were positive about their experience in the unit. Unfurnished accommodation was used sparingly.

Security measures were proportionate, and procedures to counter the availability of drugs were well developed, although neither suspicion- based nor random drug testing was being carried out.

There had been seven self-inflicted deaths since our last inspection in early 2018. Some positive changes had been made in response to recommendations from the Prisons and Probation Ombudsman, especially by the health care team, but levels of self-harm were high compared to similar prisons, and the rate had been rising in recent months. Data analysis had improved but there was not enough systematic action to reduce the rate of self-harm.

The work of assessment, care in custody and teamwork (ACCT) case managers was of a good standard, but ACCT documents varied in quality and wing staff were not always sufficiently aware of the prisoners concerned.

## Respect

Fewer than two-thirds of prisoners who responded to our survey said that staff treated them with respect. Many were exasperated at the shortfalls in confidence, competence and consistency among many prison officers, about 30% of whom were in their first 12 months of service. We observed some good interactions, but frequently saw staff together in offices, leaving prisoners unsupervised. On several occasions we witnessed a lack of challenge in response to poor behaviour, and inconsistent enforcement of rules. The house units were well designed but in many cases not sufficiently clean. Cells were well equipped and free of graffiti. Many shower rooms were in poor condition and most lacked adequate screening.

Laundry facilities on the wings were good but the supply of prison clothing was inadequate. Access to stored property and purchases remained a problem because of a lack of staff. Cell call bells were often ignored, or answered after a long delay. Prisoners were unhappy with the quality of the food, and meals were still served too early.

There had been some potentially useful consultation events and surveys, but prisoners said that improvements had not ensued, and a regular pattern of consultation was lacking. The number of complaints was high and had been rising in the past year. The tracking of data on complaints had only started recently. The applications process was weak.

Work on equality remained sparse, with limited activity in relation to protected characteristics in spite of evidence of unequal outcomes. The equality training day, written and presented jointly by prisoners and staff, was a very good innovation. Black and minority ethnic and Muslim prisoners responded similarly to others in our survey on their experience of treatment and conditions. There was not enough support for foreign nationals.

The chaplaincy had worked very hard to mitigate the impact of pandemic restrictions, and pastoral support was good. However, corporate worship remained suspended and religious classes had only recently resumed for small groups. Health services were well led by a strong clinical management team.

Effective contingencies had been implemented to manage Covid-19 and few prisoners had tested positive. There had been no outbreak until very recently.

Officers were frequently unavailable to escort prisoners to health appointments, which was extending the waiting lists. Regular nurse-led clinics were held for long-term conditions and the clinical assessment unit provided good care. The addictions team had maintained one-to-one psychosocial interventions. Medicines were generally well managed but officer support for their administration was variable, increasing the risk that medicines would be diverted.

The demand for social care was monitored through good partnership arrangements. The mental health service was stretched but delivered an impressive range of support. There were long waits for psychology interventions. The mental health day unit was a promising initiative to provide emotional support to patients with complex needs. Prisoners referred to external hospitals under the Mental Health Act invariably waited too long for an assessment, despite escalation by the team.

Dental services had continued to provide urgent care, and measures were being taken to reduce a long waiting list.

### Purposeful activity

Ofsted carried out a progress monitoring visit of the prison alongside our full inspection and the purposeful activity judgement incorporates their assessment of progress.

Time out of cell was normally limited to two hours on weekdays for many prisoners, and on two days each week, they were locked up all day except for an hour's exercise. Almost half the population was unemployed, and just 9% were receiving in-cell education.

Prisoners were offered one 45-minute session in the gym each week, during one of their domestic

periods. The library remained closed and few prisoners were borrowing books.

Leaders had been unable to deliver education, skills and work to all but a handful of prisoners during the pandemic. Too few of them had been given in-cell work packs.

On arrival, prisoners received an in-cell education induction pack including an initial educational assessment. Too many of these packs were not completed and they were not accessible to many for whom literacy or the English language was a problem.

Prisoners received support through in-cell telephones and at the cell door. Leaders had identified the programmes that they planned to implement but did not have a detailed plan for return to classroom-based teaching.

No prison workshops were in operation. Only the kitchens, waste management and gardens provided prisoners with work off the wings, and no accredited qualifications were provided.

1.36 Too often, requests for in-cell learning packs were ignored or they took too long to arrive. Tutors provided feedback, but often with long delays, so that many prisoners made slow progress or became disengaged.

### Rehabilitation and release planning

Social visits and video calls were only offered on weekdays, and take-up was low. Visitors said that they were treated with respect during their visit, and visits generally started on time. The charity PACT provided good support to visitors. Nearly all prisoners were serving long or indeterminate sentences. An effective, practical, overarching strategy for reducing reoffending among this population was lacking.

Persistent staff shortages in the offender management unit were undermining core work. The caseloads for prison/probation offender managers (POMs) were unmanageable and among the highest we have seen. There was not enough contact between POMs and prisoners.

Efforts were being made to address a small but persistent OASys (offender assessment system) backlog. In our survey, only about half the prisoners were aware of having a sentence plan. Progress against sentence plan objectives was not strong, especially in relation to offending behaviour work. Up-to-date risk management plans were in place in virtually all cases and most were of a good enough standard.

The interdepartmental risk management team met each month but attendance was poor. Targeted telephone monitoring for public protection was in disarray with a lack of management oversight. Reviews were not taking place on time and there was a significant backlog of calls for monitoring.

Some one-to-one work was taking place, but no delivery of group interventions had been possible during 2021. Waiting lists for courses were growing, and some prisoners had been released without completing key offending behaviour work designed to reduce their risk of offending. Of the few prisoners who were released, most were considered high risk. We saw evidence of effective handover and resettlement planning between prison and community staff. Covid-19 tests were completed for all prisoners before release.

### Key concerns and recommendations

Key concerns and recommendations identify the issues of most importance to improving outcomes for prisoners and are designed to help establishments prioritise and address the most significant weaknesses in the treatment and conditions of prisoners.

During this inspection we identified some areas of key concern and have made a small number of recommendations for the prison to address those concerns.

Key concern: Proactive local leadership was not bearing sufficient fruit in terms of the morale, commitment and teamwork of operational staff. Shortage of staff, inexperience and high turnover were limiting what Woodhill could achieve in many areas. Many operational staff showed a lack of confidence and competence in the everyday supervision and support of prisoners. This had a detrimental impact on many aspects of the regime and on the experience of prisoners who were often frustrated at basic tasks not being completed by staff properly, consistently or at all. More prison officers were leaving than joining. These long-standing challenges at Woodhill had not been effectively addressed.

Recommendation: There should be clear measures to train, retain and develop operational staff and to increase the confidence, competence and consistency shown by prison officers in their supervision and support of prisoners, with objective assessment of outcomes.

Key concern: Violence was high and rising. Management of violence through the CSIP process was ineffective and leaders did not give adequate scrutiny at meetings to use of force footage. There was not enough use of body-worn cameras and many staff and prisoners felt unsafe.

Recommendation: Behaviour management approaches, including CSIP, should be used by staff at all levels to reduce violence by focusing on the individual prisoner, who should be personally involved.

Key concern: There had been seven self-inflicted deaths since the previous inspection. Levels of self-harm were consistently high and higher than at similar prisons. Although there had been some

actions to improve systems, work to address the rate of self-harm had not been effective. Staff struggled to deliver support consistently for prisoners in crisis, who were locked in their cells for long periods.

Recommendation: Continued development of data analysis and monitoring should underpin effective work to reduce the rate of self-harm, with all relevant prison staff working in a consistent and coordinated way to support prisoners at risk.

Key concern: Cleaning arrangements, including access to materials and compliance with basic standards of cleaning hygiene, were not good enough. Cleaners complained of not having enough time outside the wing domestic periods to complete their cleaning duties.

Recommendation: All residential areas should be kept clean through effective systems of work, monitoring, and access to the necessary materials.

Key concern: In spite of some one-off events, the regular arrangements for prisoner consultation were not good enough. Prison council meetings were irregular, not all houseblocks were represented, and the minutes did not show meaningful progress. Consultation arrangements on the wing were inadequate with no wing forums taking place.

Recommendation: Consultation arrangements should identify prisoners' concerns effectively and should result in prompt actions.

Key concern: Time out of cell was limited to two hours five days a week for most prisoners. All jobs were full time, but 47% of the population was unemployed, and just 9% were receiving in-cell education.

Recommendation: Opportunities for work and other constructive activity should be extended to more prisoners, so that all have sufficient regular and predictable time out of cell to promote rehabilitation and mental well-being.

Key concern: The level of contacts between prisoners and prison offender managers (POMs) was among the lowest we have seen in recent inspections and was not enough to drive progress in the majority of cases that we inspected. There were staff shortages in the offender management unit and POM caseloads of up to 160 were unmanageable and among the highest we have ever seen.

Recommendation: Staff resources in the OMU should be sufficient to ensure that all POMs have caseloads which permit effective offender management and regular contact with the prisoners for whom they are responsible.

Key concern: Telephone monitoring arrangements for public protection were in disarray and lacked management oversight. Reviews were not taking place on time owing to delays in the completion of monitoring forms and there was an unknown but sizeable backlog of calls waiting to be monitored, with no clear catch-up plan.

Recommendation: Managers should ensure that public protection monitoring is timely and effective.

### Notable positive practice

We define notable positive practice as innovative work or practice that leads to particularly good outcomes from which other establishments may be able to learn. Inspectors look for evidence of good outcomes for prisoners; original, creative or particularly effective approaches to problem-solving or achieving the desired goal; and how other establishments could learn from or replicate the practice.

Inspectors found four examples of notable positive practice during this inspection.

A member of the safety team interviewed each new prisoner on their arrival at the prison, providing a valuable opportunity to identify vulnerability or unmet needs.

The Compass unit provided a supportive non-clinical environment in which vulnerable prisoners could receive support and prepare to re- integrate into prison life. (See paragraph 3.51)

An impressive, well-prepared equality training day, written and presented jointly by black and minority ethnic prisoners and staff, was being delivered to staff.

The music group facilitated by the charity 'Finding Rhythms' had fostered creativity and improved the communication skills and well-being of individuals who had previously struggled to participate in progressive pathways.

### INDEPENDENT MONITORING BOARD: Annual Report

The law requires every prison to be monitored by an independent Board appointed by the Justice Secretary; these are known as Independent Monitoring Boards (IMBs). The IMB must satisfy itself as to the humane and just treatment of those held in custody within its prison and the range and adequacy of the programmes preparing them for release; it must report annually to the Justice Secretary on how well the prison has met the standards and requirements placed on it.

### IMB Report 1 June 2020 to 31 May 2021
### Published 12 December 2021
### Executive summary
### Background to the report

The reporting year was dominated by the restrictions imposed due to the Covid-19 pandemic. For the first part of the reporting year, prisoners were confined to their cells for 23 hours a day, being allowed out only for exercise and showers. Visits, religious services, education and the gym were all stopped. Prisoners were kept in small groups and not allowed to mix, to reduce the chance of transmission of the virus.

The prison took other measures to reduce the spread of the virus, and through good planning and good fortune there was no outbreak at Woodhill. There were only two cases among prisoners, and both of those were in individuals transferred from other prisons who were already infected. The isolation measures for all transferees to Woodhill helped protect the resident population. Woodhill was reported as being the only prison that did not have an outbreak among its prisoners during the year.

At times, over 15% of staff were either off sick or isolating because they had been in contact with cases or were vulnerable. In addition, there were other staff off work for more 'normal' reasons, such as annual leave, maternity or other sickness absences. This inevitably affected the provision of the regime, including dealing with applications and complaints, prisoner monies, answering queries, and basic locking and unlocking.

The was some relaxation of the restrictions during the summer of 2020; visits restarted and time out of cell was increased to two hours a day. However, the severe restrictions were re-imposed in December 2020. They continued until May 2021, when visits resumed again and there was limited use of the gym. The prison continued to provide limited in-cell education, a wider allocation of televisions, DVD and games loans, and activity packs.

Two other themes were notable during the year: the levels of violence and the new ways of sending banned items into the prison.

Throughout the year, there were very high levels of violence, of all types, reported: assaults by prisoners on staff, assaults by prisoners on prisoners, and prisoners' self-harm. Woodhill had the highest level among comparator establishments, although there were some indications that the prison was more assiduous in reporting incidents than other prisons. The prison took several strong initiatives to tackle the problems during the second half of the year.

In response to the visiting and movement restrictions caused by Covid-19, Woodhill experienced a huge increase in the number of 'throw-overs'. There were no visitors, and prisoners could not mix outside their Covid-19 'bubble' of 20. Packages started to be propelled into an exercise yard, and were retrieved by prisoners into their cells via someone in the yard or by using a retrieval line. Many of the packages were retrieved before they got to prisoners and were found to contain mobile phones, SIM cards and drugs.

The prison responded by installing restrictors on windows, so that the packages could not be retrieved by prisoners. There was also close liaison with the local police for increased monitoring outside the perimeter, and assistance from local residents identifying suspicious people. The number of throw-overs had declined markedly, to almost nil, by spring 2021. The lack of available drugs seemed to provoke increases in self-harming and brewing 'hooch' to distract prisoners from the harsh realities of incarceration, particularly with the Covid-19 restrictions.

Finally, a note about the speed of the prison's information technology (IT) systems. While the software and programmes used in the prison are generally very good, the poor speed of the connections and processing makes them almost unusable for prison staff and the Board. Untold hours are wasted as staff sit and wait for a response to a key press, or a system process to respond. Staff productivity would be increased considerably if the speed of the IT systems matched those generally used in other organisations.

The preparation of this report has been more difficult than in pre-Covid years. The assessments made are based on observation throughout the reporting year and information obtained from the prison where it was available. However, during the Covid-19 emergency it has not always been possible to triangulate the evidence to substantiate our observations as well as we would have hoped. Thanks are due to prison staff for providing us with information despite the difficulties they faced.

## Main judgements
### How safe is the prison?
The Board judges that the prison is reasonably safe, despite:
a) the high levels of all types of violence
b) the high proportion of inexperienced staff, which results in delicate situations being mishandled, inadequate knowledge of rules and processes, and safety being compromised. There is also a small proportion of staff who appear not to care sufficiently about prisoners' welfare.

### How fairly and humanely are prisoners treated?
The Board judges that prisoners are mainly treated humanely, despite:
a) too many prisoners being held in segregation for long periods. Despite the best efforts of prison staff, prisoners are held for months waiting for referral to the CSC system, transfer to a special unit or for a progression plan to be formulated, or simply held because they cannot or will not go back to normal location and there seem to be no other options
b) continuing problems with moving prisoners'

property, principally by prisons transferring property to Woodhill. Property is frequently lost or delayed in transit
c) prisoners arriving at Woodhill who are concealing contraband, indicating that they were not properly search before leaving their former prison
d) servery facilities being poorly maintained, hygiene procedures being followed sporadically and inadequate record-keeping
e) the impact of the Covid regime restrictions on prisoners' wellbeing, essential though they may have been to protect their physical health.

### How well are prisoners' health and wellbeing needs met?
The Board judges that the healthcare services operated well, despite:
a) the severe difficulties caused by the Covid-19 restrictions
b) staffing and other resource constraints
c) the disruption caused by relocating prisoners temporarily to other premises during building works.

### How well are prisoners progressed towards successful resettlement?
The Board judges that progression has been inadequate because:
a) Covid-19 restrictions meant that there were delays in progressing parole board hearings
b) Covid-19 restrictions meant that education and library provision was curtailed c) for most of the year, there were no social visits, although video-conferencing facilities ameliorated the situation somewhat
d) there are too few offending behaviour programmes to progress prisoners towards parole release
e) there are too few workshops, education and library facilities to advance prisoners' work and qualifications.

## Main areas for development
### TO THE MINISTER
a) Again, we ask the minister to work with ministerial colleagues in the Department of Health to ensure that delays in transferring prisoners to secure mental health facilities are reduced.
b) To review the per-day funding allocation for food and to ensure that prisoners are able to access, for example, five portions of fruit and vegetables a day, in line with current Department of Health and Social Care guidance

### TO THE PRISON SERVICE
a) To increase the number of specialist units to cater for prisoners now kept in long-term segregation
b) To review and reform the property system, to

reduce delays in transportation, inconsistencies in entitlements and reduce losses

c) To ensure that prisoners are properly searched and transferred from one prison to another without contraband

d) To ensure sufficient funding for works and maintenance

e) To increase efforts to recruit and retain uniformed staff

f) To improve the speed of prison IT systems.

**TO THE GOVERNOR**

a) To continue to work with the Service to reduce the number and length of stay of prisoners placed in segregation

b) To ensure that appropriate offending behaviour programmes are reinstituted as early as possible to support the progression of prisoners

c) To expand work and education opportunities to a level where all those seeking work can be supported and ensure that education opportunities at a range of entry levels are available to all

d) To increase efforts to improve servery hygiene and maintain the food logs on each wing.

PO BOX 757
DU CANE ROAD
LONDON
W12 0AE

HM PRISON
WORMWOOD
SCRUBS    Tel: 020 8588 3200

*For the latest reports on this prison please visit:*
https://tinyurl.com/bdfh26rv

*Important Changes:* **(1) Visits:** the identification necessary to access this prison and visit for social or professional purposes has changed; (2) **Money and Gifts** new rules now apply to these. See page 16 for full details of the above.

**Task of the establishment** HMP Wormwood Scrubs is a reception and resettlement prison (category B, local) holding adult men and some young adults.

**Certified normal accommodation and operational capacity**
Prisoners held at the time of inspection: 1,079
Baseline certified normal capacity: 1,172
In-use certified normal capacity: 1,175
Operational capacity: 1,273

**Prison status and key providers**
Public
Prison Group: London

Prison Group Director: Ian Bickers
Governor/Director: Amy Frost
IMB Chair: Tanya Ossack
Physical health provider: Practice Plus Group Health and Rehabilitation Services Limited
Mental health provider: Barnet, Enfield & Haringey Mental Health Trust
Substance use treatment provider: Forward Trust
Prison education framework provider: Novus; In-House Records; Active IQ
Escort contractor: Serco

**Brief history** Wormwood Scrubs was built by prisoners from Millbank Gaol between 1875 and 1891. In 1902, the last female prisoner was transferred to HMP Holloway. In 1922, one wing became a borstal. During World War II, the prison was used by the War Department. In 1994, a new hospital wing was completed, and in 1996 a fifth wing was completed.

**Short description of residential units**
• A wing (landings 1 and 2): Workers, remand and sentenced prisoners. It holds a maximum of 207 prisoners.
• A wing (landing 3): Protective isolation unit. It holds a maximum of 80 prisoners.
• B wing: Induction, reverse cohort unit (RCU; see Glossary of terms). It holds 167 prisoners.
• Jan Wilcox unit: Induction workers. It holds 17 prisoners, in double rooms and a dormitory. This is an annexe of B wing.
• C wing (landings 1 and 2): Workers, remand and sentenced prisoners. It holds a maximum of 138 prisoners.
• C wing (landings 3 and 4): Second-stage integrated drug treatment system. It holds a maximum of 165 prisoners.
• D wing (landings 1, 2 and 3): Workers, remand and sentenced prisoners. It holds a maximum of 180 prisoners.
• D wing (landing 4): Incentivised substance-free living unit. It holds a maximum of 64 prisoners, all in single rooms.
• E wing (landings 2 and 3): Workers, remand and sentenced prisoners. It holds a maximum of 91 prisoners.
• E wing (landing 4): Elizabeth Fry unit (EFU) and off-wing workers. It holds a maximum of 55 prisoners. The EFU supports those with learning difficulties and those engaging with in-reach.
• Health care unit: Holds a maximum of 17 inpatients.
• Conibeere unit: Detoxification/stabilisation unit and RCU. It holds a maximum of 55 prisoners.
• First night centre: Holds a maximum of 36 prisoners.
• Segregation unit: 18 single cells.

## Visiting Information

Book online at: www.gov.uk/prison-visits or ring 0300 060 6511 Mon to Fri, 9am to 6pm
**Visiting times:** Mon, Wed, Thurs: 9am to 11am and 2pm to 4pm, Tues, Fri: 9am to 11am.

**Legal visits:** Email: hmppsvisitbooking@noms.gsi.gov.uk or ring 0300 060 6511 Monday to Friday, 9am to 6pm.
**Visiting times:** Everyday: 9am - 11am & 2pm - 4pm

## INSPECTIONS & REPORTS

**Date of last full inspection 7–17 June 2021**
**HMCIP Report, published 09 September 2021**

Wormwood Scrubs is a famous, category B, men's local prison in west London that held just over 1,000 prisoners at the time of our inspection, of whom a third were foreign nationals, more than half were black, Asian or minority ethnic and two-thirds were unsentenced. It has had a troubled recent history culminating in our 2017 inspection, when we described the 'intractability and persistence of failure at this prison'. When inspectors returned in 2019, they found a much-improved situation and I am pleased to say that this report shows that progress in many areas has been maintained. The prison feels calm and well-ordered and inspectors who knew the prison well noted a better atmosphere than in the past.

The prison was safer than at our last inspection. Assaults on staff and the use of force had continued to fall, while the rate of prisoner-on-prisoner assaults was one of the lowest of all local prisons. Data, though routinely collected, was not being used to analyse patterns of violence and create plans to achieve further progress in a prison that often saw gang and crime-related issues imported from the community. Reductions in violence were at least partly due to the fact that most prisoners had been locked in their cells for 23 hours a day and were at the expense of access to work, education and time to socialise. This was compounded for the 118 prisoners who had to share cramped, often ill-ventilated cells that were designed for one person, though the welcome introduction of in-cell telephones had at least allowed them to stay in regular touch with family and friends. Leaders at Wormwood Scrubs had not shown the ambition that we have seen elsewhere in increasing the amount of time prisoners were spending out of their cells.

With the support of the prison service, leaders have put much effort into improving the infrastructure of the prison with ongoing improvements to windows, serveries, the visits hall and showers. Officers were rightly proud of the cleanliness of their wings which, considering the churn in prison population, was mostly good.

It has always been difficult to recruit and retain staff members at this jail and at the time of inspection there was a large proportion of recently recruited officers who had not yet experienced anything like a normal regime. Staff training had fallen behind during the pandemic and hard work is needed to make sure that officers are fully prepared when the regime begins to open up.

The education provider had been too slow in reopening services and had done little to communicate with prisoners about the availability or range of courses. A lack of planning for a return to face-to-face education meant that classrooms were empty while prisoners were languishing behind their doors. Tutors had not made enough use of assessments to create in-cell education packs, meaning these were often of low quality and little use.

Leaders had been working to improve the quality and range of key work in the prison and, though more vulnerable prisoners were being seen regularly, there was much more to be done to make sure that every prisoner had meaningful access. The Listener scheme (prisoners trained by the Samaritans to provide confidential emotional support to fellow prisoners) was particularly impressive and, where in some prisons this vital service had withered during the pandemic, at Wormwood Scrubs it had continued to thrive. Self-harm had reduced substantially and was already on a downward trend before the pandemic. Overall, the prison was a much safer, cleaner and better organised prison than it had been in the past, but prisoners were locked in their cells for too long. The most important challenge facing leaders is to maintain and improve on the levels of safety, while significantly increasing the amount of time prisoners are spending out of their cells in education, training, work, leisure and rehabilitation activity.

Charlie Taylor, HM Chief Inspector of Prisons
June 2021

### Safety

At the last inspection of Wormwood Scrubs in 2019, we found that outcomes for prisoners were not sufficiently good against this healthy prison test.

At this inspection, we found that outcomes for prisoners were now reasonably good against this healthy prison test.

Initial risk screenings of prisoners by reception staff were brief and were not followed up with first night interviews, but health care reception assessments had improved. First night centre staff were approachable, and the induction was helpful. There was a sense of order and calm in the prison. Levels of violence had reduced substantially. The safety strategy was comprehensive, but violent incidents were not always investigated thoroughly and there was limited use of case management procedures to address antisocial behaviour or to support victims. Use of force had also reduced sharply, but a considerable amount of paperwork was outstanding and we saw little evidence of de-escalation. Batons had been drawn on seven occasions in the previous year, but paperwork indicated that this had been proportionate in each case.

The use of segregation had reduced and prisoners generally reported that they had been treated well by unit staff. Prisoners were usually reintegrated into the main population quickly and care planning for prisoners segregated for longer periods was good. The segregation unit was clean and prisoners had in-cell telephones. However, toilets had no seats or lids, and most cells had been fitted with fixed metal furniture.

Physical security arrangements were generally proportionate and aligned to risks, but some elements of procedural security were disproportionate, such as excessive handcuffing of prisoners on hospital escorts and routine strip-searching in reception and segregation.

A general theme across the management of violence, use of force, segregation and security was that good collection of data was not consistently followed by tangible action to help to improve outcomes further.

Levels of self-harm had reduced substantially and were lower than at comparable prisons. The implementation of assessment, care in custody and teamwork (ACCT) case management processes for prisoners at risk of suicide or self-harm was inconsistent, but these individuals reported positively on the care given to them. There had been three self-inflicted deaths since the previous inspection and not all Prisons and Probation Ombudsman (PPO) recommendations had been implemented effectively. In particular, each PPO investigation had highlighted similar failings during the early days in custody.

### Respect

At the last inspection of Wormwood Scrubs in 2019, we found that outcomes for prisoners were reasonably good against this healthy prison test. At this inspection, we found that outcomes for prisoners remained reasonably good against this healthy prison test.

In our survey, 62% of prisoners said that staff treated them with respect. About a quarter of staff had only started work as prison officers during the pandemic. Prisoners told us that many staff were unable to deal with their queries, and we saw several examples of staff failing to challenge low-level rule breaking. Key

work had been improving since March 2021 but remained inconsistent.

Communal areas and cells were generally clean and in reasonable repair, but poor cell ventilation, overcrowding and minimal time out of cell made conditions difficult. Prisoners had good access to showers and clean sheets, but there were ongoing problems with retrieving stored property. Cell call bell response times were improving and prison leaders had secured funding for an electronic monitoring system. Almost 80% of prisoners in our survey said that the food was bad. Meals were served too early and were provided in foil containers at cell doors rather than at serveries.

There was reasonably effective communication with prisoners, including through weekly newsletters and use of WayOut TV, and some consultation had taken place during the pandemic. Prisoners had little confidence in the complaints system, although oversight and analysis had improved. A recently appointed bail information officer provided good support to prisoners.

Strategic oversight of equality and diversity had deteriorated during the pandemic. There was insufficient response to adverse equality monitoring data, and under-identification of prisoners with disabilities. However, in our survey, prisoners in protected groups reported broadly similarly to other prisoners, and good work had been done to encourage understanding of diversity through, for example, some excellent and informative prisoner-led discussions on WayOut TV.

The well-led, energetic chaplaincy had done good work to help mitigate the impact of Covid-19 restrictions on prisoners by visiting them every week, from the outset of the pandemic. Pastoral support was good and the team continued to provide bereavement counselling.

Health services were well led by a strong management team. Decisive and effective action had been taken to manage Covid-19 outbreaks and there had been no positive prisoner cases for four months. Most clinics had restarted and had reasonable waiting times. The management of long-term conditions had improved, but support for some patient groups was insufficient and care plans were not sufficiently personalised. The inpatient unit provided a good standard of care. Prisoners with social care needs were supported in the prison, but the local authority had not responded to prison referrals for over a year. An impressive range of mental health services was provided, but high referral rates had led to long waits for routine appointments. A large number of prisoners had severe mental health problems requiring transfer to external hospitals and most had waited too long to access a bed. Prisoners

## Purposeful activity

At the last inspection of Wormwood Scrubs in 2019, we found that outcomes for prisoners were not sufficiently good against this healthy prison test. At this inspection, we found that outcomes for prisoners remained not sufficiently good against this healthy prison test.

About 300 prisoners were in some form of activity, most of it full time, but those who were not working received only one hour out of cell each day for outdoor exercise, association and showers. Prisoners could still not visit the library and there was too little use or promotion of the book delivery service. Few prisoners were yet able to use the recently reopened gym.

Ofsted carried out a progress monitoring visit of the prison alongside our full inspection, and the purposeful activity judgement incorporates their assessment of progress.

In-cell education learning packs were of variable standard and leaders had not planned early enough for the return to face-to-face teaching. A newly opened restaurant allowed a small number of prisoners to gain skills and a qualification in hospitality and catering, but there were limited opportunities overall for prisoners to complete accredited courses.

The quantity and quality of information, advice and guidance given to prisoners on the wings were insufficient. Many prisoners did not know what courses were available to them and how to access them.

Tutors did not use the results of initial assessments well enough to inform individual learning support plans. The feedback given to prisoners on their learning packs was often unhelpful and did not support them to improve their work.

## Rehabilitation and release planning

At the last inspection of Wormwood Scrubs in 2019, we found that outcomes for prisoners were not sufficiently good against this healthy prison test. At this inspection, we found that outcomes for prisoners remained not sufficiently good against this healthy prison test.

The visits hall had been refurbished and provided excellent facilities. Social visits had resumed recently and were handled sensitively by visits staff. Although the take-up of 'Purple Visits' was fairly high, too many were cancelled as a result of staff shortages. The services of the Prison Advice and Care Trust (PACT) had been reduced, but the PACT family engagement worker continued to carry a substantial active caseload. There was a thorough reducing reoffending needs analysis, but progress had been limited because

of staff shortages and the uncertainties caused by the imminent reorganisation of resettlement services delivered by the community rehabilitation company (CRC). There were not enough middle managers, and several offender management unit (OMU) staff told us that they felt insufficiently supported in their work. There was good partnership working, and work across the resettlement pathways was well coordinated. Although the backlog of offender assessment system (OASys) assessments had been reduced to reasonably low levels, only 10% of respondents to our survey were aware of a current custody plan. There was inconsistent and often very limited contact between prisoners and their prison offender manager. Most prisoners we spoke to said that it was difficult to contact the OMU. Despite reduced staffing, the public protection team was experienced and committed, and completed necessary work on time. The number of prisoners on telephone monitoring was kept realistic through a tight focus on risk. There was good communication between the prison and the community in relation to the highest-risk offenders.

There had been delays in categorisation procedures, but the backlog was improving. Progression was usually good, but those given category D status often had to wait several months for a transfer to open conditions, despite places being available. There was limited focus on the needs of indeterminate-sentenced prisoners, but monthly forums had recently restarted.

The recent needs analysis drew attention to the need to address offending behaviour for the substantial number of younger adults, many of whom may not have had the opportunity or sufficient time remaining in their sentence to be transferred to a category C training establishment. No offending behaviour programmes were available, but some useful short resettlement courses had continued to be delivered throughout the Covid-19 period by the CRC team.

There was a high level of housing need and, although few prisoners had been released homeless in the previous year, an average of only 61% had been released to permanent or settled accommodation. It was a concern that an imminent new housing contract did not include provision for the large remand population.

## Key concerns and recommendations

Key concerns and recommendations identify the issues of most importance to improving outcomes for prisoners and are designed to help establishments prioritise and address the most significant weaknesses in the treatment and conditions of prisoners.

During this inspection we identified some areas of key concern and have made a small number of recommendations for the prison to address those concerns.

Key concern: While initial assessments by health care staff had improved, the brief risk screening from reception staff was not followed up with an in-depth interview in the first night centre or reverse cohort unit to identify and address immediate needs and concerns. This was concerning, given that the PPO had been critical of the early days risk assessments preceding three self-inflicted deaths.

Recommendation: All new arrivals should have an in-depth first night interview that covers all risk factors, including self-harming behaviour. (To the governor)

Key concern: Too much use of force paperwork was outstanding and both paperwork and available video footage suggested little evidence of de-escalation. Body-worn cameras were not routinely turned on during incidents, and recordings of unplanned incidents were not retained.

Recommendation: Prison leaders should ensure rigorous oversight and accountability in relation to the use of force, including through routine use of body-worn cameras and thorough completion of paperwork. (To the governor)

Key concern: Many staff were inexperienced, had not worked in the prison outside of Covid-19 restrictions and were not confident in handling challenging behaviour. There was a large backlog in training.

Recommendation: Prison leaders should ensure that staff understand the needs of the prisoners they are supporting, and have the knowledge, skills and support to do this effectively. (To the governor)

Key concern: Too many cells designed for one were still being shared by two prisoners. This longstanding problem had persisted despite prison leaders' efforts to obtain approval from HMPPS to convert them to single accommodation.

Recommendation: Two prisoners should not be held in cells designed for one person. (To the governor and HMPPS)

Key concern: There was poor identification of prisoners in protected groups, particularly those with disabilities. Insufficient consideration of monitoring data, together with the suspension of consultation, did not provide assurance that need was properly understood. Even when identified, some evidence of consistent disproportionate treatment was not acted on adequately. For example, there had been no action in response to monitoring data showing disproportionate use of force on, and segregation of, black prisoners.

Recommendation: Prisoners in protected groups should be identified systematically and consulted regularly. Monitoring data which shows disproportionate findings should be investigated and result in suitable actions where necessary. (To the governor)

Key concern: Most prisoners were locked in their cells for 23 hours a day, which had a serious impact on their wellbeing. Leaders were taking a cautious approach to improving the inadequate regime, partly because of staff inexperience, but time out of cell could have been improved with current staff numbers and experience, even in the context of the pandemic. There was a lack of clear planning for regime recovery.

Recommendation: Prison leaders should set out a roadmap for substantially increasing prisoners' time out of cell and participation in activity, with clear milestones that are understood by prisoners and staff. (To the governor)

Key concern: In our survey, only 10% of prisoners said that they had a custody plan, and although there was some good offender management work, it was not consistent and there was not enough contact with prisoners. Some key management posts in the OMU had been vacant for some time and there was a lack of positive day-to-day leadership. Several OMU staff told us that they felt insufficiently supported in their work.

Recommendation: Day-to-day leadership in the offender management unit should be strengthened and leaders should ensure that the provision of offender management services is comprehensive and consistent. (To the governor)

**Notable positive practice**

We define notable positive practice as innovative work or practice that leads to particularly good outcomes from which other establishments may be able to learn. Inspectors look for evidence of good outcomes for prisoners; original, creative or particularly effective approaches to problem-solving or achieving the desired goal; and how other establishments could learn from or replicate the practice.

Inspectors found seven examples of notable positive practice during this inspection.

The bail information officer identified and supported prisoners who were eligible to apply for bail, providing a useful and proactive service to the large number of remand prisoners at the establishment.

The prison made particularly good use of WayOut TV to keep prisoners informed and stimulate debate through a range of thoughtful filmed presentations involving staff and prisoners alike. Content included equality and diversity-related discussions, and celebration of religious festivals and events such as Black History Month.

The chaplaincy had worked energetically to mitigate the impact of Covid-19 restrictions by conducting weekly welfare visits to all prisoners. The team of occupational therapists in the Seacole day centre provided particularly good practical and emotional support to individuals with neurodiverse needs.

A pharmacist was now placed on the first night centre, to review medicines at an early stage. This had led to earlier identification of prisoners with complex needs and addressing of any discrepancies with medication.

Prison leaders had taken a leading part in a pilot project in London prisons, to provide confirmation of identity to prisoners who did not have this, in order to access accommodation and benefits.

## INDEPENDENT MONITORING BOARD:
### Annual Report

The law requires every prison to be monitored by an independent Board appointed by the Justice Secretary; these are known as Independent Monitoring Boards (IMBs). The IMB must satisfy itself as to the humane and just treatment of those held in custody within its prison and the range and adequacy of the programmes preparing them for release; it must report annually to the Justice Secretary on how well the prison has met the standards and requirements placed on it.

### IMB Report 1 June 2020 – 31 May 2021
### Published December 2021
### Executive summary
### Background to the report

This report is, in reality, a review of a Covid-19 year at HMP Wormwood Scrubs. For the Board it has meant almost no physical contact with the prison, and for the prisoners it has meant precious little contact with the outside world – at a time when the outside world was having precious little contact with each other. For much of the reporting year it has meant a 23-hour confinement for many prisoners.

From March 2020 (before this reporting year) to August 2020, the Board stopped all visits to the prison and instituted a system of remote monitoring. With the exception of a short period from September to mid-December, when three members intermittently visited parts of the prison with great effect, that remained the case until mid-May 2021.

Remote monitoring had the advantage of maintaining contact with the prison but did not permit Board members to verify or challenge much of what they were being told. Necessarily some of what is in this year's report is information gleaned solely from the prison. This is not to say it is not accurate or reliable, but to highlight the source from which it comes.

During remote monitoring, Board members continued to receive and deal with applications from prisoners, which often assisted the Board in getting a fuller picture of the regime within the prison. Members were also able to attend meetings remotely. The Board received daily updates from the prison and also received notices to prisoners/staff and weekly prisoner newsletters.

At the end of June 2020 a new governing governor took up his post. He has attended monthly Board meetings via Zoom, and has appointed a business and communications manager – one of whose responsibilities is to directly liaise with the Board at least weekly.

### Main judgements
### How safe is the prison?

The Board reported last year a number of initiatives aimed at making the prison a safer environment: a scanner at reception, a full-time police officer within the prison, weekly meetings to review CCTV, and improvements to the assessment, care in custody and teamwork (ACCT) documentation. The introduction of those initiatives has brought positive results. There has been an overall reduction in recorded violence, following the fall in the second half of our last reporting year.

Significantly, the prison benefited during the last year from a number of safety interventions through charities: Catch22 (gang-related violence), Belong (mediation) and Safety Box (anti-knife crime). It is very disappointing to note that, because of funding cuts, only the full-time police officer and Belong remain on site.

The targeted use of the whole-body scanner based at reception assists greatly in the recovery of contraband, but reduced staff availability (often Covid-19 related) has meant that it is not always in full use.

The inadequate use of body worn video cameras (BWVCs) continues to be a concern. The prison has made them easier to access by placing them next to where officers draw their keys, but large numbers remain unclaimed each day.

The efficacy of the prison complaints system has been subject to criticism by the Board over the course of the year. The speed and completeness of responses has been seriously inept at times. A new management structure and review processes may alleviate this.

There has been a marked decrease in use of force (UoF) incidents. This may be pandemic related, but there has also been an emphasis in the prison on having a weekly review of such incidents as well as monthly UoF meetings. However, the statistics for some months show a disproportionate number of black prisoners represented in such incidents.

Following a prisoner's death in custody shortly after the prisoner's arrival, the Board remains of the view that the initial admission processes require reform. There is a review of processes in train, but this is not a new issue, and Her Majesty's Inspectorate of Prisons (HMIP) among others has highlighted it.

**How fairly and humanely are prisoners treated?**
Some renovation work continued during the pandemic, with new windows installed, redecoration on A and C wings, and refurbishment of the visits and reception areas, and of several shower blocks and serveries. However, many of the prison's facilities remain in poor condition, and it remains a source of shame that at the end of May 2021,118 prisoners were sharing cells designed for one person only. The antiquated nature of the infrastructure meant that at a point in November 2020 there was either no heating on a wing, or it was heated to an unhealthily high temperature.

Access to showers during the pandemic has occasionally been restricted. Most prisoners got a daily shower, but in October 2020 prisoners on A wing who had tested positive did not get any time out of cell or showers at all until their isolation was complete.

One of the most frequent and persistent sources of complaints received by the Board has been the quality and quantity of the food provided for prisoners. There are persistent issues relating to the equipment in the kitchens not working or not being repaired, the provision of specialist diets, the timing of meals and food hygiene.

The key worker scheme has been unable to function as originally intended and is another casualty of the pandemic. However, the prison was able to keep a skeleton scheme going by contacting prisoners through in-cell telephony. This ensured that the most vulnerable prisoners received a weekly call.

The welcome appointment of an equalities officer has provided an impetus for the development of a range of activities, from a coaching programme for black, Asian and minority ethnic staff to events around Black History Month in October 2020. Prisoner equality representatives are present on each wing, but the number of discrimination incident reporting forms (DIRFs) is low. This may be because prisoners continue to use the normal complaints procedure, but it is another area the Board will monitor closely going forward.

The vexed issue of property remains a concern. The problem of property going missing on transfer has been reduced this year as there were far fewer transfers. But a communication failure meant that one prisoner waited eight months for his property to be moved from the property store to his cell.

**How well are prisoners' health and wellbeing needs met?**
The pandemic has put a strain on many medical providers and the prison has been no different. A comprehensive plan for testing/isolating and later vaccinating was put in place very early on, and this rigorous policy led to no positive tests for Covid-19 from February 2021 to the end of the reporting year. Take up of the vaccine is lower than healthcare had hoped, but not significantly out of line with comparison groups in the community.

The mental health of prisoners however has suffered greatly, and this manifested itself in a significantly increased number of mental health referrals. Prolonged cellular confinement, necessary to control the spread of Covid-19, must be responsible in part for this increase. The Board also notes with dismay that during the pandemic the prison reported an increased number of prisoners with acute mental health problems being brought into prison, perhaps reflecting the lack of alternative provision in the community.

The consequence of this increase in mental ill-health is that although all emergency and urgent referrals have been seen within the recommended time frames (24 hours and 48 hours, respectively), routine referrals are not seen within the target of five days. Some prisoners have been made to wait as long as four weeks.

Last year the Board raised concerns about the number of cancelled external hospital appointments. This year has seen a mixed picture of cancellations due to a lack of staff to escort prisoners, but also an increase in prisoners refusing to attend. The reason for this refusal is often not noted in the documentation.

During the pandemic a community psychiatric nurse (CPN) has attended segregation rounds and provided input to the ACCT reviews. However, it is of great concern to the Board that the learning disability nurse has left, and the departure of the head of psychology and her deputy has left the prison with no psychology service. This is a huge gap in provision for a very vulnerable group and has led to a very long waiting list for therapeutic interventions.

Some drug rehabilitation interventions continued through the Forward Trust via in-cell distraction packs and contact via in-cell telephones. Mandatory drug testing was suspended in February 2020 and had not resumed by the end of the reporting period. This is said to be lower on the list of priorities as the prison moves towards re-introducing the full regime.

**How well are prisoners progressed towards successful resettlement?**
The pandemic brought about the almost complete shut-down of work, with the exception of essential

activities such as laundry and the kitchen. It also meant pausing most accredited learning – the provider (Novus) withdrew from the prison – and instead a number of in-cell learning packs were provided to prisoners who wanted to continue their education. By the end of the reporting period there was still no face-to-face teaching.

Ofsted undertook a 'virtual' inspection in March, noting that there was insufficient engagement with in-cell education, and that increased pay rates and incentive schemes had been drawn up to encourage more prisoners to access education. More encouraging was the opening of a new staff canteen named 'The Escape'. In April, a dismal room was turned into a welcoming and much improved café in which 12 prisoners undertake a 12-week catering/hospitality training course, which will equip them for employment on release. The closure of all social visits because of Covid-19 restrictions meant a huge reduction in valuable family contact for prisoners. Their gradual re-introduction along with 'Purple Visits' – video calls – has meant that prisoners have been able to see their families, albeit in a restricted way. In-cell telephony and additional phone credit have also helped to maintain family/friendship links.

## Main areas for development
### TO THE MINISTER

In our last report we urged the continuing funding of projects which have contributed to making the prison safer. What we have seen is the opposite – a reduction in funding – and we ask that the minister urgently reconsider budget cuts which will only put in peril any progress made.

We again urge the minister to make it mandatory for officers to wear and use their BWVC when they are in situations where they may have to use force against prisoners. Can the minister also tell the Board what has happened to the review of PSI 04/2017, promised in the last response by the minister to the Board in February 2021?

### TO THE PRISON SERVICE

1. When will the final (as opposed to draft) policy framework on prisoners' property, promised in February 2021 for 'wider circulation shortly' in the HMPPS response to our last report, be published?
2. In the absence of this, can there be a directive to all prisons that they should, in so far as they are able, ensure that a prisoner's property follows him when he is transferred to another prison?

### TO THE GOVERNOR

Can the Governor ensure that investigations will be undertaken to consider and monitor the disproportionate incidents in some months of use of force against black prisoners? Following such investigations can any necessary training be provided for prison officers?

Given that there is acknowledgement within the prison that the food, its production and nutritional value and its quantity are an issue, can the Governor consider with some urgency how this can be remedied? If there is to be consultation, the Board suggests that this should be done speedily.

When a prisoner refuses to attend a hospital appointment, can the reason for that refusal be noted on the relevant documentation?

### Progress since the last report

The Governor has arranged for BWVCs to be moved to a convenient place for prison officers to collect them. This should be encouraging news. However, so far it seems to have made little difference to either the number collected each day or used.

ULNES WALTON LANE
LEYLAND
PRESTON
PR26 8LW

**HM PRISON WYMOTT**    Tel: 01772 442000

*For the latest reports on this prison please visit:*
https://tinyurl.com/bdfh26rv

*Important Changes:* **(1) Visits:** the identification necessary to access this prison and visit for social or professional purposes has changed; (2) **Money and Gifts** new rules now apply to these. See page 16 for full details of the above.

**Task of the establishment** HMP Wymott is a complex category C training prison, with half of the population convicted of sexual offences and others being convicted of a wide range of offences, including violence.

### Certified normal accommodation and operational capacity

Prisoners held August 2020: 985
Baseline certified normal capacity: 1,077
In-use certified normal capacity: 1,077
Operational capacity: 1,035
(temporary reduction)

### Prison status and key providers

Public
Prison Group: Cumbria & Lancashire
Prison Group Director: John Illingsworth
Governor/Director: Graham Beck

IMB Chair: Diana Kelshaw
Physical health provider: Greater Manchester Mental Health NHS Trust
Mental health provider: Greater Manchester Mental Health NHS Trust
Substance use treatment provider:
Delphi Medical
Prison education framework provider: Novus

### Brief history

HMP Wymott is an adult male category C training prison. The population comprises approximately 40% mainstream category C prisoners and 60% prisoners convicted of a sexual offence (PCOSO). The majority of the prisoners are serving sentences of four or more years. Prior to the Covid-19 outbreak, the prison had an operating capacity of 1,174 prisoners but this was reduced to 1,020 in May 2020, to enable all prisoners to be accommodated in single cells. It has recently been increased to 1,035.

In its usual form, the accommodation comprises a number of specialist wings, including a care and reablement wing (supported by an older prisoners' activities centre (CAMEO), delivered by the Salvation Army), a drug therapeutic community wing, two psychologically informed planned environment (PIPE) units (for prisoners with personality disorders), an integrated drug treatment programme (managing prisoners on a controlled methadone programme), four wings for PCOSO and three other wings. Since March 2020, the prison has worked with Public Health England (PHE) to reconfigure the population and function of the wings, to provide a protective environment for all of the prisoners, particularly those who are exceptionally vulnerable. Wings were repurposed for shielding these prisoners, the reverse cohorting of those coming into the prison, the isolation of positive cases or essential workers' wings.

Healthcare services are provided by Greater Manchester Mental Health Trust (GMMHT). This includes primary care, dentistry, mental health care and a range of other services. The prison now has an in-house pharmacy. Delphi Medical provides the drug and alcohol recovery service.

Education is provided by Novus, and a full education programme is normally on offer, from pre-entry level up to degree level, with a particular focus on developing literacy and numeracy skills. Group classes have been suspended since March 2020 because of the pandemic, but in-cell materials have been provided for some prisoners to continue their studies.

The prison workshops can offer a range of employments, many of which lead to nationally accredited qualifications. Some of these workshops are operated on a commercial basis, providing quality services to external clients and effectively constitute a 'working prison'. Most of the workshops have been closed to prisoners throughout the reporting period, but during this time the prison has been exploring new opportunities for the prisoners through developing links with local employers.

A range of offending behaviour programmes, to help prisoners address their offending behaviour, is provided by the North-West Regional Psychology Services and the local programmes team. These too have been suspended, but a restricted service is now beginning to be offered.

As Wymott is not a designated resettlement prison, the resources for preparing prisoners for release are limited. Through-the-gate services are provided by Achieve North-West and the community resettlement company (Sodexo), which work with individuals being released outside the probation service. The prison has also developed its own pre-release support programme.

An active chaplaincy supports a range of faiths, and the full-time chaplains are assisted by sessional ministers and volunteers. Pastoral support and family liaison are provided through the chaplaincy. While collective worship has not been possible during the pandemic, the chaplaincy staff have worked tirelessly to visit individual prisoners and to provide weekly faith packs.

The PE department consists of a large sports hall, a well-equipped gym, and a full-size outdoor sports field. During the pandemic, part of the outside area was used to house a number of temporary accommodation units as a contingency, but they were never used and are now being removed.

General maintenance within the prison is provided by Amey, and the visitors centre is managed by Phoenix Futures.

### Short description of residential units

Shielding units:
- K wing (category C)
- I wing (men convicted of sexual offences (MCOSO)/older prisoners/social care)
- B wing (MCOSO, non-cellular accommodation)
- G wing (MCOSO, cellular accommodation)
Reverse cohort units:
- D wing (category C) (1 landing)
- H wing (PIPE unit - MCOSO, cellular accommodation)
Prisoner isolation unit:
- D wing (category C) (1 landing)
- H wing (MCOSO, cellular accommodation)
Workers units (essential workers):
- A wing (MCOSO)
- C wing (category C)

- F wing (PIPE unit)
- J wing (mixed MCOSO and category Cs)
- E wing (category C)

## Visiting Information

Book online at: www.gov.uk/prison-visits or ring 01772 442234 and 01772 442254 Monday to Friday, 9am to 3pm

**Visiting times:** Monday to Friday: 2:30pm to 3:30pm, Saturday and Sunday: 9:30am to 10:30am and 2:30pm to 3:30pm

## Legal visits: Email:

LegalVisits.Wymott@justice.gov.uk
**Visiting times:** Tues, Thurs: 9:30am to 10:30am

## INSPECTIONS & REPORTS

**Scrutiny visit: 18 and 25–26 August 2020, report published 29 September 2020**

This report discusses the findings from a scrutiny visit (SV) to HMP Wymott. The SV methodology developed from the 'short scrutiny visit' approach that HMI Prisons had used to provide independent oversight of custodial establishments since April 2020. Our previous approach monitored outcomes for prisoners in a small number of key areas at a time when regimes were severely restricted. While SVs are still far more limited in scope than our full inspections, they are increasing the intensity of scrutiny as prisons enter a phase of recovery. SVs examine the treatment and conditions of prisoners in greater detail and focus in particular on the pace of recovery and proportionality of treatment, while ensuring the safest possible inspection practices.

HMP Wymott, located in central Lancashire, is a category C training prison for adult male prisoners and a small number of young adults. Prisoners arrive at Wymott from all areas of England and Wales, and primarily go to there to undertake offending behaviour work and other activities aimed at helping them to reduce their risks, progress to open prisons or prepare for release. At the time of this visit, the prison held 985 prisoners, compared with 1,053 when we inspected in 2016. About half of the prisoners had been convicted of sexual offences and a third were aged over 50. The prevalence of mental health problems and physical disabilities among the population was high.

Wymott experienced an outbreak of Covid-19 very early into the restricted regime. At the peak of the outbreak, 34 prisoners were showing symptoms of the virus and almost half of the population needed to shield (see Glossary of terms) because they were vulnerable or extremely vulnerable to the risk that the virus presented. At that time, a quarter of staff were

absent from work owing to the need to shield, and, sadly, two members of staff died from Covid-19-related illnesses. The prediction for Wymott in those early days was that there would be widespread infection and the potential for a number of deaths among prisoners.

It was refreshing to find a prison and a senior management team showing a clear commitment to managing the crisis while maintaining their 'can do' attitude. They worked closely with Public Health England and the NHS to put in place robust measures to promote infection control. This included a reduction in the population by about 10%, to enable prisoners to have their own cell, and the establishment of several units, in which almost half of the prisoners who were at risk from the virus could be cohorted.

The measures had been effective to date. At the time of our visit, there had been no prisoner deaths from Covid-19-related illnesses, and none had tested positive for several weeks. The prison had cared for operational staff returning to work from shielding by allocating them to work on the shielding units, which was notable positive practice. Most staff and prisoners felt that the restrictions were necessary and proportionate, given the risks to the population. Prisoners we spoke to who were shielding were anxious that safeguards might be lifted too quickly, and, sensibly, the management team had adopted a cautious approach to this over the last few months. Reception and early days arrangements were reasonably good and the use of the two reverse cohort units (RCU, see Glossary of terms) was robust, with the exception that prisoners on these units could not access video calling with their family and friends, and that their time out of cell could be substantially reduced when the units were holding a number of small cohorts of prisoners.

The number of violent incidents had reduced since the restricted regime had started. However, despite many staff promoting the idea that self-harm had decreased sharply since the start of the restricted regime, we could find no evidence for this. When we took into account the reduced population, the rate of recorded self-harm incidents in the last four months was the same as for the four months before the restrictions were put in place. Care for those at risk of self-harm was reasonable but Listeners (see Glossary of terms) were unable to provide ongoing support to those in crisis, which needed addressing urgently. In our survey, 16% of prisoners said that they currently felt unsafe, and the reasons behind this needed exploring to understand fully what this means to prisoners.

The prison was committed to rehabilitation and reducing reoffending but the implementation of the restricted regime brought with it some unavoidable consequences, including the suspension of much of the risk reduction work. Prisoners felt the impact of the lack of progression opportunities and the lack of support from their offender managers. The governor was clear that this could not continue in the long term, and was committed to returning to the rehabilitative focus that the prison used to have. Social distancing (see Glossary of terms) was weak at times, and hand washing protocols were not always adhered to, but additional cleaning on the wings continued in order to fight the spread of the virus. Staff were responsive to prisoners' needs, and the quality of relationships and interactions was good. It was disappointing that key worker support had ended and that the use of well-being checks was not as robust as the management team would have liked.

Some aspects of strategic oversight had deteriorated because of the restrictions, including the attention given to equality and diversity. While our survey did not show many differences in outcomes for those with protected characteristics, we found some clear examples of unmet needs for prisoners with disabilities.

We found two areas of key concern with the health care provision. First, delays in prisoners receiving their medication and poor governance in pharmacy created unnecessary risks and caused severe distress for many. Secondly, owing to staff shortages, mental health provision was lacking. Both of these key concerns required immediate attention.

The regime was reliably delivered but, although time out of cell had increased, it still remained limited for most prisoners. However, the prison had plans to increase this further in the very near future. Over a quarter of the population continued to have employment on or off the wings but the lack of formal and purposeful education continued to be a significant gap. The library and gym remained closed five months after the restricted regime had been imposed, and little progress had been made in delivering effective interim provision.

It is to the credit of the staff and prisoners that the consequences of the impact of Covid-19 have been managed well, and at the time of writing this report the establishment had controlled the spread of the virus. It is perhaps now time to harness the obvious 'can do' attitude presented by Wymott, take further steps towards recovery and promote the rehabilitative culture that has, in the past, driven its ethos.

HM Chief Inspector of Prisons, September 2020

### Key concerns and recommendations

Key concerns and recommendations identify the issues of most importance to improving outcomes for prisoners and are designed to help establishments prioritise and address the most significant weaknesses in the treatment and conditions of prisoners.

During this visit we identified some areas of key concern, and have made a small number of key recommendations for the prison to address.

Key concern: Many staff we spoke to were convinced that there had been a substantial reduction in self-harm following the implementation of the restricted regime. This was not supported by evidence, and we were concerned that this misconception could inadvertently lead to staff responsible for caring for vulnerable individuals becoming complacent. Listeners were not active in their formal role, which was a serious gap in care.

Key recommendation: Data on self-harm should be used to monitor the trends in incidents during the restricted regime and this should be communicated widely to staff and prisoners. Listeners should be active throughout the prison to provide support to those in crisis.

Key concern: Key worker contact had been suspended since lockdown and there were no immediate plans for its resumption. This meant that there was no reliable method of engaging prisoners in planning for their own progression and ensuring that they were being offered the support they needed.

Key recommendation: Key worker sessions, with a focus on prisoner well-being and the restarting of purposeful rehabilitative work, should be resumed.

Key concern: There was limited strategic oversight of equality work, and there were weaknesses in the monitoring and analysis of equality data and other actions to understand the situation of prisoners with protected characteristics.

Key recommendation: Work on equality should include robust oversight, effective monitoring and action planning, to ensure that the needs of prisoners with protected characteristics are consistently identified and met. (To the governor)

Key concern: The lack of senior leadership, staffing vacancies, weak governance arrangements and the poor pharmacy working environment resulted in delays in delivering medications to prisoners, and created unnecessary risks.

Key recommendation: Managers should ensure that the pharmacy has systems in place to store and dispense medicines in a safe and timely manner, and that urgent attention is given to outstanding remedial work to the pharmacy clinical environment.

Key concern: Prisoners had no access to evidence-based psychological treatment, which resulted in long waiting lists and unmet need.

Key recommendation: Prisoners should have

timely access to psychological treatment, commensurate with that in the community.

Key concern: The education providers had been slow to put into place alternative methods of learner engagement and provision, and there was a risk that learners would lose interest or motivation. While the processes and procedures for sending, collecting and assessing work packs were under consideration, elsewhere we had seen these in place for some time.

Key recommendation: The engagement of learners should be prioritised, and education and learning opportunities specific to their needs should be provided. As a priority, a process whereby their work can be assessed should be introduced.

Key concern: For the majority of prisoners, sentence planning and risk reduction work had stopped, and for most there were no immediate plans to resume their challenge, support and supervision. The lack of key worker and prison offender manager contact, delivery of offender behaviour programmes, and therapeutic community and psychologically informed planned environment interventions meant that this had a serious impact on many prisoners' sentence progression.

Key recommendation: Prison offender managers and key workers should engage with prisoners to discuss the impact of the ongoing restricted regime on their individual sentence plan, and set realistic steps and timescales for progression.

Key concern: Resettlement planning had been undertaken remotely, and, for most, plans were developed without the prisoner being present, and often too late towards release to be meaningful and effective. Some of the resettlement agencies had advised their staff not to see prisoners in person, and most staff were still mostly working from home.

Key recommendation: Routine and timely contact with prisoners should be safely resumed, to ensure effective and meaningful release planning.

### Notable positive practice

We define notable positive practice as innovative practice or practice that leads to particularly good outcomes from which other establishments may be able to learn. Inspectors look for evidence of good outcomes for prisoners; original, creative or particularly effective approaches to problem-solving or achieving the desired goal; and how other establishments could learn from or replicate the practice.

Inspectors found the following examples of notable positive practice during this visit.

• Staff who had been away from work because of the need to shield were supported in returning to operational duties by being allocated to work on the shielding wings.

• The prison's motivational approach towards behaviour management was successful in reducing conflict and helping prisoners 'play to their strengths'.

• Managers had been creative in addressing gaps in family contact. Photographs of over 250 prisoners had been taken, printed off and sent to their families with the message, '...I'm fine, I'll see you soon...'.

• Phoenix Futures had continued to provide support for families throughout lockdown, using video technology to hold forums and provide up-to-date information on social visits and other relevant topics.

• The prison had taken extra steps to support some vulnerable prisoners on release, by driving them home or paying for a taxi to ensure that they arrived safely, rather than letting them rely on public transport during the pandemic.

### INDEPENDENT MONITORING BOARD: Annual Report

The law requires every prison to be monitored by an independent Board appointed by the Justice Secretary; these are known as Independent Monitoring Boards (IMBs). The IMB must satisfy itself as to the humane and just treatment of those held in custody within its prison and the range and adequacy of the programmes preparing them for release; it must report annually to the Justice Secretary on how well the prison has met the standards and requirements placed on it.

### IMB Report 01 June 2020 – 31 May 2021
### Published 8 October 2021
### Background to the report

Throughout the reporting period, the Covid-19 pandemic has continued to have a significant impact on the prison and on the Board's ability to gather information and discuss the contents of this annual report. The Board has therefore tried to cover as much ground as it can in these difficult circumstances, but inevitably there is less detail and supporting evidence than usual. Ministers are aware of these constraints. Regular information is being collected specifically on the prison's response to the pandemic, and that is being collated nationally.

Although Covid-19 restrictions are now beginning to be lifted in the outside community, the Prison Service has understandably had to be more cautious due to the increased risk of spread in a closed community. The lifting of restrictions nationally has been, and will continue to be, slower than that on the outside, in order to keep prisoners safe. A four-stage recovery programme is being followed, with progression from one stage to the next being subject to national approval. The prison is currently in stage 3.

The Wymott IMB withdrew from the prison at the start of the pandemic, but continued to monitor remotely. Board members returned to direct monitoring at the start of August 2020, and have attended the prison continuously since then. The prison also received a scrutiny visit from Her Majesty's Inspectorate of Prisons (HMIP) in August 2020.

### Main judgements
### How safe is the prison?

Overall, the Board considers that prisoners are relatively safe at Wymott. All of the staff have worked extremely hard, through very challenging times, and it is to their credit that no prisoners have died from Covid-19. Sadly, four members of staff have been lost. Levels of self-harm and violence have both gone down during the restricted regime Reported incidents of drug use also went down. Prisoners have regularly told Board members that they feel safer not mixing in large groups. However, there remain some serious concerns around drug-related deaths.

### How fairly and humanely are prisoners treated?

In general, prisoners at Wymott are treated with fairness and humanity, although lockdown has inevitably impacted upon time out of cell and family contact. The Board would wish to recognise the good work being done in the prison using the 'buddy' system, in association with Recoop. Rota reports have regularly noted positive interactions between staff and prisoners. The Board would also wish to commend the chaplaincy team for their sustained support for individual prisoners. There are still significant issues relating to poor handling of prisoners' complaints, and loss of prisoners' property.

### How well are prisoners' health and wellbeing needs met?

In general, prisoners' health and wellbeing needs are being met. Healthcare staff are to be commended for the efficient roll-out of the Covid-19 vaccination programme. However, certain long-standing problems remain, notably the distribution of medication, inadequacy of premises and waiting times for dental services.

### How well are prisoners progressed towards successful resettlement?

Opportunities for progression have been very limited during 2020/21, and this has been a source of frustration and anxiety for many prisoners. Offender management work was only being carried out remotely for much of the year and offending behaviour programmes ceased entirely for many months. Recategorisation reviews continued remotely, although transfers to open conditions were stopped for a time.

Parole hearings were suspended for several months and there is now a significant backlog. The Board is concerned that much of the through-the-gate work is still being done remotely, and often with only limited involvement of the prisoner.

### Main areas for development
### TO THE MINISTER

• Wymott still holds a significant number of prisoners serving indeterminate sentences for public protection. Are there any plans to give these prisoners some cause for optimism?

### TO THE PRISON SERVICE

• One wing in Wymott has already been lost because of failing to meet health and safety legislation. Other wings have been in a dire state for many years. Is funding to be made available to replace the lost accommodation? What plans are in place for the other two wings that the Board has highlighted for a number of years?

• Can Her Majesty's Prison and Probation Service (HMPPS) give any indication of a timescale for kitchen improvements at HMP Wymott?

• Can HMPPS provide assurance that the prisoners' property framework is having any impact on the amount of property still going missing across the estate?

• Is it anticipated that there will be an increase in the budget for prisoners' pay very soon.

### TO THE GOVERNOR

• The Board seeks reassurance that prisoners' complaints will be dealt with in a timely and effective manner.

• How does the prison intend to ensure that the actions identified in the action plan following Prisons and Probation Ombudsman (PPO) reports into deaths in the prison are implemented effectively?

• The Board would like to see the prison ensure that prisoners due for release are informed in a more timely manner about the arrangements in place for them.

### Progress since the last report

• Work on the main boiler house and hot water supply to the wings is now complete. As a result, there are far fewer complaints from the prisoners about issues with the heating and hot water.

• The Board is pleased to note the reduction in reported acts of violence and self-harm, and would hope to see that continue as the prison moves through the Covid-19 recovery stages.

• The pandemic has clearly hindered progress in a number of areas. The Board feels that it would be unfair to expect to have seen significant improvement during such a challenging period.

# Section 2

## Advice

2.1 Early Days in Custody
2.2 Offending Behaviour Programmes
2.3 Criminal Cases Review Commission
2.4 Requests and Complaints
2.5 Prisoner Communications
2.6 Drugs and Alcohol in Prison Institutions
2.7 The Prison Disciplinary System
2.8 Who Can Help?
2.9 Healthcare
2.10 Religion
2.11 Equality *Age, Gender, Disability & Race*
2.12 Social Security and Discharge Grants
2.13 Release and Recall
2.14 Indeterminate Sentences
2.15 Women Prisoners
2.16 Young Offenders (18-21 year olds)
2.17 Young People (15-17 year olds)
2.18 Foreign Nationals
2.19 Disability in Prison
2.20 Employment, Training & Skills
2.21 Work and Pay
2.22 Incentives and Earned Privileges
2.23 Civil Partnerships & Equal Marriage
2.24 Elderly Prisoners
2.25 Segregation
2.26 Security Categorisation

## 2.1 EARLY DAYS IN CUSTODY

**Introduction: *It's not the end of the world.***
For anyone facing the prospect of their first prison sentence, it seems like the end of the world - but the Editor of book you now hold in your hands (or are viewing on *prisonoracle.com*) - The Prisons Handbook - once spent 14 years in prison and, like thousands of others, came out the other side of it safely and made a success of life after prison too; and so can you.

For those facing their first prison sentence, from what to pack in your 'Bang Up Bag' to take with you on that first journey through the prison gates, to the vital necessity of eating your last breakfast in case, as prison folklore has it, you return to eat it another day, we recommend **The Cell Companion,** written by those who have been to prison - it is everyone's guide to serving and surviving a prison sentence in England and Wales, available from prisonoracle.com.

The early days and weeks of custody are often a difficult time for prisoners and the evidence shows they are periods of particular vulnerability for those at risk of suicide. The Prison Service has introduced reception, first night and induction processes to help identify and reduce this risk.

Some prisoners have obvious factors, such as mental ill-health, drug misuse or a lack of experience of prison, that indicate that they are at heightened risk of suicide, but fatal incident investigations too often find that staff have failed to recognise or act on them - with potentially fatal consequences.

Prison staff have a hugely demanding task. Reception, first night and induction facilities, particularly in large, local prisons, are busy places that have to manage large numbers of prisoners, many of whom have multiple risks and vulnerabilities.

Moreover, any risk assessment must always rely in large part on staff judgment, and no one is infallible. But, to be effective, risk assessment must also take account of known or readily available information associated with suicide - if you are the relative of someone in prison, and have concerns about their risk of self-harm or suicide, telephone the prison, any time, day or night, tell them you have a 'suicide or self-harm concern to communicate' and you will be put through immediately to someone who can help and who will take the matter seriously - many prisons now have a special Safety Hotline and these numbers are on The Prison Oracle and in the respective establishment entry.

In the 12 months to June 2022, there were 288 deaths in prison custody, a decrease of 27% from 395 deaths the previous 12 months. Of these, 66 deaths were self-inflicted, a 20% decrease from the 82 self-inflicted deaths in the previous 12 months.
In the most recent quarter, March 2022 to June 2022 there were 70 deaths, almost unchanged from 69 deaths in the previous quarter.

Many of these incidents took place during the early days in custody - so what do we expect our prisons to do during the first days and weeks of custody, what are the expectations, and how does HM Prison and Probation Service (HMPPS) deliver those expectations in practice?

**Expectations**
HM Prisons Inspectorate (HMIP) have the following expectations of what prisons should deliver to prisoners during their early days in custody.
Overview: Prisoners transferring to and from prison are safe and treated decently. On arrival prisoners are safe and treated with respect. Risks are identified and addressed at reception. Prisoners are supported on their first night.

Induction is comprehensive.

*1. Prisoners travel in safe, decent conditions, are treated with respect and attention is paid to their individual needs.*

The following indicators describe evidence that may show this expectation being met, but do not exclude other ways of achieving it:

• Prisoners are given sufficient notice of transfer and information about the prison to which they are being transferred *(this Handbook and The Cell Companion are ideal ways of delivering that accurate information),* subject to well evidenced security considerations.

• Escort vehicles are clean and meet the diverse needs of prisoners.

• Prisoners are not kept waiting on vehicles after arrival.

• Escorting staff are aware of the individual needs of the prisoners in their care and provide an effective briefing to receiving staff, including the person escort record.

• Prisoners are given adequate comfort breaks and refreshments during transfer.

• Prisoners arrive in sufficient time to allow reception and first night procedures to be conducted effectively.

*2. Prisoners are safe and treated with respect on their reception and first night in prison. Risks are identified and prisoners are supported according to their individual needs.*

The following indicators describe evidence that may show this expectation being met, but do not exclude other ways of achieving it:

• The needs of new prisoners are promptly assessed to ensure their safety, with particular attention to the risk of suicide and self-harm.

• Reception is a welcoming and supportive environment.

• Prisoners are not strip- or squat-searched unless there is sufficient specific intelligence and proper authorisation.

• Interviews are private, take account of all available information and identify vulnerability and risk. Reception staff provide an effective briefing to wing staff.

• Prisoners are reunited with their property on arrival and are moved quickly to designated first night accommodation.

• Prisoners know how to access help and support from staff, family and peer supporters.

• Prisoners can shower on their first night in a new prison.

• A free telephone call is offered and additional support is provided to those who have no external support.

• Prisoners receive basic equipment and supplies.

• Peer supporters are used effectively in reception and during first night arrangements.

• Regular welfare checks are carried out on new arrivals.

*3. Prisoners are promptly inducted and supported to understand life in prison.*

The following indicators describe evidence that may show this expectation being met, but do not exclude other ways of achieving it:

• Prisoners receive comprehensive information about the rules and regime in a format and language they understand.

• Induction includes a private conversation with an officer to identify and address any concerns.

• Prisoners' immediate rehabilitation needs (including debt, families, accommodation, employment) are identified on arrival and met.

• Prisoners are meaningfully occupied during induction and are allocated regime activity swiftly.

• Prisoners understand that their personal mail and telephone calls may be monitored.

• Prisoners subject to recall or eligible for bail are identified promptly and supported to exercise their legal rights.

• Prisoners who face an indeterminate sentence are identified on remand and given support. The elements and implications of an indeterminate sentence are explained to them and, where appropriate, their families.

• Prisoners are supported to arrange their first visit.

*In 2014 the Prisons Inspectorate issued a Thematic Review on* **Transfers and Escorts**, *and in November 2015 they issued a findings paper on the* **First 24 Hours in Prison**, *both of which are relevant to early days in custody although they have not been updated to date (September 2022).*

**PSI 07/2015 & OMiC (updated 13 January 2020) (See section 7.6)**

The current HMPPS instruction covering **Early Days in Custody, Reception in Custody, First Night in Custody and Induction to Custody is contained in Prison Service Instruction 07/2015.** This sets out guidance and mandatory actions for prison staff regarding reception in, first night in custody and induction procedures.

It applies only to prisoners aged 18 and over and mandates the completion of resettlement needs screening using the Basic Custody Screening Tool (BCST) and completion of a resettlement plan for all prisoners. This is reinforced in the **Managing The Custodial Sentence Policy Framework** that incorporates the delivery of the **Offender Management in Custody model (OMiC).**

The desired overall outcomes are that prisoners are received into lawful custody and treated with decency and with regard for their and others' safety and well-being. Prisoners are kept safe and supported during their first night in prison, their immediate needs are met and understand entitlements and responsibilities, and how to access support facilities.

**PSI 07/2015 Reception: Service elements**

**The key outcome of this service is that prisoners are received into lawful custody and treated with decency and with regard for their and others' safety and well-being.**

*All prisoners must be held lawfully, and their wellbeing must be the primary concern of staff throughout the reception and first night process. The guiding principle in management of reception and first night is the duty of care to prisoners.*

**Service Element: Receive from escort.**

**Output: Prisons accept lawfully detained prisoners into custody, through appropriate reception procedures that operate within agreed opening hours and exceptionally outside those hours.**

*Governors must ensure that Reception operates efficiently and effectively for all prisoners entering the establishment. Reception opening hours must be agreed with the Deputy Director of Custody (or with the Deputy Director of Contracted Custodial Services, in those contracted prisons where opening hours are not specified in the contract), and arrangements put in place to deal with prisoners exceptionally arriving outside those hours.*

**Service Element: Check detention details and identification.**

**Output: The identity and legal status of individual prisoners is validated.**

*All prisoners entering an establishment must be identified, and the validity of the warrant or other documentation authorising their detention must be verified. Warrants can be either hard copy or electronic, do not need to be signed and do not have to contain a seal. The warrant must identify:*

*a) the person(s) to whom it is directed (the Governor of the first prison receiving the prisoner from court);*

*b) the defendant against whom it was issued (the prisoner);*

*c) the reason for its issue (the charge or offence);*

*d) the court that issued it, unless that is otherwise recorded by the court officer; and*

*e) the court office for the court that issued it.*

*A list of such documents is at Annex A. If the warrant or other document is not available on arrival, but Reception staff are satisfied it exists, the prisoner must be admitted and the court or other issuing authority, or the prison where a transferred prisoner was previously held, must be requested to forward it immediately. Photocopied or faxed warrants are acceptable on arrival, but the original must be obtained as soon as possible unless an electronic warrant has been issued, in which case it should be printed for retention in the F2050. An electronic signature or emailed warrant is acceptable. If there is any doubt about the validity of the warrant (e.g., the court order appears to be incorrect, or the prisoner disputes the name on the warrant), the prisoner must be admitted and the court asked for clarification.*

Prisoners should also be allowed to contact their legal advisers for help in resolving such disputes.

*Foreign national prisoners, or prisoners who hold British passports but have lived for a substantial period in another country, must be identified. PSI 52/2011 includes guidance on establishing nationality - see Section 2.18.*

Guidance on dealing with prisoners who have been unlawfully at large is in Annex C.

**Output: A record of every prisoner's identification is kept on file and updated when necessary.**

*Details of all newly arriving prisoners must be recorded in their personal record F2050 and on Prison-NOMIS. The information recorded must include the name and contact details of the prisoner's next of kin or nominated contact, the prisoner's ethnic group, and their religion (including nil religion), using the Religion Card as an aid if necessary. If the name on the warrant is different to that used by the prisoner on a previous sentence, the current name must be used to identify him/her, and any alternative names recorded as aliases.*

*Warrants must be date-stamped on the first occasion a prisoner arrives in prison custody after the warrant is issued, to confirm that the court's order has been complied with. On subsequent entries to the prison, or moves to other establishments, it is only necessary to record details of the move on the F2050 and Prison-NOMIS (or alternative system in establishments where P-NOMIS is not available).*

*All prisoners must be photographed in accordance with the National Security Framework, and the photograph downloaded onto Prison-NOMIS. Features that will aid identification including tattoos, scars, and biometric data must also be recorded.*

**Service Element: Identification of immediate needs. First Night security information.**

**Output: Key information on individual prisoners is identified, including their eligibility for the first night in custody service, and recorded.**

The **Person Escort Record Policy Framework** (cancels PSO 1025) came into force on 19th April 2021 and was updated on 24th May 2021.

The Person Escort Record PF sets out mandatory instructions and guidance regarding completion of the Person Escort Record (PER).

The PER is a record which must be completed for all prisoners prior to any escorted external movement or transfer. It provides escort staff and establishments with relevant information on a prisoner and highlights risks they may pose during and after the movement.

The PER is not itself a risk assessment. It conveys the information about the assessed risks to others who may need to know about them.

Before any escort commences an assessment needs to be made of the risks posed by the prisoner which may impact on how the escort should be carried out and the allocation of the prisoner to court, holding cells or prison cells.

Any risks or vulnerabilities identified should be noted and acted upon by those receiving the prisoner.

PERs provide assurance that information about a prisoner on escort or transfer is available and that any identified risks/vulnerabilities, and any new risks that develop during a movement are communicated to those responsible for their custody.

Correct completion and storage of the PER will help to prevent suicide/self-harm, escapes, assaults, releases in error and other serious incidents. It will also ensure the accurate recording of prisoner's money and property and will aid investigations of prisoner allegations of mistreatment. Correct use of the PER will ensure that all escorts are carried out decently, safely and securely, and are done so in a way that protects the welfare of all those being escorted.

*The PER form that must accompany each new prisoner, and any other available documentation, must be examined in Reception to identify any immediate needs and risks already recorded. Staff should also be aware that in cases where a prisoner has been remanded by the Courts, there will be a requirement to examine the PER for any indication of a risk to witnesses/victims (this will be highlighted on Form MG6 from the police), which will necessitate restrictions being placed on their communications (see PSI 46/2011 Tackling Witness Intimidation by Remand Prisoners). The prisoner must also be interviewed, in private if possible, to discover and record any further immediate needs and risks, and any other information about the prisoner that may be relevant, particularly during their first night in custody. Alerts on Prison-NOMIS must be created and updated.*

As soon as all Reception procedures have been completed new prisoners should be moved on to the First Night Unit, or other accommodation, such as the Segregation Unit or Healthcare, as necessary, where they will spend their first night in the establishment. Prisoners who are returning to the same establishment after a temporary absence should move back to normal accommodation unless, following a revised risk assessment owing to a change in status or circumstances, they require location in healthcare or other special accommodation. Prisoners who were informed about obtaining legal services during an earlier stage of imprisonment may need further advice and support if their status changes, e.g. from remand to convicted/sentenced prisoners, or if their appeal fails.

**Output: All prisoners are risk assessed for potential harm to themselves, to others and from others.**

*The PER and any other available documentation including Suicide & Self Harm Warning Forms,*

*ACCT documents and CSRAs, must be examined, and the prisoner interviewed in Reception, to assess the risk of self-harm or harm to others by the prisoner, or harm from others. All available, relevant information must be considered including that held on OASys/Delius. Staff should liaise with the OMU where necessary. Assessments must also be made of prisoners who by-pass some Reception processes owing to their late arrival or disruptive behaviour, and those whose status and demeanour may change after a court appearance via video link.* **See PSI 64/2011 (updated July 2021) for guidance on risk to self, to others and from others and PSI 20/2015 for Cell Sharing Risk Assessment.**

**Output: Information is recorded and shared with other departments and agencies both internal and external, and actions taken are documented.**

*All relevant information available about the prisoner must be noted in the appropriate record, and forwarded to other staff as necessary, both within the establishment and externally. Actions taken in relation to this information must also be recorded and the relevant other departments and agencies informed. Local policies and procedures must make clear the options available to reception, first night and healthcare staff to keep safe and support those identified on reception as being at risk of suicide or self-harm, and how to access any additional care or healthcare, including management of drug and alcohol withdrawal. The Border and Immigration Authority must be notified of any prisoner with outstanding immigration issues. In accordance with* **PSI 52/2011** *(Immigration, Repatriation and Removal Services), once* **convicted and sentenced** *the following categories of foreign national prisoners must be referred to Criminal Casework Directorate (CCD) within five working days of sentence and before transfer to another establishment, using the CCD/ Local Immigration Team Referral Form (LIT):*

*All those recommended for deportation by a court.*

*All foreign nationals (European Economic Area and non-EEA nationals) sentenced to 12 months or more imprisonment (except Irish citizens).*

*All non-EEA nationals sentenced to less than 12 months but where the current sentence plus one or two previous sentences within the last 5 years (taking account of the most significant sentences during the period) total 12 months or more.*

*All non-EEA nationals who receive a custodial sentence for a drug offence (except possession only cases)* A copy of the completed CCD/LIT Referral Form should be kept with the prisoner's record.

A table giving examples of information, reasons it may be needed, and who needs it, is at *Annex B.*

*Governors of local prisons must ensure that Part 1 of the Basic Custody Screening is completed within 72 hours of the prisoner's details being entered onto Prison-NOMIS, for both prisoners entering and* recalled to custody. The results will be shared automatically with the CR via OASys.

Within five business days of receipt of Part 1 of the Basic Custody Screening and staff must complete Part 2 and create a resettlement plan. (The Basic Screen Custody Tool is available on prisonoracle.com

**Service Element: Search.**

**Output: Valuables and in possession property are searched and issued.**

All property in the possession of incoming prisoners, or forwarded on later from a previous location, must be searched and either returned to the prisoner to retain in possession, or else securely stored, in accordance with the National Security Framework, the Local Security Strategy, the Searching of the Person, the Searching of Prisoners' Stored Property and the Prisoners' Property. All property must be recorded on the appropriate record. All new prisoners must have a property box number allocated to them on the P-NOMIS system before they leave Reception. If any valuable items are found in a prisoner's possession on reception that appear prima facie not to be the prisoner's property - for example bank cards or identity documents in names other than that of the prisoner - this must be reported to the PIO unless this has already been done. Where the police take no action, the documents should be placed in the prisoner's stored property and returned on release.

**Service Element: Search.**

**Output: Prisoners are level B searched and undergo metal detection and are full searched on an intelligence-led basis.**

All incoming prisoners must be searched in accordance with the procedures described in the National Security Framework, the Local Security Strategy, and the Searching of the Person. In high security prisons, all male prisoners must be given a full search on reception. Female prisoners must not be routinely full searched, but only when intelligence or reasonable suspicion suggest that an item is being concealed that may be revealed by the search.

**Output: Prisoners are full searched.**

Full searches of male prisoners must be conducted in accordance with the National Security Framework, the Local Security Strategy, and the Searching of the Person.

**Output: Prisoners are given a gender specific search.**

Female prisoners must be searched in accordance with the National Security Framework, the Local Security Strategy, and the Searching of the Person PSI 07/2016.

The National Security Framework and Searching of the Person PSI 07/2016 include guidance on searching disabled or injured prisoners, transsexual / gender dysphoric prisoners, and religious or cultural searching issues.

**Service Element: Identification of immediate needs.**

**Output: Prisoners are held in reception for the minimum length of time possible.**

The reception-in procedure can be a stressful experience for prisoners, who must not be held in escort vehicles or holding rooms any longer than is necessary while waiting to complete the procedures, before moving on to their first night location.

**Output: Prisoners are placed in a waiting area in accordance with their individual needs and risk, to ensure the safety and wellbeing of all prisoners and staff.**

An initial assessment of individual prisoners' risk of harm to or from others must be made and reasonable steps taken to minimise any risk during the waiting period. If the prisoner is identified as being at risk of suicide or self-harm an ACCT must be opened and followed up as required, or an existing ACCT followed up. The environment prisoners are held in while waiting to complete reception-in procedures is likely to influence their mood at this time, and Governors should ensure, as far as possible, that holding rooms are clean and reasonably comfortable, with diversionary material such as magazines, information on the prison, or TV.

**Output: An assessment of prisoners' healthcare needs is completed.**

All incoming prisoners must be medically examined, in private if possible, by a qualified member of the Healthcare team, or a competent and trained Health Care Assistant, who has been trained in ACCT procedures, to determine whether they have any short or long term physical or mental health needs, including disability, drugs or alcohol issues, and ensure that any follow up action is taken, that anyone who needs to know about individual prisoners' ongoing healthcare requirements is informed, and that actions taken are recorded in the appropriate record. If a prisoner is identified as being at risk of suicide or self-harm an ACCT must be opened, or an existing ACCT followed up. Disability data should be entered on Prison-NOMIS, if the prisoner consents.

Prisoners spending their first night in the current prison following transfer from another establishment may undergo the detailed medical assessment on the following day, (or if this is not possible, no later than one week after arrival) unless there are urgent health issues that must be addressed on the day of arrival. Any medical records transferred with the prisoner must be examined as part of the assessment. *Service Element: Phone call.*

**Output: Prisoners are allowed access to telephones, having regard to public protection requirements.**

Newly arrived prisoners must be given access to a telephone in Reception, if available, or else in the first night location, to contact their legal adviser, or to address urgent domestic issues (e.g., childcare or other dependent care arrangements, etc, or to advise a family member where they are being held). If a prisoner wishes to make a legal call the onus will be placed on the prisoner to inform staff that they wish to make such a call. On reception calls to legal advisers must not be made via a PINphone until a prisoner's

PINphone account has been properly set up. A member of staff must first ring the number provided by the prisoner to verify that the number is a bone fide legal number.

Wherever possible prisoners must agree and sign a copy of the Communications Compact before making their first call. Failing this the Compact must be signed before the prisoner is issued with their own personal PIN number.

If the prisoner is subject to public protection restrictions (Protection from Harassment Act or Child Protection measures, and others – see Public Protection Manual) a member of staff should make the call on the prisoner's behalf, checking that the recipient is willing to receive the call in the first instance. Staff should also be aware of those prisoners on remand who are subject to restrictions on their communications under **PSI 46/2011** Tackling Witness Intimidation by Remand Prisoners.

*First Night in Custody*

**Key outcome: Prisoners are kept safe and supported during their first night in prison and their immediate needs are met.**

First Night in Custody, when family and community links are broken and the future is uncertain, is one of the most stressful times for prisoners. Many self-inflicted deaths and self-harm incidents occur within the first 24 hours, the first week, and the first month, particularly among younger prisoners. Extra emphasis placed on tackling safer custody issues during the first 24 hours and beyond is likely to produce most benefit in this early period. Listeners or other peer supporters may offer additional help to prisoners, particularly during the first night.

*Service Element: Risk assessment for cell sharing.*

**Output: Prisoners are risk assessed for potential harm to themselves, to others and from others.**

*A Cell Sharing Risk Assessment must be completed, by an appropriately trained member of staff, whenever required in accordance with national instructions (PSI 20/2015). The rating resulting from the paper based CSRA must be entered onto Prison-NOMIS before any offender is physically located in the cell. Staff must be aware of, and comply with, national and local instructions on violence reduction (PSI 64/2011 (updated July 2021) and the local Violence Reduction Strategy).*

*Service Element: Addressing immediate needs.*

**Output: Prisoners assessed as being at risk of suicide or self-harm have support identified and managed.**

*All newly arrived prisoners must be assessed as part of the reception health screen process to determine whether they are at risk of suicide or self-harm, and an Assessment Care in Custody and Teamwork (ACCT) Plan opened, or an existing ACCT continued, as*

appropriate. An ACCT alert must be updated on Prison-NOMIS when an ACCT is opened. Prisoners returning to custody are at increased risk of suicide/self-harm, and the risk occurs with transferred prisoners as well as those on initial reception into custody. Staff must be aware of, and comply with, national and local instructions on preventing suicide and managing self-harm

A list of the categories of prisoners who may be especially vulnerable to suicide or self-harm is at *Annex D.*

**Output: Prisoners are allocated to first night accommodation which:**

**1 meets national requirements;**

**2 takes account of their individual needs and risk.**

*Prisoners who are new to prison custody, or new to the current establishment, must be allocated initially to dedicated first night accommodation, if available, or to another location which meets at least the minimum national standard for certified accommodation, and which is suitable for new prisoners. Where appropriate, following medical assessment, new prisoners may be located in Healthcare or a detoxification unit, or, if appropriate, a vulnerable prisoners' unit or segregation unit.*

*When allocating prisoners to their accommodation for their first night in the establishment, and subsequently, staff must take account of the requirement to manage any risk of harm to or from others, and any risk of suicide or self-harm. They must also take account of information in the PER and other relevant documentation, and all relevant information obtained during reception, particularly in relation to any form of risk to the prisoner or others. Refer to Caremaps for prisoners transferring on an open ACCT, or in the post-closure phase.*

*Governors must ensure that arrangements are in place for staff to monitor prisoners' safety and well-being throughout the first night in the current prison, and that action is taken to address any concerns as necessary. Prisoners must be advised on how to summon help during the night, if needed. See Management and Security of Nights PSI 24/2011.*

*As far as possible convicted and unconvicted prisoners must be accommodated separately, in accordance with Prison Rule 7.*

**Output: The immediate needs of prisoners are recorded, and where required action is taken.**

*All information about prisoners' immediate healthcare needs and details of any urgent issues that require immediate intervention and resolution must be recorded in the appropriate record, and suitably followed up by the relevant staff.*

**Output: Information on women's prisons, and what to expect on first night in prison is available in courts and local police stations.**

*The Governor must liaise with the police and National Probation Service with a view to arranging for information about the prison, particularly new*

prisoners' reception and first night experience, to be provided to local courts and police stations, for issue to new prisoners likely to come to that prison.

**Output: Prisoners' hygiene needs are met.**

*All new prisoners must be given access to a bath or shower in reception or before they are locked up for the first night. All prisoners must be provided with toiletries (soap, toothpaste, toothbrush etc) sufficient to last for at least the first 24 hours. Female prisoners must be provided with appropriate sanitary items. Where appropriate, items suitable for particular ethnic groups should be available.*

*All new prisoners must be provided with clean, reasonably fitting clothing as necessary.*

**Output: All prisoners receive a hot meal and drink.**

*Prisoners who have completed the reception-in process in time must be served the normal evening meal (or lunch, if they arrive early enough). Prisoners who arrive too late for the normal evening meal must be provided with hot food and a drink in reception or wherever they spend the first night, before lock up (**PSI 44/2010**, Annex B, paragraph 4.27, and Annex A, service element 12). The food and drink provided must take account of religious, cultural and medical needs (**PSI 44/2010**, Annex B, paragraph 3.13).*

**Output: Prisoners with complex immediate needs receive a supplementary service of one to one interactive support.**

Some prisoners arriving in prison custody will need support and assistance to resolve urgent and immediate issues arising as a result of their imprisonment and which adversely affect their lives (or the lives of others) outside the prison. It is important that we help prisoners to uphold their immediate responsibilities to others by assisting them to solve immediate problems and make arrangements to cover the time they will spend in prison. For example, they may be worried about having left children or family members without an explanation of where they are or about not being able to let their employer know that they will not be at work the following day.

*During the initial interview, staff must take time to listen to prisoners and offer them help and support in resolving or managing their most urgent issues and in particular those that arise directly as a result of their imprisonment. Time and resources must be available to resolve issues that cannot be left unresolved overnight and to provide personal help and support to prisoners as needed. First night staff should be supported by the chaplain, Samaritans, Listeners and Insiders, and others in this task.*

The complete range of issues that might need immediate attention and resolution cannot be captured in a list. Possible topics that may need to be addressed on the first night include but are not limited to:

Urgent issues related to accommodation (for example where dependents are locked out or

where homes have been left unsecured);
health related issues (for example where either prisoners or dependents need access to specialist medication that is not in their possession);
issues relating to the safety or wellbeing of children or family members;
Issues relating to the prevention of harm to others.

Equally, some prisoners may need additional support and assistance in understanding and adapting to the prison environment.

*Particular care should be taken to ensure that prisoners with special needs in relation to communication or understanding receive the support and information they need to overcome immediate issues that arise. The immediate needs of prisoners with disabilities or learning difficulties must be addressed. Prisoners identified as having a disability should be issued with the 'Information Book for Prisoners with a Disability' which is also available in Easy Read format.*

**Output: Prisoners receive a First Night pack.**

*New prisoners must be issued with a pack (variously known as a reception pack, comfort pack or first night pack) containing items such as tea, milk, sugar and sweets. Prisoners aged over 18 may also be provided, on request, with tobacco ('smoker's pack'). Diversionary reading material should also be included where possible, along with writing materials and, where there is no TV access, a radio. Prisoners should be told that the cost of the pack will be recovered from their future earnings in the establishment, and they may therefore choose to refuse to accept it.*

*Prisoners must be told when and how they will be able to make purchases from the prison shop/canteen. If items routinely provided by the prison shop/canteen are needed urgently before prisoners are able to obtain then from the shop/canteen they may be provided in advance and paid for later.*

*Service Element: Health screening.*

**Output: Prisoners have additional healthcare support if required.**

Prisoners who require detoxification from the effects of drugs or alcohol, or other immediate medical needs (e.g., medication, help with disabilities) must be referred to the appropriate specialist unit or staff.

*Service Element: Provision of the relevant information.*

**Output: All prisoners new to custody and/or new to the establishment are provided with key information relevant to their first few days in the establishment.**

*All new prisoners must be provided with a pack or booklet giving essential information about what will happen during their first few days in the establishment, and including information about the Samaritans, Listeners, Insiders, and any other peer supporter initiatives. This pack or booklet will contain a brief description of what the prisoner can expect* from their Offender Supervisor and clarify that they will be allocated an Offender Supervisor during their period in custody who will work closely with their Offender Manager in the community. As far as possible, this information should be available in a variety of formats (e.g., written, video, audio) and a range of languages reflecting the make-up of the local prison population. Prisoners new to custody are likely to find the reception and first night periods confusing and even overwhelming, and while staff should try to help them settle in and overcome their anxieties, it is good practice not to overload prisoners with information when they first arrive.

Staff must reassure prisoners that safer custody (e.g., violence reduction/prisoner safety measures) is a high priority, and Governors must ensure that these measures are effective. Staff should explain to prisoners that the induction stage, which will explain more about prison life, will follow shortly. If not already clear from the reception stage, staff should enquire about the prisoner's previous prison experience and knowledge, so as to make an appropriate recommendation about a suitable individual induction programme.

All newly convicted prisoners must be advised that they are entitled to a social visit within 72 hours of their conviction.

**Output: One to one welfare support is provided within courts/custody suites to address immediate needs of the prisoner.**

This is an additional service for prisoners which may be commissioned. Its aim is to provide prisoners with complex needs with a more personal service, including advice and support ahead of their arrival at the establishment. See *PSI 64/2011 (Updated July 2021).*

**Induction to Custody**

**Key outcome: Prisoners know and understand their entitlements and responsibilities, and how to access support and facilities available to them.**

All prisoners undergoing induction must be treated decently, with full regard for equality, vulnerability, and any special needs. Safer custody requirements must be followed at all times and risks appropriately managed.

*Service Element: Induction to Custody.*

**Output: Prisoners receive the relevant Induction to Custody package at a time, and in a manner, relevant to their individual needs.**

Induction consists of two parts. The Introduction to Custody (ITC) presentation has been developed to provide a standardised process for inducting prisoners into local prisons. The Purpose of the 'ITC' presentation is to provide prisoners with all information that is mandatory under this instruction. ITC has to be completed within 5 days of a prisoner arriving into the prison. The day of Reception is counted as day

one and is therefore included in the 5 days. Part Two is a localised introduction specific to each establishment. Public sector prisons that have a 'Local' function must deliver both parts. *Outside of the local estate governors can determine how induction is delivered but they must still cover all parts of the PSI and may wish to use the model provided for local prisons.* Prisoners with wide custodial experience are likely to need less input than those comparatively new to prison, but staff should be aware that some prisoners may not retain information for very long and will need reminding. A flowchart detailing what is expected in the first 5 days in custody is contained in ***Annex F*** and for further detail about the process and presentation please see the 'Local Prisons delivery model for induction, delivery of resettlement needs screening and initial resettlement service' issued by the Business Development Group.

Every prisoner's knowledge and previous experience of custody should be explored during the reception and first night stages, and all prisoners requiring induction should be referred on to either the full Part One and Two programme, or only Part Two, as appropriate.

*Prisoners must be placed on an appropriate induction programme, as described above, as soon as they are able to benefit from it (eg, after completing a detox period if necessary) and as soon as a vacancy on a programme is available. Arrangements must be made for those whose induction is delayed to be able to obtain information in the interim. The induction package must be adapted as far as possible to take account of individual prisoners' learning abilities and language competencies, and make use of a variety of formats (eg, visual, oral, written, etc) as appropriate. The location and accessibility of the induction accommodation must be taken into account in relation to disabled prisoners.* The multi-lingual Prisoners' Information Book is a useful source of guidance for prisoners.

**Output: Prisoners are given information. Prisoners understand their entitlements and responsibilities while in custody.**

Prisoners undergoing Part One of induction should be provided with information on the following topics:

Prison or YOI Rules, and local rules or regulations. Remand prisoners should be informed of the particular rights and obligations that apply to them under the Rules;

Advice on living co-operatively with others within the prison, including sensitivity to their needs and diversity, care for the environment and personal care, safeguarding their property, suicide prevention and self-harm management, and local responses to violence;

Samaritans and Samaritan Listener scheme within the prison;

Raising the alarm and emergency situations;
Working with staff;
Making applications;
Making complaints, including the role of the Prisons and Probation Ombudsman;
Adjudications procedures;
The role of the Independent Monitoring Board;
Faith issues and the role of the Chaplaincy;
Arrangements for release (including temporary release) and (where relevant) deportation (in general – arrangements specific to the individual prisoner will come under Offender Management, not induction);
Making applications for bail and obtaining advice on legal services;
Details of active civil and criminal providers can be accessed via the following website link: https://www.gov.uk/find-a-legal-adviser
Local healthcare services;
Counselling, Assessment, Referral and Throughcare Services (CARATS), and other substance misuse services;
The Assisted Prison Visits scheme;
Voting rights for eligible prisoners (see PSO 4650 – see later in this chapter).
As far as possible, induction staff should confirm that prisoners understand the information they have been given, and know where to seek further guidance.
**Output: Prisoners are given information. Prisoners understand how to access support and facilities available to them in this establishment.**
Prisoners undergoing Part Two of induction should be provided with information on the following topics:
Prisoners' pay arrangements;
The Incentives and Earned Privileges scheme;
Safer custody issues, including suicide prevention, self-harm management, peer support (Samaritan and Listener) and violence reduction;
Health and Safety;
Any other locally relevant information likely to help prisoners integrate into the establishment (e.g., visiting arrangements, mealtimes, access to library, gym, exercise, association, work and education, and placing orders with the prison shop/'canteen');
Obtaining advice on legal services;
Explanation of the "Core Offer" of Rehabilitative Services (*further guidance and detail will be published in the revised instructions accompanying the Rehabilitative Services in Custody specification*), the role of Probation in compiling resettlement plans and providing services and of the range of "additional services" that they might be able to access whilst in prison.
Again, as far as possible, induction staff should confirm that prisoners understand the information they have been given, and know where to seek further guidance.

SENTENCE PLANNING
**The Offender Management in Custody (OMiC) Model.**
**Important Note: The practical implementation of OMiC, between 2020 and 2022, has been severely restricted by the Covid-19 pandemic and those restrictions are expected to continue well into 2023.**
Manage the Custodial Sentence Policy Framework (OMiC) November 2018.
Background:
In November 2016, the Ministry of Justice announced that it was to recruit an additional 2,500 prison officers as part of the then Prison *Safety and Reform* white paper - later scrapped and replaced by the *Prisons Strategy* white paper in December 2021.
These 'new dedicated officers, each responsible for supervising and supporting around six offenders' were at the heart of a major policy change that is known today as 'Offender Management in Custody' – or 'OMiC' for short.
HMPPS describe OMiC as a key part of the response to self-inflicted deaths, self-harm and violence in prison - all prevalent during early days in custody. OMiC is intended to improve safety by engaging with people, building better relationships between staff and prisoners and helping people settle into life in prison.
OMiC has three high level service outcomes:
• reoffending is reduced;
• the custodial sentence is managed; and
• risk of serious harm is reduced.
***OMiC in a Nutshell***
*The **Offender Management in Custody (OMiC)** model, introduced in 2019, provides that all prisoners within the male closed estate, including those remanded in custody and on a standard recall, must receive a Core Service and be allocated to a specially trained Prison Officer who will have a key worker role - for which Governors must ensure that time is made available for an average of 45 minutes per prisoner per week for delivery of this key worker role which includes individual time with each prisoner.*
*Within this allocated time, key workers can vary individual sessions in order to provide a responsive service, reflecting individual need and stage in the sentence. A key worker session can consist of a structured interview or a range of activities such as attending an ACCT review, meeting family during a visit or engaging in conversation during an activity to build relationships.*
*From September 2019 OMiC saw a move to having prison-based offender managers to manage the custodial part of sentences rather than the former system of being allocated offender managers in the community.*

The introduction of OMiC was by way of the *'Manage the Custodial Sentence Policy Framework'* document which is available on **prisonoracle.com** and this is particularly significant as it was the first in a new type of guideline being produced by the Ministry of Justice, called 'Policy Frameworks'.

Policy Frameworks is part of a move away from Prison Service Instructions in an effort to simplify the current instruction system and give greater discretion to governors. This has been a Government intention since 2015 and was also reflected in the abandoned 2016 White Paper with a commitment to 'look at each policy, and either replace it with the minimum mandatory requirements to ensure a safe, decent and lawful system, with consistency across the estate where this is deemed critical or get rid of it altogether.'

**Introduction of OMiC**

In November 2018, Her Majesty's Prison and Probation Service (HMPPS) introduced the Offender Management in Custody (OMiC) model of offender management.

Managing offenders lies at the heart of HMPPS; it is central to the aims of reducing reoffending, protecting the public and preventing victims by changing lives. It is a central pillar of the work to rehabilitate and give hope to those in prison; and it remains one of the key purposes of custodial sentencing.

The way prisoners' sentences are planned, the way they are case managed through the custodial sentence, has been revised within the OMiC model.

The purpose of the changes is to ensure that:

Every prisoner should have the opportunity to transform their lives by using their time in custody constructively to reduce their risk of harm and reoffending; to plan their resettlement; and to improve their prospects of becoming a safe, law-abiding and valuable member of society. The OMiC Model provides the framework to co-ordinate and sequence an individual's journey through custody and post release. The OMiC model places prisoners and the development of rehabilitation cultures in prisons at the heart of offender management processes and supports the reduction of re-offending in custody and the community, the rehabilitation culture and re-integration into the community.

The OMiC Model was designed to retain existing best practice developed within prisons since the first introduction of the original offender management model and incorporate evidence based practice into revised requirements.

It aims to promote procedural justice in particular considering: voice; neutrality; respect and trustworthiness which a review of research suggests influence cooperation and compliance. A process that is perceived as being applied fairly is more likely to be seen as legitimate and the final decision complied with. This can support a prison which is safe and decent.

The OMiC model provides a sound basis on which to build a rehabilitative culture and is designed to promote the positive staff prisoner relationships which support rehabilitative cultures.

**The Core OMiC Service.**

Key workers must raise any concerns with the Offender Management Unit (OMU) who will communicate with NPS offender managers if required.

The Governor must ensure there are processes in place for those individuals who will receive the core service to ensure that the relevant offender management processes (such as HDC and ROTL) are delivered in sufficient time to enable the process to be completed by the eligibility date where relevant.

The principle of assigning the same prison offender manager for all processes must be applied, where possible, in order to retain continuity and enable an effective working relationship.

*Specialised Service:*

In addition to the core service, a specified cohort will receive a specialised service and be assigned to a prison offender manager who, in addition to completing offender management core tasks, must offer one to one supervision. The specialised service will be provided to:

• All NPS allocated prisoners who have over 10 months left to serve;

• All Probation allocated prisoners with over 48 months left to serve or medium risk with over 10 months left to serve;

• All Probation allocated prisoners whilst in the open estate;

• Care leavers aged 18-25. Governors must ensure there are processes and policies in place to encourage disclosure of care leaver status.

• All standard recalled prisoners. They remain allocated to a community offender manager based within the NPS throughout the recall due to the potential to release determinate sentence prisoners at any stage under Secretary of State Executive Release.

**The Sentence Plan (OASys & OMiC)**

The sentence plan is the key tool for identifying what an offender will do during their sentence, based on an assessment of the factors associated with their offending, to achieve the aims of the sentence. This is particularly important for reducing the likelihood of reoffending and, in custodial cases, promoting resettlement.

A further important aim of the plan is to reduce the risk of serious harm the offender poses, particularly for offenders' subject to an extended determinate or indeterminate sentence, as they

*OASys is a national system for assessing the risk and needs of an offender. The decision was taken to develop a new risk assessment system because none of the existing tools and inventories fully met the requirements specified by the project team. The Prison and Probation Services have jointly designed the system.*
*OASys is designed to:*
* *assess how likely an offender is to be reconvicted*
* *identify and classify offending-related needs, including basic personality characteristics and cognitive behavioural problems*
* *assess risk of serious harm, risks to the individual and other risks*
* *assist with management of risk of harm*
* *link the assessment to the supervision or sentence plan*
* *indicate the need for further specialist assessments*
* *measure change during the period of supervision/sentence.*

have received this sentence based on an assessment of their 'dangerousness'. A key consideration for the Parole Board in determining whether to direct release will be the offender's engagement with appropriate activities and interventions in order to reduce the risk posed. However, the main consideration will be whether there is clear evidence that the offender has demonstrated positive changes in behaviour, thinking and attitudes, and that there is a clear plan in place to manage any residual risk the offender poses on release from custody.

The focus of sentence planning should be on achieving outcomes supported by defined actions or activity. The plan should cover the whole of the sentence, and define clearly:
* the overall outcomes to be achieved through the plan
* the activity needed to achieve the intended outcomes and expected timescales
* how the activity will be delivered to meet individual offender need
* what is expected of the offender in terms of the objectives they are aiming to achieve in support of an action or outcome, and
* who will have overall responsibility for the continued review and updating of the plan as it is delivered.

### Offender Assessment System: OASys

Risk assessment of offenders and keeping the public safe is at the heart of what HMPPS does. Accurately assessing the risk offenders represent is therefore of primary importance - below we look at a summary of evidence relating to offender risk assessment, risk of reoffending and risk of serious harm.

Criminal behaviour is influenced by a range of individual, social and environmental factors. People tend to interpret others' behaviour as because of the sort of person they are. We often fail to see situational, environmental or social influences. Much decision making in criminal justice needs to be informed by an assessment of

whether someone poses a risk to the public. For example, is there a risk that they might break the law again and might that be for a serious offence? Considerable effort has been made over the years to develop reliable, unbiased estimates of the risk of further offending.

The Offender Assessment System (OASys) was introduced in 2001 and built on the existing 'What Works' evidence base. It combines the best of actuarial methods of prediction with structured professional judgement to provide standardised assessments of offenders' risks and needs, helping to link these risks and needs to individualised sentence plans and risk management plans1.

There are two main types of risk:
* likelihood of future re-offending and reconviction - the probability that someone will offend, be arrested, and reconvicted within two years
* risk of serious harm - if reconvicted, the probability that the offence will be one of 'serious harm'

The Criminal Justice Act 2003 defines serious harm as: 'death or serious personal injury, whether physical or psychological'.

OASys defines serious harm as 'an event which is life threatening and/or traumatic and from which recovery, whether physical or psychological, can be expected to be difficult or impossible'.

The risk of harm posed by offenders to others has two key dimensions:
* the relative likelihood that an offence will occur
* the relative impact or harm of the offence - what exactly might happen, to what or whom, under what circumstances, and why.

Some crimes like shoplifting, have relatively little impact or harm. But, statistically, they are the most common. Others like homicide are rare but cause greatest damage.

### Risk levels

The level of serious harm is defined by the likelihood of it happening:

**Low:** current evidence does not indicate a likelihood of causing serious harm

**Medium:** there are identifiable indicators of serious harm. The offender has the potential to cause such harm. But they are unlikely to do so unless there is a change in circumstances. For example, failure to take medication, loss of accommodation, relationship breakdown, drug or alcohol misuse

**High:** there are identifiable indicators of serious harm. The potential event could happen at any time and the impact would be serious.

**Very high:** there is an imminent risk of serious harm. The potential event is more likely than not to happen as soon as the opportunity arises and the impact would be serious. 'Opportunity' can include the removal or overcoming of controls, and changes in circumstances.

### Who is at risk?

It is important to identify the person or groups of people who are specifically at risk. Risk is categorised as risk to:

• the public: either generally or a specific group, for example, the elderly, vulnerable adults, women or an ethnic minority group
• a known adult, such as a previous victim or partner
• prisoners: within a custodial setting
• children: either specific children or children in general who may be vulnerable to harm of various kinds - this includes violent or sexual behaviour, emotional harm or neglect or because they are in custody
• staff: anyone working with the offender, whether from Probation, the Prison Service, police or other agency
• self: the possibility that the offender will commit suicide or self-harm.

### What are risk and protective factors?

Risk factors are circumstances or characteristics that make criminal behaviour more likely. For example, poor temper control or an anti-social peer group. Protective factors make anti-social behaviour less likely. For example, supportive family or secure employment. Risk factors may be mitigated by protective factors. People who reoffend most often have risk factors across many areas. To reduce reoffending, we need to help people manage or overcome risk factors and develop or strengthen protective factors.

### Risk assessment can also help target services on the right people

Rehabilitative intervention is most effective when it is proportionate to the likelihood of someone's reoffending. We should focus more intensive help on those with the highest likelihood of reconviction. We should avoid directing limited resources to those unlikely to reoffend.
Alongside likelihood of reoffending, we sometimes want to estimate the risk of other future events, like absconding from prison.
We can measure likelihood of reoffending in several ways:

**Actuarial or clinical?** Actuarial assessments combine information about individuals in a structured way. This is weighted by the strength of their link with future behaviour, based on large scale research evidence. In HMPPS these are predictor tools such as the Offender Group Reconviction Sore (OGRS) or the Risk of Serious Recidivism (RSR). Clinical assessments rely on a practitioner's judgement and experience to estimate the imminence of the offending behaviour. Some risk assessment tools fall in one or other category – others use elements of both.

**Static or dynamic?** Static risk factors are fixed or past elements that will not change. These include age, gender, current offence type or childhood experiences. Dynamic factors are associated with the changing likelihood of reoffending over time. These are factors that we can support service users with to help reduce the risks. Research shows there are nine issues commonly associated with offending behaviour:
• unstable accommodation
• a lack of employment
• no positive recreation activities
• poor personal relationships
• alcohol misuse
• drug misuse
• impulsivity and poor emotional control
• anti-social peers
• attitudes that support crime
These dynamic risk factors are also sometimes called criminogenic needs. Both clinical and actuarial assessments can draw on static and dynamic elements. For example, a history of truancy and a current problem with binge drinking.

### Using risk assessments

The choice of actuarial or clinical risk assessment and static or dynamic is determined by the context and purpose of the risk assessment and will be included in the design of any risk assessment tools. An actuarial tool using only static data, can bring a swift, reliable estimate of the likelihood of reconviction. It also demands minimal staff resources. But this tells us little about that person's strengths or areas of need that we can work on. For sentence planning or risk management, we need a further assessment using dynamic information to identify:
• areas for attention
• strengths to build on and
• priorities to agree
Clinical predictions of the likelihood of reoffending are less objective and less accurate. However clinical understanding of the relevance of risk factors is important for effective sentence planning and risk management.

### Risk of what?

It is important that we are clear about the outcome that we are estimating.
Do we need to know whether the person is likely

to commit any new offence over a particular period? Typically, we look at one year or two years following the start of a community sentence or release from prison.

Or do we want to estimate the risk that the potential reoffence might be for a violent crime or for any crime likely to cause serious harm?

The core risk assessment tools that HMPPS currently uses are:

## OASys Sexual Reoffending Predictor (OSP) Policy Framework (issued 28th January 2021, updated 11 March 2022)

Implementation and use of OASys Sexual re-offending Predictor (OSP) Policy Framework is a HMPPS actuarial risk assessment tool used to assess the likelihood of further proven sexual offending by adult males.

March 2022 - Change made: OSP guidance for Practitioners updated, setting out the arrangements, mandatory requirements, and general guidance for use of the OASys Sexual Reoffending Predictor (OSP). OSP replaced Risk Matrix 2000 as the HMPPS actuarial risk assessment tool for adult males convicted of sexual/sexually motivated offences from 1 March 2021.

HMPPS plays a vital role in protecting the public from those who pose a risk of sexual offending. Effective risk assessment is a critical part of this process and informs the way in which we manage the risk of harm posed by such individuals. In addition to strengthening risk assessment, OSP will also support more effective risk management and responsive sentence planning for those who pose a risk of sexual harm.

## Offender Group Reconviction Scale (OGRS3)

Percentage likelihood of committing any offence within 2 years leading to reconviction (proven reoffending). An OGRS3 score of 50% or more means that an offender is more likely than not to commit a proven re-offence within 2 years. OGRS scores can be used to target those resources designed to reduce reoffending. Accredited offending behaviour programmes often require particular OGRS scores as part of their eligibility criteria. There is good evidence that when these programmes are delivered to participants with too low or too high a risk they are much less likely to benefit.

## OASys Violence Predictor (OVP)

Percentage likelihood of committing any violent proven re-offence within 2 years. This includes minor violent offences like common assault, harassment and criminal damage and more serious violent offences. An OVP score of 30%+ is the criterion for accredited programmes that

address violent offending behaviour. The more intensive programmes specify an OVP score of 60% or above.

## Risk of Serious Recidivism (RSR)

Percentage likelihood of committing a seriously harmful reoffence within two years. This is defined as an offence where the victim is killed or suffers trauma from which it will be hard or impossible to recover. Serious reoffending is rare. Fewer than 2% of the caseload commit a serious reoffence within two years of a release from prison or the start of a community order.

## Risk of Serious Harm (RoSH) Updated 2020

A structured professional judgement assessment based on completion of OASys. Practitioners consider risk and protective factors alongside immediate situational and relational factors. People are allocated to a Risk of Serious Harm category from 'low' to 'very high'. The RoSH assessment identifies whether the risk is to known adults, children, staff and/or the public. It also identifies whether the risk identified should be regarded as imminent. An individual who is rated as presenting a 'high' or 'very high' risk of serious harm is managed by the NPS. The core risk and need assessment tools are integrated into OASys. OGRS and RSR can be calculated outside of OASys assessment as they rely on a limited number of items available from the person's records. OVP and RoSH are normally generated as part of the OASys process. They both draw on the standardised assessment of the more dynamic features of the person's life that OASys provides. There are further tools for particular contexts. These include the Spousal Assault Risk Assessment Guide (SARA) for risk of partner violence, and the RM2000 assessment of the risk of further sexual offending.

*What makes a good risk assessment tool?*

It is important that the risk assessment tools we use are theoretically sound and provide reliable and valid estimates. Criteria for approving risk assessment tools is supported by advice from MoJ's Correctional Services Accreditation and Advice Panel (CSAAP). A sufficiently robust risk tool will demonstrate the following components: clear description of the tool(s) and its fit with the
• overall approach to assessment
• sound theoretical underpinning and credible rationale
• evidence that the tool does what it aims to do
• commitment to ongoing research and validation to ensure ongoing fitness for purpose
• assessors using the tools are competent in its use
• use of the tool is implemented as intended

*Managing risk and building hope – what next for assessment?*

A HMPPS priority is to reduce reoffending and protect the public. Until recently, we have focused on the risk presented by individuals but in future will need to understand more about areas of strength and factors that support people to desist from crime. Focusing on negative labelling and stigmatisation following conviction can hinder desistance. Desistance is how people with a previous pattern of offending abstain from crime. An effective risk assessment system can help us do both.

We will continue to evaluate and learn from evidence, and to develop more effective risk assessment tools, to help individuals to reduce their reoffending and to lead better lives.

*Further reading* - all available on The Prison Oracle (Reception to Release, Early Days in Custody) the definitive prisons website for England and Wales - prisonoracle.com

Prison, probation and rehabilitation: Public Protection Manual Guidance for prison and probation staff on managing offenders and protecting the public from harm.

The Risk Assessment Tools Evaluation Directory (RATED) provides a summary of the empirical evidence on each assessment tool included in the directory (The Risk Management Authority, Scotland).

ROSH Guidance 2020

## VOTING RIGHTS
**Restrictions on prisoner voting policy framework, issued - 11th August 2020.**
This Policy Framework sets out the rules and guidance to be followed to ensure prisoners are aware of whether or not they are eligible to vote. Where eligible prisoners wish to vote, prisons must have in place processes to support them to do so. This policy framework replaces PSO 4650.

### What are my voting rights?
Convicted prisoners serving a custodial sentence are disqualified from voting while they are detained in custody - this is printed on the warrant of committal, however, some people in prison may have the right to vote, in certain circumstances.
You may be eligible to vote if:
- You are an unconvicted prisoner.
- You are on Judges Remand - a convicted but unsentenced prisoner.
- You are a civil prisoner.
- You are serving a default term for non-payment of a fine.

- You have been committed to prison for contempt of court.
- You are in the community on home detention curfew (HDC) or released on temporary licence (ROTL). *

*\*Prisoners on HDC and ROTL are only eligible to register to vote once they are in the community and become ineligible again upon return to prison.*

If you wish to make an application to register to vote, or are unsure about whether or not you can vote, please speak to a member of staff and read the guidance within the Restrictions on Prisoner Voting policy framework.

Staff can print out voting registration forms from the staff intranet. Your eligibility to vote will still depend on whether you are on the electoral register. It remains the legal responsibility of your Electoral Registration Officer to determine applications to register to vote based on the facts of each case.

Prisoners who are registered to vote and have been released from their sentence on HDC or are in the community on ROTL will be able to vote in the same ways as any other eligible person in the community. This includes attending a polling station *where it meets the conditions of their release* or a postal or proxy vote registered to their home address.

Postal and proxy votes from prison, are not available to those on HDC or ROTL. All other eligible prisoners listed above may, if registered, apply to vote by post or by proxy from prison.

### Eligibility Criteria
The following eligible to apply to register to vote:
Un-convicted prisoners;
Convicted but un-sentenced prisoners;
Persons imprisoned for contempt of court and other prisoners classified under Prison Rule 7(3);
Fine defaulters and those on HDC or ROTL.

## PRISONERS PROPERTY
Prisoners' Property Policy Framework
Issue Date: 1 August 2022
Implementation Date: 5 September 2022
Cancels:
• PSI 12/2011 Prisoners' Property
• PSI 14/2015 Disposal of Prisoners Unauthorised Property
• Prisoners' Property Specification

### Outcomes
Prisoners' property is managed efficiently, effectively, consistently and with care and respect, recognising the potential personal and emotional significance of items.
Staff and prisoners are aware of, and comply with, the rules on what property can be held in possession or storage.

Property complies with volumetric control guidance and is consistent with local incentives schemes.

Prisoners are able to lead as normal and individual an existence as possible within the constraints of the prison environment.

Prisoners' property is checked, recorded, stored, sent out or issued correctly.

Rules and decisions about a prisoner's property are properly explained to the prisoner in a language/format they understand.

Any disposal of prisoners' property is undertaken appropriately.

Property complaints are investigated thoroughly and efficiently, with appropriate reimbursement for lost or damaged items and the avoidance of unnecessary litigation.

### Management checks

Governors / Directors should ensure management checks are undertaken to make sure that prisoners' property is being handled correctly and with care (e.g. that property cards are being accurately completed and that the volume of property held by prisoners is checked regularly and does not become excessive).

### Searching of property

For defensible, consistent and professional practice reasons, the searching of all property accompanying prisoners entering a prison (including on transfer), held in-cell and stored property, must be undertaken in line with the National Security Framework and the local searching strategy.

### Recording of information

All newly arrived prisoners must have a property box number allocated to them on the Prison NOMIS system before they leave reception.

Under Prison Rule 43, it is a statutory requirement to maintain a clear and legible inventory of a prisoner's property. This must be recorded on the appropriate property card. This is important in order to track, safely store and later locate items.

The property cards are:
• F2056A Prisoner's Property Record
• F2056B In Possession Property – Clothing Only (includes footwear)
• F2056C Stored Property
• F2056D In Possession Property
• F2056E Property Record for Transfer / Temporary Release

To be effective, and to avoid issues, complaints and litigation, property cards must include details on all:
• prisoners' property held in possession (including clothing they are wearing on arrival at the prison), apart from consumables/disposable items;

• property held in storage locally;
• property sent to the National Distribution Centre (NDC) Branston, including outsize items, the items contained in each storage box and the seal numbers;
• property owned by the prisoner but which is not for issuing to them;
• items purchased by the prisoner (e.g. via catalogues)
• security seal numbers for property that is being transferred;
• damaged seals and the replacement seal numbers;
• security seal numbers for valuable items stored locally;
• items that have been loaned to the prisoner by the prison (e.g. by Chaplaincy) and it made clear that the item is loaned;
• disability aids and, where possible, it made clear whether it is a privately purchased item or one provided by the NHS;
• confiscated items which were previously authorised;
• items donated by the prisoner to the prison;
• items that have been transferred between prisoners (see 'Transfer of property (gifting) between prisoners');
• disagreements about property due to be returned to prisoners leaving the prison, or any lost or damaged items;
• property that has been disposed of;
• cases where compensation has been paid for lost or damaged property.

Under Prison Rule 43, adult prisoners are required to sign the completed property card. Under-18s in YOIs are also expected to sign their property cards as well. The property card includes a disclaimer and it is important that all new arrivals are helped to understand both the property card and disclaimer, including the use of translation services where necessary. Where prisoners are not willing to sign, the reasons must be recorded clearly on the card. Locally produced disclaimers for property should not be used.

Property cards must be updated to reflect any changes to a prisoner's property and prisoners must be invited to sign the card as soon as possible after any changes, having a proper opportunity to see that it is correct. The greater transparency in this process, the greater trust prisoners will have that their property is being cared for properly.

When a transaction affects a number of items, the appropriate property cards will need to be updated so that the outcome is clearly recorded individually against each item. This discipline is important and will aid in response to any complaints and provide an effective audit trail for staff and management.

All entries on property cards must be appropriately detailed. Any abbreviations should be in line with those already printed on the property cards. If alternative abbreviations need to be used, a key should be included so that others can easily identify what is meant. The better the quality of the entries, the more trustworthy and effective the system will be, and the easier it will be to resolve issues.

Any property cards identified as illegible, unclear or otherwise no longer fit for purpose must be re-listed to ensure accurate and clear recording of all items of a prisoner's property.

All property records (including old completed cards), property disclaimers and cell clearance certificates must be stored securely in the prisoner's core record to allow for effective recording and management of prisoners' property. Items with brand names on them, including clothing, must be recorded as 'item marked with brand logo' rather than 'brand item'. See 'Complaints and compensation claims' for further information.

See 'Valuable property' for information on recording valuable items. Annex A provides further guidance on how to record property.

### Authorised items

When deciding whether or not a prisoner should be allowed to have a particular item, a number of factors need to be considered, including:

• Whether the item is permitted under the Offender Management Act 2007: see PSI 10/2012 Conveyance and Possession of Prohibited Items and Other Related Offences.

• Nature of the Material: The Public Protection Manual sets out materials to which prisoners must not have access and staff need to be aware of these restrictions. More generally, the Governor must temporarily confiscate, pending a decision, any publication where they consider the content presents a threat to good order or discipline or to the interests of prison or national security, or that possession of the material is likely to have an adverse effect on the prisoner's physical or mental health. Prisoners must be told the reasons for the temporary confiscation of their property with sufficient detail for this decision, and have their questions answered. This is important as such confiscations may cause frustration or anxiety, and the quality of the decision-making and explanation can help to minimise this. Decisions must be made in line with the Public Protection Manual which provides further information on the handling of confiscated items. See 'Confiscation and disposal of property' for situations where it would be appropriate to dispose of confiscated items. PSI 64/2011: Management of Prisoners at Risk of Harm to Self, to Others and from Others, provides further information on the removal of in-possession items from at-risk prisoners. When confiscating illicit items, it is important to consider any links the items might have to prisoner debt and issues of prisoner safety.

• Cash: In accordance with Prison Rule 43(3) and YOI Rule 48 (1) prisoners are not allowed to retain cash whilst in prison. Cash must be handled in line with PSI 01/2012 Manage Prisoner Finance. The HMPPS Finance Manual provides further details on the handling of foreign currency.

• Volumetric Control: The overall amount of property held by a prisoner must be within volumetric control limits unless there are exceptional circumstances where a governor permits a prisoner to exceed these limits (see 'Volumetric control', 'Locally stored property' and 'National Distribution (NDC) Branston'). A leaflet which explains these limits, and which can be given to prisoners on reception to a prison, is available at Annex B. The leaflet is available on the intranet in different languages (including Welsh) for prisons to print as required.

• Incentives: Property held in possession must be in line with local incentives schemes and it is important that all prisoners understand the differences between the levels of the scheme.

To ensure a safe, decent and respectful environment, it is important that governors impose restrictions on the display of material which could cause offence, even if an item is otherwise allowed in possession. It is not appropriate for items to be displayed where, for example, the content is indecent or violent, or where it would be inconsistent with commitments to eliminate discrimination and harassment and to promote equality. It is important that prisoners understand what content would fall into these categories and why it is not allowed.

There are a number of individual groups, or particular circumstances, in which additional practices about property are important, and are linked to ensuring that the treatment of prisoners is decent and respectful. This will include:

• To comply with PSI 05/2016 Faith and Pastoral Care for Prisoners, and taking into account guidance in the booklet for staff 'A Guide to Religious Practice in Prison' prisoners must be allowed to have in their possession, or have access to, such artefacts and texts as are required by their religion.

• Disabled prisoners and those with an identified health, social care or neurodiverse need must be allowed to have aids/reasonable adjustments in possession, or have access to them, subject to security checks and health and/or local authority social care assessment and recommendations.

• In permitting items of property, the needs of transgender prisoners must be considered with the use of Voluntary Agreements where appropriate (see The Care and Management of Individuals who are Transgender Policy Framework).

• Any additional or exceptional property required by women in prison who are pregnant or residing on a prison Mother and Baby Unit with their children. For example, maternity clothing, infant feeding equipment and baby grows. See the Pregnancy, Mother and Baby Units and Maternal Separation from Children up to the Age of Two in Women's Prisons Policy Framework for more information.

## Volumetric control

Limits on property exist to ensure safety and security and so that all property can be transferred with a prisoner on their movement to another establishment. This 'volumetric control' is applicable to all establishments.

Experience shows that misunderstanding around volumetric control can lead to significant frustration and tension. It is important, therefore, that prisoners and staff understand:

• what the volumetric control limits are

• why volumetric control exists

• why the limits are set as they are.

A prisoner's total property, whether held in possession or in storage, must fit into two standard size volumetric control boxes (a volumetric control box is 70cm x 55cm x 25cm and has a maximum weight of 15kg per box) plus half a volumetric control box for consumable items.

In addition, the following items are permitted:

• all legal papers;

• religious texts and artefacts, essential for the practice of the prisoner's religion.

• reasonable adjustment/disability aids

• reasonable amounts of items that support transgender prisoners to live in the gender with which they identify. Governors must be satisfied that the quantity held does not impede effective searching. Restrictions on such items must be based on a clear and evidenced operational, risk and/or security assessment (see The Care and Management of Individuals who are Transgender Policy Framework for further information).

• items held in possession for the care of babies in mother and baby units; Governors need to be satisfied that such items are held for this purpose, and that the quantity held does not impede effective searching;

• one set of clothing (whether prisoner's own clothing or prison issue). When considering the one set, this includes that worn by the prisoner when the volume of property is monitored;

• bedding (one set of e.g. pillow, duvet, sheet);

• one musical instrument (e.g. a guitar);

• posters etc. which are appropriate to be attached to cell walls; posters cannot be attached to external walls;

• one birdcage (in prisons where birds are permitted). However, where allowed, prisoners should be made aware at the outset that birds are not allowed in every prison establishment and if transferred they may not be able to take their bird with them. It is important in such situations that prisoners understand why individual prisons might have different rules in place.

Education materials, food, consumables, cooking utensils and cell hobbies items are not exempt from volumetric control if held in possession.

A focus on compliance with volumetric control limits is important throughout a prisoner's time in custody. Consideration must be given to how much property a prisoner already has when permitting the purchase of any further items (e.g. from catalogues). Where a prisoner exceeds volumetric control limits, staff should consider writing to the prisoner to explain this and to set out how their property can be brought back within the limits. For handling of items which exceed volumetric control limits, see 'Sending in and handing out of property', 'Locally stored property' and 'National Distribution Centre (NDC) Branston'.

## Valuable property

A local system must be in place to distinguish between valuable and non-valuable property. This is important so that valuable items can be stored securely.

Prisoners should be encouraged to hand or send out valuable items. If they do not agree to this, it must be explained carefully to them that, in the event of loss or damage, they cannot expect compensation for the purported value where they are unable to prove the cost of purchase (see 'Complaints and compensation claims'). This is supported by the disclaimer that is signed by prisoners and staff on the property card which states that the prisoner has been advised not to have any valuable items in the prison.

The expectation is that valuable property will not be held in possession. However, some items permitted under the National Facilities List (see the Incentives Policy Framework) might be valuable and of sentimental importance. Where a prisoner wants to retain such items in possession, this should only be permitted where to do so would not be a risk to good order or discipline, security and safety and the items are in line with the National Facilities List. All other valuable property must be placed in a sealed bag or bags and held securely with the storage arrangements agreed locally. It is important that prisoners

747

understand what the local storage arrangements are, in order for them to trust that these operate effectively and their belongings are safe.

Where there is any doubt as to the possible monetary value of a piece of property, staff should be cautious and treat the item as valuable property. All valuable property must be described as seen and not in accordance with statements made by prisoners which cannot be verified. The correct recording of valuable property is important to be able to identify items when needed and for the handling of any complaints which might arise in the future.

All pieces of jewellery must be recorded as, for example, yellow or white metal rather than gold or silver.

House keys must be stored as valuable property. The following information should be obtained and recorded where possible: is the prisoner the tenant or owner; who is the landlord/mortgage company; is anyone else currently living in the property; and contact details of all interested parties. This is in case any concerns about the return of the keys are raised with the prison prior to the prisoner's release. The key/s only remain the property of the prisoner whilst they have a proprietary interest (i.e. he or she remains a tenant or owner). Once the property rights have been extinguished, the right to return the key/s is either extinguished or transferred to the new owner/tenant.

All prisoners' passports, or any other identifying documentation (e.g. ID cards or driving licences) must be stored as valuable property. Prisoners in the open estate might require frequent access to their driving licences or keys for work. These must still be stored securely. Passports or other forms of identification belonging to foreign national prisoners must be scanned and a copy sent to Home Office Immigration Enforcement (HOIE) with further copies kept in the offender's core record. Foreign national offenders should not be permitted to send to a third party any passports/ID cards/driving licences held other than to their own embassy, HOIE, or the police where surrender of the passport is a condition of bail.

### Items of sentimental value

Particular care must be taken by staff when handling items of sentimental value to a prisoner. Loss or damage to such items can have a particular impact on prisoners. Where a prisoner identifies an item is of sentimental value, and even if it is comparatively inexpensive, staff should advise that the item should be kept with valuable property rather than held in-possession.

### Unconvicted prisoners

The specific rights of unconvicted prisoners must be respected. These rights are set out in Annex B of PSO 4600 Unconvicted, Unsentenced and Civil Prisoners.

### Sending in and handing out of property

The arrangements on the sending in of property must be in line with the requirements set out in the Incentives policy framework, including the particular considerations around the sending in of books. It is important that prisoners understand the arrangements, and why these exist, in order to help them to co-operate with these and not cause undue frustration or confusion.

Under Prison Rule 44(4) the Governor has discretion as to what action will be taken with articles sent in by post to convicted prisoners. The same approach will apply to items sent in by other means (e.g. via courier). Prison Rule 44(4) gives Governors the discretion on whether such items shall be given to the prisoner, placed in their stored property at the prison or returned to the sender. Where the sender's name and address are not known, or the article is of such a nature that it would be unreasonable to return it, the article can be sold or otherwise disposed of and any proceeds paid to NACRO. However, where the prisoner has been committed to prison in default of payment of a sum of money, the money shall be used to pay towards that sum unless the prisoner objects. See PSI 01/2012 Manage Prisoner Finance for the handling of money sent in by post. See PSI 49/2011 Prisoner Communication Services for the handling of correspondence sent to a prisoner.

It is important that an audit trail is maintained for the handling of any property sent into the prison, including where items have been sent in without permission, to avoid subsequent claims for loss. This audit trail must include where parcels are returned to the sender or forwarded to a subsequent prison.

Prisoners must be allowed to hand out and reduce both in-possession and stored property through social visits or through other opportunities, subject to existing rules on frequency of access to property held at NDC Branston (see 'National Distribution Centre (NDC), Branston'). This does not apply to items which are unsuitable for handing or sending out (e.g. extremist materials or other permanently confiscated items which have been identified for destruction). See 'Confiscation and disposal of property'.

Opportunities must be given to facilitate prisoners handing or sending out valuable property safely and securely.

Prisoners who are in the process of being transferred, and who hold excess property, must be allowed and encouraged to hand out excess items.

## Property on transfer between prisons

The transfer of property between prisons can be a common source of difficulty, and loss or damage of items can lead to frustration, anxiety, resentment and a loss of trust in staff and the Prison Service. It is also the cause of many complaints that staff then need to handle. The more effectively we can handle property generally, and during transfer, the more likely we can avoid these outcomes.

Only property which falls within volumetric control limits, and items which are permitted as volumetric control exemptions (see 'Volumetric control') will be transported with a prisoner when they transfer establishments or attend court. It is therefore very important that these limits are respected. See 'Transferring property outside volumetric control limits' for the handling of excess property.

When a prisoner moves to another prison, all their property cards must be sent on to the new establishment with them.

Property for transfer must be placed in a property bag secured with a security seal unique to the establishment and bearing a unique number. Each bag must not weigh more than 15kg.

On arrival at the receiving establishment, all property bag seals must be checked against the Person Escort Record. See The Person Escort Record (PER) Policy Framework.

On occasion, prisoners will arrive on transfer from another establishment with items such as a large stereo which are not permitted in the receiving establishment's facility list but were permitted at the previous establishment. Governors must consider these items on a case-by-case basis and decide whether or not they should be allowed. Unless the item is considered a risk to good order, discipline, security, safety and/or exceed volumetric control limits, the expectation will be that the prisoner should be allowed to retain it in possession. This is in recognition that the prisoner may have spent money and been permitted the item previously. However, the fact that an item was allowed on this basis does not give the prisoner any right to replace it 'like for like'. Any replacement must comply with the local facility list. If an item was previously allowed, but is not by the receiving prison, it is important that the reason(s) for this difference are explained to the prisoner. Without understanding the reasons, differences in practice can be frustrating and seem arbitrary to prisoners, which can compromise respect for staff and the legitimacy of decisions.

Where a prisoner has exceptionally large amounts of property, but which are still within volumetric control levels (e.g. significant boxes of legal papers), the prison must inform the Prisoner Escort Contractor Service (PECS) contractor using the free text comments section of the transfer request when requesting the move. The PECS contractor can use this information when considering their choice of vehicle and, where possible, utilise a larger vehicle than normal. This option is not available where property is outside of volumetric control limits.

Prisoners must retain access to, and not be deprived of, essential disability aids/reasonable adjustments. Arrangements must be made as early as possible to ensure continuity. Where the items are the property of NHS or local authority services, these services should be consulted on how continuity should be achieved, and prisoners must not be deprived of such essential items at any stage. Considerations of ownership are secondary to ensuring a prisoner has the disability aids they need at all times. See PSI 03/2016 Adult Social Care for further information about transfer and discharge arrangements for those in receipt of care and support or may require care and support on transfer or discharge.

Transgender prisoners must retain access to, and not be deprived of, items necessary to their gender expression. Prior to transfer, a copy of any Voluntary Agreement in place that details access to such items should be provided to the receiving prison in order that arrangements can be made to ensure continuity of access upon transfer.

## Transferring property outside volumetric control limits

The discharging prison must be responsible for ensuring that any property which PECS is contractually unable to take (i.e. property which is above volumetric control limits) is forwarded to the receiving establishment within four weeks of transfer unless exceptional circumstances prevent this.

The discharging prison must maintain a record of the excess property which is sent on.

The record will state the date sent, the method of transport and the property bag seal numbers.

The cost of transferring such property must be met by the discharging prison and not passed on to the prisoner.

The discharging prison must notify the receiving prison when the excess property is to be sent. If a delivery is expected, there are less likely to be issues around handling.

The receiving prison cannot refuse to accept the excess property which is sent on. The prisoner must be encouraged to send or hand out any excess items. If there is a lack of local storage, consideration should be given by the receiving prison to sending the items to NDC Branston. NDC Branston cannot, however, provide any assistance in moving on excess property between establishments.

### Discharge

With the exception of some brief temporary absences, all prisoners' in-possession property, valuables and locally stored property must accompany them (subject to volumetric control levels) when they are discharged. This includes for relevant court appearances.

Property for prisoners being discharged must be handled in line with PSI 72/2011 Discharge.

Any excess property must be:

• Kept securely at the prison in case the prisoner returns (e.g. if they return from court the same day); or

• In the event that the prisoner is not discharged from court and is returned from court to a different prison, forwarded to the prisoner's receiving establishment in line with the requirements set out under 'Property on transfer between prisons' above; or

• If the prisoner is discharged from court, retained at the establishment for a period of 12 months, unless claimed earlier by the prisoner, at which point it may be disposed of (see 'Confiscation and disposal of property').

At the end of their custodial term, prisoners must be asked to sign a disclaimer form to confirm that they are aware that any property which is left behind will be kept only for a period of 12 months before being disposed of or sold. The expectation is that prisoners will not leave any property behind. However, where this happens and the property remains unclaimed after 12 months, it may be disposed of. The disclaimer form must be kept with the prisoner's property card as it provides documentary evidence should there be a subsequent compensation claim. A sample form is at Annex D, which may be used for this purpose. When signing the discharge disclaimer form, prisoners should be encouraged to state whether they wish for item(s) of their property which they no longer require to be sold or destroyed.

Prior to a prisoner's planned discharge, staff must check if any property is held at NDC Branston. If any property is left stored at NDC Branston because the prisoner does not wish to retain it on discharge, the establishment must inform NDC Branston of the disposal date within a month of the prisoner's release. This is so that NDC Branston can arrange for disposal 12 months after the prisoner has left custody. See 'National Distribution Centre (NDC) Branston'.

All property accompanying prisoners leaving the prison for any reason, including for court appearances or transfer to another establishment, must be checked against the property record cards and discrepancies recorded. Clear and accurate recording practices will help to avoid potential future complaints and litigation, as well as demonstrating our professional standards.

Staff should discuss with prisoners whether the return of house keys is appropriate. For example, whether the prisoner is still the owner/tenant of the property. If the prisoner remains the owner/tenant, staff should only refuse to return keys if they have received evidence that they will be used for criminality and have discussed with the police.

### Foreign National Offender discharges

Where a foreign national offender is approaching their Early Removal Scheme Eligibility Date and HOIE has not indicated that they have no further interest in the offender, any stored property held at Branston should be retrieved. This will enable property to be available should the prisoner be removed at short notice. Once removal directions have been set, the prisoner should be advised of the airline's luggage weight limit and encouraged to dispose of any excess baggage. If removal does not take place, the property can continue to be stored. Property will also need to be retrieved from Branston for prisoners who are to be removed under other schemes. 'Confiscation and disposal of property' sets out the handling of property which is left behind by any prisoner.

### Locally stored property

Storing excess property at a location within the prison must be an exceptional or temporary measure and will occur only when Governors are satisfied that excess property cannot otherwise be handed out. Stored property must be kept in bags secured by the establishment's own unique property seals. It is important that prisoners understand how and why decisions on whether to allow storage of property are reached, in line with procedural justice principles.

Excess property of prisoners with less than six months remaining before discharge, and those held solely under immigration powers, must be held locally.

Any discharge clothing belonging to a prisoner must be stored locally.

### National Distribution Centre (NDC), Branston

Property which is not held in-possession, handed out or cannot be stored locally will be stored at NDC Branston. This must only occur in exceptional circumstances, since prisoners should not exceed volumetric control limits and, where they do exceed these limits, local storage must be utilised first. NDC Branston will not store unattributable property.

From the date of implementation of this policy, prisons are not permitted to send property to Branston if it will result in a prisoner having more than three boxes stored there in total. An outsize item will be regarded as the equivalent of one box. This limit should only ever be exceeded where staff have very thoroughly explored all other options with the prisoner and consider that the circumstances are so exceptional as to require additional boxes to be sent for storage.

The following procedure must be followed when excess property is sent to NDC Branston:

• Property must be bagged, sealed and packed into the storage boxes (item 1626), which have a weight limit of 15kg;

• The correct seals, which have a 7-digit serial number, must be used;

• Outsize items must be packaged, sealed and clearly labelled;

• The prisoner's anticipated release date must be included to give NDC Branston an indication of when property might become eligible for disposal if it remains unclaimed 12 months following the prisoner's release. However, where property remains at Branston following a prisoner's release, it remains the responsibility of the Governor to notify NDC Branston of the disposal date for that property within 28 days of the prisoner's release (see 'Discharge').

• Property cards updated (see 'Recording of information')

The following restrictions on items sent to NDC Branston apply:

• Only clothing which is freshly laundered may be included;

• No items subject to chemical degradation or bacteriological growth may be included.

• Batteries must not be included.

• Other than in exceptional circumstances agreed by the Governor, property cannot be accessed within 12 months of being placed into storage.

• Legal papers must not be included. These must be held locally.

Property stored locally for a period of 28 days after a prisoner has escaped or absconded and who has not returned to custody may be sent to the NDC for long term storage. This property must be designated for disposal for 12 months from the date of escape or abscond.

When recalling property, form S&T 445 must be used. If, exceptionally, urgent delivery is required, the establishment must contact the Logistics Office Team at NDC Branston to arrange delivery, using carriers where necessary. Property belonging to a prisoner who has been discharged will only be sent by NDC Branston to their last establishment for collection, and will not be delivered directly to any private address. All requests for retrieval of property must

therefore come from an establishment. As part of discharge checks, prisoners should be asked if they have property at Branston so that it can be returned to the prison in good time.

Property sent to NDC Branston is held there on behalf of the Governor of the prisoner's current establishment. If a prisoner is transferred, custody of the property moves to the Governor of the new prison.

Staff at NDC Branston will not open property, and investigation of any complaints relating to loss or damage, and any compensation claims, comes under the responsibility of the establishment recalling the property.

## Accommodation / cell clearance

Accommodation clearance can present particular issues in the handling of prisoners' property. It is therefore important that significant care is taken. The more that prisoners can be safely involved in this process, the faster accommodation can be secured and then vacated, and accurate records maintained, the more effectively this process will work. Seeing that their property is handled appropriately and with care is more likely to help prisoners see the process is fair.

Where a prisoner is made aware of an arranged move, they should be given sufficient time to pack their own possessions where possible.

Where it is not possible for a prisoner to pack their possessions, and the accommodation is single occupancy, the accommodation must be secured as soon as it is vacated. Securing shared living accommodation immediately can be more complex. Wherever possible, this should happen, but in any case as soon as possible.

Property in situ must be checked against the prisoner's property card and recorded on the Cell Clearance Certificate (F2056J) by two members of staff as soon as possible. Local versions of cell clearance certificates should not be used. A note must be made of any damaged items or of any items that become damaged during the clearance. The Cell Clearance Certificate must be kept with the relevant property card.

In shared accommodation the remaining prisoner must normally be present to identify their property. If the prisoner is briefly unavailable, consideration should be given to waiting until they can be present and the accommodation secured until that time.

Any discrepancies between items listed on the Cell Clearance Certificate and on the prisoner's property card must be recorded and investigated. Other than perishable items, the property must be placed in property bags and sealed.

If a prisoner later returns to the establishment, or to normal accommodation within it, the property bags must be unsealed in the prisoner's presence and the prisoner asked to check the contents. Any discrepancies must be recorded and investigated. This also applies when the prisoner is moved to another establishment.

If the cell clearance is due to a prisoner's escape or death, any items which may be relevant to the investigation must first be drawn to the attention of the appropriate authority. Following a death in custody, and pending the arrival of police, the cell must be sealed and all property must be preserved in situ as evidence and not removed or bagged until the police give permission.

Any property retained by the police as evidence needs to be recorded and the executor or next of kin informed. The handling of deceased prisoners' property is covered in PSI 64/2011: Management of Prisoners at Risk of Harm to Self, to Others and from Others.

**Confiscation and disposal of property**

The Governor is authorised to permanently confiscate the following items and to subsequently arrange for safe and proper destruction where:

• possession of the item would itself give rise to a criminal offence (for example, holding controlled drugs or psychoactive substances and items that can be linked to the trafficking and or misuse of drugs); or

• the item is inherently dangerous (such as a primed explosive device, for example), and could not, therefore be safely stored; or

• the storage of the item would present a proven health hazard.

In any of these events, an explanation needs to be given to the prisoner, explaining how that item comes under one of these three categories. Staff must also be mindful of any issues around prisoner debt/safety which might exist where a prisoner has been in possession of particular items. More widely, Section 42(A) of the Prison Act 1952 provides details of the items that Governors have the power to destroy or otherwise dispose of. This is where:

• An article is found in the possession of a prisoner who is not authorised to have it in their possession; or

• An article found inside the prison or in a prisoner escort vehicle where the owner of the article is a prisoner who is not authorised to have it in possession or the owner cannot be ascertained.

See Annex E for a process map and definitions for information on which property can be disposed of.

Where Governors decide to dispose of unauthorised or unattributable property which was found or confiscated after 26 March 2015, such property must be retained at the prison for a minimum of three months after it is found

before being disposed of. During this time, a prisoner must be able to make representations about how the property is dealt with and be made aware of the intended date of disposal. The exception to this three-month rule is where continued storage would present a proven health hazard or possession would otherwise give rise to a criminal offence or the item is inherently dangerous. Items must not be destroyed or disposed of while there is an outstanding dispute about how they will be dealt with (e.g. if the matter is still being considered via the complaints system). Staff should establish with the prisoner that the matter has not been referred to the PPO and the property not disposed of until any PPO investigation has concluded. A record of the items must be kept but the items must only be added to a prisoner's property card when any dispute about ownership has been resolved in the prisoner's favour.

Relevant items (see Annex E for definitions) confiscated before 26 March 2015 may be destroyed immediately.

Under Prison Rule 43 (4) and YOI Rule 48 (3), any unclaimed property belonging to a prisoner who is no longer in custody must be held for a period of 12 months after their permanent release, abscond, escape or death. If the property remains unclaimed after 12 months, it may be disposed of. Disposal within the 12 months is permissible where continued storage of an item would present a proven health hazard or possession would otherwise give rise to a criminal offence or the item is inherently dangerous.

Further to the requirements under 'Accommodation/cell clearance', all property (including valuables) belonging to a prisoner who dies in custody should be offered to their next of kin, unless there is a potential dispute as to who is entitled to this, in which case advice should be sought from the Coroner. Property belonging to prisoners with no identifiable next of kin must be kept at the prison and staff must take reasonable steps to try and trace any next of kin. All property should be disposed of or sold that is not claimed by a prisoner's next of kin after 12 months of their death or by prisoners after 12 months of their custodial term ending.

Items sent to a convicted prisoner, where the sender is unknown, can be sold or otherwise disposed of in line with paragraph 4.33 above.

The net proceeds of any sale of unauthorised or unattributable property, or any other items which are sold in line with the requirements above, must be donated to NACRO.

Where any items are disposed of, records must be maintained to provide details of the items, where they were found and the date and reasons for disposal.

## Gifting between prisoners

Prisoners must only be permitted to transfer in-possession property to the ownership of other prisoners if the Governor is satisfied that such transfers are voluntary and for acceptable reasons (e.g. not the result of bullying, prisoner debt or in exchange for illicit items) and that they will not undermine the incentives scheme or good order or discipline. Where approval is given to the transfer of an item of property, details must be recorded clearly on the relevant property cards. Any local arrangements for transferring property must be explained clearly to prisoners.

## Complaints and compensation claims

All complaints must be investigated in accordance with the Prisoner Complaints Policy Framework and the Finance Manual. NDC Branston will not investigate or process complaints, but will assist an establishment's investigating officer by providing responses to relevant specific enquiries.

Governors must ensure that property complaints and disputes are investigated thoroughly and efficiently, with prisoners being offered appropriate compensation where items have been lost or damaged. All efforts should be made to resolve issues through the various stages of the complaints process, including the PPO, and avoid unnecessary future spending on a litigation claim. The principles of procedural justice (see 'Guidance' for more information) are applicable here in how decisions/outcomes of the investigation are communicated and explained to the prisoner.

Where prisoners have transferred, establishments must liaise with each other to ensure such complaints are investigated and answered efficiently and promptly without placing unnecessary burdens on a prisoner who has transferred.

In cases where the establishment is responsible for the loss or damage to the prisoner's property, the prisoner must be fairly reimbursed and an apology given. The fact that prisoners sign a disclaimer that they hold property at their own risk cannot excuse the prison from paying compensation if the prison was clearly at fault. A common example of this relates to loss or damage to personal clothing during the laundry process. It is not reasonable to expect the prisoner to bear any loss or damage if they have handed it over to be washed in the prison laundry. Any compensation paid must come from the prison responsible for the loss or damage, rather than automatically from the prison in which the complaint is made.

Where a reimbursement or local compensation awards are being considered for lost or damaged items, prisoners should be asked to produce evidence of the item's value (e.g. a receipt). Where this is not possible, governors should compare the cost of replacing the item(s) from suppliers that are available to prisoners. If there are no such suppliers, online searches of high street retailers may be used. In either case, adjustments should be made for age/wear and tear but the offer needs to be fair.

Staff must use appropriate judgment on compensation for branded and/or valuable items. For example, it is less reasonable to expect a prisoner to be able to provide proof of purchase for typical brands of sportswear items and which they might have possessed for some time. In such cases, it would be appropriate to compensate on the assumption that the item is genuine. However, for more expensive items (e.g. designer tops, luxury brand watches) it is much more reasonable to expect that a prisoner will have retained, and will be able to provide, proof of purchase or information on the authenticity of the item. Where a prisoner is unable to do so for such items, compensation should be provided for the cost of a standard equivalent replacement (e.g. a standard watch or top) from a supplier that is available to prisoners.

Compensation for lost or damaged items must be credited to the prisoner's 'Private Cash' account. If replacement goods are to be purchased, the debit transaction can also be made from this account. This is permitted under the 'exceptional circumstances' outlined in PSI 01/2012 Manage Prisoner Finance and exceeds the limits set for prisoner spending laid out under the Incentives scheme.

## Managing locally stored property

It is advisable for staff to make regular checks through property which is stored locally at the prison. In handling such property, it can be helpful where possible to group items appropriately (e.g. clearly identify items which will be for disposal if unclaimed 12 months after the prisoner has been released). Regular checks will then ensure excessive amounts of property do not build up.

## EDUCATION

The subject of Education in prison is covered by Prison Education & Library Services for adult prisons in England Policy Framework, issued April 2019 (see section 7.4); PSI 04/2012 (Enablers of Services) & 06/2012 (Prisoner Employment, Training and Skills). Education is covered more fully in chapter 2.20.

## WORK & PAY

Work. PR 31

Unconvicted prisoners do not have to work (Prison Rule 31(5)) or attend education inside prison but may do so if they wish. Work is not always available for unconvicted prisoners. If no work is available they will receive a small amount of money each week to cover basics such as toiletries, etc. If they are given the opportunity to work they may earn a little more money, but if they are offered work and refuse it they will not receive any money at all, and the prison does not have to offer them further work. They will also be able to use their private cash unless this privilege is withdrawn as a punishment by the Governor. For more details see *Chapter 2.21, Work and Pay*.

## LIBRARY

*Background*

The subject of Library provision in prison is covered by Prison Education & Library Services for adult prisons in England Policy Framework, issued April 2019 (see section 7.4); see also PSI 02-2015 on the prison library services.

*Legal Requirements*

The Prison Rules 1999, and Young Offender Institution Rules 20009, as amended, place on the Secretary of State the responsibility for ensuring that each Prison Service Establishment has a library, and that, subject to any directions of the Secretary of State, the prisoners of those establishments have facilities to use and exchange books.

Governors must ensure as a minimum that a prisoner's statutory entitlement to library provision is met.

Article 6 of the European Convention on Human Rights includes the requirement that individuals must be afforded enough time and facilities to prepare their defence.

The Prison Rules (1999) state:

**(33). A library shall be provided in every prison and, subject to any directions of the Secretary of State, every prisoner shall be allowed to have library books and to exchange them**

*Mandatory Publications*

The following publications must be made available in prison libraries:

• Archbold's Criminal Pleading, Evidence and Practice

• The Civil Procedure Rules

• Extant Prison Service Instructions (PSIs) and Prison Service Orders (PSOs), Policy Frameworks (when published) excluding those that have restrictions placed on them.

Libraries in prisons in England and Wales may be by a range of suppliers including the local Public Library Authority (PLA); or directly by the establishment; or through other

appropriate arrangements in agreement with the Prison Governor.

Regional Library Budgets are devolved to regional or cluster Heads of Learning, Skills and Employment, who discuss and agree individual establishments' allocations with library provider managers; then ensure that this information is communicated to the Governor's Finance representative.

Part of the purpose of a prison library is to support prisoner resettlement, rehabilitation and purposeful activity. A focus on improving literacy and other barriers to effective resettlement assists prisoners in making the transition from custody to community.

*Governors must ensure as a minimum that a prisoner's statutory entitlement to library provision is met. Access to the library must be weekly, for a minimum duration of thirty minutes. Local arrangements will dictate what will be the most appropriate times for access to libraries. Prison establishments and library service providers must ensure that these arrangements are reflected in the Service Level Agreements.*

### Library Access and Environment

In line with Prison Rules, all prisoners must be allowed access to library books and other appropriate materials. The frequency of access will be tailored to establishment need. Library visits will be enabled in line with the specification set out in the SLA. Access through out-reach services to materials for more vulnerable prisoners and those less able to access the main library must be provided where possible.

Governors must ensure as a minimum that a prisoner's statutory entitlement to library provision is met. **Access to the library service must be weekly, and where the prisoner is able to attend the library, the visit should be for a minimum duration of thirty minutes.** Accessibility may be more frequent and for longer duration for prisoners wishing to research legal issues or in support of education requirements.

*Article 6 of the European Convention on Human Rights includes the requirement that individuals must be afforded enough time and facilities to prepare their defence (further guidance is attached with the Mandatory Publications List at Annex D).* While this does not place a requirement on all prison libraries to stock all legal resources which a prisoner might need, it is important to ensure that prisoners have reasonable access to legal publications.

*Prison libraries must stock Archbold's Criminal Pleading, Evidence and Practice: The Civil Procedure Rules: extant Prison Service Instructions (PSIs) and Prison Service Orders (PSOs), excluding those that have a restrictions placed on them. It will also not* necessarily be the case that the library is the only facility in which a prisoner could prepare a case but where it is, or it is the most convenient place to do so, consideration must be given to affording visits on a more frequent basis or of a longer duration. Smaller prison libraries may seek assistance from Newbold Revel and Ministry of Justice Libraries if they have difficulties in accessing Archbold's Criminal Pleading, Evidence and Practice or The Civil Procedure Rules.

*Prisoners unable to access the library must be offered the same level and duration of access to mandatory and non-mandatory legal publications, or the appropriate printed copies, as those who are able to access the prison library, via an out-reach service or other appropriate means.*

*The Library must be located in a suitable space that allows prisoners to browse the stock easily, and to access and use (for example, read and make notes from) reference materials. A wing-based or out-reach service should be provided as an alternative to or in support of the main library provision.*

All staff should encourage prisoners to use the library facilities, and help raise awareness of the services provided in the library area.

Where prisoners are unable to access the library, an alternative service should be provided that allows them to both exchange, borrow and order material at least as often as if they were able to visit the library. This should include an out-reach service where possible.

Stock should be available on some units, such as the First Night Centre, Induction Unit and Health Care Centre, where possible.

Governors may restrict an individual's access to some material on a case-by-case basis in accordance with the Public Protection Manual, for example where this is necessary in light of the prisoner's offence or offending behaviour work. *Librarians must ensure they comply with any such rulings and have an informed approach to provision of and requests for materials from the library.* Where there is doubt a senior manager in the prison should be consulted and agreement reached and recorded. The final decision will lie with the Governor.

*Prisoners are not allowed to possess or view DVDs or computer games with an 18-rated certificate within any prison. All '18' rated (or equivalent) and unrated DVDs and computer games must be removed from prison libraries and should no longer be purchased or stocked by prison libraries.*

Governors will have the final authority to decide whether material should be made available in the library or to an individual.

Decisions to proscribe materials, in compliance with the Public Protection Manual need to be linked with the management of offending behaviour or maintaining good order and discipline. All decisions on public safety, good order and offending behaviour are matters for prison staff and ultimately the Governor. Such decisions should not be made by prison library provider staff.

### Staffing

Library service providers will ensure the provision of appropriate staff. In addition, the establishment will ensure staffing levels to enable prisoner access to the library service and Prisoner Library Assistants (selected from the prisoner population) to support the library service.

Library staff and Prisoner Library Assistants should encourage and help individuals to derive the maximum benefit from the resources available in the library.

*Prisoner Library Assistants must be selected in line with usual allocation to activity procedures. They must be properly trained in their duties, supervised and, where possible, given the opportunity to gain appropriate accredited qualifications. Library service managers will arrange and supervise the training of Prisoner Library Assistants in co-operation with prison staff.*

*Governors must ensure, working with library service providers where necessary, that library staff receive appropriate training, support and guidance; that they are integrated into the prison team and are able to contribute towards quality assurance.*

*Governors must ensure that library staff are made aware of and appropriately trained in all security processes, in particular those where a breach may lead to exclusion. Where a breach occurs and a member of library staff is excluded, Governors must ensure that the reasons for the exclusion are recorded in writing and explained to the service provider; and that appropriate procedures are followed to ensure fairness in seeking a resolution.*

### Stock

The range of stock should reflect the nature and requirements of the prisoner population and the prison regime. Consideration should be given to the provision of materials in a range of languages and print sizes; and to the appropriateness of audio or visual material.

*DVDs and computer games classified as 18-rated are not permitted in Prison Libraries. Any which are currently available should be removed and no further purchases should be made of DVDs and computer games of this rating.*

*A list of publications that libraries must provide access to is given at Annex D (The Mandatory Publication List). These must be kept as reference stock. Where Governors can demonstrate that an item will be required by prisoners only rarely and may not need to be kept in stock, it must be quickly accessible should a prisoner request it. A list of supplementary publications which may be of use to prisoners pursuing legal* cases is also suggested. These do not need to be kept in stock but libraries may find it useful so to do as they may be frequently requested by prisoners. *Requests for material by inter-library loan which prisoners require to pursue legal cases should be prioritised.* Materials may also be printed from the internet by an appropriate member of staff.

*Governors must ensure that all prisoners can access materials on the Mandatory Publication List. Access to mandatory materials for more vulnerable prisoners and those less able to access the main library must be enabled in agreement and consultation with prison staff.*

*Both the establishment and the library service provider must agree on and enforce methods to minimise stock loss and damage.*

## PRISON SHOP AND PRIVATE CASH

PSI 23/2013 - updated 27th January 2020.

This PSI contains guidelines for prisons on setting up and managing a retail service for prisoners to order essential goods. It describes how the products should be chosen to meet the diverse needs of the local population, be priced fairly, and managed securely.

It covers:

• selecting products from the national product list
• maintaining security
• day-to-day running of the retail service
• running retail workshops for packing and distribution of orders
• supply and delivery of orders

This is a current PSI. It came into effect on 1 August 2013 and was last updated on 27 January 2020 when references to IEP have been changed to incentives policy framework which came into force on 13th January 2020. Policy change is at 2.16 to allow selling prices of retail products to prisoners to be changed at any time, not just quarterly as was previously stated.

*Desired outcomes*

This instruction aims to ensure that:

• Prisoners are able to spend their earnings and private cash which has been transferred into their spends account to purchase items for their own use.
• Prisoners are able to purchase items at prices not higher than recommended retail prices (rrp).
• Prison security and individual health and safety are not compromised by the ordering and delivery process.
• Good order and discipline is supported by prisoner access to items in accordance with the local incentives and earned privileges scheme.
• Items available for purchase by prisoners support decency and reflect the diverse needs and protected characteristics of the prisoner population.
• Products, prices, and operational procedures are standardised.
• Provision of retail goods to prisoners is accurate and timely.

• Purposeful activity is provided for prisoners with opportunities for them to acquire skills for resettlement.

*Prison Shop*

The prison has a small shop (sometimes called a canteen) which prisoners can sometimes visit although in many prisons shop purchases are done on a pre-order and bagging system delivered to the prisoners' cell once a week.

Prisoners' earnings can be spent in the shop on vaping requisites (in those 18+ establishments where vaping is permitted), sweets, biscuits, toiletries, batteries, stationary.

A prisoners' own money which was brought with them into prison, or which has been sent in by relatives and friends (known as 'private cash'), can be used to buy certain items. The items which convicted prisoners can purchase from private cash are restricted, and it is worth checking with the 'Facilities List', which must be reviewed annually, as to which items may be purchased from private cash.

Access to private cash is governed by the Incentives and Earned Privileges Scheme (see *Chapter 2.22*).

**How the system works**

HMPPS has a National Product List (NPL) which lists all the products prisoners can buy. The NPL (a copy of the 2021 list for information purposes is at *www.prisons.org.uk/NPLJuly2021.xlsx*). Note that the NPL has a maximum of 1,000 items on it which are reviewed quarterly - mostly it is the prices which change rather than the items. The NPL also sets a limit on the quantity of any product which an individual prisoner can buy in a single order - just because an item is on the list doesn't mean that a prisoner can purchase it through the canteen, canteen stock is a matter for each establishment to set in a Local Product List (LPL), but a canteen cannot stock any item not on the NPL.

In selecting items for their LPL governors should consult with prisoner representatives, consider equal opportunity impact, reports from the Prisons Inspectorate and consult with Chaplaincy, Healthcare and the IMB. Chilled products can only be included where chilled storage is available.

**Prisoner Ordering**

Prisoners must be issued with a retail order form in advance of the agreed collection date for the completed forms. The forms are provided by the contractor, and show the local selection made by the establishment from the NPL. Prisoner details including name, prison number, cell location, and available spends, must be printed onto the form using PNOMIS prior to issue.

Prisoners subject to disciplinary awards which

restrict retail spending must not be able to purchase items in excess of the prescribed limits. The establishment must manage this, to prevent orders containing items which have been denied being forwarded to the retail workshop.

Versions of local forms can be provided electronically on request to the agreed contractor in the alternative languages of Arabic, French, German, Spanish, Punjabi and Welsh.

Governors must have in operation local arrangements to ensure that prisoners with special needs are not disadvantaged, and are able to place orders.

Completed forms should be collated by the establishment, and left at the agreed point and time for the contractor to collect. The contractor will arrange the delivery of these to the retail workshop.

If an automated kiosk system be available for prisoners to use, then this may take the place of order forms subject to the required data being provided in an acceptable electronic format to the contractor.

*Blind Picking*

The picking process is carried out by prisoners in the workshops. In order to ensure that the person carrying out the picking does not know who any order is for, an anonymous pick slip is used, which has product details on it only. Full details of the process can be found in the Retail Operations Manual.

*Delivery of Packed Orders*

The packed orders will arrive at the serviced establishment from the designated retail workshop, to the schedule as agreed in the retail MOU. If goods are not to be immediately distributed to prisoners, then secure storage must be arranged, including suitable chilled or frozen storage facilities if applicable.

*Distribution to Prisoners*

Packed orders can be distributed to prisoners by either contractor or prison service staff, depending on local arrangement.

Products are distributed to prisoners either through a central serving point with prisoners called forward in manageable groups, or direct to their cells. The method used is decided upon according to the preference of the establishment, and set out in the retail MOU.

A system must be in place to ensure that the prisoner identity is verified and the packed order is handed to the correct prisoner. Prisoners may not collect bags on behalf of other prisoners. Prison Service staff may sign and take responsibility for orders where prisoners are not present at the time of distribution. They must check that the contents are correct before doing this.

*Receipt of purchased items by prisoners is recorded.*

Irrespective of the approach to distribution, prisoners must be given a reasonable opportunity to inspect the products being sold to them before acceptance. Prisoners may reject products according to their statutory rights. Proof of acceptance must be gained from the prisoner and the prisoner issued with a receipt clearly itemising the products that have been sold to them, the unit price paid, and the total amount charged to them. If goods are rejected, then a credit note must be given.

*Prisoners receive items they have ordered safely.*

The governor must ensure that prisoners are supervised appropriately at all times by Prison staff during the distribution of retail orders, to ensure that prisoners receive items safely and bullying is not taking place at point of service. They should also ensure that the integrity of picked and packed products is not compromised prior to acceptance.

Prisoners only purchase items for which they have funds to pay or where an advance is approved.

Goods will only be provided up to the spends value as printed on the prisoner order form. If more items have been ordered than can be afforded, then the products will be supplied in the priority order as set out by the order form. Items at the top of the list will be supplied first, working down until no further funds are available. The total amount spent by each prisoner, proof of acceptance, and copies of any credits given must be provided to the establishment in order to update the prisoner's spending account.

## ASSOCIATION AND EXERCISE

PSI 75/2011 - Residential Services

This PSI details the facilities, services and support that prisons should provide to prisoners as part of their daily routine, including:

• cell furnishings, fittings and equipment
• clothing, bedding and footwear
• toiletries, bathrooms and laundry
• time outside
• meal times
• social care, including building positive staff-prisoner relationships and good behaviour
• care for prisoners at risk of suicide and self-harm
• access to computer facilities for legal reasons

It also details specific support for prisoners with disabilities, elderly prisoners, ethnic minority prisoners and other specific groups.

This is a current PSI. It came into effect on 1 January 2012 and was last updated on 27 January 2020 when references to IEP were changed to the Incentives Policy Framework (IPF), which came into force on 13 January 2020.

Consideration needs to be given by prisons to what extent the additional requirement identified for the care and support of individual prisoners impacts on the delivery of Residential Services.

Prisoners are entitled to a minimum of 30 minutes in the open air daily, as defined in the SLA/Contract.

This provision is mandatory, subject to weather conditions and the need to maintain good order and discipline. Cancellations must be recorded by the authorised manager, as nominated by the Governor. "Time in the open air" means time spent in a situation where the prisoner is able to benefit from fresh air and natural light.

Time spent outdoors as part of a formal activity, for example outdoor work or watching or participating in sport, counts as meeting this requirement.

The time in the open air does not have to be spent in a single period, but must be in no more than two periods, which can include time in the open air moving between activities.

While it will often be difficult to provide time in the open air for prisoners attending court, Governors ought to consider making arrangements for prisoners who are at court on two or more consecutive days to get some time in the open air.

The previous mandatory requirement for prisoners on restricted regimes to have 60 minutes in the open air has been withdrawn. However, Governors will be required by their SLA/Contract to continue to provide a minimum of 60 minutes activity for such prisoners, of which at least 30 minutes must be in the open air.

### CLOTHING
#### Incentives Policy Framework July 2020
*Prisoners' opportunities to Wear Their Own Clothes*
All unconvicted, civil and foreign national prisoners held under immigration powers (IS91) must be allowed to wear their own clothes (5.46).
All convicted prisoners, including prisoners in the women's estate, must wear prison-issue clothing, as the default position, in line with the Prison Rules. However, Governors have the authority to make provision in their local incentives policy for such prisoners to wear their own clothes and can choose to include the opportunity for convicted prisoners to wear their own clothes at any incentive level, including Basic (5.47).
When deciding at which levels convicted prisoners can wear their own clothes, Governors must consider locally how to remove or minimise disadvantages suffered by people with protected characteristics, taking steps to meet any differential needs.
The Care and Management of Individuals who are Transgender Policy Framework and PSI 05/2016 Faith and Pastoral Care for Prisoners set out guidance on clothing for transgender prisoners

and those from particular faith groups. (5.48)
Certain items of clothing are NOT permitted:
• Uniform/Military style clothing
• Studded clothing
• Steel toe capped footwear (other than those issued by the prison for work or for working outside purposes)
• Team shirts, i.e. Football, Rugby, Hockey, Basketball shirts unless allowed on working out schemes
• Any clothing that is deemed to be; obscene, offensive, racist, abusive, homophobic, sexist or has inappropriate slogans or motifs
• Clothing that may lead the wearer to be mistaken for a member of staff
• Clothing that is in a poor state of repair, or has been designed to look as such.

### UNCONVICTED PRISONERS
*Property:* PSI 12/201 which referred to unconvicted prisoners' property was cancelled with effect from 5th September 2022 and replaced by the Prisoners' Property Policy Framework.
*General:* As a result of their special status, unconvicted prisoners have a number of special rights and privileges (details of which are set out in PSO 4600 Annex B).
Governors may not prevent unconvicted prisoners from having supplied to them at their own expense and for retention in possession books, newspapers, writing materials and other means of occupation, except any that appear objectionable to the IMB or, pending consideration by them, to the Governor (Prison Rule 43(1) refers).
Unconvicted prisoners are also entitled to wear clothing of their own so far as it is suitable, tidy and clean, and shall be permitted to arrange for the supply to them from outside prison of sufficient clean clothing.
It may therefore be reasonable to refuse to deliver additional clothing to an unconvicted prisoner if this results in other suitable clothing being placed in storage as this may indicate that the additional clothing is over and above what is "sufficient".
Prisoners are allowed to receive and/or exchange property through social visits…Prison Rule 23 provides for unconvicted prisoners to have sufficient clean clothing sent in to them from outside the prison (whether through visits, by post or other means).
However, in accordance with volumetric control limits and the need to reduce the amount of excess property within the system it may be reasonable to refuse to deliver to an unconvicted prisoner additional clothing if this results in other suitable clothing being placed in storage as this may indicate that the additional clothing is over and above what is "sufficient".

*Special Rights and Privileges*

As a consequence of their special status, unconvicted prisoners have a number of special rights and privileges.

*Mandatory Requirement:*

Governors must ensure that, as far as possible, unconvicted prisoners are accorded the following rights and privileges.

In brief, unconvicted prisoners are entitled to:

• Have supplied at his/her own expense, books, newspapers, writing materials and other means of occupation. [Prison Rule 43(1)]

• Have items for cell activities and hobbies handed in by relatives or friends, as well as to purchase them from private cash or pay.

• Carry out business activities

• Wear his/her own clothing, unless considered inappropriate or unsuitable. [PR 23, 40(3)]

• Send and receive as many letters as he/she wishes. [Prison Rule 35(1)] including two statutory letters at public expense per week.

• Be attended by his own registered medical practitioner or dentist, at his own expense. [Prison Rule 20(5)

• Be separated from convicted prisoners, as far as can reasonably be done. [Prison Rule (2)]

• Under no circumstances be required to share a cell with a convicted prisoner. [Prison Rule (2)]

• Unconvicted prisoners must be allowed visits on at least three days a week, which includes weekends; and

• Not to work unless he/she chooses to. [Prison Rule 31(5)]

Some of these special privileges are not absolute and can be tempered by consideration of security, operational need and practical considerations. However, when restricting an unconvicted prisoner's rights, we must be aware of these entitlements and be able to justify our restrictions should we be challenged. For example, Prison Rules allow that an unconvicted prisoner who is placed on the escape list can be required to wear E-list clothing.

## SMOKING & VAPING

*Prisons are now smoke-free*

Since September 2018 all prisons in England and Wales have been smoke-free environments.

Rechargeable vaping devices are available across the whole prison estate. Vape devices are now available through the prison shop and as a reception pack in all prisons apart from the under 18 estate.

Vaping is permitted in all over 18 establishments (note at Feltham it is permitted in Feltham B but not Feltham A).

In closed establishments vaping is only permitted in cell. In open establishments vaping is also permitted in a designated vaping area within the grounds at designated times (again on a split site such as HMP Hewell only those in open conditions can vape outside).

*The approved available product*

• The product is the Pro-Logic rechargeable vape device which can be refilled using pre-sealed capsules and is recharged using a USB adapter.

• A leaflet 'Using your E-Cigarette' detailing how to use an e-cigarette has been produced and can be found on all prison wings.

*Pricing*

• Vape products are sold separately and prisoners will need to buy a vape device, a USB charging plug and a supply of refillable capsules to get started.

• Following this they will only need to buy the refillable capsules each week. Best advice suggests that on average one capsule should last one to two days, dependent on use.

## RIGHTS IN RESPECT OF LEGAL MATTERS

• Prisoners have the right to consult a legal adviser or conduct legal proceedings in prison in relation to any matter, whether connected with their imprisonment or not

• Every prisoner convicted of an offence has a right to apply for leave to appeal to a higher court against that conviction and (with some exceptions) against the sentence imposed

• A prisoner may make requests or complaints to the Criminal Cases Review Commission on matters in connection with conviction and sentence (see *Chapter 2.3, The Criminal Cases Review Commission*)

• The Court of Appeal has decided that discussions about the substance of a legal services funding application should, apart from in exceptional circumstances, be confidential.

## CRIMINAL CASES REVIEW COMMISSION (CCRC)

With regard to communications between prisoners and the CCRC, it is mandatory policy that:

• prisoners are informed of the role and function of the CCRC

• CCRC leaflets distributed to prisons are made widely available

• all correspondence between prisoners and the CCRC is treated as privileged

• visits by staff from the CCRC are treated as legal visits

• telephone calls between prisoners and the CCRC are not monitored or recorded.

For further details see *Chapters 2.3, The Criminal Cases Review Commission and 2.5, Visits, Letters and Telephone Calls.*

## BAIL

PSI 09/2012
Policy name: Bail Accommodation and Support Service (BASS) Policy Framework
Issue Date: 21 December 2018
Cancels the following documents:
• PSI 25/2013; PI 10/2013 Accommodation and Support Service for Bail and HDC
• PSI 17/2011 Bail and Accommodation Support Service Specification Implementation
• Ministry of Justice Service Specification for Bail Accommodation and Support Service vP3.2

## APPLICATIONS FOR BAIL

*The Right to Bail*

Under s. 4 of the Bail Act 1976, on each occasion that a person is brought before a court accused of an offence, or remanded after conviction for enquiries or a report, he must be granted bail without condition, if none of the exceptions to bail apply.

Under s. 5 of the Bail Act 1976, the court or officer refusing bail or imposing conditions must give reasons for their decision.

*Exclusions to the right to bail*

The general right to bail does not apply in the following circumstances:

*Murder*

The power of magistrates to consider bail in murder cases, whether at first hearing or after a breach of an existing bail condition, is now removed by s. 115(1) of the Coroners and Justice Act 2009. This does not apply to attempted murder or conspiracy to murder.

Where a person is charged with an offence of murder or attempted murder, and has previously been convicted in the UK or court of an EU Member State of an offence of murder, attempted murder, rape or a serious sexual offence (as listed in s. 25(2) of the Criminal Justice and Public Order Act 1994), he shall only be granted bail where there are exceptional reasons, which justify it.

Section 114 of the Coroners and Justice Act 2009 amends Schedule 1 to the Bail Act 1976. Section 114(2) provides that bail may not be granted to someone charged with murder unless the court is satisfied that there is no significant risk that, if released on bail, that person would commit an offence that would be likely to cause physical or mental injury to another person. In coming to that decision, the court must have regard to the nature and seriousness of the offence, the suspect's character and antecedents and his record in relation to previous grants of bail.

*Manslaughter and Serious Sexual Offences*

Where a person is charged with an offence of manslaughter, rape or a serious sexual offence, and has previously been convicted in the UK or court of an EU Member State of an offence of murder, attempted murder, rape or a serious sexual offence (as listed in s. 25(2) of the Criminal Justice and Public Order Act 1994), he shall only be granted bail where there are exceptional reasons, which justify it.

Note: Where a person charged with one of the offences referred to above has a previous conviction for manslaughter or culpable homicide in the UK or EU court, he shall only have his right to bail restricted where he received a sentence of imprisonment or detention upon conviction.

*Class A Drug Users - Designated areas only*

In certain parts of the country, Paragraphs 6A to 6C of Part I of Schedule I of the Bail Act 1976 apply which set out the exception to bail for adult drug users where their offending is drug-related, and where they have been required to undergo drug testing but have failed to comply with that requirement.

*Exceptions to the general right to bail*

Exceptions to the above are covered in schedule 1 to the Bail Act 1976. Schedule 1 states where a person is accused, or convicted, of an offence punishable with imprisonment they may not be granted bail in the following circumstances if:
• the court is satisfied there are substantial grounds for believing that the defendant, if released on bail would:
fail to surrender to custody
commit an offence while on bail
interfere with witnesses or otherwise obstruct the course of justice
• the court is satisfied that the defendant must be kept in custody, either:
for their own protection
if they are a child or young person, for their own welfare
• the defendant is already in custody in pursuance of (as a result of) a court sentence
• it has not been possible, due to time constraints, to gather enough information to allow the court to make its decision on bail
• having been released on bail, the defendant has been arrested for absconding or breaking the conditions of their bail
• the offence is triable on indictment or either way and the defendant was on bail in criminal proceedings on the date of the offence

Where the accused is charged with an offence which is not punishable with imprisonment, schedule 1 states that bail may only be withheld if:
• the court:
is satisfied that the defendant must be kept in custody for their own protection, or if they are a child or young person, for their own welfare believes that the defendant would abscond if released on bail because they have previously failed to surrender to custody

- the defendant is already in custody in pursuance of (as a result of) a court sentence
- having been released on bail, the defendant has been arrested for absconding or breaking the conditions of their bail

*Bail from Prison*

The prison must have in place systems for ensuring that:

(i) Assistance is giving to prisoners who wish to apply for bail

(ii) Staff know and carry out the correct administrative procedures

(iii) The relevant people receive necessary notifications at the correct time

(iv) Proper records are kept.

### Grounds for appeal against a remand in custody (unconvicted prisoners).

An unconvicted prisoner's (i.e. defendant's) aim in appealing against a remand in custody is to try to prove that the reasons the court gave for refusing bail do not apply. They may include factors such as the strength of the prosecution or defence case, the defendant's own family circumstances, the availability of sureties and the length of time the defendant has spent (or is likely to spend) in custody.

### Number of applications for bail

Part 11A of Schedule 1 to the Bail Act sets out the number of applications that may be made to the various courts for bail. The court does not have to hear the same arguments for bail more than twice, so unless the defendant's circumstances change this is the number of applications the defence will normally make. Defendants who are refused bail by Magistrates' Court may apply to the Crown Court or to the High Court if they have been granted a certificate by the lower court showing that full arguments have been heard. If they have been refused bail by the Crown Court, they may make one further application (using the same arguments) to the High Court. If the High Court refuses bail, no further application may be made to another High Court judge or to a Divisional Court.

### Applications to the High Court

Applications to the High Court for release on bail must be made to a Judge in Chambers by a solicitor. Prisoners should be told that it is unlikely that a judge will entertain such an application unless it has been considered by magistrates or, if appropriate, an High Court.

The Governor should only produce the prisoner for the High Court if the Judge in Chambers or the Secretary of State authorises it.

If the Judge grants bail and orders immediate release after personally taking any recognisances or sureties which were required, the prisoner must not be allowed to leave the escort's custody until the escort has confirmed the terms of the order.

If, when granting bail, the Judge does not order immediate release, the Governor will receive a copy of the terms of the High Court order. Prisoners securities may be taken by the Governor, but their recognisances may only be entered into before the Governor if the Judge has authorised it. It must otherwise be entered into before a court or a justice of the peace.

### APPEAL AGAINST CONVICTION

1. Anyone convicted at the Crown Court you may apply for leave to appeal against sentence, conviction or both to the Court of Appeal (Criminal Division). They must lodge their appeal at the Royal Courts of Justice within 28 days of the date of sentence.

2. No one can appeal to the Court of Appeal if they were convicted and sentenced at the magistrates' court, though if they were convicted at the magistrates' court, committed for sentence and sentenced at the Crown Court they may, in certain circumstances, appeal to the Court of Appeal.

3. The Court of Appeal can consider an appeal against conviction even if they pleaded guilty, but they will have to put forward very good grounds as to why the conviction should be set aside.

Where an appeal has been rejected by the Court of Appeal, the Criminal Cases Review Commission is able to consider cases for reference back to the Court of Appeal, both in relation to conviction and sentence—see *Chapter 2.3, The Criminal Cases Review Commission.* Convicted prisoners involved in legal proceedings may have their own doctor visit in connection with those proceedings, subject to Prison Rule 20(6).

*Advice and assistance*

It is important to get professional advice before submitting an application for leave to appeal against either sentence or conviction. If an appeal is submitted without any real grounds then the Court, when it finally hears the appeal, can order that any time spent in custody 'as an appellant' shall not count towards sentence. In practice this is rarely done—though it is not by any means unheard of.

Following a criminal conviction and sentence in a Magistrates or Crown Court, the defendant's lawyers (solicitor or barrister) will provide advice as to whether or not they feel that a successful appeal can be put forward to the appellate courts. If there are no grounds for an appeal then that advice will generally be verbal. If it is felt that there are grounds for an appeal against either the conviction, sentence or both, then the barrister (referred to as Counsel) will prepare such an advice in writing along with those grounds.

The solicitor will complete the relevant forms (Form NG) and will submit all the paperwork to the convicting/sentencing court. The court will then forward the appeal application to the appellate court in London (where someone is appealing from the crown court this is usually the Criminal Court of Appeal, The Court of Appeal (Criminal Division) or The High Court).

Any crown court appeal application must usually be submitted within 28 days after sentence. There are exceptions to this rule where a request can be made for the court to allow an appeal 'out of time' (this is known as 'Leave to Appeal out of Time'). This type of application must be justified and the full reasons why the application is out of time must be explained.

The above application to appeal either the conviction and/or sentence is known as an application for 'Leave to Appeal' and that application is considered by a single Appeal Judge. He or she decides whether or not the application has a reasonable chance of succeeding. In other words, the single Judge is there to filter out all of the applications that will probably end up being unsuccessful anyway. All applications will go through this process and the single Judge will always provide reasons for the decision in writing.

If an application for Leave to Appeal is granted (by the single Judge) the application will go on to the 'Full' Court. This is where the application will be heard in full, witnesses can give evidence and the reasons (known as arguments) can be advanced. The full Court will then make its decision and the application will be granted or refused.

If the application/appeal is granted, there are a number of options open to the appellate court:

In the case of an appeal against sentence, a reduction of sentence can be made.

In the case of an appeal against conviction, the court can 'quash' (overturn) the conviction completely or they can order a re-trial.

*No Grounds of Appeal*

Where the barrister or solicitor advises that there are no grounds of appeal against conviction or sentence there are several choices available. Firstly, if a defendant feels strongly that they have grounds to appeal, they can make an application themselves. They will need to obtain from the Legal services Officer at the prison a copy of the application (Form NG) and fully set out their reasons.

Alternatively, a person who has been convicted can seek a second opinion from another lawyer. They need to write to a solicitor who will then send you some forms to sign called CDS1 and CDS2. Once the solicitor has these forms back, he or she will usually be able to come and see the client (if he or she is in prison) to discuss their case and the options available. The client's reasons can be explored and he will receive a second opinion in writing. If a solicitor thinks that the appeal may have a chance, then he or she will begin to prepare and investigate the appeal properly, and also prepare justification for the application being out of time if it is longer than 28 days since sentence. This will be the same process whether it is out of time by a week or out of time by a year or longer.

*Rejected Applications: Single Judge Rejections.*

In the case where Grounds of Appeal has been rejected at the first stage (The Single Judge Stage) there is an option available to request that the application is still put forward to the full Court regardless. However, this option needs to be considered very carefully as it can carry harsh penalties if the appeal is ultimately refused. Such penalties include the potential for any time already spent in custody (up until the point of the refusal by the Court of Appeal) to not be counted as part of the sentence. In other words, there is a risk that they would have to start their sentence again from scratch.

*Full Court of Appeal Refusals*

If an application reaches the Full Appellate Court and is not successful, there are still options available should you disagree with the Court's decision. One such avenue is to submit an application to the Criminal Cases Review Commission (C.C.R.C) who will then appoint a case worker to investigate the concerns. In the United Kingdom, this is generally the only way that a person can have their case referred back to the appellate courts.

No application can be made to the CCRC until the appeal has first been rejected by the Court of Appeal.

## COMING TO PRISON FOR THE FIRST TIME

View of one former Prisoner

*Coming into prison for the first time is, needless to say, a daunting experience. For remand prisoners, not knowing how long you may be staying there makes it even worse. All that is running through your mind (if it is not so numb that it can't function) is the family you have left behind. How will your children cope without their mother? How will you cope without your partner for comfort? Depression, anger and resentment each take their turn to roll through you until you feel emotionally and physically drained.*

*Reception is the first point of call once you are off-loaded from the 'sweatbox'. The reception staff can appear quite solemn and somewhat regimental in manner, but this is mainly because they want to get you processed and accommodated as quickly as possible. It is a national routine procedure to be strip-searched. Not a pleasant experience, but they need to check that you have not concealed any weapons, drugs, or other prohibited items on your person. In some prisons you are then give a 'prison issue' towel, soap, shampoo, toothbrush and dressing gown, and made to take a shower. The nurse comes to take your height and weight and will ask you about your general fitness, you are also usually questioned as to whether you have any suicidal tendencies. They then send you back to the care of the reception staff to have your property logged. Finally, you are permitted to put your clothes back on and collect your belongings to take with you to your allocated cell.*

*If you had started to gain comfort from getting to know the other new prisoners who came in with you, then it is soon lost as you are all split up and locked in separate cells. I remember walking down the wing hearing the prisoners shouting 'New meat!' to each other, and having to take deep breaths to steady my rapidly beating heart. The harsh sound of steel-on-steel as your cell door is slammed and locked behind you is enough to send your already delicate nerves over, or at least close to, the edge. Then you are completely alone to adjust to and take in your new surroundings. You will be given an induction on the prison's facilities, including what the gym, library and education have to offer. These can all be used to vent your pent-up emotions and feelings through the right channels, giving you a modest sense of release. Keeping yourself to yourself is best, at least until you have studied and observed how your fellow prisoners profile. For those who have been sentenced it is a good idea to 'plan' how to spend your time inside constructively. Offending behaviour courses are always beneficial and, depending on the length of your sentence, there is usually a range of educational courses available.*

*It does not generally take long to adjust to prison life. I am, not saying that it is enjoyable, far from it, but you learn to cope. For anyone who is finding it exceptionally difficult to settle, and becoming quite desperate, do not be afraid to talk to someone. If you feel that you cannot do so to an officer or any other member of the prison staff, there is a 'Listener's Scheme' in every prison, which is a group of inmates trained by the Samaritans.*

*You do not need to be told who to hang around or socialise with, this is simply a matter of common sense. The main thing always to remember is that you have to look out for yourself at all times as, believe me, no one will be doing it for you. All you need to know is that a focused mind is the key to survival!*

## 2.2 OFFENDING BEHAVIOUR PROGRAMMES 2021/2022

**Courses updated to 09 February 2021**
**Correctional Services Accreditation and Advice Panel (CSAAP)**
*Note: August 2022:* In August 2021 the MOJ said, in respect of Accredited Offending Behaviour Programmes, that with they HMPPS Interventions Team the MOJ was "exploring a refined Accredited Programmes (AcPs) suite to increase focus on quality in delivery, enable improved evaluation and, ultimately, seek to improve the impact on reduced reoffending rates."

One year on, there has been no further announcements about this.

The following are therefore the currently accredited programmes last updated in February 2021.

### ACCREDITED FOR DELIVERY IN THE COMMUNITY
**Becoming New Me + (BNM+)**
Provided by HMPPS Interventions Services
BNM+ is for high or very high-risk adult men who have learning disabilities or learning challenges and have been convicted of a sexual offence. It supports development of skills to strengthen pro-social identity and plan for an offence-free life.

**Breaking Free: Health and Justice Package**
Provided by Breaking Free Online Ltd
This comprises two accredited programmes:
Breaking Free Online. An 8-session digital behaviour change programme which addresses the underlying psychological and lifestyle difficulties behind alcohol/drug use and offending behaviour. The programme targets 70 problem substances including illegal substances, New Psychoactive Substances (NPS), and prescribed medications.
Pillars of Recovery. A 12-session behaviour change programme that targets the underlying psychological and lifestyle difficulties behind alcohol/drug use and offending behaviour.

**Building Better Relationships (BBR)**
Provided by HMPPS Interventions Services
BBR is for adult men convicted of an Intimate Partner Violence (IPV) offence. BBR is a moderate-intensity cognitive-behavioural programme which recognises that IPV is a complex problem which is likely to have multiple causes. BBR responds to individual needs and provides opportunities to develop skills for managing thoughts, emotions, and behaviours

**Building Skills for Recovery (BSR)**
Provided by HMPPS Interventions Services
BSR) is a psychosocial programme for adult men and women who are dependent on substances or alcohol. The programme aims to reduce offending behaviour and problematic substance misuse with the ultimate goal of recovery.

**Drink Impaired Drivers Programme (DIDP)**
Provided by HMPPS Interventions Services
DIDP is a cognitive-behavioural and educational programme that targets non-dependent drink-drive individuals. DIDP teaches participants about alcohol and supports development of skills to avoid future drink driving situations through:
• greater self-awareness
• self-monitoring of drinking behaviour improved planning
• greater understanding of consequence decision making

**Healthy Identity Intervention (HII)**
Provided by HMPPS Interventions Services
HII is designed for those who have committed extremist offences. It supports desistance and disengagement from extremism. It encourages stronger positive and pro-social aspects of identity. It helps individuals develop resilience and supports them to identify ways of meeting their identity needs. For example, need for belonging, need for recognition, without involvement in extremism.

**Horizon**
Provided by HMPPS Interventions Services
Horizon is designed for medium and above risk adult men who have been convicted of a sexual offence. It supports participants to develop optimism, and skills to strengthen their pro-social identity and plan for a life free of offending.

**iHorizon**
Provided by HMPPS Interventions Services
iHorizon is a version of Horizon for men whose sexual offending is internet only. Offences involve possessing, downloading, and/or distributing indecent images.

**Identity Matters (IM)**
Provided by HMPPS Interventions Services
IM is a one to one programme for adult men whose offending and harmful behaviour is motivated by their identification with a gang. It supports desistance by encouraging participants to develop a stronger individual identity and develop resilience. It identifies ways of meeting their needs without group driven offending.

**Mentalization-based Treatment (MBT)**
Provided by HMPPS/NHS Offender Personality Disorder Team
MBT is a psychoeducation programme. It is for people with some traits of Antisocial or Borderline Personality Disorder. It teaches social functioning, and addresses violent and suicidal thoughts, and risky behaviours. There are weekly psychotherapy groups, and monthly one-to-one meetings for a year.

**New Me Strengths (NMS)**
Provided by HMPPS Interventions Services
NMS is designed for medium and above risk adult men who have learning disabilities or learning challenges (LDCs) and a conviction(s) for any offence. It supports development of skills to strengthen pro- social identity and plan for an offence-free life.

**Living as New Me (LNM)**
Provided by HMPPS Interventions Services
LNM is an accredited skills maintenance (booster) programme for those individuals who have already completed NMS or BNM+ and may require further additional support.

**Resolve**
Provided by HMPPS Interventions Services
Resolve is designed for adult men with a medium to high risk of reoffending with convictions for violent offences. Resolve aims to support participants with histories of violence to reduce the use of aggression and/or violence by developing insight in to behaviours and skills to support achieving pro-social goals.

**Thinking Skills Programme (TSP)**
Provided by HMPPS Interventions Services
TSP is designed for adult men and women with a medium/high risk of reoffending. TSP supports participants to develop thinking (cognitive) skills to manage risk factors, develop protective factors, and achieve pro-social goals.

**ACCREDITED FOR DELIVERY IN CUSTODY**
**Alcohol Dependence Treatment Programme (ADTP)**
Provided by The Forward Trust
ADTP is a 6-week programme for men with a medium-high risk of reoffending, who are dependent on alcohol. Participants stop drinking and do Steps 1-3 of the Twelve Steps of Alcoholics Anonymous (AA). They can access group therapy, peer support, AA meetings, and individual support.

### Becoming New Me + (BNM+)
Provided by HMPPS Interventions Services
BNM+ is for high or very high-risk adult men who have learning disabilities or challenges and have been convicted of a sexual, Intimate Partner Violence (IPV) or general violent offence. It supports participants to develop optimism and skills to strengthen their pro-social identity and plan for an offence-free life.

### Breaking Free: Health and Justice Package (Custody)
Provided by Breaking Free Online Ltd
This comprises two accredited programmes:
Breaking Free Online: an 8-session digital behaviour change programme which addresses the underlying psychological and lifestyle difficulties behind alcohol/drug use and offending behaviour. The programme targets 70 problem substances including illegal substances, New Psychoactive Substances (NPS), and prescribed medications of abuse; and
Pillars of Recovery: a 12-session behaviour change programme that targets the underlying psychological and lifestyle difficulties behind alcohol/drug use and offending behaviour.

### Building Better Relationships (BBR)
Provided by HMPPS Interventions Services
BBR is for adult men convicted of an Intimate Partner Violence (IPV) offence. BBR is a moderate-intensity cognitive-behavioural programme which recognises that IPV is a complex problem which is likely to have multiple causes. BBR responds to individual needs and provides opportunities to develop skills for managing thoughts, emotions, and behaviours.

### Building Skills for Recovery (BSR)
Provided by HMPPS Interventions Services
Building Skills for Recovery (BSR) is a psychosocial programme for adult men and women who are dependent on substances or alcohol. The programme aims to reduce offending behaviour and problematic substance misuse with the ultimate goal of recovery.

### Challenge to Change (C2C)
Provided by Kainos Community
A six-month offending behaviour programme for men in prison. Participants live on a dedicated unit within a prison. Through cognitive behavioural therapy they learn to challenge and change their thinking, attitudes and behaviour. Participants become active members of the community, agreeing rules, meeting together, and providing peer support. Peer mentors play an important part.

### Choices, Actions, Relationships, Emotions (CARE)
Provided by HMPPS Interventions Services
CARE is for women who are medium and above risk, and have a history of violence and complex needs. CARE aims to assist women with understanding and therefore learn how to manage the risk they pose to themselves and others, and to live a more satisfying and pro-social life.

### Control of Violence for Angry Impulsive Drinkers – Group Secure (COVAID-GS)
Provided by Delight Services
A cognitive-behavioural programme for men in secure settings who are violent under the influence of alcohol. Consisting of ten group sessions with supplementary individual support sessions, it encourages individuals to understand their behaviour and practise skills for change so that risk of violence is reduced.

### Control of Violence for Angry Impulsive Drinkers – Group Secure Women (COVAID-GSW)
Provided by Delight Services
A cognitive-behavioural programme for women in secure settings who are violent under the influence of alcohol. This programme has been developed with and for women in prison.

### Democratic Therapeutic Community Model (DTC)
Provided by HMPPS/NHS Offender Personality Disorder Team
DTCs are part of the Offender Personality Disorder Pathway. They are for people with complex psychological and emotional needs, likely to meet the criteria for a diagnosis of 'personality disorder'. They provide a 24/7 therapeutic environment. Most DTC residents have committed violent offences, some of which may be sexually motivated.

### Therapeutic Communities Plus (TC+)
Provided by HMPPS/NHS Offender Personality Disorder Team
TC+ is part of the Offender Personality Disorder Pathway. These communities are for people who are eligible for but unable to participate in, mainstream DTC due to mild to moderate learning disability. TC+ services provide group and creative psychotherapies in a 24/7 living-learning environment. Most TC+ residents have committed violent offences, some of which may be sexually motivated.

### Healthy Identity Intervention (HII)
Provided by HMPPS Interventions Services
HII is designed for those who have committed extremist offences. It supports desistance and

disengagement from extremism. It encourages stronger positive and pro-social aspects of identity. It helps individuals develop resilience and supports them to identify ways of meeting their identity needs. For example, need for belonging, need for recognition, without involvement in extremism.

### Healthy Sex Programme (HSP)
Provided by HMPPS Interventions Services
HSP is designed for adult men who have a conviction of a sexual offence or an offence with a sexual element. Regardless of level of risk of sexual reoffending, HPS is designed to respond to the needs of individuals with learning disabilities and challenges and is delivered one to one.

### Horizon
Provided by HMPPS Interventions Services
Horizon is designed for medium and above risk adult men who have been convicted of a sexual offence. It supports development of skills to strengthen pro-social identity and plan for an offence-free life.

### Identity Matters (IM)
Provided by HMPPS Interventions Services
IM is a one to one programme for adult men whose offending and harmful behaviour is motivated by their identification with a gang. It supports desistance by encouraging participants to develop a stronger individual identity and develop resilience. It identifies ways of meeting their needs without group driven offending.

### Kaizen
Provided by HMPPS Interventions Services
The version of Kaizen accredited for custody is for high or very high risk adult men who have been convicted of a sexual, Intimate Partner Violence (IPV) or general violent offence. It supports participants develop the optimism, and skills to strengthen their pro-social identity and plan for a life free of offending.

### Living as New Me
Provided by HMPPS Interventions Services
LNM is an accredited skills maintenance (booster) programme for those individuals who have already completed NMS or BNM+ and may require further additional support.

### New Me Strengths
Provided by HMPPS Interventions Services
NMS is designed for medium and above risk adult men who have learning disabilities or learning challenges (LDCs) and a conviction(s) for any offence. It supports participants to develop optimism, and skills to strengthen their pro-social identity and plan for a life free of offending.

### Resolve
Provided by HMPPS Interventions Services
Resolve is designed for adult men with a medium to high risk of reoffending with convictions for violent offences. Resolve aims to support participants with histories of violence to reduce the use of aggression and/or violence by developing insight in to behaviours and skills to support achieving pro-social goals.

### The Bridge Programme
Provided by The Forward Trust
The Bridge is a 6-week programme for men with a medium to high risk of reoffending and a history of substance dependence. Participants give up drugs and do Steps 1-3 of the Twelve Steps of Narcotics Anonymous (NA). They can access group therapy, peer support, AA and NA meetings, and individual support.

### Thinking Skills Programme (TSP)
Provided by HMPPS Interventions Services
TSP is designed for adult men and women with a medium/high risk of reoffending. TSP supports participants to develop thinking (cognitive) skills to manage risk factors, develop protective factors, and achieve pro-social goals.

## 2.3 THE CRIMINAL CASES REVIEW COMMISSION

*June 2022 Update: The CCRC started work in April 1997, between then and 30th June 2022 it has:*
- *28,861 applications received (including all ineligible cases)*
- *28,059 cases completed*
- *796 cases referred to appeal*
- *774 appeals heard by the courts*
- *542 appeals allowed*
- *217 dismissed*
- *668 cases under review*
- *131 awaiting consideration*

The Criminal Cases Review Commission (CCRC) is an independent public body that was set up in March 1997 by the Criminal Appeal Act 1995. Its purpose is to review possible miscarriages of justice in the criminal courts of England, Wales and Northern Ireland and refer appropriate cases to the appeal courts.

The Commission is based in Birmingham and has about 90 staff, including a core of about 50 caseworkers, supported by administrative staff. There are 12 Commissioners who are appointed in accordance with the Office for the Commissioner for Public Appointments' Code of Practice. They work with the Senior Management

Team to ensure the Commission runs efficiently. The CCRC is completely independent and impartial and do not represent the prosecution or the defence.

## CCRC vision
To enhance public confidence in the criminal justice system, to give hope and bring justice to those wrongly convicted, and based on our experience to contribute to reform and improvements in the law

## CCRC values
Independence
Integrity
Impartiality
Professionalism
Accountability
Transparency

## CCRC aims
To investigate cases as quickly as possible and with thoroughness and care.
To work constructively with our stakeholders and to the highest standards of quality.
To treat applicants, and anyone affected by our work, with courtesy, respect and consideration.
To promote public understanding of the Commission's role.

## INTRODUCTION
The Criminal Cases Review Commission enjoys a unique position in the criminal justice system. It is independent of Government and the courts, it is impartial, and it has extensive investigative powers. Unlike many other bodies, the Commission's role is to take an investigative approach rather than an adversarial one. And crucially, the Commission does not represent the prosecution or the defence. Set up under the Criminal Appeal Act 1995 to investigate possible miscarriages of justice in England, Wales and Northern Ireland, the Commission took over the role from the Home Office and Northern Ireland Office from 31 March 1997. This chapter examines the role of the Commission, how people can apply, and the way in which the Commission deals with applications.

## Casework timelines
All cases
The CCRC aim to complete a minimum of 85% of cases within 12 months of receiving the application.
The position at the end of June 2022 was that 85.06% of cases were applicants in custody, and 79.44% of cases were applicants are at liberty. The target is 85%.

## THE COMMISSION'S PURPOSE AND ROLE
The Commission's purpose is to review possible miscarriages of justice in the criminal courts of England, Wales and Northern Ireland and refer appropriate cases to the appeal courts - since October 2009 it has also assumed responsibility for referring cases from military tribunals and Courts Martial.
In the normal criminal sense The Commission can review criminal cases that were heard in either the magistrates' court or the crown courts and refer to the appeal courts a:
• conviction
• verdict
• finding
• or sentence
where the Commission considers there is a "real possibility" that it would not be upheld. The Commission has no power to overturn convictions or sentences itself; only the appeal courts have the power to do that. Unless there are exceptional circumstances, there needs to be NEW evidence or NEW argument which was not put before the courts at the original hearing or appeal in order for a referral to be made. The Commission cannot review cases from the Isle of Man, the Channel Islands or Scotland (which has its own body, the Scottish Criminal Cases Review Commission), nor can it review cases tried in military courts. The Commission can also investigate and report on any matter referred to it by the Court of Appeal, and help the Secretary of State with the consideration of the exercise of The Royal prerogative of mercy, both by referring cases to the Secretary of State and assisting as required, although this latter power has not so far been used.

## KEY COMMISSION OFFICIALS
Twelve Commissioners are appointed in accordance with the Office for the Commissioner for Public Appointments' Code of Practice. They work with the senior management team to ensure we run efficiently.
Decisions about whether or not cases can be referred are always taken by one or more of our Commissioners who are chosen for their professional experience and ability to make important decisions in complicated matters.
Cases are generally passed to Commissioners on a 'cab rank' basis. They decide all types of cases and are appointed by the Queen on the recommendation of the Prime Minister.

**Helen Pitcher OBE (Chairman)**
**David Brown**
**Ian Comfort**
**Rachel Ellis**
**Jill Gramann**
**Johanna Higgins**

Linda Lee
Robert Ward CBE QC (Hon)
Zahra Ahmed
Joanne Fazakerley
Nicola Cockburn

### Our non-executive directors

We have three independent Non-Executive Directors (iNeds) on our Board. They are not our employees and sit on the Board in order to provide independent advice, constructive challenge and scrutiny of its decisions and performance. The iNeds sit on the Board along with the Chairman, members of the Senior Management Team, and three Commissioners who serve as Non-Executive Directors.

Andre Katz
Martin Spencer
Mark Oldham

### Our senior management team

Day-to-day operations are the responsibility of the Chief Executive, Miss Karen Kneller. Karen is supported in this by Mrs Amanda Pearce, Interim Director of Casework Operations, and Mr Peter Ryan, Director of Finance & Corporate Services. Together they make up the Senior Management Team.

Our Board is made up of the Senior Management Team, three Commissioners and two Non-Executive Directors and our Chairman. Our Chairman and all twelve Commissioners form the Body Corporate as defined in the Criminal Appeal Act 1995

### BASIC RULES

The basic rule is that the Commission can only review those cases which have either:

• already been refused leave to appeal, or
• had an appeal dismissed.

On rare occasions, it may be able to take on a case which has not been through the appeals procedure, but there would need to be exceptional circumstances. The Commission can also reconsider cases previously rejected by the Home Office.

### CASE ORDERING AND PRIORITY RANKING

The majority of cases are dealt with in order of receipt.

Cases are categorised, and the more complex and time-consuming cases wait in separate queues to be allocated to a case reviewer. Cases where the applicant is in custody take priority over cases where the applicant is at liberty.

Other considerations which affect a decision to give priority to a case include:

• the age, health of the applicant or a witness;
• the possibility of evidence deteriorating or being lost; and
• the case's impact on the criminal justice system.

### Reviewing a case

The Commission obtains all the necessary material about the original case, using its unique powers to access information held by any public body, such as the police, the Crown Prosecution Service or the NHS.

In some cases, it may be necessary to interview new witnesses or those involved in the original case. The Commission may also seek expert reports or arrange for forensic tests, such as DNA profiling. It is unusual to see applicants in person but this does happen sometimes if necessary.

The Commission can also direct bodies such as police forces to investigate specific issues on its behalf. This is sometimes done in complex or sensitive cases.

### How long does it take?

Although the majority of cases are dealt with in a matter of months, more complex applications are assessed and allocated into categories, depending on the range and complexity of the investigation required.

Each of these categories has a waiting list and the most complex cases can wait some time before the detailed review starts – more than a year in some cases.

The review starts when the case is allocated to a named case reviewer. Reviews can be very time-consuming. Complex cases can take months or even years to complete. Thoroughness is our priority.

### What happens when the review is complete?

Once a review is complete, a Commissioner, or committee of Commissioners, considers the case and decides whether or not to refer it to an appeal court. A decision to refer a case has to be made by a committee consisting of not fewer than three Commissioners.

Applicants are sent a Statement of Reasons setting out the decision and the reasons for it. If the initial decision is not to refer the case, applicants are given time to respond before a final decision is made.

If the Commissioners decide there is a 'real possibility' that a conviction would be overturned or sentence reduced, the case is sent to the relevant appeal court which must hear the appeal. It usually takes some time before the appeal hearing takes place. Whether or not a conviction is quashed or a sentence reduced is entirely a matter for the appeal court.

If an application is not referred to an appeal court a new application can be made to the Commission, but some new evidence or line of argument will usually be expected.

## DOCUMENTS AND EXPERTS

Under Section 17 of the Criminal Appeal Act 1995, public bodies holding any material relating to the review of a case are obliged to produce it for the Commission, give access to it, allow the Commission to take it away or make copies, and preserve material until the Commission withdraws its direction.

This includes material covered by Public Interest Immunity and the Official Secrets Acts. In some cases, the Commission will be able to reach a decision based on the information supplied in the application form and material relating to the original investigation.

In others, its case reviewers will need to call for further information and carry out their own investigations into aspects of a case. Experts may be instructed to report on matters which call for special knowledge.

## INVESTIGATING OFFICER

Section 19 of the Act empowers the Commission to require the appointment of an investigating officer from another public body, usually the police.

The Commission has put in place strict controls over the conduct of these investigations, setting the brief and carrying out regular monitoring of progress.

## COMMISSION RESOURCES

The Commission's most important resource is its staff. Case reviewers have to pass a rigorous recruitment process, undergo two weeks intensive induction training when they join us, and are given ongoing in-house training aimed at keeping their knowledge of legislation and developments in case law up to date. The Commission is recognised as a provider of training for professional development purposes by the Law Society and the Bar Council.

Case reviewers are supported by legal advisers (legally-trained) and investigations advisers (former senior police officers), who provide advice on matters related to cases under investigation, legal issues, the implications of judgments likely to influence case handling and the conduct and control of investigations.

## CONFIDENTIALITY

While the Commission is as open as possible about its policies and procedures, explanations about case decisions are restricted under the Act to applicants or their legal representatives, the appeal courts, and those likely to be involved in any proceedings following a reference to the appeal courts, for example, the Crown Prosecution Service.

As an investigation proceeds, the case reviewer will inform the applicant of progress, although on occasion there may be confidential matters affecting others which cannot be disclosed.

## STATEMENT OF REASONS

The Commission also provides applicants with a full explanation of its decision to refer or not to refer, known as the Statement of Reasons.

If the decision-making committee decides not to refer a case, a provisional Statement of Reasons is sent to the applicant or the legal representative, and a minimum period of 28 days allowed for comment or fresh submissions to the Commission. Only after that time has elapsed, and depending on there being no new issues raised, is the final decision made on whether or not to refer.

## COURT OF APPEAL

Once the final decision has been taken, the Commission's involvement is ended. In the case of referrals, it is up to applicants and their legal representatives to present a persuasive case to the appeal court.

Those who have been refused referral can apply again to the Commission if fresh matters significantly affecting the conviction or sentence come to light later.

## COMPLAINTS PROCEDURE

The Commission has a complaints procedure which looks into and reports on any objections to the way a case has been handled, or an applicant treated.

## HELP FROM A SOLICITOR

It is not essential to use a solicitor when applying to the Commission, but some applicants find that there are benefits to having a legal representative. Public funding for Advice and Assistance may be available under the Legal Aid scheme if the firm holds a General Criminal Contract. The lawyer will be able to assess your income and capital and advise whether you are financially eligible for such help.

## COMMISSION AIMS

The Commission's overall aims are to:
• investigate cases as quickly as possible and with thoroughness and care
• work constructively with our stakeholders and to the highest standards of quality
• treat applicants, and anyone affected by our work, with courtesy, respect and consideration
• promote public understanding of the Commission's role.

## FURTHER INFORMATION

Information packs and application forms are available. Please contact:
Criminal Cases Review Commission

23 Stephenson Street
Birmingham B2 4BH
Local rate telephone 0300 456 2669
(calls to this number from anywhere in the UK
are charged as local rate calls)
Switchboard: 0121 233 1473
Website: www.ccrc.gov.uk

## 2.4 REQUESTS AND COMPLAINTS

### 2.4.1 REQUESTS AND COMPLAINTS

*Prisoner Complaints Policy Framework issued 5th July 2019.*

*Latest update: 4th February 2022:*

*Para 4.52 updated to clarify that IMB board members can have access to locally held confidential access complaint responses as part of their statutory monitoring role and to facilitate prisoner access to the PPO.*

*The cost of photocopying complaint forms must be met by individual establishments – paragraph 4.44 refers. Those responsible for answering confidential complaints must provide the prisoner with two copies of the reply - paragraph 4.53 refers.*

*The Prisoner Complaints Framework sets out requirements and information on providing a fair and effective system for dealing with prisoner complaints, including by ensuring procedural justice and taking a problem-solving approach for both adult prisoners and young people. It also incorporates the parts of PSI 58/2010 (Prison and Probation Ombudsman) that refer to complaints.*

### I want to make a complaint. What do I do?

You have the right to make a formal written complaint on form COMP 1 at any stage, but you should think about whether speaking to a member of staff first will solve your problem. Most problems can be sorted out quickly and easily this way.

If you are not satisfied with the response to your written complaint you should appeal using form COMP 1A.

### I have made a wing application but I am still not happy. What do I do next?

You can make a formal complaint in writing. Copies of the complaint form COMP 1 should be freely available for you to pick up on your wing or in your residential area. You do not have to ask for a form. Where online systems/kiosks operate on the wing, you can use these instead of a paper form. Read the notes on the form first. Then fill in your details and say what your complaint is in the space provided. Keep your complaint brief and to the point. When you have signed and dated the form, post it in the locked complaints box on your wing or in your residential area. The box is emptied every weekday.

### Who opens the prison's complaints boxes?

Complaints boxes are opened by a designated officer who is not a residential officer on the wing.

### When will I get a response?

You should normally receive a response to your complaint to the prison within five working days. The response will be on the same form as your complaint. In some cases it might take longer to investigate a complaint. If so, you will receive a reply explaining the reason for the delay (this is called an interim reply).

### Who will respond - Reserved Subjects?

In most cases, your wing officer will respond. In some cases you might get a reply from another member of staff, depending on what your complaint is about.

Subjects - such as allegations against the Governor/Director, litigation against HMPPS, deportation, appeals against Mother and Baby Unit rejections - are dealt with only by HMPPS Headquarters. Dealing with these complaints will take longer, up to six weeks. Staff will tell you when your complaint has been sent to Headquarters. You must make complaints about reserved subjects in writing. If you have difficulty putting your complaint in writing you can make your complaint orally to a member of staff.

### What if I am not satisfied with the response?

If you are not happy with the response to your complaint, you have the right to appeal and have your complaint considered by someone at a level more senior than the person who provided the response to your original complaint. There is another form for this, COMP 1A.

Say why you are not satisfied with the response to your complaint in the space provided on the COMP 1A form. You must do this within a week of receiving the first response. Post the form in the complaints box.

You should normally receive a response within five working days, although in some cases this might take longer. If so, you will receive an interim reply explaining the reason for the delay. The response will be on the same form.

Does this apply to complaints about reserved subjects, which are dealt with at Headquarters? No. In the case of a reserved subject complaint there is no formal appeal within HMPPS. But you can send in your complaint again if you have new information which was not available when you first complained. You can also take your complaint outside the service, for example to the Prisons and Probation Ombudsman, if you wish.

### I don't want wing staff to know about my complaint. What can I do?

You can use the confidential access procedure if your complaint is about a particularly serious or sensitive matter. Confidential access allows you to write directly to the governor/director, the Prison Group Director (PGD)/Directors line manager or the Chair of the Independent Monitoring Board.

Confidential access is not a short cut for ordinary complaints. If it turns out that your complaint could have been dealt with using the normal procedures, you may be asked to use the normal procedures.

### What do the IMB do?

The Independent Monitoring Board is responsible for monitoring the treatment of prisoner to check that it is fair, just and humane. To do this, they make regular visits to each prison. They are ordinary people appointed by Ministers and are completely independent of the Prison.

### Can I go to the Independent Monitoring Board with a complaint?

Yes. You can apply at any time - using the wing IMB application system to request to speak to a member of the Board. But the Board will normally expect you to have tried to sort your problem out with prison staff first.

If you have already made a written complaint, the Board will look at the reply which you were given and any other relevant information.

The Board will tell you when you can expect to get a reply. If there is likely to be a delay, you will be told what is happening. The Board will let you know what it has decided to do about your complaint. It could, for example, ask the governor/director to think again about a decision which has been made. Or, it could bring it to the attention of the Prison Group Director/Director's Line Manager

### How do I make an application to the IMB?

Forms to make an application to the IMB should be available on the wing and you then fill out the form and put it in the box marked IMB.

### Are applications to the IMB confidential?

Yes, all applications are confidential though you may be asked to agree to the IMB consulting staff if necessary. You can ask to see a copy of the IMB privacy notice, which explains how the IMB will use your information.

### Who opens the IMB application boxes?

Only IMB members open these boxes.
Remember: you are more likely to have your complaint put right quickly if you follow the normal procedures. If you misuse confidential access you will waste time

### Under confidential access, will my complaint be completely confidential?

Investigating your complaint properly may mean that others - not just the governor/director, the Prison Group Director/Director's Line Manager or the Chair of the Independent Monitoring Board - will have to know about it. But they will keep your complaint confidential as far as possible. No-one will be told about your complaint if they don't need to know about it. Your complaint and the response will be sent in a sealed envelope.

### How do I make a confidential complaint?

Use Form COMP 2, for a confidential access complaint. Copies should be freely available for you to pick up on your wing or in your residential area, with a covering envelope for you to use.

Read the notes on the form first. If you think that your complaint is suitable for confidential access, fill in your details and say what your complaint is. Say why you are using confidential access. Place the filled-in form in the envelope and address it to the person you want to consider your complaint. This must be the governor/director, the Prison Group Director/Director's Line Manager or the Chair of the Independent Monitoring Board. Then post the sealed envelope in the complaints box.

The envelope will be opened only by the person you address it to.

### When will I get a response to my confidential access complaint?

You should receive a response from the governor/director within 5 working days, for HMPPS headquarters on behalf of the Prison Group Director/Director's Line Manager or the Chair of the Independent Monitoring Board (on the same form as your original complaint and in a sealed envelope) within about 10 working days, depending on where you addressed the complaint. If the response takes longer, you will receive an interim reply explaining why.

The governor/director, the Prison Group Director/Director's Line Manager or the Chair of the Independent Monitoring Board may decide that your complaint is unsuitable for confidential access and should go through the normal procedures. If so, he or she will return the form to you in a sealed envelope and explain why.

### What do I do if I want to withdraw a complaint?

If you want to withdraw your complaint, you can do so at any time. Just tell a member of staff. He or she will arrange for you to write on the form that you want to withdraw it.

**What if I have a complaint about the prison staff?**
If you think that a member of staff has mistreated you, you can complain to the Governing Governor/Director You can also complain directly to the Prison Group Director/Director's Line Manager, using confidential access.
Use a complaint form or a confidential access complaint form. Write down clearly what happened and say exactly what you think the member of staff did wrong. Say if someone else saw what happened and support your complaint with any evidence which you have. Post your complaint in the complaints box. If you are using confidential access, seal your form in an envelope addressed to either the governor/director or the Prison Group Director/Director's Line Manager.

**What happens then?**
The governor/director will ask a senior member of staff to look into your complaint. He or she will ask you what happened and will talk to the member of staff you have complained about. If there are other people who saw what happened, they will be spoken to as well. All this takes time, so you must be patient. The investigation has to be thorough to be fair to everyone involved.
At the end of the investigation, the governor/director will decide what, if any, action to take. If the governor/director decides that your complaint is justified, the member of staff concerned may be disciplined. If your complaint is very serious the governor/director may decide to ask the police to investigate.
The governor/director will write to you at the end of the investigation to tell you what he or she has decided. This will usually take about two weeks but may take longer. If the police have been called in, you will be told.
If you wrote to the Prison Group Director/Director's Line Manager under confidential access, he or she will send you a reply telling you what action has been taken. Unless there are exceptional circumstances, the Prison Group Director will usually ask the governor/director to investigate.
Remember: the complaints procedures are there to help you. They rely on you to complain when something goes wrong so that it can be put right. If you deliberately make false complaints, prison staff will not be able to give as much time to those that are genuine.

**Part 2: Outside the prison system**
**Can I take my complaint outside the Prison Service?**
Yes. You can complain to the Prisons and Probation Ombudsman, but you must have completed the internal complaints procedures first. You should normally send your complaint to the Ombudsman within three months of receiving the final response to your complaint from the governor/director or HMPPS Headquarters. The address is:
**The Prisons and Probation Ombudsman**
**3rd Floor**
**10 South Colonnade**
**Canary Wharf**
**London E14 4PU**
There is a separate leaflet about how to complain to the Ombudsman. You should be able to pick up a leaflet in the library or chaplaincy.

**Are there other people or organisations outside the prison system I can complain to, besides the Ombudsman?**
Yes. The Independent Monitoring Board is completely independent from the prison, see how to make an IMB application above. Other bodies are listed below.
Unlike a complaint to the Ombudsman, you do not always have to have completed the internal complaints procedures before taking a complaint to one of the organisations in the list. But remember that it will usually be quicker to try to settle the problem inside the prison system first. If you do go straight to an outside person or organisation, and they decide to take up your complaint, the prison will almost certainly be asked to investigate your complaint at some stage. This may simply mean that your complaint will then take longer to deal with than if you had raised it with prison staff in the first place.
It is a good idea to talk to a member of staff about what you plan to do, so that he or she can tell you anything else which you need to know.

**Legal advisers**
You may write to your legal adviser about a complaint.

**Letter to a Member of Parliament (MP)**
You can write to an MP. This should normally be the MP for the area where you would be living if you were not in prison. You should write to him or her at the House of Commons, London SW1A 0AA. If you do not know the name of your MP, staff will find out for you.
You should write on letter paper and make sure that you include your home address if you have one.

**Petitions to the Queen**
You can petition the Queen. You should write out your petition on letter paper. Hand your petition to a member of staff, who will send it the Prison Group Director/Director's Line Manager. You do

not have to tell staff what you are writing about, but the governor/director will be told that you have sent a petition to the Queen. A petition to the Queen does not count against your allowance of letters.

## Petitions to Parliament
You can petition Parliament. Petitions to Parliament are presented to the House of Commons by MPs. A petition must be sent to a named MP (that is, you must name the MP you are sending it to). This should normally be the MP for the area where you would be living if you were not in prison. You should ask staff for letter paper and a copy of the instructions. You must follow these instructions carefully or your petition cannot be presented.

You can ask a member of the House of Lords to present a petition to the House of Lords.

Use letter paper and ask staff for the instructions for petitions to the House of Lords. You should address your petition to a named member of the House of Lords.

## Petition to the European Parliament
You can petition your Member of the European Parliament (MEP). If you do not know the name or address of your MEP, staff will find out for you. A letter to your MEP does normally count against your allowance of letters.

## European Court of Human Rights
You can petition the European Court of Human Rights. But you should note that the Court will not generally deal with a petition until you have tried all the other complaints procedures. You should send your petition within six months of trying all the other procedures. You should address your petition to:

**The Secretary General, Council of Europe**
**European Court of Human Rights**
**67075 Strasbourg. France**
Hand your petition to staff. The governor/director will be told what your petition is about but you do not have to discuss it with staff.

## Parliamentary Commissioner for Administration (Parliamentary Ombudsman)
MPs can refer complaints to the Parliamentary Commissioner for Administration (PCA). If you want to ask the PCA to look at your case you should write to an MP and ask him or her to forward your complaint to the PCA. You can write direct to the PCA, but he cannot investigate a complaint unless an MP asks him to. The PCA will decide whether your complaint is suitable for him to investigate.

## The police
You can write to the Chief Officer of the local police force if you have evidence that a criminal offence may have been committed. If this concerns something that has happened in the prison you should consider whether you should raise the matter with a member of staff first. If necessary you can do this by writing to the governor/director using confidential access.

## Criminal Cases Review Commission
The Criminal Cases Review Commission (CCRC) is an independent body responsible for investigating suspected miscarriages of criminal justice in England, Wales and Northern Ireland. The Commission's main role is to review the convictions of those who believe they have either been wrongly found guilty of a criminal offence, or wrongly sentenced. The Commission is a last resort. It cannot normally consider any case until it has been through the appeal system.

Your prison should hold full information on the CCRC and to how to apply. The Commission's address is:

**Criminal Cases Review Commission**
**23 Stephenson Street**
**Birmingham**
**B2 4BH**

## Criminal Injuries Compensation Authority
The Criminal Injuries Compensation Authority (CICA) can award compensation for injuries directly resulting from a crime of violence. For your application to be considered, you must have been:

(a) a victim of a crime of violence, or injured in some other way covered by the Criminal Injuries Compensation Scheme; and

(b) physically or mentally injured (or both) as a result; and

(c) in England, Scotland or Wales at the time you were injured; and

(d) injured seriously enough to qualify for at least the minimum award available under the scheme. Or, you must be a dependent or relative of a victim of violence who has since died.

If you want to apply to the CICA you will be allowed to do so.

The address is:
**The Criminal Injuries Compensation Authority**
**Alexander Bain House Atlantic Quay 15 York Street Glasgow G2 8JQ**

## Equality and Human Rights Commission
You can write to the Equality and Human Rights Commission to ask for their help in making a complaint of unlawful discrimination. Their address is:

Equality and Human Rights Commission
Fleetbank House
2-6 Salisbury Square
London EC4Y 8JX

**Other organisations**
There are other organisations you can write to, such as the National Council for Civil Liberties (Liberty), the National Association for the Care and Resettlement of Offenders (NACRO), the Prison Reform Trust (PRT) and the Women Prisoners' Resource Centre. These organisations have no power to deal with your complaint but may be able to offer advice.

## 2.4.2 THE PRISONS AND PROBATION OMBUDSMAN

The Prisons and Probation Ombudsman (PPO) is appointed by and reports directly to the Secretary of State for Justice. The Ombudsman's office is wholly independent of the services in remit, which include those provided by Her Majesty's Prison and Probation Service (HMPPS), the National Probation Service for England and Wales; Prisoner Escort and Custody Services; the Home Office (Immigration Enforcement); the Youth Justice Board; and those local authorities with secure children's homes. It is also operationally independent of, but sponsored by, the Ministry of Justice (MoJ).

The roles and responsibilities of the PPO are set out in the Terms of Reference (ToR), the 2021/2022 version of which can be found below. The PPO has three main investigative duties:
• complaints made by prisoners, young people in detention, offenders under probation supervision and immigration detainees
• deaths of prisoners, young people in detention, approved premises' residents and immigration detainees due to any cause
• using the PPO's discretionary powers, the investigation of deaths of recently released prisoners or detainees

**Vision & Values**
*PPO vision*
To carry out independent investigations to make custody and community supervision safer and fairer
*PPO values*
We are:
• Impartial: we do not take sides
• Respectful: we are considerate and courteous
• Inclusive: we value diversity
• Dedicated: we are determined and focused
• Fair: we are honest and act with integrity
The Prisons and Probation Ombudsman is totally independent of the Prison Service. He and his colleagues can investigate prisoners' complaints

once they have been through all stages of the Prison Service's internal complaints system. The current Prisons and Probation Ombudsman is Sue McAllister and she can be contacted as shown below:

**Prisons and Probation Ombudsman,**
**Third Floor, 10 South Colonnade,**
**London E14 4PU**

**Email (general & complaints):**
mail@ppo.gov.uk
**Email (fatal incidents):**
PPOFIIAdmin@ppo.gov.uk

**Fax: 020 7633 4141**
**General telephone enquiries: 020 7633 4100 or lo-call 0845 010 7938**
**Media enquiries: 020 3334 0357 (media Only)**

**Brief history**
The Woolf Report into the prison disturbances of 1990 led to the creation of an independent adjudicator for prisoner complaints. The report identified a lack of an independent point of appeal as one of the causes for the disturbances and recommended that an independent arbiter be appointed who would consider applications from complainants who had not achieved satisfaction through the internal complaints system. The office of the Prisons Ombudsman was officially created in 1994.
In 2001 the Ombudsman's remit was extended to include complaints from those under probation supervision. The office was re-named the Prisons and Probation Ombudsman to reflect this change. A further extension in 2006 incorporated complaints from those in immigration detention. The fatal incidents function was introduced in 2004 adding to the Ombudsman's remit the requirement to investigate all deaths in prisons; probation approved premises, immigration detention facilities and secure training centres. The Ombudsman also has the ability to conduct ad hoc investigations on request.
The Ombudsman's post is currently vacant (September 2022) following the retirement of Sue McAllister in June 2022; she was appointed Ombudsman in October 2018.
Prisoners have confidential access to the Prisons and Probation Ombudsman. Prison Service staff cannot prevent a prisoner from referring a complaint to the Ombudsman. Telephone calls to the Prisons and Probation Ombudsman's office should be in sight, but out of hearing, of prison staff. Leaflets explaining the work of the Prisons and Probation Ombudsman, and how to complain, are available at all prisons.
**The Ombudsman:**
(September 2022) - post currently vacant

## TERMS OF REFERENCE 2022/2023

Published 13th December 2021

### The Role

1. The Prisons and Probation Ombudsman (PPO) is appointed by the Secretary of State for Justice, following recommendation by the House of Commons Justice Select Committee. The Ombudsman is therefore an administrative appointment. These Terms of Reference represent an agreement between the Ombudsman and the Secretary of State as to the Ombudsman's role.

2. The Ombudsman is wholly independent. This includes independence from Her Majesty's Prison and Probation Service (HMPPS), and any individual Local Authority, the Home Office, the Youth Justice Board (YJB), providers of secure youth accommodation, the Department for Education (DfE), the Department of Health, NHS England & Improvement and Healthcare Inspectorate Wales (HIW)[1]. This enables the Ombudsman to execute fair and impartial investigations, making recommendations for change where necessary, without fear or favour. The Ombudsman's ability to act entirely independently from the authorities in remit is an absolute and necessary function of the role.

3. The Ombudsman's office is operationally independent of, though it is sponsored by, the Ministry of Justice (MoJ). The perceived and visible independence of the Ombudsman from the sponsorship body is fundamental to the work of the Ombudsman. No MoJ official may attempt to exert undue influence on the view of the Ombudsman.

4. The bodies subject to investigation by the Prisons and Probation Ombudsman will make sure the requirements of these Terms of Reference are set out clearly to staff in internal policies, procedures and instructions.

### Matters subject to investigation

5. The Ombudsman can investigate:

i.decisions and actions (including failures or refusals to act) relating to the management, supervision, care and treatment of prisoners, detained individuals, or young people in secure accommodation[2]. The Ombudsman's remit does not depend on the authority in remit or their staff, acting or failing to act, or taking decisions, themselves. The Ombudsman will therefore also look at the decisions and actions of contractors and subcontractors and of the servants and agents of the services in remit, including members of the Independent Monitoring Board and other volunteers, where these are relevant to the matter under investigation;

ii. decisions and actions (including failures or refusals to act) relating to the management, supervision, care and treatment of offenders under probation supervision. The Ombudsman's remit does not depend on HMPPS, or their staff, acting or failing to act or taking decisions, themselves. The Ombudsman will therefore also look at the decisions and actions of contractors and sub-contractors and of the servants and agents of HMPPS, including volunteers and supply chain organisations, where these are relevant to the matter under investigation; and

iii. decisions and actions (including failures or refusals to act) in relation to the management, supervision, care and treatment of individuals detained under immigration powers, including residents of immigration removal centres, those held in short term holding facilities or pre-departure accommodation, and those under immigration escort. The Ombudsman's remit does not depend on the Home Office or their staff, acting or failing to act, or taking decisions, themselves. The Ombudsman will therefore also look at the decisions and actions of contractors and sub-contractors and of the servants and agents of the Home Office, including members of the Independent Monitoring Board and other volunteers, where these are relevant to the matter under investigation.

6. The Secretary of State for Justice may also request that the Ombudsman carries out an exceptional investigation that would normally be outside of the Ombudsman's remit. It would be for the Ombudsman to decide whether they are able to undertake the investigation.

### Right of access

7. The 'Head' of the relevant authority (or the relevant Secretary of State where appropriate) will ensure that the Ombudsman has unfettered access to all relevant material, held both in hard copy and electronically, that is required for the purpose of investigations within the Ombudsman's Terms of Reference. This includes classified material, physical and mental health information, and information originating from or held by other organisations e.g. contractors (or their sub-contractors) providing services to or on behalf of those within remit. The Ombudsman will consider representations as to the necessity of particular material being provided, the means by which provision is achieved and any sensitivity connected with future publication, but the final decision rests with the Ombudsman who will define the material required based on the context of the investigation.

8. The Ombudsman and their staff will have access to the premises of the authorities in remit, at times specified by the Ombudsman, for the purpose of conducting interviews with employees, prisoners, detained individuals and other individuals, for examining source materials (including those held electronically such as CCTV), and for pursuing other relevant enquiries in connection with investigations within the Ombudsman's Terms of Reference. The Ombudsman will normally arrange such visits in advance.

9. The Ombudsman and their staff have the right to interview all employees, prisoners, detained individuals and other individuals as required for the purpose of an investigation and will be granted unfettered access to all such individuals. This includes the staff of contractors and sub-contractors.

Complaints
10. The Ombudsman's complaints investigations will support the UK's compliance with the requirements of Article 3 (read with Article 1) of the European Convention on Human Rights, specifically by ensuring the independent investigation of allegations of torture, inhumane or degrading treatment or punishment.

11.The aims of the Ombudsman's investigations are to:
• establish the facts relating to the complaint with particular emphasis on the integrity of the process adopted by the authority in remit and the adequacy of the conclusions reached;
• examine whether any change in operational methods, policy, practice or management arrangements would help prevent a recurrence;
• seek to resolve the matter in whatever way the Ombudsman sees fit, including by mediation; and
• where the complaint is upheld, restore the complainant, as far as is possible, to the position they would have occupied had the event not occurred.

12. The Ombudsman will consider the merits of the complaint as well as the procedures involved.

Persons able to complain
13. The Ombudsman will investigate eligible complaints submitted by the following people:
i.Prisoners[3], including prisoners in the custody of the Prisoner Escort and Custody Service (PECS)[4], and young people, including those in youth detention accommodation[5] , who have failed to obtain satisfaction from the internal complaints system in place at the relevant institution;
ii. offenders who are, or have been, under probation supervision or accommodated in

approved premises and who have failed to obtain satisfaction from the probation complaints system; and
iii. individuals detained under immigration powers[6], including residents of immigration removal centres, pre-departure accommodation, short-term holding facilities and those under managed immigration escort anywhere in the UK and internationally[7], who have failed to obtain satisfaction from the Home Office complaints system;

14. The Ombudsman will normally only act on the basis of eligible complaints from those individuals set out at paragraph 13 and not on those from other individuals or organisations. However, the Ombudsman has discretion to accept complaints from third parties on behalf of individuals set out at paragraph 13, where the individual concerned is either deceased or is unable to act on their own behalf. Complaints from legal representatives (or similar) will require the written consent of the individual set out at paragraph 13, before the complaint can be considered by the Ombudsman.

15. The Ombudsman also has discretion to accept complaint referrals (that it would be inappropriate for the authority to consider under its own internal complaints procedure) direct from HM Inspectorate of Prisons (HMIP), the IMB or Lay Observers, acting on behalf of the National Preventive Mechanism under OPCAT[8] , where an individual alleges that the authority has prevented them from communicating with HMIP, the IMB, Lay Observers or PPO, or that they have been subject to victimisation or sanctions as a result of doing so[9].

Eligibility of Complaints
16. Before putting a complaint to the Ombudsman, a complainant must first seek redress through the appropriate use of the relevant prison, PECS, youth detention accommodation[10], probation or Home Office complaint procedure.

17. Complainants will have confidential access to the Ombudsman and no attempt should be made to prevent a complainant from referring a complaint to the Ombudsman. The cost of postage of complaints to the Ombudsman by prisoners, individuals detained under immigration powers and young people in detention, will be met by the relevant authority.

18. Where there is some doubt or dispute as to the eligibility of a complaint, the Ombudsman will contact the relevant authority in remit who

will provide the Ombudsman with such documents or other information as the Ombudsman considers are relevant to considering eligibility.

19. If a complaint is considered ineligible, the Ombudsman will inform the complainant and explain the reasons, in writing.

20. The Ombudsman may decide not to accept a complaint otherwise eligible for investigation, or to discontinue any ongoing investigation, where they consider that no worthwhile outcome can be achieved, or the complaint raises no substantial issue.

21. The Ombudsman may also decide to discontinue an investigation where they consider the complainant's behaviour to be unreasonable[11]. The Ombudsman will inform the complainant in writing of the reasons for this action.

Time Limits

22. The Ombudsman will consider complaints for investigation if the complainant is dissatisfied with the reply from the authority in remit.

23. The Ombudsman will also consider complaints for possible investigation if the complainant does not receive a final reply within 30 working days of making the complaint or
i. 45 working days in the case of complaints relating to probation matters; or
ii. 30 working days of making the complaint in the case of complaints from individuals detained under immigration powers, unless the complaint is a serious misconduct complaint being investigated by the Professional Standards Unit, for which the timescale is 60 working days.

24. Complainants submitting their complaint to the Ombudsman must do so within three calendar months of receiving a substantive reply from the relevant authority.

25. The Ombudsman will not normally accept complaints where there has been a delay of more than 12 months between the complainant becoming aware of the relevant facts and submitting their case to the Ombudsman, unless the delay has been the fault of the relevant authority and the Ombudsman considers that it is appropriate to do so.

26. Complaints submitted after these deadlines will not normally be considered. However, the Ombudsman has discretion to investigate those where it considers there to be good reason for the delay, or where it considers the issues raised to be of sufficient severity to warrant an exception to the usual timeframe.

Limitations on matters subject to investigation

27. The Ombudsman may not investigate complaints about:
i. policy decisions taken by a Minister and the official advice to Ministers upon which such decisions are based;
ii. the merits of decisions taken by Ministers, except in cases which have been approved by Ministers for consideration;
iii. actions and decisions (including failures or refusals to act) in relation to matters which do not relate to the management, supervision, care and treatment of the individuals described in paragraph 13 or outside the responsibility of the authorities in remit. This exclusion covers complaints about conviction, sentence, immigration status, reasons for immigration detention or the length of such detention, and the decisions and recommendations of the judiciary, the police, the Crown Prosecution Service and the Parole Board and its Secretariat;
iv. matters that are currently or have previously been the subject of civil litigation or criminal proceedings; and
v. the clinical judgement of healthcare professionals.

Fatal Incidents

28. The Ombudsman's fatal incident investigations will support the UK's compliance with the requirements of Article 2 (read with Article 1) of the European Convention on Human Rights which ensures the right to life, specifically the need for the independent investigation of all deaths in custody.

29. The Ombudsman will investigate the circumstances of:
i. the deaths, from any cause, of prisoners and young people, including those in youth detention accommodation[12] and those in Secure Children's Homes on a welfare basis. This generally includes people temporarily absent from the establishment but still subject to detention (for example, under escort, at court or in hospital);
ii. the deaths of people in the custody of PECS in HMCTS court premises
or in PECS custody on escort[13];
iii. neonatal deaths and stillbirths that occur within the prison or under prison transfer (including on prison transfer to hospital);
iv. neonatal deaths and stillbirths that occur in hospital following transfer from prison where the PPO considers it necessary to exercise their discretion to investigate;
v. the deaths of children living in a Mother and

Baby Unit within a prison;

vi. the deaths of those who have been released from prison where the PPO considers it necessary to exercise their discretion to investigate;

vii. the deaths of residents of approved premises (including voluntary residents) where the PPO considers this is necessary, including for Article 2 compliance; and

viii. the deaths of detained individuals, including residents of immigration removal centres, pre-departure accommodation, short-term holding facilities and those under managed immigration escort anywhere in the UK and internationally[14].

30. The Ombudsman will have discretion to investigate, to the extent appropriate, other fatal incidents that raise issues about the care provided by the relevant authorities in respect of paragraph 5 (i) to (iii).

31. The Ombudsman will act on notification of a death from the relevant authority and will decide on the extent and output of the investigation, which will be determined by the circumstances of the death.

32. The aims of the Ombudsman's investigations are to:

• establish the circumstances and events surrounding the death, in particular the management of the individual by the relevant authority or authorities within remit, but also including any relevant external factors;

• examine whether any change in operational methods, policy, practice or management arrangements would help prevent a recurrence;

• in conjunction with NHS England & Improvement, [15] HIW or the relevant authority in the cases of the deaths of individuals detained under immigration powers in Scotland or Northern Ireland, [16] where appropriate, examine relevant health issues and assess clinical care;

• provide explanations and insight for the bereaved relatives; and

• help fulfil the investigative obligation arising under Article 2 of the European Convention on Human Rights ('the right to life') by working together with coroners to ensure as far as possible that the full facts are brought to light and any relevant failing is exposed, any commendable action or practice is identified, and any lessons from the death are made clear[17].

Clinical issues

33. The Ombudsman's investigation includes an examination of the clinical issues relevant to each death. In the case of deaths in prisons, youth detention accommodation, Secure Children's Homes and immigration detention facilities, the Ombudsman will ask NHS England & Improvement or, in Wales, the HIW[18] to review the clinical care provided according to agreed protocols, including whether referrals to secondary healthcare were made appropriately. The Ombudsman may also ask NHS England & Improvement or the HIW to provide a clinical reviewer for other fatal incident investigations when the Ombudsman determines a clinical review is necessary. The clinical reviewer will be independent of the relevant authority's healthcare provision and will have unfettered access to healthcare information. Where appropriate, the reviewer will conduct joint interviews with the Ombudsman's investigator.

Relationship with other investigations

34. The Ombudsman may defer all or part of a complaint or fatal incident investigation, when the police are conducting a criminal investigation in parallel. If at any time the Ombudsman forms the view that a criminal investigation should be undertaken, the Ombudsman will alert the police.[19]

35. In the case of the death of a young person in custody, the Local Safeguarding Children Board in England will conduct a serious case review. In Wales, the Safeguarding Children Board may undertake a child practice review. This will normally take place in parallel to the Ombudsman's investigation. The PPO will seek to work closely with the relevant Safeguarding Board to maximise the benefit of both exercises.

36. If at any time during or following a complaint or fatal incident investigation the Ombudsman forms the view that a relevant authority in remit should undertake a disciplinary investigation, the Ombudsman will inform that authority.

37. If at any time findings emerge from the Ombudsman's investigation that the Ombudsman considers require immediate action by the relevant authority, the Ombudsman will alert the relevant authority to those findings at the earliest opportunity.

Output from the Ombudsman's investigations

38. The Ombudsman has the discretion to choose the manner in which the findings of investigations are reported but all investigations will result in a written response.

39. The Ombudsman may share an advance draft of the written response, in whole or part, to the authority in remit where there is concern over the disclosure of security issues.

40. If a draft report contains criticism of named staff or recommends that disciplinary action be considered against an identified individual, the Ombudsman will normally disclose an advance copy of the draft, in whole or part, to the relevant authority in order that they, and the staff member(s) subject to criticism, have the opportunity to make representations (unless that requirement has been discharged by other means during the course of the investigation).

41. The Ombudsman may make recommendations to the authorities within remit, the relevant Secretary of State or to any other body or individual that the Ombudsman considers appropriate given their role, duties and powers.

Complaints Investigations
42. Where a formal report is to be issued, the Ombudsman will send a draft to the head of the authority in remit and the complainant.

43. The recipient(s) will have an agreed period to draw attention to any factual inaccuracies. The relevant authority may also use this opportunity to respond to any recommendations.

44. The Ombudsman will consider any feedback on the draft report, but will exercise their own discretion on what, if any, changes to make, and issue a final report. Final reports will be issued to the complainant and the relevant authority. Additional circulation of final reports will be at the Ombudsman's discretion.

45. The authorities within remit or the relevant Secretary of State will provide the Ombudsman with a response to the final report within four weeks, indicating whether a recommendation is accepted or not (in which case reasons will be provided) and the steps to be taken by that authority within set timeframes to address the Ombudsman's recommendations, including evidence of implementation of the recommendations. The Ombudsman will advise the complainant of the response to the recommendations.

Fatal Incident Investigations
46. Where a fatal incident investigation report is to be issued, the Ombudsman will send a draft and any related documents to the head of the authority in remit, the bereaved family, the Coroner, and NHS England & Improvement or HIW.[20]

47. The recipients will have an agreed period to draw attention to any factual inaccuracies.

48. The authorities within remit or the relevant Secretary of State will provide the Ombudsman with a response, within the specified timeframe, of receiving the draft report, indicating whether a recommendation is accepted or not (in which case reasons will be provided) and the steps to be taken by that authority within set timeframes to address the Ombudsman's recommendations. Where that response has not been included in the Ombudsman's report, the Ombudsman may, after consulting the authority as to its suitability, append it to the report at any stage.

49. The Ombudsman will consider any feedback on the draft report, but will exercise their own discretion on what, if any, changes to make, and issue a final report.

50. Final reports will be issued to the relevant authority, the bereaved family, the Coroner, the Local Authority, and NHS England & Improvement or HIW[21]. Additional circulation of final reports will be at the Ombudsman's discretion.

51. In the case of a fatal incident investigation, and having considered any views of the recipients of the report and having complied with the legal obligations in relation to data protection and privacy, the Ombudsman will publish the final report on the Ombudsman's website. All references to individuals other than the deceased will be anonymised.[22]

52. The Ombudsman will consult the Coroner or relevant authority if the report is to be published before the inquest.

Reporting Arrangements
53. The Ombudsman will produce and publish an annual report, which the Secretary of State for Justice will lay before Parliament. The content of the report will be at the Ombudsman's discretion but will normally include:
• anonymised examples of complaints investigated;
• anonymised examples of fatal incidents investigated[23];
• recommendations made and responses received;
• a summary of the workload of the office, including the number and types of complaints received, investigated and upheld and the number and types of death notifications received and investigated;
• the office's success in meeting its performance targets;
• a summary of the costs of the office.

54. The Ombudsman may publish additional reports on issues relating to their investigations, such as themed learning lessons publications. The Ombudsman may also publish other information as considered appropriate.

55. The Ombudsman's targets for conducting investigations, responding to complainants and publishing reports will be set out in an annual business plan.

Disclosure

56. The Ombudsman is subject to the Data Protection Act 2018, the General Data Protection Regulation (GDPR) and the Freedom of Information Act 2000.

57. In accordance with the practice applying across government departments, the Ombudsman will follow the Government's policy that official information should be made available unless it is clearly not in the public interest to do so.

58. The Ombudsman, HM Inspectorate of Prisons and Probation, IMB and the Lay Observers will share relevant information, knowledge and expertise, especially in relation to conditions for prisoners, residents and detained individuals generally. The Ombudsman may also share information with other relevant specialist advisers and investigating bodies, such as the Independent Office for Police Conduct, to the extent necessary to fulfil the aims of an investigation. Protocols will be developed in order to describe the Ombudsman's relationship with relevant partners.

1 Referred to throughout as 'the authorities'.
2 The PPO will investigate fatal incidents in Secure Children's Homes (SCHs). This includes fatal incidents of young people placed in SCHs on welfare grounds. The Ombudsman will not investigate complaints from young people in SCHs.
3 The PPO definition of a prisoner for these purposes is an individual who is under a sentence of imprisonment,
is in prison or is on temporary release from prison.
4 Individuals in the custody of PECS can only complain if they are also a prisoner. The PPO will not investigate complaints from those in PECS custody where the complaint is regarding an event that took place on police premises.
5 For the purposes of complaints, this does not include secure children's home accommodation.
6 defined throughout as those detained under powers set out in the Immigration Acts.
7 The PPO's remit only covers individuals detained under powers set out in the Immigration Acts.
8 The Optional Protocol to the Convention against Torture and other Cruel, Inhuman or Degrading Treatment or Punishment (OPCAT) is an international human rights treaty designed to strengthen protection for people deprived of their liberty. It recognises that such people are particularly vulnerable and aims to prevent their ill- treatment through establishing a system of visits or inspections to all places of detention. OPCAT requires that States designate a 'national preventive mechanism' (NPM) to carry out visits to places of detention, to monitor the treatment of

and conditions for detainees and to make recommendations regarding the prevention of ill- treatment. The UK ratified OPCAT in December 2003 and designed its NPM in March 2009. The UK's NPM is currently made up of 18 visiting or inspecting bodies who visit places of detention such as prisons, police custody and immigration detention centres.
9 The relationship between the named bodies is described in a separate protocol.
10 For the purposes of complaints, this does not include secure children's home accommodation.
11 As defined by the PPO policy on Dealing with Unreasonable Behaviour from Complainants.
12 This covers deaths in young offender institutions, secure training centres and secure children's homes.
13 The PPO's remit does not cover deaths that occur in police premises.
14 The PPO's remit only covers individuals detained under powers set out in the Immigration Acts.
15 The National Health Service Commissioning Board and Clinical Commissioning Groups (Responsibilities and Standing Rules) Regulations 2012 confer responsibility on the NHS Commissioning Board (NHS England) for commissioning health services in prisons and custodial establishments.
16 In the case of fatal incident in Immigration Removal Centres in Scotland or Northern Ireland.
17 The relationship between the Ombudsman and the Coroners' Society is described in a separate Memorandum of Understanding.
18 In the case of fatal incidents in Immigration Removal centres in Scotland or Northern Ireland, the equivalent relevant authority.
19 The relationship between the Police and the Ombudsman is described in a Memorandum of Understanding.
20 In the case of fatal incidents in Immigration Removal centres in Scotland or Northern Ireland, the equivalent relevant authority.
21 In the case of fatal incidents in Immigration Removal centres in Scotland or Northern Ireland, the equivalent relevant authority.
22 In reports of fatal incident investigations of people under the age of 18, the deceased person's details are also anonymised.
23 Anonymised at the discretion of the Ombudsman.

## 2.5 PRISONER COMMUNICATIONS
### Letters, Visits, & Phone Calls:
### *The Importance of Family Ties*

*Policy name: Strengthening Prisoners Family Ties Policy Framework. Date: 31 January 2019*

*NOTE The Covid Pandemic seriously effected prison visits during 2020/2021, and for some establishments it has continued to cause disruption into 2022. The majority of prisons are now operating visits again, some to a limited extent, but if there are further Covid-19 outbreaks visiting may once again be affected into 2023.*

### Mobile PIN Phones

To support prisoners in maintaining contact with family and friends during the COVID-19 pandemic challenges, temporary Mobile PIN Phones were distributed to prisons without in-cell telephony via the regional Prison Group Directors network.

With each prison facing different challenges depending on numerous factors (including prisoner and staff infection rates, physical design of prison buildings etc.) establishments were encouraged to provide access to the mobile PIN phones in a way that met the needs of their own prisoner population. Prioritisation was focused around providing phone access to prisoners with COVID, isolating and clinically vulnerable prisoners, those who were not able to make use of fixed PIN phones in landing/association areas and also in temporary accommodation units where no alternative telephone communication was available.

Between April 2020 until June 2021 prisoners made over 1.3 million calls on the mobile PIN phones, suggesting they have been widely distributed and used. The mobile PIN phones were distributed according to need as assessed by Prison Group Directors offices. Where infection levels increased the central team supported individual establishments by redirecting unused stock to those prisons most in need to maintain prisoner contact with family and friends.

### In-Cell Telephony
June 2022

In-Cell Telephony pin phones are installed directly into cells which provide prisoners with easier access to telephony without the need to share communal pin phones.

This enhancement allows for privacy and flexibility to contact family, friends and support frameworks.

In-Cell Telephones are an extension of the current communal wing pin phone system which means all calls remain restricted to pre-approved numbers only, and that public protection and safeguarding factors have been considered prior to the number being approved by the prison.

All calls are recorded for the purpose of call monitoring, with the exception of legal calls and support lines such as the Samaritans. Phones are active during the agreed operating times specified by the prison.

There are 14 open prisons within England and Wales that are currently out of scope for In-Cell Telephony due to the prisons being open and offering access to communal pin phones 24/7.

There are 12 closed prisons within England and Wales where the introduction of In-Cell Telephony is intended but not currently in place. The following Public Closed Estate Prisons in England and Wales have In-Cell Telephony installed: Aylesbury, Bedford, Belmarsh, Berwyn, Brinsford, Bristol, Bullingdon, Chelmsford, Cookham Wood, Downview, Drake Hall, Durham, Eastwood Park, Elmley, Erlestoke, Exeter, Featherstone, Feltham, Foston Hall, Garth, Gartree, Guys Marsh, Hewell, Highdown, Highpoint, Hindley, Holme House, Hull, Humber, Huntercombe, Isis, Isle of Wight, Kirklevington Grange, Lancaster Farms, Leeds, Leicester, Lewes, Lincoln, Lindholme, Liverpool, Low Newton, Maidstone, Manchester, Moorland, New Hall, Norwich, Nottingham, Pentonville, Portland, Ranby, Risley, Send, Stocken, Stoke Heath, Styal, Swaleside, Swansea, Swinfen Hall, The Mount, Warren Hill, Wandsworth, Wayland, Wealstun, Werrington, Wetherby, Winchester, Woodhill, Wormwood Scrubs, Rochester, Birmingham.

The following prisons are currently at implementation stage and will complete installation by the end of 2022:
Brixton, Buckley Hall, Cardiff, Channings Wood, Coldingley, Deerbolt, Morton Hall, Onley, Preston, The Verne and Wymott.

The Private Estate Prisons in England and Wales that have In-Cell Telephony installed are: Altcourse, Ashfield, Bronzefield, Doncaster, Dovegate, Five Wells, Forest Bank, Lowdham Grange, Northumberland, Oakwood, Parc, Peterborough, Rye Hill, Thameside.

The Public Closed Prisons in England and Wales without In-Cell Telephony, but where its introduction is intended, are:
Bure, Dartmoor, Frankland, Full Sutton, Grendon, Littlehey, Long Lartin, Stafford, Usk, Wakefield, Whatton, Whitemoor

The Public Open Prisons currently out of scope to receive In-Cell Telephony are:
Askham Grange, East Sutton Park, Ford, Hatfield, Haverigg, Hollesley Bay, Kirkham, Leyhill, North Sea Camp, Prescoed, Springhill, Stanford Hill, Sudbury, Thorn Cross.

For HMP Wymott, implementation is underway, and completion is due by December 2022.

### Family Services

Since October 2017, Governors in Public Sector Prisons have held the budgets and responsibility for providing family services, giving them the authority and leverage to utilise resources to support positive relationships between prisoners, their family and significant others.

Governors were engaged in a commercial exercise to select new family services providers which are now contracted to deliver services over 3 years + 1 year - providing flexibility where an extension at the end of the contract period may be required.

### Purpose

The *Strengthening Prisoners Family Ties Policy Framework* policy supports the maintenance and development of prisoners' relationships with family, significant others and friends, by using a range of methods and interventions. Supporting prisoners' relationships outside of prison is considered to help prevent reoffending and reduce intergenerational crime.

Prisoners, their family and significant others, all internal and external staff and service providers are encouraged to work in partnership and share good practice, to enhance opportunities for prisoners to develop or enhance positive relationships. This service can include physical (visits), digital and other forms of communications such as phone calls and letters.

## Evidence

There is growing evidence that family support and maintaining family ties is not only important for the well-being of prisoners, but may also aid reintegration into the community following release from prison, and reduce reoffending. In a Ministry of Justice Surveying Prisoner Crime Reduction (SPCR) survey of almost 1500 newly sentenced prisoners in England and Wales, 40% said that support from their family, and 36% said that seeing their children, would help prevent them from reoffending.

Other research using survey data found that prisoners who received visits during imprisonment or who had a close partner were more likely to report that they had arranged employment and accommodation on release, and had a lower reconviction rate in the year after release from prison, than those who did not.

A recent study found that higher levels of emotional support were associated with significantly lower rates of recidivism among a reasonably large sample of prisoners in the U.S. This effect was stronger for incarcerated women than men.

In another UK based study positive family relationships significantly predicted less difficulty with accommodation, alcohol and drugs, better family relationships and coping ability after release.

## Outcomes

• Each prison must have a Family and Significant Other Strategy and development plan that is available to prisoners, staff and all visitors. The strategy is outward facing, published and freely available to families, prisoners and staff. It will be easy to read; avoiding any complex language or acronyms.

• Governors will identify the development aims of the Family and Significant Other Strategy and seek to report back on progress of objectives at least annually.

• A Senior Manager leads on Families and ensures that family work is an operational priority.

• Family work is prioritised and staff understand its importance in reducing reoffending keeping prisoners safe and preventing self-harm and suicide.

• All staff are fully trained in child protection/Public Protection and Safeguarding.

• Family service provision supports the development and maintenance of prisoners' family and significant other ties and outside contacts.

• Information is made available to prisoners, their family and significant others regarding the application process for accessing extended visits, where locally these are made available.

• Family learning service in partnership with the offender learning provider offer advice on how best to meet the needs of the prisoners, family/significant others.

• Governors and Directors use Release on Temporary Licence (ROTL) to enable prisoners that have been risk assessed and approved to spend time with family and significant others.

• Innovative approaches are developed to enable prisoners to engage with their family and significant relationships.

• Governors must provide contact details that prisoners' families/significant others can use to share information with the prison about risk of harm to and from prisoners.

• Governors must put effective arrangements in place to receive and act promptly on information, and to provide feedback to the individual where appropriate.

## Requirements

*Legal Requirements*

The following criteria reflect the requirements of Article 8 of the European Convention on Human Rights ("ECHR"); Respect for family life and private life.

• Under section 6 of the Human Rights Act 1998, a public authority is obliged to act compatibly with ECHR rights, including article 8. Both the Secretary of State for Justice and governors are bound by section 6 of the Human Rights Act 1998. Governors must ensure that the local prison approach to the family ties strategy is sufficient to ensure compliance with article 8.

*Prison Rules 1999*

• Each prison must ensure that it operates in accordance with rule 4 of the Prison Rules 1999 and complies regarding outside contacts.

• Special attention shall be paid to the maintenance of such relationships between a prisoner and his family or significant other, as are desirable in the best interests of both, Prison Rule 4(1).

• A prisoner shall be encouraged and assisted to establish and maintain such relations with persons and agencies outside prison as may, in the opinion of the governor, best promote the interests of his family and his own social rehabilitation, Prison Rule 4(2).

The Equality Act created the Public Sector Equality Duty (PSED), which requires that public authorities, including the Secretary of State for Justice and Governors must, in the exercise of their functions, have due regard to the need to:

- Eliminate unlawful discrimination, harassment and victimisation and other conduct prohibited by the Act.
- Advance equality of opportunity between people who share a protected characteristic and those who do not.
- Foster good relations between people who share a protected characteristic and those who do not.

*See PSI 20/2016 Implementation of Equality Analysis* According to Prison Rules 1999, HMPPS shall encourage and assist the maintenance of relationships between prisoners and their families to support their social rehabilitation. This is integral to an offender's right to family life as their rehabilitation and visits are crucial to sustaining relationships with close relatives, partners and friends where appropriate and help maintain links within the community.

All newly received prisoners and their family must be provided with information about early days in custody which include information on visits in a format that is easy to understand.

In compliance with rule 10(2) of the prison rules 1999 the governor or a designated member of staff must explain information to a prisoner (i.e. orally) if they cannot read or have difficulty understanding, so that they can understand their rights. Materials and information must also be provided in different ways for prisoners who are learning disabled, illiterate, have mental health impairments, are blind, or require a foreign language translation.

### Visits

Governors must permit prisoners to receive visits in compliance with Prison Rule 35 on personal visits, which requires that convicted prisoners must be permitted to receive visits twice every 4 weeks. Governors must also actively encourage prisoners to maintain outside contacts as may, in the opinion of the Governor, best promote the interests of his family and his own social rehabilitation. Prison Rule 4 sets out that special attention should be paid to the maintenance of relationships between a prisoner and their family as are desirable in the best interests of both; including foreign national prisoners. See PSI 16/2011 Providing Visits and Services to Visitors for details of statutory entitlements to visits and the environment that these take place in, as well as who is eligible. Guidance is provided on good practice relating to visits.

Governors need to be mindful of the fact that the visitor experience is very much determined by their first experience of attempting to book a visit. Visits booking systems rules need to be accurate, straightforward and widely advertised on the MOJ prison finder page. Consideration must be given to ensuring the prison's booking line provides adequate cover to ensure the work is remains an operational priority. Turnaround times on the simplest of visit booking requests can be lengthy and can be further delayed when a visit request isn't straightforward.

Governors must consider any potential barriers at the establishment such as the physical appearance of the visits halls, the lengthy wait time from entering the visits centre to seeing a prisoner which may reduce meaningful contact time.

Governors may wish to consider utilising the HMPPS centralised booking system which provides the prison with the opportunity to offer visitors a booking line from 9am – 6pm Monday to Friday, online bookings which can be actioned within 1 – 3 working days over 90% of the time and a dedicated email booking facility for professional visitors. While a standardised booking approach is aimed for, the service does not lose sight of the individual prison culture and population and their challenges and currently covers a range of prison establishments (such as HMP, YOIs and the Women's estate). This allows the prison to focus on their internal processes but also the visitor (and prisoner) experience at the prison.

Provision will include the following:

- Facilities should be provided for children to play whilst visiting a prisoner.
- Governors will ensure that private meetings can be facilitated between visitors and Partner Agencies
- The visitors' area caters for the needs of children and promotes a positive and safe experience.
- Visitors receive understandable basic information through a variety of media on support services for families and signposting to specialist services.
- All visitors have an opportunity to speak to a member of staff to share their concerns or discuss their family member.
- Accurate information about the Assisted Prison Visits Scheme (APVU) and establishment visiting arrangements is accessible to visitors.
- A Family Support Worker is available to support families.

### Assisted Prison Visits Scheme (APVS)

See 'Visits' below.

### Establishing a Family Strategy

Governors and Directors must develop a family and significant other strategy that includes the following Farmer family offer defined as:

(a) Visitor base/centre and visiting services;
(b) Staffing structure to ensure family work is an operational priority;
(c) Extended visits for eligible prisoners based on local policy; (e.g., Homework clubs and family days)

(d) Family learning; and

(e) 'Gateway' communication system. – (Effective arrangements for families/significant others to report safety concerns, and promotion of their use)

The Family and Significant Other Strategy may be an individual document for each prison, or an overarching group strategy which sets out how each prison will deliver on the outcomes set out in this document. The HMPPS Family and Significant Operational Guidance document is a useful tool to aid the development and maintenance of a strategy that will support the delivery a well- structured family and significant other service.

When developing the local family strategy, Governors must consider recommendations from the Farmer Review (2017), HMIP Expectations and Operations Systems Assurance Group Audit and other relevant data.

The Senior Manager responsible for family visits must monitor and review their family service provision through a formal annual review process, including a visitor feedback based on intentions listed in a published, Local Family Strategy. This information may be collected using a needs analysis and surveys. See HMPPS Family and Significant Other Operational Guidance for an example of a Visitor Survey.

## Other Requirements

*Family contact*

Governors in partnership with family service providers must make opportunities available for prisoners to interact positively with their family and significant others. This may include family days where prisoners can spend time with their families in a relaxed environment; homework clubs as appropriate depending on location, or other bespoke services to meet the identified needs of prisoners and the prison category.

Governors will establish a process that enables family members and/or other people with concerns about a prisoner's safety to contact an identified member of staff without delay. On receipt of such information:

• A member of staff will physically check to make sure that the prisoner is safe.

The information received will be used to determine:

• for a prisoner who is not being supported through the ACCT process, if to open an ACCT document, or what other action is necessary;

• for a prisoner who is being supported through ACCT, if a review is necessary.

The process must include prompt feedback to the person who raised the concerns, to confirm that the individual is safe and (with due consideration to the appropriateness of the level of information sharing) to describe what action is being taken.

This service may be required at any time, and Governors will therefore need to ensure the effectiveness of the provision at all times of the day and night, and that it is sufficiently resourced. The potential benefit of this service will include reducing the risk of self-harm and suicide, particularly after a difficult visit or phone call, or the receipt of bad news.

## Play facilities

Governors and providers must make sure that all staff delivering services to children are appropriately vetted, trained and have received clearance to work with children and vulnerable people (Disclosing and Baring Service – DBS, Security Vetting).

## Prisoners without family contact details

Governors must identify prisoners who do not have details of family or significant others or who do not receive visits. Establishments should evidence that such individuals have been encouraged and supported to establish at least one external contact.

In accordance with Prison Rule 4(2) Governors must encourage and assist prisoners to establish and maintain relations with agencies (as well as persons) which the governor thinks best promote the interests of their social rehabilitation. They should identify which type of agency, organisation or charity with the help of the family services providers could help prisoners with rehabilitation.

In compliance with Prison Rule 5, consideration must be made to the prisoner's future from the beginning of their sentence, giving assistance during their incarceration and through the gate. Where required, family services providers can support this process.

## Foreign National Prisoners

Foreign National Offenders (FNO) represent the second biggest cohort of prisoners housed in the general estate and also has its own distinct estate of three prisons; Maidstone, Huntercombe and Morton Hall.

• There should not be an assumption that because a prisoner is a foreign national and subject to deportation that they do not have family resident in the UK who can visit.

• It is important to facilitate a FNO's contact with family who reside overseas.

• Adopt a flexible approach for FNO's to access the telephone in accordance with PSI 49/2011, Prisoner Communication Services, to enable them to engage in meaningful contact with family resident in different time zones.

• FNOs are more likely to have family abroad which is an impediment to ongoing family visits.

Governors must consider ways to mitigate this disadvantage e.g. through additional provision for phone calls, additional visits when family are in the UK etc.

For Prison Service Instructions please see;

PSI 52/2011 - Immigration, repatriation and removal services

PSI 01/2015 - The allocation of prisoners liable to deportation or removal from the United Kingdom. On 15th June 2022 PSI 04/2013 was amended, Early Removal of Foreign National Prisoners to remove FNO's more quickly.

The Criminal Justice Act 2003 introduced the Early Removal Scheme (ERS) for foreign national prisoners. The scheme allows fixed-term foreign national prisoners (FNPs), who are confirmed by the Home Office Immigration Enforcement (HOIE) to be liable to removal from the UK, to be removed from prison and the country before the earliest point in the sentence when release could otherwise take place. This policy was revised on 15th June 2022 to incorporate the changes to the ERS that will be made by the Nationality and Borders Act 2022 (NABA 2022) which will be implemented on 28 June 2022. The NABA 2022 increases the ERS window from 9 months to 12 months and introduces a new 'stop the clock' provision for those who are removed under the ERS on or after 28 June 2022 and allows ERS for those recalled to custody from licence. In short therefore, NABA amends sections 260 and 261 of the Criminal Justice Act 2003 to increase the ERS window from 270 days before the earliest release point to 12 months before the earliest release point.

**Security**

The decision to allow any visit must be balanced against the need to maintain security and keep prisoners in lawful custody. The security measures that must be in place as part of the visits specification are set out in PSI 15/2011, Management of Security at Visits. Visits must be well managed, monitored, and where necessary due to suspected or proven inappropriate behaviour, terminated to maintain the good order and discipline of the prison.

**Contact with children - Family days and other activities**

Family days and other planned activities help to improve positive relationships between prisoners and their children or other family members. Regular and good quality contact time between an offending parent and their children, may prevent them from reoffending, as the responsibility and impact of separation may be an incentive for them not to re-offend.

• The loss of family days, which are in addition to the statutory minimum of 2 visits per 4 weeks,

cannot be linked to downgrading of incentive and earned privilege level • A risk assessment must be conducted for any prisoner wishing to take part in special children's visits dedicated to enabling prisoners to spend time with their children or events which includes children and their carers'. A separate assessment must be conducted for prisoners' subject to Safeguarding Children: Child Contact procedures.

• While it may be appropriate for a prisoner to have access to a named child under close supervision; irrespective of the prisoner's wishes the primary consideration must be whether it is in the child's best interests for the prisoner and/or child to take part in such a visit/event. It may be unsafe to allow the same prisoner general access to children. (See Public Protection Manual for details)

• Keeping Children Safe in Education (2018) page 77 refers to children who have a family member in prison may need support. The NICCO11 website provides information and assistance to schools which may seek to engage in active partnerships, such as; homework clubs, co-ordinating visits days and family days.

• All processes must support the prison's responsibility to safeguard children and other vulnerable people.

• Considering resources and security considerations, Governors may wish to consult prisoners and children on the format, environment and objectives for all family activities during family days. Prison staff may need to modify the programme to ensure that the needs of children and adults with a disability are met.

**Women's Estate**

PSI 49/2014, Mother and Baby Units, states that "The Governor/Director must ensure that procedures are in place to ask women on reception or at the earliest opportunity whether they are pregnant or have children under the age of 18 months". When collecting information about next of kin and family contacts when prisoners are received, Governors/Directors should include requesting details of children. This will enable appropriate services to be provided to support prisoners and their family. Governors/Directors are also advised to refer to the National Strategy for Women and Girls 2017-2020

**Close Relatives**

A close relative is defined as a spouse/partner (including a person - whether of the same or different sex - with whom the prisoner was living as a couple in an established relationship immediately prior to imprisonment) parent, child, brother, sister (including half or step brothers and sisters), grandparent, civil partner, fiancé or fiancée, or a person who has been acting in loco parentis to a prisoner, or a person to whom the prisoner has been in loco parentis i.e. where they have had/have parental responsibility for that person. Those who have clearly demonstrated the intention to register a civil partnership with the prisoner but have not yet done so may also be included within this definition of close relative for the purposes of correspondence.

### Care Leavers

5.5 Non-contact with family can be attributed to various reasons. Their crime may be associated with a family member either as a perpetrator or a victim. In such cases safeguarding is of paramount importance. Other prisoners may not have contact with family members because of they have been beneficiaries of the social care system as care leavers (see Guidance on Care Leavers). Family and significant other activities should be delivered to develop and enhance prisoners' relationships with at least one external significant person.

• Identify whether the prisoner is socially isolated – not engaging in the regime.
Offender Management in Custody process, family engagement workers, prisoner Samaritans and other support provision.

• Chaplaincy provides invaluable support regardless of the imprisoned person's faith and seeks to engage with those that are isolated. One approach is the Official Prison Visitors Scheme (OPV), although there are other variations to this across the prison estate. However, in some prisons, the nature of the prison may prevent volunteers from offering their services.

### VISITS
**Policy Frameworks:**
1. **Management of Security at Visits Policy Framework: Open Estate** 8th April 2021
   Annexes A to M
2. **Management of security at visits Policy Framework: Closed Estate** 8th April 2021
   Annexes A - O
PSI 16/2011 (updated Sept 2021 - Amendments have been made to paragraphs 5.13 & 5.15 to clarify when inter-prison visits should be allowed) This PSI supports the implementation of the Visits Bundle of specifications, which cover three linked services: Visits Booking, Conduct Visits and Services for Visitors.

### Booking a Visit
You can book a social visit online at: https://www.gov.uk/prison-visits
To use this online service to book a social visit to a prisoner in England or Wales, you will need:
• Prisoner's number

• Prisoner's date of birth.
• Dates of birth for all visitors coming with you.
*The prisoner must add you to their visitor list before you can book a visit. You'll get an email confirming your visit and it takes 1 to 3 days.*
**Visits - Contact the prison directly if you need to arrange any of the following:**
• Legal visits, for example a solicitor discussing the prisoner's case
• Official Prison Visits (visits by people approved by the Governor/Director to visit prisoners who have no other visits)
• Reception visits, for example the first visit to the prisoner within 72 hours of being admitted
• Double visits, for example visiting for 2 hours instead of 1
• Family Day visits - special family events that the prison organises.

### Secure video calls with prisoners
**Important Note.** Currently (September 2022) HMPPS is in the process of changing the national secure visits video provider from 'Purple Visits' to 'Prison Video'.
It is important to know which app is used by the prison in which your loved one is located - all 'Prison Establishment' entries on The Prison Oracle (prisonoracle.com) show which application to use for which prison, and from where to download it - just select 'Video Visits' from the Prison Oracle Home Page.

### Video Visits.
You can have a secure video call with a prisoner using your mobile phone or tablet.
Video calls last 30 minutes and each prisoner can have up to 4 people on the call.
This service is available at most prisons in England and Wales. You can check individual prison information pages on prisonoracle.com to see which are offering video calls.

### Having a secure video call with a prisoner
You can have a video call using an app on your phone or tablet. It's not possible to use a computer.

### You must make sure that:
• all video callers are on the prisoner's visitor list
• the 'main caller' is over 18 (people under 18 can be on the video call, as long as they are on the prisoner's visitor list)
Video calls will be recorded and monitored by male or female prison staff. Secure video calls are limited to 1 a month.

### What you'll need to make a video call
• mobile phone or tablet
• passport, driving license or other government-issued photo ID

- proof of address (if your ID does not include this)
- the prisoner's name, number and date of birth names, dates of birth and addresses for everyone who would like to be on the video call

## How to get set up for a video call

In August 2022 the Ministry of Justice began to change the national supplier of its video visiting application from Purple Visits to Prison Video. These two applications will be used in different prisons until the change over is complete.

It is important that you ensure that you have downloaded and installed the right application - Prison Video or Purple Visits - for the prison where your family or friend is located and registered an account with the right application.

### Step 1: Download and install the app

You can download the app by selecting 'Video Visits' from the Home Page of The Prison Oracle (prisonoracle.com). You will need to install the app on your phone or tablet.

### Step 2: Create an account in the app and add everyone who will be on the call

You need to create an account with the app provider. This involves taking a picture of your driving licence, passport or other government-issued photo ID. It can take up to 24 hours for your account to be verified.

You must include the names and dates of birth of everyone who will be on the video call. You will need to upload ID for people over 18.

Finally, add the name of the person you want to want to have the video call with as a 'contact'.

### Step 3: Make a video call request or wait for prison staff to schedule the video call

The exact process of scheduling a call will depend on the prison.

For some prisons, you will be able to select a possible date and time in the next 7 days in the app. In other prisons, prison staff will book a date and time following a request from the prisoner. Either way, you'll receive a confirmation email when your video call has been scheduled

### Step 4: Get set up for the video call

You need a reliable internet connection. Wifi is recommended, but you can also use 3G or 4G mobile data. Disconnect anything else that's connected to the internet, for example other phones or computers, as this may improve your connection. You don't need headphones for the video call, but it may help with the sound quality.

### Step 5: Have the video call

You'll be able to enter a 'waiting room' 15 minutes before the video call is scheduled. Open the purple visits app to go through the security checks and be ready for the call to begin. Call times are fixed and cannot be extended.

**Calls will be paused if anyone**:
- who is not booked on the call appears on the camera
- behaves in a way that would not be appropriate for a social prison visit
- tries to record the call or take a screenshot

If a call is paused, you will need to go through a security check before it can start again.

### Tips for a successful video call

Keep the camera still and switch off notifications Video calls may be interrupted by notifications and alerts, for example when you get a new email or sms message. Make sure they are switched off before the call starts.

Try and keep your phone or tablet as still as possible. It may be best to rest it against something.

### Good lighting and a plain background

You must have the call in a private house rather than a cafe or public space. Make sure the room is well-lit. Uneven lighting, for example sunlight, can disrupt the way the system recognises faces. It is best to sit in front of a plain wall. Pictures or patterns in the background may affect the camera being able to stay focused on your face.

### Clear sight of everyone on the call

Make sure that your whole face - and the faces of any additional people - can be seen clearly.

If there are young children on the call, make sure they either look directly at the camera or else stay out of the picture.

The call may be paused if only part of a face or the back of a head can be seen.

### Dress code and behaviour

You'll need to follow the usual prison rules around what to wear and how to behave. Remember that all calls are recorded, and prison staff may monitor calls as they are happening. The call can be paused or ended if prison rules are not followed

### Inter-prison visits

PSI 16/2011 updated October 2021.

Visits may be allowed, if approved by the governors of both establishments, between close relatives when both parties are prisoners at separate establishments.

For visits purposes 'close relatives' are defined as a spouse/partner (including a person - whether of the same or different sex - with whom the prisoner was living as a couple in an established relationship immediately prior to imprisonment) parent, child, brother, sister (including half - or step - brothers and sisters), civil partner, fiancé or fiancée (provided that the Governor is satisfied that a bona fide engagement to marry exists), or

787

a person who has been acting in loco parentis to a prisoner, or a person to whom the prisoner has been in loco parentis. Grandparents and those who have clearly demonstrated the intention to register a civil partnership but have not yet done so may also be included within this definition of close relative for the purposes of social visits. This definition of "close relative" is distinct from the interpretation of a prisoner's "immediate family" which appears in Chapter 2 Section 2 of the Public Protection Manual.

Where a request is made for an inter-prison visit between close relatives, approval should be given unless:

a. there are reasons to believe that such visits will seriously impede the rehabilitation of either prisoner; or

b. where it would be compatible with the prisoners' rights to private and family life under Article 8 ECHR and it would be necessary and proportionate on one of the following grounds, that the prisoners should be prevented from visiting:

• the interests of national security;

• the prevention, detection, investigation or prosecution of crime; o the interests of public safety;

• securing or maintaining prison security or good order and discipline in prison; o the protection of health or morals;

• the protection of the reputation of others;

maintaining the authority and impartiality of the judiciary; or o the protection of the rights and freedoms of any person;

and in either case the risks identified cannot be adequately managed by monitoring or placing other controls on the visit.

If approved by the governors of both establishments, Population Management Section may be consulted for advice as to the most suitable location for the visit. Subject to the considerations listed above, and the availability of transport and accommodation, arrangements may be made for inter-prison visits to take place at three-monthly intervals, and each prisoner must surrender one visiting order. Each visit should last as long as local circumstances permit. Where inter prison visits prove exceptionally difficult to organise Governors should consider the use of video-link facilities as an alternative. The use of video-links for legal matters and official business will continue to take precedence.

**Assisted Prison Visits**

The Assisted Prison Visits Scheme (APVS) provides a contribution towards prison visit costs for close relatives, partners or sole visitors. The visitor must be on a low income.

Help is provided for English, Welsh and Scottish prisons. Limited help is available for Channel Island prisons.

Different rules apply to Northern Ireland prisons (ask at the prison you are visiting for information). The minimum age to apply for help from the APVS is 18 years (16 years when visiting a prison in Scotland). Eligible children are included on the claim.

Claims are processed by the Assisted Prison Visits Unit in Birmingham, part of Her Majesty's Prison and Probation Service.

To get help you must be listed on both the visitor and low income list below:

Visitor:

• Husband, Wife or Civil Partner

• Partner - living as a couple before the prisoner went into prison

• Parent or Grand-parent (includes step-parent or adoptive parent)

• Brother or Sister (includes half-sibling or step-sibling)

• Son or Daughter (includes step or adoptive)

• Next of Kin (as noted by the prisoner in prison records)

• Sole Visitor (only Social visitor in the four weeks before a visit claimed)

• Escort to a qualifying adult or child (see Escort Section)

Low income:

• Income Support

• Income - based Job Seekers Allowance

• Employment and Support Allowance (Income related)

• Universal Credit

Working Tax Credits (with Disability or Child Tax)*

• Child Tax Credits*

• Pension Credit

• Hold HC2 or HC3 Certificate

If someone else claims benefits for you, make your claim online and AVPU will contact you for further details if required. If you are taking a qualifying child on behalf of a parent who is on low income, see Escort Section.

**Apply gov.uk/helpwithprisonvisits**

The online application process allows you to upload your income details, receipts and visit confirmation. Payment is made into your bank account or cashed at a Post Office.

**OFFICIAL VISITS**

*Consent to official visits*

Official visits will be subject to the consent of the prisoner with the exception of:

• visits where the prisoner is detained under immigration powers. The prisoner should be informed beforehand of the reason for the visit but it will be clearly explained to the visitor and the prisoner that the prisoner is free to refuse to make any statement;

• visits for the sole purpose of the service of legal process such as the serving of summons. Such visits will not attract legal privilege.

• certain visits by police, immigration or Customs officers

## Legal advisers

Legal visits are subject to Prison Rule 38 (YOI Rule 16) and are for the purpose of:
• discussing ongoing or possible legal proceedings to which the prisoner is a party.
• discussing other legal business such as the sale of property or making a will.
• allowing a prisoner to consult their legal adviser about a forthcoming adjudication.

A legal adviser may use a cassette recorder or another sound recording device. The sound recording device may be digital or mechanical but must not contain either a camera or mobile telephone. If recording equipment is used a written undertaking will be required from the legal adviser that the recording will be kept securely in their office and will be used solely in connection with the proceedings or legal business discussed during the course of the visit. Letters and documents handed over to or by prisoners during visits from their legal advisers are also subject to whatever monitoring procedures would have been appropriate if they had been sent through the post.

## Police officers

Interviews with police officers must be conducted, so far as possible, in accordance with the terms of the Police and Criminal Evidence (PACE) Act 1984, and of Code C of the Codes of Practice issued under the Act in relation to the conduct of interviews at police stations. Interviews will take place within the sight and, where appropriate, within the hearing of a prison officer.

Before the interview commences the prisoner will be advised of the right to consult a legal adviser unless precluded by the terms of PACE, and/or, if there are language barriers, the right to have an interpreter present during the interview. If the prisoner has a visual or hearing impairment and requires assistance in communicating this should be taken into consideration. If the prisoner is under 17 or there are grounds to believe that they may require assistance during the course of the interview an appropriate adult shall be present. A member of staff or one specifically nominated by the prisoner, if no other appropriate adult is available, may undertake such a role.

## Writers, journalists or media representatives

Detailed guidance on the handling of requests for visits by media representatives is in PSI 2010/37 – Prisoners' Access to the Media. If the visit is social, the visitor will be required to give a written undertaking before the visit takes place

that any material gained from the prisoner at any time will not be used for publication or broadcast.

## Priests or ministers

Prisoners may be allowed pastoral visits from their home minister of religion or leader of their faith with the agreement of the Chaplain and the Governor. A visiting order will not need to be used for such a visit. It may be beneficial for pastoral visits from home clergy to take place in the Chaplaincy area, but this will depend on local circumstances and arrangements, and should be discussed with the co-ordinating Chaplain.

## Equality and Human Rights Commission (EHRC)

Prisoners may request visits from representatives of the EHRC. The visit should take place within sight but not within hearing range of a prison officer.

## Members of Parliament

Members of Parliament acting in a constituency capacity may visit a prisoner with the prisoner's agreement. Similar provisions may also apply to Members of the European Parliament (MEP) and Members of the Welsh Assembly (AM) who are acting in a constituency capacity. This privilege is not extended to members of the House of Lords, who have no constituency obligations, or to local Councillors.

## Commonwealth or Consular Officials

The Vienna Convention on Consular Relations, which has been supplemented by a number of bilateral agreements between the United Kingdom and other countries, guarantees freedom of communication between consular officers and their nationals.

On induction, foreign national prisoners must be informed of this right to communicate with the appropriate consulate or High Commission. Consular officers have the right to visit any of their citizens in prison. For the purpose of this Order prisons should accept a prisoner's claim to citizenship. Further guidance about the legal obligations under the Vienna Convention and individual Bi-lateral Consular Agreements in terms of contact with embassies is contained within PSO 4630 Immigration and Foreign Nationals in Prison.

Requests for such visits by Commonwealth or Consular Officials must fall under the category of official visits and be arranged as soon as possible. Visits must take place in the sight but out of the hearing of prison staff.

## Central or local government officials

Public officials listed below may visit prisoners, in their professional capacity, without visiting orders and out of hearing of prison staff:
• an accredited agent of the Treasury Solicitor, the Director of Public Prosecutions, the Crown

Prosecution Service, or the Official Receiver in Bankruptcy, on production of the necessary authority from the department, to interview and to serve documents on a prisoner

• Offender Managers, in respect of a prisoner in whom he or she has a professional interest

• the supervising social worker, of a young offender who, on reception, was subject to a care order, or who will on discharge be placed in the care of a local authority

• an immigration officer, to interview a Commonwealth citizen or a foreign national detained under the Immigration Act 1971

• other public officials whom the Governor permits to visit.

### LETTERS

PSI 49/2011 - updated October 2021

*Letters: Desired Outcomes*

All prisoners are able to communicate with family, friends and professional advisers (Written)

Prisoners are actively encouraged to maintain contact with the outside world, which would include family, friends and where applicable professional advisers/bodies.

Prisoners may write to, and receive letters from, any person or organisation, subject to the acceptability of the contents and to the restrictions set out further in this PSI. Restrictions are necessary in order to protect the public, prevent crime and ensure the security of the prison. However, this does not necessarily mean that if a prisoner corresponds with any person or organisation, that he/she may be visited by that person or a representative of that organisation.

Prisoners may write letters in the language of their choice, but letters not written in English and which are subject to routine reading may be liable to delay while translations are obtained. Prisoners can generally write as much as they wish. At establishments where routine reading of correspondence is in force, Governors may set a limit on the length of letters, subject to a minimum of four sides of A5 paper.

Letters between prisoners and their legal advisers, as well as a number of statutory bodies/persons responsible for the welfare of prisoners while in custody, are treated as privileged and must be handled in confidence (see paragraph 14.1 below for a detailed list of those to which these provisions apply).

### Prisoners are entitled to send:

(a) Statutory Letters (free to the prisoner/paid for from public funds) - one that a prisoner is entitled to under Prison Rule 35 or Young Offender Institution Rule 10, and must not be withdrawn or withheld as part of a punishment.
(b) Privilege Letter (paid for by the prisoner) - one that a prisoner is regularly allowed to send over and above their statutory entitlement of letters.
(c) Special Letter (in exceptional circumstances) - one that is not counted against a prisoner's allocation of statutory or privilege letters and which he/she is given permission to send for some special reason (see paragraphs Special Letters below). The postage costs of some but not all of these will be paid for out of public funds.

### Allowances

Unconvicted prisoners and those held under an Immigration Detention Warrant (see list of definitions contained in Annex A of PSO 4600 – Unconvicted, Unsentenced and Civil Prisoners) may send:
(a) two Statutory Letters per week;
(b) as many Privilege Letters as they wish;
(c) a Special Letter when;
(i) they are about to be transferred to another establishment or, if this has not been possible before transfer, on reception at the new establishment;
(ii) in connection with their defence, if they cannot afford the postage costs of a privilege letter for this purpose;
(iii) to enable a prisoner to notify the relevant Council Tax Officer of his/her reception into custody.
(iv) to enable a prisoner to write to the Prisons & Probation Ombudsman.

### Convicted prisoners, including those unsentenced, may send:

(a) one Statutory Letter per week, the first letter to be issued immediately on reception;
(b) as many Privilege Letters as they wish, except at establishments where routine reading is in force, in which case Governors have the discretion to set limits on the number of privilege letters prisoners may send, subject to a minimum of at least one privilege letter per week in the case of adults and two in the case of young offenders. Prisoners should be allowed to send as many privilege letters as practicable taking account of the staff resources available to examine and read correspondence;
(c) Special Letters, in the circumstances set out below.

### Special Letters

Convicted prisoners must be issued with one or more Special Letters, in the following circumstances:
(a) when they are about to be transferred to another establishment; or on reception at the new establishment. The number of letters issued must correspond to the number of outstanding visiting orders but only in respect of those visitors who are scheduled to visit them immediately before transfer;
(b) immediately after conviction if he/she needs to settle business affairs;
(c) if necessary for the welfare of the prisoner or

his/her family, including where required as part of an at-risk prisoner's ACCT CAREMAP;

(d) in connection with legal proceedings;

(e) to enable the prisoner to write to a relevant offender manager or to an agency that is arranging employment or accommodation for him/her on release;

(f) to enable a prisoner to notify the relevant Council Tax Officer of his/her reception into custody where this has not previously been done as an unconvicted prisoner;

(g) on a discretionary basis, for additional contact with their Member of Parliament (MP) Member of the National Assembly for Wales (AM), Member of the European Parliament (MEP) or Consular representative;

(h) to enable a prisoner to write to the Prisons & Probation Ombudsman.

### Additional discretion- Letters in Lieu

In accordance with Prison Rule 35 (4) and Young Offender Rule 10 (3), a prisoner must be given an extra letter at public expense in place of any statutory visit which the prisoner does not wish to take or accumulate.

A prisoner may be given a Statutory Letter in advance of the due date of their next statutory entitlement. The date of the next letter will be calculated from the due date.

A convicted prisoner may, to the extent that the Governor considers it reasonable, accumulate his/her allowance of statutory and privilege letters.

### Letters received

At establishments where all or most correspondence is not monitored, there are no restrictions on the number of letters which prisoners may receive.

At other establishments prisoners are allowed to receive as many letters as they are allowed to send. However, if a prisoner receives an excessive number of letters either habitually or on one occasion, the Governor has the discretion to return excess letters to the sender(s) but the prisoner will be given the opportunity to select those which he/she particularly wishes to read. Similarly anyone who makes a practice of sending excessively long letters to prisoners may be asked to confine themselves to four sides of paper. If they ignore the request the Governor may return subsequent letters, in which case the prisoner should be informed accordingly.

### Inter-prison and ex-prisoner mail

PSI 49/2011 was amended on 2nd September 2021. Correspondence between convicted prisoners requires the approval of the Governors of both the prisons concerned. Where the prisoners are close relatives (as defined above) or where they were co-defendants at their trial and the correspondence relates to their conviction or sentence and subject to the provisions above, approval should be given unless:

a) there are reasons to believe that such correspondence will seriously impede the rehabilitation of either prisoner; or

b) where it would be compatible with the prisoners' rights to private and family life under Article 8 ECHR and it would be necessary and proportionate on one of the following grounds, that the prisoners should be prevented from communicating:

• the interests of national security;

• the prevention, detection, investigation or prosecution of crime;

• the interests of public safety;

• securing or maintaining prison security or good order and discipline in prison;

• the protection of health or morals;

• the protection of the reputation of others;

• maintaining the authority and impartiality of the judiciary; or

• the protection of the rights and freedoms of any person; and in either case the risks identified cannot be adequately managed by monitoring or placing other controls on the correspondence.

Accordingly, if the Governor of the sending establishment has no objections, the letter should be sent to the Governor of the recipient's establishment with a covering note inviting them to consider whether it should be issued. Where approval is given, communications may be made subject to monitoring or other controls. See The Interception of Communications in Prisons and Security Measures for further guidance.

The same considerations apply to inter- prison telephone calls for close relatives or partners.

### Postage Costs

Statutory Letters must be sent at public expense but the postage costs of Privilege Letters are paid from the prisoner's spends account. The postage costs of Special Letters for convicted prisoners should usually be met from the prisoner's spends account. The Governor may decide to pay for a Special Letter in exceptional circumstances but the prison must pay for Special Letters in the following circumstances:

(a) letters on transfer;

(b) letters to offender managers or agencies helping with employment or accommodation arrangements;

(c) letters to the Prisons & Probation Ombudsman;

(d) letters to Council Tax Officers;

All Special Letters sent by unconvicted prisoners and those who may be held under an Immigration Detention Warrant must be sent by public expense.

The cost of posting of celebratory cards may be met from the prisoner's spends account.

If prisoners pay for the postage costs of their correspondence they have the option of choosing between First and Second Class and for overseas letters Air or Sea mail. Subject to the following paragraph, letters sent at public expense will normally be sent at the cheapest rate but a prisoner may pay the difference for a higher class of postage.

Letters sent at public expense must be sent first class or by air mail if:

(a) they are Special Letters sent on transfer;

(b) they are in connection with an appeal;

(c) exceptionally, postage at the higher rate has been approved by the Governor.

The correspondents of some prisoners may wish to send them stamped addressed envelopes, bearing their return address, to encourage them to write letters and to help with the costs. This must be allowed and no deductions must be made from the private cash allowance for the cost of the stamps or envelopes received.

Additionally, correspondents may send in monies to prisoners in the form of cheques or postal orders which will be credited to their private cash account and should be managed in accordance with the guidance covered in PSO 4465 Prisoners Personal Financial Affairs.

### Correspondents

A prisoner may write to, and receive letters from, any person or organisation, subject to the acceptability of the contents and to the restrictions set out further in this PSI. However, it does not necessarily follow that because a prisoner is in correspondence with a person or organisation that he/she may be visited by that person or a representative of that organisation.

If the recipient of correspondence from a prisoner requests in writing to the prison that no further letters should be sent, the prisoner must be informed of the request, asked to co-operate by not writing and given the opportunity to discuss the matter with a member of staff. If the prisoner then hands in a further letter for posting, the prison must comply with the recipient's request and inform the prisoner that the letter and any subsequent letters to the intended recipient will not be sent. The letter will then be returned to the prisoner.

### Correspondence with children (defined as someone under 18 years of age)

If a prisoner wishes to correspond with a child, the procedures set out above in paragraph 2.19 will be applied if the person or authority having parental responsibility for the care of the child requests that the correspondence between them is stopped.

Prisoners identified as presenting a risk to children are managed under Safeguarding Children procedures and any contact with a child must comply with the Child Contact procedures contained within Chapter 2 of the Public Protection Manual. This means that any prisoner falling under this category must first apply to a member of staff in order to correspond with a child. Where these safeguarding procedures apply contact with children will only include contact with the prisoner's immediate family or children, and the children of a partner provided they were living together as partners in an enduring family relationship prior to imprisonment. Included within this definition are sons and daughters, brothers and sisters, grandchildren, stepchildren, adopted children and foster children. A prisoner may be permitted contact with other children provided the prisoner can produce a substantial case for contact and the Governor agrees that such contact would be in the interests of the child and only after a full risk assessment had been carried out.

### Correspondence with young prisoners

If the Governor considers that correspondence between a prisoner who is under 18 and any other person would not be in that prisoner's best interests, they may stop the correspondence, taking into account the views of the prisoner's parent or guardian. If the Governor proposes to exercise this discretion in relation to correspondence with a close relative this should be done in accordance with procedures in the Local Security Strategy.

A close relative is defined as a spouse/ partner (including a person - whether of the same or different sex - with whom the prisoner was living as a couple in an established relationship immediately prior to imprisonment) parent, child, brother, sister (including half or step-brothers and sisters), grandparent, civil partner, fiancé or fiancée, or a person who has been acting in loco parentis to a prisoner, or a person to whom the prisoner has been in loco parentis i.e. where they have had/have parental responsibility for that person. Those who have clearly demonstrated the intention to register a civil partnership with the prisoner but have not yet done so may also be included within this definition of close relative for the purposes of correspondence.

### Victims and public protection issues

Prisoners wishing to correspond with the victim of their offences, or the victim's family, must first apply to the Governor for permission to do so, which may be withheld if it is considered that the approach would add unduly to the victim's or family's distress. The Governor must contact any probation victim liaison officers involved

with the victim or victim's family, and take into account any concerns they raise about any such contact. Further information can be found in the Public Protection Manual in relation to protection from harassment as well as the National Security Framework. This restriction is in line with Prison Rule 34 (2) & (3) and is compliant with Articles 8 & 10 of the ECHR. This restriction does not apply where:
(a) the victim is a close relative (as defined above) and who wishes to receive correspondence;
(b) the victim has already written to the prisoner since conviction and/or they are in contact for the purposes of mediation or restorative justice;
(c) the prisoner concerned is unconvicted, unless there is evidence that they may be harassing the victim, thereby breaking any conditions imposed by the Courts, or attempting to pervert the course of justice.

### Threats to security

The Governor has the discretion to disallow any correspondence with a person or organisation if there is reason to believe that the person or organisation concerned is planning or engaged in activities which present a genuine threat to security or good order of the establishment or other prisons. This is covered under Prison Rule 34 (2) & (3) and compliant with Articles 8 & 10 of ECHR. If the Governor is disallowing correspondence between a prisoner and a close relative (defined above), this should be done in accordance with the guidance/procedures found in the Local Security Strategy.

When a prisoner has been prevented from writing to a person or an organisation, or would not be allowed to do so, communication with any other person at the same address will also be stopped unless the other person is a close relative as defined above.

### Penfriends

Any prisoner who wishes to place an advert for a penfriend(s) should first apply to the Governor for permission and approval of the text. Permission may be granted unless:
(a) the advertisement invites respondents to write to a box number;
(b) the prisoner is an adult and the publication concerned is aimed at, or read mainly by children or young people;
(c) the advertisement is to be placed in a periodical which caters for tastes or interests which may have motivated the prisoner's offence;
(d) correspondence arising from the advertisement might place respondents in danger of harm from the prisoner after release.
At establishments where all or most correspondence is monitored, it must be made clear to prisoners that Governors have discretion to withhold replies if an excessive number are received.

### PO Box numbers

Prisoners must not normally be allowed to write to a PO Box number, but if the prisoner does not know the private address of the correspondent, the Governor may, if satisfied that security is not threatened, allow the letter to be sent (this would not normally be an issue where the person/ organisation is a recognised body such as the Samaritans or Alcoholics Anonymous). Similarly, prisoners will not normally be allowed to receive anonymous letters, and the Governor has discretion to withhold letters which do not show the sender's address.

### Prisoners on "dirty protest"

If a prisoner is participating in a "dirty protest" they are still entitled to send and receive mail. However, this will have implications for the health of both staff and the public, especially postal workers. Royal Mail will not under any circumstances handle contaminated correspondence so unless a prisoner can obtain the services of a delivery agent who is willing to deliver this type of correspondence (using suitable packaging) they will not be permitted to send out such mail. This also applies to Rule 39 correspondence. Staff should refer to the detailed guidance in Prison Service Order 1700 – Segregation Dirty Protests (Guide to Contents) – (8) Regime – (b) Communications – Letters. This is currently being revised and the revised Instruction will appear under Function 2 of the National Security Framework.

### Prisoners transferred or released from custody

Correspondence received for an ex-prisoner, which arrives after he/she has been released from custody, must not be opened unless staff are not sure who it is actually addressed to. Any such correspondence must then be forwarded to the individual concerned in a plain envelope at their private address but if this is not known and they were released under the supervision of a relevant probation provider, it should be forwarded to their Supervising Officer to pass on. Failing this, correspondence should be placed back in to the postal system/returned to the Post Office.

Any correspondence which is addressed to a prisoner and received while that prisoner is unlawfully at large may be opened and read. If it is from a prohibited correspondent it should be recorded in the prisoner's record, otherwise it must be returned to the sender with a covering letter stating that the prisoner is no longer in prison custody and his/her whereabouts are unknown. If the sender's address is unknown and cannot be found it must be stored with the prisoner's property.

Any letters received for a prisoner after they have been transferred to another establishment must not be opened. The address on the front of the envelope must be amended to show the details of the new establishment and the envelope forwarded through the ordinary post. If the letter appears to be legal or from an official body, a telephone check must be made first, in order to establish that the prisoner has not moved again and this must be forwarded as a mater or urgency. If the prisoner has moved again, the prison with the letter must identify and telephone the prison holding the prisoner to confirm he or she is held there.

### Prisoners are able to send as many letters as they wish at their own expense (Written)

Prisoners are permitted to send out as many Privilege Letters (those paid for by the prisoner) as they can afford to unless there are restrictions placed on their correspondence which may limit the number being sent. This limitation would be set in those cases where active examination was required i.e. public protection or offence related monitoring or if in a High Security prison.

### The service supports arrangements for prisoners to receive Private Cash by post (Written)

In accordance with Prison Rules 43(2) and 44 (2) and YOI Rule 48 prisoners are able to have money sent into them by family and friends from outside the prison and credited to their account. This money should be processed in accordance with the guidance contained within the instructions/guidance found in Prison Service Order 7500 Finance and Prison Service Order 4465 Prisoners Personal Financial Affairs. This will also be reflected in the relevant Manage Prisoner Finance Specification and PSI.

### Prisoners who have not had a social visit will be helped to maintain family ties and outside contacts by provision of a free letter, in lieu of that one visit (Written)

In accordance with Prison Rule 35 (4) and Young Offender Institution Rule 10 (3), a prisoner must be given an extra letter at public expense in place of any statutory visit which the prisoner does not wish to take or accumulate.

### TELEPHONE CALLS
**PSI 04/2016, updated April 2021**
*Phone Calls - Desired Outcomes*
All prisoners are able to communicate with family, friends, legal and professional advisers.

### Inter-Prison telephone calls
Where prisoners who are close relatives (see 'inter-prison visits' above for a definition) are detained in different prisons, the approval of the Governors of both the prisons concerned is required before telephone contact is facilitated.

Where approved, in order to facilitate regular contact by telephone, the establishments concerned must agree between them that one prisoner may be permitted to receive a call on an official telephone at a time convenient to both prisons. Where appropriate once the number has been added to the prisoner's PIN account the outgoing call should be made using a PINphone. The call will be recorded at the originating establishment, thus meeting any security considerations.

### Reception
On first reception into prison, prisoners often need to make an early telephone call to family and friends to let them know their whereabouts. The Governor must make local arrangements to allow a call to be made within the first 24 hours of reception. Reception staff must read the Prisoner Escort Record and the police/CPS MG6 form to identify whether restrictions need to be placed on the prisoner's communications.

If the prisoner is subject to, or likely to be subject to, public protection restrictions (including an identified risk of intimidating victims or witnesses), or is provisional Category A/Category A prisoner, a member of staff should make the call on the prisoner's behalf, checking that the recipient is willing to receive the call in the first instance.

Where a prisoner is making the call a personal identification number or PIN will be required and the account credited with funds before a call can be made. A call made on reception or in the first night accommodation can be funded in two ways or a combination of both:

(a) by the use of one generic PIN account, pre-funded with credits which are paid for from public funds to enable them to make a short call;
(b) after signing the Communications Compact, the prisoner is put on the PINphone system with their own personal account and PIN credits are issued as an advance.

With both options the call will be recorded. If a prisoner wishes to make a legal call the onus will be placed on the prisoner to inform staff that they wish to make such a call. On reception calls to legal advisers must not be made via a PINphone until a prisoner's PINphone account has been properly set up. A member of staff must first ring the number provided by the prisoner to verify that the number is a bone fide legal number.

## Communications Compact

An example of a Communications Compact is set out in PSI 04/2016 (Restricted)

**Wherever possible, prisoners must agree and sign a copy of the Communications Compact before making their first call. Failing this the Compact must be signed before the prisoner is issued with their own personal PIN number. The Compact must be explained to all prisoners and if a prisoner has reading difficulties the Compact must be read to them and signed by the member of staff. The prisoner should also sign that this action has been undertaken to evidence that they were present when the Compact was explained to them.**

**Prisoners will be required to differentiate between social numbers to be placed on the "open" side of the PINphone system and legal and confidential access numbers on the "restricted" side on the Compact. It remains the responsibility of the prisoner to distinguish between social and legal/confidential access numbers in the first instance and the Compact may be used for evidential purposes to this effect. Once signed the document should be stored in such a way to ensure that it is readily accessible. This document could be stored with the prisoners' core record or security file although a consistent approach to storage across the establishment is recommended.**

**Where the Person Escort Record and the police/CPS MG6 form identifies the need for specific restrictions to be placed on the prisoner's communications the prisoner must be reminded that they must not seek to contact those named persons either by telephone or letter.**

## General access

Prisoners must be given access to the PINphone during association and at other such times as are reasonably practicable, depending on the nature of the establishment's regime. The time available for using the phones must not normally be less than two hours each day.

Phones can be scheduled to come on and off according to the prison's working day. Different schedules can be applied to different days, or the phones can be left switched on all the time. These schedules are applied centrally within the establishment.

Any prisoner on a call enabling regime will be required to have the numbers approved before the call can be made to that number. All legal and confidential numbers provided by prisoners should be checked and verified as bone fide. The checking of social numbers must be proportionate to risk and checked as necessary in accordance with the NSF and as set out in the local security strategy.

Prisoners on a call enabling regime will be allowed up to:

(a) 20 social numbers;

(b) 15 legal and confidential access numbers. If engaged in litigation prisoners may be permitted a second account of a further 15 legal numbers. Under exceptional circumstances, Governors will have discretion to allow a prisoner more than 30 legal numbers.

In addition to their personal lists prisoners will also be able to access local (establishment based) numbers and global (estate wide) numbers (e.g. Samaritans, Crimestoppers).

Telephone numbers for the courts in England and Wales are available to all prisoners. A central number for the Palace of Westminster is also contained in this list. Prisoners can ring this number and then be connected to the Member of Parliament's office of their choice.

Establishments must add their local Samaritans branch contact number to local allowed lists for all prisoners.

All prisoners subject to call enabling will only have access to telephone numbers on their personal lists that have been approved by their current establishment. A transfer from one prison to another does not require the receiving prison to automatically accept the telephone numbers on the prisoners allowed list.

Governors must not permit the insertion of any numbers submitted by a prisoner if they have any reason to believe that the number is one submitted on another prisoner's behalf, or if the prisoner cannot justify his/her need to contact the number in question. If there is any doubt, prisoners must be asked to produce further verification for any number they wish to have on their list, e.g. a letter of authorisation from the recipient that they are content to receive calls from the prisoner.

Should a prisoner wish to amend his personal list s/he must not be charged for adding to or deleting legal numbers from their PINphone account. If a prisoner loses their PIN number or allows it to become compromised the Governor may charge for the issuing of a new PIN number. Prisoners are permitted to telephone business numbers but for the sole purpose of speaking to family and friends.

## Business

Prisoners are not permitted to make any commercial enquiries or order goods using the telephone.

## Operators

Prisoners are not able to make calls to or via the operator, to other operator services and must not be given access to telephone directories. Should a prisoner need to know a particular number or an area code they must make an application to an Operational Manager, explaining why they want to call the person in question. Staff must look the number up on the prisoner's behalf.

### Additional guidance

Annex A to PSI 49/2011 contains guidance about the ways in which the PINphone system can be configured in order to restrict prisoner use and arrangements for discharge. Annex B contains some guidance for particular groups of prisoners.

### Incoming phone calls from official bodies or the courts can be facilitated (Speech)

The PINphone system does not accept incoming calls. Any arrangement to allow incoming calls must involve an official telephone. Prisoners will continue to receive pre-arranged calls on office phones from members of staff of the Prison and Probation Ombudsman's Office and the CCRC.

### Prisoners can make urgent phone calls for domestic or legal reasons at public expense (Speech)

Where there are urgent legal or compassionate circumstances, such as imminent court proceedings or a domestic crisis, Operational Managers have discretion to allow such calls to take place at public expense. Before agreeing to such an application, Operational Managers must satisfy themselves that the need could not adequately be met by means of a visit or letter. The Operational Manager must also be satisfied that the prisoner has insufficient credit within their PINphone account to make the call.

The costs of these calls must be at public expense. Such calls can be made either via an official telephone or a generic PINphone account, pre-funded with credits paid for with public funds.

### Prisoners with close family abroad who have not had a social visit in the preceding month will be helped to maintain family ties and outside contacts by provision of a free five minute phone call (Speech)

Foreign national prisoners or those with close family abroad must be permitted a free five minute call once a month where the prisoner has had no social visits during the preceding month. Consideration must be given to allowing such prisoners to have access to telephones outside normal hours to make calls to their country of origin where there is a significant time difference between their country of origin and the UK.

### Prisoners may communicate with members of the media (General)

Staff must refer to PSI 37/2010 Prisoners Access to the Media for further guidance on prisoners having legitimate access to the media.

### Prisoners are prevented from sending and receiving illicit or unauthorised articles, information or data (General/Written/Speech)

Letter paper and air letter forms should be stamped at the head with the name and address of the establishment before issue.

However, Governors may allow a prisoner to write on plain paper which does not indicate its place of origin to his or her child or, at the Governor's discretion, to any other person or organisation, and greetings cards with only a simple greeting need not show the address of the establishment.

The private postal address of the establishment must be on the outside of air letter forms.

### Restrictions on correspondence – including publication on the Internet. Correspondence may not contain the following:

(a) Material which is intended to cause distress or anxiety to the recipient or any other person, such as:
(i) messages which are indecent or grossly offensive;
(ii) a threat;
(iii) information which is known or believed to be false;
(b) Plans or material which could assist or encourage any disciplinary or criminal offence (including attempts to defeat the ends of justice by suggesting the fabrication or suppression of evidence);
(c) Escape plans, or material which if allowed would jeopardise the security of a prison establishment;
(d) Material which would jeopardise national security;
(e) Descriptions of the making or use of any weapon, explosive, poison or other destructive device;
(f) Obscure or coded messages which are not readily intelligible or decipherable;
(g) Material which is indecent and obscene under Section 85(3) of the Postal Services Act 2000;
(h) Material which, if sent to, or received from, a child might place his or her welfare at risk;
(i) Material which would create a threat or risk of violence or physical harm to any person, including incitement to racial hatred;
(j) In addition to restrictions on access to the media (see PSI 37/2010 Prisoners' Access to the Media), material which is intended for publication or use by radio, television or the Internet (or which, if sent, would be likely to be published or broadcast on these media channels) if it:
(i) is for publication in return for payment, unless the prisoner is unconvicted. However, prisoners are permitted to receive payment for pieces of artwork or work of literary merit but only if they do not contravene any of the restrictions contained within paragraphs (ii)– (v) below and only if channelled through appropriate charitable organisations. This should not be done on a regular basis so as to constitute any

form of business activity (i.e. being commissioned to write a series of books or a regular feature in a national publication). It would be for the Governor to decide if such material contravened any of these restrictions. Further guidance on this is at paragraph 2.27 of PSO 4465 - Prisoners' Personal Financial Affairs; (ii) is likely to appear in a publication associated with a person or organisation to which the prisoner may not write as a result of the restriction on correspondence in paragraphs above; (iii) is about the prisoner's own crime or past offences or those of others, except where it consists of serious representations about conviction or sentence or forms part of serious comment about crime, the criminal justice system or the penal system; (iv) refers to individual prisoners or members of staff in such a way that they might be identified; (v) contravenes any of the restrictions on content applying to letters; (k) In the case of a prisoner against whom a deportation order is in force, material constituting or arranging any financial transaction unless the Governor is satisfied that there is a genuine need for such a transaction (i.e. if in relation to the financial support of a close relative or if seeking advice in order to petition against deportation). This restriction does not apply to a prisoner whose sentence includes a recommendation for deportation but where a decision has not been made by the Secretary of State to act upon the recommendation; (l) In the case of a prisoner in respect of whom a receiving order or confiscation order has been made or who is an undischarged bankrupt, material constituting or arranging any financial transaction except: (i) on the advice of the Official Receiver; (ii) to pay wholly or in part a fine or debt in order to secure the prisoner's earlier release; (iii) to defend criminal proceedings brought against the prisoner; (iv) to meet the cost of communicating with or instructing a solicitor to act on the prisoner's behalf in bankruptcy proceedings; (v) to meet the costs of the prisoner's production in bankruptcy proceedings.

A prisoner may not ask, in writing or otherwise, another person either inside or outside the establishment they are held in, to make on his or her behalf a communication which he or she would not be allowed to make direct, or which would contravene restrictions in PSI 49/2011.

On induction, prisoners at Open, Category C, Category B training establishments, female and young offender establishments must be informed that their correspondence will not normally be read. However, in each case it must be made clear to the prisoner that they are still required to observe the restrictions contained within this order, and that if they fail to do so, the Governor may order all their correspondence to be read or take appropriate disciplinary action.

Any incoming correspondence or parcel, which is recorded/signed for or special delivery must be signed for by staff at the gate as confirmation that the item has actually been delivered to the prison by Royal Mail. Any parcel would also need to be processed in accordance with the guidance found at paragraphs 2.64 -2.66 of PSI 12/2011 – Prisoners' Property. Unless covered by the arrangements for Rule 39 or Confidential Access mail, it must then be opened and examined in the normal way for any illicit enclosures and passed to the prisoner concerned as soon as is possible. In order to prevent complaints that a valuable item has been lost, it must be opened in the presence of another member of staff. A record must be kept of the receipt of all parcels and recorded signed for/special delivery letters and any prisoner who requests the original Royal Mail receipt should be given this to keep.

Prisoners must not communicate by telephone matters that they would not be allowed to communicate by letter under the terms of the above restrictions.

**Prison Drugs Strategy: Current September 2022.**
- *prisons.org.uk/drugs-strategy.pdf*
• **PSOs 3550 & 3601,** and **PSI 32/2014.**

The Prison Drugs Strategy, published April 2019 and jointly developed by the Ministry of Justice (MoJ) and Her Majesty's Prison and Probation Service (HMPPS), sets out to tackle drugs by restricting supply, reducing demand and building recovery. This mirrors the three strands of the HM Government Drug Strategy and, through a comprehensive approach, offers the best opportunity to reduce the levels of drug misuse in our prisons.

## 2.6 DRUGS & ALCOHOL IN PRISON

### rMDT Testing 2021/2022
In the 12-months to March 2022, there were 12,396 **random mandatory drug tests (rMDT)** carried out nationally across all types of drugs, an increase from 4,738 the previous year, but this remains low compared with over 54,000 tests conducted in 2019-20.

In normal circumstances, as part of HMPPS's comprehensive drug testing regime, a random sample of prisoners (5%, or 10% in prisons with under 400 prisoners) are subject to rMDT each month. This translated to over 54,000 tests completed in the year to March 2020, across all prisons. However, because of the COVID-19 pandemic, testing was suspended across prisons from April 2020 and only partially resumed from September 2020. Establishments were required to resume testing when they were operating at Stages 2 or 1 rather than at Stages 3 and 4 of the National Framework for managing Covid. This resulted in a significant drop in the number of completed tests throughout 2020-21, continuing into 2021-22.

In the 12-months to March 2022, the latest year, there were 12,396 random mandatory drug tests (rMDT) carried out nationally, an increase from 4,738 conducted in 2020-21. However, in 2021-22 test volumes remained below pre-pandemic years, averaging approximately 1,030 per month compared to 4,500 per month in 2019-20. In addition to the low testing volumes, the number of establishments participating in testing in any one month was insufficient to make inferences about drug misuse across the estate for 2020-21 and 2021-22 - although the majority of prisons were testing in the three months from October to December 2021, testing fell sharply with the outbreak of the Omicron variant in December, and the coverage of prisons was not representative.

A more detailed guide to rMDT operates is on: *https://prisons.org.uk/facts-figures/hmpps-annual-digest/*

This includes further details on why the numbers of participating prisons and testing volumes were considered too low to produce reliable and representative estimates.

The extent to which the testing panel covers the drugs that are prevalent in prisons, in particular the latest compounds of Psychoactive Substances (PS) in use, is another determinant of the reliability of rMDT estimates. Time lags in updating the testing panel with new substances lead to underestimation of drug use because they cannot be detected. It has not been possible to draw conclusions about the level of misuse of drugs including PS for 2018-19 and 2019-20 because of two new compounds of PS in circulation in prisons which could not at the time be identified by the rMDT test.

Because of the pause and subsequent disruption to testing due to the pandemic in 2020-21 and 2021-22 and underestimation of drug use in 2018-19 and 2019-20 due to time lags in updating the testing panel for new PS, readers are referred to the findings in the HMPPS Digest for the period 2017-2018 on *prisonoracle.com* - the latest data including for 2017/18 and past trends are given in HMPPS Annual Digest: April 2019 to March 2020 edition (*https://prisonoracle.com*). This includes full details of data quality which are summarised in the Guide to this year's HMPPS Digest. In 2017-18, the percentage of positive drug tests (including PS) was 21.3%.

We will not be able to improve safety, prevent reoffending and tackle serious and organised crime without reducing the misuse of drugs in prisons. This is a complex, multi-faceted problem with no simple answer – it requires a coordinated effort to limit the supply of drugs both inside and outside prisons, encourage people away from drug misuse towards positive and productive activities, and support those requiring treatment. It is therefore crucial that our approach to tackling the problem considers the whole system, working across government and with our partners at a national, regional and local level.

The scale of the problem is significant and has become more challenging in recent years.

Between 2012/13 and 2019/20, the rate of positive random tests for 'traditional' drugs in prisons increased by 50%, from 7% to 10.5%, and drug use in prisons is now widespread, particularly in male local and category C prisons. The emergence of New Psychoactive Substances (NPS - see below) such as synthetic cannabinoids has exacerbated the problem, and these are often used in conjunction with other drugs, while we remain aware of problems with the diversion and misuse of prescription medication. The prevalence and patterns of drug misuse in prisons is shaped by patterns in the community, and the challenges faced by prisons can be exacerbated when those entering prison have an existing drug misuse issue or when drug misuse has been normalised in the community.

Evidence shows us that the prisons with the highest rates of positive random drug tests are the prisons that are the least stable. The misuse of drugs contributes to a cycle of disruption and violence, leading to a reduced or unstable regime, which through unpredictability and lack of purpose can encourage prisoners to turn to drugs and alcohol. The debt resulting from the supply, distribution and use of drugs is also a significant cause of violence, intimidation and self-harm across the estate, endangering both staff and other prisoners. Consequently, to tackle drug misuse, we need changes in all elements of this cycle, enabling prisoners to engage positively with rehabilitation, in a calm and safe environment. Reducing drug misuse is crucial to the safety of our prisons and the rehabilitation of prisoners.

The *central elements of the strategy* are:

• **Restricting the supply of drugs** by improving security, building intelligence, and targeting the criminal networks which aim to bring drugs into prison.

• **Reducing the demand for drugs** in prison by developing more meaningful regimes, providing more constructive ways for prisoners to spend their time and ensuring the balance of incentives encourages prisoners to make the right choices.

• **Working closely with health and justice partners** to build recovery for prisoners who want to overcome their substance misuse, providing prisoners who are serious about living substance free with the environment to do so successfully and enable NHS England to deliver person-centred services to ensure the right help is available at the right time.

## Impact

To achieve these objectives, HMPPS are focusing on five areas that impact the levels of drug misuse in prisons.

• **People** – that prisons have the right staff, with appropriate skills and support

• **Procedural** – that prison processes are clear, fair and effective

• **Physical** – that prison conditions are safe, clean, decent and promote well-being and recovery

• **Population** – that prisoners have positive relationships and engage in constructive activities

• **Partnership** – that all the organisations contributing to achieving our aims work together effectively.

## Categories of NPS

1. Synthetic cannabinoids (SC) include a large number of drugs, the best known and most widely used being Spice and Black Mamba
2. Depressants include such drugs as GHB (gamma hydroxybutyrate), GBL (gamma butyrolactone) and ketamine, which has dissociative effects in addition to its depressant effects
3. Stimulants include drugs like MDMA (methylene-dioxymethamphetamine), better known as ecstasy, and ecstasy variants such as PMA (paramethoxyamphetamine) and PMMA (paramethoxymethamphetamine)
4. Hallucinogens include drugs such as LSD (lysergic acid diethylamide) and assorted

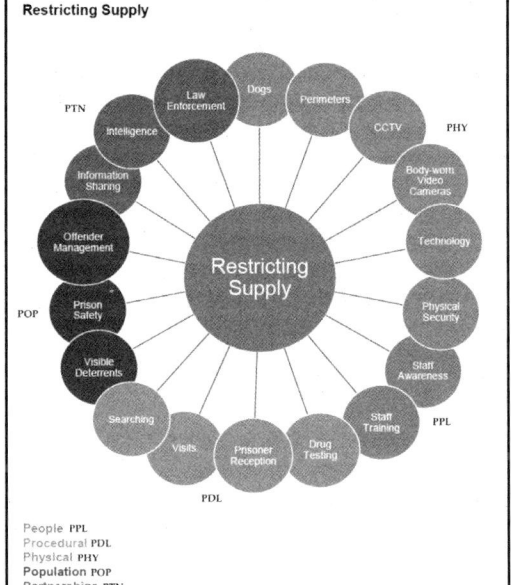

Restricting Supply

People PPL
Procedural PDL
Physical PHY
Population POP
Partnerships PTN

tryptamines and phenethylamines
The current evidence indicates that the majority of NPS circulating in the prison system are synthetic cannabinoids.

## POST RELEASE DRUG TESTING

As a result of sections 11 and 12 of the Offender Rehabilitation Act 2014, PSI 32/2014 introduced two new licence conditions and supervision requirements which may be requested by the Offender Manager to manage the offender in the community. These requirements may only be imposed where there is a reason to believe that misuse of illegal drugs (for testing this applies to specified Class A and specified Class B drugs) caused or contributed to an offence of which the person has been convicted or is likely to cause or contribute to the commission of further offences by the person; and the person is dependent on, or has a propensity to misuse illegal drugs.

## DRUG TESTING

Since 1994 it has been an offence under the Prison Rules to:

• administer a controlled drug; or
• fail to prevent the administration of a controlled drug.

The Rules also contain statutory defences to these offences:

• the controlled drug was lawfully in your possession – ie a prescription;
• the drug was administered without consent or under duress where it was unreasonable to resist;
• there was no reason to suspect or know that the drug was being administered.

| | |
|---|---|
| People | • Provide guidance and advice to all prisons on security measures including searching, prison reception, visits and new methods by April 2019.<br>• Share the Drug Diagnostic toolkit with all prisons by April 2019, alongside guidance to assist each prison in identifying improvements in their practice. |
| Procedural | • Review our approach to drug testing to ensure it is comprehensive and balanced.<br>• Launch a restructured Counter Corruption Unit to tackle corruption, including drug trafficking, by spring 2019. |
| Physical | • Extend the use of enhanced gate and perimeter security across the prison estate, particularly in local prisons.<br>• Increase the searching of all entrants to prisons, including prisoners, visitors and staff. |
| Population | • Develop the Digital Categorisation Service to provide a wider range of information on male offenders coming into prison, including those who may have the means to smuggle drugs into prison. |
| Partnerships | • Build our national and regional intelligence units to develop intelligence on those offenders who pose the greatest threat to prison security.<br>• Work with law enforcement to implement the commitments in the Serious and Organised Crime Strategy for lifetime offender management of priority organised criminals in prison, to prevent and disrupt their offending. |

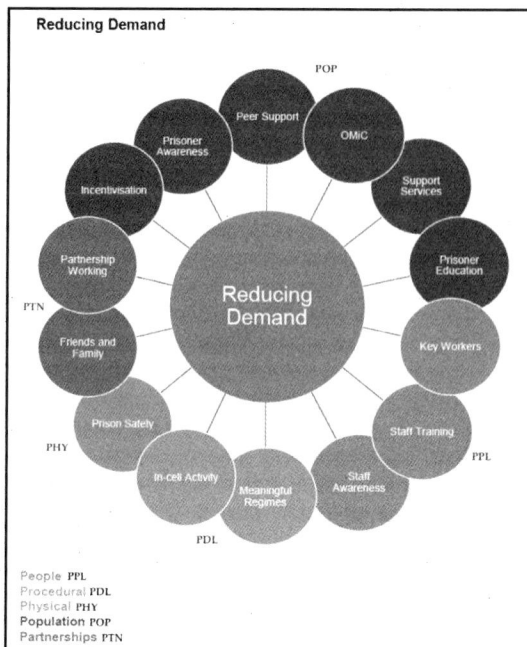

Reducing Demand

People PPL
Procedural PDL
Physical PHY
Population POP
Partnerships PTN

the prisoner and they should be asked to sign the seals. Tube A will then be sent to a laboratory contracted by the Prison Service for analysis. Tube B is the prisoner's part of the sample and is stored securely in a fridge with its seal intact for 9 months in case it is required for your own independent analysis.

*What happens when the test is positive?*

If the screening test proves negative the prisoner should be notified. If the screening test proves positive they will be charged. If they enter any other plea than a definite "guilty" the adjudication must then be adjourned for a confirmation test, which is more accurate than a screening test. The confirmation test provides results which are deemed to be 'beyond reasonable doubt'. If the confirmation test proves negative the charge will be dropped.

Prisoners can request an independent analysis through their solicitor. Once the solicitor has found a laboratory to carry out an independent test a letter must be sent to the Prison Service asking them to authorise the release of the sample. This must do this within two weeks. The prisoner then has six weeks from the adjournment of the adjudication to present their evidence; otherwise the adjudication may be reconvened and concluded on the available evidence.

Some medication can give positive results. Many pain killers, for example, contain controlled drugs and prisoners will be asked to sign a consent form to enable the medical officer to confirm whether

*Who can be tested?*

All prisoners (whether on remand or convicted) can be tested. There are three main procedures for selecting people for testing:

• computer-generated random tests are carried out on 10% of the prison population each month;
• targeted testing if there is a reasonable suspicion that drugs have been used;
• risk assessment testing in relation to privileges such as temporary release or transfer to an open prison. Any refusal will be treated as disobeying a lawful order and a charge can be laid under Prison Rule 51(22). Likewise the provision of an adulterated sample will be treated as disobeying a lawful order. Punishments for refusing are usually as severe as for a positive test.

*How should the test be carried out?*

Prisoners must be given reasons why they are being tested and be searched before providing a urine sample. Whilst providing a sample should not be in the direct view of a prison officer, indirect observation is however considered appropriate.

If a prison cannot provide a sample they may be kept segregated for up to five hours and given controlled amounts of water to drink (a 1/3 of a pint of water at the start of each hour)

If they still fail to provide a sample it is likely they will be charged with disobeying a lawful order.

Once the sample has been provided it is divided into two A and B sample tubes which should be sealed in the presence of

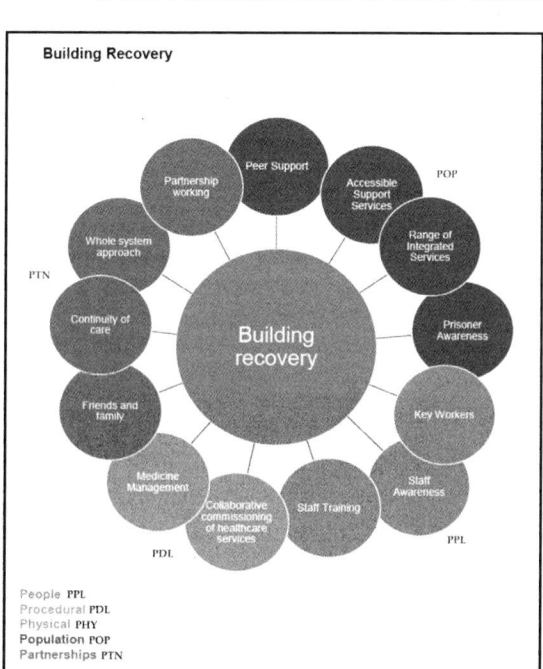

Building Recovery

People PPL
Procedural PDL
Physical PHY
Population POP
Partnerships PTN

you have been prescribed any medication.

*How often can a prisoner be tested?*

Prisoners should only be tested for periods during which they have been in continuous prison custody or released on temporary licence. After giving a positive sample there is a minimum waiting period for each drug before they can be tested again. This period depends on how long the drug stays in the system and so it will be 30 days for cannabis, 5 days for heroin, 3 days for LSD etc.

In general, prisoners cannot be found guilty at an adjudication solely on hearsay evidence. However, although the written evidence of the laboratory technician is hearsay, the courts have accepted that a prisoner can be found guilty on the basis of the report from the laboratory.

If found guilty a prisoner can receive the normal range of disciplinary punishments (up to 42 additional days if the case is heard by an independent adjudicator). If a prisoner tests positive for more than one drug, they can face a charge for each drug found in their system. The punishments should match the seriousness of the offence and, for example, repeatedly failing a test will warrant a more severe punishment.

A prisoner can appeal against a finding of guilt at an internal adjudication by submitting form DIS8 within six weeks of completion of the hearing. The prison must forward this to the Briefing and Casework Unit which will consider the review request and make a recommendation to a Deputy Director of Custody or the Director of High Security who will then decide the appeal.

The reviewer may:

a) uphold the adjudicator's decision

b) mitigate the punishment (ie: reduce it to something less severe),

c) quash the finding of guilt and punishment

If an appeal is unsuccessful, a prisoner can complain to the Prison and Probation Ombudsman within three months. The Ombudsman can make a recommendation to HMPPS which, although not binding, will usually be accepted. In very limited circumstances a prisoner could apply for judicial review of a governor's adjudication, if an aspect of the adjudication was unlawful.

A prisoner cannot appeal against a finding of guilt if the adjudication took place before an independent adjudicator, except by judicial review. They will only be able to ask the Senior District Judge that the punishment awarded be reviewed, within 14 days from the conclusion of such an adjudication.

In some cases, there may be grounds for judicial review if some aspect of the procedure or adjudication was unlawful.

*Generating random tests*

In R v the Secretary of State for the Home Department ex parte Russell (10/7/02 HC) The applicant refused a lawful order to attend a random MDT. Due to the volume of previous random tests he had disputed the randomness of the latest test and therefore the lawfulness of the order. The judge found that the governor should have investigated and established whether the test was random and then made those findings available to the applicant before proceeding with the adjudication. Because of the failure to do so the judge quashed the adjudication – and the Prison Service confirmed that in future the details of the random selection process would be made available to any prisoner selected for an MDT. A similar matter was investigated by the Prisons and Probation Ombudsman in 2002 and the complaint upheld.

**THE PRISONS (ALCOHOL TESTING) ACT 1997**

The Act was passed on 21 March 1997, and came into force in May 1997. The Act inserts section 16B into the Prison Act 1952. Section 16B gave Prison Officers, in accordance with Prison Rules and provided an authorisation is in force, the power to require any prisoner to provide a sample of breath for the purpose of testing for the presence of alcohol. Prison Rules to allow alcohol testing were introduced on April 18 2005. The introduction of an alcohol-testing regime is at a Governor's discretion on suspicion or as part of a risk assessment. There are no plans to introduce random testing. The ability to test for alcohol brings prisons in line with the existing ability to test for illicit drugs. A Testing Manual of Guidance to support the new Prison Rules was launched in December 2004 and describes policy, procedures and good practice relating to alcohol testing.

## 2.7 THE PRISON DISCIPLINARY SYSTEM - *Hamish Arnott, Solicitor*

'Prison Discipline' is governed by the contents of Prison Service Instruction 05/2018.

### *Breaking News.*

### *Update as we went to press:*

Prison Service Instruction (PSI) 05/2018 was comprehensively updated on 11th August 2022. Section 2.7 must therefore be read against the following amendments. A full updated copy of PSI 05/2018 is available on *prisonoracle.com* - and prisoners can access a copy of the updated PSI by application to the library where all PSIs, and other Orders and Policy Frameworks are mandatory publications (Prison education and Library Services Policy Framework refers.)

**Table of amendments**

| Amendment | Reference |
|---|---|
| Public sector equality duty, unconscious bias | PSI Executive Summary |
| Recovery of monies for damage to prisons and prison property | PSI Executive Summary, 2.40, 2.46 - 48, 3.12 – 3.13 Annex B, 1.91, 1.95, 2.12 Annex C |
| Immigration detainees and foreign national prisoners, Prison Rules, refusal to comply | PSI Executive Summary Annex A, 1.4 – 1.5 Annex B, 1.134 – 1.137 |
| Removal of mandatory consultation with the Adjudication Liaison Officer | PSI 2.3 |
| Crimes in Prison Referral Agreement | PSI 2.8 Annex A, 2.23 – 2.27 Annex D |
| Further guidance on assisting prisoners with communication or language difficulties or any other special needs | PSI 2.16, 2.26 Annex A, 1.21 – 1.26 |
| Timescale for adjournments to seek legal advice | PSI 2.17 |
| Disclosure of CCTV/PinPhone/body worn video camera footage and adjudication papers | PSI 2.19, 2.22 Annex A, 2.9 - 2.13 |
| Body worn video cameras | PSI 2.19 Annex A, 2.11 - 13, 2.46 Annex B, 1.146, 1.148 |
| Children and young persons | PSI 2.20, 2.35 |
| Fitness to face hearing and punishment including CC | PSI 2.27 Annex A 1.31 – 1.32 Annex B, 2.19 |
| IA hearings – referrals, independence, protocol, seriousness test, procedures, impact assessment, video link, prisoner's absence, induction of new IAs | PSI 2.32 Annex A 2.28 – 2.29 2.31 – 2.33, 2.35 – 2.39 Annex D Annex E |
| Additional days and sentence calculation requirements | PSI 2.39 Annex A, 2.75 |
| Punishments and CSRA | PSI 2.41 |
| Minor reports | PSI 2.45 |
| Discretion to adjudicate and alternative measures | PSI 3.2-3.5 |
| Timely completion of paperwork and any drug tests | Annex A, 1.2 |
| Status of accused and Rules applicable | Annex A, 1.3 |
| Safer custody guidance | Annex A, 1.14 - 17 |
| Adult safeguarding | Annex A, 1.18 - 20 |
| Segregation | Annex A, 1.27 - 30 |
| Transfers before hearing is commenced or completed | Annex A, 1.33 |
| Hearing room layout | Annex A, 2.1- 2.2 |
| Hearings in a prisoner's absence & record of hearing | Annex A, 2.3 – 4, 2.6 |
| Hearing procedures - preliminaries | Annex A, 2.5 – 2.8 |
| General Data Protection Regulation (GDPR) | Annex A 2.13, 3.36 |
| Principles of natural justice and adjournments | Annex A, 2.20 – 2.22 |
| Offences involving protected characteristics | Annex A, 2.32, 2.61 |

| | |
|---|---|
| | Annex B 1.2-1.3 |
| Witnesses and video link | Annex A, 2.41 |
| Teleconferencing | Annex A, 2.45 |
| Prisoner's defence - duress | Annex A, 2.54 |
| Punishments - ACCT | Annex A, 2.64 |
| Handing of DIS 7 to prisoner | Annex A, 2.66 |
| Additional days | Annex A, 2.73, 2.75, 2.77, 2.78 |
| Appeals - role of Prisoner Casework Section and Prison Group Director | Annex A, 3.4 – 3.8 |
| Remission (or restoration) of additional days | Annex A, 3.20 - 3.31 |
| Management oversight | Annex A, 3.32 – 3.34 |
| Retention of records | Annex A 3.36 |
| Charges, Punishments and Proof | Annex B |
| Escape and abscond definitions - charges | Annex B, 1.36 - .38 |
| Psychoactive substances - charges | Annex B, 1.46 - 50 |
| Mobile phones - charges | Annex B, 1.68 |
| Refusal to attend court - charges | Annex B, 1.128 |
| Unauthorised photographs | Annex B 1.138 |
| Incidents at height - charges | Annex B, 1.159 - 1.160 |
| Smoking related charges | Annex B 1.161, 2.4 |
| Prisoners assisting in drone related activity - charges | Annex B 1.163 |
| Visits entitlement | Annex B, 2.4 |
| Flow chart | Annex D |
| Updated case law | Annex E |
| **The below is updated as of the republishing of PSI 05/2018 on 11/08/22** | |
| Independent Adjudicators | PSI 1.14 |
| Resource Impact, Independent Adjudicators | PSI 1.18 |
| Independent Adjudicators, reasons for referral to the IA | PSI 2.32 |
| Authority to adjudicate | PSI 3.7 |
| Contents | Annex A |
| Prisoners with disabilities, mental impairments, and communication or language difficulties | Annex A 1.21 |
| Hearing room layout | Annex A 2.1 |
| Hearings in a prisoner's absence | Annex 2.3 |
| Referral to an Independent Adjudicator | Annex A 2.31-.233 |
| IAs entering prison establishments, HMPPS Chief Magistrate IA Protocol, Further good practice guidance | Annex A 2.35-2.39 – now moved to Annex J |
| Arranging IA hearings | Annex A 2.40a-2.40e, 2.41a-2.41b |
| IA hearings in a prisoner's absence | Annex A 2.42 |
| Completing IA hearings | Annex A 2.43 |
| Other witnesses | Annex A 2.47 |
| Review of adjudications – contact details | Annex A 3.4 |
| Review of IAs – Chief Magistrate's Office | Annex A 3.12 |
| Wording in race charge example | Annex B 1.8 |
| Charging guidance | Annex B 1.43 |
| Wording of prison rule and charge example | Annex B 1.46 |
| Charging guidance | Annex B 1.47-1.48, 1.51 |
| Charging guidance | Annex B 1.71 |
| Unauthorised photographs contact details | Annex B 1.138 |

| Wording of prison rule and charge example | Annex B 1.145-1.146 |
|---|---|
| Charging guidance | Annex B 1.148-1.149 |
| Introduction of virtual adjudication flow chart | Annex D |
| Updated case law | Annex E |
| Updated DIS3 form | Annex F |
| IA5 form | Annex F |
| Refusal to attend Governor and IA hearing forms | Annex F |
| Preparing for Virtual Hearings Guidance | Annex I |
| Independent Adjudicators entering prison establishments, Template IA Facility Check Sheet and Template Safe System of Work Review | Annex J |

**PSI 05/2018**                                                  **RE-ISSUED 11/08/2022**

MOJ Statistics for the latest quarter, show there were 37,102 adjudication outcomes between January and March 2022.

This has remained almost unchanged compared with the same quarter a year ago. Additional days were awarded as punishment on 582 occasions in this quarter.

Two thirds (67%) of adjudications were proven. The number of proven adjudications has remained almost unchanged (at 24,980) from the same quarter in 2021, but there was a 2% rise in the number of punishments (to 43,258).

A third (34%) of proven adjudications were for offences of 'disobedience and disrespect', with the next largest category being 'unauthorised transactions' (29%). The number of proven adjudications for 'unauthorised transactions' and 'violence' offences rose by 13% (to 7,189) and 2% (to 3,691) respectively on the same quarter of the previous year. This has been offset by a fall in other categories, in particular 'wilful damage' and 'disobedience and disrespect'. They fell by 19% (to 2,572) and 1% (to 8,601) respectively on the same quarter of the previous year.

Although the number of proven adjudications for violence increased in comparison to Q1 2021, this is still lower than the figures recorded up until 2019 where quarterly averages exceeded 5,000 offences. This increase is largely driven by the relaxing of measures implemented since March 2020 to reduce physical interactions amongst inmates and prison staff due to Covid-19.

Additional days were awarded as punishment on 582 occasions between January and March 2022; this is a 22% fall compared with the same period in 2021. A total of 9,218 days were awarded in the latest quarter – this is a 23% fall compared with the same quarter in 2021 (11,959 days between January and March 2021).

The overall number of adjudication outcomes has remained almost unchanged in comparison to Q1 2021.The quarterly volume of adjudication outcomes has continued to be below 40,000 since the start of the lockdown.

A number of policy interventions were made to suspend discipline hearings requiring an Independent Adjudicator (IA) between 23 March and 22 June 2020. Referrals to IAs have now resumed but are still held virtually and are subject to new guidelines. This impacted the number of referrals (876 for the quarter), which is far below the averages recorded before the lockdown.

In addition, other changes to the prison regime have been implemented to support operational delivery. These include new rules for governors, enabling them to: limit the movement of prisoners; implement social distancing; compartmentalise prisons to isolate symptomatic prisoners; quarantine new entrants; and so forth. These measures remain in place and taken together have reduced interactions between prisoners and staff, hence reducing the number of adjudications and related punishments.

In addition, other changes to the prison regime have been implemented to support operational delivery. These include new rules for governors, enabling them to: limit the movement of prisoners; implement social distancing; compartmentalise prisons to isolate symptomatic prisoners; quarantine new entrants; and so forth. These measures remain in place and taken together have reduced interactions between prisoners and staff, hence reducing the number of adjudications and related punishments.

More information about the trends in Adjudications between 2011 and 2018 can be found in 'The Adjudications Story' publication:

https://prisons.org.uk/reception-2-release/advice-database/7-the-prison-disciplinary-system/

**Introduction**

An adjudication has two purposes:

• To help maintain order, control, discipline and a safe environment by investigating offences and punishing those responsible;

• To ensure that the use of authority in the establishment is lawful, reasonable and

Minor report hearings are a form of adjudication and are subject to the same principles though their procedures are simpler. The role of the

adjudicator is to inquire into a report of alleged events and to decide whether an offence under Prison Rule 51 or YOI Rule 55 has been established beyond reasonable doubt. The adjudicator must investigate the charge, being prepared to question, in a spirit of impartial inquiry, the accused, the reporting officer and any witnesses. This inquisitorial role is therefore different from the one of a magistrate or judge in criminal proceedings. Adjudicators must act fairly and justly. They are responsible for the conduct of their hearings. The parts of this PSI that deal with procedure during hearings are advisory unless indicated as mandatory. If adjudicators (PS) depart from the guidance and, in doing so, compromise fairness and justice, their decisions risk being overturned. PSO 2000 For further information on the disciplinary system see: Section 4 Discipline
• Disciplinary charges PR 53, YOI 58
• Management of segregation units & management of prisoners under Rule 45 (YOI rule 49) PSO 1700
• Offences against PR 51-61, YOI 55-57
• Offences committed by young persons PR 57
• Officers, code of PR 68
Prisoners are found guilty of disciplinary charges in tens of thousands of disciplinary hearings, or adjudications, each year. If you are charged with an offence you do have important rights and if a hearing is conducted unfairly you can challenge the finding of guilt and punishment awarded. The notes below refer primarily to adult prisoners although most provisions are the same for young offenders.

**THE OFFENCES**
 The list of disciplinary offences is contained in Rule 51 of the Prison Rules 1999 (and Rule 55 of the Young Offender Institution Rules 2000): A prisoner is guilty of an offence against discipline if he -
1. commits any assault;
1A. commits any racially aggravated assault;
2. detains any person against his will;
3. denies access to part of the prison to any officer or any person (other than a prisoner) who is in the prison for the purpose of working there;
4. fights with any person;
5. intentionally endangers the health or personal safety of others or, by his conduct is reckless whether such health and safety is endangered;
6. intentionally obstructs an officer in the execution of his duty, or any person (other than a prisoner) who is at the prison for the purpose of working there, in the performance of his work;
7. escapes or absconds from prison or legal custody;
8. fails to comply with any condition upon which he is temporarily released under Rule 9;

9. is found with any substance in his urine which demonstrates that a controlled drug has, whether in prison or while on temporary release under rule 9, been administered to him by himself or by another person (but subject to rule 52);
10. is intoxicated as a consequence of consuming any alcoholic beverage (but subject to rule 52A);
11. consumes any alcoholic beverage whether or not provided to him by another person (but subject to rule 52A);
12. has in his possession
any unauthorised article, or
a greater quantity of any article than he is authorised to have;
13. sells or delivers to any person an unauthorised article;
14. sells or, without permission, delivers to any person any article which he is allowed to have only for his own use;
15. takes improperly any article belonging to another person or to a prison;
16. intentionally or recklessly sets fire to any part of a prison or any other property, whether or not his own;
17. destroys or damages any part of a prison or any other property, other than his own;
17.A. causes racially aggravated damage to, or destruction of, any part of a prison or any other property, other than his own;
18. absents himself from any place he is required to be or is present at any place he is not authorised;
19. is disrespectful to any officer, or any person (other than a prisoner) who is at the prison for the purpose of working there, or any person visiting a prison;
20. uses threatening, abusive or insulting words or behaviour;
20A. uses threatening, abusive or insulting racist words or behaviour;
21. intentionally fails to work properly or, being required to work, refuses to do so;
22. disobeys any lawful order;
23. disobeys or fails to comply with any rule or regulation applying to him;
24. receives any controlled drug, or, without the consent of an officer, any other article, during the course of a visit (not being an interview such as is mentioned in rule 38);
24. A. displays, attaches or draws on any part of a prison, or any other property, threatening, abusive or insulting racist words, drawings, symbols or other material;
a) attempts to commit,
b) incites another prisoner to commit, or
c) assists another prisoner to commit or attempt to commit, any of the foregoing
A detailed description of each offence and the evidence needed to establish guilt is contained in Annex B of PSI 5/2018

## WHO HEARS THE CHARGE?

Since the case of Ezeh and Connors v UK in 2003 there has been a two-tier system so that charges can either be heard by a governor or an independent adjudicator (District Judge -Rule 53(2)).

In summary, the more serious cases where a prisoner might have additional days awarded are referred to the independent adjudicator and are treated as being similar to criminal charges which brings them within the scope of Article 6 ECHR. A governor (or Director in private prisons, who has responsibility for disciplinary matters since the Prison Rules were amended when the Offender Management Act 2007 came into force) must first decide whether a charge is so serious that it should be referred to the police, or, if not, whether additional days would be an appropriate punishment should the prisoner be found guilty. If so the charge must be referred to an independent adjudicator (Rule 53A).

The Prison and YOI Rules were amended in 2011 to allow a charge against a prisoner who is not eligible for additional days (ie ISPs) to be referred to an independent adjudicator, where the governor determines that it is "necessary or expedient" for an IA to inquire into it (see also Smith [2009] EWCH 109).

PSI 5/2018 notes that: "This is intended to apply only in exceptional cases where the charge against the prisoner is very serious (such as a serious assault), but for some reason it is not being prosecuted in the courts" (Annex A, para 2.29). If the case is not so referred the governor proceeds to hear the charge. A referral can also be made at any stage of the process of hearing the charge (Rule 53A(3)) although if such a referral is made the adjudicator should hear the charge afresh, otherwise Article 6 could be breached (as where the prisoner is at risk of additional days the entire hearing needs to meet the Article 6 requirements).

Where a case is referred to an independent adjudicator, either at the outset, or during the course of the hearing of the charge, that independent adjudicator must first inquire into the charge (even if the case is then adjourned) within 28 days of the referral (Rules 53(3) and 53A(3)). In such cases the prisoner has a right to legal representation (Rule 54(3)). Legal aid is available, subject to the prisoner qualifying financially and the case having strong enough merits. This can be accessed through solicitors who have a prison law contract with the Legal Aid Agency. Where cases are not referred to independent adjudicators, no legal aid is available at all unless the governor allows legal representation at the hearing itself (note that legal aid is not available to give advice and assistance). Governors retain discretion to allow legal representation although this is exercised very rarely (see below).

Where Governors hear charges they are required to be able to hear the charge afresh, and so should not hear charges where they have knowledge of the charge which may prejudice consideration of the case (see Carroll and Al-Hasan v Home Secretary [2005] UKHL 13 where it was held that a Governor should not have heard charges relating to the refusal of a general order, where he had been involved in issuing the order). A governor can delegate adjudication duties to any to any other officer of the prison or YOI. In practice this means delegation to any operational member of staff at a managerial level of at least Band 7 or the equivalent in private prisons (PS1 5/2018, para 2.4).

It is important to remember that the requirements of Article 6 are much wider than just the provision of representation and an impartial tribunal and also encompass, for example, the need for the prison authorities to provide timely and adequate advance disclosure of evidence to be used at the hearing and proper facilities for preparing defences including access to witnesses. The Prison Rules already made some provision for the basic rights of prisoners charged with disciplinary offences and these apply whether or not the case is referred to an adjudicator. Rule 54 (Rule 59 of the YOI Rules) states that a prisoner should be 'given a full opportunity of hearing what is alleged against him and of presenting his own case'. This is an important Rule and most of the procedures outlined below have been introduced to ensure hearings do meet this basic requirement of fairness.

## MINOR REPORTS FOR YOUNG OFFENDERS

PSI 5/2018 continues to allow for a system of "Minor Reports" for certain charges in relation to young offenders in either YOIs or in prisons (see Annex A, paras 2.80 – 2.89). References in this chapter are to the PSI unless otherwise stated.

## PRISON DISCIPLINE MANUAL–PSI 5/2018

In February 2019 PSI 5/2018 updated and replaced PSI 47/2011. The PSI should always be made available to prisoners facing disciplinary charges. Much of the PSI reflects what the courts have held to be the requirements of fairness in all tribunals and it remains an extremely useful tool when facing a hearing in front of an independent adjudicator.

## LAYING THE CHARGE

Disciplinary charges are brought by you being given the charge sheet - Form DIS 1 (also called being 'put on report' or given a 'nicking-sheet'). The charge sheet should be given to you 'as soon as possible and, save in exceptional circumstances, within 48 hours of the discovery of the offence' (Rule 53(1) and Rule 58(1) of the YOI Rules).

The courts have interpreted 'as soon as possible' to mean any time within 48 hours and will be prepared to allow longer if a satisfactory explanation is given (Garland v Secretary of State for Justice [2011] EWCA Civ 1335). In MDT cases the discovery of the offence is generally when the screening certificate is received from the testing laboratory (Annex A, paragraph 1.1). Prison Rule 53(3) (Rule 58(3) of the YOI Rules) says that the governor should start the hearing unless he immediately refers it to an adjudicator under Rule 53A (even if it is then adjourned) no later than the day after the DIS 1 is given to you (unless that day is a Sunday or public holiday).

Rule 53(4) (Rule 58(4) of the YOI Rules) allows the governor to segregate you until this first hearing of the charge. This should not be automatic and paragraph 1.27 of the PSI says the power should only be exercised if "there is a significant risk of collusion or intimidation in the period between laying the charge and the governor's initial determination at the opening of the hearing whether to refer the case to an independent adjudicator".

Any continued segregation after the first hearing during any adjournments has to be under Rule 45 (Rule 49 of the YOI Rules). The DIS 1 should give details of what is alleged to have happened and should not just repeat the words of one of the charges under Rule 51. A failure to give sufficient detail to explain what is alleged will mean you have not been given a proper chance to prepare your defence and would therefore breach Rule 54. Once a charge has been laid against you, it cannot normally be reduced during the adjudication (see Annex A, paras 2.7) and therefore officers should lay separate charges for each suspected offence. Although separate charges can be laid from one incident, a prisoner should not be charged twice for what is essentially the same offence. For example, someone who swears at an officer should not be charged both with being disrespectful (Rule 51(19)) and with using abusive language (Rule 51(20)). During the adjudication it may be decided that you are not guilty of the offence being considered but in fact are guilty of a different offence under Rule 51. The original charge may be dropped and another charge laid against the prisoner as long as it is still within 48 hours of the discovery of the alleged offence. The proceedings will begin afresh and a new adjudicator must hear the newly laid charge.

## REFERRING OFFENCES TO THE POLICE

See **Crime in Prison Referral Agreement**, May 2019 at the end of this chapter.

Serious criminal offences which occur in prison are referred to the police to deal with (guidelines are in Annex A, paras 2.23-2.27). Except for the most serious criminal charges (murder, prison mutiny etc.) where the police are called in, the prison still lays a disciplinary charge under the Prison Rules. This must still be done within 48 hours, the adjudication opened in the normal way and then adjourned. The record of hearing that the governor completes (Form DIS 3 – formerly F256) has a specific tick-box 'referred to the police' to cover such an adjournment. If no prosecution results from the referral then the adjudicator must consider whether to proceed with the disciplinary charge. If there is a prosecution the disciplinary charge will not be proceeded with (Annex A, para 2.27). If the CPS decide not to prosecute because of insufficient evidence and the disciplinary charge is similar to and relies on the same evidence as the criminal one, then it will be difficult for the Governor to proceed. In other cases the adjudicator can proceed (for example if a witness will not co-operate with the police, but will with the governor).

## PREPARATION FOR THE HEARING

You should consider when charged whether you wish to seek advice or representation from a solicitor. Remember you have a right to legal representation where your case is referred to an independent adjudicator and even if you are thinking of pleading guilty a representative may be able to help with mitigation. You can write your defence on the back of form DIS 2 and state whether you wish to call any witnesses. Although some prisoners reasonably opt not to disclose their defence in advance, it may be wise to do so and in particular to list your witnesses in case of any dispute later as to what your defence was or whether you did call witnesses.

You should be given at least two hours before an adjudication to prepare your defence (Annex A, para 2.8). This is a minimum and if a charge is serious or complex you should be given more time. You have the right to free copies of all statements of evidence that will be used at the hearing to help prepare your defence (Annex A, para 2.9) and other relevant information (such as incident reports) should be disclosed. In a departure from previous policy, this paperwork will only be sent to the legal representative where the case has been referred to an Independent Adjudicator. For cases being heard by the Governor, the policy is to issue the papers to the prisoner who can then choose to send them on.

Interviewing witnesses should generally be allowed as should access to relevant reference books.

If you have representation your solicitor may ask for access to the prison or prison staff to enable an inspection of the area where the incident took place and/or interview potential witnesses. These requests should be dealt with by someone other than the person hearing the adjudication (Annex A, paras 2.17 – 2.18). The duty on the prison to meet such requirements will be stronger in cases where the charge has been referred to an adjudicator under Rule 53A. The prisoner's fitness for the adjudication is to be determined by the adjudicator although a list of those facing adjudication should be passed to the Healthcare Unit sufficiently in advance of any hearing to allow any relevant concerns to be passed to the adjudicator (Annex A, paras 1.31 – 1.32). The adjudicator should adjourn to obtain a health assessment of your fitness if this is considered necessary before proceeding. Prison Rule 58 requires the adjudicator (including independent adjudicators) to enquire from a medical practitioner or registered nurse as to whether there are any medical reasons as to why cellular confinement should not be imposed as punishment.

## LEGAL REPRESENTATION IN CASES HEARD BY THE GOVERNOR

It is important to understand the distinction between legal assistance and legal representation. In all adjudications, prisoners are entitled seek legal advice and the adjudicator must normally adjourn hearings to allow this to happen, subject to the prisoner taking reasonable steps to access that advice (Annex A, para 2.8).

Legal representation is where a solicitor or other representative actually appears in person at the hearing to present your case. You may still have legal representation in cases heard by a governor but this will be very rare. The courts have set down guidelines on what governors should take into account in making such a decision. In R v Secretary of State for the Home Department ex parte Tarrant [1984] 1 ALL ER 799 it was held that the adjudicator must consider the following factors:

1. the seriousness of the charge;
2. whether any points of law are likely to arise;
3. the capacity of the prisoner to present his/her own case;
4. whether or not there are likely to be any procedural difficulties;
5. the need for reasonable speed in hearing the charge;
6. the need for fairness as between prisoners and between prisoners and prison

The adjudicator is required to ask you whether you want legal representation and to record this request and reasons for refusal on the record of the

hearing (Annex A, para 2.8). Perhaps the most important category of prisoners to whom the Tarrant criteria will remain important is lifers. Their cases can only be referred to Independent Adjudicators in the most exceptional cases (see above). However, a finding of guilt against a lifer can have catastrophic effects on the timing of their eventual release, where for example it leads to a removal from open conditions prior to a Parole Board review.

If the governor does not allow representation s/he may allow you to have a 'Mackenzie friend' (so called because of the name of the case establishing the right) to sit with you during the hearing. This is someone who can attend the hearing, take notes, make suggestions to you about points you may want to raise when making submissions or questioning witnesses, generally helping you to present your case and lend support. Again, the decision is for the governor to make and this should be done using the Tarrant criteria. The governor should also consider whether the proposed Mackenzie friend (who could be a friend, relative, fellow prisoner or solicitor) is available and suitable. If your case is referred to an independent adjudicator you must be offered the opportunity to seek legal representation at the time of the referral. If neither legal representation nor the right to have a Mackenzie friend is granted or requested, an adjournment to seek legal advice should be granted if the first time the request is made is during the hearing, or if when the charge is read you have not had reasonable time to contact a solicitor. If the adjournment is for long enough, the advice may be given in writing.

However, usually the adjournment will be only sufficient to permit a telephone call to a solicitor. This will be an opportunity to get advice on the elements of the charge to be proved, which witnesses to call and whether to ask for a further adjournment to trace or interview witnesses, and other matters such as how to put forward your defence or legal arguments. Failure to properly consider requests for legal representation or advice and to record reasons for such decisions can result in successful challenges to findings of guilt. You should be told of the next date of the hearing if it is adjourned.

## THE HEARING ITSELF

PSI 5/2018 recognises that whilst Independent Adjudicators are bound by the Prison Rules, that due to their judicial independence they are not bound by the policy guidance in the PSI.

However as the guidance largely reflects the principles of fairness legally required in adjudications, breaches of its requirements may indicate that there are grounds to challenge the outcome.

PSI 5/2018 states that Governors should ensure 'an atmosphere that is generally relaxed while still formal enough to emphasise the importance of the proceedings' (paragraph Annex A 2.1). As referred cases involve charges which are criminal within the meaning of Article 6, hearings before adjudicators may be more formal and may appear more adversarial. The governor and any escorting officers should not act in an aggressive or intimidating way (Annex A, para 2.1). The adjudicator will keep a record of the hearing on form DIS 3. This does not have to be a word for word record but "Clarity and legibility are important, since the DIS 3 will be relied on in any subsequent review (including judicial review), and a case may stand or fall based on the information recorded" (Annex A, para 2.6).

If the charge is proved it must be clear from the record why the adjudicator rejected any defence put. In practice this means that large sections of evidence are not recorded. If the adjudicator does not seem to be making notes of your evidence or other important matters it is therefore important to ask that s/he does. Later on it may be your word against theirs as to whether you raised something at the time. Annex A, para 2.8 of the PSI guidance on the conduct of an adjudication. The adjudicator is firstly obliged to complete a number of formalities. These include ensuring that the prisoner understands the charge, asking whether legal assistance or representation is required, taking a plea and asking whether any witnesses are required. After these are complete, a request by a prisoner for an adjournment should be granted if it is accepted that s/he needs more time to prepare a defence, seek legal advice or representation or requires further information about the charge or procedure.

Witnesses: The reporting officer (who will have given the governor a report of his evidence on the DIS 1 at the same time as the charge was laid) will give evidence first and can be cross examined by you or your representative. The adjudicator may ask further questions and will then ask the prisoner if s/he has any defence to the charge or if s/he wants to give any explanation or evidence. If the prisoner wants to call witnesses the adjudicator may ask what evidence they will show and can only deny this request on proper grounds and not just because of administrative convenience or because s/he considers the case already proved. Refusal can be where the adjudicator considers that the request is simply an attempt to render the hearing unmanageable. The request must be noted on the record of hearing along with the reasons for refusal. An improper refusal to allow a witness to attend will give strong grounds for challenging a finding of guilt. If a witness has provided a written statement which you dispute, that witness should be called to answer questions. If the witness does not appear, then because the statement is hearsay (not evidence given in person by the witness) the written statement should not be taken into account and cannot be used to support a finding of guilt if it is contested (Annex A, para 2.49). The exception to this is the confirmation certificate following an MDT (Annex A, para 2.50).

The High Court in R v Governor of Swaleside ex parte Wynter decided that a finding of guilt could be made on the basis of the confirmation certificate alone. In making this ruling the court stated that technical rules of evidence did not apply to these kinds of adjudications and that the overriding requirement was that hearings were carried out fairly and in accordance with Prison Rule 54 (see above). If a potential witness is a member of the public (e.g. if the incident occurred in a visiting room or court complex), the governor can invite that person to attend as a witness but there is no power to compel them to do so. Copies of the letter of invitation and of the reply, if any, should be made available to the prisoner and should form part of the record of the hearing. If their evidence is deemed relevant to the hearing and yet there are compelling security reasons why they should not be admitted to the prison, or they decline to attend, the charges against you may have to be dismissed.

## WHAT NEEDS TO BE PROVED?

Before considering the evidence which has been presented by both sides the adjudicator must ask you if you have anything further to say. At the end of the adjudication you will be told whether you have been found guilty or not and the finding will be noted on the written transcript. You can only be found guilty if the adjudicator is satisfied that all essential elements of the charge are proved. Paragraphs Annex B to PSI 5/2018 contain very useful guidance on what needs to be proved in relation to the elements of all the charges (although see the comments on intent/recklessness above). A finding of guilt can only be made if the governor is satisfied that each element of the charge is proved beyond reasonable doubt (paras 2.59-2.60) - this criminal burden of proof applies whether or not your case is referred to an independent adjudicator). In relation to the 4 new charges introduced in July 2000 to deal with racist behaviour a Rule 51A states that 'words, behaviour or material are racist if they demonstrate, or are motivated (wholly or partly) by hostility to members of a racial group (whether identifiable or not) based on their membership (or presumed membership) of a racial group, and "membership", "presumed", "racial group" and "racially aggravated", shall have the meanings assigned to them by section 28 of the Crime and Disorder Act 1998'. Further guidance on these offences is provided in Annex B of the PSI. The Prison Rules do not specify what defences may be given to the charges except in the case of a charge following a mandatory drugs test under 51(9) (55(10) of the YOI Rules). The statutory defences to this charge are set out in Rule 52 (56) of the YOI Rules)-:

• The controlled drug had been, prior to its administration, lawfully in his possession for his use or was administered to him in the course of a lawful supply of the drug to him by another person;
• The controlled drug was administered by or to him in circumstances in which he did not know and had no reason to suspect that such a drug was being administered; or
• The controlled drug was administered by or to him under duress or to him without his consent in circumstances where it was not reasonable for him to have resisted.

Details on the procedures that should be followed where you want to challenge an MDT charge by obtaining an independent test on the sample were previously contained at paragraphs 6.47 to 6.59 and Annex G of PSO 2000 but are not reproduced in the new PSI. Similar defences are contained in Rule 52A in relation to charges arising from breath testing for alcohol under the new compulsory alcohol testing regime introduced in Rule 50B from 18 April 2005. From that date prisons have been able to require prisoners to submit to testing for alcohol consumption although testing will be by breath test rather than by urine sample (see annex C to PSI 15/2005).

A positive breath test cannot on its own prove guilt of intoxication under Rule 51(10) (Annex B, para 1.57) although may the offence under Rule 51(11) subject to the statutory defences. Where Article 6 applies (if your case has been referred under Rule 53A) you do not have to 'prove' these defences. You need to put forward some evidence that one of the defences applies (and this can be your account of what happened) and then the adjudicator can only find you guilty if satisfied beyond reasonable doubt that defence has not been made out. Although the Prison Rules do not contain a rule explaining general defences, such as self-defence, that prisoners will have to other charges, the same basic defences used in criminal law can be raised.

However this position is complicated by the guidance stating that intent or recklessness need only be proved where this is explicitly mentioned in the statutory offence (see discussion above). If you are found guilty you must be asked if there is any mitigating evidence

to put forward and witnesses can be called in support of your mitigation. Before considering what punishment is suitable, the adjudicator will listen to a report on your custodial behaviour. You should be given the opportunity to question the officer on anything contained in that report. Unless the adjudicator wants to adjourn the hearing to consider what the correct punishment should be, you will be told what the punishment is, whether punishments relating to multiple findings of guilt are to be consecutive or concurrent and whether a previously suspended punishment imposed at a previous hearing is to be activated.

## PUNISHMENTS

The Rules set out a different range of punishments available to governors and independent adjudicators. Governor's punishments are set out at Prison Rule 55 (60 of the YOI Rules) and the governor can impose one or more of the following (although a caution cannot be combined with any other punishment):
• caution;
• forfeiture for a period not exceeding 42 days of any of the privileges under Rule 8;
• exclusion from associated work for a period not exceeding 21 days;
• stoppage of or deduction from earnings for a period not exceeding 84 days;
• cellular confinement for a period not exceeding 21 days;
• removal from his wing or living unit for a period of 28 days
• in the case of a prisoner otherwise entitled to them, forfeiture for any period of the right, under rule 43(1), to have the articles there set out.

The punishments for Young Offenders are slightly different not including (c) and (g) above, and including removal from activities (other than education, work, training courses and physical education) for up to 21 days, 2 hours extra work a day for up to 21 days and removal from the wing or living unit for up to 21 days. Maximum periods of cellular confinement and stoppage of earnings are 10 and 42 days respectively for young offenders. In April 2000 the power to punish under 18 year olds with cellular confinement was removed from the Rules. Those serving Detention and Training Orders are also not eligible for cellular confinement.

If a prisoner serving a period of cellular confinement is found guilty of further offences, the period can be extended to up to 35 days (16 for young offenders) (Annex B, paras 2.15 – 2.16). The punishments available to adjudicators where cases are referred under Rule 53A are set out in Rule 55A. These are the same as those available to governors but include the power to impose a punishment of up to 42 additional days on prisoners or young offenders serving determinate sentences. Prisoners who cannot receive additional days are those serving indeterminate sentences (ISP's including life sentences, detention at Her Majesty's pleasure, custody for life and IPP); those subject to Detention and Training Orders (DTO); and foreign nationals who have completed a determinate sentence and are now held solely under immigration powers (although they may receive other punishments while held subject to Prison or YOI Rules). Prisoners committed to imprisonment for default on fines and confiscation orders and contemnors were eligible for additional days under provisions in the CJA 1991 (which continue to apply in respect of prisoners committed to prison before 4 April 2005) but they are not eligible for additional days if the order was made pursuant to the CJA 2003 (ie after 4 April 2005). Additional days are added to your release dates (although they cannot delay your eventual sentence expiry date) and are served in full. It is therefore important to seek legal advice where you are facing the possibility of such a punishment. Remand prisoners can be awarded prospective additional days which come into operation if they are convicted and receive a determinate prison sentence (section 257(2) Criminal Justice Act 2003). The Prison Rules 1999 provide in Rule 55(4) for there to be central guidelines on what punishments should be handed out and in October 2008 the Office of the Chief Magistrate issued guidelines for Independent Adjudicators in terms of additional days and these are periodically reviewed – see the end of this chapter.

### Challenging Governors' adjudications

The Secretary of State has the power to quash any finding of guilt and to remit any punishment awarded made by a prison governor (Prison Rule 61(1)). There is a separate review procedure for the decisions of independent adjudicators which is outlined below. At the conclusion of an adjudication, the prisoner can ask the Governor (or Director) to review the finding and the Governor retains the power to set aside the finding or remit the punishment if they agree (Annex A, para 3.2). The formal procedure for the review of a Governor's adjudication is to apply to the Prisoner Casework Section at Prison and Probation Service Headquarters for a review. This can be activated by the prisoner completing a DIS 8 form (replacing the old ADJ 1) or a legal representative writing directly to the PCS (prisonercasework@noms.gsi.gov.uk). The Governor is required to send the application together with the record of the hearing, the

charge sheet and the conduct and behaviour reports (forms DIS 1, 3, 5 & 6). PCS will then conduct the review and make a recommendation to the relevant prison group director (Annex A, paras 3.6).

### Prisons Ombudsman

All adjudications conducted by Governors and Directors can be referred to the Ombudsman once the internal complaints process is exhausted. The Ombudsman has no power to review IA cases as he has no jurisdiction over judicial decisions. The complaint can be made through confidential access or through writing to The Prisons & Probation Ombudsman. The complaint must be made within 6 months of the final decision. Outside of this time the Ombudsman can only consider complaints if there is some exceptional reasons for the delay. The courts now expect complaints to be made to the PPO before recourse is had to judicial review in most circumstances (see further below).

### Challenging independent adjudicators' hearings

The Secretary of State has no power to review independent adjudicators' hearings under Rule 61. Instead a procedure was been introduced by Prison Rule 55B whereby a prisoner may, within 14 days, request a review of the adjudication (55B(2)). The review is conducted by or on behalf of a Senior District Judge (SDJ) who will have power to reduce, substitute or quash the punishment entirely where it appears that the punishment was 'manifestly unreasonable' (55B(5)). Applications are made on form IA 4, or simply in a letter, which is forwarded by the Governor to the SDJ's office at Westminster Magistrate's Court. The review should be completed within 14 days, or faster if the additional days are being served. There is no power to quash the finding of guilt. This may be due to the fact that the courts have held that Article 6 is only engaged in the prison disciplinary system where additional days are awarded and there is no breach of the Article in refusing to quash a finding of guilt where the punishment of additional days has been remitted (Napier v Home Secretary [2004] EWHC 936 (Admin)). If a finding of guilt is being challenged, this has to be done by way of judicial review.

### Challenging adjudications generally

Paragraph 2.9 of Annex A to PSI 47/2011 allows prisoners or their solicitors to obtain copies of the transcript of the adjudication and the supporting papers. For independent adjudications this will be sent to the solicitor. For internal adjudications the PSI states that this will only be handed to the prisoner, this paperwork is usually essential when preparing representations for review. There is a time limit of 3 months for submitting a DIS 8 which will run from the date the hearing concluded and this will rarely be extended. You should explain on the form why you think the hearing or punishment was wrong or unfair. It will help to consult the PSI and look at a copy of the record of hearing when considering your reasons. Some of more common points that might be relevant are:

• Were you charged as soon as possible and in any event within 48 hours? - For MDTs this runs from the time when the screening certificate is received by the prison.

• Were there at least two hours between charging and the hearing?

• If your case was referred to an independent adjudicator, did the first hearing take place within 28 days?

• Did the charge sheet give enough particulars of the charge for you to know what was alleged against you?

• Were you given a proper opportunity to prepare (such as to consult the PSI or other books, or trace and interview witnesses)?

• Were you medically fit to go through the hearing?

• Were you given a chance to seek legal advice?

• If you requested legal representation or a Mackenzie friend was this request properly considered and reasons given for its refusal?

• Did the governor call all the witnesses you asked for and if not did he consider the request and give proper reasons for the refusal?

• Did the governor's conduct or attitude, or the behaviour of anyone else present, stop you putting your case forward properly?

• Did the governor have any involvement in the facts leading to the charge which may give rise to concerns about his/her impartiality?

• Was there evidence to prove each element of the charge against you beyond reasonable doubt? Check what needs to be proved for the charge in question in PSI 5/2018.

• Did the adjudicator improperly admit contested hearsay evidence and was this relied on in finding you guilty?

• Did the governor give reasons for his decision to find you guilty, including why s/he rejected your defence?

• Did the governor misdirect himself as to the standard or burden of proof?

• Was the punishment excessive or unreasonable?

### Judicial Review

The final remedy is to seek a judicial review of the finding of guilt. This can be done before the PCS has reviewed the adjudication although in practice, unless the matter is urgent, the High Court will normally expect you to exhaust that option first. In the important case of R v Deputy Gov. of Parkhurst ex parte Leech [1988] AC 533 HL it was confirmed that governors' adjudications could be the subject of judicial review proceedings. Over the years, a substantial body of case law has arisen and whilst many of these cases relate back to the days when Boards of Visitors were responsible for hearing the more serious charges, the principles are applicable to governors' and independent adjudicators' hearings. In the case of Gifford v Governor of HMP Bure [2014] EWHC 911 (Admin) however the court gave more detailed guidance on when prisoners challenging Governors' findings of guilt should complain first to the PPO before resorting to judicial review immediately. The case states that most adjudications will be suitable for referral to the PPO except where: an injunction is sought; there is an urgent aspect to the case, or; there is a challenge to a policy or relevant legal provision. In judicial reviews challenges have been made to both general points of principle and the constituent elements of specific charges. For example, the point that contested hearsay evidence should not form the sole basis for a finding of guilt was upheld in R v Hull BoV ex parte St Germain (No 2) [1979] 3 All ER 545 (now reflected in the PSI) - as has the right to call relevant witnesses - R v Blundeston BoV ex parte Fox Taylor [1982] 1 All ER 646. In contrast, mere technical breaches of procedure that have not affected the fairness of the hearing will not generally result in successful challenges. There is a digest of some of the key disciplinary judicial reviews in Annex E to PSI 5/2018. Proceedings for judicial review must be brought promptly and in any event within 3 months. Except in urgent cases judges will usually expect you to ask the PCS or Senior District Judge to review the decision and so the 3 months will run from the date of the BCU/SDJ response. You should get advice from a solicitor as judicial review proceedings can be complex. Proceedings are now issued on form N461 available from the Administrative Court Office at the Royal Courts of Justice in the Strand, London - the court also can provide very helpful notes for guidance on the procedure.

### Governor's remission of punishments

Prison Rule 61(2) gives a prison governor the authority to remit any punishment including additional days on the basis of good behaviour. The governor retains the power to remit (or restore) additional days even where they were imposed following an independent adjudicator's hearing. Guidance to this power is contained in Paragraphs 3.20 – 3.31 of Annex A, PSI 5/2018. Under the current guidelines applications will be considered if the prisoner remains free of adjudications (not just those that result in additional days) for a period of six months (four months for young offenders) from the date of the offence (3.20). Consideration is only given if the prisoner makes a request, a report on custodial behaviour will be obtained on form DIS 9 which should normally be disclosed to the prisoner (3.26). The application considered by the Governor, or Director in private prisons, within one month (3.28).

## CRIME IN PRISON AGREEMENT

Referral Agreement 07 May 2019

1. This document sets out the agreement between Her Majesty's Prison and Probation Service (HMPPS), National Police Chiefs' Council (NPCC) and the Crown Prosecution Service (CPS).

### Purpose of this Agreement

2. This Agreement:

• Aims to ensure that acts of criminality that occur in prison are properly addressed within the Criminal Justice system where the prison determines that the internal prison disciplinary process is insufficient, and the circumstances indicate that a criminal prosecution is appropriate or where a statutory obligation

• Establishes a common understanding of the roles and responsibilities of HMPPS, the police and the CPS relating to the referral, investigation and prosecution of crimes committed in

• Aims to achieve an improved and consistent performance in the investigation and prosecution of offences in a custodial

• Applies to all prisons, including those contracted, Young Offender Institutions and Immigration Removal Centres operated by HMPPS on behalf of the Home

• Recognises the principles agreed upon are not legally binding, and are not intended to create any legally enforceable rights or obligations. Each party will discharge its own statutory and common law obligations.

• Agree the principles outlined in this agreement reflect a national minimum expectation for all Additional guidance may be provided to each agency.

### Referral of a crime

3. The prison should contact the police immediately if there is a very serious incident such as a sudden death, life threatening injury, active escapes or serious disorder/ incident where staff require the immediate attendance of police to protect life or the integrity of establishment, in line with locally agreed contingency plans. The prison should also discuss the forensic strategy for these serious incidents with the police.

4. Any serious assault, sexual assault, escape from a secure establishment or escort, concerted indiscipline with extensive damage caused, conveyance into or out of an establishment of explosives or firearms, must be referred to the Please see Annex A for a more detailed list.

5. Whilst the views of the victim are always important and may influence the decision to refer for prosecution, the crimes in Annex A must be referred to the There may be circumstances where a case would be pursued without the victim's involvement (this is often known as a victimless or evidence-led prosecution).

6. Before reporting other incidents to the police, the prison will consider whether a case could be more appropriately dealt with by the Prison Adjudication System or whether the victim wants the crime referred to the police.

7. When an incident is referred to the police, internal disciplinary charges should be laid by the prison in the normal way within 48 hours of the incident, and an adjudication opened on the following day and adjourned pending police If the police or CPS decide not to proceed with a prosecution then the adjudication may be reconvened and the disciplinary charge heard, as long as it is fair to continue, considering the natural justice principles.

8. All crimes suitable for referral, should be referred to the police within 7 days of the incident.

9. Whilst the list in Annex A is the minimum requirement for referrals, there may be local arrangements based on current threats and risks to the prison to include additional offences. Discussions on the current threats and risks should take place regularly with the Governor, prison managers and local law enforcement.

10. In making a crime referral, the prison will:

• Provide a full description of the incident to the police, including details of offenders, victims and witnesses and including any previous relevant behaviour;

• Preserve the evidence ensuring continuity (including CCTV and body worn video cameras (BWVC)) in accordance with the Dealing with Evidence Prison Service Instruction;

• Enable access for the police to attend the prison and take witness statements;

• Provide access to the crime scene;

• Provide the police with a Prison Community Impact Statement;

• Help arrange staff to be available to provide statements to the police;

• Where prisoners have been moved to another prison, provide information of the movements of the prisoner to the police and CPS;

• Record the crimes referred to the police in the Crime in Prison Data Tracker; and

• Provide documents for disclosure to the police and CPS

11. In cases of serious crime where there is likely to be key forensic evidence, the prison will make early contact with the police to agree a clear forensic strategy.

12. If a prison determines that an offence does not meet the threshold but the victim wishes to report the crime to the police themselves, the prison must allow the victim to do so.

13. Victims, regardless of whether they are staff or prisoners, are entitled to services under the Victims Code. Special measures to support witnesses and victims may be put in place, at the discretion of the court, if the witnesses are considered to be vulnerable or at risk of intimidation.

14. The prison should assist in facilitating the provision of any Victim Personal Statement or Prison Community Impact Statement to the CPS prior to the first hearing. These can also be submitted at any time prior to sentencing. A further statement may also be submitted if the impact to the victim changes.

Investigation

15. Referring a crime to the police does not automatically mean that a full police investigation will take place or that the CPS will be consulted and a criminal prosecution take place.

16. Following a referral, the police will acknowledge receipt to the prison's Crime in Prison Single Point of Contact (SPoC) or Local Counter Corruption Manager for corruption cases, within 10 working days and advise of the next steps, this may include requesting additional information.

17. Where a decision is made that a formal criminal investigation will not take place, the police will advise the prison's Crime in Prison SPoC/ Local Counter Corruption Manager within 10 working days with the reasons for the decision not to pursue the investigation. See paragraph 26 for escalation processes.

18. Where a formal police investigation is commenced, the police investigators will update the SPoC/ Local Counter Corruption Manager and make any arrangements to progress the investigation, who will in turn keep Governors, prison managers and Adjudication Liaison Officer advised.

19. The police will keep the prison SPoC/ Local Counter Corruption Manager informed regarding the progress of the case on a regular The frequency of the update should be agreed between the police, the prison SPoC/ Local Counter Corruption Manager and the victim, however at minimum, once a month.

CPS advice and decision to charge

20. The CPS will make a charging decision in accordance with the:

• Code for Crown Prosecutors;

• Director's Guidance on Charging;

• CPS Policies, in particular Prison Related Offences and Misconduct in Public Office;

• CPS charging standards: CPS Charging standards on Assault and Assaults on Emergency Workers (Offences) Act

21. For certain offences, the police may make the charging decision.

22. Subject always to the consideration set out in the Code for Crown Prosecutors (paragraph 10) to consider each case on its own facts and merits, when reviewing cases involving assault on prison officers, and in assessing the public interest stage, prosecutors should bear in mind the impact of the offence as set out in the Prison Community Impact Statement and the impact of a decision not to prosecute.

23. In considering the public interest stage, prosecutors must have regard to the provision of the Code that states that a prosecution is more likely if the offence has been committed against a victim who was at the time a person serving the public.

24. The CPS will explain a decision to take no further action or to reduce a charge to the police, and will write to the victim in accordance with the obligations under the Victims Code. The police will inform the prison SPoC of such a decision.

25. The Sentencing Council Definitive Guidelines on Offences Taken into Consideration and Totality states that a consecutive sentence will ordinarily be appropriate where any offence is committed within the prison context.

Escalation

26. If the prison disagrees with the decision not to proceed with an investigation, this can be raised locally with the police force and their appeals process can be followed.

27. Where a decision by the CPS is not agreed upon by the police, the process of appeal under management review of charging decisions and actions will apply.

28. Where such a decision is taken by the CPS, a victim of crime in prison can invoke the Victims' Rights to Review, which enshrines a victim's right to request a review of decisions taken by the CPS not to charge, to discontinue or otherwise terminate all proceedings.

**Annex A**

Mandatory Crime Referral Criteria The crimes below must be reported to the police for investigation.

• Murder, attempted murder and manslaughter;

• Rape and attempted rape;

• Threats to kill, where evidence of genuine intent exists or there is intelligence to believe there is a threat to life or serious harm;

• Offences involving the use of a serious degree of violence or serious threats of violence;

• Offences resulting in the occasioning of serious injury and that:

1. Results in detention in outside hospital as an inpatient;

2. Requires medical treatment for concussion or internal injuries; or

3. The injury is a fracture, scald or burn, stabbing, crushing, extensive or multiple bruising.

• Assaults against a member of staff, except where there is little or no injury (see Annex B);

• Sexual offences where there has been a penetrative assault or the offence has been committed against a member of staff;

• Offences involving the throwing of bodily fluids ("potting") when it has hit a member of staff in the face or head;

• Unlawful imprisonment (hostage taking) unless there is proof of collusion between the hostage taker and alleged victim;

• Riot and offences of serious disorder, including prison mutiny;

• Any escape from an establishment or secure escort;

• Any abscond which the prisoner remains at large for more than 24 hours;

• Misconduct in Public Office;

• Robbery, involving the use or threat of serious violence or weapon;

• Possession with intent to supply drugs by prisoners, visitors or staff (including psychoactive substances);

• Possession of drugs by visitors or staff (any class of drugs or any quantity, including psychoactive substances or tobacco which is mixed with drugs);

• Conveyance into or out of a prison by any person, of other List A items, namely explosives, firearms, ammunition or offensive weapons;

• Tobacco found in possession of visitors or staff where intelligence or evidence suggests an intent to supply to prisoners;

• Mobile phones or component parts found in the possession of, or identified as belonging to, prisoners identified as high-priority either through the Prisoner Risk Assurance Service (PRAS) or subject to Lifetime Offender Management (LOM);

• Mobile phones found in possession of visitors or staff where intelligence or evidence suggests an intent to supply to prisoners; or

• Any incident of breach or attempted breach of a restraining order or injunction by a prisoner.

### Annex B
### Staff Assaults

1. Other than those less serious assaults where there is little or no injury, which are more appropriately dealt with by adjudication, all assaults on staff will be referred to the police for investigation and consideration for prosecution.

2. Dealing with minor assaults by adjudication may provide a more efficient disposal. Some examples of these offences include assaults where there is no injury (pushes or grabs) or less serious injury not requiring hospital treatment,

including minor scuffs and reddening of the skin; superficial scratches; minor bruises; small cuts, grazes or abrasions and minor swellings. If the member of staff requests the crime is referred to the police, the prison must do so.

3. Assaults occasioning transfer of bodily fluids including biting (where the skin is broken and saliva may have transferred into the wound) or spitting (where the assailant is known to have an infectious disease) should be considered for a referral to the police;

4. There may be factors which would indicate a referral to the police and each incident should be considered on a case by case basis, including considering the perpetrators offending This may include, but is not limited to:

1. Where there is clear intent to cause more serious injury than that sustained.

2. The assault was pre-planned/ premeditated rather than reckless or an immediate reaction to a particular situation;

3. The assault is part of, or linked to, organised criminal and TACT-related activity; or

4. Assaults motivated by or demonstrating hostility to the staff member based on his/her religion; race; ethnic origin; sexual orientation; gender; disability; age or political views.

5. See Annex D for the Staff Assault 8 Point Plan Assaults of Emergency Workers (Offences) Act 2018

6. Following the introduction of the Assaults on Emergency Workers (Offences) Act 2018 on 13th November 2018, police and prosecutors should cease charging the existing offences of common assault, battery, assaulting a police officer in the execution of their duty and other existing similar offences where the complainant is an emergency worker.

7. Emergency workers are defined at S.3(1) of the Act, this includes:

1. Prison officers;

2. Person (other than a prison officer) employed or engaged to carry out functions in a custodial institution of a corresponding kind to those carried out by a prison officer;

3. Prison custody officer, so far as relating to the exercise of escort functions;

4. Custody officer, so far as relating to the exercise of escort functions;

### Annex C
### Other Offences

1. There may be other offences where it is appropriate to refer to the police, however these will need to be determined on a case by case basis. Aggravating Factors

2. Each case should be determined on a case by case basis. Some things that should be considered include:

• There is intelligence or evidence to suggest the prisoner has links to serious and organised crime groups;

815

• There is intelligence to suggest the prisoner is a TACT or TACT related nominal;

• There is evidence that the crime is part of, or linked to, wider criminal activity than this offence alone;

• The victim is vulnerable or the crime was motivated by discrimination (this is often known as hate crime);

• Offences which have resulted in a high degree of damage or danger to life such as arson; or

• Offences which mirror the prisoner's index offence or there is an ongoing risk.

3. If the prison become aware or are concerned about potential TACT or extremist offences or radicalisation, they should contact the Regional Counter Terrorism Lead.

4. There may also be offences which would not usually meet the criteria, however it is appropriate to refer to the police due to the prisoner's repeat or escalating offending, or if there is belief the prisoner is adapting their offending to try to avoid a police referral. The prison should raise their concerns with their local police force and explain the circumstances of these cases.

5. This list of aggravating factors is not exhaustive and local arrangements based on current threats and risks to the prison should take place between the prison and local police force. These should be reviewed regularly due to the changing nature of the environment.

Weapons

6. Unauthorised possession of a knife, bladed or offensive weapon will be considered by the prison to determine the appropriate course of action, taking into consideration any aggravating factors.

7. A referral to the police may be appropriate if a blade or multiple weapons have been found that can be attributed to a prisoner.

8. If a prison is having a particular problem with weapons, a discussion should take place with the local police force to determine the threshold for these offences.

**Mobile phones**

9. Mobile phones present substantial risks in prisons and Mobile phones or component parts found in the possession of prisoners identified as high-priority either through the Prisoner Assurance Risk Service (PRAS) or subject to Lifetime Offender Management (LOM) or visitors or staff where intelligence or evidence suggests intent to supply to prisoners must be referred to the police.

10. Other incidents involving mobile phones should be determined on a case by case basis. Some considerations, but not limited to, are:

• If there is evidence or intelligence that the prisoner is using the phone for criminal activity or the prisoner is identified as a high-priority offender either through intelligence to the

police or HMPPS or is flagged as an organised crime nominal.

• If serious criminality is discovered during the interrogation of the phone, including serious organised crime, terrorism or extremist related offences, the interrogation should immediately be stopped and referred to the police.

**Annex D**

**Staff Assaults**

8 Point Plan HMPPS will not tolerate assaults or hate crimes on our officers, staff or volunteers. Being assaulted or abused in any way is not part of the job.

1. In line with the Crime in Prison Referral Agreement, assaults against members of staff will be referred to the police for investigation and consideration for Less serious assaults, where there is little or no injury, are more appropriately dealt with by the prison disciplinary system.

2. The Duty Manager must ensure that the Duty Governor (and designated support officer, if the prison has one) is informed to provide continuity of welfare Line managers and other staff should be notified as considered appropriate locally. The victim will also have access to the Employee Assistance Programme and the Care Team within the prison. The Prison Officers Association can also provide valuable additional support to the victim.

3. To achieve a successful prosecution, the best evidence must be presented to the police in a timely manner, including any victim and witness statements, CCTV and Body Worn Video Camera footage that can be instrumental in these cases.

4. The prison will provide a Prison Community Impact Statement to highlight significant implications for the safety, control, and order that crimes committed within a prison cause and the impact the offence itself has had on the Victim Person Statements should be used to detail the harm caused to the victim.

5. The Victims' Code applies to all victims including prison officers who have been subject to assault or hate crime. Complying with the Victims' Code means keeping the victim updated, discussing outcome options, and taking account of the victim's point of view before imposing an Special measures to support witnesses and victims may be put in place, at the discretion of the court, if the witnesses are considered to be vulnerable or at risk of intimidation. The prison will also provide appropriate after care to members of staff.

6. The assault will be reported on the Incident Reporting System. Serious assaults will also be telephoned into the National Incident Management If there has been a use of force, the relevant paperwork will also be completed.

7. The police will keep the prison updated of the progress of the enquiry. The police will provide a

full explanation to the prison if it is decided not to proceed with a case. The prison should consider any lessons learned following this feedback.

8. Victims recover better and more quickly if they receive the right welfare and supervision.

This also helps to avoid long-term negative consequences. The affected person's manager should meet with them as soon as it is practical to do so. The victim may downplay the impact on them, but managers should be aware of the potential effects of the incident, which may include the decision whether they want police involvement.

**What you can expect from the Police**

When the Police take on a crime in prison investigation they will update you at key stages of the investigation and at regular intervals. The frequency of update and preferred method of contact should be agreed between the officer and victim, default should be at least monthly or at key points such as arrest/charge. The officer in the case (OIC) will identify whether the victims are vulnerable and / or assess whether they are at risk of intimidation. The OIC will assess whether they are likely to need to attend court and if so tell them so they can receive the appropriate support. The OIC will record details of all contact or attempted contact on the appropriate crime recording system. The Police aim to deliver a high quality of service to victims and witnesses.

**What you can expect from the Crown**

Prosecution Service (CPS) CPS prosecutors when identifying the correct charge will do so in accordance with the Code for Crown Prosecutors; the Director's Guidance on Charging; CPS policy, in particular the Prison Related Offences guidance; CPS Charging Standards; and CPS Charging Standards on Assault. The prosecutor will consider each case on its own facts and merits.

The prosecutor will, when reviewing cases involving assaults on prison officers that meet the criteria within the Protocol and in assessing the public interest stage, bear in mind the impact of the offence on the safe and secure running of the establishment and the potential impact of a decision not to prosecute. When considering the public interest stage of the Code for Crown Prosecutors, prosecutors will have regard to the provisions that state that a prosecution is more likely if the offence has been committed against a victim who was at the time a person serving the public. A prison officer is a person who serves the public.

The CPS will explain a decision to take no further action or to reduce a charge to the police, and will write to the victim in accordance with the Code of Practice for Victims of Crime. This is in addition to the rights of an individual victim under the CPS Victims' Right to Review. When considering the public interest for prosecution, the likelihood

that a concurrent sentence will be imposed is not in itself sufficient to refrain from prosecuting an offence committed by a prisoner in prison.

*Edited by Hamish Arnott who specialises in public law and human rights with a particular focus on the civil liberties of prisoners and those detained under immigration laws.*

## 2.8 WHO CAN HELP?

**Introduction**

Coming into prison can be a huge culture shock for anyone but it is important to remember that there are numerous groups and individuals, from inside and outside the prison, available to answer any questions and help with difficulties you may be experiencing.

The best book you can get for simple straight forward advice, written for prisoners by prisoners, is **The Cell Companion** the latest edition of which you can purchase online at *www.prisons.org.uk*

Below is a brief introduction to people, their role, and details of how to contact them who can help. The list begins with HMPPS Staff, and then proceeds alphabetically.

*Note: Confidentiality, when discussing your situation, will normally be respected by the person you are talking to. However, if you reveal information that could threaten the security, good order or discipline of the prison, most of those listed have a duty to report such matters to the Governor.*

For a more comprehensive list of organisations that may be able to provide advice and assistance on a variety of issues, please see *Section 3* of this handbook, *The Directory*.

2.8.1 Prison Staff
    (a) Reception staff
    (b) Wing Officers
    (c) OMiC Keyworkers / Personal Officers
    (d) Equality Officers
    (e) Lifer Liaison Officers
    (f) Shared Working in Prison Officers
    (g) Governor.
2.8.2 Independent Monitoring Boards
2.8.3 Chaplaincy
2.8.4 CAB
2.8.5 Education / Library
2.8.6 Prisons Inspectorate
2.8.7 Listeners
2.8.8 MP's / Councillors
2.8.9 Prisoner Committees
2.8.10 Ombudsman
2.8.11 Prison Visitors
2.8.12 Probation Officers
2.8.13 Samaritans
2.8.14 Voluntary Organisations

Section Two

Advice
2.7 The Prison Disciplinary System / 2.8 Who Can Help?

### 2.8.1 PRISON STAFF

**Reception Staff**

Reception is the first place you enter when coming into prison. The officers will be able to assist you with any immediate needs or queries. **The Cell Companion** book will usually contain the answers to most of your questions about prison procedures and regimes, together with outlines of your rights as a prisoner. Should you have any doubts about what is happening or why, or if you need further information, you should ask staff for assistance.

Following reception, you will take part in the Prison's 'induction programme', this is designed to introduce you to the prison and the way in which it is run. You will be advised of education and work opportunities, facilities for recreation, and will get the opportunity to discuss any specific needs you may have and courses available to you. The courses vary from prison to prison but may include programmes for addiction and anger management, and more specialist courses such as the Sex Offender Treatment Programme.

**Wing officers**

Wing Officers will be able to advise directly with most enquiries regarding daily regime activities: visits procedures, property allowances, canteen, applications to see Healthcare, Probation or IMB, mail, personal cash, use of the telephones and many other issues. To avoid delay, it is best to approach the Wing officers first for assistance. If they are unable to help they will be able to refer you to others who may be better qualified to help.

**OMiC Keyworkers (often called Personal Officers or Offender Supervisors)**

Since 2019 the Offender Management in Custody (OMiC) model of offender management has been rolled out across all prisons in England and Wales - as a part of this you will be allocated a prison officer who has a keyworker role and will be responsible for you and other prisoners - see *2.1 Early Days in Custody* for more information about OMiC.

Once you enter prison you will be allocated a keyworker - normally a Prison Officer, who will be your first port of call if you need advice or have any questions or queries. Keyworkers will take time to get to know you and your individual needs. They will help you with your sentence plan (if you are an adult and serving more than 12 months, with at least six months to serve) and may be called upon to write reports about your progress.

**Governor**

The Governor and his/her deputies have the authority to decide upon most issues that may affect you. You have no absolute right to see a Governor in person, so issues unresolved by wing staff should be re-addressed through a Governor's Application. (For more information see chapter on Requests and Complaints). Governors can be approached informally, however, when 'doing the rounds' on the wings.

### 2.8.2 INDEPENDENT MONITORING BOARDS (IMB's)

The Prison Act 1952 provides that the Secretary of State appoints a IMB for every prison in England and Wales (including contracted out establishments). Each IMB is made up of members of the public from the local community. They are unpaid volunteers and, as such, are independent of HM Prison Service. The purpose of the Boards is to act as independent watchdogs, on behalf of the Home Office, to ensure the prison is run fairly and in accordance with the Prison Rules.

**The most important point to remember with Members of Independent Monitoring Boards is that they are in the prison to 'monitor' what happens - they are not there to 'manage' the place.** They have zero executive powers, they cannot make or change decisions made by prison staff, though they can make recommendations to them which may cause a decision to be amended or altered; but they cannot do this themselves.

Each IMB normally works to a rota system, where members take turns to visit the prison at least once a week. These visits are unannounced, and members have the right of access to every part of the prison, and every prisoner, at any time. The members are particularly concerned with the state of the prison and its administration, the treatment of prisoners, facilities provided, and that both staff and prisoners are treated fairly. Any matters giving cause for concern will be immediately raised with the Governor, or reported directly to the Secretary of State.

The IMB will also hear any complaints made by prisoners, you can apply to see a member of the Board, either via a written application through the wing office, or you can approach one of the Board if you can spot them 'on the hoof'; making a rota visit. They can assist and advise you on how to proceed, or may take up the complaint on your behalf. It is possible to ask to see the whole Board (a minimum of three) if a single member has been unable to assist satisfactorily. You will find more about IMBs in *section 2.4* of the handbook.

Finally, it is important to remember that though their title contains the word *'Independent'* every Member of an Independent Monitoring Board is selected by, and answerable only to, the Ministry of Justice - it is this fact that has meant that faith in their 'independence' has, perhaps unfairly in many cases, largely failed to develop among many prisoners and staff

### 2.8.3 CHAPLAINCY
Prisoners have a protected right to practice their religion whilst in prison. Each prison has a Chaplain from the Church of England, Roman Catholic or Methodist Churches. The Chaplain should see all those newly entering prison soon after arrival, as part of the Reception/Induction process. At other times you can put in a formal request via the wing office and a meeting will be arranged. The Chaplain can also arrange for Visiting Ministers from other faiths to provide pastoral care, teaching, fellowship and opportunities for worship to those of their own faith.

Maintaining contacts from outside the prison can be greatly assisted by the Chaplaincy team, as it is possible for them to work in co-operation with Probation Officers to help preserve links with your family and community. Chaplains also have a pastoral role towards the whole prison community including staff and management. It is through the Chaplain that you can arrange to see a Prison Visitor (see below).

### 2.8.4 CITIZENS ADVICE BUREAU (CAB)
CAB are a nationwide organisation which has around 1,000 branches. CAB are a comprehensive source of information and advice for your family and can help with enquiries on housing, benefits and a wide range of other issues. Several prisons have CAB advice sessions, otherwise they can be contacted by letter or phone. Please see entry under National Association of Citizens Advice Bureau, in *Chapter 3.1, The Directory.*

### 2.8.5 EDUCATION/ LIBRARY
Every prison has an education department and library. Courses available vary from prison to prison and are often provided by a local college. Usual subjects include: basic literacy and numeracy, IT skills and social skills. You should have the opportunities to study for nationally recognised qualifications, sometimes up to degree level, with courses from the Open University. A representative from the Education Department should meet with you during your induction training, to discuss your educational needs and provide full details of courses available in that prison.

The library is a good source of information and is able to order books, through inter-library loans, if they are not available at your establishment.

There are many publications required to be held within prison and YOI libraries, currently these include: *The Prisons Handbook,* HMCIP Annual and Establishment Reports, Prisoners Information Books, together with Prison Service Guides and Manuals, Council of Europe and UN Publications, Legal Guidance, and Government Reports, Statutory Instruments and Acts, such as; Prison Act 1952, Police and Criminal Evidence Act 1984 and Prison Rules. The library should have the latest and most up to date list of documents available for reference. For a full list see the *Chapter 2.1, Coming into Prison.*

### 2.8.6 PRISONS INSPECTORATE.
HMCIP works independently of the Prison Service and reports directly to the Home Secretary. HMCIP, together with a team of inspectors, have a duty to regularly inspect prison conditions and the treatment of prisoners in England and Wales. The inspections are often unannounced, but if a specific area is to be covered an announced inspection will take place. The opinions of prisoners are sought by the inspectors, which are taken in confidence.

HMCIP produces an Annual Report, and detailed reports on establishment inspections, together with Thematic Reviews on specific subjects. All of which should be available for reference through your prison's library. You will find more information about the Prisons Inspectorate, including summaries of all their latest inspection reports, in *section 6.1 of the Handbook*

### 2.8.7 LISTENERS
The Listener scheme was set up in partnership with the Prison Service and the Samaritans, and many prisons now have the scheme. The Samaritans come to the prison and train volunteer prisoners to give 24 hour support and counselling to other prisoners. The scheme works because many of the Listeners may, at some stage, have experienced similar problems. They can offer support and advice in confidence. The Listeners have regular de-briefs with the Samaritans on how to cope with stressful situations. The Listeners can be contacted via the wing office, the IMB, the Chaplain or, as the Listeners wear an identity badge, you may be able to approach them directly. If there is no Listener scheme at your prison, contact the Samaritans.

### 2.8.8 MPs AND LOCAL COUNCILLORS
Members of Parliament and local Councillors, as elected representatives, are able to advise on a wide range of issues. Usually your home address determines your MP and councillors, but whilst

in prison you may contact the constituency into which the prison falls.

Whilst in prison on remand and unconvicted, and if over 18 years of age on the date of an election, you are still entitled to vote, by post or proxy. You will need to apply to the Electoral Registration Officer well in advance of the election date, your Key Worker should be able to advise you how to do this. You will not be allowed to vote if you are convicted unless you are registered to vote *and on the date of an election* you are either Released on Temporary Licence to work in the Community or happen to be on Home Detention Curfew.

## 2.8.9 PRISONER COMMITTEES

Many prisons operate Prisoner Committees as a means of canvassing the opinions and suggestions of the prisoners. Usually there are one or two elected representatives from each wing who will meet monthly with officers and Governors to discuss issues raised by the prisoners, and to advise prisoners as to changes to the regime. If you have an issue to be raised, your wing officers will be able to tell you which prisoners are on the committee, so you can approach them directly with your suggestions. If you would like to be on the committee, wing officers, or your currently elected representative, would be able to advise you of the procedure.

## 2.8.10 PRISONS AND PROBATION OMBUDSMAN

The Prisons Ombudsman is an independent adjudicator for prisoner complaints that have failed to reach a satisfactory conclusion through the established complaints system. Set up in 1994 as a result of recommendations of the Woolf Report into prison disturbances in 1990, the Report stated that one of the main issues for prisoners was that their grievances were not being adequately resolved.

For a complaint to be investigated by the Ombudsman:

1. you have completed the internal complaints process

2. it is less than three months since you had a response to the final stage of your complaint there is a substantial issue raised

3. you are the person directly affected by the complaint you have raised (although the Ombudsman has discretion to accept complaints from third parties on behalf of individuals who are unable to act on their own behalf).

The Ombudsman cannot investigate complaints about:

1. the clinical judgement of medical professionals

2. policy decisions taken by a Minister of State

3. cases currently the subject of civil litigation or criminal proceedings

4. conviction, sentence, immigration status, reasons for immigration detention or the length of such detentions

5. decisions or recommendations of the judiciary, the police, the Crown Prosecution Service and the Parole Board and its Secretariat.

## 2.8.11 PRISON VISITORS

Prison Visitors (PVs) are independent, local, volunteer members of the public of varied age, background and ethnic origin. Each prison has a Prison Visiting Scheme that can arrange a visit for you upon request. Sometimes the scheme is used by those who have no-one to visit, others use it as a means of maintaining contact with the outside world, and some appreciate the chance to speak to someone not involved in the prison system. The visits will take place either in your cell, an interview room or the visits room. A visit from a PV does not affect your entitlement to ordinary visits and a visiting order (VO) is not needed. To arrange to see a PV, speak to the Chaplain or there may be a Prison Visitor Liaison Officer.

## 2.8.12 PROBATION SERVICE

All prisons and YOIs have a Probation Department and you will meet an offender manager shortly after arrival. Probation staff can help you to keep contact with your family, and advise you on any immediate areas of concern. They can also offer courses on offending behaviour, drug and alcohol misuse and anger management. Probation officers are involved in risk assessments for parole or home detention curfew, sentence planning, bail information and preparation for your release.

## 2.8.13 SAMARITANS

A national organisation accessible to anyone feeling anxious, distressed or alone. Samaritans are volunteers who are available to listen to your worries in a non-judgemental way and to offer support and guidance through your period of distress.

The Samaritans are completely unconnected to the PS, and, any conversations that take place are completely confidential and will not be discussed with prison staff. Most prisons maintain strong links with the Samaritans making use of the Listeners Scheme (see above), or surgeries, when volunteers come into the prison on a regular basis for one-to-one discussions. It may be possible to telephone the Samaritans in private, away from the landings, request a private visit by a Samaritan, or get a special free letter, if you are particularly distressed. Details of how to contact the Samaritans should be displayed clearly around the prison with details of the telephone number and address of the local branch. Or you could write to: Chris, PO Box 1250, Slough SL1 1ST. It is important to contact the Samaritans as soon as you feel in need, rather than allowing problems to build up. If you would like help in contacting the Samaritans ask your Wing Officer, Chaplain or member of the IMB, all will be happy to assist.

## 2.9 HEALTHCARE

**Updated from an earlier chapter by the Nuffield Trust**
**Overview 2022**
Although people in prison are deprived of their liberty, their right to health care is unaffected. But prisoners tend to be of poorer health than the general population and have complex health care needs.

Addressing inequalities between people in prison and the general population is a key policy goal, but there are challenges to making this work in practice. Prisons are overcrowded, they face particular challenges with staffing and funding has decreased since 2010. Security concerns can also have a profound impact on how healthcare is delivered in prisons.

Since 2013, prison health care has primarily been the responsibility of NHS England, which directly commissions primary, hospital and public health services for people in prison.

However, from 2024, prison health care commissioning is set to become the responsibility of integrated care systems (ICS).

All prisons have some health care services (such as primary care and mental health support) on-site and some also have dedicated healthcare wings where people can go to receive care and treatment. The exact set-up depends on the characteristics of the prison itself; there is wide variation in the services available across the prison estate.

On arrival at prison, people should receive a health care assessment. During their stay, they should be able to access primary care services, and if they need to attend an appointment off-site, at least two escorts will need to accompany them. People in prison should also get access to the same public health programmes as the general population.

But there are concerns about prisoners' access to and quality of health care. The Covid-19 pandemic has also had an impact on this and current evidence suggests there has been wide variation in people's experiences.

### Key Figures 2022
There are 119 prisons in England and Wales. Women currently represent less than 5% of the total prison population—a level which has remained consistent over the last 5 years. In line with the overall prison population, the number of women prisoners has declined over the same period. As of 15 July 2022, there were 3,219 women in prison, compared to 3,958 in February 2017—a 19% decrease. However, the Ministry of Justice predicts that the number of women in prison will increase to 4,500 by September 2026 as a consequence of the Government's commitment to employ 23,400 more police officers.

The proportion of people in prison aged over 50 increased from 7% in 2002 to 17% in March 2020 to 23% in 2021.

Her Majesty's Prison and Probation Service (HMPPS) uses age 50 to describe 'old age' in prisons, given the significant health needs of people in prison. Of the people in prison, at March 2021, 28.2% identify as minority ethnic, compared with 13% in the general population.

The average age of death of people dying in prison is 56, compared with 81 in the general population. As of 30 June 2022, 43,425 prisoners or children in custody have tested positive for Covid-19 since the start of the pandemic and 288 prisoners, children in custody and supervised individuals have died within 60 days of testing positive or where there was a clinical assessment that Covid-19 was a contributory factor in their death: HMPPS Covid-19 statistics, June 2022 published 15th July 2022.

### The Health and Care Act 2022
The Health and Care Bill received Royal Assent and came into force on 1 July 2022.

The clauses of the Bill are wide ranging and include the abolition of the NHS Trust Development Authority and Monitor, formal establishment of NHS England, and provisions to support integration of functions across NHS organisations. Further detail on the Bill can be found in the Government's White Paper, Integration and innovation: working together to improve health and social care for all, and on the Parliament website on the Health and Care Bill.

*White Paper:* tinyurl.com/26j53rne
*Health and Care Bill:* tinyurl.com/yepwvv4h

### 2023 and Beyond: Integrated Care Boards
In April 2021, 42 integrated care systems (ICSs) were established and formed from the existing local organisations. The Health and Care Bill established these systems as statutory bodies, called integrated care boards (ICBs), from July 2022.

ICBs replace clinical commissioning groups (CCGs), with CCG staff and functions transferring to the new organisations. ICBs will have broad objectives, including:
• Developing a plan to meet the health needs of their population,

• Developing capital plans for NHS providers in their geography,

• Securing the provision of health services to meet the needs of their population.

The ICBs will become responsible for commissioning primary medical care services, acute hospital services, ambulance and emergency care services, and also some of the services currently commissioned by NHS England; for example, primary dental services and some specialised services. In commissioning these services, ICBs will need to secure improvement in the physical and mental health of their population, and improve the prevention, diagnosis and treatment of illness.

ICBs will also have a duty to promote the integration of functions in such a way to improve the quality of those services and reduce inequalities in both access and outcomes. When making decisions, ICBs also have a duty to have regard to the triple aim: the health and well-being of people in England; the quality of services provided; and efficient and sustainable of the use of resources.

NHS England's objectives are to support the establishment of ICBs and move to greater integration of organisations across system footprints. Consequently, ICBs will become the default organisations for planning services.

NHS England set out the intention to strengthen joint working across NHS England's direct commissioning functions, including through joint committees, in a letter from Amanda Pritchard, NHS England's Chief Executive, in July 2021 *Letter:* https://tinyurl.com/4mzbwv4k The letter confirmed that ICBs would work with NHS England to determine, by April 2024, whether some health and justice services would be delegated to ICBs to lead. This work is underway. Full proposals for the future of health and justice services from April 2024 are in development and will be confirmed in due course.

### Provider collaboratives and place-based partnerships

NHS England issued *guidance* on provider collaboratives in August 2021 which set out the following roles for provider collaboratives: *Guidance:* https://tinyurl.com/2p8zww65

• Reducing unwarranted variation and inequality in health outcomes, access to services and experience,

• Improving resilience by, for example, providing mutual aid,

• Ensuring that specialisation and consolidation occur where this will provide better outcomes and value.

All NHS trusts providing acute and mental health services were expected to become a member of at least one provider collaborative by July 2022. However, NHS England will not prescribe the membership of provider collaboratives, or have a role in shaping their priorities and objectives.

Working with their ICB or ICBs, clinical networks, cancer alliances and others, collaboratives will agree:

• Shared goals and appropriate membership and governance,

• Alignment with the ICB's priorities,

• Objectives and priorities,

• Plans for delivery and establish programmes of work,

• How they will work together with other provider collaboratives.

The framework for provider collaboratives envisages:

• **Regional collaboratives** across a large geographic footprint, focused on (for example) highly specialised and specialised services and collaborating with specialised clinical networks.

• **Multi-system collaboratives** working across multiple ICBs focused on specialist and specialised services; community and mental health; and access to urgent and emergency care, and working closely with specialist clinical networks.

• **System collaboratives**, where services a primarily delivered on an ICB footprint. It is envisaged that most provider collaboratives will operate on this footprint, but that they should nevertheless be well-connected to service delivery and decision-making on multi-system, regional and national levels.

### Primary care networks (PCNs)

PCNs were introduced into local commissioning arrangements as part of the NHS Long Term Plan, published in January 2019. They are designed to enable GP practices to join networks with the net result of establishing fully integrated community-based healthcare delivery. They have a dedicated funding stream to support the employment of clinical pharmacists and social prescribing link workers (in the first instance) and in relation to these specifications offer a considered approach to anticipatory care and the potential to support personalised budgets for some of the patient co-hort. Elements of the PCN local to a prison establishment offers regional commissioners and providers of the services described within these specification mechanisms to support the broader patient management innovations and continuity of care pre and post release that benefit improved patient outcomes.

## Introduction

The NHS Act 2006 mandates NHS England to commission health services across prisons and other places of prescribed detention. NHS England has responsibility for commissioning healthcare services under the principle of 'equivalence' is adhered to, enabling patients' access to physical and mental health care as required in line with services offered in the community, working towards agreed health outcomes and being supported to manage their ongoing health care needs.

NHS England commissions healthcare within prisons and other secure settings via the 7 regional teams within England they undertake this by using national specifications and clinical guidelines.

There are numerous clinical guidelines and best practice documentation that describe clinical practice and processes to steer best practice in the delivery of physical healthcare for people in secure and detained environments.

People in secure and detained environments may require additional health and social care support generally. Whilst social care is not legally the responsibility of NHSE/I commissioning arrangements, there is a strong need to work collaboratively with local authorities' social care teams and other healthcare providers. This can entail a collaborative commissioning approach or the provider holding the social care contractual obligation through a separate contract.

Appropriate support must be provided to people in secure and detained environments with an identified or suspected learning disability or difficulty to enable them to cope better within the secure environment and ensure that their health needs are met.

The primary care service provider also has a role in providing general support and advising other agencies within a prison of their respective responsibilities to support patients in daily life.

For ease of reference, throughout this document the term 'learning disability', unless otherwise stated, encompasses individuals with learning disabilities (LDs), autism or other vulnerabilities. A safe and secure prison system cannot be successfully delivered without effective healthcare services, in turn, such services cannot be delivered without the full support and partnership of the prison regime and its staff. Both the physical environment within which a person lives and receives care and the service provided contribute towards general physical and mental wellbeing within the prison.

## IT and HJIS

All secure setting healthcare services use the national IT solution provided by NHSE/I health and justice information system (HJIS) as the primary clinical record for the patient.

## 1 Guiding principle

The purpose of health care in prison is to provide an excellent, safe and effective service to all patients ensuring access to and the quality of services delivered is of an equivalent standard to that of the community. Services should meet the objectives and outcomes of national frameworks and priorities and are expected to develop and implement measures to monitor these outcomes.

Services should operate from a position of 'Making Every Contact Count'. Wherever a patient presents to any health service, or via some other intervention, it is incumbent upon providers to meet immediate needs and bring appropriate provision to the patient, not 'send' the patient to another intervention.

Screening, assessment and treatment for health conditions and learning disabilities should be appropriate and address the wide range of other, often related mental and/ or substance dependency needs identified. It should have a public health perspective and focus on reducing harms and promoting recovery and rehabilitation. Care should be person centred and delivered by professionals and allied staff who are suitably competent, well led, properly supervised and operating within a clear quality and clinical governance framework supporting safe and effective delivery.

Treatment and care plans should be regularly reviewed. There should be access to suitable psychosocial and clinical interventions, as well as a focus on health promotion and supporting positive health and well-being. Where medication is indicated, its provision should be suitably safe particularly in those with difficulties achieving stability and with clear shared care between prescribers.

Clinicians should be able to adapt evidence-based treatments from the wider community to the prison estate and regime and be able to work with security staff and systems to reduce harm and to manage risk, particularly the risk of fatalities and self-inflicted harm, as well as other risks to consider such as abuse and exploitation. They should also have established links with social care providers serving the prison and contacts with the education provider for the establishment to ensure those with social care and/or communication needs receive a holistic package of care and support.

## Cross referencing commissioning responsibilities outside those of health and justice.

There are a number of areas where the commissioning for delivering care must work in conjunction with the commissioning responsibilities of other areas within NHSE/I and where health and justice direct commissioning processes must be aligned. These include services commissioned by specialised commissioning to our patient population constituting services such as anti-libidinal medication, supporting patients with serious mental health needs which ultimately require secure hospital care, care and treatment of specific blood borne viruses (BBV) conditions such as HIV infection and the specialist treatment a transgender patient would require as well as supporting the social care requirements of a patient (this is not an exhaustive list).

## 2 Frameworks and priorities

Healthcare for people in the CJS is influenced by a wide range of policy areas and developments. Healthcare deliver a prison-based community care services model (hereafter referred to as healthcare services in prison) to meet the objectives and outcomes of the various frameworks and priorities and will be expected to develop and implement measures to monitor these outcomes. These include but are not limited to:

### NHS Outcomes Framework

The NHS Outcomes Framework sets out the framework and indicators used to hold NHSE/I and commissioned services to account for improvements in health outcomes. These are not prison specific but are organisationally relevant. The outcomes and indicators can be found here: https://tinyurl.com/4t5ehvf4

### 3 NHS Long Term Plan

The NHS Long Term Plan (LTP) published in January 2019 sets out the vision for the NHS over the next decade. The entire document can be accessed here:
https://www.longtermplan.nhs.uk/
While the principles of the entire LTP apply to all health and justice commissioned services, there are five priorities related specifically to health in the justice system – in summary these are:

• Additional investment in services for people experiencing a mental health crisis will make a real difference for people who need support and will help ease pressures on police services. Adults, children and young people will receive health screening on entering prison and a follow-up appointment within seven days, or sooner as required. This will be supported by the full roll-out of the health and justice digital patient record information system across all adult prisons, immigration removal centres (IRCs) and secure training centres for children and young people. This will include the digital transfer of patient records before custody, in custody and on release.

• Health and justice services are provided to some of the most vulnerable members of our society. Many people within the justice system experience greater problems than the rest of the population but do not regularly access timely healthcare. The NHS is already working with partners across government to improve the wellbeing of people in prison, reduce inequalities and address health-related drivers of offending behaviours. A priority in services for this group of patients is improving continuity of care. The care after custody service, RECONNECT, starts working with people who meet the eligibility criteria before they leave prison and helps them to make the transition to community-based services that will provide the health and care support that they need. Over the next five years, RECONNECT will engage and support more people after custody per year.

• Since 2017, five parts of England have been testing a new Community Service Treatment Requirement (CSTR) programme. This enables courts to require people to participate in community treatment, instead of a custodial sentence. CSTR sites have provided community treatment for people who would otherwise have been sentenced inappropriately. We will build on this by expanding provision to more women offenders, short-term offenders, offenders with a learning disability and those with mental health and additional requirements. This service is commissioned as part of the overall prison health pathway and should ensure that this model supports an integrated treatment system both within the prison and onwards into the community. The service focus on delivering person-centred care within seamless and integrated clinical services in prison and facilitating arrangements through the gate into the community to ensure effective continuity of care. Close joint working with other healthcare services, as well as other departments within the prison such as education, offender management, and physical education, is imperative to the success of the delivery of this service.

1. The NHS Standard Contract is mandated for use by clinical commissioning groups (ICSs) and NHSE/I when commissioning non-primary medical services NHS-funded healthcare services. Where primary medical services are being commissioned, the appropriate form of primary medical services contract must be used in accordance with the relevant regulations and directions.

2. In certain circumstances, commissioners may commission a package of services including both primary and secondary care elements from a single provider. An example of this would be the commissioning of an integrated prisons healthcare service (for which the NHS Standard Contract must be used) and GP services (for which a general practice contract must be used). In those circumstances neither the NHS Standard Contract nor any form of primary medical services contract may lawfully be used on its own to commission that package of services. Various contractual structures may be used to deal with this. The use of Schedule 2L of the NHS Standard Contract offers a relatively simple solution, for use in appropriate circumstances.

3. If the package of services includes primary medical services and services for which the NHS Standard Contract is the mandated form of contract, commissioners may include provisions in Schedule 2L of the NHS Standard Contract to make the Contract compliant with the Alternative Provider Medical Services (APMS) Directions in relation to the provision of primary medical care services. In other words, to ensure that the contract is both an NHS Standard Contract and an APMS contract.

4. Schedule 2L is based very closely on NHSE/I model form of APMS Contract, which is available at:

www.england.nhs.uk/commissioning/gp-contract/

The service is made available to all people residing within the establishment. The provider must meet the unique needs of the establishment and take into account the needs of the population within that establishment.

Services should be familiar with the legal duties placed upon them by both the Equalities Act (2010) and the Health and Social Care Act (2012), as well as the Care Act (2014) and Mental Health Act (1983) and include such considerations into the overall approach taken and any plans made. Primary care services should be delivered as part of an integrated healthcare service (as described within the full range of health and justice service specifications). The service providers must ensure that the workforce is able to provide high quality, safe, effective, caring, responsive and well-led care to patients and that 'the right staff in the right place at the right time' are available to achieve better outcomes, better patient and staff experiences and effective use of resources.

The appropriate skill mix of healthcare staff in the prison will include the use of practitioners from a variety of disciplines e.g. GPs, nursing, paramedic, Mental health, Substance misuse support workers and assistant/associate practitioners. The workforce must have the essential and relevant qualifications and competencies to carry out their roles and responsibilities and have access to regular clinical supervision.

The providers must ensure that there is a rolling training programme to ensure staff have access to mentorship skills training to maintain skills in supporting trainees and newly appointed staff.

The service must meet the prison's specific requirements for healthcare input as stated in Prison Service Instructions (PSIs) and Prison Service Orders (PSOs).

## Clinical governance

Clinical governance arrangements and structures are in place which facilitate continuous service improvement by the utilisation and analysis of key information sources such as: risk register, critical incidents, complaints, best practice and clinical audit, audit of Deaths in Prison Serious Incident reporting, Prisons and Probation Ombudsman (PPO) reports, Serious Case Reviews and Her Majesty's Inspectorate of Prisons (HMIP) action plans. Clinical governance concerns both clinical and non-clinical staff and acknowledges everyone's contribution to the patient's experience. Good integrated governance should combine and create consensus around the concerns of clinical staff, prison staff and managers, patients and their families. Key to effective governance is the availability of information sources on which to base decisions.

The providers use a variety of effective methods to ensure that a high-quality service is provided in accordance with standard NHS practice. These will include, but not be limited to the following:
- Patient engagement.
- Waiting time surveys.
- Clinical audit.
- Audit of prescribing and medicine usage.
- Activity information.

## 4 Reconfigured adult male estate

The establishment types – reception, trainer, resettlement, open – will need to be considered when commissioning healthcare services in the reconfigured estate, as each will have different healthcare priorities. It should also be noted that most prisons will have a dual function (e.g. reception and resettlement), so the service will need to meet the needs of all patient populations within the establishment.

Local determination will be required based on the health needs assessment (HNA) for each establishment and the unique population of each site.

Below are general commissioning considerations for each type of prison function:

**Reception**
- First night reception screening.
- Ensuring the identification of immediate health, risk and safety needs.
- Appropriate care for the first 10 days in custody and the transfer of health information to receiving prison where appropriate.
- Pathways across prison patient population and cluster may be needed to ensure continuous care.
- Appropriate screening, testing and treatment, e.g. BBVs and chlamydia.
- General health screening within seven days.

**Trainer**
- Management of long-term conditions including health checks for over people over 35 years old.
- Referrals to secondary care.
- Public Health section 7a services.
- Appropriate links to social care.
- Appropriate screening, testing and treatment, e.g. BBVs.

**Resettlement**
- Discharge planning to ensure continuity of care on release.
- Healthcare contribution to resettlement planning.
- Engagement with RECONNECT programme as per eligibility criteria.

**5 Adult women's estates**

There is no reconfiguration strategy for the women's estate and as such women's prisons remain as they are with a mixed economy of patient management. The model for the women's estate includes young offender and older adult women and covers reception, resettlement, training, open and closed facilities. The women in these prisons will receive the all the healthcare as in the male estate but with the specific gender related elements taken into account in meeting the health needs of this population.

**Regulation**

The Care Quality Commission (CQC) and HM Inspectorate of Prisons jointly inspect health care services in prisons. Since April 2015, the Care Quality Commission has also been responsible for inspecting adult social care services in prisons. HM Inspectorate of Prisons' inspections are guided by the principle of 'healthy establishments', which includes a number of expectations concerning safety, respect and rehabilitation. The role of HM Inspectorate of Prisons in conducting regular inspections is important for fulfilling the UK's obligation under the United Nations Optional Protocol to the Convention Against Torture and other Cruel, Inhuman or Degrading Treatment or Punishment (OPCAT), which requires action to prevent the ill-treatment of people in prison.

The key bodies, and commissioning and regulation responsibilities, are set out in the infographic below. What health care services should be provided to people in prison?

Although there is guidance outlining the health care services that should be provided to people in prison, in practice prisoners can experience challenges accessing health services and there is variation between prisons over what services are available. In this section we provide an overview of what services should look like and then, in the following section, we highlight some of the longstanding challenges surrounding access to and quality of health care.

All prisons have some health care services on-site and some also have dedicated healthcare wings where people can go to receive care and treatment. NHS England sets out the core services that should be provided in prisons and these should be evidence-based, person-centred and delivered by appropriately trained staff. However, the exact set-up should be tailored to the characteristics of the prison and the needs of the particular prison population.

**On arrival**

Within 24 hours of arriving in prison, people should receive an initial health care assessment from a health care professional to identify their immediate needs such as ongoing medication requirements for physical or mental health problems or treatment linked to drug or alcohol withdrawal.

This should also include an assessment of any other medication needs, physical injuries and chronic health conditions (such as diabetes or asthma), as well as any recent medical appointments requiring follow-up. People in prison should also be screened for tuberculosis within 48 hours of arrival. Numerous templates exist to help with these assessments, including tools specific to identifying health needs in young people, such as the Comprehensive Health Assessment Tool (CHAT). From April 2021, prisoners should also be screened for brain injury sustained through domestic violence.

A follow-up health care assessment should take place within seven days to address any issues raised at the initial screening that require ongoing input, as well as meeting more general health care needs and giving health promotion advice. People should be told how they can access ongoing medical support, such as how to book a GP appointment.

This secondary assessment should also include screening for blood-borne viruses such as hepatitis C. Opt-out blood-borne virus testing was introduced in a pilot project in the prison estate in 2013, and it was rolled out across the whole adult estate in England in 2018.

## Information sharing between prisons and the community

Collecting, storing and sharing data across services is a key commitment of the Digital, Data & Technology Strategy, recently published by HMPPS, and the importance of data-sharing to support meeting the needs of people in prison is also noted in the overarching draft data strategy for health and social care.

On arrival at prison and with their consent, the person's medical records should be transferred from the community to the prison to ensure continuity of care. But historically, transferring records between prison and the community has been challenging.

The Health and Justice Information Services is a national programme, commissioned by NHS England, which aims to bring the information technology (IT) system in place within the secure estate in line and up-to-date with other clinical systems used in the community.

Successful implementation would enable sites to access the NHS national spine and services such as e-referrals and e-prescriptions. Patients will also be able to select the secure estate health care provider as their registered GP, enabling the electronic transfer of information between the prison and the community.

The programme is intended to improve information-sharing between prisons and the community, including on the person's release.

## During prison stay

### Primary care

People in prison should have access to primary care, as well as services such as dentistry, podiatry and ophthalmology. People can request to see a GP if they need to and some prisons have GPs on-site. Services should have staff from a range of disciplines, appropriate to the particular setting and prison population. At a minimum level, services are expected to:
- provide emergency (within two hours) and urgent (within one day) referrals
- provide an opportunity for people to book appointments up to 48 hours in advance
- have a system in place whereby people in prison can consult a GP where these are not available on-site.

### Secondary care

Some prisons may have access to diagnostic equipment such as portable fibro scanners, to assess liver cirrhosis, or dialysis machines. If someone needs to attend an appointment off-site (such as at a hospital), they require at least two escorts and may require restraint such as handcuffing, based on an individual risk assessment.

### Social care and end-of-life care

Through the Care Act 2014, social care remains the remit of local authorities and they are responsible for providing social care services to people in prison living within their area. People in prison who have a terminal illness may be eligible to apply for the compassionate early release scheme – the most common reason for early release is cancer.

### Public health

People in prison are entitled to access all appropriate cancer and non-cancer screening programmes for their age, sex and other risks factors, as well as the NHS Health Check programme. Eligibility for Health Checks in prisons starts at age 35 (as opposed to age 40 for the general population), recognising the higher prevalence of risk factors in the prison population. This is important given that cardiovascular disease is the leading cause of death for people in prison.

It is estimated that around 80% of prisoners are smokers on arrival to prison, compared with just under 15% of people in the general population. The extent to which prisoners are still smoking despite the smoking ban is unclear. A smoking ban was introduced in prisons in 2018 and smoking cessation services should be provided.

People in prisons should also be offered advice on diet, exercise, sexual health and contraception. Provision of these services should be tailored to need and exactly what this entails varies across the prison estate. People in prison should also be offered vaccinations such as the flu vaccine, in line with the clinical at-risk groups identified in the community.

### Substance misuse services

Integrated substance misuse services are an important part of health care within prisons. How services operate varies between prisons but NHS England has set out a framework highlighting the key aspects and principles, including the importance of focusing on recovery, partnership working and a comprehensive understanding of the needs of the particular population.

Although drug-taking is banned in prisons, the use of novel psychoactive substances such as 'spice' is a particular challenge within the prison estate.

## Mental health

An overhaul of what the then Prime Minister Boris Johnson described in May 2022 as "antiquated" mental health laws will make it harder to detain people with learning disabilities and autistic people in hospital.

The reforms – which were part of the Queen's speech in May 2022 and are the first big changes to the Mental Health Act in four decades – are designed to reduce the number of people being detained under current laws in England and Wales. The number of detentions rose by 40% between 2005-06 and 2015-16 and have continued to rise year on year.

Details of the new draft mental health bill were announced on Friday night by Downing Street, which said it met key manifesto commitments.

They include ending a situation in which people with learning disabilities and autistic people can be detained under the act even if the patient does not suffer from any mental health conditions. This practice will be ended by removing learning disabilities and autism as mental health disorders. While current laws allow treatment to be imposed on patients against their wishes, the draft bill will allow them to voice a preference or refuse a specific treatment where a suitable alternative is available.

Currently, NHS England is responsible for commissioning mental health services. Many people in prison experience mental health problems – 71% of women and 47% of men – and they should receive care that is person-centred, provided by appropriately trained staff and be regularly reviewed to ensure they are given the right treatment and interventions. NHS England outlines a 'stepped care' model, with self-help at the bottom and specialist mental health services for those with marked mental illness at the top.

People in prison may also meet the criteria for assessment and treatment under the Mental Health Act 1983. Importantly, mental health care should be integrated with other prison services, such as substance misuse services and care for physical health, and have a focus on rehabilitation. Guidance states that mental health services should also recognise the significance of trauma in the lives of many people who require a prison stay and its relationship with mental health (NHS England, 2018).

Some prisons have an Improving Access to Psychological Therapies (IAPT) service and some also have 'in-reach' teams, which are multidisciplinary teams of health care professionals who support the mental health needs of people in prison. NHS England and NHS Improvement have recently commissioned a mental health needs analysis of services in order to attempt to quantify the level of need and service availability in the prison estate. The Centre for Mental Health has recently published The Future of Prison Mental Health Care in England, a review commissioned by NHS England and Improvement. Although it found that the current model of mental health care is working well and there are examples of innovative good practice, it also identified a number of challenges and areas for improvement. It also noted that, in reality, there is wide variation regarding what services are available across the prison estate (Durcan, 2021). The review also highlighted concerns about the screening process for people arriving at prison with mental health needs, continuity of care for people on release and delays in transferring people under the Mental Health Act 1983.

The review put forward a number of recommendations to improve the provision of mental health care in prison, with a particular focus on:

- enhancing training for staff
- reducing short sentences and finding alternatives to prison for people with mental health problems
- fostering peer support programmes
- enhancing digital capability.

The review also emphasised the importance of enacting the recommendations of the Independent Review of the Mental Health Act, such as ensuring prisons are never used as a 'place of safety' for people who meet the criteria for detention under the Mental Health Act.

## Mother and baby units

The experiences of pregnant women and babies in prison have been highlighted due to two tragic deaths of new-born babies within 18 months, both of which are subject to ongoing investigation.

Mother and baby units exist to support women in half of the 12 women's prisons in England. The national operational capacity of these units is 64 mothers and 70 babies (to allow for twins and triplets).

A July 2020 review by the Ministry of Justice on operational policy on pregnancy - available on *prisonoracle.com* - identified a number of reforms that needed to be made to improve the treatment of pregnant women in prison, including publishing more detailed data to inform care.

A dedicated perinatal pathway is also due to be rolled out nationally across the women's estate to support continuity of care for mothers and babies, but the Covid-19 pandemic has delayed this.

## On release

Transition into the community is a significant time for people in prison and steps must be taken to ensure continuity of care, particularly where people have begun programmes or treatment within prison. Continuity of care for people in prison is a key ambition within the NHS Long Term Plan, particularly through the RECONNECT programme.

People with complex needs should have a pre-release health assessment at least one month before the release date, led by primary health care but involving multidisciplinary team members.

People should be provided with a care summary and support for ongoing medication needs, and steps should be taken to liaise with relevant community services such as substance misuse, mental health and social services. Not all people in prison are registered with a GP when they enter prison and so they should be supported to do so on their release if that is the case. The Health and Justice Information Services should help to facilitate this.

### What do we know about access to and quality of health care in prison?

In this briefing we have described what people in prison should theoretically receive with regards to health care. But, in practice, there are concerns about people's access to and quality of health care in prison. The literature review we conducted for our previous research into and accompanying analysis of prisoners' use of hospital services identified a number of issues.

Natural causes are the main cause of death for people in prison, with the leading cause being disease of the circulatory system (43%) followed by cancer (32%). However, the Independent Advisory Panel on Deaths in Custody has suggested that many are preventable and a result of failings in health care management, such as a failure to recognise deterioration or poor management of long-term conditions – this is a particular concern for older prisoners.

The charity INQUEST (2020) conducted a review of inquests and coroners' reports and identified a number of areas of concern, including cancelled or delayed appointments, poor communication between health care and prison staff, and poor understanding of appropriate procedures.

Some studies have explored prisoners' perspectives on their access to health care. Quinn and others (2018) conducted a qualitative study exploring offenders' perspectives on factors that contributed to, or worked against, enabling and sustaining their access to health care.

This highlighted the significant role of GPs in facilitating access, including the value of trusting relationships, flexibility and good communication. Edge and others (2020) explored the role of security constraints in prisoners' access to secondary care and identified a number

of challenges, including the need for escorts, stigma arriving handcuffed and a lack of confidentiality when prison officers are present at consultations.

Access to and quality of prison health care must be understood within the wider context of prison policy and practice. Ismail (2019) used a qualitative study to understand the impact of austerity on prison health by conducting interviews with a number of international policy-makers. This identified a number of issues, including the 'disappearing chain of accountability', an increase in prison instability and longer waiting times.

Another study looked at the impact in England specifically and found that a reduced workforce, increased availability of drugs, a prevalence of violence and political turnover all had an impact, among others. This wider instability has an effect on the prison's ability to deliver health care services, for example by contributing to staff shortages, increasing waiting times and increasing security concerns.

Furthermore, staff shortages (such as not enough escorts) or security emergencies can affect how services are prioritised and who can access them. Security concerns also play a significant role in people's experiences of secondary care services, including not being able to be told in advance when their appointment will be and impeding privacy during the appointment. The Covid-19 pandemic has also put extensive pressure on health care services, including within prisons, with changes to the wider prison regime impacting both the services people in prison have been able to receive as well as their long-term health care needs.

The above with grateful thanks to the Nuffield Trust.

### NHS complaints

All prisoners now have access to the NHS complaint system. The NHS can investigate any prison healthcare service, whoever the provider is. NHS England also provides advice on complaints.

### How does a prisoner complain?

Prisoners are entitled to the same range and quality of health services as the general public. This includes access to dental services.

Prison healthcare is currently (2022) overseen by NHS England. They have 10 teams across England that will commission, monitor and manage all the contracts for prison health. Even if prison Healthcare in the prison is run by a private company like Primary Plus Group, it will be overseen by NHS England.

## NHS complaints: Prisoner Information

All prisoners now have access to the NHS complaint system. The NHS can investigate any prison healthcare service, whoever the provider is. NHS England also provides advice on complaints. The first step is to complain directly to the service provider in the prison. They should have their own complaints process and be able to give you information on this. This is a different process to making a prison complaint on a COMP1.

If you remain unsatisfied you can make a further complaint to:

**NHS England
PO Box 16738
Redditch, B97 9PT
Tel 0300 3112 233**

You need to provide your name and address, details of your complaint and any letters or relevant documents. NHS England aims to respond within 20 working days. The process is different if you are complaining about a hospital or GP in the community. It is also different if you are in a prison in Wales.

*What can I do if I am unhappy with the response to my complaint?*

If you receive a response from NHS England and are unhappy with it, the final stage of the complaints system is to go through the Parliamentary and Health Service Ombudsman (PHSO). They have the same powers as a court. NHS England has to give the PHSO any information they need to help them investigate your complaint. You must normally exhaust the internal complaints process before you ask the PHSO to investigate.

You can write to the PHSO at:

**Parliamentary/Health Service Ombudsman
Millbank Tower
Millbank, London SW1P 4QP
Tel: 0345 015 4033**

*Legal Action*

If you have suffered personal injury as a result of failure to provide treatment, you may be able to make a claim for compensation. If you think you have a claim you should get advice as soon as possible from a specialist clinical negligence lawyer. Do not use the NHS complaints procedure if you are taking legal action to get financial compensation. This is not available under the NHS complaints system and your NHS complaint will not proceed if legal action is underway. You can potentially bring judicial review proceedings against the NHS if you are seriously affected by an ongoing unlawful act or decision by an NHS body. You should seek legal advice before doing this.

*Handcuffing during hospital treatment*

Prisoners may be handcuffed in public areas when on escorted visits to hospital if the prison considers they pose a risk to the public or there is a risk of absconding. The National Security Framework starts from the premise that handcuffs should be removed during treatment unless the risk of escape is too high.

The test is whether it is necessary and proportionate to use them. Handcuffs may be used even where the risk to the public and escape potential is categorised as 'low' (R. (on the application of Faizovas) v SSJ [2009] EWCA Civ 373). However, a disproportionate use of handcuffs during escorts or treatment when there is no risk to the public or of escape is likely to constitute a breach of Article 3 of the European Convention of Human Rights and be unlawful. Similarly, routine handcuffing of a prisoner at a hospital, without an assessment of individual risk, is likely to be unlawful (Mouisel v France [2004] 38 EHRR 34). Moreover, the particular nature of treatment may require handcuffs to be removed during treatment if alternative security arrangements are available (Faizovas).

*Raising concerns about fitness to practice for different healthcare workers*

**Nurses-Nursing and Midwifery Council (NMC)** - You are entitled to report concerns about the conduct of nursing staff to the NMC so they can investigate whether that nurse should be disciplined, suspended or struck-off.

If you have concerns about a registered nurse, you can write to the NMC to raise a concern or submit a complaint. The NMC investigates various allegations including misconduct, lack of competence and criminal behaviour. Their address is:

**Nursing and Midwifery Council
23 Portland Place
London, W1B 1PZ
Tel: 020 7333 9333**

**Doctors- General Medical Council (GMC)** - The GMC will investigate concerns about a doctor's practice. The types of concerns investigated are: serious or repeated mistakes in patient care; failure to respond reasonably to patient needs; violence, sexual assault or indecency; fraud or dishonesty; discrimination; and serious breaches of patient confidentiality.

If you have concerns about a doctor, you can write to the GMC to raise a concern or submit a complaint. Their address is:

**General Medical Council
Regent's Place
350 Euston Road
London, NW1 3JN**

Tel: 0161 923 6602 or:

**Paramedics and other health professional - Health & Care professions Council (HCPC)** - The HCPC regulate professionals who have designated titles that are protected by law and who must be registered to use them. These include:

- Art therapists
- Dietitians
- Occupational therapists
- Orthoptists
- Social workers
- Speech and language therapists
- Paramedics
- Prosthetists
- Psychologists
- Radiographers

The HCPC considers every concern raised individually. The HCPC investigates various allegations including: dishonesty, fraud or abuse of trust or position; exploitation of a vulnerable person; failure to act in the best interests of service users; serious breaches of a service user's confidentiality; committing reckless or deliberately harmful acts; serious or repeated mistakes; and violence, sexual misconduct or indecent behaviour. If you have concerns about a HCPC regulated professional, you can write and raise a concern or submit a complaint. Their address is:

**HCPC**
**Park House,**
**184–186 Kennington Park Road,**
**London, SE11 4BU**
**Tel: 020 7840 9814**

**Other organisations to raise concerns with Care Quality Commission (CQC)** - The CQC are an independent regulator of health and social care in England. They monitor, inspect and regulate services. They also publish reports on healthcare inspections of prisons. You are able to write to the CQC and ask for a copy of the healthcare inspection report for your prison.

The CQC consider there to be fundamental standards of care which must be met and everybody has the right to expect that standard of care to be maintained. A full list of their fundamental standards can be obtained from CQC if you write to them.

The CQC need to be made aware of the problems people face with healthcare in prison if they are to ensure fundamental standards of healthcare are being maintained. Therefore, if you have experienced poor healthcare in prison, it is important that you also make CQC aware of your experience. Please be aware however, that the CQC do not settle individual complaints. You can write to the CQC at:

**Care Quality Commission**
**Citygate, Gallowgate**
Newcastle upon Tyne
**NE1 4PA**
**Tel: 03000 616161**

If you would like legal advice about injury suffered in prison write to:
**Michael Jefferies**
**Chairman: Prison Injury Lawyers Association**
**The Triangle**
**8 Cross Street**
**Altrincham**
**Cheshire WA14 1EQ**
**Tel: 0800 808 9570**

## 2.10 RELIGION

The Prison Service recognises and respects the right of prisoners to register and practise their faith whilst in custody.

Prison Service Instruction 05/2016 (last updated September 2016) supports the Specification: Faith and Pastoral Care for Prisoners. It sets out the procedures that should be followed in the delivery of the Specification.

PSI 05/2016 specifies that chaplaincy reception visits must be on an individual basis and should take place within 24 hours (2.5), that prisoners on an open ACCT (Assessment, Care in Custody, Teamwork) are seen at least weekly (18.1) and introduces some changes to the recording of statutory duties. It provides additional guidance on through the gate work (15.5 – 15.12), provision for the numerically smaller traditions when a faith chaplain is not present (4.22 – 4.23) and on funerals (17.8 and 17.9). Changes to the faith annexes of the PSI include the introduction of Prasad for Hindu prisoners (F2), reflect the need for a shower on the day of prayers for Sikh prisoners (R3) and make clarification to the information on Islam (H) and Paganism (M).

### Extremism

For the effective delivery of PSI 05/2016, it has to link successfully with a range of other policies, (see the list below of Associated Documents) and which provide detailed instructions on their particular areas. This includes PSI 43/2011 - Managing and Reporting extremist behaviour in custody. It is recognised that a few prisoners misuse their faith to put forward an extremist narrative based on a distorted view of their religion. Chaplains have a key role to play in challenging this narrative and in guiding prisoners on their faith journey.

Information on managing the risks posed by extremism and on identifying extremist behaviours is set out in PSI 43/2011. Through the reception interview and the other elements within the PSI relating both to faith provision and pastoral care, chaplains will be alert to words or behaviours that may raise concerns under the Prevent duty and report them in line with local and national policy.

For most prisoners, their religion and its practice provides a positive framework to navigate both the prison system and their journey towards desistance and law abiding lives. Support on release from faith communities can also be instrumental in helping with the transition to life outside prison.

*Desired Outcomes*

**Denominal Balance**

Output 1 The Chaplaincy provision reflects the faith / denominational requirements of the prison. Chaplains and Chaplaincy Teams must be appointed to meet the needs and reflect the faith make up of the prison population. Chaplains must be recruited and appointed in line with national Prison Service guidelines.

**Prisoner Access**

Output 2 Prisoners have access to a member of the Chaplaincy Team on first reception into each establishment. Where their faith is not represented, arrangements are made for them to have access to a Minister of their own faith. Religious registration made upon Reception should be checked and confirmed as accurate by a Chaplain on a Reception Visit. Errors must be corrected immediately and noted as "wrongly registered". If the choice of faith does not carry a Prison Service code the prisoner should choose a registration that is closest to the preferred option or "Non Specified". Prisoners who do not wish to specify a religion or denomination should be entered as "Nil Religion" or "Non Specified.

*See further - PSI 52/2010 Early Days in Custody*

Prisoners must be treated as being of the faith by which they are registered for all their religious observance needs.

A prisoner must not be subject to any form of discrimination or infringement of their human rights by declaring themselves of any faith or religion or as belonging to none.

A case of alleged discrimination on the grounds of a prisoner's registered religion must be recorded in the Chaplaincy Team Journal and reported to the Governor. Each case will be investigated by the Equalities Manager or other appointed manager.

A prisoner must not be required to undertake such work that is unsuitable or offensive to their registered religion.

A Chaplain must see each new reception as soon as possible after they are received into prison. This may be a brief introductory visit and conducted either on an individual basis or within a group setting. It should take place within 48 hours of the prisoner being received into an establishment. Each prisoner should be offered a Chaplaincy Reception leaflet setting out the names and faith designations of each member of the Chaplaincy Team together with details of the faith provision available.

Further contact with a Chaplain and additional information can be incorporated within the subsequent Induction Programme.

If the Chaplaincy reception visit is not made by someone of the prisoner's own faith:

• The prisoner should be informed who the appropriate Chaplain is and their availability.

• If there is no specific request by the prisoner to see the Chaplain of their faith the appropriate Chaplain should be informed within seven days.

• If there is a specific request from the prisoner to see a Chaplain of their faith the appropriate Chaplain should be informed within 24 hours.

Visits to new receptions should be recorded within Chaplaincy.

All Chaplains should have the opportunity to access prisoner details on Prison-NOMIS.

Chaplains who undertake faith specific duties only should receive a weekly list (or at different intervals if this is agreed between the Co-ordinating Chaplain and the appropriate Chaplain) in advance of their visit showing all prisoners registered (if any) of their faith tradition.

**Changing Religion**

Output 3 Prisoners are able to change their religious registration

A prisoner must notify the Co-ordinating Chaplain in writing if they wish to change their religious registration. They should complete the form at Appendix One. Chaplains of the current religious registration and the intended registration should be informed and sent a copy of the prisoner's notification (Appendix One) within seven days of the change being made on Prison-NOMIS. They may wish to visit the prisoner.

The prisoner must be informed in writing that their notification to change religion has been completed. On completion of the prisoner's notification the prisoner's records should be updated to reflect the change. The prisoner must be allowed to observe the faith practice of the new registration from the time the change is made.

When considering a change of religion a prisoner should be permitted to attend acts of worship of the faith by which they are not currently registered but which they are considering changing to. This should happen with the knowledge of the appropriate Chaplains and for an agreed period of time. Consideration should be given to issues of control and security in any arrangement.

All changes in religious registration (excluding "wrongly registered") should be recorded within Chaplaincy and be available to the Governor on request.

## Corporate Worship

Output 4 Prisoners have the opportunity for corporate worship or meditation for one hour per week.

Provision must be made to enable all prisoners who choose to do so to attend the main religious observance of the week for the faith in which they are registered.

Prisoners must be treated as belonging to the faith currently entered on their record.

They must be able to attend corporate worship or meditation unless specifically excluded under:
• Rule 46 (CSC or SSU or similarly designated prisoners).
• Individual cases authorised by the Governor.

In exceptional individual cases a prisoner may be excluded from a corporate faith activity for a maximum of one month. This exclusion must then be reviewed but may be renewed. The exclusion must be authorised and recorded by the Governor.

Grounds for exclusion may be:
• Exceptional and specific concerns for the prisoners' mental or physical wellbeing.
• In agreement with the Chaplain leading worship it is judged that the prisoner has previously seriously misbehaved at a time of worship or meditation.
• The Governor judges that their presence is likely to cause a disturbance or be a threat to security or control.

The Governor should inform the Co-ordinating Chaplain, the appropriate Chaplain and the prisoner of the exclusion, giving their reasons. This should be done after the initial exclusion and again after each review and renewal of any exclusion.

Where there is a change of circumstances that justified the original exclusion an earlier review may take place and the exclusion lifted.

The Chaplain of the excluded prisoner's faith should be invited to offer a view and consideration should be given to such views.

Prisoners registered "Nil Religion" or "Non Specified" should be able to attend corporate worship or meditation by agreement with the appropriate Chaplain.

A prisoner should not normally be allowed to attend worship or meditation of more than one faith during the course of a week.

The "one hour" allowed for corporate worship or meditation should commence once the prisoner(s) expected to attend are present and the appropriate Chaplain is able to begin.

If the prison has a "split regime" there must be equality of access to corporate worship by each section of the prison population. In some establishments a single act of worship or meditation may serve all within each faith group. In other establishments separate and duplicate services will be necessary. Such duplication may not necessarily take place on the same day or be provided by the same Chaplain.

Corporate worship and meditation must be accessible to those with disabilities. This may be the provision of physical access or provision for those with impaired sight, hearing or an inability to write.

Where other regime activities or courses coincide with corporate worship or meditation or the observance of religious festivals, alternative provision for attendance at the faith activity or other activity should be made.

Prisoners must not be required to do any non-essential work on key festival days specified for the observance of their faith.

Numbers attending all faith activities should be noted in the Chaplaincy Journal and recorded in Regime Monitoring.

## Places of Worship and Meditation

Each establishment must set aside places for corporate worship and meditation. Such accommodation should be of a size to reflect the practising faith population of each faith. Places for worship and meditation must be capable of being configured to reflect the religious, cultural and symbolic requirements of each tradition.

In locating places for worship and meditation it is advisable that they:
• Are accessible.
• Are located away from undue noise or disturbance.
• Include proximity to ablution/washing facilities.
• Are convenient for staff observation and supervision.
• Are well decorated; heated; ventilated and carpeted.
• Contain suitable storage facilities for artefacts and books and religious symbols.
• Provide a shoe rack where necessary
• Fulfil the needs of all appropriate Chaplains and faith practice.
• Can be configured to accommodate those faiths that are required to worship or pray in a fixed direction.

Places for worship and meditation should be of a size to accommodate all those who wish to attend worship or meditation. Numbers allowed to attend corporate worship will be subject to:
• Health & Safety limits
• Security & Control limits

Local risk assessments will be conducted to establish upper attendance limits for corporate activities. In cases where there is insufficient capacity to allow all who wish to attend to do so at a single service other provision must be made so that no one is denied access to their main weekly act of worship or meditation. A dedicated place for worship and meditation should be available to facilitate personal and private spiritual need (e.g. bereavement; anniversaries; confession; counselling). Such need should take precedence over other use.

There should be a clear agreement within the Chaplaincy Team on how the places for worship and meditation are to be arranged for each act of worship or meditation. Religious artefacts may need to be removed or covered and replaced in preparation for other faith observance. There should be suitable storage available for faith items. The religious use of places for worship and meditation must take priority. Non-religious use of this space is at the discretion of the Governor in consultation with the Chaplaincy Team.

Places for worship and meditation must be treated with respect by prisoners and staff at all times. It is disrespectful to place items on a Communion Table/Altar or on the floor; to walk in front of the direction of prayer or across prayer mats. Staff should avoid doing so unless responding to an incident.

Secure storage is required for such items as Communion Wine and Incense.

There should be an inventory system to monitor the use of Communion Wine containing alcohol. Some traditions use non-alcoholic wine. Anglican, Roman Catholic and Orthodox traditions require the use of alcoholic wine.

Governors should take into account sensitivities when changing or introducing new security procedures or changes of purpose within faith areas. When such schemes are under consideration there should be liaison between the Governor, Co-ordinating Chaplain and the Chaplaincy Team.

Guidance on the setting up and management of places for worship and meditation are set out in a separate MoJ publication (Places for Worship and Meditation in Prison).

### Provision for smaller faith groups or where a Chaplain is not present

For some smaller faith groups there may not be an appropriate Chaplain available each week to lead corporate worship or meditation. In these circumstances, as a temporary arrangement and subject to risk assessment and appropriate supervision, prisoners from the faith concerned may be allowed to meet together for weekly worship or meditation. In these circumstances a prisoner may lead the prayers, worship or meditation. The appropriate Chaplain, where one is appointed, should agree in advance which prisoner(s) will be involved in leading worship or meditation. In the absence of an appointed appropriate Chaplain the leading of worship or

meditation should be agreed with the Co-ordinating Chaplain in consultation with the Faith Adviser. This should only ever be a temporary arrangement to be used as a contingency measure in the absence of an appropriate Chaplain.

Staff supervision must be similar to that when a Chaplain is present.

This arrangement will not normally apply to Christian or Muslim worship or prayers when a Chaplain is expected to be present. Muslim prisoners in the High Security Estate must not lead Friday Prayer. A contingency plan should be in place for emergency cover for Friday Prayer in the HSE.

### Informal unsupervised worship, religious study or meditation

Prisoners of the same faith may wish to gather for private worship (i.e. small wing-based or landing-based group not attended by a Chaplain). Staff and prisoners need clear local guidance on when, how and where this can take place. These instructions should incorporate any faith specific guidance contained in Part Two (Faith Annexes)

The number of prisoners gathering for private worship outside formal corporate worship or meditation should be in line with the number allowed for other wing / landing based activities. Any larger meetings for faith based activity unsupervised by a Chaplain must be authorised by a Governor.

Unsupervised worship or prayer should not compromise any communal area (e.g TV Lounge; Association Room or Landing).

Local Cell association policies apply to numbers for worship or study (e.g. if three prisoners are allowed in a cell for other purposes then this number should apply to worship, prayer, meditation or religious study). In the case of shared cell accommodation each occupant must be in agreement, without coercion, with others being invited into the cell for the faith activity.

Staff who have concerns about a faith activity should bring it to the attention of the Governor via the SIR system and also contact the appropriate Chaplain.

### Segregation and Healthcare

Output 5 Prisoners located in Segregation Units or Healthcare Units have the opportunity for corporate worship or meditation for one hour per week.

This section covers Segregation and Healthcare but the provision should be extended to other "smaller / special units".

Prisoners located in a Segregation Unit or Health Care Centre (or similar "smaller unit") must be able to attend the main corporate worship or meditation of their registered faith unless prevented under 4.2 or 4.3 above. A protocol must be in place to enable them to attend corporate worship or meditation.

If necessary a risk assessment must be undertaken and the appropriate Chaplain should be consulted. The prisoner should be notified by a Governor of the outcome within 7 days of the application being received by the Segregation or Health Care Manager and prior to the worship service.

Where prisoners are excluded from attending corporate faith activity under 4.2 or 4.3 above consideration should be given to alternative provision. Ideally a Quiet Room should be provided within smaller unit accommodation (Health Care Centre; Segregation Unit / Special Secure Unit) for worship and meditation. In the absence of a dedicated Quiet Room another suitable alternative room should be made available on request.

There should be the opportunity for a single individual or a small group to come together to share in those elements of corporate worship from which they are otherwise excluded or unable to attend and that are practical to provide. The Chaplain of each faith whose registered members are located in such units should, where possible, make arrangements with the unit manager (SEG/SACU/CSC/HCC) to conduct weekly worship or meditation.

This will be very important in the celebration of religious festivals.

### Religious Festivals

Output 6 Recognised religious feasts, fasts and festivals are observed.

Recognised and authorised worship; feasts; fasts and festivals must be observed in line with Part Two (Faith Annexes) to this PSI and as published annually by Chaplaincy HQ as "Religious Festival Dates"

After consultation with the appropriate Chaplain, the Co-ordinating Chaplain should publish in advance for staff the arrangements for a forthcoming religious observance. This should include a brief note regarding the meaning, relevance and importance of the occasion to the faith group concerned.

Supervisory staff must be available for the observance of the festival.

The prisoner faith group should be notified of the forthcoming observance and the arrangements that are in place to celebrate the occasion.

If the observance is to include the provision of food the kitchen should be consulted in advance and arrangements agreed.

The provision of food for religious festivals must be in line with requirements set out in the Catering PSI and Operating Manual. There must

be equitable provision, as far as practicable, across the faith traditions.

Ideally a festival should be observed on the day on which it falls. If there is variation of opinion within a faith group, the day should be agreed with the appropriate Chaplain in consultation with the Faith Adviser. If the appropriate Chaplain is unable to attend on the precise day of the festival an alternative occasion should be agreed in advance.

Provision must be made for equality of access for prisons with a split regime.

Prisoners registered as belonging to the faith being observed / celebrated must be allowed to attend the celebration unless excluded under 4.2 or 4.3 above. Prisoners are not required to work on recognised key festival days. Reference should be made to the annual Religious Festival Dates.

### Community Faith Groups

Output 7 Prisoners have the opportunity to engage with members of their faith group from the community.

Prisoners are entitled to visits from their local/home clergy or Minister (e.g Priest; Imam; Rabbi or equivalent)

Arrangements should be in place for local/home clergy or ministers to visit those prisoners who request a visit and are registered as belonging to their faith. Such visits are in addition to the statutory allowance. This is to enable the prisoner to maintain links with their home and community.

• One individual from the outside faith group should be nominated and the necessary level of security clearance obtained.

• Where the status of an individual within a religious body is unclear advice should be sought from the appropriate Chaplain, Co-ordinating Chaplain, Regional Chaplain or Faith Adviser.

• Visiting arrangements will vary according to establishment but should ensure privacy and confidentiality.

• Pastoral visits should follow local procedure and be at intervals deemed by the Governor and appropriate Chaplain to be reasonable. The visits should not normally be more frequent than one per month.

• In the event of disagreement the Governor, in consultation with the appropriate Chaplain, Co-ordinating Chaplain; Regional Chaplain and Chaplaincy HQ, will decide what is reasonable.

*See further: PSI 16/2011 Providing Visits and Services to Visitors, PSI 15/2011 Management of security at visits*

Members of outside faith communities should be encouraged and enabled to attend faith and other activities, by agreement with the appropriate Chaplain. This is intended to contribute to pro-social modelling and behaviour and assist with normalisation and re-integration of prisoners.

Those who visit regularly from the outside community must have an appropriate level of security clearance. They should be registered with the member of staff within the prison responsible for community engagement. They should have an induction programme and training appropriate to their level of responsibility and involvement.

Provision must be made for equality of access for prisoners operating a split regime.

Faith communities may be involved in the Induction process, pre-release planning and community re-integration where appropriate.

**Religious artefacts and Dress**

Output 8 Prisoners have access to authorised religious artefacts including dress and headwear. Prisoners must be allowed to possess or have access to, artefacts and religious texts that are required by their faith. Artefacts and religious texts that are allowed are agreed with the Faith Advisers at Chaplaincy HQ and are found in Part Two (Faith Annexes) of PSI 05/2016

Prisoners must be allowed to wear dress, including headdress, that accords with the requirements of their registered faith as agreed between the Faith Adviser and the Prison Service. Information on the agreed position is contained in Part Two (Faith Annexes) of PSI 05/2016 *See further PSI 67/2011 Searching of the Person, PSI 68/2011 Cell Area and Vehicle Searching* Prisoners may be allowed additional artefacts or texts not listed in the Annexes to PSI 05/2016 if they are deemed by the Governor to be no threat to security or control and agreed with the appropriate Chaplain.

In the absence of local agreement about artefacts and dress the Governor should ensure that, subject to there being no threat to security or control, a prisoner is not discriminated against. Advice can be sought from the Co-ordinating Chaplain; Regional Chaplain or Chaplaincy HQ.

Incense must be available through the Prison Facilities List for those prisoners registered:

Buddhist

Hindu

Orthodox (Christian)

Pagan

Sikh

Chinese Religions

It may be necessary to provide a variety of incense to meet the needs of different traditions within the above faith groups. The Governor may decide to make it available as a general item available to any prisoner. Prisoners who practise the above faiths should be allowed to hold incense in their cell and use it for private worship

or meditation, except where 8.7 applies. Incense in powder or granular form and carbon or iron pellets are not permitted.

Governors have the discretion to decide on the amount of incense that can reasonably be in possession.

Governors have discretion to disallow incense in a prisoner's possession if it constitutes a risk to health, safety, security, good order or discipline. If incense is withheld or withdrawn from a prisoner on these grounds a written explanation must be provided to the prisoner and the appropriate Chaplain and entered on the prisoner record.

**Access to Religious Classes and Cultural Activities**

Output 9 Prisoners have access to a programme of religious educational classes and cultural activities. A programme setting out details of the Chaplaincy educational classes and cultural activities will be agreed with the Governor and published throughout the prison.

Provision should be made for religious education and nurture within each faith group. This will contribute to the Reducing Re-offending Strategy Pathway Seven "Attitude, Thinking and Behaviour" in challenging and changing thinking and behaviour.

Attendance at religious educational classes and cultural activities is in addition to the statutory one hour of corporate worship / meditation. Classes may follow on from worship and form a unified faith / cultural session.

Religious classes and cultural activities must be accessible to those with disabilities. This may be the provision of physical access or provision for those with impaired sight, hearing or an inability to write.

Religious education classes and cultural activities will be offered as part of a Chaplaincy programme and agreed with the Governor.

**Promotion of Religious Classes and Cultural Activities**

Output 10 Prisoners and staff know what religious educational classes and cultural activities are available.

Co-ordinating Chaplains must ensure there is a published Chaplaincy programme covering all faith communities and activities. This should be included in the Service Level Agreement/ Business Plan. This should be published sufficiently in advance to allow staff and prisoners to integrate faith requirements and opportunities with other prison programmes.

The programme should be published in all staff and prisoner areas. Prisoners for whom the activity is particularly intended should be notified individually.

The Offender Management Unit and Sentence

Planning Unit must be made aware of the Religious Education Classes and Cultural Activities available within Chaplaincy and invited to consider these as appropriate for inclusion as Sentence Plan objectives.

Suitable and available facilities should be in place to accommodate the agreed Chaplaincy programme.

Supervisory staff, where required by a risk assessment, must be available for all religious classes and cultural activities agreed by the Governor. A risk assessment should be carried out where appropriate.

In arranging such a programme the Chaplaincy will need to liaise with:

Education Department
Equalities Manager
Sentence Planning Department
Programmes / Interventions Department
Gym staff
Staff Detail

**Supervision of Corporate worship or Meditation**

Output 11 Corporate worship or meditation is supervised in line with local risk assessments and agreements

Corporate worship and meditation must take place in an atmosphere of respect. It must be facilitated to ensure order and control. There is a need to risk assess faith activities in relation to:
• Numbers attending
• Security category of attendees
• Security information on individuals and / or groups
• Location of the activity

Chaplains must not be left in sole charge of a large number of prisoners (defined by a local risk assessment) without appropriate support.

Places of worship and meditation should provide areas for supervising staff to be present within or adjacent to the service. Staff should be within sight and sound of the worship and if within the service or its proximity must not talk unnecessarily; jangle keys or eat and drink during the service.

Supervision of all religious services (i.e. for any faith) may be by female or male officers.

Where a staff radio is required this must be fitted with an earpiece to avoid disturbing the service. It may be appropriate to provide overshoes for staff supervising some religious services.

The Chaplain leading corporate worship or meditation is in charge during the duration of the service. Staff should not normally intervene once a service has commenced except in exceptional circumstances – serious and immediate threat to order and control or to health and safety. Under these circumstances staff have the discretion to intervene directly to control or remove prisoners from the service. If staff are requested by the

Chaplain to remove an individual(s) or the situation is so serious they are obliged to intervene directly, this should be done sensitively and cause as little disruption as possible.

It is the responsibility of the Chaplain leading worship or meditation to set and maintain appropriate standards of behaviour.

Chaplains leading worship or meditation should have the required skills to enable them to challenge inappropriate behaviour and to maintain order and control. Advice and guidance is available from the Governor, Co-ordinating Chaplain or Regional Chaplain.

**Pastoral Care**

Output 12 All prisoners wherever they are located in the prison have access to, and be offered, pastoral care by Chaplaincy staff.

A Chaplain is able to visit all areas of the prison in which prisoners are located. This is to offer pastoral care and to contribute to decency and safer custody.

Prisoners who have made an application to see a Chaplain must be seen within 24 hours. The application should be logged by the Wing and by the Chaplaincy. When a request is made to see a Chaplain who is not immediately available that Chaplain should be notified within 24 hours and the notification recorded in the Chaplaincy Team Journal. There should be a record maintained in Chaplaincy that a prisoner has been seen following an application.

A Chaplain must not visit a prisoner against their will nor subject a prisoner to unwanted or unsolicited persuasion to change their religious affiliation. Where there is an allegation about an unsolicited visit or attempt to persuade a prisoner to change their religious affiliation this will be investigated. If upheld it may lead to disciplinary action.

Prisoners regardless of religious registration may apply to see any Chaplain.

**Segregation**

Output 13 Prisoners located in the Segregation Unit have access to a member of the Chaplaincy Team each day.

A member of the Chaplaincy Team must visit prisoners in the Segregation Unit daily. It is a statutory duty to visit all prisoners undergoing cellular confinement. This visit should be facilitated in a similar way to the Governor and Healthcare visit. Not only is this a statutory requirement but it recognises that prisoners located in Segregation can often feel isolated or depressed. They are normally removed from the routine of prison life and excluded from accessing many activities.

The visit must be recorded in:
• Segregation Unit Daily Diary
• Prison-NOMIS case notes and individual Prisoner History Sheets
• Chaplaincy Team Journal
• ACCT document (if relevant)

The prisoner may not wish to speak with the Chaplain and this must be recorded on their Prison-NOMIS case notes and individual history sheet. This should be respected and the prisoner made aware of the ongoing availability of the Chaplaincy Team.

Applications to attend corporate worship or meditation from prisoners located in a Segregation Unit should be processed in accordance with Section 5 above.

Where a Chaplain or prisoner requests it there should be a facility for a private conversation. This will be subject to a local Risk Assessment and by arrangement with the Segregation Unit Manager.

Copies of the scriptures and religious artefacts of each faith listed in Part Two of the PSI must be readily available for those located in the Segregation Unit.

Where appropriate a Chaplain should be included in the review of prisoners located in Segregation. Prisoners undergoing cellular confinement outside the Segregation Unit must be treated by Chaplains in the same way as those located within the Segregation Unit.

### Healthcare

Outcome 14 Prisoners located in the Health Care Unit have access to a member of the Chaplaincy Team each day.

A member of the Chaplaincy Team must visit prisoners in the Health Care Centre daily. Not only is this a statutory requirement but it recognises that prisoners located in Health Care can often feel isolated or depressed. They are normally removed from the routine of prison life and excluded from accessing many activities.

The Chaplaincy visit must be recorded in:
• The Health Care Centre Daily Diary
• Prison-NOMIS case notes and individual prisoner history sheets
• Chaplaincy Team Journal
• ACCT document (if relevant)

Where a prisoner requests it there should be a facility for seeing an individual in private. This will be subject to a local Risk Assessment and by arrangement with the Health Care Manager.

Copies of the scriptures and religious artefacts of each faith listed in Part Two of the PSI must be readily available for those located in the Healthcare Centre.

Prisoners located outside the HCC but regarded as "in patients" for medical purposes should receive Chaplaincy provision in the same way as those located in the HCC.

Chaplains are able to visit prisoners located in an outside hospital as part of their pastoral care. The visit should be made with the knowledge of Security and the Co-ordinating Chaplain. The visit should be recorded in the Chaplaincy Team Journal.

### Discharge

Output 15 Every prisoner has access to a member of the Chaplaincy Team before discharge at the end of their sentence.

Discharge can be a stressful event. It may be after the completion of a long sentence or mark the beginning of an uncertain future.

The discharge process may be formal and a multidisciplinary board may be convened. The Chaplain should be included in the membership.

A discharge interview should be conducted on an individual basis. The Chaplain should make contact with each prisoner in the week before release to offer support and contact with outside agencies e.g. Community Chaplaincy or Faith Community. It may be appropriate to offer a Discharge Leaflet with information about faith and community support and resources.

Chaplaincy involvement in the discharge process should be in cooperation with the Offender Management Unit and Public Protection Department. *See further PSI 25/2011 Discharge*

### Serious Illness or Death in Custody

Output 16 Arrangements are in place to support prisoners directly or indirectly affected by a serious illness or death in custody

An effective system must be in place to notify the Co-ordinating Chaplain and appropriate Chaplain immediately of the serious illness; attempted suicide or death of a prisoner.

The Governor must ensure that Chaplains are included in the Contingency Plan so that the appropriate Chaplain can be contacted immediately. The appropriate Chaplain should be given access to the dead or dying prisoner to enable the religious ritual of their faith to be carried out.

In the case of serious illness and where the prisoner is located in an outside hospital the Chaplain may wish to contact the Hospital Chaplain. The Chaplain may contact a prisoner's family with the prisoner's consent and with regard to security considerations and the wishes of the prisoner's family.

The Chaplain should be available to speak to prisoners who have been involved in or are affected by the circumstances surrounding a sick or deceased prisoner. There may be a need for an immediate response and in some cases an ongoing need for care and support.

The Chaplain should work closely with the Care Team Leader and the Family Liaison Officer following a serious incident.

The Chaplain is responsible for conducting the funeral of the deceased when there are no other arrangements in place.

### Serious Illness or Death of a Relative

Output 17 Arrangements are in place to support prisoners directly or indirectly affected by a serious illness or death of a relative.

An effective system must be in place to notify the Co-ordinating Chaplain and appropriate Chaplain immediately of the serious illness or death of a prisoner's family member.

News of the serious illness or death of a family member should be conveyed to a prisoner as soon as practical. The person best placed to do this is often a Chaplain. When a Chaplain is unavailable and another member of staff is responsible for conveying the message the Chaplaincy must be informed immediately.

If the prisoner informs a member of staff that they have received news of the serious illness or death of a family member the Chaplain must be informed immediately.

When news is received from an outside party about the serious illness or death of a prisoner's family member the accuracy of the information should always be confirmed before the prisoner is informed. When the news is received from the prisoner this should be confirmed immediately by a statutory external agency.

The Chaplain must inform staff prior to giving news of serious illness or death to a prisoner. Following receipt of the news by the prisoner the Chaplain must ensure it is recorded on Prison-NOMIS, in the Wing Observation Book and in the Chaplaincy Team Journal.

It may be appropriate to consider if the prisoner should be placed on ACCT.

The Chaplain should offer care and support to the prisoner following news of serious illness or the death of a family member.

### Self-Harm

Output 18 Arrangements are in place to support prisoners at risk of harm to self or others.

The Chaplaincy must be notified of all those for whom an ACCT document is opened, and when it is closed.

Notice of ACCT documents being opened or closed should be entered in the Chaplaincy Team Journal. Where a visit and conversation has taken place between a Chaplain and a prisoner on an open ACCT this must be noted in the ACCT document. A Chaplain should be invited to attend an ACCT review when there is pastoral contact between the Chaplain and prisoner.

A Chaplain may become an ACCT Assessor on completion of the appropriate training.

### Marriage and Civil Partnership

Output 19 Prisoners are able to marry or engage in a civil ceremony whilst in custody.

A system must be in place to allow a prisoner to enquire about marriage or civil partnership and to make a subsequent application. It is often Chaplaincy that has the lead role in processing a marriage application and arrangements for the ceremony. This will be done in cooperation with a designated manager.

Some Chaplains may wish to withdraw from processing marriage applications on religious grounds. This must be respected.

Where Chaplaincy has a significant role in the marriage application, pastoral support and advice is necessary and often welcome.

Chaplaincy will need to work with others, including:

Local Registrar

Local minister or priest

Security Department

Public Protection Manager

Sentence Planning Department

Designated Manager

in processing marriage applications.

It is recommended that Chaplaincy do not have any direct role in the processing of Civil Partnership applications in accordance with the relevant PSO. Chaplaincy may wish to offer pastoral support to the applicants.

The decision to allow a marriage or civil partnership to take place rests with the Governor. *See further PSO 4450 Marriage of Prisoners, PSO 4445 Civil Partnership Registration*

### Official Prison Visitors Scheme

Output 20 Prisoners have access to the Official Prison Visitors (OPV) Scheme.

Each establishment should have an Official Prison Visitors Scheme.

The Official Prison Visitor Scheme is not faith based and a declaration of faith is not required of anyone wishing to become an Official Prison Visitor.

Official Prison Visitors (OPVs) are volunteers appointed by the Governor. They visit prison in order to offer friendship and support to prisoners. In considering an appointment the Governor must ensure the following criteria are met:

• All applicants must be of good character.

• Applicants must not hold employment or office liable to cause embarrassment or conflict in their relations with the prison, prisoners or staff.

• Members of the Independent Monitoring Board are not eligible for appointment.

All categories of prisoner are eligible for an OPV regardless of whether they have visits from family or friends. An OPV visiting a Category A prisoner will need to undergo additional security clearance to comply with the conditions of the Approved Visitor Scheme in accordance with the National Security Framework (NSF). The prisoner receiving a visit from an OPV does not need to surrender a Visiting Order to receive a visit.

A Liaison Officer should be appointed to co-ordinate the work of the Official Prison Visitors Scheme in each establishment. Where Chaplaincy is responsible for the operation of the Official Prison Visitor Scheme there will be a nominated OPV Liaison Officer who is a member of the Chaplaincy Team.

The Liaison Officer in cooperation with the Security Department will be responsible for the recruitment; selection; training and deployment of suitable Official Prison Visitors. The final responsibility and issuing of the formal letter of appointment is made by the Governor.

The OPV Liaison Officer should produce clear local guidance on available visiting days and times; how the visit is to be booked; where the visit is to take place; how long the visit is expected to last; how many prisoners may be allocated to each OPV etc.

Where there is a local branch of the NAOPV, the OPV Liaison Officer will work with the Chair and Secretary in the operation of all aspects of the scheme.

Official Prison Visitors will be appointed and work in line with the 'HM Prison Service Handbook for Official Prison Visitors'. A copy of this handbook will be sent, together with a Letter of Appointment, to all newly appointed Official Prison Visitors. This forms part of the OPV contract with HM Prison Service.

The OPV Liaison Officer will promote the scheme within the prison ensuring that all prisoners are aware of the scheme and the way they are able to access it.

The OPV Liaison Officer will attend branch meetings, where applicable, and ensure the smooth running of all aspects of the scheme. Where there is no NAOPV local branch the OPV Liaison Officer should maintain regular contact with OPVs to ensure the transfer of relevant information and to offer support and guidance.

The National Association of Official Prison Visitors is a registered charity which promotes and maintains Official Prison Visiting in establishments throughout the Prison Service. The NAOPV is approved and supported by the Ministry of Justice with whom regular meetings are held.

It is not a requirement of appointment that an Official Prison Visitor become a member of the NAOPV. *See further PSI 16/2011 Providing Visits and Services to Visitors, PSI 15/2011 Management of security at visits*

**Resettlement**
Output 21 Prisoners have access to Resettlement Chaplaincy Scheme.
http://www.communitychaplaincy.org.uk
"Community Chaplaincies work alongside prisoners, ex-prisoners and their families, offering practical, social, relational and spiritual support within prison, through the gate and out in the community".

Community Chaplaincy schemes vary in what they provide and the extent of the provision. Each project has established an approach that is suited to local needs. Schemes normally operate under an SLA.

The Community Chaplaincy Association (CCA) is an independent organisation that has been established to support, train and equip both emerging and established Community Chaplaincies in England and Wales.

Models of Community Chaplaincy currently operating:

Prison Based: Chaplains are an integral part of the Chaplaincy Team with a specific role as Community Chaplain. They continue links with prisoners on local discharge release and refer others to support agencies elsewhere.

Community Based: Chaplains receive referrals from Chaplains and Resettlement Staff in a number of prisons. They visit prisoners as part of a pre-release scheme and continue support after release thereby enabling a holistic approach to take place.

Community Chaplaincy seeks to replicate the principles of Prison Service Chaplaincy in offering support to prisoners of all faiths and none. Some single faith schemes operate in providing support to prisoners of a single faith only. Single faith support groups may become associate members of the CCA but cannot become full members.

## 2.11 EQUALITY

**Age, Gender, Disability & Race**
PSI 32/2011
**First Principles.**
PSI 32/2011 (last updated January 2020) sets out the framework for the management of equalities issues in prison establishments (except for issues relating to the equal treatment of employees which are covered in PSI 32/2011). It builds on the successes of and learning from previous arrangements for the management of race and disability issues and extends coverage to all equalities issues.

The PSI applies to all prison establishments – all references to Governors should be taken to include the Directors of contracted establishments - and it sets out the policy approach and lists some key mandatory actions designed to ensure legal compliance. These are supplemented by comprehensive guidance in the annexes to the document.

## Protected characteristics

For something to be illegal under the Equality Act 2010 it has to relate to a 'protected characteristic'. These are described below.

## Age

This refers to a particular age group, whether this is a particular age or a range of ages.

## Disability

This covers people who have or have had a physical or mental difficulty which has a substantial and long-term negative effect on their ability to carry out normal day-to-day activities, or would have such an effect if measures were not being taken to treat or control the difficulty.

## Gender reassignment

This covers people who propose to undergo, are undergoing or have undergone a process or part of a process for the purpose of reassigning their sex by changing physiological or other attributes of sex. The process is a personal one not a medical one: it is not necessary for the person to be undergoing medical treatment.

## Marriage and civil partnership

This covers people who are either married or in a civil partnership.

## Pregnancy and maternity

This refers to when a woman is pregnant or the period of 26 weeks after the birth of her child (in particular if a woman is breastfeeding).

## Race

A racial group is a group of persons who are defined by reference to race. Race includes colour, nationality and ethnic or national origins.

## Religion or belief

This includes any religion, religious belief or philosophical belief. It also includes any lack of religion, religious belief or philosophical belief.

## Sex

This covers men and women.

## Sexual orientation

This means a person's sexual orientation: whether that person's sexual orientation is towards persons of the same sex, persons of the opposite sex, or persons of either sex.

## Prohibited conduct

As a public authority, it is unlawful for HMPPS in the exercise of its public function to do anything that constitutes discrimination, harassment and victimisation. This covers treatment of prisoners and others such as visitors. Discrimination, harassment and victimisation are defined as follows.

## Direct Discrimination

This is where someone treats another person less favourably than others because of a protected characteristic. Direct discrimination can occur when a person is treated less favourably because that person is linked or associated with someone who has a protected characteristic. It can also occur where a person is treated less favourably because it is wrongly thought that the person has a particular protected characteristic or is treated as if that person does. It should be noted that in relation to age, direct discrimination can be justified as a proportionate means of achieving a legitimate aim.

## Indirect discrimination

This is where a rule or policy is applied to everybody but would put people with a relevant protected characteristic at a particular disadvantage. However, there is no discrimination if the rule or policy can be justified as a proportionate means of achieving a legitimate aim.

## Discrimination arising from disability

This is a particular form of discrimination where someone treats another person less favourably because of something arising in consequence of their disability. However, there is no discrimination if the treatment can be justified as a proportionate means of achieving a legitimate aim.

## Harassment

This is where unwanted conduct related to a relevant protected characteristic (or unwanted conduct of a sexual nature) has the purpose or effect of violating another person's dignity or creates an intimidating, hostile, degrading, humiliating or offensive environment for another person. It also constitutes harassment if, following rejection of or submission to unwanted conduct of a sexual nature or unwanted conduct related to gender reassignment or sex, a person is treated less favourably.

## Victimisation

This is where someone is subjected to a detriment because that person does a protected act, or it is believed that that person has done, or may do, a protected act. A protected act means bringing proceedings under the Equality Act 2010, giving evidence or information in connection with proceedings under the Act, doing any other thing for the purposes of or in connection with the Act and making an allegation that someone has contravened the Act. However, people who give false evidence or information, or make a false allegation, are not protected from victimisation if they have done so in bad faith.

### Discrimination Incident Reporting

All incidents of discrimination, harassment and victimisation must be reported using the Discrimination Incident Reporting Form (DIRF). The DIRF must replace the use of Racist Incident Reporting Forms and any other locally designed forms for the reporting of other equalities incidents. In addition to the DIRF Prison staff have a responsibility to respond appropriately at the time by, for instance, challenging inappropriate behaviour, and where this is achieved the incident and the outcome should be reported.

All incidents of discrimination, harassment and victimisation must be handled in a proportionate and timely way, using appropriate systems such as adjudications and security information reporting and more serious incidents must be referred for investigation.

Prisoners and visitors must be made aware of the system for reporting incidents of discrimination, harassment and victimisation, and that staff are aware of the system and of their responsibilities in responding appropriately to such incidents. Forms must be available in all areas of the prison, with envelopes provided to ensure privacy. The system for submitting and responding to them must be private and secure.

Victims and reporters of incidents must be protected in accordance with the local violence reduction strategy.

### Incidents involving Staff

Staff witnessing or being subject to an incident of discrimination, harassment or victimisation on the basis of any of the protected characteristics should take appropriate action to address the issue. This may include challenging inappropriate behaviour. Appropriate systems should be used to address such behaviour, such as the Incentives and Earned Privileges scheme and adjudications.

If the incident involves misconduct by staff this should be reported to a manager and/or via the reporting wrongdoing process (see PSI 09/2010). Having taken action, staff should report the incident appropriately. As well as completing a DIRF, other forms of reporting may be appropriate, including a disciplinary report, an entry in the case notes section of NOMIS, a Security Information Report etc.

Discrimination Incident Reporting Forms submitted by staff should be reviewed by a manager to ensure that the action taken was appropriate. The manager should identify any further action necessary and ensure that it is completed. Where action taken was not satisfactory, they should provide feedback to the member of staff who submitted the form.

### Incidents involving Prisoners or Visitors

Prisoners witnessing or being subject to an incident of discrimination, harassment or victimisation on the basis of any of the protected characteristics may submit a complaints form or a DIRF. Visitors witnessing or being subject to an incident of discrimination, harassment or victimisation may submit a DIRF.

Complaints forms reporting incidents of discrimination, harassment or victimisation will receive an interim response and be logged on a Discrimination Incident Reporting Form for response. DIRFs concerning serious incidents and/or allegations of misconduct by staff should be referred for investigation in accordance with PSO1300 or Conduct and Discipline. The prisoner should be informed that this is what has happened, and of any outcome of the investigation that is relevant to them.

DIRFs concerning other issues should be handled by a manager. The manager should interview the prisoner or visitor to explore the issue that has been raised. They should then seek to address the issue through an appropriate means, which may include informal conflict resolution, action through systems such as IEP, adjudications etc., or specific action to expedite an outcome. A written response explaining the action taken should be sent in all cases.

### Protection of victims and reporters of incidents

Managers handling DIRFs and conducting associated investigations should ensure that appropriate measures are in place to protect victims and reporters of incidents in accordance with the local violence reduction strategy.

### Incident Logging

All DIRFs should be logged on receipt and response, and the outcome should be noted on completion. The information collected on the log must include the protected characteristic concerned. Copies of completed DIRFs should be retained.

### Senior Management Sign Off / Quality Control

In order to ensure effective responses, a sign off or quality control process involving a senior manager should be used.

## Appeals

Where a prisoner is not satisfied about the outcome of a DIRF about an incident to which they have been subject, they should submit a stage 2 complaint.

## Timeliness

The general principle is that DIRFs should be handled in accordance with the timescales for prisoner complaints (see Complaints PSO/PSI). Where a serious issue is referred for investigation it will not be possible to provide a full response within this timeframe and an interim reply will be sent. There may be some other issues that require longer to resolve, and this is acceptable provided that the reporter is kept informed of developments.

## Prisoner Confidence

It is crucial to ensure that prisoners have confidence in the DIRF process. Amongst the measures that can be taken to ensure this is external scrutiny of responses. Prisoner equalities representatives can also be useful in building prisoner confidence.

## Duties

The Act imposes the following additional duties on HMPPS as a public authority.
*Eliminate unlawful discrimination, harassment and victimisation*
Unlawful discrimination, harassment and victimisation should be eliminated.

*Provide equal opportunities*
Prisoners, visitors and others with whom we work should be provided with equal opportunities. This can be done in a number of ways:
• Removing or minimising disadvantages suffered by people who share a relevant protected characteristic that are connected to that characteristic.
• Taking steps to meet the needs of people who share a relevant protected characteristic that are different from the needs of people who do not share it.
• Encouraging people who share a relevant protected characteristic to participate in any activity in which participation by such people is disproportionately low.

*Foster good relations*
Good relations between people with a protected characteristic and people without that protected characteristic should be fostered, in particular through tackling prejudice and promoting understanding.
*See further:*
Government Equalities Office:
*(gov.uk/government/organisations/government-equalities-office)*
Equality and Human Rights Commission;
*(https://equalityhumanrights.com/en)*

## 2.12 SOCIAL SECURITY AND DISCHARGE GRANTS

### Benefits & Prison
*Overview*
Benefit payments and entitlement may change or stop if you, your partner or your child is:
• sent to prison or a young offenders' institution
• in custody awaiting trial (on remand)
•You must tell the Tax Credit Office about prison sentences.
•You cannot claim State Pension while you're in prison.

### If you're in prison or on remand
You can get help from a benefits adviser to suspend or close down benefits you're no longer able to claim if you go to prison or on remand.

### If your partner or child has gone to prison or is on remand
If your partner or child has gone to prison or is on remand, you must tell whoever pays your benefits and find out:
• if your benefit claims will be affected
• if you can claim other benefits
You may still be entitled to benefits if your partner has gone to prison, as long as you satisfy the benefit entitlement conditions in your own right.

### Benefits that stop or are suspended
Your entitlement to benefit stops if you go to prison, apart from:
• Housing Benefit for shorter sentences
• help with council tax if you're eligible
• tax credits and Child Benefit, in some cases
• Industrial Injuries Disabled Benefit, which is suspended
• You'll stop getting Carer's Allowance if the person you care for goes to prison or is on remand.

### Benefits while on remand
If you're on remand, you cannot claim:
• Jobseeker's Allowance
• Income Support - apart from help with housing costs
• Working Tax Credit - although your partner may be able to claim for an absent partner
• Disability Living Allowance
• Employment and Support Allowance or • Incapacity Benefit
• Attendance Allowance
• Pension Credit - apart from help with housing costs
• Industrial Injuries Disablement Benefit
You will not be entitled to Statutory Sick Pay or Statutory Maternity Pay from your employer.

## Benefit arrears

If you're owed any benefit arrears at the time you're sent to prison or on remand, you can make a request in writing for these to be paid to someone else.

## Benefit arrears if you're not convicted

If you're not convicted, you can get benefit arrears for:
• Contributory Employment and Support Allowance
• Incapacity Benefit
• Benefit arrears if you're convicted

If you're sent to prison and claim Industrial Injuries Disablement Benefit, you may be entitled to up to a year's arrears whenever you're released.

## Claiming benefits on release

If you're entitled to benefits, you can put in new claims as soon as you leave prison. You may also be able to get other financial and practical support. You cannot claim Job Seeker's Allowance if you're released on temporary licence (ROTL).

## Housing Benefit

You may be able to continue getting Housing Benefit or make a claim for the first time if you go to prison or on remand.

## When you will not be able to claim

You will not be entitled to claim Housing Benefit if:
• you're likely to be on remand for more than 52 weeks
• you're likely to be in prison for more than 13 weeks (including any time on remand)
• you're not intending to return home on release you're claiming as a couple and you've split up
• the property is going to be rented out

## Making a new Housing Benefit claim

You can only make a new claim for Housing Benefit if one of the following is true:
•you're getting the severe disability premium
•you got the severe disability premium within the last month and are still eligible for it
•you have reached State Pension age
•you live in temporary accommodation
•you live in sheltered or supported housing with special facilities such as alarms or wardens

### On remand
### If you're single

You can claim Housing Benefit payments for up to 52 weeks while you're on remand, if you're likely to return home in a year or less.

### If you're in a couple

You can claim joint Housing Benefit for up to 52 weeks while one of you is on remand, if it's likely to be for a year or less.

### If your child is on remand

Your Housing Benefit payments can continue for up to 52 weeks if your child's on remand, if they're likely to be away for a year or less.

### In prison
### If you're single

You can claim Housing Benefit for up to 13 weeks if you're single and go to prison and are likely to return home in 13 weeks or less - including any time on remand.

### If you're in a couple

You can claim joint Housing Benefit for up to 13 weeks if one of you has gone to prison and is likely to return home in 13 weeks or less - including any time on remand.

If your partner's been the one claiming Housing Benefit and goes to prison, you may be able to claim it instead. You may need to have your name added to the tenancy agreement, if it's not there already.

### If your child is in prison

If your child goes to prison, you'll need to contact your local council to see if your Housing Benefit entitlement will change. For example, if you rent from a private landlord, the amount of benefit paid is limited, depending on who's living with you.

### Council Tax exemption and reduction

You will not count as an adult living in a property for Council Tax if you're in prison or on remand.

### If you're single

You can apply for your home to be exempt from Council Tax if you're single, in prison or on remand, and there's no one living there. **Your home will not be exempt if you're in prison for not paying Council Tax or a fine for not paying it.**

### If you're in a couple
### On remand

You can apply or continue to get joint Council Tax Reduction if your partner's on remand and is expected home in a year or less.

### In prison

You can claim or continue to claim joint Council Tax Reduction if your partner's expected to be in prison for 13 weeks or less – including any time on remand.

### Making a new claim

You'll get a 25% discount off your Council Tax bill if your partner's going to be absent for more than 13 weeks and you're the only adult in the property. You may be able to apply for Council Tax Reduction if you do not already get it.

### Tax Credits
### Reporting changes

You must tell the Tax Credit Office about changes that affect your tax credits. They'll tell you what happens next.

*Working Tax Credit*
**If you're single**
Your Working Tax Credit will stop if you're single and:
• you're on remand
• you're sent to prison
• you're sent to a young offenders' institution
**If you're in a couple**
You may be able to continue claiming Working Tax Credit if you're in a couple and your partner goes to prison for a year or less.
You must work a certain number of hours a week to qualify.
Any work you do while you're serving a sentence or on remand will not be counted.

*Child Tax Credit*
If you're single and you go to prison
Your Child Tax Credit may stop if you're single with children and go to prison. The Tax Credit Office will decide by looking at:
• whether you're still responsible for your child
• how long you're in prison for
• if you're still in regular contact
• if your child's with you in prison
        The person looking after your child or children may be able to claim Child Tax Credit if you cannot.
**If you're in a couple and one of you goes to prison**
Your Child Tax Credit will continue if you're in a couple and one of you goes on remand or to prison.
**If your child goes to prison**
You'll still get Child Tax Credit if your child goes to prison for 4 months or less.
        You will not get Child Tax Credit for your child's sentence if it's more than 4 months.

*Child Benefit*
You can continue to claim Child Benefit when you're in prison if:
• your child is with you in prison
• the child you're claiming for is living with someone else and you pay an equivalent sum to them
You can also ask to transfer the Child Benefit payment to someone else.
**If your child is being cared for by the local council, your Child Benefit payments will stop after 8 weeks.**
**If your child goes to prison or is on remand**
Your Child Benefit payments will stop after 8 weeks if your child goes to prison or is on remand. You'll get arrears if they're cleared of the offence.
**Looking after someone else's child**
You may be able to claim Child Benefit and Guardian's Allowance if you look after your partner's child or someone else's child while they're in prison.
You may also be able to claim Child Tax Credit.

*Support for Mortgage Interest*
Support for Mortgage Interest (SMI) is no longer a benefit. It's now only available as a loan.
You cannot get an SMI loan if you're serving a prison sentence but your partner might be able to claim instead.
Your partner's name may not have to be on the mortgage to be able to claim.
**Getting an SMI loan while on remand**
If you're single and on remand, you may be able to continue getting SMI loan payments if you meet the eligibility conditions.
You cannot get an SMI loan or Income Support if you're part of a couple and on remand, but your partner can claim benefit and housing costs.
**Eligibility**
If you're on remand, you must be getting Pension Credit or Income Support to get an SMI loan.
You'll need to apply for one of these benefits if you've previously qualified for SMI by getting Income-based Job Seeker's Allowance or Employment and Support allowance.
You'll only be able to get SMI loan payments - you will not be paid Pension Credit or Income Support.
*If you get Income Support and have accepted an offer of an SMI loan, you can only get loan payments after you've been receiving the benefit for 39 consecutive weeks.*

**Discharge Grants (now called 'Subsistence Payments') & Clothing**
*In May 2021 the then Justice Secretary announced that the prison discharge grant will rise from £46 to £76 - the first rise in 25 years.*
*A Ministry of Justice spokesperson said: "Around 60,000 offenders commit a crime within a few weeks each year costing the taxpayer and creating more victims.*
*"That is why we are working to get more offenders back into employment, with education, training and skills programmes in prisons to reduce reoffending and prevent these crimes.*
*"These payments will also help to support offenders with their immediate, essential travel, food and basic needs and have been increased for the first time in 25 years."*
*Reoffending costs around £18 billion a year and accounts for around 80 per cent of the sentenced crime committed in England and Wales.*
*The change will come into effect in the summer of 2021 and increase the one-off subsistence payment from £46 to £76 reflecting the increases in the UK's Consumer Prices Index (CPI) since 1995 and bringing it in line with the current cost of living.*
*The MOJ will increase the one-off subsistence payment year on year until 2024/25 in line with the CPI.*
*The MOJ states this supports the wider work being done to reduce reoffending and protect the public, including investing extra money into drug and alcohol addiction treatment, helping prison leavers who would otherwise be homeless into temporary,*

basic accommodation on release and reforming criminal records disclosure so it's easier for ex-offenders to find work.

Rule 23(6) of the Prison Rules 1999 states that a 'prisoner may be provided, where necessary, with suitable and adequate clothing on his release.' The Discharge policy (PSI 72/2011) states, at para 2.31, that 'those prisoners who need adequate clothing for release will be given it.' The terms 'suitable' and 'adequate' are not defined within the Prison Rules nor the Discharge policy, as what is 'adequate' will vary depending on the circumstances of each prisoner and it is down to the judgement of the Governor, taking into account these circumstances.

## Am I eligible for a Subsistence Payment?

All eligible prisoners aged 18 or over who have served more than 14 days in custody after receiving a custodial sentence must be given a Subsistence Payment of £76.

Prisoners in the following categories are **NOT** eligible for a Subsistence Payment:

• Prisoners who are released from court after a period on remand, even if the time on remand was over 14 days (including those sentenced to 'time served'). Sentenced prisoners who have served 14 days or less in custody since the date of sentence.

• Those recalled from licence to prison for a period of 14 days or less

• Licence recalls who were on licence for 14 days or less before recall

• Those awaiting deportation or removal from the United Kingdom

• Those travelling to an address outside the United Kingdom. For the purpose of paying the Discharge Grant, the Channel Islands, the Isle of Man and the Republic of Ireland are included within the United Kingdom

• Those being discharged to a hospital under a Mental Health Act Section Order

• Fine defaulters and those held on further remand warrants. Convicted offenders who have completed their sentence and who qualify for a grant but remain in custody in default of payment of a fine or remanded on further charges, will receive the grant on their final release

• Civil prisoners, as defined in PSO 4600

• Those aged under 18 at the time of release

• Unconvicted prisoners

• Sentenced prisoners who are known to have in excess of £16,000 in savings (and would therefore be ineligible for Income Support under the relevant regulations)

• Stage 2 resettlement regime prisoners undertaking paid work in the community. This will not apply to those carrying out unpaid community work, those attending education or training or those whose paid employment ceases

through no fault of their own 14 days or more prior to discharge

## Discretionary Payment

At the Governor's discretion, an additional payment of up to £50 may be paid directly to a genuine accommodation provider to help the prisoner secure a release address. The payment must not be made to the prisoner or to a friend or relative of the prisoner.

## 2.13 RELEASE & RECALL

**Changes in 2022 to Release and Recall**
**New Sentence Calculation Policy Framework - 28th June 2022.**

The way sentences are calculated can be very complicated and in June 2022 a new framework was introduced to reduce sentence calculation errors - a not unexpected framework given over 360 prisoners have been released in error due to incorrect sentence calculations.

Sentence calculation has always been an area which involves lots of mistakes, but this is not surprising given the plethora of new sentencing regimes that are introduced and what the Prison Officers' Association have called the 'poor training offered to staff in those roles'.

Sentence calculations can often be complicated and is often a source of frustration for prisoners. The new framework which replaces PSI 03/2015 and introduces a requirement for staff who carry out sentence calculations to engage in a 3 part process:

1) Staff must have a 'licence to operate' in the sentence calculations role;

2) Blind checks must be carried out; and

3) There must be a 2 day check before release to be carried out by a Band 4 member of staff or above.

Governors are responsible for ensuring staff carrying out initial sentence calculations and any of the sentence calculation checks required by this policy, have obtained, or are working towards obtaining, a licence to operate by completing and passing the sentence calculation courses relevant to the type of establishment in which they operate. Staff who are working towards obtaining the licence must be mentored and have their calculations checked by a member of staff holding a licence to operate.

On implementation of this framework, if there are no members of staff in the establishment who have passed the relevant YCS or Advanced Sentence Calculations course, the Governor must identify and designate the most experienced staff to carry out the 2 day checks and mentoring and take immediate action to enrol those staff on the first available relevant course.

The framework really strengthens the process and should mean there are much fewer mistakes. The first calculation sheet completed following the initial sentence must be filed in the warrant folder after being initialled by the person who carried out the calculation. This will become the 'master calculation sheet'. Every subsequent calculation/amendment must be annotated on the 'master calculation sheet' and initialled by the member of staff who carried out the particular sentence calculation action.

Staff completing the following sentence calculation actions must carry out a 'blind calculation'.

A 'blind calculation' means carrying out a full calculation of the release dates for the sentence(s) as though it was a new initial calculation. It must be undertaken without reference to any earlier completed calculation sheets. Only on completion of the 'blind calculation' should the previously completed calculation sheet(s) be viewed. This will ensure any discrepancies in the release dates come to light and can be investigated.

Once a 'blind calculation' has been carried out:

• If the dates agree with dates on the 'master calculation sheet', there is no need to file the fresh calculation sheet (used for the blind calculation) in the warrant file, but the 'master calculation sheet' must be initialled to verify that the required 'blind calculation' has been completed.

• If the dates do not agree with those on the 'master calculation sheet', the discrepancy must be investigated and brought to the attention of a Band 4 (or above) for confirmation of the correct dates. Once the correct release dates are confirmed, the 'master calculation sheet' in the warrant folder must be updated and initialled as above.

• The sentence calculation helpline must be contacted if further advice/clarification is required to establish the correct release dates.

PNOMIS must be updated as per the guidance in chapter 7 of PSI 23/2014.

A release date notification slip must be provided to the prisoner no later than 5 working days after the imposition of a sentence, or an event requiring an amendment to the calculation. The slip must be marked provisional where further information is required before the calculation can be confirmed. Once the calculation is confirmed a revised release date notification slip must be issued.

Calculations must be checked 2 working days prior to release by a person who is different to those who carried out the initial calculation and check and different to the person who carried out the 14 day check. This must be a blind calculation. The framework requires the following documentation be considered so a release date can be accurately calculated:

• Order of Imprisonment (warrant)

• Trial record sheet
• Indictment –
• Details of prospective added days awarded on adjudication (ADAs)
• Remand warrants
• Police custody records (PACE 1984)
• Previous custodial records

The framework makes clear that time spent in police custody following remand by a court, on arrest following sentence in absence or recall from licence, for example, before being transferred to prison custody, will be treated as remand/sentenced time spent in custody irrespective of when the offence was committed or the sentence was imposed.

If a prisoner is in custody serving a determinate sentence(s) and an indeterminate sentence, release cannot take place until the prisoner is entitled to be released from both types of sentence. On occasion the Parole Board has directed release of an indeterminate sentence prisoners pending the determinate sentence being served.

Under Section 385 of the Sentencing Act 2020, Crown Courts have the power to amend a sentence when a mistake has been made only within 56 calendar days following sentencing. The amended sentence is calculated from the original sentence date, unless the court directs otherwise. There is no legal requirement for the Prison Service to check the validity of the sentence imposed by the court. However, where a warrant or sentence is ambiguous, or appears to be invalid, the sentencing court must be contacted without delay so that it has the opportunity to clarify the intention of the court and issue an amended warrant where necessary.

In addition the Early Removal of Foreign National Prisoners (ERS) PSI 04/2013 has been updated. It was revised to incorporate the changes to the ERS that will be made by the Nationality and Borders Act 2022 (NABA 2022) which were implemented on 28 June 2022. The NABA 2022 increases the ERS window from 9 months to 12 months and introduces a new 'stop the clock' provision for those who are removed under the ERS on or after 28 June 2022 and allows ERS for those recalled to custody from licence. In short therefore, NABA amends sections 260 and 261 of the Criminal Justice Act 2003 to increase the ERS window from 270 days before the earliest release point to 12 months before the earliest release point.

### Power to Detain Dangerous SDSP: July 2022.

On 14th July 2022 the Ministry of Justice published a new framework entitled "Power to Detain Dangerous Prisoners Serving a Standard Determinate Sentence Policy".

The Secretary of State for Justice (SSJ) has introduced a new provision contained within Section 132 of the Police, Crime, Sentencing and Courts (PCSC) Act 2022 which allows the SSJ to refer certain Standard Determinate Sentence (SDS) prisoners to the Parole Board instead of automatically releasing them at their Conditional Release Date (CRD).

Prisoners must meet both the legal and the policy thresholds to be eligible for consideration under this policy, which includes a dangerousness test and a public interest test. Following referral, the prisoner would then not be released until the Parole Board is satisfied that it is no longer necessary for the protection of the public that the prisoner should be confined, or the prisoner reaches the end of their sentence, or the SSJ rescinds the Notice to the prisoner or the referral to the Parole Board.

The use of this power is reserved for standard determinate sentence prisoners who were not judged to be dangerous at the point of sentence (or who may have been considered dangerous but owing to the offence committed or another reason were not eligible for an extended determinate sentence at the time of sentencing) but who are subsequently assessed to pose a significant risk of serious harm to members of the public occasioned by the commission of specified offences on release. This would include:

• Prisoners who should be considered under this policy are those who are serving a SDS custodial sentence for offences, other than a terrorism or terrorism connected offences, and

• Where there are reasonable grounds, based on new or additional information, to believe that the prisoner poses an imminent and very high risk of committing a serious specified offence on release, as set out by the PCSC Act.

Qualifying offences which include murder or specified offences including violent, sexual and terrorist related offending.

There are too many offences to set them all out here, but they include manslaughter, threats to kill, GBH with intent, GBH, Possession of a firearm with intent, affray, arson, robbery, rape, indecent assault.

Prisoners identified as potentially suitable for submission to the HMPPS Panel must also meet a test for dangerousness.

Dangerousness test – the risk presented by the prisoner would:

• cause serious harm to the public (through terrorism, death or serious injury/sexual assault) or present a national security threat if the risk were to materialise;

• be likely to materialise at or soon after the conditional release point (i.e., a degree of probability about the risk arising following release and that it may be imminent);

• be credible (the prisoner has the capability and means to commit a serious offence); and

• not be safely manageable using the normal means of applying even very stringent licence conditions, supervision and restrictions.

As part of this dangerousness test, prisoners must be assessed as being very high risk of serious harm on OASys (Asset+) meaning that there is an imminent risk of serious harm i.e., the potential event is more likely than not to happen imminently, and the impact would be serious.

Prisoners must also be identified for management at MAPPA level 3, or the equivalent of MAPPA level 3 in circumstances where, due to restrictions around the index offence(s) not allowing for MAPPA level 3 management, a bespoke MAPPA information sharing meeting has taken, or will take, place.

In addition to the dangerousness test, there is also the public interest test. The public interest test must determine whether, on balance, it is in the public interest to detain the prisoner, potentially to the end of their sentence, rather than automatically release them at their conditional release date. This must be accompanied by a deliverable plan which sets out how any extra time served in prison will be used to reduce risk of harm. This should include deliverable objectives/activities. As part of the process of identifying eligible prisoners, HMPPS's existing risk management tools will be used.

A HMPPS Panel then considers the case and determines if a case should be referred to the Parole Board for a decision on release. The referral to the Parole Board takes place if the Secretary of State believes on reasonable grounds that the prisoner would, if released, pose a significant risk to members of the public of serious harm occasioned by the commission of specified offences as above.

The discretion to refer to the Parole Board rests firmly with the Secretary of State. Prisoners will only currently be considered for referral where the reasonable grounds are based on new or additional information not available at the time of sentencing. Existing information, in particular information, which was before the sentencing Court, will not be deemed sufficient.

Prisoners who can only be released by the Parole Board cannot be made subject to the process.

This new power significantly alters the sentence and release regime for a number of prisoners. It is not clear how often this new power will be used and how many prisoners will be referred to the Parole Board.

The framework suggests there must be clear evidence of an increased risk, which can then be challenged in front of the Parole Board. The intention is that clear, credible evidence will be used and justified rather than generic comments on risk but it will undoubtedly result in developing caselaw as the theory of the policy becomes tested in practice.

**The Police, Crime, Sentencing and Courts Act 2022 made changes to the process of release for some prisoners.**

**For Termination of IPP Licences see: Managing Parole Eligible Offenders on Licence Policy Framework.** Re-Issued on 21 July 2022 and replaces PI 08/2015. Chapters 3.5 and 5.5 have been updated to reflect the changes brought in by the Police Crime Sentencing and Courts (PCSC) Act 2022.

**Generic Parole Process Policy Framework Updated 21st July 2022:**
The main changes in the revised version of the Framework are:
• Removal of all references to CRC following the Probation Service unification. All references to NPS amended to Probation Service.
• Chapters 3.2, 3.4, 3.6, 3.8, 3.10 and 5.2, 5.4, 5.6, 5.8 have been updated to reflect the changes brought in by the PCSC Act 2022 - see below for summaries.
• Additional section on Parole Board Setting Aside Powers has been added as per the changes brought in by the PCSC Act 2022.
• Additional section on Restricted Transfer Indeterminate Sentenced Prisoners (ISPs) and Moves to Open Conditions has been added.
• Additional section on Mental Capacity has been added.
**3.2:** Minimum Term Reviews for Prisoners sentenced to detention at Her Majesty's Pleasure (HMP) now allows eligible prisoners who are approaching or have passed the halfway point of their tariff to request a reduction to their tariff.
**3.4:** Pre-Tariff Reviews for Indeterminate Sentenced Prisoners. This section of the Policy Framework only applies to indeterminate sentenced prisoners. All indeterminate sentenced prisoners will have their cases reviewed by the Public Protection Casework Section (PPCS) to ascertain whether all three of the criteria in the current test for open conditions has been met (see guidance 5.8.2) and that there is a reasonable prospect of the Parole Board making a positive recommendation that they progress to open conditions. This takes place before a decision is made about whether a case should be referred to the Parole Board for a recommendation around suitability for open conditions.
**3.6:** Generic Parole Process (GPP). This section of the Policy Framework applies to all

indeterminate sentenced prisoners and all parole eligible determinate sentence prisoners. This section of the Policy Framework also applies to prisoners subject to the Power to Detain legislation found in sections 244ZB and 244ZC of the Criminal Justice Act 2003, where a standard determinate sentenced offender is found to pose a significant risk of commission of serious further offences were they to be released automatically at their conditional release date and is referred to the Parole Board instead. Guidance on this process is set out in the Power to Detain Policy Framework. Where the HMPPS Panel decides that the prisoner meets both the legal threshold and the policy criteria for referral to the Parole Board, the prisoner's case will follow the process set out in this chapter of the Framework, which may be expedited for these cases. The GPP is the standardised parole process for pre-tariff, on tariff and post-tariff ISPs and for those determinate-sentenced prisoners who are eligible to be released on licence by the Parole Board, which all parties must follow to ensure the timely referral of a prisoner's case (for guidance on timings of reviews see guidance 5.1.1). All requirements for COM /Probation Practitioner in this section will, for pre-tariff reviews, be the responsibility of the POM.
**3.8:** Setting the next review date. All indeterminate sentenced prisoners and parole eligible determinate sentenced prisoners are entitled to have their case reviewed by the Parole Board as set out in the Timing and Frequency of Parole Reviews guidance 5.6.1.
**3.10** Adverse Developments. This section of the Policy Framework only applies to indeterminate sentenced prisoners. All parties must follow the requirements below where an adverse development occurs to ensure that the prisoner is detained in the correct category of prison which reflects their risk.
**5.2** Minimum Term Reviews for Prisoners Sentenced to Detention During Her Majesty's Pleasure (HMP).
**5.4** Pre-Tariff Reviews for ISP.
**5.6** Generic Parole Process (GPP).
**5.8** Setting the next review date

## RELEASE - GENERAL

**Recall, Review and Re-Release of Recalled Prisoners Policy Framework**
**Updated 21st July 2022:** This Policy Framework has been updated by removal of all references to CRC following the Probation Service unification. All references to NPS amended to Probation Service. A number of changes have been made to the chapters **4.2** (Recalling an Indeterminate Sentenced Individual and Extended Sentenced

849

Individuals); **4.3** (Recalling all Other Determinate Sentenced Individuals); **4.9** (Return to Custody of all Recalled Prisoners); **4.10** (This section of the Policy Framework applies to determinate sentenced prisoners (including extended sentence prisoners) and indeterminate sentenced prisoners subject to standard recall provisions); **4.11** (Fixed Term Recall – Review and Re-Release); **4.17** (Parole Board Oral Hearings - This section of the Policy Framework applies to all recalled prisoners, where the Parole Board has directed that an oral hearing take place, unless otherwise stated); and **6.9** of the Framework - Standard Recall - Statutory Day 28 Review.

In addition to the above recent changes, two other major changes in the last two years to release arrangements deserve particular mention.

**The following must be read together with the provisions of the Police, Crime, Sentencing and Courts (PCSC) Act 2022**

The first is the **Terrorist Offenders (Restriction of Early Release) Act 2020.**

This Act stops individuals convicted of terrorist offences, or offences with a terrorist connection, serving a determinate sentence being automatically released prior to the end of their sentence – unusually it is retrospective so applies to those already sentenced.

Such offenders continue to remain eligible for early release, but must apply to the Parole Board for conditional release two thirds of the way through their sentence. The Parole Board must then examine the case and has the discretion to release the offender on licence if it is satisfied, after conducting a risk assessment, that the offender's incarceration is no longer necessary to protect the public.

The legislation was challenged by judicial review in July 2020 (Khan v Secretary of State for the Justice [2020] EWHC 2084 (Admin) (30 July 2020) ([2020] EWHC 2084 (Admin); From England and Wales High Court (Administrative Court) but was dismissed.

The second change to the release regime is the **Release of Prisoners (Alteration of Relevant Proportion of Sentence) Order 2019** that came into force on 1st of April 2020.

The relevant points are that for those convicted of serious violence or sexual offences and who are sentenced to more than seven years, will now serve 2/3 of their sentence and not half as previously.

There are two particular points worth noting. The first is that sentences of less than seven years will not activate the 2/3 requirement and secondly it only relates to individual sentences - not consecutive ones.

So someone sentenced for relevant offences to three years and five years consecutively, making an eight year sentence in total, will NOT activate the 2/3 requirement because neither of the sentences are longer than seven years. Similarly someone sentenced to 10 years and five years consecutive, making a 15 year sentence, will only serve 2/3 of the 10 year sentence and half of the five years sentence.

Anyone sentenced on or after 4th April 2005 comes under the Criminal Justice Act 2003 and will be released (subject to the provisions of the PCSC) at the halfway point of their sentence on licence until their sentence expires - the SED or sentence expiry date.

There are three prison sentences under this Act: a 'standard' determinate sentence (SDS) which applies to anyone sentenced after 1st February 2015 to a sentence of one day or more.

**Determinate Sentence of 12 months or more:**
• Release will be at the halfway point (earlier if released on HDC - but see the **'Power to Detain Dangerous SDS' above**).
• Released on licence and supervised by the Probation service until the sentence expiry date

**Extended Determinate Sentence**
There have been different types of Extended Sentences in place over the years and as a result that often causes prisoners a lot of confusion. Sometimes those subject to them do not have the implications of being subject to one explained to them. In this section we look at the Extended Determinate Sentence (EDS) and what the release provisions for these types of sentence are.

*Who can be subject to an Extended Sentence?*
Extended sentences of some description have been around for some time. However, Extended Determinate Sentences (EDS) were introduced by LASPO (Legal Aid Sentencing and Punishment of Offenders Act) in December 2012 and essentially replaced sentences of Imprisonment for Public Protection (IPPs) for prisoners convicted of a specified offence.

An EDS can only be imposed where **all** the following conditions are met:
• The defendant has been convicted of a specified offence (a sexual or violent offence listed in Schedule 15 of the Criminal Justice Act 2003) (whether the offence was committed before or after this section came into force).
• The court considers that the defendant presents a substantial risk of causing serious harm through re-offending by committing a further specified offence. The "significant risk" test is the same as the test for IPP therefore they must meet the dangerousness threshold.

• The court is not required to impose a sentence of imprisonment for life, and Condition A or B below is met:

Condition A: at the time the offence was committed the defendant had been convicted of a sexual or violent offence listed in Schedule 15B of the CJA 2003.

Condition B: that the current offence merits a determinate sentence of at least 4 years.

If the conditions above are satisfied then an EDS will be imposed by the Court.

*What does an Extended Determinate Sentence mean?*
An Extended Determinate Sentence comprises of a custodial sentence and an extended period on licence. The Judge is required to give a minimum of 12 months for the custodial term.

In terms of the extension period, this will be decided by the Judge based on the length of time considered necessary for the purpose of protecting members of the public from serious harm. Although there is no minimum period that can be imposed in relation to the extension period, it should be noted that this period should not exceed 5 years for a specified violent offence and 8 years for a specified sexual offence.

*Is it right the EDS replaces the IPP? If so what does that mean for those subject to IPPs?*
Although IPP sentences were essentially "scrapped" as of December 2012 those sentenced to an IPP prior to this date still remain subject to the sentence and its release provisions.

*What should you be doing to help yourself?*
In order for prisoners to be able to successfully apply for Parole they will need to evidence that they have addressed their identified risk factors to a level that can be managed safely in the community.

Prisoners are advised to engage in their sentence plan as early as possible and complete any offence focused work available. It is important for prisoners to engage with both their Offender Manager and Offender Supervisor to discuss what they can do to demonstrate a reduction in risk. This will assist the report writers when they come to prepare reports setting out recommendations regarding discretionary release by the Parole Board.

**Indeterminate Sentences for Public Protection (abolished 3 December 2012) See section 2.14**

**New "mandatory" life sentences for second serious offences**
There are two conditions which have to apply. The first is the "sentence condition":

• The person must be convicted of an offence which is set out in Part 1 of new schedule 15B28

(which the Explanatory Notes refer to as "particularly serious sexual and violent offences")
• That offence must be serious enough to justify a sentence of imprisonment of 10 years or more The second is the "previous offence condition":

• The person must previously have been convicted of an offence listed in any part of new schedule 15B29
• The person must have been sentenced to imprisonment for life or for a period of 10 years or more in respect of that previous offences

**Additional CJA 2003 Information**
• The number of days remand time to count will be directed by the court.
• No credit will be given for time spent in police custody.
• Additional Days awarded will be added to all dates except the sentence expiry date or sentence and licence expiry date if this is the same.
• Terms of Imprisonment in default of Payment or for Contempt
• For terms of imprisonment imposed before 4 April 2005, for terms of 12 months or less release is at the halfway point and if 12 months release is at the two thirds point.
• For terms of imprisonment imposed on or after 4 April 2005 release is at the halfway point.
• Release from such term is unconditional, there is no eligibility for HDC nor can credit be given for time spent in police custody or on remand.

**Additional Days**
ADAs awarded will be added to all dates except the sentence expiry date or sentence and licence expiry date if this is the same.

*Offender Rehabilitation Act (ORA)*
ORA made changes to the sentencing and releasing framework to extend probation supervision after release to offenders serving short term sentences. It also creates greater flexibility in the delivery of sentences served in the community.

The ORA came into full force on 1st February 2015. At the heart of the legislation is the extension of supervision to those who are released from short prison sentences of less than 12 months.

This means that any person whose offence was committed on or after 1st February 2015, who is sentenced to a custodial term of more than 1 day, and is 18 years old or over when released, will now receive supervision in the community.

**Introduction of a new supervision period**
The ORA introduced a new period of post sentence supervision for all offenders sentenced to less than 2 years in custody.

Offenders sentenced to less than 2 years and released on license, outlined above, will be subject to an additional period of supervision, for the purposes of rehabilitation once their license period comes to an end. The license and supervision periods will together make up 12 months.

### Drug testing and drug appointments

The ORA allows for problematic drug use to be tackled as part of an offender's period of supervision on release. It extends previous provision to impose drug testing requirements for Class A drugs to also include Class B drugs. In addition, it introduces a new power to require offenders, on release, to attend appointments designed to address their dependency on, or propensity to, misuse a controlled drug.

• Young adult offenders

Those under 18 years old at the point of sentencing but who reach 18 before release will also be subject to the new license and supervision periods. This means that young adults could receive variable sentences depending on when they reach their 18th birthday:

• Female offenders

The ORA states that in providing supervision or rehabilitation the Secretary of State must comply with the public sector equality duty under the Equality Act 2010 as it relates to female offenders and must also identify anything in the arrangements that is intended to meet the particular needs of this group.

• Breach and recall

Those subject to the new license and supervision periods outlined above, will now also be subject to sanctions if they breach their license or supervision conditions, as is the existing position for longer sentenced prisoners.

Breaches during the license period will be dealt with by the National Probation Service (NPS) who will have discretion to consider a reported breach of conditions and will be able to issue a warning to the offender, ask for a variation in license conditions (for example, by adding curfew or imposing electronic monitoring) or ultimately to recall an offender to custody. Offenders recalled to custody will generally be recalled for an automatic period of 14 days (as opposed to 28 days for prisoners sentenced to over 2 years) but where the person is assessed as presenting a risk of serious harm to the public, they can be recalled until the end of their sentence.

Offenders who breach the supervision period requirements will be brought back before the court. The court will have the power to impose the following sanctions: a fine, unpaid work, a curfew, or ultimately, a return to custody for a period of up to 14 days.

*Offenders serving community orders or suspended sentences*

The ORA creates, for community orders and suspended sentence orders, a rehabilitative activity requirement. This replaces the existing 'activity' and 'supervision' requirements.

A rehabilitation activity requirement means that the offender must comply with any instructions given to attend appointments and/or participate in activities. It must specify the maximum number of days for which the offender may be instructed to participate in activities. Instructions given under a rehabilitation activity requirement must promote rehabilitation but can also pertain to other purposes in addition to rehabilitation.

Rehabilitation activity requirements can include:
• instructions to participate in specified activities;
• instructions to go to a specified place;
• activities that form a part of an accredited programme; and
• activities with a reparative purpose, such as restorative justice. An activity is considered a restorative justice activity if:
• the participants consist of, or include, the offender and one or more victims;
• the aim of the activity is to maximise the offender's awareness of the impact of the offending concerned on the victims; and
• the activity gives a victim or victims an opportunity to talk about, or otherwise express experience of, the offending and its impact.

The previous legislation that all community orders must contain a punitive element remains in place.

Courts will determine, taking into consideration the advice in a Pre-Sentence Report prepared by the NPS, what requirements to impose in a community order or suspended sentence order. When considering the content of a rehabilitation activity requirement (including confirmation of available activities) the NPS must identify and pay proper regard to the rehabilitative and criminogenic needs of offenders, as well as an assessment of their offending behaviour and associated risks.

### HOW THE LICENCE WORKS

The word 'licence' indicates some sort of accountability to the Ministry of Justice through HMPPS until your SED. It will usually include an element of supervision by the National Probation Service.

### YOUNG OFFENDER INSTITUTION LICENCE

On release you will be under supervision on licence for at least three months, even if this takes you past your SED, unless your 22nd birthday falls within that period. Supervision means that you must report regularly to your social worker or offender manager in accordance with Home

Office National Standards 2000. If you breach your conditions you may be fined or recalled to prison.

## TEMPORARY LICENCES
**Policy name: Release on Temporary Licence (ROTL) Policy Framework**
**Revised and updated WEF 17th August 2022.**
**Purpose:** Release on Temporary Licence (ROTL) facilitates the rehabilitation of offenders, by helping to prepare them for resettlement in the community once they are released. This includes, among other examples, finding work and rebuilding family ties. It is intended that this will lead to reduced reoffending in the long-term.

There is no entitlement to ROTL but the expectation is that it will be widely used with suitable offenders in open prisons and women's prisons where the resourcing and infrastructure best enable ROTL to be undertaken. As now, closed prisons can release eligible prisoners on ROTL, but Governors will want to be assured that they have the necessary security arrangements in place to prevent contraband being brought in by returning prisoners, staff in place to carry out the required assessments and Boards, and operational enablers, before considering a wider expansion.

This policy framework deals with temporary release for adults. Instructions to practitioners on temporary release for children are given in PSO 6300, in relation to children detained in Young Offender Institutions, and in separate "Mobilities" guidance for children detained in Secure Training Centres and Secure Children's Homes. Approaches to Release on Temporary Licence and Mobility for the Youth Secure Estate are being considered separately, outside of this framework. Where a child transitions from the youth to the adult estate then the adult, ROTL provisions set out here will generally apply. Where the individual has already begun to take temporary release for resettlement purposes as a child, however, consideration should be given to maintaining access to temporary release, where this remains in line with the sentence plan and subject to risk assessment, even where the individual has yet to reach the adult ROTL eligibility date.

### Restricted ROTL and Standard ROTL
ROTL is a two-tier scheme where a more stringent scheme applies in "Restricted ROTL" cases and the remainder of offenders being subject to a "Standard ROTL" regime. In the May 2019 policy framework a number of changes have been made to the previous policy.
These include:
• Changing the threshold for Restricted ROTL so that it is focused on the most serious offenders.

• Removing the current restriction on ROTL in the first three months after transfer to open conditions, subject to individual progress and risk assessment.
• Making prisoners, including those serving indeterminate sentences, eligible to be considered for unaccompanied day release (RDR) from the point of entry to the open estate (or reaching open status in the women's estate).
• Streamlining the process so that agencies are consulted and boards sit only where necessary, the focus is on the right information, and paperwork is reduced.
• Encouraging the greater use of workplace ROTL, for example, by allowing paid work to be taken as soon as the offender is eligible for day release and removing the requirement for a prisoner on ROTL to spend at least one 24-hour period per week in prison.
• Allowing primary carers and sole carers to apply for Childcare Resettlement Licence. ROTL
• Allowing offenders with a prior abscond history (if it occurred more than two years ago and only once during the current sentence) to be risk assessed for open conditions and ROTL.
• Allowing Directors of contracted prisons to take ROTL decisions whilst the Controller will continue to monitor the Director's compliance in this area.

### Prisoner Apprenticeship Programme
This policy framework (WEF 17th August 2022) also includes the Prisoner Apprenticeship Programme.
The differing types of apprenticeships range from Intermediate Apprenticeships, where the individual needs to show that they have the ability to complete the programme as well as proficiency in English and maths to higher level, and degree level apprenticeships which require higher levels of prior educational attainment. An intermediate apprenticeship usually lasts between one to four years and we expect most of our candidates to undertake this type of apprenticeship.
An apprenticeship is a job with training and there are two types of arrangement under which an approved English apprenticeship can be achieved: an Approved English Apprenticeship Agreement (AEAA), and an alternative apprenticeship. The Apprenticeship, Skills, Children and Learning Act 2009 dictates that an AEAA is to be treated as a contract of service, which means it qualifies as a contract of employment. However, it is the policy of MoJ/HMPPS that prisoners should not have contracts of employment. This is due to the practical issues and litigation risk that would arise from the conflict between prison rules and both contract law and employment rights.
For these reasons, when prisoners currently

undertake paid work whilst on ROTL they do so under a Memorandum of Understanding made between them, the placement provider and the prison.

1.8 An alternative English apprenticeship arrangement does not necessarily qualify as a contract of employment. Such arrangements are currently available where apprentices are training to become religious ministers or police constables (as members of both these vocations are office holders, rather than employees). DfE have amended their secondary legislation to allow an alternative English apprenticeship for serving prisoners. We have also developed a Prisoner Apprenticeship Programme MOU which will operate in a similar way as the one currently in use for ROTL. Paid work undertaken as part of the Prisoner Apprenticeship Programme in the open estate will be done under a quadripartite agreement via this MOU made between the prisoner, the prison, the placement provider and the training provider.

*Outcomes*
This policy aims to ensure that:
• Prison governors and decision-makers can consider ROTL earlier and in more cases;
• Offenders who are granted ROTL will benefit from resettlement opportunities, which in turn will safely prepare them for permanent release back into the community;
• The ROTL process will be clearer, more efficient, and easier to administer;
• Offenders who are eligible for ROTL will continue to undergo a thorough risk assessment;
• ROTL will be applied consistently and fairly and in a way which supports the resettlement of the prisoner, while ensuring the protection of the public remains central to the process.
• Prison governors and decision makers will also consider prisoners for the Prisoner Apprenticeship Programme and, where prisoners are eligible, will undergo the same thorough risk assessment process.

*Legal Requirements*
Prison Rule 9 & YOI Rule 5 provide the authority for ROTL to support appropriate activities. They also set out the following requirements:
Prison Rule 9 (The Prison Rules 1999) and YOI Rule 5 (The Young Offender Institution Rules 2000) provide the authority for temporary release to support appropriate activities. They also set out the following requirements:
(4) An offender shall not be released under this rule unless the Secretary of State is satisfied that there would not be an unacceptable risk of his committing offences whilst released or otherwise failing to comply with any condition upon which he is released.

(5) The Secretary of State shall not release under this rule a prisoner serving a sentence of imprisonment if, having regard to....
(a) the period or proportion of his sentence which the prisoner has served or…the period or proportion of any such sentence he has served; and
(b) the frequency with which the offender has been granted temporary release under this rule… the Secretary of State is of the opinion that the release of the offender would be likely to undermine public confidence in the administration of justice."

**Other Requirements**
4.2. The following sections, paragraphs 4.3. to 4.10., list the key actions that must be completed throughout the ROTL process. These sections are expanded on in more detail from page 9 onwards, and in the guidance section of this policy framework.

4.3. Governors must ensure that all staff are aware of and act in accordance with the ROTL principles and procedures set out in this policy framework.

4.4. NPS offender managers and CRC responsible officers 2 must be familiar with ROTL procedures set out below and particularly with those stages that deal with offender management comments and notifications about ROTL.

4.5. Decisions on temporary release must be taken by the governor or delegate (acting on behalf of the Secretary of State) and, for any release to be acceptable, there must in all cases be an identified basis under the Prison Rules for the release.
• All resettlement ROTL must have a clear, recorded link to an objective identified in the individual offender's sentence plan and/or resettlement goals. Special purpose ROTL may be granted to enable offenders to deal responsibly with unexpected family and personal events and wider criminal justice needs.

4.6. The decision to allow temporary release must always be balanced by an active consideration, by means of rigorous risk assessment, of the need for maintaining public safety and the public's confidence in the judicial system.
• The risk assessment must take account of all the information that is available, obtaining further information where necessary and considering how that evidence bears on the offender's suitability for the proposed activity.

4.7. Governors must ensure that the impact of the release on any identified victims is taken into account before any release is authorised.

• Before any release is considered, a check must be made for any relevant information held by the HMPPS Victims' Helpline and a check must be made with the offender manager to establish the whereabouts of any identified victims and whether the victim or victim's family are participating in the NPS victim contact scheme. If so, they must be afforded a reasonable opportunity to make representations about the conditions to be attached to any temporary release and any representations must be put before the ROTL board.

• The offender manager must be informed of the outcome of the ROTL board, including any victim specific conditions in order that this can be communicated to the victims via the victim liaison officer (VLO).

4.8. Governors must provide all offenders with information outlining how this policy on temporary licence will be locally administered.

• It should be made clear to the offender what ROTL opportunities are available at the prison, when and how they may apply and how the procedure works, including the principles around funding for ROTL travel and subsistence expenses set out in the Guidance below (see 6.1). Most importantly, offenders must understand the sorts of behaviours expected of them in order to gain and maintain access to ROTL. The Incentives scheme serves a different purpose to ROTL which is primarily about facilitating resettlement, but incentives scheme factors such as prisoner behaviour and engagement in addressing offending behaviour should be considered, alongside other criteria, in ROTL suitability assessments. Local incentives policies can be linked to ROTL by making prisoners aware that abiding by the rules, addressing their offending behaviour and engaging with their sentence plan are also important factors in ROTL assessments. Progress on the incentives scheme will be taken into account in all ROTL decisions, alongside all other relevant information, and ROTL failure will lead to suspension of privileges.

Types of ROTL, eligibility dates, frequency and duration and Prisoner Apprenticeship Programme eligibility and duration.

4.9. Governors must have in place a mechanism to ensure the accurate identification of Restricted and Standard ROTL prisoners so that the appropriate procedure is applied as set out in the ROTL Procedure Table below. The following offenders are all subject to Restricted ROTL:

• Indeterminate sentence prisoners (ISPs);

• Prisoners serving Extended Determinate Sentences, or other legacy extended sentences;

• Prisoners serving sentences imposed under sections 265 or 278 of the Sentencing Code (formerly section 236A of the Criminal Justice Act 2003 - offenders of particular concern);

• Prisoners serving other custodial sentences for an offence described in section 247A(2) of the Criminal Justice Act 2003 (specified terrorist or terrorist connected offences);

• Any other offender who is currently assessed as high or very high risk of serious harm on OASys. All other offenders will be considered under the Standard ROTL regime.

Restricted ROTL includes a number of elements over and above Standard ROTL:

• Offender must be in open prison (men), assessed as suitable for open conditions (women)

• Decision must be made at Governor or deputy Governor level;

• Board must be chaired by a senior manager

• Board must see an enhanced behaviour monitoring (EBM) assessment);

• Enhanced behaviour monitoring for those who require it.

• Mandatory consultation with offender manager and police

• Mandatory comments from the offender manager

• Higher level of monitoring whilst on release

Prisons listed below have been designated as being able to provide Restricted ROTL and include all open prisons, some prisons which have both open and closed conditions on the same site and, because they all have a resettlement focus, all women's prisons. Exceptionally, Restricted ROTL may be delivered from closed, male prisons for offenders who have been assessed as suitable for open conditions but cannot transfer due to their health and/or social care needs. In such cases all the Restricted ROTL elements above apply but EBM is not available so a bespoke psychologist review must be prepared for the ROTL Board.

4.10. Governors must ensure that the purpose, eligibility, frequency and duration criteria are applied appropriately in each case.

Offenders may be released on ROTL to undertake activities that are linked to objectives in their sentence plans, for childcare reasons or in more exceptional circumstances.

**List of prisons designated as being able to provide Restricted ROTL**

Ford

Hatfield

Haverigg

Hollesley Bay

Kirkham

Kirklevington Grange

Leyhill

North Sea Camp
Norwich*
Prescoed
Spring Hill
Standford Hill
Sudbury
Thorn Cross

* = this is a dual site which provides both open and closed conditions. The offender must be located in the open part of the sites prior to being able to apply for ROTL.

All women's prisons have been designated as being able to provide Restricted ROTL for offenders who have been categorised as 'suitable for open conditions'.

### Resettlement Day Release (RDR)

4.11. Offenders may be released on RDR to undertake activities that are linked to objectives in their sentence plans. This is the key criterion and there is no list of approved activities but, in order to be lawful, its purpose must fall under one of the prescribed list of reasons for temporary release under Rule 9(3) of the Prison Rules. Primarily under this heading release must be to engage in paid or voluntary work, to receive instruction or training which cannot reasonably be provided in the prison, or to assist in maintaining family ties or transition from prison to the community. Therefore, under this heading the release should fall under one or more of the following headings:

• Paid or unpaid work placements (Including prisoner apprenticeships)
• Training or Education
• Maintaining family ties
• Prisoner Apprenticeships Pathway
• Accommodation Related
• Outside Prison Activities
• Other activities linked to sentence plan

### Resettlement Overnight Release (ROR)

4.12. The purpose of ROR is to allow offenders to spend time at their release address re-establishing links with family and the local community. Offenders can also use these temporary absences to facilitate interviews for work, training or accommodation.

### Childcare resettlement licence (CRL)

4.13. The purpose of CRL is to encourage the maintenance of the ties between primary carers and their children and to help prepare the offender for the resumption of their parental duties on release.

### Special purpose licence (SPL)

4.14. SPL is generally a short duration temporary release, often at short notice, that allows eligible offenders to respond to exceptional, personal circumstances and to wider criminal justice needs. Grounds for granting SPL include compassionate, medical or court proceedings. More details can be found in the attached guidance.

The Government have said they intend to tighten up on release from prison so please view the current ROTL Policy Framework on *prisonoracle.com* for a table that sets out the current eligibility, frequency and duration for different types of ROTL.

### HOME DETENTION CURFEW (HDC)

Policy name: **Home Detention Curfew (HDC) Policy Framework**
Issue Date: 28 March 2019
Implementation Date: 28 March 2019
**Updated 26th June 2021.**

### 1. PURPOSE

1.1. The Home Detention Curfew (HDC) scheme provides a managed transition from prison to community for offenders serving short sentences. Release on HDC should be a normal part of a sentence for most eligible offenders, and refusal of HDC for those eligible and not presumed unsuitable for release the exception.

1.2. Since 1999, a number of prison and probation instructions have been published in relation to the HDC process. The aim of this Policy Framework is to consolidate those instructions into one place and therefore completely replace all of the previous instructions, as listed above.

The requirements and approach to HDC therefore remain largely the same but the following changes are highlighted:

• Decisions on HDC may now be taken by Directors of Contracted Prisons, the Controller will continue to monitor the Director's compliance in this area.

• Decisions around presumed unsuitable offenders remain with the Governor, but there is no longer any requirement to consult or notify the HDC Policy team.

• Offenders sentenced to 4 years or more imprisonment by an overseas court but who have less than 4 years to serve after repatriation to the UK are presumed unsuitable for release on HDC.

### 2. EVIDENCE

2.1. People released early from prison on HDC are subject to an electronically monitored (EM) curfew. Research evidence about the impact on reoffending rates of using EM curfew with early release is inconclusive but promising, and it appears highly cost effective. The research suggests that the overall outcomes under HDC – especially when costs are taken into account – are preferable to keeping eligible offenders in

| Table 1: ROTL types, eligibility, frequency and duration | | |
|---|---|---|
| Type | Eligibility | Frequency and Duration |
| Resettlement Day Release (RDR) — Standard – from closed men's prisons / women not suitable for open conditions | Either 24 months before the effective release date, or once they have served half the custodial period including remand/tagged bail time (see the formula at 6.33), whichever gives the later date. | The governor must decide the frequency and duration of any release. RDR to maintain family ties should generally be limited to once in every 14 day period unless special resettlement circumstances are found to apply. |
| Standard – from open / women suitable for open conditions | Eligible to be considered from the point of entry into the prison (men)/categorisation (women), subject to appropriate risk assessment. | The governor must decide the frequency and duration of any release. RDR to maintain family ties should generally be limited to once in every 14 day period unless special resettlement circumstances are found to apply. |
| Prisoner Apprenticeship Programme – from open/women suitable for open conditions | Eligible to be considered from point of entry or from 24 months before the earliest release date which-ever is the later. | The governor must decide the frequency and duration of any release. Although an apprenticeship lasts for at least 12 months and requires 30 hours work per week. |
| Restricted | As Standard (from open) but must be assessed as suitable for open conditions and be in a prison which has been designated as being able to provide Restricted ROTL (except where the Parole Board has directed the release of an offender to supported accommodation, such as Approved Premises, or the offender is prevented from transferring to such a prison on health grounds). | The governor must decide the frequency and duration of any release. RDR to maintain family ties should generally be limited to once in every 14 day period unless special resettlement circumstances are found to apply. |
| ISP | As Restricted. | The governor must decide the frequency and duration of any release. RDR to maintain family ties should generally be limited to once in every 14 day period unless special resettlement circumstances are found to apply. |
| Resettlement Overnight Release (ROR) — Standard – from closed men's prisons/ women not suitable for open conditions | Either 6 months before the release date, or once they have served half the custodial period less half the relevant remand time, whichever gives the later date. | ROR should only take place after a period of successful RDR. ROR should be limited to one ROR session in each 28-day period during the eligibility period. The governor must decide the appropriate duration of any period of ROR – this will not usually exceed 4 nights. |
| Standard – from open prisons/ women suitable for open conditions | Eligible to be considered from the point of entry into the prison (men)/categorisation (women), subject to appropriate risk assessment. | ROR should only take place after a period of successful RDR. ROR should be limited to one ROR session in each 28-day period during the eligibility period. The governor must decide the appropriate duration of any period of ROR – this will not usually exceed 4 nights. |
| Restricted | As Standard (from open) but must be assessed as suitable for open conditions and be in a prison which has been designated as being able to provide Restricted ROTL (except where the Parole Board has directed the release of an offender to supported accommodation, such as Approved Premises, or the offender is prevented from transferring to such a prison on health grounds). | As Standard but must be in a prison which has been designated as being able to provide Restricted ROTL. |
| ISP | As Restricted. | As Standard but must be in a prison which has been designated as being able to provide Restricted ROTL. |
| Childcare Resettlement Licence (CRL) — Standard | No minimum eligibility period. Offenders are eligible when they have primary caring responsibilities for a child under 18. If the child attains the age of 18 whilst the offender remains in custody, the offender becomes ineligible for CRL. | CRL may be taken no more than once per week including one period of overnight release in every 28 day period, which must not exceed four nights away from the prison. |
| Restricted | As Standard but must be assessed as suitable for open conditions and be in a prison which has been designated as being able to provide Restricted ROTL. | CRL may be taken no more than once per week including one period of overnight release in every 28 day period which must not exceed four nights away from the prison. |
| ISP | As Restricted. | CRL may be taken no more than once per week including one period of overnight release in every 28 day period which must not exceed four nights away from the prison. |
| Special Purpose Licence (SPL) — Standard | No minimum eligibility period. | SPL will generally be issued in response to a specific event or set of circumstances that would not usually require release on a regular basis. (See attached guidance in 6.23.) |
| Restricted | There is no minimum eligibility period but offenders subject to Restricted ROTL must be assessed as suitable for open conditions and be in a prison that offers Restricted ROTL before being considered for SPL, except where a prisoner is in closed conditions and urgent medical attention is required. | SPL will generally be issued in response to a specific event or set of circumstances that would not usually require release on a regular basis. |
| ISP | As Restricted. | SPL will generally be issued in response to a specific event or set of circumstances that would not usually require release on a regular basis. |

custody at the end of the custodial element of their sentence. EM is a tool to monitor compliance with the curfew, which is part of the sentence, and so enhance supervision in the community.

2.2. In addition to electronically monitored curfew, from 1 April 2019 it will be possible to impose location monitoring requirements as part of the HDC licence conditions across England and Wales.

2.3. Research into the experience of being on EM suggests it may help some people to break habits and limit opportunities to commit crime, enhancing opportunities for employment and training, and allowing relationships, including those of mutual benefit, to develop. The evidential certainty that electronic monitoring provides may act as a deterrent and incentive to comply, although monitoring alone is unlikely to help people to think and behave differently, and successfully desist from crime, in the longer-term. Compliance while on EM may be enhanced by making the process feel as procedurally just as possible, and this means transparent, consistent decisions and procedure, and ensuring people are treated with respect and courtesy.

### 3. OUTCOMES

3.1. This policy aims to ensure that:

• Eligible offenders will be identified accurately and early.

• The process will operate to time without unnecessary delays, particularly to HDC releases.

• Release on HDC will be the norm for eligible offenders, so that most can benefit from the extra stability on release that HDC offers.

• HDC will be refused or postponed for eligible offenders by exception.

This includes:

o when there are outstanding proceedings for offences committed during the current sentence; or

o where the risk management plan cannot be put in place at the proposed release address.

• Those on HDC will be supported to complete HDC successfully by timely consideration of licence variation requests.

### 4. REQUIREMENTS

#### 4.1. Legal Requirements

4.1.1. The statutory requirements of the scheme are set out primarily in section 246 of the Criminal Justice Act 2003. Although there is no statutory entitlement to release on HDC, the policy is that offenders who are eligible and suitable for the scheme are released on, or shortly after the HDC eligibility date (HDCED), wherever possible. HDC is only available to offenders who are serving a sentence of imprisonment of at least 12 weeks but less than

four years who have served the requisite custodial period of the sentence. This is reached once the offender has served at least a quarter of the sentence, and a minimum of 28 days. The maximum period of release is 135 days. As with any sentence, the custodial period might include time on remand in custody or on bail with an EM curfew ("tagged bail"), so release can occasionally take place very soon after sentence, although the law requires at least 14 days in custody post sentence before an offender can be released on HDC.

4.1.2. On release, the offender must be subject to an electronically monitored curfew. This must be for at least 9 hours per day by law, and generally for 12 hours per day as a matter of policy, reflecting the fact that the offender is still serving the custodial element of the sentence. The curfew requirement must remain in force until what would have been the conditional or automatic release date (CRD or ARD) at the halfway point of the sentence.

4.1.3. Certain offenders are excluded in law, and therefore cannot be released on HDC under any circumstances (listed at paragraph 4.3.1.), and others are presumed unsuitable for HDC in policy (listed at paragraph 4.3.7.).

4.1.4. The scheme applies to people of any age (i.e. including those under 18) who are serving sentences of detention under section 91 of the Powers of Criminal Courts (Sentencing) Act 2000 (for certain specified serious offences). HDC does not apply to those sentenced to detention and training orders (DTOs) under section 100 of the Powers of Criminal Courts (Sentencing) Act 2000; separate early release arrangements apply to them.

#### 4.2. OTHER REQUIREMENTS

4.2.1. Section 4.2 lists the key actions that must be completed throughout the HDC process, which are expanded on in more detail in sections 4.3 to 4.11. A digital service to support the HDC process is currently in development. Once launched, this will not affect the principles in this framework but will change aspects of the process, in particular, the way in which prisons and probation providers exchange information about the proposed HDC address. Currently, communication is via a central Clearing House and this will be changed for a shared digital service. Practitioners will be given full information and any necessary training once the digital service is launched.

4.2.2. Governors must ensure there are processes in place to determine eligibility for HDC.

i. The OMU must calculate an offender's HDCED when calculating their CRD or ARD within 5 working days of reception. Within a further 5 working days, the case administrator must establish the offender's eligibility for HDC, or whether they are statutorily excluded or presumed unsuitable, and notify the offender, the responsible officer (RO) and Through the Gate (TTG) provider in the prison of the outcome using the appropriate form (all forms are provided at Annex K).

ii. At least 13 weeks before HDCED in any case where an offender's current immigration status is unclear, the prison should send the HDC – FNP form to the Home Office in order to establish the current position.

iii. The decision maker must consider any representations submitted by offenders who are presumed unsuitable for HDC.

iv. If there are any changes in circumstances which affect an offender's release dates (e.g. other remand, time spent unlawfully at large, additional days are awarded), then the offender's HDCED must be recalculated as well as all other release dates.

v. The offender must not be released on HDC where there are fewer than ten days remaining to the CRD as this will not allow sufficient time for the benefits of HDC.

vi. Where there are 28 days or fewer between the date at which the offender's eligibility has been established and the CRD, the HDC process must not start unless the Governor or delegated decision-maker has agreed to this.

4.2.3. Governors must ensure that there are processes in place to facilitate eligible offenders to propose addresses for release; that the Bail, Accommodation and Support Service (BASS) is used where necessary; and that a check of the proposed release address/area is commissioned promptly.

i. At least 10 weeks prior to the HDCED, where possible, the offender must be provided with the HDC Address form. They must be encouraged to provide more than one address if possible and prioritise them so that they can be assessed in order of preference.

ii. The prison must encourage the offender to complete the Address form and ensure that they can both understand the purpose of the form and complete it.

iii. If an offender wishes to opt out of HDC the reason why must be recorded.

iv. If an offender is unable to propose an address, they must be told about BASS accommodation and asked if they wish to proceed with an application with this accommodation. Where an offender is to be released to BASS accommodation, Governors must ensure that six weeks before release, they are referred to the Local Authority, in accordance with the duty to refer process under the Homelessness Reduction Act 2017 in England and the Housing (Wales) Act

2014. For short sentences the referral would need to be completed as soon as possible.

v. At least nine weeks before the HDCED, the case administrator must send the Address Checks form to probation providers via the HDC Clearing Office (HDC.ClearingOffice@probation.gsi.gov.uk).

4.2.4. Probation providers must have processes in place to ensure that Address Checks forms are completed fully and accurately within 10 working days of receipt, and that all HDC actions are properly recorded on nDelius.

i. In respect of the proposed address, the probation provider must confirm:

• whether the main occupier gives informed consent to HDC (further guidance to probation providers is provided in section 4.5. below, and in Annexes F and G);

• whether the address has an electricity supply;

• reporting instructions;

• any non-standard licence conditions, including any variation on the usual 7pm-7am curfew hours; e.g. to accommodate work pattern;

• whether there are any risk management planning actions that must take place prior to release to that address/area and why release cannot take place in their absence;

• if so, whether further information has been sought and when it is expected; and,

• whether this is a Victim Contact Scheme (VCS) qualifying case and, if so, whether the victims have had an opportunity to comment.

ii. The probation provider is expected to pursue the further information sought from other agencies and to provide it to the prison as soon as it becomes available.

iii. The Address Checks form must be submitted within 10 working days of receipt via the Clearing Office even where the RO is still waiting for information they consider is essential to risk management planning. Where the prison has a query about something the RO has input to (or vice versa), they must contact them directly.

iv. Probation providers must be asked to check one address at a time. If the offender's preferred address is found unsuitable then the second address may be submitted on a further Address Checks form and the RO allowed a further 10 days to complete the form, and so on. Once the proposed addresses are exhausted, BASS options should be explored.

4.2.5. Governors must ensure that suitability for release on HDC is considered consistently and promptly.

i. At least five weeks before the HDCED, where possible, once the Address Checks form has been returned the case administrator must complete sections 1 – 3 of the Assessment & Decision form, and submit to the delegated HDC decision maker.

859

ii. The decision whether or not to release an offender on HDC must be taken by the Governing Governor, who may delegate the decision to a competent member of staff. Directors may delegate this decision to Deputy Directors in the contracted estate.

iii. Before releasing any offender subject to additional criminal proceedings, there must be a check whether there is a remand warrant in relation to any outstanding charges (i.e. whether or not committed during the current sentence).

iv. The decision-maker must authorise release unless any of the exceptional grounds to refuse HDC, or to postpone the decision, listed at paragraphs 4.6.3. and 4.6.4. apply.

4.2.6. Governors and probation providers must have in place processes to ensure that decisions are notified to the offender and relevant third parties.

i. Where HDC has been authorised, the prison must notify the offender using the HDC Approved form.

ii. Where HDC has been authorised, the prison must also notify the RO, the Electronic Monitoring Field & Monitoring Service Provider (EM Provider), the National Identification Service (NIS) at New Scotland Yard and the home police service using the HDC Agency Notification form.

Notification should take place as soon as possible, ideally at least 14 days before release and release must be delayed if at least 24 hours' notice is not possible.

iii. Where the decision maker is satisfied that there are exceptional reasons to refuse HDC, or the decision is being postponed, the offender must be notified using one of the HDC Address Unsuitable/HDC Postponed/HDC Not Enough Time/HDC Refused forms at Annex K, making clear that they may submit an appeal against the refusal and/ or submit another address for consideration. Appeals are processed via the prison complaints system and should be prioritised. Reasons must be provided where HDC is refused.

iv. Where HDC has been refused the prison must copy the appropriate form to the RO.

v. On receipt of the HDC Agency Notification form, the RO must notify the Victim Liaison Officer of the outcome in VCS qualifying cases, so that the victim can be notified of the outcome and any victim focused conditions on the licence.

vi. If circumstances change after release has been agreed and the offender is no longer suitable for HDC, or the details in the HDC Agency Notification form change, notification of the change must be sent using the HDC Cancellation/Variation of Agency Notification form to the other agencies originally notified.

4.2.7. Governors must have in place processes to ensure that appropriate release arrangements are made.

i. All offenders must be released on licence using one of the templates in the Licence Policy Framework.

ii. The Governor must set the curfew hours to reflect the particular needs of the case.

iii. Before release, offenders must have the licence conditions explained to them and must sign the licence, to confirm they accept the conditions;

iv. Offenders cannot be released on HDC until the requisite period has been served. Where an offender's HDCED falls on a Weekend or Bank Holiday the offender must not be released on HDC until the next working day.

v. On the day of release the offender must be released in sufficient time to ensure that they can attend any appointment necessary on the day of release and arrive at their home address in advance of the curfew.

4.2.8. Governors must ensure there are processes in place for inter-prison transfer during the HDC process.

i. Inter-prison transfers should be done as quickly as possible to the appropriate prison. If the offender reaches the point at which HDC should be started then the holding prison must still ensure the process is commenced, keeping clear records on NOMIS.

ii. Governors must ensure that there is a process in place so that all Offender Management Unit (OMU) paperwork, including that for ongoing HDC, is sent with an offender moving to a new prison as part of a planned transfer.

iii. The responsible officer (RO) must be notified of the transfer and where the completed Address Checks form should now be sent.

iv. If process fails for any reason, the sending OMU must contact the receiving OMU to inform them of the HDC stage that has been reached and make sure that any paperwork not recorded on NOMIS and any reports received after transfer are forwarded as a priority.

v. HDC paperwork that has not travelled with the offender must be scanned and/or sent by email to the appropriate functional mailbox at the receiving prison.

4.2.9. Governors must have in place processes to consider requests to vary conditions attached to HDC licences and requests to authorise absences from curfew.

i. The Governor (or NPS RO for offenders released to Wales) must consider any request for a variation in licence conditions on its merits. Licence conditions must not normally be changed where it is reasonable to expect the offender to continue to abide by them and they do not conflict with the objective of providing a stable transition back into the community. Documentary evidence (e.g. of changes in working hours) may be required.

ii. Where the offender applies to vary the licence conditions they must be advised by the governor and the RO (if the request comes via the RO) that they must abide by the current licence conditions until the variation has been authorised.

iii. The curfew address must not be changed without an assessment of the suitability of the new address by the relevant probation provider.

iv. The EM provider may authorise one-off absences from curfew in circumstances prescribed in paragraphs 4.9.11. and 4.9.12. below but other one-off absences and any permanent changes to licence conditions must be authorised by the Governor on behalf of the Secretary of State.

4.2.10. Governors must ensure there are processes in place to drive and monitor the timeliness of the HDC process, and that records of all HDC actions are properly recorded on NOMIS.

i. Eligible offenders must be identified early and all stages of the process (see Annex B) completed in line with the timetable in Annex A.

## 4.3. ELIGIBILITY AND PRESUMED UNSUITABILITY

This section sets out the eligibility criteria, how to deal with representations from offenders presumed unsuitable for HDC and how to calculate the HDCED.

Statutory eligibility criteria

4.3.1. The following are statutorily excluded from HDC.

• Anyone sentenced to 4 years or more for any offence.
• Sex offenders required to register.
• Offenders convicted of violent or sexual offences currently serving an extended sentence.
• Offenders serving a sentence for ROTL failure to return.
• Offenders serving a sentence for breach of the curfew requirement of a Community Order.
• Foreign national prisoners (FNPs) who have been recommended for deportation by the court and those who are liable to deportation and a decision to deport has been served (i.e. not just those with a Deportation Order).
• Offenders with less than 14 days to CRD from date of sentence.
• Offenders who have ever been recalled to prison for failing to comply with the HDC curfew conditions.
• Offenders who have ever been returned to custody by the court for committing an imprisonable offence during the at-risk period.
• Offenders currently serving a recall from early release on compassionate grounds.

4.3.2. The table at Annex C provides details of the different types of recall or return to custody and the effect that this has on HDC eligibility.

Fine defaulters and contemnors

4.3.3. Fine defaulters and contemnors, whether civil or criminal, are not eligible for HDC, since they are serving a term of imprisonment, not a sentence of imprisonment. However, where an offender is serving a criminal sentence (e.g. for drugs offences or fraud) and consecutive to this criminal sentence the offender is to serve a default term for non-payment, the offender may still be considered for HDC on the criminal sentence providing there is a minimum of ten days to spend on HDC between the end of the custodial period of the default term and the CRD of the original sentence.

Presumed unsuitable offenders

4.3.4. To maintain public confidence in the scheme, certain offenders are presumed unsuitable for release on HDC. These offenders are statutorily eligible to be considered for HDC but are, as a matter of policy, presumed unsuitable for the scheme in the absence of exceptional circumstances.

4.3.5. The following offenders are presumed unsuitable.

• Anyone serving a sentence for any of the following categories of offence:
  • homicide;
  • explosives;
  • possession of an offensive weapon;
  • possession of firearms with intent;
  • cruelty to children;
  • racially aggravated offences;
  • terrorism.
• Anyone with a history of sexual offending but not required to register.
• Anyone who has been recalled for poor behaviour whilst on HDC.
• Foreign national prisoners liable to deportation but not yet served with a decision to deport.
• Offenders sentenced to 4 years or more imprisonment by an overseas court but who have less than 4 years to serve after repatriation to the UK.
• Category A offenders.

4.3.6. Offenders who are presumed unsuitable for HDC may submit representations to the governing Governor if they consider that their case is exceptional. How to determine whether there are exceptional circumstances will depend on the reason why the offender is presumed unsuitable. Once satisfied that there are exceptional circumstances, then the offender may be considered for HDC as normal.

4.3.7. Where the Governor does not accept that the representations amount to exceptional circumstances, the offender must be given clear, detailed reasons why and the avenue for appeal is via the prison complaints system.

4.3.8. Further guidance on identifying presumed unsuitable offenders and applying the exceptional circumstances test is given in annex D. A list of examples of presumed unsuitable offences is given at annex E.

Presumed unsuitability when there are multiple convictions

4.3.9. An offender is presumed unsuitable for HDC if any sentence forming part of the overall sentence envelope currently being served is in respect of a presumed unsuitable offence.

4.3.10. If one of the offences is ineligible (e.g. a failure to return from ROTL offence) then the offender cannot be released on HDC whilst that sentence is being served and will be presumed unsuitable throughout the overall sentence envelope.

4.3.11. In relation to offenders serving sentences imposed before 3 December 2012 for offences committed before 4 April 2005 - Schedule 20B of the CJA 2003 sentences (previously known as CJA 1991 sentences) - the sentences form a single term and if any sentence within that single term is a statutorily excluded sentence, the offenders will be statutorily excluded on the single term.

Notorious Offenders

4.3.12. Where, following completion of the assessment process, the Governor considers that the release on HDC of an otherwise suitable offender may seriously damage public confidence in the scheme, they must consult their Group Director and the case must be referred to the Director General Prisons for a final decision. It is expected that such cases will be extremely rare and will likely involve offenders who have been involved in a nationally notorious crime or a crime of particular concern to the public, where release would bring the scheme into disrepute.

4.3.13. Offenders whose cases are to be referred for a final decision must be informed that this rests with the Director General Prisons and that they may submit reasons to them why release should be granted.

4.3.14. Cases referred to the Director General Prisons must include all HDC assessment papers and a covering note with any relevant information that may indicate that release could undermine public confidence.

No separate penalty

4.3.15. Where an offender has been convicted of a presumed unsuitable offence but the court disposal is recorded as "no separate penalty", this should not be treated as serving a sentence of imprisonment for the purposes of considering HDC. Where the "no separate penalty" relates to a sexual offence, the effect will still be to make the offender presumed unsuitable because the presumption applies to those with any history of sexual offending and arises from any conviction for a sexual offence.

4.3.16. The eligibility date is determined by length of sentence, **as set out in the above table.**

4.3.17. Please note when using a date calculator, the 'actual date of sentence' means you use the date the sentence was imposed and not the day before as you may do for other calculations and the 'effective CRD' is the CRD after any relevant adjustments e.g. remand/tagged bail have been applied.

4.3.18. Where applying the remand time to the calculation provides an HDCED which would fall before the date of sentence, the date of sentence plus 14 days should be used as the HDCED.

**Multiple sentences**

4.3.19. Annex F sets out in detail the instructions and principles for calculating HDC eligibility and HDCED in multiple sentence cases.

**4.4 ESTABLISHING PROPOSED ADDRESS**

This section sets out key actions around encouraging completion of the Address form, as well as information on BASS accommodation.

**Encouraging completion of the Proposed Address form**

4.4.1 When encouraging completion of the form, prisons must:

• make sure the offender can read and/or understand it;

• make sure they know that the address they nominate must be assessed as suitable by the probation provider (i.e. not to submit an address they know will be found unsuitable);

• ask them to nominate an alternative address where possible;

• ensure that they give full contact details, including at least one phone number for the address – even where this is housing association or local authority (it cannot be assumed that the RO will know). The number can be a mobile telephone number or landline and they should also give their own telephone number if known); and

• encourage the offender to consider BASS as an alternative, if they have no address to nominate.

4.4.2 Governors may wish to consider the use of peer supporters/prison signpost workers to help HDC eligible offenders to complete the Address form and to promote HDC and BASS.

**The Bail, Accommodation and Support Service (BASS)**

4.4.3 BASS referrals should only take place once the probation provider has indicated that the nominated area is acceptable under the address checks process.

4.4.4 Under the BASS referral criteria, offenders will be ineligible for BASS if they:

• have a conviction, caution, a current allegation of or are under police bail for any sexual offences mentioned in Schedule 3 of the Sexual Offences Act 2003;

• have been assessed by OASys to currently pose a High or Very High risk of serious harm;

- are under 18 years of age; or
- are assessed as posing an unacceptable risk to:
  - the EM provider, their property or staff;
  - other residents of the property;
  - the service user themselves;
  - neighbours; or
  - any other person.

The BASS provider may refuse any case where they consider that there is insufficient information on which to make an adequate assessment of risk.

4.4.5 If an offender does not meet the BASS referral criteria and they have not proposed any other release address, HDC should be refused on the grounds there is no suitable address.

4.4.6 If referred to BASS and the provider confirms that there is no suitable BASS address in the proposed area, the provider may suggest a BASS address in another area. The offender should be asked whether they are content to be considered for release to that area, subject to the views of the RO. If so, the HDC process should continue. If not, or there is no address available, HDC should be refused on the grounds there is no suitable address.

4.4.7 If an offender is accepted for a BASS address but the address does not become available before there are 10 days left to CRD, then HDC should be refused on the grounds that there is no suitable address.

4.4.8 In cases where a BASS referral is successful and HDC is approved, the RO will be notified of the release and release address ideally at least two weeks before the release as part of the normal notification procedures.

4.4.9 Questions about the scheme provider should be directed to the provider, currently NACRO, on 0300 555 0264 or 07423 434032, or email referrals@wmnacro.cjsm.net.

4.4.10 Questions about BASS in general can be directed to the BASS Contract Management Team at BASS1@justice.gov.uk.

4.4.11 The latest instructions and guidance on BASS, including further detail on BASS exclusions and how to make a BASS referral, are included in the BASS Policy Framework and associated BASS Stakeholder User Guidance.

### 4.5 ADDRESS CHECKS PROCESS
See Annex G to the June 2021 updated Policy Framework available on The Prison Oracle.

This section deals with informed consent and address suitability checks requirements.

4.5.1 The first step of the process is for the prison to complete part 1 of the Address Checks form which includes the offender's details, proposed addresses and main occupier contact details, and whether a BASS Referral is to be considered. Once part 1 is completed the form should be sent

to the RO via the Clearing Office nine weeks before HDCED where possible.

4.5.2 Once they receive the Address Checks form, the RO must complete part 2, by confirming that the main occupier gives informed consent to HDC at the address, and that the address is suitable for release on HDC by confirming the requirements listed at paragraph 4.2.6. above. The RO must ensure that the form is completed and returned within ten working days of receipt.

**Informed consent**

4.5.3 The RO must contact the main occupier at the address to explain the nature of HDC so that they know what to expect and how that will impact on their lives. In multiple occupancy accommodation, where there are shared facilities, it is not expected that the RO would normally contact other residents at the address unless they will live in the same room(s) as the offender.

4.5.4 The main occupier must be invited to ask questions about HDC and to raise any concerns they have. They must also be asked to identify all the other occupants of the address and give their ages. Where there are any children under 18 at the house, the main occupier must be asked to confirm whether any of the children is known to Children's Services. They must be advised that if they have concerns during the HDC period they should raise these with the RO. The main occupier should be advised that staff of the EM provider may call at the property without advanced warning from 07:00 until 23:59:59. In addition calls will be made to the monitoring unit if it determines that the subject is not present during the curfew period, this can result in calls throughout the night.

4.5.5 All reasonable efforts should be made to establish contact with the main occupier but as soon as this point has been reached (i.e. before the 10-day deadline), the HDC Address Checks form should be suitably completed and returned, so that the prison can try to get better contact details or another address from the offender and the process can continue with the minimum of delay. **Suitability of the address and consulting the NPS victim liaison officer (VLO)**

4.5.6 It is for the RO to determine whether, based on the available information and using their professional judgement, any non-standard licence conditions and/or any other specified risk management planning actions must be taken before release, in order for the address to be considered suitable and for the offender to be managed safely at that address after release. This may include GPS location monitoring, but only where this facility is necessary to manage the offender safely; i.e. where the address would otherwise be rejected as unsuitable. Location monitoring can be used to:

• enforce an exclusion zone – the offender cannot enter a specific location or area;

• keep the offender at a given distance from a point or address, including the victim's address or that of a known criminal associate;

• monitor an offender's attendance at a certain activity – for example work or a rehabilitation programme; or

• monitor an offender's movements to support discussions with probation about an offender's lifestyle and behaviours (known as "trail monitoring").

4.5.7 When returning the form, the RO must indicate whether a home visit was conducted and why, and make clear where specific information has been requested from other agencies because they think it is essential to have the information before release. They must indicate when they expect to receive the information, arrange to chase for the information and provide it to the prison offender supervisor as soon as it becomes available.

4.5.8 Victim and families of victims of serious sexual and violent offending who have opted into the VCS operated by NPS must be afforded a reasonable opportunity to make representations about licence conditions. The RO must indicate on the relevant form if the case is VCS qualifying and victims should be given two weeks to make representations but their views must be considered whenever received and, where necessary, changes to licence conditions made.

4.5.9 Further guidance for probation providers on completing address suitability checks can be found in Annex G.

**Address Checks by one probation provider on behalf of another**

4.5.10 Where the proposed address is in a different area to the allocated RO, responsibility for returning the completed Address Checks form remains with the allocated RO even where they have asked another probation provider to conduct the check. Probation providers should work together to try to ensure that the form is returned within the ten-day time limit. To facilitate this, the provider responsible for the completion of the report should alert the area checking the address as early as possible within the ten-day time frame.

**4.6 ASSESSMENT AND DECISION**

This section sets out where HDC should be postponed or refused.

4.6.1 Once the Address Checks form has been returned to the prison, the Assessment and Decision Form must be completed by the case admin and the decision-maker.

4.6.2 The decision-maker must authorise release unless the following exceptional grounds to refuse HDC, or to postpone the decision, apply.

4.6.3 HDC must be refused where:

• it is not possible to manage the offender safely at the proposed address; or

• there are fewer than 10 days remaining to CRD.

4.6.4 The HDC decision must be postponed where:

• specific public protection measures have been identified and planned to manage risk in the community but they are not yet in place; or

• the offender has been referred to the police or other law enforcement agency or to the independent adjudicator (IA) in relation to an alleged offence committed during the current sentence and the matter remains unresolved; or

• the offender is the subject of a confiscation order and, having consulted the prosecuting/enforcement authority and regional confiscation unit (details in PSI 16/2010 Confiscation Orders), it is determined by the HDC decision-maker that there is an unacceptable risk of the offender frustrating the order of the court by, for example, going to ground, leaving the jurisdiction or hiding assets if released on HDC. Where there is evidence that the offender has frustrated proceeds of crime proceedings in order to avoid a confiscation order being imposed, HDC should also be postponed until that is resolved.

4.6.5 If the offender is under investigation and/or facing criminal or IA proceedings for an offence committed during the current sentence, the HDC assessment process may be started at the usual time so that if the case is discontinued or dismissed there is no additional delay in processing HDC. Where some time has elapsed since the matter was referred there should be a check to verify the current status before deciding to postpone the HDC decision, with regular checks thereafter. "Current sentence" in this instruction is to be taken to include the whole of the current, unbroken custodial period, including time on remand or serving civil or criminal terms of imprisonment.

4.6.6 Where the offender is found guilty by the courts or IA of an offence committed during the current sentence, they must serve the penalty imposed before they can be released on HDC.

4.6.7 Where added days are awarded, the release dates must be adjusted accordingly and the offender must be considered for release on or after the adjusted HDCED.

4.6.8 Where a further sentence of imprisonment is imposed concurrently, fresh release dates will be calculated in relation to the new sentence and, if the offender remains eligible for HDC, they must be considered for release on or after the latest HDCED. Where a further sentence is imposed consecutively, fresh release dates (including a new HDCED) will be calculated for the aggregate created. If the offender remains eligible for HDC, they must be considered for release in line with the new HDCED.

4.6.9 Such considerations of HDC against revised HDC eligibility dates must be made on the same basis as other HDC considerations for eligible offenders; i.e. the disciplinary or criminal offence will have led to additional time in custody being served, but if the offender remains eligible for HDC then the assessment of suitability for HDC, and whether to approve or refuse HDC or postpone the decision, must be made in accordance with the standard provisions of this Policy Framework.

4.6.10 Where HDC is refused because the address is unsuitable, a further address may be considered if there is time (i.e. at least four weeks to CRD).

4.6.11 Guidance on recording the HDC decision is included in Annex A.

## 4.7 NOTIFYING THE OFFENDER OF THE DECISION Guidance is set out in annex H.

## 4.8 SETTING THE CURFEW CONDITIONS Guidance is set out in annex I.

## 4.9 POST-RELEASE PROCEDURES

This section sets out the process for amending HDC licence conditions, as well as circumstances in which one-off absences can be authorised.

### General

4.9.1 Currently, the Governor is responsible for varying HDC licence conditions and dealing with requests from the offender to authorise certain one-off absences from the curfew address, except where the offender is managed by the NPS and has been released to an address in Wales. In those cases, the responsibility lies with the NPS. In due course, the arrangements in Wales will apply to all offenders released on HDC but the remainder of section 4.9 has been drafted to reflect the position that applies in the majority of cases currently.

4.9.2 Statutory probation supervision commences on the day of release, whether this is on HDC or at the CRD/ARD. Where an offender is released on HDC they are subject to the HDC conditions in addition to the supervision conditions attached to the licence.

4.9.3 Offenders must be made aware of the requirements to:

• comply with the curfew and other EM monitoring conditions set out in their licence until the date given in the licence, unless a temporary absence has been formally authorised, or until they have been formally notified by the EM provider if the Governor has amended the conditions of their licence; and

• contact the EM provider immediately when they are aware that they will have difficulties in complying with their curfew conditions. This is regardless of whether they have already contacted their offender manager/responsible officer or the prison. Depending on the circumstances, the EM provider may refer the offender to their RO and/or the prison that released them.

4.9.4 PPCS, acting on behalf of the Secretary of State, is responsible for deciding whether to authorise recall of an offender released on HDC, issue a warning letter to them or take no further action. (The EM provider may also issue warning letters for minor infringements of EM conditions). If the offender is recalled to custody, the prison will need to assist in administering any appeal process (the appeal itself is determined by the MOJ HDC Recall Appeals Team).

4.9.5 Further requirements and guidance around the HDC recall and the recall appeals process is set out in the Recall, Review and Re-release of Recalled Prisoners Policy Framework.

**One-off absences**

4.9.6 In certain, clearly prescribed circumstances the EM provider may grant one-off absences during the curfew period. The absence may be authorised only where the offender provides the EM provider with sufficient written proof of the reason for the authorised absence, either 24 hours before the absence or within 48 hours of the absence for emergency absences. EM.

4.9.7 The circumstances are:

• attending a wedding or funeral of a close relative - meaning a spouse (including a partner with whom the subject is living as a spouse), parent or child (including in loco parentis relationships), sibling (including half and step) or fiancée));

• irregular or unexpected personal medical appointments/treatment;

• irregular or unexpected medical appointments/treatment for the subject's child or adult dependents;

• attendance at job interviews, jobcentres, or elsewhere in connection with any claims for financial assistance;

• attendance as a witness in court or as required by the court; or

• other appointments involving the Subject's immediate dependents where the Subject's presence is required.

4.9.8 Emergency absence reasons (which may be authorised after the event) include:

• where emergency medical treatment for the subject or his/her immediate dependents is required and other emergencies involving the subject's immediate dependents where the subject's presence is required;

• where the offender has been required to work at short notice, the work forms part of a permanent job, is not just a "one-off" piece of work, and the

employer has provided written verification that the work was required and took place; or
• where the offender has been held in police custody during the curfew period and the police verify this.

4.9.9 The period authorised must be limited to the length of the event, plus a maximum of 1.5 hours travelling each way. The EM provider must approve the minimum required time, which must not normally exceed 8 hours and may never exceed 24 hours.

4.9.10 Where the circumstances do not fall within these prescriptions prison Governors may authorise one-off absences, and may consult the RO for advice or verification. Where the Governor authorises a one-off absence from curfew, a copy of the Licence Variation form will be sent to the probation provider, plus the EM provider and the police. In such cases there is no need for a revised licence to be issued, as this is an authorised absence rather than an amendment to the licence conditions. However, any such one-off variation must still leave at least 9 hours in the day where the offender is subject to curfew.

**Permanent changes to curfew/address licence conditions**

4.9.11 If the prison receives a request for a change of address which it considers merits assessment, it must send the HDC Licence Variation form to the probation provider to confirm that the new address is suitable for HDC. They may also contact the EM provider if further information is required about the offender's performance on curfew but the EM providers have no say in the decision or assessment.

4.9.12 In some cases, where the offender is unable to continue living at the present curfew address, a swift authorisation may be required. Further details can be found at Annex I. If the probation provider considers that an adequate assessment cannot be carried out in the time (for instance if a home visit is required), then the licence must not be changed.

4.9.13 It is essential in such cases that the EM provider is notified immediately so that they are able to inform any breach reports sent to PPCS. It is also essential that the probation provider maintains a clear record of advice given to the offender. In considering enforcement action, PPCS will consult the relevant probation provider for a view on how soon a new, suitable address will be available. If it is clear that this will lead to the offender being unmonitored for more than 24 hours, PPCS should be contacted immediately. If a suitable address cannot be found swiftly, recall to prison on the grounds of "inability to monitor" will be considered by PPCS. Such a recall will allow for the re-release of the

offender if a suitable new address can be confirmed.

4.9.14 If the offender approaches the probation provider directly requesting a change to the curfew address or times, the probation provider must contact the releasing prison and advise the offender to remain at the current address or continue with the current curfew until the variation request is approved by the prison Governor and notification of the variation is received. In submitting a request for a variation of curfew times, the probation provider should provide start/end dates as relevant and documentary evidence that the variation is necessary i.e. to enable an offender to take up employment during hours that conflict with their curfew.

4.9.15 If a licence variation relating to curfew/address is authorised:
• Where there is a permanent change to the curfew conditions a new licence is issued and a copy must be sent, along with the HDC Licence Variation form, to the EM provider, the probation provider, National Identification Service (NIS) and the home police force. Where there is an address variation the EM provider will visit the address to move the equipment.
• Where visiting the address, the EM provider will outline the licence variation and get the offender to sign electronically to confirm that this has happened Otherwise they will phone the offender to explain the changes and when they will come into effect, and have the subject repeat the changes back to ensure that they are understood. In each case, the EM provider will post a hard copy of the licence to the offender.

4.9.16 If a licence variation is refused:
• Offenders must be notified of the reasons for any refusal. Where an application to change the curfew conditions is refused, the EM provider must be informed of the outcome of the application.
• The probation provider must also be informed. The offender may appeal to the Governing Governor against the decision not to vary the licence conditions.

**Prolonged absence in hospital or for court proceedings**

4.9.17 If the offender or the EM provider informs the prison that the offender is due to spend a prolonged period in hospital, the licence must not be amended so that the offender is curfewed to the hospital. In such cases Governors have instead the discretion to instruct the EM provider to treat the absence as an allowable absence, provided the offender can provide documentary evidence as required for such absences. When notifying the EM provider, the prison should make clear how long the allowable absence is allowed to last, up to a maximum of four days. If the hospital stay lasts longer than four days, it may be necessary to issue further extensions to cover the remainder of the stay. The extension of the allowable absence does not rescind the curfew and as soon as the offender is discharged from hospital he or she is once again required to comply with their curfew at the specified address, whether or not any days remain of the allowable absence authorised by the prison.

4.9.18 If an offender is required to attend a court which it is not possible to travel to in one day from the offender's curfew address, the Governor may agree the extension of the allowable absence to cover a period of up to 3 days rather than require that a new curfew address be imposed. Again, the EM provider must be informed. Such an allowable absence must not be allowed to exceed 72 hours. If it is anticipated that the offender will be required to attend the court proceedings for more than three days, it will be necessary to amend the licence to provide for a temporary curfew to an address in the vicinity of the court. As soon as the rationale for the offender's absence ceases, he or she must once more be at their specified address during curfew hours.

## 4.10. CROSS-BORDER HDC

4.10.1. Governors must follow the requirements and guidelines set out at Annex J in relation to cross border HDC.

## 4.11. HDC FOR CHILDREN

4.11.1. The scheme applies to children who are serving sentences of detention under section 91 of the Powers of Criminal Courts (Sentencing) Act 2000 (for certain specified serious offences). All of the statutory provisions on HDC apply equally to eligible children as does the policy set out in this framework, subject to the following variations.

4.11.2. The decisions ascribed to the Governor or delegated decision-maker above must be taken by the Governor or delegated decision-maker in relation to any child held in a Young Offender Institution. Appeals against HDC decisions in YOIs, including where the Governor does not accept that there are grounds to assess a presumed unsuitable offender exceptionally for HDC, should be made via the local appeals process or prison complaints system procedures

4.11.3. In relation to a child held in a Secure Training Centre (STC) or in a local authority Secure Children's Home (SCH), these decisions must be taken by HMPPS Youth Custody Service (YCS) Release and Resettlement Team, who will also be responsible for determining HDC eligibility and the eligibility date. The YCS will also be the avenue of appeal against decisions. Where a YCS decision is appealed, the appeal must be considered by a member of YCS staff not involved in the original decision.

4.11.4. Address Checks forms must be sent directly to and completed by the youth offending team, and returned directly to the YOI or STC/SCH.

4.11.5. Records of all HDC actions should be made on NOMIS or on the Youth Justice Assessment Framework (YJAF) as appropriate.

4.11.6. The forms at annex K may be used with children, subject to appropriate adaptation reflecting the different places of detention and decision-maker, and to include details of the responsible adult.

Annex A

Timeframe for HDC process and Recording decisions on NOMIS

The following table is a guideline with recommended timings based on, for illustrative purposes, an offender serving a sentence of 40 weeks or more. Shorter sentences and remand time will mean that a shorter timetable will be necessary.

For sentence/resettlement planning purposes, it is recommended that those involved in HDC work on the assumption that the HDCED will be the release date, in all cases where the offender is eligible and not presumed unsuitable, until the point where HDC has been refused. Probation providers should work on the basis that this will be the release date when they are giving reporting instructions on the Address Checks form.

**The HDC decision should be recorded on NOMIS as follows:**

**Approved:** where there are no exceptional reasons to refuse/postpone.

**Rejected:** where it is not possible to manage the offender safely at the proposed address or there are fewer than ten days to CRD.

**Postponed** (outstanding risk): where the address has not yet been ruled out as unsuitable but it is not possible to approve release because there is a risk management planning action required before release. Once this is resolved, the Assessment and Decision Form must be updated accordingly and a decision must be taken. Once notified that the HDC decision has been postponed for these reasons, the offender may choose to withdraw this address and submit another.

**Postponed (investigation):** where the offender is under investigation and/or facing criminal or IA proceedings for an offence committed during the current sentence. Or there is an outstanding confiscation order and it has been determined that release on HDC would frustrate the order of the court.

## EARLY REMOVAL SCHEME (ERS)

See Section 2.18 Foreign Nationals - but note that Early Removal of Foreign National Prisoners PSI 04/2013 was updated on 15th June 2022 so as to increase the ERS window from 270 days before the earliest release point to 12 months before the earliest release point.

**TERS Tariff-Expired Removal Scheme**
See Section 2.18 Foreign Nationals

**LIFERS**
See Section 2.14 of the Handbook

## SEX OFFENDERS

The Sex Offender Act 1997 requires any designated (Schedule one) sex offenders to notify the police of their name and address and any changes to these details should they take place. The Act was implemented on 21 March 1997 but is not retrospective. Sex Offenders released from prison must register upon their release. The register is held on the Police National Computer. The time period for which registration applies mirrors the time periods in the Rehabilitation of Offenders Act 1974 (see separate section on Rehabilitation of Offenders Act)) and time periods commence from the date of conviction, with subsequent time in prison or hospital being discounted. For offenders below the age of 18 the registration period is halved. The details must now be given in person by a visit to a police station; they are no longer allowed in writing. The police must also be notified if the person stays at any other address for longer than two weeks in a 12-month period (s.2(2)). Any failure to comply is punishable by a fine up to £5,000 and/or a period of imprisonment up to six months. There has been continued concern that the Register is not retrospective. As a response to this concern, Sex Offender Orders were introduced in the Crime and Disorder Act 1998 section 2-4 (England and Wales) and sections 20-22 (Scotland). Applications are made by the police through the local courts. In order for an application to be successful, the individual concerned must be a convicted sex offender and must have given, through their behaviour since conviction and since the commencement of the 1998 Act, reasonable cause for the belief that the Order is necessary to protect the public from serious harm. Sex Offender Orders require that those subject to the Order register under the Sex Offences Act 1997 for their duration. The minimum length of time for an Order is five years. Breach of the Order is a criminal offence with a maximum penalty of five years imprisonment.

## DISCHARGE CLOTHING

Prisoners are usually expected to wear their own clothes on release. Rule 23(6) of the Prison Rules 1999 states that a 'prisoner may be provided, where necessary, with suitable and adequate clothing on his release.' The Discharge policy (PSI 72/2011) states, at para 2.31, that 'those prisoners who need adequate clothing for release will be given it.' The terms 'suitable' and 'adequate' are not defined within the Prison Rules nor the Discharge policy, as what is 'adequate' will vary depending on the circumstances of each prisoner and it is down to the judgement of the Governor, taking into account these circumstances.

## REHABILITATION OF OFFENDERS ACT
**Purpose**

The ROA primarily exists to support the rehabilitation into employment of reformed offenders who have stayed on the right side of the law - ROA was being revised following the implementation of changes included in the Legal Aid and Sentencing and Punishment of Offenders Act 2012.

Under the 1974 Act, following a specified period of time which varies according to the disposal administered or sentence passed, cautions and convictions (except those resulting in prison sentences of over four years and all public protection sentences*) may become spent.

As a result the offender is regarded as rehabilitated. For most purposes the 1974 Act treats a rehabilitated person as if he or she had never committed, or been charged with charged or prosecuted for or convicted of or sentenced for the offence and, as such, they are not required to declare their spent caution(s) or conviction(s), for example, when applying for most jobs or insurance, some educational courses and housing applications.

*A public protection sentence, the provisions for which are set out in Part 12 of the Criminal Justice Act 2003 and Part 8 of the Armed Forces Act 2006, means a imprisonment or detention imposed for specified sexual and violent offences. These sentences include imprisonment for public protection, extended sentences of imprisonment or detention for public protection, and extended determinate sentences

All cautions and convictions may eventually become spent, with the exception of prison sentences, or sentences of detention for young offenders, of over four years and all public protection sentences regardless of the length of sentence. Cautions are spent immediately, once a conviction has become spent under the 1974 Act, a person does not have to reveal it or admit its existence in most circumstances. Unless an exception applies (see below).

## THE ROA EXCEPTIONS ORDER

Several occupations, professions, and licenses are exempt from the above provisions under the Rehabilitation of Offenders Act 1974 (Exceptions) Order 1975. Posts which involve a significant level of trust, and positions involving work with children and vulnerable adults are among these exceptions.

You should be informed during the application process if the post you are applying for is excepted from the ROA rules. Employers for such positions are entitled to ask potential employees about spent as well as unspent convictions, and job applicants are not entitled under the Act to withhold information about spent convictions when asked. Whether an offence is spent or unspent, it is ultimately for employers to make the final decision on employment of the individual.

### Ex-offenders and employment

Employers can't turn someone down for a job because they've been convicted of an offence if the conviction or caution is 'spent' - unless an exception applies.

Job applicants don't need to tell potential employers about spent convictions or cautions.

### How long will it take before my caution or conviction becomes spent?

The rehabilitation period (the length of time before a caution or conviction becomes spent) is determined by the type of disposal administered or the length of the sentence imposed.

Rehabilitation periods for custodial sentences run beyond the end of a sentence and are made up of the total sentence length plus an additional period that runs from the end of the sentence, which is called the 'buffer period'. The law on rehabilitation periods can be complex so you should always seek individual legal advice about your own particular circumstances.

Other non-custodial rehabilitation periods start from the date of conviction or the date the penalty was imposed. *It is important to realise that buffer periods start from the end of a sentence (including any licence period) and not from the date of the offence or conviction.*

### RECALL

**Policy name: Recall, Review and Re-Release of Recalled Prisoners Policy Framework**

**Updated 21st July 2022:** This Policy Framework has been updated by removal of all references to CRC following the Probation Service unification. All references to NPS amended to Probation Service. A number of changes have been made to the chapters **4.2** (Recalling an Indeterminate Sentenced Individual and Extended Sentenced Individuals); **4.3** (Recalling all Other Determinate Sentenced Individuals); **4.9** (Return to Custody of all Recalled Prisoners); **4.10** (This section of the Policy Framework applies to determinate sentenced prisoners (including extended sentence prisoners) and indeterminate sentenced prisoners subject to standard recall provisions); **4.11** (Fixed Term Recall – Review and Re-

Release); **4.17** (Parole Board Oral Hearings - This section of the Policy Framework applies to all recalled prisoners, where the Parole Board has directed that an oral hearing take place, unless otherwise stated); and **6.9** of the Framework - Standard Recall - Statutory Day 28 Review.

## CONTENTS

1 Purpose
2 Evidence
3 Outcomes
4 Requirements
Part I
Recall
4.1 Requesting a Recall
4.2 Recalling an Indeterminate Sentenced Individual
4.3 Recalling Determinate Sentenced Individuals
4.4 Recalling an Individual subject to Home Detention Curfew (HDC)
4.5 Recalling a Young Individual
4.6 Out of Hours (OoH) Recall Requests
4.7 Rescind of Recall
4.8 Unlawfully at Large (UAL) Following Recall
Part II
Return to Custody, Review and Re-Release
4.9 Return to Custody of all Recalled Prisoners
4.10 Standard recall- Statutory Day 28 Review
4.11 Fixed Term Recall - Review and Re-release
4.12 HDC Curfew Breach - Appeal process
4.13 Young Individuals - Review and Re-release
4.14 Executive Release
4.15 Ongoing Review
4.16 Annual Review
4.17 Parole Board Oral Hearings
5 Constraints
6 Guidance
6.1 Recalling an Indeterminate Sentenced Individual
6.2 Recalling Determinate Sentenced Individuals
6.3 Recalling an Individual subject to Home Detention Curfew (HDC)
6.4 Recalling a Young Individual
6.5 Out of Hours (OoH) Recall Requests
6.6 Rescind of Recall
6.7 Unlawfully at Large (UAL) Following Recall
6.8 Return to Custody of all Recalled Prisoners
6.9 Standard Recall - Statutory Day 28 Review
6.10 Fixed Term Recall - Review and Re-Release
6.11 HDC Curfew Breach - Appeal Process
6.12 Executive Release
6.13 Ongoing Review
6.14 Annual review
6.15 Parole Board Oral Hearings
Annex A Best Practice Guide: Working with Recalled Prisoners
Annex B Information regarding section 32ZA Crime (Sentences) Act 1997 Unlawfully at Large Offence

# 1 Purpose

1. Determinate and indeterminate sentenced prisoners who are released into the community subject to licensed supervision are liable to be recalled to custody by the Secretary of State, usually where they have breached the conditions of their licence. This framework sets out the mandatory requirements that the National Probation Service (NPS), Youth Offending Teams (YOT), and prison establishments must undertake for all recalled prisoners.

# 2 Evidence

2.1 Research has been undertaken to understand the risks and needs of recalled prisoners, as well as, the experience of recall from the perspective of the recalled prisoner. The outcomes of this research have guided elements of this Framework, with the introduction of the recall information leaflets, a legal phone call for all recalled prisoners and the publication of the Best Practice Guide (Annex A of this Framework).

2. 2 Guidance is also available for staff within the "Better Outcomes of Recalled Prisoners document". This document provides guidance to support staff across the NPS, and prisons working with prisoners who have been recalled to prison custody.

# 3 Outcomes

3.1 This framework aims to ensure that there is an effective process in place which:

* enables individuals subject to licensed supervision in the community to be swiftly recalled to custody where their behaviour (including where they are out of touch) indicates that they present an increased risk of serious harm (RoSH) to the public and / or an increased risk of re-offending, such that those risks are no longer capable of being effectively managed in the community.

* notifies the police that an individual 's licence has been revoked, which provides the police with the authority needed to apprehend the individual and return the individual to prison custody.

* notifies providers of probation services, the Police National Computer Bureau (PNCB) and the relevant local police force that individuals who have not been apprehended within four weeks of their licence having been revoked have been issued with a notification of recall and are therefore liable to be prosecuted for knowingly remaining unlawfully at large.

* ensures that clear arrangements are in place for identifying which recalled determinate sentenced individuals are suitable for a fixed term recall.

* provides for the review of recalled prisoners' detention to be conducted speedily, efficiently and transparently so that all recalled prisoners are provided with clear timescales for the recall process.

* ensures that recalled prisoners are not detained any longer than is necessary to protect the public and prevent further re-offending.

* requires a recall dossier to be produced, containing a current assessment of the recalled prisoner and their response to supervision, including events which triggered a request for recall, together with clear and comprehensive proposals for the future management of the recalled prisoner in the community. The Parole Board or the Secretary of State will consider whether or not to re-release the recalled prisoner on the basis of the evidence in the recall dossier.

# 4. Requirements

## PART I - RECALL

4.1 Requesting a Recall

4.1.1 It is the responsibility of the Probation Service or Youth Offending Teams (YOT) to initiate the recall of individuals on licensed supervision through the Public Protection Casework Section (PPCS).

4.2 Recalling an Indeterminate Sentenced Individual and Extended Sentenced Individuals.

4.2.1 When assessing whether to request the recall of an indeterminate sentenced/extended determinate sentenced individual, community offender managers (COMs)/Probation Practitioners must demonstrate a "causal link" in the current behaviour that was exhibited at the time of the index offence. One of the following criteria must be met when assessing whether to request the recall of an indeterminate sentenced individual:

i. Exhibits behaviour similar to behaviour surrounding the circumstances of the index offence;

ii. Exhibits behaviour likely to give rise (or does give rise) to a sexual or violent offence;

iii. Exhibits behaviour associated with the commission of a sexual or violent offence; or

iv. Is out of touch with the COM/Probation Practitioner and the assumption can be made that any of (i) to (iii) may arise.

COMs/ Probation Practitioners must ensure that there is evidence of increased risk of harm to the public and at least one of the criteria set out above is met. Further information is available in the guidance section of this Policy Framework at paragraphs 6.1.1 to 6.1.4.

4.2.2 Where the individual's circumstances have changed, the COM/Probation Practitioner must also assess whether the risk posed as a result of this change is no longer safely manageable in the community, in line with the test above.

4.2.3 The Probation Service/YOT must take into account the extent that the individual's behaviour presents an increased risk of sexual or violent harm to others, regardless of the type of index offence for which s/he was originally convicted.

4.2.4 The decision to request recall must be based on an individual's behaviour, or change of circumstances, whilst on licence. This will not necessarily be directly linked to a breach of a specific licence condition.

4.2.5 COMs/ Probation Practitioners must consider whether to seek recall in cases where they have reason to believe that an individual is actively thinking about re-offending. Further information is available on EQuiP which can be accessed via the following link: Disclosing thoughts of re-offending.

4.2.6 Where there are allegations of further offending, the decision to request recall must be based upon the individual's reported behaviour. There is no requirement for the COM/Probation Practitioner to await the outcome of police investigations or for the individual to be charged, if they are satisfied that the reported behaviour meets the recall threshold.

4.2.7 Where there have been allegations of further offending, COMs/ Probation Practitioners must consider whether it is appropriate to request a recall, whether the individual has been remanded or not. In doing so one of the factors that must be taken into account is whether the risk presented by the individual, including where they have been remanded, can be managed, in the event that the individual is automatically released should any further charges be dropped, or whether additional risks have been identified as a result of the alleged behaviour which would warrant an assessment of suitability for re- release by the Parole Board or Secretary of State.

4.2.8 Following an allegation of further offending, where the individual is no longer remanded, if the COM/ Probation Practitioner is satisfied that they can be released immediately with no increase in RoSH to the public or risk of reoffending, then the COM/Probation Practitioner may not consider that recall is the appropriate course of action. This must be assessed on a case by case basis. The test for recall is based on the COM/Probation Practitioner's professional judgement regarding the risk the individual poses. Whether the reported behaviour has taken place does not require the criminal standard of evidence.

4.2.9 Where the current behaviour exhibited is concerning but, the judgement of the COM/Probation Practitioner is that it does not meet the threshold to recall, they should consider what additional licence conditions or alternative enforcement action can be introduced to manage the individual's risk in the community.

## Submitting the Recall Request

4.2.10 The decision to initiate the recall of an individual must be made by the responsible COM/ Probation Practitioner.

4.2.11 The COM/ Probation Practitioner must ensure that the emergency recall process is used, which is set out below in paragraphs 4.3.13 to 4.3.15.

4.2.12 The Part A report (available on nDelius) along with the mandatory supporting documents must be submitted to PPCS within 24 hours of the COM/Probation Practitioner making the initial decision to request recall.

4.2.13 COMs/Probation Practitioners must ensure that all available information, which may assist the police in locating and safely apprehending the individual, is detailed in the Part A report.

4.2.14 Where there is a victim(s) involved in the Victim Contact Scheme, COMs/Probation Practitioners must ensure that the VLO is informed of the recall request.

4.2.15 The endorsement procedures set out in the Part A report must be followed.

4.2.16 The COM/Probation Practitioner must remain contactable until PPCS has issued the revocation order. A direct dial telephone number or mobile number must be provided; availability through MS Teams is also an option. In the event that the COM/ Probation Practitioner will not be available, the contact details of a senior manager or another member of staff must be provided.

## Authorising Recall

4.2.17 PPCS, acting on behalf of the Secretary of State, is responsible for ensuring that the Part A recall report and accompanying documents provides sufficient evidence and justification to recall the individual and deciding whether to authorise recall requests. This decision must take place within two hours of receipt of the recall request and the mandatory supporting paperwork. See paragraph 6.1.5 to 6.1.7 for further guidance.

4.2.18 Where recall is authorised, PPCS must issue the revocation order to New Scotland Yard, the Police Single Point of Contact and probation services.

4.3 Recalling all Other Determinate Sentenced Individuals

### Consideration of Recall for Determinate Sentenced Individual

4.3.1 COMs/ Probation Practitioners must consider recalling an individual where one or more of the following occurs:

(i) they have breached a specific condition of their licence, or

(ii) either the behaviour being exhibited, or their change in circumstances, means that the risk posed is assessed as no longer safely manageable in the community, or

(iv) where contact between the COM/Probation Practitioner and the individual has broken down.

4.3.2 In such cases, COMs/ Probation Practitioners may consider that imposing additional licence conditions and taking alternative enforcement action will provide an acceptable and safe alternative to recall.

4.3.3 The decision to request recall must be based on an individual's behaviour or circumstances presented whilst on licence. This will not necessarily be directly linked to a breach of a specific licence condition.

4.3.4 COMs/ Probation Practitioners must consider whether to seek recall in cases where they have reason to believe that an individual is actively thinking about re-offending. Further information is available on EQuiP which can be accessed via the following link: Offenders disclosing thoughts of re-offending

4.3.5 Where there are allegations of further offending, the decision to request recall must be based upon the individual's reported behaviour. There is no requirement for the COM/ Probation Practitioner to await the outcome of police investigations or for the individual to be charged, if they are satisfied that the reported behaviour meets the recall threshold.

4.3.6 COMs/ Probation Practitioners must consider whether it is appropriate to request a recall where there has been further offending, whether the individual has been remanded or not. In doing so one of the factors that must be taken into account is whether the risk presented by the individual can be managed, in the event that the individual is automatically released

should any further charges be dropped, or whether additional risks have been identified as a result of the alleged behaviour which would warrant an assessment of suitability for re-release by the Parole Board or Secretary of State.

4.3.7 Following an allegation of further offending, where the individual is no longer remanded, if the COM/ Probation Practitioner is satisfied that they can be released immediately with no increase in RoSH to the public or risk of reoffending, then recall may not be considered appropriate. This must be assessed on a case by case basis. The test for recall is based on the COM/ Probation Practitioner's professional judgement regarding the risk the individual poses. Whether the reported behaviour has taken place does not require the criminal standard of evidence.

### Types of Recall

4.3.8 When requesting the recall of a determinate sentenced individual, the COM/Probation Practitioner must make a recommendation as to the type of recall, either a fixed term or a standard, whichever is assessed suitable in order to manage the individual's risk.

### Fixed Term Recall

4.3.9 COMs/Probation Practitioners must assess an individual's suitability for a fixed term recall in terms of the RoSH. Further information on fixed term recalls can be found in the guidance section of this Policy Framework, paragraphs 6.2.5 to 6.2.12.

4.3.10 COMs/Probation Practitioners must also follow the requirements in "Submitting the Recall Request", see paragraphs 4.3.16 to 4.3.20.

### Standard Recall

4.3.11 Where it is assessed that the individual is not suitable for a fixed term recall, the COM/Probation Practitioner must complete the Part A report recommending a standard recall. Further information on standard recall can be found in the guidance section of this Policy Framework, paragraphs 6.2.13 to 6.2.15.

4.3.12 COMs/Probation Practitioners must also follow the requirements in "Submitting the Recall Request", see paragraphs 4.3.16 to 4.3.20.

### Using the emergency recall process

4.3.13 At least one of the following criteria must be met when assessing whether to use the emergency recall process. The individual:

• Is assessed to present an imminent RoSH; or

• Is subject to an indeterminate sentence or an extended sentence

• Is subject to MAPPA level 3 arrangements, or is a Critical Public Protection Case (CPPC); or
• Is assessed to present an imminent risk of re-offending.

4.3.14 Where an emergency recall is being requested during office hours, COMs/ Probation Practitioners must alert the PPCS recall team to the emergency request by telephone for approval in advance of submitting the recall paperwork.

4.3.15 The COM/ Probation Practitioner must remain contactable until PPCS has issued the revocation order. A direct dial telephone number or mobile number must be provided. In the event that the COM/ Probation Practitioner will not be available, the contact details of a senior manager or another member of staff must be provided.

**Submitting the Recall Request**
4.3.16 The decision to initiate the recall of an individual must be made by the responsible COM/ Probation Practitioner.

4.3.17 The Part A report (available on nDelius) along with the mandatory supporting documents must be submitted to PPCS within 24 hours of the COM/ Probation Practitioner making the initial decision to recall.

4.3.18 COMs/ Probation Practitioner must ensure that all available information, which may assist the police in locating and safely apprehending the individual, is detailed in the Part A report.

4.3.19 Where there is a victim(s) involved in the Victim Contact Scheme, COMs/ Probation Practitioners must ensure that the VLO is informed of the recall request.

4.3.20 The endorsement procedures set out in the Part A report must be followed.

**Authorising Recall for Determinate Sentenced Individuals**
4.3.21 PPCS, acting on behalf of the Secretary of State, is responsible for ensuring that the Part A recall report and accompanying documents provides sufficient evidence and justification to recall the individual and deciding whether to authorise recall requests. See paragraph 6.2.16 and 6.2.18 for further guidance.
For standard and fixed term recalls, this decision must take place within 24 hours of receipt of the recall request and the mandatory supporting paperwork. PPCS will determine the recall type based on the information provided.
Where recall is requested on an emergency basis,

this decision must take place within two hours of receipt of the recall request and the mandatory supporting paperwork.

4.3.22 Where recall is authorised, PPCS must issue the revocation order to New Scotland Yard, the Police Single Point of Contact and probation services.
Further guidance is available in chapter 6.2 of the Policy Framework.

**4.4 Recalling an Individual subject to Home Detention Curfew (HDC)**

**Breach of Curfew Conditions**
4.4.1 Electronic Monitoring Companies must notify PPCS immediately where a level 1 violation occurs.

4.4.2 Electronic Monitoring Companies must issue a warning letter to the individual where a level 2 violation occurs

4.4.3 Electronic Monitoring Companies must notify PPCS immediately where two level 2 violations occur.

**Inability to Monitor**
4.4.4 Electronic Monitoring Companies must notify PPCS immediately where they are unable to monitor the individual.

**Authorising Home Detention Curfew Recall**
4.4.5 PPCS, acting on behalf of the Secretary of State, is responsible for deciding whether to authorise recall, issue a warning letter or take no further action. The decision must take place within 24 hours of receipt of the breach action request.

**Breach of Standard Conditions**
4.4.6 When requesting the recall of a HDC individual for breach of standard licence conditions, COMs/ Probation Practitioners must follow the requirements set out in "Recalling all other Determinate Sentenced Individuals", chapter 4.3 of this Policy Framework.
Further guidance is available in chapter 6.3 of this Policy Framework.

4.5 Recalling a Young Individual

**Young Individuals Serving Determinate Sentences**
4.5.1 When requesting the recall of a determinate sentenced young individual, COMs/Probation Practitioners must follow the requirements set out in "Recalling Determinate Sentenced Individuals" chapter 4.2 or Recalling an Individual subject to "Home Detention Curfew", chapter 4.3 of this Policy Framework.

## Young Individuals Serving Indeterminate Sentences

4.5.2 When requesting the recall of an indeterminate sentenced young individual, COMs/Probation Practitioners must follow the requirements set out in "Recalling an Indeterminate Sentenced Individual", chapter 4.1 of this Policy Framework.

## 4.6 Out of Hours (OoH) Recall Requests

### Using the Out of Hours Service

4.6.1 The OoH service must be used to seek recall for cases where the request for recall meets the following criteria:
• The criteria for an emergency recall (see paragraph 4.3.13) are met; and
• The case has come to light after 5pm or before 9am on a weekday or during a weekend including Bank Holidays.

### Requesting an Out-of-Hours Recall

4.6.2 The COM/Probation Practitioner must contact the out-of-hours switchboard to request recall.

### Authorising an Out -of-Hours Recall

4.6.3 PPCS, acting on behalf of the Secretary of State, is responsible for deciding whether to authorise out-of-hours recall requests. This decision must take place within two hours of the COM/ Probation Practitioner contacting the out-of-hours switchboard.

4.6.4 The COM/Probation Practitioner must ensure that the Part A report is completed and sent to PPCS the next working day with all mandatory supporting paperwork.

4.6.5 COMs/Probation Practitioners must also follow the requirements in "Submitting the Recall Request", see paragraphs 4.3.16 to 4.3.20.

## 4.7 Rescind of Recall

### Requesting a Rescind

4.7.1 Requests to rescind a recall must be submitted to PPCS on the 'Probation Service Request to Rescind Recall form' (available on nDelius or an equivalent authorised case management system). Where possible it must be submitted before the individual has been returned to custody.

4.7.2 Requests to rescind a recall must be endorsed by a senior manager who is equivalent to the former ACO grade/YOT manager or equivalent.

## 4.8 Unlawfully at Large (UAL) Offence Following Recall

### Recalled Individuals with Known Addresses

4.8.1 Where a decision is made to pursue an unlawfully at large offence then where an individual has remained UAL for more than 28 calendar days (starting from the date of the revocation order), PPCS must issue a letter to the individual notifying them of their recall to custody. The letter will be sent to the individual's last recorded address, as detailed in the Part A report, and copied to the COM/ Probation Practitioner.

4.8.2 Where the individual has failed to return to custody within 14 calendar days of the date of the letter, PPCS must notify the police by submitting an evidence bundle, copied to the COM/ Probation Practitioner, informing them that the individual is liable for prosecution.

### Recalled Individuals without Known Addresses

4.8.3 If there is no last recorded address at the point of recall or the individual is of no fixed abode whilst on licence, PPCS must issue the letter to the individual "care of" the COM/ Probation Practitioner.
The COM/ Probation Practitioner must inform PPCS via email once the individual has been notified. The email must include the date the letter was given to the individual or the date this was verbally communicated to the individual.
Where the individual is notified by telephone, the COM/ Probation Practitioner must be satisfied that it is the individual they have spoken to and advise PPCS of this. E-mails and text messages for this purpose are not permitted.

4.8.4 Where the individual has failed to return to custody within 14 calendar days of receipt of the letter from the COM/ Probation Practitioner, PPCS must notify the police by submitting an evidence bundle, copied to the COM/ Probation Practitioner, informing them that the individual is liable for prosecution.

### Recalled Individuals who are Out of Contact

4.8.5 In cases where the individual is UAL for six months or more, the COM/Probation Practitioner must notify PPCS.

4.8.6 PPCS is responsible for producing a Section 9 Witness Statement when the individual becomes 'deemed notified' and for providing it to the COM/ Probation Practitioner to complete and sign.

4.8.7 COMs/ Probation Practitioner have 28 calendar days from receipt of the statement to make all necessary checks and return the completed and signed statement to PPCS.

4.8.8 On receipt of the Section 9 Witness Statement, PPCS must notify the police by submitting an evidence bundle, copied to the COM/ Probation Practitioner, informing them that the individual is liable for prosecution.

### Charging, Sentencing and Calculation
4.8.9 COMs/ Probation Practitioners must ensure that any further information requested by the police/CPS is provided by the deadline set.

4.8.10 Where a recalled individual receives a further custodial sentence for an offence of remaining UAL, the prison must re-calculate the individual's release date. The guidance for the calculation of release dates is in "PSI 03/2015 – Sentence calculation – Determinate Sentenced Prisoners".

### PART II – RETURN TO CUSTODY, REVIEW AND RE-RELEASE
4.9 Return to Custody of all Recalled Prisoners

### Apprehending and returning a recalled prisoner to custody
4.9.1 Prisons must confirm immediately on request from the police or escort contractors whether they have space to take the prisoner.

4.9.2 Prisons must check the status of any prisoner received into custody on Prison NOMIS, to establish whether or not the prisoner is subject to a licence and may have a revocation order outstanding.

4.9.3 Where subject to a recall, the receiving prison must contact the original discharging prison and obtain the record that contains the sentencing warrant, associated sentencing documents and calculation sheets. The revocation order cancels the licence and brings the original sentencing warrant back into force; it is the sentencing warrant that enables the continuing imprisonment of the prisoner.

4.9.4 Where the prisoner is subject to recall, a new entry must be made on the original prison record. The recall status code must be used to record the reason for return to custody.

### Notification of Return to Custody to PPCS
4.9.5 PPCS will run management information reports on a daily basis that will indicate when a recalled prisoner has returned to custody. If a recalled prisoner has remained in custody for over five days and the prison have not received a copy of the recall dossier, the prison must make contact with PPCS.

4.9.6 Where the prison or community offender manager (POM/COM)/ Probation Practitioner identify concerns about a prisoner's mental capacity to participate in their recall review, PPCS must be notified as soon as possible and, ideally, at the beginning of the recall process. Where there are concerns about the prisoner's mental capacity, the process and requirements set out in the Generic Parole Process Policy Framework, chapter 3.13 must be followed.

4.9.7 Where the prison identifies that the prisoner will require documents to be translated, (including the BSL language translators) for example due to a disability or language barrier, the prison must ensure that PPCS is notified as soon as possible. Whether the prison, prisoner or anyone else informs PPCS, PPCS will notify the Parole Board at the point of referral so that where required reasonable adjustments, where possible, can be made.

### Disclosure of the Recall Dossier
4.9.8 PPCS is responsible for providing a copy of the recall dossier to the prison, and for notifying the COM/ Probation Practitioner of the recalled prisoner's return to custody, within one working day of receipt of notification of return to custody.

4.9.9 All recalled prisoners must be provided with a copy of their recall dossier and a copy of the recall information leaflet by the POM within one working day of receipt from PPCS.

4.9.10 All documents within the recall dossier must be disclosed to the recalled prisoner by the POM. The recall dossier must be disclosed in full to the prisoner. Any information subject to a non-disclosure application must only be disclosed in accordance with the outcome of the application.

4.9.11 The POM must explain the documents within the recall dossier to the recalled prisoner.

4.9.12 PPCS will issue a notification with the recall dossier to the prison/recalled prisoner, informing the prisoner that they have the right to submit representations, and the deadline for which the representations must be submitted to PPCS.

4.9.13 Where a recalled prisoner makes personal representations, and does not have a legal representative, POMs must ensure that these are returned to the relevant PPCS team.

### Legal Telephone Call
4.9.14 Prisons must ensure that all recalled prisoners are provided with the official list of legal aid lawyers and the opportunity to make a

legal telephone call within two working days of receiving their recall dossier. This is in addition to the reception telephone call. See paragraph 6.8.6 of this framework for a link to legal advisor contact details.

### Recalled Individuals in custody in Prisons in Scotland, Northern Ireland, the Channel Islands and the Isle of Man

4.9.15 Where a recalled individual is returned to prison custody in Scotland, Northern Ireland, the Channel Islands or the Isle of Man, it is the responsibility of the releasing English prison to ensure that any time spent in Scotland, Northern Ireland, the Channel Islands or the Isle of Man custody is counted towards the recall.

4.9.16 Where a recalled prisoner is being released from Scotland, Northern Ireland, the Channel Islands or the Isle of Man, the releasing English prison must provide a copy of the release licence to the Scotland, Northern Ireland, the Channel Islands or the Isle of Man prison where the recalled prisoner is being held.

*This section of the Policy Framework applies to determinate sentenced prisoners (including extended sentence prisoners) and indeterminate sentenced prisoners subject to standard recall provisions.*

### Part B Report

4.10.1 The Part B report must be completed by the COM/ Probation Practitioner who will be responsible for the management of the case when the individual is re-released.

4.10.2 The POM must provide the COM/ Probation Practitioner with information on the recalled prisoner's behaviour in custody for inclusion in the Part B report.

4.10.3 The Part B report must contain clear timescales for release plans, including availability of approved accommodation, whether release is supported or not.

4.10.4 The Part B report must contain a full up-to-date risk management plan, informed by a review of the Effective Proposal Framework (EPF) 2 plan, even where release is not supported.

4.10.5 COMs/ Probation Practitioners must follow the endorsement procedures set out in the Part B report.

4.10.6 The COM/ Probation Practitioner must submit the report to PPCS and the recalled prisoner no later than 10 working days after the recalled prisoner's return to custody (with Probation Service endorsement where appropriate).

4.10.7 On receipt of the Part B report, PPCS is responsible for assessing whether the recalled prisoner is suitable for executive release. For further information on executive release see chapter 4.14 of the Policy Framework

### Disclosure of the Part B Report to the Prisoner

4.10.8 COMs/ Probation Practitioners must ensure that the Part B report is provided to the prison no later than 10 working days after the recalled prisoner's return to custody.

4.10.9 The recalled prisoner must be provided with a copy of the Part B report by the POM within one working day of receipt.

### Statutory Day 28 Parole Board Review

4.10.10 PPCS is responsible for the collation and referral of the recall dossier to the Parole Board by the 28th calendar day of the recalled prisoner's return to custody.

4.10.11 From the point of referral, PPCS is responsible for re-compiling and disclosing the dossier to all parties for all HMPPS directions (Secretary of State, Prisons & Probation).

4.10.12 From the point of referral by PPCS, the Parole Board is responsible for re-compiling and disclosing the dossier to all parties for any third party directions See paragraphs 6.9.2 to 6.9.3 of this Policy Framework for further information.

4.10.13 PPCS will retain responsibility for all directions compliance in National Security and Extremism cases, managed by the PPCS National Security Casework Team.

4.10.14 From the point of referral by PPCS, the Parole Board is responsible for any representations from the prisoner or legal representative. All representations submitted after referral must be emailed directly to the Parole Board.

4.10.15 Where an eligible prisoner or legal representative wish to submit an application to the Parole Board to reduce the 21-day reconsideration window, this must be copied to PPCSreconsiderationteam@justice.gov.uk. The Parole Board will provide the PPCS Reconsideration Team with an opportunity to submit representations on behalf of the Secretary of State.

All parties must follow the requirements and guidance set out in the Generic Parole Process Policy Framework, chapter 3.7 Reconsideration of Parole Board decisions.

**4.10.16 Recalled indeterminate sentenced prisoners only:**

On receipt of the automatic notification from the Public Protection Unit Database (PPUD), the prison must download a copy of the recall dossier and provide a copy to the recalled prisoner within one working day.

**Parole Board Decisions - Indeterminate Sentenced Prisoners**

4.10.17 The Parole Board is responsible for issuing the Parole Board decision to all parties, including the COM/ Probation Practitioner and prison offender management unit (OMU).

4.10.18 The POM must ensure that a copy of the decision is disclosed to the recalled prisoner within one working day of receipt.

4.10.19 Where the Parole Board makes a decision regarding release, the decision will remain provisional for 21 calendar days to allow prisoners or PPCS on behalf of the Secretary of State to submit an application to the Parole Board to have the decision reconsidered where the criteria is met.

All parties must follow the requirements and guidance set out in the Generic Parole Process Policy Framework, chapter 3.7 Reconsideration of Parole Board decisions.

4.10.20 The Parole Board has the power to set aside a decision in a case if that decision meets certain criteria. This applies to all recalled prisoners. All parties must follow the requirements and guidance set out in the Generic Parole Process Policy Framework, chapter 3.6 'Setting aside Parole Board Decision', which sets out the process of how to apply to the Parole Board.

**Release of recalled Indeterminate Sentenced Prisoners**

4.10.21 Where the Parole Board directs release, PPCS is responsible for organising the release arrangements with all parties for as soon as reasonably practicable.

4.10.22 In these cases, COMs/ Probation Practitioners must provide all release information to PPCS within the deadline set.

4.10.23 PPCS is responsible for notifying all parties of the release date and issuing the release licence to the prison, New Scotland Yard and the COM/ Probation Practitioners.

4.10.24 The Prison must ensure that the recalled prisoner is provided with a copy of the release licence prior to release.

4.10.25 Prisons must ensure that the recalled prisoner is released on the date specified by PPCS.

**Other Parole Board Decisions**

4.10.26 Where the Parole Board makes a negative decision on the papers, the prison must ensure that the recalled prisoner is aware of their right to apply for an oral hearing within 28 calendar days. For further guidance see paragraph 5.6.29 of the Generic Parole Process Policy Framework.

4.10.27 Where the Parole Board decides that an oral hearing is required, the prison must ensure that the recalled prisoner understands the directions set. Further information is set out in the Parole Board Oral Hearings chapter 4.17.

**Parole Board Decisions - Determinate Sentenced Prisoners**

4.10.28 The Parole Board is responsible for issuing the Parole Board decision to all parties, including the COM/ Probation Practitioner, and prison OMU.

4.10.29 The POM must ensure that a copy of the decision is disclosed to the recalled prisoner within one working day of receipt.

**4.10.30 Recalled discretionary conditional release (DCR), extended determinate sentence (EDS), extended sentence for public protection (EPP) prisoners, special custodial sentence for offenders of particular concern (SOPC) and terrorist prisoners serving determinate sentences subject to initial release by the Parole Board (in accordance with s247A of the Criminal Justice Act 20 03) only:**

Where the Parole Board makes a decision regarding release, the decision will remain provisional for 21 calendar days to allow prisoners or PPCS on behalf of the Secretary of State to submit an application to the Parole Board to have the decision reconsidered where the criteria is met.

All parties must follow the requirements and guidance set out in the Generic Parole Process Policy Framework, chapter 3.7 Reconsideration of Parole Board decisions.

4.10.31 The Parole Board has the power to set aside a decision in a case if that decision meets certain criteria. This applies to all recalled prisoners. All parties must follow the requirements and guidance set out in the Generic Parole Process Policy Framework, chapter 3.6 'Setting aside Parole Board Decision'.

### Release of recalled prisoners

4.10.32 Where the Parole Board directs the release of a determinate sentenced prisoner, the prison is responsible for organising the release arrangements with all parties to complete the release as soon as the risk management plan is in place.

4.10.33 In these cases, COMs/ Probation Practitioners must provide all release information to the prison within the deadline set.

4.10.34 Where there are barriers to release, prisons are responsible for ensuring that all efforts are made to overcome these. Where that is not possible, prisons must escalate within the Probation Service in the first instance.

4.10.35 Where all options have been exhausted and release within the proposed timescales (as set out in the Part B/C/PB Decision) looks unlikely, the prison must escalate the case to PPCS immediately.

4.10.36 PPCS will escalate these concerns with the relevant senior manager within the Probation Service.

### Other Parole Board Decisions

4.10.37 Where the Parole Board makes a negative decision on the papers, the prison must ensure that the recalled prisoner is aware of their right to apply for an oral hearing within 28 calendar days. For further guidance see paragraph 5.9.6 of the Generic Parole Process Policy Framework.

4.10.38 Where the Parole Board makes no direction to release, it is the responsibility of the COM/ Probation Practitioner to ensure that the recalled prisoner's ongoing detention is reviewed appropriately in light of any progress or developments that may be material to whether they can be safely re-released.

4.10.39 Where the Parole Board decides that an oral hearing is required, the prison must ensure that the recalled prisoner understands the directions set.

### Parole Board Decision Summaries

4.10.40 Where a victim, who is involved in the Victim Contact Scheme, wishes to request a Parole Board decision summary (PBDS), the VLO must email the request directly to the Parole Board (summaries@paroleboard.gov.uk) copying in the COM/ Probation Practitioner. This request can be made at any time, within six months of the date of the decision.

4.10.41 The Parole Board is responsible for providing the PBDS to PPCS, the prison, the VLO and the COM/ Probation Practitioner.

4.10.42 Upon receipt of the PBDS, the VLO must ensure that a copy is disclosed to the victim as soon as possible.

4.10.43 Where the recalled prisoner is in custody, upon receipt of the PBDS, the POM must ensure a copy of it is disclosed to the recalled prisoner within one working day.

4.10.44 Where the prisoner has been released, the COM must ensure that a copy of the PBDS is disclosed to the recalled individual as soon as possible.

### 4.11 Fixed Term Recall – Review and Re-Release

**Re-release prior to the end of the Fixed Term Recall**
4.11.1 Where a COM/ Probation Practitioner assesses that a recalled prisoner is safe to be released before the end of the fixed term period, they must complete a Part B report and provide it to PPCS.

4.11.2 Where a Part B report is submitted, all parties must follow the requirements set out in 'Standard Recall – Statutory Day 28 review' in relation to the completion and disclosure of Part B reports, paragraphs 4.10.1 to 4.10.9.

4.11.3 On receipt of the Part B report, PPCS is responsible for assessing whether the recalled prisoner is suitable for executive release.

### New information undermining the initial assessment of suitability

4.11.4 The COM/ Probation Practitioner must contact PPCS immediately where a recalled prisoner has been deemed suitable for a fixed term recall, but new information subsequently comes to light that calls into question the recalled prisoner's suitability. Further information is available in the guidance section at paragraph 6.10.2.

4.11.5 PPCS is responsible for deciding if the recalled prisoner is no longer suitable for a fixed term recall and must notify the prison of the change of status to a standard recall and provide an updated recall dossier.

4.11.6 Prisons must ensure that the recalled prisoner's status on PNOMIS is updated as a 'standard recall'. The recalled prisoner must be notified by the POM immediately and provided with the updated version of the recall dossier. In these cases, the prison must ensure that the recalled prisoner is not released automatically at the end of the fixed term period.

**Prisoner Representations in respect of Recall**
4.11.7 In cases where the recalled prisoner makes representations on their suitability for re-release, prisons must ensure that the representations are provided to PPCS.

4.11.8 Upon receipt of the recalled prisoner's representations, PPCS are responsible for requesting a full Part B Report from the COM/ Probation Practitioner. This request must be copied to the senior probation officer (and functional mailbox where detailed in the Part A Report).

4.11.9 The COM/ Probation Practitioner will be required to submit a full Part B report. Due to the time constraints in fixed term recall cases, this must be provided within one working day of the request being issued.

4.11.10 Where a Part B report is submitted, all parties must follow the requirements set out in 'Standard Recall – Statutory Day 28 review' in relation to the completion and disclosure of Part B reports, paragraphs 4.10.1 to 4.10.9.

4.11.11 On receipt of personal or legal representations in respect of recall, PPCS must refer the case to the Parole Board in accordance with standard procedures.
In these cases, the prison must ensure that the recalled prisoner is re-released no later than the end of the fixed term period even if the Parole Board has not yet had the opportunity to consider the representations, or has considered them and has declined to direct release on licence.

4.11.12 From the point of referral, PPCS is responsible for re-compiling and disclosing the dossier to all parties for all HMPPS directions (Secretary of State, Prisons and Probation).

4.11.13 From the point of referral by PPCS, the Parole Board is responsible for re-compiling and disclosing the dossier to all parties for any third party directions in line with the Third Party Directions Protocol. See paragraphs 6.15.1 to 6.15.2 of this Policy Framework for further information.

4.11.14 Upon receipt of the Parole Board decision, all parties must follow the requirements set out in paragraphs 4.10.28 to 4.10.34 of this Policy Framework.

**Automatic release of Fixed Term Recall prisoners**
4.11.15 Prisons must ensure that fixed term recall prisoners are re-released automatically on licence at the end of the fixed term period, unless they reach their sentence expiry date first.

4.11.16 Where a prisoner has been released early subject to HDC and subsequently receives a 14-day fixed term recall, prisons must ensure that the recalled prisoner is released on the 14th day or the CRD, whichever is later. Where, exceptionally, re-release before CRD is directed by the Secretary of State or the Parole Board, the individual may not be re-released unless satisfactory curfew arrangements are in place.

4.11.17 Where a prisoner has been released early subject to HDC and subsequently receives a 28-day fixed term recall, prisons must ensure that the recalled prisoner is re-released on the 28th day or CRD, whichever is later. Where, exceptionally, re-release before CRD is directed by the Secretary of State or the Parole Board, the individual may not be re-released unless satisfactory curfew arrangements are in place.

## 4.12 HDC Curfew Breach – Appeal Process
Prisoner Representations
4.12.1 Where a recalled prisoner makes representations against the recall breach decision, the prison must ensure that the representations are provided to PPCS.

4.12.2 On receipt of the representations (personal or legal) PPCS is responsible for forwarding these to the HDC Recall Appeals Team.

**HDC Appeal Decision**
4.12.3 The HDC Recall Appeals Team must issue the decision directly to the prison OMU functional mailbox and the COM/ Probation Practitioner.
The prison must ensure that the recalled prisoner is provided with a copy within one working day of receipt.

**HDC Appeal Team Prisons**
4.12.4 If the appeal is allowed, PPCS must cancel the revocation of the HDC licence and the prison must generally re-release the recalled prisoner subject to HDC as soon as is practicable.

4.12.5 If the appeal is dismissed, prisons must follow the requirements in paragraph 4.12.6.

**Release from HDC Curfew Breach**
4.12.6 Where a prisoner on HDC has been recalled under s255(1)(a) CJA 2003, prisons must ensure that they remain in custody until the automatic

conditional release date (CRD), unless they successfully appeal against recall (and there is a suitable address). Where the recall is for inability to monitor under 255(1)(b) CJA 2003, prisons may re-release if there is a suitable address (see the guidance section, paragraph 6.11.2).

### Standard and Fixed Term Recall during the HDC Period

4.12.7 Where a prisoner has been released early subject to HDC and subsequently receives a standard recall under s.254 CJA 2003, prisons must ensure that they are treated like any other recalled prisoner given a standard recall, as set out in chapter 4.10 of this framework. Where, exceptionally, re-release before CRD is directed by the Secretary of State or the Parole Board, the individual may not be re-released unless satisfactory curfew arrangements are in place.

4.12.8 Where a prisoner has been released early subject to HDC and subsequently receives a 14 day fixed term recall, prisons must ensure that the recalled prisoner is released on the 14th day following return to custody or the CRD, whichever is later. Where, exceptionally, re-release before CRD is directed by the Secretary of State or the Parole Board, the recalled prisoner may not be re-released unless satisfactory curfew arrangements are in place. See chapter 4.11 for more information on fixed term recall.

4.12.9 Where a prisoner has been released early subject to HDC and subsequently receives a 28 day fixed term recall, prisons must ensure that the recalled prisoner is re-released on the 28th day following return to custody or CRD, whichever is later. Where, exceptionally, re-release before CRD is directed by the Secretary of State or the Parole Board, the recalled prisoner may not be re-released unless satisfactory curfew arrangements are in place. See chapter 4.11 for more information on fixed term recall.

4.13 Young Individuals – Review and Re-Release

### Return to custody and review of all Young Individuals

4.13.1 On return to custody of a young individual, prisons must follow the requirements set out in 'Return to Custody of all Recalled Prisoners', paragraphs 4.9.1 to 4.9.16.

4.13.2 For determinate sentenced young individuals, all parties must follow the appropriate requirements set out in the appropriate chapter:
• Standard Recall – Statutory Day 28 Review chapter 4.10;

• Fixed Term Recall – Review and Re-Release chapter 4.11; or
• HDC Curfew Breach – Appeal Process chapter 4.12.

4.13.3 For indeterminate sentenced young individuals, all parties must follow the requirements set out in 'Standard Recall – Statutory Day 28 Review' chapter 4.10.

4.14 Executive Release

### PPCS consideration of suitability for executive release

4.14.1 Where the COM/ Probation Practitioner submits a Part B / C report, PPCS is responsible for assessing the recalled prisoner's case to decide whether they are suitable for executive release.

4.14.2 Where a Part B report is submitted, all parties must follow the requirements set out in 'Standard Recall – Statutory Day 28 review' in relation to the completion and disclosure of Part B reports, paragraphs 4.10.1 to 4.10.8.

4.14.3 Where a Part C report is submitted to PPCS, the requirements set out in the below chapters must be followed in relation to the completion and disclosure of Part C reports:
• Further Review, paragraphs 4.15.4 to 4.15.13;
• Annual Review, paragraphs 4.16.2 to 4.16.13; or
• Parole Board Oral Hearing paragraphs 4.17.9 to 4.17.16 and 4.17.30 to 4.17.35.

4.14.4 PPCS may seek further information to support the release process. This must be provided by the deadline set.

### Probation Service YOT Prisons Issuing an Executive Release Decision

4.14.5 Where an executive release is agreed, PPCS is responsible for issuing the decision to the prison, COM/ Probation Practitioner, the Parole Board (where the case has been referred to them) and legal representatives (where applicable).

4.14.6 The POM must ensure that a copy is disclosed to the recalled prisoner within one working day of receipt.

4.14.7 On receipt of the executive release decision, the prison must ensure that the recalled prisoner is released from prison custody on the date specified.

### Executive Release Decision Summaries
4.14.8 Where a victim, who is involved in the Victim Contact Scheme, wishes to request an executive release decision summary (ERDS), the

VLO must email the request directly to PPCS via ExecutiveReleaseSummaries@justice.gov.uk, copying in the COM.

This request can be made at any time, within six months of the date of the decision.

4.14.9 PPCS is responsible for providing the ERDS to the prison, the VLO and the COM/Probation Practitioner.

4.14.10 Upon receipt of the ERDS, the VLO must ensure that a copy is disclosed to the victim as soon as possible.

4.14.11 Where the recalled prisoner is in custody, upon receipt of the ERDS, the POM must ensure a copy is disclosed to the recalled prisoner within one working day.

4.14.12 Where the recalled prisoner has been released, the COM/Probation Practitioner must ensure that a copy of the ERDS is disclosed to the individual as soon as possible.

## 4.15 Further Review

**This section of the Policy Framework only applies to determinate sentenced prisoners (including extended sentence prisoners) subject to standard recall provisions where the Parole Board has made no direction to release.**

### Review of suitability for re-release

4.15.1 The COM/ Probation Practitioner must ensure that a recalled determinate sentenced prisoner's ongoing detention is reviewed regularly. How regularly it will be reviewed will depend on the individual case and any possible need for a review following a change of circumstances.

4.15.2 Where there are outstanding criminal matters, it is the responsibility of the COM/ Probation practitioner to monitor progress of these and to notify PPCS immediately when an outcome is known.

4.15.3 Where criminal offences are committed whilst in custody, prisons must notify the COM/ Probation Practitioner immediately.

### Part C Report

4.15.4 Where the COM/ Probation Practitioner assesses that the recalled prisoner's risk can be safely managed in the community, they must complete the Part C Report and submit it to PPCS.

4.15.5 The Part C report must be completed by the COM/ Probation Practitioner who will be responsible for the management of the case when the individual is re-released.

4.15.6 The Part C report must contain clear timescales for release plans, including availability of approved accommodation, whether release is supported or not.

4.15.7 The Part C report must contain a full up-to-date risk management plan, informed by a review of the EPF 2 plan, even where release is not supported.

4.15.8 POMs must provide the COM/ Probation Practitioner with information about the recalled prisoner's behaviour in custody, where requested, for inclusion in the Part C report.

4.15.9 COMs/Probation Practitioners must follow the endorsement procedures set out in the Part C report.

4.15.10 On receipt of the Part C report, PPCS is responsible for assessing whether the recalled prisoner is suitable for executive release. For further information on executive release, see chapter 4.14 of this Policy Framework.

4.15.11 COMs/Probation Practitioners must ensure that all Part C reports are provided to the prison.

4.15.12 The recalled prisoner must be provided with a copy of the Part C report by the POM within one working day of receipt.

4.15.13 POMs must ensure that the prisoner is informed that they have the right to make representations and that these must be submitted to PPCS within 28 calendar days of receipt of the Part C.

## 4.16 Annual Review

**This section of the Policy Framework only applies to determinate sentenced prisoners (including extended sentence prisoners) subject to standard recall provisions.**

### Updated Reports for the Annual Review

4.16.1 POMs must ensure that recalled prisoners are aware that they have a statutory right to have their ongoing detention reviewed by the Parole Board every 12 months and that they cannot opt out of this review. PPCS will issue an initial notification to the prison/recalled prisoner, informing the prisoner that they have the right to submit representations, and the deadline for which the representations must be submitted to PPCS.

4.16.2 Prisons must provide details of the recalled prisoner's behaviour and progress in custody to the COM/ Probation Practitioner within four weeks of receipt of the notification from PPCS for inclusion in the Part C Report.

4.16.3 The COM/ Probation Practitioner must provide a completed Part C report to PPCS within four weeks of the request from PPCS.

4.16.4 The Part C report must be completed by the COM/ Probation Practitioner who will be responsible for the management of the case when the individual is re-released.

4.16.5 The Part C report must contain clear timescales for release plans, including availability of approved accommodation, whether release is supported or not.

4.16.6 The Part C report must contain a full up-to-date risk management plan, informed by a review of the EPF 2 plan, even where release is not supported (R11).

4.16.7 In extended sentence cases, the COM/ Probation Practitioner must also provide a full copy of the updated OASys.

4.16.8 COMs/ Probation Practitioners must follow the endorsement procedures set out in the Part C report.

4.16.9 On receipt of the Part C report, PPCS is responsible for assessing the recalled prisoner's case to decide whether it is suitable for an executive release.

**Disclosure of the Part C report and full dossier to the Prisoner**
4.16.10 COMs/Probation Practitioners must ensure that the Part C report is provided to the prison.

4.16.11 The recalled prisoner must be provided with a copy of the Part C report by the POM within one working day of receipt.

4.16.12 PPCS is responsible for providing a copy of the dossier to the prison.

4.16.13    The recalled prisoner must be provided with a copy of the annual review dossier within one working day of receipt from PPCS. The prison must explain the documents within the annual review dossier and the recalled prisoner's right to make representations direct to PPCS within 28 calendar days from the date of the prisoner's receipt of the annual review dossier.

**Disclosure and Referral to Parole Board**
4.16.14 PPCS is responsible for the collation and referral of the dossier to the
Parole Board by the anniversary date of the latest Parole Board decision.

4.16.15 From the point of referral, PPCS is responsible for re-compiling and disclosing the dossier to all parties for all HMPPS directions (Secretary of State, Prisons & Probation).

4.16.16 From the point of referral by PPCS, the Parole Board is responsible for re-compiling and disclosing the dossier to all parties for any third party directions. See paragraphs 6.15.1 to 6.15.2 of this Policy Framework for further information.

4.16.17 PPCS will retain responsibility for all directions compliance in National Security and Extremism cases, managed by the PPCS National Security Casework Team.

4.16.18 From the point of referral by PPCS, the Parole Board is responsible for any representations from the prisoner or legal representative. All representations submitted after referral must be emailed directly to the Parole Board.

4.16.19 Where an eligible prisoner or legal representative wish to submit an application to the Parole Board to reduce the 21-day reconsideration window, this must be copied to PPCSreconsiderationteam@justice.gov.uk. The Parole Board will provide to the PPCS Reconsideration Team, with an opportunity to submit representations on behalf of the Secretary of State.
All parties must follow the requirements and guidance set out in the Generic Parole Process Policy Framework, chapter 3.7 Reconsideration of Parole Board decisions.

**Parole Board Decisions**
4.16.20 The Parole Board is responsible for issuing the Parole Board decision to all parties.

4.16.21 The POM must ensure that a copy of the Parole Board decision is disclosed to the recalled prisoner within one working day of receipt.

4.16.22 All parties must follow the requirements set out in Parole Board Decisions – Determinate Sentenced Prisoners paragraphs 4.10.28 to 4.10.34.

4.16.23 All parties must follow the requirements set out in paragraphs 4.10.40 to 4.10.43 of this framework in relation to Parole Board Decision Summaries.

4.16.24    Where the prisoner is eligible for reconsideration, all parties must follow the requirements set out in the Generic Parole Process Policy Framework Chapter 3.7.

4.16.25 The Parole Board has the power to set aside a decision in a case if that decision meets certain criteria. This applies to all recalled prisoners. All parties must follow the requirements and guidance set out in the Generic Parole Process Policy Framework, chapter 3.6 Setting aside Parole Board Decision.

**Annual Reviews and New Sentences**
4.16.26 Where a recalled prisoner receives a new sentence, the prison must ensure that PPCS are provided with the details of the new sentence. This must include the details of the length of the new sentence, the offence the sentence was imposed for, the new sentence CRD/SED, and as well as confirmation of the SED from the recall sentence.

4.16.27 PPCS is responsible for checking whether the prisoner is eligible for an annual review, in light of the new sentence. Where the prisoner is no longer eligible or the date of the annual review has changed (in line with the CRD of the new sentence), PPCS will notify the prison (and the Parole Board if the case has been referred.) The prison is responsible for informing the prisoner.

4.16.28 Where the prisoner has outstanding police/court matters, and they are eligible for an annual review (in line with the guidance at paragraph 6.14.1), the annual review will continue as normal, until such time as the outstanding matters are concluded. In these cases, further reports will be required for the annual review in line with the requirements outlined at the beginning of this chapter and must be followed by all parties.
Where the prisoner then receives a new sentence, prisons must follow the requirements above at paragraph 4.16.26 to 4.16.27.

4.17 Parole Board Oral Hearings
**This section of the Policy Framework applies to all recalled prisoners, where the Parole Board has directed that an oral hearing take place, unless otherwise stated.**

**Directions (determinate recalls only)**
4.17.1 The Parole Board is responsible for issuing Parole Board oral hearing directions and timetables to all parties.

4.17.2 The POM must ensure that Parole Board oral hearing directions and timetables are disclosed to the recalled prisoner within one working day of receipt.

4.17.3 All HMPPS (Secretary of State, Prison & Probation) reports directed for a Parole Board oral hearing must be emailed to PPCS by the deadline set by the Parole Board panel.

4.17.4 The Parole Board is responsible for securing all third party information for the panel (including directed information) as set out in the Third Party Directions Protocol. Information and reports that are intrinsic to the Risk Management Plan will also remain the responsibility of PPCS.

4.17.5 PPCS will retain responsibility for all directions compliance in National Security and Extremism cases.

4.17.6 The Parole Board is responsible for uploading all third party directions to PPUD and ensuring that the dossier is recompiled on PPUD to ensure that all parties are notified as set out in the Third Party Directions Protocol.

4.17.7 The Parole Board is responsible for requesting representations from the prisoner or legal representative. All representations must be emailed directly to the Parole Board.

4.17.8 Where the Parole Board direct that a Part C report is completed, COMs/ Probation Practitioners must also follow the requirements set out in paragraph 4.17.30.

4.17.9 The Part C report must be completed by the COM/ Probation Practitioner who will be responsible for the management of the case when the individual is re-released.

4.17.10 The Part C report must contain clear timescales for release plans, including availability of approved accommodation, whether release is supported or not.

4.17.11 The Part C report must contain a full up-to-date risk management plan, informed by a review of the EPF 2 plan, even where release is not supported.

4.17.12 COMs/ Probation Practitioners must follow the endorsement procedures set out in the Part C report.

4.17.13 POMs must provide the COM/ Probation Practitioner with information on the recalled prisoner's behaviour in custody, where requested, for inclusion in the Part C report.

4.17.14 On receipt of the Part C report, PPCS is responsible for assessing the Part C report to determine whether the recalled prisoner is suitable for executive release. For further information on executive release, see chapter 4.14 of this Policy Framework.

4.17.15 Where a direction cannot be complied with within the required timescale or where the information is either not available or would incur disproportionate cost, the directed party must ensure that PPCS is alerted immediately so that they can consider whether to seek a variation or revocation of the direction(s) under the Parole Board Rules.

4.17.16 Where additional information comes to light during the oral hearing process, which is relevant to the assessment of risk, this must be provided in an addendum report.

### Directions (indeterminate recalls only)

4.17.17 The Parole Board is responsible for issuing Parole Board oral hearing directions and timetables to all parties.

4.17.18 POMs must ensure that Parole Board oral hearing directions and timetables are disclosed to the recalled prisoner within one working day of receipt.

4.17.19 Where the Parole Board directs that a report must be provided by the prison, prisons must ensure that the report is uploaded to the end of dossier by the deadline set by the Parole Board panel and disclosed to the recalled prisoner.

4.17.20 Prisons must ensure that the dossier is recompiled on PPUD to ensure that all parties are notified that the report has been uploaded. Further guidance is available in paragraph 6.15.3.

4.17.21 All directed reports must be emailed to PPCS by the deadline set by the Parole Board panel.

4.17.22 PPCS is responsible for uploading Probation Service and YOT reports to PPUD and recompiling the dossier to ensure that all parties are notified. Further guidance is available in paragraph 6.15.3.

4.17.23 The Parole Board is responsible for securing all third-party information for the panel (including directed information), as set out in the Third Party Directions Protocol. Information and reports that and are intrinsic to the Risk Management Plan will remain the responsibility of PPCS. Further guidance is available in the Generic Parole Process Policy Framework.

4.17.24 PPCS will retain responsibility for all directions compliance in National Security and Extremism cases.

4.17.25 The Parole Board is responsible for uploading all third party directions to PPUD and ensuring that the dossier is recompiled on PPUD to ensure that all parties are notified, as set out in the Third Party Directions Protocol.

4.17.26 The Parole Board is responsible for requesting representations from the prisoner or legal representative. All representations must be emailed directly to the Parole Board.

4.17.27 Where the prisoner or legal representative wish to submit an application to the Parole Board to reduce the 21-day reconsideration window, this must be copied to PPCSreconsiderationteam@justice.gov.uk. The Parole Board will provide to the PPCS Reconsideration Team, with an opportunity to submit representations on behalf of the Secretary of State.

All parties must follow the requirements and guidance set out in the Generic Parole Process Policy Framework, chapter 3.7 Reconsideration of Parole Board decisions.

4.17.28 On receipt of the automatic email from the PPUD, the prison must download a copy of the report and the POM must provide a copy to the recalled prisoner within one working day.

4.17.29 PPCS is responsible for disclosing all directed reports to the legal representative.

4.17.30 Where the Parole Board direct that a Part C report is completed, COMs/ Probation Practitioners must also follow the requirements set out in paragraph 4.17.41.

4.17.31 The Part C report must be completed by the COM/ Probation Practitioner who will be responsible for the management of the case when the individual is re-released.

4.17.32 The Part C report must contain a full up-to-date risk management plan, informed by a review of the EPF 2 plan, even where release is not supported.

4.17.33 COMs/ Probation Practitioners must follow the endorsement procedures set out in the Part C report.

4.17.34 POMs must provide the COM/ Probation Practitioners with information on the recalled prisoner's behaviour in custody, where requested, for inclusion in the Part C report.

4.17.35 Where a direction cannot be complied with within the required timescale or where the information is either not available or would incur disproportionate cost, the directed party must ensure that PPCS is alerted immediately so that it can consider whether to seek a variation or revocation of the direction(s) under the Parole Board Rules. All HMPPS staff, including Psychology, must send all requests to vary or revoke HMPPS directions to PPCS. PPCS are responsible for making an application to the Parole Board before the set deadline for the direction is reached.

4.17.36 Where additional information comes to light during the oral hearing process, which is relevant to the assessment of risk, this must be provided in an addendum report by the COM/ Probation Practitioner.

**Disclosure of the Part C report and other directed reports to the Prisoner (determinate recalls only)**
4.17.37 COMs/Probation Practitioners must ensure that the Part C report is provided to the prison by the deadline set by the Parole Board.

4.17.38 The recalled prisoner must be provided with a copy of the Part C report by the POM within one working day of receipt.

4.17.39 PPCS is responsible for disclosing all HMPPS directed reports to the prison, COM/ Probation Practitioner and legal representative and recompiling the dossier on PPUD

4.17.40 POMs must ensure that the Parole Board directed reports are disclosed to the recalled prisoner within one working day of receipt.

**Disclosure of the Part C report and other directed reports to the Prisoner (indeterminate recalls only)**
4.17.41 COMs/ Probation Practitioner must ensure that the Part C report is provided to the prison by the deadline set by the Parole Board.

4.17.42 The recalled prisoner must be provided with a copy of the Part C report by the POM within one working day of receipt.

4.17.43 POMs must disclose all reports directed by the Parole Board to the recalled prisoner within one working day of receipt.

4.17.44 Prisons must follow the requirements set out in paragraphs 4.17.18 to 4.17.20 and 4.17.28 of this framework in relation to disclosing Parole Board Directions to indeterminate recalled prisoners.

**Parole Board Oral Hearing Witnesses**
4.17.45 Before listing the hearing, the Parole Board will provide all potential witnesses with the opportunity to declare any dates on which they are unavailable. All witnesses must respond directly to the Parole Board within two weeks of the request.

4.17.46 The Parole Board is responsible for setting the hearing date, type of hearing, time and location. See paragraph 6.15.5 of this Policy Framework for further guidance.

4.17.47 Once the date of the hearing is confirmed, all witnesses must ensure that they attend the hearing.

4.17.48 In exceptional cases, where a witness is no longer able to attend, they must notify PPCS immediately. Where deemed appropriate PPCS are responsible for informing the Parole Board and seeking agreement from the Panel Chair for an alternative witness to attend.

4.17.49 If a witness refuses to attend, the Parole Board has the power to request a witness summons from the Civil Courts.

4.17.50 HMPPS witnesses wishing to give their evidence remotely must notify the Parole Board to seek agreement from the Panel Chair no later than 12 weeks before the date of the oral hearing (unless that oral hearing has been convened as a remote hearing).

4.17.51 The Parole Board is responsible for deciding whether to approve a request for a witness to give evidence remotely.

4.17.52 Where directed by the Parole Board, the prison must request reports from psychologists at the earliest opportunity.

4.17.53 Where directed by the Parole Board, the prison must commission reports from psychiatrists at the earliest opportunity. For further information on the commissioning of specialist reports please refer to Generic Parole Process Policy Framework section 5.6.19 to 5.6.21.

4.17.54 Where the Parole Board has directed that a particular assessment or a report is completed prior to the hearing, this must be included in the dossier.

4.17.55 If the direction is unclear or, in the expert view of the regional psychologist the assessment/report is unlikely to add value, the prison must contact the PPCS case manager at the earliest opportunity.

4.17.56 PPCS is responsible for deciding whether to or seek a variation or revocation of the direction(s) under the Parole Board Rules.

**Oral Hearing Dossier**

4.17.57 PPCS is responsible for compiling and disclosing all HMPPS (Secretary of State, Prisons & Probation) directions to all parties.

4.17.58 The Parole Board is responsible for compiling and disclosing all third party directions to all parties, as set out in the Third Party Directions Protocol.

4.17.59 The POM must ensure that the dossier is disclosed to the recalled prisoner within one working day of receipt from PPCS.

**Transfer during an Oral Hearing**

4.17.60 Where it has been agreed that a prisoner will transfer to another establishment during their recall review to access a progression opportunity in line with their sentence plan, or where transfer must take place for security reasons, the establishment must notify PPCS as soon as possible of the transfer and reasons (see guidance paragraphs 6.15.8 to 6.15.13).

4.17.61 It is even more essential that prisoners are not transferred after their oral hearing date has been listed unless this is due to exceptional circumstances and it is unavoidable. In such cases, the prison must notify PPCS and the Parole Board immediately. The receiving establishment must also ensure arrangements are made for the prisoner to attend the hearing.

4.17.62 Where a transfer is necessary during a review, the sending prison must take responsibility for completing any outstanding directions as it will normally have greater knowledge of the recalled prisoner.

4.17.63 As set out in the guidance, there may be circumstances where the receiving prison is better placed to complete the outstanding directions. Where an agreement cannot be reached, it is the responsibility of the sending prison to complete the reports. See paragraph 6.15.10 of this Policy Framework.

4.17.64 Receiving prisons must ensure that they have procedures in place for checking on the progress of the recalled prisoner's oral hearing before the decision is taken to accept a recalled prisoner during the review period.

**Parole Board Decisions**

4.17.65 The Parole Board is responsible for issuing the Parole Board decision to all parties.

4.17.66 A copy of the Parole Board decision must be disclosed to the recalled prisoner by the POM within one working day of receipt.

4.17.67 All parties must follow the requirements set out for determinate sentenced prisoners in Parole Board Decisions – Determinate Sentenced Prisoners at paragraphs 4.10.28 to 4.10.35.

4.17.68 All parties must follow the requirements set out for indeterminate sentenced prisoners in Parole Board Decisions – Indeterminate Sentenced Prisoners at paragraphs 4.10.17 to 4.10.27.

4.17.69 All parties must follow the requirements set out in paragraphs 4.10.38 to 4.10.43 of this framework in relation to Parole Board Decision Summaries.

4.17.70 Where the prisoner is eligible for reconsideration, all parties must follow the requirements set out in the Generic Parole Process Policy Framework Chapter 3.7 Reconsideration of Parole Board Decisions.

4.17.71 Where the Parole Board makes a decision regarding release or a direction not to release, they have the ability to set aside their decision if the case meets certain criteria. All parties must follow the criteria, requirements and guidance set out in the Generic Parole Process Policy Framework, chapter 3.6 Setting aside Parole Board Decision.

**5. Constraints**

**Out of Hours Rescind Requests**

5.1 Rescind decisions cannot be taken out of hours. A request to rescind an out-of-hours recall must be submitted to PPCS the next working day, in accordance with requirements in chapter 4.7 of this Policy Framework.

**Reconsideration of Parole Board Decisions - Release Decisions**

5.2 This section only applies to recalled prisoners who are subject to the following sentences:
• All Indeterminate Sentenced Prisoners
• Discretionary Conditional Release (DCR)
• Extended Sentence for Public Protection (EPP)
• Extended Determinate Sentences (EDS)
• Special Sentences for Offenders of Particular Concern SOPC)
• Terrorist prisoners serving determinate sentences subject to initial release by the Parole Board (in accordance with s247A of the Criminal Justice Act 2003)

- Any other determinate sentence subject to initial release by Parole Board.

Prisons must not release recalled prisoners eligible for reconsideration until PPCS confirm that the reconsideration process has been completed and the decision has become final (see guidance paragraph section 6.9).

### Parole Board Oral Hearings

5.3 HMPPS report writers must not contact the Parole Board directly unless it is in regard to witness availability.

### Transfer during an Oral Hearing

5.4 Prisoner may be transferred during their recall review only to access a progression opportunity in line with their sentence plan or for security reasons.

### Secretary of State Representation

5.5 Prisons must not provide a Secretary of State's Representative for an oral hearing, unless previously agreed by managers at PPCS. Any representation of the Secretary of State will be carried out by a PPCS Secretary of State Representative and only where PPCS senior managers have agreed that representation is required in order to facilitate the progress of a review.

### 6. Guidance

### 6.1 Recalling an Indeterminate and Extended Determinate Sentenced Individuals

6.1.1 Life sentenced individuals who have been released on licence can have their licence revoked and be recalled to custody at any time, since their licence will remain in force for the whole of their life - even where supervision has been suspended. IPP sentenced prisoners can have their licence permanently ended after 10 years.

6.1.2 Extended sentence individuals who have been released on licence are liable to be recalled by the Secretary of State at any point during the licence period.

6.1.3 All life sentenced individuals, extended sentence individuals - extended sentence for public protection individuals (EPP) and extended determinate sentence individuals (EDS) are ineligible for a fixed term recall.

6.1.4 All life sentenced, EPP and EDS individuals can only be recalled if their behaviour indicates they present an increased RoSH/re-offending. This can either be where the RoSH has been clearly demonstrated or where the RoSH cannot be measured e.g. where the licensee fails to report as required or is out of contact entirely.

### Authorising Recall for Indeterminate and Extended Determinate Sentenced Individuals

6.1.5 On receipt of the Part A recall report and all the mandatory supporting paperwork, PPCS will ensure that the information provides sufficient evidence and justification to support the request to recall the individual and will decide whether to authorise the recall.

6.1.6 Where PPCS considers that the information does not provide sufficient evidence and justification to support recall of the individual, or there are missing documents, they will discuss this with the Probation Service in order for a final decision to be taken.

6.1.7 For all requests to recall indeterminate sentenced and extended sentenced individuals, additional authorisation will be sought from a PPCS duty senior manager.

### 6.2 Recalling all other Determinate Sentenced Individuals

6.2.1 Determinate sentenced individuals who have been released on licence are liable to be recalled by the Secretary of State at any point during the licence period.

6.2.2. Section 184 of the Police, Crime, Sentencing and Courts (PCSC) Act 2022 provides the Police with the power to undertake an urgent arrest of a TACT or TACT-Connected individual on licence who is likely to be recalled to custody due to a breach of their licence conditions, where the police reasonably consider that it is necessary to protect the public from a risk of terrorism, to detain the individual until a recall decision is made.

6.2.3 Where the Police apprehend an individual under this power, they will make immediate contact with the Probation Service to allow them to consider recall proceedings. The police can only hold the TACT or TACT Connected offender for a limited period of time (6 hours in England and Wales and 12 hours in Scotland and N. Ireland). Therefore, it is imperative that the arrest is communicated swiftly to the Probation Service in order for recall proceedings to be considered within the custody time frame.

6.2.4 Although the Police make the decision to arrest an individual, the decision to request the recall of an individual on licence remains with the Probation Service and the usual process of recalling an individual should be followed. COMs/ Probation Practitioners should refer to the appropriate chapters within this Framework when considering whether to recall the individual. For ISP/ ESP individuals please refer to paragraph 4.2

and for other Determinate sentenced individuals please refer to paragraph 4.3.

The criteria for arresting a terrorist individual without a warrant is set out in Counter Terrorism Policing- The Police, Crime, Sentencing and Courts (PCSC) Act 2022 Additional Police Powers (Terrorism) Guidance.

**Fixed Term Recall**

6.2.5 Individuals assessed as suitable for a fixed term recall will be automatically released at the end of the fixed term period. Individuals serving custodial sentences of less than 12 months will receive a 14 day fixed term recall and those individuals serving custodial sentences of 12 months or longer will receive a 28 day fixed term recall. The fixed term recall begins on the first day of their return to custody on or after the date of recall.

6.2.6 All indeterminate sentenced individuals and extended sentenced individuals are automatically ineligible for a fixed term recall.

6.2.7 All other individuals (including Sentences of Particular Concern (SOPCs), serving standard determinate sentences are deemed to be eligible for a fixed term recall.

6.2.8 Suitability is assessed in terms of the RoSH, and for the purposes of these provisions serious harm means death or serious personal injury, whether physical or psychological. The statutory test for assessing suitability is:
• A person is suitable for automatic release only if the Secretary of State is satisfied that the person will not present a RoSH to members of the public if released at the end of that period.

6.2.9 It is important to note that this is an assessment of RoSH at the end of the fixed term period.

6.2.10 When assessing an individual's suitability for fixed term recall, the COM/ Probation Practitioner should:
• Gather all relevant information, including the events that have led up to recall, and then consider the impact on the current risk assessment and, in cases of very high, high or medium risk of harm, also consider the OASys which accompanies the recall report; and
• Identify the likely impact of a fixed term period in custody on the level of RoSH and whether that RoSH can be managed if the individual is released at the end of the fixed term period.

6.2.11 Where the individual is considered suitable for a fixed term recall, the COM/ Probation Practitioner should complete the Part

A report recommending a fixed term recall. Where the individual is not considered suitable, the COM/ Probation Practitioner should complete the Part A report recommending a standard recall. See guidance below, paragraphs 6.2.16 to 6.2.18.

6.2.12 An individual will only receive a fixed term recall if assessed as eligible and suitable by PPCS.

**Standard Recall**

6.2.13 Standard recall could result in the individual remaining in prison until their sentence expiry date (SED).

6.2.14 A standard recall will be applied in all cases where the individual is assessed as unsuitable for a fixed term recall. All indeterminate sentenced individuals and extended sentenced individuals will be recalled under standard recall provisions.

6.2.15 All recalled individuals have a statutory right to have their case referred to the Parole Board. Standard recall individuals must have their case referred to the Board within 28 calendar days of their return to custody, whether or not they request a review, to allow a speedy review of their detention and annually thereafter, if they are not released sooner.

Individuals may be re-released at any point before their SED where the Parole Board or the Secretary of State is satisfied that the risks presented by the individual can be safely managed in the community. For further details on the statutory Day 28 review see paragraph 6.9.1.

**Authorising Recall for Determinate Sentenced Individuals**

6.2.16 On receipt of the Part A recall report and all the mandatory supporting paperwork, PPCS will ensure that there is sufficient evidence and justification to authorise recall of the individual and, where appropriate, assess suitability for a fixed term or standard recall.

6.2.17 Where PPCS considers that the Part A recall Report and supporting documents do not provide sufficient evidence to recall the individual, they will discuss this with the Probation Service in order for a final decision to be taken.

6.2.18 Where PPCS, on behalf of the Secretary of State, does not agree with the recommendation (for a standard or fixed term recall) made in the Part A report, PPCS will discuss the assessment with the COM/ Probation Practitioner or senior probation officer before taking a final decision. This decision will be taken within 24 hours of receipt of the Part A report and mandatory supporting paperwork.

## 6.3 Recalling an Individual subject to Home Detention Curfew (HDC)

6.3.1 Individuals who are released subject to HDC can have their licence revoked and be recalled to custody at any time during the HDC period. Whilst the individual is within the HDC period, they are subject to additional HDC licence conditions which can be revoked by PPCS following a notification from Electronic Monitoring Contractors. Electronic monitoring companies' notifications are made without direct reference to the Probation Service/YOT but they should copy them in when sending the request to PPCS.

6.3.2 Individuals released early on HDC are liable to be recalled under Section 255 of the Criminal Justice Act 2003 where it appears to the Secretary of State that:
• There is a failure to comply with the curfew condition; or
• The individual's whereabouts can no longer be electronically monitored at the place for the time being specified in the curfew conditions.

6.3.3 Individuals released subject to HDC are also subject to standard licence conditions. If these conditions are breached during the HDC period, the licence can be revoked by PPCS at the request of the COM/ Probation Practitioner. COMs/ Probation Practitioners should follow the requirements set out in 'Recalling all other Determinate Sentenced Individuals' paragraphs 4.3.1 to 4.3.20.

### Breach of Curfew Conditions

6.3.4 Electronic monitoring companies must notify PPCS where a level 1 violation occurs (see the requirements section paragraph 4.4.1). The following constitutes a level 1 violation:
• Serious infringements of the curfew or other licence conditions such as being absent for an entire curfew period; or
• Assaulting or threatening to assault a member of the contractor's staff; or
• Intentional destruction of the monitoring equipment.

6.3.5 Electronic monitoring companies are responsible for issuing a warning letter where a level 2 violation occurs and, where two level 2 violations occur, they must notify PPCS (see the requirements section paragraphs 4.4.2 to 4.4.3). The following constitutes a level 2 violation:

• Shorter absences in one curfew period;
• Intentional tampering with the equipment (but to a lesser degree than that covered by level 1); or
• A number of very short absences over the length of the monitoring and curfew period.

### Inability to Monitor

6.3.6 Electronic monitoring companies must notify PPCS where they are unable to electronically monitor an individual subject to curfew (see the requirements section paragraph 4.4.4). Inability to monitor could arise in three ways:
• Installation failure – inability to install the monitoring equipment at the curfew address, either for technical or practical reasons;
• Monitoring failure – failure of the monitoring equipment resulting in an inability to electronically monitor an individual subject to curfew; or
• Change of circumstances – the individual subject to curfew is unable to reside at the original approved curfew address (e.g. the householder/landlord/hostel manager has withdrawn consent for the individual to remain at the address).

## 6.4 Recalling a Young Individual

Young Individuals Serving Determinate Sentences
6.4.1 Young individuals serving determinate sentences of more than one day who have been released on licence are liable to be recalled by the Secretary of State at any point during the licence period. Where an individual is subject to a three month notice of supervision, recall is not available and breach of supervision requests to must be processed through the courts. Young individuals are subject to the same recall provisions as adult individuals released on licence.

## Young Individuals Serving Indeterminate Sentences

6.4.2 Life sentenced young individuals who have been released on life licence can have their licence revoked and be recalled to custody at any time, since their licence will remain in force for the whole of their life - even where supervision and conditions may be lifted. Young individuals are subject to the same recall provisions as adult individuals released on life licence. For DPP prisoners they can have their licence ended after 10 years in the community.

## 6.5 Out of Hours (OoH) Recall Requests

6.5.1 PPCS operates an out-of-hours (OoH) service for all indeterminate and emergency determinate recall requests only. The OoH service applies to the Probation Service and YOT and is available between 5pm and 9am (weekdays) and 24 hours during the weekend (including Bank Holidays). The out-of-hours switchboard telephone number is detailed on the Public Protection Group Staff Contact List, which can be accessed via the following link: Public Protection Group.

6.5.2 When contacting the out-of-hours switchboard, the Probation Service/YOT should state that an emergency recall is being requested; specifying the individual's name, Probation Service Probation Delivery Unit (PDU)/YOT area and the contact details of the requestor including a contact telephone number.

6.5.3 The switchboard will relay this information to PPCS, who will contact the requestor to discuss the request to recall and gather the individual's information in order to complete the revocation order.

6.5.4 PPCS will require the following information:
• Individual's full name including any aliases
• Date of birth
• Prison number and NOMIS number
• MAPPA level
• Releasing prison and release date
• Index offence and length of sentence
• CRO number and PNC number
• Probation Service, PDU or YOT area
• Police SPOC area
• COM's/ Probation Practitioner details
• Authorising senior manager's details
• Last known address
• Sentence Expiry Date
• Vulnerability issues and known arrest risks

6.5.5 For requests to recall indeterminate and extended sentenced individuals, additional authorisation will be sought from a PPCS duty senior manager.

6.5.6 COMs/ Probation Practitioners should refer to the consideration for recall requirement sections in this framework to ensure that the criteria is met prior to requesting an OoH Recall. See paragraphs 4.2.1 to 4.2.8 for indeterminate sentenced individuals and extended sentenced individuals and paragraphs 4.3.1 to 4.3.5 for all other determinate sentenced individuals.

### 6.6 Rescind of Recall
6.6.1 PPCS, on behalf of the Secretary of State, has the power to rescind or cancel a recall decision in certain circumstances where the decision was based on erroneous information or the Secretary of State is satisfied that all conditions have been complied with or have been breached in circumstances beyond the control of the individual.

6.6.2 Rescind applications made after an individual's return to prison custody will only be considered where information is subsequently provided that was not available to the Secretary of State at the time the recall decision was taken.

### 6.7 Unlawfully at Large (UAL) Offence Following Recall
6.7.1 The offence of being UAL applies to those who are recalled, fail to respond to a notification of the recall and remain UAL. Individuals who remain UAL for a period of six months or more and fail to keep in touch with their COM/ Probation Practitioner are deemed notified under the 'failure to keep in touch' rule.

6.7.2 PPCS will identify individuals who have been recalled to custody and remain UAL. PPCS is also responsible for undertaking the notification procedures set out in this Policy Framework and for notifying the police and PNCB once the procedures have been complied with. See paragraph 4.8.1 and Annex B for more information.

**Recalled Individuals with Known Addresses**
6.7.3 Although PPCS will not as a rule instigate the notification process until at least 28 days after the revocation order has been issued, it can, exceptionally, instigate the process sooner if it believes that it is in the public interest to do so.

**RETURN TO CUSTODY, REVIEW AND RE-RELEASE GUIDANCE**
### 6.8 Return to Custody of all Recalled Prisoners
6.8.1 On return to custody, all recalled prisoners have a statutory right to be informed of the reasons for their recall and their right to make representations in regard to their suitability for re-release. This information is provided to the recalled prisoner in the form of the recall dossier. The requirements set out in this Policy Framework are in place to ensure this is completed in a timely, efficient and transparent manner.

**Apprehending and returning a recalled prisoner to custody**
6.8.2 If the Secretary of State decides to recall the individual, they will be liable for immediate arrest, if not in custody. Following arrest by the police, recalled individuals will be returned by the escort contractors to the nearest prison or remand centre categorised as a local for prisoners of that type (adult males, females, or young adults or young people) that serves the area where the arrest took place. The police are required to notify the prison in advance.

6.8.3 Recalled individuals should be returned to the nearest local prison as defined by Population Management Unit (PMU). The Prison Escort and Court Services (PECS) contractors are responsible for the escorting arrangements and will collect the recalled prisoner from the police station on receipt of a valid Person Transportation Request (PTR) and deliver to the nearest local prison in line with their contractual obligations. Local Function Prisons cannot refuse to accept such a recalled prisoner providing the delivery is within the agreed reception opening times - Schedule 26 of the PECS Contract. If the Local Function Prison cannot accept the recalled prisoner due to population pressures, PECS contractors must gain authority from PMU to re-direct to another prison. For details of the prison requirements see paragraphs 4.9.1 to 4.9.4 of this Policy Framework.

**Disclosure of the Recall Dossier**
6.8.4 All recalled prisoners have a statutory right to be notified of the reasons for their recall and their right to make representations seeking a review of their detention to the Parole Board, via PPCS. This information is contained within the recall dossier.

6.8.5 All recall dossiers will be provided by PPCS to the prison, normally by email to the prison OMU functional mailbox. The COM/ Probation Practitioner will be copied into this email, which will also include the date that the Part B report should be submitted to PPCS.

**Legal Phone Call**
6.8.6 Details of active civil and criminal providers can be accessed via the following website link: https://www.gov.uk/find-a-legal-adviser

Recall Information Leaflets
6.8.7 There are four recall information leaflets. These are:
• Standard Recall leaflet
• Fixed Term Recall leaflet
• Indeterminate Recall leaflet
• HDC Curfew Recall leaflet

6.8.8 PPCS will provide the appropriate leaflet to the prison with the recall dossier. Each leaflet contains information on the specific review process pertinent to the type of recall and has been written specifically for recalled prisoners. The recall leaflets are also available in Welsh.

**Recalled Individuals in custody in Prisons in Scotland and Northern Ireland**
6.8.9 Where possible, recalled individuals subject to a standard recall should be transferred to an English or Welsh prison so that they can access the Parole Board. PPCS will issue the recall dossier to the establishment where the recalled prisoner is being held (copied to the releasing prison that issued the licence and the COM/ Probation Practitioner). The review process will continue as normal. See 'Standard Recall – Statutory Day 28 Review' chapter 4.10 for more information.
When requested, Scottish/Northern Irish prisons will need to prepare reports for the Parole Board.

6.8.10 Where a fixed term recalled prisoner is held in a Scottish or Northern Irish prison they can serve the recall in that establishment. Where the individual is serving a new sentence in Scotland or Northern Ireland, the fixed term recall will be served concurrently. PPCS will issue the recall dossier to the establishment where the recalled prisoner is being held (copied to the releasing prison that issued the licence and the COM/ Probation Practitioner).

**6.9 Standard Recall - Statutory Day 28 Review**
6.9.1 All standard recalled prisoners who remain in custody 28 days after their return to custody must have their case referred to the Parole Board. Statutory Day 28 Review process apply to all recalled indeterminate and extended sentenced prisoners, as well as, all other determinate sentenced prisoners subject to a standard recall.

**Statutory Day 28 Parole Board Review**
6.9.2 Following the referral of the dossier by PPCS, where the Parole Board have directed an oral hearing or an adjournment/deferral, the Parole Board will be responsible for acquiring all third party directions, other than in the cases set out at 6.9.3.

6.9.3 Where the Parole Board have directed an oral hearing or an adjournment/deferral, all Parole Board directed HMPPS directions will remain the responsibility of PPCS, including the recompiling of the dossier and disclosing the dossier to all parties. PPCS will retain responsibility for all directions compliance for cases managed by the PPCS National Security Casework Team.

**Parole Board Decisions**
**Release of recalled prisoners (Indeterminate Sentenced Prisoners only)**
6.9.4 Where the Parole Board directs the release of a recalled indeterminate sentenced prisoner, PPCS will work with the COM/ Probation Practitioner and the releasing prison to ensure that the recalled prisoner is released as soon as possible. This includes contacting the COM/

Probation Practitioner to confirm the release arrangements and reporting instructions (the time that the recalled prisoner should report and to whom). This is to ensure the integrity of the release and risk management plan. The Parole Board decision will note the proposals of the prisoner's release which was laid out by the COM/ Probation Practitioner in the Part B/C report. This will help manage the release of the prisoner.

Where the COM/ Probation Practitioner would like to seek a variation to the licence conditions set by the Parole Board, the COM/ Probation Practitioner should provide full details of the amended licence condition wording with reasons for the variation to PPCS. PPCS will then seek a variation.

### Other Parole Board Decisions (Indeterminate Sentenced Prisoners only)

6.9.5 Where the Parole Board makes a negative decision on the papers e.g. that the recalled prisoner must stay in closed conditions, the recalled prisoner has 28 calendar days to make representations requesting an oral hearing. The decision will remain provisional until the 28 calendar days have elapsed, after which the decision will become final (unless the recalled prisoner has successfully requested an oral hearing).

6.9.6 In these cases, the recalled prisoner's case will then be managed under the Generic Parole Process (GPP), see Generic Parole Process Policy Framework (GPP) for more details. Release of recalled prisoners (Determinate Sentenced Prisoners only).

6.9.7 The Police, Crime, Sentencing and Courts (PCSC) Act 2022 removed the Parole Board's power to direct immediate or forward release decisions for recalled determinate sentenced prisoners.

6.9.8 Where the Parole Board directs the release of a recalled determinate sentenced prisoner, the releasing prison will work with the COM / Probation Practitioner to ensure that the recalled prisoner is released as soon as possible. This includes contacting the COM / Probation Practitioner to confirm the release arrangements and reporting instructions (the time that the recalled prisoner should report and to whom). This is to ensure the integrity of the release and risk management plan. The Parole Board decision will note the proposals of the prisoner's release which was laid out by the COM/ Probation Practitioner in the Part B/C report. This will help manage the release of the prisoner.

6.9.9 Where the COM/ Probation Practitioner would like to seek a variation to the licence conditions set by the Parole Board, the COM / Probation Practitioner should provide full details of the amended licence condition wording with reasons for the variation to PPCS. PPCS will then seek a variation.

### Other Parole Board Decisions (Determinate Sentenced Prisoners only)

6.9.10 Where the Parole Board make no direction to release a determinate sentenced prisoner, the recalled prisoner may be entitled to further statutory reviews as set out in the guidance (see Further Review chapter 6.14 and Annual Reviews chapter 6.15).

### 6.10 Fixed Term Recall – Review and Re-Release

6.10.1 Fixed term recalled prisoners' cases are only referred to the Parole Board in cases where the recalled prisoner submits representations before the end of the fixed term period. The COM / Probation Practitioner should provide a Part B report, where they are supporting release, or the recalled prisoner wishes to submit representations to the Parole Board.

### New information undermining the initial assessment of suitability

6.10.2 Where the COM / Probation Practitioner provides new information to PPCS which has subsequently come to light and calls into question the recalled prisoner's suitability for fixed term recall, any re-assessment can only take place within the fixed term period of custody. The new evidence will need to satisfy the below criteria:
• The information was not available at the time the decision to issue a fixed term recall was taken; and
• The information would have made the recalled prisoner unsuitable for fixed term recall at the time the assessment was made.

### 6.11 HDC Curfew Breach – Appeal Process
### Release from HDC Curfew Breach

6.11.1 Prisoners recalled under section 255 (1) (a) of CJA 2003 become statutorily ineligible for future release on HDC. This does not prevent them appealing the recall decision. If successful, the exclusion on future release on HDC no longer applies. Further information is available in Home Detention Curfew Policy Framework.

6.11.2 Prisoners recalled under section 255 (1) (b) of CJA 2003 because their whereabouts could no longer be electronically monitored (usually because they have lost their address) can apply to be re-released on HDC if suitable arrangements can be made. Further information is available in Home Detention Curfew Policy Framework.

## 6.12 Executive Release

6.12.1 PPCS, on behalf of the Secretary of State, has the power to executively release determinate sentence prisoners into the community subject to licensed supervision at any time during the recall period, including those prisoners subject to extended sentences. All such releases take place without reference to the Parole Board; in making a decision to re- release, the Secretary of State must be satisfied that the recalled prisoner's RoSH can be safely managed in the community.

6.12.2 COMs/Probation Practitioners can initiate a review of suitability for re-release at any point during the prisoner's recall by submitting an updated Part C report to PPCS. There is no requirement to wait until the next scheduled review of the case (including any directed oral hearing) to request re-release.

6.12.3 PPCS will work with the COM/ Probation Practitioner and, where appropriate, the individual supervisor to develop a robust risk management plan that addresses the risks identified, including any additional licence conditions to support compliance and protect the public. PPCS will also liaise with the COM/ Probation Practitioner in regard to the preferred timescale for re-release, taking into account availability of accommodation and other relevant factors.

6.12.4 In cases where an oral hearing is directed, any consideration of executive release must be concluded by PPCS three weeks prior to the confirmed oral hearing date. If it is not possible for executive release consideration to be concluded prior to that date, unless there are exceptional circumstances, the case must proceed to the oral hearing.

6.12.5 In cases where an oral hearing is directed, where an executive release decision is issued prior to the confirmed oral hearing date, PPCS will ensure that the Parole Board are notified so that the oral hearing can be cancelled.

## 6.13 Further Review

6.13.1 If the recalled prisoner's sentence expiry date is 13 months or more from the date of the Parole Board decision not to release, the case will be set for a statutory annual review which will take place 12 months from the date of the decision.

6.13.2 If the recalled prisoner's sentence expiry date is less than 13 months from the date of the Parole Board decision not to release, the recalled prisoner will remain in custody until their Sentence Expiry Date unless re-released at an earlier date by the Parole Board or the Secretary of State.

6.13.3 The COM/ Probation Practitioner is responsible for ensuring that a recalled determinate sentenced prisoner's ongoing detention is reviewed regularly. The review of a recalled determinate sentenced prisoner's ongoing detention should be completed in line with the Best Practice Guidance: working with recalled prisoners attached at Annex A of this Framework. There is no requirement on the COM/ Probation Practitioner to wait for a request from PPCS.

6.13.4 If the recalled prisoner is the subject of police investigations into alleged further offending, or has outstanding court matters when the Parole Board make a decision not to release, PPCS will await notification from the COM/ Probation Practitioner advising them of the outcome of those investigations or proceedings before determining whether a further review will take place. It should be noted though that, as laid out in paragraph 6.13.1, where the recalled prisoner's case is eligible for a statutory annual review, the case must proceed to the annual review and will not be delayed due to alleged further offending or outstanding court matters.

6.13.5 If any new or significant information comes to light that the Parole Board was not aware of when it made its decision, this must be provided to PPCS in an updated Part C report; in cases where release has not been directed PPCS will then take a decision as to whether a further review of the case is appropriate either by executive release or a new early referral to the Parole Board. However, if the direction is for release then it must be complied with and there can be no further referral to the Parole Board. New or significant information includes any information relating to further sentences of imprisonment, not guilty decisions at court or charges not being proceeded with.

6.13.6 Where the prisoner considers that there is new or significant information in their case that the Parole Board was not aware of when it made its last decision, this should be provided to the COM/ Probation Practitioner in written or oral representations. The COM/ Probation Practitioner will review and decide whether the representations refer to any new and significant developments, unknown at the time of the previous review, which might have a material effect upon the Parole Board decision. Where representations are received directly by PPCS, these will be forwarded to the COM/ Probation Practitioner to allow them to consider whether they constitute new or significant information that impacts on the individual's current risks and manageability in the community.

6.13.7 When reviewing the representations from the prisoner, the COM/ Probation Practitioner should consider:
• Do the representations provide any new significant and relevant information that the Parole Board were not aware of when considering the case?
• Do the representations inform or update the Parole Board about the prisoner's current risks or circumstances leading to the recall?
• Do the recommendations directly address any of the concerns the Parole Board raised in its reasons for not directing that the prisoner be re-released?

6.13.8 Where the COM/ Probation Practitioner considers that the representations do include new or significant information, the COM/ Probation Practitioner will prepare a Part C report and OASys report and submit these to PPCS. PPCS will then take a decision as to whether a further review of the case is appropriate either by executive release or a new early referral to the Parole Board.

6.13.9 Where the case is referred to the Parole Board, all parties should refer to paragraph 6.9.2 in the Standard Recall – Statutory Day 28 Review chapter.

### 6.14 Annual Review
6.14.1 All determinate sentenced individuals not released by the Parole Board or Secretary of State are statutorily entitled to have their detention reviewed annually, where there sentence expiry is 13 months or more from the date of the Parole Board decision not to release.

### Annual Reviews and New Sentences
6.14.2 The Police, Crime, Sentencing and Courts (PCSC) Act 2022 clarifies that where a recalled prisoner has received a new sentence, they will no longer be automatically eligible for an annual review for as long as that sentence being served.

6.14.3 Where a recalled prisoner receives a new sentence, the prison is required to provide the details of the sentence to PPCS. The prison will need to inform PPCS, via email, in all cases, where the prisoner has an active recall review on PPUD. This will include all types of recall reviews (including a statutory day 28 review, an oral hearing, a further review or an annual review).

6.14.4 The prison must provide PPCS with the following details:
• the length of the new sentence
• the offence the sentence was imposed for
• new sentence dates (CRD/SED); and
• confirmation of the SED from the recall sentence.

6.14.5 Upon receipt of the notification, PPCS will determine whether the prisoner is eligible for an annual review. Where the CRD from the new sentence is longer than the anniversary date of the annual review, PPCS will reschedule the annual review in line with the CRD date. When the CRD from the new sentence is longer than the SED from the recalled sentence, the prisoner will not receive an annual review.

6.14.6 In cases where the CRD from the new sentence is shorter than the anniversary date of the annual review, the annual review will take place as usual. Where the annual review is cancelled due to the new sentence or rescheduled, PPCS will notify the prison.

6.14.7 In cases where the annual review is currently underway, it will be for PPCS to decide whether the annual review should be cancelled or should proceed. This will be decided on a case by case basis.

### 6.15 Parole Board Oral Hearings Directions
6.15.1 The Parole Board will be responsible for acquiring all third party directions, as set out in the Third Party Directions Protocol, other than in the cases set out at 6.15.2. Information and reports that and are intrinsic to the Risk Management Plan will also remain the responsibility of PPCS.

6.15.2 All Parole Board directed HMPPS directions will remain the responsibility of PPCS, including the recompiling of the dossier and disclosing the dossier to all parties. PPCS will liaise with all relevant parties to ensure that the directed reports are submitted within the timescales set. PPCS will retain responsibility for all directions compliance in National Security and Extremism cases, managed by the PPCS National Security Casework Team.

6.15.3 As set out in 4.17.20 and 4.17.22, in indeterminate recalled cases only, the HMPPS directed reports will be uploaded to PPUD and an automatic email will be issued by PPUD notifying all parties that the new report is available. All parties should access the new document through PPUD. PPCS should be alerted immediately if there are any issues. For Probation Service/ YOT cases, the automatic email will be issued to the division's functional mailbox.

### Parole Board Oral Hearing Witnesses
6.15.4 The attendance of witnesses at an oral hearing is a matter for the Parole Board. Each

party (i.e. the prisoner and Secretary of State) must apply in writing to the Parole Board (copied into the other parties) for leave to call witnesses. A witness may only attend if so directed by the Parole Board.

6.15.5 The Parole Board will contact all witnesses who have been directed to attend the hearing to ascertain their availability, so that this can be taken into account when the hearing is listed. It is important that witnesses provide their availability direct to the Parole Board within the deadline set. The Parole Board is not bound by witness availabilities.

6.15.6 Witnesses not based at the prison where the hearing is being held are encouraged to apply to give their evidence by video-link or telephone conference wherever possible in order to reduce travel expenses and improve efficiency by reducing time spent out of the office.

6.15.7 Where a person wishes to attend an oral hearing as an observer, an application should be made via PPCS to the Parole Board in writing no later than 12 weeks before the oral hearing date. This request will be considered by the panel chair, who will agree or refuse any such request. The Parole Board will consult with the recalled prisoner prior to agreeing or refusing any such request.

**Transfer during an Oral Hearing**
6.15.8 Transferring a recalled prisoner during a review can cause considerable disruption and therefore this should only take place in exceptional circumstances. This may be appropriate, for example, where it is necessary to transfer the recalled prisoner to complete offending behaviour work, or for security or discipline reasons.

6.15.9 Where prisons are considering a transfer during a recall review to allow the prisoner to access a progression opportunity in line with their sentence plan, there must be a clear benefit which will support the delivery of their sentence plan objectives. It is important to bear in mind the impact that a transfer during a parole review may have on the prisoner's review.

6.15.10 As set out in the requirement section at paragraph 4.17.66 the sending prison must take responsibility for completing any outstanding directions as it will normally have greater knowledge of the recalled prisoner. Exceptionally, there may be cases where the receiving prison is better placed to complete the reports.

6.15.11 Only in cases where both prisons are in agreement, will the receiving prison take over responsibility for completing the reports.

6.15.12 If such an agreement cannot be obtained then the sending prison must complete the reports.

6.15.13 Prisons should make every effort to ensure that recalled ISPs' outstanding sentence plan requirements are considered as soon after a Parole Board decision as possible. This is to enable any necessary transfers to undertake outstanding interventions/ROTLs to take place before the next parole review commences. In circumstances where a transfer to access outstanding interventions/ROTLs is necessary to support progression during a parole review (but not after an oral hearing date is set) the transfer should be facilitated. Secretary of State Representation.

6.15.14 Where it is considered that a Secretary of State Representative should attend, PPCS will consider sending a Secretary of State Representative to attend an oral hearing but only where it has been agreed that representation is required in order to facilitate the progress of the review.

6.15.15 Where PPCS deem it appropriate for a Secretary of State Representative to attend, they will inform the prison and the Parole Board who the representative will be in advance of the hearing. Further information on Secretary of State Representation (including the criteria for Secretary of State Representative attendance) is available on Gov.uk via the following link: Secretary of State Representation

6.15.16 In addition, and entirely separate to the above, HMPPS (via the Secretary of State Victim Support Representative) also provides support to victims who choose to attend a recall hearing in order to read a Victim Personal Statement (VPS).

## THE PRISON ORACLE

*The Definitive UK Prisons Website*

*prisonoracle.com*

*44,000 pages, constantly updated, with site-wide, cancel anytime, access at less than £2.50 week, that's not even the cost of a coffee!*

## 2.14 INDETERMINATE SENTENCES

*Simon Creighton, Solicitor.*

### INTRODUCTION

The term 'life sentence' or 'indeterminate sentence' refers to a number of different types of sentence. The defining feature of all of these sentences is that there is no fixed date for automatic release and that when release does take place, the individual will be on licence for the rest of his or her life. In that sense, the sentence is 'indeterminate' as it does not automatically end in the same way as a fixed term sentence. The terms life sentence and indeterminate sentenced prisoners or can be used interchangeably and the Ministry of Justice now refers to his group of prisoners as indeterminate sentence prisoners or ISPs.

The procedures to be followed for parole reviews and the release of ISPs are set out in Generic Parole Process Policy Framework. The recall procedures are contained in Recall, Review And Re-Release Of Recalled Prisoners - all are available on https://prisonoracle.com.

Following the decisions of the European Court of Human Rights in Stafford v UK (2002) 35 EHRR 32 and the House of Lords in R (Anderson) v Home Secretary [2002] UKHL 46, all indeterminate and life sentences are administered in the same way. However, there are still some transitional arrangements in place for people convicted of murder prior to January 2004 and so it is still necessary to be aware of the different types of life and indeterminate sentence that can be imposed. The type of indeterminate sentence a prisoner is serving also has some implications when preparing for parole reviews.

### 1. Mandatory life sentence

This sentence is imposed automatically on adults convicted of murder (Murder (Abolition of Death Penalty) Act 1965). An adult is classified as a person who is aged 21 or over when the offence was committed.

### 2. Custody for life

Custody for life is imposed automatically on people convicted of murder who are aged 18 or over and under 21 when the offence was committed (Sentencing Act 2020, s275 Criminal Justice Act 1982, section 8).

At the present time, this group of lifers are treated in exactly the same way as adult mandatory lifers, except that they will normally start their prison sentence in a YOI rather than an adult prison.

### 3. Her Majesty's pleasure

Detention at Her Majesty's pleasure ('HMP') is the sentence that is imposed on people convicted of murder who were under the age of 18 when the offence was committed (Sentencing Act 2020, section 259; Children and Young Persons Act 1933, section 53(1)).

### 4. Discretionary life sentences

The courts have the power to impose a life sentence following a conviction for certain serious offences. The most common time when this sentence is imposed is following a conviction for a serious sexual offence such as rape or indecent assault. However, it can also be imposed for a whole range of violent offences such as armed robbery, manslaughter or even GBH. It is called a 'discretionary life sentence' because the judge has discretion as to whether it should be imposed (the list of offences is contained in schedule 19 of the Sentencing Act 2020).

The criteria for imposing the sentence are not set in stone. For many years, the sentence was most often used in cases where the offender was considered to have some form of psychiatric condition (often referred to as an 'abnormality of the mind') which meant that s/he posed a continuing danger to the public. However, it now appears that the sentence can be imposed in any case where the offender is considered to pose a serious danger to the public and it is not clear when this danger will cease, irrespective of whether this is accompanied by any psychiatric condition.

### Automatic life sentence (1998-2005)

This automatic life sentence was created in October 1998 following the implementation of the Crime (Sentences) Act 1997 and ceased to be operative as from April 2005 when it was replaced by the indeterminate sentence imposed for public protection (see below). It was automatically imposed following a second conviction for a 'serious offence'. The first conviction can have taken place at any time but for the second qualifying offence, the offence must have been committed after the Act came into force and defendant must have been over 18 at the time of conviction.

The list of serious offences as defined by the Act is as follows:

• attempted murder, incitement or conspiracy or soliciting to commit murder
• manslaughter
• wounding or committing GBH with intent
• rape or attempted rape
• sexual intercourse with a girl under 13
• possession of a firearm with intent to injure
• use of a firearm with intent to resist arrest
• carrying a firearm with criminal intent
• armed robbery

The sentence is called an automatic sentence because the judge had to impose it following the conviction, unless there were exceptional circumstances which would justify a determinate sentence being imposed. In R v Offen [2001] 1 WLR 253 the Court of Appeal held that the intention of Parliament was that this sentence should be imposed on dangerous offenders and that as a result, trial judges must have a sufficient discretion under the exceptional circumstances proviso to only impose the sentence where they consider the person does pose a danger to the public. Whilst it was generally be assumed that a person convicted of a second serious offence did pose a danger to the public, it was possible for the accused to rebut that presumption. The sentence was therefore very similar to the discretionary life sentence.

### 6. Indeterminate sentences for pubic protection ("IPP") (2005-2012)

In November 2016 HM Inspectorate of Prisons published a short *Thematic Review: Unintended Consequences* which looked at finding a way forward for prisoners serving sentences of imprisonment for public protection.

In March 2017 an agreed action plan was published both of which you will find on the Thematic review pages on prisonoracle.com

**Overview:** The sentence of imprisonment for public protection (IPP) and a parallel sentence of detention for public protection (DPP) for children and young people under 18 were introduced in April 2005 by the Criminal Justice Act (CJA) 2003. Section 123 of The Legal Aid Sentencing and Punishment of Offenders Act 2012 (LASPO) abolished the IPP sentence from December 3 2012. Between the introduction of the sentence in 2005 and its abolition in 2012, a total of 8,711 sentences were issued by the courts. However, the abolition was not applied retrospectively; no provision was made for sentence conversion or automatic release for people already on the sentence, meaning that those still in prison remained there subject to Parole Board approved release only. Large numbers of IPP sentence prisoners still remain in custody. Although efforts were made by the Parole Board to be more proactive when considering IPP cases and release rates seemed to improve, the Chair of the Parole Board stated in his evidence to the Justice Select Committee on 18 October 2017 that more than 50% of those release by the Board were subsequently being recalled. A statutory power was created allowing the Justice Secretary to alter the test for releasing IPP prisoners, this power has never been enacted and the courts have upheld the Justice Secretary's decision not to make any changes: R (Henley-Smith) v Secretary of State for Justice [2017] EWHC 1948 (Admin). The courts have also stated that IPP sentences which were lawful at the time of imposition will not be retrospectively reviewed (R v Docherty [2016] UKSC 62; R (Knights v Secretary of State for Justice [2017] EWCA Civ 1053). A detailed briefing paper on the history if IPP sentences is available on the Research Briefings page of the prisonoracle.com

**Background:**

IPP/DPP sentences were designed to be imposed on those who had committed specified 'serious violent or sexual offences' and who were deemed to pose a 'significant risk of serious harm' in the future (termed presumed dangerousness).

Under an IPP/DPP sentence high-risk individuals would serve a minimum term in prison (their tariff), during which time they would undertake work to reduce the risk they posed. At the point when sufficient risk reduction had been achieved, they would be released by the Parole Board. If at the end of their tariff their risk has not been reduced sufficiently, they would continue to be detained until they had satisfied the Parole Board that they had reduced the risk they posed and could be safely managed in the community.

Most IPP tariffs were relatively short, with the average of all IPP sentences being only three years and five months. Those released from an IPP or DPP sentence were also subject to a life licence, which they could apply to have cancelled after 10 years in the community. In practice, this means that the IPP sentence is identical to life sentences save for the possibility of having the licence cancelled.

The IPP sentence was applicable to 95 serious violent or sexual offences which carried a maximum sentence of 10 years or more; if an offender had previously committed one of these 95 offences, or any offence from a further list of 58 other specified offences the court was in most cases required to impose an IPP sentence based on an assessment of the risk of serious harm the individual posed to the public. This list of 58 additional offences included other offences such as affray and criminal damage with intent to endanger life, or be reckless as to whether life would be endangered. This was amended in the Criminal Justice and Immigration Act (CJIA) 2008, which removed the requirement on courts to impose an IPP sentence if the stipulated conditions were met, to remove the presumption of dangerousness and also to set a minimum tariff term of two years.

For a variety of reasons, many IPP sentence prisoners were unable to demonstrate a reduction in their risk that was sufficient for the Parole Board to direct their release. These included the prisoners not being given sufficient opportunity pre-tariff to access relevant courses, delays in them being transferred to other prisons to access programmes and inadequate support being provided to help them progress through the prison system in order to demonstrate a reduction in risk. This culminated in 2012 in a European Court of Human Rights ruling in the case of James, Wells and Lee v. The United Kingdom that detention could become arbitrary, and therefore unlawful within the meaning of Article 5.1 (a right to liberty and security) of the European Convention on Human Rights, where there was insufficient opportunity provided for an IPP sentence prisoner to demonstrate education risk at tariff expiry or soon after.

Following this and other legal challenges, Section 123 of The Legal Aid Sentencing and Punishment of Offenders Act 2012 (LASPO) abolished the IPP sentence from December 3 2012.

Between the introduction of the sentence in 2005 and its abolition in 2012, a total of 8,711 sentences were issued by the courts.

However, the abolition was not applied retrospectively; no provision was made for sentence conversion or automatic release for people already on the sentence, meaning that those still in prison remained there subject to Parole Board approved release only. Large numbers of IPP sentence prisoners still remain in custody.

The average length of tariff given was approximately three years and five months. This figure is based on data from the HMPPS live case management system which contains valid tariff information for 8,113 offenders. However, this data is incomplete and may also include duplicate or otherwise erroneous records, so it should be treated with caution. In addition, the change brought about by the CJIA 2008, which is that IPP sentences should carry a minimum tariff of two years, also affected the overall average tariff length.

Over two-thirds (69%) of unreleased IPP prisoners (i.e. excluding recalls) received an IPP sentence for offences of violence against the person or sexual offences (2,871 out of 4,129 for whom offence detail information is available).

As at 30 June 2021, there were 1,722 IPP prisoners, as compared to the peak figure of 6,080 in June 2012. The number who were recalled prisoners was 1,322 and 96% of all IPP prisoners were over their tariff period - see the Offender Management pages of the prisonoracle.com

### 7. The new "automatic life" sentence

When LASPO abolished the sentence of IPP for offences committed after 3 December 2012 it introduced a new version of the automatic life sentence into the CJA 2003 (s 244A) and this power is now contained in the Sentencing Act 2020, s 283 (NB the SA 2020 contains transitional provisions for historic offences). The sentence requires a life sentence to be imposed on those people who are:

• convicted of an offence specified in Part 1 of schedule 15 of the SA 2020;

• the sentence offence and previous conviction conditions are

The sentence condition is that the sentencing court would impose a sentence of 10 years or more for the offence, disregarding any licence extension period). Part 1 of schedule 15 contains forty three serious offences including serious offences of violence, serious sexual offences and terrorist offences. The previous conviction condition is that the person has a previous conviction for an offence listed in schedule 15 and that the sentence imposed was either a life sentence with a minimum term of 5 years or more (excluding remand time) or a determinate sentence of 10 years or more. For those who had extended sentences imposed, the 10 years refers solely to the custodial period and not the extension period.

This sentence is stated to be mandatory and does not appear to allow for any discretion on the part of the sentencing judge. The possibility that the mandatory nature of the sentence may breach the principles set out in Offen (above) is likely to be quite slim bearing in mind the far more stringent criteria that apply before it can be imposed. Presumably, in case where the sentencing judge does not think it is necessary or justified the appropriate solution is to fix the new sentence at less than 10 years.

### Tariffs Or Minimum Terms

The tariff is the part of the sentence that must be served before a lifer can be considered for release. It should now officially be described as the minimum term as this recognises that it is the shortest time a lifer will spend in prison. Release does not automatically take place once this term has been served, it simply means that release cannot be considered until that time. Following the enactment of the relevant provisions in the CJA 2003 in January 2004, all minimum terms are now set by the trial judge following conviction.

### Mandatory lifers and custody for life

Anyone who was convicted of murder prior January 2004 and had their tariff set by the Secretary of State can apply to the High Court for a judge to re-set the tariff. All adults convicted of murder since January 2004 will have had their tariff (or minimum term) set by the trial judge following conviction. The sentence can then be appealed to the Court of Appeal as with any other criminal sentence. The guidelines on the length of the sentence are contained in schedule 21 of the CJA 2003. This Act has different starting points for various types of murder – the relevant starting points for adults being 15 years, 30 years and whole life. Whole life is the starting point for cases where the prisoner was over 21 years of age and has been convicted of two or more murders where the murders contained a sadistic or sexual element, a substantial degree of planning or abduction; for the murder of a child involving abduction, sexual or sadistic conduct or where a person previously convicted of murder commits a second murder. The European Court of Human Rights held that irreducible whole life terms that allow for no possibility of future review or release are a breach of Article 3 of the ECHR (Vinter v UK (2013) 34 BHRC 605) although in the subsequent case of Hutchinson v UK (2017) 43 BHRC 667, the European Court stated that the power of compassionate release was capable of meeting the requirements of Article 3 providing it took into account the possibility of reducing the tariff based on progress in custody or a change in the penological justification for imposing the original sentence.

The 30 year starting point is for offences such as the murder of a police or prison officer, murder using as firearm or for gain, murders involving sexual or sadistic conduct and murder of two or more people, but not including the aggravating features listed above. It is also the starting point for the types of murder that would attract a whole life tariff but where the prisoner was under 21 years of age.

The 15 year starting point is for all other murders. All of these starting points are then subject to variation to take account of aggravating and mitigating features and the Court of Appeal has made it clear that the sentencing judge has a great deal of flexibility. On the issue of guilty pleas, following advice from the Sentencing Guidelines Council the maximum deduction following a conviction for murder is 1/6th of the sentence with a maximum reduction of 5 years. A guilty plea will not reduce the sentence where a whole life term is appropriate.

Those mandatory lifers whose tariffs were set before January 2004 retain the right to apply to have the sentence reconsidered on the grounds of their exceptional progress and a reduction of up to 2 years can be made if the progress is considered to be exceptional. This application is made by way of an appeal out of time to the Court of Appeal. This right does not apply to anyone sentenced after 4 December 2004 when the sentences were fixed by a judge in the first instance and there is no legal basis for these tariffs to be reduced on the grounds of exceptional progress (R v Gill [2011] EWCA Crim 2795).

## HMP tariffs

The procedure for HMP detainees convicted since 2000 is that the minimum term is set by the trial judge and can be appealed (as with adult mandatory lifers, above). The sentencing principles in the Criminal Justice Act 2003 apply. These state that the normal starting point is 12 years. Although the statutory regime specifically excludes people under the age of 21 years old from the whole life orders and people under 18 years from the 30 years starting points (see above), this does not mean that very lengthy sentences are precluded for juveniles and the Police, Crime and Sentencing Bill will introduce significantly longer sentences for juveniles convicted of murder depending on their age at the time of the offence, including the power to impose whole life orders in exceptional cases (the proposed new starting points are in s 104 of the Bill at the time of writing).

For all HMP detainees, whenever they were convicted, their sentences must also take account of the 'welfare principle' because these lifers were children when they committed their offences (R v (Smith) v SSHD [2005] UKHL 51). Although this judgment requires regular reviews to be conducted to see if there are any grounds for the tariff to be reduced, the Police, Crime, Sentencing and Courts Bill contains provisions intending to limit the power of review to those prisoners who were under the age of 18 at the date of their sentence, irrespective of their age at the time the offence was committed.

### Discretionary and 'automatic' lifers

Since the Criminal Justice Act 1991 was passed in October 1992, all life sentences imposed for offences other than murder have the tariff set by the courts. After the decision has been made to impose a discretionary life sentence, the sentencing judge must fix a tariff in open court. The proper method of doing this is first to decide what fixed term sentence would have been imposed if a life sentence had not been necessary. The judge should then set the tariff at between one half and two thirds of the equivalent determinate sentence. This period is used to reflect the time when a prisoner is eligible for parole under normal sentences. Thus, in practice, a discretionary lifer should be considered for parole at the same time as if a fixed term sentence had been imposed. It is possible to appeal to the Court of Appeal against the level at which a tariff has been set in such cases. The sentencing judge should also specify how much time is to be allowed for time spent in custody on remand as this is not automatically deducted from the sentence.

All Automatic life sentences/ Indeterminate sentences of public protection. The tariffs for these sentences are set in the same way as for discretionary lifers.

### The Life Sentence System An Overview

### What is an indeterminate sentence?

The life or indeterminate sentence is different from determinate sentences as, in all cases, indeterminate sentenced prisoners (ISPs) can only be released on the direction of the Parole Board. This means that they will be required to work on their risk factors so that they can show the Parole Board that they are safe to be released by the time the minimum term has expired. Detailed guidance on the prison service procedures for people serving life sentences can be found in the Generic Parole Process Policy Framework and recall procedures are contained in Recall, Review And Re-Release Of Recalled Prisoners. An indeterminate sentence does not have a fixed release date, although the sentencing court will set a minimum term of imprisonment (the 'tariff'). All prisoners subject to life imprisonment or Imprisonment for Public Protection (IPP) are, for the purposes of their management, classed as indeterminate sentence prisoners (ISPs).

## How and when is an ISP released?

ISPs have no automatic right to be released. They are eligible for release on licence (parole) once their tariff has expired (TED). However, ISPs will only be released if the Parole Board (PB) directs release. Once released by the PB, an ISP, unless serving an IPP sentence, will remain on licence for life, subject to recall. If serving an IPP sentence, an ISP can apply for the licence to be lifted after 10 years. The PB is an independent body. Its job is to assess the risk of serious harm a prisoner might pose to the public on licence. It acts like a court. It will only direct release if satisfied it is 'no longer necessary' for the protection of the public for a prisoner to be confined.

## Parole

Prisoners serving the following type of determinate sentences also have a PED at which point the PB can direct release (discretionary release) before the automatic release date:

Sentences of 4 years+ for violent or sexual offences, under the CJA 1991: PED is at the halfway point of the sentence;

All of the provisions for the imposition of extended sentences are now contained in the Sentencing Act 2020 (see eg: ss 279-282). The sentence has bene through a series of different versions as follows: Extended Public Protection (EPP) sentences imposed before 14 July 2008 under the CJA 2003: PED is at the halfway point of the custodial term; Extended Determinate Sentences (EDS) imposed on or after 13 April 2015: PED is at 2/3 of the custodial term. The PED for prisoners serving an EDS, who were convicted before 13 April 2015, and given a custodial term of 10 years or more or the offence was under Schedule 15B CJA 2003, is also at the 2/3 point; Sentences for Offenders of Particular Concern (SOPC) under s.236A of the CJA 2003, imposed on or after 13 April 2015 for a Schedule 18A CJA 2003 offence: PED is at the halfway point of the custodial term.

The Police, Crime, Sentencing and Courts Bill contains proposed powers for some prisoners who are eligible for automatic release to have their cases reconsidered before release to determine whether they should be made subject to the same release provisions as EDS prisoners.

## The parole process

The Generic Parole Process Policy Framework (GPP) governs the parole process. It sets out the timescales and processes for pre, on, and post-tariff reviews.

## Pre-Tariff Reviews

ISPs are eligible to have their cases referred to the PB to consider their suitability for transfer to open conditions up to three years before their Tariff Expiry Date (TED). This is called a Pre-Tariff Review (PTR). The Board can only recommend, not direct, a transfer. The Secretary of State (SSJ) can refuse the Board's recommendation.

An ISP will only get a PTR if the Secretary of State refers their case to the PB, unless an application for a Guittard review is made (see below). A referral will only happen where it is decided that there is a reasonable prospect of the Board making a positive recommendation. This decision is made at what is called a 'sift review'. The sift process starts with a pre-tariff Sentence Planning and Review Meeting (SPRM) at the prison. This will include involvement by an ISP 's offender manager and supervisor. The notes from the SPRM will be sent to the Public Protection Casework Section (PPCS) at the Ministry of Justice, which then conducts a review on behalf of the SSJ, to decide whether to refer the case to the PB.

As a consequence of the case of R (Guittard) v Secretary of State (2009) in some circumstances, the Secretary of State is required to consider an ISP's suitability for a transfer to open conditions without involvement of the PB.

However it will only be granted on the following bases:

Reports contain evidence that the ISP has made significant progress in identified risk factors; and

There is consensus amongst report writers that the ISP is suitable and safe to be transferred to open conditions; and

There are no areas of concern identified in reports, which would clearly benefit from further exploration at an oral hearing of the PB; and

The ISP has demonstrated in his/her representations that there are clear benefits to being transferred to open conditions immediately rather than following the established process.

## On-Tariff and Post-Tariff hearings

It is a statutory requirement that ISPs have their cases referred to the PB at their TED. The Framework sets out a strict timetable for the parole process. The PPCS starts compiling a dossier two weeks before review initiation. This is week '0'. The dossier will contain historical information such as the judge's sentencing remarks, previous convictions, previous parole decisions as well as reports from the prison and probation. The dossier must be completed by week 8, formally referred to the PB, and disclosed to prisoners, who have 4 weeks from the point of referral to add their representations to the dossier.

A single PB member will conduct an initial review. By week 14 a decision will be issued. The Board can decide to either refuse or direct release or, that an oral hearing is necessary. If the decision is negative, a prisoner has 28 days in which to ask the Board for an oral hearing. Otherwise the decision stands.

There is no right to an oral hearing but the case of Osborn & Others v PB [2013] decided that fairness to the prisoner should be the overriding consideration when the Board consider such a request. If granted, then the hearing should be listed no later than week 26.

## Oral hearings

Usually the Board consists of a panel of three. The panel will hear evidence from witnesses including the offender manager and supervisor as well as the prisoner. A decision must be issued within 14 days of the hearing

The Board has the power to direct release but only to recommend transfer to open conditions. If it directs release, it will then set licence conditions. If it recommends transfer, the SSJ can overturn that recommendation. The decision to confirm or refuse the recommendation must be made within four weeks. If the recommendation is refused then the Secretary of State will then set the timeframe for the next hearing.

In July 2019, new Parole Board Rules came into force. The change allows victims to ask for a review of a release decision. The Secretary of State then acts on their behalf. It also allows a prisoner or their legal representative to apply for a review of a refusal to release.

The process is designed to be quicker than judicial review but the grounds and threshold are similar; it is not a merits appeal and reviews will only be granted if the decision is deemed irrational or procedurally unfair.

Timelines are strict. Applications must be made in writing and within 21 days of a decision. Forms are available in OMU. If no application is made, the decision becomes final after 21 days. The other party to the application must respond within 7 days.

A judicial PB member will conduct the review on the papers. The decision will be available to the public. If a review is granted, it could be conducted by a new or the same panel on the papers or, at an oral hearing. If the application is refused, the original decision stands.

Summaries of parole decisions will be issued at the request of either the victim or any other person, including the media (PBR 2019, r 27), providing the request is made within 6 months of the decision. The chair of the Board can decide not to issue a summary if there are exceptional circumstances.

Although parole proceedings are otherwise held in private, amendments to the Parole Board Rules are being drafted that will give victims the right to apply to attend parole hearings.

Legal aid is available to fund representation at both pre and post tariff hearings and for review applications.

### Category A prisoners

Any male category A prisoner will be allocated to a high security prison (principally Frankland, Whitemoor, Wakefield, Full Sutton and Long Lartin, with some facilities at Belmarsh, Woodhill and Manchester). All decisions on categorisation and allocation are taken by the Director of High Security and not the governor of the jail itself.

### Juvenile male prisoners

Allocation will initially be to a secure training centre (STC) until the age of 16 or a young offenders' institution (YOI). Young people can remain a YOI until the age of 21 but may be moved earlier depending on maturity and temperament.

### Adult female prisoners

All women's prisons are either open or closed, although in 2013 the Secretary of State announced that open women's prisons would be abolished and that resettlement units would be opened in all women's prisons. No progress has been made on this proposal.

### Juvenile female prisoners

There are no discrete YOIs for young women and so it too old for the STC system, allocation will normally be to an adult women's prison.

Foreign nationals liable to deportation

The lifer system applies to foreign nationals who are going to be deported at the end of their sentence save for two important exceptions. The first is that allocation will normally be to one of the prisons designated to hold foreign nationals. The second is that at the end of the sentence, the Secretary of State can release and deport the prisoner without referring the case to the Parole Board. This change was brought in by the Legal Aid, Sentencing and Punishment of Offenders Act 2012 in April 2012 and allows the Secretary of State to remove foreign national lifers who have served their minimum terms. Under the policy guidance, removal will be assumed to be appropriate unless the Secretary of State considers the prisoner to pose a high risk or that they will attempt to re-enter the country.

### Release on Temporary Licence (ROTL)

https://assets.publishing.service.gov.uk/government/uploads/system/uploads/attachment_data/file/1011503/rotl-pf.pdfhe The Framework Document on ROTL sets out the various forms of ROTL and eligibility and all ISPs and extended sentenced prisoners are subject to restricted ROTL. This means that ISPs will not normally be permitted unescorted temporary release from prison until they are in an approved open prison.

### Open prisons

An open prison is usually seen as the last step towards release where the prisoner can be tested to ensure s/he is trustworthy and can make final plans for release. As most ISPs will have been in prison for many years, the general view in terms of risk assessment is that this period of time in an open prison is essential to readjust and prepare for life back in the community and to test trustworthiness. However, for ISPs with very short tariffs the Secretary of State and the Parole Board have agreed that there is less emphasis on the need to go to an open prison at all.

ISPs cannot normally move to an open prison until they have had their first parole review, although the Secretary of State does have the power to authorise such a move without first consulting the Parole Board in exceptional cases (R (Guittard) v Secretary of State for Justice [2009] EWHC 2951 (Admin)). The more normal route is that 3 years before the end of the tariff period, the prison will conduct what is known as a 'pre-tariff sift'. This will look at whether the individual has any real prospect of being approved for a move to open conditions. Only those cases where the prison considers that this is a realistic prospect will be referred to the Parole Board at this stage. This is assessed at a sentence planning meeting at the prison and is known as the "pre-tariff sift". If a case is not referred at this stage, the ISP will then have to wait until then end of the tariff before their case is considered by the Parole Board.

### Parole Board Reviews

ISPs can only be released at the direction of the Parole Board. The statutory test that the Board are required to apply is that it "is satisfied that it is no longer necessary for the protection of the public that the prisoner should be confined" (Crime (Sentences) Act 1997, s 28). Caselaw has established that this means the risk of causing serious harm through physical or psychological damage rather than non-violent or non-sexual offending.

Cases might be referred to the Parole Board before the tariff expires to decide upon suitability for a move to open conditions (see above) and must be referred on the expiry of the tariff. The prisoner will have a dossier of reports disclosed and has the opportunity to make written submissions about the reports and to submit any further relevant information, including any independent expert reports. The case is then considered on the papers only by a single member of the Parole Board. This is known as the MCA stage (member case assessment). The Board will then decide whether the case justifies an oral hearing. The Board had operated a policy that cases would only be referred to an oral hearing where there is a realistic chance of either release or a move to open conditions or where an oral hearing is required for some other reasons (such as to resolve an issue about the existence of a risk factor). In October 2013, the Supreme Court held in the case of Osborn and Booth [2013] UKSC 61 that this policy was too restrictive and indicated that the purpose of an oral hearing was far more wide ranging and they should be permitted more frequently. If the case is not referred to an oral hearing, an appeal can be made in writing. If it is referred, then the hearing will take place before a panel of three members of the Parole Board, usually at the prison where the ISP is located. Prisoners are entitled to be legally represented at all stages of this review procedure and public funding is available for all parole reviews. The Secretary of State had removed legal aid for pre- tariff reviews in December 2013 but it was reinstated in February 2018 following a successful legal challenge (R (Howard League and Prisoners' Advice Service) v Lord Chancellor [2017] EWCA Civ 827).

Following the challenge brought in the 'Worboys' case of R (DSD) v Parole Board [2018] EWHC 694 (Admin), the Ministry of Justice is to implement a procedure for reviewing parole decisions outside of judicial review. On 4 March 2019 a response to a public consultation was published which confirmed that legislative changes would be made to allow for a review process to be introduced in ISP and EDS cases (but not in cases involving standard determinate sentences). The parties to the review – that is the Secretary of State or the prisoner – can apply for a decision to be reconsidered within 21 days of notification. Anyone who is not a party, such as a victim, can ask the Secretary of State to make an application on their behalf. The threshold for a challenge will be the same is in judicial review and so a legal flaw in the decision or procedure will need to be identified. A judicial member of the Parole Board will then consider the case on the papers and will have the power to direct that new oral hearing takes place. Judicial review will still be available but it is likely that the courts will expect people to make use of this procedure before applying for judicial review.

## Addressing Offending Behaviour

One of the themes of the reviews and reports prepared for parole reviews is the term 'addressing offending behaviour' and this is certainly the main emphasis of a life sentence, but what does it actually mean? In virtually every case, there will be reasons why a person has committed a crime. Sometimes the person will know these reasons but in other cases, they may not be aware themselves. The first purpose of these reviews and plans is to try and identify these reasons or 'risk factors'. In some cases, the reasons may be obvious. For example, a person may have had money problems or may have had a drink or drugs problem. In other cases, a person may simply have had problems controlling his or her temper. It is impossible to generalise on this subject as each person will have their own particular background and history which will be scrutinised.

The normal method of addressing offending behaviour is through an accredited prison service course. Although the usefulness of many of these courses has been thrown into considerable doubt, they still remain a critical tool for assessing risk and are heavily relied upon by the prison and probation services and by the Parole Board. The latest list of accredited courses are here.

## Assessing Risk Factors

Before prisoners commence courses, they will normally be subject to assessments to determine their levels and areas of risk. Risk assessments can either be static – which looks at fixed historical events that cannot be changed, or dynamic – which looks at those factors that are amenable to change. Static factors will include matters such as previous convictions and the age of first conviction. Dynamic factors will look at matters such as employment, accommodation and substance abuse.

All ISPs will have an OASys completed and this contains an assessment designed to give a score on a number of static risk assessment tools such as general re- offending scales (OGRS) and violent reoffending (OVP) that will inform the likelihood of further offence being committed in a set period of time. Although these statistical findings are considered to be very accurate, it is important to remember that they can only give a percentage chance of the likelihood of re-offending and do not distinguish whether a particular individual will fall within that group or not. In more complex cases, more sophisticated tools that are designed to examine historic, clinical and risk management factors, such as the HCR-20, will be used.

In addition to these risk assessment tools, there are also a number of psychological evaluations that are used to ascertain the presence of personality traits which might be relevant to the risk of offending. The two most common are the tests to establish whether someone has psychopathic traits (the PCL-R) or personality disorders (IDPE). These are considered to be important as research has shown that conventional offending behaviour programmes may not be effective for people who demonstrate these traits.

## Cognitive Behavioural Offending Behaviour Programmes

The majority of courses are based on the cognitive behavioural method. These courses may address general problems that can lead into offending, such as poor decision making or substance abuse for example, the Thinking Skills Programme (TSP) is designed to look at general 'cognitive deficits' that results in people making bad choices. These courses do not require the participant to admit any particular crime and so can be suitable for prisoners who maintain their innocence. Other programmes will look at specific types of offences and require the participant to be able to give a detailed account of their offending. For violent offending, the two most common were the Self Change Programme (SCP) and RESOLVE but these have been gradually phased out and the work integrated into the Kaizen and Horizon programmes.

## Therapeutic Communities

There is a very different method of treating offending behaviour in a very different way which was pioneered by HMP Grendon. Grendon is run as a therapeutic community ('TC') and is designed to assist and treat individuals who have difficult psychological problems that need intensive therapy. Therapeutic wings are also in operation at a few other male prisons (eg: HMP Dovegate and Gartree) and for female prisoners at HMP Send. Selection for these communities differs from that for other prisons in that they will only accept people who want to enter into therapy. Some people have a misconception that a TC is an easy option or a short cut through offending behaviour work. In fact, TCs can be a very difficult places as they require a great deal of input and involvement from the people sent there. Also, it is not usually seen as a replacement for other offending behaviour work and most people who go there will return to a normal prison and may still be expected to complete the standard offending behaviour courses. It is quite unusual for ISPs to be moved to open prison conditions direct from a TC unless all other offending behaviour programmes have already been completed.

## DSPDs

Where prisoners are diagnosed as suffering from personality disorders, progress can be extremely difficult. In such cases, special hospitals will generally not consider that they can provide any appropriate intervention as personality disorders are not considered to be' treatable'. The prison service established two centres at Whitemoor and Frankland designed to address the problems this causes by providing treatment and intervention which is more tailored to individual problems (and there are also units in the special hospital system) through a course known as CHROMIS. Other units are being considered for prisoners in less secure conditions where there are concerns about the presence of personality disorders but where the offences omitted are not the most serious. Although the two main units have been in operation for many years, progress is painfully slow and concerns have been expressed about the manner in which prisoners are progressed after completion.

## FAQ: Are The Courses Compulsory?

No-one can be forced to attend any offending behaviour programme and it is entirely up to each individual as to whether he/she will participate. The problem that is faced is these courses are seen as the most reliable method of treating risk factors. This means that in the current climate, refusal to attend can make progress much slower. The courts have also held that it is legitimate for the prison service to make addressing offending behaviour a factor taken into account when assessing the appropriate placement on the incentives and earned privileges schemes.

## What If The Prisoner Is Innocent?

Neither the Prison Service nor the Parole Board can decide whether someone is innocent and they are legally obliged to accept the findings of the courts. Although it is unlawful to refuse to progress or release a prisoner simply because he/she maintains their innocence, it becomes very difficult to progress through the system as there will be doubts expressed as to whether the risk to the public has reduced. Sometimes it is still possible to complete a course in these circumstances by looking at areas of concern without admitting the offence. For example if someone is convicted of murder during a burglary and admits the burglary but denies the murder, he/she can complete work on the burglary and general lifestyle problems.

## What About Other Convictions?

ISPs are expected to address all aspects of their offending and lifestyle even if not directly connected to the index offence. This means that if someone is convicted of murder and has an old conviction for a sex offence, that person will be expected to address both offences. The Ministry of Justice are allowed to take this approach in law on the grounds that the test for releasing a lifer is whether that person poses any risk of serious harm to the public. This approach does not breach the European Convention of Human Rights.

## What About Unconvicted Allegations?

There has been some uncertainty on the part of the Parole Board about how to treat allegations where there has been no charge or an acquittal. In the context of a recall, the position has always been that the Parole Board can investigate all relevant matters even if there have been no criminal charges or where the person has been acquitted. This is because the Parole Board operates to the lower, civil standard of proof being the balance of probabilities, rather than the criminal standard of beyond reasonable doubt (see R (Brooks) v Parole Board [2004] EWCA Civ 80). In the 'Worboys' case (R (DSD) v Parole Board [2018] EWHC 694 (Admin)) the court considered that allegations which had not been prosecuted could be a relevant factor for the Parole Board to look into when deciding whether to release an ISP for the first time, providing this was done fairly, although it was accepted that the circumstances of that case were exceptional and that it is not the task of the Parole Board "to determine whether a prisoner had committed other offences". Subsequent caselaw has not assisted in providing clarity on how the Parole Board should approach this task and appears to support the view that the Parole Board can decide that an allegation raises concerns and to then decide what weight to give to those concerns, even where they fall short of making an adverse finding of fact. The most up-to-date guidance on how the Parole Board approached this task is contained in their publication 'Guidance on Allegations" (July 2021) (https://assets.publishing.service.gov.uk/government/uploads/system/uploads/attachment_data/file/1010818/guidance-on-allegations-v1.1-july-2021_.pdf). Previous decisions have indicated that the Parole Board has the power to disregard or exclude material if it prejudicial and cannot fairly be challenged by the prisoner (R (McGetrick) v Parole Board [2012] EWHC 882 (Admin).

## What If There Are No Places On The Courses I Need To Take?

One of the problems with the increasing reliance on these courses as a tool for assessing risk has been a lack of places being available. However, the Parole Board are very reluctant to release a prisoner who has not taken a course deemed necessary, even when the fault for this lays with the prison service and not the prisoner. Many years ago the Secretary of State accepted that there is a duty in common law to provide courses

(R (Cawser) v Home Secretary [2003] EWCA Civ 1522) but it did not appear that there was clear path available for prisoners to take action about the failure to provide those courses except in the most extreme circumstances. After a lot of litigation following the problems caused by the introduction of the IPP sentence, the ECtHR found that the failure to make enough courses available for IPP prisoners had rendered the detention of three such prisoners arbitrary and in breach of Article 5(1) (James v UK (2013) 56 EHRR 12). Following that decision, the domestic courts have looked at this issue a number of times. Although the judgments are complex, the broad principle that was established was that:
• A delay in providing a prisoner with a reasonable opportunity to demonstrate a reduction in risk can also lead to a breach of Article 5 (R (Haney and others) v Secretary of State for Justice [2015] AC 1344
• These delays do not give rise to a right to release but a right to compensation.
The courts have taken quite a hard line in cases seeking compensation for such delays. Eventually, in Brown v Parole Board for Scotland [2017] UKSC 69 the Supreme Court stated that previous decisions had wrongly concentrated on a general failure to progress a prisoner (sometimes called an ancillary Article 5 duty) but the assessment should be whether the lack of access to meaningful rehabilitation rendered detention unlawful and that this is a very high threshold to cross. In cases where it was crossed, the remedy would ordinarily be the right to take proceedings to challenge the lawfulness of that detention under Article 5(4) or damages.

### Are There Any Better Methods Of Addressing Risk?

There has been a great deal of criticism of the extent to which prison assessments of risk are influenced by prison psychologists who tend to follow rather rigid models of risk assessment and may not have a great deal of experience of risk management as opposed to risk assessment. Some studies have shown that offending behaviour courses can have very little impact of reoffending rates and other studies seem to be based on models of courses run in different countries. Nevertheless, the Parole Board tend to be very strongly influenced by their approach. Unfortunately, cases before the courts have established that where the Parole Board are faced with competing but credible expert opinions (or approaches), they are entitled to make a choice as to which they prefer.

*Simon Creighton is a consultant at Bhatt Murphy Solicitors, where he specialises in prison law. He was previously the first solicitor to work at the Prisoners' Advice Service*

## 2.15 WOMEN PRISONERS

**Policy name: Women's Policy Framework**
**Issue Date: 21 December 2018** - minor update 26th June 2021 to take account that from that date all Community Rehabilitation Company (CRC) contracts have been terminated, with the responsibility for all offender management activity transferring to the Probation Service.

**Also**
*Mother and Baby Units*
Pregnancy, MBUs and Maternal Separation in Women's Prisons Policy Framework - latest update of this Policy Framework was 5th October 2021 and please note that is cancels PSI 49/2014) see below.

**Women's Prisons 2023**
• HMP/YOI Bronzefield
• HMP/YOI Drake Hall
• HMP/YOI Downview
• HMP/YOI East Sutton Park
• HMP/YOI Eastwood Park
• HMP/YOI Foston Hall
• HMP/YOI Low Newton
• HMP/YOI Peterborough
• HMP/YOI Send
• HMP/YOI Styal
• HMP/YOI New Hall
• HMP/YOI Askham Grange

**Women in prison: A Report by the Justice Committee 26th July 2022.**
**Summary:** Women represent less than 5% of the total prison population. They are often sentenced to custody for non-violent, low-level but persistent offences, and are more likely than men to be sentenced for short periods of time. Female offenders are often the most vulnerable in society and have varied and complex needs. Many have experienced mental health problems, substance misuse, homelessness, abuse and trauma in their lives. The Ministry of Justice recognised these challenges in its 2018 Female Offender Strategy, which set out its strategic priorities to see fewer women coming into the criminal justice system; fewer women in custody (especially on short sentences); and a greater proportion of women managed in the community successfully, with better conditions for those in custody. This Report assesses its performance to date against those priorities.
Whilst the Female Offender Strategy represented a welcome step forward in the Government's recognition that a specific approach was needed to achieve outcomes for women in the criminal justice system, our Report raises concerns about the lack of progress the Government has made to

date against the aims and objectives set out in the Strategy. For example, the MoJ now predicts an increase in the female population of more than a third over present levels in the next three years. There is anecdotal evidence that sentencer confidence in community sentences has declined. And progress has been slow on the MoJ 's commitment to develop five women 's residential centres. Our Report makes recommendations across a range of areas, which we hope will help re-energise the MoJ 's ambition for delivery of its Strategy as the criminal justice system slowly begins to recover from the pandemic.

The Justice Committee has warned that limited progress has been made in developing alternatives to custodial sentences for women amid concerns that the female prison population may rise by a third in the next three years. In a report published 26th July 2022, the Committee finds that more needs to be done to address the addiction, mental health and trauma issues facing women who enter the prison system.

The report calls on the Government to ensure that strategies developed to combat problems in the system are adequately funded, rolled out efficiently and monitored for performance to create meaningful change.

The report also calls for a renewed focus on the specific challenges facing women who enter the prison system. This includes the impact it has on women who are primary carers and what more can be done to ensure that vital family relationships are maintained.

Chair of the Justice Committee, Sir Bob Neill MP said: *"It is welcome that the Government has understood that there are specific challenges around sending women to prison that need to be addressed, but it is disappointing that there is yet to be significant tangible change.*

*"The 2018 Female Offender Strategy marked an important step in recognising the needs of women in the criminal justice system, but more needs to be done to understand whether it is targeting the right areas and having a meaningful impact. Women entering the prison system often have challenging needs and they must be supported from the day they arrive to the day they leave and beyond."*

### Fewer women in prison

A key objective of the Government's Female Offender strategy is to have fewer women in prison. Overall numbers have fallen, from 3,958 in February 2017 to 3,219, in July 2022, however the Ministry of Justice now predicts that it will increase by a third over the next three years. In the strategy, the Government has indicated it intends to improve Out of Court Disposals as an alternative to custodial sentences, however there is yet to be any clear evidence that more women

are being diverted away from custody through this route. The Government should set out what funding it plans to put in place to support the development of women-specific pathways to support alternatives to prison sentences. It should also set out a timeframe for when it expects these services to be in operation.

### Dealing with self-harm

Over the past decade there has been an alarming increase in the level of self-harm in the female prison estate. The Committee welcomes that the Ministry of Justice and the Prisons Service has identified this as a serious issue, however there are concerns that current self-harm reduction programmes are seen as an outcome in themselves. It calls on the Ministry of Justice to set out how it will evaluate and measure the impact of changes to the Assessment, Care in Custody and Teamwork (ACCT) process. It should also clarify what wider work is being done alongside ACCT to ensure that there is not an over reliance on a single mechanism. The Offender Management in Custody Model, where each prisoner is allocated a keyworker, is a welcome development and the Committee supports its rolling out across the female prison estate.

### Coping with past trauma

The majority of women entering the prison system have experienced past trauma and this impacts on how they interact with the prison system. The Committee welcomes the move towards a more trauma-informed approach on the female prison estate. It calls on the MoJ to clarify which staff will be given training on supporting prisoners dealing with trauma and set out how it will monitor completion on an ongoing basis.

### Impact on family life

Sending women to prison can have a significant effect on family life, particularly when they are the primary carer. It is concerning that the MoJ does not know how many women in prison are primary carers and it is vital that data collection in this respect is improved.

The impact of placing women in prisons far from their families can be severe. While it is welcome that more work is being done to improve community alternatives, the MoJ needs to do more to raise awareness of the Assisted Prison Visits Scheme to support prisoners to maintain direct contact with loved ones. The MoJ should also clarify what wider measures have been put in place to support visits and publish information on the number of visits that have taken place across the female prison estate.

### Education

Data collection on education is poor, making it difficult to draw conclusions on whether it is meeting the specific demands of women in the prison system. If current education levels or learning difficulties are not recorded it is difficult to know if their needs are being met.

The Committee is however concerned that educational opportunities are too narrow and levels of access vary depending on length of sentence. The MoJ should look at how it can broaden educational opportunities so that they support the needs of all women in the prison system irrespective of their term in prison.

### Reintegration

Finding suitable accommodation on release is one of the most significant and urgent barriers to resettlement. The MoJ should work with partners across Government to develop a strategy that provides appropriate accommodation for women leaving prison. It should set out what accommodation is currently provided by its accommodation service and how it meets the specific needs of women prisoners. It should also set out what work is being done to support resettlement when they have been held in custody far from their homes. Continuity of care also plays a crucial role in ensuring that women are adequately supported when leaving prison and the MoJ should set out what work they are carrying out to facilitate this.

The full report, Women in Prison, is available at *prisonoracle.com*

### Facts & Figures August 2022
### Use of custody

On 5th August 2022 there were 3,210 women in 12 prisons in England and Wales.

### WOMEN'S POLICY FRAMEWORK

**Updated 26th June 2021 to take account of CRC abolition.** To be read in conjunction with 'Women's Estate Case Advice and Support Policy Framework 17th May 2021 available on prisonoracle.com

**1 Purpose**
**2 Evidence**
**3 Outcomes**
- Cross-cutting
- Court
- Community / Custody
- Custody

**4 Requirements**
- Cross-cutting
- Human trafficking and Modern day slavery
- Female Genital Mutilation (FGM)
- Court
- The Offender Rehabilitation Act 2014
- Community
- The Homelessness Reduction Act 2017

- Custody
- Family

**5 Constraints**
- Prisoner Escort and Custody Services (PECS)
- Searching
- Detention of Immigration Detainees – Pregnant Women and Mothers with Babies
- Transgender prisoners

**6 Guidance**
Annex A Breakdown of Evidence
Annex B A strategy for female offenders

### 1. Purpose

1.1 This policy framework sets out the MoJ's expectations for the delivery of services for working with women in custody and the community. This enables staff to be aware of the gender specific issues that affect women, and respond appropriately to ensure that their different needs are consistently met. This does not detract from the requirement to consider the needs of other protected characteristics. It is important that this framework is read in conjunction with its supporting Guidance on Working with Women in Custody and Community.

### 2 Evidence

2.1 In 2015 the evidence based commissioning guidance Better Outcomes for Women Offenders was published.[1] This was informed by a variety of sources, including a Rapid Evidence Assessment of robust evidence from the UK and overseas to identify what works in reducing women's offending.[2]

2.2 The best available evidence suggests that we should invest in gender-informed interventions that take into account the impact of the trauma many women offenders have experienced and address the seven priority areas of need which are outlined in. Annex A.

2.3 A gender-informed approach is an approach that is built on the theories of women's crime, taking into account the characteristics of women who offend and factors that affect the response of women to interventions.

2.4 See table in Annex A for a more detailed breakdown of evidence.

2.5 In June 2018 the Government's Female Offender Strategy was published which focuses on improving the outcomes of women in both the community and custody based on the best evidence of what works.

2.6 See Table in Annex B for evidence highlighted in the Female Offender Strategy

### 3. Outcomes

Cross-cutting
3.1 Staff who work with women are provided with gender-informed training.

3.2 Women are given help and support to maintain family ties where appropriate.

3.3 The needs of pregnant women and women who have given birth are assessed and addressed.

3.4 Women who are separated or who are separating from their children (including through fostering and adoption) are given appropriate support, including those experiencing loss or bereavement.

3.5 Women are not disproportionately disadvantaged or unable to access services due to diversity circumstances, childcare, personal circumstances etc.

**Court**

3.6 Pre-sentence reports (PSRs) are written to assist the court to determine the most suitable method of dealing with an offender and should represent the personal circumstances of each woman, taking into account their specific needs (such as impact on care and safeguarding issues).

3.7 Proposals in PSRs are clear and strong in argument to support non custodial options for the Court to consider in appropriate cases.

3.8 Licence conditions and Community Order Requirements which aim to protect the public, prevent re-offending and secure the woman's successful re-integration into the community, should also be proportionate, achievable and meet the individual and distinct needs of that woman.

3.9 Women's experience while in court cells and while travelling to and from prison is safe, decent and efficient, and serves to reassure them about their well-being and safety in custody.

**Community/Custody**

3.10 Women feel safe and reassured that they will receive appropriate help to address any urgent needs.

3.11 The Assessment, Induction and the Offender Management processes meet the specific needs of women.

3.12 Women are given access to appropriate interventions in the community and in custody.

3.13 In accordance with Public Health England's Gender Specific Standards to Improve Health and Wellbeing for Women in Prison in England, women are able to access health services, including mental health, personality disorder, substance misuse and learning disability services that meet their gender specific needs.

3.14 Women at risk of, or who are victims of, domestic abuse, sexual abuse, sexual exploitation, sex work, human trafficking and other forms of gender-based abuse, are identified and then supported according to their needs.

3.15 Women are supervised/held in trauma-informed conditions and within regimes providing rehabilitative culture where they feel safe and that meet their specific needs and which facilitate their successful resettlement.

3.16 Women are given support to find somewhere safe to live, learn how to manage their money, access education and training and improve their employability.

3.17 Approved Premises are utilised in appropriate cases for those women who are assessed as high and medium risk of serious harm, but can also be used by some low risk of harm women who are high need

3.18 Women comply with their community order/licence conditions and variation to orders and licence are made to support this.

3.19 Alternatives to breach/recall are appropriately considered.

**Custody**

3.20 Women are managed appropriately to their current risk level and complexities of need, with the aim of reducing risk as their sentence progresses. Where possible, and subject to the considerations of security, good order and addressing their offending behaviour, women are held in prisons that best enable them to maintain their family ties.

3.21 Women who self-harm are supported and cared for appropriately according to their individual needs. Establishments understand the risk factors and triggers for self-harm, and use the Assessment, Care in Custody and Teamwork (ACCT) case management process effectively, with the aim of reducing the number and severity of self-harm incidents and preventing self-inflicted deaths.

3.22 There is appropriate use of peer support arrangements.

3.23 Suitable and safe accommodation on release is identified.

3.24 Order in women's prisons is managed in an informed way with preventative actions taken to promote pro-social behaviour wherever possible.

3.25 Prisons have a Family and Significant Other Strategy in place detailing how they aim to help women maintain these relationships.

3.26 All pregnant women and women with children under 18 months are made aware of the benefits of Mother and Baby Units and are assisted in making an application for a place on such a unit, where they choose to do so.

3.27 Mother and Baby Units are operated in a way that meets the best interests of the child and which work to deliver successful resettlement for mother and child.

3.28 In custody, women are given the opportunity to access appropriate education, learning, skills (including parenting skills), and employment.

## 4. Requirements
## Cross-cutting
### The Equality Act and the Public Sector Equality Duty

4.1 The Equality Act 2010 provides protection from unlawful discrimination in relation to the following characteristics: age, disability, gender reassignment, pregnancy & maternity (which includes breastfeeding), race, religion or belief, sex, marriage and civil partnership, and sexual orientation. Guidance can be found at Equality Act 2010: Summary Guidance on Services, Public Functions and Associations

4.2 The Equality Act created the 'Public Sector Equality Duty' (PSED), which requires that public sector employers must, in the exercise of their functions, have 'due regard' to the need to:
• Eliminate unlawful discrimination, harassment and victimisation and other conduct prohibited by the Act.
• Advance equality of opportunity between people who share a protected characteristic and those who do not.
• Foster good relations between people who share a protected characteristic and those who do not.

4.3 HMPPS is a public authority to the extent that it exercises public functions within the meaning of Section 149(2) of the Equality Act 2010. As such, it is also required to meet and demonstrate compliance with the PSED when undertaking these functions.

### Human trafficking and Modern day slavery

4.4. Staff must contact a 'First Responder' if an offender indicates that they have been a victim of human trafficking, or if staff have any reason to believe this may be the case. First Responders are organisations designed to assess individuals to determine whether the person should be formally referred to the National Referral Mechanism (NRM)[3].

4.5 A list of First Responders can be found at: National Crime Agency National Referral Mechanism

### Female Genital Mutilation (FGM).

4.6 Regulated health and social care professionals and teachers in England and Wales are mandatorily required to report known cases of FGM in under 18-year-olds to the police. The FGM duty came into force on 31 October 2015.[4]

## Court
### Petherick judgment

4.7 Sentencers are required to take into account the Petherick Judgement which provided 8 general principles to be considered when sentencing Offenders with dependent children:

4.8 Sentencing of a person with dependent children engages article 8, right to a family life.

4.9 Is there an interference with article 8? If so, is it in accordance with law, pursue a legitimate aim and is proportionate?

4.10 Sentencing practice in England and Wales recognises that dependent children are a relevant factor in sentencing.

4.11 The criminal court should be informed where the family life of others will be affected and this will need to be balanced with the legitimate aims that sentencing serve.

4.12 When considering the legitimate aims of sentencing, this includes the need to punish serious crime, interest of victims, appropriate deterrence and there ought not to be unjustified disparity between defendants convicted of similar crimes.

4.13 For offenders on the cusp of custody, consideration should be given to the fact that in such cases, the interference with the family life of one or more entirely innocent children can sometimes tip the scales and mean that a custodial sentence otherwise proportionate may become disproportionate.

4.14 The interference with family life caused by imprisonment is progressively reduced as the offence is graver.

4.15 Where custody cannot proportionately be avoided, the effect on children or other family members might afford grounds for mitigating the length of sentence, but it may not do so.

4.16 Pre-sentence reports should therefore assess primary care responsibilities and the impact of a custodial sentence on dependents, including children.

### The Offender Rehabilitation Act 2014

4.17 The Offender Rehabilitation Act 2014 (ORA) came into force fully on 1st February 2015. This made a number of changes to the sentencing framework, most notably changing the law so that all offenders released from short prison sentences now receive 12 months of statutory supervision and assistance with their resettlement back in the community.

4.18 Under section 10 of the Offender Rehabilitation Act 2014 (ORA), the Secretary of State for Justice is required to ensure that contracts with providers comply with the public sector equality duty and identify anything in the arrangements that is intended to meet the particular needs of female offenders.

## Community

4.19 Probation must meet three specific requirements in relation to the management of female offenders. Female offenders should be offered the option of a female Responsible Officer/Offender Manager; when attending meetings with their Responsible Officer/Offender Manager they should be offered the option of being interviewed in a female-only environment; and they should be offered the option of not being placed in an all-male work environment as part of an Unpaid Work or Attendance Centre requirement.

### The Homelessness Reduction Act 2017

4.20 The Homelessness Reduction Act 2017 came into force on the 3rd April 2018. Under the Act housing authorities must design advice and information services to meet the needs of people within their district, including people leaving prison and victims of domestic abuse. Housing Authorities have a duty to take reasonable steps to prevent an eligible person from becoming homeless if they are threatened with homelessness within 56 days, irrespective of priority need, intentional homelessness or local connection to the area

4.21 Local housing authorities must also take reasonable steps to try and relieve homelessness for eligible people who are actually homelessness, by helping them to secure accommodation. Again this relief duty is owed whether or not the applicant has priority need or may be intentionally homeless, but if there is no local connection they may be referred to another local authority for help, if they would be safe in that area. The prevention and relief duty each last for up to 56 days.

4.22 Under the Homelessness Reduction Act 2017, the Governor or Director of a prison and providers of probation services as a public authority has a duty to refer anyone who is homeless or at risk of being homeless within 56 days to a local housing authority provided HMPPS has the person's consent and the person has identified the local housing authority they wish to be referred to. In Wales, women are subject to the Welsh Housing Act 2014.

### Custody
### Immigration Act 2016 - Pregnant Immigration Detainees

4.23 Prisons must make the Home Office Criminal Casework team aware (via their designated inbox – adultatriskpregnancy@) homeoffice.gsi.gov.uk) of any pregnant immigration detainees at the earliest possible time in compliance with section 60 of Immigration Act 2016. This requires that the detention of a pregnant foreign national woman under immigration powers must not exceed a maximum period of 72 hours (or seven calendar days with Ministerial approval), and upon expiry of these time periods the pregnant woman must be released from immigration detention. However, these provisions do not apply if the woman is to be shortly removed from the United Kingdom or there are exceptional circumstances which justify the detention.

### PSI 39/2011 - Categorisation and Recategorisation of women prisoners

4.24 Governors must follow the arrangements in PSI 39/2011 Categorisation and Recategorisation of Women prisoners. This sets out that the most dangerous or high risk women are categorised as Restricted Status (RS) and are held in one of the prisons designated as secure enough to hold such women.

PSI 23/2015 - Centralised case supervision system for restricted status women and women with complex needs

4.25 Governors must follow the arrangements in PSI 23/2015 Centralised Case Supervision System for Restricted Status Women and Women with Complex Needs. This sets out the details of the support available to prisons managing Restricted Status women and those with complex needs. The system is managed through Headquarters and provides multi-disciplinary case management and reviews.

### Family

4.26 Governors must follow the arrangements in the Strengthening Prisoners' Family Ties Policy Framework and ensure that arrangements are in place to help women build, maintain and strengthen their family ties wherever appropriate.

### Mother and Baby Units
### Pregnancy, MBUs and Maternal Separation in Women's Prisons Policy Framework - latest update 5th October 2021, cancels PSI 49/2014.

This HMPPS Policy Framework sets mandatory requirements that address the additional emotional, physical and practical needs of perinatal women and mothers in prison and how prisons support them. The policy is based on the principles of individual needs-led and multi-agency care planning, to ensure the support is in place.

The policy contains requirements applying to the three groups below in recognition of shared needs:

**Part A** - pregnancy, birth, the post-natal period and other pregnancy outcomes

**Part B** - Applying for and facilitating Mother and Baby Unit (MBU) placements (replacing PSI 49/2014 PI 63/2014 'Mother and Baby Units')

**Part C** – maternal separation from children up to the age of two, due to imprisonment

This policy is supported by operational guidance and a templates pack, containing best practice advice designed to aid implementation and the development of local policies. The guidance will be published in due course.

The policy was developed following a fundamental review between July 2019 and June 2021. A wide range of stakeholders were consulted, including women with lived experience, the health sector, children's social care sector, and voluntary sector. A summary of the review scope, consultation feedback and key reforms can be found on GOV.UK.

Governors must follow the arrangements in the Policy Framework, including making sure that women are asked on reception, or at the earliest opportunity, whether they are/could be pregnant or have children under the age of 18 months. As per the Strengthening Prisoners' Family Ties Policy Framework "When collecting information about next of kin and family contacts when prisoners are received, Governors/Directors should include requesting details of children. This will enable appropriate services to be provided to support prisoners and their family".

4.28 The Mother and Baby Unit (MBU) Policy Framework provides detailed information on the management of MBUs, the appointment of Pregnancy, Mother and Baby Unit Liaison Officers (PMBULO's) who and their deputies who must be Band 3 Prison Officers, including the application and appeal process about access to a Mother and Baby Unit that is now contained in the **Prisoner Complaints Policy Framework updated 20th September 2021.**

PSI 16/2011 - Providing Visits and Services to Visitors

Governors must follow the arrangements in PSI 16/2011 Providing Visits and Services to Visitors. This provides information on providing visits and services to visitors for pregnant women, nursing mothers, families, as well as guidance on final contact visits prior to adoption.

Notification of stillbirth, neonatal death, suspected brain injury or maternal death

Prison staff need to be aware that from April 2018, the Healthcare Safety Investigation Branch (HSIB) will investigate every case of a stillbirth, neonatal death, suspected brain injury or maternal death notified to the Royal College of Obstetricians and Gynaecologists (RCOG) Every Baby Counts programme, amounting to around 1,000 incidents per year.

## 5. Constraints
### Prisoner Escort and Custody Services (PECS) – Contractual requirements

Pregnant women must not be transported in cellular vehicles unless, exceptionally, the risk has been assessed as acceptable by a healthcare professional (in the case of movements from prison this will be the prison's healthcare manager).[6] Reception staff must be made aware of this requirement and any case of authorised use of cellular vans for a pregnant woman must be reported by the Governor to PECS.

When moving a woman from police custody or court, if the Contractor has not been advised by the Agency handing over the Prisoner that she is pregnant and the Prisoner declares herself to be pregnant, the Contractor shall seek advice from a healthcare professional and a non-cellular vehicle may be used if the healthcare professional so advises.

### Searching

Women prisoners must not be full-searched as a matter of routine but only on intelligence or reasonable suspicion that an item is being concealed on the person which may be revealed by a full search. The procedure for searching women prisoners is different to that used to search male prisoners. Governors must follow the arrangements in PSI 07/2016 Searching of the Person, which specifies the searching arrangements for women prisoners. Annex D.4 includes guidance on Searching Religious or Cultural Headwear.

In accordance with HMPPS Operational Protocol 'X-Ray Body Scanning of Prisoners' women prisoners who are or who might be pregnant must not be subjected to the x-ray body scanner process.

Any searching of babies (of mothers in Mother and Baby Units) should also be carried out in accordance with Annex I of this PSI.

### Detention of Immigration Detainees – Pregnant Women and Mothers with Babies

Section 60 of Immigration Act 2016 requires that the detention of a pregnant foreign national woman under immigration powers must not exceed a maximum period of 72 hours (or seven calendar days with Ministerial approval), and upon expiry of these time periods the pregnant woman must be released from immigration detention.

When a foreign national woman who is accompanied by her child in a Mother and Baby Unit (MBU) completes her custodial prison sentence, the Home Office can only detain the mother or child in exceptional circumstances, and only with permission from the Minister for Immigration. In general, foreign national women prisoners with babies should almost never be detained at the end of their custodial prison sentence using Immigration powers. Where an IS91 is in force and no formal release order has been issued withdrawing the authority to detain, or where there is any uncertainty about what should happen to a foreign national woman and her child at the end of the custodial sentence, prison staff should immediately contact Immigration Enforcement's Minors, Mothers and Baby Team on 0113 341 3374 for advice.

**Transgender prisoners**

New Policy Framework issued January 2020 - **The care and management of individuals who are transgender.**

1. Purpose and Scope

1.1 This Policy Framework is intended to provide staff with clear direction in the support and safe management of transgender individuals in our care, including managing risks both to and from transgender individuals, and enabling risk to be managed when an individual is placed into a prison which is different to that of their legal gender or where a Gender Recognition Certification (GRC) has been obtained.

1.2 This Policy Framework provides information and sets out mandatory actions relating to the care and management of transgender individuals in Prisons, Private Prisons, Youth Secure Estate, Approved Premises (AP), Probation and private providers who provide services on behalf of HMPPS.

1.3 The primary focus is on individuals who express a consistent desire to live permanently in the gender with which they identify, and which is opposite to the biological sex assigned to them at birth, including those who:

* wish to seek to transition permanently to a new gender;

* wish to consistently live in the gender with which they identify but do not seek to have this recognised in law;

* have gained legal recognition of their new gender.

1.4 Also included in the scope of this framework are those who identify as transgender but do not seek to acquire a new gender. They will be managed in accordance with their legally recognised gender and include those who:

* are Intersex or individuals with variations of sex characteristics who are content with their sex assigned at birth;

* do not identify with a gender (non-binary);

* have an inconsistent gender identity (gender fluid);

* are cross dressers (transvestite).

1.5 This policy framework builds on the previous instruction (PSI 17/2016) in the following key respects:

* Safeguarding and decision-making processes are strengthened via Local and Complex Case Boards (CCB)

* Risk Assessment principles within CCBs have been expanded and identified

* CCBs are convened monthly and chaired by Prison Group Directors across the men's and women's estates

* Criteria for CCBs are clearer and more specific

* Local Transgender Case Boards, for all prisons, to be chaired by an operational Band 8 (or higher) deemed competent by the Governor (or equivalent in a privately managed prison and

deemed competent by the Director), of which a small number will be allocated per prison group

* Local Transgender Case Boards to be chaired by a National Probation Service member of staff at (NPS) Band 6 (or higher) deemed competent for Approved Premise allocation

* Scope is extended to include YCS

* Advance disclosure is introduced prior to a Case Board

* All remand prisoners will be initially located in the part of the estate that matches their legal gender until the CCB has approved a transfer.

* CCB process is introduced for NPS Approved Premise allocation.

* Initial Local Transgender Case Board to be held within 14 days, not 3 days, to allow for disclosure and informed risk assessments. The new timeframe will allow for a suitable amount of time in which to collect and share relevant information.

Risk assessment and risk management

1.6 The proper assessment of risk is paramount in the management of all individuals in our care. The management of individuals who are transgender, particularly in custodial and residential settings, must seek to protect both the welfare and rights of the individual and the welfare and rights of others around them, including staff. Decisions must be informed by all available evidence and intelligence in order to achieve an outcome that balances risks and promotes the safety of all in our care and management.

Evidence - HMPPS Analytical Data

2.1 The numbers of transgender individuals held in the adult prison estate are low (approximately 1.6 transgender prisoners reported per 1,000 prisoners in custody). In a snapshot data collection held in April/May 2018 and published in November 2018, there were 139 prisoners currently living in, or presenting in, a gender different to their sex assigned at birth and who had sat a Local Transgender Case Board.

**6. Guidance**

6.1 Government policy is made in accordance with the **United Nations Rules for the Treatment of Women Prisoners and Non-custodial Measures for Women Offenders** (*'the Bangkok Rules'*).

6.2 The 70 Rules give guidance to policy makers, legislators, sentencing authorities and prison staff to reduce the imprisonment of women, and to meet the specific needs of women in case of imprisonment. **Guidance can be found at: United Nations Rules for the Treatment of Women Prisoners**

6.3 More detailed information and guidance is set out in the document Guidance on Working with Women in Custody and the Community. This guidance is available internally for HMPPS staff. This guidance outlines how practitioners working with women can deliver services to them in a way that meets their distinct needs and reflects the significance of gender to their offending behaviour.

1 MoJ. (2015). Better Outcomes for Women Offenders. Available at: https://assets.publishing.service.gov.uk/government/uploads/ system/uploads/attachment_data/file/457922/Better_Outcome s_for_Women_Offenders_September_2015.pdf

2 MoJ. (2015). Effective interventions for Women offenders: A Rapid Evidence Assessment. Available at: https://assets.publishing.service.gov.uk/government/uploads/ system/uploads/attachment_data/file/448859/effective-interventions-for-women-offenders.pdf

3 The National Referral Mechanism is a multi-agency framework designed to make it easier for agencies involved in a trafficking case to cooperate, share information about potential victims and to facilitate the individual's access to support.

4 Section 5B of the Female Genital Mutilation Act 2003, inserted by section 74 of the Serious Crime Act 2015

5.http://www.bailii.org/ew/cases/EWCA/Crim/2012/2214.html

6 Cellular vehicles contain individual cells within an escort vehicle and that the cellular nature of these vehicles means that they are not suitable for holding pregnant women or mothers with babies. As such, the escort contractor must provide a non-cellular vehicle for the transport of pregnant prisoners and those who are mothers with babies (ensuring that a baby does not travel in a cellular van).

### A strategy for female offenders

1. The Female Offender Strategy (June 2018) set out the Government's commitment to a new programme of work for female offenders, driven by our vision to see:

• fewer women coming into the criminal justice system
• fewer women in custody, especially on short-term sentences, and a greater proportion of women managed in the community successfully; and
• better conditions for those in custody.[i]

2. To reduce crime and make a difference to victims, we need to consider the underlying causes of offending and reoffending, and take an evidence-based approach to rehabilitating offenders. We know that many offenders are amongst the most vulnerable people in society and that these vulnerabilities can often contribute to their offending behaviours or how they engage and respond to interventions.[ii,iii] Female offenders can be amongst the most vulnerable of all, in both the prevalence and complexity of their needs. Many experience chaotic lifestyles involving substance misuse, mental health problems, homelessness, and offending behaviour – these are often the product of a life of abuse and trauma.[iv]

3. Although the proportion of women in the criminal justice system (CJS) is small – approximately 5% of the prison population and 15% of offenders in the community– the positive impact of addressing their needs is significant. [v]

4. On average female offenders commit less serious offences than male offenders and often pose a low or medium risk of serious harm to the public.[vi,vii] Yet the reoffending rate among women is 22.9% for the April to June 2016 cohort,

often committing non-violent, low-level but persistent offences, such as shop theft.[viii,ix] Furthermore, chaotic lives and complex needs often mean female offenders have repeated needs for services and a disrupted family life. Female offenders cost the Government approximately £1.7bn in 2015/16, including estimated police costs of £1bn. This excludes wider social costs, such as the cost of intergenerational offending.

5. It is clear, therefore, that tackling and reducing the cycle of offending amongst women could have significant benefits to victims, families, and Government, as well as to female offenders themselves.

6. Outcomes for women in custody can be worse than for men: for example, the rate of self-harm is nearly five times as high in women's prisons.[xi] This disparity is highly troubling and it is right to seek to create equal opportunity for men and women in the CJS to rehabilitate themselves. Baroness Corston's seminal report, A Review of Women with Particular Vulnerabilities in the Criminal Justice System (2007), highlighted that the factors that can lead men and women to commit crime, and to reoffend, can vary significantly, as can the way men and women respond to interventions.[xii] Our own evidence review suggests that ensuring interventions are tailored appropriately to the particular needs of women can be more effective than applying a generic approach to men and women alike.[xiii]

7. There is a clear opportunity to take an entirely different approach to this cohort – one that addresses vulnerability, acknowledges the role of gender, treats female offenders as individuals with the potential to make a positive contribution to wider society, and ultimately breaks the cycle of reoffending with all the benefits that brings for families and society as a whole.

### The Case for Change:
### Criminalising vulnerable individuals has broader negative social impacts

8. Coming into contact with the criminal justice system, and in particular custody, can undermine the ability of women to address the issues that have caused their offending. In particular, many have difficulty maintaining employment and accommodation whilst in the CJS. This can contribute to these women entering crisis, or failing to come out of it, ultimately requiring greater support from services and leading to reoffending. Furthermore, the criminalisation or incarceration of parents has a significant impact on families and children.[xiv] The incarceration of women may also have a disproportionate impact on intergenerational offending as they are more likely to be living with their children prior to custody.[xv]

## Short custodial sentences do not deliver the best results for female offenders

9. Custody is intended as a last resort, to protect the public and to punish and rehabilitate offenders. Over three quarters of women sentenced to custody receive sentences of fewer than 12 months.[xvi] 56.1% of adult women released from custody between April and June 2016 reoffended within a year, with 70.7% of women reoffending following a short custodial sentence (<12m).[xvii] There is persuasive evidence that short custodial sentences of less than 12 months are less effective in reducing reoffending than community penalties.[xviii] Custody results in significant disruptions to family life. We also know that custody can be particularly damaging for women, whose rates of self-harm are nearly five times higher than those of men.[xix] Women are also twice as likely to report suffering from anxiety and depression and more likely to report symptoms indicative of psychosis.[xx]

## Good community management works

10. Many female offenders serving short custodial sentences could be more successfully supported in the community, where reoffending outcomes are better.[xxi] Community orders also offer the opportunity to support female offenders to engage in employment, and secure stable accommodation. They can be used effectively to address other underlying causes of offending, such as substance misuse problems. The third sector network of women's services, such as women's centres, play an important role in supporting women to address their needs. Holistic support for female offenders helps minimise disruption to families and more effectively maintain female offenders within their community as productive citizens, at less cost to Government and greater benefit to themselves and society.

i MOJ (2018). Female Offender Strategy. Available at: https://www.gov.uk/government/publications/female-offender-strategy

ii The higher prevalence amongst offenders of issues with drugs, alcohol and mental health is well documented. In a 2005/06 MOJ survey, 46% of female prisoners reported having attempted suicide – more than twice the rate of male prisoners (21%). This is higher than in the general population, amongst whom around 6% have. In the same MoJ survey, 64% of prisoners reported using Class A drugs in the four weeks before custody compared to 13% of the general population, and 49% of prisoners were assessed as being at risk of suffering from anxiety and/or depression, compared to 16% of the general population. In the Adult Psychiatric Morbidity Survey of prisoners (1998), 90% of prisoners had one or more of the five psychiatric disorders studied (psychosis, neurosis, personality disorder, hazardous drink and drug dependence). MOJ (2013). Gender differences in substance misuse and mental health amongst prisoners Available at: https://www.gov.uk/government/publications/gender-differences-in-substance-misuse-and-mental-health-amongst-prisoners--2

Women's Policy Framework Issued 21 December 2018 15

iii Substance misuse has been linked to increased likelihood of reoffending. According to a MoJ survey of adult prisoners sentenced in 2005 and 2006, 62% of prisoners who reported using drugs in the four weeks before custody reoffended in the year after released compared to 30% of those who reported never using drugs. 62% of those who reported drinking alcohol every day in the four weeks before custody were reconvicted, compared with 49% of those who did not report this. Addressing mental health issues should also help offenders better address other needs more directly associated with offending, such as engaging in drug treatment or maintaining stable accommodation. MOJ (2013). Gender differences in substance misuse and mental health amongst prisoners Available at: https://www.gov.uk/government/publications/gender-differences-in-substance-misuse-and-mental-health-amongst-prisoners--2

iv The human cost of VAWG is high. Experiences of abuse have serious psychological, emotional and physical consequences and may contribute to multiple disadvantage, or a chaotic lifestyle involving substance misuse, homelessness, offending behaviour, gang involvement, prostitution or mental health problems. That 41% of the prison population have witnessed or experienced domestic abuse is illustrative of the wider social harms these crimes cause". (HM Government (2016). Ending Violence Against Women and Girls Strategy 2016-2020, p.8.) Available at: https://assets.publishing.service.gov.uk/government/uploads/system/uploads/attachment_data/file/522166/VAWG_Strategy_FINAL_PUBLICATION_MASTER_vRB.PDF

v MOJ (2018). Offender Management Statistics quarterly: October to December 2017. Available at: https://www.gov.uk/government/statistics/offender-management-statistics-quarterly-october-to-december-2017

vi MOJ (2018). Criminal Justice System statistics quarterly: December 2017. Available at: https://www.gov.uk/government/statistics/criminal-justice-system-statistics-quarterly-december-2017

vii MOJ (2018). Supporting data tables: Female offender strategy. Available at: https://www.gov.uk/government/publications/female-offender-strategy

viii MOJ (2018). Proven reoffending statistics: April 2016 to June 2016. Available at: https://www.gov.uk/government/statistics/proven-reoffending-statistics-april-2016-to-june-2016

ix MOJ (2018). Criminal Justice System statistics quarterly: December 2017. Available at: https://www.gov.uk/government/statistics/criminal-justice-system-statistics-quarterly-december-2017

x Government estimates of total costs to government in 2015/16 associated with female offenders [from police through to end of sentence], drawing on a combination of different data sources and assumptions. These are high level estimates, using a number of published and unpublished data, and there is major uncertainty in several cost estimates included.

xi MOJ (2018). Safety in custody quarterly: update to December 2017. Available at: https://www.gov.uk/government/statistics/safety-in-custody-quarterly-update-to-december-2017

xii Baroness Corston (2007). A Report by Baroness Jean Corston of a Review of Women with Particular Vulnerabilities in the Criminal Justice System. Available at: http://www.justice.gov.uk/publications/docs/corston-report-march-2007.pdf

xiii MoJ conducted a Rapid Evidence Assessment (REA) 2015 to explore the evidence on the effectiveness of interventions for adult women convicted of crime. Relative to the gender-neutral initiatives, more of the gender-informed programmes reviewed led to reductions in recidivism. MOJ (2015). Effective interventions for Women offenders: A Rapid Evidence Assessment. Available at: https://assets.publishing.service.gov.uk/government/uploads/system/uploads/attachment_data/file/448859/effective-interventions-for-women-offenders.pdf

xiv Murray and Farrington (2008) The effects of parental imprisonment on children. In Tonry (Ed), Crime and justice: A review of research (Vol 3, pp 133-206). University of Chicago Press.

xv MOJ (2014). Prisoners' childhood and family backgrounds. Available at: https://www.gov.uk/government/publications/prisoners-childhood-and-family-backgrounds

xvi MOJ (2018). Criminal Justice System statistics quarterly: December 2017. Available at: https://www.gov.uk/government/statistics/criminal-justice-system-statistics-quarterly-december-2017

xvii MOJ (2018). Supporting data tables: Female offender strategy. Available at: https://www.gov.uk/government/publications/female-offender-strategy

Women's Policy Framework Issued 21 December 2018 16

xviii MOJ (2018). Do offender characteristics affect the impact of short custodial sentences and court orders on reoffending? Available at: https://assets.publishing.service.gov.uk/government/uploads/system/uploads/attachment_data/file/706597/do-offender-characteristics-affect-the-impact-of-short-custodial-sentences.pdf

xix MOJ (2018). Safety in custody quarterly: update to December 2017. Available at: https://www.gov.uk/government/statistics/safety-in-custody-quarterly-update-to-december-2017

xx MOJ (2013). Gender differences in substance misuse and mental health amongst prisoners Available at: https://www.gov.uk/government/publications/gender-differences-in-substance-misuse-and-mental-health-amongst-prisoners--2

xxi MOJ (2018). Do offender characteristics affect the impact of short custodial sentences and court orders on reoffending? Available at:
https://assets.publishing.service.gov.uk/government/uploads/system/uploads/attachment_data/file/706597/do-offender-characteristics-affect-the-impact-of-short-custodial-sentences.pdf

## Women Prisoners: Categorisation

What do the different security categories mean? The security categories of women prisoners differ from those of male prisoners. For women, the official definitions of security categories are:

**Category A** - Prisoners whose escape would be highly dangerous to the public or the police or the security of the state and for whom the aim must be to make escape impossible.

**Restricted Status** - Any female young person or adult prisoner convicted or on remand whose escape would present a serious risk to the public and who are required to be held in designated secure accommodation.

**Closed Conditions** - Prisoners for whom the very highest conditions of security are not necessary but who are too high risk for open or for whom open conditions are not appropriate.

**Open conditions** - Prisoners who present a low risk; can reasonably be trusted in open conditions and for whom open conditions are appropriate.

### What determines my initial security categorisation?

Prison Service Instruction 39/2011 (updated 29th October 2021) sets out the principles that determine the categorisation and recategorisation of women prisoners, apart from the very few women prisoners, who are Category A or Restricted Status. These are categorised and reviewed by HMPPS Headquarters.

The purpose of categorisation is to assess the risks posed by a prisoner in terms of:

• Likelihood of escape or abscond;

• The risk of harm to the public in the event of an escape or abscond;

• Any control issues that impact on the security and good order of the prison and the safety of those within it

The prisoner is assigned to the lowest security category consistent with managing those risks.

Allocation often follows immediately after categorisation but is a separate process whose purpose is to assign the prisoner to a suitable establishment.

All prisoners, unless serving a life or an IPP sentence, when initially categorised, must be regarded as suitable for open conditions unless the following applies:

• The current sentence is 3 years or more

• The prisoner has been treated as provisional category A whilst on remand

• The current or previous sentence is for terrorist (or terrorist related) offences

• There has been a previous escape from closed prison, police custody (except arrest or post-arrest) or escort

• There is a significant history of serious offending

• There is a serious criminal association

• Further charges are outstanding (other than those of a minor nature)

• There has been a previous sentence of 7 years or more (from which the prisoner was released within the last 5 years)

• The prisoner is diagnosed with or is suspected of suffering from, serious mental health problems

• There is reasonable concern regarding risk of abscond

• There have been previous breaches/failures to surrender

• There are victim issues or issues of public confidence that mean open conditions are inappropriate

• The prisoner is subject to MAPPA level 2 or 3 management, prompting serious consideration of the individual circumstances

• An OASys risk of harm level which cannot be reasonably managed in open conditions

• The prisoner has been identified as a priority or a prolific offender (PPO)

• A Serious Crime Prevention Order has been imposed

• The prisoner is subject to a confiscation order - consideration must then be given as to whether amount and default sentence imposed, might increase risk of abscond

• A prisoner has more than 2 years left to serve

Two years is considered to be the maximum time a prisoner should spend in open conditions. However, assessment of a prisoner's individual needs and risks may support earlier categorisation to open conditions. Such cases must have the reasons for their categorisation fully documented and confirmed in writing by the Governing Governor.

Prisoners with a sentence of less than 12 months must be considered for categorisation to open conditions and allocation to open conditions as soon as possible after sentencing under a streamlined risk assessment process, subject to a requirement that they spend a minimum of seven days in closed conditions.

Life and IPP sentence prisoners can only be transferred to open conditions following a recommendation by the Parole Board and/or a decision by the Secretary of State to grant them open status.

## When will I have a categorisation review?

Women serving indeterminate sentences will be subject to sentence planning and review meetings, which must be held every 12 months, at which a woman's security category should be reviewed. Prisoners serving a determinate sentence of more than 12 months but less than 4 years, extended sentence prisoners serving a sentence of less than 4 years and prisoners in the last 24 months of their sentence, should have a review every 6 months. Determinate sentence prisoners and those serving extended sentences with a sentence of 4 years or more should have a review every 12 months until they are in the last 2 years of their sentence, when they should then have 6 monthly reviews.

Prisoners may also have their security category reviewed whenever there has been a significant change in their circumstances or behaviour that impacts on the level of security required, whether negative or positive, eg. a key piece of offending behaviour work or a detoxification or opiate substitute maintenance regime is completed.

## Who will decide on my recategorisation?

Recategorisation of all female prisoners is carried out by the OCA Unit. Decisions may be made by a board or by a single manager.

Procedures must be completed by staff specially trained and able to competently fulfil the OCA role. Staff completing the form are responsible to a senior manager as designated by the Governor.

## Can I appeal if I am not happy with the result after a review of my categorisation?

Yes. If, after a categorisation decision or review, you do not believe that you have been placed in the correct category, you should pursue your concerns via the internal complaints system. A fresh review of all the facts must then be done by a manager senior to the officer, who countersigned the original decision. For Category A prisoners, you can still use the complaints procedure but your complaint form will be sent to Prison Service Headquarters for a response, rather than being answered in the prison. If you feel your concerns have still not been addressed you can appeal to the Prisons and Probation Ombudsman (Third Floor, 10 South Colonnade, London E14 4PU). It is possible on occasion to judicially review categorisation decisions, although this is increasingly difficult, especially since 2013 when legal aid funding for categorisation cases was cut. The Prison Service has a duty to give reasons for decisions about categorisation, so in order to mount your appeal you should request a full explanation of the decision and relevant reports in writing - if you need help write to the Prisoners' Advice Service, PO Box 46199, London EC1M 4XA or call them on: 020 7253 3323 / 0845 430 8923

## 2.16 YOUNG OFFENDERS (18-21)

*This chapter is to be read in conjunction with* **Policy name: Building Bridges: A Positive Behaviour Framework for the Children and Young People Secure Estate**
*Implementation Date: 01 April 2019*
*Cancels: The Youth Justice Board (YJB) Behaviour Management Code of Practice 2012*
*Amends: Relative sections of* **PSI 08/2012 Care and Management of Young People,** *which remain active in Wales but are hereby cancelled in England.*
*These sections are as follows:*
**Sections 2.14 to 2.16, 2.18, 2.19 and 2.23: Promoting and Maintaining Good Behaviour**
**Sections 2.24 to 2.29: Managing Challenging Behaviour**
**Sections 5.14 to 5.17: Offending Behaviour Interventions**
*Note: PSI 11/2011 Incentives and Earned Privileges and PSI 05/2018 Prisoner Discipline Procedures Adjudications remain in place for YOIs.*
*The Building Bridges Policy Framework sets out the regulations and guidance for developing positive relationships and cultures across the Children and Young People Secure Estate. It includes incentivising and promoting positive behaviour, minimising behaviour that can cause harm and working effectively with unacceptable behaviour to provide a safe and controlled environment for children, young people and staff.*
*The Framework currently applies to England only. It replaces related sections of PSI 08-2012 Care and Management of Young People, which remains active in Wales. It will be reviewed in April 2020.*

## INTRODUCTION
**YOI Rules 2000 as amended - current edition available on prisonoracle.com**
In recent years there has been a move to hold young adults in prisons with adult prisoners, particularly in London and South East England, following the decision to no longer hold remanded young adults in Feltham YOI. These changes were put on hold pending the findings and recommendations of the independent review into self-inflicted deaths in custody of young adult men aged 18 to 24 led by Lord Harris.
Lord Harris' review in June 2015 (see prisonoracle.com) concluded that, "given the overwhelming evidence, it is wrong to assume that maturity will necessarily have been reached by the age of 18. The Criminal Justice System needs to recognise that young adults who are 18-24 years are still developing, and their behaviour and ability to cope with custody will depend on the level of maturity they have attained."
It also called for a "legal recognition of the concept of 'maturity'. As well as chronological age, maturity should be a primary consideration

**Table 1.3: Prison population by type of custody, age and sex**

| | 30-Jun-2021 | 30-Sep-2021 | 31-Dec-2021 | 31-Mar-2022 | 30-Jun-2022 |
|---|---|---|---|---|---|
| **Males and Females** | **78,324** | **78,756** | **79,092** | **79,773** | **80,659** |
| 15-17 | 363 | 335 | 329 | 305 | 333 |
| 18-20 | 3,520 | 3,427 | 3,391 | 3,296 | 3,240 |
| 21-24 | 8,392 | 8,276 | 8,114 | 8,172 | 8,169 |
| 25-29 | 13,138 | 13,031 | 13,077 | 13,098 | 13,132 |
| 30-39 | 25,211 | 25,628 | 25,794 | 26,064 | 26,446 |
| 40-49 | 14,569 | 14,776 | 14,954 | 15,179 | 15,504 |
| 50-59 | 8,140 | 8,214 | 8,274 | 8,399 | 8,479 |
| 60-69 | 3,339 | 3,395 | 3,466 | 3,561 | 3,602 |
| 70 and over | 1,652 | 1,674 | 1,693 | 1,699 | 1,754 |
| **Remand** | **12,727** | **12,990** | **12,780** | **12,747** | **13,409** |
| 15-17 | 175 | 150 | 133 | 132 | 157 |
| 18-20 | 1,172 | 1,201 | 1,144 | 1,102 | 1,154 |
| 21-24 | 1,772 | 1,770 | 1,695 | 1,705 | 1,752 |
| 25-29 | 2,425 | 2,391 | 2,355 | 2,306 | 2,464 |
| 30-39 | 4,141 | 4,286 | 4,275 | 4,277 | 4,436 |
| 40-49 | 1,989 | 2,087 | 2,049 | 2,085 | 2,229 |
| 50-59 | 813 | 816 | 863 | 864 | 916 |
| 60-69 | 190 | 224 | 212 | 222 | 238 |
| 70 and over | 50 | 65 | 54 | 54 | 63 |
| **Sentenced** | **64,637** | **64,746** | **65,411** | **66,167** | **66,480** |
| 15-17 | 188 | 185 | 196 | 173 | 176 |
| 18-20 | 2,321 | 2,182 | 2,210 | 2,156 | 2,064 |
| 21-24 | 6,514 | 6,387 | 6,316 | 6,370 | 6,343 |
| 25-29 | 10,506 | 10,435 | 10,530 | 10,632 | 10,521 |
| 30-39 | 20,734 | 20,995 | 21,208 | 21,482 | 21,717 |
| 40-49 | 12,376 | 12,464 | 12,716 | 12,919 | 13,105 |
| 50-59 | 7,261 | 7,336 | 7,359 | 7,468 | 7,517 |
| 60-69 | 3,137 | 3,154 | 3,241 | 3,328 | 3,348 |
| 70 and over | 1,600 | 1,608 | 1,635 | 1,639 | 1,689 |
| **Non criminal prisoners** | **960** | **1,020** | **901** | **859** | **770** |
| 15-17 | 0 | 0 | 0 | 0 | 0 |
| 18-20 | 27 | 44 | 37 | 38 | 22 |
| 21-24 | 106 | 119 | 103 | 97 | 74 |
| 25-29 | 207 | 205 | 192 | 160 | 147 |
| 30-39 | 336 | 347 | 311 | 305 | 293 |
| 40-49 | 204 | 225 | 189 | 175 | 170 |
| 50-59 | 66 | 62 | 52 | 67 | 46 |
| 60-69 | 12 | 17 | 13 | 11 | 16 |
| 70 and over | 2 | 1 | 4 | 6 | 2 |

in making decisions relating to diversion, sentencing and, where a custodial sentence must be given, how and where a young adult (18–24) should be accommodated."

In December 2015, in its official response to the Harris Review, the Government rejected the recommendation that 'young offenders' should include those aged up to 24 given the concept of maturity:

*"Maturity is recognised in Liaison & Diversion services which identify vulnerabilities, and as a mitigating factor in sentencing guidelines. Prison accommodation will be considered as part of the wider prison strategy.*

*"However, the government does not agree that legislation should currently be considered which legally recognises the concept of maturity"*

## FACTS AND FIGURES: YOUNG ADULT OFFENDERS 2023.

*The table shows the prison population by Custody, Age and Sex from the offender management statistics of June 2022, published July 2022, is from the prisonoracle.com*

## INTRODUCTION

Young offenders are those given a custodial sentence whilst under 21 years of age, but over the age of 18 years old at the time of committing the offence for which they are sentenced.

The separation of the Young People system following the introduction of the Crime and Disorder Act 1998; and the establishment of the Youth Justice Board have led to significant administrative and legislative changes in how young people under 18 years of age are dealt with.

## CUSTODIAL ARRANGEMENTS FOR YOUNG OFFENDERS

The legislation currently in force for the custody of young offenders aged 18 to 20 years. The sentences or orders that the court may impose is the Powers of the Criminal Courts (Sentencing) Act 2000 (PCCSA 00) and the sentences available to the courts are:

• custody for life—in circumstances where a sentence of life imprisonment would be imposed for a person of 21 years or over;

• detention for default or contempt;

• detention in a young offender institution—the usual custodial sentence for young persons between 18 and 20 years who have been convicted of offences.

18-year-old to 20-year-old prisoners include those who have previously been sentenced under sections 90 and 91 of the Powers of Criminal Court (Sentencing) Act 2000 – Detention at Her Majesty's Pleasure or for a specified period and who come into the young adult system at 18.

The arrangements for unsentenced or unconvicted young adults are the same as those for adults but invariably young adults are held in YOIs or in separate young offender wings of local prisons.

## WHERE ARE YOUNG OFFENDERS HELD?

Establishments in 2022/2023 designated to hold 15-21 years olds are as follows

HMP/YOI Altcourse *
HMP/YOI Askham Grange F
HMP/YOI Bedford
HMP/YOI Belmarsh HS
HMP/YOI Brinsford
HMP/YOI Bristol
HMP/YOI Bronzefield * F
HMP/YOI Bullingdon
HMP/YOI Cardiff
HMP/YOI Chelmsford
HMP/YOI Deerbolt
HMP/YOI Downview F
HMP/YOI Drake Hall F
HMP/YOI Durham
HMP/YOI East Sutton Park F
HMP/YOI Eastwood Park F

HMP/YOI Elmley
HMP/YOI Exeter
HMP/YOI Forest Bank *
HMP/YOI Foston Hall F
HMP/YOI Glen Parva
HMP/YOI Hatfield
HMP/YOI Highdown
HMP/YOI Hindley
HMP/YOI Hollesley Bay
HMP/YOI Holme House
HMP/YOI Hull
HMP/YOI Isle of Wight
HMP/YOI Kirklevington Grange
HMP/YOI Lewes
HMP/YOI Lincoln
HMP/YOI Low Newton F
HMP/YOI Manchester HS
HMP/YOI Moorland
HMP/YOI New Hall F
HMP/YOI Norwich
HMP/YOI Nottingham
HMP/YOI Parc *
HMP/YOI Peterborough F *
HMP/YOI Portland
HMP/YOI Prescoed
HMP/YOI Preston
HMP/YOI Rochester
HMP/YOI Send F
HMP/YOI Stoke Heath
HMP/YOI Styal F
HMP/YOI Swansea
HMP/YOI Swinfen Hall
HMP/YOI Thameside *
HMP/YOI Thorn Cross
HMP/YOI Wandsworth
HMP/YOI Warren Hill
HMP/YOI Winchester
HMP/YOI Woodhill HS
HMP/YOI Wormwood Scrubs
HMP/YOI Wymott
HMP/YOI Doncaster *
HMP/YOI Isis
HMP/YOI Pentonville
HMYOI Aylesbury
HMYOI Cookham Wood J
HMYOI Feltham J
HMYOI Werrington J
HMYOI Wetherby J

*Those marked 'J' have Juvenile (15-17 year old) Units, those with an '*' are private sector establishments, those marked 'HS' are part of the High Security Estate and those marked 'F' hold female prisoners.*

Young offenders should serve their sentences in young offender institutions, but the Justice Secretary retains the right to direct that young adults can be held in adult prisons (PCCSA 00-s.98). Arrangements also exist to convert a sentence of detention in a YOI where the individual reaches 21

years of age, or on direction of the Secretary of State, when a person is reported by the Independent Monitoring Boards for exercising a bad influence on other inmates or behaving in a disruptive manner. In such cases the direction includes a removal to an adult prison (PCCSA 00 –s.99).

**THE YOI RULES 2000 - see prisonoracle.com**
Young Offender Institutions were established under the Prison Act 1952 and are governed by a set of rules approved by Parliament—*The Young Offender Institution Rules* the current edition of which is available on prisonoracle.com and all young offenders are entitled to be provided with a current copy on request under **Rule 7(3).**

These rules apply to YOIs holding both young offenders and young people (although there are a number that do not apply to those under 18). If you are held in prison you will be subject to the Prison Rules, which have some special provisions for those under 21 but are generally the same as for adults.

Copies of the YOI Rules and the Prison Rules should be available in the library to which you have right of access on request. References to the 'Rules' in the remainder of this section mean the YOI Rules.

**Who Decides Where I Serve My Sentence?**
The YOI or prison you are allocated to depends upon the crime you have been convicted of, the sentence you have been given and where spaces are available. If you have been sentenced to detention under section 90 or 91 of the PCC(S)A 2000, the allocation decision will be made by the Ministry of Justice. Otherwise the decision is normally made locally. A range of factors are taken into account when making a decision, including the risk you pose. You should be placed in a YOI near to your home to allow more regular contact with your family friends and probation service and enable an easier resettlement into the community. However, this may not be possible and may result in allocation some distance away from home. On average, prisoners are held 53 miles from home.

**What Is Reception?**
Reception occurs when you are first taken into custody. In the reception area you should immediately tell the Reception Officer if you are unable to read or write or have any medical or mental health problems. You will then be given a uniform if you are male, which should be clean and well fitted.

You will be given some bed linen that should be clean. You will have to store any property that you are not allowed to have with you. You should check carefully that the list of property is

correct because you will be asked to sign a disclaimer certifying that:
• stored property is securely sealed and all stored and in-possession property is correctly recorded
• you retain at your own risk items recorded as in-possession and the Prison Service will accept no liability for loss or damage.

After this there should be a medical examination. You will then be taken to where you will be staying and given a number and a 'reception letter'. This should be sent to either a member of your family or a friend, just so they know where you are. You do not have to pay the postage for this.

### What Is Induction?

When you get to your YOI or prison a programme should be in place which makes sure you are shown around and aware of the recreational and work areas. You should be given information about bail and legal aid services and a full description of the day to day running of the YOI . This should include a copy of the YOI rules. You should be allocated a personal officer who has responsibility for dealing with issues or problems that you need help with.

### What Is A Sentence Plan?

The sentence plan should help you to identify what you can achieve in prison. It should be compiled as quickly as possible following your arrival. You will be asked a series of questions which may consider the interests you had outside of prison, any qualifications you may have, the crimes you have been convicted of and identify any health problems you may have. This could include both drug and alcohol misuse. You should be able to have a copy of your sentence plan.

A new Offender Assessment System, OASys, which is computer based, should be installed in all prisons and YOIs by the end of 2004. However, research by The Howard League for Penal Reform found that the compilation of clear and well structured sentence plans are 'something of a lottery'. If you discover you have been in custody for some time and have no sentence plan you should ask for one as it will help you to get the most out of the prison facilities and help you towards a parole application.

### What Is A Keyworker?

Everyone is given a Keyworker - sometimes called a personal officer - when they arrive in a YOI or prison; this is being rolled out nationally as part of the new Offender Management in Custody (OMiC) model. This person should be your first point of contact with any questions and problems you may encounter. They are responsible for dealing with any of your complaints and should also help you with your

sentence plan. During your sentence they are responsible for keeping your offender manager informed of the progress you make. Your personal officer is also generally responsible for making recommendations about your position within the prison's 'privileges scheme'.

### What Is The Incentives And Earned Privileges Scheme?

Rule 6 requires all YOIs to have a system of privileges. These are approved by the area manager on behalf of the Secretary of State and include a range of incentives and privileges that can be applied to inmates dependent on their behaviour and position in the scheme. There are four levels: Entry, Basic, Standard and Enhanced, although some YOIs have intermediate levels as well.

Normally, you will be placed on Entry Level as soon as you arrive and your conduct, including your participation in activities, will determine whether you are demoted to Basic, promoted to Standard, then Enhanced or remain on Entry level. Your Personal Officer will recommend any changes to your level. There is a lack of consistency in operation, and all Governors are allowed to operate their YOIs according to their own resources. You may also find minor privileges are available at your own prison. This may be where you can have your own furniture in your cell or your own bedding.        You will have to see what is on offer. You should be aware of the scheme and how it operates, but do not be too surprised if the differences between the levels are not as wide as you had hoped.

### Can I Have Visits?

On arrival you should be told how many and for how long you are allowed prison visits. According to Rule 10(1b) visits are permitted once every 14 days. This provision also allows for only two visits a month should the Home Secretary approve it. In addition, under Rule 9(1) the Home Secretary may 'impose prohibitions' on any other visits that may be considered a potential threat to discipline and good order. This would and *should* never deny you a visit from the Independent Monitoring Board, a justice of the peace or a solicitor's legal visit.

The number of visits allowed depends upon where you are presently positioned in the prison's privileges scheme. The higher up you are the more visits you may be entitled to. These visits should take place in a visitors centre which has suitable facilities for children to play in. Your family are entitled to ask to see your Personal Officer or a senior member of staff who can deal with any queries, complaints and questions they may have.

### Voluntary Associates

You may also receive visits from prison visitors such as the National Association of Prison Visitors. These people are members of the public who visit prisoners during their spare time.

You should be informed of such schemes in your prison and of the role of the Independent Monitoring Board (who you can see privately, with being heard by officers). Ask your personal officer if you are interested in seeing these people.

### Can I Send Letters?

Rule 10(1)(a) states that you are normally entitled to send one letter per week with postage paid for by the authorities. This will normally be at the rate of second class. Other postage costs must be met from your own private cash or any earnings you may have.

### Can I Make Phone Calls?

Prisoner telephones use the Pinphone system. This requires your details to be entered onto the system and sufficient credit in your account to make calls. Once a week you will be given the opportunity to purchase credits in £1 units and this will be added to your account. In some prisons (or because of the nature of the offence) you may have to provide details of the telephone numbers you wish to call so that the prison can check them. As well as dialling the number you will have to input a personal identification number (PIN) on the telephone keypad.

The prison service may monitor your calls except for legal or other similar type calls. Access to telephones is not regarded by the prison service as a right and access to telephones can be withdrawn or certain telephone numbers disallowed.

### Regime

Rule 3 states that 'The aim of a young offender institution shall be to help offenders to prepare for their return to the outside community'. To achieve this goal the Rules support the 'providing of a programme of activities, including education, training and work designed to assist offenders to acquire or develop personal responsibility, self discipline, physical fitness, interests and skills and to obtain suitable employment after release'.

### Education

Rule 38 states that education should be available to all young offenders. There is no minimal requirement for education for those over school age. Education is supposed to be provided at a level appropriate to your educational needs. Education provision in YOIs generally concentrates on improving basic skills in literacy and numeracy. But there may also be IT, art, drama and other classes available. Ask the education staff about what is on offer.

Although some young prisoners have achieved good results with a number of useful qualifications, for some time the provision for suitable education has been described by HMCIP as 'poor'. This has yet to be implemented but you should ask your Personal Officer about education classes and see what is available. You may have to wait for the education classes of your choice, but keep trying.

### Can I Train For New Skills?

Rule 39 states that training courses should be provided for young offenders. You should be able to train for new skills that will help you in your search for a job on release. You may be able to learn something about motor mechanics or welding. This will of course depend very much on the particular provision at your institution. Ask your Personal Officer about what is on offer.

### Can I Work?

Rule 40 allows young offenders to work. This is to help you 'gain practical marketable skills' during your time in custody. Some prisons have good facilities for the running of the National Vocational Qualifications (NVQ) subjects including Motor Mechanics and Welding. Ask your Personal Officer about what type of work is available. Be prepared to wait as the demand often outweighs provision. But keep trying.

### Can I Exercise Regularly?

Rule 41 provides for the provision of Physical Education (PE) at YOIs. This rule states that you should be able to participate on average of two hours of PE per week. This may take place during the evenings and weekends and ideally you should be able to exercise outside and indoors. This does not count towards your 15 hours for education. If you have any problems with PE then provision should be made for you to take part in specifically organised facilities.

### Can I Use A Library?

All YOIs have a library. Unfortunately, HMCIP noted that the facilities in these libraries varied 'from the superb to the abysmal'. Very often inmates are found not to know if their own YOI has a library and, if they know one exists they don't usually know where it is. If you are interested in reading and want to borrow books then you should make yourself familiar with the library and its opening times.

Libraries are now operated under contract and the service should be improving. But many libraries in prisons and YOIs have had to compete for funds with other priorities in replacing stock, which has meant that the number of books available to prisoners has been small. Some YOIs also operate wing or unit libraries, mainly with paperbacks or hardback fiction. If there is a book you particularly want to read, ask if you can have an inter-library loan.

### Can I Enjoy Any Free Time?

This free time is known as recreation and association. You can expect to have at least one hour of recreation per day although this can vary according to the level you have attained in the YOI privileges scheme and the facilities available. During this 'free' time you may mix with other prisoners and use the recreation facilities available in your particular institution. This may mean you can watch TV, play games and pool, take a shower and use the telephone to contact family and friends.

At weekends you may find that your YOI has more time for recreation and association.

### Can I Practice My Religion?

Rules 30 to 36 deal with religious provision in YOIs. You have a right to practice your religion and (so long as it is a recognised religion) facilities will be made available for you to attend services and take part in any other proper observances. Each year the Chaplain General publishes a list of special days for all main religions, setting out what services should be held or what special arrangements should be made. This list should be available for you to see through the chaplaincy at your prison or YOI. When you come into prison you will be asked for your religion as part of reception procedures and this information will be used by the chaplaincy to arrange contact with a minister of your religion. It is possible to change your religion after this, but you will be required to fill in a form and have an interview by the chaplaincy team.

By law the Chaplain of the YOI must be Church of England (except in Wales) but there should also be Roman Catholic and Methodist chaplains available for you to see. Most prisons and YOIs will also have an Imam for Muslim prisoners and ministers of other faiths should also be available for prisoners of their faith. All the ministers are now part of a 'chaplaincy team' and should work together to develop the religious life of the prison or YOI.

The Church of England Chaplain will conduct a service every Sunday for inmates who wish to attend. This may be in conjunction with other Christian denominations or they may have separate services on a Sunday or, sometimes, on a Saturday.

Services for other faiths should be held on the appropriate day of the week or as arranged with the respective minister of religion. All YOIs should hold a service for Muslim inmates on a Friday.

Whenever you are sick or confined to your room or cell the chaplain or minister of your religion is required to visit you.

### Can I Get Some Money?

You will receive some money that will enable you to buy items from the prison shop for your own use.

The amount will depend on the level you are at in the prison's privileges scheme. Family and friends can send money into the prison for you, usually in the form of a postal order, but the amount you are allowed in private cash will depend on where the Home Secretary has set the tariff. Your Personal Officer will tell you how much you are allowed. You may also get some money if you are working in the prison.

### Help With Drug Or Alcohol Problems

If you have problems with drugs or alcohol the CARATs (Counselling, Assessment, Referral, Advice and Throughcare services) team may be able to help you. The CARATs service should offer assessments; advice; liaison with health care both in prison and in the community; care plan assessments; one-to-one counselling and groupwork services; assessment for intensive treatment programmes in prison; and throughcare, linking with community drug treatment services for up to 8 weeks. CARATs should be easily accessible to prisoners. All prisoners who have been identified as having drug related issues/problems by any member of staff can be referred to CARATs subject to their consent.

### What Can I Do If I Am Being Bullied?

The main advice is *'Do not suffer in silence'*. Some people have committed suicide because of bullying and staff at the prison should take it very seriously.

Bullying is very common in YOIs and you may find yourself bullied to give up medication or tobacco. If you should tell someone and get help.

*Who can I tell?*

If you see or are victim to any bullying you should be able to discuss it with a:
• Keyworker/Personal Officer
• • Independent Monitoring Board member
• Medical Officer
• Chaplain
• Listener
• Older inmates.

All YOIs will have a strategy for dealing with bullying which should be well publicised.

## Racism

The Prison Service has a well publicised policy that is committed to combating all forms of racism. You should let someone know if you feel you are suffering from racial harassment, either from other inmates or from a member of staff. You should also make a complaint if you feel that the YOI is not making appropriate arrangements to cater for you, for example the range of products available from the prison shop or if you are personally being discriminated against on grounds of race from having access to particular facilities.

## Discipline And Privileges

Rule 55 covers offences against discipline in your YOI. You should be provided with a copy of the Rules when you first arrive and if you have any problems understanding them you should ask your Personal Officer for advice.

## What Is An Adjudication?

At some point you may find that you are subject to an adjudication. This is where you may have been charged with an offence against discipline. If you are charged, you are entitled to know the nature of the charge within 24 hours of the offence. A hearing will then take place where a Governor will hear details of the charge. There are two types of adjudication: a charge where added days will not be given if you were to be found guilty; a charge where you may be given added days if you are found guilty. If the governor decides that you may be given added days for the offence then you are entitled to (a) legal aid, (b) a solicitor to advise and represent you. This will not cost you anything. If the governor decides that you will not be given added days then you are still entitled to seek legal advice by telephone. If you are found guilty of the charge this could affect your early release or parole. At the hearing there will be the Governor, you and any witnesses to the offence. This may be other inmates or prison officers. You may be asked if you want to have your Personal Officer present.

There is no 'appropriate adult' scheme in YOIs. This would be of direct benefit to those inmates who have learning difficulties and do not understand the procedure before them. They may need an impartial person to help them answer questions put to them at the hearing.

If the Governor finds you guilty, they will decide if you are subject to any of the punishments set out in Rule 60. These punishments include a caution, loss of privileges, extra work, stoppage of earnings, removal from wing and loss of association.

A punishment may be suspended. Most YOIs also operate a system of *Minor Reports* for less serious offences. These will normally be heard by the wing principal officer or governor. The range of punishments does not include either removal from wing or added days.

## Pre-Release Advice

Your YOI should have pre-release classes that will help you to come to terms with your period in custody and help you understand what opportunities are available to you on release. The classes will look at custody from your point of view and that of your family and will offer practical advice on housing, employment and benefits. You may find that organisations such as NACRO will visit and give you advice on training and employment as well. You should ask your Personal Officer or someone in the prison's Education or Probation department which organisations visit. (See *Section 3, Helpful Organisations*). Although HMCIP is presently unhappy with the quality of preparation for release you may find it useful to attend these sessions should they be on offer.

## 2.17 YOUNG PEOPLE (15-17)

**Policy name: Building Bridges: A Positive Behaviour Framework for the Children and Young People Secure Estate**

*Re-issue Date: 28 March 2019 Implementation Date: 01 April 2019*

*Cancels: The Youth Justice Board (YJB) Behaviour Management Code of Practice 2012*

*Amends: Relative sections of **PSI 08/2012 Care and Management of Young People**, which remain active in Wales but are hereby cancelled in England.*

*These sections are as follows:*

***Sections 2.14 to 2.16, 2.18, 2.19 and 2.23 : Promoting and Maintaining Good Behaviour***

***Sections 2.24 to 2.29: Managing Challenging Behaviour***

***Sections 5.14 to 5.17: Offending Behaviour Interventions***

*Note: PSI 11/2011 Incentives and Earned Privileges and PSI 05/2018 Prisoner Discipline Procedures Adjudications remain in place for YOIs.*

*The Building Bridges Policy Framework sets out the regulations and guidance for developing positive relationships and cultures across the Children and Young People Secure Estate. It includes incentivising and promoting positive behaviour, minimising behaviour that can cause harm and working effectively with unacceptable behaviour to provide a safe and controlled environment for children, young people and staff.*

*The Framework currently applies to England only. It replaces related sections of PSI 08-2012 Care and Management of Young People, which remains active in Wales.*

## Youth Custodial Estate 2022/23

### Secure Training Centres (STCs)

As at August 2022 there is one STCs operating, Oakhill and a second which is closed is being considered for reopening (Rainsbrook).
• **Oakhill** (Milton Keynes) is operated by G4S. It opened in 2004 and it can currently hold up to 80 boys. The NHS does not commission services at Oakhill.

### Young Offender Institutions (YOIs)

There are five YOIs and one specialist unit operating. Three of the five YOIs are dedicated for young offenders, while two were within an existing establishment that held either adults or young adults. Any boys held on split sites are still held on their own dedicated wings or units and should be kept completely separate from both adults and young adults.
• **Cookham Wood** (Rochester, Kent) became a YOI in May 2008. It is a dedicated site with a certified normal accommodation (CNA) and operational capacity of 196.
• **Feltham A** (Middlesex) is part of Feltham YOI, a split site holding boys (Feltham A) and, separately, young adults (Feltham B). Feltham A has a CNA and operational capacity of 180. It holds both sentenced and unsentenced boys.
• **Parc** (Bridgend) is a split site, and the only prison to hold adults, young adults and boys. The boys' unit has a CNA and operational capacity of 64 and holds both sentenced and unsentenced boys. It is privately run by G4S.
• **Werrington** (Stoke-on-Trent) is a dedicated site holding both sentenced boys and boys on remand, with a CNA of 118 and an operational capacity of 128.
• **Wetherby** (West Yorkshire) is a dedicated site holding sentenced boys and boys on remand. It also includes a unit dedicated to holding boys with life or long-term determinate sentences. It has a CNA and operational capacity of 336.
• **Keppel Unit** (Wetherby) is a 48-bed specialist unit within Wetherby. It is a national resource for very vulnerable boys and those who find it hard to engage in the larger YOIs.

### What custody is like for young people

Time in custody is spent:
• in lessons
• learning skills to get a job or to return to education
• taking part in programmes to improve behaviour
• participating in sport, fitness, and other activities
There are strict rules about what young people can and can't do, and they may have to go through alcohol or drug counselling.

### Types of secure centre

There are 3 types of custody for young people:
• young offender institutions
• secure training centres
• secure children's homes

**Young offender institutions**: are run by the Prison Service and private companies are for people aged 15 to 21 (people under 18 are held in different buildings) house between 60 to 400 people, split into 'wings' of 30 to 60 people

**Secure training centres:** are run by private companies are for people aged up to 17 house between 50 and 80, split into units of 5 to 8 people give 30 hours of education and training a week, following a school day timetable **Secure children's homes:** run by local councils are for people aged 10 to 14 house between 8 and 40 people give 30 hours of education and training a week, following a school day timetable

### Introduction

In March 2012 HMPPS published PSI 08/2012 on the care and management of young people in its custody by which it seeks to deliver its obligations under Section 37 of the Crime and Disorder Act 1998 which establishes the principal aim of the youth justice system:
*Aim of the youth justice system*
(i) It shall be the principal aim of the youth justice system to prevent offending by children and young persons.
(ii) In addition to any other duty to which they are subject, it shall be the duty of all persons and bodies carrying out functions in relation to youth justice to have regard to that aim.

**PSI 08/2012 sets out how HMPPS, working in partnership with the Youth Justice Board (YJB), will achieve that aim, PSI 08/2012 has been updated twice:**
**Updated March 2019**. Parts of Chapter 2 (sections 2.14-2.16, 2.18, 2.19 and 2.23) and Chapter 5 (section 5.14-5.17) only now apply to prisons in Wales. For England, these sections have now been replaced by a Policy Framework, *Building Bridges: A Positive Behaviour Framework for Children and Young People in the Secure Estate.*

**Updated January 2020** Paragraphs 2.15-2.18 and 2.20 and 2.22 have been updated to reflect the policy contained in the Incentives Policy Framework which cancels and replaces PSI 30/2013 Incentives and Earned Privileges and PSI 11/2011 Incentives and Earned Privileges on 13 January 2020.
PSI 08/2012 principally defines the regimes for young people, both male and female, who have been sentenced to a Detention and Training Order (DTO). The PSI also applies to those sentenced under Section 91 (or 90) of the Powers

of Criminal Courts (Sentencing) Act 2000 or Section 226 or 228 of the Criminal Justice Act 2003. Additionally, PSO 4960 'Detention Under Section 92 of the Powers of Criminal Courts (Sentencing) Act 2000' sets out how regimes will need to take account of the special characteristics of those young people serving longer sentences. All parts of this PSI apply to both male and female young people, unless expressly stated otherwise. Additional guidance on the gender specific needs of women prisoners, including those aged under 18, can be found in PSO 4800 'Women Prisoners'.

The PSI does not apply to those individuals who are aged over 18 who are not held in an under 18 establishment.

All elements of the regime are applicable to all unsentenced young people. In addition, Chapter 6 of the PSI sets out separate actions that are only applicable to unsentenced young people.

The regimes described in this PSI differ from those in adult custodial settings because young people are, as adolescents, different. Young people are not yet adults and every care should be taken to ensure that both the conditions of custody and regime activities promote their well-being and healthy growth. Staff should take into account the characteristics of young people's behaviour and stage of development through appropriate role modelling, promoting and maintaining positive behaviour, and clearly defining behavioural boundaries. Staff should particularly consider:

• the importance of contact with families and carers
• the influence of peers on behaviour
• impulsivity and short term thinking
• emotional immaturity, even when a young person appears physically mature
• potential to mature and grow out of crime

Underpinning the entire PSI is the belief that custody should not just be about containment and that regimes should have a positive influence by recognising that:

• young people do change
• adults matter to young people
• young people need the right balance between care and control

### PSI 08/2012 Contents

CHAPTER 1: Introduction
CHAPTER 2: Maintaining a safe and secure environment
• Safeguarding and promoting the welfare of children and young people
• Searching of the person
• Promoting and maintaining good behaviour. These sections, sections 2.14-2.16, 2.18, 2.19 and 2.23, apply to Wales only. These sections are withdrawn in England and replaced with:

Building Bridges: A Positive Behaviour Framework for the Children and Young People Secure Estate, sections 5 .3 - 5.5, 5.7 - 5.10, 5.13-5.14.
• Managing challenging behaviour This section applies to Wales only. This section is withdrawn in England and replaced with: A Positive Behaviour Framework for the Children and Young People Secure Estate, sections 5.9 - 5.10, 5.13,5.15, 5.18 -5.21.
• Dealing with complaints and investigations
• Staff selection, processes and training
CHAPTER 3: Promoting health and building resilience
• Health and healthcare
• Substance misuse
CHAPTER 4: Enabling personal development
• Reception into custody and initial assessment
• Induction and further assessment
• Sentence management
• The personal officer or caseworker
• Involvement of the family, supervising officer and outside agencies
• Communications
CHAPTER 5: Preventing reoffending
• Provision of a full, purposeful and active day
• Learning and skills
• Offending behaviour programmes. This section applies to Wales only. This section is withdrawn in England and replaced with: A Positive Behaviour Framework for the Children and Young People Secure Estate, sections 5.13, 5.15, 5.17 & 5.18.
• Physical education
• Resettlement
CHAPTER 6: Providing for unsentenced young people

Annex A - The Legislative Framework
Annex B - Template Safeguarding Children Statement
Appendix 1 - Safeguarding Children Statement Guidance Note
Annex C - Template Child Protection Policy Statement
Appendix 1 - The Child Protection Procedure
Appendix 1A - Child Protection Procedure Flow Chart
Appendix 1B - Child Protection Key Definitions and Concepts
Appendix 1C - Child Protection Log
Annex D - Template Information Sharing Policy Statement
Annex E - Operational Procedure for Management of Young People with Missing Documentation
Appendix 1 - Checklist for Documentation to be Provided on Transfer
Appendix 2 - Enhanced Baseline Supervision Log
Appendix 3 - Guidance for Completion of T1V and T1VR
Annex F - Role of the Establishment Social Worker

Annex G - Legal Status of Young People in Relation to their Home Area Local Authority

## THE YOUTH JUSTICE BOARD

In April 2000, the Youth Justice Board (YJB) assumed responsibility for the commissioning and purchasing of all secure accommodation for prisoners under 18 ('young people'). HM Prison & Probation Service (HMPPS) is by far the largest provider of places to the YJB, providing about 85 per cent of all secure accommodation for young people. A strategic partnership between HMPPS and the YJB sets out the overarching statement of how the two organisations work together. The Agreement is underpinned by a Service Level Agreement, which sets out the agreed services to be delivered.

The main custodial sentence for a young person is the Detention and Training Order but, for more serious or dangerous offences, a young person will be given a sentence under Section 90/91 of the Powers of Criminal Courts (Sentencing) Act 2000 or Section 226/228 of the Criminal Justice Act 2003 – see below.

In November 2011 the government dropped plans, contained in the Public Bodies Bill, to abolish the Youth Justice Board.

### Standards for Children in Youth Justice 2019

These standards define the minimum expectation for all agencies that provide statutory services to ensure good outcomes for children in the youth justice system.

Published 21 February 2019

These standards replace National Standards for Youth Justice Services (2013).

They aim to:
• provide a framework for youth justice practice and ensure that quality is maintained
• encourage and support innovation and good practice to improve outcomes for children who commit crime
• ensure that every child lives a safe and crime-free life, and makes a positive contribution to society
• align with the YJB's child first principle
• assist the YJB and inspectorates when they assess whether youth justice services are meeting their statutory requirements

These standards are set by the Secretary of State for Justice on the advice of the YJB.

### View the Standards here:

*prisons.org.uk/yjs_standards_for_children_2019.pdf*

There are five standards
• Standard 1: out of court disposals
• Standard 2: at court
• Standard 3: in the community (court disposals)
• Standard 4: in secure settings
• Standard 5: on transition and resettlement

### Standard 4: in secure settings

Youth offending team (YOT) management boards and secure establishment providers (inclusive of health commissioners and providers) have mechanisms in place which provide them with assurance that:
• transport used for children, from court to their destination establishment, to and from court while in custody, or used for other destinations (e.g. health appointments), is appropriate for children, and minimises delays
• the needs and risks of children in secure establishments are identified, addressed, coordinated, and managed to enable a suitable, effective and constructive resettlement with a focus on continuing desistance
• all services, including education and health care, prioritise children's best interests and recognises their needs, capacities, rights and potential
• services take all action to address the causes of a child's offending behaviour and any unmet social, emotional, health or educational needs
• the environment that children live in is rehabilitative and safe and one where there is a culture that enables children to develop, grow and learn
• children are motivated by staff to have an opportunity to engage in appropriate, high-quality education and training that helps them to make good progress
• effective communication and information exchange is in place for the preparation and delivery of the secure and the community phase of sentences
• there is a robust approach to holding services and agencies to account in the event of insufficient planning and delivery of the transition and or resettlement plan for a child
• communication between professionals is in line with Youth Custody Service requirements
• services, plans and interventions take account of diverse needs and promote equality
• safeguarding information is conveyed to relevant parties and agencies without delay
• strategic partnerships and secure establishment providers have confidence in the quality of services and in the effectiveness of supervision of children and
• all service provision prioritises the child's best interest
• children and their parents and carers are provided with appropriate information and support during the secure phase of the sentence.

### YOTs at court must:

• when custody is the expected sentence, make sure that communications and information exchange, through use of the Youth Justice Application Framework (YJAF), are in line with Youth Custody Service requirements when custody is expected

• send the relevant post-court information within two hours of the child being sentenced Secure providers must, on arrival of the child, or as soon as possible, arrange a comprehensive assessment for the secure establishment, including, but not limited to:
• comprehensive health assessment
• safety and risk of harm
• education assessment

Staff in the establishment and the YOT must:
• instigate appropriate safeguarding procedures where necessary
• work together with the individual child to deliver an effective sentence in its entirety

This should include:
• managing a safe stay in the establishment
• the assessment, the plan, the reviews, and the management of risk
• maintaining accurate timely records as and when required through AssetPlus
• maintaining community links and contact with the key people in the child's life to develop a pro-social identity with a constructive focus on future desistance
• supporting children to fulfil their potential during the whole sentence
• identifying and planning for all transitions at the earliest opportunity
• planning for successful resettlement

Initial planning should occur promptly and take account of all views (including the child's). The purpose should be to discuss and approve the plan, the interventions and the resettlement plan in detail. Efforts meaningfully to engage the child should be demonstrated in records

All subsequent sentence planning dates should be agreed at the initial meeting to meet the needs of the child Intervention planning should review progress against the plan, and towards resettlement inclusive of:
• planning for successful resettlement
• suitability for the detention and training order early-release scheme
• home detention curfew
• temporary release (formerly release on temporary licence)
• parole, and release on licence

a plan will be in place in response to a child who is identified as a risk of harm to themselves or from others, or at risk of causing serious harm to others within the secure establishment

Resettlement preparation should identify any actions with clear lines of accountability

Final release preparation should agree the resettlement and reintegration arrangements and the contents of the licence or Notice of Supervision inclusive of risk management.

## DETENTION & TRAINING ORDER (DTO)

The DTO sentences a young person to custody. It can be given to 12-17-year-olds. The length of the sentence can be between four months and two years. The first half of the sentence is spent in custody whilst the second half is spent in the community under the supervision of the Youth Offending Team–see below.

The court can require the young person to be on an Intensive Supervision and Surveillance Programme (ISSP–see below) as a condition of the community period of the sentence. A DTO is only given by the courts to young people whose offending is so serious that a non-custodial sentence would not be appropriate.

## BREACH OF A DTO

The Legal Aid, Sentencing and Punishment of Offenders Act Part 3, Chapter 1 - Section 80.

These provisions apply to breaches (not the breach hearing) that take place after 3rd December 2012.

Breach proceedings can now be brought to court even after a DTO has finished (a summons or a warrant must be issued while the DTO is still in force).

The court retains the power to impose a period of detention in response to a breach of a DTO, and gains a new power to impose a period of supervision instead of custody for the breach. The maximum period of supervision or detention will be three months or the period beginning with the date of the failure to comply with the requirement and the last day of the term of the DTO, whichever is the shorter.

Where the court imposes a period of custody or supervision for breach, it takes immediate effect and can run concurrently with a period of supervision under the DTO. Also, if a young person continues to breach the DTO, the court can impose a further period of supervision (or custody or a fine) and this continues to be the case until the young person completes the order.

### Section 90/91

If a young person is convicted of certain serious offences - generally those for which an adult could receive at least 14 years in custody - they may be sentenced under Section 90/91 of the Powers of Criminal Courts (Sentencing) Act 2000. This sentence can only be given in the Crown Court. If the conviction is for murder, the sentence falls under Section 90, otherwise the sentence will be under Section 91. The length of the sentence can be anywhere up to the adult maximum for the same offence, which for certain offences may be life. A young person given a Section 90/91 sentence will be placed in custody. Conditional release is automatic at the half-way point of sentence irrespective of sentence length. After release, the licence period in the community lasts until the full sentence expiry date. Subject to certain exceptions, young people serving determinate section 91 sentences are eligible for release up to 135 days earlier under the Home Detention Curfew (HDC). Further information on HDC, including the eligibility criteria, can be found in Section Four of this handbook. Offenders who were sentenced, prior to 4 April 2005, to less than four years will leave custody at the halfway point of their sentence and be supervised on licence by their Supervising Officer until the three-quarters point. If certain conditions apply, these young people may be released under the HDC scheme. Young people sentenced, prior to 4 April 2005, to four years or more who are successful at their parole hearing will leave custody at the half-way point. If they are unsuccessful, they will leave at the two-thirds point. In both cases, they will be supervised by their supervising officer until the three-quarters point. There are new public protection sentences introduced by sections 226 and 228 of the CJA 2003.

### Intensive Supervision and Surveillance Programme (ISSP)

**Summary:** https://tinyurl.com/f2t5jmpd

ISSP is the most rigorous, non custodial intervention available for young offenders. As its name suggests, it combines unprecedented levels of community-based surveillance with comprehensive and sustained focus on tackling the factors that contribute to the young person's offending behaviour. Responsibility for delivering ISSP rests with a dedicated team within the YOT.

Most people spend six months on ISSP. The most intensive supervision (25 hrs per week) lasts for the first three months of the programme. Following this, the supervision continues at a reduced intensity (a minimum of five hours per week, and weekend support) for a further three months. On completion of ISSP the young person will continue to be supervised for the remaining period of their order.

**Tracking:** Staff whose job it is to track the whereabouts of young offenders, reinforce participation in their supervision programme by accompanying them to appointments, providing support and advice.

**Tagging:** Electronic monitoring of the young offender (for example to reinforce a night time curfew if that is when they are most at risk of offending).

**Voice verification:** This works by checking the voice print of the young offender over the telephone at times specified in a contact schedule, in order to confirm that they are where they are supposed to be.

**Intelligence-led policing:** The police can provide overt monitoring of movements of these young offenders at key times to reinforce the programme as well as share information with ISSP staff and the YOT.

### What are the aims of ISSP?

The aim of ISSP is to:

Provide a robust, realistic alternative to custody and reduce offending behaviour whilst meeting both the needs of the community and young offenders.

### How is this achieved?

By providing a structured programme of relevant activities including the 5 core elements:
• Offending Behaviour
• Interpersonal Skills
• Education/Training/Employment
• Family Support
• Restorative Justice

### Who is ISSP designed for?

ISSP is targeted at two main groups of offenders: The small group of prolific young offenders (aged 10-17) who commit approximately a quarter of all offences committed by young people.

Those young people who are not prolific offenders but who commit crimes of a very serious nature and who would benefit from an early and intensive intervention.

### Who qualifies for ISSP?

Young offenders are eligible for ISSP if they are appearing in court charged with or convicted of an offence, and have previously:

• Been charged, warned or convicted of offences committed on four or more separate dates within the last 12 months and received at least one a community or custodial penalty.

In addition, young offenders can also qualify for ISSP if they are at risk of custody because:

• The current charge or sentence relates to an offence which is sufficiently serious that an adult could be sentenced to 14 years or more, or

• They have a history of repeat offending on bail and are at risk of a secure remand under section 130 of the Criminal Justice and Police Act 2001.

## 2.18 FOREIGN NATIONALS

The term 'foreign national prisoner' encompasses many different people. People may have come to the UK as children with parents; they may be second generation immigrants—often from former colonies; asylum seekers; people who have been given indefinite leave to remain as refugees; European and European Economic Area nationals or Irish nationals; people who have been trafficked into the country; people who would be persecuted if they returned to their country of origin; people who were entering or leaving the UK on false documents and were arrested at port of entry/exit; people who have entered the UK illegally; people who entered the UK as students and have over stayed on their visa; visitors or workers who have got involved in the criminal justice system.

All foreign national prisoners who have been sentenced to a period of imprisonment of 12 months or more are subject to automatic deportation from the UK unless they fall within defined exceptions. People contesting their deportation because they have family in the UK are no longer entitled to legal aid.

The United Kingdom has prisoner transfer arrangements with over 100 countries and territories. The majority of arrangements however are voluntary agreements which require the consent of both states involved, as well as that of the prisoner concerned, before transfer can take place. However transfers within the EU, and to Nigeria and Albania can take place without the consent of the prisoner; the implications of the decision to leave the EU on the transfer agreement are as yet unclear. The government signed a transfer agreement with Jamaica in September 2015 and committed to provide £25m from the aid budget to help fund the construction of a new 1500-place prison—however, the prison building plan has since been rejected by the Jamaican government. Plans to construct a new 112-place prison wing in Nigeria also came to nothing.

People who have served their sentence but are not UK nationals can be held in prison after their sentence has finished, released or moved to an immigration detention centre. The Legal Aid, Sentencing and Punishment of Offenders Act introduced a new Tariff Expired Removal Scheme (TERS) for indeterminate foreign national prisoners. The scheme allows indeterminate foreign national prisoners, who are confirmed by UK Visas and Immigration to be liable for removal from the UK, to be removed from prison and the country upon, or any date after, the expiry of their tariff without reference to the Parole Board. TERS is mandatory; all indeterminate foreign national prisoners who are liable must be considered for removal under the scheme.

**Foreign Nationals - updated August 2022**
• PSI 04/2013 currently remains in force and has been updated several times as shown below since it was introduced in 2013.
**Latest Update 15 June 2022: This revision is made to incorporate the changes to the ERS that were made by the Nationality and Borders Act 2022 (NABA 2022) that was implemented on 28 June 2022.**

**The NABA 2022 increases the ERS window from 9 months to 12 months and introduces a new 'stop the clock' provision for those who are removed under the ERS on or after 28 June 2022 and allows ERS for those recalled to custody from licence.**

Update 21 May 2021 – This revision is made to incorporate the information sent out in a letter on 17 February 2020 following the commencement of the Terrorist Offenders (Restriction of Early Release) Act (TORERA) 2020. The TORERA 2020 inserted Section 247A into the Criminal Justice Act (CJA) 2003 and made those prisoners subject to the release provisions of Section 247A ineligible for early removal under the ERS. The Act was retrospective. This update also includes examples of how the ERSED is calculated for prisoners serving sentences subject to the Release of Prisoners (Alteration of Relevant Proportion of Sentence) Order 2020 which was implemented on 1 April 2020.

Update 15 October 2015 - This revision makes it a requirement to populate the Early Removal Scheme Eligibility Date (ERSED) field on NOMIS by 9 November 2015 – Paragraphs 1.17, 1.18, 1.22, 3.5, 3.20 and 3.29 refer. Amendments also reflect the current electronic referral process to refer sentenced FNPs within 10 working days to Criminal Casework only.

Update 20 December 2013 – This version has amended phone numbers in Annex F.

Post-Brexit: The removal of determinate sentenced prisoners under the Early Removal Scheme (ERS) remains dependent on decisions by the Home Office that they should be deported.

The UK's departure from the EU means that, an EEA national who commits an offence *after 31 December 2020* will be considered under the same deportation thresholds that apply to Non-EEA nationals. Steps have also been taken to ensure foreign national offenders from the EEA are able to apply for EU Settled Status under the EU Settlement Scheme (EUSS) if they meet the relevant criteria.

Summary: **England and Wales only**
**Powers to deport foreign criminals**
Deportation is a statutory power of the Home Secretary. People who are not British citizens are liable to deportation from the UK if the Home Secretary deems their deportation to be conducive to the public good under provisions of the Immigration Act 1971

In addition to the existing powers under the 1971 Act, the UK Borders Act 2007 made provision for the automatic deportation of foreign criminals. The Home Secretary **must** make a deportation order in respect of a foreign national offender sentenced to a least 12 months' imprisonment unless certain exceptions apply (e.g. where deportation would contravene the UK's obligations under the Refugee and Human Rights Conventions). Those foreign national offenders not meeting this threshold may still be liable to deportation under the 1971 Act's provisions, which operate slightly differently from those dealt with under the 2007 Act.

Prior to the UK's departure from the European Union and the expiry of the associated transition period at 23:00 GMT on 31 December 2020, the Home Secretary's ability to deport criminals from EEA Member States was restricted by the operation of EU law, which required that expulsion must be proportionate and based exclusively on the personal conduct of the individual concerned and level of 'threat' that they pose to public policy, public security or public health

## Appeals

The Nationality, Immigration and Asylum Act 2002 sets out the considerations to which tribunals and courts must 'have regard' when hearing an appeal by a foreign national offender against a deportation order.

In June 2017, the Supreme Court found the 'deport first, appeal later' rules had not been implemented in a way that was fair and lawful. Originally applied only to foreign national offenders facing deportation from the UK, the approach was extended in 2016 so that any appellant challenging an immigration decision (other than in asylum cases) could be required to leave the UK. In R (Kiarie and Byndloss) v Secretary of State for the Home Department the Supreme Court held that the Home Secretary had not established that the practical arrangements in place to support appeals under 'deport first, appeal later' struck a fair balance between the rights of the appellants and the interests of the wider community.

Foreign Nationals in prison: **Source** *prisonoracle.com* **Offender Management Statistics, 28 July 2022.**

There were 9,682 foreign nationals held in custody as at 30 June 2022; representing 13.5% of the total prison population.

A foreign national offender's citizenship status or liability for deportation does not affect the Parole Board test for release or panel procedures; but the risk assessment and decision-making processes may be informed by or constrained by certain factors when an applicant does not have an absolute right to remain in the country (a foreign national offender). In particular, foreign national offenders facing imminent deportation may not be eligible for transfer to open conditions, or may be referred for consideration of their release under risk management plans whose restrictions cannot extend beyond UK jurisdiction and which therefore would not be viable/effective following deportation.

## Key Requirements
### Parole Board Rules

2.1 The Parole Board Rules 2019 apply to all prisoners and do not explicitly refer to foreign national offenders. However, the case of a foreign national offender liable to deportation may be influenced by legal, procedural and policy implications when considered by the Parole Board.

2.2 Foreign national offenders can access an information sheet for foreign nationals in the prison system provided by the Prisoners' Advice Service. HMPPS Guidance

2.3 A series of Prison & Probation Service orders and instructions set out policy and practice concerning deportation and foreign national offenders. These include Generic Parole Process Policy Framework (January 2020); PSO 29/2014 (Release on licence for Foreign National Prisoners pending deportation); PSI 37/2014 (Eligibility for Open Conditions and for ROTL of Prisoners Subject to Deportation Proceedings; PSI 01/2015 (The Allocation of prisoners liable to deportation or removal from the United Kingdom); PSI 52 / 2011 Immigration, Removal and Repatriation Services; Recall, Review and Re-Release of Recalled Prisoners Policy Framework, April 2019; and Release on Temporary Licence (ROTL) Policy Framework, May 2019 ('the Policy Framework May 2019') .

Legislative framework

2.4 A foreign national offender is anyone remanded or convicted on criminal charges who is not a British national and is subject to UK immigration control. Even if deportation is not mentioned in court at sentencing, the case of any foreign national sentenced to a custodial term is referred to Home Office Immigration Enforcement (HOIE) for consideration. Liability to deportation does not impact the Parole Board test for release but can affect how a case is dealt with.

2.5 A person with British citizenship is not a foreign national. Those with dual nationality (when one of them is British) are to be treated as British although, in very exceptional circumstances, naturalisation may be removed where there are public protection issues. Cases of dual nationality (as well as those with indefinite leave to remain) may also be referred to HOIE. A person can only have indefinite leave to remain if they are not naturalised.

2.6 Power for deportation derives from the Immigration Act 1971 and via the UK Borders Act 2007. Under the 2007 Act, non-European

Economic Area (non-EEA) and EEA nationals sentenced to 12 months or more can be automatically deported at the sentence-end unless they can show that their deportation would meet one of six exceptions enshrined in the Act, including that it would constitute a breach of their human rights.

Those non-EEA foreign national offenders sentenced to custodial terms of less than 12 months, or in some cases who receive non-custodial penalties but are considered to have caused serious harm or to be a persistent offender, may be liable to deportation under the 1971 Act.

In addition, since 1 January 2021, EEA citizens (comprising all EU citizens and those who are citizens of Liechtenstein, Iceland, Norway and Switzerland) and their family members who are not protected by the EU Withdrawal Agreement Act 2020 are covered by the UK domestic deportation threshold as per their non-EEA counterparts for criminal or other non-conducive conduct committed after 23:000 GMT on 31 December 2020. Those who are protected by the EU Withdrawal Agreement Act 2020 are still considered for deportation on public policy, public security or public health grounds under the Immigration (EEA) Regulations 2016 where it concerns conduct (including any criminal convictions relating to it) committed before 23:00 GMT on 31 December 2020.

**Deportation Procedures**

3.1 Once an appeal against a conviction has been determined (or the deadline for appeal has passed), and the HO wishes to pursue deportation, the foreign national offender will be served with a notice of liability to deportation, with the aim of enforcing deportation at completion of sentence or as soon as practicable thereafter. The decision will inform the foreign national that they may, make representations to the Secretary of State regarding their deportation which the Secretary of State will then consider.

3.2 If the Secretary of State confirms that a decision to deport has been made, and the foreign national offender raises a protection or human rights claim and the claim is refused they will be afforded a right of appeal against the refusal. The right of appeal will be in country unless the claim is certified, in which case the appeal right will be exercisable outside the UK. The deportation process normally begins 18 months before the FNO's Early Removal Scheme eligibility date.

3.3 An appeal goes to the First-Tier Tribunal (Immigration and Asylum Chamber) and can take over six months to process. Either party may, with permission, appeal on a point of law to the Upper Tribunal. A foreign national offender can make further representations to the Secretary of State at any time. If the further representations are considered to amount to a fresh claim and the fresh claim is refused, a further right of appeal is generated.

3.4 When released automatically (on reaching ARD or CRD) or by direction of the Parole Board, a foreign national offender may be liable for detention under the Immigration Act 1971. The Secretary of State decides whether secure detention is warranted on the basis of whether the foreign national offender is likely to be removed from the UK within a reasonable timeframe. Additional factors that may be considered are the risk of harm to the public and risk of absconding. If detained, a foreign national may apply to the First-Tier Tribunal for immigration bail. If immigration bail is granted, its terms will be tailored by the tribunal around the conditions of any parole licence. If the foreign national offender re-enters the UK clandestinely and was removed through the Early Removal Scheme (ERS), the FNO will be returned to prison to serve the outstanding custodial period and will not be eligible again for the ERS during this sentence.

3.5 Once a foreign national offender is deported, there are no legislative powers to enforce parole licence conditions or provide supervision outside of the UK.

**Criteria for deportation (Criteria for deportation (public policy test and non-conducive threshold)**
**Public Policy Test**

4.1 A person entitled to remain in the UK by virtue of the Immigration (EEA) Regulations 2016 may only be removed on the grounds of public policy, public security or public health. This essentially covers EEA citizens and their family members for conduct committed before 23:00 GMT on 31 December 2020, so long as they were lawfully resident in the UK at that time.

4.2 For someone subject to the EEA Regulations 2016, the test depends on the length of residence in the UK. The Secretary of State is likely to seek deportation for someone receiving a sentence of two years or more and for a prisoner serving one year or more for a sexual, violent, or drugs-related offence.

4.3 Sections 23 and 26 of the Immigration (EEA) Regulations 2016 also allows for the Secretary of State to deport an individual who is deemed to have misused the right to residence, for example someone who as knowingly entered into a sham marriage.

4.4 Under Regulation 27, it must be demonstrated that there is a genuine, present and sufficiently serious threat affecting one of the fundamental interests of society. Commonly, this will amount to a propensity to reoffend as indicated by criminal history or expert assessment. Non-Conducive threshold

4.5 This applies to a non-EEA foreign national offender, regardless of when the conduct was committed, or EEA citizens (and their family members) for conduct committed after 23:00 GMT on 31 December 2020. Sections 32 of the UK Borders Act 2007 determines that deportation is automatic when there is a single custodial sentence of 12 months or more unless an exemption under Section 33 applies.

4.7 Section 33 of the UK Borders Act 2007 allows the following exceptions to the automatic criteria:
• where the prisoner was under 18 at date of conviction or is detained under the Mental Health Act
• where extradition proceedings are ongoing
• where a claim has been lodged, that deportation would be a breach of obligations under EU Treaties or the Refugee Convention, European Convention on Human Rights or Trafficking
• An exemption to automatic deportation does not constitute an exemption to deportation. Deportation may still be pursued under the Immigration Act 1971 where the Secretary of State considers the FNO non-conducive to the public good.

**Early removal schemes (ERS & TERS)**
**ERS**
5.1 The Early Removal Scheme (ERS) allows foreign national prisoners serving determinate sentences to leave the UK prior to the end of the requisite custodial part of their sentence. **The maximum ERS period of time that a foreign national prisoner can be deported or removed from the UK is, since 28th June 2022 (see NABA above), 365 days before the conditional release date, automatic release date or parole eligibility date.** The foreign national prisoner must serve a minimum of half of the custodial period of their standard determinate sentence, half of the custodial term for sentences for offenders of particular concern (SOPC), and one third of the custodial term for extended sentence prisoners) before being removed. Prisoners excluded from the scheme are those subject to; sentences in respect of terrorism and terrorism-related offences, Sex Offenders Register notification, recalled on Home Detention Curfew and recalled for allegedly committing another offence.

**TERS (England and Wales only)**
5.2 The Tariff Expired Removal Scheme (TERS) allows early removal of foreign national offenders serving an indeterminate sentence once their sentence has been served to date of tariff. TERS is not an automatic consideration in every case for foreign national offenders serving indeterminate sentences. TERS is considered when the foreign national offender becomes barrier-free, i.e. they are going to be deported, they have exhausted their appeal rights and there are travel documents in place.

5.3 The Parole Board takes no part in the decision to remove a foreign national offender under TERS which is within the Secretary of State's remit.

5.4 The Parole review runs in parallel with the TERS process. Neither decision is reliant on the other.

5.5 The Parole Board panel may find it helpful to direct a report from the HOIE. The HOIE report should set out the current immigration status of the foreign national offender. It should indicate date of and reasons for entry to the UK, established nationality, how the individual came to Immigration Enforcement notice, and the progress in processing deportation orders with specific details about applications, appeals, and court or tribunal decisions. Where a deportation order has been served and the offender has exhausted all appeal rights, HOIE should comment on the process for arranging travel documentation and any nationality issues. Directions to provide this information, if required, should be made at the earliest opportunity.

5.6 When a case is referred to the Parole Board, a full decision will be required even if the foreign national offender is scheduled for removal under TERS as relevant parties may benefit from the Board's assessment of risk and of absconding. The Parole Board must proceed until the referral is withdrawn.

5.7 In deciding whether to refuse removal under TERS, PPCS will consider: • "Whether the prisoner has a confiscation order made against him or is subject to confiscation order proceedings;
• Whether the prisoner has outstanding criminal charges (in which case the holding establishment must notify PPCS of any outstanding criminal proceedings or police investigations and report the outcome as soon as it is known).
• Whether there is evidence that the prisoner is planning further criminal offences, including plans to evade immigration control and return to the UK unlawfully;
• Whether the prisoner is serving a sentence for a terrorism-related offence (in considering such cases, PPCS must always consult with the HMPPS Extremism Unit before a final decision is made).
• Whether the removal of the prisoner from prison would undermine the confidence of the public in the criminal justice" – as per Paragraph 3.3.2, Generic Parole Process Policy Framework (January 2020)

5.8 Once a deportation order has been served and the appeal rights have been exhausted, the prisoner is excluded from open conditions.

5.9 In determining whether an adjournment is needed to obtain immigration documentation or for other reasons, the panel must, as in all cases, make a decision on the merits of the case. However, a panel should not adjourn or defer for a TERS decision. The decision of the Parole Board is not reliant on the TERS decision and in fact, a Parole Board release decision will supercede the TERS agreement to remove.

### Implications for Practice and Decision Making
### Notice of deportation

6.1 The term "liable to deportation" applies to prisoners who (see paragraph 6.96, the Policy Framework May 2019:

- are confirmed by the Home Office as meeting the initial criteria for deportation based on such factors as nationality and sentence length (whether the offender has been informed of this or not); or
- have received a formal notice of liability for deportation; or
- have received a deportation order with appeal rights in the UK remaining; or
- fall below the threshold for deportation but are being considered for or made subject to removal from the UK as an "administrative removal".

6.2 Deportation proceedings will generally begin eighteen months prior to the ERS eligibility date. Final decisions may not have been made when a case is referred to the Parole Board, especially for indeterminate sentence foreign national prisoners.

6.3 When a prisoner is subject to deportation proceedings, this must be flagged up by PPCS on the front sheet of the dossier. Relevant information may also be contained in the OASys assessment report.

6.4 In such a case, the MCA member, panel chair or duty member must check that there is a current report in the dossier from the HOIE. If not, a copy may be directed via PPCS. When the MCA member is directing the case to an oral hearing, an updated report from the HOIE must be directed because circumstances may have changed. A member setting panel chair directions must do likewise, if the HOIE report is not already in the dossier.

6.5 The panel's direction may extend to asking the HOIE (via PPCS) for information relating to abscond risk. For example, asking how well the foreign national offender complied with Immigration Act reporting requirements prior to sentence.

### Interpreters

7.1 For prisoners whose first language is not English and have notified of a need or preference to conduct the hearing in a foreign language, the Parole Board must enable them to use their preferred language where reasonably practical.

An interpreter should be supplied automatically (by the prison) if it is evident from the dossier that one will be needed.

7.2 The need for an interpreter or signer should be referenced in the main text of MCA, duty member or panel chair directions and flagged with the Parole Board case manager so that the attendance of the interpreter can be organised and confirmed in advance of the hearing.

7.3 It may be necessary to defer or adjourn if a fair hearing cannot take place without an interpreter present.

7.4 Please refer to the Member Guidance on Translations and Interpreters which provides information and advice relating to parole cases where the prisoner's first language is not English, and translation of documents, or an interpreter, may be needed.

### Test for release

8.1 The Parole Board must apply the statutory test for release in all cases where the question of release is part of the terms of referral from the Secretary of State. The legal test for release is clear: The Board must not give a direction [for release] unless the Board is satisfied that it is no longer necessary for the protection of the public that foreign national offender should be confined [in prison]. This is also known as the public protection test.

8.2 In ERS and TERS cases the test for release whether at oral hearing or MCA stage does not change. However, the panel may wish to consider the effect on risk of the absence of an enforceable risk management plan should ERS or TERS be implemented.

8.3 Risk of serious harm to the public includes people in the country to which deportation is proposed. This could be anywhere in the world. Case law (R v Parole Board ex p White (1994) Times 30 December) says that public safety is not limited to Britain but applies to public safety in any country outside its jurisdiction. Even if a prisoner is to be deported or removed immediately, a full risk assessment must be conducted.

### Risk Management Plans

9.1 A risk management plan must be produced and assessed for every foreign national offender as for any other parole case. This is because, following a panel's direction for release, a foreign national offender scheduled for deportation may still successfully appeal the order and be released into the community.

9.2 The MCA member or panel chair must, therefore, direct submission of a risk management plan if one is not already available.

9.3 A release plan must extend to the country to which removal is proposed. However, once an offender has been deported, there are no legal agreements between countries to enforce licence conditions, to provide supervision or any release or risk management plan which would ordinarily be provided in the UK. Equally, risk is unlikely to be subject to management by external factors. Accordingly, the panel may need to make an assessment of manageability based only upon internal factors (how the foreign national offender can manage their own risks) as the panel has a responsibility to potential victims in the country to which the foreign national offender will be deported.

9.4 If the panel wishes to obtain information from outside the UK (such as details of previous foreign convictions or an offender's home situation), a direction can be set for the Secretary of State to submit such evidence (The directions should set out the information/ material required by the panel but should not detail how the Secretary of State should obtain such information). An application may be made by PPCS to the relevant embassy. In some cases, the Secretary of State may instruct an advocate to apply for a court order in the home country for the release of material. Success in obtaining information will vary depending on cooperative relations with that country, availability of relevant evidence and timescales to access information. Consideration to directing provision of such information must be given during MCA and directions made accordingly due to the extended timescales likely to be required.

9.5 If release is directed, licence conditions which can be enforced in the UK should be considered by the panel and set even if deportation seems a likely outcome. Decision letters should make reference to those supervising the case to ensure that any immigration court considering bail has sight of the licence conditions. Normally, deportation takes place soon after the direction to release: but a delay in making removal arrangements could mean the foreign national offender is released temporarily in the UK. For example, if bailed from immigration detention, the Parole Board's release requirements may be relevant in shaping bail conditions. Alternatively, the foreign national offender might successfully appeal deportation and be released on licence in the UK.

9.6 It should be noted that Immigration Enforcement can only detain a foreign national offender where it is considered removal can take place within a reasonable timescale. If an appeal becomes protracted and /or the documentation process is lengthy and / or the returns process to the country of origin is on hold, there is a higher likelihood that the foreign national offender may be granted bail by an immigration judge or the Secretary of State.

**Processes following a direction for release**

10.1 The foreign national offender to be removed from the UK under TERS will remain on life or IPP licence when the panel directs release. If the foreign national offender returns to the UK in the future, recall on that licence will follow. At which point, the individual can be considered for TERS again, and therefore potentially deported, or the matter referred to the Parole Board as a recall case.

10.2 A deportation order carries powers to detain pending removal and applies separately from the Board's direction for release. Although directed for release, a foreign national offender subject to deportation may be detained in prison or at an immigration removal centre. These are matters for HOIE. The individual may be granted bail into the community or succeed in overturning the deportation order. For this reason, a panel directing release must consider appropriate licence conditions.

10.3 The release decision from the Parole Board remains provisional for 21 calendar days if it is eligible for reconsideration (the foreign national offender is serving an indeterminate sentence; an extended sentence; a determinate sentence subject to initial release by the Parole Board under Chapter 6, Part 12 of the Criminal Justice Act 2003 (Rule 28 (2) of the 2019 Rules) or becomes final if no application for reconsideration is received within the specified time – within 21 days of the MCA paper decision; decision on the paper after a direction for oral hearing or the decision following an oral hearing.

**Open conditions**

11.1 Panels should read the Secretary of State's referral letter in the dossier to check whether the foreign national offender is eligible for open conditions. It is also important to check what documentation, if any, is provided in the dossier from UK Immigration about the offender's deportation status, and where necessary to direct an update.

11.2 Where all appeal rights against a deportation order have been exhausted, or where the appeal rights must be exercised from abroad, the foreign national offender must not be classified as suitable for open conditions. This condition does not apply to offenders already in open conditions unless their deportation status changes whilst they are in open conditions, in which case their suitability to remain in open conditions will need to be re-assessed.

11.3 Foreign national offenders in closed conditions who are liable for deportation must be subject to a more rigorous risk assessment before open conditions is considered.

11.4 A foreign national offender not subject to deportation is treated like any other parole prisoner and standard Parole Board considerations apply.

11.5 If recommending open conditions is an option available to the Parole Board, a panel must consider carefully the risk of absconding. This should take account of all available information. In the case of a foreign national offender facing removal, this might include attitude towards deportation and the possible benefits of resettlement for a foreign national offender unlikely to be released in the UK. Such an offender will be unable to access public funds and may be subject to restrictions on employment and most forms of study.

11.6 Although the proposed release plan may be limited in scope, there may be opportunities for a foreign national offender to demonstrate application and consolidation of learning from offending behaviour programmes if transferred to the environment of an open prison. In any case, the threat of deportation may be lifted at some stage, making transfer to open conditions more productive in the longer term.

11.7 The MCA member or panel chair setting directions for additional reports or hearing requirements may include brief guidance for report writers and/or witnesses as to whether recommendations for open prison should be considered, if this is included in the referral.

Release on Temporary Licence (ROTL) Eligibility
Release on Temporary Licence (ROTL) Eligibility
11.8 The Policy Framework - Release on temporary licence - GOV.UK (www.gov.uk) - outlines the position in terms of ROTL for foreign national prisoners. Eligibility for ROTL for foreign national prisoners is linked to the prisoner's deportation status. Foreign national prisoners who meet the following criteria are statutorily excluded from ROTL (Paragraphs 6.93 and 6.94 of the Policy Framework May 2019):

• "Offenders with a Deportation Order who have exhausted all deportation appeal rights in the UK are statutorily prohibited from ROTL under Prison Rule 9 (1A) / YOI Rule 5 (1A) unless the prisoner is located in open If a notification is received that appeal rights have been exhausted then the relevant security alert, "Appeal Rights Exhausted (ARE)" must be activated on the offender's NOMIS record".

• "There may be cases where a decision has been made to release on ROTL, or the prisoner is on ROTL, when they become statutorily excluded; i.e. they exhaust their in-country appeal rights against deportation. Where the prisoner has yet to be released the decision should be rescinded. Where they are on ROTL at this point, the governor, must revoke the licence and recall the offender to prison unless they are due back from ROTL on the same day the notification is received."

11.9 Those who have not exhausted their deportation appeal rights in the UK may have their ROTL considered on an individual basis. This will be subject to an enhanced risk assessment, the principles of which are set out in paragraphs 6.97 to 6.99 of the Policy Framework May 2019, namely:

"Offenders liable for deportation must not be assessed as suitable for ROTL, unless it is judged that there is a low risk of failure to return. In making the assessment, there must be an assumption that removal from the UK will take place. The risk that the offender will use temporary release to evade not only custody, but also possible deportation action must be weighed and specific account taken of the following:

• Any evidence that the offender has sought to frustrate or evade the immigration process, for example – through their previous failure to comply with immigration restrictions, immigration bail or via the terms of leave in the UK, or because they have previously absconded from an immigration removal centre.

• Any failures of temporary release or other instance of lack of compliance with prison rules and regulations that may indicate an inclination to abuse the privilege afforded by ROTL when considered in conjunction with their deportation status.

Any evidence of this nature should normally be seen as proof of not falling within the "low risk" of abscond category.

Governors must also consider factors that might indicate lower risk of failure to return, for example, where the offender is known to be cooperative with the deportation process. Other factors indicating lower risk may include strong family ties in this country and/or other evidence to indicate that the offender would not wish to jeopardise his or her chances of successfully appealing and remaining in this country.

Where the offender is in open conditions when it is confirmed that they are liable for deportation, the offender must have their security category reviewed. Only once it has been confirmed that the offender may remain in open conditions may the application for ROTL be considered, and it may be considered under the usual and not the enhanced risk assessment process."

**Home Detention Curfew (HDC)**

Certain prisoners serving sentences of at least 12 weeks, but less than four years may be considered for early release under the HDC scheme. Those eligible and suitable for HDC may be released up to 135-day prior to their automatic release date subject to an electronically monitored (tagged) curfew. Full details of the scheme are set out in the HDC Policy Framework: Home detention curfew - GOV.UK (www.gov.uk)

Prisoners who are liable to removal from the UK as defined by section 259 of the Criminal Justice Act 2003 or section 46 of the Criminal Justice Act 1991 are statutorily excluded from HDC. No prisoner can be released on HDC who:
a. is liable to deportation under section 3 (5) of the Immigration Act 1971 and has been notified of a decision to make a deportation order; or
b. has a court recommendation for deportation; or
c. has been notified of a decision to refuse leave to enter the UK; or
d. is an illegal entrant within the meaning of section 33 of the Immigration Act 1971; or
e. is liable to removal under section 10 of the Immigration and Asylum Act 1999.

Prisoners not meeting this description but who are liable to and are being considered for deportation/removal from the UK are eligible but presumed unsuitable for HDC unless there are exceptional circumstances justifying release. For example, where Immigration Enforcement has confirmed that deportation is unlikely to be effected for the foreseeable future, and they do not intend to detain the prisoner on release from prison. Each case will be considered on its merits.

**Particular thanks are due for the updating this chapter to Adrian Chen at the Ministry of Justice and Caroline Finlayson at the Home Office. The above information only applies to England and Wales, it does NOT apply to Scotland or Northern Ireland.**

## 2.19 DISABILITY IN PRISON

**PSI 32/2011**
**INTRODUCTION**
Disability now comes under the banner of Equalities - see 2.11, but will be outlined here briefly.
PSI 32/2011 requires:
Governors must ensure that efforts are made to identify whether a prisoner has a mental or physical impairment of any form. Governors must ensure that prisoners are encouraged to disclose their disability status and that procedures are in place to record this information (both on reception and subsequently) and to treat it confidentially. Not all prisoners will be aware of their disabled status and staff must be proactive in identifying the specific needs of all prisoners (further guidance on learning disabilities is at annex H).
Governors must consider on an ongoing basis what prisoners and visitors with a range of disabilities might reasonably need and ensure that reasonable adjustments (see annex G) are made for disabled prisoners and visitors. Governors must consider whether prison policies and practices, the built environment, or a

lack of auxiliary aids and services could put a disabled prisoner or visitor at a substantial disadvantage and if so must make reasonable adjustments to avoid the disadvantage. If a request for reasonable adjustments is made by a prisoner or visitor it must be considered and the outcome documented.
Governors must ensure that where it is not possible to make the reasonable adjustments required the prisoner is transferred to another appropriate establishment. Where there is a dispute between prisons about where a disabled prisoner is best located, the Deputy Director of Custody must be contacted.
The transfer of a disabled prisoner must not be delayed or prevented on the basis of their disability (unless the proposed receiving establishment cannot provide appropriate facilities). Governors must ensure that where a disabled prisoner is required at court, the escort contractor and Clerk of Court are informed of the details of the disability and the needs of the prisoner.
The 'Disability in Prison' section in earlier copies of this Handbook explained how prisons were traditionally designed and built by and for people without disabilities. With an assumption that prisoners are usually fit, young men, little consideration was given to the possible needs of a minority of people with physical or sensory impairments.
The result was that any provision made for disabled people in prison was often ad-hoc and sometimes inadequate. Anyone with an impairment who was in prison may have been faced with barriers in one form or another which could have prevented him or her from participating fully in various activities within the prison. The last ten to fifteen years though, have seen important changes taking place for disabled people in prison.
All prisons built in recent years should have been designed to comply with guidelines laid out by the DDA 2005.
Other important policy development in terms of disability legislation and resulting changes in prison service policy will be covered in this chapter. 'A short thematic review on the care and support of prisoners with a disability' carried out in March 2009 by Her Majesty's Inspectorate of Prisons (HMIP), has since resulted in a number of policy changes, and an overview of some of these changes will be given below.
There will be information on what to do if you are a disabled prisoner, and what facilities and services you can expect, and a few of the many examples of good practice (and otherwise) concerning disability within the prison estate will be outlined. Finally, a list of contact details for some of the groups who can offer advice or

assistance to disabled people in prison is provided at the end of the chapter.

## IF YOU ARE DISABLED:
### Reception and Induction

The 2009 HMIP report recommended that all prisoners should be asked whether they have a physical, mental and/or sensory disability on arrival at a prison. The report also stated that it was found during the inspection that 'the individual needs of prisoners who arrived with a disability were mainly dealt with as they arose. Prisons should by now have reviewed induction procedures and adapted information for prisoners with a range of disabilities. The points below are some of those which cover several aspects of the induction procedures for prisons

• All prisoners should be asked whether they have a physical, mental and/or sensory disability on arrival at a prison. Reception staff to include this in initial interview with the prisoner, taking care to ensure prisoner's privacy

• All prisoners should be formally screened for potential learning disabilities or difficulties on first arrival to custody. This may take place either during the initial reception interview or at a later stage prior to induction. Care should be taken to ensure the prisoner's privacy

• Information on disabilities from assessments on arrival should be recorded, including when a prisoner indicates that they do not have a disability or opts not to disclose. This should be updated if they later disclose, learn of, or develop a disability.

• When a prisoner transfers to another prison, information about their physical, mental, and/or sensory disability, or their learning disability or difficulty, should be passed to the receiving prison.

• Formal procedures for declaring a disability after arrival should be in place, promoted and known by staff and prisoners.

• There should be formal systems for staff, including health services staff, to share relevant information.

• Reception, first night, and induction procedures should offer additional, tailored support to address the individual needs and/or anxieties of disabled prisoners.

• The induction process should cover the help available for prisoners with a disability. Staff must provide information on available help in reception and first night, and whenever it is requested

• Induction procedures, prison information, and notices should be reviewed to ensure that they can be understood by, and meet the needs of, prisoners with a disability, including those with learning difficulties.

• 'Respectful Searching' will take place for all offenders searched in Reception

It is important therefore, that on reception into prison, during induction, or as soon as possible when you go into prison, that you inform staff of any disability, especially if it could affect where in the prison you are located.

If you have a visual impairment, or are deaf or hearing impaired, the Prison Service must make arrangements to ensure appropriate assistance is offered to you. For visual impairments you might need a personal reader, or information provided in Braille, large print or in an audio format (CD or tape).

If you have dyslexia, you may benefit from having information given to you in audio (tape or CD) rather than in printed form. Prisoners who feel they could benefit from any of the above methods of receiving information should make a request for them, and advice on how to make a request is outlined in Chapter 2.4.

In June 2004, the Prison Reform Trust issued an information booklet for disabled prisoners which was updated and reissued in 2009 following the policy developments discussed above. Copies of the booklet are sent to prisons. If you were not given a copy of the booklet on reception, ask in your establishment for a copy.

The Disabled Prisoners Information Booklet is available in two versions, including one in Easyread format (Easyread makes the words simpler and uses pictures alongside the words). The booklet is also available on CD for prisoners who have difficulty reading for any reason, and in 26 languages.

### Samaritans, Listeners, Insiders and Buddies

All prisons have either 'Listener', 'Buddy' or 'Insider' schemes whereby certain prisoners are trained along the lines of the Samaritans. If any prisoner feels isolated or at a loss about how to cope in prison, they will be available to lend support to anybody who feels upset or vulnerable. Prisoners should be able to call the Samaritans using the PIN phone system if they need to. In case the information may be needed in future, it may be useful for prisoners to check with the wing office as soon as possible on this. As well as the groups mentioned above, the Prison Chaplain may also be available to offer support. This support is available not just during Induction or Reception, but throughout your sentence.

### Release (Discharge)

On or before release you should try to ensure that any benefits that will be payable to you on your return to the community are available immediately following your release. There is more information on claiming benefits including Disability Living Allowance in chapter 2.12..

There may be specific considerations when releasing disabled prisoners, for example can they manage the journey home without assistance, and/or whether they have the mobility aids they need. For example, an able-bodied prisoner may be able to get a bus to the railway station, whereas a prisoner in a wheelchair may need to be sent in an adapted taxi.

A prisoner with a learning disability may have difficulty understanding travel instructions. Any instructions and reporting requirements will need to be carefully explained if there is any concern that the prisoner might have difficulty in understanding or retaining the information. A suggestion might be to give the prisoner clearly written instructions with a simple map so that they can keep referring to it, and a list of things that they must do when they get home.

Where possible, links should be established with social services in the area to which the prisoner will be released. This is especially important where the prisoner may need to access social care in daily life. Links to support organisations in the area, introductions to day care centres or other networks will assist in resettlement. Some of these may be located by contacting RADAR or DIAL (details below).

**Disability Liaison Officer**

The role of a Disability Liaison Officer (DLO) as outlined in the now cancelled PSO 2855, may still exist in some prisons, or it may have been a function assumed by an Equalities Officer, ask a member of staff if a DLO exists or who the Equalities Officer is.

**Definitions and Explanations Concerning the DDA 1995 as amended by The DDA 2005**

If a prisoner is concerned to make a complaint about discrimination under the DDA 1995 as amended by the DDA 2005, it is important to bear in mind the importance of a 'disability' being defined as such within the definition set out by the DDA, so that what is perceived to be discrimination is also covered by the relevant sections of the Acts

A disabled person as defined by the DDA is "a person who has a physical, sensory or mental impairment which has a long term and substantial effect on their ability to carry out normal day to day activities".

'Physical or mental impairment' means: 'someone who uses a wheelchair or has difficulty in walking, someone who is deaf, someone who has significantly impaired speech, someone who is blind or partially sighted, someone who has continuing treatment for diabetes, someone with epilepsy, someone who has a learning disability or someone who has a mental illness, is considered disabled under the DDA. The person does not need to be registered as

disabled. This is not an exhaustive list as there are many more disabilities which are covered.

Also protected by the Act are people who have a severe disfigurement. And someone who has recovered from a mental illness or is in remission from a condition is still protected. The Act also covers someone whose condition might initially have only a slight effect on their ability, but is likely to get worse, such as people with cancer, HIV infection or multiple sclerosis' (HMSO DL150 Oct 96). With effect from the 2005 amendments, conditions such as cancer are covered from first diagnosis, not from the onset of symptoms.

A person will be considered to be disabled if the cumulative effects of their impairments have a substantial, adverse effect on their ability to carry out normal day to day activities. A 'substantial' effect is an effect which 'must involve a limitation that goes beyond the normal differences in ability that may exist between people'. It is an effect that is more than minor or trivial For a disability to be considered 'long term' it must have lasted, or be expected to last, for 12 months or more, or be likely to last for the rest of a person's life

The DDA states that an impairment will be treated as affecting a person's ability to carry out 'normal day to day activities' if it affects one or more of the following: mobility; manual dexterity; physical co-ordination; continence; ability to lift, carry or otherwise move every day objects; speech; hearing or eyesight; memory or ability to concentrate, learn or understand, and perception of the risk of physical danger.

Conditions excluded from the DDA include addiction or dependency on alcohol, nicotine or any other substance, except where the substance is medically prescribed, seasonal allergic rhinitis e.g. hay fever, a tendency to set fires, a tendency to steal, and tattoos and non-medical body piercing. When one of these conditions causes a disability, e.g. alcoholism causing liver disease or where the condition is a manifestation of another mental health condition, the person is likely to be covered by the DDA.

The DDA makes it unlawful to discriminate against disabled people by:

• refusing to provide (or deliberately not providing) any goods, facility or service providing service of a lower standard or in a worse manner

• failing to comply with a duty to make reasonable adjustments (under section 21 of the Act) if that failure has the effect of making it impossible or unreasonably difficult for the disabled person to make use of any such goods, facilities or services.

'Reasonable adjustment' is a 'common sense' term that can only be fully defined by a Court of

Law. As case law develops, it will form the interpretation of 'reasonable adjustments'.

The DDA 2005 introduced amendments to the DDA in addition to the extension of cover for conditions such as HIV and cancer from first diagnosis. The DDA 2005 specifically applies to public bodies like the Prison Service (under the DDA 1995 this was not clear); there is a requirement to look at all the policies which impact upon prisoners, not just to respond to prisoners' individual needs: there is a much stronger requirement not to discriminate against people with disabilities by introducing a new requirement to promote equality of opportunity: this requires statistics to be collected and monitored; and the duty to eliminate harassment and to promote positive attitudes towards people with disabilities, including hidden disabilities.

From December 2006, public authorities were required to publish a Disability Equality Scheme (DES) setting out how they will implement the Disability Equality Duty. This duty is not necessarily about changes to buildings or adjustments for individuals, it's all about including equality for disabled people in practical and demonstrable ways. This means considering disabled people and disability equality into all aspects of prison life, rather than simply focusing on individualised responses to specific disabled prisoners.

Under the Disability Equality Duty (DED) the DRC, and its successor the Equality and Human Rights Commission (EHRC (contact details below)), can take legal action against public authorities that have failed to carry out their responsibilities under the DED, by issuing compliance notices. Along with individual disabled people they can also challenge a public authority's failure to meet the general duty by seeking a judicial review in the High Court. However, the DDA was set to be replaced by the Equality Act in 2010.

**Equality Act 2010**

The Equality Act came into force from October 2010 providing a modern, single legal framework with clear, streamlined law to more effectively tackle disadvantage and discrimination.

PSI 06/12

Updated: January 2020 – References to IEP have been changed to the Incentives Policy Framework (IPF), which came into force on 13 January 2020

April 2019 - This PSI has been revised due to the introduction of the Education and Library Service for Adult (including Young Adult) Prisons in England Policy Framework, published on 1 April 2019.

The Policy Framework supersedes the following

paragraphs/sections of PSI 06/2012, in England only: Paragraph 2.1.1, Output 2.2, Paragraphs 2.3.2, 2.3.5 and 2.3.6, Sections 5 and 6.

All sections of the PSI remain applicable to Wales.

## 2.20 EMPLOYMENT, TRAINING AND SKILLS

### INTRODUCTION
**Prisoner Apprenticeships**

In February 2022 the Government announced they would introduce Apprenticeships for prisoners to cut crime.

Under the **Prisoner Apprenticeship Pathway** - that came into force in August 2022 when the rules of Release on Temporary Licence were amended to permit day release for prisoners on apprenticeship pathways (see section 2.13 Release and Recall) - prisoners are now offered apprenticeships for the first time in an unprecedented move to cut crime and address local labour shortages says the Prison Service.

Until August 2022 prisoners have been unable to take advantage of apprenticeships, which would give them access to gold-standard training they can gain the skills needed to secure work on release - with evidence showing that prison leavers in work are significantly less likely to re-offend.

The government has now changed the law so that prisoners at open prisons across England are able to apply for apprenticeship opportunities in vital industries, including hospitality and construction , providing direct routes into jobs with businesses in the community.

The scheme will initially be offered up to a hundred prisoners across England before being rolled out across the wider prison estate.

The Ministry of Justice said: The new scheme is the latest step in the government's drive to boost the number of prison leavers with jobs. Prisoners are already able to study, train and work while in jail and a further 5,000 prisoners take part in vital work in the community through release on temporary license, where they learn important skills and help shore up local labour shortages.

Prisons like HMP Ford in West Sussex partner with sectors facing staffing concerns - including construction, hospitality and agriculture - with a number of offenders also training up as HGV drivers.

The scheme will see hundreds of prisoners start an apprenticeship by 2025, with pre-apprenticeship training offered to thousands more – preparing them for a full apprenticeship scheme or a higher skilled job on release.

The new scheme applies allows prisoners to access apprenticeship opportunities while they are still serving time but are out on day release or nearing the end of their sentence.

## General

PSI 06/2012 (last updated May 2021) replaces PSO 4200 and 4205. It presents an operational context for the prisoner employment training and skills experience in custody and facilitates transition and continuity upon release. This process should enable prisoners to have a focus through effective induction, assessment, advice and guidance on the offer of relevant training and employment whilst in custody.

The activity recorded on prisoners' Individual Curriculum Learning Plans (ILP's) and the Learner Plan should be closely linked with sentence plans to ensure that employment, skills and training interventions are appropriately prioritised and sequenced within the context of other rehabilitation activities and to foster a collaborative approach to developing prisoners employment, training and skills acquisition.

A focus on making prisons increasingly places of work and industry, with more prisoners experiencing structured and disciplined working weeks is reflected within this PSI. Wherever possible, work activity should be informed and complimented by the engagement of employers and industry specialists in the design and delivery of work based learning. This will ensure that both what is taught and the qualifications that are offered are recognised by industry.

Equality of opportunities is implicit throughout delivery of this policy and must include support of prisoners with learning disabilities or learning difficulties.

### Supporting the Prisoners Employment Training and Skills Specification

**Output 1:** Prisoners are able to access employment, training and skills dependent on their identified needs, the needs of the establishment and commercial commitments

All prisoners must on entry to custody be given assessments to determine their functional skills needs which should be recorded on an Individual Learning Plan.

Provision of employment, training and skills will require partnership working with a range of stakeholders and supporting sub contractors.

The prison must give partners agreed access to resources, facilities and prisoners as set out in the Enablers PSI.

Governors/ Directors must ensure that engagement with external partners is carried out appropriately with use of service level agreements or contracts as necessary, with due regard to security, benefits to prisoners, and in accordance with relevant Prison Service Instructions:

PSO 1100 Conveyance of Unauthorised Articles and Other Related Offences

PSO 1215 Attachment - Authorisation and Risk Assessment for Disclosure of Information

PSI 2010/14 - Managing Risk in Prison Industries

PSI 2010/38 - Activities in Prisons

PSO 4190 - Strategy for Working with the Voluntary and Community Sector

PSI 43/2010 - Security Vetting

Records of prisoners transferred from other prisons should be consulted so that assessments are not repeated. Prisoners should be able to access employment, training and skills opportunities dependent upon their identified needs, regime and commercial of the prison. (See Activity Allocation PSI Pending).

**Output 2 - Wales Only:** Prisoners are able to access education; learning and skills development opportunities and those with identified needs are prioritised

### Induction

2.2.1 New prisoners will be given access to the National Careers Service (NCS) as part of the induction process. These services offer new prisoners, a basic literacy and numeracy assessment. The outcomes of the assessments, aspirations and career goals will be recorded on a negotiated curriculum Individual Learning Plan (ILP).

2.2.2 The Governor/Director must provide the NCS staff with a daily reception list and ensure that prisoners are given access to the service.

Young offenders in custody will access Information Advice and Guidance Services.

2.2.3 The Governor/Director must ensure that sequencing and combining services is considered in delivering outcomes for offenders. For example, it may be important to provide services which stabilise and motivate an individual before providing an intervention targeted at reducing their risk and reoffending.

Offenders must be assessed to ensure that the type and timing of sequencing of services meet their identified needs. Please see Commissioning Intentions 2012-13

2.2.4 Once assessed, an Individual Learning Plan (ILP) will be completed and made available to all relevant service providers in order to support the offender's progress. Both internal and external partners must have access to the plan.

2.2.5 Prisoners must be allocated to activities to maintain the prison regime and meet the requirements of commercial contracts.

2.2.6 The Governor/Director must ensure that the establishment induction timetable allows sufficient time for the information, advice and guidance provider to deliver group induction sessions.

Please see PSI 74/2011 Early Days in Custody; First Night and Induction to Custody

2.3 **Output 3:** Staff support and encourage prisoners to participate fully in employment,

939

training and skills opportunities to support the importance and benefits of the work ethic

2.3.1 The offender learning experience must include a range of activities that will support the prisoner to achieve their offender management objectives devised with the support of relevant partners such as NCS, sentence management and learning and skills needs.

2.3.2 Wales only - Some prisoners will have very basic needs while others may require access to higher education opportunities. The NCS will identify these needs and a Unique Learner Number (ULN) will be issued. Where a number has been previously allocated; progress should be recorded on the Learning Records System (LRS) by the learning and skills provider. This process allows for any potential name change to the Learner Plan.

2.3.3 Governor's/ Director's and other key prison staff have a key role in determining the skills offer in their establishments. Acting collaboratively across the cluster and working with a wide set of local stakeholders, Governors /Directors will determine a mix of learning provision that gets the most effective outcomes for offenders and is able to motivate them into engaging. In particular, these activities will lead to sustainable job outcomes after release.

2.3.4 The success of the service will depend upon partners – providers, the prison service, careers advisers, Jobcentre Plus and employers – working together to match the needs of the labour market with the needs of prisoners in order to map the skills journey to employability on release.

2.3.5 Wales only - The National Careers Advice Service and all partners contributing to the prisoner's learning must ensure that assessment outcomes, all activity targets and results are recorded on their individual learning plan (ILP). This should determine the learning type or training which prisoners can access to support their learning and skills to enhance their employability.

2.3.6 Wales only - As a general principle the focus at the start of the sentence should address basic literacy and numeracy skills needs identified in the assessment of these needs.

2.3.7 The last months of the sentence must focus on up-to-date vocational skills relevant to the labour market into which the prisoner will be released. Offender managers, advice and guidance services and other relevant interventions will inform the activity identified for offenders.

2.4 **Output 4**: Opportunities exist for prisoners to progress through employment training and skills opportunities to develop a career history with the support of appropriate advice and guidance

2.4.1 The education, training and skills services is contracted by the Skills Funding Agency and co-commissioned with the National Offender Management Service.

2.4.2 NCS will advise prisoners of learning and skills opportunities be offered to progress learning to develop a career history. This progress may include access to OU, higher education and distance learning opportunities. Open University, Higher Education and Distance Learning.

2.4.3 Where prisoners are working in a specific industry, at the appropriate time in their sentence, they should be given opportunities to gain industry recognised qualifications.

2.5 **Output 5** : Prisoners have access to an approved and published number of hours of employment, training and skills provision as part of the prison regime as defined in the SLA/Contract

2.5.1 The Governor/Director will ensure that a timetable of hours and activity is made available to staff and published for prisoners using a range of appropriate methods such as the Virtual Campus; newsletters; prison library service

2.5.2 Governors / Directors and learning and skills providers must ensure that employment training and skills is delivered, mirroring the offer in the community. Such training can often best be delivered in areas that employ prisoners.

2.6 **Output 6:** Prisoners work a full working week of up to 40 hours

**Working Prisons**

2.6.1 Breaking the Cycle Effective Punishment, Rehabilitation and Sentencing of Offenders published December 2010 refers to Working Prisons. This concept is designed to ensure that more prisoners are subject to a structured and disciplined environment where they are expected to work a full working week of up to 40 hours. Delivering this will involve a number of external and internal partners with a focus on private sector business involvement.

2.7 **Output 7**: Relevant and up to date risk assessments are in place in all prisoner employment and training areas. Identified security and health & safety checks are conducted. The Governor/Director is responsible for ensuring that the working/training environment meets Health & Safety at Work Act 1974 requirements. The Governor/Director is responsible for ensuring that annual risk assessments are conducted and that records are kept and information made available for inspection and reference.

2.7.2 The Governor/Director must ensure that prisoners engaged in regime activities that require training such as industrial cleaning and food handling receive appropriate training prior to undertaking employment. Please see the

Offender Qualifications Manual for advice on appropriate courses.

2.7.3 Prisoners must be risk assessed according to the Activity Allocations PSI guidance. Risk assessments must be recorded and ongoing monitoring and reviews conducted according to local instructions.

2.8 **Output 8**: Prisoners are supervised in all employment, training and skills places, in accordance with the Local Security Strategy

2.8.1 The Governor/Director must ensure adequate supervision in all employment, training and skills places

2.9 **Output 9**: Prisoner's are searched in accordance with the Local Security Strategy

2.9.1 Governors/Directors must in accordance with the National Security Framework (NSF), PSI 67/2011 Searching the Person ensure that operational staff conduct rub down searches as per requirements, in order to maintain the safety of the learning and work environment and reduce threats to security order and control.

2.10 **Output 10**: All tools, equipment and property used in employment, training and skills places are risk assessed, stored, controlled, issued, recorded and disposed of accurately and securely.

2.10.1 The Governor/Director must ensure that all staff must comply with local protocols for risk assessment, the management of tools and their disposal.

2.11 **Output 11**: Prisoners are provided with an induction, published job description relevant training, and where required, qualifications to enable them to complete their activity effectively and ensure their safety and others.

2.11.1 The Governor/Director must ensure that before a prisoner is allocated to an activity, they are given appropriate induction to the working environment, equipment, tools and information enabling them to work safely and efficiently.

2.11.2 The Governor /Director must ensure that the appropriate provider delivers essential accredited training as required. Some activities require specialist training prior to a prisoner being allocated such as industrial cleaning and food handling. These must be delivered and a record kept of attainments.

**Output 12**: Prisoners' attainments, attendance, performance and behaviour in work or activity is recorded and co -ordinated and informs decision making, assessment, review and the monitoring of progress.

2.12.1 All relevant Prison staff and partners must record all assessment, allocation, attendance, training activity and outcomes on the prisoner's record.

2.12.2 The Governor/Director and learning and skills providers must ensure that attendance records are kept and used to inform improvement of performance.

2.12.3 All staff must ensure that appropriate action is taken to encourage positive behaviour and where this is not reflected, appropriate action must be taken in line with prison protocol (adjudications; reporting serious incidents; prison incentives scheme)

2.13 **Output 13**: Prisoners undertake work or activities when allocated except on specified days of their registered faith or if the activity is unsuitable or offensive to that faith

2.13.1 The Governor/Director must ensure that a prisoner faith is taken into account when allocating them to work or learning and skills activity. Prisoners should not be expected to work with items that are opposed to their registered faith or work on a day that is unsuitable.

2.14 **Output 14**: All service delivery/production recruitment and targets for both the internal and external markets are met to agreed quality levels.

2.14.1 Agreed production targets must also be met to the required quality standards.

2.14.2 The employment, training and skills provider must ensure that all outcomes are recorded for audit and quality improvement purposes.

2.15 **Output 15**: Prisons running external voluntary and paid employment and training schemes agree local eligibility criteria that are published and understood by staff and prisoners

2.15.1 Where appropriate the Governor/Director must ensure that proper procedures and eligibility criteria are in place and that the respective training department or employers adhere to published instructions. Release on Temporary Licence (ROTL)

2.16 **Output 16**: Prisoners in authorised regimes are able to undertake external employment and training

2.16.1 Where appropriate The Governor/Director must ensure that local protocols are in place to permit prisoners that are authorised to undertake external employment and training and that all staff involved in this process comply.

2.16.2 For prisoners employed in the community please access link Release on Temporary Licence (ROTL). Searches must also be conducted when leaving and on return from ROTL or outside working party – closed prison, open or semi open prisons.

**Output 17**: Prisoners have the opportunity to gain industry recognised and accredited qualifications through employment, training and skills according to risk and need.

Qualifications gained are aligned with market needs and within the Qualification and Credit Framework.

2.17.1 Prisoners in industry workshops must attain relevant qualifications to safely conduct their activities

2.17.2 At the appropriate time within a sentence and in preparation for release, prisoners must

941

receive information, advice and guidance to assist them in selecting training and skills opportunities to give them a better chance of employment upon release.

2.17.3 Prisoners must be risk assessed prior to their allocation to an activity. See Activity Allocation PSI

2.17.4 Qualifications offered to prisoners must feature on the Qualifications and Credit Framework (QCF) or be recognised by the specialist sector for which they are attained.

## 3. Women

3.1 All the general principles in this PSI refer to women, but additionally staff must be aware of and respond to the issues that are more likely to arise with women. Breaking the Cycle: Effective Punishment, Rehabilitation and Sentencing of Offenders recognise that women offenders have a different profile of risks and needs. Making Prisons Work states that a range of specialist provision, such as motivational activities, might help women appreciate that education and employment might be beneficial to them. The new strategy localises the responsibility for determining and commissioning the service, giving front-line managers much more ability to shape and flex the service in order to meet the particular needs of women and of their potential employers in the areas in which they will be resettled.

3.2 Learning providers are required to have the capability of meeting the particular needs of women, taking into account the differences in learning needs and the increased likelihood that they will have childcare responsibilities and require more holistic approaches, planned and delivered in partnership with other providers and linked to community provision.

Progression for women should encompass the principles of the Gender Specific Guidance (finding security and identity, building self-esteem and confidence, gaining qualifications; preparing for work and moving into employment or self-employment).

## 4. Young People

4.1 There are different arrangements for the commissioning and delivery of employment, training and skills provision for young people. Please refer to PSI 08/2012 Care and Management of Young People for more information in this regard.

## 5. Careers Service. This section applies to Wales only

5.1 As well as identifying learning and skills needs, the NCS will ensure that careers information and advice support prisoners to make realistic and informed choices about their future learning and employment options, with particular reference to the nature of their conviction (See Rehabilitation of Offenders Act 1974).

5.2 NCS and prison staff will advise prisoners about employment training and skills opportunities available to them in the prison and, as far as is practicable, allocate them to activity that relates to their choice of career or employment. Prisoners will also receive information about opportunities available to them in the prison and area to which they will be released.

5.3 The NCS must be given access to prisoners and will be required to hold the quality professional standards required of them in delivering a high quality service of careers advice and guidance. For information regarding Advice and Guidance provision, please access (National Careers Service).

5.4 Once prisoner's literacy and numeracy skills needs are identified learning programmes will be offered from basic functional skills support to higher level opportunities such as Open University, Higher Education (HE) or Distance Learning. PSI 33/2010 Open University, Other Higher Education and Distance Learning provides a framework for prisoner's access to higher level courses.

5.5 Provision of PETS must as far as is practicable, be an authentic part of mainstream programmes, mirroring the offer that a prisoner could access in the community. This will facilitate seamless transition for offenders between prison, community learning provision or employment.

5.6 All vocational training opportunities delivery will support the prison service regime such as catering; industrial cleaning; ground maintenance. Establishment, commercial commitments and relevant targets in prison industries must be met.

## 6. Learning and Risk Assessment. This section applies to Wales only

6.1 The purpose of assessment is two fold. This PSI takes into account both the assessment of learning attainment and learning need and also the assessment of risk, associated with security (Please see the following link: NOMS National Standard for the Management of Offenders)

6.2 Learning - Assessment of learning need is conducted by the National Careers Service. In custody, the service will assess learning needs and advise the learning provider what measures should be taken to meet those identified needs.

6.3 The prison must facilitate links between all partners and departments to ensure that the prisoner receives appropriate interventions to meet their needs through custody and during transition to community.

6.4 Learning providers will look to the prison to

ensure there is appropriate sequencing and prioritisation of activity in accordance with the sentence plan. This will promote better engagement in learning by ensuring that fundamental health and drug and alcohol related needs are addressed timely and appropriately.

### 7. Learning Disability and Difficulty

7.1 The Handbook for Professionals in the Criminal Justice System working with Offenders with Learning Disabilities provides an introduction; awareness and information to help staff identify and understand their needs.

7.2 It is important that people with learning disabilities within the criminal justice system are identified as early as possible to ensure they receive the appropriate support. This also applies to those people with learning difficulties who may be especially vulnerable and unable to fully understand, or participate, without additional help. Prisoners can be referred to health and social care services for a formal assessment.

### New Day Careers Service NOMS Wales

8.1 In Wales the Newday Project aims to enhance the opportunities of offenders from North and West Wales and the Valley areas of Wales (convergence areas) to gain training, qualification and employment opportunities whilst in custody and 'through the gate' into the community.

This will be achieved through the provision of innovative services that tackle economic inactivity and increase the offender's prospect of sustained employment. The project is funded through the European Social Fund (ESF) and overseen by the Welsh European Funding Office (WEFO). Within the offender cohort there is a focus on those unlikely to engage with mainstream learning provision, which will include young people who are 'Not in Employment, Education of Training' (NEET), 'Black and Minority Ethnic' (BME) individuals, women and lone parents.

## 2.21 WORK AND PAY

### Work: Prison Rule

### 31 – Work

(1) A convicted prisoner shall be required to do useful work for not more than 10 hours a day, and arrangements shall be made to allow prisoners to work, where possible, outside the cells and in association with one another.

(2) A registered medical practitioner or registered nurse working within the prison may excuse a prisoner from work on medical grounds.

(3) No prisoner shall be set to do work of a kind not authorised by the Secretary of State.

(4) No prisoner shall work in the service of another prisoner or an officer, or for the private benefit of any person, without the authority of the Secretary of State.

(5) An unconvicted prisoner shall be permitted, if he wishes, to work as if he were a convicted prisoner.

(6) Prisoners may be paid for their work at rates approved by the Secretary of State, either generally or in relation to particular cases.

### WORK OUTSIDE PRISON: THE LEVY

Some prisoners may be eligible to work outside the prison after a determined period of sentence has been served. This contributes to resettlement. In order to do so, they must pass a rigorous risk assessment. Outside work may be considered paid employment or voluntary (PR 9 b) Prisoners may also be released to receive instruction or training which cannot reasonably be provided in the prison (PR9 d).

Since September 2011 prisoners working outside the prison and who are paid in excess of £20 per week may have to contribute 40% of the amount in excess of £20 per week to the **Prisoners Earnings Act Levy** - see below.

### TYPE OF WORK

The type of work available to prisoners will depend on the activities available within individual establishments. Work that is available in most regimes will include cleaning, catering, waste management, gardens and horticulture and gymnasium.

### PAY

### INTRODUCTION

It is Prison Service Policy (PSO 4460) that prisoners receive payment if they participate constructively in the regime of the establishment. Those who refuse to participate do not receive any pay, although prisoners are eligible for unemployment pay if they are willing to work, but the establishment cannot find suitable employment or the prisoner is unable to work.

### Local Pay Policy

Governors and Directors of contracted-out prisons must have a local pay structure which:
• reflects Prison Service priorities
• supports and encourages constructive participation in regime activities
• does not provide disincentives to participation in constructive activities which are part of a prisoner's sentence/training plan or learning plan, intended to reduce the risk of re-offending
• complies with the parameters of this PSO and the Service's Incentives and Earned Privileges policies
• rewards good performance and penalises poor performance
• is fair, open, balanced and affordable.

Governors and Directors of contracted-out prisons must ensure that:

• the prisoner pay structure in their establishment is reviewed annually as part of the business planning process, to ensure compliance with paragraph 1.2 above

• information on the pay structure is available to all prisoners

• prisoners are paid correctly and promptly each week

• procedures are in place for monitoring all aspects of prisoners' pay

• appropriate records are kept in accordance with the Finance Order PSO 7500

Whatever scheme an establishment operates, it is essential that it is reasoned and structured, the requirements of the scheme are clear to both prisoners and staff, and it is not applied in an arbitrary or discriminatory way.

## RATES OF PAY
### General

All prisoners who participate in purposeful activity must be paid. Those who refuse must not receive any pay. Prisoners may also lose earnings for disciplinary reasons. Unconvicted prisoners can work if they wish to and must be paid the same rates as convicted prisoners.

An allowance should be made in the standard working week (see paragraph 2.4.1) of each prisoner for authorised absences from purposeful activity. These may include Governor's applications, welfare interviews, sick parade etc. These will be accommodated without loss of pay provided that the allowance is not exceeded. Visits, other regime instigated absences specified by the Governor, Sundays and days of religious observance for prisoners of non-Christian faith will not be counted towards the interruptions allowance and will be accommodated without loss of pay. Periods in segregation for disciplinary reasons will not count towards the allowance or normally attract pay unless the prisoner is found not guilty at adjudication or the governor authorises payment at unemployed rate.

Home leave, temporary release except on facility licence, compassionate leave and court attendance will attract no pay.

*Rate of pay for unemployed prisoners*

Prisoners are eligible for unemployment pay if they are willing to work, but the establishment cannot find suitable employment or the prisoner is unable to work - actual rates below.

*Minimum Employed Rate for All Prisoners*

Prisoners who are employed in work, induction, education, training, or offending behaviour programmes will receive at least the minimum weekly rate of pay for employed prisoners. The minimum rate of pay does not preclude deductions for poor attendance or performance. Prisoners who incur deductions for poor attendance and/or performance may earn less than the minimum employed rate, provided that the deductions have been calculated according to the formula published by the Governor/Director.

*Standard Rates of Pay*

Prisoners are eligible for standard rate of pay if they complete the full working week and demonstrate the required level of performance/effort required in any given activity in the establishment, or in any community work outside the establishment for which they are paid by the prison (see paragraph 2.7 on working out schemes).

The full working week in prison will normally be ten morning, afternoon, or evening sessions, or five night shifts.

*Mandatory actions:*

• Governors and Directors of contracted-out prisons must set standard rates of pay for each job or other purposeful activity that occupies one or more full session per week.

• The standard rate must be at or higher than the minimum employed rate

*Piecework*

Piecework is work which is paid for according to the quantity and quality produced. Establishments may set piecework pay schemes for certain jobs rather than a standard rate of pay. Piecework schemes may include rates of pay below the minimum employed rate, but prisoners must have the opportunity to earn the minimum employed rate.

Piecework pay schemes in prisons must specify:

• the rate of pay and the minimum quantity and quality of production which is expected

• the piece or bonus rates and deductions which can be earned or forfeited, depending on individual or group productivity

*Higher Rates of Pay*

Governors may establish Higher Rates of Pay schemes for any purposeful activity that occupies one or more full session per week. Higher rates of pay schemes are a key earnable privilege under IEP, and may provide for pay differentials or restrict eligibility for certain activities based on incentive level, or a combination of both.

Higher Rates of Pay schemes must only be available to prisoners who are on enhanced or standard levels of the Incentives and Earned Privileges scheme.

*Prisoners who are Released on Temporary Licence and those on 'Working Out' Schemes*

Prisoners who are released on temporary licence are not normally entitled to earnings for the period of time they are out of the establishment except under facility licence. Prisoners released on temporary licence are, however, entitled to travel costs and subsistence grants under the terms of chapter 14 of the Prison Service Finance Order (PSO 7500).

Prisoners undertaking community or voluntary work or other unpaid purposeful activity under a facility licence must be paid at a rate set by the establishment. Prisoners in these circumstances must not be expected to meet the cost of any fares or meals required to undertake the activity. The rates of pay for these activities must be published to staff and prisoners in the prisoners' pay structure.

Where prisoners are released on temporary facility licence under Prison Rules with the main or primary purpose of allowing them to undertake work for outside employers, they will not qualify for the national minimum wage under the National Minimum Wage Act 1998 (see Annex A of PSO 4460).

However, prisoners who work for outside employers, doing a normal job (that is, one which cannot be defined as voluntary or charitable work) must be paid the appropriate rate for the job at or above the National Minimum Wage. Where prisoners work for less than the normal working week, they will be paid pro rata. It is Prison Service policy that working out arrangements must not give an unfair competitive advantage to those who employ prisoners and that prisoners must not be treated less favourably than other workers in comparable employment.

Where practicable, prisoners working out in paid employment are expected to meet the cost of their travel and subsistence while outside the establishment.

Prisoners may have the opportunity to open a bank or building society account. This is desirable in the interests of resettlement and provides an appropriate means of paying their wages if they are employed.

*Where prisoners are permitted to open an account:*
• Prisoners must give the establishment as their address and the Governor/Director or authorised staff may inspect their financial records at any time.
• Prisoners must not be permitted to open or operate bank or building society accounts which allow credit. Nor may they be permitted to acquire store cards or other credit facilities while a serving prisoner.
• Cash, bank or building society books and cheques will not normally be permitted in possession within the establishment, but must be handed over at reception.

Where it is not feasible for prisoners to operate a personal bank or building society account on these terms, establishments should deal with prisoners' monies in the normal way.

Governors and Directors of contracted-out prisons must satisfy themselves that where prisoners are employed by outside employers they are paid wages which are comparable to normal rates paid in that industry for the work they do, and that a system is in place to process the prisoners' wages.

*Tax and National Insurance Thresholds*

Prisoners earning over the normal thresholds for Income Tax and National Insurance contributions are not exempted from these payments.

Governors, Directors of contracted-out prisons and outside employers are legally required to deduct National Insurance contributions and income tax from the earnings of prisoners whose wages exceed the thresholds. They are also legally required to make employer's National Insurance contributions.

The thresholds are subject to change, and the Tax Liaison Officer within each establishment will be able to provide the latest figures.

Governors and Directors of contracted-out prisons must make arrangements to deduct the appropriate National Insurance and Income Tax contributions from prisoners who are paid from their budget, who are above the normal thresholds for Income Tax and National Insurance
• They must equally ensure that arrangements are in place to make Employers National Insurance contributions when appropriate
• Governors and Directors of contracted-out prisons must ensure that outside employers of prisoners on working out schemes are informed that prisoners are not exempt from National Insurance and Income Tax contributions

*Other liabilities*

If prisoners' earnings are high enough, they may be liable for contributions to the maintenance of their dependants, under the Child Support Act and social security regulations. If an attachment of earnings order is received, the establishment must comply if all necessary conditions are met. Queries on this issue or the benefits system should be addressed to the local Benefits Office.

*Deductions*

See 'Prisoners Earnings Act Levy' below.

## PRODUCTIVITY, ACHIEVEMENT AND ATTENDANCE BONUSES

Governors and Directors of contracted-out prisons may establish systems of bonus payments to recognise and reward productivity, achievement such as obtaining nationally recognised qualifications or reaching challenging sentence plan targets, or additional hours (attendance) in purposeful activity. Bonus payments are a privilege for prisoners, not a right.

• Governors and Directors of contracted-out prisons must publish the criteria for bonuses and ensure that they are applied consistently.

• The bonus must be recommended by the manager of the activity and approved by a senior manager or senior budget holder.

## DEDUCTIONS FOR POOR ATTENDANCE OR POOR PERFORMANCE:

• Governors and Directors of contracted-out prisons must establish systems of deductions from prisoners' pay to address poor attendance or performance.

• Governors and Directors of contracted-out prisons must publish the criteria for deductions and ensure that they are applied consistently.

• The deduction must be recommended by the manager of the activity and approved by a senior manager.

• Bad behaviour by prisoners, including abuse of staff, breach of health and safety regulations, and misuse of materials, tools and equipment and other offences against good order and discipline are serious events, and must be formally managed through IEP or the Prison Discipline system as appropriate.

• Deductions must not be made for poor performance on offending behaviour programmes unless it concerns failure to attend.

## PAY IN SPECIAL CIRCUMSTANCES

*Prisoners who are Short-Term Sick*

Prisoners who are unable to work for short periods of time up to four weeks are defined as short-term sick. Prisoners who are sick for four weeks and over are to be treated as long-term sick. Establishments must pay the minimum rate of pay for short-term sickness as set out at Annex B.

*Prisoners who are Long-Term Sick, or of Retirement Age*

PSO 4460 sets a rate of pay for prisoners who are long-term sick or of retirement age.

(i) Long-Term Sickness

This Order defines long-term sick prisoners as those who have been diagnosed as unfit for work by the Medical Officer of the establishment, and who are therefore unable to undertake employment for an extended period of time -

normally four weeks and over.

These prisoners may only be required to participate in other purposeful activity as identified by the sentence/training plan or learning plan if the Medical Officer and/or any specialists consulted by the Medical Officer agree that it is appropriate and within the prisoner's capabilities.

There are separate arrangements (see paragraph 5.4 below) for prisoners staying in outside hospital.

*Prisoners of Retirement Age*

Prisoners of state retirement age are not normally required to work. They may work for standard rates of pay if they choose, provided there are suitable activities available in the establishment. Prisoners of state retirement age can, however, be required to participate in other purposeful activity as identified by the sentence/training plan or learning plan. They should be paid at the standard rate for these sessions. Unreasonable refusal renders them liable to be classified as "unwilling to work", and therefore not to receive any pay.

Prisons must pay the rate of pay for prisoners who are long-term sick or of state retirement age as set out in Annex B to the PSO.

*Pregnant Women and Mothers caring for Babies*

PSO 4460 sets a rate of pay for maternity leave in prison. Maternity Leave may apply during pregnancy, and after the birth whilst mothers have their babies with them in prison.

A pregnant woman is, however, entitled to the standard rate for the job while she continues to work before giving birth. If she is subject to periods of short-term sickness, but wishes in principle to continue working, she must receive the rate of pay for short-term sickness.

Women staying overnight at outside hospital to give birth are not entitled to earnings, but must receive the allowance for staying overnight in outside hospital (see paragraph 5.4).

If a mother does not keep her child with her in prison, there is an expectation that she will return to work after a satisfactory post-natal check. At this point, she returns to normal rates of pay, whether employed or unemployed.

Deductions from pay must not be made for attendance at contact visits with the newly born child.

If a mother keeps her child with her in prison and is not employed, she is entitled to receive the maternity leave rate whilst her child is with her. If she is employed, she is entitled to the rate for the job, as normal.

The rate of pay for prisoners who are on maternity leave, or caring full-time for children, is set out in Annex B to PSO 4460 - see below

• Governors and Directors of contracted-out prisons which hold female prisoners must ensure that the rate of pay for prisoners who are on maternity leave or caring full-time for children is published to staff and prisoners

• The Medical Officer is responsible for confirming whether a prisoner is short-term sick, on maternity leave, or fit to return to work following pregnancy or birth

### Prisoners attending Outside Hospital

Prisoners who stay overnight in an outside hospital, whether on temporary release or under escort, are not paid earnings but are eligible for an allowance. In these circumstances prisoners may be allowed to keep the cash in their possession.

• Prisoners who stay overnight as patients must be paid a hospital allowance to cover personal expenditure.

• Establishments must pay at least the rate of allowance set out in Annex B

• If a prisoner returns to work mid-week after a stay in hospital s/he must be paid for the work s/he does

• An appointment at hospital as a day patient, which has been made or approved by healthcare staff, does not attract an allowance, but the prisoner must continue to be paid at their relevant rate of unemployed, employed or standard pay.

### Transfers

On transfer, prisoners in previously paid purposeful activity will receive not less than the minimum employed rate for the first two weeks at their establishment. After two weeks the prisoner must either continue to receive their new standard rate of pay appropriate to the activity or return to the unemployed rate of pay if no employment is available. Other prisoners will receive immediately on transfer the rate appropriate to their activity (if any) in the new establishment.

Prisoners who are transferred between establishments for accumulated visits will be paid if they work satisfactorily, while so transferred, either at the rate they were receiving prior to transfer (based on their average earnings over the previous four weeks) or at the rate that is appropriate to the activity on which they are employed after transfer, whichever is the higher. Prisoners for whom no work can be found will be paid at their standard rate prior to transfer.

If necessary, advances of pay may be given to a prisoner by the establishment. Such circumstances might include on first reception or to enable a prisoner to take up outside employment. Advances should be repaid in accordance with the Finance Order and must be completely repaid before discharge. The terms of recovery of advances must be clearly explained to the prisoner at the time of issue.

### In-Cell work

Prisoners working in their cell as part of the core day or sentence or learning plan will be paid at the standard rate for the activity. Prisoners voluntarily working in their cell outside the core day and who are producing goods or work for bona fide charities or similar organisations with the agreement of the establishment, may receive payment for their work from the outside body. In these circumstances, the money must be paid into their private cash account and will be subject to the limitations on private cash under IEP.

### NATIONAL MINIMUM WAGE ACT 1998

Under section 1(2) of the National Minimum Wage Act 1998, only UK 'workers' above a certain age are capable of qualifying for the national minimum wage. Section 54(3) defines 'worker' to mean an individual who has entered into or works under a contract of employment or other contract of work or services.

Under section 45 (reproduced in full below) a prisoner does not qualify for the national minimum wage where he or she works in pursuance of Prison Rules.

"45. (1) A prisoner does not qualify for the national minimum wage in respect of any work which he does in pursuance of prison rules.

(2) In this section -

'prisoner' means a person detained in, or on temporary release from, a prison;

'prison' includes any other institution to which prison rules apply;

'prison rules' means -

(a) in relation to England and Wales, rules made under section 47 of the Prison Act 1952;

(b) in relation to Scotland, rules made under section 39 of the Prisons (Scotland) Act 1989; and

(c) in relation to Northern Ireland, rules made under section 13 of the Prison Act (Northern Ireland) 1953."

### ANNEX B TO PSO 4460
### MANDATORY PAY RATES

*Unemployment pay*

Minimum £2-50 per week (50p a day) based on a five-day week (see section 2.2)

*Employed rate*

Minimum employed rate of pay is £4-00 per week (see section 2.3)

*Short-term sickness*

The rate of pay for short-term sickness is £2-50 per week (see section 5.1)

*Long-term sickness and retirement*

The rate of pay for prisoners who are long-term sick or of retirement age is £3-25 per week (see section 5.2)

*Maternity leave or caring full-time for children*

The rate of pay for prisoners who are on maternity leave, or caring full-time for children is £3-25 per week (see section 5.3)

*Outside hospital allowance*

The allowance for prisoners staying in hospital is £4-35 per week or 60p per day (see section 5.4). Governors have discretion to increase this allowance if it is justified.

## PRISONERS EARNINGS ACT LEVY

The Prisoners' Earnings Act 1996 (PEA) and related Rules came into force on 26 September. Under the terms of the Act, prisoners who are undertaking paid work in the community and earning in excess of £20 a week may be made subject to the imposition of a levy amounting to up to (and including) 40% of their remaining earnings ('the excess'). The levy is applied to earnings over £20 per week, so if a prisoner earns £25 per week net, the levy is made only from £5 per week, not the full £25. The levy is paid to Victim Support, a national charity which works in partnership with numerous other such groups, with a view to the support of victims and communities. The PEA defines "net weekly earnings" as weekly earnings after deduction of such of the following as are applicable, namely –

(a) income tax;

(b) national insurance contributions;

(c) payments required to be made by an order of a court; and

(d) payments required to be made by virtue of a maintenance assessment within the meaning of the Child Support Act 1991.

## THE LEVY: LEGAL CHALLENGE

In July 2012 Sales. J sitting in the High Court rejected a challenge against the levy brought by two prisoners.

The court was to apply the same margin of appreciation as the European Court of Human Rights would apply when assessing the lawfulness of Prison Service Instructions and it was clear that the guidance in two Prison Service Instructions relating to the imposition of deductions from prisoners' earnings did not violate the European Convention on Human Rights Protocol 1 art.1.

(S & KF v SSJ [2012] EWHC 1810 (Admin) QBD (Admin) (Sales J) 03/07/2012

## THE LEVY: PAYMENT, APPEALS, REDUCTIONS & EXEMPTIONS

The implementation of the Prisoners Earnings Act requires all employers to pay the wages of prisoners in future direct to HMPPS via BACS - and not to the prisoner directly. Thus the PEA will mean that prisoners will no longer be paid directly by their employer and that there could be a delay of up to 5 working days before prisoners receive payment into their personal bank account. Cheque payments will incur further delay because they will require clearing before being processed.

It is a requirement of the Act that prisoners are issued with a monthly statement. This will be provided by the Shared Services and sent to prisons for distribution. An example of a monthly statement is shown at Annex E of PSI 76/2011.

When a prisoner's release date previously notified to the Shared Services is changed, for example by the granting of Home Detention Curfew (or, in the case of an indeterminate sentence prisoner, when a release date is set), the prison must notify the Shared Services. This will ensure that any late payment made by the employer does not incur deductions and can be forwarded on to the prisoner. The Shared Services will need to know and capture release dates to ensure that the adjustment is correct.

The prisoner should be advised to inform their employer of the date of their release and details of their personal bank account, in order to ensure that there is minimal disruption on release. It would be good practice for the prison to ensure that the employer has the correct release date.

The Government's recommendation is that governors should not impose levies on prisoners with less than one month to serve at the point at which they start outside employment. This is because the administrative costs of setting up deduction arrangements for such a short period and would be disproportionate to the value of the deduction.

### Reductions and exemptions to the Levy

Where a prisoner has applied for an exemption from, or reduction in, the levy, Annex B provides guidance on some of the types of exceptional circumstances governors might wish to consider when deciding whether or not to exempt a prisoner from the levy, or to reduce the amount of levy to be imposed. Where a governor decides to levy at a rate of less than 40%, or not at all, the governor should include the total amount to be exempted from the "net weekly earnings" into the PEA001 form and forward the form to the SSC, in order for the levy to be imposed on the appropriate amount of the "net weekly earnings". The SSC will then deduct the figure provided on the PEA001 form from the net weekly wage paid by the employer and will impose a levy of 40% of the balance after the first £20, and pay the balance into the prisoner's private bank account.

### Confiscation orders

Where a prisoner is making payments towards a confiscation order the net amount on which the levy can be imposed must be reduced by the amount of the payment. This is because the payments made towards the confiscation order are a court ordered payment. Once the payments have been taken into account, if the prisoner's remaining net weekly earnings, after making confiscation order payments, are less than £20, there will be no levy. If the confiscation order payments are at a different interval than the prisoner's earnings are paid (for example if a prisoner is making monthly confiscation order payments but is paid weekly, or vice versa), then the amount to be deducted from net earnings must, of course, be multiplied or divided as appropriate. To inform the SSC of cases in which prisoners are making payments to satisfy an outstanding confiscation order, the PEA001 form must set out the amount of monies the prisoner is paying towards the order and be sent to the SSC, in order that the amount can be taken into account in terms of determining the "net weekly earnings" on which the levy may be imposed.

### Where a prisoner:

• refuses to comply with a court-ordered payment schedule that is effective at the point at which the prisoner is eligible for outside paid employment; and/or
• is not required to satisfy the order until a future date; and/or
• is not voluntarily making payments to satisfying an order which is not due to be satisfied until a future date the total amount owed in respect of the confiscation order must be ignored for the purposes of determining the "net weekly earnings". Therefore, unless the imposition of the levy is to be reduced or not imposed as a result of other circumstances, a levy of 40% will continue to be deducted from "net weekly earnings". Governors will also, of course, take the confiscation order situation into account in the risk assessment to determine whether the prisoner should be allowed out on licence to work.

Currently, the PEA001 form cannot distinguish between exemptions from / reductions in the levy related to confiscation orders and those where the Governor has exercised their discretion for other reasons. As a result, governors must ensure that, in cases where a prisoner's "net weekly earnings" have been reduced as a result of monies being paid towards satisfying a confiscation order, and where the levy is further reduced for exceptional circumstances, a single figure covering the total cash amounts of both the confiscation order and exceptional circumstances elements is inserted into the PEA001 form and forwarded to the SSC in order for the appropriate amount to be levied. The SSC will then deduct the figure provided on the PEA001 form from the net weekly wage paid by the employer and will impose a levy of 40% of the balance after the first £20.

### Prisoner complaints and appeals

Any complaints from prisoners or appeals against being required to pay the levy will fall to be dealt with under the normal prisoner complaints process (see PSO 2510).

Where a prisoner believes that the calculation of the levy is incorrect, they should raise this with the prison, which will contact the Shared Services on their behalf. Only queries regarding the calculation of the levy should be addressed to the Shared Services. Shared Services are not able to respond to enquiries direct from individual prisoners, and prisoners must not be advised to contact the SSC.

Any complaints or queries about the policy, as opposed to individual cases, should be addressed to the contact point on the front of this PSI.

### THE LEVY: NOTICE TO PRISONERS
### The Prisoners' Earnings Act 1996

The Government is committed to offenders making reparations to victims and society. The Green Paper "Breaking the Cycle: Effective Punishment, Rehabilitation and Sentencing of Offenders", published set out the aims, one of which is to implement the Prisoners' Earnings Act 1996 (the PEA).

This gives the governor a power to impose a levy on your earnings in certain circumstances. This means that if you are working outside the prison on licence you will be subject to the levy.

### What is happening and when?

When the PEA was brought into force on 26th September 2011, and providing you earn more than £20 net per week ("net" means after you have paid any tax, national insurance contributions, court-ordered and child support payments that may be due), any earnings over £20 may well be subject to a levy of up to (and including) 40%.

For instance, if you earn £25 per week, the last £5 of your earnings could be subject to a levy of 40% (£2). Your overall earnings would in that case therefore be reduced from £25 to £23.

The amount of the levy will be paid to Victim Support, a national charity which works in partnership with numerous other such groups, with a view to the support of victims and communities.

**What does this mean for me?**
To make sure that the levy is correctly calculated, you will no longer be paid directly by your employer. They will still provide you with a payslip, but your net pay will be paid first into a central bank account so that the Shared Services Centre (SSC) can administer the levy on behalf of the Governor. The SSC will then make a deduction as described above, and the balance will be transferred to your outside bank account. The process may take up to 5 days, so you should expect a delay.

However, if you are paid by cheque this may mean you could experience a longer delay as the cheque will require clearing before being processed.

The prison will provide you with a monthly statement; which will show you what your net pay was from your employer, how much was taken off by way of the levy, and how much will be transferred into your outside bank account.

**What do I need to do?**
First thing you need to check is that you have an outside bank account. If you don't then you need to arrange to set one up. Your prison will assist you to do this. You will then have to provide the prison with the following details:
Name of Bank
Name of Account Holder (usually your name)
Account Number
Sort Code Number
The prison should provide you with a proforma to complete. Please make sure that you give the prison the correct details as any mistakes could delay when you receive your pay.

If you refuse to provide your outside bank details or refuse to set up an outside bank account, you will no longer be allowed to work outside in paid employment. The SSC can pay the money into someone else's bank account if you ask them to do so, but this is at your risk.

The prison should have provided your employer with your date of release however, its important that you make them aware of the date and give them your personal bank account details nearer the time. This will make sure that you will receive your pay as usual.

**PRISONERS WITH DISABILITIES**
'Following a health and safety risk assessment, appropriate and reasonable adjustments should be made to ensure wherever possible prisoners with disabilities are not excluded from work. Where appropriate, adjustments to procedures and alternative formats for information need to be provided.

A flexible approach to work placements can often allow prisoners to participate who might otherwise be considered unable to work'. (PSO 4460 6.17)

**Education and Skills**
'Where appropriate adjustments need to be made and alternative formats provided to enable prisoners with disabilities to access education and skills provision.' Providers can use an open learning process where the teacher delivers learning at the site of the prisoner if accessibility is not possible.

'Particular attention should be made to ensuring that activities should not exclude prisoners with a learning disability or difficulty'. (PSO 4200 and 4205)

**PREPARATION FOR RELEASE**
The work conducted in prisons to rehabilitate, educate and prepare offenders for their return to society is critical in providing them with an alternative to crime.

Under sentencing arrangements that make more extensive use of community sentences, there is a stronger challenge to keep individuals in learning throughout their sentence and beyond. Key to engaging offenders in learning is ensuring that their needs are assessed properly from the very start of their sentence.

They should receive information, advice and guidance at the start of their sentence and at appropriate points throughout the remainder of it on suitable learning provision, sources of funding for learning and on options for work.

The LSC aims to ensure that offenders serving custodial sentences are helped to continue their learning after release by providing courses in prison that are of the same high quality as those in the community and which are comparable to those in the area into which they will be released. To achieve the smooth transition from learning in custody to learning in the community, Heads of Learning and Skills and learning providers, working closely with Heads of Resettlement and the Director of Offender Management to ensure that learning in the community builds upon learning completed in custody and that the offender is given adequate assistance in making contact with their local information and advice service and/or their local college or other learning provider upon release.

But the need for close liaison extends beyond the learning partner organisations described above: effective relationships with Jobcentre Plus, the Connexions Service, regional planning structures, employers and others are also of critical importance in an effective transition.

## 2.22 INCENTIVES AND EARNED PRIVILEGES

### Incentives Policy Framework
Implementation Date: - 16 August 2019 last updated July 2020: All new prisoners must join the incentives scheme on Standard level.

### Purpose
1.1 The system of privileges is a key tool for incentivising prisoners to abide by the rules and engage in the prison regime and rehabilitation, including education, work and substance misuse interventions – whilst allowing privileges to be taken away from those who behave poorly or refuse to engage. This policy sets a common framework with which local incentives policies must comply.

### 2. Context
2.1 The Incentives Policy Framework, together with other key policies, such as Adjudications, and for Young Offender Institutions (YOIs), the Building Bridges Policy Framework, allows Governors to incentivise good behaviour and tackle poor behaviour and breaches of the Prison Rules and YOI Rules, helping prisoners to make the right choices to prepare them to lead crime-free lives when they leave prison.

### 3. Evidence
3.1 There are three important areas of evidence that can help Governors to implement more effective incentives schemes. These include how fairly procedures are seen to be implemented (sometimes called procedural justice), the use of positive reinforcement, and the design and monitoring of the scheme itself. Further guidance on how to translate this evidence into everyday practice is given in Section 7 (Guidance).
3.2 Research on the impact of fair procedures, shows that:
• When people believe the process of applying rules (how a decision is made, rather than what decision is made) is fair, it influences their views and behaviour. When people feel processes are applied fairly, they have more confidence and trust in authority figures, see authority figures as being more legitimate, and they are more likely to accept and abide by decisions and rules, and comply and cooperate with authority, even if the outcome is not in their favour.
• When prisoners perceive authority to be used in a more procedurally just way, this predicts significantly less misconduct and violence, better psychological health, and lower rates of reoffending after release.
3.3 Research on behaviour change shows positive

reinforcement is more effective at shaping people's behaviour than punishing them. Punishment may be required, but on its own it does not effectively change behaviour or deter people from impulsive actions. Punishment can result in compliance, but not the internalisation of values and so works less well in securing positive lasting behaviour change. Evidence also points to a range of other challenges that can result from punishment, such as aggression and damaged relationships with the punisher. Positively reinforcing desirable behaviour, on the other hand, can produce robust gains in a variety of desired behaviours; this approach teaches an individual what to do.
3.4 Research on implementing incentive schemes shows that they work better to encourage good behaviour in prison when:
• There is a clear understanding of what the scheme is trying to encourage – i.e. what desirable behaviours it is trying to increase.
• Increasing desirable behaviour is the main focus of the scheme rather than punishing poor behaviour.
• The response to behaviour is immediate and consistent. Immediate verbal praise for good behaviour or verbal challenging of poor behaviour can support this approach.
• Staff have some basic training in behaviour management principles.
• The scheme is carefully monitored to ensure it remains consistent, transparent, fair and is focussed on positive reinforcement. Without careful monitoring, schemes can easily deteriorate into coercive regimes that work less well and can even increase anti-social behaviour.

### 4. Outcomes
4.1 Prisoners engage with their rehabilitation.
4.2 Privileges are earned by progression through incentive levels, but can also be lost by moving down an incentive level(s) for poor behaviour.
4.3 Incentive levels are reviewed within the timescales set out in the Review section, and are determined by patterns of behaviour, personal progress and engagement with the prison regime and sentence plan targets.
4.4 Local incentive policies are perceived (by prisoners and staff) as being fair, consistent and non-discriminatory, encourage good behaviour and challenge poor behaviour.
4.5 The consequences of poor behaviour are proportionate, both in terms of impact and duration, and are swiftly implemented.
4.6 Due regard is given to prisoners' journey through the prison estate in designing local incentives schemes.
4.7 All prisoners, irrespective of incentive level, continue to receive the entitlements laid down in Prison/YOI Rules and other instructions in

relation to visits, letters, telephone calls, provision of food and clothing, and any other minimum activity provided locally for all prisoners. 4.8 Local incentive policies command public confidence as being appropriate and offering value for money for the public purse.

## 5. Requirements
### Legal Requirements
5.1 Each prison or YOI must ensure a system of privileges in accordance with rule 8 of the Prison Rules 1999 or rule 6 of the YOI Rules 2000. The Equality Act 2010 requires HMPPS and Governors to comply with the Public Sector Equality Duty and have due regard when exercising functions to the need to eliminate discrimination, promote equality of opportunity and foster good relations between those with protected characteristics and those without. The protected characteristics are: age; disability; gender reassignment; marriage and civil partnership; pregnancy and maternity; race; religion and belief; sex; and sexual orientation.
5.2 All systems must be fair throughout and Governors must ensure that relevant impact assessments are in place to support the local policy, including monitoring against protected characteristics. In particular, consistent with the Public Sector Equality Duty, Governors must undertake an Equality Analysis from the outset of developing the policy, and consult with relevant stakeholders to shape it and ensure compliance. It must also be compliant with health and safety requirements and where necessary, a Data Protection Impact Assessment and the Family Test must be undertaken.
5.3 Governors must ensure their local policy reflects the legal entitlements for remand and civil prisoners where these are different to those for convicted prisoners. Please refer to sections on Eligibility to wear Own Clothes, Extra and Improved Visits, Considerations for Prisoners with Specific Requirements and PSO 4600 Unconvicted, Un-sentenced and Civil Prisoners, which sets out the rights to which these prisoners are entitled.
### Other Requirements
### Incentives Scheme Structures
5.4 Governors must include at least three incentive levels in their local policy, referred to in this Policy Framework as Basic, Standard and Enhanced. Governors may create additional levels above Enhanced.
5.5 Basic level must include as a minimum the legal entitlements to which prisoners are entitled.
5.6 Prisoners must retain their incentive level upon conviction and upon transfer, (including those transferring from other jurisdictions), if there is an equivalent level at the receiving

establishment. To ensure that prisoners retain their incentive level on transfer staff must check previous P-NOMIS entries and/or check with the sending prison and amend the status field in P-NOMIS accordingly. Where there is no equivalent level the prisoner must be placed on the level closest to it, in the opinion of the receiving prison.
5.7 New and recalled prisoners must not join the prison system below Standard level.
5.8 Governors have due regard to local incentive policies in those prisons from which their prisoners are commonly received, or to which their prisoners commonly transfer, to minimise potential disruption on transfer. Individually and collectively Prison Group Directors (PGDs) should ensure consideration is given to prisoners' journeys through the estate in the design of local incentive policies.
5.9 Local incentive policies must be reviewed annually to ensure their fairness and relevance to local priorities and population, which will include considering local behavioural expectations and whether the privileges offered are sufficiently incentivising. The review should also consider its impact on groups with different protected characteristics by reviewing the Equality Analysis.
### Criteria for Progression
5.10 Criteria for progression and moving down an incentive level(s) must be in place and include compliance with Annex A, which sets out the definitions of each incentive level and requires prisons to have a small number of simple behaviour principles which apply to all prisoners. Example behaviour principles are provided at Annex A which can be used by prisons or replaced with alternatives, allowing prisons to respond to local challenges and priorities.
5.11 Beneath the principles are example behaviour expectations which staff, including key workers where they are in place, can use to coach prisoners on the types of behaviour required to meet a principle. Governors can tailor the expectations to meet local circumstances or to set short term goals for individual prisoners, e.g. to target any specific behaviours that they want to improve – or to meet alternative behaviour principles where these are in place.
5.12 Immediate positive, verbal reinforcement for good behaviour and achievements can both recognise and incentivise progress alongside formal reviews, which should consider patterns of behaviour. Similarly, poor behaviour should also be challenged outside formal reviews.
5.13 Governors must identify and respond to the needs of those who need help to engage in the scheme, by, for example, identifying and targeting behavioural support for prisoners with

potential underlying factors for poor behaviour or non-engagement, such as traumatic brain injury, learning difficulties, low maturation and mental health issues. Section 7, Considerations for Prisoners with Specific Requirements, provides further examples of those who may need additional help.

### Role of the Keyworker

5.14 Where keyworkers are in place they must have a role in the incentives scheme including:

• Helping prisoners on their caseload to understand the behaviours that are expected of them to progress on the incentives scheme and how their behaviour is considered as part of other assessments, such as Release on Temporary Licence (ROTL).

• Supporting and encouraging prisoners to take responsibility for their progression, for example by setting short term targets on behaviour and engagement. Key workers should particularly support prisoners on Basic level to progress back to Standard.

• Contributing to incentive level reviews by providing input on positive/negative progress in behaviour and performance on the wing and at activities, and other information such as new goals or concerns.

### Reviews

5.15 An incentive level review can be held at any time, subject to all prisoners being given a review at least annually. Governors must determine the period of time between incentive level reviews and/or what triggers a review. In determining this, they should be mindful of prisoners' average length of time in the prison. Wherever possible reviews should be multidisciplinary, particularly reviews of prisoners on Basic.

5.16 All prisoners placed on Basic must be reviewed within 7 days and if they are not suitable to return to Standard level further reviews must be undertaken at least every 28 days thereafter, except for those identified as at risk of suicide and self-harm and for young people, where further reviews must be undertaken at least every 14 days thereafter. A review and upgrade to Standard level can take place at any time within these timescales, should a prisoner sufficiently demonstrate the expected behaviour and engagement.

5.17 Prisoners on Basic level must be informed of the steps they need to take to return to Standard level, making clear the specific behaviours and engagement they must demonstrate. Prisoners who have been identified as needing help to engage in the scheme, - under paragraph 5.13 - and those who have been identified to be at risk of suicide or self harm must be supported whilst on Basic level.

### Reviews for New Prisoners

5.18 An initial review can take place at any time, subject to the prison reviewing the incentive level of all new prisoners within 3 months from the time they arrive in prison or receive a prison sentence, or for young people, within 1 month.

### Other Review Requirements

5.19 To inform the review, feedback must be sought from across the establishment, including education and workshop staff, reports from any treatment programmes which have been completed as part of the sentence plan and any other staff who have close dealings with the prisoner. Governors may consider when it is appropriate to use security intelligence to inform incentives level reviews for specific prisoners. Guidance on the use of intelligence is contained in the Intelligence Collection, Management and Dissemination in Prisons and Probation Policy Framework.

5.20 Prisoners must be given the opportunity to make their case in the review process. The review outcome must be discussed with them, including reasons for any decision made, and the process for appeal explained to the prisoner. The review outcome and confirmation that the prisoner received their feedback must be entered on P-NOMIS.

5.21 An immediate incentive level review should be undertaken for serious single incidents of bad behaviour, for example such incidents that were serious enough to lead to an adjudication for an offence involving violence to staff or prisoners, drugs, possession of a mobile phone, abscond or possession of a weapon. There is a strong presumption that such incidents should lead to prisoners moving down an incentive level(s) unless there are compelling reasons to maintain the current incentive level. The review should consider outcomes which follow from adjudications in relation to the same incident to ensure that the overall response to bad behaviour is not disproportionate. If any adjudication is subsequently quashed, dismissed or not proceeded with, a further review should take place to determine the prisoner's appropriate incentives level. Further guidance on Adjudications is contained in the Guidance section.

### Appeals

5.22 An appeals process must be in place, which prisoners must be informed of and have access to, that resolves issues in reasonable timescales and includes a mechanism for prisoners to raise complaints. Appeals must be considered by a more senior member of staff than the person who took the decision that is being challenged.

### Incentives Forum for Staff and Prisoners

5.23 A forum must be in place to review the fairness and effectiveness of the local incentives policy, including the efficacy of the incentives on offer. Forums must involve staff; white, BAME and

Gypsy, Traveller and Romany prisoners and all prisoner groups with protected characteristics where present in the local population. Annex B provides guidance on establishing the forum from an equalities perspective.

**Communication**

5.24 The behaviour principles required for progression on the scheme must be effectively communicated to all prisoners and staff, using simple messages that are understandable to individual prisoners.

5.25 All prisoners must be informed of the local incentives policy during their induction and details of how to learn more about the local incentives system must be advertised effectively.

**Facilities List**

5.26 All prisoners, irrespective of local incentive level, must have access to the items listed under part 1 of the National Facilities List set out in Annex C, where requested. All items are subject to volumetric control in accordance with PSI 12/2011 Prisoners' Property.

5.27 Prisoners on Basic level must be restricted to items on part 1 of the list.

5.28 Governors can choose additional items from part 2 of the list to add to their local facilities list for Standard and Enhanced levels, and any additional levels above Enhanced. It is for Governors locally to determine what incentive level prisoners must be on to have access to these items.

5.29 Where Governors wish to, they may add to the list at Annex C.

To do this they must raise this with their Prison Group Director who will provide a single point of contact to discuss with the Operational Policy Team at the Ministry of Justice. This ensures that, where changes are agreed, the National Facilities List is updated accordingly.

**Games Consoles**

5.30 Where games consoles and games are allowed as an additional in cell privilege under the local incentives scheme, they must not be provided at public expense. Consoles are not permitted for prisoners on Basic. Governors can choose at which level to make them available, from Standard and above. 18 rated games are not permitted. Advice on permitted consoles is provided at Annex D.

5.31 Prisoners aged under 18, on Standard level or higher, may be permitted to participate in communal activities involving computer games and games consoles. Those communal activities can include use of consoles with wireless connectivity, such as Wi-Fi. Communal use of games consoles with wireless connectivity capability must only be permitted in communal areas and whilst under close staff supervision.

**Property and Transfers**

5.32 All prisoner property must be managed in accordance with PSI 12/2011 Prisoners' Property. Items held in-possession by prisoners, including items listed in part 1 of Annex C and consumables, are subject to volumetric control limits unless they are exempt in accordance with other national policies. On transfer prisons can only send property on the escort vehicles up to the volumetric control limits as well as items exempt from volumetric control. It is the prisons responsibility to arrange onward transfer of any excess property.

5.33 Where a property dispute arises, prisoners should be encouraged to follow the internal complaints process. Governors must ensure property complaints are investigated thoroughly and take steps to reduce the likelihood of disputes and litigation.

5.34 On occasion, prisoners will arrive on transfer from another establishment with items, such as a large stereo, which are not permitted in the receiving establishment's facility list but are permitted at the previous establishment. Governors must consider these items on a case by case basis. Unless the item(s) is considered a risk to good order, discipline, security, safety and/or exceed volumetric control limits the prisoner should normally be allowed to retain it in-possession. However, the fact that an item was allowed on this basis does not give the prisoner any right to replace it "like for like". Any replacement must comply with the local facility list.

**Earnable Incentives**

5.35 Governors must design their local incentives schemes according to what they understand incentivises their population and the facilities and opportunities available at their prison.

5.36 However, to provide consistency across prisons in the core incentives offered, where operationally possible, the following 6 designated earnable incentives must be included in local incentive schemes as set out below. Governors are not restricted to offering these incentives, and are encouraged to develop additional incentives.

• Access to private cash;
• Eligibility to earn higher rates of pay;
• Access to in-cell television;
• Opportunity to wear own clothes;
• Additional time out of cell;
• Extra and improved visits.

**Access to Private Cash (September 2022)**

5.37 This must be in line with updated weekly central limits detailed below.

| Level | Unconvicted | Convicted |
|---|---|---|
| Basic | £27.50 | £5.50 |
| Standard | £60.50 | £19.80 |
| Enhanced | £66.00 | £33.00 |

5.38 Where Governors introduce levels above Enhanced, they may grant prisoners access to private cash up to the Enhanced level only.

5.39 Details of how to adjust prisoners' private cash limits locally are provided at Annex G and further guidance on access to private cash is given in PSI 01/2012 Manage Prisoner Finance.

## Eligibility to Earn Higher Rates of Pay

5.40 Governors must use their local pay policy to incentivise prisoners, for example by:

• offering progressively higher rates of pay for Standard and Enhanced prisoners,

• using bonus payments for achievements or qualifications,

• rewarding activities which contribute to rehabilitation and personal progress with higher pay,

• prioritising access to the highest paying jobs for those on Enhanced or above.

5.41 Detailed guidance on prisoners' pay is set out in Prison Service Order 4460 Prisoners' Pay.

## In-cell Televisions

5.42 In-cell television is allowed as a privilege for all prisoners on Standard and Enhanced and any levels above Enhanced. Prisoners on Basic are not permitted in-cell television, except in the case of the following exemptions:

• Severely disabled prisoners and those in healthcare facilities, either unable to reach association rooms or judged to need the stimulus of TV, may be allowed in-cell TV on a case-by-case basis irrespective of incentive level, and where deemed appropriate free of charge;

• All prisoners identified as at risk of suicide or self-harm may be considered for in-cell TV irrespective of incentive level on a case-by-case basis.

• Prisoners in reception/induction/first night units may have access to in-cell television free of charge.

5.43 The standard system for digital broadcasting provides prisoners with nine free-to-view channels. Governors are permitted to make additional Free-to-view Channels available, within the constraints of the available infrastructure in their prisons. It is the Governor's responsibility to ensure the suitability of any additional channel chosen for viewing. Governors have discretion to prohibit the showing of any material they consider unsuitable, taking account of the age of the prisoner and any other local factors.

5.44 Where prisoners are provided with a TV, they must sign a compact agreeing to pay towards the cost of the TV in accordance with the national current rates (£1 in single cell and 50p in a shared cell). Prisoners who are on the Basic level who do not have a TV, or who are subjected to a disciplinary punishment of forfeiture of a TV, shall not be required to pay towards the rental cost of a TV.

5.45 Governors have the authority to remove TV sets in individual cases if in-cell television appears to be having an adverse impact, for example, undermining a prisoner's engagement with the regime or increasing the risk to the public on release.

5.46 A suggested compact for in-cell televisions is set out in Annex E.

## Opportunity to Wear Own Clothes

5.47 All unconvicted, civil and foreign national prisoners held under immigration powers (IS91) must be allowed to wear their own clothes.

5.48 All convicted prisoners, including prisoners in the women's estate, must wear prison-issue clothing, as the default position, in line with the Prison Rules. However, Governors have the authority to make provision in their local incentives policy for such prisoners to wear their own clothes and can choose to include the opportunity for convicted prisoners to wear their own clothes at any incentive level, including Basic.

5.49 When deciding at which levels convicted prisoners can wear their own clothes, Governors must consider locally how to remove or minimise disadvantages suffered by people with protected characteristics, taking steps to meet any differential needs. PSI 17/2016 The Care and Management of Transgender Offenders and PSI 05/2016 Faith and Pastoral Care for Prisoners set out guidance on clothing for transgender prisoners and those from particular faith groups

## Additional time out of cell

5.50 The amount of time prisoners are allowed to spend outside their cells to engage in additional activities or to associate together, will vary from one establishment to another, depending on the availability of constructive activities and supervisory staff. Where there is scope to do so, Governors should increase the amount of time out of cell for prisoners to engage in these activities for those on higher incentive levels.

5.51 Access to gym, exercise and well-being facilities above the minimum requirement for physical exercise in the Prison Rules and YOI Rules (one hour per week for those aged 21 and over, and two hours a week on average for under 21s) may also be used as an incentive.

## Extra and Improved Visits

5.52 Prisoners on Standard, Enhanced or levels above Enhanced may receive improved visits, which could include additional visits over their statutory entitlement, visits in better surroundings, or longer visits. This would be in addition to a prisoner's statutory entitlement. Further information on a prisoner's minimum entitlement to visits is contained in Providing Visits and Services to Visitors (PSI 16/2011).

## Handing and Sending In

5.53 Governors must allow books to be handed and sent in as long as they meet with the standards laid out in Section 11 of the Public Protection Manual, and there are procedures in place to check the books for illicit enclosures. Books can also be ordered from approved retailers. Annex F provides further guidance and a list of approved retailers.

5.54 To ensure that the incentives scheme is not undermined, and to control the amount of property in the prison estate, the general presumption will be that items for prisoners other than books will not be handed in or sent in by their friends or families unless there are exceptional circumstances. Governors have discretion to determine what constitutes exceptional circumstances; this could include for example disability/health aids or an artefact for religious observance, stamped-addressed envelopes so as to facilitate a prisoner's ability to communicate or where there is a need to replace clothing due to restricted access to laundry facilities.

5.55 Governors also have discretion to allow a one-off parcel of clothing to be handed in or sent in following conviction.

5.56 In addition, unconvicted prisoners must be allowed to have sufficient clean clothing sent in to them from outside the prison (whether through visits, by post or other means). Unconvicted prisoners can also have writing materials supplied to them at their own expense. Therefore, unconvicted prisoners are not subject to the same one-off parcel restriction that applies to convicted prisoners, nor are they subject to the 'exceptional circumstances' test referred to above in respect of stamped-addressed envelopes. Clothing for unconvicted prisoners should be refused if this results in their other suitable clothing being placed in storage as this may indicate that the additional clothing is over and above what is sufficient.

## 6. Constraints

6.1 Prisoners on Basic level have limited access to ROTL. The ROTL assessment includes consideration of prisoner performance on the incentives scheme such as behaviour and engagement in addressing offending behaviour, alongside other criteria to determine ROTL suitability. Achievement of a specific incentive level must not be used as a determining factor for eligibility or suitability for ROTL. The Release on Temporary Licence Policy Framework provides detailed guidance on ROTL.

6.2 Governors must ensure that access to family days - which bring together prisoners and their families outside their statutory visits entitlement often in more informal settings - are not part of their local incentive policy. The Strengthening Prisoners Family Ties Policy Framework provides further information on Family Days.

6.3 Issues that would undermine decency, such as limiting access to showers, must not be included in any local incentive scheme.

6.4 Governors must not offer at any incentive level: conjugal visits, and any TV channels or service, other than Free-to-view channels.

## 7. Guidance

### Evidence-based Guidance for an Effective Local Incentives Policy

Reinforcing Positive Behaviours is More Effective than Punishing Undesirable Behaviours

7.1 Evidence shows that effective incentives schemes are firmly based on reinforcing desirable behaviours, rather than punishment for undesirable behaviours. Positive reinforcement can produce robust gains in a variety of behaviours, and helps teach the person what to do (rather than just what not to do). The characteristics of positive reinforcement include;
• Make it personal, warm and encouraging.
• Identify opportunities and make it immediate - catch people being good.
• Think small, verbal reinforcement works best.
• Make it earned, meaningful and relevant.
• Make it frequent - four times as much as punishment.
• It is most valued from someone who is liked and respected.
• Include a coaching element.

### Principles of an Effective Local Scheme

7.2 The ethos and implementation of incentives schemes can affect their success. More effective local schemes will:
• Take an establishment-wide approach, characterised by strong leadership, high expectations of behaviour, supported and enforced consistently by all staff and prisoners. Provide training and support for staff implementing behavioural support strategies.
• Make sure rules and expectations are short, clear and understood by all staff and prisoners.
• Recognise that personal progress for one person will likely look different from that of another.
• Ensure that the incentives offered at each level are communicated effectively and are sufficiently attractive to provide a genuine incentive to progress. The easiest way to establish this is to ask a diverse group of staff and prisoners on a regular basis.
• Encourage and create opportunities for the behaviour we want to see. Reward positive progress or behaviour.
• Target and respond to the needs of those who need help the most, including by removing triggers to, and reinforcers of problem behaviour, identifying and addressing potential underlying factors like traumatic brain injury, learning difficulties, low maturation, mental health issues and protected characteristics. This requires time and resources to plan behavioural support, targeting and tailoring it to those people who demonstrate the most challenging behaviour

- Ensure consistency and fairness in the application of rules, and make sure consequences are proportionate and applied consistently so that people feel fairly treated. This will provide clarity on what is and is not acceptable, and increase the likelihood that moving down an incentive level will have a deterrent effect.

- Work on staff-prisoner relationships, increasing positive interactions and increasing trust and view of officers as having legitimate authority.

- Frequently monitor the effectiveness of the scheme, including the appeals process to ensure it is implemented fairly, consistently and transparently, and is incentivising prisoners.

7.3 Annex H contains a compliance checklist for prisons to check that they are delivering essential elements of the policy.

## Procedural Justice – Positive Perceptions of Fairness Increase Compliance and Cooperation

7.4 Evidence shows that when prisoners perceive the process of decision making by people in authority to be fair they view those in authority as more legitimate and trustworthy, and are more likely to cooperate with the law and the authority's decisions. Where prisoners perceive processes to be applied fairly, it is associated with lower levels of misconduct, less violence, better psychological health and lower rates of reoffending after release.

7.5 There are four principles of procedural justice, the critical ingredients that make people feel processes are fair which can be embedded into local incentive policies;

- **Voice:** Giving people a chance to present their side of the story and sincerely consider and account for this in decision making.

- **Neutrality:** being transparent and open about how the rules are applied, explaining decisions and showing decision making to be principled and unbiased.

- **Respect:** Treating people with respect, taking their issues seriously, being polite, and respecting their rights.

- **Trustworthy:** Being sincere and caring, honest about motives, listening and taking issues seriously, and trying to do what is best for everyone.

## Review Considerations - Commendations and Behaviour Warnings

7.6 A system of commendations and behaviour warnings within local incentive policies may help Governors encourage positive patterns of behaviour. Governors have flexibility as to if and how these are employed. For example, an accumulation of either commendations or warnings could prompt an incentive level review, which could lead to progression or moving down an incentive level(s). Where commendations and behaviour warnings are used, it is important to record them on P- NOMIS,

and to always give meaningful reasons for them and to allow prisoners a right to respond.

## Adjudications and Local Policies

7.7 It is important that the local incentive scheme is separate to the disciplinary system. The ability to set incentive levels enables Governors to help secure commitment to rehabilitation, purposeful activity and good behaviour. In contrast, the adjudication process helps maintain order and discipline within a prison by punishing prisoners for specific incidents.

7.8 There may, however, be occasions when behaviour results in both a disciplinary punishment for a specific act and a review and moving down an incentive level because the prisoner's behaviour falls significantly below expected standards. For example, a prisoner who assaults a member of staff or a prisoner may be adjudicated against for the offence and, also, have their incentive level reviewed. Governors have the authority to determine at a local level when the thresholds for both processes are met. However, loss of specified privileges for a defined period as a result of an adjudication is separate from the incentives system which is intended to promote positive patterns of behaviour.

## Transfers

7.9 It is good practice to advise transferring prisoners that incentives available at the receiving prison may be different from the sending prison. Similarly, if prisoners are moved because of a serious incident and need to be moved down an incentive level, best practice is to do this before they are transferred to reduce the potential for conflict on arrival at the receiving prison. If this cannot happen prior to transfer, the sending prison should inform the receiving prison of the prisoner's new level. The receiving prison should move the prisoner to their new level immediately on their arrival.

## Release on Temporary Licence and Incentives

7.10 ROTL can be used as an additional tool for incentivising good behaviour. Incentive scheme factors such as prisoner behaviour and addressing offending behaviour are considered alongside other criteria in ROTL assessments. Achievement of a specific privilege level must not be used as a determining factor for eligibility or suitability for ROTL. Local incentive polices can be linked to ROTL by;

- Making prisoners aware that abiding by the rules, addressing their offending behaviour and engaging with their sentence plan are also important factors in ROTL assessments.

- Including robust systems to gather this information so it can be fully considered as part of the wider assessment for ROTL suitability.

## Enhanced Wings

7.11 Some prisons operate enhanced wings which only prisoners with Enhanced status or above can access. Governors may consider replicating this approach, subject to the physical constraints of their buildings and considering the impact on their population as whole, e.g. considering the risk it may demotivate those who may feel it is unobtainable. Prisons with incentivised Substance Free Living wings should consider how they operate alongside or within the incentives scheme.

7.12 Effective enhanced wings include:

• Incentives and a regime which are markedly better than what is available for prisoners on a normal location. For example;

Using newer or better-quality accommodation where this is available.

Providing more comfortable furnishing in communal areas.

Increasing autonomy and time out of cell for association and additional activities, e.g. allowing prisoners to prepare their own meals, have their own room keys (where this is possible), take showers when they choose and take responsibility for managing their own time. Providing additional activities.

• Clear criteria for access to enhanced wings, ensuring that they operate for enhanced prisoners or above only and spaces are not used to accommodate other prisoners. For example, requiring prisoners to:

Consistently abide by the rules.

Meaningfully engage in their rehabilitation by addressing substance misuse issues, remaining substance free and fully engaging in the regime through education, work or offending behaviour courses.

Make a positive contribution to the prison community by maintaining communal areas, volunteering as peer supporters or Listeners, or helping others.

• Prisoners who understand what is required of them on an enhanced wing. This can include:

Use of a compact setting out what is expected and the incentives received in return.

The opportunity to have a say in how the wing operates.

A process that returns prisoners who move down an incentive level following review to a standard wing.

• Ongoing communications so that all prisoners know, and are reminded of, how to work towards being on an enhanced wing. This could be delivered through:

The prison induction process, promotion of the local incentives policy via prisoner councils/forums, and the use of information on notice boards, leaflets etc.

Ensuring wing staff and key workers, where they are in place, have a good understanding of the incentives scheme and encourage prisoners to progress.

## Considerations for Prisoners with Specific Requirements

7.13 Governors need to consider that some groups of prisoners have specific needs, including those who may find it difficult to engage in the incentives scheme. These include the following:

### Unconvicted, un-sentenced and civil prisoners:

7.14 These prisoners are to be included in local incentive policies but have additional rights that must be factored into local policies. PSO 4600 Unconvicted, Un-sentenced and Civil Prisoners provides further information.

### Prisoners Committed for Contempt of Court:

7.15 Prisoners covered by Prison Rule 7(3) (Contempt of Court) are generally treated as convicted prisoners, with the exception of clothing, letters and visits where they are treated as unconvicted prisoners.

### Foreign National Prisoners and Detainees:

7.16 These prisoners are more likely to have friends and families living outside the UK and may value extra and more flexibly timed telephone calls (including long distance) rather than extra visits. In addition, they may struggle to access incentive policies that are only published in English and so Governors should ensure that local policies are translated into any additional languages required. Immigration detainees, including those held solely on an IS91, must be treated in the same way as unconvicted prisoners.

### Older prisoners and those with disabilities:

7.17 Due to physical restrictions resulting from age and/or disability, some groups of prisoners may not have equality of access to their local incentive scheme. Whenever an incentive is offered that may not be accessible to such prisoners (for example, additional gym sessions), Governors should consider alternatives that can be offered to ensure all prisoners have access to appropriate incentives. It is also good practice to provide information in a variety of formats to ensure all prisoners can understand how the local incentives scheme operates. Reasonable adjustments, such as the availability of large print and easy read versions, may help meet the needs of some disabled prisoners. These considerations form part of the wider equality assessments that Governors need to undertake when developing local incentive policies.

### Prisoners with mental health issues, learning disabilities, those in Offender Personality Disorder (OPD), including PIPEs Services, or Democratic Therapeutic Communities (DTCs):

7.18 Decisions to place, or keep, prisoners with mental health issues or learning disabilities on Basic should be carefully considered and should, wherever possible, be taken by multiagency review panels and with the input of a mental health specialist to ensure that the approach taken is not unduly penalising the individual or having a detrimental effect on their rehabilitation.

7.19 For prisons where there are OPD services, including PIPEs or DTCs, Governors will want to agree with the local clinical teams the integration of therapeutic approaches to managing behaviour and incentives with the requirements of this Framework.

**Maturity:**

7.20 Young adults are still maturing in ways which will affect their response to incentive schemes. Up until their mid-twenties, they are developing the ability to control their impulses and propensity to take risks. Younger adults, in particular, are more likely to respond to reward and are less affected by punishment, than older adults.

They are also more susceptible to peer influence, and tend to prioritise short-term gains over longer-term losses. These characteristics should be taken into account when designing and implementing local incentive schemes.

**Prisoners held in Separation Centres (SCs):**

7.21 Although SC sites publish their Regime Documents and operate in line with the SC Operating Manual, prisoners held in SCs should be treated, in respect of incentives, in line with the requirements and guidance set out in this Policy Framework.

**Prisoners held in Close Supervision Centres (CSCs):**

7.22 Although CSCs may choose to adhere to this Policy Framework the main CSC sites publish their Regime Documents and operate in line with the CSC Operating Manual which is not within the scope of this Policy Framework.

**Women Managed Through the Centralised Casework System (CCS):**

7.23 The CCS team will work with prisons to ensure that each woman has regular multidisciplinary case reviews, up-to-date sentence plans, care plans and OASys assessments as described in PSI 23/2015 Centralised Case Supervision System. Incentive status should be considered as part of their individual care or management plan.

**Prisoners identified to be at risk of suicide or self-harm:**

7.24 Governors will want to ensure that the needs of prisoners who are identified to be at risk of suicide or self-harm are considered on a case by case basis alongside their Assessment Care in Custody and Teamwork plan, including the timing of reviews if they are on the Basic level of the incentives scheme.

**Prisoners who maintain their innocence post-conviction:**

7.25 For the purposes of applying the incentive system to prisoners who maintain their innocence post-conviction, officially recognised appellants should be considered as eligible for Enhanced. An appellant can be defined as someone whose conviction is subject to the review of a higher court. This can be through an appeal against the finding of guilt following an initial conviction or, having had that appeal dismissed, by having their case referred to the Court of Appeal via the Criminal Cases Review Commission (CCRC).

7.26 To prove appellant status a prisoner must produce evidence from the Crown Court or Criminals Appeals Office showing that their case is pending in court.

This should normally be in the form of a criminal appeal number.

7.27 Where prisoners refuse to accept their guilt, and have either had an appeal refused or are not appealing, Governors can consider eligibility for Enhanced status considering their response to personal progression, progress on their sentence plan and constructive engagement in prison life. Governors can also consider whether Enhanced status would be appropriate if the prisoner's denial results in them not being able to engage in rehabilitative activities, even if they are demonstrating suitable behaviours.

Governors are entitled to take account of the indirect effect on those prisoners, who are willing to engage in their sentence plan, in determining the best approach for their prison to those prisoners who refuse to accept their guilt but who are not officially recognised appellants.

**Behaviour Principles and Incentive Level Definitions**

Annex A

The definition of each incentive level up to enhanced is set out below. Governors can add additional criteria for any levels they create above enhanced.

**Basic level** is for those prisoners who have not abided by the behaviour principles. To be considered suitable for progression from Basic, prisoners are expected to adequately abide by them.

**Standard level** is for those prisoners who adequately abide by the behaviour principles, demonstrating the types of behaviour required.

**Enhanced level** is for those prisoners who exceed Standard level by abiding by the behaviour principles and demonstrating the required types of behaviour to a consistently high standard, including good attendance and attitude at activities and education/work and interventions.

## Behaviour Principles

Example behaviour principles are provided below which can be used by prisons or replaced with alternatives, allowing prisons to respond to local challenges and priorities. Beneath the principles are example behaviour expectations which staff, including key workers where they are in place can use to coach prisoners on the types of behaviour required to meet a principle. Governors can tailor the expectations to meet local circumstances or to set short term goals for individual prisoners, - e.g. to target any specific behaviours that they want to improve – or to meet alternative behaviour principles where these are in place

### 1. Be respectful to staff and other prisoners

Behaviour expectations; prisoners can demonstrate the principle by:
• Behaving honestly and openly with staff, and prisoners, and avoiding threatening/abusive behaviour.
• Being aware and considerate of the impact of behaviour on others.
• Respecting others' possessions, rather than taking items from others.
• Acting with decency at all times remembering prisons/cells are not private dwellings (this includes not engaging in sexual activity).

### 2. Comply with rules and compacts

Behaviour expectations; prisoners can demonstrate the principle by:
• Following rules/compacts and staff instructions, and avoiding adjudications.
• No trafficking or other criminal behaviour. It's important to look beyond superficial compliance.
• Respecting prison property, taking care of living areas and maintaining cleanliness of the prison.
• Only having items that prisoners are allowed to have.

### 3. Make progress on personal goals and on your sentence plan

Behaviour expectations; prisoners can demonstrate the principle by:
• Taking an active part in the regime and sentence plan, including work, education or interventions
• Demonstrating behaviours to show progress in areas of:
- self-management, such as managing emotions and solving problems
- interpersonal skills, such as communicating effectively with others and developing relationship skills
- personal care, such as taking showers and looking after their cell and belongings

### 4. Refrain from using drugs or alcohol

Behaviour expectation; prisoners can demonstrate the principle by:
• Giving urine/breath samples, when asked, to test for illegal drugs/alcohol/medicine not prescribed for them.
• Staying free of illegal drugs like heroin, cocaine and alcoholic liquids or medicines that were not prescribed for them by a healthcare professional
• Taking part in activities which help them not to take illegal drug/alcohol/medicines not prescribed for them

### Equalities Guidance & Principles for Implementation of Fair & Effective Incentive Forums

The Lammy Review was concluded in September 2017 and the Government endorsed its key principles (fair treatment, trust and responsibility) and 35 recommendations in December 2017, Lammy Review Final Report. Recommendation 24 concerns Incentives:

**'To increase the fairness and effectiveness of the IEP system, each prison Governor should ensure that there is a Forum in their institution for both officers and prisoners to review the fairness and effectiveness of their regime. Both BAME and white prisoners should be represented in this forum, Governors should make the ultimate decision in this area'.**

Incentive decisions are an area where there appear to be disproportionate outcomes for BAME prisoners. The establishment of Forums within Prison Councils are suggested in the Review as a suitable route but there may be others such as equality action teams where representation is appropriate. In prisons where there is not a committee or other forum able to appropriately consider any disproportionality in their incentive scheme then they must be established.

### Guidance and Principles for the operation of Incentive Forums in Prisons:

• Governors must set out a statement of how the local incentive policy will be applied in their establishments within the key principles of procedural justice (voice, neutrality, respect and trustworthy motives). This should inform the Forum with a view to improving the fairness towards and trust of BAME prisoners and other people with protected characteristics.
• Governors must determine and set out the full terms of reference, appropriate frequency and wider membership of this forum. Each forum must try to include a prison officer, BAME, an white prisoner and Gypsy, Traveller and Romany representation (if present in the prison) and must meet twice yearly as a minimum. The Forum should try to ensure that there is representation from people with all

protected characteristics which are present in the prison.

• Each forum must be minuted and informed by a range of evidence that identifies key incentive data regarding outcomes, any apparent disproportionality and concerns raised by BAME or other prisoners, staff or any other interested party.

• Where data indicates disproportionate outcomes for BAME prisoners or people with other protected characteristics then the chair/lead must take steps to investigate and explain why these discrepancies exist and set out what reforms or actions are to be put in place to address such discrepancies.

• Both the investigation and steps to be taken must be formally recorded, with actions set out within a time-bound and accountable action plan. Wherever possible prisoner representatives should be involved in the process. Such records must be available for scrutiny.

• Accountability for the fairness of outcomes sits with the operational line. Prison Group Directors with their Governors will be accountable for assuring ongoing delivery of this recommendation in all sites for which they hold responsibility.

• The Forum should consider issues such as dual discrimination e.g. BAME and faith, or other protected characteristics where there appears to be disproportionality present.

• PGDs will seek assurance from Governors on the delivery and outcomes under this recommendation through the bilateral process and annual assurance arrangements. Governors may also be asked to provide feedback and confirmation that appropriate arrangements are in place as part of a twice-yearly submission to the HMPPS equalities sub-committee.

• These key principles are to be followed in all forums. How they are achieved will vary within different establishments. Data, for example, can be sought from a variety of sources: local monitoring, the complaints system, the Performance Hub, HMPPS Annual Offender Index Review, Her Majesty's Inspectorate, MQPL, IMB reports, external sources etc.

### National Facilities List

Introduction

The National Facilities List (NFL) identifies the items that Governors need to consider when developing and operating their local incentive schemes. The items below are provided to offer a level of consistency and ensure that it provides Governors opportunities to tailor schemes for their local prison population.

The list is divided into two parts

• Part 1 – the Minimum list of items that Governors must allow each prisoner, where requested, irrespective of incentive level.

Prisoners on Basic level must be restricted to items on part 1 of the list and Part 2 – Governors can choose additional items from part 2 of the list.to add to their local facilities list for Standard and Enhanced levels or levels above Enhanced. It is for Governors locally to determine what incentive level prisoners must be on to have access to these items.

When allowing items Governors should consider whether the items chosen are suitable for in-cell use, and meet all relevant risk considerations, including fire, health and safety, and security. The NFL does not override PSI 63/2011 Management of the Local Security Strategy or any other relevant safety consideration. Furthermore, local infrastructure, including electrics, fire precautions, and health and safety considerations may impact whether certain items on the NFL can be accessed within individual prisons.

There are no set numerical limits on the numbers of each item prisoners can have in possession, but prisoners must not exceed the overall volumetric control limits as set out in national policy PSI 12/2011 Prisoners' Property.

In addition, the following items are not constrained by volumetric control:

• One birdcage (in prisons where birds are permitted) is exempt from volumetric control.

However, if allowed, prisoners should be made aware at the outset that birds are not allowed in every prison establishment and if transferred they may not be able to take their bird with them;

• one musical instrument (e.g. a guitar);

• legal papers;

• bedding up to the standard cell scale issue;

• one set of clothing (whether prisoner's own clothing or prison issue), including that worn when the volume of property is monitored;

• posters etc. which are appropriate to be attached to cell walls; posters must not be attached to external walls;

• items held in possession for the care of babies in mother and baby units; Governors must be satisfied that such items are held for this purpose, and that the quantity held does not impede effective searching;

• Reasonable amounts of items that support Transgender prisoners to live in the gender they identify with. Governors must be satisfied that the quantity held does not impede effective searching

• religious texts and artefacts, essential for the practice of the prisoner's religion.

### Games Consoles and Games

Governors are permitted to provide prisoners with access only to devices that do not provide internet connectivity in their factory state. 18 rated games are not permitted.

All prisons have previously been made aware

961

that "new generation" games consoles which, in their factory state, have built in wireless access to the internet, are not permitted in possession. HMPPS's Information Security (InfoSec) & Services Team has constructed the following list of the types of consoles that are considered to present a low threat to security as they do not, on their own, provide internet connectivity:
• Microsoft Xbox (without network adaptor & associate cabling)
• Nintendo GameCube (without modem or broadband adaptor & cabling)
• Nintendo GameBoy
• Nintendo GameBoy Colour (without infrared port)
• Nintendo GameBoy Advance
• Nintendo GameBoy Advance SP
• Nintendo GameBoy Micro
• Sony PlayStation
• Sony PlayStation 1
• Sony PlayStation 2 (without network adaptor & cabling)
• Nintendo SNES Classic
At the discretion of the Governor, and if the risk is deemed manageable, prisoners may retain consoles with disabled internet connectivity that were held in possession or which had been ordered prior to September 2014. The simple rule is that, otherwise, no games consoles with Wi-Fi capability (whether or not that connectivity has subsequently been disabled) are to be allowed in possession.
SOCT Group can provide further advice on threats to prison security presented by games consoles.

**Suggested TV Compact**
**If you would like one, you can have a TV in your room because of your positive behaviour. We are committed to recognising positive behaviour when people do things well, and to not just focus on when things don't go well.**
We will give you a colour TV and a remote control (with batteries in it). We will also give you a wall bracket to hold the TV.
If the TV breaks and it was not your fault, we will repair or replace it for you. We will do this as quickly as we can, but there can sometimes be a short delay before we can get it up and running again, or if we don't have many spare TVs in the prison.
**There are a few important things you need to know about having a TV. We ask that you agree to these before you get your TV. If you have any questions, please ask a member of staff.**
• The TV and remote control belong to the prison. If you transfer, you have to leave the TV behind.
• You need to pay £1 each week to rent the TV. This money comes from your spend account. If you share a cell with other people, then you split this cost equally with them.
• Please look after the TV and keep it in your

room at all times. You are not allowed to move it somewhere else, or lend it to other people. This is because it has been given to you in recognition of your behaviour.
• Please turn off the TV when you are away from your room, and please keep the volume down, especially at night. This is out of respect for other people who might be trying to concentrate on other things, or trying to sleep. You can use headphones – if available - if you want to use the TV at times when it might disturb others.
• If the batteries of the remote control run out, it is up to you to decide if you want to replace them. If you decide to replace them, this comes from your own spend account.
**We want you to keep having a TV, but this can be taken away for a few reasons:**
• If you damage the TV (this includes damaging the TV set, the security stickers on it, the remote control or the bracket) you will be asked to pay for some or all of the damage caused. You will only get your TV back after this money has been paid.
• If you are found guilty of breaking a prison rule, one of the punishments you can be given is that you have to give up your TV.
• If you can't pay for the £1 weekly charge.
• You are moved to another prison, or accommodation where TVs are not allowed.
• If there are security reasons, health and safety reasons, or other reasons about good order and discipline that mean you cannot have a TV in your room any more.
**If these reasons are not clear, please ask staff to explain them. We want you to keep hold of your TV, and for you to know how to do this. If your TV is taken away, but you don't understand why, please ask staff to explain.**
If you have to give up your TV, staff will come and get this from your room. This usually happens during the day, when you will be at work or doing other activities.
**Sending in and handing of books to prisoners.**
**Ordering books via approved retailers**
Friends and families of prisoners are allowed to order books from approved retailers, which source and send the books on to prisoners. Current approved retailers are:
• Prisons Org UK
• Blackwell's
• Foyles
• Waterstones
• WH Smith
• Mr B's Emporium of Reading Delights
• Wordery
• Should a prisoner decide not to accept a book that has been sent in via an approved retailer (or is not permitted to have it in possession) and wishes to return it so that the sender can be refunded, the package should be returned to the

person who ordered it. This will be at the prisoner's expense.

If the prisoner does not wish to pay for the book to be returned, they should be asked whether they want the book to be sent out (at their own expense), or kept in their stored property. Unwanted books can be disposed of or destroyed with the consent of the prisoner. If the book is suitable, prisoners should have the option to offer the book to the prison library as a donation. PSI 12/2011 Prisoners' Property (and, in particular, paragraph 2.41) sets out further information on how to handle property and the options available to Governors when excess property is received.

**Sending and handing in of books directly by families and friends**

Families and friends can also send or hand in books to prisoners irrespective of whether or not there are exceptional circumstances. Visitors are not allowed to hand books directly to prisoners; they will need to be left with staff to process.

**Number of books permitted in-cell**

There is no numerical limit on the number of books which prisoners can have in their cells. The number of books permitted is subject only to the overarching volumetric control limits on property.

**Further important points**

• All books received must be searched before being passed to prisoners.

• Prisoners will continue to be allowed to order books through existing arrangements in place in prisons.

• The sending or handing in of audio books, whether via an approved retailer or directly from families and friends, is permitted in cassette or CD format. Audio books form part of the overall general limits on the number of books that can be held in-cell. For the purposes of the facilities list, such items are categorised as books, rather than CDs or cassettes.

• Restrictions on the books which prisoners are allowed to have access to remains unchanged.

The Public Protection Manual sets out the books that no prisoner can have access to and Governors can extend this list if the nature of the particular prison's population requires it. In addition, Governors can decide whether an individual prisoner should have a particular book, taking into account the prisoner's offending behaviour.

**These arrangements apply to books only. The sending and handing in of other items, including items which might be available from the approved retailers, remain subject to the restrictions set out in this Policy Framework.**

## 2.23 CIVIL PARTNERSHIPS & EQUAL MARRIAGE

With effect from **27th February 2023** and the implementation of the Marriage and Civil Partnership (Minimum Age) Act 2022 - this Act will raise the age of marriage and civil partnership to 18 in England and Wales.

This means that 16 to 17-year-olds will no longer be able to marry or enter a civil partnership under any circumstances, including with parental or judicial consent from 26 February 2023. It will not be possible for anyone under 18 to marry or enter a civil partnership after this date.

This said to be in an effort to prevent 'forced marriage' which, according to the Government, is only an offence if the person uses a type of coercion, for example threats, to cause someone to marry, or if the person lacks capacity to consent to marry under the Mental Capacity Act. The Act will therefore also expand the criminal offence of forced marriage in England and Wales to make it an offence in all circumstances to do anything intended to cause a child to marry before they turn 18. It will therefore now be an offence to cause a child under the age of 18 to enter a marriage in any circumstances, without the need to prove that a form of coercion was used. The forced marriage offence will continue to include ceremonies of marriage which are not legally binding, for example in community or traditional settings. Everything below, after 26th February 2023 should be read in light of this legislation.

PSI 14/2016 (due to be amended as a result of the Marriage and Civil Partnership (Minimum Age) Act 2022, sets out the legal requirements, policy and procedures for facilitating prisoners' requests to marry (including same sex couples) or enter into a civil partnership in England and Wales. This will ensure that HMPPS fully meets its obligations under the relevant legislation. This instruction also makes it mandatory for all Governors to consider applications from prisoners for marriage and civil partnership.

**Legal Background**

There are three main Acts that apply to parties who are marrying or entering civil partnerships after civil preliminaries, and affect the way in which each party to a civil marriage/partnership formally notifies the registration authority of their intention to marry or form a civil partnership. These arrangements apply where either or both parties are in prison custody. The relevant Acts are:

With effect from **27th February 2023** the *Marriage*

*and Civil Partnership (Minimum Age) Act 2022* that raises the age of marriage and civil partnership to 18 in England and Wales.

### Marriage Act 1983
The Marriage Act 1983 amended the Marriage Act 1949 and enables prisoners to marry in the place of their detention. Both parties to the marriage must notify the Superintendent Registrar in person of their intention to marry. The Asylum & Immigration Act 2004 also applies and covers the procedures for persons wishing to marry where either party is subject to immigration control, again where they are marrying after civil preliminaries. In such cases, the parties must give notice of intention to marry to the Superintendent Registrar.

### Civil Partnership Act 2004
The Civil Partnership Act 2004 came into effect on 5 December 2005. The Civil Partnership Act created a legal relationship of civil partner, giving same-sex couples in the UK the opportunity to gain legal recognition for their relationships. There is specific provision in the Act for "detained persons" who meet the eligibility criteria to register a civil partnership within a prison.

### Marriage (Same Sex Couples) Act 2013
The Marriage (Same Sex Couples) Act 2013 came into effect on 29 March 2014. The main provisions of the Act enable same sex couples to marry in civil ceremonies and ensure that those religious organisations who wish to do so can opt to conduct religious ceremonies for same sex couples. The Act also protects religious organisations and their representatives from successful legal challenge if they do not wish to marry same sex couples. The provisions in the Marriage Act 1949 which enable prisoners to marry in their place of detention apply equally to same sex marriages.

There are a number of distinctions between civil partnership and marriage:
• A civil partnership is formed when the second civil partner signs the relevant document. It is only available to same sex couples and is an exclusively civil procedure.
• A marriage is formed when a couple have exchanged spoken words. Couples who marry may opt for a religious or civil marriage ceremony (in the case of same sex marriages, the Act provides for religious organisations to opt in to the arrangements).
• For both civil partnerships and same sex marriages, notice of the proposed partnership or marriage must be given in person. This is to the registration authority for civil partnerships and to the Superintendent Registrar for same sex marriages. In addition, special provisions apply where either party is subject to immigration control, including the requirement for both parties to give notice of the intended partnership or marriage together.

### What is civil partnership?
Civil Partnership is a legal relationship which can only be formed by two people of the same sex. Couples who form a civil partnership acquire a new legal status – that of "civil partner". It offers same sex couples the ability to obtain legal recognition for their relationship and also confers certain rights and responsibilities upon them.
These include:
• a duty to provide reasonable maintenance for the other civil partner and any children of the family;
• civil partners to be assessed in the same way as spouses for child support;
• equitable treatment for the purposes of life assurance;
• employment and pension benefits;
• the right to register the death of the other civil partner;
• recognition under intestacy rules;
• access to fatal accidents compensation;
• protection from domestic violence; and
• recognition for immigration and nationality purposes.

### APPLICATIONS FROM PRISONERS
### Eligibility
Where a prisoner wants to marry or enter into a civil partnership in a prison, he or she is required to obtain a statement of authority (see Annex A and Annex B of PSI 14/2016) from the prison governor which states that there is no objection to the prison being named as the place at which the marriage or civil partnership will take place - NOTE: The statement by the responsible authority is not required if the prisoner is getting married or entering a civil partnership outside the prison.
Permission for a marriage or civil partnership to take place inside a prison should be given in the following circumstances, but see PSI section 4:
• In the case of sentenced prisoners, at the time of their application, the prisoner is not expected to be released or deported, or to have the opportunity to marry or enter a civil partnership while on Temporary Release, within three months of submitting their request.
• In the case of unsentenced prisoners, the prisoner is likely to remain in custody for three months or longer after their application.
• In the case of prisoners who have less than three months to serve at the time of their application, where there are exceptional compassionate reasons for allowing the marriage/civil

partnership to take place inside the prison sooner, for example, where the marriage/civil partnership is between parents whose child is expected to be born within three months (medical evidence of the likely date of birth will be required) or in the case of someone who is terminally ill.

*Any couple wishing to enter into a civil partnership must also comply with the following:*
• *be of the same sex*
• *not already be in a civil partnership or marriage*
• *be 16 years or older*
• *not be close relatives (as in the meaning of the Act)*
• *meet the legal requirements if either proposed civil partner is subject to immigration control*
Governors should discuss with those prisoners who have an upcoming release date the possibility of postponing the giving notice to register a marriage or civil partnership until after release, where the prisoner would prefer an outside registration but it cannot be permitted for security or public protection reasons. Prisoners may prefer to wait until after release which also means they will not incur the extra cost of the Registrar visiting the prison.

### Notification of applications
*The Governor/Director must report all applications to register in the following cases:*
• *an application to register a marriage or civil partnership from a Category A prisoner must be reported to the Category A Section of the Directorate of High Security Prisons;*
• *Section 53 (1) or (2) prisoners - juveniles – must be reported to Section 53/92 Unit of the Youth Justice Board (020 7271 3033);*
• *requests to register a marriage or civil partnership from any unconvicted prisoner must be reported in writing to the local office of the Crown Prosecution Service (CPS) to see if they wish to raise any objections to the registration taking place (see Annex B for addresses).* It should be made clear that it is for the CPS to raise and defend any objection to a proposed marriage or civil partnership directly with the registration authority. In order to prevent delays, staff should check with the CPS seven days after notifying them, to see if objections will be raised.

### Fees
Prisoners wishing to enter a marriage or civil partnership are responsible for compliance with the requirements of the civil authorities, regardless of where the registration takes place. This includes production of any necessary documentation (including evidence of parental consent where this is required), and payment of any fees (which may be made from earnings, private cash, or money remitted to the prisoner from outside).

Fees will be charged for giving notice, as well as for signing the document conferring registration and the certificate itself. If the act of giving notice and the signing of the document are to take place within the establishment, the visiting registrar(s) will charge for this service. Further costs will be incurred if the signing takes place outside the establishment.

Where an authorised person from the registration authority visits the prison for the giving of notice, a set fee will be charged for attendance (currently £47), in addition to the notice fee (currently £30). At the registration there will be a fee for signing of the marriage or civil partnership document as well as attendance of the registrar. A fee will also be payable for any civil partnership certificate. There are two types of certificate, one including the addresses of the partners, and one excluding the addresses. If an additional copy is required a prisoner or their partner can apply to the registration authority where the partnership was registered. Details of the most up-to-date fees for notice and registration may be obtained from the local register office. It is the responsibility of the prisoner or their partner to obtain this information.

### Notice of intention to register
Any prisoner wishing to register a marriage or civil partnership is legally required to give formal notice of their intention to do so. Each proposed civil partner should give notice to the registration authority in whose area they have resided for at least seven days. When notice is given, both parties will be asked to state where the marriage or civil partnership registration will take place (see section 4 for decisions about location of registration). If the marriage or civil partnership is to be registered outside of the area of residence, each of the proposed partners should give notice in the area where they currently reside. When giving notice, both parties will be asked to give the date and place of the proposed registration, having first agreed this with the relevant local authority. The registration will be either at a register office or approved premises.

There is a 15-day waiting period after each person has given notice of their intention to register, before the marriage or civil partnership can be registered. During this period some details from the notice will be available in the register office for public inspection to allow for any objection to be made. The details will not include the address of either proposed civil partner. The 15-day waiting period may be reduced in exceptional circumstances.

After formal notice has been given, the registration of the marriage or civil partnership must take place within three months if it is to be registered in prison custody. This period commences from the day on which notice of a proposed marriage or civil partnership was recorded and if both parties gave notice on different days, the three month period will commence from the earlier date. If the registration is to take place in the community, the normal 12 month period will apply.

### Registration

A marriage or civil partnership is registered once the couple have signed the Registration document in the presence of a registrar and two witnesses.

### LOCATION OF REGISTRATION

Most prisoners would prefer a registration outside the prison and sympathetic consideration should be given to this, whilst taking account of any security and other public protection issues. A local record should be kept of marriage or civil partnership registrations, including the prisoner's race and ethnic identity and the reason for the decision to hold the registration inside the prison or outside.

### Security Considerations

The Governor must bear in mind the following security considerations when deciding on the appropriate venue:

• *Prisoners who are Category A, provisional category A prisoners, restricted status or on the Escape list must not be allowed to register their marriage or civil partnership outside the prison. Details of all intended guests and information about the proposed registration should be passed to the Category A Section of the Directorate of High Security Prisons as soon as they are known.*

• *Category B prisoners will not normally be allowed an outside registration and must not be allowed to do so if the Governor considers that there is a high risk of the prisoner seeking to escape and if this was successful that the prisoner would pose a serious threat to the public.*

• *Category C prisoners may be allowed to register a marriage or civil partnership outside of the establishment unless the Governor assesses that there is a high likelihood that the prisoner would seek to escape*

• *Category D prisoners should normally be permitted to register a* marriage or *civil partnership outside of the establishment*

• *Young adults and women should be risk assessed to determine whether an outside ceremony can be permitted.*

### Registrations inside the establishment

For registrations inside the establishment, it is for the prisoner to make any necessary arrangements with the registration authority. The Governor is required under the Civil Partnership Act 2004 to provide a supporting statement that clearly identifies the establishment by means of the private address and also states that he/she has no objections to the establishment being named on the notice of proposed marriage or civil partnership as the place at which the person is to register as a civil partner. The form (see Annex C of PSO4445 for example) will be issued to the prisoner or proposed civil partner by the registration authority, on request, and should be completed by the Governor and given to the prisoner for return to the registration authority. A supporting statement from the Governor should be given to the Registrar at the point of giving notice, and it should have been signed no more than 21 days beforehand. The form should give both the official name of the establishment and the private postal address. The prisoner may ask the registration authority to use only the private postal address of the establishment in the register, if they do not want it be evident that the registration took place in custody.

The registration should take place in an appropriate room, taking care to make it as pleasant as possible. *Given the secular nature of the registration, the chapel, multi faith room or any place of worship must not be used as a venue.*

### Guests

The prisoner should be informed that only a reasonable number of guests will be allowed to attend the registration, including two witnesses. The precise number will be for the Governor to decide in the light of local circumstances, including security implications and availability of staff to escort the guests. The prisoner is required to give full details of all the guests beforehand. The Governor may stipulate any conditions in the interests of security, possibly by restricting the number of guests or refusing permission for a particular guest to attend.

### REGISTRATIONS OUTSIDE THE ESTABLISHMENT
### Temporary release

*Prisoners who can be safely released to attend an outside registration without a prison escort and who meet the eligibility requirements set out in PSO 6300 must be allowed to do so subject to passing the necessary risk assessment.* If a prisoner is eligible for Resettlement Day (RDR) or Overnight (ROR) RDR/ROR within one month of their application, the prisoner should normally arrange for their registration to take place during this period.

For prisoners not eligible for RDR or ROR, temporary release may be granted under a Special Purpose Licence (see eligibility requirements in PSO 6300 – paragraph 2.6). The Governor may also grant a Special Purpose Licence on the day of the registration subject to passing the necessary risk assessment. For prisoners released on a Special Purpose Licence, the period of absence should only be long enough to enable the prisoner to attend the registration.

A prisoner who is released on temporary licence will normally be expected to arrange and pay for his/her own transport. The Governor may provide official transport but the prisoner should pay the actual cost. Again, such charges may be paid from earnings, private cash or money remitted to the prisoner.

### Escorts

For prisoners who cannot be granted temporary release, who present a low security risk and there are no other reasons to prevent an outside registration, every effort should be made to provide an escort for him/her to do so. This may involve re-deployment of staff, bearing in mind the impact on the regime of other prisoners. Prisoners will be required to meet the costs of the escort and transport, and Governors should inform them of the total cost in advance. Costs should be determined on an individual basis, taking into account the number of officers required, their hourly rate of pay, amount of time taken off normal duties and the cost of transport. It is also important to plan the resources committed to the escort so as to prevent any last minute cancellations. Information on the procedures for escorts is contained in the National Security Framework.

*The prisoner must be conveyed to the ceremony in civilian clothes and with a suitable escort, who should normally wear civilian clothes and carry out their duties as unobtrusively as is consistent with the needs of security.* However, it remains the Governor's responsibility to ensure the safe custody of the prisoner and it is a matter of judgement as to what the security arrangements should be, and whether any special arrangements with the local police are required. The prisoner must be returned to the establishment as soon as the ceremony is over.

### Location and inspection of registration venue

*Where the registration is to take place outside the establishment and under escort, it must be arranged at the nearest register office (to the prison) at which the registration may lawfully be performed.* Subject to security considerations, Governors should normally involve the couple in the decision on the date and time of the registration, although there are time constraints set by Law. The local police must be informed of the registration, including details of the venue, times, and any

other such details that they may require. This is to be done even if the presence of the police is not required on the day. Media Relations Unit should be consulted about any case that might give rise to particular public interest or concern. The Governor should arrange an on-site meeting with the relevant Registrar and, where appropriate, a representative from the local police force, to discuss any security implications of the ceremony being held in those particular premises. The Governor or security manager should conduct a thorough risk assessment in advance to determine whether it is a suitable venue. *The security assessment must cover the room in which the ceremony is to take place, as well as any other relevant parts of the building that the prisoner will have access to. Particular attention should be paid to doors and windows, which may provide a means of escape either from the room in which the ceremony is to take place or any other part of the building. Arrival and departure routes must also be checked.*

Where registrations are to be held at an outside venue that has already been assessed, contact should be made to ensure that the venue has not been recently altered. Detailed information on the location and layout of the intended premises and precise instructions on the use of restraints should be given to the escorting officer(s) as part of the initial briefing.

### PUBLIC PROTECTION ISSUES

In cases where an application to register a civil partnership is received from a prisoner who has been assessed as presenting a risk of harm to either the intended partner or their children the Governor/Director should consult with all those responsible for the risk management of the prisoner. This would include relevant prison staff, the interdepartmental risk management team, offender manager and other MAPPA responsible authorities as well as Social Services. It will then be necessary to decide whether to disclose information about the risk of harm presented by the prisoner (including their offending history) to the intended partner or another third party. It should first be established whether the prisoner consents to such disclosure. If the offender does not consent, staff should refer to National MAPPA guidance (Information sharing and Disclosure) for information on disclosing in these circumstances, and if necessary seek guidance from the HMPPS Public Protection Unit.

### CHANGE OF NAME

After registering a marriage or civil partnership, some might want to change their surname to that of their civil partner, or a couple may choose to hyphenate their names. Staff should refer to

967

procedures outlined in PSO 4455 Requests from Prisoners to Change their Name. Government departments and agencies such as the Passport Agency and the DVLA will accept civil partnership certificates in the same way that they accept marriage certificates as evidence for changing names.

## 2.24 ELDERLY PRISONERS

Older prisoners can be split into four main profiles, each with different needs:

Repeat prisoners. People in and out of prison for less serious offences and have returned to prison at an older age.

Grown old in prison. People sentenced for a long sentence prior to the age of 50 and have grown old in prison.

Short-term, first-time prisoners. People sentenced to prison for the first time for a short sentence.

Long-term, first-time prisoners. People sentenced to prison for the first time for a long sentence, possibly for historic sexual or violent offences.

Many experience chronic health problems prior to or during imprisonment as a result of poverty, poor diet, inadequate access to healthcare, alcoholism, smoking and other substance abuse. The psychological strains of prison life can further accelerate the ageing process.

In November 2020 the House of Commons Justice Committee welcomed the Government's acceptance that there should be a new strategy for dealing with the increasing number of older prisoners, but has called for more detail on that strategy and a timeframe for it. The Committee meanwhile regretted that the government had rejected its recommendation that older prisoners be systematically screened for dementia.

On the Parliamentary Select Committee Databases pages of prisonoracle.com you can read the report: 'Ageing prison population: Government Response to the Committee's Fifth Report' which was itself published in July 2020.

On prisonoracle.com you will also find a copy of the charter on dying in custody.

The number of prisoners in England and Wales aged over 60 has increased by over 240% since 2002, primarily because of an increase in the number of older men being sentenced for sexual offences. Between 2002 and 2020 the number of prisoners over 60 has grown from around 1500 to over 5000.

This increased population of older people has profound implications for the prison service. Older prisoners are more likely to have chronic diseases, disability and decreased mobility. Moreover, many of our prisons, especially those built in the Victorian era, were not designed to accommodate people with serious illnesses or mobility issues.

With these realities in mind, the Committee recommended that long-term prison estate strategy should reflect the needs of older prisoners, especially as the government is planning to build new prisons to accommodate a projected 10,000 more prisoners in the years to come. The then Minister responsible for prisons, Lucy Frazer QC MP, acknowledged these findings and told the Justice Committee she had commissioned an older offenders strategy.

The Committee expressed disappointment that the government had rejected its recommendation that older prisoners be systematically screened for dementia, and that prison officers who work with older prisoners receive related training.

The Justice Committee report published in July 2020 had noted that 85% of prisoners over the age of 60 have some form of major illness and that prisoners tend to "age" more prematurely than people in the general population because of a variety of social and physical disadvantages.

In its response, the government said only that healthcare providers would be asked to look out for symptoms and ensure they knew what to do if these arise.

The Chair of the Justice Committee, Bob Neill, said: *"When many of our jails were built, in Victorian times, it couldn't have been imagined that so many people, including prisoners, would live much longer lives. Because of this, some of these buildings are no longer fit for purpose. So while we welcome the Government's commitment to commissioning an older offenders strategy, we need more detail. We would ask the Ministry to set out the parameters. Who will it consult, for example, and how will we measure success? We would also ask the Minister for a clear timeline on this strategy.*

*"On the issue of dementia I am very disappointed that the Ministry of Justice did not agree that every older prisoner should have systematic access to screening and be treated accordingly. Left untreated, dementia can rob a person of their dignity and we should not go down that road. I would urge the Government to reconsider our proposal and to set out, on the record, what precise tools are currently in place to identify prisoners with dementia".*

The Care Act means that local authorities now have a duty to assess and give care and support to people who meet the threshold for care and are in prisons and probation hostels in their area. However inspectors found that in many prisons too little had been done to prepare and plan for these new arrangements.

### Resettlement

A National Institute for Health Research study found that release planning for older prisoners was frequently non-existent. The lack of information received by prisoners in preparation for their release caused high levels of anxiety. Many reported minimal or no contact from probation workers or offender managers.

Three out of a total of five prisons surveyed said that their health care centre helped older people to register with a GP as part of their resettlement support. However, 13 out of a total of 14 former prisoners surveyed said they had no referral to a local GP. Despite the small size of the sample, the study suggests that many older people are being released without the continuity of medical care they require.

### REQUIREMENT TO WORK PSO 4460

Prisoners' Pay (see chapter 2.21 Work & Pay) - paragraph 5.2.5 sets out the policy on retirement: 'Prisoners of state retirement age are not normally required to work. They may work for standard rates of pay if they choose, provided there are suitable activities available in the establishment.' However, para 5.2.6 states that: 'Prisoners of state retirement age can, however, be required to participate in other purposeful activity as identified by the sentence/training plan or learning plan. They should be paid at the standard rate for these sessions. Unreasonable refusal renders them liable to be classified as "unwilling to work", and therefore not to receive any pay.' The State Pension is suspended for prisoners otherwise entitled to it until the day of their release when they again become eligible. See section 2.12 for general benefits advice and section 3, The Directory for more support organisations that may be able to help.

### AGE UK- www.ageuk.org.uk

Tavis House
1-6 Tavistock Square
London WC1H 9NA
http://www.ageuk.org.uk
Freephone Information Line: 0800 169 6565
AgeUK - formerly called Age Concern - has been helping older people across the UK for more than 60 years.

*Policy Statement on Older Prisoners*
### Older Prisoners (England and Wales)

The older prison population is growing. Many of these prisoners have been found guilty of serious crimes, but this is not a reason for them to receive sub-standard support. In order to reduce the likelihood of these prisoners reoffending, it is imperative that those services which best aid rehabilitation – health and social care support, housing and pensions advice, education and training – be made available to them, both in prison and following release.

Recent figures reveal that at the end of March 2010 there were 8,120 prisoners aged over 50 in England and Wales, including 605 over 70. People aged 60 and over represent the fastest growing age group in prisons and yet no national strategy for their care and management exists.

Between 1996 and 2006, the aged 60 and over population in prisons increased 149%; the aged 50-59 population increased 74%. At any one time about 10% of the prison population is aged 50 plus. A worst case scenario is that there will be a prison population of 101,900 by 2014 – this may equate to over 10,000 older offenders in prison.

It is clear that the increases in numbers are not a one off, but part of a trend as a result of changes in attitudes within society and the criminal justice system, coupled with an aging population. However, to date no additional resources have been made available to meet the needs of this particular group of offenders, either within or outside prison. And according to HM Inspectorate of Prisons in a report from 2008, apart from short sections in the Prison Service Orders on disability and women, there remains no national strategy for older prisoners as such, supported by mandatory national and local standards.

### Public Policy Proposals

Older prisoners' forums should be established in all prisons with an older population. Older prisoners should receive the same level of basic social and health care support as non-prisoners and that which addresses their specific needs. Guidance should be developed and disseminated to Resettlement Teams outlining best practice and responsibilities in resettling older prisoners including pensions advice, housing, and accessing healthcare.

Older prisoners need appropriate choices in prison accommodation. Many older prisoners wish to remain in a mainstream wing environment; they should be supported in doing this. Voluntary sector agencies have a key role to play in improving the lives of older prisoners both inside and outside prison. More opportunities should be given to the third sector to provide these and other services to older prisoners.

### ROYAL NATIONAL INSTITUTE FOR THE BLIND. (RNIB) – www.rnib.org.uk

Royal National Institute of the Blind
105 Judd Street
London WC1H 9NE
Tel: 0303 123 9999
If you have a sight problem, we can help. If you would like to contact us, please call us on 0303 123 9999. Our Helpline offers an immediate, expert and confidential service. Many of our Helpline staff have sight problems themselves. They are trained to listen and to give reassurance and advice.

Our staff can:
• put you in touch with specialist advice services
• give you details of support groups and services in your area.

We can also provide you with free information on:
• eye conditions
• making the most of your remaining vision - magnifiers, lighting
• registering a blind or partially sighted
• benefits and your rights
• living with sight loss - what's next?

Our Helpline is open Monday to Friday 9.00am - 5.00pm. Calls are charged at local rates. Interpreters can be arranged for most languages. All calls are treated in confidence.

### ROYAL NATIONAL INSTITUTE FOR DEAF PEOPLE (RNID) www.rnid.org.uk

19-23 Featherstone Street, London EC1Y 8SL

Got a question? Our friendly helpline team are waiting for your call - we offer free confidential and impartial information on a whole range of subjects relating to deafness, hearing loss and tinnitus.

Telephone     0808 808 0123 (freephone)
Textphone     0808 808 9000 (freephone)

Our Information Line is a great place to start if you want information on any aspects of deafness, hearing loss or tinnitus, or about the work we do.

*Who we are*

We have a team of trained, dedicated and professional information line officers. We provide free, confidential and impartial information to deaf and hard of hearing people, their families, friends, and professionals.

We can provide information on a number of subjects including:

hearing aids
health care
benefits and services
deaf awareness
communication
equipment
rights
tinnitus.

We can also answer your questions about Action on Hearing Loss and the work that we do, including our vision and our values.

We will try to answer any question about hearing loss or tinnitus - give us a try.

*Action on Hearing Loss publications*

We have a wide range of publications including over eighty factsheets. Many are available in Braille, audio tape and large print. You can order by contacting the Information Line, or you can ask your establishment Equalities Officer to download them from our factsheets and leaflets area.

We also have a series of information packs, on the following subjects: Sign Language, Tinnitus, Deaf awareness; and an information pack for Brownie / Girl Guide groups. The packs can be requested from the information line using the contact details above.

## 2.25 SEGREGATION

### PSO 1700

Updated April 2022 - see below

On 29th July 2015 the Supreme Court, the highest court in the UK, handed down judgement in an important case concerning the segregation of prisoners. As a result of that case Parliament issued the Statutory Instrument 1638/2015 known as The Prison and Young Offender Institution (Amendment) Rules 2015 in response to the finding by the Supreme Court in R (on the application of Bourgass & another) v Secretary of State for Justice, that under the Prison Rules as they then were Governors could not lawfully authorise removal from association (also known as segregation) for more than 72 hours.

The purpose of the Amendment Rules was to enhance the then existing system to allow governors in a prison, or young offender institution, to authorise continuing segregation beyond 72 hours, but to provide additional safeguards including a requirement for the Secretary of State to give permission before decisions can be taken to continue segregation beyond 42 days.

### Purpose of Segregation

The Prison Rules make provision for the management of prisons, including the treatment of prisoners and conduct of prison officers.

The aim of segregation is to provide a fair and safe process by which governors are able to remove from normal association (under Prison Rule 45/Young Offender Rule 49) any prisoner who by their behaviour, presents a risk to the maintenance of good order or discipline or, who is themselves at risk of harm from other prisoners. Segregation is always a last resort option used for the shortest time necessary and the prisoner must be returned to normal location as soon as it is safe and practicable.

Following the judgment in Bourgass & another, the Secretary of State made changes to the policy of Reviewing and Authorising Continuing Segregation and Temporary Confinement in Special Accommodation in 2015, further updates were issued in 2018 and the latest updates to PSO 1700, which sets out the policy on Segregation, came into effect in April 2022 and are explained below.

All the latest updates to all Prison Service Orders, Instructions, and Policy Frameworks can be found on *prisonoracle.com*

**What's New: April 2022**
The following are the key changes to segregation review policy introduced in April 2022.
**Authorisation of Segregation Beyond 42 days – Adult Prisoners and Young Adults held in YOIs (Section 3)**

The minimum level of authority for Segregation Reviews has been revised as per the following:
• First Review prior to 42 days of continuous segregation – minimum of a Band 8 Senior Manager in the Prison Group Director's (PGD) office / Headquarters (HQ)
• Subsequent Review if segregation is to continue beyond 84 days – minimum of a Band 9 Senior Manager in the PGD's office / HQ
• Review if segregation is to continue beyond 6 months – PGD or Deputy Director
These reviews must not be delegated to a grade below which is specified above but can continue to be undertaken at higher PGD and Executive Director grades if this is determined appropriate by the Executive Director for North or Executive Director for South.

**The level of authority of Segregation Reviews for the Contracted Estate is:**
• First Review prior to 42 days of continuous segregation – A minimum of Band 8 Senior Manager from the Controller Team in a privately managed prison, including a minimum of a Band 8 from the Controller Team at the same prison where the prisoner is segregated, or a minimum of a Band 8 Senior Manager in the Head of Privately Managed Prisons Office.
• Subsequent Review if segregation is to continue beyond 84 days – A minimum of Band 9 Senior Manager from the Controller Team in a privately managed prison, including a minimum of a Band 9 from the Controller Team at the same prison where the prisoner is segregated, or a minimum of a Band 9 Senior Manager in the Head of Privately Managed Prisons Office.
• Review if segregation is to continue beyond 6 months – minimum of a Band 11 Head of Privately Managed Prisons.
These reviews must not be delegated to a grade below which is specified above and can be undertaken by a more senior grade in the Head of Privately Managed Prisons Office or HQ if this is determined appropriate by the Head of Privately Managed Prisons.
In addition, a quality assurance process must be implemented by every PGD and Head of Privately Managed Prisons Office as per the following:
• First Reviews – 10% of reviews must be quality assured by an official more senior than a Band 8, and independent to the First Review
• Subsequent Review – 10% of reviews must be

quality assured by an official more senior than a Band 9, and independent to the First Review
The amendments are only in relation to Adult Prisoners and Young Adults held in YOIs. See Section 3 for further details.
Prison and YOI Rules allow governors to authorise segregation beyond 72 hours and the Governor must obtain leave from the Secretary of State to continue segregation beyond 42 days.

**Section 1 – Introduction**
1.1 This document sets out mandatory revised policy and procedures governing the way in which continuing segregation under Prison Rule 45 (YOI Rule 49) is reviewed and authorised. The document also introduces at Section 5 a new policy on reviewing and authorising Temporary Confinement in Special Accommodation beyond 24 hours under Prison Rule 48 (YOI Rule 51).
1.2 This document should be read in conjunction with **Prison Service Order 1700** which provides comprehensive policy guidance on all aspects of segregation.
1.3 This document applies where a prisoner is segregated, and is denied normal association with the mainstream prison population under either:
• Prison Rule 45 (YOI Rule 49) – Good Order or Discipline or Own Protection (Sections 2 to 4); or,
• Prison Rule 48 (YOI Rule 51) – Temporary Confinement (Section 5).
1.4 Policy on initial segregation is set out in PSO 1700.
1.5 For completeness, other reasons for segregation (not covered by these revised arrangements) are:
• Prison Rule 53(4) (YOI Rule 58(4)) – Awaiting the start of an Adjudication (where the prisoner is segregated before an adjudication).
• Prison Rule 55(e) (YOI Rule 60(f)) – Cellular Confinement
• Prison Rule 55(h) YOI Rule 60(g) – Removal from wing / unit for a period of 28 days. (See PSI 47/2011 Prisoner Discipline Procedures: a prisoner would only be held in segregation unit under this rule if there was no other suitable alternative available)

**Section 2: Reviewing and Authorising Continuing Segregation Within Establishments**
Initial Decision to Segregate
2.1 The policy on initial segregation is set out in PSO 1700. The governor has the authority to arrange that a prisoner is to be segregated where it appears desirable for the maintenance of good order or discipline or in his or her own interest. The Secretary of State gives leave to the governor to delegate this authority to a person within the prison who meets the description of "competent operational manager".

### The Role of Segregation Review Boards

2.2 A regular review of a prisoner's segregation must be undertaken by a Segregation Review Board (SRB) within the prison. It is essential that such reviews consider carefully all the available evidence for and against continued segregation in an impartial manner. All relevant issues must be considered regarding the options of either extending segregation or removing the prisoner from segregation. Both options may have risks and benefits which must be weighed against one another carefully. Failure to carry out this function thoroughly may result in (a) harm to the prisoner should he or she be inappropriately retained in segregation, or, (b) harm to the prisoner or others in the prison, and/or a threat to control and order, if the prisoner is inappropriately returned to normal location.

2.3 The SRB is the proper place for these issues to be considered. The SRB will meet to consider a case within 72 hours of initial segregation and then at no more than 14 day intervals thereafter (see para 2.8 below). The SRB should be composed of an appropriate group of people in order to provide the necessary range of knowledge and experience and a degree of impartiality and independence from the original decision to segregate (see 2.4 below). This is particularly so for decisions to segregate beyond 14 days. Evidence suggests that 14 days is the point that some prisoners may start to suffer adverse effects of segregation. For this reason, the 14-day SRB is mandated as a multi-disciplinary board capable of reviewing a range of evidence and views on continuing segregation including, but not confined to, health and security issues. The SRB will need to be satisfied that any decisions made about segregation are objective and evidence based, and that they have not been influenced by bias.

### Composition of Review Boards

2.4 The following people must be present at both the 72-hour and subsequent SRBs
• Chairperson – given the nature of the issues to be decided (see para 2.1 above) the chairperson must be a competent Operational Manager with powers delegated by the governor to carry out this role and meeting the requirements at 2.5 below.
• Healthcare representative and/or member of the Mental Health In-Reach Team.
• ACCT case manager (where prisoner is subject to ACCT processes) or other staff member who knows the prisoner and has an understanding of their ACCT circumstances.
• Prisoner (for at least part of the Board and where appropriate – see 2.14 below).
2.5 Independence of decision making: The Chairperson will take the final decision on

whether to continue segregation but must consider fully the views of the other members of the SRB and references to decisions by the SRB in this policy should be read to mean decisions by the Chairperson acting in this way. Establishments must ensure that the role of Chairperson is rotated between operational managers in order to ensure independence of decision making. The Chairperson at the 72 hour Board and the first 14-day Review Board, must be a different person to the person who authorised initial segregation other than in exceptional circumstances. Exceptional circumstances might include where there is no other operational manager who is able to Chair the SRB within the timescales. Where, in exceptional circumstances, the person who authorises the segregation is the same person that made the initial decision to segregate, a further authorisation must be sought at the earliest opportunity from an operational manager who was not involved in the initial decision to segregate. This can be done outside of a SRB based on the last SRB papers which the second operational manager should countersign.

2.6 The following people should, where appropriate, also attend the SRB for adult prisoners:
• IMB member. The IMB must be invited to all SRBs and every effort must be made to facilitate their attendance, where possible. (See 2.13 below)
• Segregation Officer;
• Wing/Unit personal officer;
• A member of the Chaplaincy Team;
• Psychologist;
• Offender Manager.
2.7 The following must also attend SRBs for Young People as appropriate:
• Personal Officer or Caseworker;
• Youth Offending Team worker;
• Local Authority Social Worker (or Leaving Care worker if appropriate);
• Young person's family or carers (where appropriate);
• Advocacy Services (if requested by the young person);
• Safer Custody Team Representative (where appropriate).
• Psychology Team input at 21 day review point (see 4.2 below).

### Timing of Review Boards (See Annex A for an outline of the process)

2.8 For prisoners segregated under Prison Rule 45 (YOI Rule 49), an initial Segregation Review Board (SRB) must be held within the first 72 hours of a prisoner being placed in segregation.
2.9 The purpose of this initial SRB is to determine whether or not the prisoner needs to remain segregated. The SRB must examine the

initial reasons for segregation and make an assessment of the prisoner's behaviour since then; the risks the prisoner poses on normal location; the risks posed to the prisoner by others within the prison; his or her ability to cope with segregation and to set out a strategy for the future management of the prisoner with the aim of achieving his or her safe return to normal location as soon as is practicable.

2.10 If it is decided that segregation is to continue following the initial review, then a further SRB must be held within 14 days of the initial review.

2.11 Subsequent SRBs for that prisoner must then be held at least every 14 days throughout the entire period during which the prisoner is segregated. The SRB Chairperson may decide to review segregation before any 14 day period expires. More frequent reviews may be necessary depending on the circumstances of the case and particular attention should be given as to whether a review needs to take place prior to the expiration of the 14 day period in the case of vulnerable prisoners.

2.12 SRBs may authorise segregation through this process for a maximum of 42 days (6 weeks) for adults and for a maximum of 21 days for Young People from the point of initial segregation without the leave of the officials acting on behalf of the Secretary of State (see Sections 3 and 4 below). Timescales for further reviews must take place as set out below at paragraph 3.4 onwards for adult prisoners, and paragraph 4.5 onwards for Young People.

**IMB attendance at Segregation Review Boards**

2.13 IMB members play a vital role in SRBs and must be facilitated to attend wherever possible. This is particularly important for 14-day reviews which must be scheduled to allow an IMB member to attend. To assist in this, prisons should consider standardising days on which the SRBs are held. Where the attendance in person of an IMB member is not possible, consideration should be given to providing teleconference facilities. Where the IMB member cannot attend and cannot dial into teleconference facilities, then they must be afforded the facility to review the segregation paperwork and provide their views to the Chairperson who authorised the decision to segregate when they are next in the establishment.

**Prisoner attendance at Segregation Review Boards**

2.14 The prisoner must be told when an SRB will take place and must be given the opportunity to attend and make representations. Any communication difficulties which may be associated with learning disability or a specific learning difficulty or limited English should be taken into account throughout and appropriate support provided. The prisoner should be allowed to attend the whole SRB if they chose to do so, and should only be excluded from that part of the meeting where sensitive security information is being discussed.

2.15 Prisoners may only be completely excluded from attending an SRB where specific safety concerns exist (e.g. where there are concerns that the prisoner may be violent towards the Board). In such circumstances, the prisoner must be given the opportunity to make representations to the SRB in some other way such as through a member of staff or in writing using the form OT029 at Annex D3.

2.16 A prisoner on an open ACCT or who is in the ACCT post-closure phase, must be invited to attend all SRBs unless there are specific reasons why this would not be possible or appropriate. The invitation should be made through the ACCT case-manager to ensure that they are aware of the possibility that the Board could potentially heighten the prisoner's risk of self-harm.

2.17 In all cases where a prisoner has declined to attend the SRB or has been excluded for all or part of the SRB, a record must be made of the reasons.

**Segregation Review Board Procedures**

2.18 Detailed guidance about the process for continuing segregation under Rule 45 (YOI Rule 49) is provided at Annex C. The final decision on whether to authorise continuing segregation rests with the member of staff chairing the SRB. That decision and the reasons for it must be recorded on the form Segregation Review Board and Governor's Authority for Continuing Segregation (OT025) and be signed by the SRB Chair and IMB member (if attending). The OT025 has been updated with a note that the reasons for the continued segregation must also be recorded on this form (see Annex D below for the new form).

2.19 The role of the representative of the IMB is to monitor and oversee the decision making process and to be satisfied that the laid down procedures have been followed and that a reasonable decision has been reached by the Chairperson. Where the IMB attends the SRB, the Chairperson must ensure that they sign the relevant part of the form (OT025) to indicate that they were present at the SRB and whether or not they were satisfied that a reasonable decision had been reached by the Board and whether the correct procedures were followed. If the IMB member does not believe that a reasonable decision has been reached and is unable to resolve the matter with the Chairperson, then the procedures outlined at para 2.29 below should be followed. Where the IMB member cannot attend the SRB and cannot dial into teleconference facilities, then they must be afforded the facility to review the segregation paperwork and provide their views to the governor or Chairperson who authorised the decision to segregate when they are next in the establishment.

### Explaining Reasons to Continue Segregation to the Prisoner

2.20 Where the SRB decides in principle to continue segregation, the reasons must be explained to the prisoner at the Review Board. The prisoner must be given the opportunity to make meaningful representations before a final decision is made. Where a final decision is made to continue segregation, the chairperson must ensure that the prisoner is informed of the substance of the reasons on which the decision to continue segregation was based and ensure that the prisoner is informed, both orally and in writing, of meaningful reasons for the decision. This will not normally require the disclosure of the primary evidence on which the decision to continue segregation was based, but the reasons must:

• provide a clear justification for the prisoner's continuing segregation;
• clearly reference the specific circumstances of the case;
• avoid the use of generic phrases and jargon and
• be understandable to the prisoner taking into account any learning disability or speech, language or communication impairment.

2.21 The reasons must be recorded on form Notification to Prisoner of Outcome of Segregation Review Board and Segregation Privileges and Behavioural Targets (OT027). A revised copy of this form is provided at Annex D2. The reason(s) should reflect the discussions held during the SRB and noted on form OT025.

2.22 Information relevant to the decision to continue segregation may be withheld from the prisoner in certain circumstances:

• in the interests of national security;
• for the prevention of crime or disorder, including information relevant to prison security;
• for the protection of a third party who may be put at risk if the information is disclosed;
• if, on medical or psychiatric grounds, it is felt necessary to withhold information where the mental and or physical health of the prisoner could be impaired;
• where the source of the information is a victim, and disclosure without their consent would breach any duty of confidence owed to that victim, or would generally prejudice the future supply of such information.

2.23 In such cases as the above, a summary or an edited form of the information that protects the source must be provided – both orally and in writing. Where information that impacts on the segregation decision is withheld from the prisoner, the completed form (OT027) must nonetheless record a brief description of the information being withheld (i.e. Security Information Report) as far as is compatible with maintaining security/protecting other persons. Any gisted information must be consistent with the information available to the SRB and must be sufficient for the prisoner to make meaningful representations against segregation.

2.24 Form 0TO27 must also be completed to advise the prisoner of the regime/privileges to which they will have access whilst in segregation; the date of the next SRB and the targets that the Board have set for the intervening period.

### Caring for Prisoners Segregated

2.25 An ACCT case review will be completed for all prisoners who are on an open ACCT (or in ACCT post-closure phase) at the time of the SRB. Prisons must be aware of the potential effects of segregation on a vulnerable person's state of mind and begin ACCT procedures if they observe any changes in a prisoner's behaviour or circumstances, which indicate an increase in the risk of suicide and self-harm. See Annex C, paragraph 1c for further information.

2.26 Prisoners segregated for a continuous period of more than 30 days must have a care plan completed detailing how their mental well being is to be supported. For prisoners on an open ACCT or during the post-closure phase, this must also trigger an enhanced ACCT case review if they are not already subject to enhanced case review procedures.

### Other Actions Establishments May Consider

2.27 Prisoners held in segregation for long, continuous periods (i.e. 3 months or more) may be considered for assessment for a Dangerous & Severe Personality Disorder (DSPD) unit, VPU or Close Supervision Centre (CSC) where considered appropriate.

### Appeals

2.28 There is no direct right of appeal for the prisoner against the decision of a SRB. If the prisoner wishes to complain about the decision taken in his or her case then the prisoner may use the prisoner complaints process set out in Prisoner Complaints Policy Framework.

### IMB Formal Objection to Segregation

2.29 Where the IMB member has a concern that the proper process has not been followed or that the decision is irrational in the light of information available to the SRB, they should try to resolve the matter informally through approaches to the Duty Governor/Director or authorising Governor/ Director or operational manager chairing the SRB.

2.30 Where an IMB member remains concerned with the decision of the SRB, they may submit their objections to continuing segregation in writing. This paper must be sent to the Governor/Director in charge of the establishment, who is required to respond within 24 hours. Both Governors/Directors in charge of the establishment and members of the IMB should make every effort to resolve the matter at local level.

2.31 If it has not been possible to resolve the issues raised in the formal objection, a copy of the IMBs objections, the paperwork from the last SRB and a letter setting out the governor's views must be sent to the PGD (or the Head of Privately Managed Prisons). The PGD (or the Head of Privately Managed Prisons) must arrange to discuss the case with the IMB member and Governor/Director within 5 working days.

2.32 If the IMB are still concerned about the segregation decision, they should bring it to the attention of the Executive Director Public Sector Prisons North, Executive Director Public Sector Prisons South or Head of Custodial Contracts for contracted prisons.

2.33 In the event of a disagreement at this stage, the matter should be brought to the attention of the Minister and the Chief Executive Officer, HMPPS.

### Monitoring the Use of Segregation

2.34 All establishments must have in place arrangements to monitor their use of segregation. This includes use of the segregation unit and the segregation of prisoners elsewhere within the establishment. Guidance on monitoring and of mandatory issues to be considered is attached at Annex E.

2.35 Monthly data on prisoners in segregation must be sent to the PGD (or the Head of Privately Managed Prisons) within 7 days of the end of each month setting out numbers of prisoners held in segregation during that month under Rule 45 (YOI Rule 49) by the following time period – numbers in continuous segregation for: *up to 72 hrs; 72 hrs to 1 week; 1-2 weeks; 2-3 weeks; 3-4 weeks; 4-5 weeks; 5-6 weeks; 6- 12 weeks; 12-16 weeks; 16-20 weeks; 20-24 weeks; 24-28 weeks and total prisoners segregated beyond 28 weeks.*

Total numbers of prisoners in segregation under Rule 45 (YOI Rule 49) who are on an ACCT, or in ACCT post-closure phase, must also be recorded.

2.36 An interim form for this is shown at Annex D8 pending development of a national system. PGD offices must monitor levels of segregation and

longer term segregation in particular and ensure that issues are flagged to PGDs prior to visits.

2.37 A quarterly report on the use of segregation must be submitted to the Governor and the PGD highlighting the key observations and summarising the use of segregation over the previous quarter. It is also recommended that the report is sent to the Safer Custody lead. As a minimum, the report should:

• monitor adherence to relevant instructions;
• detail the use of segregation throughout the prison;
• identify the training and any developmental needs of staff;
• identify and investigate trends, for example, where the segregation of BAME prisoners is disproportionate to their representation in the general prison's population;
• identify individual prisoners whose cases may need scrutiny. For example, prisoners who have spent more than 3 months in continuous segregation; prisoners who may have spent relatively short, but frequent periods in segregation; prisoners in the segregation unit on an open ACCT or in ACCT post-closure phase; prisoners segregated despite medical recommendations to the contrary.

### Section 3: Authorisation of Segregation Beyond 42 days – Adult Prisoners and Young Adults Held in YOIs
### Authority

3.1 To allow Segregation Review Boards (SRBs) to renew authorisation for continuous segregation beyond 42 days (6 weeks) from the day the prisoner was first placed in segregation, the following reviews must be carried out by an experienced and competent senior official at the specified below grades, as a minimum. It is for the Prison Group Director (PGD) or Head of Privately Managed Prisons to determine the experience and competence of the senior official to ensure they are confident in their decision-making ability for these authorisations. Reviews can also continue to be undertaken at a higher grade if this is determined by the PGD or Head of Privately Managed Prisons.

3.2 The senior official may give such leave for the SRB to continue to renew authority every 14 days for a further period which in total amounts to up to 42 days. This new period of leave starts from the day on which leave is given. The senior official may decide to give leave for a period of less than 42 days where it is considered that continued segregation is appropriate but where the senior official feels that there is a need to review that case again sooner.

3.3 For prisoners who have transferred direct from one segregation unit to another, the 42 days in continuous segregation is calculated by including time spent in segregation in the previous establishment.

First Review – Minimum of a Band 8 Senior Manager in PGD's office/HQ or minimum of Band 8 Senior Manager from the Controller Team in a privately managed prison or minimum of a Band 8 Senior Manager in the Head of Privately Managed Prisons Office.

3.4 Where the SRB consider that it may be necessary to continue to renew authority for segregation of a prisoner beyond 42 days then the form at Annex D4 (OT030) must be prepared by an operational manager and submitted to the B8 Senior Manager in the PGD's office or HQ, or minimum of Band 8 in the Controller Team in a privately managed prison, including a Band 8 Senior Manager from the Controller Team at the same prison where the prisoner is segregated, or Band 8 Senior Manager in the Head of Privately Managed Prisons Office for privately managed prisons (the First Reviewer) in sufficient time for a First Review to be undertaken. This form must have attached any paperwork relevant to the segregation that the prisoner has not had sight of. Where the case involves a vulnerable prisoner, including a prisoner on an open or post closure phase ACCT, the prison must attach any relevant additional information, for example healthcare reports, to the form.

3.5 The purpose of the First Review is for the First Reviewer to consider whether segregation is appropriate and whether there are sufficient reasons for continuing segregation beyond the 42 day period. This First Review may be conducted by correspondence or may be undertaken during a visit to an establishment where the First Reviewer may wish to discuss the case and, if required, see the prisoner. The First Reviewer may request any further paperwork relating to the prisoner's segregation prior to making a decision. If the review is conducted at a prison visit, the form at Annex D4 (OT030) must still be completed and signed by the First Reviewer. It is the responsibility of the prison to ensure that the review is scheduled appropriately.

3.6 The prisoner must be allowed to make representations at this review stage if he or she chooses to do so. These representations may be in the form of written representations by the prisoner or made orally by the prisoner and recorded by the prison. The representations should be recorded on the form at Annex D3 (OT029).

3.7 Following the First Review, the First Reviewer may give leave for the SRB to continue to renew authorisation of segregation for a period of up to 42 days. If the First Reviewer gives leave for the SRB to continue to renew authority for segregation, the SRB must continue

to meet within 14 days intervals to authorise any further periods of segregation. The SRB must meet within 14 days of the last SRB and not 14 days from the date of the First review.

3.8 If the First Reviewer does not give leave, the prison must make arrangements to ensure that the prisoner is removed from segregation at the earliest opportunity or by the date specified by the First Reviewer on the form at Annex D4.

**Delegation of First Review Authority**

3.9 Decision making must not be delegated below a Band 8 Senior Manager, or Band 8 Senior Manager in the Controller Team in a privately managed prison or Band 8 Senior Manager in the Head of Privately Managed Prisons Office. If the usual decision maker is unavailable, for public prisons another Band 8 Senior Manager (or more senior official) working to the PGD or in HQ who the PGD has deemed experienced and competent must make the decision. For privately managed prisons, another Band 8 Senior manager in the Head of Privately Manged Prisons Office who the Head of Privately Manged Prisons has deemed experienced and competent must make the decision. The person must not however, be working in or on secondment from the prison at which the prisoner is segregated except that this person can include a member of the Controller Team in a Privately Managed prison, at the same prison where the prisoner is segregated.

**Quality Assurance of First Reviews**

3.10 Quality assurance of 10% of First Reviews should be undertaken by an official more senior than a Band 8 who is working to the PGD or in HQ, or more senior that the Band 8 in the Controller Team in a privately managed prison or Band 8 Senior Manager in the Head of Privately Managed Prisons Office. Quality assurance should consider whether decisions are fair, consistent and taken without bias; whether segregation remains desirable under Prison Rule 45 (YOI Rule 49) and whether there are sufficient reasons for the segregation. Outcomes from the quality assurance must be recorded and decision re-taken if the quality assurer disagrees with the continued segregation.

Subsequent Review – A minimum of Band 9 Senior Manager in the PGD's office or from the Controller Team in a privately managed prison, including a minimum of a Band 9 from the Controller Team at the same prison where the prisoner is segregated, or a minimum of a Band 9 Senior Manager in the Head of Privately Managed Prisons Office.

3.11 Where the SRB consider that it may be necessary to continue to renew authority for segregation of a prisoner for a further 42 days then the form at Annex D4 (OT030) must be prepared by an operational manager and submitted to the B9 Senior Manager in the PGD's office or HQ, or a minimum of Band 9 Senior Manager from the Controller Team in a privately managed prison, including a minimum of a Band 9 from the Controller Team at the same prison where the prisoner is segregated, or a minimum of a Band 9 Senior Manager in the Head of Privately Managed Prisons Office (the Subsequent Reviewer) in sufficient time for the Subsequent Review to be undertaken. This form must have attached any paperwork relevant to the segregation that the prisoner has not had sight of. Where the case involves a vulnerable prisoner, including a prisoner on an open or post closure phase ACCT, the prison must attach any relevant additional information, for example healthcare reports, to the form.

3.12 The purpose of the Subsequent Review is for the Subsequent Reviewer to consider whether segregation is appropriate and whether there are sufficient reasons for continuing segregation for a further 42 day period. This Subsequent Review may be conducted by correspondence or may be undertaken during a visit to an establishment where the Subsequent Reviewer may wish to discuss the case and, if required, see the prisoner. The Subsequent Reviewer may request any further paperwork relating to the prisoner's segregation prior to making a decision. If the review is conducted at a prison visit, the form at Annex D4 (OT030) must still be completed and signed by the Subsequent Reviewer. It is the responsibility of the prison to ensure that the review is scheduled appropriately.

3.13 The prisoner must be allowed to make representations at this review stage if he or she chooses to do so. These representations may be in the form of written representations by the prisoner or made orally by the prisoner and recorded by the prison. The representations should be recorded on the form at Annex D3 (OT029).

3.14 Following the Subsequent Review, the Subsequent Reviewer may give leave for the SRB to continue to renew authorisation of segregation for a further period of up to 42 days. If the Subsequent Reviewer gives leave for the SRB to continue to renew authority for segregation, the SRB must continue to meet within 14 days intervals to authorise any further periods of segregation. The SRB must meet within 14 days of the last SRB and not 14 days from the date of the First review.

3.15 If the Subsequent Reviewer does not give leave, the prison must make arrangements to ensure that the prisoner is removed from segregation at the earliest opportunity or by the date specified by the Subsequent Reviewer on

the form at Annex D4 (OT030).

3.16 The Subsequent Reviewer must not give leave for the Governor/Director to continue to renew authorisation for more than 84 days from the prisoner's initial segregation without carrying out a Subsequent Review. This follows the same procedures as for First Review above with the exception that a fuller set of documentation is required (see 3.17 below).

3.17 An operational manager must prepare a report for the Subsequent Reviewer to consider at the Subsequent Review stage. In addition to the information submitted for a First Review, the operational manager must also enclose all previous SRB reports including the OT026 in order to evidence the reasons why segregation is continuing; the initial segregation safety algorithm; any subsequent reports from healthcare; ACCT reports or any other reports relating to the prisoner's wellbeing; all prisoner representations to-date; any other documents which have been considered by the SRB as relevant to the decision to continue segregation.

3.18 The report must be sent to the Subsequent Reviewer to allow sufficient time for the review to be undertaken within the 84 days (12 week) minimum period.

3.19 The Subsequent Reviewer must carry out a Subsequent Review at or before each subsequent 42 day period and consider at each review whether to give leave to the SRB to continue to renew authority for segregation for a period of up to 42 days. Annex A shows a summary of the process and Annex B sets out an example of a typical timeline.

### Quality Assurance of Subsequent Reviews

3.20 Quality assurance of 10% of Subsequent Reviews should be undertaken by an official more senior than a Band 9 who is working to the PGD or in HQ, or someone more senior than the Band 9 Senior Manager from the Controller Team in a privately managed prison or Senior Manager in the Head of Privately Managed Prisons Office. Quality assurance should consider whether decisions are fair, consistent and taken without bias; whether segregation remains desirable under Prison Rule 45 (YOI Rule 49); and whether there are sufficient reasons for the segregation. The quality assurance must also consider the documents listed in 3.13. Outcomes from the quality assurance must be recorded and decision re-taken if the quality assurer disagrees with the continued segregation.

### Prison Group Director/Deputy Director Review Procedures

3.21 Where a prisoner has been in continuous segregation for a period of 6 months (182 days) a

review must be carried out by the Prison Group Director (PGD) or Deputy Director (DD), or minimum of a Band 11 Head of Privately Managed Prisons for privately managed prisons.
3.22 The first stage is for a Subsequent Review report to be prepared by the prison for the Subsequent Reviewer to consider in line with para 3.16 above. If the Subsequent Reviewer agrees with continuing segregation then the report and OT032 will be sent to the relevant PGD/DD, or Band 11 Head of Privately Managed Prisons for privately managed prisons (6 Month Reviewer) to consider using the PGD/DD Review form (OT032) at Annex D6 and leaving at least 7 days for the 6 Month Reviewer to review the segregation.
3.23 The 6 Month Reviewer must undertake this review him or herself. This cannot be delegated other than where the 6 Month Reviewer is away from duties for an extended period of time such as annual leave when a deputy of the same or higher grade may be nominated to take on this role.
3.24 If the 6 Month Reviewer gives leave for the SRB to continue to authorise segregation, the 6 Month Reviewer will specify on the form at Annex D6 when the next 6 Month Reviewer review must take place within a maximum period of 6 months (182 days). The 6 Month Reviewer may decide to give leave for continued segregation for a shorter period than 6 months. In this case the review must be referred back to the Subsequent Reviewer at the earlier stage specified and, if segregation is still required, onto the 6 Month Reviewer for further consideration. It is for the prison to ensure that these timescales are noted when the form is returned and are acted upon. The 6 Month Reviewer Review does not replace the need for a First Review at least every 42 days.

### Section 4: Authorisation of extended single separation arrangements beyond initial 21 days – Young People

4.1 This section applies to children and Young People aged 15-17 held in Young Offender Institutions (YOIs). It must be read in conjunction with the operational practice document, Separation and Segregation, issued in June 2015; the Policy Framework Managing and Minimising isolation and separation in the CYPSE and accompanying Operational Expectations for YOIs, which were both issued in April 2022.
4.2 Although the Young Offender Institution Rules as amended provide that the governor must obtain leave from the Secretary of State in writing to authorise continuing separation beyond 42 days, as a matter of policy, children

and Young People cannot be separated beyond 21 days without this leave being obtained.
4.3 The deadlines which are set out here should also apply to instances of self-isolation, which should be managed with the same oversight as separation arrangements instigated to manage risk of serious harm to the child or others.

### Authority and powers of delegation

4.2 The Deputy Director (DD) of Operations for the Youth Custody Service must give leave in writing to allow SRBs to renew authorisation for separation arrangements to remain in place for a continuous period beyond 21 days (3 weeks) from the date the child or Young Person was removed to CSU. This power cannot be delegated.
4.3 The DD may give such leave for the SRB to renew authority for further periods of up to 21 days. This 21 day period starts from the day on which leave is given. The DD may decide to give leave for a period of less than 21 days where it is considered that continued placement in a CSU is appropriate but where it is felt that there is a need to review that case again sooner by the DD.
4.4 For children and Young People who have transferred direct from one establishment to another whilst subject to separation arrangements, the continuous period for separation is calculated by including time spent subject to separation in the previous establishment.

### DD Review

4.5 Where the SRB consider that it may be necessary to continue to renew authority for a child or Young Person to be subject to separation arrangements beyond 21 days from the day that they started, then the form at Annex D5 must be prepared by an operational manager and submitted with the accompanying paperwork to the DD in sufficient time for a DD Review to be undertaken.
4.6 Accompanying paperwork will include: all previous SRB reports, the initial separation healthcare algorithm; any subsequent reports from healthcare; ACCT reports or any other reports relating to the child or Young Person's wellbeing; all representations received to-date from the child or Young Person themselves; any other documents which have been considered by the SRB as relevant to the decision to continue placement in a CSU, or not.
4.7 The purpose of the DD Review is for the DD to consider whether an extension to the separation arrangement is appropriate and whether there are sufficient reasons for continuing this beyond the 21 day period. The DD Review may be conducted by correspondence or may be undertaken during the

DD's routine visit to establishments where the DD may wish to discuss the case and, if required, see the child or Young Person. If the review is conducted during an establishment visit, the form at Annex D5 must still be completed and signed by the DD and the accompanying paperwork must still be available. It is the responsibility of the establishment to ensure that the review is scheduled appropriately.

4.8 The child or Young Person must be allowed to make representations at this review stage if he or she chooses to do so. These representations may be in the form of written or oral representations by the child or Young Person and recorded by the establishment. The representations should be recorded on the form at Annex D3.

4.9 Following a DD Review, the DD may give leave for the SRB to continue to renew authorisation of separation arrangements for a period of up to 21 days. If the DDC gives leave for the SRB to continue to renew authority, the SRB must continue to meet within 14 day intervals to authorise any further extension to separation arrangements. The SRB must meet within 14 days of the last SRB and not 14 days from the date of the DD review.

4.10 If the DD does not give leave, the establishment must make arrangements to ensure that the separation arrangements are suspended at the earliest opportunity or by the date specified by the DD on the form at Annex D5.

**Delegation of DD Authority**

4.11 The DD or equivalent (as listed in 4.2 above) must undertake these Reviews which cannot be routinely delegated. The authority of those taking the decision for prolonged segregation for young people has not been lowered. This is due to Youth Custody Service wishing to continue to have more senior oversight of the segregation of children.

4.12 In order to ensure that timescales for reviews can be adhered to, any DD or equivalent may nominate a deputy to act on his/her behalf for any CSU review whilst he/she is away from normal duties for an extended period of time such as for annual leave. The deputy must meet the criteria set out in the paragraph above.

**Executive Director (ED) Review Procedures**

4.13 Where a child or Young Person been subject to separation arrangements for a continuous period of 91 days (3 months) a review must be carried out by the Executive Director (ED) of the Youth Custody Service.

4.14 The first stage in this is for a DD Review report to be prepared by the establishment for the DD to consider in line with para 4.5 above. If the DD agrees with continuing the separation arrangements, then the report will be sent to the

ED to consider using the Director Review form at Annex D7 leaving at least 7 days for the ED to review the case. The relevant ED may carry out such a review at any point but must review each separation once in each 3 month period. The ED Review does not replace the need for a DD Review at least every 21 days.

4.15 The ED must undertake this review him or herself. This cannot be delegated other than where the ED is away from duties for an extended period of time such as annual leave when a deputy may be nominated to take on this role provided that the deputy is not performing the DD role for that review.

4.16 If the ED gives leave for the SRB to continue with separation arrangements, the ED will specify on the form at Annex D7 when the next ED review must take place within a maximum period of 91 days. The ED may decide to give leave for the SRB to continue reviewing separation arrangements for a shorter period than 91 days. In this case the review must be referred back to the DD at the earlier stage specified and if placement in a CSU is still required, onto the ED for further consideration. It is for the establishment to ensure that these timescales are noted when the form is returned and are acted upon. The ED Review does not replace the need for a DD Review at least every 21 days.

4.17 The DD and ED must receive the form at Annex D5/D7 and paperwork for any reviews in sufficient time for the review to be processed before the expiry date.

**Section 5: Authorisation for Temporary Confinement in Special Accommodation**

Use of Temporary Confinement

5.1 Temporary Confinement in Special Accommodation is authorised under Prison Rule 48 (YOI Rule 51). Special Accommodation is a dedicated cell or improvised normal accommodation from which any one (or more than one) of the following items is removed in the interests of safety: - furniture, bedding, sanitation. Special Accommodation can be located anywhere in the prison - a cell from which normal furniture has been removed and replaced with chairs for the purpose of holding several prisoners pending adjudication, is not regarded as Special Accommodation.

5.2 Special Accommodation is used for the shortest time necessary to prevent a violent or refractory prisoner injuring others (as a result of the violent or refractory behaviour), damaging property or creating a disturbance that hinders the maintenance of good order. Non-compliance is not, in itself, sufficient to justify Special Accommodation unless that non-compliance represents an immediate and serious risk of harm to the prisoner themselves, to others, to property or to the good order of the establishment.

5.3 Special Accommodation must only be used to manage prisoners who cannot be located safely in normal accommodation. If the prisoner can be held safely in normal accommodation (which includes "normal" cells in the segregation unit), the use of Special Accommodation is not appropriate.

5.4 Further details on the use and safeguards relating to Special Accommodation may be found in PSO 1700 which includes policy on who to notify when a prisoner is placed in Special Accommodation; procedures necessary to safeguard prisoners including health and ACCT issues; security and observation requirements; particular arrangements for Young People; monitoring requirements and removal from Special Accommodation.

**Authorisation Process for Temporary Confinement**

5.5 A prisoner must not be placed in Temporary

**ANNEX A1 - Flow Chart illustrating the process from April 2022**

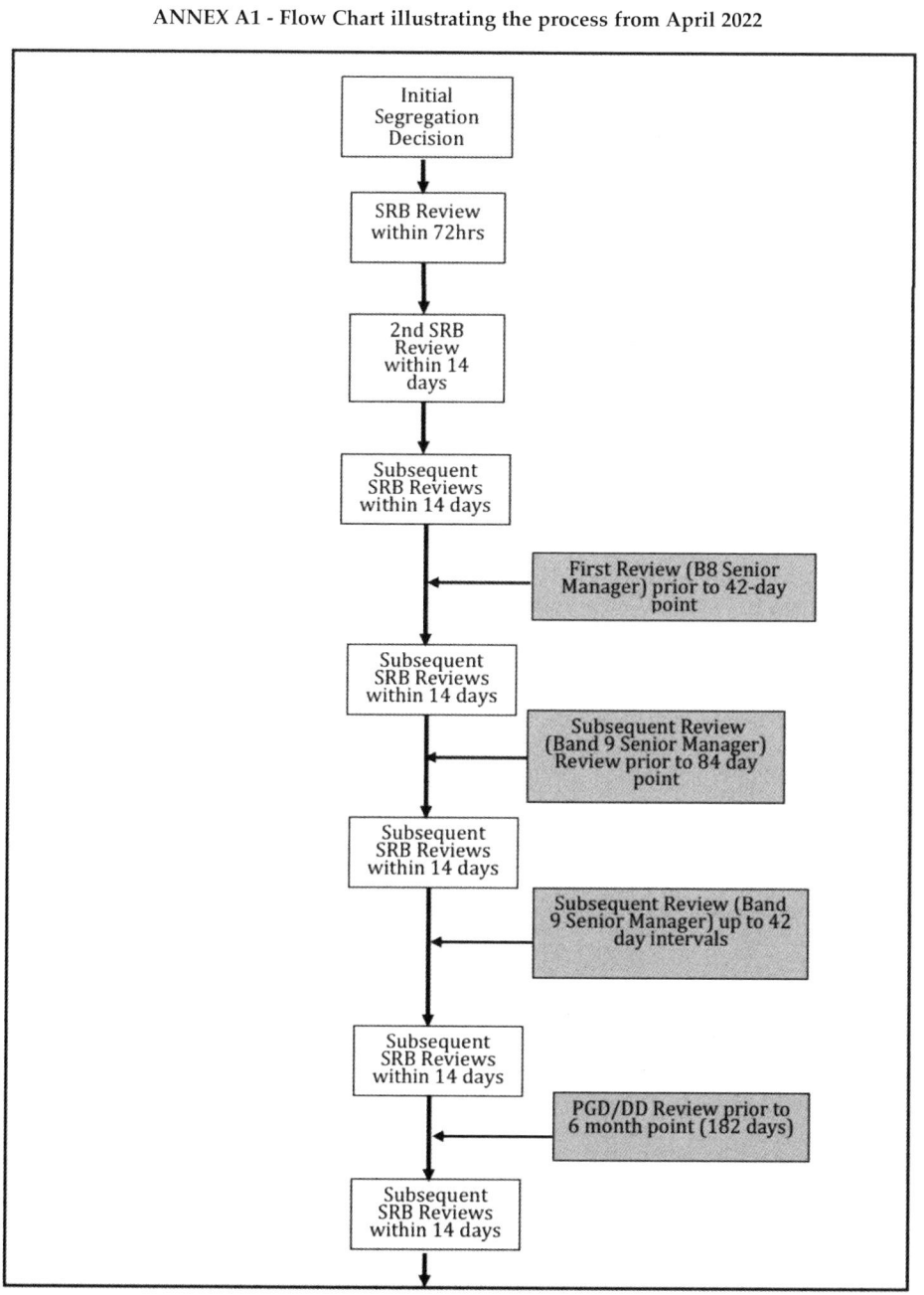

Confinement in Special Accommodation without the prior authority of the Duty Governor/Duty Director.

5.6 Special Accommodation is used for the shortest time necessary. As soon as Special Accommodation is no longer necessary, the prisoner must be removed. It is not necessary for a Review to be held in order for a prisoner to be removed from Special Accommodation.

5.7 The authority of the duty governor is valid for a maximum of 24 hours and must be recorded on Form OT013. If it is considered necessary that a prisoner remain in Special Accommodation beyond 24 hours, a direction must be obtained from the relevant PGD/DD or Head of Privately Managed Prisons using the procedures set out in the following section.

**Procedure for location in Special Accommodation beyond 24 hours**

5.8 If it is anticipated that a prisoner will need to remain in Special Accommodation beyond 24

ANNEX A2 - Flow chart comparing old and new segregation systems – Young People

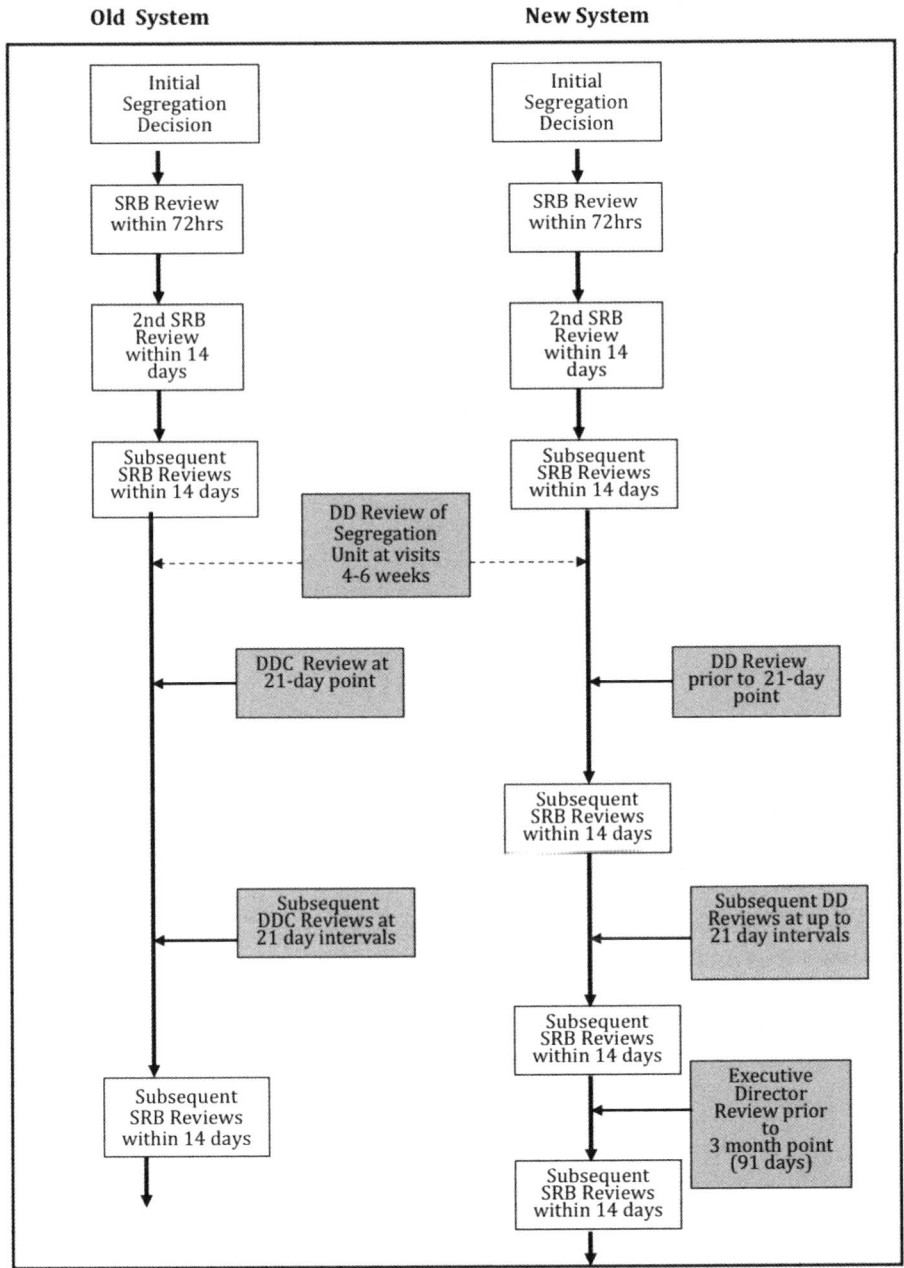

981

hours, then a direction must be obtained from the PGD. The form at Annex D1 must be submitted to the PGD/DD or Head of Privately Managed Prisons in sufficient time to enable a decision to be taken before the 24 hour point is reached.

5.9 The request to the PGD/DD or Head of Privately Managed Prisons to direct a prisoner remaining in Special Accommodation beyond 24 hours must be informed by a Case Review as set out in PSO 1700.

5.10 Any direction from the PGD/DD or Head of Privately Managed Prisons for continuing confinement in Special Accommodation will specify in writing the grounds for confinement and state the period authorised for continuing confinement. Other than in exceptional circumstances this will normally be 24 hours. The direction must be renewed prior to expiry of this period.

**Quick Summary of Review Rules**
• 1st SRB Review must be within the first 72 hours following initial segregation.
• 2nd SRB Review must be within 14 days of the 1st review.
• All subsequent SRB reviews must also be within 14 days of the last SRB review.
• In addition to the SRB cycle of reviews –
The B8 Senior Manager by way of a First Review must give leave for continuing segregation

**ANNEX B**
**Timing for Segregation Review Board Decisions**

**B1  Adult Prison example of review timing**

| | Time from Previous stage | Total time from initial segregation |
|---|---|---|
| Initial Segregation | - | 0 days |
| 1st SRB Review | 72hrs | 3 days (72hrs) |
| 2nd SRB Review | 10 days | 13 days |
| 3rd SRB Review | 14 days | 27 days |
| 4th SRB Review | 12 days | 39 days* |

First Review by Band 8 Senior Manager signed at 40 days giving leave for continuing segregation for a further 42 days up to 82 days.

| | | |
|---|---|---|
| 5th SRB Review | 12 days | 51 days |
| 6th SRB Review | 11 days | 62 days |
| 7th SRB Review | 13 days | 75 days* |

Subsequent Review by Band 9 Senior Manager signed at 81 days giving leave for continuing segregation up to 123 days.

| | | |
|---|---|---|
| 8th SRB Review | 14 days | 93 days |
| 9th SRB Review | 10 days | 103 days |
| 10th SRB Review | 13 days | 116 days* |

Subsequent Review by Band 9 Senior Manager signed at 120 days giving leave for continuing segregation up to 162 days.

| | | |
|---|---|---|
| 11th SRB Review | 14 days | 129 days |
| 12th SRB Review | 14 days | 143 days |
| 13th SRB Review | 12 days | 155 days* |

Subsequent Review by Band 9 Senior Manager signed at 160 days giving leave for continuing segregation up to 182 days which is the maximum for a Band 9 Senior Manager Review before referral to the Prison Group Director/ Deputy Director or Head of Privately Managed Prisons.

| | | |
|---|---|---|
| 14th SRB Review | 10 days | 165 days |
| 15th SRB Review | 10 days | 175 days* |

First Prison Group Director or Deputy Director Review Head of Privately Managed Prisons
**signed at 180 days giving leave for continuing segregation for a further 182 days (6 months)
(Report to go via Band 9 Senior Manager)

The cycles of SRB, Subsequent and Prison Group Director/Deputy Director reviews then repeat. The First Review is only done once.

\*      Review reports to be sent to PDG/DD offices leaving sufficient time for the reviews to take place prior to expiry of any previous leave.
\*\*    Reviews requiring Prison Group Director or Deputy Director authority must be sent via the Band 9 Senior Manager at least 7 days in advance of the previous leave for segregation expiring.

beyond 42 days of initial segregation (21 days for Young People)

The First review is not a replacement for the SRB review which must continue if the Band 8 Senior Manager gives leave for continuation of segregation.

If the Band 9 Senior Manager gives leave for continuing segregation beyond 42 days during the Subsequent Review (21 days for Young People) then this will be for a further maximum of 42 (21) days from the date of the First Review.

**The level of authority of Segregation Reviews for the Contracted Estate is:**

• First Review prior to 42 days of continuous segregation – Band 8 in the Controller Team in a privately managed prison, including a Band 8 at the same prison where the prisoner is segregated, or a Band 8 Senior Manager in the Head of Privately Managed Prisons Office.

• Subsequent Review if segregation is to continue beyond 84 days – a minimum of Band 9 Senior Manager from the Controller Team in a privately managed prison, including a minimum of a Band 9 from the Controller Team at the same prison where the prisoner is segregated, or a minimum of a Band 9 Senior Manager in the Head of Privately Managed Prisons Office.

• Review if segregation is to continue beyond 6 months – minimum of a Band 11 Head of Privately Managed Prisons.

• During that further 42 (21) day period SRBs must continue to meet on a maximum 14-day cycle from the date of the last SRB review (not from the date of the First Review which is a different type of review).

• Prior to continuous segregation of 182 days (6 months) or 91 Days (3 months) the Band 9 Senior Manager will refer the case to the appropriate Prison Group Director or Deputy Director to review.

Examples for adults and young people are shown below:

**B2 Young People Establishment example of review timing**

| | Time from Previous stage | Total time from initial segregation |
|---|---|---|
| Initial Segregation | - | 0 days |
| 1st SRB Review | 72hrs | 3 days (72hrs) |
| 2nd SRB Review | 14 days | 17 days* |

First DDC Review signed off at 21 days giving leave for continuing segregation for a further 21 days up to 42 days.

| | | |
|---|---|---|
| 3rd SRB Review | 14 days | 31 days |
| 4th SRB Review | 8 days | 39 days* |

Second DDC Review signed off at 40 days giving leave for continuing segregation up to 61 days.

| | | |
|---|---|---|
| 5th SRB Review | 7 days | 46 days |
| 9th SRB Review | 12 days | 58 days* |

Third DDC Review signed off at 60 days giving leave for continuing segregation up to 71 days.

Process continues as necessary up to 91-day point at which

The cycles of SRB, DDC reviews continue up until the 91-day (3 month) point is reached when the Director must review and give leave for continuing segregation.

First Director Review prior to 91 days giving leave for continuing segregation for a further 91 days (3 months)
(Report to go via DDC)

The cycles of SRB, DDC and Director reviews then repeat.

\* Review reports to be sent to DDC/Director offices leaving sufficient time for the reviews to take place prior to expiry of any previous leave.

\*\* Reviews requiring Director authority must be sent via the DDC at least 7 days in advance of the previous leave for segregation expiring.

983

**ANNEX C**

Further guidance for continuing segregation under Rule 45 (YOI Rule 49)

**1.** The Review Board must consider the areas set out below taking into consideration any representations the prisoner may wish to make (see 2.20 in main body above):

**a) The initial reason(s) for segregation**

The initial reason for the prisoner being segregated is an important element of defining what behaviour/attitudes need to be addressed before the prisoner may return to normal accommodation.

**b) Behaviour and attitude of the prisoner since initial segregation/last review**

Prisoners in segregation for periods of more than 72 hours should be set behaviour/attitude targets in order to start to work towards returning to normal accommodation. The extent to which the prisoner has met these targets should be discussed by the Board.

**c) Any concerns that may have come to light about how the prisoner is coping with segregation (mental health/self-harm concerns)**

This section is to specifically highlight the fact that research indicates that a person's mental health is likely to decline when they are kept in segregation. The Board must consider any observations or concerns raised by a member of staff (including Healthcare) or the prisoner about their ability to cope in segregation. The Segregation Review Board must consider additional steps to safeguard the mental health of prisoners whilst in segregation or must fully consider advice from Healthcare.

Prisoners in segregation are likely to be at an increased risk of self-harm or suicide. The Review Board should consider whether an ACCT should be opened for those prisoners located in segregation who are not already subject to ACCT procedures. PSI 64/2011 sets out further information on Safer Custody issues.

Governors should ensure that staff are aware of the potential effects of segregation on a prisoner's state of mind and begin ACCT procedures if they observe any changes in a prisoner's behaviour or circumstances, which indicate an increase in the risk of suicide or self-harm.

A prisoner does not have to have harmed themselves, or even spoken of doing so, for it to be appropriate to open an ACCT. The full range of risk factors, as set out in PSI 64/2011, including significant changes to the prisoner's behaviour or mood should be considered.

**d) Behavioural targets**

At the 72 hour review, the SRB must set targets so that the prisoner can demonstrate a willingness and ability to change the behaviour that led to segregation in the first instance. The targets should be:

• reasonable (not beyond the grasp or understanding of the 'average' prisoner)
• specific (clearly defined)
• relevant (to the reason for segregation in the first place)
• time-bound (be able to be completed before the next Review Board)

For example: If the prisoner is in segregation for repeatedly losing their temper and shouting / threatening staff and other prisoners, then behaviour targets may be:

• not raising voice at any person for the next 7 days
• not using aggressive/abusive language towards any person for the next 7 days

Intervention targets may be:

• seeing the psychologist once in the next 10 days to discuss anger management techniques
• listening to a relaxation recording provided by the library at least 3 times in the next 10 days

It is imperative that staff of all disciplines work with the prisoner during the period between reviews and provide interventions if necessary.

The Board may feel that targets set for a particular week/specified time period may need to be repeated several times before the Board will believe that a real change/willingness to change has been demonstrated by the prisoner so that it is no longer desirable to segregate them in accordance with Prison Rule 45 (YOI Rule 49). Willingness to comply with the targets set however, should lead to improved regime/ being offered to the prisoner.

**e) Rewards or incentives to be awarded or removed**

The Segregation Review Board must inform the prisoner of the regime that will be available to them. The SRB assesses the extent to which the prisoner has met or been willing to meet some/all of the targets set at the last Review Board. The Board decides whether to award any improvements to the regime & rewards/ incentives that the prisoner is currently offered. These may be granted either as rewards or incentives to encourage better behaviour.

The Review Board may feel that the prisoner has failed to meet or make any effort to meet the targets set at the last review. In such cases, the Board may decide to remove privileges or elements of the segregation regime that the prisoner currently has. A decision to remove a radio should be given careful consideration and should not be taken lightly. Further consideration should be given to the period of time the radio is removed and any changes in the behaviour/mental health the removal may have on the prisoner.

**f) Transfer to another establishment**

The Segregation Review Board should consider whether they think that the prisoner needs to be transferred to another establishment. Prisoners should be informed if they are being considered for transfer to another establishment (except on security grounds for Category A and E list prisoners). If this news is likely to lead to significant disruption or violence then the prison may decide to move the prisoner without notice. If a transfer is to take place, a copy of the Segregation Review Board notes and pre-transfer form must be sent in advance of transfer the receiving prison.

**g) Prisoners who refuse to Leave Segregation**
It is recognised that some prisoners refuse to leave segregation. The SRB must consider and make note of, the reasons for the prisoner's refusal to return to normal /other location. The actions to take in order to remove the prisoner from segregation will depend on the circumstances of the individual case, but might include giving a direct order to return to the wing with refusal leading to disciplinary action, or a review of the prisoner's IEP level. The prisoner must be made aware of the consequences of any refusal to leave segregation. Where a prisoner is refusing to leave segregation due to a genuine fear of reprisals, then consideration must be given to his or her future allocation.

**2.** Prisoners segregated for more than 30 days should be subject to care plans that detail how their mental well-being is to be supported.

**3.** Particular care should be given to authorising continued segregation of a prisoner on an open ACCT or an ACCT in post-closure phase. Continued segregation should occur only in exceptional circumstances and an ACCT case review must take place at the same time as the Segregation Review Board. If a prisoner needs to be segregated from others, but is considered to be at a high risk of suicide, the Board should increase the frequency level of observations to a minimum of 5 times an hour at irregular intervals or otherwise as stated in the ACCT care plan. This applies to the first 72 hours of segregation as well as continuing segregation beyond 72 hours.

**Paperwork the Segregation Review Board must complete**
**a.** The form Segregation Review Board – Governor's Continued Authority for Segregation will be completed by the Board and provides a record of the Board meeting and what was discussed and decided. This document must be signed by an operational manager or duty director in a contracted prison for continued segregation to be authorised.
**b.** The member of the Independent Monitoring Board (where present) signs the Review Board

form to demonstrate their attendance as an observer. The IMB member should also indicate their satisfaction or otherwise, that the correct procedures were followed by the SRB and that the decision was reasonable – Governor's Continued Authority for Segregation
**c.** The form Notification to Prisoners of Outcome of Segregation Review Board & Segregation Privileges and Behaviour Targets is completed by the Board and a copy given to the prisoner. This form tells the prisoner the basis for the decision to continue segregation and what regime / privileges they will have access to whilst in segregation, the date of the next Review Board and the targets that the Board have set for the intervening period.

**Annex D**
New or amended segregation forms (available separately)
**Amended Forms**
D1. OT019: Location in Special Accommodation - 24hr Case Review
D1.2 OT025: Authority for Continued Segregation
D2. OT027: Notification to Prisoner of Outcome of Segregation Review Board and Segregation Privileges and Behavioural Targets

**Forms**
D3. OT029: Prisoner representations against segregation
D4. OT030: First and Subsequent Review of segregation -adults
D5. OT031: DD review of separation – Children or Young People D6. OT032: PGD/DD review of segregation -adults
D7. OT033: Director review of separation – Children or Young People
D8. Interim Area Monitoring Form for Segregation – pending national system

**Annex E**
**The Monitoring Function**
Governors should ensure that a Segregation Monitoring & Review Group (SMARG) is set up in order to review and monitor segregation. The following people should be considered for membership of the monitoring group:
• Operational manager/Director with responsibility for the segregation unit;
• Segregation unit staff member(s);
• Chaplain;
• Member of the Healthcare team;
• Psychologist;
• Probation and or an offender supervisor (particularly when the prisoner is in scope of offender management);
• Safer Custody lead.
• IMB Member (in the role of observer/monitor)

985

## Mandatory Actions

Monthly data on prisoners in segregation must be sent to the PGD within 7 days of the end of each month setting out numbers of prisoners held in segregation during that month under Rule 45 (YOI Rule 49) by the following time period – numbers in continuous segregation for: *up to 72 hrs; 72hrs to 1 week; 1-2 weeks; 2-3 weeks; 3-4 weeks; 4-5 weeks; 5-6 weeks; 6- 12 weeks; 12-16 weeks; 16-20 weeks; 20-24 weeks; 24-28 weeks and total prisoners segregated beyond 28 weeks.*

Total numbers of prisoners in segregation under Rule 45 (YOI Rule 49) who are on an ACCT, or in ACCT post-closure phase, must also be recorded. An interim form for this is shown at Annex D8 pending development of a national system.

A quarterly report must be submitted to the Governor and to the PGD/DD highlighting the key observations and summarising the use of segregation over the previous quarter. A copy of the report should also be sent to the Safer Custody lead as much of the contents in SMARG crosses over with Safer Custody meetings. As a minimum, the report should:

**a.** Identify and investigate general areas of concern, for example, where the segregation unit is not meeting the PSO / Review Board timetable / where ethnic statistics on BAME prisoners on segregation give cause for concern due to being disproportionate to the general population in the establishment.

**b.** Identify individual prisoners that need scrutiny e.g. prisoners who have spent more than 3 months in continuous segregation; prisoners who have spent short but frequent periods in segregation; those on an open ACCT or in ACCT post-closure phase; prisoners who the healthcare team have indicated should no longer be segregated.

A member of the Independent Monitoring Board should be invited to attend the SMARG meetings (where held) as an observer and should be provided with a copy of the quarterly report. Members of the IMB must not take any management decisions.

The SMARG must address and record the following:
• Percentage of Initial Segregation Health Screens completed within the 2-hour time period;
• Percentage of Segregation Review Boards held within the specified time limit;
• Average number of prisoners segregated each week;
• Analysis of the reasons for segregation (GOoD/own protection/Cellular Confinement);
• Number and percentage of BME prisoners held in segregation as a proportion of their percentage in the prison as a whole and as a percentage of the total number held in segregation (investigate in cases where this appears to be disproportionate);

• Number of occasions that personal protective equipment is used;
• Number of segregated prisoners with registered disabilities;
• Equality considerations such as whether segregated prisoners' protected characteristics such as age, disability, gender reassignment, race, religion and sexual orientation (Equality Act 2010) have in some way affected the behaviour of the prisoner, or influenced the responses of staff to the prisoner.
• Any prisoner who is held in segregation for a continuous period of 42 days or more (adult) or 21 days or more (Young Person) including periods in segregation in a previous prison for prisoners transferred from another prison's segregation unit;
• Prisoners held in Special Accommodation;
• Prisoners held in segregation whilst on an open ACCT (consider separating the figures for those prisoners placed in segregation whilst on an open ACCT and those that have an ACCT opened whilst in segregation);
• The number of prisoners removed from segregation on grounds of safety;
• Prisoners who are located in segregation against medical recommendation.

## Recommended Actions

It is recommended that the SMARG addresses the following:
• Undertake quality control checks on a random sample of documents such as Initial Segregation Health Screen, Daily Occurrence Log, Review Board write-ups;
• Analysis of the length of stay of prisoners in the segregation unit/or otherwise segregated;
• Percentage of adjudications that result in Cellular Confinement;
• Number of Request & Complaints relating to segregation which are upheld;
• Number of occasions where use of force has been used (record separately where use of force has been used to prevent self-harm);
• Number and percentage of prisoners subject to a full search on initial segregation;
• Number of prisoners issued with cardboard furniture;
• Length of time each member of staff has spent working in the segregation unit;
• Monitoring that staff are up to date with their training e.g. equality matters, C&R, mental health training, suicide awareness;
• Consider other training that staff should undertake.

## Annex F
### Amended Prison Rule 45. – Removal from association (Revised 4 September 2015)

(1) Where it appears desirable, for the maintenance of good order or discipline or in his own interests, that a prisoner should not associate with other prisoners, either generally or for particular purposes, the governor may arrange for the prisoner's removal from association for up to 72 hours.

(2) Removal for more than 72 hours may be authorised by the governor in writing who may authorise a further period of removal of up to 14 days.

(2A) Such authority may be renewed for subsequent periods of up to 14 days.

(2B) But the governor must obtain leave from the Secretary of State in writing to authorise removal under paragraph (2A) where the period in total amounts to more than 42 days starting with the date the prisoner was removed under paragraph (1).

(2C) The Secretary of State may only grant leave for a maximum period of 42 days, but such leave may be renewed for subsequent periods of up to 42 days by the Secretary of State.

(3) The governor may arrange at his discretion for a prisoner removed under this rule to resume association with other prisoners at any time.

(3A) In giving authority under paragraphs (2) and (2A) and in exercising the discretion under paragraph (3), the governor must fully consider any recommendation that the prisoner resumes association on medical grounds made by a registered medical practitioner or registered nurse working within the prison.

(4) This rule shall not apply to a prisoner the subject of a direction given under rule 46(1).

### Notes:

- The Governor may delegate authority to segregate under 45(2) to any competent Operational Manager.
- The DDC will usually exercise the authority of the Secretary of State under 45(2B) and 45(2C).
- Under 45(4) - Prison Rule 46(1) refers to Close Supervision Centres
- Identical amendments have been made to YOI Rule 49.

## 2.26 SECURITY CATEGORISATION

### Security Categorisation Policy Framework

Updated 13th May 2021: Introduces a presumption that prisoners who have been convicted of specified terrorist offences will be unsuitable for Category D/Open unless there are exceptional circumstances.

Introduces a requirement, when categorising terrorist offenders, to obtain and use input to the categorisation assessment from the Regional Counter-Terrorism Team.

Clarifies existing policy on eligibility for consideration for Category D/Open for prisoners serving a determinate sentence with a Parole Eligibility Date, including Extended Determinate Sentences (EDS), sentences for offenders convicted under the Terrorist Offenders (Restriction of Early Release) Act 2020 (TORERA), and Sentence for Offenders of Particular Concern (SOPC) under s236A of the Criminal Justice Act 2003.

Includes other minor and drafting changes to clarify existing policy.

Updated 17th August 2021: Minor changes made to clarify above changes in respect of terrorist and terrorist connected offences.

### This Policy Framework, cancels:

PSI 40/2011 Categorisation/Recategorisation of Adult Male Prisoners

PSI 41/2011 Categorisation/Recategorisation of Young Adult Male Prisoners

The roles described in this document use the Offender Management in Custody (OMiC) titles. Where this is not yet fully rolled out, equivalent roles apply.

### This framework applies to the categorisation and recategorisation of:

Male determinate and Indeterminate Sentence Prisoners (ISPs) who are not Category A or Restricted Status (RS). The Category A/ Restricted Status process is set out in PSI 9/2015, ('The Identification, Initial Categorisation and Management of Potential and Provisional Category A/Restricted Status Prisoners') and in PSI 8/2013, ('The Review of Security Category – Category A/Restricted Status Prisoners').

Civil Prisoners, who are treated in the same way as convicted prisoners for the purposes of categorisation (see PSO 4600 'Unconvicted, Unsentenced and Civil Prisoners').

It must be read in conjunction with policies and guidance relating to ISPs and Category A/Restricted Status.

**It does not apply to:**

The assessment of ISPs' suitability for open conditions which normally require a recommendation from the Parole Board. All such decisions sit with officials in Public Protection Casework Section (PPCS) on behalf of the Secretary of State.

The assessment of suitability for open conditions where an individual is serving a determinate sentence at the same time as an indeterminate sentence. All such decisions sit with officials in Public Protection Casework Section (PPCS) on behalf of the Secretary of State.

Individuals released on licence and then remanded into custody on new charges but who have not formally been recalled. These individuals should be treated as unconvicted.

Individuals held solely under Immigration powers (IS91s) to whom PSI 52/2011 'Immigration, Repatriation and Removal Services' applies.

## PURPOSE

1.1 Under Rule 7 Prison Rules 1999, subject to certain exceptions, "prisoners shall be classified, in accordance with any directions of the Secretary of State, having regard to their age, temperament and record and with a view to maintaining good order and facilitating training and, in the case of convicted prisoners, of furthering the purpose of their training and treatment".

1.2 Security Categorisation is a risk management process, the purpose of which is to ensure that those sentenced to custody are assigned the lowest security category appropriate to managing their risk of:

escape or abscond;

harm to the public;

ongoing criminality in custody;

violent or other behaviour that impacts the safety of those within the prison; and

control issues that disrupt the security and good order of the prison.

1.3 Effective security categorisation is fundamental to risk management and ensuring good order is maintained. It supports HMPPS's duty to implement the sentences of the courts; protect the public; and provide a safe, secure and ordered environment that enables the provision of rehabilitative services, training, treatment and progression through the prison system.

1.4 The security categorisation process provides for a holistic assessment of risk, taking account of a broad range of information from criminal justice and law enforcement agencies where available. It supports the categorisation of individuals to security conditions best suited to managing their risks. Categorisation is neither a reward for good, compliant behaviour nor used as a punishment. Any categorisation decision must be taken on risk factors alone.

1.5 Allocation is a separate process from categorisation, the purpose of which is to assign an individual to a suitably secure establishment which meets their needs effectively insofar as pressures on the estate allow. Categorisation is an independent process, so someone may be assigned a particular category even if it is not possible to allocate them to a prison of that category immediately.

1.6 Allocation decisions should consider the individual's offending behaviour and resettlement needs (such as access to suitable training and interventions and closeness to home at the end of their sentence), their individual circumstances (such as medical requirements), and control issues (such as danger to particular staff or other prisoners). This may result in an individual being held in a prison of a higher category than their own category.

## PROCEDURAL JUSTICE

2.1 When people believe the process of applying rules (how a decision is made rather than what decision is made, and how they are treated during the process) is fair, it influences their views and behaviour. There is robust evidence, from around the world, showing that people are much more likely to respect and comply with rules and authority willingly when they believe the way the rules are applied is fair and just. This is true even if the outcomes of decisions are not in their favour or are inconvenient for them.

2.2 Research from HMPPS, and from prison services around the world, shows that when individuals perceive authority to be used in a more procedurally just way, this is associated with significantly less misconduct and violence, better psychological health, lower rates of self-harm and attempted suicide, and lower rates of reoffending after release.

2.3 This framework sets out the processes to assess an individual's security categorisation in a fair and just manner and to evidence defensible decision making.

## SECURITY CATEGORY DEFINITIONS

3.1 Individuals are categorised according to the risk they present to security, safety and public protection, and must be held in a prison providing levels of security appropriate to managing identified risks.

3.2 Closed prisons have a secure perimeter and a range of internal security measures. For adult men, they are sub-divided into: Category C prisons, providing a level of physical and procedural security capable of safely and securely managing the majority of men; and

Category B prisons, providing additional physical and procedural security suitable for managing those identified as presenting a greater level of risk.

3.3 For young adults (age 18-20), closed prisons are not sub-divided but individual prisons may be designated as suitable for holding individuals presenting higher risks.

3.4 Open prisons have minimal perimeter and physical security features and are for those who are specifically assessed as suitable for conditions of low security.

3.5 In categorising an individual to a particular security category, the risk factors to be assessed are:
escape or abscond;
harm to the public;
ongoing criminality in custody;
violent or other behaviour that impacts the safety of those within the prison; and
control issues which disrupt the security and good order of the prison.

3.6 Individuals are then assigned to the lowest security category appropriate to managing their risks:

**CATEGORY D** (Adult Men), and Open (Young Adults): Offenders who are either assessed as presenting a low risk or whose previously identified risk factors are now assessed as manageable in low security conditions.

**CATEGORY C** (Adult Men): Offenders who are assessed as requiring standard closed conditions, and do not need additional security.

**CATEGORY B** (Adult Men): Offenders whose assessed risks require that they are held in the closed estate and who need security measures additional to those in a standard closed prison.

Closed (Young Adult s): Offenders assessed as requiring standard closed conditions and are not appropriate for open conditions.

## CATEGORY A AND RESTRICTED STATUS PRISONERS

4.1 Most Category A and Restricted Status individuals will have been reported in as potential Category A following reception on remand and will have been held as provisional Category A leading up to their sentence. Staff should, however, be alert to the need to identify those individuals who, after sentencing, present as potential Category A/RS.

4.2 A member of staff identifying a potential Category A or Restricted Status prisoner should notify the duty manager immediately.

4.3 For information purposes, the relevant descriptions are:

Category A : those whose escape would be highly dangerous to the public or the police or the security of the State and for whom the aim must be to make escape impossible.

Restricted Status: any male young person or young adult, convicted or on remand, whose escape would present a serious risk to the public and who is required to be held in designated secure accommodation.

4.4 Instructions on the identification and reporting in of potential Category A/RS are included in PSI 09/2015.

## CONSTRAINTS

5.1 An individual's security category must not be adjusted to achieve a better match with available spaces within the estate.

5.2 An individual must not be allocated to a prison of a lower security category than the security category assigned to them.

5.3 Security categorisation decisions must not be influenced by any matters irrelevant to the process. The categorisation process must not discriminate against people with the personal protected characteristics protected under the 2010 Equality Act: age, disability, gender reassignment, marriage or civil partnership, pregnancy and maternity, race, religion or belief, sex and sexual orientation.

5.4 Those with 28 days or less left to serve to earliest release at the point of initial categorisation, those individuals subject to Fixed Term Recall (FTR), and those recalled (Section 255 recall) from Home Detention Curfew (HDC) for breaching curfew conditions with less than 28 days left to serve, do not need to be categorised but will generally remain in the Reception prison for the duration of their time in custody. In circumstances where it is in their interest to be allocated to an alternative establishment or where operational needs mean they must be moved, they must first be categorised using the process described in this framework.

5.5 Individuals with any of the following during the current sentence must not be categorised to Category D/Open conditions:

Currently on the Escape List (E-List);

Foreign National Offenders (FNOs) where there is both a deportation order against the individual and their appeal rights from the UK have been exhausted. These individuals are referred to as "Appeal Rights Exhausted" (ARE).

5.6 Determinate sentence individuals with an "abscond history" must not be categorised to Category D/Open. An individual has an "abscond history" for the purposes of this policy when they have: absconded from open conditions; failed to return from a period of Release on Temporary Licence (ROTL); been convicted of a criminal offence that took place while on ROTL or escaped or attempted to escape from custody and where that event:
took place within two years before the date of the recategorisation underway, the target date for the

989

next parole hearing or the first date of the proposed ROTL; or

any of these events have occurred more than once during the current sentence. Terrorist and terrorist connected offences

5.7 There is a presumption that an individual serving a determinate custodial sentence for an offence described in section 247A(2) of the Criminal Justice Act 2003 or an indeterminate sentence for a terrorist or terrorist connected offence is unsuitable for Category D/Open unless there are exceptional circumstances as set out within this framework (or the Generic Parole Process Framework where applicable).

5.8 This presumption of unsuitability for Category D/Open will apply from the date on which the sentence is imposed until the date on which it would be served in full (the sentence and licence expiry date).

5.9 Where the offender is serving consecutive or concurrent sentences, they are presumed unsuitable for open conditions if any sentence forming part of the overall sentence envelope is a specified terrorist or terrorist connected offence; and the presumption applies for the duration of the sentence envelope (including whilst released or recalled during that envelope). Where an indeterminate sentence forms part of the sentence envelope then, unless the indeterminate sentence is for a terrorist or terrorist connected offence, the presumption ends at the end of the sentence envelope for the determinate sentences. If an offender is released on licence, sentences imposed subsequently to this won't form part of this envelope and once the original envelope ends, the presumption will no longer apply (unless the new sentence is for a specified terrorist or terrorist connected offence).

5.10 The "sentence envelope" runs from the earliest start date of any of the concurrent or consecutive sentences to the latest sentence end date (the last day the prisoner is serving any of the concurrent/consecutive sentences).

**REQUIREMENTS**
**Roles and Responsibilities**
6.1 The Governor must nominate a manager whose responsibility it is to ensure that the categorisation/recategorisation process is functioning effectively; that decisions are fair, consistent and taken without bias; to provide quality assurance of decision making; to collect and analyse data in terms of protected characteristics (see paragraph 4.3) alongside other equalities data to ensure that there is a complete picture of any disproportionate impact, and to implement change where necessary.

6.2 The security categorisation assessment must be undertaken by the individual's Prison

Offender Manager (POM) or another member of staff delegated the role by the Governor and who has a similar risk assessment role. Input to the assessment may be sought from relevant sources both from within the prison and criminal justice and law enforcement agencies. The final recommendation on category is the responsibility of the staff member designated to the role, having regard to available information, assessment of intelligence, and the individual circumstances of the case.

6.3 The categorisation recommendation must be referred to a manager assigned to the role by the Governor and must either be approved or referred back to the categoriser with reasons and justifications recorded on the DCS. The manager must be someone senior to the POM and who has a risk assessment role, for example the Head of Offender Management Delivery (HOMD).

6.4 Staff completing assessments using the DCS must be competent in its use.

6.5 Where an individual who has been held as a confirmed Category A/RS prisoner in the past five years is recommended for Category C, input must be sought from the Category A Team in Headquarters. The Governing Governor of the establishment in which the individual is held must make the final decision and the reasons and justification for the decision must be recorded on the DCS (see paragraph 8.20 below, which outlines the procedure).

6.6 The Governing Governor of the establishment in which the individual is held must decide whether or not to approve any proposed categorisation to Category D/Open of: any individual recommended for the open estate outside the general eligibility period (see paragraphs 7.8 and 8.21); and

any individual serving any determinate custodial sentence, for an offence described in section 247A(2) of the Criminal Justice Act 2003. If approved, the date the approval was given and the reasons and justification for the decision must be recorded on the DCS.

6.7 The prison security department must contribute to the categorisation assessment if either the security department or the POM identifies a need to do so.

6.8 Although the individual's Key Worker is not involved in taking the categorisation decision, they have an important role in supporting an individual's engagement in rehabilitation; notifying any issues of concern to the individual's POM and providing support and guidance where an adverse categorisation outcome is received. (Disclosure section provides further information). The Key Worker may also be the first point of contact if an individual is concerned, or has questions about, their categorisation decision. The Key Worker therefore needs a general understanding of the categorisation process described in this framework and should collaborate with the individual's POM where necessary.

## INITIAL CATEGORISATION

7.1 All newly sentenced individuals, other than those who are Provisional Category A/Restricted Status or where the time left to serve to earliest release at the point of categorisation is 28 days or less, will have an initial categorisation in line with the process set out in this framework.

7.2 Individuals repatriated from abroad will also have an initial categorisation. In completing the assessment, any relevant information provided by the sending country should be taken into account.

7.3 The initial security category assessment must be completed as soon as possible to enable transfer to an appropriate prison within 10 working days of sentencing. There must be processes in place to ensure that those who need to contribute to the risk assessment do so in a timely manner.

7.4 The initial security categorisation process determines the security category which will be assigned at the outset of an individual's sentence. Because it is completed very shortly after conviction and sentencing, there will be varying levels of information available about individuals depending on whether they have been in custody on remand or during a previous sentence; from pre-sentence reports or previous OASys or from partner law enforcement agencies.

7.5 The initial security categorisation must take account of the individual's current identified risks, available information, including information about their capability to cause harm or to continue with criminality from custody.

7.6 Where an individual is serving a determinate custodial sentence for an offence described in section 247A(2) of the Criminal Justice Act 2003 or an indeterminate sentence for a terrorist or terrorist connected offence, input to the categorisation assessment from the Regional Counter- Terrorism Team must be obtained and used to inform the categorisation risk assessment.

7.7 Category C will be the most appropriate security category for most adults. Where an individual presents a level of risk that cannot safely be managed in Category C, then Category B will be appropriate (unless Category A is deemed necessary having followed PSI 9/2015). Where risk is assessed as low and the other factors identified in the following paragraphs apply, an individual may be assigned to Category D. In all cases it is vital to weigh up all available information and to arrive at a security categorisation outcome that reflects the individual circumstances of the case.

Assessment for Category D/Open Conditions

7.8 A determinate sentence individual is generally eligible for consideration for Category D/Open at initial categorisation if:

They are serving a standard determinate sentence (they do not have a Parole Eligibility Date – PED) and they have less than 3 years left to serve to automatic release (Conditional Release Date – CRD), or

They are serving a determinate sentence with a PED and have less than three years left to serve to earliest release (PED) and less than five years to automatic release (CRD), and

In either case (with or without a PED), they are not a Foreign National Offender where there is both a deportation order against the individual and their appeal rights from the UK have been exhausted (see Foreign National Offenders section).

7.9 In addition, the individual must be assessed as:
low risk of abscond
low risk of harm to the public
unlikely to continue criminality while in custody
unlikely to otherwise abuse the low security or disrupt the good order of the open estate.

7.10 Determinate sentences that have a PED include most Extended Determinate Sentences (EDS), sentences for offenders convicted under the Terrorist Offenders (Restriction of Early Release) Act 2020 (TORERA), and Sentence for Offenders of Particular Concern (SOPC) under s236A of the Criminal Justice Act 2003. It will also include those who are serving legacy determinate sentences which have a PED, including Extended Sentences for Public Protection (EPP).

7.11 Subject to constraints set out elsewhere in this framework, categorisation to D/Open in advance of PED will enable appropriate individuals to demonstrate to the Parole Board that they are suitable for release. However, these sentences are given when there are public protection issues and so any benefit to the individual must carefully be weighed against the risk to the public. There should be a clear management plan in place to allow for the risk to be managed safely. Relevant specialist units must have the opportunity to contribute to the categorisation assessment.

7.12 At initial categorisation there may be no recent custodial history and little information available to assess an individual as meeting these criteria. Every effort must be made to obtain information necessary to make an informed decision. Where there is insufficient information to determine that risks are manageable in open conditions, closed conditions are more likely to be appropriate.

7.13 Unless the risk of serious harm to the public is assessed as low, Category D/Open is not appropriate at initial categorisation given the low physical security and community-facing nature of the open estate. The degree of risk of serious harm to the public and the nature of that risk will normally be identified through an OASys assessment, but where this is not available then the risk must be assessed through other means, such as from other documents prepared for court such as the Risk of Serious Harm assessment (RoSH) or Offender Group Reconviction Score (OGRS). In circumstances where insufficient information is available at the point of initial categorisation, a period of assessment in closed conditions may be necessary.

7.14 Any individual on the E-List must not be categorised to Category D/Open.

7.15 Where an individual has previously been identified as posing a risk of escape, the assessment must consider when this was recorded and the nature of the information.

7.16 Determinate sentence individuals with an "abscond history" must not be categorised to Category D/Open. An individual has an "abscond history" for the purposes of this policy when they have: absconded from open conditions; failed to return from a period of ROTL; been convicted of a criminal offence that took place while on ROTL or escaped or attempted to escape from custody and where that event:

took place within two years before the date of the recategorisation underway, the target date for the next parole hearing or the first date of the proposed ROTL; or

any of these events have occurred more than once during the current sentence.

7.17 There is a presumption that an individual serving a determinate sentence for an offence described in section 247A(2) of the Criminal Justice Act 2003 will be unsuitable for Category D/Open unless there are exceptional circumstances and the categorisation decision is approved by the Governing Governor of the establishment in which the individual is held. If approved, the date the approval was given and the reasons and justification for the decision must be recorded in the DCS. In any such cases, input to the categorisation assessment from the Regional Counter-Terrorism Team must be obtained and used to inform the categorisation risk assessment.

7.18 The particular conditions and regime of the open estate mean that only those with less than three years left to serve to earliest release should normally be considered for open conditions. Where individual circumstances indicate that Category D/Open would be appropriate with three years or more left to serve, a recommendation for Cat D/Open should be made to the Governing Governor of the establishment in which the individual is held, who must decide whether or not to approve the recommendation. If approved, the date the approval was given and

the reasons and justification for the decision must be recorded on the DCS.

7.19 When considering anyone for Category D/Open, steps must be taken to establish whether the individual's victims have chosen to participate in the Victim Contact Scheme (VCS). The VCS is open to victims of specified violent or sexual crimes where the offender is sentenced to 12 months or more. Victims who participate in the scheme have certain statutory rights, which include being notified (through the Victim Liaison Officer - VLO) of key stages in an individual's sentence. Categorisation to Category D/Open is a key stage. Any victim who has elected to be updated about an individual's key stages i s required to be notified when an individual is being considered for Category D/Open; when the outcome of that assessment is known and again once the move has taken place. It is the responsibility of the POM to inform the VLO at each stage in the process.

## RECATEGORISATION
### Timing of Review

8.1 Categorisation reviews ensure that individuals continue to be assigned to the security category most appropriate to managing their risk throughout their time in custody. The aim is that they will, at all stages of their sentence, be held in the lowest security conditions necessary to manage the identified risk.

8.2 A non-routine review of an individual's security categorisation must take place whenever there is a material change in circumstances that impacts security risk, or information is identified (including existing information not considered before) that indicates that the individual cannot safely be managed in the current security conditions. This may be either an increase or a reduction in risk. Such reviews can take place at any time.

8.3 The maximum time between categorisation reviews is based on the individual's current category and time left to serve to their earliest release date. The earliest release date for standard determinate sentence individuals will generally be the CRD. For sentences with a PED it will be the PED.

8.4 The earliest release date for standard recalls may not be known until the Parole Board 28-day review is finalised. Where necessary, the timing of the next review should be amended once the outcome of the review is known.

8.5 Adult individuals serving a determinate sentence and held in closed conditions (Categories B and C) must be reviewed every 12 months until they have less than three years left to serve to earliest release. At this point routine reviews must be 6-monthly. Where the time left to serve to earliest release at the point of initial categorisation is less than three years, 6 monthly reviews will commence immediately.

8.6 For ISPs, including those serving a determinate sentence at the same time as an indeterminate sentence, categorisation reviews should take place in line with scheduled sentence planning reviews unless the individual needs to be able access a progression opportunity (such as training or treatment) at a prison of a lower category, in which case there will be a categorisation review at that point, outside of the planned sentence planning timetable.

8.7 Individuals assigned Category D/Open but held in the closed estate will have a routine recategorisation review in line with the timescales described above, to assess whether this category remains appropriate.

8.8 Individuals held in Category D/Open will not have routine reviews of their security category but may be recategorised to higher security at any time if risk increases, or if there is a material change in circumstances that impacts security risk, or information (including existing information not considered before) is identified that indicates that the individual cannot safely be managed in the current security conditions.

8.9 There is no mandated routine review of categorisation for Young Adults until they are turning 21 (see Young Adults section). Their categorisation can, however, be reviewed at any time if a change in circumstances indicates they would be suitable for open conditions or need heightened security measures.

8.10 Individuals subject to a standard recall, including those with further charges, will have their categorisation reviewed within 10 days of their return to custody. On reception back into custody, individuals subject to a standard recall retain the security category assigned to them on release until this categorisation review is completed and must not be marked as unclassified/unconvicted.

8.11 An individual's routine recategorisation review must not be withheld or delayed to await the outcome of a parole hearing. The review should take place at the normal time but, unless there is an urgent need to transfer the individual for security, compassionate or discipline reasons, or because the individual needs to complete necessary offending behaviour work, they should not be transferred until the parole dossier is complete (more information is available in the 'Generic Parole Process Policy' framework available from the prisonoracle.com web site. If the individual is moved before the dossier is completed, then it is the responsibility of the sending prison to complete the dossier. Moves of ISPs to open conditions will normally require a recommendation from the Parole Board and all such decisions sit with officials in Public Protection Casework Section (PPCS) on behalf of the Secretary of State.

8.12 The categorisation review must assess the individual's current risks, information about their behaviour in custody and positive efforts made towards rehabilitation, and whether the identified risks can be managed in a different (lower) level of security. At the review stage there will be a greater degree of information available including from OASys, other risk assessments as well as evidence about behaviour and rehabilitation.

8.13 There must be processes in place to ensure that information relevant to the assessment is provided by various departments (for example, Key Worker, Security, Prison Intelligence Unit, Probation, Interventions, Education and Psychology) in a timely manner.

8.14 Where an individual is serving a determinate custodial sentence for an offence described in section 247A(2) of the Criminal Justice Act 2003 or an indeterminate sentence for a terrorist or terrorist connected offence, input to the categorisation assessment from the Regional Counter-Terrorism Team must be obtained and used to inform the categorisation risk assessment.

8.15 Prisons should, wherever possible, support individuals to make representations in advance of their scheduled categorisation review. Where representations are received, these must be considered as part of the assessment process.

Recategorisation to Lower Security Conditions

8.16 Recategorisation to a lower security category is not an automatic progression or right but must be based on an assessment that the individual can safely and securely be managed in lower security conditions. For example, someone in Category B whose risk of harm to the public continues to be assessed as high but whose risk to others in custody, risk of escape or of presenting serious control issues are all assessed as low, may be suitable for Category C on the basis that that is a closed, secure prison which limits any potential to cause harm to the public.

8.17 All available information and positive aspects of behaviour must be taken into account as part of the risk assessment, including the extent to which the individual engages successfully with the prison regime, work and training opportunities. Good behaviour on its own is not, however, sufficient reason to recategorise to a lower security category. An individual displaying outwardly good behaviour may be involved in serious organised criminal activity within the prison or intimidation and bullying of others which would make them unsuitable for recategorisation to lower security conditions. The Security Department must therefore make the POM aware of any information or intelligence relevant to the categorisation assessment.

8.18 At recategorisation, knowledge of the individual and custodial history will support a fuller risk assessment than might be possible at initial categorisation. Factors to be taken into account in assessing suitability for low security conditions will include the nature of the offence; any outstanding charges or proceedings such as a Serious Crime Prevention Order or an ongoing confiscation order which the individual may seek to avoid by absconding or which could put the individual outside the eligibility timeframe for open conditions if there is a potential default sentence; custodial history including previous breaches of trust; information about ongoing criminal activity in custody; and risks highlighted by MAPPA.

8.19 In some cases, risk reduction and suitability for lower security conditions can be evidenced by successful completion of offending behaviour work, but where this hasn't been available or appropriate, staff must look to other sources of information regarding suitability for the lower security category. In assessing recategorisation from B to C consideration should be given to whether outstanding offender behaviour work can be completed in a lower category prison where there is other evidence of appropriate risk reduction.

8.20 In cases where it is proposed to recategorise an individual from Category B to C where they have been held as confirmed Category A/RS in the preceding five years, the prison must consult the HMPPS Category A Team before a decision is taken. The Category A Team will then review the relevant Category A file, the Executive Director's views at the time of the downgrade to Category B, and consider the rationale for the recommendation for Category C. The Category A Team will then make a recommendation to the Governing Governor of the establishment in which the individual is held, for a decision. The Governing Governor's decision must be recorded on the DCS with date the decision was taken and the reasons and justification for the decision.

Recategorisation to Category D/Open Conditions

8.21 To be eligible for categorisation to Category D/Open conditions, a standard determinate sentence individual (with no PED) must generally have less than 3 years left to serve to the CRD. A determinate sentence individual with a PED must generally have less than three years left to serve to PED and less than five years to automatic release and in either case, if they are a foreign national offender who is subject to a deportation order, must not have exhausted all appeal rights from within the UK against deportation (see Foreign National Offenders

section). In addition, the individual must be assessed as:

low risk of abscond;

low risk of harm to the public or has a suitable plan in place to manage identified risk; • unlikely to continue criminality while in custody; unlikely to otherwise take advantage of the low security or disrupt the good order/regime of the open estate.

8.22 Determinate sentences that have a PED include most Extended Determinate Sentences (EDS), sentences for offenders convicted under the Terrorist Offenders (Restriction of Early Release) Act 2020 (TORERA), and Sentence for Offenders of Particular Concern (SOPC) under s236A of the Criminal Justice Act 2003. It will also include those who are serving legacy determinate sentences that have a PED, including Extended Sentences for Public Protection (EPP). Any individual serving a determinate sentence with a PED will have their release at PED considered by the Parole Board who will make a direction regarding release to PPCS, but the categorisation assessment to D/Open is for the prison.

8.23 Subject to constraints set out elsewhere in this framework, categorisation to D/Open in advance of PED will enable appropriate individuals to demonstrate to the Parole Board that they are suitable for release. However, these sentences are given when there are public protection issues and so any benefit to the individual must carefully be weighed against the risk to the public. There should be a clear management plan in place to allow for the risk to be managed safely. Relevant specialist units must have the opportunity to contribute to the categorisation assessment.

8.24 An individual's OASys assessment is expected to be reviewed at points of significant change in circumstances such as before categorising a person to Category D / open conditions. The review should be used to inform and evidence the categorisation decision.

8.25 In cases where the individual is considered to present a high or very high Risk of Serious Harm to the public or to others, there must be an appropriate risk management plan in place. This must detail how the individual can safely be managed given the low physical security conditions and community-facing nature of the open estate.

8.26 An individual on the E-List must not be categorised to Category D/Open.

8.27 Where an individual has previously been identified as posing a risk of escape, the assessment must consider when this was recorded and the nature of the information.

8.28 Determinate sentence individuals with an

"abscond history" must not be categorised to Category D/Open. An individual has an "abscond history" for the purposes of this policy when they have: absconded from open conditions; failed to return from a period of ROTL; been convicted of a criminal offence that took place while on ROTL or escaped or attempted to escape from custody and where that event:

took place within two years before the date of the recategorisation underway, the target date for the next parole hearing or the first date of the proposed ROTL; or

any of these events have occurred more than once during the current sentence.

8.29 There is a presumption that an individual serving a determinate custodial sentence for an offence described in section 247A(2) of the Criminal Justice Act 2003 is unsuitable for Category D/Open unless there are exceptional circumstances and the categorisation decision is approved by the Governing Governor of the establishment in which the individual is held. If approved, the date the approval was given and the reasons and justification for the decision must be recorded on the DCS. In any such cases input to the categorisation assessment from the Regional Counter-Terrorism Team must be obtained and used to inform the categorisation risk assessment.

8.30 Determinate sentence individuals on a standard (Section 254) recall must not be categorised by the prison to the open estate until the Parole Board 28-day review is finalised.

8.31 Recalled ISPs must have their suitability for open conditions considered by the PPCS on behalf of the Secretary of State. This will normally require a recommendation from the Parole Board. The final decision sits with officials in Public Protection Casework Section (PPCS) on behalf of the Secretary of State.

8.32 The requirement that those serving a determinate sentence with a PED should generally be both within 3 years of PED and 5 years of CRD means that some, particularly those with a longer sentence, will not be in general scope for consideration for Category D until they are within one or two years of PED. Those with a very long sentence may have reached PED before they are within 5 years of CRD. Once an individual has reached PED they are eligible for consideration for Category D/Open irrespective of the time left to serve to CRD. Each case is considered on its individual merits and, where Category D/Open is recommended outside the general timescales referred to above, the categorisation decision must be taken by the Governing Governor of the establishment in which the individual is held. If approved, the

reasons and justification for the decision must be recorded in the DCS.

8.33 When considering anyone for Category D/Open, steps must be taken to establish whether the individual's victims have chosen to participate in the Victim Contact Scheme (VCS). The VCS is open to victims of specified violent or sexual crimes where the offender is sentenced to 12 months or more. Victims who participate in the scheme have certain statutory rights, which includes being notified (through the Victim Liaison Officer - VLO) of key stages in an individual's sentence. Categorisation to Category D/Open is a key stage. Any victim who has elected to be updated about an individual's key stages is required to be notified when an individual i s being considered for Category D/Open; when the outcome of that assessment is known and again once the move has taken place. It is the responsibility of the POM to inform the VLO at each stage in the process.

Recategorisation to a Higher Security Category

8.34 An increase in an individual's security category must be based on an assessment that the risks or behaviour presented can only be managed in conditions of higher security.

8.35 Recategorisation to a higher security category may be an immediate response to an incident or a material change in circumstances that impacts security risk, or information (including existing information not considered before) is identified that indicates that the individual cannot safely be managed in the current security conditions. For Category D/Open, this will usually mean the individual must quickly be transferred to closed security conditions. Where possible, the aim should be to complete the recategorisation assessment before transfer. Where operational needs mean the individual must be transferred before this can be completed or approved, then the sending prison must complete the assessment subsequently, or forward all necessary information to the receiving prison within two working days of transfer, in order that the recategorisation can be completed at the new prison.

8.36 For ISPs transferred back to closed conditions, the prison must only formally recategorise the individual once the PPCS on behalf of the Secretary of State has confirmed that the individual must be held in closed conditions.

8.37 For those in Category C, the recategorisation process must, wherever possible, be completed prior to transfer to a prison of higher security. This must include an assessment of why the risks or behaviour can only be managed in conditions of higher security. It is not enough simply to record that Category C is no longer suitable. The decision and reasons must be recorded on the DCS. If there are security concerns that prevent full disclosure of the reasons for recategorisation, particularly in cases where the recategorisation may be based on the Security Department's assessment of intelligence, then it must be recorded separately (see Withholding Information section).

### Remaining in Current Category

8.38 If it is considered that the individual needs to remain in their current security category then the reasons why these security conditions are considered appropriate must clearly be recorded, together with any recommendations for actions required to evidence a reduction in risk and progression at a subsequent review.

## GENERAL PRINCIPLES OF CATEGORISATION ASSESSMENTS

9.1 Security categorisation decisions must be made in accordance with Prison Rules, other relevant legislation, and the principles set out in this framework.

9.2 Security categorisation decisions must be based on individual security risk assessments taking account of all available information. The list is not exhaustive but may include any of the following:

Previous Convictions (if any);

Details of current offence(s);

Current custodial record;

Previous record;

Security Department assessment of relevant evidence and intelligence;

Public Protection information (MAPPA) (if eligible);

Prisoner Escort Record (PER) form;

OASys (if opened prior to sentence) or Pre-Sentence Report (PSR) or other assessments prepared for the court;

Any relevant and available information from the police or other law enforcement agency. 9.3 All categorisation decisions must be fair, objective and consistent with current policy.

9.4 It is important to consider the characteristics of the estate for which the individual is being assessed, taking account of physical and procedural security, and supervision levels. This is particularly important when considering whether to categorise to open conditions. Because of the particular characteristics of the open estate, categorisation to Category D/Open must be based on the individual's manageable risks.

Digital Categorisation Service (DCS)

9.5 The DCS is an online form and the mechanism for making, recording and justifying categorisation decisions. It supports staff in identifying relevant risk factors and reaching a decision on an individual's security needs but does not make categorisation decisions itself. It:

Provides a consistent framework for staff to record information about the various risk factors;

Automatically highlights risk information to staff where available, to reduce the amount of manual checks required during the assessment process;

Records previous categorisation assessments to support case management;

At initial categorisation, provides a suggested categorisation as a starting point, which must then be reviewed by staff and changed where appropriate.

Gathering and Sharing Information

9.6 There must be effective and lawful procedures in place for the person taking the categorisation decision to obtain relevant information including from within HMPPS and law enforcement agencies and that the use and handling of any sensitive material is in line with current guidance, including the 'Intelligence Collection, Analysis and Dissemination' Policy Framework.

### Disclosure

9.7 The categorisation decision taken is significant to the individual in question and it is important that it is relayed to them in a timely and appropriate manner. The Governor must ensure that there are processes in place to ensure that individuals understand the process for making categorisation decisions, as well as why a particular decision was made in their case. It will generally be the POM who communicates the categorisation decision to the individual who is being categorised.

9.8 Individuals may request a printed copy of their categorisation assessment. If they do so they must be provided with a copy within 3 working days, except for any restricted information (see 'Withholding Information' section).

9.9 If the individual has difficulty understanding the assessment, an explanation must be given verbally or in a manner and format which the individual understands.

9.10 An individual who knows their categorisation is being reviewed may be hoping for a favourable result. Staff involved in notifying the individual of his categorisation decision must be aware of the possibility that an adverse or disappointing outcome could lead to self-harm and suicide. It is important to be alert for any signs that the individual's risk of harm to themselves has increased. An individual who has been disappointed may also become violent to staff or other prisoners. More details of how to manage these situations are in PSI 64/2011 ('Management of prisoners at risk of harm to self, to others and from others').

### Withholding Information

9.11 All intelligence and security department assessments must be handled in line with the 'Intelligence Collection, Analysis and Dissemination' Policy Framework. Information

may be withheld from the individual where necessary in the following limited circumstances:
In the interests of national security;
For the prevention, detection, investigation or prosecution of crime or disorder, including information relevant to prison security and good order and discipline;
For the protection of a third party who may be put at risk if the information is disclosed;
If on health grounds it is felt necessary to withhold information where the mental and or physical health of the individual or a third party could be impaired;
Where the source of the information is a victim, and disclosure without their consent would breach any duty of confidence owed to that victim or would generally prejudice the future supply of such information.
9.12 Information withheld under these circumstances must be recorded separately. If it is information critical to the categorisation decision then the individual must be informed, in general terms, what the information is that has been relied on in sufficient detail to enable them to bring meaningful representations. In such cases, they must be provided with summary of the information that does not disclose the source material. The 'Intelligence Collection, Analysis and Dissemination' Policy Framework provides guidance on drafting for this purpose.

### Representations

9.13 Anyone with concerns about their security categorisation decision should be encouraged in the first instance to raise these with their Key Worker. Their Key Worker must, where the nature of the concern requires, pass these concerns onto the POM to provide a fuller explanation of the process and reasons for the decision.
9.14 If the individual wishes to challenge either the decision or the reasons given for the decision, then representations must be made to the POM using the process set out in the Prisoner Complaints Policy Framework. Representations should normally be submitted within 28 days of the individual being advised of the categorisation decision. Any complaint should be considered by a suitably qualified manager who may direct that the decision is reconsidered.
9.15 A reconsideration would be appropriate if:
Policy has not been followed, or
Relevant information available at the time was not considered, or
Information relied upon is factually incorrect, or
Any other reason is considered appropriate by the manager.
9.16 Any reconsideration will involve retaking the decision afresh looking at all the information that was available at the time of the original

decision as well as considering any further information not available when the original decision was made. This will usually be carried out by a person senior to the person who approved the original decision.
9.17 An individual who has challenged their categorisation decision will be hoping for a favourable result. Paragraph 9.10 above deals with managing adverse categorisation outcomes. The same applies when notifying an individual of the results of any representation about their category.
9.18 Prisons must keep a record of the number of complaints relating to security categorisation decisions and the outcome of the fresh consideration. This will form part of the data for analysis of fair and sound decision making.

### FOREIGN NATIONAL OFFENDERS

10.1 Foreign National Offenders (FNOs), including those subject to enforcement proceedings under the Immigration Act 1971, must be categorised/recategorised for closed conditions in the same way as all others.
10.2 Those FNOs with no liability for deportation must be categorised for Category D/open conditions in the same way as all others. These are individuals who:
do not match the initial criteria for deportation, or
have been considered for deportation by the Home Office and it has been decided that they may remain in the UK, or
are not subject to any removal procedures.
10.3 An FNO in closed conditions must not be categorised to Category D/open conditions where there is a deportation order against the prisoner under section 5(1) of the Immigration Act 1971 and no appeal is on-going, could be brought or is pending as provided in Rule 7(1A) Prison Rules 1999. Under Rule 7(1C) Prison Rules 1999, any FNO in open conditions who subsequently has a relevant deportation status must have their categorisation reconsidered as soon as practicable. These individuals are referred to as Appeal Rights Exhausted (ARE).
10.4 FNOs with a "liability for deportation" must be considered for categorisation to Category D/open conditions but that categorisation must be informed by a CCD3 completed by the Home Office and procedures must be in place to obtain this where relevant. The CCD3 will provide deportation status information relevant to the security categorisation assessment. In particular, the Home Office will advise of any individual circumstances that might increase or decrease, the incentive to abscond from open conditions in order to evade enforcement proceedings. The definition of those with a "liability for deportation" is those individuals who are:
confirmed by the Home Office as meeting the

initial criteria for deportation - whether the individual has been informed of this or not, or have received a formal notice of liability for deportation, or have received a deportation order with appeal rights in the UK remaining, or fall below the threshold for deportation but are being considered for or made subject to removal from the UK.

10.5 If an individual has been categorised to Category D/Open before their deportation status has been notified, or if their deportation status changes (including a deportation order being revoked), their categorisation must be reconsidered as soon as practicable after the prison is notified.

10.6 Where that change is that the individual has now exhausted appeal rights from the UK (ARE) any individual categorised Category D/Open but still held in the closed estate, must be recategorised to closed conditions. Any individual held in the open estate must have their categorisation reviewed but can remain in the open estate if all risks continue to be assessed as low.

## INDETERMINATE SENTENCE PRISONERS (ISPs)

11.1 ISPs being assessed for closed conditions must be risk assessed in the same way as all others: there is no requirement that they must initially be categorised to Category B if Category C is considered appropriate. The prison is not responsible for assessing ISPs for open conditions. Moves of ISPs to open conditions will normally require a recommendation from the Parole Board and all such decisions sit with officials in Public Protection Casework Section (PPCS) on behalf of the Secretary of State. Once the Secretary of State has decided an ISP is suitable for open conditions, prisons must categorise them as Category D/Open.

## RECALLS

12.1 Individuals subject to a Fixed Term Recall (FTR) will not normally be categorised. Where there is a need to reallocate a FTR from the Reception prison, a review of their category must first be undertaken.

12.2 Individuals recalled from Home Detention Curfew (HDC) for breaching curfew conditions (Section 255 recall) do not need to be categorised if they are within 28 days of release.

12.3 Individuals subject to a standard (Section 254) recall must be recategorised within 10 working days of their return to custody including where there are also further charges against the individual. In such cases, the security categorisation review must be completed with reference to the individual's previous categorisation and recategorisation assessments.

In addition, the assessment must consider: security category at release; circumstances resulting in the recall; the nature of any further charges; length of time the individual was on licence prior to recall; number of times the individual has been recalled.

12.4 Determinate sentence individuals on a standard (Section 254) recall must not be categorised by the prison to the open estate until the Parole Board 28-day review is finalised. It is open to the prison to schedule a further review of category following the Parole Board review where appropriate.

12.5 Recalled ISPs must have their suitability for open conditions considered by the PPCS on behalf of the Secretary of State.

## YOUNG ADULTS

13.1 Young Adults (18-20) will be held in Young Offender Institutions (YOIs) or dual-designated YOIs and prisons. There is no mandated routine review of categorisation for Young Adults until they are turning 21. This is because there is no sub-division of the closed estate between category C and B, and, for those unsuitable for open conditions at initial categorisation, the need to spend sufficient time in closed conditions where their behaviour can be observed. Their categorisation can, however, be reviewed at any time if a change in circumstances indicates they would be suitable for open conditions or need heightened security measures. In categorising Young Adults, particular consideration should be given to the maturity of the individual in deciding on the appropriate category.

### Recategorisation to the adult estate on turning 21

13.2 A young adult male individual held either in a YOI or a dual-designated YOI/prison must be categorised to the adult estate in the months preceding their 21st birthday so that the transition can proceed seamlessly. It should not be necessary for a young adult to be transferred from a young offender institution or dual designated YOI/prison to a local prison for categorisation and allocation, but instead they should be allocated directly to an appropriately secure prison in the adult estate

13.3 It should be the aim to transfer the individual to the adult estate on, or soon after, their 21st birthday other than where there are exceptional or compassionate reasons (such as completion of offending behaviour work; closeness to family; completion of educational work; unavailability of suitable places in the adult estate). The recategorisation assessment should be completed before the individual turns 21. Recategorisation to the adult estate ('starring up')

13.4 A young adult must only be reclassified to the adult estate in exceptional circumstances. The security and supervision afforded by the adult estate must be evidenced as necessary to meet any of the categorisation criteria set out at paragraph 1.2 of this framework. This process applies also to young adults held in a dual-designated YOI/prison.

13.5 The assessment to transfer an individual to the adult estate must involve confirmation that their sentence type does not prohibit this, consultation with the establishment's Independent Monitoring Board (IMB), the completion of a maturity assessment, an assessment of the risk of self- harm, a plan to support the individual's well -being and completion of a recategorisation assessment on the DCS. The decision to move a young adult to the adult estate must be approved in writing by the Prison Group Director (PGD) of the holding prison. The date the approval was given and the reasons in support of the decision must be recorded.

## TRANSGENDER PRISONERS

14.1 Any transgender individuals must be categorised in accordance with the security conditions applying to the estate in which they are held.

14.2 Where it is proposed to transfer a transgender individual between the male and female estates, their categorisation should be assessed in line with the policy applying to the estate to which they are moving.

14.3 For further information relating to the support and management of transgender individuals, please see 'The Care and Management of Individuals who are Transgender' policy framework.

## RETURNS FROM INPATIENT MENTAL HEALTH SERVICES

15.1 Patients returning to prison from inpatient mental health services will return to the reception prison nearest to the hospital in which they have been detained. There will be some specific cases where this does not occur; for example patients who were previously Category A prisoners must be returned to a Category A prison. Prisoners who meet Long Term High Security Estate (LTHSE) criteria will be remitted to the most suitable LTHSE prison. In all cases this will not necessarily be the same prison from which they were admitted. If for any reason, the nearest reception prison is unable to accept the patient, it is the responsibility of the Governing Governor of that prison or the relevant Prison Group Director to source an alternative prison willing to accept the patient.

15.2 The expectation is that the Reception prison will have been involved in a meeting under section 117 of the Mental Health Act 1983 prior to the patient being returned to prison custody.

15.3 The individual's security category must be reviewed within 10 working days of remittance and include an assessment of prison security and related files returned by the hospital and the hospital's own security and intelligence files relating to the individual's time in their care. The individual's core record will need to be obtained from the discharging prison.

15.4 Any Category A prisoner returning to prison custody from Special Hospital must be reported into the Category A Team at Headquarters.

# THE PRISON ORACLE - PRISONORACLE.COM

All The Definitive Prisons Information You Need From The Publisher Experts Trust

*The excellent Prison Oracle provides a window into the Prison system which is immensely valuable – and as important today as it has ever been"* Michael Spurr, CEO HM Prison & Probation Service (2010-2019)

About The Prison Oracle

Memberships from 99p a week

Advertise in our monthly newspaper

THE PRISON ORACLE
*"An Excellent Site"*
Michael Spurr
CEO HMPPS
2010-2019

Trusted by

Ministry of JUSTICE | HM Prison & Probation Service | HM PRISON SERVICE | G4S | serco | sodexo

# THE DEFINITIVE UK PRISONS WEBSITE GIVING YOU ALL THE PRISONS INFORMATION YOU NEED FROM THE PUBLISHER EXPERTS TRUST

| News Desk Membership | Basic Membership | Standard Membership | Enhanced Membership Best Value | Corporate Membership |
|---|---|---|---|---|
| £0.99 | £4.99 | £7.99 | £9.99 | £29.99 |
| per week paid monthly | per month paid quarterly | per month paid quarterly | per month paid quarterly | per month paid annually |

## LESS THAN THE COST OF A CUP OF COFFEE A WEEK: CANCEL ANYTIME!

The Prison Oracle:
*I'm impressed at how comprehensive it is.*
An excellent collection of Data and Information, I'm impressed at how comprehensive it is. A bonus is access to Reports like Woolf, Woodcock, May, Learmont and others before the Internet and difficult to otherwise access. The data is user-friendly, useful for research and easy to use with access to data on the Prison Population, Safety in Custody, and Workforce Statistics easier to access and use than on the Government's own website. A very helpful, comprehensive, user friendly source of information on prison issues.

**Phil Wheatley, CB.**
Former Director General: HM. Prison Service and NOMS

The Prison Oracle:
*'The' Go-To Place for Everything Prison Related.*
The sheer depth of available information, coupled with a simple user interface, makes The Prison Oracle *'the'* go-to place for everything that is in any way prison related. There's a vast array of publications, alongside historic reports that you simply can't find anywhere else online.
Having such a wealth of data at your fingertips, without the need to trawl the internet for hours, is exactly why I subscribed. The Prison Oracle is a tangible learning resource for anyone with an interest in the justice section; I urge you to take a look for yourself.

**Richard Rowley**
Managing Director: Census Life

The Prison Oracle:
*An excellent collection of information, data and reports*
The Prison Oracle, with everything about prisons all in one place, has long been needed and I'm delighted it's finally arrived – I 've subscribed and it's such an excellent collection of information, data and reports for practitioners, justice professionals or anyone with an interest in justice issues or reform, I've no hesitation in recommending The Prison Oracle to all my Correctional Services colleagues. An added advantage is the simple access to reports that shaped the modern Prison Service – Woodcock, Woolf, Learmont, May, Carter, and Corston.

**Tony Hassall**
Commissioner: Corrective Services Western Australia

# Section 3

## The Directory

> Government & Statutory Agencies, such as the Ministry of Justice and HM Prison & Probation Service.

### 3.1 GOVERNMENT & STATUTORY AGENCIES

#### CARE QUALITY COMMISSION (CQC)
The Chair of the Care Quality Commission is Ian Dilks OBE.
Head Office: CQC National Customer Service Centre, City Gate, Gallowgate, Newcastle upon Tyne, NE1 4PA
Telephone: 03000 616161
Web www.cqc.org.uk
Email: enquiries@cqc.org.uk
REMIT: The Care Quality Commission (CQC) is the health and social care regulator for England. It monitors, inspects and regulates health and social care in the criminal justice system to ensure that people who use services in secure settings receive the same quality of care as the rest of the population.
• The CQC published a joint report with HMIP, 'Social care in prisons in England and Wales', in October 2018:
*https://tinyurl.com/ybsl4nkg*
• How the CQC inspect health and social care in prisons and young offender institutions, and health care in immigration removal centres can be found here: *https://tinyurl.com/y3clb9uj*
• Memorandum of understanding between the CQC and HM Prisons Inspectorate can be found here: *https://tinyurl.com/y624y92h*
The services the CQC inspect range from health services that form part of youth offending teams to prison healthcare, they work in partnership with other inspectorates and use different frameworks to inspect different types of service.
Services CQC Inspect:
Youth offending teams (YOTs) are statutory bodies that include representatives from health, education, police, probation, substance misuse and social services.
Secure training centres (STCs) hold young offenders, usually over the age of 15. Offenders under 15 are normally held in secure children's homes, while those over 15 are held in STCs or young offender institutions. There are three STCs in England, two of which hold women.
Young offender institutions (YOIs) are run according to many of the same rules and policies

as prisons. There are eight YOIs that hold young males in England and Wales.
Adult prisons
Immigration removal centres
Police custody
The areas for joint work and coordination between the CQC and Prisons Inspectorate include:
• regulation and inspection of the provision of health and social care for people detained in custodial settings
• reviews, studies and reports
• advice and information to ministers, service providers and the public
• working collaboratively in fora to improve outcomes for detainees e.g. the Joint Police Programmes Board

#### CRIMINAL CASES REVIEW COMMISSION
Chair: Helen Pitcher OBE
Criminal Cases Review Commission
23 Stephenson Street, Birmingham B2 4BH
Telephone: 0121 233 1473
Web www.ccrc.gov.uk
Email info@ccrc.gov.uk
REMIT: The Criminal Cases Review Commission is the independent organisation set up to investigate suspected miscarriages of justice from magistrates courts and crown courts in England, Wales and Northern Ireland, and the Courts Martial and Service Civilian Courts.

#### CROWN PROSECUTION SERVICE
Director of Public Prosecutions: Max Hill QC
CPS Public Enquiries, 102 Petty France, London, SW1H 9EA
Tel: 020 3357 7000
Web www.cps.gov.uk
Email enquiries@cps.gov.uk
REMIT: The Crown Prosecution Service (CPS) prosecutes criminal cases that have been investigated by the police and other investigative organisations in England and Wales. The CPS is independent, and makes decisions independently of the police and government.

#### DISCLOSURE & BARRING SERVICE
Chief Executive: Dr Gillian Fairfield
DBS Customer Services, PO Box 3961, Royal Wootton Bassett, SN4 4HF
Tel: 03000 200 190
Email: customerservices@dbs.gov.uk
https://www.gov.uk/government/

organisations/disclosure-and-barring-service
REMIT: The Disclosure and Barring Service helps employers make safer recruitment decisions each year by processing and issuing DBS checks for England, Wales, the Channel Islands and the Isle of Man. DBS also maintains the adults' and children's Barred Lists and makes considered decisions as to whether an individual should be included on one or both of these lists and barred from engaging in regulated activity.

## HOME OFFICE
Head: The Rt Hon Suella Braverman QC MP, Home Secretary
Direct Communications Unit, 2 Marsham Street, London, SW1P 4DF
Tel: 020 7035 4848
Web: www.gov.uk/government/organisations/home-office
Email public.enquiries@homeoffice.gov.uk
REMIT: The first duty of the government is to keep citizens safe and the country secure. The Home Office has been at the front line of this endeavour since 1782. As such, the Home Office plays a fundamental role in the security and economic prosperity of the United Kingdom.

The Home Office is the lead government department for immigration and passports, drugs policy, crime, fire, counter-terrorism and police.

The Home Office is responsible for:
• working on the problems caused by illegal drug use
• shaping the alcohol strategy, policy and licensing conditions
• keeping the United Kingdom safe from the threat of terrorism
• reducing and preventing crime, and ensuring people feel safe in their homes and communities
• securing the UK border and controlling immigration
• considering applications to enter and stay in the UK
• issuing passports and visas
• supporting visible, responsible and accountable policing by empowering the public and freeing up the police to fight crime
• fire prevention and rescue

## HM INSPECTORATE OF PRISONS
Chief Inspector of Prisons Charlie Taylor
3rd floor, 10 South Colonnade
Canary Wharf. London. E14 4PU
Tel: 020 7340 0500
www.justiceinspectorates.gov.uk/hmiprisons/
Email: hmiprisons.enquiries@hmiprisons.gov.uk
REMIT: HM Inspectorate of Prisons for England and Wales (HMI Prisons) is an independent inspectorate led by HM Chief Inspector of Prisons. We provide independent scrutiny of the conditions for and treatment of prisoners and other detainees and report on our findings.

We inspect prisons, young offender institutions (YOIs), secure training centres (STCs), immigration removal centres (IRCs), police and court custody suites, customs custody facilities and military detention.

Our inspections are guided by the idea of 'healthy establishments', in which staff support prisoners and detainees to reduce reoffending and achieve positive outcomes for themselves and the public. In our reports, we include recommendations on how establishments can improve outcomes for prisoners.

Our work forms part of the UK's obligations under the Optional Protocol to the United Nations Convention against Torture (OPCAT). OPCAT requires member states to regularly and independently inspect places of detention.

We also work with other criminal justice inspectorates.

## HM INSPECTOR OF PROBATION
Chief Inspector of Probation: Justin Russell
HM Inspectorate of Probation
1st Floor Manchester Civil Justice Centre
1 Bridge Street West, Manchester M3 3FX
Tel: 0161 240 5336 (since March 2022 Manchester office is currently closed)
www.justiceinspectorates.gov.uk/hmiprobation/
E-mail HMIP.Enquiries@hmiprobation.gov.uk
REMIT: His Majesty's Inspectorate of Probation is the independent inspector of probation and youth offending services in England and Wales.

Our mission is to promote positive changes in these services. Our recommendations, research and effective practice guidance drive improvements at individual, local and national levels. This leads to improved outcomes for adults on probation and children in contact with youth offending services, better information and support for victims; and better protection of the public.

## HM PRISON & PROBATION SERVICE
Director General & Chief Executive: Amy Rees
102 Petty France,
London, SW1H 9AJ
Tel: 01633 630941
Web
https://www.gov.uk/government/organisations/her-majestys-prison-and-probation-service
Email: HMPPSPublicEnquiries@justice.gov.uk
REMIT: We carry out sentences given by the courts, in custody and the community, and rehabilitate people in our care through education and employment. HMPPS is an executive agency, sponsored by the Ministry of Justice.

## INDEPENDENT MONITORING BOARDS

Chair: Dame Anne Owers
Independent Monitoring Boards Secretariat
3rd Floor, Post Point 2,
10 South Colonnade, Canary Wharf,
London, E14 4PU
Web http://www.imb.org.uk
Email IMB@justice.gov.uk
REMIT: Inside every prison and immigration removal centre there is an Independent Monitoring Board (IMB) - A group of ordinary members of the public appointed by the Secretary of State for Justice to monitor the day-to-day life in their local prison or removal centre and ensure that correct and proper standards of care and decency are maintained.

## LAW COMMISSION

Chairman: Sir Nicholas Green
Law Commission, Steel House, 1st Floor, Tower, 52 Queen Anne's Gate, London, SW1H 9AG
Tel: 020 3334 0200 Fax: 020 3334 0201
http://www.lawcom.gov.uk
Email: enquiries@lawcommission.gov.uk
REMIT:—The Law Commission is a statutory independent body. We aim:
• to ensure that the law is as fair, modern, simple and as cost-effective as possible
• to conduct research and consultations in order to make systematic recommendations for consideration by Parliament, and
• to codify the law, eliminate anomalies, repeal obsolete and unnecessary enactments and reduce the number of separate statutes.

## LAW OFFICERS DEPARTMENT

Rt Hon Michael Ellis QC MP is the Attorney General and Michael Tomlinson MP is the Solicitor General.
Attorney General's Office,
102 Petty France, London, SW1H 9EA
General Inquiries: 020 7271 2492
https://www.gov.uk/government/
organisations/attorney-generals-office
E-Mail:
correspondence@attorneygeneral.gov.uk
REMIT: The Attorney General's Office (AGO) provides legal advice and support to the Attorney General and the Solicitor General (the Law Officers) who give legal advice to government. The AGO helps the Law Officers perform other duties in the public interest, such as looking at sentences which may be too low.
Responsibilities
The Attorney General's Office (AGO) is a ministerial department which supports the Attorney General and the Solicitor General (the Law Officers). The Law Officers are government ministers who:

• provide legal advice to government
• superintend, or oversee, the main independent prosecuting departments - the Crown Prosecution Service and the Serious Fraud Office
• superintend, or oversee, His Majesty's CPS Inspectorate, which inspects how cases are prosecuted
• superintend, or oversee, the Government Legal Department, which provides legal services to government
• answer questions about their work in Parliament
• perform other functions in the public interest, such as looking at sentences which may be too low - these duties are independent of government

## MINISTRY OF JUSTICE

Head: Rt. Hon Brandon Lewis MP CBE
Ministry of Justice
102 Petty France, London SW1H 9AJ
Tel: 0203 334 3555
https://www.gov.uk/government/
organisations/ministry-of-justice
REMIT: The Ministry of Justice is a major government department, at the heart of the justice system. We work to protect and advance the principles of justice. Our vision is to deliver a world-class justice system that works for everyone in society.
Responsibilities
We are responsible for these parts of the justice system:
• Courts
• Prisons
• Probation services
• Attendance centres
The organisation works together and with other government departments and agencies to bring the principles of justice to life for everyone in society. From our civil courts, tribunals and family law hearings, to criminal justice, prison and probation services.
We work to ensure that sentences are served and offenders are encouraged to turn their lives around and become law-abiding citizens. We believe the principles of justice are pivotal and we are steadfast in our shared commitment to uphold them.

## NATIONAL PROBATION SERVICE

Head: Sonia Flynn, Executive Director
Ministry of Justice
102 Petty France, London SW1H 9AJ
Telephone: 01633 630941
Email HMPPSPublicEnquiries@justice.gov.uk
https://www.gov.uk/government/organisations/
national-probation-service
REMIT: The National Probation Service is a statutory criminal justice service that supervises high-risk offenders released into the community.

On 26 June 2021, the Probation Services unified, bringing 7,000 probation professionals into our new model, either directly in the Probation Services or employed by one of the organisations appointed to deliver Commissioned Rehabilitative Services to offenders. We now have over 28,000 staff employed in the Probation Services in England and Wales and we are continuing to recruit. In June 2021, we announced the recruitment of 1,000 probation officers, meeting a government target set in July 2020.

We are now implementing the reforms to our probation services set out in our Target Operating Model, published in February 2021. These reforms will deliver a stronger, more stable probation system that will reduce reoffending, support victims of crime, and keep the public safe, while helping offenders to make positive change to their lives.

## PARLIAMENTARY JUSTICE SELECT COMMITTEE

Justice Committee
House of Commons
London
SW1A 0AA
Telephone:020 7219 8196/1280
Email: justicecom@parliament.uk
Chair: Sir Robert Neill MP
The Justice Committee is appointed by the House of Commons to examine the expenditure, administration and policy of the Ministry of Justice and associated public bodies, (to include the work of staff provided for the administrative work of courts and tribunals, *but excluding consideration of individual cases and appointments,* and excluding the work of the Scotland and Wales Offices and of the Advocate General for Scotland); and administration and expenditure of the Attorney General's Office, the Treasury Solicitor's Department, the Crown Prosecution Service and the Serious Fraud Office (but excluding individual cases and appointments and advice given within government by Law Officers).

## PAROLE BOARD

Chairman: Caroline Corby
The Parole Board for England and Wales
10 South Colonnade, Canary Wharf, London
E14 4PU
Tel: 020 3880 0885
https://www.gov.uk/government/organisations/parole-board
info@paroleboard.gov.uk
REMIT: The Parole Board is an independent body that carries out risk assessments on prisoners to determine whether they can be safely released into the community.

*Who we are*
The Parole Board is an independent body that carries out risk assessments on prisoners to determine whether they can be safely released into the community. It was established in 1968 under the Criminal Justice Act 1967 and became an independent executive non-departmental public body on 1 July 1996 under the Criminal Justice and Public Order Act 1994.

We have 246 Parole Board members who make the assessments and decisions. We employ around 120 members of staff to support them, based in 10 South Colonnade, London.

Our job is to determine if someone is safe to release. We do that with great care, and public safety is our number one priority. We deal with 25,000 cases a year, which are referred to us by the Ministry of Justice once prisoners have served the punishment determined by the courts. Parole Board decisions are solely focused on whether a prisoner would represent a significant risk to the public after release. The risk assessment is based on detailed evidence found in the dossier (a collection of documents relating to the prisoner) and evidence provided at the oral hearing.

*Our responsibilities*
Our primary role is to determine whether prisoners serving indeterminate sentences, and those serving certain determinate sentences for serious offences, continue to represent a significant risk to the public.

The main cases we oversee are for prisoners serving:
• life sentences and sentences of imprisonment for public protection (IPP), under the Crime (Sentences) Act 1997, as amended.
• extended determinate sentences (EDS), under the Criminal Justice Act 2003 (as amended by the Legal Aid, Sentencing and Punishment of Offenders Act 2012)
• sentences for offenders of particular concern, including terrorists and serious child sex offenders, under the Criminal Justice and Courts Act 2015.

We also consider:
• the re-release of prisoners who are recalled to prison for breach of their licence conditions under the Criminal Justice Act 2003.

## PRISONS & PROBATION OMBUDSMAN

Ombudsman: Kimberley Bingham (Acting Ombudsman)
3rd Floor, 10 South Colonnade, London E14 4PU
Tel: 020 7633 4100 or lo-call 0845 010 7938
www.ppo.gov.uk
Email mail@ppo.gov.uk
REMIT: The Prisons and Probation Ombudsman (PPO) carries out independent investigations

into deaths and complaints in custody. The detailed role and responsibilities of the PPO are set out in his office's Terms of Reference. The PPO has two main duties:

- to investigate complaints made by prisoners, young people in detention (prisons and secure training centres), offenders under probation supervision and immigration detainees
- to investigate deaths of prisoners, young people in detention, approved premises' residents and immigration detainees due to any cause, including any apparent suicides and natural causes.

The purpose of these investigations is to understand what happened, to correct injustices and to identify learning for the organisations whose actions we oversee so that the PPO makes a significant contribution to safer, fairer custody and offender supervision.

## SENTENCING COUNCIL

Chairman: Lord Justice William Davis
The Sentencing Council for England and Wales
The Royal Courts of Justice, East Block, Room EB16, Strand, London, WC2A 2LL
Telephone: 020 7071 5793
www.sentencingcouncil.org.uk
Email: info@sentencingcouncil.gov.uk
REMIT: The Sentencing Council for England and Wales was set up in April 2010 to promote greater transparency and consistency in sentencing, while maintaining the independence of the judiciary.

The primary role of the Council is to issue guidelines on sentencing, which the courts must follow unless it is in the interests of justice not to do so.

The Sentencing Council is an independent, non-departmental public body. We are part of the Ministry of Justice family of arm's-length bodies.

The Council has responsibility for:

- developing sentencing guidelines and monitoring their use
- assessing the impact of guidelines on sentencing practice. The Council may also be required to consider the impact of policy and legislative proposals relating to sentencing, when requested by the Government, and
- promoting awareness among the public regarding the realities of sentencing, and publishing information about sentencing practice in magistrates' courts and the Crown Court.

The Council must also:

- consider the impact on victims of sentencing decisions
- monitor the application of the guidelines, and
- when developing guidelines,

promote understanding of, and public confidence in, sentencing and the criminal justice system.

## YOUTH JUSTICE BOARD

Chief Executive: Claudia Sturt
Youth Justice Board for England and Wales
70 Petty France, London, SW1H 9EX
Press Office 020 3334 3536
https://www.gov.uk/government/organisations/youth-justice-board-for-england-and-wales
Email: YJB.Enquiries@yjb.gov.uk
REMIT: We are a non-departmental public body responsible for overseeing the youth justice system in England and Wales.
*Who we are*
We are an organisation of around 100 people and our headquarters is in London.

Our vision is for a youth justice system that sees children as children, treats them fairly and helps them to build on their strengths so they can make a constructive contribution to society. This will prevent offending and create safer communities with fewer victims.
*Our responsibilities*
One of our main functions is to monitor the operation of the youth justice system and the provision of youth justice services. Within England and Wales, we're responsible for:

- using information and evidence to form an expert view of how to get the best outcomes for children who offend and for victims of crime
- advising the Secretary of State for Justice, government departments, local authorities, those working in youth justice services and other organisations about how well the system is operating, and how improvements can be made
- identifying and sharing best practice
- promoting the voice of the child, including taking advice from our youth advisory panel of young adults who have current or previous experience of the youth justice system
- commissioning research and publishing information in connection with good practice
- monitoring the youth justice system and the provision of youth justice services
- making grants, with the approval of the Secretary of State, for the purposes of the operation of the youth justice system and services
- providing information technology related assistance for the operation of the youth justice system and services

## PRISON OFFICERS' ASSOCIATION

General Secretary: Steve Gillan
National Chairman: Mark Fairhurst
Cronin House

245 Church Street
London N9 9HW
Tel: 020 8803 0255
http://www.poauk.org.uk/
Email: general@poauk.org.uk

The POA is the largest union in the United Kingdom representing Uniformed Prison Grades and staff working within the field of Secure Forensic Psychiatric Care, with over 35 thousand members in the public and private sectors.

Its history can be traced back to 1916; in 1919 the Police and Prison Officers Union was formed, this later transformed into a Representative Committee, but it wasn't until 1939 that the Prison Officers' Association was formed and continues to this day.

The following is a current list (July 2019) of Charity Commission registered charities whose activities and/or objectives involve prisons and offenders - (*https://tinyurl.com/kuxckua*).

**For a full list of Offender and Prison related Registered Charities see the *PrisonOracle.com***

Section
Four

Legal
Prisoners and the Law

Legal
Prisoners and the Law

# Section 4

## Legal

### PRISONERS & THE LAW

The 2023 edition has been updated by Grace Cowell, Margo Munro Kerr, Natalie Csengeri, Sarah Corbett-Batson, Sarah Jane-Ewart, Hannah Webb, and Maria Liddiard of the Prison Law and Criminal Appeals Team at One Pump Court Chambers. The text is based on an earlier draft originally written by barristers Stephen Field, Rupert Wheeler, and Stefan Fox, and later updated by barristers Sharon Holloway, Stephen Knight, Angelina Nicolaou, Sophie Walker and Daniel Grütters all of One Pump Court Chambers.

**"The degree of civilization in a society can be judged by entering its prisons."**
*Fyodor Dostoevsky (1821 - 1881), Russian novelist, author of Crime and Punishment*

#### Preface to the 2023 Edition

This edition has been revised and updated to 30 June 2022.

The last 12 months has continued to show a significant decline in the treatment of prisoners as a result of the continuing COVID-19 pandemic. This must be considered alongside the grave concerns over treatment of prisoners before the pandemic, with use of force reportedly doubling against prisoners in the last decade. The pandemic led to the extension of lockdowns and restrictions on visits with family, and access to lawyers, as well as an extension of custody time limits, which at the time of publication have now been reversed. These changes, whilst designed to be temporary, continue to have a significant impact on prisoners.

In June 2022 Charlie Taylor, the chief inspector of prisons, reported concerns that prisons across the United Kingdom continue to impose 'covid-era' regimes. For example, some prisoners continue to be kept in their cells for 22-23 hours a day. This is due to multiple reasons. In particular, shortages in staffing means that prisoners often continue to experience minimal freedoms and privileges. Further to this, many prison staff who joined during the pandemic lack training and the experience of working in prisons outside of the context of the pandemic. There is concern that this contributes to the inability of prisons to "get back to normal".

The failure to return prisons and young offender institutions to more normal regimes after the Covid-19 restrictions have been relaxed, more rapidly, is a continuing criticism of the Chief Inspector - see the Report on HMP Lewes 22nd August 2022 on *prisonoracle.com*.

Separately, the introduction of new Prison & Probation Policy Frameworks is continuing, replacing many Prison Service Instructions ("PSIs"), Prison Service Orders ("PSOs") and Probation Instructions ("PIs"). The ongoing introduction of the Policy Frameworks will see further changes to the detail of prison law in the months and years to come. They are available on the Prison Oracle at *https://prisonoracle.com.*

Where relevant, this edition has also addressed the transformation of probation services in England and Wales. From 2015 to 2022, private sector Community Rehabilitation Companies ('CRC') oversaw the management and rehabilitation of medium and low-risk offenders in England and Wales. The National Probation Service (NPS), part of HM Prison and Probation Service, oversaw the management and rehabilitation of high-risk offenders only. From 26 June 2021, the NPS took over the work previously carried out by CRCs. The future of probation is on *prisonoracle.com*

This section of The Prisons Handbook though comprehensive is meant as a starting point to help prisoners to work out their legal rights and how they can challenge abuses of them. However, case law and prison rules and policies continue to develop, in new and complex ways. As such, this section necessarily cannot be exhaustive. Prisoners should think seriously about obtaining the services of a qualified Prison Law solicitor or barrister before taking legal action. Many legal issues attract time limits for taking legal action, so when issues arise it is important not to delay. Nevertheless, the case law entries serve to demonstrate the way in which prisoners have resolutely taken points of law to the courts to achieve a situation where there is now an established area of public law spanning the entirety of prison life.

The 2022 edition continues to build on the fully updated section on criminal appeals, which focuses more closely on issues that prisoners are likely to face in launching appeals against conviction and sentence. We hope that this section allows prisoners to more easily assess their legal rights when it comes to appeal, allowing them to determine the possible risks and rewards of appealing.

Features introduced in previous editions remain, such as the "A-Z of Prison Law," with key cases and key principles in any given area highlighted. Our first entry – "Access to Justice" serves as an opportunity to reflect the House of Lords decision in Raymond v Honey [1983] 1 A.C. 1; 4 March 1982, in which Lord Bridge held that:

"two basic principles [are] to be applied; first, that any act done which is calculated to obstruct or interfere with the due course of justice, or the lawful process of the courts, is a contempt of court; secondly, that a convicted prisoner, in spite of his imprisonment, retains all civil rights which are not taken away expressly or by necessary implication. To these I would add a third principle, equally basic, that a citizen's right to unimpeded access to the courts can only be taken away by express enactment".

We hope that the above statement, made more than 39 years ago, will continue to reflect the law's acceptance that even those imprisoned retain their most fundamental civil rights.

We wish to take this opportunity to thank the late Stephen Field, as well as Rupert Wheeler, Stefan Fox, Sharon Holloway, Stephen Knight, Angelina Nicolau, Daniel Grütters and Sophie Walker for their extensive commitment and contribution to the growing body of work and understanding in the area of prison law. We also thank our passionate colleagues and dedicated clerks in the Prison Law and Criminal Appeals team at One Pump Court Chambers for their support and unswerving commitment to the cause.

**Grace Cowell, Margo Munro Kerr, Natalie Csengeri, Sarah Corbett-Batson, Sarah Jane-Ewart, Hannah Webb, and Maria Liddiard**
**1st July 2022**

## PRISON & YOI RULES

**Up to date copies of both the Prison and the YOI Rules are available on The Prison Oracle –**
*https://prisonoracle.com*

**Prison Rules 1999/728**
*Preamble*
**Part I**
rule 1 Citation and commencement
rule 2 Interpretation
rule 2A Coronavirus period – transition period

**Part II PRISONERS**
**GENERAL**
rule 3 Purpose of prison training and treatment
rule 4 Outside contacts
rule 5 After care
rule 6 Maintenance of order and discipline

rule 7 Classification of prisoners
rule 8 Privileges
rule 9 Temporary release
rule 10 Information to prisoners
rule 11 Requests and complaints
**WOMEN PRISONERS**
rule 12 Women prisoners
**RELIGION**
rule 13 Religious denomination
rule 14 Special duties of chaplains and prison ministers
rule 15 Regular visits by ministers of religion
rule 16 Religious services
rule 17 Substitute for chaplain or prison minister
rule 18 Sunday work
rule 19 Religious books
**MEDICAL ATTENTION**
rule 20 Health services
rule 21 Special illnesses and conditions
rule 22 Notification of illness or death
**PHYSICAL WELFARE AND WORK**
rule 23 Clothing
rule 24 Food
rule 25 Alcohol and tobacco
rule 26 Sleeping accommodation
rule 27 Beds and bedding
rule 28 Hygiene
rule 29 Physical education
rule 30 Time in the open air
rule 31 Work
rule 31A Prescription of certain matters in respect of prisoners' earnings
**EDUCATION AND LIBRARY**
rule 32 Education
rule 33 Library
**COMMUNICATIONS**
rule 34 Communications generally
rule 35 Personal letters and visits
rule 35A Interception of communications
rule 35B Permanent log of communications
rule 35C Disclosure of material
rule 35D Retention of material
rule 36 Police interviews
rule 37 Securing release
rule 38 Visits from legal advisers
rule 39 Delivery and receipt of legally privileged material
**REMOVAL, SEARCH, RECORD & PROPERTY**
rule 40 Custody outside prison
rule 41 Search
rule 42 Record and photograph
rule 43 Prisoners' property
rule 44 Money and articles received by post
**SPECIAL CONTROL, SUPERVISION & RESTRAINT & DRUG TESTING**
rule 45 Removal from association
rule 46 Close supervision centres
rule 46A Separation centres
rule 47 Use of force

rule 48 Temporary confinement
rule 49 Restraints
rule 50 Compulsory testing for controlled drugs
or specified drugs
rule 50A Observation of prisoners by means of
an overt closed circuit television system
rule 50B Compulsory testing for alcohol
**OFFENCES AGAINST DISCIPLINE**
rule 51 Offences against discipline
rule 51A Interpretation of rule 51
rule 52 Defences to rule 51(9)
rule 52A Defences to rule 51(10) and rule 51(11)
rule 53 Disciplinary charges
rule 53A Determination of mode of inquiry
rule 54B Determination of mode of inquiry in a
Coronavirus period
rule 54 Rights of prisoners charged
rule 55 Governor's punishments
rule 55A Adjudicator's punishments
rule 55AB Requirement to pay for damage to
prison property
rule 55B Review of adjudicator's punishment
rule 56 Forfeiture of remission to be treated as an
award of additional days
rule 57 Offences committed by young persons
rule 58
rule 59 Prospective award of additional days
rule 59A Removal from a cell or living unit
rule 60 Suspended punishments
rule 61 Remission and mitigation of
punishments, variation of compensation
requirements and quashing of findings of guilt
rule 61A Enforcement of compensation requirements

**Part III OFFICERS OF PRISONS**
rule 62 General duty of officers
rule 63 Gratuities forbidden
rule 64 Search of officers
rule 65 Transactions with prisoners
rule 66 Contact with former prisoners
rule 67 Communications to the press
rule 68 Code of discipline
rule 69 Emergencies

**Part IV PERSONS HAVING ACCESS TO A
PRISON**
rule 70 Prohibited articles
rule 70A List C Articles
rule 71 Control of persons and vehicles
rule 72 Viewing of prisons
rule 73 Visitors

**Part V INDEPENDENT MONITORING BOARD**
rule 74 Disqualification for membership
rule 75 Independent monitoring board
rule 76 Proceedings of boards
rule 77 General duties of boards
rule 78 Particular duties
rule 79 Members visiting prisons
rule 80 Annual report

**Part VI SUPPLEMENTAL**
rule 81 Delegation by governor
rule 82 Contracted out prisons
rule 83 Contracted out parts of prisons
rule 84 Contracted out functions at directly
managed prisons
rule 85 Revocations and savings
Signatures
Schedule 1
para. 1
Schedule 2 Definition of specified drug
para. 1
Explanatory Note
para. 1

**Young Offender Institution Rules 2000/3371**
*Preamble*
**Part I PRELIMINARY**
rule 1 Citation and commencement
rule 2 Interpretation
rule 2A Coronavirus period – transition period

**Part II INMATES**
**General**
rule 3 Aims and general principles of young
offender institutions
rule 4 Classification of inmates
**Release**
rule 5 Temporary release
rule 5A Coronavirus Restricted Temporary Release
**Conditions**
rule 6 Privileges
rule 7 Information to inmates
rule 8 Requests and complaints
rule 9 Communications generally
rule 10 Personal letters and visits
rule 11 Interception of communications
rule 12 Permanent log of communications
rule 13 Disclosure of material
rule 14 Retention of material
rule 15 Police interviews
rule 16 Visits from legal advisers
rule 17 Delivery and receipt of legally privileged
material
rule 18 Securing release of defaulters
rule 19 Clothing
rule 20 Food
rule 21 Alcohol and tobacco
rule 22 Sleeping accommodation
rule 23 Beds and bedding
rule 24 Hygiene
rule 25 Female inmates
rule 26 Library books
**Medical Attention**
rule 27 Health services
rule 28 Special illnesses and conditions
rule 29 Notification of illness or death

**Religion**
rule 30 Religious denomination
rule 31 Special duties of chaplains and appointed ministers
rule 32 Regular visits by ministers of religion, etc
rule 33 Religious services
rule 34 Substitute for chaplain or appointed minister
rule 35 Sunday work
rule 36 Religious books
**Occupation and Links with the Community**
rule 37 Regime activities
rule 38 Education
rule 39 Training courses
rule 40 Work
rule 41 Physical education
rule 42 Outside contacts
rule 43 After-care
**Discipline and Control**
rule 44 Maintenance of order and discipline
rule 45 Custody outside a young offender institution
rule 46 Search
rule 47 Record and photograph
rule 48 Inmates' property
rule 49 Removal from association
rule 50 Use of force
rule 51 Temporary confinement
rule 52 Restraints
rule 53 Compulsory Testing for controlled drugs, pharmacy medicines and other substances etc.
rule 54 Supervision of inmates by means of an overt closed circuit television system
rule 54A Compulsory testing for alcohol
rule 55 Offences against discipline
rule 56 Defences to rule 55(10)
rule 56A Defences to rule 55(11) and rule 55(12)
rule 57 Interpretation of rule 55
rule 58 Disciplinary charges
rule 58A Determination of mode of inquiry
rules 58B Determination of a mode of inquiry in a Coronavirus period
rule 59 Rights of inmates charged
rule 60 Governor's punishments
rule 60A Adjudicator's punishments
rule 60AB Requirement to pay for damage to young offender institution property
rule 60B Review of adjudicator's punishment
rule 61 Confinement to a cell or room
rule 62 Removal from wing or living unit
rule 63 Suspended punishments
rule 64 Remission and mitigation of punishments, variation of compensation requirements and quashing of findings of guilt
rule 64A Enforcement of compensation requirements
rule 65 Adult female inmates: disciplinary punishments
rule 66 Forfeiture of remission to be treated as an award of additional days

**Part III**
**Officers of Young Offender Institutions**
rule 67 General duty of officers
rule 68 Gratuities forbidden
rule 69 Search of officers
rule 70 Transactions with inmates
rule 71 Contact with former inmates, etc
rule 72 Communications to the press, etc
rule 73 Code of discipline

**Part IV**
**Persons Having Access to a Young Offender Institution**
rule 74 Prohibited articles
rule 74A
rule 75 Control of persons and vehicles
rule 76 Viewing of young offender institutions
rule 77 Visitors

**Part V**
**Independent Monitoring Board**
rule 78 Disqualification for membership
rule 79 Appointment
rule 80 Proceedings of boards
rule 81 General duties of boards
rule 82 Particular duties
rule 83 Members visiting young offender institutions
rule 84 Annual report

**Part VI**
**Supplemental**
rule 85 Delegation by governor
rule 86 Contracted out young offender institutions
rule 87 Contracted out parts of young offender institutions
rule 88 Contracted out functions at directly managed young offender institutions
rule 89 Revocations and savings
Signatures
Schedule 1 REVOCATIONS
para. 1
Schedule 2 DEFINITION OF SPECIFIED DRUG
para. 1
Explanatory Note
para. 1

## A-Z SUBJECT INDEX

This Index has developed over many years. It was originally modelled on the Prison Service published Index to Prison Service Instructions, Orders, Standards, Prison Rules, YOI Rules & Prison Act. Headings have been added where necessary (e.g. "Access to Justice") and certain technical headings are omitted.

This "A-Z of Prison Law" is designed to identify, at a glance, the relevant statutory provisions, any relevant Prison Rule, PSO, PSI and Prison Standard, as well as providing a Case Law synopsis.

Whilst there is a full list of Standards and PSOs in Part II above, the content of selected important and relevant Prison Rules and Standards are reproduced in this Index.

Under the heading Case Law, a comprehensive list of reported cases, updated to June 2022, has been added. Key cases and words are highlighted.

Copies of most of the cases can be located on the free legal web site, Bailli.

## DEFINITIONS

ACT: Prison Act 1952 (numbers refer to sections)
AI: Instruction
CJA 1991: Criminal Justice Act 1991
CJA 2003: Criminal Justice Act 2003
CJIA 2008: Criminal Justice & Immigration Act 2008
CO: Consent Order in Judicial Review Proceedings
IG: Instructions to governors (NB only a few still important and valid are included)
IP: Information and practice paper
PSI or no prefix: Prison Service Instruction
PSO: Prison Service Order
PR: Prison Rules 1999 (numbers refer to paragraph number)
Standard: Prison Service Standard
YOI: Young Offender Institution Rules 2000 (numbers refer to paragraph number)

## ACCESS TO JUSTICE

Access to Digital Evidence Policy Framework
Re-issued 13 March 2019
This Policy Framework sets out the process for Governors/Directors in providing prisoners with access to digital equipment (Information Technology equipment), where that equipment is required for prisoners to view electronic disclosure by the Crown as evidence for the prosecution in any legal case.
Legal advice and assistance PR 38, 39.
Prison Rule 38 Legal advisers
38. - (1) The legal adviser of a prisoner in any legal proceedings, civil or criminal, to which the prisoner is a party shall be afforded reasonable facilities for interviewing him in connection with those proceedings, and may do so out of hearing but in the sight of an officer.
(2) A prisoner's legal adviser may, subject to any directions given by the Secretary of State, interview the prisoner in connection with any other legal business out of hearing but in the sight of an officer.
Prison Rule 39
Correspondence with legal advisers and courts
39. - (1) A prisoner may correspond with his legal adviser and any court and such correspondence may only be opened, read or stopped by the governor in accordance with the provisions of this rule.

(2) Correspondence to which this rule applies may be opened if the governor has reasonable cause to believe that it contains an illicit enclosure and any such enclosures shall be dealt with in accordance with the other provision of these Rules.
(3) Correspondence to which this rule applies may be opened, read and stopped if the governor has reasonable cause to believe its contents endanger prison security or the safety of others or are otherwise of a criminal nature.
(4) A prisoner shall be given the opportunity to be present when any correspondence to which this rule applies is opened and shall be informed if it or any enclosure is to be read or stopped.
(5) A prisoner shall on request be provided with any writing materials necessary for the purposes of paragraph (1).
(6) In this rule, "court" includes the European Commission of Human Rights, the European Court of Human Rights and the European Court of Justice; and "illicit enclosure" includes any article possession of which has not been authorised in accordance with the other provisions of these Rules and any correspondence to or from a person other than the prisoner concerned, his legal adviser or a court.
PSI 04/2016 The Interception of Communications in Prison and Security Measures
Re-Issued 01/04/2021
Confidential communications apply not just to a prisoner and their legal advisor. A full list of persons, bodies and organisations to which there is an 'obligation not to intercept' is set out in full at paragraph 2.22 of the PSI. This includes: Courts, Bar Council, Law Society, Official Solicitor, Criminal Cases Review Commission, Prison and Probation Ombudsman, Equality and Human Rights Commission, Embassy or Consular Officials, Samaritans, Members of Parliament etc.
In rare circumstances, a prisoner's legal and confidential communications may be monitored where those communications are believed to being used to further criminality. But such monitoring must have prior authorisation by the CEO of NOMS or another Director of NOMS in accordance with Prison Rule 35A 2A. (para 2.23) Any unintentional interception and acquisition of legal and confidential communications must be investigated by prison management. (para 2.43) Checks must be made on the authenticity of any number provided by the prisoner purporting to be a solicitor or barrister. (para 2.28)
**Case Law**
*R (on the application of Howard League for Penal Reform) v Lord Chancellor* [2017] EWCA Civ 244
The high threshold for a finding of inherent or systemic unfairness had been satisfied in respect

of the removal of legal aid for prisoners in pre-tariff Parole Board reviews, categorisation reviews of Category A prisoners and decisions on placement in close supervision centres. These changes had brought about by the Criminal Legal Aid (General) (Amendment) Regulations 2013. However, systemic unfairness was not reached in respect of decisions about offending behaviour programmes and disciplinary proceedings.

*R (on the application of SM) v The Lord Chancellor* [2021] 1 WLR 3815
The failure to provide immigration detainees held in prison access to publicly funded legal advice to the same extent as they would have if they were detained in immigration removal centres amounted to discrimination contrary to Article 14 of the European Convention of Human Rights

*Jeffrey Shane Watkins v Home Office & Ors* [2006] UKHL 17
The appellant Home Office appealed against the decision ((2004) EWCA Civ 966, (2005) QB 883) that wilful breach of a prisoner's constitutional right to receive unopened correspondence from his legal advisers or the courts amounted to misfeasance in public office that was actionable without proof of damage. W was a convicted prisoner serving a sentence of life imprisonment. He was engaged in a number of legal proceedings. The confidentiality of W's correspondence with his legal advisers and the courts was protected by the Prison Rules 1964 r.37A and then the Prison Rules 1999 r.39 . Prison officers had breached the Rules by opening and reading W's mail when they were not entitled to do so.

*R v Secretary of State for The Home Department, Ex Parte Daly* [2001] UKHL 26
A prisoner maintained three main rights whilst in custody: (i) the right of access to a court; (ii) the right of access to legal advice; and (iii) the right to communicate confidentially with a legal adviser under the seal of legal professional privilege. These rights could only be curtailed by clear and express words and then only to the extent reasonably necessary to meet the ends which justified the curtailment. A policy allowing prison staff to search a prisoner's legally privileged correspondence in his absence could not stand. (Principle applied in the Matter of an Application for Judicial Review by Louis Maguire [2012] NIQB 39 (Northern Ireland) which held that a rule requiring the presence of a prison officer patrolling the legal visits room was necessary, proportionate and in accordance with the law.)

*R v Secretary of State for the Home Department ex parte Mark Leech (no. 2) (1993)* (1994) QB 198

(1993) 3 WLR 1125 : (1993) 4 All ER 539 : Times, May 20, 1993: CA (Civ Div)
Prisoner's appeal against dismissal of his application for judicial review of r.33 Prison Rules 1964/388 concerning reading prisoners' letters which he contended was ultra vires Section 47(1) Prison Act 1952 allowed. It is an axiom of our law that a convicted prisoner, in spite of his imprisonment, retains all civil rights which are not taken away expressly or by necessary implication.

*Raymond v Honey* [1983] 1 A.C. 1
Two basic principles apply; first, that any act done which is calculated to obstruct or interfere with the course of justice, or the lawful process of the courts, is a contempt of court; secondly, that a convicted prisoner in spite of his imprisonment, retains all civil rights which are not taken away expressly or by necessary implication. To these I would add a third principle, equally basic, that a citizen's rights to unimpeded access to the courts can only be taken away by express enactment.

## ACCESS TO LEGAL REPRESENTATION
**Case law**
*R (Thakrar) v Secretary of State for Justice* [2012] EWHC 3538 (Admin)
Policies implemented by the Secretary of State for Justice under the Prison Rules 1999, supplemented by national and local guidance, in relation to communications between a prisoner in a close supervision centre and his lawyers were not unlawful, and did not breach Articles 6 or 8 of the European Convention on Human Rights. See Also under Close Supervision Centres, below.

## ACCOMMODATION
PR26
Prison Rule 26
Sleeping accommodation
26. - (1) No room or cell shall be used as sleeping accommodation for a prisoner unless it has been certified in the manner required by section 14 of the Prison Act 1952 in the case of a cell used for the confinement of a prisoner.
(2) A certificate given under that section or this rule shall specify the maximum number of prisoners who may sleep or be confined at one time in the room or cell to which it relates, and the number so specified shall not be exceeded without the leave of the Secretary of State.
Certified Prisoner Accommodation Policy Framework August 2022
1. Purpose
1.1 Certification is a legal requirement under Section 14 of the Prison Act 1952. It must be completed for all prison and young offender

institution accommodation before it can be used to confine prisoners overnight. This Policy Framework sets out the minimum requirements for certification and mandatory actions to ensure that all accommodation is properly certified.
Bail Accommodation and Supper Service (BASS) Policy Framework

**Key Note**
The 2 cases recited below are significant "slopping out" cases. The first was an unsuccessful English claim, the second was a Scottish case which gives helpful guidance on the procedural and evidential issues arising in such cases.
*(1) Desmond Grant (2) Roger Charles Gleaves v Ministry of Justice* [2011] EWHC 3379 (QB); [2012] A.C.D. 32; 19 December 2011
See "Slopping Out" below.
*Napier v Scottish Ministers* [2005] U.K.H.R.R. 268 Court of Session (Inner House, First Division) 10 February 2005
See "Slopping Out" below.

**Case Law**
*R (on the application of AN) v Secretary of State for Justice* [2009] EWHC 1921 (Admin)
Where the placement of a prisoner in a single cell for a two-week period had been a proportionate response to a genuinely and reasonably held security concern, the conditions into which he had been moved fell very far short of torture or inhuman and degrading treatment, and there was no evidence of any significant interference with the prisoner's right to private life, either in the period when he was in the single cell, or in terms of the consequences of that episode for his mental health afterwards, there had been no violation of the European Convention on Human Rights 1950 art.3 or art.8.

*Kelly v Ministry of Justice* [2014] EWHC 3440 (QB)
A high level of suffering is required to trigger ECHR art.3. A prisoner had not been able to show by direct or inferential evidence that having to use a bucket as a toilet when locked in his cell at night cause him serious suffering (e.g. physical or psychiatric injury, physiological selfharm of particularly serious distress) so as to amount to a violation of the ECHR art.3.

**ACCREDITED OFFENDING BEHAVIOUR PROGRAMMES**
**Key Note**
The failure of the Secretary of State to provide sufficient Accredited Behaviour Courses remains a contentious area of dispute within the Court system.
**Case Law**
*(1) Philip Fletcher (2) Paul Young (3) Keith Bentley V (1) Governor of Whatton Prison (2) Secretary Of State For Justice* [2014] EWHC 3586 (Admin)
The public law duty of the Secretary of State for

Justice to provide systems and resources that prisoners serving indeterminate sentences for public protection needed so as to be able to demonstrate to the Parole Board that they were no longer dangerous, confirmed in R. (on the application of Wells) v Parole Board [2009] UKHL 22, [2010] 1 A.C. 553, could not be modified or affected by the level of resources made available to prisons by the secretary of state. The secretary of state had a duty to provide sufficient resources for offender programmes to discharge the public law duty.

*R (Weddle) v Secretary Of State For Justice* [2013] EWHC 2323 (Admin)
In failing to provide a life prisoner with the means by which he could demonstrate that he constituted a reduced risk such as to enable him to progress to a lower security prison category and to become suitable for release, the Secretary of State for Justice had breached his public law duty to act rationally.

*R (on the application of M) v The Secretary of State for Justice* [2016] EWHC 2455 (Admin)
The fact that the prisoner did not have access to accredited offender behaviour programmes (OBPs) whilst in the protected witness unit (PWU) did not prevent him from accessing and benefiting from bespoke one-to-one intervention programmes comparable to OBPs, enabling him to reduce his risk to the public.

*Kaiyam v United Kingdom (Admissibility)* (2016) 62 E.H.R.R SE13
The ECtHR declined to adopt the approach of the Supreme Court ([2014] UKSC 66) that the duty to provide a reasonable opportunity for a prisoner subject to an indeterminate sentence to rehabilitate himself was an 'ancillary duty' which could not be brought within the express language of either art5(1)(a) or art 5(4) and did not therefore affect the lawfulness of the detention. The ECtHR adhered to the reasoning in the case of James v UK (25119/9). (See further application by the Supreme Court in Brown v The Parole Board for Scotland [2017] UKSC 69 at 44-45: The appropriate course is to adopt the same approach to the interpretation of article 5(1)(a) as has been followed by the ECHR since the case of James, and cease to treat the obligation in question as an ancillary obligation in article 5 as a whole. Emphasis should be placed on the high threshold to establish a violation of the obligation)

*R (on the application of Cawser) v Secretary of State for the Home Department* [2003] EWCA Civ 1522
The Home Secretary was under a duty to provide

sex offender treatment programmes for prisoners qualified by the extent of available resources and subject only to a public law duty to act rationally.

*R (on the application of Gourlay) v The Secretary of State for Justice & Ors* [2016] EWHC 1957 (Admin)
The duty to provide an opportunity reasonable in all the circumstances for a prisoner to rehabilitate himself and demonstrate that he no longer presents an unacceptable danger to the public does not extend to "everything conceivably possible".

Where a post-tariff life sentence prisoner had maintained his innocence in respect of his sexual offending, his lack of suitability for the sex offending treatment programme (SOTP) was due to his refusal to acknowledge any need for change himself. Consequently the Defendants had not breached their duty by failing to provide to the prisoner an alternative programme suitable for "deniers".

## ADJUDICATIONS

PSI 05/2018 – Prisoner Discipline Procedures (for all adjudications which commenced after 1/2/19). Note that PSI 47/2011 applies to any adjudications which commenced before 1/2/19
PSI 05/2018
3.2 "Adjudications (including a special form of hearing known as Minor Reports) are the procedures by which offences against the Prison or YOI Rules allegedly been committed by prisoners or YOs are dealt with. The adjudication systems sets out how prisons or YOs are charged with offences, the procedure for inquiring into the charge to determine the accused prisoner/YO's guilt or innocence, including their right to a defence, the punishments for those found guilty, and their right to apply for a review".
3.4 Staff should consider less formal measures in dealing with minor infringements of Prison Rules, such as Five-Minute Intervention (FMI) and informal conflict resolution techniques. Within the youth estate, those less formal mechanisms may include the Custody Support Plan (CUSP) and or engaging the young person in restorative practice via the Conflict Resolution model. The Incentives and Earned Privileges (IEP) scheme can also be used as a tool to manage low level misconduct by considering patterns of behaviour which could trigger an IEP downgrade.
**Key Note**
All Prisoners and Practitioners need to obtain a copy of the latest PSI which sets out the approach and procedures for adjudications.
The PSI includes sections on "Adjudication Procedures", and Annexes on "Before the Adjudication", "During the Adjudication", "After the Adjudication", a "Table of forms", a "Flow

Chart Basic Adjudication Procedure", "Significant adjudication case law (European Court judgements and judicial reviews)" as well as a detailed "Alphabetical Index with Paragraph Numbers".
**Case Law**
*R (Soar) v Secretary of State for Justice* [2015] EWHC 392 (Admin)
The claimant applied for judicial review of the prison adjudicator. The adjudicator had admitted medical evidence from a nurse by telephone. The prisoner, however, had not been allowed to question the nurse or adduce his own medical evidence. It was held that this was a breach of PSI 47/2001 and contrary to the rules of natural justice. It followed that the procedural irregularity rendered the adjudication unfair.

*R (Cox) v Independent Adjudicator* [2013] EWHC 2753 (Admin)
A decision of an independent adjudicator to impose an additional 13 days on a prisoner's sentence following an adjudication was quashed where the adjudicator had refused to exercise his discretion in favour of adducing CCTV footage that might have assisted, and instead relied upon the disputed evidence of the reporting officer.

*R (MA) v Independent Adjudicator* [2013] EWHC 438 (Admin)
Following a disturbance, a young offender institution had unlawfully removed five prisoners from association for three days, restricted their and two other prisoners' use of the gym, and failed to provide relevant paperwork to their legal representative before an adjudication. Deprivation of privileges, in addition to the imposition of extra days, was in line with policy and was lawful, as was the gradual reintroduction to education for risk management purposes.

*Ochechukwiw Ezeh and Lawrence Connors v United Kingdom* (2003) Application No.: 00039665/98 : 00040086/98, European Court of Human Rights (Grand Chamber) (L Wildhaber P) 9/10/2003
The Grand Chamber saw no reason to depart from the finding of the European Court of Human Rights that there had been a breach of Art.6(3) when prisoners had been denied free legal assistance in relation to adjudication hearings before their prison governor in respect of disciplinary proceedings when additional days were awardable.

## ADULT SOCIAL CARE

PSI 03/2016 AI 06/2016 PI 06/2016- "Adult Social Care"
This PSI replaces PSI 15/2015, AI 10/2015 PI 11/2015.

This PSI details changes made to NOMS Service Specifications to capture NOMS responsibilities resulting from the requirements of the Care Act 2014 and Social Services and Wellbeing (Wales) Act 2014. It provides all staff with details of the relevant elements of these Acts, which reform social care provision and clarify the responsibility of local authorities in England and Wales. These Acts ensure that social care for adults in prisons and approved premises, and for those occupying bail accommodation as a condition of criminal proceedings, is provided on the basis of equivalence to people living in the community. The relevant sections of both Acts apply to adult prisoners and young offenders aged 18 and over in England and Wales regardless of where they have lived prior to imprisonment.

It also introduces two new outputs that have been added to the relevant NOMS service specifications, to introduce a requirement for prisons to make and record appropriate referrals to the Local Authority, in order to trigger a social care needs assessment, where this is indicated (section 17).

## ADVANCES, CASH

HMPPS Finance Manual Policy Framework Re-issued 3 November 2020
HMPPS Financial Manual
13.6.8: Prisoner must only be credited with an advance to cover their first night canteen purchases at initial reception. If a prisoner has sufficient funds to cover the cost then an advance must not be issued. If a prisoner has funds to cover part of the cost the only the difference may be advanced.
13.6.9: Prisoners may be advanced funds throughout their time in custody where it can be demonstrated that there is a justified need for such funds. The advance should only be given where the repayment is guaranteed and collected in full as soon as possible.
13.6.10: Advances will be automatically deducted from the prisoner's spends account each week until fully repaid or until transfer to a private prison/release. Prison –NOMIS collects advances in sequential order of issues, so if there is more than one advance it will collect from the earliest first.

## AFTER CARE

PR 5
YOI 43
After Care (see also "Housing and Homelessness" below)
Prison Rule 5
After care
5. From the beginning of a prisoner's sentence, consideration shall be given, in consultation with the appropriate after-care organisation, to the prisoner's future and the assistance to be given him on and after his release.

## AIMS (see also "Purpose of Prison")

Prison Rule 3
Purpose of prison training and treatment
3. The purpose of the training and treatment of convicted prisoners shall be to encourage and assist them to lead a good and useful life.

## ALCOHOL AND TOBACCO

Section 16B ACT – Power to test prisoners for alcohol
Section 22 Offender Management Act 2007 – Conveyance of prohibited articles into or out of prison
YOI 21
(1) No inmate shall be allowed to have any intoxicating liquor.
(2) No inmate shall be allowed to smoke or have any tobacco except in accordance with any directions of the Secretary of State.
YOI 54A – Compulsory testing for alcohol
Prison Rule 25
(1) No prisoner shall be allowed to have any intoxicating liquor.
(2) No prisoner shall be allowed to smoke or to have any tobacco, except in accordance with any directions of the Secretary of State.
Prison Rule 50B – Compulsory testing for alcohol

## ALLOCATION

### See also "Categorisation and Allocation".
### Key Note
The Secretary of State for Justice has wide ranging powers to place a Prisoner wherever he sees fit (section 12 of the Prison Act).
Section 12 Prison Act 1952
Place of confinement of prisoners.
(1) A prisoner, whether sentenced to imprisonment or committed to prison on remand or pending trial or otherwise, may be lawfully confined in any prison.
(2) Prisoners shall be committed to such prisons as the Secretary of State may from time to time direct; and may by direction of the Secretary of State be removed during the term of their imprisonment from the prison in which they are confined to any other prison.
The Security Categorisation Policy Framework (re-issued 17 August 2021) (note this must be read in conjunction with policies and guidance relating to ISPs and Category A)
1.6: Allocation decisions should consider the individual's offending behaviour and resettlement needs (such as access to suitable training and interventions and closeness to home at the end of their sentence), their individual circumstances (such as medical requirements), and control issues (such as danger to particular

staff or other prisoners). This may result in an individual being held in a prison of a higher category than their own category.

5.7: There is a presumption that an individual serving a determinate custodial sentence for an offence described in section 247A(2) of the Criminal Justice Act 2003 or an indeterminate sentence for a terrorist or terrorist connected offence is unsuitable for Category D/Open unless there are exceptional circumstances as set out within this framework (or the Generic Parole Process Framework where applicable).

## APPEALS AGAINST CONVICTION AND/OR SENTENCE (See Part IV of this section)
### Key Note
A very common complaint is that the sentencing court was wrong to find a prisoner dangerous and/or to impose an IPP (a sentence of last resort). This area is complicated by recent statutory changes. The date of an offence is an important point to consider, particularly if a prisoner wishes to argue that an Extended sentence would have been sufficient to protect the public.

## ARTICLES, PROHIBITED
See "Prohibited articles".

## ASSAULTS
See also Civil Actions Against the Prison and/or Secretary of State

## ASSISTED PRISON VISITS SCHEME
PSI 16/2011 – Providing Visits & Services to Visitors Strengthening Prisoner's Family Ties Policy Framework (updated January 2020)

## ASSOCIATION, REMOVAL FROM
See also "Segregation".
Prison Rule 45
45.— Removal from association
(1) Where it appears desirable, for the maintenance of good order or discipline or in his own interests, that a prisoner should not associate with other prisoners, either generally or for particular purposes, the governor may arrange for the prisoner's removal from association for up to 72 hours.
PR 59A Removal from cell or living unit
YOI 49 – Removal from Association
YOI 62 – Removal from wing or living unit.
PSO 1700
### Case Law
*Donnelly v Governor of HMP Shotts* [2013] CSOH 106 (Scotland)
Decisions of the prison governor and the Scottish Ministers to remove a prisoner from association was lawful, as the governor was entitled to suspect

that the prisoner might have been attempting to introduce a controlled drug into the prison and there was an obvious risk that if he were not segregated that introduction would happen.

See *R (MA) v Independent Adjudicator* [2013] EWHC 438 (Admin), under Adjudications, above.

*R (on the application of Bary & ors) v (1) Secretary of State for Justice v Governor of Long Lartin Prison* [2010] EWHC 587 (Admin)
The claimant detainees, all Muslim Prisoners, applied for judicial review of the decision of the second defendant prison governor to change their living and working regime. The Court held that: in order effectively to restrict a detainee, who was seen to represent a significant risk to national security and have a major influence on other Muslims, and who was being held with other detainees in a self-contained unit in a high security prison, from having unmonitored contact with the prisoners in the main prison or with the outside world, it was reasonable for the prison to impose a regime which kept all the detainees in their unit.

## ASSOCIATIONS, PRISONERS' REPRESENTATIVE
PSO 4480
PSO 4480 (Extract)
Prisoners Representative Associations
SUMMARY OF POLICY
1. Article 11 of the European Convention on Human Rights guarantees the freedom of peaceful assembly and association with others. In this context "association" means the right to form or join a group with others sharing a common interest and so applies to prisoners wishing to form or join representative bodies of other prisoners. But, it is a qualified right. It can be interfered with to prevent disorder or crime, provided any interference is proportionate. In deciding how far to allow prisoners' associations to operate in their establishments, Governors and Controllers must take account of local conditions and the implications for good order or discipline (GOOD). The arrangement must be kept under review.

## ATTENDANCE
PSI 01/2017 Attendance Management Policy
AI 01/2017
PSI 01/2017
IP 4/2002

## AWARDS
See "Performance recognition".

## BAIL
Bail Accommodation and Support Service (BASS) Policy Framework

The Bail Accommodation and Support Service (BASS) provides support to courts and prisons in achieving the best use of custody through the provision of suitable accommodation in a variety of locations in England and Wales, to the following groups in the following priority:
1. Bailees
2. Individuals subject to Home Detention Curfew
3. Individuals referred because of risk to Recall to prison due to loss of accommodation; or those who could be re-released following recall due to lack of accommodation
4. Individuals subject to Intensive Community Orders with a 'residence requirement'
5. Individuals referred upon release (part of the ALC)
PSI 9/2012 Implementation of the Service Specification for Bail Services (updated 19 August 2013)
PSO 6101 - bail information schemes
PSO 6100 - The bail system (see also PSI 66/1999)
PSI 48/2000 - Amendment to PSO 6100 (replaces chapters 3&5)

## BANKING AND CASH MANAGEMENT
HMPPS Finance Manual Policy Framework
PSI 44/2011 - Identity (ID) for Bank Account Applications for all Prisoners

## BEDS AND BEDDING
YOI 23
PR 27
Prison Rule 27
Beds and bedding
27. Each prisoner shall be provided with a separate bed and with separate bedding adequate for warmth and health.

## BOARDS OF VISITORS (Independent Monitoring Board)
PR 74-80
YOI 78-84
**Case Law**
*R (on the application of Bewry) v Secretary of State for the Home Department* [2007] EWHC 2711 (Admin)
The Prison Rules 1999 r.79(3), as amended, was not ultra vires the Prison Act 1952 s.6. The claimant (B), a former member of the independent monitoring board of a prison, applied for judicial review of the decision of the defendant secretary of state to refuse to allow him access to prison files containing covert human-intelligence source material.

## BONUSES
See "Performance recognition".

## BUILDINGS, Prison Service, maintenance
PSO 5901 - Maintenance of Prison Service buildings

## BULLYING – anti-bullying strategy
**See also "Violence Reduction".**
Building Bridges: A Positive Behaviour Framework for the Children and Young People Secure Estate (27 January 2020), section 5.7.
Prisoner Complaints Policy Framework (Updated 4 February 2022) Annexes with COMP1, COMP1A and COMP2 complaints form to address bullying.

## CARATS
See "Drugs".

## CATEGORISATION AND ALLOCATION
**Key Note**
A distinction is drawn in case law between Category A Prisoners and Category B and C Prisoners. In certain circumstances a Prisoner may be able to judicially review their categorisation. The court has recognised the importance of categorisation in terms of long-term progression through the prison system to eventual release.
It is important in all instances that Prisoners use the internal complaints procedure as an appeal before considering formal Judicial Review proceedings.
The Security Categorisation Policy Framework (updated 17 August 2021) (must be read in conjunction with policies and guidance relating to ISPs and Category A).
This policy framework includes the following sections: "Initial Categorisation: Assessment for Category D/Open conditions", "Recategorisation", "Timing of Reviews" "Recategorisation to Lower Security Prisons", "Recategorisation to Category D/Open Conditions" "Re-categorisation to a Higher Security Category", "Remaining in a Current Category" and "General Principles of Categorisation Assessments"
1.4 The security categorisation process provides for a holistic assessment of risk, taking account of a broad range of information from criminal justice and law enforcement agencies where available. It supports the categorisation of individuals to security conditions best suited to managing their risks.
**Case Law**
*R (M) v Parole Board* [2013] EWHC 141 (Admin)
A Parole Board was entitled to refuse to recommend the transfer of a prisoner serving sentences for three murder offences to open prison conditions because his difficulties in interpersonal relationships and his reaction to set-backs arising from them was key to the risk he might pose to others if transferred. The prisoner was sufficiently alerted to the fact that the board was concerned about his difficulties in

relationships, but he had failed to answer those concerns adequately to persuade the board that his transfer was appropriate.

*R (Manning) v Secretary Of State For Justice* [2013] EWHC 1821 (Admin)
A prison governor who had relied on a flawed RC1 risk assessment form when approving the recategorisation of a prisoner from Category C to open conditions had been entitled to reverse his decision upon learning that the form had omitted to refer to an unsatisfied confiscation order, which meant that the prisoner was at a higher risk of absconding than previously thought. No elaborate reasons for the reversal were needed; it was acceptable simply to explain his view that the existence of the confiscation order was decisive against recategorisation.

*M v Scottish Ministers* [2013] CSOH 112 (Scotland)
See "Lifers" below.

*Osborne, Booth and Reilly* [2013] UKSC 61
See "Parole Board Oral Hearings" below.

Security Categorisation Policy Framework (Updated17 August 2021)

See also:
PSI 08/2013 – National Security Framework: Category A function: the review of security category – Category A/Restricted status prisoners
PSI 09/2015 – The identification, initial categorisation and management of potential and provisional Category A/restricted status prisoners.
PSI 73/2000 – Allocation Guide (Restricted)
**Case Law**
**See also "Category A Prisoners" Case Law below.**
*R (on the application of David Jeremy) v (1) Governor of Prescoed Prison* [2012] EWHC 1036 (Admin)
The claimant prisoner (J) applied for judicial review of a decision of the first defendant prison governor refusing to review his summary recategorisation/reallocation. J had been summarily categorised from C-D following a negative MDT. He successfully achieved the dismissal of the ensuing disciplinary charges and had been recategorised back to D and reallocated to open conditions. Since proceedings were issued he had been released from custody. He submitted that there was a continuing stain on his prison record, and if he were detained again if he committed a further offence, the prison system would treat him differently because of the recategorisation/reallocation. The Court held that the complaint was of a failure to provide an appeal from a recategorisation/ reallocation. There was a route readily available to J under PSI 03/2009 para.16.1 but he did not avail himself of it.
*R (on the application of Clive Craig) v Governor of*

*Albany Prison* [2010] EWHC 2303 (Admin)
For case summary see "Maintaining Innocence" below.

*R (on the application of Lowe) v Governor of Liverpool Prison* [2008] EWHC 2167 (Admin)
The principles of consistency and legitimate expectation had to be applied when considering the categorisation of prisoners.

**Author's Note**
This principle was successfully argued in an IEP case where a Prisoner who maintained innocence had his status lowered after several years for no apparent reason (a judicial review terminated by consent: *R on the application of W v Secretary of State for Justice* (2010) (unreported).

*R (on the application of Bryant) v Secretary of State for the Home Department* [2005] EWHC 1663 (Admin)
Unless relevant to matters of risk and security, family circumstances were not factors to be considered in the grading of prisoners into an appropriate category.

*R (on the application of Palmer) v The Home Department* [2004] EWHC 1817 (Admin); Times, September 13, 2004
The grading of a prisoner into an appropriate category was to be based on the likelihood of escape and the risk to the public if the escape was successful; other considerations such as the prospect of adverse publicity and the state of the prisoner's financial resources were not justifiable factors. There was no right for a prisoner serving a determinate sentence to make representations prior to categorisation decisions. However, there was a right to appeal which a Prisoner should exercise before initiating judicial review proceedings.

*R v Secretary of State for the Home Department, ex parte John Hirst* (2001) [2001] EWCA Civ 378; Times, March 22, 2001 : Independent, April 30, 2001
A prisoner who had served the tariff period of a discretionary life sentence was entitled to be told reasons for a proposed re-categorisation and to be afforded the opportunity to make representations on that issue and to reply to grounds put forward to re-categorise him or her. This case articulates the important relationship between categorisation and progression towards release.

*R v Secretary of State for The Home Office, Ex Parte Peries* [1997] 7 WLUK 535
Application by serving prisoner to judicially review Prison Governor's decision in relation to security re-categorisation and revocation of facility licence. Recognises rights to fairness for non Category A Prisoners.

*R v Secretary of State for The Home Department, Ex Parte Duggan* [1993] 12 WLUK 54

A prisoner is entitled to see the gist of relevant reports and the reasons for classifying him in a particular category of security risk at each annual review of categorisation by the prison governor. However, use by the decision-maker of internal advice which is not disclosed to the prisoner does not amount to procedural unfairness so long as it is not 'new' material and the gist of it is plainly known (see *R (on the application of Ferguson) v Secretary of State for Justice* [2011] EWHC 5 (Admin))

*R (on the application of Ali) v Director of High Security Prisons* [2009] EWHC 1732 (Admin)

The Claimant was a Category A prisoner with a high escape risk classification. The decision as to a prisoner's escape classification is also amenable to the common law rules of fairness. The prisoner had to be given the reasons for the decision in sufficient detail to enable him to make representations or challenge it.

## CATEGORY A PRISONERS

PSI 09/2015 - "Identification, Initial Categorisation and Management of Potential and Provisional Category A / Restricted Status Prisoners" (Replaces PSI 05/2013)

This instruction is one of a number of Prison Service Instructions (PSIs) which form the Category A function of the National Security Framework. It replaces PSI 05/2013 and provides establishments with instructions and guidelines regarding the reporting in of potential Category A prisoners to the Category A Team within the High Security Prisons Group (HSPG). All Category A instructions can be accessed via the National Security Framework website.

PSI 08/2013 The Review of Security Category – Category A / Restricted Status Prisoners

1. Executive Summary

Background

1.1 This instruction is one of a number of Prison Service Instructions (PSIs) which form the Category A Function of the National Security Framework. It is one of the two new PSIs which replace PSI 03/2010 and sets out guidelines for the procedures for reviews of Category A / Restricted Status prisoners' security category, and for deciding and reviewing the appropriate escape risk classification of Category A prisoners. All Category A instructions can be accessed via the National Security Framework.

**Case law**

*R (On the Application Of Rose) v The Secretary of State for Justice* [2017] EWHC 1826

The claimant prisoner (R) applied for judicial review of the Deputy Director of Custody High Security (Director) decision in reviewing his security categorization, not to hold an oral hearing and to remain in Category A. R was a life prisoner and had been in Category A for 27 years. Despite a highly planned escape from HMP Parkhurst in 1995 where he was unlawfully at large for several days, his escape risk classification had been downgraded to "standard" in July 2006. The Local Advisory Panel (LAP) made a recommendation to the Director for R to be downgraded from Category A to Category B, on the basis he "has made progress in all areas". In finding that the Director did not properly or fairly apply PSI 08/2013 guidance and allowing R's claim, the Court held, "Whilst oral hearings in the context of categorisation reviews will be "comparatively rare" (Hassett and Price, at 61), all save one of what are described by the policy as important factors tending in favour of an oral hearing are squarely in play in this case. Above all, this was a case where the thrust of the evidence and the LAP recommendation favoured down-grading of a post-tariff life prisoner and, if he was not down-graded, there was an impasse. This does not mean that it was not open to the Director to make a rational finding that Mr Rose should remain in Category A. But it does mean that he could not lawfully do so without giving Mr Rose an opportunity to address the points that were troubling him at an oral hearing."

*R (on the application of Bamber) v Secretary of State for Justice* [2020] EWHC 2842 (Admin)

A decision to not downgrade a category A prisoner serving a whole life sentence for the murder of five members of his family was reasonable, notwithstanding an independent forensic psychologist's conclusion that category A conditions were no longer necessary. An oral hearing had not been required as the prisoner had a fair opportunity to present his case and had been engaged in the decision-making process.

*R (Smith) v The Secretary of State for Justice* [2020] EWHC 2712 (Admin)

See this case for consideration of cases which require an oral hearing.

*Hassell & Another, R (On the Application Of) v The Secretary State for Justice* [2017] EWCA Civ 331

The Court of Appeal held that there remain material differences between the decision-making context for the Parole Board and the Director of the Secretary of State's Category A Review Team ("the CART"), such that procedural requirements are different in the two cases. Fairness will sometimes require an oral hearing by the CART/Director (Deputy Director of Custody – High Security), if only in comparatively rare cases, such as in asking the question whether upon escape the prisoner would represent a risk to the public the CART/Director, having read all the reports, were left in significant doubt on a matter on which the prisoner's own attitude might make a critical difference, the impact upon him of a decision to maintain him in Category A would be so marked that fairness would be likely to require an oral hearing. Paragraph 4.7(b) of PSI 08/2013 gives lawful general guidance regarding procedural requirements for the purposes of Category A decisions by the CART/Director. The Court concluded that it was unnecessary to consider whether the guidance in PSI 08/2013 is precisely aligned with common law fairness standards.

*R (Cain) v Secretary Of State For Justice* [2013] EWHC 900 (Admin)
The Director of High Security Prisons had been entitled to refuse to downgrade a prisoner from Category A classification to Category B because there was no cogent evidence of a significant reduction in his risk of reoffending and there was further work that could be done to address his offending within Category A conditions. The case was not one of those rare cases where it was appropriate for the Director to hold an oral hearing to consider the question of downgrading.

*R (Hussain) v Secretary Of State For Justice* [2013] EWHC 1452 (Admin)
A prisoner had not demonstrated that procedural fairness required an oral hearing of the review of his categorisation as a Category A prisoner. The proper procedure in respect of a Category A review was for the prisoner to request an oral hearing before a paper decision had been made on his categorisation

*R (Quaddy) v Governor of HMP Long Lartin* [2013] EWHC 2029 (Admin)
Although an offender's continuing denial of guilt had been a very significant factor in the decision not to recategorise a Category A prisoner, it had not been treated as the sole consideration to the exclusion of all other, and so the decision was lawful.

*R (Stromberg) v Secretary Of State For Justice* [2013] EWHC 2361 (Admin)
The decision of the Category A Review Team that a prisoner should remain Category A had not been irrational or based on an incorrect approach.

**Key Note**
A long line of cases demonstrates a shift towards fairness in Category A decision making processes. Two current issues commonly arise.

First, the disclosure of "intelligence" and secondly, the holding of an oral hearing.
A number of the following cases give guidance on the direction of recent case law on these two issues.
The entry for "Oral Hearings" is of relevance to the second issue.

**Case Law**
*R (on the application of Michael Downs) v Secretary of State for Justice* [2011] EWCA Civ 1422, 30 November 2011
The appellant prisoner (D) appealed against a decision ((2010) EWHC 3594 (Admin)) that he was not entitled to an oral hearing for a categorisation review. D had been found guilty of the murder of two elderly women, and was a Category A prisoner. The dispute between W and the prison psychologist on whether there was a sexual motivation behind the offences did not require an oral hearing to resolve because it was not a dispute that could be resolved with certainty. CART had read and understood W's reports. Its task was to decide which view it accepted on the risk posed by D, and his suitability for further sexual offenders' treatment. It did not need an oral hearing to perform that process. CART was not wrong to decide against an oral hearing where the views had been so well rehearsed, were so well known, and had not changed (paras 45, 47-52).

*Donald Mackay v Secretary of State for Justice* [2011] EWCA Civ 522
The secretary of state appealed against a decision ([2010] EWHC 2013 (Admin)) allowing an application for judicial review by the respondent prisoner (D). D had been convicted of murdering a prostitute, and had been sentenced to life imprisonment with a tariff of 20 years. He was held in Category A conditions. Twenty years later, a Parole Board concluded that a move to a Category B training prison might be constructive, but stated that there had been no significant reduction in D's level of risk. D sought an oral hearing before the Category A review team (CART), but the secretary of state rejected his requests and decided that he should remain at Category A. In relation to the substantive issue, the Court of Appeal held that a decision as to continued classification of a prisoner as Category A had a direct impact on the liberty of the subject and called for a high degree of procedural fairness. The existence of an inconsistency, for example between the views of the Parole Board and CART, could increase the likelihood of an oral hearing being required. The judge's decision rested on a single observation in the Parole Board report that a move to a Category B training prison "may be constructive". However, the Parole Board's decision taken as a whole was

clear: there had been no significant reduction in D's level of risk. The isolated comment as to the benefits of downgrading D's security categorisation did not provide sufficient foundation for concluding that an oral hearing was required. When the Parole Board's decision was considered as a whole, it was difficult to discern any significant inconsistency with CART's decision. Insofar as there was any inconsistency, it went no further than that inherent in their different spheres of interest; the Parole Board focussed on controlled, conditional release and the measures necessary to achieve it, while CART concentrated upon the risk posed by the prisoner in the event of an escape from custody. There was nothing in the Parole Board's decision which should have prompted CART to convene an oral hearing and the judge had therefore erred in law (paras 33-38). (this appeal report is also referred to as R (on the application of McLuckie) v Secretary of State for Justice EWCA Civ 522 in other reported cases)

*R(on the application of Harrison) v Secretary of State for Justice* [2020] A.C.D 17
The decision of the Deputy Director of Custody High Security not to hold an oral hearing when deciding whether to downgrade a prisoner's security classification from Category A was unlawful as he had failed to follow the secretary of state's published policy in PSI 08/2013, and common law fairness had required there to be a hearing.
*R(on the Application of Steele) v Secretary of State for Justice* [2018] EWHC 1072 (Admin) it was held an oral hearing regarding the security classification of a Category A prisoner was not an obligatory requirement under Prison Service Instruction 08/2013 following a Local Advisory Panel recommendation of security downgrading. The Court in this case held that there were no important factors in dispute or a significant dispute regarding the expert materials).

*R(on the application of Bourke) v Secretary of State for Justice* [2012] EWHC 4041 (Admin)
The Claimant prisoner (B) applied for judicial review of the decision to refuse him an oral hearing of his categorisation review. He submitted that fairness necessitated an oral hearing as his denial of guilty meant that he was at an impasse since he was unable to demonstrate a reduction in risk in the usual way by attending courses.
The Court held that it was correct for the jury's verdict to be the starting point. It couldn't be suggested that the mere existence of denial and consequent impasse would automatically entitle B to an oral hearing. Whilst the existence of an impasse might be a factor potentially in favour of the need for an oral hearing, it did not on its own

justify abandoning the normal procedure of reviewing a prisoner's security category by reference to the documents.

*R v Secretary of State for The Home Department, Ex Parte Michael Mcavoy* (1997) (1998) 1 WLR 790 : Independent, December 12, 1997 : Times, December 12, 1997
Applicant's appeal against refusal to grant judicial review on the issue of whether the procedure adopted in reviewing his prisoner categorisation was fair. The applicant, serving 25 years for robbery, submitted that full disclosure of confidential documents rather than the 'gist' of the material was the correct procedure in order to allow him to make proper representations.

## CATERING SERVICES, prison
PSI 34/1999

## CELL SHARING
PSI 20/2015 - "The Cell Sharing Risk Assessment"
This PSI provides all staff in NOMS HQ and prison establishments with updated and clearer guidance and instructions on the Cell Sharing Risk Assessment (CSRA) process. The guidance has been updated to reflect that the preceding Instruction had reached the expiry date. This guidance does not change the operation of the CSRA process or alter the thresholds for the risk levels.
Desired Outcomes: to identify, manage and support prisoners and detainees who are at risk of selfharm to others and from others. To manage and reduce violence, deal effectively with perpetrators and support victims
PSI 64/2011 (updated)
Management of Prisoners at Risk of Selfharm to Self, to Others and From Others (Safer Custody)
Re-Issue Date: 5 July 2021
This instruction replaces PSO 2700 Suicide Prevention and Self-selfharm Management, PSO 2750 Violence Reduction, and PSO 2710 Follow Up to Deaths in Custody. It sets out the NOMS framework for delivering safer custody procedures and practices to ensure that prisons are safe places for all those who live and work there.
When a prisoner, who is high risk on the cell sharing risk assessment (CSRA), requests to see a Listener, staff must make an assessment on a case by case basis as to whether or not a Listener(s) can offer support to the prisoner. In some cases, such as at night, it may be considered appropriate for two Listeners to be present. If it is decided that the prisoner should not be given access to a Listener, additional support such as the Samaritans must be offered.
**Case Law**
*R (F) v Secretary of State for the Home Department* [2012] EWHC 2689 (Admin)

Where one prisoner did not face a real and immediate risk of selfharm from a second prisoner housed in the same prison, the refusal to transfer the second prisoner did not violate the first prisoner's rights under the European Convention on Human Rights 1950 art.3. Both prisoners had rights and were entitled to have their parole and pastoral reasons for staying in that particular prison respected; neither should simply be allowed to oust the other.

## CELLULAR CONFINEMENT
See "Confinement".
PR 58
Before deciding whether to impose a punishment of cellular confinement the governor, adjudicator or reviewer shall first enquire of a registered medical practitioner or registered nurse, such as mentioned in rules 20(3), as to whether there are any medical reasons why the punishment is unsuitable and shall take this advice into account when making his decision.

## CENSUS
See "National population census".

## CHIEF INSPECTOR OF PRISONS
5A ACT – Appointment and Functions of Her Majesty's Chief Inspector of Prisons

## CHILD PROTECTION
See also "Contacts, Outside, of Prisoners".
Child protection protocol 62/2001
Public Protection Manual 18/2016 (Chapter 5c – Child Contact Procedures)
Domestic Abuse Policy Framework (2 April 2020) – Section 7 'Assessment of risk to children'

## CHILDREN
See also "Young People".
PSO 4960 - Young people serving longer sentences for serious offences
PR 57 - young persons, offences committed
Policy Framework: Building Bridges: A Positive Behaviour Framework for the Children and Young People Secure Estate (31 January 2020)
Building Bridges sets out the framework for developing positive relationships between staff and children and young people. It includes addressing the needs of children and young people who are particularly complex, with high levels of selfharm, need and vulnerability.
**Case Law**
*R (T) v Secretary of State for Justice* [2013] EWHC 1119 (Admin)
There was a breach of the Children and Young Persons Act 1933 s.31 where a 13-year-old with autism and learning difficulties, whilst detained in custody at a magistrates' court, walked from

his cell past two adult detainees and experienced a "cacophony" of sounds in the cell area.

See *Children's Rights Alliance For England v Secretary Of State For Justice* [2013] EWCA Civ 34 under "Young Offenders" below.

## CIVIL ACTIONS AGAINST THE PRISON AND / OR SECRETARY OF STATE
**Key Note**
A breach of the Prison Rules does not, in itself, give rise to a private law civil claim by a Prisoner. However, common law rules relating to claims in negligence give Prisoners a cause of action (see *Robert Michael Hartshorn (Plaintiff) v Home Office (Defendant)* (1999) 1 WLUK 584) as well as claims framed in misfeasance in a public office (see *Steven Racz v The Home Office* [1992] 12 WLUK 107). The Human Rights Act may also complement or supplant a claim in tort cases (see *Jeffrey Shane Watkins v Home Office & Ors* [2005] UKHL 17.
**Case Law**
*R (Faulkner) v Secretary of State for Justice* [2013] UKSC 23
See under "Damages Claims", below.

*Jeffrey Shane Watkins v Home Office & Ors* [2006] UKHL 17
Misfeasance in public office was not actionable without proof of material damage. In the authorities the proving of special damage had either been expressly recognised as an essential ingredient of the tort, or it had been assumed. The lack of remedy in tort did not leave W without any legal remedy. For example, breach of a fundamental human or constitutional right would, in all probability, found a claim under the Human Rights Act 1998 s.7.

*Reeves v Commissioner of the Police of the Metropolis* [2000] 1 AC 360
Article 2 ECHR places on prison authorities a positive duty to take reasonable care to safeguard the lives of prisoners and persons against the risk of avoidable selfharm. Discharge of this duty requires the putting in place of systemic precautions against suicide in prison.

See further comments in *R v Secretary of State for the Home Department, ex parte Imtiaz Amin* [2003] UKHL 51 at 30-32:
30. A profound respect for the sanctity of human life underpins the common law as it underpins the jurisprudence under articles 1 and 2 of the Convention. This means that a state must not unlawfully take life and must take appropriate legislative and administrative steps to protect it. But the duty does not stop there. The state owes a particular duty to those involuntarily in its

custody. As Anand J succinctly put it in Nilabati Behera v State of Orissa (1993) 2 SCC 746 at 767: "There is a great responsibility on the police or prison authorities to ensure that the citizen in its custody is not deprived of his right to life". Such persons must be protected against violence or abuse at the hands of state agents. They must be protected against self–selfharm: Reeves v Commissioner of Police of the Metropolis [2000] 1 AC 360. Reasonable care must be taken to safeguard their lives and persons against the risk of avoidable selfharm).

NB: aspects of this case are pending appeal.

*Regina v Her Majesty's Coroner for the Western District of Somerset and Other, ex parte Middleton* [2004] UKHL 10

"Compliance with the substantive obligations [under article 2 ECHR] must rank among the highest priorities of a modern democratic state governed by the rule of law. Any violation or potential violation must be treated with great seriousness"

*Kirkham v Chief Constable Greater Manchester Police* (1989) CA (Civ Div)

Appeal by Chief Constable of Manchester against decision awarding damages to widow of prisoner who committed suicide. By taking a man into custody the police assume a duty to pass on to the prison all information regarding his well-being. The police had been negligent in failing to tell the prison authorities o the deceased's suicidal tendencies. The Court held that the defences of volenti non fit injuria and ex turpi causa non oritur actio could not stand because the deceased was not of sound mind. He was legally sane but suffering from clinical depression impairing his judgment. Ld Denning's view in Hyde v Thameside Area Health Authority (1981) Times, April 16, 1981 that such a view was unfitting, and Euro-Diam Ltd v Bathurst (1988) 2 WLR 517 referred to.

*R v Secretary of State for the Home Department ex parte Dew* [1987] 1 WLR 881

Damages claim for delay by prison authorities not a public law claim but should be a negligence action.

*R v Board of Visitors Gartree Prison ex parte Sears* [1985] 1 WLUK 457

Irregular charge of confinement within prison is not false imprisonment. Cellular confinement wrongly ordered but no damages awarded. Variation of terms of lawful confinement not false imprisonment.

## CIVIL JUSTICE SYSTEM, Reform

PSI 31/2015 Managing Litigation Claims

This instruction updates arrangements for the management of litigation claims, including both private law claims and judicial reviews. It updates existing policy and guidance to reflect the outcomes of recent reviews and the handling of litigation in NOMS.

NOMS defends all claims robustly, as far as the evidence allows. This includes those that give rise to important points of principle. NOMS will settle cases only if there are compelling reasons why this is appropriate in all circumstances of the particular case.

PSI 06/2000 – Reform of the Civil Justice System

## CIVIL PARTNERSHIPS

See also "Marriage of Prisoners".

PSI 14/2016 Marriage of Prisoners and Civil Partnership Registration

This instruction sets out the legal requirements, policy and procedures for facilitating prisoners' requests to marry (including same sex couples) or enter into a civil partnership in England and Wales. This will ensure that NOMS fully meets its obligations under the relevant legislation.

This instruction also makes it mandatory for all Governors to consider applications from prisoners for marriage and civil partnership. Category C is now the same as Category B in relation to ceremonies.

## CIVIL PROCEEDINGS

PSO 4625 - Productions in Civil Proceedings

### Case Law

*R v Secretary of State for the Home Department, ex parte Wynn* (1993) 1 WLR 115; (1993) 1 All ER 574; Times, January 25, 1993; Independent, February 3, 1993

Prisoners' right to attend court on an appeal & liability for cost of travel & escort. Appeal against dismissal of application for declaration that it was unlawful for the Home Secretary to require a prisoner to meet the costs of his production in court dismissed. Held: A prisoner was required to make a formal request under s.29 Criminal Justice Act 1961 that he be produced before the court before the Home Secretary was required to consider whether the prisoner's production in court was desirable in the interests of justice. As appellant refused to make the request, there has never been any actual decision to be reviewed so that the question is purely hypothetical.

## CJA 1991 PRISONERS

### Case Law

*R (on the application of Darren Young) V Secretary of State for Justice* [2009] EWHC 2675 (Admin)

The disapplication of the Criminal Justice Act 1991 s.33(3) by the Criminal Justice and Immigration Act 2008 s.32 applied to prisoners who had been released on licence under the 1991 Act but recalled under the Criminal Justice Act 2003 s.254.

*R (on the application of Robinson v Secretary of State for Justice; R (on the application of Salami) v Parole Board* [2010] EWCA Civ 848
Changes to legislative provisions relating to the early release of long-term prisoners concerned the administration and execution of a sentence, rather than the sentence originally imposed. Amendments to the Criminal Justice Act 1991 which removed a recalled prisoners' automatic entitlement to early release after serving three-quarters (section 50A), did not retrospectively change the original sentence and so article 6 ECHR was not engaged.

*R (on the application of Lawrence Poku) v (1) Secretary of State for Justice (2) Parole Board* [2009] EWHC 1380 (Admin)
Amendments to the early release provisions in the Criminal Justice Act 1991 Pt II by the Criminal Justice and Immigration Act 2008 did not breach a long-term prisoner's rights under the European Convention on Human Rights 1950 art.6 and there was no unfairness caused to the prisoner by the fact that he did not fall within the amendments.

*R (on the application of Black) v Secretary of State for Justice* [2009] UKHL 1
A prisoner serving a determinate sentence was not entitled by virtue of the European Convention on Human Rights 1950 art.5(4) to a speedy judicial decision on the lawfulness of any continued period of detention once his parole eligibility date had arrived. The secretary of state's power to reject a recommendation of the Parole Board to release such a prisoner on licence at the half way stage of his term was anomalous, but was not contrary to art.5(4).

## CLASSIFICATION
### See also "Remand Prisoners".
Prison Rule 7
7.— Classification of prisoners
(1) Subject to paragraphs (1A) to (1D), prisoners shall be classified, in accordance with any directions of the Secretary of State, having regard to their age, temperament and record and with a view to maintaining good order and facilitating training and, in the case of convicted prisoners, of furthering the purpose of their training and treatment as provided by rule 3.
(1A) Except where paragraph (1D) applies, a prisoner who has the relevant deportation status must not be classified as suitable for open conditions.
(1B) If, immediately before the relevant time—

(a) a prisoner has been classified as suitable for open conditions; and
(b) the prison has received notice that the prisoner has the relevant deportation status, the prisoner's classification must be reconsidered in accordance with this rule as soon as practicable after the relevant time.
(1C) If—
(a) a prisoner has been classified as suitable for open conditions (whether before or after the relevant time); and
(b) the prison receives notice after the relevant time that the prisoner has the relevant deportation status, the prisoner's classification must be reconsidered in accordance with this rule as soon as practicable after the prison receives that notice.
(1D) This paragraph applies if a prisoner has been classified as suitable for open conditions and is located in open conditions immediately before the prisoner's classification is reconsidered, whether under paragraph (1B) or (1C) or otherwise.
(1E) For the purposes of this rule, a prisoner has the relevant deportation status if—
(a) there is a deportation order against the prisoner under section 5(1) of the Immigration Act 1971; and
(b) no appeal under section 82(1) of the Nationality, Immigration and Asylum Act 2002 ("the 2002 Act") that may be brought or continued from within the United Kingdom in relation to the decision to make the deportation order—
(i) could be brought (ignoring any possibility of an appeal out of time with permission), or
(ii) is pending (within the meaning of section 104 of the 2002 Act).
(1F) In paragraph (1E), the reference to the decision to make the deportation order includes a decision that section 32(5) of the UK Borders Act 2007 applies in respect of the prisoner.
(1G) In this rule, "the relevant time" means 5.00 p.m on 13th August 2014.
(2) Unconvicted prisoners:
(a) shall be kept out of contact with convicted prisoners as far as the governor considers it can reasonably be done, unless and to the extent that they have consented to share residential accommodation or participate in any activity with convicted prisoners; and
(b) shall under no circumstances be required to share a cell with a convicted prisoner.
(3) Prisoners committed or attached for contempt of court, or for failing to do or abstain from doing anything required to be done or left undone:
(a) shall be treated as a separate class for the purposes of this rule;
(b) notwithstanding anything in this rule, may be permitted to associate with any other class of prisoners if they are willing to do so; and

(c) shall have the same privileges as an unconvicted prisoner under rules 20(5), 23(1) and 35(1)..

(4) Nothing in this rule shall require a prisoner to be deprived unduly of the society of other persons.

## CLINICAL SERVICES FOR SUBSTANCE MISUSERS

PSO 3550 - Clinical Services for Substance Misusers

## CLOSE SUPERVISION CENTRES

See also "Separation of Prisoners".
PR 46 – Close Supervision Centres. PSI 42/2012 Close Supervision Centre Referral Manual

**Case Law**

*R (Thakrar) v Secretary of State For Justice* [2012] EWHC 3538 (Admin)

Policies implemented by the Secretary of State for Justice under the Prison Rules 1999, supplemented by national and local guidance, in relation to communications between a prisoner in a close supervision centre and his lawyers were not unlawful, and did not breach Articles 6 or 8 of the European Convention on Human Rights.

## CLOSED CIRCUIT TELEVISION, observation of prisoners by

PR 50A

## CLOTHING

YOI 19 - an inmate shall be provided with clothing adequate for warmth and health
PR 23
Prison Rule 23
Clothing

(1) An unconvicted prisoner may wear clothing of his own if and in so far as it is suitable, tidy and clean, and shall be permitted to arrange for the supply to him from outside prison of sufficient clean clothing.

Provided that, subject to rule 40(3):

(a) he may be required, if and for so long as there are reasonable grounds to believe that there is a serious risk of his attempting to escape, to wear items of clothing which are distinctive by virtue of being specially marked or coloured or both; and

(b) he may be required, if and for so long as the Secretary of State is of the opinion that he would, if he escaped, be highly dangerous to the public or the police or the security of the State, to wear clothing provided under this rule.

(2) Subject to paragraph (1) above, the provisions of this rule shall apply to an unconvicted prisoner as to a convicted prisoner.

(3) A convicted prisoner shall be provided with clothing adequate for warmth and health in accordance with a scale approved by the Secretary of State.

(4) The clothing provided under this rule shall include suitable protective clothing for use at work, where this is needed.

(5) Subject to rule 40(3), a convicted prisoner shall wear clothing provided under this rule and no other, except on the directions of the Secretary of State or as a privilege under rule 8.

(6) A prisoner may be provided, where necessary, with suitable and adequate clothing on his release.

## COMMUNICATIONS OF PRISONERS

See "Prisoner Communications"; "Human Rights – Article 10"; and "Media".

## COMMUNITY CARE

See "After Care"; "Housing and Homelessness"; and "Throughcare".

**Case Law**

*R (on the Application of NM) (Claimant) v Islington London Borough Council (Defendant) & (1) Northamptonshire County Council (2) Parole Board (Interested Parties)* [2012] EWHC 414 (Admin)

The claimant offender (N) applied for judicial review of a decision of the defendant local authority (Islington) not to conduct an assessment of his needs under the National Health Service and Community Care Act 1990 s.47. The Court held that: N was a "person for whom (Islington) may provide or arrange for the provision of community care services" within the meaning of that phrase in s.47(1). Even though N was not ordinarily resident in Islington, Islington would have the power under the National Assistance Act 1948 s.21 and s.29 to provide community care services in the form of accommodation or other services to him. The critical question was whether N was a person "who may be in need of any such services". It was necessary for N to show that there was a sufficiently concrete and likely prospect of him being in a position where community care services might need to be provided to him if he had relevant needs which would be required to be met by the provision of such services. Where it was reasonably clear that a person might be about to need the provision of such services, it was reasonable to infer that the person's needs should be assessed before arrival on the local authority's doorstep, R. (on the application of B) v Camden LBC [2005] EWHC 1366 (Admin), [2006] B.L.G.R. 19 considered.

## COMMUNICATIONS OF PRISONERS

See "Prisoner communications"; "Human Rights"; "Article 10" and "Media".

## COMMUNITY VISITS, earned

Incentives Policy Framework
5.51: Prisoners on Standard, Enhanced or levels

above Enhanced may receive improved visits which could include additional visits over their statutory entitlement, visits in better surroundings, or longer visits. This would be in addition to a prisoner's statutory entitlement. Further information on a prisoner's minimum entitlement to visits is contained in Providing Visits and Services to Visitors (PSI 16/2011) Compacts PSI 28/2010 – Custody Compacts for use in custody

## COMPASSIONATE GROUNDS, Release

Early Release on Compassionate Grounds Policy Framework (from 13 May 2022)

**Case Law**

*Bruton, R (On the Application Of) v The Secretary of State for Justice* [2017] EWHC 1967 (Admin)

The claimant prisoner (B) applied for judicial review of the Defendant's decision not to release him on compassionate grounds due the declining health of his mother. B conceded that the Defendant's decision was not perverse or irrational, rather in fell to be challenges on grounds of procedural fairness. The power to release life prisoners on compassionate grounds is found in Section 30 of the Crime (Sentences) Act which reads: "30 Power to release life prisoners on compassionate grounds (1) The Secretary of State may at any time release a life prisoner on licence if he is satisfied that exceptional circumstances exist which justify the prisoner's release on compassionate grounds. (2) Before releasing a life prisoner under subsection (1) above, the Secretary of State shall consult the Parole Board, unless the circumstances are such as to render such consultation impracticable." Part of B's complaint was that the Defendant had not disclosed essential Early Release Reports to B, and whilst that amounted to procedural unfairness, the Court held that B was aware of the essential risk assessments, and even if he had received them, his representations would not have been any different. There would have been no different outcome. The Defendant had adequate materials to make the decision and an oral hearing was not necessary. The Defendant had the power but not a duty to consult with the Parole Board and applied the correct test.

*Samantha Orobator v (1) Governor of Holloway Prison (2) Secretary of State for Justice* [2010] EWHC 58 (Admin)

The claimant prisoner (O) applied for judicial review of the second defendant Secretary of State's decision not to release her from custody. The Court held that the decision not to release a British citizen, who had been convicted by a court in Laos for a drugs offence but repatriated to the United Kingdom to serve the life sentence imposed, was appropriate where despite a number of shortcomings, she had not suffered a flagrant denial of justice on the grounds of the Lao court's lack of independence and impartiality.

*R (on the application of A) v (1) Governor of Huntercombe Young Offenders' Institute (2) Secretary of State for the Home Department* [2006] EWHC 2544 (Admin)

Where the prison service had given an apparently reliable assurance of immediate release, the circumstances were exceptional and an exercise of compassion was involved, the power under s.102(3) of the Act should be exercised unless there were good grounds for not doing so. In the instant case there were no grounds for not exercising the power and the respondents should have exercised it. Whether a court's mistake amounted to an exceptional circumstance would depend on the precise facts. In general such a mistake would not normally amount to an exceptional circumstance because of the increasing risk of their occurring. The repeated indications of immediate release had to have given rise to real feelings of upset and disappointment on X's part and it would be an act of compassion to release him.

*R v Kevin Birch* [2006] EWCA Crim 2240

Exceptional circumstances permitted the imposition of a sentence the offender had reasonably been led to expect after administrative errors made by the court when sentencing.

## COMPLAINTS PROCEDURE

**See also "Prisoner Complaints" and "Requests and Complaints".**

Prisoner Complaints Policy Framework (Updated February 2022)

Purpose: To set out requirements and information on providing a fair and effective system for dealing with prisoner complaints, including by ensuring procedural justice and taking a problem-solving approach to both adult prisoners and young people.

Prison Rule 11

11.— Requests and complaints

(1) A prisoner may make a request or complaint to the governor or independent monitoring board relating to the prisoner's imprisonment.

(2) The governor shall consider as soon as possible any requests and complaints that are made to him under paragraph (1).

(3) A written request or complaint under paragraph (1) may be made in confidence.

YOI Rule 8

**Key Note**

You may write to your legal adviser about a complaint.

Staff must apply 'balance of probabilities' as the standard of proof to investigate complaints. Deciding that something is proven on a 'balance of probabilities' means that it is more likely than not to have occurred.

Prisoners who do not have a good grasp of the English language must be allowed to submit a complaint in their own language if they wish.

## COMPULSORY TESTING FOR CONTROLLED DRUGS
See "Drugs".

## COMPUTERS
PSI 02/2017 – Working with display screen equipment

PSI 35/2010 (associated with 02/2017) – Provision of eye tests and glasses

PSO 9030 – Handling & approval of requests for IT/telephony business requirements

PSI 04/2003 – IT/telephony change requests

PSI 13/2004 – Misuse of information technology

Prison Education & Library Services for adults in prison in England Policy Framework

4.9 Governors must ensure that education providers deliver a core common curriculum including communication technology (ICT).

**Case Law**

*R (On the application of Gurkirat Singh Dhanota) v Secretary of State for the Home Department & Ors* [2003] EWHC 18 (Admin)

In relation to access to a laptop computer the Court held that at the date this application was issued the applicant had not been provided with IT equipment. A legal basis for the court to intervene is provided by Article 6 of the Convention, namely to secure the applicant's right of access to the court. The Judge directed that the defendant should arrange for facilities enabling access to his computer and storage devices Further, the defendant accepted that the applicant could have access to printing facilities at reasonable times and at a cost of 1p per page.

## CONFINEMENT
ACT 12 - Place of

PR 48/YOI 51 - Temporary

PR 58/YOI 61 - To cell or room

ACT 14 - Cells

Prison Rule 48

48.— Temporary confinement

(1) The governor may order a refractory or violent prisoner to be confined temporarily in a special cell, but a prisoner shall not be so confined as a punishment, or after he has ceased to be refractory or violent.

(2) A prisoner shall not be confined in a special cell for longer than 24 hours without a direction in writing given by an officer of the Secretary of State. Such a direction shall state the grounds for the confinement and the time during which it may continue.

## CONFISCATION ORDERS
16/2010 - Requires governors to have systems in place to ensure that establishments are compliant with the orders and sentences of the court.

## CONTACTS, Outside, of Prisoners
PR 4

Prison Rule 4

4.— Outside contacts

(1) Special attention shall be paid to the maintenance of such relationships between a prisoner and his family as are desirable in the best interests of both.

(2) A prisoner shall be encouraged and assisted to establish and maintain such relations with persons and agencies outside prison as may, in the opinion of the governor, best promote the interests of his family and his own social rehabilitation.

YOI 42

PSI 16/2011 Providing Visits and Services to Visitors (updated October 2021)

Management of Security at Visits (Open Estate) Policy Framework

**Case Law**

*Ricardo Westwater v Secretary of State for Justice* [2010] EWHC 2403 (Admin)

The claimant prisoner (W) applied for judicial review of the defendant secretary of state's decision to allow him only written contact with his 10-year-old daughter (D). The Court held that having regard to the clear terminology in the guidance issued by the secretary of state to prison governors and social services, and by the specific inter-relationship between the terminology of the Public Protection Manual, Chapter 2, Section 2, Child Contact Procedures, version 4.0, January 2009 (the PPM) and that guidance, there was only one interpretation of the policies, procedures and statutory guidance applicable to decisions about contact between prisoners and children. Prison governors had to request a written assessment from children's services, and that assessment had to be in accordance with the statutory guidance, Framework for the Assessment of Children in Need and their Families (2000). A request would trigger an initial assessment addressing parenting capacity, family and environmental factors, and the child's developmental needs. Unless the need for a more in-depth consideration was revealed, that initial assessment would suffice (see 36-38 of judgment). (2) A prisoner's right to respect for his private and family life, and thereby his contact with his children, could, subject to the principle of proportionality, be restricted, R (on the application of B) v Governor of Wakefield Prison [2001] EWHC Admin 917,

(2002) 1 FCR 445 followed ( 41). The guidance and procedures issued by the secretary of state described a careful multi-agency approach consistent with best practice assessment and child protection procedures and the balance between the child's rights and the prisoner's rights was neither disproportionate, unfair nor unreasonable. Provided the guidance and procedures were complied with, and the decision in an individual case was made on the basis of the assessments prescribed, any interference with art.8 corresponded to a pressing social need and was proportionate ( 42, 48). (3) In the instant case, however, there had been no adequate assessment and no analysis of the risks presented by more extensive contact. In those circumstances the secretary of state was not entitled to reach the conclusion he did. His decision was arbitrary and was a disproportionate interference with the W's Convention rights.

## CONTRACTED OUT PRISONS, PARTS OF PRISONS AND FUNCTIONS
PR 82-84
**See "Interface between CCG and Area Managers".**

## CONTRACTED OUT YOUNG OFFENDER INSTITUTIONS, PARTS & FUNCTIONS
YOI 86-88

## CONTROL & RESTRAINT
**See "Restraints".**

## CORRESPONDENCE
PSI 49/2011 Prisoner Communication Services

## CORRUPTION
Counter Corruption and Reporting Wrongdoing Policy Framework (Updated May 2022)
**See also "Prison Officer Corruption Prevention".**

## COSTS
**See "Judicial Review Procedure".**

## CRIMINAL CASES REVIEW COMMISSION
See Appeals section below

## CURFEW, prisoners, home detention
**See "Home Detention Curfew".**

## CUSTODIAL CARE NVQ LEVELS 2 & 3
PSO 8260

## Custodians of child protection registers
PSI 18/2016, PI 17/2016 - Public Protection Manual

## CUSTODY OUTSIDE A YOUNG OFFENDER INSTITUTION
YOI 45

## CUSTODY OUTSIDE PRISON
PR 40

## CUSTODY TIME LIMITS (Pre-Trial)
Prosecution of Offences (Custody Time Limits) (Coronavirus) (Amendment) Regulations 2020 came into force on 28 September 2020 and were repealed on 28 June 2021. The time limits temporarily extended custody time limits for most cases during the Coronavirus pandemic. These time limits have now reverted back to the limits set out in the Prosecution of Offences (Custody Time Limits) Regulations 1987. For cases in the Crown Court, the custody time limit is 112 days for those charged with either way offences and 182 days for those charged with indictable only offences). Different provisions for those in the magistrates' court and the youth court apply and are set out in the 1987 Regulations.

**Case Law**
*R (on the application of DPP) v Woolwich Crown Court, Lucima v Central Criminal Court* [2020] EWHC 3243 (Admin)
The High Court outlined a number of non-exhaustive principles relevant to determining applications for extensions of custody time limits during the coronavirus pandemic. In particular, it considered what might amount to "some other good and sufficient cause" for the purposes of the Prosecution of Offences Act 1985 Pt III s.22(3)(a)(iii):

i) Delay attributable to the pandemic, which means that it is neither practicable nor safe to hold the trial in question within the CTL, provides a good cause for an extension.

ii) Whether it provides a sufficient cause depends on an examination of the individual facts of the case and of the defendant in question.

iii) The normal requirements of exploring administratively whether a trial can be brought on elsewhere within the CTL should be followed; so too whether any non-custody cases listed for hearing can be vacated to enable a custody case to come into the list.

For the moment, neither may often be feasible but as additional court rooms come on stream the position may change.

iv) If practical arrangements cannot be made, it does not follow that it will be appropriate to extend the CTL in every case even though the need to delay a trial will be clear.

In some cases, a defendant should be released subject to exacting bail conditions. Factors which may come into play include:

a) The likely duration of the delay before trial;

b) Whether there has been any previous extension of the CTL;

c) The age and antecedents of the defendant;

d) The likely sentence in the event of conviction. A defendant should rarely be kept in custody if he had served, or come close to serving, the likely sentence were he convicted;

e) The underlying reasons why bail was refused;

f) Any particular vulnerabilities of the defendant which make remand in custody particularly difficult.

v) In multi-handed trials, consideration should be given by the parties and the court to whether delay could be reduced by separate trials.

vi) The burden is on the prosecution to satisfy the statutory criteria for the granting of an extension. No formal evidence about the impact of the pandemic will be needed in the light of the publicly available material and this judgment. All parties can be expected to be familiar with the steps taken to date by HMCTS and the courts. Judges and magistrates hearing contested applications to extend CTLs should inform the parties of the listing position at the court concerned, having regard to available and anticipated capacity, and of any inquiries made to see whether an earlier trial slot is available elsewhere.

vii) Any extension of a CTL should be for a comparatively short period, generally not exceeding about 3 months, so that the court retains the power to review the position in the light of changing circumstances.

## DAMAGES CLAIMS

### False imprisonment and Human Rights Act claims for prolonged detention

#### Case Law

*R(MA) v Secretary of State for Justice, The Governor of HMP Whatton, The Governor of HMP Stafford, MB* [2021] EWHC 1266 (Admin)

A prohibition on telephone contact and inter-prison visits between two prisoners who had married in prison was an unnecessary and disproportionate interference with their Article 8 rights and therefore unlawful. Damages were awarded on the basis that Claimant suffered substantial anxiety, frustration and distress over a period of a number of years where she was moved to HMP Stafford.

*R (Faulkner) v Secretary Of State For Justice* [2013] UKSC 23

A prisoner serving an indeterminate sentence whose detention was prolonged by the Parole Board's delay in reviewing his case following the expiry of his tariff was not the victim of either false imprisonment or a violation of the European Convention on Human Rights 1950 art.5(1). Nevertheless, damages were ordinarily to be awarded for such delay where it was established that an earlier hearing would have resulted in an earlier release.

Where that was not established, modest damages were to be awarded where the delay had caused sufficiently serious frustration and anxiety.

*R (on the application of Parratt) v Secretary of State for Justice* [2014] EWCA Civ 1478

When an offender could establish on the balance of probabilities that his period of imprisonment had been extended because of delays in Parole Board hearings which violated his rights under ECHR art.5(4), he should ordinarily receive damages as compensation. Declaratory relief alone was not just satisfaction. A period exceeding 12 months between two review hearings was not automatically an actionable delay.

*James, Wells and Lee v. The United Kingdom* (Applications nos. 25119/09, 57715/09 and 57877/09) European Court of Human Rights 18th September 2012.

See "Human Rights Article 5 rights – Freedom from Arbitrary Detention" below.

*Commissioner Of Police Of The Metropolis v (1) Thompson (2) Hsu Sub Nom Thompson & Anor V Commissioner Of Police For The Metropolis* [1997] 3 W.L.R. 403

Clarifying directions judge should include in summing up to assist jury as to damages, particularly exemplary damages, which it is appropriate to award plaintiff who succeeds in action for unlawful conduct towards them by the police.

*Mohidin v Commission of Police of the Metropolis* [2015] EWHC 2740 (QB)

Claimants who had been falsely imprisoned and assaulted by police officers and subjected to racial abuse were entitled to aggravated damages for their additional distress, humiliation and injury to feelings.

*George Lunt v Liverpool City Justices* (1991); CA (Civ Div)

An award of damages for wrongful imprisonment in the sum of £13,500 was found to be too low and was substituted with an award of £25,000 as the appellant had suffered extreme distress, humiliation and degradation whilst serving a 42-day sentence for non-payment of rates.

*R v Governor of Brockhill Prison Ex Parte Evans (No.2)* [1999] QB 1043

The court considered the damages to be awarded to an Appellant was detained unlawfully for an additional period of 59 days owing to a miscalculation of her release date which arose from a mistaken view of the law. The court held that there can be two elements to an award of damages for false imprisonment: the first being compensation for loss of liberty and the second being the damage to reputation, humiliation, shock, injury to feelings which can result from the loss of liberty. As a result of the period in which this Claimant had been lawfully detained, she had made the necessary adjustments to serving a prison sentence and so the facts of this case were different to the case of Thompson and Lunt. The court discouraged an approach of working out a daily, weekly or monthly figure and opted instead for a global amount as no two cases are the same.

## DANGEROUS INMATES, notification of release
See also "Public Protection".
PSI 76/2000 - Notification of the Release of Dangerous Inmates

## DATA PROTECTION
### Key Note
A number of prisoners take issue with information recorded against them, including Security Files and/or OASys. The Data Protection Act 2018 and the UK General Data Protection Regulation may be of assistance for obtaining information in a range of situations, particularly for obtaining one's own personal data from a data controller. The Ministry of Justice also has their own Information Charter about personal data.

There is no reported case to date on correcting misinformation held on prisoners, though applications have been made in the Administrative Court.
Information Security Policy Framework (Updated June 2021 to reflect the termination of CRC contracts)
Intelligence Collection, Analysis and Dissemination Policy Framework (Updated 31 October 2019)

### Case Law
*R(A) v Secretary of State for the Home Department* [2021] UKSC 37
The appellant was a convicted child sex offender. He suffered harassment and violence when people became aware of his convictions. He argued that the Child Sex Offender Disclosure Scheme Guidance did not go far enough in providing guidance for police forces, as to whether they are in law required to seek representations from the subject of an information request when the police are approached by members of the public with concerns about a person. The Supreme Court

held that it could not be said that the Child Sex Offender Disclosure (CSOD) Scheme Guidance, issued by the Secretary of State in accordance with her common law powers, was unlawful.

*R (XX) v Secretary of State for the Home Department* [2015] A.C.D 72
The claimant brought proceedings against various defendants in respect of the Child Sex Offender Disclosure (CSOD) scheme, the Management of Police Information Guidance and the Multi-Agency Public Protection Arrangements (MAPPA) Guidance. Through these schemes, data relating to the Claimant had been collected and held. This Claimant had been convicted of indecent assaults on children. Following his release from prison, members of the public had requested disclosure of this information, and later, the word "paedo" had been sprayed on his house and car.
He submitted that the schemes engaged his article 8 ECHR rights, and asked the Court to quash the issuing of CSOD and MAPPA guidance, as well as the decision to retain data relating to his convictions on the Police National Computer. The Court held that schemes were not arbitrary and contained safeguards against arbitrariness.
For the purposes of Article 8, the schemes were "in accordance with the law" and pursued a legitimate aim of public protection, and thus represented a proportionate and justifiable interference with his rights.

*R (on the application of Lord) v Secretary of State for the Home Department* [2003] EWHC 2073 (Admin)
Successful application by a Category A prisoner for disclosure of confidential prison reports pursuant to s.7 Data Protection Act 1998.

## DEATHS IN CUSTODY
PSI 64/2011 (updated to incorporate ACCT v6)
Management of Prisoners at Risk of Selfharm to Self, to Others and From Others (Safer Custody): Chapter 12 "Actions Following a Death in Custody"

### Case Law
*R (on the application of Maughan) v HM Senior Coroner for Oxfordshire* [2020] UKSC 46
In inquests the standard of proof that now applies to narrative and short-form conclusions of suicide and unlawful killing has changed from 'beyond reasonable doubt' (criminal standard) to 'the balance of probabilities' (i.e. civil standard)

*Tyrrell v (1) HM Senior County Durham and Darlington and (2) MOJ* [2016] EWHC 1892 (Admin)
The High Court considered the question of what article 2 ECHR requires of a coroner when a

serving prisoner dies of natural causes. The procedural obligation under article 2 does not arise when there is no reason to believe that the state failed to protect the life of the prisoner in question. However, it will arise if there has been a failure to provide timely and appropriate medical care to a detainee obviously in need of it. R (on the application of Secretary of State for Justice) (Claimant) v HM Deputy Coroner for the Eastern District of West Yorkshire (Defendant) & BK (by his Litigation Friend DF) & Ors (Interested Parties) [2012] EWHC 1634 (Admin) The court set out the test to be applied by a coroner when deciding whether to leave a particular verdict to the jury, and set out the elements which had to be proved for gross negligence manslaughter concerning a prison inmate's suicide.

*R (on the application of Lewis) V HM Coroner for the Mid & North Division of Shropshire* [2009] EWCA Civ 1403
There was no duty to require a jury, in an inquest concerning a death in custody, to consider a fact or circumstances which was only potentially causative rather than actually causative of the death.

*Savage v South Essex Partnership NHS Foundation Trust* [2010] EWHC 865 (QB)
Not a prison case, relates to failure of a hospital. The High Court awarded the claimant £10,000 in damages for a violation of article 2 ECHR in relation to the death of her mother who had committed suicide following the failure of her hospital to properly safeguard her welfare. The threshold of 'real and immediate risk to life' for triggering the duty under art.2 ECHR was high. It depended not only on what the relevant authority knew, but also what it ought to have known. The claimant only had to show that her mother had lost a substantial chance of survival as a result of the trust's actions.

**DEFAULTERS, SECURING RELEASE (YOI)**
YOI rule 18

**DELEGATION BY GOVERNOR**
PR 81, YOI 85

**DENYING GUILT**
See "Maintaining Innocence".

**DENTAL SERVICES FOR PRISONERS, strategy for modernising**
PSI 16/2003 - Strategy for Modernising Dental Services for Prisoners in England.
This PSI is to be read in conjunction with: PSI 38/2003 Basic Checks on Doctors and Dentists
Note the Service Specification for Dental Service

for prisons in England 2020 by NHS England and NHS Improvement.
"Note that the document: 'Strategy for modernising dental services for patients in England, Department of Health (2003)' 12 contains some recommendations that would not be legal under the current (2006) dental contract. Other guidance and recommendations have collectively superseded the 2003 'Strategy for modernising dental services for patients in England'" and this should no longer be used to inform dental contracting."

**DEPORTATION, prisoners liable to**
**See also "Foreign National Prisoners" below.**
See PSI 01/2015 - "The Allocation of prisoners liable to deportation or removal from the United Kingdom"

**DIABETES**
QOF and NICE Guidelines on the Care and Management of Diabetes to be included in the Service Specification Disabled Prisoners, Management.
PSI 32/2011 – Ensuring Equality (Extract)
8.1 Governors must ensure that efforts are made to identify whether a prisoner has a mental or physical impairment of any form. Governors must ensure that prisoners are encouraged to disclose their disability status and that procedures are in place to record this information (both on reception and subsequently) and to treat it confidentially. Not all prisoners will be aware of their disabled status and staff must be proactive in identifying the specific needs of all prisoners.
See also PSI 40/2011 regarding categorisation (Updated August 2021)
**Case Law**
*R (on the application of Dennis Gill) v Secretary of State for Justice* [2010] EWHC 364 (Admin)
The claimant (G) instituted judicial review proceedings seeking a declaration that the defendant secretary of state had breached both his duties under the Disability Discrimination Act 1995 and his public law duties in respect of him. G was serving a life sentence and had served more than double his five-year tariff. He had a learning disability, having an I.Q. of 65, and the secretary of state accepted that that constituted a disability for the purposes of the Act. The Parole Board had declined to direct his release and had originally recommended that he participate in offending behaviour programmes to address his areas of risk, indicating that without such participation any reduction in risk could not be measured. However, it had later acknowledged that G's learning disability made his participation in such programmes impossible. The Court held that where the

completion of offending behaviour programmes had been identified by the Parole Board as being necessary to enable a prisoner to demonstrate his safety for release, but the prisoner was prevented from participating in such programmes because of a learning disability, the secretary of state would be in breach of his statutory and public law duties if he failed to take such steps as were reasonable in all the circumstances to enable him to access such programmes in the same way as inmates who were not disabled.

## DISCHARGE OF PRISONERS

PSI 72/2011 – Discharge (Updated August 2021)
Section 30 of the Crime (Sentences) Act 1997 – Power to release life prisoners on compassionate grounds
PSI 05/2018 – Prisoner Discipline Procedures (Adjudications) (Updated May 2021)
**Key Note**
All Prisoners and Practitioners need to obtain a copy of this PSI which replaces the former Discipline Manual, PSO 2000 (and PSI 47/2011) and becomes the new "Archbold" or "Blackstone's" for Adjudications.
The PSI includes sections on "Adjudication Procedures", and Annexes on "Individual Charges offences and punishments", "Procedure for Recovery of Monies for Damage to Prison and Prison Property", a "Table of forms", a "Flow Chart Basic Adjudication Procedure", "Significant adjudication case law (European Court judgements and judicial reviews)" as well as the Chief Magistrates Sentencing Adjudication Guidelines
1.6: Bias, unconscious or otherwise, has consequences, not just in our daily interactions but in matters of importance to those in our care. We deliver our services fairly and respond to individual needs insisting on respectful and decent behaviour from our staff and prisoners. We recognise that discrimination, harassment, victimisation and bullying can nevertheless occur. Governors will take appropriate action through adjudication reviews whenever we discover them. We make daily decisions based on our own understanding of what, to us, is the correct outcome. There is a duty for all staff not to be biased or have the appearance of bias when dealing with any prisoner. These decisions may have detrimental impact on individuals with a protected characteristic.
PSI 06/2010 Conduct and Discipline (Updated January 2020)
PR 53 (updated March 2022) and/or YOI 58 – Disciplinary charges
PR 6 and/or YOI 44 – Maintenance of order and Rule 45 (YOI rule 49), PSO 1700 – Management of segregation units & management of prisoners

PR 51-61A / YOI 55-57 – Offences against discipline
PR 68 – Officers' code of discipline
Prison discipline & the European Convention on Human Rights (ECHR) guidance
YOI 58,58A,59,60,60A,63,65
PR 53, 53A,54,55,55A,56, 57,58, 59, 60, 61
Prison Rules (Extracts)
53 — Disciplinary charges
(1) Where a prisoner is to be charged with an offence against discipline, the charge shall be laid as soon as possible and, save in exceptional circumstances, within 48 hours of the discovery of the offence.
(2) Every charge shall be inquired into by the governor or, as the case may be, the adjudicator.
(3) Every charge shall be first inquired into not later, save in exceptional circumstances or in accordance with rule 55A(5), than:
(a) where it is inquired into by the governor, the next day, not being a Sunday or public holiday, after it is laid;
(b) where it is referred to the adjudicator under rule 53A(2) or 60(3)(b)], 28 days after it is so referred.
(4) A prisoner who is to be charged with an offence against discipline may be kept apart from other prisoners pending the governor's first inquiry or determination under rule 53A.
53A.— Determination of mode of inquiry
(1) Before inquiring into a charge the governor shall determine—
(i) whether the charge is so serious that additional days should be awarded for the offence if the prisoner is found guilty, or
(ii) whether it is necessary or expedient for some other reason for the charge to be inquired into by the adjudicator.
(2) Where the governor determines:
(a) that it is so serious or that it is necessary or expedient for some other reason for the charge to be inquired into by the adjudicator , he shall:
(i) refer the charge to the adjudicator forthwith for him to inquire into it;
(ii) refer any other charge arising out of the same incident to the adjudicator forthwith for him to inquire into it; and
(iii) inform the prisoner who has been charged that he has done so;
(b) that it is not so serious or that it is not necessary or expedient for some other reason for the charge to be inquired into by the adjudicator, he shall proceed to inquire into the charge.
(3) If:
(a) at any time during an inquiry into a charge by the governor; or
(b) following such an inquiry, after the governor has found the prisoner guilty of an offence but before he has imposed a punishment for that offence, it appears to the governor either that the charge is so serious that additional days should

be awarded for the offence if (where sub-paragraph (a) applies) the prisoner is found guilty or that it is necessary or expedient for some other reason for the charge to be inquired into by the adjudicator,

the governor shall act in accordance with paragraph (2)(a)(i) to (iii) and the adjudicator shall first inquire into any charge referred to him under this paragraph not later than, save in exceptional circumstances, 28 days after the charge was referred.

54.— Rights of prisoners charged

(1) Where a prisoner is charged with an offence against discipline, he shall be informed of the charge as soon as possible and, in any case, before the time when it is inquired into by the governor or, as the case may be, the adjudicator.

(2) At an inquiry into a charge against a prisoner he shall be given a full opportunity of hearing what is alleged against him and of presenting his own case.

(3) At an inquiry into a charge which has been referred to the adjudicator, the prisoner who has been charged shall be given the opportunity to be legally represented.

55.— Governor's punishments

(1) If he finds a prisoner guilty of an offence against discipline the governor may, subject to paragraph (2) and to rule 57, impose one or more of the following punishments:

(a) caution;

(b) forfeiture for a period not exceeding 42 days of any of the privileges under rule 8;

(c) exclusion from associated work for a period not exceeding 21 days;

(d) stoppage of or deduction from earnings for a period not exceeding 84 days;

(e) cellular confinement for a period not exceeding 21 days;

(g) in the case of a prisoner otherwise entitled to them, forfeiture for any period of the right, under rule 43(1), to have the articles there mentioned;

(h) removal from his wing or living unit for a period of 28 days.

(2) A caution shall not be combined with any other punishment for the same charge.

(3) If a prisoner is found guilty of more than one charge arising out of an incident, punishments under this rule may be ordered to run consecutively but, in the case of a punishment of cellular confinement, the total period shall not exceed 21 days.

(4) In imposing a punishment under this rule, the governor shall take into account any guidelines that the Secretary of State may from time to time issue as to the level of punishment that should normally be imposed for a particular offence against discipline.

55A.— Adjudicator's punishments

(1) If he finds a prisoner guilty of an offence against discipline the adjudicator may, subject to paragraph (2) and to rule 57, impose one or more of the following punishments:

(a) any of the punishments mentioned in rule 55(1);

(b) in the case of a fixed-term prisoner, an award of additional days not exceeding 42 days.

(2) A caution shall not be combined with any other punishment for the same charge.

(3) If a prisoner is found guilty of more than one charge arising out of an incident, punishments under this rule may be ordered to run consecutively but, in the case of an award of additional days, the total period added shall not exceed 42 days and, in the case of a punishment of cellular confinement, the total period shall not exceed 21 days.

(4) This rule applies to a prisoner who has been charged with having committed an offence against discipline before the date on which the rule came into force, in the same way as it applies to a prisoner who has been charged with having committed an offence against discipline on or after that date, provided the charge is referred to the adjudicator no later than 60 days after that date.

(5) Rule 53(3) shall not apply to a charge where, by virtue of paragraph (4), this rule applies to the prisoner who has been charged.

61.— Remission and mitigation of punishments, variation of compensation requirements and quashing of findings of guilt

(1) Except in the case of a finding of guilt made, or a punishment imposed, by an adjudicator under rule 55A(1) the Secretary of State may quash any finding of guilt and may remit any punishment or mitigate it either by reducing it or by substituting another award which is, in his opinion, less severe.

(1A) Where a compensation requirement has been imposed by a governor under rule 55AB(2), the Secretary of State may reduce the amount of the requirement.

(2) Subject to any directions given by the Secretary of State, the governor may, on the grounds of good behaviour, remit or mitigate any punishment already imposed by an adjudicator or governor.

**Case Law**

*R (on the application of Peter Kane) v (1) The Independent Adjudicator, (2) The Secretary of State for Justice* [2021] EWHC 673 (Admin)

Claimant challenged the Adjudicator's procedure under prison rules for not properly considering the 'so serious' test in rules 53A(1)(i). Court held that Independent Adjudicator does not have a role to review the reasons why the matter was referred to them in the first place, only to consider and adjudicate fairly on the substance of the charges. Only if the Independent

Adjudicator was on notice of something improper in the referral would they potentially examine the referral.

*R (on the application of Robert Shreeve) v Secretary of State for the Home Department (Now Secretary of State for Justice)* [2007] EWHC 2431 (Admin)
A prison service area manager had erred in upholding a deputy prison governor's finding that an inmate was guilty of having an unauthorised article in his possession, namely a sharpened stabbing implement formed from a bamboo incense holder, because, amongst other matters, it had not been established that the holder had been "sharpened", as opposed to merely being "sharp", and the requisite elements of the offence, as specified in the Prison Discipline Manual, had not been proved to the required criminal standard.

*R v Governor HMP Swaleside, ex parte James Wynter* [1998] 5 WLUK 194
Prison discipline tribunals for positive mandatory drug test cases should ensure that the prisoner was given full information on the methodology and checks in the testing procedure. Confirmation certificates were admissible hearsay.

## DISCRIMINATION
### Case Law
*R (on the application of Akbar) v Secretary of State for Justice* [2021] EWCA Civ 898
The Prison Rules (r.7(1A)), which prevented the Secretary of State for Justice from transferring any prisoner to open conditions if they were subject to a deportation order and had exhausted their rights of appeal, was not discriminatory. This rule gave preference for open conditions to those who were more likely to be released into the community. The Secretary of State has a substantial margin of judgement in discharging his responsibilities when managing prisoners.

*R (on the application of Coll) v Secretary of State for Justice* [2017] UKSC 40
The paucity of approved premises for women prisoners released from prison on licence compared with the number available for male prisoners amounted to unlawful sex discrimination which had not yet been justified.

*R (on the application of Hussein) v Secretary of State for the Home Department* [2018] EWHC 213 (Admin)
The lock-in regime at an immigration removal centre, which meant that practicing Muslims who wished to adhere to mandatory prayer times could not use the prayer room and had to pray in their rooms in the presence of other detainees and close to an unclosed lavatory, breached ECHR art.9 and constituted indirect discrimination under the Equality Act 2010, which was not justified.

*R (Cossey) v Secretary of State for Justice* [2013] EWHC 3029 (Admin)
The Secretary of State for Justice had not, contrary to the European Convention on Human Rights 1950 art.14, discriminated against a convicted prisoner who had served the minimum term for his offence but had not been paroled, by refusing to accord him some of the rights and privileges accorded to unconvicted and civil prisoners. There was no analogous comparator and his situation could not be more different to that of unconvicted and civil prisoners.

*R (Massey) v Secretary of State for Justice* [2013] EWHC 1950 (Admin)
The Legal Aid, Sentencing and Punishment of Offenders Act 2012 did not, in introducing either the "tariff-expired removal scheme" or the extended determinate sentence, discriminate against British prisoners serving indeterminate sentences of imprisonment for public protection in prisons in the United Kingdom.

*R (Bristow) v Secretary of State for Justice* [2013] EWHC 3094 (Admin)
See "Early Release of Prisoners" below.

*R (Dowsett) v Secretary of State for Justice* [2013] EWHC 687 (Admin)
The Secretary of State's policy in respect of rub-down searches of prisoners, in particular that a male prisoner could not object to being searched by a female prison officer other than where his case fell within exceptions based on religious or cultural grounds, was not discriminatory on the grounds of sex.

*R (Serrano) v Secretary of State for Justice* [2012] EWHC 3216 (Admin)
See "Home Detention Curfew", below.

*R (on the application of Dowsett) v Secretary of State for Justice* [2011] EWHC 2877 (Admin)
See "Equality and Diversity" below.

## DISINFECTING TABLETS – scheme (for drug needles)
PSI 34/2007- re-introduction of disinfecting tablets

## DISPLAY SCREEN EQUIPMENT HEALTH AND SAFETY ISSUES
PSI 02/2017 - Working with display screen equipment
AI 02/2017

## DISRUPTIVE PRISONERS, management

See also "Force, use of".

PSI 25/1999 - Management of Disruptive Prisoners

PSI 38/2000 (High Security Prisons)

## DOGS, Prison Service

Prison Dogs Policy Framework (July 2021)

## DOMESTIC ABUSE

Domestic Abuse Policy Framework (2 April 2020)

This policy framework sets out the arrangements for working with people whose convictions or behaviours include domestic abuse.

The purpose of this policy framework is to set out HMPPS' commitment to reducing domestic abuse-related re-offending and the risk of serious selfharm associated with it, to provide interventions to support rehabilitation and ensure staff at all levels understand what is expected of them, and to ensure that action is taken to safeguard adults and children at risk.

## DRUGS

PSI 47/2011 – Prison Discipline Procedures (for adjudications which commenced before 01/02/19)

PSI 05/2018 – Prison Discipline Procedures (for current adjudications and those which commenced after 01/02/19)

PR 50 – Compulsory testing for controlled drugs

Prison Rule 50

50.— Compulsory testing for controlled drugs, pharmacy medicines and other substances etc.

(1) This rule applies where an officer, acting under the powers conferred by section 16A of the Prison Act 1952 (power to test prisoners for drugs), requires a prisoner to provide a sample for the purpose of ascertaining whether he has any controlled drug, pharmacy medicine, prescription only medicine, psychoactive substance or specified substance in his body.

(2) In this rule "sample" means a sample of urine or any other description of sample specified in the authorisation by the governor for the purposes of section 16A of the Prison Act 1952.

(3) When requiring a prisoner to provide a sample, an officer shall, so far as is reasonably practicable, inform the prisoner:

(a) that he is being required to provide a sample in accordance with section 16A of the Prison Act 1952; and

(b) that a refusal to provide a sample may lead to disciplinary proceedings being brought against him.

(4) An officer shall require a prisoner to provide a fresh sample, free from any adulteration.

(5) An officer requiring a sample shall make such arrangements and give the prisoner such instructions for its provision as may be reasonably necessary in order to prevent or detect its adulteration or falsification.

(6) A prisoner who is required to provide a sample may be kept apart from other prisoners for a period not exceeding one hour to enable arrangements to be made for the provision of the sample.

(7) A prisoner who is unable to provide a sample of urine when required to do so may be kept apart from other prisoners until he has provided the required sample, save that a prisoner may not be kept apart under this paragraph for a period of more than 5 hours.

(8) A prisoner required to provide a sample of urine shall be afforded such degree of privacy for the purposes of providing the sample as may be compatible with the need to prevent or detect any adulteration or falsification of the sample; in particular a prisoner shall not be required to provide such a sample in the sight of a person of the opposite sex.

YOI 53

Section 16A of the Prison Act 1952

Sections 62-62(B) of the Criminal Justice & Court Services Act 2000: electronic monitoring conditions

PSI 45/2010 Integrated Drug Treatment System has been replaced by a new substance misuse specification April 2018

PSI 13/2001 – electronic monitoring and drug testing on licence

PSO 3601 – Mandatory Drug Testing

PSI 46/2005 - Prison drug treatment and self selfharm

PSO 3620 has been cancelled and replaced by PSI 31/2009 – Compact based drug testing (revised January 2020)

PSO 3625 - Vetting & testing of specialist external drug workers

**See also "Clinical services for substance misusers".**

**Case Law**

*R (on the application of Greenfield) v Secretary of State for the Home Department* [2005] UKHL 14

The Appellant sought damages under the Human Rights Act 1998 for breaches of his right to a fair trial. Whilst a prisoner in a private prison, he had been found guilty of a drugs offence by the deputy controller of the prison. The Respondent later accepted that the hearing before the deputy controller breached Art.6(1) and Art.6(3) as it was not a hearing before an independent tribunal and the Appellant had not been permitted to have legal representations. Damages not awarded under s.8 unless the court could be satisfied that it was necessary to do so.

*R v (1) Secretary of State for the Home Department (2) Governor of HM Prison Frankland (3) Governor of HM Prison Full Sutton, ex parte Andrew Russell* (2000); LTL 1/9/2000: Times, August 31, 2000 [2000] 7 WLUK 216

An order requiring a prisoner to submit to a random drug test could only be valid if it was truly a random test. A random process for selecting prisoners was essential to the lawfulness of the procedure.

## EARLY RELEASE OF PRISONERS
See also "Parole"; "Release, Early"; "Release, Early – Licence Conditions".
### Case Law
R (Bristow) v Secretary of State for Justice [2013] EWHC 3094 (Admin)
A prisoner repatriated from Thailand to serve the remainder of his sentence for drug offences had not been discriminated against with regard to early release as compared with other prisoners convicted abroad who were eligible for discretionary release. The legislation relating to early release for determinate sentences had changed before the prisoner had been repatriated, and there could be no possible complaint because parole had been abolished in relation to determinate offences.

## EARNINGS, prisoners'
HMPPS Finance Manual (3 November 2020)
13.9.2: Earnings must be paid in line with PSO 4460 Prisoners Pay. The Earnings Budget Holder is responsible for monitoring and management of the earnings system
13.9.4: Delays of up to 5 working days are possible before prisoners receive payment into their personal bank account. Cheque payments will incur further delay because they will require clearing before being processed.
13.9.8: Bonuses may be credited to recognise and reward productivity and achievement. Section 3.1 of PSO4460 Prisoners Pay explains the criteria for this. It is the responsibility of the Business Hub to manually credit prisoners' accounts with the bonus amounts

## EDUCATION
See also "Open University".
PR 32
YOI 38-39
Section 86 of the Apprenticeships, Skills, Children and Learning Act 2009 provides that the Secretary of State must secure the provision of such education and training facilities as he considers appropriate for education and training suitable to the requirements of persons who are subject to adult detention. Adult detention applies to persons subject to a detention order, aged 19 or over, or aged under 19 and detained in a prison or a YOI, or part of a YOI, used wholly or mainly for those aged over 18, for example persons sentenced to prison and those on remand in custody.
Section 90 of the Apprenticeships, Skills, Children and Learning Act 2009 –

Encouragement of education and training for persons aged 19 or over and other subject to adult detention
Prison Education and Library Services for Adult Prisons Policy Framework (1 April 2019):
The prison library aims to provide an accessible service which has a focus on supporting learning, improving literacy and other barriers to effective resettlement. It should promote reading as a source of pleasure and provide prisoners with opportunities for wider cultural engagement.
PSI 06/2012 Prisoner Employment Training and Skills (Updated January 2020)
PSI 32/2012 Open University, Higher Education and Distance Learning (Wales only) (Amended April 2019)
PSI 02/2015 Prison Library Service (Wales only) (Amended April 2019)
Prison Rule 32
32.— Education
(1) Every prisoner able to profit from the education facilities provided at a prison shall be encouraged to do so.
(2) Educational classes shall be arranged at every prison and, subject to any directions of the Secretary of State, reasonable facilities shall be afforded to prisoners who wish to do so to improve their education by training by distance learning, private study and recreational classes, in their spare time.
(3) Special attention shall be paid to the education and training of prisoners with special educational needs, and if necessary they shall be taught within the hours normally allotted to work.
(4) In the case of a prisoner of compulsory school age as defined in section 8 of the Education Act 1996, arrangements shall be made for his participation in education or training courses for at least 15 hours a week within the normal working week.
### Case Law
See R (MA) v Independent Adjudicator [2013] EWHC 438 (Admin) under "Adjudications".

R (on the application of Campbell and Ferguson v The Governor of HMP Wakefield [2011] EWHC 2596 (Admin)
This was the substantive hearing of an application for judicial review by each of the claimants in relation to a decision whereby the defendant, acting by his appointed representative, refused each permission to undertake an NCFE level 2 course in human anatomy and physiology. The Court held that if the claimants were to succeed they would have to demonstrate as a threshold condition that the local Wakefield protocol constituted a materially restrictive departure from the requirements of the PSI. In the Court's judgment the claimants did so.

Bullet 2 of paragraph 2.2 of the PSI requires that a prisoner "demonstrate evidence of appropriate learning and attainment at or above ... level 2 through ILP records". The Judge held that the effect of the PSI provisions was entirely clear. Compliance with the terms of the PSI was, in all material respects, mandatory. It was not an option available to either a governor or a director or his or her appointed representative to depart in any material particular from the requirements of the PSI. Any such departure would be unlawful both by operation of the terms of the PSI and the Prison Rules.

*R (on the application of BP) v Secretary of State for the Home Department* [2003] EWHC 1963 (Admin) The failure to provide the claimant with any education or training during periods of segregation, amounted to a breach of the Young Offender Institution Rules 2000 SI 2000/3371, but on the facts, there was no evidence to suggest that the conditions under which P was segregated amounted to a breach of either Art.3 or Art.8 European Convention on Human Rights.

*R v (1) Governor of HM Prison Frankland (2) Secretary of State for the Home Department, Ex Parte Lawrence Willoughby [2000]* 5 WLUK 303 The governor of a prison was entitled to refuse to allow a prisoner access to further education on the basis that it may increase his risk of re-offending. The rational decision-maker was entitled to do whatever he could to reduce the risk of re-offending and should do nothing which might increase that risk.

### EDUCATION, physical
**See "Physical education".**

### ELECTRONIC MONITORING AND DRUG TESTING ON LICENCE
PSI 13/2001
Sections 62-62(B) of the Criminal Justice & Court Services Act 2000: electronic monitoring conditions

### EMERGENCIES
PR 69

### END OF CUSTODY LICENCE
**See "Release, Early – Licence Conditions".**

### ENHANCED BEHAVIOUR MONITORING
PSI 24/2015 - "Enhanced Behaviour Monitoring (EBM)" has been replaced by the Enhanced Behaviour Monitoring Policy Framework
Enhanced Behaviour Monitoring (EBM) provides a mechanism for giving assurance that ongoing risks (e.g. of selfharm; re-offending or abscond) are being appropriately identified and managed

within open prisons and with relevant residents of women's prisons, and subsequently as individuals are permitted to spend unescorted periods of time away from the prison in the community whilst Released on Temporary Licence (ROTL)

### ENTREPRENEURIAL ACTIVITIES
HMPPS Finance Manual Policy Framework

### EQUALITY AND DIVERSITY
PSI 32/2011 Ensuring Equality (Revised Jan 2020)
1 Executive summary
Background
1.1 This instruction sets out the framework for the management of equalities issues in prison establishments (except for issues relating to the equal treatment of employees which are covered in PSI 33/2011). It builds on the successes of and learning from previous arrangements for the management of race and disability issues and extends coverage to all equalities issues.
1.2 It applies to all prison establishments – all references to Governors should be taken to include the Directors of contracted establishments.
**Case Law**
*R (Hawke) v Secretary of State for Justice* [2015] EWHC 3599 (Admin); 3 December 2015, Queen's Bench Division (Administrative Court), Holman J
The court was prevented, due to statute made by Parliament, from making a declaration that the Secretary of State for Justice had failed to comply with his equality duty under the Equality Act 2010 where the outcome would have been the same had that duty been adhered to, as neither claimant had suffered any loss as a result.

*R (on the application of (1) Campbell (2) Ferguson) v Governor of Wakefield Prison* [2011] EWHC 2596 (Admin)
See "Education" above.

*R (on the application of Dowsett) v Secretary of State for Justice* [2011] EWHC 2877 (Admin)
The claimant prisoner (D) applied for permission to apply for judicial review of the defendant secretary of state's policy on rub-down searches of prisoners. D complained that he had been subjected to a rub-down search on numerous occasions which made him feel uncomfortable or embarrassed. The Court held that although the secretary of state had not previously raised the jurisdiction argument, it was an important point with far-reaching implications and should be heard as a preliminary issue. Proceedings in the County Court might be desirable so that complex issues of fact could be assessed by a specialist tribunal, but in the instant case there were no nuanced issues to be determined. Resolution of a

dispute about whether D's claimed embarrassment was genuine did not require very much evidence. In any event, the public law challenge had properly been made in the Administrative Court and it was desirable for all claims to be heard together. D's claims were arguable. Permission to apply for judicial review was granted, and the issue of jurisdiction was to be tried as a preliminary issue (see paras 15-19, 25, 27, 29 of judgment).

## EQUALITY IMPACT ASSESSMENTS

PSI 32/2011 – Ensuring Equality (Section 5 equality impact assessments, Annex B – B1 Bullet point 2, B4 and Annex E are cancelled)
PSI 20/2016 – Implementation of Equality Analysis

## ESCAPE AND RISK CLASSIFICATION

PSI 10/2015 - "Management and Security of Escape (E-List) Prisoners
1. Executive Summary Background
1.1 This instruction is one of a number of Prison Service Instructions (PSIs) which form part of the Security Management function of the National Security Framework (NSF). All Security Management instructions can be accessed via the National Security Framework website. This PSI supports the Security Management specification.
1.2 Desired Outcomes:
• Escapes and absconds are prevented. • Threats to the security, safety, order and control of the establishment are detected and deterred. • Crime and suspected criminal activity is detected, reported and deterred. • There is effective and lawful information exchange with establishment staff. • There is effective and lawful information exchange and working arrangements with other agencies. • Security measures are applied lawfully, safely, fairly, proportionately and decently.
1.3 This PSI introduces replaces PSI 56/2011 by introducing a three classifications of E-list; Elist-Standard, E-list-Escort and E-list Heightened.
**Case Law**
*R (Khatib) v Secretary of State for Justice* [2015] EWHC 606 (Admin)
A prisoner who had been deemed a high escape risk challenged this on the basis that, in making that finding, the decision had confused the tests for security and escape classification, and had failed to take into account relevant information about his progress in prison. The Court refused to quash the decision, on the basis that the omitted information would not have materially affected the decision.

## ESCAPE, assisting prisoner to

Section 39 of the Prison Act 1952
**Case law**
*R v Perry* [2013] EWCA Crim 1598

A sentence of two months' imprisonment after a guilty plea was appropriate for an offence of escaping from lawful custody, where a serving prisoner had failed to return from permitted leave but there were no further aggravating features.

## ESCORTED ABSENCES FOR CAT. C LIFE SENTENCE PRISONERS

Release on Temporary Licence Policy Framework (update August 2021) for 'escorted ROTL' (as of May 2021 there has been the addition of specified terrorist and terrorist connected offenders to the restricted ROTL cohort)

## ESCORTS

See "Transfer of Prisoners".

## ESTATE, PRISON SERVICE

PSO 5800
PSI 38/2004 – Process for closing or re-designating industrial workshops and laundries
PSI 05/2012

## EXPENSES

HMPPS Finance Manual Policy Framework - Section 10.10 Expense Claims
Section 21 of the Prison Act 1952 – Expense of conveyance to prison
Section 51 of the Prison Act 1952 – Payment out of moneys provided by Parliament-

## EXTENDED SENTENCES

Security Categorisation Policy Framework (Updated August 2021)
**Case Law**
*R (on the application of David O'Connell) v Parole Board & Anor* [2009] EWCA Civ 575
The European Convention on Human Rights Art.5(4) did not apply to a person serving an extended sentence imposed under the Criminal Justice Act 2003 s.227 as soon as he had served one-half of the appropriate custodial term.

*Secretary of State for the Home Department v (1) William Sim (2) The Parole Board* [2003] EWCA Civ 1845; (2004) QB 1288 : (2004) 2 WLR 1170 : (2004) HRLR 15; Times, January 2, 2004
The parole board's decision to continue to detain a prisoner who had been subject to recall during an extended licence period was a decision which attracted the safeguards of Art.5 European Convention on Human Rights and therefore the detention had to be consistent with the objectives of the original sentence and would be subject to regular reviews compliant with Art.5.4. The crucial question was whether the subsequent detention after recall of a person in S's position could be said to be justified under Art.5(1)(a) because of the original sentence imposed by the

court. Where an offender was detained during the extended period of a s.85 sentence, such detention was subject to review by a judicial body. No court had ordered his detention during that period and prima facie the sentencing court took the view that he could be dealt with in the community during that period. That was the critical factor which distinguished the situation from that considered in R (Giles) v Parole Board (2003) UKHL 42 and R (Smith) v Parole Board (2003) EWCA Civ 1269, both of which were concerned with detention falling within the term of imprisonment imposed by the competent court.

In cases of extended sentences under s.85, it was the executive which decided upon an offender's recall and because that detention was not ordered by a court it had to be supervised by a judicial body. It was so supervised as provided by s.44A of the 1991 Act. Therefore Elias J was correct in his conclusion on the first issue, Art.5(4) applied to decisions to recall and detain an offender serving a s.85 extended sentence who had been released on licence.

### EX-GRATIA PAYMENTS (staff)
HMPPS Finance Manual Policy Framework
PSI 24/2008 – additional hours – payment plus

### FAITH & PASTORAL CARE FOR PRISONERS
PSI 05/2016
Executive Summary
Background
1.1  The Prison Service recognises and respects the right of prisoners to register and practise their faith whilst in custody.
1.2 This Prison Service Instruction (PSI) supports the Specification: Faith and Pastoral Care for Prisoners. It sets out the procedures that should be followed in the delivery of the Specification.
1.3 This PSI replaces PSI 51/2011 and makes some modest changes including specifying that chaplaincy reception visits must be on an individual basis and should take place within 24 hours (2.5), that prisoners on an open ACCT (Assessment, Care in Custody, Teamwork) are seen at least weekly (18.1) and introduces some changes to the recording of statutory duties.
It provides additional guidance on through the gate work (15.5 – 15.12), provision for the numerically smaller traditions when a faith chaplain is not present (4.22 – 4.23) and on funerals (17.8 and 17.9). Changes to the faith annexes of the PSI include the introduction of Prasad for Hindu prisoners (F2), reflect the need for a shower on the day of prayers for Sikh prisoners (R3) and make clarification to the information on Islam (H) and Paganism (M).

### FAMILIES, Prisoners'
See also "Human Rights – Article 8".
Strengthening Prisoner's Family Ties Policy Framework (Updated January 2020)
PR 4
Prison Rule 4
4.— Outside Contacts
(1) Special attention shall be paid to the maintenance of such relationships between a prisoner and his family as are desirable in the best interests of both.
(2) A prisoner shall be encouraged and assisted to establish and maintain such relations with persons and agencies outside prison as may, in the opinion of the governor, best promote the interests of his family and his own social rehabilitation.
YOI 42 – Outside contacts

### FINANCE
See "Prisoner Finance".

### FINES
See HMPPS Finance Manual Policy Framework

### FIRE SAFETY
PSI 11/2015 - "Fire Safety in Prison Establishments"
This PSI sets out the actions that the Responsible Persons must take to ensure that systems are in place to effectively manage the risk from fire to which relevant persons are exposed to and to ensure compliance with current legislation.

### FITNESS STRATEGY, staff
Staff Fitness Policy (intranet only version) November 2021

### FIXED TERM RECALL
Case Law
*R (on the application of Oakes) v Secretary of State for Justice & Ors* [2010] EWCA Civ 1169 The appellant prisoner (O) appealed against a decision ([2009] EWHC 3470 (Admin)) refusing his application for an order that the respondent secretary of state's refusal to release him on licence after his recall to prison was later found to be challengeable. O was recalled for breaching a licence condition. He was subject to standard recall rather than automatic recall, under which he would automatically have been released after 28 days. There was no room, on the application of that scheme, for a prisoner once lawfully not found suitable for automatic release to be assessed under the test in s.255A(5). The tests in s.255A(5) and s.255C(3) were intended to be different. The s.255C(3) test had been lawfully applied in O's case and his detention had been lawful (see paras 17, 21 of judgment). The Court of Appeal recognised that the ruling may

produce unfairness to those recalled as standard recalls where it later transpired that the circumstances of the recall were questionable.

*R (on the application of Yousef Bektas) v Secretary of State for Justice* [2009] EWHC 2359 (Admin)
Under the Criminal Justice Act 2003 s.255A(5), an offender recalled to prison while on licence would only be suitable for automatic release if the secretary of state was satisfied that they would not present a risk of serious selfharm to members of the public if released at the end of the 28 day period specified by s.255A(4).

## FLEXIBLE WORKING HOURS
### Prison Service agreement
PSO 8410 – Flexible Working Hours (replaced PSI 13/1999)

## FOOD
YOI 20
PSI 72/1999 – Food containing genetically modified soya or maize: provision of information for consumers.
PSI 29/1998 – Food Safety Act 1990
PSO 3800 – Food Safety Act 1990
PSI 34/1999- Prison catering services
PR 24
24.— Food
(1) Subject to any directions of the Secretary of State, no prisoner shall be allowed, except as authorised by a health care professional, to have any food other than that ordinarily provided.
(2) The food provided shall be wholesome, nutritious, well prepared and served, reasonably varied and sufficient in quantity.
(3) Any person deemed by the governor to be competent, shall from time to time inspect the food both before and after it is cooked and shall report any deficiency or defect to the governor.
(4) In this rule "food" includes drink.

## FORCE, use of
### See also "Disruptive prisoners, management"
PR 47
YOI 50
Prison Rule 47
47.— Use of force
(1) An officer in dealing with a prisoner shall not use force unnecessarily and, when the application of force to a prisoner is necessary, no more force than is necessary shall be used.
(2) No officer shall act deliberately in a manner calculated to provoke a prisoner.
PSO 1600
PSO 1600 (Extract)
Use Of Force
Introduction:
PSO 1600 is the policy document covering the use of force. It details the circumstances in which

force can be used and the framework for justifying the use of force. The use of force policy document covers not only Control and Restraint techniques but also de-escalation skills, personal safety techniques and the use of batons.
PSI 30/2015 (Revision)- Amends the Use of Police Policy PSO 1600
PSI 06/2014 Control and Order Function: Use of Force Implementation and Minimising and Managing Physical Restraint.

## FOREIGN NATIONALS
PSI 29/2014 (revised October 2015)- Release on licence for foreign national prisoners pending deportation
PSI 37/2014 Eligibility for open conditions and for ROTL of Prisoners subject to deportation proceedings
PSI 04/2013 The Early Removal Scheme and Release of Foreign National Prisoners
The Criminal Justice Act 2003 introduced the Early Removal Scheme (ERS) for foreign national prisoners. The scheme allows fixed-term foreign national prisoners (FNPs), who are confirmed by the Home Office Immigration Enforcement (HOIE) to be liable to removal from the UK, to be removed from prison and the country before the earliest point in the sentence when release could otherwise take place.
Updated June 2022 - This revision is made to incorporate the changes to the ERS that will be made by the Nationality and Borders Act 2022 (NABA 2022) which will be implemented on 28 June 2022. The NABA 2022 increases the ERS window from 9 months to 12 months and introduces a new 'stop the clock' provision for those who are removed under the ERS on or after 28 June 2022 and allows ERS for those recalled to custody from licence. In short therefore, NABA amends sections 260 and 261 of the Criminal Justice Act 2003 to increase the ERS window from 270 days before the earliest release point to 12 months before the earliest release point.
PSI 52/2011 Immigration, Repatriation and Removal Services
Early Release on Compassionate Grounds (ERCG) Policy Framework (May 2022), which is now applicable
### Case Law
*R (Ali) v Secretary of State for Justice* [2015] EWHC 2221 (Admin) 28 July 2015, Queen's Bench Division (Administrative Court), HHJ Heaton QC (sitting as a HCJ)
The governor of a Category A prison had not acted unreasonably in refusing to allow a Kurdish-speaking life prisoner to receive Kurdish-language audio and visual materials sent to him by his family, even though such

materials could not be obtained for him through the prison system.

*R (Hindawi) v Secretary of State for Justice* [2021] EWHC 830 (QB)
The early release provisions contained in domestic law were incompatible with the European Convention on Human Rights 1950 Art.14, in conjunction with Art.5, to the extent that they prevented prisoners liable for removal from having their cases reviewed by the Parole Board in the same manner as other long-term prisoners.

*R (Serrano) v Secretary of State for Justice* [2012] EWHC 3216 (Admin)
See "Home Detention Curfew", below.

*Vaganovs v Governor of HMP Wandsworth* [2013] EWHC 1077 (Admin)
See "Production of Prisoners" below.

*R (on the application of Shaheen) v Secretary of State for Justice* [2008] EWHC 1195 (Admin)
See "Repatriation" below.

*R (on the application of Francis) v (1) Secretary of State for Justice (2) Secretary of State for the Home Department* [2011] EWHC 1271 (Admin)
The claimant foreign national (F) applied for judicial review seeking declarations that her detention and the first defendant Justice Secretary's published policy regarding the release of foreign national prisoners were unlawful and she sought damages. The Court held that the refusal to release a foreign national prisoner under the terms of a home detention curfew scheme was not unlawful, notwithstanding that published policy incorrectly stated that a prisoner would be statutorily excluded from the scheme where detention authority had been issued, since the refusal had not been made on that mistaken basis.

### FORFEITURE OF REMISSION
PR 56, YOI 66

### FRAUD, THEFT AND IRREGULARITY and their investigation
Finance Manual Policy Framework – Risk/fraud management
PSO 1310 – Anti Fraud Strategy
PSO 1310 – Fraud Response Plan

### FREEMASON MEMBERSHIP, staff
PSI 23/2000

### GAMES CONSOLES, prisoners access to
Incentives Policy Framework, chapter 5.30 and Annex D

### GENDER
PSI 33/2011 – Establishing an appropriate staff gender mix in establishments
PSI 32/2011 (Updated January 2020) – Gender equality impact assessments (prisoners)
Care and Management of Individuals who are Transgender Policy Framework (Updated Jan 2020)

### GIFTS
Finance Manual Policy Framework, chapter 2.4 'Gifts and Hospitality'

### HEALTH AND SAFETY
PSI 06/2015 – "Policy, organisation and summary arrangements for the management of Health and Safety" (Updated March 2021)
PSI 10/2016 – Health & safety issues - consultation arrangements
PSI 44/1997 – Health & safety issues with contractors
PSI 25/2015 - "NOMS Performance Related Pay Policy"
PSI 37/2015 - "NOMS Health and Safety (HS) Arrangements for Risk Assessment"
PSI 38/2015 - "Health and Safety Arrangements for the Monitoring and Measurement of Health and Safety Performance"
PSI 10/2016 AI 09/2016 PI 12/2016 – "NOMS Health and Safety Arrangements for Consultation on Matters of Occupational Health, Safety and Fire (OHSF)" Outlines the arrangements and structures in place to ensure effective co-operation and consultation on health and safety matters between staff and managers.
PSI 11/2016 AI 10/2016 PI 13/2016 – "Health and Safety Management Arrangements for Manual Handling Operations"
MOJ, Public Health England Guidance: "Preventing and Controlling Outbreaks of Covid-19 in Prisons and Places of Detention" (Updated 21 March 2022)
"Prisoners or detained individuals with symptoms of COVID-19 should remain (in accordance with relevant powers) in single occupancy accommodation (self-isolate in their cell or room) and be tested for COVID-19 with a polymerase chain reaction (PCR) test. They should stay in their accommodation and avoid contact with other people while awaiting the results of the test.
If single occupancy accommodation is not available, possible cases should self-isolate in higher occupancy accommodation, or where demand exceeds capacity, cases may be cohorted together. The prisoner or detained individual is advised to wear a surgical face mask (Type II or IIR) while being transferred to protective isolation. Escorting staff should follow the guidance on personal protective equipment (PPE), handwashing instructions and limit close contact wherever possible."

**Prisoners or detained individuals who test positive for COVID-19**

Prisoners or detained individuals who test positive with a PCR or LFD test should self-isolate. The isolation period includes the day their symptoms started (or the day their test was taken if they do not have symptoms) and the next 10 full days. Prisoners or detained individuals may be able to end the isolation period before the end of 10 full days. They can take an LFD test from 5 days after the day their symptoms started (or the day their test was taken if they did not have symptoms), and another LFD test on the following day. The second LFD test should be taken at least 24 hours later. If both these test results are negative, and they do not have a high temperature, they may end self-isolation after the second negative test result. They should not take an LFD test before the fifth day of their isolation period, and they should only end self-isolation following 2 consecutive negative LFD tests which should be taken at least 24 hours apart, or after the full 10 days has ended.

If they take an LFD test from the fifth day of their isolation period, and the test result is positive, they should wait 24 hours before they take the next test. If both LFD test results are negative, it is likely that they were not infectious at the time the tests were taken. To further reduce the chance of passing COVID-19 on to others, if prisoners or detained individuals end their self-isolation period before 10 full days they are strongly advised to:

• 	limit close contact with other people outside of their bubble and with those in the wider population, especially in areas which are poorly ventilated

• 	not attend work where possible

• 	wear a face covering when outside of their cell or room

• 	limit contact with anyone who is at higher risk of severe illness if infected with COVID-19, including visitors

• 	follow guidance for people with COVID-19 and their contacts"

**"Prisoner routine testing**

All prisoners entering prisons are placed in RCUs. Prisoners in RCUs should be tested with LFD and PCR tests at reception and again 5 to 6 days after they arrive. They should remain in the RCU for 10 days when following this testing protocol. In cases where population pressures require more rapid transit a prisoner may be able to transfer into the general population before the 10 day RCU period ends provided:

• the individual has spent a minimum of 7 days in the RCU

• the individual has participated in the full RCU testing protocol (LFD and PCR testing on day 0/1 and day 5/6

• the individual receives 2 negative test results on day 5/6, 1 negative PCR test result and 1 negative LFD test result

The isolation period in RCUs should be maintained at 10 days for those not participating in the testing protocol.

Essential workers should be tested twice weekly with an LFD test (one of the LFD tests being mid-week).

Asymptomatic testing of prisoners using LFD should also take place:

• before release

• before a transfer to another PPD

• before a court attendance

• immediately before and after a period of ROTL" (Note that the situation with regards to COVID-19 is frequently changing and so the National Frameworks and Operational Guidance may be subject to change as and when relevant).

**HEALTH SERVICES FOR PRISONERS**
**Key Note**

In a number of recent cases, prisoners have succeeded in reinstating and/or maintaining existing medication which the prisons had intended to replace (see *R (on the application of K v the Governor of HMP Bullingdon and Secretary of State for Justice* (2008) (opiate patches); *R (on the application of M v the Isle of Wight NHS Trust and Secretary of State for Justice* (2009); *R (on the application of D v the Isle of Wight NHS Trust and Secretary of State for Justice* (2009) (opiate based medication).

PSI 24/2002 – Health promoting prisons: a shared approach, a strategy for promoting health in prisons in England and Wales

PSI 25/2002 – The protection and use of confidential health information in prisons and inter-agency information sharing

PSI 36/2002, accompanied by booklet "Developing and modernising primary care in prisons"

Finance Manual Policy Framework (Updated November 2020) – Prison healthcare: new financial reporting arrangements, see PSI 14/2005 – Handling complaints about prison healthcare

PSO 3050 – Continuity of healthcare for Prisoners
CHAPTER 1 - INTRODUCTION

1. This PSO looks at managing continuity of healthcare for prisoners and emphasises the importance of continuity in the success of clinical interventions and treatment. It focuses on the vulnerable points of the system, when the prisoner is moved in to, or out of prison such as entry into custody, leaving and re-entering prison for court visits, transfer to another prison and discharge from custody.

PSO 3100 – Clinical governance quality in prison healthcare

INTRODUCTION FROM THE DIRECTOR OF PRISON HEALTH
CLINICAL GOVERNANCE – QUALITY IN PRISON HEALTH CARE
Introduction
1. This PSO sets out requirements for Governing Governors to ensure that arrangements are being made for clinical governance in prison health care. Governors are not responsible for setting up the detailed arrangements for clinical governance – this falls to the clinical governance lead and health care team – but Governors are accountable for ensuring that the agenda is taken forward. Governors may find it helpful to use the checklist at Appendix 1, which has been based on documents used by NHS Chief Executives.
PSO 3200
Health Promotion
1. This document is introduced as a result of the formal partnership between HM Prison Service and the NHS.
2. The Prison Service in partnership with the NHS has a responsibility to ensure that prisoners have access to health services that are broadly equivalent to those the general public receives from the NHS. This means that prisons should already provide health education, patient education, prevention and other health promotion interventions to meet within that general context, this PSO sets out required actions for Governors and Directors of contracted out prisons to ensure that efforts are made to:
• Build the physical, mental and social health of prisoners (and where appropriate staff) as part of a whole prison approach.
• Help prevent the deterioration of prisoners' health during or because of custody, especially by building on the concept of decency in our prisons.
•       Help prisoners adopt healthy behaviours that can be taken back into the community upon release.
PSI 29/2015 - "First Aid"- The purpose of this instruction is to set out mandatory policy for the effective management of First Aid throughout NOMS.
Generic Parole Processes Policy Framework (Updated September 2021), para 5.6.14: Healthcare information is likely to be required by the Parole Board where the prisoner's physical or mental health is relevant to his/her risk of selfharm. For example, it may have an impact on their physical ability to commit another serious violent offence, or the prisoner may need specialist care and/or accommodation to be available before they can safely be released on licence.

Case Law
*R v Cosford* [2013] EWCA Crim 466
Nurses working in a prison were responsible not only to the prisoners, but also to the public for, so far as it was within their power to do so, the proper, safe and secure running of the prison. Therefore, they held public office, and did so even if they were employed by a private company, and could be found guilty of misconduct in public office.

*R (on the application of Roberts) v Secretary of State for Justice* [2009] EWHC 2321 (Admin)
The Secretary of State for justice had acted unlawfully in failing to publish the policy of the prison service in relation to the transfer of prisoners for hospital treatment.

*R (on the application of Nathan Brooks) v (1) Secretary of State for Justice (2) Isle of Wight Primary Care Trust* [2008] EWHC 3041 (Admin)
Prisoners had to be treated in a way which respected their right to proper medical treatment and prisoners were entitled, insofar as it was possible, to the same attention as would be provided for any person under the terms of the NHS.

*Margaret Brooks v Home Office* [1999] 2 WLUK 65
When it comes to appropriate and necessary treatment for medical conditions, Prisoners enjoy parity with non-prisoners.

**HOME DETENTION CURFEW**
Home Detention Curfew Policy Framework (Updated June 2021 to reflect the termination of CRC contracts)
1 PURPOSE
1.1 The Home Detention Curfew (HDC) scheme provides a managed transition from prison to community for offenders serving short sentences. Release on HDC should be a normal part of a sentence for most eligible offenders, and refusal of HDC for those eligible and not presumed unsuitable for release the exception.
1.2 Since 1999, a number of prison and probation instructions have been published in relation to the HDC process. The aim of this Policy Framework is to consolidate those instructions into one place and therefore completely replace all of the previous instructions, as listed above. The requirements and approach to HDC therefore remain largely the same but the following changes are highlighted:
• Decisions on HDC may now be taken by Directors of Contracted Prisons, the Controller will continue to monitor the Director's compliance in this area.
• Decisions around presumed unsuitable offenders remain with the Governor, but there is

no longer any requirement to consult or notify the HDC Policy team.

• Offenders sentenced to 4 years or more imprisonment by an overseas court but who have less than 4 years to serve after repatriation to the UK are presumed unsuitable for release on HDC.

4.3    ELIGIBILITY    AND    PRESUMED UNSUITABILITY

This section sets out the eligibility criteria, how to deal with representations from offenders presumed unsuitable for HDC and how to calculate the HDCED.

Increase in maximum home detention curfew period to 135 days

4.6 ASSESSMENT AND DECISION

This section sets out where HDC should be postponed or refused.

PSI 31/1998 – Home Detention Curfew, Funding and Planning

Bail Accommodation and Support Service (BASS) Policy Framework, accommodation and support services for bail and home detention curfew

**Case Law**

R (Foster) v Secretary of State for Justice [2015] EWCA Civ 281

Where there was evidence that a prisoner had breached a condition of his licensed release on home detention curfew, fairness did not necessitate an oral hearing when he sought to appeal the decision to recall him to prison. Home Detention Curfew operated differently from the situation where a prisoner had completed a term of imprisonment and had a statutory right to liberty, the latter of which does require an oral hearing in the event that the recall decision was challenged.

R (Jackley) v Secretary of State for Justice [2015] EWHC 342 (Admin)

Two serving prisoners challenged the Secretary of State's decision to refuse to grant them Home Detention Curfew (HDC).

The prison service had told them that they would be eligible for HDC. However, after being told, section 112 of the Legal Aid, Sentencing and Punishment of Offenders Act 2012 came into force, which rendered them ineligible for HDC as they were serving determinate sentences of over four years. They argued that they had been given a legitimate expectation by the previous statement from the prison, and that the Secretary of State had acted with procedural impropriety and in breach of their legitimate expectation by failing to notify them that they were no longer eligible for HDC by virtue of the change in the law.

The application was refused on the basis that their ineligibility was due to a change in statute, and that a legitimate expectation could not

require the Secretary of State (or any public authority) to act contrary to statute.

R (Serrano) v Secretary of State for Justice [2012] EWHC 3216 (Admin)

Under Prison Service Instruction 52/2011 foreign offenders liable to be deported were deemed unsuitable for release on home detention curfew unless exceptional circumstances were shown. That policy was lawful and did not amount to discrimination on the ground of nationality.

R (Foster) v Secretary Of State For Justice [2013] EWHC 1951 (Admin)

Justice did not dictate that the claimant prisoner should have been allowed an oral hearing as part of his appeal against his recall to prison after he had been released on home detention curfew.

Jama v Ministry of Justice [2012] EWHC 533 (QB)

Where a young offender, who was a British citizen, had stated his nationality to be Somalian to officers at a young offender institution, the prison officers had failed to take appropriate steps to have his nationality ascertained by referring him to the Immigration and Nationality Directorate. However, the offender was not entitled to damages for the extra three months he spent in detention rather than on home detention curfew as a result of the prison officers' failings.

R (on the application of Francis) v (1) Secretary of State for Justice (2) Secretary of State for the Home Department [2011] EWHC 1271 (Admin)

The claimant foreign national (F) applied for judicial review seeking declarations that her detention and the first defendant Justice Secretary's published policy regarding the release of foreign national prisoners were unlawful and she sought damages. The Court held that the refusal to release a foreign national prisoner under the terms of a home detention curfew scheme was not unlawful, notwithstanding that published policy incorrectly stated that a prisoner would be statutorily excluded from the scheme where detention authority had been issued, since the refusal had not been made on that mistaken basis.

**HOSPITALITY**
**See "Gifts".**

**HOUSING NEEDS AND HOMELESSNESS**
**See also "Resettlement".**

Homelessness Reduction Act: Duty to Refer Policy Framework

PSI 47/2003 – Rationalisation of Doctors Duties in Prisons

**Case Law**

O'Rourke (Respondent) v Mayor and Aldermen of the London Borough of Camden (Appellants) [1998] AC

188 Sub Nom O'Rourke v Camden London Borough Council (1997) HL
Appeal by Camden Borough Council against the decision of the Court of Appeal in reinstating one of the respondent's claims for damages for breaches of various statutory duties under Part III Housing Act 1985 which had been struck out by HH Judge Tibber in the Central London County Court. After the respondent's release from prison on 12/4/91 the appellant authority provided the respondent with temporary accommodation at the Northumberland Hotel. The respondent contended that this amounted to an acknowledgement that the authority owed him a duty under s.63(1) Housing Act 1985 to secure that accommodation was made available for him but he alleged that on 24/4/91 the appellant wrongfully evicted him from the hotel and did not offer him any other accommodation. The Court held, following Cocks v Thanet District (1983) the respondent had no private law action against the appellant. Thornton v Kirklees MBC (1979) QB 626 was wrongly decided. The breach of statutory duty of which the plaintiff complained gave rise to no cause of action in private law. For proceedings in the European Court of Human Rights see Peter O'Rourke v United Kingdom (2001) (Admissibility Decision).

*Crossley v Westminster City Council [2006] EWCA Civ 140; LTL 23/2/2006; (2006) HLR 26; (2006) NPC 20; Independent, March 1, 2006*
C, who was 36, grew up from the age of 3 in local authority care. Since the age of 17 he lived rough on the streets with short spells in hostels and in prison. Where a claim for housing had been made on the basis that the applicant had been vulnerable for some special reason and there were facts that had pointed towards vulnerability, where the decision maker had failed to acknowledge, take into account and evaluate those facts the decision should be reconsidered.

*R (on the application of B) v Southwark London Borough Council [2003] EWHC 1678 (Admin)*
A prison cell was not accommodation within the meaning of s.175 Housing Act 1996. Therefore a prisoner eligible for release who had no other accommodation was homeless within the definition in the Act. B considered himself homeless and applied to L for accommodation. L refused the application on the basis that since B was accommodated in prison he was not homeless within the meaning in s.175 Housing Act 1996. Prison was not accommodation within the meaning of the Act (Stewart v Lambeth (supra) considered). (2) Prison did not fall within s.175(a), (b) or (c) of the Act. For accommodation

to exist there had to be a right to occupy that was enforceable or defensible at law. A prisoner could not be said to have a right of occupation and detention was the antithesis of any such right. (3) A prison cell was not accommodation which it was reasonable to occupy within the meaning in s.175(3) of the Act. It was unrealistic to assert that the early release provisions in respect of electronic tagging were some sort of "bonus" and that therefore it was reasonable for B to occupy his cell until 19 July 2003. Objectively it was not reasonable for B to occupy a prison cell when he was entitled to release.

*R (on the application of S) v (1) London Borough of Lewisham (2) London Borough of Lambeth (3) London Borough of Hackney [2008] EWHC 1290 (Admin)*
On S's release from prison on May 12, 2004, she went to stay with a friend in the area of H under an arrangement which was intended to be temporary. On May 26, she vacated her friend's home in H and travelled by public transport to L's area, where she attended a social services office and presented a letter from her solicitors requesting urgent support under s.21. Physical presence in the area of a particular local authority was sufficient to entitle a person in need of assistance under the National Assistance Act 1948 s.21 to seek assistance from that local authority.

## HUMAN RIGHTS
*R (Chester) v Secretary of State for Justice* [2013] UKSC 63 (Scotland)
See "Voting Provisions for Prisoners" below.
**Key Note**
Human Rights issues arise in a large proportion of prisoner law cases. The following is a brief overview of common human rights issues arising in such cases.
Prison discipline & the European Convention on Human Rights (ECHR) – guidance
Howard League – The Rising Tide: Additional days for rule-breaking in prison
PSI 47/2011 – Prison Discipline Procedures (for adjudications which commenced before 01/02/19)
PSI 05/2018 – Prison Discipline Procedures (for current adjudications and those which commenced after 01/02/19)

## HUMAN RIGHTS ACT PROCEEDINGS
**Case Law**
*R (on the application of Al-Sweady & Ors) v Secretary of State for Defence [2009] EWHC 2387 (Admin)*
In judicial review cases concerning disputed breaches of human rights under the European Convention on Human Rights 1950, it was vital for the parties to consider whether there were "hard-edged" questions of fact to resolve, of the

kind described in R v Monopolies and Mergers Commission Ex p South Yorkshire Transport Ltd (1993) 1 WLR 23, as that would be relevant in determining whether the court needed to make orders for cross-examination and disclosure.

*Watkins v Secretary of State for the Home Department* [2006] UKHL 17
W was a convicted prisoner serving a sentence of life imprisonment. Prison officers had breached the Rules by opening and reading W's mail when they were not entitled to do so. Misfeasance in public office was not actionable without proof of material damage. The lack of remedy in tort did not leave W without any legal remedy. For example, breach of a fundamental human or constitutional right would, in all probability, found a claim under the Human Rights Act 1998 s.7.

### HUMAN RIGHTS: Article 2 – Right to Life (see also Deaths in Custody)
### Case Law
*R (M) v Parole Board* [2013] EWHC 1360 (Admin)
See "Media" below.

*R (on the application of JL) v Secretary of State for Justice* [2008] UKHL 68
A near-suicide of a prisoner in custody which left him with the possibility of a serious long-term injury automatically triggered an obligation on the state under the European Convention on Human Rights 1950 art.2 to institute an enhanced investigation. However, not every such investigation was required, in order to comply with art.2, to amount to the type of investigation identified in *R (on the application of D) v Secretary of State for the Home Department* (2006) EWCA Civ 143, (2006) 3 All ER 946.
*Walch v Secretary of State for Justice* [2010] EWHC 2203 (Admin)
A prisoner was refused permission to seek judicial review of the secretary of state's refusal to order an enquiry into his self-harming while in custody where there was nothing exceptional in the circumstances of the case to persuade the court that the principle established in *R (on the application of JL) v Secretary of State for the Home Department* (2008) UKHL 68, (2009) 1 AC 588 should be extended beyond cases of death or the near-death with life-threatening and permanent injuries of someone who was within the care of the state or within the state's coercive power.

*Tyrrell v HM Senior Coroner County Durham and Darlington* [2016] EWHC 1892 (Admin)
The procedural obligation for inquests into deaths in custody under ECHR art.2 did not arise in cases where it was established that death was from natural causes and there was no reason to believe that the state had failed to protect the life of the prisoner.

*R (on the application of D) v Secretary of State for the Home Department* [2006] EWCA Civ 143, (2006) 3 All ER 946
Where a vulnerable prisoner had attempted suicide whilst in custody and had sustained life-threatening injuries, any inquiry into the incident had to be held in public in order to properly discharge the state's investigative obligation implicit in the European Convention on Human Rights 1950 Art.2. It was not, however, necessary for him to be able to cross-examine witnesses.

*R v Home Office, ex parte (1) Margaret Wright (2) Moira Bennett* [2001] EWHC Admin 520 (2002) HRLR 1; (2001) UKHRR 1399; (2001) Lloyd's Med Rep 478; (2001) 62 BMLR 16
An order for an independent official investigation into the death of an inmate was permitted where it was held that his treatment had arguably been contrary to Art.2 and Art.3 European Convention on Human Rights.

### HUMAN RIGHTS: Article 3 – Freedom from Torture and Inhuman and Degrading Treatment
See also "Restraints"; & "Treatment of Prisoners".
### Case Law
*Razumas v Ministry of Justice* [2018] EWHC 215 (QB)
See "Medical Attention and Treatment" below.

*Kelly v Ministry of Justice* [2014] EWHC 3440 (QB)
A prisoner had not been able to show, by direct or inferential evidence, that having to use a bucket as a toilet when he was locked in his cell at night caused him serious suffering so as to violate the ECHR art.3.
*R (F) v Secretary of State for the Home Department* [2012] EWHC 2689 (Admin)
See "Cell sharing" above.

*R (M) v Parole Board* [2013] EWHC 1360 (Admin)
See "Media" below.

*Vinter v United Kingdom (66069/09)* [2013] 7 WLUK 244; 34 BHRC 605
See "Lifers" below.

*Krolik & Ors v Poland* [2012] EWHC 2357 (Admin)
The court gave guidance on the procedure to be followed in extradition appeals brought on the basis that extradition would be in breach of the European Convention on Human Rights article.3 by reason of Polish prison conditions.

*R (on the application of NM v Secretary of State for Justice* [2012] EWCA Civ 1182
See "Investigations" below.

**Key Note**
The first two cases recited below are significant "slopping out" cases. The first was an unsuccessful English claim, the second was a Scottish case which gives helpful guidance on the procedural and evidential issues arising in such cases:
(1) *Desmond Grant (2) Roger Charles Gleaves v Ministry of Justice* [2011] EWHC 3379 (QB); [2012] A.C.D. 32; 19 December 2011
See "Slopping Out" below.

*Napier v Scottish Ministers* [2005] 1 S.C. 307; 2005 U.K.H.R.R. 268, Court of Session (Inner House, First Division) 10 February 2005
See "Slopping Out" below.

*Hassan v Secretary of State for Justice* [2011] EWHC 1359 (Admin)
A decision to detain a prisoner in a segregation unit was justified in view of his highly disruptive and violent behaviour and evidence that he had assaulted another prisoner.
See "Segregation" below.

*R (on the application of K) v Secretary of State for the Home Department* [2009] EWCA Civ 219
The appellants were entitled to a declaration that the Secretary of State should have instituted an independent investigation into alleged violations of their rights under ECHR art.3 during a disturbance at an immigration detention centre.

*R v Bieber* [2008] EWCA Crim 1601; LTL 24/7/2008; (2009) 1 All ER 295; (2008) HRLR 43; (2009) 1 WLR 223; Times, August 11, 2008
A whole life term should not be considered as a sentence that was irreducible. Any European Convention on Human Rights 1950 art.3 challenge where a whole life term had been imposed should therefore be made, not at the time of the imposition of the sentence, but at the stage when the prisoner contended that, having regard to all the material circumstances, any further detention would constitute degrading or inhuman treatment.

*R (on the application of Graham) v Secretary of State for Justice: R (on the application of Allen) v Secretary of State for Justice* [2007] EWHC 2940 (Admin)
The handcuffing of a prisoner whilst he received chemotherapy treatment had breached his rights under the European Convention on Human Rights 1950 Art.3 not to suffer inhuman or degrading treatment as he did not represent a risk to the public and there was no risk of his escape.

*Re Mark Fulton (Application for Judicial Review)* [2000] N.I. 447; (2000): LTL 5/10/2001; (2001) HRLR 11 (Northern Ireland)

Solitary confinement or segregation of persons in detention was not per se a breach of Art.3 European Convention on Human Rights. It was permissible for reasons of security or discipline or to protect the segregated prisoner.

**HUMAN RIGHTS: Article 5 rights – Freedom from Arbitrary Detention**
*R (Sturnham) v Parole Board for England and Wales; R (Faulkner) v Secretary of State for Justice* [2013] UKSC 23
See "Damages claims" above.

*R (M) v Parole Board* [2013] EWHC 1360 (Admin)
See "Media" below.

*R (on the application of Parratt) v Secretary of State for Justice* [2014] EWCA Civ 1478
See "Damages claims" above.

*In the Matter of an Application by Martin Corey for Judicial Review* [2012] NICA 57 (Northern Ireland)
See "Recalled prisoners" below.

*Osborne, Booth and Reilly* [2013] UKSC 61
See "Parole Board Oral Hearings" below.

**Case Law**
*R (Dexter) v Secretary of State for Justice* [2020] EWHC 3184 (Admin)
Delay case. Claimant had to wait 81 days for a bed at an Approved Premises before he was released. This period coincided with the Coronavirus pandemic which meant that the prison regime was restricted and the Claimant could not work in the prison coffee shop or have family visits. Court held that it is not right that any change to an estimate release date automatically breaches Article 5(1). High threshold for establishing an Article 5 breach reiterated.

*R (on the application of Bowen & Anor) v Secretary of State for Justice* [2016] EWHC 2057 (Admin)
There was no unlawful detention or breach of Article 5 ECHR when there had been a delay in securing a place for the prisoners at a particular Approved Premises which was part of their licence conditions for release. B (a life prisoner) was released to the AP 69 days after the Parole Board decision to release; S (an IPP prisoner) was released 118 days after the Parole Board decision to release.
Having identified the appropriate AP Mandeville House as the most suitable for each prisoner (it being close to their home and family), it was not unreasonable in all the circumstances to delay release until a place was available there in each prisoners' case.

*R (on the application of Bowen) v Secretary of State for Justice* [2017] EWCA Civ 2181
An appeal by the claimants of the decision in R (on the application of Bowen & Anor) v Secretary of State for Justice [2016] EWHC 2057 (Admin) was dismissed.

*Brown v The Parole Board for Scotland, The Scottish Ministers and another* [2017] UKSC 69 (Scotland)
When a prisoner serving an extended sentence is detained during the extension period his continued detention is justified solely by the need to protect the public from serious selfharm, and not a matter determined by the original sentence of the court. In such instances the situation is analogous to life and IPP sentences. The appellant (B) had been recalled during his extended period of licence and served the remainder of the sentence in custody. In the judgment of the Court Lord Reed held, "Having regard to these circumstances - the indefinite (albeit not unlimited) duration of detention during the extension period, its preventive purpose, and the possibility of change in response to opportunities for rehabilitation - the reasoning which led the European court to decide in James, in the context of IPP sentences, that article 5(1)(a) imposed an obligation to provide the prisoner with a real opportunity for rehabilitation is equally applicable. As was explained earlier, the reasoning in James was based on the need for the conditions of detention to be related to the purpose of the detention, in order to avoid arbitrariness and hence "unlawfulness" within the meaning of article 5(1)(a). The critical feature of IPP sentences, after the prisoners had served the punishment element of their sentences, was that they were "in detention solely because of the risk they pose to the public". It followed that there must be measures in place "aimed at reducing the danger they present and at limiting the duration of their detention to what is strictly necessary in order to prevent them from committing further offences". That reasoning applies equally to prisoners detained during the extension period of an extended sentence, other than by virtue of a section 16 order or a concurrent sentence." However, in B's case, he had been provided with a real opportunity for rehabilitation but continued to be involved in violent behaviour and to abuse drugs. He had been transferred back from open to closed conditions and had reoffended when on licence resulting in his recall. Whilst there had been some delays in securing his placement on suitable courses, the general problem was not the failure of the prison authorities to provide appropriate courses, but B's own misconduct. As a result his detention during the extension period,

or at any other point during his sentence, could not have been arbitrary.

*R (on the application of Youngsam) v The Parole Board* [2017] EWHC 729 (Admin)
Delays after recall before an oral hearing of the Parole Board took place did not constitute a fresh deprivation of liberty under Article 5 (4) of the European Convention on Human Rights (ECHR) following R (Whiston) v Secretary of State for Justice [2012] EWCA Civ 1374. Turner J held, "the broad statement of principle articulated by Lord Neuberger in Whiston on the scope of Article 5(4) whilst, strictly speaking, obiter was clearly intended to, and now ought to be, followed by all courts of inferior jurisdiction." Further there was no breach in the common law duty to act in a reasonable time, notwithstanding that various delays in the process of listing an effective oral hearing had resulted in the oral hearing taking place over twelve months after the prisoner's recall.

*Kaiyam v United Kingdom (28160/15)* [2016] 1 WLUK 84, (2016) E.H.R.R. SE13
The appellant prisoners appealed against the decisions that it was lawful to continue to detain them following the expiry of their minimum terms (see directly below). Each had claimed that their progress towards post-tariff release had been undermined because the prison service had not provided them with the necessary facilities to allow for proper rehabilitation. Complaints included, for example, transfer to open conditions too close to the expiry of the minimum term to allow for immediate release, and not being able to start extended sex offender treatment programmes until after expiry of their tariffs. The Supreme Court held that James (below) could not be followed, as that would allow for the release of a prisoner who still posed an unacceptable risk. The ECtHR however did not adopt the UK Supreme Court's analysis. The ECtHR followed James but held that in Kaiyam a real opportunity for rehabilitation had been provided to the applicants.

*Brown v Parole Board for Scotland* [2015] CSIH 59; 31 July 2015, Court of Session, Lords Menzies, McGhie and Lady Clark
A prisoner's rights under Article 5 ECHR had not been infringed where he was serving a determinate sentence and the Article 5 implied ancillary duty to facilitate his progress towards release did not apply. (See also [2017] UKSC 96 above).

*R (Dixon) v Secretary of State for Justice* [2015] EWHC 2712 (Admin), 30 September 2015, Queen's Bench Division (Administrative Court), HHJ Davies (sitting as a HCJ)

Although there had been a significant delay of three to three-and-a-half months on the part of the Prison Service in the completion of a psychological risk assessment of a prisoner seeking release from custody, the delay did not give rise to a breach of Art.5 (4) ECHR. The temporary staffing difficulties which the psychology department was experiencing at the time should be taken into consideration.

*Secretary of State for Justice v James (Formerly Walker & Anor): R (on the application of Lee) v Secretary of State for Justice & Anor* [2009] UKHL 22
Where a prisoner serving an indeterminate sentence of imprisonment for the protection of the public was, after the expiry of his tariff period, unable to demonstrate his safety for release, his continued detention was not unlawful at common law. Nor did it breach the European Convention on Human Rights 1950 art.5(4), and nor did it breach art.5(1) unless there had been a period of years without any effective review.

*James, Wells and Lee v. The United Kingdom* [2012] 9 WLUK 278 (Applications nos. 25119/09, 57715/09 and 57877/09) European Court of Human Rights 18th September 2012
The ECtHR delivered a lengthy and detailed judgment on 18th September 2012 in the three applications of James, Wells and Lee. The Court analysed the factual background to each Applicant's case and set out the domestic history of the cases as well as relevant domestic law and practice. Having assessed the arguments advanced by the Applicants and the UK Government, the Court reiterated at the outset that the object and purpose of Article 5(1) is to ensure that no-one is dispossessed of his liberty in an arbitrary fashion. It has frequently emphasised the fundamental importance of the guarantees contained in Article 5 for securing the right of individuals in a democracy to be free from arbitrary detention at the hands of the authorities. The Court held that there had accordingly been a violation of Article 5(1) of the Convention in the case of all three applicants (para 222). The Court made relatively modest awards of damages (Mr James EUR 3,000 in respect of a period of five months, Mr Wells EUR 6,200 in respect of a period of twenty-one months and Mr Lee EUR 8,000 in respect of a period of thirty months (para 244). N.B. This case has mixed judicial consideration. Although sentences of Imprisonment for Public Protection ("IPP") were repealed following this judgment, this was not applied retrospectively. Furthermore, the European Court of Human Rights in the case of Kaiyam above declined to determine whether the UK has properly implemented the James judgment.

*R (on the application of MA) v (1) National Probation Service (2) Secretary of State for Justice* [2011] EWHC 1332 (Admin)
See "Human Rights: Article 8" below.

*R (on the application of Morales) v (1) Parole Board (2) Secretary of State for Justice (3) Staffordshire Probation Service* [2011] EWHC 28 (Admin)
The Parole Board constituted an independent court within the meaning of the European Convention on Human Rights 1950 art.5(4) notwithstanding its lack of powers to require the production of documents, but the failure to conduct an expeditious review of an offender's detention following his recall on licence had breached his rights under art.5(4).

*R (on the application of Faulkner) v (1) Secretary of State for Justice (2) Parole Board* [2010] EWCA Civ 1434
Where, but for unjustified delays by the Secretary of State for Justice, a former prisoner would have had a review before the Parole Board heard 10 months earlier, there had been a breach of his rights under the European Convention on Human Rights 1950 art.5(4). As the prisoner would have been released earlier if the hearing had been held earlier, he was entitled to damages to reflect the fact that he had spent 10 months in prison when he ought not to have done.

*R (on the application of Black) v Secretary of State for Justice* [2009] UKHL 1; (2009) 2 WLR 282; (2009) 4 All ER 1; (2009) HRLR 15; (2009) UKHRR 382; (2009) 1 AC 949; Times, January 30, 2009
A prisoner serving a determinate sentence was not entitled by virtue of the European Convention on Human Rights 1950 art.5(4) to a speedy judicial decision on the lawfulness of any continued period of detention once his parole eligibility date had arrived. The secretary of state's power to reject a recommendation of the Parole Board to release such a prisoner on licence at the halfway stage of his term was anomalous but was not contrary to art.5(4).

*Secretary of State for the Home Department v (1) William Sim (2) The Parole Board* [2003] EWCA Civ 1845; (2004) QB 1288; (2004) 2 WLR 1170; (2004) HRLR 15; Times, January 2, 2004
The parole board's decision to continue to detain a prisoner who had been subject to recall during an extended licence period was a decision which attracted the safeguards of Art.5 European Convention on Human Rights and therefore the detention had to be consistent with the objectives of the original sentence and would be subject to regular reviews compliant with Art.5.4. The crucial question was whether the subsequent detention after recall of a person in S's position

could be said to be justified under Art.5(1)(a) because of the original sentence imposed by the court. That was the critical factor which distinguished the situation from that considered in *R (Giles) v Parole Board* (2003) UKHL 42 and *R (Smith) v Parole Board* (2003) EWCA Civ 1269, both of which were concerned with detention falling within the term of imprisonment imposed by the competent court.

N.B. This case has mixed judicial consideration, which appears to arise out of the findings in *R (on the application of Lee Bayliss) v (1) Parole Board (2) Secretary of State for Justice* [2008] EWHC 3127 (Admin) that the test applicable to prisoners serving extended sentences was not the test to be used when deciding on the release of those sentenced to imprisonment for public protection.

*R (on the application of Giles) v (1) Parole Board (2) Secretary of State for the Home Department* [2003] UKHL 42
An extended sentence imposed under s.2(2)(b) Criminal Justice Act 1991 (re-enacted as s.80(2)(b) Powers of Criminal Courts (Sentencing) Act 2000) was not an indeterminate sentence, was the product of a judicial decision (and therefore subject to appeal), and was therefore not subject to the requirements of periodic review under Art.5(4) European Convention on Human Rights.

*R (on the application of Sim) v (1) Parole Board (2) Secretary of State for the Home Department* [2003] EWHC 152 (Admin); (2003) 2 WLR 1374; (2003) ACD 62; Times, February 21, 2003; Independent, March 17, 2003
Art.5 European Convention on Human Rights applied to the recall and detention procedures under the Criminal Justice Act 1991 for breach of an extended licence, since that Article was not satisfied by the original sentence of the court. Recall was not justifiable where the alleged risk of re-offending related to offences that were not of a similar nature to the triggering offence. In deciding whether to confirm a recall decision, the Parole Board was entitled to rely on hearsay evidence.

*R (on the application of Smith) v Parole Board for England and Wales* [2005] UKHL 1
While the common law duty of procedural fairness did not require the Parole Board to hold an oral hearing in every case where a determinate sentence prisoner released on licence resisted his recall to prison, the Parole Board's duty was not as constricted as had been held and assumed. This decision reversed the High Court's decision in Ex Parte Justin West [2002] EWHC 769 (Admin) that recall to prison after release on licence from a determinative sentence was an administrative act and therefore

neither Art 5 nor Art 6 European Convention on Human Rights were engaged.

N.B. This case has mixed judicial consideration, for instance in R (on the application of Whiston) v Secretary of State for Justice [2014] UKSC 39, which found that Smith was unsatisfactory in so far as it decided that art.5(4) was engaged. Although the relevant ECtHR cases had been cited, they had not been followed on that point, largely without explanation, and the explanation that had been given was plainly unsatisfactory. Although Giles had been referred to in argument, it had not been cited in the judgment. Further, it appeared to have been assumed, rather than decided, that art.5(4) was engaged. In relation to art.5(4), and only in relation to art.5(4), Smith had been decided per incuriam, Smith not followed. Lord Brown's obiter comments in R. (on the application of Black) v Secretary of State for the Home Department [2009] UKHL 1, [2009] 1 A.C. 949, [2009] 1 WLUK 303 implied that a United Kingdom court should hold that the reach of art.5(4) was longer than the ECtHR had held.

**HUMAN RIGHTS: Article 6 rights – Right to a Fair Trial**
**See also "Adjudications"**
**Case Law**
*R (Wood) v The Governor of HM Prison Wandsworth* [2015] EWHC 2761 (Admin); 16 September 2015, Queen's Bench Division (Administrative Court), Kerr J
It was not a breach of A.6 ECHR to offer a prisoner a read-only laptop to enable his access to justice. There was nothing so inherently complicated about his case that meant he could not correspond with the CCRC by hand.
*R (Thakrar) v Secretary of State for Justice* [2012] EWHC 3538 (Admin)
See "Access to Legal Representatives" above.

*P v Scottish Ministers* [2013] CSIH 26 (Scotland)
It was not against a prisoner's right to the presumption of innocence under the European Convention on Human Rights 1950 art.6(2) for the parole board to consider at his upcoming parole hearing material in respect of alleged offences of which he had been acquitted where the prisoner was in no sense facing a criminal charge. Proceedings before the board were not classified as being criminal in nature and were conducted with a view to making what was an administrative decision with no question of the imposition of a penalty, and the proceedings were not sufficiently linked to the prisoner's trial such as to attract art.6(2) protection.

*R (on the application of Terry Lake) v (1) Governor of Highdown Prison (2) Independent Adjudicator*

(3) Secretary of State for Justice [2007] EWHC 3080 (Admin)

Whilst an independent adjudicator had the power to require a witness to attend a disciplinary hearing involving a serving prisoner she had not been asked to exercise that power, and as a result the prisoner had not had his European Convention on Human Rights 1950 Art.6 rights infringed.

## HUMAN RIGHTS: Article 8 rights – Right to Private and Family Life

See also "Release, Early – Licence Conditions".

**Case Law**

M v Chief Constable Of Hampshire [2014] EWCA Civ 1651 18 December 2014
See "Sex offenders" below.

R (M) v Parole Board [2013] EWHC 1360 (Admin)
See "Media" below.

R (ML) v Youth Justice Board [2013] EWHC 3083 (Admin); 15 October 2013
See "Transfer of Prisoners".

R (Prothero) v Secretary Of State For The Home Department [2013] EWHC 2830 (Admin); 18 September 2013
See "Sex offenders" below.

R (Tabbakh) v Staffordshire & West Midlands Probation Trust [2013] EWHC 2492 (Admin)
See "Licence conditions" below.

R (X) v Secretary of State for the Home Department [2012] EWHC 2954 (Admin); [2013] 1 W.L.R. 2638; 24 October 2012
See "Sex offenders" below.
Main v Scottish Ministers [2013] CSOH 103 (Scotland); 26 June 2013
See "Sex offenders" below.

R (Stevenson) v Governor of HMP Wakefield [2015] EWHC 1014 (Admin)
A prisoner's Article 8 rights had not been breached when he was allocated to a prison in the north of England (his family being in the south). Visits from his family were neither difficult nor impossible.

R (on the application of Henry Max Shaheen) v Secretary of State for Justice [2008] EWHC 1195 (Admin)
See "Repatriation" below.

R (on the application of MA) v (1) National Probation Service (2) Secretary of State for Justice [2011] EWHC 1332 (Admin)
The claimant (M) applied for judicial review of a decision of the second defendant secretary of state to impose conditions on his licence following his release from prison. M had been given a determinate sentence for two offences of rape, one offence of kidnapping and one of false imprisonment. All the offences pertained to acts that M had perpetrated against his wife. Apart from mandatory standard conditions the conditions of M's licence required him not to contact his wife, to live at a particular probation hostel and to report to hostel staff every two hours between 8.00 am and 10.00 pm, unless excused from doing so by his supervising officer together with a curfew of ten hours, later reduced to seven. The reporting conditions were also later relaxed. M contended that (1) the reporting conditions, prior to their relaxation, and the initial curfew had breached his rights under the European Convention on Human Rights 1950 Article 5 and Article 8 as they had prevented him from working with various businesses that his family operated; (2) the absence of a dedicated mechanism for challenging the conditions of his licence amounted to a breach of his rights under Article 6. The Court held that M had failed to adduce evidence to show that he could not undertake work for one of his family businesses and it followed that M was at most inconvenienced in his participation in the affairs of the family business, not actually prevented from working for it. Even if the effect of the reporting requirement had been to prevent M from working for his family business the combination of that and the curfew did not amount to the deprivation of his liberty. The inconvenience caused to M might have amounted to a modest interference with M's exercise of his right to respect for his private life, but it could not be said that the level of that interference had attained the minimum level of severity as to have consequences of such gravity as to engage the operation of art.8 (see paras 22, 24-28 of judgment). (2) If art.6 was to require a dedicated mechanism for a recently released prisoner to challenge the conditions of his licence, the conditions which he wished to challenge had to have affected his civil rights in such a way that the resolution of the challenge could be said to determine his civil rights. The issue was therefore case specific. Whether the prisoner's rights which would be determined on such a challenge would amount to his civil rights within the meaning of art.6 would depend on the nature and effect of the conditions he wished to challenge. In M's case, he wished to challenge those conditions whose effect was to prevent him working in the family business. The civil right which he asserted was the right not to have his rehabilitation, career development and earning capacity impeded by his inability to work in the

family business. That issue needed to be addressed only if there was not already in existence a mechanism, not necessarily a dedicated one, which provided M with an appropriate opportunity to challenge the conditions of his licence by an art.6 compliant procedure. In the circumstances, judicial review was an appropriate existing mechanism by which M could challenge the conditions imposed on him. Whilst it could take some time for claims for judicial review to get to court, first that would apply to references to the first defendant Parole Board as well, and secondly claims which were urgent could be considered quickly if a judge ordered it, Begum v Tower Hamlets LBC [2003] UKHL 5, (2003) 2 AC 430, R (on the application of Wright) v Secretary of State for Health [2009] UKHL 3, (2009) 1 AC 739 and Tsfayo v United Kingdom (60860/00) (2009) 48 EHRR 18 ECHR considered (paras 30-39).

*Leslie Malcolm v Ministry of Justice* [2010] EWHC 3389 (QB) See "Segregation" below

*X v Secretary of State for Justice* [2010] EWHC 2507 (Admin)
The claimant prisoner (X) applied for judicial review of a refusal of the respondent secretary of state to allow him "level 4" contact with his children. The Court held that a serving prisoner's contact with his children could properly be restricted by the secretary of state. Provided that the guidance and procedures issued under the Children Act 2004 s.11(4) were complied with any interference with the European Convention on Human Rights 1950 art.8 would be proportionate and justified.

*R (on the application of Earl Francis) v West Midlands Probation Board* [2010] EWCA Civ 1470
The appellant life prisoner (F) appealed against a decision ((2009) EWHC 3747 (Admin) – see below) dismissing his application for judicial review of a refusal by the respondent local probation board (W) to transfer his supervision to a different board (X). The Court held that W had approached the transfer decision on a correct legal basis. It had not usurped the function of the parole board or acted inconsistently with any decision the parole board might make in due course. W needed to make its own assessment of the validity of the proposed transfer plan to decide, when exercising its discretionary power, whether to agree to F's request and had acted in the proper performance of its statutory functions and with due regard to the statutory aims. W had had responsibility for F's supervision for 25 years and was entitled to carefully examine whether there was good reason for the transfer. W had to form a view of the viability of the proposed release plan, which required an assessment of the risks involved in F

residing with K. If it reasonably considered that the release plan was unviable, it was entitled to take the view that the wish to put the plan forward did not provide a good reason for transfer, and in taking that approach it was exercising its functions with due regard to the Criminal Justice and Court Services Act 2000 s.2. To the extent that the decision interfered with any rights under article 8(1), it was not rendered unnecessary or disproportionate by the role of the parole board in relation to the question of release (paras 28, 32-35).

*R (on the application of (1) NW (2) YW) v Secretary of State for the Home Department* [2010] EWHC 2485 (Admin)
The claimants, a prisoner (W) and her seven-month-old daughter (X), applied for judicial review of a decision of the defendant secretary of state to maintain a 15-month period before W's next parole board hearing and refusing to expedite or shorten the parole process. The Court held that the decision of the Secretary of State for Justice to maintain a 15-month period between parole board review hearings in respect of a prisoner with a seven-month-old baby did not breach her or her child's rights under the European Convention on Human Rights 1950 art.5(4) and art.8 where there was sufficient justification for that period. The secretary of state had given careful thought to the interval between reviews and a sensible timetable been prepared for the various stages to be completed before the parole board could realistically order a change in the prisoner's status.

*R v TO* [2010] EWCA Crim 2511
The appellant (T) appealed against the terms of a sexual offences prevention order imposed on him following his convictions for 11 offences of making indecent photographs of a child and one offence of sexual activity with a child. The court varied the terms of a sexual offences order because they were too wide and represented a disproportionate interference with the offender's rights under the European Convention on Human Rights 1950 article 8. R v Mortimer (Jason Christopher) [2010] EWCA Crim 1303 considered (see paras 13-17 of judgment).

*X v Secretary of State for Justice* [2010] EWHC 2507 (Admin)
The claimant prisoner (X) applied for judicial review of a refusal of the respondent secretary of state to allow him "level 4" contact with his children. The Court held that a serving prisoner's contact with his children could properly be restricted by the secretary of state. Provided that the guidance and procedures

issued under the Children Act 2004 s.11(4) were complied with any interference with the European Convention on Human Rights 1950 art.8 would be proportionate and justified.

*R (on the application of C) v Ministry of Justice* [2009] EWHC 2671 (Admin)
The imposition of a polygraph condition on an offender released from prison on conditional licence did not amount to a breach of his rights under the European Convention on Human Rights 1950 art.8 as the condition was justified by the seriousness of the crimes for which he was convicted and his conduct.

*R (on the application of Garfield Rainford) v Secretary of State for the Home Department* [2008] EWHC 2474 (Admin)
A decision of the Secretary of State for the Home Department to certify an applicant's human rights claim as clearly unfounded was quashed as the secretary of state had not considered as a separate matter the consequences of the applicant's removal for the members of his family.

*R (on the application of A) v National Probation Service* [2003] EWHC 2910 (Admin)
The National Probation Service had erred in failing to consider the Article 8 rights of the applicant when considering him for early release on licence by deciding that a third party should be informed of the applicant's conviction. NPS had in making its risk assessment not properly addressed Z's rights or the potential selfharm that could result from the disclosure of his conviction. It had made its decision on the basis that there was a presumption of disclosure rather then that disclosure was the exception.

*R v (1) Secretary of State for the Home Department (2) Parole Board, Ex parte Stephen Craven* [2001] EWHC Admin 850
A prisoner did not necessarily lose the right to respect for family life by reason of incarceration (R v Secretary of State for the Home Department, ex parte P & Q (2001) 2 FLR 383 followed). Equally Art.8 rights were not lost on release on licence. The imposition of an exclusion zone as a condition of the applicant's release on licence from prison in order to minimise the risk of accidental contact between him and his victim's family was not unlawful because it was justified under Art.8(2) European Convention on Human Rights and it was proportionate.

*R (on the application of L) V Secretary of State for Health* (2001) 1 FLR 406; (2001) 58 BMLR 101; Times, October 26, 2000; Independent, November 20, 2000; Daily Telegraph, October 24, 2000

The Health Service Circular HSC 1999/160, which prohibited visits to a murderer in a high-security hospital by his nephews and nieces, did not breach Art.8 European Convention on Human Rights 1950.

*R (on the application of B) v Governor of Wakefield Prison* [2001] EWHC Admin 917
The governor's decision to prevent B, a discretionary life prisoner with a history of sexual offending, from being visited in prison by his young nephew was not irrational or in breach of r.4 of the Prison Rules 1999. Despite the fact that social services did not object to the visit, the governor was entitled to conclude that the difficulty over visits by B's sister due to childcare should not affect the decision relating to the overall welfare of the nephew. Further, the court did not accept that B's relationship with the nephew, who was born while B was in custody, and had visited B several times when he was very young, was sufficient to engage Article 8.

## HUMAN RIGHTS: Article 10 rights – Freedom of Expression
**See also "Media".**
*Nilsen v Governor Of HMP Full Sutton & Anor* [2004] EWCA Civ 1540; LTL 17/11/2004; (2005) 1 WLR 1028; (2005) EMLR 11; Times
Prison Standing Order 5 para.34 restricting a prisoner's rights to publish details of his crimes was not in conflict with the prisoner's freedom of expression under the European Convention on Human Rights 1950 Art.10. Application for leave to appeal to the House of Lords refused.

*Hirst v Secretary of State for the Home Department* [2002] EWHC 602 (Admin); (2002) 1 WLR 2929; (2002) UKHRR 758; (2002) ACD 93; Times, April 10, 2002
A policy that denied a prisoner the right to contact the media by telephone whenever his purpose was to comment on matters of legitimate public interest was unlawful.

## HUMAN RIGHTS: Article 11 rights – Freedom of Association
PSO 4480 (Extract)
Prisoners Representative Associations
SUMMARY OF POLICY
1. Article 11 of the European Convention on Human Rights guarantees the freedom of peaceful assembly and association with others. In this context "association" means the right to form or join a group with others sharing a common interest and so applies to prisoners wishing to form or join representative bodies of other prisoners. But, it is a qualified right. It can be interfered with to prevent disorder or crime, provided any

interference is proportionate. In deciding how far to allow prisoners' associations to operate in their establishments, Governors and Controllers must take account of local conditions and the implications for good order or discipline (GOOD). The arrangement must be kept under review.

## HUMAN RIGHTS: Article 12 rights – Right to Marry and Raise a Family
### Case Law

*R v Registrar General for Births, Deaths & Marriages, ex parte Crown Prosecution Service* [2002] EWCA Civ 1661; (2003) 2 WLR 504; (2003) 1 All ER 540; Times, November 14, 2002

The right to marry was enshrined in Art.12 European Convention on Human Rights as well as in English law. Neither the Registrar General nor a prison director had the power to prevent a proposed marriage from taking place until after the criminal trial of a man on remand, where the proposed wife was to be called to give evidence at that trial but would cease to be a compellable witness following marriage to the prisoner by reason of s.80 Police and Criminal Evidence Act 1984 (as amended). Leave to appeal to the House of Lords refused.

*R v Secretary of State for the Home Department, Ex Parte Gavin Mellor [2001] EWCA Civ 472;* (2002) QB 13; (2001) 3 WLR 533; (2001) 2 FLR 1158; (2001) HRLR 38; (2001) 59 BMLR 1; Times, May 1, 2001; Independent, April 6, 2001.

A serving prisoner did not have the right to facilities that would enable the artificial insemination of his wife. The deprivation of such facilities was a justifiable interference with the prisoner's rights under Art.8 and Art.12 European Convention on Human Rights. However there might be exceptional circumstances where facilitating artificial insemination for a prisoner could be considered. Leave to appeal to the House of Lords refused.

## HUMAN RIGHTS: Article 14 rights – Freedom from Discrimination
### Case Law

*R (Bristow) v Secretary of State for Justice* [2015] EWCA Civ 1170 17 November 2015, Court of Appeal (Civil Division), Davis and McCombe LJJ
A possible discrepancy in the management of the case of a prisoner convicted abroad for drugs offences and other prisoners convicted abroad and repatriated to the UK, relating to the date of their release on licence, had not contravened Article 14 ECHR.

*R v Nottingham Magistrates' Court, Ex Parte SR* [2001] EWHC Admin 802: Independent, December 17

The Home Office's policy of remanding boys aged 15 and 16 years old to young offender institutions, whilst girls of the same age were remanded to local authority secure units, did not violate Art.14 European Convention on Human Rights.

*R. (on the application of Stott) v Secretary of State for Justice* [2018] UKSC 59; [2018] 3 W.L.R. 1831; [2019] 2 All E.R. 351; [2018] 11 WLUK 455; [2019] Crim. L.R. 251; Times, January 14, 2019
Section 246A of Criminal Justice Act 2003, which limited the eligibility of prisoners serving extended determinate sentences to consideration of parole at the two-thirds stage of the custodial element of their sentence, was compatible with ECHR Article 14 taken in conjunction with art.5. Although the different treatment of such prisoners when compared to those serving indeterminate or other determinate sentences constituted a ground within the meaning of "other status" in Article 14, the situations were not analogous and, even if they were, there was an objective justification for the difference in treatment.

*Brown v Scottish Ministers* [2021] CSOH 123
See "Article 5" above

## HOME DETENTION CURFEW
Home Detention Curfew Policy Framework

## HYGIENE
PR 28
YOI 24
28 — Hygiene
(1) Every prisoner shall be provided with toilet articles necessary for his health and cleanliness, which shall be replaced as necessary.
(2) Every prisoner shall be required to wash at proper times, have a hot bath or shower on reception and thereafter at least once a week.
(3) A prisoner's hair shall not be cut without his consent.

## IDENTIFICATION OF PRISON STAFF WHEN ON DUTY
PSO 8805

## IDENTITY (ID) for Bank Account Applications for all prisoners
PSI 44/2011 Identity for bank account applications for all prisoners

## ILLNESS OR DEATH, notification of
Prison Rule 22
YOI 29

## ILLNESSES AND CONDITIONS
Prison Rule 21

YOI 28
ACT 28 – Power to discharge prisoners temporarily on account of ill health

## IMMIGRATION & FOREIGN NATIONALS
See "Foreign Nationals".

## IMMIGRATION ACT DETAINEES,
### management of
PSI 52/2011 - Immigration, Repatriation and Removal Services
PSI 04/2013 - The Early Removal Scheme and Release of Foreign National Prisoners (updated May 2021 to reflect the fact that terrorist offences are now ineligible for early removal under ERS)
PSI 21/2007 - Immigration and foreign nationals in prison (amended version)
PSI 49/2011 - Communication with embassies
PSI 23/2006 - Immigration checks: new mandatory procedure for staff
PSI 53/1998 - The Management of Immigration Act Detainees

## IMPRISONMENT FOR PUBLIC PROTECTION
See also "Lifers (Life Sentence Prisoners)"
See also "Human Rights: Article 5 rights – Freedom from Arbitrary Detention"
### Key Note
The imprisonment for public protection sentence was a form of indeterminate sentence introduced by section 225 of the Criminal Justice Act 2003. The sentence was composed of a punitive "tariff" intended to be proportionate to the gravity of the crime committed and an indeterminate period which commences after the expiration of the tariff and lasts until the Parole Board judges the prisoner no longer poses a risk to the public and is fit to be released. In 2012 the IPP sentence was abolished by the Legal Aid, Sentencing and Punishment of Offenders Act 2012. However, the act did not have retrospective effect and several thousand prisoners are still serving IPP sentences.
### Case Law
*Knights v Parole Board for England and Wales* [2017] EWCA Civ 1053
An offender serving a sentence of IPP appealed against a decision that the continuation of his detention did not breach the ECHR. The offender had pleaded guilty to several offences concerning indecent images of children, and had previous relevant convictions. He was sentenced three weeks before changes to the IPP regime enacted by the Criminal Justice and Immigration Act 2008 s.13 came into force. Had he been sentenced three weeks later force, he would not have been eligible for an IPP. He was released on parole in 2013 and 2014 but both times was recalled for breach of his licence conditions.
The appeal was dismissed. Regarding Article 3,

the concept of IPP did not require that the overall period the offender spent in custody had to be consistent with the gravity of the offence. IPP was a precautionary sentence. Having served the minimum tariff, the offender had become eligible for release on parole provided that he did not create a risk to the public. He had been released twice and, on each occasion, had acted in breach of licence conditions intended to protect the public. He was in custody not because of the gravity of his original offending but because of the risk that breach of his licence created for the public. The offender's suggestion that the IPP provisions had to be read subject to the maximum sentence for the offence being dealt with ignored the terms in which the legislation had been passed and the fact that it had been specifically designed to protect the public from those who were considered a risk whether or not their offence itself justified an indeterminate sentence.
Article 5(1) - As long as detention had a sufficient causal link with a lawful conviction, the detention was a matter for national authorities. The judge had found that the causal link was not broken. The offender had met the statutory test for dangerousness and posed a risk of selfharm. Far from having been allowed to languish in custody, the offender had been on courses and had twice been released before breaching the terms of his licence. It was not possible simply to add up the time spent in custody and relate it to the index offending: that ignored the part of the sentence designed to protect the public and the requirement that he learned to live within the terms of his licence. The court agreed with the judge's approach that the requirement to provide courses had to be judged against the limits on facilities and resources in the prison system, so that the overall period should be considered with allowance for inevitable delays.
Article 14 - The judge had correctly concluded that, in the light of R. (on the application of Clift) v Secretary of State for the Home Department [2006] UKHL 54, [2007] 1 A.C. 484, [2006] 12 WLUK 276, Article 14 was not triggered. Even if date of conviction could amount to sufficient status to trigger Article 14, the difference in treatment was inherent in the change in the law; if there were to be objectionable discrimination, it would be impossible to change the law.

*Henley-Smith, R (on the application of) v The Secretary of State for Justice* [2017] EWHC 1948 (Admin)
The claimant prisoner (H) sought a judicial review of the Defendant's failure to exercise his power under section 128 Legal Aid Sentencing and Punishment of Offenders Act 2012 to seek to vary the test applied by the Parole Board when

deciding where or not to direct the release of an IPP prisoner and failing to consult on such a change. When abolishing IPP sentences, Parliament had expressed its intention to maintain IPP sentences for existing prisoners. H was an IPP prisoner, convicted in 2007 to an IPP with a minimum term of 1 year and 4 months, which expired in 2008. The Parole Board had concluded on several occasions that it was necessary to continue to detain him for the protection of the public, notwithstanding he remained in prison nearly 10 years after his tariff had expired. At the time of the hearing H had been transferred to open conditions. The case rested upon whether any challenge existed to the Defendant's failures in exercising the discretion provided by LASPO 2012 to vary the release test under Crime (Sentences) Act 1997 and his failure to consult. H sought to rely on various statements made by the Defendant in Parliament. The Court held that the Defendant had a discretion to vary the test but his decision not to was legitimate and lawful, and H had not shown that the Defendant had made "a clear and unambiguous promise to consult generally about the exercise of his powers". Further, even if he had, H was unlikely to be able to rely upon it as, "serving prisoners were not a class of person whom the Minister promised to consult, or at whom the promise was directed". Nor was the failure to consult the kind of "conspicuous unfairness" that could have amounted to a breach of a common law duty to consult. The Court could not seek to fetter the discretion of the Defendant as H submitted, for that would amount to an interference by the Court with Parliamentary proceedings, which was contrary to Parliamentary privilege and the separation of powers. Rather than pursuing the power under section 128 LASPO 2012, the Defendant had instead pursued measures by way of a joint NOMS/Parole Board action plan on IPPs. Following Vintner v UK (2016) 63 EHRR 1, the Court held that H's continued detention was deemed necessary in order to protect a section of the public and did not amount to a breach of Article 3 EHCR. H had been transferred to open conditions and had access to (and completed) a large number of courses, and had the benefit of 1:1 sessions with a psychologist. He was not in a category of mentally ill or vulnerable prisoners nor those who had been unable to access courses or treatment.

*R v Docherty* [2016] UKSC 62

This Supreme Court case clarifies that there is no discrimination pursuant to Article 14 ECHR arising where the Appellant was sentenced to an IPP on 20 December 2012, having been convicted

prior to the Commencement Order of 3 December 2012 bringing in to force changes in sentencing in the Legal Aid, Sentencing and Punishment of Offenders Act 2012 (LASPO), namely the abolition of IPP.

The Court stated that for any new legislation, it was legitimate to conduct a phased introduction. Notwithstanding that D was sentenced after the date of abolition, at the time he fell to be sentenced (the date of conviction) IPP was in force, and the new regime of sentencing provisions introduced by LASPO was not therefore available to him.

The Court concluded, "the differential in treatment is clearly justified. All changes in sentencing law have to start somewhere…. The difference of treatment is inherent in the change in the law. If it were to be objectionable discrimination, it would be impossible to change the law."

*R (Bayliss) v The Parole Board* [2014] EWCA Civ 1631, 16 December 2014

A later decision by the Court of Appeal to quash the appellant's sentence of imprisonment for public protection did not render his detention pursuant to that sentence unlawful.

*James v United Kingdom (25119/09)* (2013) 56 EHRR 12

A prisoner's continued detention beyond the expiry of the minimum term of his sentence of imprisonment for public protection without access to rehabilitative courses violated article 5(1) of the ECHR. A real opportunity for rehabilitation was a necessary element of any part of the detention which was to be justified solely by reference to public protection.

*R v J* [2012] EWCA Crim 132

The appellant (J) appealed against a sentence of imprisonment for public protection with a minimum term of seven years and a Sexual Offences Prevention Order following his guilty plea to rape of a child under 13 years of age. J had been changing his two-year-old son's nappy. He became sexually aroused and penetrated his anus until ejaculation. J made full admissions during interview, admitted to having developed a sexual interest in children and pleaded guilty. A pre-sentence report noted that J's participation on a sex offender treatment programme would be crucial, his motivation to take part, that he posed a medium risk of re-offending and that if released at the date of sentencing he would pose a high risk of selfharm to children. Having examined all the facts and identifying the aggravating features of the offence, the judge concluded that there was a significant risk serious of selfharm by J and that an extended sentence would not achieve public protection. The Court held that: (1) The judge had been entitled to hold that the instant case fell outside the sentencing guidelines. J's offence was exceptionally depraved and justified a quite exceptionally long determinate sentence. The minimum term was based on a very severe starting point, but it was not manifestly excessive. (2) The principle established in *R. v Smith (Nicholas) [2011] UKSC 37*, [2011] 1 W.L.R. 1795 was that it was neither unlawful nor wrong in principle for an indeterminate sentence to be imposed on an offender who was already subject to, and serving, an earlier indeterminate sentence, Smith applied. Smith did not undermine the long-established practice that the assessment of dangerousness involved addressing the question of whether or not the offender would be dangerous when he would otherwise be released from a determinate sentence; it underlined the principle that the decision whether to make an order of imprisonment for public protection could only be made at the date of the sentence hearing, Smith applied. The question of public safety involved an assessment of the risk to the public posed through the commission of further offences by the offender subsequent to the sentencing hearing, Smith applied and *R. (on the application of Wells) v Parole Board [2009] UKHL 22*, [2010] 1 A.C. 553 considered. Smith underlined that a judge had to decide whether an offender posed the risk identified by the Criminal Justice Act 2003 s.225(1)(b) at the date of sentence hearing on the basis that an offender was not in custody. The question of whether a discretionary indeterminate sentence was appropriate in an individual case was predictive, *R. v Johnson (Paul Anthony) [2006] EWCA Crim 2486*, [2007] 1 W.L.R. 585 applied. (3) In light of the indeterminate sentence and the consequences that would follow if J was released, the Sexual Offences Prevention Order was inappropriate and fell to be quashed.

*R (on the application of Daniel Parratt) v Secretary of State for Justice* [2009] EWHC 3089 (Admin)
A prisoner sentenced to imprisonment for public protection would be entitled to a pre-tariff review determining his suitability for transfer to open conditions only if his minimum term, excluding time spent in custody on remand, was at least three years.

*R v Matthew Lee Hill* [2009] EWCA Crim 1387
A sentencing judge had been wrong to impose a sentence of imprisonment for public protection on an offender who pleaded guilty to offences of robbery and possession of an imitation firearm as he had based his assessment of dangerousness solely on the antecedent history of the offender.

*R v Robert Hicks* [2009] EWCA Crim 733
In the circumstances, a sentence of imprisonment for public protection for offences of making indecent photographs of children could not be upheld as there was insufficient information from which an assessment of significant risk of future selfharm by the future commission of specified offences could be sustained. However, the potential danger that the offender presented to young people in general was a real one and the test for making a sexual offences prevention order under the Sexual Offences Act 2003 s.104 was satisfied.

*R v Daniel Vickers* [2008] EWCA Crim 2759
A sentence of imprisonment for public protection for arson was quashed because the judge had not had sufficient information about the offender's previous convictions to find that there was a significant risk of serious selfharm to the public, nor were there sufficiently significant similarities between the arson and previous specified offences to make such a finding.

*R v (1) Michael Walker (2) Owen Morgan (3) Gilroy Goode (4) Dwaine Blake* [2008] EWCA Crim 554
Sentences of imprisonment for public protection after convictions for robberies involving firearms were quashed and replaced by determinate sentences where the trial judge had concluded that the participation in those robberies had justified the public protection sentence, but where he had failed to make any assessment of the risk to members of the public of serious selfharm by the commission of further specified.

*R (on the application of Lee Bayliss) v (1) Parole Board (2) Secretary of State for Justice* [2008] EWHC 3127 (Admin)
Life sentences included sentences of imprisonment for public protection and so the test to be applied by the Parole Board when considering, under the Crime (Sentences) Act 1997 s.28(6), the release on licence of a prisoner serving a sentence of imprisonment for public protection would be the same whether the prisoner was subject either to a sentence for public protection or to a life sentence, though in practice different considerations would bear on the application of that test.

*R v Alexander Terrell* [2007] EWCA Crim 3079
It was inappropriate to impose a sentence of imprisonment for public protection pursuant to the Criminal Justice Act 2003 s.225 on an offender

convicted of making indecent photographs of children, because the link between the offending act of downloading images and the possible selfharm to children was too remote to satisfy the requirement that the offender's reoffending would cause serious selfharm.

*R v Musa Mohammed* [2007] EWCA Crim 3450
The trial judge had erred in imposing a sentence of imprisonment for public protection following the defendant's conviction for robbery, as there was no proper factual basis for the inferences that the judge drew to justify his finding of a significant risk of serious selfharm.

*R v Stephen Howard Lang & 12 Ors* [2005] EWCA Crim 2864
The court considered and gave guidance on the principles applicable to the new mandatory sentencing provisions for the protection of the public from dangerous offenders contained in Criminal Justice Act 2003 s.224 to s.229 and the factors that judges should take into account when deciding whether one of the new sentences must be imposed. (1) The sentencing guidelines set out in the Criminal Justice Act 2003 were labyrinthine and complex. The court made the following observations, amongst others (a) to qualify for one of the new sentences, the offender had to be convicted of a "specified offence", that is one of the 153 categories of violent or sexual offences listed in Schedule 15 of the Act; (b) a specified offence might or might not be serious. If serious it might attract life imprisonment or imprisonment for public protection for an adult or detention for life or detention for public protection for those under 18 on the day of the conviction. It would attract such a sentence if the court was of the opinion that there was a significant risk to the public of serious selfharm by the commission of further specified offences; (c) significant risk had to be shown in relation to two matters: (i) the commission of further specified, but not necessarily serious offences, and (ii) the causing thereby of serious selfharm to members of the public. If there was a significant risk of both, either a life sentence or indeterminate sentence for public protection must be imposed on an adult; (d) the court was inclined to the view that parliament, when referring in s.225(2)(b) and s.226(2)(b) to the seriousness of an offence or offences being "such as to justify" imprisonment or detention for life, thereby making such a sentence mandatory, was intending to adopt the criteria for the imposition of a discretionary life sentence contained in *R v Chapman, R v Jamie Lee Chapman* (2000) 1 Cr App R 77 considered. In relation to a life sentence and imprisonment for public protection, the court

must fix a minimum term to be served in accordance with the Powers of Criminal Courts (Sentencing) Act 2000 s.82A . However there might be exceptional cases where the offence itself was so serious that an indeterminate sentence was justified irrespective of the risk to the public; (e) section 143(3) required the court to look beyond the instant offence in order to see whether there were any aggravating factors that it should have in mind when assessing the seriousness of that offence; (f) in calculating the minimum term, an appropriate reduction should be allowed for a plea of guilty and care should be taken not to incorporate in the notional determinate sentence an element for risk that was already covered by the indeterminate sentence; (g) in considering s.226 and s.228 in conjunction, the fundamental question to be addressed by sentencers would be whether an extended sentence was adequate to protect the public; (h) when s.229 and s.224 were read together, unless the information about offences, patterns of behaviour and the offender showed a significant risk of serious selfharm from further offences, it would usually be unreasonable to conclude that the assumption applied; (i) the part of the labyrinthine proposals that was most critical was s.225(1) and its echo in relation to those under 18 in s.226(1). The following factors, amongst others, should be borne in mind when a sentencer was assessing significant risk: (i) the risk identified must be significant; (ii) in assessing the risk of further offences being committed, the sentencer should take into account the nature and extent of the current offence, the offender's history of offending and whether the offending demonstrated any pattern; (iii) sentencers must guard against assuming there was a significant risk of serious selfharm merely because the foreseen specified offence was serious; (iv) if the foreseen specified offence was not serious, there would be comparatively few cases in which a risk of serious selfharm would properly be regarded as significant; (v) in relation to a particularly young offender, an indeterminate sentence might be inappropriate even where a serious offence had been committed; (vi) sentencers should usually give reasons for all of their conclusions and briefly identify the information that they have taken into account.

**INAPPROPRIATE MATERIAL REPORTS**
PSI 25/2005

**INCENSE, use for private religious practice**
PSI 05/2016 – Faith and Pastoral Care for Prisoners

## INCENTIVES & EARNED PRIVILEGES

Incentives Policy Framework

5.10 – Criteria for progression and moving down an incentive level(s) must be in place and include compliance with Annex A, which sets out the definitions of each incentive level and requires prisons to have a small number of simple behaviour principles which apply to all prisoners. Earnable incentives include:

- Access to private cash (levels updated 09/2022)
- Eligibility to earn higher rates of pay
- Access to in cell television
- Opportunity to wear own clothes
- Additional time out of cell
- Extra and improved visits

Prison Rule 8

8.— Privileges

(1) There shall be established at every prison systems of privileges appropriate to the classes of prisoners there, which shall include arrangements under which money earned by prisoners in prison may be spent by them within the prison.

(2) Systems of privileges established under paragraph (1) may include arrangements under which prisoners may be allowed time outside their cells and in association with one another, in excess of the minimum time which, subject to the other provisions of these Rules apart from this rule, is otherwise allowed to prisoners at the prison for this purpose.

(3) Systems of privileges established under paragraph (1) may include arrangements under which privileges may be granted to prisoners only in so far as they have met, and for so long as they continue to meet, specified standards in their behaviour and their performance in work or other activities.

(4) Systems of privileges which include arrangements of the kind referred to in paragraph (3) shall include procedures to be followed in determining whether or not any of the privileges concerned shall be granted, or shall continue to be granted, to a prisoner; such procedures shall include a requirement that the prisoner be given reasons for any decision adverse to him together with a statement of the means by which he may appeal against it.

(5) Nothing in this rule shall be taken to confer on a prisoner any entitlement to any privilege or to affect any provision in these Rules other than this rule as a result of which any privilege may be forfeited or otherwise lost or a prisoner deprived of association with other prisoners.

**Case Law**

*Ali v Secretary of State for Justice* [2015] EWHC 2221 (Admin)

The governor of a Category A prison had not erred in refusing to allow a Kurdish-speaking life prisoner to receive Kurdish-language CDs and DVDs sent to him by his family, even though such materials could not be obtained for him through the prison. The arguments in relation to CDs/DVDs were very different from those relating to books as discussed in R (on the application of Barbara Gordon-Jones v (i) Secretary of State for Justice (ii) Governor of HM Prison Send [2014] EWHC 3997 (Admin)

*R (on the application of Barbara Gordon- Jones) v (1) Secretary of State for Justice (2) Governor of HM Prison Send* [2014] EWHC 3997 (Admin)

This case challenged the lawfulness of Prison Service Instruction (PSI) 30/2013 which amended the Incentives and Earned Privileges Scheme (IEP) which has been in effect since 1995. The challenge relates to what are said to be unlawful restrictions on the ability of prisoners generally and the Claimant in particular to receive or have for their use books. The Judge was satisfied that in so far as it includes books in IEP schemes PSI 30/2013 is unlawful.

*R (on the application of (1) Ian Shutt (2) John Tetley v Secretary of State for Justice* [2012] EWHC 851 (Admin)

In conjoined applications for judicial review, the claimant prisoners (S and T) challenged refusals of their respective prison governors to give them enhanced status under the prison incentives and earned privileges (IEP) scheme. Both men were serving substantial determinate sentences in the Isle of Wight after having been convicted of serious sexual offences against children. They had both been assessed as suitable for a sexual offences training programme, and were willing to undertake it, but had been deemed "not ready" because of their continuing denial of the offences. National IEP policy stated that unreadiness for such a programme "could" bar a prisoner from obtaining enhanced status. Local prison policy stated that denial of guilt "should not automatically be a bar to attaining enhanced status". However, the operation of a points system within the local policy meant that convicted sex offenders who were suitable for the training programme but who were unready for it by reason of continued denial of guilt, could not accrue enough points to attain enhanced status. The issue was whether that amounted to a blanket ban, and if so, whether it was unlawful. The Court held that the natural meaning of the word "could" in the national IEP policy was that a prisoner in the same situation as S and T could be denied enhanced status, but might not be. The most natural reading of the phrase was that it would be permissible in appropriate circumstances to deny enhanced status, but that such denial would not be automatic. Thus there would need to be an informed decision as to whether a particular sex offending prisoner in denial and therefore unready, should be refused enhanced status.

*R v Secretary of State for The Home Department & Anor, Ex Parte Potter & Ors* [2001] EWHC Admin 1041
A local prison service policy that required sex offenders to admit their guilt before they could be eligible to obtain enhanced status was neither unfair nor irrational and was not inconsistent with national prison policy.

## INCIDENT MANAGEMENT MANUAL
PSI 25/1997 - Incident Reporting System

## INCOME AND RECEIPTS
Finance Manual Policy Framework chapter 8, 9

## INDUCTION
**See "Prisoner induction".**

## INFECTIONS, ZOONOTIC
PSO 3805 – Infections, zoonotic

## INFORMATION
Handling Sensitive Information Policy Framework
Information Sharing Policy Framework
Information Requests Policy Framework

## INFORMATION TECHNOLOGY
**See "Computers".**

## INFORMATION ABOUT PRISONERS
PSI 08/2016 – National Security Framework (Dealing with Evidence)
PSI 06/2016 - Information Risk Management Policy
1 Executive summary
Background
1.1 Reliable and accurate information management is critical to proper decision making across the Ministry of Justice (MoJ). Information can take many forms and may or may not have protective markings – from data sets containing personal information through to records of sensitive meetings, policy recommendations, prisoner records, case files, correspondence and historical records.
• Information is the lifeblood of our organisation, it is a critical business asset that NOMS needs to protect and get the most value from to benefit the business
• The management of information risks should be incorporated into all day-to-day operations. If effectively used it can be a tool for managing information proactively rather than reactively. It will enable NOMS to get the right information to the right people at the right time,

and help avoid incidents where data is lost or improperly disclosed.
Desired outcomes
1.2 This policy sets out NOMS commitment to the management of information risk. It also sets out what prison establishments, headquarters groups, their 'delivery partners' and third party suppliers should do to manage information risk. In doing so, this policy supports the NOMS strategic aims and objectives and should enable employees throughout the organisation to identify an acceptable level of risk and, when required, use the correct risk escalation process.

## INFORMATION TO PRISONERS
YOI 7
Prison Rule 10
10. Information to prisoners
(1) Every prisoner shall be provided, as soon as possible after his reception into prison, and in any case within 24 hours, with information in writing about those provisions of these Rules and other matters which it is necessary that he should know, including earnings and privileges, and the proper means of making requests and complaints.
(2) In the case of a prisoner aged less than 18, or a prisoner aged 18 or over who cannot read or appears to have difficulty in understanding the information so provided, the governor, or an officer deputed by him, shall so explain it to him that he can understand his rights and obligations.
(3) A copy of these Rules shall be made available to any prisoner who requests it.

## INSTRUCTIONS
**See "Prison Service Orders and Instructions"**
## INSURANCE
Finance Manual Policy Framework, chapter 2.7

## INTELLIGENCE COLLECTION, ANALYSIS AND DISSEMINATION
Intelligence Collection, Analysis and Dissemination Policy Framework

## INTELLIGENCE
**See "Surveillance".**

## INTERCEPTION OF COMMUNICATION
Prison Rule 35A

## INTERNET
PSI 25/2014 - IT Security Policy
**Case Law**
*R v The Governor Of HMP Risley & Anor, Ex Parte Gerald Cooper* [2002] EWHC 125 (Admin)
There was no failure to provide reasonable and adequate facilities for the conduct of a prisoner's legal affairs by not supplying unrestricted access to the Internet. C had not been charged with a

criminal offence, and had not provided an example of a request for material in relation to his civil proceedings that had been refused. The evidence as a whole demonstrated that a comprehensive range of facilities were available to prisoners wishing to commence litigation, to which C had access, and that the secretary of state was fully alive to the existence of the fundamental right to access to the courts. There were security implications of unrestricted internet access. C's complaint was entirely unsubstantiated.

**INTERVIEWS, POLICE**
See "Police interviews".

**INVESTIGATIONS**
PSO 1300

**INVESTIGATIONS**
CHAPTER 1: THE FRAMEWORK OF INVESTIGATIONS
1.1 Introduction
1.1.1 Whenever an incident takes place or an allegation of misconduct is made, the circumstances of the incident or allegation must be assessed by the appropriate manager who will determine whether and how the allegation or incident will be investigated.
1.1.2 Responsibility for investigations normally rests with line management, as does the decision about the level of investigation. The principles of investigation in this order apply to all members of staff. Monitors and Controllers have a statutory duty to investigate allegations against prisoner custody officers acting in pursuance of prisoner escort arrangements or custodial duties (Criminal Justice Act 1991, ss 81(2) and 85(4)b).
1.1.3 A manual detailing the full investigation process can be found in Chapter 3.
1.1.4 All investigations must be conducted according to the principles of natural justice, and also procedural fairness, which include: -
i. to correctly interpret relevant laws, rules and procedures;
ii. to take account of all relevant considerations (and not take account of irrelevant ones);
iii. to follow the correct investigatory procedures, as set out in this PSO (see Chapter 3);
iv. to act impartially;
v. to give all parties the opportunity to present their version of the facts; and
vi. to avoid applying a policy without considering whether the particular circumstances of a case merits an exception being made.
**Case Law**
*R (on the application of NM) v Secretary of State for Justice* [2012] EWCA Civ 1182
The appellant prisoner (N) appealed against a judge's ruling that an investigation into him being sexually assaulted by another prisoner complied with the prison's investigative obligation under the European Convention on Human Rights 1950 Article 3. N, who had learning difficulties, claimed that he had been sexually assaulted by another prisoner (F). N submitted that the judge erred in concluding that the prison's investigation complied with Article.3. The Court held that the judge had been right to conclude that the investigation had not been flawed. The incident, although unpleasant, was not a serious one and no systemic failure had occurred. The opportunities for learning lessons were also absent. Sufficient safeguards had been implemented in the light of N's complaint. N had been in touch with responsible officers and higher management almost immediately after his complaint to his father about the incident. Further, the penal reform charity was promptly involved, and N's wish initially to have the police involved and later not to was respected. The facts were promptly established, F was put under surveillance and his guilt was adjudicated. There had been no breach by the state pursuant to Article 3 arising out of N's vulnerabilities or a need for a formal investigation pursuant to the provisions of the PSO 1300. Breach of the investigative obligation under Article 3 would occur where the investigation conducted, out of a range of possible investigative methods and options provided by the state, was not proportionate to the seriousness and idiosyncrasies of the incident (see paras 41- 44 of judgment).

**JUDICIAL REVIEW PROCEDURE**
**Key Note**
Judicial Review is a procedure to seek a remedy for the unlawful decisions, acts and/or omissions of public bodies, including the Prison Service, prison governor, the Parole Board, NOMs, the Probation Service and the Secretary of State for Justice.
Prisoners and their advisers have fought through the years to achieve justice in the High Court where this was the only available course of action. Many of the historic, landmark cases involved Prisoners and their advisers "pushing the boundaries" to ensure that the authorities complied with their legal obligations and did not exceed their powers.
This tradition continues, and recent years have seen many important challenges which have met with varying degrees of success. What is clear is that the Court will not permit unlawful decisions, acts or omissions by the authorities given the imbalance of power faced by Prisoners. The High Court (Administrative Court) has wide ranging powers to "right wrongs", and to ensure that public bodies act lawfully.
A public body does not act lawfully if its decisions, acts or omissions are unreasonable,

irrational or perverse, nor if lawful procedures are not followed. Inconsistency of decision making and/or breach of legitimate expectation are also actionable in Prison law cases. Unnecessary or disproportionate decisions, acts or omissions are also challengeable where Human Rights issues arise.

The majority of cases cited in this entire A-Z are judicial review cases.

The procedure is not unduly difficult, but the Court expects applications to follow the Civil Procedure Rules (often abbreviated as simply CPR). Prisoners would be well advised to seek legal advice at the earliest opportunity following an objectionable decision, act or omission, given the strict time limits involved in such applications (a maximum of 3 months – though proceedings should be prepared well within that period if practicable).

Once Judicial Review proceedings have been issued, they must proceed to a decision of the Court, alternatively an agreement between the parties, sanctioned by the Court.

If a Claimant Prisoner lodges a persuasive application for Judicial Review, the Defendant(s) (eg Prison Service, Secretary of State) may concede their error. In such cases, no "case law" will be made, as the Defendant(s) will have avoided a final Court hearing.

In such cases, a Consent Order will be drawn up, agreed between the parties. Accordingly, some of Prisoners' most notable successes will not be reported. Consent Orders are public documents, and whilst not binding "legal precedents" they are powerful indicators of where a Prisoner's rights might be enforced.

**Case Law**

*Dickins v Parole Board for England and Wales* [2021] EWHC 1166 (Admin)

The High Court considered the scope of the parole board's powers to reconsider its decisions under the Parole Board Rules 2019 r.28, and when a parole board could be said to be functus officio. Reconsideration was not available on the ground of an error of law. The only grounds for reconsideration were irrationality and procedural unfairness.

*R. (McCourt) v Parole Board for England and Wales* [2020] EWHC 2320 (Admin)
See "Parole" below.

*R. (on the application of Dolan) v Secretary of State for Health and Social Care* [2020] EWCA Civ 1605
The court rejected a challenge to the vires of Regulations made on 26 March 2020 in response to the COVID-19 pandemic, subsequently amended and repealed by the Health Protection (Coronavirus, Restrictions) (No. 2) (England)

Regulations 2020. The secretary of state had power under the Regulations to impose restrictions or requirements in relation to the population generally, as well as in relation to an individual or group of persons. Moreover, the Civil Contingencies Act 2004 s.20(1) provided for the making of emergency regulations if existing legislation could not be relied upon without risk of serious delay.

*Gourlay, R (on the application of) v The Secretary of State for Justice* [2017] EWCA Civ 1003
A claimant who is successful in an application for Judicial Review against the Parole Board is not entitled to an order for costs. The principle that, unless it has acted improperly or has actively participated in the challenge, a court or tribunal is not required to pay the costs of rectifying one of its orders – whether by way of judicial review or appeal – is well-settled. It is a principle supported by many strands of public policy. The board is an independent and impartial "court" for these purposes and it was able to maintain a "neutral stance" to a judicial review challenge to one of its own decisions.

*Nathan Gifford (Claimant) v (1) Governor of Bure Prison (2) Secretary Of State For Justice (Defendants) Prison & Probation Ombudsman (Interested Party)* [2014] EWHC 911 (Admin)
The court gave guidance as to when disputes arising in connection with prisoner adjudications should be referred to the Prison and Probation Ombudsman and when it considered those disputes were more suitable for judicial review. Prisoner adjudications were generally suitable for reference to the ombudsman because of his experience of the prison service, his ability to deal with both merits and procedure, the relative speed with which he could act and the cost-effective nature of the dispute resolution service. Even if that led to an increase in the number of complaints to the ombudsman, he would still be able to address those much more quickly than the administrative court. There would be some complaints where a reference to the ombudsman would not provide a proper alternative remedy and where judicial review was the appropriate course. That would include cases where an injunction was sought and other cases where there was an urgent or emergency element; where there was a challenge with which the ombudsman could not deal, such as complaints which were, on analysis, about the underlying conviction or sentence; and where the complaint arose out of a prisoner adjudication but was properly concerned with matters of policy. The latter was not to be taken as an invitation to prisoners and their lawyers to identify some

spurious policy dispute so as to avoid a reference to the ombudsman. If a prisoner wished to challenge the outcome of adjudication by way of judicial review, he must explain in his claim form how and why the claim was not suitable for resolution by the ombudsman. It would not be enough simply to say that it concerned a matter of policy; a proper explanation of how and why the challenge concerned a matter of policy would need to be provided.

*In the Matter of an Application by Joseph Kane for Judicial Review* [2014] NIQB 118
In order to avoid last-minute claims for judicial review of prison service decisions concerning permission for prisoners to attend funerals, it would be helpful if the prison service put some structure in place to calculate how much time it required to make decisions and to inform prisoners immediately that the funeral should be planned to coincide with that time scale. The prison service should also prepare for short notice applications by preparing a bundle of relevant authorities and a skeleton argument which could be adapted for use in future cases.

*Justice for families Ltd v Secretary of State for Justice* [2014] EWCA Civ 1477
A third party application for habeas corpus could be appropriate where the prisoner was incommunicado or where the impediment preventing the prisoner from acting was ignorance or disability. It was not appropriate where the prisoner was represented by counsel throughout the proceedings which resulted in her imprisonment, or where her detention had already ended before the application for habeas corpus was made.

*R (on the application of Black) v Secretary of State for Justice* [2017] UKSC 81
A prisoner appealed against a decision that Crown premises were not covered by the prohibition on smoking in most enclosed public places and workplaces contained in Part 1 Chapter 1 of the Health Act 2006, meaning that state-run prisons were not obliged to apply the smoking ban. There was no dispute that a smoking ban was in place in the prison, but the issue was whether the prison was bound by Part 1, Chapter 1 so that the ban was backed up by criminal sanctions and other enforcement measures. The Court found that the Crown was not bound by the prohibition on smoking in public places, meaning that state-run prisons were not obliged to apply the ban. There was a presumption that Acts of Parliament only bound the Crown by express words or "necessary implication", and there were powerful indicators

in the language of the Act that the Crown was not to be bound by the ban.

*R (M) v Parole Board* [2013] EWHC 1360 (Admin)
See "Media" below.

*Children's Rights Alliance for England v Secretary of State for Justice & (1) G4S Care & Justice Services (UK) Ltd (2) Serco PLC (Interested Parties)* [2012] EWHC 8 (Admin)
The claimant charitable company (C) applied for judicial review of a decision of the respondent secretary of state refusing to provide details of former child detainees who had been subjected to unlawful restraint procedures whilst detained in secure training centres (STCs) run by the interested parties. Under the Secure Training Centre Rules 1998 r.38 the physical restraint of detainees was permitted in certain circumstances but was not permitted to ensure good order and discipline. However, it became clear during inquiries and investigations following two deaths which occurred in the STCs that in practice restraint for good order and discipline was used. C sought an order obliging the secretary of state to provide details of children who were subjected to restraint for good order and discipline and deliberately painful compliance techniques in STCs between the opening of the STCs and the introduction of a new Physical Control in Care Training Manual 2010.
C contended that the secretary of state was under a positive obligation to inform those who might have been subjected to unlawful restraint procedures that they might have been subjected to such procedures. The Court held that it was highly likely that a large number of former detainees had been the subject of unlawful force during their detention until at least 2008 when the decision in *R. (on the application of C) v Secretary of State for Justice* [2008] EWCA Civ 882, [2009] Q.B. 657 was given. Until the investigations following the deaths none of the agencies in place to monitor STCs had identified or acted to stop the unlawful nature of what happened. It was likely that there was widespread, unlawful use of restraint and very few, if any, of the children subjected to such unlawful restraint appreciated at the time that it was unlawful (see paras 76, 79, 91). (2) It could not be said that the refusal of the secretary of state to disseminate information impeded the access to justice of those potentially affected, *R. v Secretary of State for the Home Department Ex p. Leech (No.2)* [1994] Q.B. 198, *R. (on the application of Daly) v Secretary of State for the Home Department* [2001] UKHL 26, [2001] 2 A.C. 532 and *R. (on the application of Medical Justice) v Secretary of State for the Home Department* [2010]

EWHC 1925 (Admin) considered. If the common law was developed to create the remedy sought it could lead to a significant change in legal culture. The granting of a positive obligation on the secretary of state to provide information of those affected so they could, if they wished, seek redress would represent the thin end of an ever-expanding wedge without a clear appreciation of where the expansion would lead. Whilst there was a law of limitation, it possessed a degree of flexibility where those who were ignorant of material facts at the time of the unlawful acts might obtain an effective extension of time for seeking redress. Further, there was available information in the public domain about what happened within the STCs during the relevant period and steps could be taken by those affected without the need to be told about it directly by the secretary of state. Accordingly, even if it was open to the court to make the order sought by C, it was not necessary at common law to fashion that remedy in order that the former detainees, who wished to pursue redress, had access to the courts (paras 114-115, 118, 120, 139-141). (3) Equally, under the European Convention on Human Rights 1950 there was no positive obligation on the state to provide the remedy sought, *McGowan (Procurator Fiscal) v B [2011] UKSC 54*, [2011] 1 W.L.R. 3121, *Golder v United Kingdom (A/18)* (1979-80) 1 E.H.R.R. 524, *Airey v Ireland (A/32)* (1979-80) 2 E.H.R.R. 305, *R. (on the application of Ullah) v Special Adjudicator* [2004] UKHL 26, [2004] 2 A.C. 323, *R. (on the application of Al-Skeini) v Secretary of State for Defence* [2007] UKHL 26, [2008] 1 A.C. 153, *Ambrose v Harris* [2011] UKSC 43, [2011] 1 W.L.R. 2435 and *R. (on the application of Purdy) v DPP* [2009] UKHL 45, [2010] 1 A.C. 345 considered (paras 145, 147, 149, 158, 184, 186, 188, 198).

*H v Parole Board* [2011] EWHC 2081 (Admin)
The claimant life prisoner (H) applied for judicial review of the refusal of the defendant Parole Board to transfer him to open conditions. H argued that the Parole Board had reached its decision on the basis of a mistake of fact which was material: he had not been convicted of the first rape count, which was the only count alleging witnessing by his child, and the detailed allegations in relation to the violent precursor events had not been proved against him. The Court held that the relevant test had been set out in *E v Secretary of State for the Home Department* [2004] EWCA Civ 49, [2004] Q.B. 1044. First, there must have been a mistake as to an existing fact, including a mistake as to the availability of evidence on a particular matter. Second, the fact or evidence must have been "established", in the sense that it was uncontentious and objectively

verifiable. Third, the appellant (or his advisers) must not have been responsible for the mistake. Fourth, the mistake must have played a material part in the tribunal's reasoning. Each limb of that test had been made out in the instant case. The Parole Board seemed wrongly to have thought that the witnessing of the offending by H's daughter and the violent precursor events were live issues when in fact they had not been proved. Further, the mistakes which may have been made had played a material part in the Parole Board's reasoning. The Parole Board would therefore have to reconsider the matter, E v Secretary of State applied.

*R (on the application of Gibson) v Secretary of State for Justice* [2010] EWHC 342 (Admin)
The applicant prisoner (G) applied for a writ of habeas corpus. G had been released on licence half way through his sentence of imprisonment, but had been recalled to prison on September 26 following a breach of curfew. The Court held that a prisoner on licence who did not believe that his breach of curfew should have led to his recall to prison was unsuccessful in his application for a writ of habeas corpus. Habeas corpus was designed to ensure that those who were unjustifiably held in detention were released forthwith. It was not designed to compensate someone for the effect of administrative delay, nor to challenge decisions that were relevant to detention in prison, but were not themselves such as to make that detention unlawful. The Court further held that it was not customary for an applicant for habeas corpus to appear in person, but there was a narrow gap between judicial review and habeas corpus and maybe that custom was less applicable in modern circumstances.

*R (on the application of Dennis Gill) v Secretary of State for Justice* [2010] EWHC 364 (Admin)
Where the completion of offending behaviour programmes had been identified by the Parole Board as being necessary to enable a prisoner to demonstrate his safety for release, but the prisoner was prevented from participating in such programmes because of a learning disability, the secretary of state would be in breach of his statutory and public law duties if he failed to take such steps as were reasonable in all the circumstances to enable him to access such programmes in the same way as inmates who were not disabled.

*R (on the application of Rowen) v Governor of HMP Kirkham & Anor* [2009] EWHC 3756 (Admin)
A prisoner deemed unsuitable for release on home detention curfew had to be informed of the

reasons. The Court held that Prison Service Order 7600 para.7.2 required that prisoners deemed not suitable for release on home detention curfew be informed of the reasons. The decision to refuse R's request had merely recited the headings of the grounds for refusal contained in the order and had not descended to any reasons. Furthermore, para.13 required a governor to give reasons in writing for upholding, on appeal, the original decision to refuse home detention curfew. However, R had only been informed that the refusal stood. Nor could it be said that the decision would have been the same if proper procedure had been followed, since there had been material showing that R had previously been trusted to spend time in hospital without a guard. The refusal to grant home detention curfew would be quashed. See also section 3.5 above for the implications of this case on re-categorisation decisions.

*Alan Michael Houchin v Secretary of State for Justice* [2010] EWHC 454 (Admin)
The refusal of the Secretary of State for Justice to accept the advice of the Parole Board that a prisoner should be transferred to an open prison was Wednesbury unreasonable where the Secretary of State's consideration of the Board's decision was so superficial that it was clear that the views expressed by the Board had scarcely been given any consideration at all. The Court held the Secretary of State's refusal of the Board's recommendation was Wednesbury unreasonable. Although the Secretary of State was not required to enter into a point-by-point engagement with and refutation of each and every matter in which he disagreed, the decision wholly failed to have regard to the exceptional nature of the circumstances in which the advice was sought, the parole board hearing, the scrutiny given to the documentation and oral evidence and the exceptionally long and detailed nature of the decision itself. The way in which the Secretary of State stated his disagreement with the main conclusions of the Board was so cursory and lacking any supporting argument that it was evidence of only the most superficial consideration of the decision. It followed that the views expressed by the board had scarcely been given any consideration at all. That was supported by the fact that, in dealing with the assessment of risk, the Secretary of State had focused exclusively on the Board's statement that it had found the matter to be of some difficulty. He had wholly failed to take into account the way in which the Board stated it was going to deal with the matter, notwithstanding those difficulties, and the clear conclusion to which it came. The decision contained internal contradictions and confusion about the purpose of the BLB programme. The Court also ordered that H was to be transferred to open conditions immediately following his satisfactory completion of the BLB programme and a re-assessment of his suitability for and consequent completion of another rehabilitation programme, with such assessment to be conducted as soon as possible without necessarily awaiting the completion of the BLB. There was to be no requirement before his re-transfer to open conditions for any further review by the Board. Such obligations were consistent with the Board's advice that H's risk level was the same as when H was originally recommended for transfer to open conditions.

*R (on the application of Noye) v Secretary of State for Justice* [2017] EWHC 267 (Admin)
It was not open to the Secretary of State to depart from a finding of fact made by the Parole Board Panel, that the prisoner had made significant progress in changing his attitudes to violence, unless he had good reason to do so.
N had a degree of notoriety and was the subject of great media interest. In 1986 N was convicted of conspiracy to handle stolen gold relating to the Brinks-MAT robbery of 1983 in which £26,000,000 worth of gold, diamonds and cash was stolen. Whilst subject to surveillance during the Brinks-MAT investigations, N stabbed a police officer to death. He was acquitted of murder on grounds of self-defence. In 1996 Stephen Cameron was murdered in a "road-rage" incident. N fled the UK following the murder, being returned some years later as a result of extradition proceedings, and was convicted of Cameron's murder in 2000.
In coming to their conclusion that N should be moved to an open prison, the Parole Board Panel had undertaken an extensive analysis of all risk factors and conducted a thorough testing of probation officers' and the prison psychologist's views expressed in their reports, during a hearing. The Secretary of State had wrongly made alternative findings of fact regarding N's risk and attitude to violence, which he was not entitled to do. The Secretary of State's decision not to transfer the prisoner to an open prison, despite the Parole Board's recommendation to the contrary, was quashed and an order made for a fresh decision on whether or not to transfer N to an open prison.

*R. (on the application of John) v Secretary of State for Justice* [2021] EWHC 1606 (Admin)
The Secretary of State for Justice was entitled to depart from a Parole Board's recommendation for a prisoner's transfer to open conditions where he was making an evaluative assessment as to

the extent to which further consolidation work was required and where it should be undertaken.

*R (on the application of (1) John Smith (2) John Mullally) v Governor of Lindholme Prison* [2010] EWHC 1356 (Admin)
The blanket application of a policy is unlawful.
R (on the application of Hewlett) v Secretary of State for Justice [2009] EWHC 2979 (Admin)
Following the decision in Lowe [see below] the Court held that if a decision to downgrade the Incentives and Earned Privileges (IEP) status of a Prisoner was taken without there being any changed circumstances, it would arguably be irrational and a breach of legitimate expectation of consistency.

*R (on the application of Lowe) v Governor of Liverpool Prison* [2008] EWHC 2167 (Admin)
The principles of consistency and legitimate expectation had to be applied when considering the categorisation of prisoners.
This principle was successfully argued in an IEP case where a Prisoner who maintained innocence had his status lowered after several years for no apparent reason (a judicial review terminated by consent: R on the application of W v Secretary of State for Justice (2010) (unreported)).

*R (on the application of AN) v Secretary of State for Justice* [2008] EWHC 3110 (Admin)
Where a prisoner had brought judicial review proceedings against the Secretary of State for Justice over the decision to move him to a single prison cell, it was not appropriate to depart from the normal course in judicial review proceedings and allow for the cross-examination of witnesses. There were detailed witness statements and documents available that went to the essential issue of the case, on the basis of which relevant submissions could be made.

*R (on the application of E) v Secretary of State for the Home Department* [2007] EWHC 1731 (Admin)
In an appropriate case the Administrative Court had jurisdiction to intervene in an ongoing criminal trial in order to ensure a defendant's right to a fair trial. However, the trial judge had primary responsibility for the conduct of the trial and its fairness, and intervention by the Administrative Court was appropriate only in exceptional circumstances.

*R (on the application of Palmer) v The Home Department* [2004] EWHC 1817 (Admin)
The grading of a prisoner into an appropriate category was to be based on the likelihood of escape and the risk to the public if the escape was successful; other considerations such as the

prospect of adverse publicity and the state of the prisoner's financial resources were not justifiable factors. There was no right for a prisoner serving a determinate sentence to make representations prior to categorisation decisions. However, there was a right to appeal which a Prisoner should exercise before initiating judicial review proceedings.

*R (on the application of Smith) v Parole Board & Anor* [2003] EWCA Civ 1014
Where a judge hearing an application for permission to apply for judicial review had heard detailed arguments, any judge hearing the main application would require significant justification before taking a different view from that of the judge granting permission; if the judge at the main hearing came to the conclusion that there was good reason to allow argument on an additional ground, permission should be granted.

*R v Secretary of State for the Home Department, ex parte John Hirst* [2001] EWCA Civ 378
A prisoner who had served the tariff period of a discretionary life sentence was entitled to be told reasons for a proposed re-categorisation and to be afforded the opportunity to make representations on that issue and to reply to grounds put forward to re-categorise him or her. This case articulates the important relationship between categorisation and progression towards release.

*R v Secretary of State for The Home Department, Ex Parte Harrison* [2000] 7 WLUK 589
In cases where the application for review was rendered academic, it was incumbent on all parties to notify the court of circumstances which would give rise to a need for expedition, either at the time of the application or during the passage of time.

*Leech v Deputy Governor of Parkhurst Prison; Prevot v Deputy Governor of Long Lartin Prison* (1988) 136 NLJ 39; (1988) AC 533; (1988) 2 WLR 290; (1988) 1 All ER 485; (1988) 132 SJ 191 House of Lords
Prison Governor's disciplinary powers subject to judicial review. Conjoined appeals by prisoners against dismissals of appeals against denials of leave for judicial review of disciplinary decisions of prison governors, allowed. *R v Deputy Governor of Camphill Prison, ex parte King* (1984) 3 All ER 897 was wrongly decided. Where any person or body exercised a power conferred by statute, which affected the rights or legitimate expectations of citizens which was of a kind which the law required to be exercised in accordance with the rules of natural justice, the court had jurisdiction to review the exercise of that power. Governors duty to so act was never in question.

*R v Secretary of State for the Home Department, ex parte Tarrant; Sub Nom R v Board of Visitors Albany Prison ex parte Leyland; R v Board Of Visitors of Wormwood Scrubs Prison, ex parte Tagney Clark Anderson* [1985] QB 251

A prisoner has no right to be legally represented when a board of visitors is inquiring into offences against prison discipline, but the board does have a discretion to afford such a prisoner an opportunity to be so represented if he wishes.

*R v Secretary of State for the Home Department ex parte Anderson* [1984] QB 778

It was proper for there to be regulations to control prisoners' access to solicitors but following Raymond v Honey a prisoner's right of access to a solicitor to institute legal proceedings must be unimpeded in the same way as his right to sending documents for that purpose. The requirement that he must first initiate an internal complaint was ultra vires.

*O'Reilly & Ors v Mackman & Ano; Millbanks v Secretary of State for the Home Department & Ors* (1983) 2 AC 237; (1982) 3 WLR 1096; (1982) 3 All ER 1124

Civil action for declaratory relief was no alternative to judicial review proceedings where the decision of a public body was challenged.

## JUSTICE, right of to visit prison
ACT 19

## JUVENILES
**See also "Young offenders".**
PSI 07/2016 – National Security Framework 3.1 Searching of the Person
PSI 09/2000 – Regimes for Young Women under 18 Years of Old
PSO 4960 – Detention under Section 92 of the Powers of Criminal Courts (Sentencing) Act 2000: Young People Serving Longer Sentences for Serious Offences
PSI 08/2012 – Care and Management of Young People (Revised)
Building Bridges: A positive behaviour framework for the Children and Young People Secure Estate (Revised) Policy Framework

## KNIVES AND OFFENSIVE WEAPONS
PSI 10/2012 – Conveyance and Possession of Prohibited Items and Other Related Offences
NSF Function 6.3 within this PSI has been updated by PSI 21/2015
PSI 21/2015 – New Legislation – Unauthorised Possession Within Prisons of Knives and Other Offensive Weapons (Revisions to NSF Function 6.3)

## LEGAL ADVICE & SERVICES FOR PRISON SERVICE STAFF
PSI 47/2000 – Information and practice document – "The judge at your gate"

## LEGAL ADVISORS AND COURTS, VISITS AND CORRESPONDENCE TO INMATES
**See also "Access to Justice".**
PR 38-39
YOI 16-17
PSI 16/2011 - Providing Visits and Services to Visitors (Revision)
**Case Law**
*R. (on the application of Michael) v Governor of Whitemoor* [2020] EWCA Civ 29
A prison governor's decision that a category A prisoner serving a mandatory life sentence should attend the hearing of a civil claim by video link, rather than in person, did not breach his right to a fair trial under ECHR art.6. Nor had the decision-maker unlawfully fettered her discretion in refusing the prisoner's request to be produced physically at the hearing of his claim. However, the decision had been made on the basis of a fundamental misunderstanding of an important fact, and would have to be retaken in the light of up-to-date information.

## LEGAL AID, Criminal
**Case Law**
*R (on the application of Howard League for Penal Reform) v Lord Chancellor* [2017] EWCA Civ 244
The claimants (HLPR) and Prisoners' Advice Service applied for judicial review of changes to criminal legal aid for prison law which were introduced with effect from 2 December 2013 by the Criminal Legal Aid (General)(Amendment) Regulations 2013 SI 2013 No. 2790 which removed funding for pre-tariff Parole Board reviews and a number of other areas. The claimants submitted that the removal of legal aid from these areas would result in inherent or systematic unfairness.
In allowing the application in respect of three of the areas of prison law in issue, Beatson LJ stated at para 146, "We emphasise that we recognise that there may be safeguards other than legal aid and advice that will prevent inherent or systemic unfairness by enabling a prisoner to participate effectively in a category of decision-making. The government's decision to remove legal aid from the five categories of decision-making that are the subject of these proceedings by the 2013 Amendment Regulations was made because it considers that there were adequate alternative means in place to ensure prisoners can participate effectively in areas in which support has hitherto been provided by legal advice and legal representation. The consequence is that

almost no changes have been introduced to replace the gap left by the removal of legal aid. We have concluded that, at a time when ... the evidence about prison staffing levels, the current state of prisons, and the workload of the Parole Board suggests that the system is under considerable pressure, the system has at present not got the capacity sufficiently to fill the gap in the run of cases in those three areas."

As a result of the case, criminal legal aid was restored. Under the amended Criminal Legal Aid (General) Regulations 2013 (SE 2019 No. 9), Criminal Legal Aid is now available for advice and assistance regarding:

(i) when a prisoner is either entitled to be released by the Secretary of State or eligible for consideration by the Parole Board for a direction to be released;

(ii) when an offender is entitled to be released by the Secretary of State;

(iii) a review of a prisoner's classification a Category A Prisoner or as a Restricted Status Prisoner;

(iv) a prisoner's placement in a close supervision centre of a prison;

(v) a prisoner's placement in a separation centre within a prison; and

(vi) a review of an inmate's classification pursuant as a Category A Inmate or Restricted Status Inmate;

Under the amended Criminal Legal Aid (General) Regulations 2013 (SE 2019 No. 9), Criminal Legal Aid is also available for those who:

(i) require advice and assistance regarding an application or potential application to the Criminal Cases Review Commission;

(ii) require advice and assistance regarding a disciplinary hearing in a prison or young offender institution where the proceedings involve the determination of a criminal charge for the purposes of Article 6(1) of the European Convention on Human Rights; or the governor has their discretion to allow advice and assistance in relation to the hearing; and

(iii) are the subject of proceedings before the Parole Board.

## LETTERS, inmates' personal
See also "Prisoners Communications"
YOI 10 Prison Rule 35
**Case Law**
R. (on the application of MA) v Secretary of State for Justice [2021] EWHC 1266 (Admin)
A prohibition on telephone contact and inter-prison visits between two prisoners who had married in prison while serving sentences of imprisonment for public protection following their convictions for sexual offences was an unnecessary and disproportionate interference with their ECHR art.8(1) rights and therefore unlawful. The restriction on inter-prison visits was also not in accordance with published prison policy and was therefore contrary to public law.

## LIBRARIES, Prison
Prison Rule 33
33. Library
A library shall be provided in every prison and, subject to any directions of the Secretary of State, every prisoner shall be allowed to have library books and to exchange them.
PSI 02/2015 - Prison Library Service (Wales Only)
PSI 04/2012 – Enablers of Health, Library, Education and Jobcentre Plus Services in Prisons
YOI 26 Books
Prison Education & Library Service for Adult Prisons in England Policy Framework
Governors must ensure – as a minimum – that a prisoner's statutory entitlement to library provision is met. Article 6 of the European Convention on Human Rights includes the requirement that individuals must be afforded enough time and facilities to prepare their defence.

## LICENCE CONDITIONS
**See also "Release, Early – Licence Conditions".**
Licence Conditions Policy Framework
1.2 This Policy Framework aims to ensure that staff are aware of the licence conditions which apply to an individual on licence during the licence period of all custodial sentences. Further explanation is given to individual types of licence conditions and how they should be correctly applied, as well as the mandatory actions which must be undertaken when preparing and creating a licence.
1.4 Whilst this document sets out the actions for which the Parole Board is responsible, this document does not bind the Parole Board in any way as it is an internal policy document of the Ministry of Justice/Her Majesties Prison and Probation Service.
**Case Law**
R. (on the application of Latif) v Secretary of State for Justice [2021] EWHC 892 (Admin)
A prisoner who had been released on licence following his guilty plea to an offence of engaging in conduct in preparation for acts of terrorism contrary to the Terrorism Act 2006 Pt 1 s.5(1), had not been given a sufficient opportunity to make representations prior to a Multiple Agency Public Protection Arrangements meeting when it was decided that additional licence conditions would be applied to him. However, as the prisoner's representations had been taken into account at a subsequent meeting, it was not necessary to quash the decision to add new licence conditions, and declaratory relief was sufficient.

*R. (on the application of Gul) v Secretary of State for Justice* [2014] EWHC 373 (Admin)

Two licence conditions imposed on a released prisoner which were additional to the standard conditions were not tainted by procedural unfairness, ultra vires or in violation of the European Convention on Human Rights 1950 art.8, art.10 and art.11.

*Gleeson v Staffordshire & West Midlands Probation Trust* [2013] EWHC 1750 (Admin)

The Secretary of State for Justice, when imposing conditions in a release licence, was not bound by what a sentencing judge had said with regard to the terms of a sexual offences prevention order he was making, nor was he required to have regard to those terms. In the instant case, it was neither unlawful nor disproportionate to impose restrictions on a release licence where those restrictions had not been imposed on the earlier prevention order.

*R (Tabbakh) v Staffordshire & West Midlands Probation Trust* [2013] EWHC 2492 (Admin)

The procedural requirements under Article 8 of the European Convention on Human Rights had been met in the case of a prisoner upon whom additional conditions for release on licence had been imposed as the offender was able to make meaningful representations through his offender manager at the meetings to discuss the conditions that would apply to him when he was released.

## LICENCES FOR SHOWING DVD/VIDEO FILMS IN PRISONS

PSI 23/2011 – Licences for DVD / Video Films, Music and Televisions in Prisons

## LIDS DATA ENTRY

PSI 25/2006 – LIDS Data Entry 9000

PSI 3/2008 – LIDS Data Entry 9000

## LIFERS (Life Sentence Prisoners)

Managing Parole Eligible Offenders on Licence Policy Framework

### Case Law

*R. (on the application of Neville) v Secretary of State for Justice* [2021] EWHC 957 (Admin)

A prisoner whose life imprisonment sentence in Thailand had been reduced to a determinate sentence by royal pardon, and who had been transferred to the UK to serve the remainder of his sentence, was not a "transferred life prisoner" under the Criminal Justice Act 2003 s.273 who was eligible for a tariff review. That was the case even though, if he had been a life prisoner, he might have been eligible for earlier release than he was under the determinate sentence.

*R. v Esposito (Raffaele)* [2021] EWCA Crim 438

Although a life prisoner's conduct whilst serving his sentence for two counts of murder had been exemplary as evidenced by his charity and community work, law degree and policy work, it did not pass the very high threshold of exceptionality such as to justify reducing the 19-year minimum term imposed on him.

*R (Weddle) v Secretary of State for Justice* [2016] EWCA Civ 38

Had the Secretary of State for Justice treated a life sentenced prisoner's inability to recall his index offence as an absolute bar to progress in offending behaviour programmes, he would have been acting irrationally and would have failed in his public law duty to provide the prisoner with means to demonstrate that he posed a reduced risk of serious selfharm to the public. However, the secretary of state had shown that there were ways by which the prisoner could demonstrate a reduced risk of serious selfharm even if he remained unable to recall his index offence.

*R (Dunn) v The Governor of HMP Frankland* [2015] EWHC 858 (Admin)

The duty to rehabilitate a life prisoner had not been breached where he had been refused access to an offender programme, as his tariff was not due to expire until 2031 and the limited spaces on the programme meant that priority had to be given to prisoners whose tariffs would have expired sooner. In the context of a long sentence the delay in allowing him access was not excessive or a breach of duty.

*Vinter v United Kingdom (66069/09)* [2016] 63 EHRR 1

For a sentence of life imprisonment to be compatible with the Article 3 of the European Convention on Human Rights 1950, there had to be a possibility of review and a possibility of release. In introducing "whole life orders", which meant that the prisoner could not be released other than at the discretion of the Secretary of State on compassionate grounds, the United Kingdom had violated Article 3.

*M v Scottish Ministers* [2013] CSOH 112 (Scotland)

The Scottish Ministers had not acted unlawfully by failing to accommodate a prisoner in open conditions in order that he could demonstrate to the Parole Board for Scotland that it was no longer necessary for public protection for him to be confined where he had been afforded substantial opportunities to show that his risk level had lowered, the Scottish Ministers had considered all relevant factors, ignored irrelevant factors and the detention was not arbitrary.

*R v Gill : R v Eccles : R v Abu-Neigh (Formerly Wallace)* [2011] EWCA Crim 2795

In a conjoined hearing the applicants (G, E and N) sought leave to appeal out of time against the minimum terms of sentences of life imprisonment imposed on them for murder. In N's case the secretary of state had determined the minimum term, that determination having been reviewed by a High Court judge under the Criminal Justice Act 2003 Sch.22 para.3. In the cases of G and E, the minimum term had been fixed by a High Court judge under Sch.22 para.6 without any prior determination by the secretary of state. Each appeal was brought on the ground that the appellant had made exceptional progress in prison after serving several years of his sentence. The court was therefore being asked to review each sentence by assessing the conduct of each appellant long after sentence. The central questions for determination were whether (i) for the purposes of such a review, there was a distinction between terms fixed under Sch.22 para.3 and those fixed under Sch.22 para.6; (ii) the same would apply to a "modern" minimum term, namely one fixed after December 18, 2003 by a trial judge as part of the sentencing process; (iii) the Criminal Cases Review Commission could refer the matter to the Court of Appeal if the full court refused to grant an extension of time, or whether an appellant who made an application too soon was to be denied a further application. The Court held that: (1) For the purposes of a review by the Court of Appeal on the ground of exceptional progress, there was no effective distinction between a minimum term fixed under Sch.22 para.3 and one fixed under Sch.22 para.6. After the passing of the 2003 Act, the courts concluded that exceptional progress might be taken into account in respect of terms fixed by the secretary of state, *R (on the application of Cole) v Secretary of State for the Home Department* [2003] EWHC 1789 (Admin), and Caines (Setting of Minimum Term), Re [2006] EWCA Crim 2915, (2007) 1 WLR 1109 followed. That approach was subsequently applied to terms fixed under Sch.22 para.6, *R v S (Marticka Maria)* [2006] EWCA Crim 2669, Times, November 7, 2006 followed. In either case, modest allowance could be made where exceptional progress was established. When considering exceptional progress, the court was not assessing the correctness of the term fixed by the judge. Nor was it revisiting the punitive and deterrent elements of the sentence; the element of public protection; or the issues falling to be resolved by the parole board. The decision was fact-specific and was not susceptible of resolution by reference to authority. The guidance given in Caines, that mere good behaviour was not sufficient, remained good (see paras 13-14, 16-18, 28-30, 33 of judgment). (2) For sentences imposed after December 18, 2003, there was no provision for any reduction on the basis of exceptional progress. That conclusion was supported by the judgments in *R v Bieber (David Francis)* [2008] EWCA Crim 1601, (2009) 1 WLR 223 and *R v Barker (Julie)* [2008] EWCA Crim 2558, the repeal of the Crime (Sentences) Act 1997 s.29, and the absence of any corresponding provision in the 2003 Act, Bieber and Barker considered (paras 23, 27, 33). (3) A reduction to reflect exceptional progress could not realistically be considered until towards the end of the minimum period. Even if exceptional progress had been made in the first few years of a sentence, that did not necessarily indicate how the prisoner would continue to progress. In any event, exceptional progress would not lead to a reduction of more than two years. An application made more than three years before the end of the determinate period would therefore be premature. Applications would normally be made many years after the time for appeal had expired, requiring an extraordinary extension of time. Were an extension to be refused, the applicant could refer his case to the Criminal Cases Review Commission. If the Commission chose to refer the case to the court, it would be treated as an appeal, not requiring any extension of time. That seemed unnecessarily complicated and it was better for the courts simply to conduct the necessary review. That process was, however, confined to cases falling within Sch.22 para.3 and Sch.22 para.6 (paras 19-20, 33). The Criminal Cases Review Commission would continue to exercise its jurisdiction in accordance with its statutory functions. Where a defendant appealed against the minimum term on the basis that it was manifestly excessive, without reference to any progress in prison, the conclusion of that appeal would dispose of any further right to appeal against sentence. Where the question of exceptional progress genuinely arose in the context of Sch.22, but the normal appeal process had been exhausted, the case was to be referred to the Commission. In other cases where the statutory appeal process on grounds independent of exceptional progress had not been exhausted, any application for a reduction in the minimum term on the basis of exceptional progress was to be adjourned with an indication about when it would be sensible for the court to reconsider it (paras 31-33). (4) While G could be said to have made exceptional progress, E and N could not. G's appeal would therefore be allowed while E and N's would be dismissed. Applications granted, appeals allowed in part.

*R (on the application of Ian D'Cunha) v Parole Board* [2011] EWHC 128 (Admin) See "Parole" below.

*R v David Francis Bieber (AKA Coleman)* [2008] EWCA Crim 1601

A whole life term should not be considered as a sentence that was irreducible. Any European Convention on Human Rights 1950 art.3 challenge where a whole life term had been imposed should therefore be made, not at the time of the imposition of the sentence, but at the stage when the prisoner contended that, having regard to all the material circumstances, any further detention would constitute degrading or inhuman treatment.

*R v Anthony Wallis* [2005] EWCA Crim 3055

For an automatic life sentence to be imposed under s.109 of the Powers of Criminal Courts (Sentencing) Act 2000 it was necessary for a defendant to have been actually convicted of another serious offence at the time that he committed the second offence.

*R v Franklin Maynard* [2005] EWCA Crim 1820

When considering the imposition of an automatic life sentence under the Powers of Criminal Courts (Sentencing) Act 2000 s.109, it was not only necessary to consider the facts and circumstances of the previous serious offence and the present offence, but also to take into consideration a defendant's criminal record generally.

*R v Paul McMilan* [2005] EWCA Crim 222

Where an offence was not of such seriousness to disapply early release provisions to an automatic life sentence, the court was required to consider the appropriate tariff as regards seriousness without any consideration of future risk.

*R v David Wallis MacDonald* [2001] EWCA Crim 860

A mandatory life sentence passed under s.2 Crime (Sentences) Act 1997 was reduced to a term of four-and-a-half years, as it could not be said that the offender presented a real risk of selfharm to the public.

*R v Secretary of State for the Home Department, Ex Parte Myra Hindley* [2001] 1 AC 410

It was lawful for a secretary of state to impose or uphold a "whole-life" tariff on someone sentenced to life imprisonment for murder. There was no reason, in principle why a crime or crimes, if sufficiently heinous, should not be regarded as deserving life-long incarceration for the purposes of pure punishment.

## LIFERS – Setting the Minimum Term
## Case Law

For "exceptional progress" cases, see *R v Gill : R v Eccles : R v Abu-Neigh (Formerly Wallace)* [2011] EWCA Crim 2795 CA (Crim Div) 1/12/2011 in the "Lifer" section immediately above.

*In the Matter of Duncan Jackson (Setting of Minimum Term)* [2011] EWHC 1628 (QB)

The applicant (J), who had been sentenced to life imprisonment for murder, applied under the Criminal Justice Act 2003 Sch.22 para.3 to have his minimum term fixed. Although the murder had taken place in 1985, J was not arrested until 1998. He was convicted in 2000. The trial judge recommended a tariff of 15 years, while the Lord Chief Justice recommended a term of 14-15 years. In 2001, J was notified on behalf of the Home Secretary that his tariff had been set at 15 years. J argued that (1) if his case had been tried contemporaneously with the crime, he could have expected a judicial recommendation of something like 13 years, and any longer term was precluded by the European Convention on Human Rights 1950 Article 7(1); (2) the minimum term should be reduced to take into account his exceptional progress in custody. The Court held that where the court was asked to set the minimum term for an historic offence, the European Convention on Human Rights 1950 article 7(1) would not be breached simply because the court fixed a longer minimum term than would have been likely if the applicant had been convicted and sentenced shortly after the offence was committed; his rights under that provision would be infringed only if the court fixed a term which was longer than the tariff which could have been set at the time of the offence.

*R v Norman Hull* [2011] EWCA Crim 1261

The appellant prisoner (H) appealed against the determination of his minimum term of imprisonment following his transfer from prison in the Republic of Ireland to a prison in the United Kingdom. H had been convicted of murder in the Republic of Ireland and was sentenced to "imprisonment for life" under the Criminal Justice Act 1990 (Ireland) s.2. Early release from such a sentence was not set, but later authorised by the Irish Minister of Justice. Before a parole review took place, H applied and consented to be transferred to the United Kingdom to serve the remainder of his sentence in an English prison under the Repatriation of Prisoners Act 1984. His case was referred to the High Court under the Criminal Justice Act 2003 s.273(1) for the making of an appropriate sentence. Applying the decision in *Khan (Setting of Minimum Term), Re* [2006] EWHC 2826 (QB) the judge determined that the circumstances of H's offending would have provided a starting point of a term of imprisonment of 30 years but that such a sentence would exceed the period which H might reasonably have expected to serve in prison in the Republic of Ireland and that the appropriate term of imprisonment should be 18 years. The Court held that the task of the administering state when adapting a sentence was, so far as possible, to bring correspondence between the "punishment" which would have been imposed in the sentencing state and the remainder of the sentence to be served in the administering state. That required a reasoned judgment as to the likely duration of the custodial element of the sentence had the sentence been served in the sentencing state.

Hart (Review of Tariff), Re [2013] EWHC 3533 (Admin)
When reviewing a tariff imposed by the secretary of state on a life prisoner for murder, the seriousness of the offences was to be assessed in the context of the guidance in the Criminal Justice Act 2003 Sch.21, while considering the judicial recommendations made at the time of sentencing. The original tariff fixed by the secretary of state should not just be replaced by the judicial recommendation, but in the instant case the seriousness of the offender's murder offences had already been reflected in the Lord Chief Justice's recommended tariff.

R v Peter Coonan (Formerly Peter Sutcliffe) [2011] EWCA Crim 5
In determining the minimum term under the Criminal Justice Act 2003 Sch.22 for an offender who had committed a series of murders and attempted murders, a judge had been right not to take into account medical evidence of mental disorder as mitigation where the jury had rejected evidence of such disorder.

R v (1) Ricky Liam Beesley (2) Anthony Coyle: R v Zehwar Rehman [2011] EWCA Crim 1021
When sentencing for manslaughter, the judge had been right to make findings of dangerousness for the purposes of the Criminal Justice Act 2003 and sentence the offenders to imprisonment for public protection. It would be rare for the Court of Appeal to receive new psychological assessments that were not before the trial judge when considering an issue under the dangerousness provisions

R v Pitchfork [2009] EWCA Crim 963
The minimum term for an offender serving life imprisonment for the murder of two teenage girls was set on review at 28 years, which included a discount of two years for his exceptional progress in custody.

R v Malcolm Horsman [2007] 4 WLUK 513
A minimum term for life imprisonment was marginally reduced where the offender had made significant progress whilst in prison and had made excellent contributions to the prison community.

In the Matter of James Anthony Hurley [2007] EWHC 179 (Admin)
A minimum term of 11 years was appropriate in the case of an offender who had murdered his father by stabbing him in the back. It was not appropriate to reduce the tariff to reflect the progress made while in prison because the offender had not demonstrated that he had made exceptional progress.

In the Matter of John Richard Cadman [2006] EWHC 586 (QB)
A minimum term of 19 years' imprisonment was set in respect of an offender who had been sentenced to life imprisonment for three murders where the offender had made exceptional progress since his conviction.

R v Timothy Caines; R v David Roberts [2006] EWCA Crim 2915
The Court held that exceptional progress in prison could be taken into account for the purposes of resetting a prisoner's minimum term, and any reduction for such progress should be made from the fixed minimum term, not from the newly assessed notional tariff. It was held that R. v Waters (David) [2006] EWHC 355 (QB) was wrongly decided.

R (on the application of Cole; Rowland; Hawkes) v Secretary of State for the Home Department [2003] EWHC 1789 (Admin)
The Secretary of State for the Home Department could not be construed as "a court" within the meaning in para.2(1) sch.2 Criminal Appeal Act 1968 and therefore had had power to set a higher tariff than had originally been imposed following a conviction for murder after a re-trial. The secretary of state had not erred in taking into account the decision in R v Secretary of State for the Home Department, ex parte Anderson (2003) 1 AC 837 and forthcoming legislation when refusing to review the tariff of two life prisoners.

**LITIGANTS**
PSO 16
PSI 31/2015 – Managing Litigation Claims (Revision)

**LOSSES, SPECIAL PAYMENTS AND COMPENSATION**
HMPPS Finance Manual Policy Framework: Chapter 6 (Losses and Special Payments)

PSI 05/2018 – Prison Discipline Procedures (Adjudications) replaces and cancels
PSI 31/2013 - Recovery of Monies for Damage to Prisons and Prison Property

## MAGISTRATES' TRAINING VISITS TO PRISON SERVICE ESTABLISHMENTS
PSO 0160

## MAILBOXES
PSO 9050 - Functional Mailboxes
PSI 18/2008 – Use of inventory stores functional mailbox (update of PS0 9050/2006)

## MAINTAINING INNOCENCE
### Key Note
There has been something of an enduring myth to the effect that a Prisoner who maintains innocence disqualifies him or herself from progress and or Enhanced IEP status. Both published policy by the Home Office and Case Law makes it clear that a Prisoner is entitled to maintain innocence, though the prison and Parole Board are obliged to proceed on the basis of a Prisoner's guilt.

The issue is of importance at various stages in a Prisoner's progress, and has a bearing on the important issue of risk reduction.

A myth has grown up that unless a prisoner admits and expresses remorse for the crime that they have been sentenced for, they will not get parole. This is not true. It is important to get the facts right, not least for those in prison who do maintain their innocence and who may be unnecessarily affected by the myth.

Legal precedent has established that it would be unlawful for the Board to refuse parole solely on the grounds of denial of guilt or anything that flows from that (such as not being able to take part in offending behaviour programmes which focus on the crime committed). The Board is bound to take account not only of the offence, and the circumstances in which it was committed, but the circumstances and behaviour of the individual prisoner before and during the sentence.

It is important to understand that the Board is not entitled to "go behind" the conviction. That means it cannot overrule the decision of a judge or jury. That is the job of the appeal courts and the Criminal Cases Review Commission. The Board's remit extends only to the assessment of risk, and the bottom line is always the safety of the public.

### Case Law
*R v Parole Board for England and Wales, Ex Parte Oyston* [2000] EWCA Crim 3552, [2000] 3 WLUK 35
Guideline case on the factors to be considered by the Parole Board in deciding whether to grant parole and the detail to be included in the decision letter to the prisoner. In particular, maintaining innocence was not, in itself, a legitimate reason for denying release and/or progression.

The principles set out in this case have since been referred to as the "Oyston guidelines". The essential principle is set out in paragraph 43 of the judgment of Lord Bingham LCJ:

"[43] Convicted prisoners who persistently deny commission of the offence or offences of which they have been convicted present the Parole Board with potentially very difficult decisions. Such prisoners will probably not express contrition or remorse or sympathy for any victim. They will probably not engage in programmes designed to address the causes of their offending behaviour. Since they do not admit having offended they will only undertake not to do in the future what they do not accept having done in the past. Where there is no admission of guilt, it may be feared that a prisoner will lack any motivation to obey the law in future. Even in such cases, however, the task of the Parole Board is the same as in any other case: to assess the risk that the particular prisoner if released on parole, will offend again. In making this assessment the Parole Board must assume the correctness of any conviction. It can give no credence to the prisoner's denial. Such denial will always be a factor and may be a very significant factor in the Board's assessment of risk, but it will only be one factor and must be considered in the light of all other relevant factors. In almost any case the Board would be quite wrong to treat the prisoner's denial as irrelevant, but also quite wrong to treat a prisoner's denial as necessarily conclusive against the grant of parole."

*R (Quaddy) v Governor of HMP Long Lartin* [2013] EWHC 2029 (Admin)
See "Category A prisoners" above.

*R (on the application of (1) Ian Shutt (2) John Tetley) v Secretary of State for Justice* [2012] EWHC 851 (Admin)
See "Incentives and Earned Privileges" above.

*R (on the application of Clive Craig) v Governor of Albany Prison* [2010] EWHC 2303 (Admin)
The claimant (C) applied for judicial review of a decision of the defendant governor (G) refusing him a progressive move out of category B (high security) conditions. C had been sentenced to 11 years' imprisonment for rape, attempted rape and indecent assault, all against his 11 year old daughter in 2004. He sought recategorisation from category B to category C. The reason given on the relevant form RC1 for refusing recategorisation was that C was maintaining his innocence with the result that he had not participated in the sex offenders treatment

programme and there was no reduction in risk.. The Court held that the decision refusing to recategorise C from category B to category C did take into account factors independent of denial of guilt; it was clear that the prison governor could not be satisfied that there was a positive reduction in risk sufficient to merit a downgrade. The Court recognised that the authorities highlighted the continuing difficulties that prisoners who denied their guilt faced in demonstrating the necessary reduction in risk to enable progressive recategorisation, against the assumption of guilt which the prison authorities had to apply to such prisoners, *R (on the application of Roberts) v Secretary of State for the Home Department* [2004] EWHC 679 (Admin), and *R (on the application of Osborne) v Governor of Littlehey Prison* [2010] EWHC 1277 (Admin) considered.

*R (on the application of McLuckie) v Secretary of State for Justice* [2011] EWCA Civ 522
The judge had erred in finding that procedural fairness required an oral hearing before the Category A review team based on the observation by the Parole Board that a move to a Category B prison 'may be constructive'. The CoA held reading the report as a whole that single observation did not provide a sufficient foundation for concluding that an oral hearing was required.

*R (on the application of Andrew Osborne) v Governor of Littlehey Prison* [2010] EWHC 1277 (Admin)
The claimant category C prisoner (O) applied for judicial review of the refusal of the defendant prison governor to recategorise him to category D. The Court held that the prison governor had been entitled to refuse the downward recategorisation of a prisoner on the basis that in spite of the prisoner's good behaviour and educational progress his denial of the offence and consequent inability to attend offending behaviour courses did not demonstrate the prisoner's required reduction in risk of reoffending to justify recategorisation.

*Sagar v Governor of Wakefield Prison* [2010] EWHC 1378 (Admin)
The claimant prisoner (S) applied for judicial review of the defendant governor's refusal to authorise his transfer to an open prison. The Court held that the prison governor had not acted unlawfully by refusing to authorise the transfer to an open prison of a tariff-expired life prisoner who denied the offence of murder but admitted to significant violence in his past. Transfer to an open prison would allow access to offending behaviour programmes but rather than being refused because of the prisoner's denial, it had been refused because there was suitable work for him to undertake in the closed prison. Further, the act of deciding that a person would not admit that which the law had to assume, namely his guilt, was not something so central to a person's individuality as to bear proper relationship with the statuses which were otherwise plainly within art.14 of the Convention, *R (on the application of Clift) v Secretary of State for the Home Department* [2006] UKHL 54, (2007) 1 AC 484 applied. In any event, it was unlikely that art.5 of the Convention, which had to be read with art.14, would be engaged

*R (on the application of Dennis Gill) v Secretary of State for Justice* [2010] EWHC 364 (Admin)
See "Disabled Prisoners, management" and "Judicial Review Procedure" above.

*R (on the application of Hewlett) v Secretary of State for Justice* [2009] EWHC 2979 (Admin)
Exceptional circumstances must be shown if a Claimant is to succeed in arguing that he should attain IEP statues despite maintaining his innocence. There is no moment in a denier's sentence when it can be said, absent exceptional individual circumstances, that the SOTP is no longer appropriate. If the contrary is understood to have been said in either Ex Parte Potter & Ors (2001) Green (2004) [see below] it is no longer appropriate. It followed that Hewlett's challenge could only succeed if he could show that there were no appropriate changed circumstances or other good reasons to support the decision taken. His continuing denial of guilt represented good reason.

*R (on the application of Kenealy) v Secretary of State for Justice* [2009] EWHC 1503 (Admin)
A prison service director of high security was entitled to conclude that a Category A prisoner who maintained his innocence in respect of his index, sexual, offences had not demonstrated sufficient evidence of a significant reduction in his risk of sexual reoffending to warrant a downgrade in his categorisation even though he had made progress on courses aimed at his lifestyle and other types of offending.

*John Cannan v Governor of HMP Full Sutton* [2009] EWHC 1517 (Admin)
There was nothing intrinsically unfair, unreasonable or irrational in requiring a prisoner, as part of his sentence planning process, to apply for and if successful undertake certain courses notwithstanding that he maintained his innocence of the crimes of which he had been convicted and eligibility for the courses required him to admit guilt. The deliberate failure to comply with targets in the prisoner's sentence plan was, itself, a proper reason to deny the prisoner enhanced status under the IEPS.

*R (on the application of Chester) v (1) Parole Board (2) Secretary of State for Justice* [2008] EWHC 1318 (Admin)
When considering the release or recategorisation of a sex offender, the decision-maker had to consider all material relevant to risk and, in cases where the prisoner had declined to participate in sex offender training courses that might have assisted him to demonstrate a reduction in risk, it had to consider not only whether his reasons for declining to take part were indicative of risk, but also what conclusions could be drawn from the other available evidence.

*R (on the application of Dean Solomon) v Parole Board* [2006] EWHC 2639 (Admin)
A Parole Board had adopted the correct approach in deciding not to release a sex offender in the interests of public protection even though it had set out the law incorrectly in its decision letter. The error in formulation did not invalidate the decision.

*R (on the application of Peter Green) v (1) Governor of Risley Prison (2) Secretary of State for the Home Department* [2004] EWHC 596 (Admin)
It was open to a prison to refuse to grant enhanced status to a prisoner on the basis that he had failed to take part in a sex offenders treatment programme that required him to admit his guilt notwithstanding that a review of his conviction was pending at the Criminal Cases Review Commission. There was no moment in the sentence of a defendant who denied guilt when it could be said, absent exceptional individual circumstances, that the Sex Offenders Treatment Programme was no longer appropriate and any statement from this case which supports that proposition was not relied upon in *R. (on the application of Hewlett) v Secretary of State for Justice* [2009] EWHC 2979 (Admin)

*R (on the application of AT) v Probation Service* [2004] EWHC 515 (Admin)
Where a prisoner had breached a condition of his licence by refusing to take part in a sex offenders' treatment programme on the basis that he maintained his innocence, evidence to that effect went to the manifestly central issue of the reasonableness of imposing the condition and a failure to take such evidence into account when considering a later release on licence rendered the decision of the Parole Board unfair.

*R (Cavanagh and others) v Secretary of State for the Home Department and Another* [2002] EWCA Civ 334
Three convicted sex offenders were refused enhanced status at HMP Frankland because of denial and non-participation in the SOTP. The Court of Appeal held that the Prison Service was entitled to treat a prisoner as being guilty of his offence and setting targets commensurate with that presumption.

*R v Secretary of State for The Home Department & Anor, Ex Parte Potter & Ors* [2001] EWHC Admin 1041
It was not unfair or irrational for a prison to refuse to grant enhanced status to a sex offender who, by maintaining a denial of guilt, rendered himself ineligible for a SOTP. Moses J recognized that insistence that a person must attend a SOTP would at some stage become inconsistent with sentence planning on the basis that: "It can hardly be supposed that one who at first denies his sexual offences should straightaway be excused attendance on an SOTP. But if he persists in his denial, at what stage is it to be said that the denial is so entrenched that it is inappropriate to expect him to attend such a course? The question whether his denial is a good reason for non-attendance will depend upon the individual circumstances of the particular prisoner." R. (on the application of Hewlett) v Secretary of State for Justice [2009] EWHC 2979 (Admin) makes it clear that exceptional circumstances are required for denial of the offence to lead to a conclusion that the sex offenders treatment programme is no longer appropriate.

*R v Secretary of State for the Home Department, ex parte Lillycrop; Scott; Powell* [1996] 11 WLUK 402 QBD
Judicial review of Parole Board decisions not to recommend sexual offenders for early release. The Parole Board should approach any application for parole on the basis that the applicant had committed the offences of which he was convicted though a denial of guilt along with an unwillingness to address offending behaviour is a factor to which the Board must have regard in assessing the risk to the public of further offending .

*R v (1) Secretary of State for the Home Department (2) The Governor of Frankland Prison, ex parte Mohammed Zulfikar : R v (2) Secretary of State for the Home Department (2) The Parole Board, ex parte Mohammed Zulfikar* [1996] C.O.D 256; Times, July 26, 1995
Failure to acknowledge guilt was not a bar to parole and the Parole Board had to weigh each case of continued denial.

*R (on the application of Raw) v Parole Board for England and Wales* [2021] EWHC 1934 (Admin)
An appeal against the Parole Board's decision not to release a prisoner failed. The prisoner argued that the Parole Board's decision was unlawful, because a denial of guilt 'ought not to

be determinative'. The court held that it can be determinative, but this depends upon the facts of the particular case and whether the necessary balancing exercise has been carried out. The important question is whether the Board carried out the appropriate balancing exercise when reaching its decision which placed great weight on the denial of guilt and its consequences. "It is a matter for the Board to determine whether, and the extent to which, the negative outweighs the positive" [63].

## MAINTAINING ORDER IN PRISONS
**See also "Segregation".**
Prison Rule 6
6. Maintenance of order and discipline
(1) Order and discipline shall be maintained with firmness, but with no more restriction than is required for safe custody and well ordered community life.
(2) In the control of prisoners, officers shall seek to influence them through their own example and leadership, and to enlist their willing co-operation.
(3) At all times the treatment of prisoners shall be such as to encourage their self-respect and a sense of personal responsibility, but a prisoner shall not be employed in any disciplinary capacity.
Incident Management Manual in May 2022 (published 17 June 2022)

## MEMORY STICKS
**See "Removable Media".**

## MAINTENANCE
PSO 5901 – Maintenance of Prison Service Buildings
PSI 33/1999 – Prison Service Order – Technical 5900: cancelled by DOPT Nov 2018 – PSI Obsolete
PSO 0200 – Prison Service Buildings Standard: replaced by Prison Service Standards

## MARRIAGE
**See also "Civil Partnerships".**
PSI 14/2016 – Marriage of Prisoners and Civil Partnership Registration
Executive summary
This instruction sets out the legal requirements, policy and procedures for facilitating prisoners' requests to marry (including same sex couples) or enter into a civil partnership in England and Wales. This will ensure that NOMS fully meets its obligations under the relevant legislation (…). This instruction also makes it mandatory for all Governors to consider applications from prisoners for marriage and civil partnership. (…)
Desired Outcome
1.8 This PSI aims to provide advice and guidance about the legal process to enable prisoners to marry or enter into a civil partnership. (…)

3. Eligibility
3.1 Where a prisoner wants to marry or enter into a civil partnership in a prison, he or she is required to obtain a statement of authority (see Annex A and Annex B) from the prison governor which states that there is no objection to the prison being named as the place at which the marriage or civil partnership will take place.
3.2 The statement by the responsible authority is not required if the prisoner is getting married or entering a civil partnership outside the prison. (…)
4. Cases of possible concern
4.1 Under Section 27A of the Marriage Act 1949, the Governor must decide whether they have any objection to the prison being named on the notice of marriage as the place where the marriage is to be solemnized. In exercising this discretion, the Governor must be mindful of the need to make every effort possible to facilitate the prisoner's exercise of the right to marry, as per Article 12 of the European Convention on Human Rights.
**Case Law**
*R v Registrar General for Births, Deaths & Marriages, ex parte Crown Prosecution Service* [2002] EWCA Civ 1661
The right to marriage was enshrined in the Human Rights Act 1998 Sch.1 Part I Art.12 and, given that the appellant would have been free to marry if he had been on bail, there was no reason why he should be denied this right. It was further held that public policy considerations did not entitle prison directors to adopt an interventionist role in proceedings as s.27A(3) of the Marriage Act 1949 was enacted only to allow objections to prison marriages on practical and logistical grounds.

*R. (on the application of MA) v Secretary of State for Justice* [2021] EWHC 1266 (Admin)
A prohibition on telephone contact and inter-prison visits between two prisoners who had married in prison while serving sentences of imprisonment for public protection following their convictions for sexual offences was an unnecessary and disproportionate interference with their ECHR art.8(1) rights and therefore unlawful. The restriction on inter-prison visits was also not in accordance with published prison policy and was therefore contrary to public law.

## MEDIA
**See also "Prisoner Communications"; and "Human Rights – Article 10"**
*R (on the application of (1) BBC (2) Dominic Casciani)) (Claimants) v Secretary Of State for Justice (Defendant) & Babar Ahmad* [2012] EWHC 13 (Admin)

See "Prisoner Communications" below.
PSI 37/2010 – Prisoners' Access to the Media
(excerpt below)
Executive summary
1.1 This PSI replaces the guidance previously contained in Prison Service Order 4470 Prisoners' Access to the Media and provides details of the policy on prisoners' requests for access to the media by means of correspondence, telephones calls and face to face interviews by means of a visit. It sets out the exceptional circumstances under which prisoners are allowed access to the media through visits or by telephone as well as the restrictions regarding written correspondence, and provides a process for application and the consideration of applications by Governors and Directors or in the case of face to face interviews, centrally on behalf of the Secretary of State. It also gives advice on the physical conditions under which the visit or telephone conversation should take place.
1.2 Furthermore, the policy on contact via face to face interviews/visits has been relatively unchallenged since the introduction of PSO 4470 in 2005. However, in the light of continuing consideration of obligations under Article 10 (freedom of expression) of the European Convention on Human Rights, the policy needs to be clarified to reflect the fact that there are additional, exceptional circumstances in which face to face interviews may be permitted. There may be circumstances other than an alleged miscarriage of justice in which there is a sufficiently strong public interest in what is being said by the prisoner that requires a face to face interview. For example, if a prisoner alleges torture by a public official. Therefore the guidance on the consideration of applications for face to face interviews has been amended to reflect this.
Desired outcomes
1.3 This instruction will ensure that prison staff, particularly prison Media Liaison Officers, are fully aware of the policy for prisoners' access to the media and in particular the recent amendments to the criteria for consideration and handling of requests for face to face meetings with the media/journalists.
Application
1.4 From the commencement date of this instruction staff, but particularly Media Liaison Officers, must be fully familiar with the contents of this PSI.
Mandatory actions
1.5 Governors must ensure that the procedures set out in this PSI are fully implemented and ensure that staff are fully aware of the recent amendments to the criteria on applications for face to face interviews with journalists. Prisoners

who apply for visits or telephones calls should also be informed about the policy.
Resource Impact
1.6 While there may be an increase in the number of requests for visits by journalists, the impact on resources is likely to be minimal.
**Case Law**
*R (on the application of DSD) v Parole Board of England and Wales* [2018] EWHC 694 (Admin)
The Parole Board Rules 2016 r.25(1), which prohibited making information public about Parole Board proceedings, was too broad and was ultra vires the rule-making power set out in the Criminal Justice Act 2003 Pt 12 s.239(5). The Board's decision directing the release of a Category A prisoner serving an indeterminate sentence was irrational, as it should have undertaken further inquiry into the circumstances of his offending, and in particular the fact that he had admitted only to the 12 sexual offences of which he had been convicted, when there were references in the dossier to "80+ potential victims" and a key issue leading to the release decision was his openness and honesty. The further inquiry would have allowed the Board to test his account.
*R (on the application of Pearce) v Parole Board of England and Wales* [2022] EWCA Civ 4-14 Jan 2022
In an appeal against a decision upholding the Parole Board's refusal to direct a prisoner's release from prison, the Court of Appeal found that Guidance, issued by the Board in 2019 to advise its panel members regarding the consideration of unproven allegations when assessing the risks posed by a prisoner eligible for parole, was unlawful. Amendments made to the Guidance in 2021 did not rectify that error. However, the appeal would be dismissed on its merits as the judge's analysis of the Board's decision had proceeded on a different footing and was unassailable.

*Rizvi v Parole Board for England and Wales* [2020] EWHC 3877 (Admin)
In circumstances where the Parole Board had recommended moving a prisoner to open conditions, the court refused to grant permission to apply for judicial review to consider whether the Parole Board Rules 2019 r.27, which required disclosure of summary reasons only, contravened the principle of open justice. The matter had become academic and there was no good reason, in the public interest, for the court to decide the matter.

*R. (on the application of Morris) v Parole Board* [2020] EWHC 711 (Admin)
The Parole Board's refusal to direct a prisoner's release was not procedurally unfair where it had

considered unproven allegations made against the prisoner in its assessment of risk. Unproven allegations made against prisoners should be considered by the Parole Board where there was a sufficient evidential basis to allow the Board to decide that the allegations had some factual basis and make at least some findings of fact.

*R (M) v Parole Board* [2013] EWHC 1360 (Admin) The public interest in allowing media organisations to publish reports on an application by a life prisoner for judicial review of an adverse decision of the Parole Board outweighed the prisoner's rights under Articles 2, 3, 5 and 8 of the European Convention on Human Rights, with the result that a reporting restrictions order should be discharged.

*R (SF) v Secretary of State for Justice* [2013] EWCA Civ 1275 The court would only agree to a derogation from the general principle of open justice if there was clear and cogent evidence which established that such a derogation was strictly necessary in the interests of justice. The fact that the press might start a media campaign which would affect an offender's resettlement into his community could not be a general justification for banning reporting about the offender and his possible release generally.

*R (SF) v Secretary of State for Justice* [2013] EWHC 1649 (Admin) An interlocutory application for anonymity and reporting restrictions was refused pending substantive judicial review proceedings on the resettlement of a Scottish offender.

*Hirst v Secretary of State for the Home Department* [2002] EWHC 602 (Admin) A policy that denied a prisoner the right to contact the media by telephone whenever his purpose was to comment on matters of legitimate public interest was unlawful. In a democratic society, prisoners should not be wholly prevented from expressing their views to the media about matters affecting them.

*R v Secretary of State for the Home Department, Ex Parte Ian Simms : R V Same, Ex Parte Michael O'Brien* (2000) 2 AC 115; (1999) 3 WLR 328; (1999) 3 All ER 400 A convicted prisoner had a fundamental and basic right to communicate orally with the media through a journalist, in order to challenge the safety of his conviction, and the policy of the Secretary of State for the Home Department made under paragraph 37 and paragraph 37A of Section A of Prison Service Standing Order 5

was unlawful to the event that it interfered with that right.

## MEDICAL ATTENTION & TREATMENT
### See also "Health Services for Prisoners".
PSI 38/2002 – Guidance on Consent to Medical Treatment
Accompanied by Information & Practice 03/2002 "Guidance on consent to medical treatment"
PSI 46/2003 – Medical Treatment of Prison Staff by Healthcare Workers 3000
YOI 27-29
PR 20-22
20 — Health services
(1) The governor must work in partnership with local health care providers to secure the provision to prisoners of access to the same quality and range of services as the general public receives from the National Health Service.
(2) Every request by a prisoner to see a health care professional shall be recorded by the officer to whom it was made and promptly communicated to a health care professional.
(3) If an unconvicted prisoner desires the attendance of a named registered medical practitioner or dentist other than one already working in the prison, and will pay any expense incurred, the governor must, if satisfied that there are reasonable grounds for the request and unless the Secretary of State otherwise directs, allow the prisoner to be visited and treated by that practitioner or dentist, in consultation with a registered medical practitioner who works in the prison.
(4) Subject to any directions given in the particular case by the Secretary of State, a registered medical practitioner selected by or on behalf of a prisoner who is a party to any legal proceedings must be afforded reasonable facilities for examining the prisoner in connection with the proceedings, and may do so out of hearing but in the sight of an officer
(5) A prisoner may correspond, in accordance with arrangements made by the Secretary of State for the confidential handling of correspondence, with a registered medical practitioner who has treated the prisoner for a life threatening condition, and such correspondence may not be opened, read or stopped unless the governor has reasonable cause to believe its contents do not relate to the treatment of that condition.
The same provisions are mirrored in the equivalent YOI Rules.
### Case Law
*Razumas v Ministry of Justice* [2018] EWHC 215 QB The claimant prisoner (R) brought an action for clinical negligence against the Defendant for failures in his medical care during his time in

custody which ultimately led to the amputation of his left leg above the knee. In arguing the Defendant was responsible for the negligence, R submitted that the Defendant held significant responsibility for prisoners' welfare and well-being (including healthcare), for integrating health care management within overall prison and prisoner management and for securing prisoner access to healthcare. Whilst primary healthcare services for prisoners are commissioned by the Department of Health, R argued that the overall duty of care remained with the Defendant (Partnership Agreement of 2007). The Defendant accepted responsibility for the operation of the prison but not for the delivery of healthcare which was provided by the Primary Care Trust (PCT). The Defendant submitted that whilst it had a statutory duty to cooperate with the NHS, and with the PCT, that duty did not give either party control over, or responsibility for, the other's operations and the manner in which they delivered the required services to prisoners. R had developed a lump on his left calf following a fall at HMP Pentonville in 2010. Despite attending a number of hospital appointments, the lump was not diagnosed as cancerous until 2013, by which time such delays had left open the only treatment of amputation of his left leg. In the period 2010 to 2013 R had been in and out of prison, and been incarcerated in a number of different prisons. Communications about his medical appointments had been poor and the cause of many delays in R accessing treatment. R claimed this amounted to institutional and systematic failures by the Defendant that had denied him access to appropriate secondary healthcare, in particular, failing to inform R of hospital appointments and failure in the duty to enable his attendance at hospital appointments. R submitted that the successive failures to provide medical assistance for treatment of his sarcoma amounted to degrading treatment under Article 3 European Convention on Human Rights and Fundamental Freedoms (ECHR). The Court held that the test under Article 3 required a 'minimum level of severity' if it is to fall within 'inhuman and degrading treatment' following Kudla v Poland (2002) 35 EHRR 11 and Grant and Gleaves v The Ministry of Justice [2011] EWHC 3379 QB. The Defendant submitted that the matters complained of did not amount to a violation of Article 3 having regard to the minimum severity threshold; i) there was no intention to humiliate or debase Mr Razumas ii) there was no deliberate infliction of selfharm or suffering iii) R had access to a complaints system and used it iv) R also received medical treatment including pain relief, physiotherapy and treatment in the community v) there was no continuous failure because R was at liberty for significant periods; and when at liberty R could himself have sought treatment vi) The allegations were of a negligent failure to diagnose. There was no suggestion of gross negligence. The negligent failure did not reach the very high threshold for even an arguable breach of Article 3. The Court held that there were many occasions of negligence but it did not amount to gross negligence. There had not been a denial of treatment and R had neglected to take opportunities open to him to seek medical attention when he was at liberty. There was no breach of Article 3. The Court ruled therefore that R's claim failed.

*Cojanu v Essex Partnership University NHS Trust* [2022] EWHC 197 (QB)
In a clinical negligence claim brought by a remand prisoner, the recorder had erred in finding that the prisoner had been fundamentally dishonest about the cause of his injury. He had also erred in misdirecting his criticism of errors made by the prisoner's lawyers and making findings of dishonesty against the prisoner in relation to quantum. However, the recorder had not erred in dismissing the defendant's argument that the claim should be barred by reason of the prisoner's criminality.

*Ministry of Justice v Cheryl Carter* [2010] EWCA Civ 694
The appellant Ministry appealed against a decision ([(2010] EWHC 60 (QB)) that a prison doctor was negligent in failing to refer the respondent (C) to a breast cancer specialist. The lower Court had held that the failure, by a prison's medical officer, to take a prisoner's medical history at a consultation amounted to a breach of duty and was negligent in light of the prisoner's previous complaints about a breast lump and prior consultations with other medical officers. The Appeal Court held that though CC had visited three prison doctors complaining of a lump in her breast but had not been referred to a specialist, the judge had been wrong to find that the failure of the third prison doctor to take a medical history and to refer her to a specialist amounted to a breach of duty.

*R (on the application of SP) v Secretary of State for Justice* [2010] EWCA Civ 1590
The Secretary of State was not under any obligation to consider and investigate whether a patient would object to treatment where nothing in the registered medical practitioners' reports suggested that it was a live issue when making a transfer direction under s.47 of the Mental Health Act 1983

*Re W (Adult: Refusal of Treatment)* [2002] EWHC 901 (Fam)

A secure prisoner with mental capacity had the right to refuse treatment to a self-inflicted wound that was potentially life threatening. Held: The legal position was that a mentally-competent patient had an absolute right to refuse to consent to medical treatment for any reason, rational or irrational or for no reason at all, even where the decision could lead to his or her own death (In Re MB (Medical Treatment) (1997) 2 FLR 426 and Miss B v An NHS Hospital Trust) (2002) EWHC 429 (Fam) considered). (2) A person lacked capacity if some impermanent or disturbance of mental functionary rendered the person unable to make a decision whether to consent to or to refuse treatment. That inability to make a decision would occur when (a) the person was unable to comprehend and retain information which was material to the decision, especially as to the likely consequences of having or not having the treatment in question and (b) if the patient was unable to use the information and to weigh it in the balance as part of the process of arriving at a decision (as per In Re C (Adult : Refusal of Treatment) (1994) 1 WLR 290). (3) As all three psychiatrists agreed that W had mental capacity the evidence was overwhelming. There was no evidence of any substance to place in the balance against that evidence. In those circumstances the court was satisfied that W had mental capacity to choose to refuse or accept treatment at any stage, and that he had the mental capacity to refuse treatment in the future and to refuse resuscitation in the future, even if at that stage he was not in a mental capacity to make that decision.

**MENTAL HEALTH**

Generic Parole Process Policy Framework, Sections 3.12, 5.6.14 and 5.12 (excerpt below).

This Policy Framework replaced PSI 22/2015 (revised) – Generic Parole Process for Indeterminate and Determinate Sentenced Prisoners

5.12 Mental Health Cases

5.12.1 Prisoners transferred under the provisions of the Mental Health Act 1983 (MHA) do not have a right of access to the Parole Board for as long as they are deemed to require inpatient hospital treatment. While time spent in hospital counts towards the sentence for tariff purposes, in the event that a prisoner is transferred to hospital during any part of the parole review process, that review will be suspended until the remission of the prisoner to prison custody. While detained in hospital, the Secretary of State's functions under the MHA, including consideration of their discharge from hospital, come under the responsibility of the Mental Health Casework Section (MHCS) in the Public Protection Group of HMPPS.

5.12.2 Prisoners may be transferred to hospital either immediately by the trial judge when passing sentence (under s.45A of the MHA), or by order of the Secretary of State at any point during the sentence (under s.47/49 of the MHA).

5.12.3 The power to send a prisoner to hospital under either s.45A or s.47/49 may be exercised where there is evidence from two registered medical practitioners that:

• the prisoner is suffering from a mental disorder;

• detention in hospital for treatment is appropriate; and

• that appropriate treatment is available for them in hospital

5.12.4 A prisoner's suitability to remain in hospital detained under MHA is subject to regular reviews by the 'First Tier Tribunal – Health, Education and Social Care Chamber' ('the Tribunal'). Transferred prisoners may apply to the Tribunal during the second six months of their time in hospital and once in any period of 12 months thereafter. MHCS will automatically refer a restricted patient to the Tribunal after any three-year period during which the patient has been continuously detained in hospital and has not had his or her case considered by the Tribunal.

5.12.5 Where a hospital direction (with a limitation direction) or transfer direction (with a restriction direction) has been made, if the Secretary of State is notified by the responsible clinician or other approved clinician that the prisoner no longer requires treatment in hospital for mental disorder or that no effective treatment can be given, the Secretary of State may remit the prisoner back to prison under s.50 of the MHA.

5.12.6 The Tribunal cannot order the discharge of a transfer direction (with a restriction direction) or hospital direction (with a limitation direction) prisoner without the prior agreement of the Secretary of State. Once the prisoner no longer needs treatment, the Tribunal will either recommend they are discharged, and if the Secretary of State does not agree to discharge they will be remitted to prison or, if the Tribunal recommends a conditional discharge but considers that returning to prison might compromise the prisoner's mental Tribunal can recommend the prisoner remains in hospital until they can be released on licence. This is known as a section 74(1)(b) recommendation.

5.12.7 If the COM is not local to the hospital then a social worker in the hospital may agree to serve the licence but the COM is responsible for this.

Early Release on Compassionate Grounds Policy Framework (May 2022) paragraph 4.5

4.5 Prisoners who are subject to sentences of imprisonment and who have been detained in hospital are managed, on behalf of the Secretary of State, by the Mental Health Casework Section (MHCS). There are three primary scenarios that can arise where a prisoner will be subject to a sentence of imprisonment whilst they remain detained in a psychiatric hospital under the Mental Health Act 1983 (the 1983 Act):

i. A prisoner is transferred to and detained in a hospital when serving the sentence (Sections 47/49 of the 1983 Act).

ii. A prisoner was directed to hospital by a court for treatment of a mental disorder alongside a prison sentence under a hospital and limitation direction (section 45A of the 1983 Act).

iii. A prisoner who has committed an offence which has led to a sentence of imprisonment when they were already subject to a hospital and restriction order (sections 37/41 of the 1983 Act). In such cases the prisoner may have acquired the sentence whilst detained in hospital or when discharged into the community under the 37/41 hospital order.

PSI 50/2007 – Transfer of Prisoners to and from Hospital under Sections 47 and 48 of the Mental Health Act 1983 (amended by PSI 62/2011).

PSI 62/2011 – Procedure for the Transfer From Custody of Children and Young People to and from Hospital Under the Mental Health Act 1983 in England.

**Case Law**

*R. v Lall (Gurjeet)* [2021] EWCA Crim 404
A hospital order and a restriction order imposed pursuant to the Mental Health Act 1983 s.37 and s.41 on an offender who had been convicted of manslaughter by reason of diminished responsibility was not unduly lenient. The offender had paranoid schizophrenia and was unlikely to have committed the offence had he not stopped complying with his prescribed medication regime, and the medical experts agreed that a s.37/s.41 order was the most appropriate disposal.

*R. v Reynolds* [2021] EWCA Crim 10
A judge had not erred in imposing a sentence of imprisonment, with hospital and limitation directions under the Mental Health Act 1983 s.45A, where an offender had pleaded guilty to 15 child sex offences. The offender's mental disorders played a part in his offending, but could not entirely excuse or explain it so as to provide a defence. The dreadful nature of the offences and the offender's high degree of culpability for them meant that punishment, in the form of imprisonment, was necessary, rather than a hospital order under s.37.

*R. v Steele (James)* [2020] EWCA Crim 1694
A sentence of six years and eight months' imprisonment imposed on an offender following his guilty plea to aggravated burglary was manifestly excessive in light of his mental health problems and alcohol dependency syndrome, as well as his age and previous good character. A sentence of five years and four months' imprisonment was appropriate.

*R. v Nelson (Keith)* [2020] EWCA Crim 1615
The court considered the advantages and disadvantages of a hybrid order under the Mental Health Act 1983 s.45A combining imprisonment with a hospital direction and limitation direction, on the one hand, and a hospital and restriction order under s.37, with s.41, on the other. In the case of a violent offender who would always suffer from some form of mental disorder, but who had responded well to treatment and supervision in hospital, the order that would best protect the public and assist in his recovery was a hospital and restriction order.

*R. v Sowerby (Lee)* [2020] EWCA Crim 898
A sentence of life imprisonment with a minimum term of 11 years, together with a hospital and limitation direction pursuant to the Mental Health Act 1983 s.45A, imposed on a paranoid schizophrenic offender following his guilty plea to the manslaughter of his mother on the grounds of diminished responsibility was not wrong in principle or manifestly excessive. Despite the offender's illness, he retained a high level of responsibility for the offence and a s.37 hospital order with an indefinite restriction order under s.41 would not necessarily offer greater protection to the public.

*R. v Westwood (Thomas)* [2020] EWCA Crim 598; [2020] 5 WLUK 22
Where an offender had pleaded guilty to manslaughter by reason of diminished responsibility, a judge had erred in assessing his "retained responsibility" as medium to high under the sentencing guideline. Although the judge concluded that the offending was caused by the offender's anger, the psychiatric evidence clearly indicated that the most significant factor was his mental illness and that his anger at the time of the offence was not extraneous to his mental illness, but a manifestation of it. The offender's retained responsibility was low, and it was appropriate to impose a hospital order under the Mental Health Act 1983 s.37 and a restriction order under s.41.

*Rendell, R v* [2019] EWCA Crim 621
The Appellant appealed against a sentence of imprisonment for public protection imposed in

2012 following his guilty plea to wounding with intent. At the time of sentence there was no psychiatric evidence before the court. The judge found the appellant to be dangerous. While in custody between 2012 and 2015 the appellant had contact with various mental health professionals, the consensus being that he suffered from an emotionally unstable and dissocial personality disorder. In 2015, at the end of his minimum term, the appellant was transferred to a mental health centre pursuant to transfer and restriction directions under the Mental Health Act 1983 s.47 and s.49. Unlike the sentencing judge, the Court of Appeal had the advantage not only of full medical reports but of evidence of the results of the treatment to date and a future prognosis. There was evidence of the appellant's changed behaviour and his motivation and ability to maintain improvement. The instant offence was a serious one involving moderate culpability, but the appellant had been detained for twice the minimum term ordered, the equivalent of a 12-year sentence. In the unusual circumstances, the appropriate sentence was the imposition of orders under s.37 and s.41. The sentence of imprisonment for public protection was therefore quashed.

*Edwards, R v* [2018] EWCA Crim 595
Four cases were listed before the court to consider issues arising from the sentencing of mentally ill offenders to indeterminate terms of imprisonment. In each case the offenders were said to have been mentally ill at the time of the offences and it was argued that orders should have been made pursuant to ss.37 and 41 of the Mental Health Act 1983. The Court summarised the principles to assist those representing and sentencing offenders with mental health problems that may justify a hospital order, a finding of dangerousness and/or a s.45A order: i. The first step is to consider whether a hospital order may be appropriate; ii. If so, the judge should then consider all his sentencing options including a s.45A order; iii. In deciding on the most suitable disposal the judge should remind him or herself of the importance of the penal element in a sentence; iv. To decide whether a penal element to the sentence is necessary the judge should assess (as best he or she can) the offender's culpability and the selfharm caused by the offence. The fact that an offender would not have committed the offence but for their mental illness does not necessarily relieve them of all responsibility for their actions; v. A failure to take prescribed medication is not necessarily a culpable omission; it may be attributable in whole or in part to the offender's mental illness; vi. If the judge decides to impose a hospital order

under s.37/41, he or she must explain why a penal element is not appropriate; vii. The regimes on release of an offender on licence from a s.45A order and for an offender subject to s.37/41 orders are different but the latter do not necessarily offer a greater protection to the public, as may have been assumed in Ahmed and/or by the parties in the cases before us. Each case turns on its own facts.; viii. If an offender wishes to call fresh psychiatric evidence in his appeal against sentence to support a challenge to a hospital order, a finding of dangerousness or a s45A order he or she should lodge a s.23 application. If the evidence is the same as was called before the sentencing judge the court is unlikely to receive it; ix. Grounds of appeal should identify with care each of the grounds the offender wishes to advance. If an applicant or appellant wishes to add grounds not considered by the single judge an application to vary should be made. Each appeal was decided as follows.

*R v Ahmed* [2016] EWCA Crim 670
The Appellant was convicted of manslaughter on the grounds of diminished responsibility. he psychiatric evidence at trial was that X was suffering from a severe depressive episode with psychotic symptoms, but that his condition was not of such a nature or degree for him to be detained under the Mental Health Act 1983. The judge found X to be dangerous and imposed the life sentence with a minimum term of three-and-a-half years. In 2011, while in prison, X attacked another prisoner and, following almost a year in hospital under s.47 and s.49 of the 1983 Act, pleaded guilty to wounding contrary to the Offences Against the Person Act 1861 s.20. A hospital order under s.37 and a restriction order under s.41 of the 1983 Act were imposed. The fresh evidence consisted of psychiatric assessments dating from 2012 to 2015. One of the psychiatrists who gave evidence at trial had revisited his 2006 opinion and diagnosis, concluding that X suffered from schizo-affective disorder.

Since receiving appropriate treatment he had not offended, been disruptive or anti-social. Confinement and supervision in hospital, rather than prison, was the context for the change and improvement, and provided effective control of his disorder. That did not mean that he bore no responsibility for the killing, his responsibility was diminished, not eliminated, but meant that his mental health would be the fundamental issue when his release was considered by the Parole Board or the First-tier Tribunal. X's illness was life-long. The seriousness of the 2005 and 2011 offences demonstrated that when his illness was untreated he was very dangerous. Comparing the supervision regimes for release on life licence and conditional discharge under a restriction order, public safety could be better secured on X's eventual release under a restriction order.

*R v Cleland (Cameron John)* [2020] EWCA Crim 906
A sentence of life detention for attempted murder imposed on a young offender was quashed and replaced with hospital and restriction order under the Mental Health Act 1983 s.37 and s.41. The appeal court admitted fresh evidence that, at the time of the offence, the offender had been suffering from autistic spectrum disorder which was linked to the offence and which reduced his culpability.

*R v Vowles* [2015] EWCA Crim 45
Six appellants (V, B, C, O, D, M) appealed against sentence to the Court of Appeal (Criminal Division) under the Criminal Appeal Act 1968 s.23, and V appealed to the Civil Division after dismissal of her claim for judicial review (*R. (on the application of LV) v Secretary of State for Justice* [2014] EWHC 1495 (Admin), [2015] M.H.L.R. 29). The six appellants had all received indeterminate sentences specifying a minimum term. They had sought hospital orders under the Mental Health Act 1983 s.37 as amended, with a restriction under s.41. Those orders were not made and the appellants were sent to hospital under a s.47 transfer direction by the secretary of state. Consequently, decisions for their release fell to be made by the Parole Board, and their post-release regimes fell under the applicable licence provisions and the Probation Service.
Holding that a judge should consider, where the conditions in s.37(2)(a) were met, what was the appropriate disposal, and should include the extent to which treatment was needed for the mental disorder, the extent to which the offending was attributable to it, the extent to which punishment was required, and the protection of the public including the regime for deciding release and the regime post-release. There must always be sound reasons for departing from the usual course of imposing a penal sentence. The court should consider matters in the following order: whether the disorder could appropriately be dealt with by a hospital and limitation direction under s.45A and if so it should make one; if that direction was inappropriate and if the evidence satisfied s.37(2)(a), whether the conditions in s.37(2)(b) would make that the best method of disposal. It was essential that all factors under s.37(2)(b) were considered, and whether other methods of disposal were available and appropriate, including a s.47 transfer. If the court decided on a hospital order, the judge should think carefully

before making a s.38 interim order, as it would give no closure until the final order.
In Edwards (E) the appellant had a long history of mental illness and suffered from paranoid schizophrenia. She killed her elderly mother. Dr Dodge, a consultant forensic psychiatrist, who was the appellant's treating clinician said there was a clear and significant link between periods of illness and her offending; but for her mental illness her offending would not have occurred. The sentencing judge accepted that the appellant's acts were entirely attributable to her psychotic condition. He concluded that there was a definite risk of serious selfharm in the future and that the appropriate course was to pass a sentence of life imprisonment coupled with a s.45A order with a limitation direction. The judge imposed a term of life imprisonment with a minimum term of 10 years and a hospital and limitation direction under s.45A of MHA. Whilst the Court of Appeal found no basis to criticize the sentencing judge, it allowed E's appeal in part by reducing the minimum term to 5 years on the grounds that her culpability was between low and moderate, as she would not have killed but for her mental illness and her chaotic compliance with her medication was due in some measure to her illness.
In Knapper (K) the appellant had pleaded guilty to manslaughter by reason of diminished responsibility and sentenced to life imprisonment with a minimum term of 4 years and 172 days. It was further ordered that the appellant be subject to a hospital order under s.45A, including a limitation direction equivalent to that under s.41. Three forensic consultant psychiatrists agreed that at the time of the killing the appellant was suffering from paranoid schizophrenia which substantially impaired his ability to make rational judgments and exercise self-control. In considering culpability, the sentencing judge noted that there had been previous episodes of mental illness diagnosed as paranoid schizophrenia in which K knew that his condition had affected his behaviour but nonetheless the appellant had chosen to discontinue the medication that controlled his condition in March 2015 because he considered it affected his weight. Shortly beforehand he had failed to attend a doctor's appointment arranged by a care co-ordinator because of her concerns. The judge concluded that whilst his culpability was reduced by the mental illness to a large extent, K remained criminally responsible to a 'moderate' degree. The judge was satisfied that the appellant was a dangerous offender, particularly taking account of a history of non-compliance with medication. This was not a case where, once treated, the offender would cease to be a danger to the public; nor was it a case where

the offending was entirely due to the mental disorder without any culpability. For these reasons, an order under ss.37 and 41 was not appropriate. There was cause for a punitive element and measures which would effectively protect the public. The Court of Appeal held that the sentencing judge had placed K's culpability at too high a level, as his responsibility for his actions was not only substantially diminished, it was low. In allowing K's appeal the s.45A order was quashed and substituted for a hospital order under s.37 with a s. 41 restriction.

In Langley (L) the appellant was sentenced to concurrent terms of imprisonment for public protection (IPP) in respect of offences of making threats to kill with a minimum term of 1 year less 113 days spent on remand (252 days). L appealed on the grounds that a sentence of IPP was wrong in principle and that the appropriate disposal was a hospital order under section 37 of the MHA coupled with a restriction order under section 41. In allowing L's appeal, the Court of Appeal held that had the sentencing judge been aware of the L's mental disorder he would have imposed a hospital order under s.37 with a s.41 restriction. L had already served a very substantial penal element, far longer than the minimum term imposed. It was agreed that his culpability should be assessed as low. The IPP was quashed and a s37 order with a s.41 restriction imposed.

In Payne (P) the appellant was sentenced to current terms of life imprisonment for two counts of attempted murder with a minimum term of 14 years less the number of days spent on remand. He directed further that pursuant to section 45A MHA the applicant should be detained at a hospital, namely Broadmoor, and that he should be subject to the restrictions imposed by section 41. Two forensic psychiatrists gave oral evidence at the sentencing hearing with differing views. The sentencing judge had preferred the evidence of one Dr Joseph. The Court of Appeal held that the judge was entitled to prefer Dr Joseph's evidence and his opinion that P's culpability was high and to decide that the most appropriate method of disposal was a life sentence with a s.45A order. Leave to appeal was refused.

*R. v Miller (Barbara Carol)* [2021] EWCA Crim 1955
A sentence of life imprisonment imposed in 1988 on an offender following her guilty plea to manslaughter on the grounds of diminished responsibility was quashed and replaced with hospital and restriction orders. The offender, who had served more than the minimum term of her sentence, suffered from a mental disorder and fresh medical evidence established that she

had suffered from the disorder at the time of the offence and that the disorder was treatable. Recall under a restriction order would result in a return to hospital and immediate treatment, whereas release under licence carried the possibility of a recall to prison which would likely adversely affect her mental health.

*R (T) v Secretary of State for Justice* [2013] EWHC 1119 (Admin)
See "Childcare" above.

*Timothy Coombs v (1) Dorset NHS Primary Care Trust (2) Nottinghamshire Healthcare NHS Trust* [2013] EWCA Civ 471
There was nothing inherent in the Mental Health Act 1983, the National Health Service Act 2006, or by way of public policy to exclude absolutely the possibility of detained patients or their families paying for, or contributing to, the cost of their treatment or care. However, such care or treatment could not be in conflict with the recommendations of the responsible clinician.
*R (on the application of DK) v Secretary of State for Justice* [2010] EWHC 82 (Admin)
The claimant (D) applied for judicial review of a decision of the defendant secretary of state to authorise his transfer from prison to hospital. The Court held that where medical practitioners had failed to explicitly consider whether, if transferred from prison to a hospital under the Mental Health Act 1983 s.47, a prisoner could receive treatment which was likely to alleviate or prevent deterioration of his mental disorder, the secretary of state's decision to transfer him had to be quashed.

*R (on the application of P) v Secretary of State for Justice* [2010] EWHC 1124 (Admin)
The claimant (P) applied for a judicial review of a decision of the defendant secretary of state authorising his transfer from prison to a secure hospital. The Court held that the decision of the Secretary of State for Justice to direct the transfer of P from a prison to a secure hospital pursuant to the Mental Health Act 1983 s.47 was lawful. He could properly infer that appropriate treatment for P's mental disorder was available at the hospital despite that not being explicitly stated in a medical report.

*Home Office v Robert Butchart* [2006] EWCA Civ 239
Where the Home Office knew or ought to have known that a remand prisoner was vulnerable to psychiatric selfharm the duty of care that was owed to that prisoner by the Home Office included a duty to take reasonable steps to minimise the risk of psychiatric selfharm.

*R (on the application of D) v (1) Secretary of State for the Home Department (2) The National Assembly for Wales* [2004] EWHC 2857 (Admin)
Where a young offender in Wales suffered from a delay in finding a suitable secure hospital placement, the Secretary of State for the home Department and the National Assembly for Wales did not infringe the offender's rights under the European Convention on Human Rights 1950 where the delay arose from difficulties in satisfying the conditions for the exercise of the power under the Mental Health Act 1983 s.47, especially if diagnosis was uncertain and there were few places available.

*R (on the application of Abdul Miah) v Secretary of State for the Home Department* [2004] EWHC 2569 (Admin)
A prisoner's sentence and accordingly any power to impose licence conditions continued to run notwithstanding his transfer to hospital under the Mental Health Act 1983 s.47. Held: A prisoner's sentence and accordingly any power to impose licence conditions continued to run notwithstanding a transfer to hospital under s.47 of the Act. That conclusion was manifestly correct and was consistent with a concession to that effect in a case where a restriction direction had been made (*R v Secretary of State for the Home Department, ex parte T, ex parte H & Ors, ex parte Hickey (No1)* (1995) 1 WLR 830) applied). Moreover, the secretary of state's policy was that restriction directions were ordinarily imposed for the protection of the public and that was consistent with the approach that a transfer under s.47 of the Act did not affect a prisoner's sentence. In any event, it was clear that in M's case the need for licence conditions to exist had been demonstrated.

*R (on the application of S) v Secretary of State for the Home Department* [2002] EWHC 2424 (Admin)
The decision of the Secretary of State for the Home Department to revoke the licence of the claimant, who had absconded from hospital, and to recall him to prison was flawed by the failure to take into account the views of treating clinicians at the hospital.

*Keenan v United Kingdom (27229/95)* (2001) 33 EHRR 38
Mark Keenan's medical history included paranoia, aggression, violence and self-selfharm. A diagnosis of borderline personality disorder and paranoid schizophrenia was made. Whilst in prison following an assault on his girlfriend he barricaded himself in a healthcare centre protesting against a transfer to another prison. Following an adjudication hearing on 15th April 1993 a suspended punishment of 14 additional days was imposed. On 30th April he assaulted two prison officers, one seriously. On 1st May 1993 he was assessed by a medical officer with 6 months psychiatric training as an SHO, as being fit for segregation in the punishment block under Prison Rule 43. The Court held 'the lack of effective monitoring of Mark Keenan's condition and the lack of informed psychiatric input into his assessment and treatment disclosed significant defects in the medical care for a mentally ill person known to be a suicide risk. The belated imposition on him in those circumstances of a serious disciplinary punishment – 7 days segregation in the punishment block and an additional 28 days to his sentence imposed 2 weeks after the event and only 9 days before his expected date of release – which may well have threatened his physical and moral resistance, is not compatible with the standard of treatment required in respect of a mentally ill person. It must be regarded as constituting inhuman and degrading treatment and punishment with the meaning of Article 3 of the Convention. Accordingly the Court finds a violation of this provision.' There was also a breach of Article 13.

*R. (on the application of Morahan) v HM Assistant Coroner for West London* [2021] EWHC 1603 (Admin)
A coroner had not erred in deciding not to conduct an inquest which fulfilled the enhanced investigative duty required by ECHR art.2 following the death of a voluntary in-patient of a psychiatric hospital. The circumstances of the death did not automatically trigger such a duty. An NHS Trust had also not assumed responsibility for the patient and no operational duty had arisen as there had been no real or immediate risk of which the Trust should have been aware. As of June 2022, the appeal is still outstanding.

## MOTHER & BABY UNITS
Mother and Baby Units are provided in selected women's establishments to enable the mother/baby relationship to develop whilst safeguarding and promoting the child's welfare. The "best interests" of the child is the primary consideration in both policy making and individual cases.
Prison Rules 12: Women prisoners
12(1)
Women prisoners shall normally be kept separate from male prisoners.
12(2)
The Secretary of State may, subject to any conditions he thinks fit, permit a woman prisoner to have her baby with her in prison, and everything necessary for the baby's maintenance and care may be provided there.

PSI 49/2014 has now this has now been replaced by the Pregnancy, Mother and Baby Units (MBUs), and Maternal Separation from Children up to the Age of Two in Women's Prisons Policy Framework (excerpts below)

Paragraph 1.1

The Female Offender Strategy makes clear that we want fewer women serving short sentences in custody and more being managed in the community. However, for women whose offences result in a custodial sentence, including pregnant women and women with young children, it is important that the appropriate support is provided.

Paragraph 1.3

This Policy Framework directly addresses the specific and additional needs associated with pregnancy, birth, the post-natal period and stillbirth or neonatal death within 26 weeks of birth, which are protected from discrimination under the Equality Act due to the protected characteristic of pregnancy and maternity. Any discrimination of a woman because of her pregnancy or maternity outside the protected period set out in the Equality Act would be considered sex discrimination. Parental separation is a gender-neutral experience that requires consideration in relation to both men's and women's prisons. However, it is disproportionately experienced by women and therefore considered here within the context of sex discrimination against women.

Paragraph 1.4

This policy and the adjoining guidance are based on the principle of individual needs led support. 'Woman' and 'mother' are used to ensure the three cohorts addressed are easily distinguishable for readers, when being referenced. However, this policy applies to all individuals within the three cohorts who are accommodated in women's prisons, regardless of gender identity or intersex status. This includes all individuals who self-identify as transgender (trans), non-binary, or any other non-cisgender (non-cis) identity. It is essential that staff working with individuals to which this policy applies ensure no assumptions, bias or stereotyping that can result in misgendering or any other type of discrimination. For more information on supporting individuals who identify as transgender, staff can reference the Care and Management of Individuals Who are Transgender Policy Framework.

Paragraph 2.1

This Policy Framework is for Her Majesty's Prison and Probation Service (HMPPS) staff only and does not mandate actions for healthcare practitioners. It is not the role of HMPPS to provide healthcare, as this is commissioned through the health sector. The role of HMPPS is to ensure appropriate access to healthcare – including information sharing and physical access. This expectation underpins all requirements within this Framework that reference healthcare responsibilities and processes.

Paragraph 8 – Overarching Requirements

All women's prisons must appoint an operational Band 3 Pregnancy and Mother and Baby Unit Liaison Officer (PMBLO) and deputies as appropriate, who acts as a point of contact and information for women, and the liaison between them and the multidisciplinary teams and agencies supporting them. The nature of the role should be responsive to the population within each prison, and also wider supportive provisions such as family engagement workers with whom the PMBLO's role should be co-ordinated. For example, local prisons are likely to accommodate higher numbers of pregnant women so might have a greater demand for support with Mother and Baby Unit applications PMBLOs or deputy PMBLOs are required to arrange introductory meetings with women in these cohorts on reception or following identification, in order to share information on support services available, including MBU provision where a woman might be eligible. This must take place as soon as is practically possible, within a maximum of 5 calendar days following arrival or identification and followed up as appropriate. PMBLOs should consult with other prison departments, outside agencies and organisations as appropriate, to ensure the relevant follow up support can be provided.

All Pregnancy and Mother and Baby Liaison Officers, their deputy/deputies, and all MBU staff members are required to attend the 'caring for perinatal women in prison' training and these staff must complete refresher training every 3 years. A sufficient number of staff in each prison must be trained to meet demand and to provide continuity, proportionate to the needs of the prison population. The appropriate gender balance must be fulfilled where operationally viable, for decency reasons.

All prisons are required to have processes in place locally to identify and monitor women in all 3 cohorts. Data must be self-declared and processed only when consent has been given using the consent forms at Annexes B and C. Following identification data must be monitored as a matter of routine, in order to ensure women can access the relevant supportive provisions. Data collection must include monitoring of groups with protected characteristics, to ensure any specific needs or vulnerabilities relating to individuals are considered in the care they receive. If data evidences disproportionate outcomes for specific groups these must be considered, and action taken to mitigate discrimination and ensure that processes and provisions are inclusive and recognise the diverse needs of women in these cohorts.

Prisons must have a process in place to ensure that the care and safeguarding of all perinatal women (pre-birth and up to one year after birth) is considered by a multi-disciplinary team, with a review at least fortnightly. Care planning must take account of individual needs, vulnerabilities and risks, with consideration of factors such as historic trauma, mental and physical health, race, age (both young women and older women), religious and cultural needs and any other protected characteristics. Care planning teams must ensure that they routinely engage with Health, Children's Services and any other relevant agencies as part of this process, including other case management systems that might relate to the individual and impact on their pregnancy or parenting support. For example, Local Case Boards for individuals who are transgender or non-binary and for whom specific support might be required. Prisons must use the consent forms at Annex B to gain consent to share data with other agencies, and only share data without consent where there is a clear rationale for doing so, such as a safeguarding risk.

Prisons must record and where appropriate refer child safeguarding data relating to unborn children or born children on MBUs in consultation with other agencies such as Children's Services and the Police as appropriate. Where there is a suspected risk to an unborn baby this should be immediately reported via a safeguarding referral to Children's Services and a Mercury Intelligence Report (MIR). It should also be verbally communicated to a Duty Manager for consideration.

Pregnant women and mothers on MBUs must be able to store their Personal Child Healthcare Record (PCHR) - sometimes referred to as a 'Red Book' - in their room and take this to relevant appointments and meetings.

Where operationally viable, increased or adapted access to family contact provisions should be considered for women in these cohorts, including visits, phone calls and video calls, given the importance of family ties for those experiencing these life events and transitions. This must include specific consideration given to the needs of foreign national women with family overseas.

As per PSI 20/2016, consideration must be given to the religious, belief, and cultural identity of women in these cohorts, and what these factors might necessitate in relation to their perinatal or parenting needs. There are numerous differences in culture that must be recognised, particularly in relation to sleeping arrangements, bathing, and naming ceremonies/baptism and women should be asked directly about these.

Consideration must also be given to the needs of women in the cohorts who are disabled, physically or mentally, and require adjustments in order to access the appropriate perinatal or parenting support. For example, support from Local Authority Adult Social Services in relation to personal care, or specialist perinatal mental health services.

Prisons must enable women to make calls relating to childcare arrangements on reception or once identified as needed and regardless of whether they have phone credit, to ensure children are properly safeguarded

Restraints must not be used when attending medical appointments relating to these cohorts, unless there is a clear justification for doing so, in line with 6.20 – 6.32 of the National Security Framework 2015 PSI 33/2015. If restraints are required, escort chains must be used wherever possible to enable women to have confidential interactions with healthcare professionals, or to provide care to the baby where applicable.

**Case Law**

*R (on the application of WB) v Secretary of State for Justice* [2014] EWHC 1696 (Admin)
There had been a breach of the procedural rights under the European Convention on Human Rights 1950 art.8 in the refusal of the Secretary of State for Justice and a prison director to grant an application for a place in a mother and baby unit in a prison to a pregnant mother on remand. There had also been a breach of the prison director's statutory obligation under the Children Act 2004 s.11, and the secretary of state's public law obligations in accordance with *Secretary of State for Education and Science v Tameside MBC* [1977] A.C. 1014, [1976] 10 WLUK 91.

*Re L (a Child) (Interim Care Order: Mother's Imprisonment)* [2013] EWCA Civ 489
It had been inappropriate to make an interim care order where the mother had obtained a place in the prison mother and baby unit and there were no fears for the child's interim safety; an interim supervision order to the mother was granted in its place.

*R (on the application of MP) (Claimant) v Secretary of State for Justice (Defendant) & A, B , C (By G their Grandmother & Litigation Friend) (Interested Parties): R (on the application of P) (Claimant) v Governor of Downview Prison (Defendant) & (1) Secretary of State for Justice (2) R (By Her Litigation Friend E) (Interested Parties)* [2012] EWHC 214 (Admin)

The claimant female prisoners (P) applied for judicial review of decisions of the defendant secretary of state and prison governors to refuse them childcare resettlement leave (CRL). P had sole care of children aged under 16. Between 2009 and 2011, they applied for CRL when they had over two years remaining before their earliest release date and when they had been allocated to closed conditions. The secretary of state refused the applications on the ground that those factors precluded CRL under Prison Service Order 6300, which governed release on temporary licence. In 2009, a policy had been introduced that prisoners should not be allocated to open conditions more than two years from their release date. Also that year, all women's prisons were designated as either open or closed, and the designation "semi-open" was abolished. PSO 6300 was not revised to take account of those changes so far as they affected CRL. The Court held that: (1) Maintenance of the mother/child bond was not something that could be picked up in the last two years of a long sentence. CRL was not simply in preparation for the prisoner's resumption of responsibilities on release. The thorough risk assessment and decision-making process in PSO 6300 was capable of meeting the requirements of release on CRL at any stage of the sentence. The fact that CRL was "resettlement" leave did not mean that it had not been intended to be taken early in a sentence: other documents from the prison and probation services showed that resettlement work was not limited to the final stages of the custodial term. The secretary of state had misinterpreted PSO 6300 and the policy on CRL (see paras 79-87, 98, 102-110 of judgment). (2) The change in eligibility for open conditions made it more difficult for a female prisoner to become eligible for CRL. Exceptional circumstances justifying CRL could not be taken into account when considering whether there were exceptional circumstances justifying a move to open conditions more than two years before the release date. It had become an inflexible rule that the prisoner had to be within those two years to be eligible for CRL. Consideration to the potential adverse impact on eligibility for CRL had not been given in introducing the change. (3) Offending public opinion, which covered the loss of public confidence in the administration of justice under the Prison Rules 1999 r.9(5), could be a relevant factor, but not the sole factor, justifying interference with art.8 rights, *Dickson v United Kingdom (44362/04)* [2008] 1 F.L.R. 1315 and *Hirst v United Kingdom (74025/01)* (2006) 42 E.H.R.R. 41 applied. Article 8 was engaged whenever a public authority interfered with a citizen's right to respect for private and family

life. Such interference could occur as a result of a policy which restricted benefits to a particular class, *R. (on the application of P) v Secretary of State for the Home Department* [2001] EWCA Civ 1151, [2001] 1 W.L.R. 2002 and Dickson applied. (4) An inflexible policy in relation to CRL had been routinely applied which did not involve consideration of the merits of individual cases and did not permit any exceptions. That was unlawful, *R. (on the application of Cannan) v Full Sutton Prison Governor* [2003] EWCA Civ 1480, [2004] Prison L.R. 124 applied (para.186).

*CF v Secretary of State for the Home Department* [2004] EWHC 111 (Fam)

The mother had started a five-year sentence in jail with her baby sought a declaration that it had been wrong to decide that when the baby reached nine months old, it be placed with the maternal grandparents. The High Court quashed the decision by the Secretary of State because of a procedural defect in the decision-making process when the child's interests were inadequately advanced by an unprepared local authority social worker who was purportedly the child's representative. While the mother had been able to participate sufficiently in the relevant meeting prior to the decision, the daughter's interests had not been properly protected due to a lack of preparation by her representative from the local authority's social services department, who had been confused. Subjecting the Secretary of State's decision to "intense and anxious scrutiny on an objective basis", as required by Daly, he had been entitled to pay attention to the view expressed by professionals and some experts that it would be desirable for the child to live in a normal environment, Daly applied.

## MULTI-AGENCY PUBLIC PROTECTION ARRANGEMENTS (MAPPA)

PSI 40/2014 (revised) – Mandatory Use of ViSOR
Executive Summary
Background
1.1 This revised Instruction reiterates the mandatory requirements for prison establishments and the National Probation Service (NPS) in England and Wales to use ViSOR in their management of specific MAPPA (Multi Agency Public Protection Arrangements) offenders. The changes reflect the new probation structures, provide an update on the Police Vetting Unit contact details and reinforce the benefits of ViSOR quality assurance, log on audits and the need to consider ViSOR in supervision and appraisal processes. (S 2.11-2.16)
1.2 ViSOR is a national confidential database that supports MAPPA. It facilitates the effective sharing of information and intelligence on violent

and sexual offenders between the three MAPPA Responsible Authority agencies (police, probation and prisons), as well as the recording of joint risk assessments and risk management plans. ViSOR assists in the end to end management of specific offenders and improves the capacity to share intelligence and improve the safe transfer of key information when offenders move areas. ViSOR was initially an acronym for the Violent and Sexual Offender Register, but was expanded by the police to record information on some non-convicted subjects (known as potentially dangerous persons) and terrorist offenders. ViSOR is no longer an acronym but is the formal name of the database. ViSOR is to be used by MAPPA Responsible Authorities in discharging their statutory responsibilities to assess and manage the risks presented by known sexual and violent offenders.

PSI 05/2014 – Safeguarding of Children and Vulnerable Adults, 1.6

National MAPPA Team, 'MAPPA Guidance ' (Updated August 2021) (excerpt below)

1.1 The Criminal Justice Act 2003 ("CJA 2003") provides for the establishment of Multi-Agency Public Protection Arrangements ("MAPPA") in each of the 42 criminal justice areas in England and Wales. These are designed to protect the public, including previous victims of crime, from serious selfharm by sexual and violent offenders. They require the local criminal justice agencies and other bodies dealing with offenders to work together in partnership in dealing with these offenders.

1.2 This Guidance on MAPPA has been issued by the Secretary of State for Justice under the CJA 2003 in order to help the relevant agencies in dealing with MAPPA offenders. These agencies are required to have regard to the Guidance (so they need to demonstrate and record their reasons if they depart from it).

1.3 MAPPA is not a statutory body in itself but is a mechanism through which agencies can better discharge their statutory responsibilities and protect the public in a co-ordinated manner. Agencies at all times retain their full statutory responsibilities and obligations. They need to ensure that these are not compromised by MAPPA. In particular, no agency should feel pressured to agree to a course of action which they consider is in conflict with their statutory obligations and wider responsibility for public protection.

1.4 The MAPPA agencies must be free from discrimination and committed to equal access to services for all groups, particularly in relation to race, gender, gender identity, age, religious belief, sexuality, sexual orientation and disability. This means that all actions undertaken or recommended by the MAPPA agencies, and all policies and procedures, will be based on assessments of risks and needs. They will not draw on stereotypical assumptions about groups that will be discriminatory in outcome.

1.5 In undertaking their work, the MAPPA agencies will be sensitive and responsive to individual differences and needs. They will integrate this understanding into the delivery of their functions to ensure that nobody is disadvantaged as a result of belonging to a specific social group. To assist in achieving this, each Responsible Authority must have plans in place and implemented to ensure that issues of diversity are addressed.

1.6 The operation of MAPPA relies on **component bodies** working through an agreed **process** with MAPPA offenders, making provision as needed for **particular groups**, subject to **regulation and review**. These elements are briefly explored below and are developed in detail in the body of the guidance, in the chapters shown.

**Case Law**

*Westwater v Secretary of State for Justice* [2010] EWHC 2403 (Admin)

The claimant Prisoner (W) applied for judicial review of the defendant secretary of state's decision to allow him only written contact with his 10-year-old daughter (D). The Court held that having regard to the clear terminology in the guidance issued by the Secretary of State to prison governors and social services, and by the specific inter-relationship between the terminology of the Public Protection Manual (the PPM) and that guidance, there was only one interpretation of the policies, procedures and statutory guidance applicable to decisions about contact between prisoners and children. Further, a Prisoner's right to respect for his private and family life, and thereby his contact with his children, could, subject to the principle of proportionality, be restricted, *R (on the application of B) v Governor of Wakefield Prison* [2001] EWHC Admin 917, (2002) 1 FCR 445 followed (para. 41). The guidance and procedures issued by the secretary of state described a careful multi-agency approach consistent with best practice assessment and child protection procedures and the balance between the child's rights and the prisoner's rights was neither disproportionate, unfair nor unreasonable. Provided the guidance and procedures were complied with, and the decision in an individual case was made on the basis of the assessments prescribed, any interference with Article 8 corresponded to a pressing social need and was proportionate (paras 42, 48).

*Z v Z* [2021] EWFC 47

It was in the best interests of two teenage

children to have indirect, limited contact under child arrangements order with their father who was serving a prison sentence for sexual offences against children. However, the Family Court could not compel the prison governor, who opposed the order, to facilitate the contact.

*R (on the application of David Gunn) v (1) Secretary of State for Justice (2) Nottinghamshire Multi Agency Public Protection Arrangements Board* [2009] EWHC 1812 (Admin)

Stringent non-standard licence conditions imposed on an individual following his release on licence were justified by the risk of selfharm that he posed to members of the public and the assessment of the risk level that he posed could not be faulted.

**MUSLIMS, SHI'A, religious provision**

PSI 05/2016 – Faith and Pastoral Care for Prisoners

**Case Law**

*R. (on the application of Soltany) v Secretary of State for the Home Department* [2020] EWHC 2291 (Admin)

A lock-down regime that operated at an Immigration Removal Centre where detainees were locked in their rooms overnight did not breach ECHR art.5 and/or art.8. There was no religious discrimination in breach of art.9 or art.14, when read with art.9, and no indirect discrimination contrary to the Equality Act 2010 s.19, for the detainees, as practising Muslims, to pray during night lock-down in their rooms, near the toilet. The right to practise one's religion under art.9(1) was not breached in every case in which the circumstances in which an individual could practise his religion were sub-optimal.

*R. (on the application of Hussein) v Secretary of State for the Home Department* [2018] EWHC 213 (Admin)

The lock-in regime at an immigration removal centre, under which practising Muslims who wished to adhere to mandatory prayer times had to do so in their rooms, in the presence of other detainees and close to an unclosed lavatory, breached ECHR art.9 and constituted indirect discrimination under the Equality Act 2010 s.19, which was not justified.

*R (on the application of Imran Bashir) v Independent Adjudicator* [2011] EWHC 1108 (Admin)

See "Racial Justice" below.

**NATIONAL POPULATION CENSUS**

PSI 02/2011 (revised) National Population Census 2011 was cancelled in March 2018. However, no new PSI has been adopted in light of the National Population Census 2021. The following is from PSI 02/2011.

1. Executive summary

1.1 The purpose of this Instruction is to alert Governors to the forthcoming national population census on 27 March 2011, and to set out the legislative requirements under the Census Act 1920. The Census is designed to be a complete count of the population.

1.2 This Instruction includes guidance from the Office for National Statistics (ONS) on a number of points that might arise and it should be read in conjunction with the guidance leaflets which will be issued with the census questionnaires.

1.3 The ten year national census count of the population of England and Wales includes all usual residents of communal establishments, including prisons. ONS is responsible for organising this enumeration.

1.8 Governors must ensure that:

• their establishment complies with the legal requirement to take part in the census,

• they co-operate with the ONS census staff

• the CE1 questionnaire is completed, and I-questionnaires are distributed and returned to the census staff within the allotted timeframe

2. Operational Instructions

2.1 Under the terms of the Census Act 1920, each prisoner that is usually resident in the prison at midnight on the 27 March 2011 is required to complete a census I-questionnaire (copy at Annex C).

2.2 Governors have a legal duty to issue each eligible prisoner with a census questionnaire, to inform the prisoner of their legal obligation to complete the questionnaire, and warn them of the possibility of legal action if they fail to do so. If it is not clear whether an individual should receive a questionnaire they should be offered one and allowed to decide for themselves whether or not it needs to be completed. Supplementary notes for the completion of Individual questionnaires are contained in Annex A.

2.3 Every prisoner who is issued with an individual questionnaire will also be given a privacy envelope which can be used to maintain confidentiality. Envelopes should be given to prisoners after completion of the questionnaire and they are required to seal their questionnaire in the envelope. Prison staff must not look at a prisoner's answers under any circumstances unless the prisoner asks for help to complete the questionnaire.

2.4 There are penalties for breach of confidentiality. Under no circumstances, except where a request for assistance is received, should a member of the prison authorities inspect a prisoner's answers. Governors, or other persons in charge, must ensure that information provided is not divulged to any unauthorised person.

2.5 Governors must facilitate the completion of the census questionnaires as far as possible and provide assistance to those prisoners who are sight impaired, have literacy or learning difficulties and/or which addresses any special needs a prisoner with a disability may have.

2.6 For those prisoners who do not understand English, leaflets offering guidance to prisoners in some fifty-six languages and translations of the questions on the census questionnaires can be downloaded from the census website www.census.gov.uk/england/translations. Alternatively, if translation leaflets are needed discuss this with the Census Coordinator who will be able to obtain these for you. There is no provision for translators, but Annex B lists the 56 language helpline telephone numbers that can be used to help people unable to read or speak English, to complete their questionnaire.

2.7 Questionnaires in both English and Welsh will be issued to prison establishments in Wales. The prisoners have the option of completing the questionnaire in either English or Welsh but they only need to complete one questionnaire.

2.8 Governors must ensure that an I-questionnaire is distributed to all prisoners who come under the heading of usually resident.

2.9 Governors must arrange for the CE1 questionnaire (copy at Annex D) to be completed for the prison. Therefore, a local record will need to be kept of all questionnaires issued and all questionnaires returned completed. At larger prisons, the total number of questionnaires may have been sub-divided into more manageable workloads e.g. by wing or by building. If this is the case, a CE1-questionnaire will be issued and may be completed for each wing/building as appropriate.

2.10 Although in practice a Governor may delegate the task of dealing with the Census returns the Governor will still have the responsibility for seeing that the completed forms are collected back from prisoners and handed over to the census co-ordinator. The completed questionnaires should be ready for collection as soon after Census day as possible and a convenient time for their collection should be agreed with the Census Coordinator when the forms are delivered.

Annex A provides guidance on a number of issues that may commonly arise during completion of the questionnaires, but the following additional information may also be helpful;

Remand prisoners

2.11 Unconvicted prisoners will be treated as 'visitors', irrespective of how long they have been in prison or on remand. Their usual residence will be their usual family home, so there is no requirement for them to complete a questionnaire.

Immigration Detainees

2.12 Any immigration detainees within prison facilities (i.e. those who are detained under immigration powers pending their removal/deportation from the UK) will form part of the prison census if they meet the following criteria:

'Anyone from outside the UK who has stayed (or intends to stay) in the UK for at least 3 months'

Any refusals should be noted in line with paragraph 2.12.

Temporary Absence

2.13 Where a prisoner is temporarily absent from the prison establishment on 27 March 2011 but would normally be included in the census count under the 'usually resident' criteria, the governor must either arrange for a census questionnaire to be completed on the prisoner's behalf, providing key information only: name, date of birth, gender, and marital status; or the Governor can arrange for the I-questionnaires to be completed in advance of 27th March 2011.

Refusals

2.14 If a prisoner refuses to complete the questionnaire, despite being told of the legal requirement to do so and being given every opportunity possible to do so, the Governor should note on a record that the questionnaire has been issued and that the prisoner has refused to complete it. This information must be given to the Census Coordinator when he/she returns to collect the completed questionnaires.

## NATIONAL SECURITY FRAMEWORK
See also "Search".

PSI 50/2010 – National Security Framework – Covert Testing

PSI 13/2011 – National Security Framework Ref: NSF 5.2, Control of Internal Movement Function: Management and Security of Communication / Control Rooms and Internal Prisoner Movement. This PSI, together with that on the "Management and Security of Gate Services", forms the "Control of Movement" Function within the National Security Framework replacing guidance within the previous Function 2 (Accounting and Control).

PSI 14/2011 – National Security Framework Ref: NSF 5.1 Control of Internal Movement Function: Management and Security of Gate Services.

October 2020 - PSI has been revised to include the Enhanced Gate Security Policy (EGS) Operational Guidance as an Annex.

PSI 24/2011 – National Security Framework ref: NSF 8.1 Nights Function: Management and Security of Nights. Replaces existing policy contained within the National Security Framework at Function 2 (Accounting and Control), and within the Category A annex.

PSI 30/2011 – National Security Framework ref: NSF 6.8 Security Management Function: Instructions on Handling Mobile Phones and SIM Card Seizures.

Cancels PSI 47/2010 and "All existing instructions and guidance about submitting mobile phones and SIM cards for interrogation" Also see PSI 14/2015 Disposal of prisoners unauthorised property.

PSI 39/2011 – National Security Framework Ref NSF 1.2 Categorisation Function: Categorisation And Recategorisation Of Women Prisoners.

Replaces policy and guidance on categorisation and recategorisation contained in Function 1 of the National Security Framework (NSF). This guidance should be read in conjunction with PSI 3/2010 Category A and Restricted Status Prisoners: Reviews of Security Category.

13 May 2021 – updated to reflect those convicted of terrorist offences will not be suitable for open conditions.

29 Sept 2021 – the update increases the general time period before earliest release date when a female offender serving a determinate prison sentence can generally be considered for assignment to security category "Open", from two years to three years

PSI 55/2011 – National Security Framework Ref: 6.2 Security Management Function: Management and Security of Keys and Locks.

PSI 57/2011 – National Security Framework Ref: 9.2 Risk Assessment Function: Management and Security of Tools and Equipment.

PSI 63/2011 – National Security Framework Ref: 6.7 Security Management Function: Management of the Local Security Strategy (LSS).

PSI 08/2013 (Revision) – National Security Framework: Category A Function: The Review of Security Category – Category A / Restricted Status Prisoners.

PSI 06/2014 – National Security Framework – Ref: NSF 2.1 Control and Order Function: Use of Force – Implementation of Minimising and Managing Physical Restraint.

PSI 07/2014 – National Security Framework Ref: 15.1 Vetting Function – Security Vetting.

26 June 2021 – This policy has been up-dated to reflect the termination of CRC contracts

PSI 27/2014 (Revision) – National Security Framework Ref: 15.3 Vetting Function: Security Vetting – Additional Risk Criteria for Ex-Offenders Working in Prison and Community Settings.

26 June 2021 – This policy has been up-dated to reflect the termination of CRC contracts

PSI 39/2014 – National Security Framework Ref:15.5 Vetting Function: Security Vetting – Using Offenders as Mentors in the Community and in Custody.

26 June 2021 – This policy has been up-dated to

reflect the termination of CRC contracts. PSI 42/2014 – National Security Framework Ref: 15.2 Vetting Function – Exclusion of Personnel on Grounds of Misconduct.

PSI 43/2014 (Revised) – National Security Framework Ref: 12.3 Category A Function – Management and Security of Cat A Prisoners – Internal.

March 2021 – A number of alterations have been made to the policy due to changes in operating practices.

PSI 05/2015 – National Security Framework NSF 15.4 Security Vetting: Reconsideration of NOMS Central Vetting Decisions by Exception.

26 June 2021 – This policy has been up-dated to reflect the termination of CRC contracts

PSI 09/2015 – National Security Framework Ref: 12.1 Category A Function: The Identification, Initial Categorisation and Management of Potential and Provisional Category A / Restricted Status Prisoners.

PSI 10/2015 – National Security Framework Ref: 6.6 Security Management Function: Management and Security of Escape List (E-list) Prisoners.

PSI 26/2015 (Revision) – National Security Framework Ref: 7.1 External Escorts Function: Security of Prisoners at Court.

PSI 27/2015 – National Security Framework Ref: NSF 4.5a Intelligence – Regulation of Investigatory Powers Act Open Source Research on the Internet and social networking sites (Official and Official Sensitive versions).

PSI 30/2015 (Revision) – National security Framework Ref: 2.1 Control and Order Function: Amendments to use of force policy.

PSI 33/2015 – National Security Framework Ref: NSF 7.1: External Escorts – NSF: External Prisoner Movement.

The NSF is being updated in terms both of its content and overall structure, with policy being re-formatted into standard PSI format and grouped under new Function headings. This PSI consolidates in one document the escort policy contained in the NSF and in various associated notes to governors.

October 2021 - section 8 has been updated in relation to weddings and civil partnerships (and should be read in conjunction with PSI 14/2016 "Marriage of Prisoners and Civil Partnership Registration").

PSI 07/2016 – National Security Framework 3.1 Searching of the Person

PSI 08/2016 – National Security Framework Ref. NSF 3.3 Dealing with Evidence

PSI 09/2016 – National Security Framework 3.2 Cell, Area and Vehicle Searching

PSI 04/2017 – National Security Framework Security Management – Body Worn Cameras

## NEWSPAPER FUND

No reference to a fund in HMPPS Finance Manual (3 November 2020).

Paragraph 8.10.3(e) – Monies deducted from prisoners for the purchase of newspapers where an invoice is awaited from the supplier.

## NEWSPAPERS, communal

PSI 17/2005 was cancelled by OPSDR in December 2019.

## NURSING GRADES, TRADE UNION RECOGNITION

PSI 49/2000 – Trade Union Recognition for Nursing Grades 8500

## OASys

See "Offender Assessment and Sentence Management".

## OBSERVATION OF PRISONERS BY CCTV

PR 50A

50A.— Observation of prisoners by means of an overt closed circuit television system

(1) Without prejudice to his other powers to supervise the prison, prisoners and other persons in the prison, whether by use of an overt closed circuit television system or otherwise, the governor may make arrangements for any prisoner to be placed under constant observation by means of an overt closed circuit television system while the prisoner is in a cell or other place in the prison if he considers that –

(a) such supervision is necessary for –

(i) the health and safety of the prisoner or any other person;

(ii) the prevention, detection, investigation or prosecution of crime; or

(iii) securing or maintaining prison security or good order and discipline in the prison; and

(b) it is proportionate to what is sought to be achieved.

(2) If an overt closed circuit television system is used for the purposes of this rule, the provisions of rules 35C and 35D shall apply to any material obtained.

## OCCUPATIONAL HEALTH

See "Health and Safety".

## OFFENCE TYPE CATEGORIES (for risk predictor)

PSO 2200 (including appendix F) was made obsolete by Deregulation Team in March 2017. However, Annex B of PSO 2205 (see below) makes reference to the Offence Type Categories list being available on the OASys help system.

## OFFENCES AGAINST DISCIPLINE

See "Adjudications".

## OFFENDER ASSESSMENT AND SENTENCE MANAGEMENT

See also "Sentence Management and Planning".

PSO 2205 – Offender Assessment and Sentence Management – OASys

CHAPTER 1 - INTRODUCTION

OVERVIEW

1.1 This Prison Service Order provides instructions and guidance on OASys, the IT based Offender Assessment System, developed jointly by the Prison and Probation Services. It is a joint prison/probation programme, whose assessments are completed and used by both services.

1.2 This PSO applies to offenders aged 18 and over. Different arrangements, to meet the requirements of the Youth Justice Board, apply for offenders aged under 18. The YJB has a separate risk and needs assessment tool, ASSET, which is used for juveniles sentenced to Detention and Training Orders.

1.3 OASys will have a major impact in helping us to manage offenders more consistently and more effectively. It will enable staff to make sound and defensible decisions.

It will provide a comprehensive audit trail. It marks a major step towards a more joined up Criminal Justice System.

1.4 The introduction of OASys has brought significant change to the way in which many decisions about offenders are made. This will require active and enthusiastic management in Areas and establishments.

The Training Development Group (TDG) provides training for assessors and others and is available to support establishments to make implementation a success. The OASys IT application has been rolled out across the estate, Area by Area, from June 2003 to December 2004. The electronic link with the National Probation Service is planned to start in late Summer 2005 and be completed in Autumn 2005.

1.5 OASys is a risk and needs assessment tool. A new assessment system was developed because none of the existing tools and inventories fully met the requirements for consistent assessment to help practitioners make sound and defensible decisions. OASys contributes towards ensuring security and control through the identification and management of risk. OASys identifies and classifies offending related needs, such as a lack of accommodation, poor educational and employment skills, substance misuse, relationship problems, and problems with thinking and attitudes.

It also assesses the risk of selfharm offenders pose to themselves and others. From these assessments, sentence plans are drawn up within OASys to manage and reduce these risks. Thereby, OASys will help target interventions, making them more effective, and contribute towards reducing re-offending and protecting the public.

1.6 OASys has replaced the paper based sentence planning system, covered by PSO 2200 Sentence Management and Planning: an operational guide for the Prison and Probation Services. PSO 2205 on OASys replaces PSO 2200 on sentence management and planning.

1.7 This new edition of the PSO has been reduced in size to concentrate on the main issues and mandatory actions. It is designed to be used along with the OASys Guidance Document as a practitioners' guide to help staff in prisons complete assessments and should also be used in conjunction with the help provided on the IT application.

1.8 There will be a significant investment of effort in establishing systems and gaining familiarity with OASys processes. As practitioners gain experience, they will complete assessments and sentence plans more quickly. The process will be further streamlined by the build-up of easily accessed previous assessments on the individuals who have had previous dealings with the Prison and/or Probation Services.

**OFFENDING BEHAVIOUR PROGRAMMES, accredited**
See "Accredited Offending Behaviour Programmes".

**OFFICERS**
See "Prison officers".

**OLDER PRISONERS**
See "Health Services for Prisoners".

**OPEN AIR, Time in the**
PR 30
30. Time in the open air
If the weather permits and subject to the need to maintain good order and discipline, a prisoner shall be given the opportunity to spend time in the open air at least once every day, for such period as may be reasonable in the circumstances.
PSI 75/2011 (Revision) – Residential Services (extract):
1.4 The definition of the residential service is as follows:-
"Prisoners are encouraged to engage with available regimes by meeting their daily needs whilst being kept in safe, humane, decent and secure conditions. Staff will act as positive role models and ensure prisoners" domestic needs are catered for in respect of the activities of daily living including living accommodation1, cell furniture, fittings and bedding, personal hygiene and clothing.
Prisoners must be afforded time out of their

living accommodation, time in the open air and the opportunity for family contact (through phone calls).

The system of privileges aims to encourage responsible behaviour in prisoners; to encourage effort and achievement in work and other constructive activity; to encourage sentenced prisoners to engage in positive sentence management and benefit from activities designed to reduce re-offending; and to create a disciplined, controlled and safer custodial environment for prisoners, staff and visitors." (...)

1.10 Time in the Open Air PSO 4275 is cancelled and policy on time in the open air is set out in this instruction. A minimum period of time in the open air is specified for all prisoners. (...)

1.14 Prisoners must be afforded time in the open air in accordance with this Instruction. (...)

2.18 Outcome No. 21: Prisoners are afforded a minimum of 30 minutes in the open air daily, as defined in the SLA/Contract.

This provision is mandatory subject to weather conditions and the need to maintain good order and discipline. Cancellations must be recorded by the authorised manager, as nominated by the Governor.

"Time in the open air" means time spent in a situation where the prisoner is able to benefit from fresh air and natural light.

Time spent outdoors as part of a formal activity, for example outdoor work or watching or participating in sport, counts as meeting this requirement.

The time in the open air does not have to be spent in a single period, but must be in no more than two periods, which can include time in the open air moving between activities.

While it will often be difficult to provide time in the open air for prisoners attending court, Governors ought to consider making arrangements for prisoners who are at court on two or more consecutive days to get some time in the open air.

The previous mandatory requirement for prisoners on restricted regimes to have 60 minutes in the open air is withdrawn. However, Governors will be required by their SLA/Contract to continue to provide a minimum of 60 minutes activity for such prisoners, of which at least 30 minutes must be in the open air.

**OPEN CONDITIONS**
The Parole Board issues guidance on its approach to the use of the open estate: Policy on Open Conditions which is available on the *prisonoracle.com*
The Secretary of State's Directions (which apply regardless of Girling) state that most lifers should spend a period in open conditions prior to release.

The point of open conditions is not simply one of rehabilitation or curing possible institutionalism. It offers the only chance to observe a prisoner putting into practice that which he/she has learned in theory. In other words, a prisoner may well make all the right noises on an accredited programme, but the structured and sheltered nature of closed conditions, where all decisions and responsibilities are taken by others, means that prisoners cannot demonstrate that they can fend for themselves in conditions more akin to those they will face on the outside. Open conditions offers this opportunity as far as possible. It is the only true testing ground.

The overriding factor is risk to the public. The Parole Board confirms that those serving indeterminate sentences may potentially remain in prison for their natural life. It is not the role of the Parole Board to seek to help prisoners to progress towards release because of perceived shortcomings by other agencies. The Board's role is to advise the Secretary of State in line with the Directions he has imposed.

Release from closed conditions

The Board may not direct the release of any prisoner serving a sentence of life imprisonment or indeterminate sentence for public protection, unless it is satisfied that it is no longer necessary in the interests of public protection that they continue to be detained. In the majority of cases, the Board cannot ultimately be satisfied about risk until and unless a successful period of testing has been completed. Regardless of the length of tariff, where offending behaviour has been addressed in closed conditions, the prisoner has had no opportunity to demonstrate by his behaviour in conditions similar to those existing in the community that he/she can apply lessons learned in closed conditions.

It will be unusual for an indeterminate prisoner to be released direct from closed conditions. Circumstances where that may be appropriate could include

• where the Board is considering representations against recall

• where the prisoner has already successfully completed a sufficient period of testing in open conditions; AND the Board considers that the reason for removing the prisoner from open conditions was unrelated to risk

• where the case is considered on compassionate grounds

• where there are other grounds that dictate that any or further testing in open conditions is not required to satisfy the Board about the prisoners level of risk.

In determining whether the prisoner may be released from closed conditions, the Board will take into account:

• whether a previous period of testing in open conditions was cut short. If so, the expectation will be that the Board will recommend a return to open conditions for the prisoner to complete testing and monitoring

• that testing should not take place in the community. Accordingly it is not appropriate to balance risk against benefits when release is considered. Panels must acknowledge that testing, where the Board is not satisfied that risk is acceptable, may only take place in a prison environment

• where a prisoner is in closed conditions and has successfully completed all the offending behaviour work thought necessary, it is nevertheless required in the majority of cases for a testing period in open conditions to be completed before the Board can ultimately be satisfied that risk is acceptable. Panels should not be swayed by a legal representatives argument that those who have completed offending behaviour work in closed conditions must be released, unless the case falls within the exceptional category

Reasons

Where the Board directs release from closed conditions in 2 and 4 above, the reasons should state why release without a [further] period of testing in open conditions is appropriate. Every case shall be considered on its merits and nothing above detracts from the principle that if the Board is satisfied in any case that the risk to the public is acceptable, then it must direct the prisoners release.

Recommendations for transfer to open conditions

The Board recognises that the Secretary of State's Directions require the Board to balance the risk to the public against any benefits to the prisoner and the public that might accrue from the prisoners transfer to open conditions. Within that framework, the Board will take into account:

• that the normal expectation is that all offending behaviour fundamental to risk reduction must be successfully completed in closed conditions

• that only relapse prevention and booster offending behaviour work should normally be envisaged in open conditions

• that where the risk against benefits is evenly balanced, the risk to the public shall be the deciding factor

• that where the Board assesses the risk as unacceptable for a transfer to open conditions, it shall take no account of the fact that further offending work has not been identified as necessary by prison and probation staff, or that such work is not available, except to acknowledge that fact in the reasons.

**Case Law**

*R. (on the application of John) v Secretary of State for Justice* [2021] EWHC 1606 (Admin)

The Secretary of State for Justice was entitled to depart from a Parole Board's recommendation for a prisoner's transfer to open conditions where he was making an evaluative assessment as to the extent to which further consolidation work was required and where it should be undertaken. *R (Samuel) v Parole Board for England and Wales* [2020] EWHC 42 (Admin)

A Parole Board had erred in its decision not to recommend the transfer of an indeterminate-sentence prisoner to open conditions. In particular, it had failed to undertake the balancing exercise between the risks and benefits of such a transfer, as required by the directions issued pursuant to the Criminal Justice Act 2003 Pt 12 s.239(6).

The board had failed to undertake the balancing exercise between risk and benefit. Both the claimant's offender manager and supervisor had identified the benefits to the claimant of a transfer to open conditions, but there was no mention of those benefits in the board's decision, let alone any evaluation of them. If the board had directed itself in accordance with the directions issued pursuant to the Criminal Justice Act 2003 Pt 12 s.239(6) and *Green v Parole Board* [2017] EWHC 2612 (Admin), [2017] 10 WLUK 40, it would have mentioned those benefits, evaluated them and weighed them in the balance with the risk factors, Green considered. Although the board considered that the risk levels posed by the claimant remained high, it was not possible to say that it was "highly likely" that those would have outweighed the benefits of transfer. The court could not judge what the panel would have thought about the benefits had they been considered and evaluated in accordance with the correct test (see paras 22-33 of judgment).

*R. (on the application of Huxtable) v secretary of State for Justice* [2020] EWHC 2494 (Admin)

The reconsideration mechanism in the Parole Board Rules 2019, which provided that the Parole Board's decision to release a prisoner on licence would be provisional for 21 days, was not ultra vires and did not breach ECHR art.5(1) and (4).

The claimant applied for judicial review of the "reconsideration mechanism" in the Parole Board Rules 2019.

The reconsideration mechanism provided that the Parole Board's decision to release a prisoner on licence would be provisional for 21 days (or fewer days if exceptional circumstances existed, the prisoner requested it and the request was granted). During that time period, the secretary of state or the prisoner would be permitted to make representations to the board inviting it to reconsider its decision on the grounds that it was irrational or procedurally wrong. The claimant in the instant case had been sentenced to imprisonment for public protection in 2008 with a minimum term of two years and 245 days. On 21 August 2019, he was recommended for release by the Parole Board and was released 21 days later, after that decision became final. It was the claimant's case that the delay in his release had been caused by the operation of the reconsideration mechanism.

Application was refused.

*R. (on the application of Debono) v Parole Board for England and Wales* [2020] EWHC 655 (Admin)

In failing to consider the possible benefit to a prisoner of a transfer to open conditions, the Parole Board had failed to have regard to the secretary of state's 2015 Directions and had not conducted the necessary balancing exercise of the risks of transfer against those benefits.

The claimant had received two concurrent sentences of imprisonment for public protection, with a minimum specified term of eight and a half years less 323 days spent on remand, for arson with intent to endanger life. The minimum term had expired in 2014. The offences involved fire-bombing the homes of two police officers when the officers and their families, including small children, were in occupation. He had many prior convictions for offences of dishonesty, some for violence, and many involving vehicles. However, since being in custody, he had engaged in a range of rehabilitative programmes and the board described his behaviour in custody as "excellent". The board had before it a range of reports, including from a number of psychologists, his offender supervisor and his offender manager. The psychological reports indicated that he had dysfunctional personality traits and other unaddressed risk factors that were inhibiting his progress. The offender supervisor recommended a transfer to open conditions but accepted that the claimant had not fully addressed his core risk factors. The offender manager recommended that the claimant remain in closed conditions. The board concluded that the claimant's risk could probably be safely managed in open conditions but declined to order his release or recommend a transfer because there was a high probability of release if he complied with open conditions which presented an unacceptably high risk that he could commit a further offence because of his unmet treatment needs.

There was no doubt that the board had understood the matters it was required to take into account by virtue of the Directions. It had considered that the claimant's anticipated compliance with open conditions could be treated in the future as evidence that he was no longer a risk to the public when in fact there remained an unacceptably high risk because the underlying risk factors had not been addressed before moving to open conditions. The board's approach was supported by paragraph 3 of the Directions which stated that the main interventions for reducing risk factors existed principally within closed prison estate. Its conclusion that the claimant could safely be managed in open conditions and would comply with the regime, which implied that he would not abscond, showed that it had had regard to the first three factors set out in paragraph 7. However, it did not appear to have considered the benefits of transfer, including an ability for the claimant to demonstrate that he could resolve conflict without resorting to violence, resist the temptation to abuse drugs, obtain employment and enhance his personal support network without resorting to previous antisocial associates. As the board's decision made no reference to the benefits, it was not clear whether it was implicit that it had considered that the claimant's compliance with open conditions would not reduce the risk or not. Moreover, the board's decision did not provide evidence that it conducted the required balancing exercise required by the Directions. The board had failed to have regard to the Directions and failed to conduct the necessary balancing exercise, both of which were mandatory. The court considered whether the board would have reached the same decision if it had addressed the issues before it lawfully, but could not conclude that the high threshold to reach that view had been met, and so the decision was quashed and a fresh parole review was ordered.

*R. (on the application of Bowen) v Secretary of State for Justice* [2018] 1 W.L.R. 2170
On the proper construction of the Crime (Sentences) Act 1997 s.28(5), the Secretary of State for Justice was not required to release a life prisoner as soon as the Parole Board had directed his release. Where residence at approved premises was specified as a condition of a prisoner's release on licence, the obligation to release only arose once a place at the approved premises became available. The reasonableness of a period of detention pending release under a residence condition would depend entirely on the facts of the particular case. Delays in the release of two prisoners for 69 and 118 days pending the availability of beds in approved premises were not, in the circumstances, unreasonable.

*Green v The Parole Board & Anor* [2017] EWHC 2612
The claimant prisoner (G), subject to a sentence of imprisonment for public protection (IPP) of 3

years and 6 months less 38 days on remand (as amended under the slip rule), applied for judicial review of the Parole Board's (First Defendant) decision not to recommend a transfer to open conditions following an oral hearing at which no order for release was made. His next parole review was set at 18 months. The Court held that in not recommending a transfer to open conditions the first defendant had failed to carry out the necessary balancing exercise between risk and benefit; G had the benefit of three expert reports recommending transfer. In quashing the decision and remitting the case to the Parole Board for a fresh determination the Court directed an oral hearing to take place no later than 15 December 2017. In those circumstances, the challenge to the Secretary of State's (Second Defendant) setting of a parole review in 18 months' time fell away, but in any case the Court held that a review period of 18 months was unreasonable.

*R (Gilbert) v Secretary of State for Justice* [2015] EWCA Civ 802
A ministerial policy of the secretary of state, restricting the circumstances in which prisoners who absconded while on release on temporary licence would be eligible to return to open conditions, was lawful.

*R (Dilks) v Secretary of State for Justice* [2015] EWHC 11 (Admin)
The claimant had completed his minimum term and had completed all recommended offence-related courses. The Parole Board had recommended his transfer, but he had not been transferred to an open conditions until 4 ½ months later. He was also not released on temporary licence overnight in approved premises until 18 months after he was eligible for this type of release. He submitted that the Secretary of State had breached its duties under domestic law and Article 5 in failing to provide him with a reasonable opportunity to show that he no longer posed an unacceptable risk. This failure had delayed his ultimate release date. The Court held that whilst the Secretary of State had breached its public law duty to provide the claimant with an opportunity to show that he could be released on licence, in this instance the delay had not been unreasonable, and there had thus been no breach of the ancillary duty under Article 5.

**OPEN GOVERNMENT: the code of practice on access to government information**
PSO 0450 (Open Government: the code of practice on access to government information) was cancelled by DOPT April 2018 and replaced

by the Freedom of Information Act 2000.
See "Data Protection".

OPEN ESTATE
See "Categorisation and Allocation".

OPEN UNIVERSITY – Operation of the Prison Service Scheme
See also "Education".
Prison Education & Library Services for adult prisons in England Policy Framework.
Paragraph 4.5
The Governor must comply with Regulations on prisoner eligibility for tuition fee loans for higher level study (level 3 and above). See the Open University, Higher Education and distance learning guidance document for information on loan arrangements for prisoners from Wales
PSI 32/2012 (Wales Only) – Open University, Higher Education and Distance Learning
April 2019 – Amended as a result of the new Education Policy Framework to reflect provisions apply in Wales only.
1. Executive summary
Background
1.1 NOMS encourages establishments to provide prisoners with opportunities for higher education and distance learning as an important contribution to their resettlement, as well as a way to assist prisoners with long term sentences to positively engage with regimes. This instruction provides a framework through which staff must process prisoners' applications whilst ensuring that security and sifting processes are rigorous. Applications for relevant funding must also be thorough. This PSI also provides guidance on the suggested support required for successful completion of studies.
Desired outcomes
1.2 This instruction aims to ensure that Open University (OU), other Higher Education (HE) and Distance Learning (DL) courses are available to prisoners identified as likely to benefit from such study in line with assessments, resettlement requirements and aspirations. Prisoners should receive appropriate information, advice and guidance about further and higher education. The recommendation that such study is appropriate and contributes to reducing reoffending and employability objectives should be recorded on the prisoner's Individual Learning Plan (ILP) by the individual providing the advice.
Case Law
R (on the application of Stanley Matthews) v Governor of Swaleside Prison [2009] EWHC 2397 (Admin)
A prison governor had been entitled to prohibit a prisoner from submitting an assignment for a proposed study of domestic violence as part of a

university course he had started after imprisonment, where the governor had reasonable grounds to believe that the assignment was intended to be an actual research project and any reasonable prison governor would have been entitled to decide that it would not be appropriate to allow the prisoner to conduct the type of research he had outlined. The Court observed, however, that it may be that the Claimant would seek a further decision from the Defendant (or the Governor of the prison in which he now is being held) to allow him to submit the assignment on the basis that it amounted to an assessment exercise and no more. In that event the relevant Governor would have to assess the matter afresh. In the course of these proceedings the Defendant submitted that even the submission of the assignment as a pure assessment exercise properly could be refused on the basis of public perception. The argument was that the public would perceive that the Claimant was being given credit for his work when that work was inappropriate. I cannot pass final judgment on that argument since it does not arise on the factual situation as I have found it to be. Had it done so, I would have rejected it and I would have held that refusal to submit an assessment exercise that already had been completed with apparent approval was unreasonable and irrational.

OPERATIONAL SUPPORT GRADES
PSI 42/1997 – Operational Support Grades: Implementation Guidance 8600

ORAL HEARINGS
Key Note
Oral hearings can be required in a number of contexts but practitioners should be prepared to "cross-fertilise".
See "Parole Board Oral Hearings".

R. (on the application of Zaman) v Secretary of State for Justice [2022] EWHC 188 (Admin)
It had been procedurally unfair to refuse to hold an oral hearing to consider a prisoner's recategorisation from category A to category B. The reports on the prisoner's progress had been largely positive, the two adverse factors against him were disputed, and the local advisory panel had twice recommended his recategorisation but been overruled. In those circumstances, an oral hearing would have allowed the disputed matters and the secretary of state's concerns to be explored.

R (on the application of Wilson) v Secretary of State for Justice [2022] EWHC 170 (Admin)
It had been appropriate to refuse to hold an oral hearing when deciding whether to downgrade a prisoner's security categorisation. While there

was inconsistency between the refusal to downgrade and favourable recommendations, the reasoned reports were clear on their face and there was no dispute or disagreement whose nature called for an oral hearing.

*Hassett v Secretary of State for Justice* [2017] EWCA Civ 331

The guidance in Reilly's Application for Judicial Review, Re [2013] UKSC 61, [2014] A.C. 1115, [2013] 10 WLUK 277 regarding the requirements imposed by issues of procedural fairness on the Parole Board to hold oral hearings did not apply directly in the context of security categorisation decisions made by the Category A Review Team when deciding whether to maintain a prisoner's Category A status.

*R (Morgan) v Secretary of State for Justice* [2016] EWHC 2455 (Admin)

While there are many similarities between Parole Board and Category A Review Teams (CART) decisions, there are relevant differences. Parole Boards were tribunals independent of the prison service, with a specialist professional composition, performing a quasi-judicial role directly affecting the liberty of the individual to which ECHR art.5(4) applied. CART performed an internal administrative role, with no specialist professional composition and its decisions did not directly affect the liberty of the individual. It followed that there might in principle be similar cases where the common law duty of procedural fairness demanded an oral hearing in a Parole Board case where it would not in a CART case.

However, the following conclusions were also applicable to CART decisions: (a) an oral hearing should be held before determining an application whenever fairness to the prisoner required that; (b) the circumstances in which an oral hearing was necessary would often include a situation where important facts were in dispute, where it would not otherwise be possible to properly or fairly assess risk, or where it was maintained on tenable grounds that a face-to-face encounter was necessary to enable the prisoner to put his case effectively or test the views of those who had dealt with him; (c) CART should consider whether its independent assessment of risk would benefit from the closer examination which an oral hearing could provide; (d) the purpose of holding an oral hearing was not only to assist in CART's decision-making, but also to reflect the prisoner's legitimate interests in being able to participate in the decision, where he had something useful to contribute; (e) the question of whether fairness required a prisoner to be given an oral hearing was different from the question of whether he had a particular

likelihood of being released or transferred to open conditions; (f) CART had to be, and appear to be, independent and impartial; (g) CART had to guard against any temptation to refuse oral hearings as a means of saving time, trouble and expense; (h) CART's decision was not confined to its determination of whether to recommend the prisoner's release or transfer to open conditions, but included other aspects of its decision which would have an impact upon his management in prison or on future reviews; (i) it would be prudent for CART to allow an open hearing if it was in doubt about whether to do so, *McLuckie* and *Reilly* applied (see paras 23-27 of judgment). It had been lawful for the secretary of state to refuse to grant a prisoner an oral hearing prior to considering whether to downgrade his security category from category A to B: fairness did not necessitate that he be given an oral hearing, taking into account that the Defendant had no offence-related insight.

**ORDER AND DISCIPLINE**
See "Adjudications".

**ORDERS**
See "Prison Service Orders and Instructions".

**OUTSIDE CONTACTS**
See "Contacts, outside, of prisoners"

**PACKAGING: Reporting of packaging material usage – legal compliance**
Sustainable Operations Policy Framework (March 2019)

Replacement for PSI 2003/41 (Sustainable Development – Prison Service Policy and Governance); PSI 2010/07( Packaging Material Usage Legal Requirements); and PSI 2013/15 (Waste Management Data Recording).

PSI 12/2007 – Reporting of Packaging Material Usage – Legal Compliance [Producer responsibility obligations (packaging waste) regulations 2005]

PSI 06/2009 – Reporting of Packaging Material Usage – Legal Compliance

Replaced by PSI 07/2010, which was itself replaced by Sustainable Operations Policy Framework in March 2019.

**PAROLE**
See also "Recalled Prisoners".

The Parole Board is regulated by the Parole Board Rules 2019, which came into force on 22 November 2019. The Parole Board Rules 2016 and Parole Board (Amendment) Rules 2018 are revoked. Cases referred to the Parole Board before the date on which these Rules came into force continue under these Rules, and are treated as if the case was referred under these Rules (rule 3).

Under Rule 19 of the Rules, a decision on to release a prisoner can be made without an oral hearing. The Board's website contains detailed information on all aspects of Parole Board practice and procedure at http://www.paroleboard.gov.uk/

Generic Parole Process Policy Framework (Re-Issued on 17 August 2021)

Replaced and cancelled PSI 22/2015 (revised) – Generic parole process for indeterminate and determinate sentenced prisoners (GPP).

**Case Law**

*R. (McCourt) v Parole Board for England and Wales* [2020] EWHC 2320 (Admin)

The mother of a murder victim sought permission to apply for judicial review of the parole board's decision that her daughter's killer should be released. The claimant had a sufficient interest in the board's decision to challenge it, but only if she could identify an arguable basis for doing so. The board had not misdirected itself or erred by failing to apply a presumption against release.

*R. (Grinham) v Parole Board for England and Wales* [2020] EWHC 2140 (Admin)

The court quashed a decision by the Parole Board not to grant the re-release on licence of a prisoner who had been diagnosed with cancer. The expedited oral hearing of the prisoner's application had been procedurally unfair.

There were plainly serious failings in the preparation of the case for the oral hearing which resulted in real difficulty for the claimant and his solicitor on the day of the hearing:

- Late service of report by offender supervisor - The claimant's solicitor had chased the report in the week leading up to the hearing but was not provided with it until she arrived at the prison on the morning of the hearing. That afforded inadequate time for her to consider the report properly and take the claimant's instructions upon it. Although in general terms the report was favourable to the claimant in supporting his application for release, it made extensive reference to negative NOMIS entries and it was necessary for the claimant to be able to deal with those (para.64).

- Insufficient time available for hearing - The panel chair had revealed to the claimant that she had initially been unavailable to hear the matter and had only agreed to hear it on the basis that she would have to finish at around 11.30 or 12.00. She also made several references to the pressure of time and the need to get through the hearing and, when the claimant was himself giving evidence, observed that she was now sitting beyond the time when she should have been elsewhere. It was clear that the claimant himself

was adversely affected by the panel chair's disclosure of the limited time available to conduct the hearing. Pressure of time became a theme which permeated the whole hearing and was likely to affect the way he gave his evidence and undermine his ability to do himself justice. Inevitably it gave rise to a legitimate sense of grievance (paras 65-66, 70).

- Failure to comply with case management directions - The offender manager had been requested to obtain call out records for any incidents of domestic violence between the claimant and his partner, but had overlooked that request. It was regrettable that the failure to comply with the case management directions led to undue pressure of time on the morning of the hearing which was compounded by the panel chair's expressed anxiety that the hearing had to be completed by 12.00 (paras 67-68).

*R. (Stokes) v Parole Board for England and Wales* [2020] EWHC 1885 (Admin)

A reconsideration decision made by a parole board pursuant to the Parole Board Rules 2019 r.28, upholding a panel's refusal to release a life prisoner on licence, had to be quashed. The board had not given adequate reasons for its decision and had not properly engaged with the prisoner's assertion that the panel's decision was flawed by procedural unfairness.

The prisoner's second ground was made out. A parole board was entitled to reject the views of professional witnesses, but it was important that it should give adequate reasons for its decisions. The panel's reasons for rejecting the professionals' release recommendation rested on the prisoner's behaviour during his periods of release on licence. The second of those periods had ended just under a year before the oral hearing and, in the meantime, the prisoner had begun work with a psychologist and had been described as motivated and as showing a change in presentation. The evidence before the panel was that his prognosis was not poor, his relationships with professionals were good, and the professionals were concerned that the level of support he needed would not be available in open prison conditions. Those were significant developments. However, the panel did not weigh them in the balance and in that regard its reasoning fell below the acceptable standard. So too did the board's briefly expressed rejection of the challenge to that reasoning.

The prisoner's third ground of challenge was also made out. At the outset of its reconsideration decision, the board summarised the procedural unfairness challenge but thereafter the relevant paragraphs referred only to irrationality. While the decision had to be read as a whole, it was difficult to conclude that the board had considered procedural unfairness as a separate ground from irrationality or appraised the panel's recommendation in terms of procedural fairness as well as irrationality. The board lost sight of the procedural fairness challenge when it formulated its conclusion, and therefore its reconsideration decision had to be quashed.

*R. (EG) v Parole Board* [2020] EWHC 1457 (Admin) The Parole Board had failed to provide a mechanism for a prisoner who lacked capacity to conduct his parole proceedings to enable his active participation in the process, and had failed to provide him with a speedy review of the continued lawfulness of his detention contrary to ECHR art.5(4). The Parole Board Rules 2019 contained a power for the Parole Board to appoint a litigation friend to act on behalf of a prisoner who lacked capacity to understand his parole process.

*R. (Morris) v Parole Board* [2020] EWHC 711 (Admin) The Parole Board's refusal to direct a prisoner's release was not procedurally unfair where it had considered unproven allegations made against the prisoner in its assessment of risk. Unproven allegations made against prisoners should be considered by the Parole Board where there was a sufficient evidential basis to allow the Board to decide that the allegations had some factual basis and make at least some findings of fact.

## PAROLE BOARD ORAL HEARINGS

Parole Board Practice Guidance for referring cases to Oral Hearings (December 2013) (extract): 1 Overview

1.1 Following the Supreme Court's judgment in the case of Osborn & others v Parole Board [2013] UKSC 61, the Parole Board has revised its existing practice guidance on the consideration of the necessity of or suitability for oral hearings to assist both members in making their decisions, and offenders and their representatives in understanding the Board's position following the judgment.

1.2 There remains no statutory entitlement by right to an oral hearing before the Parole Board for any case other than life or indeterminate sentenced prisoners who are assessed as „not unsuitable" for release, or life or indeterminate sentenced prisoners at first review following recall. However, the UKSC judgment clearly indicated that the previous policy and practice of the Board could no longer stand. This means a fundamental change in the way the Parole Board regards the purpose of and necessity for an oral hearing in each case before it. While this does not

mean that an oral hearing will be necessary in every case, the judgment has significantly broadened the circumstances in which such a hearing will now be required.

1.3 Detailed practice guidance follows at section 3 below, but members should note the main change in the position at law following the judgment. Fairness to the prisoner is now the overriding requirement; the perceived utility of an oral hearing is not the deciding factor. Prior to the Supreme Court decision, the domestic courts had agreed with the Board's position that a relevant factor in deciding whether or not to hold an oral hearing was whether such a hearing would be likely to make a significant difference to the final outcome. In cases where it would not be likely to make a significant difference, the courts had considered that a hearing on the papers, with written representations, was procedurally fair. This is no longer the case.

1.4 It is therefore necessary for the Board to fundamentally change the way it thinks about oral hearings; where previously we might not have held an oral hearing in circumstances where resolving a dispute of fact or hearing mitigation would have no material affect on the outcome, this is no longer the position. It is purely a question of fairness to the prisoner.

*R. (on the application of Farmer) v Secretary of State for Justice* [2021] EWHC 3487 (Admin) A refusal to downgrade a prisoner from Category A to B following a period of exemplary behaviour was quashed because the decision maker had not held an oral hearing. The report writers had not expressly addressed whether the prisoner's risk to the public if unlawfully at large had significantly reduced, and as that was the focus of the test to be applied, an oral hearing should have been held to allow that issue to be explored with those authors.

*R. (on the application of Pierpoint) v Parole Board for England and Wales* [2021] EWHC 2705 (Admin) The Parole Board's refusal to order an oral hearing of a prisoner's parole review following his recall to prison after breaching his licence conditions was procedurally unfair where the community offender manager had had no contact with the prisoner, and there were disputes of fact in relation to whether the prisoner had breached a restraining order. The Parole Board had also failed to give adequate reasons for its decision.

*Knights v The Parole Board of England and Wales* [2018] EWHC 411 (Admin) A Parole Board was entitled to refuse to hold an oral hearing when the prisoner's request included a request for a deferral of his review, and the outcome of an oral hearing would have been certain. In this case the prisoner wished time to complete the Healthy Sex Programme (HSP). The prisoner accepted that an oral hearing would not consider him for release or for a move to open conditions until his successful completion of the HSP. Further, a policy of not agreeing to defer parole reviews for a period of longer than four months was not arbitrary, and the guidance maintained a degree of flexibility.

*Reilly's Application for Judicial Review, Osborn v Parole Board, Booth v Parole Board* [2013] UKSC 61 The Supreme Court gave guidance about the circumstances in which the Parole Board was required to hold an oral hearing in order to comply with its common law duty of fairness and Article 5(4) of the European Convention on Human Rights when determining a prisoner's application for release or transfer to open prison conditions. Extracts from the judgment below.

"The common law duty to act fairly, as it applies in this context, is influenced by the requirements of Article 5(4) as interpreted by the European Court of Human Rights. Compliance with the common law duty should result in compliance also with the requirements of Article 5(4) in relation to procedural fairness" (p.1133)

It also has to be borne in mind that the issues which are considered by the board are not in practice confined to the question whether the prisoner should or should not be released or transferred. As I have explained, the statutory directions given to the board require it to consider numerous matters. The board's findings in relation to these matters may in practice affect the prisoner's future progress in prison, for example in relation to the courses which he is required to undertake and his future reviews. The board may also be asked specifically to advise the Secretary of State on matters affecting the prisoner. For example, when post-tariff indeterminate sentence prisoners are referred to the board, it is generally asked to advise on the continuing areas of risk that need to be addressed. In such cases, the fair disposal of issues of that kind may require an oral hearing even if the question whether the prisoner should be released or transferred does not.

In accordance with the guidance provided in West, an oral hearing is required when facts which appear to be important are in dispute, or where a significant explanation or mitigation is advanced which needs to be heard orally if it is to be accepted"

It also has to be borne in mind that the issues which are considered by the board are not in practice confined to the question whether the

prisoner should or should not be released or transferred. As I have explained, the statutory directions given to the board require it to consider numerous matters. The board's findings in relation to these matters may in practice affect the prisoner's future progress in prison, for example in relation to the courses which he is required to undertake and his future reviews. The board may also be asked specifically to advise the Secretary of State on matters affecting the prisoner. For example, when post-tariff indeterminate sentence prisoners are referred to the board, it is generally asked to advise on the continuing areas of risk that need to be addressed. In such cases, the fair disposal of issues of that kind may require an oral hearing even if the question whether the prisoner should be released or transferred does not.

In accordance with the guidance provided in West, an oral hearing is required when facts which appear to be important are in dispute, or where a significant explanation or mitigation is advanced which needs to be heard orally if it is to be accepted" (p.1153)

Guidance – Parole Board Oral Hearings Guide (This is the guide for Parole Board oral hearings) https://www.gov.uk/guidance/parole-board-oral-hearings-guide
Parole Board Oral Hearing Administration and Attendance Policy Framework
PSI 15/2016 – Cancelled November 2021 – this has now been replaced by the Handling Sensitive Information, Including Information by Victims, for the Purpose of Parole Board Reviews Policy Framework
Policy name: Handling of Sensitive Information, Including Information Provided by Victims, For the Purpose of Parole Board Reviews Policy Framework
Paragraph 3.1 Considerations for withholding information
3.1.8 – Where the Parole Board has directed that a case be heard at an oral hearing, all HMPPS staff must ensure that PPCS is alerted to any requests to withhold information from the prisoner as soon as possible. The Parole Board Rules state that all applications for non-disclosure must be submitted to the Parole Board no later than 8 weeks before the date of the oral hearing. All non-disclosure applications must be submitted by PPCS to the Parole Board.
3.1.9 – In exceptional circumstances, where an application to withhold information is received less than 8 weeks from the oral hearing, PPCS may make a request to the Panel Chair for permission to present the application for non-disclosure and as part of the application provide reasons for the late service. The Panel Chair may decide to alter the time limit under the Parole Board Rules and

accept the late application. A clear explanation for the late application must be provided. The Panel Chair will make a final decision as to whether the application will be accepted and if so, will then consider whether it is appropriate to make a direction to withhold the information.

## Case Law

*R (on the application of Stephenson) v Secretary of State for Justice* [2010] EWHC 3134 (Admin)
The claimant prisoner (S) applied for judicial review of a decision of the prison authorities to refuse to supply him with a copy of his prison dossier for him to retain. S's request had been refused in purported application of Prison Service Order 6010. However, it was stated that he could have a copy of the documents in the dossier, provided that he paid a fee of 10 pence per sheet. S declined to pay the fee. He argued that he was entitled at common law not merely to see the dossier but to have a copy of it; in any event, he was entitled to a copy of the dossier under the Data Protection Act 1998 sections 7 and 8. The Court held that where the evidence was documentary, the party in question should "have access to the documents", *Secretary of State for the Home Department v F* (2009) UKHL 28, (2010) 2 AC 269 considered. That obligation had been fulfilled. S had been allowed access to the documents in the sense that he had been allowed to have them in his cell and to read them on every occasion on which he requested access (see para.11 of judgment). Provided that it was plain that a request was made under section 7 of the 1998 Act, the prison authorities were obliged to comply with the request to communicate to S in "an intelligible form" the information in the dossier. Further, section 8(2) obliged them to supply "a copy of the information in permanent form". In the case of documentary information, that permanent form was likely to be a document or a copy of a document. The phrase "permanent form" did not apply only to the form in which the information existed; it imported an obligation to provide a copy of the information in a form which the recipient could keep.

*R (on the application of Briggs) v(1) Parole Board (2) Secretary of State for Justice* [2009] EWHC 2761 (Admin)
There was an apparent unfairness to a prisoner at a parole hearing where it became necessary to shorten submissions made on his behalf after the judge failed to inform the parties at the outset that the hearing would be restricted to two hours to comply with the prison's lock down policy.

*R (on the application of Headley) v Parole Board* [2009] EWHC 663 (Admin)
The decision of a Parole Board not to release a prisoner on licence was vitiated by its failure to afford the prisoner an opportunity to test, by cross-examination, hearsay evidence as to the alleged incident that led to the prisoner's recall on licence.

## PAROLE BOARD DECISIONS

### Key Note

Following the parole board decision to direct the release of John Worboys (see *R (DSD) v Parole Board* below), there were calls for greater transparency in the parole system followed by a number of recent government reviews.

In April 2018, the Secretary of State for Justice published a "Review into the law, policy and procedure relating to Parole Board decisions", in particular to consider the transparency of Parole Board decision-making; whether there should be mechanism to allow parole board decisions to be reconsidered; and the involvement of victims in the process.

In March 2022 the Secretary of State for Justice published a review entitled "Root and Branch Review of the Parole System: The Future of the Parole System in England and Wales." This review builds on the work of the 2018 Review and details the government's policy commitments in relation to transparency and decision-making, as well as evaluating the overall functioning of the parole board.

The 2022 Review can be found online here:
https://www.gov.uk/government/publications/root-and-branch-review-of-the-parole-system

### Case Law

*R (on the application of Pearce) v Parole Board of England and Wales* [2022] EWCA Civ 4
The Parole Board refused to direct a prisoner's release, in part based on a consideration of allegations of sexual assault which had not resulted in convictions. The prisoner was refused permission to judicially review. On appeal against that refusal, the Court of Appeal found that the 2019 "Guidance on Allegations" issued by the Parole Board was unlawful. That Guidance, which had been issued following *DSD* (below) and was revised in 2021, advised panel members on how to consider the relevance and weight of previous unproven allegations. In particular, the Guidance suggested the panel could form an assessment of concern and risk based on those unproven allegations. The Court of Appeal was satisfied that the Guidance was unlawful – in spite of the amendments made in 2021 - although this appeal was dismissed on its own merits.

*Dickins v Parole Board for England and Wales* [2021] EWHC 1166 (Admin)
See "Judicial Review Procedure" above.

*R (on the application of DSD and NBV and Others) v The Parole Board of England and Wales and Others and John Radford* [2018] EWHC 694 (Admin)

In the opening of the judgment (Sir Brian Leveson P, Mr Justice Jay and Mr Justice Garnham) the Court stated that there had never before been a challenge to a Parole Board decision to direct the release of a prisoner nor a challenge to the Parole Board Rules 2016 (SI 2016 No. 1041) ('Rule 25'). This landmark case concerns the "black cab rapist" John Radford (aka John Worboys). Three sets of applicants were involved in the case: DSD and NBV (victims of the prisoner); the Mayor of London and News Group Newspapers Limited.

The applicants challenged the direction for the prisoner's release made by the Parole Board on 26 December 2017, and further claimed Rule 25, prohibiting the making public of information about proceedings before the Parole Board or the names of persons concerned in the proceedings, ultra vires.

### Factual background

The prisoner had been convicted on 13 March 2009 of 19 serious sexual offences against 12 victims and sentenced to an Imprisonment for Public Protection (IPP) with a minimum term of 8 years (less time on remand). Throughout the prisoner's incarceration, he had been a Category A prisoner, and maintained his innocence, including seeking to appeal his conviction and pursuing an application to the Criminal Cases Review Commission (CRCC) for his case to be treated as a miscarriage of justice. His tariff expired on 14 February 2016. Nine months before the expiry of his tariff the prisoner changed position and admitted to his offending, withdrawing his CRCC application. He completed the Sex Offender Treatment Programme (SOTP) in November 2015 and the Core Programme in October 2016. Reports began to be prepared for his review before the Parole Board which took place on 18 November 2017. The account he gave in the reports was in many respects minimizing his offending and inconsistent; questions were not put to him during the hearing challenging this account. The Court concluded, "It is a fair reading of the notes of the hearing that the credibility and reliability of Mr Radford's account was not probed to any extent, if at all". The Parole Board, in directing his release had concluded that the prisoner had taken "full responsibility" for his offending and "learnt to be open and honest with professionals."

### The claim

The victims heard the news in the media on 4 January 2018 that the prisoner's release had been directed by the Parole Board and began judicial review proceedings, notwithstanding that the details of the decision were prohibited from being made public. In declaring Rule 25 was ultra vires the Court found, "There is no objective necessity for a rule which stifles the provision of all information relating to the proceedings of the Parole Board". In respect of the information used by the Parole Board to make their decision, the Court found that whilst there was relevant information missing from the dossier, the Parole Board had made no attempt to make further enquiries of material available that could have been relevant in assessing the veracity of the prisoner's account and therefore have a bearing on the assessment of risk. Importantly, missing from the dossier was the Prosecuting Opening from the trial, the Sentencing Remarks of the trial judge and details of the victim DSD's successful claim against the Metropolitan Police for failures in the police investigation into the prisoner's offending which found breaches of her Human Rights under Articles 3 and 8 of the European Convention on Human Rights and Fundamental Freedoms (ECHR). Green J initially held [2014] EWHC 436 QB that between 2003 and 2008 the prisoner had committed in excess of 105 rapes and sexual assaults upon women in his taxi. He also found that the prisoner was, "clinical and conniving" and his methodology had become, "ever more refined". Evidence in the case had included the Prosecution Opening, a witness statement from DSD and police evidence relating to the discovery of a "rape kit" in the prisoner's car which included condoms and the sedative drug Nytol. There was also a witness statement from the prisoner confirming that he had settled civil claims of 11 victims without admitting to liability to the sum of £241,000. The decision was upheld in the Court of Appeal [2015] EWCA Civ 646 and the Supreme Court [2018] UKSC 11. Such material would have provided more extensive details of the gravity of the prisoner's offending, such that the prisoner's account could have been tested, potentially having a bearing on the assessment of risk. The Parole Board had not made enquiries to obtain any of this material.

The Court quashed the decision of the Parole Board and remitted the case back for a fresh determination.

*Wright v The Parole Board of England and Wales* [2017] EWHC 3007 (Admin)

The claimant prisoner (W) applied for judicial review of the Parole Board's failure to adjourn his third parole review, which had been previously adjourned in order that a full psychological risk assessment, including an assessment of personality disorder could be made. The assessment had not been completed for the adjourned hearing. The Court held that there was largely a consensus between three psychologists that attended the adjourned hearing (and a member of the panel was also a qualified psychologist) which provided sufficient information for the Parole Board to make the decision in assessing W's risk and refusing to make a direction to release him. There was no unfairness in failing to adjourn the hearing again.

*R (Hoffman) v The Parole Board* [2015] EWHC 2519 (Admin)
The Parole Board's decision to refuse a prisoner's transfer to open conditions was set aside where the wrong legal test had been used. An assessment of a prisoner's suitability for open conditions was a balancing test and was a completely different from an assessment of suitability for release, which was a test which requires the satisfaction of a threshold test.

*R (Khan) v The Parole Board* [2015] EWHC 2528 (Admin)
The Parole Board had failed to give adequate reasons in not recommending a prisoner's transfer to open conditions where it was not certain whether it had followed the Secretary of State's directions to the board of August 2004. The court identified that, in similar cases, the board might find it useful to list each of the directions, possibly in an annex, and specify how it had complied with the directions.

*R (D'Cunha) v Parole Board* [2011] EWHC 128 (Admin)
The claimant prisoner (D) applied for a judicial review of a decision of the defendant Parole Board in which it declined to direct D's release from custody and declined to make a recommendation to the secretary of state that he should be transferred to open conditions. D had been sentenced to imprisonment for public protection. The secretary of state referred his case to the board to consider whether it was appropriate to direct his release and, if not, to advise whether he should be transferred to open conditions. The Court held that it was implicit in the referral from the secretary of state that the board was requested to give its advice regarding transfer to open conditions in accordance with the Directions, which had been promulgated for that purpose. It followed that there was a legitimate expectation that advice would be given in accordance with the Directions. In addition, IPP prisoners were life prisoners for the purpose of the legislation and therefore there was no basis for not treating them as such for the purpose of the Directions. Further, the section

relating to the transfer of life sentence prisoners to open conditions in the Directions was mandatory. In the instant case, the board did not consider the question of transfer to open conditions as separate from the question of release, applying a balanced assessment and having particular regard to the factors in the Directions which applied specifically to open conditions. Accordingly, the decision relating to the advice as to transfer to open conditions was to be considered afresh in accordance with the relevant section of the Directions (paras 57-59, 61-62, 65).

## PAROLE - Delay in Hearing
### Case Law
*R (Bate) v Parole Board of England and Wales* [2018] EWHC 2820 (Admin)
The Parole Board had not explained or justified a delay of four months between the target date for the prisoner's hearing and the hearing itself, and this was an unlawful breach of article 5(4). When the hearing did take place, it was accepted that he would be released to a drug rehabilitation centre, and the hearing was deferred for three months so that suitable accommodation could be found; however, the board did not then hear his case again (and finally order his release) for another nine months. This was held to be a further breach of his article 5(4) rights and he was entitled to damages. A lack of resources did not excuse that breach.

*R (Hussain) v The Parole Board of England and Wales & Anor* [2017] EWCA Civ 1074
The Parole Board appealed against the decision of Hickinbottom J [2016] EWHC 288 (Admin) to grant declaratory relief to the prisoner (H) and make an award of damages for a failure by the Parole Board to convene a required hearing within the timetable set by the Parole Board Rules. The judge had decided that the systemic failure which had arisen (through a want of resources available to the Parole Board) gave rise in turn to a breach of the ancillary duty owed to the claimant by the Parole Board, occasioned by the six-month delay in listing his case for hearing. He considered that, by reference to the published guidance, and in particular paragraph 4.1 of PSI 36/2012, the Secretary of State had decided that the appropriate time to transfer indeterminate sentence prisoners to open conditions was at, or reasonably soon after, a point three years before expiry of tariff. That, as the judge saw it, was the Secretary of State's assessment of what would enable such prisoners to have an appropriate opportunity to be able to demonstrate an acceptable risk, on expiry of tariff, so as to allow for their release. The Court of

Appeal found the judge was wrong; "Paragraph 4.1 of PSI 36/2012, properly and naturally read, connotes that the three-year period (in fact, "up to" three years) there referred to relates to the eligibility to have the case referred to the Parole Board. It does not relate to the prisoner's actual transfer to open conditions. That is the plain interpretation to be given to the wording of that paragraph; and it also accords with other paragraphs within that same PSI. With respect, the judge misconstrued this guidance."

*R (Guntrip) v The Parole Board* [2014] EWHC 4180 (Admin)

The Secretary of State breached a prisoner's right to a speedy review and rights under Article 5 when it cancelled an oral Parole hearing to allow a psychiatric assessment of the prisoner to take place. The correct approach was to adjourn the oral hearing rather than cancel it, as the latter required the process to restart (and thus caused further delay). The decision to cancel had been taken unilaterally. It undermined the parole board's status as a court that was independent of the executive, and frustrated the claimant's rights under Article 5.

*R (Sturnham) v Parole Board, R (Faulkner) v Secretary of State for Justice* [2013] UKSC 23

Detention beyond the tariff period caused by delay in violation of art.5(4) did not constitute false imprisonment. The continuing detention was authorised by statute and was lawful until the board gave a direction for release. Nor was it, ordinarily, a breach of art.5(1). For continued detention to amount to a breach of art.5(1) there had to be exceptional circumstances warranting the conclusion that it had become arbitrary. Where it had been shown on a balance of probabilities that, but for the breach, the prisoner would have been released earlier, compensatory damages were ordinarily to be awarded. They would not, however, be awarded merely for the loss of a chance of early release. For an award of damages to be appropriate, it was not always necessary to show that the prisoner would have been released earlier but for the breach. The ECtHR presumed that, in any event, a failure to speedily decide the lawfulness of a detention resulted in frustration and anxiety for the prisoner, for which modest damages should be awarded. Whether a prisoner's frustration and anxiety were, in any given case, sufficiently serious to warrant an award of damages would, however, depend to some extent on the facts. While it was impossible to lay down absolute rules, damages would only be appropriate if the delay was significant. A delay of three months or more was likely to merit damages on a modest scale.

*R (Black) v Secretary of State for Justice* [2009] UKHL 1

A prisoner serving a determinate sentence was not entitled by virtue of the European Convention on Human Rights 1950 art.5(4) to a speedy judicial decision on the lawfulness of any continued period of detention once his parole eligibility date had arrived. The secretary of state's power to reject a recommendation of the Parole Board to release such a prisoner on licence at the halfway stage of his term was anomalous, but was not contrary to art.5(4).

**PAY, inmates'**
**See "Work, inmates'".**

**PAYMENTS**
See HMPPS Finance Manual (3 November 2020).

**PAYROLL**
See HMPPS Finance Manual (3 November 2020).

**P.E. EQUIPMENT – mandatory contracts**
PSI 36/2004 was cancelled in March 2018, considered out of date and was no longer used. Information is now on category specific pages on the Ministry of Justice Intranet & Procurement bulletins on the HMMPS Intranet.

**PENSION RECORDS, defective**
HMPPS Finance Manual Policy Framework.

**PERFORMANCE MANAGEMENT**
PSI 12/2013 – NOMS Policy on Managing Poor Performance
PSI 02/2014 (Revision) – NOMS Policy on Managing Performance.

**PERFORMANCE RECOGNITION**
PSI 30/2010 – Recognising Performance Policies was made obsolete and replaced with PSO 8550, Staff Grievance Procedures.

**PERSONS HAVING ACCESS TO A PRISON**
**See "Visitors".**

**PERSONS UNLAWFULLY AT LARGE**
**See "Unlawfully at Large".**

**PHARMACY SERVICES FOR PRISONERS**
PSI 28/2003 – Pharmacy Services for Prisoners 3500

**PHOTOGRAPH**
**See "Record and Photograph".**

**PHYSICAL EDUCATION**
PSI 58/2011 – Physical Education (PE) for Prisoners
Executive Summary
Background
1.1 This Instruction, including the PE Operating Manual at Annex A supports the implementation

of the Service Specification for Physical Education (PE) in prisons and sets out the mandatory instructions in order to provide effective PE for prisoners.

1.2 There are no major changes in the requirement to deliver a safe, decent and legal PE programme that helps ensure that prisoners are physically fit to engage with prison work and activity opportunities whilst maintaining physical health and mental fitness in custody and also on release.

1.3 The Prisons Act 1952 sets out the legal minimum provision of one hour per week for adults and two hours per week for young offenders.

Prison Rules 1999 (Rule 29)

Young Offender Rules 2000 (Rule 41)

1.4 The Chief Medical Officers recommendations for activity were considered by the NEMC in determining a safe and decent level of PE activity. It is essential that establishments consider their local needs when agreeing an appropriate level of PE provision..

PR 29

Prison Rule 29

Physical Education

29- (1) If circumstances reasonably permit, a prisoner aged 21 years or over shall be given the opportunity to participate in physical education for at least one hour a week.

(2) The following provisions shall apply to the extent circumstances reasonably permit to a prisoner who is under 21 years of age -

(a) provision shall be made for the physical education of such a prisoner within the normal working week, as well as evening and weekend physical recreation; the physical education activities will be such as foster personal responsibility and the prisoner's interests and skills and encourage him to make good use of his leisure on release; and

(b) arrangements shall be made for each such prisoner who is a convicted prisoner to participate in physical education for two hours a week on average.

(3) In the case of a prisoner with a need for remedial physical activity, appropriate facilities will be provided.

### POLICE INTERVIEWS
PR 36
YOI 15

### POLICE NATIONAL COMPUTER
PSO 0905 – Operation of the Police National Computer
PSO 0905 (Extract)
Operation of the Police National Computer
KEY POINTS

• The installation of PNC terminals enables establishments to gain more speedy access to prisoners' previous convictions

• Better access to Pre-Convictions, allows local prisons to categorise and allocate prisoners, serving short sentences, who sometimes remain 'Uncategorised', because Pre-Convictions are not easily obtainable

• Those establishments that do not have a PNC terminal, can ask a nearby establishment with one, to print and send them a prisoners' Schedule of Pre-Convictions, via a set procedure.

1.1.1. Police permission to use PNC within prisons is given on the understanding that : (a), only trained staff have access to the terminals (see Chapter 5 for training arrangements); (b), they adhere strictly to the Operating Procedures and Data Protection Arrangements set out in Chapter 2; and (c), they carry out systematic audit to ensure appropriate use of the information on the system (see Chapter 3).

### POLICE, production of prisoners at the request of
PS1 26/2012 – Production of Prisoners at the Request of Warranted Law Enforcement Agencies (Restricted)

### POLYGRAPH TESTING
See also "Release, Early – Licence Conditions"
Polygraph Examinations (Policy Framework) – Instructions for Imposing Licence Conditions for Polygraph on People Convicted of Sexual Offences (PCoSOs), Terrorist and Terrorist Connected Offences (3 August 2021)).
Replaces and cancels PSI 36/2014 and PI 53/2014 – Polygraph Examinations: Instructions for Imposing Licence Conditions for the Polygraph on Sexual Offenders.

### POPULATION CENSUS
See "National population census"

### POST, money and articles received by PR 44

### POST INCIDENT CARE FOR STAFF
Post Incident Care Policy Framework January 2022

### PRISON ENTERPRISES, Managing Risk
PSI 53/1999 – Managing Risk in Prison Enterprises 4101

### PRISON ESTATE, responsibility for
PSI 19/1998, was made obsolete by the Deregulation Team November 2016 as it relates to a now defunct Operations Unit.

### PRISON OFFICERS
ACT 7-11
- code of discipline PR 68

YOI 73
- communications to the press PR 67
YOI 72
- contact with former prisoners PR 66
YOI 71
- contract supplementary hours scheme 22/2001
Emergencies PR 69
General duties PR 62
YOI 67
- gratuities PR 63
YOI 68
- identification see Identification of prison staff when on duty
- internal conversion programme for Prison Service staff wishing to become prison officers Staff Resourcing Policy
PSI 7/2003 – Internal conversion programme for Prison Service staff wishing to become prison officers 8100
YOI 69
ACT 8A
- training see Point training
- transactions with inmates PR 65
YOI 70
- transfer & promotion 48/1997
- unfunded staff surpluses 85/1997
- young offender institutions YOI 67-73

**PRISON OFFICERS' ASSOCIATION,**
**engagement with establishments**
PSO 0100 – The Prison Rules 1999; The Young Offender Institution (Amendment)(No.2) Rules 1999

**PRISON OFFICER CORRUPTION PREVENTION**
PSI 01/2016 was replaced by Counter Corruption and Reporting Wrongdoing Policy Framework in April 2019.
1. Purpose
1.1. HMPPS' efforts to tackle corruption are integral to delivering a safe and secure prison and probation service – for staff, offenders and the community. Corruption facilitates the flow of drugs, mobile phones and other illicit items into prisons. These, in turn, fuel violence, debt and the illicit economy. Corruption puts the safety of offenders, staff and visitors to prisons at risk; damages the reputation of the organisation; reduces workforce morale and performance; and compromises confidence in HMPPS' ability to run safe and secure prison and probation services that protect the public and rehabilitate offenders.
1.2. We have a clear strategy for tackling corruption and a plan to continually improve our approach over time. Our ambition is to create an organisation that is resilient to the threat of corruption, can protect its hard-working staff, prevent any who might be manipulated into corruption and target those engaging in corrupt behaviour through four strategic approaches:

• PROTECT against corruption by understanding threats, having robust policies, processes and procedures in place and holding ourselves to account
• PREVENT staff from engaging in corruption by recruiting a resilient workforce, strengthening capability and professional integrity and managing corruption risks
• PURSUE and punish those involved in corruption through disciplinary and criminal justice outcomes
• PREPARE for the consequences of corrupt behaviour and support teams where corruption has occurred.

**PRISON POLICY**
**Key Note**
Unlawful Prison Policies can give rise to potential claims in a wide range of cases. In order to be lawful, policies have to comply with statute, PSIs and ECHR law, and should not be applied in an indiscriminate "blanket" fashion.

**PRISON SERVICE ORDERS & INSTRUCTIONS**
PSI 29/2012 (Revision) - The Instructions System – The Approval and Implementation of Policy and Instructions
The current system
2.4        From 1 August 2009, all new Instructions have been issued in one or more of the following formats: -
• Prison Service Instructions (PSIs) convey mandatory actions to prison establishments.
• Probation Instructions (PIs) convey mandatory instructions to Probation Trusts.
• NOMS Agency Instructions (AIs) convey mandatory instructions to NOMS HQ staff (including, where appropriate, the regional structures). A PSI or PI will not also be an AI if it is only of interest to the originating unit in HQ.
2.5        All three Instruction types have an expiry date which can be up to four years from date of issue, although they can be re-issued to extend their validity, or cancelled or amended before the expiry date if required.    Further instructions on setting expiry dates are contained in Chapter 3.
2.6        It is the responsibility of policy leads to ensure that the instructions they are responsible for are updated.    Regardless of expiry dates, instructions remain in force until specifically cancelled, marked "obsolete" or replaced and removed from the Intranet.
2.7        To help users, all instructions should be concise with the mandatory instructions easily identifiable.    Additional guidance for practitioners, which does not contain any mandatory actions, should be included in annexes which will be hyperlinked to the

relevant instructions, version controlled, and kept up to date or cancelled when necessary.

## PRISON SERVICE UNION, provision of facilities to individual members
PSI 18/1999 was made obsolete by the Deregulation team in February 2017 as it was no longer a recognised union.

## PRISONER ACTIVITIES
PSI 03/2012 – Activity Allocation
Executive Summary
Background
1.1 Prisoners engage in a range of activities during their time in custody to facilitate order and control, rehabilitation and resettlement, this includes but is not restricted to the following activities:
• Learning and skills
• Gymnasium
• Offending Behaviour Programmes
• Rehabilitation Services
• Prison Industries and other areas of prisoner employment
1.2 Where possible, the working week should be subject to a common routine and replicate a working week in the community with appointments being made during non-working hours so as to minimise disruption.
1.3 Where possible allocation should be based upon individual need and reflect the required sequencing and prioritisation of interventions identified through sentence planning. Timetabling of allocations should be planned and for the efficient operation of this PSI, effective communication systems must be established between all departments that offer activity and/or interventions to prisoners.

## PRISONERS ASSISTING OTHER PRISONERS
PSI 17/2015 (Revision) - Prisoners Assisting Other Prisoners
January 2020 – Minor changes to align with new Incentives Policy Framework.
This policy describes the principles that apply to all formal arrangements for prisoners to provide assistance, including meeting certain needs for care and support, to other prisoners. It requires every prison to have the ability to mobilise assistance from other prisoners should it be needed for a prisoner who has a care and support plan or is awaiting a care and support needs assessment.

## PRISONER COMMUNICATIONS
See also "Human Rights – Article 10; "Media"; and "Visits".
YOI 9 – 17:
YOI 9 – Communications Generally
YOI 10 – Personal letters and visits

YOI 11 – Interception of communications
YOI 12 – Permanent log of communications
YOI 13 – Disclosure of material
YOI 14 – Retention of material
YOI 15 – Police interviews
YOI 16 – Visits from legal advisers
YOI 17 – Delivery and receipt of legally privileged material
PR 34 – 39
PR 34 – Communications generally (excerpt below)
PR 35 – Personal letters and visits (excerpt below)
PR 35A – Interception of communications
PR 35B – Permanent log of communications
PR 35C – Disclosure of material
PR 35D – Retention of material
PR 36 – Police interviews
PR 37 – Securing release
PR 38 – Visits from legal advisers
PR 39 – Delivery and receipt of legally privileged material
Prison Rules 34 and 35
34.— Communications generally
(1)        Without prejudice to sections 6 and 19 of the Prison Act 1952 and except as provided by these Rules, a prisoner shall not be permitted to communicate with any person outside the prison, or such person with him, except with the leave of the Secretary of State or as a privilege under rule 8.
(2)        Notwithstanding paragraph (1) above, and except as otherwise provided in these Rules, the Secretary of State may impose any restriction or condition, either generally or in a particular case, upon the communications to be permitted between a prisoner and other persons if he considers that the restriction or condition to be imposed—
(a)        does not interfere with the convention rights of any person; or
(b)
(i) is necessary on grounds specified in paragraph (3) below;
(ii) reliance on the grounds is compatible with the convention right to be interfered with; and
(iii) the restriction or condition is proportionate to what is sought to be achieved.
(3)   The grounds referred to in paragraph (2) above are—
(a) the interests of national security;
(b) the prevention, detection, investigation or prosecution of crime;
(c) the interests of public safety;
(d) securing or maintaining prison security or good order and discipline in prison;
(e) the protection of health or morals;
(f) the protection of the reputation of others;
(g) maintaining the authority and impartiality of the judiciary; or
(h) the protection of the rights and freedoms of any person.

(4) Subject to paragraph (2) above, the Secretary of State may require that any visit, or class of visits, shall be held in facilities which include special features restricting or preventing physical contact between a prisoner and a visitor.

(5) Every visit to a prisoner shall take place within the sight of an officer or employee of the prison authorised for the purposes of this rule by the governor (in this rule referred to as an "authorised employee" ), unless the Secretary of State otherwise directs, and for the purposes of this paragraph a visit to a prisoner shall be taken to take place within the sight of an officer or authorised employee if it can be seen by an officer or authorised employee by means of an overt closed circuit television system.

(6) Subject to rule 38, every visit to a prisoner shall take place within the hearing of an officer or authorised employee, unless the Secretary of State otherwise directs.

(7) The Secretary of State may give directions, either generally or in relation to any visit or class of visits, concerning the day and times when prisoners may be visited.

(8) In this rule—

(a) references to communications include references to communications during visits;

(b) references to restrictions and conditions upon communications include references to restrictions and conditions in relation to the length, duration and frequency of communications; and

(c) references to convention rights are to the convention rights within the meaning of the Human Rights Act 1998.

35.— Personal letters and visits

(1) Subject to paragraph (8), an unconvicted prisoner may send and receive as many letters and may receive as many visits as he wishes within such limits and subject to such conditions as the Secretary of State may direct, either generally or in a particular case.

(2) Subject to paragraphs (2A) and (8) , a convicted prisoner shall be entitled—

(a) to send and to receive a letter on his reception into a prison and thereafter once a week; and

(b) to receive a visit twice in every period of four weeks, but only once in every such period if the Secretary of State so directs.

(2A) A prisoner serving a sentence of imprisonment to which an intermittent custody order relates shall be entitled to receive a visit only where the governor considers that desirable having regard to the extent to which he has been unable to meet with his friends and family in the periods during which he has been temporarily released on licence.

(3) The governor may allow a prisoner an additional letter or visit as a privilege under rule 8 or where necessary for his welfare or that of his family.

(4) The governor may allow a prisoner entitled to a visit to send and to receive a letter instead.

(5) The governor may defer the right of a prisoner to a visit until the expiration of any period of cellular confinement.

(6) The independent monitoring board may allow a prisoner an additional letter or visit in special circumstances, and may direct that a visit may extend beyond the normal duration.

(7) The Secretary of State may allow additional letters and visits in relation to any prisoner or class of prisoners.

(8) A prisoner shall not be entitled under this rule to receive a visit from:

(a) any person, whether or not a relative or friend, during any period of time that person is the subject of a prohibition imposed under rule 73; or

(b) any other person, other than a relative or friend, except with the leave of the Secretary of State.

(9) Any letter or visit under the succeeding provisions of these Rules shall not be counted as a letter or visit for the purposes of this rule.

PSI 04/2005 – Mandatory Contracts – Touchscreens Prisoner Information Systems

PSI 62/2001 – Child Protection Protocol 4950

National Offender Management Service, PUBLIC PROTECTION MANUAL 2016 Edition

PSI 16/2011 (Revision) – Providing Visits and Services to Visitors

Updated Jan 2019 as APVS elements have moved to the Strengthening Prisoner's Family Ties Policy Framework

PSI 25/2014 – IT Security Policy

26 June 2021 – This policy has been up-dated to reflect the termination of CRC contracts

PSI 49/2011 (Re-Issued) – Prisoner Communication Services (excerpt below)

Updated in November 2020 and September 2021. Revised to align with a number of policies.

Executive Summary

Background

1. This Instruction supports the implementation of the Prisoner Communication Services specification.

2. Prison Rules require prisons to actively encourage prisoners to maintain outside contacts and meaningful family ties. Prisoners also have a statutory entitlement to send and receive letters. Letters and phone calls assist in sustaining supportive relationships with family and friends. They also enable the prisoner to have access to justice through legally privileged correspondence with legal advisers and other support organisations with whom they may correspond confidentially.

3. Being able to communicate with those outside is part of providing a safe and decent

environment for prisoners and contributes to a reduction in self-selfharm and suicide. Access to communication is also crucial in helping prisoners prepare for release.

4. The duty to encourage contact must be balanced against the risks which may be associated with the ability of prisoners to communicate with those outside. Communication must be managed to prevent the trafficking of unauthorised items, ensure the protection of the public and prevent escapes.

5. The BT PIN phone system operates in every public sector prison and all but three contracted establishments. The system has been specifically designed to strike a balance between the security and good order of establishments, the need for prisoners to keep in contact with their families and friends and the protection of the public from unwanted telephone contact from prisoners. (...)

Desired Outcome

6. Prisoners can communicate and maintain ties with family and friends and communicate confidentially with legal advisers and some other organisations in a manner which does not compromise safety. The process meets minimum statutory requirements and ensures that the security and good order of the prison is maintained.

**Case Law**

*Hirst v Secretary of State for the Home Department* [2002] EWHC 602 (Admin)

A policy that denied a prisoner the right to contact the media by telephone whenever his purpose was to comment on matters of legitimate public interest was unlawful.

*R v Secretary of State for the Home Department, Ex Parte Ian Simms : R v Same, Ex Parte Michael O'Brien* (2000) 2 AC 115; (1999) 3 WLR 328; (1999) 3 All ER 400; (1999) EMLR 689; (1999) COD 520; Times, July 9, 1999; House of Lords

A convicted prisoner had a fundamental and basic right to communicate orally with the media through a journalist, in order to challenge the safety of his conviction, and the policy of the Secretary of State for the Home Department made under paragraph 37 and paragraph 37A of Section A of Prison Service Standing Order 5 was unlawful to the event that it interfered with that right.

**PRISONER COMPLAINTS**

See also "Complaints procedure" above.

The Prisoner Complaints Policy Framework, perhaps predictably, does not set out clearly that prisoners have the right to take legal advice from qualified legal advisers. In Annex E (Other Avenues of Complaint) there is no explicit reference to the important remedy of Judicial Review.

Prisoner Complaints Policy Framework (extract below)

1. Purpose

1.1 To set out requirements and information on providing a fair and effective system for dealing with prisoner complaints, including by ensuring procedural justice and taking a problem solving approach for both adult prisoners and young people. Additional requirements which apply specifically to young people are set out in PSI 08/2012: Care and Management of Young People.

Evidence 2.1

2.1 Evidence indicates that when people believe the process of applying rules (how a decision is made, rather than what decision is made) is fair, it influences their views and behaviour. This is called procedural justice. When people feel processes are applied fairly and justly, they have more confidence and trust in authority figures, see authority figures as being more legitimate, and they are more likely to accept and abide (or commit to abide) by decisions and rules, and comply and cooperate with authority, even if the outcome is not in their favour. It is also necessary in order to ensure prisoners are treated with respect and improve outcomes in terms of their daily life.

2.2 Revised complaint forms provide guidance to ensure that there is greater procedural justice within the prisoner complaints system (please see Annex A). The reason for this is that there is strong evidence that a complaints system that feels procedurally just leads to greater respect from prisoners for staff and authority, and less violence and misconduct in prison.

2.3 The guidance to staff and revised complaint forms reduce the potential impact of bias on decision making about handling complaints.

3. Outcomes

• Prisons have an effective system with a clear set of procedures for dealing with prisoners' complaints.

• Prisoners know how to make a formal complaint and have ready access to the means to do so. Complaints are managed effectively at an early stage to avoid a similar occurrence in the future and prevent the instigation of a litigation claim wherever possible. A simple investigation should identify the main issues to be considered and what remedial action needs to be taken

• Prisoners who have disabilities, literacy and learning difficulties or for whom English is not their first language are given the necessary support needed to submit a complaint.

• Prisoners have confidence in the system and believe that the decision making is fair. Responses are meaningful, considered and easily understood through a problem solving approach.

• Prisoners do not suffer detriment as a consequence of complaining.

• Complaints are answered in line with the timeliness requirements set out in this Framework.

• Complaints are considered using the 'balance of probabilities' burden of proof and appropriate action is taken when complaints are upheld.

• There is a confidential system for complaints.

• Complaint management and monitoring arrangements drive improvements across all services. Complaints Policy Framework Issue Date 13th February 2020 5

• Complaints identified as relating to Reserved Subjects (see Annex B) are passed on to the relevant people for action and processing.

• There is an avenue of appeal and Governors/Directors and all staff are familiar with the role and remit of the Prisons and Probation Ombudsman (PPO) and all prisoners entering a prison are made aware of the function and accessibility of the PPO (see Annex C for further information).

1.3 An effective system for dealing with prisoner complaints underpins much of prison life. It helps to ensure that the Prison Service meets its obligation of dealing fairly, openly and humanely with prisoners. It also helps staff by instilling in prisoners greater confidence that their needs and welfare are being looked after, reducing tension and promoting better relations. A prison's equilibrium is more likely to be maintained if prisoners feel they have an accessible and effective means of making a complaint, an outlet for their grievances and confidence that their complaints will be considered properly, with reasons given for decisions.

1.4 The aim is for resolution at the lowest level in the most expeditious manner. Prisoners do not have to use the formal complaints system set out in this Instruction to raise their concerns, although there must be no obstacle or deterrent to them doing so if they wish. However, if residential staff maintain the engagement with prisoners set out in the Residential Services specification and accompanying PSI 75/2011, many issues should be resolved informally.

4 Requirements

4.1 Prisoners are statutorily entitled to make complaints under Rule 11 of the Prison Rules 1999 and Rule 8 of the YOI Rules 2000.

4.2 Under the Prison Act 1952 it is a requirement that every prison is monitored by an Independent Monitoring Board (IMB). IMB members undertake a variety of activities in prison including receiving any complaint or request (known as an 'application') which the prisoner wishes to make to them.

4.3 In accordance with Public Sector Equality Duty (Equality Act 2010, section 149), In operating a complaints system, prison authorities must have due regard to the need to:

• Eliminate unlawful discrimination, harassment and victimisation and other conduct prohibited by the Equality Act 2010.

• Advance equality of opportunity between people who share a protected characteristic and those who do not.

• Foster good relations between people who share a protected characteristic and those who do not.

**PRISONER ESCORT RECORD FORM, introduction of**

Person Escort Record Policy Framework

**PRISONER FINANCE**

PSI 01/2012 (Revision) – Manage Prisoner Finance (excerpt below). This was amended by PSI 30/2013.

Re-issued October 2019 following publication of new HMPPS Finance Manual Policy Framework. January 2020: Minor changes to align with new Incentives Policy Framework. November 2020: Changes made to align with the Financial Investigation Unit Policy Framework.

1. Executive Summary

Background

1.1 This instruction supports the Manage Prisoner Finance Specification. However as much of the specification is about the process and not the policy, reference to NOMS Finance Manual, (Chapter 15 Prisoners' Finance) is made throughout this document.

1.2 The NOMS Finance Manual, Chapter 15 describes the processes involved in the effective recording and management of monies brought in by prisoners upon initial reception, monies sent in/out by post and the day to day expenditure undertaken by prisoners.

1.3 All transactions are accounted for, managed and reconciled.

1.4 Prisoners' financial transactions are conducted in line with IEP Scheme limits.

1.5 Money earned within the prison by prisoners is credited to their Prison-NOMIS spending account.

1.6 Prisoners are able to send money out.

1.7 Prisoners are able to conduct such personal financial affairs as are necessary and permitted in order to meet their resettlement needs.

1.8 Prisoners designated by HM Treasury as subject to asset freezing regulations have their funds managed accordingly.

1.9 Information about a prisoner's Prison-NOMIS account is available and can be provided to them upon request.

**PRISONER INDUCTION**

See PSI 07/2015 - "Early Days in Custody".

PSI 07/2015 (Revision) – Early Days in Custody – Reception in, First night in Custody, and Induction to Custody (excerpt below)

January 2020: Minor changes to align with new Incentives Policy Framework.

4. Induction to Custody

4.1 Key outcome: Prisoners know and understand their entitlements and responsibilities, and how to access support and facilities available to them.

4.2 All prisoners undergoing induction must be treated decently, with full regard for equality, vulnerability, and any special needs. Safer custody requirements must be followed at all times and risks appropriately managed.

## PRISONER RETAIL

PSI 23/2013 (Revision) – Prisoner Retail (excerpt below)

January 2020: Minor changes to align with new Incentives Policy Framework.

1. Executive Summary

1.1 This revised instruction introduces the policy of allowing more frequent price changes that mean that prices available to prisoners better reflect the reality of retail price increases (and decreases) as experienced by the general public. It will also allow prices to change in real time rather than at quarterly intervals. The policy change will also support the introduction of weekly local product lists that might include short term offers and remove items that are temporarily unavailable or withdrawn for supplier or security reasons.

Background

1.2        This instruction enacts and supports the Prisoner Retail Specification in order to provide a retail ordering service, catalogue items, and newspapers/periodicals to prisoners which meet the diverse needs of the local population, has transparent prices, does not compromise control or security, and has standardised products, prices, and operational procedures.

1.3        For prisoner retail product supply and service, the agreed contractor is DHL/Booker. The agreed contractor may change following contract expiration and re-tender.

Desired outcomes

1.4        This instruction aims to ensure that:

• Prisoners are able to spend their earnings and private cash which has been transferred into their spends account to purchase items for their own use.

• Prisoners are able to purchase items at prices not higher than recommended retail prices (rrp).

• Prison security and individual health and safety are not compromised by the ordering and delivery process.

• Good order and discipline is supported by prisoner access to items in accordance with the local incentives and earned privileges scheme.

• Items available for purchase by prisoners support decency and reflect the diverse needs and protected characteristics of the prisoner population.

• Products, prices, and operational procedures are standardised.

• Provision of retail goods to prisoners is accurate and timely.

• Purposeful activity is provided for prisoners with opportunities for them to acquire skills for resettlement.

## PRISONERS' DISCHARGE GRANTS
See "Discharge of Prisoners".
## PRISONERS' EARNINGS
See "Earnings, Prisoners"; and "Prisoners' Pay"

## PRISONERS' PAY

PSI 76/2011 (Revision) – Prisoners' Earning Act 1996 (excerpt below)

Executive summary

Update

1.1 NOMS along with all other government departments are undergoing a change to their banking arrangements. From 17 February 2016, NOMS will no longer be banking with Citi bank. The Natwest (RBS) account, which is currently only used for cheque and cash payments, will remain in place and be the only bank account used. On 31 March 2016 the Citi bank account will be closed and it is possible that any payments made to that account from then on will be returned to sender. As a result of this change, all references to the Citi bank account have been replaced with the RBS details in this PSI at paragraphs 1.13, 2.1.5 and Annex C. The Memorandum of Understanding at Annex C has also been replaced with the updated version that is in the ROTL policy (PSI 13/2015). The letter to employers at Annex F also now incorporates a reminder that they must quote the prisoner's reference on all payments to avoid delays in processing.

1.2 A reminder has also been included at paragraph 2.1.4 of the requirement on prison staff to submit PEA001 forms promptly to Shared Services. Late or no notification of amendments to the levy rate for prisoners exiting the scheme or a particular employer withdrawing from the scheme can result in over/underpayments. The former requires a process of debt recovery which is relatively simple if the prisoner is still working. However often if the prisoner has been discharged, it may need to be written off by the establishment. The latter would most often require a refund to be made to the prisoner, the calculation of which is a complex and time consuming process.

Background

1.3 The Prisoners' Earnings Act 1996 (PEA) and related Rules came into force on 26 September 2011. Under the terms of the Act, prisoners who are undertaking paid work in the community and earning in excess of £20 a week may be made subject to the imposition of a levy amounting to up to (and including) 40% of their remaining earnings ('the excess'). The levy is applied to earnings over £20 per week, so if a prisoner earns £25 per week net, the levy is made only from £5 per week, not the full £25. Levies are currently paid to such voluntary organisations concerned with victim support or crime prevention or both as may be prescribed. The PEA defines "net weekly earnings" as weekly earnings after deduction of such of the following as are applicable, namely –

(a) income tax;

(b) national insurance contributions;

(c) payments required to be made by an order of a court; and

(d) payments required to be made by virtue of a maintenance assessment within the meaning of the Child Support Act 1991.

1.4 This instruction is relevant only to prisoners working outside the prison for outside employers

PSO 4460 – Prisoners' Pay (revision) (excerpt below)

2.1.1 All prisoners who participate in purposeful activity must be paid. Those who refuse must not receive any pay. Prisoners may also lose earnings for disciplinary reasons. Unconvicted prisoners can work if they wish to and must be paid the same rates as convicted prisoners.

2.1.2 An allowance should be made in the standard working week (see paragraph 2.4.1) of each prisoner for authorised absences from purposeful activity. These may include Governor's applications, welfare interviews, sick parade etc. These will be accommodated without loss of pay provided that the allowance is not exceeded.

**Case Law**

*R (on the application of S, KF v Secretary of State for Justice)* [2012] EWHC 1810 (Admin)

The Administrative Court dismissed judicial review claims by 2 Prisoners against the imposition of the newly imposed 40% levy on Prisoners working in the community. The Claimants argued that the levy was unlawful as amounting to a retrospective penalty and as being disproportionate and discriminatory. In a lengthy judgment, the Court rejected each of these arguments.

## PRISONERS' PROPERTY

**See also "Property, Prisoners",**

PSI 14/2015 – Disposal of Prisoners Unauthorised Property. This should be read in conjunction with PSI 15/2010. In January 2020, minor changes were made to align with new Incentives PF.

PSI 08/2016 – National Security Framework Ref. NSF 3.3 Dealing with Evidence

PSI 30/2011 – National Security Framework ref:

NSF 6.8 Security Management Function: Instructions on Handling Mobile Phones and SIM Card Seizures

## PRISONS

ACT 37 – Closing of prisons.

ACT 1 – General control over.

ACT 34 – Jurisdiction of sheriff, etc.

ACT 33 – Power to provide prisons, etc.

ACT 36 – Acquisition of land for prisons.

## PRISONS OMBUDSMAN

PSI 58/ 2010 (Revised) – Prisons and Probation Ombudsman. Updated in January 2022.

## PRIVILEGES

**See also "Incentives and Earned Privileges".**

**Case Law**

*R (MA) v Independent Adjudicator* [2013] EWHC 438 (Admin)

See "Adjudications" above".

## PROBATION

Post Sentence Supervision Requirements Policy Framework (26 March 2020)

Enforcement of Community Orders, Suspended Sentence Orders and Post-sentence supervision Policy Framework (26 June 2021)

Licence Conditions Policy Framework (26 July 2021)

Travel and Transfer on Licence and PSS Outside of England and Wales (26 July 2021)

Managing Parole Eligible Offenders on Licence Policy Framework (11 November 2020)

Release on Temporary Licence (ROTL) Policy Framework (Re-issued 17 August 2021)

Polygraph Examinations – Instructions for Imposing Licence Conditions for Polygraph on People Convicted of Sexual Offences (PCoSOs), Terrorist and Terrorist Connected Offences (3 August 2021)

PSI 32/2014 – Drug Appointment and Drug Testing for Licence Conditions and Post-Sentence Supervision Requirements

## PROCEEDINGS, discontinuance of

PSI 48/2000 – Amendment to PSO 6100 – the Bail System 6100

## PRODUCTION OF PRISONERS

At police request see "Police, production of prisoners"

At civil proceedings see "Civil proceedings, productions in"

**Case Law**

*Hillman v Governor Of Bronzefield Prison* [2013] 5 WLUK 641

The failure to produce a defendant in court because of an error in the administrative process was capable of amounting to an "accident" within the meaning of the Magistrates' Courts

Act 1980 s.129(1), so as to entitle magistrates to exercise their discretion and remand her in custody in her absence.

*Vaganovs v Governor Of HMP Wandsworth* [2013] EWHC 1077 (Admin)
The claimant's application for habeas corpus failed, as he had not shown that he had not been brought before the appropriate judge under a European arrest warrant as soon as practicable; the 24-hour delay in transporting him from Bradford, where he had been arrested, to London had not been the fault of the police.

## PROFESSIONAL STANDARDS: preventing and handling staff wrongdoing
Counter Corruption and Reporting Wrongdoing Policy Framework (26 June 2021)

## PROHIBITED ARTICLES
See also "Property, prisoners'"; and "Knives and Offensive Weapons".
PSI 21/2015 – Revisions to NSF Function 6.3 New Legislation – Unauthorised Possession Within Prisons of Knives and Other Offensive Weapons
PSI 10/2012 – Conveyance and Possession of Prohibited Items and Other Related Offences. Updated in November 2021.

### Case Law
*R v Shahadat* [2017] EWCA Crim 822
The supply of drugs within the prison community was not automatically excluded from coming within category 3 of the sentencing guideline on drug offences just because it was undertaken by someone other than a prison employee. On the contrary, the supply by a prisoner selling directly to others could still fall within category 3, either because of the quantity involved or because the facts disclosed that it was street dealing. The sentence for such an offence had to reflect the highly aggravating feature of a supply within prison and a term of three years' imprisonment was appropriate following a prisoner's pleas of guilty to supplying Class A drugs and possession with intent to supply.

*R v Bayliss* [2013] EWCA Crim 1067
Sentences of 30 months' imprisonment for a prisoner who had played the dominant role in a supply of cannabis and buprenorphine into prison over two months, and 10 months each for his partner and mother, who had helped him, were appropriate.

*R v King* [2013] EWCA Crim 1599
A prison officer's sentence for three counts of misconduct in public office, which included failing to report her relationship with a former prisoner and providing him with a phone in prison, and an offence of concealing criminal property, was reduced from three years' imprisonment to 27 months' imprisonment.

## PROLIFIC AND OTHER PRIORITY OFFENDERS
PSO 4615 – Prolific And Other Priority Offenders Strategy

## PROPERTY, Prisoners'
PR43 – Prisoners Property (excerpt below)
(1) Subject to any directions of the Secretary of State, an unconvicted prisoner may have supplied to him at his expense and retain for his own use books, newspapers, writing materials and other means of occupation, except any that appears objectionable to the independent monitoring board or, pending consideration by them, to the governor.
(2) Anything, other than cash, which a prisoner has at a prison and which he is not allowed to retain for his own use shall be taken into the governor's custody. An inventory of a prisoner's property shall be kept, and he shall be required to sign it, after having a proper opportunity to see that it is correct.
(2A) Where a prisoner is serving a sentence of imprisonment to which an intermittent custody order relates, an inventory as referred to in paragraph (2) shall only be kept where the value of that property is estimated by the governor to be in excess of £100.
(3) Any cash which a prisoner has at a prison shall be paid into an account under the control of the governor and the prisoner shall be credited with the amount in the books of the prison.
(4) Any article belonging to a prisoner which remains unclaimed for a period of more than one year after he leaves prison, or dies, may be sold or otherwise disposed of; and the net proceeds of any sale shall be paid to the National Association for the Care and Resettlement of Offenders, for its general purposes.
(5) The governor may confiscate any unauthorised article found in the possession of a prisoner after his reception into prison, or concealed or deposited anywhere within a prison.
PSI 12/2011 (Revision) – Prisoners Property January 2020: Minor changes to align with new Incentives Policy Framework.

### Case Law
*R (on the application of Coleman) v Governor of Wayland Prison & Anor* [2009] EWHC 1005 (Admin)
A prison governor had no power under the Prison Rules 1999 r.43 to destroy a mobile telephone confiscated from a prisoner.

## PROPRIETY, REGULARITY AND VALUE FOR MONEY

HMPPS Finance Manual (3 November 2020) – Chapter 2.2: Regularity, Propriety, Feasibility and Value for Money.

## PROSPECTIVE AWARD OF ADDITIONAL DAYS

PR 53 – 60

## PROTECTED WITNESS UNITS,
**operating standards for**

PSI 22/2013 – The Management of Protected Witnesses in a Prison Protected Witness Unit (Restricted)

## PROVISION OF COURT TRANSCRIPTS

Generic Parole Process Policy Framework (excerpts below)

3.1.4.        PPCS are responsible for ensuring that they have received a transcript of the sentencing remarks from the court transcriber. (…)

3.1.20.      Where a parole-eligible prisoner has appealed against conviction or sentence, PPCS will acquire a transcript of the judgement, from the Court of Appeal and the application for appeal. The prison must provide PPCS with a copy of any additional documents relating to the appeal via email, pre-releaseteamA@justice.gov.uk

5.1.5.        Transcripts for ISPs are obtained by PPCS and will be loaded onto PPUD where they can be accessed by those staff in the establishment. Transcripts of sentencing remarks are not normally available until at least seven weeks after the date of sentence. Any enquiries about the provision of sentencing remarks for ISPs should be directed to PPCS.

**Case Law**

R (Alami) v Health & Care Professions Council [2013] EWHC 1895 (Admin)

The Investigatory Committee of the Health and Care Professions Council was entitled to conclude that there was no case to answer in respect of two prisoners' complaints that a psychologist had been guilty of misconduct and/or incompetence when assessing the risk that they would pose to the public if released. Whilst there might have been flaws in the committee's reasoning, and despite trenchant criticisms of the psychologist by other experts, any misconduct had not reached a sufficient level to justify sanction.

## PUBLIC PROTECTION

See also "Multi-Agency Public Protection Arrangements (MAPPA)".

PSI 18/2016 (Revision) – Public Protection Manual National Offender Management Service, PUBLIC PROTECTION MANUAL 2016 Edition

## PUBLIC PROTECTION MANUAL

See "Public Protection".

## PUBLIC RELATIONS

PSO 0050 – Public Relations (extract below) was cancelled by DOPT in January 2019.

1.1 At a national and local level there is intense public interest in crime, criminals and prisons. The media tend to reflect that interest and have a particular interest in stories, which can be presented as "scandals". This can include misrepresenting events that we would describe as normal, and through that looking to discredit the Government of the day.

1.2 Media and public relations strategies must take account of a number of factors that surround the work of the Prison Service. The work done within the Service is difficult, often involves balancing competing priorities and has at its core careful risk assessment and risk management designed to protect the public, by holding prisoners securely, and reducing the risk of re offending. The Prison Service works with many other agencies on a regular and close basis and is politically accountable through the Prisons Minister and the Home Secretary to Parliament.

1.3 Any media and public relations strategy must take account of these factors. The operation of the Prison Service will never be risk-free and therefore we need to prepare for handling some perceived "failures". Much of the good work that is done will not be readily visible simply because it consists of stopping the occurrence of events which would, if they happened, be newsworthy. Whatever we do by way of communication with the public or other agencies must be compatible with our political accountability.

## PURPOSE OF PRISON

PR 3 – Purpose of prison training and treatment

The purpose of the training and treatment of convicted prisoners shall be to encourage and assist them to lead a good and useful life.

## RACIAL JUSTICE

PSI 32/2011 (Revision) – Ensuring Equality January 2020: Minor changes to align with new Incentives Policy Framework.

R. (on the application of Eguakhide) v Governor of Gartree Prison [2014] EWHC 1328 (Admin)

To allow a Muslim prisoner to refuse to supply a urine sample for a mandatory drugs test during religious festivals such as Ramadan would undermine the random nature of the drugs testing programme and its effectiveness.

The instant case would have been different if E had tried and failed to provide a specimen of urine, R. (on the application of Bashir) v

Independent Adjudicator (below) considered. The position was different for a prisoner who had refused to provide a urine sample when ordered to do so.

*R (on the application of Imran Bashir) v Independent Adjudicator* [2011] EWHC 1108 (Admin)
The claimant prisoner (B) applied for judicial review of his conviction by the Independent Adjudicator of failure to obey a lawful order contrary to the Prison Rules 1999 r.51(22). B, who was a Muslim, had been required to provide a urine sample under the policy relating to mandatory drug testing in prisons. He had been unable to produce the minimum amount required because he was on the third day of a three-day fast as part of his preparations for a court hearing, and had refused to break the fast by drinking the water offered to him. The adjudicator held that as B was not fasting for a religious festival, the guidance in Prison Service Order PSO 3601 paras 4.70-4.75 did not apply. He found that B was free to fast at any time for reasons of particular personal significance, but that he had to bear the consequences. The High Court held that having accepted that B was maintaining a three-day fast, which he genuinely believed could not be broken, the prison had interfered with his art.9 rights by requiring him to perform an act that depended on him breaking his fast. The lawfulness of the mandatory drug testing policy in prisons remained entirely unaffected by the case-specific and fact-sensitive conclusions in the instant case (para. 34).

## RACIAL OFFENCES
PR 51, 51A    YOI 55, 57
**Case Law**
*R (on the Application of Roger Gleaves) v The Secretary of State for the Home Department* [2004] EWHC 2522 (Admin)
The prison governor's decision that the prisoner was guilty of using racially offensive language was sound even though he had not been permitted to question the victim directly. Further there was no statutory duty on the governor to give reasons for her decision and the adequacy of the reasons was not of itself a condition of the legality of the decision.

## RADIATION
PSI 18/2015 – NOMS Health and Safety Arrangements for Radiation Safety of X Ray Security Equipment
The purpose of this PSI is to ensure that Governing Governors and Heads of Groups have in place systems and protocols to protect staff, visitors, prisoners, contractors and others from the harmful effects of ionising radiation from

security x-ray equipment and to comply with the specific legal requirements around same.

## RADON GAS
PSI 19/2015 – NOMS Health and Safety Arrangements - Assessment and Control of Radon Exposure in NOMS' Custodial Premises
To define nationally the arrangements in place in NOMS to survey and assess the risk of Radon Gas exposure in NOMS

## RECALLED PRISONERS
See also "Fixed Term Recall" – also "CJA 1991 Prisoner". Recall, Review and Re-Release of Recalled Prisoners Policy Framework (Re-Issued 13 May 2021) (excerpt below)
4.2.1 Offender managers must demonstrate a "causal link" in the current behaviour that was exhibited at the time of the index offence. One of the following criteria must be met when assessing whether to request the recall of an indeterminate sentenced offender:
(i)        Exhibits behaviour similar to behaviour surrounding the circumstances of the index offence;
(ii)       Exhibits behaviour likely to give rise (or does give rise) to a sexual or violent offence;
(iii)      Exhibits behaviour associated with the commission of a sexual or violent offence; or
Is out of touch with the offender manager and the assumption can be made that any of (i) to (iii) may arise.
4.2.2 Offender managers must ensure that there is evidence of increased risk of selfharm to the public and at least one of the criteria set out above in paragraph 4.2.1 is met.
**Case Law**
*Rainey's Application for Judicial Review, Re* [2019] NICA 76
Where an offender was required to be released on licence after serving the custodial element of an extended custodial sentence, but was recalled to prison because of a change in the risk that he posed to the public, the recall amounted to a fresh detention to which ECHR art.5(4) applied.

*Vigrass, R (on the application of) v Parole Board of England and Wales* [2017] EWHC 3022 (Admin)
The claimant prisoner (V) applied for judicial review of the Parole Board's failure to fully address the notice of the Secretary of State for Justice after the prisoner was re-called. In referring the case to the Parole Board in accordance with section 32(4) of the Crime (Sentences) Act 1997 the Secretary of State requested the Parole Board to consider whether to direct the prisoner's immediate release under section 32(5) of the 1997 Act, and further that if immediate release was not directed, the Board

was asked to consider whether the offender was ready to be moved to open prison conditions. The Parole Board decided against release, but failed to address the question of open conditions. The Court held that the Parole Board had erred and made a mandatory order directed at the Parole Board requiring it to produce a further decision letter addressing the point set out in the Secretary of State for Justice's referral letter, to consider whether the offender was ready to be moved to open prison conditions.

*Goldsworthy, R (on the application of) v Secretary of State for Justice* [2017] EWHC 2822 (Admin)

The reasoning in the decision to recall the prison was unlawful as it had failed to take into account the secretary of state's own policy under PSI 30/2014. His behaviour showed no deterioration or greater risk than anticipated, but, rather, was entirely consistent with the panel chair's assessment of the type of risk which he posed, which had been judged to be insufficient to justify detention.

*R (Calder) v Secretary of State for Justice* [2015] EWCA Civ 1050

The Parole Board has an important supervisory responsibility over the secretary of state's decision to recall prisoners who had been released on licence. The Board's powers and duties stretched to reviewing the decision to recall, and are not limited to reviewing a prisoner's continued detention

## RECORD AND PHOTOGRAPH
PR 42

42.— Record and photograph

(1)        A personal record of each prisoner shall be prepared and maintained in such manner as the Secretary of State may direct.

(2)        Every prisoner may be photographed on reception and subsequently, but no copy of the photograph or any other personal record shall be given to any person not authorised to receive it.

(2A)       In this rule "personal record" may include personal information and biometric records (such as fingerprints or other physical measurements).

## REHABILITATION SERVICES SPECIFICATION – Custody

PSI 04/2015 (Revised) – Rehabilitation Services Specification – Custody

November 2019: Updated to reflect that NPS takes over from CRC's (in Wales only) from 30 November 2019

## RELEASE DATES
See also "Sentence Calculation".

**Case Law** *R. v Patel (Tristan) (and 13 Others)* [2021] EWCA Crim 231

In the case of offenders who were convicted before 1 April 2020 of a violent or sexual offence, as specified in the Criminal Justice Act 2003 Sch.15 Pt 1 or Pt.2, and sentenced after that date to fixed-term custodial sentences of seven years or more, meaning that the Release of Prisoners (Alteration of Relevant Proportion of Sentence) Order 2020 applied, changing their point of release from half to two-thirds of their sentence, it was right that their sentences were not reduced to reflect that change. The fact that their sentencing had been delayed, in most cases because of the COVID-19 pandemic, was not sufficient to make them exceptional cases where it would be appropriate to take account of the early release provisions.

*R (Abedin) v Secretary of State for Justice* [2015] EWHC 782 (Admin)

Changes in legislation relating to the release and recall of prisoners caused the claimant's automatic release date to be at the end of his full term of imprisonment rather than at the three-quarters stage. He applied for judicial review of his automatic release date, arguing that his Article 5 and 7 rights had been violated. In refusing his application, the Court held that relevant precedent from both domestic and European authorities showed that there had been no erosion in the distinction between the penalty imposed and the means of its enforcement or execution.

## RELEASE, Early
PSI 37/2011 (Transfer to the Parole Board of functions under the Criminal Justice Act 1991: Release of long-term prisoners) was superseded by PSI 30/2012, which was made obsolete by the Deregulation Team in January 2017.

PSO 6000 – Parole Release and Recall was made obsolete by the Early Release and Compassionate Grounds Policy Framework in May 2022.

**Case Law**

*R (on the application of Caron Foley) v (1) Parole Board for England & Wales (2) Secretary of State for Justice* [2012] EWHC 2184 (Admin)

The claimant (F) applied for judicial review of a decision of the defendant Parole Board refusing to release her on licence. F was serving a determinate sentence of 18 years' imprisonment imposed in 2002 for offences including arson with intent to endanger life and manslaughter. F's release was governed by the Criminal Justice Act 1991. As a long-term determinate prisoner, she was eligible for release at the half-way stage of her sentence. In deciding whether to recommend the release on licence of a prisoner undergoing a determinate sentence, the Board had to assess the risk to the public of the commission of further offences and whether any such risk was acceptable. In relation to prisoners undergoing an indeterminate sentence, the test to be applied at the expiry of the tariff, namely the half-way point of the notional determinate sentence, was whether the level of risk to the life and limb of others was more than minimal. F's case was that her rights under the European Convention on Human Rights art.14 had been breached by the application of a test which was more onerous than that applied to an indeterminate prisoner. The Court held that in the case of indeterminate sentences, the punitive element was normally regarded as having been reached at the half-way point of the sentence. Once the tariff period had expired, the Board was considering further time in custody solely on the basis of risk. There was no good reason why those who were regarded as less dangerous because they had received a determinate sentence should be subject to greater punishment than those who had received an indeterminate sentence. Nor was there any reason to prevent both types of offender from becoming eligible for release, subject to questions of risk, at the same point in their sentence. There was therefore no material difference between the two types of sentence such as to prevent their treatment as analogous and justify comparison. Accordingly, there was no objective justification for a more stringent test in relation to the early release of determinate prisoners.

### RELEASE, EARLY – Licence Conditions

See also "Multi-Agency Public Protection Arrangements (MAPPA)"; "Parole"; and "Recalled Prisoners".

**Key Note**

Many Prisoners take issue with proposed or actual licence conditions. It is possible to challenge and amend these conditions by way of Judicial Review, particularly where the conditions are unnecessary and/or disproportionate.

Licence Conditions Policy Framework (26 July 2021)

**Case Law**

R (on the application of Bentham) (Claimant) v (1) Governor of Usk & Prescoed Prison (2) Secretary of State for Justice (Defendants) [2014] EWHC 2469 (Admin)
A condition imposed following a conviction for causing death by dangerous driving which prevented a licensee from visiting his family home was disproportionate and unjustifiably infringed his right to respect for his private and family life under the European Convention on Human Rights 1950 art.8. His total exclusion from a town centre had not been necessary to prevent a chance encounter taking place between him and the victim's family.

R (on the application of Hassan Tabbakh) V (1) Staffordshire & West Midlands Probation Trust (2) Secretary Of State For Justice [2014] EWCA Civ 827
The secretary of state's policy for deciding on the conditions to be included in an offender's licence on release from prison was not inherently unfair and unlawful by reason of the omission of specific provision for an offender to be informed in advance of proposed additional licence conditions and of the basis on which their inclusion was proposed. The offender manager was the conduit through which the offender could make informed representations.

R (on the application of C) v Ministry of Justice [2009] EWHC 2671 (Admin) [2007] EWHC 1521 (Admin)
The imposition of a polygraph condition on an offender released from prison on conditional licence did not amount to a breach of his rights under the European Convention on Human Rights 1950 art.8 as the condition was justified by the seriousness of the crimes for which he was convicted and his conduct.

### RELEASE OF DEFAULTERS, securing
PR 37

### RELEASE ON TEMPORARY LICENCE
See also "Escorted absences for cat. C life sentence prisoners". PR 9
9.— Temporary release
(1)         Subject to paragraph (1A), the Secretary of State may, in accordance with the other provisions of this rule, release temporarily a prisoner to whom this rule applies.
(1A) A prisoner who has the relevant deportation status must not be released under this rule unless the prisoner is located in open conditions immediately before the time of release.
(2)  A prisoner may be released under this rule for any period or periods and subject to any conditions.
(3)  A prisoner may only be released under this rule:
(a) on compassionate grounds or for the purpose of receiving medical treatment;
(b)  to engage in employment or voluntary work;
(c)   to receive instruction or training which cannot reasonably be provided in the prison;
(d)   to enable him to participate in any proceedings before any court, tribunal or inquiry;
(e) to enable him to consult with his legal adviser in circumstances where it is not reasonably practicable for the consultation to take place in the prison;
(f) to assist any police officer in any enquiries;
(g) to facilitate the prisoner's transfer between prisons;
(h)  to assist him in maintaining family ties or in his transition from prison life to freedom.

(i) to enable him to make a visit in the locality of the prison, as a privilege under rule

(4) A prisoner shall not be released under this rule unless the Secretary of State is satisfied that there would not be an unacceptable risk of his committing offences whilst released or otherwise failing to comply with any condition upon which he is released.

(5) The Secretary of State shall not release under this rule a prisoner serving a sentence of imprisonment if, having regard to:

(a) the period or proportion of his sentence which the prisoner has served or, in a case where paragraph (10) does not apply to require all the sentences he is serving to be treated as a single term, the period or proportion of any such sentence he has served; and

(b) the frequency with which the prisoner has been granted temporary release under this rule, the Secretary of State is of the opinion that the release of the prisoner would be likely to undermine public confidence in the administration of justice.

(6) If a prisoner has been temporarily released under this rule during the relevant period and has been sentenced to imprisonment for a criminal offence committed whilst at large following that release, he shall not be released under this rule unless his release, having regard to the circumstances of this conviction, would not, in the opinion of the Secretary of State, be likely to undermine public confidence in the administration of justice.

(7) For the purposes of paragraph (6), "the relevant period":

(a) in the case of a prisoner serving a determinate sentence of imprisonment, is the period he has served in respect of that sentence, unless, notwithstanding paragraph (10), the sentences he is serving do not fall to be treated as a single term, in which case it is the period since he was last released in relation to one of those sentences under Part II of the Criminal Justice Act 1991 ("the 1991 Act" ) or Chapter 6 of Part 12 of the 2003 Act;

(b) in the case of a prisoner serving an indeterminate sentence of imprisonment, is, if the prisoner has previously been released on licence under Part II of the Crime (Sentences) Act 1997 or Part II of the 1991 Act or Chapter 6 of Part 12 of the 2003 Act, the period since the date of his last recall to prison in respect of that sentence or, where the prisoner has not been so released, the period he has served in respect of that sentence; or

(c) in the case of a prisoner detained in prison for any other reason, is the period for which the prisoner has been detained for that reason; save that where a prisoner falls within two or more of sub-paragraphs (a) to (c), the "relevant period",

in the case of that prisoner, shall be determined by whichever of the applicable sub-paragraphs produces the longer period.

(8) A prisoner released under this rule may be recalled to prison at any time whether the conditions of his release have been broken or not.

(8A) If, immediately before the relevant time, a prisoner has been released under this rule and the prison has received notice that the prisoner has the relevant deportation status, the prisoner must be recalled unless—

(a) the period for which the prisoner has been released is due to expire on 13th August 2014; or

(b) the prisoner was released from open conditions.

(8B) If a prisoner has been released under this rule (whether before or after the relevant time) and the prison receives notice after the relevant time that the prisoner has the relevant deportation status, the prisoner must be recalled unless—

(a) the period for which the prisoner has been released is due to expire on the day on which the prison receives that notice; or

(b) the prisoner was released from open conditions.

(9) This rule applies to prisoners other than persons committed in custody for trial or to be sentenced or otherwise dealt with before or by any Crown Court or remanded in custody by any court.

(10) For the purposes of any reference in this rule to an inmate's sentence, consecutive terms and terms which are wholly or partly concurrent shall be treated as a single term.

(11) In this rule:

(a) any reference to a sentence of imprisonment shall be construed as including any sentence to detention or custody; and

(b) any reference to release on licence or otherwise under Part II of the 1991 Act includes any release on licence under any legislation providing for early release on licence.

(c) any reference to a prisoner who has the relevant deportation status is to be read in accordance with rule 7(1E) and (1F); and

(d) any reference to the relevant time is to be read in accordance with rule 7(1G).

Rule 9A and YOI 5A – Coronavirus Temporary Release (see 'COVID & The Prison Rules above) Release on Temporary Licence Policy Framework (17 August 2021)

**RELEASE OF DANGEROUS INMATES**
See "Dangerous inmates, notification of release".

**RELIGION**
PR 13 & PR 19
Prison Rules 13,and 19

Religious denomination

13. A prisoner shall be treated as being of the religious denomination stated in the record made in pursuance of section 10(5) of the Prison Act 1952[6] but the governor may, in a proper case and after due enquiry, direct that record to be amended.

Religious books

19. There shall, so far as reasonably practicable, be available for the personal use of every prisoner such religious books recognised by his denomination as are approved by the Secretary of State for use in prisons.

**Case Law**

*R (on the application of Imran Bashir) v Independent Adjudicator* [2011] EWHC 1108 (Admin)
See "Racial Justice " above

## REMAND PRISONERS

PSO 4600 Unconvicted, unsentenced and civil prisoners

1.1 Unconvicted prisoners have not been tried and are presumed to be innocent, the Prison Service's sole function is to hold them in readiness for their next appearance at court. Their imprisonment should not deprive them of any of their normal rights and freedoms as citizens, except where this is an inevitable consequence of imprisonment, of the court's reason for ordering their detention and to ensure the good order of the prison. Instructions or practices that limit their activities must provide only for the minimum restriction necessary in the interests of security, efficient administration, good order and discipline and for the welfare and safety of all prisoners.

1.2 Mandatory requirement: Subject to these considerations, they must be treated accordingly and, in particular, will be allowed all reasonable facilities to:

• seek release on bail
• preserve their accommodation and employment
• prepare for trial
• maintain contact with relatives and friends
• pursue legitimate business and social interests
• obtain help with personal problems

They should receive health care appropriate to their needs, and opportunities for education, religious observance, exercise and recreation and, where possible, for training and work.

As a result of this special status, unconvicted prisoners are entitled to a number of special rights and privileges which are listed in Annex B. Further details can be found in the relevant Prison Rules and instructions which are highlighted in the Annex.

## REMAND TIME

*R (on the application of Raymond Woolley) v Ministry of Justice* [2012] EWHC 295 (Admin)
See "Sentence Calculation" below.

## REMOVAL FROM ASSOCIATION
**See "Association, removal from".**

## REPATRIATION
**See also "Foreign Nationals"; and "Transfer of prisoners".**

PSI 52/2011 Immigration, Repatriation and Removal Services – should be read in conjunction with PSI 59/2011. See "Foreign National Prisoners" above.

**Case Law**

*Bucpapa v Secretary of State for Justice* [2017] EWHC 1895 (Admin)

The claimant prisoner (B) applied for judicial review of the Secretary of State's decision to refuse to repatriate him to Albania in order to serve the remainder of his sentence in his home country. The Council of Europe's Convention on the Transfer of Sentenced Prisoners sets out the general policy framework, and The Repatriation of Prisoners Act 1984 provides the power to the Secretary of State to issue a warrant for providing the transfer of a prisoner in or out of the UK. It is dependent upon a specific agreement between the sending State and the receiving State, in this case, the Prisoner Transfer Agreement ("PTA") signed on 15 January 2013. The PTA does not provide any prisoner with a legal right to be transferred. B was originally sentenced to an indeterminate sentence with a minimum of 15 years, quashed on appeal and substituted for a determinate sentence of 30 years, enabling his automatic release on licence at 15 years. He was also subject to a Deportation Order. In refusing to repatriate B, the Secretary of State relied upon a misunderstanding of the PTA. Albania could not enforce a sentence of 30 years and therefore the Albanian Court of Appeal sought to convert the sentence to 15 years, enabling B to be released at the end of 15 years, in accordance with the mandatory non-aggravation principle of the PTA. However, the Secretary of State wrongly took in to consideration that there was a possibility of B being granted early release a the three-quarters point of his sentence, meaning it was possible he would be released 3 years and 9 months prior to the end of the period that he would otherwise have served in the UK, a factor which he considered would undermine public confidence in the transfer system. The Court held that a significant basis for the Secretary of State's Decision was the inevitable consequence of the operation of the PTA; a fact of which the Minister might well have been ignorant given his very recent appointment and the failure of the Submission to explain the basis of the Albanian Appeal Court's decision. It was irrational for the Secretary of State to rely so heavily upon what were the inevitable consequences of the operation of the PTA. B's claim was allowed and the Decision was quashed.

*R (on the application of Henry Max Shaheen) v Secretary of State for Justice* [2008] EWHC 1195 (Admin)

The claimant prisoner (S) applied for judicial review of a decision of the defendant secretary of state to refuse to consent to his transfer to the Netherlands to serve the remainder of his 16-year sentence for a drug-related offence. S, a British citizen who was 61 years old at the time of the offence, had been resident in the Netherlands for 15 years and had a Dutch wife and two teenage children. He had a heart condition and sight problems. He was convicted and sentenced in the United Kingdom with his co-accused, a Dutch national (Z), for the offence of importing Class A drugs. Both S and Z applied to be repatriated to the Netherlands to serve the remainder of their sentences there. Z's application was granted, but S's was refused. The Court held that in a case of this type, the secretary of state should be allowed a degree of discretionary judgment, but that was modest and called for careful scrutiny by the court. It was true that the secretary of state did not say at what level he rated the risk, but he did say that S had demonstrated a willingness to travel to the UK to engage in criminal activity. By saying that, he was expressing the opinion that there was a real or significant risk that if he were transferred to the Netherlands he would reoffend in the UK. His words could not bear any other meaning. The secretary of state was reasonably entitled to make that assessment.

## REPRESENTATIONS

**Key Note**

Prisoners have the right to make representations at all pivotal junctures in their prison lives, including categorisation, parole (a form will be sent to the Prisoner as appendix E to his dossier (see Rule 7 of the Parole Board Rules), recall, and oral hearings. Written representations will be most effective when they address the relevant issues set out in the Prison Rules, PSOs, Guidance, Directions etc.

**Case Law**

*R (on the Application of Francis) v Secretary of State for the Home Department : R (on The Application of Clarke) v Secretary of State for the Home Department* [2004] EWHC 2143 (Admin); (2005) 1 WLR 186

The Criminal Justice Act 1991 s.39 did not confine a prisoner who had been released on licence but recalled to prison to making only one set of written representations about his recall but it did not enable repeated further written representations to be made regardless of their merit. It was for the secretary of state to decide whether the further written representations demonstrated a material change in circumstances relevant to the recall decision so as to give rise to the duty to refer them to the Parole Board.

*R v Secretary Of State For The Home Department, Ex Parte John Hirst* [2001] EWCA Civ 378

A prisoner who had served the tariff period of a discretionary life sentence was entitled to be told reasons for a proposed re-categorisation and to be afforded the opportunity to make representations on that issue and to reply to grounds put forward to re-categorise him or her.

## REQUESTS AND COMPLAINTS

**See also "Complaints Procedure" and "Prisoner Complaints".**

PR 11

YOI 8

PF Prisoner Complaints Policy

1.1 To set out requirements and information on providing a fair and effective system for dealing with prisoner complaints, including by ensuring procedural justice and taking a problem- solving approach for both adult prisoners and young people.

## REQUESTS FROM PRISONERS TO CHANGE THEIR NAME

PSO 4455

1.1 Although there is no legal limitation on the right of prisoners to change their name, the Prison Service is under no obligation to acknowledge a new name. The Prison Service will normally officially acknowledge a name changed in the specific circumstances detailed at 1.2 below. However, Governors have discretion to refuse to recognise a name change if they have good reason. This is an important safeguard against frequent, disruptive name changes, or where issues such as public and victim protection, prison security or good order and discipline may be affected.

1.2 When Governors are considering name change requests, the following factors may be regarded as indications that the intended change is genuine and permanent, and should therefore be acknowledged officially:

• When the request is the result of a change of marital status

• When the change of name is on genuine religious grounds. If a prisoner wishes to change his/her name on such grounds, Operational Managers must obtain the views of the Chaplain (or equivalent) of the relevant faith.

• When not to acknowledge the new name may cause severe psychological selfharm to the prisoner. Medical advice should be sought.

1.3 A name change by Deed Poll is also generally an indication of genuineness on behalf of the prisoner and should be acknowledged officially. Governors may refuse a name change by Deed Poll but only in exceptional circumstances such as where the name is considered to be offensive or obscene.

1.4 When a name change request is refused, the refusal, with reasons, must be recorded on the prisoner's F2050.

1.5 In general, prisoners who change their name informally (i.e. by simply adopting another name) will continue to be known by the Prison Service by the name given when they were received into custody.

## RESEARCH

PSI 27/2015 – Open Source Research on the Internet and social networking sites

This PSI sets out the arrangements and restrictions for gathering personal information from the Internet for intelligence or investigative purposes.

PSI 22/2014 – Research Applications (updated August 2021)

1. Executive summary

Background

1.1 NOMS is committed to improving efficiency and effectiveness across probation providers and prison services, and at a time of constrained resources it is even more important that funds are spent on activities, processes and interventions that provide the greatest possible economic and social return. This requires that operational policy and delivery is based on reliable and robust evidence, for which high quality research studies and evaluations are essential. Such studies enable delivery to be improved, or can justify reinvestment or resource savings. They also contribute valuable knowledge to the policy evidence base and occupy a crucial role in the policy cycle.

1.2 This instruction applies to all studies and evaluations which apply recognisable research methods to generate quantitative and/or qualitative information (through a range of techniques, e.g. monitoring returns, observations, surveys, interviews, focus groups) in order to address specific research questions. Types of research include, but are not limited to, literature reviews, rapid evidence assessments, systematic reviews, case studies, action research studies, process evaluations, impact evaluations and economic evaluations.

## RESETTLEMENT

PSI 04/2015

Travel and Transfer On Licence and PSS outside of England and Wales Policy Framework

## RESTRAINTS

PSI 06/2014 National Security Framework – Ref: NSF 2.1 Control and Order Function: Use of Force – Implementation of Minimising and Managing Physical Restraint Rule 49, Restraints

49.— Restraints

(1) The governor may order a prisoner to be put under restraint where this is necessary to prevent the prisoner from injuring himself or others, damaging property or creating a disturbance.

(2) Notice of such an order shall be given without delay to a member of the independent monitoring board, and to a registered medical practitioner or to a registered nurse working within the prison.

(3) On receipt of the notice, the registered medical practitioner or registered nurse referred to in paragraph (2), shall inform the governor whether there are any medical reasons why the prisoner should not be put under restraint. The governor shall give effect to any recommendation which may be made under this paragraph.

(4) A prisoner shall not be kept under restraint longer than necessary, nor shall he be so kept for longer than 24 hours without a direction in writing given by an officer of the Secretary of State (not being an officer of a prison). Such a direction shall state the grounds for the restraint and the time during which it may continue.

(5) Particulars of every case of restraint under the foregoing provisions of this rule shall be forthwith recorded.

(6) Except as provided by this rule no prisoner shall be put under restraint otherwise than for safe custody during removal, or on medical grounds by direction [of a registered medical practitioner or of a registered nurse working within the prison. No prisoner shall be put under restraint as a punishment.

(7) Any means of restraint shall be of a pattern authorised by the Secretary of State, and shall be used in such manner and under such conditions as the Secretary of State may direct.

**Case Law**

*Children's Rights Alliance for England v Secretary of State for Justice & (1) G4S Care & Justice Services (UK) Ltd (2) Serco PLC (Interested Parties)* [2012] EWHC 8 (Admin)

See "Judicial Review Procedure" above.

*R (on the application of JB) v GSL UK Ltd* [2007] EWHC 2227 (Admin)

The restraint of a prisoner, including the use of

handcuffs, during medical treatment and the presence of security officers during medical consultations and treatments did not in the circumstances amount to infringements of his rights under the European Convention on Human Rights 1950 Art.3 or Art.8 as any interference was proportionate to the risk he posed.

## REWARDS
See "Performance recognition".
### RIGHTS OF PRISONERS CHARGED
PR 54
YOI 59

## RISK ASSESSMENT OF PRISONERS
The Public Protection Manual, Chapter 1

## RISK/FRAUD MANAGEMENT
PSO 1310 Preventing Fraud

## SAFER CUSTODY / SAFEGUARDING
See "Suicide and self-selfharm".
PSI 16/2015 – "Adult Safeguarding in Prison"
1.3 In England, the Care Act 2014 places Safeguarding Adult Boards (SABs) on a statutory footing. It does not require prisons to be members, and many of the safeguarding responsibilities do not apply to prisoners. However it is important to demonstrate that, as well as ensuring compliance with our duty of care, our systems also provide a level of protection for prisoners who are unable to protect themselves as a result of having care and support needs that is equivalent to that provided in the community. This instruction therefore encourages Governors to engage with SABs, both at a strategic level and as a source of advice and assistance in safeguarding prisoners who are unable to protect themselves from abuse or neglect as a result of having care and support needs.

## SAMARITANS, the role of
PSI 64/2011 – "Managing prisoner safety in custody"

## SAME-SEX RELATIONSHIPS
See also "Human Rights: Article 8" above.
### Case Law
*R (Hopkins) v Sodexo* [2016] EWHC 606 (Admin)
The prison's decision to cease to allow a prisoner to share a cell with her civil partner did not infringe Article 3 or 8, as the prison was entitled to enforce its blanket ban on not allowing women in an intimate relationship to share a cell.

*R (Bright); R (Keeley) v Secretary of State for Justice* [2015] 1 W.L.R 723
The prison had not breached the Article 8 (Right to Family Life) rights of two prisoners who were in a long term same-sex relationship when it decided to separate them. The failure of the prison to publish a policy explaining whether homosexual relationships were to be facilitated or restricted did not mean that decisions to separate prisoners in a homosexual relationship were not in accordance with the law. However, the decision to separate prisoners in a relationship did not operate in a vacuum and was subject to certain constraints.

## SEARCH
PR 41
(1) Every prisoner shall be searched when taken into custody by an officer, on his reception into a prison and subsequently as the governor thinks necessary or as the Secretary of State may direct.
(2) A prisoner shall be searched in as seemly a manner as is consistent with discovering anything concealed.
(3) No prisoner shall be stripped and searched in the sight of another prisoner, or in the sight of a person of the opposite sex.
PSI 07/2016 Searching the Person
2.12 Arrangements must be in place for keeping records of searches and finds. On completion of a search, staff must sign for all examinations they have carried out in accordance with local security strategies. As a minimum, records must be kept of all non-routine full-searches of prisoners, in circumstances where they are conducted on the basis of intelligence or suspicion (this does not include random full-searches where conducted as part of Local Searching Strategies). Records must be kept in these circumstances irrespective of whether or not an item is found during the search. Records must detail why, when and where the full search was conducted, who conducted the search and any other relevant information. A Mercury Information Report (IR) must also be completed and submitted to the security department where contraband is found as part of a search
2.23 Staff should be aware that searches, especially full searches, can be embarrassing and difficult experiences for prisoners. Staff must, in particular, bear in mind the impact searches may have on prisoners who may be at risk – see PSI 65/2011 – Safer Custody.
2.54 Women prisoners must not be full-searched as a matter of routine but only on intelligence or reasonable suspicion that an item is being concealed on the person which may be revealed by the search. Full searches must be conducted in accordance with the correct procedures, at Annex B, paragraph 24. The procedure for searching women prisoners is different to that used to search men and women visitors and staff (as set out at Annex B), and consists of two levels. Level 1 involves the removal of the woman's clothing apart from her underwear; Level 2 involves the

removal of all of the woman's clothing including her underwear (NB. The woman must never be fully naked during the search) – Annex B, paragraph 24. Level 2 of the search must only be applied if there is intelligence or suspicion that the woman has concealed an item in her underwear or if illicit items have been discovered about the woman's person during Level 1 of the search.

Annex H, para 1: Searching is arguably one of the most emotive, controversial and difficult aspects of dealing with and managing transsexual people in a prison environment. As such, it is important that a strong overall emphasis is placed on securing the cooperation of these prisoners for the purposes of searching, whilst ensuring that there are effective security measures in place which are adhered to as closely as is possible under the circumstances. Procedures must be sensitive both to the needs of prisoners and staff and they must remain proportionate and lawful.

### Case Law

*LW, KT, MC & Faulder v Sodexo Limited & Secretary of State for Justice* [2019] EWHC 367 (Admin)

The claimants were prisoners in a contracted-out prison run by the first defendant, who sought judicial review in respect of unlawful strip searches. The first defendant admitted the searches breached Article 8 ECHR and PSI 07/2016, as well as accepting there was a systemic failure within the PSI, based on its failure to train its staff. The Claimants asserted that the second defendant had a duty to put in place a supervision and monitoring framework to ensure that its conduct of searches did not violate their human rights. The Divisional Court agreed, the breaches were serious and demonstrated that the framework put in place by the secretary of state was ineffective to ensure the first defendant had adequate staff training systems. The routine strip search of female prisoners was a known and avoidable problem, and the secretary of state had a particular obligation to take effective steps to make reasonably sure that it did not happen but had not done so. The failure to do so meant he had not discharged his obligation under Article 8.

*R (BK & RH) v Secretary of State for Justice* [2015] EWCA Civ 1259, 51

"(iii)    First, the provisions of the PSI – as published policy – are to be read in a sensible and practical way. A number of authorities in this respect were cited to us. But I do not need to set them out here.

(iv) Second, the provisions of the PSI are to be read as a whole.

(v) Third, the bar is set relatively high for a challenge to a policy based on Article 3 grounds.

(vi) Fourth, there can be no doubt that strip-searching is capable in itself of engaging Article 3 (and Article 8). Certainly the application of strip searches, particularly to those who are not prisoners or reasonably suspected of having committed a criminal offence, requires rigorous adherence to prescribed procedures and the need to protect human dignity. Correspondingly, a search carried out in an appropriate manner and for a legitimate purpose may be compatible with Article 3 and Article 8: see Wainwright v United Kingdom [2009] 44 EHRR 40, at paragraphs 41 - 43.

(vii)     Fifth, and reflecting the foregoing, the prison context is of central importance in this case. That context gives rise to questions of policy, and protection and safety and security issues, on which the assessment of those entrusted with formulating such a policy should be accorded a measure of respect."

### SECURE TRAINING CENTRES

Secure training centre rules 1998 (S.I.1998 no.472)
Secure training centre (amendment) rules 2003 (S.I. 2003 no. 3005)

### SECURITY

PSI 05/2015 – "Security Vetting: Reconsideration of NOMS Central Vetting Decisions by Exception"

### SECURITY, Body Worn Video Cameras

PSI 04/2017

### SELF CARE PRODUCTS, addition to canteen lists

PSI 45/2005

### SEGREGATION PSO 1700

### Case Law

*R (Bourgass and others) v Secretary of State for Justice* [2015] UKSC 54

Decisions to continue to segregate two prisoners had been unlawful as they had not been authorised by the secretary of state and were unfair at common law. Any supposed performance of the secretary of state's function under Rule 45 by a governor or other member of staff could not be treated as performance by him.

*Leslie Malcolm v Ministry of Justice* [2011] EWCA Civ 1538, 14 December 2011

The appellant prisoner (M) appealed against a decision ((2010) EWHC 3389 (QB)) that there had been no violation of his rights under the European Convention on Human Rights 1950 art.8 during his imprisonment. M, who was serving a sentence of life imprisonment for sex offences, was detained for a period of 159 days in the segregation unit at his own request. The Prison Service Order 4275 para.2(ii) provided that governors must ensure that a prisoner in the segregation unit had the opportunity to spend a minimum of one hour in the open air each day. During the period in segregation M was provided with an average of 30 minutes in the open air each day. His claim, on the basis of, inter alia, the failure to provide him with his entitlement under the PSO constituted an unjustified interference with his art.8 rights, was dismissed. The judge held that there was no interference with his art.8(1) rights and, even if art.8(1) was engaged, any interference was justified under art.8(2). The Court held that: (1) Whilst enjoyment of exercise in the open air, particularly in the context of prison life and segregation, was capable in principle of constituting an interest protected by art.8, on the facts, art.8(1) was not engaged by the exercise regime in the segregation unit where M was imprisoned. M had around 30 minutes' exercise in the open air each day, regularly longer. An entitlement of a full hour could not be derived directly or indirectly from art.8. Even if M could establish that he had a protected interest carrying with it, for the purposes of art.8 an entitlement to one hour's exercise in the open air each day, there was not a sufficiently serious interference with that protected interest so as to engage art.8(1). The fact that M did not receive the full entitlement had no adverse effect on his physical or mental health and did not cause him any anxiety, stress or distress. It was M's choice to remain in the segregation unit, there was no good reason why he remained there and it was open to him to move to a wing where he would have received a minimum of one hour each day. Accordingly, the failure to allow him the full one hour entitlement could not be said to have been of sufficient seriousness so as to constitute an interference within art.8(1) (paras 26-27, 30 of judgment). (2) If there was an interference within art.8(1), it could not be justified under art.8(2) as it could not be shown to have been "in accordance with the law" as the prison officers failed to give effect to the mandatory requirements of the PSO (paras 31-32).

**SENTENCE CALCULATION**

See also "CJA 1991 Prisoners".

Sentence Calculation Policy Framework: determinate sentenced prisoners (implementation date 28 June 2022) This policy framework sets out what information is required and how to calculate the release dates for determinate sentenced prisoners in accordance with the relevant legislative release provisions. It explains the process to be followed, timings of required actions and who can carry out the relevant calculations and checks.

The framework replaces Prison Service Instruction 03/2015.

**Case Law**

*R (Gibson) v Secretary of State for Justice* [2018] UKSC 2; [2018] 1 Cr App R (S) 51; 24 January 2018 Where an offender serving a term of imprisonment in default, imposed at the date of a confiscation order, had made partial payments under the order, days deducted from the default term, for the purposes of the Magistrates' Courts Act 1980 s.79(2), would be calculated in proportion to the original sum excluding any interest that had accrued. The natural construction of s.79(2) was that the starting point was the sum outstanding at the time of the Crown Court order.

*R (E) v Governor Of Hatfield Prison* [2013] EWHC 775 (Admin)
The Governor was correct in not taking account the effect of a reduction in sentence on appeal when calculating the date of release from a default sentence activated by non-payment of a confiscation order in the same matter.

*R (on the application of Shields-McKinley) v Secretary of State for Justice and Lord Chancellor* [2020] 2 WLR 250
The clear intention expressed in s.243(2) was that, in the case of an extradited prisoner, s.240ZA only applied to days in detention abroad which had been specified under s.243(2), and that in the absence of such specification those days could not be taken into account under s.240ZA(3). A conforming interpretation could not be applied so as to lead to any different conclusion. The failure in the instant case to specify the days spent abroad did not render s.243 incompatible with the Framework Decision. Moreover, there was nothing in the Framework Decision to specify the domestic procedure by which the relevant days were to be identified. Parliament was therefore free to give effect to art.26 of that decision by means of s.243(2) (see paras 43-45 of judgment).

*R (on the application of Elam) v Secretary of State for Justice* [2012] EWCA Civ 29 (Civ Div) 27/1/2012
The appellant prisoner (E) appealed against a decision ((2011) EWHC 1558 (Admin)) dismissing his challenge to the respondent secretary of state's calculation of the period to be served on licence after his release from custody. E had been sentenced after the coming into force of the Criminal Justice Act 2003 to 18 months' imprisonment for an offence of perverting the course of justice committed before the Act came into force. He was also sentenced to further

consecutive sentences for offences of conspiracy to defraud. The three sentences totalled seven years. The secretary of state calculated the sentence and licence expiry date after aggregating the sentences under s.264(3) of the 2003 Act and taking into account the time spent on remand. E contended that the 18-month sentence was in respect of an offence which was committed before the 2003 Act came into force and that under the Criminal Justice Act 1991 he would have been entitled to be released after nine months with a licence period expiring after three-quarters of the sentence; that was an accrued right which was preserved by the Criminal Justice Act 2003 (Commencement No.8 and Transitional and Saving Provisions) Order 2005 Sch.2 Pt 003 para.19; therefore his licence period would end four-and-a-half months earlier than the date put forward by the secretary of state. The Court held that the Criminal Justice Act 2003 s.264(3) determined the licence expiry date in every case where a prisoner was serving consecutive terms save only where all the offences in question were committed before the coming into force of the 2003 Act, in which case the Criminal Justice Act 1991 s.37(1) served to fix the licence expiry date. E's argument produced the anomalous result that the licence expiry date would be different depending on whether the 18-month sentence was treated as being served first or last. E's argument was a tenacious attempt to re-write the statutory provisions but in the circumstances the appeal to the presumption against retrospective substantive change could not succeed, *R (on the application of Stellato) v Secretary of State for the Home Department* [2007] UKHL 5, (2007) 2 AC 70 and *R (on the application of Noone) v Governor of Drake Hall Prison [2010] UKSC 30,* (2010) 1 WLR 1743 considered (paras 20-23).

*R (on the application of Modhej) v Secretary of State for Justice : R (on the application of Smith) v Secretary of State for Justice* [2011] EWHC 2267 (Admin)
The claimant prisoners (M and S) applied for judicial review in respect of their release dates. In January 2008, M and S had been sentenced to detention/imprisonment for public protection with a minimum term of four years following their conviction for, among other things, rape and false imprisonment. They appealed against their sentences and in January 2010 the Court of Appeal replaced the sentences imposed with extended sentences. The halfway point in their custodial terms was about to be reached. The Criminal Justice Act 2003 s.247 had been amended so that a person sentenced to an extended sentence would now be entitled to release on licence automatically at the halfway point of the custodial term without reference to

the Parole Board. That amendment had been brought into force by the Criminal Justice and Immigration Act 2008 (Commencement No. 2 and Transitional and Saving Provisions) Order 2008. The issue was whether, for the purposes of Sch.2 para.2 of the Order, M and S had been "sentenced" before July 14, 2008. If they had been, they would not be able to invoke the amended s.247(2). The Court held that the ordinary and usual meaning of "sentenced" was a reference to the occasion when a first-instance court, after a plea or after the conclusion of a trial resulting in a conviction, determined the sentence to be imposed on the defendant, by reference to facts relating to the offence, the mitigating and aggravating factors and the defendant's circumstances. A defendant would in those circumstances be ordinarily referred to as a person "sentenced". A person appealing against a sentence who had his sentence reduced or increased on appeal would not in the ordinary sense of the word be a person "sentenced" on the occasion of the appeal. The fact that technically what the Court of Appeal did was to quash the original sentence and pass by way of substitution a fresh sentence did not mean that the person was "sentenced" by the Court of Appeal for the purposes of the Order. Both M and S had therefore been "sentenced" for the purposes of the Order in January 2008 (see para.14 of judgment).

## SENTENCE MANAGEMENT AND PLANNING
See "Disabled Prisoners, management" and "Judicial Review Procedure" above.
PSI 19/2014 Sentence Planning
PSO 2205 OASys
5.1 Good supervision and sentence planning is vital to ensure that the work done with the offender is appropriate and effective. By integrating supervision and sentence planning into the overall process of assessment, OASys helps the assessor by making the links between these two essential aspects of offender management.
5.2 OASys is designed so that the objectives for supervision by the Probation Service and sentence planning by the Prison Service are clearly targeted to the profile of risk and needs identified during the assessment stage. The supervision and sentence planning section allows progress against objectives to be monitored and this will, in turn, inform the re-assessment of risk of reconviction and serious selfharm.
5.3 The development of the framework for the supervision and sentence planning section of OASys was based on the previous sentence planning procedures in the Prison Service that were defined in Prison Service Order 2200 (which is replaced by this PSO) and the

framework for supervision of offenders required by the Probation Service National Standards.

**Setting objectives**

5.4 Objectives must always be achievable and reflect what opportunities are actually available. The focus must be on what the assessor is trying to change. Objectives must be Specific, Measurable, Achievable, Realistic and Time-bound – SMART – and directed towards a long-term impact, after the offender returns to the community. However, in relation to an overall objective, it may be sensible to stage the work over a period of time. This will then be reflected in the sections on how the work is to be done, and the timescales for doing it.

5.5 It is important to set objectives on which evidence of progress can be recorded when the plan is reviewed. The assessor must indicate the criteria or evidence they will use to judge whether the objective has been met. Some measures will be evident from the way in which the objectives are formulated. Self-report information from the offender may be an acceptable measure. Other objectives are more difficult and may require the use of pre- and post-test measures. If someone has attended a cognitive skills programme, for example, it is not enough to say that the programme was completed, there needs to be evidence of whether there has been cognitive change.

**Case Law**

*R (on the application of Dennis Gill) v Secretary of State for Justice* [2010] EWHC 364 (Admin)
See "Disabled Prisoners, management" and "Judicial Review Procedure" above.

**SEPARATION OF PRISONERS**

PSI 05/2017 Separation Centre Referral Manual

1. Executive Summary

1.1 This PSI introduces a Separation Centre (SC) Referral Manual. The manual aims to inform staff about the role of the SC system in the Long Term and High Security Estate (LTHSE) and to provide information and guidance to help to decide who may be suitable for SC system referral, and when and how to refer prisoners into the system.

1.2 The purpose of the referral process is to identify those prisoners who may require separation from the mainstream prison population in the interests of national security; to prevent the commission, preparation or instigation of an act of terrorism, a terrorism offence, or an offence with a terrorist connection, whether in prison or otherwise; to prevent the dissemination of views or beliefs that might encourage or induce others to commit any such act or offence, whether in prison or otherwise, or to protect or safeguard others from such views or

beliefs; or to prevent any political, religious, racial or other views or beliefs being used to undermine good order and discipline in a prison.

1.4 The Referral process is applicable to all adult male offenders in custody. Referrals from outside of the LTHSE are expected to be relatively infrequent and all referrals will require management by those working currently in the area of counter terrorism. Therefore, while all staff involved in contributing to the categorisation and allocation of adult prisoners need to be aware of the SC system and of this guidance, few key staff will require a detailed knowledge of this manual for their day to day duties.

**SEX OFFENDERS**

See also "Accredited Courses"; and "Maintaining Innocence".

**Case Law**

*R (Commissioner Of Police Of The Metropolis) v Central Criminal Court* [2013] EWHC 179 (Admin); 15 January 2013
Despite a substantial delay in applying for judicial review, it was in the public interest to quash a court's decision purporting to lift a sexual offender's notification requirements. The court lacked power to make that order, and the grant of relief upheld the rule of law and ensured that all applications to life notification requirements were dealt with under the same procedure.

*M v Chief Constable Of Hampshire* [2014] EWCA Civ 1651, 18 December 2014
The ability of the police to obtain a search warrant to enter a sex offender's home without notice under the Sexual Offences Act 2003 s.96B was compatible with his rights under Article 8 of the European Convention on Human Rights.

*R (Prothero) v Secretary Of State For The Home Department* [2013] EWHC 2830 (Admin); 18 September 2013
A sex offender's statutory obligation to provide bank account, debit and credit card details under the Sexual Offences Act 2003 (Notification Requirements) (England and Wales) Regulations 2012 did not breach his rights under Article 8 of the European Convention on Human Rights.

*R (X) v Secretary of State for the Home Department* [2012] EWHC 2954 (Admin); [2013] 1 W.L.R. 2638; 24 October 2012
The Secretary of State was required to amend the Child Sex Offender Disclosure Scheme Guidance Document, which set up a non-statutory scheme under which members of the public could ask the police to provide details of a person who had had convictions for sexual offences against children, to include a requirement that the police should

consider whether the offender should be asked if he wished to make representations, in order to safeguard the offender's rights under Article 8 of the European Convention on Human Rights.

*Main v Scottish Ministers* [2013] CSOH 103 (Scotland); 26 June 2013
The notification requirements under the Sexual Offences Act 2003 (Remedial) (Scotland) Order 2011 were a proportionate interference with Article 8 of the European Convention on Human Rights 1950, where the evidence in support of continuing risk was statistical. A fair balance had been struck between the rights of convicted offenders and the public by imposing a discharge date for notification requirements which was based on a consideration of the relevant evidence.

## SLEEPING ACCOMMODATION
**See also "Accommodation"**
PR 26
YOI 22

## SLOPPING OUT
**Key Note**
The 2 cases recited below are significant "slopping out" cases. The first was an unsuccessful English claim, the second was a Scottish case which gives helpful guidance on the procedural and evidential issues arising in such cases.
**Case Law**
*(1) Desmond Grant (2) Roger Charles Gleaves v Ministry of Justice* [2011] EWHC 3379 (QB); [2012] A.C.D. 32; 19 December 2011
The claimant prisoners (G) sought declarations that the sanitation regime in place during their detention at a certain prison was contrary to their human rights. They were detained in a closed prison, for which the defendant Ministry was responsible, and in single cells without in-cell sanitation. Each landing housed 24 prisoners, and had a recess area with toilets and washing facilities. At times when prisoners were confined to their cells, for about 13 hours each night and at certain other times, they did not have free access to a toilet. Each cell had an electronic locking system which enabled one prisoner at a time out of his cell to use the facilities. A prisoner who wished to go to the toilet might at times be locked in his cell and unable to obtain prompt release to use the facilities. For that contingency, each cell had a plastic bucket with a lid, into which a prisoner was able to urinate or defecate. In each recess area there was a sluice into which he could empty the bucket and clean it when he next had an opportunity to leave his cell. That practice was known as "slopping out". G contended that the requirement to use and thereafter slop out a bucket was degrading and

contrary to their rights under the European Convention on Human Rights 1950 art.3, and further, that it failed to respect their human dignity and private life in breach of art.8 of the Convention. The Court held that: (1) Absent any special circumstances, a domestic court should itself follow any clear and consistent jurisprudence of the Strasbourg court, *R (on the application of Holding & Barnes Plc) v Secretary of State for the Environment, Transport and the Regions* [2001] UKHL 23, (2003) 2 AC 295 applied. For treatment to amount to a breach of art.3, it required a minimum level of seriousness or severity, *Gorodnichev v Russia (52058/99) Unreported May 24, 2007 ECHR and Pretty v United Kingdom (2346/02)* (2002) 2 FLR 45 ECHR applied. Whilst any particular vulnerability of the victim, such as his subjection to state control because he was in detention, was an important factor, there was no principle that, insofar as treatment and conditions in prison were concerned, anything which was not "inherent" or necessarily part of the prison sentence, that was or might be distressing to a prisoner, was a violation of art.3, *Kalashnikov v Russia (47095/99)* (2003) 36 EHRR 34 ECHR considered. There was no lower threshold of severity for cases involving breaches of a prisoner's art.3 rights. The test for minimum severity was an objective one, to be determined on the basis of all relevant circumstances. Unless a claimant could show, by direct or inferential evidence, that ill-treatment had in fact caused him serious suffering in terms of physical or psychiatric injury, or psychological selfharm, or particularly serious evidenced distress, it would usually be difficult for him in practice to show that that objective test had been satisfied. A requirement for a prisoner to urinate or defecate into a bucket was not, necessarily and of itself, degrading and a violation of art.3: whether it was so degrading would depend upon all the circumstances of his case (see paras 22, 37, 43-44, 52, 68 of judgment). (2) On the evidence, a prisoner was not obliged to use his bucket to urinate except rarely, and not obliged to use it to defecate except extremely rarely and almost always restricted to sudden illness. Moreover, the bucket could usually be emptied promptly and the sluice area was kept clean. There was no evidence that slopping out had caused any higher degree of illness or other selfharm to any prisoner, and certainly no evidence that selfharm was caused to G, despite the size of their cells and their ventilation. There was no evidential basis upon which the court could sensibly find that G had suffered any significant selfharm as a result of the sanitation facilities at the prison. They had suffered no distress, anxiety, feelings of humiliation or other selfharm. Their claim based on a violation of art.3 had, therefore, to fail (paras 204, 209-215, 220, 226). (3) The sanitation system did not substantially interfere with the dignity or privacy of prisoners and did not interfere with G's art.8 rights. In relation to G's dignity, there was an absence of any real impact on their privacy. They did not share a cell, so did not have to perform any toilet function other than in private, and the extent to which they had to use a bucket was rare, and for defecation very rare. Neither were they obliged to empty and clean their buckets in cramped or jostling or unduly rushed circumstances; they were both given adequate time and proper facilities to do so (para.234).

*Napier v Scottish Ministers* [2005] U.K.H.R.R. 268 Court of Session (Inner House, First Division) 10 February 2005

In proceedings for judicial review brought by N, a prisoner, the Lord Ordinary found that S, the Scottish Ministers, had acted unlawfully in terms of the Human Rights Act 1998 s.6 and ultra vires in terms of the Scotland Act 1998 s.57, by acting in a manner incompatible with Sch.1 Part I Art.3 of the Human Rights Act 1998 and detaining N in conditions in which he was subjected to inhuman or degrading treatment. N was awarded damages. S reclaimed. The only issue debated was the appropriate standard of proof to be applied in civil domestic proceedings in determining whether or not there had been a breach of Art.3. Held, granting declarator, that in civil proceedings in which a finding was sought that there had been an act or a failure to act by a public authority which was incompatible with Art.3, the appropriate standard of proof was proof on a balance of probabilities.

## SMOKING
Smoke Free Policy Framework
**Case Law**
*R (on the application of Black) v Secretary of State for Justice* [2017] UKSC 81
See "Judicial Review Procedure" above.

## STAFF, Regime Management Planning
PSI 07/2017

## STAFF, Resourcing
PSI 03/2017

## SUICIDE AND SELF-SELFHARM
See also "Deaths in Custody".
**Case Law**
*R (on the application of JL) v Secretary of State for Justice* [2008] UKHL 68; [2009] 1 A.C. 588; [2008] 3 W.L.R. 1325; [2009] 2 All E.R. 521; 26 November 2008

It was common ground that, where a suicide or near-suicide in custody took place, there must be an initial investigation of the facts, and that might give rise to the requirement for a further investigation. The issues for determination were (i) whether the initial investigation must be independent, or whether it could be carried out by the prison authorities themselves; (ii) whether a further investigation must be held whenever it was not plain from the initial investigation that the state bore no responsibility for the near-suicide, or only where the initial investigation demonstrated that there was an arguable case that the state was at fault; (iii) where a further investigation was required, whether it necessarily had to be a "D-type inquiry" of the type required by *R (on the application of D) v Secretary of State for the Home Department* [2006] EWCA Civ 143, [2006] 3 All E.R. 946, [2006] 2 WLUK 747.

The House of Lords held that a near-suicide of a prisoner in custody which left him with the possibility of a serious long-term injury automatically triggered an obligation on the state under art.2 to institute an enhanced investigation. That obligation could not be discharged by an internal investigation of the facts. In some circumstances an initial investigation would satisfy the requirements of art.2. In others a further investigation would be necessary, which might well require to be a D-type inquiry. It was desirable that the initial investigation should be sufficiently rigorous to satisfy the requirements of an enhanced investigation where possible. A D-type inquiry would necessarily be more protracted and expensive. An internal investigation which did not disclose an arguable case of fault on the part of the state would not preclude the need for an enhanced investigation. This was because, firstly, the object of the investigation went beyond ascertaining whether state agents had been at fault; its primary purpose was to learn lessons for the future. Secondly, if the investigation was to be impartial and seen to be impartial, it should be carried out by a person who was independent of the prison authorities. It was unavoidable that the very first steps in investigating an incident would be internal to the Prison Service. However, the need to set up an independent investigation in compliance with art.2 would be apparent as soon as the prison authorities became aware of circumstances which suggested that a prisoner had attempted suicide and was going to be incapacitated. At that point the Prison Service should take steps to establish the independent investigation. To satisfy the requirements of art.2, besides being independent and involving the family of the victim, investigations must be initiated by the state, be promptly and expeditiously carried out, and provide for a sufficient element of public scrutiny. It was not desirable to be prescriptive beyond that point. Generally speaking there was no need for inquiries into near-suicides to take place in public, although the independent investigator's report would itself be made public. The necessity for a D-type inquiry would be comparatively rare.

## SURVEILLANCE
HMPPS Investigatory Powers Policy Framework 1.3. Legal basis for Investigatory Powers within HMPPS

HMPPS has powers under the Acts listed above and the associated Codes of Practice, to enable activity to be conducted aimed at the prevention and detection of crime, preserving order and discipline in establishments and management of risk and prevention of selfharm as well as any duty or responsibility arising from common law or other legislation. Specific to this Policy Framework are the powers to:
• Acquire Communications Data – to identify illicit communications devices being used illegally inside prisons or in contravention of licence conditions, and to help identify criminal activities in prisons through the illicit use of mobile phones.
• Conduct Surveillance – to combat criminality within prisons, maintain order and discipline, or to support the gathering of information and intelligence for the purposes of pursuing a prosecution/adjudication.
• Deploy Covert Human Intelligence Sources (CHIS) – To gather intelligence and information to assist in the detection and prevention of crime, maintain good order and discipline, and reduce the risk of selfharm to vulnerable people.
The power to intercept communications under s49 of the Investigatory Powers Act 2016 is covered by PSI 04/2016 – Interception of Communications and Security Measures in Prisons...
2.1. Policy Aims
2.1.1. All staff in HMPPS and the Contracted Estate understand what constitutes investigative activity, and their legal obligations under the relevant legislation
2.1.2. HMPPS deploys investigative powers when necessary and justified, proportionate to the outcomes being sought, including the consideration of less intrusive tactics and capabilities.
2.1.3. Applications for use of Investigatory powers are submitted in the correct manner, authorised following proper scrutiny, managed for the lifetime of the authorisation robustly, and data managed appropriately until deletion.

## TELEPHONE ACCOUNTS
In HMPPS Finance Manual, 6.5, 13.13, 13.24

## TEMPORARY CONFINEMENT
See "Confinement, temporary".

## TEMPORARY RELEASE
See "Release on Temporary Licence".

## TERMINALLY ILL PRISONERS, release
See "Compassionate Grounds, Release".

## TERRORISM
See "Separation of Prisoners".

## Therapeutic Communities, Democratic
PSO 2400
SECTION 2 – PURPOSE AND DESCRIPTION OF DEMOCRATIC TCs
Purpose: Democratic TCs provide a long term, residential, offending behaviour intervention for prisoners who have a range of offending behaviour risk areas, including emotional and psychological needs. The degree of need may prevent them from engaging fully with a shorter programme or may make shorter interventions inadequate.

## TIME LIMITS FOR SUBMISSION OF REQUESTS / COMPLAINTS
See "Requests and complaints".

## TIME IN THE OPEN AIR
Prison Rule 30
If the weather permits and subject to the need to maintain good order and discipline, a prisoner shall be given the opportunity to spend time in the open air at least once every day, for such period as may be reasonable in the circumstances.

## TRANSFER OF PRISONERS
See also "Foreign National Prisoners"; and "Repatriation".
Generic Parole Process Policy Framework – 3.3 Indeterminate Sentenced Foreign National Prisoners (IFNPs)
**Case Law**
*Re McVeigh's Application for Judicial Review* [2014] NICA 23; [2015] N.I. 146; 5 March 2014
The English High Court did not have exclusive jurisdiction to hear an application for judicial review, by a restricted transfer prisoner who had been transferred to Northern Ireland from England, challenging a decision of the Secretary of State for Justice of England and Wales not to seek advice from the Parole Board as to his suitability for open conditions. The secretary of state's office was indivisible and present throughout each part of the UK so that she had to be considered to be domiciled in Northern Ireland, and accordingly the High Court of Northern Ireland also had jurisdiction in relation to the issues raised in the judicial review claim.

R (Bristow) v Secretary of State for Justice [2013] EWHC 3094 (Admin)
See "Early release of prisoners" above.

R (on the application of Nelson) v Secretary of State for Justice [2011] EWHC 2468 (Admin).
The claimant prisoner (N) applied for judicial review of the defendant secretary of state's decision to exclude him from an early release scheme. N had been convicted of importing a controlled drug, Ecstasy, into Jersey and was sentenced to six years' imprisonment. He was transferred to a prison in England under the Crime (Sentences) Act 1997 to serve his sentence, but the Jersey authorities remained responsible for the administration of his sentence and release. Under Jersey law he was due to be released at the two-thirds point of his sentence. Jersey operated a temporary release scheme (TRS) which could have resulted in N being released four months early. However, the secretary of state refused to apply the TRS to N, and maintained that he ought to be managed under the English release on temporary licence scheme. N was later told that he was not eligible to be released on temporary licence under home detention curfew. N sought a declaration that his exclusion from Jersey's TRS was unlawful. N submitted that the Jersey TRS applied to him because it was no different to the early release scheme operated under the Prison (Jersey) Rules 2007 r.63, and early release and TRS were both made under the Prison (Jersey) Law 1957 art.29. He further argued that he should not suffer a detriment from his transfer. The Court held that the combined effect of Sch.1 para.6 of the 1997 Act and the Transfer of Prisoners (Restricted Transfers) (Channel Islands and Isle of Man) Order 1998 Sch.1 para.17 was that Jersey law applied to early release. Therefore N could not benefit from the English provision that released prisoners at the half-way point of their sentence on licence (see para.6 of judgment). (2) Nothing in the 1957 Law applied the whole of art.29 to restricted transfer cases such as N's. Article 29 contained powers to make rules encompassing a whole host of provisions which did not apply to N, for example classification and discipline. Included in that was temporary release. The TRS did not therefore apply to N. His argument that the TRS was, in substance, an early release scheme was not sustainable. The Jersey TRS was not only described as a temporary release scheme, but it was also expressly made under the power to provide for temporary release in the Prison (Jersey) Rules 2007 r.63, and therefore had to be a temporary release provision to be lawful. Even if the TRS was an early release scheme then its application to N was a matter for the Jersey

authorities and not for the secretary of state. In addition, on the evidence, N would not be eligible for the Jersey TRS in any event as it only applied to temporary release to addresses in Jersey in specified circumstances (paras 9, 12, 14). (3) In the different British Isles systems which fell within the scope of the 1997 Act, there were certain differences, not only in relation to release dates but also in other aspects, for example, temporary release, prison discipline or the prisoner serving a sentence nearer home. Within such a statutory scheme there was no room for a defendant, and much less for the courts, to begin weighing up the niceties of benefits and detriment of transfer. The court did not accept that it was an object of the 1997 Act that a prisoner should not suffer a legal or factual detriment by reason of a transfer. In any event N had not proposed release to an address in Jersey, nor were his circumstances such as to justify temporary release to an address outside Jersey. He would therefore not be eligible for the Jersey TRS even if he were in Jersey and had in fact suffered no detriment (para.14).

## TRANSGENDER PRISONERS
The Care and Management of Individuals who are Transgender Policy Framework
**Case Law**
R (H) v Secretary of State for Justice [2015] EWHC 1550 (Admin); 4 June 2015
There had been no unreasonableness or discrimination in the case of a transgender prisoner who remained detained for public protection after their minimum term had expired. In the circumstances there was no public law duty to facilitate the claimant as a transgender prisoner to complete accredited sex offender treatment programmes.

R (on the application of Green) v Secretary of State for Justice [2013] EWHC 3491 (Admin); 4 Dec 2013
The refusal to provide a male-to-female transgender prisoner with a wig, tights and a prosthetic vagina and breasts was in accordance with the relevant transsexual prisoners' policy. The prisoner had not been prevented from living in her chosen female role in prison, and the refusal to provide the requested items was justifiable and proportionate on security grounds, given that they heightened the risk of sexual abuse and assault by other prisoners, and could be used to conceal items or for escape and other illegitimate purposes.

R (on the application of AB) v (1) Secretary of State for Justice (2) Governor of Manchester Prison [2009] EWHC 2220 (Admin); [2010] 2 All E.R. 151; [2009] 9 WLUK 61; [2009] H.R.L.R. 35; 4 September 2009
A refusal to transfer a transgender prisoner from a male prison to a female prison, which

prevented the prisoner from progressing with her gender reassignment, breached her rights under the European Convention on Human Rights 1950 art.8.

## TRAVEL AND SUBSISTENCE
PSI 15/2012

## TREATMENT OF PRISONERS
### Case Law
*R (on the application of Vaclovas Faizovas (by Inga Faizovaite)) v Secretary of State for Justice* [2009] EWCA Civ 373; 13 May 2009
A judge had been entitled to conclude that the handcuffing of a prisoner whilst he received chemotherapy treatment at a hospital did not breach his rights under the European Convention on Human Rights 1950 art.3 as he represented a risk to the public and there was a risk that he would escape. The risk assessments were reasonable and the prisoner's own sense of humiliation was not sufficient to displace the importance of those assessments.

*R (on the application of Mackenzie) v Governor of Wakefield Prison* [2006] EWHC 1746 (Admin); 22 June 2006
The policy or practice of a prison governor whereby Category A prisoners were inspected at regular intervals during the night to ensure that they were still in their cells and had made no attempt to escape did not violate a prisoner's rights under Art.3 or Art.8 of the European Convention on Human Rights 1950.

## UNIFORMS
For epaulettes see PSO 8805 Identification of prison staff when on duty

## UNLAWFULLY AT LARGE
See also "Sentence calculation".
Recall, Review and Re-Release of Recalled Prisoners Policy Framework
### Case Law
*R (on the application of Steven James Ellerton) v Secretary of State for Justice* [2009] EWHC 2661 (Admin); 28 October 2009
A long-term prisoner serving concurrent sentences for offences committed both before and after 5 April, 2005, who had been released on licence after serving half his custodial sentence in the mistaken belief that the provisions of the Criminal Justice Act 2003 applied to all those sentences, had been "unlawfully at large" within the meaning of the Prison Act 1952 s.49 so as to preclude the time spent on licence from counting towards his custodial term.
*R (on the application of Lunn) v Governor of Moorland Prison* [2006] EWCA Civ 700; [2006] 1

W.L.R. 2870; 25 May 2006
See "Sentence Calculation" above.

## UNSENTENCED PRISONERS
See "Remand prisoners".

## USE OF FORCE
See "Force, use of".

## VEHICLES, use on official business
See "Travel and subsistence".

## VIDEO LINKS BETWEEN MAGISTRATES' COURTS AND LOCAL PRISONS
PSO 1030

## VISUAL DISPLAY UNITS
See "Display screen equipment health and safety issues"

## VIEWING - of prisons
PR 72
Young Offender Institutions YOI 76

## VIOLENCE REDUCTION
See also "Cell Sharing"; "Disruptive prisoners"; and "Force, use of".
PSI 20/2015
PSI 64/2011 Management of Prisoners at Risk of Selfharm to Self, to Others and From Others (Safer Custody)

## VISITORS
See also "Searches".
YOI 77 PR 70-73
Part IV PERSONS HAVING ACCESS TO A PRISON
70. Prohibited articles
No person shall, without authority, convey into or throw into or deposit in a prison, or convey or throw out of a prison, or convey to a prisoner, or deposit in any place with intent that it shall come into the possession of a prisoner, any article whatever. Anything so conveyed, thrown or deposited may be confiscated by the governor.
70A. List C Articles
A List C article is any article or substance in the following list—
(a) tobacco;
(b) money;
(c) clothing;
(d) food;
(e) drink;
(f) letters;
(g) paper;
(h) books;
(i) tools;
(j) information technology equipment;
(k) electronic cigarettes;
(l) matches;
(m) lighters.

71. Control of persons and vehicles

(1) Any person or vehicle entering or leaving a prison may be stopped, examined and searched and in addition any such person may be photographed, fingerprinted or required to submit to other physical measurement.

(1A) Any such search of a person shall be carried out in as seemly a manner as is consistent with discovering anything concealed about the person or their belongings.

(2) The governor may direct the removal from a prison of any person who does not leave on being required to do so.

72. Viewing of prisons

(1) No outside person shall be permitted to view a prison unless authorised by statute or the Secretary of State.

(2) No person viewing the prison shall be permitted to take a photograph, make a sketch or communicate with a prisoner unless authorised by statute or the Secretary of State.

73. Visitors

(1) Without prejudice to any other powers to prohibit or restrict entry to prisons, or his powers under rules 34 and 35, the Secretary of State may prohibit visits by a person to a prison or to a prisoner in a prison for such periods of time as he considers necessary if the Secretary of State considers that such a prohibition is -

(a) necessary on grounds specified in rule 35A(4); and

(b) is proportionate to what is sought to be achieved by the prohibition.

(2) Paragraph (1) shall not apply in relation to any visit to a prison or prisoner by a member of the independent monitoring board of the prison, or justice of the peace, or to prevent any visit by a legal adviser for the purposes of an interview under rule 38 or visit allowed by the board of visitors under rule 35(6).

**VISITORS, boards of**
**See "Boards of Visitors".**

**VISITS**
**See also "Visitors"; and "Searches".**
YOI 10
Management of Security at Visits (Open Estate) Policy Framework
Management of Security at Visits (Closed Estate) Policy Framework
PR35
35.  Personal Letters and Visits

35.  (1) Subject to paragraph (8), an unconvicted prisoner may send and receive as many letters and may receive as many visits as he wishes within such limits and subject to such conditions as the Secretary of State may direct, either generally or in a particular case.

(2) Subject to paragraphs (2A) and (8), a convicted prisoner shall be entitled -

(a) to send and to receive a letter on his reception into a prison and thereafter once a week; and

(b) to receive a visit twice in every period of four weeks, but only once in every such period if the Secretary of State so directs.

(2A)  A prisoner serving a sentence of imprisonment to which an intermittent custody order relates shall be entitled to receive a visit only where the governor considers that desirable having regard to the extent to which he has been unable to meet with his friends and family in the periods during which he has been temporarily released on licence.

(3) The governor may allow a prisoner an additional letter or visit as a privilege under rule 8 or where necessary for his welfare or that of his family.

(4) The governor may allow a prisoner entitled to a visit to send and to receive a letter instead.

(5) The governor may defer the right of a prisoner to a visit until the expiration of any period of cellular confinement.

(6) The independent monitoring board may allow a prisoner an additional letter or visit in special circumstances, and may direct that a visit may extend beyond the normal duration.

(7) The Secretary of State may allow additional letters and visits in relation to any prisoner or class of prisoners.

(8) A prisoner shall not be entitled under this rule to receive a visit from:

(a) any person, whether or not a relative or friend, during any period of time that person is the subject of a prohibition imposed under rule 73; or

(b) any other person, other than a relative or friend, except with the leave of the Secretary of State.

(9) Any letter or visit under the succeeding provisions of these Rules shall not be counted as a letter or visit for the purposes of this rule.

**Case Law**

*R (S) v Secretary Of State For Justice* [2013] EWHC 2889 (Admin); 6 September 2013

It was not unreasonable for the Secretary of State for Justice, in the exercise of his powers under the Prison Rule 76 to prohibit, restrict or prevent prison visits to the perpetrator by the victim of an offence, primarily because she had been his former partner and might have been under coercion.

*R v Secretary of State for the Home Department, ex parte (1) O'Dhuibhir and (2) O'Brien* [1997] C.O.D. 315; Independent, March 6, 1997; 27 February 1997 Restrictive interviewing conditions imposed in respect of high risk prisoners at a Special Secure Unit after an escape attempt in September 1994 upheld as lawful.  Appeal against dismissal of applications for judicial review of a decision of the Secretary of State for Justice on 20/6/95 that henceforward all visits, including legal visits, to prisoners classified as exceptional risk category A would normally take place under close conditions - that is with a glass screen between the visitor and the prisoner. No fundamental right of physical contact between a prisoner and his family was established.

## VOLUNTARY DRUG TESTING
See "Drugs".

## VOTING PROVISIONS FOR PRISONERS
Restrictions on Prisoner Voting Policy Framework
1. Purpose
1.1 The Government is clear that convicted prisoners detained in custody should not be able to vote. This framework replaces PSO 4650 and includes updated guidance in response to the long-standing Hirst judgment, where the Government has addressed an anomaly in the previous system, where prisoners released back in the community on licence using an electronic tag under the home detention curfew (HDC) scheme could vote, but those released in the community on temporary licence (ROTL) could not. Annex A provides updated voting eligibility criteria; under the new guidance, those on ROTL are no longer considered barred from voting.
1.2 This framework seeks to ensure that all prisoners who consider that they are (or may be) eligible to apply to vote, or to vote (and wish to do so) are appropriately supported in doing so.
[…]
Exercising the Right to Vote
4.7 Prisoners who are registered to vote and have been released from their sentence on HDC or are in the community on ROTL will be able to vote in the same ways as any other eligible person in the community. This includes attending a polling station where it meets the conditions of their release or a postal or proxy vote registered to their home address.
4.8 Postal and proxy votes from prison, are not available to those on HDC or ROTL. All other eligible prisoners listed at Annex A may, if registered, apply to vote by post or by proxy from prison.
[…]
4.10 In the limited circumstances in which prisoners are entitled to cast postal votes from prison, staff must respect the principle of the secret ballot. As set out in PSI 04/2016: The Interception of Communications in Prisons and Security Measures, correspondence between a prisoner and an ERO is handled under Confidential Access arrangements.
[…]

Annex A. Eligibility Criteria
The following prisoners are considered eligible to apply to register to vote:
• Un-convicted prisoners;
• Convicted but un-sentenced prisoners;
• Persons imprisoned for contempt of court and other prisoners classified under Prison Rule 7(3);
• Those serving a term of imprisonment in default of payment of a sum of money, adjudged to be paid on conviction;
• Prisoners that have been released from their sentence on home detention curfew (HDC); and,
• Prisoners in the community released on temporary licence (ROTL).
EDITOR'S NOTE: It is to be hoped that the conditions of release for those prisoners Released on Temporary Licence will permit them to vote at the appropriate polling station. Any release conditions which did not permit this would arguably be unlawful, and open to legal challenge.
**Case Law**
*R (Chester) v Secretary Of State For Justice* [2013] UKSC 63; [2014] A.C. 271; [2013] 3 W.L.R. 1076; [2014] 1 All E.R. 683; 16 October 2013
Although the United Kingdom's blanket prohibition on convicted prisoners voting in elections was incompatible with Protocol 1, Article 3 of the European Convention on Human Rights, the Supreme Court declined to make a further declaration of incompatibility. Further, EU law did not incorporate any right to vote on which convicted prisoners could rely.

*(1) Anthony Tovey (2) Paul Hydes & Ors v Ministry of Justice* [2011] EWHC 271 (QB); [2018] HRLR 17; 18 February 2011
The applicant secretary of state applied for summary judgment or to strike out the claim of the respondent prisoners (N) for damages for being prohibited from voting in the May 2010 general election or European Parliamentary elections and a declaration that their rights under the European Convention on Human Rights 1950 Protocol 1 art. 3 had been breached. The claim had been made on two bases. First, that N had a right to vote pursuant to Protocol 1 Art. 3 which they had been denied. Second, that the state had wrongly failed to implement the final decision in *Hirst v United Kingdom (74025/01)* (2006) 42 EHRR 41 ECHR (Grand Chamber), in which the Grand Chamber of the European Court of Human Rights had found that the United Kingdom had violated the rights of a serving Prisoner, by subjecting him to a ban on exercising the vote during his time in custody. The Court held that, applying the law as enacted by the Representation of the People Act 1983 s.3 and including the effect of the Human Rights Act 1998 s.3(2)(b) and s.6(6), a Prisoner would not succeed

before a court in England and Wales in any claim for damages or a declaration based on his disenfranchisement while serving his sentence.

*Smith v Scott* [2007] CSIH 9; 2007 SC 345; Times, February 5, 2007; 24 January 2007
A declaration of incompatibility was made by the Registration Appeal Court under the Human Rights Act 1998 s.4(5) in circumstances where there had been repeated refusals to accede to a prisoner's request to have his name added to the electoral register. Despite the ruling in Hirst v United Kingdom (74025/01) (2006) 42 EHRR 41, it was not possible to read down the Representation of the People Act 1983 s.3(1) to make it compatible with the Human Rights Act 1998 Sch.1 Part II Art.3.

*Hirst v United Kingdom* (2006) 42 E.H.R.R. 41; 6 October 2005
The automatic disenfranchisement of convicted prisoners based on what might offend public opinion offended the principle of proportionality and was a violation of the right to free elections enshrined in the Human Rights Act 1989 Sch.1 Part II Art.3.

**WELFARE OF PRISONERS, physical, and work**
PR 23-31

**WHITLEY PARTNERSHIP COMMITTEES, Local YOI 37-42**
PSI 04/2001

**WITNESS INTIMIDATION**
PSI 46/2011 Tackling Witness Intimidation By Remand Prisoners
Revised 19 May 2016
1. Executive summary
1.1 This Instruction introduces the duties that prisons must discharge to deliver NOMS' responsibilities following the recent publication of an Inter-Agency Protocol for tackling witness intimidation by defendants held in custody on remand who have been refused bail by the Courts. See Annex A for the Protocol.
1.2 The attached Protocol outlines the arrangements by which the police and Crown Prosecution Service (CPS) will notify the prison Governor of any risk to victims/witnesses so that action can be taken by staff to restrict a defendant's communications immediately on arrival in prison and throughout his/her time on remand until conviction or acquittal.
1.3 Other criminal justice organisations have been informed about the Protocol via Ministry of Justice Circular 2011/06 – Protocol for tackling witness intimidation from prisoners.
Desired outcomes

1.4 Prisoner communications are facilitated in a manner which ensures public protection, including the prevention of victim/witness intimidation Prisoner Communication Services Specification. To this end victims and witnesses should not be contacted by prisoners detained in custody on remand, who pose a risk of intimidation. In the event that contact is made, staff must take action to report this to the police and to prevent any re-occurrence.

Application
1.5 Directors/Governors of prisons, Reception staff, Public Protection Teams and those responsible for handling prisoner correspondence and Pinphone accounts.
1.6 Reception staff must read the Person Escort Record and the police/CPS MG6 form to identify whether restrictions need to be placed on the prisoner's communications. They must notify relevant colleagues in Security and/or Public Protection as well as those who deal with Prisoner Communication Services who will ensure the victim/witness is not contacted.
1.7 Staff must record the requirement to restrict the prisoner's communications on P-NOMIS and also open relevant Security and Public Protection files.
1.8 The prisoner must be informed that they must not contact the victim/witness by telephone or letter, which will be made abundantly clear on the Communications Compact they sign before being given a Pinphone Account. No details about the victim/witness other than their name should be disclosed to the prisoner.
Any changes to the victim/witness contact information must be recorded immediately and the relevant staff informed.
1.9 In cases where it has been reported that the remand prisoner has made or attempted to make contact with the victim/witness (this would not only be by Pinphone or correspondence but also the prohibited use of a mobile phone while in custody) or that the victim/witness has approached the prison with a request to be permitted to contact the offender, the matter should be drawn to the attention of the police as a matter of urgency.

**WOMEN PRISONERS**
**See also "Mother & Baby Units".**
YOI 25
PR 12
Women's Policy Framework
Prison Rule 12
Women prisoners
12. - (1) Women prisoners shall normally be kept separate from male prisoners.

(2) The Secretary of State may, subject to any conditions he thinks fit, permit a woman prisoner to have her baby with her in prison, and everything necessary for the baby's maintenance and care may be provided there.

Women's Policy Framework (Extract)

1. Purpose

1.1 This policy framework sets out the MoJ's expectations for the delivery of services for working with women in custody and the community. This enables staff to be aware of the gender specific issues that affect women, and respond appropriately to ensure that their different needs are consistently met. This does not detract from the requirement to consider the needs of other protected characteristics. It is important that this framework is read in conjunction with its supporting Guidance on Working with Women in Custody and Community.

Women's Estate Case Advice & Supporting Panel (WESCAP) Policy Framework Introduction 7.1.1 This guidance provides information on the role of the Women's Estate Case Advice and Support Panel (WECASP), formally known as the Centralised Case Supervision (CCS) system for individuals located in the women's estate. It provides guidance on the mandatory requirements above which includes what consideration should be given to make informed decisions when making a case referral, and how to complete a referral. Additionally, it provides an overview of the disciplines that contribute to this arrangement and considers how it is aligned to other operational management processes.

7.1.2 Accompanying this guidance are the necessary referral forms which must be completed as thoroughly as possible in order to evidence needs and risks and inform the decision-making process.

**Case Law**

*R v (1) The Accrington Youth Court (2) The Governor of HM Prison Risley (3) The Secretary of State for the Home Department, ex parte Claire Louise Flood* [1998] 1 WLR 156; [1998] 2 All ER 313; Times, October 10, 1997; Independent, October 3, 1997; 22 August 1997

The general policy of detaining young female offenders in prison pending their allocation to young offender institutions was unlawful and contrary to the principle contained in s.1C Criminal Justice Act 1982.

**WOODCOCK RECOMMENDATION 60**
**WORK, Inmates'**

PR 31 Work

31. - (1) A convicted prisoner shall be required to do useful work for not more than 10 hours a day, and arrangements shall be made to allow prisoners to work, where possible, outside the cells and in association with one another.

(2) A registered medical practitioner or registered nurse such as is mentioned in rule 20(3) may excuse a prisoner from work on medical grounds, and no prisoner shall be set to do work which is not of a class for which he has been passed by a registered medical practitioner or registered nurse such as is mentioned in rule 20(3) as being fit.

(3) No prisoner shall be set to do work of a kind not authorised by the Secretary of State.

(4) No prisoner shall work in the service of another prisoner or an officer, or for the private benefit of any person, without the authority of the Secretary of State.

(5) An unconvicted prisoner shall be permitted, if he wishes, to work as if he were a convicted prisoner.

(6) Prisoners may be paid for their work at rates approved by the Secretary of State, either generally or in relation to particular cases.

YOI 40

Sunday work PR 18; YOI 35

18. Arrangements shall be made so as not to require prisoners of the Christian religion to do any unnecessary work on Sunday, Christmas Day or Good Friday, or prisoners of other religions to do any such work on their recognised days of religious observance.

Prisoners' pay PSO 4460 (updated 27/01/2020)

Prisoners Pay

1. POLICY ON PRISONERS' PAY

1.1 It is Prison Service Policy that prisoners receive payment if they participate constructively in the regime of the establishment. The pay schemes and rates of pay which operate within establishments, are a matter for local management subject to the criteria below.

1.2 Governors and Directors of contracted-out prisons must have a local pay structure which:

• reflects Prison Service priorities

• supports and encourages constructive participation in regime activities

• does not provide disincentives to participation in constructive activities which are part of a prisoner's sentence/training plan or learning plan, intended to reduce the risk of re-offending

• complies with the parameters of this PSO and the Incentives Policy Framework (IPF).

• rewards good performance and penalises poor performance

• is fair, open, balanced and affordable.

1.3 Governors and Directors of contracted-out prisons must ensure that:

• the prisoner pay structure in their establishment is reviewed annually as part of the business planning process, to ensure compliance with paragraph 1.2 above

• information on the pay structure is available to all prisoners

- prisoners are paid correctly and promptly each week
- procedures are in place for monitoring all aspects of prisoners' pay
- appropriate records are kept in accordance with the Finance Order PSO 7500

1.4 Whatever scheme an establishment operates, it is essential that it is reasoned and structured, the requirements of the scheme are clear to both prisoners and staff, and it is not applied in an arbitrary or discriminatory way.

RATES OF PAY

2.1 General

2.1.1 All prisoners who participate in purposeful activity must be paid. Those who refuse must not receive any pay. Prisoners may also lose earnings for disciplinary reasons. Unconvicted prisoners can work if they wish to and must be paid the same rates as convicted prisoners.

2.1.2 An allowance should be made in the standard working week (see paragraph 2.4.1) of each prisoner for authorised absences from purposeful activity. These may include Governor's applications, welfare interviews, sick parade etc. These will be accommodated without loss of pay provided that the allowance is not exceeded.

2.1.3 Visits, other regime instigated absences specified by the Governor, Sundays and days of religious observance for prisoners of non-Christian faith will not be counted towards the interruptions allowance and will be accommodated without loss of pay. Periods in segregation for disciplinary reasons will not count towards the allowance or normally attract pay unless the prisoner is found not guilty at adjudication or the governor authorises payment at unemployed rate.

2.1.4 Home leave, temporary release except on facility licence, compassionate leave and court attendance will attract no pay.

2.2 Rate of pay for unemployed prisoners

2.2.1 Prisoners are eligible for unemployment pay if they are willing to work, but the establishment cannot find suitable employment or the prisoner is unable to work.

[...]

ANNEX B TO PSO 4460

MANDATORY PAY RATES

Unemployment pay

Minimum £2-50 per week (50p a day) based on a five-day week (see section 2.2)

Employed rate

Minimum employed rate of pay is £4-00 per week (see section 2.3)

Short-term sickness

The rate of pay for short-term sickness is £2-50 per week (see section 5.1)

Long-term sickness and retirement

The rate of pay for prisoners who are long-term sick or of retirement age is £3-25 per week (see section 5.2)

Maternity leave or caring full-time for children

The rate of pay for prisoners who are on maternity leave, or caring full-time for children is £3-25 per week (see section 5.3)

Outside hospital allowance

The allowance for prisoners staying in hospital is £4-35 per week or 60p per day (see section 5.4). Governors have discretion to increase this allowance if it is justified.

Process for closing or re-designating industrial workshops and laundries PSI 38/2004

**YOI 37-42 WHITLEY PARTNERSHIP COMMITTEES, Local**
PSI 04/2001

**YOUNG OFFENDERS**
**Case Law**
*Children's Rights Alliance For England v Secretary Of State For Justice* [2013] EWCA Civ 34; [2013] 1 WLR 3667; 6 February 2013

Where young people had been subjected to unlawful restraint techniques while detained in secure training centres, but had not appreciated that the techniques were unlawful, the Secretary of State was under no obligation to tell them that they had been unlawfully restrained so as to enable them to seek legal redress.

*R (ML) v Youth Justice Board* [2013] EWHC 3083 (Admin); 15 October 2013

It had been unfair and therefore unlawful not to give a vulnerable young offender the opportunity to make representations in respect of a prospective move from a secure training centre to a young offender institution. Given his behaviour, however the decision had been proportionate and so had not breached his rights under Article 8 of the European Convention on Human Rights.

*R (MA) v Independent Adjudicator* [2013] EWHC 438 (Admin); 7 March 2013

See "Adjudications" above".

*R (R) v Tower Hamlets London Borough Council* [2013] EWHC 2802 (Admin); 18 July 2013

The claimant prisoner (R) applied for judicial review of decisions by the defendant local authority surrounding its provision of assessments, support and accommodation for him upon his possible release from detention. When aged 14, R had been convicted of rape and sexual assaults on children aged seven to nine. He was given two sentences of detention for public protection. R was currently 21 and had served the tariff periods of his sentences. His release was therefore in the Parole Board's hands, and a parole hearing was imminent. The local authority had provided R with a pathway plan, indicating that he would be accommodated by the probation service if released. R obtained an independent psychiatric assessment recommending that, upon release, he should be placed in a facility offering therapeutic programmes and support. The local authority declined to accept that recommendation, and it was also rejected by the relevant social worker. The local authority then conducted an assessment under the National Health Service and Community Care Act 1990 s.47 and concluded that R did not have any mental health needs and was not eligible for support on that basis. R's offender manager reported that R was likely to be accommodated at probation-approved premises if released, then moving into the local authority's housing programme. An independent social worker reported that R's needs were substantial, requiring the local authority to provide supported accommodation. The local authority maintained its position that it was unable to fund R's care in a therapeutic facility. R contended that the local authority had acted unlawfully in that (1) it had failed to make provision for his eligible needs and provide supported accommodation under the National Assistance Act 1948 s.21; (2) its assessment of his needs was irrational; (3) it had failed to determine the nature and extent of the services he required on release and failed to draw up a clear care plan; (4) there was a breach of statutory duty owed to him as a care leaver wishing to pursue education; (5) it had failed to make arrangements for his accommodation; (6) it had failed to carry out an assessment under s.21 of the 1948 Act.

(1) The local authority had fulfilled its role in assessing R's needs as liable to be met initially by the probation service, having balanced his welfare needs against the need for public safety. The local authority was, however, obliged formally to set out in writing precisely what its position was so that that could be considered before the Parole Board hearing. (2) The local authority had taken a principled, detailed and considered view of R's needs. The fact that its conclusion was different to R's view did not render it irrational. The local authority had exercised its judgment carefully. (3) The local authority had determined the nature and extent of R's needs in its s.47 assessment. A more detailed care plan could be arrived at later. (4) A local authority was only obliged to support a care leaver in education until he was 21. R was over 21 and was not currently enrolled on any educational course, he had only indicated an intention to do so. There was no breach of duty in that respect. (5) The local authority had made

arrangements for R's accommodation needs in that they would be met by the probation service; he would later be accommodated under housing legislation. (6) Having made a s.47 assessment the local authority was not also required to make a s.21 assessment, especially since that would not add any additional weight to R's claim. (7) It followed that R's application failed, save to the extent that, as part of its obligation to provide support, the local authority had to provide formal written material for the Parole Board.

## YOUNG PEOPLE
See also "Childcare"; and "Young Offenders".
Building Bridges: A Positive Behaviour Framework for the Children and Young People Secure Estate Policy Framework (27/01/2020)
PSI 08/2012 Care and Management of Young People (revised 27/01/2020)
Executive summary
The purpose of this PSI is to define the principles upon which Governors of establishments holding young people must operate regimes, where they differ from adult regimes, and to provide additional guidance that is relevant only to establishments holding young people. Governors should continue to apply all NOMS policies, unless they expressly state that they do not apply to young people. This PSI also defines the key features of regimes for young people and the outcomes required. Its purpose is not to prescribe in great detail but to provide sufficient information for direction and, where appropriate, to ensure consistency. Scope is left for Governors to determine how the regimes are to be delivered operationally.
This PSI is issued to update PSI 28/2009, issued in October 2009, which it replaces. The main purpose of this revised edition is to take account of policy changes that have occurred since the last review.

## ZOONOTIC INFECTIONS
PSO 3805

## APPEALS

### Authors' Note
Since the 2019 edition this part was completely re-written in order to focus more closely on the issues which prisoners are likely to face if bringing appeals; we will retain this approach in all subsequent editions.
This part, like the preceding part, is only intended to be an introductory guide to the highly detailed rules of practice and procedure relating to Criminal Appeals. The Court of Appeal (Criminal Division) will not interfere lightly with the verdicts of juries, or the sentences imposed by judges, unless there is a

clear error in the Crown Court. Convictions and sentences imposed by magistrates' courts are more easily overturned, but experience shows that overturning convictions is often a difficult and time-consuming process.

### Resources

The rules for preparing and conducting a criminal appeal are contained in the Criminal Procedure Rules parts 34-44 and Criminal Practice Direction IX, which can be found at https://tinyurl.com/y4796lhh.

"The Court of Appeal Criminal Division Guide to Commencing Proceedings" (July 2021) is essential guidance that must be read by anyone preparing an appeal to the Court of Appeal (Criminal Division). It is available via https://tinyurl.com/y26uvgcg.

### Appeals against conviction from the Crown Court to the Court of Appeal
### Procedure

Where a defendant is convicted or pleads guilty in the Crown Court, their route of appeal against conviction will be to the Court of Appeal (Criminal Division). The same route of appeal also applies to defendants who wish to appeal against a finding that they are not guilty by reason of insanity (Criminal Appeal Act 1968 s.12) or that they are under a disability and did the act alleged (Criminal Appeal Act 1968 s.15).

In order to appeal against conviction, the defendant will normally have to apply to the Court of Appeal for permission to appeal (referred to as "leave to appeal"). The time limit to apply for permission to appeal is 28 days from conviction. The Criminal Appeal Act 1968 s.1 sets out the right to appeal as follows:

"1.— Right of appeal.
(1) Subject to subsection (3) below a person convicted of an offence on indictment may appeal to the Court of Appeal against his conviction.
(2) An appeal under this section lies only—
(a) with the leave of the Court of Appeal; or
(b) if, within 28 days of the date of the conviction, the judge of the court of trial grants a certificate that the case is fit for appeal."

There are three exceptions to the requirement to have permission to appeal.

Firstly, permission to appeal is not required if within 28 days of conviction the trial judge has certified that the case is fit for appeal.

Secondly, permission to appeal is not required if the Criminal Cases Review Commission has referred the case to the Court of Appeal.

Thirdly, permission to appeal is not required for appeals against convictions for contempt of court (Criminal Appeal Act 1968 s.18A). However, all other rules about lodging an appeal with the Court of Appeal continue to apply for convictions for contempt of court.

The application for leave to appeal is made on Form NG. There is a different Form NG for each of appeals against conviction, sentence, and confiscation. Form NG for appeals against conviction can be found at

http://www.justice.gov.uk/courts/procedure-rules/criminal/docs/october-2015/2018-appeal-forms/form-ng-conviction.doc or
https://tinyurl.com/y4dzadj4.

Form NG must be accompanied by Grounds of Appeal. The Grounds of Appeal should allow the Single Judge to understand quickly the facts and issues in the case. There are detailed requirements for how the Grounds of Appeal must be set out. In this regard, the Criminal Procedure Rules rule 39.3(2) states as follows:

"(2) The grounds of appeal must—
(a) include in no more than the first two pages a summary of the grounds that makes what then follows easy to understand;
(b) in each ground of appeal identify the event or decision to which that ground relates;
(c) in each ground of appeal summarise the facts relevant to that ground, but only to the extent necessary to make clear what is in issue;
(d) concisely outline each argument in support of each ground;
(e) number each ground consecutively, if there is more than one;
(f) identify any relevant authority and—
(i) state the proposition of law that the authority demonstrates, and
(ii) identify the parts of the authority that support that proposition; and
(g) where the Criminal Cases Review Commission refers a case to the court, explain how each ground of appeal relates (if it does) to the reasons for the reference."

Form NG, along with the Grounds of Appeal, must be submitted to the Registrar of Criminal Appeals in the Court of Appeal (Criminal Division). Electronic service is encouraged, with large attachments being sent in clearly marked separate emails. The documents should be sent as attachments by email to

**criminalappealoffice.applications@ hmcts.x.gsi.gov.uk.**

Alternatively, documents can be served by post to the following address:

The Registrar
Criminal Appeal Office
Royal Courts of Justice
Strand
London
WC2A 2LL

The time limit to make an application for leave to appeal to the Court of Appeal against conviction in the Crown Court is 28 days from the date of conviction, even if the applicant is to be sentenced later. In this regard, the Criminal Appeal Act 1968 s.18 states as follows:

"18.— Initiating procedure.

(1) A person who wishes to appeal under this Part of this Act to the Court of Appeal, or to obtain the leave of that court to appeal, shall give notice of appeal or, as the case may be, notice of application for leave to appeal, in such manner as may be directed by rules of court.

(2) Notice of appeal, or of application for leave to appeal, shall be given within twenty-eight days from the date of the conviction, verdict or finding appealed against, or in the case of appeal against sentence, from the date on which sentence was passed or, in the case of an order made or treated as made on conviction, from the date of the making of the order.

(3) The time for giving notice under this section may be extended, either before or after it expires, by the Court of Appeal."

Further, the Criminal Procedure Rules rule 39.2 states as follows:

"39.2. The appellant must serve an appeal notice on the Registrar—

(a) not more than 28 days after—

(i) the conviction, verdict, or finding,

(ii) the sentence,

(iii) the order (subject to paragraph (b)), or the failure to make an order, or

(iv) the minimum term review decision under section 274(3) of, or paragraph 14 of Schedule 22 to, the Criminal Justice Act 2003 about which the appellant wants to appeal;

(b) not more than 21 days after the order in a case in which the appellant appeals against a wasted or third party costs order;

(c) not more than 28 days after the Registrar serves notice that the Criminal Cases Review Commission has referred a conviction to the court."

Any application for leave to appeal which is made after the 28-day time limit must be accompanied by an application for an extension of time. The application for an extension of time will need to give good reasons why the application for leave to appeal is late, and why an extension should be allowed. Even very short delays in applying for leave to appeal require clear justification. In this regard the Criminal Procedure Rules rule 36.4 states as follows:

"Application for extension of time

36.4. A person who wants an extension of time within which to serve a notice or make an application must—

(a) apply for that extension of time when serving that notice or making that application; and

(b) give the reasons for the application for an extension of time."

**R v Wilson [2016] EWCA Crim 65; 9 February 2016**

On 25 February 2005 the applicant was convicted of murder and a very serious offence of conspiracy to supply class A drugs. He had earlier pleaded guilty to possession with intent to supply. Between 2005 and 2013 the applicant sought the advice of new solicitors. Only in July 2015 was an application for leave to appeal and for an extension of time made.

The Court of Appeal held that it must receive details of the delay and an explanation for it, before considering whether it will grant an extension of time. It will need to be satisfied as to the reasons for the delay and whether there is anything that justifies an extension long after the event.

Decisions on applications for leave to appeal, or applications to extend time for any application for leave to appeal, are usually made by a single judge on the papers ("the Single Judge"). In this regard the Criminal Appeal Act 1968 s 31 states as follows:

"31.— Powers of Court which are exercisable by single judge.

(1) There may be exercised by a single judge in the same manner as by the Court of Appeal and subject to the same provisions—

(a) the powers of the Court of Appeal under this Part of this Act specified in subsection (2) below;

[…]

(2) The powers mentioned in subsection (1)(a) above are the following:—

(a) to give leave to appeal;

(b) to extend the time within which notice of appeal or of application for leave to appeal may be given;

(c) to allow an appellant to be present at any proceedings"

The Single Judge may be a judge of the Court of Appeal or the High Court. In practice, most decisions on leave to appeal are made by High Court judges. As such, the judge may or may not have particular experience of the detail of criminal law, and so any grounds of appeal should be drafted with this in mind. In this regard the Criminal Appeal Act 1968 s 45(2) states as follows:

"45. Construction of references in Parts I and II to Court of Appeal and a single judge.

(2) The references in sections 23A, 31 to 31C, 44 and 44A of this Act to a single judge are to any judge of the Court of Appeal or the High Court."

The Single Judge may grant leave to appeal, may refuse leave to appeal, or may refer to the judges of the Court of Appeal (referred to as "the Full Court") the decision on whether to grant leave to appeal.

If an application for leave to appeal, or an

application for an extension of time, is refused by the Single Judge, then within 14 days the applicant may renew their application to an oral hearing before the Full Court. In this regard the Criminal Procedure Rules rule 36.5 provides as follows:

"Renewing an application refused by a judge or the Registrar

36.5.—(1) This rule applies where a party with the right to do so wants to renew—

(a) to a judge of the Court of Appeal an application refused by the Registrar; or

(b) to the Court of Appeal an application refused by a judge of that court.

(2) That party must—

(a) renew the application in the form set out in the Practice Direction, signed by or on behalf of the applicant; and

(b) serve the renewed application on the Registrar not more than 14 days after—

(i) the refusal of the application that the applicant wants to renew; or

(ii) the Registrar serves that refusal on the applicant, if the applicant was not present in person or by live link when the original application was refused."

The Full Court is usually composed of 3 judges, but often the judges include judges of the High Court. The Full court may even include a Circuit Judge who would usually sit in the Crown Court but who is permitted to act as a judge of the Court of Appeal for the purpose of the appeal (Senior Courts Act 1981 ss 9(1) and 55(6)).

The prosecution will not usually be represented at an oral application for leave to appeal. However, they may provide a Notice and Grounds of Opposition to Appeal (Criminal Procedure Rules rule 39.6).

At the hearing of the application for leave to appeal the applicant or their representative will argue why leave to appeal should be given. If the Full Court considers that the appeal is arguable then leave to appeal will be granted. If the Full Court concludes that the appeal is not arguable, then leave to appeal will be refused.

If the Full Court refuses leave to appeal, or refuses an application to extend time, the appeal itself will not be heard.

If leave to appeal is granted either by the Single Judge on the papers, or by the Full Court at an oral hearing, or if the case is referred by the Single Judge to the Full Court for a decision on whether to grant leave to appeal, then the case will be listed for a full hearing of the appeal. Notice of the hearing will be given, and the prosecution may be represented at the appeal hearing.

If an appeal is unsuccessful at any stage or is abandoned by the appellant, then the appellant will not have a right to appeal again to the Court of Appeal. In such circumstances, the only way to have a second appeal will be to apply to the Criminal Cases Review Commission.

There are minor exceptions to this rule where:

• The abandonment of an appeal by an appellant is a nullity; or

• The dismissal of the first appeal involved a procedural irregularity, which means the dismissal should be treated as a nullity.

### Abandonment of an appeal

An appeal or an application for permission to appeal may be abandoned at any time before the hearing without leave. This is done by the appellant completing and lodging Form A. An oral instruction or letter indicating a wish to abandon the appeal is insufficient. At the hearing, an application or appeal can only be abandoned with the permission of the Court of Appeal. In this regard, the Criminal Procedure Rules rule 36.13 provides in particular as follows:

"36.13.—(1) This rule applies where an appellant wants to—

(a) abandon—

(i) an application to the court for permission to appeal, or

(ii) an appeal; or

(b) reinstate such an application or appeal after abandoning it.

(2) The appellant—

(a) may abandon such an application or appeal without the court's permission by serving a notice of abandonment on—

(i) the Registrar, and

(ii) any respondent

before any hearing of the application or appeal; but

(b) at any such hearing, may only abandon that application or appeal with the court's permission."

An appeal or application which is abandoned is treated as being a final determination of the Full Court (CrimPR 36.13(4)(c)). A notice of abandonment cannot be withdrawn, nor can it be conditional. A person who wants to reinstate an application or appeal after abandonment must apply in writing to the Registrar of the Court of Appeal with reasons (CrimPR 36.13(5)). The Court of Appeal has power to allow reinstatement only where the purported abandonment can be treated as a nullity and the applicant must provide the Court with the relevant information to determine the application.

### R v Medway (1976) 62 Cr App R 85; 6 Nov 1975

The Court of Appeal held that it only has jurisdiction to give leave to withdraw a notice of abandonment of application for leave to appeal where such notice can be regarded as a nullity. For something to be a nullity it will need to not be the result of a deliberate and informed decision. Giving the judgment of the Court, Lawson J stated "We do not think that a deliberate decision to abandon taken as a result of advice which is founded on a mistaken view of the law is in itself capable of vitiating the effectiveness of the notice to abandon so as to enable the court to treat it as a nullity."

### R v Smith [2013] EWCA Crim 2388; [2014] 2 Cr. App. R. 1; 18 December 2013

The appellant was convicted of murder and appealed against the conviction. The appellant then received further advice that his appeal could not succeed, and as a result he signed a notice of abandonment. The Court of Appeal held that the advice which led him to abandon his appeal was perfectly reasonable and could not be characterised as wrong for the purposes of the defendant's application, even if some lawyers took a different or more optimistic view. Thus when the defendant abandoned his appeal on the basis of that advice, he was not relying upon incorrect legal advice.

### Bail pending appeal

The Court of Appeal has the power to grant bail pending appeal. However, in practice this power is rarely used. The powers of the Court of Appeal also include revoking bail granted by the Crown Court, and varying the conditions of bail. The power of the Court of Appeal in this regard is set out in the Criminal Appeal Act 1968 s 19 as follows:

"19.— Bail

(1) The Court of Appeal may, subject to section 25 of the Criminal Justice and Public Order Act 1994 , if they think fit,—

(a) grant an appellant bail pending the determination of his appeal; or

(b) revoke bail granted to an appellant by the Crown Court under [ paragraph (f) of section 81(1) of the Senior Courts Act 1981 ] 3 [ or paragraph (a) above ] 4 ; or

(c) vary the conditions of bail granted to an appellant in the exercise of the power conferred by either of those paragraphs

(2) The powers conferred by subsection (1) above may be exercised—

(a) on the application of an appellant; or

(b) if it appears to the registrar of criminal appeals of the Court of Appeal (hereafter referred to as "the registrar") that any of them ought to be exercised, on a reference to the court by him"

### The effect of a successful appeal against conviction

When an appeal against conviction succeeds, the Court of Appeal quashes the conviction. The Court of Appeal will then decide whether to order a retrial under the Criminal Appeal Act 1968 s 7. If a retrial is not ordered, then the verdict is changed to not guilty. In this regard, the Criminal Appeal Act 1968 s 2 provides as follows:

"2.— Grounds for allowing appeal under s. 1...

(2) In the case of an appeal against conviction the Court shall, if they allow the appeal, quash the conviction.

(3) An order of the Court of Appeal quashing a conviction shall, except when under section 7 below the appellant is ordered to be retried, operate as a direction to the court of trial to enter, instead of the record of conviction, a judgment and verdict of acquittal."

If a retrial is ordered, then this will take place in the Crown Court as a fresh trial. The successful appellant can only be prosecuted for offences of which he could have been found guilty at the original trial. In this regard, the Criminal Appeal Act 1968 provides as follows:

"7.— Power to order retrial.

(1) Where the Court of Appeal allow an appeal against conviction and it appears to the Court that the interests of justice so require, they may order the appellant to be retried.

(2) A person shall not under this section be ordered to be retried for any offence other than—

(a) the offence of which he was convicted at the original trial and in respect of which his appeal is allowed as mentioned in subsection (1) above;

(b) an offence of which he could have been convicted at the original trial on an indictment for the first-mentioned offence; or

(c) an offence charged in an alternative count of the indictment in respect of which no verdict was given in consequence of his being convicted of the first-mentioned offence."

If the Court of Appeal has ordered a retrial and the defendant is then convicted again at the re-trial, the sentence imposed after re-trial may not be more severe than the sentence originally imposed by the Crown Court. In this regard the Criminal Appeal Act 1968 s 8(4) and Schedule 2 para 2(1) provide as follows:

"8.— Supplementary provisions as to retrial.[...]

(4) Schedule 2 to this Act has effect with respect to the procedure in the case of a person ordered to be retried, the sentence which may be passed if the retrial results in his conviction and the order for costs which may be made if he is acquitted."

"Schedule 2: PROCEDURAL AND OTHER PROVISIONS APPLICABLE ON ORDER FOR RETRIAL [...]

2 (1) Where a person ordered to be retried is again convicted on retrial, the court before which he is convicted may pass in respect of the offence any sentence authorised by law, not being a sentence of greater severity than that passed on the original conviction."

The factors which the Court of Appeal will take into account when deciding whether or not to order a retrial will include the length of time which has elapsed between the appellant's original conviction and the successful appeal, the impact of the sentence already served, and the extent to which any fresh evidence received by the court undermines the strength of the case against the appellant.

If an appeal succeeds (usually on a technical basis), then instead of quashing a conviction or ordering a retrial, the Court of Appeal can in some cases substitute a guilty verdict in respect of a different offence. This will occur where the jury's verdict demonstrates that the jury must have been satisfied of facts which proved the appellant guilty of another offence. In this regard the Criminal Appeal Act 1968 s 3 provides as follows: "3.— Power to substitute conviction of alternative offence.

(1) This section applies on an appeal against conviction, where the appellant has been convicted of an offence to which he did not plead guilty and the jury could on the indictment have found him guilty of some other offence, and on the finding of the jury it appears to the Court of Appeal that the jury must have been satisfied of facts which proved him guilty of the other offence.

(2) The Court may, instead of allowing or dismissing the appeal, substitute for the verdict found by the jury a verdict of guilty of the other offence, and pass such sentence in substitution for the sentence passed at the trial as may be authorised by law for the other offence, not being a sentence of greater severity."

If an appellant had originally pleaded guilty to an offence, but the conviction was quashed on appeal, the Court of Appeal has the power to substitute a conviction for an alternative offence. This power will be exercised in circumstances where the successful appellant would necessarily be guilty of some other offence with which they were originally charged, but not the offence to which they pleaded guilty. The Court of Appeal is then enabled to impose a sentence in respect of the conviction for the substituted conviction. However, that sentence may not be more severe than the sentence originally imposed. In this regard, the Criminal Appeal Act 1968 s 3A provides as follows: "3A Power to substitute conviction of alternative offence after guilty plea

(1) This section applies on an appeal against conviction where—

(a) an appellant has been convicted of an offence to which he pleaded guilty,

(b) if he had not so pleaded, he could on the indictment have pleaded, or been found, guilty of some other offence, and

(c) it appears to the Court of Appeal that the plea of guilty indicates an admission by the appellant of facts which prove him guilty of the other offence.

(2) The Court of Appeal may, instead of allowing or dismissing the appeal, substitute for the appellant's plea of guilty a plea of guilty of the other offence and pass such sentence in substitution for the sentence passed at the trial as may be authorised by law for the other offence, not being a sentence of greater severity."

If an appellant has been convicted in the Crown Court of a number of offences and the Court of Appeal quashes some of the convictions but not others, the court is entitled to resentence the offender on the counts on which he remains convicted. However, the Court of Appeal may not pass a sentence which is more severe than that which was originally passed by the Crown Court. The Court of Appeal may resentence even on those counts for which the Crown Court imposed no separate penalty. In this regard the Criminal Appeal Act 1968 s 4 provides as follows: "4.— Power to re-sentence where appellant remains convicted of related offences.

(1) This section applies where—

(a) two or more related sentences are passed,

(b) the Court of Appeal allow an appeal against conviction in respect of one or more of the offences for which the sentences were passed ("the related offences"), but

(c) the appellant remains convicted of one or more of those offences.

(2) Except as provided by subsection (3) below, the Court may in respect of any related offence of which the appellant remains convicted pass such sentence, in substitution for any sentence passed thereon at the trial, as they think proper and is authorised by law.

(3) The Court shall not under this section pass any sentence such that the appellant's sentence (taken as a whole) for all the related offences of which he remains convicted will, in consequence of the appeal, be of greater severity than the sentence (taken as a whole) which was passed at the trial for all the related offences.

(4) For the purposes of subsection (1)(a), two or more sentences are related if—

(a) they are passed on the same day,

(b) they are passed on different days but the court in passing any one of them states that it is treating that one together with the other or others as substantially one sentence, or

(c) they are passed on different days but in respect of counts on the same indictment.

(5) Where—

(a) two or more sentences are related to each other by virtue of subsection (4)(a) or (b), and

(b) any one or more of those sentences is related to one or more other sentences by virtue of subsection (4)(c), all the sentences are to be treated as related for the purposes of subsection (1)(a)."

## The Court of Appeal Test against conviction

The test applied by the Court of Appeal when deciding whether an appeal against conviction will be allowed is whether the conviction is "unsafe". In this regard, the Criminal Appeal Act 1968 s 2 provides as follows:

"2.— Grounds for allowing appeal under s. 1.

(1) Subject to the provisions of this Act, the Court of Appeal—

(a) shall allow an appeal against conviction if they think that the conviction is unsafe; and

(b) shall dismiss such an appeal in any other case.

(2) In the case of an appeal against conviction the Court shall, if they allow the appeal, quash the conviction.

(3) An order of the Court of Appeal quashing a conviction shall, except when under section 7 below the appellant is ordered to be retried, operate as a direction to the court of trial to enter, instead of the record of conviction, a judgment and verdict of acquittal."

### *R v Cooper* [1969] 1 Q.B. 267; 8 November 1968

The classic analysis of what it means for a conviction to be unsafe was set out by Lord Widgery:

"[This is] a case in which every issue was before the jury and in which the jury was properly instructed, and, accordingly, a case in which this court will be very reluctant indeed to intervene. It has been said over and over again throughout the years that this court must recognise the advantage which a jury has in seeing and hearing the witnesses, and if all the material was before the jury and the summing-up was impeccable, this court should not lightly interfere.

Indeed, until the passing of the Criminal Appeal Act 1966 [which somewhat widened the court's powers to quash a conviction] it was almost unheard of for this court to interfere in such a case. However, now our powers are somewhat different, and we are indeed charged to allow an appeal against conviction if we think that the verdict of the jury should be set aside on the ground that under all the circumstances of the case it is unsafe or unsatisfactory.

That means that in cases of this kind the court must in the end ask itself a subjective question, whether we are content to let the matter stand as it is, or whether there is not some lurking doubt in our minds which makes us wonder whether an injustice has been done.

This is a reaction which may not be based strictly on the evidence as such; it is a reaction which can be produced by the general feel of the case as the court experiences it." (p 271C–G)

## Appeal against Conviction after a guilty plea

The fact that a defendant has pleaded guilty to an offence does not prevent them from appealing against conviction. The test for whether an appeal against conviction should be allowed by the Court of Appeal remains the same: whether the conviction is safe. However, the fact that a defendant pleaded guilty to an offence will be powerful evidence that their conviction is in fact safe. If a person was fit to plead, was represented, and had made an unequivocal and intentional plea of guilty then this would obviously be relevant to the Court of Appeal's decision about whether their conviction was safe. The Court of Appeal may be persuaded to allow a conviction following a guilty plea to be overturned in the following circumstances:

• Where a judge decided a legal issue wrongly against the defendant, and the determination of the legal issue by the judge removed any defence the defendant would have had.

• Where there is new evidence which shows that the defendant is not guilty.

• Where the defendant pleaded guilty based on negligent legal advice.

## Common grounds of appeal against conviction
### Fresh evidence

New evidence may come to light after a conviction, which may cast doubt on the safety of the conviction. If the fresh evidence renders the conviction unsafe, then the conviction will be quashed. However, there are restrictions on when fresh evidence may be relied on in an appeal.

Where grounds of appeal rely upon fresh evidence that was not adduced at trial, an application under the Criminal Appeal Act 1968 s 23 must be made. In this regard the Criminal Appeal Act 1968 s 23 provides as follows (except that, s 23(5) will not apply until 25 September 2022):

"23.— Evidence.

(1) For the purposes of an appeal, or an application for leave to appeal, under this Part of this Act the Court of Appeal may, if they think it necessary or expedient in the interests of justice—

(a) order the production of any document, exhibit or other thing connected with the proceedings, the production of which appears to them necessary for the determination of the case;

(b) order any witness to attend for examination and be examined before the Court (whether or not he was called in the proceedings from which the appeal lies); and

(c) receive any evidence which was not adduced in the proceedings from which the appeal lies.

(1A) The power conferred by subsection (1)(a) may be exercised so as to require the production of any document, exhibit or other thing mentioned in that subsection to—

(a) the Court;

(b) the appellant;

(c) the respondent.

(2) The Court of Appeal shall, in considering whether to receive any evidence, have regard in particular to—

(a) whether the evidence appears to the Court to be capable of belief;

(b) whether it appears to the Court that the evidence may afford any ground for allowing the appeal;

(c) whether the evidence would have been admissible in the proceedings from which the appeal lies on an issue which is the subject of the appeal; and

(d) whether there is a reasonable explanation for the failure to adduce the evidence in those proceedings.

(3) Subsection (1)(c) above applies to any evidence of a witness (including the appellant) who is competent but not compellable.

(4) For the purposes of an appeal, or an application for leave to appeal, under this Part of this Act, the Court of Appeal may, if they think it necessary or expedient in the interests of justice, order the examination of any witness whose attendance might be required under subsection (1)(b) above to be conducted, in manner provided by rules of court, before any judge or officer of the Court or other person appointed by the Court for the purpose, and allow the admission of any depositions so taken as evidence before the Court.

(5) A live link direction under section 22(4) does not apply to the giving of oral evidence by the appellant at any hearing unless that direction, or any subsequent direction of the court, provides expressly for the giving of such evidence through a live link.

(6) In this section, "respondent" includes a person who will be a respondent if leave to appeal is granted."

If the fresh evidence is provided by a witness, the appellant or their representatives must obtain a statement from the witness. Insofar as is relevant, the Criminal Justice Act 1967 s 9 provides the conditions that must be followed for the making of the statement as follows:

"9.— Proof by written statement.

(1) In any criminal proceedings, a written statement by any person shall, if such of the conditions mentioned in the next following subsection as are applicable are satisfied, be admissible as evidence to the like extent as oral evidence to the like effect by that person.

(2) The said conditions are—

(a) the statement purports to be signed by the person who made it;

(b) the statement contains a declaration by that person to the effect that it is true to the best of his

knowledge and belief and that he made the statement knowing that, if it were tendered in evidence, he would be liable to prosecution if he wilfully stated in it anything which he knew to be false or did not believe to be true […]"

If the fresh evidence is documentary evidence (for example, business records which contain bank statements relevant to a fraud case) or real evidence (for example, a knife used in a murder), the appellant or their representatives should obtain statements from all those involved formally exhibiting the evidence. A Form W should be lodged in respect of each witness dealing with the fresh evidence. The Registrar or Single Judge may direct the issue of a witness order but only the Court hearing the appeal may give leave for a witness to be called and then formally receive the evidence under the Criminal Appeal Act 1968 s 23.

Form W is available on gov.uk

Further, a supporting witness statement (in the form required by Criminal Justice Act 1967 s 9), or an affidavit from the appellant's solicitor must accompany the fresh evidence and Form W, setting out why the evidence was not available at trial and how it has come to light. This is referred to as a Gogana affidavit (after the case of R v Gogana The Times, July 12, 1999; see also R v James [2020] Crim LR 571). In cases where new lawyers are acting, a waiver of privilege will also usually always be required to enable the Registrar to seek the comments of the trial lawyers as to why the evidence was not available at trial (R v Singh [2017] EWCA Crim 466).

The approach to issues of non-disclosure of material that ought to have been disclosed by the prosecution should be the same as in a case of fresh evidence. It is for the Court of Appeal to decide whether the material that has not been disclosed causes it to doubt the safety of the conviction. The Court of Appeal will in practice apply the same test as it would in relation to the admission of fresh evidence. The Court of Appeal will consider the impact the withheld material might have had on the jury. This allows the Court of Appeal to "test its view" of the safety of a conviction.

**Changes in the law, in particular joint enterprise**

An apparent change in the law may, in rare circumstances, have retrospective effect. This may apply where the law has been applied incorrectly for years, and the incorrect application of the law was only appreciated later. This section uses the situation with regard to joint enterprise as an example of how this works in practice, as well as other cases where it was argued that the law was incorrectly applied.

*R v Jogee* [2016] UKSC 8; [2017] AC 387; 18 February 2016

The Supreme Court corrected a mistake in the law made decades ago in the case of Chan Wing-Siu [1985] AC 168; 21 June 1984. In summary, in Chan Wing-Siu the courts had wrongly widened the scope of "joint enterprise", a legal doctrine which makes one person liable for a crime committed by another person.

The classical example of this is a bank robbery. Two robbers walk into a bank, and a getaway driver waits outside. All three of them have agreed to rob the bank (Crime A), and so all of them are guilty of conspiracy to rob (and of robbery when they commit the offence). However, one of the robbers carries a shotgun with him. The other two know about this. When a security guard tries to stop the robbery, the robber with the shotgun shoots and kills the guard (Crime B). The robber who fired the shot is obviously guilty of murder (unless an unusual defence such as diminished responsibility or insanity applies). The question then arises of whether the other robbers are also guilty of murder.

Under *Chan Wing-Siu*, if the other robbers had foreseen the possibility of a person being caused serious selfharm in the course of the robbery, they would have been guilty of murder as well. This would be the case even if they had not agreed to it, and even if they had objected to killing anyone. Participation in Crime A knowing Crime B was possible meant being guilty of Crime B.

However, this was corrected by the Supreme Court in *Jogee*. The Supreme Court agreed that this test was wrong in law and was not justified as a matter of public policy. The law went back to what it had been before *Chan Wing-Siu*: for a person to be guilty, they would have to agree to some serious selfharm being caused, even if this agreement was conditional on something going wrong. For example, if one of the robbers had not agreed to the weapon being used, or even had argued against it being used, they may not be guilty of murder, even if they foresaw that a person might be caused serious selfharm. This means that foresight of Crime B is no longer sufficient on its own, but foresight of Crime B may be evidence of intent in relation to Crime B. In other words, the court should still take foresight into account when deciding whether or not the other robbers had agreed to Crime B, but just having foresight no longer means that they are automatically guilty of Crime B.

Many hundreds of people have been convicted under joint enterprise principles when they were incorrectly applied. The Supreme Court foresaw that many of them would want to apply to have their convictions overturned. However, they noted that the Court of Appeal may only grant leave to appeal "if substantial injustice be demonstrated". The Supreme Court did not define "substantial injustice", so any appeal on those grounds will be specific to an individual's case.

*R v Johnson (Lewis) and others* [2016] EWCA Crim 1613; [2017] 4 W.L.R. 104; 31 October 2016

This was the first full set of appeals after the case of Jogee. The court there dealt with the issue of demonstrating substantial injustice. All appellants in that case were either denied leave to appeal or had their appeals dismissed, and all convictions were therefore upheld.

To persuade the Court of Appeal that a substantial injustice has occurred an applicant will have to persuade them that they would not necessarily have been convicted even if the correct legal test had been applied. The Court of Appeal did make clear that, "If there was a substantial injustice, it is irrelevant whether that injustice occurred a short time or a long time ago. It is and remains an injustice."

Demonstrating that there was a substantial injustice has proved a difficult hurdle for applicants to overcome, even if the legal direction on joint enterprise was wholly wrong. Only one case has successfully challenged this decision.

*R v Crilly* [2018] EWCA Crim 168; [2018] 4 WLR 114; 30 January 2018

The Appellant was convicted of a murder which took place in the course of a burglary. It was agreed by the participants that no weapons were used, and the 71-year-old victim was killed by a forceful blow to the head by Mr Crilly's co-accused. Mr Crilly understood that the house was empty when he agreed to go with the co-accused to burgle the house and did not intend to cause very serious selfharm to the victim. The Court of Appeal concluded at para 42 that the evidence against Mr Crilly "was not so strong that we can safely and fairly infer the jury would have found the requisite intent to cause really serious bodily selfharm".

Examples of other cases (not involving joint enterprise) where it was argued that the law was incorrectly applied are as follows:

*R v Ordu* [2017] EWCA Crim 4; [2017] 1 Cr App R 21; 20 January 2017

The applicant was a former asylum seeker who had entered the UK using a false passport, and who pleaded to an offence of possession of false identity documents. As the law was then understood to be, the defendant, having stopped en route in a safe country, had no defence. The House of Lords subsequently held, in another case, that a defence was available where a refugee had, in the course of flight, passed through safe countries. Eight years and three months after his conviction the defendant applied for an extension of time in which to appeal against conviction.

However, despite accepting that the fact that the applicant was applying late was not the applicant's fault, the Court of Appeal refused to grant an extension of time and as such his conviction was not quashed. The Court of Appeal held "that he has now lived through all the adverse consequences of the conviction and emerged to a happier, more settled and safe life in the UK. The conviction and sentence is now a long time ago and quashing the conviction will not remedy the unpleasant memories which are now its only legacy. On the information before us, quashing the conviction would actually make no real difference to the defendant's life at all, and in those circumstances it is impossible to say that a substantial injustice will occur if this appeal is not allowed to proceed."

The Court of Appeal's conclusions are questionable, as the applicant was left with a conviction for a serious offence on his record, which would continue to have impacts throughout his life, for example preventing him from applying for British citizenship, and affecting his right to travel abroad. This shows the blinkered and restrictive approach which the Court of Appeal takes to the question of whether there is a "substantial injustice".

### R v Uthayakumar [2014] EWCA Crim 123; 15 January 2014

The appellants appealed against convictions following their guilty pleas to charges of causing death by driving while uninsured. They had been incorrectly advised that there was no element of fault required for them to be guilty of the offence. They were not told that, at the time, the law on this point was in a 'state of flux' as the point of law was going to appeal. Subsequent to their guilty pleas the Supreme Court found that an element of fault was a necessary part of the offence. The prosecution had struggled to produce any case of fault and had simply speculated about where fault may lie. The Court of Appeal held that "we are satisfied that a substantial injustice would be caused if we refuse these applications and dismiss the appeals. We cannot ignore the fact that both appellants were advised to plead guilty to a very serious offence of causing someone's death, an offence of homicide, on the basis that each had no defence. That was wrong. They do have a defence." The Court of Appeal ordered that there would not be retrials and the appeals were allowed. The Court of Appeal made it clear that they considered that this was 'an exceptional case where we should intervene, despite the pleas of guilty'.

### Negligence of trial representatives

Convicted defendants are sometimes dissatisfied with the representation that they received at trial and wish to appeal based on claims that their legal team, whether barristers, or solicitors, or both, acted negligently in the conduct of their case. Such appeals are possible but are often not well-received by the Court of Appeal.

The Court of Appeal is not generally interested in determining whether an appellant's trial lawyers were negligent. Rather, the Court of Appeal will need to determine whether negligence affected the safety of the appellant's conviction. For example, a defendant's lawyers could have acted negligently in failing to have evidence excluded, in turning up to court late every day, and then falling asleep in court, but if the appellant then entered a guilty plea without pressure being placed on them to do so then their conviction would probably still be regarded as safe.

Sometimes prospective appellants will have available to them evidence which shows that their legal team were negligent. For example, the trial lawyers' notes might be available in the papers from the trial. In such circumstances they can be reviewed and might show that the lawyers fundamentally misunderstood the case, failed to read the papers, or that they ignored the appellant's instructions.

However, in the great majority of cases it will be necessary to instruct a lawyer to take a detailed look at the papers from the trial and the court's records to discover whether suspicions of negligence are correct. Such cases can be extremely time consuming for the lawyers conducting the review, as the reviewing lawyer will need to understand ever single detail of the case to work out why the trial representatives took the tactical decisions they did. It is rare that such exercises do in fact produce evidence of negligence by trial representatives.

Finally, in some cases there will be evidence in the form of written "endorsements" between the client and their trial lawyers, i.e. a written note of the advice given by the lawyer, and the instructions given by the client. Where an appellant has been provided with advice by their lawyer and they have followed it, even if it is not the best advice, this will usually be a strong defence to any charges that the lawyer has acted negligently.

In any appeal involving criticism of the trial lawyers the Court of Appeal will require the new representatives to contact the trial lawyers to ensure that the factual basis of the appeal is accurate, unless there are in exceptional circumstances good and compelling reasons not to do so (see R v McCook [2014] EWCA Crim 734; [2016] 2 Cr. App. R. 3; 10 April 2014).

**R v Clinton [1993] 1 WLR 1181; 9 March 1993**

The Court of Appeal stated that the conduct of an advocate during a trial could only very rarely form the basis for an appeal, but that *Clinton* was undoubtedly one of those exceptional cases. The defendant had not been advised by his barrister on the importance of him giving evidence, and as a result he had not done so and no evidence was called on his behalf. The Court of Appeal held in particular as follows at pages 1186-1187:

"At the same time we are acutely aware that the circumstances in which a court is entitled to overset a jury's verdict when the grounds advanced consist wholly or substantially of criticisms of defence counsel's conduct of the trial, or of matters preparatory thereto, must of necessity be extremely rare…

[C]ases where the conduct of counsel can afford a basis for appeal must be regarded as wholly exceptional.

[W]here counsel had made decisions in good faith after proper consideration of the competing arguments, and, where appropriate, after due discussion with his client, such decisions could not possibly be said to render a subsequent verdict unsafe or unsatisfactory. Particularly does this apply to the decision as to whether or not to call the defendant. Conversely, we stress, exceptionally, where it is shown that the decision was taken either in defiance of or without proper instructions, or when all the promptings or reason and good sense pointed the other way, it may be open to an appellate court to set aside the verdict…"

**R v Ullah [2000] Crim LR 108; 14 October 1999**

Defence counsel disclosed at the end of the trial that he had in his possession tape recordings of telephone conversations between the complainant and another prosecution witness that were detrimental to the complainant's credibility. The Court of Appeal allowed the appeal against conviction on the grounds that counsel's failure to disclose the existence of such evidence undermined the safety of the conviction. The Court of Appeal said that ineptitude on the part of counsel or solicitor was a primary requirement in such a case, and that for significant fault to exist, the decision by counsel or solicitor had to be so unreasonable that it would not have been open to a reasonable counsel or solicitor to have reached it (akin to Wednesbury unreasonableness).

**R v Thakrar [2001] EWCA Crim 1096; 9 May 2001**

There were multiple allegations of incompetence on the part of solicitors in advance of trial. In particular, there was an allegation that the defendant's solicitor had told him to give the same account as the co-accused, but this allegation was not accepted by the Court of Appeal (paragraph 22). However, the Court of Appeal did accept that there was nearly a complete absence of preparation of the case by the solicitor (paragraph 23). Nevertheless, the appeal did not succeed, as the Court of Appeal took the view that the "reprehensible" shortcomings of the solicitor did not prejudice the defendant or render his trial unfair (paragraph 42). In setting out the applicable test, at paragraphs 34-35 the Court of Appeal held as follows:

"34. We have already indicated that we find that the appellant's solicitors did fall below the level of reasonably competent solicitors in the way in which they prepared this case for trial on behalf of the appellant. That however is not enough to determine this appeal against conviction. The mere fact that an appellant's solicitors may have failed to carry out their duties to the appellant in a proper manner does not itself mean that a conviction is automatically unsafe. Nor is a conviction to be quashed as a means of expressing the court's disapproval of the solicitor's failures. The test is whether, in all the circumstances, the conviction is safe. Nonetheless, if such failures have prevented an appellant from having a fair trial, within the meaning of Article 6 of the European Convention on Human Rights, that will normally mean that the conviction is unsafe and should be quashed: *Togher* [2001] CLR 124.

35. Therefore the first question is whether the appellant received a fair trial or whether such a trial was prevented by the failings in preparation on the part of his solicitors. Such an issue is to be determined by considering the proceeding as a whole, as the jurisprudence of the European Court of Human Rights makes clear, and it follows that one cannot confine one's attention merely to the solicitor's preparations in isolation. As this court said in Nangle [unreported but dated 1 November 2000] if the conduct of an accused's legal advisors has been such that the objective of a fair trial is not met, then this court may be compelled to intervene."

**R v Bolivar & Lee [2003] EWCA Crim 1167; 14 April 2003**

The Court of Appeal considered a case where a barrister had been pre-occupied by criminal investigations against him. At paragraph 52 of their judgment (handed down on 14 April 2013, 2 days before a different constitution of the Court considered the case of *Day*, below) the Court of Appeal held that:

"Professionalism requires that a barrister should do his job properly, disregarding such matters. Of course, if his performance on behalf of a client is affected by such matters, different considerations apply. Hence, in our judgment, the test to be applied in relation to a barrister's conduct, is: was it *Wednesbury* unreasonable and such as to affect the fairness of the trial?"

**R v Day [2003] EWCA Crim 1060; 16 April 2003**
The Court of Appeal set out the test which is now to be applied in most cases of appeals on the basis of incompetent representation, as follows:
"While incompetent representation is always to be deplored; is an understandable source of justified complaint by litigants and their families; and may expose the lawyers concerned to professional sanctions; it cannot *in itself* form a ground of appeal or a reason why a conviction should be found to be unsafe. We accept that, following the decision of this court in Thakrar [2001] EWCA Crim 1096, the test is indeed the single test of safety, and that the court no longer has to concern itself with intermediate questions such as whether the advocacy has been flagrantly incompetent. But in order to establish lack of safety in an incompetence case the appellant has to go beyond the incompetence and show that the incompetence led to identifiable errors or irregularities in the trial, which themselves rendered the process unfair or unsafe…"

**R v Adams [2007] EWCA Crim 1; [2007] 1 Cr App R 34; 12 January 2007**
A conviction for murder was found to be unsafe as a result of failures by the appellant's legal representatives. The appellant's representatives had not carried out essential pre-trial preparation, which resulted in a failure to adduce evidence that would have assisted the appellant's case. The Court of Appeal held in particular as follows:
"155 None of the evidence which was not deployed on these three topics can be described as fresh evidence. It was all available to the defence before trial. But the failure to use this evidence, in our judgment, demonstrates that, for whatever reason, the legal advisers at trial had failed in those respects in their pre-trial preparations. The reason for this is not hard to see. The principal cause of these failures was, in our view, the late return of their instructions by counsel first instructed. At the date when the briefs were returned much preparatory work remained to be done. Some confirmation for this finding is to be found in a note made by Mr Cosgrove for the conference to be held on April 8, 1993 to which we have referred above (see [48]). We find that not all of the essential preparatory work was carried out. It was this deficiency in pre-trial preparation which caused the failures which we have identified. It would be unfair to blame Mr Fordham and Mr Menary alone for all these failures. We have no doubt that they did their best.

We have also no doubt that they believed that everything that ought to have been done had been done. But in our judgment they underestimated the time needed to complete the work.
156 It is difficult to conclude that the criticisms and failures which we have found in respect of any one of the individual topics were on their own sufficient to render the verdict unsafe but we are quite satisfied that taken together, cumulatively they were sufficient to render the verdict unsafe. Each of these topics was important. The relevance of the Kevin Thompson unused material was, as Mr Menary conceded to the CCRC "crucially important". The West Road stop was a very important part of the prosecution case. It went largely unchallenged by the defence at trial. The ability meaningfully to probe it in the way suggested is in our view significant. Finally, the Coalway Lane getaway evidence represented an opportunity further to undermine Kevin Thompson's evidence of his alleged assistance given to the appellant and Hands in carrying out the murder."

**Teeluck and John (Jason Ellis) v The State of Trinidad and Tobago [2005] UKPC 14; [2005] 1 WLR 2421**
There is an alternative strand of cases which focus not so much on the unfairness of the conviction, but on the failure by the representative amounting to an absence of due process in the case. The Judicial Board of the Privy Council held:
"There may possibly be cases in which counsel's misbehaviour or ineptitude is so extreme that it constitutes a denial of due process to the client. Apart from such cases, which it is to be hoped are extremely rare, the focus of the appellate court ought to be on the impact which the errors of counsel have had on the trial and the verdict rather than attempting to rate counsel's conduct of the case according to some scale of ineptitude."

**R v Ekaireb [2015] EWCA Crim 1936; 16 December 2015**
A defence barrister's closing speech in a murder trial was ill-judged, patronising, and contained inappropriate attempts at humour and unprofessional observations about prosecuting counsel. The Court of Appeal referred the defence barrister to the Bar Standards Board to consider disciplinary action against him. However, it did not reach a level of incompetence that called into question the fairness of the trial or the safety of the conviction. The Court of Appeal held, "We have considered the entirety of the evidence and see no reason to doubt the safety of the conviction. There were very telling points against the appellant such as the inherent unlikelihood of the wife leaving the

flat on an October night with a suitcase given the location of the flat in Hampstead, the failure of the appellant to make inquiries about his wife though she was bearing his child, the refurbishment of the flat and the finding of the ring."

## Wrongful admission or exclusion of evidence

The rules of evidence dictate what evidence may be placed before the jury during a trial. The trial judge may make rulings allowing or prohibiting certain evidence to be placed before a jury. Prime examples of this are hearsay evidence, or bad character evidence. An incorrect decision to allow or refuse evidence to be placed before a jury may mean that a conviction is unsafe.

The fact that an appellant or their advocate did not object to the judge's ruling may lead the Court of Appeal to conclude that any incorrect decision by the trial judge was not sufficiently prejudicial to make the conviction unsafe. This is particularly the case where the Court of Appeal concludes that the decision not to object to the admission or exclusion of evidence was taken as a tactical decision.

### Stirland v DPP [1944] A.C. 315; 21 June 1944

The appellant, on trial for forgery, was wrongly asked in cross-examination questions suggesting that on a previous occasion he had been "questioned about a suggested forgery" by his former employers. The House of Lords held that the questions should have been disallowed as irrelevant and unfair. However, they also held that no reasonable jury could have failed to convict him, so the conviction would not be quashed. The House of Lords also held that there is no universal rule that a conviction cannot be quashed on the ground of improper admission of evidence prejudicial to the defendant unless defence counsel applied for the jury to be discharged. However, "The failure of counsel to object may have a bearing on the question whether the accused was really prejudiced. It is not a proper use of counsel's discretion to raise no objection at the time in order to preserve a ground of objection for a possible appeal".

### Incorrect exercise of discretion

Trial judges are granted a wide discretion in how trials are run. As such, the Court of Appeal is very reluctant to find that a conviction is unsafe on the basis of an incorrect exercise of a discretion by a trial judge. Even where the Court of Appeal would have acted differently, this will only lead to a quashing of a conviction if it means that the conviction is unsafe.

Limited circumstances where an incorrect exercise of discretion may lead to the quashing of a conviction might include where the judge has failed to take relevant matters into account or taken irrelevant matters into account.

### R v Cook [1959] 2 Q.B. 340; [1959] 2 W.L.R. 616; [1959] 2 All E.R. 97; (1959) 43 Cr. App. R. 138; 23 March 1959

Devlin J giving the judgment of the Court of Criminal Appeal stated that "It is well settled that this court will not interfere with the exercise of a discretion by the judge below unless he has erred in principle or there is no material on which he could properly have arrived at his decision."

However, the Court also made clear that where there had been a failure to exercise a discretion at all, because the trial court believed they had no discretion to exercise, then the appeal court would exercise its own discretion on the matter.

### R v Quinn [1996] Crim. L.R. 516; 1 December 1995

The Court of Appeal stated that a position set out in the legal text Archbold 1996 at paragraph 4-252a was correct, in that in relation to an exercise of discretion the Court of Appeal would only interfere in a conviction if there has been a failure to exercise any discretion, a failure to take into account a material consideration or a taking account of an immaterial consideration. In such event, the Court of Appeal would itself consider how the discretion should have been exercised. If the result of this exercise is that a different conclusion is reached to that of the trial judge, it does not necessarily follow that the conviction will be quashed: the Court of Appeal will still have to ask itself whether the conviction is unsafe. So, for example, if the Court of Appeal concludes in relation to an objection to the admissibility of certain evidence made under the Police and Criminal Evidence Act 1984 s 78 that the judge should have excluded the evidence, the Court of Appeal will be faced with the same decision as it faces in a case where legally inadmissible evidence has been wrongfully admitted.

### R v McCann (1991) 92 Cr. App. R. 239; 27 April 1990

"To reverse the judge's ruling it is not enough that the members of this court would have exercised their discretion differently. We must be clearly satisfied that the judge was wrong; but our power to review the exercise of his discretion is not limited to cases in which he has erred in principle or there is shown to have been no material on which he could properly have arrived at his decision. The court must, if necessary, examine anew the relevant facts and circumstances to exercise a discretion by way of review if it thinks that the judge's ruling may have resulted in injustice to the appellants."

*R v Denton* [2001] 1 Cr. App. R. 16; 19 October 2000
The judge failed to give reasons for his decision to exercise his discretion to admit statements into evidence. This could be seen as a breach of the defendant's right under Article 6 of the European Convention on Human Rights, to which the courts are required by the Human Rights Act 1998 to give effect. However, even though reasons were not given, the discretion was in fact properly exercised. Accordingly, the convictions were not unsafe.

### Defects in the indictment

Where the indictment charges an offence not known to law, the conviction will be quashed. That will be the case even if the defendant pleads guilty or no point is taken at trial.
There are a number of different challenges to the safety of a conviction which can be made by reference to defects in the indictment. These may occur where, for example, counts were not properly included on the indictment, or because a single count on the indictment alleges multiple crimes (referred to as "duplicity").

*R v Whitehouse* [1977] Q.B. 868; [1977] 2 W.L.R. 925; [1977] 3 All E.R. 737; (1977) 65 Cr. App. R. 33; 18 February 1977
The appellant had pleaded guilty to an offence of inciting his 15-year-old daughter to commit incest with him. The prosecution conceded that since a girl under 16 years was incapable of committing the crime of incest with her father, the appellant could not be guilty of inciting her to do so. The conviction was quashed.

### Inconsistent Verdicts

The Court of Appeal will quash a conviction based on apparently inconsistent verdicts only if no reasonable jury could have reached the conclusions that it did.

*R v Durante* [1972] 1 W.L.R. 1612; [1972] 3 All E.R. 962; (1972) 56 Cr. App. R. 708; 20 June 1972
The defendant was charged with handling a stolen cheque and endeavouring to obtain money on a forged instrument (being the same document). The charges arose out of the defendant's attempts to pass the cheque in a pub, and his defence to both was that he had been too drunk to form the necessary intention. The jury acquitted him of one offence but convicted him of the other offence.
The Court of Appeal reviewed the relevant authorities and concluded that "the burden is on the defendant to show that verdicts on different counts are not merely inconsistent but are so inconsistent as to demand interference by an appellate court." In that case they were so inconsistent, and the conviction was quashed.

*R v Fletcher* [2017] EWCA Crim 1778; 15 November 2017
Where the complainant's credibility is in issue and their evidence is uncorroborated, verdicts are not to be regarded as unsafe just because the jury had also returned not guilty verdicts on other counts based on that complainant's evidence.

*R v Andrews-Weatherfoil Ltd* [1972] 1 WLR 118; 11 October 1971
When persons concerned in a single offence are tried separately, there are inconsistent verdicts, and the difference in the evidence consists of additional material favourable to the accused being called at the second trial, the first accused should seek to call that evidence in the Court of Appeal and not rely merely on inconsistent verdicts.

### Conduct of the Trial Judge

Excessive judicial intervention during the course of the evidence of the accused has sometimes led to the quashing of a conviction.

*R v Hulusi and Purvis* (1974) 58 Cr. App. R. 378; 14 December 1973
Interventions by the judge during a trial which lead to the quashing of a conviction occur
(i) when they have invited the jury to disbelieve the evidence for the defence in such strong terms that the mischief cannot be cured by the common formula in the summing-up that the facts are for the jury, and that they may disregard anything said on the facts by the judge with which they do not agree;
(ii) when they have made it impossible for defending counsel to do his duty in conducting the defence;
(iii) when they have effectively prevented the defendant or a witness for the defence from telling his story in his own way.

*R v Naz* [2017] EWCA Crim 482; [2018] 4 W.L.R. 28; 11 April 2017
A conviction for racially aggravated intentional harassment, alarm or distress was quashed where the judge had gone beyond the grounds of permitted intervention designed to control counsel and manage the case effectively. The interventions, which effectively gave approval to the complainant's evidence and cast doubt on the veracity of the defendant's evidence, had combined to create unfairness. The Court then held that if the matters complained of rendered the trial unfair, then the strength of the case against the defendant was totally irrelevant. "Every defendant, including a defendant faced with a strong prosecution case, is entitled to a fair trial. That is an absolute right irrespective of the strength of the evidence".

### Late change of nature of prosecution case

If the prosecution opens its case to the jury on one basis, a late change in the basis on which it puts its case may prevent the defendant from properly putting their defence. This may lead to a finding that any resulting conviction is unsafe.

### Adverse publicity

It is possible for a conviction to be quashed because bad publicity makes a fair trial impossible. However, pre-trial publicity does not usually make a fair trial impossible.

### *R v Abu Hamza* [2006] EWCA Crim 2918; 28 November 2006

The fact that adverse publicity could have risked prejudicing a fair trial was no reason for not proceeding if the judge had concluded that it was possible to have a fair trial. The judge had correctly concluded that the fairness of the trial was put at risk by publicity during the period between the commission of the offence and the case coming to trial. However, he had also correctly assessed that he could discharge the task of neutralising the effects of those matters by appropriate directions, guidance and summing up. As such, the convictions were safe.

### *R v Taylor and Taylor* (1994) 98 Cr. App. R. 361; 11 June 1993

Adverse publicity of the case was "unremitting, extensive, sensational, inaccurate and misleading". The Court of Appeal found that despite the judge's warnings it was impossible to say that the jury had not been influenced by it. The nature of the publicity was such that a retrial would not be appropriate.

### Bias

A conviction may be quashed where the judge or jury show that they are biased or show the appearance of bias. This is most obviously the case where members of CPS staff, or certain police officers or police staff, are selected to sit on juries. There is no general ban on CPS staff or police officers or police staff sitting on juries. However, there are strict controls on when they are allowed to do so.

### *Porter v Magill* [2001] UKHL 67; [2002] 2 AC 357; 13 December 2001

The test for bias has been authoritatively stated by the House of Lords in paragraph 103 in the speech of Lord Hope of Craighead: "The question is whether the fair-minded and informed observer, having considered the facts, would conclude that there was a real possibility that the tribunal was biased."

### *Re Medicaments and Related Classes of Goods (No. 2)* [2001] 1 WLR 700; 21 December 2000

The relevant principles for deciding cases involving allegations of bias and appearance of bias were summarised as follows at paragraph 83: "(1) If a judge is shown to have been influenced by actual bias, his decision must be set aside. (2) Where actual bias has not been established the personal impartiality of the judge is to be presumed. (3) The court then has to decide whether, on an objective appraisal, the material facts give rise to a legitimate fear that the judge might not have been impartial. If they do the decision of the judge must be set aside. (4) The material facts are not limited to those which were apparent to the applicant. They are those which are ascertained upon investigation by the court. (5) An important consideration in making an objective appraisal of the facts is the desirability that the public should remain confident in the administration of justice".

### *Hanif and Khan v the United Kingdom* (2012) 55 E.H.R.R. 16; 20 December 2011

The European Court of Human Rights affirmed the need for all members of the jury to be impartial, and that the presence on the jury of a police officer with a similar service history to a witness could render a trial unfair. It held in relevant part as follows:

"148. The Court is of the view that, leaving aside the question whether the presence of a police officer on a juror [sic] could ever be compatible with Article 6, where there is an important conflict regarding police evidence in the case and a police officer who is personally acquainted with the police officer witness giving the relevant evidence is a member of the jury, jury directions and judicial warnings are insufficient to guard against the risk that the juror may, albeit subconsciously, favour the evidence of the police. In the present case, A.T. had known M.B. for ten years and although not from the same station, had on three occasions worked with him in the investigation of the same incident (see paragraph 12 above). Further, the other witnesses who supported M.B.'s account of events were also police officers (see paragraph 11 above). The Court recalls the conclusion of the Court of Appeal that the first applicant's defence witness was not a witness of good character and that his explanation for the records of the use of his mobile phone and the discovery of heroin in his car "bordered on the farcical" (see paragraph 25 above). However, it is not for this Court to make its own assessment of the evidence presented at trial and, in particular, of the first applicant's explanation for the evidence against him. Such assessment was for the members of the jury, who were required pursuant to Article 6 to be impartial.

149. The Court accordingly finds that there has been a violation of Article 6 § 1 of the Convention in respect of the first applicant as he was not tried by an impartial tribunal."

### R v Abdroikov and others [2007] UKHL 37; [2007] 1 WLR 2679; 17 October 2007

The House of Lords made two important points for the present case. Firstly, their Lordships made clear that the test in Article 6 is the same as the test at common law:

"There is, as Lord Steyn on behalf of the House ruled in Lawal v Northern Spirit Ltd [2003] ICR 856, para 14, now no difference between the common law test of bias and the requirement under article 6 of the European Convention of an independent and impartial tribunal. As Lord Hewart's aphorism recognises and later case law makes clear, justice is not done if the objective judgment of a judicial decision-maker (whether judge or juror) is shown to be vitiated by actual partiality or prejudice towards any of the parties. But actual bias, hard as it usually is to prove, is rarely alleged, and is not alleged in any of the cases before the House. Neither of the police officers, nor the Crown prosecutor, is alleged by the respective appellants to have leant in favour of the prosecution side for any improper reason. The appellants rely on the second part of Lord Hewart's aphorism: that justice should manifestly and undoubtedly be seen to be done. This condition, the appellants say, is not met where one of those charged to decide whether the appellant was guilty or not, is employed full-time by a body dedicated to promoting the success of one side in the adversarial trial process."

Their Lordships then went on to consider the situation of police officers and prosecutors who sat on juries. Convictions were quashed in two cases, one involving juror who was a solicitor employed by the CPS (which was the prosecuting authority), and one involving a juror who was a police officer who, although not known to the police officer on the jury, shared the same local service background with a police sergeant whose evidence was challenged. Their Lordships stated in particular as follows:

"27 In the case of the third appellant [Williamson], no possible criticism is to be made of Mr McKay-Smith, who acted in strict compliance with the guidance given to him and left the matter to the judge. But the judge gave no serious consideration to the objection of defence counsel, who himself had little opportunity to review the law on this subject. It must, perhaps, be doubted whether Auld LJ or Parliament contemplated that employed Crown prosecutors would sit as jurors in prosecutions brought by their own * authority. It is in my opinion clear that justice is not seen to

be done if one discharging the very important neutral role of juror is a full-time, salaried, long-serving employee of the prosecutor. This is a much stronger case than Pullar v United Kingdom 22 EHRR 391 : it is as if, on the facts of that case, F had been employed in the department of the procurator fiscal. Had that been so, one may be sure the court would have agreed with the commission. The third appellant was entitled to be tried by a tribunal that was and appeared to be impartial, and in my opinion he was not. The consequence is that his convictions must be quashed. This is a most unfortunate outcome, since the third appellant was accused of very grave crimes, of which he may have been guilty. But even a guilty defendant is entitled to be tried by an impartial tribunal and the consequence is inescapable. I would allow the appeal and remit the case to the Court of Appeal with an invitation to quash the convictions and rule on any application which may be made for a retrial. [...]

53 In the Green case [involving a police officer juror] there are two factors which make the connection between the police and prosecution too close for comfort. One is that the victim of the alleged crime was himself a police officer and the case depended to some extent on his evidence of how the defendant was searched and what was said at the time. The officers were serving in the same borough at the time of the trial although not in the same police station. Another is that the juror was posted to a police station which committed its cases to the Crown Court where the case was tried. Officers in his station will have had regular dealings with the CPS conducting prosecutions in the same court."

### R v Pintori [2007] EWCA Crim 1700; [2007] Crim LR 997; 13 July 2007

A member of civilian police staff sat on a jury. After the conclusion of the trial she remarked to a police colleague that in relation to 3 of the police witnesses "I knew them and because I am in this job, I just found him guilty." The 3 police witnesses had been in her previous team, albeit she claimed that she did not know them socially. She also stated that she met another police witness by chance in a takeaway. Their Lordships remarked at paragraph 21: "This was no mere casual acquaintanceship. The juror knew the officers in the case well and worked with them as a team. In our view, this knowledge alone would have led the fair-minded and informed observer to conclude that there was a real possibility of bias on her part." The conclusion of their Lordships was therefore as follows:

"22. Mr Charlton submits that there was no such possibility because there was no significant evidential issue as between the officers and the appellant. The case did not turn on whether the jury preferred the evidence of the police to that of the appellant. The real issue in the case was whether the appellant knew that the drugs were secreted in his drawers. We accept that this was the real issue in the case. But there was a subsidiary issue of fact relating to the circumstances of the police entry into the appellant's flat. If the jury preferred the evidence of the police officers on this issue, that might have influenced them in reaching a conclusion as to his credibility generally and therefore in deciding the central issue in the case.

23. But more fundamentally, the fair-minded observer would have concluded that there was a real possibility that the juror was disposed to find the appellant guilty simply because she knew the officers, had worked with them and therefore wished (consciously or subconsciously) to support them in this prosecution. In R v Abdroikov and others [2005] EWCA Crim 1986, this court rejected the suggestion that police officers should, because of their occupation, be automatically regarded as being disqualified from serving on a jury (para 25). This was because a fair-minded and informed observer would not conclude that there was a real possibility that a juror was biased merely because his occupation was one which meant that he was involved in some capacity or other in the administration of justice (para 30). At para 33, however, the court said: "The position is, however, different if the juror has a special knowledge either of individuals involved in the case or as to the facts of the case part from that provided by the evidence." We agree with this observation, which has particular application to the present case.

24. It seems to us that the fact that the juror knew the officers in the case reasonably well and had worked with them is enough to satisfy the bias test as regards the individual juror. There was a real possibility that she would be influenced by these factors in reaching her verdict". In the circumstances, the conviction was not safe.

### R v F [2009] EWCA Crim 805

A conviction for rape was rendered unsafe when there was a real risk that conversations between two jurors and a law student who had been observing the case had acted as an extraneous influence on the jurors.

### R v Edgar and others [2018] EWCA Crim 1857; 19 July 2018

The Court of Appeal overturned convictions for murder where one of the jurors was in a long-term relationship with the son of a police liaison officer who assisted the victim's family and attended court on at least one occasion, and where the juror also knew the sister of the victim through the juror's job as a teaching assistant at a school that the victim's sister's child attended. The juror and the police officer took steps to mislead the Court and investigators about their relationship. Treacy LJ held in particular as follows:

"2. In the circumstances of this case it is not necessary for us to set out the facts underlying the convictions in any great detail. If a defendant has not had the benefit of a fair trial to which he is entitled, then the strength of the case for the prosecution is irrelevant. If the trial has not been fair, then there has been no real trial at all and a conviction cannot be sustained by reference to the strength of a case against an accused.

[...]

9. The approach of this court to the question of bias is not controversial. Bias may be actual or subjective on the one hand; on the other hand, it may be apparent to a fair-minded observer, or objective. The question will be whether a fair-minded and informed observer would conclude that there was a real possibility or real danger that the juror was biased. We have considered In Re Medicaments and Related Classes of Goods (No 2) [2001] 1 WLR 700 and Porter v Magill v Weeks [2001] UKHL 67. It is agreed that if only one member of the jury panel was biased in the way described, that would be sufficient to taint the whole panel."

### Misdirection on Law

A misdirection that causes the conviction to be unsafe will be quashed

### R v Stoddart (1909) 2 Cr. App. R. 217; 21 May 1909

The Lord Chief Justice said the following in relation to how the Court of Criminal Appeal treated complaints as to misdirections in summing up:

"Probably no summing up, and certainly none that attempts to deal with the incidents as to which the evidence has extended over a period of twenty days, would fail to be open to some objection. [...] Every summing-up must be regarded in the light of the conduct of the trial and the questions which have been raised by the counsel for the prosecution and for the defence respectively. This Court does not sit to consider whether this or that phrase was the best that might have been chosen, or whether a direction which has been attacked might have been fuller or more conveniently expressed, or whether other topics which might have been dealt with on other occasions should be introduced. This Court sits here to administer justice and to deal with valid objections to matters which may have led to a miscarriage of justice" (at pp 245–246).

*R v Johnson and others* [2016] EWCA Crim 1613; [2017] 4 W.L.R. 104; 31 October 2016

The Court of Appeal confirmed that "it is not sufficient only for there to have been some misdirection or error in the conduct of the trial. What is critical is that the verdict is thereby rendered unsafe." The Court of Appeal therefore concluded that "a misdirection of law which was not, in reality, in relation to a true (or real) issue in the trial, does not thereby (and certainly not necessarily) render a conviction unsafe."

### Wrongful withdrawal of issues from the jury

If a trial judge fails to direct a jury as to an issue of fact going to an element of the offence, the conviction may be quashed if it is, as a result, unsafe. This is particularly the case if the judge wrongly actually withdraws an issue of fact from the jury, so preventing the jury from considering it. This can occur particularly where a judge wrongly withdraws a defence from the jury.

*Sheaf* (1927) 19 Cr App R 46, 2 November 1925

Avory J said "When we once arrive at the conclusion that a vital question of fact has not been left to the jury, the only ground on which we can affirm a conviction is that there has been no miscarriage of justice, on the ground that if the question had been left to the jury, they must necessarily have come to the conclusion that the appellant was guilty."

### Misdirection on Facts

A misstatement or omission of a fact in the course of the summing-up may lead to the quashing of a conviction if the fact was of such importance that, if it had been correctly stated, the jury may not have reached the same verdict.

### Appeals against sentence from the Crown Court to the Court of Appeal

### Procedure

Where a defendant is sentenced in the Crown Court (either following a guilty plea or verdict of guilty in the Crown Court, or following having been committed to the Crown Court by the magistrates' court for sentence), their route of appeal against sentence will be to the Court of Appeal (Criminal Division). In this regard, the Criminal Appeal Act 1968 ss 9 & 10 state insofar as is relevant as follows:

"9. Appeal against sentence following conviction on indictment.

(1) A person who has been convicted of an offence on indictment may appeal to the Court of Appeal against any sentence (not being a sentence fixed by law) passed on him for the offence, whether passed on his conviction or in subsequent proceedings.

(1A) In subsection (1) of this section, the reference to a sentence fixed by law does not include a reference to an order made under section 321 of the Sentencing Code in relation to a life sentence (as defined in section 324 of that Code) that is fixed by law.

(2) A person who on conviction on indictment has also been convicted of a summary offence under paragraph 6 of Schedule 3 to the Crime and Disorder Act 1998 (power of Crown Court to deal with summary offence where person sent for trial for indictable-only offence) may appeal to the Court of Appeal against any sentence passed on him for the summary offence (whether on his conviction or in subsequent proceedings) under subsection (7) of that section or sub-paragraph (4) of that paragraph.

10.— Appeal against sentence in other cases dealt with at assizes or quarter sessions.

(1) This section has effect for providing rights of appeal against sentence when a person is dealt with by the Crown Court (otherwise than on appeal from a magistrates' court) for an offence of which he was not convicted on indictment.

(2) The proceedings from which an appeal against sentence lies under this section are those where an offender convicted of an offence by a magistrates' court—

(a) is committed by the court to be dealt with for his offence before the Crown Court, or

(b) having been given a suspended sentence or made the subject of—

(i) an order for conditional discharge,

(ii) a youth rehabilitation order within the meaning given by section 173 of the Sentencing Code, or

(iii) a community order within the meaning given by section 200 of that Code, appears or is brought before the Crown Court to be further dealt with for the offence.

(3) An offender dealt with for an offence before the Crown Court in a proceeding to which subsection (2) of this section applies may appeal to the Court of Appeal against any sentence passed on him for the offence by the Crown Court."

In order to appeal against conviction, the defendant will normally have to apply to the Court of Appeal for permission to appeal (referred to as "leave to appeal"). The time limit to apply for permission to appeal is 28 days from conviction. The Criminal Appeal Act 1968 s 11 sets out the right to appeal as follows:

"11.— Supplementary provisions as to appeal against sentence.

(1) Subject to subsection (1A) below, an appeal against sentence, whether under section 9(1) or under section 10 of this Act, lies only with the leave of the Court of Appeal.

(1A) If, within 28 days from the date on which

the sentence was passed, the judge who passed it grants a certificate that the case is fit for appeal under section 9 or 10 of this Act, an appeal lies under this section without the leave of the Court of Appeal.

(2) Where the Crown Court, in dealing with an offender either on his conviction on indictment or in a proceeding to which section 10(2) of this Act applies, has passed on him two or more sentences in the same proceeding (which expression has the same meaning in this subsection as it has for the purposes of section 10), being sentences against which an appeal lies under section 9(1) or section 10, an appeal or application for leave to appeal against any one of those sentences shall be treated as an appeal or application in respect of both or all of them.

(2A) Where following conviction on indictment a person has been convicted under section 41 of the Criminal Justice Act 1988 of a summary offence an appeal or application for leave to appeal against any sentence for the offence triable either way shall be treated also as an appeal or application in respect of any sentence for the summary offence and an appeal or application for leave to appeal against any sentence for the summary offence shall be treated also as an appeal or application in respect of the offence triable either way."

There are three exceptions to the requirement to have permission to appeal.

Firstly, permission to appeal is not required if within 28 days of sentence the trial judge has certified that the case is fit for appeal.

Secondly, permission to appeal is not required if the Criminal Cases Review Commission has referred the case to the Court of Appeal.

Thirdly, permission to appeal is not required for appeals against sentence for contempt of court (s 18A Criminal Appeal Act 1968). However, all other rules about lodging an appeal with the Court of Appeal continue to apply for convictions for contempt of court – see below.

The application for leave to appeal is made on Form NG. There is a different Form NG for each of appeals against conviction, sentence, and confiscation. Form NG for appeals against sentence can be found at https://www.gov.uk/guidance/criminal-procedure-rules-forms

Form NG must be accompanied by Grounds of Appeal. The requirements as to the content of the Grounds of Appeal are set out in the section above on Appeals against conviction from the Crown Court to the Court of Appeal.

Form NG, along with the Grounds of Appeal, must be submitted to the Registrar of Criminal Appeals in the Court of Appeal (Criminal Division). The details of how to do this are set out in the section above on Appeals against

conviction from the Crown Court to the Court of Appeal.

The time limit to make an application for leave to appeal to the Court of Appeal against sentence in the Crown Court is 28 days from the date of sentence (Criminal Appeal Act 1968 s 18, and Criminal Procedure Rules rule 39.2, set out above). Any application for leave to appeal which is made after the 28 day time limit must be accompanied by an application for extension of time, as set out in the section above on Appeals against conviction from the Crown Court to the Court of Appeal.

The procedures in relation to the decisions on whether to grant leave to appeal and whether to extend time are also as set out in the section above on Appeals against conviction from the Crown Court to the Court of Appeal.

## Powers of the Court of Appeal on appeal against sentence

When an appeal against sentence is lodged, it is treated as an appeal against all linked sentences that are imposed on an appellant. In this regard the Criminal Appeal Act 1968 s 11 states:

"(2) Where the Crown Court, in dealing with an offender either on his conviction on indictment or in a proceeding to which section 10(2) of this Act applies, has passed on him two or more sentences in the same proceeding (which expression has the same meaning in this subsection as it has for the purposes of section 10), being sentences against which an appeal lies under section 9(1) or section 10, an appeal or application for leave to appeal against any one of those sentences shall be treated as an appeal or application in respect of both or all of them.

(2A) Where following conviction on indictment a person has been convicted under section 41 of the Criminal Justice Act 1988 of a summary offence an appeal or application for leave to appeal against any sentence for the offence triable either way shall be treated also as an appeal or application in respect of any sentence for the summary offence and an appeal or application for leave to appeal against any sentence for the summary offence shall be treated also as an appeal or application in respect of the offence triable either way.

(2B) If the appellant or applicant was convicted on indictment of two or more offences triable either way, the references to the offence triable either way in subsection (2A) above are to be construed, in relation to any summary offence of which he was convicted under section 41 of the Criminal Justice Act 1988 following the conviction on indictment, as references to the offence triable either way specified in the notice relating to that summary offence which was given under subsection (2) of that section."

The Court of Appeal may quash any sentence imposed on the appellant, and substitute any other sentence or order that it deems appropriate, provided that the substituted sentence could lawfully have been passed by the Crown Court and provided also that the appellant is not dealt with more severely when the case is viewed as a whole. The Court of Appeal may not impose a mandatory sentence which a Crown Court has failed to impose or if it would mean treating the appellant more severely. In this regard the Criminal Appeal Act 1968 s 11(3) states:

"(3) On an appeal against sentence the Court of Appeal, if they consider that the appellant should be sentenced differently for an offence for which he was dealt with by the court below may—

(a) quash any sentence or order which is the subject of the appeal; and

(b) in place of it pass such sentence or make such order as they think appropriate for the case and as the court below had power to pass or make when dealing with him for the offence;

but the Court shall so exercise their powers under this subsection that, taking the case as a whole, the appellant is not more severely dealt with on appeal than he was dealt with by the court below."

### Sentences that are manifestly excessive

Most appeals to the Court of Appeal relate to cases where a sentence is said to be manifestly excessive. The Court of Appeal is very reluctant to interfere with sentences just because they are severe. As such, harsh sentences given out by Crown Court judges may well not be overturned on appeal. However, sometimes the Court of Appeal recognises that sentencing judges do go too far or do make mistakes. In such cases, there is a right of appeal, which can result in a sentence being reduced.

### R v Nuttall (1909) 1 Cr App R 180; 16 Nov 1908

The Court of Appeal today continues to follow the comments of Mr Justice Channell who said:

*"This court will… be reluctant to interfere with sentences which do not seem to it to be wrong in principle, though they may appear heavy to individual judges."*

### Gumbs (1927) 19 Cr App R 74; 19 January 1926

Lord Hewart, the Lord Chief Justice, made the point even more clearly:

"…this court never interferes with the discretion of the court below merely on the ground that this court might have passed a somewhat different sentence; for this court to revise a sentence there must be some error in principle."

### Sentences that are wrong in law

Appeals to the Court of Appeal in cases where a sentence is said to be wrong in law are often quite clear cut: either the sentence is wrong in law or it is not. Examples may be where a judge has imposed a sentence which is higher than the statutory maximum; where a judge has imposed an extended determinate sentence despite the conditions not being met; or where a judge has imposed a sentence of imprisonment for public protection ("IPP") for an offence committed before IPPs were introduced. In these cases, the prosecution may even agree that the sentence was wrong in law and may support the appeal. The Court of Appeal will then look at how to restructure the sentence to make it right in law.

In other cases, there may be debate about whether a sentence was in fact wrong in law. For instance, the question of whether the criteria for the imposition of an IPP sentence were met may be open to debate (note that IPP sentences were abolished in 2012 although there are still prisoners serving IPP sentences that were imposed before then).

### Sentences that give rise to a sense of grievance

The Court of Appeal will intervene when the appellant has a justifiable sense of grievance at the sentence imposed upon him following events preceding sentence.

### Gillam (1980) 2 Cr App R (S) 267; 15 July 1980

When a judge intentionally postpones sentence so that an alternative to prison can be examined and that alternative is found to be a satisfactory one in all respects the court ought to adopt the alternative; a feeling of injustice is otherwise aroused.

### R v Page [2005] EWCA Crim 406

When the case was adjourned for reports, the judge indicated that a drug treatment and testing order (DTTO) would be likely if she was deemed to be suitable, and that if she received a custodial sentence, it would be no more than 12 months. She was sentenced to a total of two years' imprisonment. Following *Gillam*, the Court of Appeal indicated that if, when adjourning for reports, a judge indicated that a favourable report would lead to a DTTO and omitted to say that all sentencing options were open, there would be an expectation of a DTTO. However, in this case the appellant has already served more than a 12-month sentence so the Court of Appeal considered the second point and agreed that she had a legitimate expectation of a sentence of no more than 12 months. The two year sentence was quashed and a 12 month sentence was substituted.

### Appeals on the basis of disparity of sentence

There has been some inconsistency in the approach taken by the Court of Appeal to the question of the circumstances in which a difference in sentence between co-accused can form a ground of appeal against sentence. Sentences are rarely reduced on this basis.

### R v Stroud (1977) 65 Cr App R 150; 18 April 1977

The Court of Appeal pointed out that if there are sentences imposed which have glaring disparities, then if the more serious sentence is not manifestly excessive, to reduce that sentence would involve "the proposition where you have one wrong sentence and one right sentence, this Court should produce two wrong sentences."

### Fawcett (1983) 5 Cr App R (S) 158; 9 May 1983

The Court of Appeal held that where a defendant had received a lawful sentence but which was more severe than the sentence imposed on a co-defendant, the Court of Appeal would ask itself "whether right thinking members of the public, with full knowledge of all the relevant facts and circumstances, would consider that something had gone wrong with the administration of justice." In this case the Court of Appeal was of the opinion that the public would say that something had gone wrong, and as such the Court of Appeal reduced the sentences under appeal.

### R v Thomas [2020] EWCA Crim 822

The court reduced the length of a community order where the defendant was 17 years old at the time of the offence, but was 18 at the time of sentence. His co-defendants had received much more lenient sentences in the Youth Court despite one of them being only three months younger and pleading guilty to a far more serious offence. The Court of Appeal said that "the difference in age which led to his being sentenced as an adult was not so great as to justify the discrepancy".

### Failure to distinguish between offenders

The failure of the court of sentence to distinguish between offenders when one has powerful mitigation and the other does not can give rise to a successful ground of appeal against sentence.

### Risks of appealing to the Court of Appeal

Before filing an appeal against sentence, it is important to bear in mind that if the Court of Appeal considers that the appeal is plainly without merit, there are a number of sanctions available to it. In particular, the Court of Appeal can make a loss of time order or make an order that the applicant pays costs related to the appeal.

### Loss of time orders

Where the Single Judge refuses leave to appeal, they will indicate on Form SJ whether the case is without merit such that the Court of Appeal should consider using the power to make a loss of time order if the refused application is renewed to the Full Court. The reverse side of Form SJ is used by applicants to renew their applications for permission to appeal. Space is provided for the applicant to give reasons why a loss of time order should not be made, whether or not an indication has been given by a Single Judge. This should be completed in all cases, as loss of time orders can be made even where the Single Judge does not indicate that one should be considered.

A "loss of time" order is an order that some or all of the time spent in custody by an applicant will not count towards their sentence. The practical effect of this is to increase the length of the applicant's sentence. Although this power has rarely been used in practice, its use is becoming more common. Even if an applicant has been advised by their lawyers that they have grounds of appeal, the power can still be used. In this regard, the Criminal Appeal Act 1968 s 29(1) provides as follows:

"29.— Effect of appeal on sentence.

(1) The time during which an appellant is in custody pending the determination of his appeal shall, subject to any direction which the Court of Appeal may give to the contrary, be reckoned as part of the term of any sentence to which he is for the time being subject."

### R v Hart and others [2006] EWCA Crim 3239; [2007] 1 Cr. App. R. 31; 13 December 2006

The Court of Appeal decided that the power to make a loss of time direction would be exercised more frequently in the future than it had been in the past. The mere fact that counsel had advised that there were grounds of appeal would not always be a sufficient answer to the question of whether an application was without merit. In Hart, the power was exercised against two of the applicants in respect of whom the Single Judge had indicated clearly that there was no merit in the grounds of appeal, and to whom no support had been given by counsel to the effect that there were arguable grounds.

The Court of Appeal held in particular that they hoped applicants and counsel would "heed the fact that this court is prepared to exercise its power and will do so more frequently in the future than it has done so in the past."

### R v Brind and others [2008] EWCA Crim 934; 16 April 2008

The Court of Appeal listed 5 renewed applications for leave to appeal together in order to reiterate its powers to make loss of time orders. In giving the judgment of the court, the Vice-President Lord Justice Latham stated that, where the single judge had indicated on Form SJ that the application was without merit, "the would-be applicant must expect that this court will order that time served should not count."

### R v Gray and others [2014] EWCA Crim 2372; [2015] 1 Cr App Rep (S) 197; 7 October 2014

The court gave guidance as to the use of loss-of-time orders, stating that orders would be imposed whenever applications for leave to appeal were renewed against all warnings and the fact that an application had been renewed on the advice of counsel would not necessarily prevent an order being made. The Court of Appeal went on to make loss of time orders despite counsel having advised in favour of appeal. The Vice-President, Lady Justice Hallett, stated as follows:

"2. [...] Unmeritorious renewal applications take up a wholly disproportionate amount of staff and judicial resources in preparation and hearing time. They also waste significant sums of public money, for example in obtaining transcripts, especially in applications for leave to appeal against conviction. [...] The more time the Court of Appeal Office and the judges spend on unmeritorious cases, the longer the waiting times are likely to be.

3. The only means the court has of discouraging unmeritorious applications which waste precious time and resources is by using the powers given to us by Parliament in the Criminal Appeal Act 1968 and the Prosecution of Offences Act 1985."

### R v James and others [2018] EWCA Crim 285

Loss of time orders of 60 days were made where applications were deemed totally unmeritorious and 'fresh grounds' should not have been advanced. The Court of Appeal commented that "unmeritorious applications take up the precious time and resources of the staff and judges of the Court of Appeal Criminal Division".

### Costs orders

A costs order may be made by the Court of Appeal when the Court of Appeal dismisses an appeal or an application for permission to appeal. This may include any relevant costs of the case including the costs of obtaining transcripts of the trial. In this regard, the Prosecution of Offences Act 1985 s 18 provides as follows:

"(2) Where the Court of Appeal dismisses—
(a) an appeal or application for leave to appeal under Part I of the Criminal Appeal Act 1968;
[...]
it may make such order as to the costs to be paid by the accused, to such person as may be named in the order, as it considers just and reasonable.
[...]
(6) Costs ordered to be paid under subsection (2) [or (2A)] above may include the reasonable cost of any transcript of a record of proceedings made in accordance with rules of court made for the purposes of section 32 of the Act of 1968."

### R v Nolan [2017] EWCA Crim 2449; 30 November 2017

The Court of Appeal held that where the Single Judge has not indicated that the Full Court should consider making a loss of time order because the defendant has already been released, the Single Judge should consider what, if any, costs have been incurred by the Registrar and the Prosecution and should make directions accordingly. The applicant, who was in receipt of state benefits, was ordered to pay half his savings towards the cost of obtaining transcripts for hearings of unmeritorious renewed applications.

### Disposal of groundless appeal without argument

As an alternative or addition to exercising its powers to make a loss of time direction or direct an order for payment of costs, the Court of Appeal may summarily dismiss an appeal or application for leave to appeal. It may do this without either of the parties being called on to attend if the Court of Appeal considers the appeal to be frivolous or vexatious. In this regard the Criminal Appeal Act 1968 provides as follows:

"20. Disposal of groundless appeal or application for leave to appeal.

If it appears to the registrar that a notice of appeal or application for leave to appeal does not show any substantial ground of appeal, he may refer the appeal or application for leave to the Court for summary determination; and where the case is so referred the Court may, if they consider that the appeal or application for leave is frivolous or vexatious, and can be determined without adjourning it for a full hearing, dismiss the appeal or application for leave summarily, without calling on anyone to attend the hearing or to appear for the Crown thereon."

### R v Taylor [1979] Crim LR 649; 1 January 1979

A ground of appeal is "frivolous or vexatious" if it is so unmeritorious that there is no realistic prospect of it succeeding after full argument.

### Appeals against conviction and sentence from the magistrates' court

The right to a trial by a jury is considered a fundamental right in English law, and a protection for the individual against oppression by the state. Jurors bring the values of ordinary, reasonable people into the courtroom, meaning that defendants who have a jury trial are tried by their equals. Unfortunately, over 90% of criminal cases never reach a jury. Instead they are tried in the magistrates' court, by either three magistrates, or a single district judge. For a whole series of reasons, magistrates are considerably more likely to convict defendants than juries are. However, there are a greater number of routes of appeal against decisions by magistrates' courts than against decisions by the Crown Court.

## Appeal to the Crown Court

A defendant convicted after trial or sentenced in a magistrates' court has the right to appeal to the Crown Court against either their conviction and sentence, or their sentence alone. It is not possible to appeal to the Crown Court only against conviction.

The appeal must be filed within 21 days of sentence. If the appeal is filed late then an extension of time to appeal can be applied for, but this might not be granted by the court. In this regard the Magistrates' Court Act 1980 s 108 states:
"108.— Right of appeal to the Crown Court.
(1) A person convicted by a magistrates' court may appeal to the Crown Court—
(a) if he pleaded guilty, against his sentence;
(b) if he did not, against the conviction or sentence."
The appeal in the Crown Court is heard by a judge and two magistrates. Despite this being a Crown Court, there is no jury. If the appellant appealed against conviction and sentence, then the Crown Court holds a complete re-trial, just like the trial in the magistrates' court. At the end of the trial, the appellant can be found guilty or not guilty. If the appellant is found not guilty then the case comes to an end.

If the appellant is found guilty on an appeal against conviction and sentence, or if the appellant only appealed against sentence, then the Crown Court will re-sentence the appellant from scratch. That means that the appellant can be given a lower sentence, the same sentence, or even a higher sentence than that which they received in the magistrates' court.

The maximum sentence that can be imposed in the Crown Court on appeal is the same as the maximum sentence that could have been imposed in the magistrates' court. This means that appealing can sometimes be a big risk, if the appellant received a relatively lenient sentence in the magistrates' court.

## Appeal by way of case stated or appeal through judicial review

If the reason that the appellant wishes to appeal is because the magistrates' court made an error of law, or because the Crown Court on appeal made an error of law, then an appeal may be made by way of "case stated" to the High Court. This application has to be filed within 21 days of the decision appealed against.

If the court which convicted the appellant, or which refused the appellant's appeal, declines to state a case to the High Court, then the appellant can apply directly to the High Court for a judicial review of the refusal to state a case, and at the same time can pursue the arguments they would want to run in the appeal by way of case stated. If the application to state a case is filed late then if the application is to the Crown Court, the applicant can apply for an extension of time.

A case stated only looks at the law. If the appellant wishes to challenge any of the evidence, this can only be done by a re-hearing in the Crown Court.

It is important to be aware that if the magistrates' court makes an error of law, and the appellant then appeals to the Crown Court, the appellant cannot then make a further appeal by way of case stated against the decision of the magistrates' court. If the Crown Court did not make the same error of law, then the appellant would lose their right to appeal by way of case stated.

## Apply for bail pending appeal

People who have been sent to prison by the magistrates' court can apply for bail pending appeal (Magistrates' Court Act 1980 s 113(1)). This is rarely granted, but it is almost always worth asking for it. This is because it can take many weeks or months for an appeal to be heard. If an appellant does not ask for bail, then they can spend their whole sentence in prison waiting for an appeal.

## Appeals against sentence to the Crown Court

As set out above, under s 108(1)(b) Magistrates' Courts Act 1980 there is an automatic right of appeal against sentence from the magistrates' court to the Crown Court. This means that if a defendant is dissatisfied with their sentence they can try again in front of a Crown Court judge and two lay magistrates, in a complete re-hearing: they do not have to show that the sentence imposed by the magistrates' court was manifestly excessive or otherwise wrong in law. However, the Crown Court sentences from scratch. This means that on appeal from the magistrates' court to the Crown Court a sentence can be made more serious.

Despite this, there are limits to the sentence the Crown Court can impose. Firstly, unlike the Court of Appeal, the Crown Court cannot make a "loss of time" direction. Secondly, the Crown Court cannot pass a sentence which is higher than the statutory maximum sentence that the magistrates' court could have passed.

*R v Bullock* [1963] 3 All ER 506; [1964] 1 Q.B. 491; 30 July 1963

The High Court held that in "either-way" cases (cases that can be tried in the magistrates' court or the Crown Court) the Crown Court cannot commit a person to itself for sentence, in order to be able to use the higher powers of sentence that the Crown Court would have if the trial had taken place in the Crown Court.

### Costs consequences of appeals

An unsuccessful appellant can be made to pay the costs of the prosecution's response to the appeal. A successful appellant will often recover costs in respect of any private legal fees, and transport.

### Applications to the Criminal Cases Review Commission

The Criminal Cases Review Commission is the independent organisation set up to investigate suspected miscarriages of justice from magistrates' courts, the Crown Court in England, Wales, and Northern Ireland, and the Court Martial and Service Civilian Court. The CCRC was set up as an independent investigative body after a series of high-profile miscarriages of justice came to light in the 1980s and 1990s. There is a separate Scottish CCRC.

Any person who has been convicted of or pleaded guilty to an offence may apply to the CCRC for a review of their conviction or sentence. The CCRC may then refer their conviction or sentence back to either the Crown Court (for convictions in the magistrates' court) or the Court of Appeal (for convictions in the Crown Court).

### Process

Every year, hundreds of people make applications to have their convictions reviewed, but only a small proportion are referred to the Court of Appeal. Applicants do not require legal representation to have their cases considered by the CCRC. However, an application by a lawyer with a proper grasp of the relevant procedure is considerably more likely to allow the CCRC to fully understand every aspect of the submissions made.

Although there is no form which has to be used in order to apply to the CCRC, the CCRC has published a form which can be used to ensure that applicants provide all the necessary details of their case.

The CCRC will either gather the papers on the applicant's case and start the review or decide that the applicant's case cannot be reviewed. The CCRC may make such a decision not to review a case if they think that the application does not raise any significant new points that might allow them to send the case for an appeal. If they think this is the case with an application, they will write to the applicant to explain why. They will ask the applicant to tell the CCRC about anything which the applicant thinks might change the CCRC's minds. The CCRC will give at least 28 days for the applicant to reply and will not make a final decision in the applicant's case until they have considered the applicant's submissions.

If the CCRC does commence a review of a case, they may have questions about the application. Rather than rejecting the application immediately, they will either refer back to the applicant's representatives, or conduct their own investigations.

If the CCRC decides against making a referral of the case to the appeal court, they will usually give a Provisional Statement of Reasons. This sets out the reasons for their decision and allows the applicant to respond. However, in some cases where the CCRC's decision is not to refer, and where no purpose would be served by issuing a provisional decision to the applicant, the CCRC will immediately send the applicant a Final Statement of Reasons explaining why it has not been possible to refer their case to an appeal court. If the CCRC decides that there are grounds on which an applicant's case can be referred, a Final Statement of Reasons will be issued, explaining the reasons for this, and the case will be sent to the appeal court for a new appeal to be heard. In the appeal court it will proceed as if it was for all purposes a normal appeal against conviction or sentence. However, sentences cannot be increased by the Crown Court after a reference from the CCRC (Criminal Appeal Act 1995 s 11(6)).

### Investigative powers of the CCRC

The CCRC has the power to carry out investigations in order to determine whether to refer a case to an appeal court. Under the Criminal Appeal Act 1995 s 17, public bodies are required to provide to the CCRC such material as it requires them to provide to it. Further, under the Criminal Appeal Act 1995 s 18A, the CCRC can obtain an order from the Crown Court to gain from any person not serving in a public body access to any material it requires to perform its functions.

Where the CCRC has carried out investigations, it must consider whether it should then disclose the material that results from its investigations. Where the CCRC has under s 17 Criminal Appeal Act obtained material from a public body in the exercise of its functions, the Criminal Appeal Act s 25 provides for there to be an opportunity for the public body supplying the material to withhold consent for disclosure. However, whether or not the permission is withheld, the CCRC must provide such disclosure to an applicant as is necessary for the applicant to be able to properly present their case.

*R v Secretary of State for the Home Department ex parte Hickey and others (No. 2)* **[1995] 1 W.L.R. 734; 28 November 1994**

The Home Secretary used to exercise the functions now exercised by the CCRC. The disclosure obligations of the Home Secretary were considered by Simon Brown LJ who set down the guiding principle as follows:

"The guiding principle should always be that sufficient disclosure should be given to enable the petitioner properly to present his best case. That can only be done if he adequately appreciates the nature and extent of the evidence elicited by the Secretary of State's inquiries." (p 746E)

Simon Brown LJ went on to consider what would in fact require disclosure, by reference to the cases then before him. In regard to expert reports, he stated in particular as follows:

"I do not say that fairness will always and inevitably demand prior disclosure of full experts' reports. This is not an area where it is either possible or appropriate to lay down hard and fast rules. A less sweeping and absolute approach is called for than has been introduced into the Parole Board regime following *Reg. v. Parole Board, Ex parte Wilson* [1992] Q.B. 740. Almost without exception, however, I suggest that so far as experts are concerned this be done. Why not?" (p 749H)

"This sort of evidence, above all others, is surely most fairly (and indeed most conveniently) dealt with by way of verbatim disclosure. Questions of confidentiality or intimidation can hardly arise. And rather than risk the problems and delays of misunderstanding, it must surely be better to allow the petitioners' experts to see precisely what the Secretary of State's experts have said than to attempt instead a summary of their views. They, after all, will have had the benefit of the petitioners' experts' reports in full." (p 750A)

"I repeat, it is difficult to see why experts' reports should not routinely be disclosed." (p 750C)

Simon Brown LJ then took a more nuanced approach to other witnesses, stating that "As for police witnesses, prison officers and the like, there may again be compelling reasons for verbatim disclosure, but not necessarily so" (p 750D).

Simon Brown LJ further held that in the case under consideration where fresh evidence was obtained from the complainant it "cried out for verbatim disclosure" (p 757B).

The CCRC accepts the principles set out in Hickey as the basis of decision-making related to disclosure. It then notes a presumption in favour of disclosure at para. 6.3.1 as follows:

"As a general rule, all material which supports the decision for referral or non-referral together with any further information that may assist the applicant in making his best case will be disclosed."

The CCRC's Disclosure by the CCRC Casework Policy anticipates that some redaction or provision only of the "gist" of a document may take place, but provides limited guidance as to when this would happen. At para. 6.3.2 it states:

"Redaction, summarising or disclosure of the gist of a document may be undertaken for the practical purpose of simplifying the material to be disclosed. All key points will normally remain, and no information relevant to the applicant's case will be excluded. Such material may be appear in summary form within the Statement of Reasons, or in its amended form within a separate document, depending on which method will best assist full understanding of the reasons for the CCRC's decision and the material to be disclosed."

In relation to the provision of expert evidence, following Hickey it then provides a general rule in favour of disclosure, as follows at para. 6.7:

"Expert reports will generally be disclosed in full. It will be acceptable for the CCRC to disclose a summary or the gist of an expert's report if doing so satisfies the interests of fairness."

In relation to the withholding of consent it considers factors relevant to reasonableness as follows at para. 5.4:

"Factors relevant to reasonableness will include (and this is not an exhaustive list):

(i) The purpose for which the CCRC wishes to disclose the information. If it provides the main reason or a significant reason for referral or non-referral, that will generally raise a strong argument in favour of disclosure.

(ii) The reason why the public body wishes to prevent disclosure to another person or body. Examples might include sensitive, protected or personal information, or information provided in confidence. Each time such a reason is put forward to the CCRC by a public body, it will be considered on its own facts.

(iii) The extent to which withholding consent to disclosure would prevent the CCRC from complying with the requirements of the Criminal Appeal Act 1995 and/or the common law principle in Hickey.

(iv) Whether the information falls within a class of information traditionally recognised by the courts as subject to public interest immunity (for example, police reports, informant information and social services documents)."

It notes that the CCRC may withhold material which may benefit the applicant's case, but which should nevertheless not be disclosed on public interest immunity principles (para. 13).

At para. 12.1 it provides in relation to material which the CCRC in its opinion considers

irrelevant then the CCRC need not disclose it:
"If the information being considered for disclosure would not assist the applicant to make his best possible case, then there is no duty on the CCRC to disclose. This may apply, for example, to a line of enquiry which the CCRC decides to pursue on its own initiative, but which proves to be a "cold trail", or information which has no bearing whatsoever on the issues in the case or the decision made. Every such situation will be assessed on its own particular facts, but fairness to the applicant will be the general guiding principle."

### Conditions for making a reference to the Court of Appeal

The CCRC has the power to refer cases to the Court of Appeal on the ground that (i) there is new evidence or new argument not previously raised in the proceedings or any appeal or application for leave to appeal; or (ii) even if evidence or argument has been raised before, there are exceptional circumstances which justify making the reference anyway. Further, the CCRC will only make a reference to the Court of Appeal if there is a real possibility the conviction would not be upheld. In this regard the Criminal Appeal Act 1995 s 13 sets out the test as follows:

"13. Conditions for making of references.

(1) A reference of a conviction, verdict, finding or sentence shall not be made under any of section 9 to 12B unless—

(a) the Commission consider that there is a real possibility that the conviction, verdict, finding or sentence would not be upheld were the reference to be made,

(b) the Commission so consider—

(i) in the case of a conviction, verdict or finding, because of an argument, or evidence, not raised in the proceedings which led to it or on any appeal or application for leave to appeal against it, or

(ii) in the case of a sentence, because of an argument on a point of law, or information, not so raised, and

(c) an appeal against the conviction, verdict, finding or sentence has been determined or leave to appeal against it has been refused.

(2) Nothing in subsection (1)(b)(i) or (c) shall prevent the making of a reference if it appears to the Commission that there are exceptional circumstances which justify making it."

The CCRC has provided guidance on how it applies the exceptional circumstances test in its Exceptional Circumstances in "No Appeal" cases Casework Policy.

At para. 1.2, the Exceptional Circumstances in "No Appeal" cases Casework Policy states that "exceptional circumstances (ECs) can by-pass the need for a previous appeal in relation to a conviction, verdict, finding and sentence."

Although the CCRC used to provide a list of exceptional circumstances which it accepts, these have now been replaced by a case-by-case consideration of the circumstances.

### Judicial review of the Criminal Cases Review Commission

The government has cut the funding for the CCRC to very low levels. This means there are large pressures on its time and resources. Its case workers and commissioners try their hardest, but sometimes make mistakes, in particular making decisions without proper consideration of the applications made to them. Unfortunately, far too often this leads to the CCRC making "irrational" or "Wednesbury unreasonable" decisions, or decisions which fail to consider all elements of the application or consider irrelevant material.

Such decisions of the CCRC are open to challenge in the High Court by way of judicial review. Judicial review proceedings are claims in the civil courts. In a judicial review, the Queen on behalf of the applicant to the CCRC becomes the claimant, and the CCRC becomes the defendant.

### Resources

This section is only able to give a very brief overview of the process of judicial review. However, the following materials may provide some assistance.

The "Administrative Court Judicial Review Guide 2021" is essential guidance to be read by anyone preparing an application for judicial review. It is available at tinyurl.com/y8tk6rob.

The rules for a judicial review are contained in the Civil Procedure Rules. The relevant rules, Part 54, are available at tinyurl.com/y395osok

The relevant practice direction, PD 54A, is available at tinyurl.com/y4o7hugf.

The Judicial Review Handbook by Michael Fordham QC remains the most comprehensive practitioner text on the subject of judicial review. The text is currently in its seventh edition (published December 2020).

### Pre-Action

The process for judicial review is commenced by the claimant sending to the CCRC a pre-action protocol letter (a "PAP letter", also called a "letter before claim"). The PAP letter must set out the reason that the claimant asserts that the CCRC's decision is wrong in law. The CCRC will then respond to the PAP letter explaining whether they accept that they are wrong, or whether they will oppose a judicial review claim.

If the CCRC accept that they are wrong, then they will make a fresh decision. In settling any claim with the CCRC, it is advisable to include a time limit by which the CCRC will agree to make a fresh decision.

## Commencing proceedings

If the CCRC deny they are wrong then the claim will need to be filed with the Administrative Court, which is a part of the Queen's Bench Division of the High Court.

The court proceedings themselves commence when a claim form is served at the Administrative Court Office. There is a strict time limit of 3 months from the date of the CCRC's decision for the claimant to serve a claim form, although applications must also be made "promptly".

The claimant must file at the Administrative Court the claim form (Form N461) along with a Statement of Facts and Grounds of Judicial Review, and any supporting documents, which must include the decision which is the subject of the application for judicial review. A fee must be paid by a claimant in order to file the application. The claimant will need to ensure that the application and all supporting documents are served on the CCRC. The form is available at: https://www.gov.uk/government/publications/form-n461-judicial-review-claim-form-administrative-court

The CCRC will then serve an Acknowledgment of Service and Summary Grounds of Defence which set out the reason why they are opposing the claim. The CCRC will also set out the costs that they will apply for if permission to apply for judicial review is refused.

## Decisions on permission to apply for judicial review

A single High Court judge considers whether to grant permission to apply for judicial review.

If permission is not granted the claimant will normally be able to renew the application for permission in an oral hearing at the High Court. At this hearing the claimant and the CCRC will be represented.

In certain cases where the application for permission to apply for judicial review is refused, the application will also be certified by the single High Court judge as "totally without merit". In such cases, the only way to continue the claim is to appeal the certification and refusal of permission to the Court of Appeal.

## Final hearing and remedies

If permission to apply for judicial review is granted, either on the papers or at an oral hearing, the claim will continue to a full hearing, in front of the High Court.

If the High Court grants the application for judicial review, the CCRC will have to re-make their decision. If the High Court refuses the application for judicial review, this means that the CCRC's decision will remain in force.

More resources and organisations that exist to help prisoners and their families are listed in Section 3: The Directory.

### The Prison Oracle

*The definitivie website for UK Prisons.*

https://prisonoracle.com

A subscription site where everything is in one place, where the site contains over 44,000 pages (2022) of constantly updated information, and full site-wide, cancel-anytime access is less than £2.50 a week.

The Prison Oracle also hosts The Institute of Prison Law whose separate web site is at https://prisonlaw.org.uk

### HM Prison & Probation Service

HMPPS carries out sentences given by the courts, in custody and the community, and rehabilitates people in their care through education and employment.

You can visit the website at:

https://www.gov.uk/government/organisations/her-majestys-prison-and-probation-service

Prisons and Probation Ombudsman

The Prisons and Probation Ombudsman (PPO) carries out independent investigations into deaths and complaints in custody. You can visit the website at:

www.ppo.gov.uk

### Howard League for Penal Reform

The Howard League for Penal Reform is the oldest penal reform charity in the UK.

You can visit the website at:

www.howardleague.org

### Prison Advice & Care Trust

The Prison Advice & Care Trust (pact) is an independent charity which supports people affected by imprisonment. PACT work with children and families of prisoners, and with prisoners inside and on release.

You can visit the website at:

www.prisonadvice.org.uk

### Prisoners Advice Service

The Prisoners' Advice Service is an independent registered charity. PAS provides legal advice and information to prisoners in England and Wales regarding their rights, particularly the application of the Prison Rules and conditions of imprisonment.

You can visit the website at:

www.prisonersadvice.org.uk

### NACRO

The National Association for the Care and Resettlement of Offenders (NACRO). NACRO is an independent voluntary organisation working to prevent crime.
You can visit the website at:
www.nacro.org.uk

### Prison Reform Trust

The state of our prisons is a fair measure of our society. The Prison Reform Trust works to ensure they are just, humane and effective.
You can visit the website at:
www.prisonreformtrust.org.uk

### Joint Enterprise Not Guilty by Association ("JENGbA")

JENGbA are a grassroots campaign, run by volunteers. As with all grassroots campaigns the work behind opposing the might of the legal establishment has been an uphill battle. It was a role taken on mainly by women (mothers, sisters, aunties and cousins but also heartbroken dads and uncles) who will not rest while their loved ones are serving mandatory life sentences for crimes committed by others.
You can visit the website at:
http://jointenterprise.co/

### ConVerse

The national monthly newspaper for prisoners.
You can visit the website at:
https://prisons.org.uk/
The independent website dedicated to informed coverage of the penal system of England and Wales, they publish the main prison publications for England and Wales - including the largest circulation national monthly prisons newspaper; Converse.
You can visit the website at:
www.prisons.org.uk/publications/

# Section 5

## Something to say?

### 5.1 FORWARD THINKING
*Gordon Brockington, Managing Director*
*G4S Care & Rehabilitation Services*

The British penal system has come a long way since the birth of the first national state prison in 1816 and G4S is proud to be involved in managing prisons in England and Wales. For 30 years we have been at the forefront of developing pathways that provide an alternative to reoffending and the opportunity for prisoners to break this often pernicious cycle.

Today G4S-managed prisons in England and Wales offer meaningful opportunities for rehabilitation, so that prisoners can learn and develop new skills to give them the confidence they need to turn away from crime and seek stable employment when they eventually leave custody. Building on our 30 years of expertise, G4S will continue to work with the Ministry of Justice and Her Majesty's Prison and Probation Service to provide top-tier facilities and expand on our knowledge in this sector, which you can read about in this, The Prisons Handbook 2023.

G4S manages five prisons in England and Wales on behalf of the Ministry of Justice (MoJ): HMPs Altcourse in Liverpool, Five Wells in Northamptonshire, Oakwood near Wolverhampton, Parc in Bridgend, South Wales and Rye Hill, near Rugby.

It's humbling to see the dedication of my team of more than 2,600 people every day. All of the work they do is fundamentally about helping the prisoners at our establishments turn away from crime when they leave prison. We take them through the journey of settlement - into prison life and routine - rehabilitation and then working towards what they need to successfully resettle into society when they leave.

I've been the Managing Director of G4S Care & Rehabilitation Services since November 2020, and I have seen the prisons from different angles in the senior roles I have held within the Care & Justice business unit since I joined in March 2015.

G4S has managed prisons in the UK now for 30 years, with the opening of The Wolds in 1992, which was originally managed by Group 4 and then GSL, a company acquired by G4S.

Amongst my colleagues across our prisons, there is an enormous wealth of experience in managing really good establishments and working hard to continuously improve them:

these are people who have worked in both the public and private sector.

What we believe collectively, more strongly than ever, is that the private sector has brought significant change, competition, bold and often ground-breaking innovation to the Prison Service. We see ourselves as public servants employed by a private company, no different from our colleagues in publicly-run prisons up and down the country.

Some people hold ideological opposition to the existence of the private sector in the prison estate, where an incredibly sensitive public service is offered to protect society at large. To those people I would say, come and spend a day in one of our prisons and see what we do. You will see the dedication, the empathy and the high standards we aspire to always achieve. And you will also see our people making a difference.

It's fair to say that no prison exists as an island, when there are problems with drugs, violence, self-harm and mental health issues, not a single prison can eradicate those challenges completely. And issues that exist in society are always reflected in the population of prisoners that are held by the Prison Service. But there is plenty that we can do to understand these issues and find new and better ways to address them.

We've had challenges along the way and learnt lessons from them, to become a better provider. And we've also introduced, built and expanded some initiatives that have changed the lives - not only of some of the prisoners - but also their families, which in turn has the collective power to positively impact whole communities.

The name of the business I manage was changed in 2020, from Custodial & Detention to Care & Rehabilitation Services, somewhat belatedly, to try to describe and reflect what my teams up and down the country actually do.

Unlocking and locking up people in our care every day and running a respectful and purposeful establishment is not easy. For me, the magical ingredient that no prison can operate properly without is relationships.

Interactions, however small between our officers and the people in our care, happen minute after minute and hour after hour. A prison officer learns about the prisoner he sees every day. His likes, dislikes, his hopes, fears, when his daughter is sitting her GCSEs, what he wants to do when he gets out, what his pet dog at home is called and how much he misses him.  And

1167

perhaps, what he'd like to spend his money on in the prison shop after a long week of work in the prison garden or kitchen.

And as that relationship deepens, even why he did what he did, how he feels about the damage he has done, the impact that's had on his victim and his own family.

These interactions are all about our humanity and they are so critical. Going to prison is their punishment for what they have done but once they are there it is getting them ready to re-enter society ready to contribute - which is why settlement, rehabilitation and resettlement must be our focus.

Our initiatives in prison start with the solid foundation of those relationships and then go well beyond them - take for example our Peer-led initiatives (PLIs) which started at HMP Oakwood and have now been replicated across a number of our prisons, with great success.

The senior leadership team at Oakwood, some years ago, took the courageous step of listening to prisoners and their ideas about how they could help other prisoners, based on their often many years of experience as a prisoner.

Led by the then Director (our equivalent of a Governor) John McLaughlin OBE, who is now Director of HMP Five Wells, his inspirational leadership exemplified the idea that when given space to innovate and take chances, to test and learn from our action, we can come up with initiatives that truly change lives for the better. John was recognised for his visionary work at Oakwood in the Queen's Birthday Honours in 2022.

John would say the success is all down to the prisoners and their motivation, but it was his belief in them and that of Sean Oliver, previously his Deputy Director and now the current Director at Oakwood, as well as their bravery in the power of respect and trust, that made all the difference.

Those relationships drove each prisoner forward, building their self-esteem. PLIs have delivered some amazing results for all involved.

Prisoners were given the confidence to speak up and come to the senior team at Oakwood with ideas that would help other prisoners to turn away from crime, get support, improve themselves and build relationships with other prisoners.

In a report by Her Majesty's Inspectorate of Prisons (HMIP) published in September 2021, the Chief Inspector of Prisons Charlie Taylor commented that he was impressed by the extensive network of PLIs.

He said: "Without direct staff supervision, prisoners ran and organised a workshop that built tables, benches, bird boxes and hanging baskets that were sold to the local community. PLIs were also responsible for the maintenance of the grounds and a market garden that grew food for the prison and sold plants and vegetables."

"I was consistently struck by the positive way that prisoners talked about the prison, welcoming the levels of trust that they were given and describing, with very few exceptions, a professional and supportive staff team."

Nobody knows better what it's like to be a prisoner than another prisoner. That support has provided so many people in our care with someone to talk to and someone to help them believe it is possible to break whatever destructive cycle they are in.

But it works both ways, the prisoner who wanted to lead an initiative, which then becomes a success, feels a real sense of achievement, his confidence improves and he is even more motivated to help others.

PLIs have been introduced and embraced by Altcourse, in Liverpool, a category B, 1164-place, local prison with mentoring programmes and prisoner consultation on decisions made about the prison.

Something that the prisoners there really appreciate and enjoy is the prison radio station, run by prisoners for prisoners, which keeps the population both entertained and informed. Under the pioneering leadership of Director Steve Williams, this prison, with its multitude of programmes and interventions for a range of prisoners facing different challenges, including those with drug problems, has been praised by HMIP inspectors for bucking the trend of rising violence and anti-social behaviour seen in other local prisons, with a high turnover of men on remand.

Rye Hill, a 600-place category B men's prison for sex offenders led by Director Peter Small, was praised for the constructive and supportive relationships between staff and prisoners in the latest HMIP from February 2020. Inspectors noted they were encouraged further by well managed key worker and very useful peer worker schemes.

The chief inspector said: "At Rye Hill we found a well-led establishment working hard to promote the well-being of its prisoners, to sustain a credible community ethos and to create a meaningful rehabilitative culture."

The leadership at Rye Hill has sought innovative ways of trying to reach prisoners. A few years ago they forged a partnership with the organisation Pets as Therapy (Pat) to allow prison officers to bring their Pat-assessed pets into the establishment. Dozens of dogs now routinely accompany their owners to work at the prison and at HMP Altcourse too. The impact on prisoners has been profound and far reaching in a number of respects. It's been such a success that we have extended this across most of our prisons. There are a number of ways in which it has had a really important impact. Firstly, it has further improved relationships between prisoners and staff. The interaction that happens between a person stroking a dog and a dog owner is focused on the dog. They have something in common to talk about and bring them together. This builds a mutual bond. This in turn has reduced stress levels in both prisoners and officers, it's been a calming influence for everyone.

Secondly, 'normalisation' - which is a fundamental cornerstone of my vision of our rehabilitation work. What I mean by this is that prison is a constructed and largely artificial society and can be unfamiliar to those new to it but also it's not a realistic reflection of society for those who have been incarcerated for many years. The more that we can try and recreate certain elements of real society in prisons, the less of a shock it will be when they eventually leave - and most of them will. This 'normalisation' helps our work with prisoners coming towards the end of their sentence, where our ultimate goal is their resettlement back into society.

Another inspiring programme has been the bird of prey care initiative at Altcourse. This has given those prisoners involved the opportunity to focus on looking after another living being and to take responsibility for their welfare. The reported impact on improved mental health amongst those struggling is really encouraging.

For human beings any period of transition - moving house, moving school, moving job - is unsettling and can be stressful: It's a time of change and adjustment and comes with its ups and downs.

Leaving prison is essentially an enormous transition for a man who has been inside for a long time and if everything is alien - the existence of pets, modern technology such as smartphones, tablet computers, new ways of paying for goods to name just a few - it would be understandably overwhelming. The better we can prepare prisoners to cope with a modern society outside, the more likely they are to cope and choose a life without crime.

However difficult or complex the challenges are that we face, we will never stop trying to innovate and improve lives. HMP Parc has, on multiple levels, embodied this aspiration and its achievements are outstanding, even more so given its size and complexity.

In March 2020 the Chief Inspector of Prisons praised Parc for its achievements against the healthy prison tests. It improved its grading on Safety to 'Reasonably Good' since the previous inspection, 'Reasonably Good' on Respect and the highest rating of 'Good' was maintained for purposeful Activity and Rehabilitation and Release planning.

He commented: "These are impressive findings for this kind of prison, particularly given the challenging environment in which so many prisons have been operating over the past few years. The improved grade in safety was a significant achievement in the current context across the custodial estate. Parc had managed to buck the trend in terms of the overall and very large increases in violence that have been recorded."

More than 10 years ago at Parc the concept of the family intervention model was developed, based on the principle that the family should be at the heart of prisoner reform.

By connecting prisoners with their families and encouraging family ties, we seek to break the vicious cycle of reoffending, as well as intergenerational offending.

Invisible Walls Wales (IWW) has been an exceptionally successful project, which has had a hugely positive impact on the lives of the prisoners and families who participate. It has grown and grown and has been replicated in other countries and received international acclaim.

It's our belief that this approach has the potential to have a nationally and internationally significant impact. IWW was described as "cutting-edge" by Lord Farmer in his report on the importance of strengthening family ties for rehabilitation. Again, the success of this programme as with all our initiatives, has relationships at its heart.

Each G4S prison now has a Family Interventions Team, who provide prison visits and ensure the visiting facilities are family focused and friendly. The impact on children, connecting with their parent in prison and removing some of the stigma associated with that, has seen measurable improvement in the performance and achievement of the children involved at school. It's a sad fact that when a parent goes to prison the negative impact on a child and their schoolwork can be profound. The team at Parc, led by Corin Morgan-Armstrong, has worked tirelessly with more than 50 local schools in the Bridgend area to bring parents evenings to fathers at Parc.

In January this year, Parc was the first prison to be awarded Advanced Autism Accreditation by the National Autistic Society. Since Parc first opened its doors to the Cynnwys unit - meaning Inclusion in Welsh - the UK's first dedicated wing for offenders with Learning Difficulties (LD), Autism Spectrum Conditions (ASC) and significant brain injuries, the multidisciplinary team has worked hard to transform the lives of the prisoners affected by these conditions.

The results are impressive. There has been a significant reduction in reportable and violent incidents, self-harm (by 75%), adjudications and substance misuse. This is largely down to the support and interventions of the team. These findings have helped set out the pathway for LD and ASC services in custody and to support HMIP and MoJ in the development of research and policies for best practice for the support and management of offenders with neurodiverse conditions.

Director of HMP & YOI Parc Janet Wallsgrove was awarded an OBE in the Queen's New Year's Honours List 2022 for her contribution to the Prison Service, a recognition she thoroughly deserves for her committed leadership and many years of public service.

In early 2022, we opened HMP Five Wells, a new build prison and a model of the change in design and tone the whole estate will be following in years to come.

With a capacity of 1,680 spaces when it is full, which it is expected to reach towards the end of 2022, Five Wells is a world away from Victorian prisons.

HMP Five Wells is investing in the Wellingborough area, working closely with surrounding businesses, suppliers and community groups, and by the end of 2022 will have created 700 new jobs for local people.

It is the UK's first purpose-built resettlement prison, preparing prisoners for their transition back into society, providing them with skills and qualifications. The prison benefits from the latest design and technology to enhance security and rehabilitation, and fosters a purposeful environment that reflects life in the wider community.

With barless windows in cells and large hallways, a real emphasis is placed on bringing the community into the prison. We intend to achieve this through a greater focus on release on temporary license and partnerships for work with local businesses within the prison. This means that on release, men have a real stake in the local community. This is the rehabilitation theory that we hope will drive reoffending rates down.

### CONCLUSION:

The hard work and progress that G4S colleagues and prison staff have made over the past three decades is, in my opinion, outstanding and at the forefront of how to run a modern prison. However, we know that we cannot rest on our laurels and must continue to use the latest technology and expertise to continue to drive down reoffending when prisoners leave one of our five prisons.

The fact that many members of our team have been praised and have received honours for their hard work is testament to the public service they undertake. Running a prison is not possible without the officers, catering staff and other key workers. To all of them I am incredibly grateful. Finally, I am confident that our efforts will leave a lasting legacy on the people who leave our prisons.

*Gordon Brockington*
*Managing Director*
*G4S Care & Rehabilitation Services.*

## 5.2 THE MUSINGS OF A CHIEF INSPECTOR
*Charlie Taylor, HM Chief Inspector of Prisons*

**How good leadership can transform prisons**

It is almost three years since my predecessor Peter Clarke announced an Urgent Notification for HMYOI Feltham A following an unannounced inspection. He pointed to a "dramatic decline" in performance at the YOI and "numerous significant concerns about the treatment and conditions of children" held there. I remember it well because, as it happened, I was having coffee that day with another former Chief Inspector of Prisons, Lord Ramsbotham, who told me to read his report on Feltham from 1998. Doing so was a depressing experience. Huge chunks could have been cut and pasted between the two reports and no one would have noticed. The same issues – violence, demotivated, disengaged staff, lack of purposeful activity and unsanitary conditions – stood out in both, with few meaningful improvements in the intervening two decades.

One might be forgiven for believing that this suggests delivering improvement is impossible, particularly in institutions with a long history of problems. But I am pleased to say that our recent experience at Feltham and two other prisons we have inspected shows that positive change is possible – and, for me, the key ingredient is effective leadership.

During the pandemic, we conducted a scrutiny visit of the jail so we knew things were getting better, but we were still unprepared for just how much progress Feltham had made under the excellent leadership of the governor. There were genuine and immediate incentives for boys to improve their behaviour, such as more time unlocked, access to additional spending money and the chance to get involved in popular vocational activities. The Alpine unit was an impressive place where a well-trained and united staff team had created a therapeutic unit to support some of the most troubled children, who would in the past have spent time in and out of the segregation unit.

We also saw reductions in levels of violence, improved relationships between children and officers, and a leadership team focused on providing a more open and progressive regime. Our healthy prison test scores gave an unprecedented six-point rise across the board.

The week before the Feltham visit, I joined our inspection at HMP Bedford where in 2018, our report described it as a prison that was "fundamentally unsafe", with an alarming rise in drug-related violence. This time we found some big improvements: the prison was safer, better organised and had a much healthier staff culture. Staff were working well with local police to reduce the supply of drugs.

There were also encouraging initiatives to improve the experiences of black and minority ethnic prisoners and to create a new unit to support younger prisoners, who were often disproportionately involved in violence.

Although there is a long way to go in both prisons – which are fragile places at the best of times – the work and commitment it has taken to make these improvements was impressive.

While HMP Doncaster had never hit the lows of Feltham and Bedford, our 2016 inspection report still described it as "very poor." This month's report reveals a much-improved prison with "a general sense of order and calm".

Excellent leadership is the common factor that underpins these more positive inspections. In each, leaders knew and understood their prison through good use of data and by spending time on the wing and talking to prisoners and staff. They all had a clear idea of what needed to improve and were able to articulate their vision and priorities to their staff.

Leaders had used lockdowns from some serious COVID-19 outbreaks to resettle their prisons, using the time to focus on staff training. The prisons had all employed new, enthusiastic but inexperienced officers who needed clear direction and support to do their difficult and complex job with confidence. The director at Doncaster, in particular, had harnessed the potential of his young staff to become an enthusiastic and motivated team.

All of the three jails had focused on getting the basics right such as ensuring prisoners had toiletries, bedding and clean clothes. Leaders had also sought to improve the culture by making sure that officers were polite and respectful and there were high expectations of prisoner behaviour.

A year on from our first inspections of leadership, here is my list of what I think are the habits of the best prison leaders. It is, of course, by no means exhaustive, but I hope it sets out some of the most important qualities – all of which were reflected in these three, positive reports.

The best leaders understand their prison – by using data and by listening to prisoners and staff. They prioritise by identifying those things in the prison that need to improve in the short and long term.

They have clear expectation of their staff and prisoners and create plans for improvement.

They monitor that progress is being made against their priorities.

They communicate with their teams and with prisoners to make sure that everyone in the prison understands their vision and the part they must play in achieving it.

They improve their team by supporting and training staff and identifying and promoting those with potential. They make their staff accountable for their area of responsibility.

They are a visible presence around the jail, knowing who people are and what they do.

They set an example to staff, modelling the behaviour they want to see, praising good performance and refusing to tolerate any fall in standards.

### Why don't prisoners learn to read?

As a former teacher, I often ask prisoners how they got on in school; the answer, perhaps unsurprisingly, is often 'not well'. Many describe having struggled through but survived primary school, only to be expelled in their first two or three years of secondary school. Others never spent much time in education at all, having somehow through slipped through the net, often because of frequent changes of address or time spent overseas. A large proportion of prisoners also have a learning difficulty that added to their problems at school.

One prisoner I met in his mid-50s cried as he told me he had been in and out of prison all his life, spending more than 20 years behind bars and yet, to his shame, never having learned to read.

It is clear that a large proportion of those in prison struggle with reading – an assessment in August 2021 by HMPPS put the number of adult prisoners with a reading age below that expected of an 11-year-old at around 57%. This hampers the progress they can make while they are serving their sentences and hugely restricts their opportunities on release.

Many non-readers in prison have learned to mask their difficulties due to the stigma surrounding illiteracy, but their experience is diminished as a result. They have to find alternative ways to complete basic prison tasks, such as getting their cellmates to fill out their menus or officers to help them with legal letters. The stigma of being unable to read means that prisoners can be reluctant to seek the help that they require.

At the end of last year, HMI Prisons and Ofsted began a joint thematic inspection into the way that reading was taught in prisons. We visited six jails of different categories, including male and female, as well as both public and private sector establishments. The findings were far worse than I had expected–with those prisoners with the most need receiving the least support.

The problem began with the initial assessments; during COVID-19 restrictions these were long, photocopied questionnaires that were put under cell doors. The third question to one I saw was, 'do you find it hard to fill out forms?' In the pile I looked through around a third had ticked this box, before they had to wade through pages of further questions.

Prisoners told us they were fed up with doing the same assessment whenever they moved prison, often because the prison they were coming from had lost or failed to send on the result. The accuracy of assessments was also questionable because to qualify for many prison jobs, prisoners needed to demonstrate the reading skills of a Level 1 qualification. Non or poor readers therefore frequently got their cell mates to fill out the form for them so they could get work. The pay rates in prison constituted a further disincentive, given that prisoners were paid more for work than for education. Governors have the ability to increase pay for those in education to parity with those in work, but few appear to use it, meaning prisoners are better off walking round the wing wiping cells doors with a damp cloth than acquiring the skills they need to succeed on release.

The incentives to the education contractors in prison seem to be uniquely focused on prisoners gaining as many qualifications as possible. Prisoners who could not read were unlikely to acquire a qualification and consequently given no help at all – instead they were referred to a third sector organisation such as the Shannon Trust, which runs reading mentoring schemes in prison.

There is no formal relationship between the Shannon Trust and prisoner education providers, and progress that prisoners make with their mentors is not shared, monitored, or recorded by the education department. The reality, especially during lockdowns, has been that many reading mentors have been stuck in their cells for up to 23 hours a day. While prison workers are prioritised and unlocked to do their jobs, Shannon Trust mentors are not. This means they are only able to work with their mentees during the short daily association time when most prisoners will want to shower, telephone family or get some fresh air. Unsurprisingly, then, few reading sessions actually take place.

Most shocking was that almost none of the teachers we spoke to had any idea how to teach

reading. They had not been trained in the use of phonics – the established and well-researched method for teaching reading in English schools, involving sounding out letters or combinations of letters and building these into words. Most reading we saw being done in class was from photocopied sheets rather than actual books. Once again, the goal was to do just enough to gain the qualification, rather than to learn and take pleasure from reading.

Most prison libraries had some books for lower-level readers, but these were limited in number and subject content, the latter of which was unlikely to be of interest to most prisoners. During the pandemic most libraries were closed, and some are still only providing a trolley service to the wings, further limiting the range on offer for the weaker readers.

The fact that so many prisoners start and finish their sentences unable to read is a terrible indictment of the prison service and of education providers. It is crucial that these services come together to make sure that not only are non-readers taught to read, but that all prisoners have the opportunity to improve their literacy skills while in custody. There are far too many prisoners stuck in their cells whiling away their time sleeping or watching daytime television. If prisons took reading seriously, prisoners would spend their sentences productively, gaining the skills to find work when they are released and the chance to lead productive, crime-free lives.

**Why the Prisons Inspectorate is proposing to stop making recommendations**

When I first became a head teacher, my school was in a troubled state. Some established staff members had just left, the children were anxious and physical restraint had become the first rather than the last resort. There were many things that needed to be fixed, but I knew that if we did not get the basics right, we would never make progress. For the first six months I had three main priorities: find and recruit effective staff, keep the children in the classroom (they were in the habit of jumping over the fence) and rigorously enforce our behaviour management policy, establishing clear expectations and making sure that rewards and sanctions were consistently applied.

While schools and prisons are not the same, there are some common principles for leaders who are trying to improve or transform an institution. One of the most important is not trying to do too much at once. Leaders who try to solve every problem straight away are likely to solve none of them. They will spread their time too thinly in too many areas and will only be able to pay superficial attention to each issue, leaving their staff confused, overwhelmed and exhausted.

That is why, in recent years, HMI Prisons has reduced the overall number of recommendations in its reports from more than 150 to nearer 30, with a distinction between the recommendations that come from a key concern, and general recommendations to solve less urgent problems. But now we think we need to go further.

Currently, in response to our reports, governors must come up with an action plan that explains how they will deal with each of the recommendations. This process can create a blizzard of paperwork for both the prison and the prison service and can distract governors from getting on with the actual job. Our recommendations are fed into a long list to which the prison must respond, including those from the Independent Monitoring Board (IMB), the Prison and Probation Ombudsman (PPO) and the prison service's own internal monitoring.

There is a temptation for leaders to concentrate on the recommendations that are easiest to achieve, rather than those which address the most complex key concerns. The distinction that we make between the importance of different recommendations – those that will do most to improve prisoner outcomes – appears to have been lost, with the focus instead on the number of recommendations achieved as the measure of success.

Last year we introduced a self-assessment report (SAR) for governors as part of our focus on leadership. In the SAR we expect them to assess their establishment against our four healthy prison tests and to list no more than six main priorities. The number of priorities is low because we know that, with limited time and resources, their focus should be on the things that matter most, particularly in prisons that are in challenging circumstances. Governors have quite reasonably asked why, if we expect them to have no more than six priorities, do we make so many recommendations?

There is also an inherent difficulty in making a single, static recommendation to solve what are often complex problems. For example, where inspectors raise a concern that violence is too high on a particular wing, the reasons for this and the subsequent solutions may be multifaceted, such as staff-prisoner relationships, the regime, the mix of prisoners, a lack of incentives, the condition of the accommodation or the quality of leadership.

We are proposing that inspection reports will no longer include recommendations but will instead report up to 15 concerns from which inspectors will select up to six (but usually around three) priority concerns. Priority concerns will be those areas that we believe should be given the most urgent attention by prison leaders. If an independent review of progress (IRP) takes place at a prison, inspectors will focus mainly on the progress the prison has made against priority concerns when we return to the jail within a year. Each concern will be set out clearly and succinctly at the beginning of each report, with more details contained in the main text. We will still expect the prison to create an action plan which responds to our concerns.

There will be other areas prisons need to improve, but which do not reach the threshold of concerns or priority concerns. This does not mean that they are trivial or can be ignored by the prison – they will be described in the main report and inspectors will assess progress against them as part of their healthy prison assessments at the next inspection.

Since I became Chief Inspector in 2020, I have made the quality of leadership in prisons my particular focus. By moving away from making recommendations, HMI Prisons is raising its expectations of prison leaders. We will point out what needs to be fixed, but it is for governors, directors and their teams to use their knowledge and expertise to find the solutions.

**Are lockdowns the solution to prison violence?**

Recent statistics on violence in jails appear to support the old prison saying that 'happiness is door shaped'. COVID-19 restrictions meant that most prisoners, apart from a small number who were working, were locked in their cells for 22 or more hours a day. They were only unlocked in small groups that were not allowed to mix. Gyms, education, libraries and communal worship were all suspended.

Unsurprisingly, the result was a big reduction in prisoner-on-prisoner assaults from March 2020 to the following spring. This took levels of violence to where they were between 2005 and 2015, before the dramatic increases that came in the subsequent five years. The rate of assaults on officers however, fell more modestly to levels similar to 2017/18 (a year which had the third highest rate this century). Since prisons began to open up last summer, the rate of assaults between prisoners has shown a small increase, though the restrictions imposed in response to the Omicron wave will likely precipitate another fall.

Some major factors drove the increases in prison violence between 2015 and 2019. Data shows that between 2010 and 2015 the number of officers at bands 3–5 (the grades that do most frontline work) fell from 24,830 to 18,222. Surprisingly, perhaps, the rate of violence did not rise significantly during this period. In the following four years however, the rate of prisoner-on-prisoner assaults doubled, despite the number of band 3–5 officers increasing to 22,630 by 2019.

The other big change between 2015 and 2019 was not just in the number of officers, but in their levels of experience. In 2015, 92% of officers had completed three or more years of service, but by 2019 – the most violent year on record – this number had fallen to just 58%.

The proportion of officers with at least three years' experience has recently increased to 70% and this may have contributed to the small, pre-pandemic reduction in violence in 2019/20. This is not to say that officers who are inexperienced are not effective – on inspection, we see many outstanding professionals who are in their first or second year of service. But experience certainly counts in a difficult job, where de-escalating conflict is a key skill.

There is an undoubted link between drugs, debt, intimidation and violence. During the worst years, high levels of psychoactive substances (synthetic drugs such as Spice) found their way into prisons as sophisticated criminals exploited demand from many vulnerable prisoners for drugs that got them through their sentence – known in prison parlance as 'bird killers'. New body and mail scanners have certainly, recently, helped to reduce the flow of drugs and the associated violence.

Violence itself also generates its own momentum. Prisoners who have a tendency towards aggression are more likely to behave this way in an environment where their peers are more violent. This creates a cycle that leads to prisoners feeling less safe and more likely to react violently to a real or perceived threat – if you think someone is coming for you, you may decide to get your retaliation in first.

Lockdowns provided an opportunity to reboot the system and break the alarming cycle of violence. Since the pandemic began, we have heard much talk of new prison regimes that will retain the small groups in which prisoners lived during lockdown to keep prisons safer. However, if prisons continue with this policy it is inevitable that most prisoners will continue to spend long periods of time behind their doors – unless there is an extension of the core day. In most jails, prisoners are locked up for the night at around 5pm. To keep prisoners active until later in the evening would require more officers on duty and potentially an increase in spending. Money is being spent on new prisons, to hold more prisoners in England and Wales, but it is unlikely that we'll see a significant increase in the staff-prisoner ratio.

This takes us back, therefore, to the vital importance of allowing prisoners out of cells to receive visits, attend work, training and education, take exercise and prepare for eventual release under the supervision of experienced staff, with the essential 'jail-craft' that they can impart to newer officers.

Suppressing violence through lockdowns is not the long-term answer to violence. Before 2015, violence levels were consistently lower, despite prisoners generally being out of their cells for longer. Recent inspections have shown wide variation in the amount of time prisoners spend out of their cells, even in establishments of the same category. This has been dependent on the staffing situation, levels of COVID-19 risk tolerance and above all, the ambition and quality of the governor and the senior leadership team.

What the data and our reports show is that rather than returning to more restricted regimes, violence is likely to reduce where there are enough experienced officers in post and strong leadership. This is complemented by a robust strategy for preventing drugs coming into prisons and meaningful opportunities for prisoners to work, learn and socialise in a way that helps them to prepare for a successful life on release.

**Trust**

A prison chaplain recently asked me what I thought were the most important ingredients in creating a successful jail. I offered up a fairly predictable list of the things we see in the best places: effective leadership, a committed staff team, a set of values that pervades the prison, partnership with contracted services such as education and health, cleanliness, a consistent daily regime and effective support for the most disruptive or vulnerable. In the end, though, I settled for one vital element: trust.

Trust is essential in every tier of a prison system. It should run from ministers to senior leaders in HM Prison and Probation Service (HMPPS), on to prison group directors (PGDs) and to governors and directors. Within prisons, trust should also pass from governors to the senior team, to custody managers, senior officers, prison officers and finally to prisoners themselves. Trust, however, cannot just flow one way. For a prison to be successful, the prisoners need to trust it.

We see many instances where prisoners do not trust the prison. Property gets lost, applications disappear, the regime is inconsistent, activities get cancelled, recategorised prisoners do not get to move to more open conditions. Prisoners, often stuck in long-term negative patterns of behaviour, need incentives to do the right thing, but I have lost count of the times I have been told the incentives scheme does not work and does not motivate them. Why bother to work for your category D status, when it will not get you moved to an open prison?

In the most effective jails, prisoners see the

benefits of doing the right thing. In our inspection of HMP Oakwood, we commented on the many prisoner-led initiatives. One man, serving a very long sentence, told me that the wood workshop he had set up for some of the most vulnerable prisoners had given a new meaning to his and their lives.

When carrying out my review of the youth justice system in 2015, one of the things that surprised me was how little autonomy prison governors had, compared with head teachers. In my school, I was able to decide on my staffing structure, recruit and train my staff, set the rules, create the behaviour management system, commission health services and tender for building work. These freedoms are not generally afforded to prison governors. Of course, I did not have an entirely free rein: I was accountable to Ofsted, the local authority and my governing body and I had to follow policies on safeguarding, HR and finance. But if the outcomes for my pupils were good, I was trusted to get on with the job.

Prisons are not the same as schools and greater central control and oversight is necessary. It has, however, always puzzled me that the best governors in public sector prisons have only a little more autonomy than those that are the least effective or experienced, especially as directors of private sector prisons tell me they have much more independence. We see this further down the prison hierarchy, where the most effective functional heads or middle leaders work to the governor's vision but are trusted and supported to get on with the job. In our recent inspection of HMP/YOI Swinfen Hall, for instance, a brilliant custody manager ran the induction wing. She set high standards for prisoners and staff and held them to account if they let things slip.

Trust cannot just be handed out, of course. It must be earned. Whether it's prisoners or prison staff, they have to understand that being trusted also means being accountable. If prisoners were given unearned trust, then some would misuse it with serious consequences and governors (or head teachers) who were unfettered from any accountability could cause enormous problems. The aim, however, should be to pass as much trust downwards as possible and give people as much freedom as they can cope with. It involves those in authority taking a risk, because inevitably things will go wrong, but without trust, people and institutions will not flourish.

While central control can mandate minimum standards, trust is needed to unleash excellence.

## 5.3 CHANGE IS COMING:
### The mental health needs and experiences of young adults in two London remand prisons
Dr Varinder Panesar
Lead Forensic Psychologist HMP Pentonville

My interest in the experiences of young adults in prisons comes from moving from HMYOI Feltham to HMP Pentonville and HMP Wandsworth, two local remand prisons in London built in the mid-1800s and capable of housing approximately 1500 individuals. Over the last few years, the Children and Young Peoples Estate (CYPE) committed to embedding SECURE STAIRS, a trauma-informed and integrated care approach as a joint venture[1].

This cultural shift in the way we respond to the needs of the young people and prison staff was commended in HMYOI Feltham's last inspection[2]. In addition to the call for trauma-informed practice in prisons, the importance of Compassion Focused Therapy (CFT) in the forensic world is increasingly recognised[3]. Many young people housed at HMYOI Feltham will step up to the adult remand estate mainly due to serious charges and lengthy delays in their cases because of the global pandemic. Differences in the physical environment, resources, and care approach to meeting the needs of young men between HMYOI Feltham and HMP Pentonville/Wandsworth are stark and a shock to the system in every way imaginable.

Young adults (18-24 years) form 19% of the population in prison[4]; however, they have poorer outcomes compared to their older peers. This group has higher social, emotional, cognitive, mental health, and neurodevelopmental needs than the general population[5] and reoffends at a higher rate than older adults[6]. Concerns for the wellbeing of this group has been repeatedly expressed alongside an increasing sense of hopelessness and concern about how adequately their needs are met.

At the time of writing (August 2022), a national strategy for this cohort of the prison population was in its final draft. This will be welcomed as in its absence, the delivery of interventions for young adults so far has relied on the passion, commitment, and creativity of individual professionals who tend to work in silo. For example, Time4Change (a 12-week structured group programme) was developed by a Custodial Manager to address the gap at HMP Pentonville for 18-25-year-olds. It is a novel and creative initiative that has recently been recognised by the Butler Trust; however, it can come with a heavy emotional and physical cost to one individual responsible for coordinating the service. HMP Wandsworth commissions Pathways2Progress, an important and successful external organisation where 18–35-year-olds involved in serious violence can receive bespoke 1:1 or group intervention from practitioners over an 8-12-week structured programme. However, as an external initiative, there can be several barriers to consistently having access to the young men referred to the programme.

It felt important to hear the voices of young adults through focus groups so we could understand the narrative behind poor outcomes in the adult estate for this group and identify gaps in service provision with the long-term aim of being able to improve services for them. I joined one wing's Time4Change group at HMP Pentonville for four weekly sessions, two of which dedicated to using a CFT[3/7], approach to helping the group attendees learn about our evolved brains and emotions. This psychoeducation was well received and resulted in rich discussions about how adverse childhood experiences impact on an already tricky brain and body. The third session involved a focus group with eight of the young men who had regularly attended the previous sessions – here; we explored their experiences of mental health struggles and access to services. The final session was a half-day to celebrate those who had successfully completed the programme alongside their family members and loved ones. I also met with seven young adults in HMP Wandsworth for a similar focus group; however, there was no prior established therapeutic relationship with these young men and the group was co-facilitated by operational colleagues. Themes from the young men's responses to questions about their experiences are summarised below along with related research.

*1. Have you ever struggled with your mental health?*
"We don't realise it's trauma as it is normal to us"
There was an acknowledgement that the young adults had all struggled with their mental health at some point even if this was not recognised overtly. They described feeling low, anxious, hypervigilant, lacking in drive, and "irrational thinking and decisions" as symptoms they have experienced in the community. Struggles were dealt with by "keeping the lid on" and being "too distracted to face these things" either due to "pride" or believing "no one cares". The prevalence of poor mental health in the young adult population and its impact on maturation processes is highlighted in the evidence base because this adds complexity to screening, assessment, and diagnosis in this group[8].

*2. Have you gone to someone to talk about it?*
"Growing up, talking was dangerous…"
The young adults said that they have not spoken to professionals in the community – in addition to the expectation to provide for loved ones and difficulties in sharing vulnerabilities due to a sense of pride, they also described having to navigate a community of threats which made it unsafe to attend appointments. One young adult said that in prison it was "difficult and near enough impossible" to talk to professionals from the mental health team. They acknowledged the value of sharing concerns with friends and families in the form of a "therapeutic conversation" or offering a listening ear to a peer – this was described well by one young man as "if I can't step outside of it myself, I can listen to someone else's story and relate." This reinforces the powerful role of peer support models in supporting young adults' wellbeing in prison8. Another young man insightfully shared that "growing up, talking was dangerous…social services came in" so his safety strategy understandably became "don't talk" with an unintended consequence of withdrawing from professionals when support is offered.

*3. What do you think when you hear 'psychologist'?*
"Something is wrong with you"
There was a mixed response to this question, with some young adults reflecting on the potential helpful role of psychologists (e.g., it is "how you think…chats to you about wellbeing"). One young adult shared that he had initially thought that psychologists worked with "crazy people" but had experienced a friend benefiting from therapy which had helped him to shift his view. Others shared negative connotations of working with a psychologist e.g., that it indicates a sense of weakness which elicits embarrassment. There was caution about the agenda of psychologists who were thought to "read and analyse me… extract information that I don't want to give." One young adult highlighted the word 'therapist' is difficult to feel comfortable with because of a perception that they will have to "open up about my innermost secrets." Another young man used a brilliant metaphor in stating "even worse is psychotherapist!" Asked why, he explained that 'psycho' indicates "crazy" and when combined with 'therapist' (who will elicit your innermost secrets against your will), these two words "go together like a nuclear bomb." We reflected on the powerful imagery that this combination of words can elicit and agreed that no one would want to go anywhere near a nuclear bomb! Perhaps these narratives help us understand why young adults are underrepresented in prisons' mental health and psychological therapies caseloads[5].

**4. What was it like coming into HMP Pentonville/Wandsworth for the first time?**

*"More under threat…overwhelming…unsafe…guard up all the time…who am I going to see?"*

The young men said they had little support and "no one to talk to about how you are feeling" upon their arrival. High levels of anxiety ("nerve wrecking") and hypervigilance were acknowledged by the young adults, particularly in moving from induction (where they tend to mix in smaller groups) to main residential wings (where they mix with the whole landing of up to 200 people). They described feeling unprepared for main wings which felt "too big and too understaffed" with an inconsistent regime. They thought more could be done by the prison to support cell sharing with similar young adult peers to help with this transition.

One young man highlighted that "prison sounds are just different" and reflected on not only having to "shout to have your voice heard" but also struggling with the constant auditory sensory overload of keys jingling, gates banging, and others shouting. He said hearing "grown men" screaming in the night was a haunting experience which interfered with sleep and triggered past traumatic memories. Furthermore, adjusting to the space difference in a cell (e.g., he can stretch his arm out from his bed to reach for a drink) and sharing that small space with a stranger whose "poo you have to smell" was described as a humiliating and dehumanising experience. One young man reflected on how uncomfortable it is to know that faecal particles released in the air from his cellmate surround the food he will consume.

Stepping up from the CYPE was also acknowledged as a difficult adjustment with descriptions of these secure settings as "homey" and "fair" with "more understanding and guidance" from operational staff who are "more willing to help." This felt lost in the adult environment where the young men experienced staff as less caring which resulted in feeling "forgotten" behind their doors and needing to engage in extreme behaviours to be heard. For example, one young man said, "If I ask for help, it's a no, but if I jump on the netting, it's a yes….and they wonder why he self-harms and sets fires." They reflected that the global pandemic and lock down made this experience worse for them as there was no access to activities. Digital differences between the CYPE or newer prisons compared to HMP Pentonville/Wandsworth were also highlighted as difficult to adjust to, as this resulted in longer waiting time for phone credit to called loved ones and feeling more isolated.

**5. What did you notice about how this affected you and how did you cope?**

*"How did I get here?"*

The young men shared a range of ways in which they were affected - feeling low in mood, shocked, uncontained, isolated, low in confidence, and "like I don't matter." Appetite and sleep were negatively impacted due to "overthinking" and feeling "drained." High anxiety about conflicts with peers in the prison environment was also a shared feeling. Staying connected to family was described as important but also tough to navigate as emotional health suffered more when there was a death of a loved one. Some young men described looking forward to social visits and a sense that they have "so much to share" but then when sat with their loved one, feeling "blank… everything I want to say is just gone." Another described the impact of interacting with officers who have limited skills and experience in having young people in their care as "painful".

One young man spoke of self-blame, disappointment, and anger at self, and both groups shared a range of coping strategies that highlight the brain and body's inbuilt flight, fight, and freeze survival defences[3]: withdrawing from others, neglecting their self-care, sleeping all day, arguing with loved ones on the phone, fighting on the wing, self-harming, and using drugs. This helps us to understand the story behind poor outcomes highlighted in publications – i.e., compared to their older peers, young adults spend more time in the Care and Separation Unit, more time in their cells, are restrained more and are less motivated by the IEP scheme[5].

Helpful safety strategies were also highlighted in the form of getting to know others on the wing, talking to cellmates (provided this feels safe), exercise, meditation, praying, eating healthy food, receiving canteen, and putting apps in for support. However, it was difficult to experience a lack of response from services when help was sought via apps – one young adult described this as "I'm left on hold without a response, it puts me off from asking again".

Another young man shared that although he had coped effectively with the adjustment to HMP Pentonville, witnessing "desperate things people have to do to get attention" brought up shame and embarrassment – as his imagination contemplated "will there come a time I will need to do this?"

**6. Do you remember the screening process? How did it feel to answer questions about your mental health?**

*"No one really cares…this is our life, and this is their job – it's a huge difference"*

Estimations indicate that screening in reception misses about 75% of mental health need[9]. Many young men said they had no recollection about the second day screening; however, interestingly but unsurprisingly (because of somatic memory), they recalled physical health checks e.g., administration of covid-19 tests. Some recalled being asked repetitive questions in police custody and in prison but acknowledged that the clinician was "doing their job" and that mental health can change between these settings. Those who recalled the screening process in prison found it to be "quick…tick box…you are just a number" and for one empathic young adult, he decided it would be more helpful for the busy clinician if he said "no" to all questions so they would not have more paperwork to complete. The screening stage was deemed an unsafe environment to share feelings in, with a sense that they would be judged for doing so, particularly when combined with operational staff in the area who reinforced the stigma attached to mental health – with one young man sharing that a prison officer had commented "this ain't the time or place to get all emotional."

### 7. Why is it harder for young adults to access mental health services compared to over 25s?
*"Nah, it's not mental health…man's good"*
Not being aware of support on offer, pride, and fears about how they are perceived by others ("weak minded" or "there is something wrong with you") were described as barriers to accessing mental health support in prison. Some reflected on the "massive" negative connotations that continue to be attached to seeking mental health support compared to going to see the GP or dentist which made it feel safer to "push through on my own" or only accept support "if someone comes to you" instead of seeking it out. A few reflected that they had asked their partners or mothers to contact the prison to request support as they were either unsure of the self-referral processes or did not feel comfortable reaching out for help.
One young man reflected that "we know we're adults on paper but we're still gang banging and having fun with this even though it is taking our lives down a tunnel". Others shared that life changing events such as becoming a father or the death of a loved one can lead to a realisation that "something needs to change." There was also a view that around the age of 25, there can be a reflection such as "is this what I've made of my life?" which can trigger a drive towards helpful, not harmful choices. This feedback is consistent with our knowledge of brain development[10] which has highlighted the need to assess young men's 'psychosocial maturity[11]' and resulting impact on emotional control, impulsivity, influence by peers, response to authority and adherence to the prison rules.

The young adults noted that loss of youth clubs in their communities resulted in less help and "not hearing enough that you can talk to us." This idea generalises to different contexts, which makes it hard to talk to others in prison. They also shared that when they have expressed struggling with their mental health to peers when under the influence of cannabis, it is much easier to later say "nah, that's just the weed" or to describe a peer sharing his struggles with mental health as someone who is "bugging out…tapped…not like us" than to acknowledge that "he is not coping". This is because of "fear of the unknown" (i.e. being unaware of typical trauma reactions to adverse life experiences).

### 8. Why is it harder for racialised communities to access mental health services compared to their White peers?
*"That's not me, that's a White person thing"*
73% of the young men in the focus groups were from Black, Asian, or Minority Ethnic backgrounds which is consistent with their disproportionate representation in the Criminal Justice System[12]. The young men shared that culture plays a significant part in reinforcing a narrative that "mental health doesn't run in our family" i.e., that mental health difficulties are purely hereditary and there is limited awareness of the role of the environment. Limited culturally sensitive resources together with little experience of accessing generic health services in the community were described as drivers to discomfort in seeking support. Finally, one group reflected that "people delivering support are White…this can make it hard to feel comfortable with the person asking questions." This feedback is consistent with findings that mental health needs were more frequently met in White than Black, Asian, or Minority Ethnic prisoners, partly because of perceived barriers between the majority culture and that of particular ethnic groups[13].

### 9. What has been helpful about learning about our tricky brains/tricky bodies and the impact of trauma?
*"Learning about my brain is very important"*
Compassion Focused Therapy reinforces an important notion - the brain that emerges at the end of adolescence is the perfect neural combination for the environment it grew up in3. Given the prevalence of trauma in the prison population, this invites us to move away from using deficit-based language to viewing individuals who offend as highly skilled at surviving a hostile world; however, these skills are now being used out of context so become harmful. The young men in HMP Pentonville who were part of CFT psychoeducation shared

that these sessions had helped them better understand "why certain things happen in my body...why I feel certain ways about certain things in this environment...why certain thought processes happen." Having the Time4Change Custodial Manager in the group helped further the insight because of his established relationship with the young men which allowed examples to be used in a "real" way. The young men said they valued that the knowledge was shared in a "very friendly" manner and that it also helped them to "understand how other people are thinking."

### 10. What can HMP Pentonville/Wandsworth do to make it easier to access mental health support in prison?

*"You don't get help until you fall"*

The focus groups noted the importance of clarity and raising awareness about who forms part of the mental health team and their remit, and that this information is presented in an accessible manner via leaflets, posters, pop up clinics, induction reps, and use of the prison TV and radio.

The HMP Pentonville group also recognised the value of someone from the mental health team attaching to existing groups and programmes for young adults e.g., Time4Change. Young adults who had been part of the CFT psychoeducation not only found this knowledge empowering and valuable, but also described a sense of care from a mental health professional and reported more confidence in seeking further support if needed– one young man summarised "I learnt more in one month than I thought I would, I feel like you're here for us, without you joining Time4Change, we wouldn't have accessed psychology and I wouldn't know how to get support". Another young adult appreciated that the CFT psychoeducation was communicated simply because "it is about us making the connections for ourselves." This feedback highlights the importance of mirroring creative and alternative approaches used by wellbeing services in the voluntary and community sector to make mental health conversations engaging and less stigmatising than a 'conventional' mental health service8.

One young man suggested that mental health services should develop a "mental health key worker system" for young adults which focuses on building a relationship first "so we can feel comfortable to start expressing our needs...make it appetising to engage...like playing cards first, then we will open up slowly."

Finally, the young men also highlighted the importance of through the gate support so that services are set up to support continuity of care in a proactive manner, instead of only becoming involved once things deteriorate.

*Psychological Therapies will take the following lessons forward across HMP Pentonville and Wandsworth based on the feedback from the focus groups:*

a. We will create a 'Young Adult Board' consisting of a multidisciplinary team of each discipline that works in the prison, young adults, and peer mentors. This board will move away from siloed working to an integrated care approach by creating or adapting local operational policies and strategies (based on the new Model for Operational Delivery), setting targets, and reviewing progress and barriers regularly. Co-production with young adults will be at the heart of this board.

b. We will take a whole prison approach to committing to trauma informed practice, i.e. mental health staff providing training on development and impact of adverse childhood experiences, supporting staff in their work through supervision and reflective practice, working in a way that helps officers to see the young adult behind the behaviour, understanding how and why someone's early life experience may have impacted them and what might trigger them in prison, and working in a way which ultimately seeks to reduce the chance of retraumatisation and promotes healing.

c. We will invest in diversifying the backgrounds of our staff group and ensure information about our services is advertised, more visible and feels accessible to young adults on induction wings (e.g., through pop up clinics, leaflets, prison TV/radio slots). Based on the feedback received from the young adults, this will include information on preparing for the impact of transitioning to a bigger and noisier wing.

d. We will aim to empower prison officers to become specialist young adult keyworkers through training in modules such as child & adolescent development, trauma, and attachment so they understand why every interaction matters. We hope this will mirror the Custody Support Plan (CuSP) embedded in the CYPE14. The keyworker role was suspended through the pandemic and is slow to return due to ongoing staff shortages. However, young adults in the focus groups identified this role as crucial to supporting their mental health.

e. We will invest in training all reception and induction staff in line with the first NHS Improvement recommendation8 to increase safety in prisons. This sense of relational safety was highlighted in the focus groups as crucial at the reception stage so that young men can experience care and containment from staff who are helping them to navigate their first night in prison.

f. Psychological Therapies will regularly join existing programmes such as Time4Change and

Pathways2Progress to build relationships and overcome the stigma and fear associated with seeking help. From an attachment perspective, this highlights the important role of staff in offering proximity at times of stress and threat. We will advocate for young men accessing structured interventions to be placed on hold to minimise unpredictable discontinuity of care which mirrors early losses and adverse experiences.

g. In line with NHS guidance[15], we will support young men with neurodevelopmental needs to access an adapted environment with dedicated and trained officers. HMP Pentonville has recently opened a specialised landing for neurodevelopmental needs and HMP Wandsworth is committed to doing so in the future. Collaboration between healthcare and the prison will be key to opening and sustaining this landing.

h. We will integrate Compassion Focused Therapy as an approach to psychoeducation about mental health. Particularly in a remand prison where timescales are unlikely to allow for long-term therapy, psychoeducation from this lens is valued as it offers a shift from "there is something wrong with me" to "this is my tricky brain doing what it was designed to do". It can also make it more likely for young adults to continue engaging with mental health services when transferred or released into the community.

i. The young adults at HMP Pentonville particularly appreciated being able to celebrate their graduation from Time4Change with loved ones in an informal and relaxed environment. The protective nature of a family network has been well documented[16]. We will therefore increase opportunities to maintain links with loved ones via regular family days which offer a different experience to seeing family members in social visits.

j. We will adopt a whole prison approach to helping voluntary and community services have access to young adults in prison to build relationships at reachable moments before they transition to the community. This will also allow young men to receive support in a timely manner, instead of when in crisis.

k. If we are not successful at using prison as a last resort for young adults, then ideally, remand prisons in the future will mirror the SECURE STAIRS framework in the CYPE – i.e., they will have specialised landings on each wing with dedicated officers who use trauma-informed approaches; however, the current reality is that the prison service is short staffed and without an adequate support and governance structure, staff working on such landings will burn out quickly. The New Models of Care by NHS England are investing resources to better support an individual's early days in custody and their

release or transfer; however, the wellbeing of young adults in HMP Wandsworth and Pentonville is everyone's responsibility, not just the responsibility of the NHS. Commitment for a cultural shift in a remand environment where stays are short and unpredictable may be a big ask, made even more difficult as doing so goes against punitive mainstream media and political views. The idea to make prisons more therapeutic was introduced almost 50 years ago[17]; however, sadly only in recent years has there been a drive to achieve this, which has focused mainly on the young people's and women's estates. We owe the young adults we serve in remand prisons an opportunity to experience care, containment, support, and acceptance in an environment that is harsh, daunting, and chaotic. If we want levels of isolation, self-harm, and violence by young men in prison to reduce and for young adults to make helpful, not harmful choices when returned to their communities, we must take a whole prison approach in helping them to (a) navigate the adjustment to prison (b) seek support without judgement and (c) make sense of life experiences they did not choose, but which have shaped them and created unintended harmful consequences.

### Acknowledgements

A special thank you to all 15 young adults who shared their important views in the focus groups. Thank you to Custodial Manager Ricardo Lafuente-Dyer who facilitated access to the young men and has consistently advocated for Psychological Therapies to work collaboratively with Time4Change at HMP Pentonville. Thank you to Governor Robert Cunningham who organised the focus group at HMP Wandsworth and shared the draft Model for Operational Delivery for Young Adults. Finally, thank you to Twilight Bey who took the time to share how Pathways2Progress works as well as aspects of his life story that make him passionate about the programme at HMP Wandsworth.

1 The Five Year Forward View for Mental Health (england.nhs.uk) 2016
2 HMYOI Feltham A report (PDF) (476 kB), Report on a scrutiny visit to HMYOI Feltham A by HM Chief Inspector of Prisons (9 and 17 February 2021)
3 Taylor & Hocken (2021). Hurt people hurt people: using a trauma sensitive and compassion focused approach to support people to understand and manage their criminogenic needs, The Journal of Forensic Practice, Vol. 23 No. 3, pp. 301-315
4 Draft Model for Operational Delivery: Young Adult Males, 2022
5 Outcomes for Young Adults in Custody: A thematic review by HM Inspectorate of Prisons (2021). London, HM Inspectorate of Prisons
6 Achieving Better Outcome for Young Adult Men: Evidence Based Commissioning Principles (2015). National Offender Management Service
7 Gilbert (2010). An introduction to compassion focused therapy in cognitive behaviour therapy, International Journal of Cognitive Therapy, Vol.3 No.2, pp. 97-112
8 Durcan, G., 2021. The future of prison mental health care in England: A national consultation and review 2021 - Centre for Mental Health. London, Centre for Mental Health, pp. 1-43
9 House of Commons Committee of Public Accounts (2017) Mental health in prisons: Eighth Report of Session 2017–19. London. House of Commons
10 Johnson, S. B., Blum, R. W. et al., (2009). Adolescent maturity and the brain: The promise and pitfalls of neuroscience research in adolescent health policy. Journal of Adolescent Health, 45, 216-221.
11 Steinberg, L. & Cauffman, E. (1996). Maturity of judgement in adolescence: Psychosocial factors in adolescent decision-making. Law and Human Behavior, 20,

249-272

12 Uhrig, N. (2016). *Black, Asian and Minority Ethnic disproportionality in the Criminal Justice System in England and Wales*. London, Ministry of Justice.

13 McKenzie N, Killaspy H, Jakobowitz S, Faranak H, Bebbington P. *Assessing needs for psychiatric treatment in prisoners: 3. Comparison of care received by black and minority ethnic prisoners and by white prisoners. Soc Psychiatry Psychiatric Epidemiol. 2019 Jul;54(7):883-886*

14 *Action Plan: HMYOI Feltham (A) Children's Unit Action Plan (2019). A Response to the HMIP Inspection report on an unannounced inspection at HMYOI Feltham A Children's Unit. HM Prison & Probation Service.*

15 *Meeting the Healthcare Needs of Adults with a Learning Disability and Autistic Adults in Prison (Version 1, 2021). London, NHS England and NHS Improvement.*

16 Salvatore, C. & Taniguchi, T. A. (2012). *Do social bonds matter for emerging adults? Deviant Behavior, 33, 738-756.*

17 Scott, P. D. (1974). *Solutions to the problems of the dangerous offender. British*

## 5.4 PRISON MEDICINE: On The Critical List? *A health professional service-user's view of prison medicine*

By Doctor, Prisoner, Campaigner: Dr Tim Kerr

### Past Medical History

It's Friday night on the assessment suite in the Royal Victoria Infirmary. Patients swell through the doors, and line the corridors. Sent in by their GP, who agonised over whether to send them in, but did so in their best interests. They have suspected disease which needs further attention within the hospital. It could be serious. A stroke or a heart attack.

My job, as the junior doctor, is to clerk them. They've already been seen by a nurse, who is equipped to triage them on to me. I take them to a side room, to ensure confidentiality despite the place being full to capacity.

I try and ascertain why they are here, what medications they take, and what treatment they now need. They bring with them bags of medications, and a prescription if I'm lucky. But it's important that I go through them. Prescribing certain drugs incorrectly is a never event, meaning it should never happen under any circumstances. I could be referred to the regulator, that patient would have every right. I would tell them my GMC number. The standards are that high even for such a routine task as this. Another patient, in a bay down the corridor, starts getting irate. His shouts and yells echo down the corridor. But the nurse looking after that bay knows how to diffuse the situation. The anger comes from the uncertainty, the long waits, and the pathology that put him here. She knows this, from experience. She speaks with him calmly, and offers clear instructions and a plan of action. No alarm is pressed. The security guards by the entrance relax.

It only gets busier, as I do this for the next twelve hours. It is routine. Unremarkable. I refer people who make attempts on their own life to liaison psychiatry, and they are seen promptly. I explain things as best I can to those on new medications, and where they'll go next on their journey through the hospital. I force through requests for

scans and consults, time is of the essence, and early treatment can save lives. I send some home, with a discharge summary immediately written, so their GP knows what to do next.

It doesn't strike me that there is any other way to practise medicine, but to do it to the best of my abilities. Patients come to us in their most vulnerable state, and trust in us that we will treat them as we would a close family member.

Unfortunately, I broke this trust. My professionalism didn't extend beyond the hospital doors. I sold drugs to fund and fuel my addiction to cocaine and alcohol. I was arrested, in that same hospital trust, and sent to prison a year later.

### Withdrawal

I was naïve to think I could live the double life of a doctor and drug dealer. I entered prison equally naive about the situation that awaited me within. I assumed that the prison service, a big, state-run organisation with bureaucracy and lanyards and badges, would function just like the NHS. That prisoner's healthcare needs would be looked after in the same way. To the same standards I was taught at medical school were universal. This naivety didn't last long.

I arrive in reception, hungry but inquisitive of my new home. The local category B, specifically designed for accepting people fresh from court. I go through various questionnaires, with some attempts to screen me for mental health issues by prison officers. Like many who enter here, I have psychiatric disease in depression, and am stable on medication. So important to me is my newfound mental stability, that I brought three months' worth of Venlafaxine with me. Sealed in pharmacy bags, prescription alongside.

But it's Friday, I'm told, as I eat a cheese baguette. There is no pharmacy cover over the weekend. I won't receive my medication until at least Monday. I don't believe them when they say this. There will be systems in place.

Not for the first time, I am wrong. I sit in my cell all weekend, withdrawing from this medication. The last remnants of it leaving my body into the toilet situated a metre away from my cellmate. He offers me weed, and I briefly consider taking it, if only to relieve me from the insomnia, headaches, and brain zaps I'm now experiencing. Monday comes, and I work out that I am supposed to go to a medication hatch to get my drug. I queue up, in a tiny corridor. I can hear everything said to others at the hatch, the drug names spoken aloud for all to hear. My turn arrives, but I am told it's not been prescribed. They'll put a note on, they say, but there is nothing they can do. Another day without.

An idea starts to form through the fog, that this may not be a one-off error. That this sort of negligence is inherent to the running of this place. At lunch, I talk to others of my plight. My hope diminishes as one man tells me he didn't get his anti-epileptic medication for six weeks. Not even a seizure was enough to prompt them. Eventually, I do get my medication, so long as I am able to go to the hatch each morning, which is by no means guaranteed.

I'm summoned to healthcare one afternoon, unexpectedly. So I sit in the healthcare waiting room with many others, avoiding eye contact. Another prisoner walks in. He is slightly agitated, in contrast to the rest of us waiting here. He asks loudly, of the nurse behind toughened glass, when his appointment will be. The nurse tells him to shut up, that he missed his earlier appointment, and he'll have to wait his turn. His eyebrows furl. He says it wasn't his fault that he missed the appointment. That the wing staff failed to release him. She calls him a liar, and baits him, telling him he'll be thrown out if he doesn't shut up. Of course, he rises to this taunt, as she knew he would. He punches the glass, she doesn't flinch, as his slender fist rebounds off. He is smothered by two officers nearby, and bundled away. The nurse smiles, as though pleased she's reduced the waiting list.

I should have said something. But I was too meek. Already it seemed like this was just the way things were done round here, and who was I to complain. Instead I look around the walls of this room, for any posters from the regulators, suggesting how I might complain about this issue. But I can't see the Nursing Midwifery Council's (NMC) details. Nor those of the General Medical Council (GMC) and Care Quality Commission (CQC). The only thing I see, is a paper stuck to the toughened glass, with the number of missed appointments this month written on it. Apparently, this is our fault.

Eventually I go through, and they say I need an electrocardiogram, ECG, to check my heart. But they put the leads in the wrong places. I let them know at the time, pointing at the diagram on the machine. But I'm mistaken, the healthcare assistant says. I do complain, in writing this time. But I receive my complaint back, weeks later, to state that they were correct, and that in fact I was in the wrong. There is no appeal process.

Not with G4S health, who have their own separate healthcare complaints system.

Over the following months I start to see the dark side of this place. The end result of a healthcare provider insisting it is always right, yet with standards far below what is required. The effects of the inability to get the care one needs. I see people slash their skin with blades at the slightest anguish. I see people when they attempt to take their own life, but I can't refer them on to anyone here. And there are those I don't see, trapped behind their cell door by their own fear of what's outside.

### Stuck

Christmas comes, and I'm comparing a quiz on my wing. But half the page I am reading from suddenly goes blank. I look up, and half the room is missing. I know it's one of two diagnoses – migraine or a transient ischaemic attack, a precursor to stroke. The blood supply to my visual cortex interrupted by a clot.

I know what I would do, were I in the community. But here, I can't just go to A+E. There'll be no GP in today. There's now an intermediary, between me and healthcare, in the shape of a prison officer. It's unfair on them to be placed in this position. They aren't medically trained. They know it will drain resources if I am sent to hospital in an ambulance. And so, I don't want to bother the staff, who will likely tell me to wait until a normal day. So, I just continue the quiz, and hope it passes. My mind flitting between debate about whether Boris Johnson had said letterbox or post-box, and the idea that my visual cortex is slowly dying.

I think back to an incident which occurred only weeks ago. The man who had a heart attack, locked in his cell overnight. His pressing the buzzer with crushing chest pain, and it not being answered for quite some time. He had to be resuscitated by a gym officer at one point. They shook hands, but the prisoner died weeks later.

I see the GP when I can. But it's not a transient ischaemic attack, he says, confidently. And I believe him. Maybe I'm misremembering the NICE guidelines. I believe him until the moment it happens again, and again. And I start to wonder if it was the four different scans, and four separate hospital trips, required to rule out this disease, that put him off this diagnosis. The only scanners in here are those to detect drugs.

Fortuitously, I am moved prisons. To a category C as my sentence progresses. I can try my luck with a different healthcare provider. Perhaps the shoddy healthcare in the last place was just a one off.

My new cellmate here has ADHD. On our first night together, upon discovering that I am a doctor, he stops flicking through the nine TV channels for a moment, to show me a blister of the pills they gave him – Atomoxetine. He's usually on Concerta (Ritalin or Methylphenidate to many), but they switched him, and didn't explain why. The leaflet in the drug packet only worries him with an enormous list of side effects. So has stopped taking it. I tell him that they switch it as Concerta has a resale value, and guidelines prohibit its use in prisons. He looks at me, face scrunched. "Ritalin's shit", he says, perplexed. "Why would anyone here want to snort that?"

He lies back on his bunk, above me. Now he just sucks on a vape all evening, or he would, but keeps running out of cartridges. It's still far cheaper than Nicorette. Then I pick up a feint burning smell, as small embers float downwards past me and onto the floor. The TV channels stop switching, and I realise he has knocked himself out with spice. He doesn't even need to pay for it. There is so much of it here that it is given out for free.

One day, I arrive back at the cell, and my cellmate tells me that I have to see the doctor about my vision. This isn't something I've told him between spice comas. Instead, a slip of paper from healthcare arrived under our door, informing me of my appointment. And he read it, and now knows I'm maybe not well.

When I go to see the doctor here, I'm pleased to see the healthcare is run by an NHS trust. My hopes are raised by the big NHS logo, that I'll receive healthcare akin to what I practised, within that same NHS.

But here too, in an all to brief appointment, the GP insists it's not TIA or stroke. Even me dropping in phrases like Amaurosis Fugax and Hemianopia aren't enough to sway him, as he ushers me out the door.

It's here that I really start to worry. That this place will delay my treatment so much that I end up having a full-blown stroke. That part of my brain will not leave prison with me. All because I'm stuck in here, with a single healthcare option, and not out there. Those NHS logos not signalling the standards they should espouse.

## Open

Fortunately for me, I arrive at open prison early in my sentence. This is because of who I am, and my ability to navigate prison bureaucracy with relative ease. My literacy standard, backed with years of form filling as a doctor, have paid dividends in this strange world. Those less fortunate remain stuck in higher category prisons, health suffering as a result.

And finally, the GP here admits it might be a stroke. He puts me on anticoagulants, which I am able to pick up that same day. I am able to go to external healthcare appointments alone, unsupervised, on temporary licence. That not so subtle reluctance of prisons to send people to external appointments no longer influencing healthcare staff to alter their practise. They can now address the needs of the prisoner, rather than the prison.

In the local hospital, the stroke consultant I finally get to see, says what I am experiencing is typical of stroke, and I must be investigated. He

is concerned, and asks why it took so long. He shares that naivety that I once had, in a similar position. I shrug, and say "That's prison".

## Final Year

In my last year inside, now adequately treated and without the worry that had previously gripped me, I start to really reflect on the differences in healthcare, between that in prison and outside. It's still hard to get hold of information, even in here, an open prison. But I do learn of this standard of equivalence that healthcare is supposedly held to in prisons. The idea that the healthcare received in here, should be the same as that received in the community. The same healthcare I used to practise.

Like many in here, I think back to where it all started to go wrong for me. The heavy drinking and drug use in medical school. But I think then of those sleepy afternoon medical ethics lectures, in first and second year. The standards that medical practise should be held to. Things that seemed obvious at the time. Beneficence; to offer the best treatment. Non-Malfeasance; not to allow patients to come to harm. Autonomy; to respect patient's wishes. And Justice; that access to healthcare was a right for all.

These principles were imprinted on me, and guided my practice, back in the Royal Victoria Infirmary.

But these principles, if applied to prison, show up its grotesque flaws.

Here, in prison, people necessarily come to harm, and are not offered the best treatments. It is baked in, that successful treatment is stopped, not for medical reasons, but for operational reasons. The prison dictates what can be done, be it through changes to medications for security reasons, or not being referred to specialists the guidelines stipulate you should see, because they aren't available, or because the prison isn't equipped to do so.

Autonomy is obviously rescinded, but it is not adequately replaced. You can't choose your doctor in here. Choices of treatment are limited to what the prison can offer. Requests for treatment must now go through an intermediary, a prison officer, with obvious, tragic results, as you lie behind the door suffering.

Further, you have little to no information to make decisions with what little autonomy remains. Few public health measures designed to better one's life make it through the walls. Smoking cessation costs the prisoner money. The nutritional content of meals is lacking. But you are welcome to eat all the ultra-processed, obesogenic junk you wish, and use all lung traumatising tobacco products you like. The prison service will happily profit at your expense.

And finally, ironically, justice. Despite housing a population with such high burdens of psychiatric and physical disease, this high level of need is not met. Access to medical care is instead prefaced on the lottery of who you are, and what prison you are in. It is jarringly unjust, in a place existing to preserve and promote justice.

### Release

I wonder, in my last few weeks of prison, as I think more about the outside world, where the public and professional concern is. Why this longstanding inadequacy in prison healthcare persists.

Ignorance will play its part. My GP won't have had any idea that my Venlafaxine prescription wasn't being acted upon. My stroke physician seemed shocked at the difficulties in being referred. And I certainly had little idea how bad it was in prisons, all those years ago when I was practicing.

But perhaps it is more sinister. That there is a societal acceptance that prisoners should be treated less well than their community peers. It's prison, after all. A punishment. That the public are just like I was, when I sat in my chair in the waiting room two years ago, as the nurse baited the impulsive prisoner. Seeing this practise as wrong, and yet, not quite bad enough to want to do anything about it.

Pessimistically, I begin to think it would just be easier if we all admitted that it is not possible to have equivalence of healthcare between prisons and society. For sentencing remarks to henceforth state that included as part of the punishment, will be a deterioration of health. That you might even die, because of this sentence. I leave prison in October 2020. It's an experience that has shaped me. I cannot leave it behind. Unlike my medical records, which of course were not forwarded to my GP upon release.

Pleasingly, since release, my pessimism has turned to hope. I have discovered that there are in fact pockets of healthcare professionals dedicated to improving the state of healthcare within prisons. That there is a growing movement within the NHS, and other healthcare bodies, setting about to fundamentally change the way healthcare is practised in prisons. To finally change the way healthcare sits within prisons. Not as an adjunct to a static Victorian prison model. But inherent to the functioning of the prison.

Crucially, they will use the lived experience of those like me and the many others who have traversed prison, to fuel this movement. Removing that veil of ignorance surrounding prisons, that has hamstrung previous efforts to do the same. We can offer unparalleled insights into the failings of prison healthcare, and offer novel solutions.

I'm unlikely to practice medicine again. I will

only ever be entering hospitals as a patient. Gone are the days of directly improving people's health. But the memory of those places, and the standards they upheld, inspire me to work now to instil the same standards into prisons. To take prison healthcare off the critical list, and into a new, compassionate era where those detained are always viewed as patients first, and prisoners a long way second.

## 5.5 A DECENCY AGENDA OF A DIFFERENT SORT: *The Health and Wellbeing of Prison Governors and Operational Managers.* Harrison, K; Smith, L; Mason, R; Nichols, H; Saunders, G; Hall, L. *The Universities of Lincoln & Hull (UK)*

### Introduction

In his foreword to the 2022 edition of The Prisons Handbook, Sir Martin Narey discusses how one of the enduring challenges for HMPPS is the need to make prisons "consistently moral and decent places" (Leech 2022: 38). He also quotes Duncan McLoughlin, a retired Governor from Northern Ireland, who argues "if a prison is to be a positive influence on a prisoner, then that can only be achieved if we treat prisoners with respect, that we provide decent living conditions, that we make the prison a place where there is dignity, an absence of fear, and where there is a sense of self-worth and self-respect" (Leech 2022:38). Key aspects for both contributors, therefore, are decency, dignity, respect and worth, because without it, little in prisons can be achieved. Of course, both of these quotations are in the context of how we should treat prisoners and whilst we do not wish to detract from these important aims, this is not what this article is about. Rather, we are interested in how these concepts are relevant and applicable to the working lives of prison governors and operational managers and whether there is a need for a more encompassing decency agenda.

Research on the wellbeing of prison officers is not plentiful, although what does exist suggests real concern. In 2017, for example, 1,474 UK prison officers completed a survey asking about role demands, resources, and mental health. Of these participants, 74% presented as likely to have a mental health problem with this being caused by a combination of factors including "job demands, poor interpersonal relationships, role ambiguity . . . low job control and poor management of change" (Kinman, et al. 2017: 456). More recent research, based on survey data from 1,956 UK prison officers, shows that many officers work when unwell, with this being a "key risk factor for mental wellbeing and job performance" (Kinman and Clements 2022: 3389). Similar work has also been undertaken elsewhere, with one literature analysis in the US concluding that correctional officers "experience high levels of stress, burnout, and a variety of other mental health related consequences as a result of their employment" (Ferdik and Smith (2017:2). What is more difficult to find, however, is research which specifically relates to prison governors and operational managers.

Recognising this gap in the literature, a multidisciplinary team from the Universities of Lincoln and Hull, decided to contact the Prison Governors Association (PGA), in early 2021 to see whether there was any appetite to conduct research into the health and wellbeing of their members. While they had previously surveyed their membership, which had shown high workloads and high levels of stress, in-depth interviews to understand more about the factors influencing these concerns had never been undertaken. Between June-November 2021, the team completed 63 interviews, talking to members across England, Wales and Scotland. Some interviews only lasted 35 minutes, while others exceeded two and a half hours. Many participants told us that they found the experience cathartic, that this was the first time that they felt listened to and their feelings validated. While unintended by the researchers, for some participants it had felt therapeutic. It is also important to note that the data collection took place during the Covid-19 pandemic, a time when there were significant concerns that prisons could become high-risk settings for outbreaks resulting in high levels of mortality. Despite this context, participants were keen to express that many of the issues raised were not specific to the pandemic, although some had been further exacerbated by it.

In total, we spoke to 43 (68%) men and 20 (32%) women, with an age range of 28-61 years and an average (mean) age of 49.7 years. Our participants had an average (mean) length of service of 24.2 years with the range spanning from 2-35 years. While we only spoke to a small percentage (6%) of the total membership, those we did speak to were representative in terms of age, gender, and length of service when compared against PGA membership monitoring data. We also spoke to members from a variety of settings including all four HMPPS male prison security categories, the women's estate, the youth secure estate and HMPPS headquarters. Participants were thus from a range of roles including Governing Governor, Controller, Deputy Governor, Head of Function (including, but not limited to, Operations, Security, Residence, Safety, Reducing Offending) and a

range of headquarters strategic leadership and project-specific roles. For ease, we use the term Governor to represent all of these roles. Unsurprisingly, we collected a vast amount of data from the interviews which we arranged into 12 core themes and 33 sub-themes during our analysis. This article focuses on four key aspects of the research, namely: workload, work life balance, macho culture and not feeling valued.

**Workload challenges**

All interviews started with a very general question, asking participants how they would describe their health and wellbeing at work over the past 12 -18 months. While some said they felt they were coping, this was the minority view, with other more negative responses including "it has been very challenging" (PGA 51), "really stressful . . . I've never been this stressed before where it's just non-stop" (PGA 55) and "I'm not sleeping well . . . I'm just permanently tired" (PGA 40). Many attributed this to their workloads, with participants often reporting that they worked well over their contracted hours in order to complete their required tasks. One told us how:

. . . there just isn't sufficient hours in the working week to do everything I need to do. I'd love to work 37 hours a week . . . or even a 42-hour week, but it's never that, it's significantly more (PGA 4).

Another described how when they had previously worked in a prison and prior to the Covid-19 pandemic, they were "easy doing 60 hours . . . but it's what you needed to do to get you through . . . the week" (PGA 12). Later in the interview they explained how this overworking had been the reason they had left an operational prison:

I was teetering on the edge . . . I was just like, oh, my God, this is ridiculous . . . And I said, I'd never go back there and do it again. However, I see colleagues doing it. And it's like, you don't get any extra pay. You don't get, you don't win any prizes. But it's almost like a thing (PGA 12). This expectation to work such long hours was echoed by several others, with one stating: "they do say that operational managers are all hours worked, but we're not work all hours. And I just think it's built into the culture, an expectation, that this is your job description. And that's how things are" (PGA 21). Another explained how this expectation had become discriminatory for working parents:

I want a job that I can do in 40 hours a week. And that job in [prison name] was probably at least 50 and could have been a hell of a lot more. And I just don't want my kids to pay that price . . . in general terms, I think there are clear equality problems with jobs that take more than 40 hours a week, because they will discriminate against parents and mothers in particular (PGA 1).

The pandemic and the need for all to stay as safe as possible had certainly exacerbated the problem of extra work, but participants further explained how it was not just the long hours but the intensity of the work that was problematic. Many spoke about the layers of bureaucracy that they were expected to deal with and how, with reference to emails and telephone calls, "it never stops and everything pings" (PGA 7). One Governor explained how they felt:

quite overwhelmed by [their] inbox. It just keeps building up and building up and I don't have time to knock it down, because I'm doing my work, as well as . . . duty governor and the adjudications and night visits and weekends and God knows what else . . . I've got 2,000 emails sat there. If I could do one work from home day a week, it would help me clear my inbox because I have less interruptions, and also for example, my phone is right behind this iPad and I've put it on silent, and it hasn't stopped ringing. It hasn't stopped going for the 45 minutes I've been talking to you. And I've seen people peering through my office window as well, trying to see if I'm available. I don't get two minutes to myself (PGA 16).

**Work life balance**

Having such excessive workloads obviously impacted on the work life balance that individuals were able to achieve, with this being another factor which participants commonly raised. This resulted in two main issues; time at home was rarely sacrosanct and even when there was some protected time, participants were often not able to relax to properly enjoy it. One explained how "even when I'm off, I'm on call or taking phone calls . . . [or] having to read a load of gumpf because I don't have time in my working day" (PGA 4). Others highlighted "my quality time away from work is getting less. I'm still focusing on work away from work more than I ever have in the past" (PGA 40) and "by the time I went home, I was so tired, home life didn't really exist" (PGA 15). Another explained how they were unable to switch off, even when at home:

I don't believe when you're a strategic manager . . . that you can leave that work at work. One aspect of being a manager is that you've got the ability to reflect on previous issues and incidents and conversations and actions. And . . . home indeed is a good time to do that . . . I think it's the level of the work that we do that prevents you from switching off . . . while we're at home, while we're going out for a run, while we're taking the dog for a walk, rather than relaxing and enjoying the things we will be reflecting because if we don't do that, that's going to cause us additional stress. I

don't know if some people think that we're all machines, and we can just switch on and just switch off, [but] that's impossible (PGA 21).

Others spoke about how their work impacted on their families and children and how they felt that they were being pulled in opposing directions:

. . . one of the things that I struggled with was that when my kids were home learning, it would be on a rare day where I was working from home, and I had to just leave them to it. And yet I saw all of these images and heard all these stories about the mum sat at the table actually becoming a teacher and teaching the children and talking them through their lessons. And I couldn't do that. And so, I think the way in which my time away from work was spent, was fuelled by a degree of guilt because I wasn't doing what I felt other people were doing. Because I was trying to be 100% here and 100% there (PGA 3).

Others spoke about how, because of stress and tiredness, they would often "get snappy with the kids and wife" (PGA 38). Perhaps one of the more extreme examples of how work life had bled into home life was provided by one participant who said how they would "sit on a toilet in the evening and do emails on [their] smartphone" (PGA 31) in an attempt to try and create more time for their son. This allowed them to "chisel out bits of time" (PGA 31) to protect their family life.

**A macho culture**

On top of an excessive workload and little time in which individuals could properly switch off, some participants also spoke about the additional pressures of having to fit in with a macho culture "that doesn't want to accept that we suffer from stress or anxiety" (PGA 46). Another, who had worked for the prison service for 24 years, spoke of "toxic masculinity . . . that's just the culture" (PGA 37). Fitting in with this culture had meant that despite the stress and trauma that prison officers experience across all grades, Governors were expected to deal with such issues alone:

You have to say you're alright. You see somebody or you cut somebody down from hanging or slitting their wrists and somebody will ask if you're alright because that's process and then, you know, this male dominated environment you go, 'yes, I'm alright.' And then . . . you go home, and you struggle at home. So, we're not good. We're not good at coming forward and talking about our issues (PGA 40).

One Governor explained how their "manner of dealing with it is a classic sort of male approach . . . An issue goes in a box . . . and it gets put in that cupboard" (PGA 36). This was also echoed by other participants who explained how "we all have to come to work and pretend we're made of Teflon" (PGA 3) and how "especially being in the prison service, you have to have armour" (PGA 49). Dealing with such trauma in this way is, however, problematic, "Unfortunately, sometimes the lid comes off the box. And eventually it's inevitable that lids will come off most of the boxes . . . the lids have been rattling quite a lot over the last year (PGA 36).

Going against this culture, for some, was not an option, with one Governor explaining how if they "were to open up and say something, you could potentially affect your reputation, or your career, or your progression" (PGA 17). Another stated how they had "spoken out, I'd taken the big step to kind of ask [for help] and then in the end got punished for it" (PGA 43). The expectation was rather a dog-eat-dog world where it is "almost understood that you will potentially stand on people on the way up" (PGA 36). This competitiveness was also emphasised by another participant who explained how "the relationships from the top downwards can be quite bullying, vicious, controlling, as well as all the positive stuff" (PGA 2). This left most officers feeling that they were forced to put on their "big girl pants" (PGA 12) and "just get on with it" (PGA 26).

### Not feeling valued

It is unsurprising that such experiences have led to many Governors feeling undervalued. One described themselves as "just a cog in a machine . . . [where] you'll just be replaced tomorrow by somebody else" (PGA 40), with this echoed by another who viewed themselves as "a five-digit number on a spreadsheet" and therefore as "disposable as the food containers from last night's food" (PGA 43). Others felt undervalued more specifically with reference to the colossal efforts that had been invested to cope with the Covid-19 pandemic, with one explaining how they had "cancelled leave as we were encouraged to be in work more often and again without being thanked" (PGA 38). Others explained how any appreciation they did feel came not from their employers, but from external sources:

Every prisoner was getting these comfort packs. Why couldn't they have just put a little bit of something in there for the staff? . . . just send a little bit of something for them. I do know, for example, when it came to Easter, we got given easter eggs, but they were donated by Mars and Cadbury's (PGA 11).

This has led, for some, to a path of disenchantment with some thinking of leaving the Service in the near future. This shift in thinking was illustrated by many with examples including, "I have got to a place where enough is

enough, and you're not taking any more, whereas before I would just keep giving, giving, giving. But now, no, because there's nothing coming back" (PGA 4) and "When I started the job, I was proud. Proud of the service. Now, I wouldn't recommend the job to anybody" (PGA 40). Another summed up the situation perfectly: I've seen it, I have dealt with death, I have knocked on people's doors to say that their son, their husband, has died. I've done all that. I've been covered in blood. I've seen people hanging. I've seen people covered in shite. I've been spat at. I've had all that and it doesn't matter. But I'm probably now at a stage where I can see where we are, and the service takes that for granted. And I'm not asking for a big golden hello or goodbye, all I'm asking for is to be treated with fairness and decency (PGA 49).

### Conclusion

While this article only presents a fraction of our findings, hopefully it has shared enough to illustrate that, overall, the health and wellbeing of prison governors and operational managers is not good. Similarly to findings found with prison officers in the UK, stress levels are high, workloads are excessive, downtime is insufficient, and due to the macho culture of the working environment, people feel unable to ask for support. While in the past the decency agenda only applied to prisoners, we argue that it should now extend to include all those who live and work within prison establishments. To return to one of the opening quotes, prison staff of all grades deserve to work in an environment "where there is dignity, an absence of fear, and where there is a sense of self-worth and self-respect" (Leech 2022:38).

Watch this 5-minute video: 'Just Get On With It'. **www.youtube.com/watch?v=lfrX3iMAtPM**

### References

Ferdik, F and Smith, H. (2017) Correctional Officer Safety and Wellness Literature Synthesis. Washington: National Institute of Justice.

Kinman, G. and Clements, A. J (2022) 'Sickness Presenteeism in Prison Officers: risk factors and implications for wellbeing and productivity', Inter J Environ Res Public Health, 19(6): 3389, doi: 10.3390/ijerph19063389.

Kinman, G., Clements, A. J. and Hart J. (2017) 'Job demands, resources and mental health in UK prison officers', Occupational Medicine, 67: 456-460.

Leech, M. (2022)

# THE PRISON ORACLE - PRISONORACLE.COM

Trusted by

    serco sodexo

# THE DEFINITIVE UK PRISONS WEBSITE GIVING YOU ALL THE PRISONS INFORMATION YOU NEED FROM THE PUBLISHER EXPERTS TRUST

| News Desk Membership | Basic Membership | Standard Membership | Enhanced Membership<br>Best Value | Corporate Membership |
|---|---|---|---|---|
| £0.99 | £4.99 | £7.99 | £9.99 | £29.99 |
| per week paid monthly | per month paid quarterly | per month paid quarterly | per month paid quarterly | per month paid annually |

## LESS THAN THE COST OF A CUP OF COFFEE A WEEK: CANCEL ANYTIME!

**The Prison Oracle:**
*I'm impressed at how comprehensive it is.*
An excellent collection of Data and Information, I'm impressed at how comprehensive it is. A bonus is access to Reports like Woolf, Woodcock, May, Learmont and others before the Internet and difficult to otherwise access. The data is user-friendly, useful for research and easy to use with access to data on the Prison Population, Safety in Custody, and Workforce Statistics easier to access and use than on the Government's own website. A very helpful, comprehensive, user friendly source of information on prison issues.

**Phil Wheatley, CB.**
Former Director General: HM.
Prison Service and NOMS

**The Prison Oracle:**
*'The' Go-To Place for Everything Prison Related.*
The sheer depth of available information, coupled with a simple user interface, makes The Prison Oracle *'the'* go-to place for everything that is in any way prison related. There's a vast array of publications, alongside historic reports that you simply can't find anywhere else online.
Having such a wealth of data at your fingertips, without the need to trawl the internet for hours, is exactly why I subscribed. The Prison Oracle is a tangible learning resource for anyone with an interest in the justice section; I urge you to take a look for yourself.

**Richard Rowley**
Managing Director: Census Life

**The Prison Oracle:**
*An excellent collection of information, data and reports*
The Prison Oracle, with everything about prisons all in one place, has long been needed and I'm delighted it's finally arrived – I 've subscribed and it's such an excellent collection of information, data and reports for practitioners, justice professionals or anyone with an interest in justice issues or reform, I've no hesitation in recommending The Prison Oracle to all my Correctional Services colleagues. An added advantage is the simple access to reports that shaped the modern Prison Service – Woodcock, Woolf, Learmont, May, Carter, and Corston.

**Tony Hassall**
Commissioner: Corrective Services Western Australia

# Section 6

## Reports

6.1 Introduction to the Prisons Inspectorate

6.2.1 HM Prison & Probation Service Annual Report 2021/2022 (unpublished September 2022)

6.2.2 Prison & Probation Ombudsman's Annual Report 2021/22

6.2.3 HM Chief Inspector of Prisons Annual Report 2021/22

6.2.4 Parole Board For England & Wales Annual Report 2021/22

6.2.5 Criminal Justice Joint Inspection - The impact of the Covid-19 pandemic

6.2.6 Criminal Justice Joint Inspection - Individuals with mental health needs & disorders

## 6.1 INTRODUCTION TO THE PRISONS INSPECTORATE

For general enquiries email:
hmiprisons.enquiries@hmiprisons.gov.uk

Contact details:
HM Inspectorate of Prisons
3rd floor, 10 South Colonnade
Canary Wharf, London, E14 4PU
Tel: 020 7340 0500
Media enquiries: 020 7340 0500 / 07973 755397

What we do

HM Inspectorate of Prisons for England and Wales (HMI Prisons) is an independent inspectorate led by HM Chief Inspector of Prisons. We provide independent scrutiny of the conditions for and treatment of prisoners and other detainees and report on our findings.

We inspect prisons, young offender institutions (YOIs), secure training centres (STCs), immigration removal centres (IRCs), court custody suites and military detention.

Our inspections are guided by the idea of 'healthy establishments', in which staff support prisoners and detainees to reduce reoffending and achieve positive outcomes for themselves and the public. In our reports, we include recommendations on how establishments can improve outcomes for prisoners.

Our work forms part of the UK's obligations under the Optional Protocol to the United Nations Convention against Torture (OPCAT). OPCAT requires member states to regularly and independently inspect places of detention. We also work with other criminal justice inspectorates.

HMIP Staff 2022-2023
Chief Inspector of Prisons
Charlie Taylor
Deputy Chief Inspector of Prisons
Martin Lomas
Terms of Reference
https://www.justiceinspectorates.gov.uk/hmiprisons/about-hmi-prisons/terms-of-reference/

About our inspections

Prisons are inspected at least once every five years, although we expect to inspect most establishments every two to three years. Some high-risk establishments may be inspected more frequently, including those holding children and young people. Other types of custodial sectors have different inspection cycles. The inspection of facilities is predicated on a dynamic risk assessment, taking into account issues such as time since the last inspection, type and size of establishment, significant changes to the establishment or changes in leadership, and intelligence received.

The vast majority of inspections are full and unannounced, assessing progress made since previous inspections and undertaking in-depth analysis.

In exceptional circumstances, and on the basis of risk, some inspections will be announced and the prison will be informed in advance of the visit. On our unannounced inspections, the inspection team visits without notifying the establishment in advance. On all inspections, inspectors have the right to carry out inspections and cannot be refused entry by the establishment.

Covid-19

In March 2020, HMI Prisons' planned inspection schedule was suspended due to the COVID-19 pandemic. During 2020 and spring 2021, we conducted short scrutiny visits and scrutiny visits. These visits, which operated under the 'do no harm' principle, allowed HMI Prisons to fulfil its statutory duty to report on treatment of and conditions for prisoners and detainees, while making sure that the health of prisoners and detainees, establishment staff and HMI Prisons staff was not compromised.

In light of the falling number of COVID-19 infections both in the community and in prisons, and with a large proportion of the population now being vaccinated, we have decided to return to full inspections.

Full inspections will normally be carried out over two weeks, with a two-day visit by four or five members of HMI Prisons' staff to carry out a detainee survey in week one. This will be followed by a five-day visit by approximately 10 HMI Prisons and partner inspectorate staff the following week.

All full inspections will be undertaken on the basis of risk and following robust health and safety protocols.

Inspections of court custody facilities were suspended in March 2020, in line with other types of establishments. In September 2020, we returned to full inspection of court custody facilities, following a bespoke methodology and health and safety guidance.

**About our inspections**

Prisons are inspected at least once every five years, although we expect to inspect most establishments every two to three years. Some high-risk establishments may be inspected more frequently, including those holding children and young people. Other types of custodial sectors have different inspection cycles. The inspection of facilities is predicated on a dynamic risk assessment, taking into account issues such as time since the last inspection, type and size of establishment, significant changes to the establishment or changes in leadership, and intelligence received.

The vast majority of inspections are full and unannounced, assessing progress made since previous inspections and undertaking in-depth analysis.

In exceptional circumstances, and on the basis of risk, some inspections will be announced and the prison will be informed in advance of the visit. On our unannounced inspections, the inspection team visits without notifying the establishment in advance. On all inspections, inspectors have the right to carry out inspections and cannot be refused entry by the establishment.

*The establishments that we inspect are:*
Prisons
Young offender institutions
Secure training centres
Immigration removal centres
Short-term holding facilities
Military detention
Court custody

**Prisons**

Inspections of prisons, young offender institutions holding young adults (those aged 18 to 21), and specialist units take place at least every five years, but usually more frequently, and on a risk-assessed basis.

The majority of inspections are unannounced and are scheduled proportionate to risk. Inspectors undertake in-depth analysis of the four 'healthy prison' areas: safety, respect, purposeful activity and rehabilitation and release planning, as well as following up recommendations from previous inspections.

Some inspections are announced and the prison is informed in advance of the visit.

Prison inspections normally span two weeks, with two days of preparation and research during the first week. The Inspectorate collects information from many sources, including the people who work there, those who are imprisoned or detained there, and visitors or others with an interest in the establishment. Inspection findings are reported back to the establishment's managers.

**Young offender institutions**

Some of these are juvenile establishments that hold children under the age of 18. Other establishments hold young adults over the age of 18. Juvenile establishments are inspected annually.

**Secure training centres**

These are purpose-built establishments that hold young offenders up to the age of 17. Secure training centres are inspected every year. Ofsted lead these inspections, accompanied by HMI Prisons inspectors.

**Immigration removal centres**

Immigration removal centres (IRCs) hold foreign nationals who do not have a legal right to remain in the United Kingdom but decline to leave.

Every IRC will be inspected at least once every four years, on a risk-assessed basis. If the centre holds children they are inspected more frequently.

**Escort inspections**

Escorts are usually chartered flights which escort immigration detainees who are being removed from the United Kingdom to their countries of origin. The Inspectorate conducts two to three escort inspections every year.

**Short-term holding facilities**

Short-term holding facilities hold people waiting to be removed to an immigration removal centre or awaiting deportation. Non-residential short-term holding facilities are inspected at least once every six years. Residential short-term holding facilities are inspected at least once every four years. Inspections are scheduled on a risk-assessed basis.

**Military detention**

At the request of the Ministry of Defence, we inspect service custody facilities. These custody facilities are cells where Navy, Air Force and Army police hold military personnel who have been arrested.

Military facility inspections are conducted every two to three years by agreement and invitation from the military.

## Court custody

Court cells detain people who are awaiting trial or sentence. The Inspectorate undertakes three court custody inspections a year. Inspectors visit all courts containing cells within the region they are inspecting.

All reports are published within 14 weeks of inspection. The establishment is then expected to produce an action plan, based on the report's recommendations, within a short period following publication. For more information see our Inspection Framework.

## Reporting inspection findings
### From recommendations to concerns

From 3 May 2022, HMI Prisons will report up to 15 key concerns following inspection, rather than the 30–35 recommendations previously reported. Of those 15 key concerns, three to six will be identified as priorities. The change aims to encourage leaders to act on inspection reports in a way which generates real improvements in outcomes for those detained.

The change applies to prison, young offender institution and court custody reports. Piloting and consultation for immigration detention settings is ongoing.

HM Chief Inspector of Prisons, Charlie Taylor said: "I am very pleased to introduce this change which encourages leaders to focus on the issues most likely to lead to improvements in conditions for and the treatment of prisoners and detainees. The Inspectorate will continue to expect clear and effective plans to be developed and implemented following an inspection. We hope that this, together with our focus on leadership, will lead to real, sustained change in prisons and custody."

## Consultation process and changes

The change was introduced following a consultation process during which HMI Prisons discussed the proposed approach with around 400 individuals from five groups:
- *inspectors and other inspectorates*
- *inspected bodies*
- *contract managers*
- *the voluntary sector*
- *academics and other interested parties*

A range of feedback was provided. Inspectors, other inspectorates and those from inspected bodies said that the approach of reporting 30 or more recommendations made it difficult to decide which to prioritise. They were largely in favour of the proposed change, provided that an action plan would continue to be required and HMI Prisons would still measure progress in addressing concerns at a subsequent independent review of progress or inspection.

The contract managers we spoke to were generally positive but were concerned that the loss of recommendations could reduce their ability to hold establishments to account for poor performance. HMI Prisons was able to share examples of the way that concerns would be reported as part of the consultation which, in most cases, allayed this concern.

The feedback from the remaining groups was more mixed. Most respondents were positive, but others wanted us to use stronger language to report inspection findings. They wanted it to be more apparent that we expect a response to our concerns.

Most positive feedback focused on the limited impact of our current approach and the need to give local managers the responsibility for rectifying concerns. Respondents were generally positive about limiting the number of issues that we raise as concerns.

In response to the feedback, we changed the way that we will present our concerns in our inspection reports. We made several changes to the section of the report which details our priority and key concerns, including moving this section to the start of our reports, immediately following the Chief Inspector's introduction, to increase its prominence. We also changed the name of the section to 'What needs to improve at [name of the establishment]' to make clear that our concerns need to be addressed, and amended the introductory text of the section to state that priorities need to be addressed first and that an action plan should be produced and sent to HMI Prisons.

We thank all those who took the time to participate in the consultation for their contributions. An evaluation of the impact of this change will be carried out in 2023.

## 6.2 ANNUAL REPORTS

Below we provide the online address from which can be downloaded the most recent Annual Reports when they are published and, for serving prisoners who, of course, do not have internet access, we have provided a template letter (below) by which they can request a copy of the respective Annual Report under the Freedom of Information Act and a postal address from which they can request it.

**PRISONERS' TEMPLATE LETTER**

Dear Sir,

**Freedom of Information Act request.**

I am currently a serving prisoner. I do not have internet access and therefore information that would otherwise be readily available to me by the internet is not something I have any access to at all. I therefore write pursuant to the Freedom of Information Act to request that a copy of the following document(s) be sent to me by post at the following address:

*[Insert the name and address of the prison here].*

**Request:**
Can I please have a copy of:
[Here insert name the document(s) you are requesting, it is important to be specific - for example
*1. A copy of the HM Prison and Probation Service Annual Report and Accounts 2021/2022"*

Yours sincerely,
*[Insert your name and prison number]*

## 6.2.1 HIS MAJESTY'S PRISON AND PROBATION SERVICE (HMPPS) ANNUAL REPORT AND ACCOUNTS

The HMPPS 2021/2022 annual report had not been published as we went to press in September 2022 - when published it will appear here:
**https://www.gov.uk/government/organisations/ her-majestys-prison-and-probation-service**

**For Serving prisoners:** Send your written request for a copy to:
**Ministry of Justice, Disclosure team, Postal Point 10.25, Floor 10. 102 Petty France London SW1H 9AJ**

## 6.2.2. PRISONS AND PROBATION OMBUDSMAN'S ANNUAL REPORT 2021/2022

**For the Public:** You can download the 2020/2021 Annual Report from:
**https://www.ppo.gov.uk/document/annual-reports/**

**For Serving prisoners:** Send your written request to:
**Freedom of Information Team Prisons and Probation Ombudsman, Third Floor, 10 South Colonnade, London E14 4PU**

## 6.2.3 HIS MAJESTY'S CHIEF INSPECTOR OF PRISONS FOR ENGLAND AND WALES: ANNUAL REPORT 2021/2022

'We have been struck by the long hours which many inmates have to spend locked in their cells in boredom. In several local prisons a proportion of the population, including unconvicted prisoners, were locked up for twenty-two hours or more each day, for weeks on end. In some training prisons, where a full working day was intended to be central to the life of the establishment, we found some of the population without any work and others employed on work which was unsatisfactory in nature or which was insufficient to support the number of prisoners allocated to it. We believe there are powerful reasons why Prison Department must ensure that an inmate does not spend day after day in blank inactivity; he should be kept occupied for a normal working day at work, education, or some other constructive activity.'

It is 40 years since this passage was published in the first annual report from HM Chief Inspector of Prisons and it remains as relevant now as it did in 1982. Each of my six predecessors has found a new form of words to describe this seemingly intractable problem.

In many of the prisons we visited since we resumed full inspections in May 2021, prisoners were locked up for even longer than they were in 1982: some for 23 hours a day or more. In category C training prisons, in spite of their remit, the situation was often little better, with prisoners spending their time sleeping or watching daytime television rather than engaged in the work, education or training that would help them to resettle successfully in the community on release. For many prisoners during COVID-19, the only available work was the desultory wiping down of wings with a damp cloth or leaning on a mop.

Throughout the year prisoners told us that their mental health was suffering, with 51% of men and 76% of women saying they had mental health difficulties. We do not yet know what the longer-term effect of lockdowns will be on prisoners, but there is no doubt that there will be a price to pay for the loss of family visits, the limited chance to socialise with other prisoners, the lack of education, training or work, the curtailing of rehabilitative programmes, the cancellation of group therapy and the dearth of opportunities for release on temporary licence (ROTL). In the last year, more prisoners than ever before will have left custody after spending almost their entire sentence locked in their cells – blank inactivity indeed.

Some of the most disheartening inspections were at prisons with large proportions of young men, where the, often extensive, grounds and workshops remained mostly empty and just a handful of prisoners were receiving any face-to-face teaching. The failure to fill the gaps in the skills and education of these prisoners and the low expectations of their abilities and potential meant they were learning to survive in prison rather being taught how to succeed when they were released. Unless these men are given the support that they need, there is the potential that they will lead long lives of criminality – creating victims, disrupting their communities and placing a huge burden on the state.

The lack of purposeful activity could, in part, be put down to the COVID-19 pandemic that continued to affect prisons across the country, particularly during the winter months where the arrival of the Omicron variant meant that all prisons were returned to stage 3 of the COVID-19 National Framework for Prison Regimes and Services. However, inspectors saw an increasingly wide variation in how individual prisons were interpreting guidance from both the prison service and Public Health England. There appeared to be no good reason why most prisoners at one category C training prison should have been locked up for 22 hours a day, while two-thirds of those at a category B local jail were out of their cells for five hours a day during the week.

There were similar differences in the youth estate. At two young offender institutions (YOIs) we found children had recently been allowed out of their rooms for up to six hours, while at another, where we conducted a scrutiny visit earlier in the year, children were unlocked for 10 hours a day. Similarly, at the two public sector YOIs, classroom education had only recently returned, while at Parc it had carried on throughout almost all of the pandemic. This was despite the historically low numbers in the youth prison population.

Restrictions often remained in place in prisons even where infection levels were low and many of the most vulnerable prisoners had been vaccinated. Overall there was not enough ambition from some governors or the prison service to restart activity. Those who wanted to move more quickly to get prisoners back into education were often hampered by the apparent reluctance of some providers to come back into prisons and begin face-to-face education. As time went on and restrictions began to lift, it was reasonable to expect prisons to be able to deliver more in this area. Yet, in conjunction with colleagues from Ofsted, we found a depressing picture of poor outcomes for prisoners and low purposeful activity scores.

The shocking findings of our joint thematic report with Ofsted into the teaching of reading were particularly depressing and demonstrated the lack of ambition for prison education. Inspectors found that that assessment of prisoners was inadequate, that teachers did not know how to teach prisoners to read, and that information was not being shared between prisons when prisoners moved. The teaching of reading was largely being left to Shannon Trust mentors, but this relied on prisoners being unlocked and suitable space found for the programme to continue. It is an astonishing failing that people can leave prison unable to read any more fluently than when they went in. The prison service must take urgent action to respond to our findings.

Too often we saw prisons fail to motivate prisoners to behave well. Those on the highest tier of incentives schemes frequently complained that they did not receive the rewards they had earned. For example, extra gym sessions for prisoners on an enhanced regime were cancelled because officers had been cross-deployed to other work. Some prison staff seemed to have forgotten one of the basic lessons of behaviour management – that giving a sought-after reward for good behaviour is a powerful way to motivate people. I have lost count of the number of times prisoners have told me that those who throw their weight around and make the most noise get what they want, while those who behave are ignored.

Similarly, if prisoners see that their peers are not sanctioned for poor behaviour, they understandably wonder why they themselves should be compliant. Yet we found widespread inconsistency in the way that rules were applied. There is no better way to undermine officers' legitimacy or erode standards than allowing people to be seen actively breaking the rules. If a rule matters, it should be enforced; if it does not, it should be abolished. Inconsistency is the enemy of a successful behaviour management system.

Perhaps the biggest challenge facing the prison service is recruiting enough staff and stemming the flow of resignations that have, in some jails, become a flood. As the economy began to open up after the lockdowns of 2020 and 2021, employment opportunities and wages grew, and prisons in more economically buoyant parts of the country found the pipeline of new officers drying up and increasing numbers leaving the service. This led to inexperienced officers supervising new recruits and meant that in jails with long-serving populations, prisoners knew much more about prison life than staff. Prison officers often told inspectors that their work had become monotonous and unfulfilling, consisting largely of unlocking doors and chivvying small numbers of prisoners into the exercise yard, the showers, the servery and then back into their cells, before opening up the next group. They said that under this constant pressure to maintain multiple regimes on one wing, relationships had become distant and transactional. They were not able to engage with prisoners or offer them the personal support that they needed. Many assaults on staff were precipitated by prisoners' frustration with not being able to complete daily tasks.

In some prisons, far too many officers leave within the first year, which suggests that in its haste to fill vacancies, HM Prison and Probation Service is not doing enough to filter out unsuitable candidates or make sure new recruits understand what the role entails. One governor told me that a new officer explained, as she handed in her notice, that her application form had been filled in by her mother.

### Concerns for the well-being of women increase

We inspected five women's prisons using new Expectations that put greater focus on support for women, who are often themselves victims of exploitation and crime and may be suffering the effects of traumatic events in their lives. A large proportion of women experience poor mental health, and the pandemic restrictions were particularly difficult for this group. When we inspected one women's prison in May 2021, prisoners were still not allowed physical contact with their children. One woman told me she had taken the impossible decision not to see her son because she was unable to hug him. Thankfully this restriction on physical contact was lifted soon afterwards, but it clearly made it even more difficult to try to maintain normal family contact in an environment that already puts a strain on relationships.

We were very concerned to see acutely mentally unwell women being sent to prison due to a lack of community provision. We found profoundly distressed women in the health centre at Low Newton, where staff were doing their best to look after patients who should have been in hospital. In October 2021 I wrote to the Minister of State to advise her of this situation, noting my concerns that prison was not a suitable place of safety, and recommending that the prison service should begin to monitor the number of women entering custody through this route as a first step towards making sure that there was better provision in the community.

During the year, we published a short paper that highlighted some of the challenges we saw in women's prisons. Most concerning was the issuing of our lowest grade for safety at Foston Hall, where levels of self-harm were the highest in the women's estate and over 1,000 calls were being made to the Samaritans each month. However, restrictions in the women's prisons we inspected were less severe than in the men's estate and we were pleased to see a return to some pre-pandemic activity.

Finding suitable accommodation for women leaving prison remains a huge challenge, and the data produced by the Ministry of Justice seems to present a much more positive picture than we have seen on the ground. Resettlement planning was further hindered by the unification of the probation service, which had created uncertainty about future provision of resettlement services.

### Children let down

Both of our joint inspections of secure training centres (STCs) with Ofsted resulted in Urgent Notifications being sent to the Secretary of State. At Rainsbrook, this was the second time we applied the process within a year, after the Youth Custody Service and the STC failed to make adequate progress. At both Rainsbrook and Oakhill, levels of violence were far too high, while expectations of children's behaviour were much too low, with insufficient boundaries. Leaders had failed to make sure that basic safeguarding processes were in place and staff were demoralised and often ineffectual. Both centres were suffering from difficulties with staffing levels: poorly led, inexperienced staff were leaving because the working environment was so challenging.

After the Urgent Notifications were issued, the Youth Custody Service removed all children from Rainsbrook and ended the contract with the provider. Meanwhile, a monitoring visit of Oakhill in January 2022 showed that there had been some progress in stabilising the centre. Girls from Rainsbrook who were refused placement in a secure children's home were transferred to

Wetherby YOI, which opened a new female unit. Although this arrangement was not ideal, when we inspected Wetherby we found that the prison had put in place suitable provision and the girls told us they were getting better care in the YOI than they had done at the STC.

Wetherby generally remained a safer place than in recent years, but the Keppel unit, designed for the most vulnerable children, had lost its way and was operating as little more than another wing of the YOI. We found a much more worrying picture at Cookham Wood YOI, with very high levels of violence between the boys and towards staff. The YOI was failing to keep cells well maintained, clean and free of graffiti, despite having some of the newest accommodation in the youth estate.

### Haphazard immigration arrangements on the south coast

The number of detainees in immigration detention began to rise throughout the year. Our scrutiny visit to one immigration removal centre (IRC) and full inspection of another showed that the centres were doing a reasonable job in providing for detainees, although some bleak, prison-like buildings did not contribute to a positive environment. The disengagement from Home Office staff both in IRCs and in prisons with high numbers of foreign national offenders meant that detainees spent longer in custody than needed, and were left anxious and uncertain about the future. Those who had been assessed as needing community support for mental health difficulties continued to be kept in custody.

I remain very concerned about the haphazard arrangements in place for those who have crossed the Channel in small boats. Promised facilities in Dover had not materialised when we inspected in November 2021, and we found that some families were sleeping on the floor in flimsy tents with inadequate bedding or crammed into facilities where some basic safeguards were not in place. With the recent increases in small boat arrivals, we have seen insufficient preparation to provide for vulnerable adults and children. Given the difficulties in maintaining adequate provision for new arrivals, we will be looking to see significant improvements at the new facility at MOD Manston.

### A mixed picture in court custody

Our inspections of court custody this year reported on dirty cells that frequently contained graffiti and possible ligature points. The care by individual staff in court custody continued to be impressive where, in a busy and often bleak subterranean environment, they did their best to make sure detainees got the help they needed. Many staff members had some understanding of basic safeguarding for the most vulnerable detainees, but we were concerned that services were inadequate for detainees who did not speak English.

The new Prisoner Escort Custody Services contract meant that children were brought to and from court in much more suitable vehicles – a significant improvement. Staff shortages in London, however, meant that children in court custody did not get the attention and support they required. Too many women were still being transferred from court in cellular vehicles with men.

### Looking to next year – the importance of leadership and ambition

The pandemic has led to a reduction in governor autonomy and some of the most ambitious leaders have been frustrated by the restrictions they face. Effective leaders have managed to make progress despite the many difficulties that the pandemic has caused. The high turnover of governors in public sector prisons has had the effect of stalling some of the more profound, necessary cultural change. The challenge for the prison service is to make sure that it identifies talent and promotes the most capable to leadership positions.

Since I came into post in November 2020, there has been much talk within the prison service of new regimes that will build on the learning from the pandemic. Although it is not yet clear what these will entail, there is the suggestion that prisoners may continue to be unlocked in smaller groups, with the aim of maintaining the reduced levels of violence that occurred during the pandemic. The risk is that prisoners will continue to remain behind their doors for much longer than in the past.

A look at the data over the last 20 years shows that more time spent behind a cell door does not actually result in lower levels of violence. For the first decade of the century, prisoners were unlocked for much longer than they are now, yet levels of violence were substantially lower. Although the rate of assaults fell by 37% to 239 incidents per 1,000 prisons in the 12 months to March 2021, the effect of lockdown on reducing violence should not be overstated as this was still a far higher rate than a decade ago.

The welcome lifting of all national prison restrictions on 9 May 2022 means that there is now no reason why prisons cannot return to regimes at least as open as they were before the pandemic. There is the chance to reset after a difficult two years. If prisons are to be an essential component of a successful justice system that is trusted by the public to keep them safe, the ambition must also be to go further, making sure that governors and education providers create opportunities for prisoners to develop vital skills that they can use when they return to the community. A new drive to increase release on temporary licence is essential, so that prisoners have the chance to experience a more normal working life that will help them to resettle successfully on release.

In a year's time, it would be refreshing not to have to repeat the Chief Inspector's stark words from 1982.

*Acknowledgements*

I would like to pay tribute to the staff of HM Inspectorate of Prisons who have continued to work with such dedication and professionalism over the last year. I also want to acknowledge the work of governors, directors, officers and other prison, immigration removal centre, custody and third sector staff who have continued to keep the service going in spite of the difficulties caused by COVID-19.

**Charlie Taylor**
**Chief Inspector of Prisons**

**For the Public:** You can download the 2020/2021 Annual Report from:

**https://assets.publishing.service.gov.uk/govern ment/uploads/system/uploads/attachment_data /file/1089500/hmip-annual-report-2021-22.pdf**

**For Serving prisoners:** Send your written request for a copy to:

**Freedom of Information Team**
**Prisons Inspectorate,**
**Third Floor, 10 South Colonnade,**
**Canary Wharf, London E14 4PU**

## 6.2.4 PAROLE BOARD FOR ENGLAND & WALES ANNUAL REPORT 2021/2022

### Chair & CEO foreword
*Statement*

The Parole Board faced another challenging year as the continuation of COVID-19 was felt throughout much of 2021/22. Despite this, the Parole Board has fully embedded remote hearings into its work, with the vast majority of cases continuing to be heard via video or telephone. Of course, where required, a small number of cases were heard face-to-face inside prisons. The decision on whether or not a case is heard remotely or face-to-face is based purely on the needs of the case.

Regardless of the method of hearing, cases continued to move through the system effectively without any significant backlog emerging. The Parole Board would like to record its thanks to HM Prison Service for its rapid improvements in its virtual hearing capacity, to ensure cases continued to be heard.

Crucially, despite changes to its operating model, the Board's release rate has remained stable at roughly 25%. That is around 1 in 4 prisoners reviewed by the Parole Board meet the test for release, which is set by Parliament. The Parole Board has maintained its strong record on public protection, which is and always will be its top priority. During 2021/22, fewer than 0.5% of prisoners released by the Parole Board were charged with a Serious Further Offence (SFO).

This compares favourably with other parole jurisdictions around the world; however, each SFO is one tragedy too many and each case is thoroughly reviewed to ensure that any changes or improvements needed are actioned properly and speedily.

By the end of the reporting year:
*8,834 oral hearings were conducted*
*6,336 oral hearings were concluded*
*2,353 prisoners were refused release at oral hearing*
*3,434 prisoners were directed for release at oral hearing*
*556 prisoners were recommended for open at oral hearing*
*9,054 prisoners were refused release at the MCA review*
*705 prisoners were released at the MCA review*
*12 prisoners were recommended for open at the MCA stage*
*In total 11,407 prisoners were refused release and 4,139 prisoners were released.*

The Board also carried out a huge amount of other important work:
*22 more panel chairs trained and accredited*
*19 new members recruited*
*Extensive member training has continued to be delivered including vital further training around handling Terrorist Act cases*
*Several pieces of updated guidance have been issued including; transgender prisoners, restorative justice, licence conditions, interventions and specialist reports*
*Number of summaries issued this financial year is 1,706*
*Number of reconsideration decisions received in 2021/22 is 262. 69 were ineligible and 195 were eligible. 39 were granted and 156 refused*
*The Parole Board has continued to contribute and provide input to the Root and Branch Review of the parole system.*

Finally, the Parole Board would like to record its thanks to its members and staff. 2021/22 has not been an easy year and everybody has responded to the challenges in an exemplary fashion. The Board also thanks member Simon Ash for his contribution on the Management Committee (MC) before stepping down from the role in 2021, and welcomes members Maneer Afsar and Cassie Williams as well as Non-Executive Director Julie Dent on to MC.

*Caroline Corby, Chair of the Parole Board*
*Martin Jones CBE, CEO of the Parole Board*
*Date 12 July 2022*

## Headlines from 2021/22
### i) Root and Branch Review
The Parole Board saw the publication of the Ministry of Justice's Root and Branch Review of the parole system in March 2022. Legislative change is required for some of the proposals in the Root and Branch Review, which will, of course, require careful scrutiny in Parliament. The Board is committed to working closely with colleagues in the Ministry to ensure they are supported with all the data and information they require.

### ii) Transparency
Transparency is one of the Parole Board's key priorities and one which it has taken significant strides in improving in recent years. There is still work to be done in this area and openness and transparency continues to be embedded across all aspects of the Parole Board's work. Transparency around process and decision making is absolutely key and, as such, this year, 1,706 summaries of its decisions were issued, primarily to victims but also to the media and members of the public. The Parole Board welcomes proposals to go even further and as per the direction of the Root and Branch Review, the Parole Board is committed to facilitating public hearings in the few cases where this is requested and would be in the interests of justice. The Board is also working with the Ministry of Justice (MoJ) in an effort to progress plans to improve victim access to its hearings, provided there are appropriate support systems in place to avoid retraumatising victims. There is no doubt it is crucial for public confidence that the parole system is as open as possible.

### iii) Remote hearings
The Parole Board continues to hold the majority of its hearings via video-link, and to a lesser extent telephone. The Board conducted 75% of all oral hearings via video-link, 22% were telephone hearings, 2% hybrid hearings and just 1% face-to face hearings. As the effects of COVID-19 on accessing prisons has lessened, a growing number of cases have been heard inside prisons, although in relatively small numbers as we have found our new virtual ways of working to be safe and effective.

### iv) Dealing with terrorist cases
Ensuring the Parole Board is able to deal effectively and fairly with those convicted of terrorism offences goes right to the heart of its role in protecting the public. Following the Terrorist Offenders (Restriction of Early Release) Act 2020, the Parole Board has ensured that increased numbers of members are specially trained and ready to deal with these cases. This experienced cohort of members go through intensive ongoing training specific to terrorist cases and is made up of members from backgrounds such as former and serving judges, chief constables, prison governors, prosecutors, psychologists and psychiatrists. The Parole Board has also forged strong links with other agencies across the criminal justice system to ensure that decisions are informed by the fullest available information on risk.

### v) Member recruitment
The Parole Board recently recruited 19 new specialist members to work specifically on Terrorist Act cases. Due to the critical public protection nature of these cases, the Board saw fit to bolster its expertise in this area and we now have around 70 members out of a total of 346 handling such cases. The Parole Board envisages a further recruitment drive for independent members in the coming year including members with a law enforcement background.

### vi) Member training
There is an established programme of required learning for members in place which includes topics such as effective questioning, terrorism, extremism and radicalisation. In addition, separate training is given on unconscious bias and panel chair training.

### vii) Guidance updates
The Parole Board continues to progress its Guidance Project, updating and bringing together all of its published guidance for panel members in one place. The Board would like to extend its gratitude to members who have supported and continue to support the development of the various pieces of guidance whether by drafting sections or peer reviewing. Amongst our published work, there is guidance on Representation, Prisoners who are Transgender and Restorative Justice, Member Case Assessment (MCA), Licence Conditions, Interventions, Specialist Reports, Risk Assessments, Children, Young Adults and Mental Capacity & Litigation Friends

## 6.2.5 CRIMINAL JUSTICE JOINT INSPECTION - THE IMPACT OF THE COVID-19 PANDEMIC

*The impact of the Covid-19 pandemic on the criminal justice system – a progress report, May 2022*

The Covid-19 pandemic and high infection rates continue to have a major impact across the criminal justice system (CJS) in England and Wales. Last year, we reported on the many changes that had been introduced in a short space of time to comply with new laws/restrictions and to protect the health of individuals.

The impact of the pandemic on the criminal justice system, as with other aspects of public and private life, was unprecedented. However, now that restrictions have eased, some parts of the CJS are not responding quickly enough to reverse changes or restore performance to pre-pandemic levels. Throughout the pandemic, restrictions have differed between England and Wales. While the constraints on daily life have now been dropped, the CJS is a long way from recovery and in some parts continues to operate at unacceptable levels. Prisoners still spend 22.5 hours a day in their cell; hundreds of thousands of hours of unpaid work go uncompleted in the Probation Service; and Crown Court backlogs remain high. The public expects the Crown Prosecution Service (CPS), police, prisons, probation and youth offending services to work seamlessly, efficiently and effectively to prevent and respond to crime, and in so doing to protect them. We have found that justice is delayed, denied or disrupted in far too many instances.

This is against a backdrop of an increasing demand on the CJS. From 01 October 2020 to 30 September 2021, the overall crime rate increased by 14 per cent compared with two years previously. (Crime in England and Wales - Office for National Statistics (ons.gov.uk)) This was fuelled by a major increase in fraud and computer misuse, but also included the highest number of rapes and sexual offences ever recorded by the police in a 12-month period. Police forces have made good progress towards the government's ambition to recruit 20,000 new police officers by March 2023, but this will do little to address the lack of experienced detectives and digital forensic specialists that are much needed today. Workloads remain high, and the thin blue line stretched.

The Covid-19 pandemic has also exacerbated existing resource challenges in the CPS, prisons and probation services. In the CPS, staffing budgets had increased, but some Areas struggled to recruit and to cover for staff leaving or abstracted for the same reasons as affected all the criminal justice agencies, such as illness, shielding or home schooling. The work of inducting, training and mentoring new staff added to the burdens of managers and more experienced colleagues. The nationwide recruitment for prosecutors is ongoing and the CPS reports that while a small number of Areas continue to struggle to recruit, at the end of March 2022 the CPS had an overall vacancy rate for Senior Crown Prosecutors of 1.5 per cent.

Many junior barristers left the independent bar in the early days of the lockdown and have not returned, hampering the ability of the CPS to cover court hearings with external advocates. This results in the CPS having to use its own staff to deal with the significant increase in casework from rising caseloads and court backlogs, as well as covering courts that in the past would have been covered by external advocates. This is adding significant burden. In the magistrates' courts, backlogs have reduced, and some Areas, but not all, have seen live caseloads reduce back to pre-pandemic levels. The CPS published data for Q3 (October to December 2021) indicates that the magistrates' courts live caseload has dropped at an average rate of 11.5 per cent over the past year. In the last quarter receipts outnumbered case finalisations, even so overall caseloads in the magistrates' court remain about 20 per cent higher than pre-pandemic levels but geographically there are major inconsistencies.

Last year, we also reported on significant Crown Court backlogs. By the end of December 2021, 25 per cent of cases (14,612 cases) had been waiting for a year or more to come to court. (Criminal court statistics quarterly: October to December 2021 - GOV.UK)The number of cases waiting longer than a year has increased by more than 340 per cent since March 2020. (Committee of Public Accounts. (2022). Reducing the Backlog in Criminal Courts. Available at https://publications.parliament.uk/pa/cm5802/cmselect/cmpubacc/643/report.html.) When Crown Court trials get under way, the average (mean) that a case has been outstanding is 282 days. The latest CPS data shows a live Crown Court caseload some 54 per cent higher than its pre-pandemic caseload, and trial effectiveness rates are not as good as before the pandemic, meaning that many cases are adjourned - thereby increasing the overall backlogs.

The prospect of waiting years for justice is likely to be traumatising for victims and their families and has a damaging impact on justice itself, making it more likely that victims will drop out of cases. The burden on police, the CPS and court staff of the live caseloads and backlogs in the courts is immense. Ensuring, over extended periods, that cases are and stay ready for trial, that serious or complex cases and custody cases are prioritised, and that victims and witnesses are kept on board is very challenging.

Probation services have undergone a major structural change over the past year, as all services across England and Wales have been unified and are now delivered by a single, public-sector organisation. The new Probation Service has inherited issues from its predecessors, including a lack of qualified and experienced probation officers in some regions. Although the Probation Service was able to make some return to 'normal' working over the course of 2021, large numbers of court orders remain uncompleted and progress in tackling these backlogs has been disappointingly slow. Concerningly, inspectors continue to find that public protection remains the weakest area of performance and early inspections of the newly unified service have been disappointing.

Youth offending services seem to have dealt better with the pandemic, with over two-thirds of those inspected in 2021 rated as 'Good' or 'Outstanding', helped by smaller caseloads and greater flexibility over local operating models. However, while the number of children given a caution or sentence may be falling, the needs of the children coming into contact with the CJS have become more acute. The pandemic has made life even harder for these children, many of whom already have complex and multiple needs. Leaders have reported problems in accessing mental health services and in supporting children to engage with education and training.

In prison, recovery from the pandemic has been slow and inconsistent. The lengthening time it takes to dispose of cases in the Crown Court means that defendants are having to spend longer waiting for a conclusion to the proceedings against them, and for those in custody, the impact is particularly acute. Too many prisoners are still spending 22.5 hours locked up every day – in sharp contrast to the lifting of restrictions beyond the prison walls.

The lack of social contact, including with families, has had a dire effect on the wellbeing of prisoners. Long spells locked up have also limited opportunities for education, training or rehabilitation. There must be greater expectations of what can be achieved. If prisoners are successfully to rejoin the wider community when they are released, they need to be educated and trained for work, allowed to maintain contact with their families and given the support they need to address their offending behaviour by an effective and well-trained staff team.

Staff shortages in prisons and secure training centres have limited the ability of staff to deliver meaningful and constructive relationships with those they care for. In both prisons and probation services, the shortage of trained staff has hampered the delivery of rehabilitation programmes. As a result, people are leaving prison and/or finishing community sentences without addressing their offending behaviour – this is both a wasted opportunity and a failure to deliver the will of the court.

While there are still many issues as a result of the impact of the pandemic, we have seen instances where the pandemic has brought about a greater degree of strategic thinking, across agencies, about the challenges that Covid-19 presented. For example, joint recovery boards established by local criminal justice boards helped to bring local criminal justice agencies together, with a clear common purpose in the face of the pandemic. However, there does not seem to be an overarching plan for how the CJS will recover to pre-pandemic levels. Instead, each part of the system is operating in isolation and left to determine its own course. Taken together, this presents a very mixed picture.

We commend the hard work and commitment of staff delivering these services over the past two years. Their work is often unglamorous and unsung. We hope this report, and our ongoing inspections, continue to highlight areas of effective practice as well as providing senior leaders with recommendations to rebuild and restore our CJS.

## 6.2.6 CRIMINAL JUSTICE JOINT INSPECTION - INDIVIDUALS WITH MENTAL HEALTH NEEDS & DISORDERS

*A joint thematic inspection of the criminal justice journey for individuals with mental health needs and disorders, November 2021*

In 2009, the Bradley Report (Bradley, 2009) provided a comprehensive review of the experience of a person with mental health and learning disabilities in the criminal justice system (CJS). According to its author, 'failure to adequately address the mental health needs of offenders is a fundamental cause of the chronic dysfunction of our criminal justice system'. In the same year a joint criminal justice inspectorate report focusing on the services provided before sentence made five recommendations and echoed a number of the Bradley review findings. This new inspection was a significant undertaking, with input from the four criminal justice inspectorates and the healthcare inspectorates in England and Wales. It follows the progress of individuals through the CJS from first contact with the police to release from prison. Over 300 cases were reviewed in total and some 550 professionals interviewed. Penal Reform Solutions, a user engagement consultancy, interviewed 67 individuals with mental health problems who had progressed through the CJS as arrestees or convicted persons. A report of their findings is published alongside this one. Our combined work highlights some disappointing findings and makes clear that not enough progress has been made in the 12 years since the Bradley review and our last joint inspection.

There continues to be no common definition of mental health used in the CJS and this leads to individuals' needs being missed as they progress through the system. The absence of a common definition affects how cases are flagged in different agencies, with a number of individuals being missed early in the process. Information from the police to the Crown Prosecution Service about an individual's mental health needs is often not clearly communicated or transferred at all, even when it is identified. This makes timely and appropriate charging decisions more difficult and can have an impact on court proceedings. Following court, the mental health flagging system used by the probation service is not helping practitioners to fully identify the risk and level of need presented.

Strategic leaders across the CJS must make better use of the data that is available but not always systematically collected or used to inform service delivery on the ground. Incorrect interpretation of data protection regulations means that important information is not exchanged, leading to poorer assessments and poorer mental health outcomes. A Memorandum of Understanding on information-sharing needs to be agreed urgently with all partners involved in managing this journey through the CJS.

Courts face concerning delays in the timely production of psychiatric reports. There is a shortage of good-quality mental health provision and unacceptable delays in accessing services. Judges expressed frustration and concern that defendants with mental ill-health sometimes had to be remanded in prison to await an assessment or receive other support due to a lack of appropriate alternatives.

Further, and most distressingly, acutely unwell prisoners who require urgent transfer to a secure mental health inpatient hospital for treatment experience long waits in prison. Seriously mentally unwell prisoners are being held in conditions that worsen their mental health.

Mental ill-health can pose significant challenges for criminal justice agencies, particularly at the front-end. There have been some improvements since Lord Bradley's review – in particular, the roll-out of mental health liaison and diversion services in police stations and courts and a reduction in the use of police custody as a 'place of safety' for people in mental health crisis, through the use of 'section 136' beds. And we found that police officers had a good understanding that minor crime, particularly crime caused by the mental health crisis itself, could be swiftly discontinued in favour of a health care approach.

The Covid-19 pandemic has undoubtedly had a significant impact on staff and on services to support wellbeing. All inspectorates acknowledge the challenges this has created and recognise the humanity with which staff have carried out their work. Staff recognise the impact that poor mental health can have and how it can increase offending. However, in every agency, there are learning and development needs which, if addressed well, will support better mental health outcomes.

We hope that our findings, while challenging, will act as a driving force to bring about changes in practice and performance.

*Justin Russell, HM Chief Inspector of Probation*
*Dr Rosie Benneyworth BM BS BMedSci MRCGP, Chief Inspector of Primary Medical Services and Integrated Care Quality Commission*
*Andrew T. Cayley, His Majesty's Chief Inspector of the Crown Prosecution Service Inspectorate*
*Alun Jones, Interim Chief Executive Healthcare Inspectorate Wales*

Charlie Taylor,
*His Majesty's Chief Inspector of Prisons*
Wendy Williams CBE,
*His Majesty's Inspector of Constabulary*

## Executive summary

Why should the Criminal Justice System be concerned with the mental health of those passing through the system?

We know that rates of mental ill-health are high among those who pass through the CJS. Around a third of people[11] who find themselves in police custody have some form of mental health difficulty, as do 48 per cent of men and 70 per cent of women in prison.[12] Some 38 per cent of people on probation supervision are recorded as having a mental health issue.[13]

## But why does this matter?

First, because people with a mental illness need and deserve treatment. Entry into the CJS can provide a second chance for people who have been missed by other services to access that treatment and an incentive for them to take up that offer.

Second, because mental illness and the symptoms associated with it can trigger criminal behaviour and therefore bring a person into contact with the CJS. Decisions then need to be made on whether a criminal charge is in the public interest or whether an alternative disposal (such as diversion into mental health treatment) would be more appropriate.

Third, mental illness, particularly the more severe forms, can affect an individual's ability to understand and participate in the criminal justice process. They may need additional support to understand the questions put to them during an investigation or at trial or they may lack the mental capacity to plead or stand trial.

Fourth, the criminal justice process itself, for example the experience of custody, can have a severe and negative impact on someone's mental health, particularly if they are already suffering a mental illness. In these circumstances, there is a duty of care to try to mitigate these wherever possible. This includes a duty to reduce the risks of suicide and self-harm, which we know to be high in criminal justice populations.

For all these reasons, it is essential that those with a mental health condition or disorder are identified as early as possible in their journey through the CJS, particularly where that problem is severe. Once the mental health issue is identified, information relevant to that issue must be shared between agencies so that appropriate support and treatment can be offered, and the right decisions made at each step of the journey from arrest to sentence and post-sentence supervision in custody or in the community.

This inspection, the first on this topic to involve all of the criminal justice inspectorates, and to consider post-sentence supervision, as well as the period leading up to trial, focuses on these critical issues:

• Are people with a mental illness identified when they first come into the CJS?

• Is this information passed on through the rest of the system from the police and defence lawyers to the Crown Prosecution Service (CPS) and the courts or from the courts to the probation and prison services so that the right decisions can be made about next steps?

• Are people with a mental illness entering the CJS being properly assessed and then referred for help or treatment where this is identified as necessary?

• What is the quality of support they are getting? Is it timely and adequately resourced or are people having to wait many months to get it?

• Are the most seriously mentally ill people being looked after in appropriate settings and places of safety, or is custody still having to be used?

## Methodology

This joint inspection looked at the work carried out by each part of the CJS at six locations: Birmingham, Croydon, Durham, Exeter, Greater Manchester (Bolton) and Gwent, Newport. It covered the corresponding CPS areas, police forces, liaison and diversion (L&D) schemes, probation services and prisons. Due to the Covid-19 pandemic, most of the inspection was completed remotely, with interviews and focus groups conducted online over video platforms like MS Teams. In total, 45 cases were jointly inspected by all four criminal justice inspectorates, with a further 270 cases being reviewed by single inspectorates. We interviewed some 550 staff working across the different agencies. These included operational staff (such as police officers, probation practitioners, prison officers, and key workers) middle managers (such as police sergeants, lawyers, and service provider managers) senior leaders (including judges and prison governors), and commissioners.

Children being supervised by youth offending teams, witnesses and victims were not included in the scope of this inspection.

In addition, the organisation Penal Reform Solutions was contracted to undertake remote interviews with individuals journeying through the CJS as arrestees, defendants or convicted persons. Its consultants interviewed 67 individuals (of whom nine were women and 12 identified as black, Asian or minority ethnic). A copy of their report is published separately. A detailed breakdown of our methodology can be found in Annexe 2.

### Joint inspection findings

There is no common definition of mental health used across the CJS. This leads to inconsistencies in identification along all stages of an individual's criminal justice journey. When mental ill-health is identified at one stage, at the next stage it is often not. In too many instances mental ill-health is only partially identified when it should be fully identified. This results in poorer assessments and needs not being met. It also means that there is no accurate picture of the numbers of people with mental health needs and disorders in the CJS. The mental health flagging system used by probation services is muddled and the application of flagging varies considerably from one part of England and Wales to another. The registration of flags is not appropriately reviewed, and the same flags stay on case files for years without explanation. Agencies that have face-to-face contact with individuals use a range of different screening and assessment tools but do not always fully explain the purpose of the questions being asked of individuals. Therefore, the quality of the information they receive varies, leading to inaccurate decisions.

### Poor information exchange

Significant problems in information exchange occur in every agency in the CJS and at every stage of an individual's criminal justice journey. This part of the system is broken and needs to be fixed urgently. The transfer of mental health information, where available, by the police to the CPS to support charging decisions is generally weak. Officers often do not include relevant material and, when the CPS asks for further information, this inevitably causes delay. This then has a negative knock-on effect in court.

There appears to be some confusion among agencies in all sectors about the General Data Protection Regulation (GDPR) restrictions. Partners need to produce a joint national Memorandum of Understanding and resolve these issues if they are to achieve better mental health outcomes. Probation practitioners are often hindered in their work by community mental health service providers who do not 'allow' them access to information held on individuals they are working with. Similarly, where there are different commissioning arrangements for custodial and community-based mental health services, information exchange is not seamless and those being released or taken into prison do not receive the timely interventions they need.

### Committed staff but many need better training and supervision

Staff are committed, passionate, resilient and want to help people to lead more fulfilling and happy lives. They show considerable humanity to individuals who have often reached the lowest point in their personal circumstances. Many, during the pandemic in particular, have gone the 'extra mile' to ensure that basic needs are met and that no one is ever alone. Some staff disclosed their own mental health struggles during the pandemic, and this was appreciated by those going through the CJS. For them, a trusting and healthy relationship with a professional, and a safe environment to talk about their traumas, help them to grow into a better life. These thoughts and feelings must be heard and used to inform effective practice.

While differing learning and development opportunities for staff exist across the CJS, not all of these are making a difference to better equip practitioners and managers to deliver high-quality services. Police officers whose primary role it is to investigate offences had received little specific input on the mental health of suspects and how this may affect decision-making. Lawyers are familiar with the CPS Code for Crown Prosecutors and the revised policy and they have access to mental health leads and policy experts if they need specific guidance. Although the guidance is clear, having some specific face-to-face training, particularly to enhance the practical aspects of identifying and dealing with these cases, would be helpful. Probation practitioners lack effective motivational interviewing skills to help individuals struggling with their emotions, and prison officers are not supported well in their continuous professional development in working with prisoners with mental health vulnerabilities. During the past 12 months, remote learning has been made available but not all has been at a sufficient level and standard to meet the needs of all CJS staff.

The personal support that staff receive from their managers is generally good. However, the quality of clinical supervision is variable and management oversight of work is not always effective. This often leads to individuals going through the CJS not obtaining the care and treatment they need. For practitioners, opportunities for learning are missed and they continue to make similar mistakes in their practice repeatedly.

### Court reports need improvement and more sentences should include treatment

Information provided to courts, for example by L&D assessment reports, pre-sentence reports and psychiatric reports, varies in quality. Far too many reports contain very little analytical information about mental health needs and disorders. The exploration of trauma caused by life events is inadequate. Furthermore, the reports do not give enough attention to each individual's diverse needs and rely far too much on self-reporting. These deficits need to be removed. Some judges consider that the sentencing recommendations in the reports often lack detail about how mental health needs will be addressed. Sentencers do not consider Rehabilitation Activity Requirement conditions to be a credible way of dealing with mental health needs and disorders. However, Mental Health Treatment Requirement orders are viewed far more favourably. We are pleased that the number of Community Sentence Treatment Requirement sites are increasing. We endorse the expansion of these sites and the making of Mental Health Treatment Requirements and combined orders, where appropriate, to address dual diagnosis needs.

The alternative delivery pre-sentence report model being piloted across a number of magistrates' courts in England and Wales is welcomed. It should result in mental health needs and disorders being identified much earlier in the sentencing process and support better mental health outcomes. The process may also help to cement partnership working and more effective information-sharing.

**Assessment and diversion services in police custody have improved but they need to link to the rest of the criminal justice system**

There is very good coverage of L&D services across England and Wales in police custody. L&D provision in courts is not always on site and, indeed, during the pandemic the majority of assessment work has been carried out remotely. Assessments completed by L&D staff are not widely shared with partner agencies in the CJS. This causes strain. L&D teams need to be better engaged with court user groups to improve relationships. This will strengthen cross-system integration, which is much needed. The effectiveness of L&D service delivery during Covid-19 has been impeded by the loss of community mental health services. However, where L&D and community mental health services are provided by the same trust/board, service delivery has been better .

Triage services, where mental health professionals and/or social workers support policing with the initial response to incidents, exist in many locations. The provision varies between forces and few schemes are established and settled. Many are in flux and, in particular, there has been

considerable withdrawal of street services in favour of control room services for efficiency reasons. The control-room-based services offer a good service, provide added value and are appreciated by police officers. The inconsistency and instability of these services is a concern, as they are considered an important tool for all forces and partners. This needs to be addressed.

**A shortage of good-quality mental health provision and unacceptable delays to access it. This has worsened during the pandemic.**

Individuals reported that probation and prison are the two agencies most likely to give them the mental health support they need. However, help is often not timely and access to services has been a substantial problem during the pandemic. With some notable exceptions, a shortage of good-quality mental health services, combined with cases being closed, has resulted in very few interventions being delivered. There is a shortage of specialist services for ethnic minority people, such as culturally informed interventions, and little has been done to rectify this problem for many years.

Offender Personality Disorder (OPD) pathways have been used in the National Probation Service (NPS) to help practitioners better understand the mental health needs of individuals. These are providing some benefits, especially in the current environment. However, the Community Rehabilitation Companies (CRCs) did not have this facility. Following unification of these separate probation services into a single national service at the end of June 2021, there is an opportunity to make these pathways available to all who need them. Psychologists based in these OPD teams have led additional remote learning related to mental health, but this has not yet improved the overall quality of work. The Intensive Intervention and Risk Management Service, available in a number of regions, is now working much more effectively. We welcome this additional investment.

Prisons continue to be used as a place of safety, and Mental Health Act transfers out of prison custody are taking far too long. This is totally unacceptable. Shortages of local mental health beds for longer-term care remain a problem in a number of areas. This leads to vulnerable individuals with complex needs being kept in prison custody for far too long without timely assessments.

**Mental health provision in prison has improved but post-release treatment and support are poor**

Healthcare practitioners appropriately use nationally approved screening tools to assess the mental health needs of prisoners arriving in custody. Referrals for services generally follow thereafter. The impact of Covid-19, however, has resulted in long waiting lists for interventions. In-cell telephones were used extensively by mental health services to provide support during the restrictions; however, not all prisoners had access to an in-cell telephone.

Psychologically informed interventions, when delivered, are impressive and helping those in custody. Relationships with providers of mental health and substance misuse services are good and this presents a foundation from which to address comorbidity issues. Prisoners who are extremely unwell and need an urgent transfer to a secure mental health inpatient hospital for treatment continue to experience unacceptable waiting times. This needs to be remedied.

The continuity of mental health care from custody into the community is generally poor. Waiting lists for services in the community are long, leaving very vulnerable people having to cope without the help they need. They often reoffend and return to prison not long after being released. RECONNECT Care after Custody is a positive initiative and needs to be nationally embedded.[14]

### Cross-system management and leadership need to be better

Each agency in the CJS has a range of management information systems, but cross-system data is not systematically collected and analysed to promote joint working and improve mental health outcomes. Much more needs to be done to fully realise the benefits of data to inform and drive change.

Agencies across the CJS have a range of strategic intentions and governance structures linked to mental health. These are informed by policies and procedures but are not always effective in delivering positive mental health outcomes. Vulnerability is well understood. Partners come together at a number of boards. Health boards provide a focus for mental health coverage and generally work better. The impact on service delivery, however, too often depends on individual relationships with commissioners and partners rather than a drive for planned change.

*Note on terminology*

Our 2009 joint inspection on work prior to sentence with offenders with mental disorders (Criminal Justice Joint Inspection, 2009) noted that there was no universal agreement on the definition of an offender with a mental disorder, something that caused challenges in getting consistent estimates of the number of these offenders in the CJS. As such, for the purpose of the inspection it was decided to use the definition initially put forward by the National Association for the Care and Resettlement of Offenders (NACRO), one that was later adopted by Lord Bradley in his review of people with mental health problems and learning difficulties in the CJS (Bradley, 2009):

*'Those who come into contact with the criminal justice system because they have committed, or are suspected of committing, a criminal offence, and who may be acutely or chronically mentally ill. It may also include those in whom a degree of disturbance is recognised even though it may not be severe enough to bring it within the criteria laid down by the Mental Health Act 1983 (now 2007)'.*

11 *Figure based on a cohort of 134 people. Samele, C. et al. (2021). 'The prevalence of mental illness and unmet needs of police custody detainees', Criminal Behaviour and Mental Health, 31(2), pp. 80–95.*

12 *Prisoner survey 01 April 2019 and 30 June 2020 (HMI Prisons).*

13 *HM Inspectorate of Probation. (2019). The availability and delivery of interventions (probation services).*

14 *Information on RECONNECT Care after Custody is available on the NHS website: https://www.england.nhs.uk/ltphimenu/wider-social-impact/reconnect-care-after-custody*

# Section 7

## Annexes

7.1 Parliamentary Questions
7.2 Transparency & FOI Releases
7.3 Deaths in Prison Service Custody
7.4 Policy Frameworks, PSIs, PSOs
7.5 Staff Awards & Prizes
7.6 Basic Custody Screening Tool

## 7.1 PARLIAMENTARY QUESTIONS 2022

**Reoffending Rates: Friday Releases**
5th July 2022.
*Bob Blackman Conservative, Harrow East*
What assessment he has made of the impact of ending Friday releases on reoffending rates.
*Victoria Atkins The Minister of State, Ministry of Justice*
I know that accessing timely support on release can be particularly challenging on a Friday and that that can increase the risk of reoffending. That is why the Government have committed to pursuing legislation when parliamentary time allows to enable the release of prisoners up to two days earlier when a release date falls on a Friday or before a bank holiday. I welcome the fact that my hon. Friend Mark Jenkinson has introduced a private Member's Bill on the issue. I look forward to that.
*Bob Blackman Conservative, Harrow East*
What is key is that if we release ex-criminals and ex-offenders on a Friday, they are likely to return to their former habitat, reconnect with individuals whom they committed crimes with and reoffend. Equally, if they are homeless, they will not get any service from the local authority. I therefore commend the moves to change the position so that we can encourage people to rebuild their lives after being in prison.
*Victoria Atkins The Minister of State, Ministry of Justice*
I thank my hon. Friend, who has a long record of tackling homelessness. We are particularly conscious of the impact that homelessness can have on ex-offenders released from prison, so, in addition to our commitment to legislate on Friday releases, by 2024-25 we will invest an additional £200 million a year to transform our approach to rehabilitation, including expanding our transitional accommodation service across England and Wales. Ex-offenders need a home, a job and a support network, and we are determined to help them to gain all three.

**Lammy Review**
5th July 2022.
*Kate Osamor Labour/Co-operative, Edmonton*
What recent progress he has made on the implementation of the recommendations of the Lammy review.
*James Cartlidge Parliamentary Under Secretary of State (Ministry of Justice), Assistant Whip*
We have implemented almost all the actions that we committed to in response to the Lammy review and our work continues on the longer-term recruitment targets for HMPPS. That work is firmly embedded in the HMPPS race action programme: a significant three-year investment to deliver long-term change in inequality. We recognise that the Lammy review was an important start, not a complete solution, and our work has evolved considerably. Central to that are our commitments in the inclusive Britain strategy.
*Kate Osamor Labour/Co-operative, Edmonton*
The Government's offensive Sewell report sought to dismiss evidence of institutional racism in Britain, yet we know that systematic discrimination remains rife in the criminal justice system, such as the proportion of prisoners from ethnic minority backgrounds on remand. Will the Minister commit to publishing further progress updates on the Lammy recommendations so that the Government's progress can be publicly held to account?
*James Cartlidge Parliamentary Under Secretary of State (Ministry of Justice), Assistant Whip*
The hon. Lady makes a fair point. We obviously want to be held to account, and I am more than happy to write to her with further details of the progress that we are making. To give just one example, in our inclusive Britain strategy, we committed to a special pilot in police stations that is ensuring that juveniles receive legal advice. As she knows, many juveniles—and, it must be said, particularly those from ethnic minority backgrounds—were not engaging with the system; in the pilot, they must proactively choose to opt out. I have personally been to Wembley police station and to Brixton, where the trial is happening, and I am pleased to say that so far the results are incredibly encouraging: they suggest less time in custody for those juveniles who are participating. Most importantly, some of them are more likely to have an out-of-court disposal. We are trying to break that chain of getting stuck in the criminal justice—[Interruption.]

*Lindsay Hoyle Speaker of the House of Commons, Chair, Speaker's Committee for the Independent Parliamentary Standards Authority, Chair, Speaker's Committee for the Independent Parliamentary Standards Authority, Chair, House of Commons Commission, Chair, Speaker's Committee on the Electoral Commission, Chair, Speaker's Committee on the Electoral Commission*
Keep going.

*James Cartlidge Parliamentary Under Secretary of State (Ministry of Justice), Assistant Whip*
It would appear that it happens whenever I am speaking, Mr Speaker. I do not know if it is personal. I am grateful to the hon. Lady for that important question. As I said, I will write to her with further details and update her.

### Prison Officers: Pension Age
**5th July 2022**
*Mary Foy Labour, City of Durham*
What discussions he has had with Cabinet colleagues on the effect of the pension age of prison officers on staff (a) recruitment and (b) retention.

*Victoria Atkins The Minister of State, Ministry of Justice*
The Government are committed to recognising the extraordinary public service carried out by our hard-working prison staff and officers, and to ensuring that we have a modern employment offer that attracts and retains the very best. I am listening to and working with officers, staff and trade unions on all employment matters.

*Mary Foy Labour, City of Durham*
The Minister agreed more than six months ago in this place and on a number of other occasions to meet with the professional trades union for prison, correctional and secure psychiatric workers—the Prison Officers Association—to discuss prison officer pension age as a standalone issue. Yet I am informed that that meeting is yet to happen or even to be scheduled. Does the Minister understand that making promises to prison officers and then breaking them is an insult to hundreds of my constituents in Durham, but entirely consistent with the way this Government treat those brave and loyal workers?

*Victoria Atkins The Minister of State, Ministry of Justice*
I thank the hon. Lady for raising this matter. I have in fact met the Prison Officers Association; indeed, I was delighted to attend its conference in Eastbourne a couple of months ago. I note in passing that sadly the Opposition were not able to accept the union's kind invitation to attend that same conference. In terms of pensions, I am determined to have a good employment offer for all our officers. I will continue to meet the POA union and the other unions that work in our prison estate. I emphasise both to officers and to staff that we want to ensure that the hard work they put in to our prison service is reflected in the coming months in the offer we put to our staff.

### Reoffending Rates
**5th July 2022**
*Jason McCartney Conservative, Colne Valley*
What steps he is taking to reduce reoffending rates.

*Selaine Saxby Conservative, North Devon*
What steps he is taking to reduce reoffending.

*Dominic Raab Deputy Prime Minister, The Lord Chancellor and Secretary of State for Justice*
Let me take the chance, on behalf of those on the Conservative Front Bench and, I believe, on all the Benches behind me, to offer our condolences to the shadow Justice Secretary on the passing of his father.
The overall reoffending rate has decreased by 5 percentage points from 31% in 2009-10 to 26% in 2019-20. Over that period, reoffending rates for robbery, criminal damage, arson, drug offences and sexual offences have all fallen.

*Jason McCartney Conservative, Colne Valley*
I very much welcome the work that is being done to reduce reoffending rates. I vividly remember visiting Armley Jail and hearing about the work being done there. A big part of this work is transitioning ex-offenders into work. What role does my Right Hon. Friend see apprenticeships playing in that work?

*Dominic Raab Deputy Prime Minister, The Lord Chancellor and Secretary of State for Justice*
My hon. Friend is right: the work that we are doing on skills and education right the way through to getting offenders into work is vital. I am very pleased, as he may know, that, working with the Department for Education, we are introducing a statutory instrument to introduce apprenticeships in prison. That SI will pass in September, and we will start the first apprenticeship straight away.

*Selaine Saxby Conservative, North Devon*
The top 10 repeat offenders being dealt with by police in North Devon have committed 108 offences in April to June this year. As the police themselves say, many of these individuals have previously been in prison—some on multiple occasions—but the offending cycle continues. What more can be done to reduce repeat offending, as, locally, the current system is clearly not delivering that desired outcome?

*Dominic Raab Deputy Prime Minister, The Lord Chancellor and Secretary of State for Justice*
By 2024-25, we will be investing £200 million a year, in dealing with skills and work, as I have already said, and also with drug rehabilitation, particularly sustainable absence-based drug rehabilitation. The further action that we are

taking on resettlement passports will avoid that potential cliff edge when an offender leaves prison, and makes sure that the wraparound care is there as they transition.

*Sally-Ann Hart Conservative, Hastings and Rye*
Sussex prisoners' families have highlighted how important families of offenders, particularly prisoners, are in reducing offending. Prisoners' families are often forgotten about in the criminal justice system, but research shows that if prisoners have a supportive family, they are less likely to offend. What steps is my Right Hon. Friend taking to support such families, thereby helping to make our communities stronger and safer?

*Dominic Raab Deputy Prime Minister, The Lord Chancellor and Secretary of State for Justice*
My hon. Friend is absolutely right; research shows that the odds of reoffending are 39% higher for prisoners who did not have visits from family or friends while they were inside prison. That is why the new builds, Five Wells and the others, have not only in-cell technology that can facilitate dialogue and close family ties, but family centres to ensure that the ties that bind, and can cut crime by reducing reoffending, are strengthened and not weakened.

*Kate Green Labour, Stretford and Urmston*
Careful parole decisions are important to minimise reoffending. Can the Justice Secretary explain why new Parole Board rules will mean that expert report writers will be forbidden to provide a view on suitability for release of the most serious offenders?

*Dominic Raab Deputy Prime Minister, The Lord Chancellor and Secretary of State for Justice*
At the moment, when the vital question of risk is assessed, there is a risk that separate reports, whether from psychiatrists or probation officers and those who manage risk, may give conflicting recommendations. Therefore, in those serious cases that the hon. Lady refers to, there will be one overarching Ministry of Justice view, so that the Parole Board has a very clear steer and we make sure—the hon. Lady shakes her head, but I think she agrees with me—that the overriding focus is on public safety and protecting the public.

*Lindsay Hoyle Speaker of the House of Commons, Chair, Speaker's Committee for the Independent Parliamentary Standards Authority, Chair, Speaker's Committee for the Independent Parliamentary Standards Authority, Chair, House of Commons Commission, Chair, Speaker's Committee on the Electoral Commission, Chair, Speaker's Committee on the Electoral Commission*
I call the shadow Secretary of State.

*Steve Reed Shadow Secretary of State for Justice*
I thank you, Mr Speaker, the Secretary of State

and other hon. Members for their condolences on the passing of my dad, Roy Reed, a few days ago. Everyone's very kind words were a great comfort to our family at a very difficult time.
Community payback is vital for reducing reoffending and giving justice to victims, but the number of hours completed by offenders has been falling since 2017. It fell in 2018 and again in 2019, before anyone had heard of covid-19. Please can the Secretary of State explain why?

*Dominic Raab Deputy Prime Minister, The Lord Chancellor and Secretary of State for Justice*
There is renewed investment going in to community payback. There has been a covid effect since the years the hon. Gentleman mentions; I know he has raised the issue of those obligations being discharged from home, but that will all be phased out by the autumn. This is a valuable scheme for restorative justice, so that the public see those who have committed crimes making recompense.

## Support for Victims of Crime
### 5th July 2022
*Jonathan Gullis Conservative, Stoke-on-Trent North*
What plans he has to improve support for victims of crime.

*Tom Pursglove Parliamentary Under Secretary of State (Ministry of Justice and Home Office)*
Our landmark victims Bill will improve support for victims and help to give them confidence that if they report a crime the criminal justice system will treat them in the way that they should expect. We have increased the funding for victim and witness support services to £192 million by 2024-25—quadruple the level in 2009-10. With this funding we are increasing the number of independent sexual and domestic violence advisers to over 1,000— a 43% increase over the next three years—and introducing a 24/7 support line for victims of rape and sexual violence.

*Jonathan Gullis Conservative, Stoke-on-Trent North*
Last June, a six-year-old girl was tragically killed when a car hit her and her father as they walked along a road in Stoke-on-Trent North. The victim's mother has had to wait over a year, suffering in silence, because the defendant took so long to give permission for his blood sample to be tested. If a person has done nothing wrong they should have nothing to fear. That is why I am campaigning for an amendment to section 7 of the Road Traffic Act 1988 for blood testing to take place without permission, required where loss of life has occurred, to give victims the answers they deserve and need quicker. Would my hon. Friend support such a change?

*Tom Pursglove Parliamentary Under Secretary of State (Ministry of Justice and Home Office)*

I am grateful to my hon. Friend for raising this terrible tragedy in the House today. The impact on the family is unthinkable and what has happened is just awful. He will recognise that the measures introduced in the Police, Crime, Sentencing and Courts Act 2022—with his support—came into force last week, tightening the offences and reflecting the culpability of offenders and the devastating harm that these crimes cause, as well as introducing a new offence of causing serious injury by careless driving. The Department for Transport is about to launch a call for evidence looking at motoring offences, and I know it is keen to engage with my hon. Friend on that.

**Simon Jupp Conservative, East Devon**

The draft victims Bill is a huge step forward to help victims recover from the impact of crime. Does my hon. Friend agree that proper funding for victim support services in Devon and elsewhere is also essential?

**Tom Pursglove Parliamentary Under Secretary of State (Ministry of Justice and Home Office)**

I hope that I can reassure my hon. Friend that the victims Bill focuses on delivering improvements to the quality and consistency of victim support services, backed up by more funding than ever before, with £192 million by 2024-25—a four times increase on 2009-10—as well as a multi-year commitment that gives victim support services confidence to plan for the future. That will benefit people in East Devon, and it is fair to say that this Government are committed to delivering on our promises.

**Dr Caroline Johnson Conservative, Sleaford and North Hykeham**

With the victims Bill, a quadrupling of money for support services and the lengthening of sentences, it is clear that this Government are on the side of victims. One key expectation of victims is that justice will be served and prisoners will not escape, yet twice this year violent sexual offenders have escaped from a Lincolnshire prison, causing anxiety and danger to my constituents. What is the Minister doing to ensure that that does not happen again?

**Tom Pursglove Parliamentary Under Secretary of State (Ministry of Justice and Home Office)**

I am hugely grateful to my hon. Friend for her support for the measures we are introducing through the victims Bill, and I know that the prisons Minister, my hon. Friend Victoria Atkins would be willing to speak to her about the specific issue of absconding. What I can say is that we are tightening the rules governing open prisons with a tough three-step test and greater ministerial oversight, which I hope will give her confidence on this issue.

**Mark Pawsey Conservative, Rugby**

I would also like to raise the case of a constituent, because in an act of outstanding bravery, Sheila Whitehouse went to the aid of a neighbour who was being viciously attacked by a dog. The owner had no insurance, and when the case came to court, Sheila was awarded just a token sum. She suffered life-changing injuries, but had no compensation through the Criminal Injuries Compensation Authority. Will the Minister review the eligibility for compensation for those injured in such circumstances as Sheila's?

**Tom Pursglove Parliamentary Under Secretary of State (Ministry of Justice and Home Office)**

I am very sorry to hear about this particular incident, and I commend, as my hon. Friend did so brilliantly, Sheila's bravery in stepping in to help the individual affected. The criminal injuries compensation scheme exists to compensate for serious physical or mental injury attributable to being a direct victim of a crime of violence. The scheme is publicly funded, which means that there are strict eligibility criteria. An animal attack will amount to a crime of violence only where the animal was used deliberately to inflict injury. In 2020, we had a consultation on proposals to make claiming compensation simpler for victims of violent crime. We set out that expanding the definition of a crime of violence would go far beyond the original intention of the scheme, but we will be publishing a response in due course.

**Karl Turner Labour, Kingston upon Hull East**

I am afraid to tell the Minister that victims of crime are being further let down by the Government's terrible handling of the Criminal Bar Association dispute. I know that a Minister has now finally agreed to meet the Bar Council and the Criminal Bar Association, and I think that meeting is tabled for next week, but what they need to know at that meeting is when the Department will set a timetable for implementing the money that Sir Christopher Bellamy said was needed urgently. Incidentally, Sir Christopher Bellamy, who I have a great deal of respect for, is now a member of the House of Lords. When is that money coming?

**Tom Pursglove Parliamentary Under Secretary of State (Ministry of Justice and Home Office)**

No doubt the Under-Secretary of State for Justice, my hon. Friend James Cartlidge, will be answering questions on that from Members on both sides of the House. I have heard what the hon. Gentleman said, but I note that the Opposition backed the Bellamy review and its outcomes, which we are getting on with delivering.

**Lindsay Hoyle Speaker of the House of Commons, Chair, Speaker's Committee for the Independent Parliamentary Standards**

Authority, Chair, Speaker's Committee for the Independent Parliamentary Standards Authority, Chair, House of Commons Commission, Chair, Speaker's Committee on the Electoral Commission, Chair, Speaker's Committee on the Electoral Commission

We now come to the shadow Secretary of State.

*Steve Reed Shadow Secretary of State for Justice*
As we have heard, Members on both sides of the House want victims' needs to be put first, so why did the Secretary of State tour the TV studios to defend the Prime Minister for ignoring the victim of predatory sexual behaviour by a former Foreign Office Minister when he promoted him to Deputy Chief Whip, despite having been alerted to that behaviour by the permanent under-secretary and despite the Minister in question having admitted to the behaviour?

*Tom Pursglove Parliamentary Under Secretary of State (Ministry of Justice and Home Office)*
My clear understanding is that the hon. Gentleman is wrong about that, but of course it is right that the processes that have been set out should be allowed to run their course. All hon. Members take a very dim view of people being ill-treated and it is right that due process can now be followed. What is not in question is the Government's determination to ensure that outcomes for victims are better; the funding and the measures in the Bill are there, and we will get on and deliver that.

### Reoffending Rates: Friday Releases
### 5th July 2022

*Bob Blackman Conservative, Harrow East*
What assessment he has made of the impact of ending Friday releases on reoffending rates.

*Victoria Atkins The Minister of State, Ministry of Justice*
I know that accessing timely support on release can be particularly challenging on a Friday and that that can increase the risk of reoffending. That is why the Government have committed to pursuing legislation when parliamentary time allows to enable the release of prisoners up to two days earlier when a release date falls on a Friday or before a bank holiday. I welcome the fact that my hon. Friend Mark Jenkinson has introduced a private Member's Bill on the issue. I look forward to that.

*Bob Blackman Conservative, Harrow East*
What is key is that if we release ex-criminals and ex-offenders on a Friday, they are likely to return to their former habitat, reconnect with individuals whom they committed crimes with and reoffend. Equally, if they are homeless, they will not get any service from the local authority. I therefore commend the moves to change the position so that we can encourage people to rebuild their lives after being in prison.

*Victoria Atkins The Minister of State, Ministry of Justice*
I thank my hon. Friend, who has a long record of tackling homelessness. We are particularly conscious of the impact that homelessness can have on ex-offenders released from prison, so, in addition to our commitment to legislate on Friday releases, by 2024-25 we will invest an additional £200 million a year to transform our approach to rehabilitation, including expanding our transitional accommodation service across England and Wales. Ex-offenders need a home, a job and a support network, and we are determined to help them to gain all three.

### Topical Questions
### 5th July 2022

*Caroline Ansell Conservative, Eastbourne*
If he will make a statement on his departmental responsibilities.

*Dominic Raab Deputy Prime Minister, The Lord Chancellor and Secretary of State for Justice*
Since the last oral questions the Police, Crime, Sentencing and Courts Act 2022 has entered into force, I published the Bill of Rights and we submitted our victims Bill to pre-legislative scrutiny.

*Caroline Ansell Conservative, Eastbourne*
I thank my right hon. Friend for his response. For as many years as I have served as Eastbourne's Member of Parliament, Eastbourne residents have expressed to me their dismay, their outrage even, that foreign national offenders—dangerous criminals—have used the right to family life to frustrate their deportation, a deportation ordered for public safety. How will the Bill of Rights address that?

*Dominic Raab Deputy Prime Minister, The Lord Chancellor and Secretary of State for Justice*
I thank my hon. Friend; she is absolutely right. The Bill of Rights is now published and she will see, explicitly and squarely in relation to article 8, clear guidance and prescription on interpretation to prevent the ever-elastic interpretations of the right to family life, the shifting goalposts, that allows those offenders to trump the overwhelming public interest in their deportation.

*Lindsay Hoyle Speaker of the House of Commons, Chair, Speaker's Committee for the Independent Parliamentary Standards Authority, Chair, Speaker's Committee for the Independent Parliamentary Standards Authority, Chair, House of Commons Commission, Chair, Speaker's Committee on the Electoral Commission, Chair, Speaker's Committee on the Electoral Commission*
I call the shadow Minister, Anna McMorrin.

*Anna McMorrin Shadow Minister (Justice)*
Seven years on, we do not have a victims Bill in

statute. Thousands of victims are trapped in court backlogs and domestic abuse victims are still being cross-examined by their abuser in family courts, despite that being made illegal last year. Not only does the abuse continue, but the Government have facilitated it by deciding that that provision will not apply to domestic abuse victims who are already in the system. Will the Government ensure that that will apply to them and explain why victims should think that they are anything but an afterthought for the Government?

*Dominic Raab Deputy Prime Minister, The Lord Chancellor and Secretary of State for Justice*

Again, an Opposition Front Bencher is denigrating the important—albeit incremental—reforms that we are making for victims. In fact, a victims law is currently subject to pre-legislative scrutiny and it will be introduced. We are increasing the victims surcharge by 20% and are changing the way that the Crown Prosecution Service communicates. Since the last Labour Government, we have quadrupled the amount of funding that goes to victims services, and we have rolled out section 28. She is right to say that we have prioritised rape and serious sexual violence. [Interruption.] We will get on to that. In fact, the reality is that the number of rape convictions has increased by two thirds over the past year. We have also taken action through the Police, Crime, Sentencing and Courts Act 2022 on domestic abuse, which the hon. Lady voted against.

*Gagan Mohindra Conservative, South West Hertfordshire*

I recently had the pleasure of visiting HMP The Mount in my constituency, where I learned about its excellent work to provide inmates with practical work skills for life after prison. What steps is my right hon. Friend taking to ensure that when individuals leave prison, they are given the tools and skills to successfully rehabilitate themselves back into society—as they are at HMP The Mount—and get back into work, and not to fall back into a life of crime?

*Dominic Raab Deputy Prime Minister, The Lord Chancellor and Secretary of State for Justice*

I have fond memories of playing Sunday league football in my younger years in The Mount prison against the offenders. They won fairly convincingly—something tells me that they were not out on the Saturday night in the way that my team was.

My hon. Friend asks a serious question: what are we doing? In the past year, we have seen a 67% increase in offenders leaving prison being in work within six months. That is a big step change and we are restless to go further. We are doing that with the roll-out of employment advisory boards—I am very grateful to James

Timpson for driving that forward—employment hubs in prison, and critically, the drugs strategy, which will stop offenders languishing on methadone, at which point they are no good for anything.

*Lindsay Hoyle Speaker of the House of Commons, Chair, Speaker's Committee for the Independent Parliamentary Standards Authority, Chair, Speaker's Committee for the Independent Parliamentary Standards Authority, Chair, House of Commons Commission, Chair, Speaker's Committee on the Electoral Commission, Chair, Speaker's Committee on the Electoral Commission*

I call the Scottish National party spokesperson, Anne McLaughlin.

*Anne McLaughlin Shadow SNP Spokesperson (Justice), Shadow SNP Spokesperson (Immigration, Asylum and Border Control)*

Last week, Russia followed the UK Government's lead in ignoring a ruling from the European Court of Human Rights, telling the Court: "Russia no longer complies with the prescriptions of the ECHR—that's all there is to say".

When the Lord Chancellor sees that kind of behaviour, does he ever have second thoughts about the type of company that he is taking the UK into as a result of his proposals? How does he think that will be viewed by the international community?

*Dominic Raab Deputy Prime Minister, The Lord Chancellor and Secretary of State for Justice*

I am not sure what the hon. Lady thought she was referring to in the sense that we have ignored any rulings. We have one of the highest compliance records in the Council of Europe. Frankly, I think she has a problem with her moral compass if she is equating our approach with that of President Putin. [Interruption.]

*Anne McLaughlin Shadow SNP Spokesperson (Justice), Shadow SNP Spokesperson (Immigration, Asylum and Border Control)*

I am sorry to laugh—[Interruption.]

*Lindsay Hoyle Speaker of the House of Commons, Chair, Speaker's Committee for the Independent Parliamentary Standards Authority, Chair, Speaker's Committee for the Independent Parliamentary Standards Authority, Chair, House of Commons Commission, Chair, Speaker's Committee on the Electoral Commission, Chair, Speaker's Committee on the Electoral Commission*

Order. It is one thing for an hon. Member to come in to the Chamber very late, but it is another for them to start shouting. If they want to shout, shout outside.

*Anne McLaughlin Shadow SNP Spokesperson (Justice), Shadow SNP Spokesperson (Immigration, Asylum and Border Control)*

Thank you, Mr Speaker. This really is a tale of two countries.

In Scotland, legislation passed by the Scottish Parliament is not law if it is incompatible with the rights defended in the Human Rights Act. That is also woven through the devolution settlement. If the UK removes the Human Rights Act, but the Scottish Parliament refuses consent, what will the Government do? What options exist, other than voting yes to independence, to retain our human rights protections in Scotland?

**Dominic Raab Deputy Prime Minister, The Lord Chancellor and Secretary of State for Justice**

This always comes back round to independence rather than the bread-and-butter issues that the people of Scotland face. The hon. Lady should vote for our Bill of Rights because the people of Scotland are frustrated, as are people across the United Kingdom, when they hear of cases—such as those raised by my hon. Friend Caroline Ansell—of people committing serious offences, but who are not able to be deported because they claim ever-elastic interpretations of the right to family life.

**Simon Baynes Conservative, Clwyd South**

Does the Minister agree that the many people who give their time free of charge to act as magistrates are a fantastic asset to this country? They are the backbone of our justice system: without them, it could not function effectively.

**James Cartlidge Parliamentary Under Secretary of State (Ministry of Justice), Assistant Whip**

My hon. Friend is absolutely right that magistrates are the backbone of our criminal justice system. When the pandemic hit, output completely collapsed in the magistrates courts, but individual magistrates, their legal advisers and staff in our magistrates courts have worked incredibly hard to recover the position. In March, we had the highest number of disposals in magistrates courts since before the pandemic.

We have taken two key measures to strengthen magistrates: we have increased their sentencing powers from six months to 12 months, and launched a £1 million recruitment campaign. I am pleased to say that we have had 33,000 expressions of interest so far, which bodes well for the next generation of our volunteer judiciary.

**Liz Twist Opposition Whip (Commons), Shadow Minister (Scotland)**

Prosecutions for rape cases are at an appallingly low 1.3%—even an increase of two thirds still translates to less than 2%, which is truly shocking—and drop-out rates are at more than 40% because of court delays and onerous evidence requirements. What is the Minister of State doing for victims of rape, to significantly increase the number of prosecutions and convictions?

**Victoria Atkins The Minister of State, Ministry of Justice**

A huge body of work is going on across every part of the criminal justice system, from the police to the Crown Prosecution Service and through to the courts. It involves the recruitment of more independent sexual violence advisers, who can make such a difference not only to victims' recovery, but to their willingness and ability to continue with a prosecution. In particular, we are introducing enhanced measures for specialist support within three pilot courts to support victims who are taking forward these very difficult cases. We are working with the judiciary, the police and the CPS to ensure that we measure and identify what is working so that we can replicate it across the country.

**Caroline Dinenage Conservative, Gosport**

When it comes to female offenders, trauma-informed and gender-responsive programmes are the only way to break a cycle of crime and incarceration. Tomorrow, the brilliant charity One Small Thing will be here in Parliament to discuss the latest research on the intergenerational traumatic impact of maternal imprisonment. I would really love all Justice Ministers, but particularly my hon. Friend the Minister of State, to come along and hear how the justice system could better be formatted to support women and children.

**Victoria Atkins The Minister of State, Ministry of Justice**

I thank my hon. Friend for that kind invitation; I would be delighted to attend. On the impact of intergenerational trauma, one of the many reasons we are piloting the first residential women's centre in Wales is that we want to see how women who should not be receiving the very short sentences that can be imposed can benefit from an intensive residential course rather than prison. I will be watching the results with interest.

**Lloyd Russell-Moyle Labour/Co-operative, Brighton, Kemptown**

There is only one legal aid provider for immigration in Brighton and the surrounding area of Sussex: BHT, which is currently operating a waiting list and is only prioritising unaccompanied minors. Lawstop, a legal aid provider in other areas, has applied to the Legal Aid Agency for immigration legal aid support, but has been told that there is no demand in the area. How can that be, if the only other provider has to operate a waiting list and is only able to help unaccompanied minors? Is it not now time to change how legal aid contracts are given, so that all those who request it can get access to legal aid?

*James Cartlidge Parliamentary Under Secretary of State (Ministry of Justice), Assistant Whip*
We are making a significant investment in additional funding for legal aid in immigration cases. I am happy to write to the hon. Gentleman with the full details of that important step change. On the wider issue of access to legal aid, I spoke earlier about our consultation on civil legal aid reform and the means test, which will enable 2 million more people to have access to civil legal aid and 3 million more people to have access to legal aid in the magistrates courts. Combined with the £135 million that we are investing in criminal legal aid in response to the Bellamy review, that is a significant investment, by any measure, in legal aid in all our constituencies.

*Robert Buckland Conservative, South Swindon*
Further to the question that my hon. Friend Sir Robert Neill asked, I commend the courts Minister for his announced intention to meet representatives of the criminal Bar. May I press him to do so at the earliest opportunity? Will he make the subject matter of that meeting the implementation of the rest of the Bellamy reforms, notably the reforms to the advocates' graduated fee scheme and the composition and remit of the advisory board?

*James Cartlidge Parliamentary Under Secretary of State (Ministry of Justice), Assistant Whip*
My right hon. and learned Friend has made an extremely good point. He is aware of the article to which I referred in my answer to my hon. Friend the Member for Bromley and Chislehurst—the Chairman of the Select Committee—in which I made clear my wish to engage with the Criminal Bar Association on the next stage of reform, which includes the advocates' graduated fee scheme and some of its core elements that were not in the first phase. As I have said, we adopted that two-phase approach precisely in order to deliver the initial increase in fees as soon as practicable, and it will be introduced in September: a 15% increase for criminal barristers working in magistrates courts and police stations and for those in the AGFS. We think that that is a very generous offer, and we hope the members of the CBA will think about it and stop their disruption of our courts.

*Grahame Morris Labour, Easington*
I understand that the Government have now received the recommendations from the Prison Service pay review body for a rise in prison officers' wages. I do not know whether the Secretary of State chats to any security guards on the House of Commons estate, but many of them are former prison officers who left the service because of poor pay and bad terms and conditions in our prisons. When will the

Secretary of State respond to those recommendations, and will he agree to follow them in full and not pick and choose, which is what has been done for the past three years?

*Dominic Raab Deputy Prime Minister, The Lord Chancellor and Secretary of State for Justice*
The hon. Gentleman has raised an important issue. I am considering the recommendations very carefully, and will respond shortly.

*Kevin Hollinrake Conservative, Thirsk and Malton*
Given that 40% of crime is now economic crime, it is disappointing that the Law Commission has recommended restricting corporate criminal liability for failing to prevent economic crime to fraud, and leaving out key crimes such as money laundering and false accounting. Will my right hon. Friend agree to meet me to discuss the benefits of a review with a much wider scope?

*Kit Malthouse The Minister of State, Home Department, The Minister of State, Ministry of Justice, Minister of State (Ministry of Justice and Home Office)*
Yes.

*Jeff Smith Shadow Minister (Digital, Culture, Media and Sport)*
In the wake of legal aid cuts and, now, cuts in a few charitable services—such as Support Through Court, which, as we heard earlier, has had its core funding cut—and given the cost of living crisis, how do the Government expect people who cannot afford lawyers to navigate court if the last remaining services that could help them are lost?

*James Cartlidge Parliamentary Under Secretary of State (Ministry of Justice), Assistant Whip*
As I have just made absolutely clear, as a result of our consultation we will be increasing access to legal aid. Two million more people will have access to civil legal aid, 3 million more will have access to legal aid in the magistrates courts, and there will be £135 million of additional funds for criminal legal aid following the independent inquiry conducted by Sir Christopher Bellamy, now Lord Bellamy. We think that this is a significant and positive reform, which, incidentally, will help to drive wider reform of the criminal justice system and civil legal aid.

*Theresa Villiers Conservative, Chipping Barnet*
The Government are consulting on SLAPPs—strategic lawsuits against public participation. How will this ensure that action is taken against candidates who seek to use litigation and threats of it in an oppressive way to shut down debate during elections?

*Dominic Raab Deputy Prime Minister, The Lord Chancellor and Secretary of State for Justice*
We issued a call for evidence on a suite of proposals, and we are gathering the responses and formulating proposals to ensure that those

with deep pockets—oligarchs and the like—who try to silence the voices of transparency cannot do so in this jurisdiction. I will be seeking a legislative vehicle to implement those proposals.

**Dan Jarvis Labour, Barnsley Central**

The International Criminal Court has just issued arrest warrants for three men on suspicion of abduction, torture and other war crimes during Russia's invasion not of Ukraine, but of Georgia. This is a reminder that Putin's barbarity stretches back many years, and that prosecuting such barbarity also takes many years. Can the Secretary of State ensure that our commitment to delivering justice for those who have suffered in Ukraine will endure for the longer term?

**Dominic Raab Deputy Prime Minister, The Lord Chancellor and Secretary of State for Justice**

The hon. Gentleman is right to raise this issue. We have been there at the outset supporting the ICC. I remember, as a young lawyer in The Hague, negotiating the UK-UN agreement on sentence enforcement, which, just last year, enabled us to take Radovan Karadžić into this country. That is exactly the kind of staying power that we will need in the case of Ukraine.

**Rob Butler Conservative, Aylesbury**

An inspection report on Oakhill Secure Training Centre has been published today. The centre has a very poor recent record. I am pleased to see that there are signs of improvement, but much remains to be done to achieve a sustained high standard. Will the Minister commit herself to ensuring that both the Ministry of Justice and Her Majesty's Prison and Probation Service continue to focus strongly on ensuring that Oakhill can enable children to truly turn their lives around?

**Victoria Atkins The Minister of State, Ministry of Justice**

Very much so. As my hon. Friend knows from occasions when I have given evidence to the Justice Committee, we are keeping this under close review. We want the children who are held at Oakhill to be held in a way that is safe but also decent, and we want to rehabilitate those young people so that when they are released they can lead productive lives that are free from crime. I welcome my hon. Friend's focus on this issue, and believe you me, it is absolutely mirrored in the Ministry.

**Chris Bryant Chair, Committee on Standards, Chair, Committee on Standards**

The Justice Secretary said this morning on television and on the radio, on the basis of conversations that he had had with the Prime Minister in the last 24 hours, that Lord McDonald's claim that the Prime Minister had been directly and personally informed and briefed, in person, on the allegations that were

substantiated at the Foreign Office, while he was Foreign Secretary, against Christopher Pincher was untrue. Has the Justice Secretary had further conversations with the Prime Minister, and is that still his position?

**Dominic Raab Deputy Prime Minister, The Lord Chancellor and Secretary of State for Justice**

That is not what I said.

**Jamie Stone Liberal Democrat Spokesperson (Armed Forces), Liberal Democrat Spokesperson (Defence), Liberal Democrat Spokesperson (Digital, Culture, Media and Sport)**

Could I have a reassurance from Her Majesty's Government that any proposal for an independence referendum coming forward from the Scottish Government, or indeed any proposed extrapolation of a general election result, will be closely examined within the context of United Kingdom law?

**Dominic Raab Deputy Prime Minister, The Lord Chancellor and Secretary of State for Justice**

I can reassure the hon. Gentleman that the Government's position has not changed. We do not think that now is the right time for a second referendum, given all the pressures and challenges and given the outcome of the first. I think what the people of Scotland want to see is both their Governments—in Edinburgh and in Westminster—working closely together.

## Prison Officers: Training
**4th July 2022**

*Ellie Reeves Shadow Minister (Justice)*

To ask the Secretary of State for Justice, how many hours a prison officer is permitted to spend on training each year.

*Victoria Atkins The Minister of State, Ministry of Justice*

There are no set training hours for prison officers however all HMPPS staff are able to access the online e-learning platform MyLearning which hosts a variety of training, which can be accessed at any time.

To become a fully trained prison officer, each learner must undertake a Level 3 Custody & Detention Apprenticeship, which is a total of 441 hours completed over the initial 16-18 month period.

All prison officers are able to undertake a variety of operational training as part of their continued professional development. Our e-learning platform MyLearning is available to all HMPPS employees and includes all essential learning.

## Prisoners' Release: Wales
**4th July 2022**

*Liz Saville-Roberts Shadow PC Spokesperson (Home Affairs), Shadow PC Spokesperson (Women and Equalities) , Plaid Cymru Westminster Leader, Shadow PC Spokesperson*

(Justice), Shadow PC Spokesperson (Business, Energy and Industrial Strategy), Shadow PC Spokesperson (Transport), Shadow PC Spokesperson (Attorney General)

To ask the Secretary of State for Justice, how many prison leavers in (a) 2020 and (b) 2021 had an origin address in Wales, by prison establishment.

*Victoria Atkins The Minister of State, Ministry of Justice*

Please note that where the number released from an establishment was 5 or fewer, the specific figure has not been given, in order to avoid the risk of identifying individuals.

The numerical information provided has been drawn from administrative IT systems which, as with any large-scale recording system, are subject to possible error with data entry and processing. The available information is shown in the table below.

| Prison Name | 2020 | 2021 |
|---|---|---|
| Altcourse | 75 | ≤5 |
| Ashfield | 9 | |
| Askham Grange | ≤5 | |
| Belmarsh | ≤5 | |
| Berwyn | 538 | 116 |
| Birmingham | 7 | |
| Brinsford | ≤5 | |
| Bristol | 11 | ≤5 |
| Brixton | ≤5 | |
| Bronzefield | ≤5 | |
| Bullingdon | ≤5 | |
| Cardiff | 1032 | 169 |
| Channings Wood | ≤5 | ≤5 |
| Chelmsford | ≤5 | |
| Coldingley | ≤5 | |
| Dartmoor | ≤5 | |
| Deerbolt | ≤5 | |
| Doncaster | ≤5 | ≤5 |
| Dovegate | ≤5 | |
| Downview | 7 | |
| Drake Hall | 10 | ≤5 |
| Eastwood Park | 225 | 38 |
| Elmley | ≤5 | |
| Erlestoke | ≤5 | |
| Exeter | ≤5 | ≤5 |
| Featherstone | ≤5 | |
| Feltham | ≤5 | |
| Ford | ≤5 | |
| Forest Bank | 6 | ≤5 |
| Foston Hall | ≤5 | |
| Garth | ≤5 | |
| Guys Marsh | ≤5 | |
| Haverigg | ≤5 | ≤5 |
| Hewell | 11 | 6 |
| High Down | ≤5 | |
| Hindley | 10 | ≤5 |
| Hollesley Bay | ≤5 | |
| Holme House | ≤5 | |
| Hull | ≤5 | ≤5 |
| Humber | ≤5 | ≤5 |
| Huntercombe | 9 | ≤5 |
| Isis | ≤5 | |
| Kirkham | 27 | 7 |
| Lancaster Farms | ≤5 | ≤5 |
| Leeds | ≤5 | |
| Lewes | ≤5 | ≤5 |
| Leyhill | 17 | ≤5 |
| Lincoln | ≤5 | |
| Lindholme | ≤5 | |
| Littlehey | | ≤5 |
| Liverpool | ≤5 | |
| Low Newton | ≤5 | |
| Lowdham Grange | ≤5 | |
| Maidstone | ≤5 | |
| Moorland | ≤5 | |
| Mount | ≤5 | |
| New Hall | ≤5 | |
| North Sea Camp | 7 | |
| Northumberland | ≤5 | |
| Nottingham | | ≤5 |
| Oakwood | 20 | ≤5 |
| Parc | 619 | 158 |
| Pentonville | 11 | |
| Peterborough | ≤5 | |
| Peterborough (female) | | |
| | | ≤5 |
| Portland | 6 | ≤5 |
| Prescoed | 148 | 30 |
| Preston | ≤5 | ≤5 |
| Ranby | ≤5 | ≤5 |
| Risley | 20 | ≤5 |
| Rochester | ≤5 | |
| Rye Hill | ≤5 | |
| Send | ≤5 | ≤5 |
| Spring Hill | ≤5 | |
| Stafford | 22 | 6 |
| Stoke Heath | 28 | ≤5 |
| Styal | 54 | ≤5 |
| Sudbury | ≤5 | |
| Swansea | 670 | 93 |
| Swinfen Hall | ≤5 | ≤5 |
| Thameside | ≤5 | |
| Thorn Cross | 13 | ≤5 |
| Usk | 66 | 15 |
| Verne | ≤5 | ≤5 |
| Wandsworth | ≤5 | |
| Warren Hill | | ≤5 |
| Wayland | ≤5 | ≤5 |
| Wealstun | ≤5 | |
| Werrington | ≤5 | ≤5 |
| Wetherby | ≤5 | |
| Whatton | 7 | ≤5 |
| Winchester | ≤5 | |
| Woodhill | ≤5 | |
| Wormwood Scrubs | ≤5 | |
| Wymott | 10 | |

## Probation: Qualifications
### 4th July 2022
*Ellie Reeves Shadow Minister (Justice)*

To ask the Secretary of State for Justice, how many applications there were to (a) the PQiP scheme and (b) vacancies for prison officers in the last 12 months.

*Victoria Atkins The Minister of State, Ministry of Justice*

Between 1 June 2021 and 31 May 2022 inclusive, 5,614 applications to the PQiP scheme were submitted and 78,890 applications to prison officer vacancies were submitted.

*Notes:*

*1. This data comes from the Oleeo Recruitment Database. Figures do not include recruitment campaigns managed by external companies.*

*2. Oleeo is a live system so figures may be subject to change. Data regarding prison officer applications was extracted on 2 June 2022.*

*3. The total number of applications include both external and internal applicants.*

*4. The prison officer data only includes recruitment for Public Sector Prisons.*

*5. Youth Justice Worker applications are included in the count of prison officer applications.*

*6. The count of prison officer applications covers Bands 3-5.*

*7. The prison officer figure excludes applications to the "Unlocked Graduate Scheme" but includes applications to Operational Support Grade to prison officer / Youth Justice Worker fast track campaigns.*

## Prison Accommodation
### 1st July 2022.
*Matt Vickers Conservative, Stockton South*

To ask the Secretary of State for Justice, what progress his Department has made in creating new prison places.

*Victoria Atkins The Minister of State, Ministry of Justice*

We have already delivered over 3,100 additional prison places through a combination of refurbishments, installing temporary accommodation, repurposing the Morton Hall Immigration Removal Centre back into a prison and the opening of HMP Five Wells earlier this year.

## Parole
### 1st July 2022.
*Matt Vickers Conservative, Stockton South*

To ask the Secretary of State for Justice, what steps he is taking to reform the parole system.

*Kit Malthouse The Minister of State, Home Department, The Minister of State, Ministry of Justice, Minister of State (Ministry of Justice and Home Office)*

The Root and Branch Review of the Parole System was published on 30 March 2022 and set out a number of reforms to the parole system. Key reforms include: refining the statutory release test and adding criteria which Parole Board panels must consider; creating a 'top-tier' of the most serious offenders, who will be subject to increased ministerial oversight, including the ability of the Secretary of State to refuse their release; and increasing the number of panel members with law enforcement experience, mandating that these members sit on 'top-tier' cases. We will legislate for these proposals as soon as parliamentary time allows.

We have already implemented a tougher test and increased ministerial oversight when considering the most serious offenders for a move to open prison conditions. In addition, a Statutory Instrument has recently been laid in Parliament, which will amend the Parole Board Rules to allow for some parole hearings to be heard in public. It will also provide for the Secretary of State to present the Parole Board with a single view on the suitability of a prisoner for release, which will allow for ministers to put in their view to the Board in the most serious cases. All of these measures aim to enhance public protection and improve confidence in the parole system.

## Prisons: Arts and Education
### 30th June 2022
*Lord Hylton Crossbench*

To ask Her Majesty's Government what steps they are taking to restore (1) education programmes, and (2) access to (a) training, and (b) the arts, for prisoners, where those have been restricted by (i) COVID-19, and (ii) staff shortages.

*Lord Bellamy The Parliamentary Under-Secretary of State for Justice*

Staff recruitment was suspended from March 2020 until August 2020 whilst we implemented Covid-19 secure practices in response to Government guidelines on social distancing and non-essential travel. While this created a gap in our pipeline of new officers, once the process restarted, we used initiatives such as the accelerated launch of 60+ recruitment campaigns and the use of targeted overtime and mutual aid across prisons, to ensure establishments facing the greatest challenges received the most support.

Although face-to-face teaching was temporarily suspended due to safety concerns at the start of the pandemic, education continued via remote learning. With the pandemic National Framework for Prison Regimes and Services having been lifted on 9 May 2022, we are now getting increasing numbers of learners back in the classroom and participating in activities, like the arts, that support rehabilitation where it is safe to do so.

As set out in the Prisons Strategy White Paper, published on 7 December 2021, we are committed to improving education in prisons and we are delivering a Prisoner Education Service within this Parliament to raise prisoners' levels of numeracy, literacy, skills and qualifications with the aim of helping them secure jobs upon release and drive down reoffending. This work includes investment in digital infrastructure, more training that delivers the skills employers need, more education experts to support Governors and improved support for prisoners with additional learning needs.

### Prison Sentences
**30th June 2022.**
*Jim Shannon Shadow DUP Spokesperson (Human Rights), Shadow DUP Spokesperson (Health)*
To ask the Secretary of State for Justice, what recent assessment he has made of the adequacy of prison sentences given to offenders; and what assessment he has made of the potential impact of longer sentences for offenders.
*James Cartlidge Parliamentary Under Secretary of State (Ministry of Justice), Assistant Whip*
The government's top priority is protecting the public; it is essential that we have a sentencing framework that delivers this and ensures victims and the wider public have confidence that the punishment fits the crime in every case.
In 2020, the Government published a Sentencing White Paper and consequently delivered measures in the Police, Crime, Sentencing and Courts Act which received Royal Assent on 28 April 2022. Measures include ending automatic halfway release from prison for serious crimes, making a Whole Life Order the starting point for a premeditated murder of a child and a new power to refer high-risk offenders to Parole Board in place of automatic release.
While prisons keep people safe by taking dangerous criminals off our streets, we recognise that they can only bring down crime and keep the public safer in the longer-term if they properly reform and rehabilitate offenders. We therefore published the Prisons Strategy White Paper in December 2021 where we re-iterated our commitment to help individual turn their backs on crime and we will spend £200 million a year by 2024-25 to improve prison leavers' access to accommodation, employment support and substance misuse treatment.

### Offenders: Rehabilitation
**30th June 2022**
*The Bishop of St Albans Bishop*
To ask Her Majesty's Government what plans they have to introduce (1) a Community Sentence Treatment Requirement for gambling addiction, or (2) a Gambling Treatment Requirement, similar to community sentence treatments for offences where alcohol, drugs or mental health issues were an underlying factor.
*Lord Bellamy The Parliamentary Under-Secretary of State for Justice*
Offenders with a gambling addiction may be suitable for a Mental Health Treatment Requirement (MHTR) as part of a community or suspended sentence order where mental health has been identified as an underlying factor.
The MHTR clinical practitioner assessment would identify an individual's vulnerability (for example gambling addiction) and this would determine the psychological interventions suitable for them. Due to the complexity of gambling addiction, different approaches are used to enhance therapeutic effectiveness.
HM Prison and Probation Service (HMPPS) is committed to increasing awareness of the hidden harms of addiction to gambling and helping to support those with a problem, at all stages of the criminal justice system. To this end, a needs analysis is planned so that we can better understand the size of the issue. The results will inform the development of an HMPPS national gambling strategy, designed to raise awareness of problem gambling and ensure that our probation officers have the confidence to help identify and signpost individuals into the most appropriate care.
I refer the noble Lord to the answer given to HL980 for a more detailed account of the work in hand to raise awareness and knowledge of problem gambling with prison staff, probation and the police.

### Radicalisation in Prisons (2)
**28th June 2022.**
*Unmesh Desai Labour*
In 2020, you warned that prisons are 'warehouses where people are radicalised more or learn more things from a university of crime rather than being rehabilitated and punished'. Has the Government made enough progress on improving prisons in London since then and if not, what more needs to be done?
*Sadiq Khan Mayor of London*
Some progress is being made by central government and the recent Prison Strategy consultation response outlines more plans to improve security and further links to work and employment after release, but much more still needs to be done, especially in London. The huge increase in prison violence (a 268% increase in violence to staff between 2009-19), over-crowding and poor facilities in London prisons remain significant problems. There is also a

consistent lack of investment in programmes to reduce the risk of violence and reoffending following release.

I will continue to build on the success of the recently completed Prison Pathfinder pilot, to ensure that those who pose the highest risk of violence have effective work done in custody to protect the public. My report on Countering Violent Extremism in London, 'A Shared Endeavour', found that radicalisation in prisons remains a key concern. I am pleased that the Ministry of Justice are working on the improvements recently suggested by the Independent Reviewer of Terrorism Legislation. The progress of this work will be reviewed by the London CONTEST Board, chaired by my Deputy Mayor for Policing and Crime.

## Prison Governors
### 27th June 2022
*Ellie Reeves Shadow Minister (Justice)*
To ask the Secretary of State for Justice, what progress his Department has made on the policy details for the new deal for prison governors set out in the Prisons Strategy white paper.
*Victoria Atkins The Minister of State, Ministry of Justice*
In the Prisons Strategy White Paper, we committed to delivering the 'New Deal' for governors based on clear expectations and accountability, but with greater freedom and autonomy to shape delivery in prisons. In April 2022, we introduced Key Performance Indicators (KPIs) to drive improved outcomes by measuring progress with annually published performance ratings for each prison. At the end of June 2022, we will issue guidance to governors restating their existing local freedoms. We are committed to launching Earned Autonomy in early 2023 which will empower our highest performing operational leaders to innovate locally and improve outcomes.

## Prisons: Discipline
### 27th June 2022
*Ellie Reeves Shadow Minister (Justice)*
To ask the Secretary of State for Justice, what steps his Department is taking to ensure that the fast-track adjudications process does not have disproportionate impacts on protected groups.
*Victoria Atkins The Minister of State, Ministry of Justice*
The Prisons Strategy White Paper set out our ambition to introduce a fast-track adjudications system with rehabilitative interventions for lower-level offences.
We will complete a full impact and equalities assessment for this policy, and we will take the appropriate steps to ensure that prisoners with protected characteristics are not disproportionately negatively impacted by the changes.

## Prisons: Video Conferencing
### 27th June 2022.
*Ellie Reeves Shadow Minister (Justice)*
To ask the Secretary of State for Justice, if he will increase the current entitlement of prisoners to make video calls.
*Victoria Atkins The Minister of State, Ministry of Justice*
We remain committed in continuing to offer social video calls, as we have clear evidence that these, alongside face-to-face visits, telephone calls, voicemail and email, help maintain contact with families and significant others. Maintaining such ties is not only important for the well-being of prisoners but has also been shown to reduce reoffending.
At present, we are operating this offer in accordance with our interim policy which enables one free 30-minute call per prisoner, per month. Additional calls are also available at the discretion of Governors.
A longer-term policy is being developed to support our commitment to sustaining social video calling and we are considering options in line with our commitments in the Prison Strategy White Paper.

## Prisoners' Release: Temporary Accommodation
### 27th June 2022
*Ellie Reeves Shadow Minister (Justice)*
To ask the Secretary of State for Justice, if his Department will take steps to ensure that new temporary accommodation to support prison leavers at risk of homelessness will be situated in places that are not likely to increase the risk of further reoffending.
*Kit Malthouse The Minister of State, Home Department, The Minister of State, Ministry of Justice, Minister of State (Ministry of Justice and Home Office)*
This Government is determined to continue driving down reoffending rates, to make our streets safer and reduce the £18bn annual cost of reoffending. The overall reoffending rate has already fallen from 31% in 2009/10 to 26% in 2019/20.
The provision of temporary accommodation for prison leavers is a key part of our work to further reduce reoffending - we know that offenders are around 50 per cent more likely to commit crimes again if released without somewhere to stay. The provision of more temporary accommodation for prison leavers forms part of our plans to spend £200m a year by 2024-25 to reduce reoffending. As part of this, HM Prison and Probation Service (HMPPS) has launched a service providing up to

12 weeks' basic accommodation and support for those leaving prison at risk of homelessness. Originally launched in 5 probation regions, the provision is being fully rolled out across England and Wales this year, supporting the thousands of prison leavers who leave prison each year who would otherwise lack stable accommodation. We launched the competition for new contracts on 18 May 2022.

In terms of the locations of new temporary accommodation, the provider of the accommodation must obtain HMPPS' approval for new accommodation before it can be used. Information received by the Authority from the police or local authority helps to inform the decision, and a Community Probation Practitioner will risk assess whether the accommodation is suitable for the offender. In this way, it is ensured that new temporary accommodation is in appropriate locations.

## Prisons
### 27th June 2022.
*Ellie Reeves Shadow Minister (Justice)*
To ask the Secretary of State for Justice, what steps he is taking to improve conditions for those living and working in prisons.
*Victoria Atkins The Minister of State, Ministry of Justice*
We are investing £675m over the period 2022 to 2025 in capital projects across the prison estate to improve conditions for prisoners and staff, safeguard capacity, and improve sustainability. Over the same period we are also investing £3.8bn to make significant progress in delivering 20,000 prison places. These will provide modern, safe and decent accommodation and workplaces for prisoners and staff.

## Prisoners: Apprentices
### 27th June 2022
*Lord Taylor of Warwick Non-affiliated*
To ask Her Majesty's Government what plans they have to allow businesses to direct the apprenticeship levy towards prison rehabilitation schemes.
*Baroness Barran The Parliamentary Under-Secretary of State for Education*
The department fully supports preparing prisoners for employment upon their release and recognises how important this is. We are working with the Ministry of Justice to introduce an apprenticeship programme for those in prison and who are close to being released, in order for these individuals to benefit from the enhanced skills and employment prospects that apprenticeships bring.
We expect to make the necessary changes to legislation by the autumn to allow the first

apprenticeship starts later on this year. Initially, up to 100 prisoners a year will be supported to begin an apprenticeship in custody.

The introduction of apprenticeships for serving prisoners later this year will allow levy-paying employers to use their levy funds to support apprenticeships for those in custody. Levy payers can already employ prisoners as apprentices upon their release and can use their levy funds to support these apprenticeships.

We do not have plans to allow businesses to direct levy funds intended for apprenticeships towards prisoner rehabilitation schemes. The Ministry of Justice is responsible for, and receives funding to deliver, prisoner education and rehabilitation services.

## Prisoners' Release
### 22nd June 2022
*Ellie Reeves Shadow Minister (Justice)*
To ask the Secretary of State for Justice, when his plans to reduce Friday release will be implemented.
*Kit Malthouse The Minister of State, Home Department, The Minister of State, Ministry of Justice, Minister of State (Ministry of Justice and Home Office)*
This Government will legislate to enable offenders who are at risk of reoffending to be released up to two days earlier, where a release date falls on a Friday or before a bank holiday, when Parliamentary time allows.
We will continue to consider the views of stakeholders, including operational colleagues, prison staff and the third sector to shape the policy to ensure that legislative change reduces risk of reoffending, protects the public and effectively manages risk.

## Theft: Remand in Custody
### 21st June 2022
*Steve Reed Shadow Secretary of State for Justice*
To ask the Secretary of State for Justice, how many offenders were held on remand awaiting trial for theft; and for what length of time those offenders were held on remand in each prison in England and Wales in each of the last five years.
*James Cartlidge Parliamentary Under Secretary of State (Ministry of Justice), Assistant Whip*
The number of prisoners who were held on untried remand for alleged theft and the length of time those prisoners were held on remand, in each prison in England and Wales, as at 30 June in each of the last five years, is shown in the attached tables.
When the court is making a remand decision, the Bail Act 1976 provides a presumption in favour of bail, recognising that a person should not be deprived of their liberty unless necessary for the

protection of the public or the delivery of justice. The courts decide on a case-by-case basis whether a defendant presents such a bail risk as to warrant custody. Bail can only be refused where there is justification, as prescribed in Schedule 1 to the Bail Act, such as substantial grounds for believing that the defendant, would abscond, commit further offences, interfere with witnesses or otherwise obstruct the course of justice.

The overall remand population has increased in recent years as a result of the Covid-19 pandemic. The Government is committed to supporting the recovery of the courts and we continue to take action to tackle the impact the pandemic has had on the system. We have extended 30 Nightingale courtrooms beyond the end of March 2022 and have again removed the limit on the number of days the Crown Court can sit this financial year. To secure enough capacity to sit at the required levels in 2022/23 and beyond, we are also expanding our plans for judicial recruitment.

### Prison Officers
**20th June 2022**
*Baroness Blower Labour*

To ask Her Majesty's Government what recent estimate they have made of the levels of (1) retention, and (2) cumulative experience, of prison officers.

*Lord Bellamy The Parliamentary Under-Secretary of State for Justice*

HM Prison and Probation Service (HMPPS) does not have a standard definition of 'retention rates', however we do publish information on leaving rates which can be used as a proxy. The leaving rate is the number of staff who have left the department in the previous 12 months divided by the average number of staff in post over the same period.

In the 12 months to 31 March 2022, the leaving rate for Band 3 Prison Officers, Band 4 Supervising Officers/Prison Officer specialists and Band 5 Custodial Managers was 14.5%.

Band 3 to 5 covers all operational grades including all Prison Officers.

As at 31 March 2022, there were 22,002 FTE band 3-5 prison officers in post who together held a cumulative length of service of 238,195 years. In terms of headcount, there are 22,972 prison officers and so this gives an average of 10.4 years per prison officer.

A full breakdown of prison officer numbers by length of service is published in Table 4 of HMPPS workforce Statistics bulletin, the March 2022 publication is available at this link: https://www.gov.uk/government/statistics/her-majestys-prison-and-probation-service-workforce-quarterly-march-2022. Figures have been reproduced below.

*Table 1: HMPPS staff by length of service, for Band 3-5 Prison Officers as at 31 March 2022 (Full Time Equivalent)*

| Grade | Completed years of service | 31.3.22 |
|---|---|---|
| Band 3-5 Officers | | |
| | 0 | 3,272 |
| | 1 | 1,715 |
| | 2 | 1,432 |
| | 3 | 2,522 |
| | 4 | 2,425 |
| | 5-9 | 2,581 |
| | 10-14 | 1,639 |
| | 15-19 | 2,670 |
| | 20-24 | 1,344 |
| | 25-29 | 1,131 |
| | 30+ | 1,272 |
| *Total* | | **22,002** |

### Prisons: Telephones
**10th June 2022**
*Matthew Offord Conservative, Hendon*

To ask the Secretary of State for Justice, how much the Government has spent on installing in cell telephones on the prison estate in the last five years.

*Victoria Atkins The Minister of State, Ministry of Justice*

The Government has spent £36.34m on installing in cell telephony on the prison estate in the past 5 years. This technology is vital in boosting prisoners' rehabilitation prospects, as it helps them maintain family ties and access the support they need to stay away from crime on release.

In-cell telephony has also reduced the need for prisoners to share communal pin phones, which can be potential trigger points for violence, arising from prisoners queuing for public phones on the landings. Disagreements around communal phones can in turn fuel demand for illicit mobile phones.

All calls remain restricted to pre-approved numbers only, and public protection and safeguarding factors have been considered prior to the number being approved by the prison. All calls are recorded for the purpose of call monitoring, with the exception of legal calls and support lines such as the Samaritans. Phones are active during the agreed operating times specified by the prison.

### Prison Sentences
**24th May 2022**
*Lord Moylan Conservative*

To ask Her Majesty's Government, further to the Written Answer by Lord Wolfson of Tredegar on 4 April (HL7159) which said there would be greater ministerial scrutiny of the moves of indeterminate sentence prisoners to open conditions", whether this policy has already been put into effect and, if so, from what date; if the policy has not been put into effect, on what date it will come into force; which minister will be charged with undertaking the scrutiny referred to; what criteria will determine which cases are considered; against what criteria they will assess the case for a move to open conditions, and if these will differ from the criteria currently applied by officials; and what documentation the minister will receive and consider in order to reach a decision in the cases they consider personally.

*Baroness Scott of Bybrook Baroness in Waiting (HM Household) (Whip)*

Following a decision by the Deputy Prime Minister last year, there will now be greater scrutiny of Parole Board recommendations on open prison moves. The test for considering a recommendation for open conditions for Indeterminate Sentence Prisoners (ISPs) will change, and I will write to the noble Lord in due course to provide an update.

Our primary responsibility is to protect the public and it remains the case that the independent Parole Board will grant those serving indeterminate sentences release only once they have demonstrated they will no longer pose a significant risk to the public.

## Prisons: Education
### 16th May 2022

*Liz Saville-Roberts Shadow PC Spokesperson (Home Affairs), Shadow PC Spokesperson (Women and Equalities) , Plaid Cymru Westminster Leader, Shadow PC Spokesperson (Justice), Shadow PC Spokesperson (Business, Energy and Industrial Strategy), Shadow PC Spokesperson (Transport), Shadow PC Spokesperson (Attorney General)*

To ask the Secretary of State for Justice, with reference to the Answer of 28 March 2022 to Question 144980, Prisons: Education, how many meetings his officials in his Department has held with representatives of relevant trade unions on the Prisoner Education Service.

*Victoria Atkins The Minister of State, Ministry of Justice*

We are delivering a Prisoner Education Service within this Parliament to raise prisoners' levels of numeracy, literacy, skills and qualifications with the aim of helping them secure jobs or apprenticeships on their release. To do this, we must give prisons the tools they need to succeed. We will invest in digital infrastructure, more training that delivers the skills employers need, more education experts to support Governors and improved support for prisoners with additional learning needs.

To deliver this vision, we are currently running a series of engagement events, drawing on the expertise of stakeholders across the education and justice sectors.

HMPPS holds regular meetings with its recognised trade unions to share information and invite feedback on operational developments and proposals. As prison education staff are not employed by HMPPS, their union representatives are not part of these regular consultations. We have engaged with these representatives, however, as part of our wider engagement activity.

## Prisons and Probation: Standards
### 27th April 2022

*Baroness Burt of Solihull Liberal Democrat*

To ask Her Majesty's Government what progress they have made in establishing (1) an estate-wide set of non-mandatory best practice standards in prisons in England and Wales, and (2) best practice probation standards, further to the Joint IPP Action Plan published by Her Majesty's Prison and Probation Service and Parole Board in June 2019.

*Lord Wolfson of Tredegar Conservative*

The IPP Action Plan is regularly reviewed to ensure that it is responsive to the needs of those serving IPP sentences, whether in prison or in the community. A large number of IPP prisoners have been released each year since the IPP Action Plan was first introduced in 2016, and the Plan will be refreshed, reviewed and republished after careful consideration of the forthcoming Justice Select Committee's Report and recommendations. The Public Protection Casework Section in HM Prison and Probation Service (HMPPS) HQ has implemented active case management, which is directed towards ensuring that probation and prison staff comply with directions from Parole Board Panels in a timely fashion.

Best practice ideals, based on an initiative that started in prisons in the East of England Region, were developed and rolled out for use in a number of prisons prior to the pandemic. The roll out was then unavoidably disrupted by the exceptional delivery models which had to be implemented on the grounds of public health. Progress of the best practice ideals will be reviewed as part of the wider action plan following consideration of the Justice Select Committee's report and recommendations.

Offenders subject to IPP sentences are eligible for electronic monitoring following release on licence, where considered necessary and proportionate by the Parole Board. The additional investment of £183m in the expansion of electronic monitoring will also increase the availability of electronic monitoring for IPP offenders. Those whose risk is linked to alcohol are eligible for alcohol monitoring on licence, which was introduced in Wales in November and will be rolled out to England this summer. IPP releases will also be eligible for a project targeting high-risk domestic abuse perpetrators, where they will have their whereabouts monitored using GPS tags to protect victims, and potential future victims, from further trauma. The project will begin in 2023 and we expect to tag around 3,500 offenders.

HM Prison and Probation Service has developed a dataset and data dashboard, which is shared on a quarterly basis with Probation Regions and Prison Groups to support them in their efforts to monitor and manage their IPP populations, both in prisons and the community. The dashboard is still evolving and kept under review, as we identify new ways to capture additional key management information and present it in such a way as to be the most helpful to the operational line.

The following table shows the number of progression panels (lifers and IPPs) that have taken place in each Probation region by year since June 2019*: During the COVID-19 pandemic, and in accordance with measures mandated in the interests of public health, HM Prison and Probation Service (HMPPS) implemented exceptional delivery models which inevitably had some impact on all operational work.

**Sentencing**
**25th April 2022**
*Alex Cunningham Shadow Minister (Justice)*
To ask the Secretary of State for Justice, with reference to page 52 of the White Paper, A Smarter Approach to Sentencing, what steps his Department is taking to help encourage the use of deferred sentencing.

*James Cartlidge Parliamentary Under Secretary of State (Ministry of Justice), Assistant Whip*
Sentencing in individual cases is entirely a matter for our independent courts, taking into account all the circumstances of the case.

The Sentencing White Paper, A Smarter Approach to Sentencing, published in September 2020, set out a package of reforms to ensure that the most serious offenders are kept in prison for longer and to deliver tougher, better monitored and more effective community sentencing which punishes offenders, tackles the underlying drivers of offending, and provides support for those who want to turn their lives around. As part of this package of reforms, the Sentencing White Paper set out our aim to encourage the use of deferred sentences, where the court has the capacity.

Reforms within the Police, Crime, Sentencing and Courts Bill, currently before Parliament, deliver on many of the commitments made and,

| Probation Region | The number of progression panels held (Lifers and IPPs) | | | | |
| --- | --- | --- | --- | --- | --- |
| | 01/06/2019 to 31/12/2019 | 2020 | 2021 | 01/01/2022 to 22/03/2022 | Total |
| East Midlands Region | 114 | 466 | 241 | 23 | 844 |
| East of England | 224 | 715 | 554 | 107 | 1,600 |
| Greater Manchester | 294 | 472 | 291 | 36 | 1,093 |
| Kent Surrey Sussex Region | 129 | 529 | 426 | 79 | 1,163 |
| London | 236 | 551 | 629 | 134 | 1,550 |
| National Security Division | - | * | 4 | * | 9 |
| North East Region | 117 | 423 | 196 | 33 | 769 |
| North West Region | 298 | 710 | 447 | 85 | 1,540 |
| South Central | 156 | 271 | 328 | 79 | 834 |
| South West | 111 | 469 | 197 | 137 | 914 |
| Wales | 174 | 197 | 150 | 16 | 537 |
| West Midlands Region | 304 | 868 | 522 | 126 | 1,820 |
| Yorkshire and The Humber | 170 | 635 | 422 | 72 | 1,299 |
| Unknown Region | 3 | * | - | * | 16 |
| **Total** | **2,330** | **6,322** | **4,407** | **929** | **13,988** |

*Notes:
1. Panels without a recorded outcome (from the point that an outcome was required to be recorded) were assumed to not have taken place.
2. Due to probation restructures in 2020 and 2021, a small number of panels could not be assigned to a region. These are recorded as 'Unknown Region'.
3. **Disclosure control.** An asterisk (*) has been used to suppress values of one or two. This is to prevent the disclosure of individual information. Further disclosure control may be completed where this alone is not sufficient.
4. **Data sources and quality.** The figures in these tables have been drawn from the Probation Case Management System, National Delius administrative, which, as with any large scale recording system, are subject to possible errors with data entry and processing.

beyond the Bill, we are taking forward various initiatives to progress the plans we set out.

### Parole
**19th April 2022**

*Steve Reed Shadow Secretary of State for Justice*

To ask the Secretary of State for Justice, whether his plans to reform the parole process will consider preventing released offenders living near their victim where that is against the victim's wishes.

*Kit Malthouse The Minister of State, Home Department, The Minister of State, Ministry of Justice, Minister of State (Ministry of Justice and Home Office)*

As we announced in our Root and Branch Review of the Parole System, published on 30 March, our focus is to enhance public protection and improve the system for victims – giving them greater access and a more prominent voice in the parole process. It is already the case that upon release from prison, and for the duration of their licence period, offenders must only reside at an address approved by the Probation Service. Failure to comply with such conditions can result in the offender being recalled to prison.

The victim's wishes are taken into account in developing the offender's release plan. Victims signed up to the Victim Contact Scheme have the statutory right to request licence conditions in advance of a prisoner's release and the Probation Service will consider what conditions may be required to protect victims and their families against unwanted contact. These could include a non-contact condition or an exclusion zone, prohibiting the offender from entering areas where the victim lives and works, or to which the victim travels frequently.

Protecting the public and victims is the government's priority. Under our proposed reforms, we will ensure that victims' wishes and concerns are given more prominence in the parole process, including plans to require the Parole Board to take account of submissions from victims.

### Prisons: Drugs
**7th April 2022**

*Lord Bradley Labour*

To ask Her Majesty's Government how much they have spent on drug rehabilitation for (1) men, and (2) women, in prison, in (a) England, and (b) Wales, in each year since 2010.

*Lord Kamall The Parliamentary Under-Secretary for Health and Social Care*

The information is not held in the format requested. Due to the way NHS England commissions integrated services across the secure and detained estate, it is not possible to determine specific expenditure on mental health services and substance misuse services.

In England, spending on health services in prisons has increased from £400 million in 2016/17 to approximately £496 million in 2020/21. Integrated spending on substance misuse and mental health services in prisons has increased from £148 million in 2016/17 to £203 million in 2020/21. This expenditure relates to both the male and female adult secure estate.

Information on health care spending in Wales is not held as this is a devolved matter.

### Sexual Offences: Sentencing
**4th April 2022**

*Lord Garnier Conservative*

To ask Her Majesty's Government what progress they have made in establishing a progression unit for prisoners subject to Imprisonment for Public Protection (IPP) sentences with a sexual offence, further to the Joint IPP Action Plan published by Her Majesty's Prison and Probation Service and the Parole Board in June 2019.

*Lord Garnier Conservative*

To ask Her Majesty's Government what progress they have made to ensure that contracted sites are compliant with national strategies for management and progression of prisoners subject to Imprisonment for Public Protection (IPP) sentences, further to the Joint IPP Action Plan, published by Her Majesty's Prison and Probation Service and the Parole Board in June 2019.

*Lord Wolfson of Tredegar The Parliamentary Under-Secretary of State for Justice*

The IPP Action Plan is regularly reviewed to ensure that it is responsive to the needs of those serving IPP sentences, whether in prison or in the community. During the COVID-19 pandemic, and in accordance with measures mandated in the interests of public health, HM Prison and Probation Service (HMPPS) implemented exceptional delivery models which inevitably had some impact on all operational work. A large number of IPP prisoners have been released each year since the IPP Action Plan first introduced in 2016, and the Plan will be refreshed, reviewed and republished after careful consideration of the forthcoming Justice Select Committee's Report and recommendations.

A progression unit for prisoners serving IPP sentences with a conviction for a sexual offence has been open at HMP Littlehey for the last three years. The unit provides an environment where prisoners feel safe and receive support to focus on their progression. As with the other workstreams within the IPP action plan, HMPPS will review the progress of the unit this year, which will also take account of any relevant aspects of the report and recommendations of the Justice Select Committee.

HMPPS continue to engage with senior managers in prisons run under contract, to ensure that the IPP Action Plan initiatives are reflected in their delivery plans. For example, each contracted site has an IPP single point of contact for Psychology Services.

## Offenders: Employment
### 31st March 2022
*Steve Reed Shadow Secretary of State for Justice*
To ask the Secretary of State for Justice, pursuant to the Answer of 28 March 2022 to Question 144920 on Offenders: Employment, what steps he is taking to increase the number of prisoners finding work following their release from the worst performing prisons.

*Kit Malthouse The Minister of State, Home Department, The Minister of State, Ministry of Justice, Minister of State (Ministry of Justice and Home Office)*
It is a priority for this government to increase the proportion of prison leavers in employment following release. We will deliver a presumption in favour of offering offenders the chance to work in prison, on Release on Temporary Licence and on release.

We will hold Governors to account for the opportunities and outcomes to participate in work related activity they achieve for prisoners. In return, we will deliver a new digital tool to inform governors and commissioners about progress and what interventions are working in their prison.

We are also rolling out dedicated Employment Advisors in all resettlement prisons, to improve how we identify candidates and match them to jobs. This will mean that there is a named person in those establishments accountable for improving these outcomes. Alongside this, we are establishing 'Employment Hubs' which are the equivalent of a 'job centre in a prison'. Prisoners can find out about opportunities sourced by New Futures Network and other partners, as well as access support with applications. There are 23 in operation currently and we plan to have a further 13 by the end of June.

Last month the government also announced that it would change the law so that prisoners are able to apply for apprenticeship opportunities in vital industries, including hospitality and construction. Overall, we will publish an annual dashboard, showing performance against Key Performance Indicators, and league tables to increase transparency around prison performance.

## Parole System: Public Protection
### 30th March 2022
*Dominic Raab Deputy Prime Minister, The Lord Chancellor and Secretary of State for Justice 1:29 pm, 30th March 2022*
Today I am publishing the root and branch review of the parole system, and copies have been deposited in the Library.

I start by paying tribute to the chief executive officer and the chair of the Parole Board for England and Wales, Martin Jones and Caroline Corby, and to all the staff who work so tirelessly to discharge their important responsibilities. They are dedicated and committed public servants.

Before I address the detail of the statement, and with your forbearance, Madam Deputy Speaker, I will update the House on this morning's news. In the light of the Parole Board's direction to release Tracey Connelly, and having carefully read the decision, I have decided to apply to the Parole Board seeking its reconsideration.

More generally, the role of the Parole Board in deciding on the appropriateness of releasing a criminal offender from prison, including many convicted of very serious violent and sexual offences, is clearly of paramount importance to protecting the public and to maintaining and sustaining public confidence in our justice system. It is the first duty of Government to protect the public.

In recent years, a number of decisions to release offenders who committed heinous crimes have led to disquiet, concern and, regrettably, an erosion of public confidence. Take the case of John Worboys, who is serving a discretionary life sentence for rape and other sexual offences. The Parole Board's decision in January 2018 to release him on licence caused deep concern among his victims and the wider public. It was subject to a successful legal challenge, after which the Crown Prosecution Service successfully prosecuted him for attacking four further women.

I know that hon. Members on both sides of the House have raised the case of Colin Pitchfork, who was convicted of the rape and murder of Lynda Mann and Dawn Ashworth. The Parole Board decided to release Pitchfork in 2021, and it rejected the challenge by the then Justice Secretary, my right hon. and learned Friend Sir Robert Buckland. The understandable public anxiety was further compounded when Pitchfork was recalled to prison just two months after release for approaching women in breach of his licence conditions.

I make a broader point that in these kinds of cases, and in many others that do not attract the same level of media attention or public interest, victims feel their trauma and raw fear are neither recognised nor understood. Likewise, the public inevitably begin to question the reliability of decision making when serious offenders are recalled to prison for breaches of their licence or for committing further offences on release.

To give the House a sense of scale, in 2020-21 the Parole Board's annual report stated that 27 offenders went on to be charged with a serious further offence following release directed by the Parole Board panel. There were 40 cases of serious further offences being charged in each of the preceding two years. Placed in context, it is fair to say this is only a fraction of all cases, but more than once a fortnight an offender goes on to commit a serious offence while subject to supervision.

At present, victims who wish to challenge a decision by the Parole Board to release a prisoner have the option of asking the Justice Secretary to apply for the decision to be reconsidered, which is an important innovation that I exercised today for a person convicted in the harrowing case of Baby P. There have been 39 interventions since the challenge mechanism was set up two years ago, with four leading to a change in the release decision.

Following the review published today, I believe the case for reform is clear and made out. In arriving at this conclusion, it is worth pausing to acknowledge the shift in the Parole Board's approach over time. The statutory test was established in 1991 and states

"The Parole Board must not give a direction"—for release—

"unless the Board is satisfied that it is no longer necessary for the protection of the public that the person should be confined."

It is clear from this that the overriding test focuses on public protection. However, in the absence of further guidance from Parliament, the way in which the release test has been interpreted and applied over time has shifted, moving away from Parliament's original intention. In fact, as early as the Bradley judgment in 1991, the High Court concluded:

"The Parole Board have to carry out a balancing exercise between the legitimate conflicting interests of both prisoner and public."

To summarise, the statutory test has morphed over time from a strict public protection test to a balancing exercise between, on the one hand, the responsibility of the state to protect the public and, on the other hand, the rights of the prisoner. Whatever the rights and wrongs, that was palpably not the original intention of Parliament. I make it clear that I am not criticising the courts, which have sought to apply a generic statutory test without more prescriptive guidance from Parliament, nor am I criticising members of the Parole Board, as I hope I have made clear. It is worth saying that, contrary to public perception, it

is often fiendishly difficult to come to a reliable assessment of an offender's risk many years after their original crimes. Although psychiatric assessments and social science can offer guidance, risk assessments in such cases are inherently uncertain and imprecise. We need to be more honest and open about that in our public debate.

In any case, I believe the focus in this critical decision making has become adrift from its original moorings. This Government will again anchor Parole Board decision making on the cardinal principle of public protection. When it comes to assessing the risk to victims and public safety, we will introduce a precautionary principle to reinforce public confidence in the system. In cases involving those who have committed the most serious crimes, we will introduce a ministerial check on release decisions, exercised by the Justice Secretary.

The package of reforms published today will strengthen the focus on public protection at every stage. First, we will revise the statutory test for release and replace the current approach that balances the rights of dangerous offenders against public safety with an overriding focus on public protection, by providing in primary legislation further detailed criteria for the application of the statutory test.

Secondly, we will make sure that the Parole Board is better equipped to make credible and realistic assessments of risk. It is striking that, as of last year, only 5% of all Parole Board panel members come from a law enforcement background. Again, I make no criticism of the current panel members, but that is a significant deficit. I believe the deficit is wrong, and our reforms will ensure that the people we charge with making finely balanced assessments of future risk have greater first-hand operational experience of protecting the public from serious offenders. We will change this imbalance by mandating the Parole Board to recruit more members with operational law enforcement experience, and the Ministry of Justice will run a recruitment campaign to bolster its numbers. Critically, in Parole Board cases involving the top-tier cohort of serious violent and sexual offenders, we will require by law that at least one of the three panel members has a law enforcement background.

The third key reform is that, for the top-tier cohort of high-risk offenders who have committed the most serious offences, we will introduce ministerial oversight of Parole Board decisions to release such offenders back into the community, based on our assessment of the dangerousness of the offender, the risk of serious further offending and public confidence. These top-tier offenders will comprise those serving sentences for murder, rape, terrorism and causing or allowing the death of a child. In those cases, we will make two specific changes. The Parole Board will be able to refer a case to the Justice Secretary if it cannot confidently conclude whether, on the evidence, the statutory test for release has been met. In addition, we will introduce ministerial oversight over any decision to release any offender in the top-tier cohort of serious offenders. Under our reforms, in that top tier of cases the Justice Secretary will have the power to refuse release, subject to judicial challenge, on very clearly prescribed grounds, in the upper tribunal. I believe that is warranted as an extra check and safeguard to protect the public. I have not yet ruled out entirely an alternative model that could establish a three-person panel chaired by the Justice Secretary with the same power to refuse release, subject to judicial review in the normal way. We will consider further detail of the mechanism in order to strike the most effective balance.

We are making these reforms because the concept of risk is notoriously difficult to assess in these kinds of cases. We are doing it because the public expect their safety to be the overriding consideration and because, ultimately, it involves a judgment call about public protection, and the public expect Ministers to take responsibility for their safety. Let me be equally clear that there is no such thing as a risk-free society; we cannot guarantee that no one released from prison will go on to commit a serious crime. Let us be very clear about that as we have a more honest debate about the assessment of risk. Nevertheless, I believe that these measures are necessary to reinforce public safety and public confidence, and we will legislate for them as soon as possible. I should also say that we will do so alongside our proposed Bill of Rights, to ensure that the will of Parliament and that focus on public protection is not undermined by the Human Rights Act. Indeed, our reforms to parole yet again highlight the compelling case for a Bill of Rights.

Our fourth reform will increase victim participation in parole hearings, thereby delivering on this Government's manifesto commitment. I recognise that parole decisions will be immensely and acutely traumatic moments for many victims, as they are forced to remember, go through and revisit the ordeal and suffering that they have already been through. Some will not wish to be involved, whereas others will want their voices to be heard, and I believe they should have that right. So we will give victims the right to attend a parole hearing in full, for the first time, should they wish to do so. In addition, we will require the board to take into account submissions made by victims

and allow victims to ask questions through those submissions. The voice of victims will be at the centre of the process, not just some lingering afterthought.

Finally, although separate from parole decision making, similar considerations of risk and public concern have arisen in the context of decisions to transfer prisoners to prisons in open conditions. That is why in December 2021 I changed the process to introduce a ministerial check on such decisions, guided by similar principles to those that I have already set out. That is what led to my decision this month to reject the Parole Board's recommendation to move Steven Ling, who raped and killed a woman, to an open prison. I declined the move in the interest of public protection and public confidence.

In sum, our reforms will ensure that those offenders who present the highest risk to public safety are reviewed more rigorously, with additional ministerial oversight. Protecting the public is the Government's top priority. The proposals in this review will reinforce public safety. I commend this statement to the House.

*Steve Reed Shadow Secretary of State for Justice 1:43 pm, 30th March 2022*

I thank the Secretary of State for advance sight of his statement earlier today. It is hugely timely, given the disturbing news about the potential release of Baby P's killer. I fully support the Secretary of State in seeking a review of that. In broad terms, I welcome his statement too. It is crucial that public protection is paramount and that victims are right at the heart of the criminal justice system. Currently, too many victims feel that their views are not taken sufficiently into account, either in parole decisions or in sentencing, and that leads directly to public safety concerns, which must be taken more seriously. Labour will put public safety at the core of our contract with the British people. Sadly, the same cannot be said of this Government.

It is less than two months since the convicted sex abuser Paul Robson walked out of a low-category open prison in Lincolnshire. After he escaped, the public were warned that Robson was a serious danger to women and children. He clearly should never have been in a low-security prison in the first place. The Parole Board made that recommendation, but it was the Secretary of State who approved it. He or his predecessors already had the necessary powers, they just did not use them. So what will stop him making serious mistakes like that again when he exercises his new check and oversight powers in, potentially, hundreds more cases? Labour wants victims to have the right to make a new personal statement saying how they would feel if the prisoner is released. We would like any assessment of the risk to the public to include the risk of re-traumatising the victim, and to prevent released prisoners from living near their victim if that is against the victim's wishes. Will the Secretary of State consider those additional proposals?

The appalling decision to release the multiple rapist John Worboys was only stopped after the Centre for Women's Justice sued the Government, using rights established by the last Labour Government. Sir Peter Gross's review made sensible proposals to improve these rights, including the UK's margin of appreciation over interpretations we would all object to. But the Secretary of State will be throwing the baby out with the bathwater if he uses that concern as an excuse to take away British rights that protect British people from dangerous criminals, as they did in that case. Too many victims of crime do not get a say over what happens to criminals because those criminals are never prosecuted in the first place. That is because this Conservative Government cut 21,000 police officers and still have not replaced them, despite imposing the highest rates of personal taxation for 70 years —that is 21,000 people with law enforcement experience that his party sacked, whom he might now approach to sit on parole boards, as he suggests.

The Secretary of State spoke about rape cases in this statement, but only 1.5% of reported rape cases ever make it to court. Those that do now take more than 1,000 days, on average, before the trial starts—these are the longest delays in British legal history. What message does he think that sends about public safety and public protection? Under this Government, prosecution rates for crimes including burglary, robbery, car crime and fraud are so low that they have, in effect, been decriminalised. There are so few police left that victims are told to fill in a form online and hardly any of them ever hear anything again. It is no wonder that the Government stand accused of going soft on these crimes. Does he recognise that letting criminals get away with crime damages public safety and erodes confidence in the justice system, which is something he is telling us this afternoon that he wants to strengthen? The Victims' Commissioner has called on the Government to establish a new victims' right to review. That would give victims the power to challenge decisions by the police and the Crown Prosecution Service not to prosecute or to drop prosecutions. The Secretary of State did not mention that in his statement, so will he tell us whether he intends to introduce proposals along those lines in future?

Public protection requires victims to be active participants throughout the criminal justice process, including in parole decisions. Their insights strengthen public safety and public confidence in

the system. Today's statement is a step forward and it recognises some of the Government's mistakes, but it could have been bigger.

*Dominic Raab Deputy Prime Minister, The Lord Chancellor and Secretary of State for Justice*
Let me start by thanking the hon. Gentleman for his support for the decision taken today in the Tracey Connelly case. I think he also gave wholesale backing to the reforms I set out in my statement, which is important. I want to welcome what I therefore hope will be cross-party support when we come to legislate for them; he cannot support the aims and then not will the means, and I hope that that becomes clear as we take the proposals through the House.

The hon. Gentleman asked about absconds, which is an issue of significant concern. I should say to him that between 2009-10 and today, the level of absconds from prisons has fallen to a third of the level it was under the last Labour Government. He might want to think a little about that before he makes unfounded assertions. In fairness, the hon. Gentleman did ask about the case of Shane Farrington, who absconded on 24 March but was rearrested on 26 March. He is ineligible for a return to open conditions for two years. The hon. Gentleman made a point about our being empowered to do something; actually, that took place in October and I changed the rules in December, as I have made clear to the House.

I welcome what the hon. Gentleman said about the role of victims. We are making important changes and I welcome his support for them. I gently point out that, even before the spending review, the level of victims funding was three times the level it was at under the Labour Government. He talks about victims; our record is infinitely better, but we are restless to do far more. More generally, the history of the reforms we are undertaking took place on Labour's watch, because in 2008 Labour gave up the power to block the release of prisoners who had been sentenced to more than 15 years and then legislated to make the changes—in fairness, they were forced on that Government by the Human Rights Act—permanent. As a result, the number of those recalled on life licence skyrocketed, going up almost sevenfold. The hon. Gentleman should, then, have a little more humility about where the problem came from.

The hon. Gentleman criticised our approach to the Bill of Rights, but it is clear that we cannot pursue the reforms I have set out and reverse the challenges that were made under the Human Rights Act without our Bill of Rights. Again, the question for the Labour party is going to be whether it just wills the ends or is willing to back the means.

Last month, I picked up my copy of the Daily

Mirror, as I do, and read through it. I read that the hon. Gentleman had said that under the previous Labour leader, Jeremy Corbyn, Labour had appeared to care "more about criminals than their victims".

That is a greater measure of humility, but the hon. Gentleman should take a bit of responsibility for his record. He and the shadow Cabinet voted against extra funding for more police officers. They voted against the tougher sentences for dangerous offenders in the Police, Crime, Sentencing and Courts Bill—the kind of thing that would protect victims and the public. I am glad that, on this issue at least, the hon. Gentleman is showing that he is willing to support measures that will stand up for victims and protect the public. The proof of the pudding will be in how the Opposition vote when all the measures come before the House.

### Julian Lewis Chair, Intelligence and Security Committee of Parliament

The statement was excellent. My right hon. Friend is clearly revelling in an area of policy in which he has a great deal of expertise. One aspect of which I did not hear mention was the concept of punishment. Some offences, particularly the sort we are dealing with in this context, are absolutely heinous. It baffles the public as to why, for example, someone who led a home invasion in the New Forest that resulted in the burning alive of an entire family, although not until after the woman had been repeatedly raped, should be considered for release at the end of what is admittedly a long sentence. Most people would feel that people forfeit their right to liberty when they commit offences of that gravity. Where does punishment fit into all this?

### Dominic Raab Deputy Prime Minister, The Lord Chancellor and Secretary of State for Justice

I totally understand the point that my right hon. Friend makes. In truth, parole is about risk and, rightly, public protection. Either the tariff or the overall sentence should deal with the element of punishment, rather than parole. Nevertheless, my right hon. Friend makes an important point. He will know that whether it was Harper's law, Tony's law or the wider reforms to sentencing that we are making in the PCSC Bill, we have strengthened sentencing, in the teeth of opposition from Opposition Members.

In fairness, I do need to draw a distinction in respect of the reforms I have set out: they are really about public protection and the amorphous concept of risk in these cases. That itself also goes to the issue of public confidence in relation to the tariff and the punishment element that my right hon. Friend mentioned. Both are important, but with parole we focus on risk. I say that because I want to be clear that we

are not adding another sentence on top of a sentence. The question, from the point at which an offender becomes eligible for parole, is whether they satisfy the statutory criteria. Is it safe to release them, or do they present an ongoing risk to public protection? That is the core focus of the reforms I have announced today, but I heed my right hon. Friend's wider point.

### Steve McCabe Labour, Birmingham, Selly Oak

I thank the Secretary of State for his statement and welcome the broad thrust of his recommendations. I notice that the second reform deals with the assessment of risk. The Secretary of State's proposal is to employ more people with a law and order background, which I am quite happy to accept. I also notice that the report by the charity Justice published in January this year recommended:

"Enhancing the Parole Board's programme of training to include"— among other things— "critical analyses of offending behaviour programmes and risk management tools".

Does the Secretary of State have any plans to take that recommendation on board?

### Dominic Raab Deputy Prime Minister, The Lord Chancellor and Secretary of State for Justice

I thank the hon. Gentleman for his constructive and reasonable question. We will look at everything on training. The truth is that the members of the Parole Board come with a vast depth of experience; my question is whether we have the range right. Psychiatrists and psychologists have a critical role to play, and judges and lawyers inform the process, but if we say that our overriding focus is public protection and we have finely balanced questions of risk in relation to people who have committed a so-called index offence many years previously, I would have thought that, particularly for top-tier cases, the public would want to know that the grizzled police officer, for example, who has seen such cases before and knows the pattern of behaviour is also there to provide that dimension of critical thinking.

The hon. Gentleman is right in what he says about critical thinking. We need to make sure that the Parole Board panels, particularly for the serious, top-tier cohort, have a broad diversity of experience so that we can take a precautionary approach and protect the public.

### Siobhan Baillie Conservative, Stroud

I thank my right hon. Friend for his statement and continue to be impressed by how he and the Ministry of Justice are gripping so many complex justice matters all at once. This is about not only public safety but the perception of public safety. The public rightly care about law and order. I hear strong words from those on the Opposition Front Bench, but we can see from the lack of turnout among Labour MPs that they prefer to politick on this issue rather than to do the hard graft of scrutiny.

On scrutiny, I really welcome that my right hon. Friend is putting victims at the heart of Parole Board decisions and allowing them input. Will he say a little more about how the Parole Board has taken to those proposals? How can we support victims as they go through that process? Some of them will find those steps distressing even if they want to take them.

***Dominic Raab Deputy Prime Minister, The Lord Chancellor and Secretary of State for Justice***
I thank my hon. Friend for her tenacity on these issues. She makes the same point as the one my right hon. Friend Dr Lewis made about public confidence. There is no escaping that, particularly if we think of the history of parole and licence conditions and of how we ended up with life terms after the abolition of the death penalty. The public need to have confidence that sentences match the crime and that their safety is of paramount importance.

My hon. Friend asked about how we will help victims through the process; that is critical, because it must be gruelling and traumatic for them. I know from the consideration that I have given the matter and from the evidence I have seen how difficult it will be. We have already made some improvements in the process for victims: in 2018, we introduced written decision summaries to improve transparency for victims; in 2019, we introduced the reconsideration mechanism, which I exercised today; and in 2021, we announced our intention to enable public hearings and for victims to be able to attend them as observers, and we are now giving them a much fuller role, as I explained in my statement. On top of that, of course, is the statutory release test. When the Parole Board considers that test, it will take clear account of victims' submissions and victims will be able to ask questions through their submissions.

***Jim Shannon Shadow DUP Spokesperson (Human Rights), Shadow DUP Spokesperson (Health)***
I thank the Lord Chancellor for the statement; I am encouraged by the steps he has introduced today to address what one victim said to me was a "reprehensible" parole system. That lady contacted me after the murderer of her son was released and she saw him in the local Tesco. She received no warning that he had been released early. Will the Lord Chancellor confirm that the legislation will include a legal obligation to inform victims and their close family? Will he be in touch with the Minister in the Northern Ireland Assembly to discuss the legislation proposed for this place that can also be introduced in Northern Ireland?

***Dominic Raab Deputy Prime Minister, The Lord Chancellor and Secretary of State for Justice***
The root and branch review will set out all the victims' rights in the process. The hon. Gentleman will be able to see that. Copies are now available in the House. Of course we respect the devolved settlements on this, but we are always willing to engage with the devolved Administrations around cross-cutting issues and those of common concern.

***Rob Butler Conservative, Aylesbury***
The public will rightly expect that their protection is the overriding concern when serious offenders are assessed either for release by the Parole Board or, indeed, for transfer to an open prison, a subject on which my right hon. Friend touched. I know from my own time as non-executive director at Her Majesty's Prison and Probation Service that open prisons can be an extremely important part of an offenders' rehabilitation, especially at the end of a very long sentence. We have seen recent cases where the current test has clearly not worked effectively. Does my right hon. Friend agree that time in an open prison should always be regarded as a privilege, certainly never an automatic right? Will he confirm that the measures that he has already introduced, and that he is going on to introduce later today, will result in a more cautious approach that will make sure that the public is always safe?

***Dominic Raab Deputy Prime Minister, The Lord Chancellor and Secretary of State for Justice***
I agree with everything that my hon. Friend said. I do not think that there is a trade-off. In fact the two things go together: we want to protect the public as well as identify those who can be released into open conditions or into society— those who are ready to play the right role, to reintegrate back into society, to work, to look after their families and to stay clean of drugs. All of those things go together. Ultimately, our objective is to protect the public, drive down crime and reduce reoffending.

***Dehenna Davison Conservative, Bishop Auckland***
I thank my right hon. Friend for his statement and for engaging with me over my one-punch awareness campaign, something about which I am deeply passionate. Victim support is at the very heart of that campaign, because, as we all know, the victims of crime and their families do not stop suffering the moment the crime stops being committed; they can suffer for months, years and even the lifetime that follow. That is why the victims of crime need to be at the very heart of our criminal justice system to ensure that they receive the support, protection and reassurance they need. Can my right hon. Friend confirm that these proposals will improve victim

support and public protection, particularly for victims of the most serious crimes?

**Dominic Raab Deputy Prime Minister, The Lord Chancellor and Secretary of State for Justice**
I pay tribute to my hon. Friend for her tenacious campaign and say that I know how difficult that must be for her. None the less, it is very important, and she brings a huge amount of experience, particularly personal experience, to the Chamber and to the changes that we are making. I agree with what she has said. I have set out for the House the changes that we are making for victims in relation to the parole decision-making process, but they are only one element of a much broader strategy, and we will, of course, be introducing a victims' law. Again, I hope the whole House can rally around that, so that victims feel that they are front and centre of this, that they are listened to, that they are taken into account, and that they are part of the criminal justice system, not an appendix to it.

**Matt Warman Conservative, Boston and Skegness**
When Paul Robson escaped from the North Sea Camp open prison in my constituency, the sudden presence of this violent rapist in the community was deeply traumatic not just for his victims, but for all those people who live in and around the area that the prison occupies. By definition, although the Parole Board does immensely difficult work, the fact that he absconded means that he was in the wrong place. Will my right hon. Friend reassure me that what he has announced today makes it far less likely for a convict such as Paul Robson to be in those conditions and to place the public at risk in the way that he did when he absconded?

**Dominic Raab Deputy Prime Minister, The Lord Chancellor and Secretary of State for Justice**
I can reassure my hon. Friend on that. The changes that we made in December should give him some reassurance. There is no risk-free approach here. What we do is try to create safeguards to mitigate as best we can while maintaining a free society. I also note that, under successive Conservative Governments, the number of absconds has fallen, from 296 in 2009-10 to 101 in 2020-21—a third of the level. We have the security right, but we will continue to make sure that we reinforce it.

**David Johnston Conservative, Wantage**
I warmly welcome my right hon. Friend's statement today. Does he agree that, in those most serious of cases, the public do not expect politicians to throw up their hands and say, "Well, it was a decision for the Parole Board"? They expect them, as the ones accountable for keeping them safe, to step in and do so because it is their No.1 job.

**Dominic Raab Deputy Prime Minister, The Lord Chancellor and Secretary of State for Justice**
My hon. Friend is absolutely right. On that decision making, the frustration is that if we delegate from this place or from accountable Ministers, particularly when we are talking about judgment calls, not things that require a purely technocratic or scientific approach—psychiatry and psychology can only take us so far—the public feel that we have abdicated our responsibility. We are taking back control to provide a safeguard in those high-risk cases, and that is exactly what the public already expect of us.

**Paul Bristow Conservative, Peterborough**
I congratulate my right hon. Friend on his statement. We sometimes forget that the most important reason for having prisons is not necessarily as a punishment, but to keep the public safe. I know that my constituents in Peterborough would want the Parole Board always to be risk averse on public protection when it comes to releasing criminals found guilty of serious crimes. Can he reassure the good people of Peterborough that he understands their concern and that public protection is at the heart of these proposals?

**Dominic Raab Deputy Prime Minister, The Lord Chancellor and Secretary of State for Justice**
My hon. Friend is right: public protection must be the overriding priority. Moreover, it is important that the credibility of measures such as open conditions and release on licence is sustained as well. The rehabilitative work that we do—encouraging offenders into work and getting off drugs—is critical to reducing reoffending and also to protecting the public. The credibility will be eroded if we do not make sure that we have the safeguards right.

**Andy Carter Conservative, Warrington South**
I welcome the Lord Chancellor's statement. Last week, two prisoners absconded from Thorn Cross prison in my constituency, bringing the total to five so far in the first three months of this year. Shane Farrington, as the Lord Chancellor has already mentioned, was one of those who absconded. He was sentenced for killing another prisoner and for escaping from custody in 2018. Understandably, people living in Appleton Thorn in my constituency are asking what he was doing in an open prison in Warrington. Can the Lord Chancellor confirm that the changes being announced today will prioritise the safety of people living close to open prisons, and assure me that the Government's priority is to cut the number of absconds from open prisons, such as the one in Warrington South?

*Eleanor Laing Deputy Speaker and Chairman of Ways and Means, Chair, Standing Orders (Private Bills) Committee (Commons), Chair, Standing Orders (Private Bills) Committee (Commons)*

Order. Just before the Lord Chancellor answers that question, may I say that, although I appreciate that the hon. Gentleman has been waiting a long time to ask his question, he made a preamble and then asked two questions. That is not what this is about. Each person has the chance to ask one question. We do not need a preamble. The preamble comes from the Minister who is making the statement. We do not need all of that stated over and over again. I am making this point now before we come to the next statement, which I appreciate will be controversial. We will have short questions and as short as possible answers. I appreciate that the Minister has to give a full answer, but we do not need a preamble. It is not a speech; it is a question.

*Dominic Raab Deputy Prime Minister, The Lord Chancellor and Secretary of State for Justice*

Thank you, Madam Deputy Speaker. I heed your advice, as always. We have already cut the number of absconds by a third. Of course the measures that I introduced in December—not the ones that I have announced today—will further allow an extra safeguard, which, I hope, will give my hon. Friend's constituents some reassurance.

*Eleanor Laing Deputy Speaker and Chairman of Ways and Means, Chair, Standing Orders (Private Bills) Committee (Commons), Chair, Standing Orders (Private Bills) Committee (Commons)*

I thank the Lord Chancellor for his thorough answers. We will now move onto the next statement. I will pause to allow people to enter and to leave the Chamber. I also remind hon. Members that, after this item of business, we have six hours of very important consideration of Lords amendments. That will take us well into the evening.

*Reoffenders: Costs*
*14th March 2022*

Steve Reed Shadow Secretary of State for Justice
To ask the Secretary of State for Justice, what estimate he has made of the cost to the public purse of the (a) economic and (b) social effects of reoffending by area in England in each of the last five years.

*Kit Malthouse The Minister of State, Home Department, The Minister of State, Ministry of Justice, Minister of State (Ministry of Justice and Home Office)*

The economic and social cost of reoffending in England and Wales is approximately £18 billion per year. However, this figure cannot be broken down by geographical area.

The Prisons Strategy White Paper, published in December 2021, sets out the Government's

ambitious plans to reduce reoffending. We will spend £200 million a year by 2024-25 to improve prison leavers' access to accommodation, employment support and substance misuse treatment and further measures for early intervention to tackle youth offending. This builds on the Beating Crime Plan, published in July 2021, in which this Government committed to beat crime and swiftly bring criminals to justice.

We will also introduce new personalised Resettlement Passports, which will be set up prior to release and will bring together the key information and services that an individual needs to resettle into society.

This investment will protect the public, help individuals turn their backs on crime and reduce the cost of reoffending to society.

**Prisoners on Remand: Suicide**
**7th March 2022**
*Lord Patten Conservative*

To ask Her Majesty's Government what was the (1) number, and (2) ratio, of prisoners held on remand in England who have (a) committed suicide, and (b) attempted to commit suicide, in each of the last 10 years.

*Lord Patten Conservative*

To ask Her Majesty's Government whether, and if so how, their policies towards suicide prevention in prisons differ between remand and convicted prisoners.

*Lord Wolfson of Tredegar The Parliamentary Under-Secretary of State for Justice*

The table below sets out the number of self-inflicted deaths of remand prisoners in the ten years to December 2021. It also shows the percentage of all such deaths that were of remand prisoners.

Our figures refer to self-inflicted deaths, rather than suicides. Self-inflicted deaths include any death of a person who has apparently taken his or her own life, irrespective of intent. This includes not only suicides but also accidental deaths as a result of the person's own actions. We use this classification because we cannot always know whether someone intended to take their own life. Those are ultimately decisions for coroners, who investigate all deaths in custody. For similar reasons, we cannot identify "attempted suicides" separately from other forms of self-harm, as we may not know the prisoner's intention.

HM Prison & Probation Service does not operate a different approach to the prevention of suicide and self-harm among remand prisoners. All prisoners at risk of self-harm and suicide are supported equally, regardless of their situation. We recognise that remand is a known risk factor for self-harm and support is tailored to prisoners' needs, particularly in the early days and weeks of custody. Following the unavoidable closure of courts in response to Covid-19, we are taking positive action to ensure more cases are heard and therefore to reduce the number of remand prisoners. This includes extending 32 nightingale courtrooms this year, installing video link equipment in all courts and increasing its capacity in prisons, removing the limit on Crown Court sitting days during 2021/22, and continuing to give priority to cases involving custody time limits.

Self-inflicted deaths of remand prisoners, 2012 to 2021

| year | number of self-inflicted deaths | % of all self-inflicted deaths |
|---|---|---|
| 2012 | 18 | 30% |
| 2013 | 29 | 38% |
| 2014 | 26 | 29% |
| 2015 | 36 | 40% |
| 2016 | 33 | 27% |
| 2017 | 73 | 21% |
| 2018 | 27 | 29% |
| 2019 | 24 | 28% |
| 2020 | 19 | 28% |
| 2021 | 32 | 37% |

# 7.2 TRANSPARENCY & FREEDOM OF INFORMATION RELEASES

Selected Transparency and Freedom of Information Act Successful Requests, made between 15 July 2021 to 12th August 2022, can be accessed at *https://tinyurl.com/yc7jzpmv* and some examples are shown below.

Prisoners, without internet access (which should be made clear in the request along with the fact that it is a request made under the Freedom of Information Act), can request access to Ministry of Justice information under the Freedom of Information Act by making a written application to the prison who must then pass it "promptly" to the Ministry of Justice Disclosure Team under section 4.13 of the Information Requests Policy Framework which states:

*4.13 A freedom of information request must be made in writing, either in hard copy via letter or digitally via email, or social media. Anyone, anywhere within HMPPS can receive a request, but it should be promptly brought to the attention of the Disclosure Team via data.access@justice.gov.uk by the area that received it. As soon as the request is received by a business area in HMPPS the timescales start so it is important these are dealt with quickly. A contact name and address (an email address [or a prisoner's name and number] is sufficient) must be provided by the requester of the information. Anyone, anywhere in the world can make a request – it doesn't matter who they*

*are. Guidance from the Information Commissioner's Office stipulates that [HMPPS should be both applicant and motive blind. This means [HMPPS] cannot let who the individual is or why they would request particular information influence how we handle the request or the response [they] provide. The request does not have to specify it is made under the terms of the FOIA. It is up to [HMPPS staff], as a public authority, to identify a FOIA request and deal with it correctly.*

**Prison population figures: 2022**
Latest prison population figures for 2022.
From: Ministry of Justice
Updated: 12 August 2022

**Government Major Projects Portfolio – Accounting Officer Assessments Ministry of Justice**
Accounting officer assessment summaries for the Ministry of Justice (MoJ) programmes and projects in the Government Major Project Portfolio.
From: HM Treasury and 1 other
Updated: 11 August 2022

**Education, children's social care and offending**
An examination of the education and social care background of children cautioned or sentenced for an offence.
From: Department for Education and 1 other
Updated: 11 August 2022

**FOI releases for August 2022**
Freedom of Information releases by Ministry of Justice for August 2022.
From: Ministry of Justice
Updated: 9 August 2022

**MOJ: spending over £500 on a GPC 2021**
Reports on departmental spending over £500 with a government procurement card (GPC).
From: Ministry of Justice
Updated: 9 August 2022

**Funds in Court in England & Wales Account 2021 to 2022**
The annual report and accounts of the Funds in Court outline its performance in 2021 to 2022 alongside audited accounts for the year.
From: Ministry of Justice
Updated: 3 August 2022

**MOJ major projects: appointment letters and addendums for Senior Responsible Owners**
Ministry of Justice (MOJ) appointment letters for Government Major Projects Portfolio (GMPP) Senior Responsible Owners (SROs).
From: Ministry of Justice
Updated: 29 July 2022

**MoJ Government Major Projects Portfolio data, 2022**

Ministry of Justice (MoJ) March 2022 Government Major Projects Portfolio data that supports the 2022 Infrastructure and Projects Authority (IPA) annual report.
From: Infrastructure & Projects Authority and 1 other
Updated: 20 July 2022

**Ministry of Justice: spend control data for January 2022 to March 2022**

Centrally approved new spending on property, advertising, consultancy, technology and recruitment.
From: Ministry of Justice
Updated: 14 July 2022

**MOJ Business Appointment Rules**

Summary of advice given under the business appointment rules to applicants at SCS2 and SCS1 level and equivalents.
From: Ministry of Justice
Updated: 14 July 2022

**Ministry of Justice data: special advisors hospitality, gifts, and meetings, January 2022 to March 2022**

Special Advisers gifts, hospitality and meetings returns from January 2022 to March 2022.
From: Ministry of Justice
Updated: 14 July 2022

**Ministry of Justice data: ministers hospitality, gifts, travel and meetings, January 2022 to March 2022**

Minister's gifts, hospitality, travel and meetings returns from January 2022 to March 2022.
From: Ministry of Justice
Updated: 14 July 2022

**Ministry of Justice data: senior officials hospitality, travel and meetings, January 2022 to March 2022**

Senior Officials hospitality, travel and meetings returns from Q4 (January 2022 to March 2022).
From: Ministry of Justice
Updated: 14 July 2022

**Ministry of Justice Register of Board members' interests**

A register of the private interests declared by Ministry of Justice Board members as at July 2022.
From: Ministry of Justice
Updated: 14 July 2022

**Use of closed material procedure report: 25 June 2020 to 24 June 2021**

Annual report on the use of the closed material procedure under the Justice and Security Act 2013.
From: Ministry of Justice
Updated: 13 July 2022

**Employment Rates following Release from Custody - Ad Hoc Release**

Ad Hoc Statistical Release on Employment at 6 weeks and 6 months following Release from Custody, April 2021 to March 2022
From: Her Majesty's Prison and Probation Service and 1 other
Updated: 30 June 2022

**MOJ arm's length bodies spending over £25,000: November 2021**

Reports on departmental spending over £25,000.
From: Ministry of Justice
Updated: 30 May 2022

**MOJ arm's length bodies spending over £25,000: October 2021**

Reports on departmental spending over £25,000.
From: Ministry of Justice
Updated: 30 May 2022

**MOJ arm's length bodies spending over £25,000: September 2021**

Reports on departmental spending over £25,000.
From: Ministry of Justice
Updated: 30 May 2022

**MOJ arm's length bodies spending over £25,000: August 2021**

Reports on departmental spending over £25,000.
From: Ministry of Justice
Updated: 30 May 2022

**MOJ arm's length bodies spending over £25,000: July 2021**

Reports on departmental spending over £25,000.
From: Ministry of Justice
Updated: 30 May 2022

**MOJ arm's length bodies spending over £25,000: June 2021**

Reports on departmental spending over £25,000.
From: Ministry of Justice
Updated: 30 May 2022

**MOJ arm's length bodies spending over £25,000: May 2021**

Reports on departmental spending over £25,000.
From: Ministry of Justice
Updated: 30 May 2022

**MOJ arm's length bodies spending over £25,000: April 2021**

Reports on departmental spending over £25,000.
From: Ministry of Justice
Updated: 30 May 2022

**Her Majesty's Prison & Probation Service spending over £25,000: 2021**
Reports on departmental spending over £25,000.
From: Ministry of Justice
Updated: 30 May 2022

**Legal Aid Agency spending over £25,000: 2021**
Reports on departmental spending over £25,000.
From: Ministry of Justice
Updated: 30 May 2022

**HMCTS spending over £25,000: 2021**
Reports on departmental spending over £25,000.
From: Ministry of Justice
Updated: 30 May 2022

**Ministry of Justice spending over £25,000: 2021**
Ministry of Justice (MOJ) HQ spending over £25,000 data for 2021.
From: Ministry of Justice
Updated: 30 May 2022

**Workforce management information: MOJ**
Information on the Ministry of Justice, its agencies and executive non-departmental public bodies' pay bills (see the 'details' section located at the bottom of page for more information).
From: Ministry of Justice
Updated: 24 May 2022

**MOJ arm's length bodies spending over £25,000: February 2021**
Reports on departmental spending over £25,000.
From: Ministry of Justice
Updated: 22 April 2022

**MOJ arm's length bodies spending over £25,000: January 2021**
Reports on departmental spending over £25,000.
From: Ministry of Justice
Updated: 22 April 2022

**MOJ arm's length bodies spending over £25,000: December 2020**
Reports on departmental spending over £25,000.
From: Ministry of Justice
Updated: 22 April 2022

**MOJ arm's length bodies spending over £25,000: November 2020**
Reports on departmental spending over £25,000.
From: Ministry of Justice
Updated: 22 April 2022

**MOJ arm's length bodies spending over £25,000: October 2020**
Reports on departmental spending over £25,000.
From: Ministry of Justice
Updated: 22 April 2022

**Her Majesty's Prison & Probation Service spending over £25,000: 2020**
Reports on departmental spending over £25,000.
From: Ministry of Justice
Updated: 22 April 2022

**Legal Aid Agency spending over £25,000: 2020**
Reports on departmental spending over £25,000.
From: Ministry of Justice
Updated: 22 April 2022

**HMCTS spending over £25,000: 2020**
Reports on departmental spending over £25,000.
From: Ministry of Justice
Updated: 22 April 2022

**Ministry of Justice spending over £25,000: 2020**
Ministry of Justice (MOJ) HQ spending over £25,000 data for 2020.
From: Ministry of Justice
Updated: 22 April 2022

**MOJ arm's length bodies spending over £25,000: March 2021**
Reports on departmental spending over £25,000.
From: Ministry of Justice
Updated: 22 April 2022

**Ministry of Justice Commercial Pipeline**
Information about the status of current and future procurement opportunities.
From: Ministry of Justice
Updated: 13 April 2022

**Ministry of Justice: spend control data for October 2021 to December 2021**
Centrally approved new spending on property, advertising, consultancy, technology and recruitment.
From: Ministry of Justice
Updated: 1 April 2022

**Ministry of Justice data: senior officials hospitality, travel and meetings, January 2021 to March 2021**
Senior Officials hospitality, travel and meetings returns from Q4 (January 2021 to March 2021).
From: Ministry of Justice
Updated: 31 March 2022

**Ministry of Justice data: senior officials hospitality, travel and meetings, October 2021 to December 2021**
Senior Officials hospitality, travel and meetings returns from Q3 (October 2021 to December 2021).
From: Ministry of Justice
Updated: 31 March 2022

**Ministry of Justice data: special advisors hospitality, gifts and meetings, October 2021 to December 2021**
Special Advisers gifts, hospitality and meetings returns from October 2021 to December 2021.
From: Ministry of Justice
Updated: 31 March 2022

**Ministry of Justice data: ministers hospitality, gifts, travel and meetings, October 2021 to December 2021**
Minister's gifts, hospitality, travel and meetings returns from October 2021 to December 2021
From: Ministry of Justice
Updated: 31 March 2022

**Ministry of Justice non-consolidated performance related pay 2019 to 2020 and 2020 to 2021**
Non-consolidated performance related pay (NCPRP) data by the Ministry of Justice.
From: Ministry of Justice
Updated: 31 March 2022

**National Mental Capacity Forum: Chair's annual reports**
Annual reports by the chair of the National Mental Capacity Forum.
From: Ministry of Justice
Updated: 24 February 2022

**HMPPS evidence to Prison Service Pay Review Body: 2022**
HMPPS written evidence submission to the Prison Service Pay Review Body (PSPRB) for the 2022 to 2023 pay round. This outlines HMPPS pay proposals for all operational prison staff.
From: Her Majesty's Prison and Probation Service and 2 others
Updated: 23 February 2022

**Ministry of Justice's evidence to the Senior Salaries Review Body: 2022**
Ministry of Justice's evidence to the Senior Salaries Review Body, February 2022.
From: Ministry of Justice and 1 other
Updated: 23 February 2022

**UK National Preventive Mechanism annual report: 2020 to 2021**
Twelfth Annual Report of the UK's National Preventive Mechanism: Monitoring places of detention during COVID-19.
From: Ministry of Justice
Updated: 22 February 2022

**Ministry of Justice: spend control data for July 2021 to September 2021**
Centrally approved new spending on property, advertising, consultancy, technology and recruitment.
From: Ministry of Justice
Updated: 27 January 2022

**Ministry of Justice data: special advisors hospitality, gifts and meetings, July 2021 to September 2021**
Special Advisers gifts, hospitality and meetings returns from July 2021 to September 2021.
From: Ministry of Justice
Updated: 27 January 2022

**Ministry of Justice data: ministers hospitality, gifts, travel and meetings, July 2021 to September 2021**
Minister's gifts, hospitality, travel and meetings returns from July 2021 to September 2021.
From: Ministry of Justice
Updated: 27 January 2022

**Ministry of Justice data: senior officials hospitality, travel and meetings, July 2021 to September 2021**
Senior Officials hospitality, travel and meetings returns from Q2 (July 2021 to September 2021).
From: Ministry of Justice
Updated: 27 January 2022

**Prison performance data 2020 to 2021**
Supplement to the HMPPS Annual Report and Accounts 2020 to 2021.
From: Her Majesty's Prison and Probation Service and 1 other
Updated: 27 January 2022

**Ministry of Justice gender pay gap report: 2021**
The Ministry of Justice Gender Pay Gap Report analyses mean and median gender pay gaps and gender bonus gaps.
From: Ministry of Justice
Updated: 27 January 2022

**MOJ Welsh Language Scheme Annual Monitoring Report 2020 to 2021**
This report is a self-assessment of how the Ministry of Justice has delivered its commitments under its Welsh Language Scheme between April 2020 and March 2021.
From: Ministry of Justice
Updated: 23 December 2021

## MOJ Welsh Language Scheme Annual Monitoring Report 2019 to 2020

This report is a self-assessment of how the Ministry of Justice has delivered its commitments under its Welsh Language Scheme between April 2019 and March 2020.
From: Ministry of Justice
Updated: 23 December 2021

## Ministry of Justice Annual Report and Accounts 2020 to 2021

A report on MoJ's performance, governance arrangements and use of resources for the year ended 31 March 2021.
From: Ministry of Justice
Updated: 16 December 2021

## Judicial Pensions Scheme Annual Report and Accounts 2020 to 2021

A report of the Judicial Pensions Scheme, governance arrangements and use of resources for the year ended 31 March 2021.
From: Ministry of Justice
Updated: 16 December 2021

## Ministry of Justice: spend control data for April 2021 to June 2021

Centrally approved new spending on property, advertising, consultancy, technology and recruitment.
From: Ministry of Justice
Updated: 26 October 2021

## Ministry of Justice: spend control data for January 2021 to March 2021

Centrally approved new spending on property, advertising, consultancy, technology and recruitment.
From: Ministry of Justice
Updated: 26 October 2021

## Ministry of Justice data: special advisors hospitality, gifts and meetings, April 2021 to June 2021

Special Advisers gifts, hospitality and meetings returns from April 2021 to June 2021.
From: Ministry of Justice
Updated: 21 October 2021

## Ministry of Justice data: ministers hospitality, gifts, travel and meetings, April 2021 to June 2021

Minister's gifts, hospitality, travel and meetings returns from April 2021 to June 2021.
From: Ministry of Justice
Updated: 21 October 2021

## Ministry of Justice data: senior officials hospitality, travel and meetings, April 2021 to June 2021

Senior Officials hospitality, travel and meetings returns from Q1 (April 2021 to June 2021).
From: Ministry of Justice
Updated: 21 October 2021

## Funds in Court in England & Wales Account 2020 to 2021

The annual report and accounts of the Funds in Court outline its performance in 2020 to 2021 alongside audited accounts for the year.
From: Ministry of Justice
Updated: 12 October 2021

## Judicial salaries and fees 2021 to 2022

Schedules setting out judicial salaries and fees from 1 April 2021.
From: Ministry of Justice
Updated: 27 September 2021

## MOJ: spending over £500 on a GPC 2020

Reports on departmental spending over £500 with a government procurement card (GPC).
From: Ministry of Justice
Updated: 20 September 2021

## Ministry of Justice data: ministers hospitality, gifts, travel and meetings, January 2021 to March 2021

Minister's gifts, hospitality, travel and meetings returns from January 2021 to March 2021.
From: Ministry of Justice
Updated: 15 July 2021

## Ministry of Justice data: special advisors hospitality, gifts and meetings, January 2021 to March 2021

Special Advisers gifts, hospitality and meetings returns from January 2021 to March 2021.
From: Ministry of Justice
Updated: 15 July 2021

## MoJ Government Major Projects Portfolio data, 2021

Ministry of Justice (MoJ) March 2021 Government Major Projects Portfolio data that supports the 2021 Infrastructure and Projects Authority (IPA) annual report.
From: Infrastructure and Projects Authority and 1 other
Updated: 15 July 2021

## 7.3 DEATHS IN PRISON SERVICE CUSTODY

Below is a breakdown of deaths in prison in England and Wales by calendar year (January-December). These tables were published on 27 January 2022. Publication of 2022 figures will be in January 2023. For the latest statistics view The Prison Oracle Deaths in Custody at:

https://tinyurl.com/yckw966f

Table 1.1: Annual Deaths in Prison Custody Summary Statistics by apparent cause by calendar year since 1978, England and Wales

Table 1.2: Deaths arising from incidents in prison custody but occurring elsewhere by apparent cause since 1999, England and Wales

Table 1.3: Self-inflicted deaths in prison custody by time in custody and current prison since 1999, England and Wales

Table 1.4: Self-inflicted deaths in prison custody by offence since 1999, England and Wales

Table 1.5: Self-inflicted deaths in prison custody by ethnicity since 1999, England and Wales

Table 1.6: Self-inflicted deaths in prison custody by nationality type since 1999, England and Wales

Table 1.7: Self-inflicted deaths in prison custody by sentence type since 1999, England and Wales

Table 1.8: Self-inflicted deaths in prison custody by method since 1999, England and Wales

Table 1.9: Self-inflicted deaths in prison custody: Ligatures used in hanging/self-strangulation since 1999, England and Wales

Table 1.10: Self-Inflicted deaths in prison custody: Ligature points used in hanging/self-strangulation since 1999, England and Wales

Table 1.11: Self-inflicted deaths by establishment since 1978, England and Wales

Table 1.12: Natural cause deaths by establishment since 1978, England and Wales

Table 1.13: Deaths by establishment since 1978, England and Wales

Table 1.14: Dates of opening/closing and major re-roles of prisons from 2001, England and Wales

Table 1.15: Notes on Data and Methodology

# Table 1.1: Annual Deaths in Prison Custody Summary Statistics by apparent cause by calendar year since 1999, England and Wales

| | 1999 | 2000 | 2001 | 2002 | 2003 | 2004 | 2005 | 2006 | 2007 | 2008 | 2009 | 2010 | 2011 | 2012 | 2013 | 2014 | 2015 | 2016 | 2017 (c) | 2018 (c) | 2019 (c) | 2020 (c) | 2021 (p) |
|---|---|---|---|---|---|---|---|---|---|---|---|---|---|---|---|---|---|---|---|---|---|---|---|
| **MALES AND FEMALES [3]** | | | | | | | | | | | | | | | | | | | | | | | |
| Total | 149 | 146 | 142 | 164 | 183 | 208 | 175 | 153 | 185 | 166 | 169 | 198 | 192 | 192 | 215 | 243 | 257 | 354 | 295 | 325 | 300 | 318 | 371 |
| Homicide | 0 | 0 | 0 | 0 | 0 | 2 | 0 | 0 | 1 | 3 | 1 | 1 | 2 | 2 | 4 | 3 | 8 | 8 | 3 | 3 | 3 | 2 | 4 |
| Natural Causes | 58 | 61 | 68 | 66 | 85 | 101 | 89 | 83 | 89 | 99 | 104 | 126 | 122 | 123 | 131 | 145 | 147 | 206 | 193 | 168 | 176 | 222 | 247 |
| Self-inflicted | 91 | 81 | 73 | 95 | 95 | 96 | 78 | 66 | 91 | 61 | 61 | 58 | 57 | 61 | 76 | 89 | 90 | 124 | 75 | 96 | 86 | 67 | 86 |
| Other[7] | 0 | 4 | 1 | 3 | 3 | 9 | 8 | 4 | 4 | 3 | 3 | 13 | 11 | 6 | 4 | 6 | 12 | 16 | 24 | 58 | 35 | 27 | 34 |
| *of which* | | | | | | | | | | | | | | | | | | | | | | | |
| *Other/Non-natural[8]* | 0 | 4 | 1 | 3 | 3 | 9 | 8 | 4 | 4 | 3 | 3 | 13 | 11 | 6 | 4 | 6 | 12 | 16 | 24 | 56 | 27 | 24 | 4 |
| *Awaiting further information* | 0 | 0 | 0 | 0 | 0 | 0 | 0 | 0 | 0 | 0 | 0 | 0 | 0 | 0 | 0 | 0 | 0 | 0 | 0 | 2 | 8 | 3 | 30 |
| **PRISON POPULATION Males and Females** | 64,771 | 64,593 | 66,229 | 70,861 | 73,038 | 74,658 | 75,980 | 78,151 | 80,380 | 82,636 | 83,559 | 84,725 | 85,951 | 86,634 | 84,249 | 85,307 | 85,626 | 85,348 | 85,632 | 83,296 | 82,935 | 80,366 | 78,536 |
| **Deaths per 1,000 prisoners** | | | | | | | | | | | | | | | | | | | | | | | |
| Total | 2.3 | 2.3 | 2.1 | 2.3 | 2.5 | 2.8 | 2.3 | 2.0 | 2.3 | 2.0 | 2.0 | 2.3 | 2.2 | 2.2 | 2.6 | 2.8 | 3.0 | 4.1 | 3.4 | 3.9 | 3.6 | 4.0 | 4.7 |
| Natural Causes | 0.9 | 0.9 | 1.0 | 0.9 | 1.2 | 1.4 | 1.2 | 1.1 | 1.1 | 1.2 | 1.2 | 1.5 | 1.4 | 1.4 | 1.6 | 1.7 | 1.7 | 2.4 | 2.3 | 2.0 | 2.1 | 2.8 | 3.1 |
| Self-inflicted | 1.4 | 1.3 | 1.1 | 1.3 | 1.3 | 1.3 | 1.0 | 0.8 | 1.1 | 0.7 | 0.7 | 0.7 | 0.7 | 0.7 | 0.9 | 1.0 | 1.1 | 1.5 | 0.9 | 1.2 | 1.0 | 0.8 | 1.1 |
| Other | 0.0 | 0.1 | 0.0 | 0.0 | 0.0 | 0.1 | 0.1 | 0.1 | 0.0 | 0.0 | 0.0 | 0.2 | 0.1 | 0.1 | 0.0 | 0.1 | 0.1 | 0.2 | 0.3 | 0.7 | 0.4 | 0.3 | 0.4 |
| **MALES** | | | | | | | | | | | | | | | | | | | | | | | |
| Total | 140 | 136 | 134 | 152 | 168 | 188 | 168 | 147 | 177 | 161 | 162 | 190 | 187 | 188 | 209 | 231 | 249 | 332 | 287 | 314 | 292 | 311 | 365 |
| Homicide | 0 | 0 | 0 | 0 | 0 | 2 | 0 | 0 | 1 | 3 | 1 | 1 | 2 | 2 | 4 | 3 | 8 | 8 | 3 | 3 | 3 | 2 | 4 |
| Natural Causes | 54 | 59 | 66 | 63 | 85 | 94 | 87 | 80 | 88 | 96 | 100 | 122 | 119 | 120 | 127 | 136 | 145 | 200 | 187 | 162 | 175 | 217 | 247 |
| Self-inflicted | 86 | 73 | 67 | 86 | 81 | 83 | 74 | 63 | 84 | 60 | 58 | 57 | 56 | 60 | 74 | 86 | 85 | 112 | 73 | 93 | 81 | 65 | 83 |
| Other[7] | 0 | 4 | 1 | 3 | 2 | 9 | 7 | 4 | 4 | 2 | 3 | 10 | 10 | 6 | 4 | 6 | 11 | 12 | 24 | 56 | 33 | 27 | 31 |
| *of which* | | | | | | | | | | | | | | | | | | | | | | | |
| *Other/Non-natural[8]* | 0 | 4 | 1 | 3 | 2 | 9 | 7 | 4 | 4 | 2 | 3 | 10 | 10 | 6 | 4 | 6 | 11 | 12 | 24 | 56 | 27 | 24 | 4 |
| *Awaiting further information* | 0 | 0 | 0 | 0 | 0 | 0 | 0 | 0 | 0 | 0 | 0 | 0 | 0 | 0 | 0 | 0 | 0 | 0 | 0 | 0 | 6 | 3 | 27 |
| **PRISON POPULATION Males** | 61,523 | 61,251 | 62,502 | 66,562 | 68,613 | 70,209 | 71,513 | 73,703 | 76,006 | 78,222 | 79,277 | 80,489 | 81,763 | 82,481 | 80,359 | 81,402 | 81,741 | 81,493 | 81,657 | 79,450 | 79,140 | 77,004 | 75,353 |
| **Deaths per 1,000 prisoners** | | | | | | | | | | | | | | | | | | | | | | | |
| Total | 2.3 | 2.2 | 2.1 | 2.3 | 2.4 | 2.7 | 2.3 | 2.0 | 2.3 | 2.1 | 2.0 | 2.4 | 2.3 | 2.3 | 2.6 | 2.8 | 3.0 | 4.1 | 3.5 | 4.0 | 3.7 | 4.0 | 4.8 |
| Natural Causes | 0.9 | 1.0 | 1.1 | 0.9 | 1.2 | 1.3 | 1.2 | 1.1 | 1.2 | 1.2 | 1.3 | 1.5 | 1.5 | 1.5 | 1.6 | 1.7 | 1.8 | 2.5 | 2.3 | 2.0 | 2.2 | 2.8 | 3.3 |
| Self-inflicted | 1.4 | 1.2 | 1.1 | 1.3 | 1.2 | 1.2 | 1.0 | 0.9 | 1.1 | 0.8 | 0.7 | 0.7 | 0.7 | 0.7 | 0.9 | 1.1 | 1.0 | 1.4 | 0.9 | 1.2 | 1.0 | 0.8 | 1.1 |
| Other | 0.0 | 0.1 | 0.0 | 0.0 | 0.0 | 0.1 | 0.1 | 0.1 | 0.1 | 0.0 | 0.0 | 0.1 | 0.1 | 0.1 | 0.0 | 0.1 | 0.1 | 0.1 | 0.3 | 0.7 | 0.4 | 0.4 | 0.4 |
| **FEMALES** | | | | | | | | | | | | | | | | | | | | | | | |
| Total | 9 | 10 | 8 | 12 | 15 | 20 | 7 | 6 | 8 | 5 | 7 | 8 | 5 | 4 | 6 | 12 | 8 | 22 | 8 | 11 | 8 | 7 | 6 |
| Homicide | 0 | 0 | 0 | 0 | 0 | 0 | 0 | 0 | 0 | 0 | 0 | 0 | 0 | 0 | 0 | 0 | 0 | 0 | 0 | 0 | 0 | 0 | 0 |
| Natural Causes | 4 | 2 | 2 | 3 | 0 | 7 | 2 | 3 | 1 | 3 | 4 | 4 | 3 | 3 | 4 | 9 | 2 | 6 | 6 | 6 | 1 | 5 | 0 |
| Self-inflicted | 5 | 8 | 6 | 9 | 14 | 13 | 4 | 3 | 7 | 1 | 3 | 1 | 1 | 1 | 2 | 3 | 5 | 12 | 2 | 3 | 5 | 2 | 3 |
| Other[7] | 0 | 0 | 0 | 0 | 1 | 0 | 1 | 0 | 0 | 1 | 0 | 3 | 1 | 0 | 0 | 0 | 1 | 4 | 0 | 2 | 2 | 0 | 3 |
| *of which* | | | | | | | | | | | | | | | | | | | | | | | |
| *Other/Non-natural[8]* | 0 | 0 | 0 | 0 | 1 | 0 | 1 | 0 | 0 | 1 | 0 | 3 | 1 | 0 | 0 | 0 | 1 | 4 | 0 | 0 | 0 | 0 | 0 |
| *Awaiting further information* | 0 | 0 | 0 | 0 | 0 | 0 | 0 | 0 | 0 | 0 | 0 | 0 | 0 | 0 | 0 | 0 | 0 | 0 | 0 | 2 | 2 | 0 | 3 |
| **PRISON POPULATION Females** | 3,247 | 3,342 | 3,727 | 4,299 | 4,425 | 4,449 | 4,467 | 4,448 | 4,374 | 4,414 | 4,283 | 4,236 | 4,188 | 4,154 | 3,890 | 3,905 | 3,885 | 3,854 | 3,975 | 3,847 | 3,795 | 3,362 | 3,183 |
| **Deaths per 1,000 prisoners** | | | | | | | | | | | | | | | | | | | | | | | |
| Total | 2.8 | 3.0 | 2.1 | 2.8 | 3.4 | 4.5 | 1.6 | 1.3 | 1.8 | 1.1 | 1.6 | 1.9 | 1.2 | 1.0 | 1.5 | 3.1 | 2.1 | 5.7 | 2.0 | 2.9 | 2.1 | 2.1 | 1.9 |
| Natural Causes | 1.2 | 0.6 | 0.5 | 0.7 | 0.0 | 1.6 | 0.4 | 0.7 | 0.2 | 0.7 | 0.9 | 0.9 | 0.7 | 0.7 | 1.0 | 2.3 | 0.5 | 1.6 | 1.5 | 1.6 | 0.3 | 1.5 | 0.0 |
| Self-inflicted | 1.5 | 2.4 | 1.6 | 2.1 | 3.2 | 2.9 | 0.9 | 0.7 | 1.6 | 0.2 | 0.7 | 0.2 | 0.2 | 0.2 | 0.5 | 0.8 | 1.3 | 3.1 | 0.5 | 0.8 | 1.3 | 0.6 | 0.9 |
| Other | 0.0 | 0.0 | 0.0 | 0.0 | 0.2 | 0.0 | 0.2 | 0.0 | 0.0 | 0.2 | 0.0 | 0.7 | 0.2 | 0.0 | 0.0 | 0.0 | 0.3 | 1.0 | 0.0 | 0.5 | 0.5 | 0.0 | 0.9 |

(1) Deaths in prison custody figures include all deaths of prisoners arising from incidents during prison custody. They include deaths of prisoners while released on temporary license (ROTL) for medical reasons but exclude other types of ROTL where the state has less direct responsibility.

(2) Due to the number of deaths that remain unclassified (awaiting further information) in recent years, and the latest year particularly, caution should be used when comparing with earlier periods.

(3) Apparent cause is based on the HMPPS classification of deaths in prison custody. The self-inflicted deaths category includes a wider range of deaths than suicides. Similarly, the homicide category includes a wider range of deaths than murder. When comparing figures with other sources it is important to determine whether the narrower suicide or broader self-inflicted deaths approach is in use.

(4) All classifications of deaths remain provisional until confirmed at inquest.

(5) Figures include incidents at HMPPS run Immigration Removal Centres and during contracted out escorts

(6) Figures do not include incidents at Medway STC. For more information on Secure Training Centres, please see Youth justice annual statistics at https://www.gov.uk/government/collections/youth-justice-annual-statistics

(7) A proportion of the most recent two years' figures for 'other' deaths are expected to be re-classified as natural causes or self-inflicted deaths.

(8) In the case of drug related deaths where no intent to self-harm has been discovered, the death has been classified as "Other: Non-natural".

*Data Sources and Quality*
*These figures are derived from the HMPPS Deaths in Prison Custody database. As classification of deaths may change following inquest or as new information emerges, numbers may change from time to time.*

## Table 1.2: Deaths arising from incidents in prison custody but occurring elsewhere by apparent cause since 1999, England and Wales

| | 1999 | 2000 | 2001 | 2002 | 2003 | 2004 | 2005 | 2006 | 2007 | 2008 | 2009 | 2010 | 2011 | 2012 | 2013 | 2014 | 2015 | 2016 | 2017 | 2018 | 2019 (r) | 2020 (r) | 2021 (p) |
|---|---|---|---|---|---|---|---|---|---|---|---|---|---|---|---|---|---|---|---|---|---|---|---|
| **DEATHS IN PRISON CUSTODY** | | | | | | | | | | | | | | | | | | | | | | | |
| **Total** | 149 | 146 | 142 | 164 | 183 | 208 | 175 | 153 | 185 | 166 | 169 | 198 | 192 | 192 | 215 | 243 | 257 | 354 | 295 | 325 | 300 | 318 | 371 |
| Homicide | 0 | 3 | 0 | 0 | 1 | 2 | 3 | 0 | 0 | 3 | 0 | 1 | 2 | 0 | 4 | 3 | 3 | 4 | 3 | 4 | 3 | 2 | 1 |
| Natural Causes | 58 | 61 | 68 | 66 | 86 | 101 | 89 | 83 | 89 | 99 | 104 | 126 | 122 | 123 | 131 | 145 | 147 | 206 | 193 | 168 | 176 | 222 | 250 |
| Self-inflicted | 91 | 81 | 73 | 95 | 96 | 96 | 78 | 66 | 91 | 61 | 61 | 58 | 58 | 76 | 76 | 89 | 90 | 124 | 73 | 93 | 86 | 67 | 86 |
| Other[5] | 0 | 1 | 1 | 3 | 1 | 9 | 5 | 4 | 5 | 3 | 4 | 13 | 10 | 8 | 4 | 6 | 12 | 21 | 26 | 60 | 35 | 27 | 34 |
| *of which* | | | | | | | | | | | | | | | | | | | | | | | |
| *Other non-natural[6]* | 0 | - | 1 | - | 1 | 9 | 5 | 4 | 4 | 3 | 4 | 13 | 10 | 8 | 4 | 6 | 12 | 19 | 26 | 56 | 27 | 24 | 4 |
| *Awaiting further info* | - | - | - | - | - | - | - | - | - | - | - | - | - | - | - | - | - | 2 | - | 4 | 8 | 3 | 30 |
| **OF WHICH OCCURRING IN HOSPITALS, HOSPICES OR NURSING HOMES** | | | | | | | | | | | | | | | | | | | | | | | |
| **Total** | 45 | 36 | 33 | 40 | 63 | 70 | 65 | 55 | 55 | 69 | 55 | 83 | 67 | 73 | 74 | 62 | 103 | 163 | 147 | 118 | 134 | 154 | 209 |
| Homicide | 0 | 0 | 0 | 0 | 1 | 1 | 2 | 0 | 0 | 1 | 0 | 0 | 0 | 0 | 1 | 0 | 3 | 0 | 0 | 2 | 2 | 2 | 1 |
| Natural Causes | 34 | 32 | 32 | 34 | 54 | 62 | 48 | 43 | 48 | 66 | 53 | 75 | 58 | 64 | 61 | 51 | 73 | 124 | 116 | 106 | 137 | 137 | 175 |
| Self-inflicted | 11 | 3 | 5 | 7 | 5 | 12 | 12 | 5 | 2 | 3 | 5 | 3 | 8 | 9 | 11 | 0 | 22 | 33 | 20 | 18 | 10 | 13 | 25 |
| Other[5] | 0 | 0 | 0 | - | 1 | 2 | 3 | 0 | 2 | 0 | 1 | 5 | 1 | 1 | 1 | 0 | 5 | 5 | 10 | 10 | 4 | 3 | 6 |
| *of which* | | | | | | | | | | | | | | | | | | | | | | | |
| *Other non-natural[6]* | 0 | 0 | 0 | - | 1 | 2 | 3 | 0 | 2 | 0 | 1 | 5 | 1 | 1 | 1 | 0 | 5 | 5 | 10 | 10 | 4 | 3 | - |
| *Awaiting further info* | - | - | - | - | - | - | - | - | - | - | - | - | - | - | - | - | - | - | - | - | - | - | 6 |
| **PERCENTAGE DEATHS IN HOSPITALS, HOSPICES OR NURSING HOMES** | | | | | | | | | | | | | | | | | | | | | | | |
| **All Causes** | 30% | 25% | 23% | 24% | 34% | 34% | 37% | 36% | 30% | 42% | 33% | 42% | 35% | 38% | 34% | 26% | 40% | 46% | 50% | 36% | 45% | 48% | 56% |
| Natural Causes | 59% | 52% | 47% | 52% | 63% | 61% | 54% | 52% | 54% | 67% | 51% | 60% | 48% | 52% | 47% | 35% | 50% | 60% | 60% | 52% | 60% | 62% | 70% |
| Self-inflicted | 12% | 4% | 1% | 5% | 7% | 5% | 15% | 18% | 5% | 3% | 2% | 5% | 14% | 15% | 14% | 12% | 24% | 27% | 27% | 19% | 24% | 19% | 29% |

*(1) Deaths in prison custody figures include all deaths of prisoners arising from incidents during prison custody. They include deaths of prisoners while released on temporary license (ROTL) for medical reasons but exclude other types of ROTL where the state has less direct responsibility.*

*(2) Due to the number of deaths that remain unclassified (awaiting further information) in recent years, and the latest year particularly, caution should be used when comparing with earlier periods.*

*(3) In addition to deaths in prison custody which actually occur in hospitals, hospices or nursing homes a small proportion will occur while in an ambulance on the way to hospital, while on escort.*

*(4) Apparent cause is based on the HMPPS classification of deaths in prison custody. The self-inflicted deaths category includes a wider range of deaths than suicides. Similarly the homicide category includes a wider range of deaths than murder. When comparing figures with other sources it is important to determine whether the narrower suicide or broader self-inflicted deaths approach is in use.*

*(5) A proportion of the most recent two years' figures for 'other' deaths are expected to be re-classified as natural causes or self-inflicted deaths.*

*(6) In the case of drug related deaths where no intent to self-harm has been discovered, the death has been classified as "Other: Non-natural".*

*Data Sources and Quality*
*These figures are derived from the HMPPS Deaths in Prison Custody database. As classification of deaths may change following inquest or as new information emerges, numbers may change from time to time.*

**Table 1.3: Self-inflicted deaths in prison custody by time in custody and current prison since 1999, England and Wales**

| | 1999 | 2000 | 2001 | 2002 | 2003 | 2004 | 2005 | 2006 | 2007 | 2008 | 2009 | 2010 | 2011 | 2012 | 2013 | 2014 | 2015 | 2016 | 2017 (r) | 2018 (r) | 2019 (r) | 2020 (r) | 2021 (p) |
|---|---|---|---|---|---|---|---|---|---|---|---|---|---|---|---|---|---|---|---|---|---|---|---|
| **TIME IN CUSTODY** | | | | | | | | | | | | | | | | | | | | | | | |
| Total | 91 | 81 | 73 | 95 | 95 | 96 | 78 | 66 | 91 | 61 | 61 | 58 | 58 | 61 | 76 | 89 | 90 | 124 | 73 | 93 | 86 | 67 | 86 |
| On day of arrival | 3 | 2 | 2 | 0 | 1 | 3 | 0 | 2 | 1 | 3 | 8 | 0 | 0 | 2 | 1 | 1 | 2 | 2 | 0 | 0 | 1 | 0 | 1 |
| 1st or 2nd full day[4] | 10 | 12 | 3 | 9 | 9 | 10 | 11 | 3 | 3 | 4 | 4 | 3 | 4 | 2 | 8 | 4 | 6 | 7 | 4 | 4 | 6 | 4 | 6 |
| 3 days to 7 days | 14 | 7 | 4 | 14 | 10 | 10 | 2 | 2 | 6 | 3 | 7 | 5 | 6 | 3 | 5 | 9 | 8 | 3 | 5 | 5 | 7 | 3 | 2 |
| 8 days to 30 days | 10 | 14 | 18 | 22 | 11 | 16 | 14 | 5 | 10 | 5 | 5 | 8 | 8 | 5 | 14 | 9 | 11 | 14 | 9 | 11 | 5 | 7 | 9 |
| 31 days to 3 months (90 days) | 15 | 14 | 15 | 12 | 18 | 18 | 10 | 10 | 11 | 8 | 6 | 11 | 12 | 8 | 10 | 16 | 17 | 15 | 10 | 14 | 5 | 8 | 13 |
| 3 months to 6 months (91 to 182 days) | 18 | 13 | 8 | 10 | 12 | 6 | 14 | 8 | 16 | 8 | 10 | 8 | 5 | 12 | 10 | 8 | 12 | 20 | 7 | 10 | 14 | 10 | 13 |
| 6 months to 1 year | 9 | 7 | 7 | 7 | 7 | 15 | 8 | 11 | 9 | 16 | 9 | 6 | 8 | 6 | 10 | 13 | 12 | 22 | 7 | 12 | 12 | 10 | 11 |
| Over one year | 12 | 12 | 16 | 26 | 27 | 18 | 19 | 25 | 35 | 21 | 19 | 16 | 15 | 24 | 22 | 29 | 24 | 41 | 28 | 37 | 34 | 25 | 30 |
| Not known | 0 | 0 | 0 | 0 | 0 | 0 | 0 | 0 | 0 | 0 | 0 | 0 | 0 | 0 | 0 | 0 | 0 | 0 | 0 | 0 | 2 | 1 | 1 |
| **TIME IN CURRENT PRISON** | | | | | | | | | | | | | | | | | | | | | | | |
| Total | 91 | 81 | 73 | 95 | 95 | 96 | 78 | 66 | 91 | 61 | 61 | 58 | 58 | 61 | 76 | 89 | 90 | 124 | 73 | 93 | 86 | 67 | 86 |
| On day of arrival | 5 | 2 | 2 | 1 | 2 | 4 | 0 | 2 | 1 | 3 | 0 | 0 | 0 | 0 | 2 | 1 | 2 | 2 | 0 | 0 | 0 | 0 | 0 |
| 1st or 2nd full day[4] | 11 | 16 | 4 | 12 | 13 | 13 | 13 | 3 | 4 | 4 | 9 | 4 | 4 | 4 | 9 | 5 | 7 | 7 | 4 | 4 | 7 | 4 | 9 |
| 3 days to 7 days | 16 | 7 | 8 | 17 | 12 | 13 | 3 | 3 | 11 | 3 | 10 | 6 | 9 | 6 | 6 | 11 | 10 | 9 | 10 | 5 | 5 | 5 | 5 |
| 8 days to 30 days | 14 | 14 | 22 | 22 | 16 | 23 | 17 | 11 | 17 | 10 | 16 | 7 | 8 | 6 | 17 | 18 | 20 | 19 | 18 | 16 | 11 | 13 | 15 |
| 31 days to 3 months (90 days) | 17 | 20 | 15 | 20 | 18 | 19 | 12 | 20 | 23 | 15 | 16 | 16 | 17 | 17 | 14 | 22 | 18 | 26 | 14 | 19 | 12 | 13 | 19 |
| 3 months to 6 months (91 to 182 days) | 18 | 11 | 9 | 12 | 16 | 9 | 20 | 12 | 15 | 12 | 13 | 8 | 12 | 11 | 9 | 9 | 16 | 22 | 5 | 12 | 18 | 10 | 13 |
| 6 months to 1 year | 8 | 7 | 8 | 8 | 16 | 12 | 4 | 7 | 9 | 8 | 5 | 8 | 8 | 6 | 9 | 12 | 9 | 24 | 9 | 15 | 15 | 17 | 7 |
| Over one year | 2 | 4 | 5 | 3 | 12 | 3 | 10 | 8 | 11 | 5 | 2 | 10 | 7 | 8 | 8 | 11 | 10 | 18 | 11 | 17 | 19 | 8 | 16 |
| Not known | 0 | 0 | 0 | 0 | 0 | 0 | 0 | 0 | 0 | 0 | 0 | 0 | 0 | 0 | 0 | 0 | 0 | 0 | 0 | 0 | 2 | 0 | 1 |

(1) Deaths in prison custody figures include all deaths of prisoners arising from incidents during prison custody. They include deaths of prisoners while released on temporary license (ROTL) for medical reasons but exclude other types of ROTL where the state has less direct responsibility.

(2) Due to the number of deaths that remain unclassified (awaiting further information) in recent years, and the latest year particularly, caution should be used when comparing with earlier periods.

(3) Time in custody refers to time spent on current offence/prison number. Some prisoners may have previously spent time in prison custody for a different offence with a different prison number but this is not included.

(4) Prisoners who die on the date of arrival will typically have been in the prison for less than 12 hours. The one to two days category includes any death after midnight on the date of arrival and before midnight on the second complete day in the prison. Care needs to be taken when interpreting numbers of deaths in the early days of custody as the actual number of deaths in precise 24 hours time slots is not known accurately due to uncertainty about the exact time of incident/death.

*Data Sources and Quality*
*These figures are derived from the HMPPS Deaths in Prison Custody database. As classification of deaths may change following inquest or as new information emerges, numbers may change from time to time.*

**Table 1.4: Self-inflicted deaths in prison custody by offence since 1999, England and Wales**

| | 1999 | 2000 | 2001 | 2002 | 2003 | 2004 | 2005 | 2006 | 2007 | 2008 | 2009 | 2010 | 2011 | 2012 | 2013 | 2014 | 2015 | 2016 | 2017 | 2018 | 2019 (r) | 2020 (r) | 2021 (p) |
|---|---|---|---|---|---|---|---|---|---|---|---|---|---|---|---|---|---|---|---|---|---|---|---|
| **MALES AND FEMALES** | | | | | | | | | | | | | | | | | | | | | | | |
| **Total** | 91 | 81 | 73 | 95 | 95 | 96 | 78 | 66 | 91 | 61 | 61 | 58 | 58 | 61 | 76 | 89 | 90 | 124 | 73 | 93 | 86 | 67 | 86 |
| Violence against the person | 21 | 21 | 21 | 24 | 27 | 32 | 22 | 25 | 32 | 13 | 24 | 26 | 23 | 27 | 26 | 28 | 33 | 46 | 30 | 32 | 24 | 26 | 35 |
| Sexual offences | 7 | 8 | 7 | 8 | 9 | 5 | 10 | 12 | 11 | 12 | 4 | 7 | 10 | 13 | 11 | 11 | 11 | 10 | 4 | 12 | 15 | 12 | 6 |
| Robbery | 9 | 10 | 8 | 15 | 14 | 11 | 9 | 5 | 9 | 4 | 6 | 8 | 6 | 5 | 5 | 8 | 11 | 19 | 8 | 8 | 8 | 11 | 6 |
| Theft offences | 23 | 26 | 18 | 21 | 21 | 18 | 18 | 11 | 12 | 7 | 6 | 5 | 5 | 8 | 17 | 17 | 15 | 25 | 11 | 11 | 17 | 11 | 7 |
| Criminal damage and arson | 9 | 3 | 3 | 9 | 3 | 9 | 5 | 2 | 8 | 2 | 6 | 2 | 4 | 2 | 6 | 3 | 4 | 8 | 2 | 8 | 6 | 3 | 5 |
| Drug offences | 3 | 3 | 4 | 7 | 7 | 4 | 4 | 0 | 7 | 5 | 2 | 1 | 2 | 0 | 1 | 6 | 3 | 1 | 4 | 9 | 5 | 1 | 7 |
| Possession of weapons | 2 | 1 | 1 | 1 | 3 | 2 | 3 | 4 | 2 | 4 | 4 | 3 | 5 | 2 | 7 | 4 | 3 | 3 | 2 | 1 | 0 | 0 | 0 |
| Public order offences | 3 | 3 | 1 | 2 | 1 | 2 | 3 | 0 | 4 | 3 | 2 | 1 | 5 | 2 | 2 | 6 | 3 | 0 | 2 | 0 | 0 | 0 | 0 |
| Miscellaneous crimes against society | 3 | 2 | 2 | 5 | 0 | 5 | 4 | 2 | 5 | 5 | 0 | 3 | 3 | 1 | 5 | 5 | 3 | 11 | 13 | 6 | 10 | 4 | 16 |
| Fraud offences | 2 | 0 | 5 | 4 | 5 | 3 | 2 | 4 | 2 | 1 | 3 | 1 | 0 | 1 | 0 | 7 | 2 | 0 | 0 | 0 | 0 | 0 | 0 |
| Summary non-motoring | 5 | 2 | 2 | 4 | 2 | 4 | 1 | 2 | 0 | 9 | 5 | 0 | 1 | 0 | 5 | 0 | 3 | 3 | 0 | 1 | 0 | 1 | 1 |
| Summary motoring | 4 | 2 | 0 | 0 | 2 | 0 | 2 | 2 | 0 | 0 | 1 | 0 | 0 | 0 | 0 | 0 | 0 | 0 | 0 | 0 | 0 | 0 | 0 |
| Offence not recorded | 0 | 0 | 0 | 0 | 0 | 0 | 0 | 0 | 0 | 0 | 0 | 0 | 0 | 0 | 0 | 0 | 1 | 0 | 2 | 0 | 0 | 1 | 2 |
| **MALES** | | | | | | | | | | | | | | | | | | | | | | | |
| **Total** | 86 | 73 | 67 | 86 | 81 | 83 | 74 | 63 | 84 | 60 | 58 | 57 | 56 | 60 | 74 | 86 | 85 | 112 | 71 | 90 | 81 | 65 | 86 |
| Violence against the person | 21 | 20 | 19 | 20 | 23 | 28 | 24 | 24 | 29 | 13 | 24 | 26 | 23 | 27 | 25 | 28 | 33 | 43 | 29 | 31 | 23 | 24 | 35 |
| Sexual offences | 7 | 8 | 7 | 8 | 9 | 5 | 10 | 12 | 11 | 12 | 4 | 7 | 10 | 13 | 11 | 11 | 11 | 9 | 4 | 12 | 15 | 12 | 6 |
| Robbery | 8 | 10 | 6 | 8 | 9 | 10 | 9 | 5 | 9 | 4 | 6 | 8 | 4 | 6 | 5 | 8 | 11 | 18 | 8 | 8 | 7 | 11 | 6 |
| Theft offences | 21 | 21 | 16 | 20 | 17 | 16 | 17 | 10 | 10 | 7 | 5 | 4 | 5 | 8 | 11 | 17 | 14 | 21 | 6 | 11 | 15 | 7 | 5 |
| Criminal damage and arson | 9 | 2 | 3 | 7 | 4 | 5 | 4 | 0 | 8 | 5 | 2 | 1 | 2 | 0 | 6 | 3 | 4 | 7 | 2 | 9 | 5 | 3 | 7 |
| Drug offences | 3 | 2 | 4 | 8 | 3 | 7 | 4 | 1 | 1 | 3 | 4 | 2 | 2 | 0 | 1 | 6 | 2 | 2 | 2 | 5 | 5 | 1 | 7 |
| Possession of weapons | 2 | 1 | 1 | 1 | 2 | 2 | 3 | 4 | 4 | 2 | 2 | 2 | 5 | 2 | 7 | 4 | 3 | 4 | 4 | 1 | 0 | 0 | 0 |
| Public order offences | 3 | 2 | 1 | 2 | 1 | 2 | 3 | 0 | 3 | 3 | 2 | 0 | 2 | 2 | 2 | 6 | 3 | 0 | 2 | 0 | 0 | 0 | 0 |
| Miscellaneous crimes against society | 3 | 2 | 1 | 4 | 2 | 5 | 4 | 2 | 5 | 5 | 0 | 3 | 3 | 1 | 5 | 5 | 3 | 10 | 13 | 6 | 10 | 4 | 16 |
| Fraud offences | 1 | 0 | 0 | 0 | 0 | 2 | 1 | 0 | 1 | 0 | 2 | 1 | 0 | 1 | 0 | 7 | 2 | 0 | 0 | 1 | 0 | 1 | 0 |
| Summary non-motoring | 5 | 2 | 5 | 4 | 5 | 3 | 2 | 4 | 2 | 8 | 5 | 0 | 0 | 1 | 6 | 6 | 2 | 3 | 0 | 0 | 0 | 0 | 1 |
| Summary motoring | 3 | 2 | 2 | 0 | 2 | 0 | 0 | 2 | 0 | 0 | 0 | 0 | 0 | 0 | 0 | 0 | 0 | 0 | 0 | 0 | 0 | 0 | 0 |
| Offence not recorded | 0 | 0 | 0 | 0 | 0 | 0 | 0 | 0 | 0 | 0 | 0 | 0 | 0 | 0 | 0 | 0 | 1 | 0 | 2 | 0 | 0 | 1 | 2 |
| **FEMALES** | | | | | | | | | | | | | | | | | | | | | | | |
| **Total** | 5 | 8 | 6 | 9 | 14 | 13 | 4 | 3 | 7 | 1 | 3 | 1 | 2 | 1 | 2 | 3 | 5 | 12 | 2 | 3 | 5 | 2 | 0 |
| Violence against the person | 0 | 1 | 0 | 4 | 4 | 4 | 2 | 1 | 3 | 0 | 3 | 0 | 0 | 0 | 1 | 1 | 2 | 3 | 1 | 1 | 1 | 2 | 0 |
| Sexual offences | 0 | 0 | 0 | 0 | 0 | 0 | 0 | 0 | 0 | 0 | 0 | 0 | 0 | 0 | 0 | 0 | 0 | 0 | 0 | 0 | 0 | 0 | 0 |
| Robbery | 1 | 0 | 2 | 2 | 2 | 1 | 1 | 0 | 0 | 0 | 0 | 2 | 2 | 0 | 0 | 0 | 0 | 1 | 0 | 1 | 0 | 0 | 0 |
| Theft offences | 2 | 5 | 2 | 1 | 4 | 2 | 1 | 1 | 2 | 0 | 1 | 1 | 0 | 0 | 0 | 0 | 1 | 4 | 1 | 0 | 2 | 0 | 0 |
| Criminal damage and arson | 0 | 0 | 0 | 1 | 0 | 4 | 1 | 0 | 2 | 0 | 0 | 0 | 0 | 0 | 0 | 0 | 0 | 1 | 0 | 1 | 0 | 0 | 0 |
| Drug offences | 0 | 1 | 0 | 1 | 0 | 0 | 0 | 0 | 2 | 2 | 0 | 0 | 0 | 0 | 0 | 0 | 1 | 1 | 1 | 2 | 0 | 0 | 0 |
| Possession of weapons | 0 | 0 | 0 | 0 | 1 | 0 | 0 | 0 | 0 | 2 | 0 | 0 | 0 | 0 | 0 | 0 | 0 | 0 | 0 | 0 | 0 | 0 | 0 |
| Public order offences | 0 | 1 | 0 | 0 | 0 | 0 | 0 | 0 | 1 | 0 | 0 | 1 | 0 | 0 | 0 | 0 | 0 | 0 | 0 | 0 | 0 | 0 | 0 |
| Miscellaneous crimes against society | 0 | 0 | 1 | 1 | 0 | 0 | 0 | 0 | 0 | 0 | 0 | 0 | 0 | 0 | 0 | 0 | 0 | 1 | 0 | 0 | 0 | 0 | 0 |
| Fraud offences | 1 | 0 | 0 | 1 | 0 | 0 | 1 | 0 | 0 | 1 | 0 | 0 | 0 | 0 | 0 | 0 | 0 | 0 | 0 | 0 | 0 | 0 | 0 |
| Summary non-motoring | 0 | 0 | 0 | 0 | 2 | 1 | 0 | 0 | 0 | 1 | 0 | 0 | 0 | 0 | 0 | 1 | 0 | 0 | 0 | 0 | 0 | 0 | 0 |
| Summary motoring | 1 | 0 | 0 | 0 | 0 | 0 | 0 | 0 | 0 | 0 | 0 | 0 | 0 | 0 | 0 | 0 | 0 | 0 | 0 | 0 | 0 | 0 | 0 |
| Offence not recorded | 0 | 0 | 0 | 0 | 0 | 0 | 0 | 0 | 0 | 0 | 0 | 0 | 0 | 0 | 0 | 0 | 0 | 0 | 0 | 0 | 0 | 0 | 0 |

(1) Deaths in prison custody figures include all deaths of prisoners arising from incidents during prison custody. They include deaths of prisoners while released on temporary license (ROTL) for medical reasons but exclude other types of ROTL where the state has less direct responsibility.

(2) Due to the number of deaths that remain unclassified (awaiting further information) in recent years, and the latest year particularly, caution should be used when comparing with earlier periods.

*Data Sources and Quality*

These figures are derived from the HMPPS Deaths in Prison Custody database. As classification of deaths may change following inquest or as new information emerges, numbers may change from time to time.

**Table 1.5: Self-inflicted deaths in prison custody[1,2] by ethnicity[3] since 1999, England and Wales**

| | 1999 | 2000 | 2001 | 2002 | 2003 | 2004 | 2005 | 2006 | 2007 | 2008 | 2009 | 2010 | 2011 | 2012 | 2013 | 2014 | 2015 | 2016 | 2017 | 2018 (r) | 2019 (r) | 2020 (r) | 2021 (p) |
|---|---|---|---|---|---|---|---|---|---|---|---|---|---|---|---|---|---|---|---|---|---|---|---|
| **MALES AND FEMALES** | | | | | | | | | | | | | | | | | | | | | | | |
| Total | 91 | 81 | 73 | 95 | 95 | 96 | 78 | 66 | 91 | 61 | 61 | 58 | 58 | 61 | 76 | 89 | 90 | 124 | 73 | 93 | 86 | 67 | 86 |
| White | 81 | 72 | 66 | 85 | 86 | 85 | 61 | 57 | 72 | 50 | 56 | 51 | 51 | 49 | 60 | 80 | 78 | 105 | 63 | 80 | 76 | 57 | 75 |
| Asian | 3 | 1 | 2 | 3 | 5 | 5 | 4 | 3 | 6 | 7 | 3 | 4 | 3 | 3 | 6 | 3 | 3 | 8 | 5 | 2 | 2 | 3 | 7 |
| Black | 5 | 8 | 4 | 5 | 3 | 5 | 11 | 5 | 11 | 1 | 0 | 2 | 2 | 4 | 8 | 4 | 3 | 7 | 1 | 5 | 3 | 2 | 4 |
| Mixed | 0 | 0 | 0 | 0 | 0 | 1 | 2 | 0 | 1 | 2 | 2 | 1 | 1 | 4 | 2 | 2 | 3 | 3 | 2 | 1 | 3 | 2 | 0 |
| Other | 2 | 0 | 1 | 2 | 1 | 0 | 0 | 1 | 1 | 1 | 0 | 0 | 1 | 0 | 0 | 0 | 1 | 1 | 2 | 5 | 2 | 3 | 0 |
| **MALES** | | | | | | | | | | | | | | | | | | | | | | | |
| Total | 86 | 73 | 67 | 86 | 81 | 83 | 74 | 63 | 84 | 60 | 58 | 57 | 56 | 60 | 74 | 86 | 85 | 112 | 71 | 90 | 81 | 65 | 86 |
| White | 76 | 67 | 61 | 78 | 72 | 73 | 57 | 54 | 65 | 49 | 53 | 50 | 49 | 48 | 58 | 77 | 74 | 95 | 62 | 78 | 71 | 55 | 75 |
| Asian | 3 | 1 | 2 | 3 | 5 | 4 | 4 | 3 | 6 | 7 | 3 | 4 | 3 | 3 | 6 | 3 | 5 | 8 | 4 | 2 | 2 | 3 | 7 |
| Black | 5 | 5 | 3 | 3 | 3 | 5 | 11 | 5 | 11 | 1 | 0 | 2 | 2 | 4 | 8 | 4 | 3 | 7 | 1 | 4 | 3 | 2 | 4 |
| Mixed | 0 | 0 | 0 | 0 | 0 | 1 | 2 | 0 | 1 | 2 | 2 | 1 | 1 | 5 | 2 | 2 | 2 | 1 | 2 | 1 | 3 | 2 | 0 |
| Other | 2 | 0 | 1 | 2 | 1 | 0 | 0 | 1 | 1 | 1 | 0 | 0 | 1 | 0 | 0 | 0 | 1 | 1 | 2 | 5 | 2 | 3 | 0 |
| **FEMALES** | | | | | | | | | | | | | | | | | | | | | | | |
| Total | 5 | 8 | 6 | 9 | 14 | 13 | 4 | 3 | 7 | 1 | 3 | 1 | 2 | 1 | 2 | 3 | 5 | 12 | 2 | 3 | 5 | 2 | 0 |
| White | 5 | 5 | 5 | 7 | 14 | 12 | 4 | 3 | 7 | 1 | 3 | 1 | 2 | 1 | 2 | 3 | 4 | 10 | 1 | 2 | 5 | 2 | 0 |
| Asian | 0 | 0 | 0 | 0 | 0 | 1 | 0 | 0 | 0 | 0 | 0 | 0 | 0 | 0 | 0 | 0 | 0 | 0 | 0 | 0 | 0 | 0 | 0 |
| Black | 0 | 3 | 0 | 2 | 0 | 0 | 0 | 0 | 0 | 0 | 0 | 0 | 0 | 0 | 0 | 0 | 0 | 0 | 0 | 1 | 0 | 0 | 0 |
| Mixed | 0 | 0 | 0 | 0 | 0 | 0 | 0 | 0 | 0 | 0 | 0 | 0 | 0 | 0 | 0 | 0 | 1 | 2 | 0 | 0 | 0 | 0 | 0 |
| Other | 0 | 0 | 0 | 0 | 0 | 0 | 0 | 0 | 0 | 0 | 0 | 0 | 0 | 0 | 0 | 0 | 0 | 0 | 0 | 0 | 0 | 0 | 0 |

(1) Deaths in prison custody figures include all deaths of prisoners arising from incidents during prison custody. They include deaths of prisoners while released on temporary license (ROTL) for medical reasons but exclude other types of ROTL where the state has less direct responsibility.

(2) Due to the number of deaths that remain unclassified (awaiting further information) in recent years, and the latest year particularly, caution should be used when comparing with earlier periods.

(3) Ethnicity is based on self-reporting by prisoners and has not been independently validated.

"Data Sources and Quality"
These figures are derived from the HMPPS Deaths in Prison Custody database. As classification of deaths may change following inquest or as new information emerges, numbers may change from time to time.

**Table 1.6: Self-inflicted deaths in prison custody[1,2] by nationality type[3] since 1999, England & Wales**

| | | | | | | | | | | | | | | | | | | | | Number of deaths | | | |
| | 1999 | 2000 | 2001 | 2002 | 2003 | 2004 | 2005 | 2006 | 2007 | 2008 | 2009 | 2010 | 2011 | 2012 | 2013 | 2014 | 2015 | 2016 | 2017 | 2018 | 2019 (r) | 2020 (r) | 2021 (p) |
|---|---|---|---|---|---|---|---|---|---|---|---|---|---|---|---|---|---|---|---|---|---|---|---|
| **MALES AND FEMALES** | | | | | | | | | | | | | | | | | | | | | | | |
| Total | 91 | 81 | 73 | 95 | 95 | 96 | 78 | 66 | 91 | 61 | 61 | 58 | 58 | 61 | 76 | 89 | 90 | 124 | 73 | 93 | 86 | 67 | 86 |
| UK National | 84 | 77 | 68 | 86 | 87 | 89 | 72 | 60 | 67 | 52 | 56 | 52 | 45 | 57 | 67 | 74 | 74 | 104 | 59 | 85 | 79 | 59 | 76 |
| EEA Foreign National[4] | 4 | 3 | 2 | 4 | 2 | 2 | 1 | 2 | 7 | 1 | 3 | 1 | 6 | 2 | 6 | 7 | 10 | 10 | 10 | 5 | 2 | 5 | 9 |
| Non EEA Foreign National | 3 | 1 | 3 | 5 | 6 | 5 | 5 | 4 | 17 | 8 | 2 | 5 | 7 | 2 | 3 | 8 | 6 | 10 | 4 | 3 | 5 | 3 | 1 |
| **MALES** | | | | | | | | | | | | | | | | | | | | | | | |
| Total | 86 | 73 | 67 | 86 | 81 | 83 | 74 | 63 | 84 | 60 | 58 | 57 | 56 | 60 | 74 | 86 | 85 | 112 | 71 | 90 | 81 | 65 | 86 |
| UK National | 79 | 69 | 62 | 78 | 73 | 76 | 68 | 57 | 60 | 51 | 53 | 51 | 43 | 56 | 65 | 71 | 70 | 92 | 57 | 82 | 75 | 57 | 76 |
| EEA Foreign National[4] | 4 | 3 | 2 | 4 | 2 | 2 | 1 | 2 | 7 | 1 | 3 | 1 | 6 | 2 | 6 | 7 | 9 | 10 | 10 | 5 | 2 | 5 | 9 |
| Non EEA Foreign National | 3 | 1 | 3 | 4 | 6 | 5 | 5 | 4 | 17 | 8 | 2 | 5 | 7 | 2 | 3 | 8 | 6 | 10 | 4 | 3 | 4 | 3 | 1 |
| **FEMALES** | | | | | | | | | | | | | | | | | | | | | | | |
| Total | 5 | 8 | 6 | 9 | 14 | 13 | 4 | 3 | 7 | 1 | 3 | 1 | 2 | 1 | 2 | 3 | 5 | 12 | 2 | 3 | 5 | 2 | 0 |
| UK National | 5 | 8 | 6 | 8 | 14 | 13 | 4 | 3 | 7 | 0 | 3 | 1 | 2 | 1 | 2 | 3 | 4 | 12 | 2 | 3 | 4 | 2 | 0 |
| EEA Foreign National[4] | 0 | 0 | 0 | 0 | 0 | 0 | 0 | 0 | 0 | 0 | 0 | 0 | 0 | 0 | 0 | 0 | 1 | 0 | 0 | 0 | 0 | 0 | 0 |
| Non EEA Foreign National | 0 | 0 | 0 | 1 | 0 | 0 | 0 | 0 | 0 | 0 | 0 | 0 | 0 | 0 | 0 | 0 | 0 | 0 | 0 | 0 | 1 | 0 | 0 |

(1) Deaths in prison custody figures include all deaths of prisoners arising from incidents during prison custody. They include deaths of prisoners while released on temporary license (ROTL) for medical reasons but exclude other types of ROTL where the state has less direct responsibility.
(2) Due to the number of deaths that remain unclassified (awaiting further information) in recent years, and the latest year particularly, caution should be used when comparing with earlier periods.
(3) Nationality is based on self-reporting by prisoners and has not been independently validated.
(4) The European Economic Area (EEA). For definition of the countries, please see: https://www.gov.uk/eu-eea

*Data Sources and Quality*
*These figures are derived from the HMPPS Deaths in Prison Custody database. As classification of deaths may change following inquest or as new information emerges, numbers may change from time to time.*

**Table 1.7: Self-inflicted deaths in prison custody[1,2] by sentence type since 1999, England and Wales**

| | 1999 | 2000 | 2001 | 2002 | 2003 | 2004 | 2005 | 2006 | 2007 | 2008 | 2009 | 2010 | 2011 | 2012 | 2013 | 2014 | 2015 | 2016 | 2017 | 2018 (r) | 2019 (r) | 2020 (r) | 2021 (p) |
|---|---|---|---|---|---|---|---|---|---|---|---|---|---|---|---|---|---|---|---|---|---|---|---|
| **MALES AND FEMALES** | | | | | | | | | | | | | | | | | | | | | | | |
| **Total** | 91 | 81 | 73 | 95 | 95 | 96 | 78 | 66 | 91 | 61 | 61 | 58 | 58 | 61 | 76 | 89 | 90 | 124 | 73 | 93 | 86 | 67 | 86 |
| **Remand** | 59 | 47 | 32 | 53 | 49 | 49 | 40 | 21 | 40 | 25 | 30 | 32 | 23 | 18 | 29 | 26 | 36 | 33 | 21 | 27 | 24 | 19 | 32 |
| Untried | 44 | 41 | 24 | 35 | 36 | 34 | 28 | 16 | 29 | 20 | 23 | 29 | 20 | 16 | 25 | 20 | 22 | 24 | 11 | 13 | 21 | 19 | 27 |
| Convicted Unsentenced | 15 | 6 | 8 | 18 | 13 | 15 | 12 | 5 | 11 | 5 | 7 | 3 | 3 | 2 | 4 | 6 | 14 | 9 | 10 | 14 | 3 | 0 | 5 |
| **Sentenced** | 32 | 34 | 41 | 42 | 43 | 47 | 38 | 45 | 51 | 35 | 31 | 26 | 35 | 43 | 47 | 61 | 53 | 90 | 48 | 65 | 62 | 47 | 52 |
| Less than or equal to 6 months | 11 | 5 | 7 | 5 | 5 | 3 | 3 | 5 | 3 | 3 | 3 | 1 | 3 | 3 | 6 | 6 | 7 | 13 | 5 | 8 | 6 | 7 | 4 |
| Greater than 6 months to less than 12 months | 0 | 8 | 2 | 3 | 0 | 3 | 1 | 5 | 3 | 3 | 1 | 0 | 3 | 2 | 4 | 1 | 0 | 0 | 3 | 1 | 6 | 1 | 2 |
| 12 months to less than 4 years | 9 | 8 | 14 | 10 | 16 | 15 | 12 | 17 | 9 | 11 | 10 | 7 | 9 | 8 | 12 | 15 | 17 | 23 | 11 | 15 | 16 | 16 | 15 |
| 4 years or more (excluding indeterminate sentences) | 8 | 9 | 9 | 15 | 11 | 18 | 13 | 14 | 14 | 11 | 7 | 5 | 11 | 14 | 10 | 24 | 15 | 35 | 17 | 28 | 23 | 16 | 16 |
| ISPP[3] | 0 | 0 | 0 | 0 | 0 | 0 | 0 | 0 | 6 | 6 | 3 | 4 | 4 | 6 | 6 | 8 | 9 | 4 | 7 | 8 | 9 | 2 | 3 |
| Life | 4 | 4 | 9 | 9 | 11 | 8 | 9 | 6 | 18 | 6 | 8 | 8 | 5 | 10 | 9 | 8 | 9 | 12 | 8 | 5 | 9 | 5 | 12 |
| **Immigration Detainee** | 0 | 0 | 0 | 0 | 3 | 0 | 0 | 0 | 0 | 1 | 0 | 0 | 0 | 0 | 0 | 2 | 1 | 1 | 4 | 1 | 0 | 1 | 2 |
| **MALES** | | | | | | | | | | | | | | | | | | | | | | | |
| **Total** | 86 | 73 | 67 | 86 | 81 | 83 | 74 | 63 | 84 | 60 | 58 | 57 | 56 | 60 | 74 | 86 | 85 | 112 | 71 | 90 | 81 | 65 | 86 |
| **Remand** | 54 | 44 | 28 | 48 | 45 | 44 | 39 | 21 | 37 | 24 | 30 | 32 | 23 | 18 | 28 | 25 | 36 | 32 | 20 | 27 | 23 | 19 | 32 |
| Untried | 41 | 38 | 20 | 30 | 36 | 32 | 27 | 16 | 27 | 19 | 23 | 29 | 20 | 16 | 24 | 19 | 22 | 23 | 11 | 13 | 20 | 19 | 27 |
| Convicted Unsentenced | 13 | 6 | 8 | 18 | 9 | 12 | 12 | 5 | 10 | 5 | 7 | 3 | 3 | 2 | 4 | 6 | 14 | 9 | 9 | 14 | 3 | 0 | 5 |
| **Sentenced** | 32 | 29 | 39 | 38 | 33 | 39 | 35 | 42 | 47 | 35 | 28 | 25 | 33 | 42 | 46 | 59 | 48 | 79 | 47 | 62 | 58 | 45 | 52 |
| Less than or equal to 6 months | 11 | 5 | 7 | 3 | 3 | 1 | 3 | 3 | 3 | 3 | 2 | 1 | 3 | 3 | 5 | 5 | 7 | 8 | 5 | 7 | 6 | 7 | 4 |
| Greater than 6 months to less than 12 months | 0 | 5 | 2 | 3 | 0 | 3 | 0 | 5 | 3 | 1 | 0 | 0 | 3 | 2 | 4 | 1 | 0 | 0 | 3 | 1 | 6 | 1 | 2 |
| 12 months to less than 4 years | 9 | 13 | 13 | 14 | 13 | 12 | 12 | 16 | 7 | 11 | 6 | 6 | 8 | 8 | 12 | 15 | 15 | 20 | 10 | 14 | 15 | 15 | 16 |
| 4 years or more (excluding indeterminate sentences) | 8 | 9 | 9 | 14 | 9 | 16 | 13 | 13 | 13 | 11 | 7 | 5 | 10 | 14 | 9 | 23 | 15 | 34 | 17 | 27 | 23 | 23 | 16 |
| ISPP[3] | 0 | 0 | 0 | 0 | 0 | 0 | 0 | 0 | 6 | 6 | 3 | 4 | 4 | 6 | 6 | 8 | 9 | 4 | 7 | 8 | 8 | 2 | 3 |
| Life | 4 | 4 | 8 | 8 | 8 | 7 | 7 | 6 | 17 | 6 | 6 | 8 | 4 | 9 | 9 | 7 | 3 | 12 | 7 | 8 | 8 | 5 | 12 |
| **Immigration Detainee** | 0 | 0 | 0 | 0 | 3 | 0 | 0 | 0 | 0 | 1 | 0 | 0 | 0 | 0 | 0 | 2 | 1 | 1 | 4 | 1 | 0 | 1 | 2 |
| **FEMALES** | | | | | | | | | | | | | | | | | | | | | | | |
| **Total** | 5 | 8 | 6 | 9 | 14 | 13 | 4 | 3 | 7 | 1 | 3 | 1 | 2 | 1 | 2 | 3 | 5 | 12 | 2 | 3 | 5 | 2 | 0 |
| **Remand** | 5 | 3 | 4 | 5 | 4 | 5 | 1 | 0 | 3 | 1 | 0 | 0 | 0 | 0 | 0 | 1 | 0 | 1 | 1 | 0 | 1 | 0 | 0 |
| Untried | 3 | 3 | 4 | 5 | 0 | 2 | 1 | 0 | 2 | 0 | 0 | 0 | 0 | 0 | 1 | 1 | 0 | 1 | 0 | 0 | 1 | 0 | 0 |
| Convicted Unsentenced | 2 | 0 | 0 | 0 | 4 | 3 | 0 | 0 | 1 | 1 | 0 | 0 | 0 | 1 | 0 | 0 | 0 | 0 | 1 | 0 | 0 | 0 | 0 |
| **Sentenced** | 0 | 5 | 2 | 4 | 10 | 8 | 3 | 3 | 4 | 0 | 3 | 1 | 2 | 1 | 2 | 2 | 5 | 11 | 1 | 3 | 4 | 2 | 0 |
| Less than or equal to 6 months | 0 | 0 | 0 | 2 | 2 | 2 | 1 | 0 | 0 | 0 | 0 | 0 | 0 | 0 | 1 | 0 | 1 | 5 | 0 | 1 | 2 | 0 | 0 |
| Greater than 6 months to less than 12 months | 0 | 3 | 0 | 0 | 0 | 0 | 1 | 0 | 0 | 0 | 0 | 0 | 0 | 0 | 0 | 0 | 0 | 0 | 0 | 0 | 0 | 0 | 0 |
| 12 months to less than 4 years | 0 | 2 | 1 | 0 | 3 | 3 | 2 | 1 | 2 | 0 | 0 | 1 | 1 | 0 | 1 | 0 | 2 | 3 | 1 | 1 | 1 | 1 | 0 |
| 4 years or more (excluding indeterminate sentences) | 0 | 0 | 0 | 1 | 2 | 0 | 0 | 1 | 1 | 0 | 0 | 0 | 1 | 0 | 1 | 1 | 0 | 1 | 0 | 1 | 0 | 0 | 0 |
| ISPP[3] | 0 | 0 | 0 | 0 | 0 | 0 | 0 | 0 | 0 | 0 | 0 | 0 | 0 | 0 | 0 | 0 | 0 | 2 | 0 | 0 | 0 | 0 | 0 |
| Life | 0 | 0 | 1 | 0 | 3 | 1 | 2 | 1 | 1 | 1 | 3 | 0 | 1 | 0 | 0 | 1 | 2 | 0 | 0 | 0 | 1 | 1 | 0 |
| **Immigration Detainee** | 0 | 0 | 0 | 0 | 0 | 0 | 0 | 0 | 0 | 0 | 0 | 0 | 0 | 0 | 0 | 0 | 0 | 0 | 0 | 0 | 0 | 0 | 0 |

(1) Deaths in prison custody figures include all deaths of prisoners arising from incidents during prison custody. They include deaths of prisoners while released on temporary license (ROTL) for medical reasons but exclude other types of ROTL where the state has less direct responsibility.
(2) Due to the number of deaths that remain unclassified (awaiting further information) in recent years, and the latest year particularly, caution should be used when comparing with earlier periods.
(3) The indeterminate sentence of Imprisonment for Public Protection (ISPP) was introduced in 2005. It was intended for people considered 'dangerous' but whose offence did not merit a life sentence.

*Data Sources and Quality*
These figures are derived from the HMPPS Deaths in Prison Custody database. As classification of deaths may change following inquest or as new information emerges, numbers may change from time to time.

## Table 1.8: Self-inflicted deaths in prison custody[1,2] by method since 1999, England and Wales

### MALES AND FEMALES

| | 1999 | 2000 | 2001 | 2002 | 2003 | 2004 | 2005 | 2006 | 2007 | 2008 | 2009 | 2010 | 2011 | 2012 | 2013 | 2014 | 2015 | 2016 | 2017 | 2018 | 2019 (r) | 2020 (r) | 2021 (p) |
|---|---|---|---|---|---|---|---|---|---|---|---|---|---|---|---|---|---|---|---|---|---|---|---|
| Total | 91 | 81 | 73 | 95 | 95 | 96 | 78 | 66 | 91 | 61 | 61 | 58 | 58 | 61 | 76 | 89 | 90 | 124 | 73 | 93 | 86 | 67 | 86 |
| Arson | 0 | 1 | 0 | 0 | 2 | 0 | 1 | 3 | 1 | 0 | 0 | 0 | 1 | 0 | 0 | 0 | 0 | 0 | 0 | 0 | 0 | 0 | 0 |
| Cutting | 2 | 2 | 2 | 1 | 0 | 2 | 2 | 3 | 1 | 0 | 5 | 2 | 2 | 2 | 4 | 2 | 2 | 3 | 3 | 4 | 8 | 4 | 3 |
| Electrocution | 0 | 0 | 0 | 0 | 1 | 0 | 0 | 0 | 1 | 0 | 0 | 0 | 0 | 0 | 0 | 0 | 0 | 0 | 0 | 0 | 0 | 0 | 0 |
| Falling | 0 | 0 | 0 | 0 | 0 | 0 | 0 | 0 | 0 | 0 | 0 | 0 | 0 | 0 | 0 | 0 | 1 | 1 | 1 | 0 | 0 | 0 | 0 |
| Food refusal | 0 | 0 | 1 | 0 | 0 | 0 | 0 | 1 | 0 | 0 | 2 | 0 | 0 | 0 | 0 | 0 | 0 | 0 | 0 | 0 | 0 | 0 | 1 |
| Hanging | 86 | 72 | 65 | 89 | 83 | 86 | 68 | 58 | 84 | 57 | 51 | 52 | 51 | 53 | 65 | 78 | 84 | 109 | 65 | 79 | 71 | 55 | 71 |
| Overdose | 2 | 4 | 2 | 3 | 4 | 4 | 5 | 1 | 2 | 1 | 1 | 1 | 1 | 2 | 1 | 5 | 1 | 6 | 0 | 4 | 1 | 1 | 1 |
| Poison | 0 | 0 | 0 | 0 | 0 | 0 | 0 | 0 | 1 | 0 | 1 | 0 | 0 | 0 | 0 | 0 | 0 | 0 | 0 | 0 | 1 | 0 | 0 |
| Refused Medication | 0 | 0 | 0 | 1 | 0 | 0 | 0 | 0 | 0 | 0 | 0 | 0 | 0 | 0 | 0 | 0 | 0 | 0 | 0 | 0 | 0 | 0 | 0 |
| Self-strangulation | 1 | 1 | 0 | 0 | 3 | 2 | 2 | 2 | 0 | 0 | 0 | 2 | 2 | 3 | 1 | 3 | 0 | 2 | 1 | 0 | 1 | 6 | 5 |
| Suffocation | 0 | 1 | 2 | 0 | 0 | 2 | 0 | 1 | 0 | 1 | 1 | 1 | 1 | 0 | 1 | 4 | 1 | 0 | 0 | 1 | 0 | 2 | 2 |
| Other | 0 | 0 | 0 | 0 | 0 | 0 | 0 | 0 | 0 | 0 | 0 | 0 | 0 | 1 | 1 | 0 | 1 | 2 | 3 | 5 | 5 | 3 | 3 |

### MALES

| | 1999 | 2000 | 2001 | 2002 | 2003 | 2004 | 2005 | 2006 | 2007 | 2008 | 2009 | 2010 | 2011 | 2012 | 2013 | 2014 | 2015 | 2016 | 2017 | 2018 | 2019 (r) | 2020 (r) | 2021 (p) |
|---|---|---|---|---|---|---|---|---|---|---|---|---|---|---|---|---|---|---|---|---|---|---|---|
| Total | 86 | 73 | 67 | 86 | 81 | 83 | 74 | 63 | 84 | 60 | 58 | 57 | 56 | 60 | 74 | 86 | 85 | 112 | 71 | 90 | 81 | 65 | 86 |
| Arson | 0 | 1 | 0 | 0 | 2 | 0 | 0 | 0 | 1 | 0 | 0 | 1 | 1 | 0 | 2 | 0 | 0 | 0 | 0 | 0 | 0 | 0 | 0 |
| Cutting | 2 | 2 | 2 | 1 | 0 | 2 | 2 | 3 | 1 | 0 | 4 | 2 | 2 | 2 | 4 | 1 | 2 | 3 | 3 | 4 | 7 | 4 | 3 |
| Electrocution | 0 | 0 | 0 | 0 | 1 | 0 | 0 | 0 | 1 | 0 | 0 | 0 | 0 | 0 | 1 | 0 | 0 | 1 | 1 | 0 | 0 | 0 | 0 |
| Falling | 0 | 0 | 0 | 0 | 0 | 0 | 0 | 0 | 0 | 0 | 0 | 0 | 0 | 0 | 0 | 0 | 1 | 1 | 0 | 0 | 0 | 0 | 0 |
| Food refusal | 0 | 0 | 1 | 0 | 0 | 0 | 0 | 1 | 0 | 0 | 2 | 0 | 0 | 0 | 0 | 0 | 0 | 1 | 1 | 0 | 0 | 0 | 1 |
| Hanging | 81 | 66 | 59 | 80 | 74 | 75 | 66 | 55 | 78 | 56 | 49 | 51 | 50 | 53 | 63 | 77 | 79 | 100 | 63 | 76 | 67 | 53 | 71 |
| Overdose | 2 | 4 | 2 | 3 | 4 | 4 | 4 | 1 | 2 | 1 | 1 | 1 | 2 | 2 | 5 | 5 | 1 | 5 | 4 | 4 | 4 | 2 | 1 |
| Poison | 0 | 0 | 0 | 0 | 0 | 0 | 0 | 0 | 1 | 0 | 1 | 0 | 0 | 0 | 0 | 0 | 0 | 0 | 0 | 0 | 1 | 0 | 0 |
| Refused Medication | 0 | 0 | 0 | 1 | 0 | 0 | 0 | 0 | 0 | 0 | 0 | 0 | 0 | 0 | 0 | 0 | 0 | 0 | 0 | 0 | 0 | 0 | 0 |
| Self-strangulation | 1 | 0 | 1 | 0 | 0 | 1 | 1 | 2 | 0 | 0 | 0 | 2 | 1 | 2 | 1 | 3 | 0 | 2 | 1 | 0 | 1 | 6 | 5 |
| Suffocation | 0 | 0 | 2 | 0 | 1 | 1 | 0 | 1 | 0 | 1 | 1 | 1 | 0 | 0 | 1 | 3 | 1 | 0 | 0 | 1 | 0 | 2 | 2 |
| Other | 0 | 0 | 0 | 0 | 0 | 0 | 0 | 0 | 0 | 0 | 0 | 0 | 0 | 1 | 1 | 0 | 1 | 1 | 3 | 5 | 5 | 3 | 3 |

### FEMALES

| | 1999 | 2000 | 2001 | 2002 | 2003 | 2004 | 2005 | 2006 | 2007 | 2008 | 2009 | 2010 | 2011 | 2012 | 2013 | 2014 | 2015 | 2016 | 2017 | 2018 | 2019 (r) | 2020 (r) | 2021 (p) |
|---|---|---|---|---|---|---|---|---|---|---|---|---|---|---|---|---|---|---|---|---|---|---|---|
| Total | 5 | 8 | 6 | 9 | 14 | 13 | 4 | 3 | 7 | 1 | 3 | 1 | 2 | 1 | 2 | 3 | 5 | 12 | 2 | 3 | 5 | 2 | 0 |
| Arson | 0 | 0 | 0 | 0 | 0 | 0 | 0 | 0 | 0 | 0 | 0 | 0 | 0 | 0 | 0 | 0 | 0 | 0 | 0 | 0 | 0 | 0 | 0 |
| Cutting | 0 | 0 | 0 | 0 | 0 | 0 | 0 | 0 | 0 | 0 | 0 | 0 | 0 | 0 | 0 | 0 | 0 | 0 | 0 | 0 | 1 | 0 | 0 |
| Electrocution | 0 | 0 | 0 | 0 | 0 | 0 | 0 | 0 | 0 | 0 | 0 | 0 | 0 | 0 | 0 | 0 | 0 | 0 | 0 | 0 | 0 | 0 | 0 |
| Falling | 0 | 0 | 0 | 0 | 0 | 0 | 0 | 0 | 0 | 0 | 0 | 0 | 0 | 0 | 0 | 0 | 0 | 0 | 0 | 0 | 0 | 0 | 0 |
| Food refusal | 0 | 0 | 0 | 0 | 0 | 0 | 0 | 0 | 0 | 0 | 0 | 0 | 0 | 0 | 0 | 0 | 0 | 0 | 0 | 0 | 0 | 0 | 0 |
| Hanging | 5 | 6 | 6 | 9 | 9 | 11 | 2 | 3 | 6 | 1 | 2 | 1 | 1 | 0 | 2 | 1 | 5 | 9 | 2 | 3 | 4 | 2 | 0 |
| Overdose | 0 | 0 | 0 | 0 | 2 | 0 | 1 | 0 | 0 | 0 | 1 | 0 | 0 | 0 | 0 | 0 | 0 | 1 | 0 | 0 | 0 | 0 | 0 |
| Poison | 0 | 0 | 0 | 0 | 0 | 0 | 0 | 0 | 0 | 0 | 0 | 0 | 0 | 0 | 0 | 0 | 0 | 0 | 0 | 0 | 0 | 0 | 0 |
| Refused Medication | 0 | 0 | 0 | 0 | 0 | 0 | 0 | 0 | 0 | 0 | 0 | 0 | 0 | 0 | 0 | 0 | 0 | 0 | 0 | 0 | 0 | 0 | 0 |
| Self-strangulation | 0 | 0 | 0 | 0 | 0 | 1 | 1 | 0 | 0 | 0 | 0 | 0 | 1 | 1 | 0 | 0 | 0 | 0 | 0 | 0 | 0 | 0 | 0 |
| Suffocation | 0 | 1 | 0 | 0 | 1 | 1 | 0 | 0 | 0 | 0 | 0 | 0 | 0 | 0 | 0 | 1 | 0 | 0 | 0 | 0 | 0 | 0 | 0 |
| Other | 0 | 0 | 0 | 0 | 0 | 0 | 0 | 0 | 0 | 0 | 0 | 0 | 0 | 0 | 0 | 0 | 0 | 1 | 0 | 0 | 0 | 0 | 0 |

(1) Deaths in prison custody figures include all deaths of prisoners arising from incidents during prison custody. They include deaths of prisoners while released on temporary license (ROTL) for medical reasons but exclude other types of ROTL where the state has less direct responsibility.

(2) Due to the number of deaths that remain unclassified (awaiting further information) in recent years, and the latest year particularly, caution should be used when comparing with earlier periods.

Data Sources and Quality
These figures are derived from the HMPPS Deaths in Prison Custody database. As classification of deaths may change following inquest or as new information emerges, numbers may change from time to time.

**Table 1.9: Self-inflicted deaths in prison custody[1,2]: Ligatures[3] used in hanging/self-strangulation since 1999, England and Wales**

| | 1999 | 2000 | 2001 | 2002 | 2003 | 2004 | 2005 | 2006 | 2007 | 2008 | 2009 | 2010 | 2011 | 2012 | 2013 | 2014 | 2015 | 2016 | 2017 (r) | 2018 (r) | 2019 (r) | 2020 | 2021 (p) |
|---|---|---|---|---|---|---|---|---|---|---|---|---|---|---|---|---|---|---|---|---|---|---|---|
| **MALES AND FEMALES** | | | | | | | | | | | | | | | | | | | | | | | |
| Total | 87 | 73 | 66 | 89 | 86 | 88 | 70 | 60 | 85 | 57 | 51 | 54 | 53 | 56 | 66 | 78 | 84 | 111 | 66 | 79 | 72 | 61 | 76 |
| Bedding | 56 | 44 | 40 | 63 | 59 | 61 | 57 | 42 | 65 | 43 | 40 | 38 | 37 | 40 | 46 | 60 | 57 | 87 | 52 | 60 | 52 | 48 | 62 |
| Belt | 1 | 6 | 2 | 1 | 2 | 3 | 1 | 3 | 2 | 0 | 5 | 3 | 2 | 3 | 4 | 3 | 4 | 4 | 2 | 2 | 4 | 3 | 1 |
| Clothing | 12 | 6 | 3 | 6 | 7 | 2 | 3 | 2 | 6 | 2 | 1 | 1 | 0 | 1 | 5 | 3 | 6 | 3 | 4 | 7 | 6 | 2 | 6 |
| Shoelace | 15 | 15 | 14 | 14 | 13 | 18 | 9 | 9 | 6 | 8 | 2 | 5 | 5 | 5 | 6 | 5 | 8 | 14 | 3 | 7 | 6 | 4 | 2 |
| Other[4] | 3 | 2 | 7 | 5 | 3 | 4 | 0 | 2 | 2 | 1 | 0 | 3 | 5 | 4 | 4 | 7 | 8 | 3 | 4 | 3 | 4 | 4 | 4 |
| Not recorded | 0 | 0 | 0 | 0 | 2 | 0 | 0 | 2 | 4 | 3 | 3 | 4 | 4 | 3 | 1 | 0 | 1 | 0 | 1 | 0 | 0 | 0 | 1 |
| **MALES** | | | | | | | | | | | | | | | | | | | | | | | |
| Total | 82 | 66 | 60 | 80 | 74 | 76 | 67 | 57 | 78 | 56 | 49 | 53 | 51 | 55 | 64 | 77 | 79 | 101 | 64 | 76 | 68 | 59 | 76 |
| Bedding | 54 | 43 | 35 | 59 | 55 | 54 | 55 | 40 | 60 | 43 | 40 | 38 | 37 | 40 | 46 | 59 | 55 | 85 | 50 | 59 | 52 | 46 | 62 |
| Belt | 1 | 5 | 2 | 1 | 2 | 2 | 1 | 3 | 1 | 0 | 4 | 3 | 2 | 3 | 3 | 3 | 3 | 2 | 2 | 2 | 4 | 3 | 1 |
| Clothing | 11 | 4 | 3 | 6 | 5 | 1 | 2 | 2 | 5 | 1 | 1 | 1 | 0 | 1 | 5 | 3 | 5 | 3 | 4 | 5 | 4 | 2 | 6 |
| Shoelace | 14 | 13 | 13 | 11 | 9 | 15 | 9 | 8 | 6 | 8 | 2 | 4 | 4 | 5 | 6 | 5 | 8 | 9 | 3 | 7 | 5 | 4 | 2 |
| Other[4] | 2 | 1 | 7 | 3 | 3 | 4 | 0 | 2 | 2 | 1 | 0 | 3 | 5 | 3 | 3 | 7 | 7 | 2 | 4 | 3 | 3 | 4 | 4 |
| Not recorded | 0 | 0 | 0 | 0 | 0 | 0 | 0 | 2 | 4 | 3 | 2 | 4 | 3 | 3 | 1 | 0 | 1 | 0 | 1 | 0 | 0 | 0 | 1 |
| **FEMALES** | | | | | | | | | | | | | | | | | | | | | | | |
| Total | 5 | 7 | 6 | 9 | 12 | 12 | 3 | 3 | 7 | 1 | 2 | 1 | 2 | 1 | 2 | 1 | 5 | 10 | 2 | 3 | 4 | 2 | 0 |
| Bedding | 2 | 1 | 5 | 4 | 4 | 7 | 2 | 2 | 5 | 0 | 0 | 0 | 0 | 0 | 0 | 1 | 2 | 2 | 2 | 1 | 0 | 2 | 0 |
| Belt | 0 | 1 | 0 | 0 | 0 | 1 | 0 | 0 | 1 | 0 | 1 | 0 | 0 | 0 | 1 | 0 | 1 | 2 | 0 | 0 | 0 | 0 | 0 |
| Clothing | 1 | 2 | 0 | 0 | 2 | 1 | 1 | 0 | 1 | 1 | 0 | 0 | 0 | 0 | 0 | 0 | 1 | 0 | 0 | 2 | 2 | 0 | 0 |
| Shoelace | 1 | 2 | 1 | 3 | 4 | 3 | 0 | 1 | 0 | 0 | 0 | 1 | 1 | 0 | 0 | 0 | 0 | 5 | 0 | 0 | 1 | 0 | 0 |
| Other[4] | 1 | 1 | 0 | 2 | 0 | 0 | 0 | 0 | 0 | 0 | 0 | 0 | 0 | 1 | 1 | 0 | 1 | 1 | 0 | 0 | 1 | 0 | 0 |
| Not recorded | 0 | 0 | 0 | 0 | 2 | 0 | 0 | 0 | 0 | 0 | 1 | 0 | 1 | 0 | 0 | 0 | 0 | 0 | 0 | 0 | 0 | 0 | 0 |

(1) Deaths in prison custody figures include all deaths of prisoners arising from incidents during prison custody. They include deaths of prisoners while released on temporary license (ROTL) for medical reasons but exclude other types of ROTL where the state has less direct responsibility.

(2) Due to the number of deaths that remain unclassified (awaiting further information) in recent years, and the latest year particularly, caution should be used when comparing with earlier periods.

(3) In many cases, confirmation of ligature types has to await the results of investigations. For this reason there are more un-recorded cases in recent years. These numbers reduce over time as reports are received. In some cases may not be identified

(4) The 'other' category includes ligatures not easily classified in one of the other categories. It also includes cases where multiple ligatures were used e.g. bedding and shoelace etc.

*Data Sources and Quality*
*These figures are derived from the HMPPS Deaths in Prison Custody database. As classification of deaths may change following inquest or as new information emerges, numbers may change from time to time.*

Table 1.10: Self-inflicted deaths in prison custody[1,2]: Ligature points used in hanging/self-strangulation since 1999, England and Wales

| | 1999 | 2000 | 2001 | 2002 | 2003 | 2004 | 2005 | 2006 | 2007 | 2008 | 2009 | 2010 | 2011 | 2012 | 2013 | 2014 | 2015 | 2016 | 2017 | 2018 | 2019 (r) | 2020 (r) | 2021 (p) |
|---|---|---|---|---|---|---|---|---|---|---|---|---|---|---|---|---|---|---|---|---|---|---|---|
| **MALES AND FEMALES** | | | | | | | | | | | | | | | | | | | | | | | |
| Total | 87 | 73 | 66 | 89 | 86 | 88 | 70 | 60 | 85 | 57 | 51 | 54 | 53 | 56 | 66 | 78 | 84 | 111 | 66 | 79 | 72 | 61 | 76 |
| Bed | 11 | 18 | 10 | 16 | 16 | 7 | 8 | 9 | 12 | 7 | 13 | 11 | 9 | 7 | 18 | 21 | 17 | 12 | 9 | 20 | 14 | 14 | 14 |
| Conduits/piping | 0 | 2 | 1 | 2 | 2 | 4 | 0 | 2 | 0 | 1 | 2 | 0 | 1 | 0 | 0 | 7 | 1 | 1 | 2 | 1 | 0 | 0 | 0 |
| Door/cell gate | 12 | 1 | 7 | 6 | 3 | 6 | 3 | 5 | 7 | 1 | 1 | 3 | 1 | 1 | 7 | 7 | 9 | 12 | 3 | 5 | 0 | 3 | 4 |
| Light fitting | 2 | 2 | 2 | 8 | 3 | 4 | 7 | 3 | 8 | 2 | 4 | 4 | 8 | 8 | 6 | 5 | 10 | 13 | 6 | 9 | 12 | 4 | 10 |
| Privacy screen, furniture etc.[3] | 0 | 1 | 1 | 2 | 2 | 2 | 6 | 4 | 5 | 2 | 1 | 6 | 6 | 2 | 2 | 4 | 4 | 6 | 4 | 0 | 6 | 3 | 7 |
| Toilet/sink fittings/recess[3] | 0 | 7 | 3 | 8 | 5 | 8 | 6 | 4 | 3 | 5 | 5 | 5 | 8 | 6 | 3 | 7 | 4 | 3 | 3 | 4 | 5 | 3 | 5 |
| Wall fittings/mountings | 1 | 1 | 2 | 3 | 3 | 8 | 2 | 3 | 5 | 2 | 1 | 0 | 4 | 4 | 2 | 4 | 3 | 6 | 3 | 3 | 3 | 6 | 4 |
| Window | 58 | 40 | 38 | 44 | 49 | 54 | 39 | 29 | 40 | 39 | 23 | 28 | 26 | 18 | 23 | 31 | 35 | 46 | 30 | 30 | 23 | 25 | 28 |
| Other | 0 | 0 | 0 | 0 | 0 | 0 | 0 | 0 | 0 | 0 | 0 | 0 | 0 | 0 | 3 | 0 | 0 | 3 | 4 | 11 | 4 | 0 | 2 |
| Not recorded/confirmed | 2 | 0 | 1 | 0 | 0 | 0 | 0 | 1 | 4 | 0 | 0 | 0 | 0 | 0 | 1 | 1 | 0 | 0 | 5 | 0 | 0 | 0 | 2 |
| Not applicable | 1 | 1 | 1 | 0 | 3 | 1 | 0 | 0 | 1 | 0 | 0 | 2 | 1 | 1 | 0 | 0 | 0 | 0 | 1 | 0 | 1 | 1 | 0 |
| **MALES** | | | | | | | | | | | | | | | | | | | | | | | |
| Total | 82 | 66 | 60 | 80 | 74 | 76 | 67 | 57 | 78 | 56 | 49 | 53 | 51 | 55 | 64 | 77 | 79 | 101 | 64 | 76 | 68 | 59 | 76 |
| Bed | 11 | 17 | 9 | 13 | 15 | 6 | 7 | 9 | 11 | 7 | 13 | 11 | 9 | 7 | 18 | 20 | 17 | 12 | 9 | 19 | 14 | 13 | 14 |
| Conduits/piping | 0 | 2 | 1 | 2 | 2 | 3 | 0 | 1 | 1 | 1 | 2 | 0 | 1 | 1 | 0 | 7 | 1 | 1 | 2 | 1 | 0 | 0 | 0 |
| Door/cell gate | 11 | 1 | 6 | 6 | 3 | 4 | 5 | 5 | 5 | 1 | 1 | 3 | 3 | 3 | 7 | 5 | 7 | 10 | 3 | 5 | 9 | 3 | 4 |
| Light fitting | 2 | 1 | 2 | 8 | 3 | 4 | 7 | 3 | 8 | 2 | 4 | 4 | 3 | 8 | 6 | 7 | 10 | 13 | 6 | 9 | 9 | 4 | 10 |
| Privacy screen, furniture etc.[3] | 0 | 6 | 1 | 1 | 1 | 1 | 6 | 4 | 3 | 2 | 1 | 6 | 4 | 6 | 2 | 3 | 3 | 4 | 4 | 0 | 6 | 3 | 7 |
| Toilet/sink fittings/recess[3] | 6 | 2 | 2 | 7 | 5 | 6 | 4 | 4 | 5 | 2 | 4 | 4 | 4 | 8 | 4 | 3 | 2 | 8 | 3 | 3 | 5 | 3 | 5 |
| Wall fittings/mountings | 1 | 1 | 3 | 3 | 3 | 2 | 2 | 4 | 2 | 2 | 4 | 0 | 4 | 4 | 3 | 3 | 5 | 3 | 3 | 3 | 3 | 5 | 4 |
| Window | 54 | 36 | 35 | 40 | 44 | 50 | 38 | 28 | 39 | 39 | 23 | 27 | 25 | 18 | 22 | 31 | 35 | 43 | 29 | 28 | 23 | 25 | 28 |
| Other | 0 | 0 | 0 | 0 | 0 | 0 | 0 | 0 | 0 | 0 | 0 | 0 | 0 | 0 | 3 | 0 | 0 | 2 | 4 | 11 | 4 | 0 | 2 |
| Not recorded/confirmed | 2 | 0 | 1 | 0 | 0 | 0 | 0 | 1 | 4 | 0 | 0 | 0 | 0 | 0 | 3 | 1 | 0 | 3 | 4 | 0 | 0 | 1 | 2 |
| Not applicable | 1 | 0 | 1 | 0 | 0 | 1 | 0 | 0 | 0 | 0 | 0 | 2 | 1 | 1 | 0 | 0 | 0 | 0 | 0 | 0 | 1 | 1 | 0 |
| **FEMALES** | | | | | | | | | | | | | | | | | | | | | | | |
| Total | 5 | 7 | 6 | 9 | 12 | 12 | 3 | 3 | 7 | 1 | 2 | 1 | 2 | 1 | 2 | 1 | 5 | 10 | 2 | 3 | 4 | 2 | 0 |
| Bed | 0 | 1 | 1 | 3 | 1 | 1 | 1 | 0 | 1 | 0 | 0 | 0 | 0 | 1 | 0 | 1 | 0 | 0 | 0 | 1 | 0 | 1 | 0 |
| Conduits/piping | 0 | 1 | 0 | 0 | 0 | 0 | 0 | 0 | 0 | 0 | 0 | 0 | 0 | 0 | 0 | 0 | 0 | 0 | 0 | 0 | 0 | 0 | 0 |
| Door/cell gate | 1 | 0 | 1 | 0 | 2 | 3 | 0 | 1 | 2 | 0 | 0 | 0 | 0 | 0 | 0 | 0 | 2 | 2 | 0 | 0 | 0 | 0 | 0 |
| Light fitting | 0 | 0 | 0 | 0 | 0 | 0 | 0 | 0 | 0 | 0 | 0 | 0 | 0 | 0 | 0 | 0 | 0 | 0 | 0 | 0 | 0 | 0 | 0 |
| Privacy screen, furniture etc.[3] | 0 | 1 | 1 | 1 | 1 | 1 | 0 | 0 | 2 | 0 | 1 | 0 | 1 | 0 | 0 | 0 | 1 | 2 | 1 | 0 | 0 | 1 | 0 |
| Toilet/sink fittings/recess[3] | 0 | 0 | 0 | 0 | 0 | 0 | 1 | 0 | 0 | 1 | 0 | 0 | 0 | 0 | 0 | 0 | 0 | 0 | 0 | 0 | 0 | 0 | 0 |
| Wall fittings/mountings | 4 | 4 | 3 | 4 | 5 | 4 | 1 | 1 | 1 | 0 | 0 | 1 | 0 | 0 | 1 | 0 | 0 | 3 | 1 | 2 | 0 | 0 | 0 |
| Window | 0 | 0 | 0 | 0 | 0 | 0 | 1 | 0 | 1 | 0 | 0 | 0 | 0 | 1 | 0 | 0 | 0 | 1 | 0 | 0 | 0 | 0 | 0 |
| Other | 0 | 0 | 0 | 0 | 0 | 0 | 0 | 0 | 0 | 0 | 0 | 0 | 0 | 0 | 0 | 0 | 0 | 1 | 1 | 0 | 0 | 1 | 0 |
| Not recorded/confirmed | 0 | 1 | 0 | 0 | 3 | 1 | 0 | 0 | 1 | 0 | 0 | 0 | 0 | 0 | 0 | 0 | 0 | 0 | 0 | 0 | 0 | 0 | 0 |
| Not applicable | 0 | 0 | 0 | 0 | 0 | 0 | 0 | 0 | 0 | 0 | 0 | 0 | 0 | 0 | 0 | 0 | 0 | 0 | 0 | 0 | 0 | 0 | 0 |

(1) Deaths in prison custody figures include all deaths of prisoners arising from incidents during prison custody. They include deaths of prisoners while released on temporary license (ROTL) for medical reasons but exclude other types of ROTL where the state has less direct responsibility.

(2) Due to the number of deaths that remain unclassified (awaiting further information) in recent years, and the latest year particularly, caution should be used when comparing with earlier periods.

(3) The 'Privacy screen furniture etc.' and 'Toilet/sink fittings/recess' categories were added in 2004 and ligature points reclassified. However, there may be some under reporting against this category in the early years.

*Data Sources and Quality*
*These figures are derived from the HMPPS Deaths in Prison Custody database. As classification of deaths may change following inquest or as new information emerges, numbers may change from time to time.*

# Table 1.11: Self-inflicted deaths by prison¹ since 1999, England and Wales (continued on next page)

| Prison | 1999 | 2000 | 2001 | 2002 | 2003 | 2004 | 2005 | 2006 | 2007 | 2008 | 2009 | 2010 | 2011 | 2012 | 2013 | 2014 | 2015 | 2016 | 2017 (r) | 2018 (r) | 2019 (r) | 2020 (r) | 2021 (p) |
|---|---|---|---|---|---|---|---|---|---|---|---|---|---|---|---|---|---|---|---|---|---|---|---|
| Aldington | - | - | - | - | - | - | - | - | - | - | - | - | - | - | - | - | - | - | - | - | - | - | 4 |
| Altcourse | 3 | 0 | 0 | - | 2 | 0 | 4 | 0 | 3 | 3 | 1 | 0 | - | 2 | 2 | 1 | 2 | 2 | 1 | 2 | 0 | 1 | 0 |
| Appleton Thorn | 0 | - | 0 | 0 | 0 | 0 | 0 | 0 | 0 | 0 | 0 | 0 | - | 0 | 0 | 0 | 0 | 0 | 0 | 0 | 0 | 0 | 0 |
| Ashfield | 0 | - | 0 | 0 | 0 | - | 0 | 0 | 0 | 0 | 0 | 0 | 0 | 0 | 0 | 0 | 0 | 0 | 0 | 0 | 0 | 0 | 0 |
| Ashford | - | - | - | - | - | - | - | - | - | - | - | - | - | - | - | - | - | - | - | - | - | - | - |
| Ashwell | 0 | 0 | 0 | 0 | 0 | 0 | 0 | 0 | 0 | 0 | 0 | 0 | 0 | - | - | - | - | - | - | - | - | - | 0 |
| Askham Grange | 0 | 0 | 0 | 1 | 1 | 0 | 0 | 0 | 2 | 1 | 0 | 0 | 2 | 0 | 0 | 0 | 0 | 0 | 0 | 0 | 1 | 0 | 1 |
| Aylesbury | 3 | 2 | 0 | 0 | 1 | 0 | 0 | 2 | 2 | 1 | 0 | 2 | 4 | 0 | 0 | 0 | 0 | 0 | 2 | 0 | 2 | 1 | 1 |
| Bedford | 1 | 0 | 3 | 3 | - | 1 | 1 | 2 | 4 | 1 | 0 | 2 | 2 | 2 | 1 | 1 | 1 | 4 | 2 | 0 | 2 | 2 | 0 |
| Belmarsh | 1 | 1 | 0 | - | 3 | 1 | 1 | 1 | - | 0 | 3 | 3 | 0 | 3 | 1 | 0 | 1 | - | 0 | 2 | 0 | 0 | 0 |
| Berwyn | - | - | - | - | - | - | - | - | - | - | - | - | - | - | - | - | - | - | - | 2 | 0 | 1 | 1 |
| Birmingham | 2 | 3 | 0 | 0 | 4 | 1 | 1 | 1 | 2 | 2 | 0 | 6 | 0 | 0 | 0 | 0 | 2 | 6 | 1 | 0 | 0 | 0 | 0 |
| Blantyre House | 0 | 0 | 0 | 0 | 0 | 0 | 0 | 0 | 0 | 0 | 0 | 0 | 0 | 0 | 3 | 0 | 0 | 0 | 0 | - | - | - | - |
| Blundeston | 0 | 1 | 0 | 0 | 0 | 0 | 1 | 0 | 1 | 0 | 2 | 0 | 0 | 1 | 0 | - | - | - | - | - | - | - | 1 |
| Brinsford | 2 | 3 | 2 | 2 | 0 | 0 | 1 | 0 | 1 | 0 | 1 | 2 | 2 | 0 | 0 | 0 | 0 | 0 | 1 | 1 | 1 | 2 | 0 |
| Bristol | 2 | 2 | 2 | 3 | 0 | 1 | 1 | 3 | 3 | 1 | 1 | 0 | 1 | 1 | 2 | 0 | 2 | 0 | 0 | 0 | 0 | 2 | 0 |
| Brixton | 4 | 2 | 2 | 1 | 2 | 2 | 0 | 0 | 0 | 0 | 0 | 0 | 0 | 0 | 0 | 2 | 0 | 0 | 0 | 0 | 1 | 0 | 0 |
| Bronzefield | 0 | 0 | 0 | 0 | 0 | 1 | 1 | 0 | 0 | 0 | 0 | 0 | 0 | 0 | 0 | 0 | 0 | 1 | 0 | 0 | 0 | 0 | 0 |
| Buckley Hall | 0 | 0 | 0 | 3 | 0 | 0 | 0 | 2 | 0 | 0 | 0 | 0 | 0 | 2 | 2 | 0 | 0 | 0 | 0 | 0 | 2 | 0 | 2 |
| Bullingdon | 0 | 0 | 1 | 0 | 1 | 0 | 0 | 0 | 0 | 1 | 1 | 2 | 0 | 2 | 2 | 2 | 3 | 1 | 1 | 0 | 2 | 1 | 0 |
| Bullwood Hall | 0 | 1 | 0 | 0 | 0 | 0 | 0 | 0 | 0 | 0 | 0 | 0 | 0 | 0 | - | - | - | - | - | - | - | - | 0 |
| Bure | 0 | 0 | 0 | 0 | 1 | 1 | 0 | 1 | 1 | 0 | 1 | 0 | 0 | 0 | 0 | 0 | 0 | 0 | 0 | 0 | 0 | 2 | 0 |
| Canterbury | 1 | 1 | 1 | 1 | 0 | 0 | 0 | 1 | 3 | 3 | 3 | 1 | 4 | 1 | 0 | 1 | 1 | 1 | 1 | 0 | 1 | - | 3 |
| Cardiff | 1 | 0 | 3 | 1 | 2 | 1 | 1 | 2 | 1 | 0 | 0 | 0 | 2 | 0 | 0 | 1 | 0 | 2 | 1 | 0 | 1 | 1 | 0 |
| Channings Wood | 0 | 1 | 0 | 0 | 0 | 0 | 0 | 0 | 0 | 0 | 3 | 2 | 2 | 3 | 3 | 0 | 3 | 3 | 1 | 4 | 2 | 0 | 3 |
| Chelmsford | 1 | 1 | 1 | 1 | 0 | 0 | 1 | 0 | 3 | 4 | 0 | 0 | 0 | 1 | 1 | 1 | 0 | 0 | 1 | 1 | 0 | 0 | 0 |
| Coldingley | 0 | 0 | 0 | 0 | 0 | 0 | 0 | 0 | 0 | 0 | 1 | 0 | 0 | 0 | 0 | 0 | 0 | 0 | 0 | 0 | 0 | 0 | 0 |
| Cookham Wood | 0 | 0 | 0 | 1 | 0 | 0 | 0 | 0 | 0 | 0 | 0 | 0 | 0 | 0 | 0 | 0 | 0 | 0 | 0 | 0 | 1 | 0 | 1 |
| Dartmoor | 0 | 0 | 1 | 0 | 1 | 0 | 0 | 0 | 0 | 4 | 0 | 1 | 0 | 0 | 0 | 0 | 0 | 0 | 0 | 2 | 0 | 0 | 0 |
| Deerbolt | 1 | 5 | 2 | 2 | 1 | 0 | 0 | 1 | 0 | 0 | 0 | 2 | 2 | 0 | 2 | 0 | 0 | 2 | 0 | 1 | 0 | 0 | 0 |
| Doncaster | 0 | 0 | 0 | 2 | 1 | 0 | 0 | 1 | 1 | 0 | 0 | 2 | 0 | 1 | 1 | 2 | 1 | 0 | 1 | 2 | 3 | 0 | 4 |
| Dorchester | - | 0 | 3 | 0 | 2 | 0 | 1 | 0 | 0 | 0 | 0 | 0 | 0 | 3 | 0 | 0 | 0 | 2 | 3 | 0 | 1 | 0 | 0 |
| Dovegate | - | - | 0 | 3 | 0 | 0 | 0 | 0 | 0 | 1 | 1 | 1 | 0 | 1 | 0 | 0 | 1 | 0 | 0 | 0 | 0 | 0 | 0 |
| Dover | 0 | 0 | 0 | 0 | 0 | 0 | 0 | 0 | 0 | 0 | 0 | 0 | 0 | 4 | 4 | 0 | 0 | 0 | 0 | 0 | 0 | 0 | - |
| Downview | 0 | 0 | 0 | 0 | 1 | 0 | 0 | 0 | 0 | 0 | 0 | 1 | 1 | 0 | 0 | 1 | 1 | 1 | 0 | 1 | 0 | 1 | 0 |
| Drake Hall | 0 | 0 | 0 | 0 | 0 | 0 | 0 | 0 | 0 | 0 | 4 | 0 | 1 | 0 | 3 | 2 | 2 | 0 | 3 | 2 | 0 | 0 | 0 |
| Durham | 3 | 1 | 0 | 6 | 5 | 3 | 2 | 2 | 0 | 0 | 0 | 1 | 1 | 3 | 0 | 0 | 1 | 1 | 0 | 3 | 4 | 0 | 0 |
| East Sutton Park | 0 | 3 | 1 | 1 | 0 | 0 | 0 | 0 | 1 | 0 | 0 | 0 | 0 | 0 | 0 | 0 | 0 | 0 | 0 | 0 | 0 | 0 | 1 |
| Eastwood Park | 0 | 0 | 0 | 1 | 0 | 2 | 2 | 0 | 0 | 0 | 1 | 1 | 0 | 0 | 0 | 1 | 0 | 3 | 0 | 0 | 1 | 0 | 0 |
| Edmunds Hill | 1 | 0 | 1 | 0 | 1 | 0 | 1 | 1 | 0 | 1 | 0 | 0 | 1 | 1 | 1 | 1 | 0 | 1 | 1 | 0 | 0 | 0 | 0 |
| Erlestoke | 0 | 0 | 0 | 0 | 0 | 0 | 0 | 0 | 0 | 0 | 0 | 0 | 0 | 0 | 1 | 1 | 1 | 0 | 0 | 0 | 4 | 0 | 0 |
| Everthorpe | 0 | 0 | 1 | 0 | 0 | 0 | 0 | 1 | 0 | 0 | 0 | 1 | 0 | 0 | 0 | 1 | 0 | 0 | 0 | 0 | 0 | 1 | - |
| Exeter | 0 | 1 | 2 | 2 | 3 | 0 | 0 | 2 | 2 | 2 | 2 | 1 | 1 | 0 | 3 | 3 | 4 | 4 | 5 | 2 | 2 | 1 | 3 |
| Featherstone | 0 | 1 | 0 | 3 | 0 | 0 | 1 | 1 | 1 | 3 | 0 | 0 | 0 | 0 | 0 | 2 | 0 | 0 | 0 | 3 | 1 | 0 | 1 |
| Feltham | 0 | 1 | 1 | 0 | 0 | 0 | 0 | 0 | 0 | 0 | 0 | 0 | 1 | 0 | 0 | 0 | 1 | 0 | 0 | 1 | 1 | 1 | 0 |
| Ford | 0 | 0 | 0 | 1 | 1 | 0 | 0 | 0 | 0 | 0 | 0 | 0 | 0 | 0 | 0 | 0 | 0 | 0 | 0 | 2 | 0 | 0 | 0 |
| Forest Bank | 0 | 3 | 0 | 1 | 0 | 0 | 0 | 1 | 1 | 1 | 1 | 0 | 0 | 0 | 1 | 1 | 1 | 2 | 3 | 0 | 2 | 0 | 0 |
| Foston Hall | 0 | 0 | 0 | 0 | 0 | 2 | 1 | 0 | 0 | 0 | 0 | 1 | 0 | 0 | 0 | 0 | 0 | 0 | 0 | 0 | 0 | 0 | 0 |
| Frankland | 0 | 0 | 1 | 1 | 1 | 0 | 0 | 1 | 0 | 1 | 1 | 0 | 1 | 0 | 0 | 1 | 0 | 0 | 0 | 1 | 0 | 1 | 1 |
| Full Sutton | 0 | 0 | 0 | 0 | 0 | 0 | 0 | 0 | 0 | 0 | 0 | 0 | 0 | 0 | 0 | 0 | 1 | 2 | 0 | 0 | 0 | 0 | 0 |
| Garth | 1 | 0 | 0 | 2 | 0 | 0 | 0 | 1 | 2 | 0 | 1 | 1 | 0 | 0 | 0 | 0 | 1 | 0 | 0 | 0 | 1 | 0 | 1 |
| Gartree | 0 | 1 | 0 | 0 | 0 | 0 | 1 | 1 | 1 | 0 | 2 | 0 | 1 | 0 | 3 | 2 | 0 | 0 | 0 | 2 | 1 | 0 | 0 |
| Gaynes Hall | - | - | 0 | 0 | 0 | 0 | 1 | 0 | 1 | 0 | 0 | 0 | 0 | 1 | 0 | 0 | 0 | 0 | 0 | 1 | 1 | 0 | 3 |
| Glen Parva | 1 | 1 | 0 | 3 | 0 | 3 | 2 | 0 | 1 | 0 | 1 | 2 | 3 | 2 | 2 | 1 | 2 | 1 | 0 | 2 | 0 | 0 | 0 |
| Gloucester | 2 | 1 | 3 | 1 | 0 | 0 | 4 | 0 | 0 | 0 | 0 | 0 | 1 | 0 | 1 | 2 | 0 | 1 | 0 | 1 | 0 | 0 | 0 |
| Grendon/Spring Hill: Grendon | 0 | 0 | 0 | 0 | 0 | 0 | 0 | 0 | 0 | 0 | 0 | 0 | 0 | 0 | 0 | 0 | 0 | 0 | 0 | 0 | 1 | 0 | 0 |

LEGEND

*"-" Not applicable - prison not in operation*

*(1) Caution should be used when comparing the number of deaths from one year to the next due to low numbers which are subject to fluctuation. This table should be read in conjunction with table 14 which outlines some of the major changes to prisons that will have affected numbers.*

*Data Sources and Quality*

*These figures are derived from the HMPPS Deaths in Prison Custody database. As classification of deaths may change following inquest or as new information emerges, numbers may change from time to time.*

**Table 1.11: Self-inflicted deaths by prison[1] since 1999, England and Wales (continued on next page)**

| Prison | | | | | | | | | | | | | | | | | | | | | | | |
|---|---|---|---|---|---|---|---|---|---|---|---|---|---|---|---|---|---|---|---|---|---|---|---|
| Grendon/Spring Hill: Spring Hill | 0 | 0 | 0 | 0 | 0 | 0 | 1 | 0 | 0 | 0 | 0 | 0 | 0 | 0 | 0 | 0 | 0 | 0 | 0 | 0 | 0 | 0 | 0 |
| Guys Marsh | 0 | 0 | 2 | 1 | 1 | 2 | 0 | 0 | 0 | 0 | 0 | 0 | 0 | 0 | 0 | 1 | 0 | 2 | 0 | 0 | 0 | 0 | 0 |
| Haslar | 0 | 0 | 0 | 0 | 0 | 0 | 0 | 0 | 0 | 0 | 0 | 0 | 0 | 0 | 0 | 0 | 0 | 0 | - | - | - | - | - |
| Haverigg | 0 | 1 | 0 | 0 | 1 | 0 | 0 | 0 | 0 | 0 | 0 | 1 | 0 | 0 | 0 | 0 | 0 | 0 | 0 | 0 | 0 | 0 | 0 |
| Hewell | - | - | - | - | - | - | - | - | - | - | 3 | 0 | 0 | 0 | 2 | 0 | 2 | 3 | 3 | 0 | 1 | 0 | 0 |
| Hewell: Blakenhurst | 2 | 3 | 3 | 3 | 2 | 0 | 1 | 0 | 0 | 3 | - | - | - | - | - | - | - | - | - | - | - | - | - |
| Hewell: Brockhill | 1 | 2 | 0 | 0 | 2 | 0 | 0 | 0 | 0 | 0 | - | - | - | - | - | - | - | - | - | - | - | - | - |
| Hewell: Hewell Grange | 0 | 0 | 0 | 0 | 0 | 0 | 0 | 0 | 0 | 0 | - | - | - | - | - | - | - | - | - | - | - | - | - |
| High Down | 0 | 1 | 2 | 2 | 2 | 3 | 0 | 0 | 0 | 0 | 0 | 0 | 0 | 1 | 0 | 2 | 3 | 0 | 0 | 1 | 2 | 0 | 0 |
| Highpoint | 1 | 2 | 0 | 1 | 2 | 1 | 1 | 0 | 0 | 0 | 0 | 0 | 1 | 0 | 0 | 1 | 1 | 0 | 0 | 0 | 0 | 0 | 0 |
| Hindley | 0 | 0 | 0 | 1 | 2 | 1 | 0 | 3 | 1 | 0 | 0 | 0 | 0 | 0 | 0 | 0 | 0 | 0 | 0 | 0 | 0 | 0 | 0 |
| Hollesley Bay | 0 | 0 | 0 | 0 | 0 | 0 | 0 | 0 | 0 | 0 | 0 | 0 | 0 | 0 | 0 | 0 | 1 | 0 | 0 | 0 | 0 | 1 | 0 |
| Holloway | 2 | 3 | 2 | 0 | 2 | 0 | 0 | 1 | 0 | 0 | 1 | 0 | 0 | 1 | 0 | 0 | 0 | 0 | 0 | 0 | 0 | 0 | 0 |
| Holme House | 3 | 1 | 1 | 1 | 0 | 4 | 3 | 0 | 2 | 2 | 4 | 2 | 0 | 0 | 1 | 2 | 2 | 1 | 0 | 2 | 2 | 4 | 0 |
| Hull | 0 | 1 | 0 | 0 | 1 | 0 | 0 | 0 | 0 | 2 | 1 | 0 | 0 | 1 | 1 | 1 | 0 | 3 | 4 | 3 | 0 | 0 | 1 |
| Huntercombe | 0 | 0 | 0 | 0 | 0 | 1 | 0 | 0 | 0 | 0 | 0 | 0 | - | - | - | - | - | - | - | - | - | - | - |
| Isis | - | - | - | - | - | - | - | - | - | - | - | 0 | 0 | 0 | 0 | 0 | 1 | 1 | 0 | 1 | 0 | 1 | 0 |
| Isle of Wight | - | - | - | - | - | - | - | - | - | - | - | 1 | 0 | 1 | 0 | 2 | 0 | 0 | 0 | 0 | 0 | 2 | 0 |
| IoW: Albany | 0 | 0 | 0 | 0 | 0 | 0 | 1 | 0 | 2 | 0 | 0 | - | - | - | - | - | - | - | - | - | - | - | - |
| IoW: Camp Hill | 0 | 0 | 1 | 0 | 0 | 2 | 0 | 0 | 0 | 2 | 1 | - | - | - | - | - | - | - | - | - | - | - | - |
| IoW: Parkhurst | 0 | 1 | 0 | 1 | 0 | 0 | 0 | 0 | 0 | 1 | 0 | - | - | - | - | - | - | - | - | - | - | - | - |
| Kennet | - | - | - | - | - | - | - | - | - | - | 0 | 0 | 0 | 0 | 0 | 0 | 0 | 0 | - | - | - | - | - |
| Kingston | 0 | 0 | 0 | 0 | 1 | 0 | 0 | 1 | 0 | 0 | 1 | 0 | 0 | - | - | - | - | - | - | - | - | - | - |
| Kirkham | 0 | 0 | 0 | 0 | 0 | 0 | 0 | 0 | 0 | 0 | 0 | 0 | 0 | 0 | 0 | 0 | 0 | 0 | 0 | 0 | 0 | 0 | 0 |
| Kirklevington | 0 | 0 | 0 | 0 | 0 | 0 | 0 | 0 | 0 | 0 | 0 | 0 | 0 | 0 | 0 | 0 | 0 | 0 | 0 | 0 | 0 | 0 | 0 |
| Lancaster Castle | 0 | 0 | 0 | 0 | 0 | 0 | 0 | 0 | 1 | 0 | 0 | 0 | 1 | 1 | - | - | - | - | - | - | - | - | - |
| Lancaster Farms | 0 | 1 | 0 | 1 | 3 | 2 | 1 | 0 | 0 | 0 | 0 | 0 | 0 | 0 | 1 | 0 | 0 | 0 | 0 | 0 | 0 | - | - |
| Latchmere House | 0 | 0 | 0 | 0 | 2 | 0 | 2 | 1 | 1 | 0 | 0 | 0 | 0 | - | - | - | - | - | - | - | - | - | - |
| Leeds | 5 | 3 | 4 | 4 | 4 | 2 | 3 | 2 | 2 | 0 | 1 | 0 | 3 | 2 | 2 | 4 | 0 | 2 | 2 | 0 | 0 | 0 | 0 |
| Leicester | 3 | 4 | 0 | 2 | 0 | 1 | 1 | 0 | 0 | 0 | 0 | 2 | 1 | 0 | 3 | 0 | 0 | 3 | 0 | 0 | 0 | 0 | 0 |
| Lewes | 3 | 2 | 2 | 5 | 0 | 0 | 0 | 0 | 0 | 0 | 3 | 2 | 0 | 1 | 1 | 2 | 0 | 1 | 0 | 0 | 0 | 0 | 0 |
| Leyhill | 0 | 0 | 0 | 0 | 0 | 0 | 0 | 0 | 0 | 0 | 0 | 0 | 0 | 0 | 0 | 0 | 0 | 0 | 0 | 0 | 0 | 0 | 0 |
| Lincoln | 0 | 0 | 0 | 0 | 0 | 2 | 0 | 3 | 2 | 2 | 0 | 1 | 2 | 0 | 3 | 0 | 0 | 0 | 0 | 0 | 0 | 0 | 0 |
| Lindholme | 0 | 0 | 0 | 1 | 2 | 1 | 1 | 1 | 0 | 1 | 0 | 0 | 1 | 0 | 0 | 3 | 0 | 1 | 0 | 0 | 0 | 0 | 0 |
| Littlehey | 1 | 0 | 0 | 0 | 1 | 0 | 0 | 0 | 0 | 0 | 1 | 1 | 0 | 1 | 0 | 0 | 0 | 0 | 0 | 0 | 1 | 0 | 0 |
| Liverpool | 0 | 2 | 2 | 3 | 2 | 0 | 0 | 0 | 0 | 2 | 2 | 2 | 2 | 4 | 0 | 3 | 2 | 0 | 1 | 0 | 0 | 0 | 0 |
| Long Lartin | 0 | 3 | 0 | 1 | 0 | 0 | 3 | 0 | 1 | 3 | 0 | 0 | 3 | 2 | 0 | 5 | 0 | 0 | 0 | 0 | 0 | 0 | 0 |
| Low Newton | 0 | 0 | 0 | 0 | 0 | 0 | 0 | 0 | 4 | 0 | 0 | 0 | 0 | 0 | 0 | 0 | 0 | 0 | 0 | 0 | 0 | 0 | 0 |
| Lowdham Grange | 0 | 0 | 0 | 0 | 1 | 0 | 0 | 0 | 1 | 0 | 0 | 1 | 0 | 0 | 0 | 0 | 0 | 0 | 0 | 0 | 0 | 2 | 0 |
| Maidstone | 8 | 1 | 1 | 2 | 4 | 2 | 6 | 0 | 4 | 1 | 2 | 3 | 2 | 0 | 1 | 4 | 4 | 0 | 0 | 0 | 0 | 0 | 0 |
| Manchester | - | 1 | 1 | 0 | 0 | 0 | 1 | 0 | - | - | - | 3 | 3 | 0 | 0 | 0 | 0 | 1 | 0 | 0 | 2 | 1 | 0 |
| Medomsley | 0 | 0 | 0 | 0 | 0 | 0 | 0 | 0 | 0 | 0 | 0 | 0 | - | - | - | - | - | - | - | - | - | - | - |
| Moorland | 0 | 0 | 1 | 2 | 1 | 0 | 0 | 1 | 0 | 0 | 0 | 0 | 0 | 1 | 0 | 0 | 0 | 2 | 0 | 0 | 0 | 0 | 0 |
| Moorland Open (Hatfield) | 0 | 2 | 2 | 3 | 3 | 2 | 0 | 3 | 0 | 0 | 0 | 0 | 0 | 0 | 0 | 0 | 0 | 0 | 0 | 0 | 0 | 0 | 0 |
| Morton Hall | 0 | 3 | 0 | 1 | 0 | 3 | 0 | 1 | 0 | 0 | 0 | 1 | 0 | - | - | - | - | - | - | - | - | - | - |
| Mount | 1 | 0 | 1 | 0 | 0 | 2 | 3 | 0 | 1 | 0 | 1 | 0 | 0 | 0 | 0 | 1 | 0 | 1 | 1 | 0 | 1 | 0 | 0 |
| New Hall | 0 | 0 | 0 | 0 | 2 | 0 | 0 | 0 | 0 | 0 | 0 | 0 | 0 | 0 | 0 | 0 | 0 | 0 | 0 | 0 | 0 | 0 | 0 |
| North Sea Camp | 0 | 0 | 0 | 0 | 2 | 0 | - | - | - | - | 1 | 0 | 0 | 0 | 0 | 0 | 0 | 0 | 0 | 0 | 0 | 0 | 0 |
| Northallerton | - | - | - | 2 | 0 | 2 | 0 | 0 | - | - | 0 | 0 | 0 | 0 | 1 | 0 | 0 | 1 | 0 | 0 | 0 | 0 | 0 |
| Northeye | - | - | - | - | - | - | - | - | - | - | - | - | - | - | - | - | - | - | - | - | - | - | - |
| Northumberland | - | - | - | - | - | - | - | - | - | - | - | - | - | - | 2 | 0 | 2 | 0 | 3 | 0 | 0 | 2 | 0 |
| Northumberland: Acklington | 0 | 1 | 2 | 0 | 0 | 2 | 1 | 2 | 0 | 0 | 0 | 1 | 0 | 1 | - | - | - | - | - | - | - | - | - |
| Northumberland: Castington | 1 | 1 | 0 | 2 | 1 | 0 | 1 | 1 | 0 | 1 | 0 | 0 | 0 | 0 | - | - | - | - | - | - | - | - | - |
| Norwich | 2 | 3 | 1 | 3 | 2 | 2 | 3 | 3 | 2 | 4 | 3 | 3 | 1 | 1 | 1 | 0 | 1 | 0 | 1 | 2 | 2 | 3 | 0 |
| Nottingham | 1 | 3 | 3 | 0 | 1 | 3 | 1 | 1 | 0 | 4 | 1 | 0 | 0 | 0 | 3 | 1 | 2 | 3 | 0 | 0 | 2 | 6 | 0 |
| Oakwood | - | - | - | - | - | - | - | - | - | - | - | - | - | 0 | 1 | 0 | 0 | 0 | 0 | 0 | 1 | 2 | 0 |
| Onley | 0 | 0 | 0 | 1 | 0 | 1 | 0 | 0 | 0 | 0 | 0 | 0 | 0 | 0 | 0 | 0 | 0 | 0 | 0 | 0 | 0 | 0 | 0 |

LEGEND
"-" Not applicable - prison not in operation

(1) Caution should be used when comparing the number of deaths from one year to the next due to low numbers which are subject to fluctuation. This table should be read in conjunction with table 14 which outlines some of the major changes to prisons that will have affected numbers.

Data Sources and Quality
These figures are derived from the HMPPS Deaths in Prison Custody database. As classification of deaths may change following inquest or as new information emerges, numbers may change from time to time.

# Table 1.11: Self-inflicted deaths by prison[1] since 1999, England and Wales

| Prison | 1999 | 2000 | 2001 | 2002 | 2003 | 2004 | 2005 | 2006 | 2007 | 2008 | 2009 | 2010 | 2011 | 2012 | 2013 | 2014 | 2015 | 2016 | 2017 | 2018 | 2019 | 2020 |
|---|---|---|---|---|---|---|---|---|---|---|---|---|---|---|---|---|---|---|---|---|---|---|
| Oxford | - | - | - | - | - | - | - | - | - | - | - | - | - | - | - | - | - | - | - | - | - | - |
| Parc | 1 | 1 | - | - | - | 3 | - | - | 2 | 0 | 0 | 0 | 0 | 0 | 2 | 0 | 0 | 1 | 0 | 1 | 0 | 1 |
| Pentonville | 1 | 1 | 2 | 3 | 3 | 3 | 0 | 2 | 1 | 1 | 2 | 0 | 1 | 2 | 0 | 2 | 2 | 0 | 0 | 2 | 2 | 2 |
| Peterborough | - | - | - | - | 1 | - | - | 0 | 0 | 2 | 0 | 0 | 0 | 1 | 1 | 0 | 0 | 1 | - | 0 | 1 | 0 |
| Peterborough Male | - | - | - | - | - | 1 | 1 | 0 | - | 0 | 1 | 0 | - | - | - | - | - | - | - | 0 | - | - |
| Peterborough Female | - | - | - | - | - | - | - | 0 | - | 0 | 0 | - | - | - | - | - | - | - | - | 0 | 0 | - |
| Portland | - | 0 | 0 | 0 | 0 | 0 | 0 | 1 | 0 | 1 | 1 | 0 | 0 | 0 | 1 | 0 | 1 | 0 | 0 | 0 | 0 | 0 |
| Preston | 3 | 2 | 1 | 2 | 3 | 2 | 0 | 0 | 0 | 1 | 0 | 0 | 1 | 3 | 0 | 1 | 0 | 0 | 3 | 0 | 0 | 1 |
| Pucklechurch | - | - | - | - | - | - | - | - | - | - | - | - | - | - | - | - | - | - | - | - | - | - |
| Ranby | 1 | 0 | 0 | 0 | 0 | 0 | 2 | 0 | 0 | 1 | 0 | 0 | 0 | 0 | 0 | 4 | 1 | 0 | 1 | 0 | 0 | 0 |
| Reading | 0 | 0 | 0 | 1 | 0 | 1 | 0 | 0 | 0 | 0 | 0 | 0 | 0 | 1 | 0 | 0 | 0 | 0 | 0 | 0 | 0 | 0 |
| Risley | 0 | 1 | 0 | 1 | 1 | 0 | 0 | 3 | 0 | 2 | 0 | 1 | 0 | 0 | 1 | 0 | 0 | 0 | 0 | 0 | 0 | 0 |
| Rochester | 0 | 0 | 0 | 0 | 0 | 0 | 0 | 0 | 0 | 0 | 1 | 0 | 0 | 1 | 1 | 0 | 0 | 0 | 1 | 1 | 0 | 0 |
| Rye Hill | - | - | - | - | - | 0 | 0 | 0 | 0 | 0 | 0 | 0 | 0 | 0 | 0 | 0 | 0 | 0 | 0 | 0 | 0 | 0 |
| Send | 0 | 0 | 0 | 0 | 0 | 0 | 2 | 0 | 2 | 0 | 3 | 0 | 2 | 0 | 0 | 0 | 0 | 0 | 0 | 0 | 0 | 0 |
| Sheppey: Elmley | 0 | 0 | 2 | 0 | 0 | 2 | 5 | 0 | 1 | 2 | 0 | 2 | 1 | 0 | 0 | 5 | 0 | 0 | 0 | 0 | 1 | 0 |
| Sheppey: Standford Hill | 0 | 0 | 0 | 0 | 0 | 0 | 0 | 0 | 1 | 0 | 1 | 0 | 1 | 0 | 0 | 0 | 0 | 0 | 0 | 0 | 0 | 0 |
| Sheppey: Swaleside | 0 | 2 | 2 | 0 | 0 | 2 | 0 | 0 | 0 | 2 | 2 | 0 | 0 | 1 | 0 | 0 | 0 | 2 | 0 | 0 | 0 | 0 |
| Shepton Mallet | 0 | 0 | 0 | 0 | 4 | 1 | 0 | 0 | 0 | 0 | 0 | 0 | 0 | 0 | 0 | 0 | 0 | 0 | - | - | - | - |
| Shrewsbury | 0 | 0 | 0 | 1 | 0 | 0 | 0 | 0 | 1 | 0 | 0 | 0 | 1 | 5 | 0 | 0 | 0 | 0 | - | - | - | - |
| Stafford | 2 | 1 | 0 | 0 | 0 | 0 | 0 | 1 | 0 | 0 | 2 | 1 | 0 | 1 | 0 | 0 | 1 | 0 | 1 | 0 | 0 | 0 |
| Stocken | 1 | 0 | 0 | 0 | 0 | 1 | 1 | 1 | 0 | 0 | 0 | 0 | 0 | 0 | 0 | 0 | 0 | 0 | 0 | 0 | 0 | 0 |
| Stoke Heath | 0 | 1 | 0 | 4 | 0 | 2 | 0 | 3 | 0 | 0 | 1 | 0 | 0 | 0 | 0 | 0 | 0 | 2 | 2 | 3 | 2 | 1 |
| Styal | 0 | 0 | 1 | 0 | 1 | 4 | 0 | 0 | 1 | 0 | 2 | 0 | 0 | 0 | 0 | 0 | 0 | 0 | 0 | 0 | 0 | 0 |
| Sudbury | 0 | 0 | 0 | 1 | 0 | 0 | 0 | 0 | 0 | 0 | 0 | 0 | 0 | 0 | 0 | 0 | 0 | 0 | 0 | 0 | 0 | 0 |
| Swansea | 0 | 0 | 1 | 0 | 1 | 1 | 0 | 0 | 0 | 0 | 0 | 2 | 0 | 1 | 0 | 0 | 0 | 0 | 0 | 0 | 5 | 2 |
| Swinfen Hall | 0 | 0 | 0 | 0 | 0 | 0 | 0 | 0 | 0 | 1 | 0 | 1 | 0 | 0 | 0 | 0 | 0 | 1 | 0 | 0 | 2 | 0 |
| Thameside | - | - | - | - | - | - | - | - | - | - | - | - | - | - | - | - | - | - | - | 0 | 0 | 1 |
| Thorn Cross | 0 | 0 | 0 | 0 | 0 | 0 | 0 | 0 | 0 | 0 | 0 | 0 | 0 | 0 | 0 | 0 | 0 | 0 | 0 | 0 | 0 | 0 |
| Usk/Prescoed: Usk | - | - | - | - | - | 0 | 0 | 0 | 0 | 0 | 0 | 0 | 0 | - | 0 | 0 | 0 | 0 | 0 | 0 | 0 | 0 |
| Usk/Prescoed: Usk | - | - | - | - | 1 | 5 | 0 | 0 | 0 | 0 | 0 | 0 | 0 | 0 | 0 | - | - | 0 | 0 | 0 | 0 | 0 |
| Verne | 2 | 0 | 0 | - | 1 | 0 | 1 | 1 | 1 | 1 | 0 | 0 | 1 | 1 | 0 | 0 | 1 | 1 | - | 0 | 0 | 0 |
| Wakefield | 2 | 0 | 0 | 0 | 0 | 3 | 0 | 5 | 1 | 2 | 2 | 0 | 1 | 0 | 0 | 0 | 0 | 0 | 0 | 4 | 0 | 0 |
| Wandsworth | 0 | 7 | 0 | 3 | 3 | 0 | 5 | 0 | 4 | 0 | 3 | 0 | 2 | 5 | 5 | 3 | 0 | 0 | 0 | 0 | 0 | 0 |
| Warren Hill | 0 | 0 | 0 | 1 | 0 | 0 | 0 | 0 | 0 | 0 | 0 | 0 | 0 | 2 | 0 | 0 | 0 | 0 | 0 | 0 | 0 | 0 |
| Wayland | 0 | 0 | 0 | 0 | 2 | 0 | 0 | 0 | 0 | 2 | 0 | 0 | 2 | 0 | 0 | 0 | 0 | 2 | 0 | 0 | 0 | 0 |
| Wealstun | 0 | 0 | 2 | 0 | 0 | 0 | 0 | 1 | 1 | 0 | 1 | - | 1 | 0 | 1 | 0 | 0 | 0 | 3 | 0 | 0 | 0 |
| Weare | 0 | 0 | - | - | - | - | - | - | - | - | - | - | - | - | - | - | - | - | - | - | - | - |
| Wellingborough | 0 | 0 | 1 | 0 | 0 | 0 | 0 | 1 | 0 | 0 | 0 | 0 | 0 | 0 | 0 | 0 | 0 | 0 | 0 | 0 | 0 | 0 |
| Werrington | 0 | 0 | 0 | 0 | 0 | 0 | 0 | 0 | 0 | 0 | 0 | 0 | 0 | 0 | 0 | 0 | 0 | 0 | 0 | 0 | 0 | 0 |
| Wetherby | 1 | 1 | 1 | 0 | 1 | 0 | 0 | 0 | 0 | 0 | 0 | 0 | 0 | 0 | 0 | 1 | 0 | 0 | 0 | 0 | 0 | 1 |
| Whatton | 0 | 1 | 0 | 0 | 0 | 0 | 0 | 1 | 1 | 0 | 0 | 1 | 0 | 1 | 4 | 0 | 1 | 0 | 0 | 0 | 2 | 1 |
| Whitemoor | 0 | 0 | 0 | 0 | 0 | 0 | 0 | 4 | 0 | 4 | 0 | 0 | 0 | 0 | 0 | 0 | 0 | 0 | 0 | 0 | 0 | 0 |
| Winchester | 2 | 4 | 3 | 1 | 1 | 0 | 0 | 3 | 0 | 0 | 0 | 0 | 1 | 2 | 0 | 1 | 3 | 0 | 0 | 1 | 0 | 0 |
| Wolds | 1 | 1 | 0 | 0 | 4 | 0 | 1 | 1 | 2 | 0 | 0 | 0 | 0 | 0 | 0 | 0 | 3 | 2 | 2 | 0 | 1 | 1 |
| Woodhill | 0 | 2 | 2 | 0 | 0 | 3 | 0 | 0 | 3 | 1 | 2 | 1 | 2 | 1 | 4 | 5 | 0 | 0 | 0 | 0 | 5 | 2 |
| Wormwood Scrubs | 1 | 1 | 3 | 0 | 2 | 3 | 1 | 0 | 1 | 0 | 0 | 0 | 0 | 0 | 2 | 0 | 2 | 2 | 3 | 3 | 1 | 1 |
| Wymott | 1 | 0 | 0 | 1 | 1 | 2 | 0 | 1 | 0 | 0 | 0 | 0 | 0 | 0 | 0 | 0 | 0 | 0 | 0 | 0 | 2 | 0 |
| ESCORT AREAS | 5 | 0 | 0 | 0 | 0 | 1 | 0 | 0 | 0 | 0 | 0 | 0 | 0 | 0 | 0 | 0 | 0 | 0 | 0 | 0 | 0 | 0 |
| **Total** | **91** | **81** | **73** | **95** | **95** | **96** | **78** | **66** | **91** | **61** | **58** | **58** | **61** | **76** | **89** | **90** | **124** | **73** | **93** | **86** | **67** | **86** |

LEGEND
"-" Not applicable - prison not in operation

(1) Caution should be used when comparing the number of deaths from one year to the next due to low numbers which are subject to fluctuation. This table should be read in conjunction with table 14 which outlines some of the major changes to prisons that will have affected numbers.

Data Sources and Quality
These figures are derived from the HMPPS Deaths in Prison Custody database. As classification of deaths may change following inquest or as new information emerges, numbers may change from time to time.

## Table 1.12: Natural cause deaths by prison[1] since 1999, England and Wales (continued on next page)

| Prison | 1999 | 2000 | 2001 | 2002 | 2003 | 2004 | 2005 | 2006 | 2007 | 2008 | 2009 | 2010 | 2011 | 2012 | 2013 | 2014 | 2015 | 2016 | 2017 | 2018 | 2019 | 2020 (r) | 2021 (p) |
|---|---|---|---|---|---|---|---|---|---|---|---|---|---|---|---|---|---|---|---|---|---|---|---|
| Aldington | 1 | 0 | 3 | 1 | - | 2 | - | 1 | 0 | 2 | 2 | 2 | 2 | 2 | - | - | 5 | 5 | 3 | 5 | 7 | 7 | 5 |
| Altcourse | - | 0 | - | 1 | 2 | 0 | 2 | 1 | 0 | 2 | 2 | 2 | 1 | 0 | 2 | 1 | 2 | 2 | 0 | 1 | 1 | 1 | 2 |
| Appleton Thorn | - | 0 | 0 | 0 | 0 | 0 | 0 | 0 | 0 | 0 | 0 | 0 | 0 | 0 | 0 | 1 | 1 | 0 | - | - | - | - | - |
| Ashfield | - | 0 | 0 | 0 | 0 | 0 | 1 | 0 | 0 | 0 | 1 | 0 | 0 | 0 | 0 | 0 | 0 | 0 | 0 | 0 | 0 | 0 | 0 |
| Ashford | - | 0 | - | 0 | 0 | 0 | 0 | 0 | 0 | 0 | - | - | - | - | - | - | - | - | - | - | - | 0 | 2 |
| Ashwell | 0 | 0 | 1 | 0 | 0 | 0 | 0 | 0 | 0 | 0 | 0 | - | - | - | - | - | - | - | - | - | - | 0 | 0 |
| Askham Grange | 0 | 0 | 0 | 1 | 0 | 0 | 0 | 0 | 0 | 0 | 1 | 0 | 0 | 0 | 0 | 0 | 0 | 0 | 1 | 0 | 1 | 0 | 3 |
| Aylesbury | 0 | 0 | 0 | 2 | 3 | 0 | 0 | 0 | 0 | 2 | 0 | 3 | 0 | 0 | 0 | 0 | 3 | 3 | 2 | 2 | 1 | 2 | 0 |
| Bedford | 0 | 1 | 1 | 1 | 2 | 2 | 2 | 1 | 0 | 1 | 1 | 0 | 0 | 1 | 0 | 3 | 0 | 0 | 2 | 4 | 0 | 3 | 3 |
| Belmarsh | 3 | 1 | 2 | 0 | 1 | 1 | 1 | 4 | 4 | 3 | 1 | 4 | 4 | 1 | 1 | 3 | 6 | 6 | 6 | 3 | 3 | 3 | 5 |
| Berwyn | - | 0 | 0 | 1 | 0 | 0 | 0 | 0 | 0 | 0 | 0 | 0 | 0 | 0 | 0 | 2 | 0 | - | - | - | - | 0 | 0 |
| Birmingham | 0 | 0 | 0 | 0 | 0 | 0 | 0 | 1 | 0 | 0 | 0 | 0 | 0 | 0 | 0 | 0 | 0 | 0 | 0 | 0 | 0 | 0 | 2 |
| Blantyre House | 1 | 1 | 0 | 1 | 0 | 0 | 1 | 2 | 2 | 2 | 0 | 1 | 2 | 0 | 0 | 1 | 2 | 0 | 2 | 0 | 2 | 0 | 0 |
| Blundeston | 0 | 3 | 0 | 0 | 0 | 0 | 2 | 0 | 0 | 0 | 0 | 0 | 0 | 1 | 0 | 0 | 2 | 1 | 1 | - | - | 0 | 4 |
| Brinsford | 0 | 0 | 0 | 0 | 0 | 0 | 0 | 2 | 0 | 0 | 1 | 1 | 0 | 0 | 0 | 0 | 2 | 2 | 2 | 0 | 0 | 0 | 6 |
| Bristol | 0 | 0 | 0 | 1 | 1 | 0 | 0 | 0 | 0 | 0 | 0 | 0 | 1 | 1 | 0 | 1 | 2 | 2 | 5 | 0 | 3 | 3 | 2 |
| Brixton | 1 | 0 | 1 | 1 | 0 | 1 | 0 | 2 | 2 | 1 | 0 | 2 | 3 | 0 | 0 | 0 | 0 | 2 | 1 | 0 | 3 | 3 | 3 |
| Bronzefield | - | 0 | 0 | - | 1 | 0 | 1 | 0 | 0 | 0 | 2 | 0 | 0 | 4 | 0 | 0 | 2 | 2 | 1 | 1 | 3 | 0 | 0 |
| Buckley Hall | 0 | 0 | 0 | 0 | 0 | 2 | 0 | 0 | 0 | 0 | 0 | 0 | 2 | 4 | 1 | 3 | 2 | 2 | 1 | 2 | 0 | 0 | 0 |
| Bullingdon | 0 | 0 | 1 | 1 | 1 | 1 | 1 | 2 | 0 | 0 | 1 | 1 | 1 | 0 | 0 | 1 | 2 | 2 | 2 | 0 | 1 | 0 | 4 |
| Bullwood Hall | 0 | 0 | 0 | 0 | 0 | 0 | 0 | 0 | 0 | 0 | 0 | 0 | 0 | 0 | 0 | - | 2 | 2 | 2 | 0 | - | - | - |
| Bure | - | 0 | 1 | 0 | 0 | 0 | 0 | 0 | 0 | 0 | 0 | 0 | 0 | 1 | 1 | 2 | 2 | 2 | 5 | 0 | 3 | 6 | 6 |
| Canterbury | 1 | 0 | 0 | 1 | 1 | 1 | 0 | 0 | 0 | 0 | 0 | 1 | 0 | 0 | 1 | 0 | 0 | 0 | 1 | - | - | 1 | 2 |
| Cardiff | 0 | 0 | 0 | 1 | 1 | 0 | 0 | 2 | 2 | 1 | 2 | 1 | 3 | 2 | 0 | 0 | 0 | 2 | 2 | 0 | 3 | 3 | 2 |
| Channings Wood | 0 | 0 | 1 | 1 | 1 | 1 | 0 | 2 | 1 | 0 | 0 | 0 | 2 | 4 | 2 | 3 | 2 | 2 | 1 | 2 | 1 | 3 | 3 |
| Chelmsford | 0 | 0 | 0 | 0 | 0 | 0 | 1 | 0 | 0 | 0 | 0 | 0 | 1 | 1 | 0 | 0 | 1 | 0 | 1 | 2 | 3 | 0 | 0 |
| Coldingley | 0 | 2 | 2 | 0 | 0 | 3 | 0 | 0 | 1 | 0 | 0 | 0 | 2 | 0 | 0 | 2 | 0 | 0 | 0 | 0 | 0 | 2 | 4 |
| Cookham Wood | 0 | 0 | 1 | 0 | 0 | 0 | 0 | 1 | 1 | 1 | 0 | 1 | 0 | 0 | 0 | 0 | 0 | 0 | 0 | 0 | 0 | 0 | 0 |
| Dartmoor | 1 | 2 | 1 | 0 | 0 | 1 | 0 | 0 | 0 | 1 | 1 | 1 | 0 | 1 | 0 | 0 | 2 | 3 | 3 | 2 | 0 | 2 | 0 |
| Deerbolt | 0 | 0 | 0 | 0 | 0 | 0 | 0 | 0 | 0 | 0 | 0 | 1 | 1 | 0 | 0 | 0 | 0 | 2 | 3 | 0 | 1 | 0 | 0 |
| Doncaster | 0 | 0 | 0 | 2 | 0 | 0 | 2 | 2 | 4 | 1 | 0 | 0 | 1 | 1 | 1 | 0 | 3 | 2 | 5 | 3 | 4 | 7 | 0 |
| Dorchester | 0 | 0 | 0 | 2 | 2 | 1 | 1 | 0 | 0 | 0 | 0 | 2 | 2 | 2 | 1 | 1 | 2 | 1 | 0 | 3 | 2 | 2 | 2 |
| Dovegate | - | 0 | 0 | 2 | 1 | 1 | 1 | 0 | 0 | 2 | 3 | 0 | 1 | 0 | 0 | 0 | 0 | 0 | 0 | 3 | 0 | 2 | 3 |
| Dover | 0 | 0 | 0 | 0 | 0 | 0 | 0 | 0 | 0 | 0 | 0 | 0 | 0 | 1 | 0 | 2 | 2 | 0 | 0 | - | - | 0 | 0 |
| Downview | 0 | 0 | 0 | 0 | 0 | 1 | 1 | 0 | 0 | 0 | 1 | 0 | 3 | 0 | 1 | 0 | 0 | 0 | 0 | 0 | 0 | 0 | 3 |
| Drake Hall | 0 | 1 | 0 | 0 | 1 | 0 | 0 | 0 | 0 | 0 | 0 | 0 | 3 | 0 | 0 | 1 | 2 | 2 | 6 | 0 | 2 | 2 | 1 |
| Durham | 3 | 3 | 1 | 0 | 1 | 3 | 1 | 1 | 0 | 4 | 5 | 2 | 2 | 0 | 1 | 2 | 3 | 3 | 0 | 0 | 0 | 0 | 0 |
| East Sutton Park | 0 | 0 | 1 | 1 | 0 | 3 | 0 | 0 | 0 | 0 | 1 | 1 | 2 | 0 | 2 | 0 | 0 | 0 | 0 | 2 | 0 | 0 | - |
| Eastwood Park | 0 | 0 | 0 | 1 | 1 | 0 | 0 | 0 | 0 | 0 | 0 | 0 | 0 | 0 | 0 | 0 | 0 | 1 | 0 | 0 | 0 | 0 | 1 |
| Edmunds Hill | 0 | 0 | 0 | 0 | 1 | 1 | 1 | 1 | 1 | 0 | 1 | 0 | 1 | 0 | 0 | 0 | 0 | 1 | 1 | 1 | 0 | - | - |
| Erlestoke | 0 | 0 | 0 | 0 | 0 | 0 | 0 | 2 | 1 | 0 | 0 | 0 | 0 | 0 | 0 | 0 | 0 | 0 | 0 | 0 | 0 | 0 | 0 |
| Everthorpe | 0 | 0 | 2 | 2 | 0 | 0 | 1 | 0 | 2 | 2 | 0 | 2 | 2 | 0 | 1 | 4 | 4 | 9 | 4 | 2 | 5 | 4 | 1 |
| Exeter | 0 | 1 | 0 | 0 | 0 | 0 | 0 | 0 | 0 | 0 | 0 | 0 | 0 | 2 | 2 | 0 | 6 | 2 | 2 | 3 | 3 | 3 | 4 |
| Featherstone | 0 | 0 | 0 | 0 | 0 | 1 | 1 | 0 | 0 | 0 | 0 | 0 | 3 | 0 | 0 | 0 | 0 | 2 | 0 | 0 | 0 | 0 | 3 |
| Feltham | 0 | 0 | 1 | 0 | 0 | 0 | 0 | 0 | 0 | 0 | 0 | 0 | 0 | 0 | 0 | 1 | 1 | 1 | 0 | 0 | 1 | 0 | 0 |
| Ford | 0 | 0 | 0 | 0 | 1 | 0 | 0 | 0 | 2 | 0 | 0 | 3 | 2 | 2 | 0 | 2 | 2 | 1 | 4 | 0 | 2 | 2 | 3 |
| Forest Bank | 0 | 0 | 0 | 1 | 0 | 0 | 0 | 0 | 0 | 0 | 0 | 3 | 0 | 0 | 0 | 3 | 0 | 0 | 0 | 2 | 0 | 0 | 0 |
| Foston Hall | 0 | 6 | 3 | 4 | 1 | 3 | 3 | 1 | 0 | 4 | 5 | 7 | 6 | 6 | 4 | 3 | 3 | 4 | 4 | 4 | 6 | 12 | 3 |
| Frankland | 1 | 1 | 0 | 0 | 2 | 1 | 0 | 3 | 0 | 3 | 1 | 2 | 5 | 2 | 3 | 3 | 0 | 2 | 4 | 1 | 3 | 3 | 3 |
| Full Sutton | 1 | 1 | 0 | 1 | 1 | 1 | 0 | 3 | 1 | 0 | 3 | 2 | 2 | 4 | 4 | 0 | 3 | 4 | 4 | 1 | 3 | 3 | 3 |
| Garth | 2 | 1 | 2 | 0 | 0 | 0 | 1 | 1 | 2 | 2 | 1 | 0 | 3 | 1 | 0 | 1 | 2 | 2 | 4 | 0 | 2 | 2 | 4 |
| Gartree | 0 | 1 | 0 | 2 | 0 | 0 | 0 | 1 | 4 | 0 | 0 | 1 | 1 | 1 | 2 | 1 | 3 | 3 | 1 | 2 | 2 | 4 | 4 |
| Gaynes Hall | - | 0 | 0 | 2 | 1 | 0 | 0 | 0 | 0 | 0 | 0 | 0 | 0 | 0 | 0 | 0 | 0 | 0 | 0 | 0 | 0 | 0 | 0 |
| Glen Parva | 0 | 1 | 0 | 1 | 1 | 1 | 1 | 1 | 1 | 1 | 1 | 0 | 0 | 0 | 0 | 0 | 0 | 0 | 1 | - | - | 0 | 0 |
| Gloucester | 0 | 0 | 0 | 1 | 0 | 0 | 0 | 0 | 0 | 0 | 0 | 1 | 0 | 0 | 0 | - | - | - | - | - | - | - | 0 |
| Grendon/Spring Hill: Grendon | 0 | 0 | 0 | 1 | 0 | 0 | 1 | 0 | 1 | 1 | 0 | 0 | 0 | 0 | 0 | 3 | 1 | 0 | 1 | 1 | - | 0 | 5 |

LEGEND
"-" Not applicable - prison not in operation

(1) Caution should be used when comparing the number of deaths from one year to the next due to low numbers which are subject to fluctuation. This table should be read in conjunction with table 14 which outlines some of the major changes to prisons that will have affected numbers.

Data Sources and Quality
These figures are derived from the HMPPS Deaths in Prison Custody database. As classification of deaths may change following inquest or as new information emerges, numbers may change from time to time.

# Table 1.12: Natural cause deaths by prison1 since 1999, England and Wales
## (continued on next page)

The table lists natural cause deaths by year (columns, unlabelled in this crop) for the following prisons:

- Grendon/Spring Hill: Spring Hill
- Guys Marsh
- Haslar
- Haverigg
- Hewell
- Hewell: Blakenhurst
- Hewell: Brockhill
- Hewell: Hewell Grange
- High Down
- Highpoint
- Hindley
- Hollesley Bay
- Holloway
- Holme House
- Hull
- Humber
- Huntercombe
- Isis
- Isle of Wight
- IoW: Albany
- IoW: Camp Hill
- IoW: Parkhurst
- Kennet
- Kingston
- Kirkham
- Kirklevington
- Lancaster Castle
- Lancaster Farms
- Latchmere House
- Leeds
- Leicester
- Lewes
- Leyhill
- Lincoln
- Lindholme
- Littlehey
- Liverpool
- Long Lartin
- Low Newton
- Lowdham Grange
- Maidstone
- Manchester
- Medomsley
- Moorland
- Moorland Open (Hatfield)
- Morton Hall
- Mount
- New Hall
- North Sea Camp
- Northallerton
- Northeye
- Northumberland
- Northumberland: Acklington
- Northumberland: Castington
- Norwich
- Oakwood
- Onley
- Oxford

LEGEND
"-" Not applicable - prison not in operation

(1) Caution should be used when comparing the number of deaths from one year to the next due to low numbers which are subject to fluctuation. This table should be read in conjunction with table 14 which outlines some of the major changes to prisons that will have affected numbers.

Data Sources and Quality
These figures are derived from the HMPPS Deaths in Prison Custody database. As classification of deaths may change following inquest or as new information emerges, numbers may change from time to time.

## Table 1.12: Natural cause deaths by prison[1] since 1999, England and Wales

| Prison | | | | | | | | | | | | | | | | | | | | | | | |
|---|---|---|---|---|---|---|---|---|---|---|---|---|---|---|---|---|---|---|---|---|---|---|---|
| Parc | 1 | 1 | 1 | - | 1 | 2 | 2 | 2 | 1 | 2 | 0 | 3 | 2 | 5 | 3 | 3 | 4 | 6 | 1 | 4 | 5 | 5 | 4 |
| Pentonville | 2 | 1 | 3 | 4 | 1 | 0 | 2 | 2 | 0 | 0 | 3 | 1 | 3 | 1 | 0 | 3 | 0 | 3 | 0 | 1 | 0 | 1 | 3 |
| Peterborough | - | - | - | - | - | - | - | - | - | 5 | 0 | - | - | - | - | - | - | - | - | - | - | - | - |
| Peterborough Male | - | - | - | - | - | - | - | - | - | - | - | - | - | - | - | - | - | - | - | - | - | - | - |
| Peterborough Female | - | - | - | - | - | - | - | - | - | - | - | - | - | - | - | - | - | - | - | - | - | - | - |
| Portland | 0 | 0 | 0 | - | 0 | 0 | 0 | 0 | 0 | 0 | 0 | 0 | 0 | 0 | 0 | 0 | 0 | 2 | 0 | 0 | 0 | 0 | 0 |
| Preston | 1 | 1 | 2 | 2 | - | 2 | 2 | 0 | 1 | 0 | 0 | 2 | 0 | 0 | 1 | 1 | 4 | 0 | 2 | 0 | 1 | 0 | 2 |
| Pucklechurch | - | - | - | - | - | - | - | - | - | - | - | - | - | - | - | - | - | - | - | - | - | - | - |
| Ranby | 0 | 2 | 0 | 0 | 0 | 2 | 0 | 2 | 0 | 2 | 1 | 1 | 0 | 2 | 2 | 2 | 0 | 5 | 6 | 2 | 3 | 0 | 3 |
| Reading | 0 | 0 | 0 | 0 | 2 | 0 | 0 | 0 | 0 | 0 | 0 | 0 | 0 | 0 | 0 | 0 | 0 | 2 | 3 | 0 | 0 | 0 | 1 |
| Risley | 0 | 0 | 4 | 0 | 0 | 2 | 0 | 2 | 0 | 2 | 1 | 0 | 0 | 0 | 0 | 1 | 2 | 6 | 5 | 0 | 5 | 4 | 6 |
| Rochester | 0 | 4 | - | - | 0 | 0 | 0 | 0 | 0 | 1 | 0 | 0 | 2 | 3 | 0 | 0 | 0 | 0 | 0 | 7 | 0 | 0 | 1 |
| Rye Hill | - | - | 0 | 1 | 0 | 3 | 4 | 0 | 0 | 0 | 2 | 0 | 2 | 0 | 1 | 0 | 0 | 6 | 6 | 2 | 2 | 0 | 6 |
| Send | 0 | 0 | 1 | 0 | 2 | 0 | 0 | 0 | 0 | 0 | 2 | 0 | 2 | 4 | 0 | 0 | 0 | 6 | 0 | 0 | 0 | 0 | 4 |
| Sheppey: Elmley | 1 | 0 | 1 | 2 | 2 | 3 | 0 | 3 | 0 | 0 | 0 | 3 | 0 | 0 | 4 | 3 | 3 | 3 | 6 | 2 | 2 | 0 | 6 |
| Sheppey: Standford Hill | 1 | 3 | 3 | 2 | 2 | 4 | 1 | 1 | 1 | 1 | 1 | 0 | 3 | 2 | 0 | 1 | 0 | 0 | 2 | 7 | 0 | 5 | 0 |
| Sheppey: Swaleside | 1 | 2 | 0 | 2 | 2 | 0 | 1 | 2 | 0 | 2 | 2 | 0 | 0 | 0 | 3 | 0 | 0 | 0 | 0 | 3 | 3 | 3 | 4 |
| Shepton Mallet | 0 | 0 | 0 | 0 | 0 | 2 | 0 | 1 | 2 | 0 | 1 | 1 | 0 | 0 | 2 | 1 | 1 | 1 | 1 | 2 | 0 | 0 | 0 |
| Shrewsbury | 1 | 1 | 1 | 0 | 1 | 1 | 0 | 0 | 2 | 0 | 1 | 1 | 2 | 1 | 2 | 3 | 0 | 0 | 0 | 0 | - | - | - |
| Stafford | 1 | 0 | 0 | 2 | 0 | 2 | 0 | 0 | 2 | 0 | 2 | 1 | 0 | 0 | 0 | 1 | 5 | 5 | 7 | 3 | 0 | 0 | 0 |
| Stocken | 1 | 0 | 0 | 1 | 0 | 0 | 0 | 0 | 0 | 2 | 0 | 0 | 0 | 0 | 0 | 7 | 2 | 0 | 6 | 3 | 5 | 1 | 2 |
| Stoke Heath | 0 | 0 | 4 | 0 | 0 | 0 | 1 | 0 | 0 | 0 | 0 | 0 | 0 | 0 | 1 | 3 | 0 | 0 | 2 | 2 | 1 | 0 | 0 |
| Styal | 1 | 0 | - | 0 | 0 | 0 | 0 | 0 | 0 | 2 | 0 | 3 | 0 | 0 | 0 | 1 | 0 | 1 | 0 | 0 | 0 | 0 | 4 |
| Sudbury | 0 | 0 | 0 | 0 | 2 | 0 | 0 | 1 | 0 | 0 | 0 | 0 | 0 | 0 | 0 | 0 | 0 | 0 | 0 | 0 | 5 | 6 | 0 |
| Swansea | 0 | 0 | 0 | 0 | 0 | 0 | 1 | 1 | 0 | 0 | 0 | 2 | 0 | 0 | 1 | 0 | 0 | 0 | 0 | 3 | 5 | 0 | 3 |
| Swinfen Hall | 0 | 0 | 0 | 0 | 0 | 0 | 0 | 0 | 0 | 0 | 1 | 0 | 0 | 0 | 0 | 0 | 0 | 0 | 0 | 1 | 0 | 0 | 0 |
| Thameside | 0 | 0 | - | - | 0 | 0 | 0 | 0 | 0 | 2 | 0 | - | 0 | 0 | 0 | 2 | 3 | 2 | 3 | 3 | 2 | 2 | 0 |
| Thorn Cross | 0 | 0 | 0 | 0 | 0 | 1 | 0 | 1 | 0 | - | 1 | 1 | 0 | 2 | 3 | 0 | 1 | 0 | 0 | 2 | 1 | 1 | 1 |
| Usk:Prescoed | - | 1 | 1 | 0 | 1 | 0 | 0 | 0 | 0 | 0 | 0 | 1 | 0 | 0 | 0 | 0 | 0 | 2 | 0 | 0 | 2 | 1 | 0 |
| Usk:Prescoed: Usk | 5 | 0 | 0 | 1 | 0 | 0 | 2 | 0 | 0 | 0 | 3 | 1 | 0 | 0 | 0 | 3 | 7 | 5 | 0 | 7 | 3 | 8 | 2 |
| Verne | 2 | 1 | 5 | 6 | 4 | 3 | 1 | 0 | 5 | 1 | 1 | 1 | 1 | 1 | 1 | 1 | 3 | 11 | 2 | 3 | 3 | 9 | 7 |
| Wakefield | 0 | 1 | 1 | 1 | 1 | 0 | 0 | 3 | 3 | 1 | 2 | 2 | 6 | 6 | 2 | 5 | 0 | 0 | 2 | 3 | 2 | 0 | 0 |
| Wandsworth | 0 | 3 | 3 | 0 | 0 | 0 | 0 | 0 | 0 | 0 | 0 | 0 | 2 | 2 | 0 | 1 | 7 | 2 | 0 | 3 | 3 | 2 | 3 |
| Warren Hill | 0 | 0 | 0 | 0 | 0 | 0 | 0 | 0 | 2 | 0 | 0 | 0 | 0 | 0 | 1 | 0 | 1 | 0 | 0 | 0 | 0 | 0 | 0 |
| Wayland | 0 | 0 | 0 | 0 | 0 | 0 | 1 | 0 | 1 | 0 | 0 | 1 | 1 | 0 | 0 | 0 | 0 | 0 | 1 | 0 | 2 | 2 | 2 |
| Wealstun | 0 | 1 | 0 | 1 | 0 | 0 | 0 | 0 | 0 | - | 1 | 0 | 0 | 0 | 0 | 0 | 0 | 2 | 0 | 4 | 2 | 0 | 0 |
| Weare | 0 | 0 | 0 | 0 | 0 | 0 | 0 | 0 | - | - | - | - | - | - | - | - | - | 0 | 1 | 4 | 4 | 0 | 0 |
| Wellingborough | 0 | 0 | 0 | 0 | 0 | 0 | 0 | 0 | 1 | 0 | 0 | 1 | 0 | 0 | 0 | 0 | 0 | 0 | 0 | 0 | - | - | - |
| Werrington | 0 | 0 | 0 | 0 | 0 | 0 | 0 | 0 | 0 | 0 | 0 | 0 | 0 | 0 | 0 | 0 | 0 | 0 | 0 | 0 | 0 | 0 | 0 |
| Wetherby | 0 | 0 | 0 | 0 | 2 | 0 | 0 | 0 | 0 | 0 | 0 | 0 | 0 | 0 | 0 | 0 | 0 | 0 | 4 | 2 | 5 | 9 | 5 |
| Whatton | 1 | 2 | 2 | 2 | 3 | 0 | 1 | 0 | 0 | 0 | 4 | 3 | 3 | 5 | 7 | 3 | 7 | 4 | 6 | 6 | 0 | 6 | 3 |
| Whitemoor | 0 | 1 | 1 | 0 | 0 | 1 | 3 | 1 | 0 | 1 | 0 | 0 | 1 | 1 | 0 | 1 | 2 | 2 | 3 | 0 | 0 | 0 | 3 |
| Winchester | 0 | 2 | 2 | 0 | 2 | 2 | 0 | 0 | 0 | 0 | 0 | 2 | 1 | 0 | 3 | 0 | 2 | 4 | 2 | 0 | 2 | 2 | 3 |
| Wolds | 0 | 0 | 1 | 1 | 0 | 3 | 1 | 4 | 0 | 2 | 0 | 3 | 2 | 0 | 0 | 0 | 0 | 0 | 0 | 0 | 2 | 0 | 0 |
| Woodhill | 0 | 2 | 0 | 0 | 1 | 0 | 2 | 1 | 4 | 0 | 2 | 0 | 3 | 0 | 1 | 0 | 1 | 0 | 4 | 4 | 2 | 0 | 0 |
| Wormwood Scrubs | 1 | 1 | 2 | 3 | 0 | 3 | 1 | 2 | 1 | 2 | 1 | 3 | 0 | 3 | 0 | 2 | 0 | 2 | 2 | 6 | 0 | 6 | 6 |
| Wymott | 3 | 4 | 1 | 2 | 3 | 2 | 7 | 5 | 1 | 4 | 1 | 0 | 4 | 3 | 8 | 0 | 2 | 7 | 0 | 6 | 4 | 6 | 11 |
| ESCORT AREAS | 0 | 0 | 0 | 1 | 0 | 0 | 0 | 0 | 0 | 0 | 0 | 0 | 0 | 0 | 0 | 0 | 0 | 0 | 0 | 0 | 0 | 0 | 0 |
| **Total** | **58** | **61** | **68** | **66** | **86** | **101** | **89** | **83** | **89** | **99** | **104** | **126** | **122** | **123** | **131** | **145** | **147** | **206** | **193** | **168** | **176** | **222** | **250** |

LEGEND
"-" Not applicable - prison not in operation

(1) Caution should be used when comparing the number of deaths from one year to the next due to low numbers which are subject to fluctuation. This table should be read in conjunction with table 14 which outlines some of the major changes to prisons that will have affected numbers.

Data Sources and Quality
These figures are derived from the HMPPS Deaths in Prison Custody database. As classification of deaths may change following inquest or as new information emerges, numbers may change from time to time.

# Table 1.13: Deaths by prison[1], since 1999 England and Wales (continued on next page)

| Prison | 1999 | 2000 | 2001 | 2002 | 2003 | 2004 | 2005 | 2006 | 2007 | 2008 | 2009 | 2010 | 2011 | 2012 | 2013 | 2014 | 2015 | 2016 | 2017 | 2018 | 2019 (r) | 2020 (r) | 2021 (p) |
|---|---|---|---|---|---|---|---|---|---|---|---|---|---|---|---|---|---|---|---|---|---|---|---|
| Aldington | 4 | 0 | 3 | 2 | 4 | 0 | 6 | 2 | 0 | 5 | 3 | 3 | 3 | 3 | 4 | 5 | 4 | 7 | 4 | 7 | 3 | 8 | 9 |
| Altcourse | | | | | | | | | | | | | | | | | | | | 1 | 1 | 1 | 2 |
| Appleton Thorn | 0 | 0 | 0 | 0 | 0 | 0 | 0 | 0 | 0 | 0 | 0 | 0 | 0 | 0 | 0 | 0 | 2 | 2 | 1 | 1 | 2 | 2 | 0 |
| Ashfield | 0 | 0 | 1 | 0 | 1 | 0 | 1 | 0 | 0 | 0 | 1 | 0 | 0 | 0 | 0 | 0 | 0 | 0 | 0 | 0 | 0 | 0 | 0 |
| Ashford | | | | | | | | | | | | | | | | | | | | | | | 3 |
| Ashwell | 0 | 0 | 0 | 0 | 0 | 0 | 0 | 0 | 0 | 0 | 0 | 0 | 0 | | | | | | | | | | |
| Askham Grange | 3 | 2 | 0 | 0 | 0 | 1 | 0 | 0 | 1 | 1 | 0 | 2 | 0 | 0 | 0 | 0 | 0 | 0 | 0 | 0 | 1 | 1 | 3 |
| Aylesbury | 1 | 2 | 0 | 4 | 1 | 1 | 4 | 2 | 4 | 3 | 1 | 4 | 1 | 1 | 3 | 2 | 4 | 4 | 3 | 4 | 4 | 4 | 3 |
| Bedford | 1 | 2 | 1 | 1 | 6 | 3 | 4 | 4 | 1 | 1 | 5 | 2 | 1 | 3 | 2 | 2 | 4 | 4 | 0 | 5 | 3 | 3 | 6 |
| Belmarsh | 5 | 5 | 5 | 0 | 5 | 2 | 2 | 5 | 7 | 5 | 12 | 0 | 2 | 4 | 4 | 4 | 7 | 7 | 0 | 8 | 6 | 3 | 6 |
| Berwyn | | | | | | | | | | | | | | | | 0 | 0 | 1 | 7 | 3 | 3 | 3 | 3 |
| Birmingham | 0 | 2 | 0 | 0 | 0 | 0 | 0 | 0 | 0 | 0 | 0 | 0 | 1 | 0 | 1 | 0 | 3 | 0 | 1 | 3 | 1 | 1 | 0 |
| Blantyre House | 3 | 3 | 2 | 2 | 2 | 6 | 1 | 2 | 3 | 2 | 3 | 3 | 1 | 2 | 0 | 4 | 4 | 0 | 0 | 3 | 0 | 1 | 3 |
| Blundeston | 4 | 5 | 2 | 2 | 0 | 3 | 2 | 5 | 4 | 2 | 0 | 1 | 1 | 1 | 2 | 1 | 1 | 2 | 2 | 2 | 2 | 2 | 2 |
| Bronsford | 0 | 0 | 0 | 0 | 0 | 0 | 2 | 0 | 0 | 0 | 0 | 0 | 0 | 0 | 0 | 0 | 0 | 0 | 0 | 0 | 0 | 0 | 0 |
| Bristol | 0 | 0 | 0 | 4 | 2 | 0 | 1 | 0 | 1 | 0 | 2 | 0 | 2 | 2 | 3 | 1 | 0 | 4 | 2 | 3 | 2 | 0 | 1 |
| Brixton | 0 | 0 | 0 | 0 | 0 | 1 | 1 | 4 | 5 | 1 | 0 | 3 | 0 | 5 | 0 | 3 | 1 | 4 | 3 | 5 | 5 | 5 | 4 |
| Bronzefield | | 0 | 3 | 5 | 1 | 6 | 0 | 2 | 0 | 1 | 5 | 4 | 4 | 5 | 2 | 3 | 1 | 4 | 3 | 1 | 4 | 2 | 0 |
| Buckley Hall | 0 | 0 | 0 | 2 | 0 | 2 | 0 | 0 | 0 | 1 | 0 | 2 | 3 | 0 | 2 | 1 | 1 | 4 | 2 | 2 | 2 | 2 | 3 |
| Bullingdon | 0 | 1 | 1 | 2 | 2 | 4 | 1 | 4 | 1 | 1 | 2 | 3 | 2 | 2 | 3 | 2 | 0 | 0 | 1 | 3 | 0 | 0 | 0 |
| Bullwood Hall | 1 | 2 | 0 | 0 | 1 | 0 | 0 | 0 | 0 | 0 | 0 | 0 | 0 | 0 | 0 | | | | | | | | |
| Bure | | | | | | | | | | | 0 | 0 | 0 | 0 | 0 | 4 | 1 | 1 | 0 | 5 | 0 | 0 | 6 |
| Canterbury | 2 | 0 | 2 | 0 | 0 | 0 | 1 | 2 | 0 | 2 | 0 | 3 | 0 | 0 | 0 | | | | | | | | |
| Cardiff | 1 | 2 | 3 | 2 | 0 | 2 | 1 | 4 | 5 | 1 | 5 | 4 | 5 | 5 | 2 | 3 | 3 | 4 | 4 | 0 | 4 | 0 | 5 |
| Channings Wood | 1 | 2 | 1 | 1 | 1 | 0 | 1 | 2 | 1 | 1 | 1 | 1 | 0 | 3 | 2 | 1 | 4 | 4 | 3 | 1 | 5 | 4 | 4 |
| Chelmsford | 0 | 0 | 2 | 0 | 0 | 0 | 2 | 0 | 4 | 4 | 5 | 4 | 3 | 3 | 3 | 3 | 4 | 4 | 2 | 7 | 4 | 2 | 0 |
| Coldingley | 0 | 0 | 1 | 2 | 0 | 0 | 0 | 0 | 0 | 0 | 0 | 0 | 1 | 0 | 0 | 0 | 0 | 1 | 0 | 2 | 2 | 3 | 0 |
| Cookham Wood | 1 | 2 | 2 | 2 | 2 | 0 | 2 | 2 | 2 | 0 | 2 | 0 | 0 | 0 | 0 | 0 | 5 | 3 | 4 | 0 | 5 | 0 | 3 |
| Dartmoor | 3 | 2 | 2 | 2 | 6 | 0 | 1 | 5 | 3 | 0 | 0 | 0 | 0 | 0 | 2 | 0 | 0 | 1 | 0 | 1 | 0 | 0 | 5 |
| Deerbolt | 0 | 0 | 0 | 0 | 0 | 0 | 0 | 0 | 0 | 0 | 0 | 0 | 0 | 0 | 0 | 4 | 0 | 0 | 0 | 0 | 0 | 0 | 0 |
| Doncaster | 4 | 2 | 0 | 4 | 3 | 2 | 2 | 3 | 4 | 2 | 2 | 5 | 5 | 2 | 2 | 3 | 5 | 3 | 2 | 4 | 4 | 4 | 4 |
| Dorchester | 1 | 2 | 3 | 5 | 2 | 0 | 1 | 1 | 5 | 2 | 3 | 2 | 4 | 1 | 0 | 5 | 5 | 1 | 1 | 6 | 1 | 1 | 1 |
| Dovegate | 0 | 0 | 0 | 0 | 0 | 1 | 0 | 1 | 1 | 0 | 5 | 2 | 4 | 0 | 2 | 0 | 0 | 1 | 1 | 0 | 1 | 0 | 3 |
| Dover | 0 | 0 | 0 | 0 | 0 | 0 | 2 | 0 | 0 | 0 | 0 | 0 | 0 | 0 | 2 | 0 | 0 | 2 | 1 | 0 | 0 | 1 | 0 |
| Downview | 0 | 0 | 0 | 0 | 0 | 1 | 1 | 2 | 2 | 3 | 0 | 0 | 0 | 0 | 0 | 0 | 1 | 0 | 1 | 4 | 1 | 0 | 3 |
| Drake Hall | 0 | 3 | 0 | 0 | 0 | 0 | 0 | 0 | 0 | 0 | 0 | 5 | 0 | 2 | 0 | 0 | 0 | 3 | 9 | 0 | 0 | 0 | 1 |
| Durham | 3 | 4 | 1 | 6 | 6 | 6 | 3 | 2 | 1 | 2 | 6 | 3 | 4 | 2 | 4 | 2 | 1 | 3 | 0 | 4 | 8 | 7 | 3 |
| East Sutton Park | 0 | 0 | 0 | 1 | 4 | 3 | 1 | 1 | 1 | 1 | 0 | 5 | 0 | 0 | 0 | 3 | 0 | 3 | 0 | 0 | 0 | 0 | 1 |
| Eastwood Park | 3 | 3 | 2 | 2 | 3 | 3 | 2 | 1 | 4 | 4 | 7 | 7 | 3 | 8 | 0 | 0 | 0 | 7 | 1 | 7 | 2 | 0 | 0 |
| Edmunds Hill | 1 | 0 | 1 | 2 | 0 | 0 | 2 | 2 | 2 | 0 | 3 | 3 | 6 | 3 | 1 | 1 | 0 | 1 | 1 | 0 | 6 | 12 | 4 |
| Erlestoke | 0 | 3 | 0 | 0 | 0 | 0 | 0 | 0 | 1 | 1 | 0 | 3 | 3 | 0 | 0 | 0 | 0 | 0 | 1 | 4 | 1 | 4 | 4 |
| Everthorpe | 0 | 2 | 3 | 0 | 2 | 0 | 2 | 2 | 2 | 2 | 0 | 2 | 0 | 0 | 2 | 0 | 2 | 0 | 1 | 0 | 0 | 4 | 4 |
| Exeter | 0 | 1 | 0 | 3 | 0 | 2 | 2 | 5 | 5 | 2 | 3 | 4 | 5 | 0 | 5 | 10 | 13 | 3 | 9 | 4 | 0 | 2 | 5 |
| Featherstone | 0 | 2 | 0 | 3 | 0 | 0 | 1 | 0 | 1 | 0 | 0 | 0 | 0 | 2 | 0 | 2 | 0 | 3 | 4 | 0 | 0 | 0 | 6 |
| Feltham | 0 | 1 | 0 | 0 | 0 | 0 | 0 | 0 | 0 | 3 | 0 | 0 | 1 | 0 | 0 | 0 | 0 | 0 | 0 | 1 | 1 | 1 | 0 |
| Ford | 0 | 2 | 0 | 0 | 1 | 0 | 0 | 0 | 0 | 0 | 0 | 4 | 3 | 2 | 2 | 3 | 3 | 2 | 2 | 4 | 4 | 4 | 0 |
| Forest Bank | 0 | 0 | 4 | 6 | 0 | 3 | 3 | 2 | 2 | 2 | 3 | 4 | 2 | 2 | 2 | 0 | 2 | 4 | 2 | 2 | 0 | 0 | 1 |
| Foston Hall | 0 | 0 | 0 | 0 | 0 | 0 | 0 | 1 | 1 | 0 | 0 | 7 | 3 | 0 | 0 | 3 | 0 | 2 | 0 | 0 | 0 | 1 | 3 |
| Frankland | 0 | 6 | 3 | 5 | 3 | 1 | 0 | 1 | 1 | 4 | 7 | 7 | 4 | 8 | 3 | 4 | 6 | 4 | 2 | 4 | 2 | 2 | 4 |
| Full Sutton | 1 | 1 | 0 | 1 | 3 | 1 | 0 | 1 | 0 | 0 | 3 | 3 | 3 | 3 | 0 | 2 | 6 | 3 | 4 | 2 | 4 | 2 | 5 |
| Garth | 3 | 0 | 2 | 2 | 0 | 2 | 0 | 1 | 2 | 1 | 1 | 3 | 0 | 3 | 0 | 0 | 1 | 4 | 5 | 7 | 7 | 6 | 6 |
| Gartree | 1 | 0 | 0 | 3 | 0 | 1 | 2 | 2 | 2 | 2 | 1 | 1 | 0 | 0 | 2 | 3 | 2 | 5 | 1 | 2 | 5 | 5 | 0 |
| Gaynes Hall | 1 | 2 | 3 | 5 | 0 | 4 | 2 | 3 | 3 | 3 | 3 | 3 | 2 | 2 | 2 | 7 | 2 | 3 | 1 | 8 | 3 | 3 | 3 |
| Glen Parva | 2 | 1 | 2 | 0 | 0 | 0 | 5 | 0 | 2 | 1 | 0 | 0 | 1 | 1 | 2 | 2 | 10 | 3 | 4 | 0 | 0 | 1 | 0 |
| Gloucester | 2 | 2 | 4 | 0 | 0 | 3 | 0 | 0 | 0 | 2 | 1 | 1 | 0 | 1 | 2 | 2 | 0 | 2 | 0 | 0 | 0 | 0 | 0 |
| Grendon/Spring Hill: Grendon | 0 | 0 | 0 | 0 | 0 | 0 | 0 | 0 | 0 | 0 | 0 | 0 | 0 | 1 | 0 | 0 | 2 | 3 | 2 | 4 | 4 | 2 | 0 |
| Grendon/Spring Hill: Spring Hill | 0 | 0 | 0 | 0 | 0 | 0 | 1 | 0 | 1 | 0 | 1 | 0 | 0 | 0 | 0 | 0 | 0 | 0 | 0 | 2 | 2 | 0 | 0 |
| Guys Marsh | 0 | 0 | 0 | 1 | 0 | 0 | 0 | 0 | 0 | 0 | 2 | 2 | 0 | 0 | 0 | 3 | 2 | 1 | 1 | 2 | 0 | 1 | 1 |
| Haslar | 0 | 0 | 0 | 0 | 0 | 0 | 0 | 0 | 0 | 0 | 0 | 0 | 0 | 0 | 0 | 0 | 0 | 0 | 0 | | | | |
| Haverigg | 0 | 0 | 0 | 0 | 0 | 0 | 0 | 0 | 0 | 0 | 0 | 0 | 0 | 0 | 0 | 0 | 0 | 0 | 0 | 0 | 0 | 0 | 0 |
| Hewell | | | | | | | | | | | 4 | 4 | 7 | 2 | 5 | 7 | 4 | 3 | 7 | 6 | 3 | 3 | 6 |
| Hewell: Blakenhurst | 2 | 1 | 3 | 3 | 5 | 4 | 2 | 3 | 2 | 2 | | | | | | | | | | | | | |
| Hewell: Brockhill | 1 | 2 | 2 | 0 | 0 | 2 | 5 | 0 | 3 | 5 | | | | | | | | | | | | | |
| Hewell: Hewell Grange | 0 | 0 | 0 | 1 | 0 | 0 | 0 | 0 | 0 | 0 | 2 | | | | | 4 | 4 | 1 | 4 | 7 | 4 | 4 | 2 |
| High Down | 0 | 1 | 0 | 1 | 2 | 1 | 1 | 0 | 2 | 4 | 1 | 1 | 4 | 0 | 4 | 3 | 1 | 1 | 4 | 1 | 1 | 4 | 2 |
| Highpoint | 1 | 0 | 0 | 0 | 0 | 0 | 0 | 3 | 3 | 0 | 1 | 1 | 1 | 1 | 4 | 2 | 3 | 1 | 3 | 2 | 3 | 2 | 0 |

LEGEND
"-" Not applicable - prison not in operation

(1) Caution should be used when comparing the number of deaths from one year to the next due to low numbers which are subject to fluctuation. This table should be read in conjunction with table 14 which outlines some of the major changes to prisons that will have affected numbers.

Data Sources and Quality
These figures are derived from the HMPPS Deaths in Prison Custody database. As classification of deaths may change following inquest or as new information emerges, numbers may change from time to time.

**Table 1.13: Deaths by prison[1], since 1999 England and Wales (continued on next page)**

| Prison |
| --- |
| Hindley |
| Hollesley Bay |
| Holloway |
| Holme House |
| Hull |
| Humber |
| Huntercombe |
| Isis |
| Isle of Wight |
| IoW: Albany |
| IoW: Camp Hill |
| IoW: Parkhurst |
| Kennet |
| Kingston |
| Kirkham |
| Kirklevington |
| Lancaster Castle |
| Lancaster Farms |
| Latchmere House |
| Leeds |
| Leicester |
| Lewes |
| Leyhill |
| Lincoln |
| Lindholme |
| Littlehey |
| Liverpool |
| Long Lartin |
| Low Newton |
| Lowdham Grange |
| Maidstone |
| Manchester |
| Medomsley |
| Moorland |
| Moorland Open (Hatfield) |
| Morton Hall |
| Mount |
| New Hall |
| North Sea Camp |
| Northallerton |
| Northeye |
| Northumberland |
| Northumberland: Acklington |
| Northumberland: Castington |
| Norwich |
| Nottingham |
| Oakwood |
| Onley |
| Oxford |
| Parc |
| Pentonville |
| Peterborough |
| Peterborough Male |
| Peterborough Female |
| Portland |
| Preston |
| Pucklechurch |
| Ranby |
| Reading |
| Risley |
| Rochester |
| Rye Hill |
| Send |
| Sheppey: Elmley |
| Sheppey: Standford Hill |
| Sheppey: Swaleside |
| Shepton Mallet |
| Shrewsbury |

LEGEND
"-" Not applicable - prison not in operation

(1) Caution should be used when comparing the number of deaths from one year to the next due to low numbers which are subject to fluctuation. This table should be read in conjunction with table 14 which outlines some of the major changes to prisons that will have affected numbers.

Data Sources and Quality
These figures are derived from the HMPPS Deaths in Prison Custody database. As classification of deaths may change following inquest or as new information emerges, numbers may change from time to time.

# Table 1.13: Deaths by prison[1], since 1999 England and Wales
(continued on next page)

| Prison | 1999 | 2000 | 2001 | 2002 | 2003 | 2004 | 2005 | 2006 | 2007 | 2008 | 2009 | 2010 | 2011 | 2012 | 2013 | 2014 | 2015 | 2016 | 2017 | 2018 | 2019 | 2020 | 2021 |
|---|---|---|---|---|---|---|---|---|---|---|---|---|---|---|---|---|---|---|---|---|---|---|---|
| Stafford | 3 | 1 | 0 | 0 | 2 | 2 | 0 | 3 | 0 | 0 | 1 | 2 | 1 | 2 | 1 | 2 | 1 | 5 | 6 | 4 | 3 | 6 | 8 |
| Stocken | 2 | 0 | 0 | 2 | 0 | 0 | 1 | 1 | 0 | 2 | 0 | 0 | 2 | 0 | 0 | 0 | 2 | 2 | 2 | 3 | 0 | 3 | 3 |
| Stoke Heath | 1 | 0 | 0 | 1 | 0 | 0 | 1 | 1 | 0 | 2 | 0 | 1 | 0 | 0 | 1 | 0 | 2 | 1 | 4 | 0 | 2 | 1 | 1 |
| Styal | 1 | 1 | 1 | 0 | 4 | 0 | 1 | 0 | 0 | 3 | 0 | 1 | 0 | 3 | 0 | 1 | 1 | 1 | 1 | 2 | 0 | 3 | 0 |
| Sudbury | 0 | 0 | 0 | 0 | 0 | 1 | 1 | 1 | 2 | 0 | 0 | 0 | 1 | 0 | 0 | 2 | 0 | 2 | 2 | 0 | 2 | 1 | 1 |
| Swansea | 0 | 0 | 1 | 0 | 3 | 1 | 0 | 0 | 0 | 2 | 2 | 0 | 0 | 3 | 0 | 0 | 1 | 3 | 0 | 1 | 0 | 3 | 0 |
| Swinfen Hall | 0 | 0 | 0 | 0 | 1 | 0 | 0 | 2 | 0 | 0 | 0 | 1 | 0 | 1 | 1 | 0 | 1 | 0 | 1 | 0 | 1 | 0 | 2 |
| Thameside | - | - | - | - | - | - | - | - | - | - | - | - | 0 | 2 | 2 | 2 | 1 | 0 | 1 | 3 | 0 | 4 | 0 |
| Thorn Cross | 0 | 0 | 0 | 0 | 0 | 0 | 0 | 0 | 0 | 2 | 1 | 0 | 0 | 3 | 2 | 3 | 0 | 5 | 1 | 0 | 0 | 1 | 0 |
| Usk/Prescoed | 0 | 0 | 1 | 0 | 0 | 1 | 0 | 0 | 0 | 0 | 0 | 1 | 0 | 0 | 1 | 0 | 0 | 1 | 0 | 0 | 0 | 1 | 2 |
| Usk/Prescoed: Usk | - | - | - | - | - | - | - | - | - | - | - | - | - | - | - | - | - | - | - | - | - | - | - |
| Verne | 5 | 0 | 1 | 1 | 0 | 3 | 1 | 2 | 2 | 0 | 2 | 3 | 1 | 0 | 2 | 3 | 2 | 0 | 2 | 2 | 0 | 1 | 1 |
| Wakefield | 4 | 1 | 5 | 2 | 6 | 4 | 2 | 6 | 1 | 3 | 0 | 1 | 0 | 7 | 7 | 4 | 0 | 11 | 8 | 8 | 12 | 2 | 3 |
| Wandsworth | 0 | 8 | 4 | 6 | 7 | 2 | 7 | 1 | 7 | 5 | 3 | 6 | 7 | 4 | 10 | 10 | 5 | 3 | 1 | 5 | 4 | 5 | 9 |
| Warren Hill | 0 | 0 | 0 | 3 | 4 | 7 | 0 | 0 | 0 | 0 | 0 | 0 | 2 | 0 | 1 | 0 | 3 | 0 | 0 | 1 | 1 | 0 | 3 |
| Wayland | 0 | 0 | 2 | 0 | 0 | 0 | 0 | 0 | 2 | 2 | 0 | 1 | 0 | 1 | 0 | 1 | 1 | 4 | 1 | 1 | 0 | 2 | 3 |
| Wealstun | 0 | 0 | 0 | 1 | 0 | 0 | 0 | 0 | 0 | 0 | 2 | 0 | 1 | 0 | 2 | 1 | 0 | 0 | 1 | 1 | 1 | 1 | 0 |
| Weare | 0 | 0 | 0 | 0 | 0 | 1 | 0 | 1 | 1 | - | - | - | - | - | - | - | - | - | - | - | - | - | - |
| Wellingborough | 0 | 0 | 0 | 1 | 1 | 0 | 0 | 0 | 0 | 0 | 0 | 0 | 0 | 1 | 1 | 0 | 0 | 0 | 0 | 0 | 0 | 0 | 0 |
| Werrington | 0 | 0 | 0 | 0 | 0 | 0 | 0 | 0 | 0 | 0 | 0 | 0 | 0 | 0 | 0 | 0 | 0 | 0 | 0 | 0 | 0 | 0 | 0 |
| Wetherby | 1 | 1 | 0 | 0 | 0 | 4 | 3 | 0 | 4 | 0 | 0 | 0 | 3 | 3 | 7 | 3 | 0 | 0 | 4 | 5 | 0 | 0 | 0 |
| Whatton | 1 | 0 | 0 | 2 | 4 | 2 | 0 | 6 | 2 | 4 | 3 | 0 | 2 | 5 | 1 | 4 | 0 | 0 | 0 | 3 | 5 | 9 | 4 |
| Whitemoor | 3 | 5 | 0 | 3 | 2 | 2 | 2 | 5 | 5 | 3 | 2 | 2 | 3 | 1 | 4 | 4 | 0 | 0 | 4 | 3 | 3 | 3 | 1 |
| Winchester | 1 | 0 | 2 | 2 | 0 | 0 | 0 | 3 | 0 | 0 | 0 | 3 | 2 | 0 | 4 | 0 | 2 | 2 | 2 | 1 | 1 | 0 | 0 |
| Wolds | 2 | 0 | 0 | 0 | 0 | 2 | 0 | 0 | 0 | 2 | 2 | 0 | 0 | 1 | 0 | 0 | 0 | 0 | 4 | 5 | 5 | 4 | 3 |
| Woodhill | 1 | 0 | 4 | 4 | 6 | 6 | 3 | 2 | 4 | 4 | 3 | 5 | 0 | 1 | 3 | 5 | 0 | 4 | 2 | 6 | 6 | 4 | 3 |
| Wormwood Scrubs | 2 | 2 | 3 | 3 | 4 | 4 | 4 | 5 | 5 | 4 | 6 | 3 | 0 | 6 | 6 | 3 | 5 | 3 | 3 | 2 | 4 | 2 | 11 |
| Wymott | 3 | 5 | 1 | 4 | 8 | 3 | 3 | 1 | 6 | 1 | 3 | 6 | 0 | 9 | 1 | 6 | 3 | 7 | 7 | 8 | 4 | 7 | 0 |
| ESCORT AREAS | 5 | 0 | 1 | 2 | 0 | 1 | 2 | 2 | 2 | 0 | 0 | 0 | 2 | 0 | 1 | 0 | 0 | 0 | 0 | 0 | 0 | 0 | 0 |
| **Total** | **149** | **146** | **142** | **164** | **183** | **208** | **175** | **153** | **185** | **166** | **169** | **198** | **192** | **192** | **215** | **243** | **257** | **354** | **295** | **325** | **300** | **318** | **371** |

*LEGEND*
*"-" Not applicable - prison not in operation*

*(1) Caution should be used when comparing the number of deaths from one year to the next due to low numbers which are subject to fluctuation. This table should be read in conjunction with table 14 which outlines some of the major changes to prisons that will have affected numbers.*

*Data Sources and Quality*
*These figures are derived from the HMPPS Deaths in Prison Custody database. As classification of deaths may change following inquest or as new information emerges, numbers may change from time to time.*

Table 1.14: Dates of prisons opening/closing from 1978 and major[1] re-roles of prisons from 1997 (continued on next page)

| PRISONS OPENING/CLOSING (1978-1996) | | | |
|---|---|---|---|
| Wymott | | 1979 | Opened |
| Warren Hill | | 1982 | Opened |
| Appleton Thorn | | c1982 | CLOSED (Site used for Thorn Cross) |
| Morton Hall | | 1985 | Opened |
| Stocken | | 1985 | Opened |
| Wayland | | 1985 | Opened |
| Thorn Cross | | 1985 | Opened |
| Lindholme | | 1985 | Opened |
| Mount | | 1987 | Opened |
| Full Sutton | | 1987 | Opened |
| Littlehey | | 1988 | Opened |
| Garth | | 1988 | Opened |
| Downview | | 1989 | Opened |
| Whitemoor | | 1991 | Opened |
| Belmarsh | | 1991 | Opened |
| Brinsford | | 1991 | Opened |
| Ashford | | 1991 | Amalgamated with Feltham |
| Northeye | | 1992 | CLOSED (Limited use from 1986) |
| Kirklevington | | 1992 | Opened |
| Holme House | | 1992 | Opened |
| Woodhill | | 1992 | Opened |
| Elmley | | 1992 | Opened |
| Wolds | | 1992 | Opened |
| Lancaster Farms | | 1993 | Opened |
| Blakenhurst | | 1993 | Opened |
| Doncaster | | 1994 | Opened |
| Wealstun | | 1995 | RENAMED (Formerly Thorp Arch and Rudgate) |
| Escort Areas | | 1995 | Escort areas begin to be reported separately |
| Pucklechurch | | 1996 | CLOSED |
| Oxford | | 1996 | CLOSED |
| Eastwood Park | | 1996 | Opened |

# Table 1.14: Dates of prisons opening/closing from 1978 and major1 re-roles of prisons from 1997

| PRISONS OPENING, CLOSING AND MAJOR RE-ROLES | | | |
|---|---|---|---|
| Parc | | 1997 | Opened |
| Altcourse | | 1997 | Opened |
| Foston Hall | July | 1997 | Changed from male to female prison |
| Weare | | 1997 | Opened |
| Lowdham Grange | | 1998 | Opened |
| Send | | 1998 | Changed from male to female prison |
| Aldington | | 1999 | Closed |
| Risley | April | 1999 | Changed from male and female prison to male only |
| Low Newton | September | 1999 | Changed from male and female prison to female only |
| Ashfield | | 1999 | Opened (On site of former HMP Pucklechurch) |
| Rye Hill | | 2001 | Opened |
| Dovegate | | 2001 | Opened |
| Downview | September | 2001 | Changed from male to female prison |
| Morton Hall | | 2001 | Changed from male to female prison |
| Haslar | April | 2002 | Changed from prison to Immigration Removal Centre |
| Dover | April | 2002 | Changed from prison to Immigration Removal Centre |
| Rochester | | 2002 | Changed from adult male prison to YOI |
| Buckley Hall | April | 2002 | Changed from male to female prison |
| Buckley Hall | September | 2005 | Changed from female to male prison |
| Wolds | | 2003 | Changed from male local to male training prison |
| Canterbury | | 2003 | Changed from male local to male training prison |
| Bronzefield | | 2004 | Opened |
| Winchester | April | 2004 | Changed from male and female prison to male only |
| Weare | March | 2005 | Closed |
| Peterborough | | 2005 | Opened |
| Durham | | 2005 | Changed Cat A /female Cat B local to male local |
| Edmunds Hill | January | 2005 | Changed from female to male prison |
| Buckley Hall | | 2005 | Changed from female to male prison |
| Onley | | 2005 | Changed from YOI to YOI + cat C training prison |
| Swinfen Hall | | 2005 | Changed from YOI to YOI + cat C training prison |
| Brockhill | July | 2006 | Changed from female to male prison |
| Bullwood Hall | June | 2006 | Changed from female to male prison |
| Kennet | | 2007 | Opened |
| Cookham Wood | | 2007 | Changed from female and 15-17 to male prison only |
| Hewell Cluster | | 2008 | Hewell, Blakenhurst and Brockhill merged |
| Bure | | 2009 | Opened |
| Isle of Wight | April | 2009 | Albany, Camp Hill and Parkhurst merged. Only reporting as Isle of Wight from 2013 |
| Isis | | 2010 | Opened |
| Northumberland | | 2011 | Acklington and Castington merged |
| Ashwell | March | 2011 | Closed |
| Highpoint | April | 2011 | Edmunds Hill merged with Highpoint |
| Morton Hall | June | 2011 | Changed from female prison to Immigration Removal Centre holding male only |
| Latchmere House | September | 2011 | Closed |
| Lancaster Castle | | 2011 | Closed |
| Thameside | March | 2012 | Opened |
| Oakwood | April | 2012 | Opened |
| Brixton | July | 2012 | Changed from Cat B to Cat C prison |
| Wellingborough | December | 2012 | Closed |
| Bullwood Hall | March | 2013 | Closed |
| Canterbury | March | 2013 | Closed |
| Gloucester | March | 2013 | Closed |
| Kingston | March | 2013 | Closed |
| Shepton Mallet | March | 2013 | Closed |
| Shrewsbury | March | 2013 | Closed |
| Ashfield | June | 2013 | Changed from YOI to Cat C sex offender prison |
| Downview | October | 2013 | Temporarily closed pending re-role from female to male prison |
| Verne | October | 2013 | Changed from Cat C prison to Immigration Removal Centre |
| Blundeston | December | 2013 | Closed |
| Dorchester | December | 2013 | Closed |
| Reading | December | 2013 | Closed |
| Northallerton | December | 2013 | Closed |
| Warren Hill | January | 2014 | Changed from YOI to male adult prison |
| Humber | April | 2014 | Everthorpe and Wolds merged |
| Blantyre House | March | 2015 | Temporarily closed |
| Haslar | April | 2015 | Decommissioned places for detainees. Temporarily closed pending re-role |
| Dover | October | 2015 | Decommissioned places for detainees. Temporarily closed pending re-role |
| Downview | May | 2016 | Reopened as a female prison |
| Holloway | June | 2016 | Closed |
| Kennet | December | 2016 | Closed |
| Berwyn | February | 2017 | Opened |
| Holme House | May | 2017 | Changed from local to Cat C prison |
| Glen Parva | June | 2017 | Closed |
| The Verne | December | 2017 | Decommissioned places for detainees. Temporarily closed pending re-role |
| Birmingham | July | 2019 | Changed from private to public |

(1) The list here shows years of opening/closing and major re-roles of establishments. However, prisons are constantly
evolving as new wings open and old ones close for refurbishment. Even a relatively minor change in a prison has the potential
to affect the distribution of safer custody risk, for example, the opening or closing of a special unit. When interpreting figures for
particular establishments there is no substitute for knowledge of local factors likely to affect the distribution of risk.
For additional information on prisons, see the latest HM Inspector of Prisons inspection reports which can be found here:
http://www.justice.gov.uk/publications/inspectorate-reports/hmi-prisons/prison-and-yoi

### 1.15. Notes on Data and Methodology

1) Revisions: Figures for earlier years have been revised throughout these tables where numbers and classifications have been revised following inquests or where further information are available. These changes affect a number of tables in this publication.

2) Prison population: figures are averaged across 12 months. See MoJ's Offender Management annual statistics Table A1.2.

3) Data Sources and Quality: these figures are derived from the HMPPS Deaths in Prison Custody database. As classification of deaths may change following inquest or as new information emerges, numbers may change from time to time.

4) Deaths in prison custody include all deaths of prisoners arising from incidents during prison custody. These include deaths of prisoners while released on temporary license (ROTL) for medical reasons but exclude other types of ROTL where the state has less direct responsibility. In recent years, approximately half of the overall deaths in prison custody occur in hospitals or hospices (see Table 4).

5) Classification of deaths: Apparent cause of death is based on the HMPPS classification of deaths in prison custody. Self-inflicted deaths includes a wider range of deaths than suicides. Similarly the homicide category includes a wider range of deaths than murder. When comparing figures with other sources it is important to determine whether the narrower suicide or broader self-inflicted deaths approach is in use.

6) Time in current prison: '3 months' is defined as 90 days, '3 to 6 months' is defined as 91 to 182 days. Care needs to be taken when interpreting numbers of deaths in the early days of custody as number of deaths in precise 24 hours time slots is not known accurately due to uncertainty in the exact time of death

7) Ethnicity is based on self-reporting by prisoners and has not been independently validated.

8) Nationality is based on self-reporting by prisoners and has not been independently validated.

### Revisions

The deaths data tool which is published quarterly has been expanded to include age of the prisoner. The deaths data tool has therefore become the most up-to-date source for information on deaths by age, and the tables giving an age breakdown have therefore been removed from the annual deaths tables. Tables 1.3, 1.6 and 1.15 from the historic annual deaths tables included breakdowns of deaths by age now available from the tool, and have been removed from the annual deaths tables from this release.

In addition, three tables on the classification of deaths have been consolidated into Table 1.1, which now includes a breakdown by gender and death rates due to 'Other' causes. This will reduce duplication and make the presentation of this data more consistent with the Summary death statistics (Table 2) in the other quarterly Safety in Custody publications. Tables 1.1, 1.2 and 1.5 from the historic annual deaths tables included breakdowns of deaths by classification and gender, and have been removed from the annual deaths tables from this release. Table 1.1 in the new list of tables includes a detailed breakdown by gender and classification.

# 7.4 PRISON SERVICE INSTRUCTIONS, ORDERS & MINISTRY OF JUSTICE POLICY FRAMEWORKS AS AT 1ST AUGUST 2022

In April 2017, when the National Offender Management Service (NOMS) became HM Prison and Probation Service (HMPPS), one consequence of this was the transfer of policy-making powers from NOMS to the Ministry of Justice (MOJ).

Prior to 2017 prisons had been administered by way of Prison Service Instructions and Orders (PSIs and PSOs), however following the transfer of policy making powers to the MOJ the Ministry is moving away from issuing Instructions and Orders and is, instead, issuing Policy Frameworks. Below we list those PSIs, PSOs and Policy Frameworks which are currently in force at 17th August 2022. Those which have been cancelled, replaced or made obsolete are not shown, and some of these documents, particularly those relating to the National Security Framework or Incident Management, are classified as Restricted and are not publicly available.

All publicly available PSI's, PSO's and Policy Frameworks are available on the MOJ web site... but...

*A note of caution.*

*Documents shown on the MOJ web site, that purport to be 'in force' may not be - there is a considerable lag, up to a year or more in some cases, before cancelled documents are removed from the MOJ web site, or amended versions of current in force documents are uploaded.*

*Whereas the **Prisons Org UK** web site, available to Members by subscription, is constantly updated - visit www.prisons.org.uk and learn more about the benefits of Membership - subscriptions start at just £4.99 a month, and you can cancel at any time.*

## POLICY FRAMEWORKS

**A-Z List of current Policy Frameworks correct to 1st August 2022 -** *a summary of each framework follows the list.*

Access to Digital Evidence
Bail Accommodation and Support Service (BASS)
Building Bridges: A Positive Behaviour Framework for the Children and Young People Secure Estate
Business Continuity
Care and Management of Individuals who are Transgender
Case Transfer
Certified Prisoner Accommodation
Counter Corruption and Reporting Wrongdoing
Domestic Abuse
Early Release on Compassionate Grounds
Early & Late Release for Detention & Training Orders
Enforcement of Community Orders, Suspended Sentence Orders and Post-sentence supervision
Enhanced Behaviour Monitoring
Financial Investigation Unit

Generic Parole Process
Handling of Sensitive Information, Including Information Provided by Victims, for the Purpose of Parole Board Reviews
HMPPS Child Safeguarding
HMPPS (Interim) Compartmentalisation and Protective Isolation
HMPPS Finance Manual
HMPPS Flu Pandemic – interim
HMPPS Health and Safety Arrangements for the Management of Workplace Transport
HMPPS Investigatory Powers
Home Detention Curfew
Home Visits
Homelessness Reduction Act: Duty to Refer
Implementation & use of OASys Sexual reoffending Predictor (OSP)
Incentives
Information Requests
Information Security
Information Sharing
Intelligence Collection Management & Dissemination
Licence Conditions
Manage the Custodial Sentence
Management of Security at Visits (Closed Estate)
Management of Security at Visits (Open Estate)
Managing Extremism and Terrorism Amongst Offenders in Custody and the Community
Managing Parole Eligible Offenders on Licence
Minimising and Managing Use of Separation and Isolation in the Children and Young People Secure Estate
Multi-Agency Lifer Risk Assessment Panel (MALRAP)
Notification & Review Procedures for Serious Further Offences
Occupational Health and Employee Assistance Programmes
Parole Board Oral Hearing Administration & Attendance
Person Escort Record
Polygraph Examinations
Post Incident Care Policy Framework
Post Sentence Supervision Requirements
Power to detain dangerous standard determinate sentence prisoners
"Pregnancy, Mother & Baby Units (MBUs), & Maternal Separation from Children up to the Age of Two in Women's Prisons"
Prison Dogs
Prison Education & Library Services for adult prisons in England
Prisoner Complaints
Probation Service Management of MAPPA Level 1 Cases

Probation Service Management of Young Adults Progression Regime

Recall, Review & Re-release of recalled Prisoners

Release on Temporary Licence

Reporting and reviewing deaths under probation supervision

Restrictions on Prisoner Voting

Secure Social Video Calling

Security Categorisation

Sentence Calculation: determinate sentenced prisoners

Separation Centres Policy Framework

Serious and Organised Crime

Smoke Free

Strengthening Prisoners Family Ties

Sustainable Operations

Transition of Young People from the Children and Young People Secure Estate to Adult Custody

Travel and Transfer on Licence and Post Sentence Supervision Outside of England and Wales

Use of CCTV (Overt Closed-Circuit Television system)

Use of Narcotics Detection Equipment on Correspondence

Use of X-Ray Body Scanners (Adult Male Prisons)

Women's Estate Case Advice & Supporting Panel (WECASP)

Women's Policy Framework

### Summaries

### Access to Digital Evidence (A2DE)

This Policy Framework explains the process for prison staff around the provision of Access to Digital Evidence Equipment (A2DE).

Policy name: *Access to Digital Evidence Policy Framework*

Re-issue Date: 13 March 2019

Implementation Date: 21 December 2018

This Policy Framework sets out the process for Governors / Directors in providing prisoners with access to digital equipment (Information Technology equipment), where that equipment is required for prisoners to view electronic disclosure by the Crown as evidence for the prosecution in any legal case. Equipment provided for these purposes is termed Access to Digital Evidence Equipment (A2DE), previously called Access to Justice Equipment (A2J).

### Bail Accommodation and Support Service (BASS)

Rules and referral instructions to prison and probation staff on how to refer to the Bail, Accommodation and Support Service (BASS).

Policy name: *Bail Accommodation and Support Service (BASS) Policy Framework*

Issue Date: 21 December 2018

Implementation Date: 18 June 2018

Replaces the following documents (e.g. PSIs, PSOs, Custodial Service Specs) which are hereby cancelled:

• *PSI 25/2013; PI 10/2013 Accommodation and Support Service for Bail and HDC*

• *PSI 17/2011 Bail and Accommodation Support Service Specification Implementation*

• *Ministry of Justice Service Specification for Bail Accommodation and Support Service vP3.2*

The Bail Accommodation and Support Service (BASS) provides support to courts and prisons in achieving the best use of custody through the provision of suitable accommodation in a variety of locations in England and Wales, to following groups in the following priority:

1. Bailees;

2. Individuals subject to Home Detention Curfew;

3. Individuals referred because of risk to Recall to prison due to loss of accommodation; or those who could be re-released following recall due to lack of accommodation.

4. Individuals subject to Intensive Community Orders with a residence requirement;

5. Individuals referred upon release (part of the ALC). Governors must ensure that any new local policies that they develop because of this Policy Framework are compliant with relevant legislation, including the Public-Sector Equality Duty (Equality Act, 2010).

### Building Bridges: A Positive Behaviour Framework for the Children and Young People Secure Estate

Policy name: *Building Bridges: A Positive Behaviour Framework for the Children and Young People Secure Estate*

Re-issue Date: 27 January 2020

Implementation Date: 01 April 2019

Replaces the following documents:

*The Youth Justice Board (YJB) Behaviour Management Code of Practice 2012*

Introduces amendments to the following documents: *Relative sections of PSI 08/2012 Care and Management of Young People, which remain active in Wales but are hereby cancelled in England. These sections are as follows:*

*Sections 2.14 to 2.16, 2.18, 2.20 and 2.23: Promoting and Maintaining Good Behaviour*

*Sections 2.24 to 2.29: Managing Challenging Behaviour*

*Sections 5.14 to 5.17: Offending Behaviour Interventions*

*Note: The Incentives Policy Framework (IPF) and PSI 05/2018 Prisoner Discipline Procedures Adjudications remain in place for YOIs.*

Building Bridges has been commissioned and agreed by the YCS Behaviour Management Steering Group, which includes representation from the Youth Custody Service (YCS), the Youth Justice Board (YJB), NHS England, Medway STC, MTCNovo, GEO/Amey, G4S, the Secure Accommodation Network (SCH's), MOJ Commissioning, HMI Prisons, Ofsted, HMPS Effective Practice, Care and Quality Commission, The Association of Youth Offending Team Managers and Unlocked Org.

The population of children and young people in custody has reduced significantly over the last five years, resulting in a proportionate increase in those convicted of more serious offending. These children and young people are likely to have more complex needs and to be suffering the harmful effects of adverse childhood experiences (ACE) or trauma in one or more forms

Building Bridges has been informed by:

• The Framework for Integrated Care (SECURE STAIRS), which is being led by NHS England and delivered in partnership with Department of Education, Youth Justice Board, Her Majesty's Prison and Probation Service, Youth Custody Service and the Ministry of Justice. This is introducing trauma-informed care which is formulation-driven, evidence-based and takes a whole-systems approaches to supporting children and young people within the Children and Young People Secure Estate (CYPSE) One of the core principles of the SECURE STAIRS framework is that the day-to-day staff are at the centre of the intervention, recognising that they have a pivotal role in developing the environmental and relational conditions that can manage risk, promote positive behaviour and safety (relational security) and create change with the children and young people. As such, the environment and the relationships within it are proposed as the primary agents of change for children and young people within secure settings. Additionally, the framework explicitly acknowledges and addresses the day-to-day stresses experienced by primary caregivers, and the need to support them in their role with children and young people. The creation and maintenance of a trauma-informed therapeutic milieu is therefore a critical and essential task in its own right.

• The psychologically informed Public-Sector Youth Custody Service and NHS England Behavioural Management Strategy.

• Feedback from a group of young people in Wetherby Young Offenders Institute (YOI) and the YJB's Youth Advisory Panel

### Care and Management of Individuals who are Transgender

This framework replaces and builds on Prison Service Instruction (PSI) 17/2016: The care and management of transgender offenders, published in 2016.

The aim of this Policy Framework is to detail the minimum mandatory requirements which are needed to care for and manage individuals who are transgender.

In doing this there is an emphasis on adopting a balanced approach which considers the safety and needs of those who are transgender whilst ensuring that decisions do not have any negative impact on the wellbeing and safety of others, particularly in custodial settings such as in women's prisons.

The framework supports Governors, National Probation Directors and all providers of services on behalf of HM Prison & Probation Service (HMPPS) to ensure they are compliant with the relevant legislation including the Public Sector Equality Duty (Equality Act 2010).

### Case Transfer

Policy name: *Policy Framework for Case Transfers (including transfer as a result of escalation in risk of serious harm) for offenders subject to statutory supervision either pre-release or in the community*

Issue Date: 26 June 2021

Implementation Date: 26 June 2021

Replaces the following documents (e.g. PSIs, PSOs, Custodial Service Specs) which are hereby cancelled:

• *PI 57/2014 - Process for Community Rehabilitation Companies to refer cases in custody or the community to National Probation Service for Risk Review, including escalation.*

• *PI 07/2014 - Case Transfers for Offenders Subject to Statutory Supervision Either Pre-Release From Custody or Whilst Completing an Order Or Licence*

This policy framework (PF) sets out the arrangements for:

• The transfer of supervised individuals due to a geographical move, whether temporary or permanent, including between Probation Delivery Units within the same region.

• Transfer of cases between officers and teams (including National Security Division cases) as a result of an assessed escalation in risk of serious harm. It replaces the previous probation instructions relating to Case Transfer (PI 07/2014) and Risk Escalation and Risk Review (PI 57/2014).

Detailed information in relation to transfers in and out of jurisdiction (e.g. Scotland) can be found in Annex A of this document.

Youth to adult transition is out of scope for this framework, however national protocol and links to relevant guidance can be found in Annex B.

This document aims to ensure that there are key principles to inform decision-making; standard processes to give effect to decisions; and a consistent interpretation of the case transfer framework; and a more collaborative approach supporting supervised individuals when there is a change of responsible officer.

For the purposes of this PF the term 'Responsible Officer' (RO) is used to refer to a probation practitioner allocated to a named individual to be managed on a community sentence (as per sections 213 and 299 of the Sentencing Act 2020). For those in custody, who will be managed through Offender Management in Custody

(OMiC), distinction is made between OMiC roles (Prison Offender Manager - POM / Community Offender Manager - COM) to align with their agreed roles and responsibilities.

From 26 June 2021, all RO's will be part of the unified Probation Service. However, existing NPS and CRC team structures and operating models will in many respects continue for a transitional period after this date. This framework uses the terms 'legacy CRC' and 'legacy NPS' when referring to these structures and ways of working.

### Certified Prisoner Accommodation

Certification is a legal requirement under Section 14 of the Prison Act 1952 that must be completed for all prison and young offender institution accommodation before it can be used to confine prisoners overnight.

Certification is the responsibility of the Prison Group Director (for Public Sector Prisons), Executive Directors (for Wales and YCS), Deputy Director (for Long Term High Security) or Head of Custodial Contracts (for contracted prisons) and cannot be delegated.

8 This PF sets out the minimum requirements for certification and the mandatory actions for Authorising Directors and Governors to ensure that all accommodation they are responsible for is properly certified. The higher technical specifications to which all modern accommodation will be built can be accessed by emailing moj_ed_technicalstandards@justice.gov.uk.

### Counter corruption and reporting wrongdoing

Rules and guidance for prison and probation staff on tackling wrongdoing and corruption.

Policy Name: *Counter corruption and reporting wrongdoing policy framework*

Re-Issue Date: 26th June 2021

Implementation Date: 26th June 2021

Replaces the following documents (e.g. PSIs, PSOs, Custodial Service Specs) which are hereby cancelled:

- *PSI 01/2016 Corruption prevention – how to identify, report and manage staff corruption in prisons and headquarters*
- *PI 05/2016 – Corruption prevention – how to identify, report and manage staff corruption in the Probation Service*
- *PSI 21/2013 - Reporting wrongdoing*
- *PI 41/2014 – Probation Service reporting wrongdoing*

HMPPS' efforts to tackle corruption are integral to delivering a safe and secure prison and probation service – for staff, supervised individuals and the community. Corruption facilitates the flow of drugs, mobile phones and other illicit items into prisons. These, in turn, fuel violence, debt and the illicit economy. Corruption puts the safety of supervised individuals, staff and visitors to prisons at risk; damages the reputation of the organisation; reduces workforce morale and performance; and compromises confidence in HMPPS' ability to run safe and secure prison and probation services that protect the public and rehabilitate supervised individuals.

We have a clear strategy for tackling corruption and a plan to continually improve our approach over time. Our ambition is to create an organisation that is resilient to the threat of corruption, can protect its hard-working staff, prevent any who might be manipulated into corruption and target those engaging in corrupt behaviour through four strategic approaches:

• PROTECT against corruption by understanding threats, having robust policies, processes and procedures in place and holding ourselves to account

• PREVENT staff from engaging in corruption by recruiting a resilient workforce, strengthening capability and professional integrity and managing corruption risks

• PURSUE and punish those involved in corruption through disciplinary and criminal justice outcomes

• PREPARE for the consequences of corrupt behaviour and support teams where corruption has occurred

HMPPS oversees a proud and professional prison and probation service. We drive a culture of professional standards and are committed to addressing wrongdoing sensitively and fairly, and at the earliest stage, preventing it escalating into corruption. Where corruption does take place however, HMPPS will provide a robust response. This Policy Framework sets out a range of activities that will help prevent corruption before it takes place and outlines a clear process for pursuing corrupt staff to appropriate HR and criminal justice outcomes.

Staff at all grades, and in all roles, have a responsibility to protect the resilience of this service against wrongdoing and corruption. While this Policy Framework sets out the important minimum mandatory actions for staff, it is vital that staff behave professionally in everything they do. In particular, staff must consciously maintain professional boundaries as they develop supportive and rehabilitative relationships with supervised individuals, and speak confidently to line managers or local counter corruption staff if they are concerned they have overstepped the line.

The Counter Corruption Unit (CCU) also plays a key role in supporting staff, managers and leaders to tackle corruption throughout the organisation. It is responsible for HMPPS' counter corruption policy and procedures, leading counter corruption capability raising, and most fundamentally, supporting the organisation to pursue corruption where it takes place. This document also sets out the mandatory actions for the CCU at regional and national level. This Policy Framework clarifies:

• the definition of corruption and how it can manifest in prison and probation services;

• the mandatory processes and procedures to tackle corruption;

• the remit and responsibilities of staff and teams with dedicated counter corruption roles;

• the relationship between counter corruption processes and relevant HR procedures and contract management; and

• the relationship between counter corruption processes, procedures and other policies and requirements (e.g. safeguarding, Intelligence Collection, Management and Dissemination, Data Protection, Anti-Fraud Policy).

As a result of this Policy Framework, staff should understand how they support the delivery of HMPPS' protect, prevent, pursue and prepare objectives. Staff should understand:

• the importance of behaving professionally and ethically in everything we do;

• what corruption is, how it can happen, how to prevent it taking place;

• what to do if they suspect wrongdoing and corruption, including what and how to self-disclose and / or report other concerns;

• the roles of local counter corruption staff, the CCU and its regional teams to tackle corruption;

• the new process for investigating corrupt activity including case management and prioritisation and how to effectively work in partnership with law enforcement agencies; and,

• what steps must be taken to help manage known corruptors.

This Policy Framework is supported by the Counter Corruption Handbook and a Memorandum of Understanding (MoU) between HMPPS and the National Police Chiefs' Council regarding corruption in prisons and probation, which are available to staff counter corruption roles only. The Handbook provides guidance and best practice and its use is encouraged, although not mandated. The MoU outlines the agreed ways of working with the police on corruption matters. This Policy Framework, the Counter Corruption Handbook and the MoU will be regularly reviewed and updated to inform operational responses, training and communications relating to counter corruption activity in prison and probation services.

It is likely that staff involved in investigating suspected corruption may need to work with intelligence, and therefore must adhere to the Intelligence Collection, Analysis and Dissemination Policy Framework.

**Domestic Abuse**

Policy name: *Domestic Abuse Policy Framework* Re-Issue Date: 2 April 2020
Implementation Date: 2 March 2020
Associated documents:
*Risk of Serious Harm Guidance 2020*
*HMPPS Interventions Referral and Suitability Guide (May 2019)*
*NOMS Domestic Abuse Guidance (August 2016)*
*Women's Policy Framework*
*PSI 18/2016 - Public Protection Manual P*
*SI 04/2016 - The Interception of Communications in Prisons and Security Measures*
*PI 04/2016 - Determining Pre-Sentence Reports - Sentencing within the new framework*
*PI 19/2015 - Health and safety arrangements for the risk management of home / community visits*
*PI 09/2015 - Licence Conditions and Temporary Travel Abroad*
*PI 48/2014 - Victim Contact Scheme Guidance Manual*
*AI 14/2014, PI 13/2014, PSI 19/2014 - Sentence Planning*
*Manage the Custodial Sentence Policy Framework*
*PI 05/2014, PSI 14 2014 - Case Allocation*
*PI 57/2014, PSI 41/2014 - Process for Community Rehabilitation Companies to refer cases in custody or the community to National Probation Service for Risk Review, including escalation Home Detention Curfew (HDC) Policy Framework*
*Release on Temporary Licence (ROTL) Policy Framework*
*CRI 019 - Registrations*

This policy framework (PF) sets out the arrangements for working with people whose convictions or behaviours include domestic abuse. It also recognises there are individuals in our care and supervision who have been victims of domestic abuse. Her Majesty's Prison and Probation Service (HMPPS) has a key role to play in tackling domestic abuse by bringing together prisons, probation providers and partners as part of its wider role of protecting the public and reducing re-offending.

The purpose of this policy framework is to set out HMPPS' commitment to reducing domestic abuse-related re-offending and the risk of serious harm associated with it, to provide interventions to support rehabilitation and ensure staff at all levels understand what is expected of them, and to ensure that action is taken to safeguard adults and children at risk.

In order to support the ambitions of the cross government Ending Violence Against Women and Girls (VAWG) strategy, this PF has been developed to address the work in prisons and in the community. The term Responsible Officer (RO) is used to refer to staff allocated a named individual to be managed on a community sentence. For those in custody who will be managed through OMiC distinction is made between OMiC roles (Prison Offender Manager - POM /

Community Offender Manager - COM) to align with their agreed roles and responsibilities. In this document the term Governor also applies to Directors of Contracted Prisons.

### Early Release on Compassionate Grounds

This Policy Framework sets out the criteria and process for making an application for Early Release on Compassionate Grounds (ERCG) for determinate and indeterminate sentenced prisoners, children and young people.

The Policy Framework combines and replaces Chapter 12 in PSO4700 and Chapter 12 in PSO6000. It covers:

The eligibility criteria for the scheme

Guidance for applications due to health/social care needs

Guidance for non-medical related applications

Refusal/approval of an application

Release and recall processes

Application forms

### Early and Late Release for Detention and Training Orders

This Policy Framework sets out rules and guidance for staff involved in the administration of the early and late release process for children serving Detention and Training Orders of 8 months or more.

The aim of the scheme is to encourage and motivate children from the point of entry into custody and throughout their custodial journey to engage meaningfully with their resettlement plans and shift their identity from pro offending to pro social. Early release supports effective resettlement planning involving education, training and supervision arrangements upon release so that children are given the best chance of succeeding with the scheme and sustaining the positive progress made in custody when they return to their communities.

In this Framework, Resettlement Practitioners/ caseworkers are encouraged to fully embrace the key principles of procedural justice which has been built into the administration of the entire process to ensure a fair, consistent and transparent approach to assessing release applications.

### Enforcement of Community Orders, Suspended Sentence Orders and Post-sentence supervision

Policy name: Enforcement of Community Orders, Suspended Sentence Orders and Post-sentence supervision Policy Framework

Re-Issue Date: 26 June 2021

Implementation Date: 26 June 2021

Replaces the following documents which are hereby cancelled:

• *PI 24/2014 – Enforcement of the Post-Sentence Supervision Requirements*

• *PI 06/2014 – Enforcement of Community Orders and Suspended Sentence Orders*

Effective enforcement of any sentence of the court is essential in ensuring sentencer and public confidence in the management of individuals subject to Probation supervision. This policy framework sets out the mandatory actions for PS, and EM providers to ensure that the enforcement of Community Orders (COs), Suspended Sentence Orders (SSOs) and Post-sentence supervision (PSS) is both appropriate and timely.

### Enhanced behaviour monitoring

Rules and guidance for prison and probation staff on the Enhanced Behaviour Monitoring scheme.

Policy Name: *Enhanced Behaviour Monitoring (EBM) Policy Framework*

Issue Date: 16 May 2019

Implementation Date: 16 May 2019

Replaces the following documents which are hereby cancelled:

*PSI 24/2015/ PI 16/2015 Enhanced Behaviour Monitoring (EBM)*

Enhanced Behaviour Monitoring (EBM) provides a mechanism for giving assurance that ongoing risks (e.g. of harm; re-offending, or abscond) are being appropriately identified and managed within open prisons and with relevant residents of women's prisons, and subsequently as individuals are permitted to spend unescorted periods of time away from the prison in the community whilst Released on Temporary Licence (ROTL).

### Financial Investigation Unit

No information available to the public.

### Generic Parole Process

Policy name: *Generic Parole Process Policy Framework*

Re-issue Date: 13 May 2021

Implementation Date: 27 January 2020

Replaces the following documents:

*PSI 22/2015 - PI 2015-14 – AI 11/2015 - Generic Parole Process for Indeterminate and determinate sentenced prisoners (GPP)*

*PSI 18/2012 – PI 11/2012 - AI 05/2012 - Tariff Expired Removal Scheme (TERS)*

*PSI 12/2016 – Writing Healthcare Reports for The Parole and Recall Process*

*PSI 36/2013 – Transcripts of Sentencing Remarks (Court Transcripts)*

The purpose of this Framework is to set out the mandatory actions which the National Probation Service, Youth Offending Team and Prison establishments must complete for all parole eligible prisoners to ensure the timely and efficient completion of the Generic Parole Process (GPP).

## Handling of Sensitive Information, Including Information Provided by Victims, for the Purpose of Parole Board Reviews

This policy framework sets out the mandatory requirements and guidance for all HMPPS staff involved in handling sensitive information for parole eligible and recalled prisoners' Parole Board reviews. The framework provides clear requirements and guidance for staff to enable the correct handling of sensitive information to ensure that the Parole Board is provided with all relevant risk-related information, even where the material is too sensitive to disclose to the prisoner. This is vital to the parole and recall processes.

The framework provides requirements for the process of applying to the Parole Board for victim personal statements (VPS) to be withheld from the prisoner, if requested by the victim, allowing victims and/or the victim's family to provide information to the Parole Board without having to reveal personal information to the offender. Getting this process right is of the utmost importance to ensure transparency, provide the Parole Board with relevant risk information, while maintaining information security and allowing victims to provide their views to the Parole Board.

## HMPPS Child Safeguarding

This Policy Framework (PF) also includes a comprehensive guidance section to support staff in their work to promote the safety and wellbeing of children.

It sets out how Her Majesty's Prison and Probation Service (HMPPS) will deliver on our statutory responsibility to safeguard and promote the welfare of children, as set out in section 11 of the Children Act 2004, as amended by the Children and Social Work Act 2017, and, the Social Services and Wellbeing (Wales) Act 2014. This PF provides operational staff and strategic leads with a summary of what they are required to do as part of their safeguarding responsibilities and includes a guidance section which provides general information and advice on child safeguarding expected practice. This document applies to all permanent and temporary employees and contractors. This PF does not apply to HMPPS staff who work directly with children within the Youth Custody Service.

This policy will be reviewed annually.

## HMPPS (Interim) Compartmentalisation and Protective Isolation

This policy framework provides for the isolation in custody of people who have or may have a disease which presents a significant risk to human health. It sets requirements for their safe and supportive management.

This is an interim Policy Framework. It is subject to review and revision and feedback on its application is welcome.

The Policy should be read in conjunction with the supporting HMPPS operational guidance and the Public Health guidance for prisons and places of detention.

Separate guidance is provided for Secure Children's Homes.

## HMPPS Finance Manual – update 31st Oct 2019

Policy name: *HMPPS Finance Manual*
Re-issue Date: 3 November 2020
Implementation Date: 1 October 2019
Replaces the following documents
*PSI 2013-37 / AI 2013-15 - NOMS Finance Manual*
This Finance Policy Manual is intended as a single central source for financial policies and procedures within Her Majesty's Prison and Probation Service (HMPPS). It applies the guidance contained within HM Treasury's (HMT) Managing Public Money and reminds staff of the need for propriety and regularity in the control of all government expenditure and income.

## HMPPS Flu Pandemic – interim

No information available to the public.

## HMPPS Health and Safety Arrangements for the Management of Workplace Transport

This particular set of arrangements bring together and update a range of national guidance on the management of the risk of workplace transport in public sector prisons and establish the standards and good practice elements to be achieved at local level in managing this significant risk.

They do not extend to the management of driver and vehicle safety where driving is being undertaken on public roads by HMPPS employees for work purposes (known as Occupational Road Risk). They do not extend to unpowered vehicles.

## HMPPS Investigatory Powers

Policy name: *Investigatory Powers*
Issue Date: 1st June 2021
Implementation Date: 1st June 2021
Replaces the following documents which are hereby cancelled:
*PSI 22-2012 Covert Surveillance;*
*PSI 23-2012 CHIS;*
*PSI 04-2014 Acquisition of Communications Data;*
Introduces amendments to the following documents: Service Specifications altered as noted in Appendix 5.2.
*Purpose of Policy Framework*
The policy will ensure consistent application of powers available to HMPPS under the

Regulation of Investigatory Powers Act 2000 (RIPA) and the Investigatory Powers Act 2016 (IPA).

*Guidance and additional instructions for Operational staff*

Detailed guidance for operational staff working in any areas affected by this Policy Framework will be provided via a restricted Operations Manual which has been restricted in order to protect HMPPS tactics from exposure. This will be provided to relevant staff by the National Intelligence Unit.

*Legal basis for Investigatory Powers within HMPPS*

HMPPS has powers under the Acts listed above and the associated Codes of Practice, to enable activity to be conducted aimed at the prevention and detection of crime, preserving order and discipline in establishments and management of risk and prevention of harm as well as any duty or responsibility arising from common law or other legislation. Specific to this Policy Framework are the powers to:

• Acquire Communications Data – to identify illicit communications devices being used illegally inside prisons or in contravention of licence conditions, and to help identify criminal activities in prisons through the illicit use of mobile phones.

• Conduct Surveillance – to combat criminality within prisons, maintain order and discipline, or to support the gathering of information and intelligence for the purposes of pursuing a prosecution/adjudication.

• Deploy Covert Human Intelligence Sources (CHIS) – To gather intelligence and information to assist in the detection and prevention of crime, maintain good order and discipline, and reduce the risk of harm to vulnerable people. The power to intercept communications under s49 of the Investigatory Powers Act 2016 is covered by PSI 04/2016 – Interception of Communications and Security Measures in Prisons.

Assurance and Governance for Investigatory Powers within HMPPS

Each of the powers available to HMPPS is overseen by a Senior Responsible Owner (SRO), who are supported in this role by a function which provides the central retrievable record.

• The Senior Responsible Owner for powers under RIPA 2000 is the Director of Security, Order and Counter Terrorism (SOCT) or other nominated Senior Civil Servant. The central record function is provided by the National Intelligence Unit.

• The Senior Responsible Owner for Communications Data and Internet and Intelligence Investigations is the Deputy Director (National Security Group) of SOCT, or other nominated Senior Civil Servant or delegated official. The central record function is provided by the National Intelligence Unit.

**Home detention curfew**

Policy name: *Home Detention Curfew (HDC) Policy Framework*

Re-issue Date: 26th June 2021

Implementation Date: 26th June 2021

Replaces the following documents which are hereby cancelled:

*PSO 6700 Home Detention Curfew.*

*PSI & PI 01/2018 Home Detention Curfew Assessment Process.*

*PSI 43/2012 Home Detention Curfew,*

*PSI 17/2008 Amendments to PSO 6000; PSO 6300 and PSO 6650, in relation to calculation of release dates for DCR prisoners.*

*PSI 41/2008 Introduction of Cross Border Arrangements between England and Wales and Scotland for Home Detention Curfew purposes.*

*PSI 49/2007 Bail and HDC Support Services.*

*PSI 31/2006 Impact of CJA 2003 & consolidation of guidance (and guidance on presumed unsuitability).*

*PSI 31/2003 Changes to HDC (guidance on presumed unsuitability).*

*PC 82/1998 HDC – Accommodation and outstanding HDC issues.*

*PC 44/1998 HDC: The Role of the Probation Service Policy Statement: Safeguarding and Promoting the Welfare of Children; Probation Service Policy Statement: Safeguarding Adults at Risk.*

The Home Detention Curfew (HDC) scheme provides a managed transition from prison to community for supervised individuals serving short sentences. Release on HDC should be a normal part of a sentence for most eligible supervised individuals, and refusal of HDC for those eligible and not presumed unsuitable for release the exception.

Since 1999, a number of prison and probation instructions have been published in relation to the HDC process. The aim of this Policy Framework is to consolidate those instructions into one place and therefore completely replace all of the previous instructions, as listed above. The requirements and approach to HDC therefore remain largely the same but the following changes are highlighted:

• Decisions on HDC may now be taken by Directors of Contracted Prisons, the Controller will continue to monitor the Director's compliance in this area.

• Decisions around presumed unsuitable supervised individuals remain with the Governor, but there is no longer any requirement to consult or notify the HDC Policy team.

• Offenders sentenced to 4 years or more imprisonment by an overseas court but who have less than 4 years to serve after repatriation to the UK are presumed unsuitable for release on HDC.

### Home Visits

This policy framework forms part of the arrangements to help minimise risks to the health and safety of employees undertaking home visits in accordance with the Probation Service's duty to ensure the safety of its employees so far as reasonably practicable.

It aims to ensure that there is clear guidance to inform decision-making and a consistent interpretation of the instruction to support staff in the undertaking of a home visit to people on probation in the community - both subject to licence conditions and community orders.

It is intended for operational probation practitioners who undertake home visits to people on probation.

This policy framework sets out the mandatory requirements, instructions and guidance in relation to the undertaking of home visits and refers readers to other relevant policies and practice guidance to assist them with the undertaking of the most effective home visits.

### Homelessness Reduction Act: Duty to refer

Policy name: *The Homelessness Reduction Act 2017: Duty to Refer (England only)*

Issue Date: 08 April 2021

Implementation Date: 1 July 2021

Since 1st October 2018 specified public sector bodies, including all Prisons and Probation services, in England have been subject to the "Duty to Refer" (under section 213B of the Housing Act 1996, as amended by section 10 of the Homelessness Reduction Act 2017). They are required to refer anyone who is homeless or at risk of becoming homeless to a Local Housing Authority (LHA) of the service user's choice. This policy framework sets out how those bodies must comply with their statutory responsibilities and sets out a referral process that should be followed when complying with this duty. Prisons, Probation services and Local Authorities must work together to ensure these processes work locally and adapt as necessary.

### Implementation and use of OASys Sexual reoffending Predictor (OSP)

Her Majesty's Prisons and Probation Service plays a vital role in protecting the public from those who pose a risk of harm from sexual offending. Effective risk assessment is a critical part of this process and informs the way in which we manage the risk posed by such individuals. Risk assessment relies on the analysis of static and dynamic risk factors. Actuarial sexual offending risk assessment tools provide predictively valid estimates of how likely individuals are to be reconvicted for a sexual offence – the first step in the risk assessment process. We are committed to reviewing the risk assessment tools that we use and making changes to these tools when more efficient and digitally-enabled ones become available, to make sure that we are using those that best support our risk assessments of this cohort.

Policy name: *Implementation and use of OASys Sexual reoffending Predictor (OSP)*

Re-Issue Date: 03 August 2021

Implementation Date: 01 March 2021

Associated Documents:

• *Risk of Serious Harm Guidance 2020*
• *PI 53/2014 Polygraph Examinations: Instructions for Imposing Licence Conditions for the Polygraph on Sexual Offenders*
• *PI 09/2015 Licence conditions & temporary travel abroad*
• *PI 10/2015 Release on Temporary Licence*
• *The Care and Management of Individuals who are Transgender*
• *Programme Needs Assessment guidance 2017*
• *Programme Needs Assessment supplementary guidance 2020*

Actuarial assessments inform overall risk assessments and contribute to resources being targeted where they are most likely to have the greatest effect. Risk Matrix 2000 (RM2000) has long been the actuarial tool used by HMPPS and the police to assess the likelihood of repeat sexual reconviction. The Ministry of Justice (MOJ) has developed OSP (OASys Sexual [proven] reoffending Predictor) - a static actuarial assessment tool for adult men who have been convicted of sexual or sexually motivated offences (MCoSOs). OSP predicts the likelihood of proven reoffending for a sexual offence, distinguishing between likely reconviction for a contact sexual offence (using OSP/C) or a further noncontact offence relating to indecent images of children (using OSP/I), a distinction not made in RM2000.

The implementation of OSP will ensure that sexual reoffending measures are based on the most recent OASys data using a tool which is more efficient and scored more accurately. The move to OSP will also enable static risk scores to be recorded in a way that will better support data retrieval and performance management and will allow the score to be accessed across prisons and probation. Police have previously committed to adopting OSP but have held back so that they did not adopt ahead of HMPPS. Now that we have a clear implementation date, we will work with them with a view to aligning our assessment tools.

This policy framework provides instructions on the implementation and use of OSP, including the process for when a case with an existing RM2000 score should be recalculated.

Governors of public sector prisons and contracted prisons and Probation Service regional directors must ensure that local procedures are in place to ensure that OSP is used by staff in accordance with the instructions detailed within this framework.

### Incentives

Updated 8th July 2020.
Update: This updates Annex C and D in relation to the use of Nintendo and Xbox game consoles.
Policy Framework Name: *Incentives Policy Framework*
Re-issue Date:8 July 2020
Implementation Date: -
*16 August 2019: Use of Entry level ceases. All new prisoners must not join the incentives scheme below Standard level and all prisoners on Entry level must be moved to Standard level. Paragraphs 1.8 and 4.7-4.11 of PSI 30/2013 will no longer apply from this date. 27 September 2019: Incentive Forums must be in place and comply with 5.23 of this Policy Framework. 13 January 2020: A local policy must be in place which fully complies with this Policy Framework.*
Replaces the following documents which are hereby cancelled with effect from 13 January 2020:
*PSI 30/2013 Incentives and Earned Privileges*
*PSI 11/2011 Incentives and Earned Privileges*
*Residential Services Service Specification; Outputs 4, 5, and 6.*
The system of privileges is a key tool for incentivising prisoners to abide by the rules and engage in the prison regime and rehabilitation, including education, work and substance misuse interventions – whilst allowing privileges to be taken away from those who behave poorly or refuse to engage. This policy sets a common framework with which local incentives policies must comply.

### Information Requests

Policy name: *Information Requests Policy Framework*
Issue Date: 2 August 2021
Implementation Date: 2 August 2021
Replaces the following documents which are hereby cancelled:
*PSI 03/2018, PI 03/2018, AI 02/2018*
This Policy Framework (PF) sets out how to comply with information legislation and how to respond to requests for information under the Freedom of Information Act 2000 (FOIA), Environmental Information Regulations 2004 (EIRs) and under the data protection laws (the Data Protection Act (2018) and UK General Data Protection Regulation (UKGDPR)). It informs staff of the process for the handling of FOIA and EIR requests for information through the Knowledge and Information Liaison Officers (KILOs) network throughout Her Majesty's Prison and Probation Service (HMPPS) and of the handling process for subject access requests under the data protection laws through Information Access Representatives (IARs). It

aims to further embed FOI, EIR, and the UK's data protection laws in the organisation and to ensure compliance with our statutory obligations under these statutes.

The Ministry of Justice (MOJ) has a statutory requirement to respond to valid requests made under the data protection laws, FOIA and EIR. Building on experience in other areas of the organisation, we have established processes for how we deal with requests for information. Two networks, KILOs and Information Access Representative (IAR), have been established across the business. This places the primary responsibility for responding to requests on the area responsible for the subject matter of the request. The Disclosure Team – part of the Information Services Division (ISD), Security Services and Information Governance Group in MOJ – actively supports KILOs and IARs in their duties by logging cases and providing expert advice, training, guidance and procedural management of requests made under information legislation.

The Branston Offender subject access request (SAR) team handles SARs received from offenders (prisoners and probation service users) for the MOJ.

### Information Security

All information asset owners, information asset custodians, senior managers, delivery partners and third-party suppliers. Governors must ensure that any new local policies that they develop because of this Policy Framework are compliant with relevant legislation, including the Public-Sector Equality Duty (Equality Act, 2010). This Policy Framework has been revised to remove reference to CRCs only, as all CRC contracts terminated on 26 June 2021.
Policy Name: *Information Security Policy Framework*
Re-Issue Date: 26 June 2021
Implementation Date: 26 June 2021
Replaces the following documents which are hereby cancelled:
• PSI 24 /2014 - AI 18/2014 - PI 18/2014
Information Security is the practice of managing risks related to the use, processing, storage, and transmission of information or data. It is also ensuring the systems and processes used for those purposes are in line with the organisational policies.
• Information is the lifeblood of our organisation, it is a critical business asset that HMPPS needs to protect and get the most value from to benefit the business.
• It is important that only authorised sources have access to HMPPS information, at the right time and the correct details

## Information Sharing

Policy name: *HMPPS Information Sharing Policy Framework*

Issue Date: 28 May 2021

Implementation Date: 28 May 2021

Replaces the following documents which are hereby cancelled:

• PSI 16/2016, AI 12/2016, PI 15/2016 Information Sharing Policy

The purpose of this framework is to recognise that the sharing of personal data is a process integral to meeting the HMPPS business objectives. This framework provides guidance and support to practitioners in establishing agreements to make the process as straight forward as possible. Any sharing of personal data – whether small or large scale – needs to be done in accordance with the provisions of the Data Protection Act 2018 (DPA) and the General Data Protection Regulation (GDPR). The DPA provides a framework for how personal data should be correctly handled. The DPA neither promotes nor prohibits the sharing of personal data, but its principles apply to data sharing as they apply to any other form of processing of personal data. Following a Cabinet office review, it has been agreed that a Memorandum of Understanding (MOU) will suffice between Government Ministries instead of an Information Sharing Agreement (ISA). The MOU should cover all aspects of the data sharing arrangement between the Government Ministries however a legally binding ISA is not required.

## Intelligence collection, management and dissemination in prisons and probation

Rules and guidance for prison and probation staff on the collection, management, and sharing of intelligence about offenders.

Policy name: *Intelligence Collection, Analysis and Dissemination Policy Framework*

Re-Issue Date: 31 October 2019

Implementation Date: 18 March 2019

Purpose of Policy Framework

The policy will ensure consistent approaches to the collecting, handling, analysis and dissemination of intelligence by HMPPS. It sets out the purposes for which intelligence is collected, how it should be handled, and where/with whom that intelligence can be shared. Compliance with the policy will enable staff to have confidence that they are acting in a lawful manner, and using intelligence appropriately.

Definitions

Intelligence, for the purposes of this document, is defined as information which has been collected and analysed. Any information which has been subjected to an evaluation of the reliability of the source, the reliability of the information and the value of onward dissemination of the information, can be considered to be intelligence. Where information has been assigned an evaluation and handling code such as a 5x5x5 or 3x5x2 code, then this information should be regarded as intelligence.

Guidance for Operational staff

An accompanying restricted Intelligence Operations Manual for staff will be circulated to Establishments and Probation Local Delivery Units (LDUs) on request via intelligence. projectspolicy@noms.gsi.gov.uk to provide detailed guidance on processes and tactics.

Intelligence Operations within HMPPS

HMPPS collects information for a variety of purposes, including to support offender management, for the prevention and detection of crime, preserving order and discipline in establishments, management of risk and prevention of harm, and any duty or responsibility arising from common or statute law.

Within HMPPS any information which provides an indication of the likely or actual behaviour/conduct of an offender or staff member could potentially be used as intelligence, as defined above. It is sourced from a variety of places, and will be documented, considered and shared in a range of environments depending on the context and detail of the intelligence. Examples of intelligence can include but are not limited to:

• Observations of offender behaviour submitted by staff

• Information passed to HMPPS by another party, such as the police, victims or family members, detailing concerns about an offender's behaviour.

• Confirmed information about inappropriate/criminal activity, such as concerns that a staff member is in an inappropriate relationship with an offender.

• Anonymous information submitted by the public (e.g. Crimestoppers), such as reporting an offender in a location from which they have an exclusion area.

• Images collected by non-directed CCTV, such as video of a pass of illicit items taking place in a visits hall, or throw overs into an establishment.

• Conversations overheard by, or directly held with a HMPPS staff member (or non-directly employed staff member) where an offender volunteers information, such as a good source of drugs on a wing.

• Formal disseminations from other agencies regarding particular offenders or groups of offenders, such as a form of words indicating reasonable grounds for suspicion of criminal activity by an offender on licence, leading to consideration of recall

It is important that HMPPS staff are aware of how to appropriately collect, record, assess and act promptly on intelligence. By doing this, intelligence can be used in order to assist the prevention of crime, protect individuals and/or the organisation from harm, or promote rehabilitation, both in the community and custodial environments. For example:

• Acting on intelligence which is assessed to be reliable, prisons can combat conveyance of illicit items through targeted cell searches, or by making directed surveillance applications.

• Acting on intelligence about inappropriate behaviour/associations by an offender on licence can reduce the risk of harm through alteration of licence conditions such as increased curfews etc.

### Licence conditions

Policy name: *Licence Conditions Policy Framework*
Issue Date: 26 July 2021
Implementation Date: 2 August 2021
Replaces the following documents which are hereby cancelled:
• *PI 09/2015 Licence Conditions and Temporary Travel Abroad;*
• *PSI 12/2015 Licences, Licence Conditions and Licence and Supervision Notices;*
• *The Service Specification: Offender Management - Manage the Custodial & Post Relief Periods (outputs 33, 34, 35, 36, 37, 43 and 44)*

The aims of the licence period are to protect the public, to prevent re-offending and to secure the successful re-integration of the offender into the community. Licence conditions must be preventative as opposed to punitive and must be proportionate, reasonable and necessary.

This Policy Framework aims to ensure that staff are aware of the licence conditions which apply to an individual on licence during the licence period of all custodial sentences. Further explanation is given to individual types of licence conditions and how they should be correctly applied, as well as the mandatory actions which must be undertaken when preparing and creating a licence.

It also reflects a further type of licence condition for the first time, the compulsory licence condition. This concerns the compulsory inclusion of an electronic monitoring condition on the licence of individuals required by an order of the Secretary of State. This makes a total of four types of licence condition; standard, compulsory, additional and bespoke.

Whilst this document sets out the actions for which the Parole Board is responsible, this document does not bind the Parole Board in any way as it is an internal policy document of the Ministry of Justice/Her Majesties Prison and Probation Service.

### Manage the custodial sentence (OMiC)

Mandatory actions for prison and probation staff managing those sentenced or remanded in custody.
Policy name: *Manage the Custodial Sentence Policy Framework*
Re-issue Date: 28 November 2018
Implementation Date: 06 September 2018
Introduces amendments to the following documents:
*This Policy Framework incorporates most of the Service Specification for Manage the Custodial and Post Release Periods, which will remain in place until otherwise notified.*

This Policy Framework sets out high level requirements and outputs for staff in prisons and probation case managing prisoners throughout the custodial sentence.
It includes actions for:
• *those held on remand pre-sentence*
• *foreign national prisoners held in the prison system*
It does not apply to Immigration Removal Centres or to young people under the age of 18.
It incorporates the actions required to deliver the Offender Management in Custody model.
There are separate Policy Frameworks and Prison Service Instructions providing greater detail for offender management processes such as parole, licences, Release on Temporary Licence (ROTL) and Home Detention Curfew (HDC).

### Management of security at visits: Closed estate

Policy name: *Management of Security at Visits Policy Framework (Closed Estate)*
Issue Date: 06 April 2021
Implementation Date: Upon publication, this Policy Framework will immediately replace PSI 15/2011 with the exception of the revised visitor ID requirements (Annex A). An 8 week transitional period will be allowed for social visitors, from the recommencement of such visits in 2021. A transitional period of one calendar month will be allowed for official visitors, from the publication of this Policy Framework. During this time the acceptable forms of ID set out in PSI 15/2011 will be sufficient. This is to allow visitors time to make the necessary arrangements to obtain suitable ID under the new requirements, where necessary.
Replaces the following documents which are hereby cancelled:
• *PSI 15/2011 Management of Security at Visits*
• *Conduct Visits Service Specification – Outputs 7 and 19*
• *Visits Booking Service Specification – Outputs 4 and 5*
The purpose of social visits is to actively encourage prisoners to maintain outside contacts and meaningful family ties. This is integral to the prisoner's rehabilitation. Visits are crucial to sustaining relationships with close relatives, partners and friends, and help prisoners maintain links with the community. HMPPS

aims to encourage and assist the maintenance of relationships between prisoners and their families to support their social rehabilitation.

As such, HMPPS have a responsibility to appropriately balance effective, dynamic security and support for family contact. This balance should be maintained by efficient management of security processes to minimise delays, disruption and difficulty accessing visits, and the ability of staff involved in security processes to conduct these in a way that reflects procedural justice and engages good interpersonal interactions with prisoners and visitors. In order to support these interactions, and to promote procedural justice, Governors should ensure that prisoners and visitors are consulted about the impact and conduct of security procedures. For more information, please see the useful resources in section 7.

This Policy Framework sets out the minimum measures that must be taken to maintain security at visits.

## Management of security at visits: Open estate

Policy name: *Management of Security at Visits Policy Framework - Open Estate*

Issue Date: 06 April 2021

Implementation Date: Upon publication, this Policy Framework will immediately replace PSI 15/2011 with the exception of the revised visitor ID requirements (Annex A). An 8 week transitional period will be allowed for social visitors, from the recommencement of such visits in 2021. A transitional period of one calendar month will be allowed for official visitors, from the publication of this Policy Framework. During this time the acceptable forms of ID set out in PSI 15/2011 will be sufficient. This is to allow visitors time to make the necessary arrangements to obtain suitable ID under the new requirements, where necessary.

Replaces the following documents which are hereby cancelled:
• *PSI 15/2011 Management of Security at Visits*
• *Conduct Visits Service Specification – Outputs 7 and 19*
• *Visits Bookings Service Specification – Output 4 and 5*

The purpose of social visits is to actively encourage prisoners to maintain outside contacts and meaningful family ties. This is integral to the prisoner's rehabilitation. Visits are crucial to sustaining relationships with close relatives, partners and friends, and help prisoners maintain links with the community. HMPPS aims to encourage and assist the maintenance of relationships between prisoners and their families to support their social rehabilitation.

As such, HMPPS have a responsibility to appropriately balance effective, dynamic security and support for family contact. This balance should be maintained by efficient management of security processes to minimise delays, disruption and difficulty accessing visits, and the ability of staff involved in security processes to conduct these in a way that reflects procedural justice and engages good interpersonal interactions with prisoners and visitors. In order support these interactions, and to promote procedural justice, Governors should ensure that prisoners and visitors are consulted about the impact and conduct of security procedures. For more information, please see the useful resources in section 7.

This version of the Management of Security at Visits Policy Framework has been created for the open estate only and caters only to the specific needs of open prisons, and their operation of visits.

## Managing Extremism and Terrorism Amongst Offenders in Custody and the Community

No information available to the public.

## Managing Parole Eligible Offenders on Licence

The Framework has been revised to incorporate the changes brought in by commencement of the Police, Crime, Sentencing and Courts Act (2022). The framework sets out the mandatory requirements and guidance which must be followed by the National Probation Service (NPS) and the Public Protection Group (PPG) for all indeterminate sentenced individuals and parole eligible determinate sentenced individuals in the community on licence.

The framework mandates the processes for:
managing all indeterminate sentenced individuals in the community (including frequency of reporting)
varying the licence conditions of indeterminate and parole eligible determinate licences in the community
applying for the suspension and re-imposition of supervision of all indeterminate sentenced individuals in the community
applying for the licence to be terminated for those individuals subject to indeterminate sentences of Imprisonment for Public Protection (IPP) and Detention for Public Protection (DPP)

The framework replaces PI 08/2015- Managing Indeterminate Sentenced Offenders on Licence.

Minimising and Managing Use of Separation and Isolation in the Children and Young People Secure Estate.

## Multi Agency Life Risk Assessment Panel

This policy framework sets out the mandatory process of Multi Agency Life Risk Assessment Panels (MALRAP).

Policy name: *Multi-Agency Lifer Risk Assessment*

Panel (MALRAP) Policy Framework
Issue Date: 4th April 2019
Implementation Date: 4th April 2019
Replaces the following documents which are hereby cancelled:
*MALRAP policy is covered within PSI 36/2010 – updated chapter 4 of the Indeterminate Sentence Manual. The Manual (PSO 4700) has been cancelled, with the exception of Chapter 12 – Compassionate Release. This Policy Framework now covers the MALRAP which remains a mandatory requirement.*

This policy framework is aimed at staff working with prisoners who have recently been convicted of murder who have received a mandatory life sentence. A similar meeting may take place for other types of life sentenced prisoners on a discretionary basis.

The MALRAP meeting is a mandatory requirement for management of prisoners convicted of offences of murder, and takes place as soon after sentencing as is reasonably possible. The purpose of the meeting is to gather useful risk management information from the police.

MALRAP provides an opportunity for the senior police officer who investigated the case to share any relevant risk related information with prison staff, to enable the prisoners to be managed as effectively and safely as possible.

MALRAPs are not a new process and have been in operation in prisons for many years. The reason for the publication of this policy framework is that the Indeterminate Sentence Manual has recently been cancelled, and MALRAP remains one of the only mandatory areas within the manual which isn't already covered by other published policies.

The MALRAP process is mandatory and as such there are mandatory requirements associated with it.

**Notification & Review Procedures for Serious Further Offences**
This HMPPS Policy Framework sets out the requirement to complete a SFO review when a supervised individual is charged and appears in court for a qualifying offence. It includes mandatory actions and guidance to operational staff and specifically the regional SFO Teams, including the completion of the notification, review, action plan, outcome documents and engaging with victims.

**Occupational Health and Employee Assistance Programmes**
**Parole Board Oral Hearing Administration & Attendance**
Policy name: *Parole Board Oral Hearing Administration & Attendance Policy Framework*
Issue Date: 4th November 2019

Implementation Date: 4th November 2019
Replaces the following
• *PSI 35/2013 – Parole Board and Prison Service Oral Hearing Standards;*
• *PI 21/2014 – Giving Evidence via video link to a Parole or Recall Oral Hearing*
This framework applies to Parole Board oral hearings for all prisoners, including those subject to the Generic Parole Process and recall cases. It sets the expected standards for the provision and facilitation of all Parole Board oral hearings, including requirements. The framework confirms the appropriate escalation routes for both establishments and Parole Board members should these standards not be met, as well as the involvement of PPCS, where appropriate. The framework also contains guidance for staff who are required to attend hearings to give evidence and outlines the different means by which an oral hearing may be conducted, including the use of remote hubs, teleconference and video-link, as well as providing guidance on security measures of which witnesses will need to be aware, such as ID and requirements for IT devices.

**Person Escort Record**
The Person Escort Record (PER) was launched alongside the relevant Prison Service Order (PSO) in 2009 (PSO1025) and is now being formalised into a policy framework The purpose of the (PER) is to capture and transfer information which in turn will helps to manage risk. It is not a risk assessment tool. A review of the Person Escort Record (PER) document was commissioned in response to criticisms by Her Majesty's Chief Inspectorate of Prisons (HMIP), the Prisons and Probation Ombudsman and Coroners. The redesign clarifies areas of risk and gives more opportunities for risk information to be transferred effectively but still requires knowledgeable users, with an understanding of the process and what information needs to be included. The document allows for the changing nature of risk, ensuring that it is dynamic, with a red flag page to highlight changes in risk. A suicide and self-harm (SASH) warning form is included within the new booklet to enable effective information sharing on prisoners at risk of suicide or self-harm. There is a new health and social care page for health risks, social care needs, other vulnerabilities and details of medication. Impacts Given that this policy framework is only formalising work that is already carried out and covered by existing staff, there will be no change to benchmark staffing figures required as a result and no impact on staff resourcing.
Policy name: *The Person Escort Record (PER) Policy Framework*
Issue Date: 19 April 2021

Implementation Date: 19 April 2021
Replaces the following documents which are hereby cancelled:
*PSO 1025 Person Escort Record (PER)*
This Policy Framework sets out mandatory instructions and guidance regarding completion of the Person Escort Record (PER).

The PER is a record which must be completed for all prisoners prior to any escorted external movement or transfer. It provides escort staff and receiving establishments with relevant information on a prisoner and highlights risks they may pose during and after the movement.

The PER is not itself a risk assessment. It conveys the information about the assessed risks to others who may need to know about them.

Before any escort commences an assessment needs to be made of the risks posed by the prisoner which may impact on how the escort should be carried out and the allocation of the prisoner to court, holding cells or prison cells. Any risks or vulnerabilities identified should be noted and acted upon by those receiving the prisoner. PERs provide assurance that information about a prisoner on escort or transfer is available and that any identified risks/vulnerabilities, and any new risks that develop during a movement are communicated to those responsible for their custody. Correct completion and storage of the PER will help to prevent suicide/self-harm, escapes, assaults, releases in error and other serious incidents. It will also ensure the accurate recording of prisoner's money and property and will aid investigations of prisoner allegations of mistreatment. Correct use of the PER will ensure that all escorts are carried out decently, safely and securely, and are done so in a way that protects the welfare of all those being escorted.

## Polygraph examination licence condition

Her Majesty's Prison and Probation Service is committed to reducing sexual and terrorist offending and the risk of serious harm associated with those offences. The use of polygraph examination for those convicted of serious sexual offences, terrorist offences and those offences with a terrorist element, is one of the strategies being utilised to monitor and manage those who pose a risk of committing further offences. It is also used to support effective risk management and assist in reducing the number of new victims that are created.
Policy Name: *Polygraph Examinations – Instructions for Imposing Licence Conditions for Polygraph on People Convicted of Sexual Offences (PCoSOs), Terrorist and Terrorist Connected Offences*
Issue Date: 03 August 2021
Implementation Date: 24 June 2021
Replaces the following documents which are hereby cancelled:

- *PSI 36/2014 and PI 53/2014 - Polygraph Examinations: Instructions for Imposing Licence Conditions for the Polygraph on Sexual Offenders*
Associated Documents:
- *Generic Parole Process Policy Framework (issued February 2020)*
- *Recall, Review and Re-Release of Recalled Prisoners Policy Framework (issued February 2020)*
- *PI 09/2015 – Licence Conditions and Temporary Travel Abroad*
- *PSI 12/2015 – Licences, Licence Conditions and Licence and Supervision Notices*
- *National Standards for Counter Terrorism Polygraph Examinations*

Polygraph examination is used to support effective management of licences for PCoSOs who are assessed as posing a high or very high risk of re-offending and a high risk of harm and those convicted of terrorist and terrorist connected offences who are assessed as presenting a very high or high risk of harm.

This policy framework sets out the arrangements for imposing a licence condition requiring certain people convicted of sexual offences (PCoSOs) and terrorist and terrorist connected offences sentenced to a term of imprisonment of 12 months or more to undergo polygraph examinations. It details how probation practitioners should identify which of those individuals convicted of a sexual, a terrorist or terrorist connected offence must be made subject to the polygraph examination condition. This must be in accordance with the criteria specified by HMPPS within this Policy Framework which requires that tests be arranged for all relevant people on probation. It includes instructions for identifying those meeting the mandatory criteria, and advice on the process Probation Service regions and NSD Units will need to put in place to enable testing on a small number of discretionary cases.

## Post Incident Care Policy Framework

HMPPS has a legal duty under the Health and Safety at Work etc. Act (1974) to ensure as far as reasonably practicable, the health, safety and welfare of its staff.

It is reasonably foreseeable that the duties of HMPPS employees working in operational areas of the business place them at a higher risk of exposure to serious and potentially traumatising incidents in the workplace than those of employees in most other organisations.

The management and control of threats to staff from prisoners is dealt with under security and intelligence procedures whereas this policy is about the treatment, care and support for staff who may be significantly distressed and or traumatised by events in the workplace or arising from their work. Most notably but not exclusively such events will include incidents of self-harm, physical assault and verbal abuse and threats. It extends as well to the potential distress caused by exposure to extreme materials, for example relating to sexual abuse.

Response, care and support including observations of a colleague's mood and behaviour is expected initially at team and line manager level. Trained Staff Care Teams are present in all public sector prisons to provide additional independent support and to signpost services that may be beneficial.

Ultimately, clinically qualified interventions are available from HMPPS' Occupational Health and Employee Assistance Services.

This Instruction highlights the mandatory actions expected at each level. It reflects current best practice and explains how HMPPS will meet its duty of care to staff. It replaces existing post-incident care policy and reflects the current, revised arrangements in place to support staff.

Revised July 2018 – Minor updates including: references to General Data Protection Regulation; referral to Occupational Health now via portal; and updates to a Functional Mail Box.

**Post Sentence Supervision Requirements**

Policy name: *Post Sentence Supervision Requirements Policy Framework*
Issue Date: 26 March 2020
Implementation Date: 26 March 2020
Associated documents:
• *PI 09/2015 Licence Conditions and Temporary Travel Abroad*
• *PSI 12/2015 Licence Conditions, Licences and Licence and Supervision Orders*
• *PI 30/2014 PSI 32/2014 Drug Appointment and Drug Testing for Licence Conditions and Post Sentence Supervision Requirements*
• *PI 24/2014 Enforcement of Post Sentence Supervision*

This Policy Framework aims to ensure that staff are aware of the post sentence supervision (PSS) requirements which apply to an offender during their PSS period. Furthermore, this framework intends to highlight that the licence and PSS periods are two similar but separate periods undertaken by the offender through the management of a probation provider in the community.

**Power to detain dangerous standard determinate sentence prisoners**

This Policy Framework sets out duties, rules and general guidance on the new provision set out in section 132 of the Police, Crime, Sentencing and Courts (PCSC) Act 2022. This provision enables the Secretary of State for Justice to refer certain Standard Determinate Sentence prisoners to the Parole Board instead of automatically releasing them at their Conditional Release Date. Prisoners must meet both the legal and the policy thresholds to be eligible for consideration under this policy, which includes a dangerousness test and a public interest test.

**Pregnancy, Mother & Baby Units (MBUs), & Maternal Separation from Children up to the Age of Two in Women's Prisons**

This HMPPS Policy Framework sets mandatory requirements that address the additional emotional, physical and practical needs of perinatal women and mothers in prison and how prisons support them. The policy is based on the principles of individual needs-led and multi-agency care planning, to ensure the appropriate support is in place.

The policy contains requirements applying to the three groups below in recognition of shared needs:
Part A - pregnancy, birth, the post-natal period and other pregnancy outcomes
Part B - Applying for and facilitating Mother and Baby Unit (MBU) placements (replacing PSI 49/2014 PI 63/2014 'Mother and Baby Units')
Part C – maternal separation from children up to the age of two, due to imprisonment

This policy is supported by operational guidance and a templates pack, containing best practice advice designed to aid implementation and the development of local policies. The guidance will be published in due course.

The policy was developed following a fundamental review between July 2019 and June 2021. A wide range of stakeholders were consulted, including women with lived experience, the health sector, children's social care sector, and voluntary sector. A summary of the review scope, consultation feedback and key reforms can be found on GOV.UK.

**Prison Dogs**

The Prison Dogs Policy Framework underpins the professional practice and oversight of HMPPS dog operation and adherence to it will ensure consistent application of training and licensing standards, retention, deployment and decision-making to dog team resources. It is further supported by, and should be read in conjunction with, the Prison Dogs Supplementary Guidance document.

This policy framework provides instructions for managers and front-line staff to ensure that training, care and deployment of prison dogs always operates within the boundaries of authority set out in this framework. The Operational Response and Resilience Unit (ORRU) will ensure that it is reviewed regularly, and that it remains aligned to departmental priorities, reflects regulations and law, and includes the latest evidence lead practice.

### Prison Education and library services for adult prisons in England

This Policy Framework details the minimum mandatory requirements which are needed to deliver education and library services in adult prisons in England.

Policy Name: *Prison Education & Library Services for adult prisons in England Policy Framework*

Issue Date: 01/04/2019

Implementation Date: 01/04/2019

Replaces the following documents (e.g. PSIs, PSOs, Custodial Service Specs) which are hereby cancelled:

*PSI 20/2000 Education Key Performance Indicator: Measuring basic skills attainment.*

Introduces amendments to the following documents:

The education related elements of the following PSIs and Output 2 from the Prisoner Employment, Training & Skills Service Specification no longer apply to prisons in England – please note that they do still apply in Wales and the elements not related to education, e.g. employment, are still applicable in England and Wales:

*PSI 06/2012 Prisoner employment, training and skills*

*PSI 32/2012 Open University, Higher Education and distance learning*

*PSI 02/2015 Prison Library Service*

*Prisoner Employment, Training & Skills Service Specification, Output 2*

Education

Education in prisons aims to give individuals the skills they need to unlock their potential, gain employment and become assets to their communities. It should also build social capital and improve the wellbeing of prisoners during their sentences and once released.

Prison Library

The prison library aims to provide an accessible service which has a focus on supporting learning, improving literacy and other barriers to effective resettlement. It should promote reading as a source of pleasure and provide prisoners with opportunities for wider cultural engagement.

### Prisoner Complaints

UPDATED: 13 February 2020.

In compliance with the Data Protection Act 2018 and the General Data Protection Regulation a requirement for written confirmation that a prisoner has agreed to the sharing of personal information for the purposes of a PPO investigation – paragraph 4.44 and Annex C

amended. Template for prisoner consent form added – Annex K

UPDATED: 3 November 2020.

Paragraph 4.48 has been deleted. Amendments made to Annex A (COMP 2) and Annex K. There is no requirement to obtain consent for the IMB to access prisoner records for the purposes of investigating a complaint.

Inclusion in Annex B of the action and processing required for appeals against decisions made by the Financial Investigations Unit.

Policy name: *Prisoner Complaints Policy Framework*

Re-Issue Date: 03 November

Implementation Date: 1st August 2019

Replaces the following documents:

*PSI 02/2012 Prisoner Complaints*

*Processing and Resolution of Prisoner Complaints Specification*

Introduces amendments to the following documents:

*PSI 58/2010 Prisons and Probation Ombudsman (replaces sections covering Complaints)*

To set out requirements and information on providing a fair and effective system for dealing with prisoner complaints, including by ensuring procedural justice and taking a problem-solving approach for both adult prisoners and young people. Additional requirements which apply specifically to young people are set out in PSI 08/2012: Care and Management of Young People.

### Probation Service Management of MAPPA Level 1 Cases

This Policy Framework sets out mandatory instructions as well as guidance for Probation Practitioners managing MAPPA Level 1 cases. It aims to ensure the right offenders are managed at Level 1 and that Probation Service management of them is based on effective information sharing and partnership working, ensuring issues are responded to effectively to minimise risks and support rehabilitation. This Policy Framework will support Practitioners in ensuring all reasonable steps are taken to protect the public.

### Probation Service Management of Young Adults

This Probation Service Policy Framework sets out the requirements for Probation Practitioners when working with Young Adults aged between 18 and 25 years old, who are in contact with the Probation Service. It also provides supplementary guidance and signposts to other resources that support work with this age group of People on Probation.

### Progression regimes

Policy name: *Progression Regime Policy Framework*

Re-issue Date: 13th May 2021

Implementation Date: 4th April 2019

Progression Regimes have been developed for

male Indeterminate Sentences Prisoners (ISPs) who are: excluded from open conditions, serving the recall period of their licence in custody, or having difficulty progressing through their sentence via the usual routes. At the time of the publication of this document, there are four PRs in operation at HMPs Warren Hill, Buckley Hall, Humber and Erlestoke. There are only a very small number of women ISPs affected by the criteria above and, according to the aims of the Women's Estate Review, we aim to keep women as close to their home areas as possible, whilst ensuring the Women's strategy for ISPs is fit for purpose.

This framework, therefore, describes a PR for males and a Progression Approach for women that can be taken in any women's prison, in order to help ISPs reduce their risks in a closed prison environment. The purpose of a PR is to re-introduce the responsibilities, tasks and routines associated with daily life in the community, to test prisoners' readiness to respond appropriately to the trust placed in them, and to actively pursue activities and relations which support rehabilitation.

### Recall, Review And Re-Release Of Recalled Prisoners

Policy name: *Recall, Review and Re-Release of Recalled Prisoners Policy Framework*
Re-issue Date: 13 May 2021
Implementation Date: 1 April 2019
Replaces the following documents:
*PSI 30/2014, AI 22/2014, PI 27/2014 – Recall Review and Re-Release of Recalled Offenders on licence*
*PSI 28/2015, AI 18/2015 - PI 20/2015 - Unlawfully at Large after Recall Offence Protocols*
Determinate and indeterminate sentenced prisoners who are released into the community subject to licensed supervision are liable to be recalled to custody by the Secretary of State, usually where they have breached the conditions of their licence. This framework sets out the mandatory requirements that the National Probation Service (NPS), Youth Offending Teams (YOT), Community Rehabilitation Companies (CRCs) and prison establishments must undertake for all recalled prisoners.

### Release on temporary licence

Policy name: *Release on Temporary Licence (ROTL) Policy Framework*
Re- issue Date: 8th June 2021
Implementation Date: 16th May 2019
Replaces the following documents:
*PSI 13/2015 Release on Temporary Licence*
Release on Temporary Licence (ROTL) facilitates the rehabilitation of offenders, by helping to prepare them for resettlement in the community once they are released. This includes, among other examples, finding work and rebuilding family ties. It is intended that this will lead to reduced reoffending in the long-term.

There is no entitlement to ROTL but the expectation is that it will be widely used with suitable offenders in open prisons and women's prisons where the resourcing and infrastructure best enable ROTL to be undertaken. As now, closed prisons can release eligible prisoners on ROTL, but Governors will want to be assured that they have the necessary security arrangements in place to prevent contraband being brought in by returning prisoners, staff in place to carry out the required assessments and Boards, and operational enablers, before considering a wider expansion.

This policy framework deals with temporary release for adults. Instructions to practitioners on temporary release for children are given in PSO 6300, in relation to children detained in Young Offender Institutions, and in separate "Mobilities" guidance for children detained in Secure Training Centres and Secure Children's Homes. Approaches to Release on Temporary Licence and Mobility for the Youth Secure Estate are being considered separately, outside of this framework. Where a child transitions from the youth to the adult estate then the adult, ROTL provisions set out here will generally apply. Where the individual has already begun to take temporary release for resettlement purposes as a child, however, consideration should be given to maintaining access to temporary release, where this remains in line with the sentence plan and subject to risk assessment, even where the individual has yet to reach the adult ROTL eligibility date.

A number of changes have been made to the previous policy in order to allow governors to consider ROTL earlier and in more cases within a robust risk assessment framework. These include:
• Changing the threshold for Restricted ROTL so that it is focused on the most serious offenders.
• Removing the current restriction on ROTL in the first three months after transfer to open conditions, subject to individual progress and risk assessment.
• Making prisoners, including those serving indeterminate sentences, eligible to be considered for unaccompanied day release (RDR) from the point of entry to the open estate (or reaching open status in the women's estate).
• Streamlining the process so that agencies are consulted and boards sit only where necessary, the focus is on the right information, and paperwork is reduced.
• Encouraging the greater use of workplace ROTL, for example, by allowing paid work to be taken as soon as the offender is eligible for day release and removing the requirement for a

prisoner on ROTL to spend at least one 24-hour period per week in prison.

• Allowing primary carers and sole carers to apply for Childcare Resettlement Licence.

• Allowing offenders with a prior abscond history (if it occurred more than two years ago and only once during the current sentence) to be risk assessed for open conditions and ROTL.

• Allowing Directors of contracted prisons to take ROTL decisions whilst the Controller will continue to monitor the Director's compliance in this area.

## Reporting and reviewing deaths under probation supervision

This Policy Framework sets out the mandatory actions following the death of a person under probation supervision. It describes the information to be gathered, recorded and shared and explains the roles of probation practitioners, their line managers and staff with specific responsibilities for deaths under supervision. It acknowledges the emotional impact that a death may have and describes the process for ensuring that the welfare needs of staff and others are considered. It explains how we use learning from deaths to improve our service and our approach to preventing deaths.

## Restrictions on Prisoner Voting

Policy name: *Restrictions on Prisoner Voting Policy Framework*

Issue Date: 11 August 2020.

Implementation Date: 11 August 2020.

Replaces the following documents which are hereby cancelled:

*PSO 4650 Prisoners' Voting Rights*

The Government is clear that convicted prisoners detained in custody should not be able to vote. This framework replaces PSO 4650 and includes updated guidance in response to the long-standing Hirst judgment, where the Government has addressed an anomaly in the previous system, where prisoners released back in the community on licence using an electronic tag under the home detention curfew (HDC) scheme could vote, but those released in the community on temporary licence (ROTL) could not. Annex A provides updated voting eligibility criteria; under the new guidance, those on ROTL are no longer considered barred from voting.

This framework seeks to ensure that all prisoners who consider that they are (or may be) eligible to apply to vote, or to vote (and wish to do so) are appropriately supported in doing so.

## Secure Social Video Calling (Interim)

Policy name: *Secure Social Video Calling (Interim) Policy Framework*

Issue Date: 26 February 2021

Implementation Date: 26 February 2021

Replaces the following documents which are hereby cancelled: This Policy Framework replaces the internal document: Video Calls: *Interim Policy Framework*

Social video calls were introduced as an emergency measure to help maintain family contact for those held in custody (referred to as prisoners and young people in this policy framework) whilst physical visits are impacted by the restrictions of COVID-19. The social video calls currently operate alongside, not as a replacement for, face-to-face social visits in line with the COVID-19 National Framework for Prison Regimes and Services.

This policy framework does not intend social video calls to be a substitute for face-to-face visits, where face-to-face visits can safely be delivered prisons must seek to facilitate these. Providing access to social video calls for prisoners and young people as a supplement to existing communications through letters, phone calls and social visits helps to maintain and strengthen family ties and is a key recommendation of the 2017 and 2019 Lord Farmer Reviews. There are however security risks associated with all prisoner communications and there may be circumstances where it is necessary and proportionate to place restrictions or conditions on social video calls. As per the direction of the Secretary of State laid out in PSI 04/2016 Interception of Communications in Prisons and Security Measures all social video calls will be intercepted and recorded. This framework provides Governors direction on these policy areas and sets out how they should make decisions in a lawful manner for the duration of the COVID19 restrictions.

## Security Categorisation

Policy name: *Security Categorisation Policy Framework*

Re-issue Date: 13 May 2021

Implementation Date: 20 February 2020

Replaces

*PSI 40/2011 Categorisation and Recategorisation of Adult Male Prisoners**

*PSI 41/2011 Categorisation and Recategorisation of Young Adult Male Prisoners**

Under Rule 7 Prison Rules 1999, subject to certain exceptions, "prisoners shall be classified, in accordance with any directions of the Secretary of State, having regard to their age, temperament and record and with a view to maintaining good order and facilitating training and, in the case of convicted prisoners, of furthering the purpose of their training and treatment".

Security Categorisation is a risk management process, the purpose of which is to ensure that those sentenced to custody are assigned the lowest security category appropriate to managing their risk of: • escape or abscond; • harm to the public; • ongoing criminality in custody; • violent or other behaviour that impacts the safety of those within the prison; and • control issues that disrupt the security and good order of the prison.

Effective security categorisation is fundamental to risk management and ensuring good order is maintained. It supports HMPPS's duty to implement the sentences of the courts; protect the public; and provide a safe, secure and ordered environment that enables the provision of rehabilitative services, training, treatment and progression through the prison system.

The security categorisation process provides for a holistic assessment of risk, taking account of a broad range of information from criminal justice and law enforcement agencies where available. It supports the categorisation of individuals to security conditions best suited to managing their risks. Categorisation is neither a reward for good, compliant behaviour nor used as a punishment. Any categorisation decision must be taken on risk factors alone.

Allocation is a separate process from categorisation, the purpose of which is to assign an individual to a suitably secure establishment which meets their needs effectively insofar as pressures on the estate allow. Categorisation is an independent process, so someone may be assigned a particular category even if it is not possible to allocate them to a prison of that category immediately.

Allocation decisions should consider the individual's offending behaviour and resettlement needs (such as access to suitable training and interventions and closeness to home at the end of their sentence), their individual circumstances (such as medical requirements), and control issues (such as danger to particular staff or other prisoners). This may result in an individual being held in a prison of a higher category than their own category.

### Sentence Calculation: determinate sentenced prisoners

This policy framework sets out what information is required and how to calculate the release dates for determinate sentenced prisoners in accordance with the relevant legislative release provisions.

It explains the process to be followed, timings of required actions and who can carry out the relevant calculations and checks

The framework replaces Prison Service Instruction 03/2015.

### Separation Centres Policy Framework

The Separation Centre Policy Framework provides guidance to staff on how to refer, assess, select, manage and deselect prisoners into and out of separation centres.

The Secretary of State of Justice may direct that a prisoner be placed in a separation centre where desirable on one or more of the following grounds of Prison Rule 46A:

a. The interests of national security

b. To prevent the commission, preparation or instigation of an act of terrorism, a terrorism offence, or an offence with a terrorist connection, whether in a prison or otherwise

c. To prevent the dissemination of views or beliefs that might encourage or induce others to commit any such act or offence, whether in a prison or otherwise, or to protect or safeguard others from such views or beliefs, or

d. To prevent any political, religious, racial or other views or beliefs being used to undermine good order and discipline in a prison.

This Separation Centre Policy Framework replaces PSI 05/2017 Separation Centre Referral Manual and the Separation Centre Operating Manual 2017.

### Serious and Organised Crime

Policy name: *Serious and Organised Crime Policy Framework*

Issue Date: 30 September 2019

Implementation Date: 30 September 2019

The Government's Serious and Organised Crime (SOC) Strategy 2018 makes a commitment to relentlessly target and disrupt serious and organised crime offenders in our communities and in our prisons. Ongoing criminal activity by SOC offenders undermines safety, security and public protection. The majority of SOC offenders under HMPPS supervision have diverse crime portfolios and can adapt their offending behaviour dependent on their situation.

Effective management of SOC offenders is required to minimise the risk of them using their time in custody or under supervision to develop new capabilities, expand their criminal networks or exploit new revenue streams (including orchestrating illicit supply into prisons). We know that SOC offenders are more resistant to rehabilitation, meaning they more often leave custody with specific risk factors that need robust management.

The criminal activities of the highest threat SOC offenders frequently provide sizeable illicit wealth, a sense of identity and a support network and for some offenders this will have been a lifetime in the making. For this cohort, it is important to be mindful that the successful pathway out of SOC may take some time and will need a holistic approach that address the issues highlighted above.

The HMPPS SOC Strategy states we will undermine and disrupt serious and organised crime in prisons and across probation provision. We will work with Law Enforcement Colleagues (e.g. Home Office, Police, National Crime Agency (NCA), Regional Organised Crime Unit (ROCU) and others) to prioritise, target and robustly manage SOC nominals through four strategic objectives:

• PROTECT prison and probation services from SOC with stronger organisational capability.
• PREVENT SOC offenders from engaging in SOC in prisons and probation.
• PURSUE SOC nominals to disrupt their criminality and the threat they pose to prison stability and civil society.
• PREPARE for the harm caused by SOC in prisons and probation with greater organisational resilience.

HMPPS is committed to deliver that ambition and has established a Serious Organised Crime Unit (SOCU) to oversee and drive our SOC strategy. The unit is made up of a small national team and 5 regional teams who will provide direct support to staff across prisons and probation. It is responsible for our serious and organised crime policy and procedures, leading SOC capability, raising and most fundamentally, supporting the organisation to pursue SOC activity where it is taking place. This document sets out the mandatory actions for the SOCU and HMPPS staff at local, regional and national level. This Policy Framework clarifies:

• The HMPPS definition of SOC offenders and how their criminal activity manifests itself in prisons and probation services.
• The mandatory processes and procedures to manage serious and organised criminals.
• The role of SOCU and how to access their specialist capability.

This new Policy Framework is supported by the HMPPS Handbook on Managing SOC. Due to the handbook containing advice and guidance on disrupting SOC offenders it is marked as OFFICIAL SENSITIVE and is only available to staff who have access to the SOCT Security Information Hub or via their regional SOCU contact. The Handbook provides guidance and best practice and its use is encouraged, although not mandated. This Policy Framework and the SOC Management Handbook will be regularly reviewed and updated by the Serious Organised Crime Unit to inform operational responses, training and communications relating to serious and organised crime in prisons and probations services.

**Smoke Free Policy**
Policy name: *Smoke Free Policy Framework*
Issue Date: 27 January 2020

Implementation Date: 1 May 2018.
Replaces the following documents:
*PSI 09/2007 Smoke free legislation*
*PSI 09/2007W Smoke Free legislation Welsh Prisons*
The Prison and Young Offender Institute (Amendment) Rules 2018 allows for a smoke free prison estate in order to improve air quality and to minimise the dangers from passive smoking whilst promoting a healthier lifestyle. It is our intention to maintain a totally smoke free environment in the closed estate whilst allowing prisoners to smoke in the open estate at designated times and in designated areas.

**Strengthening Prisoners Family Ties**
Policy name: *Strengthening Prisoners' Family Ties Policy Framework*
Re-issue Date: 27 January 2020
Implementation Date: 31 January 2019
Replaces the following documents:
• *NOMS Service Specification:*
o *Social Visits - Conduct Visits Outcome 23.*
o *Services to Visitors, Outcomes; 6, 7,11,13 and 14.*
Introduces amendments to the following documents:
• *PSI 16/2011*
This policy supports the maintenance and development of prisoners' relationships with family, significant others and friends, by using a range of methods and interventions. Supporting prisoners' relationships outside of prison is considered to help prevent reoffending and reduce intergenerational crime.

Prisoners, their family and significant others, all internal and external staff and service providers are encouraged to work in partnership and share good practice, to enhance opportunities for prisoners to develop or enhance positive relationships. This service can include physical, digital and other forms of communications such as phone calls and letters.

**Sustainable operations**
Policy name: *Sustainable Operations*
Issue Date: 15 March 2019
Implementation Date: 15 March 2019
Replaces the following documents:
*PSI 2003/41 Sustainable Development – Prison Service Policy and Governance,*
*PSI 2010/07 Packaging Material Usage Legal Requirements,*
*PSI 2013/15 Waste Management Data Recording*
This Policy outlines aims and approach of the Ministry of Justice (MoJ) and Her Majesty's Prisons and Probation Service (HMPPS) to sustainable operations. It makes clear that these organisations are committed to running their estates as sustainably as possible and that they have committed to achieving challenging

sustainability targets. It goes on to outline how Governor/Directors and individual members of staff can contribute to this.

## Transition of Young People from the Children and Young People Secure Estate to Adult Custody

Transitioning in the context of this Framework is when a young person moves from the children and young people secure estate (CYPSE) to the adult estate. This move involves a significant change in environment, regime and peer group for those in custody and can be unsettling for many young people who may be particularly vulnerable during this stage of their custodial journey, with potential for any stresses to be exacerbated should transition not be managed effectively. Where necessary, this Framework should be read in conjunction with the, 'Joint National Protocol for Transitions in England', the 'Youth to Adult Transitions Principles and Guidance Wales', and the Royal College of Paediatrics and Child Health 'Healthcare Standards for Children and Young People in Secure Settings'.

## Travel and transfer on licence and PSS outside of England & Wales

Policy name: *Travel and Transfer on Licence and PSS Outside of England and Wales*
Issue Date: 26 July 2021
Implementation Date: 2 August 2021
Replaces the following documents which are hereby cancelled:
• *PI 09/2015 Licence Conditions and Temporary Travel Abroad;*
• *PI 07/2015 PSI 08/2015 Permanent Resettlement Outside of England and Wales*
This Policy Framework aims to ensure that staff are aware of the three different means under which an individual on licence or post sentence supervision (PSS) can travel/transfer outside of England and Wales either on a temporary or permanent basis and the criteria which applies in each case.

## Use of CCTV (Overt Closed-Circuit Television system)

This Policy Framework sets out the legal requirements of the management, operation and use of overt closed-circuit television (CCTV) systems across Her Majesty's Prison and Probation Service (HMPPS). It also includes guidance on the use of CCTV for staff.

## Use of Narcotics Trace Detection Equipment on Correspondence

Policy name: *Use of Narcotics Trace Detection Equipment on Correspondence Policy Framework*

Issue Date: 01 April 2021
Implementation Date: 01 April 2021
Replaces the following documents which are hereby cancelled:
• *Rapiscan Itemiser Guidance, Security Risk Unit, December 2018 (updated July 2019)*
• *Security Briefing Note: Conveyance of drug laced paper and illicit items via correspondence, November 2018 (updated July 2019)*
• *Interim Itemiser guidance on the use on correspondence – Issued June 2020*
The purpose of this Policy Framework is to provide mandatory instructions around the use of narcotics trace detection equipment when testing correspondence. This policy also sets out the constraints in which this equipment must be used. Results produced by narcotics trace detection equipment must not be used on their own as evidence. They must be used to contribute towards a wider intelligence picture and inform decisions about correspondence and other evidence and intelligence.

Governors must ensure that the use of all narcotics trace detection equipment is consistent with both this policy framework and other policies concerning correspondence and prisoner property, whilst also ensuring that processes and arrangements for their use are reflected in their Local Searching Strategy.

This framework is to be used alongside official and mandatory training. It applies to Governors, Directors, Heads of Security, Security departments and mailroom staff. This framework must be read in conjunction with:
Section 42A Prison Act 1952
Prison Rule 34
Prison Rule 35A
Prison Rule 39
Prison Rule 43
Prison Rule 44
PSI 49/2011 - Prisoner Communication Services
PSI 04/2016 – The Interception of Communications in Prisons and Security Measures
PSI 16/2011- Providing visits and services to visitors

## Use of X-Ray Body Scanners (Adult Male Prisons)

Policy name: *Use of X-Ray Body Scanners (Adult Male Prisons).*
Issue Date: 18 May 2020
Implementation Date: 18 May 2020
This Policy Framework provides end-to-end instruction and guidance on the procurement, installation and use of X-ray body scanners in Adult male prisons to detect if prisoners are attempting to conceal contraband internally. The mandatory requirements in this document set out the minimum required for a prison to be compliant with legislation and HMPPS's Requirements for Practice for Prisons.

## Women's Estate Case Advice and Support Panel

Policy name: *Women's Estate Case Advice and Support Panel (WECASP) Policy Framework*

Issue Date: 11 May 2021

Implementation Date: 11 May 2021

Replaces the following documents which are hereby cancelled:

*PSI 23/2015 – Centralised Case Supervision system for Restricted Status women and women with complex needs*

The purpose of this Policy Framework (PF) is to set out the mandatory requirements which HMPPS staff, including prisons and probation providers, must complete for those individuals who are being considered for a referral to the Women's Estate Case Advice and Support Panel (WECASP). It also sets out the mandatory requirements that are expected of the core members who form the WECASP Board. This Policy Framework aims to ensure that there is an effective process in place to support prisons in the management of individuals displaying complex and challenging behaviour.

The Women's Estate Case Advice and Support Panel guidance provides further detail and clarity on the role of the WECASP and sets out the processes and templates for referring those within the women's estate to the WECASP for discussion. The guidance also offers additional information on the WECASP boards, the disciplines who are closely aligned and involved in this process and information sharing and recording actions.

## Women's Policy Framework

Gender specific rules and guidance for prison and probation staff on how to manage and support women in custody and the community.

Policy name: *Women's Policy Framework*

Issue Date: 26 June 2021

Implementation Date: 26 June 2021

Replaces the following documents which are hereby cancelled:

*PSO 4800*

This policy framework sets out the MoJ's expectations for the delivery of services for working with women in custody and the community. This enables staff to be aware of the gender specific issues that affect women, and respond appropriately to ensure that their different needs are consistently met. This does not detract from the requirement to consider the needs of other protected characteristics. It is important that this framework is read in conjunction with its supporting Guidance on Working with Women in Custody and Community.

PRISON SERVICE INSTRUCTIONS 'IN FORCE' 1st August 2022

Activities in prison

Additional risk criteria for ex-offenders working in prison & community settings

Adult social care

Allocating prisoners to activities

Amendments to the use of force policy

Arrangements for the monitoring & measurement of health & safety performance

Assessment and control of radon exposure

Caring for young people in custody

Case allocation

Categorising adult male prisoners

Categorising women prisoners

Categorising young adult male prisoners

Cell sharing risk assessments

Centralised case supervision system for restricted status women and women with complex needs

Certifying prisoner accommodation

Checking the barred status of prisoners

Close supervision centre (CSC) referral manual

Communications and security during internal prisoner movements

Compact based drugs testing

Confiscation orders

Consulting on occupational health, safety and fire issues

Controlling banned (prohibited) items

Covert testing

Crown copyright and licences

Custody compacts for use in custody

Data gateway service: approval of data collections

Dealing with evidence

Deducting money from prisoner wages

Disposing of unauthorised property

Drug appointments and drug licence conditions

Early days in custody

Early removal of foreign national prisoners

Enablers of services in prisons

Ensuring equality

Ensuring the safety of radiation equipment when transferring healthcare

Exclusion of personnel for misconduct

Faith and pastoral care for prisoners

Fire safety in prisons

First aid

Food Safety Act

Guidance on consent to medical treatment

Handling complaints about prison healthcare

Handling mobile phones and SIM cards found in prison

Handling prisoner applications to marry or form a civil partnership

Health and safety arrangements for risk assessment

Health and safety arrangements for workplace inspection

Health and safety issues with contractors

Health & safety management arrangements for manual handling operations

Housing benefit continuance forms

Identifying potential high security prisoners

Implementation of equality analysis

Implementation of the deliver accredited programmes specification

Implementation of the service specification for "Manage the sentence: pre and post-release from custody"

Implementation of the service specification for bail services

Information risk management

Information sharing agreements

Install, maintain and use prison radio equipment

Introduction of Brent equipment

Investigating incidents of serious self-harm or assault

IT Security Policy

Keeping adult prisoners safe

Manage and keep prison keys and locks secure

Management and security of prisons at night

Managing accidents and injuries in prison

Managing health and safety

Managing litigation claims

Managing prison gates

Managing prison visits

Managing prisoner property

Managing prisoner safety in custody

Managing prisoners who pose an escape risk

Managing prisoners' money

Managing risk in prison industries

Managing the local security strategy

Managing tools and equipment securely in prisons

Mandatory use of the violent and sex offender register (ViSOR)

Medical emergency response codes

Medical treatment of prison staff by healthcare workers

Model induction framework for healthcare staff

Monitoring & managing prisoner communications

Mother and baby units

Night workers health assessment

Open prison and temporary release for prisoners who may be deported

Open source research on the internet and social networking sites

Open University higher education distance learning

People under supervision leaving England & Wales

Performance hub data quality policy

Pharmacy services for prisoners

Physical education for prisoners

Placing prisoners who may be deported

Playing films, television and music in prison

Prison adjudications policy

Prison adjudications policy (cases before Feb 2019)

Prison bedding fire standards

Prison discharge policy

Prison drug treatment and self harm

Prison security passes

Prison service library

Prison-NOMIS

Prisoner communications policy

Prisoner meals

Prisoner rehabilitation services

Prisoner retail

Prisoners assisting other prisoners

Prisoners' access to the media

Procedures for searching cells, areas and vehicles

Procedures for searching people

Process for opening, closing or re-designating workshops and laundries

Providing prisoners with ID for bank applications

Provision of offender risk information to Home Office immigration enforcement

Psychologist report format (SPR E)

Public protection manual

Radiation safety of X-ray equipment

Rationalisation of doctors' duties in prisons

Reconsideration of NOMS central vetting decisions by exception

Records information management policy

Referring probation cases for risk review

Regime management planning

Reintroduction of disinfecting tablets

Release on licence of foreign national prisoners pending deportation

Releasing prisoners with travel restriction orders

Removable media

Repatriation and removal of foreign nationals

Research applications

Resettlement

Residential services

Restricting access to prison server and PABX rooms

Reviewing the categorisation of high security prisoners

Searching stored property

Security of prisoners at court (cancelled WEF 22/9/2022)

Security vetting

Sentence planning

Separating prisoners from the general population

Sharing sensitive information with the Parole Board

Strategy for promoting health in prisons

Tackling witness intimidation by remand prisoners

Taking prisoners outside the prison (escorts) (cancelled WEF 22/9/2022)

The bail system

The instruction system: the approval & implementation of policy & instructions

The Prisons and Probation Ombudsman

The protection and use of confidential health information in prisons

Touchscreen prisoner information systems

Transferring children and young people between custody and hospital under the Mental Health Act

Transferring prisoners between custody & hospital under the Mental Health Act

Unauthorised possession of knives & other

offensive weapons in prison
Update to PSI 47/2003: Rationalisation of doctors' duties in prisons
Use of body cameras
Use of force form part 1
Use of force form part 2
Use of force in the young people's estate
Using offenders as mentors in the community and in custody
Visits security
Work and learning opportunities for prisoners

## PRISON SERVICE ORDERS CURRENTLY 'IN FORCE' 1ST AUGUST 2022

| | |
|---|---|
| 9050 | Functional mailboxes |
| 9030 | Handling and approval of requests for IT |
| 8525 | Enabling agreement on change proposals & resolving disputes |
| 6300 | Release on temporary licence (ROTL) from young offender institutions (YOIs) |
| 6101 | Providing bail information for prisoners on remand |
| 5901 | Maintaining prison buildings |
| 5400 | Prison transport manual |
| 4960 | Managing young people convicted of serious crimes |
| 4625 | Producing prisoners at court for civil proceedings |
| 4600 | Treatment of unconvicted, unsentenced and civil prisoners |
| 4480 | Prisoner representative associations |
| 4460 | Paying prisoners for work & other activities |
| 4455 | Handling requests from prisoners to change their name |
| 4350 | Creating and running prisoner interventions |
| 3805 | Zoonotic infections |
| 3802 | Management of inadvertent exposure to asbestos |
| 3800 | Food Safety Act 1990: agricultural business enterprise |
| 3625 | Testing of external drug workers |
| 3601 | Mandatory drug testing |
| 3550 | Treating prisoners for substance misuse |
| 3200 | Promoting healthy behaviours in prison |
| 3100 | Ensuring clinical governance in prison healthcare |
| 3050 | Ensuring continuity of healthcare for prisoners |
| 2600 | Legal issues relating to prisoners |
| 2400 | Democratic therapeutic communities for prisoners |
| 1700 | Management of segregation units |
| 1600 | Use of force in prisons |
| 1310 | Preventing fraud |
| 1300 | Investigations |
| 1025 | Sharing risks & information about a prisoner escort or transfer |

| | |
|---|---|
| 905 | Using the police national computer |
| 160 | Hosting magistrates' training visits |
| 101 | Changes to young offender institution rules |

## 7.5 STAFF AWARDS & PRIZES 2022

**BUTLER TRUST**
*www.butlertrust.org.uk/people/awards/our-winners/*
**The Butler Trust**
**Southbank House**
**Black Prince Rd**
**London**
**SE1 7SJ**
**Tel: 020 8688 6062**
**Email: info@butlertrust.org.uk**

### ABOUT THE BUTLER TRUST

The Butler Trust was set up in 1985 by former prison governor, Rev Peter Timms OBE and Veronica Linklater, later Baroness Linklater of Butterstone.

We are named after Richard Austen Butler (RAB), later Lord Butler of Saffron Walden, and the Butler family have been closely involved with the Trust throughout.

As Home Secretary (from 1957 to 1962), RAB introduced a series of reforms to improve the management, care and rehabilitation of offenders. To further the scientific understanding of criminality, he set up the Home Office Research Unit, and helped set up the Cambridge Institute of Criminology. He also gave the go-ahead for Grendon, as the world's first dedicated psychotherapeutic prison.

And the 1975 Butler Report (which RAB oversaw after leaving office) led to significant improvements in the management and care of offenders with a mental illness.

### HRH THE PRINCESS ROYAL

HRH is a long-standing champion of the #HiddenHeroes working in our prisons, IRCs, probation and youth justice settings, and has been a Patron of the Trust since its inception in 1985. The Princess has hosted and presented the Butler Trust Annual Awards every year since 1985.

In addition to presenting our Awards, HRH has, over the years, visited almost every prison across the UK (many of them more than once), as well as many probation and youth justice offices, to see the work of our Award Winners and their #HiddenHeroes colleagues first-hand, and to thank them for all they do.

### CHARITABLE OBJECTS

The Butler Trust was launched as a charity in 1985. In 2012 we became incorporated as a charitable company, limited by guarantee (charity number: 1145182; company number: 07844810).

*Our charitable objects are –*

To further and promote practice among those working in the penal system in the United Kingdom which contributes to:

• the rehabilitation of offenders and the prevention of crime;

• the promotion of the social inclusion of offenders by facilitating their integration and constructive engagement in society;

• the advancement of the health, safety and psychological wellbeing of offenders and those who work with them.

The Butler Trust is committed to promoting equality, fairness and respect, and opposes all forms of unlawful and unfair discrimination, victimisation, harassment, bullying, and insulting or abusive behaviour.

*The Trust aims to ensure that:*

• diversity is encouraged within the Trust, creating an environment in which individual differences and the contributions of all are recognised and valued;

• the working environment within the Trust, and the way we carry out our work, promotes dignity, respect and fairness to all;

• no one is unlawfully or unfairly discriminated against on grounds of age, disability, gender reassignment, race, religion or belief, sex, sexual orientation, marriage or civil partnership, pregnancy or maternity, or any other irrelevant factor.

**2021-22 Award Winners & Commendees**

**Award Winners**

**ANDREW BLACKMORE**
**(HMP & YOI Woodhill)**

Andrew wins an Award, as an Officer at HMP/YOI Woodhill, for his diligence, decency, and unwavering positivity; for his outstanding de-escalation skills with prisoners, and support and encouragement of colleagues; and for producing a guide for new staff which is now being taken up elsewhere.

**GRAHAM DUNCAN**
**(HMP Channings Wood)**

Graham receives an Award as a "role model for prisoners and staff" in his work as a Supervisory Officer at HMP Channings Wood, as "an exemplar of compassion for others", and in particular for his truly exceptional contribution to staff well-being in the prison, which is now widely recognised as best practice.

**LES EGAN**
**(HMP & YOI Hatfield)**

Nominated as a Custodial Manager at HMP/YOI Hatfield, after 40 years in the Service, Les's Award is for his remarkable and unfailing commitment to rehabilitation and resettlement, his outstanding support for prisoners and staff, and his "enthusiasm, drive and determination, [which] knows no bounds".

**NATHAN GREWAL**
**(HMP & YOI Brinsford)**

Described as "inspirational" by the Governor, Nathan receives an Award for his "groundbreaking" work, as a Prison Officer at HMP/YOI Brinsford, helping to tackle gang-related violence in the jail – employing his drive and "fantastic rapport with prisoners" to achieve "outstanding results".

**MATT HILLARD**
**(HMP & YOI Cardiff)**

A teacher at HMP/YOI Cardiff, Matt wins an Award for his work on Knox TV – a station he set up, from scratch and with no prior experience, to help keep the prisoners educated and entertained during Covid; and for which he produced most of the content, much of it in his own time.

**JULIE JONES**
**(HMP & YOI Parc)**

Julie wins an Award, as the Schools & Prisons Family Coordinator at HMP/YOI Parc, for her tireless dedication, skill and compassion – evidenced in testimonies from many of those with whom she's worked – in her groundbreaking work with prisoners and their children.

**CHRIS MACINNES**
**(HMP & YOI Isis)**

Chris is granted an Award for all-round excellence as a Prison Officer at HMP/YOI Isis, where he is widely respected by colleagues and prisoners alike, for his positive attitude, outstanding jail-craft, and "Zen-like calm" – in the words of the Governor, Chris "embodies all that is good about Prison Officers".

**SHONA PATE**
**(HMP Edinburgh)**

Already regarded as an "inspirational" manager of HMP Edinburgh's Visitors' Centre, Shona's Award is for the remarkable outreach service she put in place to support vulnerable families, including food parcels, home visits, and welfare checks, when prison visits, and many social care services, were closed by Covid.

**VICKY WALTON**
**(North East National Probation Service)**

In a nomination supported widely, including in

moving testimony from service users who describe her as "brilliant" and a "superstar", Vicky receives an Award for being quite simply exceptional, in all aspects of her role, as a Probation Services Officer for the NPS in Middlesbrough.

## PAUL WOOD
### (West Sussex Youth Offending Team)
Paul is granted an Award for his exceptional work with West Sussex Youth Offending Team. Winning widespread praise from colleagues for his "enthusiasm", "compassion", and "creativity", he "has a heart of gold" according to one young person, while to one of their parents "what Paul does is beyond words".

### Commendees
At *HMP Maghaberry, Amanda Wilson* is revolutionising accessible visits for disabled children – 'There was barely a dry eye in the house', while in HMP Pentonville it's Eve Brotzel's 'magic' helping vulnerable prisoners communicate and deepen Officers' understanding. For HMP Exeter, a challenging resident getting 'Enhanced' says everything about Bridgette Setters.

*HMP Doncaster's Emily Hazard* 'smashed it and left a legacy' by reinventing an Early Day Centre with peer 'Insiders' (reinventing them, too); HMP Full Sutton's Mel Walker 'changed everything', brilliantly solving tough problems; and HMP Preston's Ann Donnellon, with 'absolute dedication, each & every day' turned decline into transformation.

*East Midlands NPS's Myra Hogan's* 30 years giving magnificent admin support makes her the 'irreplaceable' 'Queen of Probation'. At West Midlands NPS 'quiet, determined, and gracious' Audrey Beckford brings excellence everywhere, including serious further offences practice, while 'outstanding leader' Natalie Hill has forged a new level of 'best' in staff support. HMP/YOI Isis's Chineme Mgbeike has 'unwavering personal integrity' as 'a role model, mother figure, and great example of care for staff and prisoners'.

For 45-year years, *Hackney YOT's Horace Dawkins* has used 'heart, passion, and values' while 'teaching Love to young people, love of themselves, and others.' Steven Swan, formerly at Merseyside CRC and now at North West NPS, 'gives people hope', bringing 'magic' to connecting with young men. Oakhill STC residents say Sharon Arnold 'is like my mum in prison' – their touching nominations showing her impact . HMYOI Werrington call Alice James a 'heart amongst hearts', 'the soul of the prison',

but for the boys, 'she's like your Mum and your Nan all in one'. HMP/YOI Grendon 'shining star' Gemma Grahame-Wright had 21 nominations recognising 'an absolute force of nature'.

*HMP Bronzefield's Simeon Sturney* goes the extra mile by walking alongside newly released women: 'one mile to make the difference'. HMP Lewes has had hard miles but had Gary Offen 'present at all the right moments', bringing tireless compassion to all. HMP Liverpool's Imam Talha Ahmed revived a Chaplaincy, shining light into darkness: they're 'all proud to call him our friend.' Daniel Crawley's 'courage of a lion', always calm under pressure, means 'Liverpool is lucky to have him.' HMP Wymott's Martin Wilsdon has faced crisis through grit and compassionate leadership, and 'epitomises all that we stand for.'

### TALHA AHMED
#### (HMP Liverpool)
Talha receives a Commendation for all-round excellence as Managing Chaplain at HMP Liverpool, for driving cultural change and religious understanding, and as an unwavering champion of equality and decency for all.

### SHARON ARNOLD
#### (Oakhill Secure Training Centre)
Nominated by one of the young people at Oakhill STC, and described as "exceptional" by her Director, Sharon is Commended for her extraordinary compassion and skill in supporting even the most complex children in her care.

### AUDREY BECKFORD
#### (West Midlands National Probation Service)
Audrey's Commendation is for her outstanding work with West Midlands NPS' Further Serious Offence Team, for the leadership and support she provides to colleagues, and for driving best practice across the region and beyond.

### EVE BROTZEL
#### (HMP & YOI Pentonville)
Eve is Commended for her work as a Speech and Language Therapist at HMP/YOI Pentonville; praised for her skill and sensitivity, she is described, by colleagues and clients alike, as "exceptional", "magic", and "amazing".

### DANIEL CRAWLEY
#### (HMP Liverpool)
Daniel's Commendation is for his remarkable "courage", "calm", and "compassion", and his willingness to "go the extra mile" – even learning Spanish to communicate better with one man –

as an Officer on HMP Liverpool's Care & Separation Unit.

### ANN DONNELLON
### (HMP & YOI Preston)

Ann is Commended for her professionalism, compassion, and dedication as an Officer and Custodial Manager at HMP/YOI Preston, and in particular for her outstanding and transformational leadership of her wing during the Covid pandemic.

### GEMMA GRAHAME-WRIGHT
### (HMP Grendon)

Nominated by more than 20 prisoners, who describe her as "exceptional" and "a shining star", Gemma is granted a Commendation for her outstanding work as an Officer in HMP Grendon's Therapeutic Community.

### NATALIE HILL
### (West Midlands National Probation Service)

Described as "an exceptional leader", Natalie's Commendation is for her exemplary management and support of staff dealing with a critical incident, and its aftermath, in her role as Head of Staffordshire NPS.

### ALICE JAMES
### (HMYOI Werrington)

Described by her Governor as "a heart amongst hearts", Alice is Commended for her outstanding care and compassion towards colleagues and prisoners at HMYOI Werrington, over more than 20 years as an Officer and Senior Manager.

### CHINEME MGBEIKE
### (HMP & YOI Isis)

Chineme is Commended for her "kindness", "calmness", and "compassion" towards prisoners and staff at HMP/YOI Isis, her "integrity" and steadfast commitment to best practice, and as an exemplary role model to her colleagues.

### GARY OFFEN
### (HMP & YOI Lewes)

OSG Gary's Commendation is for the truly exceptional support he provided to staff and their families during the pandemic, including when two of his colleagues sadly died, in his voluntary role as Joint Care Team Leader at HMP Lewes.

### BRIDGETTE SETTERS
### (HMP & YOI Exeter)

Bridgette is Commended as "a superb role model", "who changes lives for the better", as an Officer at HMP/YOI Exeter, and for her remarkable, life-transforming work with one especially troubled and challenging individual.

### STEVEN SWAN
### (Merseyside CRC / North West NPS)

Steven is Commended for his work as a Probation Services Officer in Merseyside, in particular for his tireless efforts, and ability to inspire hope and change, with some of the most challenging young men in the area.

### MEL WALKER
### (HMP Full Sutton)

Mel's Commendation is for her outstanding leadership in transforming the Close Supervision Centre, and Separation & Segregation Unit, at HMP Full Sutton, praised by the Regional Director, HMI Prisons and the prisoners themselves.

### MARTIN WILSDON
### (HMP & YOI Wymott)

Martin is Commended for his remarkable courage, leadership and determination throughout Covid, as Catering Manager at HMP/YOI Wymott, including, at the start of the pandemic, when his team suffered the death of a much-loved colleague.

**PSI 07/2015 has been revised to take into account the changes introduced as a result of the Transforming Rehabilitation programme (see section 2.1).**
It sets out guidance and mandatory actions for prison staff and CRCs regarding reception in, first night in custody and induction procedures.
It applies only to prisoners aged 18 and over and extends the requirements for conducting resettlement needs screening on all offenders using the Basic Custody Screening Tool and introduces the new standardised 'Introduction to Custody' process for inducting prisoners into local prisons. All subsequent references to Governors in this PSI should be taken to include Directors of contracted out prisons.

| Basic Custody Screening | For NOMS Internal use only | Official -Sensitive |

This printable version of the BCS is for use when access to the live application is not available or is not appropriate.

**Please complete all details so this can be read as a stand alone document.**

The format follows the online application as closely as possible.
To allow for additional information to be included if using this version continuation sheets are available.

INDEX
Page 2     Case Identification and Sentencing Information
Page 4     Offending Information
Page 6     Accommodation
Page 8     Education Training and Employment
Page 10    Finance
Page 11    Relationships
Page 13    Health and Well-being
Page 14    Thinking and behaviour
Page 15    Communication Issues
Page 16    Risk Screening
Page 18    Resettlement Plan

| Purpose of Assessment | |
|---|---|
| ☐ | Basic Custody Screening - Start |
| ☐ | Basic Custody Screening - Review |
| ☐ | Review Resettlement Plan |

| Reception Date | |
|---|---|

Basic Custody Screening     For NOMS Internal use only     Official -Sensitive

OASys (Offender Assessment System) **Basic Custody Screening**
This is an open document. Enter only information that can be shared with the offender

## Case Identification

| | | | |
|---|---|---|---|
| Surname Name | | Forename(s) | |
| Gender | | DOB | |
| Police National Computer (PNC) Number | | Prison Number (LIDS) | |
| Prison NOMIS Number | | Ethnic Category | |
| Tier Level | □ 1 □ 2 □ 3 □ 4 | White | □ British<br>□ Irish<br>□ Any other white background |
| Preferred Spoken Language (if not English) | | | |
| Interpreter Required | □ Yes □ No | Mixed | □ White & Black Caribbean<br>□ White & Black African<br>□ White & Asian<br>□ Any other mixed background |
| Has this offender been identified as a Prolific or other Priority Offender? (Effective September 2004) | □ Yes □ No | | |
| Have they been a member of the armed services? | □ Yes □ No | Asian or Asian British | □ Indian<br>□ Pakistani<br>□ Bangladeshi<br>□ Any other Asian background |
| NI Number | | Black or Black British | □ Caribbean<br>□ African<br>□ Any other black background |
| NHS Number | | | |
| Has the offender been in the care of local authority children's services at any time? | □ Former relevant child (under 21) □ former relevant child (under 25)<br>□ person qualifying for assistance and advice<br>□ care experience<br>□ No<br>□ Don't know | Chinese or other ethnic group | □ Chinese<br>□ Any other ethnic group |
| Sentence Date | | Not Stated | □ |
| Sentence Type | □ Remanded<br>□ 0-3 Months | Court Name | |

Basic Custody Screening     For NOMS Internal use only     Official -Sensitive

| | ☐ 4-6 Months<br>☐ 7-12 Months<br>☐ Over 12 Months | Court Type | |
|---|---|---|---|

| Date of actual release | / / | | |
|---|---|---|---|
| Home detention curfew date | Automatic release date | Conditional release date | |
| / / | / / | / / | |
| Parole eligibility date | Non parole date | Licence expiry date | |
| / / | / / | / / | |
| Facility licence eligibility date | Resettlement licence eligibility date | Sentence expiry date | |
| / / | / / | / / | |
| Post Sentence Supervision Expiry Date | | | |
| / / | | | |

| Prison | |
|---|---|
| LDU | |
| Team | |
| BCS Screener Name | |
| Assessor Position | |
| Screening Date | / / |

| Please state if screening cannot be completed and state reason | |
|---|---|

| **Current Event** | |
|---|---|
| Category of Offence* | |
| Offence* | |
| Code | |
| Subcode | |
| Count | |

Basic Custody Screening | For NOMS Internal use only | Official -Sensitive

| Additional Offence | |
|---|---|
| Category of Offence* | |
| Offence* | |
| Code | |
| Subcode | |
| Count | |

| Additional Offence | |
|---|---|
| Category of Offence* | |
| Offence* | |
| Code | |
| Subcode | |
| Count | |

| Additional Offence | |
|---|---|
| Category of Offence* | |
| Offence* | |
| Code | |
| Subcode | |
| Count | |

| Additional Offence | |
|---|---|
| Category of Offence* | |
| Offence* | |
| Code | |
| Subcode | |
| Count | |

| Additional Offence | |
|---|---|
| Category of Offence* | |
| Offence* | |
| Code | |
| Subcode | |
| Count | |

**Please note that the screener is not required to complete the OGRS questions.**

| B1.1 | |
|---|---|
| Number of court appearances at which convicted aged under 18 years | |
| Score | |

Basic Custody Screening | For NOMS Internal use only | Official -Sensitive

| B1.2 | |
|---|---|
| Number of court appearances at which convicted aged 18 years and over. Do not include current appearances | |
| Score | |
| B1.3 | |
| Number of formal cautions, reprimands and final warnings | |
| Score | |
| B1.4 | |
| Age first in contact with police: first recorded caution, reprimand or final warning (record in years) | |
| B1.5 | |
| Age at first conviction (record in years) | |

Please use the OGRS3/OGP/OVP spreadsheet calculator to provide the figures below.

| OGRS 3 | | Rating /Cat |
|---|---|---|
| General offending% within 1 year of discharge | % | V.H / H / M / L |
| General offending% within 2 years of discharge | % | V.H / H / M / L |

Basic Custody Screening        For NOMS Internal use only            Official -Sensitive

| Question Number | Question | |
|---|---|---|
| B3.1 | What was your accommodation status before prison? | ☐ Permanent<br>☐ Temporary<br>☐ NFA |
| B3.2 | What was your address before you came into prison?<br>*Only complete this question if you answered 'Permanent' or 'Temporary' to question B3.1 above* | |
| | What was your postcode?<br>*Only complete this question if you answered 'Permanent' or 'Temporary' to question B3.1 above* | |
| B3.3 | What local authority did you live in before you came into prison?<br>*Only complete this question if you answered 'Permanent' or 'Temporary' to question B3.1 above* | |
| B3.4 | What type of housing did you live in before you came into prison?<br>*Only complete this question if you answered 'Permanent' or 'Temporary' to question B3.1 above* | ☐ Council, Housing Association<br>☐ Private<br>☐ Own Home<br>☐ Hostel<br>☐ Traveller<br>☐ B&B-Hotel<br>☐ NFA |
| B3.5 | Was this accommodation from a supported housing provider?<br>*Only complete this question if you answered 'Permanent' or 'Temporary' to question B3.1 above* | ☐ Yes<br>☐ No<br>☐ Not Applicable |
| B3.6 | Are you claiming Housing Benefit?<br>*Only complete this question if you answered 'Permanent' or 'Temporary' to question B3.1 above* | ☐ Yes<br>☐ No<br>☐ Don't know |
| B3.7 | Have you got somewhere to live when you leave prison? | ☐ Yes<br>☐ No<br>☐ Don't know |
| B3.8 | Is it the same address as the one you were living at before you came into prison (B3.2 above)?<br>*Only complete this question if you answered 'Yes' to question B3.7 above* | ☐ Yes<br>☐ No<br>☐ Don't know |
| B3.9 | Are there any tenancy or rental issues with this address because you are in prison? | ☐ Yes<br>☐ No<br>☐ Not Applicable |

Basic Custody Screening        For NOMS Internal use only            Official -Sensitive

| | | |
|---|---|---|
| B3.10 | Where will you live when you leave prison?<br>*Only complete this question if you answered 'No' to question B3.8 above* | |
| | What is the postcode?<br>*Only complete this question if you answered 'No' to question B3.8 above* | |
| B3.11 | Which local authority will you be living in when you are released?<br>*Only complete this question if you answered 'No' to question B3.8 above* | |
| B3.12 | Is this an issue which needs addressing? [For the screener to consider] | ☐ Yes<br>☐ No |
| B3.13 | Evidence and any further information<br>[For the screener to consider] | |

Basic Custody Screening          For NOMS Internal use only          Official -Sensitive

| Question Number | Question | |
|---|---|---|
| B4.1 | Before coming to prison were you in:<br>1) Education, or<br>2) Apprenticeship or traineeship? | □ Yes<br>□ No |
| B4.2 | What qualifications do you have? | |
| B4.3 | Do you find it easy to read and write? | □ Yes<br>□ No<br>□ Don't know |
| B4.4 | Have you got a learning difficulty or disability? | □ Yes<br>□ No<br>□ Don't know |
| | If yes, please specify | |
| B4.5 | Have you attended a special school? | □ Yes<br>□ No |
| B4.6 | Do you find understanding English easy? | □ Yes<br>□ No |
| B4.7 | Do you find reading English easy? | □ Yes<br>□ No |
| B4.8 | Do you find writing English easy? | □ Yes<br>□ No |
| B4.9 | Do you find speaking English easy? | □ Yes<br>□ No |
| B4.10 | Do you find maths easy? | □ Yes<br>□ No<br>□ Don't know |
| B4.11 | Do you feel you need any help to make you able to work? | □ Yes<br>□ No |
| B4.12 | Were you working before you came to custody? | □ Yes<br>□ No<br>□ Don't know |
| B4.13 | Do you need help to keep your job while in prison?<br>*Only complete this question if you answered 'Employed' to question B4.12 above* | □ Yes<br>□ No<br>□ Don't know |

Basic Custody Screening          For NOMS Internal use only          Official -Sensitive

| | | |
|---|---|---|
| B4.14 | Were you on any sort of work programme before you came into prison? | □ Yes<br>□ No |
| | If so, which provider was it with? | |
| B4.15 | Is this an issue which needs addressing? [For the screener to consider] | □ Yes<br>□ No |
| B4.16 | Evidence and any further information [For the screener to consider] | |

| Question Number | Question | |
|---|---|---|
| B5.1 | Do you get money every week/month? | ☐ Yes<br>☐ No |
| B5.2 | Do you get benefits? | ☐ Yes<br>☐ No<br>☐ Don't know |
| B5.3 | Do you have any debts? If so, tell me about them? | |
| B5.4 | Do you have a bank/post office/credit union account? | ☐ Yes<br>☐ No<br>☐ Don't know |
| B5.5 | Is this an issue which needs addressing?  [For the screener to consider] | ☐ Yes<br>☐ No |
| B5.6 | Evidence and any further information [For the screener to consider] | |

| Question Number | Question | |
|---|---|---|
| B6.1 | Are you in a relationship, or single? | ☐ In a relationship – living together<br>☐ In a relationship – not living together<br>☐ Not in a relationship |
| B6.2 | How many children live at home? | |
| B6.3 | If there are children at home, how many are boys, and how many are girls?<br>*Only complete this question if the answer to question B6.2 is 1 or more* | |
| B6.4 | If there are children at home, how old are they?<br>*Only complete this question if the answer to question B6.2 is 1 or more* | |

Basic Custody Screening · For NOMS Internal use only · Official -Sensitive

| B6.5 | Are you the main carer for any of the children?<br>*Only complete this question if the answer to question B6.2 is 1 or more* | |
|---|---|---|
| B6.6 | Who is caring for your children while you are in prison?<br>*Only complete this question if the answer to question B6.2 is 1 or more* | |
| B6.7 | Are social services involved with your family? | □ Yes<br>□ No<br>□ Don't know |
| B6.8 | If so, what is the name of your social worker and where is their office? | |
| B6.9 | Do you live with others? | □ Yes<br>□ No<br>□ Don't know |
| B6.10 | Tell me who these people are.<br>*Only complete this question if you answered 'Yes' to question B6.9 above* | |
| B6.11 | How many people over 18 live with you?<br>*Only complete this question if you answered 'Yes' to question B6.9 above* | |
| B6.12 | Who are men? Who are women?<br>*Only complete this question if the answer to question B6.11 is 1 or more* | |

| B6.13 | How old are they?<br>*Only complete this question if the answer to question B6.11 is 1 or more* | |
|---|---|---|
| B6.14 | Are you the main carer for any adults? | □ Yes<br>□ No<br>□ Don't know |
| B6.15 | Who is caring for them while you are in prison?<br>*Only complete this question if you answered 'Yes' to question B6.14 above* | |

| B6.16 | Are you in contact with any family and friends? | ☐ Yes<br>☐ No<br>☐ Don't know |
|---|---|---|
| | *Refer to prison visitors scheme?* | |
| B6.17 | Would you like to be referred to someone who can help with sexual abuse issues? | ☐ Yes<br>☐ No |
| B6.18 | Would you like to be referred to someone who can help with domestic violence issues? | ☐ Yes<br>☐ No |
| B6.19 | Would you like to be referred to someone who can help with childhood abuse issues? | ☐ Yes<br>☐ No |
| B6.20 | Have you ever been involved in prostitution? | ☐ Yes<br>☐ No<br>☐ Don't know |
| B6.21 | Is this an issue which needs addressing? [For the screener to consider] | ☐ Yes<br>☐ No |
| B6.22 | Evidence and any further information [For the screener to consider] | |

| Question Number | Question | |
|---|---|---|
| B8.1 | Has the health care screening been completed on reception? | ☐ Yes<br>☐ No<br>☐ Don't know |
| B8.2 | Are you registered with a GP? | ☐ Yes<br>☐ No<br>☐ Don't know |
| B8.3 | Have you ever received support from Social Services or Social Care Services? | ☐ Yes<br>☐ No<br>☐ Don't know |
| B8.4 | Have drugs and /or alcohol ever been a problem for you? | ☐ Alcohol<br>☐ Drugs<br>☐ Both<br>☐ No |
| B8.5 | Have you ever had any contact with a drug or alcohol agency? | ☐ Yes alcohol only<br>☐ Yes drugs only<br>☐ Yes Both<br>☐ No |

| | If yes, please specify | |
|---|---|---|
| B8.6 | Have you ever had any contact with mental health services? | ☐ Yes<br>☐ No<br>☐ Don't know |
| B8.7 | Do you have any care or health problems for which you require immediate attention or medication, or which might impact on your dayto-day ability to engage with the prison regime? | ☐ Yes<br>☐ No |
| B8.8 | If yes, what help do you need with these? | |
| B8.9 | Is this an issue which needs addressing? [For the screener to consider] | ☐ Yes<br>☐ No |
| B8.10 | Evidence and any further information [For the screener to consider] | |

Basic Custody Screening                For NOMS Internal use only                Official -Sensitive

| Question Number | Question | |
|---|---|---|
| B11.1 | Do you need help to manage your temper? | □ Yes<br>□ No<br>□ Don't know |
| B11.2 | Do you need help to manage impulsivity? | □ Yes<br>□ No<br>□ Don't know |
| B11.3 | Is this an issue which needs addressing? [For the screener to consider] | □ Yes<br>□ No |
| B11.4 | Evidence and any further information [For the screener to consider] | |

Basic Custody Screening                For NOMS Internal use only                Official -Sensitive

| Question Number | Question | |
|---|---|---|
| B12.1 | Thinking about this interview as a whole in your view is there any evidence of any speech, language or communication difficulties? [For the screener to consider] | □ Yes<br>□ No<br>□ Don't know |
| | If yes, please specify | |
| B12.2 | Is this an issue which needs addressing? [For the screener to consider] | □ Yes<br>□ No |
| B12.3 | Evidence and any further information [For the screener to consider] | |

Basic Custody Screening          For NOMS Internal use only          Official -Sensitive

**The BCS Part 1 contains a Risk screening but this will not be completed as a part of the BCS process and should remain blank.**

**Risk Screening**

| Question Number | Question | |
|---|---|---|
| BR1 | To your knowledge, has the offender ever been convicted of any serious offence? Blackmail, Harassment, Stalking, Child neglect/abuse, Abuse of a vulnerable adult, Child pornography (inc possession), Abduction, Death by dangerous driving, Terrorist offences, or Serious organised crime | □ Yes<br>□ No |
| BR2 | Is offender subject to any restraining orders? | □ Yes<br>□ No<br>□ Further checks required |
| BR3 | Type. | |
| BR4 | Details for above. | |
| BR5 | Have there been any significant events in the past? | □ Yes<br>□ No<br>□ Don't know |
| BR6 | Details for above | |
| BR7 | Are there any concerns in relation to children? | □ Yes<br>□ No<br>□ Further checks required |
| BR8 | Is there evidence the offender is a perpetrator of domestic violence? | □ Yes<br>□ No<br>□ Further checks required |
| BR9 | From what you know about this offender have there been or are there currently any concerns about risk of suicide? | □ Yes<br>□ No<br>□ Don't know |
| | Check ACCT or open a new one | |
| BR10 | From what you know about this offender have there been or are there currently any concerns about risk of self harm? | □ Yes<br>□ No<br>□ Don't know |
| BR11 | From what you know about this offender have there been or are there currently any concerns about vulnerability? | □ Yes<br>□ No |

Basic Custody Screening          For NOMS Internal use only          Official -Sensitive

| BR12 | Is there a current ACCT (Assessment, Care in Custody and Teamwork)? | □ Yes<br>□ No |
|---|---|---|
| | Enter date and number of ACCT in Evidence free text box | |

---

Basic Custody Screening  For NOMS Internal use only  Official -Sensitive

| BR13 | Is this an issue which needs addressing? | ☐ Yes<br>☐ No |
|---|---|---|
| BR14 | Evidence and any further information | |

| BCS Screener Signature | | Date | / / |
|---|---|---|---|
| BCS Screener Position | | | |
| BCS Screener Team | | | |
| BCS Screener Establishment | | | |

**Resettlement Plan**

| Area of Concern | □ Accommodation<br>□ Education Training & Employment<br>□ Finance<br>□ Relationships | □ Health & well-being<br>□ Thinking & Behaviour<br>□ Communication Issues<br>□ Risk Screening |
|---|---|---|

| Problem Area | Action Required | Person Responsible | Date Opened | Completion Date | Complete |
|---|---|---|---|---|---|
| □ Accommodation<br>□ Education<br>□ Employment<br>□ Finances<br>□ Relationships<br>□ Drug Misuse<br>□ Alcohol Misuse<br>□ Thinking & Behaviour<br>□ Communication Issues<br>□ Risk Screening □ Other | | | | | □ Yes<br>□ No |
| □ Accommodation<br>□ Education<br>□ Employment<br>□ Finances<br>□ Relationships<br>□ Drug Misuse<br>□ Alcohol Misuse<br>□ Thinking & Behaviour<br>□ Communication Issues<br>□ Risk Screening □ Other | | | | | □ Yes<br>□ No |
| □ Accommodation<br>□ Education<br>□ Employment<br>□ Finances<br>□ Relationships<br>□ Drug Misuse<br>□ Alcohol Misuse<br>□ Thinking & Behaviour<br>□ Communication Issues<br>□ Risk Screening □ Other | | | | | □ Yes<br>□ No |
| □ Accommodation<br>□ Education<br>□ Employment<br>□ Finances<br>□ Relationships<br>□ Drug Misuse<br>□ Alcohol Misuse<br>□ Thinking & Behaviour<br>□ Communication Issues<br>□ Risk Screening □ Other | | | | | □ Yes<br>□ No |

Basic Custody Screening     For NOMS Internal use only     Official -Sensitive

| Problem Area | Action Required | Person Responsible | Date Opened | Completion Date | Complete |
|---|---|---|---|---|---|
| □ Accommodation<br>□ Education<br>□ Employment<br>□ Finances<br>□ Relationships<br>□ Drug Misuse<br>□ Alcohol Misuse<br>□ Thinking & Behaviour<br>□ Communication Issues<br>□ Risk Screening □ Other | | | | | □ Yes<br>□ No |
| □ Accommodation<br>□ Education<br>□ Employment<br>□ Finances<br>□ Relationships<br>□ Drug Misuse<br>□ Alcohol Misuse<br>□ Thinking & Behaviour<br>□ Communication Issues<br>□ Risk Screening □ Other | | | | | □ Yes<br>□ No |
| □ Accommodation<br>□ Education<br>□ Employment<br>□ Finances<br>□ Relationships<br>□ Drug Misuse<br>□ Alcohol Misuse<br>□ Thinking & Behaviour<br>□ Communication Issues<br>□ Risk Screening □ Other | | | | | □ Yes<br>□ No |
| □ Accommodation<br>□ Education<br>□ Employment<br>□ Finances<br>□ Relationships<br>□ Drug Misuse<br>□ Alcohol Misuse<br>□ Thinking & Behaviour<br>□ Communication Issues<br>□ Risk Screening □ Other | | | | | □ Yes<br>□ No |

| Basic Custody Screening | For NOMS Internal use only | | | Official -Sensitive |
|---|---|---|---|---|
| □ Accommodation<br>□ Education<br>□ Employment<br>□ Finances<br>□ Relationships<br>□ Drug Misuse<br>□ Alcohol Misuse<br>□ Thinking & Behaviour<br>□ Communication Issues<br>□ Risk Screening □<br>Other | | | | □ Yes<br>□ No |

| | |
|---|---|
| Actions on offenders identified as high risk of reconviction or high risk of serious harm (without OASys sentence plan) | |
| Pre-release activities completed | □ Yes |
| Comments | |

| | | | |
|---|---|---|---|
| **Resettlement Officer Signature** | | Date | /    / |
| **Resettlement Officer Position** | | | |
| **Resettlement Officer Team** | | | |
| **Resettlement Officer CRC** | | | |

Basic Custody Screening       For NOMS Internal use only       Official -Sensitive

| CONTINUATION SHEET     (Print out this page as required and index as required) | | | |
|---|---|---|---|
| Section/Question | | Offenders Name | |
| | | | |

# Section 8

## Prison Staff: Officers & Governors

**8.1 OFFICERS** - *Custody & Detention Professional Apprenticeships 2022/2023*
**8.2 GOVERNORS** - *Justice Leaders Course*
**8.3 PROMOTION** - from bottom to top
**8.4 HMPPS Workforce Statistics: August 2022**
**8.5 HMPPS Annual Staff Equalities Report**
**8.6 Pay Scales 2022/2023**
**8.7 Statement by the Justice Secretary**

### 8.1 OFFICERS Custody & Detention - Professional Apprenticeships

Since Summer 2021 all new prison officers starting in establishments in the North and Midlands region of England have begun their career by completing a Custody and Detention Professional Apprenticeship which should take 12 – 18 months to complete.

**Level 3 Apprenticeship Custody and Detention**
The Level 3 Apprenticeship Custody and Detention programme has been designed to provide Prison Officers with the confidence and competence to complete their role - it was launched in September 2021.
The delivery of the apprenticeship focuses on a practise perfect methodology, set within a framework of adult learning principles, allowing learners to become confident and competent in the practical and theoretical content of an officer role.
The apprenticeship will help HM Prison Service grow talent and develop a motivated, skilled and qualified workforce.
The apprenticeship will take, on average, 12-15 months to finish.
At the end of this time they will receive a Level 3 award, which is nationally recognised and is the equivalent of two 'A' Levels as well as a Diploma in Custodial Care.
Trainees will also receive functional skills awards in English and Maths, if they don't already have these qualifications.

**Week 1 to 10:** following a local induction at your 'home' prison you will go on a foundation training programme at a designated learning centre. This will usually be close to your 'home' prison location.

**Week 11 to 25:** you will be back at your 'home' location where you will carry on with your training with regular support from apprenticeship coaches.

You will also have 2 checkpoints to review your progress:

**Checkpoint 1 (weeks 25 to 28)**
This will include 1 week of portfolio work outside of your regular working area and 1 week at a Learning and Development Centre.

**Checkpoint 2 (weeks 44 to 47)**
You will spend 1 week at a designated learning centre. This week is an opportunity to reflect on your current progress and prepare for the Gateway at the end of your apprenticeship.

**You will receive full pay and expenses.**

**Apprenticeship coach**
You have access to an apprenticeship coach who will be an experienced operational prison officer. You will regularly meet your apprenticeship coach to check your progress and ensure you are supported throughout the apprenticeship programme.

**The Gateway**
After one year you will be eligible for the Gateway. The Gateway refers to the standard requirement that needs to be met before you start the end point assessment (EPA).
At this stage, you'll need to have completed a learning portfolio and be at the required level to undertake your English and Maths functional skills.
You will have discussions with your line manager and apprenticeship coach to see if you are ready to pass through the Gateway.

**End point assessment (EPA)**
This will take place within 3 months after passing through the Gateway.
The EPA consists of 2 parts (a project and a professional discussion) and must be passed to complete the apprenticeship.
The professional discussion makes up the bulk (71%) of the end point assessment. It will last between 90 -120 minutes and mainly consist of a small panel asking about scenario-based prison officer questions that will be linked to your portfolio of work.
The remainder of the end point assessment (29%) consists of a 1,500 word project report that will be marked by a 3rd party assessor.
When you pass the end point assessment you

will have completed your Level 3 Custody and Detention Officer apprenticeship.

You will be invited to a graduation ceremony to celebrate your success with your fellow apprentices. You have now completed your apprenticeship but this is only the beginning of your prison officer career. There will be lots of opportunities for you to continue to learn and progress.

## Top questions about the apprenticeship

*Are apprenticeships only for young people or school leavers?*

No. An apprenticeship is an enhanced programme of work-based learning for people of all ages who want to be a highly trained and professional prison officer.

The Custody and Detention apprenticeship programme offers prison officers a new approach to training and development throughout your first 12 months.

This includes support from an apprenticeship coach and opportunities to reflect and build on your skills and knowledge – getting your career off to the best possible start.

*How long does the programme take to complete?*

The prison officer apprenticeship typically takes 12 – 18 months but will be completed at your own pace and we will ensure you are fully supported throughout the programme,

*How do you apply for the apprenticeship programme?*

If your application to be a prison officer is successful you will be automatically enrolled onto the programme.

*What is the style of learning?*

You will learn a range of modules. These will be delivered by online, self-paced learning supported by face-to-face sessions with your apprenticeship coach. You will also have the opportunity to apply your learning on-the-job.

*Where will training take place?*

At the start of your apprenticeship you will complete an eight week foundation course at a dedicated learning centre.

The purpose of this course is to teach you the essential skills you need for the role of a prison officer.

Following this your training will be mainly based in your 'home' prison location and delivered via a mix of workbooks, practical assessments and case studies.

You'll receive support from your apprenticeship coach and benefit from taking part in group sessions to discuss the expert skills

*Are there any entry requirements to enrol on the apprenticeship?*

So long as you are not currently enrolled in another apprenticeship or already possess a qualification in the justice sector then there are no other entry restrictions that are specific to the apprenticeship. You will however have to achieve the required level of skills in English and Maths by the end of the apprenticeship to obtain the qualification.

## Prison officers starting in the South

Prison officers starting their career in the South of England or Wales will complete the same training as the apprenticeship (listed above) but will work towards a Professional Vocational Diploma in Custodial Care.

*What to expect during training*

The apprenticeship prepares you for life as a prison officer. You will learn and practise all the key skills and behaviours that are vital to the role including:

• how to look after people in custody
• search and security procedures
• de-escalation techniques

You will receive an NVQ Level 3 Diploma in custodial care and, for those starting in adult prisons from Summer 2021, a level 3 professional apprenticeship qualification in Custody and Detention when you complete the course.

## Opportunity and progression

Training continues throughout your probation. There may be a further 2-week residential course if you work in a high security prison.

Training is available throughout your career. You could choose to specialise in working with vulnerable prisoners, become a dog handler or train as a physical education instructor.

## Benefits of an apprenticeship

**Level 3 Custody and Detention Professional Apprenticeship** gives you the opportunity to gain specialist training alongside your regular day-to-day prison officer duties.

You can learn expert skills and behaviours to become a high performing prison officer including:

• gain a recognised qualification (equivalent to an A level)
• work with expert and experienced coaches
• additional training to reach standards in English and Maths (if required)
l• earn key transferrable skills and knowledge

As a professionally trained prison officer you will be given important skills and knowledge that will stand you in good stead throughout your prison service career.

## Custody and Detention officer

To work in custody and detention is to ensure that individuals are held in a secure, safe decent and fair environment and work as part of a team to ensure that safety of everyone in custody and detention centres is a priority.

You will operate in a secure environment such as Prisons, Detention Centres, Custodial Establishments and Custodial Services are unique and often challenging places to work.

The environment could vary from a Women's unit or treatment prison to a male resettlement prison. The people in your care will have a variety of different needs and display varied It is your role to work to ensure those individuals are treated with dignity and respect and helped to find a new way of life whilst maintaining a safe, secure and structured environment.

These environments rely and operate on routine, which you'll need to be part of, however they can often be volatile challenging places to work and officers must be able and agile enough to respond quickly to a variety of incidents whilst maintaining professional standards throughout.

You will also play a key role in rehabilitation of those in your care, acting to build commitment to change to reduce reoffending and to coach people in skills such as problem solving and management of emotions.

You will be expected to positively influence the lives of those in your care, by working with them on a daily basis in ensuring they take responsibility for their actions and welfare.

This may include maintaining links with their families, addressing offending behaviours which may have contributed to their situation and to seek positive resolution to circumstances that will affect their re-integration to society.

Officers are frontline staff who have a duty to enforce and uphold legal decisions and follow process and procedure with integrity, honesty and professionalism.

Roles in this environment will involve working a variety of shifts 365 days a year including evenings, nights, weekends and holiday periods. Examples of roles in this sector are Prison Officer, Custodial Officer, Detention Officer and Escorting Officer

### Entry Requirements

Apprentice's must be over 18 due to legal restrictions. The Apprentice must already hold a level 2 qualification in literacy and numeracy or achieve it by prior to gateway assessment

### Level: 3

*Duration: 12 - 18 months*

**As a Custody and Detention officer you must know and understand:**

• The tasks and responsibilities of the role such as keeping individuals secure, preparing them for release, authorised physical control and restraint. Including how that is relevant to the context in which you are working, how it fits within the organisation and how it interacts with other relevant organisations and agencies such as the NHS and Police

• Policies and procedures relevant to the custodial environment in which you are working and how to operate these within the remit of your role

• The key and critical aspects of security, how they contribute to the overall security of the establishment and wider service

• The causes of crime, and how you can help people turn their lives around

• The importance of having and demonstrating the values and behaviours that keep custodial environments safe and enable the people in them to concentrate on rehabilitation

• Rights and responsibilities of those in custodial care or detention

• Recognise and understand the impact of mental health issues on individuals and be able to access support as appropriate. An example of this would be sign posting effective support services, which may assist in the prevention of self-harm by others

• The importance of caring for vulnerable people who are at risk of self-harm or violence using recognised procedures and good interpersonal skills

• How you recognise the signs of substance misuse and its impact on individuals and be able to access support as appropriate

• Key principles/theories of violence reduction

• Understand the behaviour patterns of an individual during

• The importance of good communications, the use of different communication styles and knowing when to use them. An example of this might be how you motivate individuals to take part in organised activities to address offending behaviour

• Understand health and safety procedures and how to reduce the risk of harm or injury to yourself, your colleagues and those is your care by using the positive risk management processes

• How to search individuals, vehicles and buildings in the custodial setting

**As a Custody and Detention officer you must be able to:**

• Contribute actively to promote a rehabilitative culture

• Undertake incident management and " first on scene" response appropriately

• Recognise and be able to take steps to defuse potential conflict situations

• Conduct all searching appropriately, examples being the searching of individuals, buildings, vehicles and areas for the detection of illicit or prohibited items

• Explain processes, procedures and decisions to individuals in custody and detention so that they understand what will happen to them and why

• Maintain and update documentation, reports, records and supporting systems in-line with local, national and organisational requirements

• Work professionally within the custodial environment, including maintaining your own professional standards and development

• Work collaboratively with external stakeholders for example the Police, courts, National Probation Service and Community Rehabilitation Companies

• Work effectively as part of a team by positively contributing to team dynamics and being a trusted team member

• Identify risks and respond dynamically, for example carry out fire prevention protocols, or in the case of severe need, carry out a full evacuation plan in co-operation with others

**Behaviours: you will be able to**

• Adapt your personal behavioural style to suit the situation

• Act with legitimate authority so that people feel safe and treated fairly

• Act as a positive role model in terms of conflict resolution, problem solving and emotional management

• Recognise and respect diversity and cultural differences

• Be able to apply strong personal resilience and maintain personal wellbeing

• Behave openly, honestly, directly and with integrity

• Behave in a professional manner and be committed to organisational values

• Challenge individuals appropriately

• Industry specific requirements: Apprentices must attain the Ministry of Justice Commissioners license to practice prior to gateway assessment

**Where every day is different and every prison officer is too.**
There's no such thing as a typical prison officer and no such thing as a typical day.
You will work with people from all walks of life and perform a wide range of roles as a key worker – from keeping the prison safe and secure to helping vulnerable people through a difficult time in their lives.

**It's hard work but it matters.**
There is no such thing as a typical day. Life can depend on the prison, its level of security and the prisoners.

**Shifts**
Most prisons work with a changing shift pattern of 39 hours a week. This can include some nights, weekends and public holidays (these days are added to your holiday allowance).
Shifts usually follow regular hours although the start and finish time may vary depending on your prison. An example shift pattern is shown below.

|  | Start | Finish |
|---|---|---|
| Early | 7.00am | 12.30pm |
| Late | 12.00pm | 8.00pm |
| Main | 8.00am | 5.00pm |
| All day | 8.00am | 8.00pm |
| Nights | 8.45pm | 7.30am |

**Benefits**
• 25 days of annual holiday (rising to 30 days after 10 years service)
paid time off for public holidays and 1 extra privilege day
• Civil Service pension of up to 20% of your salary
• cycle to work scheme, travel loans and other benefits

**Pay**
Your pay depends on where you work in England and Wales, and your weekly shift hours. You will start on a 37 hour contract until your initial training is complete. After this you can choose to increase your hours to 39 or 41 hours a week.
You can also earn more if overtime is available in your prison.

**Example starting salary for a 39 hour week - but see further into this chapter for the payscales from April 2022 announced in August 2022 and backdated.**
The following examples include 17% unsocial hours allowance.
Inner London £31,728*
Outer London £30,149 – £32,149*
South and South East £27,118 – £29,118*
Other locations £24,118

*Your training will include the following:*
**ACCT - Assessment, Care in Custody and Teamwork**
*Key topics: ACCT Documents, Concern and Keep Safe Form*
*Learning Outcomes*
• Identify the triggers and concerns resulting in the need to open an ACCT document
• State how they would ensure that the prisoner is kept safe once a concern has been identified
• Demonstrate how to complete the Concern and Keep Safe form

• State what they would do with the ACCT Plan once the Concern and Keep Safe form has been completed

*Description*

Learners look at a case study of David who has become increasingly withdrawn and is showing signs of being upset. It transpires that a few days ago he had some upsetting news -the death of a relative. He was very close to this person, who was the only person that visited or wrote to him. He now feels miserable and alone. The learners are invited to discuss what they would do next, and to practice filling out a Concern and Keep Safe form. They then receive a hand out of a second case study for which they complete a further Concern and Keep Safe form.

### Accommodation fabric checks (AFCs)

*Key topics: Cell Call Alarm Bells*

*Learning Outcome*

• Describe and demonstrate the organisational procedures for an Accommodation Fabric Check (AFC)

*Description*

Learners look at the importance of AFCs and when they should be carried out. This session includes practice of conducting AFCs.

### ASPECT

*Key topics: Extremism, Radicalisation, Terrorism*

*Learning Outcomes*

• To provide staff working in prisons with an improved understanding of extremism, radicalisation, and extremist ideologies

• For staff to take this learning back into your work environment and use it in their day-to-day relationships with prisoners, including how to identify, report and challenge extremist behaviours

• To improve staff confidence in challenging behaviours that are contrary to our fundamental values

*Description*

This session has been developed by the Counter Terrorism group. It aims to provide an introduction to extremism within prisons.

### Authority of a prison officer

*Key topics: Arrest, Powers of the Constable, Serious Organised Crime and Police Act*

*Learning Outcomes*

• State the purpose of an arrest

• Name the two acts the powers of arrest derive from

• Demonstrate an understanding of a constable's power of summary arrest

• List the nine reasons for making a constable's arrest necessary

• State the procedures for arrest and recall the caution

*Description*

This session aims to provide an understanding of the authority of a prison officer regarding the

power of arrest and procedures involved. Learners are taught the purpose of an arrest; that while acting as such, a prison officer has all the powers of a constable; and the Serious Organised Crime and Police Act 2005 (SOCAP). The session also covers under what circumstances making an arrest might be necessary, and learners are taught the acronym ID COP PLAN to remember these by: Investigation, Disappearance, Child, Obstruction, Physical Injury, Public Indecency, Loss, Address, and Name.

### Body worn video cameras (BWVCs)

*Key topics: Security, Legal Requirements, Footage*

*Learning Outcomes*

• To understand the aims of BWVCs

• To have a better understanding of the use of BWVCs

• To ensure compliance with all security and legal requirements relating to the use, storage and downloading of material

*Description*

This session aims to introduce learners to BWVCs. It provides learners with information on how and when to use BWVCs, what happens to the footage, and how it is stored.

### Cell fire safe systems of work and respiratory protective equipment (RPE) initial

*Learning Outcomes*

• Explain how to raise the alarm and give warning of fire in the workplace

• Demonstrate an understanding of how to carry out a DRA

• Demonstrate how to use an RPE set, don and doff the set correctly and explain an understanding of all of the warning signals associated with the use of RPE

• Demonstrate how to use an inundation key to remove an inundation port

• Demonstrate safe cell door entry procedures in accordance with the Cell Fire Safe Systems of Work

• Demonstrate how to search for and safely remove an offender in accordance with the Cell Fire Safe Systems of Work

• Demonstrate appropriate management of physically aggressive and abusive behaviour using safest possible methods of persuasion and de-escalation, giving potentially lifesaving advice to the offender

• Explain the operation of extinguishing medium (methods) including Water Mist and Water Hose Reels demonstrating an understanding of how tenability of life is affected by the inundation process

• Explain how a cell fire would be resolved, if the offender was non-compliant, in an appropriate time frame ensuring the safety of both staff and offender

## Cell searching
*Key topics: Unauthorised Articles, Searching Equipment, Reporting*
*Learning Outcomes*
• Demonstrate methodical searching techniques during cell searching in accordance with the National Security Framework, whilst maintaining dignity and respect of the prisoner and their property
• State the different types of cell search, when, why and how they are carried out
• Describe how to deal with any unauthorised articles found during a cell search
• Describe why it is important to inform prisoners about the search procedure and to ask them to declare any unauthorised articles prior to the search
• Describe how to deal appropriately and sensitively with religious items whilst maintaining the security of the establishment
• State how to deal with confidential material such as legal papers
• State the search equipment that may be used when searching accommodation
*Description*
This session aims to give new staff the understanding, knowledge and skills needed for cell searching, demonstrating respect and dignity for the prisoner whilst carrying out a cell search. It looks at what routine, routine-plus, and intelligence-led cell searches involve and how to deal with any unauthorised articles.

## Communicable diseases
*Key topics: Health and Safety at Work, Control of Substances Hazardous to Health, Infectious Diseases, Bio-Hazard Cleaning*
*Learning Outcomes*
• State three factors which amplify the transmission of any infectious disease in prisons
• State the three main blood borne viruses prevalent in prisons
• State two ways staff may become infected with a blood borne virus in the operational environment
• State three ways you can protect yourself against Hepatitis B
• State what to do if you are exposed to blood or body fluid in the event of an incident
• Describe how to deal with a small blood spillage
• Describe how TB is spread and what kind of duties in prisons would place staff most at risk
*Description*
This session aims to provide learners with information on communicable disease in prisons and what steps they need to take to protect their own health and the health of others.

## Conditioning, manipulation and corruption prevention awareness
*Key topics: Corruption, Conditioning, Manipulation, Conflict of Interest, Misconduct in Public Office*
*Objectives*
• Define corruption
• Identify why staff become corrupted
• Give examples of strategies to prevent conditioning and manipulation
• State the potential consequences of becoming corrupt
• Explain how to report corruption
• Explain what Misconduct in Public Office means and give three examples
• List three examples that must be reported on the Conflict of Interest Register
• List five offences (other than conveying) against the Offender Management Act
*Description*
This module looks at how to maintain professional boundaries within the custodial environment. It aims to raise awareness of conditioning and manipulation and the consequences thereof. It includes the video 'Don't Cross the Line' which presents cases of corruption. Learners are required to respond to questions on each case presented and engage in discussions around them.

## Custodial health and safety 1
*Key topics: Risk, Legal Duties, Protection, HMPPS Policies on Stress*
*Learning Outcomes*
• List three pieces of legislation regarding work place safety
• State the five requirements under the Health and Safety at Work Act 1974 that employers must provide to look after the Health and Safety of their employees
• Describe legal duties to colleagues and others in respect of health and safety
• List the key duties of all staff in relation to HMPPS National Health and Safety Policy AI 04/2015
• Describe the difference between a hazard and a risk
• Be able to state the key health and safety risks to which they will be exposed in custodial operations
• Describe the risk control hierarchy and give an example for each
• Describe the reasons why accidents and injuries at work happen in custodial settings
• Explain the reporting process in the case of an accident, near miss or work related illness
*Description*
This session aims to provide learners with an understanding of custodial health, safety, fire and wellbeing management and how it relates to their work in the prison service. it also covers how the control of health and safety risk is an intrinsic part of operational tasks and thinking of an officer and HMPPS health and safety policy

and arrangements for managing health and safety risk.

## Custodial health and safety 2
*Key topics: Hazards, Risks, Risk Control Hierarchy, People, Plant, Premises, Procedures*
*Learning Outcomes*
• State at least five health and safety considerations they have made during the and how the health and safety principles are linked to other aspects of their training and practice.
• Explain what the term reasonably practicable means
• Define a hazard and a risk and explain how this risk can be mitigated
• Complete a risk assessment form using examples of hazards within normal wing operations
• Explain the Swiss cheese risk control model
*Description*
This session includes a description of hazards, risks and risk assessments and how these form an intrinsic part of operational tasks and the thinking of an officer.

## Decision making model
*Key topics: Defensible Decisions, Reactive Decision Making, Proactive Decision Making, IPS, Pro-Social Modelling*
*Learning Outcomes*
• Explain the five stage decision making model and how it relates to their duties
• Demonstrate, via selected exercise scenarios, the ability to follow the decision making model and make clear, justified and defensible decisions
*Description*
This aims to enable learners to make justified and defensible decisions using the decision making model. It was developed to help staff identify, prioritise and justify every decision they take, be it routine or one in relation to incidents and emergencies.

## Emergency first aid at work
• Understand the role and responsibilities of an Emergency First Aider
• Know how to assess an incident
• Manage an unresponsive casualty who is breathing normally
• Manage an unresponsive casualty who is not breathing normally
• Recognise and assist a casualty who is choking
• Manage a casualty who is wounded and bleeding
• Manage a casualty who is in shock
• Understand how to manage a casualty with a minor injury
*Description*
This session aims to provide all learners with the skills and knowledge to provide the organisation with Emergency First Aider's that can provide treatment to their casualties in a prompt, safe and effective manner.

## Equalities 1
*Key topics: Equality Policy Statement, Protected Characteristics, Legal Responsibilities, Equalities Act 2010, Victimisation, Stereotypes, Prejudice, Discrimination*
*Learning Outcomes*
• State the three duties the Equality Act imposes on HMPPS
• State the nine protected characteristics
• Define discrimination and harassment
• Define stereotyping and prejudice
• Describe the actions to be taken when witnessing an incident of discrimination, harassment or victimisation on the basis of the protected characteristics
*Description*
This session aims to give learners an understanding of the Equality Act and how it relates to their work in the prison service. Learners explore how as members of staff they are required to work and behave in a way that is consistent with the equality policy statement and legal responsibilities to eliminate discrimination and to promote equality and good relations.

## Equalities 2
*Key topics: Protected Characteristics, Harassment, Hate Crime*
*Learning Outcomes*
• Consider equality issues raised in case studies and discuss solutions to these issues
• Define disability hate crime
• State the definition of a learning disability and state three conditions common in prison establishments
*Description*
This session follows on from Equalities 1, continuing to give learners an understanding of the Equality Act. It covers additional duties of staff: to eliminate unlawful discrimination, harassment and victimisation; provide equal opportunities and foster good relations.

## Escorts, restraints and vehicle search
*Key topics: Escapes, Escort Bag, Escape Pack, Person Escort Record, Bed Watches, Cuffing, Escorts, Approved Restraints, Escapes, Unauthorised Articles, Safety and Decency, Risk*
*Learning Outcomes*
• Demonstrate knowledge of procedures for carrying out an escort and correct technique for use of restraints
• Explain the five key areas for a vehicle search
• Demonstrate the application of handcuffs for single cuffing, double cuffing and the escort chain
• State how to minimise risk when searching a vehicle

*Description*

This session aims to build on previous learning of the procedures and security measures required to carry out an escort of prisoners outside the establishment by using practical skills exercise, and to give new staff an understanding of the knowledge and skills necessary to carry out an effective vehicle search.

### Five minute interventions (FMI)

*Key topics: Every Contact Matters, Making Conversations Count, Pro-Social Behaviour, Communication, Interpersonal Skills, Rehabilitation, Socratic Questioning, Listening, Hope, Learning, Change, Respect, Practical Skill-Set, Safety & Decency, Attitudes, Goals, Self-Responsibility*

*Learning Outcomes*

• Explain the 10 FMI skills and the six targets
• Describe what behaviour will enable others to trust them
• State what the term active listening means
• Explain why it is important to give people hope and show they are able to do this in conversations
• State how to create space in difficult situations
• Demonstrate Socratic questioning
• Explain how to encourage people to seek reliable information
• Demonstrate language and questioning techniques which helps individuals move from the negative to positive
• Describe why it is important to encourage commitment to change
• Explain two strategies that will help when rolling with resistance
• State one example of giving and receiving feedback

*Description*

This session aims to introduce learners to the benefits of five minute interventions – using five minute conversations to make a difference. It will help learners to recognise that this involves consistently demonstrating that we believe in rehabilitation and that pro-social attitudes and behaviour are important, valued, respected, and a successful and rewarding way of living life. Learners are introduced to a particular set of skills to help prisoners change the ways of thinking and feeling that have got them into crime in the past.

### The 10 FMI Skills

Building trust, confidence and rapport
Active listening
Giving people hope
Creating space
Socratic questioning
Teaching people to seek reliable information
Moving from negative to positive
Commitment to change

Rolling with resistance
Giving and receiving feedback
It involves practical group exercises to explore these skills and to put them into practice.
The aim throughout the FMI training is for trainers to model FMI skills as much as possible. This includes encouraging learners to participate in their own learning and modelling a positive, encouraging and motivational attitude towards change and learning.

### Foreign national offenders

*Key topics: Stigma, Cultural Issues, Legal Support, Racism, Human Trafficking*

*Learning Outcomes*

• Define the term foreign national offender
• List six problems that foreign nationals may experience in prison
• List six things an officer can do to aid a foreign national offender
• Describe human trafficking and the National Referral Mechanism (NRM)

*Description*

This session aims to provide learners with an understanding of the needs and problems facing foreign national offenders. It explores some of the challenges which individuals in the prison system may face, including: language barriers, potential isolation, mental health and cultural differences.

### Full search

*Key topics: Officer's Powers of Search*

*Learning Outcomes*

• Explain the legal and organisational requirement for searching
• Demonstrate methodical full searching techniques in accordance with the National Security Framework, whilst maintaining dignity and respect of the prisoner and their property
• Describe how to deal with any unauthorised articles found during a rub down or full search
• Describe why it is important to inform prisoners about the search procedure and to ask them to declare any unauthorised articles prior to the search
• Describe how to deal appropriately and sensitively with religious items whilst maintaining the security of the establishment

*Description*

This session aims to give learners an understanding of the knowledge and skills necessary to carry out full searches whilst communicating effectively and demonstrating respect for the individual's dignity and rights. It covers the legal requirements which must be upheld during a full search, and how to deal with unauthorised articles.

## Incentives and earned privilege (IEP) national policy framework

*Key topics: Rehabilitation, Level Reviews, Pro-Social Modelling*

*Learning Outcomes*

• Explain why we have an IEP national policy framework
• List five positive behaviour expectations that prisoners must demonstrate in order to progress through the IEP framework
• Define the four levels of IEP status
• List the six key earnable privileges
• Outline the IEP review procedure

*Description*

This session aims to provide an understanding of the Incentives and Earned Privilege policy framework and how local schemes are used to encourage a commitment to rehabilitation, responsible behaviour and participation in constructive activity. It covers what the IEP framework expects prisoners to do, the different levels in the IEP framework, and the key earnable privileges.

## Induction to the Prison Service

*Description*

This covers the legal responsibilities of HMPPS staff to meet high standards of professional and personal conduct, and the HMPPS Equality Statement:

*HMPPS is committed to fairness for all. We treat our staff properly and ensure equality of opportunity. We deliver our services fairly and respond to individual needs. We insist on respectful and decent behaviour from staff, offenders and others with whom we work.*

## Interviewing techniques

*Key topics: Negative Behaviours, Cross-Cultural Differences, Motivational Skills, Empathetic Listening*

*Learning Outcomes*

• List the skills required to be an effective interviewer
• Describe what security measures must be in place before interviewing an offender
• Describe motivation techniques used during the interview process

*Description*

This session aims to provide the skills required for effective communication when interviewing and motivating prisoners. It covers the four stages of an interview: Preparation, Introduction, Facilitative questioning and Active listening, and Finishing. It also looks at interview room security, alerts and personal safety. Learners engage in practical interviewing role plays and are encouraged to use the 5WH model (Who, What, When, Where, Why, How?).

Learners identify passive and active listening techniques and blocks to effective communication. They learn that as an interviewer they have a purpose to increase the motivation of the offender to address offending behaviour. The session explores four motivational interviewing principles, how to: Express empathy, Develop change, Avoid argument, and Support self-responsibility. Learners are encouraged to reflect, clarify, shift focus and provide personal assurance to handle resistance. The importance of avoiding giving certain responses and making assumptions while interviewing is also explored.

## Introduction to mental health

*Key topics: HMPPS Equality Statement, Mental Illness, Mental Health Continuum, Stigma, Anxiety, Depression, Bi-Polar Disorder, Psychosis, Schizophrenia, Personality Disorders, ACCT Document*

*Learning Outcomes*

• Define mental health and mental illness
• List three groups of factors that can cause mental ill-health
• Describe the difficulties associated with social labelling
• List three examples of how a prisoner suffering mental ill-health may present

*Description*

This session aims to give staff an introduction to mental health issues in prisons. It compares and contrasts physical and mental health problems and looks at the prevalence of mental health disorders in prison. Learners look at the most prevalent disorders found in prison: anxiety states, depression, bi-polar disorder, psychosis and schizophrenia, and personality disorders. The session also covers how a prisoner's mental health might affect how they present themselves and how an officer might interact positively with prisoners with different disorders.

## Introduction to rehabilitation and building a rehabilitative culture

*Key topics: What is rehabilitation?, What does a rehabilitative culture look like in a prison environment?, why should we rehabilitate prisoners?*

*Learning outcomes*

• State what rehabilitation is
• Describe the costs of re-offending
• State the five components of the rehabilitative triangle
• Describe what benefits rehabilitation and a rehabilitative culture can bring to prisoners, staff and society

*Description*

This session introduces learners to the concepts of rehabilitation, rehabilitative culture and the important role prison officers play in these.

### Introduction to security

*Key topics: Procedural Security, Physical Security, Dynamic Security, Escape Risks, Terrorism, Security Measures*

*Learning Outcomes*

• State the differences between procedural and physical security
• State the definition of dynamic security
• Explain the four security categories applicable to adult male prisoners and the definition of each category
• Explain the four security categories applicable to female and young person/young adult prisoners
• State the three escape risk classifications
• Describe the difference between escape and abscond
• Describe the three levels of response to a terrorist threat

*Description*

This session provides learners with an overview of security within the custodial environment. It covers physical, procedural and dynamic security. Learners look at the different categories of prisons and the purpose of categorisation. They also learn about E-list prisoners, escapes, absconds, and different security measures.

### Introduction to suicide and self-harm prevention

*Key topics: Mental Health, Triggers, Active Listening, Closed Questions, Open Questions, Socratic Questions, Communication*

*Description*

These sessions aim to provide learners with an understanding of the triggers and causes that can bring about distress and prompt a prisoner to attempt self-harm or suicide. For those identified as being at risk know how to support them to reduce the risk including how the effective use of the ACCT process can assist with this aim.

*Session 1 Learning Outcomes*

• Outline why people self-harm and attempt suicide
• Describe six high risk situations within the prison environment
• Identify six trigger factors within prisons
• Describe how to recognise distress
• Describe six methods of self-harm

*Session 2 Learning Outcomes*

• List four common components of communication
• Describe five skills of an effective listener
• List four barriers to communication
• List three qualities needed to deal with conflict and difficult situations
• Outline approaches to effective questioning
• Demonstrate effective communication skills

### Introduction to suicide and self-harm prevention (continued)

*Key topics: Resilience, Stigma, Unconscious Bias, FMI, Support Mechanisms, ACCT Plan*

*Session 3 Learning Outcomes*

• Demonstrate/issue correctly opened ACCT document
• Completion of keep safe and care form
• How to action opened document
• Input for case reviews
• Completion of ongoing records

*Session 4 Learning Outcomes*

• List four internal support services and how to refer them
• List four external support services and how to refer them
• Describe the importance of maintaining family contact

*Session 5 Learning Outcomes*

• Identify potential bias associated with suicide and self-harm
• Identify potential signs of stress in self and others
• Identify support that is available for members of staff

### Law and policy

*Key topics: Human Rights Act, Breaches, Fundamental Rights and Freedoms, NSF, LSS, Risk Analysis, Audit, Searching of Staff, Rehabilitation, Consequences of Actions, Safety, Good Order and Discipline*

*Learning outcomes*

• Explain what the Human Rights Act (HRA) is and why it was introduced
• Explain the purpose of prison rules
• Explain the purpose of Prison Service Instructions (PSI) and Prison Service Orders (PSO)
• Explain the purpose of the National Security Framework (NSF) and the Local Security Strategy (LSS)

*Description*

This session gives learners a brief outline of law, policies and what governs HMPPS.

### Manual handling

*Learning Outcomes*

• Understand the reasons for safe manual handling
• Understand how manual handling risk assessments contribute to improving health and safety
• Understand the principles, types of equipment and testing requirements associated with manual handling safety
• Be able to apply safe manual handling principles

### Key worker (offender management)

*Key topics: Key Worker, Progression Plan, FMI, Cycle of Change, Reinforcing Positive Change*

*Session 1 Learning Outcomes*

• State the two new offender management roles

- List three of the five key features of the new model
- State the difference between a CRC or NPS allocated prisoner
- State the desired outcomes of the key worker role

Session 2 Learning Outcomes
- List the different stages of the person's journey
- Explain the difference between an indeterminate and a determinate sentence
- List the types of indeterminate sentence
- Explain the tasks a key worker can undertake to increase the likelihood of success during the person's journey

Session 3 Learning Outcomes
- State the definition of risk
- Describe the three key risk assessments undertaken in the criminal justice sector
- State five of the dynamic factors considered when assessing the risk of reoffending
- State three of the static factors used when assessing the risk of reconviction

Session 4 Learning Outcomes
- Conduct a key worker session using the national script format
- Facilitate an individual to develop their own progression plan utilizing all available sources of information
- Use appropriate styles of questioning to explore an individual's motivation, recognise barriers or resistance and consider ways to help individuals overcome this
- Manage a difficult conversation with an individual
- Recognise and celebrate an individual's achievements in an appropriate way

Description
Session one aims to introduce learners to the offender management model and the role of the key worker. Session two aims to introduce learners to the journey through custody and release and how this will involve them as key workers. Session three explores risk within the criminal justice sector and aims to help learners recognise and respond to this within the custodial environment. Session four consolidates the learning from prior sessions with practical skills training on conducting key worker sessions.

## Personality disorders
Key topics: Features, Myths, Reactions, Responses, Strategies, Diagnosis, Biopsychosocial Model
Learning Outcomes
- Describe what personality disorder means
- Explain what influences the development of personality difficulties/disorder
- Describe the impact personality difficulties/disorder might have on a prisoner and how they can be supported
- Explain how to respond to challenging behaviour
- Explain why it is important to build supportive relationships and emotional communication

Description
This session aims to provide learners with an introduction to some of the key ideas about personality disorder and to encourage them to think about what their role as a prison officer is in supporting someone who might experience difficulties. It introduces and gives a simple definition of personality disorders. Learners are taught the common features of personality disorders and "the three Ps": Problematic, Persistent, and Pervasive. The session also covers the biopsychosocial model of health, patterns of attachment and some case studies. Learners look at: the primary presenting factors of some disorders; potential positive and negative effects of diagnosis; common myths, reactions and responses; and some helpful strategies.

## Placing a prisoner on report and adjudications
Key topics: Fairness, Impartiality, Hearings, Legal Requirements, Records
Learning Outcomes
- Explain the purpose of the adjudication process, the roles and responsibilities in relation to it, and the records that must be completed
- State the considerations prior to placing the prisoner on report ensuring fairness and impartiality
- Describe two alternatives to placing a prisoner on report
- State five offences that require adjudications
- Draft charges that are justifiable, verified, within agreed timescales and meeting legal requirements
- State the roles of all those involved in the adjudication process and the appropriate way to inform people about charges against them
- Take part in an adjudication role-play

Description
This session aims to provide learners with an understanding of the procedures to place a prisoner on report and the adjudication process. The session covers questions which should be asked before placing a prisoner on report and potential alternatives. After covering the theory, learners have the opportunity to practice their new skills through the use of role play adjudication scenarios.

## Procedural justice perceptions (PJP) in prisons
Key topics: Violence Reduction, Safety, Rehabilitation
Learning Outcomes
- Describe what procedural justice perceptions (PJP) are
- Describe the four principles of PJP
- Identify specific behaviours relating to these four principles
- Explain why perceptions of fair and just treatment achieve better outcomes. What procedural justice is

*Description*

This session aims to explore what it means to be perceived as procedurally just, which behaviours contribute to being perceived as procedurally just, and what effects procedural justice perceptions can have in a prison environment.

**Pro-social modelling & interpersonal skills 1**

*Key topics: Rehabilitation, Attitudes, Behaviours, Communication, First Impressions, Perception, Adaptive Unconscious (or unconscious bias), Confirmation Bias, In Group Advantage*

*Learning Outcomes*

• Explain what the term pro-social modelling means
• Describe five measures you can consider in order to make an appropriate first impression on those you meet
• Give three examples of appropriate language that encourages pro-social modelling
• List the four common components of communication that are essential for giving and receiving clear helpful and appropriate information
• Describe three barriers to communications and how to overcome them
• Describe what 'adaptive unconscious', 'confirmation bias' and 'in group advantage' are and how they relate to your work

*Description*

This session aims to provide learners with an understanding of pro-social modelling, how their behaviours are perceived by others within an operational setting, and the implications this can have for themselves, their colleagues, and the offenders we work with, as well as the public at large.

**Pro-social modelling & interpersonal skills 2**

*Key topics: Responsible Authority, Respect, Belief in Change, Social Learning, Betari Box*

*Learning Outcomes*

• List six positive behaviours that reflect pro-social role modelling
• Briefly explain how your behaviour will influence prisoners and others who you come in contact with
• List six behaviours that do not reflect pro-social role modelling

*Description*

This session aims to introduce the concept of pro-social modelling and establish a clear understanding of what it is and what it is not.

**Pro-social modelling & interpersonal skills 3**

*Key topics: Relationships, Team Building, Valuing Diversity, Promoting Equality, Rapport*

*Learning Outcomes*

• State who we have relationships with and why we build relationships
• State what makes a good relationship

• State the benefits of valuing diversity and promoting equality/good relations
• Identify the five levels of RAPPORT
• Give a definition of TEAM and list the stages of team development
• Take part in team building exercise, building effective working relationships with other course members

*Description*

This session aims to give a basic understanding of the concepts of relationship building, team building and team development. It includes a team building activity.

**Pro-social modelling & interpersonal skills 4**

*Key topics: Environmental Influence, Person Influence, Personal Choice, Responsibility, Attitudes, Approaches, Betari Box, Open Questioning*

*Learning Outcomes*

• Explain how your own attitude and behaviour affects the attitude and behaviour of others
• Describe the importance and impact of pro-social modelling in custody, and how this links to the needs of the organisation
• Describe and use techniques to reinforce and promote pro-social attitudes and behaviour
• Describe and use pro-social techniques to challenge anti-social attitudes and behaviour
• Understand and describe methods which promote choice and self-responsibility

*Description*

This session aims to explore how we build on pro-social skills and knowledge in order to promote pro social attitudes and behaviour in offenders, and how to challenge anti-social attitudes and behaviour.

**Public protection and MAPPA**

*Key topics: Offender Assessment System, Multi Agency Public Protection Arrangement, ViSOR, Critical Information*

*Learning Outcomes*

• State the link that our statement of purpose has with public protection
• Explain the officer's role in public protection
• Explain how prisoners in custody can still cause harm to the public
• List at least three public protection issues that offenders may present
• State three methods of sharing information about prisoners
• Describe the purpose of MAPPA

*Description*

This session aims to give new staff an understanding of their role in public protection and the reporting systems in place to raise concerns. It covers some methods used by prisoners to cause harm to the public including letters, telephone calls and visits, and considers ways these are monitored. Learners look at how the public are protected following release of an individual and the role of staff in this. The composition of MAPPA, its purpose, and who is managed by MAPPA are also covered.

## Purpose of HMPPS
*Key topics: Ministry of Justice, HMPPS, National Probation Service, Community Rehabilitation Companies, Statement of Purpose, Rehabilitation*
*Learning Outcomes*
• Explain the values and statement of purpose of HMPPS
• Describe how HMPPS fits within MOJ
• Summarise the role of HMPS
• Summarise the role of the NPS in HMPPS
•Summarise the role of CRC in HMPPS
*Description*
This session enables learners to have an understanding of the purpose of HMPPS and their role within the Prison Service. It explores the management structure of the organisation and how its different components link together, along with the prison services' statement of purpose, vision, objective and principles.

## Radio 1 and 2
*Key topics: Radio Set-Up, Net Procedures, Phonetic Alphabet*
*Learning Outcomes*
• Check and demonstrate that their radio is set up and working properly
• State and demonstrate the correct use of the phonetic alphabet
• State at least five standard expressions
• State at least five designated call-signs
• Apply the acronym SAD when using the radio
• Demonstrate the use of the radio when moving prisoners around the establishment
• Understand radio procedures in the deployment of fixed posts
• Demonstrate the correct procedure for the deployment of fixed posts
*Description*
Radio 1 aims to give new staff an introduction to radio and net procedures used in the prison service. It covers the key components of the radio network and the standard expressions used by staff to communicate by radio. New prison officers learn how to join the prison net, how to respond to net test calls and how to leave the net.
Radio 2 aims to develop radio skills in order to meet operational requirements through practical activities.

## Radio 3 and 4
*Key topics: Urgent Message, Suspicious Package, Incident Report*
*Learning Outcomes*
• Apply the mnemonic "AIR" to urgent message situations
• Explain the procedure when dealing with a suspect package
• Send an "urgent message" during an exercise scenario in line with the organisations policies and procedures
• Complete an accurate and effective incident report
*Description*
Radio 3 aims to provide learners with the knowledge of, and ability to carry out, urgent message procedures. This session involves practical activities using radios. It includes when an Urgent Message would be required and what information should be transmitted in an urgent message. It also covers what actions should be taken if a suspicious package is found.
Radio 4 is highly practical and aims to provide learners with skills to effectively manage an urgent message situation using correct radio procedures.

## Reception, first night unit and induction
*Key topics: Treatment, Procedures, Humanity, Courtesy, Risk, Property, Individual Needs*
*Learning Outcomes*
• State the purpose of the reception process
• Explain the checks that need to be made to ensure a prisoner can be held legally
• Identify at least four functions of the person escort record (PER)
• Describe the purpose of the Cell Share Risk Assessment (CSRA) process
• Name the relevant colour codes on a prisoner property card
• Take part in a practical exercise for the reception process using a prisoner profile case study
• State five potential risks or needs of a prisoner on their first night in custody
• Identify ways to manage the concerns of a prisoner during the first night in custody and induction process
*Description*
This session is a practical session that covers the procedures for receiving offenders into custody, providing an overview of first night units and inductions. Learners look at the treatment of offenders, the 5 point warrant check, the PER, the Suicide and Self-Harm Warning Form, Cell Share Risk Assessment, and further checks. It also includes meeting individual needs and risks, and examples of phase 1 and 2 induction topics such as "making applications and complaints" and "obtaining advice on legal services".

### Reflective learning sessions

*Description*

The aim of these sessions is to provide learners with a safe and controlled environment to put into practice the skills they have gathered throughout their training.

The sessions are an opportunity for learners to practice their techniques and ask questions focused around key behaviours such as: rehabilitative skills, five-minute interventions, interpersonal skills, first on scene, incident handling, violence reduction, rehabilitative culture, conflict resolution, and further skills learned on the course.

### Regime management planning

*Key topics: Safety, Health & Safety, Risk*

*Learning Outcomes*

• Explain what a regime management plan (RMP) is, and why is it required
• Describe the purpose of RMP
• Outline the relationship between health & safety, risk assessments and safe systems of work, and the RMP
• State what minimum staffing levels (MSL) are and their importance
• State the importance of the alarm response

*Description*

This session aims to provide prisoner-facing staff with an understanding of safe operating procedures in order to support the stability of the regime within an establishment.

### Responding to incidents / first on scene including hostage

*Key topics: Preservation of Evidence, Vigilance*

*Learning Outcomes*

• Describe HMPPS' four main objectives for dealing with serious incidents
• Explain the difference between a minor and a serious incident
• State the command mode/structure that is put in place in the event of a serious incident
• Explain the purpose of contingency plans
• Explain the mnemonic STORM in relation to being first on scene at an incident
• State the initial actions to be followed by the first on the scene at a serious incident
• Explain the process for preservation of evidence
• State the procedures to be followed by the first on the scene at a hostage incident
• Describe the strategies which should be adopted if taken hostage

*Description*

This session aims to provide staff with an awareness of the prison service strategy for dealing with serious incidents including hostage. It covers HMPPS' strategy: to preserve life, to prevent escape, to demonstrate that hostage taking does not work, and to maintain public confidence.

### Restraints

*Key topics: Cuffing, Escorts, Approved Restraints*

*Learning Outcomes*

• Explain the importance of professional working relationships
• State the three main different types of approved restraints
• State the appropriate use of restraints
• Demonstrate the correct procedure for single cuffing
• Demonstrate the correct procedure for double cuffing prisoner to officer
• Demonstrate the correct procedure for double cuffing prisoner to prisoner
• Demonstrate how to correctly apply an escort chain when the prisoner is handcuffed to an officer
• Demonstrate how to correctly apply an escort chain when a prisoner is handcuffed to another prisoner

*Description*

This session aims to enable learners to apply mechanical restraints effectively, including demonstrating the appropriate interpersonal skills. It covers pre-cuffing procedures, professional working relationships, and the importance of considering how the prisoner might be feeling based on why they are leaving the establishment, e.g. to attend a funeral. It highlights the importance of remaining alert, regardless of the type of escort. Also during the session new officers will learn about the three main different types of approved restraint: standard handcuffs, ratchet handcuffs, and escort chains.

### Role of the prison officer

*Key topics: Rehabilitation, Integrity, Decency, Attitude, Behaviour, Interpersonal Skills, Resilience, Use of Legitimate Authority*

*Learning Outcomes*

• Describe five main characteristics required to be an effective prison officer and what each means
• List five examples of how staff can work as part of a team within their establishment

The session emphasises that the role of the prison officer is one that requires many different skills and qualities, and that developing themselves is continual process which will begin during their foundation training. It aims to give learners an understanding of the role of a prison officer and what qualities are needed to be the ideal officer. It outlines key behaviours including: being morally conscious, using legitimate authority, being rehabilitative, being resilient, and being interpersonally courteous.

### Roll checks, locking and unlocking

*Key topics: Physical Security, Personal Safety*

*Learning Outcomes*

• Describe and demonstrate the organisational procedures for a roll check

• Demonstrate the organisation's locking and unlocking procedures

*Description*

This session aims to provide new staff with an understanding of physical security, roll checks and locking & unlocking procedures within the custodial environment. Learners are taught the purpose of a roll check and how to carry out a roll check.

## Rub down search

*Key topics: Officers' Powers of Search, Legal Requirements*

*Learning Outcomes*

• Explain the legal and organisational requirement for searching

• Demonstrate methodical rub down searching techniques in accordance with the National Security Framework, whilst maintaining dignity and respect of the prisoner and their property

• Describe the procedure for searching children and babies

• Demonstrate how to use a hand-held metal detector

• Describe how to deal with any unauthorised articles found during a rub down search

• Describe why it is important to inform prisoners about the search procedure and to ask them to declare any unauthorised articles prior to the search

• Describe how to deal appropriately and sensitively with religious items whilst maintaining the security of the establishment

*Description*

This session aims to provide learners with an understanding of the knowledge and skills required to carry out a rub down search including communicating effectively and demonstrating respect for the individual's dignity and rights. It covers key legal requirements related to when and how a prisoner should be searched.

## Safeguarding

*Key topics: Child Safeguarding, Domestic Abuse, Duty of Care, Violence, Neglect, Risk Factors, Reporting, Coercion*

*Learning Outcomes*

• List the four main types of child abuse

• List four triggers that may indicate that a child is subject to neglect or harm

• State three factors that are widely recognised as putting children more at risk of harm

• State who staff can report concerns to

• List three ways to make a written record of a safeguarding concern

• List the five main types of domestic abuse

• List four triggers that may indicate that an individual is subject to domestic abuse

• List four triggers that may indicate that an

individual is a perpetrator of domestic abuse

• List two behaviours exhibited by children who witness domestic abuse

*Description*

This session aims to give new staff an understanding of the duty placed on organisations by the Children Act 2004. To safeguard and promote the welfare of children and statutory guidance: Working Together to Safeguard Children, which supports organisations in fulfilling that duty. It also aims to give new staff an awareness of domestic abuse, as defined by the cross-government definition, and their responsibilities in relation to it.

## The Shannon Trust

*Key Topics: Reading Plan, Turning Pages, Support, Impacts*

*Learning Outcomes*

• Identify potential impacts of not being able to read in the prison environment

• Explain what the Shannon Trust Reading Plan (Turning Pages) is

• Describe steps staff can take to help prisoners who cannot read

*Description*

This session has been created by the Shannon Trust, registered charity 1117249. The session aims to provide learners with a knowledge of the Shannon Trust Reading Plan (Turning Pages), the prevalence of reading difficulties across the prison estate, and how staff can best help those in prison who cannot read.

## Security and wing duties 1

*Key topics: Supervision, Communication, Procedures, LSS, Nights, ACCT, Residential Handovers, Roll Checks, Unlocking*

*Learning Outcomes*

• Describe the differences between day and night security states

• Describe the organisation's residential handover procedures

• State the purpose of a roll check

• Describe a range of relevant wing documentation for prisoners/staff and explain who to pass them on to

*Description*

This session aims to give learners an understanding of wing duties and their responsibility toward security within the residential areas of the custodial environment.

### Security and wing duties 2

*Key topics: Prisoner Complaint Procedure, High Risk Prisoners, Roll Checks, Exercise*

*Learning Outcomes*

• Describe the purpose of the prisoner complaint procedure

• State the stage one and stage two response times for prisoner complaints

• Explain the reasons why a prisoner may use confidential access to make a complaint

• Describe three security measures that need to be considered during the movement of prisoners

• State two additional security measures that need to be considered when moving high risk, Category A or E list prisoners

• Describe why it is important to maintain the roll

• State the reason why a stand fast role check may be called

• Describe five security measures that need to be considered during prison exercise

*Description*

This session continues on from Wing Duties and Security 1. It covers: the prisoner complaint procedure, the preparation for and movement of prisoners; category A, high risk, and E list prisoners; roll checks; and exercise.

### Security and wing duties 3

*Key topics: Tools, Shadow Boards, Servery, Menus and Meals, Prison Rule 24, Food Hazards, Slips and Trips*

*Learning Outcomes*

• Describe how to account for tools and utensils in the workplace

• Describe the tally system for accounting for tools and utensils

• Explain measures to ensure that food is transported, stored and served safely

• Explain what due diligence means

• Describe a range of checks servery officers can make to ensure that food handlers under their supervision comply with the law

• List the written audit checks that need to be completed on a daily basis

• Complete the level 1 food safety exam

• Explain the British Institute Cleaning science (BICs) colour coding chart for cleaning

• Explain the safety considerations that need to be made when supervising the cleaning of floors and stairs

*Description*

This session continues on from Wing Duties and Security 2. It covers tools and their storage, Prison Rule 24 on food, serving temperatures, and the Workplace Regulations 1992. New officers also learn about personal protective equipment, cleaning, and food hazards (microbiological, physical, chemical, and allergenic).

### Stress management, resilience and wellbeing

*Key topics: Wheel of Stress, Five Ways to Wellbeing, Support Networks, Pressure, Attendance, Physical and Mental Wellbeing, Health and Safety at Work Act*

*Learning Outcomes*

• Define stress and list its impact on health and wellbeing

• State the difference between pressure and stress and list the factors which can cause stress in any work (especially in prison operations) and in your personal life

• State the role you have in responding to stress in yourself and colleagues and the value of maintaining physical and mental health

• Define the concept of personal resilience

• List the various measures in place in HMPPS to prevent, identify and respond to cases of stress

• Describe possible strategies to combat personal stress

*Description*

This session aims to provide learners with an introduction of how to increase and maintain their wellbeing and resilience through positive behaviours and how to deal with stress. It explores the short- and long-term effects of stress, recognising stress, and stress and the law. It provides strategies for dealing with stress, the role of employers and employees in managing stress, and covers the five ways to wellbeing. It also explores resilience and its contribution towards mental wellbeing.

### Substance misuse

*Key topics: Psychoactive Substances, Paraphernalia, Testing*

*Learning Outcomes*

• List some of the reasons why people take drugs

• List substances commonly used in prison

• Describe what a drug is and list the four main groups of drugs and their effects

• List methods of drug taking

• Identify items used in drug taking

• Describe some of the health harms arising from licit and illicit substance use

• Signpost prisoners into relevant treatment/recovery services

• List the four priorities of the cross-Government Drugs Strategy 2010

• State the different types of drug testing undertaken in establishments

• Describe the strategies that are in place to reduce supply and demand of drugs in prison

*Description*

This session aims to give new staff a basic understanding of substance use/misuse in prisons and some of the health harms arising from licit and illicit use and how this issue is dealt with in prisons. It covers the procedures in place to test for drug/alcohol misuse and understand why demand and supply strategies should be mutually reinforcing. It aims to provide staff with the confidence to recognise drugs and drugs paraphernalia and understand the effects drugs can have on individuals.

## Use of force - theory

*Key topics: Defensible Decision Making, Health and Safety, Communication, Resolution, Managing Conflict*

*Learning Outcomes*

The Law:
• Outline legislation and organisational policies that underpin the use of force

Managing conflict through communication:
• Identify barriers to communication and ways to overcome these
• Identify early warning signs of aggression and ways to reduce the build-up of aggression

Decision making process:
• Describe the decision-making process
• Outline resolution strategies, based on risk assessment for specified scenarios

Application of techniques:
• Apply all approved restraint techniques safely and in line with associated law and policy
• Apply all approved additional restraints safely and in line with associated law and policy

Medical:
• Identify the potential medical complications of approved use of force techniques
• Identify pre-existing conditions that may be exacerbated by using force
• Name possible causes of restraint asphyxia
• List the signs and symptoms of asphyxia
• Demonstrate the actions to be taken in response to a medical emergency

Report writing:
• Define the term 'use of force'
• Outline the purpose of writing use of force reports

Learning:
• Enable learning through demonstrations and instructions

## Use of force – practical

After completing the use of force theory sessions, learners will undertake eight practical sessions before they are assessed to a level of competence.

## Violence reduction

*Key topics: Victimisation, Anti-Social Behaviour, Racism, Physical Assault, Risks, Triggers*

*Learning Outcomes*
• Explain the meaning of a violent incident
• List four forms of violence
• State five known triggers which may increase violence in prison
• State the aim of the violence reduction strategy
• List the six key principles of the violence reduction strategy

• State three responsibilities of an officer in successfully managing violence in prisons

*Description*

This session aims to provide learners with information on reducing violence in prisons. It covers the definition of a violent incident, forms of violence, triggers of violent episodes, and the effects of violence. Learners also look at the crucial risk factors for managing violence in prisons: individual, situational and social approaches. The session explores the violence reduction strategy and how to improve challenging behaviour. It includes role plays to practice the skills developed in class.

## Visits (maintaining family ties)

*Key topics: Legal and Professional Visits, Social Visits, Entitlements, Surveillance, Searching, Visitor Exit Procedures*

*Learning Outcomes*
• Identify the key outcome requirements for the service from visits
• Identify different types of establishment visits
• State the security measures to be in place prior to/ during and after a visits session
• State what impacts having a parent/ guardian in prison may have upon a child
• State how the public protection and safeguarding measures relates to visits

*Description*

This session aims to provide new staff with an understanding of policy requirements relating to visits procedures, and how they complement the regime and routine of the establishment. It explores the impact on families and children of having a relative in prison.

## 8.2 GOVERNORS - JUSTICE LEADERS COURSE 2022/2023

**Prison**
**Probation**
**Youth Custody**
**You can influence it all**
**Transform the future of the justice system on a unique new leadership scheme.**

## The path to leadership

*Justice Leaders* is an exciting, brand new fast-track scheme that spans the whole of His Majesty's Prison and Probation Service (HMPPS). It is the first of its kind to develop future leaders in operational offender facing roles, with the ability to work across Prison, Probation, and the Youth Custody Service.

HMPPS carries out sentences given by the courts, helping people lead law-abiding and useful lives, both while they are in prison and after they are released. We support people in our care on their road to rehabilitation through education and employment.

Over four years, you will experience a diverse variety of exciting placements across Prison, Probation and Youth Custody while completing a bespoke Masters qualification. These placements will provide a foundation for your future leadership roles. You will help to improve the experiences of people moving through the system, bringing about positive change through your inspirational attitude, engagement, and commitment to making a difference to the lives of those in your care.

### Placements & Scheme Structure
### Years 1 and 2

The first three months of the scheme are spent experiencing the journey of somebody moving through the criminal justice system. You will spend time with the Police, Courts, Prison and Probation. During this time, you will also complete your seven-week Prison Officer Entry Level Training. This is the operational training required to become a Prison Officer and includes a combination of practical and theoretical learning on everything from personal protection to identifying people at risk of self-harm.

You will then go on to spend three months working in a prison as a Prison Officer. In this role you will develop your understanding of the prison system, building confidence and working directly with prisoners. Expect to encounter people from all walks of life and perform a wide range of roles as a key worker – from keeping the prison safe and secure to helping vulnerable people through a difficult time in their lives.

The next stage of the scheme will involve 17 months of varied work across Prison and Probation. During this time, you focus on completing the Professional Qualification in Probation (PQiP) element of the Masters and learning how we support people as they complete or serve their sentences in the community.

### Years 3 and 4

At the end of two years, you will sit a Career Development Panel. This will be an opportunity to discuss your progress and to choose whether to specialise in Prison, Probation or Youth Custody. At this point the pathways diverge and offer different kinds of experience and training over the following two years. However, all participants pursue the same Masters qualification.

### Masters Qualification

The HMPPS Justice Leadership Masters is a bespoke new qualification created specifically for the Justice Leaders scheme to develop the first

## JUSTICE LEADERS SALARY 2022

| YEARS 1 AND 2 | | |
|---|---|---|
| **National** | **Outer London** | **Inner London** |
| £27,121 £21,693 basic salary + additional allowances for additional and unsocial hours | £30,488 £24,689 basic salary + additional allowances for additional and unsocial hours | £32,244 £26,111 basic salary + additional allowances for additional and unsocial hours) |

| YEAR 3 | | | |
|---|---|---|---|
| £37,276 £30,453 basic salary + additional allowances for additional and unsocial hours) | £40,536 £33,116 basic salary + additional allowances for additional and unsocial hours) | £42,236 £35,234 basic salary + additional allowances for additional and unsocial hours) | Probation Career Pathway switch at year 3 + 4 months as below: £37,276 – £37,174 (basic salary + marked time balance of £102) Additional London Allowance (where applicable) of £3,889 = total pay £41,165 |

| YEAR 4 | | | |
|---|---|---|---|
| £37,276 £30,453 basic salary + additional allowances for additional and unsocial hours | £40,536 £33,116 basic salary + additional allowances for additional and unsocial hours) | £42,236 £35,234 basic salary + additional allowances for additional and unsocial hours | Probation Career Pathway £37,276 – £37,174 (basic salary + marked time balance of £102) Additional London Allowance (where applicable) of £3,889 = total pay £41,165 |

| ONCE OFF THE SCHEME |
|---|
| Candidates will be required to apply for their chosen role through fair and open competition. Where successful, those who are pursuing the prisons career pathway will have their pay calculated as a promotion from Band 3 under whichever prisons pay on promotion policy is in place at the time. If this results in lower pay than in year 4 of the scheme, the necessary upward adjustment will be made to ensure no detriment. Because there are no recognised grade equivalencies between prisons and probation, those pursuing the probation career pathway will be placed at the pay range minimum for the role successfully applied for. If this results in lower pay than in year 4 of the scheme, the necessary upward adjustment will be made to ensure no detriment. Staff then becoming subject to either the prisons or probation pay awards (depending on chosen career pathway) annually. |

cohort of future leaders with the skills and experience to work across HMPPS. You will study a range of topics such as safeguarding in childcare, risk management, rehabilitation, protecting the public, critical thinking, understanding crime and criminal behaviour and leadership.

### Youth Custody

Prison Officers who work in the Youth Custody Service are called Youth Justice Workers. Working with Children is a specialism and so requires specialist knowledge. The new Masters takes several of the most salient modules from the existing qualification that Youth Justice Workers must complete.

### Support while on the scheme

We understand the pressures of undertaking such an intensive period of development. We will ensure you are well supported in both your operational work and your academic learning.

You will be offered several career development panels during the scheme. This is designed to be a supportive process, which gives you an opportunity to discuss your ambitions, progress and how you can make the most difference in your career.

To ensure you get the most out of Justice Leaders you will be expected to be proactive, taking ownership and responsibility of your personal development. There will be mentoring and coaching available from colleagues and managers, and you will also have the support and guidance of your line manager and the central Justice Leaders team.

## 8.3 PROMOTION

Current assessment model at each level:
**Band 3 or 4 Prison Officer on promotion to Band 5 Custodial Manager will need to:**
• Have a minimum 2 years' service as a substantive Prison Officer
• Have completed the Development Workbook to at least 70%
• Once applications open, complete the Readiness Assessment in conjunction with Line Manager
• Readiness Assessment to be signed off by Governor/Head of Group
• Application to be endorsed and signed off by Prison Group Director, in line with assessment spaces per Prison Group
• On the day of the Custodial Manager Assessment Centre (CMAC), three parts, each lasting up to 1.5 hours over one day:
• Custodial Manager Part A (In-tray Exam)
• Custodial Manager Part B (Operational Simulations)
• Custodial Manager Part C (People Management Exam)

• Legacy candidates or those who hold part-accreditation from the pre-2017 staged style of assessments will only complete either Parts B & C, or Part C only. Please refer to the most current assessment NTS for more details
• Once the CMAC has been passed staff can then apply for any Custodial Manager vacancies that come up

**Band 5 Custodial Manager on promotion to Band 7 and 8 Head of Function will need to:**
• Have a minimum 1 years' as a substantive Custodial Manager
• Have completed the Development Workbook to at least 70%
• Once applications open, complete the Readiness Assessment in conjunction with Line Manager
• Readiness Assessment to be signed off by Governor/Head of Group
• Application to be endorsed and signed off by Prison Group Director, in line with assessment spaces per Prison Group
• On the day of the Head of Function Assessment Centre (HFAC), three parts, each lasting up to 1 hour over one day:
• Head of Function Part A (In-tray Exam)
• Head of Function Part B (Operational Simulations)
• Head of Function Part C (People Management)
• Legacy candidates or those who hold part-accreditation from the pre-2017 staged style of assessments will only complete either Parts B & C, or Part C only. Please refer to the most current assessment NTS for more details
• Once a candidate has successfully passed the HFAC, they will be required to pass the Incident Management Silver Command (IMSC) exam to achieve full accreditation. This consists of four days training including practical assessment and exam on day five lasting approximately 1.5 hours.
• Once both the HFAC and IMSC have been passed staff can then apply for any Head of Function vacancies that come u

**Band 7 and 8 Head of Function on promotion to Band 8 and 9 Deputy Governor will need to:**
• Have a minimum of 2 years' as a substantive Head of Function at either band 7 or 8 Deputy Governor
• Have completed the Development Workbook
• Once applications open, complete the Readiness Assessment in conjunction with Line Manager
• Readiness Assessment to be signed off by Governor/Head of Group
• Two day Deputy Governor Assessment Centre (DGAC), day 1: Training for Incident Management Silver Command and day 2: four parts:
• Deputy Governor Part A (Situational Judgement Test)

• Deputy Governor Part B (Operational Simulations)
• Deputy Governor Part C (Group Exercise)
• Deputy Governor Part D (IMSC assessment)
• Once all parts of the DGAC (including the IMSC) have been passed staff can then apply for any Deputy Governor vacancies that come up

**Band 8 and 9 Deputy Governor on promotion to Band 10 and 11 Governing Governor will need to:**
• Have a minimum of 2 years' as a substantive band 8 Deputy Governor
• Have completed the Development Workbook
• Once applications open, complete the Readiness Assessment in conjunction with Line Manager
• Readiness Assessment to be signed off by Governor/Head of Group
• Two day Governor Assessment Centre (GAC), day 1: Training for Incident Management Silver Command and day 2: four parts:
• Governor Part A (Situational Judgement Test)
• Governor Part B (Operational Simulations)
• Governor Part C (Group Exercise)
• Governor Part D (IMSC assessment)
• Once all parts of the GAC (including the IMSC) have been passed staff can then apply for any Governor vacancies that come up.

## 8.4 HMPPS - Workforce Statistics

**His Majesty's Prison and Probation Service (HMPPS) Workforce Statistics Bulletin, as at June 2022 published 18th August 2022**
*58,343 FTE (full time equivalent) staff in post*
This is a similar number of staff in post to 30 June 2021 and a minimal change of 95 FTE (0.2%) since 31 March 2022. Of the staff in post, there were 33,893 FTE in Public Sector Prisons (PSP), 17,710 FTE staff in the Probation Service, 5,198 FTE staff in HQ and Area Services, and 1,543 FTE in the Youth Custody Service (YCS).
*21,725 FTE band 3-5 prison officers in post*
This is a slight decrease of 318 FTE (1.4%) since 30 June 2021 and a slight decrease of 276 FTE (1.3%) prison officers compared to 31 March 2022.
*5,094 FTE band 2 operational support staff in post*
This is no substantial change of 13 FTE (0.3%) since 30 June 2021 and no substantial change of FTE operational support staff since 31 March 2022.
*4,542 FTE band 4 probation officers in post*
This is a slight increase of 85 FTE (1.9%) since 30 June 2021 and an increase of 204 FTE (4.7%) compared to 31 March 2022. In addition to the band 4 probation officers, there were 5,811 FTE band 3 probation services officers: a slight increase of 94 FTE (1.7%) since 30 June 2021 and a decrease of 293 FTE (4.8%) since 31 March 2022.
*Leaving rate of 15.3% amongst band 3-5 prison officers*
This is a slight increase of 0.8 percentage points compared to the year ending 31 March 2022. The overall leaving rate across HMPPS over the past 12 months stood at 13.0%, which is no substantial change (0.4 percentage points) compared to the year ending 31 March 2022.
This publication provides details of staffing levels, staff inflows and outflows, sickness absence rates, and protected characteristics for the directly employed workforce of HMPPS. Information presented covers PSP, the Probation Service, the YCS, and HMPPS headquarters, which includes Area Services that provide direct operational support to prisons. Technical details and explanatory notes can be found in the accompanying Guide to HM Prison and Probation (HMPPS) Workforce Statistics.

**Statistician's comment**
In this publication we are reporting on the HMPPS workforce as at 30 June 2022.
As at June 2022 there were 58,343 FTE staff in post, an increase of 288 FTE over June 2021.
Leaving rates fell during the COVID-19 pandemic, possibly due to increased uncertainty in the employment market. Leaving rates have now increased and are continuing the upward trend seen from March 2016 to March 2020.
HMPPS staff sickness accounted for an average of 14.4 working days per person lost for the 12 months to the end of June 2022. This is the highest in the time series and is 4.2 working days higher than the predominantly COVID-19 free year ending 31 March 2020. For the 12 months to the end of June 2022. the main reason for sickness was mental and behavioural disorders (30.3% of absences) followed by epidemic/pandemic (22.9%) of absences.

**Points to note**
*His Majesty's Prison and Probation Service*
HMPPS is focused on supporting operational delivery and the effective running of prison and probation services across the public and private sectors. HMPPS works with a number of partners to carry out the sentences given by the courts, either in custody or the community. This publication covers the reporting period up to 30 June 2022 and therefore considers in detail quarterly staffing levels and staff inflows and outflows, for HMPPS and its predecessors, since 2016.
For ease, the statistics in this publication will be referred to as those of the HMPPS workforce (i.e. staff working in HMPPS and with a contract of employment with HMPPS, excluding those on career breaks and those on secondment or loan outside of HMPPS but including staff on secondment or loan into HMPPS).
Staff employed by private sector establishments, community rehabilitation companies and other contractors are excluded.

### Coronavirus (COVID-19)

Figures relating to effect of the coronavirus (COVID-19) on HMPPS staff are published alongside this edition of the bulletin as a separate annex. They are experimental statistics and include information about COVID-19 related testing, sickness and deaths of HMPPS staff.

### Annex on Prison Officer recruitment diversity

As noted in previous bulletins, the annex with experimental statistics on Prison Officer and Operational Support Grade (OSG) recruitment has been moved to a six-monthly production cycle.

### Annex on Probation Officer Vacancies and Trainees

As of the June 2019 publication, this annex has been added to this bulletin which presents figures on Probation Officers in post, and their required staffing level, in addition it shows the number of trainee and qualified Probation Officers.

### Recent Organisational Changes

• In June 2022 around 1,000 Approved Premises staff were moved out of HQ directorates and back into Probation Service. This reverses a move from November and December 2019, when over 1,200 NPS staff moved to the Community and Interventions directorate, part of HMPPS HQ and Areas Services. Figures for all historical periods have been revised to reflect this change.
• The Prison region of Immigration Removal Centre and Foreign National Centre (IRCs and FNCs) group was officially disbanded at the end of March 2021 and the prisons within it were moved to be managed by their respective geographical regions:

Morton Hall - East Midlands
Huntercombe - South Central
Maidstone - Kent, Surrey and Sussex

• In late June 2021, more than 7,000 staff from private sector Community Rehabilitation Companies (CRC) came together with probation staff already in the public sector in the new Probation Service. Records are still being updated following this change, resulting in some entries being classified as 'unknown' in the accompanying tables. In addition, many of the new staff had not been able to update their voluntary declarations on diversity information at the time of joining, which has led to an initial drop in recorded declaration rates for many of the indicators, as can be seen in Table 5d, of the accompanying tables.
• From April 2021 the Probation Service has been undergoing a reorganisation, with staff moving into new Probation Delivery Units (PDUs).
• Medway Secure Training Centre closed on 31 March 2020.

### Future Plans

For future publications we are considering ways in which we can improve the bulletin, and some of the issues we may look into are as follows:

• How to make the tables and presentation of the figures more user-friendly.
• Whether to and how to expand the range of information provided.

If you have any particular comments or views on the above, or any other aspects you would like to be considered about this bulletin, please contact us at the address given at the end of the publication.

## 1. Total HMPPS staff in post

*58,343 FTE staff in post (as at 30 June 2022)*

This is a similar number of staff in post since 30 June 2021 and a minimal change of 95 FTE (0.2%) since 31 March 2022. Of the staff in post, there were 33,893 FTE in Public Sector Prisons (PSP), 17,710 FTE staff in the Probation Service, 5,198 FTE staff in HQ and Area Services, and 1,543 FTE in the YCS.

As at 30 June 2022, there were 58,343 FTE staff in post in HMPPS on a full time equivalent (FTE) basis (Figure 1). This includes 33,893 FTE staff in PSP (making up 58.1% of all HMPPS staff),17,710 FTE in the Probation Service (30.4% of all HMPPS staff), 5,198 FTE in HMPPS HQ and Area Services (8.9% of all HMPPS staff), and 1,543 FTE in the YCS (2.6% of all HMPPS staff).

Compared to 30 June 2021, the overall staff numbers remained broadly consistent: FTE in PSP slightly decreased by 478 (1.4%), FTE in the Probation Service slightly increased by 190 (1.1%), FTE in HQ and Area Services increased by 564 (12.2%), and FTE in the YCS slightly increased by 14 (0.9%).

As at 30 June 2022, there were 27,844 FTE (47.7% of HMPPS staff) operational prison service staff (including YCS staff). This is a slight decrease of 264 FTE staff (0.9%) compared to 30 June 2021. Non-operational roles across PSP, YCS, and HMPPS HQ accounted for 12,492 FTE staff (21.4% of HMPPS staff), which is an increase of 323 FTE (2.7%) since 30 June 2021. There were 18,007 FTE staff[footnote 1] in the Probation Service (30.9% of all HMPPS staff): a slight increase of 230 (1.3%) FTE since 30 June 2021.

Figure 1 shows a big increase in Probation Service staff in June 2021, which was due to more than 7,000 staff from private sector CRCs coming together with probation staff already in the public sector in the new Probation Service.

### 1.1 Length of Service

Length of service information has been calculated for HMPPS staff from the most recent hire date. Where staff have transferred in from another government department or have transferred in through HMPPS taking over a function, length of service is calculated from entry to HMPPS. Across HMPPS overall, 27.7% of FTE staff in post had less than 3 years' service,

**Figure 1: Number of HMPPS staff in post on an FTE basis, 31 March 2017 to 30 June 2022 (Source: Table 1)**

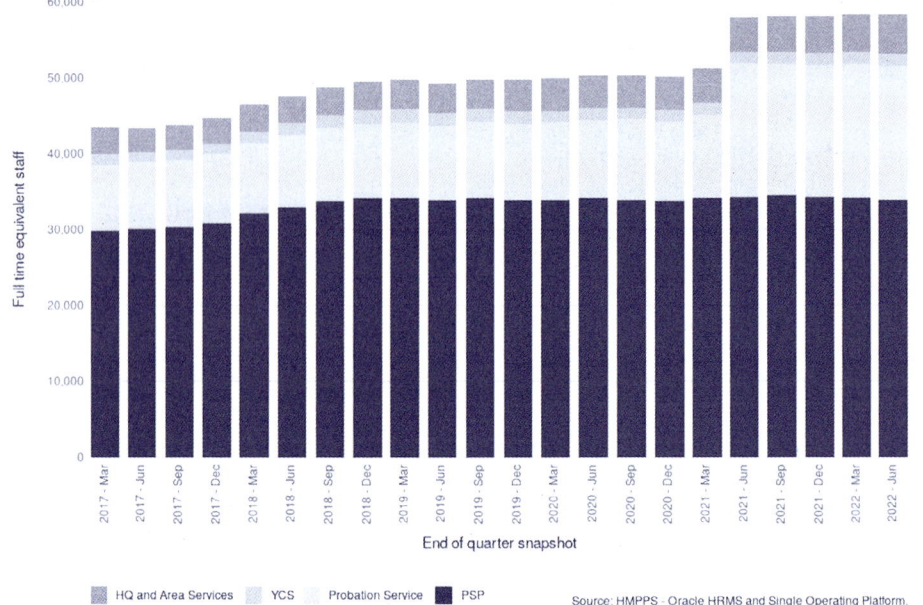

which was a slight decrease from 28.7% at 30 June 2021 and no substantial change from 27.2% at 31 March 2022. 33.1% of HMPPS FTE staff in post had 10 years or more of experience, representing a decrease from 35.7% at 30 June 2021 and a slight decrease from 33.8% at 31 March 2022.

It should be noted, that the National Probation Service was created on 1 June 2014 and the service of Probation Service staff in Probation Trusts prior to the creation of the Probation Service is not included. Therefore, the figures relating to the length of service of Probation Service staff, which are included in the HMPPS overall figures, do not necessarily represent their full experience but rather the length of service from entry to HMPPS. The situation is different for the over 7000 staff who transferred from the CRCs in June 2021 and for them their service prior to their date of transfer is included.

Excluding the Probation Service, 27.3% of FTE staff in post across HMPPS had less than 3 years' service as at 30 June 2022. This is a slight decrease of 0.7 percentage points compared to 30 June 2021. The non-Probation Service staff with 10 years' experience or more made up 40.6% of the workforce, which is a 3.3 percentage points decrease compared to 30 June 2021.

**2. Band 3-5 prison officers and band 2 operational support staff**
*21,725 FTE band 3-5 prison officers in post (as at 30 June 2022)*
This is a slight decrease of 318 FTE (1.4%) in FTE

since 30 June 2021 and a slight decrease of 276 FTE (1.3%) prison officers compared to 31 March 2022.
*5,094 FTE band 2 operational support staff in post (as at 30 June 2022)*
This corresponds to no substantial change of 13 FTE (0.3%) since 30 June 2021 and no substantial change of FTE operational support staff since 31 March 2022.

The key operational grades in public sector prisons are the band 3 to 5 prison officers. They consist of band 3 prison officers, band 4 officer specialists, band 4 supervising officers, and band 5 custodial managers.

The proportion of band 3-5 prison officers with less than 3 years' service at 30 June 2022 fell to 29.9% compared to 30.8% as at 30 June 2021. The proportion of band 3-5 prison officers with between 3 to 9 years of service increased by 7.2 percentage points from 27.0% at March 2021 to 34.2% at 31 March 2022. The proportion of officers in post with 10 years or more of experience decreased by 3.8 percentage points from 39.5% at 30 June 2021 to 35.8% at 30 June 2022. This corresponds to 7,768 FTE staff with 10 years or more of experience at 30 June 2022, which is a fall of 942 FTE, or 10.8% since 30 June 2021.

The proportion of band 2 OSG FTE staff with less than 3 years' service increased from 38.6% at 30 June 2021 to 43.4% at 30 June 2022, and the proportion of those with 10 years or more of experience decreased from 38.5% at 30 June 2021 to 33.4% at 30 June 2022.

Figure 3 shows a quarterly trend of band 3 to 5 appointments and leavers since 2016/17. Over

**Figure 2: Number of band 3-5 prison officers in post on an FTE basis, 31 March 2017 to 30 June 2022 (Source: Table 3)**

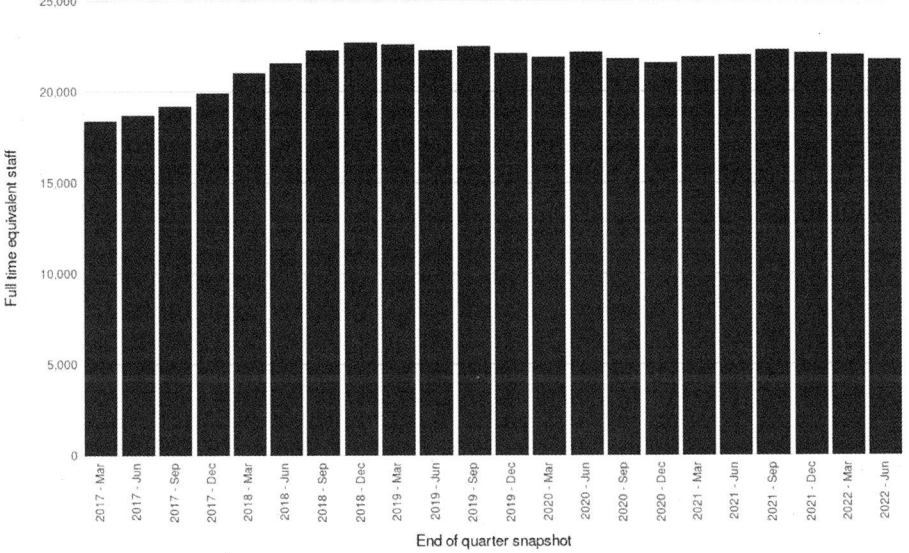

Source: HMPPS - Oracle HRMS and Single Operating Platform.

the year to 30 June 2022, 4,060 band 3 to 5 officers were appointed (consisting of direct new recruits and existing staff who converted to a band 3 officer grade), an increase of 1,280 (46.0%) compared to 2,780 in the previous year. Looking at the quarterly figures, the headcount of new band 3 to 5 officer appointments decreased by 228 (21.9%) from 1,039 between January and March 2022 to 811 between April and June 2022 (Table 17).

The headcount of band 3 to 5 prison officers who left HMPPS in the year ending 30 June 2022 was 3,558, which is an increase of 1,264 (55.1%) compared to the year ending 30 June 2021. This is actually lower than previous quarters. Leaving rates fell during the COVID-19 pandemic, possibly due to increased uncertainty in the employment market. Leaving rates in the last year have increased and are continuing the upward trend seen from March 2016 to March 2020. Examining reasons for leaving, 74.5% of prison officers who left in the year ending 30 June 2022 resigned from their roles (up from 61.9% in the year ending 30 June 2021). Of the other prison officers who left HMPPS, 10.7% were dismissed and 6.4% retired in the year ending 30 June 2022: the proportion dismissed are down from 14.5% compared to previous year while the number retiring are similar.

The number of band 2 OSG staff who joined HMPPS in the year ending 30 June 2022 was 1,464: an increase of 178 (13.8%) compared to the previous year ending 30 June 2021. There was a slight increase of 26 (1.8%) since the year ending

31 March 2022. The headcount number of band 2 OSG staff who left HMPPS was 1,026, which is an increase of 344 (50.4%) compared to the year ending 30 June 2021 and an increase of 44 (4.5%) compared to the year ending 31 March 2022.

Joiners and leavers are not the only movements into and out of the band 3 to 5 officer grouping. There are also typically differences in the proportion of new joiners and older officers who work part time as well as movements between grades. For these reasons, the change in FTE does not directly reflect the difference between the number of joiners and leavers. Changes such as staff switching from full time to part time have the effect of reducing the FTE of officers available as they progress through their career.

### 3. Probation practitioners and senior probation officers

*4,542 FTE band 4 probation officers in post (as at 30 June 2022)*

This figure is a slight increase of 85 FTE (1.9%) since 30 June 2021 and an increase of 204 FTE (4.7%) probation officers compared to 31 March 2022. In addition to the band 4 probation officers, there were 5,811 FTE band 3 probation services officers: a slight increase of 94 FTE (1.7%) since 30 June 2021 and a decrease of 293 FTE (4.8%) since 31 March 2022 .

Key grades in the Probation Service include band 3 probation services officers, band 4 probation officers (collectively known as probation practitioners), as well as band 5 senior probation officers. Staff who are training to be a probation

**Figure 3: Newly appointed band 3 to 5 prison officers and band 3 to 5 prison officer leavers, April 2016 to 30 June 2022 (Source: Table 17)**

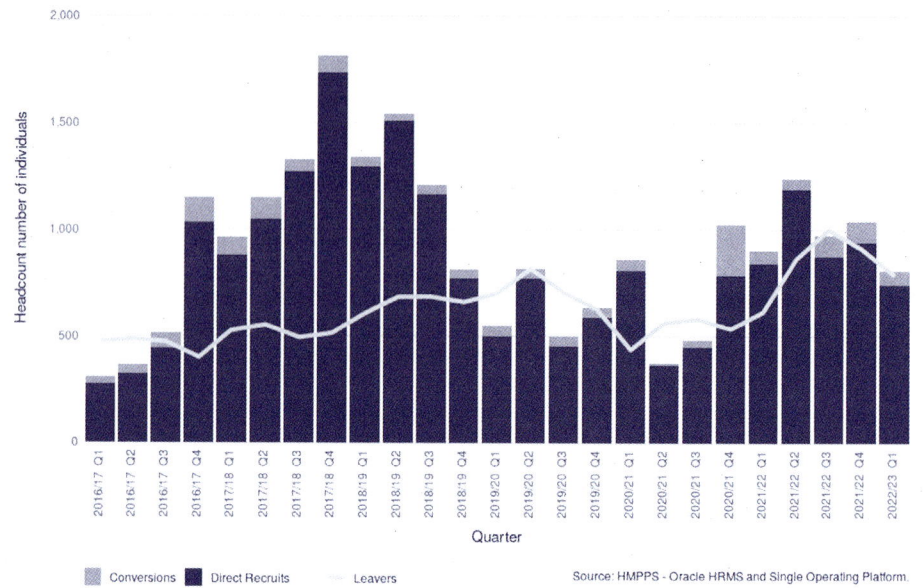

officer work as a probation services officer during their training, so a proportion of the probation services officers in post will be working towards the professional probation officer qualification.

As of the June 2019 publication, an experimental statistics annex has been added to this bulletin which presents figures on Probation Officers in post, their required staffing level, in addition to the number of trainee and qualified Probation Officers. As at 30 June 2022 there were 5,811 FTE band 3 probation services officers in post, a slight increase of 94 FTE (1.7%) over the past year and a decrease of 293 FTE (4.8%) over the quarter; 4,542 FTE band 4 probation officers, representing a slight increase of 85 FTE (1.9%) over the past year and an increase of 204 FTE (4.7%) compared to the previous quarter; and 1,261 FTE band 5

**Figure 4: Number of probation officers, probation services officers and senior probation officers in post on an FTE basis, 31 March 2017 to 30 June 2022 (Source: Table 3)**

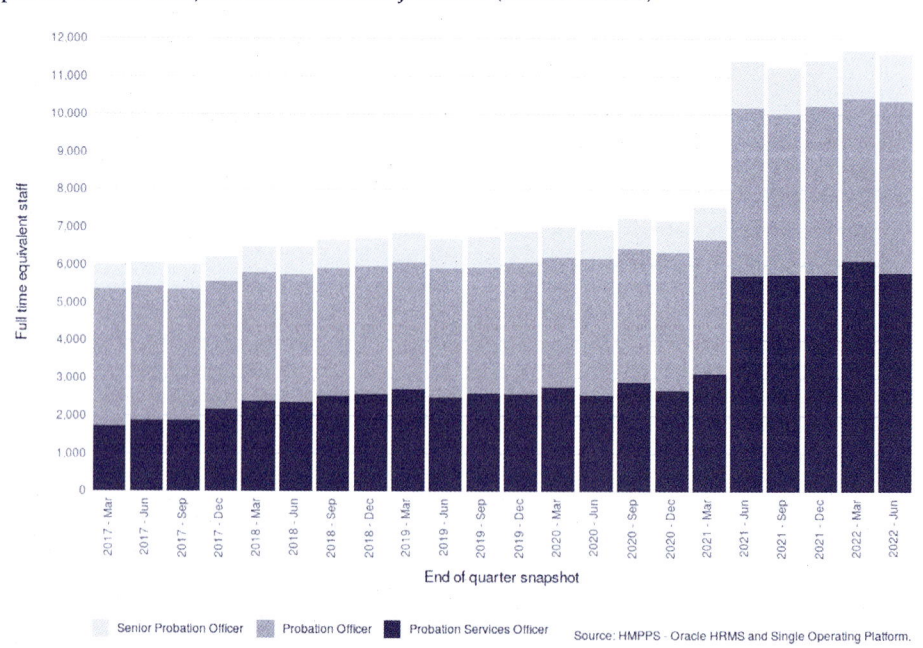

senior probation officers, showing a slight increase of 18 (1.4%) over the previous year and a slight increase of 12 (1.0%) since the last quarter (Figure 4).

In the past year, 1,432 probation services officers were appointed, some of whom will be training to become qualified probation officers. This is an increase of 532 (59.1%) compared to the year ending 30 June 2021 and an increase of 190 (15.3%) compared to the number appointed in the year ending 31 March 2022. Within the Probation Service, there were 4,470 FTE probation officers in post, a shortfall of 1,692 FTE against the required staffing level of 6,162 FTE. There were 1,790 staff, equivalent to 1,783 FTE, undertaking the PQiP training at the end of June 2022 (please refer to the Probation recruitment annex for more details). In the past year, 835 probation services officers left the service. This is an increase of 563 (207.0%) compared to the year ending 30 June 2021 and an increase of 113 (15.7%) compared to the number who left in the year ending 31 March 2022.The number of leavers has increased considerably since June 2021, which is likely attributable to competition in the labour market.

## 4. Joiners and Leavers

*Leaving rate of 15.3% amongst band 3-5 prison officers (for the 12 months ending 30 June 2022)*
This is a slight increase of 0.8 percentage points compared to the year ending 31 March 2022. The overall leaving rate across HMPPS over the past year stood at 13.0%, which is similar (0.4

percentage points) compared to the year ending 31 March 2022 of 12.6%

Over the past year, 8,351 staff joined HMPPS, which is an increase of 2,195 (35.7%) compared to the year ending 30 June 2021. These joiners consisted of 5,638 across PSP, 294 in the YCS, 2,122 in the Probation Service, and 297 in HMPPS HQ and Area Services. Compared to the year ending 30 June 2021 these numbers of joiners represent an increase of 36.0% for PSP, an increase of 57.2% for YCS, an increase of 40.3% for Probation Service, and a decrease of 4.8% for HMPPS HQ and Area Services.

There were 8,249 leavers in the year ending 30 June 2022, an increase of 3,204 (63.5%) compared to the year ending 30 June 2021. This includes 5,521 leavers from PSP (an increase of 48.2%), 219 from YCS (an increase of 59.9%), 2,114 from the Probation Service (an increase of 136.7%), and 395 from HMPPS HQ and Area Services (an increase of 36.7%).

### 4.1 Leaving Rates *[footnote 2]*

The overall HMPPS leaving rate for the year to 30 June 2022 was 13.0%, which is broadly the same as for the year to 31 March 2022 (Figure 5), which was of 12.6%, a change of 0.4% . For the year up to 31 March 2021 the increased uncertainty in the employment market following the COVID-19 pandemic may have contributed to the drop in the number of resignations during most of the year, therefore impacting on the overall reduced leaving and resignation rates. The latest leaving rates are now higher than pre-pandemic levels

**Figure 5: Annual leaving rates of permanent staff in key operational grades (excluding VEDSR), from the 12 months to 31 March 2017 to the 12 months to 30 June 2022 (Source: Table 11)**

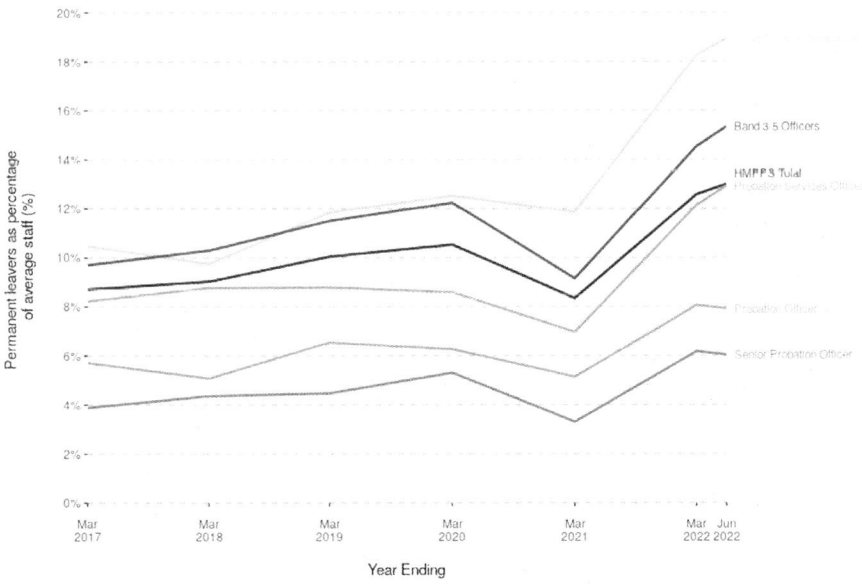

Source: HMPPS - Oracle HRMS and Single Operating Platform.

**Figure 6: Annual resignation rates of permanent staff in key operational grades, from the 12 months to 31 March 2017 to the 12 months to 30 June 2022 (Source: Table 12)**

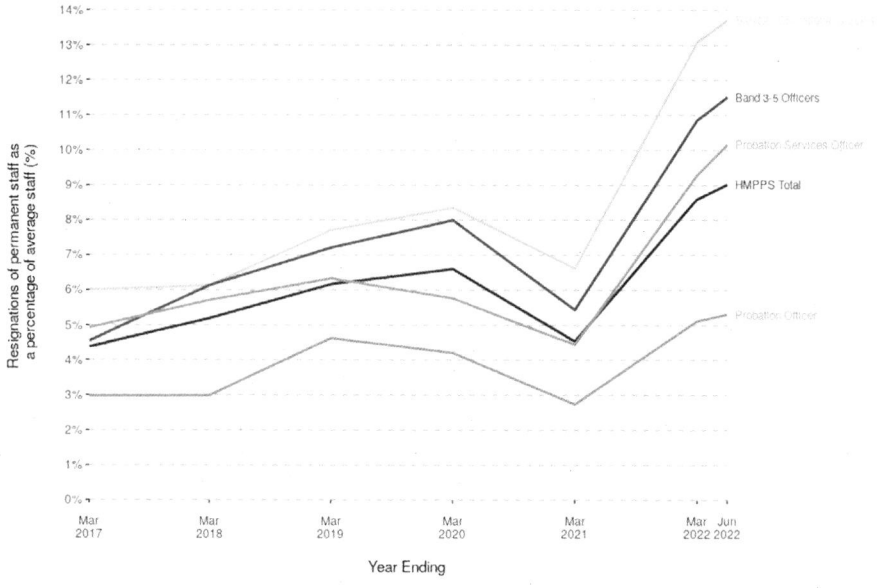

Source: HMPPS · Oracle HRMS and Single Operating Platform.

and are continuing the upward trend seen from March 2016 to March 2020. For band 3 to 5 prison officers, the leaving rate of 15.3% in the year ending 30 June 2022 represented a slight increase of 0.8 percentage points since the year ending 31 March 2022. The leaving rate for band 2 OSG staff was 18.9% in the year ending 30 June 2022, which is a slight increase of 0.7 percentage points compared to the year ending 31 March 2022.

**4.2 Resignation Rates** *[footnote 3]*

The overall HMPPS resignation rate for the 12 months to 30 June 2022 was 9.0%, which is broadly the same (8.6%) as for the year to 31 March 2022 (Figure 6). For band 3-5 officers, the resignation rate was 11.5% in the year ending 30 June 2022, which is a slight increase of 0.7 percentage points since the year ending 31 March 2022. The resignation rate for OSG staff was 13.7% for the year ending 30 June 2022, which is a slight increase of 0.6 percentage points since the year ending 31 March 2022.

For Probation Service overall, the resignation rate was 7.3% for the year ending 30 June 2022. This represents no substantial change (0.4 percentage points) compared to the year ending 31 March 2022. Amongst the operational grades within the Probation Service, probation services officers had the highest resignation rate at 10.2%, (a slight increase of 0.9 percentage points) since the year ending 31 March 2022. Resignation rates for probation officers stood at 5.3% (no substantial change (0.2 percentage points) since the year ending 31 March 2022).

**5. Sickness absence**

*HMPPS staff lost an average of 14.4 working days to sickness absence in the 12 months ending 30 June 2022 (including COVID sickness)*

This represents an increase of 0.7 Average Working Days Lost (AWDL) compared to the year ending 31 March 2022.

Since June 2021 these sickness absence figures include COVID-19 AWDL sickness numbers, including a revision to all AWDL figures since the start of the pandemic. In addition, please see the annex with experimental statistics on COVID-19 and HMPPS staff, which includes information about staff absent due to COVID on given days.

In the year ending 30 June 2022, HMPPS staff lost an average of 14.4 working days to sickness absence. This is an increase from 13.8 average working days lost for the year ending 31 March 2022, and an increase of 3.1 days compared to the predominantly COVID-19 free year ending 31 March 2020.

YCS staff had the highest sickness absence rate at 19.3 AWDL, followed by PSP (15.9 AWDL), Probation Service (13.5 AWDL), and HQ and Area Services (6.0 AWDL) (Figure 7). Compared to the year ending 31 March 2022, these represent an increase of 1.0 days for YCS, an increase of 0.8 days for PSP, an increase of 0.6 days for Probation Service, and an increase of 0.3 days for HQ and Area Services staff.

The most common category of sickness absence in terms of days lost was mental and behavioural disorders, corresponding to 30.3% of absences in

**Figure 7: Average working days lost to sickness absence, 12 months to 31 March 2017 to 12 months to 30 June 2022 (Source: Table 18)**

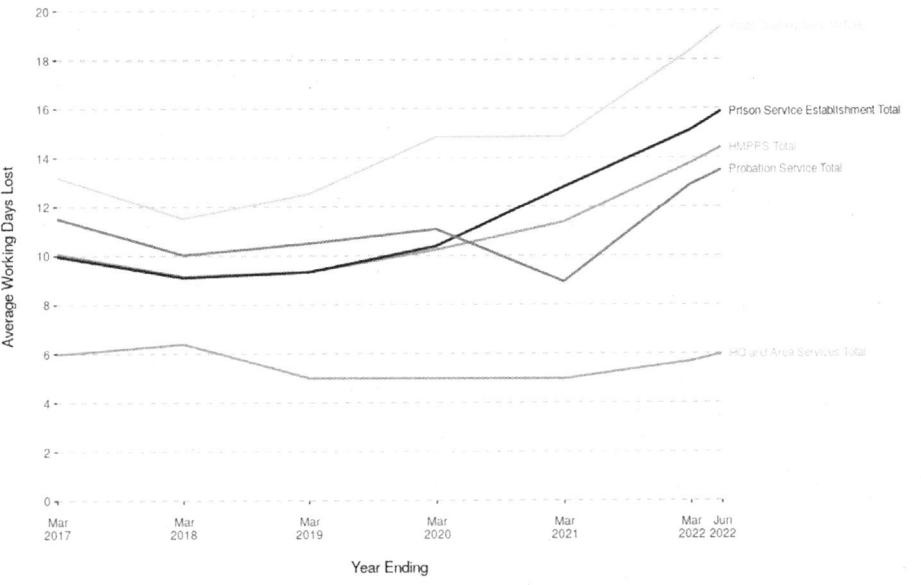

Source: HMPPS - Oracle HRMS and Single Operating Platform.

the past year. This category was most prevalent for probation officers, where 50.0% of working days lost were attributed to mental and behavioural disorders.

For HMPPS overall the category that accounted for the second largest proportion of working days lost was epidemic/pandemic (22.9%). Together the top two categories accounted for 53.2% of all working days lost.

**Further Information**

*Accompanying files*

As well as this bulletin, the following products are published as part of this release:

• A technical guide providing details of the HMPPS workforce structure as well as how the data are collected and processed. Information on the revisions policy and disclosure relevant to HMPPS staffing data is also included.

• A set of summary tables for the latest quarter and year as well as over time.

• A supplementary annex presenting experimental statistics on Probation Officers in post, their required staffing level, and the number of trainee and qualified Probation Officers.

• A supplementary annex on the effect of the coronavirus (COVID-19) on HMPPS staff. They are experimental statistics and include information about COVID-19 related testing, sickness and deaths of HMPPS staff.

*Official statistics*

The statistics in this bulletin are classified as official statistics. The Statistics and Registration Service Act 2007 defines 'official statistics' as all

those statistical outputs produced by the UK Statistics Authority's executive office (the Office for National Statistics), by central Government departments and agencies, by the devolved administrations in Northern Ireland, Scotland, and Wales, and by other Crown bodies (over 200 bodies in total). The statistics in this bulletin comply with all aspects of the Code of Practice for Official Statistics. The Code encourages and supports producers of statistics to maintain their independence and to ensure adequate resourcing for statistical production. It helps producers and users of statistics by setting out the necessary principles and practices to produce statistics that are trustworthy, high quality and of public value.

*Experimental Statistics*

The statistics in the Recruitment annex, Probation Officer annex and the annex on the effect of the coronavirus (COVID-19) on HMPPS staff are experimental statistics. Experimental statistics are a subset of newly developed or innovative official statistics undergoing evaluation. They are developed under the guidance of the Head of Profession for Statistics (HoP) and published to involve users and stakeholders in the assessment of their suitability and quality at an early stage. Therefore, we would like to receive feedback as to how useful they are, whether a different analysis would be preferable, or any other comments about them. If you wish to send any views you may have about these experimental statistics, please use the contact details below.

*Contact*

Press enquiries should be directed to the Ministry of Justice press office:

Tel: 020 3334 3536

Email: newsdesk@justice.gov.uk

Other enquiries about these statistics should be directed to:

Bryce Millard

Corporate Data Sharing Lead

Data and Evidence as a Service

Ministry of Justice

10 South Colonnade

London

E14 4PH

Email: statistics.enquiries@justice.gsi.gov.uk

*1. This includes staff in Probation Service grades working in other parts of HMPPS.*
*2. Percentage of staff with a permanent contract of employment who left HMPPS, including individuals who have retired early, but excluding staff who left due to voluntary early departure schemes and redundancy (VEDSR).*
*3. Percentage of staff with a permanent contract of employment who resigned from HMPPS.*

## 8.5 HMPPS - Annual Staff Equalities Report

**His Majesty's Prison and Probation Service (HMPPS) Annual Staff Equalities Report 2021**
**Ministry of Justice**
**Published 25th November 2021**

**Main Points**

*54,296 (headcount) staff in post as at 31 March 2021*

This was an increase of 2.6% compared to the same point in 2020. Females represented 50.0% of staff, and 10.9% of staff who declared their ethnicity were Black, Asian and minority ethnic.

*5,803 (headcount) new recruits to HMPPS in 2020/21*

This was 597 (11.5%) more than in 2019/20. Females accounted for 55.6% of joiners and more than half of joiners (50.8%) were aged under 30 years old.

*3,052 staff (6.3%) were receiving temporary cover allowances (TCA)*

This was an increase of 0.8 percentage points compared to 31 March 2020. TCA rates were higher for females (6.4%) compared to males (6.2%).

*3.8% of permanent staff were promoted, an equivalent of 2,004 promotions*

A decrease from the rate of 4.6% (2,409 promotions) in 2019/20. The promotion rate for female staff was higher in 2020/21 at 4.4% (1,146) than for males at 3.2% (858). Black, Asian and minority ethnic staff had a higher promotion rate at 4.2% than White staff at 4.0%.

*763 staff raised grievances, representing 1.4 per 100 staff*

These resulted in 911 cases of which 380 (41.7%) were upheld/ partially upheld. The number of grievance cases raised during the year decreased compared to 2019/20 (from 1.7 per 100 staff), but the percentage of cases being upheld/partially upheld increased by 3.5 percentage points (from 38.2%).

*Overall rate of conduct & discipline cases was 1.5 per 100 staff*

An increase from 1.2 per 100 staff in for 2019/20. In 2020/21, the rate was higher for male staff (at 2.1 per 100 male staff) compared to female staff (at 0.9 per 100 female staff).

*HMPPS staff lost an average of 11.4 working days due to sickness*

An increase from 10.2 days for 2019/20. For 2020/21, the average was higher for male than female staff (11.8 and 10.7 days respectively) and was higher for Black, Asian and minority ethnic staff (12.9 days) compared to White staff (11.0 days). This publication considers staffing profiles and processes of the directly employed HMPPS workforce from an equalities perspective. Technical details and explanatory notes can be found in the accompanying Guide and Glossary to the annual HMPPS Staff Equalities Report.

Please send any feedback you may have related to the content of this publication to: statistics.enquiries@justice.gov.uk

**Statistician's comment**

The headcount of HMPPS as of 31 March 2021 was 54,296, this was an increase of 2.6% compared to the same point in 2020. Females represented 50.0% of staff, and 10.9% of staff who declared their ethnicity were Black, Asian and minority ethnic.

There were 5,803 (headcount) new recruits to HMPPS in 2020/21. This was 597 (11.5%) more than in 2019/20. Females accounted for 55.6% of joiners and more than half of joiners (50.8%) were aged under 30 years old.

The impact of COVID-19 throughout 2020/21 has meant that the staff appraisal assessment was suspended due to the challenges of managing the COVID-19 pandemic. In addition, staff bonuses in 2020/21 included a range of COVID-19 special payment schemes which were set up for frontline prison and probation staff, this has resulted in bonuses increasing substantially compared to last year.

For this release the 2019/20 working days lost to sickness has been updated to include COVID-19 sickness. For 2020/21 HMPPS staff lost an average of 11.4 working days due to sickness, an increase from 10.2 days for 2019/20.

**Points to note**

*Her Majesty's Prison and Probation Service*

On 1 April 2017, Her Majesty's Prison and Probation Service (HMPPS) replaced the National Offender Management Service (NOMS), an agency of the Ministry of Justice. HMPPS is focussed on supporting operational delivery and the effective running of prison and probation services across the public and private sectors. HMPPS works with several partners to carry out the sentences given by the courts, either in custody or the community. This report considers profiles and processes of the HMPPS workforce from an equalities perspective.

HMPPS delivers services directly through public sector prisons, the youth custody service and the National Probation Service. The statistics in this publication relate to staff working within HMPPS with a contract of employment with HMPPS, who are all civil servants. Staffing in private sector establishments, Community Rehabilitation Companies (CRCs) and other contractors are excluded.

During June 2021 more 7,000 staff from private CRCs came together with 3,500 probation officers already in the public sector in the new Probation Service. Since the transfer of CRC staff occurred in June 2021, the CRC staff are out of scope for this report.

The equality objectives of HMPPS are stated, along with progress and achievements, in the HMPPS Annual Report and Accounts 2019/20. The 2020/21 report is due to be published shortly. https://www.gov.uk/government/publications /hmpps-annual-report-and-accounts-2019-20

**There are many interactions between characteristics of staff that influence outcomes on staff processes. These include interactions between protected characteristics, such as between age and race, as well as other factors such as grade level. It is not possible within a report of this size to explore these interactions. Important considerations, such as differences in grade levels and how they may affect different groups of staff are highlighted, but no detailed analysis is included that removes the interactions and allows the unique contribution of protected characteristics to be isolated.**

Values of 2 or fewer or other values which would allow values of 2 or fewer to be derived by subtraction are suppressed. Please see our technical guide for further information on suppression.

Workforce statistics for HMPPS (and NOMS prior to 1 April 2017) are also published through the HMPPS Quarterly Workforce Bulletin:

www.gov.uk/government/collections/national-offender-management-service-workforce-statistics

This report covers staff processes with reference to protected characteristics as set out below.

*Staff Process*
Total Staff in Post
Joiners
Temporary Cover
Promotions
Staff Appraisals
Special bonuses
Grievances
Investigations
Conduct and Discipline Cases
Sickness Absence
Leavers

*Protected Characteristic*
Sex
Age
Race
Disability
Sexual Orientation
Religion / Belief

An accompanying report relating to Offender Equalities statistics for 2020/21 will also be published on 25 November 2021 and available at: https://www.gov.uk/government/statistics/an nouncements/hm-prison-and-probation-service-offender-equalities-report-2020-to-2021

Protected characteristics information is recorded for HMPPS staff on gender, age, race, disability, sexual orientation, religion/belief, and work pattern. Caution should be exercised in attempting to make comparisons between the composition of the HMPPS workforce and the wider population of England and Wales based on protected characteristics. There is substantial regional variation of these distributions in the general population, and HMPPS staff are not distributed across England and Wales in the same proportions as the general population, this may render such comparisons invalid.

Data on the protected characteristics race, disability, sexual orientation and religion/belief were collected from self-declared, non-compulsory fields on the Human Resources Management System (HRMS) until December 2016 and from the Single Operating Platform (SOP) from January 2017 onwards. With lower declaration rates, the risk of bias increases greatly, and the accuracy of a representation rate based on known declarations falls rapidly. Consequently, when a declaration rate falls below 60%, no representation rate is provided.

Race, disability, religion and sexual orientation are all self-declared, optional fields. Since the introduction of SOP in January 2017, there was a large drop in the declaration rates of new joiners to HMPPS. It is likely that the very low declaration rates are due to issues with the user-friendliness of SOP when it was first introduced. Over the past couple of years there has been a large increase in declarations, meaning that some of these characteristics have reached the threshold to allow for meaningful analysis of new recruits by these protected characteristics.

The Ministry of Justice is looking at ways to address these issues and improve these declaration rates further.

**1. Total Staff in Post**

There were 54,296 staff in post as at 31st March 2021, 2.6% more than at the same date in 2020. Females accounted for 50.0% of staff, the age band with the largest proportion of staff was 50-59 year olds (26.2%) and 10.9% of staff who declared their ethnicity were Black, Asian And Minority Ethnic.

As at 31 March 2021, there were 54,296 staff (headcount) in HMPPS, an increase of 1,368 (2.6%) on the previous year. This consisted of 29,255 staff in operational grades, 12,171 in the National Probation Service grades, and 12,869 in non-operational grades.

Figure 1 shows the make-up of the workforce across the available protected characteristics. Representation rates are only illustrated where information is recorded for over 60% of staff. Additional details on staff in post can also be found in tables 1a and 1b of the Equalities Report. Females accounted for 50.0% (27,144) of HMPPS staff as at 31 March 2021, an increase of 1.0 percentage point on their representation for the previous year when it was 49.0% (25,948 females). Overall 41.1% (92) of senior leaders in public prisons and HMPPS HQ (Senior Civil Servants and operational managers including governors) were female. Furthermore, females accounted for 37.7% (326) of operational manager bands 7-9, 29.1% (6,659) of prison officer bands 3-5, and 47.9% (2,536) of Operational Support Grades (OSGs).

In contrast, there were more female than male staff in non-operational grades (in prisons, HMPPS HQ and Area Services); 56.6% in non-operational manager grades (up by 1.5

percentage points from 55.2% in March 2020), and 64.9% in non-operational grades below management level (down 0.2 percentage points from 65.1% since the previous year) were female. The National Probation Service[footnote 1] had higher female representation than the other parts of HMPPS. Females predominated in the National Probation Service at all levels, comprising of 67.5% (141) of staff in senior NPS roles (NPS bands A-D), 72.7% (958) in NPS bands 5-6, and 78.0% (8,304) in NPS grades below management level (which includes probation officers at band 4).

As at 31 March 2021, the age band with the largest proportion of staff was those aged 50-59, comprising of 26.2% (14,206) of all staff. The proportion of those aged 40 or over as at 31 March 2020 stood at 56.4% (30,623), a decrease of 0.6 percentage points since the previous year whilst those aged under 30 represented 19.6% (10,638) of the HMPPS workforce, compared to 19.5% last year.

By grade, the 50-59 age band had the highest proportion of staff across all the grades, except for band 3-5 officers (23.4% (5,352) compared to 27.0% (6,166) aged 30-39), those at NPS management grade band 5-6 (25.9% (341) compared to 38.4% (506) aged 40-49), and those at NPS grades below management level (22.6% (2,405) compared to 24.0% (2,554) aged 30-39).

As at 31 March 2021, 85.8% of staff had declared their ethnicity. Of these, 10.9% (5,075) were in a Black, Asian or Minority Ethnic group. There were some differences between the groups within the Black, Asian and minority ethnic category, with 4.7% of staff being from a Black background compared to 0.5% of staff who declared as Other Ethnic. By grade, the lowest Black, Asian and minority ethnic representation

**Figure 1: HMPPS staff by protected characteristic, as at 31 March 2021**

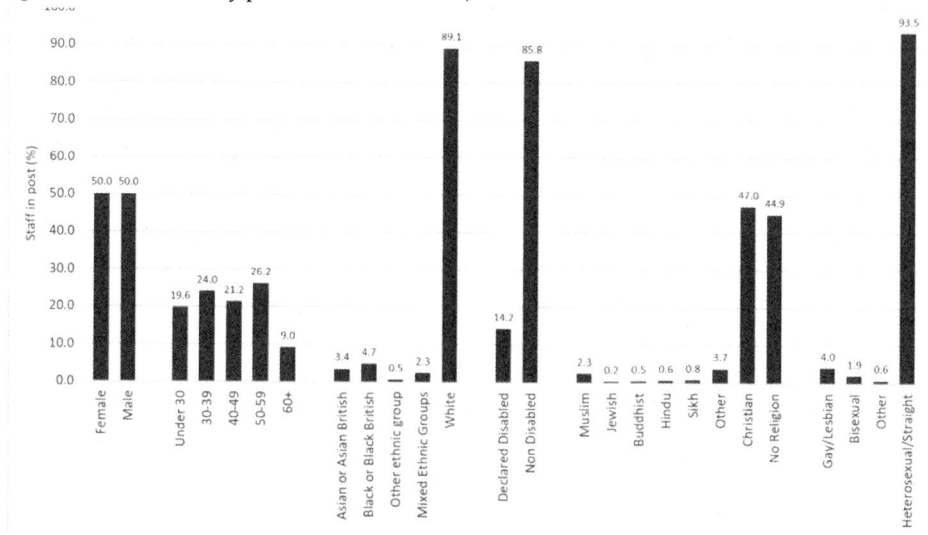

**Figure 2: HMPPS new joiners by protected characteristic, 1 April 2020 to 31 March 2021**

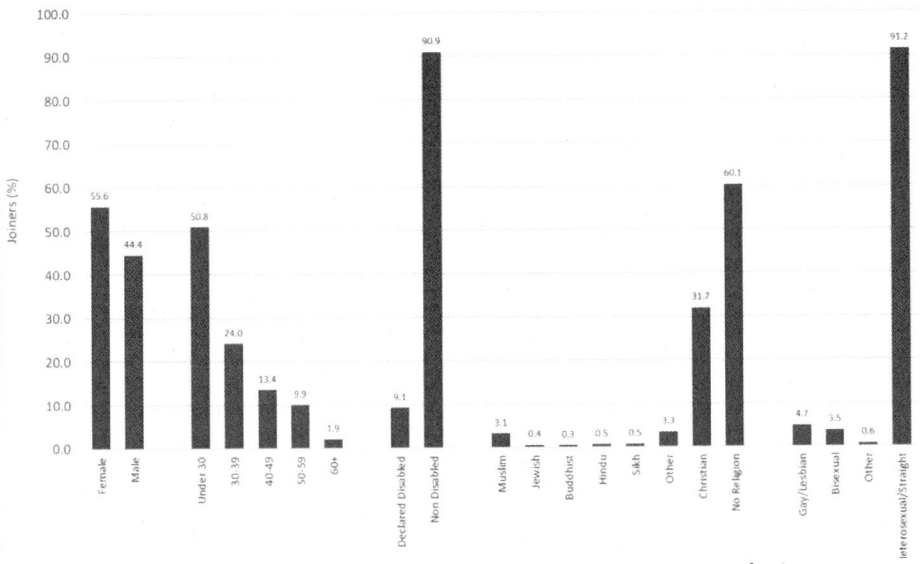

was for operational managers bands 7-9 at 5.5% (46), an increase of 0.1 percentage points compared to the previous year (5.3%).

Overall 77.3% of staff had declared their disability, which was above the 60% threshold at which meaningful representation rates can be considered. Similarly, 73.2% of staff had declared their religion, and 74.1% their sexual orientation. As of 31 March 2021, there were 14.2% of staff who declared themselves as disabled compared to 85.8% who declared themselves as non-disabled. The lowest disability representation rate was for band 3-5 officers at 9.5% (1,565), and the highest representation rate was for NPS below management grade at 20.9% (1,969).

Of the 73.2% of staff who had declared their religion, 47.0% were Christian, 44.9% had no religion and 8.1% were non-Christian. There were some differences between the groups within the non-Christian Religion category, with most non-Christian staff being Muslim or Other at 2.3% and 3.7% respectively, compared to 0.2% of staff who declared as Jewish

Of those who had declared their sexual orientation as at 31 March 2021, 93.5% were heterosexual/straight compared to 6.5% of staff declaring themselves as LGB (Lesbian, Gay, Bisexual and Other).

## 2. Joiners

There were 5,803 (headcount) new recruits to HMPPS in 2020/21; 597 more than in 2019/20 and a 11.5% increase. Females accounted for 55.6% of joiners and more than half of joiners (50.8%) were aged under 30 years old.

The number of staff appointed to HMPPS increased from 5,206 in 2019/20 to 5,803 in

2020/21, a 11.5% increase. The largest group of recruits were band 3 to 5 officers, with 2,410 appointed in the 12 months to 31 March 2021. Figure 2 shows a breakdown of joiners across the available protected characteristics; additional details can also be found in the tables 2a and 2b. *Note: Black, Asian and minority ethnic breakdowns are not shown due to low declaration rates.*

Overall, 44.4% of those who joined HMPPS were male and 55.6% were female. This varied by grade with band 3-5 officer joiners being the only grade where staff were largely male (62.0%) compared to other grades such as National Probation Service below management level where the majority of joiners were female (78.3%). More than half of new joiners (50.8%, equivalent to 2,950 individuals) in 2020/21 were aged under 30 whilst 25.2% (1,461) were aged 40 or older. Specifically, 56.3% (1,358) of staff who joined as band 3-5 officers were aged under 30.

Declaration rates are high enough for disability, religion and sexual orientation to allow meaningful analysis by these protected characteristics, the declaration rate for race is still too low.

Of the 61.2% of joiners that declared their disability status in 2020/21, 9.1% were self-declared as being disabled compared to 90.9% of non-disabled staff.

There was a higher proportion of joiners who declared themselves as having no religion (60.1%) compared to those belonging to a religious group (39.9%, of which 31.7% were Christian and 8.1% were non-Christian).

Of those who had declared their sexual orientation, a higher proportion of recruits were heterosexual/straight at 91.2% compared to 8.8%

**Figure 3: Temporary cover allowances (TCA) per 100 staff, as at 31 March 2021**

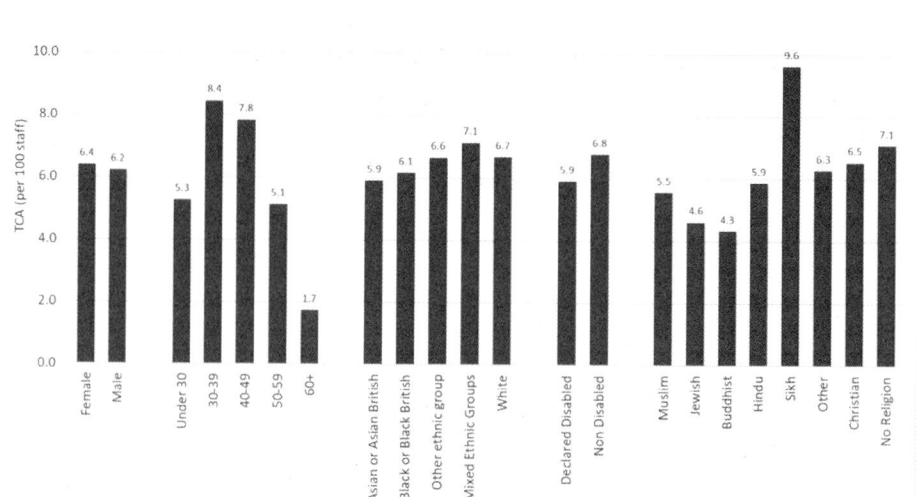

who were Lesbian, Gay, Bisexual and Other (LGB). Of the LGB categories, Gay/Lesbian staff made up the largest proportions of joiners at 4.7 compared to bisexual and 'other' (3.5% and 0.6% respectively).

### 3. Temporary Cover

*As at 31 March 2021, 3,052 staff (6.3%) were receiving temporary cover allowances (TCA).* TCA rates were higher for females, those aged 30-39 years old, mixed ethnicity staff, non-disabled staff, and non-religious staff.

Temporary cover payments are a system that enables staff to work temporarily in a more senior role and receive an additional payment while this work is undertaken. Although temporary cover payments tend to be received for a considerable duration while an individual covers a role at a higher grade on a temporary basis, these figures are based on snapshots at a moment of time at the end of a financial year. As such, they may not accurately represent the rates of those receiving cover payments during the financial year.

As at 31 March 2021, 3,052 staff were receiving Temporary Cover Allowances for filling posts of a higher grade on a temporary basis. This represents 6.3% of staff, an increase from 5.5% of staff as at 31 March 2020. The rate of temporary cover allowances is illustrated in figure 3, with additional details in tables 3a and 3b.

*Note: Sexual orientation breakdowns are not shown due to low declaration rates.*

As at 31 March 2021, 6.4% of females were on temporary cover compared to 6.2% of males. For operational and non-operational staff, rates for TCA were higher for female staff. The TCA rates among female and male staff in probation service grades were very similar.

Temporary cover payments were most prevalent amongst those aged 30 to 39 and 40 to 49 (8.4% and 7.8% respectively), compared to 5.3% of under 30s, 5.1% of 50 to 59 year olds, and 1.7% of staff aged 60 or over.

As at 31 March 2021, 6.3% of Black, Asian and minority ethnic staff were receiving temporary cover payments compared to 6.7% of White staff. Last year, 5.3% of Black, Asian and minority ethnic staff and 5.9% of White staff were on temporary cover. Numbers within the Black, Asian and minority ethnic subset groups were low, so some caution is advised when viewing rates. However, within the Black, Asian and minority ethnic category, staff who declared as Mixed Ethnic groups had the highest rate of receiving TCAs at 7.1%.

The proportion of staff receiving temporary cover allowances was lower amongst disabled staff compared to non-disabled (5.9% and 6.8% respectively as at 31 March 2021).

As at 31 March 2021, 6.2% of non-Christian staff were receiving temporary cover payments, compared to 6.5% of Christian staff and 7.1% of staff with no religion. Within the non-Christian religion subset groups, 9.6% of those who self-declared as being Sikh were receiving TCA.

Declaration rates for sexual orientation were too low for any meaningful analysis to be carried out.

### 4. Promotions

*In 2020/21, 3.8% of permanent staff were promoted, an equivalent of 2,004 promotions.* The rate of promotions was higher for: females, those aged 30-39 years old, mixed ethnic groups, non-disabled, non-religious staff and staff who identified as gay or lesbian. Promotions relate to staff moving to a more senior grade through an

**Figure 4: Promotions per 100 staff, 1 April 2020 to 31 March 2021**

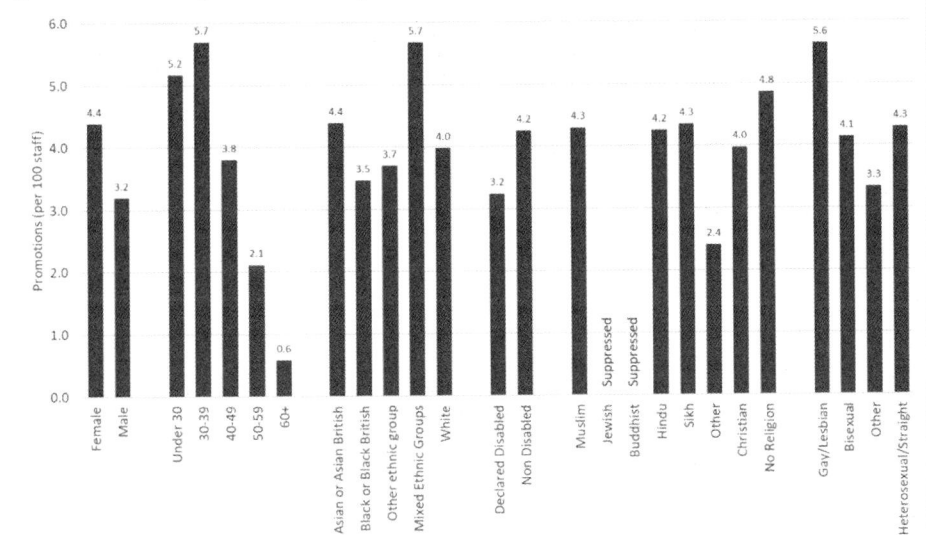

internal process. Operational Support Grade staff who convert to become prison officers are known as 'conversions' and not defined as promotions and so this specific grade change does not appear in this report. Promotions are reported in terms of the grade of the staff prior to promotion rather than the grade they were promoted into. Similarly, rates are calculated in relation to the number of staff in the lower grade.

In 2020/21, 3.8% of staff were promoted (the equivalent of 2,004 promotions within the year), a decrease from the rate of 4.6% (2,409 promotions) in 2019/20.

The rate of promotions, which represents the number of individuals promoted per 100 staff, in 2020/21 across all protected characteristics is illustrated in figure 4. Additional details on promotions can also be found in tables 4a and 4b. The promotion rate for female staff was higher in 2020/21 at 4.4% (1,146) than for males at 3.2% (858). Over the past 4 years, promotion rates have been consistently higher among female staff compared to male staff.

The rate of promotions generally declines as the age of staff increases. In 2020/21, staff aged under 30 had a promotion rate of 5.2% while staff aged 30 to 39 had the highest rate of promotion at 5.7% of staff in post, compared to 3.8% for staff aged 40 to 49, 2.1% for the 50-59 age group and 0.6% for staff aged 60 and over.

In the 12 months ending 31 March 2021, Black, Asian and minority ethnic staff had a slightly higher promotion rate at 4.2% than White staff at 4.0%. Within the Black, Asian and minority ethnic groups, those identifying as mixed ethnicity had the highest rate at 5.7%.

In 2020/21, the rate of promotion between staff who declared themselves disabled was lower than that of non-disabled staff, at 3.2% and 4.2% respectively. This pattern was seen across all grades apart from OSG staff but this is based on a small number of promotions as the most common upward move for OSG staff is to Band 3-5 prison officers which is not recorded in these statistics.

In 2020/21, the promotion rate was lower in non-Christian staff (3.2%) compared to Christian staff (4.0%) or those with no religion (4.8%). Staff who identified themselves as LGB (lesbian, gay, bisexual or other) had a higher rate of promotion compared to heterosexual staff (5.0% and 4.3% respectively).

### 5. Staff Appraisals

For the year 2020/21 the normal appraisal reporting was suspended due to the COVID-19 pandemic.

In HMPPS, the system of staff appraisals is called the 'Staff Performance and Development Record' (SPDR). There is an annual cycle or appraisals and marks are awarded at the mid-year and then the end-year. It is the end-year markings that are shown within the data tables.

For the financial year 2019/20, the usual process for SPDR assessment at year end in HMPPS was suspended due to COVID-19, with the aim of relieving staff of some of the administrative burden around the end of year performance management process at a difficult time. Given the exceptional circumstances, managers were only required to record a rating for those staff assessed as 'outstanding'. This means that the majority of staff would have been awarded with a 'good' marking, including those whose performance may have dipped to 'improvement required'. Therefore, for those two markings analysis and comparison with previous years are not possible. Staff on formal Managing Poor

Performance measures were recorded separately and this process continued as usual.

For the financial year 2020/21 the normal reporting process was suspended due to the challenges of managing the COVID-19 pandemic. Managers were not required to complete appraisal reports or input performance markings. As in 2019/20, staff on formal Managing Poor Performance measures were recorded separately and this process continued as usual.

Further detail on appraisal ratings in previous years can be found in tables 5a and 5b.

## 6. Special Bonuses

*In 2020/21, a range of COVID-19 special payment schemes were set up for frontline prison and probation staff.* These special payment schemes were processed as special bonuses which resulted in the 2020/21 bonus figures being much higher than those for previous years. The figures show total bonus value awarded to staff in 2020/21 was £47.5m compared to £1.3m in 2019/20. The rate of special bonuses awarded to staff, including COVID 19 special payment schemes, in 2020/21 was 64.3 per 100 staff.

The rate of bonuses awarded was higher for White staff (at 67.2 per 100 staff) compared to Black, Asian and minority ethnic staff (at 52.6 per 100 staff), and non-disabled staff (at 65.4 per 100 people) compared to disabled staff (at 50.7 per 100 people).

During 2020/21, special payments were paid to frontline prison and probation staff, with band 3-5 prison staff receiving higher rates of bonuses

than probation staff. Band 3-5 prison staff are more likely to be male (71% male) whereas probation staff were more likely to be female (77% female). In addition, probation staff had a higher rate of disability (18%) compared to band 3-5 prison officers (10%). Therefore, when reviewing special bonuses by protected characteristics, please take into consideration the grade of those who were awarded special bonuses, which is available in table 6b(ii).

Special bonuses allow local management the opportunity to recognise and reward any member of staff for exceptional performance in a particularly demanding task or situation through a one-off non-consolidated lump sum payment of up to £2,000 (or up to £20,000 with CEO approval). In 2020/21 a range of COVID-19 special payment schemes were set up for frontline prison and probation staff. The special payment schemes were developed to support the staffing for prisons and probation through the COVID-19 pandemic in recognition of the exceptional circumstances in which they were working. The special payments schemes were processed in the same way as special bonuses and cannot be separated from special bonuses. This has resulted in the 2020/21 figures showing a significant increase compared to previous years. During 2020/21 the total bonus value awarded to staff was £47.5m compared to £1.3m in 2019/20. As the 2020/21 data contains these extra COVID-19 special payments, please treat any comparisons to previous years with caution.

The rate of special bonuses awarded to staff, including the special payment schemes, in

**Figure 5: Average value of special bonuses awarded, 1 April 2020 to 31 March 2021**

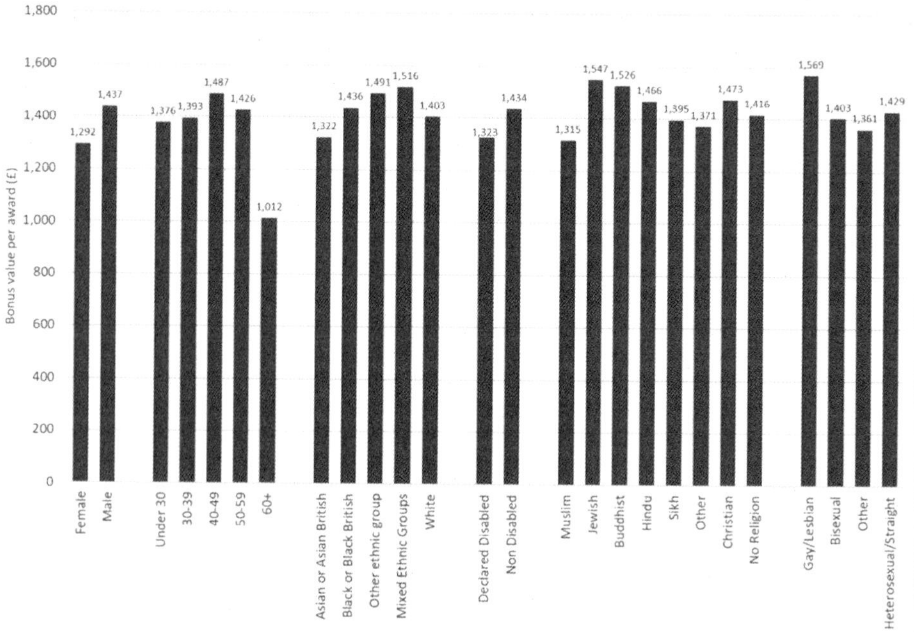

2020/21 was 64.3 per 100 staff, compared to 3.6 in 2019/20. The average value of the awards per staff member increased from £661 in 2019/20 to £1,384 in 2020/21.

Across the grades, the rate of bonuses awarded was higher for managerial positions than for junior positions. In operational grades, operational managers were awarded bonuses at a rate of 96.9 per 100 staff compared to the more junior operational positions of band 3-5 officers at 93.9 per 100 staff, and OSGs at 86.2 per 100 staff. A similar pattern was seen for non-operational and NPS grades too; non-operational managers were awarded bonuses at 57.3 per 100 staff compared to more junior non-operational positions at 55.2 per 100 staff, and NPS management grades were awarded bonuses at 8.0 per 100 staff compared to NPS below management grades at 2.9 per 100 staff.

The average value per award across protected characteristics are illustrated in figures 5 below, and bonus statistics can be viewed in tables 6a, 6b(i) and 6b(ii).

The rate of special bonuses awarded in 2020/21 was higher for males at 80.7 per 100 staff than for females at 47.6 per 100 staff. The average value of the bonuses was also higher for males who received an average of £1,437 compared to females who received an average of £1,292. The rate of special bonuses awarded was higher for males than females across all grades except non-operational manager and NPS roles (both managers and junior positions).

In 2020/21, staff in the 50-59 age group had the highest rate of bonuses awarded at 66.6 per 100 staff, and the average value of bonuses for this age group was the second highest compared to the other age groups at £1,426. Staff aged 40-49 had the lowest rates of bonuses at 60.3 per 100 staff but it was also the age group with the highest average value of awards at £1,487.

In 2020/21, the rate of bonuses awarded to Black, Asian and minority ethnic staff was lower compared to White staff (52.6 compared to 67.2 per 100 staff respectively), but the average value of bonuses awarded was similar with an average of £1,425 for Black, Asian and minority ethnic staff and £1,403 for White staff. There were differences between the rates and average value of bonuses awarded to different groups of Black, Asian and minority ethnic staff. Staff who declared themselves as 'other ethnic groups' were awarded the highest bonuses at a rate of 68.1 per 100 staff, with an average value of £1,491. In contrast, staff who declared themselves as 'Asian or Asian British' were awarded the lowest bonuses at a rate of 48.4 per 100 staff and had a lower average value of £1,322.

The rate of bonuses awarded in 2020/21 to those who declared as disabled was 50.7 per 100 staff, compared to 65.4 per 100 staff for non-disabled staff. Moreover, the average value of these awards was slightly lower for those declared disabled at £1,323, compared to non-disabled at £1,423.

In 2020/21, the rate of bonuses awarded to those who declared as Christian (64.2 per 100 staff) was lower compared to those with no religion (67.7 per 100 staff) but higher than those affiliated with non-Christian religions (57.5 per 100 staff). Staff who declared themselves as LGB (Lesbian, Gay, Bisexual and Other) were awarded bonuses at a higher than heterosexual staff (73.2 per 100 staff compared to 64.6 per 100 staff), as well as having a higher average value of the awards (£1,503 for LGB staff compared to £1,429 for heterosexual/straight staff).

## 7. Grievances

In 2020-21, 763 staff raised grievances resulting in 911 cases. Of these cases, 41.7% were upheld/partially upheld. The raising of grievances was higher for: Black, Asian and minority ethnic staff (at 2.4 per 100 staff) compared to White staff (at 1.3 per 100 staff) and disabled staff (at 2.9 per 100 staff) compared to non-disabled staff (at 1.2 per 100 staff)

A grievance is defined as any concern, problem or complaint raised by an individual member of staff relating to his or her employment. Only grievances that have gone through the formal procedure are analysed here. Grievances resolved locally or through mediation are not recorded centrally. Further details on grievances can be found in tables 7a, 7b(i) and 7b(ii).

In 2020/21, there were 763 staff who raised grievances, resulting in 911 cases. Of these cases, 41.7% (380 cases) were upheld or partially upheld, an increase of 3.5 percentage points compared to the previous year. The overall figure for the number of grievances raised in 2020/21 represented 1.4 per 100 staff, a decrease from 2019/20 (1.7 per 100 staff). Across grade breakdowns, operational managers had the highest rate in terms of raising a grievance at 2.4 per 100 staff.

Figures 6 and 7 show the rate per 100 staff raising grievances and the percent of cases upheld or partially upheld, split by protected characteristic. Overall, female staff raised grievances in 2020/21 at the same rate as males at 1.4 per 100 staff. Across grades, females raised fewer grievances per 100 staff compared to males in National Probation Service grades (both manager and junior grades), but not in operational grades (operational managers, band 3-5 officers, OSGs and for both non-operational manager and non-operational below management grades) where female staff raised a higher rate of grievances than male staff. The largest difference between rates of female and male staff who a raised

**Figure 6: Number of staff per 100 staff raising grievances, 1 April 2020 to 31 March 2021**

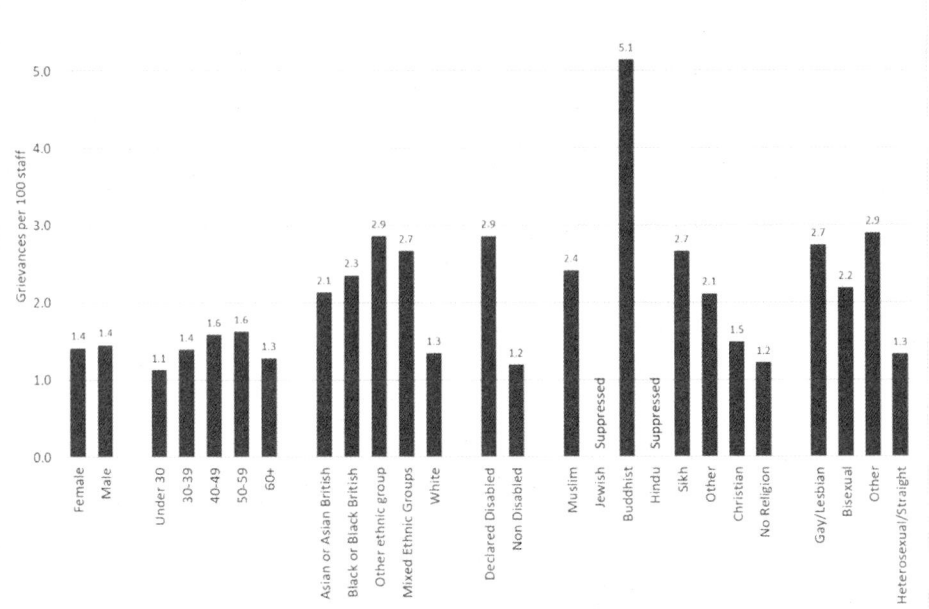

**Figure 7: Percent of cases upheld or partially upheld, 1 April 2020 to 31 March 2021**

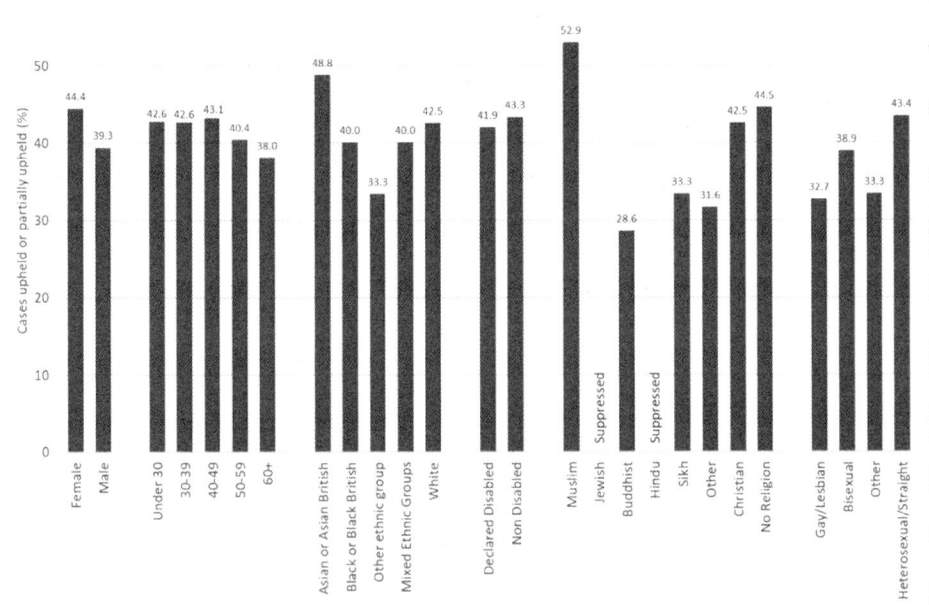

grievance was for the operational manger grade group (at 3.0 and 2.1 per 100 staff respectively). The percentage of cases upheld or partially upheld in 2020/21 was higher for females (44.4%) than for males (39.3%).

In 2020/21, there was a tendency for the rate of grievances to increase with age, except for those aged 60 or over. Staff under 30 had a grievance rate of 1.1 per 100 staff compared to 1.6 per 100 staff aged between 50-59, with those aged 60 and over having a grievance rate of 1.3 per 100 staff.

The overall rate of grievances raised per 100 staff was higher amongst Black, Asian and minority ethnic staff compared to White staff, at 2.4 per 100 and 1.3 per 100 staff respectively. The percentage of cases upheld or partially upheld was higher for White staff at 42.5% compared to Black, Asian and minority ethnic staff at 42.1%. Overall, self-declared disabled staff raised more grievances, at a rate of 2.9 per 100 staff, than non-disabled staff, at 1.2 per 100 staff. This pattern was seen across all grades.

Non-Christian staff raised more grievances than Christian staff, at 2.3 and 1.5 per 100 staff respectively. Considering grades where numbers are large enough to disclose, this pattern was seen across all grades except for non-operational grades below management level. Christian staff had a higher proportion of cases being upheld or partially upheld at 42.5% compared to non-Christian staff at 40.2%.

Staff who identified themselves as LGB raised more grievances, at a rate of 2.6 per 100 staff, compared to heterosexual staff, as at a rate of 1.3 per 100 staff. The percentage of cases upheld or partially upheld was higher for heterosexual staff at 43.4% compared to LGB staff at 34.2%.

**8. Investigations and Conduct & Discipline cases**
*In 2020/21, the overall rate of investigated staff was 3.4 per 100 staff.* The rate was higher amongst male staff (4.7 per 100 males) compared to female staff (2.1 per 100 females), Black, Asian and minority ethnic staff (3.8 per 100 staff) compared to White staff (3.1 per 100 staff), and those under 30 (5.1 per 100 staff) compared to staff in other age bands.

*In 2020/21, the overall rate of conduct and discipline cases was 1.5 per 100 staff.* The rate was higher for; male staff (2.1 per 100 male staff) compared to female staff (0.9 per 100 female staff). Black, Asian and minority ethnic staff (1.4 per 100 staff) and White staff (1.4 per 100 staff) had the same rate of conduct & discipline cases.

Investigations into staff conduct are designed to establish the truth of the case and to determine whether conduct and discipline

action is recommended. A conduct and discipline case imposes a penalty on a member of staff for wrong-doing. In cases of summary dismissal, it is not always possible to have had a full internal investigation.

Both investigations and conduct and discipline cases may involve multiple charges and may have multiple outcomes for the different parts of the case. More than one member of staff can also be charged and penalised in a single case. For the purpose of this report, a case is defined as a charge or set of charges being brought against an individual. Where more than one individual is charged together, they are counted as multiple cases in this report.

Further details on investigations and conduct and discipline cases can be found in tables 8a, 8b(i) and 8b(ii), and 9a, 9b(i) and 9b(ii).

In 2020/01, 1,806 staff faced at least one investigation, representing a rate of 3.4 investigated staff per 100 staff, an increase from 2.9 investigated staff per 100 for 2019/20. Of the 1,937 cases, 1,223 (63.1%) had further action recommended. In 2020/21, band 3-5 officers had a higher rate of investigations than staff in other grades (5.9 investigated staff per 100 staff, with all other grades with a rate of 2.8 or below).

Overall, male staff were investigated at more than double the rate of female staff in 2020/21, at 4.7 investigated staff per 100 males compared to 2.1 investigated staff per 100 females. The rate of investigations for male staff was higher across all grades except for non-operational managers . The percentage of cases with further action recommended was slightly higher for females at 64.0% compared to 62.8% for males.

**Figure 8: Staff subject to at least one investigation per 100 staff in post, 1 April 2020 to 31 March 2021**

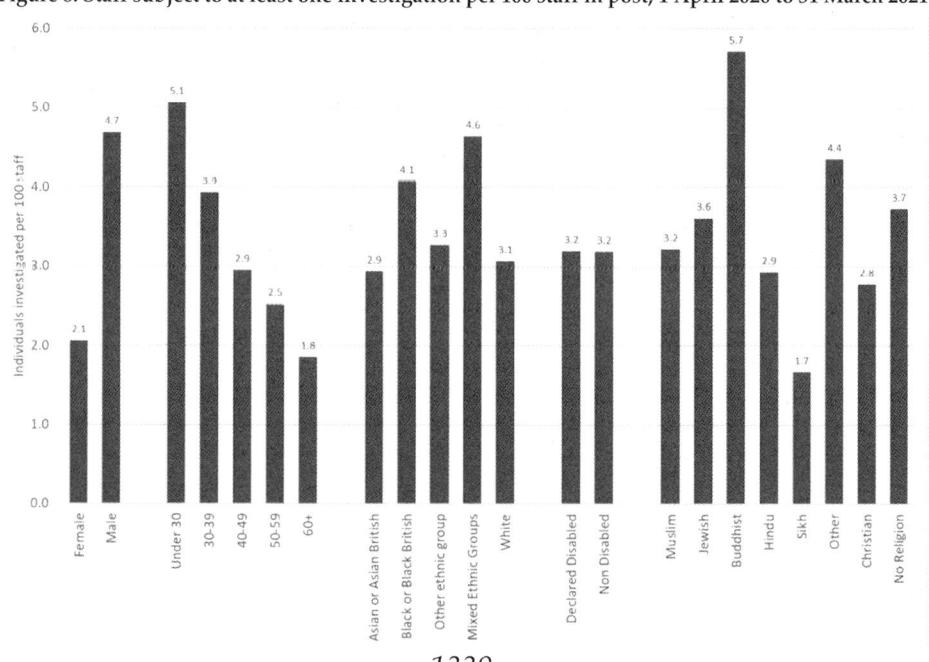

Figure 9: Proportion of Investigations where further action was recommended, 1 April 2020 to 31 March 2021

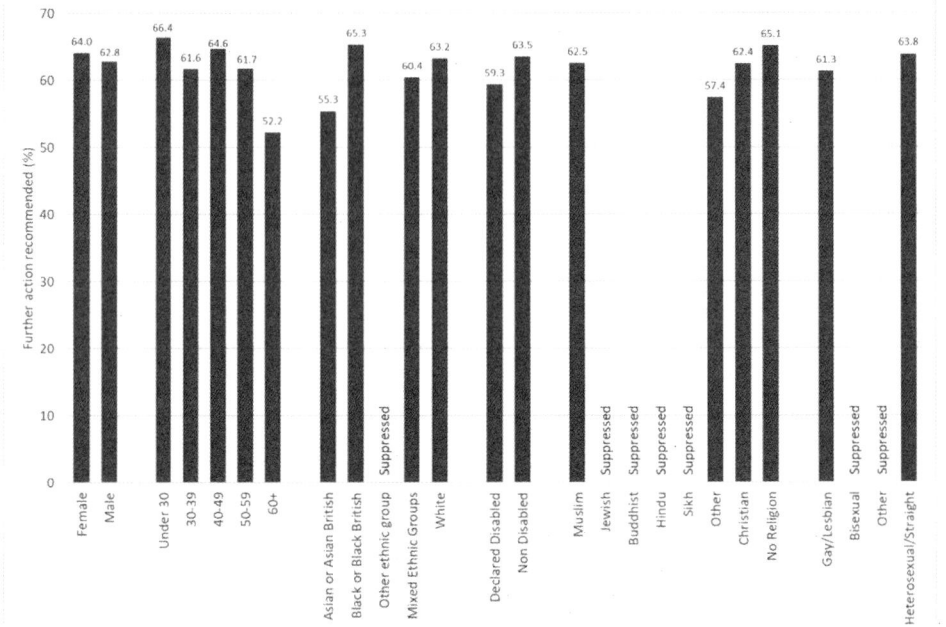

Figures 8 and 9 show the rates per 100 staff who were investigated in 2020/21 and the proportion of cases where further action was recommended, split by protected characteristic.

*Note: Sexual orientation breakdowns are not shown due to low declaration rates.*

In 2020/21, there was a tendency for the rate of investigations to decrease with age from 5.1 investigated staff per 100 staff for those aged under 30, to 1.8 investigated staff per 100 staff aged 60 and over.

The proportion of Black, Asian and minority ethnic staff investigated in 2020/21 was higher than the proportion of White staff investigated, 3.8 investigated staff per 100 staff compared to 3.1 investigated staff per 100 staff. The percentage of cases with further action recommended was lower for Black, Asian and minority ethnic staff (61.4%) than for White staff (63.2%).

In 2020/21, the proportion of staff with non-Christian religious beliefs investigated was

Figure 10: Staff per 100 staff subject to conduct and discipline action, 1 April 2020 to 31 March 2021

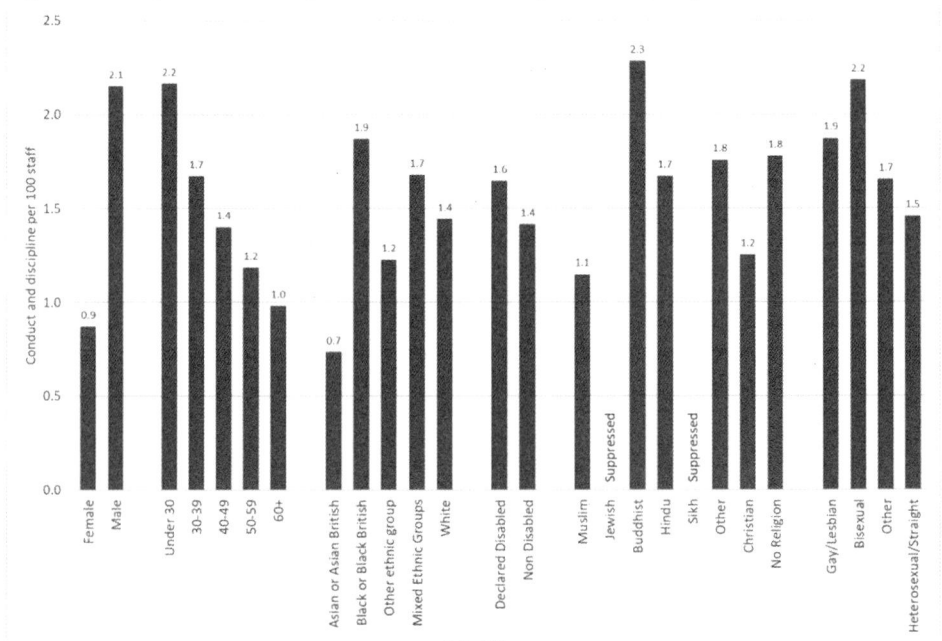

**Figure 11: Percentage of conduct cases leading to dismissal, 1 April 2020 to 31 March 2021**

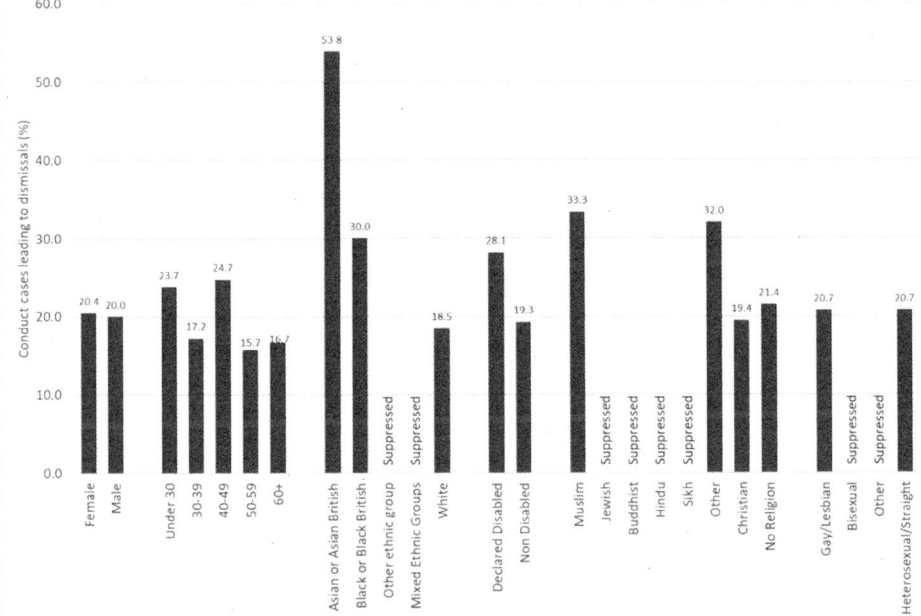

higher than for Christian staff, at 3.7 investigated staff per 100 staff, compared to 2.8 investigated staff per 100 staff for Christian staff. Non-Christian staff had a lower proportion of cases with further action recommended (60.3%) compared to Christian staff or those with no religion (62.4% and 65.1% respectively).

There were 810 staff subject to conduct and discipline action in 2020/21, a rate of 1.5 per 100 staff. There was a total of 835 conduct cases and of these 20.1% resulted in the penalty of dismissal[footnote 2]. The rate of conduct cases was highest amongst band 3-5 prison officers at 2.5 per 100 staff.

Figures 10 and 11 show the rates per 100 staff who were subject to conduct and discipline action and the proportions of conduct cases leading to dismissal in 2020/21, split by protected characteristics.

The rate of conduct cases involving male staff was more than double the rate for female staff, 2.1 per 100 male staff compared to 0.9 per 100 female staff. The proportions of cases resulting in dismissal were higher for female staff compared to male staff (20.4% and 20.0% respectively).

In 2020/01, the rate of conduct and discipline cases was highest among staff aged under 30 at 2.2 per 100 staff and decreased with age where those aged 60 plus had a rate of 1.0 per 100 staff. In 2020/21 Black, Asian and minority ethnic staff and White staff had the same rate of staff subject to conduct and discipline action per 100 staff with 1.4 per 100 staff respectively. The percentage of dismissals resulting from conduct cases was higher for Black, Asian and

minority ethnic staff at 31.5% compared to White staff at 18.5%.

There was a slightly higher proportion of staff subject to conduct and discipline among those who declared themselves as disabled, 1.6 per 100 staff, compared to non-disabled staff, 1.4 per 100 staff. The percentage of cases resulting in dismissals was higher for disabled staff compared to non-disabled staff (28.1% and 19.3% respectively).

In 2020/21, staff with non-Christian religious beliefs, 1.4 per 100 staff, were subject to conduct and discipline action at a higher rate than Christian staff, 1.2 per 100 staff. Non-Christian staff had a higher proportion of cases which resulted in dismissals (34.0%) compared to Christian staff (19.4%) or those with no religion (21.4%).

The rate of conduct and discipline cases was higher for staff who identified as LGB compared to Heterosexual staff (1.9 per 100 staff and 1.5 per 100 staff respectively).

### 9. Sickness Absence

In 2020/21, HMPPS staff lost an average of 11.4 working days due to sickness, a 1.1 average working day increase compared to 2019/20. The average working days lost due to sickness increased with age and was higher for males, Black, Asian and minority ethnic staff, and those that declared themselves as disabled, non-Christian, or LGBT.

Sickness absence is represented in this section by the average working days lost (AWDL) due to sickness per employee per year. Comparisons to the figures for the period 1 April 2017 to 31

March 2018 should be interpreted with caution due to an under-recording of sickness absence records during migration of data to the Single Operating Platform. To note, 2019/20 and 2020/21 financial year sickness absence data both include figures relating to the effect of COVID-19 on HMPPS staff in the publication. In the previous year's publication, COVID-19 figures are not included, hence why the 2019/20 figures differ from this year's. For further information on sickness reason, please see our HMPPS workforce release.

In 2020/21, the AWDL due to sickness absence was 11.4, a 1.1 percentage point increase from 10.2 in 2019/20. The average working days lost to sickness absence was higher for male staff at 11.8 days, than for female staff at 10.7 days. This was seen across all NPS below management grades but not in operational grades, non-operational grades, NPS below management grades and NPS management grades.

Figure 12 illustrates the AWDL in 2020/21 across all protected characteristics. Further details on sickness absence can be found in tables 10a and 10b.

In 2020/21, the average working days lost to sickness absence increased with age from 10.3 days for those aged 30-39, increasing through each age group to the over 60s who had the highest AWDL at 13.9 days. This pattern was seen across many of the grades, except for band 3-5 officers (where those aged 50-59 had the highest AWDL at 15.0).

In 2020/21, across operational, non-operational and NPS roles the AWDL was lower for senior staff compared to grades below management level. Operational, Non-Operational and NPS grades below management level had the highest levels of AWDL; 13.8 days for officers, 12.9 days

for OSGs, 9.8 days for non –operational below manager and 9.3 days for NPS staff below management grade.

In 2020/21, the AWDL was 12.9 days for Black, Asian and minority ethnic staff and 11.0 days for White staff. There were some differences in the AWDL between the groups within the Black, Asian and minority ethnic category, with Black or Black British staff having the highest rate of 13.5, followed by Mixed Ethnic Groups staff at 12.8, Asian or Asian British staff at 12.3 and Other ethnic group staff at 11.7. Compared to 2019/20, there was an increase in the AWDL among White staff at 1.1 percentage points and an increase for Black, Asian and minority ethnic staff of 0.8 percentage points. By grade, in the 12 months ending 31 March 2021, the AWDL rate was higher for Black, Asian and minority ethnic staff in all staff positions, apart from Operational Managers (7.5 AWDL for White staff compared to 3.8 for Black, Asian and minority ethnic staff). For 2020/21, those who declared themselves as being disabled had more working days lost, on average, than that of non-disabled staff, at 17.1 days compared to 10.0 days respectively. Disabled staff had a higher AWDL compared to non-disabled staff across all grade groups where the declaration rates were above the 60% threshold.

In 2020/21, staff who declared themselves as being a non-Christian had a higher rate of AWDL of 13.4 days compared to Christian staff (11.3 days) and staff with no religion (10.1 days). Of the non-Christian religions, Sikh staff had the highest AWDL of 14.4 days. Staff who declared themselves as LGB had the highest rate of AWDL of 13.2 days compared to an AWDL of 10.7 days in heterosexual/straight staff.

**Figure 12: Average working days lost due to sickness absence, 1 April 2020 to 31 March 2021**

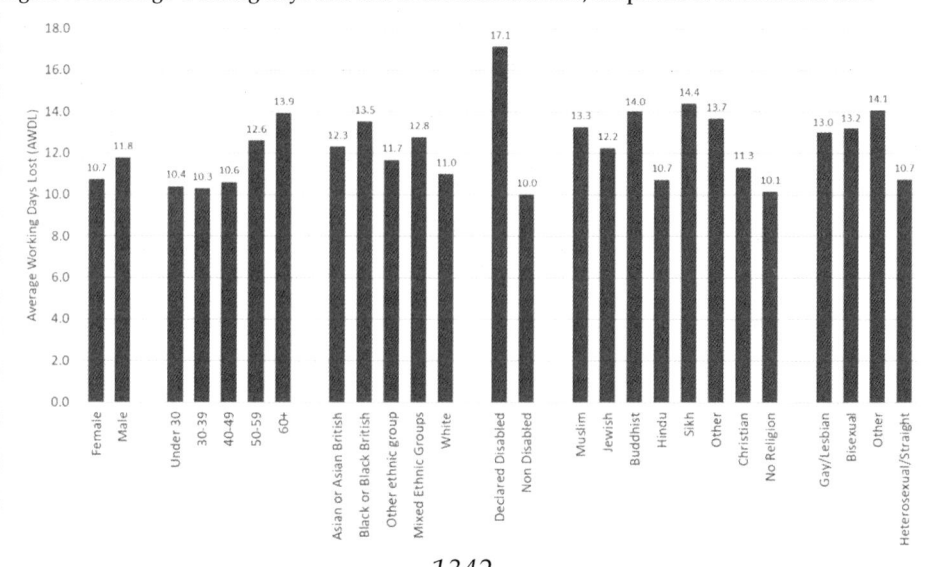

## 10. Leavers

In 2020/21, the leaving rate of HMPPS staff was 8.3%, a decrease of 2.2 percentage point since 2019/20. Leaving rates were higher amongst male staff (8.8%) compared female staff (7.9%). By age, the highest leaving rate was for those aged 60 and over (16.5%), followed by those aged under 30 (12.7%).

In the 12 months ending 31 March 2021, 4,428 permanent staff (headcount) left HMPPS. The leaving rate stood at 8.3%, representing a decrease of 2.2 percentage point from the previous year's rate of 10.5%. The rates presented include retirement but exclude voluntary exits under the Voluntary Early Departure Scheme and redundancies (VEDSR).

Leaving rates for each protected characteristic are shown in figure 13. Further details on leavers can be found in tables 11a to 11c.

The leaving rate for female staff was lower in the 12 months ending 31 March 2021 at 7.9% than the rate for male staff at 8.8%, a decrease of 1.8 and 2.5 percentage points respectively compared to the previous year.

Considering gender splits of leaving rates by grade group, in 2020/21, operational below management grades had the largest leaving rates; OSGs had a leaving rate of 11.9%, a decrease from 12.5% in 2019/20, and band 3-5 officers had a leaving rate of 9.1%, a decrease from 12.2% in 2019/20. Band 3-5 prison officers and non-operational managers were the only grades where females had a higher leaving rate than males; a rate of 9.6% compared to 9.0%, respectively for band 3-5 officers, and a rate of 5.8% compared to 5.5%, respectively for non-operational managers. NPS management grades had the largest gender

difference with the rate for male leavers at 5.1% compared to 2.9% for females.

As leaving rates include retirement it would be expected that those aged 60 and over would have the highest leaving rates. Accordingly the leaving rate for those aged 60 and over was the highest at 16.5% in the 12 months to 31 March 2021, a decrease of 1.4 percentage points compared to the previous 12 months. Those aged under 30 had leaving rates of 12.7%, which was a decrease of 4.2 percentage points compared to the 12 months to 31 March 2020.

In 2020/21, the leaving rate was lower for Black, Asian and minority ethnic staff at 6.6%, compared to White staff at 7.3%. Within the Black, Asian and minority ethnic subgroups, those who declared themselves as other ethnic group or mixed ethnic groups had the highest leaving rates at 8.2% and 7.5%, respectively. Staff who had declared themselves as disabled had a leaving rate of 8.2% which was higher than the leaving rate of non-disabled staff at 7.1%.

Declaration rates for religion and sexual orientation are above the level at which meaningful consideration can be made. In 2020/21, staff who declared themselves as having no religion had a higher leaving rate of 7.7% compared to non-Christian staff (7.3%) and Christian staff (6.7%). Staff who declared themselves as LGB had a higher leaving rate of 7.6% than heterosexual/straight staff leaving rate of 7.1%.

### Further Information
### *Accompanying files*

As well as this report, the following products are published as part of this release: A technical guide and glossary providing details of the data

**Figure 13: Permanent staff leaving rates (excluding VEDSR), 1 April 2020 to 31 March 2021**

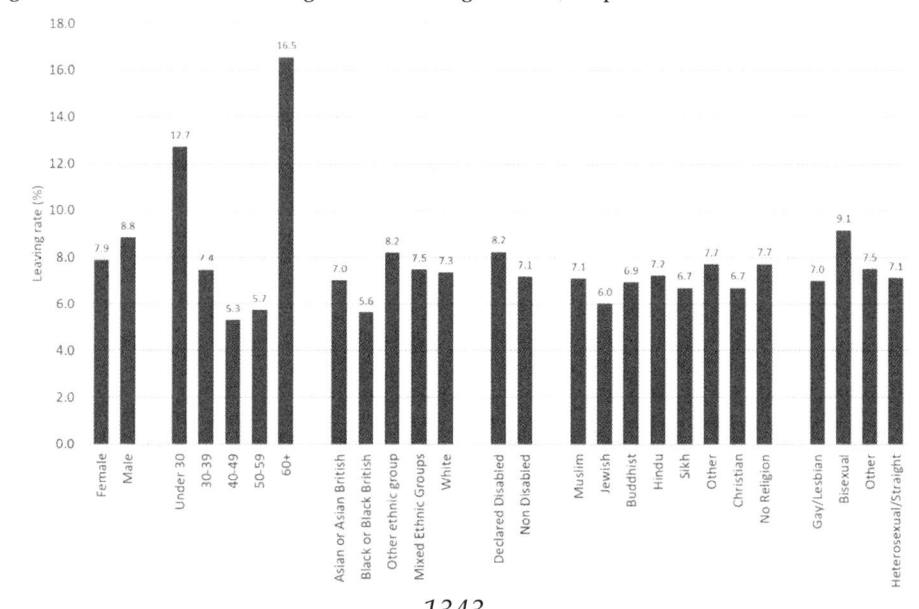

sources and quality. Information on the revisions policy and disclosure relevant to HMPPS staffing data as well as a definition of terms used is also included. A set of tables for the year as well as over time.

*Official Statistics*

The statistics in this bulletin are classified as official statistics. The Statistics and Registration Service Act 2007 defines 'official statistics' as all those statistical outputs produced by the UK Statistics Authority's executive office (the Office for National Statistics), by central Government departments and agencies, by the devolved administrations in Northern Ireland, Scotland and Wales, and by other Crown bodies (over 200 bodies in total). The statistics in this bulletin comply with all aspects of the Code of Practice for Official Statistics. The Code encourages and supports producers of statistics to maintain their independence and to ensure adequate resourcing for statistical production. It helps producers and users of statistics by setting out the necessary principles and practices to produce statistics that are trustworthy, high quality and of public value.

**Contact**

Press enquiries should be directed to the Ministry of Justice press office:
Tel: 020 3334 3536
Email: newsdesk@justice.gov.uk
Other enquiries about these statistics should be directed to:
Chris Casanovas
Corporate Data Sharing Lead
Data and Evidence as a Service
Ministry of Justice
10 South Colonnade
London
E14 4PH
Email: statistics.enquiries@justice.gov.uk
URL:
www.gov.uk/government/collections/national-offender-management-service-workforce-statistics

© Crown copyright

1. *In this report National Probation Service staff are reported according to grade and therefore vary slightly from the total number of staff in the National Probation Service. This is due to the small number of National Probation Service staff in non-Probation Service grades.*
2. *Details of appeals are not included in the analysis so a number of the penalties may have been overturned on appeal.*

## 8.6 PAY SCALES

**Prison Service Pay Review Body 2022 report on England and Wales**
**Executive Summary: July 2022**
**This report sets out our recommendations on pay and allowances for operational prison staff. Our recommendations for 2022 are:**

**Recommendation 1:** We recommend that from 1 April 2022, the Fair and Sustainable National Band 3 to 5 base pay points, the Band 7 to 11 base pay minima and maxima, and all closed grade spot rates and base pay points be increased by 4% (including the closed grade Required Hours Addition/Allowance cash element), as set out in Appendix D. This award to be consolidated and pensionable for all staff.

**Recommendation 2:** From 1 April 2022, we recommend that the consolidated, pensionable salary for Prison Auxiliary and Night Patrol staff be increased to the National Living Wage or by 4%, whichever gives the greater amount.

**Recommendation 3:** We recommend that from 1 April 2022 the Fair and Sustainable National Band 2 spot rate be increased by £1,500. This award to be consolidated and pensionable for all staff. On 1 April 2022, this fully erodes the market supplements for those Band 2 staff who currently receive them.

**Recommendation 4:** We recommend that from 1 April 2022, the Fair and Sustainable Band 12 spot rate be increased by 5%, as set out in Appendix D.

**Recommendation 5:** We recommend that from 1 September 2022, the Fair and Sustainable National Band 3 base pay points increase by £2,500 giving a total consolidated and pensionable award of £3,000 when the 20% unsocial hours payment is included. On 1 September 2022, this erodes the 'amber' market supplement and £3,000 of the 'red' and 'red plus' market supplements for those Band 3 staff who currently receive them.

**Recommendation 6:** We recommend that from 1 April 2022, the Fair and Sustainable Bands 3 and 5 be shortened from five to three pay points as per HMPPS's proposals.

**Recommendation 7:** We recommend that from 1 April 2022, Fair and Sustainable Band 4 become a spot rate by removing all pay points below the maximum.

**Recommendation 8:** We recommend that all staff (except those subject to formal poor performance procedures) on Fair and Sustainable Bands 3 and 5 who are in post on 31 March 2022 and do not automatically receive an uplift as a result of pay band restructuring should progress by one point, effective from 1 April 2022.

**Recommendation 9:** We recommend that all staff (except those subject to formal poor performance procedures) on Fair and Sustainable Bands 7 to 11 who are in post on 31 March 2022 receive a consolidated and pensionable progression increase of 4%, capped at the 2022 band maximum.

**Recommendation 10:** We recommend that from 1 April 2022, the fixed cash pay differentials for the Fair and Sustainable Outer and Inner London zones be increased by 4% and continue to be applied consistently across all bands, positioning maxima at £2,836 and £4,314 respectively above the base 37 hour National zone pay. We also recommend adjusting minima and intermediate points so that progression steps are the same percentage as on the National bands. The increase to be consolidated and pensionable.

**Recommendation 11:** We recommend that from 1 April 2022, the percentage uplift on base pay for the Unsocial Working Hours allowance be increased to 20% for Bands 2 to 5 and is applied to all contracted hours worked.

**Recommendation 12:** We recommend that from 1 April 2022, the percentage uplift on base pay for the Required Hours Addition/Allowance be increased to 20% for Bands 7 to 11.

**Recommendation 13:** We recommend that from 1 April 2022, the Care and Maintenance of Dogs allowance be increased to £2,434 per annum for those with responsibility for a single dog. We further recommend that the rate for multiple dogs is set at 25% above the single dog allowance.

**Introduction**

i. While writing our report this year, restrictions put in place during the coronavirus (Covid-19) pandemic were starting to be cautiously lifted in prisons. Her Majesty's Prison and Probation Service (HMPPS) has been widely praised for its response to the pandemic but as the Prison Service tries to return to a normal operating state we are left with a very troubling picture. Despite a temporary reprieve due to increased economic uncertainty and limited opportunities in the labour market during the pandemic, staff leaving rates have resumed their upward trajectory and have now not only returned to but have exceeded pre-2020 levels. When finalising our decisions at the beginning of June 2022, additional statistics published by HMPPS covering the year to March 2022 were released. This data indicated a further worsening of leaving rates for all groups of operational staff and in particular Band 2 Operational Support Grades (OSG) and Band 3 to 4 Prison Officers.

ii. The strong conclusion we drew from the evidence this year is that HMPPS is facing a crisis in the recruitment and retention of Band 2 and 3 staff and that pay, in particular take home pay, is a significant contributory factor to this. The lack of action in recent years to improve the market position of these staff has led to increasing numbers leaving the Service year on year. This is having a major impact on our remit group and the stability of public sector prisons.

iii. We are not alone in our concerns. This year HMPPS took the unusual step of making changes to the market supplements during the middle of the pay round due to serious concerns about several prisons where the number of leavers were exceeding joiners.

However, it is evident to us that market supplements not only fail to address but in fact reinforce more serious structural issues in the pay system. Moreover, in the past two years, HMPPS has become over reliant on an increasing number of complex allowances and payments that have further exacerbated the fundamental problems with the current pay structure.

iv. We ask that the Government carefully consider the recommendations we make this year, and the clear and substantial evidence on which they are based. It is crucial that HMPPS invests in its pay structures now, not only to recruit, retain and train the staff it needs in front-line operational roles, but also to deliver on its commitments in the Prison Strategy White Paper and to ensure a stable and effective Prison Service.

v. Our priorities this year are to give all staff a meaningful consolidated base pay increase and to target additional investment at the lowest paid operational grades. Taken together, our recommendations will provide investment where it is most critically needed, whilst ensuring that all our remit group receive a fair and affordable pay award.

*Role of the Prison Service Pay Review Body*

vi. The Prison Service Pay Review Body (PSPRB) was established under statue in 2001 to examine and report on matters relating to the rates of pay and allowances to be applied in the public sector prison services in England and Wales, and in Northern Ireland. The PSPRB was set up by the Government as a compensatory mechanism for the remit group's loss of the right to take industrial action of any form.

This was reinforced in the 336th report of the International Labour Organization in 2005, in which the Government gave a clear and unequivocal commitment to depart from the PSPRB's recommendations only in "exceptional circumstances" and agreed that such recommendations would be complied with in practice.

Despite having rejected a number of significant recommendations over the past four years, the Government continues to reaffirm this commitment.

*Our remit and approach this year*

vii. On 2 December 2021, the Minister of State for Prisons, Victoria Atkins MP, wrote to us asking us to commence our work for the 2022-23 pay round. The Minister asked that affordability be a critical part of our considerations and that we should be mindful of the evidence from Her Majesty's Treasury (HMT) setting out the economic, labour market and financial context within which the Pay Review Bodies have been asked to consider their recommendations. Within this evidence, HMT noted that public sector earnings growth over the next three years should retain broad parity with the private sector. The Minister's activation letter further drew our attention to the Prison Service's need to recruit and retain the best public servants.

viii. We received written submissions from the POA, the Prison Governors' Association (PGA), the Public and Commercial Services Union and HMPPS. Unfortunately, our visits this year were again restricted by Covid-19 but in late 2021 and early 2022 we held virtual discussion groups with prison staff via telephone and video conferencing. These virtual visits allowed us to meet and hear evidence from remit group staff at all levels on a wide range of issues.

**2022 pay award**

ix. In determining the headline increase for staff this year, we are mindful of the difficult economic backdrop against which we are making our recommendations. We recognise the impact both of the rate of inflation and the resulting increases in the cost of living on our remit group, particularly those on the lowest incomes. However, in determining the quantum of the headline award, our principal focus has been on the workforce data, particularly trends in recruitment and retention, as well as the relative market position of operational Prison Service pay. We have also considered data on average earnings growth and median pay settlements across the whole economy that were available to us at the time of making our decisions.

x. From the outset this year, we recognised that all staff should receive a consolidated uplift to base pay. We therefore recommend a consolidated, pensionable increase of 4% for all staff in Bands 3 to 11, along with all closed grade staff (including closed grade OSGs). This will deliver the same headline award to staff irrespective of whether they are on Fair and Sustainable or closed grades.

xi. This year HMPPS proposed a cash award of £1,500 for staff in Fair and Sustainable Band 2. We welcome the proposal by HMPPS to provide a substantial increase to the Band 2 spot rate to improve the market position for these staff. We

support this proposal and therefore recommend that the Fair and Sustainable National Band 2 spot rate be increased by £1,500. This increase will be used to fully erode the market supplements, where paid to Fair and Sustainable Band 2 staff.

xii. This is the first year we have made recommendations for the newly created Fair and Sustainable Band 12. HMPPS proposed a headline award for Band 12 that was 1% higher than that for Bands 3 to 11. HMPPS informed us that this was because there is no separate Required Hours Addition/Allowance (RHA) payment for Band 12 staff and a slightly higher increase was required to keep their pay ahead of Band 11 pay. We recognise the need to keep a reasonable differential between the two bands to maintain a coherent pay structure and have applied this rationale to our headline pay award as a result. We therefore recommend that the Fair and Sustainable Band 12 spot rate be increased by 5%.

*Fair and Sustainable Band 3*

xiii. In analysing the evidence available to us, we concluded that it was even stronger this year in supporting the need for significant additional investment in Band 3 Prison Officer pay. The extent of the issue the Service is grappling with in regard to recruiting and retaining Prison Officers is clear in all the evidence we have reviewed and it all points to a deterioration year after year. We believe that the number of leavers at Band 3 will continue to get worse unless action is taken to address the insufficiently competitive levels of pay at this grade. Our own analysis of the relative position of Band 3 pay shows that it continues to lag behind a number of comparable occupations.

xiv. The lack of an effective pay strategy for Band 3 pay has become more apparent this year due to the contradictory approach to market supplements. Although we welcome the commitment from HMPPS to start eroding the market supplements we do not believe this is compatible with the supplements being increased and extended to more prisons. These measures may help to reduce the flow of officers out of the Service in the very short term, but it is clear to us that their continued and repeated extension is evidence of its limited effectiveness. We believe staff need certainty and confidence in their pay and the Service must act now to provide a competitive base salary. We accept the aspiration of HMPPS not to rely on market supplements, as it has demonstrated in its approach to Band 2. However, we believe the Service must, given the scale of the recruitment and retention issues it faces, move further and faster to do so.

xv. Our own aspiration remains that all Prison Officers in closed and Fair and Sustainable grades should be paid a single rate for the job, set at an appropriate position against the relevant market comparators. This is consistent with the overarching principle of the HMPPS Fair and Sustainable framework. Our recommendation this year takes a substantial step to close the gap between the maxima of the two pay structures. However, we recognise that our recommendations alone may not bring Band 3 Prison Officer pay up to a competitive relative market position or completely resolve equal pay risks at this grade. It may take several years to achieve this.

xvi. We therefore recommend that from 1 September 2022, the 'amber' market supplement is consolidated into pay, resulting in a £3,000 increase in pensionable pay for all Band 3 staff on the National Fair and Sustainable Band 3 pay scale. This £3,000 increase should be paid to all staff in Band 3, including those working at 'red' and 'red plus' market supplement sites. We further recommend that HMPPS continue to pay an amended non-consolidated 'red' market supplement of £2,000 (reduced from £5,000) and a 'red plus' market supplement of £3,500 (reduced from £6,500) a year to those Band 3 Prison Officers who are currently eligible to receive them. We will review these payments in the future in line with our longer-term aspirations for Band 3 Prison Officer pay.

*Pay band restructuring*

xvii. HMPPS informed us that one of its key priorities this year was to achieve a complete structural reform across the Fair and Sustainable pay structure to incentivise progression through the pay scale and remove the "leap frogging" of newly promoted staff over experienced colleagues. It provided us with a number of proposals to reduce pay ranges and move some bands to spot rates.

xviii. We were pleased to see HMPPS make a serious attempt to start addressing some of the structural problems in the pay framework. However, we were not convinced that in every case its proposals were the best approach. We believe that the changes are designed to fix an immediate recruitment and promotion problem facing the Service, by incentivising staff to move through the grades, but that this could have a number of unintended and adverse longer-term consequences, such as a reduction in progression through the range that could adversely affect retention.

xix. We were disappointed that HMPPS did not discuss these proposals with the unions in advance of submitting them to us. When we sought views from the unions on the proposals during oral evidence, they were mixed. Although the unions largely favoured the proposed changes for the officer grades there were concerns raised by the PGA about the consistency in approach for the operational manager grades.

xx. We have always been wary about unpicking proposals which both HMPPS and the unions support, and we therefore endorse the structural proposals for Bands 3 to 5. Our concerns were more profound for operational manager grades, particularly as we struggled to see any compelling rationale for introducing spot rates for these grades, when it takes time for individuals to become fully competent in the role. We understand however, that this is a real concern for HMPPS particularly at Band 7 and therefore encourage HMPPS to work with the PGA to agree on and implement a solution for these grades outside of the pay round and as soon as possible.

*Performance management and pay progression*

xxi. This year HMPPS introduced a new performance management system that effectively ends the link between end of year markings and progression through the pay ranges. While we welcome the move towards a new system, we have considerable concerns about how the new system will function in an operational service such as HMPPS. It is crucial for HMPPS to consider how it will build staff and trade union confidence in the new system and ensure that there is adequate time for staff to administer it.

xxii. This year we will not make recommendations on pay progression for Band 2 or Band 4 as they are, or have been recommended to move to, a spot rate. In line with the approach taken in previous years, we recommend that staff on Fair and Sustainable Bands 3 and 5, who do not automatically receive an uplift as a result of pay band restructuring, progress to the next pay point following the pay uplift unless they are subject to formal poor performance procedures.

xxiii. In the absence of a performance link and clear information from HMPPS about our role in recommending pay progression under the new performance management system, it has been difficult to determine appropriate pay progression for Fair and Sustainable Bands 7 to 11 this year. We continue to believe however that operational managers should still be able to progress through their respective pay ranges from minima to maxima within five years.

We therefore recommend that staff in Bands 7 to 11 receive a consolidated and pensionable progression increase of 4%, capped at the 2022 band maximum. This should be adjusted to reflect any shortening of the pay range that is agreed between HMPPS and the PGA to remain consistent with managers progressing through the pay range within five years.

*Allowances*

xxiv. In our 2021 report we set out our concerns that many allowances had not been considered or changed for some considerable time. We recommended that all allowances should be reviewed in depth via a fixed rolling review over a five-year period, and that any allowance that had a fixed cash value that compensated staff for undertaking a particular duty throughout the year should be uprated each year in line with the headline rate. Despite the Government's decision not to respond to this recommendation in 2021, our position has not changed this year. We do not think it is right to let the value of an allowance be eroded over time leaving staff insufficiently remunerated.

xxv. In accordance with the timetable for our five year rolling review, this year we conducted a review of the Care and Maintenance of Dogs allowance and both the Unsocial Working Hours (UWH) allowance and RHA. We asked the parties to provide us with a wide range of information on the allowances, as well as their views on the appropriateness of the current allowance levels and clear rationale for any proposed changes.

xxvi. We received proposals from HMPPS, the POA and PGA on UWH and RHA. However, from the evidence presented to us we cannot be certain about the extent of unsocial hours worked by staff. The proposals from the parties demonstrated to us the fragility of the basis on which UWH and RHA are paid, largely relying on a historical equal pay settlement from 18 years ago to determine what percentage of salary could legitimately be attributed to operational staff working unsocial hours. While we endorse the proposal to increase both UWH and RHA to 20%, we would encourage the parties to look again in more detail at the payment of these allowances to ensure that they are set at appropriate levels.

xxvii. The second allowance we reviewed this year was the Care and Maintenance of Dogs allowance, for which we received proposals from HMPPS and the POA. We decided that there was a strong case to match the current Police dog handlers' allowance as we considered that both roles are broadly comparable. We therefore recommend that from 1 April 2022 the Care and Maintenance of Dogs allowance for those with responsibility for a single dog be increased to £2,434 a year. This value aligns the allowance with the 2021 Police dog handlers' allowance of £2,340 a year, uprated by the headline pay award of 4% (in line with our intention to uprate allowances of a compensatory nature with a fixed cash value by the headline award each

year). We recommend that the multiple dog rate remains set at 25% above the single dog allowance.

xxviii. We received many other proposals for increases to allowances and payments this year and although we were sympathetic to some of them, we ultimately had to prioritise the funds available this year and recommend investing them where we felt they were most needed and would make the most difference. We therefore recommend no further changes to other allowances and payments this year.

xxix. As part of our five year rolling review of allowances, we will review Payment Plus and OSG overtime next year. However, we wish to remind all parties that we remain willing to consider any allowance outside of the review period should they think it is required.

*Cost of our recommendations*

xxx. We estimate that our recommendations will result in an increase of approximately 8.5% (£111 million) to the total paybill for our remit group, excluding pay progression iv. This equates to 2% of HMPPS's £5.6 billion annual budget for operational expenditure v as of 2020-21. We estimate that HMPPS's proposals cost £66 million, excluding pay progression.

As we have set out in previous reports, we do not include the cost of pay progression or contractual performance awards when calculating the cost of the annual pay award.

iv This percentage takes account of both our recommended increase to pay scales, restructuring and those elements of the paybill that are not subject to any increase. It also takes account of the non-payment of market supplements, given that the £3,000 increase will be used to erode existing market supplements for Band 3 staff currently receiving them.

v HMPPS, (2021). HMPPS Annual Reports and Accounts 2020-21. (online) Available at: https://www.gov.uk/government/publications/hmpps-annual-report-and-accounts-2020-21[accessed on 10 June 2022].

xxxi. We consider that our recommendations this year offer value for money and will deliver long-term productivity savings to the Prison Service through increased retention and lower recruitment and training costs that will offset some of the cost of this award.

*Looking ahead*

xxxii. Looking ahead to the next pay round, we have asked the parties to address several issues in evidence for our 2023 report so that we may consider them more fully. These cover a range of data requests as well as evidence about recruitment and retention, motivation and morale, performance management, equality and diversity and HMPPS's short- and medium-term strategies for moving towards a coherent and cohesive pay structure.

xxxiii. We also ask HMPPS and Government to consider the position in relation to non-operational staff who are not in our remit group but who HMPPS maintain are affected by our pay recommendations. In recent years this read across has become more prominent as it has played a part in HMPPS's deliberations on whether our recommendations are affordable, despite the non-remit group not being part of our terms of reference or considerations.

We are therefore put in a difficult position each year whereby the Government's approval of our recommendations is influenced by a group of staff who are not in our remit. We do not think this is a sensible or logical situation and we ask the parties to bring forward proposals on how this can be resolved in the future.

*Conclusion*

xxxiv. The evidence we received this year demonstrated that uncompetitive pay levels and serious long-running recruitment and retention problems are putting the Prison Service in an unsustainable position that risks the stability of prisons due to inadequate staffing levels and experience. Although we recognise the financial pressures that HMPPS faces within its current budget, we believe it cannot afford to continue with the current approach of short term, time limited measures. The crisis the Service is facing will only worsen unless there is significant and immediate investment in pay to improve the competitiveness of the Prison Service's employment package.

xxxv. We believe that our recommendations this year offer a fair and meaningful pay award to staff and, importantly, target investment where it is needed most. Our recommendations provide a significant step towards establishing one single market facing rate for each grade.

However, we must stress that we have taken a proportionate approach, considering carefully what is affordable this year, and that it may take some time to fully resolve the fundamental issues in the pay structure. We look forward to continuing to work collaboratively with all the parties to achieve this in the future.

Tim Flesher CB (Chair)

Mary Carter

Luke Corkill

Judith Gillespie CBE

Leslie Manasseh MBE

Paul West QPM DL

## 8.7 STATEMENT BY THE JUSTICE SECRETARY

**Full Statement by the then Justice Secretary Dominic Raab MP, 19th July 2022**

I am today confirming the Government's decision on pay awards for prison staff. Throughout the pandemic and beyond, our officers (alongside all prison service staff) have gone above and beyond to protect the public and give prisoners the best possible chance at a new start. Their efforts are hugely appreciated.

We have carefully considered the Prison Service Pay Review Body's (PSPRB) recommendations on the 2022/23 pay award, given the economic context, and I am announcing that we are accepting in full the recommendations made by the review body for all prison staff between Operational Support Grade and Governing Governor for implementation in this financial year. For clarity, this means accepting all recommendations from the Prison Service Pay Review Body, excluding recommendation 4.

This will deliver a pay rise of at least a 4% base pay increase for all prison staff between Operational Support Grade and Governors (Bands 2-11). This pay award will be paid this autumn and will be backdated to 1 April 2022.

In addition, a number of targeted pay rises will be made for our lowest paid staff.

Band 2 Operational Support Grades on modernised terms and conditions will receive an increase of £1,500 (recommendation 3). This fully replaces the market supplements for those Band 2 staff who currently receive them.

Band 3 prison officers will receive a base pay increase of £2,500 (£3,000 for operational staff when the linked unsocial hours payment is included) from September 2022 (recommendation 5), offset against Market Supplement payments for those that receive them.

This reflects my commitment to supporting the recruitment and retention of prison staff and recognises the essential contribution they make every day.

Pay awards this year strike a careful balance between recognising the vital importance of public sector workers, whilst delivering value for the taxpayer, not increasing the country's debt further, and being careful not to drive even higher prices in the future. Sustained higher levels of inflation would have a far bigger impact on people's real incomes in the long run than the proportionate and balanced pay increases recommended by the independent Pay Review Bodies now. These pay awards should be viewed in parallel with the £37 billion package of support the Government has provided for the cost of living, targeted at those most in need.

I will not be accepting the PSPRB's recommendation for a 5% pay increase for Prison Group Directors (Band 12), recommendation 4. Such an increase would be inconsistent with the approach taken for other senior roles across the public sector. However, I am pleased to announce that Prison Group Directors will still receive a 3% pay rise, to ensure parity and fairness with their contemporaries in the civil service.

Most overall pay awards in the public sector are similar to those in the private sector. Survey data suggests median private sector pay settlement, which is the metric most comparable to these Pay Review Body decisions, was 4% in the 3 months to May. Median full-time salaries are higher in the public sector, and public sector workers also benefit from some of the most generous pensions available.

I would like to thank the Prison Service Pay Review Body for their valuable advice and response to the Government's evidence.

The report has been laid before Parliament today, 19 July, and a copy is attached. I am grateful to the Chair and members of the Review Body for their report.

*Rt.Hon Dominic Raab, Secretary of State for Justice and Lord Chancellor, 19th July 2022*

*Appendix D*

# *Appendix D*: Current and recommended pay levels

## Current and recommended pay levels for *Fair and Sustainable* grades

### *Fair and Sustainable ranges – National*

### Band 7 to 12 – National

Current and recommended pay (£ per annum) from 1 April 2022

*The pay ranges for Bands 7 to 11 shown below are based on the existing pay structures, and do not include any restructuring. The values from the 1 April 2022 represent the current pay ranges, uplifted by the headline award (Recommendations 1 and 4) and are subject to further change based on discussions between HMPPS and the unions.*

| Grade/Pay Band | Current pay ranges | | From 1 April 2022 | |
|---|---|---|---|---|
| | 37 hour base pay | 37 hour inc 17% RHA | 37 hour base pay | 37 hour inc 20% RHA |
| Prison Group Director (Band 12) (spot rate) | 103,000 | – | 108,150 | – |
| Governor (Band 11) Max | 81,584 | 95,453 | 84,848 | 101,818 |
| Governor (Band 11) Min | 67,987 | 79,545 | 70,707 | 84,848 |
| Governor (Band 10) Max | 72,127 | 84,389 | 75,013 | 90,016 |
| Governor (Band 10) Min | 60,102 | 70,319 | 62,507 | 75,008 |
| Deputy Governor (Band 9) Max | 65,518 | 76,656 | 68,139 | 81,767 |
| Deputy Governor (Band 9) Min | 54,599 | 63,881 | 56,783 | 68,140 |
| Deputy Governor/Head of Function (Band 8) Max | 51,154 | 59,850 | 53,201 | 63,841 |
| Deputy Governor/Head of Function (Band 8) Min | 42,626 | 49,872 | 44,332 | 53,198 |
| Head of Function (Band 7) Max | 43,870 | 51,328 | 45,625 | 54,750 |
| Head of Function (Band 7) Min | 38,148 | 44,633 | 39,674 | 47,609 |

Notes:
1. The Band 7 to 11 ranges do not have fixed incremental pay points.
2. Base pay ranges are calculated by rounding up to the nearest £ after the uplift is applied. Pay with Required Hours Addition (RHA) is presented as rounded to the nearest £.
3. The 37 hour base pay salaries are the basis from which other rates are calculated.
4. RHA is pensionable and is calculated as 20% of base pay (previously 17% prior to 1 April 2022).
5. The Band 7 to 11 pay ranges may be subject to future change following discussions on HMPPS's proposed changes with the Prison Governors' Association (PGA).

## Custodial Manager (Band 5) – National

Current and recommended pay (£ per annum) from 1 April 2022

| Current pay ranges | | | From 1 April 2022 | | |
|---|---|---|---|---|---|
| 37 hour base pay | 37 hour inc 17% unsocial | 39 hour inc 2xACHP & 17% unsocial | 37 hour base pay | 37 hour inc 20% unsocial | 39 hour inc 2xACHP & 20% unsocial |
| 31,176 | 36,476 | 38,161 | 32,424 | 38,909 | 41,012 |
| 30,453 | 35,630 | 37,276 | 31,672 | 38,006 | 40,061 |
| 29,748 | 34,805 | 36,413 | 30,938 | 37,126 | 39,132 |
| 29,058 | 33,998 | 35,569 | Removed | Removed | Removed |
| 27,697 | 32,405 | 33,902 | Removed | Removed | Removed |

## Supervising/Specialist officers (Band 4) – National

Current and recommended pay (£ per annum) from 1 April 2022

| Current pay ranges | | | From 1 April 2022 | | |
|---|---|---|---|---|---|
| 37 hour base pay | 37 hour inc 17% unsocial | 39 hour inc 2xACHP & 17% unsocial | 37 hour base pay | 37 hour inc 20% unsocial | 39 hour inc 2xACHP & 20% unsocial |
| 27,381 | 32,036 | 33,516 | 28,477 | 34,172 | 36,020 |
| 26,852 | 31,417 | 32,868 | Removed | Removed | Removed |
| 26,334 | 30,811 | 32,234 | Removed | Removed | Removed |
| 25,826 | 30,216 | 31,612 | Removed | Removed | Removed |
| 24,619 | 28,804 | 30,135 | Removed | Removed | Removed |

Notes:
1. Base pay for Band 2 to 5 staff is based on a 37 hour week and is the basis from which other rates are calculated. These staff may qualify for an additional unsocial hours payment of 20% which is pensionable (previously 17% prior to 1 April 2022).
2. Base pay scales are rounded up to the nearest £. Those which include 17%/20% unsocial working hours and those including Pensionable Additional Committed Hours (ACHP) are rounded to the nearest £ at the end of the calculation.
3. From 1 April 2022 ACH and ACHP also attract unsocial hours payments of 20%, which are pensionable.

*Prison Staff: Officers & Governors*

## Prison Officer (Band 3) – National

Current and recommended pay (£ per annum)

| Current pay ranges | | | From 1 April 2022 | | |
|---|---|---|---|---|---|
| 37 hour base pay | 37 hour inc 17% unsocial | 39 hour inc 2xACH & 17% unsocial | 37 hour base pay | 37 hour inc 20% unsocial | 39 hour inc 2xACH & 20% unsocial |
| 21,963 | 25,697 | 27,122 | 22,842 | 27,410 | 29,139 |
| 21,547 | 25,210 | 26,608 | 22,409 | 26,891 | 28,587 |
| 21,137 | 24,730 | 26,101 | Removed | Removed | Removed |
| 20,737 | 24,262 | 25,607 | 21,567 | 25,880 | 27,512 |
| 19,781 | 23,144 | 24,427 | Removed | Removed | Removed |

## Operational Support Grade (Band 2) – National

Current and recommended pay (£ per annum)

| Current pay ranges | | | From 1 April 2022 | | |
|---|---|---|---|---|---|
| 37 hour base pay | 37 hour inc 17% unsocial | 39 hour inc 2xACHP & 17% unsocial | 37 hour base pay | 37 hour inc 20% unsocial | 39 hour inc 2xACHP & 20% unsocial |
| 17,855 | 20,890 | 21,855 | 19,355 | 23,226 | 24,481 |

Notes:
1. Base pay for Band 2 to 5 staff is based on a 37 hour week and is the basis from which other rates are calculated. These staff may qualify for an additional unsocial hours payment of 20% which is pensionable (previously 17% prior to 1 April 2022).
2. Base pay scales are rounded up to the nearest £. Those which include 17%/20% unsocial working hours and those ACHP or Additional Committed Hours ((ACH) – not pensionable but has a 1.2 multiplier) are rounded to the nearest £ at the end of the calculation.
3. From 1 April 2022 ACH and ACHP also attract unsocial hours payments of 20%, which are pensionable.

## Fair and Sustainable ranges – Outer London

Outer London covers – Belmarsh, Downview, Feltham, High Down, Isis and the controllers' offices at Bronzefield and Thameside.

## Band 7 to 12 – Outer London

Current and recommended pay (£ per annum) from 1 April 2022

*The pay ranges for Bands 7 to 11 shown below are based on the existing pay structures, and do not include any restructuring. The values from the 1 April 2022 represent the current pay ranges, uplifted by the headline award (Recommendations 1 and 4) and are subject to further change based on discussions between HMPPS and the unions.*

| Grade/Pay Band | Current pay ranges | | From 1 April 2022 | |
|---|---|---|---|---|
| | 37 hour base pay | 37 hour inc 17% RHA | 37 hour base pay | 37 hour inc 20% RHA |
| Prison Group Director (Band 12) (spot rate) | 103,000 | – | 108,150 | – |
| Governor (Band 11) Max | 84,310 | 98,643 | 87,684 | 105,221 |
| Governor (Band 11) Min | 70,258 | 82,202 | 73,071 | 87,685 |
| Governor (Band 10) Max | 74,853 | 87,578 | 77,849 | 93,419 |
| Governor (Band 10) Min | 62,374 | 72,978 | 64,871 | 77,845 |
| Deputy Governor (Band 9) Max | 68,244 | 79,845 | 70,975 | 85,170 |
| Deputy Governor (Band 9) Min | 56,871 | 66,539 | 59,147 | 70,976 |
| Deputy Governor/Head of Function (Band 8) Max | 53,880 | 63,040 | 56,037 | 67,244 |
| Deputy Governor/Head of Function (Band 8) Min | 44,898 | 52,531 | 46,696 | 56,035 |
| Head of Function (Band 7) Max | 46,596 | 54,517 | 48,461 | 58,153 |
| Head of Function (Band 7) Min | 40,520 | 47,408 | 42,141 | 50,569 |

Notes:
1. The Band 7 to 11 ranges do not have fixed incremental pay points. The ranges are calculated by setting the range maximum at a value equal to the equivalent National pay band maximum plus the Outer London differential £2,836 from 1 April 2022 (previously £2,726 from 1 April 2021). Minima are then calculated so that they are the same proportion of the maximum as is the minimum of the equivalent National range.
2. Base pay ranges are calculated by rounding up to the nearest £ after the uplift is applied. Pay with RHA is presented as rounded to the nearest £.
3. The 37 hour base pay salaries are the basis from which other rates are calculated.
4. RHA is pensionable and is calculated as 20% of base pay (previously 17% prior to 1 April 2022).
5. The Band 7 to 11 pay ranges may be subject to future change following discussions on HMPPS's proposed changes with the PGA.

## Custodial Manager (Band 5) – Outer London

Current and recommended pay (£ per annum) from 1 April 2022

| Current pay ranges | | | From 1 April 2022 | | |
|---|---|---|---|---|---|
| 37 hour base pay | 37 hour inc 17% unsocial | 39 hour inc 2xACHP & 17% unsocial | 37 hour base pay | 37 hour inc 20% unsocial | 39 hour inc 2xACHP & 20% unsocial |
| 33,902 | 39,665 | 41,498 | 35,260 | 42,312 | 44,599 |
| 33,117 | 38,747 | 40,537 | 34,443 | 41,332 | 43,566 |
| 32,352 | 37,852 | 39,601 | 33,645 | 40,374 | 42,556 |
| 31,603 | 36,976 | 38,684 | Removed | Removed | Removed |
| 30,124 | 35,245 | 36,873 | Removed | Removed | Removed |

## Supervising/Specialist officers (Band 4) – Outer London

Current and recommended pay (£ per annum) from 1 April 2022

| Current pay ranges | | | From 1 April 2022 | | |
|---|---|---|---|---|---|
| 37 hour base pay | 37 hour inc 17% unsocial | 39 hour inc 2xACHP & 17% unsocial | 37 hour base pay | 37 hour inc 20% unsocial | 39 hour inc 2xACHP & 20% unsocial |
| 30,107 | 35,225 | 36,852 | 31,313 | 37,576 | 39,607 |
| 29,526 | 34,545 | 36,141 | Removed | Removed | Removed |
| 28,957 | 33,880 | 35,445 | Removed | Removed | Removed |
| 28,399 | 33,227 | 34,762 | Removed | Removed | Removed |
| 27,072 | 31,674 | 33,137 | Removed | Removed | Removed |

Notes:
1.  These scales are calculated by setting the scale maximum at a value equal to the equivalent National pay band maximum plus the Outer London differential – £2,836 from 1 April 2022 (previously £2,726 from 1 April 2021). Other points are then calculated so that they are the same proportion of the maximum as the equivalent point on the equivalent National scale.
2.  Base pay for Band 2 to 5 staff is based on a 37 hour week and is the basis from which other rates are calculated. These staff may qualify for an additional unsocial hours payment of 20% which is pensionable (previously 17% prior to 1 April 2022).
3.  Base pay scales are rounded up to the nearest £. Those which include 17%/20% unsocial working hours and those including ACHP (pensionable) or ACH (not pensionable but has a 1.2 multiplier) are rounded to the nearest £ at the end of the calculation.
4.  From 1 April 2022 ACH and ACHP also attract unsocial hours payments of 20%, which are pensionable.

## Prison officer (Band 3) – Outer London

Current and recommended pay (£ per annum)

| Current pay ranges | | | From 1 April 2022 | | |
|---|---|---|---|---|---|
| 37 hour base pay | 37 hour inc 17% unsocial | 39 hour inc 2xACH & 17% unsocial | 37 hour base pay | 37 hour inc 20% unsocial | 39 hour inc 2xACH & 20% unsocial |
| 24,689 | 28,886 | 30,487 | 25,678 | 30,814 | 32,757 |
| 24,222 | 28,340 | 29,911 | 25,192 | 30,230 | 32,137 |
| 23,762 | 27,802 | 29,343 | Removed | Removed | Removed |
| 23,312 | 27,275 | 28,787 | 24,247 | 29,096 | 30,931 |
| 22,238 | 26,018 | 27,460 | Removed | Removed | Removed |

## Operational Support Grade (Band 2) – Outer London

Current and recommended pay (£ per annum)

| Current pay ranges | | | From 1 April 2022 | | |
|---|---|---|---|---|---|
| 37 hour base pay | 37 hour inc 17% unsocial | 39 hour inc 2xACHP & 17% unsocial | 37 hour base pay | 37 hour inc 20% unsocial | 39 hour inc 2xACHP & 20% unsocial |
| 20,581 | 24,080 | 25,192 | 22,191 | 26,629 | 28,069 |

Notes:
1. These scales are calculated by setting the scale maximum at a value equal to the equivalent National pay band maximum plus the Outer London differential – £2,836 from 1 April 2022 (previously £2,726 from 1 April 2021). Other points are then calculated so that they are the same proportion of the maximum as the equivalent point on the equivalent National scale.
2. Base pay for Band 2 to 5 staff is based on a 37 hour week and is the basis from which other rates are calculated. These staff may qualify for an additional unsocial hours payment of 20% which is pensionable (previously 17% prior to 1 April 2022).
3. Base pay scales are rounded up to the nearest £. Those which include 17%/20% unsocial working hours and those including ACHP (pensionable) are rounded to the nearest £ at the end of the calculation.
4. From 1 April 2022 ACH and ACHP also attract unsocial hours payments of 20%, which are pensionable.

## Fair and Sustainable ranges – Inner London

Inner London covers – Brixton, Pentonville, Wandsworth, Westminster headquarters and Wormwood Scrubs.

## Band 7 to 12 – Inner London

Current and recommended pay (£ per annum) from 1 April 2022

*The pay ranges for Bands 7 to 11 shown below are based on the existing pay structures, and do not include any restructuring. The values from the 1 April 2022 represent the current pay ranges, uplifted by the headline award (Recommendations 1 and 4) and are subject to further change based on discussions between HMPPS and the unions.*

| Grade/Pay Band | Current pay ranges | | From 1 April 2022 | |
|---|---|---|---|---|
| | 37 hour base pay | 37 hour inc 17% RHA | 37 hour base pay | 37 hour inc 20% RHA |
| Prison Group Director (Band 12) (spot rate) | 103,000 | – | 108,150 | – |
| Governor (Band 11) Max | 85,732 | 100,306 | 89,162 | 106,994 |
| Governor (Band 11) Min | 71,443 | 83,588 | 74,303 | 89,164 |
| Governor (Band 10) Max | 76,275 | 89,242 | 79,327 | 95,192 |
| Governor (Band 10) Min | 63,599 | 74,411 | 66,102 | 79,322 |
| Deputy Governor (Band 9) Max | 69,666 | 81,509 | 72,453 | 86,944 |
| Deputy Governor (Band 9) Min | 58,055 | 67,924 | 60,379 | 72,455 |
| Deputy Governor/Head of Function (Band 8) Max | 55,302 | 64,703 | 57,515 | 69,018 |
| Deputy Governor/Head of Function (Band 8) Min | 46,082 | 53,916 | 47,927 | 57,512 |
| Head of Function (Band 7) Max | 48,018 | 56,181 | 49,939 | 59,927 |
| Head of Function (Band 7) Min | 41,756 | 48,855 | 43,426 | 52,111 |

Notes:
1. The Band 7 to 11 ranges do not have fixed incremental pay points. The ranges are calculated by setting the range maximum at a value equal to the equivalent National pay band maximum plus the Inner London differential – £4,314 from 1 April 2022 (previously £4,148 from 1 April 2021). Minima are then calculated so that they are the same proportion of the maximum as is the minimum of the equivalent National range.
2. Base pay ranges are calculated by rounding up to the £ after the uplift is applied. Pay with RHA is presented as rounded to the nearest £.
3. The 37 hour base pay salaries are the basis from which other rates are calculated.
4. RHA is pensionable and is calculated as 20% of base pay (previously 17% prior to 1 April 2022).
5. The Band 7 to 11 pay ranges may be subject to future change following discussions on HMPPS's proposed changes with the PGA.

## Custodial Manager (Band 5) – Inner London

Current and recommended pay (£ per annum) from 1 April 2022

| Current pay ranges | | | From 1 April 2022 | | |
|---|---|---|---|---|---|
| 37 hour base pay | 37 hour inc 17% unsocial | 39 hour inc 2xACHP & 17% unsocial | 37 hour base pay | 37 hour inc 20% unsocial | 39 hour inc 2xACHP & 20% unsocial |
| 35,324 | 41,329 | 43,238 | 36,738 | 44,086 | 46,469 |
| 34,506 | 40,372 | 42,237 | 35,886 | 43,063 | 45,391 |
| 33,708 | 39,438 | 41,260 | 35,055 | 42,066 | 44,340 |
| 32,927 | 38,525 | 40,305 | Removed | Removed | Removed |
| 31,385 | 36,720 | 38,416 | Removed | Removed | Removed |

## Supervising/Specialist officers (Band 4) – Inner London

Current and recommended pay (£ per annum) from 1 April 2022

| Current pay ranges | | | From 1 April 2022 | | |
|---|---|---|---|---|---|
| 37 hour base pay | 37 hour inc 17% unsocial | 39 hour inc 2xACHP & 17% unsocial | 37 hour base pay | 37 hour inc 20% unsocial | 39 hour inc 2xACHP & 20% unsocial |
| 31,529 | 36,889 | 38,593 | 32,791 | 39,349 | 41,476 |
| 30,920 | 36,176 | 37,847 | Removed | Removed | Removed |
| 30,324 | 35,479 | 37,118 | Removed | Removed | Removed |
| 29,740 | 34,796 | 36,404 | Removed | Removed | Removed |
| 28,351 | 33,171 | 34,703 | Removed | Removed | Removed |

Notes:
1. These scales are calculated by setting the scale maximum at a value equal to the equivalent National pay band maximum plus the Inner London differential – £4,314 from 1 April 2022 (previously £4,148 from 1 April 2021). Other points are then calculated so that they are the same proportion of the maximum as the equivalent point on the equivalent National scale.
2. Base pay for Band 2 to 5 staff is based on a 37 hour week and is the basis from which other rates are calculated. These staff may qualify for an additional unsocial hours payment of 20% which is pensionable (previously 17% prior to 1 April 2022).
3. Base pay scales are rounded up to the nearest £. Those which include 17%/20% unsocial working hours and those including ACHP (pensionable) are rounded to the nearest £ at the end of the calculation.
4. From 1 April 2022 ACH and ACHP also attract unsocial hours payments of 20%, which are pensionable.

## Prison officer (Band 3) – Inner London

Current and recommended pay (£ per annum)

| Current pay ranges | | | From 1 April 2022 | | |
|---|---|---|---|---|---|
| 37 hour base pay | 37 hour inc 17% unsocial | 39 hour inc 2xACH & 17% unsocial | 37 hour base pay | 37 hour inc 20% unsocial | 39 hour inc 2xACH & 20% unsocial |
| 26,111 | 30,550 | 32,244 | 27,156 | 32,587 | 34,642 |
| 25,618 | 29,973 | 31,635 | 26,642 | 31,970 | 33,987 |
| 25,131 | 29,403 | 31,033 | Removed | Removed | Removed |
| 24,656 | 28,848 | 30,447 | 25,642 | 30,770 | 32,711 |
| 23,520 | 27,518 | 29,044 | Removed | Removed | Removed |

## Operational Support Grade (Band 2) – Inner London

Current and recommended pay (£ per annum)

| Current pay ranges | | | From 1 April 2022 | | |
|---|---|---|---|---|---|
| 37 hour base pay | 37 hour inc 17% unsocial | 39 hour inc 2xACHP & 17% unsocial | 37 hour base pay | 37 hour inc 20% unsocial | 39 hour inc 2xACHP & 20% unsocial |
| 22,003 | 25,744 | 26,933 | 23,669 | 28,403 | 29,938 |

Notes:
1. These scales are calculated by setting the scale maximum at a value equal to the equivalent National pay band maximum plus the Inner London differential – £4,314 from 1 April 2022 (previously £4,148 from 1 April 2021). Other points are then calculated so that they are the same proportion of the maximum as the equivalent point on the equivalent National scale.
2. Base pay for Band 2 to 5 staff is based on a 37 hour week and is the basis from which other rates are calculated. These staff may qualify for an additional unsocial hours payment of 20% which is pensionable (previously 17% prior to 1 April 2022).
3. Base pay scales are rounded up to the nearest £. Those which include 17%/20% unsocial working hours and those including ACHP (pensionable) or ACH (not pensionable but has a 1.2 multiplier) are rounded to the nearest £ at the end of the calculation.
4. From 1 April 2022 ACH and ACHP also attract unsocial hours payments of 20%, which are pensionable.

## Pay levels for *Fair and Sustainable* Band 3 from 1 September 2022

### *Fair and Sustainable scale – National*

| From 1 April 2022 | | | From 1 September 2022 | | |
|---|---|---|---|---|---|
| 37 hour base pay | 37 hour inc 20% unsocial | 39 hour inc 2xACH & 20% unsocial | 37 hour base pay | 37 hour inc 20% unsocial | 39 hour inc 2xACH & 20% unsocial |
| 22,842 | 27,410 | 29,139 | 25,342 | 30,410 | 32,328 |
| 22,409 | 26,891 | 28,587 | 24,909 | 29,891 | 31,776 |
| Removed | Removed | Removed | Removed | Removed | Removed |
| 21,567 | 25,880 | 27,512 | 24,067 | 28,880 | 30,702 |
| Removed | Removed | Removed | Removed | Removed | Removed |

Notes:
1. Base pay for Band 2 to 5 staff is based on a 37 hour week and is the basis from which other rates are calculated. These staff may qualify for an additional unsocial hours payment of 20% which is pensionable (previously 17% prior to 1 April 2022).
2. Base pay scales are rounded up to the nearest £. Those which include 20% unsocial working hours and those ACHP or Additional Committed Hours ((ACH) – not pensionable but has a 1.2 multiplier) are rounded to the nearest £ at the end of the calculation.
3. From 1 April 2022 ACH and ACHP also attract unsocial hours payments of 20%, which are pensionable.

### *Fair and Sustainable scale – Outer London*

Outer London covers – Belmarsh, Downview, Feltham, High Down, Isis and the controllers' offices at Bronzefield and Thameside.

| From 1 April 2022 | | | From 1 September 2022 | | |
|---|---|---|---|---|---|
| 37 hour base pay | 37 hour inc 20% unsocial | 39 hour inc 2xACH & 20% unsocial | 37 hour base pay | 37 hour inc 20% unsocial | 39 hour inc 2xACH & 20% unsocial |
| 25,678 | 30,814 | 32,757 | 28,178 | 33,814 | 35,946 |
| 25,192 | 30,230 | 32,137 | 27,697 | 33,236 | 35,332 |
| Removed | Removed | Removed | Removed | Removed | Removed |
| 24,247 | 29,096 | 30,931 | 26,762 | 32,114 | 34,140 |
| Removed | Removed | Removed | Removed | Removed | Removed |

Notes:
1. These scales are calculated by setting the scale maximum at a value equal to the equivalent National pay band maximum plus the Outer London differential – £2,836 from 1 April 2022 (previously £2,726 from 1 April 2021). Other points are then calculated so that they are the same proportion of the maximum as the equivalent point on the equivalent National scale.
2. Base pay for Band 2 to 5 staff is based on a 37 hour week and is the basis from which other rates are calculated. These staff may qualify for an additional unsocial hours payment of 20% which is pensionable (previously 17% prior to 1 April 2022).
3. Base pay scales are rounded up to the nearest £. Those which include 20% unsocial working hours and those including ACHP (pensionable) are rounded to the nearest £ at the end of the calculation.
4. From 1 April 2022 ACH and ACHP also attract unsocial hours payments of 20%, which are pensionable.

Prison Staff: Officers & Governors

## *Fair and Sustainable ranges – Inner London*

Inner London covers – Brixton, Pentonville, Wandsworth, Westminster headquarters and Wormwood Scrubs.

| From 1 April 2022 | | | From 1 September 2022 | | |
|---|---|---|---|---|---|
| 37 hour base pay | 37 hour inc 20% unsocial | 39 hour inc 2xACH & 20% unsocial | 37 hour base pay | 37 hour inc 20% unsocial | 39 hour inc 2xACH & 20% unsocial |
| 27,156 | 32,587 | 34,642 | 29,656 | 35,587 | 37,831 |
| 26,642 | 31,970 | 33,987 | 29,150 | 34,980 | 37,186 |
| Removed | Removed | Removed | Removed | Removed | Removed |
| 25,642 | 30,770 | 32,711 | 28,166 | 33,799 | 35,931 |
| Removed | Removed | Removed | Removed | Removed | Removed |

Notes:
1. These scales are calculated by setting the scale maximum at a value equal to the equivalent National pay band maximum plus the Inner London differential – £4,314 from 1 April 2022 (previously £4,148 from 1 April 2021). Other points are then calculated so that they are the same proportion of the maximum as the equivalent point on the equivalent National scale.
2. Base pay for Band 2 to 5 staff is based on a 37 hour week and is the basis from which other rates are calculated. These staff may qualify for an additional unsocial hours payment of 20% which is pensionable (previously 17% prior to 1 April 2022).
3. Base pay scales are rounded up to the nearest £. Those which include 20% unsocial working hours and those including ACHP (pensionable) or ACH (not pensionable but has a 1.2 multiplier) are rounded to the nearest £ at the end of the calculation.
4. From 1 April 2022 ACH and ACHP also attract unsocial hours payments of 20%, which are pensionable.

Prison Staff: Officers & Governors

## Pay levels for non-*Fair and Sustainable* grades

*We note that some pay points below are not occupied by our remit group staff (see footnotes below). We will remove these pay points in our next report.*

### Non-*Fair and Sustainable* operational manager scales

Current and recommended pay (£ per annum)[83]

| Grade | Current pay | Pay From 1 April 2022 |
|---|---|---|
| Senior Manager A | 91,246 | 94,896 |
| Senior Manager B | 88,567 | 92,110 |
| Senior Manager C[84] | 79,762 | 82,953 |
| Senior Manager D (pre-2009 scale) (RHA inclusive)[85] | 73,277 | 76,209 |
| Senior Manager D (post-2009 scale) | 67,310 | 70,003 |
| Manager E | 50,664 | 52,691 |
| Manager F | 42,977 | 44,697 |
| Required Hours Addition (pensionable)[86] | 5,967 | 6,206 |

---

[83] We understand that former HMPs Wolds and Birmingham, along with Medway Secure Training Centre (the latter is now closed), operational manager grades previously run by G4S are on individual salaries.
[84] No staff within our remit group occupy this pay scale, however HMPPS may still employ non-operational staff on this pay scale.
[85] No staff within our remit group occupy this pay scale, however HMPPS may still employ non-operational staff on this pay scale.
[86] This applies to the following grades: post-2009 Senior Manager D, Manager E, Manager F.

## Non-*Fair and Sustainable* support and officer grades

Current and recommended pay (£ per annum)

| Grade[87] | Current pay | Pay From 1 April 2022 |
|---|---|---|
| Principal Officer | 36,622 | 38,087 |
| Senior Officer | 34,066 | 35,429 |
| Prison Officer | 31,649 | 32,915 |
| Prison Officer 2[88] | 19,025 | 19,786 |
| G4S Prison Custody Officer[89] | 26,370 | 27,425 |
| Operational Support Grade | 20,920 | 21,757 |
| Night Patrol[90] | 20,465 | 21,820 |
| Prison Auxiliary[91] | 18,139 | 19,341 |
| G4S Security Officer[92] | 20,618 | 21,443 |

## Non-*Fair and Sustainable* HMP Birmingham grades

Following the transfer of HMP Birmingham back to HMPPS, staff TUPE transferred on G4S pay and grading arrangements. Staff are therefore on several different pay scales and individually negotiated rates of pay, therefore no pay rates will be covered in this appendix. Staff will be treated as closed non-*Fair and Sustainable* grades and are entitled to any pay award applied to the non-*Fair and Sustainable* closed grades as recommended in this report. Those staff that have opted in to *Fair and Sustainable* will be covered under the National *Fair and Sustainable* rates of pay.

---

[87] The pay shown in this table is based on a 39 hour week, except for the Prison Officer 2 and Night Patrol grades. Only those pay points occupied are shown.

[88] 37 hour base pay shown. Those at this grade may also work and qualify for an additional unsocial hours payment of 17%.

[89] This grade was formerly part of HMP Wolds run by G4S.

[90] 44 hour base pay shown. Pay uplifted by the headline recommendation or by the National Living Wage, whichever gives the greater amount.

[91] Pay uplifted by the headline recommendation or by the National Living Wage, whichever gives the greater amount.

[92] This grade was formerly part of HMP Wolds run by G4S.

## *Appendix E*: Locality Pay Allowance rates

We recommend no change to legacy Locality Pay Allowance (LPA) rates for the closed, pre-*Fair and Sustainable* grades so the rates remain as below. These rates are pensionable and are only payable to those staff in post at 31 March 2012.

| Rating structure | £ a year | Establishments/sites covered: |
|---|---|---|
| Rate 1 | 4,250 | Brixton, Pentonville, Wandsworth and Wormwood Scrubs |
| Rate 2 | 4,000 | Feltham, Huntercombe, The Mount and Westminster headquarters |
| Rate 3 | 3,100 | Belmarsh, Bronzefield[93], Coldingley, Downview, High Down, Isis and Send |
| Rate 4 | 2,600 | Aylesbury, Bedford, Bullingdon, Chelmsford, Grendon/Springhill and Woodhill |
| Rate 5 | 1,100 | Lewes and Winchester |
| Rate 6 | 250 | Birmingham[94], Bristol, Littlehey, Long Lartin and Onley |

---

[93] Payable to eligible staff in the controller's office at this establishment.

[94] There may be a number of former HMPPS staff that were TUPE transferred to G4S at this establishment who have now TUPE transferred back to HMPPS, that may also be in receipt of this LPA rate.

Prison Staff: Officers & Governors

## *Appendix F*: Allowances and payments

We make one change to allowances, to both rates of the Care and Maintenance of Dogs allowance. Below are the continuing rates from 1 April 2022.

| Allowances and payments | Closed grades From 1 April 2022 | *Fair and Sustainable* grades From 1 April 2022 |
|---|---|---|
| Care and Maintenance of Dogs95 Rate 1 – single dog | £2,434 a year | £2,434 a year |
| Care and Maintenance of Dogs Rate 2 – multiple dogs | £3,043 a year | £3,043 a year |
| Specialist allowance (pensionable): Healthcare Officers | £1,296 a year | Not applicable |
| Specialist allowance (pensionable): Caterers, Patrol and Search Dog Handlers, Librarians, Physical Education Instructors, Trade Instructors and Works Officers | £1,200 a year | Not applicable |
| National Tactical Response Group allowance | £6,670 a year | £6,670 a year |
| National Dog and Technical Support Group allowance | £6,670 a year | £6,670 a year |
| Operation Tornado payment (officers) | £24.86 per hour | £24.86 per hour |
| Operation Tornado payment (OSG) | £19.00 per hour | £19.00 per hour |
| Payment Plus | £22.00 per hour | £22.00 per hour |
| Dirty Protest allowance: four hours or less per day | £10.00 per day | £10.00 per day |
| Dirty Protest allowance: over four hours per day | £20.00 per day | £20.00 per day |
| On-call (radio pager): Weekdays | £5.67 per period of more than 12 hours | Not applicable |
| On-call (radio pager): weekends and privilege holidays | £16.13 per 24 hour period or proportionately for periods of less than 24 hours | Not applicable |

---

[95] We introduced a second rate for the Care and Maintenance of Dogs allowance in our 2016 report. This means there are now two rates – one for care of a single dog (amount is £2,434 a year) and one for care of multiple dogs (amount is 25% more than the single rate – £3,043 a year).

| Allowances and payments | Closed grades From 1 April 2022 | *Fair and Sustainable* grades From 1 April 2022 |
|---|---|---|
| On-call (radio pager): public and bank holidays | £20.41 per 24 hour period or proportionately for periods of less than 24 hours | Not applicable |
| On-call (home): weekdays | £7.09 per period of more than 12 hours | Not applicable |
| On-call (home): weekends and privilege holidays | £20.17 per 24 hour period or proportionately or periods of less than 24 hours | Not applicable |
| On-call (home): public and bank holidays | £25.47 per 24 hour period or proportionately for periods of less than 24 hours | Not applicable |
| On-call (home)[96]: weekdays and privilege holidays | Not applicable | £9.00 per period of 12 hours or more |
| On-call (home) weekends and public holidays | Not applicable | £25.00 per period of 24 hours or more or proportionately for periods of less than 24 hours |
| On-call (home) (hourly rate) | Not applicable | (£1.04 per hour whilst on call outside of normal office hours) |
| Stand by (office): weekdays | £13.43 per period of more than 12 hours | Not applicable |
| Stand by (office): weekends and privilege holidays | £38.46 per 24 hour period or proportionately for periods of less than 24 hours | Not applicable |
| Stand by (office): public and bank holidays | £48.26 per 24 hour period or proportionately for periods of less than 24 hours | Not applicable |

[96] For staff on Fair and Sustainable grades the on-call payments are payable as two rates only: (a) work days and (b) rest days or weekends and bank or public holidays.

Prison Staff: Officers & Governors

## *Appendix G*: Rolling review programme for Prison Service staff allowances

The table below outlines our rolling review programme and which allowances will be considered in detail in which report and year.

| PSPRB Report | Allowances to be considered |
|---|---|
| Twenty Second (2023) | Payment Plus<br>OSG overtime |
| Twenty Third (2024) | Operation Tornado payments<br>Dirty Protest payments |
| Twenty Fourth (2025) | National Tactical Response Group<br>National Dog and Technical Support Group |
| Twenty Fifth (2026) | Closed grade specialist allowances<br>On-call allowances (both pay structures) |
| Twenty Sixth (2027) | Unsocial hours payments in *Fair and Sustainable*<br>Care and Maintenance of Dogs |

## *Appendix H*: Recommendations from the 2021 England and Wales report

- Her Majesty's Prison and Probation Service provide to a comprehensive pay strategy, including short-, medium- and long-term objectives, for the next pay round to address the structural issues in the pay system. This should incorporate Recommendation 3 from the 2020 report, modified as necessary by the developing evidence.

- All those staff identified by Her Majesty's Prison and Probation Service as being eligible should receive the Government's £250 pay uplift, or an award to remain compliant with the National Living Wage from 1 April 2021.

- All staff (except those subject to formal poor performance procedures) on *Fair and Sustainable* Bands 3 to 5 who are in post on 31 March 2021 progress by one pay point, effective from 1 April 2021.

- All staff (except those subject to formal poor performance procedures) on *Fair and Sustainable* Bands 7 to 11 who are in post on 31 March 2021 receive a consolidated and pensionable progression increase of 4%, capped at the 2021 band maximum.

- All the allowances in Appendix F of the 2020 report (except closed grade specialism allowances) are increased in future years by the headline percentage pay award. In future years all allowances are considered as part of a fixed rolling review with individual allowances considered every five years (as per Appendix G of the 2020 report).

## *Appendix I:* Summary of PSPRB headline pay award recommendations from 2014 to 2020

- **2020** – a consolidated 2.5% increase for all *Fair and Sustainable* and closed grades from 1 April 2020. From 1 September 2020 the *Fair and Sustainable* National Band 3 base pay points increase by £2,564 giving a total consolidated and pensionable award of £3,000 when the 17% unsocial hours payment is included.

- **2019** – a consolidated 2.2% increase for all *Fair and Sustainable* and closed grades, except *Fair and Sustainable* Band 3, which was recommended a 3.0% consolidated pay increase.

- **2018** – a consolidated 2.75% increase for all *Fair and Sustainable* and closed grades, except *Fair and Sustainable* Band 3 and 4, which were recommended increases of 5.25% and 3.5% respectively. Rejected by the Government and reduced to a 2.0% consolidated and 0.75% non–consolidated award for all *Fair and Sustainable* and closed grades.

- **2017** – a consolidated flat cash award of £400 to all uniformed grades (both those on *Fair and Sustainable* and closed grades) and an increase of 1% to the maxima of the *Fair and Sustainable* National Bands 7 to 11.

- **2016** – an increase of 1% to the maxima of the *Fair and Sustainable* National bands and non-consolidated awards of £300 for Prison Officers and support staff, £325 for Senior Officers and £350 for Principal Officers.

- **2015** – an increase of 1.8% to the maxima of the *Fair and Sustainable* National bands but no recommended pay awards for those on closed grades. The Government then provided non-consolidated retention bonus payments (£300 for Prison Officers and support staff, £325 for Senior Officers and £350 for Principal Officers) shortly after the publication of our 2015 report.

- **2014** – a 1% consolidated pay increase for all officers and support staff on all pay structures and changes to some *Fair and Sustainable* National Band 7 to 11 pay structures to provide 2% to staff who opted in.

# Section 9

## Research Briefings

All briefings contain Parliamentary information licensed under the Open Parliament Licence (v3.0). All of the Research Briefings listed below are available to view in full on: *prisonoracle.com*

### A-Z

Accusations of racism in the Metropolitan Police Service

Adjudications: Subsequent custodial misconduct following disciplinary adjudications

Analytical report brief intervention women serving short sentences

Approved: Food fraud

Autism – overview of UK policy and services

Black Lives Matter protests: UK reaction to the killing of George Floyd

Brexit next steps: The European Arrest Warrant

Cannabis: Medical use 9th December 2021

Categorisation of prisoners in the UK

Code of Practice for Victims of Crime

Commons Library Analysis: The Prisons and Courts Bill

Comparative Prison Sentences in the EU

Contracting out of probation services

Coronavirus Act: Elections

Coronavirus: FAQs on postponed elections

Coronavirus: Parliamentary consent for the lockdown in England

Coronavirus: Prisons (England and Wales)

Corporate criminal liability 6th May 2021

Counter-Terrorism and Sentencing Bill 2019-21

Counter-Terrorism and Sentencing Bill: Briefing for Lords Stages

COVID-19 misinformation

COVID-19 outbreak: What data or information do experts want the UK Government to release?

COVID-19: Insights from behavioural science

Covid-19. Risking a rise in online child sexual abuse?

Covid-19: The impact on human trafficking

Crime, justice, policing and COVID-19: What are experts concerned about?

Criminal Justice & Courts Bill – Lords Amendments

Criminal Memoirs

Cryptocurrencies

Current Affairs Digest: World Affairs (June 2020)

Cyber security in a digital age

Delivering public services: The growing use of Payment by Results

Drug crime: Statistics for England and Wales (24th October 2021)

Drugs Review: summary (18th September 2020)

Drugs Review: summary

Drugs Review: evidence pack

Drugs Strategy 2019

Early release of prisoners in England and Wales - an overview

End of Custody Licence

Exploring Extremism in 3 Prisons (2nd September 2021)

Exploring the role of the Internet in radicalisation and convicted extremists (16/9/2021)

Exploring substance use in prisons: a case study approach (26 October 2020)

Extradition (Provisional Arrest) Bill [HL]: Briefing for Lords Stages

Extradition (Provisional Arrest) Bill 2019-21

Extremism in prisons: Are UK de-radicalisation programmes working?

Firearm Crime Statistics: England & Wales (24th September 2021)

Firearms

Fishmongers' Hall - a Preventable Tragedy. (7th June 2021)

Focus on Women's Prisons (9th February 2022)

Food fraud

Foreign National Offenders - Deportation: January 2020

Hate Crime

Hate Crime - spreadsheet

Health and Safety of Prison Staff

Helen's Law - Parole for murderers who conceal their victims' remains

Indeterminate Sentences for Public Protection

Inequalities Faced by Gypsy, Roma and Traveller Communities

Insights for the new Parliament (plus BSL video)

Introducing "Payment by Results" in Offender Rehabilitation

Is the criminal justice system fit for purpose?

Judicial Review and Courts Bill

Key Issues for the 2015 Parliament

Knife crime statistical briefing

Legal aid, Sentencing and Punishment of Offenders Bill No 205 of 2010-12

Local government in England: structures

Magnitsky legislation

Meeting the need of older prisoners

Ministry of Justice Areas of Research Interest

Misuse of Civilian Drones & Prisons

Nitrous oxide: No laughing matter?

Non-Custodial Sentences

Offender Rehabilitation Bill

Online Safety Bill - draft: A Reading List (10th April 2022)

Police, Crime, Sentencing and Courts Bill:

Progress of the Bill 25th March 2022

Police Detention Powers 27th July 2021

Police personnel: recruitment, training & welfare

Police powers: an introduction

Police powers: detention & custody (21st Nov 2020)

Police powers: stop and search (11th March 2021)

Policing and crime- Opposition Day Debate

Policing in the UK (4th June 2021)

Policing in the UK: Serious and Organised Crime

Police powers: detention and custody

POST Fellowships 2020/2021

Prison Estate December 2019

Prison Reform: Recent Developments

Prison Statistics, England and Wales

Prisons (Substance Testing) Bill 2019-21

Prisoners (Disclosure of Information about Victims) Bill 2019-20

Prisoners: Incentives & Earned Privileges Scheme

Prisoners: transfers to other prisons in England and Wales

Prisoners' Release on Temporary Licence

Prisoners' voting rights (2005 to May 2015)

Prisoners' voting rights: developments to August 2020

Prisons (Interference with Wireless Telegraphy) Bill 2017-19

Prisons and Terrorism

Prisons: The role of the private sector

Probation reforms 2014

Public service pension age - including Prison Officers (12th Nov 2021 - page 27)

Racial Bias is Pulling Black Young Adults Into Crisis and Crime

Reducing reoffending: the "what works" debate

Registration and Management of Sex Offenders (4th March 2021)

Regulating online harms (13th August 2021)

Rehabilitation of Offenders Act 1974 (2nd Feb 2021)

Release from Prison - and plans to change it

Release from prison in England and Wales

Retention and Disclosure of Criminal Records

Review of Drugs: Part One and Part Two - Professor Dame Carol Black

ROTL Statistics

Rough Sleepers (10th April 2021)

Safety in Custody December 2019

Safety in Custody December 2019 - Spreadsheet

Safety in prisons in England and Wales

School Exclusions

Self-Defence Training in Schools

Sentences of Imprisonment for Public Protection

Sentencing for emergency service deaths: Calls for change

Sentencing Repeat Offenders (Word -21st June 2022)

Serious violence and knife crime: Law enforcement and early intervention

Service Police review

Sexual harassment in education

Sexual Reoffending Predictors (26 January 2021)

Short Guide to the Criminal Justice System (12 January 2022)

Short prison sentences: Calls for change

Substance use in prisons (26 October 2020)

Suicide Prevention: Policy and Strategy - Full Report (22nd April 2021)

Suicide Prevention: Policy and Strategy

Support for Women Leaving Prison (6th Mar 2021)

Tackling anti-social behaviour

The Target Operating Model for Probation Services in England and Wales

Terrorist Offenders (Restriction of Early Release) Bill 2020 (Feb 2021)

The 2020 Spending Review envelope

The Bail Accommodation and Support Service

The Checkpoint Programme

The Compliance Officer for IPSA

The disturbance at HM Prison Ford on 1 Jan 2011

The Independent Inquiry into Child Sexual Abuse and background

The Intelligence and Security Committee (4th December 2021)

The Parole System of England and Wales (21st June 2022)

The Prisons (Interference with Wireless Telegraphy) Bill

The Prisons (Property) Bill

The Prisons (Property) Bill: Committee Stage Report

The Prisons Substance Testing Bill (16 Dec 2020)

The Psychoactive Substances Bill 2015-16: Report on Committee Stage

The Supreme Court 24 June 2022

The Troubled Families programme (England) 27 November 2020

Transgender Prisoners

UK Prison Population Statistics

UN Convention on the Rights of the Child: a brief guide

Unexplained Wealth Orders (24th February 2022)

Undercover Policing in England and Wales (6 November 2020)

Unification of probation services (8th June 2021). See here pp-211-219 for offices

Voting age

Who can vote in UK elections?

Why is police bail being reviewed again?

Women in prisons: a select bibliography

Worker exploitation in UK clothing supply chains

Young Offenders: What Next

Youth Custody (27th April 2022)

### Accusations of racism in the Metropolitan Police Service

Published Thursday, 09 July, 2020

This article looks at accusations of racism in the Metropolitan Police Service, both towards officers and in its interactions with the public. The action being taken to address racism in the Metropolitan Police Service is the subject of an oral question in the House of Lords on 15 July 2020.

The recent killing by US police of George Floyd, an unarmed black man, has sparked discussion about racism in the UK's police forces. Media articles have highlighted racism faced by ethnic minority police officers. Concerns about the police's use of stop and search against black people, and its use of force against black people in custody, have also received attention.

This article provides an overview of some of the issues relating to racism in the Metropolitan Police Service (the Met).

## Racism towards officers
### Representation
London's Metropolitan Police has a lower proportion of police officers from ethnic minorities than the community it serves. However, it has a higher proportion of police officers from ethnic minorities than any other police force in England and Wales. In 2019, 15% of the Met's police officers were from Asian, black, mixed and other non-white backgrounds. This compares to 40% of London's population who come from these backgrounds. 3.5% of the Met's officers are black, and 5.9% are Asian.

The proportion of police officers from ethnic minorities in senior roles is much smaller. Data from 2019 show that only 4% of senior officers in England and Wales were from Asian, black, mixed and other non-white backgrounds, and this proportion has not increased since 2013.

### Disciplinary procedures against officers from ethnic minorities
It has been alleged that police officers from ethnic minorities are unfairly overrepresented in misconduct and disciplinary procedures. The Met commissioned research to examine whether there was any disproportionality in misconduct allegations and cases. This research was based on misconduct data from 2010 to 2015 and was undertaken by the Mayor's Office for Policing and Crime (MOPAC). It found that Metropolitan police officers from ethnic minorities were more likely to be subject of misconduct allegations than white officers. They were also more likely to have a misconduct allegation against them substantiated. This disproportionality is driven by complaints from other officers and members of Met staff. The research found no difference in the proportion of complaints from the public against white and non-white officers.

There are several theories about why this disproportionality may exist, though the true cause is not known. The MOPAC research listed three possible explanations:
• conscious or unconscious bias;
• fear of being accused of racism (and therefore

not addressing incidents informally); and
• failure to deal with difference.

## Anecdotal evidence of racist behaviour
Some current and former officers have made public their experiences of racism in the Met. Writing in the Independent, Kevin Maxwell, a black former officer, says that the force was found guilty of "racial discrimination, harassment and victimisation" towards him a few years ago. The BBC has reported the experiences of Shabnam Coundhri, an Asian former officer, who says she experienced racism during her tenure with the Met.

An anonymous current officer, who describes herself as black, wrote about her experiences in the Guardian. She says that over the last year she has "been likened to confectionery, heard racist language passed off as a joke and witnessed BAME [black, Asian, and minority ethnic] officers in plain clothes accused of being intruders or told they look like they've just left the custody suite by other officers".

## Racism directed at the public
The Met has also been accused of racism in its policing. Concerns about racist policing include overuse of stop and search powers against black men and overuse of force. The reasons for the overall over-representation of black people in the criminal justice system are widely recognised to be complex and multi-faceted.

## Confidence in police
Londoners from black, Asian and minority ethnic backgrounds view the police less favourably than white Londoners. For example, 61% of young (16- to 24-year-old) black and minority ethnic Londoners have confidence that the police do a 'good job', compared with 70% of white 16- to 24-year olds. Similarly, the MOPAC User Satisfaction Survey found a "sizeable and enduring" gap in levels of satisfaction with police service between white and ethnic minority victims of crime.

## Stop and search
A police officer has powers to stop and search a person if they have 'reasonable grounds' to suspect the person is carrying illegal drugs, weapons or stolen property. Stop and search without 'reasonable grounds' must be approved by a senior police officer. In this case, the police officer must suspect that serious violence could take place or the person is carrying a weapon or has used one. Stop and search without 'reasonable grounds' is also allowed in specific locations for time-limited periods.

Black, Asian and minority ethnic Londoners are 2.5 times more likely to be stopped and searched than white people. This rises to ten times more likely for vehicle stops. Almost one in three of all searches, 32%, result in an illegal object found or a relevant crime detected. Approximately one in five searches results in an arrest. This is an increase on 8% of searches which resulted in an arrest in 2011.

### Use of force and deaths in custody
In the period April 2019 to March 2020, 32.4% of recorded incidents in London where police used force were against black males. Approximately 13% of London's population identify as black.

Figures for deaths in custody by ethnicity are not available for London alone. In England and Wales, in the ten years between April 2009 and March 2019, 164 people died in or following police custody. Of these people, 13 were black and 10 were from other ethnic minority groups. The numbers include deaths that occurred where injuries that contributed to the death were sustained during the period of detention, and deaths that occurred as a result of injuries or other medical problems that were identified or that developed while a person was in custody.

Compared to the proportion of the overall population, black people are twice as likely to die in custody as white people. However, of people who are arrested, white people are approximately 25% more likely to die in custody than black people.

In 2017/18 and 2018/19, data show that 17 deaths in police custody involved or followed the use of force. Of these 17 people, twelve were white and five were black.

A 2017 independent review of deaths and serious incidents in police custody found that potential examples of racial stereotyping, such as young black men being seen as "dangerous, violent and volatile", were not explored when deaths in custody were investigated. It recommended that the Independent Police Complaints Commission "ensure that race and discrimination issues are considered as an integral part of its work".

Nazir Afzal, a former chief crown prosecutor, has drawn attention to the fact that only one police officer has been convicted for their role in the death of someone in their care since 1969.

### Oral question in Lords
The action being taken to address racism in the Metropolitan Police Service is the subject of an upcoming oral question in the House of Lords: "Lord Paddick to ask Her Majesty's Government what discussions they have had with the Metropolitan Police Service about the steps being taken to address racism within its ranks".

*An evaluation of a brief intervention to reduce reoffending among women serving short sentences*

### Summary
This report documents the results of a randomised control trial testing a brief intervention that aimed to reduce reoffending among women serving short sentences in one prison in England.

Over the course of a year, 255 women serving sentences of under 12 months, and who were in the last 6-8 weeks of their sentence, agreed to take part in the trial. Participants were randomly assigned to an intervention or control task. The intervention task consisted of three exercises: i) a daily goal-setting task, which required women to set a goal they could achieve that day, and to review it, and set another the following day, ii) a "Best Possible Self" task, which asked women, in the week prior to their release, to articulate what their life would look like in five years' time if everything had gone as they would like it to, including the steps they would have taken to achieve this, and iii) providing peer support to ("buddying") a fellow participant, helping them to complete their tasks during the intervention period. Women in the control group were asked to complete a list, daily, of the things they had done that day.

Two-hundred and twenty-eight women went on to start the trial and of these, 28-29% in both the experimental and control groups dropped out. Most commonly women chose to drop out; the second most common reason for attrition was early release on home detention curfew. Randomisation was successful, creating two comparable groups, and for the most part, the trial was implemented as intended. However, due to logistical issues on site, less than half of the women (48.8%) in the experimental condition took on the role of the 'buddy' for someone else. In addition, while just under half of the women who took part in the daily review (n = 39) stuck to using this as a listing task, 41 women used the task as a diary, including some reflection and emotional expression, as well as some (limited) goal setting.

Wherever possible, analysis proceeded on an intent-to-treat basis, comparing the outcomes of those assigned to each condition, regardless of whether or not they received or completed the intervention. This approach minimises the risk that it is differences between the characteristics or situation of the experimental and control groups that are responsible for any difference in outcome, rather than the intervention. The analyses involving data from post-treatment questionnaires, however, included only a small number of non-completers (n = 6); the majority of non-completers did not complete the second set of questionnaires, therefore were excluded from analyses that used these data. Analyses compared women in the experimental and control groups on measures of future orientation (the extent to which someone is engaged with the notion of their future and a future self), self-efficacy (believing one can achieve one's goals), self-esteem, self-reported resettlement plans, and official records of proven reoffending a year after release. Results suggest that the brief intervention led to more comprehensive resettlement planning, and had a small impact on time offence-free up to 18 months post release. The rates of proven reoffending across both groups of women was high, with just over 70% going on to commit another offence, in line with the national average for women serving short sentences.

While, for the whole sample, the comprehensiveness of resettlement plans was not related to one-year proven reoffending (frequency or rates), women who had no fixed address to go to on release, who did not feel that their accommodation was safe and secure or who did not report any family contact, had statistically significantly higher proven reoffending rates than those who did. Women reporting a substance use issue just prior to release had much higher rates of proven reoffending than those who did not; 81.3% of the women who participated in the trial reported a problem with substance use. Reconviction for a new offence within a year of release was predicted by number of previous convictions, whether education, training or employment was set up in advance of release, lack of family contact and level of future orientation just prior to release.

The findings highlight the importance and security of accommodation, family contact, proper and sustained support for substance use problems, and education, training and employment for women seeking to (re)integrate into the community following a prison sentence. The trial suggests that a brief intervention for women serving short sentences can have merit in the short-term by improving the breadth of resettlement planning, but that any impact on time offence-free is small. Brief psychological interventions for women in prison, while promising, may struggle to make a difference in the face of the structural disadvantages they can face on release. The study emphasises the need for comprehensive and continued support to help women manage the transition from prison to the community.

### Approved: Food fraud

Published Thursday, 21 May, 2020

Food fraud encompasses a range of activities including intentional adulteration or substitution of ingredients and mislabelling of food products.

Although it is difficult to quantify the impact of food fraud, estimates of the annual global trade in counterfeit food and drink range from $6.2 billion to $40 billion. Modern food supply chains and manufacturing infrastructure have greatly increased opportunities for it to occur, its scale and impact.

Examples of high-profile cases of food fraud include the addition of undeclared horsemeat to a variety of beef products in the UK and Europe in 2013, addition of melamine to baby formula in China in 2008 and the presence of other ingredients (including olive and myrtle leaves) in around one in four UK samples of oregano in 2016.

Key Points

• Foods that are commonly reported to be adulterated include herbs and spices, coffee, seafood, honey and olive oil.

• In addition to affecting consumer choice and confidence, food fraud may pose a public health risk. In 2016, a restaurant owner was sentenced to prison after substituting almond powder with mixed nut powder containing peanuts, resulting in the death of a customer.

• Other impacts on consumers include loss of nutrition and inadvertent consumption of foods that are normally restricted for ethical or religious reasons.

• Businesses may suffer financial losses following food fraud incidents due to factory closure, product recalls or destruction of contaminated ingredients or products. Companies may also suffer reputational damage.

• A range of UK laws and regulation contribute to preventing food fraud. The majority of law relating to food in the UK is based on the Food Safety Act 1990, which prohibits food which is not of the nature, substance or quality that consumers would expect, and describing or presenting food in a false or misleading way.

• Public bodies responsible detecting and mitigating food fraud include local authorities, government departments and regulators. In England, Defra is responsible for policy and legislation on food labelling and composition. It is also responsible for the Government's food authenticity research programme, which identifies risks to food authenticity and develops and validates food testing methods.

• Strategies to detect and prevent food fraud broadly fall into two categories: scientific analysis to test the authenticity of foods and broader mitigation strategies including intelligence gathering, vulnerability assessments and economic analysis strategies.

• Each food business has its own approach to testing the authenticity of its products. Food retailers often have contractual agreements with suppliers that require them to carry out authenticity testing of their ingredients. Large food retailers, such as supermarkets, typically have their own routine monitoring programmes.

• There are a variety of analytical techniques that can be used to test for adulterated food and drink and often a combination of methods will be used.

• Testing can be targeted (whereby the analysis looks for a pre-defined characteristic, such as a specific adulterants or section of DNA), or non-targeted (whereby multiple measurements of a sample are taken using a variety of techniques to obtain a sample's 'chemical fingerprint')

• Barriers to tackling food fraud relate to the cost and capability of authenticity testing, perpetrators changing their mode of operation, and a complex regulatory enforcement system.

• The Food Standards Agency (FSA) has said that there is no evidence to suggest the UK will be at more risk from food crime after the Brexit transition period. However, some stakeholders have raised concerns that EU exit may impact the UK's vulnerability to food fraud.

• Concerns relate to checks on food imports, the UK's food testing capacity and the extent of UK access to EU food fraud intelligence networks.

*Autism – overview of policy and services*
22 January 2020

**Summary**

This briefing provides an overview of policies and services for people with autism spectrum disorder in England.

It is now over ten years since the passing of the Autism Act 2009, which is still the only disability-specific piece of legislation in England. The Act required the Government to introduce an adult autism strategy, which was published in 2010 and refreshed in 2014. The accompanying statutory guidance sets out requirements for the NHS and local authorities to implement the strategy, in areas such as training for staff, identification and diagnosis, transition planning when people move from children to adult services, employment and criminal justice.

The Government is now undertaking a comprehensive review of the autism strategy and will be extending it to include children and young people for the first time. A consultation was launched in March 2019, and the Government is due to publish its response. The revised strategy was originally due to be published towards the end of 2019, however no update has yet been given for an expected publication date.

There have been successive health policies to improve outcomes for people with autism. Most recently, the NHS Long Term Plan (2019) provides several objectives for people with autism, including: the introduction of a 'digital flag' in the patient record by 2023/24, to ensure staff know a patient has autism; ensuring reasonable adjustments are made so that wider NHS services can support people with learning disabilities or autism; and piloting the introduction of a specific health check for people with autism.

There are however concerns around diagnosis, particularly for children, with increasing waiting times from referral to diagnostic assessment in some areas. NICE guidance recommends a maximum waiting time of 3 months from referral to assessment however the latest local authority self-assessment (2018) found that the median reported waiting time from referral to diagnostic assessment was 30 weeks. In a recent debate, the Minister for Care said that this "postcode lottery" must end and explained that new data on autism waiting times would help hold local authorities to account.

The Government and NHS have also focused on reducing levels of inpatient care for people with a learning disability and/or autism. The Department of Health and Social Care has said that hospitals are not where people should live and committed to move people to community-based support. However, ambitions for this have been postponed. The most recent target, as detailed in the NHS Long Term Plan, is for a reduction in inpatient provision of 50% (compared to 2015 levels) by 2023/24.

The Government has also committed to introducing mandatory training on learning disabilities and autism for health and social care staff. Trials will begin in health and social care settings by April 2020, and report by March 2021, after which wider roll-out of training is expected for all staff. This note focuses on policies in England. Health is a devolved matter so each of the devolved administrations are responsible for setting their own policies in this area. However, the note briefly outlines strategies implemented by the Governments in Scotland, Wales and Northern Ireland in section 8. This note also describes policies in the areas of employment, education and social security.

*Black Lives Matter protests: UK reaction to the killing of George Floyd*
Published Thursday, 04 June, 2020

This Insight outlines the background to the Black Lives Matter movement and the reaction in the UK to the death of George Floyd.

During the past two weeks protesters have taken to the streets across the UK in solidarity with protesters in the US, reacting to the death of George Floyd, a 46-year-old black man.

George Floyd died on 25 May after a police

officer knelt on his neck for almost nine minutes. The officer is currently awaiting trial for murder; other officers present are also facing charges. The event sparked a wave of protests across the US that spread globally.

While many of the protests have not been organised by any one group, they are associated with the Black Lives Matter movement. In the UK, the Prime Minister said those exercising their right to protest should do so in line with social distancing rules.

This Insight outlines the background to the Black Lives Matter movement and the reaction in the UK to the death of George Floyd.

### What is the Black Lives Matter movement?

Black Lives Matter (BLM) is an anti-racist and human rights movement that originated in the US in 2013 from a hashtag – #BlackLivesMatter. The hashtag was circulated following the acquittal of a neighbourhood watch coordinator who shot an unarmed black teenager, Trayvon Martin.

The movement gained momentum in the wake of successive black deaths, often as a result of police shootings in the US.

The phrase "black lives matter" can refer to the protest slogan, the overarching movement or one of a collection of chapters of the Black Lives Matter Global Foundation, an organisation that operates across the US, UK and Canada.

While BLM has been likened to the American civil rights movement, campaigners often shirk the comparison, highlighting the relatively decentralised nature of BLM, without prominent figureheads.

The recent protests show this lack of hierarchy: they are often organised via social media, by multiple campaign groups, without any central spokesperson. While some protests in the US have turned violent, researchers have in the past cautioned against delegitimising the BLM movement by associating it with protest violence outside its control.

### The UK reaction to the killing of George Floyd

On the weekend of 30-31 May protests took place in London, Manchester and Cardiff. On 3 June thousands of protesters marched in London from Hyde Park to Victoria Station and then to Westminster, where they gathered outside Parliament.

UK protesters have highlighted their own experiences of racial violence and discrimination. They have drawn attention to events such as the Windrush scandal and the recent death of Belly Mujinga. Mujinga died with Covid-19 after reportedly having been spat at while working at Victoria Station. The subsequent investigation found no evidence of anyone spitting or of the death being linked to the incident. A recent review led by Public Health England found that death rates from Covid-19 were highest among people in Black, Asian and Minority Ethnic groups.

The campaign group Stand Up to Racism called for people to "take the knee" on their doorsteps and in their communities. The London protests were accompanied by people around the country responding to this call. The gesture traces back to 2016, when American football players knelt during the national anthem to raise awareness of racial injustice. It has now acquired a new significance in light of the circumstances of George Floyd's death.

### How has Parliament responded?

SNP and Labour Members of Parliament have sponsored an Early Day Motion, tabled on 2 June, stating: "This House supports the Black Lives Matter campaign."

Members of Parliament have also tabled several parliamentary questions to ask the Secretary of State for Foreign and Commonwealth Affairs, what contact his department has had with the US Administration on the civil unrest following the death of George Floyd.

During Prime Minister's Questions on 3 June the Leader of the Opposition, Sir Keir Starmer MP, said the death of George Floyd: "shone a light on racism and hatred experienced by many in the US and beyond." He called on the Prime Minister to convey to President Trump "the UK's abhorrence about his response to the events."

The Prime Minister said he thought what had happened in the US was "appalling and inexcusable," although cautioned that the protests "should take place in a lawful and reasonable way."

Later that day, during the Downing Street press conference, the Prime Minister said: "racist violence has no place in our society," and that while people in the UK were exercising their right to protest, they should do so "in accordance with the rules on social distancing."

### Protesting during coronavirus

Under lockdown laws currently in force across the UK, certain gatherings are prohibited for public health reasons. The rules on gatherings are different in the UK's four nations. In England, indoor gatherings are completely prohibited, as are outdoor gatherings of more than six people. The police have new public health powers to disperse gatherings taking place in public spaces but cannot use these powers for public order purposes. This means they can only break up protests using their lockdown powers when they are concerned about the risk of coronavirus spreading.

The police also has a duty to facilitate peaceful protests. Officers policing protests must now balance this duty with their new task of enforcing lockdown laws.

Senior police leaders have asked protesters to "work with officers at this challenging time." Police present at protests that took place over the last weekend chose not to break up the gatherings but did arrest some protesters for lockdown offences.

Further reading

blacklivesmatter.com

Coronavirus: Which key workers are most at risk? House of Commons Library

Coronavirus: Which workers are economically impacted? House of Commons Library

*About the authors: Doug Pyper is Head of the Home Affairs Research Section and Jennifer Brown is a researcher specialising in policing and crime at the House of Commons Library.*

### *Brexit next steps: The European Arrest Warrant*
Published Thursday, 20 February, 2020

The European Arrest Warrant (EAW) is a simplified system for extradition between EU Member States. As a member of the EU the UK has used the EAW since 2004. Under the Withdrawal Agreement (WA) this will continue until the end of the transition period.

This Insight explains how the EAW works. It sets out what will happen during the transition period and examines the prospects for new arrangements.

### What is the EAW?
The EAW is a fast track extradition procedure between EU Member States. A Member State can make a request when they want to prosecute or imprison a person who is in another Member State. The EAW is based on the principle of 'mutual recognition' of judgments between Member States.

Mutual recognition means the authorities in one Member State can arrest and 'surrender' a person to another Member State. They do this on the basis of a request from a judicial authority in the other Member State. The process is concluded with minimal inquiry into the basis of that request. The EAW was a response to the free movement of people within the EU. It recognised the possibility that criminals might try to evade justice by moving between Member States. Before the EAW's introduction, extradition arrangements were notable for their complexity and potential for delay.

According to data from the National Crime Agency, extradition requests to the UK under the EAW increased from 1,865 in 2004 to 12,613 in 2015. Requests made by the UK to other Member States have gone up from 96 to 228 per year over the same period. According to Government statistics, in 2018/19 15,540 requests were made under the EAW process, and 1412 EAW related arrests were made.

### What space is there for negotiations?
The UK and the EU aim to negotiate new arrangements for criminal justice cooperation. These will include extradition. The new arrangements would come into force at the end of the transition period.

No countries outside the EU or the EEA currently have extradition arrangements that are equivalent to the EAW. The EU has said that access to the EAW is linked to allowing freedom of movement. The UK Government has rejected the possibility of maintaining freedom of movement at the end of the transition period.

### What will happen during the transition period?
Under the WA, the UK and Member States can continue to use the EAW, provided the process is initiated before the end of the transition period. However, the WA allows Member States to refuse to surrender their own nationals to the UK using the EAW during the transition period. Some Member States have constitutional rules that prohibit the extradition of their own nationals to countries outside the EU. The UK has the option to reciprocate by refusing to extradite its own nationals to any EU country that exercises this option.

Germany, Austria and Slovenia have said that they will no longer extradite their own nationals to the UK. If a national from one of these countries commits a crime in the UK and subsequently leaves, it will only be possible to prosecute them if the authorities in their own country are willing to do so.

The Home Affairs Select Committee has raised concerns about this exemption. The committee pointed out that victims of serious offences committed in the UK might need to travel to EU countries to take part in trials if the accused is not extradited. It suggested that the Government should be open with Parliament and the public about what this means for access to justice for victims. It also called for practical arrangements to be put in place to support the prosecution of EU nationals in their own countries.

### What happens after transition if no agreement is reached?
If no new agreement is reached the UK will fall back on previous arrangements. These are contained in a 1957 Council of Europe Convention on Extradition. This will require amendments to domestic legislation. The UK will also be reliant on other Member States making equivalent

amendments because some have repealed legislation that gave effect to the Convention since the EAW. Unlike the EAW, the Convention does not impose time limits and requests are made through diplomatic rather than judicial channels. There are also more grounds on which extradition can be refused than under the EAW.

The May Government published an assessment of the impact of there being no agreement on extradition arrangements. It stated that relying on the 1957 Convention would mean that requests would be subject to a longer and more complex process, and extraditions would be more difficult. It also noted that prior to the implementation of the EAW, the UK extradited fewer than 60 people each year. It pointed to the example of Rachid Ramda, whose 2005 extradition to France on terrorism charges took 10 years from the original request.

### The Extradition (Provisional Arrest) Bill

The Extradition (Provisional Arrest) Bill was introduced in the House of Lords by the Government in January 2020. It would provide police with the power to arrest without a warrant for the purposes of extradition. Currently the Bill only applies to certain non-EU countries. This is because the power already exists under the EAW and is therefore not needed for Member States during the transition period. The Government has said the power could be extended to EU countries in the future if the UK lost access to the EAW. However during the second reading debate in the House of Lords the minister stated that the Bill was not an "attempt… to replicate the capability of the EAW". The police has requested this power as part of its contingency planning if no agreement is reached.

### Will replacing the EAW be difficult?

The Political Declaration (PD) on the future relationship between the UK and the EU says both parties should have streamlined procedures and time limits that allow them to surrender those suspected or convicted of crimes efficiently and quickly.

The PD also raises the possibility of waiving the requirement of 'double criminality'. This is a feature of most extradition agreements. It means the offence a person is being extradited for must be an offence in both countries involved.

The EU's draft negotiating mandate notes that arrangements for future law enforcement and judicial cooperation will need to take into account the fact that the UK will be a non-Schengen third country. The UK will no longer allow the free movement of persons. And the draft negotiating mandate states that a third country cannot enjoy the same rights and

benefits as Member States. The EU mandate also proposes that any agreement reached should be terminated if the UK were to denounce the European Convention on Human Rights (ECHR), and suspended if the UK repealed domestic legislation that gives effect to the ECHR (namely the Human Rights Act 1998).

The UK Government's written statement on the future relationship suggests: "it is in the UK's and the EU's mutual interest to reach a pragmatic agreement" on law enforcement and judicial cooperation. However, the UK Government position states that EU law must not "constrain the autonomy of the UK's legal system in any way".

### Can the EAW be replaced with a 'surrender agreement'?

A 'surrender agreement' between the EU, Norway and Iceland (non-EU countries but in the Schengen zone) came into force in November 2019. It mirrors the EAW in most respects and is the first extradition agreement with a non-EU country to do so. However, it contains a similar exemption for the extradition of a country's own nationals as in the WA. Norway, Iceland and the EU first agreed in principle to these arrangements in 2006 but the completion of necessary legal formalities by all the states concerned took a considerable length of time.

The Home Affairs Select Committee has suggested that the Home Office is "overly-optimistic" about the ease with which replacement arrangements can be negotiated, given how long it took for Norway and Iceland to negotiate an agreement.

*Further Reading*
*Home Office preparations for the UK exiting the EU, Home Affairs Select Committee.*
*UK-EU security cooperation after Brexit: Follow-up report, Home Affairs Committee.*
*Brexit: the proposed UK-EU security treaty, EU Home Affairs Sub-Committee.*
*UK-EU security cooperation after Brexit, Home Affairs Select Committee.*
*Extradition (Provisional Arrest) Bill [HL]: Briefing for Lords Stages, House of Lords Library.*

### Categorisation of prisoners in the UK
29 December 2015

### Summary

The relevant prison rules for England and Wales, Scotland and Northern Ireland provide for prisoners to be assigned a security category or supervision level.

This briefing offers a short guide to prisoner categorisation in each jurisdiction.

Categorisation of prisoners in England and Wales centres around an assessment of risk and particularly the risk (and potential consequences) of escape. Categorisation in Scotland and Northern Ireland works in a broadly similar way.

At one end of the scale for adult male prisoners in England and Wales, Category A is for prisoners whose escape would be highly dangerous to the public or the police or the security of the State and for whom the aim must be to make escape impossible. At the other end of the scale, Category D is for those prisoners who present a low risk, can reasonably be trusted in open conditions and for whom open conditions are appropriate.

Although instructions to prison governors in England and Wales state very plainly that prisoners should not be recategorised simply to enable them to be moved to where there are spaces within the prison estate, the Prison Officers' Association has been alleging for some time that the recategorisation process is flawed, with unsuitable prisoners being sent to open conditions. This briefing also describes that controversy.

Another controversial issue has been the removal of legal aid from many areas of prison law in England and Wales, as part of ongoing reforms to legal aid. Legal aid is no longer available for challenges to recategorisation decisions, although is available for judicial review. It has been argued that this both leads to poorer quality decisions and makes it more difficult for prisoners to challenge those decisions.

*Further briefings about prisons are available on Parliament's topic page for prisons.*

*Further briefings about legal aid are available on Parliament's topic page for legal aid.*

### Code of Practice for Victims of Crime in England and Wales
November 2020
**Summary of Victims' Rights**

*Right 1:* To be able to understand and to be understood you have the right to be given information in a way that is easy to understand and to be provided with help to be understood, including, where necessary, access to interpretation and translation services.

*Right 2:* To have the details of the crime recorded without unjustified delay You have the Right to have details of the crime recorded by the police as soon as possible after the incident. If you are required to provide a witness statement or be interviewed, you have the Right to be provided with additional support to assist you through this process.

*Right 3:* To be provided with information when reporting the crime You have the Right to receive written confirmation when reporting a crime, to be provided with information about the criminal

justice process and to be told about programmes or services for victims. This might include services where you can meet with the suspect or offender, which is known as Restorative Justice.

*Right 4:* To be referred to services that support victims and have services and support tailored to your needs You have the Right to be referred to services that support victims, which includes the Right to contact them directly, and to have your needs assessed so services and support can be tailored to meet your needs. If eligible, you have the Right to be offered a referral to specialist support services and to be told about additional support available at court, for example special measures.

*Right 5:* To be provided with information about compensation Where eligible, you have the Right to be told about how to claim compensation for any loss, damage or injury caused as a result of crime.

*Right 6:* To be provided with information about the investigation and prosecution You have the Right to be provided with updates on your case and to be told when important decisions are taken. You also have the Right, at certain stages of the justice process, to ask for decisions to be looked at again by the relevant service provider.

*Right 7:* To make a Victim Personal Statement You have the Right to make a Victim Personal Statement, which tells the court how the crime has affected you and is considered when sentencing the offender. You will be given information about the process.

*Right 8:* To be given information about the trial, trial process and your role as a witness If your case goes to court, you have the Right to be told the time, date and location of any hearing and the outcome of those hearings in a timely way. If you are required to give evidence, you have the Right to be offered appropriate help before the trial and, where possible, if the court allows, to meet with the prosecutor before giving evidence.

*Right 9:* To be given information about the outcome of the case and any appeals You have the Right to be told the outcome of the case and, if the defendant is convicted, to be given an explanation of the sentence. If the offender appeals against their conviction or sentence, you have the Right to be told about the appeal and its outcome.

*Right 10:* To be paid expenses and have property returned If you are required to attend court and give evidence, you have the Right to claim certain expenses. If any of your property was taken as evidence, you have the Right to get it back as soon as possible.

*Right 11:* To be given information about the offender following a conviction Where eligible, you have the Right to be automatically referred to the Victim Contact Scheme, which will provide you with information about the offender and their progress in prison, and if/when they become eligible for consideration of parole or release. Where applicable, you also have the Right to make a new Victim Personal Statement, in which you can say how the crime continues to affect you.

*Right 12:* To make a complaint about your Rights not being met If you believe that you have not received your Rights, you have the Right to make a complaint to the relevant service provider. If you remain unhappy, you can contact the Parliamentary and Health Service Ombudsman.

*Commons Library Analysis: The Prisons and Courts Bill*

## The Prisons and Courts Bill

### Summary

The Prisons and Courts Bill covers a number of policy areas that fall within the Ministry of Justice's remit, from prisons to whiplash to online criminal convictions. The Bill, which is composed of six parts, deals with four discrete areas:

• Part 1 on prison reform
• Parts 2 and 3 on reforming the court and tribunal system
• Part 4 on the judiciary and the Judicial Appointments Commission
• Part 5 on whiplash.

The Bill is due to have its second reading on 20 March 2017.

### Where does the Bill extend to?

Most of the Bill extends to England and Wales only. However, some aspects of the prison reforms also extend to Scotland and Northern Ireland, because Her Majesty's Inspectorate of Prisons and the Prisons and Probation Ombudsman have functions relating to immigration detention, and this is a reserved matter. In relation to court reform, Parts 2 and 3 of the Bill are relevant to Scotland and Northern Ireland in so far that they make changes to the way in which reserved tribunals are administered.

### Prison reform

Part 1 of the Bill concerns prison reform. The Government's November 2016 white paper, Prison Safety and Reform, set out a range of proposals to deal with increasing levels of violence and self-harm in prisons and the persistently high levels of reoffending. A central proposal was greater autonomy for prison governors, currently being piloted in six "reform prisons".

Many of these reforms do not need primary, or indeed any, legislation. As a result, there is actually very little in the Bill on prisons. Clause 1 sets out a new statutory purpose for prisons promised by the white paper (similar declaratory provisions exist in legislation for probation and youth justice) and amends the Secretary of State's duties to include reporting on the extent to which prisons are achieving that purpose. Clause 2 puts Her Majesty's Inspectorate of Prisons on a statutory footing (the Chief Inspector is already provided for in statute), and provides inspectors with some additional powers. Clauses 4-20 would put the Prisons and Probation Ombudsman on a statutory footing. There were attempts to do this in 2004 and 2008, but these were abandoned.

The provisions on prison security in chapter 3 of Part 1 build on recent legislation to help deal with two major challenges to prison security: illicit mobile phones and psychoactive substances. A 2012 Act already allows prison governors to interfere with wireless telegraphy in prisons in order either to block mobile phones or detect their use. Clause 21 would allow the Secretary of State to authorise telecoms and internet service providers to do this. Legislation in 2015 and 2016 was brought in to deal with New Psychoactive Substances (NPSs), including introducing a new offence of possession in a custodial setting. Clause 22 would allow for prisoners to be tested for the use of NPSs without each individual substance needing to be specified separately.

### Reforming the Court and Tribunal System

Parts 2 and 3 of the Prison and Courts Bill will make significant changes to the courts and tribunals system in England and Wales.

The provisions includes reforms to the criminal courts, civil courts, the family courts and tribunals in England and Wales. The provisions in Parts 2 and 3 predominantly relate to Her Majesty's Court and Tribunal's (HMCTS) Reform Programme, which was launched in March 2014. (Lord Chief Justice of England and Wales, Senior President of Tribunals and Lord Chancellor and Secretary of State for Justice, Joint Letter (2014)) The programme, and this Bill, aim to modernise the justice system and improve access to justice, through a series of reforms designed to integrate technology and enhance efficiency. The aims and principles of the programme were set out in a joint statement by the Lord Chancellor, the Lord Chief Justice and the Senior President of Tribunals, titled Transforming Our Justice System, which was published in September 2016. The proposed reforms to the criminal courts focus on expanded use of technology, in particular by providing for more hearings and decisions to be conducted in writing (including electronically) or virtually via audio and video links. The proposals that have attracted most comment are those to enable "fully virtual" court hearings, and those to introduce a new automated online conviction procedure for certain low-level non-imprisonable offences.

Part 2 of the Bill also provides the legal foundations for the introduction of new online procedures and online dispute resolution (ODR) for the civil courts, family courts and tribunals. The clauses enable the creation of a new online court that could deal with low value money claims below £25,000, as was recommended by Lord Justice Briggs' Civil Courts Structure Review. (Lord Justice Briggs, Civil Courts Structure Review: Final Report (2016) p) The clauses would allow new online procedures to apply to existing civil courts, family courts and tribunals. The Government's Transforming our justice system paper indicates that the Social Security and Child Support Tribunal is going to be one of the first "to be moved entirely online, with an end-to-end digital process that will be faster and easier to use for people that use it". (Transforming our justice system: summary of reforms and consultation (September 2016) Cm 9321 p10)

### Judiciary and the Judicial Appointments Commission

Part 4 of the Bill concerns judicial terms and conditions, and the role of the Judicial Appointments Commission. The former provisions of the Bill largely follow from the Ministry of Justice's consultation on Modernising Judicial Terms and Conditions, while the latter follow from certain recommendations in the Triennial Review of the Judicial Appointments Commission. There are also minor changes to the law on deployment of judges and the remuneration of Employment Tribunal members.

At present, some leadership roles are held on a fixed term basis whereas others are not. Many leadership judge positions are non-statutory, and thus can already be held on a fixed-term basis without the need for legislation. Clause 56 amends the law to allow the remaining statutory judicial leadership positions to be held on a fixed-term basis, in line with the conclusions of the Ministry of Justice's consultation. The Government claim that this will create a clearer career path and improve diversity in the judiciary. The Bill does not specify how long the term will be for any such appointments, as this is left to the Lord Chancellor to decide following consultation with the judiciary. Proposals to appoint all fee-paid judges on fixed-term appointments were included in the consultation but are not being taken forward in the Bill.

Clause 60 amends the law to allow the Lord Chancellor to direct the Judicial Appointments

Commission (JAC) to provide its advice on appointments both within and without the United Kingdom, even where those appointments are non-judicial in nature. The JAC is also empowered to set up a charging model to recoup the costs of providing this advice. This is following a recommendation in the Triennial Review that these duties were formalised, as they were already being sought out due to the JAC's expertise in the realm of appointments.

### Whiplash

Against a background of rising motor insurance premiums and the perception (not universally accepted) of the existence of a "compensation culture", there has been a focus on the incidence of personal injury claims for whiplash injuries, insurance fraud more generally, and the extent to which this has affected the cost of motor insurance. The Government remains concerned about the number and cost of whiplash claims and has consulted on ways to address the issue. It now intends to proceed with a range of reforms aimed at capping whiplash compensation payments and banning settlement of claims without medical evidence.

Part 5 of the Bill deals with whiplash, including the definition of whiplash; damages for whiplash injuries; an uplift, in exceptional circumstances, to the amount of damages; banning settlement of claims before medical report; and regulation of the ban on premedical settlement. Much of the detail would be included in secondary legislation, which, in many cases, would be subject to the affirmative resolution procedure.

In general, lawyers' groups, including the Law Society and the Association of Personal Injury Lawyers, are among those who have raised concerns about the Government's proposals, while the Association of British Insurers has welcomed them.

The Government considers that the reforms would lead to savings of about £1bn and expects this to be passed on to motorists, resulting in an average saving per motor insurance premium of £40. Others disagree that the savings will be passed on and also consider it unfair that the reforms would reduce the compensation payable to genuine claimants, and leave victims to conduct claims without legal advice. There is also disagreement about whether the number and cost of whiplash claims has increased.

### *Comparative Prison Sentences in the EU*
Published Monday, 08 June, 2015

Whilst most countries within the European Union have a similar basic structure to their criminal justice system, recognising a range of alike offences stemming from a common law origin, difficulties in the comparison of specific crimes or legal provisions reflect the complex nature of the varying legal traditions between nations.

These difficulties extend to the process by which an accused may be deemed to have committed an offence, the way that the offender is punished and the severity of the punishment received. Furthermore, in trying to make comparisons between countries, it is important to note that legal systems do not necessarily follow recognised state borders and can create significant variations in criminal justice within a country: one such example of this phenomenon is the different legal systems which exist within the UK between England and Wales, Northern Ireland and Scotland.

As regards the variation in prison sentence given for similar crimes across Europe, there are limited sources available for making any meaningful comparison. However, one is worthy of note:

• HEUNI, European Sourcebook of Crime and Criminal Justice Statistics 2014, 5th Edition (Helsinki, 2014)

The result of a collaboration between the European Institute for Crime Prevention and Control and the University of Lausanne, the European Sourcebook seeks to provide a range of comparable data across European countries with statistics on police, prosecution, convictions and correction, probation and victim surveys.

Included in the European Sourcebook are a set of tables showing the percentage of persons convicted by length of unsuspended custodial sanction imposed by offence in 2010. Using this data the House of Commons Library has produced the Comparative prison sentences in the EU visualisation tool.

This tool may be downloaded as an excel file using the link below. It allows for quick and easy comparison between two countries of the percentage of convicted offenders receiving different lengths of custodial sentence for 9 offence types. These are:

• Intentional Homicide (including attempts)
• Completed Intentional Homicide
• Robbery
• Theft (total)
• Theft (burglary)
• Rape
• Sexual Assault
• Assault (with injury)
• Drug Offences

Also included is an index of available data and a table showing the modal average of each offence by country.

The graph and results are designed to be indicative of sentencing practises across the EU

rather than read as absolute values. Great care should be taken in making inter-country comparisons with criminal justice statistics; for more information the European Sourcebook should be consulted.

*Contracting out probation services*
20 May 2019
**Summary**

Background In the 2010 Coalition agreement, the Government said it would introduce a "rehabilitation revolution that will pay independent providers to reduce reoffending". On 9 May 2013, the MoJ published Transforming Rehabilitation: A Strategy for Reform, announcing its plans to invite providers from the voluntary and private sectors to bid for rehabilitation services.

One of the main new changes was splitting the probation service in two, with the public sector National Probation Service (NPS) managing high risk offenders and providing services to the courts, and the new Community Rehabilitation Companies (CRC) managing low and medium risk offenders. In September 2013, the MoJ invited bids to run 21 CRCs across England and Wales, worth a combined £450 million. The list of new owners of CRCs was released on 18 December 2014. Only one of the CRCs was won by an organisation outside the private sector.

**Implementation**

Payment by Results (PbR) is an outcome-based payment scheme central to the Government's reforms. Under the contracts, a proportion of a provider's payment is determined by the reductions in reoffending they achieve. The Transforming Rehabilitation strategy document said this would create an incentive for providers to "focus relentlessly on driving down reoffending".

Transforming Rehabilitation introduced a nationwide "Through the Gate" resettlement service. The intent was to give most offenders continuous support, usually by the CRC, from custody into the community. CRCs began providing "Through the Gate" services from 1 May 2015.

**Inspections**

Her Majesty's Inspectorate of Probation (HMIP) produced five reports evaluating the reforms as they progressed. The final report, published in May 2016, found improvements in joint working and communication between the CRCs and the NPS, particularly in dealing with breaches or increased risk of harm. However, there were problems with court work, staff training and morale. In its thematic inspections, HMIP said that the 'Through the Gate' services were so poor that if they were removed the impact would be "negligible". HMIP also found in a separate report that the reforms had meant services for women offenders were less focused. In a further report, HMIP found that CRC enforcement decision making in relation to community orders, suspended sentence supervision orders and post-sentence supervision was poor. HMIP began individual area inspections in summer 2016. They have found overall that CRCs are performing below expectations, with particular criticism for some CRCs monitoring offenders by telephone.

### Coronavirus: Elections

Published Wednesday, 14 April, 2021

The coronavirus pandemic has had significant implications for elections in both 2020 and 2021. Local elections due in England in May 2020 were postponed. Early in 2021 there was speculation that the elections might be delayed again.

In February 2021 the UK government confirmed that the 2021 scheduled polls in England and those delayed from 2020 would go ahead on 6 May 2021. It also published a delivery plan to assist electoral administrators plan for those polls. The Scottish and Welsh governments also stated their intentions that the devolved elections, for the Scottish Parliament and Senedd Cymru, scheduled for May 2021, should go ahead.

This briefing explains how the elections due in 2020 were postponed. It also examines the impact of the pandemic on preparations for the 2021 English local elections and devolved elections, including the measures put in place in England, Scotland and Wales, to allow the elections to go ahead.

These measures include encouraging voters to apply early for postal and proxy votes. The deadline to apply for a postal vote for the elections in England and Wales is 5pm on Tuesday 20 April. The deadline in Scotland has been brought forward (see section 2.2) to 5pm on Tuesday 6 April.

The deadline to apply for a proxy vote is 5pm on Tuesday 27 April in all three countries. Voters must already be registered to vote. The deadline to register to vote for elections on 6 May is 23:59 on 19 April 2021.

Going to a polling station and working on the election, either in a polling stations, count venues or in related roles are legitimate reasons to leave your home if coronavirus restrictions are in place. Voters should wear a face covering in polling stations.

If a voter is ill or self-isolating as a result of coronavirus then they can make use of an emergency proxy in order to vote. Rules for emergency proxies have been temporarily

altered. Normally they are only granted if you fall ill or are required to go away for work at short notice and applications must have supporting evidence from an employer or health professional. For the elections in May voters who fall ill because of Covid, or a required to self-isolate because coronavirus, will be able to apply for an emergency proxy without needing to provide additional evidence. Emergency proxy applications can be made up to 5pm on polling day.

Candidates will need fewer signatures in support of nomination papers. This is aimed at reducing the amount of contact required between people. However, nomination papers still need to be delivered in person to the relevant returning officer within the specified times set out in law.

Campaigners will also need to take note of the separate guidance in England, Scotland and Wales on the need to maintain social distancing and what is allowed during campaigning:

Government's approach to elections and referendums during COVID-19 (applies to England)

Coronavirus (COVID-19): Scottish Parliament Election 2021 – campaign activity

Guidance to persons undertaking election campaigning activities in Wales during the Coronavirus pandemic

The combination of so many polls and the different voting systems in place mean that these will be some of the most complex polls ever held, particularly in England.

The local elections delayed from 6 May 2020 are:

• PCC elections in England and Wales for/in 39 police force areas (it was originally 40 but the West Yorkshire PCC powers will be transferred to the elected mayor for West Yorkshire). In Essex, North Yorkshire, Northamptonshire and Staffordshire the role of PCC also now includes responsibility for fire and rescue services;

• Local elections for 115 principal councils (34 metropolitan boroughs, 59 district and 22 unitary authority council areas) in England.

• Greater London Authority (GLA) elections for London mayor and all seats on the London Assembly;

• Metro-mayoral elections in Greater Manchester, Liverpool City Region, Tees Valley and West Midlands;

• Single-authority mayoral elections in Bristol, Liverpool, and Salford.

• Parish council elections in some areas.

Some local referendums and council by-elections were also scheduled to take place on the same day. The elections that are already scheduled for May 2021 are:

• Elections for all seats in the Scottish Parliament and Senedd Cymru;

• Whole county council elections in 21 two-tier counties and six unitary counties in England;

- Whole council elections in Doncaster and the Isles of Scilly;
- Three combined authority mayors (West of England, West Yorkshire, and Cambridgeshire and Peterborough) and two single authority mayors (Doncaster and North Tyneside);
- Parish council elections in some parts of England

### Coronavirus: FAQs on postponed elections
Published Wednesday, 06 May, 2020
This is a fast-moving issue and should be read as correct at the date of publication (06.05.20).
Thursday 7 May 2020 should have been local election day in England and Wales. Parliament passed emergency legislation to delay the elections because of the ongoing coronavirus pandemic.
This Insight gives answers to some FAQs on the postponed elections.

### Which elections are affected?
The Coronavirus Act 2020 postponed the elections for:
- 40 Police and Crime Commissioners (PCC) in England and Wales;
- London Mayor and members of the Greater London Authority (GLA);
- Councillors in 118 English councils;
- Local authority mayors in Bristol, Liverpool and Salford;
- 4 combined authority mayors (Greater Manchester, Liverpool, Tees Valley, and West Midlands); and
- Parish council elections in some parts of England. Some local referendums were also due to be held. For example there was meant to be a council tax referendum in Warwick (which has now been cancelled).

### When will they be held instead?
These elections will now take place on 6 May 2021. This date is set by the Coronavirus Act.

### What happens to those currently serving in these seats/posts?
The PCCs, councillors, mayors and GLA members affected by the delay would normally be coming to the end of their four-year terms. Instead they will continue in post for an extra 12 months.
When the elections for these seats are held next year, the winning candidates will serve three years instead of the normal four years. This will allow those elections to revert to their original four-year cycle.
The four 'metro mayors' for Greater Manchester, Liverpool, Tees Valley, and West Midlands were first elected in 2017. They would have been coming to the end of their first term of three years. The winning candidates in 2020 were meant to serve four years with subsequent elections every four years. Instead the winning candidate in 2021 will serve a three-year term with elections every four years from 2024.

### What about the areas where local government has been reorganised?
In Buckinghamshire the existing county and district councils were abolished on 1 April 2020. All the councillors from the former districts and the county became councillors of the new unitary authority of Buckinghamshire.
Councillors will continue to serve until May 2021, when all seats will become vacant. All councillors elected in May 2021 then will serve four year terms and whole council elections will then be held every four years from 2025.
In Northamptonshire, councillors were due to be elected to two new shadow unitary authorities. They will take over the running of the county in April 2021. These councillors will now be elected in May 2021 and replace all existing councillors. Those elected in 2021 will serve four-year terms and, like Buckinghamshire, will serve four years before whole council elections occur every year from 2025.

### What about the local elections already scheduled for 2021?
Local elections in England are already due to take place on 6 May 2021. They will be for all seats on 24 county councils, six unitary county councils, Doncaster Council and the Isles of Scilly. The councillors elected for these seats will be elected for their normal four-year term.
Voters may be voting in two or more elections in May 2021 as a result of combining this year's delayed polls with those already scheduled next year. In Cambridge and Liverpool voters will have four different elections on the same day.
Holding several elections on the same day is cost-effective and convenient. On the other hand, holding several elections on the same day has the potential to confuse voters with the number of ballot papers. This is especially true when there are different voting systems on different ballot papers.
General elections are also scheduled to take place for the Scottish Parliament and the Senedd Cymru on 6 May 2021. In Wales, the current rules prevent a PCC election from being combined with a general election for the Senedd Cymru. Combining polls administratively allows voters to vote in both elections in the same polling station at the same time.
Polls that cannot be combined but that are held on the same day may cause confusion for voters and may involve voters being asked to vote in two separate polling stations. The Welsh and Westminster governments will need to work with returning officers to reach a solution.

## What about by-elections?

By-elections for most local elections and mayoral elections must normally take place within 35 days of the vacancy arising. Parliament has approved regulations to delay these too. These will also now take place on 6 May 2021.

The Government has said it will keep these arrangements under review. If the pandemic restrictions can be eased it may be possible to hold elections earlier. This could mean that pending by-elections might be allowed before 6 May 2021. Rallings and Thrasher, the elections experts, recorded 224 local council by-elections across the UK in the last 12 months.

## What about other elections?

The next scheduled UK general election is currently May 2024, although the current Government has committed to abolishing the Fixed-term Parliaments Act 2011. There are currently no by-elections due for seats in the House of Commons.

There is no set time limit for by-elections to the House of Commons to be held. If a seat becomes vacant, it will be for the party that previously held the seat to decide when to hold the by-election.

The Coronavirus Act makes no changes to the dates of scheduled elections to the Scottish Parliament and the Senedd Cymru/Welsh Parliament due on 6 May 2021. The regulation of these elections is devolved and it will be for the Scottish Parliament and the Senedd Cymru to approve any changes to the dates if required.

The Coronavirus Act does, however, allow for by-elections for constituency seats in the Scottish Parliament or the Senedd Cymru to be delayed. The law normally says constituency by-elections must be called within 3 months of the vacancy arising. The Coronavirus Act allows the presiding officers in each Parliament to delay any constituency by-elections arising.

Local council by-elections arising in Scotland and Wales will also be delayed.

Elections in Northern Ireland are an excepted matter, which means they remain the responsibility of ministers in the UK Government. The next scheduled elections in Northern Ireland are likely to be the Assembly elections in May 2022 and local elections in May 2023.

*Further reading: Coronavirus Act: Elections, House of Commons Library*

## Coronavirus: Parliamentary consent for the lockdown in England

Published Monday, 04 May, 2020

This is a fast-moving issue and should be read as correct at the date of publication (04.05.20).

Today (Monday 4 May) MPs will consider a motion to approve the legislation that underpins the current 'lockdown' in England: The Health Protection (Coronavirus, Restrictions) (England) Regulations 2020 and The Health Protection (Coronavirus, Restrictions) (England) (Amendment) Regulations 2020. These regulations are already in force. This Insight explains why MPs are only approving them now and what might happen to these regulations as the Government's response to coronavirus progresses.

## What do the emergency regulations do?

The regulations have given the police extraordinary powers to enforce a lockdown across England. They have three main effects:

• They significantly restrict the free movement of people by making it an offence be outside without a "reasonable excuse" and (with some exceptions) to gather in groups of more than two.

• They require all non-essential retail, hospitality and entertainment businesses to close.

• They give police officers powers to take people flouting the lockdown back to their homes.

The police has adopted a co-operative approach. Those who break the rules are encouraged to return home before they resort to enforcement. The police can issue Fixed Penalty Notices (FPNs) to those who commit an offence under the regulations. Forces in England issued 8,877 FPNs between 27 March and 27 April 2020.

## Why are MPs considering the regulations now?

The regulations were made under emergency powers in public health legislation. Regulations made under this public health legislation normally require parliamentary approval before they can be brought into force.

Due to the coronavirus pandemic, the Secretary of State for Health and Social Care, Matt Hancock declared the regulations were needed urgently, and brought into force without prior parliamentary approval. They came into force on Thursday 26 March 2020, after Parliament had risen early for the Easter Recess due to the crisis.

The regulations cannot remain in force indefinitely without parliamentary approval. Under the Public Health (Control of Disease) Act 1984, parliamentary approval is required within 28 days (excluding certain times when both Houses of Parliament are not sitting). The regulations will therefore cease to have effect on the 19 May if they aren't approved before.

## Why is there an amendment regulation?

The Health Protection (Coronavirus, Restrictions) (England) (Amendment) Regulations 2020 came into force on 21 April 2020.

They were also introduced using the Government's emergency public health powers. They mostly make minor changes to the original regulations that don't have a significant effect. However, there is one amendment that is more substantial.

Before they were amended, the regulations created an offence of: "leaving the place where they are living without reasonable excuse." The amendment regulations changes this. It's now an offence to "leave or be outside of" the place you are living without reasonable excuse.

The original wording might have created a curious defence for the new offence. Theoretically, those accused of being outside without a reasonable excuse could have claimed to have left home with a reasonable excuse but got waylaid by something 'unreasonable'.

The Government says this amendment: "put beyond doubt that a person commits an offence if they remain outside of the place where they are living without reasonable excuse." However, some legal commentators have criticised the Government for amending the meaning of the offence without fully acknowledging the change.

### What about relaxing the lockdown?

Last Thursday (30 April) the Prime Minister said the Government would be, "setting out a comprehensive plan," for relaxing the lockdown once the 'five key tests' on the spread of the virus have been met.

It's not clear how the Government intends to legislate for future changes to the lockdown rules. It may revoke these regulations and make fresh regulations under public health legislation. It could also further amend the regulations being considered by Parliament today.

The current regulations require a government review the need for the lockdown every 21 days. The next such review is due to take place on Thursday (7 May).

*Further reading : Policing the coronavirus lockdown, House of Commons Library.*

### Coronavirus: Prisons (England and Wales)
### 1. The situation in prisons
March 2020

In March 2020 the Justice Secretary told the Justice Committee that the pressure on prisons in England and Wales due to coronavirus was acute.[1] The Chair of the Justice Committee described prisons as "a potential hotbed for viral transmission", stating that "they are overcrowded, understaffed and often dirty".[2] The Head of the Prison Governors Association told the Guardian:

… a combination of prison overcrowding, prisoner lockdown and staff shortages as a result of prison workers needing to isolate themselves meant that the system was facing unprecedented pressure.[3]

The physical health of the prison population, across a broad range of conditions, is much poorer than that of the general population.[4] The proportion of prisoners aged over 50 increased from 7% in 2002 to 16% in March 2019.[5] Living conditions across much of the prison estate are poor. As at February 2020, 60% (70) of prison establishments were crowded.[6] These 70 prisons accommodated around 60,000 prisoners or 71% of the total prison population.

### April and May 2020

On 27 April 2020 the Justice Secretary said that the numbers of coronavirus cases and deaths in prisons were lower than had been originally predicted and that "while we are not out of woods", prisons were coping and dealing well with the threat of covid-19.[7] A press release from the Ministry of Justice on the 28 April 2020 said that "jails are successfully limiting deaths and the transmission of the virus within the estate".[8] As of 12 May, 404 cases had been confirmed amongst prisoners. 21 prisoners and 7 members of prison staff had died.[9]

Public Health England (PHE) reported on 24 April 2020 that data it had collected "suggests that the 'explosive outbreaks' of COVID19 which were feared at the beginning of the pandemic wave are not being seen. Instead, there is evidence of containment of outbreak".[10] PHE's report stated that because access to testing for prisoners has been limited and variable, the number of confirmed cases reported "does not represent the true burden of infection in the prison system". It states that in addition to the 304 laboratory-confirmed cases in prisoners in England and Wales (at the time the report was written) data showed there had been also over 1,783 possible/probable cases.

Looking to the future, the report said:

In the absence of a vaccine or effective treatment, risks of large outbreaks in the prison estate will remain. These risks may be escalated later in the year relating to relaxation of wider community restrictions, some return of normal police and court activities, with consequent impacts on prisoner flow.

### 2. Measures being taken

The Ministry of Justice has said HM Prison and Probation Service is working closely with Public Health England, the NHS and the Department of Health and Social Care to manage the challenges prisons face.[11]

The prison system has been placed in "command mode", whereby the response to a major incident can be coordinated nationally.[12]

*2.1 Measures in prisons*

Within prisons, restrictions on movements of

prisoners have been put in place. The Justice Secretary has said efforts are being made within the prison estate to separate as many people as possible and create different cohorts of prisoners, so that, for example, new prisoners are not mixed with the existing population and that those who are particularly vulnerable, some of whom were convicted of serious and grave offences, are safe. [13]

Prisoners are spending more time in cells, gyms are closed, and non-essential work has been cancelled.[14] The Chief Inspector of Prisons, Peter Clarke, described the extreme restrictions for prisoners in local prisons visited by inspectors:

The vast majority were locked up for nearly the whole day with usually no more than half an hour out of their cells. We found some examples of even greater restrictions. In one prison, a small number of symptomatic prisoners had been isolated in their cells without any opportunity to come out for a shower or exercise for up to 14 days.[15]

From 15 May 2020 amendments were made to the rules for prison and young offender institutions to allow them to continue to implement a restricted regime to manage the effects of coronavirus.[16]

Concerns are now being raised about how purposeful and rehabilitative activities can be resumed within prisons, particularly in light of PHE's assessment of risks of large outbreaks remaining in the absence of a vaccine or treatment. Peter Clarke has said that prisons face potentially greater challenges in the coming months as they try to ease restrictions and reintroduce more purposeful regimes.[17]

### 2.2 Visits suspended

On 24 March 2020 all visits to prisons were suspended. People can stay in touch with prisoners by using the Prison Voicemail Service, the email a prisoner service and by writing letters. HM Prison and Probation Service said prisons across the estate would receive 900 secure phone handsets as part of plans to maintain family contact. [18] Prisons are providing extra phone credit to prisoners. Secure video calls are also being provided in some prisons and young offender institutions.[19]

A gov.uk page Coronavirus (COVID-19) and prisons provides guidance for families and friends of those in prison.

### 2.3 Temporary prison accommodation

The Ministry of Justice said in early April it was "working to identify publicly owned sites that could be used to house temporary prison accommodation to ease pressure on the permanent estate, further separate prisoners and

reduce the spread of the virus".[20]

The Ministry announced on 9 April that work to install 500 temporary, single occupancy cells within the existing, secure, prison estate had begun.[21] On 29 April the Ministry announced that the recently closed Medway Secure Training Centre, would be temporarily reopened as an annex to nearby HMP Rochester, housing up to 70 category D adult prisoners.[22]

### 2.4 Early release for some prisoners

**Pregnant prisoners and women in prison with their children**

On 31 March 2020 the Government announced that pregnant women and prisoners with their children in Mother and Baby Units would be temporarily released from prison where they were assessed not to pose a high risk of harm to the public.[23] As at 12 May 2020, 21 pregnant women had been released.[24]

On 24 April 2020 the Ministry of Justice published the criteria for potential compassionate temporary release, which could include prisoners who are pregnant.

### Low risk offenders within two months of release date

On 4 April 2020 the Government announced that selected risk-assessed prisoners who are within two months of their release date would be temporarily released.[25] A press release said:

• Selected low-risk offenders, within weeks of their release dates, will be electronically tagged and temporarily released on licence in stages

• Offenders can be recalled at the first sign of concern

• Violent and sexual offenders and those of security concern will not be considered

The Government estimated that up to 4000 prisoners would be eligible for the scheme.

### Amendments to the Prison and Young Offender Institution Rules

A statutory instrument was laid on 6 April 2020 amending the Prison and Young Offender Institution Rules to allow for early release due to the Coronavirus: The Prison and Young Offender Institution (Coronavirus) (Amendment) Rules 2020.

It authorises the Secretary of State to make a direction describing specified prisoners, or classes of prisoners and to subsequently release those prisoners on coronavirus restricted temporary release. The Secretary of State's direction may be made by reference to whatever matters are deemed appropriate. This could include, but is not restricted to, named prisons, named prisoners, or a group of prisoners within a specified description.

The new rules specify which prisoners may be released:
• those serving a standard determinate sentence, with an automatic release date and no Parole Board involvement; and,
• those committed to custody in default of payment of a sum adjudged to be paid by a conviction, or for contempt of court.[26]

Those whose initial release is subject to Parole Board discretion must not be released. The following are therefore excluded:
• those serving indeterminate sentences, extended sentences or sentences for offenders of particular concern; and,
• offenders serving sentences for terrorist and terrorist related offences' Other prisoners excluded from release under the scheme are:
• those excluded from Release on Temporary Licence;
• those committed to custody for trial or remanded by the courts;
• those who have committed offences whilst at large following temporary release;
• those who are being removed from the United Kingdom and who have exhausted their "in-country" rights of appeal against removal;
• those who will be subject to the notification requirements of Part 2 of the Sexual Offences Act 2003 ("registered sex offenders") and
• prisoners whose security classification is Category A (males) or Restricted (females and young adults).

A prisoner released under this scheme may be recalled at any time, whether or not any conditions of release have been breached.

A further statutory instrument was laid to provide that prisoners released under the new scheme may be accommodated in Approved Premises.[27] An Explanatory Memorandum has been published. These instruments came into force on 7 April 2020.[28]

On 24 April 2020 the Ministry of Justice published an overview of the eligibility criteria and the process for offenders to be released under the scheme, which it has called "End of Custody Temporary Release".

**Initial responses**

The measures for temporary early release were welcomed, including by the Prison Reform Trust and the Howard League for Penal Reform. They had written a joint letter to the Justice Secretary on 1 April 2020 stating that decisive action to release a substantial number of prisoners in England and Wales was required "in order to prevent loss of life on an unprecedented scale".

Some raised questions and concerns about the Government's plans. There was concern about whether there is sufficient suitable accommodation for those being released. The

Prison Governors Association (PGA) questioned whether it was necessary to tag all prisoners being released early under this scheme and whether there was sufficient capacity to do so:

The decision to tag all early releases seems excessive, when at the normal release date this would not happen. We believe that currently tagging capacity is only around 2,000 and this decision will build in delay when we need to move at pace to make a difference.[29]

The Justice Secretary responded to the question of the necessity of tagging those released early saying that tagging gave the public the reassurance they naturally looked for when the exceptional step of releasing prisoners on temporary licence was taken. On capacity he was confident of the ability to scale up tagging and said the Ministry of Justice was working with providers.[30]

The PGA stated that the scheme would not result in enough prisoners being released to sufficiently ease overcrowding. The PGA urged the Government to "be braver and make significant reductions". The PGA said the 4,000 figure was not achievable given the strict criteria set out and estimated that 2,000 would be released. It said this was nowhere near enough to free up the spaces in jails necessary. The PGA stated that official advice said 15,000 prisoners would have to be released to safeguard other inmates and prison staff.

Jo Farrar, Chief Executive of HM Prisons and Probation Service acknowledged this concern when she appeared before the Justice Committee on 7 April 2020. She said that the release of up to 4,000 prisoners was not the only plan in place. She said there would be new accommodation in some prisons from the next week to provide enhanced facilities for vulnerable people, with better health care provision and more isolation and shielding. She said the strategy was a mixed plan of release, extra accommodation and more staffing.[31]

Jo Farrar said that between 10,000 and 15,000 prisoners would have to be released to achieve single cell occupancy, but that PHE advice was that it was best not to send prisoners between prisons to achieve single cell accommodation.

The Justice Secretary, Robert Buckland, said that he was seeking in some cases to accelerate release with suitable licence conditions, accommodation and other provision, in order to speed up efforts within the prison estate to separate as many people as possible. He said he was exercising powers such as compassionate release for those with life threatening illness or medical reasons for some prisoners who were vulnerable.

## Temporary suspension

The end of custody temporary release scheme was temporarily suspended on 16 April before being restarted a few days later. The suspension was a response to 6 prisoners being released by mistake as a result, the Ministry of Justice said, of an administrative error. The prisoners who were mistakenly released all returned to prison.[32]

## Concern about delay and numbers released

Alarm has been growing about the delay in releasing prisoners and the low numbers released. On 27 April the Justice Secretary said he admitted progress had been careful and slow. He said 33 prisoners had been released altogether, including pregnant women.[33]

On 12 May the Prisons Minister, Lucy Frazer, told the Justice Committee that 81 prisoners had been released early during lockdown. Of these 81 prisoners, 55 were released on the temporary release scheme, 21 were pregnant women and 5 were released on compassionate grounds.

The Howard League for Penal Reform and the Prison Reform Trust wrote to the Justice Secretary on 17 April stating that they were proposing to make an application for judicial review of the Government's response to coronavirus in prisons.[35] Following a response from the Government on 28 April, the charities decided that the information provided meant that it would not, at that time, be necessary for them to proceed to a judicial review.[36]

The Government's letter stated that as of 28 April 2020 a further 200 people in prison had been approved for temporary release under the scheme and a further 300 prisoners were being considered with further information being awaited before a final decision could be made. The charities have published the information provided to them by the Government and stated that they will continue to monitor the situation closely.[37]

Both charities continue to call for further releases which they say are needed to create the space to "manage the transition towards active regimes, rather than simply warehousing people".[38]

## Support for released prisoners

The Justice Secretary said he was making sure accommodation was ready for those released and was working with the Department for Work and Pensions on universal credit provision, which was not previously available for those on temporary licence.[39] He said people were being sent out with £80 extra allowance to help them.

### 2.5 Testing

Prison staff have access to testing. The Justice Secretary said on 27 April 2020 that prison staff

had been made a priority by the Secretary of State for Health and Social Care. He said he hoped testing would be extended to prisoners too, once capacity allowed.[40]

### 2.6 Changes to inspections

HM Inspectorate of Prisons (HMIP) has announced "an adapted approach" to prison inspections, involving "short scrutiny visits – of one-day duration, involving two or three inspectors". They said:

Inspectors will focus on issues which are essential to the safety, care and basic rights of those detained in the current circumstances. These include: healthcare, nutrition and hygiene; contact with families, friends and the outside world; legal rights; use of time and the need for meaningful human contact; support for those at risk of selfharm and suicide; and support and risk management for those being released.[41]

HMIP has published an Alternative approach to scrutiny during the COVID-19 pandemic.

Reports on the short scrutiny visits undertaken are being published:

• Report on visits to young offender institutions holding children, 7 May 2020

• Report on visits to local prisons, 18 May 2020.

## 3. Calls for further action

### 3.1 Reducing flow of people into prisons

There have been calls to reduce the number of people being sent or returned to prison. The Prison Reform Trust has said that alongside releases, it is vital that "the flow of people into prisons is also drastically reduced".[42]

The Centre for Crime and Justice Studies notes that governments in other countries have opted to postpone or suspend new prison sentences for some, or in some jurisdictions, all of those sentenced to immediate custody.[43]

## Recalls to prison

Frances Crook, CEO of the Howard League for Penal Reform, has said guidance on avoiding unnecessary recalls should be strengthened.[44] The Prison Reform Trust has said people should not be recalled to prison "in all but the most dangerous of circumstances".

## Short sentences

David Gauke, the former Justice Secretary, has called for a suspension on the use of short prison sentences. The Guardian reported:

"The advantage of not sending people inside for short sentences is that it reduces the churn," Gauke said. "That is really important. There is a lot of churn in prisons, with people coming in and out. That creates a risk.[45]

Frances Crook has said the Government should

send a message to judges and magistrates to consider avoiding short sentences, particularly for breaches, time in lieu for nonpayment of fines and for non-violent and non-sexual offences.[46]

The thinktank Reform has called for the use of short sentences to be suspended. It proposes preventing sentencers from passing a sentence of six months or less, with exemptions for violent and sexual offenders.[47]

The Justice Secretary told the Justice Committee on 7 April 2020 that it was tempting to use the crisis as a pretext to change policy on sentencing. He said he was not persuaded that the short sentence option should be abolished. He said work on ensuring that community alternatives were as meaningful as possible would be done through a sentencing white paper and bill this year.[48]

### Remand

Frances Crook has said the Government should send a message to judges and magistrates that any decision to remand to custody should be subject to anxious scrutiny in light of the virus.[49]

### Children

The Howard League for Penal Reform highlights the difficulties for children in custody caused by the severely restricted regimes. Their briefing states that, were the severely restricted regimes to continue in the long term, children's rights would be contravened:

A continuation for up to a year of the severely restricted regimes that have been in place in child prisons since the end of March contravene children's rights under the UN Convention on the Rights of the Child and they are simply untenable long-term.[50]

The Howard League argues that children should not be detained in such severely restricted conditions:

Unless and until arrangements are made to ensure children are guaranteed humane conditions in custody, they should not be detained, either on remand or under sentence.

### 3.2 Home Detention Curfew

Currently Home Detention Curfew (HDC) enables eligible prisoners serving between 12 weeks and just less than 4 years to be released up to 135 days before the half-way point in their sentence, subject to an electronically monitored curfew. The prisoner must have served at least a quarter of the sentence, and a minimum of 28 days.[51]

There have been calls for the use of HDC to be reviewed further. The think tank Reform argues that:

Government should consider using emergency legislation to transfer all prisoners currently serving a sentence of less than six months into the HDC population.[52]

The Government had already planned to increase the amount of time eligible prisoners can spend on HDC from four and a half to six months. A Statutory Instrument was laid to implement this change in July 2019 and then withdrawn prior to the 2019 election.[53] A further statutory instrument was laid in March 2020.[54] It was due to come before the House on 12 May 2020 but did not. Prisons Minister, Lucy Frazer, was asked on 12 May why the plans had been "pushed back or dropped".

She told the Justice Committee:

HDC is already in operation. It is an effective scheme that works well and is part of the toolkit we have. We are committed to the rehabilitation that it offers, but at the moment we are concentrating on dealing with covid in our prisons. The capacity issue has significantly changed since that instrument was laid.[55]

1 Justice Committee, Oral Evidence, The Work of the Lord Chancellor, HC 225, 24 March 2020

2 Bob Neill, We must help our prisons in the fight against coronavirus, The House, 19 March 2020

3 Release inmates or face jail pandemic, say prison governors, Guardian, 25 March 2020

4 See Health and Social Care Committee, Prison health, 1 November 2018

5 Library briefing, UK Prison Population Statistics, July 2019

6 For further detail see the Library briefing, The Prison Estate, December 2019 and the National Audit Office report Improving the Prison Estate, February 2020. Prison population figures which can be used to estimate crowding are released monthly, with the latest as of 8 April 2020 being those for February 2020

7 HC Deb 27 April 2020 c93

8 Gov.uk, Update on COVID-19 in prisons, 28 April 2020

9 PQ42884, 14 May 2020

10 Dr Éamonn O'Moore, Briefing paper- interim assessment of impact of various population management strategies in prisons in response to COVID-19 pandemic in England, 24 April 2020

11 Prisons: Coronavirus: Written question – 30086, 19 March 2020

12 Release inmates or face jail pandemic, say prison governors, Guardian, 25 March 2020

13 Justice Committee, Summarised note of meeting with the Lord Chancellor, 7 April 2020

14 Gov.uk, Coronavirus (COVID-19) and prisons

15 HM Inspectorate of Prisons, press release, Local men's prisons during COVID-19 – communications key to prisoner acceptance of severe restrictions, 18 May 2020

16 The Prison and Young Offender Institution (Coronavirus) (Amendment) (No.2) Rules 2020

17 HM Inspectorate of Prisons, press release, Local men's prisons during COVID-19 – communications

key to prisoner acceptance of severe restrictions, 18 May 2020

18 Gov.uk, press release, Prison visits cancelled, 24 March 2020

19 Gov.uk, press release, Secure video calls to help prisoners maintain family ties, 15 May 2020

20 Gov.uk, press release, Measures announced to protect NHS from coronavirus risk in prisons, 4 April 2020

21 Gov.uk, press release, Prison estate expanded to protect NHS from coronavirus risk, 9 April 2020

22 Gov.uk, press release, Further expansion of prison estate to protect NHS, 29 April 2020

23 Gov.uk, press release, Pregnant prisoners to be temporarily released from custody, 31 March 2020

24 Justice Committee, Oral evidence: Ageing prison population, 12 May 2020, Q144

25 Gov.uk, press release, Measures announced to protect NHS from coronavirus risk in prisons, 4 April 2020

26 The new rules make the same provision for young offenders with the addition that those serving a Detention and Training Order may also be released

27 The Offender Management Act 2007 (Coronavirus) (Approved Premises) (Amendment) Regulations 2020

28 The Explanatory Notes note that these instruments both breach the 21 day rule for laying in Parliament because they are emergency legislation, see para 3.1

29 Prison Governors Association, press release, Early Release of Prisoners Announcement, 4 April 2020

30 Justice Committee, Summarised note of meeting with the Lord Chancellor, 7 April 2020

31 Justice Committee, Summarised note of meeting with the Lord Chancellor, 7 April 2020

32 UK coronavirus prison plan on hold after six inmates freed in error, Guardian. 18 April 2020

33 HC Deb 27 April 2020 c92

34 Justice Committee, Oral evidence: Ageing prison population, 12 May 2020, Q144

35 Prison Reform Trust, press release, Judicial Review: PRT and Howard League issue government with letter before action, 17 April 2020

36 Prison Reform Trust, press release, Government responds to PRT and Howard League letter before action, 29 April 2020

37 Prison Reform Trust, press release, PRT and Howard League publish government Covid-19 documents and call for further urgent action, 6 May 2020

38 Prison Reform Trust and Howard League for Penal Reform, Letter to Robert Buckland: Covid19 and prisons: the next phase, 6 May 2020

39 See: The Social Security (Coronavirus) (Prisoners) Regulations 2020

40 HC Deb 27 April 2020 c92. Further detail was given in a letter from the Prisons Minister to the Justice Committee on 4 May 2020.

41 HM Inspectorate of Prisons, COVID-19 update, 8 April 2020

42 Prison Reform Trust, Early release of prisoners, 25 March 2020

43 Centre for Crime and Justice Studies, Helen Mills, Prison sentencing needs to be part of the 'new normal', 11 May 2020

44 Howard League for Penal Reform, Frances Crook's blog, Coronavirus in prison: Measures that could be considered, 18 March 2020

45 Prisons 'could see 800 deaths' from coronavirus without protective measures, Guardian, 21 March 2020

46 Howard League for Penal Reform, Frances Crook's blog, Coronavirus in prison: Measures that could be considered, 18 March 2020

47 Reform, Reducing the prison population: Extending Home Detention Curfew and scrapping short sentences, 20 March 2020

48 Justice Committee, Summarised note of meeting with the Lord Chancellor, 7 April 2020

49 Howard League for Penal Reform, Frances Crook's blog, Coronavirus in prison: Measures that could be considered, 18 March 2020

50 Howard League for Penal Reform, Children in prison during the Covid-19 pandemic: A briefing from the Howard League for Penal Reform, May 2020

51 HM Prison and Probation Service. Home Detention Curfew (HDC) Policy Framework, 28 March 2019

52 Reform, Reducing the prison population: Extending Home Detention Curfew and scrapping short sentences, 20 March 2020

53 The Criminal Justice Act 2003 (Early Release on Licence) Order 2019

54 The Criminal Justice Act 2003 (Early Release on Licence) Order 2020

55 Justice Committee, Oral evidence: Ageing prison population, 12 May 2020, Q145

### Corporate criminal liability

5 May 2021

**Summary**

Corporates in themselves can't think or act – it's their members, employees or directors that do so. But they generally are legal persons, so can commit crimes.

As crime is devolved in Scotland and Northern Ireland, this briefing focuses on England and Wales. In England and Wales there are three ways a corporate can be prosecuted for a criminal offence committed by those acting on its behalf:

1 Where Parliament has created a specific criminal offence for corporates, such as under the Bribery Act 2010 or the Criminal Finances Act 2017;

2 Through vicarious liability, which is generally used for regulatory offences that don't require proof of mental fault; and

3 Through the identification doctrine, when someone who can be said to be the "directing mind and will" of a corporate commits the offence. Successfully prosecuting large corporates in particular has been challenging, leading to concern that the UK is falling behind

internationally in tackling corporate crime. The identification doctrine has been interpreted narrowly by the courts, as shown in the recent Barclays case, and vicarious liability is limited in its scope. As a result there has been pressure from politicians and campaign groups to expand the first option - for Parliament to intervene and reform corporate criminal liability.

In its response to a Call for Evidence on this issue in November 2020, the Government said it had not identified a clear consensus on the best path for reform, and has asked the Law Commission to undertake a review, that will include examining whether the identification doctrine is fit for purpose. The Law Commission expects to report back with an Options Paper in late 2021.

In the meantime, there has been continued pressure on Government from within Parliament to move more rapidly, most recently through unsuccessful amendments tabled during the passage of the Financial Services Act 2021.

For wider information about economic crime in the UK, see our briefing Economic crime in the UK: a multi-billion pound problem.

## 1. What is corporate criminal liability?
### What is a crime?
Defining "crime" is hard, but at its heart a criminal offence is an act punishable by the State. It is tried in the criminal courts and the punishment imposed for committing it might include imprisonment and fines. Sometimes, in addition to or instead of the power to bring criminal prosecutions, regulators – like the Financial Conduct Authority – are granted powers to impose punishments like fines, but these aren't crimes – they are regulatory penalties. The process for imposing them differs from criminal offences.

As an example, section 146 of the Policing and Crime Act 2017 empowers the Office of Financial Sanctions Implementation (OFSI), a department within the Treasury, to impose monetary penalties for breaches of financial sanctions. To impose the penalty OFSI doesn't need to prove a breach to the criminal standard of being "sure that the defendant is guilty"[1] – it needs to prove it to the civil standard of "balance of probabilities" (i.e. more likely than not).[2]

### What is a corporate?
When we talk about "corporates", we usually mean companies. But the definitions used in law are wider than this. For example, the corporate criminal offence of failure to prevent bribery under section 7 of the Bribery Act 2010 applies to a "relevant commercial organisation" which includes:

• bodies incorporated in the UK;

• those incorporated outside the UK that carry on business in the UK; and

• partnerships (which by their nature are not incorporated).

## 2. When can a corporate be criminally liable?
Corporates in themselves obviously can't think or act – it's their members, employees or directors that do so. But there are three ways a corporate can be prosecuted for a criminal offence committed by those acting on its behalf:

*1. Parliament creates a specific criminal offence for corporates*

Sometimes Parliament passes a law creating a criminal offence specifically intended for corporates. One example is corporate manslaughter,[3] a criminal offence applying to organisations whose activities are managed in a way that breaches duties it owes (for example to its employees) and causes a person's death. Since it's of course not possible to imprison a corporate, the punishment for committing these offences would typically be a fine. Separately, there is also the reputational damage caused to a company for being found to have committed a crime.

Other examples include offences under the Bribery Act 2010 and the Criminal Finances Act 2017, discussed further below.

*2. Vicarious liability*

Vicarious means "experienced as a result of watching, listening to, or reading about the activities of other people, rather than by doing the activities yourself". In some cases, even though a criminal offence might not specifically be made for companies, the law considers it appropriate for a corporate to be held vicariously liable for criminal acts done by its employees or agents. A court might consider, looking at the language and purpose of a law, that it is appropriate for employers to take criminal responsibility for offences committed by its employees.[4] So for example an employer that owns shops can be held vicariously criminally liable if one of its employees sells lottery tickets to an underage person.[5]

In theory vicarious criminal liability is not based on fault – the corporate is found to be liable because it is appropriate for it to take responsibility, not because it has done anything wrong. That is why it is usually found in "strict liability" areas of the criminal law like environmental and consumer protection offences, which often don't require the person who committed the offence to be at fault – it is enough that the act was done.

Using the lottery example above, an employer can be held vicariously liable for their employee selling tickets to an underage person even if they weren't aware that the sale had happened, and even if the employee who sold the ticket didn't know they were selling the ticket to an underage person. The idea in such cases is not necessarily to punish people who have done something wrong but to "encourage greater vigilance in preventing the commission of the prohibited act".[6]

Vicarious liability is a narrow concept since it is used for regulatory offences, and so would not for example currently be used for economic crimes like fraud, which need proof of being at fault. For a crime like fraud the only current way of prosecuting a corporate is through the identification doctrine.

### 3. The identification doctrine

This is when someone who is the "directing mind and will" or "an embodiment" of a corporate commits the criminal offence.[7] The idea is that a person committed the offence in circumstances where it would be a fiction to try and distinguish between them and the company. It applies to all criminal offences which can be punishable by a fine (as a company clearly cannot be imprisoned) and which can sensibly be said to be committed by someone within the scope of their authority.[8] It might include for example fraud committed by the members of the board of a company.

It's unclear how senior someone must be within a company to be "identified" with it. By requiring that only the most senior persons can be the "directing mind and will" of a company, it's arguable that large companies are let off the hook, since many key decisions will be decentralised away from the most senior management.

### The Barclays case and the identification doctrine

The recent high-profile Barclays case shows the limits of the identification doctrine. The case is from 2018 but the judgements were only released in 2020 after reporting restrictions were removed. This was the only prosecution of a bank to emerge from the 2007/08 financial crisis.[9] In the Barclays case, senior executives of Barclays, including the Chief Executive (CEO) and Finance Director (CFO), attracted funds from Qatari investors to avoid having to be bailed out by the UK Government.

The Serious Fraud Office (SFO) alleged that the true commissions (fees) paid to the Qatari investors were far higher than had been publicly announced – and that the Barclays executives deliberately hid this to make their position seem stronger than it was, and to avoid having to pay similarly high commissions to other investors. The SFO argued that the alleged criminal dishonesty of the senior executives could be identified with the company, and prosecuted

Barclays for conspiracy to commit fraud alongside the more technical offence of unlawful financial assistance.

However, the SFO's attempt failed in both the Crown Court and the High Court (which was effectively acting as an appeal court to the Crown Court decision). Both courts rejected the view that the senior executives could be the "directing mind and will" of Barclays, because although they occupied senior roles, they did not have the authority of the company to conclude the relevant agreements. The powers which they exercised had been entrusted to the board of directors, or the Barclays Board Finance Committee (BFC). The judge sitting in the High Court (Lord Justice Davis) concluded that since they did not have ""full discretion" to act independently and they were responsible to another person [viz the BFC] for the manner in which they discharged their duties…they could not be regarded as the directing mind and will for the purpose of performing the functions in question".[10] He also questioned the justification for prosecuting Barclays:

In the present case, as I gather, Barclays is currently the subject of a regulatory investigation (albeit stayed, pending the criminal proceedings). It has also, I gather, been served with civil proceedings for financial redress by aggrieved parties claiming to have suffered loss as a result of what has occurred. Yet further, the individuals within Barclays itself said to have been responsible for what has happened are, as I have recorded, the subject of ongoing criminal prosecution. So why prosecute Barclays itself (the more so perhaps when, if there were a conviction, the resultant, presumably heavy, fine would in practice be borne by the innocent shareholders)? The answer I was given was that it was to promote deterrence and good corporate governance.

This, however, leads to another consideration. It is always open to Parliament to draft statutory offences with the position of corporations in mind. […][11]

The judge in the Barclays case therefore suggested keeping the identification doctrine narrow in its scope, at least partly on the basis that if Parliament wanted corporates to be prosecuted more easily it could do so by creating a new corporate criminal offence.

### 3. Recent reforms

Bribery Act 2010 Concern that the existing law on corporate liability for economic crime (essentially, the identification principle) was insufficient to tackle bribery led to the passing of the Bribery Act 2010, which obtained Royal Assent shortly before the 2010 general election.[12] Section 7 of the Bribery Act 2010 introduced a new corporate offence of failure to prevent bribery. It applies where someone associated with the organisation bribes someone. It is an offence of "strict liability", which applies even if the organisation itself wasn't aware of the bribery that happened. The company has a defence if it can show that it had in place adequate procedures to prevent bribery.

The first prosecution under section 7 took place in 2016, relating to a UK-based company which failed to prevent bribes paid by its subsidiary in the United Arab Emirates. The offender was ordered to pay over £2m.

### Deferred Prosecution Agreements

The Crime and Courts Act 2013 then created Deferred Prosecution Agreements (DPAs), which had been available in the United States for some time.

DPAs were partly a response to difficulties involved in the prosecution of companies as a result of the high threshold needed under the "identification" principle.[13] They are a tool that allow corporates charged with certain offences relating to fraud and dishonesty to avoid prosecution. Instead, the corporate will enter into an agreement with prosecutors, under the supervision of a judge, to do certain things like paying a financial penalty, and co-operating relating to the future prosecution of individuals for the offence. When deciding whether to offer a DPA rather than to prosecute, prosecutors will take a number of factors into account including the seriousness of the offence and the level of co-operation it has received from the company.[14] So long as the corporate abides by the DPA the matter will then be concluded without prosecution.[15] The first DPA was in 2015, concerning section 7 of the Bribery Act 2010, involving payments made to the Government of Tanzania, and they have been used a number of times since.[16]

### Criminal Finances Act 2017

At the March 2015 Budget the Government announced that it would introduce a new corporate offence relating to the facilitation of tax evasion, again partly in response to concerns about the shortcomings of the "identification" principle.[17] The result was the Criminal Finances Act 2017, which represents the most recent reforms in this area.

Sections 44 and 45 established the corporate criminal offences of failing to prevent the facilitation of tax evasion (both in the UK and overseas). It might apply for example to a company whose employee agreed with a supplier that it could issue false invoices to the company to evade tax. These offences were also added to the list of offences that could be dealt with by DPA.[18]

Modelled on section 7 of the Bribery Act 2010, it imposes criminal liability on organisations that fail to prevent persons associated with them from facilitating tax evasion. A defence will be available for corporates who show they had reasonable procedures in place, or that it was reasonable to expect them to have had procedures in place.

As of 13th October 2020 there were 13 live investigations relating to these offences but no charges or prosecutions.[19]

## 4. The future of corporate criminal liability

### Recent Government action

In December 2014 the Government published its Anti-Corruption Plan, that tasked the Ministry of Justice with examining the case for a new offence of corporate failure to prevent economic crime.[20] In May 2016, Prime Minister Cameron announced a consultation to consider the extension of the corporate liability "failure to prevent" model to a wider range of economic crimes such as fraud and money laundering.[21] The Ministry of Justice Call for Evidence in this area was published in January 2017, following David Cameron's announcement, while the then-Criminal Finances Bill was going through Parliament.

It asked whether it was worth building on the corporate criminal offences created relating to bribery and tax evasion, in response to corporate wrongdoing that had occurred (particularly) in the financial services sector. It explained the shortcomings in the "identification" principle and summarised the problem faced by prosecutors:

Tom Hayes, the Libor-fixer employed by UBS, was held to account in a criminal court in England but UBS, a large multi-national bank could not be prosecuted in the UK. The SFO [Serious Fraud Office] did not have sufficient admissible evidence that a person who was identified as a directing mind was party to Hayes's conduct and therefore could not conclude that there was a realistic prospect of conviction.[22]

It's worth noting that regulatory sanctions are sometimes available where criminal ones are not, so whereas UBS could not be prosecuted for a crime relating to LIBOR manipulation, the Financial Conduct Authority did impose a £160 million fine on UBS.[23]

### Call for Evidence: options for reform

In the Call for Evidence, the Ministry of Justice put forward a number of (not mutually exclusive) options for expanding corporate criminal liability to areas other than bribery and tax evasion (like fraud and money laundering):

1 Legislating to amend the "identification"

principle so that it was more able to hold large companies to account;

2 Create a new "strict liability" offence based on the principle of vicarious liability. The offence would therefore apply to employees/agents of the company but the company could be prosecuted because of vicarious liability;

3 Create a new "strict liability" offence which was not based on vicarious liability, and therefore would be specifically targeted at corporates. To benefit from a defence that the corporate had adequate procedures in place, the burden of proof would be on the defence (the corporate). Out of the options, this is most similar to the section 7 of the Bribery Act 2010 offence;

4 Option 3 above but require the prosecution to prove that the company had not taken adequate steps to prevent the unlawful conduct, rather than the defence; or

5 Leave the criminal law as it is but look at reforming the regulatory regime (for example FCA powers).

### Call for Evidence: response

The response to the Call for Evidence was published in November 2020. The response concluded that:

There was no clear consensus from respondents on what corporate liability offence should be created if the identification doctrine was replaced. Equally, some responses disclosed significant opposition to reform given the potential adverse impact of new criminal liability on growth and competition. Others questioned whether there was a need for further criminal sanctions at all in the already heavily regulated financial services sector. In general, however, although a range of divergent and often conflicting views were expressed, there was no new or significantly persuasive evidence submitted by the CfE respondents to support the case for a change to the law.[24]

Some key points emerging from the response to the Call for Evidence (which obtained 62 responses) are that:

• A slim majority of respondents did not believe the existing framework provides sufficient deterrent;

• None of the five options mentioned above obtained majority support from respondents;

• 34.5% of respondents felt that reform of the law might adversely impact UK competitiveness and/or growth;

• 73.6% felt that there were examples of corporate criminal conduct where a purely regulatory response would not be appropriate (and therefore criminal sanctions should be available);

• A slim majority said there was a case for introducing a corporate failure to prevent

economic crime offence along the lines of section 7 of the Bribery Act 2010; and

• Two-thirds felt that adopting expanded "failure to prevent" offences would improve corporate conduct.

The response therefore considered the evidence received "inconclusive". Recent reforms in this area have also not yet been fully implemented, allowing their outcomes to be assessed, including:

a. the failure to prevent offences relating to tax evasion introduced under the Criminal Finances Act 2017 described above;

b. the introduction of the Senior Managers & Certification Regime (a regulatory regime replacing the existing "approved persons regime". It, for example, requires senior managers of financial services firms to be approved by the regulators); and

c. the Money Laundering, Terrorist Financing and Transfer of Funds (Information on the Payer) Regulations 2017 (which introduced requirements on financial institutions and "gatekeepers" to the financial system such as tax advisers, to help prevent money laundering and terrorist financing. Failure to comply with these obligations is a criminal offence),

(for more information on these recent reforms, see paragraphs 67 to 70 of the Response to the Call for Evidence). Therefore, the Government felt that more time was needed to allow these reforms to show their impact and then properly assess what is needed.

### Law Commission review

In the meantime, the Government has commissioned an "expert review" of the identification principle from the Law Commission (which last properly considered the issue in 2010), which is estimated to take around 12 to 15 months. Once the Law Commission's work has concluded, expected to be in late 2021, the Government will evaluate it alongside the impact of the recent reforms it has made to "inform" any future decision in this area.[25]

### 5. Financial Services Act 2021: corporate crime amendments

During the passage of the Financial Services Act 2021 through the Houses of Commons and Lords, amendments were tabled seeking to introduce a new corporate criminal offence.

### House of Commons
*Second Reading*

During the Second Reading debate on 9 November 2020, backbench MP Kevin Hollinrake (Conservative, Thirsk and Malton) pressed for the introduction of a new corporate economic crime offence:

Another area that was mentioned in an earlier intervention was the Government's commitment to make the failure to prevent economic crime a corporate offence. It is great that they have said they will do that, and that will start with a Law Commission review to see how best it can be done. As the Law Commission rightly said, if we do not change the rules on that, the UK risks falling behind international standards, which I am sure we would not want. That is clearly something to bring forward, but it could be done more hastily in the Bill, with a framework added on later, which would expedite the process. That would make a huge difference.

The Serious Fraud Office has tried to take forward many cases—those involving Serco, Barclays and Olympus, for example—but it could not do that because it had to establish a directing mind principle for the people at the top of those organisations before it could proceed with the offence of corporate fraud. The proposed measure would make that much easier. It is great that the Government are willing to take it forward, but they could do so more quickly.[26]

*Committee Stage*

The issue was also raised during Committee Stage. In written evidence, campaign group Spotlight on Corruption wrote:

Spotlight on Corruption believes that there are several important reasons for the urgent introduction of a failure to prevent economic crime offence as outlined in this amendment. These reasons are:

· to promote strong corporate governance and deter wrongdoing in the financial sector after the UK leaves the EU (protection of market integrity);
· to create a level playing field for how large and small companies are held to account for economic crime, particularly in response to the burgeoning fraud crisis resulting from COVID-19 (fairness);
· to ensure that the UK does not fall behind international standards on prosecuting economic crime (equivalence); and
· to create a level playing field on how liability is attached to companies across different economic crimes within the UK (consistency).[27]

In oral evidence, Dr Susan Hawley from Spotlight on Corruption argued:

Just to explain the problem we think needs addressing, fundamentally at the moment, particularly after the judgment in the Barclays case, which was the only prosecution for financial crime following the last financial crisis, there is increasing legal commentary that large financial institutions are beyond the reach of prosecutors for certain economic crimes. Legal attempts to resolve this have failed—in fact, the Barclays judgment has now made it even more

difficult for prosecutors to prosecute large financial institutions—and only action by Parliament can change that.[28]

Asked whether he would support the introduction of a "failure to prevent economic crime" corporate criminal offence, Duncan Hames from campaign group Transparency International replied:

Yes, we would. That is separate to the discussions about the identification doctrine, on which, as I am sure you will be aware, the director of the Serious Fraud Office has frequently shared views and on which now the Law Commission has been invited to bring forward its own options for reform. These are complementary measures.

We now have a "failure to prevent" offence in relation to two areas of offending: one, the Bribery Act and, two, failure to prevent the facilitation of tax evasion. Applying a "failure to prevent" offence more widely, while still considering reform of the identification doctrine in regard to the substantive offence, would be entirely complementary, rather than the House having to consider doing one or the other.[29]

The Labour frontbench (Pat McFadden, Abena Oppong-Asare and Jeff Smith) subsequently tabled an amendment (New Clause 24)[30] that would create a new criminal offence for corporates who facilitate economic crime or fail to take steps to prevent economic crime by a person acting in its name (similar in its approach to Option 3 in the Ministry of Justice "Options for reform"). It would apply to fraud, false accounting and the main money laundering offences under the Proceeds of Crime Act 2002.

Mr McFadden said: What would creating an offence of failure to prevent economic crime do? It would create a level playing field between small and large companies; it would send out a strong signal about the kind of financial sector that we want as we come to the end of the transition period; and it would equalise how different kinds of economic crimes are treated, because such a liability—I stress that it would be a corporate liability—already exists when it comes to, for example, bribery or tax evasion. Why should the ignorance defence be available for some offences but not for bribery or tax evasion? The Treasury would never accept it if senior members of a company said, "Oh, we didn't know we were supposed to pay those taxes." That would not be a legitimate defence, and yet it can be used for some other kinds of wrongdoing.[31]

Economic Secretary to the Treasury John Glen responded that stronger evidence would be needed before a new offence could be supported: Before any broader new "failure to prevent"

1395

offence for economic crime is introduced, there needs to be strong evidence to support it. It will also be important that any new offence is designed rigorously, with specific consideration given to how it sits alongside associated criminal and regulatory regimes and to the potential impacts on business. The scope of who a new offence applies to must also be holistically worked through.

The Law Commission's work will take some time, but it is clear that we are zoning in on that aspect of the problem. In the light of that response, I ask the right hon. Gentleman to withdraw the new clause.[32]

Mr McFadden subsequently agreed to withdraw the amendment, though he said he suspected "the Minister might meet a very similar amendment later in proceedings on the Bill."[33]

*Report Stage*

Two amendments seeking to create new corporate crime criminal offences were tabled for Report Stage on 13 January 2021.

New Clause 4 was a cross-party amendment in the names of Dame Margaret Hodge and five other Members. It would create a new criminal offence for financial services firms (those authorised or registered with the Financial Conduct Authority) to facilitate economic crimes, or to fail to take steps to prevent economic crimes committed by people acting on their behalf (such as employees). New Clause 30 was similar in substance but was tabled by members of Labour's Socialist Campaign Group. The focus of these amendments on financial services is likely driven by the procedural requirement that amendments must be within the scope of the bill's subject matter.

Neither of these amendments were selected for a vote by the Speaker. Economic Secretary to the Treasury John Glen explained why the Government opposed them:

Before any broader new "failure to prevent" defence for economic crime is introduced, there needs to be strong evidence to support it, as there was when similar bribery and tax evasion offences introduced in 2010 and 2017 respectively took place. A new offence will also need to be designed rigorously, with specific consideration given to how it sits alongside associated criminal and regulatory regimes and to the potential impacts on business.

The proposed new offences in this amendment would lead to a discrepancy in treatment between FCA-regulated businesses and other businesses under criminal law. The 2017 call for evidence did not provide any evidence to suggest financial services businesses should be specifically targeted with a new offence. Indeed,

many of the examples provided related to businesses in other sectors.[34]

### House of Lords
*Second Reading*

At Second Reading in the House of Lords on 28 January 2021, Lords Hendy (Labour), Rooker (Labour), Garnier (Conservative) and Hodgson (Conservative), and Baronesses Bennett (Green) and Bowles (Liberal Democrat) all spoke in favour of a new corporate criminal offence.

For example, Lord Garnier, a former Solicitor-General, said:

Finally, we must reform the law relating to corporate criminal liability. The noble Lord, Lord Hendy, is right and I profoundly agree with him. I have been writing and speaking about the need to do this for years. The concept of the directing mind and will as the basis for corporate criminal liability, which the Americans abandoned before the First World War, worked for the small family businesses of the 19th century, but is now long outdated. Today, companies can operate in many different countries with national, regional and global boards and with hundreds of thousands of employees engaging in multi-jurisdictional trade in goods and services. Locating the directing mind and will of these vast conglomerates is difficult, if not impossible, and the current law does not reflect the reality of modern business life. It is an affront to common sense and justice. As in the United States, we need to introduce vicarious liability into our corporate criminal law.[35]

*Committee Stage*

Four corporate crime amendments were tabled at Lords Committee Stage. Amendments 81, 82 and 83 (in the name of Lord Garnier and three others) each sought to create a new corporate "failure to prevent" criminal offence. Amendment 84 (in the name of Baroness Bowles and three others) sought to create a new corporate offence of committing or facilitating financial crimes.

In support of her amendment, Baroness Bowles argued:

I know there is some reluctance in the Ministry of Justice, which sat on its hands for ages after its call for evidence on corporate liability, to which I made a submission, and then said there is no new evidence. That was really a bit rich, given that the call for evidence background document itself gave a good exposition of how bad matters are and of many of the reasons why evidence of failures in prosecutions is relatively scant. That is exactly why there is no new evidence—because prosecutors know they cannot succeed against large companies and give up.[36]

In rejecting these amendments, Lords Government Whip Baroness Penn responded:

I appreciate that this is a long-running issue, but before any broader, new "failure to prevent" or facilitation offence for economic crime is introduced, there needs to be strong evidence to support it. A new offence will also need to be designed rigorously with specific consideration given to how it sits alongside associated criminal and regulatory regimes and to the potential impact on business. Unlike with bribery and tax evasion, there are already extensive regimes, both criminal and regulatory, to hold both individuals and corporates to account for money laundering. Further, the "failure to prevent" offences introduced in respect of bribery and facilitation of tax evasion are both formulated to tackle very specific and precise circumstances. Wider economic crime offences present more complications. Fraud, for example, covers a much wider range of activity and business areas. The complexity of a broader economic crime offence is why the Government want to await the conclusions of the Law Commission's review.[37]

Ultimately, Amendments 81 to 84 were not pressed to a vote,[38] and no corporate criminal offence amendments were proposed at Report Stage. The Bill gained royal assent on 29 April 2021 and did not include a new corporate criminal offence.

## 6. Stakeholder views

The 62 responses to the Ministry of Justice Call for Evidence (which are summarised above) came from law firms, financial services firms, trade and industry bodies, civil society organisations (non-profit interest groups), police organisations, prosecutors, academics, individuals and Parliamentarians.[39]

The consultation response doesn't match up the organisations to the responses they provided, but it provides a useful understanding of the general sentiment.

*Treasury Select Committee*

In March 2019 a report published by the Treasury Select Committee (TSC), then chaired by Nicky Morgan, said that:

The Government's proposals on reforming the law on corporate liability around economic crime have stalled…Without reform in this area, multi-national firms appear beyond the scope of legislation designed to counter economic crime. That is manifestly unfair, and weakens the deterrent effect a more stringent corporate liability regime may bring.[40]

The TSC report examined in detail the views of different stakeholders:

In his evidence Mark Thompson [then interim director of the SFO] also provided a glimpse into the potential factors the Government may be considering around whether or not to legislate for these changes to the legislative framework:

"The Government continue to consider whether it is necessary. My understanding of the Foreign Office's position, for example, is that it was not necessary because the regulatory regime around senior persons in the City was sufficient to address a lot of this."

Colin Bell, of HSBC, also argued that the FCA's Senior Managers Regime effectively bound those in financial services:

"As an approved person under the senior managers regime, with accountability for financial crime risk within HSBC, I feel that accountability very keenly. I feel bound by that statement of responsibilities. I think my colleagues and peers feel the same way. There has been a sea change in the way that is tackled, and we feel it. We really do feel it."

However, in its evidence, the SFO argued that a regulatory response alone was not enough:

"Regulation has an important part to play, but it does not meet the challenge. Regulation only covers a limited section of corporate activity and cannot affect non-regulated sectors and the SFO has several investigations underway into non-regulated businesses that illustrate this point. Regulation also tends to focus on procedures and record keeping rather than on the end goals of preventing and punishing offending. In addition, a regulatory sanction does not carry the weight or impact of a criminal conviction or the terms of a DPA [Deferred Prosecution Agreement]"

The Solicitor General also appeared unsympathetic to any attempts by industry to forestall reform. He told us that:

"In any development of policy you are going to have debate, but in response to that I would say this. Companies and corporates have already brought in measures to deal with failing to prevent bribery and tax evasion and, if they have not, they ought to get on with it, because this is the law of the land. Frankly, if they brought in mechanisms and systems to deal with those particular aspects of criminality, it would not be a leap in the dark to extend them to economic crime more generally."[41]

The report went on to say:

When the Committee queried whether preparations for the UK's departure from the EU had hampered work in this area, the Solicitor General replied: "I have been rather busy on Brexit, as have my colleagues. Although some people think I have unbounded energy, I have to prioritise. This is a very important priority for me.[42]

The report also described the SFO's proposals for reform:

Having identified the problem with the UK's regime, the SFO argued for "two equally favoured and parallel options". It called for:

1. Replacing the identification doctrine with a new principle for the attribution of corporate liability. This would set out the circumstances in which a company would be liable for the substantive criminal offence. The SFO's proposal is that a company would be guilty of the substantive offence if a person associated with it commits that offence intending:

• To obtain or retain business for the company; •
To obtain or retain a business advantage for the company; or

• Otherwise to (financially) benefit the company. This solution would provide a principled basis on which all companies would be liable for all substantive offences.

2. The introduction of a new offence of failing to prevent economic crime. This solution aligns well to the provisions of section 7 Bribery Act 2010, as well as the new Criminal Finances Act offence of failure to prevent tax evasion, and promotes consistency across the wider economic crime landscape. Section 7 of the Bribery Act has been proven to be effective in its application. This would allow for a quicker and consistent solution to this urgent problem.[43]

The TSC is conducting an inquiry to "review what progress has been made in combatting economic crime" since its last inquiry. The new inquiry explicitly includes corporate liability for economic crime. A call for evidence closed on Friday 27 November 2020[44] and the first oral evidence session was held on 25 January 2021 in the presence of officials from the National Crime Agency, City of London Police, and Police Scotland. Labour MP Siobhain McDonagh asked the witnesses whether "creating corporate liability for economic crime" would "be a helpful deterrent to offences such as money laundering". Angela McLaren from City of London Police said it would, and Graeme Biggar from the National Crime Agency said there "would be value in introducing" a failure to prevent offence for fraud.[45]

*Media coverage*

The Financial Times reported on the day the Ministry of Justice's response to the consultation was published, 3 November 2020, criticism from stakeholder groups of the "slow pace" of reform.[46] Among the stakeholders quoted are:

• Susan Hawley, director at campaign group Spotlight on Corruption, who said there was "a real danger that this decision kicks reform into the long grass, and will result in corporate impunity for large banks and companies for several more years". Of course, the current law does not provide for literal corporate impunity, but it does set a high threshold for corporate prosecution of economic crime because of the "identification" doctrine;

• Barry Vitou, a partner at US law firm Greenberg Traurig, who welcomed the review sought from the Law Commission but said it was "long overdue", pointing out that the government had first issued a call for evidence in 2017; and

• David Green QC, who in 2013 (then director of the UK Serious Fraud Office), called for changes so that companies could be held to account for failing to prevent any kind of economic crime, not just bribery. With reference to the Barclays case mentioned above, David Green, now a consultant at law firm Slaughter and May, is quoted as criticising the identification doctrine, saying "It is almost impossible to find a controlling mind and prove that controlling mind is complicit in any criminality… The email chain tends to dry up at middle management level.[47]

Lisa Osofsky, current Director of the SFO, has said that the identification doctrine was a "standard from the 1800s when 'mom and pop' ran companies – that is not at all reflective of today's world".[48]

A former senior prosecutor was quoted the Financial Times in March 2020, referring to possible legal reform of the "identification doctrine":

You've got to ask how attractive this will be to Boris [Johnson] and his post-Brexit Britain…The prime minister is not going to want to be seen to be adding red tape to business right now. If they want to hold corporates accountable, they need to make this change, but will probably kick it into the long grass and give it to the Law Commission to consider…[49]

*Financial Action Task Force*

The Financial Action Task Force (FATF) sets international standards for countering money laundering and terrorist financing. It is an intergovernmental body set up in 1989 which now has 37 members (including the UK).[50] In its last analysis (Mutual Evaluation) of the UK's standards in 2018, it said:

Where legal persons are involved in offending, the UK will wind up shell or front companies and pursue prosecution of the natural persons or civil or regulatory actions. Complicit legal persons are investigated as part of the broader investigation, but rarely convicted. This is because the UK's ability to prosecute large legal persons for criminal ML [money laundering] offences under POCA and notable predicates such as fraud remains limited due to difficulties in proving criminal intent. Under the 'Identification Doctrine' established in UK case law, a criminal act can only be attributed to a legal person where the natural person committing the offence can be said to represent the "directing mind and will" of the legal person. In large companies with diffused decision-making responsibilities, proving this is extremely difficult, as was acknowledged by the NCA and the SFO. In response to this issue, the UK has made legislative changes to ease the intent requirements with respect to certain offences, including bribery and corruption and, with the enactment of the Criminal Finances Act 2017, tax evasion. The UK opened a call for evidence on making similar changes to corporate liability for economic crime offences in January 2017 and as at March 2018, was analysing the feedback.[51]

The FATF report was cited by Pat McFadden in making the case for a new corporate economic crime offence as part of the Committee Stage of the Financial Services Act 2021. He noted that "The lack of such an offence was also pointed out in the Financial Action Task Force 2018 UK evaluation, which pointed out the difficulties in proving criminal intent."[52]

## 7. International comparisons
### United States

Because of its wider treatment of the concept of vicarious liability, the United States is often used as a comparator. The TSC report summarises the position:

The United States provides an interesting comparator to the UK due to its differing framework for corporate liability. Naomi Hirst outlined the following advantages of the US system: "There is a debate to be had about what that offence looks like. It is worth considering that the DOJ [Department of Justice] in the United States have a definition of vicarious liability that they can use very easily, very successfully, and we are very far away from that. That is to the point where, from the outside, it might look like the UK is actually outsourcing some of our corporate prosecutions to other jurisdictions that can do this much easier than we can."

Mark Thompson, then Interim Director of the SFO, also noted the implications of this difference in the law between the US and the UK: "They have significant advantages, particularly in respect of dealing with companies and corporate entities because their system relies on vicarious liability. If an employee of a bank is involved in money laundering, the bank is pretty much liable. We do not have that here, which makes it more difficult for British regulators and prosecutors to take the same action that our American colleagues take."

Mr Thompson noted that "there are some corporate criminal fraud offences that could be prosecuted with a different regime".

The United States example was also explored by the Solicitor General:

"Nobody can deny that [the United States] is not anything other than a very vigorous free market economy, and yet its criminal rules on corporate liability are very tight indeed. They have a system of vicarious criminal liability, which means that the corporate is responsible for the acts of the individual, even if the corporate has taken steps to stop or prevent the individual from wrongdoing. That is a model we need to look at that very carefully."

However, the Solicitor General did note some potential drawbacks to the position taken by the US:

"In going down the path of enhanced corporate criminal liability, we must not take away from the fact that there will be cases of rogue individuals who behave in a way that a well-intentioned company did not intend or wish. It would be a false choice for us to make, when it comes to prosecution, between corporates and individuals. This is one area where we need to have our cake and eat it. [...] ] What draws me away from the American vicarious liability model is that it tends to focus very much on the corporate and not on the individual, in a way that the public would be concerned about."[53]

Expanding vicarious liability along the lines of the US model, so that it extends beyond "regulatory" offences, would be roughly equivalent to option 2 in the Ministry of Justice's Call for Evidence described above.

### Germany and the EU

Germany has for some time been considered an outlier in not providing for any form of corporate criminal liability[54], but that appears likely to change soon. In August 2020 law firm Pinsent Masons wrote:

Although there is no corporate criminal law in Germany yet, fines of up to €10m can be imposed on companies if managers commit criminal or administrative offences, including the failure to take compliance measures. Alternatively, a forfeiture order can be issued. [...]

The [German] Federal Ministry of Justice has recently published the draft Corporate Sanctions Act which would introduce corporate criminal liability in Germany, and make enforcement action against companies mandatory in cases of reasonable suspicion. The draft law aims to provide incentives for compliance measures and the investigation and disclosure of compliance violations and provides for monetary sanctions of up to 10% of the annual worldwide group turnover. [...]

It should be noted that contrary to other corporate sanction laws, such as the UK Bribery Act, the German draft Corporate Sanctions Act does not only apply to specific crimes like bribery and anti-money laundering, but to each and any illegal act that would comprise to a criminal offence in Germany or abroad, in that sense it is more similar to the UK's failure to prevent the facilitation of tax evasion offence which criminalises a corporate's failure to prevent any act that amounts to dishonest facilitation.[55]

The new law could come into force in Germany "in the course of 2021".[56]

The EU's Sixth Money Laundering Directive[57] required Member States to "take the necessary measures to ensure that legal persons can be held liable"[58] for money laundering crimes. The UK Government decided not to opt in on the basis that the "UK's domestic legislation is already largely compliant with the Directive's measures" and in fact "goes much further"[59] in some areas.

In oral evidence to the Financial Services Act 2021 Public Bill Committee, Susan Hawley from Spotlight on Corruption said:

Under the EU's sixth anti-money laundering directive, all states must have corporate criminal liability and must impose criminal and non-criminal sanctions that are proportionate and dissuasive. We are already seeing countries such as Germany taking really strong steps to implement that. It has a corporate sanctions Bill coming up, which has a clause that requires prosecutors to investigate suspicions of corporate crime. It is a very strong Bill. Before that, Germany was the outlier and had no proper corporate criminal liability. We see it in the Netherlands as well, where increasing levels of corporate fines are being imposed for money laundering, and there is a very strong corporate liability framework there as well. In Ireland, the Irish Law Commission has recommended changes to the law on corporate liability. We are seeing a raising of standards across the EU that the directive will bring in the context of money laundering.[60]

*Law Commission 2010 review*

The Law Commission's last review of this area (now slightly dated, from 2010) considered the models adopted in different countries. After explaining that some countries operated a "general liability" scheme (where corporate criminal liability used the same principles for all different types of crimes) and some adopted different models for different criminal offences, it said:

Most jurisdictions adopt a general liability scheme. Many have a generic – one size fits all –

model that applies to all types of offence. So for example the USA, Austria, Belgium, France, and South Africa apply the same model whatever the type of offence... Australia...and Canada on the other hand have a general liability scheme but apply different models according to the fault element of the offence...It is thus possible to develop a relatively simple scheme which caters for the full range of types of offences within it (as in Australia and Canada). This has the advantage that the jurisprudence in relation to corporate liability can develop independently of other principles of criminal liability.

England and Wales has a complex scheme combining both different liability models applying to types of offence together with some exempt offences to which specific rules apply. Examples of [these] are the stand-alone offence of corporate manslaughter and the Law Commission proposal in relation to bribery [which became section 7 of the Bribery Act 2010].[61]

*1 Crown Prosecution Service, The Code for Crown Prosecutors, 26 October 2018, para 4.7*

*2 See Lord Nicholls in the case of In re H (Minors) [1996] AC 563, para 73*

*3 Under section 1 of the Corporate Manslaughter and Corporate Homicide Act 2007*

*4 See for example the case of Mousell Brothers Ltd v London & North Western Railway Co [1917] 2 KB 836, 845*

*5 A criminal offence under the National Lottery etc. Act 1993*

*6 Harrow London Borough Council v Shah And Another [2000] 1 W.L.R 83, p88*

*7 See Tesco Supermarkets Ltd. v Nattrass [1972] AC 153*

*8 So would obviously not apply to a crime like rape, for example. See CPS, Corporate Prosecutions*

*9 Herbert Smith Freehills, No "directing mind and will" found in SFO prosecution of Barclays, 5 May 2020*

*10 SFO v Barclays [2018] EWHC 3055 (QB), paras 118 and 119*

*11 Ibid, paras 102 and 103*

*12 Law Society, Bribery Act 2010, 25 November 2019*

*13 Ministry of Justice, Consultation on a new enforcement tool to deal with economic crime committed by commercial organisations, May 2012, para 26*

*14 CPS, Deferred Prosecution Agreements Code of Practice*

*15 See Serious Fraud Office, Deferred Prosecution Agreements*

*16 Serious Fraud Office, About us, section of Deferred Prosecution Agreements*

*17 HMRC, Tackling tax evasion: legislation and guidance for a corporate offence of failure to prevent the criminal facilitation of tax evasion, April 2016, para 1.4*

*18 See para 26A of Schedule 13 to the Crime and Courts Act 2013*

19 Gov.uk, FOI release, Number of live Corporate Criminal Offences investigations, 21 October 2020
20 Gov.uk, UK anti-corruption plan, 18 December 2014
21 The Guardian, The fight against corruption begins with political will, David Cameron, 11 May 2016
22 Ministry of Justice, Corporate Liability for Economic Crime, Call for evidence, January 2017, p14
23 Ibid, p15, and see FCA, UBS fined £160 million for significant failings in relation to LIBOR and EURIBOR, published 19 December 2012
24 Ministry of Justice, Corporate Liability for Economic Crime, Call for Evidence: Government Response, 3 November 2020, para 15
25 Ibid, paras 73 to 75
26 HC Deb 9 November 2020, vol 683, col 677
27 Financial Services Act, Written Evidence submitted by Spotlight on Corruption, 19 November 2020
28 Official Report, Public Bill Committee, Financial Services Act, p80
29 Ibid, p99
30 Public Bill Committee Proceedings, Financial Services Act, Thursday 3 December 2020, p22
31 Ibid, p405
32 Ibid, p407
33 Ibid
34 HC Deb 13 January 2021, Vol 687
35 HL Deb 28 January 2021, vol 809, col 1857
36 HL Deb 3 March 2021, vol 810, col 399GC
37 Ibid, col 416GC
38 See HL Deb 8 March 2021, vol 810, col 559GC
39 Ministry of Justice, Corporate Liability for Economic Crime, Call for Evidence: Government Response, 3 November 2020, para 12
40 Treasury Committee, Economic Crime - Anti-money laundering supervision and sanctions implementations, 4 March 2019, para 28
41 Ibid, paras 191 to 193
42 Ibid, para 197
43 Ibid, para 188
44 See UK Parliament, Call for evidence, Economic crime
45 Treasury Committee, Oral Evidence: Economic crime, HC917, 25 January 2021, Q73 and 74
46 Financial Times, Campaigners criticise slow pace of reform to UK corporate crime law, 3 November 2020
47 Financial Times, Barclays: the legal fight over a company's 'controlling mind', 9 March 2020
48 Ibid
49 Ibid
50 Financial Action Task Force, FATF Members and Observers
51 Financial Action Task Force, United Kingdom Mutual Evaluation Report, December 2018, p71
52 Official Report, Public Bill Committee, Financial Services Act, p406
53 Treasury Committee, Economic Crime - Anti-money laundering supervision and sanctions implementations, 4 March 2019, paras 189 and 190
54 See the useful liability map produced by law firm Clifford Chance, dated April 2016
55 Pinsent Masons, Germany to strengthen criminal liability for acts committed in UK, 4 August 2020
56 Legal Business, Corporate criminal liability in Germany, sponsored briefing by Alexander Cappel (Norton Rose Fulbright), 30 April 2021
57 OJ L 284/22, 12 November 2018
58 See Article 7, para 1 of the Directive
59 Home Office and Ministry of Justice, Eighth Annual Report to Parliament on the Application of Protocols 19 and 21 to the Treaty on European Union (TEU) and the Treaty on the Functioning of the Union (TFEU) in Relation to EU Justice and Home Affairs (JHA) Matters (1 December 2016 – 30 November 2017), February 2018, p7

### Counter-Terrorism and Sentencing Bill 2019-21

Published Monday, 08 June, 2020

In the Queen's Speech in December 2019, the Government said it would legislate to "ensure the most serious terrorist offenders stay in prison for longer".

Following the attacks at Fishmongers Hall in November 2019 and in Streatham in February 2020 the Terrorist Offenders (Restriction of Early Release) Act 2020 was passed as emergency legislation to change release arrangements for certain terrorist offenders (in England and Wales and Scotland). At that time the Justice Secretary said wider measures would follow.

The Government has said the purpose of this Bill is to better protect the public from terrorism by strengthening the law which governs the sentencing, release and monitoring of terrorism offenders.

The Bill would:

• Introduce a new sentence for terrorist offenders; the "serious terrorism sentence", made up of a minimum of 14 years in custody and a 7 to 25 year period of extended licence. Courts would be required to impose the sentence for specified offences where certain conditions are met unless exceptional circumstances apply.

• Remove the possibility of release at the two thirds point of the custodial part of an extended sentence for relevant terrorist offenders and provide that offenders serving a serious terrorism sentence cannot be released until the end of the custodial part of their sentence.

• Increase from 10 to 14 years the maximum sentence available for the offences of: membership of a proscribed organisation, inviting or expressing support for a proscribed organisation and attendance at a place used for terrorist training.

• Allow for any non-terrorist offence with a maximum sentence of over 2 years to be found to have a terrorist connection.

• Expand the list of offences which can result in an extended sentence and increase the maximum period of the extended licence for certain terrorist offenders from 8 to 10 years (in England and Wales and Northern Ireland, it is already 10 in Scotland).

• Expand the list of offences that can result in a Sentence for Offenders of Particular Concern (SOPC) and create new sentences, the equivalent of a SOPC, for Scotland and Northern Ireland and for under 18s UK wide.

• Provide for polygraph testing of certain terrorist offenders when released on licence.

• Revise the scheme for imposing Terrorism Prevention and Investigation Measures (TPIMs) on those suspected of involvement in terrorism, by lowering the standard of proof required; expanding the range of measures available; and removing the two year time limit.

• Enable the police to apply for Serious Crime Prevention Orders (SCPOs) in terrorism cases.

• Remove the statutory deadline for conducting an independent review of the Prevent Strategy.

The Government has published Explanatory Notes. A Gov.uk page for the Bill provides links to a Fact sheet, Equality Statement, European Convention on Human Rights Memorandum and an Impact assessment.     There is also a Bill page on the Parliament website.

The provisions of the Bill extend and apply to England, Wales, Scotland and Northern Ireland. Counter-terrorism is a reserved matter, although sentencing (including release provisions) is devolved to Scotland and Northern Ireland. For details see the Explanatory Notes, page 15 and Annex A.

Some provisions of the Bill would come into force on commencement, some two months after the Act is passed and others on a day to be set out in regulations. See the Government's Fact sheet and the Explanatory Notes, page 42, for details.

### Counter-Terrorism and Sentencing Bill: Briefing for Lords Stages

Published Wednesday, 02 September, 2020

The Counter-Terrorism and Sentencing Bill would provide for changes in the sentencing, release and monitoring of terrorism offenders, including:

• introducing a new serious terrorism sentence;

• removing the possibility of release at the two-thirds point of a custodial sentence for certain categories of terrorism offenders, and ensuring those serving a serious terrorism sentence cannot be released until the end of the custodial part of their sentence;

• increasing the maximum sentence available for certain terrorism-related offences;

• enabling a court to deem that any non-terrorist offence that carries a maximum sentence of over two years can be considered to have a terrorist connection and can receive a more severe penalty as a result, amongst other measures;

• expanding the list of offences that can result in an extended sentence and increasing the maximum extension period that can be given as part of an extended sentence for certain terrorist offenders;

• expanding the list of offences that can result in a 'sentence for offenders of particular concern' (SOPCs). SOPCs are given to those whose offences were not serious or dangerous enough for the court to impose a life sentence or extended determinate sentence, but yet whom the Government argues should be recipients of a punishment that is more severe than a standard sentence. The bill would also create new sentences, the equivalent of a SOPC, for Scotland and Northern Ireland and for under 18s UK wide; and

• providing for polygraph testing of certain terrorist offenders when released on licence.

In addition, the bill would change existing terrorism prevention and investigation measures (TPIMs). These would change through lowering the standard of proof required, through expanding the range of conditions available to include polygraph and drug testing, and by removing the two-year time limit on TPIMs. It would also enable the police to apply for serious crime prevention orders (SCPOs) in terrorism cases. In addition, it would remove the statutory deadline for conducting an independent review of the Prevent strategy.

The bill received cross-party support in the House of Commons. However, MPs raised concerns about matters including: the new serious terrorism sentences for adults aged 18 to 21; restricted eligibility of release on licence for terrorist prisoners in Northern Ireland; effectiveness of strategies to deal with lone terrorists; use of polygraph testing; and changes to TPIMs such as the lowering of the standard of proof. No opposition amendments were made to the bill during its passage through the House of Commons. Minor and technical government amendments were agreed without votes at both committee and report stage.

### COVID-19 misinformation

Published Thursday, 23 April, 2020

• According to a recent study from Ofcom, 46% of respondents have encountered false or misleading coronavirus information since the lockdown.

• Most cases of misinformation are found on social media.

• Misinformation can lead to public mistrust, endangerment of public health, as well as hate crime and exploitation.

• Different approaches are being implemented to fight misinformation including content moderation, myth-busting, and a focus on education.

• This is part of our rapid response content on

COVID-19. You can view all our reporting on this topic under COVID-19.

The volume of inaccurate information circulating around the COVID-19 outbreak has prompted a global 'infodemic'.

Widespread misinformation has included proposed underlying causes of the virus (such as 5G radio waves), conspiracies around the actions of public bodies and unverified treatments and preventative measures.

An Ofcom survey of over 2,000 people found that, within the first week of the 'stay at home' measures, 46% encountered false or misleading information. Within this group, 66% reported that they were seeing COVID-19 misinformation at least once a day and 55% said that they did nothing about it.

So where does this false information come from? What are the consequences? And what can be done to counter harmful misinformation?

## Sources of COVID-19 misinformation

Misinformation may be passed on in many ways, including discussions with family and friends, through the media and online. A study by the Reuters Institute of Journalism (a UK-based think-tank) and Oxford University recently analysed 225 items of COVID-19 misinformation and found that 88% appeared on social media. Social media content can be posted instantly without verification or editorial judgement, which allows misinformation to be produced rapidly and disseminated widely.

The Reuters Institute found that 56% of misinformation around COVID-19 appears to have been based upon true information which has been reconfigured. For example, the NHS recommends that washing bed linen in temperatures of 60 degrees Celsius will help prevent germs outside of the body from spreading. This may have evoked false claims that people can protect themselves from COVID-19 by taking hot baths or using hairdryers.

Misinformation can arise from genuine misconceptions around terms and statistics. For example, the term 'coronavirus' refers to a family of viruses, some of which can cause the common cold. The term is not limited to the virus which causes COVID-19.

References to coronavirus date back to the 1960s, which has fuelled conspiracies that the current pandemic was expected. A photo of a disinfectant bottle label, which claims to 'kill human coronavirus' has been shared on Facebook over 2500 times, which has led users to speculate that the product's manufacturers knew about COVID-19 ahead of the public. Misinformation may also be spread through parody or satirical content, which some people may interpret as fact.

In other instances, some people may publish deliberately misleading information about COVID-19. This could be motivated by financial gain (for example, to sell products), or to promote political interests. People may also publish misleading 'click-bait' in order to gain widespread viral attention.

This is potentially further fuelled by the algorithms that underpin online platforms: when a user views online content, the hosting website displays adverts to generate revenue. Algorithms attempt to direct users to content they are likely to view, in order to increase engagement and hence revenue. Sensationalist content, which may contain misinformation, is more likely to be viewed by users and be recommended by the algorithms.

## Harmful consequences of misinformation

The spread of COVID-19 misinformation can be harmful in many ways. It can fuel mistrust in public authorities, enable criminal activity and lead to severe health consequences.

### Public mistrust

The Reuters Institute's analysis of COVID-19 misinformation found that 39% of false claims were about the actions of public authorities (such as government, the World Health Organisation or the United Nations), which was the single largest category of claims within the sample.

This can decrease the public's trust in public authorities' actions. For example, false reports of secret mass cremations provoked upset and gave the impression that the severity of the situation was being concealed from the public. This can have severe consequences for public cooperation with government guidelines. A recent study from King's College London found that people who believe in COVID-19 conspiracy theories (such as 5G radiation being connected to symptoms) are more likely to neglect public health guidance on social distancing.

### Health implications

COVID-19 misinformation, unsupported by medical evidence and masquerading as official health guidelines, may contradict official health advice. As a result, individuals are more likely to endanger themselves and others. There is evidence that misinformation can cause humans to take greater risks, such as sharing food with ill people and failing to wash their hands. In some cases, acting on misinformation can pose a risk to life. It has been reported that in Iran more than 300 people have died after drinking methanol (which is highly toxic), following false claims that it be used to treat COVID-19.

*Crime*

A UN official has commented that misinformation that attempts to blame particular organisations, or individuals, presents a 'risk of stigma and fear'. Researchers suggest that misreporting around the origins of the virus has spurred an increase in xenophobic abuse against people of Asian descent since the outbreak of COVID-19.

Criminals have also exploited public uncertainty for fraudulent purposes. People have received phishing-scam texts claiming to be from the UK Government, notifying them that they must pay a £35 fine for breaching social distancing measures. Google has reported that scammers are sending 18 million hoax emails about COVID-19 every day. Action Fraud (the UK's national reporting centre for fraud and cybercrime) recorded losses of over £1.6 million due to COVID-19 related fraud.

*Box 1*

In 2019, the Government put forward proposals to address disinformation in its Online Harms White Paper. The White Paper outlined proposals to establish a duty of care for internet companies that will make clear companies' responsibilities around online harms. So far, attempts to address these issues have largely been industry-led. However, stakeholders including the House of Commons Digital, Culture, Media and Sport Committee have called for further action from government and technology companies.

The Government has committed to work with social media companies to combat false information during the pandemic. In March 2020 it set up a Counter Disinformation Unit (part of the Department for Digital, Culture, Media and Sport), specifically to identify and respond to COVID-19 misinformation and scams. The Government has reported that the Unit is identifying and resolving up to 70 incidents per week.

**Preventing and challenging COVID-19 misinformation**

Digital platforms have attempted to address the spread of misinformation. This includes moderating content, fact checking services and 'myth busting' false claims about the virus, and education and guidance for users on how to recognise misinformation.

*Content moderation by digital platforms*

In March 2020, Facebook, Google, Twitter, YouTube, LinkedIn, Reddit and Microsoft released a joint statement announcing their collaboration in preventing online misinformation and fraud around coronavirus. Some of the approaches

taken by these platforms and others include:

Content removal, deprioritising and labelling: Online platforms are not currently obliged to remove content containing misinformation in the UK (see Box 1). However, private companies may choose to remove or deprioritise content. Content can be removed or demoted by human moderators, or can be detected and removed automatically.

Several of the major social media platforms are taking steps to remove or demote content containing COVID-19 misinformation. Facebook is removing all COVID-19 related content that could cause imminent physical harm to users. Misinformation that does not directly result in physical harm is referred to a fact checking system. If the content is rated as false, it is demoted so that it ranks lower in users' news feeds. In some cases it is tagged with a warning label. In April 2020, YouTube announced it would remove conspiracy theory videos linking coronavirus to 5G.

Prioritising and promotion of official information: Some social platforms and search engines have implemented measures to direct users to official information, including information from national governments and health services.

NHS England has collaborated with Twitter and other social media platforms to provide users with easy access to NHS guidance on the virus. When users search for COVID-19 or related terms on Twitter, a banner is displayed that provides them with links to the NHS website and the Department for Health and Social Care Twitter account.

Similarly, when users carry out a Google search on COVID-19, an information panel appears linking to UK Government and NHS information. Some platforms have collaborated with health authorities, including the World Health Organization (WHO), to set up dedicated COVID-19 information hubs. Facebook recently launched a COVID-19 Information Centre, available in several countries. The WHO has launched a chatbot on Facebook Messenger and WhatsApp to provide instant information on COVID-19.

Advertising bans: Some platforms, including Twitter and Google, have placed restrictions on hosting certain adverts that mention COVID-19, including adverts for certain products related to the virus (such as hand sanitisers, face masks and testing kits).

Messenger service restrictions: In April 2020, WhatsApp imposed restrictions on message forwarding as a way to prevent the spread of misinformation via the app. The new restrictions mean that messages that have already been forwarded multiple times can only be forwarded on to one chat at a time (rather than five).

One of the challenges of using automated tools to identify misinformation is the potential for social media algorithms to incorrectly flag legitimate information as misinformation. For example, in March 2020, a bug in Facebook's software led to some news articles about COVID-19 being incorrectly labelled as spam.

It has also been suggested that, in some cases, labelling content as misinformation could be counterproductive. This is because it may draw additional attention to it and result in the misinformation being amplified. Some commentators have also raised concerns that removing conspiracy theory content may fuel further conspiracy theories by making users feel they are being censored.

### Fact-checking and myth busting

The number of fact checking organisations globally has increased in recent years. The majority are independent or civil society organisations, although many are linked to established news institutions such as Channel 4 News or the BBC.

Some examples of UK-based fact checking organisations include:

- Full Fact
- Channel 4 News' FactCheck
- BBC's Reality Check
- Fact Check NI (Northern Ireland)
- Ferret Fact Services (Scotland)

Fact checking organisations are carrying out an increasing number of checks on information related to COVID-19, with many now directing resources to debunking false claims about the pandemic. One analysis estimated that there had been a 900% increase in English language fact checks from January to March 2020. Some fact checking organisations have reported that tackling COVID-19 misinformation is causing a strain on staff capacity.

Reports rated false by fact checking organisations may be removed from the platform on which they are hosted or have a warning label attached to them to make users aware that the content might be false or misleading.

The Reuters Institute and the University of Oxford found that there had been a varying response to fact checked posts by social media platforms. On Twitter, 59% of posts rated as false remained up on the site with no warning label. 27% remained up on YouTube and 24% on Facebook.

The International Fact-Checking Network aims to bring together fact-checking bodies worldwide. The organisation has created a database of COVID-19-related fact checks, which pools together debunked misinformation

published across 70 countries. The WHO has added a 'myth busters' section to its online resources about the virus, and UNESCO is promoting the use of hashtags such as #thinkbeforeyouclick.

### Education and guidance

Commentators suggest that educating people about misinformation and improving their ability to appraise information critically could reduce some of its negative impacts. A number of organisations, including the UK Government, have produced guidance to help prevent the spread of misinformation about COVID-19.

The Centre for Countering Digital Hate (CCDH, a UK based charity), recently produced guidance called 'Don't Spread The Virus'. It encourages social media users not to share or comment on false information they see online, even if they want to point out that it is wrong, to prevent the content from appearing in other users' social media feeds.

Instead, users are encouraged to block people who are sharing misinformation and report the content to the platform. The guidance also suggests that users can help to 'drown out' misinformation by posting and sharing information and advice from official sources.

The UK Government has relaunched its 'Don't Feed The Beast' campaign. This is a public information campaign first launched in 2019, which aims to empower users to question information they read online. The campaign includes a five-step checklist to help the public identify whether information may be misleading:

1. Source: make sure information comes from a trusted source.
2. Headline: always read beyond the headline.
3. Analyse: check the facts.
4. Retouched: does the image or video look as though it has been doctored?
5. Error: look out for bad grammar and spelling.

### COVID-19 outbreak: What data or information do experts want the UK Government to release?

Published Wednesday, 03 June, 2020

- Over 1,100 experts have shared with us their concerns about COVID-19 and COVID-impacted areas in the immediate and longer-term future.
- This report includes data or information experts would like to see the Government release in order to understand the decisions that underpin its approach to the COVID-19 outbreak.
- Generally, experts have highlighted five key areas of concern in the way the UK Government has released information. These include:
o Transparency of decision-making mechanisms.
o The quality, quantity and range of types of evidence used.

1405

o The justification of the Government's decisions.
o The need for accessible and understandable information.
o And the need to publish data as soon as its available.
• Experts have also called for additional information to be released by the Government including:
o Academic studies, models and Government data sets used to make decisions.
o All data being collected during the COVID-19 outbreak.
o Government guidance to departments, public bodies and public services.
o And recovery strategies from the Government and other public bodies.
• You can find all our horizon scanning work on COVID-19 here.

Our survey of over 1,100 experts asked them about their most important concerns relating to the COVID-19 outbreak. Their responses were analysed and synthesised into 15 reports in different areas. Our survey also asked experts what data or information they would like to see the Government release in order to understand the decisions that underpin its approach to the COVID-19 outbreak. There were 672 responses to this question (submitted between 3 and 30 April). These have been analysed and synthesised in this report. The first section of this report details the general principles that experts suggest the Government should follow when using data/information for making decisions and explaining these decisions to the country. The second section lists the specific data and information that experts want the UK Government to release in 13 different policy areas.

### General principles

Over 120 responses focus on general principles for how the UK Government should release data and information relating to the COVID-19 outbreak. Experts suggest that these principles have not been routinely followed and this makes scrutinising the evidence base behind Government decisions more difficult. Experts' responses centred on five main principles:

### Transparency

Experts emphasise the need to be transparent about what data/information is being collected during the COVID-19 outbreak and what data/information the Government is using when making decisions. Some experts also suggest that the full list of members of the Scientific Advisory Group for Emergencies (SAGE) and related subgroups should be public. Others suggest that minutes from SAGE, the Civil Contingencies Committee (COBR) and any other relevant meetings should be released.

### Type of evidence

Experts raise concerns about the quality, quantity and range of data/information used by the Government to make decisions. They suggest that some publications released by the Government contain very few academic studies, considering the scale of the decisions being made. Other experts express concern that there has been an overreliance on a small number of studies and experts. Some suggest that the Government should consult experts from a wide range of institutions and disciplines to ensure they are using the maximum amount of information in their decision-making. There are a variety of concerns around the use of computational modelling in Government decisions. These include that Government decisions did not account for the uncertainty in the models and that important information about the models was not available publicly. Experts suggest that if models are used in Government decisions then their full code should be published alongside the data used for the model. They also suggest there should be a clear explanation about the assumptions made and the level of uncertainty in the output. Experts note that this allows others to replicate and test the models, permitting better scrutiny and potential improvements to the models.

### Justification

Experts suggest that the Government should publish all the data/information they have consulted along with clear justifications for why decisions have been made, on what evidence these decisions were based and what are the contingencies if the decisions do not have the intended results. They also suggest that other policy opinions that were considered and rejected should be made public, along with the reasons they were not taken. Experts also want the UK Government to publish an overall strategy so the reasons for decisions are clearer to the general public and can be scrutinised.

### Accessibility

Experts note that UK citizens may feel they have a right to know about what data/information the UK Government is consulting and what data/information they are collecting. They suggest that this information should be easily accessible and understandable for the public. Experts provide a number of ways this could be improved. They suggest that publications should be accessibly written so that anyone (not just experts) can understand the data/information and decisions made. For example, they note that better use of graphics could help to explain key concepts. They also suggest that studies used in decisions should be made open access (not behind a pay wall) so that anyone can read them. Some suggest that all the data/information about the COVID-19 outbreak should be published in one easily searchable place on the Government website.

*Timeliness*
Experts suggest that the UK Government should publish data/information as soon as it is available. They note that there have been delays in publishing decisions and strategies relating to the COVID-19 outbreak, which has reduced potential scrutiny. Experts also suggest that data/information should be regularly updated and decisions should be amended to include emerging evidence. They also suggest that detailed data/information should be systematically collected during the COVID-19 outbreak to allow for future scrutiny and learning. In particular, experts want to see more data disaggregated by protected characteristics (such as sex or ethnic background), region, occupation, and income level.

*Example of a typical response in this area: The government need to be clear about what scientific evidence they have been using – not just via this [gov.uk] website but it also needs to be represented clearly on news programmes or other easily accessible formats to help gain trust and improve public understanding of what decisions have been made and why.*

*Information wanted in different areas*
Nearly 550 responses focus on the data/information that experts want the Government to release across 13 different policy areas. Across all the policy areas, experts want the Government to release four types of information publicly:

1. The data/information being used to make decisions during the COVID-19 outbreak, including academic studies, models and Government data sets.

2. The data being collected during the COVID-19 outbreak in a format that allows easy analysis by others (such as in a raw form in spreadsheets) and includes the maximum amount of detail possible (such as geographical granularity).

3. The guidance that has been given by the Government to departments, public bodies, public services and others relating to the COVID-19 outbreak.

4. The strategies being drawn up by Government departments and other public bodies for how the UK will recover after the COVID-19 outbreak.

Economy and finance
Nearly 40 responses focus on the data/information experts want the Government to release about economy and finance. In particular, experts want to see any models that assessed the economic impact of different responses to the COVID-19 outbreak. For example, they want to know what assumptions were made about how lockdown would affect productivity and long-term health costs, including how excess deaths from non-COVID-19 causes were factored in. Experts also want to know what the Government's long-term economic predictions are and its strategy for reviving the economy after the COVID-19 outbreak eases. Other experts suggest that the data and information that were used to decide the economic rescue plan for businesses should be released. For example, they want to know what data were used to set the rate of pay for furloughed workers and how many businesses were predicted to apply for Government support. Additionally, they want to know what the strategy is for financing this economic support, including any long-term plans for taxation or borrowing.

*Example of a typical response in this area: I would like to see more information about the estimated short, medium and long-term likely economic and financial costs of current policy and alternative approaches.*

Business and trade
Nearly 40 responses focus on the data/information experts want the Government to release about business and trade. Experts want more data on supply chains and how imports/exports are being affected by the COVID-19 outbreak. They also want data released on the number of businesses that have applied for Government funding and the number of business going into receivership during this period. Other information they suggest should be public include details of the contracts granted to companies by the Government to make vital equipment (such as ventilators). Some experts suggest that there should be data released regularly on productivity and manufacturing output during the outbreak. There are also calls for data on how the current situation has affected foreign investment in the UK. Experts also suggest that the UK Government could liaise more with private companies to collect industry data that may help track the effects of the outbreak. For example, data collected by supermarkets, delivery companies or search engines may provide insights into the stages of the outbreak.

*Example of a typical response in this area: I would like to see an analysis of the UK's food security based on an analysis of short, medium and long-term impacts of the pandemic.*

## Work and employment

Over ten responses focus on the data/information experts want the Government to release about work and employment. Experts want data to be released more regularly on unemployment figures during the outbreak and the number of people claiming benefits. They also want the Government to publish a strategy on how they will support employment in the long-term.

*Example of a typical response in this area: To understand the consequences of this, it is important to have data that can be used to track the changing demographics of economic vulnerability.*

## Research and innovation

Over 80 responses focus on the data/information experts want the Government to release about research and innovation. Most responses in this area are experts requesting the Government to release all the research evidence that they consulted in their decisions during the COVID-19 outbreak. This includes the evidence used to decide when the UK went into lockdown, why face masks were not initially recommended, how to operate testing, how to develop and use contact tracing phone apps, and which indicators should inform an exit strategy from lockdown. Eight experts want the UK Government to address why their recommendations and strategy differ from advice given by the World Health Organization (WHO) and what research evidence supports the UK Government's different approach. Some experts also want regular updates from the Government about financial investment and progress in research for new treatments, tests and vaccines for COVID-19.

*Example of a typical response in this area: A key element for an effective response and monitoring of the illness was the testing capabilities available to track contact with the virus: There is still a lack of information on what methodology, tests and data analysis they are using to track people who have antibodies and are potentially immune for future outbreaks.*

## Health and social care system

Nearly 40 responses focus on the data/information experts want the Government to release about the health and social care system. Experts want various data relating to the health system to be made available, including the current NHS budgets and level of spending related to COVID-19 by local area, the types of treatments currently being used in hospitals for COVID-19 and the patient outcomes, the stock levels of personal protective equipment (PPE) and other equipment for COVID-19 by local area, patient figures for non-COVID-19-related services compared to figures in the same period in previous years, and NHS workforce figures (such as current staffing capacity, number of staff on sick leave, and the number of staff who have tested positive for COVID-19). Experts also want various data relating to the social care system to be made available, including figures on the number of referrals to social care services during this period and the number of people who have tested positive for COVID-19 in the social care system (particularly staff and residents in care homes). Other information that experts want published in this area includes all Government guidance given to hospitals, GPs and care homes relating to COVID-19 and the long-term strategy for how the health and social care system will manage ongoing COVID-19 cases.

*Example of a typical response in this area: Location, quantity, quality and accessibility of the resources required to implement different elements of the response.*

## Public health

Over 150 responses focus on the data/information experts want the Government to release about public health. The majority of these responses urge the Government to release daily data on the number of people tested, the number of confirmed COVID-19 cases in hospitals and the community, figures on many people are in hospital with COVID-19 and how many are in intensive care, the number of deaths from COVID-19, and the number of deaths from other conditions. Experts particularly express the need for these data to be in a format allowing easy analysis (such as being published in a spreadsheet) and to be as detailed as possible. They suggest that the data should contain as much detail on cases as possible, including protected characteristics (such as sex and ethnic background), income level, occupation, other health conditions, and specific region (ideally at postcode-level rather than by local authority). Experts also want to know what information the UK Government is currently collecting on the mental health and well-being of the population and want this to be published publicly.

Experts want the Government to publish all of the research evidence and data used to plan its exit strategy along with any strategies it has for the long-term effects of the outbreak. They also urge the Government to publish all the emergency planning, protocols and policies that were in place before the COVID-19 outbreak. They also want full details of all previous pandemic planning exercises and strategies. In addition, they suggest the Government should publish a report on what lessons have been learned during the current outbreak and how this will change emergency planning for the future.

*Example of a typical response in this area: Accurate statistics on infection levels, death rates, recovery rates, IC [intensive care] capacity, tests carried out, arranged by geography, occupation, age and setting (hospital/community/family/workplace).*

International affairs

Nearly 40 responses focus on the data/information experts want the Government to release about international affairs. The majority of these responses focus on cooperation and information sharing between the UK and other nations. Experts want the Government to publish a summary of the data and information that they received from other countries and justify why this was or was not used to inform UK strategies. They also want to know how countries are coordinating data collection so that it is globally comparable. Other experts want the Government to publish what the UK's strategy is for supporting international development during the COVID-19 outbreak. Some experts want to see the research evidence used to decide that airports in the UK should remain open and that there would not be international travel restrictions.

*Example of a typical response in this area: An analysis of the procedures adopted from other countries could help in decision making for Government and in the evaluation of the most effective approaches.*

Law and human rights

There are ten responses focusing on the data/information experts want the Government to release on law and human rights. Experts want the Government to publish its human rights and equality impact assessments for the responses to the COVID-19 outbreak (including for lockdown, designations of 'key workers' and schools closing/reopening). They also want to know what legal advice the Government received on human rights and discrimination when making decisions. Some experts want regular updates on the number of employment tribunals throughout the course of the outbreak. Other experts want to know what guidance has been given to prisons for managing the outbreak and how many prisoners and prison workers have been infected.

*Example of a typical response in this area: The legal advice for the measures which have had the most impact on a range of European Convention rights of the UK public.*

Society and community

Over 30 responses focus on the data/information experts want the Government to release about society and community. The majority of these responses concern the collection and publication of data relating to inequalities. Experts want to

know what data are being collected by the Government to measure how responses to the COVID-19 outbreak affect different groups. They want to know how potential social, economic and health inequalities are being measured. They note that detailed data should be collected to see what effect protected characteristics, vulnerabilities and other factors have on people's experiences of the COVID-19 outbreak. Experts also want more data published on individuals living in detention centres and those classified as homeless (including how and where local authorities have housed these individuals). Experts also want information about how voluntary organisations have assisted during the outbreak, such as what roles volunteer groups have taken on and how many people have been volunteering.

*Example of a typical response in this area: Data, where appropriate, needs to take into account the impact of Covid-19 in relation to the protected characteristics included in the Equality Act.*

Media and communications

Over 40 responses focus on the data/information experts want the Government to release about media and communications. Experts want to know what research evidence and data were used to create the Government communications strategy. They also want to know what data are being collected to assess how well the public understands the policies in place and how much they are adhering to any restrictions. Experts also want to know if the Government is tracking misinformation about COVID-19 and want publications debunking false claims and guidance about how to deal with misinformation. In general, experts suggest that the public need more guidance written in a clearer way and covering a wider variety of topics.

*Example of a typical response in this area: Data related to the behaviour of society in terms of adhering to government advice / regulations, and public information search / seeking (e.g. online).*

Crime, justice and policing

Nearly 20 responses focus on the data/information experts want the Government to release about crime, justice and policing. Experts want data to be released regularly about arrests and fines relating to COVID-19. They also want data on the level of other crimes during this period, especially domestic abuse, public disorder and cyber-crime. Some experts also want the Government to release all guidance given to police forces relating to COVID-19, especially any that outlines how they may use new powers.

*Example of a typical response in this area: Data on alternative powers used to enforce the regulations should also be published, with a marker placed on all coronavirus-related out of court disposals, arrests and prosecutions whether under the regulations or other powers (e.g. Public Order Act) so that these can be subsequently analysed.*

Education

Over 20 responses focus on the data/information experts want the Government to release about education. Experts want data published on how the predicted grades being received by students this year compare to the actual grades achieved in previous years. They also want data on whether some groups (such as young people from Black and Minority Ethnic backgrounds) have fared worse than usual. Experts also want data on how many schools are providing online education, how they are providing it, and how many children and young people do not have the technology required to access online education. Some experts want the Government to publish any safeguarding guidance given to educational organisations relating to managing the COVID-19 outbreak.

Experts want to know what data are being collected to measure the impact of educational disruption on children and young people. Experts also want to know what the long-term strategy is for supporting services like the National Careers Service, as young people are likely to graduate into a difficult employment market. Experts also want data released on the number of nurseries and childcare services that have shut down during the COVID-19 outbreak. Some experts suggest that figures about the number of university applications as well as number of students who have deferred should be published publicly.

Experts also urge the Government to publish any research evidence or data on how the virus spreads in schools and how risks can be best managed.

*Example of a typical response in this area: How the qualifications that pupils have been given this year based on teacher assessment have been received by the pupils, higher education and industry.*

Infrastructure

Over ten responses focus on the data/information experts want the Government to release about infrastructure. The majority of these responses are about transport. Specifically, experts want regular data published on the use of public transport and road traffic during the outbreak. They also want the Government to publish the research evidence and data they have consulted about how the virus spreads in public transport. Experts also want the Government to publish data on telecoms usage during the outbreak. Some experts want data to be released on how infrastructure has been maintained

during this period and about the current state of key UK infrastructure.

*Example of a typical response in this area: Impact of public transport on the spread of the virus.*

### 21. COVID-19: Insights from behavioural science
Published Monday, 30 March, 2020

• On 20th March, the Scientific Advisory Group for Emergencies (SAGE) released the evidence behind the government response to Coronavirus disease (COVID-19). This series of short articles summarises these 32 documents. You can view all our reporting on this topic under COVID-19.

• This article goes over insights from behavioural science such as the risk of public disorder and adherence to household isolation.

The Scientific Pandemic Influenza group on Behaviour (SPI-B) is a group of experts that advise SAGE. This advice is limited to anticipating and helping people adhere to the interventions proposed. Group members vary by the topic that is being considered. They have included health psychologists, social psychologists, anthropologists and historians. Experts from Government departments also input to discuss the issues they are facing.

SPI-B provided advice on the use of behavioural and social interventions (COVID-19: Behavioural and social interventions). They have also reported on risk of public disorder and guidance for self-isolation.

The evidence base available to make behavioural recommendations is limited. Studies have shown that the psychological and public responses to the 2009 influenza pandemic varied between countries. For self-isolation and quarantine, a rapid review of the evidence was conducted. This looked at both the psychological impact of quarantine, and ways to improve adherence. For school closures a further rapid evidence review was used.

**SPI-B: Return on risk of public disorder (25 February 2020)**

SPI-B, the behavioural subgroup of SAGE, was asked to consider the risk of public disorder. This was defined as opportunistic crime, community tension and rioting.

Their conclusions were:

• Large scale rioting is rarely seen in these situations.
• Acts of altruism will predominate.
• Public disorder is usually linked to perception of the Government response not the outbreak itself.

Specific issues facing the police may be:

• Low police numbers due to workplace absences.
• Police actions appearing to control rather than support the public.

The recommendations of SPI-B to further reduce the risk of public disorder were:

- Provide clear and transparent reasons for different strategies.
- Set clear expectations on how the response will develop.
- Promote a sense of "we are all in this together". In particular the public needs to understand why the UK response may be different to other countries. SPI-B recommended focusing early messaging on why actions are being taken. Clear expectations of how the response will develop also need to be laid out. This messaging should be coupled with reinforcing a sense of community. This will avoid creating tensions between groups and promote social norms around behaviours.

### SPI-B: Insights on self-isolation and household isolation (9 March 2020)

SPI-B was asked to advise Public Health England on guidance for self-isolation of people with COVID-19 symptoms.

In particular they considered:
- What are the barriers and facilitators to isolation?
o Do these change for vulnerable groups?
- How can altruism towards isolated groups be promoted?
- What communication strategies should be used to discourage attendance at schools and workplaces?

SPI-B provided Public Health England with advice on its draft guidance for home isolation. In particular they recommended considering more the specific needs of different audiences. They also recommended providing guidance on mental and physical well-being.

An area of difficulty with adherence is where people with symptoms are worried about staying at home. In particular they may worry that they will infect other members of the household. There is a need to understand the increased risk to other household members compared with isolating elsewhere.

Ways to increase adherence and reduce presenteeism (i.e. going to workplaces) could include:
- Emphasise the civic duty of isolating.
- Change social norms – allow others to express disapproval.
- Consider the organisations to which individuals belong e.g. health workforce.
- Emphasise how others are isolating.
- Try to give control and choice to individuals.
- Provide specific guidance to individuals in difficult circumstances.
- Community organisations will be important for providing support.

### 22. Covid-19: Risking a rise in online child sexual abuse?
Published Wednesday, 10 June, 2020

In recent years, various organisations have highlighted the issue of online-facilitated child sexual abuse and exploitation (CSAE). The current outbreak of coronavirus has led to many children spending more time online. As a result, various governmental agencies and children's charities have raised concerns that there is an increased risk of online-facilitated CSAE. This article explores these concerns and what the UK Government has done to reduce the risks.

### What is the problem?
Following an investigation into online-facilitated CSAE, the Independent Inquiry into Child Sexual Abuse found that the internet has enabled individuals to:
- distribute indecent images of children;
- groom and manipulate children to commit sexual acts on them; and
- live stream the sexual abuse of children from around the world.

The inquiry also reported that there are millions of indecent images of children in circulation, with most sites hosting the material found on the open web. Research by the National Crime Agency (NCA) has supported this, finding that indecent material of children can be found in just three clicks.

### What are the concerns around Covid-19?
Many organisations have raised concerns that the pandemic could lead to an increased risk of online-facilitated CSAE. For example, Europol, the European Union's law enforcement agency, has argued that children spending more time unsupervised online could mean that they may:
- be more exposed to offenders through various channels, including online gaming, chat apps and social media;
- be more inclined towards making explicit material to exchange with peers; and
- become lonely and isolated, which offenders may try to benefit from.

The NCA has warned of a spike in online child sex offending during the pandemic. It urged children, parents and carers to ensure they know how to stay safe online. It said that there was a minimum of 300,000 individuals in the UK that pose a sexual threat to children. The NCA also reported that offenders in online chats have been discussing opportunities to abuse children during the crisis. The Australian e-safety commissioner also found that child abusers had created and shared an online grooming manual describing ways to manipulate and exploit children online during the pandemic.

Research by the Internet Watch Foundation has supported these concerns. On 20 May 2020, it reported that more than eight million attempts to

Research Briefings

access child sexual abuse material online had been made in the UK during the lockdown. However, it said this was a conservative estimate as the data used came from only three companies. The National Society for the Prevention of Cruelty to Children (NSPCC) has also argued that a shortage of moderators who combat online sexual abuse combined with children spending more time online has created a "perfect storm" for abusers to take advantage of the pandemic. It has raised concerns that moderators working from home would not be able to moderate the most harmful content due to data protection. In addition, the charity highlighted concerns about the impact of working from home on moderator's mental health. The Government also raised these fears in evidence to the House of Commons Home Affairs Committee.

### What is the Government doing to address the issue?

*Funding announcements*
In answer to a recent written question, James Brokenshire, Minister for Security, said that the Government was working with law enforcement, the UK intelligence community, safeguarding partners and the third sector to tackle offending and provide protection for vulnerable children.

Setting out funding commitments, Mr Brokenshire said that the Government had made £1.6 million available immediately to the NSPCC to expand and promote its national helpline for adults. He also said that the Home Office would distribute a further £7.8 million in emergency support for charities helping vulnerable children who had been impacted by the virus.

*Guidance and resources*
In April 2020, the Government published advice on how to help people, particularly children, stay safe online during the coronavirus outbreak. This guidance set out a four-point plan, recommending people:
• review security and safety settings;
• check facts and guard against disinformation;
• be vigilant against fraud and scams; and
• manage the amount of time spent online.
It also recommended that parents make use of parental controls to manage what children can access and have conversations with children to encourage them to speak to a trusted adult if they come across anything online that makes them uncomfortable.

The Government has highlighted the NCA's #OnlineSafetyAtHome campaign and its ThinkUKnow resources, in addition to interim safeguarding guidance for schools and colleges issued by the Department for Education. It also

said it was working with the Five Country partners to "galvanise industry action".

*Online harms white paper*
The Government set out plans to tackle online CSAE in April 2019 when it published its Online Harms White Paper. The paper detailed harms, both legal and illegal, linked to internet use. Included in this list was the issue of CSAE. The Government argued that the issue presented a growing threat, with both the scale and severity of this type of offending increasing.

The white paper set out a programme of actions aimed at tackling the harms described. This included a plan to become the first country to establish a regulatory framework to tackle online harms. Detailing this, it said that it would establish a new statutory duty of care to make companies take more responsibility for the safety of their users and tackle harm caused by content or activity on their services. An independent regulator—proposed to be Ofcom—would oversee compliance with this duty and set out how companies should comply in codes of practice.

On CSAE, the Government said it would require companies to take "particularly robust action". It said that it would introduce new powers, including the ability to direct the regulator on the content of the code of practice for CSAE. It also said that it would produce an interim code of conduct for CSAE while the regulator was established. In addition, from September 2020, the Government said it would require both primary and secondary schools to have lessons focusing on how to keep children safe online.

Providing an update on the progress of these proposals, Oliver Dowden, Secretary of State for Digital, Culture, Media and Sport, said in June 2020 that the Government would publish a full response to the white paper this year and would introduce a bill later in this session. Some opposition MPs have been critical of this time scale, arguing that online harms legislation is needed sooner. For example, Chi Onwurah, Shadow Minister for the Department for Digital, Culture, Media and Sport, said "parents, the NSPCC and three Select Committees all say we need legislation now".

### Covid-19: The impact on human trafficking
Published Friday, 10 July, 2020
There are concerns that the Covid-19 pandemic could make people more vulnerable to exploitation by human traffickers and could make victims less able to access help. This issue is the subject of an oral question to be asked in the House of Lords on 16 July 2020: "The Lord Bishop of Bristol to ask Her Majesty's

Government what assessment they have made of the impact of the COVID-19 pandemic on human trafficking in the United Kingdom."

## What is human trafficking?

Human trafficking is a specific offence under the Modern Slavery Act 2015. The Act also outlaws slavery, servitude and forced or compulsory labour. Home Office guidance on the Act explains that "the essence of human trafficking is that the victim is coerced or deceived into a situation where they are exploited". Forms of exploitation include sexual exploitation, forced labour or domestic servitude, slavery, financial exploitation or the removal of organs. Child human trafficking does not need to involve any element of coercion or deception.

The Home Office guidance explains that trafficking is a process comprising a number of interrelated actions. Once initial control is secured, victims are generally moved to a place where there is a market for their services, often where they lack language skills and other basic knowledge that would enable them to seek help. These actions can take place within one country or across international borders.

The Human Trafficking Foundation explains that smuggling and trafficking are not identical. In smuggling cases, asylum seekers and migrants pay people to help them enter the country. Smugglers provide an illegal service rather than treating a person as a commodity. However, trafficking victims may start out believing they are being smuggled but end up in a potentially exploitative situation where they are forced to work to pay off their 'debts'.

## What impact might Covid-19 have on human trafficking?

Charities, law enforcement agencies and other bodies are concerned that the Covid-19 pandemic could make people more vulnerable to exploitation and could make victims of human trafficking less able to access help.

In a preliminary assessment of the impact of the pandemic on human trafficking published in May, the United Nations Office on Drugs and Crime (UNODC) concluded that measures around the world such as lockdowns and travel restrictions might drive crime further underground and cause traffickers to adjust their business models. It was concerned that at the same time, the pandemic would impact capacity to provide essential services to the victims of trafficking. UNODC also argued that the coronavirus outbreak had "exacerbated and brought to the forefront the systemic and deeply entrenched economic and societal inequalities that are among the root causes of human trafficking".

Similarly, Interpol reported in June that smugglers and traffickers were finding ways to get around measures intended to prevent the spread of the disease. It also concluded that the economic consequences of the pandemic could impact the incentives and opportunities for criminals to profit from illegal migration. It said that the novel coronavirus "has only pushed human trafficking deeper into the dark and its victims further from possible detection and assistance".

The British Institute of International and Comparative Law is undertaking a research project, funded by the US Department of State, into the impacts of Covid-19 on efforts to combat human trafficking around the world. Its early findings are that not only will Covid-19 exacerbate vulnerability to human trafficking, but at the same time financial and other resources allocated to anti-trafficking efforts are likely to decrease.

Sara Thornton, the UK's Anti-Slavery Commissioner, warned in May that as lockdown measures ease, traffickers could seek to profit from industries looking to recruit low-paid workers, such as the hospitality industry. She was also concerned about the whereabouts and wellbeing of people who had been trafficked to the UK to work in informal sectors such as nail bars and car washes. She feared they could be pushed into "more perilous, insecure and risky work" as their 'debts' to their traffickers continued to mount and they were unable to work during lockdown.

The Salvation Army operates the Government's victim care contract for victims of modern slavery. It reported in early July that after an initial lull in the immediate aftermath of lockdown, it had started receiving calls again to its modern slavery referral helpline.

*Tracking the scale of the issue in the UK*

It may be too early for government data to reflect any impact the pandemic has had on human trafficking in the UK, and in any case measuring the scale of trafficking is challenging. The Office for National Statistics (ONS) published an article on modern slavery in the UK in March 2020, in which it noted that the crime's hidden nature makes it difficult to produce an accurate measure. Currently there is no definitive source of data. Instead, the ONS article brought together a range of available data sources on known victims and cases to provide a better understanding of the extent and nature of this crime. For example, it reported there were 5,144 modern slavery offences recorded by the police in England and Wales in the year ending March 2019, an increase of 51% from the previous year. The number of potential victims referred through the UK national referral mechanism (NRM) increased by 36% to 6,985 in the year ending December 2018.

Most of the figures in the article pre-date the coronavirus pandemic. However, more recent figures were published in June 2020, showing the number of referrals to the national referral mechanism from 1 January 2020 to 31 March 2020. During this period, 2,871 potential victims of modern slavery were referred to the NRM across the UK; this was a 14% decrease from the previous quarter, but a 33% increase from the same quarter in 2019.

The Government said in October 2019 that the most robust estimate to date of the scale of modern slavery in the UK was produced by the Home Office in 2014. This suggested there were between 10,000 and 13,000 potential victims of modern slavery in 2013.

### Government support to victims of human trafficking

Adults who are potential victims of modern slavery can be referred for support through the national referral mechanism, with their consent. All potential victims under 18 must be referred to the NRM. Under the NRM, adults have access to specialist tailored support services for at least 45 days while their case is considered. Support may include:

• Access to legal aid for immigration advice

• Access to short-term government-funded support through the victim care contract (accommodation, material assistance, translation and interpretation services, counselling, advice)

• Outreach support if already in local authority accommodation or asylum accommodation

• Assistance to return to their home country if not a UK national

Support for children is provided through local authorities and independent child trafficking guardians.

The Government has acknowledged that victims of modern slavery may be "especially isolated and hidden from view during the coronavirus outbreak". It said it recognised that "there are greater vulnerabilities for potential victims during Covid-19, as social distancing means there is a risk that they are not identified by first responders and may find it harder to access support". The Home Office published guidance on support for the victims of modern slavery on the coronavirus pages of the UK Government website. The Government also set out steps it has taken to provide support to the victims of modern slavery during the pandemic: "We announced on 6 April 2020, that all individuals in accommodation provided by the government-funded specialist modern slavery victim care contract, will not be required to move on from their accommodation for the next three months.

"We have also secured £1.73 million of the funding for charities, announced by the Chancellor last month, to provide emergency support to victims of modern slavery who have been impacted by the coronavirus outbreak. This funding will assist individuals supported through the victim care contract and will ensure victims are able to stay in government-funded safe accommodation, access financial assistance, access support services remotely, and make sure we manage additional demand on services during this period."

Individuals provided with accommodation under the victim care contract are usually able to access accommodation for at least 45 days and would then be assisted to move on. The Government announced on 7 July 2020 that it is extending the temporary policy change to the 'move on' period for another month, allowing people to stay in their accommodation until 6 August 2020, although they can move on earlier if they wish.

The Government held an online summit on 'hidden harms', including modern slavery, in May. The Home Office said that the summit had brought key decision makers together to help agree an approach for tackling these crimes as the easing of lockdown measures began.

Charities have reported their concerns that some victims of modern slavery, particularly those who are receiving outreach support, have had their financial support cut during lockdown.

The Helen Bamber Foundation, which works with survivors of modern slavery, has called on the Government to take further actions to support them during the pandemic, such as providing survivors with greater certainty about their immigration status, refraining from issuing negative decisions on NRM referrals or asylum applications while the public health crisis is ongoing and increasing financial support to ensure that survivors have internet access.

### Crime, justice, policing and COVID-19: What are experts concerned about?

Published Friday, 22 May, 2020

• Over 1,100 experts have shared with us their concerns about COVID-19 and COVID-impacted areas in the immediate and longer-term future.

• This report outlines crime, justice and policing concerns.

• On policing, experts are concerned about how the police are monitoring and enforcing adherence to Government restrictions. This includes the inadvertent criminalisation of certain communities and the risk for civil disorder.

• Experts are also concerned about the potential

increase of certain types of crime during the outbreak, such as organised crime, corruption, domestic abuse and cybercrime.

• On the criminal justice system experts worry about a backlog of cases in courts which were put on hold due to the pandemic. They are also worried about a surge of news cases as a result of the pandemic. Finally there are concerns about the health of prisoners at this time and want to know about plans for early releases.

• You can find all our horizon scanning work on COVID-19 here.

Our survey of over 1,100 experts asked them what their most important concerns were in the short (next 3 months), medium (next 3 to 9 months) and long-term (beyond the next 9 months) relating to the COVID-19 outbreak. Their responses were analysed and synthesised. This synthesis comes from survey responses submitted between 3 and 30 April. Experts raised 85 concerns relating to crime, justice and policing. Below are the areas of concerns that experts have relating to this area.

## Policing

Experts raised over 40 concerns about policing during the COVID-19 outbreak. Experts are concerned about how the police are monitoring and enforcing adherence to Government restrictions. They want to know what powers the police are using and how this is being measured. There are concerns that police are unable to monitor adherence in all areas because they do not have the number of officers required. Other concerns include that the police may inadvertently criminalise certain groups who are less able or less likely to observe Government guidance. For example, young people who live in unsafe housing may be more likely to be in public spaces more often. Some experts express concern that there could be a rise in tensions between the police and certain communities if people feel they are being unduly monitored compared to others. In the medium and long-term, experts are concerned about how police behaviour during the COVID-19 outbreak will affect public trust in the police and perceptions of their legitimacy.

Experts are also concerned about a potential rise in civil disorder in the medium and long-term. They suggest that people may experience frustration at restrictions and that police may struggle to contain civil unrest if there are widespread violations of restrictions, or protests. Experts want to know how the Government will maintain social order in the medium and long-term.

*Example of a typical medium-term concern in this area: What will be the impact of policing enforcement policy and lockdown on the perceived legitimacy of policing and with community relations?*

## Crime rates

Nearly 20 concerns focus on the effect of the COVID-19 outbreak on crime rates in the short, medium and long-term. In the short and medium-term, experts are concerned about potential increases in some types of crime. For example, experts suggest that organised crime and corruption is likely to increase during the COVID-19 outbreak because police will have less time to monitor these crimes. Experts also suggest that domestic abuse cases are likely to increase in the short and medium-term. Experts want to know how police will be supported in investigating these crimes alongside their work in enforcing Government guidance.

Experts also note that an increase in the number of people using digital technologies will also create an increase in the level of cybercrime. They note that police forces are generally less equipped and less well-trained to deal with cybercrime. They question how the police will be supported in dealing with increased numbers of cases involving cybercrime and how they can be trained quickly to deal with these crimes. Some experts are also concerned that misinformation on social media about the origins of the virus may lead to an increase in hate crime. They want to know how the Government will act against hate crime and counter racist and xenophobic messages being spread by social media.

Although some types of crime have reduced during the COVID-19 outbreak, experts are concerned that there could be a rise in crime in the long-term. For example, they suggest that unemployment could lead to increases in various types of theft.

*Example of a typical short-term concern in this area: Increase of domestic violence and child abuse incidents, possibly leading to fatalities – the unseen victims of COVID19 [sic].*

## Criminal justice system

There are over 20 concerns relating to the effects of the COVID-19 outbreak on the criminal justice system in the short, medium and long-term.

Experts want to know how jurors and people working in courts will be protected from catching the virus in the short and medium-term. They want to know what guidance is being given to courts to help them enforce social distancing. In the medium and long-term, experts are concerned that there will be a backlog of cases in courts because they have been unable to work at normal capacity. They also suggest there could be a surge in legal cases resulting from the COVID-19 outbreak in the medium and long-term. There are concerns that the criminal justice system was overstretched before the outbreak and it is unlikely to be able to cope with the surge in cases. This may mean that people are unable to get justice in a timely manner.

Some experts raise concerns around prisons in the short and medium-term. They want to know what the plans are for early release of prisoners during the outbreak. Experts also note that releasing prisoners while restrictions are in place may make it harder for prisoners to reintegrate into society. They suggest parole officers need more support during this period. Another concern raised by experts in the short and medium-term is the risk of a COVID-19 outbreak within prisons. Experts want to know how the Government is ensuring that prisons are being kept safe for officers and prisoners. They also want to know what measures are in place to enforce social distancing without violating prisoners' human rights.

*Example of a typical medium-term concern in this area: That policing and criminal justice agencies can maintain their conventional functions in addition to responding to emergencies, such as maintaining order and also being able to investigate and prosecute wrongdoers.*

### Criminal Justice and Courts Bill – Lords Amendments [Bill 120 of 2014-15]]

Introduction The Criminal Justice and Courts Bill was introduced in the 2013-14 session and carried over to the 2014-15 session. Progress of the Bill together with relevant documentation can be found on the Criminal Justice and Courts Bill. This includes the following Commons and Lords Library Papers, prepared for earlier stages:

• Commons Library Research Paper 14/8 (20 February 2014) prepared for second reading in the Commons

• Library Standard Note 6882 (12 June 2014) prepared for report stage in the Commons

• Library Note 2014/022 (26 June 2014) prepared for second reading in the Lords

This paper is designed to provide background information for Consideration of Lords Amendments of the Criminal Justice and Courts Bill, which is due to take place on 1 December 2014. The amendment numbers throughout refer to those listed in the latest Bill document, Lords Amendments to the Criminal Justice and Courts Bill [Bill 120 of 2014-15]. Unless stated otherwise, references to clause numbers are to the Bill as introduced in the Lords (HL Bill 30).

There were many Government amendments to the Bill. The Ministry of Justice has produced extensive and useful Explanatory Notes on the Lords Amendments. This paper does not seek to replicate these or to discuss every amendment.

Lords Amendments opposed by the Government Excluding boys under 15, and girls, from secure colleges

Clauses 29 and 30 would add "secure colleges" to the list of types of establishments where young offenders could be accommodated, and allow for the contracting out of the provision and running of them. Background is given on pages 20-23 of Library Research Paper 14/8.

Lords Amendment 74 would exclude all girls, and boys aged under 15, from the secure colleges. Moving the amendment, the Shadow Justice Spokesperson Lord Beecham said that safeguarding plans for the colleges were inadequate, and that there were so few girls in custody they could easily be accommodated in smaller, more appropriate Secure Children's Homes.[1] The Crossbench peer, Lord Ramsbotham, described the proposed "pathfinder" secure college at Glen Parva as a "cost-saving exercise based on presumed economies of scale".[2] Lord Carlile of Berriew also criticised the physical plans for the pathfinder college (involving locking down part of the site from older students whilst girls and younger boys are moved) and cited the lack of nearby residential mental health facilities with educational provision. The Justice Minister Lord Faulks said that the Government had "gone to considerable lengths" in their designs "to ensure that the younger and more vulnerable groups could be accommodated in separate small units".[3] Secure colleges would "provide the right environment where healthcare professionals" could care for young people. The amendment was narrowly agreed to on division, by 186 votes to 185.

Judicial Review

Part 4 of the Bill would bring in a number of reforms to judicial review following a Government consultation on proposals with the aim of "reducing the burden of judicial review".[4] Background is given on pages 49-56 of Library Research Paper 14/8.

Lords Amendments 97-107 were added to the Bill as a result Government defeats on the third day of Report,[5] following heated debate of similar amendments in Committee (which were withdrawn).[6]

The amendments fall into three groups. On report, Labour's Lord Beecham described them as together "dispensing with the fetters on judicial discretion which the Bill would otherwise apply."[7]

Likelihood of substantially different outcome for the applicant

Clause 64 would require the High Court or Upper Tribunal to refuse to grant a remedy or permission on an application for judicial review if it considers it "highly likely" that defendant's conduct in the matter in question would not have affected the outcome for the defendant. At present the court has discretion to refuse to grant permission or a remedy if it is "inevitable" that the failure complained of would not have made a difference to the outcome.

Lords Amendments 97 to 98 would give the High Court or Upper Tribunal discretion over whether they should refuse a remedy if it appears highly likely that the outcome for the applicant would not have been substantially different if the conduct complained of had not occurred. Lords Amendment 99 would give the High Court discretion to consider, if asked to do so by the defendant, whether it was highly likely that the outcome would not have been substantially different. Lords Amendment 100 would give the High Court discretion to refuse permission for judicial review if they were satisfied that the outcome would have not have been substantially different. Lords Amendments 101-102 would make equivalent provision for the Upper Tribunal. At report stage, Lord Pannick said that the clause ignored the fact that one of the central purposes of judicial review is to identify unlawful conduct by the Government or other public bodies. To introduce an initial stage of considering "what would have happened if the defendant had acted differently" would be time-consuming, expensive and extremely difficult.[8] Lord Beecham said that the proposals had been "roundly condemned by the Constitution Committee, by the Delegated Powers and Regulatory Reform Committee, by 11 Police and Crime Commissioners and, of course, by the Joint Committee on Human Rights".[9]

The Conservative peer Lord Horam highlighted delays he said that judicial review was causing to infrastructure projects, the costs and examples of abuse.[10] For the Government, Lord Faulks said that "judicial review, when used properly, is an essential component of the rule of law", but that it could delay "crucial projects with direct implications for jobs."[11] The lead amendment was agreed to on division by 247 votes to 146.[12]

Information about financial resources

Clause 65 provides that permission to proceed with a judicial review cannot be granted unless the applicant provides information about the financing of judicial review. Lords Amendment 103 would give the High Court discretion over this, and Lords Amendment 104 does the equivalent for the Upper Tribunal. Clause 66 provides that, when considering liability for costs in judicial review proceedings, the relevant courts must have regard to the financial information provided under clause 65. Lords Amendments 105 and 106 would, again, give these courts discretion over this.

In the debate at report stage, Lord Pannick said

that these clauses would have a "severely inhibiting effect on judicial review", [13] and Labour's Baroness Lister of Burtersett also referred to their "the chilling or deterrent effect".[14] For the Government, Lord Faulks said that the clauses were "about transparency" and would prevent a third party from using a "front man" to shield themselves from incurring their share of the costs.[15] The lead amendment was agreed to on division by 228 votes to 195.[16]

Interveners and costs

Clause 67 would establish a presumption that interveners in a judicial review will pay their own costs (and any costs incurred by any other party because of the intervention) except in exceptional circumstances. Lords Amendment 107 would give courts discretion over this. Lord Pannick, who moved the amendment at report stage, said that courts would be denied assistance from public interest bodies with knowledge and experience which may help them to resolve legal issues, including government departments who make a number of interventions in judicial review cases.[17] Lord Faulks said that the Government thought it "right that people who intervene in judicial reviews should have a fairer financial stake in the case and do so in a way that does not cause the true parties to the judicial review additional costs".[18] The amendment was agreed to on division by 219 votes to 186.

Other Lords Amendments accepted by the Government

Knives

Clause 25 would amend the sentencing for second offences for those aged 16 or over in possession of a weapon or bladed article in public, or on school premises. A previous conviction for threatening with a knife or an offensive weapon would count as a first strike. The minimum custodial sentence would be six months for those aged 18 or over, and a four month Detention and Training Order for those aged over 16 but under 18. This was added to the Bill at report stage, following the passing of an amendment sponsored by Conservative MP Nick de Bois.[19] The clause was controversial in the Lords. In committee a number of peers spoke against it in the clause stand part debate, citing erosion of judges' discretion amongst other arguments. However, others supported it because of the deterrent effect of a known penalty. On division, it was agreed that the clause should stand part (228 votes to 159.)[20]

At report stage, Baroness Browning (who in 2011 was a Home Office minister with responsibility for gang and knife crime) introduced some technical and drafting amendments to the clause.[21] These are now listed as Lords Amendments 48 to 67 and 124. See pages 6-7 of the Explanatory Notes for details.

Arrested Juveniles

Currently section 37 of the Police and Criminal Evidence Act 1986 (PACE) defines an "arrested juvenile" as a person who "appears to be under the age of 17". This means that 17 year olds are not treated in the same way as 10-16 year olds under Part 4 of PACE. In particular, where a younger child who is arrested and charged is not released, they will be transferred where practicable to local authority accommodation, whereas a 17 year old would be kept in police custody.[22]

The different treatment of 17 year olds from that of younger teenagers under PACE Codes (statutory guidance for police) has been highlighted in a number of cases where 17 year olds killed themselves after being arrested.[23] In April 2013 Hughes Cousins-Chang, a 17 year old who had been detained as an adult, successfully challenged the policy through judicial review.[24] The High Court ruled that the Home Secretary's refusal to revise Code C so as to distinguish the procedures applicable to a 17-year-old detainee in police custody from those applicable to an adult was unlawful.[25] As a consequence, the PACE code was revised.

Lord Listowel (Crossbench) moved amendments in committee and at report stage to change the definition of an arrested juvenile to include 17 year olds.[26] At report stage, Lord Ashton of Hyde (for the Government) explained that an internal Home Office review following the Cousins-Chang case was examining other primary legislation which might need to be amended.[27] Lord Listowel withdrew his amendment. However, he moved it again at third reading. Lord Faulks said that that the Government had "listened to his plea":

The Government have now concluded their review and have arrived at a very clear conclusion: the provisions in PACE that relate to the treatment of 17 year olds should be amended as soon as possible so that they are treated as children.

I must point out that this is a very complex area and the Home Office review was very wide-ranging—more so than the amendment that has been tabled today. This means that the amendment only partially affects the change in relation to the treatment of 17 year olds. However, in the limited time available, this amendment makes the most substantial change, that relating to the overnight detention of children charged and denied bail. The effect of

the amendment would be that 17 year olds, as with 12 to 16 year-old children, must be transferred to suitable local authority accommodation overnight in these circumstances. The amendment has the full backing of the police. The Home Office will work with forces to help them prepare for implementation.[28]

Government Amendments made in the Lords
Recall adjudicators

There was debate in Committee in the Lords about the impact of various provisions in the Bill upon the work of the Parole Board,[29] particularly in the context of the recent Supreme Court Judgement on the issue of when the Parole Board should offer an oral hearing to determine prisoners' release or transfer to open conditions.[30] Lords Amendments 5 to 35 and 121 to 123 are the Government's response to another judgement, and aim to reduce some of the burden on the Parole Board. Currently, prisoners on determinate sentences who are recalled to prison must be referred to the Parole Board to have their detention reviewed. This is because the Parole Board is a "court-like" body. On 2 July 2014, the Supreme Court overturned previous case-law by finding that determinate sentence recall cases do not engage Article 5(4) of the European Convention on Human Rights.[31]

The Government's amendments, which were introduced at report stage[32] would provide a power for the Secretary of State to appoint "Recall Adjudicators" to review the detention of recalled determinate sentence prisoners. Further information is given in the Ministry of Justice's Impact Assessment, Recall Adjudicator for recalled determinate sentence prisoners, (15 October 2015).

"Revenge pornography"

Lords Amendments 70 and 71 would create a new offence of disclosing private sexual photographs and films with intent to cause distress. The offence, which will extend to England and Wales, will be triable either way and punishable with a maximum custodial sentence of two years. Lords Amendment 126 would insert a new schedule to deal with "information society services"[33]

The issue of revenge pornography was raised at Lords Committee stage. Lord Marks of Henley-on-Thames (Liberal Democrat) moved amendments to make it an offence to publish a sexually explicit or pornographic image without consent. Lord Marks explained the problem as follows:

…the term "revenge pornography" refers to the publication, usually but not always, on the internet, of intimate images of former lovers without their consent. This thoroughly nasty behaviour generally involves the perpetrator in taking advantage of his or her possession of sexually explicit images, generally taken or obtained in private during the course of an intimate relationship in circumstances where the parties, and certainly the party photographed, had every right to expect that the images would remain private.[34]

He called for the practice to be criminalised. The Minister of State at the Ministry of Justice, Lord Faulks, said that the Government was "carefully considering" what needed to be done to combat revenge pornography:

If new legislation is required, we must ensure that we address all the issues involved to ensure that we properly target the material that is causing concern and that we capture only the relevant behaviour. This requires detailed consideration and care, as has been widely acknowledged during the debate. Although there is a degree of consensus about what evil we are trying to seek out and criminalise, exactly how we capture it is a complex problem. This debate will certainly help the analysis that will take place in the month or two that follow, and I would of course be happy to see any of those concerned to ensure that we capture adequately and appropriately the behaviour at which these amendments are directed. We will take away these amendments and return to the House with our conclusion at a later stage of the Bill…[35]

Lord Marks withdrew his amendments, although he returned to the subject at report stage,[36] when the Government moved its own amendments to introduce the new offence.[37] Lord Faulks summed this up as follows:

The current law can already punish instances of this behaviour in certain circumstances. A number of offences can be used, and the recently updated guidance from the CPS has made clear that, where intimate images are used to coerce victims into further sexual activity, offences in the Sexual Offences Act 2003 can be used both where the victim is an adult and where they are a child. This offence, however, will target very different behaviour: namely, the malicious disclosure of private sexual photographs or films. The offence seeks to target material, the disclosure of which would have the potential to cause the most harm to an individual. It will therefore apply to the disclosure of private sexual photographs or films of people, such as those which show them engaged in sexual activity or depicted in a sexual way where what is shown is not the kind of thing usually seen in public. In determining whether the picture is sexual, the court will be required to take into account both the nature of

what is shown and the context provided by the whole of the pictures' content. To commit the offence, the disclosure must take place without the consent of at least one person featured in the image and with the motivation of causing that person distress.[38]

Lord Marks said that he was "content that the government amendments represent an effective way of dealing with this despicable behaviour."[39]

Personal injury claims: cases of fundamental dishonesty

Clause 45 of Bill 30 was added at Report stage in the House of Commons. The clause would require a court to dismiss in its entirety any personal injury claim where it was satisfied that the claimant had been fundamentally dishonest, unless it would cause substantial injustice to the claimant to do so.[40] Lord Faulks had previously stated that, under the current law, the courts have discretion to dismiss a claim entirely for fraudulent behaviour, but will only do so in very exceptional cases, and will generally still award the claimant compensation in relation to the "genuine" element of the claim.[41] A Government factsheet provides information about the mischief Clause 45 is intended to address: Tackling unjustified personal injury claims.[42]

Sub-clause (5) of Clause 45 deals with the amount of the defendant's costs a court might require the claimant to pay when it dismisses a claim. At committee stage, Lord Hunt of Wirral asked for clarification of how this sub-clause would operate, querying whether it "simply undoes the good work of the rest of the clause".[43] In reply, Lord Faulks said that the sub-clause would ensure that, when a court dismisses a claim under the clause, it could award costs against the claimant only to the extent that these exceeded the damages that would otherwise have been awarded. However, he said that he would consider the drafting of sub-clause (5) before Report stage.[44]

Lords Amendment 84 is a Government amendment, agreed at report stage without vote, which would replace sub-clause (5) of Clause 45 and which, Lord Faulks said, would clarify the position. Revised sub-clause (5) would apply when the court was assessing costs in proceedings where the claim had been dismissed because of the claimant's fundamental dishonesty. The court would be required to deduct the amount of damages that it would have awarded to the claimant from the amount which it would otherwise order the claimant to pay in respect of the defendant's costs. Lord Faulks set out the underlying intention of the provision:

…to ensure that claimants are not excessively sanctioned by both losing the genuine element of the award of damages and having to pay the defendant's costs without any credit for what the defendant has saved by avoiding payment of the genuine element of the award. I should add that one of the main intentions behind this provision is to deter people from bringing these claims at all, or at least deter them from being dishonest when advancing them.[45]

Lord Faulks said that it was not the Government's intention to interfere more generally with the court's discretion on whether to make a costs order and, if so, in what terms.

Rules against inducements to make personal injury claims

Lords Amendments 85 to 88 and 117 are Government amendments which would ban the offer by a regulated person (as defined) of monetary and non-monetary inducements to potential claimants as an incentive to bring personal injury claims (now Clauses 57 to 60 of the Bill as amended on Report).[46]

Lord Faulks said that the measures would complement other Government reforms intended to control the costs of civil litigation. He said it was necessary to stop the practice of offering inducements in order to protect both consumers and the reputation of the legal profession. A Government fact sheet set out the Government's concern that the offer of inducements by some law firms was helping to encourage exaggerated or fraudulent personal injury claims, wasting time and money. The Government expressed concern about the impact such claims could have on motor insurance premiums.[47]

At committee stage, Lord Faulks indicated that a ban on the offer of inducements had cross-industry support and had been endorsed by the House of Commons Transport Committee.[48] The new provisions were supported by the Opposition.

New clauses were agreed without vote at Committee stage.[49] Government amendments to the new provisions were agreed without vote at Report stage;[50] these amendments are intended to prevent regulated persons avoiding the ban by offering inducements through third parties, and were introduced in response to an amendment tabled (but not moved) by Lord Hunt of Wirral at Committee stage.

The amendments would define what is considered to be an inducement, and other relevant terms. Regulators set out in a list would be required to monitor and enforce the ban, and would have power to make rules for that purpose. Breach of the ban would not be a criminal offence and would not give rise to a right of action for breach of statutory duty.

The Lord Chancellor would have power to make regulations by statutory instrument – the affirmative resolution procedure would apply to regulations made under the new clause inserted by Lords Amendment 85 (Rules against inducement to make personal injury claims) and the negative resolution procedure would apply to regulations made under the new clause inserted by Lords Amendment 87 (Inducements: interpretation).

The new provisions would extend only to England and Wales.

Appeals from the Court of Protection

Section 53 of the Mental Capacity Act 2005 (MCA 2005) sets out the routes of appeal for cases in the Court of Protection and provides that rules of court may specify that appeals from certain levels of judge lie to another (higher) judge within that Court, rather than to the Court of Appeal.

The Crime and Courts Act 2013 added to the categories of judicial office holders who are eligible for nomination to sit in the Court of Protection, but omitted to address the subject of appeals from this extended range. This means that appeals from decisions of judges in the wider range have to go to the Court of Appeal.

Lords Amendments 89 and 110 are Government amendments agreed without vote at Report stage. They would deal with this omission and provide that rules of court could allow appeals from decisions of any specified description of person to be heard within the Court of Protection rather than by the Court of Appeal. Lord Faulks said that this would prevent the Court of Appeal being "unnecessarily burdened by a significant increase in cases" and would allow the Court of Protection the flexibility to deal with resources efficiently.[51] The new clause would come into effect on the same day as Royal Assent.

Meeting a child following sexual grooming

Lords Amendment 73 was a Government amendment agreed to after a brief debate in committee. It would amend the existing offence in section 15 of the Sexual Offences Act 2003. At present, the offence occurs where a person has met or communicated with the child "on at least two occasions" and subsequently meets (or travels to meet) the child intending to commit sexual offences. The amendment would mean the perpetrator would only have had to meet or communicated with the child on "one or more" occasions rather than "at least two". There was a brief debate, and all those who spoke welcomed the change. [52]

## Other Government amendments

There were many other Government amendments in the Lords which did not occasion much, if any, debate. These include:

- Lords Amendments 1-4, which make minor changes to the new sentencing scheme for serious offences. These were agreed in committee without division or much debate. [53]
- Lords Amendment 36 on rehabilitation of offenders in Scotland, which is "required in order to address a legal competence gap that has been identified by the Scottish Government in relation to the exercise of enabling powers in Schedule 3 to the Rehabilitation of Offenders Act 1974"[54]
- Lords Amendment 124 which increases the time limit for bringing prosecutions for offences under Section 127 of the Communications Act 2003. Section 127 makes it an offence to send grossly offensive, indecent, obscene or menacing material over a public telecommunications network.[55]
- Lords Amendments 83, 108 and 109, designed clarify the operation of the mode of trial used for low-value shoplifting (following the introduction of section 176 of the Anti-social Behaviour, Crime and Policing Act 2014)[56]
- Lords Amendments 95 which would allow the President of the Supreme Court of the United Kingdom to make written representations to Parliament about the Supreme Court and its jurisdiction in the same way as the Lord Chief Justice of any part of the United Kingdom can do[57]
- Lords Amendment 95 which would allow the Supreme Court to appoint judges to the judges to the Supplementary Panel within two years of their retirement, provided that they are under the age of 75.[58]

## Clauses which the Government removed from the Bill

In committee, the Government explained that it would not be proceeding with what had been clauses 51 and 52 of the Bill designed to reform the law of strict liability contempt:

These clauses were included in the Bill at introduction to implement recommendations by the Law Commission intended to reform the law of strict liability contempt. The purpose was to remove the burden on publishers to monitor online archives for potentially contemptuous material, while protecting a defendant's right to a fair trial. However, the Government have received representations from media organisations making it clear that they oppose the measures. The Joint Committee on Human Rights also commented on the issue in its 14th report of this Session. The Government have carefully considered those concerns. We remain

of the view that the proposals are balanced and measured but we are satisfied that the existing law will continue to provide satisfactory protection to the integrity of legal proceedings.

Since the measures were intended to assist the media but the media do not want them, we see no purpose in proceeding with the clauses. The then Attorney-General therefore announced in a statement on 30 June, and I also gave notice at Second Reading, that the Government had decided not to pursue the measure and would seek to omit the clauses from the Bill. Amendment 86 is consequential to the omission of Clause 51, since there is no purpose in defining its extent. I urge the Committee to agree that Clauses 51 and 52 should not stand part of the Bill.[59]

1 HL Deb 22 October 2014 c666
2 Ibid
3 HL Deb 22 October 2014 c674
11 HL Deb 27 October 2014 cc973-4
12 HL Deb 27 October 2014 c978
13 HL Deb 27 October 2014 c982
14 HL Deb 27 October 2014 c983
15 HL Deb 27 October 2014 c986
16 HL Deb 27 October 2014 c988
17 HL Deb 27 October 2014 c993
18 HL Deb 27 October 2014 c996
19 HC Deb 17 June 2014 c1013
20 HL Deb 21 July 2014 c955
21 HL Deb 20 October 2014 cc502-9
22 Section 38(6) of PACE
23 See for example "Joe Lawton's parents in reform plea over his death" BBC News 8 March 2013
24 "Teenager wins ruling on detention of 17-year olds", BBC News, 25 April 2013
25 R. (on the application of HC) v Secretary of State for the Home Department, [2013] EWHC 982 (Admin);
26 HL Deb 22 October 2014 cc726-9
27 Ibid c728-9
28 HL Deb 10 November 2014 c20
29 See HL Deb 14 July 2014 cc379-385
30 Reilly's Application for Judicial Review, also known as Osborn v Parole Board and Booth v Parole Board, [2013] UKSC 61, 9 October 2013
31 R. (on the application of Whiston) v Secretary of State for Justice, [2014] UKSC 39, , 02 July 2014
32 HL Deb 20 October 2014 cc451-4
33 Defined as in Article 2(a) of the E-Commerce Directive as covering "any service normally provided for remuneration, at a distance, by means of electronic equipment for the processing (including digital compression) and storage of data, and at the individual request of a recipient of a service" (see paragraph 6 of the Schedule introduced by Lords Amendment 126.
34 HL Deb 21 July 2014 c969
35 HL Deb 21 July 2014 c979
36 HL Deb 20 October 2014 cc517-532

37 *Ibid c537*
38 *Ibid cc523-4*
39 *Ibid c519*
40 *HC Deb 17 June 2014 cc1066*
41 *HL Deb 9 June 2014 cc26-7WS*
42 *Gov.UK website [accessed 27 November 2014]*
43 *HL Deb 23 July 2014 c1260*
44 *HL Deb 23 July 2014 c1268-9*
45 *HL Deb 22 October 2014 cc742*
46 *HL Bill 49 2014-15*
47 *Gov.UK, Criminal Justice and Courts Bill: fact sheet: Banning inducements to issue personal injury claims [accessed 27 November 2014]*
48 *HL Deb 23 July 2014 c1272*
49 *HL Deb 23 July 2014 c1271-5*
50 *HL Deb 22 October 2014 cc744-6*
51 *HL Deb 22 October 2014 cc746-50*
52 *HL Deb 21 July 2014 cc960-2*
53 *HL Deb 14 July 2014 c378*
54 *HL Deb 14 July 2014 c469*
55 *HL Deb 20 Oct 2014 cc526-7*
56 *HL Deb 23 July 2014 cc1229-31*
57 *HL Deb 22 Oct 2014 cc748-9*
58 *Ibid*
59 *HL Deb 28 July 2014 cc1424-6*

### Criminal memoirs

Last updated: 23 May 2012

There is no law prohibiting convicted criminals from publishing their autobiographies or other writings in which their crimes may be described, or from selling their stories to newspapers or biographical writers. However, there are restrictions on criminals profiting from such activities. These are set out in Part 7 of the Coroners and Justice Act 2009, which came into force on 6 April 2010. The Act established a civil recovery scheme that enables the courts to order criminals to pay an amount in respect of assets or other benefits derived from the exploitation of accounts of their crimes. Sums received are then paid into the Consolidated Fund (the Government's general bank account at the Bank of England). Special rules apply to serving prisoners, who under the Prison Rules and Prison Standing Orders may be prevented from publishing material relating to their crimes while in custody. In the case of a life sentence prisoner serving a whole life term, the application of the Rules may effectively prevent any such publication during his or her lifetime. There are also various media codes of practice advising broadcasters and journalists on making payments to criminals: public interest is the key factor.

### 1 Background

There have been several examples in recent years of criminals who have reportedly profited from published accounts of their crimes. Although these incidents are relatively rare, some of them have attracted considerable public outrage.

In 1998, it was reported that Mary Bell, who killed two toddlers when she was eleven, was receiving payment for helping with a book about her life, Cries Unheard by Gitta Sereny.[1] There were many reports that Mary Bell had received £50,000 for her contribution, although this was disputed at the time. The book was also serialised in the Times.

In 2003, there was public concern that Tony Martin, who shot and killed a young burglar, had sold his story to the Mirror for £125,000; however the Press Complaints Commission ruled that there had been no breach of the relevant code of practice, instead taking the view that the payment was necessary and that the story was in the public interest.[2] In 2005, the BBC paid £4,500 to Brendan Fearon, the surviving burglar in the Tony Martin case, and argued that the programme was in the public interest. The programme maker stated that Fearon's participation in the programme ensured "balance".[3]

### 2 The civil recovery scheme: exploitation proceeds orders

#### 2.1 Background

In 1998, the furore surrounding Mary Bell's paid collaboration on her biography led Jack Straw, the then Home Secretary, to ask officials to "consider whether the law relating to criminal memoirs might sensibly be strengthened".[4] A review was conducted by an interdepartmental working group, and in October 1999 Lord Bassam of Brighton (then a junior Home Office minister) announced that the review had been completed and publication of the outcome was likely to follow in the very near future.[5] In the event, no conclusions were actually published; however, the work of the 1998/9 review was incorporated into a later review, the results of which were published as a green paper in November 2006.[6]

The green paper presented four proposals:

• make receipt by and/or payment to convicted criminals for publications about their crimes a criminal offence;

• introduce a new civil scheme for the recovery of profits based on the provisions of the Proceeds of Crime Act 2002;

• extend the self-regulatory approach (i.e. codes of practice) governing the press to other groups such as book publishers and film-makers; or

• do nothing.

Following analysis of the responses to the consultation,[7] the Ministry of Justice (which took over policy responsibility for this area from the Home Office in 2007) announced that it would be proceeding with the second of these options: namely a civil recovery scheme.

2.2 The Coroners and Justice Act 2009 The civil recovery scheme is set out in Part 7 of the Coroners and Justice Act 2009, which came into force on 6 April 2010.[8] An overview of the scheme is set out in a Ministry of Justice circular: Part 7 of the CJA 2009 introduces a civil scheme, through which the High Court can order a qualifying offender to pay a sum of money to the enforcement authority in respect of exploitation proceeds obtained from a relevant offence. A person obtains exploitation proceeds from an offence where they derive a benefit from exploiting material pertaining to a relevant offence or from any steps taken or to be taken in the future with a view to such exploitation. This new kind of order is known as an 'exploitation proceeds order'.[9]

A "qualifying offender" is a person convicted of a relevant offence by a court in the UK, or by a foreign court provided the individual in question is a UK national or resident (or was a UK resident at the time the offence was committed). In respect of foreign convictions, the offence must be one that would also have constituted an offence if it had been committed in the UK. Service offenders are also covered, as are people found not guilty of an offence by reason of insanity.

A qualifying offender can "exploit material" by any means, including by publishing material in written or electronic form, by using any media from which visual images, words or sounds can be produced, or by live entertainment, representation or interview. Benefits derived for the benefit of a third party, for example a family member of the offender, are also covered. It is irrelevant whether the material is exploited or the benefit derived in the UK or overseas: both scenarios are caught.

Only material "pertaining to a relevant offence" will be liable to the scheme:

It is this type of material that is likely to cause the most concern to victims or bereaved families. Offenders who write about prison life or the steps they have taken to rehabilitate themselves will not therefore fall within the scheme, unless their work also includes material pertaining to the offence itself.[10]

"Relevant offences" are defined as serious offences triable only on indictment. The scheme is therefore targeted at offenders convicted of offences such as murder, manslaughter, rape and robbery, rather than offenders convicted of lower level crimes.

The scheme applies to all qualifying convictions regardless of whether they were incurred before or after 6 April 2010; however, it does not apply to any benefits derived before this date and does not, therefore, enable retrospective recovery of payments received prior to this date.

The court can only make an order following an application by a relevant enforcement authority: in England, Wales and Northern Ireland the relevant authority is the Serious Organised Crime Agency (SOCA). SOCA may only apply for an order with the consent of the Attorney General. The Ministry of Justice circular envisages that "cases are most likely to come to light following reports in the media, which in turn may trigger correspondence from members of the public or MPs". It advises that correspondence should be directed in the first instance to the Ministry of Justice.[11]

Once SOCA has made an application, the court uses its discretion to decide whether to make an order (and, if so, for how much). The 2009 Act sets out a range of factors that the court must consider:
(a) the nature and purpose of the exploitation from which (or intended exploitation in connection with which) the [offender] derived the benefit;
(b) the degree to which the relevant material was (or was intended to be) integral to the activity or product and whether it was (or was intended to be) of central importance to the activity or product;
(c) the extent to which the carrying out of the activity or supplying of the product is in the public interest;
(d) the social, cultural or educational value of the activity or product;
(e) the seriousness of the relevant offence to which the activity or product relates;
(f) the extent to which any victim of the offence or the family of the victim is offended by the [offender] obtaining exploitation proceeds from the relevant offence.[12]

The court may take other matters into account if it thinks them relevant.

If the court decides to make an order, the recoverable amount cannot be greater than the total value of the benefits derived by the offer (including any secured for a third party). The order should also not exceed the "available amount", which is the amount the offender can actually afford to pay: in the words of the explanatory notes that accompanied the Coroners and Justice Bill as first introduced, "it is not the intention of the scheme to cause bankruptcy".[13]

Any funds recovered are paid into the Consolidated Fund (the Government's general bank account at the Bank of England): the money does not go to the victim (if any) of the offence.

The Regulatory Impact Assessment on these provisions projected that they would be sparingly used, and that proceeds would be unlikely to exceed enforcement costs:

At most it is projected that two cases a year will arise, with an estimated annual cost to SOCA of around £280,000. The scheme will also have minor cost implications for the civil courts and also for the Community Legal Service if public funding were granted to defend any recovery action. On the basis of two cases per year, the financial impact is estimated to be under £90,000 per annum.

Benefits

Any proceeds recovered by the scheme are unlikely to exceed enforcement costs unless the criminal's memoirs are widely read and generate significant amounts of profit. Any money recovered will be paid into the Consolidated Fund.

Although we anticipate only a small number of cases, in terms of public perception that crime does not pay the scheme is an important one which justifies its existence even if it rarely needs to be used.[14]

The Assessment also summarised the human rights implications of the scheme, particularly under Article 10 of the European Convention of Human Rights relating to the right to freedom of expression:

Article 10 is a qualified right under the ECHR and interference with the right may be justified in pursuance of certain aims. These include the aims of protecting the rights of others and the protection of morals. The restriction is necessary in a democratic society, that is, it is compatible with the characteristics of a democratic society, specifically because of the public concern where criminals profit from their crimes, which amounts to a "pressing social need" justifying legislative action. We consider that the scheme is proportionate to the aim being pursued, particularly as it only relates to those who have committed crimes and would not prevent publication altogether, but would apply to recover the benefit from the publication. In addition, a court considering an application for an order has a discretion as to whether or not to make the order and, if so, the sum to be paid. In exercising that discretion, the court must take into account a list of factors which including the public interest in the publication and its social, cultural or educational value. Furthermore, an application for an order may not be made without the consent of the Attorney General.[15]

An article in the Guardian in December 2008 described a considerable amount of hostility to the measure from publishers and publishing bodies: Publishing trade body the Publishers Association described the plans as "disproportionate", "impractical" and "unnecessary" in its response, saying they would "set a highly dangerous precedent for state control of publishing, putting at risk the UK's enviable and hard-won freedom of speech", and would be "impossible to implement in practice".[16]

3 The Prison Rules

The Prison Rules 1999, SI 1999/728 (as amended) enable the Secretary of State to impose restrictions or conditions on permitted communications between a prisoner and other persons on grounds such as national security, crime prevention, and protecting the health, morals or reputation of others. Such restrictions must be proportionate and compatible with rights under the European Convention on Human Rights.

Paragraph 7.1(10) of Prison Service Order 4411 provides that prisoner correspondence may not contain any of the following:

(10) Material which is intended for publication or use by radio or television (or which, if sent, would be likely to be published or broadcast) if it:

(a) is for publication in return for payment, unless the prisoner is unconvicted. However, prisoners are permitted to receive payment for pieces of artwork or work of literary merit but only if they do not contravene any of the restrictions contained within paragraphs 10(b)–(e) and only if channelled through appropriate charitable organisations. This should also not be done on a regular basis so as to constitute any form of business activity (i.e. being commissioned to write a series of books or a regular feature in a national publication). It would be for the Governor to decide if such material contravened any of these restrictions.

(...) ;

(...)

(c) is about the prisoner's own crime or past offences or those of others, except where it consists of serious representations about conviction or sentence or forms part of serious comment about crime, the criminal justice system or the penal system;

(...).[17]

In a case involving the manuscript autobiography of Dennis Nilsen, who murdered six men, the court rejected arguments that confiscation of the manuscript was incompatible with his right to freedom of expression under Article 10 of the European Convention on Human Rights.[18] Nilsen's subsequent appeal was dismissed, the Court of Appeal saying:

We do not believe that any penal system could readily contemplate a regime in which a rapist or murderer would be permitted to publish an article glorifying in the pleasure that his crime had caused him.

(...)

[Strasbourg jurisprudence] did not establish that it was disproportionate for imprisonment to carry with it some restrictions on freedom of expression...[19]

4 Self-regulation: media codes of practice

Various guidelines and codes of practice are in place regarding the payment of convicted criminals by journalists and broadcasters.

The Ofcom Broadcasting Code states that no payments should be made to criminals unless it is in the public interest:

No payment, promise of payment, or payment in kind, may be made to convicted or confessed criminals whether directly or indirectly for a programme contribution by the criminal (or any other person) relating to his/her crime/s. The only exception is where it is in the public interest.[20]

The Press Complaints Commission code of practice imposes a similar restriction, again subject to exceptions where payment is demonstrated to be in the public interest:

Payment to criminals

i) Payment or offers of payment for stories, pictures or information, which seek to exploit a particular crime or to glorify or glamorise crime in general, must not be made directly or via agents to convicted or confessed criminals or to their associates – who may include family, friends and colleagues.

ii) Editors invoking the public interest to justify payment or offers would need to demonstrate that there was good reason to believe the public interest would be served. If, despite payment, no public interest emerged, then the material should not be published.[21]

The BBC's editorial guidelines state:

The BBC does not normally make payments, promise to make payments or make payments in kind, whether directly or indirectly (such as through fixers or intermediaries), to criminals, or to former criminals, who are simply talking about their crimes. In general the same should apply to families or relatives of criminals or former criminals. This is to protect our reputation, and the credibility of our interviewees and sources, as well as respecting the sensitivities of the victims of crime.

Any proposal to pay criminals, former criminals, their families or their associates (directly or indirectly) for interviews or other contributions relating to their crimes, must be referred to Director Editorial Policy and Standards. Payment of an actual fee will only be approved for a contribution of remarkable importance with a clear public interest which could not be obtained without payment. In such cases, only actual expenditure or loss of earnings necessarily incurred during the making of a contribution will normally be reimbursed. Note that this is not intended to inhibit the rehabilitation of criminals or prevent payment to people with a criminal conviction who are making a contribution not about their crime.

People who may not have committed a crime but whose behaviour is clearly anti-social must not normally be paid for interviews or other contributions about their behaviour. Nor normally must people whose activities have attracted such notoriety that any payment might be inappropriate, regardless of the nature of the contribution. Any proposal to make such payments, including payments in kind, must be referred to Director Editorial Policy and Standards.[22]

1 "Hounding of Mary Bell : Child killer forced into hiding after tabloids track her down", Guardian, 30 April 1998

2 Press Complaints Commission, Adjudicated complaint: PCC Investigation - Daily Mirror, 2 October 2003

3 "BBC row over Martin burglar fee", BBC News website, 4 March 2005

4 HC Deb 22 July 1998 c548

5 HL Deb 11 October 1999 c7

6 Home Office/Scottish Executive/Northern Ireland Office, Making sure that crime doesn't pay: proposals for a new measure to prevent convicted criminals profiting from publishes accounts of their crimes, November 2006

7 Ministry of Justice, Making sure that crime doesn't pay – a new measure to prevent convicted criminals profiting from published accounts of their crimes: response to consultation, CP(R) 11/06, January 2009

8 Coroners and Justice Act 2009 (Commencement No. 4, Transitional and Saving Provisions) Order 2010, SI 2010/816

9 Ministry of Justice circular 2010/08, Coroners and Justice Act 2009 – commencement of Part 7 ('Criminal Memoirs, etc.'), March 2010

10 Ibid, para 11

11 Ibid, para 27. The address is Criminal Law Policy Unit (re: criminal memoirs), Ministry of Justice, 7.41, 102 Petty France, SW1H 9AJ.

12 Coroners and Justice Act 2009, section 162

13 Coroners and Justice Bill 2009: Explanatory Notes, para 663

14 Ministry of Justice, Impact Assessment of new scheme to prevent convicted criminals profiting from accounts of their crimes, 15 December 2009, p6

15 Ibid

16 "Publishers angry at plans to hit criminals' memoirs", Guardian, 5 December 2008

17 Prison Service Order 4411, Prisoner Communications: Correspondence, para 7.1(10)

18 R v Governor of Full Sutton Prison ex p Nilsen [2003] EWHC 3160 (Admin)

19 R v Governor of Full Sutton Prison ex p Nilsen [2004] EWCA Civ 1540

20 Ofcom, Ofcom Broadcasting Code 2011, para 3.3

21 Press Complaints Commission, Code of Practice, rule 16

22 BBC website, Editorial guidelines (section 8): reporting crime and anti-social behaviour, paras 8.4.20-1 [accessed 21 May 2010]

*Cryptocurrencies*

Published Wednesday, 19 February, 2020

'Cryptocurrencies' are often talked about but they're not well-understood. In 2019, 73% of the UK population said they didn't understand the idea.

## What are cryptocurrencies?

'Cryptocurrencies' are a digital means of financial exchange. This briefing focuses on the 'decentralised' model used by Bitcoin, which is still dominant. In traditional currencies, governments and central banks guarantee to maintain confidence. Bitcoin replaces this with a public algorithm and technology. But being 'decentralised' means that there is nobody to take responsibility when things go wrong.

Most cryptocurrencies are very volatile in value and not suitable for everyday financial transactions. They are often used for speculative investment, and the overall market is comparatively small. It may be better to call them 'crypto-assets', 'exchange tokens' or 'unregulated tokens'.

## How do they work?

Users of cryptocurrencies receive public and private cryptographic keys and a 'public address'. These enable them to make and accept transfers and to withdraw funds. Accounts are usually anonymous.

All cryptocurrencies use distributed ledger technology (DLT) to verify transactions. This involves multiple confirmations of transactions that are than added to a permanent record – the blockchain in the case of Bitcoin. Multiple checking is meant to make fraud next to impossible.

## Benefits and challenges

• Cryptocurrencies may have been over-hyped. They may be a solution looking for a problem. But many financial services and authorities are interested in DLT.

• Most cryptocurrencies are extremely volatile. They may be more attractive in countries in economic chaos. More regulation and uptake may help to reduce this volatility.

• Approving transactions may be slow and open to premium charges. This undermines some of the improvements to traditional systems that they were meant to offer.

• Running Bitcoin relies on vast amounts computer processing power. This is unlikely to be sustainable for continued expansion. By January 2020, Bitcoin processing was using as much electricity as Austria.

• The decentralised nature of most cryptocurrencies has made them attractive to organised crime and tax evasion. But the public ledger can enable audit and tracing of criminal transactions.

• Cryptocurrencies can present major risks to consumers. There is little or no guarantee for protecting investment. There is a wide range of scams that take advantage of the mystique of the cryptocurrency.

## Political and regulatory responses

The Bank of England and other authorities have strongly highlighted the consumer risks of cryptocurrencies. They have tended to play down their threat to established systems.

The Financial Conduct Authority (FCA) regulates some types of crypto-assets that function like shares or investments. Cryptocurrency exchanges must register with the FCA and follow anti money laundering regulations. The FCA can offer little further consumer protection.

## Facebook and the Libra

In June 2019, Facebook announced the proposed launch of a new cryptocurrency, the Libra. They aimed to overcome some of the drawbacks described above. But the political and regulatory response has been very critical. Many partners have since withdrawn from the project.

*Current Affairs Digest: World Affairs (June 2020)*

Published Friday, 19 June, 2020

## Coronavirus in Africa

Coronavirus has affected informal workers significantly in Africa. This article reports that 86% of jobs in Africa are in the informal or traditional work sector, and in Nigeria 60% of the country's GDP is made up from informal work.

Brice Ngameni considers the impact on the sector. The author writes that government-imposed measures intended to stop the spread of coronavirus have had a negative impact on informal workers' income. These measures have included:

• The need for workers to regularly spend money on new masks or face coverings;

• A reduction in the number of passengers able to ride in taxis; and

• Early curfews, limiting daily working hours.

In addition to challenges associated with coronavirus, workers in the food supply chain in East Africa have had to contend with plagues of locusts destroying their crops.

In order to make up for lost revenue and help informal workers in the future, Ngameni says governments should pursue measures to pump capital into small businesses. His recommendations include:

• Lending through non-traditional channels;

• Suspension of rent payments and some

assistance for utility bills; and

• Suspension of back taxes and an exemption of tax payments for the first few years.

He argues that these benefits should only be offered to workers who agree to register with the state. This will bring a whole group of workers under the state's remit for the first time, which Ngameni believes will be the first step towards "a stronger and more resilient Africa".

Read the full article: Brice Ngameni, 'Coronavirus: Now is the time to build a future for Africa's informal workers', The Africa Report, 3 June 2020

## Understanding Iran and Venezuela

This article looks at the historic relationship between Iran and Venezuela and uses this to urge international policymakers not to overreact to Iran's shipment of fuel tankers to Venezuela in late May 2020. The author explains that Iran's decision to send fuel went against the US's current sanctions against Venezuela, a country facing fuel shortages. The author discusses how international onlookers may view the two countries' relationship as concerning, as they have both "consistently harboured anti-U.S. sentiment".

The author explains that Iran and Venezuela's diplomatic and commercial relationship began before the former's revolution in 1979. He argues that the two countries were closest during the presidency of Hugo Chávez in Venezuela from 1999 to 2013. In 2012, he states that Iran's investments in Venezuela were valued at $15 billion. In return, Venezuela's cooperation helped Iran make further relationships with Latin American countries such as Ecuador, Bolivia and Nicaragua.

He notes, however, that this relationship has not yielded particularly prosperous outcomes, as initiatives were not seen through to completion. Since the death of President Chávez in 2013, the article states that the two countries' relationship has declined. But he views the fuel shipment as "a renewed commitment" between the two states that have found themselves to be otherwise internationally isolated.

Ultimately, the author argues that the world should not see this cooperation as a threat, as Iran cannot be relied upon to deliver the goods or services needed to sustain Venezuela long-term.

Moises Rendon and Antonio de la Cruz, 'Understanding the Iran-Venezuela relationship', Centre for Strategic and International Studies, 4 June 2020

## US Protests

Many commentators have linked the protests in the US, following the death of George Floyd in police custody, to those during the summer of 1968. In this piece, Julia Azari states that comparisons can be drawn from several events in US history.

First, Azari considers the links between recent events and those of 1968. She notes that both protests had similar goals and that the rhetoric of "law and order" from President Nixon and President Trump has been similar.

The article then discusses events during the 1990s; for example, the beating of Rodney King by police officers in 1991 that was caught on a hand-held video recorder. Azari states that the recording of the event, as with the video of George Floyd, prompted wider recognition of police brutality.

The author also looks at the Reconstruction era (1865–77). Despite the recent abolition of slavery, Azari states that a number of practices were used to undermine the freedoms of black Americans. The author again compares President Trump with his precedent, President Andrew Johnson, who Azari says "allowed" this treatment of black Americans to continue.

Finally, Azari highlights the work of black activists during the 1900s. This period saw the creation of groups such as the NAACP and a move towards using the courts to force policy changes. The author compares the current actions of the US Senate to stall a bill intended to make lynching a hate crime, with similar efforts to pass the same bill in the early twentieth century. Read the full article: Julia Azari, '1968 isn't the only parallel for this political movement', Fivethirtyeight, 9 June 2020

## *Cyber security in a digital age*

Published Wednesday, 15 January, 2020

Cyber threats from foreign states and criminal groups are growing more frequent and sophisticated. Cyber attacks continue to feature in the news, including prominent incidents in the last year affecting WhatsApp and British Airways. Cyber security relates to the protection of devices, data, and services from unauthorised access, harm or misuse.

Use of online services and 'smart' consumer devices connected to the internet is also increasing. This means that cyber security is not just an issue for the security services or big business, but also for small businesses and individuals.

This Insight will cover threats to UK cyber security. This includes two key cyber security issues for the new Parliament: telecoms infrastructure and consumer devices.

## Where do cyber threats come from?

The Conservative Government's National Cyber Security Strategy 2016–2021 (NCSS) identified the key actors that pose a threat to UK cyber security. They are generally classified by their motive for engaging in malicious cyber activity. These include:

• Cyber criminals. Much of the most serious cyber-crime is enacted by financially-motivated Russian-language organised crime groups in eastern Europe. The threat also emanates from other countries and regions, including from within the UK. The NCSS identifies emerging threats from south Asia and west Africa as an increasing concern.

• States and state-sponsored groups. These actors regularly attempt to penetrate UK networks. This can be for political, diplomatic, technological, commercial and strategic advantage. According to the NCSS, few states have the technical capability to pose a serious threat to the UK's overall security. But many more are seeking to develop cyber espionage capability through the use of 'off the shelf' hacking tools. A small number of hostile foreign states have developed and deployed offensive cyber capabilities, such as the ability to access an opponent's networks with the intention of causing disruption, damage or destruction.

• Terrorists. Terrorist groups aspire to conduct damaging cyber activity against the UK and its interests. However, technical capability of terrorist groups is judged to be low by the NCSS. The volume and sophistication of cyber attacks may increase if new, more technologically literate generations engage in extremism.

There is a graphic that explains the above and which you can view on the Research tab of The Prison Oracle - tinyurl.com/2cjfe6yd

### Which groups are the most active?

According to the 2018 Threat Landscape Report by ENISA, the EU's Agency for Cyber Security, cyber criminals remained the most active group engaging in malicious cyber activity.

Nation states engaging in malicious cyber activity occurred several times within the EU. This was due to geopolitical developments/ tensions, most notably involving China, the USA, North Korea, Russia, Germany and the UK. Terrorism and malicious cyber activity continued to converge, motivated by the desire to launch cyber attacks, as well as fundraise and recruit.

There is a graphic that explains the above and which you can view on the Research tab of The Prison Oracle - tinyurl.com/2cjfe6yd

### Securing UK infrastructure

The UK's critical national infrastructure, including utilities, health, transport and communications, is at risk from state-sponsored cyber attacks. It is also increasingly at risk from criminal groups, which can now acquire sophisticated cyber tools.

With some key exceptions, the majority of critical infrastructure in the UK is privately owned. This raises questions regarding how far the Government should intervene in the operations of private companies to ensure that UK national security interests are prioritised.

The cyber security of UK telecoms networks has been in the spotlight in the last year. The May Government found that a stronger statutory framework for telecoms security is required. In particular, there is an outstanding decision on whether parts supplied by Chinese company Huawei and other 'high-risk' suppliers should be allowed in UK 5G networks. The Intelligence and Security Committee urged the incoming Prime Minister in July 2019 to take a decision on which companies will be involved in the 5G network, and suggested that debate on the issue had damaged the UK's international relationships.

### How secure are our smart devices?

Use of 'smart' devices connected to the internet is increasing in UK households. This includes tech products like fit bits and smart speakers as well as everyday household items like fridges, lightbulbs and toys. Although bringing many economic and social benefits, many smart devices lack basic security features. Security weaknesses in these devices can undermine the privacy and safety of individuals. Vulnerabilities also pose wider risks, for example, if devices are harnessed en masse to carry out larger attacks.

Currently there is no specific regulation setting cyber security standards for consumer products. As a result, there is little incentive for manufacturers to prioritise security in the design of products, which comes at a cost. This places the burden on consumers, often with limited technical knowledge, to make decisions about cyber security. For example, will the device be updated automatically to fix security flaws?

The May Government developed a voluntary code of practice and labelling scheme for consumer devices that set minimum security standards for manufacturers and retailers. The Government was considering making parts of the code and labelling scheme mandatory. This would require new powers in primary legislation to be brought before the next Parliament.

*Further reading*
• National Cyber Security Strategy 2016-2021, HM Government.
• Annual Review 2019, National Cyber Security Centre.
• Cyber Security and the UK's Critical National

Infrastructure (PDF, 709KB), Third Report of Session 2017–19, Joint Committee on the National Security Strategy, November 2018.
• Progress of the 2016-2021 National Cyber Security Programme, National Audit Office.
• Cyber security in the UK (PDF, 270KB), Ninety-Ninth Report of Session 2017–19, House of Commons Public Accounts Committee, June 2019.

**Insights for the new Parliament**
This article is part of our series of Insights for the new Parliament. This series covers a range of topics that will take centre stage in UK and international politics in the new Parliament.
• Browse all Insights for the new Parliament

*Delivering public services: The growing use of Payment by Results*
Last updated: 26 April 2013
The Payment by Results (PbR) approach to delivery of public services is not new — indeed, it was announced in the Labour government's plans for NHS reform more than a decade ago. PbR projects fall into two types: those run on the prime provider model (such as the Work Programme) and those using Social Impact Bonds (such as the pilot scheme at Peterborough Prison to finance rehabilitation work with short term prisoners, the first project operating under a SIB).
Nor is PbR without controversy. Advocates of the PbR approach tend to depict its advantages in terms of reforming and improving public services, by delivering more for less and by bringing in a wider range of service providers from the public, private and third sectors. Critics of the PbR approach, though, express concerns about whether it will by its nature tend to favour larger providers, thus squeezing out small and medium-sized providers (such as local charities and third sector organisations) and whether it will induce providers to "cream" the more tractable cases and "park" the less tractable ones. There is debate, too, about what constitutes a "result", by which service providers will be paid. This note examines some of the arguments for and against PbR and looks at current and planned projects in rehabilitation, welfare to work, the NHS, children's social services and with rough sleepers and with vulnerable young people.

**Drug crime: Statistics for England and Wales**
26 October 2020
**Summary**
*Recorded crime*
In 2019/20, there were around 175,000 drug offences recorded by the police in England and Wales. This is 13% higher than 2018/19. National totals exclude figures from Greater Manchester

for the years ending March 2019 and 2020 and are not directly comparable with previous years.
*Drug crime by police force area*
Merseyside recorded the highest rate of drug offences 8.3 per 1,000 population in 2019/20, up from 6.1 in 2018/19. Warwickshire had the lowest rate of 1.6 offences per 1,000 individuals (the same as the previous year).
*Proven offences and offenders*
In 2018/19, there were around 48,800 disposals given (cases dealt with) for drug offences. Between 2008/09 and 2018/19, the proportion of drug offenders receiving a caution fell from 46% to 30%, while the proportion receiving a custodial sentence increased from 9% to 16%.
*Hospital admissions*
There were 13 hospital admissions per 100,000 population due to drug related mental and behavioural disorders in England in 2018/19, and 19 per 100,000 in Wales. In the same year, there were also 32 hospital admissions per 100,000 due to poisoning by drug misuse in England and 32 per 100,000 in Wales.
*Drug related deaths*
Drug related deaths have increased year on year from 2,652 in 2011 to 4,393 in 2019 (representing a 66% increase). Data prior to 2011 is not directly comparable. Between 2017 to 2018 (the most recent data available) saw the largest annual increase in deaths (16%) since the time series began.

**Background**
*Legislation*
The Misuse of Drugs Act 1971 regulates the production, supply and possession of "controlled" drugs.
Controlled drugs are listed in Schedule 2 to the 1971 Act and are divided into three Classes – A, B and C – with Class A drugs considered the most harmful. Controlled drugs also include any substance or product specified in a temporary class drug order as a drug subject to temporary control. Drug crime is divided between 'trafficking in controlled drugs' and 'possession of drugs' offences. Possession of controlled drugs offences were split with effect from April 2004 into possession of Cannabis and possession of drugs other than Cannabis. 'Other drug offences' also fall under the possession category, consisting of offences related to permitting the use of premises for the supply or production of a drug, or the possession of a psychoactive substance with intent to supply (covered by the Psychoactive Substances Act 2016).
The above offences are all "either way" offences, meaning they can be tried in either a magistrates' court or a Crown court depending on the seriousness of the offence. However, offences

relating to the production and supply of Class A drugs are rarely tried in magistrates' courts due to their higher minimum sentences.

Maximum sentences for drug offences can range between a fine and life imprisonment depending on the class of the drugs involved and the seriousness of the crime.

### Drugs Review: Summary

Updated 17 September 2020
Dame Carol Black, February 2020
Summary of key findings

The illicit drugs market is big business, worth an estimated £9.4 billion a year. Around 3 million people took drugs in England and Wales last year, with around 300,000 in England taking the most harmful drugs (opiates and/or crack cocaine).

Drug deaths have reached an all-time high and the market has become much more violent. Taking the health harms, costs of crime and wider impacts on society together, we estimate the total costs of drugs to society are over £19 billion, which is more than twice the value of the market itself.

The drugs market consists of a number of distinct but overlapping product markets. Most drugs consumed in the UK are produced abroad. The supply of drugs has been shaped mostly by international forces, the activities of Organised Crime Groups and advances in technology.

The demand for opiates and crack/cocaine, and deaths from misuse of these substances, is closely associated with poverty and deprivation. There is an ageing population of heroin users with severe health needs, some of whom are using crack cocaine too, but there is also a new population of younger crack cocaine users that do not use heroin.

The heroin and crack cocaine retail market has been overtaken by the county lines model, which is driving increased violence in the drugs market and the exploitation of young people and vulnerable drug users.

The demand for powder cocaine is closely linked to that for other recreational drugs, such as ecstasy and amphetamines. Increased use of powder cocaine has been driven by those under 30. The demand for these drugs is strongly linked to the night-time economy and alcohol.

The use of new psychoactive substances among the general population has fallen but has increased in vulnerable populations such as those sleeping rough and those in prison.

Government interventions to restrict supply have had limited success. The key institutions involved are Border Force, the National Crime Agency (NCA) and police forces. All have faced budgetary constraints in the past decade and competing priorities. Even if these organisations were sufficiently resourced it is not clear that they would be able to bring about a sustained reduction in drug supply, given the resilience and flexibility of illicit drug markets.

There has been a renewed focus in recent years by the NCA and police forces on drugs in response to the serious violence caused by the county lines model.

More than a third of people in prison are there due to crimes relating to drug use (mostly acquisitive crime). These prisoners tend to serve very short sentences, have limited time in prison treatment and poor hand-offs back into the community. They are very likely to re-offend.

Drugs within prisons are widely available, with around 15% of prisoners testing positive to random drug tests. The problems are greatest in male local and category C prisons. New psychoactive substances have become increasingly problematic in prisons. Drug use in prisons is closely linked to the amount of purposeful activity available to prisoners.

Treatment in the community is the responsibility of Local Authorities. Spending on treatment has reduced significantly because Local Government budgets have been squeezed and central Government funding and oversight has fallen away. There is significant local variation, with some Local Authorities having reduced treatment expenditure by 40%.

Local Authorities commission treatment from NHS Trusts and third sector providers. A prolonged shortage of funding has resulted in a loss of skills, expertise and capacity from this sector. Treatment providers often have to prioritise the severe needs of the long-term heroin using population, meaning that services for other drug users have had less investment.

Even if more funding became available for treatment (which is vital), there would be a lot of work to do to build up capacity and expertise in this market. In addition to dedicated funding, the re-introduction of incentives and levers, and locally held joint responsibility and accountability, would go a long way to regenerate and vitalise the system.

Recovery is about more than just treatment. Other factors are equally important, particularly housing and employment. Central Government has funded some excellent pilots to address the complex housing and employment needs of long-term drug users but these are time-limited and small-scale.

Young people and children have been pulled into drugs supply on an alarming scale, especially at the most violent end of the market. There are strong associations between young people being drawn into county lines and increases in child poverty, the numbers of children in care and school exclusions. Social media has played a facilitating role.

There is a considerable increase in children using drugs, after a long period of a downward trend. Those seeking treatment have a number of complex needs, including mental health needs, that can only be met through a combination of specialist treatment and wider social and health care.

## Drugs Review: Summary
February 2020
See 32 above

## Drugs Review: evidence pack
Dame Carol Black, February 2020
Summary of the market analysis
There is a four-page graphic with grids that provide a summary of an analysis of the drugs market in England, covering five widely used substances; heroin, crack-cocaine, cocaine powder, cannabis and synthetic cannabis such as MDMA and amphetamines which you can view on the Research tab of The Prison Oracle - tinyurl.com/2cjfe6yd

For each one it follows the path from production to the end user, identifying the main distribution routes, the costs and harms as well as international comparisons and emerging risks.

## Drugs Strategy 2019
Introduction
The misuse of drugs in prison is one of the biggest challenges facing our criminal justice system today. Drug misuse is prevalent and contributes to violence, crime and vulnerability within prisons, which threatens safety and the ability of our hard-working prison staff to deliver effective regimes. We will not be able to improve safety, prevent reoffending and tackle serious and organised crime without reducing the misuse of drugs in prisons. This is a complex, multi-faceted problem with no simple answer – it requires a coordinated effort to limit the supply of drugs both inside and outside prisons, encourage people away from drug misuse towards positive and productive activities, and support those requiring treatment. It is therefore crucial that our approach to tackling the problem considers the whole system, working across government and with our partners at a national, regional and local level.

The scale of the problem is significant and has become more challenging in recent years. Between 2012/13 and 2017/18, the rate of positive random tests for 'traditional' drugs[1] in prisons increased by 50%, from 7% to 10.6%, and drug use in prisons is now widespread, particularly in male local and category C prisons. The emergence of psychoactive substances such as synthetic cannabinoids has exacerbated the problem, and these are often used in conjunction with other drugs, while we remain aware of problems with the diversion and misuse of prescription medication. The prevalence and patterns of drug misuse in prisons is shaped by patterns in the community, and the challenges faced by prisons can be exacerbated when those entering prison have an existing drug misuse issue or when drug misuse has been normalised in the community.

Evidence shows us that the prisons with the highest rates of positive random drug tests are the prisons that are the least stable. [2] The misuse of drugs contributes to a cycle of disruption and violence, leading to a reduced or unstable regime, which through unpredictability and lack of purpose can encourage prisoners to turn to drugs and alcohol. The debt resulting from the supply, distribution and use of drugs is also a significant cause of violence, intimidation and self-harm across the estate, endangering both staff and other prisoners. Consequently, to tackle drug misuse, we need changes in all elements of this cycle, enabling prisoners to engage positively with rehabilitation, in a calm and safe environment. Reducing drug misuse is crucial to the safety of our prisons and the rehabilitation of prisoners.

This strategy has been developed by the Ministry of Justice (MoJ) and Her Majesty's Prison and Probation Service (HMPPS), working with other partners across government. It sets out our plans to reduce the misuse of drugs in our prisons, and will provide direction to assist all stakeholders in this. We are also releasing detailed guidance for prisons to support them in identifying issues and share best practice. Together, we will focus on restricting the supply of drugs by improving security, building intelligence, and targeting the criminal networks which aim to bring drugs into prison. We will also reduce the demand for drugs in prison by developing more meaningful regimes, providing more constructive ways for prisoners to spend their time and ensuring the balance of incentives encourages prisoners to make the right choices. We will work closely with our health and justice partners to build recovery for prisoners who want to overcome their substance misuse, providing prisoners who are serious about living substance free with the environment to do so successfully. It is crucial that we deliver all three strands of this strategy in unison to make a meaningful, positive difference to both prisoners and staff.

1 Rates of positive drug tests are split between 'traditional' drugs – controlled substances defined in the Misuse of Drugs Act 1971, such as opiates and cannabis – and 'psychoactive substances' – substances initially defined in the Psychoactive Substances Act 2016, such as synthetic cannabinoids, but many of

*which have now been controlled by the Misuse of Drugs Act 1971.*

2 *Ministry of Justice, (2016), Prison Safety and Reform White Paper,*

*https://assets.publishing.service.gov.uk/government/ uploads/system/uploads/attachment_data/fil e/565014/cm-9350-prison-safety-and-reform- _web_.pdf, p. 41.*

There is a graphic that explains the above and which you can view on the Research tab of The Prison Oracle - tinyurl.com / 2cjfe6yd

### Early Release of Prisoners in England & Wales - an overview
24 January 2020

**Summary**
When a person in England and Wales is given a sentence of imprisonment for a period of time they will not usually spend all of that time in prison. The law allows for prisoners to be released on licence to serve the last part of their sentence in the community. Depending on the type of prison sentence the person is given, they can be:
• released from prison automatically at the halfway point of their sentence;
• released at the two thirds point of their sentence if the Parole Board decides it is no longer necessary to keep them in prison for the protection of the public; or
• released after the end of the minimum term of a life sentence if the Parole Board decides it is no longer necessary to keep them in prison for the protection of the public.

A person released on licence will be supervised by probation staff and must comply with certain conditions. If they breach the conditions of their licence they can be returned (recalled) to prison to serve part, or all, of the remainder of their sentence in prison.

The law on the point at which a prisoner can be released and whether the Parole Board is involved has changed over the years.

Various reasons have been put forward for having systems of releasing prisoners into the community before the end of their term of imprisonment. These include pragmatic reasons such as reducing overcrowding in prisons. Release part way through a sentence can also serve a rehabilitative purpose, allowing for supervision of prisoners in the community.

In both the October and December 2019 Queen's Speeches the Government set out plans for a Sentencing Bill, which would increase the automatic release point for certain serious violent or sexual offenders from the halfway point to the two-thirds point. The Government has said it will publish a white paper before introducing the Sentencing Bill.

The Government laid a draft order in October 2019 which provides that prisoners would be released automatically at the two thirds point of their sentence if they had been:
• convicted of a relevant violent or sexual offence for which the maximum penalty is life; and
• sentenced to a standard determinate sentence of seven years or more.

The Government has explained it is seeking to make this change now, by statutory instrument, ahead of wider reforms in a sentencing bill because not to do so would mean "continuing with a system which fails properly to ensure that serious offenders serve sentences that reflect the gravity of their crime".

The Government says this change would provide greater assurance to victims and the public that sentences will reflect the severity of their crime. Critics of the proposed change argue it will not meet these aims.

A debate on the draft order in the Lords raised questions regarding the impact on prison overcrowding and conditions. Concerns were also raised about a lack of public consultation and how the measure would fit with other Government policies on sentencing. It was noted that under the proposals, individuals would spend less time under probation supervision.

The draft order will be debated in the Commons on 28 January 2020.

### End of Custody Licence
The End of Custody Licence (ECL), which has just been abolished by the Government with effect from 12 March 2010, was introduced in June 2007 as part of the Government's response to prison overcrowding. Under the scheme, eligible prisoners serving sentences of between four weeks and four years could be released under temporary licence up to 18 days before their automatic or conditional release date. The list of disqualifying offences was extended in March 2008 to include certain terrorism-related offences, following the early release of two convicted terrorists. Guidance on the scheme is contained in Prison Service Instruction 42/2007. As at 31 January 2010, nearly 80,000 prisoners had been released on ECL, of whom 3% have allegedly reoffended during the period on the licence.

The Government have said that they intend the scheme to be a temporary one – indeed the Justice Secretary, Jack Straw said in February 2009 that it was "not satisfactory", and would end as soon as the prison system had sufficient capacity. Then in February 2010, the government announced that it would be abolished. The Conservatives had pledged to abolish the scheme, and the Liberal Democrats had also criticised it.

The End of Custody Licence is just one form of early release from prison. Information on others can be found in Prison Service Order 6000, and in Library Standard Note SN/HA/5199, Early Release of Prisoners: An Overview.

### The scheme's introduction

The End of Custody Licence was first announced by the then Lord Chancellor, Lord Falconer, in a statement on prison population, during which he announced an additional 1,500 prison places. Lord Falconer emphasised that this was a temporary measure:

In addition to the increased prison capacity, I have today authorised the issuing of guidance to prison governors to allow them to make wider use of the prison rules provisions to authorise release on licence for offenders who are coming to the end of their sentence. The guidance will authorise the release on licence, in accordance with existing prison rules, up to 18 days before their release date to those who have been sentenced to a determinate prison sentence of four years or less. This is a temporary measure.

Release on licence is not the same as executive release. Releasing people on licence means their sentence continues and will be granted only to those who meet the eligibility criteria, set out in the guidance which I will place in the Library of the House. The criteria exclude offenders convicted of serious sexual or violent crimes, those who have broken the terms of temporary licence in the past and foreign national prisoners who would be subject to deportation at the end of their sentence. It will apply only to those who are not released on home detention curfew. While on licence, the offender will remain the subject of his sentence and will be liable to recall.[1]

The scheme started on 29 June 2007, following press reports that Lord Falconer had been "trying desperately to avoid ordering the early release" in the face of rising prison populations.[2] Just weeks before its introduction, the day before taking responsibility for prisons under the new Ministry of Justice, Lord Falconer had been reported as ruling out an early release scheme to Sky News.[3] The scheme's introduction prompted a number of hostile press articles. For example, the Daily Express reported it as follows:

NEARLY 1,200 prisoners will spill out on to the streets of Britain today after being released early. Jails across the country will open the door for burglars, drug dealers and other crooks.

They will be freed up to two and-a-half weeks early after officials decided against staggering the controversial measure.

It means hundreds of convicted criminals being let back in to our communities at once and, in an added insult, each will have up to £172 in cash to spend. [4]

1 HL Deb 19 June 2007 c98
2 "Jailing fewer people 'is only way to solve overcrowding'", Times, 31 May 2007
3 "Falconer denies report of early prisoner releases", Guardian, 7 May 2007
4 "1,200 prisoners let out early hit the streets today", Daily Express, 29 June 2008

### Exploring extremism in three prisons
First published 2021

#### Summary

*Study aims*

This exploratory qualitative study explores the extent and nature of prisoner radicalisation in three high security prisons in England, how the establishments were managing extremist prisoners and responding to the risk of radicalisation.

#### Approach and interpreting findings

Interviews were conducted, between January 2014 and January 2015, with 83 male prisoners and 73 staff from a range of disciplines, including, prison wing officers, security staff, psychologists, offender supervisors and chaplains across the three establishments. Interview material was analysed using thematic analysis. The findings should be viewed with a degree of caution as the views presented may not be representative of all prisoners or staff.

#### Key findings

While the study aimed to examine all forms of extremism, only Islamist extremism was reported by respondents, as this was considered to be the most prevalent extremist ideology in prisons at the time of the fieldwork. This study found that, despite their small number, those convicted of Islamist extremist offences had a disproportionately disruptive influence in the prisons, exerting power and influence over other prisoners. However, not all were interested in pursuing an Islamist extremism agenda. They tended to either be motivated by an extremism agenda or interested in orchestrating anti-establishment and criminal activities of what was frequently described as a 'prison gang'. Those who were motivated by extremism were making attempts to radicalise others. While some prisoners outside of these groups were reported to express sympathies with Islamist extremism, there was little suggestion they would act upon this when released. Prisoners who were considered to be more susceptible to Islamist radicalisation were those thought to be most vulnerable within prison, who had the strongest sense of loss, loneliness, and alienation. They also tended to have grievances against society and the prison system, channelling their anger and frustration into extremism.

While it was reported by those interviewed that some prisoners were converting to Islam (with conversions to Islam reported to be higher than for any other faith), they were perceived, on the whole, to be doing so to help them survive in prison, with the Muslim faith offering the benefits of friendship and support. Religious behaviour did not typically compromise security and was identified by respondents as a useful aid to rehabilitation.

The study highlighted the importance of fostering a supportive environment in countering the risk of Islamist radicalisation, where staff were able to build relationships with prisoners. It was thought that this could be facilitated by ongoing staff training to increase their understanding of the Muslim faith and ensuring there were sufficient staffing levels to allow officers time to interact with prisoners. Media reporting was thought to increase divisions between Muslim prisoners and staff, with negative stereotypes of Muslims being perpetuated, especially in the tabloid press. The need for strong counter arguments to challenge these stereotypes was recognised.

It was generally thought that the strategies used by the prison service to disrupt the influence of extremists were largely effective. Management of extremists included moving problematic prisoners to different establishments to disrupt their influence and power base and gathering and disseminating intelligence on extremist activity. Imams were also thought to play an important part in countering extremism. However, it was recognised that their role was challenging and had expanded over time. The need to provide prison Imams with sufficient support so they are able fulfil their many, different functions was highlighted.

**Placing findings within a contemporary policy and operational context**

Since conducting the fieldwork for the study in 2014–2015, the operational and policy context has changed considerably. The terrorist offender population has more than doubled in number and its profile has become more complex, with increasingly diverse drivers of offending and a significant increase in Extreme Right Wing prisoners numbers. Alongside this, HMPPS has significantly strengthened its approach to managing terrorist and terrorist risk offenders. In 2016, a new Security, Order and Counter Terrorism Directorate (SOCT) was established to manage national security threats, maintain good order, and support operational partners more effectively to tackle criminality. A Home Office and HMPPS Joint Extremism Unit (JEXU), created in 2017, works within this directorate and is the strategic and operational centre for all counter terrorism work across prison and probation.

The counter terrorism operating model in HMPPS is delivered through a dedicated network of CT staff operating a specialist end-to-end offender case management process. The purpose of this work is to both manage and reduce the risk that terrorist offenders present and to prevent individuals from being drawn into terrorism. A range of control measures support this work, including Separation Centres for the most influential extremists, communications monitoring and restrictions, and the removal of extremist literature from the prison estate. A range of assessments and rehabilitative interventions are also applied to the terrorist and terrorist risk cohort. Since this research was conducted, HMPPS has trained and supported a cadre of prison chaplains to deliver theological and ideological interventions to terrorist and terrorist risk prisoners, with positive results reported in a number of cases.

Following the terrorist attacks in 2019 and 2020 involving serving offenders, HMPPS has further reviewed its counter terrorism policies and operations and made significant further investment in this area to better manage national security risk. This has strengthened the full range of HMPPS' counter terrorism capabilities and enabled better partnership working with other agencies. For example, it has delivered a new multi-agency intelligence hub to co-ordinate quicker and better information and intelligence exchange between operational partners and enable better detection and disruption of the terrorist risk in prison and those under probation supervision in the community. It is also introducing a dedicated counter terrorism assessment and rehabilitation centre, where psychologists and specialist staff will deliver a comprehensive assessment and rehabilitation strategy, underpinned by the latest research and thinking. In addition, the programme is rolling out new and professionalised training to staff across the sector to better understand and respond to the signs of radicalisation and terrorism risk across the range of ideologies. Further improvements to counter terrorism work in the sector will be informed by the various inquests, inquiries and reviews that have been set up in response to the attacks and are yet to conclude.

Most relevant to this report, HMPPS will continue to prioritise work to understand radicalisation in prisons and to develop effective responses and stronger operational safeguards. Given the changes to the policy and operational context since this research was conducted, this will include work to assess the feasibility of undertaking another study on radicalisation in prisons.

*Exploring the role of the Internet in radicalisation and offending of convicted extremists*
16th September 2021

**Executive Summary**

The aim of the study was to establish the role of the Internet in radicalisation[1] processes and offending of those convicted of extremist offences[2] in England and Wales by comparing radicalisation pathways across three groups: those who primarily radicalised online; those who primarily radicalised offline; and those radicalised through both online and offline influences. Four key areas were investigated: first, whether the Internet plays a prominent role in radicalisation; second, whether those taking different radicalisation pathways differ in their internet use; third, whether differences exist in demographic profiles and type of offences committed by those taking different radicalisation pathways; and fourth, whether the pathway taken impacts on professionals' perceptions of risk of committing future violent extremist offences.

Detailed post-conviction assessments were reviewed, which included 267 Extremism Risk Guidance (ERG22+) and two Structured Risk Guidance (SRG[3]) reports. Both the ERG22+ and SRG assessments are risk and need formulation tools intended for use with individuals who have been convicted of any extremist or extremist-related offence. The sample of reports included within the study comprised all that were available on the convicted extremist population in England and Wales from October 2010 to December 2017. Online behaviours commonly associated with radicalisation, demographic information and offence characteristics were coded for all cases. Professional ratings for overall levels of engagement, intent and capability to commit violent extremist acts were also included. Statistical analyses were used to compare all three radicalisation pathway groups. A key strength of the study was the data-driven approach utilising a unique dataset, with this being the first time that SRG and ERG22+ assessments have been available to those studying the role of the Internet by convicted extremists. This needs to be weighed against several limitations: only the convicted extremist population was represented; there was potential for missing data due to the purpose of these reports, as well as a general disparity in length and detail of reports accessed; and the number of offenders who primarily radicalised online was comparatively small – all of which should be borne in mind when interpreting findings.

**Key findings**

During the time period under investigation, up until 2017, the Internet appeared to play an increasingly prominent role in radicalisation processes for those convicted of extremist offences in England and Wales, reflecting general trends of widespread internet use in today's society. The types of websites, platforms and applications used by convicted extremists had changed over time, with a move from using specific extremist websites to open social media platforms.

The internet-related behaviours that were found to contribute most to a differentiation of pathway groups were general online activities relating to extremist activity, namely learning from others online and the use of open social media platforms. More specialised activities, such as the use of encrypted applications, were less predictive, possibly due to their low frequency of occurrence.

In terms of general profile and vulnerability factors, several differences between pathway groups were identified. Those who primarily radicalised online were less likely to be socially connected in the context of the offence and they were more likely to display signs of mental illness or personality disorder, compared against the other two pathway groups. Conversely, those who primarily radicalised offline were more likely to take on the role of attacker and they were less likely to follow an Islamist ideology, compared against the other two pathway groups. Most importantly, differences were found in assessed levels of engagement, intent and capability, with those who primarily radicalised online considered the least identified with an extremist group or cause, and least willing and able to perpetrate violent extremist acts. Based on the findings of this study, five recommendations for counter-terrorism policy and practice are proposed.

1 *Radicalisation is being defined as, "the process by which a person comes to support terrorism and extremist ideologies associated with terrorist groups" (HM Government, 2015, p. 21).*

2 *Extremist offending is defined as, "any offence committed in association with a group, cause, and/or ideology that propagates extremist views and actions and justifies the use of violence and other illegal conduct in pursuit of its objectives" (HM Prison and Probation Service, 2019, p. 8).*

3 *Following independent evaluation (see Webster, Kerr & Tompkins, 2010), the SRG was revised and was formally renamed the ERG22+ in 2011.*

*Exploring Substance Use in Prisons: A case study approach in five closed male English prisons*
26th October 2020

**Summary**

Substance use is a significant issue in prisons across England and Wales and it affects the regime stability along with resident and staff health and well-being. This research used case study methodology to identify factors associated with substance use in five English prisons – all of them closed prisons for men. The aim was to explore the wider cultural features of the prisons which, according to the recovery literature, may have an impact on levels of drug use, and has not been investigated in prior research. Observations, interviews, documentation analysis and data gathering were carried out. A total of 78 staff members and 61 residents across the five prisons were interviewed. Using thematic analysis, themes to explore factors associated with substance use across the prisons were generated.

There are some limitations with case study designs; whilst qualitative methodology enables the exploration of rich, in-depth information it is difficult to generalise the findings and to explore causal relationships. The learning made may not be relevant to all staff and residents or to other prison sites – particularly to prisons at lower or higher security level or those holding women or younger people. It is also unlikely that the five selected sites will have identified all of the possible factors associated with substance use. Another limitation was that the final site selection may have been biased to sites who were more willing to be involved in research.

Nine themes emerged from the qualitative analyses, which were clustered into three domains. The first domain was entitled 'descriptions of drug use' comprising themes which described the extent and consequences of drug use. This included a theme around the 'epidemic' nature of drug use, which encapsulated the perceptions that the extent of substance use was widespread, had major impacts on the prison, staff and residents, and was akin to an epidemic in prisons. Psychoactive substances were the most problematic drug reported. Also identified was a theme around the reasons for drug use, entitled 'escapism', to reflect the most commonly cited reason for drug use across the five prisons, as well as a theme entitled 'prison type and population', which grouped together perceptions of different contextual factors which impact on drug use, including the specifics of the population held at the prison, the prison type, the regime and staffing levels. The second domain was 'rehabilitative focus', and contained three themes: relationships, hope and prison culture. Relationships between staff and residents, and within staffing groups were perceived as fundamental, and differed between prisons with higher levels of substance use and those with lower levels of substance use. In prisons with a more prominent drug problem and amongst

those who reported using drugs, there was a real sense of hopelessness and helplessness amongst both staff and residents. The culture of the prisons also seemed to be related to substance use, with more punitive cultures existing in the prisons with greater levels of substance use. The third domain was called 'enablers of a more effective response to drug use' and included themes around resources (e.g. staff numbers and time), treatment provision, and prison regime/activity, all of which were factors which could help better address substance use. Resourcing was perceived to be key in dealing with the issue of drug use in prisons. Particularly in prisons with higher levels of drug use, many staff said that they did not have the time to devote to meaningful activity with residents, being instead overrun with paperwork, and managing processes and the consequences of drug use. There was limited treatment provision for substance use across all five prisons, and services were often observed to be quite separate from the rest of the prison rather than an integral part. The provision and availability of purposeful activity and a full regime were deemed important to support the reduction of substance use in prisons.

Recommendations arising from this predominantly qualitative analysis included recognising the extent of drug use, the need to focus on 'recovery capital', and adopting a prison wide approach. Improving and strengthening staff and residents' relationships, a greater use of rehabilitation over a solely punitive stance, better training for staff, a focus on improving procedural justice, and improving communication between staffing groups regarding Substance Misuse Services (SMS) and healthcare services were also recommended.

*Extradition (Provisional Arrest) Bill [HL]: Briefing for Lords Stages*
Published Monday, 27 January, 2020
The Extradition (Provisional Arrest) Bill [HL] was announced in the December 2019 Queen's Speech. Its primary purpose is to create a power of arrest, without warrant, for the purpose of extraditing people for serious offences. This would apply to certain countries specified by the bill. In cases where these specified countries make a valid extradition request (as defined under the bill) a designated authority in the UK would be able to issue a certificate in respect of the request. The issuing of this certificate would allow a constable, customs officer, or a service police officer to arrest the individual specified without the need to apply to a court. The Government intends for the designated authority in the UK to be the National Crime Agency.

Were the UK to lose access to the European arrest warrant, provisions in the bill would allow for the Government to apply the new power of arrest to extradition requests made by some or all EU member states.

The bill would also make consequential amendments and create a power for the Government to make further consequential amendments to primary legislation through regulations. The bill consists of two clauses and one schedule.

### Extradition (Provisional Arrest) Bill 2019-21
Published Friday, 19 June, 2020

The Extradition (Provisional Arrest) Bill was introduced in the House of Lords by the Government in January 2020. It completed Third Reading on 15 June and is due to have Second Reading in the House of Commons on 22 June.

Extradition is the legal process by which a person accused or convicted of a crime is surrendered from one state to another to stand trial or serve a sentence. It is governed by the Extradition Act 2003, which implements the European Arrest Warrant for EU Member States, and sets out the procedure to be followed in the case of other territories with which the UK has formal extradition agreements.

The Bill would amend the 2003 Act to provide police with the power to arrest without a warrant for the purposes of extradition. According to the Government this is necessary to address a capability gap that exists at present where the police become aware of a person wanted by a non-EU territory, usually through the system of Interpol alerts, but are unable to arrest them without obtaining a warrant from a court. This gives rise to a risk that the wanted person might abscond or offend before the police are able to detain them.

Currently the Bill only applies to extradition requests from certain non-EU countries: Australia, Canada, Liechtenstein, New Zealand, Switzerland and the USA.

The Government has said that this is because the UK has a high level of confidence in these countries as extradition partners, in their criminal justice systems, and in their use of extradition. It also reflects the fact that the power already exists under the European Arrest Warrant (EAW) and is therefore not needed for nationals of EU Member States before the end of the Brexit transition period.

Further territories could be added to the list in the future by regulations, and the Government has said the power could be extended to EU countries if the UK lost access to the EAW. However during debates in the House of Lords the minister stated that the Bill was not an attempt to replicate the capability of the EAW.

The House of Lords was broadly supportive of the aims of the Bill but amended it to introduce additional safeguards to the process of adding further territories in the future. This reflects concerns about the possibility of countries with poor human rights records abusing the extradition system.

### Extremism in prisons: Are UK deradicalisation programmes working?
Published Thursday, 11 June, 2020

The effectiveness of deradicalisation programmes in UK prisons is coming under increased public scrutiny. Government, parliament, and criminal justice agencies have discussed the programmes' efficacy following recent UK terrorist attacks.

In February 2020, police shot a man in Streatham, south London. The attacker was a convicted terrorist who had recently been released from prison. He injured three people during the attack. In December 2019, two people were fatally stabbed near London Bridge. The attacker was also a convicted terrorist who had recently been released following a sentence of imprisonment. The Streatham attacker was reported by the BBC to have "refused to engage with attempts to turn him away from violence" whilst in prison. The London Bridge attacker had attended two counter-terrorism programmes during his eight-year prison sentence and following his release.

The Home Secretary, Priti Patel, said that the Government had been confronted "with some hard truths about how [it] deal[s] with terrorist offenders" following the London Bridge attack. The Prison Officers' Association also said that a "fundamental review" of deradicalisation programmes in the UK was needed.

#### Has radicalisation in prisons increased?
Extremism in prisons is not a new concern. In 2016, Ian Acheson led a review into Islamist extremism in prisons, probation and youth justice. The then Justice Secretary, Michael Gove, commissioned the review. The review found that Islamist extremism in prisons was growing. It called for a central strategy to monitor and counter this extremism.

In March 2020, Baroness Hussein-Ece (Liberal Democrat) questioned the Government about steps it was taking to address radicalisation in prisons in England and Wales. She suggested there was evidence that showed the "overcrowded and "understaffed" prison system was failing to rehabilitate and deradicalise terrorist prisoners. The Government said it used tailored interventions and a network of counterterrorism prison and probation specialists to facilitate disengagement. For example, the

Government has, amongst other things, recently recruited 22 specially trained imams to engage with Islamist extremist prisoners and assist the delivery of the programmes.

Following the Streatham attack, former chief prosecutor Nair Afzal spoke of the need to have effective rehabilitation processes in place. Mr Afzal said:

"[…] there is a real problem with deradicalisation and disengagement programmes. […] There's no formal mechanism to risk assess [prisoners], they will commit this crime unless something is done about this in prison. Yes, longer sentences will have an impact, but it just delays the inevitable."

### What are the UK deradicalisation programmes?
There are several deradicalisation programmes in the UK for those who have been involved in extremist activity. This includes the 'Healthy Identity Intervention' and the 'Desistence and Disengagement Programme'. The 'Channel' programme provides support to those identified as vulnerable to being drawn into terrorism.

### Healthy Identity Intervention
The Healthy Identity Intervention ('HII') is one of the main programmes. It was one of the first behaviour offender programmes to be delivered to extremists in England and Wales.

HII seeks to address two areas: the reasons why people are motivated to offend, and the beliefs that enable them to offend. The programme aims to prevent extremist offending by minimising an individual's engagement within a specific group or ideology.

The intervention is delivered on a one-to-one basis. The programme is open to those convicted of Islamist terrorism offences and those jailed for "extreme right-wing violence".

### Desistence and Disengagement Programme
The Desistance and Disengagement Programme ('DDP') is another deradicalisation intervention. It forms part of the Prevent strand of the Contest strategy ('Contest'). Contest is the Government's counter-terrorism strategy. Contest has four strands for countering terrorism: Prevent, Pursue, Protect and Prepare. Prevent aims to stop people becoming terrorists or supporting terrorism.

DDP supplements HII. DDP provides a range of "intensive, tailored interventions and support designed to tackle drivers of radicalisation". The programme includes mentoring, psychological support, theological and ideological advice. The Government said DDP is designed to introduce "protective factors" to support individuals to disengage from terrorism and reintegrate into society. DDP can be offered to prisoners and those released on licence.

### Channel programme
The Channel programme ('Channel') provides support to individuals who are identified as vulnerable to being drawn into terrorism. It is available within communities and is not specific to prisons. There are some instances where Channel is available to individuals serving a prison sentence. Circumstances include where an individual is shortly due to be released and there is a need to put appropriate support in place.

Individuals can be referred by anyone, including by a family member or colleague. Referrals are assessed by a panel who decides what support can be offered. Participation in Channel is voluntary and not a criminal sanction.

### Programme evaluations
HM Prison and Probation Service ('HMPPS') piloted HII in 2011. The results of the pilot said that HII had "overwhelmingly positive" reactions from participants and facilitators. However, no full evaluation of HII has been completed. In 2018, a process evaluation of the HII pilot was published. HMPPS confirmed that it was developing an impact evaluation of HII to "explore outcomes over the longer term and across national delivery". Christopher Dean, a forensic psychologist involved in creating HII, was reported by the BBC to have said:

HII could not currently be tested like other rehabilitation programmes […] because there were too few offenders to get a scientifically-robust assessment of what worked.

The BBC has also reported that no evaluation of the DDP programme has been undertaken since its launch in 2016. Government officials say that the schemes have not been in operation for long enough for the results to be assessed. A government spokesperson was reported by the BBC to have said:

"All [of] our offender behaviour programmes are monitored, evaluated and kept under constant review to ensure that they are effective in reducing reoffending and protecting the public."

The Home Office commissioned an evaluative study of deradicalisation programmes in 2018. The study, conducted by the Behavioural Insights Team, reported that 95% of deradicalisation programmes were "ineffective". Following the findings, Diane Abbott, the then Shadow Home Secretary, asked the Home Secretary to publish the findings of the study. Ms Abbott also made reference to the Prevent strategy being a "tainted brand". Ms Abbott said:

"I suggest that those two facts—that Prevent is a tainted brand and that so many of the deradicalisation programmes are ineffective—are not unrelated."

In 2019, the Government announced an independent review of Prevent. The review will look at different aspects of the delivery of Prevent, including a review of the Channel process. Lord Carlile left his post as independent reviewer in December 2019. The Government is still to announce who will lead the review.

A Centre for Research and Evidence on Security Threats ('CREST') guide previously highlighted the challenges of assessing the success of interventions such as deradicalisation programmes. It said the complexity and diverse nature of extremist motivations makes it difficult to create broad evaluation measures.

## What are the next steps?

The Government announced a £90 million package of measures to counter extremism in January 2020. As part of this package, £3 million is for specialist intervention. This includes counter-terrorism programmes and intervention centres. The Government also said that prison officers will receive training to help them respond to incidents.

The Government also committed to introducing a new Counter-Terrorism Bill during the first 100 days of the new government. Amongst other things, it said the bill would "overhaul the terrorist licensing regime". The bill would also increase the number of specialist counter-terrorism probation officers.

The bill was introduced to the House of Commons on 20 May 2020. It was debated at second reading on 9 June 2020 and has now been sent to a Public Bill Committee, which is due to report by 14 July 2020.

The Terrorist Offenders (Restriction of Early Release) Act 2020 became law in February 2020. The Government said that the purpose of the Act was to ensure that terrorist offenders were not automatically released on licence before the end of their custodial term without the Parole Board's prior agreement. During the second reading debate in the House of Lords, peers highlighted a need to keep the effectiveness of deradicalisation programmes under continuous review.

The potential impact that the coronavirus pandemic may have on the timetable for introducing the Government's counter-terrorism package remains unknown. The Government announced measures to protect NHS services from becoming overwhelmed by a coronavirus outbreak in prisons. Measures include temporarily releasing low-risk offenders on licence where they are close to their release date.

*Firearm Crime Statistics: England & Wales*
22 September 2021
**Summary**
Statistics on the number of police recorded firearm offences are published by the ONS in the Crime in England & Wales bulletin. Gun related crime statistics are published by the ONS in the Offences involving the use of weapons: data tables.
*Recorded non-air firearm offences*
In the year ending 31 March 2020, there were a total of 6,622 non-air firearm offences recorded in England & Wales. This was a decrease of -4% compared with 6,884 offences recorded during the year ending 31 March 2019, which was the highest recorded since 7,040 in 2010/11.
*Homicide*
The most recent data suggests that there were 30 homicides committed by shooting in the year ending 31 March 2020 – 4% of all homicides. Of these 30 victims, 20% were female and 80% were male.
*Types of firearm offences by firearm type*
In the year ending 31 March 2020, Criminal damage and Violence Against Person (VATP) offence categories respectively accounted for 30% and 24% of air and non-air firearms offences combined. Robbery and Possession of Weapons offences each represented 15%.
*Type of non-air firearm used*
Since 2010/11, handguns have remained the most commonly used non-air firearm type, accounting for 40% of non-air firearm offences in 2019/20. The use of imitation firearms has increased the most among non-air firearm offences, from 23% of all non-air firearm offences in 2010/11 to 28% in 2015/16, before falling back to 23% in 2019/20. Rifles have remained the least common non-air firearms type, accounting for around 1% of all offences over the period.
*Non-air firearm offences by Police Force Area*
In 2019/20, the Metropolitan Police Service (MPS) recorded the largest number of non-air firearm offences - accounting for 27% of all non-air firearm offences in England & Wales. However, West Midlands Police had the highest rate of non-air firearm offences per 100,000 population, at 24, followed by MPS at 20.

*Firearms*
Published Wednesday, 13 January, 2021
In the UK firearms are heavily regulated. Not all guns can be licensed. Individuals seeking to own licenced guns are vetted and approved by the police.
As at March 2020 around 590,000 people legally owned firearms in England & Wales. Criminal offences involving firearms account for less than 1% of all recorded crime. In 2018/19 there were around 6,700 recorded offences in which a firearm was the principal weapon. The Library briefing

Firearm crime statistics: England & Wales provides further information.

The principal piece of legislation which regulates the possession of firearms and ammunition in Great Britain is the Firearms Act 1968 (as amended). However, there are many more pieces of legislation which contain provisions relating to firearms.

The Home Office has published various pieces of guidance relating to firearms ownership, a collection of which can be found on the webpage: Firearms licensing.

## Firearms licensing

In 2015, the Inspectorate of Constabulary (HMIC, now called HMICFRS) published a critical inspection of the firearms licensing functions of police forces: Targeting the risk: An inspection of the efficiency and effectiveness of firearms licensing in police forces in England and Wales. HMIC found several inconsistencies in the way forces dealt with firearms licensing. They recommended that the Home Office enhance the status of guidance on firearms licensing law, which currently has no statutory footing. Groups representing gun owners have also raised concerns with the licensing system, particularly with the way requirements to disclose medical information are dealt with.

The Police and Crime Act 2017 introduced powers for the Secretary of State to bring forward statutory guidance to police on their firearms licensing functions. The Home Office opened a consultation on draft statutory guidance in July 2019. The consultation closed on 17 September 2019, but the Government has yet to respond.

## Firearms safety

In June 2018 the Government introduced the Offensive Weapons Bill 2017-19 to Parliament. The Bill, as introduced, proposed tighter restrictions on certain high-powered and rapid-firing rifles. During the passage of the Bill, various Members of Parliament raised concerns with aspects of its firearms provisions and other issues relating to firearms regulation. Subsequently, the Offensive Weapons Act 2019 placed restrictions on rapid-firing rifles and required the Secretary of State to bring forward secondary legislation to specify how licence holders of high-powered rifles must safely store their weapons. During debates on the Bill, the Government committed to launch a public consultation on 'firearms safety'.

The consultation opened on 24 November 2020 and will close on 16 February. It asks for views on:
• setting prospective statutory rules for holding high powered rifles at "level three" security measures.
•amending existing air weapons regulations concerning the possession of air weapons by children.
• requiring people who run rifle ranges/ shooting galleries where only miniature rifles are used to hold a firearms licence.
• creating a new offence associated with the possession of the component parts of ammunition with intent manufacture.

### Air weapons

Air weapons are largely exempt from the firearms licensing scheme in England and Wales, although they are subject to licensing controls in Scotland and Northern Ireland. There have been longstanding concerns about the safe regulation of air weapons. A recent Government review the legislation resulted in proposals for reform of the statutory framework. This briefing paper does not discuss air weapons regulation, a separate Library briefing: Air Weapons discusses the issue.

## Antique firearms

Antique weapons are largely exempt from firearms licensing regulations, so long as they are held as a curiosity or ornament. In 2015 the Law Commission, the independent body which reviews legislation in England and Wales, published a wide-ranging review of Firearms legislation: Firearms Law – Reforms to Address Pressing Problems. The Law Commission raised concerns that the law poorly defined antique weapons and that this provided a loophole by which criminals could easily obtain dangerous weapons.

Provisions in the Police and Crime Act 2017 allows the Secretary of State to bring forward regulations to specify the definition of "antique weapons". This is intended to close the loophole identified by the Law Commission. A Government consultation on regulations to be brought under the Act closed in December 2017,the Government published its response in November 2020 and made the Antique Firearms Regulations 2020. The regulations provide a formal definition for 'antique firearm'. As a result, an estimated 26,000 more guns will now require a firearm licence to hold.

### Fishmongers' Hall: A Preventable Tragedy
Peter Clarke CVO OBE QPM
### Executive Summary
On 29th November 2019 the Learning Together programme of the Cambridge University Institute of Criminology organised a celebration of their 5th anniversary to be held at the Fishmonger's' Hall in the City of London. The programme is intended to bring serving prisoners and undergraduates together in a learning environment. On this occasion one of

the invitees was Usman Khan, who had been released from prison some 11 months previously after serving 8 years of a sentence imposed for terrorist offences.

It transpired that Khan had travelled to the event having equipped himself with knives and an imitation suicide belt. He attacked and killed Jack Merritt and Saskia Jones, both of whom were working with the Learning Together programme. Khan was subsequently killed by armed police officers.

The inquest into the appalling tragedy of the deaths of Mr Merritt and Ms Jones has exposed a catalogue of failures on the part of virtually every organisation involved with the management and monitoring of Khan in the lead up to, and following his release from prison in December 2018. Vital intelligence about his possible intention to mount a terrorist attack was not properly shared with those who needed to be aware of it. The Multi-Agency Public Protection Arrangements meetings did not receive crucial information, despite those who were aware of it being present at their meetings. Neither the police nor the probation officers assigned to monitor and manage Khan had the training or experience needed to deal with such a dangerous and deceitful terrorist.

The process and structures for managing terrorists both in prisons and after release needs to be thoroughly overhauled. This inquest has exposed extraordinary systemic failings that had unspeakably tragic consequences.

The case of Usman Khan is not an isolated one of terrorists mounting violent attacks on the public following their release from prison. The essential role that prisons should fulfil in contributing to public safety, both by holding prisoners safely and preparing them for safe release back into the community should be recognised by returning their management to the Home Office from the Ministry of Justice. There should also be urgent reviews of the use of Separation centres in prisons and the management and monitoring of released terrorists should be removed from local police and probation officers into an entirely new structure.

## Policy recommendations

• That responsibility for managing Her Majesty's Prison and Probation Service should be transferred from the Ministry of Justice to the Home Office, enabling closer alignment with all aspects of law enforcement and intelligence, and emphasising the essential role of prisons in protecting the public both during a prisoner's sentence and in preparing for safe release into the community.

• That there should be a distinct and separate structure for managing the treatment and risk of all offenders convicted of terrorism or terrorist related offences. This should be organised on a regional or national basis, and its staff should be trained and experienced in dealing with the specific risks presented by terrorist offenders, particularly those who are ideologically inspired.

• That there should be an urgent review of the use of Separation Centres in prisons to ensure that they fulfil the function of protecting both vulnerable prisoners and ultimately the public from being exposed to the risks posed by prisoners who have been radicalised while serving their sentences.

### Focus on Women's Prisons

This briefing paper describes the findings, best practice and key areas for improvement from inspections of five women's prisons: HMP Send, HMP & YOI Low Newton, HMP & YOI Downview, HMP & YOI Styal and HMP & YOI Foston Hall. (9th February 2022)

### Food fraud

Published Thursday, 21 May, 2020

Food fraud encompasses a range of activities including intentional adulteration or substitution of ingredients and mislabelling of food products. Although it is difficult to quantify the impact of food fraud, estimates of the annual global trade in counterfeit food and drink range from $6.2 billion to $40 billion. Modern food supply chains and manufacturing infrastructure have greatly increased opportunities for it to occur, its scale and impact.

Examples of high-profile cases of food fraud include the addition of undeclared horsemeat to a variety of beef products in the UK and Europe in 2013, addition of melamine to baby formula in China in 2008 and the presence of other ingredients (including olive and myrtle leaves) in around one in four UK samples of oregano in 2016.

### Key Points

• Foods that are commonly reported to be adulterated include herbs and spices, coffee, seafood, honey and olive oil.

• In addition to affecting consumer choice and confidence, food fraud may pose a public health risk. In 2016, a restaurant owner was sentenced to prison after substituting almond powder with mixed nut powder containing peanuts, resulting in the death of a customer.

• Other impacts on consumers include loss of nutrition and inadvertent consumption of foods that are normally restricted for ethical or religious reasons.

• Businesses may suffer financial losses following food fraud incidents due to factory closure, product recalls or destruction of contaminated ingredients or products. Companies may also suffer reputational damage.

• A range of UK laws and regulation contribute to preventing food fraud. The majority of law relating to food in the UK is based on the Food Safety Act 1990, which prohibits food which is not of the nature, substance or quality that consumers would expect, and describing or presenting food in a false or misleading way.

• Public bodies responsible detecting and mitigating food fraud include local authorities, government departments and regulators. In England, Defra is responsible for policy and legislation on food labelling and composition. It is also responsible for the Government's food authenticity research programme, which identifies risks to food authenticity and develops and validates food testing methods.

• Strategies to detect and prevent food fraud broadly fall into two categories: scientific analysis to test the authenticity of foods and broader mitigation strategies including intelligence gathering, vulnerability assessments and economic analysis strategies.

• Each food business has its own approach to testing the authenticity of its products. Food retailers often have contractual agreements with suppliers that require them to carry out authenticity testing of their ingredients. Large food retailers, such as supermarkets, typically have their own routine monitoring programmes.

• There are a variety of analytical techniques that can be used to test for adulterated food and drink and often a combination of methods will be used.

• Testing can be targeted (whereby the analysis looks for a pre-defined characteristic, such as a specific adulterants or section of DNA), or non-targeted (whereby multiple measurements of a sample are taken using a variety of techniques to obtain a sample's 'chemical fingerprint')

• Barriers to tackling food fraud relate to the cost and capability of authenticity testing, perpetrators changing their mode of operation, and a complex regulatory enforcement system.

• The Food Standards Agency (FSA) has said that there is no evidence to suggest the UK will be at more risk from food crime after the Brexit transition period. However, some stakeholders have raised concerns that EU exit may impact the UK's vulnerability to food fraud.

• Concerns relate to checks on food imports, the UK's food testing capacity and the extent of UK access to EU food fraud intelligence networks.

### Foreign National Offenders - Deportation: Jan 2020

**Summary**

Powers to deport foreign criminals Deportation is a statutory power of the Home Secretary. People who are not British citizens are liable to deportation from the UK if the Home Secretary deems their deportation to be conducive to the public good.

The UK Borders Act 2007 made provision for the automatic deportation of foreign criminals. The Home Secretary must make a deportation order in respect of a foreign criminal unless certain exceptions apply (e.g. where deportation would contravene the UK's obligations under the Refugee and Human Rights Conventions).

The Home Secretary's ability to deport criminals from EEA Member States is restricted by the operation of EU law, which requires that expulsion must be proportionate and based exclusively on the personal conduct of the individual concerned and level of 'threat' that they pose to public policy or public security.

The position of EEA citizens will change after Brexit, when EEA citizens and their family members will come within the scope of UK domestic law on deportation. The timeframe for the changes to be implemented will depend on the type of exit the UK has from the EU.

*Appeals*

The Nationality, Immigration and Asylum Act 2002 sets out the considerations to which tribunals and courts must 'have regard' when hearing an appeal by a foreign national offender against a deportation order.

In July 2017 the Supreme Court found the 'deport first, appeal later' rules to be unfair and unlawful. Originally applied only to foreign national offenders facing deportation from the UK, the approach was extended in 2016 so that any appellant challenging an immigration decision (other than in asylum cases) could be required to leave the UK. In R (Kiarie and Byndloss) v Secretary of State for the Home Department the Supreme Court held that the Home Secretary had not established that 'deport first, appeal later' struck a fair balance between the rights of the appellants and the interests of the wider community.

*Operation Nexus*

Operation Nexus is a joint operation between the Home Office's Immigration Enforcement Directorate and several police forces. It was launched in London in 2012. Described as a means of more effectively tackling offending by foreign nationals, its focus was said to be on identifying 'high harm' offenders. However the initiative has attracted criticism for facilitating the deportation of people with no criminal convictions based on untested police reports or conduct that led to a criminal charge but did not result in a conviction. Critics say its mission has widened considerably since its inception, targeting specific groups for deportation.

An unsuccessful legal challenge was brought by the AIRE Centre in 2017, and their subsequent appeal was dismissed in 2018.

*Deportation with assurances*

As both the Refugee and Human Rights conventions prohibit deportation when there is a real risk of torture or inhuman or degrading treatment or punishment in the receiving state, the UK has pursued a policy of deportation with assurances [DWA] in the cases of foreign nationals suspected of terrorism.

The policy has been criticised by both human rights advocates and by those who feel the strict conditions imposed by the European Court of Human Rights infringe upon British sovereignty. David Anderson QC, former Independent Reviewer of Terrorism Legislation, was tasked by the Coalition Government with reviewing the process of deporting foreign nationals suspected of terrorism. His report, co-authored with Clive Walker QC, professor emeritus of criminal justice studies at Leeds University, was published in July 2017.

**Scrutiny**

The Home Affairs Select Committee criticised the Home Office's decision to set targets for deportation in their 2018 report into the Windrush Generation.

In its June 2016 report on the work of the Immigration Directorates, the Home Affairs Committee focussed on efforts to deport foreign national offenders with EU citizenship, concluding that the Government 'should have done better'. In its response the Home Office argued that the number of foreign national offenders removed from the UK in 2015-16 was the highest since records began.

The lack of progress and inefficient approach 'dismayed' the Public Accounts Committee. The Committee noted in 2015 that over a third of failed deportations were within Home Office control. It pointed out that the number of British citizens returned to UK prisons through prison transfer agreements to serve the remainder of their sentences in the UK was broadly double the number of foreign national offenders removed from the UK. It called for a full end-to-end review of the deportation process.

The NAO's 2014 report described slow progress in deporting foreign national offenders despite both Labour and Coalition Governments having put greater effort and resources into removals. Its investigation found legal processes and administrative factors exacerbating problems caused by a lack of joint working and administrative errors. It recognised the Government's belief that the Immigration Act 2014 would reduce the number of appeals against deportation orders.

*Hate Crime Statistics*
10 December 2020

**Hate Crime Summary**

Police Recorded Crime Police recorded crime figures in 2019/20 show that there were 105,090 offences where one or more of the centrally monitored hate crime strands were deemed to be a motivating factor. This represented a 8% increase on figures for 2018/19. Figures from Greater Manchester Police (GMP) were not included in this year's release due to the implementation of new IT systems affecting data supply.

The increase in police recorded hate crime over the years has partly been attributed to better recording methods used and greater awareness in reporting hate crimes.

**Covid -19 Pandemic**

In October 2020, the Home Office published provisional trends in racially or religiously aggravated offences under Covid-19 restrictions in England and Wales, up until July 2020.

Data from the GMP was excluded and provisionally shows that in March, April and May 2020 the levels of racially or religiously aggravated offences recorded by the police were lower than the same period in 2019, but that in June and July 2020 they were higher – in June by as much as one third.

**Police Force Area Data**

The highest rate of hate crimes for all offences recorded by the police per 100,000 population in 2019/20 (excluding the GMP whose figures were not included this year) was in the West Yorkshire Police Force Area (359). The lowest rate was found in North Yorkshire (78). The rate for England and Wales including the British Transport Police was 177.

West Yorkshire was the only police force to appear amongst the 10 highest rates recorded for each hate crime strand.

*Hate Crime - spreadsheet*
*https://prisons.org.uk/facts-figures/research-briefings/*

*Health and safety for prison staff*
16 March 2020
**Summary**

A Westminster Hall debate on health and safety for prison staff is scheduled for Wednesday 18 March 2020 at 9.30am. The Member leading the debate is Grahame Morris MP.

**1. Background**

1.1 Safety in prisons Chief Inspectors of Prisons, the Prison and Probation Ombudsman,

Independent Monitoring Boards and the Justice Committee have all repeatedly expressed concern about a decline in prison safety since 2012.

Various factors have been identified as contributing to the decline in safety, including:
• a link between violence and the number of staff
• drugs misuse and psychoactive substances
• limitations to prison regimes and
• poor day-to-day living conditions, including crowding

For more information see the Library briefing Prison Safety in England and Wales.

*Assaults on staff*

A recent National Audit Office report, Improving the prison estate, noted that between 2015 and 2018, among adult prisoners, key indicators of poor safety in prisons reached all-time highs. There was a 110% increase in prisoner assaults on staff. The number of assaults on staff has been rising consistently since the start of 2015, reaching a peak of 10,424 assaults on staff in the year ending June 2019.[1] Before 2015, there were around 3,000 recorded assaults on staff per year.

The rise in assaults has begun to slow down, with the number being fairly level since mid-2018 (albeit rising slightly in 2019). The most recent figures at the time of writing show a slight fall, to 10,059 assaults on staff in the year ending September 2019.

The prison population does vary from year to year, so these figures need to be put in context. In the year ending September 2019, there were 121 assaults on staff per 1,000 prisoners, compared with 54 per 1,000 prisoners in 2015 and 35 per 1,000 prisoners in 2010.

The statistics also indicate the 966 of the assaults in the year ending September 2019 were classified as 'serious assaults'.[2] The number of serious assaults per year has risen in line with the rising number of all assault, so they made up around 10% of assaults on staff in each year.

*Overall level of violence in prisons*

The level of violence in prisons in general has been rising. The annual number of assaults by prisoners, which includes assaults on staff, more than doubled between 2010 and 2019, and was around 33,000 in the year ending September 2019.[3] Self-harm incidents reached a record high of 61,461 incidents in the 12 months to September 2019, up 16% from the previous 12 months. Self-harm incidents have followed the same trend as assaults, having been level at around 25,000 per year up until 2015, when they started to rapidly rise.

HMPPS releases annual statistics showing the number of recorded incidents of protesting behaviour. There were nearly 2,200 incidents involving barricades, hostage-taking, or concerted indiscipline or around 27 per 1,000 inmates. This was nearly four times the equivalent number ten years previously (just over 560).[4]

*Exposure of staff to psychoactive substances*

The Health and Social Care Committee, in a 2018 report, Prison health, noted that the increasingly widespread use of novel psychoactive substances was a serious risk to the health and safety of users, fellow prisoners and staff alike.

*Hiring and staff retention*

The number of prison officers fell by a quarter between 2010 and 2014, going from around 25,000 to 18,000. Between 2014 and 2017, the number stayed at around 18,000 before increasing again to nearly 23,000 in 2019 as the result of a recruitment drive.[5]

The result of the changes of the last decade is that, although the number of prison officers is almost back at its 2010 level, the collective level of experience within the workforce has decreased substantially. In 2010, 7% of prison officers had been in post for less than 2 years compared with 35% in 2019. The proportion with 10 years' experience or more went from 56% of officers to 46% in the same period.

The workforce statistics also suggest a problem of new recruit retention. As the number of joiners has risen since 2017, the number of leavers has also risen. The result is that a larger-than-ever proportion of leavers have served less than one year. The proportion over time can be seen in the chart in the margin.

Looked at differently, the proportion of new recruits who leave after less than one year has also risen in recent years. The latest rough estimate is that one in five new prison officers (bands 3-5) leaves after less than one year.[6] It is worth noting that this proportion was similar between 2010 and 2014 but was lower in the years since, until 2019.

*Sickness absence*

In 2018/19, an average of 9.3 days were lost to sickness absence per full-time equivalent staff member. This was around the same as in the previous year and lower than the average of around 11 days in 2013/14 and 2014/15. The number of days lost to absence is consistently highest in the Youth Custody Service, with 12.5 days lost per full-time equivalent staff member in 2018/19.[7]

There is no routinely published data on the reasons for sickness absence, although some has been published in response to PQs. In 2018/19, 1,939 prison officers in public sector prisons took sick leave due to 'mental and behavioural disorders'.[8] This was the highest number recorded in any year (the series begins in 2010) and a 43% increase on the previous year. Note that these figures might not be a complete count of prison officers who took leave for these reasons because in some cases a reason might not have been recorded.

## 1.2 The Joint Unions in Prisons Alliance – Safe Inside

The Joint Unions in Prisons Alliance (JUPA) has raised concerns about health and safety conditions for prison staff. JUPA includes a number of trade and professional organisations with members working to provide services inside prisons. JUPA's May 2019 position statement listed their key concerns:

- Unsafe staffing
- Work-related violence
- Impact of exposure to psychoactive substances
- Working conditions and overcrowding.

JUPA's June 2019 report, Safe Inside states that health and safety is now the preeminent concern of members. The report provides the results of a survey of staff working in prisons and concludes that the results "present a picture of a prison system that is failing to meet the basic health and safety needs of the prison workforce". JUPA calls for:

1. Tougher responses to violent incidents
2. Better health and safety reporting, including a single reporting system
3. Action to prevent exposure to psychoactive substances
4. Joint work to examine the causes and effects of violence against staff
5. More prison officers to ensure safe staffing levels

JUPA has developed a Safe Inside Prisons Charter. An EDM tabled on 25 February 2020 notes the high levels of violence against prison staff and welcomes the Safe Inside Prisons Charter, calling on the Government to adopt it.

## 1.3 Government policy

The Justice Secretary was asked in a PQ in July 2019 what recent steps he had taken to improve the health and safety of prison staff. Robert Buckland replied:

The health and safety of our staff and those in our care remains our top priority. Risks to staff are continually assessed, and suitable controls are implemented accordingly. The effectiveness of those controls is monitored at local and national level, and through joint audit work with prison unions.

HMPPS recognises that the physical, emotional and social wellbeing of employees is paramount. All HMPPS staff have access to an occupational health service and employee assistance programme. This includes 24 hour, 365 days a year access to signposting and counselling, and trauma support services.

It is a priority to ensure that prisons are places of safety and reform and the government has invested an additional £70 million investment in safety, security and decency. This has included £16 million to improve conditions for prisoners and staff and £7 million on new security measures, such as security scanners, improved searching techniques, phone-blocking technology and a financial crime unit to target the criminal kingpins operating in prisons.[9]

In August 2019 the Government announced £100 million to fund airport-style security to "reduce illicit items which fuel violence and hinder rehabilitation".[10] The first sixteen prisons to receive scanners were identified in January 2020.[11]

In July 2019 Robert Buckland said the prison service had started research on the effects on prison staff of second-hand exposure to psychoactive substances, in particular across 10 prisons. He said:

That testing programme will be extended. We have also established a drugs taskforce, because the best way to deal with the risk is to minimise the use of drugs in prisons.[12]

The Government has said prison officers are being given tools to help them do their job more safely.[13] The Ministry of Justice announced in October 2018 that prison officers would be issued with incapacitant spray, PAVA. A press release stated that the national roll out, to prisons for adult males, followed a successful pilot at four prisons.[14] Rigid Bar handcuffs are being provided to prison officers in the adult male estate.[15]

## 1.4 Coronavirus

On 12 March 2020 Prisons Minister, Lucy Frazer, made a statement on preparedness to deal with coronavirus (COVID-19) in prisons.

The Government is doing everything it can to combat the COVID19 outbreak, based on the very latest scientific and medical advice. This includes in our prisons, where we are working closely with Public Health England, the NHS and the Department of Health and Social Care to manage the challenges we face.

The safety and wellbeing of staff, prisoners and visitors is paramount and at the heart of our approach.

Prisons have existing, well-developed policies and procedures in place to manage outbreaks of infectious diseases. This means prisons are well prepared to take immediate action whenever cases or suspected cases are identified, including isolating individuals where necessary.

Basic hygiene is a key part of tackling the virus and good practice is being promoted on posters throughout the estate. Handwashing facilities are available to all prisoners – not just in cells but other shared areas such as education blocks and kitchens. Staff and visitors also have access to handwashing facilities and we have worked closely with suppliers to ensure adequate supply of soap and cleaning materials.

We understand that prisoners and their loved ones might be concerned about the situation. But we can assure them that we will continue to operate normal regimes, with the minimum disruption, for as long as we can. This will include visits to prisoners but, in line with Public Health advice for the general public, we urge any friend or family member not to come to a prison for visit if they have any symptoms associated with COVID19 - a fever or new, persistent cough. We are also looking into ways to keep prisoners in close contact with their families in all eventualities, and will share further information as and when necessary.

We have procedures agreed with our public health colleagues for protecting staff in the workplace but, like any member of the community, some prison staff may need to self-isolate in line with public health advice, or may become infected. We are taking steps to boost staff availability and so enable us to look after prisoners properly and minimise the impacts on prison regimes of staff absences.

There is a huge amount of work taking place, and I want to thank all those who have been striving tirelessly to make sure we are ready to do all we can to respond over the coming weeks.[16]

1 Ministry of Justice, Safety in Custody quarterly: update to September 2019, 30 January 2020

3 Ministry of Justice, Safety in Custody quarterly: update to September 2019, 30 January 2020

4 HMPPS, HMPPS Annual Digest 2018 to 2019, chapter 8

5 These figures refer to prison officers in bands 3-5 which includes prison officers (including specialists), supervising officers, and custodial managers.

6 HMPPS, HM Prison and Probation Service workforce quarterly: June 2019, tables 8 and 13.

7 HMPPS, HMPPS Annual Digest 2018 to 2019, chapter 15

8 HC 281606, 24 July 2019

9 Prisons: Industrial Health and Safety: Written question   277823, 22 July 2019

10 Gov.uk, £100 million crackdown on crime in prison, 13 August 2019

11 Gov.uk, press release, 16 jails to receive X-ray scanners, 24 January 2020

12 HC Deb 9 July 2019 c136

13 Prison Officers: Resignations: Written question – 24344, 11 March 2020

14 Gov.uk, Prison officer safety equipment rolled out, press release, 9 October 2018

15 Prison Officers: Restraint Equipment: Written question – 14687, 13 February 2020

16 Gov.uk, Coronavirus (COVID-19) prison preparedness: Lucy Frazer statement, 12 March 2020

## "Helen's Law" - Parole for murderers who conceal the whereabouts of victims' remains
1 February 2017

**Summary**

'Helen's Law' refers to a proposal that the law should be changed to prohibit the release on parole of offenders who were convicted of murder and have failed to reveal the location of the body of their victim.

The campaign for 'Helen's Law' is led by Marie McCourt whose daughter, Helen, was murdered in 1988. Ian Simms, who was convicted of Helen's murder, has to date not revealed the location of her body.

The change.org petition calling for Helen's law has been presented to the Government by Marie McCourt. As at 1 February 2017, it had over 390,000 signatures.

Conor McGinn introduced a Ten Minute Rule Bill, Unlawful Killing (Recovery of Remains) Bill 2016-17 which was given a first reading on 11 October 2016. The Bill has not yet been published. In theory, it is due to receive its Second Reading on 3 February 2017, but it may well not be reached. Amongst other proposals, the Bill would deny parole to murderers for as long as they refuse to disclose the whereabouts of their victim's remains. Mr McGinn has called for the Government to support his proposal or incorporate it into its legislative programme.

The Government has written to the Parole Board asking it to review its guidelines on the issue. This is part of a wider review of Parole Board guidance, the results of which have not yet been published. The Government also points out that, in sentencing and parole decisions, the courts and the Parole Board already take refusal to reveal the location of victims' remains into account.

## Indeterminate Sentences for Public Protection
6 June 2019

**Summary**

*What are IPPs?*

Sentences of Imprisonment for Public Protection (IPPs) were introduced by the last Labour Government from 2005. They were designed to ensure that dangerous violent and sexual offenders stayed in custody for as long as they presented a risk to society. Under the system, a person who had committed a specified violent or sexual offence would be given an IPP if the offence was not so serious as to merit a life sentence. Once they had served their "tariff" they would have to satisfy the Parole Board that they no longer posed a risk before they could be released.

## Criticisms of the sentence

The main concerns about IPPs were that:

• Some less serious offenders were given very short tariffs but then have been kept in prison for a long time after these have expired

• The prison and parole systems could not cope with the need to give all these short-tariff prisoners appropriate access to rehabilitative and resettlement programmes so that they could demonstrate they were no longer a risk to society

• The administrative delays resulted in uncertainty and perceived injustice for prisoners and litigation

• The rapid increase in the numbers of those on IPPs contributed to prison overcrowding, which in turn exacerbated the problems with providing rehabilitation

## IPPs were abolished in 2012, but not for existing prisoners

The Coalition Government abolished sentences of imprisonment for public protection for offenders convicted on or after 3 December 2012, calling the system "not defensible". It replaced them with different sentences for dangerous offenders. However, the change was not made retrospective. It didn't apply to existing prisoners serving those sentences at the time. At the end of March 2019 there were still around 2,400 prisoners serving IPPs.

## Pressure for further change

Former Justice Secretaries Ken Clarke and Michael Gove have called for reforms. The then Chairman of the Parole Board, Nick Hardwick, set out in November 2016 how the Board could reduce the numbers of IPP prisoners but also suggested possible ways that the Government could take action if it wanted further reductions. This could be done by revising the risk test (either for all IPP prisoners or for those with short tariffs) or releasing IPP prisoners who have now served longer than the maximum current sentence for their offence.

In a thematic review, Her Majesty's Chief Inspector of Prisons, Peter Clarke, said it was "widely accepted that implementation of the sentence was flawed" and that "decisive action" was needed for reasons of cost, "fairness and justice" and to relieve pressures on the system.

Government statements have pointed to "encouraging progress" with reducing the numbers serving IPPs but point out the need to balance this progress with the potential dangers such prisoners can pose.

Recently concerns have been raised about the numbers of recalls to prison of IPP prisoners following their release.

## Inequalities Faced by Gypsy, Roma and Traveller Communities

Published Monday, 17 February, 2020

• The House of Commons Women and Equalities Committee published the findings of its inquiry into inequalities faced by Gypsy, Roma and Traveller communities on 5 April 2019.

• Among the committee's key findings were that these communities have the worst outcomes of any ethnic group across a range of areas, including education, health, employment, criminal justice and hate crime.

• The committee also found that there has been a persistent failure by national and local policymakers to tackle these inequalities in a sustained way, leading to services that are ill equipped to support Gypsy, Roma and Traveller people. In turn, this has led to a lack of trust in these public services. It further noted issues within these communities, such as a high level of domestic abuse and violence against women and girls.

• Among the committee's recommendations were that the Cabinet Office create a specific workstream within the Race Disparity Unit for eliminating Gypsy and Traveller inequalities, and that every relevant government department have a strategy for tackling these issues.

• Further, the committee called for more analysis on the scale of the issues faced by Gypsy, Roma and Traveller communities, including by those of school age who may be 'missing' from local authority registers or facing challenges in accessing the right educational provision.

• In its response published on 2 July 2019, the Government agreed with the committee's findings on the level of discrimination faced by these communities. It pointed to the results of its own Race Disparity Audit, which found that Gypsy, Roma and Traveller communities were significantly worse off than the general population on almost every measure.

• As announced on 6 June 2019, the Government said it would be developing a cross-departmental national strategy on tackling Gypsy, Roma and Traveller inequalities. It added that it agreed with the committee that health and education inequalities are considerable and must be tackled. Further, the Government said it would seek to develop proposals addressing the levels of violence against women and girls.

• A response from Ofsted was also included as an appendix to the Government's report, where it said it would look for signs that any pupil has been 'off-rolled', and that its new inspection framework will allow better identification and reporting.

*Insights for the new Parliament*

Published Friday, 24 January, 2020

Insights for the new Parliament is a landmark collection of topical briefings. Produced by our impartial researchers, the articles cover the topics MPs will need to know about in the coming months and years. Below is a summary in British Sign Language and text, along with links to download the PDF booklet or as individual articles.

## A summary of the key issues facing the new Parliament

Insights for the new Parliament provides impartial analysis of some of the key issues that parliamentarians will have to address. Prepared during the general election campaign, the publication covers a range of domestic and international policy areas which have been chosen by Commons Library researchers.

It begins with an overview of the Brexit process and the options still available. It also looks at how, in the event the UK leaves, the future relationship agreement with the EU will be negotiated and the option of extending the transition period.

## Living and working in the UK

Chapter one, Living and working in the UK, examines key areas of daily life.

In the housing sector the most pressing challenge will be to achieve a sustained increase in house building and tackle the backlog of housing need. In the utilities sector, there has been a rise in public and political interest in how companies are managed and regulated. Using the water industry as an example, we look at what changes might be considered in the coming years. The new Parliament is likely to consider critical changes to building regulations and safety in the coming years. This is driven by the Grenfell Tower fire and the need to reduce emissions from housing. The future of rail services will be informed by the anticipated awaited Williams Review, which is likely to recommend improving accessibility and regional accountability. However, political parties differ over the role of the private sector.

Brexit could affect the protection of human rights in the UK, as the European Charter on Fundamental Rights will cease to have effect after the UK leaves the EU. We examine key legislation and the role of human rights in the UK's future relationship with the EU.EU citizens living in the UK who want to stay after Brexit will need to apply for a new immigration status and can do so via the EU Settlement Scheme. Deadlines to apply may vary depending on the Brexit process.

For the UK's workforce, the Good Work Plan has introduced a range of proposals to tackle insecure work but many of the key proposals are yet to be implemented. For UK farmers, the new Parliament could see the biggest changes to farm policy for decades. Leaving the EU means the UK could develop new policies to support farming.

## Health, social care and welfare

Chapter two, Health, social care and welfare, looks at how those in our society are cared for.

It considers proposals to reform the NHS to offer more integrated care in England and whether new legislation is needed to achieve this. It also looks at NHS waiting times, which reached record highs in 2019, and the demand for NHS services, including overnight beds and capacity issues. Shortages within the health and social care workforce have a knock-on effect on care. We explore how the new Parliament might address this.

Social care will be a key issue for the new Parliament. Social care is not generally provided for free and its funding needs to be examined. We look at whether reform is likely to happen. Pressure to address mental health with the same urgency as physical health has gained prominence in the last decade. The new Parliament is likely to look at how to improve services and break down barriers to improving mental health care.

Universal Credit, which is replacing means-tested benefits and tax credits for people of working age, is being rolled out across the UK. There have been concerns over the process of moving people over, including how the monthly assessment and single monthly payments work. Within pension policy, there is cross-party support for key areas.As people are being given more control over their savings pots, Parliament will need to consider what measures need to be taken to ensure that pensioners are adequately provided for throughout their retirement.

## Education

Chapter three, Education, considers issues shaping how children and young people are educated.

The level and distribution of school funding in England has been a major focus of debate in recent years, and this looks set to continue. The funding of further and higher education is of similarly longstanding concern. The recent Augar review made proposals to reduce university tuition fees and enhance support for other post-18 courses. Reforms to support for children and young people with special educational needs and disabilities made in 2014 are now embedded, but recent reports have questioned whether they have been implemented well enough, and funded sufficiently, to succeed.

## Environment

Chapter four, the Environment, looks at the plans for net zero emissions and meeting environmental challenges.

Following Parliament's 2019 declaration of a 'climate emergency,' the Government legislated for net zero greenhouse gas emissions. Debate in the new Parliament is likely to consider what sectors, including transport, energy, and agriculture can do to reduce emissions. We look at what areas are likely to lead the debate in the new Parliament to achieve this. An exploration of environmental challenges for 2020 and beyond highlights five areas of environmental concern: environmental governance, flooding, air quality, biodiversity loss and resource use.

## Trade and the economy

Chapter five, Trade and the economy, focuses on the issues facing the UK economy.

We turn first to slowing economic growth and consider how low levels of productivity have meant that while employment has been rising, real wages have not. The form that Brexit takes could have a significant impact on the UK's economic outlook. Once the UK leaves the EU, it will gain greater responsibility for formulating an independent trade policy. We look at the decisions the UK will have to take on issues such as tariffs, product safety standards, assistance to developing countries and its place in the WTO. Trade in services are particularly important to the UK economy, ranging from financial and business services to tourism and IT. We consider how EU membership allows the free movement of services and what the UK will need to do to ensure future services trade is as frictionless as possible.

Government spending was already set to increase and during the campaign all parties made further spending pledges. We look at the challenges facing public spending, including Brexit, rising health and social care bills and the prospect of a future recession.

## Crime and cyber security

Chapter six, Crime and cyber security, looks at key areas of safety and security.

There is a consensus that domestic abuse legislation is needed. When Parliament was dissolved in November, the Domestic Abuse Bill fell. We examine what the legislation might look like and how far the previous Parliament got with the bill. Knife crime has been on the rise in England and Wales, although some of the reported increase is due to improvements in police recording practices. We look at the use of stop and search powers, and approaches to early intervention.

There is increasing concern about harmful content and activity on social media. We look at what regulation might be needed and what select committees and charities have said. Cyber threats from foreign states and criminal groups are growing more frequent and sophisticated. The new Parliament will need to consider key cyber security issues, including in the telecoms infrastructure and consumer devices.

Although recent years have seen an increase in recorded crime, the number of prosecutions has fallen. There are also concerns that legal aid changes are compromising defendants' access to justice. We examine key areas of the criminal justice system including the Ministry of Justice and the Crown Prosecution Service. It has long been recognised that the process which dictates how funding is allocated to police forces requires reform. We look at how police forces are currently funded, and how much they receive.

## Foreign affairs

Chapter seven, Foreign affairs, considers the UK's armed forces and place in the wider world.

Relationships with the European Union and the United States will be at the heart of decision-making in UK foreign policy, following Brexit developments and ahead of the US presidential election in 2020. The UK faces challenges around the world, including tensions in the Strait of Hormuz, ongoing counter-terrorist operations against ISIS, and in its relationship with Russia. The UK's defence in the 2020s will be shaped by the Strategic Defence and Security Review due in 2020, as well as challenges in recruitment and expenditure on military equipment. Debates can also be expected on the prosecution for alleged historical offences by military personnel. The replacement of the UK's nuclear deterrent will move into its next phase in this Parliament, with a decision due on whether to replace the current nuclear warhead, which is expected to be retired in the late 2030s.

## Parliament and the constitution

Chapter eight, Parliament and the constitution, looks at key legislation affecting Parliament and the UK's relationship with the EU, Northern Ireland, Wales and Scotland.

One of the major hurdles in negotiating a Brexit settlement has been the need to keep an open border between Ireland and Northern Ireland. Brexit has also led to challenges and tensions for the relationship between Westminster and the Scottish Parliament, National Assembly for Wales and Northern Ireland Assembly.

The Fixed-term Parliaments Act sets a five-yearly interval between general elections. It is due for a review in 2020, and Labour and the Conservatives have both promised to abolish it. The Parliamentary Works Sponsor Body will be responsible for the restoration of the Palace of Westminster. It starts operations in earnest in April 2020.

### Introducing "Payment by Results" in Offender Rehabilitation and other reforms
24 October 2013

Concerns about reoffending and what works in rehabilitation are longstanding. Driven (in part at least) by such concerns, there has been a series of reforms to probation in recent years.

The previous Government introduced significant reforms, including a purchaser/provider split. The present Government too has ambitious plans for the rehabilitation of offenders and has published a number of consultation documents. The first, Breaking the Cycle (December 2010) proposed a payments by results (PbR) model to reduce reoffending. The Government then published a further consultation document in March 2012, Punishment and Reform: Effective Probation Services, advocating a "stronger role for public sector Probation Trusts as commissioners of competed probation services." In October 2012, Lord Chancellor and Secretary of State for Justice, Chris Grayling, announced that the Government now intended to apply PbR to the majority of rehabilitation work conducted with offenders in the community, as part of broader reforms. The Ministry of Justice's strategy document Transforming Rehabilitation: A Strategy for Reform (published on 9 May 2013 as its response to the consultation Transforming Rehabilitation: A revolution in the way we manage offenders) again set out a number of proposed reforms to the rehabilitation system in both custody and the community. Proposals relating to rehabilitation in the community include legislating to introduce a minimum of 12 months' mandatory supervision for all offenders sentenced to less than two years in custody and changes to the conditions that can be imposed as part of a Community Order or Suspended Sentence Order (as set out in the Offender Rehabilitation Bill [HL Bill 2] 2013-14).

Perhaps the source of greatest controversy is the proposal to invite a range of new providers from the voluntary and private sectors to bid for contracts to provide rehabilitation services to all but the most high risk offenders, to be paid according to a system of PbR. A new public sector probation service would be created to directly manage high risk offenders. This note provides a summary of the strategy's main proposals and reaction to them.

### 1 Background
According to the Ministry of Justice, £3bn a year is spent on prisons, and almost £1bn a year on

delivering sentences in the community, including £800m on probation. Figures also show that spending on probation increased by over 70% between 1998/99 and 2010/11.[1]

Concerns about high rates of reoffending and the effectiveness of rehabilitation – especially in the light of expenditure on dealing with crime and repeat offending – are long-standing. Driven (in part at least) by such concerns, there has been a series of reforms to probation in recent years.

### 1.1 Labour's reforms
The National Probation Service was formed in 2001, as part of a major reorganisation. Two years later, in 2003, the Carter Review of Correctional Services proposed further reform.[2] The Carter report proposed the integration of the prison and probation services in a new Offender Management Service, "end to end" management of offenders, "contestability" from private and voluntary providers and a purchaser/provider split. The National Offender Management Service was duly launched in 2004, with Regional Offender Managers (ROMs) commissioning services from April 2006. Further background on these reforms is available in Library Research Paper 06/62.[3]

At first, the statutory duty to arrange provision of probation services was the responsibility of local probation boards. To encourage the growth of "contestability", the Offender Management Act 2007 transferred this responsibility to the Secretary of State. Thus, the Secretary of State could commission most services directly, not only from public sector providers, but also from the private and voluntary sectors.

Following a further report from Lord Carter, on 1 April 2008, the National Offender Management Service was established as an agency, merging the Prison Service and NOMS.[4]

### 1.2 Current government's consultations on rehabilitation and probation
In the May 2010 coalition agreement, the Government said it would introduce a "rehabilitation revolution" with payments to independent providers to reduce reoffending.[5] In June 2010, the then Lord Chancellor and Secretary of State for Justice, Kenneth Clarke, said prison was a "a costly and ineffectual approach that fails to turn criminals into law-abiding citizens" and that "we must now ... shut off this revolving door of crime and reoffending.[6] There followed a series of consultations.

### Breaking the Cycle
In December 2010, the Ministry of Justice published the consultation paper, Breaking the Cycle: Effective Punishment, Rehabilitation and Sentencing of Offenders, in which it committed

to introducing PbR to all providers of services for offenders by 2015.[7]

*Competition Strategy for Offender Services*
The Competition Strategy for Offender Services was published in July 2011. It set out the Government's proposals for competition in eight prisons, in PbR pilots, community payback and electronic monitoring. On non-custodial services, the strategy advocated competition:

The starting point here is different, as the use of competition in delivering core probation services is far less developed, as is the market for providing those services. However, we believe that we can learn from those areas of non-custodial work where we have more experience in using competition, and where there is a market, including electronic monitoring, and bail accommodation and support services.[8]

The Justice Committee, in a 2011 report, noted several similarities between this and the previous Government's approaches, but remarked that they differed over models of commissioning and the current Government's emphasis on PbR.[9]

*Punishment and Reform: Effective Probation Services*
Further consultation came in March 2012, with the publication of Punishment and Reform: Effective Probation Services[10] and a parallel consultation on community sentences. Elements of its "core proposition" covered some now-familiar themes:

• A stronger role for public sector probation trusts as commissioners of competed probation services.
• Devolving to probation trusts the budget for community offender services, from which trusts would commission services to meet local need and circumstances.
• In the interests of value for money, some services — such as electronic monitoring of curfew requirements — might continue to be commissioned at national level
• Probation trusts would retain responsibility for providing, in the case of all offenders, advice to court on sentencing and the enforcement of those sentences and would be responsible for making certain 'public interest' decisions for all offenders
• All probation services not directly provided by probation trusts would be opened up to competition.
• The participation of the voluntary, private and public sectors would be encouraged, alongside new models for delivering public services
• Probation trusts might choose to compete for services as separate entities, independent of those probation trusts which are responsible for commissioning, giving advice to court, managing higher risk offenders and taking public interest decisions.
• Local probation presence would be strengthened as the front line of offender management.
• Over time, other public bodies, such as local authorities or, with a broadened statutory role, Police and Crime Commissioners might take responsibility for probation services.[11]

*Transforming rehabilitation – a revolution in the way we manage offenders*
On 9 January 2013, the Ministry of Justice launched another consultation, Transforming Rehabilitation - a revolution in the way we manage offenders. This consultation took place between 9 January and 22 February 2013. Key points included:
• The Ministry of Justice intended to introduce supervision for prisoners released after sentences of less than 12 months. (Currently the probation service only supervises those with sentences of 12 months' imprisonment or more).
• Competition would open up the market and bring in a more "diverse mix of providers"
• Providers would only be paid in full when they reduced reconviction rates in their area
• The public sector probation service would retain ultimate responsibility for public protection and would directly manage high risk offenders
• However, the great majority of community sentences and rehabilitation work would be delivered by the private and voluntary sectors, to be paid by results.
Lord Chancellor and Secretary of State for Justice, Chris Grayling, described his proposals in a Written Ministerial Statement at the launch of the consultation:[12]
The consultation document explored a number of issues:

*How will smaller organisations be able to compete for contracts?*
One such issue was how the Ministry of Justice proposed to retain the expertise of small and medium-sized organisations in the contracting process. This would be done, the document stated, through the "emerging social investment market" and through sub-contracting arrangements:
One issue on which respondents to the 'Punishment and Reform: Effective Probation Services' consultation were almost universally agreed was that the effective interventions delivered by small and medium-sized enterprises (SMEs) and the VCS must be preserved within the system. We recognise the significant expertise and dynamism of many VCS providers and that they have a crucial role to play in embedding work with offenders into local initiatives and communities.[13]
A Ministry of Justice press release on 24 January 2013 announced that a third sector organisation had been granted £150,000 out of a £500,000 pot to draft an action plan with voluntary organisations on overcoming the barriers to

participation into PbR contracts.[14] Lord McNally, Minister of State at the Ministry of Justice, also drew attention to the £500,000 funding pot to assist voluntary organisations in getting ready to take on work and for creating partnerships with private companies.[15]

*What will be left for the public sector?*

Transforming Rehabilitation made it clear that there would still be a role for the public sector in retaining overall responsibility for public protection and in managing high risk offenders:

The public sector probation service will retain responsibility for public protection. For the highest risk offenders, this will mean direct offender management responsibility. For all other offenders, the public sector will have responsibility for ensuring contracted providers are effectively managing the risk of harm posed to the public. The public sector deserves recognition for the professional standards it has demonstrated in protecting the public from serious harm, and we intend to maintain and build on that expertise.

(...)

All other offenders will be managed by contracted providers, but the public sector probation service will continue to have responsibility for ensuring the risk of harm to the public posed by these offenders is properly managed.[16]

*Delivery structure*

The consultation document invited views on the best ways of structuring services, although the Ministry of Justice proposed "bundled" services in around 16 areas, covering wider geographical areas than the current 35 probation trusts in England and Wales:

We expect most contracts to cover geographical areas larger than the current Probation Trusts. The public sector will be organised in the most efficient manner for delivery of its new responsibilities – this will require fewer Trusts or a different structure (such as a single national probation trust or direct delivery on behalf of the Secretary of State). We intend to begin the transition to the new operating structure in 2013.[17]

*The role of Police and Crime Commissioners*

The consultation document also proposed that Police and Crime Commissioners would play a "crucial role":

PCCs bring an opportunity for collective local leadership to galvanise police, local authorities, the Crown Prosecution Service and courts to work together to prevent crime and reduce reoffending. Our rehabilitation services need to be responsive to these changes and by designing

contract package areas which align with the PCCs' police force boundaries we want to ensure that measures to reduce crime and rehabilitate offenders can be integrated effectively to achieve the best results.

PCCs will also play a crucial role locally by holding local partners to account via the Community Safety Partnerships and we envisage that the public, private and voluntary sectors might form part of these partnerships. PCCs will also commission services at a local level with other local agencies (for example, local health commissioners).[18]

1 Ministry of Justice, *Transforming Rehabilitation: A Strategy for Reform*, Cm 8619, May 2013, p44

2 Patrick Carter, *Managing Offenders: Reducing Crime*, 11 December 2003

3 Library Research Paper 06/62, *The Offender Management Bill*

3 Lord Carter's Review of Prisons, *Securing the Future: Proposals for the efficient and sustainable use of custody in England and Wales*, December 2007

5 *The Coalition: our programme for government*, May 2010, p23

6 "Justice Secretary plans 'radical' prison policy change", BBC, 30 June 2010

7 Ministry of Justice, *Breaking the Cycle: Effective Punishment, Rehabilitation and Sentencing of Offenders*, Cm 7972 ,December 2010, p11

8 Ministry of Justice *Competition strategy for offender services*, July 2011: page 15

9 Justice Committee, *The role of the Probation Service*, 27 July 2011, HC 519-I 2010-12

10 Ministry of Justice Consultation Paper CP7/2012, *Punishment and Reform: Effective Probation Services* March 2012

11 bid: page 8

12 HC Deb 9 January 2013 cc19WS 1

13 Ministry of Justice, *Transforming Rehabilitation - a revolution in the way we manage offenders*, January 2013, Cm 8517, p16

14 Ministry of Justice, *Transforming rehabilitation - unlocking the voluntary sector*, 24 January 2013.

15 "Probation service reform will help offenders turn their lives around", Guardian, 25 January 2013.

16 Ministry of Justice, *Transforming Rehabilitation - a revolution in the way we manage offenders*, January 2013, Cm 8517, p21

17 Ibid, pp 24-25

18 Ibid, pp 26-7

**Is the criminal justice system fit for purpose?**

Published Wednesday, 15 January, 2020

Although recent years have seen an increase in recorded crime, the number of prosecutions has fallen. The Home Affairs Committee has noted this trend could risk "both a serious decrease in public safety and in confidence in the police and the Crown Prosecution Service."

In the year ending March 2019, 5.3 million crimes were recorded by police in England and Wales, compared with 3.9 million in 2011/12. The figures are not directly comparable over time, as recording practices change, although there has evidently been a rise in recorded crime. Over the same period, the number of prosecutions brought by the Crown Prosecution Service (CPS) fell by 46%.

There are also concerns that legal aid changes are compromising defendants' access to justice.

## Ministry of Justice funding

In 2017, the Institute for Fiscal Studies calculated that in the decade from 2010/11, the Ministry of Justice's (MoJ) budget would be cut by around 40%. Spending plans have been revised upwards since then, so that in 2019/20 the total MoJ budget was only around 25% lower than in 2010/11.

The distribution of funding across the various stages of the criminal justice process is important. In November 2019 the Public Accounts Committee warned of potential "downstream impacts" for courts, prisons and probation services if extra police officers were recruited. It concluded it was "far from certain" that these services were sufficiently resourced to cope if caseloads increased.

The Director of Public Prosecutions (DPP), Max Hill QC, called for a "thematic approach" to criminal justice funding in evidence to the Justice Committee in December 2018. He said it was important "not to create a bulge in one part of the system, or still worse a blockage in another part of the system, but to resource all parts equally so that they can meet an increase in demand."

There is a graphic that explains the above and which you can view on the Research tab of The Prison Oracle - tinyurl.com/2cjfe6yd

## The Crown Prosecution Service

The DPP has described the CPS as a "classic demand-led organisation." It does not generate its own caseload but decides whether suspects investigated by the police should be charged with an offence. It is generally accepted that the CPS is dealing with an increasingly complex caseload, including violent and sexual offences and a high volume of digital evidence.

However, CPS funding and staff numbers have fallen in recent years. In 2018/19, there were 5,684 full-time equivalent CPS staff in post compared with 8,094 in 2010/11.

In 2018 the Justice Committee warned that the collapse of a number of high-profile cases due to the failure of police and prosecutors to disclose key evidence to the defence was "symptomatic of a criminal justice system under significant strain."

The DPP said additional CPS funding announced by the Government in August 2019 would provide increased capacity to enable the CPS to respond to "the surge in violent crime" and "the explosion of digital evidence", and to cope with any increase in caseload as a result of increased police numbers. However, the FDA – the trade union that represents CPS lawyers – said that although this funding was welcome, it was "not enough to undo all the damage that has been done by years of cuts."

There is a graphic that explains the above and which you can view on the Research tab of The Prison Oracle - tinyurl.com/2cjfe6yd

## Defendants' access to legal advice

Between 2010/11 and 2018/19, criminal legal aid expenditure fell by over a third (35%).

There are concerns that current remuneration rates are threatening the sustainability of criminal defence work, which may mean suspects struggle to find local legal representation. The Law Society says the problem is particularly acute with duty solicitors, who provide free advice to suspects detained by the police.

The number of providers of police station advice covered by legal aid has fallen by 20% since 2011/12. The number of people receiving telephone advice from a duty solicitor while at a police station has fallen by more than 40%, despite the level of police recorded crime having risen.

In 2018 the Justice Committee noted "there is compelling evidence of the fragility of the Criminal Bar and criminal defence solicitors' firms." It said underfunding of the criminal justice system not only threatens its effectiveness but "undermines the rule of law and tarnishes the reputation of the justice system as a whole."

Defendants who are not eligible for legal aid may choose to represent themselves, which raises questions about 'equality of arms' before the court. Alternatively, such defendants may opt to pay for private representation. However, if they are acquitted then under current rules the state will only reimburse their private legal costs at legal aid rates. Any difference between these rates and the defendant's actual legal costs – sometimes dubbed the 'innocence tax' – must be borne by the defendant. The Bar Council has described this as "desperately unfair."

A Government review of criminal legal aid is underway and is due to report towards the end of summer 2020.

*Further reading*
• Disclosure of evidence in criminal cases, House of Commons Justice Committee.
• Criminal Legal Aid, Twelfth Report of Session 2017–19, House of Commons Justice Committee.

*Judicial Review and Courts Bill*
[AS INTRODUCED]

## CONTENTS

PART 1
JUDICIAL REVIEW
1 Quashing orders
2 Exclusion of review of Upper Tribunal's permission-to-appeal decisions
PART 2
COURTS, TRIBUNALS AND CORONERS
CHAPTER 1
CRIMINAL PROCEDURE
Written procedures for dealing with summary offences
3 Automatic online conviction and penalty for certain summary offences
4 Guilty plea in writing: extension to proceedings following police charge
5 Extension of single justice procedure to corporations Offences triable either way: determining the mode of trial
6 Written procedure for indicating plea and determining mode of trial: adults
7 Initial option for adult accused to reject summary trial at hearing
8 Written procedure for indicating plea and determining mode of trial: children
9 Powers to proceed if accused absent from allocation hearing Transfer of cases between courts
10 Sending cases to Crown Court for trial
11 Powers of Crown Court to remit cases to the magistrates' court
12 Powers of youth court to transfer cases if accused turns 18 Miscellaneous and consequential provision
13 Involvement of parent or guardian in proceedings conducted in writing
14 Removal of certain requirements for hearings about procedural matters
15 Documents to be served in accordance with Criminal Procedure Rules
16 Power to make consequential or supplementary provision
17 Consequential and related amendments

CHAPTER 2
ONLINE PROCEDURE
18 Rules for online procedure in courts and tribunals
19 "Specified kinds" of proceedings
20 Provision supplementing section 18
21 The Online Procedure Rule Committee
22 Powers of the Online Procedure Rule Committee
23 Power to change certain requirements relating to the Committee
24 Process for making Online Procedure Rules
25 Power to require Online Procedure Rules to be made
26 Power to make amendments in relation to Online Procedure Rules
27 Duty to make support available for those who require it
28 Power to make consequential or supplementary provision
29 Amendments of other legislation
30 Judicial agreement to certain regulations
31 Interpretation of this Chapter

CHAPTER 3
EMPLOYMENT TRIBUNALS AND THE EMPLOYMENT APPEAL TRIBUNAL
32 Employment Tribunal Procedure Rules
33 Composition of tribunals
34 Saving for existing procedural provisions
35 Exercise of tribunal functions by authorised persons
36 Responsibility for remunerating tribunal members

CHAPTER 4 CORONERS
37 Discontinuance of investigation where cause of death becomes clear
38 Power to conduct non-contentious inquests in writing
39 Use of audio or video links at inquests
40 Suspension of requirement for jury at inquest where coronavirus suspected
41 Phased transition to new coroner areas

CHAPTER 5
OTHER PROVISIONS ABOUT COURTS
Local justice areas
42 Abolition of local justice areas

Courthouses in the City of London
43 The Mayor's and City of London Court: removal of duty to provide premises
44 The City of London Magistrates' Court: removal of duty to provide premises

PART 3
FINAL PROVISIONS
45 Regulations
46 Extent
47 Commencement and transitional provision
48 Short title Documents to be served in accordance with Criminal Procedure Rules
Schedule 1 — Documents to be served in accordance with Criminal Procedure Rules
Schedule 2 — Criminal procedure: consequential and related amendments
Schedule 3 — Practice directions for online proceedings
Part 1 — Civil proceedings and family proceedings in England and Wales
Part 2 — Proceedings in the First-tier Tribunal and Upper Tribunal
Part 3 — Proceedings in employment tribunals and the Employment Appeal Tribunal
Schedule 4 — Online procedure: amendments

Schedule 5 — Employment Tribunal Procedure Rules: further provision
Part 1 — Making and content of Employment Tribunal Procedure Rules
Part 2 — Other amendments of the Employment Tribunals Act 1996
Part 3 — Related amendments of other legislation
*https://prisons.org.uk/facts-figures/research-briefings/*

## Key issues for the 2015 PARLIAMENT
### Foreword
We live in a world where information is ever more abundant and accessible. This is a good thing: democracy and political debate can have no life or meaning if it is not well-informed.

But such availability and abundance may not be making your lives as Members of Parliament any easier! Increasingly, you are expected to be in command of detail and accurate in presentation: mistakes and misunderstandings can be identified and publicised in a matter of minutes. And the task of sorting through the profusion of data, news, views and research, assessing its provenance and veracity, and reaching informed conclusions, can be difficult.

The House of Commons Library offers Members extensive resources not only to access information, but to help them understand and act on it. In addition to its vast range of books, press and parliamentary material, it provides a dedicated research service consisting of 60 experts, experienced in providing impartial and authoritative briefing for Members from all sides of the House. They are able to separate fact from fiction; to bring expert knowledge and judgement to bear on today's policy issues; in short, to help navigate and understand the wealth of information and data at our fingertips. In the last Parliament, the research service provided substantive responses to 110,000 questions asked of them by Members and their staff. The range of work undertaken varies enormously: from a statistic needed within minutes for use in the Chamber, to a detailed analysis of a policy issue; from advice on a constituency matter, to a country briefing for a visit overseas. But whatever your question, you can be confident that all responses will have certain qualities in common.

• They will be reliable. We understand the importance of accuracy, and the consequences of mistakes, in public debate.

• They will be tailored to the question you have asked, to the deadline you have set, and to the context in which it will be used.

• They will be confidential and not shared beyond your office.

• They will be impartial. We are asked so many questions because our customers are confident that they will get a balanced and non-partisan response. It is a reputational asset that we prize very highly.

The research service also publishes pre-prepared briefings on topical issues and in-depth analysis of every major piece of primary legislation. Though they are available publicly on the Parliament website, they are written with the needs of MPs and their staff in mind, and are underpinned by the same principles of impartiality and accuracy.

In this book, you will find examples of the kind of work at which the Library excels. I hope it proves a useful and topical guide to the issues of interest to the new Parliament, and an insight into the quality of work you can expect from our research service.

Penny Young
Librarian and Director General,
Information Services
May 2015
*https://prisons.org.uk/facts-figures/research-briefings/*

## Knife Crime in England and Wales
30 September 2021
### Summary
### Recorded crime
In the year ending March 2021, there were around 41,000 (selected) offences involving a knife or sharp instrument in England and Wales (excluding Greater Manchester Police Force). This was 15% lower than in 2019/20 and 27% higher than in 2010/11. Recent trends in knife crime have been affected by undercounting in the Greater Manchester Police Force area prior to 2018/19. Increases in recorded offences since 2018/19 are directly related with improvements in recording practices.

### Homicide
In the year ending March 2021 there were 224 homicides (currently recorded) using a sharp instrument, including knives and broken bottles.

### Knife crime by police force area
The West Midlands Police Force recorded the highest rate of 156 offences involving a knife per 100,000 population in 2020/21, a 41% increase on a rate of 118 recorded in 2019/20. Durham had the lowest rate of 22 offences per 100,000 individuals (down from 26 in 2019/20).

### Proven offences and offenders
In the year ending March 2021, there were 18,553 disposals given for possession of a knife or offensive weapon. Juveniles (aged 10-17) were the offenders in 19% of cases.

## Hospital admissions

There were 4,091 finished consultant episodes (FCE) recorded in English hospitals in 2020/21 due to assault by a sharp object. This was 14% lower than in 2019/20 but 12% higher than in 2014/15.

## Background

"Knife" crime, a crime involving an object with a blade or sharp instrument, is a persistent concern and disproportionately impacts the young and disadvantaged. Various remedies have been tried over the years.

The Library Briefing Paper Knives and Offensive Weapons (SN00330) discusses the legislation which governs the carrying (possession) and sale of knives and other offensive weapons. To summarise the main possession offences: [1]

• It is an offence under Section 1 of the Prevention of Crime Act 1953 for a person to have "with him in a public place any offensive weapon without lawful authority or reasonable excuse". Section 1(4) of the 1953 Act defines "offensive weapon" as:

any article made or adapted for use for causing injury to the person or intended by the person having it with him for such use by him or by some other person.

• Under Section 139 of the Criminal Justice Act 1988 it is an offence for a person to have "with him in a public place... any article which has a blade or is sharply pointed", except a folding pocketknife with a cutting edge of three inches or less, without good reason or lawful authority.

• Under Section 139A of the Criminal Justice Act 1988, it is an offence for a person to have an offensive weapon or a bladed or pointed article on school premises without good reason or lawful authority.

The above offences are all "either way" offences, meaning they can be tried in either the magistrates' court or the Crown court depending on the seriousness of the offence.

The maximum sentence for each of these offences is up to six months' imprisonment and/or a fine following summary conviction in the magistrates' court, or up to four years' imprisonment and/or a fine following conviction on indictment in the Crown Court. Mandatory minimum custodial sentences apply if an offender is aged 16 or over.

1 "Making threats" and sale/supply offences are also described in Knives and offensive weapons (SN00330)

## Legal Aid, Sentencing and Punishment of Offenders Bill

27 June 2011

### Summary

The Legal Aid, Sentencing and Punishment of Offenders Bill had its first reading on 21 June 2011, was published the following day and will have its second reading on 29 June 2011.

The Bill's provisions cover a diverse range of issues:

Legal aid: The Bill would reverse the position under the Access to Justice Act 1999, whereby civil legal aid is available for any matter not specifically excluded. The Bill would take some types of case out of scope for legal aid funding and cases would not be eligible for funding unless of a type specified in the Bill. As it stands, the Bill would allow the Lord Chancellor by order to omit services from this list but confers no power to add new services. The Bill paves the way for further changes (through secondary legislation) to the financial criteria for eligibility for civil legal aid and extends the scope for means-testing for criminal legal aid. The Bill would also abolish the Legal Services Commission.

Litigation funding and costs: The Bill makes various provisions in respect of civil litigation funding and costs, taking forward the recommendations of the Jackson Review and the Government's response to that review. The Bill's provisions cover (amongst other things) conditional fee agreements, damages-based agreements and other matters relating to civil litigation funding and costs in divorce and dissolution proceedings. It also deals with costs that might be awarded from central funds in criminal cases.

Sentencing: Following the consultation in the Green Paper Breaking the Cycle: Effective Punishment, Rehabilitation and Sentencing of Offenders, the Bill makes changes to sentencing provisions. Examples include: giving courts an express duty (rather than the current power) to consider making compensation orders where victims have suffered harm or loss; reducing the detailed requirements on courts when they give reasons for a sentence; allowing courts to suspend sentences of up to two years rather than 12 months; and amending the court's power to suspend a prison sentence. New powers would allow curfews to be imposed for more hours in the day and for up to 12 months rather than the current six, and courts would have more discretion with regard to various orders for young offenders. In addition, the Bill would repeal provisions in the Criminal Justice Act 2003 which would have increased the maximum sentence a magistrate's court could impose from six to 12 months. These were part of plans to introduce a new form of sentence ("Custody Plus") for people with sentences of under a year. However, they never came into force because of resource constraints. There are also changes to remove some of the restrictions on the use of recalls to prison.

*Bail and remand:* changes in the Bill on bail and remand aim to reduce the number of those who are unnecessarily remanded into custody. Under the new "no real prospect" test, people would be released on bail if they would be unlikely to receive a custodial sentence. There were mixed reactions when this was proposed, with many welcoming the move, but some questioning whether the outcome of a court case could be predicted at the outset in this way. Where a person aged under 18 has to be remanded into custody, the Bill would ensure that in most cases they would be remanded into local authority accommodation.

*Release on licence:* The Bill amends provisions relating to the release and recall of prisoners. The Bill's provisions include (amongst other things) the simplification of the calculation of crediting periods of remand on bail, additional restrictions for early release on Home Detention Curfew and the supervision of young adult prisoners released from sentences of less than 12 months.

*Prisoners' pay and employment:* The Bill gives the Secretary of State new powers to make prison rules about prisoners' employment, pay and deductions from their pay. The intention is that prisoners should make payments which would support victims of crime.

*Out of court disposals:* Here, the Bill introduces a penalty notice with an education option and provision for conditional cautions to be given without the need to refer the case to the relevant prosecutor. New conditions could be attached to a conditional caution given to a foreign national offender without leave to enter or stay in the United Kingdom. There would also be a new kind of youth caution, and youth conditional cautions would be amended.

*Knives:* The Bill would create a new offence of threatening with an offensive weapon or an article with a blade or point thereby creating an immediate risk of serious physical harm. A minimum sentence of 6 months imprisonment would normally be given to persons over 18 found guilty of this offence.

### Local government in England: structures
Published Monday, 08 June, 2020
This note contains basic details of the structure and functions of English local government. It outlines the system of counties, districts and unitary authorities), and other bodies such as fire and rescue authorities, combined authorities, and Police and Crime Commissioners.

Section 3 explains the system of local government elections, including the systems of electing by 'halves' and 'thirds' used in many local authorities. It also provides details of the local government franchise (those eligible to vote).

Section 4 provides details of the legal process for structural change in English local government. This includes the merger of district councils and the creation of 'unitary authorities' to replace 'two-tier' local government – i.e., county and district councils. Section 4 provides details of current restructuring plans and recent changes, and discusses Government guidance on proposals for unitary local government. The Appendix provides a breakdown of the division of responsibilities between county and district councils in two-tier areas.

Section 5 provides brief details of the financing of English local government, including an explanation of the annual Local Government Finance Settlement. Additional details can be found in the Library briefing Local government finances, and details of the 2020-21 settlement process can be found in the Library briefing on the Local Government Finance Settlement 2020-21.

### Magnitsky legislation
Published Monday, 20 July, 2020
#### Magnitsky
Sergei Magnitsky was a Russian lawyer who uncovered large-scale tax fraud. While working for Hermitage Capital, a firm based in London and run by the US-born financier Bill Browder, he discovered that millions of dollars of Hermitage tax payments had been syphoned off into the pockets of Russian officials. He was arrested but refused to withdraw his testimony and died in 2009, after mistreatment in jail.

Bill Browder, now a UK citizen, started a campaign to have sanctions imposed on the officials involved – to get the officials banned from visiting the US and using the US financial system. A Magnitsky Act naming the Russians involved was passed by the US Congress in 2012. It was later broadened to become the Global Magnitsky Act of 2016, applying to gross human rights abusers anywhere. Other countries, including Canada, Lithuania and Estonia have introduced their own versions of the legislation.

#### Pressure in the UK
There was increasing pressure for the UK to follow suit. Various pieces of legislation came before Parliament, in the form of Private Members' Bills and amendments to Government Bills, although "Magnitsky" did not appear in their official titles and they did not refer to Russia. Arguments used against introducing Bills or changing existing law to provide Magnitsky

legislation included questions about the definition of 'gross human rights abuse' and the suggestion that powers to sanction gross human rights abusers are already there in existing legislation. There are some who question the effectiveness of Magnitsky legislation: there are countless powerful officials who commit gross human rights abuses; choosing who to impose sanctions is likely to be a subjective business. Inconsistencies in application would make designations even more likely to be litigated.

The Magnitsky amendments to UK legislation were broadly welcomed, however. Two major pieces of legislation had 'Magnitsky' elements added to them: the Proceeds of Crime Act 2002 and the Sanctions and Anti-Money Laundering Bill (now the Sanctions and anti-Money Laundering Act 2018).

The Criminal Finances Act 2017 amended the Proceeds of Crime Act 2002 to expand the definition of 'unlawful conduct' to include gross human rights abuse or violation. After Opposition and Government amendments, the Sanctions and anti-Money Laundering Act 2018 includes gross human rights violation as a reason for imposing sanctions on a person or an entity.

After the passage of the 2018 Sanctions Act, the Government said it would bring forward more detail on Magnitsky sanctions in the form of secondary legislation using the powers in that Act.

**Magnitsky sanctions announced**

The Government announced the first new sanctions using the Sanctions Act in July 2020. They imposed asset freezes and travel bans on Saudi citizens alleged to have been involved in the murder of Jamal Khashoggi, the Saudi journalist murdered in the Saudi Embassy in Istanbul. Also targeted were Russian officials allegedly involved in the mistreatment of Sergei Magnitsky in a Moscow jail.

Other countries have introduced Magnitsky-style sanctions legislation or are working on it. The European Commission started organising EU Magnitsky legislation in December 2019.

*Meeting the needs of older prisoners*
9 May 2013

In recent years, the population of older prisoners (defined variously as those aged over 50, 60 or 65) has increased dramatically. The Department of Health's National Service Framework for Older People applies to prisoners as it does to older people in the community and emphasises the need for partnership working between the NHS and the prison service. Nonetheless, concerns have been expressed that the National Offender Management Service (NOMS) is ill-equipped to deal with an ageing prison population. Although HM Inspectorate of Prisons and others have found some instances of good practice, concerns remain that the physical fabric of prisons, their regimes, their provisions for health and healthcare and arrangements for release and post-release care are geared towards the young and the able-bodied and do not adequately meet the needs of older prisoners.

This note discusses some of the issues raised by the growing number of older offenders in prison in England and Wales, such as the availability (or not) of suitable accommodation for those with mobility problems and the involvement (or not) of social care agencies in providing appropriate care and services.

*Ministry of Justice: Areas of Research Interest*
December 2020
**Foreword**

The Ministry of Justice (MoJ) is a major government department, working to protect and advance the principles of justice and deliver a world-class justice system that works for everyone. Our responsibilities are significant, wide-ranging and have implications for some of the most vulnerable people in society. They range from building and maintaining the prisons, youth and courts estate, to developing interventions that reduce reoffending and protect the public, to ensuring children's needs are put first in legal decisions about their care.

It is imperative that robust research and analysis underpins this remit. We need to understand who, why and how people come into contact with our system and what we can do to improve their experiences and outcomes. As a department, we are committed to enhancing the way data and evidence is used, to shape policy and operational decisions and drive improvements to justice outcomes.

We are proud to be working with a diverse community of analysts at MoJ, including economists, operational and social researchers, statisticians and data scientists. Our combined methodological expertise, policy and operational knowledge and drive to continually enhance the analysis we provide makes for better decision-making. We want to strengthen this with a more comprehensive, dedicated and coordinated approach to engagement with our external partners. Only by drawing on the wealth of their knowledge and expertise, can we make sure the department is maximising the role of evidential insights.

The Areas of Research Interest (ARI) publication reflects this ambition. It will be used as the basis for ongoing conversations, collaboration and challenge with experts in academia, research organisations and funding bodies. Our aim is to increase the available evidence against our priorities, enhance our combined strategic research capabilities, and reinforce the impact of evidence at all stages of policy and operational development and evaluation.

Our ambitious and pioneering data-linking programme, Data First, is one way we are demonstrating our commitments; representing the most substantial investment across Whitehall by Administrative Data Research UK (ADR UK). Data First is unlocking the potential of the wealth of our data by linking administrative datasets from across the justice system and beyond and enabling researchers to access the data in an ethical and responsible way. By facilitating justice system research, we are creating opportunities for new insights on our users and their needs, pathways and outcomes across a range of public services. We are excited to share our lessons from this project as we pave the way across government to collaborate with experts and make progress against our research priorities. The unprecedented challenges caused by the Covid-19 pandemic have only underlined the need for robust, timely and relevant research and data. Our aims as a department align with the wider government ambition, outlined in the UK Research and Development Roadmap, to make significant investments in science and research to deliver benefits for society across the UK. The National Data Strategy further makes the case for developing a coherent approach for the UK to build a world-leading data economy, ensuring people can access data when they need it and trust how it is used.

We are pleased to see the publication of this ARI. As we move forwards, we are excited about what we can accomplish through positive engagement, collaboration and constructive challenge from our wider research community. We look forward to working with you.

Alexy Buck and Rachel Dubourg
MoJ Chief Social Researchers

## Misuse of civilian drones & prisons
January 2020

Drones are increasingly used for photography, agriculture, delivery and emergency response. However, travel disruption at UK airports due to drone sightings has renewed debate about their use. This note looks at civilian drones and their applications, focusing on potential misuse and possible responses.

## Background

Aerial drones, also known as unmanned aircraft, are flying systems that do not carry a pilot. They may be controlled remotely by a pilot or fly with various levels of autonomy following pre-programmed flight plans. Drones may be fully autonomous, meaning that a pilot is unable to intervene during flight. Drones can have fixed wings, rotary blades or a combination. They are one component of an unmanned aircraft system, comprising the drone, a controller and a communications system.

Drones can have civilian or military uses. This note focuses on civilian uses. Drone use for recreational and commercial purposes is growing, as technology becomes cheaper and more sophisticated. A 2018 survey found that 11% of adults in England had used a drone at least once. The Civil Aviation Authority (CAA) reported that permissions obtained for commercial drone operators in the UK doubled to over 5,000 from February 2017 to May 2019. A drone operator is a person or organisation who manages a drone but may not directly control it or be present during flight. One projection suggests that more than 76,000 drones, operated by government and commercial organisations, may be in use in the UK by 2030, increasing UK gross domestic product by around £42 bn in public services, construction and manufacturing. Publicly available data about the number of recreational drones in use in the UK are limited. Forecasts of the global market vary from £2.4–25.8bn by 2025.14 This compares with projections for the global commercial drone market of £1.2–6.9 bn by 2025.

Greater drone use affords many potential social and economic benefits. Drones can also present new challenges for safety and security. For example, reports of near-misses between aircraft and drones rose from 71 in 2016 to 125 in 2018. However, these figures have been challenged by some in the industry as overestimates. A 2016 study using laboratory tests and computer modelling found that mid-air collisions with drones could cause critical damage to manned aircraft. The Commons Science and Technology Committee recently raised concerns about a lack of consensus in the aviation community on the likely consequences of a drone-aeroplane collision.

In 2018, the Government introduced new limits on where drones can be flown and new registration and education requirements for drone operators and pilots. It also announced up to £125m for a Future Flight Challenge to support the development of electric and autonomous aircraft by 2025. Before the 2019 General Election, the Government published a strategy for tackling malicious drone use. In January 2020, the new Government introduced a bill that included new police powers for enforcing aviation laws. The EU is standardising rules for drone operations across Member States and published a regulatory framework for drone use in 2019.

## Overview

■ Drone use for commercial and recreational purposes offers many potential social and economic benefits, including for aerial observation, transport and sport.

■ Yet, drones pose potential challenges for safety, security, privacy and noise, and may facilitate crime.

■ Technology can help detect, control, seize, disable or destroy drones that are being misused. However, this may be by-passed or inappropriate in some settings.

■ Widespread commercial adoption would need further technological innovation and changes to legislation.

## Nitrous oxide: No laughing matter?

Published Monday, 20 July, 2020

On Tuesday 21 July MPs will discuss the misuse of nitrous oxide (commonly known as laughing gas) in an adjournment debate. This Insight explains what nitrous oxide is and how its use as a recreational drug is currently policed.

There is a graphic that explains the above and which you can view on the Research tab of The Prison Oracle - tinyurl.com/2cjfe6yd

## The science

### Legitimate uses of nitrous oxide

Nitrous oxide (N2O) is a colourless gas discovered by Joseph Priestly in 1772. In human and veterinary medicine, it is used with oxygen as an anaesthesia due to its pain-relieving effects. It is often referred to as 'laughing gas' because it can give those who inhale it a euphoric mood.

Other legitimate uses of nitrous oxide include as a fuel additive and as an approved food additive when used as a propellant for whipped cream.

### Use as a recreational drug

Recreational users typically inhale via a balloon inflated with the gas. There are health risks associated with the recreational use of nitrous oxide.

The Government-funded drugs advice service FRANK emphasises that inhaling nitrous oxide directly from the canister is "very dangerous because the gas is under such high pressure. It can cause a spasm of the throat muscle and stop a person breathing."

FRANK also says that nitrous oxide can cause:

• severe headache
• dizziness
• stop people thinking straight
• short-lived but intense feelings of paranoia.

The Advisory Council on the Misuse of Drugs advises the Government on the control of dangerous drugs. It says that long-term use of nitrous oxide can lead to vitamin B12 deficiency. In severe cases this can lead to neurological changes.

## The law

Nitrous oxide is normally treated as a "psychoactive substance" under the Psychoactive Substances Act 2016. Producing, supplying and importing/exporting psychoactive substances for human consumption is illegal. It's not illegal to possess psychoactive substances unless it's with intent to supply. Possession of such a substance in prison is also an offence. However, the application of the 2016 Act in cases involving nitrous oxide has not always been straightforward.

### Psychoactive substances

A psychoactive substance is anything capable of producing a "psychoactive effect" in those who consume it, assuming it's not exempt. Illegal drugs, alcohol, tobacco, caffeine, medicine and food are all exempted under the 2016 Act.

Last year two nitrous oxide "intent to supply" cases collapsed when questions were raised as to whether the gas is exempted because it is consumed as food in whipped cream. In 2017 an appeal against a conviction for intent to supply nitrous oxide was denied when the court decided nitrous oxide wasn't exempted as a "medical product."

### Police powers

Police have a range of powers which help them enforce the law. They can stop and search those they suspect are committing an offence under the 2016 Act. Police can also get a warrant to search premises for psychoactive substances. Finally, they can seize substances they find if they suspect they are drugs meant for recreational use.

### Supplying nitrous oxide

Those selling psychoactive substances can be found guilty of supplying the drug when they are "reckless" as to whether it is being consumed by people. Even if someone advertises the sale of a psychoactive substance for a legitimate purpose, if they know (or ought to know) it is being bought for recreational purposes they can be found guilty. Those found guilty could face up to six months in prison or an unlimited fine.

## The statistics

The 2016 Act was formally reviewed in 2018. The review found:

"the use of nitrous oxide (among all adults) does not appear to have been affected by the Act, although there are limited time series data to draw comparisons from."

Data for 2018/19 shows that 2.3% of adults aged 16-59 had used nitrous oxide in the last 12 months (around 763,000 people) up from 2% in 2012/13. Nitrous oxide use is more prevalent in young people. 8.7% of 16 to 24-year olds had used the drug in 2018/19 down from 9% in 2016/17 but up from 6.1% in 2012/13.

A one-off data release from the ONS shows the number of deaths associated with nitrous oxide between 1993 and 2017. Although the numbers are very small, there are signs of an increased trend. If we examine the rolling average number of deaths for 5-year periods, the average number peaked at just below 5 deaths per annum on average for 2013-2017.

## The concerns

There are concerns about the health impact of recreational nitrous oxide. There are also concerns about anti-social behaviour associated with the drug's use. Some are worried about the disturbance caused by those using the drug in public. Littering of empty cannisters on the street is also a problem. Local authorities, like Middlesbrough and Tower Hamlets, have stepped up their efforts to discourage the use of the drug in response to these concerns.

Local authorities can prohibit people from taking psychoactive substances in a specific place by making a public space protection order (PSPO). In order to do so they must show that the persistent use of psychoactive substances is causing a "detrimental effect on the quality of life of those in the locality."

Those who break a PSPO could be issued a 'fixed penalty notice' fining them up to £100. Scarborough and Lambeth have both made PSPOs banning the consumption of nitrous oxide. It's hard to assess their impact because we don't have enough data about them.

## The proposed solution

A petition currently before Parliament asks the Government to make the recreational use of nitrous oxide an offence. Given its widespread use for legitimate purposes, such a prohibition might be difficult to police. The Government says it has no plans to change the criminal law regarding to nitrous oxide. The Royal College of Nursing have called for better public information about the dangers of nitrous oxide misuse.

## Non-custodial sentences

January 2020

Non-custodial sentences are those that do not include imprisonment. They can include discharges, fines and community orders. In England and Wales, the vast majority of sentences are non-custodial. This POSTnote presents trends in sentencing and describes the non-custodial sentences being used in England and Wales. It also reviews evidence on the effectiveness of non-custodial sentences and current policy considerations.

## Background

When sentencing an individual, criminal courts judge whether an offence is serious enough to impose a custodial sentence (immediate imprisonment or a suspended sentence) or a noncustodial sentence. Criminal justice is devolved, so this POSTnote focuses on non-custodial sentences in England and Wales. The Criminal Justice Act 2003 reserves custodial sentences for the most serious offences. Most sentences imposed in England and Wales are non-custodial (90% of all sentences in the year ending June 2019).

In 2019, the Commons Justice Committee suggested that a rise in custodial sentences (in both length and as a proportion of all convictions) has contributed to the increasing prison population in England and Wales. This roughly doubled in size between 1990 and 2017 but has remained relatively stable since 2012. In 2019 there were 139 prisoners per 100,000 people in England and Wales, one of the highest rates in Europe.

There is general consensus that increasing the proportion of non-custodial sentences is unlikely to reduce the prison population due to other contributory factors (such as sentence length). But, non-custodial sentences may provide other benefits, especially compared with short custodial sentences (less than 12 months). These include reducing reoffending and causing less disruption to a sentenced person's life. In May 2019, the Ministry of Justice (MoJ) announced more funding for voluntary and private sector organisations to deliver rehabilitation services. These services will be delivered on behalf of the National Probation Service, which supervises both those receiving some types of non-custodial sentence and those released from prison into the community on probation.

Non-custodial sentences include discharges, fines and community orders. Evidence on their effectiveness varies, with most research focussing on the effect of community orders on reoffending. This POSTnote presents sentencing trends and describes the non-custodial sentences currently used for adults and young people in England and Wales. It also reviews evidence on the effectiveness of non-custodial sentences and discusses policy considerations.

## Overview

■ Non-custodial sentences include discharges, fines and community orders.

■ In the year ending June 2019, 90% of people sentenced in England and Wales were given non-custodial sentences.

■ The types of sentence given to individuals from different demographics (such as young people or women) vary.

■ Research shows that reoffending rates tend to be lower for non-custodial sentences than for custodial sentences.

■ There is less evidence on the effectiveness of these sentences on other outcomes, such as making up for any harm caused.

■ Policy considerations include public opinion, potential unintended effects on prison population, and cost.

### Offender Rehabilitation Bill
6 November 2013
This Bill would extend the mandatory supervision of offenders released from custodial sentences to provide that all offenders would be subject to at least 12 months of supervision in the community. It would also introduce new requirements, including drug appointments and residence requirements, which could be applied to offenders subject to such post-release supervision as well as those subject to community and suspended sentence orders.
John Bardens
Gabrielle Garton-Grimwood
Aliyah Dar

### Summary
The Offender Rehabilitation Bill [HL Bill 88 2013-14] seeks to amend the law relating to the release, and supervision after release, of offenders released from short custodial sentences. It would also make some changes to community sentences. The Bill represents the legislative parts of the Ministry of Justice's Transforming Rehabilitation strategy (see below). The Bill can be (broadly speaking) separated into three parts:
• The first part, which consists of clause 1 alone, concerns the MoJ's controversial proposals for reform of the probation services. Opponents of the proposed reforms have argued, among other things, that they would create perverse incentives for new contracted providers and lead to increased risks to public protection. These were not included in the Bill as introduced, as the MoJ said it would make the changes using existing powers. Clause 1, a non-Government amendment, would require any change to the structure of the "probation service" to be approved by both Houses of Parliament first.
• The second part, clauses 2-13, deals with the supervision of offenders released from short custodial sentences. All offenders released from sentences of less than two years would be subject to at least 12 months of mandatory supervision in the community. Many commentators have welcomed the proposals, but some have argued that they could lead to an increase in the use of short custodial sentences and an increase in recalls to prison.

The Bill would also put on a statutory footing the requirement to have regard to the special needs of female offenders when making supervision arrangements. It would also introduce new drug appointment requirements and expand the categories of drugs that can be tested for.
• The third part, clauses 14 -18, would amend the community sentencing framework. It would introduce a new "rehabilitation activity requirement" for community orders and suspended sentence orders and make amendments to allow private providers to be responsible officers for the supervision of offenders subject to such orders. It would also introduce a new mandatory requirement that offenders subject to such orders seek permission from their responsible officer before changing their place of residence.

### Territorial extent
Most of the provisions of the Bill consist of amendments to existing legislation which applies to England & Wales only.

### 70. Online safety bill – draft: A Reading List
1 October 2021
### Background
This reading list collates a selection of media coverage, stakeholder responses and other material relevant to the draft Online Safety Bill. The draft Bill, announced in the Queen's Speech, was published on 12 May 2021. It sets out Government plans to impose duties of care on providers of online content sharing platforms and search services. A Library Paper, Regulating online harms (CBP 8743), provides policy background.
*https://prisons.org.uk/facts-figures/research-briefings/*

### Online Safety Bill - A Reading List
The Bill was introduced in the House of Commons on 17 March 2022. This reading list provides a selection of media coverage, stakeholder responses and material relevant to the Bill. (10th April 2022)

### Police, Crime, Sentencing and Courts Bill: Progress of the Bill
This research paper summarises the Commons stages of the Police, Crime, Sentencing and Courts Bill and the Lords amendments to the Bill. (25th March 2022)

### Police powers: detention and custody
19 August 2021
### Summary
The police have powers, set out in Part IV and Part V of the Police and Criminal Evidence Act 1984 (PACE), to detain those they have arrested

on suspicion of committing a crime. The police have separate powers to detain those suspected of terrorism offences under Part V and Schedule 8 of the Terrorism Act 2000.[1] The detention of a suspect is often crucial to a police investigation. It allows officers to question them and collect their biometric details. This information helps the police decide whether they have grounds to charge a suspect with a crime.

The police also have powers to detain adults for their own (or other's) safety under section 136 of the Mental Health Act 1983. Adults detained under section 136 of the 1983 Act can only be held in a police station in exceptional circumstances.

The police detain people in custody suites which are normally situated within large police stations. There are around 200 custody suites across England & Wales. Individual police forces are responsible for deciding how many custody suites to operate and where to situate them.

Her Majesty's Inspectorate of Constabulary, Fire & Rescue Services (HMICFRS) and Her Majesty's Inspectorate of Prisons (HMIP) jointly inspect police custody. They measure forces against their expectations for police custody. They also monitor compliance with statutory guidance on detention powers (PACE Code C) and College of Policing (the body responsible for professional standards in policing) has also published guidance on detention and custody.

### Vulnerable people in custody

There were longstanding concerns with the delivery of police custody and particularly the treatment of vulnerable people in custody. In 2015 HMICFRS (then HMIC) published a thematic inspection of the welfare of vulnerable people in police custody, which was followed in 2017 by Dame Elish Angiolini independent review into deaths and serious incidents in police custody. Both Dame Elish and HMICFRS recommended major changes to the police's approach to vulnerable people and suggested that other public services should play a greater role in caring for vulnerable people who come into contact with the police.

Since Dame Elish's Review the Government have legislated to minimise the use of police custody for those with severe mental health needs. It has asked the College of Policing to revise its guidance on detention and custody and are working to ensure that every custody suite has access to 'liaison and diversion services' for those with mental health needs or substance addiction. Despite significant political scrutiny on custody since Dame Elish's Review, concerns have persisted. HMICFRS and HMIP have said that "most forces...continue to improve their custody services" but that they "weren't seeing much

improvement in outcomes for detainees". The Inspectorates said the "capacity of other agencies to help forces meet the needs of detainees, and meet their own statutory responsibilities, remained a difficult problem."

*1 Note: This research briefing does not discuss police powers to detain those suspected of terrorism offences.*

### Police personnel: pay, recruitment, training and welfare

29 September 2021

**Summary**

There are four main types of personnel that work in police forces: police officers, police specials (volunteer police officers), Police Community Support Officers (PCSOs) and civilian support staff. Police officers are 'office holders' rather than employees, holding the Office of Constable. They are prohibited from joining a trade union. Instead, there are 'staff associations' which represent officers. 'Rank and file' officers are represented by the Police Federation. The Police Superintendents Association represents senior officers. Police chiefs and their deputies are represented by the Chief Police Officers' Staff Association.

The College of Policing (the College) is the professional body for English and Welsh policing. It sets policing standards, including recruitment and training standards for police officers. Each police force in the UK organises its officers using a standardised rank structure which denotes their seniority and responsibilities. Officers can work their way up the rank structure, others may be fast tracked to leadership roles either through a graduate programme or a talent identification scheme.

Police forces divide their personnel into teams known as police units. Most police units fall into one of two categories: local response teams work in shifts to respond to emergency calls whilst centralised specialist units investigate specific types of crime.

Police personnel can specialise in different types of policing. The most notable specialism is 'investigations' where detectives spend their time investigating crimes rather than patrolling and responding to emergency calls. There are many unique police specialisms. For example, police officers may specialise in public order, neighbourhood, or undercover policing (amongst other things). Others are trained to work with police animals like sniffer dogs and horses. The College has issued policing professional profiles which describe the responsibilities and functions of generic roles across the policing profession.

### Police uplift programme

In July 2019, in his first speech as Prime Minister,

Boris Johnson pledged to put "another 20,000 police on the streets" by March 2023. The work to meet this pledge is known as the "police uplift programme". An estimated 50,000 police officers will need to be recruited to meet the pledge. The police are targeted to increase officer numbers by 6,000 by March 2021 and a further 6,000 by March 2022.

The Home Office is releasing regular information about the progress of the programme on its webpage police officer uplift statistics. As at 30 June 2021, 9,814 police officers have been recruited through the uplift programme.

### Policing covenant

The Government is introducing a 'Police Covenant' to recognise the sacrifices of those who work in policing. The Police Covenant will focus on three key areas: the health and wellbeing of police personnel, the physical protections they need on the job and support for their families.

The Government published detailed proposals for the covenant in September 2020. It proposed the following wording for the covenant:

This Covenant acknowledges the sacrifices made by those who serve or have served in our Police Forces, either in a paid or voluntary capacity, whether as an officer or as a member of staff. It is intended to ensure that they and their families are not disadvantaged as a result of that commitment and seeks to mitigate the impact on their day to day life or in their access to justice. Police officers are required at all times to uphold the important principles of policing by consent, the foundation of their long-standing relationship with the public. We ask a great deal of our police and we expect the highest standards to be maintained. In return, we have a responsibility to provide protection and support to the police.

The Covenant recognises that working within policing comes with a high level of personal accountability, duty and responsibility requiring courage and personal risk both on and off duty. This recognition extends to all those who support police forces in upholding the principles and practices of their vocation. Recognising those who have served in policing unites the country and demonstrates the value of their sacrifice. This has no greater expression than in upholding this Covenant.

Clause one of the Police, Crime, Sentencing and Courts Bill would require the Home Secretary to report annual on the principals of the covenant. Part 1 of the PCSC Bill includes other provisions connected to the protection of the police. The Library's briefing paper on Part 1 includes further information.

### Police pay

Police officer pay is set annually by the Home Office on the advice of the Police Remuneration Review Body (PRRB). Each year the Home Secretary sends a remit letter to the PRRB setting out the considerations it wants it to take into consideration when making its annual recommendations. The PRRB takes evidence from stakeholders across the policing system and publishes a report in response to its remit letter.

In 2021, in line with Treasury policy, all police officers earning below £24,000 received a consolidated pay award of £250. All other officers experienced a pay freeze. The pay deal was widely criticised by those in policing. In response both the Police Federation and the Police Superintendents Association withdrew their support for the PRRB arguing that it was not truly independent of government and therefore lacked credibility.

### Police Powers - an introduction

See below & https://prisons.org.uk/facts-figures/research-briefings/

### Police powers: detention and custody

21st November 2020

This briefing forms part of a series about police powers. The briefing police powers: an introduction provides an overview of police powers and links to other relevant briefings.

The police have powers, set out in Part IV and Part V of the Police and Criminal Evidence Act 1984 (PACE), to detain those they have arrested on suspicion of committing a crime. The police have separate powers to detain those suspected of terrorism offences under Part V and Schedule 8 of the Terrorism Act 2000. The detention of a suspect is often crucial to a police investigation. It allows officers to question them and collect their biometric details. This information helps the police to determine whether to charge a suspect with a crime.

The police also have powers to detain adults for their own (or other's) safety under section 136 of the Mental Health Act 1983. However, adults detained under section 136 of the 1983 Act can only be held in a police station in exceptional circumstances.

The police detain people in custody suites which are normally situated within large police stations. There are around 210 custody suites across England & Wales. Individual police forces are responsible for how many custody suites they have and where they are situated.

Her Majesty's Inspectorate of Constabulary, Fire & Rescue Services (HMICFRS) and Her Majesty's Inspectorate of Prisons (HMIP) jointly inspect police custody. They measure forces against their expectations for police custody. They also monitor compliance with statutory guidance on detention powers (PACE Code C) and College of Policing (the body responsible for professional standards in policing) guidance on detention and custody.

## Vulnerable people in custody

There have been longstanding concerns with the delivery of police custody and particularly the treatment of vulnerable people in custody.

In 2015 HMICFRS (then HMIC) published a thematic inspection of the welfare of vulnerable people in police custody, which was followed in 2017 by Dame Elish Angiolini independent review into deaths and serious incidents in police custody. Both Dame Elish and HMICFRS recommended major changes to the police's approach to vulnerable people and suggested that other public services should play a greater role in caring for vulnerable people who come into contact with the police.

Since Dame Elish's Review the Government have legislated to minimise the use of police custody for those with severe mental health needs. They asked the College of Policing to revise its guidance on detention and custody and are working to ensure that every custody suite has access to 'liaison and diversion services' for those with mental health needs or substance addiction.

Despite significant political scrutiny on custody since Dame Elish's Review, concerns have persisted. HMICFRS and HMIP have said that "forces continue to improve their custody services" but that they "weren't seeing much improvement in outcomes for detainees". The Inspectorates said the "capacity of other agencies to help forces meet the needs of detainees, and meet their own statutory responsibilities, remained a difficult problem."

## Police powers: stop and search

10 March 2021

Summary

This briefing provides information for England and Wales only This briefing paper is part of a series which discuss police powers in England and Wales. The series is introduced by the briefing police powers: an introduction. The police have a variety of legislative powers to stop and search those they suspect have certain items. Their stop and search powers allow them to "allay or confirm" their suspicions without making an arrest. There are three types of stop and search powers:

• powers which require officers to have "reasonable grounds" to conduct the search, sometimes known as 'section 1' searches;

• a power which allows officers to search

without reasonable grounds, sometimes known as 'no suspicion' or 'section 60' search. This power can only be used when authorised by a senior officer based on certain 'pre-conditions'.

• a power officers can use to search those they 'reasonably suspect' are terrorists.

This terrorism power is not discussed in this briefing.

Officers must use a specific legislative power every time they carry out a stop and search. They must use the correct power for the circumstances of each search. They cannot rely on someone's consent alone to search them.

The Home Office maintains statutory guidance on the most frequently used stop and search powers in PACE Code A. The College of Policing (the body responsible for professional standards in policing) maintains an Authorised Professional Practice (APP) on stop and search. All English and Welsh police forces have subscribed to follow, at least in part, additional Home Office guidance on the best use of stop and search.

## Use of stop and search

Police forces have reduced their use of stop and search over the past ten years, but the number of searches has recently increased. Around 577,000 searches were conducted in 2019/20. 58% fewer than in 2009/10 but 52% higher than in 2018/19.

The reduction in the use of stop and search was the result of reforms bought forward between 2013 and 2016. At the beginning of the 2010s there were concerns that the police were overusing their stop and search powers and conducting poorly targeted searches. This was resulting in some ineffective and unlawful use of stop and search. Reforms were introduced to police guidance which encouraged forces to ensure their use of stop and search was based on robust intelligence and information.

The current Government and policing leaders have argued that stop and search should form part of the response to violent crime. The Home Office has relaxed voluntary guidance on the use of pre-condition search introduced during the 2013-2016 reform period and encouraged forces to use their search powers more frequently.

The use of pre-condition search has increased markedly over the last three years. Most searches are conducted using reasonable grounds powers (97% in 2019/20) but the number pre-condition searches increased from 622 in 2016/17 to 18,081 in 2019/20. Pre-condition searches accounted for around 5% of the overall increase in the use of stop and search between 2017/18 and 2020/19.

## Tactical use

A small number of forces conduct most stop and searches. The Metropolitan Police Service (MPS) conducted almost half of all searches in 2019/20 (48%). 64% of all searches were conducted by just five forces: the MPS, Merseyside, West Midlands, Essex and South Yorkshire.

Most searches are conducted to find drugs. Around 63% of all reasonable grounds searches were conducted to find drugs in 2019/20 with around 16% conducted to find offensive weapons. In its February 2021 spotlight report on the disproportionate use of stop and search and the use of force, Her Majesty's Inspectorate of Constabulary and Fire & Rescue Services (HMICFRS) found that drug searches contributes to "ethnic disproportionality" in stop and search rates "despite evidence that there is no correlation between ethnicity and rates of drug use". HMICFRS says the high prevalence of drug possession searches indicates that "enforcement efforts are not being effectively focused on force priorities".

### Fair use?

Evidence suggests that police practice did improve during the 2013-16 reform period. However, recently police watchdogs (including HMICFRS and the Independent Office for Police Conduct) have raised concerns that some searches are not conducted lawfully and effectively. In February 2021 HMICFRS published findings of a review of 9,378 search records. 14% of those records had "recorded grounds that were not reasonable". The inspectorate said the "vast majority" of search records had weak recorded grounds (80%). HMICFRS has repeatedly called on forces to do more to monitor and scrutinise their use of the powers.

### Impact of stop and search

Those in policing claim that when stop and search is targeted and conducted in line with the law and guidance, they can confiscate dangerous and prohibited items without undermining public trust in the police. Those opposed to stop and search argue that a history of poor use demonstrates it is a fundamentally flawed police power. They note that the long-standing disparity in the search rate by ethnicity continues to ensure that Black and Minority Ethnic (BME) people are disproportionately affected by the negative effects of stop and search.

BME people were four times more likely to be searched than white people in 2019/20. The difference was particularly pronounced for black people, who were nine times more likely to be searched than white people. HMICFRS says no force "fully understands the impact of the use of [stop and search] powers" and "no force can satisfactorily explain why" ethnic disproportionality persists in search records.

Poorly targeted and conducted stop and search is widely acknowledged to damage police community relations, whilst evidence regarding the impact of stop and search on crime is mixed. There is little evidence to suggest that stop and search provides an effective deterrent to offending. Stop and search is more effective at detecting criminals, but most searches result in officers finding nothing. Only around 20% of searches in 2019/20 resulted in a criminal justice outcome (an arrest or out of court disposal) linked to the purpose of the search.

### Policing and crime- Opposition Day Debate
28 January, 2020

Police forces in England and Wales are emerging from a period of financial pressure. They are responding to evolving crime threats including digital crime, county lines drug dealing and serious violence.

Her Majesty's Inspectorate of Constabulary and Fire & Rescue Services (HMICFRS) has reported that the police have responded well to these challenges. However, they have raised continued concerns about the resourcing of police forces and called for fundamental reform of police governance which facilitates better collaboration at a regional and national level. These concerns have been shared by several stakeholders and commentators.

In September 2019 the previous Johnson Government committed to undertake a "formal review of the powers, capabilities, governance and funding" needed by police services. The new Johnson Government has committed to establishing a Royal Commission on the criminal justice system. It is not clear to what extent the Commission will look at the governance and funding of police services. It is also not clear if/ when the review committed to last September will be launched.

On the 23 January 2020 the Government announced the 2020/2021 police funding settlement which increased the funding available for Police and Crime Commissioners in England and Wales from £12.1 billion in 2019/20 to a provisional £13.1 billion in 2020/21.

### Policing in the UK
29 September 2021

#### Summary
Police services in the UK are organised around two legal entities: the 'Office of Constable' and the police force.

Police officers (no matter their rank) each individually hold the Office of Constable. The Office of Constable grants them powers to detect, prevent and investigate crime.

Every police officer is a member of a police force. The police force organises and coordinates their crime fighting. As members of police forces, officers (and other police personnel) are under the "direction and control" of their chief officer. Chief officers are ultimately responsible for the operation of their force.

There are 48 civilian police forces in the UK: 43 territorial police forces in England and Wales, a national police force in both Scotland and Northern Ireland and three specialist police forces (the British Transport Police, the Civil Nuclear Constabulary and the Ministry of Defence Police).

Policing is (by and large) a devolved matter in Scotland and Northern Ireland. The Scottish Government and the Northern Ireland Executive are responsible for deciding how most police services are organised and managed in their nations. Policing culture is very similar throughout the UK and Police Scotland and the Police Service Northern Ireland share many of the characteristics of English and Welsh forces.

The term British model of policing is sometimes used to describe policing culture in the UK. There is no formal definition of the British model, but it is typically understood though three interlinked concepts: The Office of Constable, operational independence and policing by consent.

## Force performance

Data from the Crime Survey for England and Wales (CSEW) suggests that around 55% of people think their police force is doing a "good" or "excellent" job. This figure is often known as the confidence level. The confidence level has fallen over the last two years (from around 62% in 2017/18 to 55% in 2019/20).

Her Majesty's Chief Inspector of Constabulary and Fire & Rescue Services inspects forces and scores them against three assessment pillars (effectiveness, efficiency and legitimacy). Forces receive one of four 'judgements' for each pillar: outstanding, good, requires improvement and inadequate. It maintains an online dashboard displaying all force scores. HMICFRS also provide a detailed written assessment of each force which can be found by navigating through the online dashboard. There were no inspections in 2020 owing to the pandemic. Therefore HMICFRS PEEL scores are still the latest given as at 2018/19. HMICFRS has tended to judge forces better on effectiveness and legitimacy, giving slightly lower scores on efficiency. Overall, most forces are judged to be performing well by the Inspectorate across all three measures. However, there is growing divergence between the performance of forces. The Inspectorate has said this is the result of some forces rising to the twin challenges of rising demand and falling resources better than others.

The Government began measuring 'National Crime and Policing Measures' (data points associated with certain crime types) in the summer of 2021. It is expecting "significant" national improvements against these measures within three years. It is also committed to working with HMICFRS to publishing police force "league tables" for 101 and 999 call responsiveness. However, it is yet to announce when the first league tables will be published.

## Policing in the UK: Serious and Organised Crime
16 January, 2020

Serious and organised crime (SOC) is criminal activity that is planned, coordinated and committed by people working individually, in groups, or as part of transnational networks. It usually centres on acquiring money, profit, influence and power. Sexual gratification is also a motivator in some cases. Such offences are often committed by organised crime groups (OCGs), who use violence, corruption and intimidation to protect their criminal activities.

The National Crime Agency (NCA) has stated that SOC affects more UK citizens, more often, than any other national security threat. It has a daily impact on citizens, public services, businesses, institutions, national reputation and infrastructure. In the UK, no single official or body is in overall charge of the response to SOC. Rather, there are over 100 government departments, law enforcement bodies, agencies and other organisations involved in tackling this type of crime. Operationally, the NCA leads and coordinates the UK's response. It also publishes an annual national strategic assessment on the issue, highlighting key findings and trends.

The UK Government and the devolved administrations in Northern Ireland and Scotland are responsible for policy, including serious and organised crime. In England and Wales, the Home Office has overall responsibility for policy, strategy and funding, including the publication of the Serious and Organised Crime Strategy. In October 2019, the UK Government announced an independent review, led by Sir Craig Mackay, to support the implementation of the SOC strategy.

There is no dedicated funding stream for tackling serious and organised crime. The work is financed through several unconnected funding streams by sources that are subject to annual bidding and decision processes.

Both the National Audit Office and the House of Commons Public Accounts Committee have recently looked at the UK Government's strategic response to serious and organised crime, arguing that while there are examples of good work, "there remain some significant and avoidable shortcomings". In addition, the director general of the National Crime Agency, Lynne Owens, has called for an increase to the amount of funding aimed at tackling serious and organised crime.

### Police powers: detention and custody
19 August 2021

**Summary**
The police have powers, set out in Part IV and Part V of the Police and Criminal Evidence Act 1984 (PACE), to detain those they have arrested on suspicion of committing a crime. The police have separate powers to detain those suspected of terrorism offences under Part V and Schedule 8 of the Terrorism Act 2000.[1] The detention of a suspect is often crucial to a police investigation. It allows officers to question them and collect their biometric details. This information helps the police decide whether they have grounds to charge a suspect with a crime.

The police also have powers to detain adults for their own (or other's) safety under section 136 of the Mental Health Act 1983. Adults detained under section 136 of the 1983 Act can only be held in a police station in exceptional circumstances.

The police detain people in custody suites which are normally situated within large police stations. There are around 200 custody suites across England & Wales. Individual police forces are responsible for deciding how many custody suites to operate and where to situate them.

Her Majesty's Inspectorate of Constabulary, Fire & Rescue Services (HMICFRS) and Her Majesty's Inspectorate of Prisons (HMIP) jointly inspect police custody. They measure forces against their expectations for police custody. They also monitor compliance with statutory guidance on detention powers (PACE Code C) and College of Policing (the body responsible for professional standards in policing) has also published guidance on detention and custody.

### Vulnerable people in custody
There were longstanding concerns with the delivery of police custody and particularly the treatment of vulnerable people in custody. In 2015 HMICFRS (then HMIC) published a thematic inspection of the welfare of vulnerable people in police custody, which was followed in 2017 by Dame Elish Angiolini independent review into deaths and serious incidents in police custody. Both Dame Elish and HMICFRS recommended major changes to the police's approach to vulnerable people and suggested that other public services should play a greater role in caring for vulnerable people who come into contact with the police.

Since Dame Elish's Review the Government have legislated to minimise the use of police custody for those with severe mental health needs. It has asked the College of Policing to revise its guidance on detention and custody and are working to ensure that every custody suite has access to 'liaison and diversion services' for those with mental health needs or substance addiction. Despite significant political scrutiny on custody since Dame Elish's Review, concerns have persisted. HMICFRS and HMIP have said that "most forces…continue to improve their custody services" but that they "weren't seeing much improvement in outcomes for detainees". The Inspectorates said the "capacity of other agencies to help forces meet the needs of detainees, and meet their own statutory responsibilities, remained a difficult problem."

*1 Note: This research briefing does not discuss police powers to detain those suspected of terrorism offences.*

### POST Fellowships 2020/2021
Published Tuesday, 11 February, 2020
All you need to know to apply for a POST Fellowship in 2020/2021. Fellowships are available for postgraduate students and, in the case of some schemes, researchers with PhDs.
• 8 PhD Fellowship schemes will be accepting applications in 2020/2021
• All dates are provisional and subject to change
• Last updated 9 March 2020
POST provides training to the next generation of policy shapers through a range of fellowship schemes. In partnership with their funder, successful PhD students are invited to UK Parliament to work at POST.
While fellows typically get to help us with the production of a POSTnote or POSTbrief, this once in a lifetime opportunity to view the epicentre of policy-making from the inside may also include a secondment to a Select Committee or the House of Commons or House of Lords Libraries.
By the end of their time at POST, our fellows learn how to write for policy with balance and impartiality. They also develop a unique understanding of Westminster and forge important relationships with key stakeholders, while often delving into a novel and exciting topic of research.
All POST Fellows need to be able to work in the UK. POST Fellowships can only be confirmed after successful security vetting. This includes a Counter Terrorist Check.
Below you can find POST fellowships that will accept applications in 2019/2020. You will find eligibility criteria and provisional application opening and closing dates.

**The Nuffield Foundation**
Applications reopen November 2020
Applicants will be:
• doing a PhD in a UK university,
• doing a PhD on a scientific or quantitative social science field, and
• in their last or second to last year of study.
Nuffield Fellows have worked on topics such as:
• Early interventions to reduce violent crime
• Creating age-friendly cities
• Obesity treatments
For more information, see the 2019/2020 call for applications.

**The Royal Society of Chemistry**
Applications now open for 2020/2021.
Applicants will be:
• doing a PhD or have completed a PhD in the last six months,
• be a member of the Royal Society of Chemistry (RSC) or submit an application for RSC membership alongside their fellowship application.
RSC Fellows have worked on topics such as:
• Climate change and infrastructure (in production)
For more information, see the 2020/2021 call for applications.

**The Wellcome Trust**
Applications now open for 2020/2021
Applicants will be:
• holders of a Doctoral Studentship, or
• a Research Fellowship in Humanities and Social Science, or
• a Research Fellowship for Health Professionals, or
• be a PhD student funded by the Investigator Awards in Humanities and Social Science, or
• a PhD student funded by the Collaborative Awards in Humanities and Social Science.
Wellcome Fellows have worked on topics such as:
• Improving witness testimony
• Advances in cancer treatment
• Electronic health records
For more information, see the currently open 2020/2021 call for applications.

**The British Ecological Society**
Applications reopen June/July 2020
Applicants will be:
• doing a PhD in a UK university,
• in their 2nd, 3rd or 4th year of full-time study or part-time equivalent,
• members of the British Ecological Society (BES).
Wellcome Fellows have worked on topics such as:
• Climate change and agriculture
• Managing UK fisheries
• Environmental crime
For more information, see the 2019/2020 call for applications.

**The Institute of Food Science and Technology**
Applications reopen April/May 2020
Applicants will be:
• IFST Fellows have worked on topics such as:
• Compostable food packaging
• Plastic food packaging waste
• Intellectual property and plants
For more information, see the 2019/2020 call for applications.

**The British Psychological Society**
Applications reopen June/July 2020
Applicants will be:
• postgraduate students registered for a doctoral degree in a psychology-related subject e.g. PhD/MPhil or taught practitioner doctorates (DClinPsy etc) at a UK HE institution,
• in their last or second to last year of their studies,
• in part or full-time study at the time of the start of their placement at POST, and
• at least graduate members of the British Psychological Society (BPS)
BPS Fellows have worked on topics such as:
• Autism
• Academic evidence on selective secondary education
• Policing domestic abuse
For more information, see the 2019/2020 call for applications.

**UK Research and Innovation**
Applications reopen July/August 2020
Applicants will be:
• doing a PhD funded by the Research Councils of UK Research and Innovation (AHRC, BBSRC, ESRC, EPSRC, MRC, NERC and STFC),
• able to start their fellowship before the end of their funded period of study
UK Research and Innovation Fellows have worked on topics such as:
• Brain-computer interfaces
• Non-custodial sentences
• Human germline genome editing
For more information, see the 2019/2020 call for applications.

*Prison Estate*
8 October 2021
**Summary**
The prison estate in England and Wales contains 117 prisons holding people who have been sentenced or are on remand awaiting trial for a range of crimes. The prison estate has a mixture of publicly and privately-run institutions some of which are newly built, while others date back to the Victorian era.
**Concerns about conditions**
There has been growing concern that the prison estate is unfit for purpose. The estate includes many dilapidated and overcrowded prisons.

There is a backlog of maintenance work in prisons that has been estimated at around £1 billion.

Reports from the Chief Inspector of Prisons in 2017-19 said that conditions in this period were some of the most disturbing and squalid the inspectorate had ever seen. The inspectorate reported that in 2019-20, prior to the Covid19 pandemic, some prisons had improved living conditions, but conditions remained poor and overcrowded for many prisoners. The current Chief Inspector of Prisons in his 2020-21 annual report stated that the pandemic had exacerbated some underlying problems and unacceptable conditions that inspections have previously criticised.

### Government prison estate programmes

The Government ran a 'Prison Estate Transformation Programme' from 2016- 2019 with the aim of building 10,000 new prison places, investing in repairs and renovations and reorganising the functions of individual prisons. In 2020 the National Audit Office and Public Accounts Committee published reports that were critical of the attempts made by the Ministry of Justice and HM Prison and Probation Service (HMPPS) to improve the prison estate. The Public Accounts Committee said that despite promises to create 10,000 new-for-old prison places by 2020, just 206 new places had been delivered, and prisoners continued to be held in unsafe, crowded conditions that did not meet their needs.

A New Prison Programme was created in 2019. In August 2019 the Government announced that it would spend up to £2.5 billion to create 10,000 prison places. In the 2020 Spending Review the Government stated it would spend more than £4 billion towards delivering 18,000 prison places across England and Wales by the mid-2020s. The 18,000 places would include the 10,000 places at four new prisons (announced in August 2019), the expansion of a further four prisons, the refurbishment of the existing prison estate and the completion of ongoing prison builds at Glen Parva and Five Wells (Wellingborough).

The 2020-21 Spending Review also included £315m capital funding which HMPPS said would be used to make a start on critical refurbishment projects. The Public Accounts Committee has said the £315 million is significantly below what is required to maintain the prison estate.

### Responses to the Government's approach

Prison reform organisations have been critical of the Government's approach. They argue that instead of increasing prison places the Government should reduce the prison population thereby reducing overcrowding and freeing up resources for rehabilitation.

In January 2021 the Government announced that up to 500 prison places would be built in existing women's prisons. The plans have been criticised by prison reform organisations who have commented that they undermine the Government's commitments to reduce the women's prison population and go against the Government's own evidence that most women in prison do not need to be there.

This briefing discusses the prison estate in England and Wales.

### Prison Reform: Recent Developments
5 December 2017

**Summary**
The 2015-17 Conservative government published a white paper on Prison Safety and Reform in November 2016. It set out proposals which aimed to deal with increasing levels of violence and self-harm in prisons and the persistently high levels of reoffending. A central proposal was greater autonomy for prison governors which was being piloted in six 'reform prisons'. Other key proposals included were:
• 'sharper' inspection and scrutiny arrangements
• Additional funding with 2500 more prison officers by 2018
• More extensive drug testing, including on entry to and exit from prison
• New prison league tables covering public protection, safety and order, time out of cells and prisoners' progress in education, health and work
• A stronger role for Her Majesty's Inspectorate of Prisons
• A new duty for the Secretary of State to intervene when prisons are failing
• All prisoners to be allocated a dedicated officer to oversee their progression through custody.

The white paper was followed by the introduction of the Prisons and Courts Bill published in February 2017. The Bill contained provisions relating to a number of the reforms set out in the white paper which required legislation. The Bill had second reading in March 2017 but did not complete committee stage, falling at the dissolution of Parliament in May 2017.

The Prisons and Courts Bill 2016-17 contained clauses concerning:
• the statutory purpose of prisons;
• the role of the Secretary of State in relation to prisons;
• the role and powers of Her Majesty's Inspectorate of Prisons;
• the status and powers of the Prisons and Probation Ombudsman;
• disruption of unlawful mobile phone use; and
• testing for new psychoactive substances.

For detail regarding the Bill see the Library briefing The Prison and Courts Bill – Prison aspects, 15 March 2017, prepared for second reading. Also: Justice Committee, Prison reform: Part 1 of the Prisons and Courts Bill, HC 1150, 28 April 2017.

The Conservative party manifesto for the 2017 general election included measures on prison reform. No prison reform legislation was announced in the 2017 Queen's Speech on 21 June 2017. Some expressed disappointment, including the Chief Inspector of Prisons who called it a missed opportunity. In an open letter published on the same day the newly appointed Justice Secretary, David Lidington, said that work on prison reform would continue. In October 2017 he stated that the Government was developing an update to the 2016 white paper and would soon be publishing a prison safety strategy and action plan.

Prisons policy is a devolved matter in Scotland and Northern Ireland.

### Prisons Statistics, England and Wales
6 December 2017

**Summary**

This paper provides background statistics on prisons in England and Wales ahead of the Backbench Business debate on a motion on prison reform and safety (Robert Niell MP) on 7 December 2017.

Commons Briefing Paper SN04334: UK Prison Population Statistics (currently being updated) explores prison population data for England and Wales in more depth and includes data for the rest of the UK.

### Prison Population

As at 30 September 2017:
• The total prison population was 85,997.
• The most frequent length of sentence being served was a sentence over 4 years.
• Violence against the person (VATP) offences accounted for the highest proportion (25%) of prisoners. Sexual, theft and drug offences each accounted for approximately 15% of the reason offenders were in prison.
• There were just under 10,000 foreign nationals within the prison population. Those originating from the European Union (excluding the UK) accounted for 41% of all foreign nationals in prison and just under 5% of the total prison population.
• As at October 2017, 67% (78) of prison establishments were overcrowded.

### Prison Safety

In the 12 months to June 2017:
• There were just over 27,000 prisoner assault incidents within prisons, a 14% increase the figure to June 2016.
• There were 7,437 assaults on prison staff, 798 of

which were serious. There was a rise of 25% from the twelve months ending June 2016.
• There were over 41,103 self-harm incidents. This was an increase of 77% compared to the 12 months to June 2007 and an increase of 12% compared to the 12 months to June 2016.
• In the 12 months to September 2017 there were 300 deaths of prisoners in custody. Around 63% of the deaths were through natural causes, 26% were self-inflicted, 10% were classed as other (including those waiting for further information on cause of death) and 1% were the result of homicide.
• The number of prisoner escapes has reduced since 1995/96 when 52 prisoners escaped. There were four KPI prisoner escapes in 2016/17 and two in 2015/16.

### Prisons (Substance Testing) Bill 2019-21
16 December 2020

**Summary**

The Prisons (Substance Testing) Bill 2019-21 was introduced to the House of Commons on 5 February 2020. It is a Private Members' Bill introduced by Dame Cheryl Gillan. It had second reading on 16 October 2020. Committee stage took place on 2 December 2020. Report stage and third reading are due to take place on 22 January 2021. The Bill has Government support. Explanatory Notes have been prepared by the Ministry of Justice.

HM Prisons and Probation Service (HMPPS) in its Prisons Drugs Strategy, April 2019, described the misuse of drugs in prison as "one of the biggest challenges facing our criminal justice system today".

The law in England and Wales currently allows for mandatory drugs testing in prisons. Prisons Minister, Lucy Frazer, has said that drug testing is a "crucial part" of the strategy as it provides "robust evidence on the prevalence of drug misuse and can be used to support security measures, identify and signpost into drug treatment, monitor treatment compliance and act as an incentive to engage in treatment and recovery".

Issues have been identified with the current legislation which provides for drug testing in prisons. The chemical composition of psychoactive substances is subject to rapid change. New psychoactive substances are often created with slight alterations to the chemical make-up of existing psychoactive substances. Currently, where the chemical composition of a psychoactive substance is changed, a change in the law to include that new substance is required. Amending the law for each new substance is time-consuming and can cause delays in detection. Another issue with the law on drugs testing in prisons is that not all prescription and pharmacy medicines are included in the list of specified drugs prisons can test for. Also, there is currently no legislative basis for prevalence testing, an anonymised process to help identify any new substances being found routinely.

The Bill seeks to address these issues. It would:

• Amend the provision that allows for mandatory drug testing in prisons so that it uses the generic definition of a psychoactive substance from the Psychoactive Substances Act 2016, thereby removing the need for repeated changes to the law for newly identified substances to be individually added;

• Create powers for testing of prisoners for prescription only and pharmacy medicines; and

• Set out a statutory framework for prevalence testing

The Bill extends to England and Wales only. It would come into force on a date to be appointed by the Secretary of State.

### Prisoners (Disclosure of Information About Victims) Bill
29 September 2020

**Summary**

The Prisoners (Disclosure of Information about Victims) Bill 2019-21 was introduced in the House of Commons on 8 January 2020. It completed all stages in the House of Lords on 8 September 2020. At report stage in the Lords one new clause, moved by Baroness Kennedy of Cradley (Non-Affiliated), was agreed on division. The new clause agreed by the Lords would require the Parole Board to create and maintain a new database. The database would contain details of family members of victims in cases covered by the Bill where a prisoner refuses to disclose information about the whereabouts of a victim's body or the identity of a child in an indecent image. The Parole Board would be required to contact those on the database to provide specified information about an offender's parole application.

The Bill is due to return to the Commons on 6 October 2020 for consideration of this Lords amendment.

The Bill as introduced would place a statutory obligation on the Parole Board to take into account an offender's non-disclosure of certain information when making a decision about the release from prison of certain prisoners. The Parole Board would be required to take into account a prisoner's non-disclosure of information about a victim's remains or the identity of child victims in indecent images.

Parole Board guidance currently advises panel members to consider any failure or refusal by an offender to disclose the whereabouts of a victim's remains when assessing suitability for release. It is also established Parole Board practice to consider the non-disclosure of relevant information by offenders in cases involving living victims. The Government has said the Bill would ensure that the Parole Board take such matters into account by placing the guidance and practice into law.

The statutory obligation would apply to prisoners serving:

• a life sentence for murder, manslaughter, or the offence of taking or making an indecent photograph or pseudo-photograph of a child;

• an extended determinate sentence (or a similar predecessor sentence) for manslaughter or taking or making an indecent photograph or pseudo-photograph of a child.

The obligation to take into account the non-disclosure would apply to all such sentences, including those that were imposed before the coming into force of the provisions contained in this Bill. The obligation would apply to decisions about a first release, not any subsequent releases following recall to prison.

The Bill responds to the campaign for "Helen's law", led by Marie McCourt, whose daughter, Helen, was murdered in 1988. Helen McCourt's body has never been found. The Bill also responds to the case of Vanessa George, a nursery worker who was convicted of multiple counts of sexual abuse and taking and distributing indecent images of children and refused to name the victims.

Some have questioned whether the provisions of the Bill will make any difference in practice given the guidance already followed by the Parole Board.

The Ministry of Justice has published papers concerning the Bill, including a factsheet, equalities statement and European Convention on Human Rights memorandum. See: Gov.uk, Prisoners (Disclosure of Information about Victims) Bill. Information about the Bill can also be found on the page for the Bill on the Parliament website. Explanatory Notes were published for the Bill as brought from the Commons to the Lords. Explanatory Notes have also been published for the Lords amendment.

The provisions of the Bill extend and apply to England and Wales only. Prisons and sentencing (including release provisions) are devolved to Scotland and Northern Ireland. For further detail see paragraph 8 and annex A of the Explanatory Notes.

The Bill would come into force on a date to be specified by the Secretary of State by statutory instrument.

### Prisoners: Incentives & Earned Privileges Scheme
31 July 2014

In November 2013, the National Offender

Management Service revised the Incentives and Earned Privileges scheme for prisoners – this was the first review of the policy for 10 years. When coming to his role as Justice Secretary, Chris Grayling announced that the current policy was in need of an overhaul. He said that he wanted to ensure that the new policy properly addressed the issue of reoffending and was something that the public would have confidence in.

The changes have been controversial, particularly in relation to prisoners' ability to have steel-stringed guitars in their possession or to receive books sent from outside prison.

It was reported on 29 July 2014 that, in response to feedback from prison governors, the ban on steel-stringed guitars had been reversed, although the ban on receiving books would remain.

1 Background to the IEP prison scheme

1.1 What is the "Incentives and Earned Privileges scheme" for and why was it introduced?

The Incentives and Earned Privileges (IEP) system was introduced in 1995. It is a tool of prison management. As stated by the Prison Reform Trust, the scheme:

promotes conforming behaviour through rational choice. Enabling people to earn benefits in exchange for responsible behaviour encourages prisoners to engage with sentence planning and ensures a more disciplined and controlled environment which is safer for staff and prisoners. Other outcomes include a reduced risk of self-harm and improved staff-prisoner relationships.[1]

The IEP scheme for prisoners was revised in November last year. Details of the scheme can be found under paragraph four of the Prison Service Instruction (PSI) 30/2013, Incentives and Earned Privileges. The IEP scheme now comprises four levels – an increase from three: Basic, Entry (the new level), Standard and Enhanced. Basic level is for prisoners who have not demonstrated a sufficient commitment to rehabilitation or who have behaved badly; Entry level is the level applied to all newly convicted prisoners received into custody on or after 1 November 2013; Standard level is for those prisoners who have successfully completed the 'Entry' level requirements and who are considered to be meeting rehabilitation expectations and behaving well; and the Enhanced level is for prisoners who have demonstrated for a minimum of three months a commitment to their rehabilitation and adherence to the regime.

A press release from the Ministry of Justice described the changes to the scheme as "significant reforms" and summarised some of those changes:

When taking up the role of Justice Secretary, Chris Grayling made it clear that the current

policy needed a thorough and detailed review to ensure that it properly addresses reoffending as well as being something the public can have confidence in.

A full review of the policy – the first for 10 years – was ordered by Ministers last year and was completed in April. From today the absence of bad behaviour will no longer be enough to earn privileges – prisoners must also actively work towards their own rehabilitation.

Other key changes include:

• The introduction of a new IEP level – "Entry" – where privileges are restricted.

• Certificate 18 DVDs and subscription channels banned from all prisons.

• A national standardised list of items available for each level.

• An automatic IEP review for bad behaviour, with a presumption of downgrading.

• TVs turned off when prisoners should be engaged in work or other productive activity.

• Prisoners who misbehave will lose their TV.[2]

The Prisoners' Advice Service has published an information sheet on the IEP Scheme. A National Offender Management Service guide to changes to the scheme was also published in the prisoners' newspaper, Inside Time.[3]

1 Prison Reform Trust Incentives and Earned Privileges, [accessed 3 June 2014]

2 Ministry of Justice press release Major shake-up to prisoner incentives, 1 November 2013

3 NOMS guide to changes to the IEP scheme, Inside Time, November 2013

### Prisoners: transfers to other prisons in England and Wales

Published Monday, 07 October, 2013

The National Offender Management Service does (broadly speaking) seek to help prisoners to maintain family ties. There may, though, be many reasons — including (amongst other things) the prisoner's security categorisation, availability of prison places, remoteness of the prisoner's home or the prison and the need to move prisoners around the prison estate to ease population pressures — why prisoners may be held in a prison which is not the closest to their home. There is no requirement that prisoners should be held within a fixed distance of their home and nothing to prevent a prisoner being transferred to another prison; indeed, the Secretary of State has discretion to hold prisoners "in any prison". Where family members are finding it difficult to visit a relative in prison, the prisoner may apply for accumulated visits, a temporary transfer to a prison closer to home to receive visits there or a transfer to another prison. Information about any of these should be available in the prison.

## Prisoners' Release on Temporary Licence
11 July 2019

**Summary**

Release on Temporary Licence (ROTL) allows prisoners to be released temporarily into the community for specific purposes such as to engage in employment, to maintain family ties or to receive medical treatment.

According to the Ministry of Justice's Policy Framework, ROTL facilitates the rehabilitation of offenders by helping to prepare them for resettlement in the community once they are released.

Not every prisoner is eligible to be released on temporary licence. Some, such as those posing the highest security threat are barred altogether. There was controversy concerning the policy on ROTL in 2013/14 when there were a number of serious incidents in which prisoners released on temporary licence committed offences. This led to a review undertaken by HM Inspectorate of Prisons. In response to these incidents, the then Justice Secretary, Chris Grayling, announced that the rules for ROTL would be tightened. A new scheme of "restricted ROTL" for those prisoners who had committed serious offences in the past, with more stringent risk assessment and more robust monitoring arrangements was introduced.

In May 2019 the Government revised the rules on ROTL to allow more prisoners to become eligible for ROTL, earlier in their sentence. The Ministry of Justice said that the changes would give prison governors greater autonomy and would allow prisoners more opportunities to work and train with employers while serving their sentence.

Changes made to the previous policy included:

• Changing the threshold for restricted ROTL to focus on the most serious offences;

• Removing the restriction on ROTL in the first three months after transfer to open conditions, subject to individual progress and risk assessment; and

• Allowing offenders with a prior abscond history (if it occurred more than two years ago and only once during the current sentence) to be risk assessed for open conditions and ROTL.

This briefing paper covers England and Wales. Information about the various temporary release schemes which operate in Scotland and Northern Ireland can be found on the websites of the Scottish Prison Service and the Northern Ireland Department of Justice:

• Scottish Prison Service, People Affected by Crime: Frequently Asked Questions

• Department of Justice, Temporary Release Schemes and Home Leave Scheme

## Prisoners' voting rights (2005 to May 2015)
11 February 2015

Prisoners serving a custodial sentence do not have the right to vote under UK law. Prisoners on remand are able to vote under the provisions of the Representation of the People Act 2000.

This Standard Note provides a narrative of events from the judgment of the European Court of Human Rights (ECtHR) on 6 October 2005, in the case of Hirst v United Kingdom (No 2), to the May 2015 General Election. For analysis of recent developments, the House of Commons Library Briefing Paper, Prisoners' voting rights: developments since May 2015, covers the period from May 2015.

For information about the European Convention on Human Rights and compliance with the Court's rulings see Library Standard Notes SN/IA/5936, The European Convention on Human Rights and the Court of Human Rights: issues and reforms, and SN/IA/5941, European Court of Human Rights rulings: are there options for governments?

Two consultations were held by the Labour Government in the 2005-10 Parliament; but no legislation was forthcoming. In the 2010-15 Parliament the issue continued to be contentious.

In December 2010 the Government announced that, in response to the judgment in Hirst, it would bring forward legislation to allow those offenders sentenced to a custodial sentence of less than four years the right to vote in UK Parliamentary and European Parliament elections, unless the sentencing judge considered this inappropriate. No timetable was announced for this proposed legislation.

A backbench debate was subsequently held in the House of Commons on 10 February 2011: the motion, which supported the continuation of the current ban, was agreed on a division by 234 to 22. On 1 March 2011 the Government referred the latest ECtHR ruling on the issue, the Greens and MT judgement, to the Grand Chamber of the European Court of Human Rights. This in effect appealed the Court's decision that the UK had six months to introduce legislation to lift the blanket ban. On 11 April 2011 this request for an appeal hearing was dismissed and the Court gave the UK Government a deadline of six months from this date to introduce legislative proposals.

On 6 September 2011 the Government announced that it had requested an extension to this deadline to take account of the referral of Scoppola v Italy (No 3) (a case similar to that of Greens and MT) to the Grand Chamber. The Court granted an extension of six months from the date of the judgment in the case. The United Kingdom Government made submissions to the Grand Chamber as a third party intervener in the case.

The Grand Chamber's judgment in the case of Scoppola v Italy (No 3) was announced on 22 May 2012. The Grand Chamber confirmed the judgment in the case of Hirst (no 2) (which held that a general and automatic disenfranchisement of all serving prisoners was incompatible with Article 3 of Protocol No 1); but it accepted the UK Government's argument that member states should have a wide discretion (or 'margin of appreciation') in how they regulate a ban on prisoners voting. The delivery of the judgement in the Scoppola case meant that the UK Government had six months from 22 May 2012 to bring forward legislative proposals to amend the law.

On 22 November 2012 the Government published a draft Bill, the Voting Eligibility (Prisoners) Bill, for pre-legislative scrutiny by a Joint Committee of both Houses. The Committee published its report on 18 December 2013 and recommended that the Government should introduce legislation to allow all prisoners serving sentences of 12 months or less to vote in all UK Parliamentary, local and European elections. The Lord Chancellor and Justice Secretary, Chris Grayling, made a brief response to the Committee's report on 25 February 2014; but the Government have not responded substantively and did not bring forward a Bill with the 2014 Queen's Speech.

On 16 October 2013 the UK Supreme Court dismissed the appeals of George McGeoch and Peter Chester, both prisoners serving life sentences for murder, who had brought domestic law proceedings in 2010 challenging the ban. The Supreme Court rejected a separate head of claim that the blanket ban was incompatible with European Union law. However, the Supreme Court also maintained the position determined in Strasbourg that the UK's blanket ban was contrary to the European Convention on Human Rights; although it refused to make a further 'declaration of incompatibility' with the Human Rights Act 1998, considering that it was unnecessary in the circumstances.

In two recent judgments in August 2014 and February 2015 (Frith and others v UK and McHugh and others v UK) relating to a large number of outstanding claims by prisoners, the European Court of Human Rights noted the continuing violation of Article 3 to Protocol No. 1 to the Convention, but did not award the applicants any compensation or legal expenses.

In December 2014, the Government announced that prisoners would not be enfranchised prior to the General Election of 2015.

*Prisoners' voting rights: developments since August 2020*

19 November 2020

**Summary**

In 2005 the European Court of Human Rights (ECtHR) ruled that the UK was in breach of Article 3 of Protocol No 1 of the European Convention on Human Rights in relation to prisoner voting rights. The issue remained unresolved for over a decade.

In December 2017 the UK Government came up with proposals that the Council of Europe said were sufficient to signify compliance with the 2005 ruling. The Council finally closed the case in September 2018.

Post-Brexit, the UK remains a member of the Council of Europe and remains a signatory to the European Convention on Human Rights.

This briefing gives a summary of events before May 2015 and examines the debate since May 2015. It also gives details of the provisions to allow some prisoners to vote in local and devolved elections in Scotland and Wales.

For more detail on events before 2015, see the Library briefing paper Prisoners' voting rights (2005 to May 2015)

**The ban**

The disenfranchisement of prisoners in Great Britain dates back to the Forfeiture Act 1870 and was linked to the notion of 'civic death'. The 1870 Act denied offenders their rights of citizenship.

The current provisions are set out in Section 3 of the Representation of the People Act 1983, as amended, and prevent convicted prisoners serving a custodial sentence from registering to vote. The Representation of the People Act 2000 allowed prisoners on remand to register to vote.

**The challenge**

In 2001 the ban was challenged by three convicted prisoners. The domestic courts rejected the challenge and one of the prisoners, John Hirst, then took his case to the ECtHR.

On 6 October 2005, in the case of Hirst v United Kingdom (No 2), the ECtHR ruled that the UK's current ban on all serving prisoners from voting, as defined by the 1983 Act, contravenes Article 3 of Protocol No 1 of the European Convention on Human Rights (ECHR), which provides that signatory states should "hold free elections … under conditions which will ensure the free expression of the opinion of the people".

The central element to the ECtHR ruling was that the UK's blanket ban on prisoner voting was indiscriminate and disproportionate.

**The debate**

The Hirst (No 2) judgment set off a political

debate. This debate has largely focused on the constitutional issues raised by the judgment, in particular: the UK's relationship with the ECtHR; reform of the Human Rights Act 1998; and the importance of parliamentary sovereignty.

Hirst (No 2) is regarded by some as an example of the ECtHR overstepping its proper role and encroaching upon Parliament's legislative authority. The judgment has also been criticised by some as an example of the misuse of human rights, in the sense that the ECtHR's interpretation of Article 3 of Protocol No 1 went beyond the drafters' intentions.

### The responses

The 2005 Labour Government considered the ban on prisoners voting was appropriate but was conscious of the need to meet its obligations under international law to rectify the contravention of Article 3. In the 2005 Parliament, the Labour Government issued two consultations, one in 2006 and one in 2009. It did not bring forward final proposals before the 2010 General Election.

In 2012, the Coalition Government of 2010-15 published a draft Bill which gave three options for the right to vote in UK Westminster Parliamentary and European Parliament elections: the status quo – an outright ban; a ban for prisoners sentenced to 4 years or more; or a ban for prisoners sentenced to more than 6 months.

In 2013, a Joint Committee scrutinising the Bill recommended that all prisoners serving sentences of 12 months or less should be entitled to vote in all UK parliamentary, local and European elections. The Government did not formally respond, and these proposals were not taken forward.

The Conservative Government's Queen's Speech in May 2015 did not refer to any plans to change the existing legislative position, and David Cameron subsequently implied that the blanket ban on prisoners' voting rights would not be changed while he remained Prime Minister.

In October 2015, in the case of Thierry Delvigne v Commune de Lesparre-Médoc and Préfet de la Gironde, the Court of Justice of the European Union (CJEU) ruled that a French law, which deprived certain convicted prisoners of the vote, was not an unlawful breach of the right of EU citizens to vote in elections for the EU Parliament, as protected by the Charter of Fundamental Rights of the European Union.

The CJEU's judgment also explained that the French law in question was lawful because it was proportionate, which in these circumstances meant that the law took into account "the nature and gravity of the criminal offence committed and the duration of the penalty".

In December 2015, Michael Gove indicated that the Government would, in 2016, produce a substantive response to the 2013 report by the Joint Committee on the draft Voting Eligibility (Prisoners) Bill, after the publication of the consultation on reform of the Human Rights Act 1998. Neither a response to the Committee nor a consultation on the Human Rights Act was published.

### The solution

Following further calls from the Council of Europe's Committee of Ministers to resolve the impasse, the then Secretary of State for Justice, David Lidington, published proposals in November 2017. These proposals were more limited in scope than those included in previous proposals. The main change proposed was to allow prisoners on Temporary Licence to vote. In December 2017 the Council of Europe welcomed the proposals, agreeing to them as an acceptable compromise that would address the criticisms raised by Hirst (No 2).

The Government intended to implement the proposed changes by the end of 2018. It agreed to report back to the Council of Europe's Committee of Ministers by September 2018. The Council of Europe confirmed that the case was closed at its meeting of September 2018.

### Scotland and Wales

Although the dispute between the UK Government and the ECtHR appears to have been resolved, responsibility for local and devolved elections in Scotland and Wales is now devolved.

In March 2019, the Scottish Government completed a consultation on prisoner voting and how it can ensure compliance with ECtHR judgements. The Scottish Government opposed lifting the ban entirely and favoured allowing prisoners serving shorter sentences, 12 months or shorter, to be allowed to vote. The consultation sought views on what the appropriate length of sentence should be.

The Scottish Government introduced legislation in the Scottish Parliament to extend voting rights to some prisoners. The Bill was passed in February 2020 and extends voting rights to prisoners serving sentences of 12 months or less at Scottish Parliamentary and local elections.

The Welsh Government consulted on the issue of prisoner voting in summer 2017 as part of a wider consultation on local election reform. The Welsh Government's Local Government and Elections (Wales) Bill was introduced into the National Assembly on 18 November 2019. One of its key changes will be to lower the voting age for local government elections in Wales to 16. The Bill as introduced made no mention of prisoner voting. The Welsh Government had intended to amend the Bill to allow prisoners sentenced to less than four years to register to vote in time for scheduled council election in 2022. The intended amendments were dropped, with the Welsh Government saying its focus on the coronavirus pandemic meant it could not devote time to drafting amendments.

The National Assembly for Wales Commission also consulted on prisoner voting. Following the consultation, the Llywydd wrote to the Assembly's Equality, Local Government and Communities Committee asking if it would conduct an inquiry into prisoner voting. The Committee agreed and subsequently reported in June 2019. It could not find consensus on a prison sentence threshold, but it recommended that prisoners serving sentences of less than four years should be entitled to register to vote in Assembly elections. Legislation to lower the voting age and to rename the Assembly the Senedd Cymru/Welsh Parliament, passed in November 2019, did not address the issue of prisoner voting.

### Prisons (Interference with Wireless Telegraphy) Bill 2017-19
22 June 2018
#### Summary
The Prisons (Interference with Wireless Telegraphy) Bill 2017-19 is a Private Member's Bill, sponsored by Maria Caulfield (Conservative). It would create a new power for the Secretary of State to authorise public communications providers (for example mobile phone network operators) to interfere with wireless telegraphy to disrupt unlawful mobile phone use in prisons.

The provisions of this bill replicate those contained in the Prisons and Courts Bill 2016-17. That Bill fell at the dissolution of Parliament for the 2017 general election. The Government, referring to pressures on legislative time, has said that though there will be new bills to cover some aspects of the bill that was lost, the prisons aspects will not be included. Therefore, the Government is supporting this Private Member's Bill to seek to ensure that these provisions, concerning the disruption of unlawful mobile phone use in prisons, are passed into legislation. The Explanatory Notes to the Bill have been prepared by the Ministry of Justice with the consent of Maria Caulfield.

### Prisons and Terrorism: Extremist Offender Management in 10 European Countries
22nd July 2020
#### About this Study
• This report offers a wide ranging analysis of the role prisons can play in radicalising people – and

in reforming them. Building on a 2010 study that used the same methodology, it examines the policies and approaches of 10 European countries, identifying trade-offs and dilemmas but also principles and best practices that can help governments and policymakers spot new ideas and avoid costly and counterproductive mistakes.
• It paints a picture of countries trying to grapple with a challenging – and rapidly changing – situation. Over the past decade, many European countries have had to deal with a significant increase and diversification of their extremist offender populations, raising systemic questions about prison regimes, risk assessments, probation schemes, and opportunities for rehabilitation and reintegration that had previously often been dealt with on a case by case basis.

#### The Extremist Offender Population
• Throughout Europe, the extremist offender population has changed profoundly over the past decade:
1) There are more inmates convicted of terrorism related offences than at any point since the turn of the millennium.
2) They have more varied backgrounds – including more women and a rapidly growing prisoner population from the far right.
3) They are serving a wider range of sentences, many of them relatively short term.
• Combined, these three developments mean that managing extremist offenders is even more urgent – and more challenging – an issue.

#### Planning and Plotting
• A new development is the occurrence of terrorist attacks within prisons, of which there have been six known cases in the ten European countries surveyed since 2015. Attacks typically target prison officers, and most have been carried out by inmates with a violent past.
• Over the same period, there have been 22 prison related plots: for example, attacks that followed an inmate's release, plots the perpetrators of which met in prison; or attempts to coerce authorities into releasing prisoners. Some 12 of these plots involved jihadists who were only recently released from prison.
• Prison based recruitment remains an issue. As with 'traditional' prison gangs, extremists target vulnerable inmates such as those who are isolated or new to prison. Targeting often involves the offer of material benefits and 'protection'.

#### Preventing Radicalisation and Recruitment
• Although countries have intensified training efforts, they have also recognised that it is neither reasonable nor practical to expect all prison officers to have an up to date and sophisticated

knowledge of extremist movements. This has led to the creation of centralised 'Extremism Units', which provide expertise and input where needed.

• Extremism specific risk assessment tools are now used in a majority of the countries surveyed. Many are relatively new and still need to be thoroughly evaluated. Their accuracy also depends on the skills and experience of those who use them.

• 'False compliance' seems to have become more widespread, especially among jihadist prisoners, though its true extent is unknown. This can be a major issue in relation to risk assessment and release arrangements.

### Prison Regimes

• There are three broad categories of regimes for convicted terrorists:

1) Placing all extremists together ('concentration');
2) Dispersing them among the regular criminal population ('dispersal');
3) Isolating them from each other and the regular criminal population ('isolation').

• While full and permanent isolation is illegal, prison services across Europe have experimented with different regimes and it has become increasingly popular to have a mixed approach, which involves concentrating or separating the most dangerous inmates while dispersing the remainder.

• There is no single, perfect solution. The examples provided in this study make clear that every type of prison regime involves trade-offs; what works for one kind of extremist prisoner population may not necessarily be effective for another. Prison services are, generally, flexible in their approach.

### Promoting Reintegration and Rehabilitation

• Nearly all the European countries surveyed have, in recent years, considered rehabilitation programmes for extremists. Most schemes follow the same basic principles: they begin with a risk assessment, are individually tailored and involve a variety of interventions, such as cognitive behavioural therapy, mentoring and structured dialogue tools. They all recognise that disengagement takes time and will not always be successful.

• However, there are also significant differences, especially in relation to: whether they are compulsory; the role of mentors; post release arrangements; the emphasis on ideology; and evaluation.

• There are significant differences when it comes to the processes and procedures whereby extremist offenders are released and the (probation) arrangements they are subjected to once they return to society. Only a small number

of countries have an integrated approach towards prison and probation.

### Recommendations

• The issues raised in this report should therefore prompt policymakers and practitioners to assess how to best respond to these phenomena. Our recommendations are:

1) Avoid overcrowding and understaffing;
2) Develop expertise and train staff;
3) Share information;
4) Evaluate risk assessment tools and determine what 'success' looks like;
5) Assess and adapt prison regimes;
6) Link up prison and probation;
7) Pay attention to emerging challenges.

• Although we recognise that spending money on prisons is unpopular, politicians, policymakers and the wider public need to understand that maintaining safe and orderly prisons are key investments in countering crime and terrorism. No clever piece of software or risk assessment tool can compensate for the absence of sufficient staff, space and basic resources.

• Not least, governments must always treat extremist offenders fairly and with respect. Whatever the prison regime, its foundation should be professionalism, respect and core values, such as human rights and the rule of law.

### *Prisons: The role of the private sector*
30 January 2014

The first contracted (private sector) prison in the UK – HM Prison Wolds – opened in 1992 and since then the role of the private sector in running prisons has grown steadily. Two other contracted prisons (Buckley Hall and Blakenhurst) returned to the public sector in 2000, and the Wolds returned to the public sector in 2013, and so there are now 14 prisons in England and Wales run by the private sector, holding 17% of the prison population. The contracts are shared between three companies: G4S Justice Services, Serco Custodial Services and Sodexo Justice Services.

The contracting-out of imprisonment to the private sector remains controversial. Some argue that the involvement of the private sector has created a diverse market, driving up standards and promoting efficiencies, while others argue that imprisonment is a function which the state should not delegate and prisons should not be for profit. Debate about whether contracted prisons perform better or worse or represent better value for money than their counterparts in the public sector continues apace.

The Ministry of Justice has indicated that it will use a benchmarking approach to maximise savings in public sector prisons. In November

2013, the privatisation of three prisons in south Yorkshire was abandoned, as the leading bidder was under investigation for alleged overcharging on other contracts for the tagging of offenders. Recently, following HM Inspectorate of Prisons' critical inspection report of HM Prison Oakwood, shadow Lord Chancellor and Secretary of State for Justice, Sadiq Khan, has said that Labour would take failing private prisons back into the public sector.

This note offers an overview of some of the main areas of controversy and debate.

## Probation reforms 2014
9 September 2014

There has been a series of reforms to probation in recent years, summarised in Library Standard Note 6665 Introducing "Payment by Results" in Offender Rehabilitation and other reforms. (24 October 2013) This Note looks at the current position in relation to the Government's policy on Offender Rehabilitation and the role of Payment by Results (PbR).

In October 2012, Lord Chancellor and Secretary of State for Justice, Chris Grayling, announced that the Government now intended to apply PbR to the majority of rehabilitation work conducted with offenders in the community, as part of broader reforms. The Ministry of Justice's strategy document Transforming Rehabilitation: A Strategy for Reform (published on 9 May 2013 as its response to the consultation Transforming Rehabilitation: A revolution in the way we manage offenders) again set out a number of proposed reforms to the rehabilitation system in both custody and the community. Proposals relating to rehabilitation in the community include legislating to introduce a minimum of 12 months' mandatory supervision for all offenders sentenced to less than two years in custody and changes to the conditions that can be imposed as part of a Community Order or Suspended Sentence Order (as set out in the Offender Rehabilitation Act 2014.

A new public sector probation service has been created to directly manage high risk offenders known as the National Probation Service. This began operating from 1 June 2014. Library Standard Note 6894 Privatisation of the probation service :what's happened so far? (20 May 2014) gives further details on the contracting out process. Standard Note 6665. Introducing "Payment by Results" in Offender Rehabilitation and other reforms (24 October 2013) provides a summary of developments in probation reform since 2001.

## Racial bias is pulling Black young adults into the revolving door
### Introduction

In April, we published a briefing that showed how young adults are dragged into the criminal justice system for relatively minor and non-violent offences[1] primarily driven by profound and persistent experiences of trauma and poverty. In our consultation with young adults we heard numerous accounts of two other significant factors that compound and exacerbate the chances of a young adult being pulled into the criminal justice system – and those are racism and discrimination.

This is not a grand revelation. We owe much to multiple inquiries and reviews which have laid bare the racial disparities in our criminal justice system. In the past ten years alone, the Harris Review showed the disproportionate levels of self-inflicted deaths among imprisoned Black men; the Young Review argued for the probation and resettlement services to acknowledge and address the over-representation of and poor outcomes experienced by Black and Muslim young adult men, and called for culturally sensitive, data-driven, lived-experience led practice; the Lammy review provided clear evidence that people from Black and Minority Ethnic backgrounds are over-represented in the criminal justice system and that this "starts long before a young man or woman ever enters a plea decision, goes before a magistrate or serves a prison sentence".

This briefing focuses on a very specific group of people in the criminal justice system – young adults who are, or at risk of being, in the revolving door. These young adults come into the criminal justice system for relatively minor and non-violent offences. We reviewed the evidence on racial disparities among this group, because we believe that if we can predict inequalities, we can prevent the revolving door too.

In looking at the evidence, we noticed Black young adults are more likely to be pulled into the revolving door than any other group of young adults. For that reason, this paper focuses explicitly on the racial disparities experienced by Black young adults.

We drew on a range of published data in this briefing, and in doing so faced one of the most common obstacles in any reviews of this nature: the data is incomplete, out of date, unpublished, or otherwise problematic. For example, it was not possible for us to get a picture of young adults from Gypsy, Roma, and Traveller communities; or to compare different faith groups; or to get a more granular level analysis for young Black women in this analysis. We aim to be vigilant in getting this data wherever possible and scrutinising it.

The evidence presented in this briefing helps us to understand the complexities, but it also raises questions. We have listed some of the big unknowns in Section 6, and we believe these are the issues that we need to understand to effectively predict and prevent young adults entering the revolving door.

1 *The full list of offences included in this analysis can be found in Appendix-1.*

### Reducing Reoffending: The "What works" Debate
22 November 2012

The remanding and sentencing of people alleged to have been involved in the riots in England in August 2011 caused the prison population to rise again, before falling back to pre-riot levels. It now stands at around 86,300 (below the record high of 88,179 on 2 December 2011). That surge in the prison population made the debate about prison and whether it "works" all the more urgent. Evidently, while they are in prison, offenders cannot commit further offences in the community, but what happens when they are released? Are they less likely to reoffend? Does prison help offenders to "go straight"? If not, what might? Is prison, in fact, an expensive way of making bad people worse?

This paper examines the evidence for the effectiveness of prison and programmes in the community aimed at reducing reoffending and some of the claims and counter-claims for whether "prison works".

Gabrielle Garton Grimwood

Gavin Berman

**Summary**

For decades, one of the preoccupations of criminologists, politicians and commentators has been whether, as it has been claimed, "prison works". This paper therefore examines the evidence for the effectiveness of prison and programmes in the community aimed at reducing reoffending and some of the claims and counter-claims for whether "prison works". The main focus of this paper is the high prison population and austere financial climate in England and Wales, the challenges these present for the National Offender Management Service (NOMS) and particularly HM Prison Service, and the emerging evidence of "what works" in reducing reoffending. Some of the research, though, has been conducted outside the UK and so some of the evidence cited is international.

The purposes of imprisonment are often cited as incapacitation, punishment, retribution, deterrence and rehabilitation, but views differ as to the relative importance and priority of each. There is a broad consensus that, for the most serious offences, a custodial sentence is likely to be the most appropriate one. Prison also offers the public some respite, by taking offenders off the streets and so, in that sense, "prison works". That much is fairly widely agreed.

Where the consensus breaks down is over the use of short prison sentences and the imprisonment of those convicted of less serious offences. Here, arguments rage over whether prison is the best option: does it help prisoners to "go straight" any better than a non-custodial sentence might? At a time of financial austerity, is the huge financial cost of prison justified by its results in rehabilitating offenders? Or is prison, in fact, an expensive way of making bad people worse? And what of the political dimension? Attitude surveys highlight public concern about crime and law and order and suggest that alternatives to prison do not inspire public confidence. Commentators have suggested that there has been political competition over sentencing, whilst the divisions between the main political parties over criminal justice policy have become blurred.

Amidst the welter of Ministry of Justice statistics for reoffending rates, there are figures to indicate that reoffending rates for offenders serving community orders are lower than for those sentenced to imprisonment. There are sizeable differences too between prisons in the reoffending rates of prisoners on release. Evidence drawn from the UK's trial of two "boot-camps" for young offenders and American research into reoffending according to the prisoner's security level suggests that harsher prison conditions do not reduce reoffending and may, indeed, even increase it. Also from the United States comes much of the research and commentary casting doubt on the value of mass incarceration. A study in the Netherlands of the effect of first-time imprisonment concluded that going to prison made it more (not less) likely that an offender would reoffend in the three years after release.

A recent study of offending by teenagers has suggested that youth crime may be driven more by a lack of moral and cognitive development than by opportunism, with implications for policing and the youth justice system. Another recent British study of acquisitive crime as recorded by the police concluded that longer sentences could prevent (for example) 4800 burglaries a year, although (it remarked) the justice system had other goals besides crime reduction.

The Government has promised a "rehabilitation revolution" which will, it claims, break the cycle of repeated offending. The new Lord Chancellor and Justice Secretary, Chris Grayling, has echoed the remarks of his predecessor, Kenneth Clarke, about the need to break the cycle of reoffending.

*Registration and Management of Sex Offenders*
3 February 2021

**Summary**
Part 2 of the Sexual Offences Act 20031 provides various measures that enable the police in England and Wales to monitor and manage sex offenders living in the local area.

**Notification Requirements: The "sex offenders register"**
Certain sex offenders are required to notify the police of personal information such as their name, address and bank and credit card details, and to update the police whenever this information changes. The police record of this information is commonly referred to as the "sex offenders register". There is no general public access to the "sex offenders register". The child sex offender disclosure scheme allows parents, carers and guardians to formally ask the police to tell them if someone has a record for child sexual offences. The notification requirements are imposed automatically on offenders convicted of certain offences in the UK, but can also be imposed by way of court order on offenders convicted overseas.

The notification requirements are imposed for a fixed or indefinite period, depending on the sentence received. The penalties for breaching notification requirements range from a fine to imprisonment for up to five years.

Those offenders subject to an indefinite notification period can apply to the police for a determination that they no longer pose a risk and should no longer be on the register. The earliest point at which such an application can be made is 15 years after the date of the offender's first notification (or eight years, for those aged under 18 when convicted).

**Sexual Harm Prevention Orders and Sexual Risk Orders**
There are other civil orders available to manage sex offenders and those who pose a risk of harm: Sexual Harm Prevention Orders (SHPOs) and Sexual Risk Orders (SROs). These orders can place a range of restrictions on individuals depending on the nature of the case, such as limiting their internet use or preventing travel abroad. The penalties for breach range from a fine to imprisonment for up to five years.

These orders have replaced, in England and Wales, the civil orders that were previously available (namely Sexual Offences Prevention Orders, Foreign Travel Orders, and Risk of Sexual Harm Orders).

*Regulating online harms*
12 August 2021

**Summary**
There is increasing concern about harmful content and activity online. This includes cyberbullying, material promoting violence and self-harm, and age inappropriate content. The Covid-19 pandemic has seen groups using social media platforms to spread anti-vaccine misinformation.

Critics, including parliamentary committees, academics, and children's charities, have argued that self-regulation by internet companies is not enough to keep users safe and that statutory regulation should be introduced.

**The Online Harms White Paper (April 2019) – a new regulatory framework?**
An Online Harms White Paper (April 2019) argued that existing regulatory and voluntary initiatives had "not gone far or fast enough" to keep users safe. The Paper proposed a single regulatory framework to tackle a range of harms. At its core would be a duty of care for internet companies, including social media platforms. An independent regulator would oversee and enforce compliance with the duty. A consultation on the proposals closed in July 2019.

The White Paper received a mixed reaction. Children's charities were positive. However, some commentators raised concerns that harms were insufficiently defined. The Open Rights Group and the Index on Censorship warned that the proposals could threaten freedom of expression.

**Government response to the White Paper consultation (December 2020)**
An initial response to the consultation was published in February 2020. This stated, among other things, that the Government was minded to make Ofcom the regulator for online harms.

A full response was published in December 2020. This confirmed that a duty of care would be introduced through an Online Safety Bill and that Ofcom would be the regulator. Reaction was again mixed. Some commentators continued to argue that the framework would threaten freedom of expression and privacy. Others raised concerns about the definition of harm.

**Draft Online Safety Bill (May 2021)**
A draft Online Safety Bill was included in the Queen's Speech of 11 May 2021. The draft Bill was published the following day, along with Explanatory Notes, an Impact Assessment and a Delegated Powers Memorandum.

A Joint Committee of both Houses has been established to consider the draft legislation. The Committee must report by 10 December 2021.

In line with the Government's December 2020 response to its Online Harms consultation, the draft Bill would impose duties of care on providers of online content-sharing platforms and search services. Ofcom would enforce compliance and its powers would include being able to fine companies up to £18 million or 10% of annual global turnover, whichever is higher, and have the power to block access to sites.

The Government has said that the draft Bill would protect freedom of expression, but critics remain unconvinced.

For a selection of comment on the draft Bill, see the Library Paper, Reaction to the draft Online Safety Bill: a reading list (CBP 9243).

### Rehabilitation of Offenders Act 1974
1 February 2021
**Summary**
Rehabilitation periods and spent convictions
The Rehabilitation of Offenders Act 1974 aims to give those with convictions or cautions the chance – in certain circumstances – to wipe the slate clean and start afresh.

Under the Act, eligible convictions or cautions become "spent" after a specified period of time known as the "rehabilitation period", the length of which varies depending on how the individual concerned was dealt with.

Prison sentences of over 4 years are excluded from the scope of the Act and can therefore never become spent. The rehabilitation periods for other types of sentence vary according to whether the person was cautioned or convicted and, if the latter, the type of sentence imposed. Rehabilitation periods are generally shorter for those aged under 18 when they were convicted.

Once the conviction or caution becomes spent, the person is regarded as rehabilitated and (for most purposes) is treated as if they had never committed the offence.

However, there are a number of exceptions to this general approach. For example, for some types of employment a person can be required to disclose details of both unspent and spent convictions or cautions.

**Proposals for changes to rehabilitation periods**
In a White Paper, A Smarter Approach to Sentencing, published in September 2020, the Government set out plans to amend the current law. The Government intends to legislate to reduce the rehabilitation periods that apply before a conviction becomes spent. The changes proposed would also allow for some convictions resulting in a custodial sentence of more than 4 years to become spent. Convictions for serious sexual, violence and terrorist offences would be excluded from this change. The charity Unlock has welcomed the

proposals made but has criticised the reforms as being too limited to achieve the Government's goal of reducing barriers to employment.

**Earlier changes**
The 1974 Act was amended previously by section 139 of the Legal Aid, Sentencing and Punishment of Offenders Act 2012, which was brought into force on 10 March 2014 and made two key changes. The first change was to extend the scope of the Act to cover custodial sentences of up to 48 months (previously prison sentences over 30 months never became spent), and the second was to change the length of some of the rehabilitation periods (in most cases by reducing them). This briefing applies to England and Wales.

### Release from prison - and plans to change it
24 January 2020
**Summary**
When a person in England and Wales is given a sentence of imprisonment for a period of time they will not usually spend all of that time in prison. The law allows for prisoners to be released on licence to serve the last part of their sentence in the community.

Depending on the type of prison sentence the person is given, they can be:
• released from prison automatically at the halfway point of their sentence;
• released at the two thirds point of their sentence if the Parole Board decides it is no longer necessary to keep them in prison for the protection of the public; or
• released after the end of the minimum term of a life sentence if the Parole Board decides it is no longer necessary to keep them in prison for the protection of the public.

A person released on licence will be supervised by probation staff and must comply with certain conditions. If they breach the conditions of their licence they can be returned (recalled) to prison to serve part, or all, of the remainder of their sentence in prison.

The law on the point at which a prisoner can be released and whether the Parole Board is involved has changed over the years.

Various reasons have been put forward for having systems of releasing prisoners into the community before the end of their term of imprisonment. These include pragmatic reasons such as reducing overcrowding in prisons. Release part way through a sentence can also serve a rehabilitative purpose, allowing for supervision of prisoners in the community.

In both the October and December 2019 Queen's Speeches the Government set out plans for a Sentencing Bill, which would increase the automatic release point for certain serious violent or sexual offenders from the halfway point to the two-thirds point. The Government has said it will publish a white paper before introducing the Sentencing Bill.

The Government laid a draft order in October 2019 which provides that prisoners would be released automatically at the two thirds point of their sentence if they had been:

• convicted of a relevant violent or sexual offence for which the maximum penalty is life; and

• sentenced to a standard determinate sentence of seven years or more.

The Government has explained it is seeking to make this change now, by statutory instrument, ahead of wider reforms in a sentencing bill because not to do so would mean "continuing with a system which fails properly to ensure that serious offenders serve sentences that reflect the gravity of their crime".

The Government says this change would provide greater assurance to victims and the public that sentences will reflect the severity of their crime. Critics of the proposed change argue it will not meet these aims.

A debate on the draft order in the Lords raised questions regarding the impact on prison overcrowding and conditions. Concerns were also raised about a lack of public consultation and how the measure would fit with other Government policies on sentencing. It was noted that under the proposals, individuals would spend less time under probation supervision. The draft order will be debated in the Commons on 28 January 2020.

### Release from prison in England and Wales
24 January, 2020

When a person in England and Wales is given a sentence of imprisonment for a period of time they will not usually spend all of that time in prison. The law allows for prisoners to be released on licence to serve the last part of their sentence in the community. Depending on the type of prison sentence the person is given, they can be:

• released from prison automatically at the halfway point of their sentence;

• released at the two thirds point of their sentence if the Parole Board decides it is no longer necessary to keep them in prison for the protection of the public; or

• released after the end of the minimum term of a life sentence if the Parole Board decides it is no longer necessary to keep them in prison for the protection of the public.

A person released on licence will be supervised by probation staff and must comply with certain conditions. If they breach the conditions of their licence they can be returned (recalled) to prison

to serve part, or all, of the remainder of their sentence in prison.

The law on the point at which a prisoner can be released and whether the Parole Board is involved has changed over the years.

Various reasons have been put forward for having systems of releasing prisoners into the community before the end of their term of imprisonment. These include pragmatic reasons such as reducing overcrowding in prisons. Release part way through a sentence can also serve a rehabilitative purpose, allowing for supervision of prisoners in the community.

In both the October and December 2019 Queen's Speeches the Government set out plans for a Sentencing Bill, which would increase the automatic release point for certain serious violent or sexual offenders from the halfway point to the two-thirds point. The Government has said it will publish a white paper before introducing the Sentencing Bill.

The Government laid a draft order in October 2019 which provides that prisoners would be released automatically at the two thirds point of their sentence if they had been:

• convicted of a relevant violent or sexual offence for which the maximum penalty is life; and

• sentenced to a standard determinate sentence of seven years or more.

The Government has explained it is seeking to make this change now, by statutory instrument, ahead of wider reforms in a sentencing bill because not to do so would mean "continuing with a system which fails properly to ensure that serious offenders serve sentences that reflect the gravity of their crime".

The Government says this change would provide greater assurance to victims and the public that sentences will reflect the severity of their crime. Critics of the proposed change argue it will not meet these aims.

A debate on the draft order in the Lords raised questions regarding the impact on prison overcrowding and conditions. Concerns were also raised about a lack of public consultation and how the measure would fit with other Government policies on sentencing. It was noted that under the proposals, individuals would spend less time under probation supervision.

### Retention and disclosure of criminal records
10 February 2021

**Summary**
*Information held by the police*
Criminal records information is held on two main systems. The first is the Police National Computer (PNC), which records details of convictions, cautions, reprimands, warnings and arrests. The second is the Police National Database (PND),

which records "soft" local police intelligence, for example details of investigations that did not lead to any further action.

Chief constables "own" the data that their force has entered on to the PNC. They can exercise their discretion, in exceptional circumstances, to delete non-court disposals (e.g. cautions) which are owned by them and held on the PNC as well as any non-conviction outcome. Individuals can, in some circumstances, apply for the removal of a record from the PNC.

*Criminal records checks*

Cautions, reprimands and warnings and some convictions become "spent" after a certain period of time. Once a record becomes spent it does not usually need to be declared to employers or voluntary organisations. When a person applies for a so-called "excepted position", they may be required to provide details of their criminal record, both spent and unspent, by way of a standard or enhanced criminal records check from the Disclosure and Barring Service. Excepted positions cover, for example, work with children or vulnerable adults or roles in certain licensed occupations or positions of trust.

The information in this briefing about disclosure relates to England and Wales. For information about Scotland see Disclosure Scotland and for information regarding Northern Ireland see AccessNI.

A standard check contains details of all spent and unspent convictions, cautions, reprimands and final warnings (as held on the PNC) except those which, under the filtering rules, should no longer be disclosed (see below). An enhanced check includes the same information as a standard check together with details of relevant and proportionate non-conviction information, for example details of arrests recorded on the PNC or police intelligence recorded on the PND. Disclosure of such information is not automatic but is done on a case-by-case basis following the exercise of police discretion.

*The disclosure of non-conviction information and old and minor convictions*

There has been some debate over two particular issues relating to criminal records checks: the disclosure of non-conviction information and the disclosure of old and minor convictions.

The Government legislated, via the Protection of Freedoms Act 2012, to introduce new safeguards relating to the disclosure of non-conviction information, such as a new independent disputes process.

Legislation introducing a new filtering mechanism to restrict the disclosure of old and minor convictions came into force in May 2013.

This followed a Court of Appeal ruling in January 2013 that the mandatory and blanket disclosure of convictions as part of a criminal records check was incompatible with Article 8 of the European Convention on Human Rights (right to respect for private life).

A judgment of the Supreme Court in January 2019 said that two specific aspects of the filtering mechanism, concerning multiple convictions and the disclosure of warnings and reprimands received by children, were disproportionate and therefore incompatible with Article 8. The Government amended the filtering rules in November 2020 to remove the automatic disclosure of youth cautions, reprimands and warnings and the 'multiple conviction' rule.

*Calls for wider reform of disclosure*

There have been calls for wider reform of criminal records disclosure, including from the Law Commission, the Justice Committee, Charlie Taylor in his review of youth justice and David Lammy in his review into the treatment of and outcomes for BAME individuals in the criminal justice system.

The Government in its September 2020 White Paper, A Smarter Approach to Sentencing, said that it wanted to "go further on criminal records disclosure to support those who offended in the past to move on with their lives and in particular to improve access to employment for those with criminal records". In addition to the changes to the filtering rules, the Government proposed changes to the rehabilitation periods that govern the length of time before a conviction becomes "spent".

*Review of Drugs Part One and Part Two – Professor Dame Carol Black*
### Review of Drugs
Executive Summary
Dame Carol Black
February 2020

**Summary of key findings**

1. The illicit drugs market is big business, worth an estimated £9.4 billion a year. Around 3 million people took drugs in England and Wales last year, with around 300,000 in England taking the most harmful drugs (opiates and/or crack cocaine).
2. Drug deaths have reached an all-time high and the market has become much more violent. Taking the health harms, costs of crime and wider impacts on society together, we estimate the total costs of drugs to society are over £19 billion, which is more than twice the value of the market itself.
3. The drugs market consists of a number of distinct but overlapping product markets. Most drugs consumed in the UK are produced abroad.

The supply of drugs has been shaped mostly by international forces, the activities of Organised Crime Groups and advances in technology.

4. The demand for opiates and crack/cocaine, and deaths from misuse of these substances, is closely associated with poverty and deprivation. There is an ageing population of heroin users with severe health needs, some of whom are using crack cocaine too, but there is also a new population of younger crack cocaine users that do not use heroin.

5. The heroin and crack cocaine retail market has been overtaken by the county lines model, which is driving increased violence in the drugs market and the exploitation of young people and vulnerable drug users.

6. The demand for powder cocaine is closely linked to that for other recreational drugs, such as ecstasy and amphetamines. Increased use of powder cocaine has been driven by those under 30. The demand for these drugs is strongly linked to the night-time economy and alcohol.

7. The use of new psychoactive substances among the general population has fallen but has increased in vulnerable populations such as those sleeping rough and those in prison.

8. Government interventions to restrict supply have had limited success. The key institutions involved are Border Force, the National Crime Agency (NCA) and police forces. All have faced budgetary constraints in the past decade and competing priorities. Even if these organisations were sufficiently resourced it is not clear that they would be able to bring about a sustained reduction in drug supply, given the resilience and flexibility of illicit drug markets.

9. There has been a renewed focus in recent years by the NCA and police forces on drugs in response to the serious violence caused by the county lines model.

10. More than a third of people in prison are there due to crimes relating to drug use (mostly acquisitive crime). These prisoners tend to serve very short sentences, have limited time in prison treatment and poor hand-offs back into the community. They are very likely to re-offend.

11. Drugs within prisons are widely available, with around 15% of prisoners testing positive to random drug tests. The problems are greatest in male local and category C prisons. New psychoactive substances have become increasingly problematic in prisons. Drug use in prisons is closely linked to the amount of purposeful activity available to prisoners.

12. Treatment in the community is the responsibility of Local Authorities. Spending on treatment has reduced significantly because Local Government budgets have been squeezed and central Government funding and oversight has fallen away. There is significant local variation, with some Local Authorities having reduced treatment expenditure by 40%.

13. Local Authorities commission treatment from NHS Trusts and third sector providers. A prolonged shortage of funding has resulted in a loss of skills, expertise and capacity from this sector. Treatment providers often have to prioritise the severe needs of the long-term heroin using population, meaning that services for other drug users have had less investment.

14. Even if more funding became available for treatment (which is vital), there would be a lot of work to do to build up capacity and expertise in this market. In addition to dedicated funding, the re-introduction of incentives and levers, and locally held joint responsibility and accountability, would go a long way to regenerate and vitalise the system.

15. Recovery is about more than just treatment. Other factors are equally important, particularly housing and employment. Central Government has funded some excellent pilots to address the complex housing and employment needs of long-term drug users but these are time-limited and small-scale.

16. Young people and children have been pulled into drugs supply on an alarming scale, especially at the most violent end of the market. There are strong associations between young people being drawn into county lines and increases in child poverty, the numbers of children in care and school exclusions. Social media has played a facilitating role.

17. There is a considerable increase in children using drugs, after a long period of a downward trend. Those seeking treatment have a number of complex needs, including mental health needs, that can only be met through a combination of specialist treatment and wider social and health care.

## Review of drugs part two: prevention, treatment, and recovery
Updated 2 August 2021

### Executive summary
*What this review set out to achieve*

The review aims to help government reduce demand for illegal drugs. Problem drug users, including an estimated 300,000 opiate and crack users, need high-quality treatment and recovery services, alongside pathways into treatment and away from the criminal justice system. For recreational drug users, we need to find ways to change attitudes and behaviour.

This problem and its solutions span many government departments, local government and other organisations. So, this review makes a large number of recommendations that fall to different players within the system. These should be seen as a package of reforms that are interdependent and mutually reinforcing.

*Reform of central government leadership*
Tackling the demand for illegal drugs must start with clear central government leadership and oversight. Responsibility for this agenda spans multiple departments. People with drug dependence are a small part of the much wider populations that departments serve, so tend not be prioritised in policy and funding decisions. There is no systematic way for departments to co-ordinate plans so that they cohere when implemented on the ground.

We recommend the formation of a central Drugs Unit, sitting in whatever department or joint arrangement seems appropriate, with clear ministerial sponsorship. This unit should take the lead in setting clear objectives and targets for the rest of government, and translate these into a new National Outcomes Framework, with the sponsoring minister reporting annually to Parliament on progress.

*Increased funding for drug treatment and wider recovery support*
Local authorities are responsible for drug treatment. Spending on treatment has recently reduced significantly because local government budgets have been squeezed and central government funding and oversight have fallen away.

We have concluded, based on current evidence of prevalence, that an additional £552 million is needed from DHSC by year 5 on top of the baseline annual expenditure of £680million from the public health grant, to provide a full range of high-quality drug treatment and recovery services, as follows:
• year 1: £119 million
• year 2: £231 million
• year 3: £396 million
• year 4: £484 million
• year 5: £552 million
An additional £15 million by year 5 is needed from DWP for employment support, as follows:
• year 1: £6 million
• year 2: £11 million
• year 3: £16.5 million
• year 4: £15.9 million
• year 5: £15.1 million
This would allow for increased capacity for under-served groups, including non-opiate users and young people, and for larger numbers to be diverted away from the criminal justice system. Further work needs to be carried out by MHCLG before the next Spending Review to identify how much additional funding is required to provide

housing support to people in treatment who lack adequate housing.
In parallel, we recommend additional investment by NHS England (NHSE) in high quality physical and mental health for this group. Given fiscal pressures, government may have to take a long-term view and fund this programme over a time frame longer than 5 years. If this is the case, I strongly recommend ensuring the whole package is delivered immediately, with all its components, to those areas in greatest need.

*Allocating and protecting funding*
Additional investment in treatment and recovery cannot be allowed to disappear to fund other local priorities. We recommend that funding for drug treatment be allocated to local authorities based on a needs assessment and then protected. Where relevant, other government departments should protect funding at local level for their wider recovery services.

*Commissioning*
Many local authorities do not commission the full range of services required and there are important gaps in provision, such as suitable treatment services for non-opiate users. We recommend that DHSC should develop a national Commissioning Quality Standard, based on clinical guidelines, to help specify the full range of treatment services that should be available in each local area.
This national Commissioning Quality Standard should exist alongside strong local leadership, with local authorities working closely with NHS organisations and wider recovery partners. Joint local plans should be produced across all local organisations involved in treatment and recovery. Commissioners should also work more collaboratively with providers and introduce longer commissioning cycles of at least 5 years, to encourage service stability and improvements to quality. Commissioning arrangements should mirror NHS practice where there is a move away from competition towards collaboration.

*Strengthening local authority accountability*
With more investment in treatment and recovery, there must be greater accountability for this spend. We recommend that the new Office for Health Promotion use the new National Outcomes Framework and the national Commissioning Quality Standard to hold local authorities and partner agencies to account.

*Rebuilding services: workforce*
Sufficient capacity and quality in treatment services depend on a suitably trained workforce.

However, the drug treatment and recovery workforce has deteriorated significantly in quantity, quality and morale in recent years, with excessive caseloads, decreased training and lack of clinical supervision. DHSC should commission Health Education England (HEE) to devise a workforce strategy for substance misuse treatment and give it sufficient new funding to support the required training. In parallel, DHSC should support structured peer-led recovery networks in every local area, to complement the professional workforce.

### Rebuilding services: treatment

Local authorities should commission a full range of evidence-based harm reduction and treatment services to meet the needs of their local population. However, some services have all but disappeared and will not automatically return even with higher funding and better commissioning. High cost but low volume services, such as inpatient detoxification, are too costly for a single local authority to procure and should be covered by a new regional or sub-regional approach to commissioning.

More funding needs to be available to improve capacity and quality of specialist substance misuse services in response to increased drug use among children and young people. The national Commissioning Quality Standard should ensure that these services are linked with other local services for vulnerable young people.

### Rebuilding services: recovery support

DHSC and the Office for Health Promotion should support local areas to ensure that thriving communities of recovery are linked to every drug treatment system, working to standards on quality and governance developed by the government's Drug Recovery Champion and the Office for Health Promotion.

### Diverting more offenders into treatment and recovery services

Too many people with addictions are cycling in and out of prison, without achieving rehabilitation or recovery. The recent sentencing white paper committed to greater use of police diversions and community sentences with treatment as an alternative to custody. This must now be put into action, alongside extra funding for treatment places to accommodate the extra demand.

In prisons, MoJ should work with DHSC and NHSE to improve the experience of treatment, with prisoners always taken to their treatment appointments. On release from prison, prisoners must have ID and a bank account and the ability to claim benefits on the day of release. Those with drug dependence should be helped to continue with drug treatment in the community as soon as possible.

### Employment support

Employment is an essential part of recovery, both for financial stability and to offer something meaningful to do. Intensive, employer-focused employment support inside treatment centres has shown promising results, based on a recent trial of Individual Placement and Support (IPS) in 7 local authorities. The IPS model should be rolled out in treatment settings across the whole of England. DWP should also introduce peer mentors in each Jobcentre Plus to help people with drug dependence to receive more tailored and sympathetic support.

### Housing

Drug dependence can be both a cause and consequence of homelessness and rough sleeping. MHCLG has estimated that almost two-thirds of people who sleep rough have a current drug or alcohol problem. PHE's drug treatment data shows that one-fifth of adults starting treatment in 2019 to 2020 reported a housing problem, increasing to one-third of people in treatment for opiates.

MHCLG and DHSC have secured welcome substantial additional funding to improve treatment services for people who sleep rough. We know that housing and housing support have a crucial role to play in the success of drug treatment and that many of those entering treatment report a housing need. MHCLG should work with DHSC to assess the types and levels of housing related needs among people with substance misuse problems.

### Mental health

For many people, mental health problems and trauma lie at the heart of their drug and alcohol dependence. However, they are too often excluded from mental health services until they resolve their drug problem and excluded from drug services until their mental health problems have been addressed. DHSC and NHSE should work together to set out a plan to solve this problem.

The workforce in both services should be trained to better respond to co-existing drug and mental health problems. This should be a key component of HEE's competency and training requirements for the workforce.

### Physical healthcare

Many drug users have poor overall health. The NHS is poor at engaging with the wider health needs of drug users with medical co-morbidities (for example, hepatitis C, HIV, heart and lung disease), many of whom are ill-equipped to navigate complex pathways, and feel stigmatised. DHSC and NHSE should work together to develop an action plan on improving access to physical healthcare.

*Prevention and early intervention*

Preventing drug misuse is more cost-effective and socially desirable than dealing with the consequences of misuse. The Smoking, Drinking and Drug Use among Young People in England survey has shown that drug use among children (aged 11 to 15) has increased by over 40% since 2014, reversing a previous long-term downward trend.

The Department for Education (DfE) must ensure that schools seize the major prevention opportunity presented by the statutory guidance for Relationships, Sex and Health Education (RSHE). This guidance came into force in England from September 2020 and sets out requirements in relation to teaching about tobacco, alcohol, prescription drugs and illicit drugs.

It is equally important that children attend school and have rewarding, fulfilling activities available to them outside of school. They also need adequate support services, particularly for mental health. We recommend that the DfE and Department for Digital, Culture, Media and Sport (DCMS) lead investment in age-appropriate evidence-based services and support all young people to build resilience and avoid substance misuse. Local authorities should identify, and provide additional support to, those young people most at risk of being drawn into using illicit substances or involvement in supply.

*Research*

Research in many areas of addiction is underdeveloped and under-resourced, with the exception of opioid substitution treatment. The research infrastructure in local authorities is far less developed than it is within the NHS, and current service models often do not provide the stability, expertise or right staff mix to undertake high quality research.

We recommend that DHSC and the Department for Business, Energy & Industrial Strategy (BEIS) encourage and facilitate research into what works to combat substance misuse, across supply, prevention, treatment and recovery. DHSC should promote innovative research on addiction and its implementation in practice by offering incentives or rewards to companies and other organisations for effective developments in this field. For example, pharmaceutical advances.

There is also a lack of evidence on what works to deter people from taking drugs recreationally. The majority of recreational drug users do not see themselves as having a drug problem and it is a difficult population to influence. However, this misuse carries risks and fuels the illicit drug market. We recommend HO invests now in an innovation fund to test out which marketing and behavioural interventions could work in the UK to diminish recreational drug use, building on evidence from abroad.

### ROTL Statistics
**Offender Management Statistics quarterly: April to June 2021**

Detailed quarterly statistics on offenders in custody (including offence groups, sentence lengths and nationalities), and quarterly and annual statistics on prison receptions, prison releases, adjudications, licence recalls and offenders under probation supervision.

**Quarterly: April to June 2021**
**Prison population: 30 September 2021**
**Main Points**

*78,756 prisoners in England and Wales as at 30 Sep 2021*
The total prison population was 1% lower than the same point in the previous year.

*15,206 first receptions into prison between April and June 2021*
The number of first receptions represents a rise of 21% compared to the same period in 2020.

*11,623 releases from sentences between April and June 2021*
This was 13% lower than the same period in 2020. As the prison population shifts towards those serving longer sentences, we would expect fewer releases in each period.

*36,659 adjudication outcomes between April and June 2021*
This was a fall of 5% compared to the same period in 2020. Additional days were awarded as punishment on 607 occasions.

*5,362 licence recalls between April and June 2021*
This was a 9% decrease on the same quarter in 2020.

*230,578 offenders on probation at the end of June 2021*
This number increased by 3% compared to the number of offenders supervised as at 30 June 2020.

This publication provides offender management annual and quarterly statistics for the latest date available and provides comparisons to the previous year.

For technical detail please refer to the accompanying guide, 'Guide to offender management statistics'

*Statistician's comment*
In this publication we are reporting on the prison population as at 30 September 2021, with comparisons to the same point in 2020. Over this 12-month period, the total prison population has fallen slightly (1% decrease).

The increasing remand population trend that we have seen since early 2020 has continued (a 6% increase between 30 Sep 2020 and 30 Sep 2021), but all of this increase over the past 12 months has been in the 'convicted unsentenced' remand population (the 'untried' population is virtually unchanged compared to 30 Sep 2020). This likely reflects the impact of partial court recovery following COVID-19 restrictions, resulting in an increase in the number of convicted prisoners awaiting sentence.

Between September 2020 and 2021, the sentenced population has fallen by 2%. This is much smaller than the decreases we have seen over recent quarters (there was a 10% decrease from March 2020 to March 2021, and a 4% decrease from June 2020 to June 2021). As with the remand population mentioned above, this reflects that the normal flow of individuals from the remand to the sentenced population (after sentencing at court) is continuing to recover following COVID-19 restrictions.

On the topic of COVID-19 recovery, the prison population has not yet returned to pre-pandemic levels; the 30 Sep 2021 prison population is still more than 5,000 below the level of 30 Sep 2019, and more than 4,000 below the level of 31 Mar 2020.

The prisoner flows data in this publication cover the period April to June 2021, which means that for the first time we are comparing prisoner flows data between two 'COVID-19 periods' (the comparison period being April to June 2020). The spring 2020 COVID-19 lockdown dramatically affected the normal Criminal Justice System processes – as such, during the April to June 2020 quarter, prisoner first receptions fell to around 12,600 (compared to around 17,000 in the previous quarter). In the latest quarter, there were around 15,200 first receptions – which reflects a 21% increase compared to April to June 2020.

Due to the COVID affected figures seen between April and June 2020, there are several very large annual percentage changes in this current publication (covering the period April to June 2021) – though these tend to be for specific prisoner reception types (i.e. for certain offence groups and sentence lengths).

To illustrate some examples, the number of sentenced first receptions for determinate sentences of '4 years or more' has increased by 405% (i.e. is more than 5 times as high) compared to the same period in 2020 – though this is simply a reflection of a return to pre-COVID levels (of around 400 per quarter). The same is true for the number of immediate sentenced admissions for 'sexual offences' – which is 194% higher than (i.e. almost three times the level seen) in April to June 2020, but again simply reflects a return to pre-COVID levels (of around 700 per quarter).

Similar large percentage changes are apparent for the number of Release on Temporary Licence (ROTL) incidences in the latest quarter – which has increased by 304% (i.e. is more than 4 times as high) compared to April to June 2020; and the number of Prisoner Transfers (123% higher than; i.e. more than double) the level seen in April to June 2020. This is associated with changes in operational practices, moving away from COVID-19 restrictions that had been imposed on the prison regime.

### Rough Sleepers: Enforcement Powers (England)
9 April 2021

The 2020 autumn count in England recorded 2,688 people sleeping rough, representing a fall of 37% on 2019 but 52% higher than the number recorded in 2010.[1] The 2020 count coincided with a national lockdown in response to the Covid-19 pandemic, which is likely to have impacted the numbers recorded.

Rough sleeping is often associated with nuisance activities such as begging, street drinking and anti-social behaviour. Homelessness is a complex issue and entrenched homelessness presents particular difficulties; addictions and criminal and offending behaviour may be a symptom of homelessness as well as an underlying cause.[2]

Nuisance activities can have a negative impact on local communities. The police and local authorities have a range of powers to tackle these activities. However, homelessness organisations are concerned that the use of these powers criminalises rough sleeping and does not address the root cause of the problem.

1. *Ministry of Housing, Communities and Local Government, Rough sleeping snapshot in England: autumn 2020, 25 February 2021*

2. *2 Department for Communities and Local Government, Evidence review of the costs of homelessness, August 2012*

### Safety in Custody: December 2019
### Prison Safety in England and Wales
28 November 2019
#### Summary
*A decline in safety*

There has been a decline in prison safety since 2012. Assaults and incidents of self-harm are at record highs and the number of self-inflicted deaths has risen. Chief Inspectors of Prisons, the Prison and Probation Ombudsman, Independent Monitoring Boards and the Justice Committee have all repeatedly expressed concern.

The urgent notification process was introduced at the end of 2017. It allows the Chief Inspector to bring urgent concerns to the attention of the Secretary of State who is then required to respond with an action plan. It has been used five times for adult prisons.

In the year ending September 2019, there were close to 61,000 recorded incidents of self-harm in prisons, which was equivalent to 732 per 1,000 prisoners.[1] This number was over a fifth higher than in the previous year and more than double the number ten years previously.

There were 90 apparent suicides in prisons in the year ending September 2019, although 58 deaths had not been classified. The most suicides in one year, once all deaths had been classified, was 124 in the year ending December 2016. [2]

In the year ending June 2019, there were 34,000 recorded assaults in prisons, the highest ever recorded, which was equivalent to 412 per 1,000 prisoners.[3] This was more than double the number recorded ten years prior, although the rise has entirely been since 2012.

In the year ending March 2019, there were 2,200 recorded incidents of protesting behaviour in prisons, which includes forming barricades, taking hostages, and concerted indiscipline.[4] This was nearly four times the equivalent number ten years previously.

*Reasons for the decline and measures taken to improve safety*

Various factors have been identified as contributing to the decline in safety.

The Ministry of Justice acknowledged in its 2016 white paper, Prison Safety and Reform, that there was a link between violence and the number of staff and committed to recruiting more staff. Staff numbers have risen since 2016 but have not returned to pre2010 levels.[5] There are now concerns about the experience of staff and about retention. The Ministry of Justice has piloted issuing staff with PAVA incapacitant spray as a measure to reduce violence and is rolling out its use.

Drugs misuse and psychoactive substances have been identified factors in the decline in safety. Drug debt leads to bullying and violence. Prisoners taking psychoactive substances can be violent. The Prison Drugs Strategy published in April 2019 set out measures to restrict supply and the Ministry of Justice is funding measures such as x-ray scanners to deal with security in prison. Prisons involved in the Ten Prisons Project which focussed on reducing violence including through increasing security against drugs saw a reduction in the percentage of positive results from random mandatory drug tests. The Justice Committee has considered how limitations to prison regimes and poor day-today living conditions, including crowding, can both negatively impact on safety. The Chair of the Independent Monitoring Boards emphasised the link between safety and purposeful activity and

this link was recognised by the Justice Secretary. The Committee repeated its call for a dual focus on improving safety and rehabilitative initiatives saying prisons would not become less violent without proper investment in purposeful activity for prisoners. In August 2019 the Government announced up to £2.5 billion of funding to create 10,000 additional prison places.

The Chief Inspector and the Prisons and Probation Ombudsman have been critical of the quality of support for prisoners in crisis, delivered through Assessment, Care in Custody and Teamwork (ACCT) case management. The Ministry of Justice is developing a new version of the ACCT case management process and has rolled out a revised and improved suicide and self-harm prevention course for staff.

*Failure to learn lessons and implement recommendations*
HM Inspectorate of Prisons, the Prison and Probation Ombudsman, Independent Monitoring Boards, and the Independent Advisory Panel on Deaths in Custody have all expressed serious concerns at the seeming inability of prisons to take action as a result of their reports, in terms of learning lessons, implementing changes, and sustaining resulting improvements.

*Government strategy*
HM Prisons and Probation Service has a national strategy for safety. The Justice Committee has called for an overarching and integrated prisons strategy.

1 Ministry of Justice, Safety in custody: quarterly update to June 2019, summary table 3.

2 Ibid, summary table 2.

3 Ibid, summary table 4.

4 HMPSS, HMPPS Annual Digest 2018 to 2019, table 8.1.

5 Ibid., Chapter 14.

**Safety in Custody: December 2019 - Spreadsheet**
**Safety in Custody Statistics - Summary tables**
**Self-harm and assaults to December 2019**
**Deaths in prison custody to March 2020**
These tables are part of the Safety in Custody Statistics Bulletin
*https://prisons.org.uk/facts-figures/research-briefings/*

Contents

Table 1: Annual Safety in Custody Summary Statistics, England and Wales

Table 2: Annual Deaths in Prison Custody Summary Statistics, England and Wales

Table 3: Annual Self-harm Summary Statistics, England and Wales

Table 3a: Annual Self-harm Summary Statistics, Youth estate, England and Wales

Table 4: Annual Assaults Summary Statistics, England and Wales

Table 4a: Annual Assaults Summary Statistics, Youth estate, England and Wales

Table 5: Deaths in prison custody by apparent cause by quarter, England and Wales

Table 6: Self-harm incidents by quarter, England and Wales

Table 7: Assault incidents by quarter, England and Wales

Table 8a: Assault incidents by month, year and prison, 2003 - December 2019, England and Wales

Table 8b: Serious assault incidents by month, year and prison, 2003 - December 2019, England and Wales

Table 8c: Prisoner on Prisoner assault incidents by month, year and prison, 2003 - December 2019, England and Wales

Table 8d: Serious Prisoner on Prisoner assault incidents by month, year and prison, 2003 - December 2019, England and Wales

Table 8e: Assault on Staff incidents by month, year and prison, 2003 - December 2019, England and Wales

Table 8f: Serious assault on Staff incidents by month, year and prison, 2003 - December 2019, England and Wales

Table 8g: Assault incident rates by month, year and prison, 2003 - December 2019, England and Wales

Table 9a: Self-harm incidents by month, year and prison, 2004 - December 2019, England and Wales

Table 9b: Self-harm incidents requiring hospital treatment by month, year and prison, 2004 - December 2019, England and Wales

Table 10: Assault incidents and assault rate in the ten prisons, June/August 2018 - October/December 2019

Date of next publication: 30 July 2020

### Safety in prisons in England and Wales
28 November 2019

See opposite page.

### School Exclusions
Published Monday, 24 February, 2020

This pack sets out current policy on school exclusions, statistical information, recent parliamentary proceedings, and related research and news. It mostly relates to England, but also includes some statistical and other information on Scotland, Wales and Northern Ireland.

Schools in England can exclude pupils on a temporary or permanent basis, but only for disciplinary reasons.

In 2017/18, England's permanent exclusion rate was 0.10 per cent – equivalent to 10 per 10,000 pupils. The rate increased between 2012/13 (0.06 per cent) and 2017/18 (0.10 per cent). The most common reason for permanent exclusion in 2017/18 was physical assault against another pupil. There have been a number of reviews and reports relating to school exclusion in recent years. These include:

• Edward Timpson's review, published in May 2019 – to which the then-Government simultaneously published a response. This promised that schools would be made accountable for the outcomes of pupils they permanently excluded.

• The All-Party Parliamentary Group on Knife Crime's report on school exclusions, published in October 2019.

The 2019 Government has said that it has an "ambitious programme of action on behaviour, exclusion and alternative provision".

### Self-Defence Training in Schools
Published Tuesday, 10 March, 2020
**Physical Education (PE)**

PE is a compulsory subject under the National Curriculum at all key stages; National Curriculum programmes of study outline what should be taught at each key stage. Local authority-maintained schools are required to follow the National Curriculum; academies and free schools do not have to follow it but are required to provide a broad and balanced curriculum that promotes the physical development of pupils. The national curriculum details the competencies that pupils are expected to develop in each key stage but does not set out compulsory sports and activities that schools must teach (with the exceptions of swimming and dance).

The activity content for GCSE and A-Level PE was last revised in September 2019, and does not currently include self-defence. Explaining a previous revision carried out to the list, the then-Minister Robert Goodwill Minister in 2017 said that "as part of these revisions, the activity list was reviewed to ensure that all activities could be assessed reliably, were of comparable demand amongst pupils, and were manageable for schools to assess. The inclusion or non-inclusion of sports does not represent a view on the legitimacy or value of the activity" (PQ 109945, 31 October 2017).

In 2019 Sport England published the second set of data from its Active Lives Children and Young People Survey. The report summarised the activity levels of 5-16 year olds in England in the 2018-19 academic year. However, it does not include data on the take up of self-defence within schools.

*News Articles & Reports*
Ellie Gould: Murdered Girl's Friends Call for Self-Defence Lessons, BBC News, 3 February 2020 Primary School Students Getting Self-Defence Classes for Knife Attacks, The Telegraph, 3 November 2019
London Schools Teach Self-Defence and First Aid to Protect Pupils from Knife Crime, The

Independent, 2 December 2018
Self-Defence Lessons for Girls Should be on the Curriculum, says Teacher, Times Education Supplement, 7 August 2014
Corinna Seith and Liz Kelly, Achievements Against the Grain: Self-Defence Training for Women and Girls in Europe, London Metropolitan University, 2003, esp. sections 3.1.2-3.1.4

*Sentences of Imprisonment for Public Protection*
6 June 2019

**Summary**

*What are IPPs?*
Sentences of Imprisonment for Public Protection (IPPs) were introduced by the last Labour Government from 2005. They were designed to ensure that dangerous violent and sexual offenders stayed in custody for as long as they presented a risk to society. Under the system, a person who had committed a specified violent or sexual offence would be given an IPP if the offence was not so serious as to merit a life sentence. Once they had served their "tariff" they would have to satisfy the Parole Board that they no longer posed a risk before they could be released.

*Criticisms of the sentence*
The main concerns about IPPs were that:
• Some less serious offenders were given very short tariffs but then have been kept in prison for a long time after these have expired
• The prison and parole systems could not cope with the need to give all these short-tariff prisoners appropriate access to rehabilitative and resettlement programmes so that they could demonstrate they were no longer a risk to society
• The administrative delays resulted in uncertainty and perceived injustice for prisoners and litigation
• The rapid increase in the numbers of those on IPPs contributed to prison overcrowding, which in turn exacerbated the problems with providing rehabilitation

*IPPs were abolished in 2012, but not for existing prisoners*
The Coalition Government abolished sentences of imprisonment for public protection for offenders convicted on or after 3 December 2012, calling the system "not defensible". It replaced them with different sentences for dangerous offenders. However, the change was not made retrospective. It didn't apply to existing prisoners serving those sentences at the time. At the end of March 2019 there were still around 2,400 prisoners serving IPPs.

*Pressure for further change*
Former Justice Secretaries Ken Clarke and Michael Gove have called for reforms. The then

Chairman of the Parole Board, Nick Hardwick, set out in November 2016 how the Board could reduce the numbers of IPP prisoners but also suggested possible ways that the Government could take action if it wanted further reductions. This could be done by revising the risk test (either for all IPP prisoners or for those with short tariffs) or releasing IPP prisoners who have now served longer than the maximum current sentence for their offence.

In a thematic review, Her Majesty's Chief Inspector of Prisons, Peter Clarke, said it was "widely accepted that implementation of the sentence was flawed" and that "decisive action" was needed for reasons of cost, "fairness and justice" and to relieve pressures on the system.

Government statements have pointed to "encouraging progress" with reducing the numbers serving IPPs but point out the need to balance this progress with the potential dangers such prisoners can pose.

Recently concerns have been raised about the numbers of recalls to prison of IPP prisoners following their release.

*Sentencing for emergency service deaths: Calls for change*
Published Thursday, 10 September, 2020
The sentencing of offenders whose crimes lead to the death of an emergency service worker can vary depending upon the conviction received. The Harper's Law campaign has called for life sentences to be imposed in instances where an emergency service worker is killed as a direct result of a crime. This article discusses life sentences, minimum terms, and recent calls for change to sentencing in England and Wales. This is due to be the subject of an oral question in the House of Lords on 1 October 2020.

Sentences for offenders who commit crimes that lead to the death of an emergency service worker are coming under increased public scrutiny.

The Harper's Law campaign, originally named 'Andrew's Law', wants anyone who is found guilty of killing an emergency service worker as a direct result of a crime to receive a life sentence. Harper's Law would deem emergency service workers to include police officers, firefighters, nurses, doctors, prison officers and paramedics.

Lissie Harper launched the campaign following the death of her husband PC Andrew Harper. PC Harper was killed whilst on duty when responding to an incident in Berkshire in August 2019. The defendants Henry Long, Jessie Cole and Albert Bowers were found guilty of manslaughter following a trial at the Old Bailey. Henry Long was convicted for 16 years, whilst Jessie Cole and Albert Bowers received 13 years each. The Attorney General has since referred the sentences to the Court of Appeal to consider if they were unduly lenient.

A similar campaign launched by PC Harper's mother, Andrew's Law UK, is also seeking to change sentencing in England and Wales. Andrew's Law UK is calling for a minimum sentence of 20 years for offenders who seriously injure or kill a police officer whilst committing a crime.

Lord Brownlow of Shurlock Row (Conservative) is due to ask the Government what plans it has to introduce a new sentencing tariff for those who commit a crime and kill a member of the emergency services as a result. This oral question is scheduled to take place on 1 October 2020.

### What is the "minimum term" or "tariff" of a sentence?

Where a court imposes a life sentence, it must set a minimum term, also known as a 'tariff'. This is the minimum amount of time that an offender must spend in prison before becoming eligible to apply to the Parole Board for consideration of release.

When a court imposes a life sentence on a defendant who has been convicted of murder, a judge will decide the minimum term based on guidance set out in the Criminal Justice Act 2003. Offenders who are convicted of manslaughter do not always receive a life sentence. In cases where a life sentence is imposed for manslaughter, judges will consider the same guidance when determining the minimum term for a life sentence for those convicted of manslaughter, as determined by the case of R v Wood [2009] EWCA Crim 651.

### What is a life sentence?

The term 'life sentence' refers to several types of sentences that are given to offenders convicted of the most serious crimes. A life sentence means that an offender will be subject to that sentence for the rest of their life, although it does not necessarily mean they will serve the rest of their life in prison. The two main types of life sentence are mandatory life sentences and discretionary life sentences.

### Mandatory life sentences

A mandatory life sentence must be given to all offenders found guilty of murder in England and Wales. This has been the case since the suspension of the death penalty in 1965. For mandatory life sentences, courts will set a minimum term that an offender must serve in prison before being considered for release. The offender will only be released once this minimum term has been served and with the Parole Board's approval. If the Parole Board gives permission for release, the offender will spend the rest of their life on licence in the

community. The offender can be recalled to prison if the National Probation Service considers them to be a risk to the public. They do not need to have committed another offence.

For the year 2016, the Government said that the average minimum term given to offenders who received mandatory life sentences for murder was 21.3 years.

Offenders who are convicted of the most serious cases of murder can receive a whole life order. This is sometimes referred to as a 'whole life tariff' and means the offender will never be released from prison. Notable offenders who have received whole life orders include Peter Sutcliffe ('the Yorkshire Ripper') and Harold Shipman ('Dr Death'). In June 2020, the Ministry of Justice offender management statistics showed that there were 63 offenders serving whole life orders at the end of June 2020.

Prior to November 2002, the Home Secretary had the power to set the minimum term for mandatory life sentences. Following a successful appeal in Anderson v Secretary of State [2003] 1 AC 837, this practice was declared unlawful. The Criminal Justice Act 2003 now requires minimum terms to be set by the courts.

### Discretionary life sentences

There are several serious offences, such as manslaughter, rape or robbery, for which the maximum sentence available is life imprisonment. Discretionary life sentences are not automatically imposed, but are available if a judge believes that the circumstances of an offence warrant such a sentence.

Similar to mandatory life sentences, a judge will set a minimum term that an offender subject to a discretionary life sentence must serve in prison. Once the minimum term has been completed, the offender can be released on licence into the community with the permission of the Parole Board. The offender can be recalled to prison if they are considered a risk to the public or if licence conditions are broken.

### Offences against emergency service workers

In England and Wales, there are examples of provisions that apply to offences committed against the emergency services. This includes instances where a police officer or prison officer is murdered in the course of their duty. Schedule 21 of the Criminal Justice Act 2003 provides the starting points that courts should consider when determining the minimum term of a mandatory life sentence for murder. The guidance states that, for offenders aged over 21 who murder a police or prison officer in the course of their duty, the court's starting point for the minimum term should be a whole life order. The court will then assess aggravating and mitigating factors to determine the final minimum term.

Legislation was also introduced in 2018 for assaults against the emergency services. The Assaults on Emergency Workers (Offences) Act 2018, the Crown Prosecution Service said, was to ensure a more "effective investigation and prosecution of cases where emergency workers are the victim of crime". The act enables anyone who is found guilty of assaulting an emergency service worker to be given a maximum sentence of 12 months imprisonment. Prior to this, the maximum sentence available was six months imprisonment. Following the commencement of the act, the Government launched a consultation in July 2020 seeking views on whether the maximum penalty available for the offence of assaulting an emergency service worker should be increased to two years' imprisonment. The Government is yet to publish the outcome of the consultation.

### Next steps

Since its launch, the Harper's Law campaign has received support from the Police Federation of England and Wales. A petition in support of the campaign has also attracted over 654,000 signatures. The Deputy Chief Constable from Cumbria Constabulary, Mark Webster, is also cited by the News and Star as welcoming any legislation that would protect emergency workers. Lissie Harper met the Home Secretary and Justice Secretary to discuss the campaign's proposals on 2 September 2020. The BBC cites Ms Harper as saying "[…] clearly [the Home Secretary and Justice Secretary] want to support [Harper's Law] in trying to achieve this so I am very encouraged". To date, the Government has not published an official comment.

### *Sentencing Repeat Offenders*

When an offender is sentenced, there is a statutory requirement that the court treat any previous convictions as an aggravating factor, providing it considers that it is reasonable to do so. The court will consider the nature of the offence and its relevance to the current offence and how recently the offender was convicted of the previous offence. The presence of an aggravating factor can increase the severity of a sentence. (21st June 2022)

### *Serious violence and knife crime: Law enforcement and early intervention*

Published Tuesday, 14 January, 2020

Knife crime has been on the rise in England and Wales over the past few years. Although some of the reported increase is due to improvements in police recording practices, there have been some real rises.

Between April 2018 and March 2019 around 47,500 offences involving a knife or sharp instrument were recorded in England and Wales. This is 82% higher than in 2013/14 according to Office for National Statistics data, which excludes data collected by Greater Manchester Police, due to the force undercounting knife crime. Since the publication of their Serious Violence Strategy in April 2018, Conservative Governments have been trying to tackle knife crime by investing in law enforcement and 'evidence-based early interventions.'

There is a graphic that explains the above and which you can view on the Research tab of The Prison Oracle - tinyurl.com/2cjfe6yd

### An increase in use of stop and search powers

Since July 2017, the Home Office and the National Police Chiefs Council have been running 'weeks of action' to prevent knife crime, called Operation Sceptre. Although Operation Sceptre has not been entirely about stop and search, it has been a key component. For example, a March 2019 operation saw officers conduct around 1,900 searches.

The Home Office has also been encouraging forces to use stop and search powers more frequently in their day-to-day operations. Between March and July 2019, it slowly repealed strict guidance restricting 'no suspicion' stop and search powers introduced when Theresa May was Home Secretary in 2014. These powers allow officers to stop and search anyone in a specific area affected by serious violence, for a time-limited period, without a reasonable suspicion that they may have a weapon.

With more freedom and encouragement to use stop and search powers, the number of searchers increased for the first time since 2009/10 in 2018/19, though it is still much lower than at the beginning of the decade.

### Does stop and search lead to a reduction in knife crime?

Senior police officers have linked stop and search to recent reductions in knife crime. However, the effectiveness of the power is not clear. Home Office statistics show that most searches (around 60% in 2018/19) were conducted to find drugs rather than offensive weapons like knives. When officers did search for offensive weapons, they didn't always find what they were looking for. Only around one in 10 of these searches resulted in an outcome linked to the reason for the search. Long-term studies, including one of Metropolitan Police data, show that stop and search has only a marginal impact on crime reduction.

## Who is more likely to be stopped and searched?

Black people were 10 times more likely than white people to be searched in 2018/19.

In August 2019, the Johnson Government released an Equality Impact Assessment of the recent changes to guidance on 'no suspicion' searches. It concluded that it is "possible that this disparity is at least in part a result of discrimination/stereotyping on the part of officers and forces carrying out searches." The assessment acknowledged that this could negatively impact the relationship between black people and the police. The Government expects senior police officers to pay "continued attention to the issue of community relations, public trust and racial disparities" to mitigate this potential impact.

There is a graphic that explains the above and which you can view on the Research tab of The Prison Oracle - tinyurl.com/2cjfe6yd

## The Government has prioritised early intervention to prevent crime

Alongside increased law enforcement, the Conservative Governments (from April 2018 onwards) have been increasing funding for projects that aim to divert young people away from crime. Inspiration has been taken from Scotland, which established a public health approach to violent crime in the mid-2000s. This approach has seen the Scottish Violence Reduction Unit (VRU) try to tackle the root causes of violence through co-ordinated multi-agency projects. In May 2019, the May Government set aside £35 million to fund 18 VRUs in English and Welsh police forces.

In October 2018 the May Government announced it was investing £200 million over ten-years to the Youth Endowment Fund. The Fund provides direct funding to individual early-intervention projects across England and Wales and evaluates these projects to inform future policy making.

There has been growing cross party consensus supporting early intervention projects and treating knife crime as a public health problem. In July 2018, the Youth Violence Commission, a cross-party group of MPs, published its interim report advocating the approach. In July 2019, the Home Affairs Select Committee praised the Government for taking a public health approach. However, there has been some scepticism of how the Government has been implementing this approach. The Home Affairs Select Committee argued in July 2019 that the Government needs to give more thought to "what sustained and coherent preventative measures should look like, and how to ensure that public funding is diverted towards the most effective approaches."

## What might the new Parliament do?

The new Parliament will likely be looking at how the police can effectively prevent knife crime and how the public and third sectors can work together to address its root causes. It looks set to scrutinise the use of stop and search powers. The Labour Party manifesto pledged to "eliminate institutional biases against BAME communities." The Labour Party has said that a disproportionate use of stop and search against black and Asian men is "poisoning relations between the police and the local communities they serve." The Conservatives have pledged to back the "increased use of stop and search as long as it is fair and proportionate."

Both major parties have been supportive of multi-agency early intervention polices. The Labour Party's 2019 manifesto stated that "effective policing" requires forces to work "collaboratively with youth workers, mental health services, schools, drug rehabilitation programmes and other public agencies." The May Government published legislative proposals to create a legal duty on local services to implement a public health approach in July 2019. The Conservative Party manifesto committed to introducing this legalisation if re-elected.

*Further reading*

• How is the Government implementing a 'public health approach' to serious violence? House of Commons Library.
• Early Interventions to Reduce Violent Crime, Parliamentary Office of Science and Technology.
• Knife crime statistics, House of Commons Library.
• Police stop and search powers, House of Commons Library.

*Service Police review*
Published Tuesday, 30 June, 2020
**Who are the Service Police?**
The Service Justice System provides a legal framework that ensures Service personnel are subject to a single disciplinary code that applies wherever they are serving.

The disciplinary systems of the three services – the Army, the Royal Navy and the Royal Air Force – were drawn together under a common system by the Armed Forces Act 2006. While the Service Justice System mirrors the criminal law in England and Wales as closely as possible it also provides an avenue to enforce standards that are distinctive to the Armed Forces.

Each of the three services has its own police force: The Royal Military Police (RMP) in the Army, the Royal Air Force Police (RAFP) and the Royal Navy Police (RNP). Collectively they are known as the Service Police. They are empowered by the Armed Forces Act 2006 to investigate service offences.

Service offences include all criminal offences under the laws of England and Wales, as well as some additional disciplinary offences unique to the military, for example absence and misconduct.

**The Service Police Review**
The Ministry of Defence published a review of the Service Police and the Service Justice System in early 2020.
The review will inform the next Armed Forces Bill, which must be passed by Parliament in 2021. The Service Policing: Service Justice review Policing review was led by the former Chief Constable for Merseyside, Sir Jon Murphy. He made 24 recommendations in total. The policing review also included an audit of the process of domestic abuse and serious sexual offences investigated by the Service Police.
The review supported retaining three separate Service Police organisations but recommended the creation of a Tri-Service defence serious crime unit. The review also recommended Service Police should no longer be responsible for investigating the most serious offences (murder, rape and manslaughter) in the UK. This recommendation is in alignment with the recommendation by HH Shaun Lyons, in his review of the Service Justice System, for the Crown Prosecution Service (CPA) become responsible for the prosecution of the most serious crimes committed in the UK, rather than the Service Prosecuting Authority (SPA). The MOD originally rejected this, but in June announced that the Defence Secretary had decided to give "fresh consideration" to this recommendation.
The review also recommended that all incidents of domestic abuse that are brought to the attention of the Chain of Command should be reported to the service police.

**The Service Justice System Review**
The Library will publish a paper on the Service Justice System Review at a later date. The Review was commissioned in preparation of the next Armed Forces Bill, which must be passed by Parliament in 2021.

*Sexual harassment in education*
Published Monday, 21 June, 2021
**Schools and colleges**
All schools in England must have a child protection policy in place, including measures in relation to protecting children from sexual harassment, whether from staff members or their peers. Relevant policies are in place relating to behaviour at school, bullying, and the Public Sector Equality Duty.
Keeping Children Safe in Education is the statutory guidance to which all schools and

colleges in England must regard when carrying out their duties to safeguard and promote the welfare of children. The most recent version came into force in September 2019.
Advice for schools on Sexual violence and sexual harassment between children in schools and colleges sets out more direct information for schools and colleges on how to deal with incidents and allegations.
Statutory Relationships Education at primary school, and Relationships and Sex Education at secondary level, became compulsory in all English schools from September 2020. Statutory guidance has been published on the reformed subjects.
In March 2021, the Government asked Ofsted to undertake an immediate review of safeguarding policies in state and independent schools with relation to sexual harassment and abuse. The review was published in June 2021. It depicted widespread sexual harassment in schools, and made recommendations for action in schools, government, and Ofsted to combat the problem.
This briefing provides an overview of the relevant policies schools are expected to have in place on sexual harassment, and recent policy developments.
The same guidance for schools also applies to colleges, but some different considerations may apply where the students involved have turned 18, depending on context. Issues relating to over-18s are explored further in later sections.
Education policy is a devolved area, and this briefing focuses on the position in English schools. Links are provided to relevant policies in place in Scotland, Wales, and Northern Ireland.

**Further and higher education**
Universities and FE colleges face different challenges to schools with regard to the welfare and protection of students as most students are adults. The situation is complicated on campuses where students are living and socialising together. Higher and further education institutions have a duty to ensure that students have a safe environment in which to live and work. They also have a duty under the Equalities Act 2010 to eliminate discrimination, to promote equality, and to foster good relations between groups. These duties however must be implemented whilst allowing adult students freedom and autonomy. This can be a difficult balance to achieve.
There have been concerns that sexual harassment is increasing in universities. A BBC report in 2019 showed that reports of rape, sexual assault, and harassment at UK universities had trebled in three years. In 2015, Universities UK set up the Taskforce on Sexual Violence and Harassment, which published guidelines to assist Higher

Education Providers with drafting policies on sexual harassment and hate crime. Most colleges and universities now have processes and procedures in place to address harassment (including sexual harassment), violence, and hate crime.

This paper gives an overview of the issue of sexual harassment in colleges and universities, and sets out the legal duties of institutions and their responses to the problem of rising incidents of sexual harassment and violence.

## Sexual Reoffending Predictors
26 January 2021

### Comparing two predictors of sexual recidivism: the Risk Matrix 2000 and the OASys Sexual Reoffending Predictor

Philip Howard and Helen Wakeling Ministry of Justice, and Her Majesty's Prison and Probation Service

### Summary

This study aimed to inform decisions about the risk assessment of men convicted of sexual offences. It did this by testing the predictive validity for sexual reoffending – the ability to separate lower- and higher-risk individuals – of two actuarial risk instruments, the OASys Sexual Reoffending Predictor (OSP) and the Risk Matrix 2000/s.

Previous research has found OSP to be a slightly better predictor of proven contact sexual reoffending than a simulated version of RM2000/s. This study re-examined this issue using full RM2000/s scores and minor revisions to OSP's scoring. It also compared a further OSP scale, developed for indecent image reoffending, with RM2000/s. Finally, the study examined whether length of time without offending in the community (on release from prison) affected contact sexual reoffending rates and whether this should be considered in determining individuals' risk ratings. It examines these issues using a sample of men released from custody in the 2000s.

### Approach

A prison sample of 2,728 men who had been convicted of at least one sexual offence and who had been risk assessed for participation in an offending behaviour programme, was utilised, and rates of proven reoffending were examined. RM2000/s, OSP/Contact (OPS/C) and OSP/Indecent images (OSP/I) risk categories were produced for each individual in the sample, and the predictive validity of the tools were examined. Caveats with the current study include the fact that the sample is historic, and that most had contact sexual offences as their index offence.

### Results

• OSP/C was a slightly better predictor of proven contact sexual reoffending than RM2000/s.
• By far the best predictor of proven indecent images reoffending was OSP/I.
• Analysis, based on a small sample, indicated that those contact sexual offenders who had been in the community offence-free for a five-year period had a lower risk of reoffending beyond the five-year point. These results, therefore, lend some support to the recent guidance proposing the reduction of risk by one category for every five years an individual convicted of a sexual offence has been in the community offence-free.

### Conclusions

The results provide further support for the use of OSP over RM2000/s in assessing the risk of proven contact sexual reoffending in men with a sexual offending history. OSP has a number of advantages over RM2000/s: it focuses on specific types of sexual reoffending, it has a simpler scoring process, there is no age restriction on its use and it has better predictive validity for its two outcomes.

### Short Guide to the Criminal Justice System

This Library Briefing provides information on the system for investigating and prosecuting criminal cases. It outlines each stage of the process up to the point of conviction (11th January 2022).

### Short prison sentences: Calls for change

Published Wednesday, 17 June, 2020

Short prison sentences are the focus of the following oral question to the Government in the House of Lords on 29 June 2020: "Lord German to ask Her Majesty's Government what plans [it] has to reduce the number of short prison sentences".

The effectiveness of short-term prisons sentences has been debated for several years. Those in favour of reform say that such sentences are an ineffective deterrent that increase criminality. Opponents to reform argue that the abolition of such sentences would result in criminal individuals, who would otherwise be incarcerated, being free to commit further crime. Both sides of the argument are explored in this blog.

### History of calls for reform to short prison sentences

Calls for reform of the use of short prison sentences in England and Wales are not new.

In July 2001, the Making Punishments Work review, also known as the Halliday Review, looked at the sentencing framework in England and Wales. It found that shorter prison sentences were "ill-equipped to do anything to tackle the factors of underlying criminal behaviour, by comparison with any other sentence [...]".

The Coalition Government's transforming rehabilitation reforms in 2013 also considered, amongst other things, the use of short prison sentences and their reduction on reoffending.

Five years later, the House of Commons Justice Committee issued its Transforming Rehabilitation report in 2018. The committee recommended that the Government introduce a presumption against short prison sentences. The Government welcomed this, saying it was "currently exploring options [...]". In a follow-up report in July 2019, the committee noted the Government's stated intention to move away from short custodial sentences.

The Conservative manifesto for the 2019 election did not explicitly include plans to reduce the use of short prison sentences.

### What has the Government recently said?

A Ministry of Justice analytical series study from 2019 referred to evidence that suggested prison sentences of under 12 months, without supervision on release, were associated with higher levels of reoffending than sentences served in the community.

During his time as Justice Secretary, David Gauke advocated for the criminal justice system to move away from using short prison sentences of up to six months. Mr Gauke referred to research suggesting that the replacement of certain short prison sentences with community orders could lead to 32,000 fewer proven reoffences per year. He argued, amongst other things, that short prison sentences did not offer enough time to address problems such as drug misuse.

Mr Gauke's successor, Robert Buckland, announced that short sentences of under six months would not be abolished. Speaking to the House of Commons Justice Committee in October 2019, Mr Buckland said he did not believe abolishing short sentences was the right way forward:

"My own experience as a recorder teaches me that there are times when, however reluctantly, [short term prison sentences] should be available to judges and magistrates. For example, repeat offenders who fail to comply with community orders ultimately need the sanction of custody."

### What are the arguments on short prison sentences?

In March 2019, Ellie Reeves (Labour MP for Lewisham West and Penge) led a Commons debate about the cost and effectiveness of prison sentences of under 12 months. Ms Reeves said that short sentences often resulted in limited opportunity to address the needs of the prison population. She provided examples of limited access to education, work, and offending behaviour programmes.

Robert Neill (Conservative MP for Bromley and Chislehurst) agreed with Ms Reeves, referring to the purpose of prison being, not just punishment, but a place for reform and rehabilitation. Marion Fellows (SNP MP for Motherwell and Wishaw), highlighting the economic costs of short prisons sentences during the debate, said:

"[...] if prisons are full of people on short sentences, there will be less time and money available for real rehabilitative work within the prison system."

In contrast, John Hayes (Conservative MP for South Holland and The Deepings) argued that the removal of short prison sentences could send out the wrong signal. Mr Hayes said that the Government should instead focus on reforming prisons:

"Prison is of course about trying to put people straight, but it is also about punishing people for the harm they have done. That is an entirely respectable part of criminal justice, and it is what our constituents expect of us and of the Government."

In February 2019, a report by think tank Civitas stated that ending prison sentences of below six months would see 34,000 individuals receive non-custodial sentences each year. The report's author and founder of the Centre for Crime and Prevention, Peter Cuthbertson, said:

"The Government must now consider the evidence, rather than proceed any further with plans for an effective amnesty for burglars, shoplifters and other prolific criminals."

Andrew Neilson, the director of campaigns for Howard League for Penal Reform, was quoted by Sky News as describing the Civitas study as "scaremongering". In a blog written by Frances Crook, chief executive of Howard League for Penal Reform, in July 2019, Ms Crook spoke of reasons why short prison sentences should stop. Her reasoning included their ability to "embed criminality" and link to recidivism.

In 2018, the Prison Reform Trust called on the UK Government to follow Scotland and introduce a presumption against short prison sentences. A presumption against the use of sentences of three months or less was first introduced into Scotland in 2011. This came into force as an amendment to the Criminal Justice and Licensing (Scotland) Act 2010. The presumption against such sentences was extended to short sentences of less than 12 months in July 2019. An evaluation of Scotland's extended presumption in February 2020 noted a decrease in the use of short sentences in Scotland.

### Coronavirus and short prison sentences

The coronavirus pandemic has ignited calls to temporarily reduce the use of short prison sentences.

On 1 April 2020, the Revolving Door charity argued that the Government should temporarily suspend prison sentences of six months or less for certain non-violent and non-sexual offences. This call was supported by a coalition of members from the House of Lords, police and crime commissioners, academics and more. Matthew Ellis, the Police and Crime Commissioner for Staffordshire said:

"There are practical reasons during the current pandemic to reduce pressure on our prison service by releasing low-risk, non-violent individuals serving short sentences […]."

On 7 April 2020, the Government began the end of custody temporary release scheme ('ECTR'). This allows 'risk-assessed prisoners' who are within two months of their release date in England and Wales to temporarily released. The aim of the ECTR was to limit the spread and impact of coronavirus on the prison estate. As at 29 May 2020, 95 prisoners had been released under the ECTR in England and Wales.

On the same day that the ECTR came into operation, the House of Commons Justice Committee asked the Justice Secretary whether the coronavirus pandemic had thrown into perspective the need to consider short sentences. In response, Mr Buckland said "it was tempting to use the crisis as a pretext to change policy on sentencing", but he was not persuaded that short sentences should be abolished.

*Read more*
• Reform, The Prison System: Priorities for Investment, January 2020.
• Centre for Crime and Justice Studies, "Stopping Short?' Sentencing Reform and Short Prison Sentences', UK Justice Policy Review, August 2019.

*Substance use in prisons*
26 October 2020
**Exploring Substance Use in Prisons: A case study approach in five closed male English prisons**
Dr Helen Wakeling (Her Majesty's Prison and Probation Service), and Kieran Lynch (Public Health England)

**Summary**
Substance use is a significant issue in prisons across England and Wales and it affects the regime stability along with resident and staff health and well-being. This research used case study methodology to identify factors associated with substance use in five English prisons – all of them closed prisons for men. The aim was to explore the wider cultural features of the prisons which, according to the recovery literature, may have an impact on levels of drug use, and has not been investigated in prior research.
Observations, interviews, documentation analysis and data gathering were carried out. A total of 78 staff members and 61 residents across the five prisons were interviewed. Using thematic analysis, themes to explore factors associated with substance use across the prisons were generated.

There are some limitations with case study designs; whilst qualitative methodology enables the exploration of rich, in-depth information it is difficult to generalise the findings and to explore causal relationships. The learning made may not be relevant to all staff and residents or to other prison sites – particularly to prisons at lower or higher security level or those holding women or younger people. It is also unlikely that the five selected sites will have identified all of the possible factors associated with substance use. Another limitation was that the final site selection may have been biased to sites who were more willing to be involved in research.

Nine themes emerged from the qualitative analyses, which were clustered into three domains. The first domain was entitled 'descriptions of drug use' comprising themes which described the extent and consequences of drug use. This included a theme around the 'epidemic' nature of drug use, which encapsulated the perceptions that the extent of substance use was widespread, had major impacts on the prison, staff and residents, and was akin to an epidemic in prisons. Psychoactive substances were the most problematic drug reported. Also identified was a theme around the reasons for drug use, entitled 'escapism', to reflect the most commonly cited reason for drug use across the five prisons, as well as a theme entitled 'prison type and population', which grouped together perceptions of different contextual factors which impact on drug use, including the specifics of the population held at the prison, the prison type, the regime and staffing levels. The second domain was 'rehabilitative focus', and contained three themes: relationships, hope and prison culture. Relationships between staff and residents, and within staffing groups were perceived as fundamental, and differed between prisons with higher levels of substance use and those with lower levels of substance use. In prisons with a more prominent drug problem and amongst those who reported using drugs, there was a real sense of hopelessness and helplessness amongst both staff and residents. The culture of the prisons also seemed to be related to substance use, with more punitive cultures existing in the prisons with greater levels of substance use. The third domain was called 'enablers of a more effective response to drug use' and included

1499

themes around resources (e.g. staff numbers and time), treatment provision, and prison regime/activity, all of which were factors which could help better address substance use. Resourcing was perceived to be key in dealing with the issue of drug use in prisons. Particularly in prisons with higher levels of drug use, many staff said that they did not have the time to devote to meaningful activity with residents, being instead overrun with paperwork, and managing processes and the consequences of drug use. There was limited treatment provision for substance use across all five prisons, and services were often observed to be quite separate from the rest of the prison rather than an integral part. The provision and availability of purposeful activity and a full regime were deemed important to support the reduction of substance use in prisons.

Recommendations arising from this predominantly qualitative analysis included recognising the extent of drug use, the need to focus on 'recovery capital', and adopting a prison wide approach. Improving and strengthening staff and residents' relationships, a greater use of rehabilitation over a solely punitive stance, better training for staff, a focus on improving procedural justice, and improving communication between staffing groups regarding Substance Misuse Services (SMS) and healthcare services were also recommended.

*Suicide Prevention: Policy & Strategy Full Report*
21 April 2021
**Summary**

This paper set out suicide prevention policies in England.

The national suicide prevention strategy, Preventing Suicide in England: A cross-government outcomes strategy to save lives, was first published in 2012. Its key aims are to reduce the suicide rate in the general population in England and better support those bereaved or affected by suicide. It was updated in 2017 to including tackling self-harm as an issue in its own right. To support the strategy, the NHS asked that all CCGs should deliver local multi-agency suicide prevention plans.

The strategy included a commitment to reduce the rate of suicides in England by 10% by 2020/21 (compared to 2015 levels). The most recent progress report, published January 2019, showed that there was a 9.2% reduction in suicides. The Government will measure success against this target based on the suicide registrations for 2020, expected to be published by the ONS in 2021.[1]

The NHS Long-term Plan (January 2019) reaffirmed the NHS's commitment to make

suicide prevention a priority over the next decade. It committed to rolling out funding to further Sustainability and Transformation Partnership (STP) areas, implementing a new Mental Health Safety Improvement Programme, and rolling out suicide bereavement services across the country.

The Cross-Government suicide prevention workplan (January 2019) also commits every area of Government to taking action on suicide and sets out clear deliverables and timescales to monitor progress against the key commitments set out in the Suicide Prevention Strategy.

The Government has allocated funding of £57 million for suicide prevention work up to 2023/24.[2]

A fifth progress report was published in March 2021. This sets out additional Government support and funding for suicide prevention to address additional pressures caused by the COVID-19 pandemic. This includes £5 million to support suicide prevention voluntary and community sector organisations in 2021 to 2022. The report also notes that, although full data is not yet available, early indications do not suggest a rise in the number of suicides when comparing pre- and post-lockdown figures, for January to August 2020.

**Suicide rates**

Section one of this briefing paper provides a statistical overview of suicide rates throughout the UK over time, using the latest data published by the Office of National Statistics in September 2019. This shows that in 2018 there were 6,507 recorded suicides in the United Kingdom. This number of deaths equates to an age-standardised suicide rate of 11.2 deaths per 100,000 population, which is a significant increase on previous years and the highest rate recorded since 2002. It is also, nevertheless, lower than rates recorded in the 1980s and 1990s.

**Suicide prevention in different policy areas**

This paper covers the following policy areas:
• Health services – with details of suicide prevention measures and mental health support in the NHS Long Term Plan (January 2019) and other NHS England reports. It also covers local suicide prevention plans, and NHS support for high risk groups;
• Education – setting out suicide prevention measures taken by educational institutions, including schools and the mental health services they provide, as well as further and higher education institutions which have a legal duty under the Equality Act 2010 to support their students, including those with mental illness conditions;
• Employment – outlining policies designed to

keep people who suffer from mental health problems in work, including implementation of a Government strategy for support for people with health conditions in the workplace called 'Improving Lives', as well as a recent consultation on proposals to reduce ill-health related job loss;

• Social security – outlining support for benefit claimants with mental health problems, training and guidance for DWP staff, the risks in ESA and PIP assessments, and concerns about the impact of conditionality and sanctions on people with mental health conditions;

• Transport – detailing suicide prevention measures for railways and roads undertaken by the British Transport Police (BTP) and the Department of Transport, as well as suicide prevention strategies developed by Samaritans, BTP, Network Rail, Highways England, and other parts of the transport sector;

• Prisons – outlining current prison service policy and health services for prisoners, Government policy to prevent suicide in prisons, as well as concerns about the levels of self-harm and suicides in prisons;

• Media – outlining issues connected to the reporting of suicide, as well as the role of the internet and social media;

• Armed forces – providing information on suicide in the UK regular armed forces, the Ministry of Defence Mental Health and Wellbeing Strategy (July 2017), concerns around suicide among veterans; and

• Coroners' conclusions – explaining how the civil standard of proof – i.e. "on the balance of probabilities" – applies for suicide conclusions, rather than the higher threshold applied by the criminal courts – i.e. proof "beyond all reasonable doubt".

### Suicide prevention in the devolved nations

The latest suicide prevention plans for the devolved administrations, covered briefly in this paper, are:

• Scottish Government – Suicide Prevention Action Plan: Every Life Matters, August 2018;

• Welsh Government – Talk to me 2: Suicide and Self Harm Prevention Strategy for Wales 2015-2022, June 2015; and

• Northern Ireland Department of Health – Protect Life 2: Strategy for Preventing Suicide and Self Harm in Northern Ireland 2019-2024, September 2019.

1 HM Government, Preventing suicide in England: fourth progress report of the cross-government outcomes strategy to save lives, January 2019, page 9
2 PQ 54973 [on suicide: males], 4 June 2020

*Suicide Prevention: Policy and Strategy*
21 April 2021
*See 132 and https://prisons.org.uk/facts-figures/research-briefings/*

*Support for Women Leaving Prison*
6 March 2021
**Debate Research Briefing: Support for Women Leaving Prison**
This briefing provides an overview of the support given to prison leaving prison - ahead of the Westminster Hall debate on 'support for women leaving prison' scheduled for 9 March 2021, from 2.30pm.

The debate will be led by Carolyn Harris MP.

As at December 2020, 96% of prisoners were male (75,044) and 4% were female (3,136) (both in remand and sentenced). In December 2019, 95.5% were male (79,165) and 4.4% were female (3,703). Women typically serve shorter sentences than men. View the national statistics on Women and the Criminal Justice System on the Facts and Figures tab.

In 2019, the average custodial sentence length for male offenders was 19.7 months compared to 11.3 months for female offenders. A greater proportion of female offenders are sentenced for offences that tend to receive shorter sentences.

Short sentences can pose challenges for rehabilitation and resettlement. An August 2020 report by the Independent Monitoring Boards (which provide independent oversight of prisons and places of immigration detention) commented that short sentences mean (page 4):
maximum disruption to lives and minimum time available to provide meaningful rehabilitation and resettlement … Prisons and their partners have little time to address offending related needs and struggle to provide more than the most basic assistance.

Stakeholders have voiced particular concern about women leaving prison to rough sleeping and homelessness. The Independent Monitoring Board report noted (p5).

Prisoners and resettlement staff identified finding suitable housing as the main challenge. In addition to increasing the likelihood of reoffending, living on the streets is a poor option for vulnerable women often with underlying mental health issues, victims of domestic and sexual abuse and suffering from previous trauma. All of these issues are over-represented in the female prison population.

In June 2018 the Government published a Female Offender Strategy, which had been promised in the 2016 Prison Safety and Reform white paper. The Strategy's introduction acknowledged the particular vulnerability of female offenders, noting that their vulnerabilities can "often contribute to their offending behaviours or how they engage and respond to interventions". It stated that "many experience chaotic lifestyles involving substance misuse, mental health problems, homelessness, and offending behaviour" and noted that these are often the product of a life of abuse and trauma.

In the Strategy the Ministry of Justice made three immediate commitments as a "first step". It committed to:

• invest £5 million of cross-Government funding over two years in community provision for women
• work with local and national partners to develop a pilot for 'residential women's centres' in at least five sites across England and Wales
• reduce the number of women serving short custodial sentences.

The Strategy also committed the Government to developing a concordat which would (p9) "set out how local partners and services should be working together in partnership to identify and respond to the often multiple and complex needs of women as they journey through the criminal justice system".

In December 2020 a Concordat was published and describes the case for a 'whole system approach' that (p18):

• promotes multi-agency working involving criminal justice agencies, other statutory services (especially those related to health, including mental health and substance misuse; accommodation; domestic abuse; and employment), and voluntary sector women's services;
• builds on existing local landscape and partnership working;
• creates strong governance to embed new working practices and ensure on-going collaboration;
• takes a gender- and trauma-informed and - responsive approach, requiring an understanding of the gender-specific disadvantages faced by women using services and the impact of past violence, abuse, and trauma on these women; and
• makes a mutual commitment amongst partner agencies to avoid unnecessary duplication of work through improved communication, information sharing and related joint working.

The co-signatories to the Concordat (including various government departments – listed at Annex A of the Concordat) have committed to working together to improve outcomes for women who have already encountered the criminal justice system or are at risk of doing so. In response to a Parliamentary Question on 22 September 2020, the Government indicated that approximately 4% of female prison releases are to rough sleeping and 14% are homelessness. On 14 December 2020 Lucy Frazer MP, then Minister for Prisons and Probation, outlined government funding to provide support to women leaving prison:

Reducing reoffending is a complex issue and needs to be a combined effort across government and local partners in order to help ex-offenders secure employment, find a home, get treatment for a drug addiction and support for mental health issues.

And we remain committed to delivering the Female Offender Strategy's objectives of fewer women coming into the criminal justice system and reoffending, fewer women in custody (especially on short-term sentences) and a greater proportion of women managed in the community successfully, and better conditions for those in custody.

The Government recognises the important role played by women's community services in supporting women leaving prison. Following the publication of the Female Offender Strategy, the Government invested £5.1 million over two years in women's community sector organisations, including women's centres. Thirty different organisations across England and Wales received funding, which included the creation of six new women's centres. On 5 May, the Government announced further funding of £2.5 million for the sector.

On 23 January 2021, a government press release announced an additional £2 million in government funding to help support organisations that work to reduce female offending. The press release noted that:

Around half of women in prison have a mental health issue and a similar proportion have a history of drug use. Dealing with these underlying issues can help reduce the chance of women entering the criminal justice system in the first place and reduce reoffending rates when they do. This requires a whole host of different agencies, local and national, to work together to help each individual offender, whether that be, getting into addiction treatment, finding a stable home or escaping an abusive partner.

*Tackling anti-social behaviour*
Published Tuesday, 21 April, 2020
Anti-social behaviour (ASB) encompasses a wide range of behaviours that cause nuisance and harm to others. Local authorities, the police and social landlords share responsibility for tackling ASB at a local level. These public bodies have a range of powers, set out in Parts 1 to 4 of the Anti-social Behaviour, Crime and Policing Act 2014, to tackle ASB. Local public services may also tackle ASB with informal remedies.

There is a graphic that explains the above and which you can view on the Research tab of The Prison Oracle - tinyurl.com/2cjfe6yd

## ASB powers

Parts 1 to 4 of the Anti-social Behaviour, Crime and Policing Act 2014 provide six ASB powers to local public services. These powers (summarised in the table below) are a consolidation of nineteen that existed prior to the 2014 Act. Taken together, they provide a broader enforcement regime than in the past in which local agencies have stronger powers they can use in more circumstances.

There are no centrally collated and published statistics on the use of these powers. Without robust data, it is hard to assess how they are being used and what impact this is having on ASB.

Civil rights groups have expressed concern that these powers are being used to criminalise vulnerable groups such as homeless people and young adults. There has been particular concern at the inappropriate use of Public Space Protection Orders (PSPOs). In December 2017 the Government revised its statutory guidance to frontline professionals on the powers in order to emphasise that PSPOs should not be used to target "behaviour that is neither unlawful nor antisocial."

## Putting the victim first?

The 2014 Act also provides two mechanisms which aim to empower ASB victims and involve them in the response to ASB. These are:

• Community resolutions: A form of 'out of court disposal' in which victims are provided an opportunity to influence how their perpetrator is punished.

• The Community Trigger: A mechanism by which victims (or those close to them) can request that the relevant authority review how their ASB case was handled.

These mechanisms are key to the Government's priority to put the 'victim at the heart of the response to ASB'. Despite this emphasis, the Victims Commissioner said in April 2019 that victims of ASB were 'being let down' by local public services who were not adequately prioritising ASB. The Victims Commissioner and the charity ASB Help have called on the Government to provide more oversight on how local public services are running their Community Trigger schemes.

## The Target Operating Model for probation services in England and Wales

### The purpose of probation

As set out in law, probation services have multiple aims that relate to protecting against further offences (protecting the public, empowering those that commit crimes to want to make positive changes and reducing the likelihood of reoffending) and addressing the harm caused by the original offence (highlighting the effects of crime on victims and facilitating appropriate punishment).

These aims are not mutually exclusive and there is overlap across them. For example, by challenging and empowering people to embrace the opportunity to make lasting changes to their lives, Probation Practitioners will, in turn, advance the key aim of protecting the public by reducing reoffending. Indeed, a renewed focus on change work forms part of the Government's broader approach to the Criminal Justice System, particularly through the ambition (set out in the White Paper 'A Smarter Approach to Sentencing') to make greater use of robust and effective community sentences as a credible alternative to custodial sentences. Through increasing the use of appropriate community sentencing options, we will be better equipped to address the complex needs of supervised individuals and to target the underlying causes of offending behaviour, thereby breaking the cycle of offending and keeping the public safer.

Our reform of probation services offers a valuable opportunity to not only stabilise the probation landscape, reinforce its ethics[1] and ensure that core services are properly delivered, but also to innovate and improve the way these services are delivered such that we can better achieve probation's key aims. In defining the future operating model, we have, therefore, considered the foundations of a strong probation service to be able to achieve this and have distilled it into a simpler description of 'Assess, Protect and Change'.

Probation's statutory aims revolve around three distinct groups with differing perspectives (those that commit crime, victims and the public). We have, therefore, outlined in Figure 1 (below) what Assess, Protect, Change means in the context of both probation services themselves and those that they are intended to serve.

In Chapter 3, we further consider the implications of Assess, Protect, Change on the role of the Probation Practitioner in the context of delivering advice to court, Sentence Management and resettlement support.

## Our vision and the HMPPS Business Strategy

The new probation model is grounded in the overarching HMPPS Business Strategy which sets out our vision to work together to protect the public and help people lead law abiding and positive lives. It outlines four principles that inform the way in which we deliver the role of probation services to 'Assess, Protect, Change', namely:

• enabling people to be their best – Investing in our people to make sure they have the tools to do their jobs well and reach their full potential.

• transforming through partnerships – Working closely with our partners to deliver a more holistic service that elicits positive change and keeps the public safe.

• an open, learning culture – Consulting with our colleagues and stakeholders, including supervised individuals, to learn from each other and looking externally at good practice to improve services.

• modernising our estates and technology – Making our working environment safe and flexible and harnessing data and technology to facilitate more effective working practices.

**What we want to achieve**

The shortcomings of the existing system have been well documented and the need for reform called out by several external bodies including the Justice Select Committee, National Audit Office and Her Majesty's Inspectorate of Probation.

This has resulted in us being able to make a strong case for reform and further investment in the system. We estimate that once the new model is in place fully, total annual spending on probation services will be around £155m more than current annual spend.

Our starting point in considering how we can reform the current system most effectively has been to consider the desired outcomes of those that use, are involved in or impacted by probation services. The diagram at Figure 2 outlines what each group wants from a reformed service, and these have fed into the benefits we want to achieve as well as specific elements of the new target operating model.

We anticipate that, longer-term, our reforms and increased investment will deliver the following strategic benefits:

• Consistent supervision and targeted rehabilitation.
• Trusted contribution to the delivery of justice in courts.
• A skilled, responsive and resilient workforce.
• A flexible, responsive and collaborative system.

We have identified a series of intermediate benefits that we expect the target operating model to achieve as we phase in reforms further post Day 1 and which will feed into achievement of our strategic benefits:

• Improved Sentence Management.
• Improved assessment of service users' needs, risks and characteristics.
• Improved sentencer[2] confidence in the new probation service and contracted probation services.
• Improved quality of pre-sentence advice.
• Increased staff capacity to meet demand.
• Improved staff engagement.
• Improved quality of programmes, interventions and Unpaid Work.
• More successful delivery of programmes, interventions and Unpaid Work.

• Increased local and partnership-based delivery of probation services.

These intermediate benefits will be measured and monitored in order to ensure that they are fully realised as the new model is established and embedded. They are likely to begin to be realised from 2022 (particularly as baseline measures for new approaches are established). More detail on how these intermediate benefits will be measured can be found in the relevant sections of Chapter 3.

We anticipate that implementation of the new model will generate financial efficiency savings as well as benefits which will improve outcomes and the effectiveness of probation services.

Anticipated efficiencies can be categorised into four broad areas:

• Removal of unproductive activities: This includes unification of probation services resulting in a reduction in hand offs and duplicative activities.

• Preventing breaches and recall: The model aims to reduce the amount of enforcement actions needed, for example, through regular case reviews.

• Increased productivity: We anticipate that this will be achieved through greater investment in staff and their working environments as well as improvements to digital services that will drive efficiencies and improvements in the way we work.

• Structural cohesion: Bringing decision making under one organisation will bring efficiencies including reducing work required to maintain communications across multiple organisations.

Efficiency savings made will be reinvested in service delivery and enable us to improve the quality of probation services to get better outcomes, and to meet increases in demand.

*1 The Probation Institute owns and regularly updates the Code of Ethics for Probation and Rehabilitation, which can be found here: https://www.probation-institute.org/code-of-ethi*

*2 We are using the term 'sentencer' as a generic term to describe sentencing judges and magistrates.*

**Terrorist Offenders (Restriction of Early Release) Bill 2019-2020**

11 February 2020

**Summary**

The Terrorist Offenders (Restriction of Early Release) Bill 2019-20 was introduced on 11 February 2020. All stages in the House of Commons are due to take place on 12 February 2020.

The Bill has been introduced in response to the terrorist attacks on London Bridge in November 2019 and in Streatham in February 2020. The offenders in each of these attacks had been released from prison automatically without the involvement of the Parole Board.

The Government has said the Bill should be fast tracked through Parliament because legislation is needed urgently to put appropriate safeguards in place before further terrorist offenders, including some due for automatic release before the end of February 2020, are released from prison.

Currently prisoners serving a standard determinate sentence are automatically released from prison at the half way point of their sentence to serve the rest of their sentence in the community on licence. Prisoners serving extended sentences imposed before 2015 may be released automatically on licence at either the two thirds or half way point. Prisoners serving sentences for offenders of particular concern may be released on licence from the halfway point at the discretion of the Parole Board.

The Bill would change release provisions so that offenders given a determinate sentence for a relevant terrorism offence do not become eligible for release until the two thirds point of the sentence. Release at the two thirds point for these offenders would not be automatic. They would be referred to the Parole Board to decide if they are safe to release on licence.

The changes would apply not only to those sentenced for the relevant offences in the future but also to those currently in custody serving sentences for these offences. This has led to some debate as to the compatibility of the Bill with the European Convention on Human Rights, which prohibits the retrospective imposition of criminal penalties. The Government's position is that the changes relate to the administration of the penalty, rather than its scope, and that the Bill is therefore compatible with the Convention.

The Bill does not address concerns about the management of terrorist offenders within prisons. It is not clear whether the interventions used in prisons with extremist offenders are effective. Separation centres set up for some extremist offenders have been little used.

The Government has said it intends, in the coming weeks, to introduce a further bill making provision for the sentencing and release of terrorism offenders.

The provisions of the Bill would extend and apply to England, Wales and Scotland. Counter-terrorism is a reserved matter, although prisons and sentencing (including release provisions) are devolved to Scotland and Northern Ireland. The Government states that a Legislative Consent Motion will be required from the Scottish Parliament. For detail on the territorial extent and application of the Bill see page 7 and Annex A of the Explanatory Notes.

The Bill would come into force on Royal Assent. The Government has published Explanatory Notes. A Gov.uk page for the Bill provides links to a Factsheet, Equality Statement, European Convention on Human Rights Memorandum and an Impact Assessment. There is also a Bill page on the Parliament website.

*The 2020 Spending Review envelope*
Published Thursday, 19 March, 2020
In the 2020 Spring Budget, Chancellor Rishi Sunak announced the official start of the 2020 Comprehensive Spending Review.

This was originally intended to be the second of this year's trilogy of big financial events (the other two being the Spring Budget we have just had, and the autumn Budget). However, given the rapidly changing nature of the coronavirus outbreak, it now seems likely that the plans will have to change. The timings of these events may be affected, and there may be a series of further financial measures to help to cope with the impact of the outbreak, in addition to the ones already announced at the Budget and on 17 March.

**Background to the Spending Review**
Every few years, the Treasury sets long-term budgets for each of the government departments. The idea is to give each department certainty about how much money it will have, so they can plan what they want to do.

Spending Reviews are not just important because departments need money to deliver public services. They also give an overall picture of a government's priorities and goals for its time in office. In this case, the Budget lists four priority areas:
• Levelling up economic opportunity across all nations and regions of the country by investing in infrastructure, innovation and people, to drive productivity and spread opportunity
• Improving outcomes in public services, including supporting the NHS and taking steps to cut crime and ensure every young person receives a superb education
• Strengthening the UK's place in the world
• Reducing carbon emissions and improving the natural environment
The most recent full Spending Review was in 2015 and planned out spending up to the current year. A one-year Spending Round last year extended the plans to 2020/21. The new review, which the Chancellor has just announced, is planned to run until July this year (although recent events may mean that this changes). It will set out plans until 2023/24, and until 2024/25 for long-term investment spending.

There is a graphic that explains the above and which you can view on the Research tab of The Prison Oracle - tinyurl.com/2cjfe6yd

**The new spending envelope**
The Budget also included the 'envelope' for this

year's Spending Review. This is the total amount of money the Treasury plans to allocate between departments over the years covered by the Review. These spending figures were announced before the recent financial package to cope with the economic effects of coronavirus, so the final figures are likely to be somewhat different. How different they are will depend on how long the outbreak lasts, and how long the effects of these financial interventions last.

Even without taking extra coronavirus spending into account, the envelope announced represents a large amount of money – over £1.5 trillion over three years.

*See Table above:*

*Note: Spending figures are total Departmental Expenditure Limits (DEL) – that is, resource DEL excluding depreciation plus capital DEL.*

*Source: HM Treasury, Budget 2018 table 1.9 and Budget 2020 table 1.10*

However, several large spending commitments have already been made:

• The NHS Funding Act 2020 sets out funding commitments of between £130 billion and £150 billion for the NHS in every year of the new Spending Review period.

• New funding for schools was laid out at last year's Spending Round. This lasts until 2022/23 (when it reaches £52 billion).

• The Government has repeatedly confirmed it intends to stick to its current targets of spending at least 2% of GDP on defence, and 0.7% of national income on overseas aid.

Adding these up, and assuming (as in the 2019 Spending Round) that no other departments will see real-terms cuts in their budgets, leaves comparatively little money for new spending.

*Note: Spending figures are resource Departmental Expenditure Limits (RDEL) excluding depreciation. NHS and schools funding estimated for the years after their settlements end by assuming flat real-terms growth. Source: Library calculations, using data from HM Treasury, Spending Round 2019 and Budget 2020; OBR, Public finances databank and Economic and fiscal outlook*

The 'headroom' shown in the chart above is the money left over for everything else, after all of these commitments have been accounted for. It amounts to between £13 billion and £19 billion in each year of the Spending Review period.

This is still a large amount of money, but represents only about 3-5% of the total envelope. The Institute for Fiscal Studies has done some similar analysis, taking into account that the UK will be replacing funding currently coming from the EU. It concludes that even less money will be available for other departments not covered by commitments already made.

This may help to explain why the Budget also mentions: "an exercise across departments to identify savings and projects that do not provide value for money" or which do not fit with the four priority areas listed above. The message seems to be that although there is new money on offer, there will still be tight control over the purse strings.

**How people can have their say**

Negotiations between departments and the Treasury are likely to take place over the next few months to determine how the money will be divided up.

This is not a process that takes place only within Government. The Treasury has invited interest groups, individuals and representative bodies to submit representations that suggest new ideas for this money. Submissions are open until 20 May 2020.

Although Parliament has no formal role in the Spending Review process, it can also have an impact. Mel Stride MP, the Chair of the Treasury Committee, has written to the chairs of all departmental committees asking them to help scrutinise the process and raise important issues.

*The Bail Accommodation and Support Service*
Published Friday, 18 December, 2015
What is BASS?

The Labour Government introduced the Bail and Accommodation Service (BASS) in England and Wales in 2007. This is a scheme to accommodate people on bail and on Home Detention Curfew. They are adults who need a suitable address, or some support, so that they can be released. Certain people are not eligible;

• those convicted/charged with a sexual offence listed in Schedule 3 to the Sexual Offences Act 2003;

• those who pose a significant risk to the public, to BASS staff or to others in a shared house;

• those under 18 years of age; or

• those unable to pay rent or claim housing benefit

Why does the Government use the scheme?

The Government's aim in having this scheme is to reduce offending, use resources efficiently and free up prison places. The service, it argues, provides a cost effective alternative to custody or custodial remand for people who would be living in the community anyway if they had alternative accommodation.

**Who runs BASS?**

At first a company called ClearSprings had the contract for BASS. Since 2010 Stonham, a social housing provider, has run the service. It provides around 650 bed spaces in the community in small houses or flats – typically with two or three people sharing.

BASS accommodation is not the same as "probation hostels", known officially as "approved premises". Approved premises are much larger and provide intensive supervision for higher risk offenders.

**Where are these properties?**
There was controversy at the beginning of the scheme, not least because of the very limited information about the location of properties being used. The Ministry of Justice does not provide information about the private addresses of those on bail or who have been released on Home Detention Curfew.

**Are local residents consulted?**
Stonham does not have to consult local residents before using a property under BASS. It does, however, consult police, local authorities and probation providers. It also informs immediate neighbours and provides contact details. As these are normal residential properties being used for this purpose, there is no need for planning permission.

*Further information*
There is further information on Stonham's BASS website, and FAQs and contact details for people with concerns on a separate BASS website.
Policy information is in a National Offender Management Service (NOMS) Service Specification Document and NOMS Probation Instruction, Accommodation and Support Service for Bail and HDC.
This Briefing Paper covers England and Wales only.

*The Checkpoint Programme*
Published Thursday, 20 February, 2020
• Durham Constabulary introduced the Checkpoint programme in 2015 as an alternative to prosecution for low-level crime.
• Checkpoint is a four-month management programme which aims to tackle underlying issues, such as alcohol or drug misuse or the offender's mental health.
• Offences deemed eligible for the scheme include theft, criminal damage, fraud, or common assault. Hate crimes are not accepted for Checkpoint.
• As part of the programme, offenders agree to an individually tailored contract. If the contract is completed without the offender reoffending then no further action will be taken against them. If they fail to complete the contract, then the offender may face prosecution.
• Initial analysis by Cambridge University, published in Policing journal, has found that individuals who took part in Checkpoint had a lower re-arrest and reoffending rate compared to offenders who had been given other types of out of court disposals (eg community service). The

full study into Checkpoint is expected to be published in 2022.
• A similar trial scheme, Operation Turning Point, was run in the West Midlands between 2011 and 2014. West Midlands police also reported reductions in reoffending as a result of the scheme.
• The use of out of court disposals has been advocated by the National Police Chiefs' Council. In its 2017–21 national strategy, the Council provides guidance on how to use out of court disposals and highlights the Checkpoint programme and Operation Turning Point as effective methods to reduce re-offending rates.
• The Government stated in response to a written question in July 2019 that the use of out of court dispersals are an operational matter for the police.
• Research from the Centre for Justice Innovation suggests that there is moderate evidence in the UK that out of court punishments for low level crime reduces reoffending. Civitas has claimed that using out of court punishments over sentences would mean more victims of burglary and shoplifting, drink-driving and knife crime.

*The Compliance Officer for IPSA*
Published Wednesday, 29 April, 2020
This briefing paper sets out the legislative background to the post of Compliance Officer, created in the Parliamentary Standards Act 2009, as amended. The Compliance Officer investigates complaints about expenses claimed by Members of Parliament and reviews claims that the Independent Parliamentary Standards Authority does not allow. The briefing paper outlines the procedures the Compliance Officer follows in undertaking investigations and reviews.
The Compliance Office for IPSA ('Compliance Officer') is an independent statutory office holder, responsible for investigating complaints about MPs' claims for business costs and expenses paid to MPs by the Independent Standards Authority (IPSA).
The procedures for conducting investigations are determined by IPSA, following consultation. The current Procedures have operated since January 2015.
The Compliance Officer also undertakes reviews, upon the request of an MP, of a determination by IPSA to refuse an MP's expense claim in whole or in part.
Tracy Hawkings – the former Head of Crime and Public Protection Command at Essex Police Headquarters – has been the Compliance Officer for IPSA since May 2018.
The current Compliance Officer works 2 days a week.
In 2018/19, the total cost of staffing, legal costs, expenses and consultancy for the Compliance Officer amounted to £95,000, with the

Compliance Officer's salary in the range of £25,000-£30,000.

### The disturbance at HM Prison Ford on 1 Jan 2011
24 March 2011

Prison Service Orders require that prisoners should be categorised objectively according to the likelihood that they will seek to escape and the risk that they would pose should they do so. The process of categorisation starts from a presumption that a prisoner will probably be suitable for a low (C or D) categorisation unless there is evidence, such as the nature of the offence and/or the length of the sentence, to suggest otherwise.

Updated guidance on re-categorising prisoners to category D, suitable for open conditions, was issued in 2009 and emphasises that, in making such decisions, prison governors should bear in mind "the particularly challenging management issues associated with the low physical security and supervision levels of the open estate". Nonetheless, the Prison Officers' Association and National Association of Probation Officers have for some time been alleging that prisoners are being inappropriately downgraded to category D, to enable spaces in the category D estate to be filled at a time of population pressures. In 2009, HM Chief Inspector of Prisons described the smuggling of alcohol into Ford prison (an open prison in West Sussex) as a "significant problem". This note discusses some of the controversy surrounding the re-categorisation of prisoners to category D and examines what is known about the disturbance at HM Prison Ford, which is subject to two ongoing investigations.

### The Independent Inquiry into Child Sexual Abuse and background
11 August 2016

**Summary**

On 4 February 2015, the then Home Secretary, Theresa May, announced that a new, statutory, inquiry would take place into child sexual abuse. An Inquiry Panel was formed, led by the New Zealand judge, Lowell Goddard, although she subsequently resigned on 4 August 2016. Professor Alexis Jay, a panel member of the inquiry, was announced as the new Chair on 11 August 2016.

The Inquiry Panel was formally established by Mrs May on 12 March 2015, and following preparatory work the Inquiry was formally opened by the then Chair on 9 July 2015.

Justice Goddard described the Inquiry's task as "daunting" and hoped that the Inquiry's work will be concluded before the end of 2020. In the mean-time, the Inquiry Panel would published annual reports from 2016 and updates on its work.

The inquiry is limited in scope to England and Wales (with some exceptions) but as a statutory inquiry has the power to compel people to give evidence. Exemptions from the Official Secrets Act 1989 for whistle-blowers has been granted by the Solicitor General.

The Inquiry Panel wishes to hear from survivors of child sexual abuse:
• an online form is available to submit evidence at: https://www.iicsa.org.uk/share-your-experience
• a guide on submitting evidence is available, entitled Truth Project – Sharing your experience: what to expect.

The current Inquiry replaced the previous, non-statutory, Inquiry established in July 2014. As well as having less powers than the current Inquiry, its terms of reference limited it to matters dating from 1970; there is no cut-off date for the current Inquiry.

In addition, the previous Inquiry lacked a Chair for most of its existence: the two Chairs of the Panel who were appointed both resigned over concerns from victims and survivors of alleged links they had with individuals under the remit of the investigation.

### The Parole System
The Parole Board is an executive non-departmental public body, responsible for the parole system. The Parole Board carries out risk assessments on these prisoners to determine whether they can be safely released into the community. It is governed by the Parole Board Rules, secondary legislation that sets out the procedures that must be followed when determining parole cases. (21st June 2022)

### The Parole System of England and Wales
9 September 2019

**Summary**

The parole system determines which prisoners, who have been sentenced to indeterminate and certain determinate sentences, can be released early subject to certain conditions.

In England and Wales this system is overseen by the Parole Board. This organisation is responsible for:
• The release of certain prisoners, including approving licence conditions; • Reviewing the circumstances in which some prisoners have been recalled and deciding whether those prisoners should be re-released; and
• Making recommendations to the Secretary of State for Justice for the transfer of indeterminate sentence prisoners from a closed (high or medium security) prison to an open (low security) prison.

The Parole Board undertakes hearings, either based on paper evidence or in person, to determine whether an offender can be released back into community without posing a risk of serious harm to the public.

The work of the Parole Board has increased significantly in recent years following a Supreme Court ruling in 2013 that oral hearings should be undertaken in a much wider range of cases. The number of oral hearing increased from 4,628 in 2012-13 to 8,137 in 2017-18.

Following the controversial decision to release John Worboys in November 2017 and the subsequent judicial review of the decision in the High Court, which quashed the original decision to release Mr Worboys, there was much criticism about the lack of transparency in how the Parole Board arrived at a decision, as well as the fact that a Parole Board decision could, at that time, only be challenged through judicial review.

In May 2018, the Parole Board Rules, secondary legislation governing the working of the Parole Board were amended to enable the Parole Board to provided summaries of its decisions to victims and other interested parties. Between May 2018 and March 2019, the Parole Board provided summaries for 1,171 decisions.

In February 2019, the Government published details of its proposals for a reconsideration mechanism. This allows victims, via the Secretary of State for Justice, as well as prisoners, to ask the Parole Board to reconsider its original decision. This came into force for decisions made after 22 July 2019.

## The Prisons (Interference with Wireless Telegraphy) Bill
13 September 2012

Sir Paul Beresford's Private Members' Bill, the Prisons (Interference with Wireless Telegraphy) Bill would allow the Secretary of State to authorise prison governors to interfere with wireless telegraphy in order either to block mobile phones or detect their use. It was published on 28 June 2012, had a formal second reading without debate, and was referred to a Public Bill Committee. The first session is expected to be on 17 October 2012. The Bill has government and cross-party support. Mobile phones and similar devices in prisons have long been associated with problems such as organised crime, drug supply, bullying and harassment of victims. The previous Government introduced criminal offences of bringing unauthorised electronic communications devices into or out of prisons, and of possessing a mobile phone in prison without authorisation, to add to the existing disciplinary offence of possessing an unauthorised article.

Mobile phone jamming in prisons presents technical and legal challenges, not least ensuring that it does not affect phones outside the prison perimeter. The National Offender Management Service has been trialling the use of equipment, which the Government says have demonstrated that the technology can work, although it is "not a quick, simple or cheap solution." For security reasons the Government does not publish information about which prisons are involved.

The Bill would enable the authorisation of the use of such equipment rather than requiring its use. No additional funding is being sought. The Explanatory Notes say the Bill will impose no financial obligations on the public sector, and that no full Regulatory Impact Assessment has been produced.

The Bill extends to Scotland as well as England and Wales, and a Legislative Consent Motion has been tabled in the Scottish Parliament.

## The Prisons (Property) Bill
13 September 2012

The Prisons (Property) Bill is a Private Members' Bill which had its first reading on 20 June 2012 but was not published until 9 September. It is due to have its second reading on 14 September 2012. Stuart Andrew is the Member in charge of the Bill. It has government support, and the Ministry of Justice has provided Explanatory Notes.

Currently prison governors can confiscate unauthorised items such as mobile phones or alcohol. They also have the power to sell or otherwise dispose of unclaimed items of prisoners' property. However, they do not have an express power to destroy prisoners' property. In 2009 the High Court rejected the argument that governors had a common law power to do this. There was speculation at the time that this could lead to compensation claims from other prisoners whose property had been destroyed. The Government was given leave to appeal, but did not do so.

The result is that items which are confiscated must be stored by the prison authorities and may be returned to the prisoner on release. The cost of storing such property is met by the National Offender Management Service (NOMS).

The Bill would allow a governor or director of a prison to destroy unauthorised property found in prisons, or dispose of it in other ways including selling it.

### 1 Introduction and background

The Prisons (Property) Bill is a Private Members' Bill which had its first reading on 20 June 2012 but was not published until 9 September 2012. It is due to have its second reading on 14 September 2012.

Stuart Andrew is the Member in charge of the Bill, but it has government support, and the Ministry of Justice has provided Explanatory

Notes.

The Bill would allow a governor or director1 of a prison to destroy unauthorised property found in prisons, or dispose of it in other ways including selling it.

1.1 What powers do prison governors[1] have to confiscate unauthorised items?

The history of prisoners seeking to get hold of things which those holding them prisoner do not want them to have is probably as long as the history of imprisonment itself. Much of the effort in maintaining the security of prisons is concerned with ensuring that prisoners do not gain access to things which might be used in a bid to escape or might otherwise jeopardise security. It has, for example, long been a criminal offence to bring tobacco or alcohol into a prison or unlawfully to introduce letters or other articles. The Labour Government updated the law and introduced new explicit criminal offences of bringing various items such as drugs, firearms and mobile phones into prisons.[2] The Offender Management Act 2007 made it a criminal offence to convey mobile phones and associated equipment into or out of a prison, or to transmit sounds or images from within a prison, without authorisation.[3] Library Research Paper 06/62, which was written for the Bill's second reading, discusses the provisions relating to prison security.[4]

It has long been a disciplinary offence under the Prison Rules to possess an "unauthorised article".[5] Again, the Labour Government made it a criminal offence to possess an unauthorised mobile phone inside a prison. [6]

Under rule 43 of the Prison Rules, Governors have the power to confiscate unauthorised items. They also have the power to sell or otherwise dispose of unclaimed items of prisoners' property:

4) Any article belonging to a prisoner which remains unclaimed for a period of more than one year after he leaves prison, or dies, may be sold or otherwise disposed of; and the net proceeds of any sale shall be paid to the National Association for the Care and Resettlement of Offenders, for its general purposes.

(5) The governor may confiscate any unauthorised article found in the possession of a prisoner after his reception into prison, or concealed or deposited anywhere within a prison. What they do not have, at present, is the express power to destroy property, even unauthorised property, which prisoners want back.

1.2 The Coleman Case

The position regarded prison governors' powers to dispose of unauthorised possessions was tested in the High Court in April 2009.[7] A former prisoner had been found guilty under the prison rules of possessing an unauthorised mobile phone, and the phone was later destroyed. In the case, lawyers for the Secretary of State argued that the governor had the power in section 43 of the 1952 Act to confiscate the item, but also that the governor had a power at common law to destroy the phone. The Court found that the governor had no such power. Comments by human rights lawyers in the press speculated that the case could open the way for many other ex-prisoners to seek compensation for similar destruction of mobile phones and other property.[8] At the time the judge gave leave to appeal the judgement, but no appeal was made.

1.3 The Government's explanation of the background to the Bill: The Explanatory Notes set this out as follows:

(..) there are restrictions on the property that prisoners may bring into and possess in prison. Although provisions in the Prison Act 1952 and in rules made under that Act provide for the confiscation of unauthorised property, they do not provide for the destruction of confiscated property.

6. This means that, at present, unauthorised property found in the possession of a prisoner and which is subsequently confiscated must be stored by the prison authorities and may be returned to the prisoner on release. The cost of storing property until a prisoner's release is met by the National Offender Management Service (NOMS).

7. One of the most commonly confiscated items is mobile telephones, of which a large number are currently stored by NOMS. Many of the phones held in storage are not attributable to individual prisoners and, in any event, very few prisoners have sought the return of these items upon their release. Other commonly confiscated items include authorised items which have been adapted for unauthorised uses and items of property which have been smuggled into prison or stolen or coerced from another prisoner.

8. When controlled drugs and other illegal items such as weapons are found inside prisons, these are generally referred to the police (and are not therefore stored by NOMS). However there is currently no express power for the destruction or disposal of other property of the types described. The Bill is designed to address this situation and to ensure there is a clear legal basis for the destruction or other disposal of unauthorised or unattributable property.

*1 Private prisons have "directors" rather than Governors*
*2 The Offender Management Act 2007: Library Research Paper 06/62, which was written for the Bill's second reading, discusses the provisions relating to prison security on pages 52-3*
*3 sections 21-22*

4 *pp52ff*
5 *Rule 51, Prison Rules 1999 SI 1999/728; see also Prison Rules 1964 SI 1964/388*
6 *Section 45 of the Crime and Security Act 2010. This is discussed in more detail in Library Standard Note 6414, The Prisons (Interference with Wireless Telegraphy) Bill*
7 *R. (on the application of Coleman) v Governor of Wayland Prison [2009] EWHC 1005 (Admin).*
8 *See for example "Compensation floodgates may open after judge rules prison unlawfully destroyed inmate's smuggled mobile phone was destroyed", Daily Mail, 3 April 2009 and "Prison 'wrong' to destroy phone", BBC News, 3 April 2009*

### The Prisons (Property) Bill Committee Stage Report
23 November 2012
*See 146 The Prisons (Property) Bill*

### The Prisons (Substance Testing) Bill 2019-21
16 December 2020

**Summary**

The Prisons (Substance Testing) Bill 2019-21 was introduced to the House of Commons on 5 February 2020. It is a Private Members' Bill introduced by Dame Cheryl Gillan. It had second reading on 16 October 2020. Committee stage took place on 2 December 2020. Report stage and third reading are due to take place on 22 January 2021. The Bill has Government support. Explanatory Notes have been prepared by the Ministry of Justice.

HM Prisons and Probation Service (HMPPS) in its Prisons Drugs Strategy, April 2019, described the misuse of drugs in prison as "one of the biggest challenges facing our criminal justice system today".

The law in England and Wales currently allows for mandatory drugs testing in prisons. Prisons Minister, Lucy Frazer, has said that drug testing is a "crucial part" of the strategy as it provides "robust evidence on the prevalence of drug misuse and can be used to support security measures, identify and signpost into drug treatment, monitor treatment compliance and act as an incentive to engage in treatment and recovery".

Issues have been identified with the current legislation which provides for drug testing in prisons. The chemical composition of psychoactive substances is subject to rapid change. New psychoactive substances are often created with slight alterations to the chemical make-up of existing psychoactive substances. Currently, where the chemical composition of a psychoactive substance is changed, a change in the law to include that new substance is required. Amending the law for each new substance is time-consuming and can cause delays in detection. Another issue with the law on drugs testing in prisons is that not all prescription and pharmacy medicines are included in the list of specified drugs prisons can test for. Also, there is currently no legislative basis for prevalence testing, an anonymised process to help identify any new substances being found routinely.

The Bill seeks to address these issues. It would

• Amend the provision that allows for mandatory drug testing in prisons so that it uses the generic definition of a psychoactive substance from the Psychoactive Substances Act 2016, thereby removing the need for repeated changes to the law for newly identified substances to be individually added;

• Create powers for testing of prisoners for prescription only and pharmacy medicines; and

• Set out a statutory framework for prevalence testing.

The Bill extends to England and Wales only. It would come into force on a date to be appointed by the Secretary of State.

### The Psychoactive Substances Bill 2015-16: Report on Committee Stage
15 January 2015

**Summary**

The Psychoactive Substances Bill 2015-16 was introduced in the House of Commons on 21 July 2015. It received its Second Reading on 19 October 2015.

The Bill was debated in Committee on 27 and 29 October 2015, there were three sittings. It is tabled for Report Stage on 20 January 2016.

A background to the Bill, a summary of Lords consideration and an overview of the bill as introduced to the House of Commons is provided in the Commons Library briefing paper, Psychoactive Substances Bill 2015.

The Psychoactive Substances Bill intends to introduce a blanket ban on the production, supply, possession with the intent to supply, and import and export, of psychoactive substances. Simple possession is not an offence under the Bill. A number of substances will be explicitly exempted from the controls in the Bill and the Bill provides order-making powers for the Secretary of State to add substances to this list. It includes a range of civil and criminal sanctions.

The Bill was introduced in the Queen's Speech in May 2015 after recommendations from the Home Office appointed expert panel report on new psychoactive substances.

**Government amendments**

Government amendments tabled at Committee Stage included:

• To introduce a new offence of possession of a psychoactive substance in a custodial institution;

• To add exemptions to offences under the Bill

for healthcare professionals acting in the course of their work, and for activity conducted in the course of approved scientific research;

• To change the definition of medicinal product under the list of exempted substances to that in the Human medicines Regulations 2012;

• To repeal the Intoxicating Substances Act 1985. These were all agreed and added to the Bill without division. Other amendments Opposition and other amendments tabled at Committee Stage included:

• To change the definition of psychoactive substances under the Bill;

• To add Alkyl Nitrites to the list of exempted substances;

• To exclude social supply of psychoactive substances from the controls under the Bill;

• To add statutory aggravating factors to the offence of supply, or offer to supply:

− To aggravate the offence if the person knew, or had reason to believe the substance would cause harm

− To aggravate the offence if the supply was in the vicinity of a premises intended to accommodate vulnerable children;

• To introduce a new clause to make personal, social and health education a foundation subject in the National Curriculum in England;

• To add a requirement that the review of the implementation of the Bill include a report on progress made in improving the education about new psychoactive substances (NPS);

• To give powers to police officers and local authority officers to require a premises to cease trading where a premises notice had been breached. None of these amendments were added to the Bill, but it was indicated that a number may be tabled again at Report Stage.

This paper summarises the Committee debate, following a short summary of debate during Second Reading. It will also provide some information about the Home Affairs Committee Report on psychoactive substances that was published before Committee Stage.

### The Supreme Court

The UK Supreme Court (UKSC) was established in October 2009 under the Constitutional Reform Act 2005 (CRA 2005). It was created as part of a push to strengthen the separation of powers in the UK constitution, by removing the judiciary (the Law Lords) from the upper house of the UK legislature (the House of Lords). The 12-member Court is the final court of appeal for civil matters throughout the UK and for criminal matters in England and Wales and in Northern Ireland. It also has a special role in relation to the devolution statutes in Scotland, Wales and Northern Ireland: it adjudicates on devolution

"issues" raised and "references" made under those statutes. (24th June 2022)

### The Troubled Families Programme (England)
27 November 2020

**Summary**

The Troubled Families Programme (TFP) is a programme in England administered by the Ministry of Housing, Communities and Local Government (MHCLG). The programme conducts targeted interventions for families experiencing multiple problems, including crime, anti-social behaviour, truancy, unemployment, mental health problems and domestic abuse.

The programme has had two iterations since its introduction in 2012: the first programme ran from 2012 to 2015 and the second was due to run from 2015 to 2020. The Spending Review in November 2020 announced £165 million to extend the TFP to 2021-22. This was in addition to the £165 million confirmed for 2020-21 in January 2020.

### 2012-15 Programme
The previous 2012-15 programme aimed to "turn around" 120,000 families in England. Department for Communities and Local Government figures stated 116,654 of the 117,000 identified families had achieved this outcome by May 2015.

Based on the accompanying report, Benefits of the TFP to the taxpayer (2015), the Department estimated that the average gross cost saving to the taxpayer per family was £12,000, more than twice the average cost of the programme's intervention at £5,493. The programme had a central government budget of £448 million.

The 2016 Public Accounts Committee report, Troubled families: progress review, criticised the Government's evaluation. The Committee said the term "turned around" was "misleading" as the outcomes measured were short-term. The Committee also said the Department had "not demonstrated that the programme has provided genuine financial savings". The Government, in its response to the report, agreed with the Committee's recommendations and adopted new methodologies for evaluating the post-2015 TFP.

### 2015-21 Programme
Funding In 2013, the then-Coalition Government announced that a second programme would run from 2015/16. A total of £1.1 billion of funding has been committed to March 2021. The programme intended to help up to 400,000 families "achieve significant and sustained progress against all their multiple problems and make work and ambition for all families" by 2020. The programme is primarily a payment by

results scheme, where local authorities claim payment when their work with families results in significant and sustained progress against their identified problems, or achieve continuous employment. Funding is allocated to local authorities based on the level of need. From 2018, 14 authorities moved to an upfront funding model known as "earned autonomy".

The County Councils Network in May 2020 called upon the UK Government to make TFP funds available "now to scale up family support services" and to set out a long term financial settlement in the forthcoming Spending Review, as it expected rising pressure on services due to the Coronavirus outbreak. £165 million of funding was announced in the November 2020 Spending Review to continue the programme to 2021-22. This was in addition to the £165 million confirmed for 2020-21 in January 2020.

## Who does the programme aim to support?

To be eligible for the TFP, each family must include dependent children and/or expectant parents, and have at least two of the six problems prescribed by the MHLCG. These relate to crime and antisocial behaviour, education, life chances, living standards, domestic abuse and mental and physical health.

Analysis in the MHCLG's Annual report of the TFP 2019-20 (June 2020) shows that the most common problems faced by families related to children needing help (88%), worklessness (58%) and health (48%). Of the families on the programme, 49% had at least one child under the age of five at the start of the intervention. 74% of families were assessed as experiencing between two and four problems.

## Who does the programme work for?

The MHCLG's Annual Report of the TFP 2019-20 (June 2020) said that successful family outcomes numbered around 350,000 by 5 April 2020. Of these, around 30,000 families have adults who moved into continuous employment.

MHCLG analysis said the TFP was having a positive impact on offending outcomes for those families with a recent criminal history and for those who have been involved with children's social care in the year before joining the programme. The impact of the TFP on employment, school attendance and domestic violence were either less significant or could not be established as a direct result of participation in the programme.

*Transgender Prisoners*
19 September 2018
**Summary**
In November 2016, the National Offender Management Service (NOMS) published a revised policy on transgender prisoners.[1] NOMS had initiated a review of the issue early in 2015. However, late in 2015 its scope was broadened following the deaths of two transgender inmates, and another case where a transgender woman was first sent to a male prison, but was later transferred to a women's prison after a public petition.

2011 policy guidelines for England and Wales had stated that prisoners should normally be located in the prison estate of their gender as recognised by UK law. For transgender prisoners, a Gender Recognition Certificate (GRC) would normally be necessary before a person could be placed in a prison corresponding to their acquired gender. However there was some flexibility for trans prisoners who were "sufficiently advanced in the gender reassignment process".

The Women and Equalities Committee looked at the issue of transgender prisoners as part of their wider report on Transgender Equality, published in January 2016. The Committee said there was a "clear risk of harm" where trans prisoners are not located in a prison "appropriate to their acquired/affirmed gender".

The Government published a report on their policy review in November 2016 which acknowledged that the treatment of transgender people in the criminal justice system had not kept pace with wider social views. Whilst earlier 2011 guidelines had emphasised the role of GRCs and medical interventions, the report noted that many transgender people successfully lived their lives without these. The new policy needed to "take as its starting presumption a wish to respect someone in the gender in which they identify".

The new policy guidelines, Prison Service Instruction 17/2016 state that "all transgender prisoners (irrespective of prison location) must be allowed to express the gender with which they identify". Such prisoners must be asked their view of the part of the prison estate that reflects this; however a decision to locate them in a prison which does not accord with their legal gender can only be made following a Transgender Case Board. Those who wish to be placed in a prison location which is not consistent with their legally recognised gender must provide evidence of living in the gender with which they identify. Assessments will be made on a case by case basis.

Also in November 2016, the Ministry of Justice published the first official statistics on transgender prisoners. A data collection exercise in March/April 2016 showed that there were 70 transgender prisoners in 33 of the 123 public and private prisons in England and Wales.

A Ministry of Justice report published in November 2017 said there were 125 transgender prisoners in England and Wales who had had a local transgender case board when data was collected in March/April 2017. 47 of the prisons in England and Wales said that they had 1 or more transgender prisoners.

In Scotland, policy guidelines state that the social gender in which the prisoner is living should be fully respected, regardless of whether or not they have a GRC.

The Northern Ireland Prison Service has no recent record of any prisoners who have self-identified as transgender. Their needs would be considered on a case by case basis, to include arrangements for where they would be accommodated and how they would engage in the prison regime.

*1. On 1 April 2017 NOMS became Her Majesty's Prison and Probation Service (HMPPS)*

### UK Prison Population Statistics
3 July 2020

**Summary**

This briefing paper explores data on the UK prison population, including the population size and change over time, the demographic profile of prisoners, safety in prisons, and the cost per prisoner. Prisons are a devolved, so UK prison statistics are published separately for England and Wales (the Ministry of Justice), Scotland (the Scottish Government), and Northern Ireland (the Department of Justice). This briefing also compares the UK with other countries.

Weekly prison population data are available for England, Wales and Scotland and quarterly data are available for Northern Ireland.

The latest available data show a current prison population of approximately 87,900, comprising
• 79,453 in England and Wales[1],
• 7,004 in Scotland[2], and
• 1,484 in Northern Ireland (these at the end of June 2019).[3]

The prison population has fallen since lockdown measures were introduced in response to the Covid-19 pandemic. Since the end of February, the UK prison population has shrunk by around 5,500 people or 6%.[4]

In addition to these snapshots, all jurisdictions publish the average annual prison population, which was approximately 82,935 in England and Wales in 2019, and 7,789 in Scotland and 1,448 in Northern Ireland for the financial year 2018/19.

There is a general underlying, increasing trend in the number of people held in prison. The graph below shows prison population change relative to 1900 (and relative to 2000 for Northern Ireland).

The prison population of England & Wales quadrupled in size between 1900 and 2018, with
around half of this increase taking place since 1990. The Scottish prison population almost doubled in size since 1900 and rose 60% since 1990. The data series for Northern Ireland begins in 2000. Between 2000 and 2018/19 the prison population of Northern Ireland increased by 36%, although the prison population is currently lower than at its peak of around 1,800 in 2014/15. To put the prison population in context, it is possible to calculate the number of prisoners per 100,000 people in the general population. At the most recent count there were:
• 173 prisoners per 100,000 of the population in England and Wales in 2019
• 162 per 100,000 in Scotland (2018/19) and
• 96 per 100,000 in Northern Ireland (2018/19).[5]
In each jurisdiction, prison population projections are made on a regular basis. At the most recent estimate, the prison population in 2022 is projected to be around 81,400 in England and Wales, 7,800 in Scotland, and 2,251 in Northern Ireland (approximately 96,000 in total).[6]
There are many other statistics on the prison population available for England and Wales which are published in the Ministry of Justice's Offender Management Statistics Quarterly.
The key findings are that, at March 2020:
• The prison population is ageing: in 2002, 16% were under the age of 21 compared with 6% in 2020 and the number over the age of 50 went from 7% in 2002 to 17% in 2020;
• Prison sentences were longer in 2020 than in 2010, with 48% being over 4 years compared with 33% in 2019[7];
• Foreign nationals made up 11% of the prison population;
• People of minority ethnicities made up 27% of the prison population compared with 13% of the general population.
In May 2020,
• 49% of prisons in England and Wales were over-crowded. [8]
Each jurisdiction also publishes data on the cost per prisoner or prison place. In 2017/18, the average cost per prison place was £39,385 in England and Wales, £35,601 in Scotland, and £54,893 in Northern Ireland.[9]

*1. Ministry of Justice Offender Management Statistics Quarterly: October to December 2019*
*2 Scottish Prison Service Prison Population*
*3 Department of Justice Weekly Situation Reports*
*4 Based on end of week population: 28 Feb 2020 compared with 26 June 2020.*
*5 These are based on the population aged 15 and over.*
*6 Ministry of Justice Prison population projections 2019-24, Scottish Government Prison statistics and population projections Scotland 2013/14, Northern Ireland Prison Service FOI Case No. 13:454*
*7 Excludes indeterminate-length sentences*

8 MoJ, Population bulletin: monthly May 2020

9 MoJ, Prison performance statistics 2018/19; Scottish Prison Service, Annual report and accounts 2017/18, appendix 8a; Northern Ireland Prison Service, Annual Report and Accounts 2018/19, p.14
There is a graphic that explains the above and which you can view on the Research tab of The Prison Oracle - tinyurl.com/2cjfe6yd

### UN Convention on the Rights of the Child: a brief guide
29 November 2016

**Summary**

This Commons Library briefing gives an overview of the 1989 UN Convention on the Rights of the Child, what it covers and how it is enforced.

### What is the Convention?

The Convention on the Rights of the Child is a multilateral treaty designed to promote the protection of children worldwide. It is one of the core UN human rights treaties, and is the most rapidly and widely ratified of them all. The UK ratified it in 1991.

The Convention has been hailed as a victory for the children's rights movement. However, it is only as effective as its implementation, and has been criticised for endorsing only Western values.

### What does the Convention cover?

The rights set out in the Convention are wide-ranging, encompassing civil and political rights as well as economic, social and cultural ones, for all children under 18. They have been categorised as rights to provision, rights to protection and rights to participation, with the last of these often considered the Convention's main achievement (although implementation is often particularly problematic).

The Convention also says what governments, public authorities and adults must do to ensure all children can enjoy all their rights.

Two optional protocols added to the Convention in 2000 concern children in the armed forces, and commercial sexual exploitation. A 2011 optional protocol provides a quasi-judicial process for children whose rights have been violated. The UK has ratified the first two but not the third optional protocol.

### How is it enforced?

All treaties bind the States that have ratified them, under international law, but this does not necessarily mean that they are implemented and enforced.

The Convention on the Rights of the Child established a Committee on the Rights of the Child to oversee and report on States' implementation. Its latest report on the UK was published in May 2016. The Committee can also hear complaints from individual children whose Governments have ratified the 2011 optional protocol on individual complaints (the UK has not). However, the Committee's recommendations are not legally binding.

UNICEF, the United Nations Children's Fund, is specifically named in the Convention as a source of expert assistance and advice on implementation. Independent National Human Rights Institutions (NHRIs), non-governmental organisations (NGOs) and national reporting and follow-up mechanisms can also have a direct role. The extent to which the Convention forms part of national law and can be enforced by national courts varies. Generally speaking the UK Government has preferred to take a sector-by-sector approach to implementing the Convention. In Wales and Scotland Ministers and public authorities have some new general duties in relation to children's rights. But there have been many calls for the UK to incorporate the Convention directly into domestic law.

### Unexplained Wealth Orders
1 October 2021

**Summary**

For some time the UK has been accused of being a hub for dirty money - especially London's prime property market.

The Proceeds of Crime Act 2002 introduced Civil Recovery Orders (CROs) to help tackle the problem. CROs permitted the confiscation of criminal property using a lower "civil" standard of proof. Instead of needing to prove a crime was committed, law enforcement bodies only needed to show a court that on the balance of probabilities (or "more likely that not") unlawful conduct had occurred, and the property was obtained as a result of that unlawful conduct.

However, use of CROs was limited to exceptional cases where the prospect of criminal prosecution was unavailable or undesirable. It didn't help in the most difficult cases, such as where concrete evidence was hard to obtain because the alleged launderer was part of, or had the support of, a foreign regime.

The Criminal Finances Act 2017 therefore introduced Unexplained Wealth Orders (UWOs). Nicknamed "McMafia Orders" (after the book and TV series of the same name), these went a step further than CROs. Targeted at people linked with serious crime or who hold public office outside of Europe, they allow law enforcement to apply for a court order requiring someone to explain their interest in property and how they obtained it. If that person failed to comply, law enforcement could then apply to the court for a CRO with the benefit of a presumption that the property should be confiscated.

In theory, therefore, UWOs provide an opportunity to confiscate assets without ever having to prove that the property was obtained from criminal activity.

Available from January 2018, the use of UWOs has been limited so far, having only been obtained in four cases as of June 2021. There have been high-profile successes and failures.

A Government money laundering risk assessment concluded in December 2020 that money laundering has probably increased since 2017, suggesting that UWOs are yet to have the desired impact.

Wider action on money laundering has been set out in the Government's Economic Crime Plan 2019 to 2022, as discussed in our briefing Economic crime in the UK: a multi-billion pound problem.

### Unexplained Wealth Orders

Unexplained Wealth Orders allow for the confiscation of property without proving criminality, by reversing the burden of proof. This briefing discusses their introduction, how they work, and their use so far (22nd February 2022)

### Undercover policing in England and Wales
5 November 2020

### Summary

Police forces use undercover police officers in a variety of operational deployments. The use of undercover police officers is governed by Part II of the Regulation of Investigatory Powers Act 2000 (RIPA). RIPA sets out the legal framework for the use of 'covert human intelligence sources' by public authorities, including the police, the security and intelligence services, and customs officials.

The Investigatory Powers Act 2016 created a new single oversight body for all investigatory powers, the Investigatory Powers Commissioners Office (IPCO). IPCO regularly inspects and monitors the use of undercover policing and has raised several concerns about the authorisation and oversight of undercover policing. In its first annual report (published January 2019) IPCO acknowledged that there had been "significant public disquiet" about the past actions of undercover police officers.

### Concerns with past undercovering policing

In the early 2010s a series of revelations about the practices of undercover officers came to light raising serious concerns about undercover policing in England and Wales.

Several undercover officers were found to have had multiple intimate relationships with those they were investigating. Some of these officers fathered children in these relationships. Historic undercover policing units were found to have routinely used the identities of dead children to construct undercover personas for officers. There have also been questions about the effectiveness of undercover policing and the appropriateness of its use against certain protest movements. A major trial against climate protestors who attempted to occupy a Ratcliffe-on-Soar power station collapsed when evidence collected by an undercover officer was mishandled. There have also been serious concerns about the use of undercover officers to monitor those associated with the campaign for justice for Stephen Lawrence.

### Proceedings against the police

Two high profile officers, Mark Kennedy (who was the officer involved in the collapse of the Ratcliffe power station trial) and Jim Boyling (an officer who had several intimate relationships with those he was tasked to investigate) left the police. Jim Boyling was dismissed for 'Gross Misconduct'. Mark Kennedy had left before his involvement was exposed. The police have also come to financial settlements with several women who had intimate sexual relationships with undercover officers. The police have issued a public apology to these women in which they described the intimate sexual relationships as "abusive, deceitful, manipulative and wrong" and "a gross violation" of personal privacy.

However, attempts to bring criminal charges against individual officers have failed. The CPS have decided not to prosecute officers for sexual offences and this decision was upheld after judicial review.

One of the women who had a relationship with Mark Kennedy has bought a human rights claim against the police. The police have admitted that her human rights were violated, but the legal proceedings are ongoing.

### The Undercover Policing Inquiry

On 12 March 2015 former Home Secretary Theresa May announced a public inquiry into undercover policing. This followed several other independent reviews into aspects of undercover policing. The Mitting Inquiry (so named after its current chair Sir John Mitting) has been beset by controversy and delay since it was announced. It began taking oral evidence in November 2020.

### Reform of undercover policing

There has been recent reform of the governance of undercover policing and police practice. The Investigatory Powers Act 2016 established an independent single oversight body for all investigatory powers.

The Inspectorate of Constabulary reviewed undercover policing in 2014 and recommended that new guidance be drafted for undercover officers. New guidance was published in October 2020.

## Unification of probation services
7 June 2021
### Summary
Probation services Probation practitioners supervise offenders in the community and oversee their rehabilitation. People on probation are supervised while serving a noncustodial sentence or following their release from prison on licence.

### The new model
A new model for probation services in England and Wales will be brought in from June 2021 when current contracts for Community Rehabilitation Companies end. Under the new model, from 26 June 2021, all sentence management for low, medium and high-risk offenders will be carried out by the National Probation Service. Unpaid work, accredited programmes, other interventions and resettlement services will also be delivered by the National Probation Service.

The National Probation Service will be able to commission some services from the private and/or third sectors. The Dynamic Framework, a commissioning mechanism, will allow regional probation directors to procure rehabilitation services, for example, in relation to accommodation, employment and training.

Probation services will be organised around 12 regions (including Wales) and overseen by a Regional Probation Director with accountability for both the National Probation Service and contracted delivery. In Wales sentence management was unified in December 2019 when all case management activity moved to the National Probation Service.

The new model has been broadly welcomed with many expressing the hope that it will bring some stability to probation services.

### Reversal of earlier reforms
The new model will largely reverse the heavily criticised reforms of probation services that took place from 2014. These reforms, known as "Transforming Rehabilitation" divided the probation service into two: The National Probation Service and Community Rehabilitation Companies.

### The transition
Concerns have been raised about the transition from the old to new model. The Chief Inspector of Probation said the timeline was ambitious

and that the pandemic had added further complexity to the schedule. In May 2021 HM Inspectorate found that the reforms were broadly on track but raised some concerns regarding staffing and services.

*See also*
*The Target Operating Model for probation services in England and Wales*
### Introduction
This chapter provides the context for our target operating model, outlining what we hope to achieve through our reforms and the additional investment being made. It also sets out some key considerations that have informed our proposals, including alignment with the HMPPS Business Strategy, how we can create a more equitable, diverse and inclusive system, and how our proposals link to wider changes and improvements to the criminal justice system.

### About this document
This document supersedes the document 'A Draft Target Operating Model for the Future of Probation Services in England and Wales,' published in March 2020. It sets out the further design detail and key design changes that have developed since then.

It is aimed at staff and stakeholders involved in probation delivery and is intended to establish a common understanding of our aspirations for the future of probation services in England and Wales.

Its focus is, therefore, on how we anticipate the key features of the model working once we have implemented the reforms. We recognise that it will take time to get there, not least given the challenges presented by COVID-19 and the subsequent recovery work needed to get probation services onto a stable footing. The position as of June 2021 – when Community Rehabilitation Company (CRC) contracts end – will, therefore, look quite different, as our focus will be on the smooth transition of services. We provide an overview in Chapter 2 of what services will be in place as of June 2021 ('Day 1') and key milestones post Day 1 to get us to our target operating model.

In accordance with the HMPPS Business Strategy principle of an open, learning culture, we will need flexibility to update this target operating model to be able to apply lessons learned from how it is working in practice. The experience of the COVID-19 pandemic has also highlighted that events or wider changes outside our direct control may impact on how our probation system operates. We therefore expect that there will be further iterations of this target operating model following the transition to the new model.

We have used language intended to resonate with stakeholders and best reflect the intentions behind the new model and the benefits that we are seeking to achieve. In describing the new probation system, this document will, therefore, and as far as possible, use:

• 'Probation Practitioner' to denote the formerly-used terms 'Offender Manager'/'Responsible Officer' and 'Officer.'

• 'Sentence Management' to denote the formerly-used term 'Offender Management.'

Learning from the more progressive approach CRCs have taken, we will also move away from the term 'offender' in those contexts where it is an unhelpful label, instead referring in this document to supervised individuals or individuals.

Exceptions to this approach will be either to denote a specific Criminal Justice Context (such as Responsible Officer when referring to key legislation requirements) or when referring to parallel programme features, such as Offender Management in Custody.

*Voting age*

Published Thursday, 19 November, 2020

Under current legislation, a person must be 18 or over to vote in elections to the UK Parliament. The voting age for devolved and local election in Scotland and Wales has been lowered to 16. This Note gives details of calls for a change in the law to reduce the voting age to 16 in recent years.

There are two distinct franchises, the Parliamentary franchise and the local government franchise. There are also separate electoral registers for each franchise but in practice they are maintained, as far as is practicable, as a single register.

There is a graphic that explains the above and which you can view on the Research tab of The Prison Oracle - tinyurl.com/2cjfe6yd

**UK Parliamentary elections**

The voting age for UK Parliamentary elections remains at 18 for the whole of the UK and changes to the Parliamentary franchise are a reserved matter for the UK Parliament. The current Government is opposed to lower the voting age for Parliamentary elections.

**Local and devolved elections**

*England*

The voting age for local elections in England, including mayoral and police and crime commissioner elections, is 18. The UK Government has no plans to lower the voting age for local elections in England.

*Scotland*

Scotland has lowered the voting age to 16 for local and devolved elections. This followed the extension of the vote to 16- and 17-year olds to allow them to take part in the 2014 referendum on Scottish independence. The law was subsequently changed in Scotland to lower the voting age to 16. This applies to elections to the Scottish Parliament and local government elections in Scotland.

*Wales*

The Wales Act 2017 gave the National Assembly for Wales and the Welsh Government legislative competence for the administration of Assembly and local government elections in Wales, including the franchise for those elections.

The National Assembly for Wales passed the Senedd and Elections (Wales) Act 2020 at the end of 2019 and it received Royal Assent on 15 January 2020. It amended the law to allow 16- and 17-year olds to register to vote at Senedd Cymru/Welsh Parliament elections held on or after 5 April 2021. The next scheduled elections are May 2021. The Act also renames the National Assembly for Wales the Senedd Cymru or Welsh Parliament. The new names took effect on 6 May 2020.

A Bill to allow 16- and 17-year olds to vote in local government elections in Wales has now also been passed. The Local Government and Elections (Wales) Bill was introduced to the Senedd on 18 November 2019 and included provisions to lower the voting age for local government elections in Wales. The Bill passed its final stage in a year later, on 18 November 2020. The next scheduled local council elections in Wales are in May 2022.

Police and Crime Commissioner elections are a reserved matter and the voting age remains at 18 for PCC elections in Wales.

*Northern Ireland*

Elections in Northern Ireland are an excepted matter and remain the responsibility of UK ministers in Westminster. The voting age is 18 for all election in Northern Ireland.

**Party policy**

The Labour Party, the SNP, the Liberal Democrats, Plaid Cymru, the Green Party, the Alliance Party of Northern Ireland and Sinn Féin all support voting at 16 for all elections.

Historically the Conservative Party has been opposed to reducing the voting age and the Government currently has no plans to lower the voting age for local elections in England or for Parliamentary elections.

However, a number of senior Conservatives, such as Baroness Morgan of Cotes and Sir Peter Bottomley, now support votes at 16. In Scotland the reduction of the voting age for local government and Scottish Parliamentary elections was passed with the support of the Scottish Conservatives.

During the 2010-15 Parliament, the Political and Constitutional Reform Committee produced a report on voter engagement. The committee did not take a view one way or the other but the report, published in November 2014, called on the Coalition Government to lead a national discussion on reducing the voting age and to allow the House of Commons a free vote on the issue.

## Who can vote in UK elections?
Published Tuesday, 21 September, 2021

All democratic countries have rules about who has the right to vote, known as the franchise, in their elections. This is usually based on nationality, age and residence.

In recent years the rules on who can vote in which election in the UK have diverged depending which bit of the UK you live in.

### UK Parliamentary elections
Across the whole of the UK, to vote in a UK Parliamentary election a person must be must:
• be registered to vote in the constituency;
• be of voting age – 18 years old on polling day;
• be either a British, qualifying Commonwealth citizen or a citizen of the Republic of Ireland; and
• Not be subject to any legal incapacity to vote – Peers in the House of Lords, prisoners serving a prison sentence or having been convicted of committing certain electoral crimes.

### Local elections in England and Northern Ireland
For local elections in England and Northern Ireland the rules are the same as they are for UK Parliamentary elections with two main exceptions. Peers in the House of Lords and EU citizens resident in the UK may also vote in local elections as long as they meet the age and residency requirements.

### Local and devolved elections in Scotland and Wales
In Scotland and Wales, you must be registered to vote in the area but there are now different rules on nationality and age, and the ban on some prisoners voting has been removed.

In Scotland, the main differences for local and Scottish Parliament elections are:
• Registered 16- and 17-year olds can vote;
• All legally resident foreign nationals can also register to vote (not just EU nationals);
• Convicted prisoners who are detained and serving a sentence of 12 months or less may now register to vote in local and Scottish Parliamentary elections.

In Wales the franchise has been changed for Welsh Parliament/Senedd Cymru and local elections:
• Registered 16- and 17-year olds can vote;
• All legally resident foreign nationals can also register to vote (not just EU nationals).

16- and 17-year olds and qualifying foreign nationals will only be able to vote in the next scheduled local elections on 5 May 2022 and not in by-elections held before May 2022.

These changes do not cover police and crime commissioner elections in Wales as these elections are reserved. Voting age will remain at 18 for PCC elections in Wales and only registered British, qualifying Commonwealth and Irish citizens will be able to vote.

All convicted prisoners serving a prison term are still prohibited from voting in Senedd Cymru and Welsh local elections.

### Non-British Citizens
The right of some non-British residents, namely Commonwealth and Irish citizens, to vote in UK elections is a result of historic ties with the UK.

Citizens of the Republic of Ireland who are resident in the UK are eligible to register for, and vote in, all elections in the UK.

Qualifying Commonwealth citizens who are resident in the UK are eligible to register for, and vote in, all elections in the UK.

A qualifying Commonwealth citizen is someone who is resident in the UK and who has leave to remain in the UK or does not require leave to remain. Electoral registration officers can check the immigration status of applicants from a Commonwealth nation.

EU national citizens legally resident in the UK may currently register to vote in all elections that use the local government franchise. However, the Government has recently proposed changes to legislation as a result of the UK's exit from the EU.

Provisions included in the Elections Bill 2021-22 would restrict voting rights for EU citizens living in England and Northern Ireland who entered the UK after the end of the Implementation Period, 31 December 2020, to those from countries where a bilateral agreement has been agreed between the UK and individual member states. So far this covers Spain, Portugal, Poland and Luxembourg.

EU citizens who were living in the UK prior to the end of the Implementation Period will maintain their local voting and candidacy rights in England and Northern Ireland, provided they retain lawful immigration status.

EU citizens living in Scotland and Wales will retain their existing voting rights as all legally resident foreign nationals can register to vote for local and devolved elections.

## Why is police bail being reviewed again?
Published Monday, 06 January, 2020

On the day before Parliament dissolved to hold the general election (5 November), the

Government announced a review of police bail legislation. This review comes only a few years after the last reform of police bail (in 2017) and has the potential to overhaul how suspects are released from police custody again. So why is police bail being reviewed again?

This Insight describes what police bail is, explains why the review into police bail legislation has been announced and considers arguments for the current legislation being amended.

### What is police bail?

Police bail, officially known as 'pre-charge bail', is used when police have arrested a suspect but do not have enough evidence to charge them with a crime. If it is deemed necessary and proportionate, the police can release the suspect on 'pre-charge bail' whilst they continue their investigation.

When on bail suspects are required to report to the police when asked. Those on bail may also be subject to specific conditions about where they can go and who they can associate with. These rules help the police protect victims and witnesses, preserve evidence and mitigate the risk of suspects committing crime.

### How was police bail reformed in 2017?

Provisions in the Policing and Crime Act 2017 overhauled police bail by introducing strict rules about when and for how long it can be used.

Before the 2017 Act, if police wanted to continue an investigation against a suspect they could no longer detain without charge, they essentially had to release them with bail. Now there is a presumption against the use of police bail in such circumstances. As set out in official police guidance, if further time is needed to investigate a suspect the police should now release them without bail "in almost all cases."

Under the 2017 Act, police bail can only be justified if an Inspector deems it "necessary and proportionate." The 2017 Act did not define what "necessary and proportionate" means but the intention was for the bar to be quite high. Police guidance lists protecting "national security" or the "economic well-being of the UK" as possible reasons bail might be "necessary".

The 2017 Act limited the use of bail to an initial 28 days with extensions up to three months requiring authorisation from a senior officer. Any extension beyond three months now needs permission from the courts. Police guidance advises officers to make a clear investigative plan to ensure police bail is used for "the minimum period required."

The police should now release most suspects they need more time to investigate with a new status: released 'under investigation' or RUI for short. The police have no powers to require RUI suspects to

report to them, no powers to place conditions on them and no time limits within which to complete their investigation against them.

### Why was police bail reformed?

The 2017 police bail reforms came after a period of turmoil for police custody officers. In 2011 the High Court unexpectedly ruled that time spent on bail counted towards a suspect's detention without charge. Assuming they have permission from the courts, the police can legally detain a suspect without charge for a maximum of four days. By establishing that bail counted towards this time limit, the High Court effectively imposed a four-day deadline on investigations against arrested suspects. Those who couldn't be charged within the time limit would have to be released. The police would only be able to re-arrest them if they found new evidence.

The 2011 ruling cast doubt on the status of thousands of people on bail at the time. In response, the Coalition Government introduced emergency legislation to restore the police's powers to bail suspects for longer than four days. But some serious concerns with police bail had been highlighted. It became clear that many suspects were being kept on police bail for long periods of time. This was concerning for two reasons:

• It was detrimental to suspects' civil liberties. Suspects could have stringent conditions placed on their lives for long periods without being charged.

• It was encouraging lethargic justice. Both suspects and victims could be waiting months, possibly years, for a case to be resolved following an arrest.

By 2015 the now Conservative Government was proposing reforms to police bail to create "speedier justice" and a "fairer system." These proposals would eventually be incorporated into the Policing and Crime Act 2017.

### What has prompted the new review?

Since the 2017 reforms, stakeholders throughout the criminal justice system have questioned whether they are having unintended consequences. Her Majesty's Inspectorate of Constabulary, Fire and Rescue Services (HMICFRS) raised concerns that without the use of police bail conditions, vulnerable victims (particularly victims of domestic abuse) are not being protected properly. Practitioners from Women's Aid told HMICFRS that victims of domestic abuse are being forced into precarious housing because police bail conditions are not being used to prevent their alleged abuser from returning to their home. In response the National Police Chiefs Council issued interim guidance to police forces "reinforcing pre-charge bail as a legitimate tool" when investigating domestic abuse cases.

Lawyers are concerned that, just as under the old police bail regime, suspects are being left with uncertainty for long periods of time. The London Criminal Courts Solicitors' Association reported that in a sample of 109 RUI cases, more than 69 had been ongoing for between 18 months and two years.

However, there is a lack of quality evidence about the impact of the 2017 reforms. Police forces are not yet required to report data on when and why they used RUI or pre-charge bail. We simply don't know how many suspects have been released using these powers, what they were arrested for and for how long they have remained under investigation.

To gather better evidence HMICFRS has committed to conduct a thematic inspection of RUI and pre-charge bail. It is also working with police forces and the Home Office to establish how reliable data can be collected on RUI and pre-charge bail.

### Is further legislation needed?

Some have already argued that the legislation needs reforming again.

The Law Society say the police should be required to explain to suspects who have been 'under investigation' for more than four months why there is a delay in their case.

The Joint Committee on the Draft Domestic Abuse Bill (which would become the Domestic Abuse Bill 2017-19) recommended legislation create a presumption that suspects in domestic abuse cases are released from custody on pre-charge bail, unless it is clearly not necessary for the protection of the victim.

### What next?

The Government announcement in November did not say when the review into police bail will officially launch. Nor did it say whether the review is intended to propose legislation. For now, we wait for further announcements from the Home Office.

*Further reading*

Police detention powers, House of Commons Library.

*Women in prisons – a select bibliography*
4 July 2011

### 1 Official sources

HM Prison Service webpage, Female Prisoners

Ministry of Justice, Adult re-convictions: results from the 2009 cohort England and Wales, March 2011 Ministry of Justice statistics bulletin March 2011

Ministry of Justice, Breaking the Cycle: Effective Punishment, Rehabilitation and Sentencing of Offenders, December 2010

Prison Service Order 4801, The Management of Mother and Baby Units, Forth Edition, last updated April 2010

Ministry of Justice, A Report on the Government's Strategy for Diverting Women Away from Crime, December 2009

Ministry of Justice, Delivering the Government Response to the Corston Report: A Progress Report on Meeting the Needs of Women with Particular Vulnerabilities in the Criminal Justice System, December 2008

Ministry of Justice, Women and the criminal justice system, January 2010

Ministry of Justice, National Service Framework for Women Offenders, May 2008

HM Prison Service, Women prisoners, Prison Service Order 4800, last updated April 2008

Home Office, A report by Baroness Jean Corston of a review of women with particular vulnerabilities in the criminal justice system [The Corston Report] March 2007

### 2 Parliamentary material

All Party Parliamentary Group on Women in the Penal System (chaired by Baroness Corston), Women in the penal system: Second report on women with particular vulnerabilities in the criminal justice system, 2011

All Party Parliamentary Group on Women in the Penal System (chaired by Baroness Corston), Response to the Government's green paper 'Breaking the cycle: effective punishment, rehabilitation and sentencing of offenders', February 2011

### 3 Reports by charities and NGOs

Prison Reform Trust, Reforming Women's Justice: Final report of the Women's Justice Taskforce, 2011

Prison Reform Trust, Bromley Briefings: Prison Factfile, July 2010

Fawcett Society, Engendering Justice – from Policy to Practice: Final report of the Commission on Women and the Criminal Justice System, May 2009

Sanfilippo, Lisa, Unlocking Value: How we all benefit from investing in alternatives to prison for women offenders, New Economics Foundation, November 2008

National Association for the Care and Resettlement of Offenders (NACRO), Policy briefing: Criminal justice liaison and diversion schemes: A focus on women offenders, September 2008

Rutherford, Max, The Corston Report and the government's response: The implications for women prisoners with mental health problems,

Sainsbury Centre for Mental Health, January 2008

Gelsthorpe, L et al, Provision for women offenders in the community, Fawcett Society, July 2007

Howard League for Penal Reform, Prison Information Bulletin 2: Women and girls in the penal system, August 2006

Plugge, Emma et al, The Health of Women in Prison Study, University of Oxford, 2006

NACRO, Policy report: Women who challenge - Women offenders and mental health issues, January 2005

NACRO Policy report: Women beyond bars - A positive agenda for women prisoners' resettlement, January 2001

Wedderburn, Dorothy. Justice for women the need for reform: the report of the committee on women's imprisonment, Prison Reform Trust 2000

**4 Periodical articles**

Trammell, R, 'Relational Violence in Women's Prison: How Women Describe Interpersonal Violence and Gender', Women & Criminal Justice, Volume 19, Issue 4, 2009, pp 267 – 285

Worrall, A and Gelsthorpe, L, "What works' with women offenders: The past 30 years', Probation Journal, Vol 56(4), 2009, pp 329-345

Player, E, 'Remanding Women in Custody: Concerns for Human Rights', The Modern Law Review, Volume 70, Number 3 (May 2007), pp. 402-426 (full text Ebsco)

**5 Books**

Carlen, P, A Criminological Imagination: Essays on Justice, Punishment, Discourse, Ashgate, 2010

Sandler, M and Coles, D, Dying on the Inside: Examining Women's Deaths in Prison, Inquest, 2008

Carlen, P. and Worrall, A, Analysing Women's Imprisonment, Willan Publishing, 2004,

*Worker exploitation in UK clothing supply chains*
Published Wednesday, 08 July, 2020

This Insight discusses exploitation in UK garment factories, how workers' rights are enforced, and the calls to make companies responsible for rights violations in their supply chains.

On Saturday (4 July), the Government imposed a local lockdown in Leicester following a significant rise in the number of Covid-19 cases in the area. Campaign groups argued that poor working conditions in garment factories contributed to the spread of the virus.

This has re-ignited a debate about worker exploitation in the garment sector. According to the Sunday Times, the Government has asked the National Crime Agency to investigate for modern slavery in certain Leicester garment factories. However, commentators argue such exploitation was revealed over three years ago

and have criticised the Government for failing to take up reforms.

This Insight discusses exploitation in UK garment factories, how workers' rights are enforced, and the calls to make companies responsible for rights violations in their supply chains.

**Exploitation in garment factories**

Worker exploitation in clothing supply chains is not a new issue. A global response was triggered however in 2013, when the collapse of the Rana Plaza garment factory in Bangladesh, that made clothes for brands like Primark, killed over 1,100 workers.

Problems in UK garment factories came to public attention more recently. In 2019, the Environmental Audit Committee found that many brands were moving production from Asia back to the UK, especially to Leicester. Earlier investigations by Channel 4 and Financial Times journalist Sarah O'Connor exposed exploitation in small Leicester factories. They found that many workers were being significantly underpaid, often as little as £3 or £4 an hour, and that working environments were often unsafe with a number of fire hazards.

The investigations showed that cost and time pressures placed on suppliers by leading brands were a major contributor to these exploitative working conditions. Campaign group Labour Behind the Label has shown that a large proportion of workers in Leicester garment factories were born outside of the UK and that many came from South Asia. They argued that a worker's limited English language skills or issues with their immigration status can make them particularly vulnerable to exploitation.

This problem is not confined to Leicester or to garment factories. The charity Focus on Labour Exploitation (FLEX) argues that exploitation occurs in various supply chain arrangements, including outsourcing, subcontracting and offshoring.

**How are employment rights enforced?**

In the UK, employment rights are normally enforced by individual workers bringing action against their employer in a court or tribunal. In 2018 the Trades Union Congress argued that many workers were unaware of their rights and lacked union representation. It also noted that the 'hostile environment' immigration policy deterred many migrant workers from bringing claims.

Some employment rights are enforced by the state. This includes the minimum wage, which is enforced by HMRC, and health and safety, which is enforced by the Health and Safety Executive. The Gangmaster and Labour Abuse Authority investigates cases of serious exploitation, including modern slavery.

There are limitations here too. In the 2018/19 Labour Market Enforcement Strategy, the Director of Labour Market Enforcement (DLME) found that state enforcement bodies lacked resources, couldn't always impose sufficient penalties and didn't work together enough.

In the December 2019 Queen's Speech the Government committed to set up a single enforcement body for employment rights.

## What responsibility should companies have for their supply chains?

Workers in the UK can normally only bring claims against their direct employer. Groups like FLEX have argued this means companies can often avoid responsibility for conditions in their suppliers' factories, even if they are contributing to it by insisting on extremely low costs.

Under the Modern Slavery Act 2015, companies with a turnover of more than £36 million must publish an annual statement on transparency in its supply chains. This can include information about its modern slavery policies and due diligence processes. However, this only applies to modern slavery, which includes slavery, forced labour and human trafficking but not to other forms of exploitation like underpayment. A Government-commissioned independent review found that publication of these statements is not monitored and there are no penalties for not doing so.

In the 2018/19 Labour Market Enforcement Strategy the DLME said UK employment law was failing to keep up with increasing use of supply chains. This was contrasted with countries like Germany and Italy where companies at the head of a supply chain can be jointly liable for workers' rights violations. The DLME rejected the argument for joint liability but proposed a model of joint responsibility. Under this proposal, companies at the head of a supply chain would be notified about breaches by suppliers and would be publicly named if they failed to rectify it. Only the direct employer would face sanctions. The DLME also proposed a 'hot goods' model, which exists in the USA, where products can be temporarily embargoed if workers' rights were violated in their production.

The Government's response agreed that companies should take responsibility for exploitation in their supply chains but suggested enforcement bodies should work with companies privately. It also said it would consider 'hot goods' rules. The Government sought views on these issues in its consultation on the single enforcement body.

### Other models for supply chain liability

There have been a number of other recent proposals for protecting workers' rights in supply chains.

FLEX has called for a worker-driven social responsibility model. In this, companies enter binding contracts with workers' organisations to only source products from suppliers that respect employment rights.

In a recent book Criminality at Work, law professors Alan Bogg and Paul Davies highlight an Australian model of 'accessory liability' where companies can face penalties if they cause or influence a breach of employment rights by a supplier.

Sandhya Drew, a barrister and law lecturer, noted on the Oxford Human Rights Hub blog that French law requires companies to be transparent about any human rights violations in their supply chains. It also requires companies to publish detailed plans for how they will address such issues.

*Further Reading*

Insecure work: the Taylor Review and the Good Work Plan, House of Commons Library.

Fixing Fashion: Clothing consumption and sustainability, Environmental Audit Committee.

Dark factories: labour exploitation in Britain's garment industry (free to read), Financial Times.

Worker-driven social responsibility: Exploring a new model for tackling labour abuse in supply chains, Focus on Labour Exploitation (FLEX).

### *Young offenders: What next?*
23 October 2013

The problem of youth crime, and how best to respond to it, has attracted political attention for decades. More than 30 years ago, for example, the 1979 Conservative party manifesto promised to make more use of attendance centres for "hooligans" and to give a "short, sharp shock" to young offenders.

The Labour Government introduced wide-ranging reforms to youth justice, intended to deal with the perceived inefficiency and ineffectiveness of the old system. These included the creation of the Youth Justice Board and a system of local, multi-disciplinary Youth Offending Teams. Evaluations of these reforms identified improvements, but there were also criticisms, with some calling for more prevention work (particularly through other services such as local authority children's services) and less criminalisation of young people.

The Coalition document, published in May 2010, announced a review of sentencing and the consultation (green) paper on punishment and rehabilitation, published in December 2010, promised to "break the cycle" of reoffending. In

February 2013, the Ministry of Justice published a further consultation (green) paper Transforming Youth Custody: Putting education at the heart of detention, which put forward proposals based around the concept of Secure Colleges. That consultation closed at the end of April 2013 and the Lord Chancellor and Secretary of State for Justice, Chris Grayling, has recently said that an announcement on the Government's plans for rehabilitating young offenders will be made "in the very near future".

### Introduction

The perceived problem of youth crime, and how best to respond to that problem, has attracted political attention for very many years. More than 30 years ago, for example, the 1979 Conservative party manifesto promised to make more use of attendance centres for "hooligans" and to give a "short, sharp shock" to young offenders.

In the ensuing decades, the issues surrounding crime in general and youth crime in particular have received no less attention from legislators and the media. It has been argued, too, that increased crime levels in the 1980s and high profile cases — such as the murder of James Bulger in 1993 — fuelled political competition over sentencing. In 1993, Tony Blair promised the Labour party conference that he would be "tough on crime and tough on the causes of crime", while Michael Howard told the Conservative party conference that "prison works".

Certainly, there has been a historically large number of criminal justice acts since 1994 and in this time, the prison population has risen sharply; the Ministry of Justice's most recent population briefing puts the prison population at 85,828.[1] The growth of the prison population and some of the ensuing questions about reoffending and rehabilitation are discussed in the Library Research Paper 12/71 Reducing reoffending: The "what works" debate.[2]

The criminologist Lorraine Gelsthorpe offers an account of the changes in youth justice in England and Wales since the Children and Young Persons Act 1969. She points to the complex relationship between law, politics and civil society:

Conceptions of offenders and changes in legislation reflect social and political debates and struggles and are inextricably bound up with changes occurring in the social and political order, and with political debates within which that social order (re)produces itself. (...) Thus debates about 'youth crime' or 'juvenile justice' are rooted in what Antonio Gramsci would call 'civil society' ... rather than in the political realm, but the underlying message undoubtedly remains political.[3]

1 Including those in NOMS-operated immigration removal centres. Population and capacity briefing – 18 October 2013, from Prison Population Figures: 2013 on gov.uk website
2 RP12/71, 22 November 2012
3 Lorraine Gelsthorpe "Recent changes in youth justice policy in England and Wales" in Ivo Weijers and Antony Duff (eds) Punishing juveniles: principles and critique, 2002: page 45

### Youth Custody
31 January 2020

**Summary**

In England and Wales children (those aged under 18) remanded to custody or sentenced to custody are placed in one of three types of institution:
• a Young Offenders Institution (YOI);
• a Secure Training Centre (STC) or
• a Secure Children's Home (SCH).

In 2018/19, 73% of those in youth custody were placed in a YOI, 17% in an STC and 10% in a SCH. There was an average of 859 under-18-year olds in youth custody at the end of any given month. Just over a quarter of the youth custody population in 2018 was being held on remand. The remainder had been sentenced to custody.

Concerns have been raised about the current provision of youth custody. These include:
• a lack of safety;
• the use of restraint and force including the use of pain inducing techniques; • the segregation of children away from others;
• a lack of purposeful activity and time out of cells;
• the disproportionate number of BAME children in custody; and
• the distance away from home that children are sometimes held.

The Government initiated a review of youth justice in 2016. Charlie Taylor's review included proposals for the reform of youth custody by the introduction of secure schools. The Government accepted this proposal and started implementation with the creation of the first secure school on the site of the current Medway STC. Interested groups have raised concerns about the model of secure schools and about the use of the Medway site.

### Youth Custody

Children remanded or sentenced to custody are placed in a Young Offenders Institution, a Secure Training Centre or a Secure Children's Home. Concerns have been raised about the current provision of youth custody, The Government has accepted proposals to introduce secure schools. (27th April 2022)

# Index

A2DE, 1260

Access to Justice, 49, 1010, 1260, 1456

Accommodation, 14-15, 30, 37, 41, 51, 78, 93, 95, 122, 130, 135, 160, 215, 225, 229, 285, 290, 355, 441, 474, 485, 500-501, 510, 540, 545, 586, 607, 686, 751-752, 760, 856, 859, 862, 970-971, 979-982, 985-986, 1012-1013, 1016-1017, 1044, 1259-1260, 1266, 1287, 1291, 1299-1301, 1307, 1370, 1506-1507

Adam Connolly, 31, 328

Adjudications, 59, 87, 330, 739, 804, 916, 922, 951, 953, 957, 1014, 1016, 1032, 1036, 1073, 1114, 1138, 1260, 1369

Adult female prisons, 5, 12

Adult male prisons, 5, 11, 1280

After Care, 297, 446, 1015

Alan Scott, 30, 32

Alcohol Dependence Treatment Programme (ADTP), 764

Ali Barker, 32, 671

Alison Clarke, 33, 503, 555, 597, 611

Alli Black, 31, 392

Allocation, 133, 177, 267, 400, 480-481, 682-683, 901, 915, 929, 939, 942, 988, 1015, 1018, 1031, 1109, 1263, 1278

Altcourse, 13, 28, 31-32, 67-70, 72-74, 781, 917, 1167-1169, 1214

Amanda Corrigan, 31, 158

Amanda Hughes, 31, 119

Amy Dixon, 31, 219, 238

Amy Frost, 32, 718

Amy Rees, 30, 1002

Andrea Coomber, 5, 45-47

Andy Davy, 31, 244

Andy Hudson, 31, 196

Andy Lattimore, 27, 33, 148, 251, 314, 376, 586, 702

Andy Lund, 31, 303

Andy Sleight, 31, 555

Angelina Nicolaou, 1007

Anne Owers, 474, 1003

Annual Staff Equalities Report, 1303, 1330-1344

Ashfield, 13, 29, 31-32, 62, 74-77, 781, 1214

Askham Grange, 12, 27-28, 31, 33, 78-80, 781, 905, 917, 1214

Assaults, 156, 254, 446, 500, 547, 557, 719, 814-816, 1444, 1489-1490, 1494

Assisted Prison Visits Scheme, 783, 788

Association, 52-53, 85, 105, 774, 816, 819, 831, 834, 840, 846, 920, 1006, 1016, 1115, 1166, 1185, 1204, 1206, 1208, 1212, 1260, 1291, 1346, 1378, 1380, 1385, 1387, 1390, 1424, 1437, 1463-1464, 1508, 1510, 1521

Awards, 6, 49, 1283, 1469

Aylesbury, 18, 20, 29, 31, 33, 80-86, 88, 781, 918, 1213, 1228

Babafemi Dada, 31, 307

Bail, 51, 53, 229, 510, 607, 760-761, 859, 862, 1013, 1016-1017, 1044, 1114, 1143, 1218-1219, 1259-1260, 1266, 1370, 1457, 1506-1507

Band 2, 1344-1347, 1349

Band 3, 911, 1086, 1219, 1321, 1324, 1335-1336, 1343-1349

Band 4, 846, 1219, 1344, 1347

Band 5, 1219, 1321

Band 6, 912

Band 7, 806, 1321, 1344, 1347

Band 8, 912, 971, 976, 983, 1321-1322

Band 9, 971, 976-977, 983

Band 11, 971, 978, 983, 1346

Basic Custody Screening Tool, 6, 732, 1287

Becoming New Me + (BNM+), 765

Bedford, 18, 27, 29, 31-32, 45, 91-93, 95-96, 98, 781, 917, 1171

Belmarsh, 18, 28, 31, 33, 100-103, 105-109, 381, 781, 901, 917, 1214

Berwyn, 18, 27-29, 31, 109-113, 781, 1214

Birmingham, 6, 12, 18, 27, 29, 31, 33, 44, 113-116, 118, 515, 766, 770, 773, 781, 788, 1001, 1201, 1214, 1227

Bob Neill MP, 906

Bonuses, 1036, 1336

Boris Johnson, 828, 1182, 1464

Brandon Lewis, 1003

Breaking Free Online:, 765

Breaking Free: Health and Justice Package (Custody), 765

Brian Ward, 31, 624

Brinsford, 27, 29, 31, 33, 119-120, 123-125, 514, 781, 917, 1214, 1284

Bristol, 18, 27, 29, 31-32, 62, 74-75, 107, 125-130, 227, 241, 781, 917, 1214, 1382-1383, 1412

Brixton, 16, 27-28, 31, 33, 130-134, 136-138, 781, 1205, 1214

Bronzefield, 13, 29, 31-32, 138-142, 144, 781, 905, 917, 1114, 1214, 1285

Buckley Hall, 27-28, 31-32, 145-148, 781, 1276, 1478

Building Better Relationships (BBR), 763, 765

Building Skills for Recovery (BSR), 764-765

Bullingdon, 13, 27, 29, 31, 33, 148-151, 153, 781, 917, 1042, 1214

Bure, 27, 29, 31-32, 154-157, 781, 812, 1062

Carats, 1017

Cardiff, 18, 29, 31, 33, 62, 158-161, 624, 781, 917, 1214, 1284, 1375

Care Quality Commission, 545, 826, 831, 1001, 1200

Carl Hardwick, 31, 227

Caroline Vine, 32, 691

Case Transfer, 1259, 1261

Categorisation, 5, 49, 142, 172, 234, 244, 450, 455, 463, 529, 568, 659, 731, 910, 915, 987-1000, 1015, 1017-1019, 1038, 1092, 1098, 1260, 1277-1278, 1369, 1377-1378

Category A Prisoners, 1017-1018

Category B, 90, 113, 244, 259, 314, 363, 413, 423, 465-467, 549, 623, 657, 710, 797, 966, 989, 991, 993-994, 998, 1017, 1019-1020, 1023, 1074

Category C, 9, 20, 24, 145, 161, 191, 251, 279-280, 292, 376, 428, 455, 466, 472, 492, 797, 966, 988, 990-991, 993-995, 998, 1018, 1023

Category D, 20, 24, 256, 312, 322, 328, 559, 574-575, 966, 987, 989-998, 1016-1017, 1378

Cathy Robinson, 27

Cell Sharing Risk Assessment, 736, 1021

Cellular Confinement, 986

Challenge to Change (C2C), 765

Channings Wood, 13, 27, 29, 31-32, 161-165, 781, 1214, 1284

Charities, 1413-1414

Charlie Taylor, 5, 14, 47, 49, 68, 92, 96, 101-102, 114, 132, 140, 155, 166, 183, 198, 239, 245, 252-253, 261, 270, 275, 282, 287, 316, 330, 342, 352, 365, 369, 373, 378, 410, 420, 429, 441, 445, 451, 461, 478, 487, 508, 522, 532, 539, 557, 565, 569, 580, 612, 616, 630, 637, 641, 645, 680, 703, 712, 719, 1002, 1007, 1168, 1170, 1189, 1191, 1196, 1201, 1524

Chelmsford, 19, 27, 29, 31-32, 165-174, 781, 917, 1214

Chief Inspector of Prisons, 6, 8, 13-14, 41, 47, 49, 68, 76, 79, 83, 92, 96, 101, 111, 114-116, 127-128, 132, 137, 140, 147, 150, 155, 159, 163, 166, 193, 207, 215, 220, 229, 239, 242, 245, 252, 261, 267, 270, 275, 279, 282, 287, 298, 301, 305, 308, 316, 319, 324, 330, 338, 342, 348, 352, 356, 361,

365-366, 369, 373, 378, 382, 387-388, 393, 397, 400, 406, 410, 420, 425, 429, 434, 438, 441, 445, 451, 457, 469, 474, 478, 485, 487, 494, 499, 505, 508, 517-518, 522, 527, 532, 534, 539, 542, 547, 551, 557, 565, 569, 576, 580, 587, 590, 594, 598, 602, 605, 612, 625, 637, 641, 645, 653, 655, 669, 677, 680, 687, 692, 697, 703, 712, 719, 728, 1002, 1022, 1168-1170, 1180, 1189, 1191-1192, 1196, 1201, 1386, 1470-1471, 1508

Child Protection, 736, 924, 1110

Civil Partnerships, 5, 49, 731, 963-968, 1076

Civil Prisoners, 748, 790, 952, 958, 987

Civil Proceedings, 1023

Classification, 1008-1009, 1024, 1258

Close Supervision Centres, 959, 1012, 1025

Closed Conditions, 915

Coldingley, 27, 29, 31, 33, 44, 174-181, 781, 1214

Colin Hussey, 31, 486

Community Rehabilitation Companies, 1276

Compassionate Grounds, 1026, 1040, 1080, 1131, 1259, 1264

Complaints, 5, 48, 62, 84, 103, 208, 211, 273-274, 376, 586-587, 638, 641, 662, 731, 746-747, 753, 770-780, 818, 842-843, 911, 974, 986, 997, 1017, 1026, 1048, 1111-1112, 1122, 1259, 1275, 1372, 1422, 1425

Complaints Policy Framework, 770, 911, 974, 997, 1017, 1026, 1111-1112, 1275

Complaints Procedure, 1122

Computers, 1060

Confinement, 488, 970-971, 979-981, 986, 1010, 1022, 1082, 1131

Confiscation Orders, 864

Cookham Wood, 29, 31, 33, 181-191, 781, 918, 923, 1195

Coronavirus, 433, 435, 658, 1008-1010, 1028, 1047, 1062, 1120, 1323, 1369, 1376, 1382-1386, 1389-1390, 1410, 1426-1427, 1445-1446, 1498, 1513

Counter Corruption and Reporting Wrongdoing, 1028, 1115, 1259

COVAID-GS, 765

COVAID-GSW, 765

Covid, 8, 13, 59, 68-69, 72, 76-77, 79-81, 88-89, 91, 96-98, 101-102, 106-107, 109, 111-118, 120-121, 123-124, 126, 128-129, 136-137, 139-144, 147-161, 163-164, 166-168, 170-171, 173-175, 179-184, 187-190, 192-199, 202-205, 207, 209-212, 215-216, 218-221, 223-227, 229-230, 233-234, 236, 238-240, 242-243, 245, 249-250, 252-255, 258-260, 262-264, 268-271, 274-277, 281, 283-286, 288-289, 291-296, 299-303, 305-307, 309-317, 320-322, 327-331, 333-338, 340, 342-344, 348-354, 356-357, 359, 361-363, 365-367, 369-379, 382, 384-385, 393-394, 397-398, 400-403, 406-407, 409-410, 412, 417-419, 422-423, 425-432, 437, 439-441, 443-444, 446-451, 453-454, 457-458, 460-462, 465-467, 469-471, 474, 477, 479, 482-483, 485-496, 499-500, 502, 505-506, 508, 512-515, 519, 527-530, 535-536, 538, 541, 550-558, 561-562, 564-567, 569-570, 573-574, 577-585, 587-588, 590-591, 595-597, 599-600, 602-603, 605, 608-609, 612, 614-616, 619-621, 623-625, 627-635, 637-642, 645-651, 653-654, 657-659, 662, 665-666, 669, 672, 674, 676, 678, 682, 687-694, 696-700, 704, 707-709, 712-717, 720-730, 739, 780, 798, 804, 821, 828-829, 1007, 1041, 1185, 1187, 1189, 1198-1201, 1204, 1215, 1219, 1231, 1284, 1286, 1345-1346, 1369, 1375, 1382, 1390, 1409, 1411-1414, 1443, 1459, 1481, 1489, 1514, 1522

Craig Smith, 31, 611

Criminal Cases Review Commission, 731, 759, 761, 766-770, 773, 1001, 1011, 1068, 1070, 1073, 1140-1142, 1157, 1162

Criminal Evidence, 789, 819, 1054, 1151, 1462, 1464, 1468

Criminal Records, 51, 1370

Crown Prosecution Service, 51, 777, 813, 820, 1001, 1054, 1076, 1200-1201, 1211, 1226, 1400, 1449, 1452-1453, 1494, 1496

Curfew, 52, 58-59, 820, 856, 869, 873, 879-880, 889, 891-892, 927, 931, 934, 948, 989, 998, 1017, 1028, 1034, 1041, 1043-1044, 1054, 1259-1260, 1263, 1266, 1270, 1389-1390, 1457, 1506-1507

Custodial Care, 49, 1303-1304

Damages Claims, 1022

Damian Evans, 31

Dan Cooper, 31, 550

Dangerous Inmates, 1030

Daniel Grütters, 1007-1008

Darren Finley, 31, 297

Dartmoor, 27, 29, 31-32, 43, 62, 191, 193-195, 781, 1214

Data Protection, 51, 780, 802, 952, 1030, 1098, 1103, 1107, 1263, 1268-1269, 1274-1275

Dave Nicholson, 32, 667

David Bamford, 31, 636

David Bourne, 32, 651

David Daddow, 31, 354

David Redhouse, 31, 376

Dawn Mauldon, 31, 455

Dean Gardiner, 31, 568

Deaths in Custody, 829, 1021, 1046, 1130, 1236, 1490

Declan Moore, 31, 496

Deerbolt, 27-28, 31, 33, 196-198, 202-205, 360, 781, 917, 1214

Democratic Therapeutic Community Model (DTC), 765

Deportation, 861, 928-932, 934, 1121, 1369, 1442-1443

Diabetes, 509, 512, 1031

Diane Lewis, 32

Disability, 5, 48-49, 51, 130, 731, 735, 737, 788, 840-841, 843, 935-938, 943, 1031, 1181, 1331

Disabled Prisoners, 936, 1031, 1074, 1127-1128

Discharge Grants, 5, 48, 731, 843-846

Discharge of Prisoners, 1113

Discipline, 574, 801, 805, 842, 916, 922, 946, 971, 1010, 1014, 1032, 1034-1035, 1045, 1073, 1217, 1260, 1312, 1331, 1339

Disclosure and Barring Service, 1002, 1484

Disruptive Prisoners, 1035

Diversity, 327, 367, 558, 587, 644, 1034, 1314

Dogs, 1035, 1259, 1274, 1345, 1348

Domestic abuse, 1263

Domestic Abuse Policy Framework, 1022, 1035, 1263

Dominic Raab, 1206-1207, 1209-1213, 1223, 1226-1230, 1349-1350

Doncaster, 6, 12-13, 19-22, 28, 31-32, 206-211, 322-323, 428, 468, 781, 918, 1171, 1214, 1285, 1383

Dougie Graham, 31, 386

Dovegate, 13, 27, 29, 31-32, 212-215, 217-218, 514, 781, 903, 1214

Downview, 27, 29, 31, 33, 219-220, 224-226, 243, 781, 905, 917, 1087, 1214, 1441

Drake Hall, 27, 29, 31, 33, 227-230, 781, 905, 917, 1127, 1214

Drugs, 5, 48, 110, 191, 342, 572, 666, 731, 797-801, 1017, 1027, 1135, 1222, 1295, 1318, 1369-1370, 1413, 1429-1432, 1460, 1471, 1484-1486, 1490, 1511

DSPD, 974

Durham, 19-20, 22, 27-28, 31, 33, 196-197, 199, 227, 231-234, 236-237, 297, 360-361, 444, 495, 781, 917, 1030, 1046, 1201, 1206, 1455, 1507

Earnings, 943, 945, 948-949, 1036, 1113

East Sutton Park, 12, 27, 29, 31, 33, 79, 238-240, 781, 905, 917

Eastwood Park, 19, 27, 29, 31, 33, 240-244, 781, 905, 917, 1214

Ed Cornmell, 32

Education, 7, 51-52, 55, 89, 104, 109, 129, 145, 151, 153, 171, 189, 222, 237, 272, 288, 290, 317, 322, 329, 344, 362, 376, 384-385, 421, 433, 436, 442, 444, 451-452, 479, 483, 488, 491, 493, 500, 514, 525, 543, 551, 556, 574, 586, 589, 597, 609, 613, 637, 642, 647, 650, 660, 726, 747, 753-754,

775, 785, 817, 819, 837, 856, 907, 920, 922, 927, 938, 940, 942-943, 950, 993, 1008, 1010, 1027, 1036-1037, 1068, 1080, 1087, 1098, 1106-1107, 1206, 1216, 1218, 1220, 1231, 1259, 1261, 1275, 1287, 1292, 1299-1301, 1405, 1410, 1412, 1448, 1487-1488, 1491-1492, 1496-1497, 1500

Elderly Prisoners, 5, 49, 731, 968-970

Electronic Monitoring, 873

Elmley, 13, 29, 31, 33, 244-251, 781, 918, 1214

Emergencies, 1009, 1108, 1406, 1410

Emily Martin, 31, 341

Emily Thomas, 31, 380

End of Custody Licence, 1369, 1432-1433

Enhanced behaviour monitoring, 855

Entry Level Training, 150, 1320

Equality, 5, 47-48, 51-52, 84, 104-105, 170, 184, 186, 192, 209, 221, 252, 271, 273, 287, 327, 359, 377, 389, 429, 442, 474, 479, 523, 534, 538, 542, 586, 614, 618, 644, 652, 681, 697, 731, 773-774, 782-783, 789, 817, 840-843, 852, 909, 938-939, 952, 986, 989, 1011, 1031, 1034, 1037-1038, 1086, 1090, 1112, 1116, 1260-1261, 1268, 1309, 1311, 1314, 1402, 1409, 1477, 1495-1496, 1500, 1505, 1513

Erlestoke, 14, 19, 27, 29, 31, 33, 251-259, 781, 1214, 1276

Escape, 725, 796, 803, 966, 989, 1038, 1092, 1309, 1312

Exeter, 19, 27, 29, 31-32, 191, 227, 259-265, 781, 918, 1201, 1214, 1285-1286

Extended Sentences, 991, 994

Featherstone, 18-19, 22, 27, 29, 31, 33, 119, 266-267, 269, 514, 781, 970, 1214

Feltham, 20, 27-28, 31, 33, 269-272, 274-279, 759, 781, 916, 918, 923, 1170-1171, 1175, 1180-1181, 1214

Feltham YOI, 916, 923

Finance Manual, 746, 753, 1015, 1017, 1036-1039, 1041-1042, 1060, 1072, 1106, 1112, 1116, 1131, 1259, 1265

Financial management, 51

Fire Safety, 1039

Five Wells, 6, 8-9, 13, 29, 31, 279-280, 312, 781, 1167-1168, 1170, 1207, 1215, 1470

Fixed Term Recall, 850, 869, 872, 878-880, 888, 891-892, 998, 1117

Food, 73, 106, 208, 403, 568, 681, 1008-1009, 1040, 1281, 1283, 1318, 1369, 1373-1374, 1441-1442, 1469

Ford, 20, 27, 29, 31, 33, 281-285, 781, 855, 938, 1214, 1370, 1508

Foreign Nationals, 5, 29, 731, 867-868, 927-935

Forest Bank, 13, 20, 28, 31-32, 285-290, 292, 312, 466, 781, 918, 1214

Fosse Way, 6, 8, 13, 32

Foston Hall, 27, 29, 31, 33, 293-295, 781, 905, 918, 1214, 1441

Frances Crook, 5, 44-45, 47, 1388-1390

Frankland, 27 28, 31, 33, 297-298, 781, 901, 904, 1035, 1037, 1069, 1075

Fraud, 53, 1003-1004, 1041, 1124, 1263, 1392-1393, 1395, 1397-1398, 1400, 1404

Full Sutton, 20, 28, 31, 33, 299-303, 781, 901, 1035, 1053, 1074, 1285-1286, 1425

Games Consoles, 954, 961

Gareth Sands, 31, 300

Garry Newnes, 31, 165

Garth, 27-28, 31, 33, 304-306, 781, 1214

Gartree, 20, 29, 31, 33, 307-314, 781, 903, 1023, 1116

Gary Monaghan, 27, 32, 91, 154, 433, 496, 670

Gary Price, 31, 593

Gavin O'Malley, 33

Gender, 5, 48, 731, 840-841, 908, 912, 914-915, 942, 1041, 1234, 1281, 1288, 1513, 1522

Generic Parole Process, 849, 875-878, 882-884, 886, 892, 896, 900, 929, 931, 993, 1080, 1100, 1116, 1131, 1259, 1264, 1272-1273

Generic Parole Process Policy Framework, 849, 877-878, 883-884, 886, 896, 900, 931, 1080, 1100, 1116, 1131, 1264, 1273

Gifts, 1041, 1044

Giles Mason, 33, 109, 158, 521, 525, 624, 644

Glen Parva, 6, 8, 13, 62, 918, 1416

Glossary of Terms, 5

Gordon Brockington, 5, 47, 49, 1167, 1170

Grace Cowell, 49, 1008

Graham Beck, 32, 725

Graham Spencer, 31, 281

Grendon, 20, 27, 29, 31, 33, 314-317, 586, 588, 781, 903, 1283, 1285-1286

Guys Marsh, 27, 29, 31-32, 318-320, 781, 1214

Hamish Arnott, 801, 817

Handcuffing, 830

Handling Sensitive Information, 1060

Hannah Lane, 31, 414

Hatfield, 20, 22, 27-28, 31, 33, 322-328, 468, 781, 855, 918, 1126, 1284

Haverigg, 20, 27-28, 31-32, 329-335, 781, 855, 1214

Head of Function, 1185, 1321

Health Services, 67, 395, 521

Healthy Identity Intervention (HII), 764-765

Healthy Sex Programme (HSP), 766

Heather Whitehead, 33

Helen Clayton-Hoar, 31, 91, 293

Helen Judge, 33, 322, 364, 372, 404, 428, 468, 676

Helga Swidenbank, 27, 30, 33, 182, 269, 277, 679, 686

Hewell, 20, 27, 29, 31, 33, 336-340, 759, 781, 1214

High Down, 27, 31, 33, 341-346, 1214

Highpoint, 13, 20, 27, 29, 31-32, 346-347, 349, 781

Hindley, 13, 27-28, 31-32, 350-354, 781, 918, 1071, 1214

HM Inspectorate of Prisons, 82, 166, 369-370, 407, 453, 503, 529, 567, 671, 776, 826, 897, 1002, 1180, 1189, 1388-1390, 1479, 1490

HM Prisons Inspectorate, 585, 731, 1001

HMPPS estate, 5, 9, 12

HMPPS Finance Manual, 746, 1015, 1017, 1036-1039, 1072, 1106, 1112, 1116, 1131, 1259, 1265

Hollesley Bay, 27, 29, 31-32, 354-359, 669-670, 781, 855, 918, 1214

Holme House, 21, 27-28, 31, 33, 360-361, 363, 781, 918, 1214

Home detention curfew, 93, 142, 172, 200, 222, 234, 256, 447, 510, 523, 571, 582, 607, 663, 682, 934, 1266, 1289

Home Visits, 1259, 1267

Homelessness, 859, 907, 910, 1015, 1044, 1259, 1267, 1489

Homelessness Reduction Act, 907, 910, 1044, 1259, 1267

Horizon, 764, 766, 903

Hospitality, 1041

Hull, 6, 21, 27-28, 31, 33, 364-367, 369-370, 781, 812, 918, 1071, 1184-1185, 1208, 1214

Human Resources, 52, 1331

Human Rights, 47, 52, 773-774, 776-778, 782, 789, 830, 843, 896, 898, 904, 931, 1011-1012, 1014, 1016, 1022, 1024-1025, 1029, 1032, 1034-1035, 1037-1038, 1041, 1045-1054, 1061-1062, 1064, 1068-1069, 1071, 1076-1079, 1085, 1102, 1104, 1106, 1110, 1119, 1125, 1128-1130, 1133, 1135-1136, 1138, 1149, 1152-1153, 1210-1211, 1225, 1312, 1377, 1402, 1417-1418, 1424, 1442-1443, 1472, 1474-1476, 1484, 1505, 1522-1523

Huntercombe, 9, 21, 27, 29, 31-33, 376-380, 472, 781, 784, 1026, 1214, 1323

Huw Sullivan, 31, 162

Hygiene, 1008-1009, 1054

Ian Bickers, 33, 130, 341, 380, 529, 659, 718

Ian Blakeman, 30-31, 529

Ian Walters, 31, 318

Ian West, 31, 589

Ian Whiteside, 31, 139
Identity Matters (IM), 764, 766
Immigration Removal Centres, 780, 813, 1237
Incense, 834, 836
Incentives, 5, 49, 245, 731, 739, 746-748, 753, 756-758, 842, 855, 916, 919, 922-923, 938, 943-944, 951-963, 1014, 1025, 1041, 1059, 1066, 1073, 1109, 1112-1116, 1137, 1259-1260, 1268, 1311, 1370, 1472-1473
Incentives & Earned Privileges, 1370, 1472
Incentives and Earned Privileges, 5, 731, 739, 756, 916, 922-923, 943, 1059, 1066, 1073, 1268, 1473
Incentives Policy Framework, 747, 757-758, 951, 1025, 1041, 1059, 1109, 1112-1113, 1115-1116, 1137, 1260, 1268
Incident Management, 1076, 1259, 1321-1322
Indeterminate Sentences, 5, 49, 731, 851, 896-905, 1276, 1369, 1446
Induction, 48, 83, 134, 136, 158, 175, 200, 232, 254, 261, 270, 307, 336, 364, 383, 433, 452, 550, 661, 681, 718, 732, 738, 755, 819, 832, 836, 908, 919, 924, 936, 939, 1112-1113, 1311
Information Book, 737-738
Information Requests, 1060, 1231, 1259, 1268
Information Security, 962, 1030, 1259, 1268
Information Security Policy Framework, 1030, 1268
Information Sharing, 924, 1060, 1259, 1269
Information Technology, 52, 1260
Inmates, 1010, 1030
Inspectorate of Prisons, 9, 52, 82, 99, 118, 156, 166, 174, 243, 262, 316, 369-370, 407, 415, 453, 503, 529, 549, 567, 649, 671, 724, 730, 776, 826, 897, 1002, 1180, 1189, 1196, 1272, 1379, 1388-1390, 1463-1464, 1468, 1470, 1479, 1490
Inspectorate of Probation, 164, 1002, 1204, 1381, 1504
Internet, 4, 52, 459, 796, 1060, 1092, 1123, 1266, 1369, 1411, 1435
Investigatory Powers, 1092, 1131, 1259, 1265-1266, 1516
IPP, 52, 56, 60, 148, 157, 180, 210, 216, 259, 306, 312, 320, 334-335, 340, 358-359, 402, 413, 423, 427, 432-433, 470-471, 501, 506, 566, 578, 584, 597, 658, 668, 679, 811, 849-851, 887, 897-898, 900, 905, 915, 933, 1004, 1016, 1047-1049, 1055-1056, 1084, 1097, 1104-1105, 1158, 1220-1223, 1271, 1446-1447, 1492
Isis, 27-28, 31, 33, 380-382, 384, 781, 918, 1214, 1284-1286
Isle of Wight, 27, 29, 31, 33, 48, 386-389, 781, 918, 1043, 1059
James Bourke, 32, 702
James Lucas, 33, 174, 244, 281, 414, 455, 568, 593
Janet Wallsgrove, 31, 521, 525, 1170
Jeannine Hendrick, 27, 32, 162, 191, 260, 318
Jennifer Willis, 31, 468
Jenny Louis, 31, 100
Jim Donaldson, 31, 408
Jo Farrar, 1387
John Hewitson, 31, 206
John Huntington, 31, 600
John Illingsworth, 27, 32, 328, 392, 398, 550, 725
Jonathan French, 31, 285
Judicial Review Procedure, 1074, 1103, 1123, 1127-1128, 1130
Julia Spence, 31, 78, 484
Juveniles, 1418, 1455
Kaizen, 766, 903
Karen Harrison, 6, 47, 49
Karen Head, 31, 472
Katie Price, 32, 659
Keith Attwood, 32, 679
Kirkham, 21, 27-28, 31-32, 391-395, 781, 855, 1023, 1064, 1214
Kirklevington, 21, 27-28, 31, 33, 360-362, 395-398, 781, 855, 918
Kirklevington Grange, 27-28, 33, 360-362, 395-398, 781, 855, 918
Lancaster Farms, 27-28, 31-32, 399-401, 781, 1214

Laura Sapwell, 31, 148
Laura Whitehurst, 31, 266
Law Commission, 1003, 1212, 1391, 1394-1396, 1398, 1400, 1421, 1440, 1484
Leeds, 21, 27-28, 31, 33, 47, 404-407, 686, 781, 1214, 1443
Legal Services, 1456
Leicester, 14, 21, 29, 31-32, 408-413, 781, 1522
Lewes, 21, 27, 29, 31, 33, 414-418, 781, 918, 1007, 1214, 1285-1286
Leyhill, 27, 29, 31-32, 77, 419, 421-423, 781, 855, 1214
Libraries, 433, 647, 754-755, 920, 1468
Licence Conditions, 1036-1037, 1051, 1068, 1107, 1114, 1119, 1197, 1259, 1263, 1267, 1270, 1273-1274, 1280
Lifers, 1018, 1046, 1055
Lincoln, 6, 21-22, 31-32, 47, 49, 412, 423-427, 472-473, 781, 918, 1184-1185, 1214
Lindholme, 21, 27, 31, 33, 323, 428-429, 431-432, 468, 781, 1066, 1214
Littlehey, 27, 29, 31-32, 432-436, 781, 1074, 1214, 1222
Liverpool, 18, 21, 27, 31-32, 67, 353, 436-439, 781, 1018, 1029, 1066, 1167-1168, 1214, 1285-1286, 1382-1383
Living as New Me, 764, 766
Long Lartin, 29, 31, 33, 440-444, 781, 1016, 1020, 1066, 1073
Low Newton, 27-28, 31, 33, 444-449, 781, 905, 918, 1214, 1441
Lowdham Grange, 13, 29, 31-32, 450, 452-455, 1214
Maidstone, 9, 19, 22, 29, 31-32, 455-459, 472, 781, 784, 1214, 1323
Manchester, 18, 20, 22-23, 25, 27-28, 31-33, 62, 145, 285-286, 288, 290-292, 303-304, 350, 353, 436, 459-463, 465-467, 563, 604, 640, 726, 781, 901, 918, 1002, 1023, 1132, 1201, 1221, 1375, 1382-1383, 1429, 1443, 1455, 1494
Manchester Prison, 20, 22, 460, 1132
MAPPA, 52, 86, 105, 134-135, 150, 156, 177, 185-186, 193, 209, 248, 256, 323, 327, 332, 368-369, 400, 429, 510-511, 524, 554, 633, 705, 848, 873, 890, 915, 967, 994, 996, 1030, 1088-1089, 1116, 1119, 1259, 1275, 1314-1315
Marcella Goligher, 31, 372
Margo Munro Kerr, 1007-1008
Maria Liddiard, 1007-1008
Mark Allen, 31, 80
Mark Creaven, 31, 579
Mark Greenhaf, 31, 628
Mark Hanson, 31, 212, 217
Mark Icke, 31, 615
Mark Leech, 3-5, 43, 48, 65, 1012
Mark Livingston, 31, 436
Marriage, 5, 49, 731, 839, 841, 963-968, 1023, 1076, 1092
Martin Booth, 31, 450
Martin Jones, 31, 74, 1197, 1223
Martin Narey, 43, 1184
Matt Spencer, 31, 423
Matthew Tilt, 31, 515
Media, 34, 774, 789, 796, 967, 1025, 1046-1047, 1051, 1053, 1063, 1076-1077, 1109, 1116, 1189, 1212-1213, 1371, 1398, 1404, 1409, 1412, 1434, 1488, 1501
Medical Attention, 1046
Michael Spurr, 672
Michelle Jarman-Howe, 30, 32
Michelle Quirk, 31
Michelle Quirke, 604
Mick Mills, 31, 322
Moorland, 27-28, 31, 33, 468-472, 599, 781, 918, 1133, 1214
Mother & Baby Units, 1136, 1259
Mother and Baby Units, 785, 905, 908, 910, 1085-1086, 1274, 1386, 1521
Natalie Csengeri, 1007
Natalie McKee, 31, 350

Natasha Wilson, 31, 269, 277

National Insurance, 945

National Population Census, 1090

National Probation Service, 85-86, 88, 142, 475, 495, 774, 852, 912, 1003, 1053, 1203, 1261, 1263, 1271, 1285-1286, 1306, 1315, 1331-1332, 1344, 1381, 1450, 1461, 1479, 1493, 1517

National Security Framework, 733, 735, 745, 793, 840, 941, 967, 1018-1019, 1038, 1060, 1067, 1091-1092, 1114, 1123, 1259, 1308, 1312

Neil Richards, 27, 30, 32, 67, 74, 139, 206, 212, 217, 280, 285, 450, 492, 507, 537, 540, 575, 636

Neil Thomas, 31, 597

New Hall, 22, 27-28, 31, 33, 484-485, 781, 905, 918, 1214

New Me Strengths, 764, 766

Niall Bryant, 31

Nick Leader, 31

Nicki Smith, 31, 563

Nicola Marfleet, 32, 710

Nigel Smith, 31, 346

North Sea Camp, 29, 31-32, 486-487, 489-492, 781, 856, 1214

Northern Ireland Prison Service, 9, 40, 63, 1514

Northumberland, 13, 28, 31-32, 328, 362, 492-493, 781, 1045, 1214

Norwich, 18, 22, 27, 29, 31-32, 154, 227, 496-502, 672, 781, 856, 918

Nottingham, 22, 24, 27-29, 31, 33, 450, 503-505, 781, 918, 1054, 1214

Nursing Grades, 1093

Oakwood, 6, 12-13, 29, 31-32, 119, 507-511, 513-515, 781, 1167-1168, 1175, 1214

OASys, 51, 53, 75, 82, 86, 88, 93, 104, 106, 111, 122, 135, 150, 153, 163, 172, 177, 209, 214, 234, 247, 267, 279, 298, 301, 306, 326, 348, 361, 378, 382, 384-385, 396, 400, 415, 425, 430, 434, 437-438, 456, 471, 479, 492, 498, 501, 518, 531, 547, 554, 559, 561, 576, 587, 601, 603, 619, 625, 633, 635-636, 650, 663, 677, 705, 714, 721, 734-735, 740-741, 743, 848, 855, 862, 882, 888, 894, 903, 915, 919, 932, 959, 991, 993-994, 996, 1030, 1093-1094, 1127, 1259, 1267, 1288, 1301, 1497

Occupational Health, 1041, 1259, 1274

Offence Type Categories, 1093

Offending Behaviour Programmes, 5, 731, 763-766, 1109

Older Prisoners, 969

Olivia Phelps, 31, 433

Onley, 23, 29, 31-32, 515-520, 781

Open Estate, 786, 1027, 1134, 1259, 1271

Open Government:, 1097

Open Prisons, 781

Open University, 238, 362, 647, 940, 942, 1036, 1098, 1275, 1282

Operational Support Grades, 1098, 1332, 1349

Oral Hearings, 850, 869, 877, 883, 887, 894, 1018, 1020, 1047, 1101-1102

Parc, 13, 27, 29, 31, 33, 521-529, 781, 918, 923, 1167, 1169-1170, 1193, 1214, 1284

Parliamentary Questions, 6, 49, 1205-1231

Parole, 6, 26, 49, 53, 56, 180, 320, 328, 334-335, 349, 492, 535, 668, 730, 741, 777, 808, 820, 847-851, 869-872, 875-888, 891-905, 915, 928-934, 987-988, 990-995, 998, 1004, 1012-1013, 1016-1021, 1024-1026, 1029, 1031-1032, 1036, 1038-1039, 1041, 1043, 1046-1053, 1055-1057, 1061-1069, 1071, 1073-1075, 1077-1078, 1080, 1082-1083, 1094-1106, 1114, 1116-1119, 1122, 1127, 1131, 1138-1139, 1163, 1189, 1196-1198, 1207, 1215-1216, 1220, 1222-1225, 1227-1229, 1259, 1264-1265, 1270-1274, 1282, 1289, 1369-1370, 1387, 1418, 1421, 1432, 1439, 1446-1447, 1472, 1482-1483, 1492-1493, 1504-1505, 1508-1509

Parole Board, 6, 26, 49, 56, 320, 334-335, 349, 492, 741, 777, 820, 847-851, 869, 871-872, 875-880, 882-888, 891-895, 897, 900-905, 915, 928-934, 988, 991-995, 998, 1004, 1012-1013, 1017-1021, 1024-1026, 1029, 1031-1032, 1038-1039, 1041, 1043, 1046-1051, 1053, 1055-1057, 1061-1069, 1071, 1073-1075, 1077-1078, 1080, 1082-1083, 1094-1106, 1117-1118, 1122, 1127, 1131, 1138-1139, 1163, 1189, 1196-1198, 1207, 1215, 1220, 1222-1225, 1227-1229, 1259, 1265, 1270, 1272, 1274, 1282, 1387, 1418, 1421, 1432, 1439, 1446-1447, 1472, 1482-1483, 1492-1493, 1504-1505, 1508-1509

Paul Cawkwell, 32, 408, 423, 472, 486, 515, 691

Paul Crossey, 32, 476

Paul Newton, 31, 113

Paul Woods, 32, 125, 419, 545, 651

Paul Yates, 31, 503

Pay, 5-6, 49, 93, 731, 754, 843, 943-950, 955, 969, 1036, 1041, 1113-1114, 1137, 1234, 1303, 1306, 1344-1350, 1478

Payments, 845, 1072

Pentonville, 5, 14, 27-28, 31, 33, 47, 49, 529-537, 781, 918, 1079, 1175-1180, 1214, 1285

Person Escort Record, 733, 749, 795, 1112, 1136, 1259, 1272-1273, 1309

Pete Francis, 31, 398

Pete Gormley, 32, 686

Peter Small, 31, 575, 1168

Peterborough, 13, 23, 29, 31-32, 537-545, 696, 781, 905, 918, 1214, 1229, 1383, 1429

Phil Copple, 30, 32

Phil Husband, 31

Photograph, 4, 1106

Physical Education, 1106-1107, 1491

Pia Sinha, 33, 78, 219, 227, 238, 241, 293, 444, 484, 579, 604

Pillars of Recovery, 763, 765

PJ Butler, 31

POELT, 150, 309, 554

Police National Computer, 868, 870, 1107, 1288, 1483

Policy Frameworks, 6, 14, 49, 740, 786, 801, 970, 1007, 1205, 1259-1283

Polygraph examination licence condition, 1273

Portland, 23-24, 27, 29, 31-32, 545-549, 651-652, 781, 830, 918, 1214

Post Sentence Supervision Requirements, 1114, 1259

Pregnancy, 747, 841, 905, 910-911, 1086, 1259, 1274

Prescoed, 27, 29, 32-33, 549, 644-650, 781, 856, 918, 1018, 1119, 1214

Preston, 21, 23, 27, 31-32, 395, 549-555, 781, 918, 1214, 1285-1286

Prison & YOI rules, 5

Prison Disciplinary System, 5, 731, 801-817

Prison Estate, 8, 18-26, 1370, 1389, 1469-1470

Prison Group Director, 14, 27, 32-33, 53, 67, 78, 80, 91, 100, 113, 119, 125, 130, 139, 145, 148, 154, 158, 162, 165, 174, 182, 191, 196, 206, 217, 227, 231, 238, 241-242, 244, 251, 260, 266, 269, 277, 280-281, 293, 297, 300, 303, 307, 314, 318, 322, 328, 336, 341, 346, 350, 354, 360, 364, 372, 376, 380, 386, 392, 395, 398, 404, 408, 414, 419, 423, 428, 433, 436, 440, 444, 450, 455, 459, 468, 472, 476, 484, 486, 496, 501, 503, 515, 521, 525, 529, 545, 547, 550, 555, 563, 568, 579, 586, 589, 593, 597, 600, 604, 611, 615, 624, 628, 636, 640, 649, 651, 654, 659, 667, 670, 676, 679, 686, 691, 695, 702, 710, 718, 725, 771-772, 971, 975, 977, 983, 999, 1321

Prison Officers, 38, 53, 816-817, 911, 1006, 1187, 1206, 1219, 1284, 1303, 1321, 1345, 1347, 1378, 1437, 1446, 1508

Prison Officers Association, 816, 1206

Prison Service Instructions, 740, 754, 785, 825, 939, 948, 1010, 1108, 1259, 1270, 1312

Prison Service Orders, 49-50, 240, 658, 754, 969, 1007, 1312, 1508

INDEX

Prison Shop, 756

Prisoner Communications, 5, 48, 731, 780-797, 1025, 1076-1077

Prisoner complaints, 949

Prisoner Complaints Policy Framework, 770, 911, 974, 1017, 1026, 1111, 1275

Prisons and Probation Ombudsman, 53, 62, 99, 103, 121, 139, 151, 212, 221, 246, 320, 366, 368-369, 405, 462, 484, 533, 557, 601, 661, 730, 739, 770, 772, 774-775, 801, 1004, 1165, 1192, 1272, 1275, 1282

Prisons Inspectorate, 5-6, 13, 43, 48-49, 65, 585, 731-732, 756, 817, 1001, 1189, 1196

Prisons Ombudsman, 5, 62-65, 774, 811, 820

Private Cash, 753, 794, 954

Private sector prisons, 5, 12-13, 16

Production of Prisoners, 1041, 1107

Professional Standards, 777

Progression Regimes, 1275

Public Relations, 1116

Purpose of Prison, 1015

Purposeful activity, 69, 75, 85, 93, 104, 121, 133, 141, 171, 176, 184, 200, 208, 221, 233, 247, 255, 272, 288, 325, 331, 367, 447, 463, 479, 510, 523, 558, 570, 581, 606, 618, 632, 646, 662, 682, 705, 714, 721, 756, 1113

Race, 48, 53, 170, 328, 519, 731, 840-841, 1331, 1447

Race Relations, 53

Radiation, 1117, 1282

Ralph Lubkowski, 31, 336

Ranby, 27-29, 31, 33, 555-559, 562-563, 781, 1214

Rebecca Newby, 395

Recall, 49, 56, 731, 846-896, 900, 929, 938, 989, 998, 1017, 1050, 1084, 1117-1118, 1133, 1260, 1264, 1272-1273, 1276, 1418

Recalled Prisoners, 850, 865, 869-870, 875, 890, 896, 929, 1117, 1119, 1273, 1276

Release, 7, 48, 51-53, 55, 58, 70, 114, 127, 185, 225, 272, 282, 289, 326, 337, 361, 488, 510, 565, 571, 594, 601, 608, 625, 668, 731, 740, 744-745, 782, 846-896, 898, 900, 902, 922, 928-929, 934, 936, 938, 941, 953, 956-957, 964, 987, 989, 991, 994, 1009, 1026, 1030, 1034, 1038, 1040, 1043, 1051, 1055, 1080, 1095, 1114, 1117-1118, 1120, 1133, 1169, 1197, 1223, 1232, 1259-1261, 1263-1264, 1266-1267, 1270, 1272-1274, 1276, 1282-1283, 1370, 1387, 1389-1390, 1401, 1432-1433, 1439, 1457, 1474, 1482-1483, 1489, 1504-1505

Release on Temporary Licence, 7, 53, 668, 853, 902, 934, 938, 941, 957, 989, 1038, 1114, 1120, 1223, 1260, 1263, 1267, 1270, 1276, 1370, 1387, 1474

Religion, 48, 731, 733, 831-841, 921, 1331, 1333

Remission, 803, 1009-1010, 1033

Repatriation, 734, 929, 988, 1040-1041, 1051, 1055, 1071, 1121, 1282

Reporting Wrongdoing, 1028, 1108, 1115, 1259

Resettlement, 18-26, 70, 93, 108, 134, 172-173, 193, 204, 206, 209, 239, 241, 266, 269, 272, 280, 292-293, 322, 347, 349, 352, 355, 368, 411, 487-488, 494, 506, 511, 561, 582, 603, 624, 658, 663, 682, 729, 774, 826, 840, 853, 856, 867, 924, 926, 950, 966, 968-969, 1115, 1166, 1194, 1204, 1230, 1264, 1277, 1280, 1282, 1287, 1289, 1299, 1301, 1510, 1521

Resolve, 320, 525, 679, 764, 766

Restraints, 1009-1010, 1087, 1123, 1309, 1316

Restrictions on prisoner voting, 744

Reverse Cohort Unit, 53

Richard Luscombe, 31, 260

Richard Suttle, 32, 640

Richard Vince, 30

Risley, 23, 27-28, 31-32, 563-567, 604, 781, 1060, 1075, 1137, 1214

Rob Denman, 32, 644

Rob Kellett, 31, 428

Rob Knight, 31, 459

Rob Luxford, 31, 545

Rob Young, 31, 444

Robbie Durgan, 31, 145

Rochester, 19, 23, 27, 29, 31, 33, 568-575, 781, 918, 923, 1214, 1386

ROTL Policy Framework, 856

Ruth Stephens, 32, 695

Rye Hill, 13, 29, 31-32, 575-578, 781, 1167-1168, 1214

Samantha Pariser, 31, 492

Sarah Coccia, 30, 32

Sarah Corbett-Batson, 1007

Sarah Jane-Ewart, 1007

Scottish Prison Service, 34-35, 38, 1474, 1514-1515

Sean Oliver, 31, 507, 1168

Sean Ormerod, 31, 360

Search, 735, 1008-1010, 1310, 1317

Secure Schools, 9

Secure Social Video Calling (Interim), 1277

Secure Training Centres, 5, 9, 12, 853, 923, 1237

Security categorisation, 989, 996

Security Categorisation Policy Framework, 987, 1015, 1017-1018, 1038, 1277

Segregation, 5, 49, 68, 92, 100, 119, 131, 149, 169, 197, 206, 246, 249, 304, 336, 341, 360, 399, 441, 474, 484, 497, 501, 507, 563, 569, 606, 656, 718, 731, 734, 793, 802, 834-835, 837-838, 970-987, 1047, 1052, 1286

Send, 23, 27, 29, 31, 33, 219, 579-585, 759, 781, 903, 905, 918, 920, 1059, 1192, 1196, 1198, 1214, 1315, 1441

Sentence Calculation, 846, 1118, 1121, 1126, 1133, 1260

Sentence Planning, 837, 839, 1127, 1263

Sentencing Council, 814, 1005

Serious and organised crime, 1467

Sex Offenders, 868, 931, 1075, 1370, 1481

Sharon Holloway, 1007-1008

Shaun Mycroft, 31, 364

Simon Cartwright, 32, 165, 346, 354, 476, 667

Simon Creighton, 896, 905

Simon Drysdale, 31, 182

Simon Rhoden, 31, 154

Simon Walters, 31, 404

Smoke Free, 1130, 1260, 1279

Smoking, 803, 1183, 1488

Social Security, 5, 48, 731, 843-846, 1380, 1390

Sonia Brooks, 31, 130

Sophie Walker, 1007-1008

Spring Hill, 314, 585-586, 856, 1214

SSV, 530, 550

Staff Awards & Prizes, 6

Stafford, 19, 23, 27, 29, 31, 33, 226-227, 589-592, 781, 896, 1029, 1214

Standard Recall, 850, 869, 872, 878-880, 888, 891, 894

Standford Hill, 27, 31, 33, 593, 595-596, 620, 622-623, 856

Steve Cross, 31, 440

Steve Gillan, 1005

Steve Hodson, 31, 419

Steve Mead, 31, 191

Steve Williams, 31, 67, 1168

Stocken, 23, 27, 29, 31, 33, 597-600, 781

Stoke Heath, 27, 29, 31, 33, 600-603, 781, 918, 1214

Strengthening Prisoners Family Ties, 780-781, 1260

Styal, 23, 27, 29, 31, 33, 604-611, 781, 905, 918, 1214, 1441

Sudbury, 23, 27, 29, 31, 33, 293, 611-615, 781, 856, 1214

Susan Howard, 33, 196, 231, 360, 395

Swaleside, 27, 29, 31, 33, 615-623, 781, 809, 1034, 1098

Swansea, 24, 27, 29, 31, 33, 623-628, 781, 918, 1214

Swinfen Hall, 27, 29, 31, 33, 628-633, 635-636, 781, 918, 1175, 1214

Temporary Release, 58, 745, 964, 1009, 1387, 1474

Ten Prisons Project, 1490

Teresa Clarke, 27, 33, 113, 119, 266, 336, 589, 600, 628

Thameside, 13, 28, 31-32, 636-639, 781, 918, 1023, 1214

The Bridge Programme, 766

The Mount, 27, 29, 32, 476-479, 482-483, 781, 1210

The Verne, 9, 27, 29, 32, 651-654, 781

Theft, 56, 1381

Therapeutic Communities, 765, 903, 958

Therapeutic Communities Plus (TC+), 765

Thinking Skills Programme (TSP), 764, 766

Thorn Cross, 27-29, 32, 640-643, 781, 856, 918, 1214

Through the Gate, 610, 1381

Throughcare, 51, 739, 921

Tim Allen, 27, 32, 145, 350, 436, 563, 640

Tim Kerr, 6, 47, 49, 1181

Tim Knight, 31, 251

Time Limits, 777, 1028

Tobacco, 815

Tom Wheatley, 32, 654

Transfer of Prisoners, 1051, 1081, 1132

Transport, 439, 1046, 1129, 1208, 1214, 1220, 1259, 1420, 1443, 1467, 1501

Treatment of Prisoners, 15

Urgent Notification, 43, 91, 114-115, 126-127, 166-167, 260, 274, 416, 437, 533, 1170

Usk, 27, 29, 32-33, 549, 643-650, 781, 1119, 1214

Vacant, 774

Varinder Panesar, 5, 47, 49, 1175

Violence Reduction, 1021, 1313

Visits, 16, 40, 67, 70, 86, 89, 91, 100, 104, 106, 121, 124-127, 131, 145, 151, 153-154, 158, 179-180, 189, 191, 194-195, 204, 213, 217, 227, 231, 265, 272, 286, 305, 308, 311, 315, 317, 321, 331-332, 337, 349, 353, 374, 376, 381, 391-392, 407, 409, 426-427, 429, 445-446, 448, 451, 458, 465, 468, 470, 479, 482, 486, 489, 501-502, 510, 512-513, 515, 529, 535, 537, 541-542, 555, 565, 584-585, 588, 592-593, 621, 638-639, 649, 652, 666, 675, 678, 686, 689-690, 701-702, 708, 711, 716, 721, 725, 739, 759, 780, 783, 785-789, 803, 832, 835, 840, 906, 911, 919, 944, 952, 955, 1008-1009, 1016, 1025-1027, 1051, 1067, 1073, 1109-1110, 1134, 1138, 1259, 1267, 1270-1271, 1279, 1283, 1319, 1386

Wakefield, 22, 24, 27-28, 32-33, 484, 654-659, 781, 901, 1027, 1036-1037, 1051, 1053, 1074, 1089, 1133

Wandsworth, 27-28, 32-33, 48, 659-667, 781, 918, 1041, 1050, 1115, 1175-1177, 1179-1180, 1214

Warren Hill, 27, 29, 32, 355, 668-670, 781, 918, 1214, 1276

Wayland, 13, 27, 29, 32, 670-675, 781, 1115, 1214, 1511

Wealstun, 27, 32-33, 676-679, 781, 1214

Werrington, 24, 27-29, 32-33, 679-685, 781, 918, 923, 1214, 1285-1286

Wetherby, 24, 27-28, 32-33, 204, 676, 685-690, 781, 918, 923, 1195, 1214, 1261

Whatton, 24, 27, 32, 690-695, 781, 1013, 1029, 1214

Whitemoor, 27, 29, 32-33, 695-702, 781, 901, 904, 1067

Who Can Help?, 5, 48, 731, 817-821

Will Styles, 33, 80, 100, 386, 440, 615, 695, 710

Winchester, 24, 27, 29, 32-33, 390, 702-710, 781, 918, 1214

Witness Intimidation, 734, 736, 1136

Women in Custody, 907, 912, 1281, 1522

Women Prisoners, 5, 731, 905-916, 924, 1092

Woodhill, 27, 29, 32-33, 710-718, 781, 901, 918, 1214, 1284

Workforce Statistics, 6, 1303, 1322-1330

Wormwood Scrubs, 27-28, 32-33, 718-725, 918, 1067, 1214

Wymott, 27-28, 32, 725-730, 781, 918, 1214, 1285-1286

Wyn Jones, 6, 13, 292

X-ray, 309, 520, 666, 1280, 1282, 1446

Young Adults, 971, 993, 998, 1180, 1197, 1260, 1275, 1370

Young Offenders, 5, 9, 26, 29, 35-36, 39, 49, 52, 731, 810, 916-927, 1022, 1026, 1261, 1370, 1524

Youth Custody Service, 12, 27, 30, 182, 187, 269-270, 277, 679, 685-687, 690, 867, 925, 978-979, 1194, 1260-1261, 1265, 1321-1322, 1444

Youth Justice Board, 25, 54, 74, 774-775, 916-917, 922-923, 925, 1005, 1051, 1093, 1138, 1260-1261, 1523

Zoe Short, 31, 241

Zoonotic, 49, 1283

# October 2022

| | | |
|---|---|---|
| 1 | Sa | |
| 2 | Su | |
| 3 | Mo | Wk 40 |
| 4 | Tu | |
| 5 | We | |
| 6 | Th | |
| 7 | Fr | |
| 8 | Sa | |
| 9 | Su | |
| 10 | Mo | Wk 41 |
| 11 | Tu | |
| 12 | We | |
| 13 | Th | |
| 14 | Fr | |
| 15 | Sa | |
| 16 | Su | |
| 17 | Mo | Wk 42 |
| 18 | Tu | |
| 19 | We | |
| 20 | Th | |
| 21 | Fr | |
| 22 | Sa | |
| 23 | Su | |
| 24 | Mo | Wk 43 |
| 25 | Tu | |
| 26 | We | |
| 27 | Th | |
| 28 | Fr | |
| 29 | Sa | |
| 30 | Su | |
| 31 | Mo | Wk 44 |

# November 2022

| | | | |
|---|---|---|---|
| 1 | Tu | | |
| 2 | We | | |
| 3 | Th | | |
| 4 | Fr | | |
| **5** | **Sa** | | |
| **6** | **Su** | | |
| 7 | Mo | | Wk 45 |
| 8 | Tu | | |
| 9 | We | | |
| 10 | Th | | |
| 11 | Fr | | |
| **12** | **Sa** | | |
| **13** | **Su** | | |
| 14 | Mo | | Wk 46 |
| 15 | Tu | | |
| 16 | We | | |
| 17 | Th | | |
| 18 | Fr | | |
| **19** | **Sa** | | |
| **20** | **Su** | | |
| 21 | Mo | | Wk 47 |
| 22 | Tu | | |
| 23 | We | | |
| 24 | Th | | |
| 25 | Fr | | |
| **26** | **Sa** | | |
| **27** | **Su** | | |
| 28 | Mo | | Wk 48 |
| 29 | Tu | | |
| 30 | We | | |
| | | | |

# December 2022

| 1 | Th | |
|---|---|---|
| 2 | Fr | |
| **3** | **Sa** | |
| **4** | **Su** | |
| 5 | Mo | Wk 49 |
| 6 | Tu | |
| 7 | We | |
| 8 | Th | |
| 9 | Fr | |
| **10** | **Sa** | |
| **11** | **Su** | |
| 12 | Mo | Wk 50 |
| 13 | Tu | |
| 14 | We | |
| 15 | Th | |
| 16 | Fr | |
| **17** | **Sa** | |
| **18** | **Su** | |
| 19 | Mo | Wk 51 |
| 20 | Tu | |
| 21 | We | |
| 22 | Th | |
| 23 | Fr | |
| **24** | **Sa** | |
| **25** | **Su** | Christmas Day |
| **26** | **Mo** | Boxing Day        Wk 52 |
| **27** | **Tu** | Substitute day |
| 28 | We | |
| 29 | Th | |
| 30 | Fr | |
| **31** | **Sa** | |

# January 2023

| | | |
|---|---|---|
| 1 | Su | New Year's Day |
| 2 | Mo | Wk 1 |
| 3 | Tu | |
| 4 | We | |
| 5 | Th | |
| 6 | Fr | |
| 7 | Sa | |
| 8 | Su | |
| 9 | Mo | Wk 2 |
| 10 | Tu | |
| 11 | We | |
| 12 | Th | |
| 13 | Fr | |
| 14 | Sa | |
| 15 | Su | |
| 16 | Mo | Wk 3 |
| 17 | Tu | |
| 18 | We | |
| 19 | Th | |
| 20 | Fr | |
| 21 | Sa | |
| 22 | Su | |
| 23 | Mo | Wk 4 |
| 24 | Tu | |
| 25 | We | |
| 26 | Th | |
| 27 | Fr | |
| 28 | Sa | |
| 29 | Su | |
| 30 | Mo | Wk 5 |
| 31 | Tu | |

INDEX

# February 2023

| | | | |
|---|---|---|---|
| 1 | We | | |
| 2 | Th | | |
| 3 | Fr | | |
| **4** | **Sa** | | |
| **5** | **Su** | | |
| 6 | Mo | | Wk 6 |
| 7 | Tu | | |
| 8 | We | | |
| 9 | Th | | |
| 10 | Fr | | |
| **11** | **Sa** | | |
| **12** | **Su** | | |
| 13 | Mo | | Wk 7 |
| 14 | Tu | | |
| 15 | We | | |
| 16 | Th | | |
| 17 | Fr | | |
| **18** | **Sa** | | |
| **19** | **Su** | | |
| 20 | Mo | | Wk 8 |
| 21 | Tu | | |
| 22 | We | | |
| 23 | Th | | |
| 24 | Fr | | |
| **25** | **Sa** | | |
| **26** | **Su** | | |
| 27 | Mo | | Wk 9 |
| 28 | Tu | | |
| | | | |
| | | | |
| | | | |

# March 2023

| | | |
|---|---|---|
| 1 | We | |
| 2 | Th | |
| 3 | Fr | |
| **4** | **Sa** | |
| **5** | **Su** | |
| 6 | Mo | Wk 10 |
| 7 | Tu | |
| 8 | We | |
| 9 | Th | |
| 10 | Fr | |
| **11** | **Sa** | |
| **12** | **Su** | |
| 13 | Mo | Wk 11 |
| 14 | Tu | |
| 15 | We | |
| 16 | Th | |
| 17 | Fr | |
| **18** | **Sa** | |
| **19** | **Su** | |
| 20 | Mo | Wk 12 |
| 21 | Tu | |
| 22 | We | |
| 23 | Th | |
| 24 | Fr | |
| **25** | **Sa** | |
| **26** | **Su** | |
| 27 | Mo | Wk 13 |
| 28 | Tu | |
| 29 | We | |
| 30 | Th | |
| 31 | Fr | |

# April 2023

| 1 | Sa | |
|---|---|---|
| 2 | Su | |
| 3 | Mo | Wk 14 |
| 4 | Tu | |
| 5 | We | |
| 6 | Th | |
| 7 | Fr | Good Friday |
| 8 | Sa | |
| 9 | Su | |
| 10 | Mo | Easter Monday    Wk 15 |
| 11 | Tu | |
| 12 | We | |
| 13 | Th | |
| 14 | Fr | |
| 15 | Sa | |
| 16 | Su | |
| 17 | Mo | Wk 16 |
| 18 | Tu | |
| 19 | We | |
| 20 | Th | |
| 21 | Fr | |
| 22 | Sa | |
| 23 | Su | |
| 24 | Mo | Wk 17 |
| 25 | Tu | |
| 26 | We | |
| 27 | Th | |
| 28 | Fr | |
| 29 | Sa | |
| 30 | Su | |
| | | |

# May 2023

| 1 | Mo | Early May Bank Holiday | Wk 18 |
|---|---|---|---|
| 2 | Tu | | |
| 3 | We | | |
| 4 | Th | | |
| 5 | Fr | | |
| **6** | **Sa** | | |
| **7** | **Su** | | |
| 8 | Mo | | Wk 19 |
| 9 | Tu | | |
| 10 | We | | |
| 11 | Th | | |
| 12 | Fr | | |
| **13** | **Sa** | | |
| **14** | **Su** | | |
| 15 | Mo | | Wk 20 |
| 16 | Tu | | |
| 17 | We | | |
| 18 | Th | | |
| 19 | Fr | | |
| **20** | **Sa** | | |
| **21** | **Su** | | |
| 22 | Mo | | Wk 21 |
| 23 | Tu | | |
| 24 | We | | |
| 25 | Th | | |
| 26 | Fr | | |
| **27** | **Sa** | | |
| **28** | **Su** | | |
| 29 | Mo | Spring Bank Holiday | Wk 22 |
| 30 | Tu | | |
| 31 | We | | |

INDEX

# June 2023

| 1 | Th | |
|---|----|---|
| 2 | Fr | |
| **3** | **Sa** | |
| **4** | **Su** | |
| 5 | Mo | Wk 23 |
| 6 | Tu | |
| 7 | We | |
| 8 | Th | |
| 9 | Fr | |
| **10** | **Sa** | |
| **11** | **Su** | |
| 12 | Mo | Wk 24 |
| 13 | Tu | |
| 14 | We | |
| 15 | Th | |
| 16 | Fr | |
| **17** | **Sa** | |
| **18** | **Su** | |
| 19 | Mo | Wk 25 |
| 20 | Tu | |
| 21 | We | |
| 22 | Th | |
| 23 | Fr | |
| **24** | **Sa** | |
| **25** | **Su** | |
| 26 | Mo | Wk 26 |
| 27 | Tu | |
| 28 | We | |
| 29 | Th | |
| 30 | Fr | |
| | | |

# July 2023

| 1 | Sa | |
|---|---|---|
| **2** | **Su** | |
| 3 | Mo | Wk 27 |
| 4 | Tu | |
| 5 | We | |
| 6 | Th | |
| 7 | Fr | |
| **8** | **Sa** | |
| **9** | **Su** | |
| 10 | Mo | Wk 28 |
| 11 | Tu | |
| 12 | We | |
| 13 | Th | |
| 14 | Fr | |
| **15** | **Sa** | |
| **16** | **Su** | |
| 17 | Mo | Wk 29 |
| 18 | Tu | |
| 19 | We | |
| 20 | Th | |
| 21 | Fr | |
| **22** | **Sa** | |
| **23** | **Su** | |
| 24 | Mo | Wk 30 |
| 25 | Tu | |
| 26 | We | |
| 27 | Th | |
| 28 | Fr | |
| **29** | **Sa** | |
| **30** | **Su** | |
| 31 | Mo | Wk 31 |

INDEX

# August 2023

| | | | |
|---|---|---|---|
| 1 | Tu | | |
| 2 | We | | |
| 3 | Th | | |
| 4 | Fr | | |
| **5** | **Sa** | | |
| **6** | **Su** | | |
| 7 | Mo | | Wk 32 |
| 8 | Tu | | |
| 9 | We | | |
| 10 | Th | | |
| 11 | Fr | | |
| **12** | **Sa** | | |
| **13** | **Su** | | |
| 14 | Mo | | Wk 33 |
| 15 | Tu | | |
| 16 | We | | |
| 17 | Th | | |
| 18 | Fr | | |
| **19** | **Sa** | | |
| **20** | **Su** | | |
| 21 | Mo | | Wk 34 |
| 22 | Tu | | |
| 23 | We | | |
| 24 | Th | | |
| 25 | Fr | | |
| **26** | **Sa** | | |
| **27** | **Su** | | |
| **28** | **Mo** | August Bank Holiday | Wk 35 |
| 29 | Tu | | |
| 30 | We | | |
| 31 | Th | | |

# September 2023

| | | |
|---|---|---|
| 1 | Fr | |
| **2** | **Sa** | |
| **3** | **Su** | |
| 4 | Mo | Wk 36 |
| 5 | Tu | |
| 6 | We | |
| 7 | Th | |
| 8 | Fr | |
| **9** | **Sa** | |
| **10** | **Su** | |
| 11 | Mo | Wk 37 |
| 12 | Tu | |
| 13 | We | |
| 14 | Th | |
| 15 | Fr | |
| **16** | **Sa** | |
| **17** | **Su** | |
| 18 | Mo | Wk 38 |
| 19 | Tu | |
| 20 | We | |
| 21 | Th | |
| 22 | Fr | |
| **23** | **Sa** | |
| **24** | **Su** | |
| 25 | Mo | Wk 39 |
| 26 | Tu | |
| 27 | We | |
| 28 | Th | |
| 29 | Fr | |
| **30** | **Sa** | |
| | | |

# ONE PUMP COURT

## BARRISTERS WORKING FOR YOU

**Your Appeals and Prison Law Team**

The Appeals and Prison Law Team at One Pump Court was established by Stephen Field in 2008. The team is now being led by Rebecca Martin and Terry Pedro, who worked alongside Stephen since the team's inception and continue its commendable work in his memory.

**Rebecca Martin & Terry Pedro** are both highly experienced criminal defence barristers, with practices encompassing serious crime of all varieties in the Crown Court, High Court and Court of Appeal. They particularly specialise in advising on appeal against conviction and sentence, frequently appearing in the Court of Appeal on behalf of those who have contacted us through this page. They also conduct parole hearings and judicial review proceedings in prison or parole matters. Terry also undertakes Direct Access Work.

**Angelina Nicolaou** has a mixed practice within the crime, prison, immigration and inquest/inquiries team. She represents claimants in civil actions against public bodies, including prisons and police, as well as representing families in inquests. She is a contributor to the Prison Handbook and Prison Law Index.

**Natalie Csengeri** is a criminal defence barrister, specialising in mental health issues. She can assist in appeals against conviction and sentence, as well as represent individuals at parole hearings. She is direct access accredited.

**Stephen Knight** works in crime and immigration, and can be of particular help where the two issues interact. He has a large appeals caseload and is able to assist on a direct access basis if a solicitor cannot act for you if legal aid is unavailable.

**Sophie Walker** has a wide practice spanning civil and criminal law. She represents claimants in civil actions against prisons and other public bodies, as well as families in inquests.

**Grace Cowell** is a barrister working in criminal defence, prison and family law, who specialises in cases concerning mental health issues. She is a contributor to the Prison Handbook and Prison Law Index and can assist in appeals against conviction and sentence.

### About One Pump Court

The Appeals and Prison Law Team represents prisoners in prison law matters, including pre-tariff reviews, categorisation disputes, adjudications, parole hearings and judicial review.

Our members also provide advice on appeal against conviction and sentence following trial and pursue those appeals where appropriate. We specialise in advising on and conducting appeal proceedings on behalf of those represented by other counsel at trial, frequently appearing in the Court of Appeal in such matters.

**If you have a problem we can help with, just contact us at: One Pump Court Chambers, Elm Court, Temple, London, EC4Y 7AH**

**E: clerks@onepumpcourt.co.uk**